MW01123318

The Edinburgh Encyclopaedia

The Edinburgh Encyclopaedia

Volume XVI

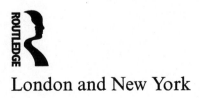

London and New York

First published 1830
by William Blackwood

Reprinted 1999
by Routledge
11 New Fetter Lane, London EC4P 4EE

Simultaneously published in the USA and Canada
by Routledge
29 West 35th Street, New York, NY 10001

Reprinted 1999 by Pear Tree Image Processing Limited, Stevenage,
Herts. SG1 2PT

All rights reserved. No part of this book may be reprinted or
reproduced or utilised in any form or by any electronic, mechanical,
or other means, now known or hereafter invented, including
photocopying and recording, or in any information storage or retrieval
system, without permission in writing from the publishers.

British Library Cataloguing in Publication Data
A catalogue record for this book is available from the British Library

Library of Congress Cataloging in Publication Data
A catalogue record for this book has been requested

ISBN 0–415–18026–0 (18 volume set)

Publisher's note
These reprints are taken from original copies of each book. In many
cases the condition of these originals is not perfect, the paper, often
handmade, having suffered over time, and the copy from such factors
as inconsistent printing pressure resulting in faint text, show through
from one side of a leaf to the other, the filling in of some characters,
and the break-up of type. The publisher has gone to great lengths to
ensure the quality of these reprints, but wishes to point out that
certain characteristics of the original copies will, of necessity, be
apparent in reprints thereof.

THE

EDINBURGH ENCYCLOPÆDIA;

CONDUCTED BY

DAVID BREWSTER, LL.D.

F. R. S. LOND. AND EDIN. AND M. R. I. A.

CORRESPONDING MEMBER OF THE ROYAL ACADEMY OF SCIENCES OF PARIS, AND OF THE ROYAL ACADEMY OF SCIENCES OF
PRUSSIA; MEMBER OF THE ROYAL SWEDISH ACADEMY OF SCIENCES; OF THE ROYAL SOCIETY OF SCIENCES OF DENMARK; OF
THE ROYAL SOCIETY OF GOTTINGEN, AND OF THE ROYAL ACADEMY OF SCIENCES OF MODENA; HONORARY ASSOCIATE OF THE
ROYAL ACADEMY OF SCIENCES OF LYONS; ASSOCIATE OF THE SOCIETY OF CIVIL ENGINEERS; MEMBER OF THE SOCIETY OF THE AN-
TIQUARIES OF SCOTLAND; OF THE GEOLOGICAL SOCIETY OF LONDON, AND OF THE ASTRONOMICAL SOCIETY OF LONDON; OF THE
AMERICAN ANTIQUARIAN SOCIETY; HONORARY MEMBER OF THE LITERARY AND PHILOSOPHICAL SOCIETY OF NEW YORK, OF THE
HISTORICAL SOCIETY OF NEW YORK; OF THE LITERARY AND PHILOSOPHICAL SOCIETY OF UTRECHT; OF THE PHILOSOPHICAL
SOCIETY OF CAMBRIDGE; OF THE LITERARY AND ANTIQUARIAN SOCIETY OF PERTH; OF THE NORTHERN INSTITUTION, AND OF
THE ROYAL MEDICAL AND PHYSICAL SOCIETIES OF EDINBURGH; OF THE ACADEMY OF NATURAL SCIENCES OF PHILADELPHIA; OF
THE SOCIETY OF THE FRIENDS OF NATURAL HISTORY OF BERLIN; OF THE NATURAL HISTORY SOCIETY OF FRANKFORT; OF THE
PHILOSOPHICAL AND LITERARY SOCIETY OF LEEDS, OF THE ROYAL GEOLOGICAL SOCIETY OF CORNWALL, AND OF THE PHILOSOPHICAL
SOCIETY OF YORK.

WITH THE ASSISTANCE OF

GENTLEMEN EMINENT IN SCIENCE AND LITERATURE.

IN EIGHTEEN VOLUMES.

VOLUME XVI.

EDINBURGH:

PRINTED FOR WILLIAM BLACKWOOD;

AND JOHN WAUGH, EDINBURGH; JOHN MURRAY; BALDWIN & CRADOCK;
J. M. RICHARDSON, LONDON; AND THE OTHER PROPRIETORS.

M.DCCC.XXX.

THE

EDINBURGH ENCYCLOPÆDIA.

ORISSA, an extensive province of Hindostan, situate between the 16th and the 23d degree of north latitude; extending about 530 miles in length from north-east to south-west, and 90 at its average breadth. It is bounded by Bengal on the north; by the river Godavery on the south; by the bay of Bengal on the east; and by the province of Gundwana on the west. It was formerly known by the name of Utcala or Odradesa; and was then inhabited by a powerful martial race, who were at last extirpated by the kings of Magadha. In more recent times, it was governed by a dynasty of Hindoo princes of the race of Gijaputty, who were conquered in 1592 by the Emperor Acber's viceroy in Bengal. It was never completely occupied by the Mahommedans: and it is still one of those provinces in which the Hindoo manners are preserved in their greatest purity. Three-fourths of the province are under the British government, and the remainder is possessed by a number of petty native chiefs, who are in a state of perpetual hostility with each other, but in some measure subject to the Nagpoor Mahrattas. The principal modern divisions of this province are Cicacole, Rajumundry, Cuttack, Mohurbunge, Konjeur, and Midnapoor. The maritime districts are equal in fertility to any territory in the south of India; but the province in general may be described as barren in comparison with Bengal. The interior in particular remains in a very savage state, consisting chiefly of rugged hills, uninhabited jungles, and deep water courses, surrounded by pathless forests. These tracts are extremely unhealthy, and are traversed only during the dry season by the inland carriers.

The population varies very much in the different districts. Midnapoor, one of the richest divisions, contains one million and a half of souls; but the population of the whole province does not exceed four millions and a half. In the back parts of the province, beyond the British dominion, the natives are a fierce and intrepid people. They are armed with bows and arrows, and swords of a peculiar shape, broad in the end and narrow in the middle, which they usually carry without a scabbard. Those again who are under the Company's jurisdiction, are a quiet inoffensive race, resembling the other Hindoos, who live under the British government. The language of the province, and the character in which it is written are termed Ooreeah. The most remarkable place in the province is JUGGERNAUTH, described in Vol. XII. p. 387. (q)

ORKNEY ISLANDS.*

ORKNEY ISLANDS, or ORCADES, are a group of small islands in the ocean which washes the northern extremity of Scotland, included between the parallels 58° 44', and 59° 25' N. Lat. and within the meridians 0° 19' E. and 0° 17' W. Long. from Greenwich. They are irregularly scattered over a space of about forty-one geographic miles in length, by twenty-five in breadth. Their number, including the uninhabited islets, or, as they are called in the dialect of the country, *holms*, amounts to sixty-seven. Of these, twenty-nine are inhabited, and the rest are wholly dedicated to pasturage, and the manufacture of kelp. The following are the modern and ancient names of the inhabited islands. The orthography of the former is according to the native mode of pronouncing them, that of the latter is derived from old authors.

	Modern.			Ancient.
1.	Pomona, or Mainland		.	Pomona.
2.	Lambholm	.	.	
3.	Burrey	.	.	Borgarey.
4.	South Ronaldshey		.	Rognvalldsey.
5.	Swaney		.	Sviney.
6.	Pentland Skerry		.	
7.	Flota	.	.	Flotey.
8.	Cava	.	.	Cavey.
9.	Fara	.	.	
10.	Rissa	.	.	
11.	Waas	.	.	Kalfey.
12.	Hoy	.	.	Haey.
13.	Græmsey	.	.	Grimsey.

* The Editor has been indebted for this Article to Thomas Stewart Traill, M.D. F.R.S. Ed.

A

	Modern.			*Ancient.*
14.	Damsey	.	.	Daminsey.
15.	Gairsey	.	.	Garegsey.
16.	Weir	.	.	Færoe.
17.	Enhallow	.	.	Eyinhelga.
18.	Rousey	,	.	Rolfsey.
19.	Egilshey	.	.	Eigilsey.
20.	Westrey	.	.	Vesturey.
21.	Papa Westrey	.	.	Papey.
22.	North Ronaldshey	.	.	Rognvalldsey.
23.	Sandey	.	.	Sandey.
24.	Edey	.	.	Eidey.
25.	Fairey	.	.	Fridarey.
26.	Stronsey	.	.	Strionsey.
27.	Papa Stronsey	.	.	Kolbensey.
28.	Shapinshey	.	.	Skipensey.
29.	Copinshey	.	.	Kiolbensey.

The general aspect of the Orkney Islands is not very diversified. With the exception of Hoy and Rousey, none of them deserve the name mountainous. The western division of Pomona, Edey, and a part of Westry, and South Ronaldshey, are the only parts of the group which can be considered as hilly. The general surface of the rest is low and undulating; in some instances green or cultivated to a considerable extent, especially along the shores; but in general they present a monotonous surface of heath or coarse pastures, here and there interspersed with spots of cultivated land, destitute of trees, or even of tall shrubs, except in the gardens of a few gentlemen in the neighbourhood of Kirkwall. The coasts are often indented by spacious and secure havens, where the largest ships may anchor; sometimes they slope gradually to the water; but often they are girt with stupendous cliffs, especially where exposed to the fury of the Western Ocean. The mixture of fantastic precipices, with basins of transparent water, produce a highly picturesque effect, though in this respect the Orkneys are far inferior to the sister Zetland Isles.

We shall shortly notice the inhabited islands, and briefly describe the most remarkable objects in each, commencing with the largest of the group.

Sect. I.—*The Islands in General.*

The islands in general. *Pomona*, or *Mainland.*—Its extreme length is about 19 geographic miles, and its greatest breadth, from Costa-head to Howton-head, 14; but its coasts are so deeply cut by extensive bays, that its area does not probably exceed 150 square miles. It is divided into 14 parishes; most of which are grouped in pairs, that have only one clergyman between them, who preaches in each on alternate Sundays; but there are two clergymen in the united parishes of Kirkwall and St. Olave; and service is performed twice on every Sabbath in the well preserved ancient Cathedral of St. Magnus, which towers over the royal burgh of Kirkwall, the capital of these islands. KIRKWALL is in latitude 58° 33′ N. Long. 0.25 W: on a wide bay which affords good anchorage for shipping. The western side of the town is washed by a small arm of the sea, which at one time formed a lake; but by an injudicious attempt to drain it, the tide now has free access. Kirkwall consists chiefly of one narrow street, about a mile in length, winding and ill paved, having something of a foreign aspect from the gables of the houses being chiefly turned to the street. The burgh, by the census of 1821, contains a population of 938 males, and 1274 females; or a total of 2212 persons. A spirit of improvement has manifested itself of late years in this

remote corner, and is visible in the superior comfort of the habitations of the people, in the lighting of the streets, in the institution of a subscription library, and in the construction of a very commodious harbour. Two substantial piers have been built at an expence of L.4963, 12s. Sterling, of which L.1800 was paid by government, and the remainder from the funds of the burgh, and the voluntary subscriptions of the inhabitants.

The architectural antiquities of Kirkwall probably surpass those of any small town in the British islands. The vast Cathedral, dedicated to St. Magnus, a canonized Earl of Orkney, is an entire and fine specimen of that style of Gothic, which has been denominated Saxon or heavy Norman by our archaiologists. The length of this building, which is in the form of the Latin cross, is 232 feet; its breadth 56 feet 9 inches. The arms of the transept are each $22\frac{1}{2}$ feet in length, and 30 feet 8 inches in breadth. It has three aisles, divided by very massy round piers without any mouldings, except a simple fillet above, and a sort of flat torus below, which give them the general appearance of heavy Tuscan columns. The piers are surmounted by two rows of plain semicircular arches; but in the transept are smaller arches, with mouldings and mullions, such as are seen in many ancient cathedrals in England. The piers amount to 28; but some of those inclosing the space for the high altar are different from those of the nave. The four central piers which support the steeple, and belong to the most ancient part of the buildings, are beautifully ornamented with deep and well cut mouldings running from the base into lofty pointed arches of great boldness; which are distinguished by the zig-zag and tooth-like ornaments that characterize the Gothic architecture of the twelfth century.

The roofs of all the aisles are of stone, ribbed with intersecting arches, the key-stones of which, especially in the choir, are carved with foliage of great delicacy. This fine vault is elevated 71 feet above the pavement of the church. The handsome tower, over the central piers, is disfigured by a low pyramidal roof, which has long supplied the place of an elegant wooden spire, consumed by lightning in 1670. The central portion of this cathedral was founded in 1138, by Earl Rognvalld or Ronald, in honour of his recently sainted kinsman. Two considerable additions were made to it by two different prelates of the See of Orkney. Bishop Edward Stewart enlarged it considerably towards the east, and gave it a most elegant window, divided into five lights by slender mullions, and surmounted by a circular one divided into 12 compartments. The whole window is 36 feet high, and 12 feet in breadth, and is externally surrounded by very bold mouldings. There is also a fine window in each end of the transept; that on the south is circular, and is more modern than the lancet-shaped double light in the north end. Bishop Robert Reid enlarged the cathedral by adding three piers to the west end about 1545. The pointed window in this part shows the decay of the art, more than the ornamented porch, which serves for the central door of the Cathedral.

The highest elevation of the present steeple is 140 feet. It is furnished with a fine chime of four well toned bells, three of which are of vast size, the gift of Bishop Maxwell. The following inscription round the largest bell, " *Robert Borthwick made me in the Castle of Edinburgh,*" shows that they were cast by the celebrated founder whose cannon are mentioned by the

Scottish historians. This venerable pile fortunately suffered little injury from the rude hands of the reformers; but the ravages of time and of neglect were too apparent on it till of late years. It narrowly escaped demolition from an Earl of Caithness in 1614: but was saved by the spirit of the bishop and the inhabitants. Since the days of Episcopacy, the only funds for its support and repair were derived from a small portion of the voluntary contributions received weekly at the church doors, and the trifling fees exacted on burials; which together seldom exceeded from L.10 to L.20. The rigidly economical application of these by the kirk session, have been sufficient to prevent dilapidation. The increased revenues of the church enabled them to appropriate something even toward beautifying the cathedral, and considerable improvements on it were commenced about 1802; under the superintendence, and directed by the taste of the present senior clergyman, the Rev. Robert Yule; but the munificent bequest of the late Gilbert Meason, Esq. of L.1000, the interest of which is to be applied to the ornament and repair of this noble pile, has already contributed much to its restoration. This fund, under the judicious management of Mr. Yule and the trustees, has already produced the restoration of all the fallen pinnacles, and the reopening of 67 windows, out of the 95 which light the Cathedral.

In this church repose the ashes of several of the Norwegian, and of some of the Scottish earls, and the bones of the patron saint were here enshrined, as well as those of his nephew St. Ronald, the founder. A coffin containing bones, in a rich pall, was discovered about 40 years ago, in an upright position, in one of the piers of the choir. After a hasty examination, they were restored to their original niche; and there is some reason to believe, that they were the remains of the MAID OF NORWAY, who died in Orkney in 1290, on her way to mount the throne of her ancestors.

The ruins of the once strong castle of Kirkwall are reduced to some insignificant vestiges, on the west side of the wide street, in front of the cathedral. It was founded by Henry St. Clair, the first of the Scottish Earls, and a descendant of the Norwegian line. Gilbert Balfour, its governor, shut its gates against the infamous Bothwell. It subsequently was held out by the valiant *bastard* of Orkney, for his father Earl Patrick, against the Earl of Caithness, at the head of a party of the king's forces, aided by artillery, for the space of three weeks; and, when taken, was demolished by order of the privy council.

The bishop's palace appears to have been built and altered at different times. It consisted of several lofty square, and one vast round tower, connected by strong walls, and inclosing some large apartments. The walls of the towers are of enormous thickness. The whole was built of a sort of sandstone flag in thin layers, united by so excellent a cement, that large masses of wall fell unbroken to the earth. The angles and windows were faced with red freestone.

The date of its commencement is uncertain; but it must have been a place of note in the 13th century; for it was the winter quarters of king Hacon of Norway, after his disastrous expedition to Scotland; and in one of its apartments, that monarch expired in 1263. The round tower, which was repaired, or rebuilt, by Bishop Reid, is still pretty entire. Its height to the parapet is $58\frac{1}{2}$ feet: its external circumference below the parapet is 91 feet. Though externally round, it is square within; and such is the solidity of its walls, that the apartments it contains are but 14 feet square. It is a handsome tower, and has in its N.W. wall a stone tablet with an alto relievo of the founder.

The extreme length of the whole palace seems to have been 91 feet, its breadth 27 feet. The hall = 49 feet by 21 feet. The most wanton destruction of a great part of this building has been made within the last 30 years, and, until lately, it was regarded only as a convenient quarry.

The Earl's palace stands on the opposite side of a spacious court. It might have still been habitable, had not a barbarian clothed with temporary authority, in the last century, unroofed the building to sell the materials, and even pulled down a part of its walls to inclose an adjoining field. It is in that style of architecture which prevailed in Scotland about the time of James V. Regularity of design was less studied than variety; yet, the effect of the hanging turrets of considerable size at the angles, the fine masonry of its massy walls, its ornamented doors, and the spacious *mullioned* windows of its great hall, gave it an air of magnificence. It was built by Earl Patrick Stewart, who appears to have united it to the Bishop's palace, so as to form a hollow quadrangle of buildings of different styles, which measures 240 feet by 200 feet; exceeding in magnificence any other habitation of the proudest Scottish noble of that day. This extravagance may have been one cause of the difficulties which precipitated this Earl into the criminal methods of repairing his desperate fortunes that ultimately proved his ruin. The following are the dimensions of what remains: East side, = 89 feet by 26 feet. South side = $53\frac{1}{2}$ feet by 22 feet. Extreme length of the west front, including the breadth of its wings = 101 feet. The great hall 58 feet by 20 feet, was lighted by four large mullioned windows, and warmed by two fire places, one of which is not less than 15 feet wide. The grand entrance is through a curious anteroom, which is gained by a very spacious staircase of three easy flights of steps.

Kirkwall was created into a royal burgh by James III. on his obtaining possession of the islands; and it was honoured by a visit of James V. in one of his useful progresses through his scattered dominions. The government of the burgh is vested in a provost, four baillies, a dean of guild, a treasurer, and fifteen councillors, annually chosen. Kirkwall, in conjunction with Wick, Dornoch, Tain, and Dingwall, sends a representative to the imperial parliament. Besides a parochial school, there is an endowed grammar school, where the classics, mathematics, and the more usual branches, are taught to numerous scholars.

The country parish of St. Ola, or St. Olave, which is united to Kirkwall, contains 1034 persons, and exhibits considerable marks of a spirit of agricultural improvement. No vestige remains of the ancient church of St. Olave. The Antiburgher dissenters have a large place of worship in this parish. The deep ditches, and shapeless mounds of a fort, thrown up by the soldiers of Cromwell, to command the harbour of Kirkwall, are still visible. Several of those subterranean retreats called *Pict's*, or *Pik's houses*, have been here discovered; the most remarkable of which was found at Quanterness, near the borders of Firth, in 1803. It consisted of a central quadrangular chamber $21\frac{1}{2}$ feet long, by six in breadth, which communicated with six smaller apartments of the same shape. They were lined with masonry without mortar—and the roof of the largest apartment was formed by the gradual approximation of the upper layers of the stone work, giving a height to the room of 11½ feet. In one of the smaller chambers, a human skeleton was found lying on its face, but not buried in the earth.

In this parish is a very strong chalybeate spring, in which the iron is suspended by carbonic acid. It issues from a boggy soil about two miles from Kirkwall; and was formerly in some repute, but is now neglected.

Two extensive bays divide the island of Pomona into two unequal parts, connected by an isthmus about two miles in width. The western part comprehends the united parishes of Firth and Stennis, Evie, and Rendal, Birsay and Harray, Sandwick and Stromness, and the single parish of Orphir. This division is more hilly than the eastern. The hills inclose some pretty extensive and fertile valleys, possessing a rich loamy soil; but the principal cultivation here, as in the smaller islands, is along the coast, where an abundant supply of sea weed thrown up by the waves, affords, at little expense, a valuable manure. Much of this district remains in a state of nature, and regular inclosures are scarcely known. It contains several fresh water lakes, or *lochs*, as those of Orphir, Stennis, Skaill, Birsay, and Aikerness, giving rise to considerable streams, abounding with various species of trout; but Orkney, as might be expected, has no river, and the true salmon is rarely caught. The extensive heaths in the western parishes afford shelter to immense numbers of red grous, plovers, and snipes. Neither partridges, nor hares, nor foxes, are found in Orkney; though the white hare was once indigenous in Hoy. That the stag once browsed on these hills is manifest, from the numerous instances of their horns found in the peat bogs. These wastes also bear evidence of their having once been covered with woods of the smaller kinds of trees; and this has been confirmed by the discovery of an ancient submerged wood, of some extent, exposed by a heavy surf at Skaill, on the western side of Pomona. The hills feed a vast number of sheep; a branch of rural economy, till lately extremely ill managed in Orkney. Formerly the sheep of a parish were permitted to run wild among the hilly districts, which are separated from the cultivated land by an insecure wall of turf, forming a general fence to the whole parish. Once a year they were collected to be shorn, and to receive certain marks on their ears or on their nose, a barbarous mode of ascertaining the property of each individual owner in the general flock. Latterly, a better system has been introduced. Merino rams have been imported, and care has been taken to improve the breed of sheep. The commons feed also large herds of swine, of a diminutive and ill favoured breed, which are very destructive when accident permits them to enter the cultivated townships.

The western coasts of Pomona are, in general, very bold, presenting mural cliffs, covered with innumerable sea-fowl, and often hollowed out into caverns, or perforated by natural *arches*. A magnificent instance of the latter occurs near Skaill, and not far from the pavement of *figured stones*, as it has been named, which is conspicuous in the early descriptions, but which modern inquiry has reduced to a very common instance of partial disintegration in a ferruginous sandstone. In fine weather, this lofty arch, which perforates a little promontory, may be safely entered; but when the storm rages, the waves burst through it with surprising fury. Along this western coast, the approach of a storm is usually indicated, several hours before it happens, by a sudden rolling of vast waves from the ocean. Enor-

mous stones are hurled against the rocks; and the raging of the waves against the caverned precipices may be distinctly heard, on such occasions, at the distance of eighteen miles.

The western parts of Pomona contain the scanty remains of the once independent Udallers, or allodial proprietors of Orkney. The usurpations of the Scottish earls, who laboured to introduce feudal tenures, and the injustice of the Scottish government, which transferred to itself the spoliations committed on the people by the earls, and altered the laws which it had solemnly promised to retain inviolate, have reduced the Udallers to a very small number of little proprietors, who chiefly reside in Rendal and Harray. The names of many of these men proclaim their pure Scandinavian descent, though they have now totally lost the *Norse* language, which, about eighty years ago, was the common tongue in Harray.

The parish of Stennis obtains its name from some remarkable antiquities in the vicinity of its large *loch*. The figure of this piece of water is winding. It communicates with the head of the bay of Stromness, or Kairston, by a wide channel, over which the road from Kirkwall to Stromness is carried on a bridge formed of wooden beams, resting on piers of stone. The lake, by much the largest in Orkney, is nearly divided into two by a tongue of land projecting through its centre. The united lengths of both portions of the lake is about ten miles, while its medial breadth is about a mile. Its shores are flat, and tolerably cultivated; but deserve notice here, only on account of the remains of an ancient place of assembly, or temple, second only to the stupendous monument on Salisbury plain, which has so long exercised the ingenuity, and baffled the researches of our antiquaries.

The *Stones of Stennis*, or of Stonehouse, consist of two groups of rude pillars, formed of single stones, placed perpendicularly in the earth. On a slight elevation, on the above-mentioned peninsula, stands the largest of these, arranged in a circle 300 feet in diameter. When entire, it appears to have consisted of thirty-five upright stones, thirteen only of which now retain their erect position. The distances between them seem to have been in some places irregular, and a considerable space on the east side of the circle appears never to have been occupied by any; yet many of them are planted at regular intervals of 17 feet. The tallest of the remaining pillars is 16 feet high, and the lowest is 10 feet; their breadth varies from 2½ feet to 5 feet. The circle is surrounded by a circular ditch; which is still 12 feet deep, and 20 feet broad. The earth of this excavation seems to have been carried away, probably to form four large tumuli at a little distance on the west and east sides of the circle; and may have contributed to the numerous smaller mounds which are scattered around. Whether we are to regard this as a place of assembly, or *Ting*, or as a temple, it must have been a work of great labour, and therefore a place of great consequence in the eyes of the early inhabitants of Orkney. From the extremity of the peninsula, a series of loose stones forms a rude sort of bridge, or foot path, across the narrowest part of the lake. This is also probably of high antiquity, as it forms the communication between the circle and a semicircle of similar construction, which stands close to the eastern side of the lake. The diameter of the latter is 96 feet. Only two of the pillars now remain erect; but the circumference is well marked by a surrounding mound of earth, and the remains of some of the overthrown stones. The pillars of this monument are a little larger than those of the former, measuring 17½ feet in height. A third stone, which was lately pulled down, had two feet only buried in the earth; but it had been firmly wedged by several blocks of stone fixed around its base. This stone measures 18½ feet by 5 feet, and is 22 inches in thickness. In the centre lies a large horizontal slab, which has been conjectured to be the altar for Scandinavian sacrifice; and probably was that which smoked with the blood of the unhappy Halfdan, son of Harold, king of Norway, who was offered up to Odin by the command of Earl Einar I.

At a little distance there were two or three other upright stones, through one of which was a hole, consecrated from time immemorial by a native superstition, which gave an inviolable sanctity to every promise made between those who joined hands through the magic aperture. The plighted vows of love, and the rude contracts of the natives, were, even lately, more firmly sealed by the promise of Odin, as this ceremony was named. The awe with which this vow was regarded, its name, the site, and the worn appearance of the hole, give colour to the local tradition, that this was the pillar to which the victims, about to be offered to the fierce deity of the north, were bound, preparatory to the horrid sacrifice.

The antiquary will learn with much regret, that this venerable relic of antiquity, as well as two of the pillars of the semicircle, were, in 1814, wantonly destroyed by the stupid barbarity of a neighbouring farmer, who, a stranger to the country, and regardless of its antiquities, but vexed at the damage his pastures sustained from the frequent pilgrimages to the stone, shivered it and another in pieces, and employed the materials in the construction of a pig stye. The hand of sacrilege was arrested by the exertions of the late Malcolm Laing, Esq. the historian of Scotland, a native of these islands. The remaining parts of these monuments, especially on the eastern side of the loch, have a venerable appearance from their age, and their shaggy covering of luxuriant tufts of the *Lichen calicaris*. Stennis contains 596 people.

On the confines of the parishes of Stennis and Orphir is Summerdale, the scene of a battle of some note in Orkney history. In this place an Earl of Caithness lost his life; and the adjacent marsh of Bigswell is found to have been the grave of his defeated followers.

STROMNESS.—This is the only place in Orkney besides Kirkwall, which deserves the name of a town. It lies at the foot of a rugged granitic hill, skirting the west side of a beautiful and excellent haven, where ships of considerable size are secure from every blast. The town is very irregular, the houses having been placed without any regard to symmetry, or even general convenience. The streets are badly paved, and are impassable to wheel carriages. The best houses are built on small wharfs, at which vessels of moderate burthen may discharge their cargoes. Stromness has been created by the excellence of its port, which is continually the resort of numerous ships navigating the north seas. By the returns of 1821, the population amounted to 940 males and 1296 females, or to 2236 persons, having more than doubled itself in twenty years. It is still, however, united into one cure with the parish of Sandwick, so that the inhabitants have public worship among them only on every second Sunday. Until the middle of the last century, Stromness was considered as under the control of the magistrates of Kirkwall, who, not exercising their authority meekly, caused the

inhabitants to appeal to the Court of Session; and the decision of that body in their favour was confirmed, in 1758, by the House of Lords. Stromness was erected into a burgh of barony in 1817, and is now under a corporation of two baillies, nine councillors, a town-clerk, a fiscal, and seventy-two burgesses. The spirit of improvement is in full activity in this thriving community, and the establishment of a public library by voluntary subscription affords a good omen of future progress. The approach from Kirkwall affords a picturesque view of Stromness, backed by the magnificent mountain skreen of Hoy, with its stupendous wave-worn cliffs.

A large portion of Sandwick is devoted to open pasturage; yet it is a populous parish, containing, with the part of Stromness not included in the burgh, 1614 persons. The improvements introduced into this parish are chiefly due to Mr. Watt of Skaill, who has successfully introduced the cultivation of flax, and established the first tannery erected in Orkney.

The united parishes of Harray and Birsay are populous; the latter district containing 1526, the former 719 persons. Harray long retained the use of the Norse tongue; but not one individual now speaks a language, which within a century was there the vulgar dialect. Birsay was long a favourite residence of the Norwegian race of earls, whose ancient castle was greatly enlarged by Earl Robert Stewart, a natural son of James V. of Scotland. It still testifies, though in ruins, the pride and magnificence of that prince. This building is a hollow oblong of 158 feet by 100 feet, with a flanker of 20½ feet square at each angle of the main front, to strengthen the entrance. Another square tower of more ancient workmanship is at the north-west angle. The principal gateway is 4½ feet wide and 7 feet high; but it is most remarkable for the Latin inscription, in which, probably by a grammatical error, the founder, arrogates to himself the crown of Scotland: *Dominus Robertus Stuartus filius Jacobi Quinti Rex Scotorum, hoc opus instruxi,*—a circumstance, it is said, which actually urged on the trial of his son as evidence of treasonable intentions. His palace was not a place of strength, but secure against a *coup-de-main*. Its walls are thirty feet high, of two stories, and it had a well in the centre of the court.

The curious stone over the burial-place of the fabulous Orkney prince Belus, is no longer seen in the church-yard of Birsay, as it was in the days of Dr. Wallace.

The parish of Evie is in part well cultivated. Along its shores are numerous examples of those structures called *Pik's houses*. The parish of Rendal is generally hilly; and though the low lands have generally a good soil, they are ill cultivated. The first parish has a population of 811, the latter of 518 persons. A deep bay divides these from the parish of Firth, which is little cultivated, and only contains 545 inhabitants. A range of undulating hills divides this parish from Orphir. The south-west parts of the latter are tolerably cultivated. At Howton, the Scandinavian earls had a strong castle, of which no remains are now to be traced. A fulling mill was formerly wrought in this parish. Its population, including the little island of Cava, = 906 persons.

The eastern division of Pomona contains the fertile parish of Holm, and the united parishes of St. Andrew's and Deerness.

Holm, or *Ham*, is one of the best cultivated tracts in these islands. The culture of flax has here been long known; and the introduction of the linen manufacture has had a favourable effect on its agriculture. Besides a considerable quantity of yarn annually sold, upwards of 20,000 yards of linen have been sent in one year from Holm to the English market. Its population is 773 persons.

St. Andrew's and Deerness.—These parishes, united into one cure, are separated by an extensive bay, which affords good anchorage to vessels, and is often their refuge in storms. St. Andrew's has a considerable extent of cultivation; but the system of agriculture is little to be commended. The present incumbent, Mr. Smellie, has successfully shown the utility of planting an orchard, and that the soil and climate are extremely well adapted to the production of apples and the smaller fruits. The population = 857. Deerness is nearly an island, presenting a bluff headland to the Northern Ocean. One proprietor here, Captain Richan, R. N. has introduced some agricultural improvements. This parish once contained woods of the smaller trees, as is proved by the contents of the peat bogs; and the authority of Ben, who found, in 1683, " a little wood, about two butts in length and one in breadth," principally of low salices. Population = 691 persons. The whole mainland contains 15,062 inhabitants.

South Isles.

Lambholm lies near Holm. It is a small green island, inhabited by only one family, and well adapted to the pasturage of sheep.

Burrey, olim *Borgarey,* is four miles in length by two in breadth. It is flat and fertile, producing much natural clover. A portion is sandy, and breeds innumerable rabbits. The pastures feed the finest cattle in Orkney. Its inhabitants are 245. It is part of the parish of

South Ronaldshey, olim *Rognvalldsey, Ronald's Island,* a contiguous island, better peopled than any other part of Orkney, in proportion to its extent. Its square surface is estimated at eighteen square miles, and its inhabitants 1949. A considerable quantity of grain, beyond the consumption of the island, is raised; and the system of farming is better than usual in Orkney. This island owes much to the excellence of its havens, and its situation near the entrance of the Pentland Firth. St. Margaret's Hope and Widewall are harbours well known to the northern navigator. The furious currents which wash its southern extremity, abound with the finest cod fish; and the people are also engaged in fishing. An opulent English company carry on, in this neighbourhood, an extensive fishery, for the purpose of supplying London with cod and lobsters, which are carried alive to the metropolis in *welled smacks* of about seventy tons burden. South Ronaldshey possesses some antiquities. The How of Hoxa appears to have been a strong hold of some consequence, and is of high antiquity. There are several considerable Pik's houses. On the summit of a hill are three monumental stones, only one of which is now erect; and a single one, sixteen feet high, occurs in another part of the island. It was in this island that St. Olave, of Norway, compelled the Pagan Earl of Orkney and his followers to embrace Christianity, by threats of instant death in case of refusal. To this island the post-office mail, from all parts of Britain, crosses the Pentland Firth four times a week in an open boat; yet with such skill do the natives manage their frail barks, that only one instance of the loss of the mail boat has occurred in about eighty years. This island has a well endowed school, a mu-

nificent donation from Governer Tomason of the Hudson Bay Company's establishment.

Swaney, olim *Swiney, Swine Island,* is a small islet, only remarkable for the perilous eddies which encircle it at particular times of the tide; but which, like Scylla and Charybdis, have lost much of their ancient terrors. This islet, and the next, have a population of thirty-seven persons.

Pentland Skerries are two rocky islets in the eastern jaws of the Firth of that name. On the largest, an excellent light-house has been long erected, and is well kept up.

Flota or *Flotey, Flat Island,* is about three miles long, and one in breadth. It is nearly severed by a good haven, which, from the salt-works once established on its shores, is named Panhope. This isle is fertile; and with the little isle of *Fara,* contains 297 people.

Cava, or *Cavey, Cheese Island,* obtained its name from the excellence of its pastures. Here also were salt-works, until the severity of the revenue laws destroyed this branch of industry. The island supports three families.

Fara and *Rissa* are chiefly dedicated to pasture.

Waas, Kalfey, Calf Island, is celebrated from its most noble haven, Longhope, where the largest fleets might safely ride at anchor. In time of war, it is the usual rendezvous of our north-bound fleets. The island possesses two other good havens, Orehope and Kirkhope. The southern part of *Waas* is flat and well cultivated. The continual resort of shipping to Longhope, and the produce of the cod fishery, have rendered the inhabitants comparatively opulent. The western part is mountainous; affording pasture to vast flocks of sheep, to many horses, and an excellent breed of black cattle. The population, = 949 persons. This island is really joined by a narrow isthmus to

Hoy, Haey, High Island, which consists of a picturesque group of three rugged mountains of grand outline. The central one is the highest land in Orkney; and though estimated at only 1600 feet above the sea, the steepness of its bold front and its general form, give it considerable sublimity. The western mountain appears as it were the half of a hill, severed from its summit to the base by some terrible convulsion, which buried the other portion in the ocean. Here the precipices, the haunts of the eagle, are of the most stupendous grandeur, towering to the height of 800 or 900 feet, and presenting vast detached pillars, insulated amid foaming waves. The valleys of Hoy are narrow and steep, and afford much scope for botanical research. In one of the most gloomy of these, lies a large mass of sandstone, artificially hollowed out into a small circular chamber, with two recesses or beds on the opposite sides. This is the *Dwarfie stone* which is so celebrated in the recent novel, the Pirate. The native tradition ascribes it to the *Trows* or *Drows,* a species of amphibious demons of diminutive stature, but great powers, who occasionally mingle in the affairs of men, are dangerous friends, and not less formidable enemies. The name and size of the excavation sufficiently refute the idea promulgated by some strangers to the country, who have supposed the trows giants. What the purpose of the maker might have been, it is difficult to discover. Its dimensions are too small to have rendered it more than a temporary shelter to human beings. It has however been cut out with some care, and the marks

Orkney
Islands.

of the chisel are very apparent in the beds. The circular chamber is not above seven or eight feet wide; it has a hole in the roof and a square entrance: the bed, with a stone pillow, is five feet eight inches long, and two feet broad ; and the other recess is somewhat larger.

The sandstone, of which these mountains wholly consist, have been explored in the hope of profitable veins of galena; but the quantity found has never repaid the expence of extraction, and the mines have therefore been abandoned.

A strong current sets through the narrow channel, which flows between Hoy and Pomona. When the west wind rages, the conflict between it and the ebb tide produces, in the entrance of this strait, a tremendous sea, that excites very awful sensations of sublimity. The pretty green island,

Græmsey, or *Græme's Island*, lies within the strait. Its length is only 1½ miles, its breadth 1 ; yet it supports 220 inhabitants, who are very expert and adventurous fishermen.

North Isles.

In the bay of Firth lie two small islets, named *Damsey, Daminsey*, or *Dame's Island*. Both are covered with verdant turf, and produce very delicate natural pasture. The largest one was the site of a strong castle, a favourite retreat of some of the Norwegian Earls, of which no vestiges now remain.

Gairsey, Garegsey, Garrick's Isle, is a considerable conical hill, the eastern slope of which is well cultivated, and supports 79 inhabitants.

Weir, olim *Færoe*, or *Isle of Danger*, probably so named from its position in the midst of rapid currents, has a poor soil, and a population of 80 persons, who remedy the sterility of the land by the copious supply of sea-weed afforded by the shores. Near the centre of this island are the ruins of the castle of *Cubbirow*, topping a green knoll. It was a strong hold of an Orkney chief, Kolbeinn Hruga, who was conspicuous in the history of the islands in the twelfth century. What remains show it to have been a massy tower of fifteen feet square, with walls seven feet thick, and defended by ditches and outworks. It was considered in these times a place of great strength, and stood a siege of several months without being taken.

In the strait which divides Rousey from Pomona is *Enhallow*, olim *Eyinhelga, Holy Islet*. It is a pretty verdant islet, with a population of only 11 persons. It was formerly the scene of various miracles, which have long ceased, as well as the antipathy between its soil and rats and mice. If these vermin do not infest it, this exemption is due to the smallness of the isle, and its remote situation; but the supposed virtue of the soil has failed, as might have been anticipated, to rid other places of the nuisance, when carried thither for the purpose.

Rousey, Rolfsey, Rolf's, or *Rollo's Island*, consists principally of lofty but not rugged hills. Some of the valleys are picturesque, and would be fertile, but the principal population is collected near the shores, and much good inland is left in a state of nature. The island supports horses, and black cattle, with immense herds of swine, and many sheep. Its western shores are precipitous, but its eastern, northern, and southern slopes are green and easy of access. Monumental stones, Pik's houses, and tumuli, are not rare. Near the house of Westness are considerable ruins, which probably belonged to the castle of Earl Sigurd II. the hero of Clontarf. Not far off are graves that have been found to contain human bones, arms, and trinkets, which, with the name of Sweindrow, preserve the memory of the slaughter of Earl Paul's faithful attendants, when that unfortunate prince was treacherously seized by Swein, the son of Asleif. Rousey contains 834 inhabitants.

Egilshey, probably derives its name from *Ecclesia*, as here was the first considerable church in these islands, and it was the birth-place of St. Magnus, as well as a favourite abode of the Orkney prelates of later times. It is a flat and very verdant islet, 1½ miles long, and 1 in breadth, surrounded by rapid currents and rocky sloping shores; it is extremely productive of excellent kelp, and a constant supply of shells, and affords a valuable manure. The ancient church of St. Magnus is the only existing specimen of a true Scandinavian church in the British dominions. It has a round tower-like steeple at one end; and though small, had the reputation of high sanctity from the martyrdom of Magnus, once an Earl, and now the tutelar saint of Orkney, having taken place near it. Here his body was first deposited; but his bones were afterwards enshrined at Kirkwall.

Westrey, or *Vesturey, Western Island*, is one of the largest of the northern group. A range of moderately high hills skirt its west side, and terminate in magnificent precipices, the resort of innumerable sea-fowl, which at certain seasons become the prey of the natives, who suspend themselves over the cliffs by small ropes, in order to obtain them. The rest of the island is nearly level, or gently sloping from its centre. The island has generally a rich soil, and much of what is left in a state of nature is capable of improvement; but it labours under the serious disadvantage of a great deficiency of peat for fuel; and this necessary article is, with much risk and labour, carried from the neighbouring island, Edey. It has two havens; one of which affords indifferent anchorage, the other is tolerably safe, though rather open. From the northern part of the island, some boats go to fish cod and ling, with encouraging success. The shores produce abundance of excellent kelp, which has turned the attention of the proprietors too much from agricultural improvement. Much fine land has been overwhelmed by sand-blowing, particularly near Tuquoy and Treneby. This destructive accident, occasioned by the little attention paid to preserve the *arundo arenaria*, and similar plants, has caused some curious discoveries. A vast many graves, which had for ages been deeply buried under hills of sand have been exposed. Several of them were opened by the writer of this article. They are generally constructed of four flags placed on a fifth, so as to form a rectangular chest, and appear to have been covered with a sixth. Most of the graves contained human bones, mingled with fragments of armour, battle-axes, two-handed swords, chains, fibulæ of brass, and often blue glass beads. Occasionally the bones are found in very entire urns of coarse pottery, rudely ornamented on the outside with zig-zag patterns. In one grave were found a glass cup, capable of holding half an English pint, and a piece of polished marble cut into a perfect circle, two inches and a half in diameter. In another, probably a still more ancient grave, was a short sword with a blade of fish bone ; and stone hatchets have been often discovered. The frequency of the sepulchral urns show that the burning of the body was very generally practised. Local traditions have not pre-

served any distinct traces of the origin of these antiquities; but the memory of very fierce contests between the natives and plundering bands of roving West-
Highlanders, is yet preserved by oral chronicles.
The numerous scattered graves in different parts of
this island countenance the idea that they mark fields
of battle; and the care with which some of the obsequies have been performed, are probably memorials of
valiant natives, who fell in the cause of their country.

This island possesses a solitary monumental stone of
considerable height, concerning which tradition is silent.
The castle of Noltland is a spacious structure in the
northern part of Westrey. The main building, of an
irregular form, is 86 feet long by 32 feet in breadth,
and the height to the parapet, which is supported on
corbells of hewn stone, and runs round the main structure, is 46 feet, while the gables rise 18 feet above the
parapets. The eastern part contains two chambers
18 feet square, the lowest of which communicates with a
handsome hall on the first floor, 42 feet by 23 feet. Over
its wide fire place is a tablet, with the defaced armorial
bearing of the Balfours. It communicates by a narrow
staircase with a vast arched hall, 64 feet long by 20½ feet
wide. This seems to have been the great hall, or kitchen, having a wide chimney, 17 feet 10 inches wide,
and an oven, still almost entire. The walls are of very
perfect masonry, seven or eight feet thick; and from
this, and the smallness of the external apertures, it was
evidently intended as a place of no mean strength. A
strong wall on the south incloses a court 63½ feet by
38½ feet. The entrance to the castle is through this
court. The gate is 4½ feet wide and 7 feet high. A
handsome spiral staircase leads to the upper hall, and
36 of its steps, 7 feet 3 inches wide, yet remain entire,
though the building is much dilapidated. We have
no document to show the date of this building. Vulgar tradition assigns it to Gilbert Balfour, master of
the household to Queen Mary and Darnley, who is said
to have built it as a place of refuge for Bothwell; but
the MS. Journal of Ben notices it as " excellentissima
arx sive castellum, sed nondum tamen adhuc completa" in
the year 1529; i. e. in the middle of the reign of
James V. and long before the birth of Mary.

A small cavern in the high cliffs of Rapness, of
dangerous access, was the refuge of several Orkney
gentlemen, who in 1745 espoused the cause of the
house of Stuart. Here they were concealed for several months, while a vigilant search was made for them
through the islands by a party of the king's troops.
They endured much hardship in that interval. Their
food was daily supplied by a faithful female. Their
houses were burnt; but this proved fortunate; for
government afterwards, ashamed of this circumstance,
not only granted indemnity, but gave them better
houses than had been destroyed. The population of
Westrey is 1650 persons.

Papa Westrey, or *Little Westrey*, is a small island
contiguous to the last, of extreme fertility. In summer, its natural meadows are covered with luxuriant
crops of red and white clover. Its length is about
four miles, and its breadth not more than a mile. In
a small loch is the ruins of the little chapel of St.
Tredwell, covering an islet that once was occupied by
a Pik's house. At the distance of two miles from the
north end of this isle, commences a most prolific fishing bank of vast extent, which has only of late attracted the attention of the British public, though long well
known to the inhabitants of this sequestered isle.

North Ronaldsey, *Ronald's Island*, a low and fertile

spot, which is the most northern of the whole group.
Notwithstanding the low state of agricultural practice,
it produces good crops of oats and bear. What is
rare in these islands, the number of males exceeds that
of females; the population return being 213 of the
former to 207 of the latter, in all 420 persons. North
Ronaldshey forms part of the parish of Ladykirk in
Sandey; but in the tempestuous season of the year,
the visits of the pastor are necessarily few. A light-
house of great importance marks this extremity of the
Orkneys. A single monumental stone in the centre of
a plain, is still the resort of the inhabitants on New
Year's day, when they indulge in innocent festivity.
The island contains several tumuli: One of these was
opened a few years ago, and discovered a small building, externally circular, but square within, containing
a human skeleton in an upright posture.

Sandey, Sandy Island, is of a very irregular form,
being deeply indented by the sea. Its length is about
12 miles; but its mean breadth is not more than a
mile and a half. With the exception of a ridge of
about 250 or 300 feet high, at its western side, this isle
is extremely flat. It has a light sandy soil, which is remarkably fertile; and it is much better cultivated than
any other Orkney island. The crops are not so subject to blight from sea-spray, as in those islands with
precipitous shores; and its flat coasts afford a plentiful supply of sea-weed for manure. The farmers here
are of a superior class: and it is not only the granary
of Orkney, but produces about one-fifth of all the
kelp made in this country: but it is totally destitute of
fuel; and the expence of transporting peats from
other islands, reduces many of the poorer inhabitants
to use dried cow-dung and sea-weed as fuel. The
flatness of the land, and the extensive shoals which
line its coasts, have made Sandey the terror of sailors;
but the recent erection of a light-house on the Start
Point, has diminished the number of shipwrecks of
late years. The sea appears here to have encroached
on the land, and high tides threaten to sever it between
Otterwick and Kettletoft. The former bay, a corruption of Odinswick, is traditionally believed to have
been a wooded plain overwhelmed by the sea.

A remarkable isolated mass of granite or gneiss,
about 14 tons in weight, lies on the sandstone flag
formation, near the church of Burness. It probably
was transported by some such accident as removed
the ancient land-mark near Castle Stewart, in Inverness-shire.

The antiquities of Sandey consist in one or two
ruined chapels, and some considerable Pik's houses.
The population in the three parishes of this island, =
1860 persons.

Edey, or *Eidey*, the isle of solitude, is, generally
speaking, hilly and little cultivated, except towards
the eastern side, which is flat and fertile. Calf Sound
is a commodious haven, and near it is Carrick, a village, erected into a burgh of barony, during the time
of its founder Lord Carrick, a son of Earl Robert
Stewart. Salt was there manufactured in considerable quantity; and this art lingered among the inhabitants until of late years. The inhabitants of Edey
are expert fishermen; a considerable quantity of fish
oil is here prepared; and many lobsters are caught
on its coasts. It was in this island that the pirate
Gow was seized by a spirited proprietor M'Fea, who
was almost ruined by this act, which ought to have secured a national reward. The population of Edey,
including the next island, = 643 persons; yet it makes a

Orkney
Islands.

part of the parish of Stronsey, an extremely injudicious allotment, which deprives it of the due attention of a clergyman during the severe season of the year.

Fairey, or *Fridarey*, *Isle of Reconciliation*, lies close to Edey, is fertile, but of trifling extent.

Stronsey, *Strionsey*, or *Strunsey*, *Deceitful Island*, may have been named from its appearing at a little distance like three detached isles, and from the violent currents which surround it. This island is flat; and though much remains in a state of nature, agriculture has made considerable improvement, which will probably be aided by Mr. Neill's discovery of a bed of limestone, a substance rarely found in Orkney. This lies in the sandstone formation, between Odness and Kirbuster. Agriculture might also avail itself of a large bed of shell sand, accumulated near Odness by the waves. The antiquities of this island are some Pik's houses; and a building at Lamb Head has very massy circular walls, containing small chambers within the thickness of the rude masonry. Tumuli occur here as elsewhere. Two promontories, Odness and Torness, are certainly named in honour of the northern deities, Odin and Thor. A small creek also bears the name of Gio-Odin, where the *Fucus palmatus* is supposed to have sanative qualities to those who eat it.

Papa Stronsey, or *Little Stronsey*, is a green and fertile islet, which lies near the former, and is occupied by a farmer, who resides there with his people. Though it has not a circumference of three miles, yet such was the care of souls in Popish times, that it had two chapels; while at present this, and the three parishes of the larger island, are united with Edey in one cure. The Stronseys have a population of 1013 persons.

Shapinshey, olim *Skipensy*, or *Ship Island*, is about seven miles long and five in breadth; but its coasts are indented with bays and creeks. A large portion of this island is in a state of nature, and much of it is ill cultivated; but the southern part of it, under a judicious proprietor, has assumed an appearance of cultivation and order, that surpasses any thing in Orkney. A better husbandry, rotation of crops, a superior breed of cattle, and regular inclosures, mark improvements introduced by the late Colonel Balfour, and continued under his son. The stimulus given to the industry of the island by their residence, created a village on the excellent haven of Ellwick, which is sheltered by the green islet, Ellerholm, from the east wind. The Rev. Dr. Barry, historian of Orkney, was clergyman of this parish. The shores of Shapinshey abound with Pik's houses, which appear to have been exploratory edifices. There is one upright monumental stone in the island, numerous tumuli, and a mass of stone, lying on the shore opposite to Stronsey, which still is named the black stone of Odin, and is said to mark the place of his descent on Shapinshey. A bed of limestone occurs near How, which has long been worked with advantage. The population =779 persons.

Copinshey, olim *Kiolbenshey*, or *Kolben's Island*, is the last of the group which we shall describe. It presents lofty rugged cliffs to the eastern ocean, and rapidly slopes towards the mainland. It is the residence of two families, who raise some grain with advantage; but it is chiefly used as pasturage. Near this island an aerolite descended about 1676, and fell into a fishing boat, to the great terror and danger of the people. This meteor seems to have occurred not far from the spot where the extraordinary hail storm of 1819, which is described by Mr. Neill, appeared to commence.

SECT. II. *Natural History.*

Geology. The mineral history of Orkney is singularly monotonous and uninteresting; the whole islands, with slight exception, consisting of horizontal, or slightly inclined strata of sandstone, flag, and a species of slaty-clay, occasionally intermixed with thick beds of red and grey sandstone, and in a few places, containing beds of limestone, with some traces of marine remains.

The chief exception to this structure occurs in the vicinity of Stromness; where a small-grained granite, with gneiss, and mica-slate, containing hornblende rock, form a small district of two or three miles in extent. These rocks constitute the rugged hill above Stromness, and may be traced to the mill of Kairston, where they are seen dipping under a breccia composed of fragments of the same rocks; and farther to the west, they are covered by indurated shale, which is distinctly stratified, and nearly horizontal. This shale in some places has the appearance of a coarse *greywacke-slate*, and is little disposed to split into thin layers. At no great distance from the granite formation, the shale is traversed by veins of sulphate of barytes, mixed with calc-spar and detached masses of sulphuret of lead. In one of these veins, Dr. Traill discovered a compound of carbonate of strontia, and sulphate of barytes, which is so perfectly homogeneous, even when examined by a lens, that he considered it as a mineral species, and gave it the name of *Stromnite*. In that neighbourhood, some attempts have been made to open mines; but the quantity of galena obtained, did not offer a sufficient inducement to continue the excavations. Similar attempts were made in South Ronaldshey, in Hoy, and Shapinshey, with similar results. Sandstone of a red colour occurs in thick beds in the island of Edey, on the west side of Inganess bay, in Pomona, and on the south side of Hoy. Sandstone occurs in other places of all intermediate shades between yellow and grey. Occasionally it becomes so hard, as to form tolerable millstones, with which Orkney is chiefly supplied from the vicinity of Skaill, on the south-west coast of Pomona. The sandstone flag often readily splits into such layers, as to render it very suitable for building. This rock and indurated shale constitute by far the greatest part of Orkney; and being often readily acted on by the elements and the ocean, give an air of ruin to many of the lofty precipices which gird the coasts. These rocks are often indurated, and when lime cement is employed, form very durable edifices. Limestone is rare in Orkney. A bed of it in Shapinshey, another in Stronsey, and one of fetid limestone at Yesnaby, in Pomona, are all that are at present known in these islands; forming beds in the sandstone-flag. The occurrence of trap rocks is also uncommon. At Yesnaby, basalt occurs in the form of veins traversing the sandstone flag, and often containing large crystals of hornblende. A bed of basaltic rock occurs also in Shapinshey. A hard sort of wacke is found in the eastern part of Waas, and the same substance has been observed in Copinshey.

In the little islet Ruskholm, slate is found so impregnated with bitumen, as to afford some heat when mixed with other fuel; and something of the same sort occurs in Waas.

Hoy, though the highest point of Orkney, consists wholly of sandstone, and sandstone flag. A few veins in the latter afford scattered masses of galena, and in one place some rich iron hæmatite. Bog iron ore is not uncommon on the hills, in some parts of Orkney,

B

and sulphuret of iron is often disseminated in the sandstone; but no trace of copper has been hitherto detected in Orkney.

Botany. Dr. Barry's history contains a considerable Flora Orcadensis, chiefly compiled from the manuscript notes of the Rev. George Low, a zealous naturalist, who was pastor of Birsay, where he died in 1795. Dr. Barry's catalogue contains 312 species of indigenous plants. We are indebted to Mr. Neill for a correction of this list, from which six species are to be rejected as erroneous, and also for an addition of no less than 156 species; so that the Flora Orcadensis now contains 462 plants; to which an able botanist with sufficient leisure, might probably add many more.

Zoology. The zoology of Orkney has been very ably treated in the *Fauna Orcadensis* of Low, a work which shows the author to have been an able and diligent observer of nature. A short notice of it has been given by Dr. Barry. Mr. Low's industry has left little to be added to the classes mammalia, aves, and pisces; but no author has given us any account of the lower animals which inhabit the Orkney islands. We shall endeavour briefly to supply these defects, from such materials as are within our reach; premising that the writer of this article has paid little attention to insects, and has not been in Orkney for many years.

MAMMALIA.—*Phoca barbata* has been often shot in Orkney, and probably also *Phoca hispida. Cervus tarandus,* rein deer, was introduced, and seemed to thrive in Orkney, notwithstanding the dampness of the climate; but it was found to be an inconvenient addition to a country little inclosed, and the whole have been shot. To the cetacea, we have to add *Balæna rostrata,* caught in Scapa bay; and *Delphinus deductor,* or *D. melas,* both figured in Scoresby's Arctic Regions. This last species is very numerous in the Orkney seas, and probably is the *bottle-nose whale* of Low. Perhaps we ought to add the *Monodon monoceros,* and *Delphinus leucas,* to the list of Orkney cetacea, as they certainly have been seen in the neighbouring seas.

AVES.—*Strix nyctea,* the snowy owl, and *Picus major,* the greater spotted wood-pecker, are occasional visitors. *Scolopax gallinula,* the jack snipe, is found in Westrey. *Scopopox Phæopus,* the whimbrel, is not rare; *S. glottis,* the green shank, rare; *Tringa lobata,* the grey phalarope, not rare; *Rallus chloropus,* the water hen, and *Fulica atra,* the coot, are found in several lakes. *Alca pica,* the black-billed auk, very common. *Procellaria glacialis,* the fulmar, and *Mergus serrator,* the red breasted goosander, are often found. *Anas ferina,* the pochard, and *Anas glacialis,* long tailed duck, are common birds.

PISCES.—Order *Cartilagini; Chimera borealis,* the northern chimæra, is rare. *Squalis canicula,* the panther shark, very common. *Syngnathus hippocampus,* seahorse pipe-fish, is occasionally found dead on the shores. To this order must be referred that extraordinary animal which was cast on the beach of Stronsay in 1808. From the evidence of respectable persons, some of them personally known to the writer of this article, it measured 55 feet, though a part of the tail was broken off. Sir E. Home imagined it to be a basking shark; but its enormous length, its attenuated form, and, still more, an inspection of the skull and vertebræ, preserved in the Museum of the University of Edinburgh, show that it is totally different from any species of animal described by modern naturalists. The sea-snake of Pontoppidan has probably had such a prototype; and the singular animal seen since near Coll, and also

the American sea-snake, belong in all probability to this new species. An Orkney gentleman assured the late Dr. Barry, that he had once observed a slender whitish animal, many fathoms in length, passing, with a slow motion, beneath his boat, while fishing off Sandey.

INSECTA.—There are a considerable number of *coleopterous* insects in Orkney. The *Hemiptera* are not so numerous. Of these, the *Cimex lectularius* was, till lately, unknown, and is said to be confined to Kirkwall. Different species of *Aphides* are not uncommon. Of *Lepidoptera,* the genus *Papilio* is not numerous; but there are many *Phalænæ.* Of the *Neuroptera,* the most common are Ephemera vulgata, E. horaria, and Hemerobius perla. Of *Hymenoptera,* there are several species of Ichneumon, especially I. glomeratus; two species of Vespa; Apis terrestris, and Apis muscorum, are common. Of *Diptera,* there are some Œstri, and many Tipulæ, especially T. oleracea. The Muscæ are numerous, especially M. domestica, M. carnaria, M. vomitoria, M. scybalaria, M. stercoraria. The Tabanus bovinus, T. pluvialis, Culex pipiens, and Culex pulicans, are troublesome. Of *Aptera,* we may mention Podura aquatica, Pediculus humanus, P. pubis, and a great variety of Pediculi on many birds. Pulex irritans, common.—*Articulata : Arachnides.* Acarus siro, A. reduvius, A. ricinus, A. littoralis, A. coleopteatorum, A. passerinus; Aranea of several species. Phalangium. Oniscus; O. asilus, O. entomon, O. marinus, O. oceanicus, O. armadillo, Scolopendra forficata.

CRUSTACEA.—The following have been observed: Cancer pisum, C. minutus, C. latipes, C. mænas, C. depurator, C. pagurus, C. platycheles, C. araneus, C. maja, C. bernhardus, C. squilla, C. crangon, C. Norvegicus, C. pulex, C. locusta.—*Monoculus.* M. quadricornis, M. conchaceus. Both these last are given on Mr. Low's authority, from a MS. work on microscopic investigations, full of beautiful drawings by that ingenious author, among which there is a drawing of another, which probably is non-descript.

VERMES.—*Intestina.* Ascaris vermicularis, A. lumbricoides, besides several in the lower animals. *Fasciola,* several species. *Taeina solium* is not rare in those who have lived in Hudson's Bay; and others exist in different animals, especially in dogs.—*Gordius.* G. aquaticus, G. marinus, in the muscle of ling and cod. —*Lumbricus.* L. terrestris, L. marinus.—*Planaria.* P. viridis?—Hirudo-sanguisuga. The medicinal one is not indigenous in Orkney.—*Mollusca.* Limax. L. ater, L. cinereus, L. agrestis.—Doris. D. papillosa?—Aphrodita. A. acculeata?—Amphitrite. A. auricoma. —Nereis. N. noctiluca, a minute red species described in Low's MS.; perhaps it is the N. rufa of Pennant.— Ascidia. A. rustica, A. mentula, A. conchilega.—Actinia. A. rufa, A. crassicornis.—Lernæa spectoralis. —Sepia. S. loligo, S. media.—Medusa. M. simplex, M. æquorea, M. purpurea, M. undulata. M. hæmispherica.—Beroe. B. fulgens, B. ovata.—Asterias. A. glacialis, A. rubens, A. aculeata, A. caput medusæ.— Echinus. E. esculentus, E. cidaris, E. placenta, E. lacunosus?—*Testacea.* Lepas. L. balanus, L. balanoides, L. anatifera, on wrecked timber, L. fascicularis? of Fleming.—Pholas teredo, in drift wood.—Mya. M. truncata, M. arenaria.—Solen. S. vagina, S. siliqua, S. ensis.—Tellina Ferroensis, T. crassa, T. vitrea, T. compressa.—Cardium. C. edule, C. aculeatum, C. echinatum.—Mactra. M. solida, M. stultorum, Arca, Glycymeris, *Neill.*—Venus. V. Islandica, V. verucosa, V. rugosa vel striatula.—Pecten. P. maximus, P. opercularis, P. obsoletus.—Ostrea sinuosa, (found in

Stroma, *Wallace*.) O. edulis.—Mytilus. M. edulis, M. modiolus, M. pellucidus, M. rugosus.—Pinna ingens, dredged from the depth of thirty or forty fathoms. —Cypræa pediculus vel arctica.—Bulla?—Buccinum. B. undatum, B. lapillus, B. minutum.—Murex erinaceus, M. antiquus, M. turricula? M. costatus? M. rufus.—Trochus. T. zizyphinus, T. umbilicatus.—Turbo. T. littoreus, T. clathrus, T. terebra, T. ulvæ?— Helix. H. albella vel ericitorum, H. lapicida.—Nerita. N. glaucina, N. littoralis.—Patella. P. vulgata, P. pellucida, P. lævis?—Serpula. S. spirorbis, S. intricata, S. contortuplicata. Teredo navalis, in wrecked timber.—Sabella. S. rudis, S. alocolata.

ZOOPHYTA.—Milleporà. M. compressa, M. truncata, M. cellulosa, M. polymorpha.—Isis. I. heppuris.—Gorgonia. G. lepadifera.—Tubipora. T. catenularia, T. serpens, T. fascicularis.—Spongia. S. ventilabrum, S. infundibileformis, S. tomentosa, S. palmata, S. compressa.—Alcyonium. A. digitatum, A. cydonium, A. gelatinosum.—Flustra. F. foliacea, F. truncata, F. pilosa, F. hispida, F. membranacea, F. lineata.—Tubularia. T. indivisa.—Corallina officinalis, C. cristata. Pennatula; P. mirabilis.

SECT. III.—*History of the Islands.*

THE earliest inhabitants of these islands appear to have been Picts, or Piks, a tribe originally Scandinavian, who, at an unknown period before the Christian æra, established themselves in the northern and western parts of Scotland. Diodorus Siculus mentions Cape *Orcas* as one of the extremities of Britain; and the *Orcades* are first named in the second century by Pomponius Mela, who states their number at thirty. Pliny augments them to forty; but Ptolemy makes them thirty: differences which are easily reconciled, by supposing that the Roman naturalist included all the considerable islands, while the other writers attended only to those inhabited. Tacitus asserts that the Orcades were discovered and subdued by Agricola— which implies that they were then inhabited; yet Solinus, at a subsequent period, says of them, " *vacant homines;*" but little reliance on this subject can be placed in an author who states their number at *three.*

The origin of the name is undoubtedly Teutonic, and is probably derived from ORKN, a large marine animal, and has been applied both to whales and seals; ORKNEY, therefore, means, *Land of Whales or of Seals.*

The Orcades seem to have been esteemed of considerable importance in the time of Constantine, as they are especially mentioned with Gaul and Britain as the patrimony of his youngest son. Little is known of the Orcades from that time until the convulsions in Norway, which ended in the elevation of Harold the Fair Haired to the undivided sovereignty of that country. The discontented chiefs sought for new settlements in the Orkneys, in the Hebudæ, and even in Iceland, whence they issued in piratical fleets to harrass and plunder the coasts of his kingdom. Harold pursued them, and added the Western Isles and Orkney to his dominions; and the management of the latter was intrusted to Rognvalld, or Ronald, Count of Merca, the father of Rolf or Rollo, the successful invader of Normandy, and the great great grandfather of William the Conqueror. From this distinguished family spring the ancient Scandinavian jarls (earls) of Orkney,—a race of hardy and intrepid *reguli*, who affected, and generally maintained, the character of independent princes. The habits of the dark ages rendered plundering excursions, and the warfare of petty

chiefs, honourable pursuits. The earls of Orkney subdued, and for a long period maintained possession of Caithness and Sutherland, and made their power to be felt in Rosshire, Moray, and various parts of the western coasts of Scotland. There are several instances of their descents on Ireland; and the fall of Sigurd II. in the battle of Clontarf, near Dublin, is celebrated in a wild ode, which has been translated by Gray under the title of *The Fatal Sisters.* In the Norwegian expeditions against England and Scotland the earls occasionally bore a share; and their followers formed part of those predatory hosts, who were confounded under the general name of Danes, and recognized as the scourges of Britain. That these earls were potent, is obvious from their intermarriages, not only with the daughters of the petty kings of Ireland, but with the royal families of Norway and Scotland. Their hosts in all probability were not wholly derived from their hereditary dominions; but when a *sea king* planned an expedition, he was probably joined by many independent adventurers, allured by the prospect of war and plunder. The dependence of Orkney on the crown of Norway appears in general to have been little more than nominal, unless when the reigning monarch came to claim the allegiance of the earls; but a short time before the cession to Scotland, the Orkney earls had regular investiture from the king of Norway. The early history of Orkney is detailed at length in the *Orkneyinga Saga,* and in Torfæus. The *Orcades* of the latter were compiled by him from the ancient Sagas, and such documents as the Danish records could furnish. In this, as in other works, he sustains the character of a faithful historian; and the facts which he details are probably as authentic as the early records of any portion of the British empire, while he has enabled us to correct several errors in the commonly received account of the affairs of Scotland. We must refer the reader to the original work, or to the abridgment of it in Dr. Barry's history, where the succession of the Scandinavian earls of Orkney is carried down from A.D. 920 to about 1325, when the direct line failed, and the earldom passed to a collateral branch in Malis, earl of Strathearne, and afterward into the family of St. Clair, about 1379. In the year 1468, Orkney and Zetland were impignorated to James III. of Scotland, as a portion of the dowry of his Danish queen. The sum for which Orkney was pledged was 60,000 florins, and it was redeemable on the repayment of that sum. The islands, however, were formally annexed to the crown of Scotland by that monarch; and the earldom having been purchased from the St. Clair family by the government, the crown lands were at first leased by, and afterwards conferred upon, court favourites. This departure from the wise resolution of James III. has been the source of many grievances to Orkney and Zetland. Queen Mary alienated them in favour of her natural brother, Lord Robert Stewart; and though the grant was several times recalled, he was at length invested with the earldom of Orkney and all the crown lands. He exchanged his temporalities as abbot of Holyrood with the bishop of Orkney; and having obtained the right of summoning and adjourning the Great Fowde Court, he became most absolute master of the country. This more than regal power was grossly abused. Most of the lands in Orkney were held by *udal*, or allodial tenure. Udal lands were free of all taxes to the crown, and the udaller acknowledged not himself the vassal of any lord superior. Udal possessions could not be alienated, except by what was called a *shynde bill*, obtained with the consent of all heirs, in the Fowde Court. They were equally divided, at the death of the possessor, among all his children, and no fine was levied on the entry of heirs. It was the great object of the earls of the Stewart family to destroy this system, and introduce feudal tenures into Orkney. The courts of justice were perverted by the introduction of the earl's creatures; the refractory udallers were overawed and silenced by a licentious soldiery retained by the earl; and the possession of the temporalities of the bishopric, afforded a pretext for exacting fines from those landholders who fell under church censure. By these means much landed property fell into the hands of the earl, and of his son and successor Patrick Stewart; and many of the proprietors were terrified into acknowledging themselves the vassals, and taking out charters of the earls. The rents of the earldom were chiefly paid in kind; and, under those two earls, the weights used in the country were twice arbitrarily altered in value. The *mark* was originally 8 ounces, and the *lispund* 24 marks, or 12 lbs. Robert raised the mark to 12 oz. and consequently the lispund to 15 lbs. and Patrick still farther increased them respectively to 12 oz. and 18 lbs. Multiplied oppressions of the inhabitants produced such representations to the throne, that earl Robert was recalled; and earl Patrick suffered a long imprisonment, which only ended in his death. The crimes of this unfortunate man were probably exaggerated by his enemies at court; and there can now be little doubt, that however great his injustice to the people of Orkney had been, his execution at Edinburgh, in 1612, was a foul judicial murder, instigated by those who longed to possess his inheritance. There seems, however, little foundation for the surmise that has been drawn in his favour, from the circumstance of 500 persons aiding his son the bastard of Orkney, to support the claims of his imprisoned father. These probably were the military retainers of the family, who would anxiously seek every opportunity of regaining lost consequence.

The injustice to the islands, however, was not confined to the earls. The lands were not immediately declared to be forfeited on the attainder of the earl, under the pretext that it might injure those who had taken charters from him. This suggestion alarmed the Orkney proprietors into the wished-for measure of taking out charters from the crown in the usual feudal form. This completed the ruin of the udal tenures; and the country learnt with grief and astonishment, that on the annexation of the Orkneys to the crown " for ever," the rental of earl Patrick was declared to be the rule for the future; and no surrender was made of lands that had been unlawfully seized by the last earls.

The revenues of the crown were for some time managed by commissioners who oppressed the people. In 1643, Charles I. granted them to Lord Morton; but they were redeemable on the liquidation of an alleged debt of £30,000. His son mortgaged them to assist Charles, and they were confiscated by Cromwell. Charles II. again granted the islands to the Morton family, and, under the arbitrary control of Lord Morton's chamberlain, Douglas of Spynie, the Fowde Court was totally abolished; but, in 1669, Orkney and Shetland were again " for ever" annexed by act of parliament to the domains of the crown. In 1707, Queen Anne once more alienated them, with a reserved rent of £500 a year, to James, earl of Morton, who was created admiral, and hereditary steward and justiciary over them. At that time the crown revenues were

computed at £3000 Sterling per annum; yet Lord Morton, in 1742, had sufficient influence to get an act of parliament, declaring them his property irredeemably, on the pretext that the rents did not equal the interest of the alleged mortgage. Within five years he received £7500, as a compensation for his hereditary jurisdiction; and, in 1776, he sold the estate to Sir Lawrence Dundas for £60,000. Before this last transaction, the Orkney proprietors made a judicial attempt to have their grievances redressed, as far as related to the increase of weights; but, after a long lawsuit, they failed in their object. Soon after the last sale, Sir Lawrence Dundas conceiving himself entitled to powers considerably beyond those exercised by Lord Morton, instituted an expensive lawsuit, in which he was finally defeated. The islands have since remained in the family of his descendant, Lord Dundas, between whom and the Orkney proprietors several important legal questions are now at issue.

Sect. IV.—*Present State.*

Political State.—Orkney and Zetland form one stewartry or county, and one member of parliament is understood to represent both; but by a strange anomaly, the member is solely returned by the freeholders of Orkney; and the proprietors of Zetland are excluded from all exercise of the elective franchise. The cause of this loss of rights is usually stated to be the want of any valuation of the lands in Zetland, by which the qualification of a freeholder could be ascertained. The valuation of Orkney is by no means very correct; and the mode of apportioning the public burdens between the two parts of the county is extremely imperfect. In all assessments of public burdens, the cess of Zetland has been usually taken at one-half that of Orkney; or the former has paid one-third, the latter two-thirds, of the whole impost. This practice was adopted, on account of the want of a valuation of lands in Zetland. For a long period no attempts were made by the proprietors of that part of the county to obtain a share in the elective franchise; but latterly they have been inclined to seek parliamentary redress. The long period during which their right has been dormant, may be an obstacle in the way; but the confessedly defective state of the Orkney valuation seems to call loudly for inquiry and redress. The original valuation-book of Orkney has been either lost or purloined; and the recent attempts to supply the defect, have not been founded on correct principles. The representative system of these islands claims an early attention from the legislature; and it will probably be found necessary to authorize a new valuation of the whole county, as the basis of a better system, which shall afford to the proprietors of both its divisions a just share in returning a member to parliament, and correcting some glaring abuses which have crept into the freehold qualifications of Orkney.

Population.—By the census in 1821, Orkney contains, males 12,469, females 14,710, or 27,179 inhabitants, which are included in 5746 families. Of these there are

Families engaged in agriculture, including kelp-making, 3152
Families engaged in traffic, . . . 1274
Families which fall not under any of these denominations, 1320

The population is thus distributed in the islands.

	Males.	Females.	Inhabitants.	Houses.
Pomona contains	6670	8392	Total 15,062,	2759
South Isles . . .	1854	2141	 3995	737
North Isles . . .	3945	4177	 8122	1435

Agriculture.—The defects in the system of Orkney farming, pointed out by Dr. Barry, still remain too visible; and probably the estimate he made twenty years ago, of the proportion between the cultivated and waste land, is not yet very far from the truth. The whole islands have been estimated at 150,000 square acres, of which about

90,000 are uncultivated commons.
30,000 are *infield* pastures and meadow.
24,000 land in tillage.
4,000 covered by fresh-water lakes.
2,000 occupied by buildings and gardens.

The quantity of the first denomination is probably diminished; because extensive commons have been inclosed and subdivided, but these have in general not added much to the quantity of the land in tillage.

It is true, that since the publication of Dr. Barry's history, very considerable improvements have been made, especially by the spirited exertions of some enterprising proprietors and farmers in the vicinity of Kirkwall, and in a few of the islands: but these laudable examples of agricultural skill have not been so generally followed as might have been expected. The rude one-stilted plough has indeed almost wholly disappeared, and the other implements of husbandry have been considerably improved; but much of the land under cultivation is not regularly fenced, nor divided into separate fields. The lands of a whole township are frequently protected from the depredations of sheep and swine, only by a rude wall, usually of turf, which divides the township from the commons, and forms a general fence for the whole. In many places, the lands of different farmers, or even of different proprietors, are cultivated and reaped in common, or in alternate ridges. Very little attention is bestowed on manuring the soil, or on introducing a rotation of crops; the rearing of artificial grasses, and raising of turnips for cattle, are not generally followed, and the making of hay is not well understood. The spirit of improvement is however abroad in these islands. Some large commons have been divided, and regular inclosures are becoming more frequent. The example of a few resident proprietors and enterprising farmers has shown the advantage of turnip husbandry, of the cultivation of artificial grasses, and of a proper rotation of crops; and they are slowly followed by the smaller farmers. The general use of the two-stilted plough, drawn by two horses *abreast*, without a driver, might shame the slovenly agriculture of the west of England. Even a few thrashing-mills have been erected in Orkney. A great source of improvement would be the encouragement, by the resident gentlemen, of cottage gardens, and superior neatness in their habitations among the poorer farmers and cottagers.

The grain almost exclusively cultivated in Orkney, is of two kinds; oats and *bear*, an inferior sort of barley. The oat chiefly cultivated is *Avena strigosa*, which is thought less liable than any other species to be shaken by the furious gales, which too often attend an Orkney autumn. The frequent occurrence of gales at that season, the danger of blights from the spray of the sea, and the general humidity of the climate, render Orkney less favourable for the cultivation of grain than for the rearing of black cattle and sheep, for which the peculiar mildness of the winter, in a country where frost is rarely of three or four days continuance, is extremely well adapted. This advantageous branch of rural economy would probably have become general in Orkney, but for the peculiar tenure on which the lands are now held. Most

of the proprietors in Orkney hold their estates, subject to most enormous *feu-duties, payable in kind to the lord superior.* In many cases, these are so extravagantly high, that the lands would long ago have fallen into the hands of the superior, but for the fortunate discovery of the value of the kelp produced on the shores. In many places this forms the sole value of an Orkney estate to the proprietor; the feu-duty swallowing up all the rest. The payment of such duties *in kind*, is a manifest injury to agriculture, by encouraging the production of an inferior grain. If the farmers neglect to raise as much as will maintain their servants, and liquidate the claims of the lord superior, the county price of grain is enhanced, and they must make good the deficiency by payment of the price thus artificially raised. It is therefore the interest of the farmer to devote a large portion of his agricultural adventure to raising a quantity of inferior grain, and thus his means are diverted from the adoption of what would be most expedient for the climate and situation.

The union of the farmer and kelp-maker has also been unfavourable to agriculture. As this species of manufacture is uniformly carried on in Orkney by the tenants, for the benefit of the proprietor, who, in granting land, stipulates in the lease or verbal agreement, to pay the tenant a certain price per ton for the kelp produced on the shores of his estate; and as this substance is the immediate product of living vegetables, it may be considered under this head with almost as much propriety as hay-making or the preparation of flax.

Kelp is produced by the incineration of different fuci. Those chiefly employed for this purpose, in Orkney, are F. digitatus, F. vesiculosus, F. serratus, F. nodosus. The last usually grows on the rocks, which lie nearest *high water-mark*, while the first grows on rocks that are only uncovered at the lowest ebbs. These plants are cut with sickles, attached to long handles, and are either carried up immediately on hand-barrows, or are floated up in rope-nets, prepared for the purpose. The fuci are spread out in favourable weather to dry, and are then burnt in circular pits, which are usually about ten inches deep, and four or five feet in diameter. A small peat fire is kindled in the pit, and the half dried fuci are added by degrees; fuel soon becomes unnecessary, as the fuci themselves are sufficient to support the requisite degree of heat, and the fire is kept up until the ashes are sufficient to fill the pit: the fire is then permitted to subside, and the semi-fluid ashes are well stirred with iron rakes, and left to cool; after which the cake of kelp is broken into three or four pieces, and deposited in a storehouse until a sufficient quantity to send to market is burnt. Should much rain fall during the drying of the fuci, they lose their salt taste, and become so poor in alkali, as to be of little value. This would incline us to believe that the alkali is formed by the decomposition of the muriate of soda in the pores of the plant during the time it is incinerated. A kelp pit usually contains about 6 cwt. or $\frac{1}{4}$ ton of kelp. The average quantity of this article produced in Orkney, for many years, has been about 2700 marketable tons, which, during the late war, might average £9 per ton, after deducting the cost of sending it to market at Dumbarton or Newcastle; and hence this manufacture brought into the country about £24,000 a-year. The proprietors pay to the kelp burners from £1. 15s. to £3 per ton, according to the nature of the shores where it is made. The average may be stated about £2 per ton, with certain allowances of meal, &c.; so that the labourers received about £5400 a-year from that source, for about six weeks work in the height of summer. The number of persons actually engaged in kelp-making, perhaps does not exceed 2500; but as almost all the agricultural population are more or less interested in kelp, we cannot state the number of those connected with this important manufacture, at less than 13,000 persons in Orkney alone.

Besides these products of an Orkney estate, we must mention the cultivation of flax, which for seventy years has been raised in some quantity in the parish of Holm, and has been more recently introduced in a few other places.

Manufactures.—Kelp has been already noticed as the staple article of Orkney.

The *spinning of flax*, and the *linen manufacture*, afford employment to numerous individuals. Some years ago the export of linen yarn amounted annually to 100,000 spindles; besides which, 50,000 yards of excellent linen were woven in Orkney, as appears by the stamp-books. This was partly from native flax, but chiefly from what was imported.

Straw plaiting was introduced in Orkney about twenty years ago; and for several years it gave partial employment to between 6 and 7000 persons, chiefly young females; and was computed to bring into the country £20,000 per annum. But the caprice of fashion in the southern part of Britain has reduced the number of people employed to 3000, and their annual gains to £2000. The fluctuating demand for this article is a serious objection to the encouragement of the manufacture, even if by congregating a large number of young and thoughtless individuals, it had not been prejudicial to their morals. It certainly produced in these islands a laxity of morals and decorum till then fortunately rare. No such objections lie against the extension of the linen manufacture, which may advantageously be carried on in the bosom of a private family; and it thus avoids the contamination incident to large assemblages of manufacturers.

Woollen manufactures of the coarser kinds were once of some extent; but at present there is nothing in these islands that deserves the name.

There are two licensed distilleries in Kirkwall, and one in Stromness; besides a few public breweries on a small scale.

Trade.—There are 46 registered vessels belonging to Orkney; and measuring 2841 tons, and employing about 300 seamen. A single ship of 279 tons register goes annually to Greenland, with a crew of 50 men. The success has not been very encouraging. She has averaged since 1814 about 100 tons of blubber, and 3½ tons of whalebone, annually. The visits of the Scotch and English whale-ships were once a source of wealth to the country. From 50 to 60 of these vessels annually touched at Stromness; and about 50 of them received 12 additional men to their crews. The wages of these men averaged about £20 for the voyage; and brought into the country £12,000; but the trade has been gradually declining. In 1822, fifty whalers touched at Orkney; of these 24 shipped 12 men each, whose average wages amount to £9 per man, or will produce £2592. The decline of this trade is the more to be regretted, as it was the nursery of excellent seamen, many of whom, during the last war, fought the battles of their country.

The Fisheries.—Until a few years ago, the fisheries were unaccountably neglected by the inhabitants, and

are still in their infancy. After a long slumber, the herring fishing was lately revived, chiefly by the enterprise of Samuel Laing, Esq. who set an example to his countrymen. In 1820, no less than 17,989 barrels of herrings were exported from Orkney, which divided among the fishermen of the country about £10,000. Since that period, this branch of industry has greatly declined, chiefly owing to the discouraging state of the markets in the southern part of the empire. Swarms of herrings have, for some years, set into the bays of Orkney, and tempt numerous vessels from the west coast of Scotland to resort thither; but the products of that industry is not included in the above estimate. The periodic migrations of the herring offer a curious field of inquiry to the naturalist, which is as yet little understood. It is fortunate, that their recent desertion of some parts of the western coast of Scotland should be, in some measure, compensated by their unusual numbers round the Orkney Islands.

The cod and ling fishery has been strangely neglected by the natives of these islands; though a London Company, for half a century, has employed ten or twelve *welled smacks*, at an expence of about £60 or £70 per month, to carry live cod and lobsters to the markets of the metropolis. These fish are caught within a few miles of the coast, yet it has never stimulated to any considerable exertion among the natives, to avail themselves of this fertile source of wealth. In a few of the islands some of the people were addicted to this fishing; but the most extensive fishing banks, where, in a short time, we have seen 500 or 600 of the finest fish caught by *hand lines*, have only of late attracted attention. In this respect the people of Orkney are far behind their Zetland brethren. In 1820, 55 ton of cod and ling were exported from Orkney, and this species of industry promises soon to become of great magnitude.

The lobster fishing is carried on by the natives. The lobster is caught in wicker traps, on the principle of the *live-mouse-trap*. These are baited with any sort of flesh or fish. The lobsters, when removed from the trap, have their claws secured by twine, to prevent their fighting, and are inclosed in a deal chest, perforated with holes, which is anchored in a gentle current, where they are kept until the fishing-smacks come to purchase them. The present current price to the fishers is twopence halfpenny a-piece. About 65,000 are annually sent to London from Orkney, and return to the country £800 a-year.

Orkney derives some advantage from the Hudson Bay Company's trade. For many years the ships have touched at Stromness, and carried away 50 or 60 persons annually. These are of the class of labourers, who remit to the country from £2000 to £3000 annually. Some of them return home with little fortunes, acquired by years of privation and honest industry.

Orkney has also derived considerable advantage from the residence of four companies of Veterans, from 1809 to the end of the war. Their pay brought £9000 a-year into the country; and their example was, in many instances, of use to the natives. Since the peace, about fifty of them have fixed their abode in Orkney, which derives about £900 per annum from their half-pay.

During the war, the *monthly money* to the families of Orkney sailors in the navy produced £940 a-year, and the annual *navy bills* about £500 more; *Greenwich chest* and *pension bills* £200; Greenwich *prize bills* £105; and *pilotage* for ships of war about £50.

We shall close this article by the following extracts from the custom-house books:

Duties on Imports, including Wrecked Property.

In the year 1812	. .	£3823 18 6
1813	. .	2240 4 9
1814	. .	1046 19 0
	3	7111 2 3
Average for 3 years		£2370 7 5

Duties on Exports.

In the year 1814	. .	£7 3 1¾
1815	. .	8 13 7
1816	. .	24 10 0½
1817	. .	14 0 3
	4	54 7 8¼
Average for 4 years		£13 14 9

The reason of this small export duty is too obvious to require comment. Orkney, it may be added, exports a considerable surplus of grain and other produce annually. In the year 1816, were exported of bear, 4028 quarters; of oatmeal, 1063 bolls. In 1817, of bear 140 quarters; no oatmeal. In 1818, of bear, 550 quarters; of oatmeal, 84 bolls. In 1819, of bear, 2782 quarters; of oatmeal, 501 bolls; of rabbit skins, 2165 dozens. In 1820, of bear, 4745 quarters; of oatmeal, 2562 bolls; of rabbit-skins, 2090 dozens.

See *Orkneyinga Saga. Torfœi Orcades. Voyage of Hakon,* Icelandic and English. Wallace's *Description of Orkney.* Ben's *Descriptio,* MS. Mackaile's *Account of Orkney,* MS. Jameson's *Mineralogy of the Scottish Isles.* Barry's *History.* Neill's *Tour.* Sheriff's *Agricultural Survey.* Gifford's *Shetland.* Edmonston's *Zetland.* Hibbert's *Shetland.* Peterkin's *Notes on Orkney. Papers relating to the Pundler Process. Grievances of Orkney. Papers relating to the Law-suit against Sir L. Dundas.* Low's *Fauna Orcadensis.* Low's *MS. Microscopic Observations. Various MS. Notes.*

ORLEANS, anciently *Aureliana Civitas,* a city of France, and capital of the department of the Loiret, is agreeably situated at the base of a declivity, washed by the Loire. The town is of an oblong shape, extending along the north bank of the Loire. The streets are in general straight, but narrow and inconvenient. The squares, or open places, are four in number, the central one being the handsomest. The Rue Royale, which is the handsomest street, extends from north to south from the central square to the bridge. The houses are built in the ancient style, but are tolerably good. The principal public buildings are the cathedral, which is a very elegant Gothic edifice, with a handsome spire; the bridge over the Loire, which consists of nine arches; the town-house, the court of justice, the mint, the theatre, and twenty-two parish churches and convents. There is also here an academy, a high school, and a public library, containing 30,000 volumes. The city, which was formerly surrounded by a wall and ditch, is 2396 toises in circuit. Besides the public walk along the ramparts and quay, there is a mall 2890 feet long. The principal manufactures of Orleans are woollen goods, stockings, hats, and leather, refining of sugar, &c. The principal exports are corn, wine, brandy, and fruits. The environs of Orleans are beautiful. There is an extensive forest to the north of the town. Population 36,165. East Long. 1° 54′ 41″, North Lat. 47° 54′ 12″.

ORLEANS, the name of the middle county of the three northern ones in the state of Vermont, in the United States of North America. It is bounded on the north by Canada; on the east by Essex county; on

the south-east by Caledonia county; on the south by Washington county; and on the west by Franklin county. The chief towns are Craftsbury, Irasburg, and Brownington. It contains 832 square miles, and twenty-three towns. Its population in 1800 was 1437, and in 1810, 5830. The land is very elevated, and hence its waters flow in every direction. A part of the lake Memphremagog projects into the country from Canada. The Clyde, the Barton, and Black Rivers, empty themselves into lake Memphremagog. The waters of the numerous streams of the Missiscoui, the La Moelle and the Onion rivers, which have their origin in this county, fall into Lake Champlain; while those of Mulhegan and Pasumpsick run into Connecticut river. See Morse's *Gazetteer,* &c.

ORLEANS is also the name of a county in the state of Louisiana. It consists of the parish of Orleans, the city and suburbs of New Orleans, the precincts of New Orleans, and the parish of Placquemine. It contains 1300 square miles; and, in 1810, the population was 24,552.

The climate of this county is by no means good. The most sickly season is in August, when the adjacent ponds begin to evaporate and send forth their pestilential effluvia. The number of births and deaths in the city of New Orleans, from March, 1807 to March, 1808, was, births 456, deaths 769. Of the births, 137 were whites, and 319 persons of colour; of the deaths, 318 were whites of adult age, and 56 children; and 286 persons of colour and of adult age, and 109 children.

Rice is cultivated below New Orleans, (in places unfit for any other grain,) where the ground can be laid under water. The nett value from 100 acres, cultivated by 50 workmen, is estimated at 700 barrels, which, at 6 dollars per barrel, gives 4200 dollars, or 84 for each labourer. The following is an estimate of produce received annually at New Orleans.

Cotton, bales,	60,000
Sugar, hhds.	11,000
Molasses, gallons,	500,000
Tobacco, hhds.	7,000
——— carrots,	10,000
Flour, in barrels,	75,000
Corn in ear, barrels,	60,000
Meal, barrels,	1,000
Rice, barrels,	9,000
Beans, do.	3,000
Beef, do.	5,000
Pork, do.	4,000
Bacon, lbs.	700,000
Hemp, cwt.	3,000
Yarns, reels of 1000 lbs.	2,000
Cordage, cwt.	5,000
Baling, coils,	3,000
Bagging, pieces,	10,000
Linen, coarse, do.	2,500
Whisky, gallons,	200,000
Gin, do.	50,000
Taffia, do.	180,000
Rum, do.	
Beer, barrels,	1,000
Horses,	300
Cider, barrels,	1,000
Apples, do.	5,000
Potatoes, do.	5,000
Butter, lbs.	10,000
Lard, do.	250,000
Soap, boxes,	10,000
Candles, do,	2,000
Tallow,	
Bees wax, lbs.	30,000
Saltpetre, do.	50,000
Gun-powder, barrels,	4,500
Linseed oil, do.	300
Potashes	
Indigo, lbs.	7,000

Orleans
‖
Ormskirk.

Kettles and castings, points,	200,000
Lead, cwt.	6,000
Shot, cwt.	1,000
Bark, tanners cords,	4,000
Nails, lbs.	50,000
Tar, barrels,	7,000
Pitch, do.	3,000
Rosin, do. Turpentine, do.	1,000
Masts and spars, Planks, Staves,	
Furs, Deer skins,	
Hides,	5,000
Bear skins,	4,000
Hogs,	1,000

What is called the island of New Orleans, is a tract of land formed on one side by the river Mississippi, and on the other by the lakes of Pontchartrain and Maurepas, together with the river Ibberville, which is an outlet of the Mississippi. It is about 100 miles in length, and from 3 to 50 in breadth. It produces sugar, lemons, oranges, and figs. The river Bayou St. John, which is navigable for small vessels that pass between New Orleans and Mobile, and Pensacola, forms a communication between New Orleans and lake Pontchartrain. For farther information respecting this county, see LOUISIANA, and NEW ORLEANS, Vol. XV. p. 351.

ORLEANS, ISLE OF, is an island in the middle of the river St. Lawrence, a little below Quebec, and remarkable for the richness of its soil. The navigable channel is on the south side of the island, that on the north being incapable of admitting even shallops at full tide. The south-west end of the island is called Point Orleans. The island itself is 25 miles long and 5 broad, and is next in size to that of Montreal. The coast is rocky for a mile and a half within the south channel, but in general the shores slope gradually to the beach. Large spaces of low meadow land, sometimes crossed by spots of excellent arable land, extend from the foot of the slope. The centre of the island is thickly wooded, but no timber of great value is produced. The little river Dauphin, the rivulet Maheux, and a few smaller streams, water the island very scantily. They drive two mills, which are often without water in summer. The island is surrounded with a good road, which is crossed by several others. The island of New Orleans is considered an extremely delightful spot, and is frequented by numerous visitors, who find accommodation in a group of very neat houses erected on the western point of the island. Population about 4000, West Long. 70° 28′, and North Lat. 47° 5′.

ORLEANS, NEW. See NEW ORLEANS, Vol. XV. p. 351.

ORMSKIRK, a market-town of England, in the county of Lancaster. It consists of four principal streets, crossing each other nearly at right angles. The principal public building is the church, which is an ancient structure, with a tower at one end, and a spire entirely detached from it. There are several monuments in the interior in honour of the earls of Derby. Besides two chapels of ease, there is here a chapel for dissenters, and another for Methodists. Great quantities of cotton, and thread for making sail cloth, were manufactured here both by the hand and by machinery. The following was the population of the township in 1821.

Number of houses,	738
Number of families,	782
Employed in agriculture,	67
In other trades,	490
Males,	1812
Females,	2026
Total population,	3838

See the *Beauties of England and Wales*, vol. ix. p. 218.

ORMUZ, an island of Asia, at the entrance of the Persian Gulf. It is about six miles long and four broad, about five miles from the continent of Persia, and twenty-five from that of Arabia. The island is traversed by a high mountain running from east to west, which is supposed to have been a volcano. It is very barren and rocky, and contains quantities of rock salt, which is so hard that it is said to be used for building houses. The soil consists principally of white sand, which was once imported into Europe. There is no water in the island but what is collected in cisterns.

The ancient city of Ormuz is a mass of ruins, the reservoirs of water being the only buildings that are still in a perfect state. It contains only a fort and a wretched suburb with about 500 inhabitants.

The only natural productions of the island are sulphur, salt, and red earth, for which vessels occasionally come. The black shining sand of the island is much esteemed in India.

Ormuz once contained a city, which became the most splendid in Asia, from its being the principal magazine of Indian commerce. Albuquerque attempted in vain, in 1508, to take the island, which was defended by 30,000 men; and had in its harbour 400 vessels, 60 of which were brigs, and having in all 2500 men on board. He returned, however, in 1514, with an overwhelming force, and having obtained possession of the island, he erected a strong fort. It remained in their possession for 120 years, and advanced so rapidly in wealth and splendour, that it was deemed the richest spot in the world. In 1622, it surrendered to the combined arms of the English and Persians. Having thus fallen into the hands of the Persians the place fell into decay, and its trade was transferred to Gombroon. East Long. 56° 40′, North Lat. 27° 12′.

ORNANS, a town of France in the department of the Doubs. It is situated on the small river Louve, 12 miles south-east of Besançon. There is a remarkable spring in the vicinity, which in rainy weather overflows to such a degree, as to inundate the surrounding district. There are large iron works in the neighbourhood, which give employment to many of the inhabitants. There are also in the town manufactories of paper and leather. Population 3100.

ORNE, the name of a department in the north of France, which derives its name from the principal river which rises in it. It was formed out of the part of Normandy which comprehended the diocese of Seez, and a part of Perche. It is bounded on the north by the department of Calvados and Eure, on the west by that of La Manche, on the south by those of the Mayenne and the Sarthe, and on the east by those of the Eure and Loire and the Eure. The principal rivers are the Orne, the Sarthe, and the Huisne, which passes by Nogent-le-Rotrou. The department contains about 2500 square miles. The chief productions are wheat, rye, barley, oats, buck wheat, hemp, flax, &c. Iron is wrought in various parts of the department to the amount of 5000 tons of cast, and 3000 of wrought iron annually. The other articles of manufacture are linen, lace, leather, knives. The principal towns are,

	Population.
Alençon	12,407
Domfront	1548
Argentan	5618
Mortagne	5720

The forests occupy about 135,000 acres, about two-thirds of which belong to the nation. Contributions in 1803, 3,666,903 francs. Population in 1815, 422,000. Alençon is the capital of the department.

Ormuz
‖
Orne.

ORNITHOLOGY*.

Ornitho-
logy.
⁓
Definition
of the term.

ORNITHOLOGY is composed of two Greek words, name-
ly, ορνις, a *bird*, and λογος, *discourse*, and, consequently,
denotes that department of zoological science which
treats of birds. The latter are furnished with two feet,
covered with feathers, and provided with wings, by
means of which most of them are enabled to fly in the
air. Although they have warm blood, a heart with
two auricles and two ventricles, and although they
breathe by lungs, they are distinguished from the mammiferous tribes by their feet, feathers, wings, horny
bill, and oviparous production.

Exposition of the Class.

Limited
survey of
the subject.

From the mass of authentic information relative to
the natural history of birds, which has been accumulated in the course of ages, the unavoidable limitation of
our plan constrains us to select only the more prominent
portions, and to reduce them within the narrowest possible compass of space. Hence we are less solicitous to
present our readers with a complete technical vocabu-
lary, than with leading and important views of the
principal families, genera, and species, with their manners, dispositions, and uses. It may likewise be proper
to premise, that of many of the foreign species little is
hitherto known beyond the names, or scientific definitions; and that Gmelin, and other systematists, have
often confounded species and varieties, or been misled
by want of due consideration to the appearances induced by sex or age, and have thus, unconsciously, extended their catalogues by superfluous references, so
that many of our omissions will be found, on close examination, to be only apparent.

ORDER I.

ACCIPITRINE, or RAPACIOUS BIRDS.

Accipi-
tres.
Physical
and moral
characters
of the or-
der.

The birds belonging to this division are at once distinguished by their hooked bill and claws, the width of
their nostrils, the largeness of their head, the strength
of their muscles, their piercing vision, and their power
of elevated flight. Their stomach is somewhat analogous to that of carnivorous quadrupeds; but its cavity
is more a continuation of the œsophagus, and the solvent
glands are more numerous and conspicuous. The car-
diac portion of their stomach is also very distinct from
the pyloric.

Rapacious birds are naturally addicted to pursue their
prey, and to feed on raw flesh. They lead a roaming
and solitary life, generally associating only in pairs, af-

fecting sequestered mountains, or deserted rocks, in the
crevices of which, or on the tops of the loftiest trees, they
build their nests. Though less fertile than most of the
other families, Linné and Temminck have too rashly asserted, that they lay no more than four eggs at a time; for
the number has been known to vary from one to seven.
Their harsh, unsocial, and even ferocious dispositions,
seem to be the unavoidable result of those constitutional
propensities by which they are impelled to rapine and
slaughter, in order to gratify the cravings of appetite.
Their depredations are less extensive on the land than
on the waters; but, as in no country the water animals are wholly protected from their ravages, and as
their own carcasses afford no salutary food to man, they
have been regarded as nuisances by the thoughtless,
and even by those accustomed to reflection. Yet a very
ordinary degree of discernment may suffice to convince
us, that the multitudes of animals which fall victims to
their more powerful assailants, are absolved from the
protracted torments of age, or lingering disease; that
the balance of the races on which the welfare and comfort of all living beings depend, could not be maintained if the predacious tribes were exterminated; that
the produce of our fields would be devoured by vermin, and that the air would be tainted with pestilence
and death.

Ornitho-
logy.
⁓

Systematic
distribution
of the or-
der.

The extrication of the species of this order is involved in considerable obscurity, both because the individuals which compose them frequent remote or inaccessible retreats, and because they are liable to more remarkable changes after the first three moultings than
most birds of the other orders. They have generally
been divided into the *diurnal* and *nocturnal,* the former
hunting for their food during the day, and the latter
during the night.

Diurnal.

The diurnal birds of prey have the eyes situated on
the sides of the head; the cere covering the base of the
beak; three toes before, and a featherless one behind,
the two exterior almost always united at their base by
a short membrane; the plumage closely arranged; the
quill-feathers strong; the stomach, with few exceptions,
membranous; the intestines of moderate dimensions;
the *cœcum,* or blind gut, particularly short; the *sternum,* or breast bone, large, and completely ossified, to
afford more extensive attachments to the muscles of the
wings; and the forking semicircular, and very wide,
in order to resist the violent depressions of the hume-
rus in rapid flight.

VULTUR. Illig. Temm. VULTURE.

Vultur.
Characters.

Bill thick and strong, much more elevated than
broad, the base covered with a cere; the upper mandi-

---

* The contributor of the ensuing article had prepared it for the press on a scale more commensurate with the nature and extent of the
subject; but circumstances connected with the plan of the work for which it was destined, have induced him, however reluctantly, to suppress the preliminary and general dissertation on the structure, economy, and diseases of birds, the chronological notices of eminent ornithologists, and the details of specific, sexual, and other distinctions. Such of his readers as may be desirous of supplying these unavoidable
omissions, will find much valuable and satisfactory information in the disquisitions prefixed to the article *Ornithologie,* in the French En-
cyclopédie Méthodique, in the Introduction to Montagu's Ornithological Dictionary, and in the last edition of the *Manuel d'Ornithologie,*
by Temminck, whose divisions are here generally adopted.

Ornitho-
logy.

ble straight, curved only towards the tip; the under mandible straight, rounded, and inclined towards the tip; head naked, or covered with a very short down; nostrils naked, lateral, and diagonally pierced near the margin of the cere; legs robust, furnished with claws slightly hooked; the middle toe very long, and united to the outer at the base; wings long, the first quill short, and the sixth the longest.

As the strength of their claws does not correspond with the size of their bodies, vultures have most frequently recourse to their beak for seizing and tearing their prey. When glutted with food, their crop projects from above their breast, a fetid humour exudes from the nostrils, and they fall into a state of listlessness, bordering on stupidity. They are much more common in warm than in cold climates. When compared with eagles and hawks, they are cowardly and ignoble, seldom killing their prey from choice, but in general devouring only such animals as are either dying, or found dead and putrid. Though often put to flight by birds much inferior to themselves, if not molested, they will prey in the midst of cities. In some of the battles of the east, in which an extensive slaughter of elephants, horses, and men, takes place, voracious animals crowd to the field from every quarter, particularly jackals, hyænas, and vultures. Even in regions where the last mentioned are at other times seldom observed, the plains will, on these occasions, be found covered with them; and multitudes of them will be seen descending from the air on every side, insomuch that the Indians believe they have a presentiment of slaughter some days before the event.

Fulvus.

V. fulvus, Gmel. &c. *Fulvous Vulture.* Grey or brown, inclining to fulvous; down of the head and neck cinereous; collar white, sometimes mixed with brown; feathers of the wings and tail brown; bill and legs plumbeous. The body is larger than that of the golden eagle, measuring four feet in length, the legs are more than a foot long, and the neck is seven inches. The body of the male is smaller than that of the female.

The fulvous vulture is pretty generally diffused on the mountains of the old continent, as in Turkey, the Archipelago, Silesia, the Tyrol, the Alps and Pyrenees, and throughout Africa. It is said to be common in the neighbourhood of Gibraltar. It builds its nest on precipitous cliffs. The eggs are of a grey-white, marked with some spots of rufous-white. The individuals of this species kept in the Parisian menagerie generally live quietly, and in apparent harmony with one another, in their narrow confinement; but they occasionally manifest much agitation and discontent.

The academicians, who dissected two females, have observed, that the bill is longer and less curved than in the eagles; that at the base of the beak are placed the two nostrils, each six lines long and two broad, which affords an ample space for the external organs of smell; that the tongue is hard and cartilaginous, scooped near the tip, and the edges elevated into serrated ranges, pointing towards the gullet; that the œsophagus dilates below, and forms a large sac, differing from the crop of fowls only by the interspersed ramifications of a great number of vessels; that the gizzard is neither so hard nor so thick as in the gallinaceous tribe; that the intestines and cœcum are small, &c. Now, from these observations we may infer, that, though vultures feed on flesh as eagles do, they have not the same conformation in the organs of digestion, and that in this last respect they approach much nearer to poultry, and other birds that live on grain; so that they are perhaps occasionally granivorous or omnivorous.

The present species, we should remark, is synonymous with *V. leucocephalus*, Meyer; *V. percnopterus*, Daudin; and *V. trenkalos*, Bechst.

V. auricularis, Lath. &c. *Auriculated Vulture.* Neck naked; skin of the ears elongated; general plumage brown. This species takes its name from the remarkable projection of the skin round the ears, and which is also continued to some little distance down the neck on each side. It is a very large bird, being three feet high, and measuring ten feet from tip to tip of the outstretched wings. Its general colour is brown; but the throat is black, and covered with coarse hairs. Native of the southern parts of Africa and of the East Indies; and, contrary to the nature of the fiercer birds of prey, is of a gregarious disposition, being often seen in large flocks, and sitting in great numbers about the caverns of rocky mountains, in which it breeds. The nests, too, are often placed very near one another, each generally containing two, and sometimes three eggs, of a white colour, and not disagreeable to the taste. During incubation, the male watches before the entrance of the cavern in which the female sits, and may be regarded as a certain indication of the nest: but this last is usually of very difficult access. "However," says Levaillant, "I have sometimes, with the aid of my Hottentots, surmounted all difficulties, and often risked my life, that I might examine the eggs of this bird, whose retreat is a sink of disgusting pollution, and contaminated by an insupportable odour. It is the more dangerous to approach these obscure recesses, because their entrance is beset with filth, and this always in a liquid state, by reason of the moisture produced by the water which incessantly oozes from the rocks, so that, by sliding on the points of these rocks one runs the hazard of tumbling over hideous precipices, on the top of which the *oricous* preferably establish their abodes." At sunrise, flocks of these birds may be seen perched at the entry of their gloomy habitation, and sometimes studding at intervals an entire mountain range. As an instance of their voracity, the author whom we have just quoted mentions, that having wounded one of them, when busily engaged on the carcass of a hippopotamus, the oricou still tore off morsels of its prey in its attempts to escape, and encumbered with six pounds and a half of meat in its stomach. Embarrassed with this quantity of food, and detained by its wound and its gluttony, it allowed the traveller and his attendants time to come up with it, and to assail it with the butt end of their muskets. For a long time the bird defended itself with singular intrepidity, and seemed even to make some impression on the barrels of the fowling-pieces. It is only, however, in such cases of emergency that it displays real courage; for, notwithstanding its great strength and dimensions, it is naturally indolent and sluggish, seldom attacking the weakest animals, provided it can gorge itself with their spoils, and the fragments of corruption.

V. papa, Lin. &c. *King of the Vultures.* Of a whitish rufescent hue, with naked variegated head and neck; nostrils furnished with a loose orange-coloured caruncle, and the neck with a grey ruff. One of the most elegant of the tribe, and well figured by Edwards. The extreme length of the body does not exceed twenty-nine inches and a half, and it is not thicker than that of the hen turkey. It is a native of the plains, and other hot

Ornitho-
logy.

Auricularis.

Papa.

FALCO IMPERIALIS
Imperial Eagle

PARADISEA MAJOR
Great Bird of Paradise

MENURA SUPERBA
Superb Menura

STRIX PASSERINA
Little Owl

PIPRA CARUNCULATA
Carunculated Chatterer

GLAUCOPIS CINEREA
Cinereous Wattlebird

VULTUR GRYPHUS
Condor

SERPENTARIUS AFRICANUS
Snake Eater

BUCEROS RHINOCEROS
Rhinoceros Hornbill

Engraved for the Edinburgh Encyclopædia by J. Moffat Edinr.

regions of South America, and, it is also said, of the West Indies; but it is not met with in the East Indies, as they who make a traffic of showing birds would induce us to believe. It lives on rats, lizards, snakes, carrion, and all sorts of excrementitious matters, exhaling a most offensive odour, which the stuffed skin has been known to retain for upwards of twenty years. The feathers, fantastically arranged and painted, are used by some of the American Indians as a sacred ensign both of peace and war. When extensive plains have been set on fire either by lightning, or by the natives for the purpose of rousing the game, and immense tracts of dry herbage have been consumed, the ashes have scarcely cooled, when this vulture alights on them in quest of scorched snakes and other vermin, which are then so intent on feeding, and apparently so fearless of danger, as to be easily dispatched.

Aura.

V. aura, Lin. &c. *American*, or *Carrion Vulture, Turkey Buzzard, Carrion Crow of Jamaica*, &c. The specific designation is from the Brasilian *ouroua*, so that the expression, *Regina aurarum*, or *Queen of the Gales*, applied to this species by some of the elder ornithologists, proceeds on a misconception. The American vulture is blackish, with purple and green reflexions; the head and neck are red, naked, papillous, and wrinkled. It occurs throughout the continent of America; but is more common in the warmer parts of it. In Europe it haunts the Grison Alps, Silesia, Poland, and some other countries, but not Great Britain. It is also met with in Asia. Its length is about four feet and a half, and its average weight between four and five pounds.

By some navigators, this species has been mistaken at a little distance for the turkey, as happened to one of the officers engaged in the expedition round the world, under Woodes Rogers. In the island of Lobos immense numbers of them were seen; and, highly delighted with the prospect of dainty fare after a long and tedious voyage, the officer would not even wait till the boat could put him ashore, but, with his gun in his hand, leapt overboard, and swam to land. Coming near to a large assemblage of the birds, he fired among them; but, on seizing his game, he was sadly disappointed to find that they were not turkeys, and that their stench was almost insupportable. Though much addicted to carrion, they will also kill lambs; and snakes are an usual article of their food. Flocks of them may be observed roosting on tall dead pines, or cypress trees, and with their wings spread open in the morning for several hours together. In other regions they are seen in flocks of forty or fifty, perched on the cocoa trees; for they range themselves in files, to sleep together, like poultry; and such is their indolence, that they go to roost long before sunset, and awake not till far on in the morning. In some regions of the torrid zone they haunt the towns in great multitudes, as Carthagena, for example, where they perch on the roofs of the houses, or even stalk along the streets, and are of infinite service to the inhabitants, as they devour all manner of filth and refuse. When food fails them in the cities, they seek for it among the cattle of the adjoining pastures; for if an animal is unfortunate enough to have a sore on its back, they alight on it without ceremony, and attack the part affected, nor quit their hold until they have completed the creature's destruction. In some parts of South America, where the hunters kill beasts merely for the skins, vast numbers of these vultures

follow in their train; and, were it not for their assiduous voracity, the many flayed carcasses exposed to the air would speedily generate disease. We need not wonder, therefore, that the Spanish and Portuguese dealers in hides should protect the carrion vultures, and allow them to feed with their dogs. These birds likewise contribute to repress the multiplication of alligators, by preying on their eggs the moment that they are consigned to the sand, and left by the parent. Their sloth, foulness, and voracity, are such as almost to exceed belief. Whenever they alight on a carcass which they can tear at their ease, they leave the bones as if they had been scraped with a knife, and they often continue feeding till they are incapable of flight. On the pressure of danger, however, they have been known to rid themselves of a burdened stomach by disgorging.

In the month of October, the female of this species lays two white eggs slightly spotted with reddish. The young, on their exclusion, are covered with a white down, and their eyes are closed. The nest consists of an artless excavation in the ground, or of brushwood, on the borders of forests, without any regular distribution of materials.

Iribu.

V. iribu, d'Azara. *Iribu Vulture*. Head remarkably flat. This species, which the Guaranis, a tribe of South American Indians, call the *Iribu*, by way of eminence, has been inadvertently confounded with the preceding by some of our most celebrated ornithologists, and particularly by Buffon and Cuvier. The head and upper part of the neck are destitute of feathers, and much wrinkled. It is not found farther south than the parallel of Buenos Ayres; and for a considerable time after the conquest of America, it was unknown at MonteVideo, whither it passed, in following the course of ships and boats.

During the greater part of the day, the iribu takes its station on trees or palings, to watch if any person stops for the purpose of easing nature, of throwing away the relics of dried meat, or of killing a sheep. Several usually congregate on the same tree; and as nobody harasses them, they live in tranquillity and safety. When assembled on a mass of carrion, if any noise or object alarms them, they suddenly send forth their only cry, which is the sound of the syllable *hoo*, uttered with a very nasal intonation. Whether alone or in company, they never attack or molest any living creature; and, when several of them fall on a dead one, of small size, every one endeavours to tear off a bit, without quarrelling with his competitors. They begin by devouring the eyes, then proceed to the tongue, and next to the intestines, when they can extract them by the vent. If the carcass has a very hard skin, and has not been touched by a dog, or some carnivorous animal, they abandon it; but if they meet with any opening, they gnaw off the flesh to the very bones, leaving the skin spread over them. They sometimes follow the track of travellers, or boats, to pick up the offals and filth that are thrown out. On feeling themselves wounded, they disgorge the contents of their stomach. The female constructs no regular nest, but deposits two white eggs in the hole of a rock or tree. The young, at birth, are covered with a white down.

Gryphus.

V. gryphus, Lin. &c. *Condor, Cundur, Cuntur,* or *Great Vulture of the Andes*. Blackish spot on the wings, and ruff white. Besides the upper caruncle, which is large, and without indentations, the male has another under the beak ; but the female is destitute of both. In the early stage of its existence, this bird is of a fulvous brown, and wants the ruff. There is reason to believe that, in mature age, it is liable to considerable varieties of colour, which may partly account for the discordant reports of different writers. This circumstance, however, will not explain the diversity of statements with respect to its dimensions and strength ; for its extent of wing has been reckoned from eight to eighteen feet ; and, while Frezier asserts that it can carry off a sheep or a boy of ten years of age, Marco Polo more undauntedly affirms, that it can raise an elephant high enough from the ground to kill it by letting it fall. Humboldt acquaints us, that he never saw an individual of the species that measured more than three feet three inches in length, and eight feet nine inches from tip to tip of the wings : he admits, however, that it may sometimes exceed these dimensions, and that it may perhaps attain to eleven or twelve feet in extent of wing. The expanded wings of a preserved specimen, in the Leverian Museum, measured ten feet. When seated on the point of a rock, and viewed from below, its form being then contrasted with the clear sky above, appears considerably larger than it really is, and thus may have given rise to the exaggerations of the early describers.

The condur preys both on living and dead animals, marking with wonderful sagacity its victim at a distance, and pouncing on it with astonishing boldness. A couple of them will lay hold on a heifer, and begin their work of destruction by picking out its eyes, and tearing out its tongue.

The usual residence of these birds is in lofty rocks, in the regions of the Andes, and just beneath the boundary of perpetual snow ; but they are capable of soaring beyond the reach of human vision. In the rainy or cold season, they sometimes repair to the sea-shore, especially towards the approach of evening, and return again to their mountainous haunts in the morning, unless detained by some of the larger fishes that have been stranded by the tempest. In Peru and Quito, they are not unfrequently taken alive in the following manner : A cow or horse, which is of little value in those countries, is killed and exposed ; and, in a short time, the condurs are seen suddenly to emerge from quarters where their existence was not even suspected. They always begin with the eyes and tongue, and then proceed to devour the entrails, &c. When gorged, they are too heavy and indolent to fly ; and the Indians easily capture them in nooses. Sometimes, again, a person covers himself with the hide of a newly flayed animal, goes into the fields, and so counterfeits the gait of a quadruped, that one of these birds will frequently attempt to attack him, whilst other persons, purposely concealed, rush forward to his assistance, and at once overpower and kill the assailant. Sometimes traps and springs are employed with success ; and sometimes the cunning natives will work up a piece of viscous clay into the form of an infant, on which the condur darts with so much vehemence, that his claws are entangled in the mass. When surprised by any of these modes, they are dull and timid for nearly an hour, and then become extremely ferocious : and, being very tenacious of life, they will for a long time survive such wounds as might be supposed to prove immediately fatal. Such, too, are the fulness of their plumage, and the thickness of

their skin, that a musket ball does not always dispatch them. They make their nests in the most inaccessible rocks ; and the female lays two white eggs, which are larger than those of the turkey-hen.

V. percnopterus, Lin. &c. ; *Cathartes percnopterus*, Temm. ; *V. leucocephalus*, Lath. ; *V. stercorarius*, La Peyrouse ; *Neophron percnopterus*, Savig.; *Ourigourap* of Le Vaillant ; *Rachamach* of Bruce, &c. *Ash-coloured*, or *Alpine Vulture, Pharaoh's Hen, Aquiline*, or *Egyptian Vulture*, &c. Male white ; female brownish, with lengthened narrow beak, naked face, and black wing feathers, edged with grey. The colouring of the plumage varies considerably, according to age. The full-grown bird is about the size of a stork, measuring about two feet and a half in length, and about eight feet from tip to tip of the wings. Percnopterus.

Both the male and female are of a repulsive and ignoble aspect, and the constant flow of rheum from the nostrils, and of saliva from the two openings in the bill, are little calculated to weaken the impression produced by their haggard and disproportioned form. During the summer months, flocks of them range the rocky heights of the Alps and Pyrenees, and in winter resort to the plains of the south of France and Spain. As they delight in carrion and excrementitious matters, and prey on serpents and other noisome reptiles, they are protected and cherished in some countries of the east, particularly in Egypt, where they were anciently held in such veneration, that any person who destroyed them was punished with death. At this day, immense flocks of them are observed over all the principal towns of Egypt, Syria, and Persia, mingling with other animals of similar appetites and propensities, and clearing away all those relics which would otherwise be left to putrify, and to infect the air with the most noxious effluvia. In consequence of the long experienced protection of man, they have become fearless of his approach, and feed with the greatest familiarity, even in the streets of the most populous towns. At Cairo their skins are sold, and converted into very comfortable dresses.

V. barbatus, Lin. &c. ; *Gypaetus barbatus*, Cuv. Temm. ; *Phene ossifraga*, Sav. ; *V. barbatus*, Lath. ; *V. leucocephalus*, Meyer ; *Falco barbatus*, Gmel. ; *Nisser*, Bruce, &c. *Bearded* or *Golden Vulture*. Black-brown above, somewhat fulvous beneath ; head and neck covered with lanceolate whitish plumes, and the under part of the bill bearded. Barbatus.

This species is a native of many of the wilder regions of Asia and Africa, and exists also, though more sparingly, in Europe, as in the Swiss Alps and Pyrenees, and in the mountains of Tyrol and Hungary. The German appellation of *Laemmer Geyer*, or *Lamb Vulture*, has been applied to it, as to other large birds of prey. It is one of the largest of European vultures, measuring between four and five feet in length, and between eight and nine of outstretched wing. Specimens of still more ample dimensions have been occasionally shot ; and one is cited, by the Abbate Fortis, which was twelve feet in stretch of wing. This enormous bird had haunted the precipitous rocks that skirt the Cettina, in Dalmatia, where the bearded vultures carry off in their talons, and convey to their eyries, not only sheep, lambs, calves, kids, marmots, &c. but also children, if they find them unprotected. According to Pallas, they arrive, for breeding, in the granitic mountains of Odon Tschelon, in Siberia, during the month of April. The individual particularized by Mr. Bruce, who terms it an *Eagle*, was considerably larger than that described by Edwards, and weighed twenty-two pounds.

The bearded vulture is said to build its nest in the inaccessible cavities of lofty rocks, and to lay two eggs, whose rough surface is white, marked with brown spots. It obviously forms a connecting link between the vultures and eagles, and seems to have suggested the exaggerated tales relative to the *Roc* of oriental writers.

Falco, Lin. &c. Falcon.

Falco.

Head covered with feathers; beak hooked, and generally curved from its origin; a coloured cere, more or less hairy at its base, the under mandible obliquely rounded, and both the mandibles sometimes notched; nostrils lateral, rounded, or ovoid, pierced in the cere, and open; tarsi covered either with feathers or scales; three toes before, and one behind, the outermost frequently connected at its base by a membrane to the middle toe; claws pointed and sharp, much hooked, moveable, and retractile.

This numerous division of the diurnal birds of prey has been conveniently distributed into several sections. Besides the characters which we have just stated, they are distinguished by a projection of the eye-brows, which gives their eyes the appearance of being deepseated in their orbits, and imparts to their physiognomy a very different aspect from that of the vultures. Their first plumage is often differently coloured from that of the mature bird, which is not induced till the third or fourth year, or even later,—a circumstance which has betrayed many ornithologists into an erroneous multiplication of the species. The female is usually about one-third larger than the male, and has been providently endowed with superior strength, because it is necessary that she should both protect and feed her voracious offspring; whereas the smaller dimensions of the male are more adapted to the rapidity and loftiness of his flight; and he is, accordingly, more esteemed by falconers. Though they are all carnivorous, they seldom feed on carrion, except when pressed by hunger, which they are capable of enduring for a long time. They have a very acute sense of sight, and pounce down on their prey with surprising force, promptitude, and accuracy; manifesting, however, very different degrees of courage in pursuit of their game. Owing to their great strength, they are capable of carrying birds or other animals, nearly as heavy as themselves, to a considerable distance, sometimes forty miles or upwards, for the nourishment of their young. Many of the species eat fish, and others feed principally on the smaller birds, snakes, and reptiles. They never associate in flocks; and, except during the breeding season, even two of them are seldom seen together. Most of them build their nests or eyries in lofty and inaccessible places; but a few form them on the ground. They void by the mouth the indigested exuviæ and bones that happen to be swallowed along with their food, and which are formed in the stomach into round balls or pellets. Upwards of one hundred and fifty alleged species have been described; but of these, many are little known, and not a few are mere varieties, resulting from age, sex, climate, &c.

Hawks, properly so called.

Hawks.

Beak short and curved from its base; a sharp denticulation on each side of the upper mandible, which fits

into a corresponding notch in the lower; legs robust; toes strong, long, and armed with hooked and pointed claws; tarsi short; wings long and pointed, so as to weaken their efforts in a vertical direction, rendering their flight, in a tranquil atmosphere, very oblique, and constraining them, when they are desirous of rising directly, to fly against the wind. As most of them are endowed with a certain degree of docility, and are capable of being trained to the diversion of falconry, they have been denominated *noble birds of prey*. They show great address and activity in surprising and seizing their prey, and build their nests among the crevices of rocks or forsaken ruins. The accurate discrimination of the species is attended with considerable difficulty; and Temminck proposes as the least fallible criteria the measurement of the total length, the length of the wings compared with that of the tail, and the colour of the feet, cere, and eyebrows.

F. peregrinus, Temm. Gmel. Lath.; *F. abietinus*, Bechst.; *F. communis*, of various authors; *Peregrine* or *Common Falcon*. Brown above, with rufous undulations; tail marked with dusky bars; breast and belly whitish, with dusky spots. The length of the mature male is a foot and two or three inches, and that of the female a foot and four or five inches, with three feet and a half of expanse of wing.

Peregrinus.

This falcon is a native of the temperate and colder parts of Europe, ranging from Iceland to the islands of the Mediterranean, frequenting high and rocky mountains, and building its nest, about the end of February, in precipitous cliffs, with a southern aspect. The eggs are generally three or four, and white, spotted with brown. It is rarely found in champaign countries, and never in those of a marshy description. It abounds in Germany and France, is pretty common in Holland and England, but is seldom met with in Switzerland. There is hardly any part of our coasts, from north to south, where the cliffs rise to three or four hundred feet, in which they are not found scattered in the breeding season, and from which they seldom retire, except as occasional migrants, or when the young are driven to seek for fresh quarters. The insulated rock on which the castle of Dumbarton stands, has been particularly quoted for a breed of the peregrine falcon. So rapid is the growth of the young, that, in three months, they are said to equal their parents in size. We may also remark, that they are very courageous birds, darting suddenly, perpendicularly, and with great rapidity, on their prey, which principally consists of partridges, pheasants, quails, wood-pigeons, &c. and the smaller quadrupeds. They also attack the kite, and compel it to relinquish its victim, but spare its life, as if in contempt of such a dastardly adversary. Various instances are recorded of their fleetness of flight; thus, one that eloped from its master, in the county of Forfar, on the 24th of September, 1772, with four heavy bells at its feet, was killed on the morning of the 26th of the same month, at Mostyn, in Flintshire. Another, belonging to a Duke of Cleves, flew out of Westphalia into Prussia in one day; and, in the county of Norfolk, one was known to make a flight at a woodcock of nearly thirty miles in an hour. A still more remarkable example is that of a falcon which belonged to Henry IV. king of France, and which, having escaped from Fontainebleau, was found, twenty-four hours after, in Malta, the space thus traversed being not less than 1350 miles, and corresponding to a velocity of fifty-seven miles an hour, supposing the bird to have been on wing the whole time. But, as these hawks never fly by night, such a rate of progress would amount to seventy-five miles an hour, supposing the day to have been at the longest, or to have lasted eighteen hours. It is probable, however, that he neither had so many hours of light in the twenty-four, nor that he was re-taken the moment of his arrival, so that we may fairly conclude much less time was occupied in performing such a distant flight.

The female peregrine falcon is, in the terms of fal-conry, always called *Falcon,* while the male is deno-minated *Tercel ;* the female, when a year old, is term-ed a *Red Falcon,* and the male, a *Red Tercel ;* and, when thoroughly bred, they are called *Gentil* or *Gentle Hawks.* This last expression has also been sometimes applied to the young of the goshawk, and, more vaguely, to such birds as are manageable in the sport.

For the mode of using and training hawks in falcon-ry, see HUNTING.

Islandicus.

F. Islandicus, Bech. Temm.; *F. hierofalco,* Cuv. ; *F. Islandicus candicans,* Gmel. Lath. Meyer ; *F. rusticolus,* Gmel. *Iceland falcon, jerfalcon, White jerfalcon, Brown jerfalcon,* &c. Ground of the plumage white, with nar-row brown bands on the upper parts and tail, and the under parts white, marked with small brown tear-like spots.

The native abodes of the Iceland falcon are the north of Europe and Asia, particularly Norway and Iceland. An instance occurs of its having been shot in the coun-ty of Aberdeen ; and it has been occasionally observed in the north of Scotland, and in the Orkneys. Though indigenous only to the colder latitudes, it perfectly ac-commodates itself to the more temperate and warm climates, when transported to them. At no very dis-tant period, it was in training in this country. Next to the eagle, it is reputed the most formidable and active, as well as the most prompt and intrepid of all our pre-dacious birds ; and it is still the most esteemed for fal-conry, being conveyed from Iceland and Russia into France, Italy, Turkey, and Persia. The female boldly attacks the largest of the feathered race, the stork, heron, and crane, being its easy victims, and it kills hares by directly darting on them. The male is used chiefly to catch the kite, the heron, and the crow. But unless treated with patient gentleness and care, in the course of discipline, this species becomes refrac-tory and unmanageable. In a state of liberty, it preys on other birds, and especially on pigeons ; and such is its ardour for the chace, that when it has seized and lacerated one victim, it will fly off in pursuit of another. The female breeds in the north among lofty and inac-cessible rocks.

Laniarius.

F. Laniarius, Lin. &c. *Lanner.* Wings terminating at two-thirds of the tail, the middle toe shorter than the tarsus, beneath the eye a black stroke, which dis-appears with age, or at least is nearly obliterated ; legs bluish ; the two first quills with their beards truncated at the extremity. We have adopted those characters from Temminck, as being less equivocal than those usually quoted, and less apt to confound the present species with the peregrine falcon, especially as the markings of the young of both are nearly similar.

The lanner is found in many parts of Europe, inha-bits Iceland and the Feroe Islands, Denmark, Sweden, the Tartarian deserts, and is said to breed in the vici-nity of Astrachan. In this island it is rarely met with ;

but it is reported to breed in Ireland. It is pretty common in Hungary, Poland, Russia, Austria, and Styria. The nest is generally placed in hilly situa-tions, and either on rocks, or among trees and brush-wood. Though the lanner is a bold bird, and was formerly used in falconry, few particulars are recorded of its habits and manners.

F. subbuteo, Lin. &c. *Hobby.* Bluish-dusky above, white beneath, with oblong black spots, and the cheeks marked on each side by a descending black spot. Length of the mature male, one foot two inches, and weight, seven ounces. The female measures one foot four inches in length, and weighs nine ounces.

Subbuteo.

The hobby is a native of Great Britain, Sweden, France, Germany, the deserts of Tartary, and Siberia, &c. and is destructive of small birds, particularly of larks and quails. It may also be trained to hunt the partridge. It commits its depredations chiefly on plains that confine on forests, flies easily, and even higher than the lark, and, when it captures its prey, retires with it into the forest, and perches on the loftiest trees. In these last it makes its nest, or occupies that which has been deserted by a crow, the female laying two or three whitish eggs, dotted with brown, and marked with some larger spots of black. It leaves us about the latter end of October, and is known to winter about Woronetz and Astrachan. Notwithstanding its diminutive size, it yields to none of its congeners in courage and ad-dress ; and is therefore trained for hawking, but more commonly for taking partridges and larks with a net, which is termed *daring ;* for the hobby being cast off, so frightens the birds, that they readily suffer a net to be drawn over them. When pouncing on a call-bird, it is sometimes entangled in the fowler's snare, when it lays itself on its back, and will not suffer itself to be handled, without exerting its bill and claws to the ut-most, and scratching the person who lays hold of it, to the effusion of his blood.

F. æsalon, Lin. &c.; *F. cæsius,* Meyer ; *F. lithofalco,* Gmel. *Merlin,* or *Stone Falcon.* Cere and legs yellow ; head ferruginous, body bluish-grey, with ferruginous spots, and streaks above, and yellowish-white, with oblong spots beneath. The mature male weighs nearly five ounces and a half, is twelve inches in length, and about twenty-five inches in extent of wing. The fe-male weighs about nine ounces, and is twelve inches and a half long. Both are subject to vary in their co-louring. The wings are not so long and pointed as in the hobby, for, when closed, they do not reach to the end of the tail by an inch and a half.

Æsalon.

The merlin is a migratory species, resorting to the north in spring, for the purpose of breeding, and re-turning to the south on the approach of winter. Ac-cording to Mr. Pennant it does not breed in England ; but Mr. Latham, on the authority of a highly respecta-ble observer, assures us that it has twice produced young in Cumberland, placing its nest on the ground, in the manner of the ring-tail ; and, in Northumber-land, Colonel Montagu found three young ones about half grown, in the middle of a high clump of heath, in which they were so well concealed, that they would not have been discovered, but for a setting dog, which made a point at them. The eggs are said to be of a plain chocolate colour, to vary in number from three to six, and to have been found occasionally in a desert-ed crow's nest. According to Temminck, they are whitish, and mottled at one of the ends with greenish

Ornitho-
logy.

brown. On the Continent the merlin is usually observed to affect hilly and woody situations, and is supposed to breed in trees, or crevices of rocks. It preys on larks and other small birds. It was often trained for hawking, especially for taking partridges, which it will kill by a single pounce on the head or neck. Though of a bold spirit, it flies low, and may be seen along the sides of roads, skimming from hedge to hedge in quest of prey. Partridges and their young are so terrified at its approach, that they have been known to squat down at the fowler's feet.

Tinnuncu-
lus.

F. Tinnunculus, Lin. &c.; *Kestril*. Provincially, *Stonegall, Stannel, Windhover*, &c. Crown of the head bluish-grey, upper parts ferruginous, sprinkled with black angular spots; under parts white, slightly dashed with reddish, and marked with oblong brown spots; the tail cinereous, with a broad black band near the white extremity. The beak is bluish, and the cere, iris, and legs, are yellow. The male measures 14 inches in length, two feet five inches in expanse of wing, and weighs about seven ounces.

The kestril is by far the most elegant of the small British hawks. Including two or three varieties which do not exactly accord with the preceding description, it may be said to inhabit Europe, Siberia, and the more temperate regions in North America. In Sweden it is migratory, remaining in that country only during summer, appearing with the white wagtail, when the crocus, snow-drop, and violet blossom, and quitting the country in September, nearly about the same day on which the white wagtail takes its departure. It breeds in old towers and ruins, and sometimes in the woods, when it will occasionally content itself with the deserted nest of a rook or magpie. Its own is made of sticks, and lined with wool, or other soft materials. The eggs, which are four or five in number, are rather inferior in size to those of the sparrow-hawk, and of a dirty white, blotched with rust colour of various shades, and sometimes wholly covered with a deep rusty red. The kestril is a common inhabitant of our own country, especially about our rocky coasts, or in high or ruinous towers, proclaiming its presence by a loud, tingling, and grating noise. In clear weather it is frequently observed fixed, as it were, in one place, and fanning the air with its wings, being then intent on its prey, such as moles, field-mice, frogs, &c. on which it shoots like an arrow. It also preys on birds; and such is the violence with which it directs its horizontal flight, either in flying from some more powerful enemy of its own tribe, or in the ardent pursuit of distant game, that it has been known to break through a pane of glass, and fall stunned into the middle of a room in which were two opposite windows. After it has secured its prey, it plucks the feathers very dexterously from the birds, but swallows the mice entire, and discharges the hair at the bill, in the form of round balls. It has been often trained to the pursuit of the smaller kind of game, and is said to have been excellent in the chase of partridges and quails, and sometimes even of pheasants. When taken young, and fed on raw meat, it is easily tamed.

Sparverius.

F. sparverius, Lin. &c.; *Little Falcon, St. Domingo Falcon, New York Merlin, American Merlin*, &c. Ferruginous, with black and blue-grey variegations, and white throat: the female coloured like the female kestril. An elegant species, in general appearance closely allied to the preceding, but of considerably smaller size, and the male more diversified in its mark-

ings. Like others of its tribe, it is extremely liable to assume different colourings at different stages of its growth, and has thus given rise to several imaginary species. It is a native of North and South America, and of the West Indies. In the north of the United States, where it is called *little sparrow-hawk*, it is much more rare than in the south; and it is particularly abundant in St. Domingo, where the facility with which it procures small lizards, its favourite food, seems to have rendered it less active and more sociable than on the continent; for in the warmer latitude of the island it occurs in flocks; and the male manifests much attachment to its mate. The female makes its nest on the top or in the hollow of trees, or in the galleries of churches, and lays from two to four eggs, which are white, and spotted with rufous.

Ornitho-
logy.

Ignoble birds of prey are so denominated, because they are not easily trained to falconry. They are a very numerous tribe, distinguished by the length of the fourth quill, and the shortness of the first, so that the wing appears as if obliquely truncated. Their beak is destitute of a lateral tooth near the point, and has only a slight projection in the middle of its length.

Ignoble
birds of
prey.

Eagles, properly so called.

Beak strong, of considerable length, and hooked towards the extremity. Legs strong and nervous, and covered with feathers, or naked; toes robust, and armed with powerful and very crooked claws. Their flight is elevated and rapid, and their courage yields to that of no other bird. Some of them prey on the smaller quadrupeds and birds, whilst others pounce on fishes, and some attack only reptiles and insects. Although it is commonly alleged that they never drink, and it is certain that they can dispense with water for a great length of time, yet when it is presented to them they plunge and bathe in it, and even drink of it like other birds. According to Spallanzani they have a very decided antipathy to bread, and refuse to eat it even after long fasting; but when it is forced into their stomach, it is digested like any other aliment.

Eagles.

F. imperialis, Bechst. Temm.; *F. mojelnick*, Gmel.; *Aquila heliaca*, Savig. *Imperial Eagle*. Crown of the head and occiput furnished with acuminate sub-rufous feathers, edged with bright rufous, of a very dark glossy brown above, of a very dusky brown beneath, with the exception of the abdomen, which is yellowish rufous; some of the scapular feathers always pure white.

Imperialis.

The imperial eagle is diffused over Hungary, Dalmatia, and Turkey, and is more common in the eastern and southern parts of the world than in any other quarter, abounding in Egypt and on the coast of Barbary; but it is rare in the centre of Europe. It preferably resides in the extensive forests of hilly countries, preying on stags, roebucks, foxes, and other mammiferous animals, and often on large birds. The female breeds in lofty trees or elevated rocks, and lays three or four eggs of a dirty white. The cry of this species is loud and sonorous, owing, it is alleged, to the very solid and approximated rings of which the wind-pipe is composed.

F. fulvus, Gmel. Tem. &c.; *F. niger*, Gmel. Lath.; *F. chrysætos*, Lin. &c. (the female;) *F. aquila*, and *F. communis*, of different authors. *Royal or Common Eagle; Ring-tail Eagle* of Willoughby; *White-tail Eagle* of Edwards; *Ring-tail* and *Golden Eagle* of Latham; *Black Eagle* of Pennant, &c. Crown of the head and nape with acuminate feathers, of a bright rufous and golden tinge;

Fulvus.

all the other parts of the body of an obscure brown, more or less blackish, according to age. The male is about three feet long, and the female three feet and a half, the wings stretching to between seven and eight feet.

The royal eagle is pretty generally scattered over the world; for it haunts the high mountain ranges of Europe, Asia Minor, Tartary, the north of Africa, and the prominent crests of Atlas, Persia, Arabia, Russia, Siberia, Kamtschatka, Hudson's Bay, Carolina, Louisiana, &c. It occurs in the mountains of England, Wales, Scotland, and Ireland, but not so commonly as is generally believed; for the osprey is often mistaken for it; and in some districts every large eagle is called the *golden*, or *eagle of the sun*. An overgrown specimen of the present kind was shot at Warkworth, whose out-stretched wings measured eleven feet three inches.

In a clear sky, the royal eagle soars to a great height, but he flies lower in cloudy weather. He rarely quits the mountains to descend into the plains; and his muscular force enables him to encounter the most violent winds. When Ramond had reached the summit of Mont Perdu, the highest of the Pyrénées, he perceived no living creature but an eagle, which passed above him, flying with inconceivable rapidity in direct opposition to a furious wind from south-west. When far aloft, and no longer discernible by the human eye, its cry, which in that situation has been compared to the squeaking of a puppy, may still be heard; and such is the wonderful acuteness of its sight, that from the same elevation it will mark a hare, or even a smaller animal, and dart down on it with unerring aim. The male and female usually hunt together, and the mountaineers allege, that the one beats the bushes, and that the other pursues the started game. Each pair live in an insulated state, establishing their quarters on some high and precipitous cliff, at a respectful distance from others of the same species, and occasionally interrupting their silence by a sharp, piercing, and lugubrious cry. They are extremely tenacious of life, whence probably originated the eastern notion, that they possessed the power of renewing their youth. Keysler alludes to an individual, which lived a hundred and four years at Vienna, though in a state of confinement. Nor is it less remarkable for enduring abstinence, especially when deprived of exercise; for one, taken from a fox-trap, refused food for five weeks, when it was killed. Redi likewise informs us that he kept two alive, the one for twenty-eight, and the other for twenty-one days without food. In old age, individuals of this species become more or less hoary, or partially of a pure white; and similar changes are induced by disease, and protracted captivity or hunger. From their solitary and domineering habits they keep all other birds of prey at a distance from their haunts, and delight in combats and rapine; but they seem to be averse to carrion, and to disdain the insults of weak and petty animals, attacking and bearing away lambs, kids, young gazelles, &c. Their strength chiefly resides in the beak, talons, and wings; and there is scarcely any animal that is a match for them, as they are capable of giving the most terrible annoyance without much danger to themselves, insomuch that a single flap of their wing has struck a man dead in an instant. Unless taken when quite young, they are scarcely to be tamed. In the depth of winter they sometimes descend from the mountains and take refuge in the forests, as in those of Orleans and Fontainebleau. When they regale on their mangled prey,

a dirty bluish liquor, secreted from peculiar glands, has been observed to ooze from the nostrils, and, flowing along the beak, to enter the mouth, where it may possibly assist in preparing the due concoction of the food. It would appear, however, from the experiments of Spallanzani, that their breath is not fetid. In Scotland they are still destructive of deer, which they seize between the horns, and soon subdue by incessantly beating the harassed quadruped with their wings. In the island of Rume, according to Pennant, they have nearly extirpated the stags: and in Shetland they are general plunderers, robbing the rock-birds, especially gulls and cormorants, of their young. In the Orkneys, the nest of a pair has been observed on the same spot from time immemorial. Another pair seem to have once bred in Tintholm, one of the smallest of the Faroe islands, according to the testimony of Landt, who relates the following distressing incident. An eagle one day darted on an infant, who was lying at a little distance from its mother, and carried it to its nest, which was placed on a rock so steep towards the summit, that the boldest bird-catchers had never ventured to climb it. The mother, however, contrived to ascend it; but she arrived too late, for the child was dead, and its eyes torn out. Again, in the year 1737, in the parish of Norderhougs, in Norway, a boy, upwards of two years of age, was running from the house to his parents, who were at work in the fields at no great distance, when an eagle pounced on him, and carried him off in their sight, in spite of all their screams and efforts. Anderson, in his History of Iceland, asserts, that in that island children of four or five years of age have experienced the same cruel fate; and Ray mentions, that in one of the Orkneys an infant of a year old was seized in the talons of an eagle, and conveyed about four miles to its eyry; while the mother, knowing the spot, pursued the bird, found her child in the nest, and took it home unhurt.

The nest is usually placed horizontally, in the hollow or fissure of some high and abrupt rock, and is constructed of sticks of five or six feet in length, interlaced with pliant twigs, and covered with layers of rushes, heath, or moss. Unless destroyed by some accident, it is supposed to suffice, with occasional repairs, for the same couple during their lives. It is said that a peasant once got a comfortable subsistence for himself and family out of an eagle's nest; and that he protracted the assiduity of the old birds, by clipping the wings, and thus retarding the flight of the young, as also by binding the latter, so as to increase their cries, and thus stimulate the urgency of the parents to supply their wants. It was lucky for him, however, that the old ones did not happen to encounter him, as their resentment might have proved fatal. An Irish peasant, who had determined to rob an eagle's nest on one of the islands of the lake of Killarney, was less fortunate. He swam over, indeed, when the old birds were gone; but on his return, while still up to the chin in water, they fell on him, killed him on the spot, and rescued their offspring.

The female of the present species usually lays two, sometimes only one, and rarely three eggs, of a dirty white, speckled with rufous or reddish. The incubation lasts thirty days. The eaglets are at first covered with a white down; and their early feathers are of a pale yellow. Like the rest of the tribe, the royal eagle drives off the young from its nest as soon as they are able to shift for themselves,—a circumstance which

Pliny states like an elegant philosopher, and Thomson describes in the genuine spirit of poetry.

European falconers have long since desisted from attempting to press the eagle into their service, both on account of its weight, (from 16 to 18 pounds,) which renders it inconvenient to carry on the hand, and of its untractable and malevolent dispositions. Yet, in some regions of Persia and India it is tutored to the hunting of deer and antelopes; and the Kirgis, a nomadic horde, who pitch their tents to the east of the Caspian Sea, are as knowing in young eagles, as our jockeys are in horses, and will give the Russian dealers a fine horse or a sheep in exchange for an eagle suited to their purpose, while they will scarcely offer the most contemptible trifle for another that gives no indication of possessing the proper qualities. Here, then, we have an illustration of an important zoological position, that individuals of the same species widely differ from one another in respect of temper and talents. The independent Tartars have long been accustomed to discipline this species to the chace of hares, foxes, antelopes, and even wolves; and the practice is at least as old as 1269, when Marco Polo contemplated, with admiration, the diversions of the Grand Khan of Tartary, who had several eagles that were devoted to this kind of sport. This, however, like other eagles, has a very imperfect sense of smell, and hunts merely by its exquisite sight. Although it frequently gets fat in winter, and its flesh contracts no offensive flavour, it is, nevertheless, too tough and stringy to be used as food.

From its stately demeanour, and the altitude of its flight, the eagle was denominated by the ancients the *Celestial Bird,* and regarded in their mythology as the *Messenger of Jove,* and worthy of bearing the thunderbolts in its talons. Its figure, in gold or silver, and placed on the end of a spear, was the military ensign of the Romans and of the Persians; and it has been adopted in modern heraldry as an emblem of power.

Nævius.

F. nævius, Gmel. &c. including his *Maculatus; Aquila planga,* Vieill.; *Spotted, Rough-footed,* or *Plaintive Eagle.* Body, head, wings, and tail, of a glossy brown, of various degrees of intensity, according to age.

Although not numerous in any particular district, the spotted eagle is spread over Europe, with the exception, it is alleged, of Denmark, Sweden, and Norway; but it is not uncommon in Russia, Siberia, and even Kamtschatka. It occurs likewise in Asia Minor, Persia, Arabia, and in Africa; and a variety, with an imbricated tail, is found in New Holland. The female builds her nest on lofty trees, and lays two white eggs, streaked, at wide intervals, with red. Ducks, pigeons, rats, and large insects, are its principal prey. It is of less spirited dispositions than other eagles, and is remarkable for its plaintive cry. Being more easily tamed than most of the race, it has sometimes been used in falconry, but seldom with much success, on account of its want of courage; for it has been subdued and brought to the ground by a sparrow-hawk.

Armiger.

F. armiger, Shaw; *F. bellicus,* Lath.; *Griffard,* Levaill.; *Griffard,* or *Warlike Eagle.* Grey-brown above, white beneath; hind-head crested, the smaller wing-feathers and tail crossed with whitish bars. The male differs from the female, chiefly in the greater darkness of its colouring. About the size of the royal eagle. It is a very fierce and ravenous species, preying on the young of antelopes, hares, and other small quadrupeds, and driving predacious birds from its domain. When he has slain his victim, troops of crows and vultures flock from different quarters, to participate of the spoil;

but, standing on the dead body, his haughty and menacing attitude suffices to ward off the band of greedy and importunate plunderers. The female builds her eyry either on very tall trees, or on abrupt points of rock, constructing a large platform, strong enough to bear the weight of a man. The eggs, which are two in number, are almost spherical, and perfectly white. During incubation the male caters for the family; but, when the young have grown a little, their ravenous appetite consumes the supplies of both parents. The griffard is, in fact, uncommonly voracious. Levaillant preserved one alive, which he had lamed in the wing, and which, during three days, refused every kind of nourishment; but it then became insatiable, was thrown into a state of extreme agitation whenever meat was presented to it, and would often swallow an entire lump of nearly a pound weight. Even when its crop was filled, it refused nothing, and bolted, indiscriminately, every kind of flesh, not excepting that of other birds of prey. It is a native of Africa, particularly of the Namaquas, and is conspicuous for strength, courage, and ferocity.

Haliaëtus.

F. haliaëtus, Lin., &c. including *F. arundinaceus,* Gmel.; *Bald Buzzard, Fishing Eagle, Fishing Hawk,* and *Osprey Eagle,* of some of the English writers; although, to prevent confusion, we would restrict the latter to *F. ossifragus.* The Linnæan specific name, we may also remark, is not sufficiently appropriate, as the bird haunts fresh in preference to salt water. Brown above, white beneath, with whitish head, and blue cere and legs. The minuter markings vary considerably, according to age. The male is one foot, and nine or ten inches long; the female two feet, and measures five feet and a half from tip to tip of the expanded wings. The legs are short and strong; the outer toe turns easily backwards, and the claw belonging to it is larger than that of the inner one, by which contrivance the slippery prey is more easily secured. Many of the elder ornithologists have erroneously alleged, that it has one foot sub-palmated. It makes its nest in the crevices of rocks, or on the tops of tall trees, and occasionally on the ground, among reeds, laying from two to four white eggs, spotted with reddish, rather smaller than those of the domestic hen. Colonel Montagu once saw a nest belonging to a pair of this species, on the top of a ruined chimney on an island in Loch Lomond. It was large and flat, formed of sticks laid across, lined with flags, and resting on the sides of the chimney. From an expression which occurs in some old acts of parliament, there is reason to believe that the bald buzzard was once trained to fishing in England. It is now rarely met with in that country, residing chiefly near water, especially large rivers and lakes, and feeding principally on fish, which it catches with great eagerness, and on which it pounces with astonishing rapidity, sometimes plunging two feet under the surface of the water, carrying off its capture, and devouring it at leisure at some distance. In the breeding season, it is frequently seen about the Lake of Killarney in Ireland. It is found in most of the countries of Europe, from Sweden to Greece, and is very common in Siberia, where the inhabitants foolishly believe, that a single scratch of its talons is highly poisonous. It has been, moreover, ascertained to inhabit Egypt, Nigritia, Barbary, and Louisiana. These birds are almost always observed in pairs, except during the prevalence of severe frost, when the waters are congealed, and when they usually separate in quest of milder skies. During the spring and summer months, the bald buzzard is frequently seen hovering over the large rivers in America, or resting on the wing for several minutes at a time, then suddenly darting down, and seldom emerging without a fish in its talons. It then shakes off the water, like a mist, and shapes its course to the woods. The white-headed eagle, which, on those occasions, is usually on the watch, instantly gives chace, and endeavours to soar above it, when the bald buzzard, alarmed for its own safety, drops the fish, which the eagle never fails to catch before it reaches the ground.

There are several varieties of this species, among which may be included those of Carolina and Cayenne.

Ossifragus.   *F. ossifragus,* Gmel. and Lath. including *Albicilla* and *Albicaudus,* which only denote changes of sex and age. *Sea Eagle,* or *Osprey.* Grey brown, spotted with darker brown above ; breast and belly brown grey, spotted with blackish ; the great wing feathers blackish, and those of the tail of a blackish grey outwardly, and deep cinereous, on the inner side. A sort of beard, or tuft of feathers, depends from the base of the under mandible. In the old birds, the tail is pure white. Length of the male two feet four inches, and of the female two feet ten inches at most, and the extent of wing seven feet. It is a native of Europe, and also of North America ; but the American variety is the larger of the two. It is very frequent in Kamtschatka, and is found, during summer, even on the arctic coasts. It is likewise common in Russia and Siberia, and far from rare about the Caspian Sea, where it breeds in the highest trees. It chiefly affects sea coasts, and the vicinity of lakes and rivers. Though it can neither swim nor dive, it pounces with great rapidity on fish, as they happen to come near the surface of the water, falling down on them like a lump of lead, with a loud sousing noise and scream, carrying them off in its talons, and devouring them in some place of security. In attempting to catch overgrown fish, however, it is sometimes drowned, being dragged forcibly under water when unable to disengage its talons. Buffon adverts to its alleged imperfection of vision, noticed by Aristotle, and which he traces to the addition of a membrane in the eye, which appears like a speck, but which does not materially impede the transmission of light, since the bird hunts for its prey both in the twilight and during the night. This species is not unfrequent in Scotland and the Orkney islands, where it is known by the name of *Erne,*—an appellation, however, which is vaguely bestowed on the *golden,* and some other sorts of eagles. The osprey is also frequently confounded with the golden eagle. The female breeds on high trees, or cliffs on the sea-shore, and lays two roundish white eggs, thinly sprinkled with reddish spots.

The Greenlanders, who kill these birds with arrows, or catch them by snares laid on the snow, eat their flesh, make under garments or beds of their skins sewed together, and use the beak and claws as amulets in the treatment of various complaints.

Vocifer.   *F. vocifer,* Shaw. *Vociferous Eagle.* Brown ferruginous, undulated with black ; head, neck, breast, and tail, white. The craw, which is slightly visible, is covered with long frizzled down. The female is stronger than the male, but less brilliant in her attire. The sexes are inseparable companions, hunting, flying, and resting together. They subsist chiefly on fish, darting down from the air with inexpressible celerity on such as they perceive, striking the surface of the water with a loud noise, and even submerging their whole body to secure their prize. They also devour a sort of large lizard, which abounds in some of the African rivers,

and occasionally antelopes, but never birds. Their loud and clamorous call resounds through the vast solitudes of Southern Africa. They are rare at the Cape of Good Hope, and seldom met with till about sixty or eighty leagues in the interior of the country ; but the district in which they most frequently occur is about the Bay of Lagoa. Like most other eagles they place their nest either on the top of lofty trees, or on the points of rocks, and line it with wool, feathers, &c. The eggs are shaped like those of the turkey, but larger, and also whiter.

Albescens.   *F. albescens,* Daud. *Blanchard,* Levaill. *Albescent Eagle.* Whitish, variegated above with yellowish brown ; tail black, barred with white ; back of the head slightly crested. About a third smaller than the golden eagle, and of a more slender shape. First observed by Levaillant in the regions of Africa that confine on the Cape of Good Hope. The albescent eagle pursues its game with such agility that hardly any bird can outstrip it. It is partial to a sort of wood pigeon, whose flight is also very rapid, but which rarely escapes its fangs. It likewise subsists on wood partridges, and on a very diminutive kind of antelope, which occurs only in the forests. There, concealed behind the thick branch of a tree, this eagle watches his prey, which he seizes by rushing down on it with noise. No sooner has he accomplished the capture, than all the crows in the neighbourhood flock around him to share in the spoil ; but he defies alike their approach and their clamour, so that they are contented to remain under the tree on which he makes his repast, and pick up the fallen fragments. He never eats his game on the ground, but always bears it to some lofty station, and plucks off the feathers before he dispatches it. " But what is very extraordinary," observes Levaillant, " and seems difficult of belief in a bird whose ordinary food consists of birds, is, that the smallest of them may fly, or remain near him with impunity, and even alight on his eyry ; for he not only does them no harm, but becomes their protector, and defends them against other birds of prey." But he suffers no ravenous bird to approach his domain, chasing and harassing it till it retires. When tranquil, and sated with food, he repeats, for hours together, a weak and shrill cry. The nest is placed on the top of the highest trees, and contains two white eggs, as large as those of the turkey hen, and rounder. The male and female perform, alternately, the functions of incubation.

Goshawks.

Beak curved from the base.

Goshawks.   *F. palumbarius,* Lin. &c. including the *gallinarius* and *gentilis* of Gmel. and Lath. *Goshawk.* Upper *Palumba-* parts bluish-cinereous ; a broad white stripe above *rius.* the eyes ; the under parts white, with transverse bars, and longitudinal lines of dark brown ; tail cinereous, with four or five blackish brown bars. The beak is bluish black, the cere yellowish green, and the iris and the feet are yellow. Length of the female about two feet ; size of the male about one-third less. In the female the brown prevail over the bluish shades, and the number of small brown bars under the breast is greater. Like others of the falcon tribe, the goshawk is sometimes entirely white, or nearly so, and sometimes the head white, and the rest of the body marked as usual, or with occasional variations. It is a native of every quarter of the globe, being found in Iceland, Russia, Poland, Denmark, Great Britain, France, Switzerland, Germany, Italy, Greece, Persia, Armenia, and in various parts of Africa and North America. In this island, it principally occurs in Scotland. It breeds on the tops of high trees, the female laying four or five eggs, of a bluish white, spotted with fulvous. It flies low, proves very destructive to game, pigeons, and poultry, and dashes through the woods with great impetuosity after its quarry; but if it cannot almost immediately catch the object of its pursuit, it desists, and perches on a bough, till some other opportunity occurs. In the days of falconry, it was held in higher estimation than any of the short-winged hawks, and was used for the larger sorts of game, as it still is in the great sporting excursions of the emperor of China.

Cachin-
nans.

F. cachinnans, Lin. &c. *Niacagua* of Azara. *Laughing Falcon.* Cere and legs yellow; eye-lids white; body variegated with brown and whitish; top of the head black, surrounded by a white ring. Native of Paraguay, Cayenne, and other regions of South America, haunting flooded savannahs and marshy grounds, and perching on dried and elevated branches of trees, whence it is conjectured to feed on fish, frogs, lizards, and other reptiles. It is of gentle dispositions, and rather a stupid bird, occasionally uttering a sound, which is expressed by its vernacular appellation, and, when disturbed, emitting a shrill and sudden cry, as if laughing.

Sparrow-hawks,

Sparrow-
hawks.
Nisus.

Denote such of the present tribe as have long and slender tarsi.

F. nisus, Lin. &c. *Sparrow-hawk.* Bluish-cinereous above; a white spot on the nape, white beneath; with brown undulations; tail ash-grey, with five bars of blackish cinereous. The colouring, however, is very liable to vary, and specimens entirely milk-white have been sometimes observed.

This species is well known for its depredations among poultry, and is numbered by falconers among the short winged hawks, or such in which the wings, when closed, fall short of the end of the tail. The length of the male is usually about twelve inches, its extent of wing twenty-three inches, and its weight scarcely five ounces, whereas the female measures about fifteen inches in length, and weighs about nine ounces. She builds in lofty trees, old ruins, or high rocks, frequently occupying the old nest of a crow, and laying from four to six eggs, of a dirty white, and sometimes of a bluish tinge, blotched at the large, and sometimes, though rarely, at the narrow end, with rust colour. Though it flies low, it is very fierce and predacious. It more or less abounds in almost every quarter of the world, being found as high as Sondmor, and in the Faroe Isles, though not, as alleged, in Siberia, and again, as far south as Africa. In this country, it is common in most of the wooded or inclosed parts of the kingdom, but is of less frequent occurrence in the more champaign districts. In some parts of Europe it seems to be a partial migrant; for Belon, long ago, witnessed their passage, as Sonnini more recently did, when at sea, between Italy and Barbary. On the approach of winter, legions of them move southward, to the dismay of the smaller and weaker migratory bands, on which they prey with cruel assiduity, and from which circumstance the mariners in the Mediterranean term them *corsairs.* In Egypt, they are stationary throughout the year, and many of them are habituated to a town life, usually taking up their abode along with kites and vultures, on the terraces of the houses, and sparing, as if by implied contract, the turtle-doves. Indeed, we should remark, that, notwithstanding its

bold and ravenous propensities, the sparrow-hawk is more easily tamed than most birds of prey, and not unsusceptible of attachment. The young bird, it is alleged, may be used as food.

Ornitho-
logy.

F. minullus, Lath. &c. *Dwarf Sparrow-hawk.* Brown above, white beneath, breast marked with descending brown streaks, and the abdomen with descending brown bars. Although this small species does not exceed the size of the blackbird, it is by no means deficient in courage or assiduity; for it drives the butcher-bird from its neighbourhood, and fears not to attack the kite and the buzzard; but crows are the most marked object of its persecution; for it chases them with eager impetuosity, uttering a cry which has been compared to that of the kestril. The smaller birds are its ordinary food; but when a sufficiency of these cannot be procured, it has recourse to some of the larger sorts of insects, particularly of the mantis and locust tribes. The female, which is nearly twice the size of the male, but with plumage of duller tints, forms its nest in rather a coarse style, of small twigs, intermixed with leaves and moss, and lined with leaves, moss, or wool: in this she lays four or five eggs. As Levaillant was sitting at a table, engaged in preparing some birds lately killed, one of these hawks suddenly stooped, and, seizing one of the recently stuffed specimens, and flying with it to a neighbouring tree, began to plume and tear it open, but finding nothing but moss and cotton, seemed indignant at the disappointment, and at length contented itself with devouring the head, the only part which remained in its natural state.

Minullus.

F. musicus, Daud. and Lath. *Chaunting Sparrow-hawk.* Grey above, with brown undulations beneath, black wing feathers, and brown wedge-shaped tail, barred with white. An elegant species, of the size of the common falcon, observed by Levaillant in the interior of Africa, where it builds in woods, laying four white and nearly round eggs. The female is a third larger than the male, and both commit great havock among the smaller kind of game, as quails, partridges, &c. They even attack hares, and will, like the buzzard, feed on moles, rats, field-mice, &c. In the breeding season, the note of the male is much more musical than that of any bird of prey, and is heard at the dawn of day, or in the dusk of the evening, and, not unfrequently, during the greater part of the night. It sings out in a loud tone for more than a minute, and, after an interval, begins anew. During its song, it is so regardless of its own safety, that a person may approach very near to it; but at other times it is extremely suspicious, and takes flight on the most trifling cause of alarm. Should the male be killed, the female may also be shot without difficulty; for her attachment to him is such, that she continues flying round with the most plaintive voice, and often passes within a few yards of the fowler. If, however, the female should happen to be shot first, the male retires to the top of some distant tree, and, without ceasing his song, becomes uncommonly shy and wary.

Musicus.

Kites,

Kites.

Have short tarsi, weak toes and claws, and a beak small and weak in proportion to their size. Their long wings and forked tail enable them to fly with great ease and rapidity.

F. furcatus, Lin. &c. *Swallow-tailed Falcon.* White; with the back, wings, and very long forked tail, purplish black. About two feet long, and of very elegant proportions and plumage, the whole bird, on a

Furcatus.

Ornitho-
logy.

general view, having the appearance of some gigantic species of swallow; but the curved bill, and lengthened plumes on the thighs, denote its true station in the system. It feeds principally on insects, which it catches in its flight; but it also preys on the smaller kinds of snakes, lizards, &c. and is often observed to tear off the nests of wasps as it glides along the trees on which they are fixed. Found in Carolina, Louisiana, &c. but migrates to South America on the approach of cold weather.

Milvus.

F. milvus, Lin. &c. *Common Kite.* Prov. *Glead, Greedy Glead*, and *Puttock.* Variegated with brown, and ferruginous; head whitish, and streaked with brown, tail ferruginous, and much forked. The male weighs about two pounds six ounces, and measures two feet two inches in length, and upwards of five feet in extent of wing. The female is somewhat larger.

The kite is a native of most of the countries of Europe, and of various regions of Siberia and of Africa. It likewise occurs in some of the provinces of America. Although it has been traced to the south of Norway, there is reason to believe that many of those which breed in Europe retire into Egypt, or other hot latitudes, during the cold season. Their appearance in Greece, during the spring, is alluded to by Aristophanes. It is, nevertheless, certain, that not a few in this and other countries of Europe, are stationary throughout the year. The species is partial to hilly and wooded situations. Early in spring the female makes a nest in a fork of some large tree, composing it of sticks, and lining it with such soft materials as chance may happen to throw within its reach, as wool, the inner bark of some tree, hair, bits of cloth, &c. The eggs, which are commonly three, and rarely four, are larger than those of the domestic hen, and of a dirty white, with a few rusty spots at the large end, though sometimes quite plain.

The most ordinary observer of our native birds must be acquainted with the elegant appearance of the kite, while sailing aloft in its circling flight, and maintaining its equipoise by a slight exertion of its pinions at distant intervals. It is then watching the surface of the soil for prey; and it occasionally descends from its airy height on some bird, or other creature, within its view; its depredations being limited to animals on the ground, as young rabbits, hares, game of all kinds, poultry, and young birds, incapable of flight. It will also destroy young lambs, and feed greedily on carrion; but, in default of these, it readily eats mice, worms, insects, and even snakes. It frequently resorts to the neighbourhood of towns, to pick up offals, which it also sweeps from the surface of the water with great dexterity. Were it not such an unmerciful invader of the poultry-yard, it would be welcomed as the harbinger of fine weather and clear skies, with which its principal excursions coincide, whereas its clamours are said to presage rain and storms. So cowardly is it in its dispositions, that it is often insulted and pursued by the crow, and that, notwithstanding its vehement appetite for chickens, the anger of the brooding hen will drive it away. At times, however, it is so completely absorbed in the gratification of feeding, that it will allow a person to approach near it, or even knock it down.

In the towns of Upper Egypt, where this bird is not only tolerated but cherished, it abounds on the terraces of the houses, and lives in perfect harmony with vultures, thus rendering a most important service to the community, by acting as scavengers, or policemen. At Constantinople they are equally protected, and consequently so tame, that they fly towards those who whistle on them. Busbequius mentions, that he ordered the insides of a sheep to be cut into small pieces, and whistled to the kites, when many flew about him, and, as he threw the bits of meat into the air, they would catch them before they fell to the ground. In the days of King Henry VIII. as appears from the observations of Clusius, even the British metropolis swarmed with kites, which were attracted by the various kinds of offals thrown into the street, and were so fearless as to snatch up their prey in the midst of the greatest crowds; for it was forbidden to kill them.

Buzzards.

These are characterized by their long wings, even tail, and the beak suddenly curved from the base.

F. apivorus, Lin. &c. *Honey Buzzard*, Prov. *Capped Bird.* Brown, with cinereous bands on the wings; under parts white, with transverse sub-ferruginous bars, the space between the eye and the bill covered with feathers very compactly arranged, in the form of scales. This last circumstance is more characteristic than the disposition of the colours, which varies considerably, according to sex, age, and accidental modifications. The total length of the full grown male is about two feet, the extent of wing four feet one inch, and the weight about thirty ounces.

Although the honey buzzard has many of the propensities of the kite, it does not, like it, soar aloft, but flies from tree to tree, and from bush to bush, or runs along the ground, in quest of field-mice, frogs, lizards, caterpillars, &c. It feeds its young with the larvæ of wasps, and perhaps of bees. It builds in trees, forming its nest of small twigs, lined with wool, and laying, for the most part, two eggs, but sometimes only one, smaller, and not so round as those of the buzzard, of a dirty white, and blotched all over with rust colour, but sometimes dotted at each end with small red spots, and surrounded in the middle with a broad blood-coloured zone. The female occasionally makes good her lodging in the old nest of another bird, particularly in that of the kite. This species occurs, though sparingly, in England, and in France; its numbers have been much reduced, but it abounds in some of the northern and eastern parts of the world, as in the open regions of Russia and Siberia, particularly on the borders of Lake Krasnojark, where the most ordinary articles of its food are toads and lizards. In winter, the young birds are caught in snares, being then fat, and reputed fit for the table, having less of the alkaline and ammoniacal flavour than most birds of prey, and which usually yields to the application of the vegetable acids, as of vinegar.

F. lagopus, Gmel. Lath.; *F. plumipes*, Daud.; *F. Sclavonicus*, Lath. *Buse Gantée*, of Levaill. *Rough-legged Falcon.* Feet feathered to the toes, a large brown patch on the belly, and a considerable portion of the tail white from its origin. These characters are sufficiently discriminative; and the more general markings are liable to vary. The male is about nineteen, or twenty inches in length, and the female two feet three inches. It occurs in the North of Europe, in North America, and also in the heart of Africa, frequenting the outskirts of woods, in the neighbourhood of waters and marshes, and feeding on small quadrupeds, game, and reptiles. It is more fierce and sanguinary than others of its tribe, nestles in large trees, and lays four

Ornitho-
logy.

Buzzards.

Apivorus.

Lagopus.

Ornitho-
logy.

Buteo.

or five eggs, marked with reddish undulations. It has sometimes been shot in England.

F. buteo, Lin. &c. *F. communis fuscus. F. variegatus, F. albidus,* and *F. versicolor,* Gmel. *Common Buzzard,* Prov. *Puttock.* Varied with brown and ferruginous above, with white and ferruginous beneath; cere and legs yellow; tail banded with brown. The subordinate details of the colouring are so very variable, that scarcely any two individuals exactly resemble each other. The female is generally of darker hues than the male, weighs about thirty ounces, and measures about twenty-one inches in length, and four feet one inch in extent of wing. It is the *Falco ranivorus* of Shaw, the *Grenouillard* of Levaillant, and the *Busard Roux* of Vieillot. The big head, short neck, thick body, clumsy limbs, and large lifeless eyes, sufficiently bespeak the sluggish dispositions of the buzzard. Too heavy and indolent to hunt by flight, it will continue motionless, for hours together, on a tree, bush, stone, or clod of earth, till some game passes within its spring, when it dashes on, and devours it. Small birds, young rabbits and hares, moles, field-mice, lizards, frogs, toads, &c. constitute its ordinary fare; but, in default of these, it will eat worms, beetles, and even carrion. In the breeding season, it is more active, and will soar to a considerable height, ascending in a spiral direction. The female makes her nest in the fork of a tree, with large sticks, and lines it with wool, hair, or other soft substances, and sometimes takes possession of a deserted crow's nest, which it enlarges, and accommodates to its purpose. She usually deposits two, not unfrequently three, and seldom four eggs, rather larger than those of a hen, of a dirty white, or greenish, and most commonly spotted with rust-colour, chiefly at the larger end. The young, when in the nest, are covered over with a yellowish down; and they begin to perch on bushes about the middle of July, when they utter a shrill and plaintive cry. It has likewise been observed, that they accompany the old birds for some time after quitting the nest, a circumstance unusual in other birds of prey, which generally drive off their young as soon as they can fly. Ray affirms, that if the hen should happen to be killed, the cock buzzard will hatch and rear the brood. The eyes of this bird are readily dazzled by a strong light; and it seems to welcome the setting of the sun, especially in summer, by its stridulous call, thus approaching to the nocturnal birds of prey. It is one of the most common birds of the hawk kind that we have in this country, and is, indeed, very generally spread over the world, exhibiting many varieties, several of which have been inadvertently described as separate species. Although of little service in falconry, it is capable of being trained, in a certain degree, to habits of domestication.

Ærugino-
sus.

F. æruginosus, Lin. &c. *Moor Buzzard,* Prov. *Duck-Hawk,* or *White-headed Harpy.* Brown; crown of the head luteous; cere and legs yellow. The prevailing hue is chocolate brown, tinged more or less with ferruginous, and brightest in the male. The female weighs about twenty-eight ounces and a half, and is twenty-three inches and a half in length; the male is somewhat less, weighing about twenty-one ounces, and measuring twenty-one inches in length; but both are subject to considerable varieties in their markings. They chiefly affect swampy moors, and barren situations in the neighbourhood of pools, rivers, and lakes. Instead of perching on lofty trees, like several of their congeners, they watch for their prey on the ground, on a stone, or a bush; they fly heavily, horizontally, and at a little

Ornitho-
logy.

distance from the surface of the soil, attacking water fowls, fish, frogs, toads, and aquatic vermes; their long legs enabling them to wade on the margins of the waters. They have likewise recourse to rabbits, and other small game; nor do they disdain lizards, and some of the larger insects. Being bolder and more active than the common buzzards, when pursued, they face about, and make a vigorous defence; and both the hobby and the kestril shun their approach. Although the nest is sometimes met with in the fork of a large tree, it is much more commonly made on the ground, among short wood, furze, or fern, and composed of sticks, rushes, or coarse grass. In this the female deposits three or four eggs, considerably smaller than those of the common buzzard, and, according to Montagu, who observed them in the nest, " perfectly white, without any spots," whereas Vieillot asserts, that they are whitish, with brownish spots, intermingled with some others of a decided brown." In the breeding season, when the female is employed in incubation, the male will soar to a considerable height, and remain suspended on wing for a long length of time. The moor buzzard is but sparingly dispersed over most of the countries of Europe, although it seems to abound in some particular districts; thus, Montagu remarks, that it is the most common of the falcon tribe about the sandy flats of the coast of Carmarthen, where he saw no fewer than nine of them regaling on the carcass of a sheep; and Cetti acquaints us, that it has greatly multiplied in Sardinia. In former times, it was used by falconers, for the chace of rabbits, partridges, and quails; but it has long since been rejected, as a bird of ignoble flight.

Cyaneus.

F. cyaneus, Lin. &c. including *Pygargus,* which is now proved to be the female; and one or other of these designations comprises *F. albicans, F. communis,* E, *albus* of Frisch, *F. montanus,* B, *griseus, Bohemicus, Hudsonius,* and *Buffonii,* Gmel. *F. rubiginosus,* and *ranivorus,* Lath. *F. europhigistus,* Daud. and *F. strigiceps,* Nilson. *Blue Hawk,* of Edwards; *Ring-tail,* and *Hen Harrier,* of Pennant and others, and *Katabilla* of the Orcadians. M. Temminck proposes, as two discriminating characters, the termination of the wings at three fourths of the length of the tail, and the equal length of the third and fourth quills. The technical definition of the male is, whitish-grey, with a collar of stiffish brown and white feathers, and dusky quill feathers; and that of the female brown, with ferruginous variegations, a collar of stiffish brown and white feathers, white rump, and dusky quill feathers. But the varieties of marking, induced by age and other circumstances, are too numerous and minute to be detailed, and have contributed to involve the history of the species in mystery, paradox, and incongruity. The question relative to the specific identity of the two sexes has been ably discussed by the judicious Latham, in the Supplement to his Synopsis; but the interesting facts, briefly recorded by Colonel Montagu, in the Supplement to his Ornithological Dictionary, from a more extended communication, inserted in the ninth volume of the *Linnean Transactions,* must be allowed to be decisive.

This species occurs, more or less diffused, and variously modified, from the polar regions to the heart of Africa. In France, Germany, and Great Britain, it is sufficiently common, as likewise in Southern Siberia, and Hudson's Bay. It flies low, skimming along the surface, in quest of prey; delights in marshy situations, and feeds on lizards, and other small reptiles and birds.

It has its English appellation from its persecutions in the poultry-yard.

M. Gérardin relates, that he procured two young ones from the nest of a Hen-Harrier, placed in the fork of a tree; so that it does not invariably nidificate on the ground, or in bushes, though it sometimes selects rushes, or grain that has been sown in winter. The nestlings were, at first, reared on the livers of calves and oxen, of which they were very greedy, and of which they swallowed morsels as large as walnuts. One of them, however, soon died, on the shooting of its first quill-feathers; the other, which was a female, lived for the space of a year, eating all kinds of meat, either raw or cooked, and also small birds, which it deplumed very neatly before eating them. Its familiarity, which was at first very amusing, afterwards degenerated into a troublesome and outrageous deportment, which ultimately cost it its life. When admitted, for example, into the dining-room, it would spring on the table, survey the dishes, and, in a twinkling, bear off in its talons a lump of boiled beef, of which it was passionately fond, fly precipitately out at the door, and devour its morsel in a corner, at leisure. When scarcely six months old, it exercised despotic government in the house, driving the cats from their meals, and attempting to pick out their eyes. A friend of M. Gérardin happening one day to call at the house, accompanied by his pointer, the hawk no sooner perceived the latter, than it sprang on the poor animal, seized him by the throat, and, with a single stroke of its bill, deprived him of an eye, when the owner of the dog inflicted summary vengeance, by dispatching the aggressor with a blow of his cane on the head.

SERPENTARIUS, Shaw, &c.; VULTUR SERPENTARIUS, Lin. GYPOGERANUS, Illig. and Temm.; *Messenger, Secretary,* &c. Bill shorter than the head, thick, strong, curved from near its origin, furnished with a cere at the base, and depressed at the point; nostrils somewhat remote from the base of the bill, lateral, inserted in the cere, diagonal, oblong, and open; legs very long and slender; the tibia feathered, the tarsus long, and more slender below than above; the toes short, warty beneath, the fore ones united at the base by a membrane, the hinder articulated on the tarsus; wings long, and armed with obtuse spurs. There is only one species, whose characters, consequently, are those of the genus.

S. Africanus, Shaw, &c.; *Vultur serpentarius,* Lin. &c.; *Snake-eater, African Snake-eater, Secretary, Sagittarius, Secretary Vulture,* &c. Cinereous; hind-head crested; tail wedge-shaped, with the middle tail-feathers lengthened. The bill is black, and the crest capable of being erected or depressed. From this bunch of ten-feathers behind the head, the Dutch gave the bird the name of *Secretary,* because in Holland, clerks, when interrupted in their writing, stick their pen in the hair, behind the right ear. This species inhabits the dry plains in the lower parts of Africa and the Philippine islands. Being almost always obliged to run in pursuit of its prey, it seldom avails itself of its power of flight; and it frequently kills, or at least wholly disables, a snake, by breaking the vertebræ with a single stroke of the wing. In its natural state it is very wild, and not easily approached. The male and female rarely quit each other. Those which frequent the neighbourhood of the Cape construct a very large nest, on the top of some high thicket, and line it with wool and feathers; but towards the regions of Natal, they build on lofty trees. The eggs, which are two

or three in number, are about the size of those of a goose, and white, with reddish specks.

When taken young, the snake-eater may be easily tamed, and kept with poultry in the farm-yard, where it is serviceable in destroying rats and other noxious animals. It may be fed with meat, either raw or dressed, and will readily eat fish; but, if allowed to fast too long, it is apt to seize on small chickens and ducklings, which it swallows whole. It is not, however, of a malignant disposition, and is generally observed to interpose its authority in appeasing the quarrels that take place among the other birds. When in a domesticated state, scarcely any kind of food comes amiss to it; and, if young birds are presented to it, it will take them by the bill foremost, and swallow them entire. Levaillant tells us, that he witnessed an engagement between a secretary vulture and a serpent, and which was conducted with obstinacy and address on both sides. The latter, feeling at length the inferiority of his resources, employed, in attempting to regain his hole, all that cunning which is ascribed to his race, while the bird, apparently guessing his design, stopped him on a sudden, and cut off his retreat by placing herself before him at a single leap. On whatever side the reptile endeavoured to effect his escape, his adversary still appeared before him. He then erected himself boldly, to intimidate the bird, and, hissing vehemently, displayed his menacing throat, inflamed eyes, and a head swollen with rage and venom. This threatening aspect sometimes produced a suspension of hostilities; but the bird soon returned to the charge, and covering her body with one of her wings, as a buckler, struck her antagonist with the bony protuberance of the other. He then staggered and fell, and the conqueror, with a single stroke of her beak, laid open his skull. At this instant, the traveller fired at and killed her. In her crop he found, on dissection, eleven tolerably large lizards, three serpents as long as his arm, eleven small tortoises, most of which were about two inches in diameter, and a number of locusts and other insects. In addition to this mass of food, the crop contained a sort of ball, as large as a goose's egg, formed of the vertebræ of serpents and lizards, shells of different tortoises, and wings, claws, and shields of different sorts of beetles, destined, no doubt, to be disgorged, as in other birds of prey.

The young snake-eaters remain a long while in the nest, until they are capable of supporting themselves on their slender limbs. Even when four months old, they may be seen to walk, resting on the heel, which gives them a very awkward appearance: but, at the age of seven months, when they have attained their full growth and size, they display much grace and ease in their motions. It is a singular circumstance, that, in all their contests, these birds strike forwards with their legs, and not backwards, like others of their class.

The birds of prey denominated *nocturnal*, have generally a large head, very large and prominent eyes, surrounded by slender feathers, and a thick but light skull, in which are several cavities. Their soft and downy feathers make little or no noise during flight; and their outer toe may be directed forward or backward at pleasure. Their eyes are so constructed, that they are able to see much more distinctly in the dusk of the evening than in the broad glare of day. Most animals, by the contraction and dilatation of the pupil of the eye, have, in some degree, the power of shutting

Ornitho-
logy.

out, or admitting light; but in the owls this property is observed in singular perfection, besides an irradiation on the back of the organ, which greatly aids their vision in the obscure places which they frequent. Incapable of seeing their prey, or of avoiding danger sufficiently, in the full blaze of sunshine, they shrink from its influence in silence and solitude; or, if compelled to come abroad, every thing dazzles and distracts them. Legions of birds flock around them, and single them out as objects of derision and contempt. The unfortunate wanderer patiently sits, and suffers all their indignities with real or apparent stupidity. Although none of the nocturnal birds of prey are materially hurtful to mankind, and although they are instrumental in the destruction of vermin, which might otherwise disappoint the hopes of the husbandman, yet in almost every age and country, they have been regarded by the vulgar as creatures of evil omen, and the heralds of death.

The whole family are included under the genus

STRIX, or OWL,

STRIX. of which some of the principal characters are, bill-hooked, without a cere; nostrils oblong, covered with recumbent setaceous feathers; head, eyes, and ears large, tongue bifid, and exterior toe reversible, or moveable backwards. They may be conveniently divided into the *horned* and *hornless*, or *smooth-headed*; the former comprising such as have lengthened feathers on each side of the head, resembling horns or ears, and capable of being more or less erected at the bird's pleasure; and the latter, such as are destitute of those lengthened plumes. Other minute divisions and subdivisions of the race have been instituted, but without sufficient attention to the approximating gradations of the foreign species, which connect most of the family by imperceptible links. We should likewise remark, that several of the sorts, previous to their first moulting, exhibit various degrees of darkness on the face, and have thus been described by some ornithologists as distinct species.

Otus. *S. otus*, Lin. &c.; *Long-eared*, or *Horn-owl.* Yellow ferruginous, with black and grey variegations; ear-tuft, consisting of six plumes, of a brownish-fulvous, barred with black. The length of the female is about fifteen inches, the extent of its expanded wings three feet four inches, and its weight ten ounces. The male is a little smaller in its dimensions.

The long-eared owl seldom takes the trouble of constructing a nest, but seizes on that of a magpie, buzzard, or other large bird, in which it deposits four or five rounded white eggs. The young are at first entirely covered with white down, but begin to acquire their appropriate colours at the expiration of fifteen days. This bird frequents extensive woods, and wooded or rocky solitudes, manifesting a partiality to plantations of fir, box, or holly, in which it more readily conceals itself by day, during all seasons of the year. In France, however, and some other countries of Europe, in which it is by no means uncommon, it often quits the forests and caverns in winter, and comes down to the plains, when it will even approach houses. Its cry is loud, and heard at a very considerable distance, being a grave and protracted moaning, incessantly reiterated during the night; but, on commencing its flight, it also emits a sharp sobbing-like sound, which has been attributed to the violent contraction of the pectoral muscles. It is found in all the quarters of the world; and is common at Hudson's Bay, where

it preys by night with much clamour, and often approaches the dwellings of the inhabitants. In Britain, it is not of very ordinary occurrence, but it has been met with in the north of England, Cheshire, and Cornwall. Unless taken when very young, it refuses food in confinement. It is occasionally used as a call-bird, to decoy others.

S. brachyotos, Lath. Gmel. Tem. &c.; including the *Ulula* of the two former, the *Accipitrina* of Pallas, and the *Stridula, Palustris, Brachyura, Tripennis, Arctica,* &c. of different writers. *Short-eared, Brown,* or *Caspian Owl;* provincially, *Mouse-hawk, Hawk-Owl, Woodcock-Owl,* &c. Yellow-ferruginous, varied with brown; ear-feathers narrow, and the tail marked with sub-ocellated spots. Until lately, this and the *Ulula* were conceived to be distinct species, an error which originated in the minuteness of the ear-feathers, which are often not erected, and never after death; so that the same bird was described by different ornithologists as horned or hornless, according to the state in which it happened to be examined. Mr. Pennant, who first introduced it into the British Fauna, and who has described it in a manner which should have protected him from the misplaced and uncourteous criticism of Buffon, is nevertheless mistaken, when he asserts that it has only one feather erectable on each side of the head. The length of the short-eared owl is fourteen or fifteen inches, the extent of wing three feet, and the weight fourteen ounces.

These birds make their appearance in this island in October, about the same time with the woodcocks, and depart with the latter in March. They are supposed to breed in the Orkneys, and probably in Norway. In Holland it is very common in the months of September and October; and it is alike spread over Europe and North America, visiting Hudson's Bay in May. During the day it generally lies concealed among old long grass; and, when disturbed, it seldom flies far, but will alight, and sit staring at one, in which attitude the horns are distinctly visible. It has not been observed to perch on trees; and, in dark or hazy weather, it will hunt for its food in the day time. As it rids the fields of mice, moles, &c. its presence is welcomed by the unprejudiced husbandman. No fewer than twenty-eight of them have been reckoned in a turnip field. The nest is said to consist of dried grass, placed on the ground, either on some small elevation, or in a marshy spot among tall herbage, and to contain three or four round white eggs, of the size of those of the wood-pigeon. Though naturally a bold bird, it is tamed without difficulty.

S. nebulosa, Lath. &c. *Barred Owl.* Transversely fasciated with brown and whitish above, with oblong, ferruginous spots beneath. Length of the male sixteen inches; extent of the wings four feet, and the weight three pounds. The female is twenty-one inches long. On the upper parts, the whole bird is beautifully barred with numerous brown bands, on a yellowish white ground, or, as it might also be expressed, with white on a brown ground, the spaces between the two colours being nearly equal. Native of the regions of the arctic circle, from which it seldom deviates; and, though it occurs in Sweden and Norway, it is more abundant in North America, particularly in Hudson's Bay and New York, where it preys on hares, rats, and various sorts of grouse. It nestles on trees, and lays from two to four white eggs, of a very rounded form.

S. flammea, Lin. &c. *Common, Screech, White,* or *Barn Owl.* Provincially, *Gillihowlet, Howlet, Madge*

Ornitho-
logy.

Brachyotos.

Nebulosa.

Flammea.

Howlet, Church Owl, Hissing Owl, &c. Sub-fulvous, with grey variegations; black and white spots down the shafts of the feathers, white breast and abdomen, and glaucous eyes. The common occurrence of this bird, on the one hand, and the superstitious apprehensions of the uninstructed, on the other, have contributed to the neglect of the downy softness, and the uncommon elegance of its plumage. Its usual weight is eleven ounces, its length between thirteen and fourteen inches, and its stretch of wing three feet. It is very commonly diffused over Europe, in North and South America, in the deserts of Tartary, in Persia, Indostan, and even in Australasia. It is likewise met with at the Cape of Good Hope, where it builds a regular nest among the rocks, forming it of a few twigs and dried leaves, and laying seven or eight oblong whitish eggs. In Europe, it chiefly frequents inhabited districts, and deposits from two to six eggs in the hole of a wall, under the eaves of buildings, in a decayed tree, &c. without any formal construction of a nest. While the young remain in their hole, their parents alternately sally out in quest of food, make their circuit, beat the fields with the regularity of a spaniel, and drop instantly on their prey in the grass. One of them seldom stays out above five minutes, when it returns with its game in its claws; but as it is necessary to shift it into the bill, it always alights for that purpose before it enters the nest. As the young remain long in this state of protection even after they can fly, several hundreds of mice will scarcely suffice to their maintenance.

The barn owl usually haunts churches, towers, barns, maltings, farm houses, &c. and its most ordinary food consists of rats, mice, and small birds. That it has no aversion to the flesh of the shrew-mouse, to which deleterious qualities have been foolishly ascribed, is abundantly obvious from the fact that Mr. Montagu extracted no fewer than five from the stomach of one of the present species. In a state of nature, and in fine weather, it generally leaves its haunts about twilight, skimming along the ground, exploring the neighbouring woods for prey, and returning before sunrise, not hooting, but repeating a sort of blowing noise, like the snoring of a man who sleeps with his mouth open. It expresses alarm by forcibly striking its mandibles together. When it flies, or alights, it, moreover, doles out certain lugubrious and sharp notes, which, added to the solemnity and stillness of the scene, especially when near church-yards, are apt to inspire awe and apprehension in the minds of the ignorant, and are often interpreted by the sick and the superstitious, especially in some of the country districts of France, as the presage of approaching dissolution. Yet the poor barn owl is a very harmless creature, and such an excellent mouser as to deserve the protection of every farmer and good housewife. It is easily caught in a small net, placed at its hole, and, if taken young, becomes very tame; but it is not easily supported in confinement, on account of its incessant calls for fresh mice. A gentleman who resides in Yorkshire, and who is very conversant in ornithology, having observed the scales of fishes in the nest of a pair of this species, in the neighbourhood of a lake, was induced one moonshine night, to watch their motions, when he was agreeably surprised to see one of them plunge into the water and seize a perch, which it bore to its nest.

S. aluco, Lin. &c. *Stridula* of Gmel. and Lath. and *Sylvatica* of Shaw. *Grey, Brown, Wood*, or *Tawny Owl, Common Brown Ivy Owl*, or *Howlet, Screech Owl*,

&c. Ferruginous, or grey-brown, wing coverts spotted with white, eyes glaucous. The length of the female is fifteen inches, its extent of wing two feet eight inches, and its weight about nineteen ounces. It is a native of most of the countries of Europe, and is also found in Newfoundland, and in South America, preferably frequenting large and dense forests, and concealing itself in the thickest recesses. Occasionally it settles on the ground, but if disturbed, takes shelter in a neighbouring tree. Unless forced from its haunts, it is rarely seen on wing during the day; and so imperfectly does it perceive objects in a bright day, that it is no uncommon thing for boys to hunt it down with sticks and stones. It breeds in the hollows of trees, and sometimes in barns and granaries, in which it is welcomed by the farmer, on account of the numbers of the murine race which it destroys; but it is a far less acceptable visitor in pigeon-houses, in which it commits serious devastation. It scarcely prepares the form of a nest, but drops from two to four eggs, of a dull white, and of a roundish shape, on the decayed wood, and sometimes in the abandoned nest of a rook, jay, or other large bird. In Devonshire, it not unfrequently nidificates in an ivy bush, or on the stump of an old pollard, apparently from the want of better accommodation. The young are covered with a light-coloured down, and are, at first, very shy, but soon become tame, if fed from the hand. If put out of doors, within hearing of the parent birds, they retain their native shyness; for the latter visit them at night, and supply them with ample provision. This is the most common of our British owls, and the only one of them which hoots, inflating its throat, at the same time, to the size of a hen's egg, besides which it makes a disagreeable screaming noise, and has, in most countries, been regarded as a bird of evil omen. It is very rapacious, making great havock among young rabbits, hares, and partridges, and skinning mice with great dexterity before it eats them. It seizes its game with great fierceness, and, beginning at the head, tears it violently in pieces, but usually leaves the hinder parts untouched. It is not difficult to catch it in traps, or it may be easily shot, in the evening, by any person who can allure it by imitating tolerably well the squeaking of a mouse. It is bold and furious in defence of its young.

S. bubo, Lin. &c.; *Great Owl, Great Eared*, or *Great* Bubo. *Horned Owl, Eagle Owl, Stork Owl*, &c. *Katogle* of the Orcadians. Rufous, variegated with black, brown, and cinereous spots and freckles. Length, from the point of the beak to the extremity of the tail, four feet eleven inches. The great quantity of feathers with which the body is invested, makes it appear much larger than it really is, and has caused it to be compared to the eagle in bulk. The whole plumage is a mixture of brown, fulvous, and sub-rufous, disposed in spots and bands; the brown of the upper parts and wings is darker than that of the belly and abdomen, and the breast is whitish. But this general description admits of considerable diversity, and there are several foreign varieties which have been exhibited by some as distinct species.

As this bird can bear both heat and cold, it is found in the north and south of both continents; for it has been observed in the arctic regions, in Kamtschatka, Siberia, &c. in the neighbourhood of Astrachan, on the borders of the Elephant river, in Africa, in South America, and as far as north as Hudson's Bay. It is very common in the wooded tracts of Russia, Hungary, Germany, and Switzerland, but less so in France.

Ornitho-
logy.

Though rare in Britain, it has been shot in Yorkshire, Sussex, and Scotland; and in the Orkneys its presence is attested by its destruction of red grouse and rabbits, which abound in some of the islands. It seldom perches on trees; but haunts mountainous, rocky, and desolate situations, as deserted towers, precipices, and lonely crags. Although more capable of supporting the light of day than many of its congeners, its most successful excursions are performed in the silence of the night, when it seizes on leverets, young rabbits, moles, mice of all descriptions, serpents, lizards, toads, frogs, and even bats. After breaking, with its beak, the head and bones of a mouse, it swallows it entire, and, in the course of a few hours, rejects by the mouth the hair, bones, and skin, in the form of balls. At all times an active hunter, it is particularly murderous during the breeding season, that it may supply the voracious cravings of its progeny. Its presence in the dark is announced by the doleful cry of *hehoo, hoohoo, boohoo, heohoo;* but when it cries through pain or fear, the sound is exceedingly strong and grating. Its nest is nearly three feet in diameter, composed of small branches of dry wood, interwoven with pliant roots, and strewed with leaves. It seldom lays more than two eggs, but sometimes three, and very rarely four, which are round, large as those of a hen, and mottled, like the bird which they inclose. The parents are vigilant in providing subsistence for the young, which they procure in silence, and with more agility and courage than we might be apt to suppose; for they often fight with the buzzard, and compel it to surrender its spoil. Although their wings are shorter than those of most soaring birds, they can rise to a great height, especially about twilight; but at other times they generally fly low, and to short distances. They have been frequently employed in falconry, to allure the notice of the kite. For this purpose, it is customary to append a fox's tail to the owl, to enhance the singularity of its appearance. Thus equipped, it skims along the surface of the ground, and alights on the plain, without venturing to perch on a tree. The kite perceives it from a distance, and advancing to examine it, generally hovers about unguardedly, till it is surprised by the sportsman, or caught by some of the birds that are flown at it. The breeders of pheasants likewise frequently keep a great eared owl, which they put into a cage among rushes, in an open place, to attract the crows and ravens, that they may be more speedily dispatched with a cross-bow, which does not, like the report of a fowling-piece, scare the young pheasants. In a state of captivity this species will readily subsist on raw flesh and bullock's liver; nor does it reject small and middle sized fish. It can long dispense with drink, but sometimes indulges in it as if by stealth. Its gastric juice, according to Spallanzani, is quite incapable of digesting vegetable substances, however triturated or masticated. A variety of the present species was venerated by the Athenians, as the bird of Minerva, and the emblem of wisdom; but, in most other communities, the solemn aspect and lugubrious clamour of the bird have contributed to associate it with ideas of gloom and repulsion.

Nyctea.

S. nyctea, Lin. &c.; *Candida,* Lath. *Snowy, Hermit,* or *Great White Owl.* Snow-white, spotted with black; bill black; irides yellow. The head is less in proportion than that of other owls. The whole plumage is of a snowy whiteness, sometimes pure, but more frequently marked with dusky spots. The full grown bird measures about two feet in length, and in size

nearly equals the preceding; but the weight is said to vary from one and a half to three pounds. It sustains, throughout the year the utmost rigour of the northern regions, being very common in Hudson's Bay, Norway, and Lapland, and shrinking not from the accumulations of ice in the centre of Greenland. In America, it seldom strays so low as Pennsylvania or Louisiana. It abounds in Kamtschatka; but is scarce in Prussia, becomes more common on the Uralian ridges, all over the north and east of Siberia, and even in the hot latitude of Astrachan. It is not uncommon in Iceland; and has, of late years, been observed, though sparingly, in one or two of the Shetland and Orkney islands. It preys on grouse, hares, rabbits, carrion, &c. nestles in craggy rocks, or old pines, and lays two white round eggs, which, according to Vieillot, are spotted with black. Its cry has been compared to that of a man in deep distress. Among the Kalmuc Tartars it is deemed a crime to kill one of them, because they are considered to be the oracles of good or bad fortune, according as they fly to the right or to the left.

Passerina. *S. passerina,* Lin. &c. *Pygmœa,* of Bechstein. *Passerine,* or *Little Owl.* Sub-olivaceous brown, with whitish spots above; whitish, with brown spots beneath; wing feathers barred with white; irides yellow. About the size of the missel thrush, but varies considerably in dimensions, as from six to eight and a half inches in length. It is also subject to diversity in the cast of its colours, and in the hues of the iris. The feet are feathered to the claws. It resides throughout the year in North America, from Hudson's Bay to New York, frequenting the pine forests, building its nest half way up a tree, and laying from two to six roundish eggs, spotted with yellow and white. It is frequent in Russia, but less so in Siberia; and in some parts of Greece it is migratory, appearing in great numbers early in April, and, after breeding, retiring with the storks. In Italy, it is used for the purpose of decoying small birds to limed twigs. It is rare in France, and still more so in England, though sometimes found in Yorkshire, Flintshire, Devonshire, and the neighbourhood of London. In Carniola it builds in chimneys, and in some other countries in the holes of rocks and walls. It is an elegant species, and the smallest of our British owls; naturally shy and solitary, keeping close for the most part in its retreat during the day, but very active in catching mice, &c. during the night.

Scops. *S. scops,* Lin. &c.; *Zorca* and *Carniolica,* Gmel.; *Zorca* and *Giu,* Lath. *Scops Eared,* or *Scops Horned Owl.* Grey brown, with sub-ferruginous and black variegations above, and grey, with black variegations beneath; the tail crossed by four narrow white bands, and the feet feathered to the toes. From six to eight inches long, and scarcely exceeding the size of a quail, being of a short and thick form, but variable both in its dimensions and in the shading of its plumage. The auricular plumes, which Linné represents as only one on each side, are in reality composed of six on each side; but being only six or seven lines in length, they are sometimes inconspicuous, and, in the dead bird, they are not easily discerned.

This species is a native of the warmer and more temperate parts of Europe, and of a roaming disposition. In the department of the Vosges, in France, it arrives in spring, in bands, sometimes consisting of several hundreds, and retires again in autumn. The inhabitants, instead of hailing its appearance as the harbinger of the fine season, and a pledge of the destruction of the moles, rats, and mice, with which their

fields would otherwise be overrun, regard it with superstitious apprehensions, and seem to be afraid even
of its harmless cry. In Italy, its favourite residence is
in gentle wooded acclivities. During the day, it continues in the shade of woods, perched motionless on
the branch of a tree, and with its ear-tufts erected, in
which state it will permit a very near approach before
it retires to hide itself afresh. Towards the dusk of
evening it emerges from its retreat, perches on a tree
in some open spot, and begins its cry, which consists
of a quick and often repeated whistle, somewhat like
the word *keevee*. Without constructing any nest, it deposits from two to six white eggs in the hollows of
trees, or the fissures of rocks. The young are fully
fledged by the beginning of July, when they follow
their parents during the night for food, until they are
able to provide for themselves, and to pursue insects
and the minuter quadrupeds. In Italy, they remain
till October, when they are in their plumpest state, and
were it not for their disagreeable smell, would be reckoned delicate eating.

Other species, of a diminutive size, have been particularized, but not with sufficient distinctness to detain
us.

ORDER II.

OMNIVOROUS BIRDS.

Beak middle-sized, robust, sharp on the edges, the
upper mandible more or less notched at the point; feet
furnished with four toes, namely, three before and one
behind, wings moderate, with the quill feathers terminating in a point.

The birds which compose this order usually live in
flocks; a single female suffices for a male; they nidificate on trees, in the holes of old ruins and towers, or
in natural holes in trees or rocks; the male and female
incubate alternately; they live on insects, worms,
offals, grains, fruits, &c. and their flesh is generally
hard, tough, and unsavoury.

Corvus, Lin. &c. Crow Tribe.

Bill strong, upper mandible a little convex, edges
cultrated, and in most species slightly notched near the
tip; nostrils covered with bristles reflected over them;
tongue divided at the end; three toes forward, one
backward, that in the middle joined to the outer, as far
as the first joint; feet formed for walking. The characteristics of the family ought, however, to be viewed
with a considerable degree of limitation, especially since
recent ornithologists have added many species that are
but imperfectly known. Some of the tribe are found
in almost every climate. They are social and clamorous, nidificate in trees, and live on grain, seeds, insects,
worms, &c. Some of them are apparently prejudicial
to the interests of the husbandman; but their service
in diminishing the quantity of noxious vermin, probably more than counterbalances the waste with which
they are chargeable. Their voice, or note, is generally
hoarse, and, to most ears, far from pleasant; but some
species possess a considerable degree of docility, and
may be taught to articulate in the manner of parrots.
For the most part they are sagacious, active, and faithful to one another, living in pairs, and forming a sort
of society, in which there appears something like a regular government and concert in the warding off
threatened danger.

C. Corax, Lin. &c. *Raven, Corby,* of the Scotch.

Deep black, the upper parts with a bluish gloss, tail
somewhat rounded. The young, when hatched, incline
to whitish. The ordinary length of the bird is about
twenty-two inches and a half, its stretch of wing about
three feet, and its weight thirty-five or thirty-six
ounces, the female being three or four ounces heavier.
Like birds of prey, it is furnished with a strong bill,
and with long vigorous wings.

As the raven has a lofty flight, and is capable of sustaining every temperature, the wide world is open to
its range; and it is found from the polar circle to the
Cape of Good Hope, and the island of Madagascar.
The crews of the *Mascarin* and *Castries* killed ravens
in every respect similar to those of France, on the
southern point of Van Diemen's Land, and Vancouver
found them at Port Bodegu, in the same country. Their
voracity is scarcely less indiscriminate than their residence. In Greenland, they usually haunt the neighbourhood of the sea, assembling in troops, during winter, around the huts of the natives, plundering the provisions, devouring the offals, or even, from hunger,
pulling the leathern canoes to pieces. On the north-
west coast of Hudson's Bay, in Kamtschatka, &c. they
prey in concert with the white bear, the arctic fox,
and the eagle, greedily seizing the eggs of other birds,
shore-fish, and such testaceous and crustaceous animals as happen to be within their reach. With these
last they will soar into the air, and drop them on a
rock, so as to break the shells, and get at the contents,
but when famished, they swallow shells and all. In
their attempts to plunder the eggs of puffins and oys-
ter-catchers, they often meet with determined, and
even fatal enemies in the parent birds. By picking
out the eyes of young lambs, they readily dispatch
them, and gorge themselves with their prey; for,
though they can resist for a considerable time the
importunate calls of hunger, they will glut themselves
when an opportunity offers, retire to digest, and return
again to feed. They are known to frequent woody
places, in the neighbourhood of towns, for the sake of
carrion, and other refuse on which they feed. They
are also unsparing of ducklings and chickens, and have
even been known to destroy sickly sheep. The alleged instances of their extraordinary acuteness of
smell may perhaps be more satisfactorily explained,
from their uncommon quickness and power of vision,
which enable them to perceive prey and other objects
almost instantaneously, and from a great distance. Insects and earthworms are their more ordinary fare;
but their habits have often been confounded with those
of the carrion crow. The genuine mountain raven is
not a bird of passage, but manifests, on the contrary,
an attachment to the rock on which it was bred, or
rather to that on which it has paired, which is its ordinary residence, and which it never entirely abandons. When it descends into the plains, it is for the
purpose of procuring subsistence; and this happens
more rarely in summer than in winter. These birds
do not, like the carrion crows, pass the night in the
woods, but select among the mountains a retreat, sheltered from the northern blast, under the natural alcoves
that are formed by the recesses and projections of the
rocks. Thither they retire in the night, in flocks of
fifteen or twenty, and sleep on the bushes that grow
between the rocks. In February or March, they build
their nests in the crevices, or in holes of walls, on the
tops of deserted towers, or in the forks of large trees.
The nest, which is very large, consists of three distinct
layers of materials; the first, or outermost, being com-

posed of branches and roots of shrubs ; the second, of the fragments of the bones of quadrupeds, and other hard substances ; and the third of a soft lining of grass, moss, or other stuffing. The female lays from two to six, and even sometimes eight eggs, of a pale bluish green, marked with numerous spots and streaks of brown and ash-colour, and somewhat larger than those of the carrion crow. The incubation lasts about twenty days, during which period the male assiduously waits on his mate, and not only provides her with abundance of food, but relieves her in turn, taking her place in the nest during part of the day. The female, however, according to the observations of Otho Fabricius, sits on the eggs all night, and the male roosts in the immediate neighbourhood. The same pair nestle, it is alleged, in the same situation every year, unless much molested, or driven from their haunts. The young are hatched with a portion of the yolk of the egg included in the abdomen, and which flows insensibly into the intestines by a particular duct ; but, after a few days, the mother feeds them with the proper aliments, which undergo a preparation in her crop, and are then disgorged into their bills, in a manner similar to what takes place with pigeons. The male, meanwhile, not only caters for the family, but watches for its safety. If he perceives a kite, or other rapacious bird, approaching the nest, the danger stimulates his courage, he takes wing, soars above the invader, and, dashing downwards, strikes violently with his bill ; both contend for the mastery, and sometimes mount entirely out of sight, until, overcome with fatigue, one or both will fall to the ground.

Gesner informs us, that he fed young ravens with raw flesh, small fishes, and bread soaked in water. They are very fond of cherries, and swallow them greedily with the stones and stalks, but digest only the pulpy part, and in two hours afterwards vomit the rest. Although they rapidly arrive at maturity, they are capable of living to a great age, some well authenticated cases being on record, of their having completed a century. The ancients, who laid great stress on auguries, studied with the most scrupulous attention the history and manners of the present species, and, besides the more minute discriminations of its voice, reckoned no fewer than sixty-four distinct inflexions. Besides its native notes and calls, however, the raven possesses the talent of imitating the cry of other animals, and even human discourse, a quality which is said to be improved by cutting the ligament of the tongue. Vieillot's tame raven, however, which had never submitted to this ceremony, not only pronounced its words very distinctly, but even associated ideas with them ; for, when it wished its neck to be scratched, it incessantly repeated, *gratte colas*, and evinced its satisfaction by erecting its feathers, bending its head, and inclining its neck. Scaliger heard one, which, when hungry, called on *Conrad*, the cook ; and, he adds, that the same bird, having met with a sheet of music, pricked with its bill, as if it were reading and beating time. The raven, at all events, is not insensible to music ; and Dr. Goldsmith was fortunate enough to hear one sing the "Black Joke," with great distinctness, truth, and humour. That trained by Debes, took a lesson of two hours every morning on his knee, and repeated what it had learned the preceding evening, spelling syllable by syllable, till it could pronounce the whole word, as children learn to read at school. Many examples might also be quoted of the propensity evinced by the raven for mimicking

and gesticulation, as well as of its capability of being trained to hunt game. Like some of its congeners, it is likewise notorious for hoarding and pilfering, not only provisions, but whatever tickles its fancy, especially if it be of a shining or glossy appearance. Thus, one at Erford had the assiduity to carry, one by one, and conceal beneath a stone, in a garden, a quantity of small pieces, amounting to five or six florins.

Notwithstanding the injury which these birds occasion to the farmer, they are often useful in destroying noxious insects and vermin ; and in hot countries, in particular, they are of signal service, in the neighbourhood of towns, by devouring the carcasses and refuse which would otherwise prove a serious nuisance. When they croak three or four times, repeatedly extending their wings, and shaking the leaves of the tree on which they are perched, they are said to foretell serene weather. Linné informs us, that, in the southern provinces of Sweden, the ravens, in fine weather, soar to an immense height, and make a clangorous noise that is heard at a great distance ; and Mr. Pennant adds, that, in this case, they generally fly in pairs. The Greenlanders observe, that when they roam about in a restless manner, making a noise in the air, they presage a violent south wind and tempest.

The large quills of the raven sell for upwards of twelve shillings a hundred, being of great use in tuning the lower notes of harpsichords, and in drawing fine strokes, or executing delicate writing. Few persons, even among the savage tribes of mankind, eat the flesh ; yet, in Greenland, it forms an article of food ; and the skin, with the feathers on, is preferred to most other substances as a warm under garment, while the beak and claws are used as amulets.

C. corone, Lin. &c. *Carrion,* or *Common Crow.* In old English, *Gor-crow,* or *Gore-crow.* In the north of England, and some parts of Scotland, it is called *Midden Crow,* or *Black-nebbed Crow.* Bluish-black ; tail rounded, tail feathers acute. Length, eighteen inches, stretch of wing, twenty-six ; weight about nineteen ounces. The female is somewhat smaller than the male, and her plumage of a less shining lustre.

Birds of this species are more numerous than, and as widely diffused as, the raven, being common in most parts of the world ; though we are informed, on the testimony of Linné, that they are almost unknown in Sweden ; yet they occur in the diocese of Drontheim, and in the Faroe Isles. They generally pass the summer in extensive forests, from which they occasionally emerge to procure subsistence for themselves and their infant brood. They feed on flesh, eggs, worms, insects, and various sorts of grain ; but they are particularly fond of carrion. In spring, they greedily devour the eggs of quails and partridges, and are so dexterous as to pierce them and carry them on the point of their bill to their young. Even fish and fruits are not unsuitable to their palate. They often attack the eyes of dying animals, destroy weakly lambs, and, when pressed with hunger, will even pursue birds on the wing. They are notorious for the havock which they occasion among young game and poultry, and in rabbit-warrens, where they kill and devour the young. When hens lay their eggs in hedge-bottoms, or farm-yards, crows are often caught in the act of devouring them : but, when they happen to be satiated, they will frequently hide their food, till hunger becomes more urgent. The late Mr. Watt, of Heathfield, whose capacious intellect embraced almost every object of human pursuit, mentioned to the writer of this article, that he saw a crow take up a crab a considerable way into the air, let it fall down on a rock, to break the shell, then pounced instantly down on it, and bore it away for immediate consumption. In like manner, a friend of the late Dr. Darwin saw, on the northern coast of Ireland, above a hundred crows preying at once on muscles, which they dispatched by a similar process. Near the Cape of Good Hope, they have been observed to dispose in the same way of land tortoises. We read, too, of an ill-starred philosopher, of ancient times, who was killed by an oyster impinging on his bald pate, which a crow had mistaken for a block of stone.

During the winter, these birds consort with the rooks and hooded crows, and sometimes intermingle with the latter, so as to give rise to a hybrid race. In this season, numerous flights of various species of the first genus assemble about our dwellings, keeping much on the ground, sauntering among the flocks and shepherds, hovering near the tracks of the labourers, and sometimes hopping on the backs of pigs and sheep, with such apparent familiarity, that they might be taken for domestic birds. At night they retire into the forests, to lodge among the large trees, resorting to the general rendezvous from every quarter, sometimes from the distance of nine miles all around, and whence they again sally out, in the morning, in quest of subsistence. As long as this association lasts, the hooded and carrion crows are observed to grow very fat, while the rooks continue always lean. Towards the close of winter, the latter also remove into other regions, whereas the carrion crows resort to the nearest large forests, where they pair, and seem to divide their territory into districts of about three quarters of a mile in diameter, each of which is allotted to the maintenance of its appropriate family, an arrangement which is said to subsist inviolate during the lives of the respective parties. The female lays from four to six eggs, of a bluish green, marked with large and black spots, of cinereous grey and olivaceous, and weighing about five drachms each. She sits about three weeks, during which time the male supplies her with food.

The carrion crow often wages war with the lesser species of hawks; but it is especially courageous in the breeding season; nor will it suffer the kite, buzzard, or raven, to approach its nest with impunity. The young do not finally break off connection with the parents till the commencement of a new brood. As they naturally attack small game, when wounded, or exhausted, they have, in some countries, been bred for falconry, as in Turkey, where gentry of inferior quality paint them of different colours, carry them on their right hand, and call them back by the frequent repetition of the syllable *hoob*. Although their flight is neither easy nor rapid, they generally mount to a very great height, and indulge much in a whirling motion. Their croaking in the morning is said to indicate fine weather. As they are exceedingly cunning, have an acute scent, and commonly fly in large flocks, it is difficult to get near them, and still more so to decoy them into snares. Some of them, however, are caught by imitating the screech of the owl, and placing limed twigs on the high branches of a tree; or they are drawn within gun-shot by means of an eagle-owl, or such other nocturnal bird, raised on perches, in an open spot. They are destroyed, too, by throwing to them garden beans, in which rusty needles are concealed. They are likewise caught by cones of paper, baited with raw flesh. As the crow introduces his head to devour the bait, which is near the bottom, the paper, being besmeared with bird-lime,

sticks to the feathers of the neck, and he remains hooded; unable to rid his eyes of the bandage, he rises almost perpendicularly in the air, the better to avoid striking against any thing, until, quite exhausted, he sinks down, always near the spot from which he mounted. These, and other modes of ensnaring crows, are chiefly practised in the winter season, when the ground is covered with snow, or bound up in frost; for then they more readily approach human habitations, and seek to pick up some subsistence from the dung of animals that have passed along the highways. But many of them are killed, at all seasons, in various parts of the Continent, by strewing over the grounds which they frequent, pellets of minced meat, mixed with the powder of Nux vomica.

Like the raven, and other congenerous birds, the carrion crow may be domesticated, and taught to articulate several words. It has been also observed to manifest the same disposition to hoard provisions and glittering trinkets.

C. cornix, Lin. &c. Hooded, *Royston*, or *Grey Crow*; in provincial English, *Duncrow*, *Scare-crow*, and *Bunting-crow*; *Hoody* of the Scots. Ash-coloured; head, throat, wings, and tail, black. Length, twenty-one inches; spread of wing, twenty-three; weight, about twenty-two ounces.

Like the rook, this bird associates in numerous flocks, and is, perhaps, still more familiar with the haunts of man, preferring, especially in winter, the vicinity of our farms and hamlets, and picking up its food in the kennels and dunghills. Like the rooks, also, in several countries, it changes its abode twice a-year, appearing in flocks in the middle or at the end of autumn, and departing, in a northerly direction, about the beginning of spring. It visits the south of England in October, or the beginning of winter, arriving and departing with the woodcock, and retiring north, to breed, in the beginning of April. In the northern parts of the island, it is more frequent than in the south; and in the Orkneys, Hebrides, and Shetland islands, it is the only genuine crow, the rook and carrion being there unknown. In these districts, and in some parts of Scotland and Ireland, it is resident throughout the year. Where opportunities offer, it breeds in the pines and other large trees, in default of which it nestles in the cavities of rocks. The female, which is rather smaller than the male, and of less lively hues, usually lays four, five, or six eggs, of a greenish-blue, marked with many spots of blackish-brown. It pairs during the whole of the breeding season; and both parents are much attached to their offspring. They are remarked for their double cry, of which one is hollow and well known, and the other shrill, and somewhat resembling the crowing of a cock. When other food is wanting, they will eat cranberries, and other mountain fruits; in open fertile countries, they live much on grain, worms, and carrion; but they often resort to the sea-shores, and prey on the various animal matters thrown up by the tide. Frisch observes, that they are expert at picking fish-bones, and that, when water is discharged from ponds, they quickly perceive the fish which are left in them, and lose no time in darting on them. They not only attack the eyes of lambs and diseased sheep, but of horses that have got entangled in bogs. In the Faroe Isles, where they abound, they are particularly mischievous, picking the seed from the fields, digging up the newly planted potatoes, destroying the barley before it is ripe, and carrying off goslings and ducklings, or the fish which is hung up to dry, to their

Ornitho-
logy.

young. In some parts of these islands, they assemble to about the number of two hundred in one place, and at one time, as if by concert. A few of the congregation sit with drooping heads, others seem as grave as judges, and others, again, are very bustling and noisy. The meeting breaks up in the course of an hour; and it is not uncommon to find one or two dead on the spot. These, according to the insinuation of Landt, are either *criminals punished for their offences*, or invalids that have died of some disorder. Low observes, that, in the Orkneys, they meet together in spring, as if to deliberate on the important concerns of summer, and, after flying about in this collected state for eight or ten days, separate into pairs, and betake themselves to the mountains.

Frugilegus.

C. frugilegus, Lin. &c. *Rook*, or *Rook Crow*. Black, front ash-coloured; tail somewhat rounded. According to Mr. Pennant, the weight and the length nearly coincide with those of the carrion crow; but the extent of wing exhibited by the rook is greater by two inches and a half. These congeners, in fact, pretty nearly resemble each other; but the plumage of the rook is rather more glossy, and its tail-feathers somewhat broad and rounded; its bill is more straight and slender, and has its base encircled by a naked white skin, which is scaly, and sometimes scabby, and takes place of those black projecting feathers, or bristles, which, in the other species of crow, extend as far as the opening of the nostrils. The belly, too, is not so thick or strong as in the crow, and has a rasped-like appearance. But some of these peculiarities of the rook obviously result from its mode of life; for as grain, roots, worms, and insects, form its proper food, and as in search of these it scratches deep in the ground with its bill, the latter becomes rough, and the feathers at the base are worn off by continual rubbing, or at least only a few straggling ones are left.

The rook is a native of most of the temperate regions of Europe, but is not found much farther north than the south of Sweden, where it breeds, but from which it is driven by the severity of winter. In Russia, and the west of Siberia, it is far from rare, emigrating early in March to the environs of Woronetz, and mingling with the common crows. In England, they are stationary; but in France, Silesia, and many other countries, most of them are birds of passage. In France, they are the forerunners of winter, whereas in Siberia they announce the summer. Their flights are sometimes so dense as to darken the air, being frequently joined, not only by the common crow and the jackdaw, but also by troops of starlings. Every spring they resort to breed on the same trees, preferring the loftier branches, and building sometimes ten or twelve nests, which rise above one another on the same tree, whilst a great many trees thus furnished occur in the same forest, or rather in the same district. They seek not retirement and solitude, but rather settle near our dwellings. When a pair are employed in constructing the nest, one remains to guard it, while the other is procuring the suitable materials; for otherwise the structure would, it is alleged, be instantly pillaged by the other rooks which have fixed on the same tree, each carrying off a twig to its own dwelling. Rookeries are sometimes the scene of violent contests between the old and the new inhabitants, whether the intruders be of the same, or of different species. A pair which had in vain attempted to establish themselves in a rookery at no great distance from the Exchange of Newcastle-upon-Tyne, having

Ornitho-
logy.

been compelled to abandon their purpose, took refuge on the spire of that building; and, though constantly interrupted by others of their own species, succeeded in completing their nest on the top of the vane, and reared their young, apparently regardless of the noise of the people underneath. The nest, and its inhabitants, were, in course, turned round by every change of the wind; and yet the parents persevered in maintaining the same station for ten years, when the spire was taken down. As soon as rooks have finished their nest, and before they lay, the males begin to feed the females, which receive their bounty with a fondling tremulous voice, fluttering wings, and all the little blandishments that are expected by the young, while in a helpless state. This gallant deportment of the males is continued through the whole season of incubation. The female lays four or five eggs, which are smaller than those of the raven, but marked with broader spots, especially at the large end. After the young have taken wing, there is a general desertion of the nest trees, but the families return to them again in October to roost, and to repair their dwellings. On the approach of winter, however, they usually seek some more sheltered situation at night, but generally assemble first in the usual place, and then fly off together. Their autumnal exercises of departing on their foraging excursions in the morning, and returning in the evening, are familiar to ordinary observation, and have been well described by White and others. Though the forest may be said to be their winter habitation, they generally visit their nurseries every day, preserving the idea of a family, for which they begin to make provision early in spring, the business of nidification being usually accomplished in the month of March.

The rook has but two or three notes, and makes no great figure in a *solo*; but when he performs in *concert*, which is his chief delight, these notes, though rough in themselves, being intermixed with those of the multitude, have, as it were, their ragged edges worn off, and become harmonious, especially when softened in the distant air. So marked is their dread of a fowling-piece, that the country people allege they even smell gunpowder; but if the gun be carefully concealed from their view, a person with his pockets full of powder, may approach very near them. Among the favourite articles of their food is the grub of the chafer, or dor-beetle, which, if allowed to multiply unchecked, would lay waste whole meadows and corn fields. It must not be dissembled, however, that rooks themselves are sometimes very injurious to new sown wheat, just when it begins to germinate. The severity of winter, when accompanied by a heavy fall of snow, sometimes drives them down to the sea-shore, when they are observed to feed on small shell-fish, particularly the common periwinkle. Having raised these last into the air, to about the height of fifty feet, they let them fall among stones, stooping instantly after their prey. If the shell is unbroken, they lift it again and again; and when the wind happens to carry it out of the perpendicular direction, they toil much and gain little. Frauds in the mode of procuring their livelihood, as well as in that of building their nests, are sometimes attempted among them, but which, when discovered, meet with instant and condign punishment. Indeed, we can scarcely doubt that these sagacious birds have ideas of property, unknown to many of the inferior animals, as each pair, year after year, assert their claim to the same nest; and an attempt to invade them, on the part of

E

others, would, as often happens, be punished, not merely by the aggrieved individuals, but by the combined efforts of the society, which clearly proves that they consider it as an offence against the community. When tamed they evince both confidence and attachment.

The young of this species are, by some, reckoned good for the table, but those habituated to better fare will probably esteem them somewhat coarse.

Monedula. *C. monedula*, Lin. &c. *Jackdaw*, or *Daw, Kae* of the Scots. Dusky, back of the head hoary, wings and tail black.

This species inhabits many of the temperate parts of Europe, occurs as far north as Sondmor, and is sometimes seen in the Faroe Isles. From Smoland and East Gothland it migrates as soon as harvest ends, and returns in the spring, accompanied by the starlings. It winters about Upsal, and passes the night in large flocks, in ruined towers, especially those of the old town. It is common all over Russia and Western Siberia. In the south of Russia and in Great Britain it is stationary throughout the year, but in France, some parts of Germany, &c. it is at least partially migratory, though a number of them continue in these countries during summer. Such of them as migrate form themselves into large bodies, like the rooks and hooded crows, whose phalanxes they sometimes join, continually chattering as they fly. Yet they observe not the same periods in France and in Germany; for they leave the latter in autumn, and appear not again till the spring, after having wintered in France. In general they frequent old towers, ruined buildings, and high cliffs, but they also occasionally breed in the holes, or even on the branches of trees, especially if in the neighbourhood of a rookery. In some parts of Hampshire, owing probably to the want of towers and steeples, they frequently build in the burrows of a rabbit-warren, and in the Isle of Ely, from a similar cause, they take up their abode in chimneys. Their nest is made of sticks, and lined with wool, and other soft materials; and the eggs are generally five or six, smaller and paler than those of the crows, of a bluish or greenish ground, spotted with black or brown. After the young are hatched, the female watches, feeds, and rears them with an affection which the male seems eager to share. Some authors affirm that they have two broods in the year; but this, we have reason to believe, is by no means uniformly the case. During the season of courtship they prattle incessantly, woo each other's society, and even kiss. Even in captivity they refrain not from these marks of tender attachment. Many pairs usually nestle in the same neighbourhood. They feed principally on worms and the larvæ of insects, and are very fond of cherries. Their voice is shriller than that of the rook or crow, and appears to be capable of different inflexions. They are easily tamed, and seem so fond of domestication as seldom to attempt their escape. They may be fed on insects, fruit, grain, and even small pieces of meat. With no great difficulty they may be taught to articulate several words; but they are mischievous and tricky, and will secrete not only portions of their food, but pieces of money, jewels, &c.

Jamaicen-sis. *C. Jamaicensis*, Lath. &c. *Chattering Crow.* Of a uniform deep black. This scarcely differs in appearance from the European carrion crow, but utters a peculiar chattering note. A native of Jamaica, where it frequents mountainous situations, and feeds principally on berries.

C. pica, Lin. &c. *Pica Europœa*, Cuv. *Pica Melanoleuca*, Vieill. *Magpie*, or *Pianet*, Prov. *Hagister*. Black, with purple and green reflexions, the scapulars, breast, belly, and inside of the wing-feathers white; tail lengthened and cuneated. The black, especially on the feathers of the wings and tail, exhibits, in certain dispositions of the light, very fine reflexions of green, blue, purple, and violet, a circumstance of which superficial observers are little aware; nor can he who has only examined a dirty specimen in confinement, form any adequate notion of the native beauties of the bird. It is about eighteen inches long, twenty-four in extent of wing, and weighs between eight and nine ounces. The female differs from the other sex only in being somewhat less, and in having a shorter tail. Among the more remarkable varieties to which it is occasionally liable, we may notice that of whiteness, almost pure, cream, or buff colour, and white, streaked with black.

The magpie is generally diffused in England, France, Germany, Sweden, and most of the countries of Europe, and it also occurs in Asia as far as Japan, in China, as well as in Siberia, Kamtschatka, and the adjacent islands, whence it has possibly passed into the northern parts of America; for it is seen, though rarely, in Hudson's Bay, and on the borders of the Mississippi. In Europe, it is found as far north as Wardhuis, in Lat. 71½, and as far south as Italy; but it seldom abounds in hilly regions. Being smaller than the rook, and with wings proportionally shorter, its flight is neither so lofty nor so well supported; neither does it undertake long journies, but only flies from tree to tree, at moderate distances; yet it is seldom at rest for any length of time, but skips and hops about, and shakes its long tail, almost incessantly. Though naturally shy and distrustful, yet it is seldom found remote from human habitations. Magpies generally continue in pairs throughout the year, and if they sometimes unite into small flocks, it is only for some temporary purpose. They are clamorous and mischievous, reject hardly any species of animal food, or fruits, and devour grain, when nothing else is within their reach. They will prey on birds caught in snares, on nestlings, rats, field mice, young poultry, leverets, feathered game, carrion, fish, insects, &c. Lambs, and even weakly sheep they attempt to destroy, by first plucking out their eyes. They are notorious pilferers and hoarders, and will conceal either provisions, or any glittering objects, with great address, pushing them into a hole, until they are no longer visible. Their winter store of food is usually collected in the middle of a field, and is sometimes indicated by two of the species contending for the hoard. Though crafty, they are also familiar; and, though naturally addicted to chatter, they are still more so when their tongue is untacked, so that, especially when taken young, they may be taught to pronounce words, and even short sentences, and will imitate any singular noise. In their natural state, they proclaim aloud any apparent danger, insomuch that no fox, or wild animal, can appear without being noticed and haunted; and thus even the fowler is frequently deprived of his sport; for all birds seem to know the magpie's alarming chatter. The nest, which is placed on the top of a tree, in a thick bush or hedge, and sometimes at no great distance from the ground, bespeaks much skill and artifice. The male and female work at it conjointly, or alternately, beginning in February, and usually continuing their labours for six weeks or two months. It is, for the most part, constructed on a fork, or on a junction of branches, and

Ornitho-
logy.

composed of twigs, young shoots of trees, and a thick covering of leaves, strengthened outwardly with long and flexible sticks, plastered over with mud, the upper part being covered with thorny branches, closely matted, so as to secure a retreat from the intrusion of other birds, a hole being left in the side barely sufficient for the admission and egress of the parent birds. The inside is furnished with a sort of matrass, composed of the fibres of roots, wool, and other soft materials, being only six inches in diameter, whereas the whole edifice measures at least two feet in every direction. Should the eggs be destroyed, the female abandons a construction which had cost her and her partner so much trouble, and will lay a second, and even sometimes, if again disturbed, a third time, the number of eggs diminishing at each hatch. On these occasions she does not build a new nest, but takes possession of, and refits an unoccupied one that has belonged to a rook, or else finishes one of those imperfect structures which are occasionally to be found in her neighbourhood, as if purposely reserved for cases of emergency. But, if unmolested, there is but one brood, which generally consists of seven or eight. The eggs are of a bluish or pale green, spotted with brown and cinereous. The male and female incubate alternately, and, in the course of about fourteen days, the young are brought forth blind, and continue so for some days. The parents rear them with great solicitude, and for a considerable length of time. During winter nights, magpies assemble in great numbers in some coppice or thicket to roost; but they separate again in the day time. When the young are taken from the nest for training, they may be fed with bread, curdled milk, or new cheese. Their flesh is considerably inferior to that of the young rook. In almost every country, the appearance of the magpie is, in the minds of the vulgar, associated with superstitious and ominous notions. In some parts of Lorraine this bird is regarded as a witch; in certain northern latitudes, one of them perched on the church denotes the death of the parson, or, if on the castle, that of the governor of the district; in some parts of the north of England, a magpie, flying by itself, forebodes ill luck; two together augur good fortune; three indicate a funeral; four, a wedding, &c.

Glandari-
us.

C. glandarius, Lin. &c. *Garrulus glandarius,* Cuv. and Vieill. *Jay.* The body of a wine buff colour; the head white, with black streaks; the wing coverts marked with blue and black bars, and the tail black. Length of the body about thirteen inches, extent of wing twenty-two, and weight from seven to nine ounces. This bird, which is of a moderately thick and stout form, is the most elegant of the tribe that is indigenous to Great Britain. Owing to the wideness of its gullet, it swallows acorns, filberts, and even chesnuts entire. Its treatment of the flower-cup of a pink is, however, very different; for, if one be thrown to it, it will seize it greedily, and, if others be offered, it will continue to snatch them till its bill can hold no more. When it wants to eat these, it lays aside all but one, holds it with the right foot, and plucks off the petals, one by one, keeping a watchful eye all the time, and casting a glance on every side; at length, when the seed appears, it devours it eagerly, and proceeds to pluck a second flower. These birds are great consumers of fruit and grain, especially of those already mentioned, as well as beech-mast, peas, sorbs, cherries, &c. They also frequently plunder the nests of smaller birds of their eggs and young, and sometimes even pounce on the old birds, and on mice. When they feed on the former, they begin by tearing out the eyes and

brain. It is commonly alleged that they hoard acorns for the winter; but their supposed magazines in the woods belong to squirrels, or some of the murine tribe. Yet it is by no means improbable that they pillage these stores, when they happen to fall in with them; and it is well known that in the domestic state, like others of the family, they not only conceal their superfluous provisions, but purloin any glittering object within their reach. If they perceive in the wood a fox or other ravenous animal, they utter a shrill scream to alarm their companions, which quickly assemble, as if solicitous to appear formidable by their noise and number. On seeing a sportsman, a jay will sound the same note of alarm, and thus frustrate his aim.

This species occurs in various temperate parts of Europe and the corresponding latitudes of Asia, frequenting wooded tracts, but not in flocks. It commonly breeds once or twice a year, in woods remote from human dwellings, preferring high coppices, or hedges, or branchy oaks, whose trunks are entwined with ivy. Here, in the month of May, or near the end of April, they build their nests, which are hollow hemispheres, formed of sticks, with small interlaced roots, open above, without any soft lining, or exterior defence. The eggs, which are from four to seven, are smaller than those of a pigeon, and somewhat resemble those of the partridge, being grey, with more or less of a greenish tint, and with small olivaceous brown spots, faintly marked. The incubation lasts thirteen or fourteen days. The young undergo their moulting in July, and generally keep company with their parents till spring, when they separate, and form new pairs. By this time, too, the blue plate on their wings, which appears very early, has attained its highest beauty. When full grown, the jay is extremely shy; but, if taken from the nest, it evinces great docility. Its common notes bespeak a wonderful flexibility of throat; for it naturally imitates the sounds with which it happens to be most familiar, as the bleating of a lamb, the mewing of a cat, the cry of a kite or buzzard, the hooting of an owl, the neighing of a horse, &c. These imitations, Col. Montagu observes, are so exact, even in the wild state, that he has been often deceived by them. We need not wonder, then, that it is capable of being taught to articulate various words, and that it is frequently procured for that purpose. The French allege that *Richard* is the name which it learns to repeat with the greatest readiness. In the Greek islands, in particular, it is often tamed on account of its singular loquacity. Its keen sensations and quick movements seem to be intimately connected with the petulance of its disposition. In its frequent sallies of rage, it hurries into danger, and often entangles its head between two branches, and dies, thus suspended in the air. When conscious of restraint, its violence exceeds bounds, and hence, in a cage, it is constantly rumpling, wearing, and breaking its feathers. During winter, jays seem to pass much of their time in the hollows of trees, but they come forth in the mild days that occasionally happen in that season. They likewise sometimes migrate in quest of a warm climate. In certain parts of the Levant, they arrive in troops about the beginning of autumn, and depart early in the spring. In a domestic state, the jay has been known to live from ten to eighteen years; but it is said to be subject to epilepsy. Its flesh, though eatable, is not generally relished: but if first boiled, and afterwards roasted, it is said to taste like goose, and, when young, and in plump condition, it sometimes passes at French tables for the thrush.

C. cristatus, Lath.; *Garrulus cristatus,* Cuv. and Cristatus.

Vieill.; *Blue Jay* of Catesby and Edwards. Crested, blue above, sub-rosaceous beneath, collar black, wings and cuneated tail barred with black. A most elegant species, ten inches nine lines long; not less lively and petulant than the preceding, but destitute of its hoarse clamour, its note being far from disagreeable, although very remote from the song ascribed to it by Pennant. Its general manners correspond with those of the European jay. It is pretty generally spread over North America, from the Floridas to Canada, as also on the north-western coasts, and in New California. These jays retire, in autumn, from the more northerly regions, and arrive, in large flocks, in Pennsylvania, where some of them pass the winter, whilst others advance more to the south. In the cold season, they approach houses, and are easily ensnared. The nest is usually placed in covered situations, that are watered by small streams. The eggs, which are four or five, are olivaceous, spotted with blackish-grey. The blue crest of the female is less conspicuous than that of the male. These birds feed on worms, serpents, chesnuts, &c. and are particularly injurious to maize-fields.

C. caryocatactes, Lin. &c.; *Nucifraga caryocatactes*, Temm.; *Nut-cracker*, or *Spotted Crow*. Rusty brown, with triangular white spots; crown and wings blackish; tail blackish, and tipt with white, and the middle feathers as if worn. Length of the body thirteen inches; extent of wing twenty-one inches; and the general size about that of the magpie. To the latter and the jay, it is closely related; but it is distinguished from both by the shape of the bill, which is straighter and blunter, and composed of two unequal pieces. Its instinct is also different; for it prefers the residence of high mountains; and its disposition is not so much tinctured with cunning and suspicion. The iris is hazel; the bill, feet, and nails, are black; the nostrils round, shaded with whitish feathers, which are straight, stiff, and projecting; the feathers in the wing and tail are blackish, without spots, but, for the most part, only terminated with white. Besides the brilliancy of its plumage, the nut-cracker is remarkable for the triangular white spots which are spread over its whole body, and which are smaller on the upper part, and broader on the breast. There are, however, some diversities in the different individuals, as well as in the different descriptions, which seems to confirm the opinion of Klein, that there are two races, or varieties; the one speckled like the stare, with a strong angular bill, and a long forked tongue; and the other of inferior size, with a more slender and round bill, and the tongue deeply divided, very short, and almost lost in the throat. Both live much on hazel nuts; but the former breaks, and the latter pierces them. They likewise feed on acorns, wild berries, the kernels of pine-tops, and even on insects. It should seem that, when pressed by hunger, they likewise prey on small birds. They have the hoarding propensity of the raven, &c. concealing what they cannot consume. Their cry resembles that of the magpie. They nestle in the holes of trees, the female laying five or six eggs of a fawn-grey, with thinly scattered spots of a clear grey-brown. As they haunt remote, and not very accessible spots, we know little of their incubation, the training of their young, or the duration of their lives. When taken young, they are capable of being tamed; but all attempts to domesticate the adults, have, it is alleged, proved abortive, as they soon languish and die, in consequence of the obstinate rejection of food.

This species inhabits many parts of Europe, and is found even in Siberia and Kamtschatka, but is very rare in this island. Though not statedly birds of passage, they sometimes fly from the mountains to the plains; and Frisch observes, that flocks of them are frequently seen to accompany other birds into different parts of Germany, especially where there are pine forests. In some particular years, large flocks of them have emigrated to different parts of France, in a half starved and emaciated state; the wild fruits on which they mostly fed having failed from drought in their more ordinary places of resort. They are unfriendly to the health of large trees, by piercing their trunks. This bird is admirably figured by Edwards.

C. graculus, Lin. &c.; *Fregilus graculus*, Cuv.; *Coracias erythroramphos*, Vieill.; *Pyrrhocorax graculus*, Tem.; *Red-legged Crow*, or *Cornish Chough*, Prov.; *Cornish Daw, Cornwall Kae, Chouk, Daw, Market Jew Crow*, and *Skilligrew*. Violaceous black; bill and legs red. Weighs about fourteen ounces; measures nearly seventeen inches in length; and stretches its wings to twenty-six inches. Native of the Alps and Pyrenees, Norway, Austria, and various countries of the continent of Europe. In this island it seems to be principally limited to Devonshire, Cornwall, and Wales; but it is also found in some parts of Scotland and the Hebrides. It appears in immense flocks in Egypt, towards the end of the annual inundation of the Nile, when it feeds, with the storks and falcons, on the reptiles which then overrun the land. With us, they are stationary throughout the year. According to Scopoli, they are particularly fond of locusts and grasshoppers, and are observed to feed much on juniper-berries. They appear to be partial to sea-shores, inhabiting cliffs and ruined towers, or castles; but they are not constant to their places of abode, deserting them occasionally for a week or ten days at a time. They commonly fly very high, are seldom seen abroad except in fine weather, and make a more shrill and stridulous noise than the jackdaw. Their nest, which is composed of sticks, and lined with a great quantity of wool and hair, is usually built about the middle of the cliffs, or in the most inaccessible parts of ruins. The eggs, which are commonly four or five, are somewhat larger than those of the jackdaw, and of a dull white, sprinkled with light-brown and ash-coloured spots, mostly at the larger end. The ordinary food of these birds consists of grain and insects, though, in confinement, they show no aversion to flesh. They are easily tamed, but crafty and capricious; nor should they be trusted where articles of value are kept; for they are taken with glittering objects, and are apt to snatch up bits of lighted sticks, with which they have been known to set fire to a house. With their long bills, they will also tear holes in the thatch of roofs, in search of worms and insects, and, by thus admitting the rain, accelerate the decay of the thatch. The Cornish peasantry often keep them tame in their small gardens. The appearance of any thing strange or frightful makes them shriek aloud; but when applying for food, or desirous of pleasing those who usually fondle them, they render their chattering very soft and engaging. In this domesticated state, they are docile and amusing, and very regular to their hours of feeding; but however familiar they may be with their more immediate friends, they are impatient of the approach of a stranger.

BUCEROS, Lin. &c.; CALAO or HORNBILL. Bill convex, curved, sharp-edged, of large dimensions, serrated at the margins, with a horny protuberance near the base of the upper mandible; nostrils behind the base of the

Ornitho-
logy.

bill; the tongue short, and situated at the bottom of the throat. By the form of their enormous bill, the birds of this family are allied to the toucans, while their deportment and habits assimilate them to the crows, and the structure of their feet approximates them to the bee-eaters and king-fishers. The large prominence on the upper mandible differs in shape in the different species; and in a few it is wanting. The hornbills feed not only on various berries, and other vegetable substances, but also on many of the smaller animals, as mice, birds, &c. though more commonly on insects, and not even disdaining carrion. They are inhabitants of the warmer regions of Asia and Africa. Their large bills are not solid, but of a cancellated internal structure. As the process or appendage to this instrument does not exhibit its genuine form till the full growth of the bird, and the difference between the males and females is very considerable, the determination of the species has been attended with no small degree of difficulty. Buffon has not failed to descant on the mal-conformation of the bill, and on its liability to bruises and fractures; but he was not aware of the fact, that these injuries are annually repaired by an inherent reproductive power, so that even the missing serratures are replaced at every moulting. These birds walk little, and awkwardly, and generally perch on trees, especially such as are dead, in the hollows of which they breed.

Rhinoce-
ros.

B. rhinoceros, Lin. &c.; *Rhinoceros Hornbill, Horned Indian Raven*, or *Rhinoceros Bird*. Black, tail tipped with white, beak yellowish, recurved casque red above. General size that of a hen turkey, but more slender in proportion; extent of wing nearly four feet; the neck of moderate length; and the tail slightly cuneated. The plumage black, but exhibiting, when exposed to a strong light, a slight bluish gloss; but the lower part of the abdomen and the tail are white. The bill measures about ten inches in length, and is of a slightly curved form, sharp-pointed, serrated in a somewhat irregular manner on the edges, and furnished at the base of the upper mandible with an extremely large process, continued, for a considerable space, in a parallel direction with the bill, and then turned upwards, in a contrary direction, in the style of a reverted horn. This appendage, which is eight inches long, and four in width at the base, is divided into two portions by a longitudinal black line. Though apparently a formidable weapon, this singular bill is by no means so in reality; for Levaillant assures us, that he often put his hand into it, without feeling the slightest pain, though the bird exerted all its endeavours to wound him. The young is destitute of the horn-like excrescence on the bill.

This species occurs in the Philippine islands, in Java, Sumatra, and various countries of India. The individuals belonging to it have a melancholy wild air, a heavy gait, hop instead of walking, and are of a timid and stupid disposition. In a wild state, they live on flesh and carrion, and are known to accompany the hunters of boars, wild cows, and stags, to pick up the intestines, and other refuse of these animals which are resigned to them. In Sumatra, when kept in confinement, they are fed on rice and soft meats; and, in various parts of India, they are domesticated for the purpose of catching rats and mice. When they have got one of the latter, they squeeze it in their bill to soften it, throw it up into the air, and then receive it entire into their capacious gullet. That described by Levaillant never manifested any thing like sprightli-

ness, but when its food was presented, it advanced with extended wings, and uttered a slight scream of joy. It was fed with biscuit steeped in water, flesh, either raw or dressed, rice, &c. When presented with some newly killed small birds, it readily swallowed them entire, after bruising them for some time in its bill.

Ornitho-
logy.

B. niger, Vieill. *Crescent Hornbill*. Black; thighs base, and tip of the tail white, bill yellowish, and the casque lunated upwards. About the size of the preceding, which it considerably resembles; but the casque of the bill is shaped like a crescent or boat, longitudinally affixed by its bottom to the ridges of the upper mandible. It is not concave at the top, but flattened, and the two ends rise up, the one before and the other behind the base of the mandible; that in front somewhat exceeding the length of the other. It is a native of Java, where it is said to frequent large woods, uniting in troops, in order to devour carrion. The female wants the patch of red brown between the shoulders, which characterizes the male, and is, besides, somewhat smaller than the latter.

Niger.

B. monoceros, Shaw; *B. Malabaricus*, Lath. *Unicorn Hornbill, Indian Raven, Horned Crow, Horned Pie*, &c. Slightly crested, and black abdomen, and sides of the tail-feathers white, bill yellowish, with compressed casque, black above, and pointed in front. About the size of a raven, and measuring nearly three feet of outstretched wing. The curious structure of its bill is detailed by Buffon. The female is rather smaller than the male, and has the casque less elevated and its point less prominent.

Monoceros.

These birds frequent high woods, perching on large trees, especially on the dead boughs. They nestle in the hollows of decayed trunks, and lay about four eggs, of a dirty white. The young are at first quite naked, and their bills have merely a slight ridge, three or four lines high, and which is not clearly defined till the space of three months, when they take their flight; and the point does not project till they are fully grown, and have assumed their mature plumage. This part, it has been remarked, is subject to frequent accidents, from striking against the branches of trees, when the bird is endeavouring to detach the bark, in order to obtain the insects, small lizards, tree-frogs, &c. which lurk beneath. The individual described by Buffon hopped with both feet at once, forward and sideways, like a magpie or jay. When at rest, its head seemed to recline on its shoulders: when molested, it swelled, and raised itself with an air of boldness; but its general gait was dull and heavy. It swallowed raw flesh, and would also eat lettuces, which it first bruised with its bill. It caught rats, and devoured a small bird that was thrown to it alive. Its ordinary voice was a short hoarse croak; and it likewise uttered at intervals a sound exactly similar to the clucking of a hen. It was fond of warmth, spreading its wings to the sun, and shivering at a passing cloud or gale. It lived only three months, dying before the end of summer.

B. violaceus, Levail. *Violaceous Hornbill*. Violaceous black; sides of the wing, and tail-feathers, white; bill whitish; casque compressed, obtuse in front, and marked by a black spot. Nearly resembles the unicorn species, but is of a smaller size. When viewed in a full light, it is very richly glossed with violet, green, and purple reflexions, though, when viewed in the shade, it appears of a greenish black. It is a native of Ceylon. Levaillant mentions that he saw one which had been brought to the Cape of Good Hope. It showed

Violaceus.

much attachment and docility to its keeper, was fed with meat, either raw or dressed, and with various kinds of vegetables. It pursued and readily caught both rats and mice, which it swallowed entire, after having rubbed them in its bill. Whenever a quarrel arose among any of the other birds, it immediately ran to them, and, by the strokes of its bill, enforced a suspension of hostilities. It even kept the larger birds in awe, and would make an ostrich take to its heels, pursuing it, half flying, and half running. It imposed, in short, on the whole menagerie, more, we may presume, by the size of its enormous bill, than by any intrinsic strength or courage.

B. Abyssinicus, Lath. *Abyssinian Hornbill.* Black, with white primary quills, the secondaries ferruginous; bill black, and casque abruptly orbicular. According to Mr. Bruce, who has distinctly described this species, it is of a blackish fuliginous hue, measuring three feet ten inches in length, and six feet in extent of wing. On the neck are several protuberances, as in the turkey, of a light blue, changing, on various occasions, to red. It occurs in Abyssinia, generally among the fields of *taff,* feeding on the green beetles that frequent that plant. As it has a fetid smell, it has been erroneously supposed to subsist on carrion. It usually runs on the ground, and does not hop, like most of its congeners; but, when raised, it flies both strong and far. It is supposed to be very prolific, as it has been seen with eighteen young ones attending it. It builds in large thick trees, making a curious nest, like that of the magpie, but four times larger than that of the eagle, placed firm on the trunk, at no great distance from the ground, and with the entrance always on the east side. The young, according, to Levaillant, are of a brownish black colour, with the larger wing feathers rufous white; and such seems to have been the specimen described by Buffon.

Of the species which want the horn-like appendage, we shall notice only two.

B. nasutus, Lin. &c. *Senegal,* or *Red-billed Hornbill.* Black and white, with a simple red bill, and red legs. Size not superior to that of a magpie; length rather more than twenty inches. Common in Senegal, where it is known by the name of *Tock.* When young, it is very simple and unsuspicious, and will suffer itself to be approached and taken, but it gradually becomes shy as it advances in age. It frequents woods, the old birds perching on the summits of the trees, and often soaring, with lofty and rapid flight, while the young generally remain in the lower parts of the trees, sitting motionless, with the head contracted between the shoulders. In their native state, they live on wild fruits, and, in confinement, on almost any thing that is presented to them.

B. coronatus, Levail. *Crowned Hornbill.* Black, with the abdomen, stripe on each side of the hind head, and tip of the tail, white; bill red, and slightly crested. Native of Africa, and described, for the first time, by Levaillant, who saw a flock of more than 500 of them in the company of crows and vultures, and preying on the remains of slaughtered elephants. The female deposits four white eggs in the hollows of trees.

PRIONITES, Ill. MOMOT.

Feet and carriage of the bee-eaters; but the bill is stronger, with the margins of both mandibles notched; and the tongue is barbed, or feathered, like that of the toucans.

P. Brasiliensis, Cuv. *Ramphastos momota,* Lin. *Mo-*

mota Brasiliensis, Shaw. *Momotus Brasiliensis,* Lath. *Baryphonus Cyanocephalus,* Vieill. *Brasilian Momot,* or *Brasilian Saw-billed Roller.* Green above, buff-coloured beneath; crown-blue, marked with a black spot, and the two middle tail-feathers elongated. Head large, bill black, legs black, and claws hooked. Length, from the tip of the bill to that of the tail, about a foot and a half. Edwards, in his minute description of this bird, remarks, that the two long feathers in the middle of the tail seem as if they were stripped of their webs on each side, for the space of an inch, a little within their tips; and Buffon seizes on this peculiarity as an excellent distinctive character, although he admits that it is only observable in the adult birds. Some have supposed that the defect is occasioned by the bird itself tearing off that portion of the web, after every moulting; but it is by no means probable, that every individual would be instinctively guided to such a capricious and useless practice; and the circumstance may, perhaps, be accounted for by some unknown habit peculiar to the bird. This species inhabits the hotter regions of South America, particularly Guiana and Brazil. In the former country, it is known by the name of *Hootoo,* which is expressive of the bird's cry, a sound which it utters distinctly and abruptly, as often as it leaps, and which is heard early in the morning, before all the other birds are awake. Naturally shy, it courts the recesses of the forest, and lives in solitude. It is chiefly seen on the ground, or on some low branch of a tree, taking short flights, when disturbed. The female makes a nest of stalks and dry grass on the ground, frequently in the deserted hole of an armadillo, cavy, or other quadruped, and usually lays two eggs. It feeds on insects and raw flesh, the fragments of which it macerates in water. When caught, it strikes violently with its bill.

P. Cyanogaster, Blue-bellied Momot. Green above, blue beneath, tail cuneated. Length fourteen inches and a half. Has the habits of the preceding. Its usual cry is *too, too, too,* but it also utters *hunu* in a more feeble tone. In confinement, it readily eats raw meat, and little bits of bread, frequently striking them against the ground before swallowing them, as if it believed them to be endued with life. It gives chase to small birds, of which it is very fond; and, when it catches them, it beats them, in like manner, against the ground, and continues to do so even for some time after they are dead; and it then swallows them entire, beginning with the head. It treats mice in the same manner; but it refuses to meddle with birds that are too large to be swallowed at once. It is a native of Paraguay.

GLAUCOPIS, Gmel. &c. WATTLE BIRD. CALLÆAS, Bech.

Bill incurvated, arched, the lower mandible shortest, with a caruncle below at the base; nostrils depressed, and half covered with a membrane, nearly cartilaginous, cut at the point, and fringed; feet gressorial, or formed for walking. A single species is known, namely, the

G. cinerea, Gmel. &c. *Cinereous Wattle-bird.* Blackish, with blue eyes and red wattles. Irides blue, and very large; tail long, and wedged; legs long, hind claws longer than the others. Fifteen inches long, and about the size of a jay. Inhabits New Zealand, where it is often seen walking on the ground, and sometimes, though more rarely, perched on trees. It feeds on various sorts of berries and insects, and even, according

Ornithology.

Abyssinicus.

Nasutus.

Coronatus.

PRIONITES.

Brasiliensis.

Ornithology.

Cyanogaster.

GLAUCOPIS.

Cinerea.

Ornitho-
logy.

to some, on small birds. Its note approaches to a whistle, and sometimes to a kind of rather pleasing murmur. Its flesh is eatable, and by some esteemed savoury.

BUPHAGA, Lin. &c. BEEF-EATER.

BUPHAGA.
Africana.

Bill straight, squarish, gibbous, entire; feet gressorial.
B. Africana, Lin. &c. *African Beef-eater*, or *Oxpecker.* Ferruginous-brown above, pale beneath; tail feathers sub-acuminated. Size of a lark, and eight inches in length. The female differs from the male in being rather smaller, and in having the bill of a paler cast. It resides in the hotter parts of Africa, and is said to be frequent in Senegal, where its chief food consists of the larvæ of œstri, or gad-flies, which it picks out of the skin of the larger cattle. According to Levaillant, who observed it in the country of the Great Namaquas, it is usually seen in small flocks, of six or eight together. But it is extremely shy, and will not easily admit of a near approach. The strength of the beak is very great, and well adapted to the purpose of extracting larvæ from the hide of animals; but it also feeds on various insects in their perfect state. It has a sharp cry, in no respect approaching to a song.

BOMBYCILLA, Brisson. AMPELIS, Lin. &c. CHATTERER.

BOMBY-
CILLA.

Bill short, straight, elevated; the upper mandible faintly curved towards the extremity, with a very marked indentation; nostrils basal, ovoid, open, concealed by rough hairs directed forward; three toes before, and one behind, the outer consolidated with that in the middle; wings of moderate size, with the first and second quills the longest.

Garrula.

B. garrula, Ampelis garrulus, Lin. &c. *Bohemica,* Brisson. *Waxen Bohemian,* or *Silk-tail chatterer,* or *Bohemian Wax-wing.* Back of the head crested; length nearly eight inches; size about that of a starling.

Though found in Europe, Northern Asia, and America, the original country of this bird is doubtful; for every where it seems to roam, and in no region has its mode of breeding been ascertained. Linné, and others, have conjectured that the species is propagated farther north than Sweden, and it is supposed to build its nest in the holes of rocks. The epithet *Bohemian* is by no means appropriate, for it only migrates into Bohemia, as it does into many other countries. In Austria it is conceived to be a native of Bohemia and Styria, because it enters by the frontiers of those regions; but, in Bohemia it might with equal propriety be called the *bird of Saxony,* and in Saxony the *bird of Denmark,* or of other countries on the shores of the Baltic. They occasionally abound in Prussia, and visit Poland and Lithuania; and Strahlenberg informed Frisch, that they have been met with in Tartary, in the holes of rocks. After a period of three years, or more, they are said to leave Bohemia entirely; and they are not found there in winter. The few, on the contrary, which stray into France and Great Britain, appear in the depth of the winter, but always in small parties, as if they had parted from the great body by some accident, whereas immense numbers have, at particular epochs, been seen to arrive in Italy, where, in former times, their congregated legions were deemed ominous of war or pestilence. In Sweden they sometimes pass in such dense bands as to intercept the light. They are partial to melting juicy fruits, to grapes, berries of various descriptions, almonds, apples, &c. They are

Ornitho-
logy.

easily tamed, affectionate, sociable, and susceptible of particular friendships among themselves, independently of sexual attachment; but they languish and die in strict confinement. They utter a sort of chirrup when they rise, but are quite mute in a cage. Réaumur will not even allow that they can chant, while Prince d'Avensperg asserts that their notes are very pleasing. The truth, perhaps, is, that, during a short period in the breeding season, they may warble, and only chirp and chatter at other times. Authors likewise differ as to the edible qualities of their flesh, which probably vary according to the prevailing diet of the bird.

CORACIAS, Lin. &c. ROLLER.

CORACIAS.

Bill strong, compressed towards the extremity, bent in at the point, with the base naked of feathers; nostrils oblong; feet short, stout, and formed for walking; wings long, with the first quill somewhat shorter than the second. Most of the family are conspicuous rather for brilliancy than harmony of colouring, and in their general manners they seem to be nearly allied to the crows.

Garrula.

C. garrula, Lin. &c. *Galgulus garrulus,* Vieill. *Common, European,* or *Garrulous Roller.* Sea-green, with nearly even tail; wings varied with blue, sea-green, and black; back testaceous; rump blue. The shoulders, or parts invested by the smaller wing-coverts, are of a rich ultra-marine blue; the back and scapular feathers testaceous, or pale chesnut; and the rump ultra-marine; the whole vying with some of the parrots, and on this account, as well as on that of its chattering propensity, the bird has been sometimes denominated the *German parrot.* It is about the size of a jay, measuring thirteen inches in length, and two feet from tip to tip of the outstretched wings. The young do not acquire their splendid colours till the second year; and Montbeillard suspects that the two long tail feathers are the attribute of the male.

This is the only one of the family known in Europe. It roams as far north as Sweden, and a few stragglers have been met with in England. In France it is far from common; but it occurs more frequently in Germany, Italy, Sicily, Malta, &c. and appears preferably to haunt the warmer regions of the old continent, particularly Africa. In some of the European countries it is said to migrate in the months of May and September. In districts in which it abounds, it is seen to fly in large flocks in the autumn, and to frequent cultivated grounds, in the company of rooks and other birds, searching for worms, small seeds, roots, &c. It breeds among birch trees, and sometimes, as in Malta, in a hole in the ground, laying from four to seven eggs, of a glossy greenish white. It feeds on moles, worms, beetles, acorns, grain, &c. is fond of fruit, and, in case of necessity, does not reject carrion. Its note is noisy and chattering. It is publicly sold in the market in Sicily, Malta, &c. and is said to taste like turtle.

ORIOLUS, Lin. &c. ORIOLE.

ORIOLUS.

Bill in the form of a lengthened cone, horizontally compressed at the base, and sharp-edged, the upper mandible surmounted by a ridge, notched at the point; nostrils basal, lateral, naked, and horizontally pierced in a large membrane; tarsus shorter than, or of the same length as, the middle toe, the outer united to the latter; wings of moderate dimensions, with the first quill very short, and the second shorter than the third.

The birds included within the reduced limits of this generic term, inhabit the woods and thickets of the old continent, living in pairs, and migrating in families. They feed on berries, soft fruits, and insects. The prevailing colour in the plumage of the males is yellow, and of the females greenish, or dull yellow. The young, in their first stage, resemble the females.

Galbula. *O. galbula*, Lin. &c. *Golden Oriole*, or *Witwall*. Body, and tip of the tail gold-yellow; wings, tail, and cere, black. There are several marked varieties in different quarters of the world, as the *Black-headed*, and the *Motled*; at Madras, the *Chinese* and the *Indian*.

In France, and other parts of the European continent, the golden oriole summers and breeds, appearing in the neighbourhood of Paris about the end of May, and departing in the beginning of September. On their first arrival, they are so exhausted and emaciated, that they allow the fowler to approach within gunshot of them, as they are feeding on insects. Yet, soon after, they commence pairing. In Malta, they are observed in September, on their passage to more southern regions; returning the same way in spring, to their northerly abodes. According to Retzius, they visit even Swedish Finland about the end of May, and retire in September; whereas, in England, there are not many well authenticated instances of their appearance. They live on caterpillars, worms, insects, berries, and other fruits, and are particularly fond of cherries. Their nest is a neat, and highly finished structure, supported by the edge or rim, having the appearance of a shallow purse or basket, suspended from the forked extremity of some slender branch. Wreathing the two branches of the fork round with straws, grasses, or other vegetable fibres, suited to the purpose, the bird at length connects the two extremities of the fork, in order to form the verge of the nest; then, continuing the straws of the one side to the other, giving the whole a proper depth, and crossing and interweaving the materials, as the work proceeds, forms the general basket, or concavity, which is afterwards thickened with the stems of the finer grasses, intermixed with mosses and lichens; and, finally, lined with still more delicate substances, as the silken bags of the chrysalids of moths, down, spiders' webs, &c. On this luxurious couch the female deposits four or five eggs of a dirty white, scattered with small blackish-brown spots, which are most numerous at the larger end. The incubation lasts twenty-one days. The parents fetch caterpillars, by ten, or a dozen at a time, to their nascent progeny, in whose defence they will boldly fly in the face of danger. The hen bird has sometimes submitted to be captured along with the nest, and died in the act of incubation. This beautiful bird has a loud, shrill, and rather a disagreeable note, preceded by a sort of mewing. It is tamed with considerable difficulty, and seldom survives two years in captivity, being generally carried off by a goutish affection in the feet. When fattened with its favourite fruits, as figs, grapes, cherries, &c. it is deemed a delicacy at table.

Icterus, Daud. Temm. Troupial.

Icterus. Bill larger than, or as long as, the head, straight, prolonged with a cone, pointed, a little compressed, without any distinct ridge, the base projecting among the front feathers; the point sharp and piercing, without a notch; margins of the mandibles more or less bent inwards; nostrils basal, lateral, longitudinally cleft in the corneous mass of the bill, and covered above by a horny rudiment; tarsus as long as, or longer than, the middle toe; wings long.

Nigricollis. *I. nigricollis*, Cuv. *Pendulinus nigricollis*, Vieill.

Oriolus capensis, Gmel. and Lath. and the female of *Oriolus spurius*, Gmel. *Black-necked Troupial*, or *Cape Oriole;* but this last is an unfortunate appellation, as the bird is not a native of Africa. Spot between the bill and the eye, the middle of the throat, and the front of the neck, black. Length six inches two lines; but the female is only five inches seven lines; has no black in her plumage, and the throat yellow. These birds pass the summer in North America, frequenting copses and orchards. The song of the male is sonorous and melodious, but the air short and little varied. They make their nest of the fibrous parts of hemp, and other analogous materials, giving it the form of a small platter or saucer, and fixing it to the extremities of two branches of a tree, by the projecting edges; and yet so compact are its texture and fastenings, that it braves the violence of the winds. The hatch consists of four or five white eggs, with black zig-zag markings at the larger end.

Domini- *I. Dominicensis*, Cuv. *Oriolus Dominicensis*, Lath. censis. *Pendulinus flavigaster*, Vieill. *St. Domingo Troupial*, or *St. Domingo Oriole*. Bill, feet, and general plumage black, with the exception of the smaller wing-coverts, the lower parts of the back, the rump, and the abdomen, which are of a beautiful yellow. Rather more than seven inches long. The female differs only in having less brilliant colours. Native of South America and the West India Islands; building in lofty trees, a pendulous purse-shaped nest. The young have often been described as a separate species.

Sturnus, Lin. &c. Starling.

Sturnus. Bill of a middle size, straight, in the form of a lengthened cone, depressed, slightly obtuse, base of the upper mandible projecting on the forehead, the point much depressed, and without a notch; nostrils basal, lateral, half concealed by an arched membrane; wings long, the first quill merely visible, the second and third the longest. Many birds used to be arranged under this designation, though destitute of the bill and the manners of genuine starlings, whilst other American species, whose legitimacy cannot be questioned, have been classed along with other families.

Starlings feed principally on insects; nestle in the holes of trees, under the tiles of roofs, and in the holes of walls. Like many of the omnivorous order, they consort and travel in large flocks. They frequently attend on cattle, and pick up their food in meadows and gardens. The males and females differ little in general aspect; but the young of the first year are very dissimilar to the mature birds; whilst, even in these last, the double and periodical change of colour in the beak and legs, and in the tints and decorations of the plumage, is superinduced without the aid of a second moulting, the habit of friction, and the influence of the air and light apparently obliterating the ends of the webs of the feathers, and the numerous spots which are so conspicuous in autumn. They are found in every quarter of the globe.

Vulgaris. *S. vulgaris*, Lin. &c. *S. varius*, Meyer. *Common Starling* or *Stare*. Prov. *Chep Starling*, or *Chepster*. Bill yellowish; body shining brassy black, spotted with white. The sexes nearly resemble each other, but the male is the heaviest of the two, weighing about three ounces, the length of the body being eight inches and three quarters, and the extent of wing fourteen inches. As the males only are susceptible of education, the bird-catchers recognise them by a minute blackish spot under the tongue. Among the numerous varieties to

Ornitho-
logy.

which this species is subject, we may mention, that of a white cast, with reddish legs and bill, between which and the common appearance it is found in different stages. In some the ground is cream-coloured, spotted with pure white; and in others, the upper parts are of a rufous-ash, inclining to yellow, and the breast slightly spotted. The young differ so materially from the old birds, and so much resemble the female of the solitary thrush, that the late Colonel Montagu, with all his acuteness of discrimination, has described one of them as such.

The stare occurs abundantly in the old continent, from Norway to very southern latitudes. A few remain all the winter in Norway, in the fissures of a rocky isle near Stavanger, and come forth to bask in the sunny days. Vast flocks of them are met with in all parts of Russia and western Siberia; but they are very scarce beyond the Jenisei. From the very northern countries, their passage has been traced to Poland, the Crimea, the Ukraine, and back again, by the same route, or through Lithuania. Of those which breed in the south of Europe, many winter in Egypt. In many parts of this country, they are stationary; but, from others they migrate in large flights, after the breeding season. During very severe winters, they have also been observed to retire westward, into Devonshire and Cornwall, and to return eastward with the breaking up of the frost. In the early days of spring, when the pairing commences, the males fight fiercely for their mates, and the latter submit to the conquerors. They breed in the hollows of trees, or rocks, among rubbish, in old towers, under the eaves of houses, dovecots, &c. and not unfrequently in the deserted nest of a bird of some other species; as, for example, of the woodpecker, which sometimes returns the compliment. The nest is artlessly made up of straw, coarse hay, leaves, feathers, &c. in which the female drops from four to seven eggs, of a pale greenish ash. The male participates with her the cares of incubation, which lasts eighteen or twenty days; and the young do not quit the nest till they are very completely fledged. In our temperate climates, starlings breed only twice in the year. Linné mentions that a lame one had been observed, for eight successive summers, to nestle in the hollow of the same alder tree, though it regularly left the country in winter. The young do not acquire their permanent colours during the first year, but are of a dusty brown, and might be readily mistaken for thrushes, or blackbirds. Their general food consists of insects and their larvæ, snails, earthworms, the *cancer pulex*, grains, seeds, berries, grapes, cherries, &c. By some they are accused of preying on the eggs of pigeons; and, in a state of confinement, they will eat meat of almost any kind. Fifty-seven individuals of this species were once killed at a single shot, near Kirkwall, where they are as common as sparrows elsewhere, and flocks of them perch on every wall and chimney top.

In the evening, these birds appear in the greatest numbers, assembling in marshy places, where they roost among the reeds, which, in the fens of Lincolnshire, are broken by their weight, and thus rendered unfit for being used as thatch. The flight of stares is not undulatory, but smooth and even; and they walk very easily in the manner of a wagtail; but, when they assemble in flocks, their movements are noisy and tumultuous, describing a sort of vortex, combined with an advancing progress. So attached are they to society, that, immediately after breeding, they not only consort with those of their own species, but also with birds

of a different kind, and may be frequently seen in company with redwings, fieldfares, &c. and even with pigeons, jackdaws, and owls. They chatter much in the evening and morning, both when they assemble and when they disperse. On the approach of predacious birds, they rally in close array, and usually succeed in driving them off. The kings of Persia used to have starlings trained to hunt butterflies; but they are principally tamed for the sake of the warble which they are capable of acquiring in confinement, and to amuse their owners by their various feats of mimicry. For these purposes, it is recommended to take them from the nest three or four days after birth; for, if they remain in it much longer, they seldom get entirely rid of their shrill and disagreeable twitter. At this very tender age, they should be carefully kept in a small box, furnished with moss, which should be changed every day; cleanliness being of the greatest consequence. They should be fed with little shreds of sheeps' heart, cut in the form of caterpillars, and presented at the end of a small stick, till they can feed themselves, when they may be served with the same paste that is given to nightingales. Their food, indeed, may be considerably varied; as, in this respect, they are very accommodating. It should likewise be noticed, that they will readily enough breed in bird pots, affixed to a tree, or the walls of a house. Their pliant throat quickly catches the most varied accents and intonations, so that they can distinctly articulate the letter R, and may be taught to prattle words, and even sentences, in different languages. "The young Cæsars," says Pliny, "had stares and nightingales, docile in the Greek and Latin languages, and which made continual progress, and assiduously prattled new phrases of considerable length." When M. Gérardin visited his friend, M. Thirel, in Paris, he was agreeably surprised and astonished by hearing a stare articulate a dozen of consecutive sentences, with the same precision as if some person had uttered them in the next room; and, when the mass bell rang, it called on its mistress by name, and thus distinctly addressed her: *Mademoiselle, entendez-vous la messe que l'on sonne? Prenez votre livre, et revenez vîte donner à manger à votre polisson.* ["Mademoiselle, don't you hear the summons to mass? Take your book, and return quickly, to feed your little rogue."] This pleasing tattle it enlivened by whistling two or three flageolet airs, which it improved by various graces, and imperceptible transitions of its own. In a wild state, the starling is supposed to live eight or ten years; and, in confinement, it has sometimes dragged out its existence to twenty. When kept and hampered in cages, it is, like many other birds similarly circumstanced, liable to epilepsy; and its flesh was formerly very absurdly believed to be an *antidote* to that complaint in the human subject. As an article of cookery, it is generally dry, bitter, and unpalatable.

PARADISEA, Lin. &c. PARADISE BIRD.

These birds, like the crows, have the bill straight, compressed, strong, and notchless, and the nostrils covered, but with feathers of a velvety or metallic lustre, with a singular and splendid development of the plumage of several parts of the body. Although they occur in Japan, China, Persia, and various regions of India, they are believed to be originally natives of New Guinea. Their history, till of late, was involved in fable; for they were said never to alight on the ground, from their birth to their death, to subsist entirely on dew, and to be produced without legs. The circum-

Ornitho-
logy.

PARADI-
SEA.

stance which gave rise to the last-mentioned tale was merely accidental, the legs and coarser parts of the wings having been pulled off, in the course of preparing the birds as an ornamental article of dress. The Dutch used to procure them chiefly from Banda, and propagated the story of their want of limbs, with a view to enhance their value. The Portuguese navigators to the Indian Islands called them *Passaros da Sol*, or *Birds of the Sun*, in the same manner as the Egyptians regarded the imaginary phœnix as a symbol of the annual revolution of the great luminary. The inhabitants of the island of Ternate call them *Manu-co-Dewata*, or *Birds of God*, which Buffon has Frenchified into *Manucode*. But his countryman, Vieillot, has more satisfactorily illustrated the tribe, in a magnificent publication entitled *Histoire Naturelle des Oiseaux de Paradis*. As no intelligent European, however, has watched their proceedings in a state of nature, their habits and economy are still obscure.

P. major, Shaw; *Apoda*, Lin. &c.; *Great Bird of Paradise*. Of a cinnamon hue, crown luteous; throat golden green, or yellow; side feathers very long and floating. We have adopted Dr. Shaw's specific epithet, because that of Linné being deduced from fable, might tend to consecrate error. The length of this species, from the point of the bill to the end of the real tail, is about twelve inches; but, if measured from the tip of the bill to the termination of the long hypochondroid feathers, the result will be nearly two feet.

Pigafetta having had ocular demonstration of the existence of the legs in this species, and of the natives cutting them off previously to selling them, recorded the facts in his journal; but so rooted was the contrary notion in Europe, that Aldrovandus charged Pigafetta with an audacious falsehood, and the acute Scaliger still adopted the popular persuasion. It was, moreover, supposed, that these birds perpetually floated in the atmosphere, or suspended themselves, for a short time, by the naked shafts, that they never descended to the earth till their last hour, and that all which had been procured, had fallen from their aerial elevation, during the moments immediately preceding their fate.

The great birds of paradise are found in the Molucca Islands, and in those surrounding New Guinea, particularly Papua and Aru, where they arrive with the westerly, or dry monsoon, and whence they return to New Guinea, on the setting in of the easterly, or wet monsoon. They are seen, going and returning, in flights of thirty or forty, conducted by a leader, which flies higher than the rest, and crying like starlings in their progress, preserving their light and voluminous plumage in proper trim, by invariably moving against the wind. In consequence of a sudden shifting of the wind, however, their long scapular feathers are sometimes so much discomposed, as to preclude flight, when they fall to the ground, or are lost in the water. In the former case, they cannot easily reascend, without gaining an eminence, and are taken by the natives, and killed on the spot. They are likewise caught with bird-lime, shot with blunted arrows, or intoxicated, by putting the berries of *Menispermum cocculus* into the water which they are accustomed to drink. Their real food is not known with certainty; according to some, they eat the red berries of *Ficus benjamina*, or the waringa tree, whilst others allege, that they are particularly fond of nutmegs; some, again, assert, that they live on the larger moths and butterflies, and others, that they prey on small birds; and it is not improbable, from the structure of their

bill and claws, that they subsist both on animal and vegetable food. It is only for ornament that they are coveted by the inhabitants of the east, the chiefs wearing them on their turbans. The grandees of Persia, Surat, and the East Indies, use them as egrets, and even adorn their horses with them. A specimen of the greater paradise bird was once brought to England in a living state, but it had entirely lost its beautiful floating feathers, and did not long survive its arrival.

A smaller variety, by some regarded as a distinct species, termed *Minor*, is found in the Papua Islands.

P. rubra, Cuv. &c.; *Red Bird of Paradise*. Side feathers red; shafts broad, and concave on one side. Length, from the extremity of the beak to that of the tail, about nine inches, and to that of the side feathers, fourteen or fifteen. Another elegant species, and presumed to inhabit the same regions with the preceding.

P. alba, Cuv. &c.; *Falcinellus resplendescens*, Vieill. *White Bird of Paradise*. Side feathers white, tinted with yellow. The filaments issue, not from the rump, but from the extremities of the side feathers, and are of the strength and thickness of a horse's hair, about ten inches long, nearly naked, and twisted in different directions. The length of the bird, from the tip of the bill to the extremity of the tail, is nine inches and a half. The primary quill feathers are conformable to those of the other species, but the accidental circumstance of their being wanting in the specimen in the Parisian Museum, misled M. Cuvier, who represents them as short, and far less numerous than in the other birds of paradise.

P. regia, Lin. &c.; *Cicinurus regius*. Vieill. *Royal Bird of Paradise*, or *King Paradise Bird*. Red chesnut, with a golden green pectoral band; the two middle tail feathers filiform, with lunated feathered tips. The smallest of the tribe, not exceeding the size of a lark, and usually measuring five inches, or five inches and a half, in length, without reckoning the two middle tail feathers, which are about six inches long, in the form of naked shafts, divaricating as they extend, and each terminating in a moderately broad gold green web, rising from one side only of the shaft, and disposed into a flat spiral, of nearly two convolutions. It is a scarce and shy bird, not associating with its congeners, nor perching on tall trees, but flitting from bush to bush, in quest of wild berries. It occurs in the islands of the Indian Ocean, and returns to New Guinea in the rainy season.

P. magnifica, Lath. &c.; *Magnificent Bird of Paradise*. Chesnut coloured above, shining green beneath, each side of the neck tufted with yellow plumes. The general shape of this singular and splendid species, considerably resembles that of *P. major*, to which it is somewhat inferior in size.

P. sexsetacea, Lath. & Shaw; *P. aurea*, Gmel.; *Parotia sexsetacea*, Vieill. *Six-shafted*, or *Golden-breasted Bird of Paradise*. Velvet-black, hind-head and breast gold-green, side feathers lengthened, and loose-webbed, and the head furnished on each side with three naked shafts, five or six inches in length, and terminating in broad oval webs. This, which is also a gorgeous species, and from ten to eleven inches in length, is said to inhabit New Guinea.

P. superba, Lath. &c. *Sophorina superba*, Vieill. *Superb Bird of Paradise*. Black, with a wing-like series of feathers on each side of the body, and bright green pectoral plumes, diverging and lengthening on each side. The predominant colour is black, with green reflexions; but the bird may be at once discriminated by the semblance of a forked tail hanging from the breast, and produced by a band of blue-green feathers. It inhabits that part of New Guinea called *Serghile*, and can seldom be found entire; for the natives tear off the wings and tail, dry the birds in smoke, and put them in bamboos to carry them to market.

ORDER III.

INSECTIVOROUS BIRDS.

Bill middle sized, or short, straight, rounded, faintly sharp-pointed, or awl-shaped, upper mandible curved and notched at the point, most frequently furnished at the base with some rough hairs, pointing forwards; feet with three toes before and one behind, articulated on the same level.

The voice of these birds is distinguished by its harmony and cadence; most of them chiefly subsist on insects, especially during the breeding season, but many of them have likewise recourse to berries. They have usually more than one brood in the year; they inhabit the woods, bushes, or reeds, in which they build solitary nests.

LANIUS, Lin. &c. SHRIKE, or BUTCHER-BIRD.

Bill middle-sized, robust, straight from its origin, and much compressed; upper mandible strongly compressed towards the tip, which is hooked, the base destitute of a cere, and furnished with rough hairs, pointing forwards; nostrils basal, lateral, almost round, half closed by an arched membrane, and often partly concealed by hairs; tarsus longer than the middle toe.

Most of the birds of this family are so remarkable for their courage and voracity, that they have by many been classed in the Predacious Order; but their claws, their voice, their diet, residence, &c. more strictly assimilate them to the thrushes, and the other tribes of the present division. They have been called *butcher-birds*, from their habit of killing several victims before they begin to feed. They live in families, fly unsteadily and precipitately, and utter shrill cries. They nestle on trees, with great attention to cleanliness, and are tenderly careful of their young.

L. excubitor, Lin. &c. *Great Cinereous Shrike, Grey Shrike,* or *Greater Butcher-Bird.* Prov. *Shriek, Shrike, Mattages, Wierangle, Night-jar, Murdering Bird, Murdering Pie, Mountain Pie, French Pie,* &c. In some parts of America it is denominated the *Nine killer,* and in others, *White Whisky John.* Grey above, white beneath, wings wedge-shaped, tail and stripe across the eyes black, side tail feathers white. The bill is black, strong, and much hooked at the end; the irides are dusky, and the mouth is beset with strong bristles; the tail consists of twelve feathers of unequal length; and the legs are black. Weight rather more than two ounces, length from nine to ten inches, and extent of wing about fourteen inches. The female has nearly the same dimensions as the male, with lighter shadings above, and dirty white, with numerous semicircular brown lines beneath. A variety occurs that is almost entirely white, and others are more or less so.

The Greater Butcher Bird is a native of several countries in Europe and North America; it is particularly common in Russia; but there is reason to suspect that it is only an accidental visitant of this island. In France it remains all the year, haunting the woods in summer, and frequenting the plains and even approaching human habitations in winter. In the month of May it places its nest sometimes in the branchings or forkings of detached trees, and sometimes in prickly hedges or thickets, forming the frame work of small twigs, which it twists and interweaves with fibrous roots and moss, and lines with a profusion of feathers, down, wool, or gossamer, the whole so neatly arranged and compacted as scarcely to be affected by wind or rain. The eggs, which vary in number from four to eight, are probably not uniform in their markings; for Pennant represents them as of a dull olive green, spotted at the large end with black, while Latham says they are of a dull white, with dusky spots at the large end. Vieillot describes them as of a grey-white, spotted with pale olive-green, and cinereous. Gérardin asserts that they are white, spotted with dirty brown over most of the shell, but with black at the broad end; and Temminck states that they are white, with spots of a dirty brown. As the young are brought forth without down, the soft and warm casing of the nest supplies the want of it. The parents besides manifest the most tender solicitude for their welfare, feeding them with insects, and affectionately associating with them till the following spring. During autumn and winter they may be observed flying about in little domestic parties, which never commingle. They may be distinguished by their shrill cry—*troole, troole*—which is heard at a considerable distance, and which they incessantly repeat when perched on the top of trees, or flying. The latter motion is performed neither obliquely nor on the same level, but always up and down, by successive jerks and vibrations. They perch on the very extremity of the highest and most insulated branches, a position naturally suggested by their mode of catching their prey, because, as from the shortness of their wings, they fly with difficulty, it was of importance that they should be able to dart down, at once, and with force, on their destined victims, and compel them to take to the ground, when they are quickly dispatched by a violent compressure of the neck. Hence the Germans call the shrikes *Suffocating Angels.* When perched, and spying their prey, they constantly raise and depress the tail. After killing a bird, or large insect, they affix the carcass to some sharp thorn, in order possibly to devour it more readily and more at leisure; for these birds want the strength of the hawk to retain their quarry in their claws, and pull it with their bill. In dispatching a bird, they usually begin by opening the skull, and regaling on the brains. They are partial to field mice and chafers, without ever injuring the crops, and should therefore be protected by the farmers. They likewise spit the larger insects on thorns, before devouring them, reserving them, according to some, as store in case of need, and using them, according to others, as a decoy to the insectivorous birds. The two purposes are not incompatible; but, from M. Heckenwelder's interesting letter on this subject, inserted in the fourth volume of the *American Transactions,* and to which we beg leave to refer the curious reader, the alluring of birds appears to be the predominant motive. It has been, moreover, asserted, that, besides their own sharp note, they occasionally adopt those of other birds, with a view to draw them within their reach. Instances are on record of their having been bred to the flight of game; and, in Sweden, they are still employed to discover sparrow-hawks.

L. minor, Lin. &c.; *L. Italicus,* Lath. *Lesser,* or *Italian Grey Shrike.* Cinereous above; throat white; breast and flanks rose-coloured; the black bands near the eyes united on the forehead into a broad fillet. A little smaller than the preceding, and now proved from its habits, and other circumstances, to be a distinct species. The female is somewhat rufous beneath. Occurs not only in Italy, but also in France, Spain, and Russia. It may be readily distinguished from the preceding, by its rapid, straight, and easily sustained flight; by its cry, its habit of frequently halting on the ground, a stone, or some little eminence; by its expression of anxiety and suspicion, and by its escaping out of sight when approached. The female lays five or six oblong eggs, of a greenish white, and encircled about the middle with dots of greenish-brown, and cinereous-grey. This species readily learns to imitate the song of other birds.

Ruficollis. L. ruficollis, Gmel. &c.; *L. rufus*, Lin.; *L. rutilus*, Lath.; *L. Pomeranus* Lin. and Gmel. *Wood-chat Shrike.* Black and white, with the front and eye-stripe black; back of the head and upper part of the neck ferruginous. Not very uncommon in some parts of Europe and Africa, but so extremely rare in this country, that hardly a single specimen exists among our collections. It has many of the habits of the *Excubitor* and *Collurio*, with the last of which it was long confounded as a variety; but the recent observations of Levaillant, Sonnini, Montagu, and Vieillot, no longer permit us to hesitate in ranking it as a separate species. Length, seven inches, and stretch of wing about a foot and a half. The woodchat shrike is a bold and undaunted bird, and endowed with such strength of bill as to pierce the hand through a double glove. The bird catchers in Egypt, accordingly, who sell it as an article of food, are in the habit of tying its bill as soon as it is taken. Like the grey shrike and the flasher, it preys on small birds, vermin, and the larger insects, transfixing them on the thorns of the trees and bushes which they frequent, and also inveigling birds by an accurate imitation of their song. It appears in France in the spring, where it breeds, and departs in autumn, though several remain during the year; and, in Africa, where they abound, they seem to be quite stationary. The nest, which is somewhat smaller than that of the grey shrike, is constructed of analogous materials, and with not less art and neatness. The eggs are generally five or six, of a somewhat rounded form, and whitish-green, with some large, and a great many small cinereous spots. Neither the colours of the bird, nor its habits, appear to suffer any alteration from the influence of climate; for Levaillant, a very competent judge, could discern no difference in these respects between those of Lorraine and those of Africa.

Collurio. L. collurio, Lin. &c.; *L. spinitorquens*, Bechst. *Red-backed Shrike*, *Lesser Butcher-Bird*, or *Flasher*. Head grey; eye-streak black; back and wing-coverts ferruginous; breast sub-roseate. The male weighs eight drachms, and the female ten; and the former measures six inches and one fourth in length, and the latter seven inches. In the male, the quills are brown, and the tail is composed of twelve feathers, longest in the middle, more or less white at the base, black towards the end, and faintly tipt with white, except those in the middle, which are wholly black. In the female, all the upper parts are of a ferruginous brown; the back of the neck is dashed with grey; beneath the eye there is a brown streak; the breast and sides are dirty white, marked with numerous semicircular dusky lines; the middle of the belly and the vent are white, the quill and tail feathers brown, and the outer web of the exterior feathers of the tail white.

The red-backed shrike is diffused in the north and south of Europe, in Senegal, and the south of Africa, and has been observed at Pondicherry. It visits us in May, and departs in September, and is supposed to be somewhat local, being not uncommon in Devonshire, Wiltshire, Gloucestershire, and Shropshire. It is partial to the outskirts of forests, and to inclosed moist situations, and grounds that abound in bushes. In other respects it evinces many of the habits of its congeners. It usually makes its nest in some thick hedge, composing it of moss and fibrous roots, put together with wool, and lined with hair. It lays five or six eggs, rather blunt at the ends, and either pink-coloured, with rufous spots, or yellowish, with spots of greenish-ash in the form of a zone. According to other accounts they are white, or bluish-white, with dusky spots; so that we may suppose they are liable to vary. There are two broods in the year, and the eggs of the second are said to have smaller, and more thinly scattered spots. If any person approach the nest, the female makes an importunate and chattering noise. The male has a chirping note, not very dissimilar from that of the house sparrow, and he sometimes attempts a sort of song. Seated behind the thick foliage of a bush, he will occasionally succeed in deceiving young birds by his mimic strains; but the old ones, it is alleged, are not to be so trepanned. He transfixes the larger insects, particularly the chafer, on a thorn, and tears off the body, leaving the wing-cases, wings, and head. Colonel Montagu kept a young brood of this species for some time; but though they lived in amity for about two months, they then became very pugnacious, and two out of four were killed. The other two, which were chained, as goldfinches often are, were extremely docile, and would come at a call for the sake of a fly, of which they were particularly fond. When raw meat was given to them, they would endeavour to fasten it to some part of their cage, in order to tear it; and they would eat mice and small birds chopped in pieces, with the feathers, fur, and bones, which they disgorged like the hawk tribe. One of them fell a sacrifice to swallowing too large a quantity of mouse-fur, which strangled it; and the other, which had become pampered, died of epilepsy, while feeding on insects.

Collaris. L. collaris, Lin. &c. *Collared Shrike. Fiscal* of Levaillant. Black above, white beneath; white scapulars, and cuneated tail, edged with white. This last colour runs from each side of the lower part of the neck, behind the shoulder, and meets on the lower part of the back. The bill and legs are black. Twelve inches in length, and of a somewhat more slender form than the European sorts. Native of the interior of Africa, and very common at the Cape of Good Hope, where it may be observed in the gardens, and sometimes in the street. According to Levaillant, when it sees a locust, a mantis, or a small bird, it springs on it, and instantly carries it off, to impale it on a thorn, and with such dexterity that the spine always passes through the head of the victim; or, if a thorn cannot readily be found, it fixes, with great address, the head of the captured animal between a division of two small branches. Every creature which it seizes undergoes exactly the same process, and it thus continues to kill, and to store up its bloody acquisitions all day long, transfixing many more carcasses than it ultimately devours. It generally practises so to perch on the top of trees, especially on dry branches, that it pounces indiscriminately on all that comes in its way; and, when hungry, it visits its gibbets, and selects what it prefers. It is bold, vindictive, and very clamorous, chasing even birds of prey from its domain. Yet many of the predacious tribes profit by its collections, which are so widely scattered that it is impossible to preserve them all. It flies low, mounting and descending by jerks; nestles in the fork of a tree, and lays four or five eggs. The male shares with the female the cares of incubation, and neither abandons the young till they have acquired sufficient strength to provide for themselves. In early age these birds are very unlike what they are destined to become, in so much that one would take them for some very different species. The males, it has been observed, often wage furious and deadly conflicts with one another, especially when two of them contend for a female.

TURDUS, Lin. &c. THRUSH.

Bill middle-sized, sharp-edged; tip compressed and recurved; upper mandible notched near the point, detached hairs at the opening of the mandibles; nostrils basal, ovoid, lateral, half concealed by a naked membrane; tarsus longer than the middle toe, to which last the outer is united at the base.

Most of the species live principally on insects, especially during the breeding season, but they are also very fond of berries. They migrate in large flocks, whilst others are sedentary, especially in the south of Europe. Many of them have been remarked for their warbling strains, and most of them are reckoned delicate eating.

T. viscivorus, Lin. &c. *Missel, Missel Bird*, or *Missel Thrush*, Prov. *Throstle-Cock, Screech-Thrush, Holm-Thrush, Misseltoe-Thrush*, &c. Grey-brown above, whitish-yellow beneath; varied with dusky spots, the three outer tail-feathers tipt with white. Quill and tail feathers brown, with pale edges; legs yellow, and claws black. The female is somewhat lighter coloured above, and inclining to rufous beneath. The bird varies with more or less of white, and with brown, or rufous ash spots. It is the largest of the European thrushes, weighing five ounces, and measuring eleven inches in length, and sixteen and a half in extent of wing. It inhabits Europe as far northward as Norway, and is common in Russia, but not found in Siberia. In most of the temperate parts of Europe, it is partly migratory, and partly stationary. We gladly welcome it as one of the first heralds of spring; for, in the fine days of February, the male, perched on the top of a lofty tree, warbles in a strain of sweetly varied notes, and which, though strong, are generally admired. If the weather happens to prove mild, it will even begin to sing in January, but ceases as soon as the thermometer sinks below forty degrees; its voice, however, is often heard in windy and showery weather, whence, in Hampshire and Sussex, the people call it the *Storm-cock* or *Storm-fowl*. When disturbed or agitated, it utters a shrill grating scream, which is its usual note in autumn and winter, and is the same with that of the female. The pairing takes place in January, and continues during the breeding season. About the middle of March, the female makes a nest in the fork of a tree, especially if overgrown with lichen, sometimes on a lofty ash, but more frequently on one of moderate height, particularly an apple tree, in an orchard, or garden, constructing the fabric of white moss and coarse grass, interwoven with earth, outwardly fortified with pieces of stick, and lined with fine grass, hair, or wool. The number of eggs rarely exceeds four or five; and they are flesh-

coloured, with dark and rust-coloured spots. The male shares the duties of incubation, but ceases his song when the young are hatched. Both parents feed the latter with caterpillars, small worms, slugs, and snails, of which last they break the shells. After this first brood, they frequently have a second, when all the family unite, and vegetable food, as berries, cherries, grapes, &c. are superadded to their diet. To these, in winter, succeed the berries of the juniper, holly, ivy, buckthorn, and, above all, of the *misseltoe*, from which they have their name. As these berries are frequently propagated after passing through the bird, it was believed in ages of ignorance, that this was the only mode in which the plant was disseminated; and hence the proverb, *Turdus malum sibi cacat*. If the young are taken away, the male continues his song as before; and, if his mate be snatched from him, he is tuneful all summer. The missel thrush is very bold during the breeding season, driving other birds from the neighbourhood of the nest, and even attacking the magpie and jay. Montbeillard, strangely enough, applauds the pacific and harmonious dispositions of these birds, whereas they are very quarrelsome, and often fight with one another, either for food or a companion; nor do their combats, which are urged with great obstinacy, cease, until the weakest have relinquished the object of contention, and the haunts of the conquerors. Such of them as settle in orchards, are vigilant sentinels to the poultry, warning them of the approach of birds of prey, nay, seeming to take under their protection all the small birds which breed in their neighbourhood; for, if the kestril, sparrow-hawk, raven, magpie, or jay, appears within their purlieus, the males announce the enemy's presence by their cries of alarm, in which they are instantly joined by the indignant clamour of the females, when a legion of smaller birds, especially of finches, accompany them, in pursuit of the invader, and put him to flight. Being shy and wary, these thrushes are not easily caught in snares. In order to have them properly tamed, they should be taken from the nest when fledged, and fed, for some time, on crumbs of bread, soaked in water, and mixed with the yolk of eggs; and when they can feed themselves, they should be served with worms, snails, various sorts of berries, bruised apples, &c. Their song is louder than that of the throstle, but far inferior in harmony. Their flesh too, is less in request than that of several of their congeners, especially when they happen to be restricted to the berries of the northern countries. In default of these, they have sometimes recourse to the roots of plants, particularly to those of *Arum maculatum*, or *Lords and Ladies*.

T. pilaris, Lin. &c. *Fieldfare*, or *Fieldfare Thrush*, Prov. *Feldfare*, and *Pigeon Fieldfare*. Brown-red above, varied with dusky beneath; tail feathers black, the outer one with the interior edge whitish at the tip; head and rump hoary. There are, besides, three or four varieties. Length, ten inches; extent of wing, sixteen; and weight, about four ounces.

The fieldfare occurs in Europe, Syria, and Siberia; but, in many countries, it is only a bird of passage, visiting them in the winter, and retiring in spring. It is generally supposed to breed in the northern regions, as in Norway, Sweden, Russia, Poland, Lower Austria, and Siberia, building its nest in large trees, laying from four to six eggs, of a sea-green, spotted with rufous brown. In this country, they generally arrive about Michaelmas, or in October, in numerous flocks, blended with the red-wing, and frequently remain till the

Ornithology.

beginning of April, though they often take their departure in March. In France they seldom appear before November or December, and some of them occasionally loiter till the end of April, when they are observed to pair, though not to breed. With us, besides insects, they readily partake of haws, the berries of the holly, juniper, &c.; and they are passionately fond of the fruit of the service. In very severe weather, they migrate farther south; but should a sudden fall of snow arrest their progress, in crossing over the sea, many of them perish with cold and hunger. In the winter of 1798, a very heavy snow fell in the northern and eastern parts of England, when prodigious flocks of fieldfares appeared in the west; but, as the snow followed in their train, and remained a considerable time on the ground, they became too weak to move southwards, and thousands that had been starved to death were picked up in Devonshire. If rigorous weather comes on more gradually, and food becomes scarce, few are seen with us after Christmas; but they appear again, in small flocks, on their return northwards to breed. They seem to be of a more sociable disposition than either the throstle, or missel, or else from notions of common protection in regions where they are only visitants, they congregate for mutual safety; for, although they are sometimes seen singly, they generally form very numerous flocks, and fly in a body; and, though they often spread themselves through the fields in quest of food, they seldom lose sight of one another, but, when alarmed, fly off, and collect together on the same tree. When a person approaches a tree that is covered with them, they appear to continue fearless, until one, at the extremity of a branch, rising on its wings, utters a loud and peculiar note of alarm, when they all fly, with the exception of a single individual, which remains till the person comes still nearer, and then it, too, flies off, repeating the note of alarm. On their arrival in this island, they are generally observed to alight just before dark, and to take up their abode on the heath, or in woods; and they commonly roost on the ground. The song of the male, if he has any, during the breeding season, is, in course, unknown in this country; but his rallying cry of alarm is not distinguishable from that of the female. Linné, in his *Fauna Suecica*, alludes to a fieldfare, which was bred in the house of a wine merchant, and had become so familiar as to run along the table, and drink the wine out of the glasses, in consequence of which habit it lost the feathers on the head; but it recovered them, on being kept from its favourite beverage. Frisch ascribes the bitter relish of the flesh of this species to the bird's feeding on juniper berries. Some epicures prefer the flavour of those which have been fed only on insects; but the ancient voluptuaries, who included the present species under *Turdus*, appear to have been much more extravagant in their admiration of its properties as an article of cookery; for Varro tells us, that they fattened these birds with crumbs of bread, mixed with minced figs, and various kinds of food, to improve the delicacy of their flesh, and that the people employed for this purpose kept thousands of them in successive states of preparation for the table. The aviaries in which they were kept, were so contrived, as to admit barely enough of light to direct them to their food, whilst every object that might contribute to remind them of their former liberty, was carefully kept out of view, such as the fields, woods, birds, or whatever might disturb the repose deemed requisite for enhancing their value in the eyes of the cook. When prepared under this system

of management, they were sold for about two shillings each.

T. musicus, Lin. &c. *Throstle*, or *Song Thrush*. In some parts called *Grey-Bird*, or *Stormcock*, and in Scotland *Mavis*. Grey-brown above, whitish-red beneath, varied with dusky spots; inner base of the quills ferruginous. Weight three ounces, length nine inches, and extent of wing thirteen inches and a half. The colour so nearly resembles that of the missel thrush, that when we state its smaller size, and the yellow tinge of the inner wing-coverts, we may be said to have completed its description. The female is somewhat smaller, with the yellowish tint of the breast clearer, and the rufous extremity of the wing-coverts less conspicuous. White, brown, and intermediate varieties, also occur.

The throstle inhabits Europe as far north as Sondmor, and is found in most parts of Russia where the juniper grows, especially about the river Kama, but not in Siberia. Towards the approach of the vintage, innumerable flocks of the thrush tribe quit the northern regions; and such is their abundance on the southern shores of the Baltic, that, according to Klein, the city of Dantzic alone consumes ninety thousand brace of them. The different species, however, do not travel simultaneously; for the throstle appears first, and the red-wing, fieldfare, and missel, succeed in order. They halt in different districts, particularly in such as afford to them the most copious and easy subsistence. Thus, prosecuting their route southward, many reach certain stations sooner or later, according to the direction of the winds, and the variable changes of temperature, as has been remarked of all the feathered tribes that are driven from the north by the cold. Of the roaming throstles, some advance no farther than the islands of the Mediterranean, and others steer their course into Africa. According to Sonnini, they arrive in Egypt in the month of October, and leave it again in March, keeping at no great distance from human dwellings, and affecting the shade of the orange and lemon trees, which embellish some of the districts of Lower Egypt. Many of the species, however, do not undertake such extensive journeys, being content to pass the winter, or even to breed, in far more temperate quarters, braving, for example, our British winters, under hedges, in woods, or near houses. We need scarcely observe, that it is generally admired for its song, which, for fulness and clearness of tone, is perhaps excelled by none of our warblers, and which, for plaintiveness, compass, and execution, is much superior to that of the blackbird. Its notes agreeably enliven the woods and thickets during nine months in the year; but they are too powerful to be pleasing in a room. A variety which does not visit us till March, and departs in autumn, is still more prized for its song by the bird-fanciers. It is distinguished from the common sort by its shorter make, its more solitary habits, and by its frequenting only open and heathy grounds, whence it is known by the appellation of *Heath Thrush*; but in this country it is very rare. The throstle breeds twice, and sometimes thrice in the season, and consequently continues long in song. In March the female makes her nest, composing it externally of dried grass and green moss, and plastering it within with a mixture of rotten wood and cow dung, or clay, and that with such compactness as to retain water,—a circumstance which, in a rainy season, sometimes proves fatal to the eggs. The nest is sometimes placed on the stump of a tree, very near the ground, or against the side of one, and frequently in a hedge, or solitary bush. The female lays from three to

Ornithology.

Musicus.

Ornitho-
logy.

six eggs, of a pale blue, verging on green, with large and small rufescent and black spots, especially towards the broad end. Both sexes participate the cares of incubation. Their food consists of insects and berries in general; and they are particularly fond of grapes and of snails, whose shell they break by repeated strokes against a stone. If teased, they manifest their resentment by snapping their bill. In order to rear the male in a cage, he should be caught young, and fed with crumbs of bread, bruised rape and hempseed, and minced meat; and this sort of diet may be varied with grapes, olives, or other favourite fruits. They are very susceptible of discipline, and may be taught to whistle several airs, and even to articulate words. In confinement they will live seven or eight years.

Iliacus. *T. iliacus*, Lin. &c. *Red-ning, Red-wing Thrush, Swine-pipe,* or *Wind Thrush.* Grey-brown above, whitish beneath, with brown spots; wings ferruginous beneath; eye-brows whitish. This species has been frequently confounded with the preceding; but it is smaller, weighing only two ounces and a quarter, and measuring eight inches in length; its colours, too, are more glossy, its bill blacker, the spots on the breast more numerous, and the wings are orange red underneath. Its manners nearly correspond with those of the field-fare and the throstle; and it is pretty generally spread over Europe. In this country it appears in September, and has only a piping note; but in Sweden, where it breeds, especially in the maple forests, it will perch on a tree, and sing very sweetly. It likewise breeds in the neighbourhood of Dantzig; and, according to Nozeman, in some parts of Holland, selecting such grounds as yield plenty of elder-berries and sorbs. In the course of April, May, and June, it has two broods, each of which consists of about four or six eggs, of a greenish-blue, spotted with dusky. The nest is usually placed on shrubs or hedges. Contrary to the commonly received opinion, both this species and the fieldfare have been observed in large flocks with us so late as June, though many of them certainly quit the country in spring. Nozeman asserts, that both parents swallow the dejections of the young as long as they remain in the nest,—a habit to which they are addicted in common with many other birds; but the excrementitious matter is retained at the entrance of the gullet, until it is disgorged at some considerable distance from the nest, as if to remove all suspicion of the place which conceals their offspring. In default of worms, caterpillars, and insects, the red-wings fall on cherries, grapes, and other succulent fruits, when their flesh acquires that delicacy which procures it such a cordial reception at the table of the epicure. The injury which they occasion to the orchard and the vineyard, is more than compensated by the quantities of insects and their larvæ which they destroy, especially in spring and summer. A variety, discovered in the Pyrenees, by Picot la Peyrouse, and designed by him *Mauvis Blond*, is of a rufescent white hue; and, in the British Museum, there is a specimen of a cream-coloured brown, with all the markings of a pale colour, and the bill and legs nearly white.

Torquatus. *T. torquatus*, Lin. &c.; *Ring-Ouzel*, or *Ring-Thrush*, Prov. *Rock*, or *Mountain Ouzel, Tor-Ouzel, Michaelmas Blackbird*, or *Heath Throstle*. Dusky, with a white collar, and yellowish bill. Weight four ounces; length eleven inches; extent of wing seventeen.

The economy and habits of the ring-ouzel are pretty analogous to those of the blackbird, but its note is much weaker. It affects wild, mountainous, and woody or heathy districts; appears in some countries of Europe, as, for example, in France, only in spring and autumn, fattens on its erratic expedition, and haunts the hilly regions of Sweden, Britain, Switzerland, Greece, &c. besides many parts of Asia and Africa. In this country, it stately visits the isle of Portland every spring and autumn, on its arrival and departure; and it breeds in Wales, Cornwall, Devonshire, &c. During their passages on the Continent, these birds proceed in small groups, along woods and hedges, feeding as they advance. If molested in the breeding season, they are very clamorous; but they are, on the whole, less shy than the blackbird; and they are tamed without difficulty if taken young. Their fattened flesh is reckoned delicate eating. The *Turdus saxatilis*, or *Rock-Thrush* of some authors, is only the young of the present species.

Merula. *T. merula*, Lin. &c.; *Black-Ouzel, Blackbird*, or *Blackbird Thrush.* Prov. *Amsel.* Black, with the bill, eyelids, and feet, tawny yellow.

The common blackbird inhabits the greatest portion of the temperate regions of Europe and Asia. In Russia it migrates in the dead of winter; and there is reason to believe that it partially shifts its station in other countries, or at least that the females do so. Its habits are solitary, for it associates only with its mate, and often lives singly. Yet, though shy and suspicious, it is more easily tamed than the thrush, and more willingly resides and nestles near houses. At the same time, owing to the acuteness of its sight, it spies the fowler at a distance, and is not easily approached. The male begins his song in the first fine days of spring, and, except during the period of moulting, continues it till the commencement of winter. This species breeds twice or thrice in the year, placing its nest in thick bushes, at a moderate height from the ground, or on old trunks of pollards. Moss, which always occurs on the trunk that is selected, and mud, which is to be found at the foot of it, and which the bird works with moisture like the swallows, are the materials which form the body of the nest, the moss being outermost, and stalks of grass, small roots, feathers, &c. are the substances with which they line it. By the co-operation of the male and female, the whole is usually constructed in the course of eight days, when it becomes the receptacle of from four to six eggs, of a bluish-green hue, with frequent but inconspicuous spots of rust-colour. Montbeillard has stated, that, during incubation, the male merely supplies his partner with food; but Vieillot has frequently seen him on the nest, from ten or eleven till two or three o'clock in the afternoon. Naturally jealous and distrustful, these birds have been frequently known to abandon or devour the first laid eggs, or even the newly hatched young, if they happened to be touched by any person. But, even when unmolested by importunate visitors, the first brood frequently fails, in consequence of the severity of the weather. Both parents feed their young with earth-worms, caterpillars, and the larvæ of all sorts of insects; but, as soon as they can shift for themselves, they give way to their natural unsocial propensities, and each individual becomes insulated, superadding to its former diet, berries and fruits of every description. In winter, they select the most sheltered situations, commonly settling in the thickest woods, especially when supplied with permanent springs, and consisting of evergreens, as firs, pines, laurels, cypresses, myrtles, junipers, &c. which at once afford them subsistence and protection against the rigour of the season. They also occasionally seek for food and corn in our gardens and shrubberies. Olina fixes the term of their life at seven or eight years. Their flesh is much esteemed as an article of food. Persons who are desirous of rearing them for the sake of their song, or with a view to train them to whistle airs, or to prattle, should take them from the nest as soon as they are fledged, and accommodate their fare to the state of their growth.

Cyanus.

T. cyanus, Lin. &c.; *T. solitarius,* and *Manillensis,* Lath.; *Blue, Solitary,* or *Pensive Thrush.* Blue, with the margin of the feathers grey; mouth and eye-lids yellow; rather smaller than the blackbird. In the female, the blue of the upper parts is blended with brown and cinereous. Native of the mountainous districts of the south of Europe. Nestles in the holes of inaccessible rocks, or in old deserted towers, or even in the hollows of trees, laying four or six eggs of a greenish and spotless white, though, according to some, they are mottled with blackish. It has most of the habits of the other thrushes. Its song, which has been compared to that of the nightingale, is louder and stronger, and is heard in greatest perfection before sunrise. When confined, it requires nearly the same treatment as the nightingale; but it is easily prevented from exerting its musical powers, being remarkably shy and capricious.

Orpheus.

T. orpheus, polyglottus, Dominicensis, Lin. &c.; *Mocking Thrush, Mock Bird, Mimic Thrush, St. Domingo Thrush,* &c. Grey-brown above, greyish-white beneath; lateral tail-feathers, and spot on the wings white. The bill is blackish-brown, the irides are yellow, the supercilia white, the rump grey-blue, and the legs in some black, and in others cinereous. About the size of the throstle, but of a more slender shape. There is a large variety, of a dusky-brown above, and grey-white beneath; that of St. Domingo inclines to cinereous above, and to white beneath; and there are some more diversified in their markings than any of those which we have just specified. The female has the same dimensions as the male, but brown is her prevailing colour above, and dirty white beneath.

This species occurs in North America, especially in its more temperate regions, and in several parts of the West Indies, manifesting a preference to moist shady woods, where, in a tree of moderate height, or else in a fruit-tree or bush near houses, the female places her nest, composing it of dry sticks or twigs, mixed with straws, hay, pieces of wool and tow, lining it with a thick layer of light brown fibrous roots, and fencing the under part externally with spines. The eggs are generally four or five, as large as those of the blackbird, of an ashen blue, and sprinkled with rufous dots and blotches, especially towards the larger end. The female sits fourteen days, and has usually two, or, if disturbed, three broods in the year. Bold and courageous, especially in the breeding time, the mocking bird makes war against the lesser shrikes, and expels the smaller birds of prey from its haunts. Its residence is seldom remote from the dwellings of man, to whose society it is so little averse, as naturally to sing in his presence, and to be trained under his guidance to various exhibitions. At the same time it is so easily scared from its nest, that if a person only look at it, the bird is said immediately to abandon it; if a cat, on the contrary, happens to approach, the parent bird will fly at the head of the animal, and, with a hissing noise frighten it away. The young are fed chiefly with grasshoppers; but the old ones, besides insect

food, eat cherries and berries of various kinds. After making every rational abatement for the exaggerated accounts of their song, it seems to be generally admitted that they not only possess native notes, which are truly musical and plaintive, but that they are, moreover, endowed with the faculty of imitating the tones of other birds, those of quadrupeds, and various sorts of noises. Thus, one of them confined in a cage, has been heard to mimic the mewing of a cat, the chattering of a magpie, and the creaking of the hinges of a sign-post in high winds. It is one of the few singing birds of America that can be compared with those of Europe; but it is ridiculous to allege that its strains are superior, or even equal to those of the nightingale. In the warmer parts of America, it continues musical from March to August, and warbles both day and night, beginning with its own compositions, and frequently finishing with borrowed descants. It accompanies its warbling with appropriate action and expression, and may sometimes even be said to dance; for, when excited into a kind of ecstasy by its own music, it gradually raises itself from the place where it stood, and, with extended wings, drops down to the same spot, whirling round and performing many amusing gesticulations. On account of the diversified and imitative character of its notes, the Mexicans call it by a name which signifies *the bird of a hundred tongues.* Its native strains are, however, too loud for a room, and are heard to most advantage at a little distance in the open air. If taken young, and treated with great care, it may be reared in captivity, so as to become both familiar and docile, and to afford much amusement by its interesting feats; but scarcely more than one in ten of such attempts proves successful. When first confined, it will endeavour to escape through the wires of the cage, and will kill itself if the upper part be not made of wood, so as entirely to obstruct its view. In some places, and particularly at Philadelphia, it is in high request for the table; and a fine bird has been sometimes known to fetch upwards of a hundred dollars.

Roseus.

T. roseus, Lin. &c. *Roseate Thrush,* or *Rose-coloured Ouzel.* Pale pink; head, wings, and tail, black; hind head crested. This beautiful species of thrush is rather less than the blackbird. It appears to be diffused in the hottest and coldest regions of our continent, Forskael having remarked it in the burning soil of Arabia, and in the fields of Aleppo, in the months of July and August, Levaillant in the latitude of 24°, and other naturalists in Bengal; whereas Pallas encountered it in the northern districts of Siberia, on the hilly banks of the Irtisch, where it breeds among the rocks; and Linné asserts, that it is found in Lapland. It is common on the shores of the Caspian, near Astrachan, and all along the Volga, passing, in very numerous flocks, into the southern parts of Russia. In France, it is only a temporary visitant, along with other birds of passage. Considerable troops of this species were seen to traverse Piedmont and Provence, in the autumn of 1817, and they have been repeatedly observed in Burgundy. They are rarely met with in England; but a few specimens are said to be shot almost every year about Ormskirk, in Lancashire. On account of its incessant warfare against the locust, this bird was regarded as a divine blessing by the ancients; and, even at the present day, the inhabitants of Arabia and Aleppo invoke the *Samarmar,* or *Locust-bird,* to protect the invaded crops; nor will the Turks allow any person to kill it in their presence. We have to add, that, in its

Ornitho-
logy.

habits, it manifests considerable analogy to the starling, associating with cattle, picking insects from their hair and skin, flying in bands, and nestling in the holes of the rocks. In default of insects, it eats berries and tender fruits. According to Forskael, its only note is a uniform reiteration of *tr, tr, tr*, which is, certainly, far from musical.

Novæ Guinensis.

T. Novæ Guinensis, Cuv. *Paradisea Gularis,* Lath. *Paradisea Nigra,* Gmel. and Levail. *Astrapia Gularis,* Vieill. *New Guinea Thrush, Gorget Thrush,* or *Gorget Paradise Bird.* Black, glossed with purple; back, and under parts blackish golden green; throat golden copper-coloured; tail extremely long and cuneated. This singular and showy bird was first accurately described by Latham, from a specimen in the possession of the late Sir Joseph Banks. The female is mostly black, and both smaller and less splendid in its garb than the male.

MYRMOTHERA, Illig. Temm. &c. ANT-EATER.

MYRMOTHERA.

This genus has been detached from *Corvus* and *Turdus,* the birds belonging to it being distinguished by their tall legs and short tail, and their addiction to the eating of ants.

Brachyura.

M. Brachyura, Corvus Brachyurus, Lin. *Short-tailed Ant-Eater, Short-tailed Crow,* or *Short-tailed Pie.* Green above, luteous beneath; three black stripes on the head; blue shoulders and tail-coverts, and red vent. This is a bird more beautiful in its colouring than elegant in its proportions; the body appearing thick, and the tail disproportionately short. It is a native of Ceylon, and the Molucca Isles; is about the size of a blackbird, and exhibits several varieties, of which the most remarkable has the head and neck entirely black, without any appearance of stripes.

Tinniens.

M. tinniens, Turdus tinniens, Lin. *Alarum Ant-Eater,* or *Thrush.* Brown above, white beneath; breast clouded with dusky. Between six and seven inches in length. The female is similar in colouring to the male, but large. The species has its name from its shrill and loud tinkling cry, which has been compared to the alarum of a clock, and is continued for nearly the space of an hour during the mornings and evenings. It is common in Cayenne, where Sonnini mentions that he often saw it, and partook of it at table, before he was aware that such a small bird was the cause of so much noise.

Cantans.

M. cantans, Turdus cantans, Lin. *Musician Ant-Eater, Arada,* or *Musician Thrush.* Reddish-brown above, transversely striped with dusky, whitish beneath; a black patch, sprinkled with white dots, under the eyes; cheeks, and lower part of the neck reddish orange. Only four inches in length. Native of the forests of Cayenne, of a solitary disposition, feeding principally on ants, and uttering a beautiful song, which consists of tones and accents at once solemn, sweet, and tender, and vocal as the sound of the flute. At times, it also whistles in such a manner as to be mistaken for a man. As it breeds twice or thrice in the year it continues long in song; yet that song, which is rarely equalled in compass and pathos by any of the warblers of the grove, never cheers the busy haunts of men, being limited to deep and abandoned forests, so that Sonnini, who was agreeably surprised by it in his lonely peregrinations, emphatically denominated this bird the musician of the wilderness.

Tintinna-
bulata.

M. tintinnabulata, Turdus tintinnabulatus, Lin. *Turdus campanella,* Steph. *Chiming Ant-Eater,* or *Thrush.* Brown above, reddish-orange beneath and

on the rump; throat white; top of the head and cheeks white, spotted with black; supercilia, and stripe behind the eyes black; length of the preceding; native of the forests of Cayenne and Guiana, but not very abundant, assembling in small flocks of six or eight, and uttering a remarkable note, which conveys the idea of a chime of three bells, and which is often continued for hours together.

Ornitho-
logy.

CINCLUS, Temm. &c. WATER-OUZEL.

CINCLUS.

Bill middle-sized, sharp-edged, straight, elevated, compressed, and rounded at the extremity; the point of the upper mandible inflected on the lower; nostrils basal, lateral, concave, longitudinally cleft, invested by a membrane; head small, tapering upwards, forehead elongated, and terminating at the nostrils; tarsus longer than the middle toe; the first quill very short, and the third and fourth the longest.

C. aquaticus, Bech. Tem. *C. Europæus,* Shaw, *Sturnus cinclus,* Lin. *Turdus cinclus,* and *Turdus gularis,* Lath. *Water Ouzel, Penrith Ouzel, European Water Ouzel,* &c. Prov. *Water Crake, Crow,* or *Piet, Water Colly, Dipper,* &c. Black; breast white; chin white; belly ferruginous; legs pale blue before, and black behind.

Aquaticus.

This singular species inhabits the Alps and Pyrenees, Sweden, Holland, Jutland, the Faroe Islands, Russia, Siberia, and even Kamtschatka, and the hilly districts of France, Spain, Italy, Sardinia, the north of Persia, &c. Acerbi, indeed, denies its existence in Italy; but his assertion is not corroborated by either Sonnini or Vieillot. In this island it is not uncommon, in its favourite haunts of hill and rock, by clear running and brisk streams, as in Scotland and Wales. The nest is very large, and yet carefully concealed, formed, externally, of water-plants and moss, and lined with dry oak leaves, in shape resembling that of the wren, but less deep in proportion, and furnished with a dome and portico. As Colonel Montagu has seen this unusual structure, we must believe that he has accurately stated the particulars. M. Gérardin's correspondent, on the contrary, who furnished him with several breeding pairs of this species, along with their eggs, mentions, that the materials of the nests were so rudely huddled together as to be incapable of carriage. But more or less skill may, possibly, be employed, according to situation, climate, and other circumstances. It is placed in holes already excavated in the banks of rivulets, in cavities of rocks, or in the fissures of walls, situated in the neighbourhood of waters. The female deposits four or five eggs, of a semi-transparent pure white, long, and very pointed at the narrow end. When disturbed, this bird flirts up the tail, and makes a chirping noise; and some ornithologists, who have only heard the latter, affirm that it has no other note; but Colonel Montagu assures us, that it sings sweetly, early in spring, and even during intense frost. In general, however, it is not only silent, but solitary and unsocial, never consorting even with a mate, unless when breeding. Although destined to subsist on small fish and aquatic insects and their larvæ, it is incapable of swimming, or diving, in the manner of web-footed fowls, but walks into the water, up to the head, then lowers its wings, and continues advancing till completely immersed, moving along the bottom in pursuit of its prey, and frequently remaining under water for upwards of a minute at a time. In these subaqueous excursions, its plumage is not only defended by an oily varnish, but seems to be surrounded by air-bubbles, like the *hydrophili* and *ditisci.* The observations of Herbert and

Ornitho-
logy.

Gérardin, who repeatedly witnessed the manœuvres which we have described, permit us not to doubt of their reality. Colonel Montagu, indeed, proposes theoretical difficulties ; but facts are not to be controverted by suppositions. In most countries in which it has been observed, this bird is not migratory. It is capable of flying rapidly in a straight line, and grazes the surface of water like the king-fisher. As it requires to see its prey, it never frequents water that has an oozy or slimy bottom. In France, and other countries, it is reckoned delicate eating. The *Penrith Ouzel* of Pennant is merely a larger variety of the present species.

Menura, Shaw, &c.

Menura.

Bill of moderate dimensions, straight, somewhat slender, conico-convex, inclined at the point of the upper mandible, and furnished at the base with setaceous plumes, pointing forwards, the lower mandible shortest ; nostrils oval, large, covered with a membrane, and situated in the middle of the bill. Only one species has been hitherto discovered, namely,

Superba.

M. superba, Shaw ; *M. Novæ Hollandiæ*, Temm. *Superb*, or *Mountain Menura*, which has been minutely described by Major-General Davies.

This remarkable species inhabits hilly and rocky situations, in New South Wales, perches on trees, and alights on the ground in pursuit of food, when, it is presumed, the males keep their tail erect, as its feathers have not been observed to be injured. Little, however, is known relative to its economy and modes of life.

Pipra, Lin. &c. Manakin.

Pipra.

Bill compressed, more deep than broad, and notched ; nasal fossæ large ; tail short ; two exterior toes united at about half their length.

Rupicola.

P. rupicola, Lin. &c. *Crested*, or *Rock Manakin*, or *Hoopoe Hen*. Body saffron-coloured ; tail-coverts truncated ; crest erect, with purplish margin. This elegant and shy bird, which is about the size of a common pigeon, is found in many rocky situations, in South America, where it makes a nest of dry bits of sticks, in dark sequestered recesses, and lays two white and round eggs. Like some of the gallinaceous order, the female is said to assume the plumage of the male, after she has ceased to breed.

Peruviana.

P. Peruviana, Lath. &c. *Peruvian Manakin*. Body of a reddish saffron cast ; greater wing-coverts ash-coloured ; quills and tail black ; tail-coverts not truncated. Larger than the preceding, which, in several respects, it considerably resembles. Native of Peru.

Aureola.

As exemplifications of the uncrested manakins, we may select, *P. aureola*, Lin. &c. *Red* and *Black Manakin*. Body black ; head and breast crimson ; front of the quill-feathers with a white spot. It is the most common of this numerous and showy family, and measures only three inches and a half in length. The female is olivaceous above, olive-yellow beneath, and has the crown of the head encircled by a red filament. Native of Guiana.

Monacus.

P. monacus, Lin. &c. *Black-capped Manakin*. Black above, white beneath ; spot on the neck and wings white. Found in the out-skirts of the large forests of Guiana ; and usually on the ground, or perched on a low branch of a tree ; living in families, but not consorting with its congeners ; often hopping about, indicating restlessness ; feeding on insects, especially ants, and making a chattering noise, like that produced by nut-crackers.

Ornitho-
logy.

Ampelis, Lin. &c. Cotinga, Tem. &c. Chatterer.

Ampelis.

Bill short, somewhat depressed, deeper than broad, hard, solid, three-cornered at the base, compressed and notched at the point, a little convex above, and suddenly inflected at the point ; nostrils basal, lateral, half-closed by a membrane, and imperfectly concealed by the hairs on the forehead ; legs middle-sized ; tarsus as long as, or shorter than, the middle toe ; wings moderate ; the second quill larger than the first. There are few birds more conspicuous than those of this family, for the delicacy and variety of their colours, the beauty and glossiness of their plumage, shades of violet, purple, blue, orange, red, pure white, and velvet black, being lavished on them in gay profusion, sometimes softening, with great delicacy, into one another, and sometimes very strikingly contrasted ; while the changeable hues which the same feathers exhibit, in different points of light, produce a splendour of effect, which neither the pen can express, nor the pencil pourtray. Many of them are destroyed, both for the sake of their feathers and of their flesh, which is reckoned delicate food.

Rubricollis.

A. rubricollis, *Muscicapa rubricollis*, Lath. *Querula rubricollis*, Vieill. *Purple-throated Cotinga*, *Purple-throated Fly-catcher*, &c. Black ; the chin, and a large spot on the throat purple. The female wants the purple mark on the throat. Length eleven or twelve inches. Associates with the toucans in the forests of Cayenne, always announcing its presence by the sharp note of *pee, ho, ho,* fluttering about with great activity, and subsisting on insects and fruits.

Militaris.

A. militaris, *Coracias militaris*, Shaw. *Crimson Chatterer*, or *Crimson Roller*. Crimson, with black wings and tail. The female differs in being grey-brown above, and white beneath. This highly beautiful bird, which is well delineated in Levaillant's Natural History of New and Rare Birds from America and the Indies, is scarcely inferior in size to a crow. Inhabits the forests of Cayenne and Surinam, where it lives on insects and berries, and is said to be very wild.

Carnifex.

A. carnifex, Lin. &c. *Red Chatterer*. Red, with a band through the eyes, and the tips of the quills and tail feathers black. Different shades of red predominate in the male, which is about seven inches long. The female is brown-red, more or less dashed with reddish, or with olive green, in different parts. Gmelin has described this species under the designations of *Carnifex* and *Coccinea*. It is very common in Cayenne, Guiana, Brazil, and New Spain, where the colonists call it *Cardinal*, and sometimes *Ooett*, from its note.

Pompadora.

A. Pompadora, Lin. &c. *Pompadour*, or *Grey Chatterer*. Purple, with the feathers of the greater wing-coverts sword-shaped. The tail is composed of twelve feathers, and exceeds the wings by seven or eight lines ; the length of the bird being seven inches and a half. The Pompadour chatterer is erratic, appearing in Guiana, in the neighbourhood of inhabited places, in the months of March and September. The natives call it *Pacapaca*.

Cotinga.

A. cotinga, Lin. &c. *Purple-breasted Chatterer*. Splendid blue above, purple beneath, wings and tail black. Length, nearly nine inches. The female has all the upper parts of the body of a fine blue, the throat, neck, and breast, purple, and the belly and vent blue, in some places varied with black. But various sportings of colouring are quoted.

Variegata.

A. variegata, Lath. *Variegated Chatterer*. Grey,

with black, spear-shaped wattles on the throat. Sonnini's description of the male bird is only applicable to its first attire. In its mature state, it is of a light grey hue, approaching to white, with the wings black, and a great many flattened caruncles, at least an inch long, and a line in breadth, on the naked throat. Levaillant and Cuvier have very unaccountably ranked this species as only a variety of the *Cayana*, to which it bears hardly any resemblance, and which has no wattles on the throat. The Portuguese of Brazil term the variegated chatterer, *Averano*, or *Summer Bird*, because it exerts its loud and disagreeable cry in December and January, summer months in that quarter of the world. This cry is, at times, peculiarly grating, like the sound produced by striking a block of iron with a sharp instrument, at other times it may be compared to that of a cracked bell.

A. carunculata, Tem. &c. *Carunculated Chatterer.* White, with the rump quills and tail-feathers inclining to yellowish, forehead naked, with an elongated caruncle. Twelve inches in length. The note of this bird, which consists of only the two syllables, *ang, ong,* uttered in a drawling kind of tone, is, nevertheless, loud enough to be heard at the distance of half a league.

EDOLIUS, Tem. DRONGO, DICRURUS, Vieil.

Bill depressed, and notched at the end, like that of the *fly catchers*, but both mandibles slightly arched through their length; nostrils covered with feathers and long hairs, in the form of whiskers.

Latham, Gmelin, and others, have dispersed the members of this family among the crows, shrikes, and fly-catchers, to all of which they are more or less allied; and one of them has even been stationed among the cuckoos. The African drongos, observed by Levaillant, live in society, and congregate at the close of day. They are very restless and clamorous, feed on insects, particularly bees, nestle in trees, and generally lay four or five eggs.

E. forficatus, Lanius forficatus, Lath. *Lanius drongo,* Shaw. *Fork-tailed Drongo.* Greenish-black, with upright frontal crest, and forked tail; bill and legs black. Its song, which is strong and steady, is heard only in the breeding season. It hunts for bees, especially after sun-set and before sun-rise, when small bands cross one another in all directions, emitting a cry, which Levaillant expresses by *pia griach, griach.* Native of China, Madagascar, and the Cape of Good Hope.

E. musicus, Dicrurus musicus, Vieil. *Musical Drongo.* Black, blended with brown, and bluish-black; tail moderately forked. Smaller than the fork-tailed species, and the female somewhat smaller than the male. Its evening and morning song resembles that of our common thrush. The nest is composed of slender and flexible splinters of wood, but with such wide interstices, that the eggs may be seen and counted from the bottom of the tree. They are usually four in number, and of a white ground, varied with black square spots. Native of the Cape of Good Hope.

TODUS, Lin. &c. TODY.

Bill long, formed of two thin plates, broader than deep, with a distinct ridge; point of the upper mandible straight, divided at the extremity, the lower obtuse and truncated; nostrils on the surface of the bill, distant from its base, open, and rounded; base of the mandibles furnished with long hairs; feet moderate, lateral, toes unequal; wings short, with the fourth quill the longest.

T. viridis, Lin. &c. *Green Tody, Green Sparrow,* or *Humming Bird* of Edwards. Green above, breast red. Total length three inches nine lines. A beautiful little species, of the size of a wren, which occurs in many of the West India islands, and in the warmer regions of the American continent. In St. Domingo it is known by the name of *Ground Parrot,* on account of its green attire, and of its breeding on the ground. It feeds on flies and other insects, which it seizes with much address; is of a shy and solitary disposition, being seldom seen except by itself, or as one of a family, affecting the lonely portions of moist tracts of country, where it is observed to sit with its head drawn in between the shoulders, and apparently so stupid as almost to allow itself to be caught by the hand. Its note, which it frequently repeats, is plaintive and monotonous; and its range of flight is very limited. The nest is often placed in rifts of the ground, near the margin of rivers, or scooped out of soft soil by the bird's own claws and beak, and skilfully enough lined with pliant straw, moss, cotton, and feathers. The female lays four or five small bluish-grey eggs, spotted with deep yellow.

Several other species, which were formerly classed with the todies, have been lately transferred to other categories.

MUSCIPETA, Cuv. and Tem. FLY HUNTER.

Bill much depressed, broader than deep, often somewhat dilated at the sides; upper mandible with a sharp ridge, hooked, and incurved on the lower, and most generally notched; lower mandible very depressed, pointed at the extremity, the base furnished with long hairs, which frequently project beyond the bill; nostrils basal at the surface of the bill, and open; feet middle-sized, or short and feeble; lateral toes unequal; wings moderate, the first three quills graduated, and the fourth or fifth the longest.

M. regia, Todius regius, Lath. *Royal Fly Hunter,* or *Royal Tody.* Brown above, whitish, with brown undulations, beneath; crest ferruginous, and tipt with black; chin and eye-lids white, bill dusky-brown, legs flesh-coloured. This singular and beautiful species, which is seven inches long, is a native of Cayenne, where, however, it is very rare.

M. paradisi, Paradise Fly Hunter, Crested Long-tailed Pie, Pied Bird of Paradise, &c. Crest on the head bluish-green, body white, tail wedge-shaped, with the two middle feathers very long in the male, but considerably shorter in the female. The body measures about six inches in length, and the tail fourteen. It is, however, very liable to vary; for it occurs of smaller dimensions also, with most of the upper parts pale-chesnut, likewise with the breast bluish-ash, &c. Hence it has been thrice described by Brisson under different designations; and hence the *Muscicapa paradisi,* and the *Todus paradisiacus* of Gmelin, are both the female of the present species. Klein mistook it for a crested thrush, Mœhring for a *Monedula,* and Linné for a *Corvus.* Native of the Cape of Good Hope, Senegal, and Madagascar, where it haunts the mangroves, or the borders of rivers, &c.

M. pristrinaria, Vieil.; *Miller Fly Hunter.* Rufescent-brown, dashed with an olive tint above, white beneath; bill and legs dark-brown, and eyes of a lively orange. It is called *Molinar* by the colonists of the Cape of Good

[marginal notes: Ornithology. Carunculata. Edolius. Forficatus. Musicus. Todus. Ornithology. Viridis. Muscipeta. Regia. Paradisi. Pristrinaria.]

Hope, because the incessant chattering of the male much resembles the voice of the mills used in that quarter of the world for grinding grain. It is about the size of the coal titmouse, and haunts thick bushes.

Many more species might here be quoted; but, as they differ more from one another in colouring than in habits, a long series of mere characters would occupy much space, without conveying any important information to our readers.

MUSCICAPA, Lin. &c. FLY CATCHER.

Bill middle-sized, strong, angular; depressed at the base, more or less broad; compressed towards the point, which is strong, hard, curved, and much notched, the base furnished with long and stiff hairs; nostrils basal, lateral, ovoid, partly covered by hairs projecting forward; the tarsus as long as, or a little longer than, the middle toe, and the lateral toes almost always equal.

In Europe, these birds are migratory, arriving late in the spring, and departing early in autumn. They subsist almost entirely on flies and other winged insects, which they catch in the air, more rarely picking them off the leaves of trees. They perch on the tops of trees, and lead a solitary life in the forests. The species are very numerous, and spread over all temperate countries.

M. grisola, Lin. &c. *Spotted Fly-catcher*, Prov. *Beam-bird, Bee-bird, Rafter, Cobweb, Chanchider,* and *Cherry-sucker.* Brownish above, whitish beneath; neck longitudinally spotted; vent rufous. The bill is dusky; the irides are hazel; the sides under the wings tinged with dull orange; and the legs short and black. Size of the tit-lark, and scarcely six inches long. It is rare in the north, but very common in the southern countries of Europe, arriving in May, and disappearing in September. This species is either very susceptible of cold, or very liable to privation of food on a sudden reduction of temperature, as a few days of frost commonly prove fatal to the new comers. They mostly frequent woods, orchards, and gardens, and are seldom seen on the ground. It is a prevailing notion in Kent, that they suck the cherries; but individuals who have daily watched their proceedings in the French orchards, could never perceive that they attacked that fruit, though frequently allured to the trees by the presence of insects. By sudden jerks and turnings, they will often lay hold on one of the latter that seemed to have eluded their pursuit; but, in general, they appear to be shy, melancholy, and stupid birds. Their nests, which is laboriously constructed, and which they seem to be little careful of concealing, is by no means a model of neatness. The materials are usually vegetable fibres, moss, wool, &c. interwoven with spiders' webs, and lined with wool; and the situation is in trees or bushes, or the limb of a fruit tree, nailed to a wall; in holes in the walls of out buildings, or on the end of a beam, rafter, &c. The eggs are four or five, and not unlike those of the red-breast, being-bluish white, with rust coloured spots, but the latter more distinct, and not so much confined to the larger end, where, however, they are of a deeper tint. Both sexes share the care of incubation. As soon as the young leave the nest, they are conducted by their parents to some neighbouring wood or grove where insects abound, and where they may be seen darting, in every direction, in pursuit of flies. As the note of this species is a simple weak chirp, seldom uttered till the young have fled, the bird is less readily discovered than the red-start, and other summer

migrants, which are perhaps less common. The spotted fly-catcher has been frequently noticed in Cornwall and Devonshire.

M. atricapilla, Lin. &c. *M. albicollis*, Tem. *M. collaris*, Bechst. *Pied Fly-catcher*, or *Cold Finch*, apparently a corruption of *Coal* or *Cole Finch.* Black above, under parts, forehead, spot on the wings, and lateral tail feathers, white. Nearly five inches long, and about the size of a linnet. If Pennant and Vedeman be correct, the spotted fly-catcher, though migratory in the south of Europe, is stationary in the north, even as high as Sondmor; and, according to Dr. Reeves, defies the Norwegian winter, during which it repairs to houses, and subsists on flesh dried in the smoke. Vieillot appears to have identified it with one of the *Beccaficos*, or *Fig-eaters*, of the Italians. Mr. Bewick adverts to an alleged instance of a nest of this species having been found in the hole of a tree, in Axwell Park, on the 18th of June; but the circumstance of its containing a *very great number of young*, is somewhat suspicious, the number of eggs not having been known to exceed six. The Rev. Mr. Dalton of Copgrove, in the West Riding of Yorkshire, procured a specimen of the nest and eggs for Colonel Montagu, in May, 1811. The nest was taken from the hole of a tree, and was composed of dried leaves, intermixed with broad pieces of the interior bark of the same tree, and a little hay, with a few long hairs, and lined with only three or four feathers, the whole very slenderly connected. The eggs were five in number, and of a very pale blue. We have been induced to enter into these details, because the bird in question is, in this country, very rare, and very local, and because its general history is still involved in some degree of confusion and obscurity. In Yorkshire, Lancashire, and Derbyshire, it is said to affect wild and uncultivated tracts, overrun with furze, and to court solitude. In Lorraine, and some other parts of France, it chiefly frequents the forests, living entirely on flies and other winged insects. It has no regular song, but a very shrill plaintive accent, which turns on the sharp sound *crree, crree.* Though generally of a dull and melancholy aspect, its attachment to its progeny inspires it with activity, and even with courage. After the young are hatched, the parents frequently go in and out of the nest, diligently catering for the brood.

M. tyrannus, Cuv. *Lanius tyrannus*, Lin. &c. *Tyrant Fly-catcher, Tyrant shrike,* or *Tyrant of Carolina.* Grey-brown above; whitish beneath; crown black, and marked by a longitudinal fulvous stripe. The tail is black, with a white tip; about the size of a thrush, measuring eight inches in length; but it varies both in respect of dimensions and colours. In the province of New York, it appears in April, constructing, in low bushes, a nest of wool and moss, lined with the small fibres of roots, and laying five flesh-coloured eggs, marked at the larger end with spots of dark pink, and a few black ones. In August, it retires southward. It is found in Carolina, and other parts of the United States. According to Catesby, this little creature pursues and puts to flight all kinds of birds that come near his station, from the smallest to the largest, but when the young are flown, it is as peaceable as other birds.

SYLVIA, Lath. Temm. WARBLER.

Bill straight; slender, awl-shaped; the base more elevated than broad; point of the upper mandible frequently notched; the under one straight; nostrils basal, lateral, ovoid, and half-closed by a membrane;

Ornitho-
logy.

tarsus longer than the middle toe; the first quill very short, or almost imperceptible, and the second scarcely exceeding the third; the great wing-coverts much shorter than the quill-feathers.

The members of this family, which comprizes most of the small woodland songsters of Europe, are generally of shy and recluse habits. They subsist on flies and worms, which they do not catch when on wing, but which they pick from the ground, or from trees and bushes, hopping from spray to spray, and visiting the leaves. Most of them visit us in spring, and depart early in autumn; but a few are stationary, and have two broods in the year. As many of them appear to be in ceaseless motion, they have, by some of our later writers, been denominated *Motacilla*. Among them are included most of those small birds which the Italians call *Beccaficos*, and which are so much relished by the epicures of the south of Europe. At Cerino, and in many of the villages of Cyprus, the people catch them in great numbers, in autumn, on their passage from more northern countries. After plucking off all the feathers, they boil them, for a few minutes, in very pure water, then dry them very carefully, and, lastly, put them into vinegar, or Cyprus wine, in which they will keep very well for twelve months. Those thus prepared in Cyprus are exported, in earthen pots, to Marseilles, Leghorn, Venice, and many of the towns of Italy.

Rubicola.

S. rubicola, Lath. *Motacilla rubicola*, Lin.; *Saxicola rubicola*, Bech. Tem. *Stone Chat, Stone Chatter,* or *Moor-titling*. Prov. *Stone-Smith*, or *Blacky-Top*. Grey above, reddish beneath, with a white spot on each side of the neck; about the size of a linnet, measuring five inches in length, and eight in extent of wing; inhabits Europe, from Great Britain as far south as Italy and Greece; occurs also in Siberia, and is stationary in Africa. In France, it is migratory, and partially so in this country; for we do not see so many of them in winter as in summer. It is a shy and solitary bird, being observed in pairs only during the breeding season, which is early in spring. At that period, it sings very prettily, springing into the air, and suspending itself for some time on wing; but it ceases its tuneful notes after the young are hatched; and its ordinary clattering cry has been aptly compared to the clicking of two stones on each other, or to the noise of a mill clack. It chiefly affects hedges, vineyards, moorish tracts of country, and furzy commons, perching on the extremities of vine-props, or the more elevated sprays of bushes, darting at every passing fly. It delights most in dry grounds, flies low, is restless and agile, and feeds on worms and insects. The nest is neatly composed of moss and bents, lined with hair, and sometimes mixed with small feathers. It is usually situated in waste-lands, at the foot of bushes, under their roots, the covering of a stone, &c.; and the female quits and approaches it in such a cunning and circuitous manner that it is not easily discovered. She lays five or six eggs, of a whitish green, with small faint rufous spots at the broad end. In defence and protection of their young, both parents are bold and clamorous; and they are singularly anxious and assiduous in tending and feeding them, screaming when any person invades the nest, or when any of their little family venture at first to leave it. In captivity, they are dull, languid, and intractable. When fattened, they are reckoned delicate eating.

Rubetra.

S. rubetra, Lath. *Motacilla rubetra*, Lin. *Saxicola rubetra*, Bech. Tem. *Whin-Chat, or Whin-Chat Warbler,* Prov. *Furze-Chat*. Dusky, with white eyebrows; a white spot on the wings; throat and breast yellowish; weighs about four drachms and a half, and is fully five inches in length. Inhabits the same countries, and often the same districts, as the preceding, with which it has many habits in common; but it is more decidedly migratory, appearing with us about the middle of April. In Kent, however, and some parts of the south of England, it is occasionally met with in winter. The female places her nest on the ground, among the grass, at the bottom of a bush or mole-hill, very artfully concealed, and composed of dried grass and stalks, with very little moss externally, and lined with fine dried grass. The eggs are commonly from five to seven, entirely sky-blue, according to Latham, Montagu, and others, while Buffon asserts that they are of a dirty white, spotted with black, and Vieillot describes them as bluish-green, with a few inconspicuous spots at the larger end. During the breeding period, the male sings sweetly, not unfrequently suspended on wing over the furze. In autumn, it acquires a considerable degree of fatness, when it is reckoned little inferior to the ortolan for the table; but it should be dressed on the day that it is killed.

Œnanthe.

S. œnanthe, Lath. *Motacilla œnanthe*, Lin. *Vitiflora œnanthe*, Ray, &c. *Saxicola œnanthe*, Bechst. Tem. *Wheat-ear, White-rumped Wheat-ear, White-rump, Grey-Wheat-ear* of Pennant. Prov. *Fallow-Finch, Fallow-Smich, White-tail, Chickell, Hedge-Chicker, Chack-bird, Snorter,* &c. *Chack,* or *Check,* of the Scots. Back hoary; forehead, eyebrows, rump, and base of the tail, white; a black band through the eyes; the length is nearly six inches and a half, and the weight about six drachms and a half. It is a native of Europe, Asia, and Africa. In Sweden, it appears with the blowing of the wood anemone; in Orkney, it arrives in April, and disappears in winter, notwithstanding the persecution of old and young, who, from some wanton prejudice, or aversion, destroy as many, both of the birds and of the eggs, as happen to come within their reach. The males, usually preceded by the females about ten days or a fortnight, arrive on the shores of England in March, or the beginning of April, and from that time till late in May. About the end of September they assemble and depart, the last flight retiring in October. When the season is mild, a few remain throughout the winter. Though dispersed in small groups over the island, they chiefly abound in certain districts of the coasts of Sussex and Hampshire. In Greenland, they frequent rivulets, and feed on worms, among the graves, for which reason they are abhorred by the natives. In general, they are partial to high countries, upland plains, and downs. They dart on their insect food by a rapid succession of short hops. If approached, or disturbed, they move from one clod to another, always flying low, and never enter the woods, nor perch higher than the hedges or bushes. When seated, they wag their tail, and chirp with a sound, which Buffon expresses by *titreû, titreû,* and, when they fly, they seem to pronounce, with a stronger voice, *far, far, far, far,* in rapid succession. They breed under tufts and clods, in newly ploughed fields, under stones, in fallow grounds, near quarries, in old rabbit burrows, or in holes in stone fences. The nest is neatly constructed of moss, or tender grass, and lined with feathers, or wool, having a sort of cover placed above it, and being stuck to the stone or clod under which the fabric is formed. The eggs, which are commonly five or six, are of a light bluish-white, with a circle of duller blue

ORNITHOLOGY.

at the larger end. The female incubates with so much ardour, that she may be frequently taken on the nest; and, like other vigilant brooders, loses all the feathers on the middle of the stomach. The male not only relieves her about noon, but incessantly watches for her safety, and that of the nascent family; fetching ants and flies, making a chattering noise on the approach of danger, and running or flying before a passenger, endeavouring to attract notice, till the person has got to a sufficient distance, when he returns, by a circuit, to the nest. He sings very sweetly, and, not unfrequently, on wing, hovering over his mate, and sometimes displaying his tail in a singular manner.

The average number of these birds annually taken in the neighbourhood of Eastbourne has been computed at upwards of 1800 dozen, and 84 dozen are recorded to have been captured on the South Downs, by a single shepherd, in one day. They are caught by placing two turfs on edge, in the form of the letter T; at each end a small horse-hair noose is fastened to a stick, which the birds, either in search of food, or on the appearance of a hawk, or the motion of a cloud, get under for shelter, and are certain to be entangled in the noose. These traps are always set on St. James's day, the 25th of July, and the greatest number of birds are taken during the prevalence of a westerly wind, against which they fly. They are mostly young ones; and, early in the spring, a few old birds only are to be seen. In Mr. Pennant's time they were sold at the rate of sixpence per dozen; but now the charge is from five to fifteen shillings for the same number, owing not only to the depreciation of money, but to the crowds of visitors that resort from the metropolis and elsewhere to the coast of Sussex in the bathing season. It was also the custom for the inhabitants in the neighbourhood of the traps, to visit them, take out the birds, and leave a penny for the shepherd, which was never touched by any other person; but such indications of pastoral simplicity and honesty have passed away. Many of these birds, which are sometimes called *English Ortolans*, are pickled, and sent up to the London poulterers, and many are potted. " Wheat-ears," remarks Mr. Pennant, " are much fatter in a rainy season than in a dry one; for they not only feed on insects, but on earth-worms, which come out of the ground in greater numbers in wet weather than in dry."

S. imitatrix, Œnanthe imitatrix, Vieil. *Motacilla imitatrix*, Gmel. *Mimic Warbler.* Forehead, eyebrows, throat, fore part of the neck, under part of the body, and upper-tail coverts, white; top of the head, bill, feet, tail, and wings, black. The colours of the female are less pure and vivid. The economy of this bird is very analogous to that of the preceding; but it is, moreover, endowed with a remarkable imitative propensity, insomuch that it can counterfeit the crowing of the cock, the clucking of the hen, the cackling of geese, the bleating of sheep, the barking of dogs, &c. It is a native of Africa, and the Dutch colonists call it *Nightingale*.

S. rubicola, Lath. Tem. *Motacilla rubicola*, Lin. *Red-Breast, Robin Red-Breast, Red-Breast Warbler,* or *Ruddock.* Grey, with the throat and breast ferruginous.

Although this species is familiar to the observation of mankind, it is still undetermined whether it belongs to the migratory or stationary class of birds. Scopoli asserts, that it stately visits and quits Carniola; and Buffon was of opinion that it migrates individually, but

not in flocks. As the severity of the season chiefly forces them on our notice, there can be no doubt that many of them, at least, remain with us during the winter; but it is not improbable that others, on the reduction of their insect food, may repair to more congenial latitudes. If, however, they change their quarters singly, and not in troops, the circumstance must be regarded as very anomalous. Their habits, however, are naturally solitary; and they guard their respective domestic circles with pugnacious jealousy, insomuch, indeed, that two of a different brood are never seen on the same bush or tree. They breed in spring under the new spread foliage, and make their nest about the beginning of April, near the ground, on the roots of young trees, on herbs that are able to support it, or on some bush or out-house, intermixing with hair and oak-leaves, and lining these materials with feathers. After it is built, the bird will often strew leaves over it, reserving only a narrow winding entrance under the heap, and closing even the mouth of the nest with a leaf, when she goes abroad. The eggs, which generally vary in number from four to seven, are of a dirty white, with waving spots and streaks of rust-colour, and cinereous. During the whole time of incubation, the male cheers and soothes his mate, with his sweet, delicate, and tender warbling, enlivened by some brilliant modulations, and broken by gracefully melting accents. The red-breast is partial to shady and humid abodes, feeds in the spring on worms and insects, which it hunts skilfully and nimbly, fluttering like a butterfly about a leaf on which it perceives a fly; and, on the ground, it advances by small leaps, and darts on its prey, clapping its wings. It takes a worm, by one extremity, in its bill, and beats it on the ground, until the inner part comes away, and then, seizing it, in the same manner, by the other end, it cleanses the outer part, which alone it eats. In autumn and the vintage season, when it is fattest, it likewise eats black-berries, grapes, sorbs, &c. It is one of the most wakeful of birds, commencing the music of the groves at early dawn, protracting it to the latest hour, and fluttering about in the evening. Owing to its restlessness or curiosity, it is easily decoyed, being attracted by similated sounds, and hurrying on every kind of snare. It will often approach almost within reach of a person's hand, and seems to take pleasure in accompanying the traveller through the forest. In every country of Europe it prefers the woods and mountains for its spring and summer residence; but, on the approach of cold, and when thick snow covers the ground, it courts the habitations of man. In November, 1788, an individual of this species, shivering with cold, pecked on the outside of one of M. Gérardin's windows, and, when admitted, perched without ceremony on the back of an elbow chair near the fire. Its first exertions were to snap at some flies, which had been kept alive by the heat of the room; and during the rest of winter it lived very contentedly on crumbs of bread, and little bits of boiled beef. Every morning at day-break it saluted the family with a song, which was sometimes prolonged for hours together. As a proof of its familiarity, M. Gérardin mentions that, when he was writing at his desk, it would hop on the paper, or alight on his left hand. On the return of spring the window was allowed to be opened, and three days after his gentle and playful guest took final leave, and fled directly to the forest. Instances are likewise on record of red-breasts returning, for successive winters, to houses in which they were treated with kindness, and of their building their nest, and rearing their young, in the bustle of people at work. Its song is the more valuable, as it is occasionally heard even in winter and the earliest part of spring. So quick, too, are its powers of imitation, that a young red-breast, bred under a very fine nightingale, which already began to be out of song, and was perfectly mute, in less than a fortnight, sang three parts of four of the nightingale's notes. The red-breast is likewise serviceable to mankind by the destruction which it occasions of hurtful insects. In Lorraine, where these birds abound, they are taken by the fowlers, and packed up for the Parisian market, being in great request among the lovers of delicate fare; and yet the inhabitants of Lorraine conceive that they have completely lost their relish if kept more than twenty-four hours.

Suecica. *S. Suecica*, Lath. Temm. *Motacilla Suecica*, Lin. &c. *Blue-throated Warbler.* Rust-coloured; breast striped with blue; tail feathers brown, and rusty towards the base. Nearly the size of the preceding, with which many of its habits also coincide. Instead of living in the heart of the woods like the red-breast, this species affects their outskirts, and haunts marshes, moist meadows, and places that abound with willows and reeds. After passing the summer months in its sequestered retreats, it visits gardens, orchards, avenues, and hedges, previous to its departure to southern latitudes. Towards the close of summer, it often alights in fields sown with the larger sorts of grain. Frisch notices its partiality to pease fields, and even alleges that it breeds in them; but its nest is at least more commonly found among willows and osiers, and such bushes as grow in wet situations, and not unfrequently on the dwarf birch. It is composed of dried grass, matted together, and lined with soft materials, on which are deposited five or six greenish-blue eggs. In the amorous season, the male ascends to some little height in the air, chanting as he rises, and then whirls round, and drops back on his bough. His song is also heard in the night. As it constantly varies, and is, for the most part, an imitation of almost every note within the hearing of the bird, the Laplanders designate the latter by an expression which means *a hundred tongues*; and Acerbi hesitates not to prefer its music for a room to that of the nightingale, being less strong and shrill. It occurs from Sweden to the Pyrenees, but not in this island; nor is it so frequent on the continent of Europe as the red-breast, though it may be traced in the lower parts of the Vosges, in Germany and Prussia, and even in Siberia. When plump it is caught in the noose, and much esteemed for the delicacy of its flesh.

Phœnicurus. *S. phœnicurus*, Lath. Tem. *Motacilla phœnicurus*, Lin. &c. *Red Start*, or *Red Start Warbler*, Prov. *Red Tail*, or *Brown Tail.* Head and back hoary; throat black; belly and tail red. The ordinary length of the bird is five inches three lines, and its alar extent eight inches. It is migratory, visiting most of the countries of Europe in spring, and returning in autumn. The French call it *Rossignol de Muraille;* but its song has neither the extent nor variety of that of the nightingale, although it partakes of the same modulations, blended with an air of tenderness and melancholy. It pours forth its notes from towers, deserted buildings, the top of a May-pole, &c. Though found in the heart of forests, and of shy dispositions, it also haunts peopled districts, and is sometimes seen in towns. It flies nimbly, and, when it perches, gives a feeble cry, incessantly quivering its tail in a horizontal direction, and as if by a convulsive motion. It breeds both in the town and the country, in walls, crags of rocks, on the top of

a cottage, or in holes of trees. The nest is composed of moss, with a lining of hair and feathers, and contains from four to eight eggs, of a light blue colour, and in other respects resembling those of the hedge sparrow, except that they are rather more elongated at the smaller end. While the process of incubation lasts, the male chants from some neighbouring eminence; and its music is softest at day-break. In some mountainous districts, its matin song summons the shepherd and labourer from their repose. In this island it is rarely observed farther to the north than Yorkshire, or farther west than Exeter. In the wild state it feeds on insects. If taken in the mature state, it either refuses sustenance, and pines to death, or is sullen, silent, and intractable; but the nestlings may be reared in a cage, and require to be treated as nightingales.

Sialis. *S. sialis*, Lath. *Motacilla sialis*, Lin. &c. *Œnanthe sialis*, Vieill. *Blue Warbler, Blue Bird, Blue Redbreast, or Blue-backed Red-breast.* Blue above, red and white beneath; length five inches ten lines. The blue warbler shuns forests and thick copse woods, occurring in open districts, cultivated fields, and orchards. It seizes with address the winged insect that flutters within its reach, and darts with surprising velocity on such as alight on the grass, or as run along beaten tracks, or on ploughed fields, seeking its prey on the ground. It appears in flocks in Carolina and in Virginia very early in spring, and moves southward in autumn, its known range reaching from New York to the Bermuda Islands. It nestles in the holes of a tree or wall; and, although it has only a slight plaintive note, the inhabitants, who are partial to its melody, fix boxes to their houses, in which it may breed. In default of insects, it approaches farm-houses, to pick up grass-seeds, or any thing else that it can swallow.

Calliope. *S. Calliope*, Lath. *Motacilla Calliope*, Gmel. *Kamtschatka Thrush*, or *Ruby-throated Warbler.* Rusty-brown above, yellowish-white beneath; throat vermillion, bordered with black and white; lora black, and eye-brows white. Inhabits the eastern provinces of Siberia and Kamtschatka; is fond of perching on high trees; is an excellent songster, and warbles during the night.

Luscinia. *S. luscinia*, Lath. Tem. *Motacilla luscinia*, Lin. &c. *Nightingale*, or *Nightingale Warbler.* Red-grey above, cinereous-white beneath; tail brownish-red.

Both male and female occasionally vary in size; but there is no marked disproportion between them. Different varieties of the species, among which one entirely white is noted, have been particularized by ornithologists; but these we are unwilling to enumerate and define, both for want of room, and because we have reason to believe that they have been somewhat needlessly multiplied. Even the three alleged races of *country, mountain,* and *aquatic* nightingales, appear to M. Vieillot, gratuitous. The name of *nightingale* has been, moreover, improperly applied to several species of foreign birds, remarkable for their tuneful notes. That now under consideration is limited to the old continent, and ranges over Europe, from Italy and Spain to Sweden; occurring likewise in Siberia, Kamtschatka, China, and Japan; but it betrays local preferences which are not easily explained, being met with, for example, in higher latitudes and colder countries than Scotland, whilst it is, nevertheless, a stranger to the latter, to a large portion of the north of England, and to Ireland. In England, it seems not to have advanced farther north than Yorkshire, nor farther west than the eastern borders of Devonshire, whereas it is plentiful both in Somersetshire and Dorsetshire. Though

4

unknown in Lincolnshire, it has been heard on the confines of that county, near Peterborough. In a large district of Bugey, in France, in most of Holland, &c. it is equally an alien. Some of the territories which it disdains to visit, are, doubtless, deficient in wood and inclosures, to which it is partial; and they may, possibly, be less abundantly provided with some of the favourite insects on which it feeds. In Europe the nightingale is migratory, arriving in spring, and departing in autumn, sooner or later, according to the temperature of the latitude. They are said not to travel in flocks, but singly; yet, as their numbers increase on the southern shores of Europe, previous to their departure, it is probable that, notwithstanding their natural shyness, they may unite for the common defence. It was long generally supposed that they repaired to Asia for their winter residence; but Sonnini has distinctly traced them to Africa, particularly to Egypt. This learned traveller recognised them, in winter, in the fresh and smiling plains of the Delta, and witnessed their passage to the islands of the Archipelago. He likewise remarks, that they are common in winter, in some parts of Asia Minor, as in Natolia, where they pass the season in the forests and groves, but undistinguished by their song; which, in their free condition, is appropriate to the period of breeding.

These birds have a sort of vibratory motion, and raise and depress their body by turns; and they oscillate the tail upwards and downwards. As the ancients believed that they passed the night in singing, so they alleged that they never slept, that their flesh had a soporific quality, but that the heart and eyes laid under a person's head would keep him awake. On these erroneous surmises the nightingale became the emblem of vigilance; but the moderns, who have observed with greater accuracy, have found that, in the season of love, it sleeps during the day, and even dreams. On their first arrival in the provinces of Europe, these birds affect the bottoms of hedges and inclosures, which are calculated to afford them at once concealment, protection from the cold, and insect food; but as soon as the forests begin to assume their verdure, they retire into the thickest recesses, and take up their residence under the covert of a hill, or in the neighbourhood of a brook, or of an echo, with the reverberation of which they appear to be delighted. The male selects two or three favourite trees, from which he loves to pour forth his lays, in the most perfect style, particularly from that which is nearest to the nest. When once coupled, he allows none of his fellows to intrude on his chosen domain. The extent of the latter is regulated by the quantity of subsistence requisite for the family; for it has been observed, that in those situations in which food abounds, the intervals between the nests are much more limited. Fierce and deadly contests sometimes ensue for the possession of the females; and it has been repeatedly asserted that the males greatly exceed the other sex in number,—a position from which Colonel Montagu is strongly inclined to dissent; but as the males arrive about ten days sooner than the females, and consequently none but males are caught at first, he supposes that this circumstance suggested the notion of the disparity. Each couple work at the construction of their respective nest, which, after all, is so loosely put together, as scarcely to bear transporting from one place to another. The external materials employed are quantities of coarse grass and dried leaves of the oak, and the lining consists of hair, fibrous roots, down, or other soft

substances. It is usually placed near the ground, in bushes, at the foot of a hedge, or of a row of hornbeams, or on the undermost branches of some tufted shrub. Hence the eggs, the young, and sometimes the mother, are known to fall a sacrifice to dogs, foxes, pole-cats, weasels, &c. The hatch generally consists of from four to six eggs, of an olivaceous green. In this country there is seldom more than one brood in the year, and in France seldom more than two, unless some accident befals the first. The female, though a close and ardent sitter, is said to be sometimes relieved by the male. From the moment that the young are hatched, both parents attend them with much assiduity; but it is a mistake to suppose that, like the canaries, they disgorge for them, in the form of pellets, the food which they had previously swallowed; for, having no crop, they merely stuff their bill to the œsophagus, with young worms, smooth caterpillars, and the larvæ of ants, and of other insects, which they share, in equal portions, among the brood; or, if abundance of food be near at hand, they are contented to fetch it at the end of their bill, as they do in aviaries. The young are fledged in less than a fortnight, and quit the nest before they are capable of flight, hopping after their parents from twig to twig; but from the moment that they can use their wings, the male alone takes charge of them, and the female prepares the nest for a second hatch. As soon as the young come forth from the shell, the male ceases his song, which he seldom resumes during the second breeding; but, if by accident his female is taken from him, or killed before the accomplishment of the first hatch, he is again musical, and will continue to sing very late in the summer, or till he finds another mate. Both parents, however, have a clamorous note of anxiety and alarm, which they frequently repeat, especially if danger threatens the nest, and which serves as a signal to the young to remain silent and motionless. About the end of August, or even sooner, if their stock of provisions begin to fail, both old and young resort to the hedges, orchards, newly turned up fields, &c. where they find more abundant fare, and add to their ordinary diet elder berries and other soft fruits, on which they fatten. In some countries they are then snared, and reckoned as dainty as ortolans.

The nightingale, we need scarcely observe, excels all birds in the softness and mellowness, as well as in the duration, of its warble. Though heard to most advantage in the stillness of a fine evening, it also sings in the day time, but its tones are then blended with those of the other choristers of the grove, and, consequently, not so readily distinguished. Mr. John Hunter discovered that the muscles of the larynx are stronger in this than in other species of birds, and that they are strongest in the male, which is the principal songster. The Hon. Daines Barrington, who kept a very fine nightingale for three years, and bestowed particular attention on its musical faculties and exertions, ascertained, that the sound of its song filled the circle of an English mile in diameter, which is equal to the power of the human voice. When it *sang round*, in its entire compass, he remarked sixteen different beginnings and closes, at the same time that the intermediate notes were commonly varied in their succession with so much judgment, as to produce the most pleasing variety. It would sometimes continue its warble for twenty seconds without a pause; but whenever respiration became necessary, it was taken as skilfully as by an opera singer. Kircher and Barrington both attempted to note the nightingale's song in technical form; but, although the notes were played by an excellent performer on the flute, they bore no resemblance to the native warble of the bird, owing, as Mr. Barrington conjectured, to the impossibility of marking the musical intervals; for the measures are so varied, the transitions so insensibly blended, and the succession of tones so wild and irregular, as to soar beyond the fetters of method. These birds, however, differ very much in regard to the quality of their song; for, in some, it is so indifferent, that they are not reckoned worth keeping, and it is even pretended that their warble is not the same in every district. The bird-fanciers in England, for example, prefer the nightingales of Surrey to those of Middlesex, as they give a preference to the chaffinches of Essex, and the goldfinches of Kent. At times, even a female has been heard to sing, though less powerfully than the male, a circumstance which may rescue Virgil and Milton from the criticism of having improperly attributed to her the prerogative of the other sex. That the male nightingale is naturally endowed with a decided musical propensity, cannot be questioned, and might be exemplified by many anecdotes; but we shall cite only the following: Bartolomeo Ricci, in a letter to Giambatista Pigna, when describing the readiness with which Silvio Antoniano acted the part of an *improvisatore*, and accompanied his verses with the lyre, relates, that a nightingale, attracted by his music, took its station at no great distance, answered with its notes to the lyre, and seemed to contend with the poet in the song. Silvio no sooner perceived this than he changed his theme, and celebrated the praises of the nightingale. The Rev. Dr. Black, author of the Life of Tasso, conjectures, that this incident may have suggested the contest of the lyrist and the nightingale, in the beautiful poem, in which Strada, in his *Prolusions*, professes to imitate Claudian. " An intelligent Persian," (says the late Sir William Jones, in his Dissertation on the Musical Modes of the Hindus,) " declared he had more than once been present, when a celebrated lutanist, surnamed Bulbul, (the nightingale,) was playing to a large company in a grove near Schiraz, where he distinctly saw the nightingales trying to vie with the musician; sometimes warbling on the trees, sometimes fluttering from branch to branch, as if they wished to approach the instrument, and at length dropping on the ground in a kind of ecstasy, from which they were soon raised, he assured me, by a change in the mode." When M. Gérardin happened to saunter in the *Jardin des Plantes*, at Paris, in a fine evening of spring, his ear was regaled with the melodious accents of two nightingales. He instantly returned the compliment by some passages of tender airs, on the German flute, when his feathered musicians approached him, first in silence, but, after listening for a while, they sung in unison to his instrument, and soon surpassed its powers. On raising his key, first one-third, and subsequently a whole octave, they shrunk not from the challenge, and acquitted themselves in such a style, as, by M. Gérardin's own confession, to merit the palm of victory.

The nightingale may be domesticated, though not without considerable pains and difficulty. For this purpose it must be treated with tenderness, and with favourite food, as the nymphæ of ants, meal-worms, and certain pastes, prepared by the dealers. In consequence of careful management, its warble is rendered much superior to that of the wild nightingale, and will be uttered all the year round, except during moulting.

In many parts of Russia, and particularly at Moscow, the art of taming and rearing nightingales is practised on an extensive scale; and, according to the observation of that intelligent and entertaining traveller, Dr. Clarke, these birds are heard throughout the night, " making the streets of the city resound the melodies of the forest." When once reconciled to captivity, these little songsters will appropriate the notes of other birds, from imitation, or rivalship, and will even chant the stiff airs of a nightingale-pipe. Nay, they may be instructed to sing, in alternation, with a chorus, and to repeat their couplet at the proper time. They may also be taught to enunciate words, though not, we may presume, to conduct trains of discourse in the marvellous manner recorded by Pliny and Gesner. Their attachments, though slowly acquired, are strong and permanent; they distinguish the step of their master, and welcome his approach with the music of joy; and some of them have pined to death on the loss of their benefactors. One that was presented to a gentleman, no longer seeing the lady who used to feed him, became sullen, refused to eat, and was soon reduced to that state of weakness, that he could no longer support himself on his perch; but, on being restored to his former mistress, he quickly revived, ate, drank, returned to his perch, and was well in twenty-four hours. Buffon makes particular mention of a nightingale, which, by feeding on a prepared paste, lived to the age of seventeen years, and, though hoary, yet happy and gay, warbling as in early youth, and caressing to the last the hand which fed it.

S. arundinacea, Lath. Tem. *Motacilla arundinacea*, Gmel. *Reed Warbler*, *Reed Wren*, or *Lesser Fauvette*. Olive-brown above, whitish beneath; lora and orbits brownish-white; angle of the wings brownish-yellow beneath; tail slightly wedged and brown. At the corner of the mouth, there are three strong bristles; and the irides are hazel. Length scarcely five inches and a half, extent of wing eight inches eight lines, and weight nearly three drachms. This bird may be at once distinguished from the *Salicaria*, with which it has been so often confounded, by the base of the bill being broader, by the want of the light stroke over the eye, and by having all the upper parts of one plain colour. The nest and eggs are also different. The former is curiously suspended between three or four reeds, or on some plant overhanging the water, being fastened by means of dead grass, of which and reeds it is principally composed on the outside; and the lining consists of the flowery tufts of reeds, dead grass, and a few horse hairs. Its great proportionate depth affords security to the contents; for, as it is perpetually swinging about with the wind, every gust forces it near the water, and might otherwise throw out the eggs or the young. The eggs, which are usually four or five, are larger than those of the sedge warbler, of a greenish-white, blotched with green and brown spots, which are most numerous at the larger end. The young ones, though tender and unfledged, are apt to desert the nest if it be touched, or too nearly inspected. But, when taken young, they are easily reared, and their song and sprightly manners are very engaging. Bewick erroneously makes this species synonymous with the *Passerina*. It is a native of Europe. In this country it is a much more local bird than the *sedge warbler*, though sometimes they are found together. In England it occurs along the coasts of Kent and Sussex, from Sandwich to Arundel, among the reedy pools and ditches, especially on Romney Marsh,

Ornitho-
logy.

Turdoides.

also near Uxbridge, in the fens of Lincoln, and in great abundance near the river Coln, in Buckingham-shire. It arrives about the end of April, or the beginning of May, and departs in September.

S. turdoides, Meyer and Tem. *Turdus Arundinaceus*, Lin. &c. *River Warbler*, or *Red Thrush*. Ferruginous brown above, whitish testaceous beneath; quill-feathers fuscous, tipped with whitish. Length seven inches, alar extent upwards of ten inches. Native of the greater part of Europe, from Gibraltar to Russia and Poland, but not indigenous to Britain. It haunts the reedy and rushy margins of lakes, rivers, and pools, flies heavily, and has a loud and powerful, but rather shrill and disagreeable note. The nest is very ingeniously constructed of the dried leaves of reeds, interwoven with pliant fibrous roots, lined with soft materials, and so loosely suspended by a sort of rude rings to the stems of reeds or rushes, that it is supposed to rise or fall with the level of the water. It is about six inches deep, and very thick at the bottom. In this receptacle the female deposits four or five eggs, of a yellowish-white, spotted with brown. During incubation, she is serenaded day and night by the male, who pours forth his clamorous music at a little distance from the nest, accompanied with a very brisk tremulous motion of the whole body. It has been sometimes confounded with the preceding.

Salicaria.

S. salicaria, Lath. *Motacilla Salicaria*, Lin. &c. *Sedge-Bird*, or *Sedge Warbler*, *Reed Fauvette*, or *Willow Wren*, Prov. *Sedge Wren*, or *Lesser Reed Sparrow*. Cinereous above, white beneath, with white eye-brows. This is an elegant species, weighing about three drachms, and measuring from five and a half to six and a half inches. The nest, which is composed of moss and dried stalks, lined with dried grass and a few hairs, is sometimes fastened to two or three reeds or sedges, or on a low bush, or willow stump, and it contains five or six light-brown eggs, varied with darker shades. During the whole of summer this bird may be seen darting from among the reeds, to catch the dragon-flies, and other insects which buzz on the surface of the water. It often warbles and sings in the warm nights of spring. From the variety of its notes it has obtained the appellation of the *English mock-bird;* for it counterfeits the song of the sky-lark and swallow, and even the chatter of the domestic finch. Its warble has been often attributed to the *Reed Bunting*, which appears conspicuous on the upper branches, while the real songster, concealed in the thickest branches, is heard aloud.

Atricapilla.

S. atricapilla, Lath. Tem. *Motacilla atricapilla*, Lin. &c. The fem. *Motacilla mosquita*, Gmel. *Black-cap*, or *Black-cap Warbler*, Prov. *Nettle Creeper*, *Nettle Monger*, or *Mock Nightingale*. Testaceous above, ash-coloured beneath; top of the head obscure. Length five inches five lines; alar extent eight inches and a half; weight about four drachms. In the male the upper part of the head is black; the hind part of the neck cinereous brown; the back greyish-brown, with a tint of green; the quill feathers and tail are dusky, edged with dull green; the breast and upper part of the belly light ash colour; and the legs plumbeous. The female is somewhat superior in size, and has the crown of the head of a dull rust colour. A variety has been found in Sardinia, with a red band over the eyes; another with a rufous crown; another with the whole plumage marked with black and white; and another still with the upper parts deep dusky, the throat white, and the sides grey.

This species, which is migratory, is common in Italy, France, Germany, &c. and even in Sweden, but is much more rare in Britain. The males arrive in the first days of April, but the females not till the middle of that month. If, at that early season, a return of cold should deprive them of their insect food, they have recourse to the berries of spurge-laurel, ivy, privet, and hawthorn, which are also the resource of the few which are precluded, by a tardy hatch, or other accidental cause, from undertaking their stated migration southward. Immediately on the arrival of the females, these birds are busied in preparing their nests, the males selecting the most suitable spots, and, when they have fixed on them, intimating their choice by more tender and attractive strains than usual. The favourite situations are in eglantine or hawthorn bushes, at the height of two or three feet from the ground, on the border tracks of forests, or in woods or hedges. The nest is small and shallow, usually made of dried stalks, grass, and wool, lined with fibrous roots and horses hair. That described by Mr. Pennant was placed in a spruce-fir, about two feet from the ground; the inside was composed of dried stalks of the goose grass, with a little wool, and green moss round the verge, and the lining consisted of fibrous roots, thinly covered with horses hair. It contained five eggs, of a pale reddish brown, mottled with a deeper colour, and sprinkled with a few dark spots. The male manifests the most tender assiduity to his mate, takes his turn of sitting on the eggs, from ten o'clock in the morning till four or five in the evening, and caters worms and insects for the family. The young are produced without any down, but are covered with feathers in a few days, and very soon quit the nest, especially if molested. They then follow their parents, hopping from spray to spray, and the whole family assemble on one branch to pass the evening, the male at one end, the female at another, and the young in the middle, all huddled together, as close as possible for the sake of warmth, and exhibiting a scene truly domestic. To the first brood a second, especially in warm climates, usually succeeds, and sometimes even a third, if any accident has befallen the second. The black cap sings sweetly, and so much in the style of the nightingale, that in Norfolk it is called the *Mock Nightingale*. Its airs are light, and executed with apparent ease, consisting of a succession of modulations harmoniously blended, especially when the bird sits calmly, and prolongs its song; for frequently its notes are desultory, and the strain of short continuance. In confinement, it soon becomes attached to its keeper, greets him with a peculiar accent, and flutters against the cage-wires to get in contact with him. From the warmth of its affections, Mademoiselle Des Cartes could not help remarking, that, with all deference to her uncle, it was endowed with sentiment.

Hortensis.

S. hortensis, Lath. Bech. Tem. *Motacilla hortensis*, Lin. &c. *Petty Chaps*, *Greater Petty Chaps*, or *Garden Warbler*. Grey-brown above, reddish-white beneath; quill feathers grey-brown, edged with grey; tail feathers fuscous, and the outer whitish on the exterior web, and towards the tip, within. Base of the under mandible yellowish, irides hazel, orbits white, legs bluish-brown. Length six inches; alar extent eight inches ten lines; weight about five drachms. Another European migrant, which arrives in this island about the end of April, or the beginning of May, and leaves us in autumn, for the islands of the Archipelago, Lower Egypt, &c. Though its principal food is insects, it

ORNITHOLOGY.

PLATE CCCCLIV.

ORIOLUS GALBULA
Golden Oriole

TROCHILUS MINIMUS
Least Humming Bird

FRINGILLA PARADISEA
Whidaw Bunting

ORIOLUS BALTIMORE
Baltimore Oriole

PARUS PENDULINUS
Penduline Titmouse

PSITTACUS CRISTATUS
Broad-Crested Cockatoo

SYLVIA REGULUS
Golden Crested Wren

LOXIA CURVIROSTRA
Crossbill

HIRUNDO FUCIPHAGA
Esculent Swallow

PSITTACUS ALEXANDRI
Alexandrine Parrakeet

UPUPA EPOPS
Hoopoe

RAMPHASTOS VIRIDIS
Green Toucan

ALCEDO GIGANTEA
Giant King Fisher

Engraved for the Edinburgh Encyclopædia by J Moffat Edin.

likewise contrives to subsist on soft berries and fruits. It frequents gardens and orchards, and generally takes up its abode in thick hedges, in which, or among the sticks of peas, and near the ground, it preferably places its nest, composing it of dried goose grass, and other fibrous plants, flimsily put together, with the occasional addition of a little green moss externally. It lays from four to six eggs, about the size of those of the hedge sparrow, of a dirty white, blotched with light-brown, and spots of cinereous. The late Sir Ashton Lever first recognised it as a native of England, in Lancashire; but it has since been noticed in Wiltshire, Devonshire, Somersetshire, &c. Its song is reckoned little inferior to that of the nightingale, some of the notes being sweetly and softly drawn, others quick, lively, loud, and piercing, reaching the distant ear with pleasing harmony, somewhat resembling the whistle of the blackbird, but in a more hurried cadence, and frequently uttered after sunset. Mr. Pennant erroneously makes the present article synonymous with *Beam-bird*, which is one of the popular denominations of the *Spotted Fly-catcher*, and he adds to the confusion by quoting *Motacilla hippolais*, Lin. which is the *Lesser pettychaps*.

Cinerea.

S. cinerea, Lath. Tem. *Motacilla sylvia*, Lin. &c. *White-throat*, or *White-throated Warbler*, Prov. *Muggy*, or *Nettle-creeper*. Cinereous above, white beneath, with the outer tail-feathers longitudinally half white, and the next tipt with white. Bill dusky-brown above, whitish beneath; irides yellowish; legs pale-brown. Weight about four drachms; length five inches and three-quarters. The male has a roseate tint on the breast, and purer colouring than the female. Several varieties have been observed. Occurs from Sweden to Italy, and is diffused over most of Russia and Siberia. In this country it is very common in all inclosed districts, appearing about the middle of April, and enlivening our hedges with its song. It prefers smooth caterpillars, and other larvæ, to full-formed insects, and is partial to hedges and bushes; but in the summer it brings its brood into gardens and orchards, for the sake of cherries, currants, and other fruits, among which it makes serious havock. The nest is generally placed in some low bush, among nettles or other luxuriant herbs, and made of goose-grass, lined with fibres, and sometimes a few long hairs; but it is of such a slight texture, that it can afford little warmth to the eggs or young. The former are greenish-grey, with numerous rufous and olivaceous spots. The note of this bird, which is constantly repeated, and often accompanied with odd gesticulations on the wing, is harsh and displeasing. Both sexes are shy and wild in the breeding season, avoiding neighbourhoods, and haunting lonely lanes or commons, where there are bushes or covers.

Modularis.

S. modularis, Lath. *Motacilla modularis*, Lin. *Accentor modularis*, Cuv. Temm. *Hedge-sparrow*, or *Hedge-warbler*, Prov. *Tilling*, or *Dunnock*. Grey-brown above; tips of the wing-coverts white; breast grey-blue. Belly dusky-white, sides and vent tawny-brown. Bill dusky, irides light hazel. Length nearly six inches; alar extent eight; weight six drachms; and size about that of the red-breast. The female has less of ash-colour about the head and breast; the under parts pale-cinereous, and the belly more spotted. The hedge-sparrow inhabits most of the temperate, and some of the colder regions of Europe, and is one of the few of the warbler tribe that remain with us all the year. In France, however, it arrives when most of the other migrants are retiring southward. In this country it is

a very common and familiar bird, beginning its pleasant song, if the weather is mild, with the beginning of the year. It seems to prefer situations near human dwellings, and breeds early, making, in March, a nest of green moss and wool, lined with hair, in some low ever-green shrub, thick bush, cut hedge, or faggot-piles, and laying four or five light-blue eggs. It is chiefly in the morning and evening that it utters its feeble and plaintive, but not unpleasing song. It may likewise be recognised by its little tremulous cry of *tit*, incessantly repeated, from which it has got the name of *Titling*. The male assists his mate in the construction of the nest, the cares of incubation, and the rearing of the brood. The hedge-sparrow, when taken young, is easily tamed, and indicates affection to those who cherish it. Instances occur of its breeding in aviaries and orangeries. Though well furnished with plumage, it is seldom found fat.

S. regulus, Lath. Tem. *Motacilla regulus*, Lin. &c. Regulus. *Regulus vulgaris*, Steph. *Golden-crested Wren*, or *Common Gold Crest*, Prov. *Marigold Finch, Wood Titmouse* and *Tidby Goldfinch*. Cheeks pure cinereous, without any indication of white bands; crest of the male orange-yellow; bill very feeble, and awl-shaped. This is the least of British, and, perhaps, of European birds, weighing only seventy-six grains, and being three inches and a half long; the wings extending only to five. When stripped of the feathers, it is scarcely an inch in length. In consequence of this diminutive size, it glides through the wires of cages, and the meshes of snares, and, if let loose in a chamber, the smallest opening will allow it to escape. From other birds it may be readily distinguished, not only by its minuteness, but by its beautiful crest, which is composed of a double series of feathers, arising from each side, and almost meeting at the points, the exterior ones being black, and the inner bright orange-yellow.

Notwithstanding its apparent delicacy, the golden-crested wren braves the rigours of northern winters; for it not only remains with us all the year round, but is found in as high a latitude as Drontheim in Norway; and, though rare in Russia, it is frequent in Siberia, about the banks of the Jenisei. It crosses annually from the Orkneys to the Shetland Islands, where it breeds, and returns again before winter—a long flight for so small a bird. It is also found in Pennsylvania, New York, and some of the northern parts of America; and Latham mentions a specimen received from Cayenne with black legs. As it has also been found in Bengal, it seems to be a true cosmopolite. It delights in wooded parts of the country, particularly where oaks and firs abound; and it is more common than is generally supposed, its minuteness often concealing it from view among the foliage, so that it is more readily observed in winter, when it flits among the naked sprays. Its feeble, but not disagreeable song, is repeated at intervals during the day, in spring, but is discontinued during the rearing of the young. It subsists on insects, small worms, and seeds. In summer, it seizes its prey nimbly, on the wing; in winter, it explores the holes and crevices in which it finds dead insects, or dormant larvæ, and frequently eats till it is surfeited. It is very agile, and almost constantly in motion, fluttering from bough to bough, creeping on the trees, or clinging, indifferently, in every situation, and often hanging by the feet, like the titmice, ferreting in all the cracks of the bark for its tiny prey, or watching it as it creeps out. The nest is not constructed with an opening on one side, as alleged by some, but in form and elegance resembles that of the chaffinch, being composed of green moss, interwoven with wool, and invariably lined with small feathers, with which it is so well bedded as to conceal the eggs. It is sometimes placed against the body of a tree covered with ivy, but more commonly beneath the thick branch of a fir. The eggs are from six to eleven, about the size of large peas, of a pinkish white, and rather darker at the larger end. It has been remarked that the female, from some cause which has not been satisfactorily explained, is frequently destroyed during the time of incubation, and the nest with the eggs left to decay. A nest, containing ten young, was placed in a small basket, near the window of Colonel Montagu's study, for the purpose of enticing the old birds, which soon made their appearance, and became very familiar, the mother attending even when the nest was placed far in the room, or held in the hand. The male constantly accompanied his mate as far as the outside of the window, but would not venture in; nor did he utter any note except his partner was in sight, and then only a slight chirp. The hen bird repeated her visits, every two or three minutes, for full sixteen hours daily, each time loaded with food, which her offspring greedily devoured, consuming above their own weight in four days. In autumn, these wrens being plump and delicate, are in some countries taken by a call, and sold for the table: the market of Nuremberg in particular is abundantly stocked with them during that season.

S. trochilus, Lath. Tem. *Motacilla trochilus*, and *M. acredula*, Lin. *Sylvia titis*, Bechst. *Yellow Wren*, or *Yellow Warbler*, Prov. *Willow Wren*, *Ground Wren*, *Ground Huck-muck*. Grey-green above; the wings beneath and the quill feathers yellowish; eye-brows yellow; bill dusky above, yellowish beneath; irides hazel; legs light brown. Weight nearly three drachms, and length five inches and one-fourth. The under parts of the female are less purely tinted, and less yellowish. This species is very plentiful in some wooded situations, especially where willows abound; and it is frequently found in company with the wood wren, but does not generally extend so far west in England, being rarely met with in Cornwall. It visits us early in April, and soon begins its song, which has three or four variations, beginning with a slender broken cluck, which is succeeded by a series of detached silvery sounds, like the clinking of crown-pieces that are told over, and then commences the full song, which is soft, pleasing, and well sustained. This, its spring and summer warble, gives place in autumn to a tender whistle, expressed by *tweet, tweet*, and nearly corresponding to that of the red-tail and nightingale. The yellow wren is a very active bustling bird, incessantly and busily fluttering from branch to branch, or creeping up and down the trunks of trees, searching for, and darting on insects. It likewise exhibits slow and regular oscillations of the tail upwards and downwards. These birds arrive in small flocks of fifteen or twenty, but immediately separate into pairs. Shortly after their appearance, they are sometimes surprised by frost, and drop down dead; and yet they pervade Europe from Sweden to Greece. In the northern regions it settles on the loftiest branches of the birch trees, and makes the air resound with its melodious song. About the latter end of April, or beginning of May, it makes an oval-shaped nest, composed of moss and dried grass, and lined with feathers, with a small opening near the top, placed in the hollow of a ditch, or in a low bush, close to the ground. The female lays six or seven white eggs, spotted with light rust colour, especially towards

the large end. We shall here take occasion to observe, that the eggs of the next species in order are invariably spotted with dark purple, which is one sure mark of distinction, to which we may add the superior dimensions of the trochilus, and the colour of the legs; for otherwise the two birds are with difficulty discriminated. An individual of the present species had nestled in the bank of one of Mr. White's fields, near Selborne. That gentleman and a friend had observed the bird as she sat on the nest; but they were particularly careful not to disturb her, although she eyed them with some degree of jealousy. Some days after, as they passed the same way, they were desirous of remarking how the brood went on; but no nest could be found, until Mr. White happened to take up a large bundle of long green moss, thrown as if at random over the nest, in order, no doubt, to mislead the eyes of intruders.

S. hippolais, Lath. Tem. *Motacilla hippolais*, Lin. &c. *Lesser Petty-chaps*, or *Petty-chaps Warbler*, Prov. *Chip-Chop*, *Chiff-Chaff*, *Choice and Cheap*. Greenish-ash above, yellowish beneath; belly whitish; eye-brows white. This hardy little bird, which is one of our earliest warblers, appears in March, and remains till October, and sometimes all winter. It is the smallest of our migrants, weighing only about two drachms, and scarcely exceeding four inches and a half in length. As its general plumage singularly coincides with that of the yellow wren, they have been often confounded. The present species is common in many parts of Europe, and is much diffused in England, especially in the neighbourhood of woods and hedges, although, from the smallness of its size, and the shyness of its manners, it is supposed by many to be of rare occurrence. On its arrival, it commences its note, which is continued through the summer, and long after the yellow wren is silent. It prepares its nest early in spring, placing it on or near the ground, in a tuft of grass or low bush, forming it of an oval shape, with a small aperture near the top, and composing it of coarse dry grass and dry leaves externally, and fine downy feathers within. On these last are deposited five or six white eggs, sprinkled with purplish red, especially at the larger end. It chiefly subsists on small winged insects.

S. sibilatrix, Bechst. Tem. *S. sylvicola*, Lath. *Wood Wren*, *Green Wren*, *Yellow Willow Wren*, or *Large Yellow Wren*. Greenish above, yellowish beneath; eye-brows yellow; abdomen and vent snow white. Weighs about two drachms and forty grains, and measures upwards of five inches in length. The female is rather larger than the male, but has the same description of plumage. Although noticed by Mr. White in his *Natural History of Selborne*, this species is described by Mr. Lamb in the second volume of the *Linnean Transactions* as new; and Colonel Montagu communicates a more detailed account of it in the fourth volume of the same work. Owing to its resemblance to the yellow wren and to the lesser petty-chaps, with both of which it has been frequently confounded, it has been little noticed as a distinct species; yet it is far from rare either in England, or in various countries of the continent of Europe. The males arrive towards the latter end of April, ten days or a fortnight before the females, and both depart in September. They seem to be partial to oak and beech woods, in which they may be discovered by their peculiar note, which has been compared to the word *twee*, drawn out to some length, and repeated five or six times in succession, terminating with the same, delivered in a hurried manner, and accompanied with a shaking of the wings during the incubating season. They make their nest on the ground, beneath the shade of trees or bushes, constructing it of dried grass and of a few dead leaves, mixed with a little moss, and lined with finer moss and a few long hairs. The eggs, which are commonly six, have a dull white ground, and are sprinkled all over with rust-coloured spots, which are occasionally confluent, and form a circle near the obtuse end.

Pensilis.

S. pensilis, Lath. *Motacilla pensilis*, Lin. &c. *Pensile*, or *Hang-nest Warbler*. Grey above, yellow beneath; abdomen and eye-brows white; lora spotted with yellow; wing-coverts with alternate bars of black and white. An elegant little creature, measuring four inches and three quarters in length, and inhabiting St. Domingo and some of the West India islands, where it feeds chiefly on insects and fruits, and continues its delicate song throughout the year. The female does not fix the nest at the forking of the branches, as is usual with most other birds, but suspends it to binders hanging from the netting which she forms from tree to tree, especially those which fall from branches that hang over the rivers and deep ravines. The fabric consists of dry blades of grass, the ribs of leaves, and exceedingly small roots, interwoven with the nicest art, and it is fastened on, or rather worked into, the pendent strings, forming, in fact, a small bed rolled into a ball, so thick and compact as to exclude the rain; and it rocks in the wind without receiving any harm. But the elements are not the only enemies against which this bird has to contend. With wonderful sagacity it provides for the protection of its nest from intrusion. The opening is not made on the top, nor on the side, but at the bottom. Nor is the entrance direct; for, after the bird has made its way into the vestibule, it must pass over a kind of partition, and through another aperture, before it descends into the abode of its family. This lodgement is round and soft, being lined with a species of lichen which grows on the trees, or with the silky down of plants.

Troglodites.

S. troglodites, Lath. Tem. *Motacilla troglodites*, Lin. &c. *Troglodites Europæus*, Leach. *Wren, Common*, or *European Wren*. Grey, with the wings waved with black and grey. Length about three inches nine lines; alar stretch nearly six inches; and weight two drachms and three quarters. It inhabits Europe and Asia, and is by no means unfrequent in Great Britain, where it remains throughout the year; but it is rare in Sweden and Russia, and is said never to penetrate into Siberia. Its song is much admired, being, though short, a very pleasing warble, and much louder than might be expected from the size of the bird. This chant it continues throughout the year; and it will even sing, with apparent unconcern, during a fall of snow. Its music is also heard late in the evening, though not after dark; and it is one of the first songsters that is awake in the morning. It readily associates with the red-breasts; but the male wrens are jealous of one another, and solitary in the season of courtship. They feed on small worms, flies, and other little insects and their larvæ, which they procure in sufficient quantity to support life, even in the severest winters. The wren is a sprightly little bird, sometimes showing itself on a morning on a heap of dried wood, and the next instant entering into it and disappearing: for a moment it may be seen on the edge of the thatch, but quickly conceals itself under it, or in some hole in the wall; and, as soon as it comes out again, it frisks

among the thickest of the neighbouring bushes, always erecting its tail. Its flight is quick and irregular; and it flaps its little wings with such rapidity, that their vibrations are scarcely perceptible. In winter, it frequents the banks of unfrozen streams, retiring occasionally into the hollow portions of decayed trees, in which no fewer than twenty have sometimes been found together, as if to keep one another warm. The nest is curiously constructed, and not begun at the bottom, as is commonly the case, but first traced in an oval frame work, and equally fastened in all its parts to a tree, or other support, and afterwards inclosed on the sides and top, with the exception of a small opening for entrance. If placed under a bank, the top is first begun, and well secured, in some small cavity, from which the fabric is suspended. The materials, too, are generally adapted to the nature of the situation; for if built, for example, against the side of a hay-rick, the nest is composed of hay; if against a tree, covered with lichen, it is made of that sort of moss, &c. but is invariably lined with feathers. The number of eggs varies very considerably, being seldom fewer than seven, nor more than eighteen. They are very small, white, and marked at the larger end with a band of rust-coloured dots. When the wren approaches our habitations in winter, it seems to be confident, familiar, and even prying and inquisitive; yet it is with difficulty caught, as the smallness of its size, and the nimbleness of its movements almost always enable it to elude the eye and the grasp of its enemies. It is also too delicate to be easily reared in a cage; but the attempt will best succeed by keeping it warm in the nest, allowing it to eat often, and little at a time, of sheep's or calf's heart, minced very small and mixed with flies. When it feeds thus alone, a little corner of the cage should be hemmed in with red cloth, to which it is partial, and under which it may retire at night. When kept alive and healthy by such attentions, it amply repays them by its enlivening song in winter.

Alba.

S. alba, Motacilla alba and *cinerea*, Lin. *Motacilla albida*, Gmel. *White Wagtail*, or *Collared Wagtail*, Prov. *Water-wagtail, Black* and *White Water-wagtail, Pied Water-wagtail, Dishwasher*, or *Washerwoman*. Breast black; the two lateral tail feathers obliquely half-white.

The white wagtail is so generally diffused over the old continent, that it is met with in Europe, Siberia, Africa, and Indostan. Its elegant form, sprightly manners, and nimble and frisking movements, are familiar to common observation. Its note is sweet, but feeble, and in autumn degenerates into a sort of murmur. In flight it moves its tail in a horizontal, and, when on the ground, in a perpendicular direction. These birds run lightly, and with short, but very precipitate steps, along the margins of streams; and their legs admit of their wading into the water to the depth of a few lines; but they more frequently take their station on a stone, or other little elevation. From the numbers which are sometimes seen together resorting to sheep-folds and newly turned up fields, we may presume that they are gregarious in their flights. In autumn they appear with us in numerous bands, spreading over the country through the day, and retiring towards evening into the osier holts, and among the willows on the banks of canals and rivers, where they keep up an incessant petty chattering till night-fall. Many of them leave us in October, when they may sometimes be heard, passing along, high in the air, their ceaseless chattering being still audible; and others pass from the northern to the southern parts of the island in winter. In that season they abound in Egypt, Senegal, &c. along with the swallows and quails, re-appearing in the north about the end of March, and penetrating even to the Faroe islands and Iceland. In the breeding season, they seem to prefer pleasure-grounds that are constantly mowed, on which they run unencumbered, and where the insects have not sufficient cover to evade their sight. The nest is found in various situations, as on the ground, under some roots, or the turf of pastures, but more frequently on the sides of streams, among stakes, near rivers, in heaps of stones, in the hole of a wall, or even on the top of a pollard tree. It is composed of dried grass, fibrous roots, and moss, rather carelessly put together, but abundantly lined with feathers and hair. Among the laurels in the Botanic Garden at Upsal, a pair of white wagtails were observed to breed for six successive seasons, and so tame as to appear fearless of the spectators. The eggs are usually from four to six, of a bluish-white, spotted with brown and ash-colour, and resembling those of the cuckoo. Gérardin mentions an instance of a female of this species laying thirty eggs, in consequence of a person withdrawing them gradually from the nest, till pity overcame curiosity, and the poor bird was permitted to hatch the usual number without further molestation. The white wagtail frequently builds twice in the season, and the male relieves his mate, during some hours in the day time, from the cares of incubation. Both parents defend their young with the greatest boldness, flying out on those who approach the nest, and plaguing and hovering about them, so as to insult or scare them. If the invader removes their offspring, they flutter over his head, turning constantly round him, and uttering incessant lamentations. It has been likewise remarked, that they tend their brood with the utmost care and solicitude, and carry off every kind of dirtiness to some distance from the nest, a proceeding which has been noticed in regard to some other species of birds, and which may be designed not only to preserve cleanliness, but to keep the nest better concealed. When the new family are capable of flying, both parents still attend and feed them during three weeks or a month, when they wage incessant war on insects, seizing and devouring them with astonishing promptitude, as if they scarcely allowed themselves time to swallow them. In general, they are far from shy, and they appear to be more apprehensive of birds of prey than of mankind, seldom retiring to any distance, even on the discharge of a fowling-piece, and easily falling into the different snares that are laid for them. The full-grown birds, however, cannot be reared in a cage; and, when confined, usually die in the course of twenty-four hours; but the nestlings may be domesticated, if trained like young nightingales. In Egypt, these birds are said to be preserved for the table by being dried in sand.

Flava.

S. flava, Motacilla flava, Lin. &c. *Motacilla chrysogastra,* Bech. *Yellow Wagtail,* Prov. *Summer* or *Spring Wagtail.* Breast and abdomen yellow, and the two outer tail-feathers obliquely half white at the tips; length about six inches and a half; weight five drachms. This species is diffused throughout Europe, Russia, and Siberia, and has been found in moist situations in Madeira. In Devonshire it appears in autumn, but not in spring; nor is it known to breed in that county, whereas in Hampshire it is said to be stationary. In many of the temperate regions of Europe it appears early in spring, and departs late in autumn: and, in

France, it is even a partial resident during winter. In autumn, it congregates in numerous bands, which then preferably frequent upland and champaign arable fields, and sometimes uncultivated land, interspersed with furze. They are also partial to bean-fields, and breed in such situations; being more indifferent about water than the white or the grey species. They familiarly mingle with flocks and herds, and seem almost willing to consort with man; yet they are so impatient of bondage that they quickly die in confinement, unless they be taken young, and reared like nightingales; and even this treatment they seldom survive three or four years. The female places her nest in meadows, or corn fields, and sometimes on the brink of a stream, under the root of a tree, composing it, outwardly, of dried grass and moss, and lining it with abundance of feathers, hair, and wool. She lays from six to eight rounded eggs, of an olivaceous-green, with bright flesh-coloured spots according to some, and dirty-white, or pale-brown, sprinkled all over with a darker shade, according to others; their markings perhaps not being invariable. The male assists both in constructing the nest, and in hatching the young. It has a very shrill note, but which can scarcely be called a song.

S. boarula, Motacilla boarula, Lin. Lath. *Motacilla melanope,* Pallas. *Grey Wagtail* of Pennant, &c. *Yellow Wagtail,* of Albin. Prov. *Winter Wagtail.* Cinereous above, yellow beneath, with the whole of the first tail-feather, and the inner web of the second, white. This species, which has been often confounded with the preceding, is more entitled than it to the epithet *yellow,* in as much as it has more of that colour on its plumage. The grey wagtail is of more rare occurrence than the preceding, and seems to be of solitary habits, more than two being seldom seen together. It is indigenous, however, to various countries of Europe, and is said to breed in Cumberland. The female makes her nest in heaps of stones, coarse gravel, or in a hole in the earth, and constructs it of dried fibres and moss, which it lines with hair, feathers, or wool. The eggs are from five to eight in number, of a dirty white, marked with reddish spots. This bird is much in motion, constantly flirts its tail, seldom perches, and affects the neighbourhood of waters. According to Latham, it is first seen in this country in April, and departs again in October. In France, few are seen during the winter, many of them, on the approach of that season, migrating far southward. Adanson remarked, that they were very plentiful, in the winter months, in Senegal, where they were very fat, and captured like ortolans, being esteemed great delicacies.

S. provincialis, Gmel. Tem. *Motacilla provincialis,* Lin. &c. *Sylvia Dartfordiensis,* Lath. *Dartford Warbler.* Dusky reddish brown above, breast and belly deep ferruginous, middle of the belly white. Inhabits Provence, and rarely England; but it is not uncommon in Spain, and in the south of Italy. It is rather larger than the common wren, and about five inches in length. The shortness of the wing, and the length of the tail, give it a singular manner of flying, which is in short jerks, with the tail thrown up. Its note is a weak but shrill piping noise, several times repeated. It picks small insects and caterpillars from cabbages, furze, &c. and shily lurks and creeps among leaves or bushes, when in the least alarmed. The female makes her nest in a thick bush of furze, composing it externally of dry grass and little bits of twigs, and lining it with wool and feathers. The hatch consists of four or five eggs, of a

Boarula.

Provincialis.

Ornitho-
logy.

slightly greenish-white, with dots of olivaceous and cinereous brown, very numerous and dense, and sometimes exhibiting a band at the larger end.

ANTHUS. Bech. Tem. Vieill.

ANTHUS.

Bill straight, slender, cylindrical, awl-shaped near the tip, edges inflected towards the middle ; base of the upper mandible ridged, point slightly notched ; nostrils basal, lateral, and half-closed by an arched membrane ; the hind claw more or less bent, and generally longer than the hind toe, the third and fourth quills the longest.

Birds of this family were long united with the larks, on account of the length of their hind claw ; but their slender and notched beak approximates them to the warblers.

Pratensis.

A. pratensis, Bech. Tem. *Alauda pratensis*, Lath. *Alauda mosellana*, Gmel. *A. sepiarius*, Vieill. *Pipit Lark.* Tail feathers brown, the outer one half white, the second with a wedge-shaped spot, of the same colour, at the tip, and a double white line on the wings. Weight about five drachms and a half, and length six inches and a half. The bill is dusky ; the sides and base of the upper mandible are dull yellow, and the irides are hazel. The male sings flying, or perched on the twig of a bush, when he erects his body, half opens his bill, and unfolds his wings. His warble is simple, but sweet, harmonious, and clearly uttered. When raised, he pronounces, like his mate, the syllable *pee*, three or four times, successively, and alights at a short distance from the spot which he left. M. Vieillot, who has watched the manners of this bird in Upper Normandy, where it abounds, could never perceive it perch on a tree, but occasionally on the top of a small bush, and that only for a short time ; in the breeding season, he never encountered it in the champaign country, but on hills covered with turf, and sprinkled with dwarf shrubs. He found the nest sometimes under a tuft of herbage, and sometimes at the foot of a low shrub, composed of stalks of grass, moss, and hair, and containing four or five eggs, of a dull white, marked with irregular brown spots, most numerous at the broad end, and in the form of dots near the smaller.

Arboreus.

A. arboreus, Bechs. Tem. *Alauda pratensis*, Lin. *Alauda trivialis*, Gmel. *Tit Lark, Teeting* of the Scots. Greenish-brown above, with the two outer tail feathers externally white, and the eye-brows of the same colour. Inhabits the whole of Europe, though more plentifully in some countries than in others. In many parts of this island it is very common, and remains with us throughout the year, affecting barren situations, whether swampy or moorish, and placing its nest on the ground, among furze, or long grass, constructing it of bents, dry grass, and stalks of plants, and lining it with fine grass and horse-hair. The eggs are generally five or six, but vary considerably in size and marking, some being of a dark brown, others whitish, speckled with rufous brown, or of a paler brown, tinged with red. During the period of incubation, the male sits on an adjoining tree, and pours forth his short but pleasing song, which some rank next to that of the nightingale. It likewise sings on the ground, or in the air, increasing the loudness of its descant as it approaches the branch on which it is going to perch. In Scotland, it is almost the only bird that frequents the extensive heath-tracts in which it breeds. In winter these birds haunt the low grounds in search of worms and insects, and fly in small troops ; and, in the Orkneys, they resort to the

sea-shores. In Italy, they fatten in the vineyards, and are included among the *Beccaficos*.

Ornitho-
logy.

Rufescens.

A. rufescens, Tem. *A. campestris*, Bech. *A. rufus*, Vieil. *A. campestris*, Meyer *A. mosellana*, Lath. *Marsh Lark*, or *Willow Lark.* Red, varied with brown above ; rufescent beneath ; the breast spotted with brown, and three brown stripes beneath the eyes. Length, six inches and a half. Native of France and other countries of the European continent, where it affects stony and sandy hillocks, or moorish and heathy grounds, in which it nestles, under a clod of turf, or sometimes beneath a bush ; but it neither frequents rivers nor marshes, as some of its synonymes would seem to intimate, and some of which have originated in Montbeillard having confounded it with the *Anthus aquaticus* of Vieillot, or *Alauda campestris*, var. A, of Latham. The female lays from four to six eggs, of a pale bluish tint, on which are scattered small purple and brown-red lines and spots.

ORDER IV.

GRANIVOROUS BIRDS.

GRANIVO-
ROUS
BIRDS.

Bill strong, short, thick, more or less conical ; the mandibles most frequently without a notch ; feet with three toes before and one behind, and the anterior divided ; wings of moderate size.

The birds ranged under this denomination live in pairs, and are migratory or sedentary, according to the climates in which they breed ; but most of them statedly pass and repass from one country to another at appointed seasons, and assemble in large flocks previously to commencing their annual flights. They feed principally on grains and seeds, from which many of them detach the husk ; but they have frequently recourse to insects, especially for their young. All of them may be maintained in confinement, on grains alone. Next to the pigeons, or gallinaceous fowls, they are most susceptible of enduring the approach and discipline of mankind. Most of the foreign species moult twice a-year ; the males are gaily or splendidly attired in the season of love, but assume the modest livery of the females in winter.

ALAUDA, Lin. &c. LARK.

ALAUDA.

Bill straight, short, conical ; upper mandible arched, of equal length with the under, and without a notch ; nostrils at the base of the bill ovoid, and covered by small feathers, projecting forward ; the three anterior toes quite divided, and the claw of the hind one longer than the toe ; the third quill the longest ; feathers of the head more or less lengthened, and capable of erection.

The larks live on the ground in the fields ; do not vibrate the tail, and sing as they mount perpendicularly into the air. They nestle on the soil, roll in the dust, and are easily reared in confinement. They moult only once a-year, and the females and young are not very dissimilar in appearance from the males.

Calandra.

A. calandra, Lin. &c. *A. sibirica*, Pallas. *Calandre Lark.* Breast with a fuscous band ; web of the exterior tail-feathers, and the second and third, at the tip white. Larger than the sky-lark, which it considerably resembles, both in appearance and manners. It has been observed throughout a great part of Europe, and over large tracts of Asia, frequenting the deserts of Tartary, and most of the Russian empire. It forms its nest after the manner of the sky-lark, and lays four or five clear purple eggs, marked with large cinereous spots, and dark brown dots. It is seldom seen in flocks. As it has not only a note of its own, superior to that of the sky-lark, but will imitate that of many other song birds, it is often caught young, and trained to sing in confinement. In winter it is very fat, and much esteemed for the table.

Cristata.

A. cristata, Lin. &c. *Crested*, or *Greater Crested Lark*. Head crested, tail feathers black, but the two outer white on their exterior edges. Length about seven inches, and expanse of wing ten inches and a half. The number of feathers which compose the crest varies from seven to ten; and the bird can lower them at pleasure. The male has a larger head and stronger bill than the female, and more black on the breast. In both the tongue is large, and slightly forked. Native of the continent of Europe, from Russia to Greece, but not of Great Britain. According to Vieillot, it has been seen in Egypt. In winter, it frequents the margins of streams and highways, and may sometimes be seen among a flight of sparrows, picking the undigested grains from horses' dung, &c. Its most ordinary haunts are fields and meadows, the banks of ditches, the ridges of furrows, and sometimes the entrance to woods. Not unfrequently it affects the neighbourhood of villages, and will even enter them, and alight on dunghills, garden walls, or the roofs of houses. It does not fly in troops, soars to a moderate height in the air, and remains a short time without alighting. It is a somewhat familiar bird, uttering its sweet notes on the approach of man. It seldom ceases to sing in fine weather; but rain, or a cloudy sky, often reduces it to silence. Its voice is not so powerful as that of the field lark, but it more readily acquires lessons in music, so as often to forget its native warble; and yet it seldom long survives a state of captivity. The female nestles on the ground, and sometimes in a juniper-bush, very early in spring, and has two broods in the season, laying at a time four or five eggs, of a bright ash-colour, sprinkled with many brown and black spots. These birds are snared in autumn, when they are in their plumpest condition: but they have other enemies than man; for the smallest of the rapacious birds assail them, and, when threatened with such attacks, they have been known to throw themselves on the mercy of the fowler, or to remain motionless in a furrow till they were caught by the hand.

Arvensis.

A. arvensis, Lin. &c. *Field Lark*, or *Sky Lark*, Prov. *Laverock*. Varied with dusky-grey, reddish and white above, reddish-white beneath, with the outer webs of the two exterior tail-feathers white, and the two middle ones with their edges ferruginous. Length about seven inches, stretch of the wings nearly a foot, and weight one ounce and a half. The male is somewhat larger and browner than the female; has a sort of blue collar; more white at the tail, and the hinder claw longer. The stomach in this species is fleshy and large, when considered in relation to the size of the bird. The present species, whose song ushers in the spring, is too well known to require any detailed description; but we may remark, that varieties occasionally occur, either white, for example, or nearly so; or dusky, or almost black, or of some of the intermediate shades. Others, which have been observed in Russia, are remarkable for the length of their legs; and Gérardin mentions his being in possession of an individual, the mandibles of whose bill crossed each other, and constrained it to pick up its food in an awkward manner. It is not improbable that some

of the cream-coloured and hoary specimens owe their peculiarities of hue to age, which produces considerable changes on the plumage of larks.

The sky-lark inhabits all parts of Europe, even as high as Nordland, beneath the arctic circle; but, in some parts of Scandinavia it is migratory. It is likewise met with in all parts of Russia and Siberia, reaching even Kamtschatka. It abounds, too, in other tracts of Asia, and in Africa; but it seems to be unknown in America. With us, it is most common in the open and upland cultivated districts, allotted to corn, being rarely seen on extensive moors remote from arable land. The nest is placed on the ground, often between two clods of earth, among grass, clover, turnips, or corn, and is formed of dry grass, and other vegetable stalks, or roots, or hair, and lined with grass of a finer quality. The eggs, which are generally four or five, have a greyish ground, and are spotted with brown. The incubation lasts fourteen or fifteen days; and, in the temperate parts of Europe, two broods are produced in the course of the summer: but, in some of the southern regions, as, for example, in Italy, three young families are brought forth, namely, the first early in May, the second in July, and the third in August. Even in this country the bird will lay as late as September, if its nest happens to be destroyed. When the young are hatched, the mother watches over them with the most tender solicitude for about a fortnight, feeding them with the chrysalids of ants, with worms, insects, and, in some countries, with the eggs of locusts. Hence, in the island of Lemnos, where these last-mentioned insects occasionally pullulate, and commit great havock on the vegetable produce, the sky lark is deemed a sacred bird. In their mature state, these birds live chiefly on seeds, herbage, and many other vegetable substances. They are easily tamed, and become so familiar as to eat off the table, and even to alight on the hand; but they cannot readily cling by the toes on account of the form of the hind one, which is too long and straight. The instinctive warmth of attachment which the female bears to her young, often betrays itself at a very early period, and even before she is influenced by the cares of maternity.

The sudden appearance of immense flocks of sky larks in Egypt and other countries, at particular seasons, and the circumstances of their being occasionally observed in a very emaciated and exhausted state, and of their being noticed at sea, leave no doubt with respect to the fact of their partial migration; but it is equally certain, that they do not all quit the countries in which they breed; and thus we are enabled to reconcile the discordant sentiments of ornithologists; at the same time, the motives which induce only a portion of the species to shift their abode do not readily suggest themselves to conjecture. The lark is one of those few birds which chant on wing, becomes tuneful early in spring, and continues so throughout the summer. Its enlivening song is chiefly heard in the morning and evening. We need scarcely remark, that he mounts almost perpendicularly, and by successive springs, into the air, where he hovers at a great height, and whence he descends in an oblique direction, unless menaced by some ravenous bird, or attracted by his mate, when he darts down to the earth like a stone. When he first leaves the earth, his notes are feeble and interrupted; but, as he rises, they gradually swell to their full tone; and they are sometimes still distinctly heard when he is scarcely visible. These birds cease to be musical in winter, when they assemble in flocks, grow

Ornithology.

fat, and are taken in multitudes by the bird-catchers. Thus, four thousand dozen have been captured in the neighbourhood of Dunstable, between September and February; and Keysler informs us, that the excise on larks alone produces about £900 a-year to the town of Leipsic, whose neighbourhood, like those of Naumburg, Merseburg, Halle, &c. is celebrated for larks of a peculiarly delicate flavour.

Arborea.

A. arborea, Lin. &c. *A. nemorosa*, Gmel. *A. cristatella*, Lath. *Wood Lark*, or *Lesser Crested Lark*. Varied with dusky-grey, and reddish; the head with an annular stripe, bordered with white. This considerably resembles the preceding, but the tail is much shorter, and the feathers on the head are longer. Length between five and six inches; weight eight drachms. It inhabits Europe, as far north as Sweden, and is met with, though sparingly, in various parts of this country, particularly Devonshire, where it seems to abound more than in any other part of England. According to Pennant, it occurs in Siberia and Kamtschatka. It sings delightfully on wing, but rarely when sitting on the ground, though sometimes when perched on a tree. Although its song does not consist of so great a variety of notes as that of the sky-lark, it is much more melodious, and frequently uttered during the night, insomuch that it has been mistaken for the nightingale. With the exception of June and July, when it is silent, it is more or less musical all the year round, for it will sing even after Christmas, in frosty weather, if there be sunshine about mid-day. It does not ascend into the air perpendicularly, and continue hovering and singing over the same spot as the preceding, but it will soar to a great height, and keep flying in large irregular circles, singing with little intermission, and will thus continue for an hour together. The nest is usually placed in a hollow on the ground, covered with grass or heath, or in the middle of thick moss, composed externally of the dried stalks of grass, and lined with soft herbage and hair. The eggs, to the number usually of four or five, are of a dirty white, tinged with brown, and spotted with reddish. During incubation, which takes place in April, the male serenades his mate with his sweetest notes; but when the young are hatched, he pauses from his lays, and assists in the cares of rearing the new family. There is occasionally a second brood. In spring, these birds frequent dry sloping grounds, interspersed with bushes or briars, but always on the verge of woods. In winter, they prefer stony fields, and are observed to unite in compact bands, consisting of from thirty to fifty individuals, which never mingle with any other species. If they alight, they keep close by one another; and, if scared, they rise awkwardly, and with apparent reluctance, frequently descending on the spot from which they were started. During the same season, however, separate pairs may also be seen; and it seems to be ascertained, that, like the sky-lark, they are partial migrants. They are easily decoyed by the call of one of their kind; but the mature birds are so strongly attached to their family habits, that they soon pine and die in a cage.

Arenaria.

A. arenaria, Vieill. *A. calandrilla*, Bonelli. *A. brachydactyla*, Tem. *Sand Lark*, or *Lesser Calandre Lark*. Above, reddish ash-coloured, spotted with black; beneath, white, with a black band of spots on the breast, interrupted in the middle; tail black, but the outer feathers white towards their tips. Length nearly five inches and a half. The young have a mottled livery, like that of the sky-lark. Native of Italy, Spain, and the countries that confine on the Mediterranean, as also

of the Canary Islands, and not advancing farther north than Champagne. In the latter province, it arrives in great numbers about the end of April, frequenting arid and sandy districts. As Bonelli first described it in the *Memoirs of the Academy of Turin*, and it has been only recently recognised as a distinct species, it was probably long confounded with the sky-lark, although its characters and habits proclaim a difference. It has two, and sometimes three broods in the year. The nest is placed on the ground, in the print of a horse's hoof, in a small rut, or other depression of the surface, and composed chiefly of bits of grass, being arranged with great simplicity. The female lays three or four grey eggs, covered with brown-grey spots, which are confluent at the large end. When the young of all the broods are able to fly, the assembled families forsake the sandy moors, associate in very considerable flocks, and resort to the shady and arable districts. They quit Champagne about the end of August, and do not return till spring. In the morning and evening, all the males of the plain assemble aloft in the air, and give a concert, which is distinctly heard, though they themselves are beyond reach of the naked eye. Their warble is more agreeable and melodious than that of the sky-lark; but it is seldom heard in the middle of the day, and never when the bird is on the ground. So fond are they of rolling in sand, that when it is presented to one of them in a cage, the little creature manifests its joy and gratitude by a sweet, and often repeated note, by the precipitate agitation of its wings, and by the bristling of all its feathers. It then plunges into the sand, as another bird would do into a bathing vessel—remains in it for a long time, rolls about in every direction, and never desists till it is so completely besanded, that its plumage is scarcely discernible.

Parus, Lin. &c. Titmouse.

Parus.

Bill short, straight, strong, conical, compressed, terminating in a sharp point without a notch; the base furnished with small hairs; nostrils basal, rounded, and concealed by projecting feathers; legs stout, toes divided to their origin, the hind one the strongest and most bent; the fourth and fifth quills the longest.

These are very small, but very lively and active birds, being constantly in motion, and possessing a great degree of strength and courage for their size; many of them venturing to attack birds three times larger than themselves, and pursuing even the owl, and aiming at its eyes. They likewise attack sickly birds, which they more easily dispatch; and when they have effected their conquest, they pierce a hole in the skull, and eat the brains. They are also partial to flesh and fat, which they eat with great avidity. Their principal food, however, consists of insects, which they obtain in the spring by biting off the open buds, and in the summer by searching in cracks and crevices of trees. They likewise feed on the seeds of plants and grain, which they sometimes hoard in magazines. Their voice is generally unpleasant. Their nests are constructed with peculiar elegance and ingenuity. They are prolific even to a proverb; and they occur in all the regions of the old world, and many of them throughout the American continent, the West India Islands, New Zealand, &c. In confinement, their manners are amusing; but on account of their sanguinary dispositions it is not safe to introduce them into an aviary.

Major.

P. major, Lin. &c. *Great Titmouse*, or *Ox-eye*, Prov. *Black-cap*, or *Great Black-headed Tom-tit*. Olive-green above, yellowish beneath; head black, temples white, top of the neck yellowish. The great tit-mouse weighs about ten drachms, and measures five inches and three quarters in length, and eight inches four lines in expanse of wing. It is widely diffused over Europe, Asia, and Africa; and, in some of the colder climates it appears to be a bird of passage. In many parts of this country, especially in hilly situations, it is not uncommon, frequenting woods, copses, gardens, and orchards, where it searches, with unceasing activity, for caterpillars or insects. It is likewise a notorious bee-eater, and has been known to depopulate hives. It feeds also on the seeds of panic-grass, beech-mast, hazel nuts, and almonds, grasping these last in its little claws, breaking their shell by repeated strokes of its sharp bill, and dexterously picking out the substance. The nest is made of moss, feathers, or other downy and delicate matters, lined with hair, and placed in the hollow of a tree, or in a wall. Colonel Montagu mentions, that he once found it in the barrel of a garden pump; and he has found the eggs in the hole of a decayed tree, on the rotten wood, without the least appearance of a nest. The male assists both in the construction of the nest and in the cares of incubation. There are usually two broods in the year. The female lays from six to ten or twelve eggs, which are yellowish-white, spotted with rust-colour, especially at the larger end, and scarcely to be distinguished from those of the nuthatch. The young continue blind for some days, after which their growth is very rapid, so that they are able to fly in about a fortnight. After quitting the nest, they perch on the neighbouring trees, incessantly call on one another, and continue together till the approaching spring invites them to pair. Before the first moulting, the male may be distinguished by his superior size, and more ardent temperament. In the space of six months, the new race are fully grown, and four months after moulting, they are fit for breeding. A couple, when once paired, continue faithful, it is alleged, for life. The common cry of the species is a sort of grating chatter, and has been compared to the filing of iron, or the whetting of a saw; but, in February, when they pair, they utter more joyful notes, which cease with incubation. The approach of these birds to houses and villages is supposed to denote a rigorous degree of cold. In deep snows, they may be observed, with their back downwards, drawing straws, lengthwise, from the eaves of thatched houses, in order to pull out the flies concealed between them, and this so often repeated, as to deface the thatch, and give it a ragged appearance. Though seldom domesticated, because their song is not generally admired, yet they are easily tamed, and grow so familiar as to eat out of the hand; they are also expert in performing the little feat of drawing up the bucket. They will even breed in captivity. Their ordinary term of life is five or six years, and their death is sometimes preceded by gout, and a rheum in the eyes. During the spring, titmice are frequently observed searching for the *tortrices*, so abundant among the opening buds of fruit-trees, and thus benefiting man in a very considerable degree; but their services are no better repaid than those of other small birds; and the thoughtless gardener, supposing them the enemies of his blossoms, destroys them without mercy. An uncommon variety of the present species is described and delineated by Lewin. The general colour of the plumage was much darker than in the common sort; and both the mandibles were elongated, curved, and crossed. This singular specimen was taken up before it was quite dead, in the street of Feversham, in Kent, after having been wounded by shot.

P. ater, Lin. &c. *Colemouse*, or *Cole-Titmouse*. Back ash-coloured; head black, occiput white. Weighs two drachms and a quarter, and measures four inches and a quarter in length. The nest is placed in some hole, either in a wall or a tree, and is composed of moss and wool, and lined with hair. The eggs are six or seven, sometimes as numerous as ten, pure white, and spotted with rusty-red. That the present species subsists entirely on insects, appears to be an erroneous opinion; for Labillardière, who observed it at the Cape of Good Hope, admired the lightness with which it hovered about the *Agave vivipara*, whilst it fed on the saccharine liquor which exudes from the basis of the corolla of that plant; and we may add, that it will eat the seeds of the sun-flower with great greediness. In the neighbourhood of Paris, according to Vieillot, the colemouse appears to be a bird of passage, and yet it winters even beyond the Lena in Siberia. Frisch says, that in Germany it inhabits the pine forests; but in Sweden, according to Linné, it prefers the alders. It is likewise known to haunt woods in general, especially such as contain evergreens, and to be partial to vineyards and gardens. Like the rest of its congeners, it creeps and runs on the trees, and although next to the long-tailed species, it is the smallest of the tribe; it is also reputed the least timorous and cunning, not only allowing a person to approach very near it, but even to ensnare it more than once.

P. palustris, Lin. &c. including *P. autricapillus*, Gmel. *Marsh Titmouse*, Prov. *Black-cap, Black-capped Titmouse*, or *Little Black-headed Tom-tit*. Head black, back ash-colour, temples white. The markings are, however, subject to vary. In general the black on the head extends downwards on the nape. Length four inches and a half, weight two drachms and a half. In the female, the black on the head is of a lighter shade than in the male, and on the throat very faint, with spots of grey. Though found throughout Europe, and even enduring the hardest frosts of Siberia, it is at least a partial migrant in some parts of France; flocks of them approaching houses in that country in September and October, and apparently passing into Italy. Though more common than the colemouse, it is by no means so much so as either the great or the blue species. With the latter it partakes of flesh, and haunts the oat-ricks. Besides ants, wasps, bees, and other insects, it devours with avidity the seed of hemp, sun-flower, &c. and it lays up a store of seed against a season of want. Early in February it begins two quaint notes, like the whetting of a saw. It particularly affects low wet grounds, especially where old willow trees abound, in which, and in old apple and pear trees that are near water, it often nestles. They have been seen excavating the decayed parts of a willow-tree, carrying the chips in their bill to some distance, always working downwards, and making the bottom, for the reception of the nest, larger than the entrance. The nest is composed of moss and thistledown, or feathers, and lined with down. The female lays five or six white eggs, spotted with rusty-red, chiefly at the larger end.

P. cœruleus, Lin. &c. *Blue Titmouse*, or *Tom-tit*, Prov. *Blue Cap, Nun, Titmal, Tinnock*, or *Willow Bitter*. Olive-green above, yellowish beneath; quills blue, outer margin of the primaries white; forehead white; and crown blue. The line from the bill to the eyes, that surrounding the temples, and legs and claws, black.

Ater.

Palustris.

Cœruleus.

Length, about four inches and a half, and weight, three drachms. Belon, Klein, and Kolben are, therefore, mistaken, in representing it as the smallest of the family. The female is rather smaller than the male, and has less of blue on the head. In the young birds, the white is replaced by yellowish, the blue by cinereous-brown, and the olive-green and yellow by duller shades.

This species, which would probably be more admired for its beauty, were it less common, inhabits the whole of Europe, southern Russia, but not Siberia, and is met with on the coast of Africa, and in the Canary Islands; but, in these warmer latitudes the blue approaches to black, and the other hues are less distinctly marked. By ridding our orchards and gardens of insects and their larvæ, it renders us an important service, but which is sometimes counterbalanced by the tender buds which it destroys in hunting for them, and by picking the full formed fruit, which it carries to its receptacle for provisions. In winter it frequents houses for the sake of plunder, and it will greedily devour flesh whether recent or putrid. So cleanly does it pick the bones of the birds which it subdues, that Klein proposed to employ its services in preparing skeletons of this class of animals. It is a constant attendant where horse-flesh is kept for hounds, and also in the farm-yard, being fond of oats, which it plucks out of the ear, and, retiring to a neighbouring bush, fixes between its claws, and hammers with its bill to break the husk. Mr. White observes, that it frequently picks bones on dunghills, is a great admirer of suet, and frequents butchers' shops. "When a boy," he says, " I have known twenty in a morning caught with snap mouse-traps, baited with tallow or suet. It will also pick holes in apples left on the ground, and be well entertained with the seeds on the top of a sun-flower." Its ordinary retreat is a hollow tree, or a hole in a wall, selected in some warm situation, in winter, but in one more cool, and of more difficult access in summer. In this dwelling the female constructs her nest, composed of moss, and lined with a great quantity of feathers and hair. The number of eggs, according to Montagu, who examined many of the nests, is six or seven, and rarely eight. Montbeillard again mentions having seen seventeen in one nest; and ornithologists have generally asserted that they sometimes amount to twenty, or even to twenty-two. They are of a reddish-white, and speckled with rust-colour at the larger end. Should they be touched, or a single one broken, the dam forsakes the nest, and breeds again; but otherwise she makes but one hatch in the year; and after the young have been produced, she is so tenacious of her nest, that she will often suffer herself to be taken rather than quit it, and will return to it after having been removed from it. She menaces every intruder in a singular manner, hissing like a snake, bristling all her feathers, and uttering a noise like the spitting of a cat, at the same time biting severely if handled, and defending herself to the last gasp. As soon as the young brood can fly, they associate with their parents, quit the woods, resort to gardens and orchards, and often mingle with the great titmice. The pairing commences in January, and although their chirp is singular and little varied, yet we hear it with no unpleasing emotion, as one of the early harbingers of spring. At other seasons these birds have no regular song, but utter a shrill note, quickly repeated. A full-grown bird, when taken, rejects not the food that is offered to it, and soon becomes familiar, nor does it seem to dislike the place of its confinement, provided it be somewhat spacious, and furnished with lurking holes, in which it may occasionally conceal itself, and pass the night; but few of them, even when treated with the utmost attention, survive the close of winter.

P. cristatus, Lin. &c. *Crested Titmouse.* Reddish-grey above, white beneath; collar black; head furnished with a crest. This is a shy and solitary bird, and being chiefly limited to the pine forests of Europe, or to desolate heaths, overrun with juniper bushes, is not generally known. Its retreat and its caution, for the most part, save it from the fowler's snares, or, if surprised, it refuses food, and, spurning every soothing attention, soon expires in confinement. It has been observed in Sweden, some parts of the north of France, and in the western and temperate parts of Russia, but not in Siberia. Though not found in England, it has been met with in the pine forests of the north of Scotland, particularly in that of Glenmoor, the property of the Duke of Gordon. According to Meyer, it nestles in the hollow of a tree, the rent of an old wall, or among stone heaps, and sometimes in the forsaken abode of a squirrel, and lays from eight to ten eggs, of a beautiful white, spotted or dashed with bloody red. It is said to exhale the odour of the juniper, and of other resinous trees, among which it principally resides.

Cristatus.

P. caudatus, Lin. &c. *Long-tailed Titmouse.* Prov. *Bottle Tom, Long-tail Pie, Long-tail Mag, Long-tail Capon, Huck-muck,* and *Mug-ruffin.* Varied longitudinally with white, rose-colour, and black; crown white, and tail long. The last character is sufficiently discriminative; for the tail is longer than the body; yet both together measure only five inches and a quarter; and, though the rumpled and discomposed, or rather bristling state of the feathers, imparts somewhat of an inflated appearance to the bird, its body is very small, the whole weighing only two drachms. The male has more of the rose colour than the female; but, in both, the markings are liable to vary. It is a native of the woods and thickets of Europe, is very abundant in Holland, and by no means uncommon in many districts of our own island. In spring, it has a pleasing song; but at other times only a shrill call. The young birds remain with the parents during winter, assembling at night, and roosting on the branch of a tree, closely huddled together. They feed like the rest of the genus. The nest is singularly curious and elegant, being of a long oval form, with a small hole in the side, and sometimes with an opening near the top, at each side, so that in certain situations, the dam can go in and out, without injury to its long tail, which is but loosely put together, and easily discomposed. The situation is generally the forking of a tree, overgrown with lichens, about three or four feet from the ground. The outside is formed of moss, woven or matted together with the silken shrouds of the aureliæ of insects, and covered all over with tree and stone lichens, fixed with fine threads of the same silken material. From this covering the rain trickles off, without penetrating the fabric; while, from its similarity in colour and appearance to the bark on which it is placed, it is not readily perceived. The inside is thickly furnished with feathers, the soft webs of which are all laid inwards, and the quills or points stuck into the outward part of the structure. In this comfortable little mansion, which is fashioned neither after the manner of those of the family which breed in trees or walls, nor after that of the hang-nest sorts, the female

Caudatus.

deposits from ten to sixteen or seventeen eggs, little larger than peas, some of them pure white, others white and delicately speckled with red, and all assuming a fine red blush, when held between the eye and the light, owing to the transparency of the shell, which shows the yolk. From the circumstance of many of them being almost entirely concealed among the feathers, some have supposed that the hatch is less numerous than a careful examination has proved it to be. Some writers maintain, that these birds are permanent residents in the countries in which they breed: and others that they migrate, statements not irreconcilable, if we suppose that they are addicted to partial migrations, varying their range according to circumstances, and changing when they want a better. They are seldom caught in traps ; nor are they deemed fit for the table.

Bicolor. *P. bicolor*, Lin. &c. *Toupet Titmouse* of Pennant, *Crested Titmouse* of Catesby, Latham, and Wilson. Head crested, forehead black ; body ash-coloured above, and reddish-white beneath. Crest of a deep cinereous ; tail slightly forked ; the female similar to the male, but less bright in its hues. Length between five and six inches : native of North America, and the South of Greenland. It has a singular flight, frequently folding up its wings. It inhabits the forests of Carolina and Virginia the whole year, and feeds principally on insects. It nestles early in May, in the hole of a tree, which it sometimes scoops out by its own exertions. The hatch usually consists of six white eggs, marked with a few small red spots, near the broad end. The male is remarkable for the varied compass of his notes, which are sometimes as feeble as the chirp of a mouse, and sometimes a clear and sonorous whistle, which resounds in the woods for nearly half an hour, and which he always accompanies with a precipitate movement of his wings. When captured and confined, this bird will eat hempseed, cherry-stones, apple-seeds, and similar substances, if broken in small fragments. It likewise soon becomes very familiar ; but, if put into a wooden cage, it soon effects its escape.

Biarmicus. *P. biarmicus*, Lin. &c. including the *Russicus* of Gmel. *Bearded Titmouse*, or *Least Butcher Bird* of Edwards. Rufous, with a hoary crown ; head bearded ; vent black ; tail longer than the body. This elegant bird is about six inches one quarter in length, of which the tail makes one-half. It is pretty numerous in Holland, less so in Denmark and Sweden, but common on the borders of the Caspian Sea, and the Palus Mœotis, not advancing farther north in Asia. Its invariable haunts are reedy marshes, which are seldom accessible, and, consequently, the history of the bird has been but imperfectly unfolded. It has been ascertained, however, that it breeds in some parts of England, and that it remains with us all the year. The nest is placed near the ground, among reeds or rushes, compactly formed of the tops of dry grass, mixed with reeds and rushes, and interspersed with small oblong leaves, and always above the highest water mark. The female lays from five to eight reddish eggs, with large brown spots, which are very numerous about the larger end.

**Penduli-
nus.** *P. pendulinus*, Lin. &c. including *Narbonensis*, Gmel. *Penduline Titmouse*, or *Remis, Mountain Titmouse* of Albin. Head sub-ferruginous, black band beneath the eye ; quills and tail feathers brown, and margined on each side with rust colour.

The penduline titmice inhabit Poland, Russia, Hungary, some parts of Germany, Italy, the south of France, and also Siberia, haunting marshes, concealing them-

selves among the rushes, and conducting themselves with so much craftiness as to be hardly ever taken in snares. But the most interesting fact which has been ascertained with respect to their natural history is the superior sagacity and skill with which they arrange and construct their nests. With their bill they entwine the light and filamentous down that is found in the buds of the willow, poplar, and aspen, on thistles, cotton-grass, dandelion, flea-bane, &c. and form it into a thick close tissue. This they strengthen outwardly with fibres and small roots, which penetrate into the texture, and in some measure compose the frame-work of the nest. They line the inside with the same sort of down, but without weaving it, that their young may lie soft. They shut it above, to confine the warmth ; and they suspend it by nettles, hemp, &c. from the cleft of a small pliant branch, hanging over the stream, at once for the sake of security, and that it may rock more gently, being assisted by the pliancy of the twig. In this situation, the brood are well supplied with insects, and at the same time, protected from lizards and other reptiles. The nest varies considerably in its form, sometimes resembling an elongated bag, sometimes a short purse, and sometimes a flattened bagpipe, &c. The aperture is made in the side, and is almost always turned towards the water, generally round, and often, though not always, surrounded by a brim. These nests are found in the fens of Bologna, Tuscany, the department of the Upper Garonne, and Languedoc, Germany, Lithuania, Poland, and even Siberia, in some of which countries the peasants regard them with superstitious veneration, one of them being suspended near the door of every cottage, as a charm against lightning. Cajetan Monte has given us a figure of one of them, and Daniel Titius of two ; and it is remarkable that these three sorts differ not only from one another, but from that figured by Bonani, both in respect of size and form. The largest was seven inches long, and four and a half wide, and was found suspended at the fork of a small branch, with hemp and flax ; the smallest was five inches and a half long, of the same breadth at its upper part, and terminated in an obtuse point ; while that of Monti was pointed both above and below. Titius was led to suspect that the penduline titmice make only a rude essay in constructing their first nest ; that the sides are then thin, and the texture loose ; but that they improve in each subsequent attempt ; and that, as their diffidence and mistrust grow on them, they add firmer coats on the outside, and softer ones within. About the end of December, 1691, near Breslaw, a female siskin was found in one of those nests, with a young one, and three eggs not yet hatched, so that we may presume that the nests of the penduline titmouse subsist from year to year. Titius adds, that we need not wonder to find the siskin hatching in winter, since the crossbill does the same. The remiz lays from four to six white transparent eggs, with a remarkably thin shell, about the size of those of the wren, and marked with some rufous spots.

P. Capensis, Gmel. Lath. &c. *Cape Titmouse.* Cine- **Capensis.** reous-grey ; quills black, margined with white ; tail black above, and white beneath. Inhabits the Cape of Good Hope. The male assists his mate in the construction of a luxurious nest, chiefly composed of the down of a species of *Asclepias.* Near the upper end projects a small tube, about an inch in length, with an orifice of about three-fourths of an inch in diameter. Immediately under the tube is a small hole in the side, that has no communication with the interior. In this hole the male sits at night; and there both he and the female are secured from the weather. In working at the nest, the former strikes his wings forcibly against the sides of it, and thus reduces it into the form of a compact elongated ball. The eggs are placed in the centre, where they are safest and warmest.

EMBERIZA, Lin. &c. BUNTING.

**EMBE-
RIZA.**

Bill strong, short, conical, compressed, sharp edged, and notchless; the upper mandible narrower than the under, the edges of both bent inwards, and in the inside of the upper there is a large bony knob, of great use in breaking the kernels and hard seeds on which the family subsist; nostrils basal, rounded, surmounted and partly covered by feathers in front; tail forked, or slightly rounded.

The buntings feed chiefly on farinaceous seeds, but also eat insects. Most of them live in woods and gardens, and nestle among bushes and thickets. Such of them as are furnished with a long hind toe haunt rocks and plains. The sexes are generally very different in their garb; and some of the foreign species moult twice in the year. In general they are not gifted with much foresight, and are easily ensnared.

Citrinella.

E. citrinella, Lin. &c. *Yellow Bunting, Yellow Hammer*, or *Yellow Yowley.* Tail feathers blackish, the two outer, or the inner webs, marked with an acute white spot. The ordinary weight of the yellow bunting is about seven drachms, the length six inches three lines, and its extent of wing nine inches two lines. It inhabits Europe from its southernmost point at least as far north as Sondmor, and it is likewise found in the west of Siberia. In this and many other countries it is of very common occurrence. Its song is as little attractive as that of the common bunting, consisting merely of a repetition five or six times of the same note, and terminating in one more lengthened and shrill. But, besides this native note, it has two particular calls, the one that of rallying, which it commonly utters when flying, and on the approach of evening during summer; and the other expressive of its uneasiness when offended, especially when one comes near its nest or its little ones. Many of them are supposed to travel southward during the autumn; such as remain congregate in winter, and mingling with sparrows, chaffinches, and other small birds, approach houses in the day time, or even towns, or frequent highways, picking up little grains, and extracting them from the dung of horses, &c. This combination of different species, intent on catering, lasts only during the day; for some hours before night-fall the family separate, and retire to their respective haunts, the buntings previously perching on the tops of trees, from which they do not descend till after sun-set. From the same elevation the male pours forth his note in the season of love, remaining sometimes for hours together without changing his position. In spring and summer they frequent hedges and copses, but rarely the interior of forests. They fly rapidly, alight suddenly, and for the most part amidst thick foliage. The female does not breed till late in the spring, and yet has two, and sometimes three hatches in the season. The nest, which is large, flat, and rather artlessly composed, is generally placed near the ground, sometimes under a clod, but more frequently in some low bush or hedge, and consists of straw and various dried stalks, lined with fine grass and long hair. The eggs vary in respect of colour and size, some being nearly white, and others having a purplish hue, but all more or less marked with hair-like streaks, and terminated with a

roundish speck; and their number varies from three to five. The dam incubates with such ardent attachment, that she may be frequently caught by the hand. During her short absence for food, the male takes her place in the nest. The young are fed with small seeds and insects. In captivity these birds will live for six or seven years; but they are liable to epilepsy; and their music is too little engaging to repay the trouble of rearing them. In Italy, where small birds of almost every description are used for the table, the yellow bunting is often fattened for the market.

E. miliaris, Lin. &c. *Common Bunting*, or *Bunting*, Prov. *Bunting Lark.* Grey above, spotted with black beneath; orbits red. Weight nearly two ounces; length seven inches and a half; alar expanse, eleven inches four lines.

Miliaris.

This species is spread over most of Europe, in various parts of which it is migratory; but it remains the whole year in England. In Shetland, it has been observed in small flocks in winter, but it retires in spring. It evinces a preference to champaign countries that abound in corn and meadows, being rarely found in uncultivated tracts, or even in grass fields that are remote from arable land. It may be frequently seen on the highest part of a hedge, or uppermost branch of a tree, uttering its harsh and dissonant cry, which it repeats at short intervals. In this situation these birds are seen and heard during the greater part of summer, after which they are met with in flocks, and continue so during most of the winter. While the female is busied with incubation, the male sits on a neighbouring tree, and cheers her with his rude song, occasionally taking her place at noon, when she is said also to sing, perched in her turn. The nest is placed among tall herbage, on the ground, or else in a very low shrub, about three or four inches above the surface of the soil, formed externally of straw, lined with fibrous roots or dry grass, and sometimes finished with long hair or wool. The eggs are from four to six, of a dirty white, spotted and veined with reddish-brown and ash colour. The young quit the nest before they can fly, being fond of running on the ground; and the parents continue to guard and feed them till they are fledged; but their anxiety for the safety of their brood not unfrequently betrays them; and if a person happens to approach the spot, they wheel round his head in a doleful manner. These birds are sometimes brought to market, and sold for larks, to which, as an article of food, they are nothing inferior, but from which they may be easily distinguished by the form of the bill, and the tooth-like knob on the palate. The old lean birds are dry and tough; but the fat ones are reckoned delicate. At Rome, they are fattened, like the ortolan, with millet. Bird-catchers use them as calls in autumn; and they entice not only the foolish buntings, but many other small birds of different kinds into the snare. For this purpose they are put into low cages without bars or roosts.

E. schœniculus, Lin. &c. *E. arundinacea* of some authors, and *E. passerina* of others, this last applying to the young. *Reed Bunting, Black-head Bunting*, or *Reed Sparrow.* Head black; body black and grey; outer tail feathers with a wedge-shaped white spot. Weight nearly five drachms and a half; length six inches; and alar extent nine inches. The female is a little less than the male, has the upper part of the head varied with rufous, shows less of black on the fore part of the neck, and wants the white ring on the head. It is found as far north as Denmark, is rare in Sweden, but not uncommon in the marshy and reedy districts

**Schœnicu-
lus.**

of the rest of Europe, and of southern Siberia. A brown variety occurs at the Cape of Good Hope, and a white one at Astrachan. Although these birds delight in fenny situations, they sometimes resort to the high grounds in rainy seasons. In spring they are seen by the sides of roads, and in August they feed in the corn fields, when they manifest a decided predilection for millet. In general they seek their food, like the other buntings, along the hedges and in cultivated spots, resorting to their marshes in the evening. They keep near the ground, and seldom perch except on the bushes; neither do they assemble in large flocks, scarcely more than four or five being seen together. They jerk their tail upwards and downwards as quickly as the wagtails, and with fully more animation. They seem to be abundantly vigilant; and when they descry a fowler, or other object of alarm, they make an incessant teasing cry, which is apt to frighten away game. In this country they are mostly stationary; but in France, and other parts of the Continent, they are partial migrants, arriving in Lorraine in April, and departing in autumn. It is somewhat extraordinary, that the economy of this bird should have so long remained in obscurity. Even modern authors assure us that it is a songster, warbling after sun-set, and describe its nest as suspended over the water, and fastened between two or three reeds. There can be no doubt, however, that the nest, as well as the song of the sedge warbler, have been mistaken for those of the present species, whose tune consists only of two notes, the first repeated three or four times, and the last single and more shrill, and this it continues to deliver, with small intervals, from the same spray for a considerable length of time when the female is sitting. The nest is most commonly placed on the ground near water, but sometimes in a bush, at a little distance from the ground, and at other times in high grass, reeds, sedges, or even in furze, considerably remote from any water; but in none of these situations is it fastened or suspended, as authors have related. It is composed of stalks of grass, or other dry vegetable substances, sometimes partly of moss, and lined with fine grass, to which long hair is occasionally added by way of finish. The eggs, which are four or five, are either of a dirty bluish-white, or purplish-brown, with numerous dark-coloured spots and veins much resembling those of the chaffinch.

Hortulana. *E. hortulana,* Lin. &c. *Ortolan Bunting,* or *Ortolan.* Quill feathers black, three outer feathers with whitish margins; tail feathers black, the two lateral ones externally white. In size the ortolan is somewhat smaller than the yellow-hammer, being in length six inches and a quarter, and stretching its wings to nine inches. Though not found in Great Britain, it occurs in various parts of Europe, as Italy, France, Germany, and even Sweden, migrating in spring and autumn, when great quantities of them are caught, and fattened for the market, being proverbially celebrated for the delicacy of their flavour. That they may more speedily acquire the requisite degree of plumpness, they are shut up in a room, from which the external light is excluded, but in which are placed a few lanterns, to enable them to see to run about, and pick up the millet and oats that are regularly strewed on the floor. Under this regimen they soon get so fat, that they would speedily die if not removed by the dealers. It is pretended, that those from the plains about Toulouse are superior to those of Italy. In some districts of the latter country where they are plentiful, as, for example,

in Lombardy, they are not only prepared for the table, but trained to sing; and Salerne observes, that there is considerable sweetness in their song. If allowed to associate, especially when young, with other birds, they adopt some of their notes. The female makes her nest in a low hedge, or a vine, or on the ground, especially among corn, composing it carelessly of bents, mixed with leaves and dry or green rushes. She lays four or five greyish eggs, with a very pale tinge of purple, and sprinkled with very small blackish spots. There are usually two broods in the year.

Oryzivora. *E. oryzivora,* Lin. &c. *Passerina oryzivora,* Vieil. *Rice bird,* or *Rice bunting,* Prov. *Bob Lincoln, Coquelde, White-backed Maize Thief,* &c. Brown above; black beneath; nape of the neck rufescent; tail feathers pointed. The female is nearly all rufous, with a change of brown on some parts. Length six inches eight lines. The colouring varies considerably with the season; and the species undergoes two moultings in the year. Native of America. Haunts moist meadows; sings on the ground; and rarely perches for a little on the branch of a bush or tree. Except in pairing time, these birds, which are of a very sociable disposition, live in numerous flocks, arriving in the centre of the United States about the end of April or the beginning of May, and remaining till September, when they commence their erratic excursion. In autumn these flocks are composed of males and females; but when they return in spring, the sexes separate, and form into distinct bands. The maturity of the rice regulates their movements towards the end of summer, the young advancing first, and then the old ones, along with the late broods, and the individuals which breed in the north of the United States, all being attracted to the regions in which their favourite food abounds. They travel during the night; and, as their incessant clamour gives intimation of their passage, they may be perceived in moonshine, although at a great elevation in the air. They rest during the day in the fields, feeding on the seeds of various plants indigenous to their native abodes. The syllable *tweet,* pronounced in an abrupt and shrill tone, is both their rallying cry previous to departure, and their note of uneasiness and alarm. Such of them as inhabit the island of Cuba quit it in August, when the rice crops are gathered in, for they seldom attack that grain when quite ripe, but whilst it is yet milky. They then resort to Georgia and Carolina, where the same grain is still immature, and, combining with those which arrive from the north, commit rapid and extensive havock among the crops. Montbeillard alleges that they winter as far north as Canada; but this has been found to be a mistake, as they all proceed southward on the approach of winter, some of them halting in the West Indies, and others in Mexico; nor are they ever seen in Canada before the fine weather sets in, namely, in the month of May. In this northern province they breed, and then depart in August for Georgia and Carolina, where their meagre bodies are rapidly fattened by the quantities of rice which they devour, and they are then reckoned a delicate morsel for the epicure. When in a state of confinement, they are wakeful at the stated periods of their journeys, and frequently utter their rallying cry during the night. Their usual movements seem to depend on the appearance of certain insects; for, after they arrive in Florida, about the beginning of April, they remain till the *May-fly,* and a species of locust on which they preferably feed, have been extir-

Ornitho-
logy.

pated. Although the males and females travel separately in the spring, Catesby is mistaken when he asserts that the autumnal birds are composed cnly of females, for Vieillot found them to consist of both sexes; but at that season of the year their attire is similar, so that an ordinary observer may be easily misled. The female builds her nest at the foot of tall herbage, forming the outside of some of the coarser grasses, and the inside of a large quantity of the finer sorts. She lays four or five bluish-white eggs, spotted with brown, and of the size of those of our common bunting. The note of the male is shrill, singularly varied, and characterized by abrupt transitions, as if expressive of anger or passion.

Cirlus.

E. cirlus, Lin. &c. *E. eleathorax*, Bechs. *Cirl Bunting*. Varied above; yellow beneath; and the two outer tail feathers marked with a white wedge-shaped spot. The cirl bunting is six inches and a half in length. It is a native of France, Italy, and other warm parts of Europe, frequenting newly-ploughed lands, feeding on grains, worms, and insects, which last it picks out of the ground. Though not uncommon in many parts of Cornwall and Devonshire, it was first recognised as appertaining to the British Fauna by Colonel Montagu, who met with it among flocks of yellow buntings and chaffinches. It generally builds in furze, or some low bush, the nest being composed of dry stalks, roots, and a little moss, and lined with long hair and fibrous roots. The eggs are four or five in number, cinereous white, with irregular, long, and short curved lines, frequently terminated with a spot at one end. The birds pair in April, and begin laying early in May. The females might, at a little distance, be readily mistaken for the same sex of the yellow bunting, but are obviously different when nearly compared. The note of this species is also similar to that of the yellow bunting, but shorter, less shrill, and the final part not drawn out to such a length. The female has only a gentle, plaintive chirrup. The principal food of the young birds appears to be insects, especially grasshoppers; and they will likewise eat various seeds, of which canary is the favourite. They are easily tamed, and will live about six years in confinement.

Nivalis.

E. nivalis, Lin. &c. The young have been described by Gmelin and Latham as distinct species, under the titles *Mustelina, Montana*, and *Glacialis*. *Snow Bunting, Sea Lark* of Ray, *Great Pied Mountain Finch*, or *Brambling*, of Willoughby, *Pied Mountain Finch*, and *Pied Chaffinch* of Albin. Prov. *Snow bird, Snow-flake, Snow-fowl*, and *Oat-fowl*. Quills white; primaries black outwardly; tail feathers black, with the exception of the three outer ones, which are white. In winter, the whole body of the snow bunting, with the exception of the back and middle coverts, often becomes white, or more or less so according to the climate; and in this state it has been sometimes mistaken for a white lark. It is somewhat larger than the chaffinch; weighs about one ounce and a quarter; measures nearly seven inches in length, and stretches its wings to ten or twelve inches. In summer it inhabits, in vast flocks, the north of Europe, Asia, and America, in the highest latitudes that have been explored; but in winter it often moves to some warmer regions. Large bands of this species issue from Lapland, and spread over Podolia to the Carpathian mountains, returning to their more northerly haunts in February and March. In America they advance no farther south than Virginia. Myriads of them have been seen on the ice on the coasts of Spitzbergen, and they are known to breed in Greenland,

Ornitho-
logy.

where the female nidificates in the fissures of the mountain rocks. The northern parts of this island abound with them; and they have been traced in various districts of Northumberland and Yorkshire, but scarcely, we believe, farther south. Many thousands of them winter in the Orkneys, and part of them breed in the Highlands of Scotland; but flocks also migrate from that quarter by the Orkneys, Shetland, and Faroe Islands, to the extreme north—a wonderful flight for such small birds. When they first arrive in the north of Scotland they are much emaciated, but soon get plump; and though they are distinct from the genuine ortolans, for which they have been mistaken, they may be termed the *ortolans of the north*; for they are caught by the Laplanders and others in great quantities, and are reckoned very delicate food. Their arrival in this island is supposed to betoken a severe winter, or heavy falls of snow. These birds do not perch, but continue on the ground, and run about like larks, which they also resemble in size, and in the length of their hind claws, and by some authors they have been accordingly ranged with that family; but, from the peculiar structure of the bill, they are now, with more propriety, referred to the tribe of buntings. They are very wakeful, sleeping little during the night, and in the months of June and July, beginning to hop about with the earliest dawn. The male sings feebly during the breeding season; his calling note is more agreeable, but that of alarm or anxiety is, on the contrary, loud and shrill. He sings from the middle of May till the end of July, and often during the night, which they always pass on the ground. The female builds in the crevices of rocks, constructing a nest of grass and feathers, lined with the hair or wool of the arctic fox, or other quadruped, and laying five reddish-white eggs, spotted with brown, and nearly spherical. The male assists in the duty of incubation.

TANAGRA. Lin. &c. TANAGER. TANGARA of Tem. &c.

Tanagra.

Bill short, strong, hard, triangular at the base, slightly depressed, more or less conical, much compressed at the point, which is bent, the upper mandible longer than the under, and notched, edges of the mandibles bent inwards, ridge elevated, under mandible straight, and somewhat inflated towards the middle; nostrils basal, lateral, rounded, and partly concealed by projecting feathers in front; tarsus of the same length with the middle toe; wings of moderate dimensions, with the second and third quills longest.

The tanagers have the habits of the sparrow tribes, and subsist on seeds, berries, and insects. Of upwards of fifty species which have been ascertained, most are conspicuous for the brilliancy of their plumage, and all are foreign. They frequent woods, and are generally shy; and some of them remarkable for their euphonious strains.

Violacea.

T. violacea, Lin. &c. *Golden Tanager, Golden Titmouse* of Edwards. Dark violet above, under parts and back of the head fine yellow, middle quills, and the lateral tail-feathers, with their inner webs, white. Common in Guiana, Surinam, and Brazil, where it frequents soil that has been brought into culture, near houses, subsisting principally on the berries of shrubs, but also making depredations on the rice-crops. Its hemispherical nest resembles that of the Pacarini, though of a less compact structure, and composed of reddish herbs. It is often kept in cages by the natives.

and cheerfully submits to confinement, especially if five or six of them are shut up together.

T. musica, Pipra musica, Lin. *Tuneful Tanager* or *Organist.* Dusky above, fulvous beneath; throat and cheeks black; top of the head, and nape of the neck, blue; forehead yellow. In the female the upper parts of the body are olive-green, the throat is cinereous, and the under parts are olivaceous. Native of St. Domingo. It is an active and amusing bird, four inches in length. Like the woodpeckers and creepers, it shifts itself round the branches of trees with such rapidity, that it is not easily shot. Vieillot confirmed to Sonnini the extraordinary fact, that its song is the complete octave, which it repeats, note after note, for a considerable time together. According to Dupratz, its strains are so varied, so melodious, and warbled in such a tender and impressive style, that those who have heard it are less captivated with the nightingale. As it sang, perched on an oak, near the house in which he lived, that traveller had an excellent opportunity of appreciating its musical talents.

T. cristata, Lin. *Crested Tanager.* Dusky, with an orange crest, and fulvous throat and rump. The crest is raised only when the bird is agitated. About the size of the house sparrow. Abounds in Guiana, but is not found in the woods, frequenting only the more open situations.

T. Mississippiensis, Lin. *Mississippi Tanager.* Entirely red, with the wings and tail darkest. Native of the borders of the Mississippi. Dupratz informs us, that this elegant species will collect a large quantity of maize against winter, and that it is so extremely tenacious of its hoard, that it will seldom stir from the spot, except to drink. This store, which has been known to equal a Parisian bushel, it carefully covers over with leaves. Its note is disagreeable, loud, and piercing.

PLOCEUS. Cuv. Tem. WEAVER.

Bill stout, hard, conical, sharp, inflected, and compressed at the point, without a notch, edges of the mandibles bent inwards; nostrils basal, near the surface of the bill, ovoid, and open; tarsus of the same length as the middle toe, the three anterior toes united at the base; the fourth quill the longest.

P. Philippinus, Cuv. Vieil. *Loxia Philippina,* Lin. &c. *Philippine Weaver* or *Philippine Grossbeak.* Brown above, whitish-yellow beneath, crown of the head and breast yellow, throat brown. Length, five inches and a quarter. The female has the upper parts brown, edged with rufous. Native of the Philippine Islands, India, and Abyssinia. It is said to feed on fire-flies. It forms a very curious nest, in the shape of a long cylinder, swelling out at the middle, composed of the fine fibres of leaves and grass, and fastened by the end to the branch of a high tree, which is, generally, the *Palmyra,* or Indian fig-tree. This nest has two or three compartments, the eggs being deposited in that which is in the globose portion in the middle, and the entrance being at the bottom of the long cylinder, and thus, in a great measure, concealed. The whole is generally suspended over water. The eggs, which resemble pearls, have the white part transparent, when boiled, and are reckoned particularly delicate by the lovers of nice eating. The Philippine weaver may be rendered so very tame, as to come and perch on its master's hand, or to fetch and carry, like a dog, at command.

In India, where it is very common, it is called *Baya.*

P. textor, Cuv. Vieil. *Oriolus textor,* Lin. Lath. &c. *Weaver,* or *Weaver Oriole.* Fulvous yellow, head brown, with a shade of golden; quill and tail-feathers blackish, edged with fulvous. The young do not acquire their full colouring till two years; and the shadings of the adult birds vary considerably, according to the season. The weaver is somewhat less than the starling, and is found in Senegal, and in the kingdoms of Congo and Cacongo. It utters a singular and cheerful note, and attempts to construct its curious nest, even in confinement.

P. Abyssinicus, Cuv. *P. Baglafecht,* Vieil. *Loxia Abyssinica,* Gmel. *Loxia Philippensis,* var. Lath. *Beglafecht, Abyssinian Weaver,* or *Abyssinian Grossbeak.* Yellow, with the crown, cheeks, throat, and breast, black; wings and tail brown. Size of the hawfinch, and a native of Abyssinia. This bird forms an ingenious nest, of a pyramidal shape, which is suspended from threads of branches, like the nest of some others of this tribe. The opening is on one side, facing the east, being opposite to that from which the rain proceeds; the cavity is separated in the middle, by a partition of half its height, up which the bird mounts perpendicularly, and then, descending on the other side, forms its nest in the further chamber. By these means the brood is defended from snakes, squirrels, monkeys, and other mischievous animals, besides being secured from the rains, which, in that country, sometimes last for five or six months together.

P. pensilis, Cuv. *P. Nelicourvi,* Vieil. *Loxia Pensilis,* Lin. Lath. *Pensile Weaver,* or *Pensile Grossbeak.* Green above, grey beneath; vent rufous, with the head and lower parts of the neck yellow; quills and tail-feathers black. Size of the common sparrow, above five inches in length, and a native of Madagascar. It constructs a hanging nest of straw and reeds, shaped like a bag, with an opening beneath, on one side of which is the true nest. The bird does not choose a new situation every year, but fastens a fresh nest to the end of the last, so that five may sometimes be seen hanging from one another; and no fewer than four or five hundred may be sometimes observed on a single tree. This species seldom produces more than three young at a brood.

P. socius, Cuv. *Loxia socia,* Lin. Lath. *Sociable Weaver, Sociable Grossbeak,* or *Republican.* Reddish brown above, yellowish beneath; capistrum black; tail short. About the size of a bullfinch. Inhabits the interior parts of the Cape of Good Hope, where it was first discovered by Mr. Paterson. These birds build their nests in a species of *Mimosa,* which grows to an uncommon size, and which, from its ample head, and strong wide spreading branches, is well calculated to admit and support their dwellings. The tallness and smoothness of its trunk are also a perfect defence against the invasions of the serpent and monkey tribes. In one tree discovered by Mr. Paterson, there could not be fewer than from 800 to 1000 nests under one general roof. Mr. Paterson calls it a *roof,* because it resembles that of a thatched house, and projects over the entrance of the nest below in a very singular manner. This species also constructs its nest on the acacia trees, and on the *Aloe dichotornes,* which grows to a very large size. Mr. Barrow notices one of them which had steps cut out on its sides, to enable a person to climb up to the nests.

LOXIA. CROSS-BILL.

Bill compressed, and the two mandibles so incurvated as to cross one another near the point, sometimes on one side, and sometimes on the other.

L. curvirostra, Lin. &c. *Curvirostra vulgaris*, Steph. *Cross-bill, Cross-beak, Shell-apple*, or *Sheld-apple*. Bill long, slightly curved, five lines broad at the base, of the length of the middle toe, and the crossed point of the lower mandible projecting beyond the upper edge of the bill. Body of a variable red; quills and tail-feathers brown; tail forked. The red of the male is varied with brown and green, and the female is olive-green, mixed with brown: but both sexes appear very different at different times of the year, and at different ages. Such, indeed, is their disposition to vary in the colours of their plumage, that, among a great number of individuals, scarcely any two can be found that are perfectly similar. The size of the cross-bill nearly corresponds to that of the lark; for it measures about six inches and a half, and weighs an ounce and a half.

This species is found in Europe, Asia, and America, affecting cold and mountainous latitudes, and traced as far north as Greenland. It breeds in Russia, Poland, Sweden, Germany, &c. and among the Alps and Pyrenees, whence it migrates, in vast flocks, into other countries, but apparently with no systematic regularity; for it appears in great numbers in some years, and scarcely at all in others. In 1791, these birds were seen in almost every part of England and Scotland, and remained till September. In various districts, they are more or less plentiful, in the fir and pine forests, from June to the latter end of the year, feeding on the seed by dexterously dividing the scales of the cones. They are sometimes met with in orchards in autumn, when they will readily divide an apple to get at the kernels. They have been observed to hold a pine-cone in one claw, like the parrot, and, when kept in a cage, they have all the actions of that bird, climbing, by means of their hooked bill, from the lower to the upper bars; and hence, by some, they have been called the *German Parrot*. Many of them are taken with bird-calls and limed twigs, and others by a horse-hair noose, fixed to a long fishing-rod; for so intent are they on picking out the seeds of the cone, that they will suffer themselves to be taken by the noose being put over their head. They breed even in the northern countries so early as the month of January, on the tops of the pine trees, making their hemispherical nest of twigs, and of the *Sphagnum arboreum*, two inches and a half thick, and lining it with the *Lichen floridus*. It is fixed to the bare branch by the resinous matter that exudes from the tree, and it is besmeared on the outside with the same substance, so as to be impermeable to the melted snow and the rain. In this warm and secure retreat the female deposits four or five greenish-grey eggs, spotted and streaked with red-brown, especially towards the thicker end. The cross-bills are of placid dispositions, and not intractable in confinement. Dr. Townson, when at Göttingen, kept several of them, which, in consequence of gentle treatment, soon became so tame, that he suffered them to be loose in his study, and to exhibit their proceedings without constraint, so that they would often come to his table, when he was writing, and carry off his pencils, little chip boxes, in which he occasionally kept insects, and other small articles, and would tear them to pieces almost instantly. When he gave them almonds in their shells, they quickly got at the kernels. Notwithstanding the ap-

parent awkwardness of the bill, therefore, it is admirably adapted to their mode of feeding; and, as they can bring the mandibles point to point, they can at any time pick up and eat the smallest seeds.

PYRRHULA. BULLFINCH.

Bill short, hard, conico-convex, thick, gibbous at the sides, compressed at the tip and towards the ridge; the upper mandible always bent, the under more or less so; nostrils basal, lateral, rounded, and most frequently concealed by feathers in front; the tarsus shorter than the middle toe, the anterior toes divided to their origin; wings short, the fourth quill the shortest; tail rather long, and either slightly rounded or square.

Most of the species belonging to this genus reside in the cold and temperate climates of the globe, subsist on hard grains and seeds, and undergo a double moulting.

P. enucleator, Temm. *Loxia enucleator*, Lin. &c. *Corythus enucleator*, Cuv. *Strobilifaga enucleator*, Vieil. *Pine Hard-beak, Pine Gross-beak*, or *Greatest Bullfinch*. Dull roseate, varied with brown and grey, with a double white line on the wings, and the tail-feathers entirely black. The length of the greatest bullfinch is upwards of seven inches, and its weight rather more than two ounces. Inhabits the northern regions of Europe, Asia, and America, but sometimes visits the more temperate latitudes during winter. It particularly affects the pine-forests of the north; and, in this island, it occurs only in the north of Scotland, where it is also supposed to breed. It is likewise found in the pine-forests of Siberia, Lapland, and the northern parts of Russia. In autumn, it is very common about St. Petersburgh, where it is caught for the use of the table. In Hudson's Bay it feeds not only on pine-cones, but on the buds of the willow. There, in May, it makes its nest of sticks and feathers, at a little distance from the ground, laying four white eggs, which are hatched in June. The young brood for some time remain of a dull blue. In spring the male sings sweetly, and during the night, but it ceases to be musical early in summer.

P. vulgaris, Cuv. Tem. *Loxia Pyrrhula*, Lin. &c. *Bullfinch*, or *Bullfinch Gross-beak*, Prov. *Alp, Nope, Pope, Monk, Thick-bill, Red-Hoop, Tony-Hoop, Coaly-hood*, &c. Cinereous; head black, wing-coverts and hind-part of the quills white. The cheeks, breast, and belly, are crimson, and the tail is black. The female is of a dirty brown, with the exception of the crown of the head, which is black, and of the rump which is white. The young birds, when first hatched, very much resemble the female, except that they have no black on the head, which, with the crimson on the breast of the male, appears about two months after they leave the nest. The bullfinch sometimes changes its plumage, and becomes quite black during confinement, especially when fed with hemp-seed. In the Leverian Museum there was an entirely white variety; and one nearly so was shot in Nov. 1801, by Mr. Spearman of Wharton. Nestlings perfectly white have been known to assume their ordinary hues when full grown. The usual length of this bird is scarcely six inches; but there is a race, or variety, somewhat larger, and much prized by the bird-fanciers. The species inhabits Europe and Siberia. In summer it affects woods, especially such as are situated in hilly districts; but in winter it approaches nearer to culti-

Ornitho-
logy.

vated places, and feeds on seeds, winter berries, &c.; in the spring it frequents orchards and gardens, where it hunts the worms and insects that are lodged in the tender buds of the trees. On perceiving a bird of prey, or other object of alarm, it plunges into the thickest bush within reach, and remains perfectly silent and tranquil till the cause of its apprehension has disappeared. Bullfinches are not gregarious, but may be generally seen in pairs or broods. They remain with us throughout the year. The nest is composed of small dry twigs, lined with fibrous roots, or hair, and placed in some thick bush, particularly in the hawthorn, either in woods or hedges. The female, aided by the male, begins building it about the latter end of April, or the beginning of May, and has, for the most part, two hatches in the year, each consisting of from three to six bluish-white blunt eggs, marked at the larger end with a band of brown and purple spots. When the female is seated on them, the male fetches her food, and shows her every mark of tender attachment. The native notes of the bullfinch are few, simple, and not very audible, but remarkable for softness; and, in confinement, especially if caught young, it may be taught a considerable variety of tunes. " I know a curious person," says the author of *Adonologie*, " who, having whistled some airs quite plain to a bullfinch, was agreeably surprised to hear the bird add such graceful turns, that the master could scarcely recognise his own music, and acknowledged that the scholar excelled him." It must, however, be admitted, that if the bird be ill directed, it acquires harsh strains with the same facility. Thus Buffon mentions the case of one which had never heard any person but carters whistle; and it whistled like them, and with all their strength and coarseness. It likewise learns to articulate words and sentences, and utters them with such delicacy of accent, that we might almost suppose it felt their emphasis. These birds are, besides, susceptible of attachment both strong and durable; for some of them, after having effected their escape, and passed a whole year in the woods, have been known to recognise the voice of their former mistress, and to return to forsake her no more; and others have pined, and even died of melancholy, on being removed from the object of their first affection. From their docility they may be trained to many amusing tricks, as to alight on their master's shoulder at a call, &c. There are even instances of two of them having been taught to sing in parts; and, according to Lewin, the females may be taught to pipe musical notes. The male will occasionally couple with the hen canary, and be very attentive to her during incubation; but he occasionally kills the young by piercing their skull with his bill.

FRINGILLA, Illig. Tem. GROSS-BEAK.

FRINGIL-
LA.

Bill short, stout, straight, and conical; upper mandible gibbous, a little inclined at the point; nostrils basal, round, placed near the forehead, and partially concealed by the feathers in front; tarsus shorter than the middle toe, and the front toes entirely divided; wings short, the third and fourth quills the longest.

Professor Illiger and M. Temminck have judiciously arranged, under this category, a great variety of species, which Cuvier, Vieillot, and others, had distributed under several genera, but without sufficient regard to the insensible gradations and common habits by which they are all so closely allied. They subsist on all sorts of seeds and grains, which they open with their bill, while they reject the husk; and they rarely

partake of insect food. They are very generally scattered over the face of the earth, but are most numerous in the warm and hot latitudes. Many of them are subject to a twofold moulting, in which case the male takes in winter the livery of the female.

Ornitho-
logy.

F. coccothraustes, Tem. *Loxia coccothraustes*, Lin. &c. *Coccothraustes vulgaris*, Cuv. and Vieil. *Grossbeak, Hawfinch, Haw-gross-beak, Hawfinch-gross-beak, or Cherry Finch*. Cinereous chesnut; a white line on the wings, middle-quill feathers rhomboid at the tip, lateral tail-feathers black at the base. The length of this species is nearly seven inches, its extent of wing ten inches eight lines, and its weight about two ounces. The female resembles the male, but her colours are less vivid; and the space between the eye and the bill is usually grey instead of black. In some individuals the head is wholly black, in others the whole upper portion of the body is of that colour, whilst others have been met with which are white, with the exception of the wings. The other subordinate shades are innumerable; for it is rare that any two exactly resemble one another.

Cocco-
thraustes.

These birds inhabit Europe, as far as Sweden northwards, and usually appear in this island in autumn, continuing till April, and flying about in small flocks of four or five; but they are not regular migrants with us, though they have sometimes been known to breed about Bath. They are much more plentiful in Germany, France, Italy, &c.; and they breed in Burgundy in April. To some of the districts of Lorraine they seem to be attracted in multitudes, by the profusion of the cherry-trees, for they feed on the pips of that fruit with great voracity. They are likewise partial to juniper berries, pine cones, beech-mast, the kernel of the almond, walnut, &c. breaking the hardest of them with their bill as easily as other birds break the seed of hemp. The nest, which is commonly placed in the fork of a tree or bush, about ten or twelve feet from the surface of the ground, is of a hemispherical form, composed externally of dried fibres, intermixed with lichens, and lined with finer materials, as hair or wool. The eggs, which vary from three to five, are roundish, and of a bluish-green tinge, spotted with olive-brown, and a few irregular black markings. The young are fed with insects, chrysalids, and other soft nutritious matters. The note of the male is shrill, and, according to some, rather grating: but Colonel Montagu acquaints us, that he has heard it sing pleasantly in low plaintive notes, even in winter, when the weather happened to be unusually warm. In summer the gross-beaks chiefly haunt the woods and mountains; but in winter they descend into the plains, and approach houses. In most countries they are partial migrants. When about to be robbed of their offspring, they make a vigorous defence, and bite fiercely. In some parts of France, they are caught for the table; but they are said to be dry and unsavoury.

F. chloris, Tem. *Coccothraustes chloris*, Cuv. *Loxia chloris*, Lin. &c. *Green Gross-beak, Green Finch*, Prov. *Green Linnet*. Yellowish-green, with the primary quills in front, and the four lateral tail-feathers, yellow. The bill thick and whitish; the head and back yellowish-green; edges of the feathers greyish, inclining to ash-colour, about the sides of the head and neck; rump and breast yellow; tail slightly forked. The plumage of the female is less bright, inclining to brown and olivaceous. An albino, or white variety, sometimes occurs. Rather larger than the housesparrow; length six inches and a half, expanse of

Chloris.

wing nine inches, weight nearly eight drachms. Inhabits Europe and Kamtschatka, and is very common in most parts of this country; in summer frequenting woods, orchards, and gardens, or haunting the highways, feeding on seeds and grain, becoming gregarious in winter, and associating with chaffinches and yellowhammers; but in severe cold it migrates from particular districts. It is rather a late breeder. The nest is composed of small dry twigs, bents, and moss, interwoven with wool, and lined with hair and feathers. It is commonly placed in ivy that surrounds a tree, or in some hedge or low bush. The female lays from four to six greenish-white eggs, with detached spots of brown and purple. She is such a close sitter, that she may sometimes be caught on the nest; and during incubation the male is very attentive in fetching her food. This species readily intermingles with the canary. Its native song is trifling, but in confinement it will catch the notes of other birds. It is, besides, easily tamed, especially if held on one's fingers in the dark, and treated with gentleness, when it may be taught various little tricks and manœuvres; but if much exposed to the sun, it is apt to become blind.

Petronia.

F. petronia, Tem. Lin. &c. *Coccothraustes petronia*, Cuv. *Ring-Finch, Ring-Sparrow, Foolish, Speckled,* and *White-tailed Sparrow;* for, with its accidental varieties, it includes *F. leucura, stulta,* and *Bononiensis* of Gmelin and Latham. Grey, with white supercilia, luteous throat, and a white spot towards the tip of the exterior tail-feathers. Length nearly six inches. It abounds most in Germany, but is also found in a large portion of Europe, especially in its southern regions. It has the figure and some of the manners of the common sparrow; but it usually resides in woods, and often falls a sacrifice to severe cold in winter. It nestles in the holes of trees, and has but one hatch in the year, consisting of four or five brown eggs, speckled with white. As soon as the young have acquired sufficient strength to follow their parents, the families unite in flocks, and are inseparable till spring, when each male selects his partner. They are said to be migratory in the northern, but stationary in the southern countries.

Domestica.

F. domestica, Lin. &c. *Pyrgita domestica*, Cuv. *Domestic,* or *House-Sparrow,* or *House-Finch.* Quill and tail-feathers fuscous, body black and grey, and a single white band on the wings. The ordinary weight of the house-sparrow is about seven drachms, its length nearly six inches, and its extent of wing eight inches eight lines. It is stationary in Europe, Asia, and Africa, supporting alike the heat of Egypt and the cold of Siberia; but in the latter country not advancing beyond the line of cultivated crops. It is, indeed, never found in desert wastes, or remote from the dwellings of man, on the produce of whose labours it seems principally to subsist, residing in towns and villages, about granaries, barns, court-yards, pigeon-houses, wherever, in short, grain happens to be accumulated or scattered. So decided, too, is its partiality for cherries, that it is with difficulty scared from them. Buffon, Sonnini, and others, have loudly inveighed against the extent of their depredations; and, in some parts of Germany they are a proscribed race; but Mr. Bradley also reminds us that they are great consumers of insects; for he ascertained that the parents carried to the nest forty caterpillars in the space of an hour; so that, on the supposition of their entering the nest only during twelve hours each day, they would occasion a daily destruction of 480 caterpillars,

4

or 3360 in a week. But their usefulness is not limited to this circumstance alone, for they likewise feed their young with butterflies and other winged insects, each of which, if not dispatched in this manner, would be the parent of hundreds of caterpillars. Though familiar with the haunts of human society, they are very crafty, and generally avoid, with great cunning, the traps and snares that are set for them in summer; but they are more easily caught in the autumn and winter by a batfowl net, when they collect in great numbers on trees; whereas, in summer, they seldom or never congregate. Their flight is short and laborious; and they will rise at once, with noise, and in a flurry, nor ascend to any considerable elevation. They have no native song; and, for the most part, only a disagreeable chirp; but one may discriminate their calls of affection and alarm; and they are capable, when in confinement, of acquiring the notes of the linnet, and of some other birds within hearing. They are, for the most part, easily domesticated, but are less affectionate to their keepers than the canaries, and several other small birds. In autumn they are often gregarious, but more steadily so in winter. The males are very ardent in courtship, and fight obstinately for the possession of their mates. Like the wren and titmouse, the sparrow carefully secures for itself a nest in which it may roost during the winter, and from which, in very severe cold, it sometimes does not go out, even during the day. The female constructs her breeding nest conformably to the place which she selects for incubation, as in the hole of a wall, in thatch, under the eaves or gutters of a house, or in the nest of a martin, or other bird, and especially in the bottom of that of a rook. In some of these cases, it is rather carelessly made up of hay and feathers; but, when placed on the top of a tree, it is usually as large as a man's head, with a cover to keep off the rain, composed chiefly of hay and straw, and warmly lined with feathers and fragments of thread, or worsted, bits of cloth, or any refuse material of that description that can be picked up about houses. If the nest should be destroyed, another is reared in the course of twenty-four hours. The female lays from four to six or eight greenish-white eggs, thickly dotted with dusky and cinereous, and usually breeds thrice in the year, which accounts for the great multiplication of the species. In some parts of France, particularly in the departments of the Meurthe, the Meuse, and the Vosges, the people, both in the towns and in the country, are accustomed to hang on the outside of their houses earthen pots, in which the sparrows breed, and which supply the family with young ones for the table. The kings of Persia have these birds trained to hunt the butterfly. It is worthy of remark, that the white variety is persecuted even by its own species; and that, from its conspicuous appearance, it is very liable to be devoured by birds of prey. Gérardin mentions an instance of a tame sparrow which lived eighteen years, and died in consequence of the rigorous cold of 1788; but, near the close of its life, it exhibited every symptom of age, had grown grey, became fretful, and bit with great keenness. Mr. Donovan mentions having in his possession a specimen of the house sparrow, in which all the fore toes are double; so that each foot is furnished with six toes in front; and the back toe, which is single, as usual, on one side, is treble on the other, except which there is no material appearance of distortion, every toe being distinctly formed, and armed with its proper claw.

F. montana, Lin. &c. *Pyrgita montana*, Cuv. *Loxia Montana, Hamburgia*, Gmel. *Tree,* or *Mountain Finch, Tree* or

Mountain Sparrow, Hamburgh Gross-beak, Hamburgh Tree Creeper, &c. Quill and tail-feathers fuscous, body black and grey, with a double white band on the wings. This species is by no means so plentiful in Yorkshire, Lancashire, and Lincolnshire, as has been represented; every house sparrow which happened to breed in a tree having been confounded with it. In this island it has not been observed farther north than the counties just mentioned; but it is a native of North America, and not uncommon in some of the temperate parts of Europe, and even Siberia. It is considerably inferior in size to the preceding, though the difference in weight is only about a drachm. Its note is similar to that of the house sparrow, but somewhat more shrill. The nest, which is composed of hay, feathers, horse hair, &c. is made in holes and cavities of trees, and never among the branches, nor in buildings. The eggs are from five to seven, of a cinereous white, minutely dotted and speckled with reddish and ashen spots.

The tree sparrow is a lively active little bird; and when it alights on the ground, or on a bough, it has a variety of motions, whirling about, and jerking its tail. The young may be reared in a cage; but they are not remarkable either for their musical talents or their docility. According to Frisch, it will breed with the canary, and the mongrel offspring may have contributed to perplex the history of the genuine lineage.

Serinus.

F. serinus, Lin. &c. *Carduelis serinus*, Cuv. *Serin Finch.* Greenish; the lower mandible whitish; sides of the back spotted with fuscous, and a yellow band on the wings. Length four inches eight lines. The female is a little more slender than the male, but her plumage is nearly similar. Native of Spain, Italy, Austria, Turkey, the south of France, &c. According to Scopoli, who ranges it with the *Loxiæ*, it is gregarious in the spring, frequenting orchards, often taking sudden flights upwards, and, after fluttering and warbling in the air for some time, alighting, with expanded wings, nearly on the same spot whence it rose. It eats a great variety of small seeds, but is partial to those of hemp and cabbage. It nestles in osiers planted on the banks of rivers, in fruit trees, beeches, oaks, &c. employing chiefly hair and moss, and lays four or five white eggs, marked at the larger end with a ring of brown and reddish spots. Its note is strong and varied; and it willingly borrows graces from the air of the goldfinch, to which it appears to be much attached.

Cœlebs.

F. cœlebs, Lin. &c. *Chaffinch*, Prov. *Beech-Finch, Horse-Finch, White-Linnet, Pink, Twink, Shilfa, Scobby, Skelly,* and *Shell-Apple.* Quills white on each side; the three first purely so; the two outer tail-feathers obliquely white. The very various markings of this well-known bird, which also change considerably according to the season, need not to be here detailed. The female is dull-green above, has the breast and belly yellow, wants the red on the breast and other parts, and is less sprightly in her attire. A white, and other varieties, sometimes occur; and, even among those of the same district considerable differences may sometimes be remarked.

The chaffinch is rather less than the house sparrow, and measures six inches four lines in length, and nine inches ten lines in extent of wing. It is generally spread over Europe, from Sweden to Gibraltar, and has been also observed on the coast of Africa, and in some parts of Asia. With us, most of the species, at least, continue all the year round; but the females migrate from Sweden to Holland in autumn, leaving the males behind them, and return to them in the spring. Mr.

White observes, that great flocks of chaffinches, consisting mostly of females, appear in the neighbourhood of Selborne about Christmas. In France, and possibly in various other countries, they appear to be partial migrants. They begin their short and frequently repeated carol early in spring, and continue it till the summer solstice, after which they only chirp. In confinement they are capable of acquiring the notes of the canary, nightingale, &c. and even the articulation of a few words; and since it has been discovered that they sing most and in greatest perfection, when blind, there are found individuals inhuman enough to deprive them of sight. According to Frisch, the prelude of the chaffinch's song is composed of three similar notes, or strokes, the quaver of seven different notes descending, and the close of two notes; and Lottinger has remarked, that, in anger, its air is simple and shrill; in fear, plaintive, short, and often repeated; and in joy, lively, and terminating with a sort of burden. Both sexes have a monotonous call-note, which has been represented by *twink* and *pink.* The male likewise emits a rough rattling sound during rain. These birds chiefly subsist on small seeds, of various kinds, especially in the winter; but they also eat insects and their larvæ, with which they likewise feed their young. They manifest great dexterity in removing the husk from wheat, oats, &c. before devouring the mealy part. From their sprightly manner, incessant motions, and elegant plumage, has been deduced the proverbial expression, *as gay as a chaffinch.* They more frequently sit squatted than perched, and never walk hopping, but trip lightly along the ground, and are constantly busy in picking up something. Their flight is unequal; and, when their nest is attacked, they hover about, screaming. The males frequently maintain obstinate combats for their mates, and fight till one of them is vanquished, and compelled to give way. The nest is nicely composed of green moss, curiously mixed with lichens, interwoven with wool, or the fibres of roots, and lined with feathers, hair, and spiders' webs. It is often placed against the side of a tree, particularly in ivy, or in some forked branch of a bush; and not uncommonly in our orchards and gardens, or apple-trees, overgrown with moss and lichens, and so assimilated to the surrounding materials and colour as not to be readily perceived. The male is very assiduous in his attendance during hatching time, seldom straying far from the nest, and then only to procure food. The eggs are four or five, of a greenish-blue, or dirty-white, tinged with purple, and marked with coffee-coloured streaks and spots, particularly at the larger end. Birds of this species, destined for confinement, should be taken from the nest, for the old ones will scarcely submit to captivity.

Montifrin-gilla.

F. montifringilla, Lin. &c. including the *Lulensis* of Gmelin. *Mountain Finch, Bramble, Brambling,* or *Kate.* Black above, with the feathers margined with rufous; under parts and vent white; throat and breast rufescent, lateral tail-feathers blackish, and externally margined with white. The female is somewhat less bright in the colouring, and smaller in dimensions, than the male; the total length of the latter is six inches and a half; its alar expansion ten inches, and its weight about an ounce. It inhabits Europe and Asia, breeding in the beech and pine forests of the northern regions. Edwards observed some that were brought from Hudson's Bay, under the name of *Snow-Birds;* and people who traded to that country assured him that they were the first birds which appeared every year on the return of spring, before even the snows were melted. In some years, they arrive in the temperate regions of Europe in immense flocks. The time of their passage is the autumn and winter, when they frequently return again in eight or ten days, but sometimes remain till spring. During their stay, they consort with the chaffinches; and, like the latter, court concealment in the thick foliage. In the winter of 1765, more than six hundred dozen of these birds were killed every night in the pine forests situated four or five leagues from Sarbourg, in Lorraine. The people were not at pains to shoot them, but knocked them down with switches; and, although this massacre lasted the whole winter, the congregated mass was scarcely perceptibly thinned. But no where are they known to appear so regularly as in the forests of Weissenburg, which are plentifully stocked with beeches, and consequently afford abundance of mast, of which they are so fond that they eat it day and night. They also live on all sorts of small seeds. When they arrive from the north, they are far from shy, and allow persons to come near them. They fly close together, and alight and rise in the same compact body. When they feed in the fields, they are observed to perform the same manœuvres as the pigeons. When the winter is severe, they are sometimes seen in large flocks on the coast of Kent and Sussex, and occasionally so exhausted as to suffer themselves to be taken up. They are also found in the interior parts of the kingdom during that season consorting with chaffinches and yellowhammers; and, in hard winters, they frequently resort to the neighbourhood of Edinburgh. Their song is far from being so pleasing as that of the chaffinch, and has been compared to the screech of the owl, and the mewing of a cat. They have two cries, one a sort of chirping, and the other, which they utter when they sit on the ground, resembles that of the stone-chat, but is neither so strong nor so clear. Yet they are susceptible of the same degree of instruction; and, when kept near another bird, whose warble is more agreeable, their song is gradually mellowed, and more or less assimilated to that which they hear. About the end of April they begin to build their nest, pretty far up in the more branchy pines, composing it, outwardly, of hypna and long mosses, and inwardly of hair, wool, and feathers. The female lays four or five whitish eggs, spotted with yellowish; and the young may be seen flitting from branch to branch, about the end of May. The flesh, though eatable, is frequently bitter, owing, it is supposed, to their feeding on the seeds of the broom. According to Olina, the brambling lives about five years.

Cannabina. *F. cannabina*, Lin. &c. including the *Linota* of Gmelin. *Common*, or *Brown Linnet, Grey Linnet, Greater Redpole, Greater Redpole Finch, Red-headed Linnet*, or *Red-breasted Linnet*. The markings of this species so nearly approach to those of the *Montium*, that we gladly adopt the specific definition of Temminck, especially as the colourings of both species are liable to great varieties. Bill strong and blackish, of the breadth of the forehead; throat whitish, marked in the middle with some brown spots. Length five inches one line; alar extent eight inches eight lines. This species inhabits Europe and America, and is very partial to vineyards. In many parts they haunt the sea-shore, and, in the breeding season, often resort to vineyards, furzy commons, &c. They fly in flocks during the autumn and winter, when many of them are caught in particular countries. They fly very crowded, alight and rise

together, perch on the same trees, and, about the beginning of spring, they all chant at once. They lodge, during the night, in oaks and elms, whose leaves, though withered, have not yet fallen. They are likewise seen on the linden and poplars, on the buds of which they feed, as well as on various small seeds, as of flax, hemp, thistles, rape, raddish, millet, plantain, poppy, &c. Their walking is a sort of hop, but their flight is continuous and uniform. They sometimes place the nest on the ground, sometimes between the vine props, or in the vine itself, in a juniper, furze, or gooseberry bush, in hazel trees, hedges, copses, &c. It is composed outwardly of small fibrous roots and dried leaves, interwoven with wool, and lined with feathers, hair, and a large quantity of wool. The number of eggs usually varies from four to six, and they are of a dirty or bluish-white, with numerous reddish-brown, or flesh-coloured specks, and short lines. For the most part there are two broods, the first of which is hatched in May; but, if the nest is destroyed, the female will continue breeding till August. During incubation, the male serenades his partner with his sweeter notes; but he sounds alarm by a different call, and expresses manifest uneasiness when she is threatened by invaders, flying to a little distance, and then returning with apparent anxiety and agitation: they then both fly off, and do not return for about an hour, unless the hatching is on the point of taking place, when their absence is shortened. The female is destitute of song, and even the adult males, taken out of the nest, seem not to profit by instruction, the male nestlings alone being susceptible of musical education. They are very familiar, and so easily tamed as to appear quite cheerful five minutes after they are taken. When brought up under the nightingale, goldfinch, wood lark, &c. they acquire the respective songs of those birds. Nay, they may be taught to articulate a few words with distinctness, and are extremely playful and caressing, evincing the strongest attachment to those who have the charge of them, and sometimes recognising them even by the sound of their step in an adjoining room. An instance is recorded by Gérardin of one which possessed these winning properties in an eminent degree, and which was accidentally drowned at the age of sixteen.

F. montium, Lin. &c. *Mountain Linnet, Twite*, or Montium. *Twite Finch*. The bill forming a complete triangle, the throat rufous, without any spot, and the legs black. The top of the head and rump are red. It is larger than the preceding, with which it occasionally associates. It is a native of Europe, and builds in hilly districts, making its nest of moss and roots of plants, mixed with heath, and lined with finer headed and fibrous roots. The eggs are bluish-white, faintly spotted with purplish-red at the larger end. The note of these birds is short, trifling, and unmusical; and the syllable *twite*, which they seem frequently to repeat, has given rise to their popular name. In the south of England, large flights of them may be observed during the winter, feeding on such plants as remain and ripen their seeds, on the sea-walls and marshes; and, as they come from the French coast, they are commonly called *French Linnets*. The plumage of the female is dull brown.

F. spinus, Lin. &c. *Siskin*, or *Aberdevine*. Fuscous, Spinus. with yellowish bill; feathers of the breast tipped with rose colour; tail slightly forked. Length nearly five inches. Inhabits many parts of Europe, and is plentiful in the western and southern parts of Russia, but is not met with in the Uralian chain, nor in Siberia.

Ornitho-
logy.

One of the varieties is said to reside in Silesia, and another in South America. Though migratory in most places, it seems to observe no regular periods; and it is sometimes seen in large, and at other times in very small flocks. According to some writers, the great flights happen only once in the course of three or four years. Kramer informs us, that in the forests bordering on the Danube, thousands of young siskins are frequently observed that have not dropped their first feathers, and that yet it is rare to meet with one of their nests. But this need the less to surprise us, when we consider that they are birds of elevated flight, and accustomed to breed on the tops of pines and firs, in mountainous situations. The nest is placed in the fork of a tree, and composed of dry bents, mixed with leaves, and amply lined with feathers. The female lays from three to five eggs, of a greyish-white, dotted with purple brown. This species rarely approaches houses or villages, living in woods, and among juniper bushes, in summer, and in alder groves in winter, associating with the lesser redpole, and subsisting on the catkins of the alder, the seeds of the hop, &c. In Germany it is sufficiently numerous to injure the hop gardens, and in France it nips the blossoms of apple trees. In some parts of the south of England it is called the *barley bird*, from its appearing when that grain is sown. Its song, though not so loud and powerful as that of the canary, is pleasing, and considerably varied. Though taken when full grown, the siskin is familiar, cheerful, and docile in captivity, and will imitate the notes of other birds, even to the chirping of a sparrow. Like the goldfinch, it may be easily taught to draw up its little bucket with water or food, to eat from the hand, to alight on a person, on the ringing of a bell, &c. It drinks frequently, and takes pleasure in sprinkling water over its feathers. The male breeds freely with the hen canary, and is assiduous in his attentions to her, carrying and arranging the materials of the nest, and, during incubation, regularly supplying her with food. Such, indeed, is the benignity of temper manifested by the species, that they not only abstain from quarrelling with other birds, in a volery, but even fetch food to such of them as have become the objects of their intimacy.

Linaria.

F. linaria, Lin. &c. *Linaria borealis*, Vieil. including the *Flavirostris* of the *Fauna Suecica*, which is the young before the second moulting. *Lesser Redpole, Lesser Red-headed Linnet*, or *Lesser Redpole Finch*. Bill a lengthened cone, compressed, slender, and very sharp pointed, throat black. Length five inches, weight about two drachms and a half. Native of the northern and temperate regions of Europe, Asia, and North America, preferably haunting alder groves, breeding as far north as Greenland, placing their nest in the trunk of an alder, or between the branches of a bush, and composing it of three layers, the first consisting of bents and a few small sticks, the second of feathers and moss, and the third of the down of the cotton grass, in which last the female deposits four or five eggs of a bluish-white, thickly sprinkled with reddish spots, especially at the larger end. In this country these birds are known to breed in Scotland, Wales, and the north of England. Mr. Pennant found one of their nests on an alder stump. " The bird," he adds, " was so tenacious of her nest, as to suffer us to take her off with our hand, and we found after we released her, she would not forsake it." It was lined with hair. Lewin alludes to another which was lined with the down of thistles. Such diversities in the structure of the nest, and in-

stances of which might be greatly multiplied, would indicate that, in the process of forming them, birds are not impelled by blind undeviating instinct.

The lesser redpoles quit the arctic regions in October, and do not re-appear till April; yet they seldom migrate far southward; for they are not found in the south of France, except during very severe winters; nor in America do they pass beyond Pennsylvania, not even visiting that province, till the winter has fairly set in, and all the ground is covered with snow, whence their American name of *snow-bird*, which, however, has been vaguely applied to all the small birds which reside in the central states only in winter. They are partial to the catkins of the alder, and, when picking them, hang, with their back downwards, like the titmice, and may then be easily taken by means of a twig fastened at the end of a long pole, and smeared with bird-lime. They feed likewise on the buds of the oak, and on the seed of bromegrass, centaury, flixweed, &c. They run with great vivacity along the branches of birches, poplars, oaks, &c. or cling to them with their backs downwards. In winter, when they are assembled in flocks, many are caught in the neighbourhood of London, under the denomination of *storm redpoles*. Their note is feeble and plaintive, and during flight, or when hunting for food, they keep up an incessant chattering.

Carduelis.

F. carduelis, Lin. &c. *Carduelis vulgaris*, Cuv. *Goldfinch, Gold Spink*, or *Thistle Finch*. Quills in front yellow, the outer one immaculate; the two outer tail-feathers white in the middle, and the rest of the same colour at the tip. The goldfinch is rather less than the chaffinch, being five inches three lines in length, and nine inches in stretch of wing. It is plentiful in various parts of Europe; but less so in Asia and Africa. It flies low, but with an evenly continued motion, and not, like the sparrow, by jerks and bounds. It is active and laborious; gentle and affectionate to those of its own species, but given to quarrel with canaries and linnets. The species begin to congregate in autumn, when they are caught among the birds of passage that pillage gardens. In winter they fly in numerous flocks, so that six or eight may be killed at a shot. They subsist on the seeds of the thistle, hemp, wild succory, poppy, burdock, and capitated plants, and, when young, on those of groundsel, chickweed, &c. That they also eat insects and caterpillars, as has been alleged, appears more doubtful; and Vieillot is of opinion that they are entirely granivorous. In winter they approach the highways in quest of food, and shake off the snow, to obtain the seeds of plants. In Provence they lodge, in great numbers, among the almond trees; and, when the cold is intense, they seek the cover of thick bushes, and always in the vicinity of their appropriate food. The males begin their warble early in March; and their music is in greatest perfection in May, when, perched on the top of some moderately-sized tree, they pour out their lay at day-break, and are vocal till sunset. They continue in song during the whole of the genial season, and even in winter, when kept in apartments in which they enjoy the temperature of spring. Though their native notes are seldom quite pure in a cage, Aldrovandus reckons it the second among the singing birds; but the Hon. Daines Barrington assigns to it only the sixth place; and both he and Salerne have remarked, that it acquires the song of the wren with more readiness than that of any other bird. Their nest excels even that of the chaffinch in neatness and compactness, and is placed, sometimes in copses, bushes, or hedges, but more commonly in ever-

Ornitho-
logy.

green or fruit trees, and on the weakest branches, which vibrate most. It is constructed of bents, fibrous roots, moss, or lichens, interwoven with wool, and lined with wool and hair, covered with thistle-down, willow-cotton, or other delicately soft substances. The female begins to lay about the middle of May, and has two or three broods in the season. Each hatch consists of three, four, five, or, at most, of six eggs, of a bluish-white, with a few small reddish-brown spots, chiefly at the larger end. On these the mother sits with such ardour of attachment, that, when they are on the point of being hatched, she patiently encounters wind and heavy rain, and will rather be bruised by hail-stones than desert her charge. The male watches over her, when she is engaged in hatching and rearing the common offspring. The goldfinch may be induced to unite with the canary and other congenerous birds; but this intermixture succeeds best between the cock goldfinch and the hen canary, the issue resembling the male parent in the shape of the bill, and in the colours of the head and wings, and the female in the rest of the body. Though apparently more vigorous than their progenitors, it is doubtful if these hybrids are productive. In confinement, the goldfinch has often been known to live sixteen or eighteen years. Gesner saw one at Mentz, which had attained to twenty-three; but the people of the house were obliged once a-week to scrape its nails and bill, that it might eat, drink, and sit on its bar. It had subsisted principally on poppy seeds; it was incapable of flying, and all its feathers had become white. M. Gérardin mentions, that he saw an individual of this species, which a friend of his had kept during twenty years, during the last of which it was quite blind; and such was the alteration which confinement and old age had produced on its plumage, that all the red portions had become completely black, and the yellow white. It has been remarked, that caged goldfinches are liable to epilepsy, which seems to be frequently induced by feeding too exclusively on hemp-seed; they are likewise subject to inflammation of the bowels, and to be seriously, and sometimes fatally, affected by moulting. They are readily tamed after being caught, and are remarkable for their extreme docility, and the attention which they pay to instructions. It requires, for example, very little trouble to teach them to perform several movements with accuracy, to fire a cracker, and to draw up small cups containing their food and drink. For this last purpose, they must have fastened round them a small belt of soft leather, two lines broad, with four holes, through which the feet and wings are passed; and the ends, joining under the belly, are to be held by a ring, which supports the chain and cup. Some years ago, the Sieur Roman exhibited in this country the wonderful performances of his goldfinches, linnets, and canary birds. One appeared dead, and was held up by the tail or claw without indicating any signs of life; a second stood on its head, with its claws in the air; a third imitated a Dutch milk-maid going to market, with pails on its shoulders; a fourth mimicked a Venetian girl looking out at a window; a fifth appeared as a soldier, and mounted guard as a sentinel; a sixth was a cannonier, with a cap on its head, a firelock on its shoulder, and a match in its claw, with which it discharged a small cannon; it also acted as if it had been wounded, and, after being wheeled in a barrow, as to the hospital, it flew away before the company; a seventh turned a kind of wind-mill; and the last stood in the midst of some fire-works, which were discharged all around it,

without its betraying the least sign of apprehension. In solitude, the goldfinch delights to view its image in a mirror, fancying possibly that it sees another of its own species; and it will pick up hemp-seed, grain by grain, and advance to eat it at the mirror, from the conviction, we may presume, that it is thus feeding in company.

C. canaria, Lin. &c. *Canary Bird,* or *Canary Finch.* Beak and body whitish-yellow; quills and tail feathers green. In its wild state, as observed by Labillardière and others, it exhibits a brown hue, mixed with various others; and its plumage is not so attractive as it becomes in confinement. In consequence of long domestication, it has, like the dog, assumed an almost endless series of varieties, twenty-nine of the principal of which are indicated by Buffon. The colours of the female are of a more feeble tint than those of the male. This bird is somewhat longer than the siskin, measuring about five inches and a half. In its native condition it principally occurs in the Canary islands, frequenting damp places; and at Palma, Fayal, Cape Verd, and Madeira. From the Canary islands they appear to have been brought into Europe about the beginning of the fourteenth century, and have been generally diffused over almost every civilized country, owing to the powerful attractions of their song, combined with the gracefulness and tenderness of their manners, and their great docility. The interesting exhibition of their family economy has been transferred from the fields to the habitations of man; and such a complete revolution have their habits undergone, that the wild and domestic sorts do not sexually unite. Their voice is better adapted to a chamber than that of the nightingale, and is also more pliable to instruction; for they will learn various notes and airs, and even the articulation of words. When imported from their native abodes they are often silent, or have but an indifferent song; and the fine warble to which our ears are so familiar, is usually modelled on that of the tit-lark or of the nightingale. Most of those from the Tyrol have been educated under parents, whose progenitors were instructed by a nightingale; but our English bred Canary birds have more of the tit-lark's notes. Entire treatises have been written on the mode of rearing them; and to these we must beg leave to refer the curious reader, particularly to that by Hervieux, and to the article *Serin,* in the *Nouveau Dictionnaire d'Histoire Naturelle.* Great numbers of these birds are still nursed and disciplined in the Tyrol; and four men used to fetch annually from that country to England about sixteen hundred of them, which cost about £20 on the spot; and, though they carried them a thousand miles on their backs, they could afford to sell them at five shillings a-piece. Some of the families will breed four or five times in the year, and lay from four to six eggs at each hatch. The male assists in collecting and arranging the materials of the nest, provides food for the young, and chants his lively and impassioned strains. Seeds of various kinds, as of canary-grass, hemp, rape, oats, with chickweed, &c. form their principal food; and they are very fond of sugar. They will readily propagate with some of their congeners; and the progeny, in some cases, is fertile. As a proof of their teachable disposition, we may mention that some of them have been trained at a given signal to perch on the head of a cat, to sing aloud in that situation, and to receive a kiss from their natural enemy. Often have their enlivening strains, caressing manners, and little playful antics, soothed the hours of

Ornitho-
logy.

Canaria.

Cardinalis.

languor and disease, and beguiled the solitude of the prison and the cloister. Under careful management they will live fifteen or sixteen years; but they are liable to various disorders, part of which have probably been entailed on them by habits of confinement and too luxurious fare.

F. cardinalis, Coccothraustes cardinalis, Cuv. and Vieil. *Loxia cardinalis,* Lin. *Cardinal Gross-beak, Red Gross-beak* of Albin. Crest red; capistrum black; bill and feet red; rest of the plumage fine red, but not so bright on the quills and tail. Female almost entirely of a reddish-brown; length about eight inches. It is met with in several parts of North America, appearing in New York and the Jerseys about the beginning of April, frequenting the Magnolia swamps in summer, and departing in the autumn towards Carolina. In spring, and during part of summer, it sits on the tops of the highest trees, and makes the forest echo with the melody of its song, which has procured for it in some districts the name of *nightingale.* In autumn, it lays up its winter store of maize and buck wheat, of both of which it is very fond. In its retreat has been found nearly a bushel of the former grain, artfully covered with leaves and twigs, and only a small hole left for the entrance of the bird. In confinement it may be fed on millet, and it is very greedy of hemp-seed, but this last is apt to shorten its days. Being easily tamed, it readily sings, and, with a short interval, will continue its music during the greater part of the year.

Regia.

F. regia, Emberiza regia, Lin. and Lath. *Vidua regia,* Cuv. *Shaft-tailed Finch, Shaft-tailed Widow,* or *Bunting.* Four middle tail feathers very long, even, and webbed only at the tip; beak red; the head, back, rump, and the wing and tail feathers are of a beautiful black, and a fine aurora tint covers the cheeks, throat, breast, and belly, while the abdomen and inferior tail-coverts are pure white. The female wants the brilliant colouring of the male. The length of the latter is from twelve to thirteen inches, reckoning from the point of the beak to the extremity of the shafts. Native of the coast of Africa, and frequently kept at Lisbon in a domesticated state, on account of the beauty of its plumage and its song. In a large and well-heated volery, furnished with evergreens, the suppleness and grace of its motions, its cheerful disposition and fine warbling, are exhibited to the greatest advantage; and when thus accommodated it has been known to live ten years in France.

Paradisea.

F. paradisea, Vieil. *Emberiza paradisea,* Lin. &c. *Vidua paradisea,* Cuv. *Red-breasted Long-tailed Finch, Whidaw Widow,* or *Whidaw Bunting.* Brown, breast red; the four middle tail feathers elongated and acuminated, the two outer very long; bill black. The two middle tail feathers are four inches in length, very broad, and terminate in a long thread; the next two are thirteen inches or more in length, very broad in the middle, narrower at the end, and rather pointed; from the middle of the shaft of these last arises another long thread. The legs are flesh-coloured. The female is wholly of a deep brown, approaching to black, but does not acquire her full plumage till the third year. This species consists of two races, one of which is considerably smaller than the other; but both inhabit Africa, although Olina has described one as an African, and the other as an American species. The warble of the male is considerably varied, but somewhat shrill. These birds are cheerful and sprightly, and easily fed on chickweed, endive, &c. but they are with difficulty induced to breed in Europe.

F. longicauda, Vieil. *Vidua longicauda,* Cuv. *Emberiza longicauda,* Lath. *Long-tailed Widow,* or *Orange-shouldered Bunting, Yellow-shouldered Oriole* of Brown. Black; shoulders fulvous, margined with white; six middle tail feathers very long; size of the song thrush. The tail of the male, when in his full attire, is actually double, the upper portion being composed of six feathers, the longest of which measures thirteen inches, and the under portion of twelve, which are nearly equal, and pretty long. This remarkable appendage, along with his velvet black hue, and orange on the shoulders, he retains only during six months of the year; and, when divested of them, he can with difficulty be recognised for the same bird. It is remarkable that the female, when past breeding, assumes the gaudy attire of the male; and it is equally deserving of notice, that these birds are polygamous, two males sufficing for thirty or forty females, which breed in domestic societies, their nests being all contiguous.

COLIUS, Gmel. &c. COLY.

This family is nearly allied to the preceding. The birds belonging to it have a short, thick, and conical bill, somewhat compressed, and the mandibles arched, without one exceeding the other in length; their tail feathers are imbricated, and very long; their hind toe may, as in the martins, be turned forwards; and their fine and silky feathers are generally characterized by their cinereous tints. They are natives of Africa or the Indies; climb somewhat in the manner of parrots, live in troops, build numerous nests on the same bushes; and sleep, suspended on the branches, with their head downwards, and pressed close to one another. They live on fruits; but little else is known relative to their habits.

C. Capensis, Gmel. &c. *Loxia Capensis,* Lin. *Cape Coly.* Outer edges of the exterior tail feathers white; body cinereous above, whitish beneath. Size of a chaffinch. Inhabits the Cape of Good Hope. The *Paroyensis, striatus,* and *erythropus,* are now accounted only varieties of the present; and the others which have been defined are very limited in number, and have been hitherto discriminated only by differences of aspect.

CASSICUS. Cuv. CASSIQUE.

Bill large, quite conical, thick at the base, nicely whetted at the point; the junction of the mandibles in a broken line, or forming an angle, as in the starlings; nostrils small and round, and placed on the sides of the bill. These are American birds, in manners approximating to the starlings, living, like them, in flocks, often constructing their nests near one another, and with singular skill and artifice. They live on seeds and insects; and their numerous flocks frequently occasion serious injury to the cultivated fields. Their flesh has, for the most part, a very indifferent relish.

C. cristatus, Cuv. Vieil. *Oriolus cristatus,* Lath. *Crested Cassique,* or *Crested Oriole.* Black, crested; lower part of the back, rump, and vent chesnut; lateral tail feathers yellow. The colours of the female are less distinctly pronounced. Length of the body from eighteen to twenty inches, and extent of wing twenty-nine inches. This species, which is the largest of the tribe, occurs in Brazil, Guiana, and Paraguay; varies considerably both in dimensions and colours; lives both on insects and fruits, and is particularly fond of those of the *Passiflora latifolia,* and of a grain,

Colius.

Capensis.

Cassicus.

Cristatus.

which gives a yellow tinge to its dung. Its flesh exhales a very strong odour of castoreum. When it utters its very varied and singular cry, which is not often the case, it is perched on the sloping branch of a tree, with its body stretched out, its head lowered, and its wings expanded, and smartly agitated. It is most generally observed solitary, or in pairs, but sometimes in flocks of about a hundred, which fly and work in common, keep time with the beating of their wings, and occasionally halt on the tops of trees. Six of their hanging nests may be seen on the same tree, owing perhaps to the scarcity of the particular description of trees suited to their purpose; for they uniformly select only such as are dispersed on the outskirts of the woods, and have the trunk quite smooth to the height of thirty or forty feet, before they throw out their many horizontal branches. To the extremity of one of those branches, and at a great distance from the trunk, they suspend their nest, which is about thirty-six inches long, and resembles a purse or pouch, with the lower end hemispherical, and ten inches wide. The male and female jointly manufacture it, by interlacing or knitting shreds of the bark of a species of aloe, termed *caraguata*, small rushes, and old man's beard, and lining the bottom with a thick layer of large dried leaves, plucked from the tree itself. In this rocking cradle the female lays three eggs, and feeds her young with worms. When they have attained maturity, they greedily feed on the orange and pine-apple.

C. hemorrhous, Cuv. Vieil. *Oriolus hemorrhous*, Lath. *Red-rumped Cassique*, or *Oriole*. Black, with the lower part of the back, rump, and vent, crimson. An elegant species, though of plain colouring. Length about eleven inches. Native of South America, particularly of Guiana. Builds its nest on branches which project over water, composing it of dried bents, and giving it the form of a narrow cucurbit with its alembic, the bottom in which the eggs are deposited being much thicker than the rest; the entrance is a little under the upper part, and the passage oblique, so that rain cannot gain admission from whatever quarter it proceeds. The nest, which is suspended by the upper part, measures externally about eighteen inches in length, and the internal cavity is about ten inches.

C. icteronotus, Vieil. *Oriolus Persicus*, Lin. *Oriolus Cacicus*, Shaw. *Grand Troupiale* of Azara. *Black and Yellow Cassique*, *Black and Yellow Oriole*, *Persian Pie*, &c. Black, with the lower part of the back, spot on the wing-coverts, and base of the tail feathers, yellow. Size of a blackbird. The female is somewhat larger than the male, and has less brilliant plumage. The epithet *Persian* is quite inapplicable to the present species, which is found only in South America, and particularly in Cayenne. It is of a gregarious disposition, like the rooks in Europe, great numbers building near one another, insomuch that no fewer than four hundred nests have been seen on the same tree. They are shaped like an alembic, and about eighteen inches in length. The upper portion by which they are fastened to the branch is of a compact substance, the lower or purse forming the true nest. The whole is composed of dried grasses, and the fibres of the parasitical plant called *Tallandsia usneoides*, or *old man's beard*, which, in its dried state, bears a strong resemblance to horse hair. The eggs are dirty white, with small pale brown spots. This species is prolific, having three hatches in the year. They feed on grain and insects, perch on trees, and, by the variety of their native whistle, and the different expressions of their

warble, with which they blend imitative sounds, one would suppose that they were mocking the people who listen to them. They are very easily tamed, and very amusing in confinement, as they readily learn different tunes, and counterfeit the cries of various animals, the barking of a dog, the laughing of a man, &c. Like the crested species, they smell strongly of castoreum.

XANTHORNUS, Cuv. CAROUGE.

Differs from the preceding genus only in the circumstance of the bill being quite straight.

X. icterus, Cuv. *Oriolus icterus*, Lin. &c. *Pendulinus longirostris*, Vieil. *Icteric Carouge, Icteric Oriole*, or *Large Banana Bird*. Fulvous, with black head, throat, wings, and tail; the wings marked by two white bars. Nine inches and a half long. A beautiful species, which inhabits the lower parts of North, and many districts of South America, as well as the West India islands, particularly Jamaica. In its wild state it is agile and gregarious, building a large cylindrical nest, suspended to the end of a slender branch of a tree, with a view to remove its young from the attacks of snakes and other animals. Of these nests several may sometimes be seen near one another. The icteric carouge is often domesticated in America for the sake of destroying insects of various kinds; and it is also said sometimes to attack and prey on other birds. It is naturally of a lively disposition, and, when domesticated, manifests a high degree of docility, following those who have the charge of it, descending from a tree or a house on being called by its name, and delighting to be handled and caressed in the manner of a lap-dog.

X. phœniceus, Cuv. *Oriolus phœniceus*, Lin. &c. *Agelaius phœniceus*, Vieil. *Red-winged or Red-shouldered Carouge*, or *Oriole, Scarlet-feathered Indian Bird, Red-winged Starling, Red Bird*, &c. Black, with crimson shoulders, margined with yellow. Size of a starling. The female is of a dusky or brown hue, with the edges of the feathers whitish or pale, and with a less distinct appearance of red on the shoulders. We need not, therefore, wonder that she should have been frequently described as a separate species, under the epithet *Melanoleucus*. The males themselves are liable to vary in their aspect at different periods of their life, and have sometimes been found of a uniform cream colour. This species occurs in North America, from Mexico to Nova Scotia, and still farther north, but not in the West Indies. It winters in the southern states, and returns, early in March, to the central provinces, the males uniformly arriving first, and the females some days later. But both sexes and the young migrate in autumn to Louisiana in such dense multitudes, that 300 may be captured at one drag of the net; and an instance is recorded, of a single individual having collected in one winter 40,000 of the red patches which discriminate the males, and which were formerly in great request for ornamenting ladies' gowns. On their return to the states of New York and New Jersey, these birds frequent the salt marshes, for the sake of feeding on the grains of *Zizania aquatica*. As they advance farther northward, their bands augment in numbers, as each resorts to its birth-place, and breeds among aquatic plants. During the day they haunt the fields and meadows, but towards evening betake themselves to the marshes and reeds, among which they pass the night. Their nest, which they often place in the most inaccessible situations, is suspended, as it were, between two reeds, the leaves of which they interlace, and form into a sort of shed or covering, while they impart solidity and thickness to its circumference and base by dry grasses, bound together with mud; and they line it with the fibres of roots, and the softest and most delicate herbage. This nicely constructed cradle is always raised above the highest state of the water over which it impends. In default of reeds suited to their purpose, these birds will build between the branches of a bush or shrub, but always in swampy situations. Each hatch, for they have usually two in the season, consists of five or six eggs, of a grey-white, irregularly spotted with black.

The red-winged carouges attack the maize fields at two different periods, namely, when the grain begins to germinate, and a little before the plant attains to maturity, and, either by themselves, or in the company of the purple grakle, commit great havock on the crop. They are very bold, and not to be terrified by a gun; for, although the sportsman should make great slaughter among a flock, the remainder will take a short flight, and settle again in the same field, and often with increased numbers. The farmers sometimes steep the maize before they sow it in a decoction of white hellebore, which stupifies the birds, and enables people to kill them in great numbers. From the greediness with which they devour this grain, they are popularly termed *maize thieves.* But it should also be recollected, that they destroy myriads of insects and their larvæ; and that their complete extirpation would probably be followed by more serious consequences than any which result from letting them alone. They are fond of singing, and exceedingly playful, either when confined, or when suffered to run about the house. When placed before a looking-glass, they will erect the feathers of the head, and hiss at their own image, then lowering the crest, they will set up their tail, quiver their wings, and strike at the figure with their bill. When taken, either young or old, they become immediately familiar. Though often killed for the table, their flesh is not reputed delicate.

Baltimore. X. *Baltimore,* Cuv. *Oriolus Baltimore,* Lin. &c. *Yphantes Baltimore,* Vieil. *Baltimore Carouge, Baltimore Oriole,* or *Baltimore Bird.* So named from a similarity in its colours to those in the arms of the Baltimore family. Blackish; the under parts of the body, and the band on the wings, tawny; bill lead colour; greater wing-coverts black, tipt with white; first quill feathers dirty white, edged with white; two middle tail feathers black; the rest black on the lower part, and orange above. The female has the head, neck, shoulders, and back, varied with olive-green and brown; the throat, breast, belly, and inferior tail-coverts, yellow; the smaller wing-coverts black, externally margined with deep olive green; the greater coverts and quills fringed with white, the tail grey-olive, and the legs black. The young resemble the females, but exhibit fainter hues. These birds are found in many parts of America, from Carolina to Canada, occupying the northern regions in summer, advancing to Montreal in May, and returning southward in winter, during which season they are seen in Maryland and Virginia. They make their nest of tough vegetable filaments, curiously interwoven, mixed with wool, and lined with hair. In shape it somewhat resembles a pear, is open at top, and furnished with a hole on the side, for the purpose of more expeditiously feeding the young; and it is attached, by vegetable threads, to the extreme forks of the tulip-tree, plane, or hiccory. The eggs are spotted with red. The country people call the Baltimore carouges *fire birds,* or *fire hang*

nests, because, when in high plumage, their motions from branch to branch present the semblance of a flash of fire.

Dacnis, Cuv. Pit-pit.

Bill conical and pointed; birds small. The characters, in other respects, coincide with those of the preceding family.

D. Cayana, Cuv. *Motacilla Cayana,* Lin. *Sylvia Cayana,* Lath. *Cayenne Pit-pit, Cayenne Warbler, Blue Manakin,* &c. Blue, with the capistrum, shoulder, wings, and tail, black; but its plumage is variable, especially during the two first years of its life, a circumstance which has given rise to several superfluous specific distinctions. Inhabits Guiana, where it resides in the woods, perching on the tops of the lofty trees, and flying in flocks. The few others which belong to this genus are little known, but are presumed to have similar manners and habits.

ORDER V.

ZYGODACTYLOUS BIRDS.

Bill of various forms, more or less arched, or much hooked, and often straight and angular; feet constantly furnished with two toes before, and two behind, and the outer hind toe frequently capable of being turned forwards.

The distinctive character of birds of this order, is the disposition of the toes in pairs. Many of them chiefly or exclusively live on caterpillars, worms, and insects, but others on soft or hard fruits; and most of them nidificate in the holes of decayed trees.

Musophaga, Tem. Touraco, or Plantain-eater.

Bill short, stout, broad, ridge arched and elevated, notched at the point, extremity of the lower mandible forming an angle; nostrils basal, and often concealed by the front feathers; legs stout, tarsus equal in length to the middle toe; the fourth and fifth quills the longest.

M. persa, Opœthus persa, Vieill. *Cuculus persa,* Lath. *African Touraco.* Head crested, body greenish-blue, quill feathers red. The head, throat, neck, upper parts of the back, breast, part of the belly and sides, are covered with soft silky feathers, of a fine deep green. The feathers on the crown are lengthened into a crest, tipped with white, and which the bird can erect or depress at pleasure. But the general plumage is so liable to vary, that the species has been needlessly multiplied. The female is somewhat smaller than the male, and of less brilliant hues. This species occurs at the Cape of Good Hope, in the extensive eastern forests, and on the confines of the country of the Anteniquois. Levaillant represents it as of a disposition so familiar and curious, that it spontaneously approaches a man, or an animal, leaping from tree to tree, and uttering its cry of satisfaction, which is expressed by the syllable *cor,* uttered with a prolonged and guttural pronunciation, and with a quiver of the tongue, especially on the letter *r.* Its love-call has been represented by the word *corouw,* uttered eight or ten times in succession; and, lastly, its note of alarm has been assimilated to the abrupt sounds of military trumpets. The female lays four bluish-white eggs in the large holes of trees.

Indicator, Vieil. Tem. Levail. Honey Guide.

Bill strong, conical, dilated at the base, narrow to.

wards the tip; the upper mandible bent and carinated, the lower recurved at the tip; nostrils slightly covered with feathers; the outer hind toe longest, and armed with a short claw. The birds of this very limited family have their designation from directing the natives to the repositories of wild honey. Their skin is so tough and compact, as to be with difficulty pierced with a pin, an admirable provision against the stings of bees, which, nevertheless, contrive to attack them near the eyes, and thus often destroy them.

Major. I. *major*, Vieil. *Cuculus indicator*, Gmel. and Lath. *Great Honey Guide*, *Honey Cuckoo*, or *Moroc*. Olive green above, yellow beneath; rump and tail coverts white; upper wing coverts white, varied with olive. The forepart of the neck and breast are pale yellow, and the middle of the neck is varied with black spots, which ascend to the throat. The female, described as the *I. Sparrmanni* by some, is rusty grey above, and white beneath. Inhabits the interior of Africa, at a considerable distance from the Cape of Good Hope. This bird is very fond of honey and bee maggots; but, being unable by its own efforts to procure them from the hollows of trees, it points out to man, and to the animal called *ratel*, the nests of wild bees. The morning and the evening are its principal meal times; or, at least, it is then that it shows the greatest inclination to come forth, and, with a grating cry of *cherr, cherr, cherr*, to excite the attention of the ratel, as well as of the Hottentots and colonists. Somebody then generally repairs to the place whence the sound proceeds, when the bird, continually repeating its cry, flies on slowly, and by degrees, to the quarter where the bees have taken up their abode. The persons thus invited follow accordingly, taking great care, at the same time, not to frighten their guide by any unusual noise, but rather to answer it now and then by a soft gentle whistle, by way of letting the bird know that its call is attended to. When the bees' nest is at some distance, the bird often makes long stages or flights, waiting for its sporting companions between each movement, and calling to them again to come on; but it flies to shorter distances, and repeats its cry more frequently, and with greater earnestness, in proportion as it approaches the nest. When the bird has, sometimes in consequence of its impatience, got too far a-head of its attendants, but particularly when, on account of the unevenness of the ground, they have not been able to keep pace with it, it will fly back to meet them, and, with redoubled cries, seems to chide their tardiness. When it arrives at the nest, whether the latter is placed in the cleft of a rock, or in a hollow tree, or in some cavity in the soil, it hovers over the spot for a few seconds, then sits in silence, and, for the most part, concealed, in some neighbouring tree or bush, in expectation of the result, and with a view of receiving its share of the booty. Nor is it disappointed; for the hunters, in reward for its services, leave it a considerable portion of that part of the comb in which the bees are hatching. Mr. Barrow corroborates these details, and adds, that the moroc intimates to the inhabitants, with equal certainty, the dens of lions, tigers, hyenas, and other beasts of prey, or noxious animals. Mr. Bruce, on the contrary, by confounding the present species with another, which is peculiar to Abyssinia, has indulged in some very misplaced strictures on the accounts of Sparrmann and Lobo. Levaillant mentions, that the Hottentots are very partial to the moroc, on account of its good offices; and that once, when he was on the point of shooting one,

they entreated him to spare its life. According to the same author, the female nestles in the hollows of trees, into which she climbs like the wood-pecker, and lays three or four eggs of a dirty white, the male participating in the cares of incubation. A nest, which was shown to Dr. Sparrmann, as belonging to the moroc, was composed of slender filaments of bark, woven together in the form of an inverted bottle; and a string was suspended across the opening, and fastened by the two ends, perhaps for the birds to perch on. But such an apparatus was probably the production of some of the hang-nest tribe.

CUCULUS, Lin. &c. CUCKOO.

Bill of the same length as the head, compressed, and *Cuculus.* faintly arched; mandibles notchless; nostrils basal, pierced in the margins of the mandible, and surrounded by a naked and prominent membrane; legs feathered under the knee; tail long, and more or less graduated; wings of moderate size, the third quill the longest.

The cuckoos are a shy and solitary race of birds, which live chiefly on insects and caterpillars, and are remarkable for depositing their eggs, one by one, in the nests of some of the smaller birds. Only one species is a native of Great Britain, and very few belong to Europe. The limits of the genus have been recently considerably circumscribed.

C. canorus, Lin. &c. *Common Cuckoo*, Prov. *Gowk*. *Canorus.* Head, neck, and throat, cinereous; breast and belly whitish, transversely striated with fuscous; back and wings blackish, tail-feathers blackish, externally spotted with whitish, as is the middle of the intermediate quills. When young, the whole body is brownish, and the feathers are edged with white. The female is somewhat smaller than the male, but has generally the same markings. The details of colouring, however, in both sexes, are so subject to vary, that M. Gérardin assures us, that, in his numerous collection of individuals, scarcely any two are marked alike; and this circumstance has proved the source of more confusion and perplexity in the extrication of the genus, than we can stop to particularize.

This well known species inhabits Europe, Asia, and Africa, is found as high as Finmark, within the arctic circle, and as far east as Kamtschatka. It is a stated migrant, arriving, for the purpose of breeding, in different countries, earlier or later in the season, according as the temperature of the climate unfolds the insects on which it feeds. With us it usually makes its appearance pretty early in April, is silent for a few days, and begins to utter the cry from which it has derived its name, in almost every language, about the middle of the month. This, which is the note of the male, ceases about the close of June. The female makes only occasionally a chattering noise, which bears some resemblance to the cry of the dabchick. From the silence of the male, it had been supposed that the old birds directed their course southwards, early in July; but their silence is occasioned by the approach of their moulting, and most of them take their departure between the first and 15th of September. Such as are observed later are the tardy young of that year, or wounded or sickly stragglers. A person worthy of credit assured Linné, that, very late in the autumn, he saw a cuckoo perched on a hop-pole, and *singing*. On which occasion the celebrated naturalist remarks, that birds in autumn are sometimes visited with the gay associations of the spring. In general, the first sensations of cold, or the failure of insects and soft fruits,

which last they will eat in default of the former, induce the cuckoos to pass into the warmer regions of
Africa. In Malta, and the Greek islands, where they
are seen twice a-year on their transit, they arrive with
the turtle doves, and as they are far less numerous than
the latter, the natives call them their leaders or guides.
During these migrations the cuckoo is no longer a solitary bird, but associates in flocks with its own species, and even unites with those of others. No longer
impelled also by the desire of reproducing its kind, the
male is mute. Love, therefore, alone is possibly the
cause of the insulation of the individuals in spring,
and the early part of summer; for, after that period,
young and old have been seen together in flights of
ten or twelve. When on the ground they have a hopping march; but they seldom alight on the soil, owing
probably to the shortness of their legs and thighs.
When young, they seem not to make use of their legs
in walking, but drag themselves along on their belly by
means of their bill, as parrots do in climbing.

Cuckoos for the most part haunt woods, and manifest a preference to those which are situated on shelving grounds and hills, frequenting the neighbourhood,
and constantly returning into the circuit which they had
selected for their summer quarters. They are then
unusually solitary, and have the appearance of being
restless, as they are perpetually flitting from one spot
to another, and are every day a considerable time on
wing, without, however, taking long flights at once,
being impelled to these movements in search of their
most suitable food. They ramble about in all directions, sometimes halting on the tops of trees, sometimes
plunging into the thickest coverts, and every where
pursuing insects, and picking up caterpillars. They
likewise eat the eggs of small birds, and discover, with
singular sagacity, the best concealed nests. A single
cuckoo is not easily approached, and, by flitting from
tree to tree without removing to any great distance,
will often exhaust the patience of the sportsman.

With the natural history of this species much fable
and absurdity have been blended, which we have
neither room nor inclination to state or to confute.
That part of its economy which we have presently to
unfold, is sufficiently anomalous, without superadding
to it the tales of ignorance and superstition. We do
not even assert absolutely, that the cuckoo never builds
a nest, or takes charge of her young, like almost all
other birds. On the contrary, a few well-authenticated
instances of its breeding in the ordinary manner are
on record. Thus the Hon. Daines Barrington informs
us, that, as the Rev. W. Stafford was one day walking
in Blossopdale, Derbyshire, he saw a cuckoo rise from
its nest, which was on the stump of an old tree that
had been felled some time, and nearly resembling the
colour of the tree. In this nest were two young birds,
one of which he fastened to the ground by means of
a peg and line; and, for a few days, very frequently
saw the old cuckoos feeding them. The same writer
quotes two other examples of a similar nature; one of
which occurred within a few miles of London, and the
other on the south-west coast of Merioneth. Mr. Wil-
mot, of Morley, in Derbyshire, mentioned to Dr. Darwin, that he observed a cuckoo for some time on its
nest before and after the eggs were hatched; and also
bringing food to the young ones, to which it showed
great attachment. It is at the same time certain, that
by far the greater number of the species make no nest,
and leave their eggs to be hatched by other birds. Dr.
Edward Jenner, one of the greatest benefactors of man-

kind, in a paper inserted in Vol. LXXVIII. of the
Philosophical Transactions, and Dr. Lottinger, who
devoted much of his time to investigate the manners of
the present species, have proved this remarkable fact
beyond all dispute. The nest which the female cuckoo
selects is most commonly that of the hedge-sparrow,
though sometimes that of the water-wagtail, yellow
wren, tit-lark, yellow-hammer, green-linnet, or some
other small insectivorous bird. It is, at first sight, difficult to conceive how such a large bird as the cuckoo
should insinuate its egg into the nest of a wren, for
example, without in the least discomposing so delicate
a structure; but Levaillant mentions, that he has seen
the female of an African species of this genus swallow
the egg, and retain it in the œsophagus, till she dropped it into the nest; and a person worthy of credit
assured M. Vieillot that he witnessed the same proceeding in the female of the present species. According to Dr. Jenner, while the hedge-sparrow is laying
her eggs, which generally occupies four or five days,
the cuckoo contrives to deposit one of her own among
them, an intrusion which is seldom unattended with
inconvenience; for the old sparrow, while sitting, not
only throws out, at intervals, some of her own eggs,
but occasionally injures them in such a way, that they
become addle, so that often not more than two or three
of the parent birds' eggs are hatched with that of the
cuckoo; and, what is very remarkable, it has never
been observed that the sparrow has thrown out or
injured that of the latter. When she has sat her usual
time, and disengaged the young cuckoo and some of
her own offspring from the shell, her young ones, and
any of the eggs that remain unhatched are soon turned
out, when the young cuckoo remains in full possession
of the nest, and is the sole object of the future care of
its foster parent. The mode by which it contrives to
eject the legitimate occupants of the nest is truly curious; for, by the aid of its rump and wings, it gets the
young sparrow on its back, and, making a lodgement
for the burden, by elevating its elbows, clambers back
with it, up the side of the nest, till it reaches the top,
where, resting for a moment, it throws off its load with
a jerk, and quite disengages it from the nest. It then
remains for a little time in that situation, and feels
about with the extremities of its wings, to be convinced
that the business is properly executed, after which it
drops into the nest again. Dr. Jenner made several
experiments on different nests, by repeatedly putting
in an egg to the young cuckoo, which was always disposed of in the same manner; and it is very remarkable that nature seems to have provided for this singular disposition of the cuckoo in its formation at this
period; for, unlike every other newly-hatched bird,
its back, from the scapulæ downwards, is very broad,
with a considerable depression in the middle, as if intended for giving a more secure position to the egg of
the hedge-sparrow, or young one that is cast out.
When it is about twelve days old, this cavity is quite
filled up; and, at this time, its disposition for expelling its companion entirely ceases. As the same cuckoo
deposits only one egg in a nest, it has been hastily inferred that she laid no more; but it has been found, on
dissection, that her ovary contains several; and we
may reasonably presume that they are deposited in
different nests. When two are included in the same
nest, as sometimes happens, they are probably deposited by different individuals; and, if they are both
hatched, the extruded birds contend fiercely for the
mastery till one of them is killed. From Dr. Lottin-

ger's observations, it seems to result that the parent cuckoos sometimes hover about in the vicinity of the nest, occasionally visiting their offspring, and that they recognize them when they take wing. But had this been uniformly the case, it could scarcely have escaped Dr. Jenner's notice. The attempt of the parent cuckoo to introduce her egg into the nest is sometimes successfully resisted by the proprietor, but the usurpation is generally effected in the temporary absence of the latter. No satisfactory reason has been hitherto assigned for this peculiarity in the economy of the cuckoo: for the anatomical argument advanced by Herrisant, and deduced from the conformation of the stomach and sternum, turns out to be quite unfounded; nor does the alleged short residence of the parents in the breeding latitudes afford any better solution of the phenomenon, it having been now ascertained that the old and young birds migrate at the same time. The egg of the cuckoo is about the size of that of the butcher bird, having a very thin shell, of a round form, and of a dirty white ground, marked with reddish dots, and some black lines, irregularly dispersed. Sepp has erroneously figured it as that of the goatsucker. The young, which are very clamorous for the insect food, brought to them by their foster parents, grow rapidly, and continue for three weeks in the nest. If molested, they will bristle up their feathers, and assume a fierce and pugnacious attitude. In their stomach are often found small balls of horsehair, which they have a trick of detaching from the nest in which they are reared. Balls composed of a more delicate hairy substance are met with in the stomach of the adult birds, obviously proceeding from the hairy caterpillars on which they feed; for, in place of rejecting these, they seem to be partial to them. Although the young are long of manifesting much sagacity, they are capable of being tamed; and, when in confinement, they will eat bread, milk, fruit, insects, eggs, and even flesh, either raw or dressed. In its natural state, however, it is by no means a carnivorous bird, although it has been often described as such. Neither does it long survive captivity; for it rarely lives beyond the first winter, and most frequently dies in the course of it. Confinement seems also to suppress the growth of its mature plumage, and its vernal song. The Romans greatly valued this bird as an article of food; and the French and Italians eat it at this day. When fattened, it is said to be as delicate as the land-rail.

C. *Americanus*, Lath. Cuv. *Coccyzus pyropterus*, Vieil. *Carolina cuckoo.* Body cinereous above, white beneath; lower mandible yellow; tail wedge-shaped. The upper parts of the female are of a faint brown-grey. Size of the black-bird, and ten inches eight lines in length. Inhabits the western world, from Jamaica to Canada, and is not uncommon in Carolina. It arrives in the United States in May, but departs in October, to winter in the West Indies. It generally haunts the thickest recesses of forests, but approaches houses during the season of ripe cherries, when it frequents orchards and groves, attracted by the fruits and wild berries of autumn. The male and female are seldom seen together, even during the breeding season. The note of the male is sometimes analogous to that of the European species, but so feeble that it is audible only at a small distance. The nest, which is placed in a tree, is outwardly composed of dried twigs and roots, and within, of fine grass and hair;

and the hatch consists of four or five bluish-brown eggs.

PTEROGLOSSUS, Illig. Tem. ARACARI.

Bill cellular, slender, longer than the head, depressed at the base, bent like a sickle, suddenly inflected at the tip, edges of the mandibles regularly dentated; nostrils basal, pierced in two deep notches, orbicular and open; tarsus of the same length as the outer toe, and the two front toes united to the second articulation; wings short and concave; tail long and much cuneated.

P. viridis, Illig. *Ramphastos viridis*, Lin. &c. *Green Aracari*, or *Green Toucan*. Blackish-green, with black head and neck, yellow abdomen, red rump, and cuneated tail. In the female, the head and neck are chesnut, and the bill is shorter. Length, fourteen inches. Native of Cayenne.

RAMPHASTOS, Lin. &c. TOUCAN.

Bill enormously large, light, cellular within, convex, serrated outwardly, and slightly curved at the tip; nostrils behind the base of the bill; orbits naked; tongue long, narrow, and feather-shaped.

The toucans are chiefly indigenous to the warmer regions of South America. Like the hornbills, they are distinguished by the huge size of their beaks, which, in some species, is nearly equal to that of the whole body. It is composed, however, of a light cellular substance, and so soft as to be compressible between the fingers. The tongue is of a highly singular form, being of a somewhat horny or cartilaginous nature, and divided on each side into innumerable short and close-set fibres; in consequence of which structure it is described, by some of the old naturalists as a real feather, supplying the place of a tongue. They feed on fruit, especially that of the palm-trees, and sometimes on insects and buds of trees; but they also destroy a great many small birds, attacking them with their overgrown bills, expelling them from their nests, and even in their presence devouring their eggs and their young. If a nest be constructed of clay, they refrain from attacking it until it is softened by rain, when they demolish it by repeated blows. From this propensity to seize small birds and their eggs, Azara has classed them with birds of prey, although their general structure and habits are very different. They swallow their food entire, previously tossing it in the air. They are generally met with in small flocks of eight or ten, moving from place to place in quest of food, and advancing northward or southward in proportion as the fruits ripen, though they are not properly migratory, and are very impatient of cold. Sonnini compares their flight to that of the magpie. They easily mount to the top of the highest trees, on which they delight to perch. They are vigilant and jealous of what is passing around them, and rarely alight on the ground, but when they do, they are observed to hop obliquely and with their legs astride. They make their nests in the hollows of trees, abandoned by woodpeckers, the structure of their bill not allowing of the efforts necessary to make, or even to enlarge a hole in the most tender timber. They are supposed to lay two eggs, and to breed more than once a-year; but so wary are they in concealing their breeding haunts, that no traveller has been enabled to mention the size or colour of the eggs, and that Azara and Sonnini, both zealous ornithologists, and who resided for years in South America, were never fortunate enough to see one of them. If caught

Picatus.

when young, they are easily tamed, and become very familiar. Their flesh is tough, but eatable. We shall particularize only one of the species.

R. picatus, Lath. *Red-bellied*, or *Preacher Toucan*, or *Brazilian Pie*. Upper parts of the body glossy black, with a tinge of green, breast fine orange, belly, sides, thighs, and the short tail feathers bright red, remainder of the tail black, tipt with red. Nearly twenty inches in length. Native of Guiana and Brazil. The red-bellied toucan feeds chiefly on fruits, but when tamed will eat almost any thing that is offered to it. Pozzo, who had one perfectly domesticated, informs us, that it leaped up and down, wagged its tail, and cried with a voice like that of a magpie. It fed on the same things as parrots, but was most covetous of grapes, which, when plucked off, and thrown to it one by one, it would with great dexterity catch in the air, before it fell to the ground. As this species is easily tamed, it is in great request in South America, both for the delicacy of its flesh and the beauty of its plumage, particularly of the feathers on the breast. The Indians pluck off the skin from this part, and glue it, when dry, to their cheeks, as, in their estimation, an irresistible addition to their beauty. In several districts of South America those birds are denominated *preachers*, from the habit of one of their flock perching on the top of a tree, above its fellows, when they are asleep, and making a continued noise, resembling ill-articulated sounds, moving its head to the right and left, in order, it is supposed, to deter birds of prey from approaching to the spot.

CROTOPHAGA, Lin. &c. KEEL-BILL, or ANI.

CROTO-
PHAGA.

Bill smooth or furrowed, curved, entire, laterally compressed, angular on the margins, keeled at the top; nostrils basal, lateral, pervious, and oval; tongue compressed, pointed at the tip; wings short; tail composed of eight feathers.

The birds of this family are called *Ani* by the natives of Brazil; but they have various popular and provincial names in different parts of South America. Their wings are feeble, and their flight is very limited, so that many of them perish in hurricanes. So powerful are their social propensities, that they are almost invariably observed in flocks, the smallest of which usually consists of eight or ten, and the largest of twenty-five or thirty individuals, which keep together, whether flying or at rest, and when they perch on the branch of a tree, they are always clustered as closely as possible. This mutual harmony dates from their birth; for they are nursed and live in common. In the month of February they are conscious of the influence of the tender passion, but although then more animated than usual, their courtships are conducted without jealousy or disturbance. The males and females labour together in constructing a large nest, which accommodates several breeders at once. The first that is ready to hatch waits not for her companions, who enlarge the dwelling while she is busied with incubation. The common hatching proceeds with perfect amity. The females take their stations close by one another; and, if the eggs happen to get mixed, or too closely pressed, a single female hatches those of other birds along with her own, and pushes them together, that the heat may be equally distributed over them, without being dissipated. The same good understanding is maintained when the young are extruded; for the mothers who have incubated, feed, in succession, every one of the

nascent family, the males assisting in providing the supplies. But such females as have hatched separately, rear their young apart, yet without umbrage or molestation. They construct a rude but very solid nest, with twigs of shrubs, matted together with the filaments of plants, and internally strewed with leaves. This fabric is very wide, and elevated on the edges, being sometimes eighteen inches in diameter, and its capacity proportioned to the number of incubating females. The few which breed separately make a small partition in the nest with stalks of grass, that their eggs may be kept apart. All cover them with leaves or grass as soon as they are laid; and they repeat this precaution during incubation, as often as they are obliged to leave them to snatch their own food. Each female has several broods in the course of the year. These birds live both on animal and vegetable food; but they manifest a predilection to small serpents, lizards, and other reptiles, caterpillars, worms, the larger sorts of ants and termites, and other insects. They likewise alight on cattle, to pick up the ticks, caterpillars, and insects that lodge in their skin or hair. In default of animal nourishment, they will eat various sorts of grains, as maize, millet, rice, wild oats, &c. When on the ground, or perched, they are observed to carry their heads drawn in, or close to the shoulders, sitting near one another, and uttering a constant chattering cry, somewhat in the manner of starlings. They are neither shy nor timid, never fly to any distance at a time, and as they are not scared by the noise of fire-arms, many of them may be shot without much trouble; but the rankness of their flesh, and their offensive odour, even when alive, naturally repel the sportsman's ardour. For the rest, they are of gentle dispositions and easily tamed, and when taken young they may be taught to speak like the parrots. They abound in Guiana, Mexico, Brazil, St. Domingo, &c. generally frequenting places that are open or slightly shaded, and never in woods of any considerable extent. Two of the species particularized by Latham, namely, the *Varia* and *Ambulatoria*, are recorded from imperfect descriptions, and seem to appertain to some other family.

C piririgua, Vieil. *Cuculus guira*, Lath. *Piririgua Keel-bill*, or *Brazilian Crested Cuckoo*, of Latham. Crested, body whitish-yellow; head, neck, and wing-coverts, varied with brown and yellowish; tail-feathers brown, with white tips. Fifteen inches long. Native of Brazil, where it is called *Piririgua*, or *Piririta*, both being imitative of its ordinary cry, which it often repeats, whether on wing or on the ground. It picks up its food in all directions, in plantations, inclosures, thickets, among cattle, &c. and devours crickets, grasshoppers, small lizards, &c. It sometimes mingles with flocks of congenerous species, and breeds in common with them; but, more frequently a troop of its own species form a nest for themselves, placing it on high and thick bushes, and giving it a flattened form. The eggs are elongated, as large at one end as at the other, and of a bluish-green, with white veins, which are effaced by a slight rubbing. During incubation, the female is very courageous, and will put to flight any bird which threatens to molest her.

Piririgua.

TROGON, Tem. &c. CURUCUI.

Bill much shorter than the head, furnished with bristles at the base, broader than deep, serrated on the margins, curved at the point; nostrils round, situated

TROGON.

Ornitho-
logy.

near the origin of the bill, and covered by the bristles; tongue short, triangular, and pointed; gape wide; legs short, and covered with down. The serratures of the bill are not apparent in the young birds.

The appellation of *Trogon* was first suggested by Mœhring, and that of *Curucui* is from the popular name *Coorookoo*, well known in Guiana, and expressive of the natural cry of the family. The plumage of the birds belonging to this genus is rich and varied, and usually more or less adorned with metallic lustre; but their short neck and feet, and their long and broad tail, impart to them a heavy and shapeless aspect. Their multiplied, long, slender, and thickly webbed feathers, augment their apparent dimensions; but they are so loosely affixed to the body as to be very easily detached, and the skin is so weak and slender, that it tears on the least degree of stretching. The curucuis are of very solitary dispositions, never frequenting open or inhabited tracts of country, but delighting in the silence of the desert, where they even shun one another, and seek the recesses of the thickest forests, in which they reside throughout the year. They may sometimes be seen on the tops of trees, but they more usually station themselves about the middle, without alighting on the ground, or even on the lower branches, and lying in ambush during part of the day, for the insects which pass within their reach, and which they seize with much address. Their flight is quick, short, vertical, and undulating. If they conceal themselves in the foliage, it should seem to be from no feeling of suspicion or distrust, for, when visible, one may approach very near them before they fly off, and may even knock them down with a stick. Except in the breeding season, they are rarely heard to cry, and their note is strong, sonorous, monotonous, and plaintive. They nestle in the holes of decayed trees, which they enlarge with their bill, so as to be able to turn freely round in the cavity. The female lays from two to four eggs, and has several hatches in the year. The male is very attentive to her wants during incubation, fetching her food, and soothing her by a plaintive warble, which, to human hearers, seems insipid, but to her has, no doubt, its charms. Vieillot says it may be expressed by the syllable *peoo*, repeated several times in succession, with a strong and mournful accent, and reminding one of the whining of a strayed child. The young are produced quite naked, but acquire their feathers in the course of a few days. As soon as they can dispense with the attentions of their parents, they disperse, and commence that insulated existence to which they are so decidedly partial. Their food consists of the larvæ of insects, beetles, &c. and berries, which they swallow whole. As the male at different periods of his age, the female and the young are variously attired, the species have been superfluously multiplied. After the preceding short sketch of their general habits, we shall particularize only one of the most conspicuous.

Roseigaster. *F. roseigaster*, Vieil. *Trogon curucui*, Gmel. &c. *Red-bellied Curucui.* Golden-green above, fulvous-red beneath; throat black; wing-coverts, and the three exterior tail feathers white, striped with black. Rather less than a magpie. Length ten inches and a half. The female is characterized by the prevalence of a slate-grey hue, which is lighter on the under parts. The plumage of this species is said to vary very much. The sexes pair in April, and again in August or September. If there is no decayed dust already in the hole in which the eggs are to be deposited, they pro-

cure a supply of the powder of the sand-wood, which they prepare with their strong and powerful bill. At St. Domingo they are called *Caleçon Rouge, Demoiselle, Damoiseau, Dame Anglaise,* &c. They are likewise found in Cayenne, Brazil, Mexico, and Peru. All attempts to tame them have hitherto proved fruitless; for they obstinately reject food till they expire.

Ornitho-
logy.

Bucco, Gmel. &c. Barbet.

Bill strong, pointed, laterally compressed, covered with strong bristles, or bearded at the base; the apex emarginated and incurved, gape reaching below the eyes; nostrils covered with recumbent feathers, and the feet formed for climbing. The birds of this family are all inhabitants of Africa, and the warmer parts of Asia and America. Their head is very large; and they are a stupid solitary race, mostly living in sequestered forests, and chiefly feeding on insects.

Bucco.

B. tamatia, Gmel. &c. *Tamatia maculata*, Cuv. *Spotted-bellied Barbet.* Reddish-brown above, reddish-white and spotted with black beneath, throat fulvous, neck with a lunated collar, composed of black and rufous; a black spot behind the eyes. Length six inches and a half. Native of Cayenne and Brazil. It is a clumsy heavy-looking bird, and, in disposition, fond of retirement, pensive, and silent, haunting those places which are remote from human habitations, particularly woods, where it fixes on some low branch well covered with foliage. On this it will perch for a long time together, with its huge head leaning on its shoulders; and, as it is very little inclined to activity, it may be easily killed, for it will suffer itself to be repeatedly shot at without attempting to escape. Its principal food is insects, particularly beetles. The natives sometimes eat it, though its flesh is not very palatable.

Tamatia.

Psittacus, Lin. &c. Parrot.

Bill hooked, upper mandible moveable, and, for the most part, covered with a case; nostrils rounded, basal; tongue, in most of the species, fleshy, obtuse, and entire; feet formed for climbing.

Psitta-
cus.

This splendid genus, which includes about one hundred and fifty species, is peculiar to the warmer regions of the globe, but not restricted to the limits assigned by Buffon, namely, a zone of twenty-five degrees on each side of the equator, for some of them have been found in latitudes as far as forty or even forty-five from the line. Some species equal the domestic fowl in size, whilst others are not larger than a sparrow. They resemble the accipitrine tribes in the form of their bill, but in that of their feet, and in their manners, they coincide with the other genera of this order. They climb easily, assisting themselves with their bill, associate in pairs or in flocks, feed on the seeds and fruits of various plants, often attain to a great age, and, by means of their obtuse tongue, and the conformation of their larynx, may be taught to imitate human speech. Their roosting stations are usually in the woods of islands, situated in rivers, which traverse extensive forests, or in places of difficult access. Each troop, it is said, has its sentinel, and all are very clamorous before they go to rest, and when they awake in the morning; but, when engaged in pillaging fruit, they pause from their chattering. Their general character, in some respects, accords with that of the monkey among quadrupeds, for they are capricious, mischievous, and prone to imitation. In Europe, the female will sometimes lay eggs, but very rarely hatches them, unless a temperature be kept up corresponding to that of her native climate. In their wild state, the male and female sit on their eggs alternately. The flesh of the full-grown birds is generally reckoned tough and unsavoury, but that of the young of some of the species is in more request. Buffon and others have divided the tribe into various sections, but it will suffice for the very limited nature of our illustrative exposition to adopt the two-fold Linnean distinction of *Macruri*, or those which have the tail more or less long, and the *Brachyuri*, or those which have it more or less short, and even feathered, without pretending to draw a precise line of demarcation between them, which possibly does not exist.

A. *With comparatively long and pointed tails.*

P. Macao, Lin. &c. *Macrocrecus Macao*, Vieil. *Scarlet*, or *Blue* and *Red Maccaw*. Scarlet, with blue wings; wing-coverts varied with yellow, cheeks white, naked, and wrinkled. The upper mandible white, tail long and red, with the feathers blue at the sides. Size of a capon, and about two feet seven inches in length. Inhabits Brazil, Guiana, and other regions of South America, affecting moist palm woods, and living on the fruit of the trees. These birds generally appear in pairs, and but seldom in flocks. Sometimes, however, they congregate, and the clamour of their united bands is then heard at a great distance. They are the best flyers of all the parrot tribe, and are always observed to perch on the summits of trees, or on the highest branches. During the day they wander two or three miles from their favourite spot or home, but always return in the evening. They build in the hollows of large trees, widening the cavity when too narrow, and lining it with feathers. Like all the other American parrots, they have two hatches annually, each consisting of two eggs, which are said to be of the size of those of a pigeon, and spotted like those of the partridge. The males and females sit alternately on the eggs, and cherish the young, never deserting their charge so long as their assistance is required, and always perching near the nest. When necessitated to feed on the manchineel apple, their flesh is poisonous, though the birds themselves apparently experience no inconvenience from it. The strength of their bill is sufficient to break a peach stone with great ease. The young are readily tamed, and are even taught to speak, but the old birds are clamorous, unmanageable, and troublesome, snapping the bars of chairs, and pulling the brass nails from every article of furniture. They are, nevertheless, capable of being domesticated, though not of acquiring articulate sounds, and are, consequently, seldom caught for the purpose of confinement. Like others of the genus, they are subject to epileptic fits when kept in houses, notwithstanding which they frequently attain to a considerable age. Though their flesh is hard, black, and unsavoury, it makes good soup, and furnishes a considerable portion of the food of the inhabitants of Cayenne, as well as of other parts of South America.

P. severus, Lath. &c. *Maracana*, or *Brazilian Green Maccaw*. Green, with naked cheeks, purple-brown front, and blue wings and tail-feathers, which are dusky red beneath. Size of a pigeon, and about seventeen inches long. Native of Brazil, where it appears in large flocks, and proves injurious to the coffee plantations. It soon becomes familiar with persons whom it sees frequently, and is pleased in receiving and repaying their caresses; but it has an aversion to strangers, and also particularly to children, and flies at them with great fury. It is exceedingly jealous, and, on seeing a young child sharing the caresses of its mistress, it

tries to dart at the infant, but, as its flight is short and laborious, it can only exhibit its displeasure by angry gestures and restless movements, and continues in evident torment till the child is let go, and the bird received again into favour by being placed on its owner's finger. It is then overjoyed, murmurs satisfaction, and sometimes makes a noise exactly like the laugh of an old person. It is likewise very impatient of the company of other parrots, insomuch, that if one be lodged in the same room with itself, it seems to enjoy no comfort. It eats almost every article of human food, and is particularly fond of bread, beef, fried fish, pastry, and sugar. It cracks nuts with its bill, and picks them dexterously with its claws. It does not chew the softer fruits, but sucks them by forcing the tongue against the upper mandible, but the harder sorts of food, as bread, pastry, &c. it bruises by pressing the tip of the lower mandible on the most hollow part of the upper.

P. Guianensis, Lath. *Pavouane Parrot*, or *Pavouane Parrakeet*. Green, with naked whitish orbits; ridge of the shoulders, and under wing-coverts red, and quill and tail-feathers yellowish beneath. Of the length of twelve inches. Native of Cayenne and the Antilles, where it is not uncommon, assembling in large troops, and making the air incessantly resound with their shrill and piercing cries. They are particularly fond of the fruit of *Erythrina corallodendron*, and make great havock in the coffee plantations, as they eat the pulp of the berry, and, like the other parrots, reject the bean, which they drop on the ground. Though not easily reclaimed, they have sometimes been rendered familiar and taught to speak; and Levaillant quotes one which was so docile as to lie on its back, with its feet clasped together, and, in this attitude, repeat the Lord's Prayer in Dutch. The same author remarks, that the pavouane parrot varies considerably, both in size and colour, according to the regions in which it occurs. He, moreover, makes an important observation relative to the long-tailed tribe of the family in general, namely, that in a state of domestication, it not unfrequently happens, that the genuine shape of the tail is so materially injured or altered in its proportions, by moulting, as to create a degree of uncertainty to which of the divisions the species belongs. Hence many of the mistakes into which Buffon has been betrayed in his exposition of this department of ornithology; and hence the propriety of obtaining, if possible, specimens in their truly natural or wild state.

P. Alexandri, Lin. &c. *P. docilis*, Vieil. *Alexandrine*, or *Ring Parrakeet*. Green, with red hind collar and shoulder stripe, and black fore collar and throat. Size of a common pigeon, and general length about fifteen inches. This elegant species, which has long maintained a distinguished reputation for its docility and imitative powers, is supposed to have been the only bird of the parrot kind known to the ancient Greeks and Romans, having been brought from Ceylon after the Indian expeditions of Alexander the Great. In the reign of Nero, the Romans first became acquainted with other species, which they obtained from various parts of Africa. They lodged these birds in superb cages, ornamented with silver, tortoise-shell, and ivory; and the price of a parrot often exceeded that of a slave. It was in commemoration of one of the present species belonging to Corinna, that Ovid composed his celebrated elegy. So ardent are the male and female in their attachment, that Vieillot entertains little doubt of their breeding in Europe, provided a tropical temperature

Ornitho-
logy.

be maintained in the aviary. There are several varie-ties, as the *Rose-ringed, Double-ringed, Purple-ringed, Blue-collared, Javan, Blue-headed, Jonquil, Sulphur,* &c.

B. *With tails more or less short and even.*

Gigas.

P. gigas, Lath. *Cacatua aterrima,* Vieil. *Black Cockatoo,* or *Great Black Cockatoo.* Grey-black; head crested; cheeks red and naked. The female is of a paler cast. Equal in size to the great scarlet maccaw. The tongue is hollow at the tip, so as to constitute a sort of tube or trunk, assisting the bird in the act of taking its food, and of penetrating into the substance of fruits, &c. In cold weather the bird covers the bare space on each side of the bill, by lowering over it the plumes of the crest. It is a native of Ceylon.

Cristatus.

P. cristatus, Lin. Lath. including *P. rosaceus* of the latter. *Broad-crested Cockatoo, Great Red-crested Cock-atoo, Yellow-crested Cockatoo,* or *White-crested Parrot* of Aldrovandus. White, with expansile crest, that of the male red beneath. This is an elegant species, of the size of the common domestic fowl, with a very light tinge of rose-colour on the head and breast, and of yel-low on the inner wing-coverts and tail feathers. On the head is a very ample crest, consisting of large and long feathers of different extent, arched over the whole head, and which the bird can raise or depress at plea-sure. Native of the Malacca islands. It is of a mild and gentle disposition, but can rarely be tempted to articulate any other word than *cockatoo,* which, like some of its congeners, it does with great distinctness.

Erithacus.

P. erithacus, Lin. &c. *Ash-coloured, Hoary,* or *Com-mon Grey Parrot.* Grey, with naked white orbits and bright red tail. General size that of a small pigeon, and length about twelve inches. This well-known species is remarkable for its docility, the distinctness of its articu-lation, and its unrestrained loquacity, readily imitating every sound within its hearing, especially during the three first years of its life; for, after that period, it learns lessons with much more difficulty. It is generally brought from Congo and Angola, but is common also in other regions of Africa.

Buffon informs us, that the grey parrot has been known to breed in France. A gentleman of Marmande, in that country, had, it seems, a pair, which, for five or six years together, produced young ones, that were successfully reared. They made their nest in spring in a cask, filled with saw-dust; and the number of eggs was four, but only three productive. According to Labat, a similar instance once occurred at Paris.

Like many others of its tribe, the grey parrot often lives to a great age; and we are told of individuals at-taining to fifty, sixty, or even one hundred years. Ac-cording to Levaillant, one which lived in the family of Mr. Meninck-Huyser, at Amsterdam, for thirty-two years, had previously passed forty-one with that gentleman's uncle, who bequeathed it to his nephew; and there can be little doubt, that it must have been at least two or three years old at the time of its arrival in Europe. When Levaillant saw it, the bird was in a state of complete decrepitude, and, having lost its sight and memory, had lapsed into a sort of lethargic condi-tion, and was fed at intervals with biscuit dipped in Madeira. In the days of its vigour it used to speak with great distinctness, repeat many entire sentences, fetch its master's slippers, call the servant, &c. At the age of sixty its memory began to fail, and, instead of acquiring any new phrases, it began very perceptibly to lose those which it had learned, and to intermix, in a discordant manner, the words of its former language.

It moulted regularly once a-year, till the age of sixty-five, when the red feathers of the tail were supplied by yellow ones, after which no other change of plu-mage took place.

Amazoni-us.

P. Amazonius, Shaw, *P. æstivus,* Lin. *Amazon Parrot, Common Green Parrot* of Willoughby, &c. Green, with the edges of the shoulders red; a red patch on the wings; crown yellow; and frontal bar blue. The varieties are very numerous, and have given rise to a voluminous catalogue of names. These birds are natives of South America, especially of that extensive territory which is watered by the river Amazon. In Surinam, they occasion much injury in the plantations. They build in the midst of thick forests, the female laying four white eggs in the hollow of a tree. The young are at first quite naked, and then covered with a whitish-grey down, which is gradually succeeded by the plumage. On issuing from the nest, the male and female resemble each other.

The wonderful parrot which held a conversation with Prince Maurice, as commemorated by Locke and Sir William Temple, appears to have belonged to one of the varieties of the present species, as also that which Col. O'Kelly bought at Bristol for a hundred guineas. This last not only repeated a great number of senten-ces, but would answer questions, and whistle a great variety of tunes. It also beat time with all the ap-pearance of science, and if by chance it mistook a note, it would revert to the bar where the slip was made, correct itself, and, still beating regular time, go through the whole with wonderful exactness.

Pullarius.

P. pullarius, Lin. &c. *Guinea Parrot, Red-headed Guinea Parrakeet, Ethiopian Parrot,* &c. Green, with red face, blue rump, and orange-red tail, crossed by a black bar. A highly beautiful species, about five inches and a half in length, and a native of Guinea, where it is of common occurrence. It is also found in Ethiopia, Java, and the East Indies. In those countries it preys on the corn and fruits, as the sparrow does in Europe. The trading vessels seldom fail to bring away consi-derable quantities of them in cages; but they are so delicate that most of them die in their passage to our colder climates. It has also been observed, that the firing of a vessel's great guns is fatal to many of them, which drop down dead from fear. Although very im-itative of the manners of other birds, it is difficult to teach them to articulate words. They are extremely kind and affectionate to one another.

A male and female of this species were lodged toge-ther in a large square cage. The vessel that held their food was placed at the bottom. The male usually sat on the same perch with the female, and close beside her. Whenever one descended for food, the other al-ways followed; and, when their hunger was satisfied, they returned together to the highest perch of the cage. In this state of confinement they passed four years, when the female became languid, and her legs swelled, and were knotty, as if symptomatic of gout. It was no longer possible for her to descend, and take her food as formerly; but the male assiduously brought it to her, carrying it in his bill, and delivering it into hers; and he continued to feed her in this manner for four entire months. The infirmities of his mate, how-ever, increased every day, so that at length she was no longer able to sit on the perch, but remained crouched at the bottom, making from time to time a few fruit-less efforts to regain the lower perch, while the male, who remained close by her, seconded these her feeble attempts with all his power, sometimes seizing with his

M

bill the upper part of her wing, to try to draw her up to him; sometimes taking hold of her bill, and attempting to raise her up, repeating his efforts several times. His countenance, his gestures, his continual solicitude, indicated in this affectionate bird the most ardent desire to aid the weakness, and to alleviate the sufferings, of his companion. But the scene became still more interesting, when the female was on the point of expiring. Her unfortunate partner then went round and round her without ceasing; he redoubled his assiduities and his tender cares; he attempted to open her bill, in order to give her some nourishment; he went to her, and returned with the most agitated air, and with the utmost inquietude; at intervals he uttered the most plaintive cries, while at other times, with his eyes rivetted on her, he preserved a sorrowful silence. His faithful companion at length ceased to breathe; and from that time he languished, and died in a few months.

Picus, Lin. &c. Woodpecker.

Picus.

Bill angular, straight, wedged at the tip; tongue round, vermiform, very long, bony, missile, beset at the point with reflex bristles; tail feathers ten, hard, rigid, and pointed. In search of insects and their larvæ, the birds of this genus climb trees, especially such as are decaying, or already dead. For this exercise nature has formed them with short and robust legs and feet, stout toes, hooked, strong, and pointed claws, which are thicker than broad, a thick and muscular rump, the tail feathers concave, and very strong and elastic at the points, so that they easily cling to trees with their feet, and sustain their creeping and upward movements by their tail. The strokes of their beak are sometimes repeated in such rapid succession, that it is impossible to reckon them. If they perceive that a caterpillar is lodged beneath the bark, and observe no hole by which it can get out, they strike with more force, but less rapidity, as is likewise their practice when they scoop out a hole for their nest; and such is their perseverance, that they have been known to excavate the thickest trunks to the very centre. All the woodpeckers have an offensive smell, owing perhaps to their constantly living on worms and insects. Very few of them are capable of walking on the ground for any length of time. Some of them live in families, some in pairs, and others are solitary. By means of their hard and sharp bill they bore the wood, and expose the retreats of their prey, and then, with a motion inconceivably quick, darting at their victims with their long tongue, which is tipt with a sharp bony process, dentated on both sides, and smeared over with a viscous fluid, transfix them with this formidable weapon, and draw them within their mouths. They have a membranous stomach, and are destitute of a cœcum. In many places they are unjustly persecuted, from a notion that they are injurious to trees, whereas they in fact prevent the multiplication of their most insidious enemies. We should observe, however, that some of them also eat fruit; and that sound trees are sometimes affected by their perforations. None of them have a musical note; nor do they appear to have been destined for social intercourse, being almost incessantly occupied in picking the bark of trees for their sustenance.

Martius.

P. martius, Lin. &c. *Black Woodpecker, Great*, or *Greatest Black Woodpecker*. Black, with the crown scarlet. Bill nearly two inches and a half long, of a dark ash-colour, and whitish on the sides; irides pale yellow. Size of a jackdaw; length seventeen inches; alar extent upwards of two feet; and weight about

eleven ounces. In the female the hind-head only is red, and the whole plumage has a tinge of brown. In some instances the red on the head is entirely wanting. The young males have the upper parts of the head marked with red and blackish spots. It occurs in Europe, Siberia, and Chili; but few well-authenticated instances are on record of its having been observed in Great Britain. It appears, however, to have been once shot in Lancashire, and perhaps once or twice in Devonshire. Some writers allege that it is migratory; but Gérardin assures us, that in Lorraine, though far from numerous, it remains throughout the year. It is not found in Italy, but is said to be common in Germany, and in some parts of southern Russia and Siberia, affecting the solitary and extensive forests of hilly regions, and exhibiting most of the habits of the green species. So hostile is it to bees, that where many of these insects are hived in the trees, the people are obliged to take every precaution to guard the mouth of the hive, which is generally done with sharp thorns, though not always with sufficient effect. The black woodpecker makes its nest deep in some tree, which it has excavated for the purpose, and lays two or three eggs, which, like those of most of the genus are white and glossy.

Viridis.

P. viridis, Lin. &c. *Green Woodpecker*, Prov. *Woodspite, High-hoe, Haw-hole, Awl-bird, Yappingale, Yaffle, Yaffler, Woodwall*, and *Popinjay*. Wallis, in his *History of Northumberland*, observes, that it is called by the common people, *Pick-a-tree*, and also *Rainfowl*, from its being most loud and noisy before rain; and, for the same reason, it was included in the *Pluviæ Aves* of the Romans. Green, with a scarlet crown. Nearly the size of a jay; weight six ounces; length thirteen inches; and alar extent eighteen inches six lines. The young, on coming from the nest, have very little red on the head. Among the accidental varieties, some are of a light straw-colour, with the head only tinged or spotted with red, and others are more or less sprinkled with white. Inhabits Europe, and is far from uncommon in the wooded parts of England. Its note is harsh, and its flight undulating. It feeds on insects, and is partial to ants and bees. It is frequently seen climbing up a tree, dislodging the larvæ of a numerous tribe of the coleopterous insects, as well as the fetid caterpillar of the *Goat-moth* (*Phalæna cossius,*) of which it frequently smells. In spring and summer it is more commonly observed on the ground than its congeners, being strongly attracted by ant-hills. Laying its long extensile tongue in the path of the little occupants, who seem to take it for a worm, whenever it is sufficiently loaded with them, it suddenly draws it in and swallows them. Should cold or rain benumb or confine the ants, the woodpecker breaks down their habitation by the combined efforts of its bill and feet, and consumes both the insects and their chrysalids at leisure. The hole which it makes in a tree is as perfect a circle as if it had been traced by a pair of compasses. It is curious to observe it trying every part of the dead limb of a tree, till it has discovered the most sonorous; and then its strokes are reiterated with such velocity that the head is scarcely perceived to move, and the sound may be distinctly heard at the distance of half a mile. Dr. Plott ludicrously exaggerates this noise, and erroneously attributes it to the nuthatch. The softer kinds of wood, such as the elm, the ash, and especially the aspen, are most commonly selected for the purpose of nidification; and they are perforated only where they exhibit symptoms of decay. In the course of the boring process the male and female labour by turns. The excavations are often deep, to give security to the eggs, which are generally four or five, of a transparent white or greenish hue, marked with small black spots, and placed on the rotten wood, without any formal nest, usually at fifteen or twenty feet from the ground. Occasionally, however, moss or wool is employed as a bed for the eggs. During breeding time the sexes seldom separate, retire early to rest, and remain in their retreat till day-break. The young ones are able to climb before they can fly; and they roost very early in the evening. Even at a very tender age, if fed with caterpillars from the dunghill, put into milk, and mixed with crumbs of bread, they will not only submit to confinement, but become sufficiently tame, and evince attachment to their feeder. A jarring noise, which has been compared to a hurried and continuous laugh, and which is sometimes heard in the forests in spring, is said to be the sexual call of this species, which also emits a plaintive and protracted clamour, expressed by the syllables *pleu, pleu,* on the approach of rain. A person may often come nearly within reach of the green woodpecker when it is occupied in beating on a tree; but it frequently makes an abrupt turn round to the opposite side of the trunk or branch, to seize on any insects which, alarmed at the noise, may have issued from their retreats.

Major. *P. major,* Lin. &c. *Greater Spotted Woodpecker,* Prov. *Witwall.* Varied with black and white; back of the head and vent red. Female without red on the hind-head. Weight about two ounces and three quarters, length nine inches, and extent of wing between thirteen and fourteen inches. The bill is dusky, and an inch and a quarter long; and the irides are reddish-brown. Inhabits most parts of Europe, and is also found in Siberia and about Astrachan. It is less common in England than the green species, to which it is much allied in habits and manners, except that it more rarely descends to the ground; but it creeps, with wonderful facility and in all directions, on the branches of trees, and is so very shy and wary as to be with difficulty aimed at; for if it perceive a person in the neighbourhood, it instantly skulks behind a bough, eyeing the stranger all the while, and regulating its motions so as to be constantly disguised from him. It resides in the woods in the summer season, but may frequently be seen in gardens and orchards in winter, picking its food from the fruit trees. It strikes on trees with great loudness and violence; nestles at about twenty feet above the ground, in a hole of its own excavation, in a tree, without any arrangement of soft materials, except of the powder of the rotten wood; and lays four or five glossy white eggs, from which, or her young, the dam is not easily detached, as she will sometimes rather suffer herself to be taken than abandon her charge. Both sexes utter the loud and discordant noise to which we have alluded in our notice of the green species. The *medius* of Linné is the young of the present species.

Minor. *P. minor,* Lin. &c. *Lesser Spotted Woodpecker,* Prov. *Hickwall* and *Crank-bird.* Varied with black and white, crown red, vent testaceous. The female has no red on the head; and the parts which are black in the male are in her of a washy brown. A pure white, or a cream-coloured variety, sometimes occurs. It is the smallest of the European woodpeckers, being scarcely so large as a house sparrow, about five inches and a

half in length, nine in stretch of wing, and scarcely five drachms in weight. Though diffused over the north of Europe, and not uncommon in some parts of Russia and Siberia, it is of rather rare occurrence in France, and is not often met with in Britain. Specimens, however, have been obtained both from Gloucestershire and Wiltshire. In its habits it pretty nearly corresponds with the preceding, frequenting woods in the fine season, but in winter drawing near houses and vineyards, yet by no means of easy capture. Like its congeners, it breeds in the holes of decayed trees, and will sometimes dispute possession with the colemouse, which it compels to relinquish its lodging. The lesser spotted woodpecker has the same discordant note as the greater, but of a more feeble tone.

Campestris. *P. campestris,* Vieil. *Field Wren.* The head crested with black and long feathers, a white spot extending over the nostrils to beyond the eyes, and one of pure yellow from the ears to the fore part of the neck; all the hinder parts whitish, and transversely striped with blackish. The throat is black in the female, and marbled with white in the male. Length eleven inches two lines. This species, according to Azara, never penetrates into woods, nor climbs on trees, but seizes its insect food in the open plains, which they traverse with a precipitate step on their long legs. By forcibly striking the turf once or twice with their bill, they bring forth earth-worms and insects from their retreats. They likewise attack ant-hills when softened by rain, and pick up the ants and their larvæ. They perch occasionally, however, on the trunks or branches of trees, or on stones, sometimes in a horizontal, sometimes in a vertical, and sometimes in a climbing attitude. They live in pairs or in families, and nestle at the bottom of holes, which they dig in the mud of deserted walls, on the steep banks of rivulets, &c. and the female lays from two to four eggs of a very glossy white.

Tridactylus. *P. tridactylus,* Lin. Tem. *Picus hirsutus,* Vieil. *Picoides hirsutus,* Cuv. *Tridactylia hirsuta,* Steph. *Three-toed Woodpecker, Northern Three-toed Woodpecker, Downy Woodpeckeret,* &c. Varied with black and white; the tarsi feathered half way down. Nearly nine inches in length, but varies both in size and markings. The female resembles the male in every respect except the colour of the crown, which in the male is yellow, and in the female white. It is an inhabitant of the colder climates of Europe, as Sweden, Lapland, and Russia, as far as the Don. Towards the south it extends to Austria and Switzerland, in the last of which it appears to be most frequent, the species delighting in the highest mountainous situations. Though so widely diffused, it is not common, and is extremely rare in this island; but is said to have been once shot in the north of Scotland. It is reported to occur in Hudson's Bay, and other parts of North America. It breeds in the natural holes of trees; and the female lays four or five glossy white eggs.

We might easily multiply the list of foreign woodpeckers; but, as they differ chiefly in some unimportant points, and their habits are presumed to be very similar, their exposition would prove at once irksome, and incompatible with the limits of the present article.

YUNX, Lin. &c. WRYNECK.

Yunx. Bill short, straight, in the form of a depressed cone, and very slender at the tip; the mandibles unnotched, nostrils basal, naked, partly closed by a membrane;

Ornithology.

the two fore toes united at their origin, the hind ones divided; the tongue capable of elongation, as in the woodpeckers, but not barbed.

The wrynecks have many of the habits of the preceding family, but are not so capable of climbing trees, and chiefly fix on the bark, to extract insects from the crevices. They are also frequently observed on ants' nests, preying on the ants and their larvæ. There are only three known species.

Torquilla.

Y. torquilla, Lin. &c. *Wryneck*, Prov. *Long-tongue*, or *Emmet Hunter*. Grey, varied with black and fuscous above; abdomen rufescent white, with blackish spots; tail feathers spotted, and barred with waving black striæ. No pen or pencil can furnish a perfect idea of the minute and elegant markings of this bird, which is about the size of a lark, measures seven inches in length, and nine and a half in stretch of wing, and weighs about ten drachms. The hues of the female are rather paler than those of the male. A pure white, and a yellowish-white variety, sometimes occur.

The wryneck is so called, from the singular manner in which, especially when surprised, it turns its head over its shoulders, perpetually looking about, while the black list on the back of the neck gives it a twisted appearance. On such occasions it also erects the feathers on the head. It inhabits Europe, Asia, and Africa, occurring from Greece and Italy to Sweden, and even Lapland, in Siberia, and Kamtschatka, and, according to Kolben, at the Cape of Good Hope; and Edwards assures us that it is met with in Bengal. It is not uncommon in the southern and eastern parts of England, but is more scarce on the western side of the island, and is rarely, if ever, found in Cornwall. It is partial to poplar, and to old and decayed pollard elms, and will perch on a detached tree in a hedge, usually frequenting woods, or thick inclosed countries; yet, towards the close of summer, it may be observed hopping alone, in the pathways which traverse fields of wheat, barley, or oats, when it becomes excessively fat, and is reckoned a great delicacy for the table. Its food principally consists of ants and other insects, of which it finds abundance lodged in the bark and crevices of trees, or in other retreats. So shy and unsocial are these birds, that, except during the breeding season, they are never found in the company even of their partners, and, when the domestic union is dissolved in September, they retire, and seem to migrate by themselves. The female lays from eight to ten very white and transparent eggs, for the most part on the dust of a hole, in a decayed tree, which she scrapes together with her bill and feet; but sometimes she constructs on it an artless nest of dried grass. The entrance into the hole is so small as scarcely to admit the fingers; so that the eggs are not readily procured. During incubation the male fetches ants and other insect food to his mate. If surprised in her nest, the female stretches herself at full length, erects the feathers on the crown of the head, and exhibits a snake-like motion, in which she is imitated by the young, who moreover emit a hissing sound; and thus intruders are sometimes scared, believing that they have come in contact with a brood of serpents. In spring, the wryneck frequently repeats a sort of noise, like that of the smaller species of hawks.

ORDER VI.

ANISODACTYLOUS BIRDS.

Aniso-dacty-lous Birds.

Bill more or less arched, often straight, always subulate, filiform, and slender; feet with three toes before and one behind, the outer united at the base to that in the middle, the hinder one generally long, and all provided with pretty long and hooked claws.

The birds of this division have more or less the manners and habits of those of the preceding order; for almost all of them are climbers, and insectivorous.

SITTA, Lin. &c. NUTHATCH.

Sitta.

Bill straight, prismatic, pointed, and fitted for opening the bark of trees; the tail composed of twelve feathers.

Europæa.

S. Europæa, Lin. &c. *European Nuthatch*, Prov. *Nutjobber*, *Nutbreaker*, or *Woodcracker*. Plumbeous above, sub-ferruginous beneath; a black streak across the eyes, and black lateral tail feathers, whitish near the tips. Weight nearly an ounce, length five inches three quarters, and alar expanse nine inches. The tints of the female are weaker than those of the male, especially about the sides and thighs. This species inhabits Europe and Asia, and seems to be little affected by the influence of climate. In this island, as in most other countries, it is stationary, but local, and chiefly affects wooded and inclosed situations, frequently selecting the deserted habitation of a woodpecker for its nest. In this case the entrance to the hole is first contracted by a plaster of clay or mud, to exclude larger birds, and leaving only sufficient room for itself to pass in and out. The male and female jointly labour at the construction of the nest, which usually consists of dead leaves and moss heaped together without much order, and sometimes lined with the dust of the decayed tree in which the nest is placed. The number of eggs is generally six or seven, and they are of a dirty white, with dusky spots, being scarcely distinguishable from those of the greater titmouse. If the plaster at the entrance be destroyed when there are eggs in the nest, it is speedily replaced. During incubation the female is assiduously attended by the male, who regularly supplies her with food. Though easily driven from her nest at other times, she sits on her eggs with great pertinacity, striking the invader with her bill and wings, and hissing like a snake; and after every effort has been practised in vain, she will rather suffer herself to be taken than desert her charge. The eggs are hatched in May; and there is rarely more than one brood in the season. After the young can provide for themselves, the family separates, and all seek retirement, though they are occasionally observed to mingle with titmice and woodpeckers. Although the nuthatch spends much of its time in climbing or creeping on trees, its motions are nimbler than those of the sparrow, as well as smoother and more connected; for it makes less noise in flying. In climbing it is more expert than the woodpecker; for it runs up and down a tree in all directions. When employed in breaking a nut, its favourite position is with the head down. In the autumn, it is no uncommon thing to find in the crevices of the bark of an old tree a great many broken nut shells, the work of this bird, which repeatedly returns to the same spot for this purpose. When it has fixed the nut firm in a chink, it turns on all sides to strike it with most advantage. This, with the common hazel nut, is a work of some labour; but it strikes a filbert with ease. Whilst at work, it makes a rapping noise, which may be heard at some distance. In default of nuts or seeds, this bird searches for insects and their larvæ among moss or old trees, or walls, thatch, &c. In winter it picks the larvæ of beetles from under the bark of trees, and has recourse to the magazine of nuts, and the seeds of sun-flower, hemp, &c. which it is known sometimes to lay up against the cold season. Sometimes it is met with in vineyards, orchards, or gardens; and in the cyder season it has been observed culling the seeds from the refuse of the pressed apples. Though silent during the greater part of the year, it has in spring a remarkably loud and shrill whistle, which ceases after incubation, and gives place in autumn to a double reiterated cry; but the singular jarring noise produced by some species of woodpeckers, by repeated strokes of the bill against the decayed limb of a tree, has been erroneously ascribed to the nuthatch.

CERTHIA, Lin. &c. CREEPER.

CERTHIA. Bill long, or of moderate size, more or less arched, triangular, compressed, and slender; nostrils basal, naked, pierced horizontally, and half closed by an arched membrane; the outer toe united at its base to the intermediate; claws much hooked, that on the hind toe the longest; tail graduated, and furnished with stiff and sharp-pointed shafts; wings middle-sized, the fourth quill the longest.

The birds of this genus climb on trees like the woodpeckers, supporting themselves by the stiff-pointed feathers of the tail. They nestle in the chinks and holes of trees, and live principally on small insects and seeds. The limits of the genus have of late been considerably abridged. Only one species is indigenous to Europe; for the alleged *Brachydactyla* of M. Brehon, of Saxony, proves to be only one of those accidental varieties, which, in this instance, are considerably multiplied. But the sexes and the young are less dissimilar from one another than in most species of the feathered race.

Familiaris. *C. familiaris*, Lin. &c. *Common Creeper*, Prov. *Ox-eye Creeper*, or *Tree Creeper*, or *Tree Climber*. Chesnut, varied with black and whitish above, white beneath; tail sub-fulvous, and pointed. The weight of the full grown bird is only about two drachms, and its length five inches. Except the crested wren it is the smallest of British birds; but the length of its feathers, and its manner of ruffling them, make it appear larger than it is in reality.

The common creeper inhabits Europe, Asia, and North America, especially the neighbourhood of Philadelphia, where it is very common. It runs with great quickness and facility round trunks and limbs of trees in search of insects and their eggs, which it also picks up from among moss, and which constitute its principal food. Though pretty common, it is not readily perceived, from the ease with which, on the appearance of any person, it glides to the opposite side of the tree. Its nest is composed of dry grass and the inner bark of wood, loosely put together, and lined with small feathers; and it is usually placed in some hole, or behind the bark of a decayed tree. The eggs are from six to eight, whitish, or ash-coloured, and minutely speckled with bars and spots of bright rust colour. During incubation the male caters for his partner. His note is weak, monotonous, and delicately uttered, but rarely heard in winter. This little bird

seems to be not averse to the society of mankind; for it haunts trees on public walks near towns; and, in some parts of the world it is protected by human care from motives of interest. Thus, from observing its usefulness in destroying insects, it has long been customary in several districts of the United States, to fix a small box at the end of a long pole in gardens and about houses, as a receptacle for its nest. In these boxes the birds readily form their nests, and hatch their young, which the parent feeds with a variety of different insects, particularly those species which are injurious to the produce of the garden.

TICHODROMA, Illig. Tem. PETRODROMA, Vieil. CERTHIA, Lin.

TICHO-DROMA. Bill very long, slightly arched, slender, cylindrical, triangular at the base, tip depressed; claw on the hind toe very long; tail rounded, with weak shafts.

Muraria. *T. muraria*, Illig. *T. phœnicoptera*, Tem. *Petrodroma muraria*, Vieill. *Certhia muraria*, Lin. *Wallcreeper*, or *Spider-catcher*. Cinereous, with black wings and tail, wing-coverts rose-colour, as are the edges of the quills. The under part of the neck is whitish, the quill-feathers are black, those of the tail whitish; and the claws, particularly the hind one, are very strong. About the size of a sparrow, seven inches in length, and nine in stretch of wing. The male and female are alike. Inhabits the temperate countries of Europe and Asia. Though found in Austria, Silesia, Poland, Switzerland, and Lorraine, it courts milder latitudes in winter. Aldrovandus informs us, that it is not uncommon in the territory of Bologna, flying in the manner of a hoopoe, frequently shaking its wings like that bird, and never resting long in one place. In Spain and Portugal it is said to be by no means rare. It is found in Mount Caucasus, and has been fetched from China. Though gay and sprightly, it is so solitary in its habits, that, according to Scopoli, it migrates singly. Its note is loud, but not unpleasing; and its manners are similar to those of the common creeper, except that, in place of haunting trees, it affects rocks, old walls, ruined edifices, arches, &c. feeding on insects, and manifesting a partiality to spiders. It nestles in the holes of walls, and the crevices of high rocks.

NECTARINIA, Illig. Tem. NECTAR SUCKER.

NECTARI-NIA. Bill long, or as long as the head, weak, subulate, and more or less curved, widened and depressed at the base, trigonal, compressed, and very slender at the point; tongue long, extensile, tubular, and bifid; nostrils near the base, lateral, closed above by a large naked membrane; the third and fourth quills the longest. The species, which are pretty numerous, are all exotic: Some of them are of small dimensions and brilliant hues, and others are larger. They have their designation from sipping the sweet juice of flowers.

Cyanea. *N. cyanea*, *Certhia cyanea*, Lin. *Coereba cyanea*, Vieill. *Cyanean Nectar-sucker*, or *Cyanean-creeper*. Deep blue, with beryl-coloured crown, black wings and tail, and yellow under coverts. This elegant little bird, which is more minutely described by Edwards, measures about four inches and a quarter, is a native of South America, particularly of Brazil and Cayenne. The female is said to differ in having the insides of the wings yellowish-grey, and the young males are at first greenish above, except on the wings and tail, and of a paler or yellowish cast beneath. They afterwards become varied, or patched with black, blue, and green, with a mixture of rufous on some parts. We notice these dif-

Rufa.

ferences, because by some writers they have been stated as so many varieties or species.

N. rufa, Merops rufus, Lath. *Turnarius rufus,* Vieill. *Rufous Nectar-sucker,* or *Rufous Bee-eater.* Rufous above, with brown quill feathers, rufous on the edges. The throat, fore part of the neck, breast, and belly, are of a beautiful white. Length seven inches two lines. This species, which is a native of South America, readily frequents cultivated fields, and approaches small towns, villages, and hamlets, preferably breeding near houses, and sometimes within them. Though they reside in bushes and thickets, they come abroad into the open fields, never penetrating into extensive woods nor haunting elevated situations. They associate in pairs, and are not observed in families or flocks. As their wings are somewhat short, and far from strong, they fly to a little distance at a time. They always build their nest in some open situation, as on a large leafless branch of a tree, or on the window of a house, or on a paling or stake at several feet from the ground. The nest, which is shaped like a baker's oven, is constructed of mud or clay, and is sometimes completed in two days, the male and female jointly working, each fetching in turn a pellet of the materials of the size of a hazel nut, which they arrange and adjust into a fabric, six inches and a half in diameter, with the opening on the side twice as high as broad. The interior is divided into two parts by a partition, which begins at the side of the entrance, and terminates circularly, so as to leave a passage into a sort of chamber, in which, on a lid of grass, are deposited four white eggs, dotted with rufous, and somewhat pointed at the narrow end. The same nests, if not destroyed by the rain, will serve the same pair for more than one season; and if they find it occupied by a bird of another species, which sometimes happens, they generally succeed in expelling the usurper. Azara notices a tame individual of this species which was allowed to go at large, and, when hungry, would eat pounded maize, but always preferred raw meat; and if the bit was too big to be swallowed at once, it would press it on the ground with its foot, and tear it with its bill. Its walk was alternately grave and majestic, and quick and precipitate, with the head and neck erect. When it sung, it stretched out its body, lengthened its neck, and beat its wings. The note, which is common to both sexes, and is continued all the year round, consists in the loud and frequent repetition of the syllable *shee,* at first uttered at intervals, and then pronounced pretty smartly, until it forms a continuous burden or cadence, which is heard at the distance of half a mile.

Sannio.

N. sannio, Certhia sannio, Lath. *Melithreptus sannio,* Vieill. *Mocking Nectar-sucker,* or *Creeper.* Olive, with the wings and slightly forked tail brown. Bill black, and legs lead-colour. Size of the thrush, length about eight inches and a half. Native of New Holland. It is reported to have a fine note, and to acquire with great facility those of other birds. So remarkable too is its propensity to vary its song, that, when in hearing of it, a person is apt to suppose that he is surrounded by many birds of different species. The crown of the head has often a purple tint, occasioned by thrusting it against the stamina of certain flowers, of which it extracts the sweets.

TROCHILUS, Lin. &c. HUMMING-BIRD.

TROCHI-
LUS.

Bill subulate, filiform, tubular at the tip, and longer than the head; the upper mandible sheathing the lower;

the tongue filiform, having its two threads coalescing, and tubular.

The birds of this family are of very small dimensions, and, with a very few exceptions, inhabit the southern regions of America. Their bill and feet are weak; but the former is very long in proportion to the size of the body; the nostrils are minute, and the tongue is capable of being thrust a great way out. They fly very rapidly, take their food on the wing, and suck the honied juice of flowers without discomposing them. As they are spread to the 35th degree of southern latitude, and occur in the neighbourhood of the Plata, in situations which, during winter, are destitute both of groves and flowers, we may infer that they are capable of sustaining a considerable degree of cold, and of living on other food than nectar. Azara accordingly observed them visiting the webs of spiders, and, as he supposed, eating the spiders themselves; and Father Isidore Guerra, a man worthy of credit, and who amused himself with rearing humming birds, has fully confirmed his conjecture. The strength of their rump and tail feathers enables them to turn in the air, and to stop short in the midst of their fleetest career, as if suspended before a flower, flapping their wings with inconceivable quickness, darting their tongue into the nectary, and holding their body in a vertical position, as if stuck fast by the bill. They roost on the branch of a tree during the night, and the hottest part of the day, and pass the rest of their time in fluttering from flower to flower. When they are engaged in extracting the juices from the blossoms of a tree, one may approach pretty near them without driving them away. Their note, which is very seldom heard except when they remove from one flower to another, is expressed by *taïre,* more or less shrilly, but feebly pronounced. Two of them are seldom seen together, or even on the same tree. Notwithstanding their very diminutive size, they are bold and pugnacious, and make a louder humming noise by the motion of their wings than by their voice. Their fierce conflicts often terminate by their sudden disappearance, without the spectator being able to ascertain which of the combatants has had the advantage. They construct an elegant hemispherical nest of the down of a species of thapsus, and suspend it over branches of trees, where it is concealed by the leaves, the female laying two white eggs of the size of peas, and which are hatched, in consequence of the alternate incubation of the parents. The latter manifest unusual courage in driving intruders from their nest; and they sometimes assail and chase other birds without any apparent motive. They are taken by firing at them with sand, aspersing them with water from a syphon, or entangling them in delicate nests; for the finest shot would blow them to pieces, and rods smeared with bird-lime would destroy their plumage. The unrivalled brilliancy of their colours has been aptly compared to the richest metallic hues, or to the changeful reflexions of gems; and in sunshine they glow with peculiar splendour. It is not, however, to be imagined, that all the species of humming birds are thus magnificently decorated; for some are even obscure in their attire, and instead of the prevailing gaudiness of the family, exhibit only a faint appearance of a golden green tinge diffused over the brown or purplish shade of the back and wings.

Several people in South America have kept humming-birds in their houses. Not many years ago, Don Pedro Melo, governor of Paraguay, had one full grown, which lived with him for four months, and was allowed to

Ornitho-
logy.

range in the house. This little flutterer was perfectly attached to his master, whom he would kiss, and playfully importune for a little syrup, or a nosegay. Thus he lived, healthy and apparently happy, till, in the Don's absence, he perished from the negligence of the servants.

This numerous and interesting genus has been commodiously divided into two sections, the first including those with curved, and the second those with straight bills, corresponding to the *colibris* and *oiseaux-mouches* of the French; yet the precise limits of the two divisions are not very easily assignable.

A. *Curved-billed Humming-birds.*

Pella.

T. pella, Lin. &c. *Topaz-throated Humming-bird*, or *Long-tailed Red Humming-bird*. Purple-red, with black head, topazine throat, and the two middle tail-feathers very long. The male is the most conspicuous of its section, both its size and the brilliancy of its plumage distinguishing it above the rest. Its body is equal in size to that of a wren, but if measured from the extremity of the bill to that of the middle tail-feathers, its length is from eight to ten inches. This species, which occasionally varies in the sportings of its rich colourings, is a native of several parts of South America, but is principally met with in Surinam and Guiana, where it preferably affects the banks of rivers and brooks, especially in the interior of the country. It commonly perches on the lower branches of such trees as overhang the stream, or on such as, from decay, have fallen into the water. During their flight they skim the surface of the water, like swallows.

Mango.

T. mango, Lin. &c. *Mango Humming-bird*. Copper-green, with the stripe on the throat, and the abdomen black, wings violet-brown, and the tail ferruginous and edged with black. Length four inches and a quarter. In the female, the back and the two middle tail-feathers are golden-green. Native of South America, particularly of Brazil, and is said also to occur in Jamaica, St. Domingo, and some other of the West India islands. Dr. Latham informs us, that a pair of young humming-birds, supposed to be of this species, are reported, on unexceptionable testimony, to have been brought alive to England, having been hatched during their voyage from Jamaica, where the parent bird, while sitting on her eggs, was discovered by a young gentleman, then on the point of leaving the island. Having cut off the twig on which the nest was placed, he brought it on board the ship. The female soon became sufficiently tame to suffer herself to be fed with honey, and during the passage hatched two young ones, but did not long survive that event; but the young were so successfully managed, as to be conveyed in good health to England, where they were presented to Lady Hammond. The Doctor adds, that Sir Henry Englefield, Bart. and Colonel Sloane, are both witnesses to these little birds readily taking honey from the lips of Lady Hammond with their bills. One of them lived at least two months from the time of its arrival, but the other not many days.

B. *Straight-billed Humming-bird.*

Cristatus.

T. cristatus, Lin. &c. *Crested Humming-bird*, or *Crested Green Humming-bird* of Edwards. Golden-green above, cinereous beneath, with golden-blue pointed crest, and violet quill-feathers and tail. Length about three inches. Edwards, who describes the bird, has given a good figure both of it and of the nest. The female wants the crest. It is rare at Cayenne, but

numerous in Martinique, Guadaloupe, and some other of the West India islands. In its general manners and character it seems to resemble the red-throated species, being of a bold disposition, attacking larger birds, and expelling them from its haunts. It frequents orchards and gardens, and fears not to breed even in towns. It often builds its nest on the twig of an orange tree, lemon tree, or jasmine, and sometimes on the projecting straws of the roof of a cottage; and if the nest and young be taken into a house, the female will follow, and rear her charge in confinement.

Colubris.

T. colubris, Lin. &c. *Red-throated Humming-bird*, or *Humming-bird* of Catesby. Gold-green above, white beneath, with gold-red throat, and purple-brown wings and tail. This most beautiful species usually measures about three inches and one-third from the tip of the bill to that of the tail.

The red-throated humming-bird inhabits America, continuing in the southern parts of that continent the whole year, and appearing in the northern provinces, as far as Canada, in the summer only, arriving in the month of May, when the peach-trees are in blossom, and breeding in Carolina, the Floridas, &c. but, on the approach of winter migrating to Mexico and the West Indies. In autumn it frequently perishes, in consequence of having been detained by the late brood, at a time when the flowers begin to be destroyed by frost, and of its being weakened by cold weather, when it can no longer execute the movements of its wings with the necessary degree of rapidity to keep it suspended in the act of sucking its food. In such a state of the atmosphere, it is observed to fly with less velocity, to perch often, sometimes to rest on the ground, and gradually to sink under the cold. The late broods, too, are often exposed to this fate, and are found dead during the autumnal season. During the warmer days of summer, this charming little creature flies so swiftly that the eye is incapable of pursuing it, and the motion of its wings is so rapid as to be imperceptible to the nicest observer. It never feeds but on the wing, suspended over the flower from which it extracts its nourishment; and, like the bee, having exhausted the honied liquor of one flower, it wanders to the next in quest of new sweets. It is most partial to those flowers that have the deepest nectaries, as the balsamine, scarlet monarda, &c.; so that, in those countries which these birds inhabit, whoever sets plants of this description before his window, may depend on being visited by them in multitudes. M. Vieillot having observed them often perch on the dry twigs of trees, and wishing to contemplate them in full sunshine, inserted several small sticks among the flowers which they frequented, and had thus the pleasure of seeing them, while sitting, dart their tongue into the nearest flowers, and trying every tube by thrusting in their bill. If they found the flower already rifled, they would frequently, in a fit of rage, pluck it off, and throw it on the ground, or even tear it in pieces. Numbers would also sometimes contend very fiercely for the possession of the same flower; and, in the course of warfare, they would frequently pursue the fugitives into the apartments of those houses whose windows happened to be left open, make a turn round the room, as flies do with us, and then suddenly regain the open air. When feeding, they will allow a person to come within two yards of them; but, on a nearer approach, they dart off with wonderful swiftness. Their nest is most commonly placed in the middle of a branch of a tree, and is so small as not to be noticed by a person standing on the ground. The male assists in fetching the materials, and the female arranges them. The structure is quite round, the outside being, for the most part, composed of the green moss common on old poles and trees, and the inside of the softest vegetable downs, as that of the sumach, or of the great mullein. They sometimes, however, vary the texture, using flax, hemp, hairs, and other similar substances. At other times they will fix on some low bush, on a stalk of the tobacco plant, or even on the side of an ocra pod, as a station for their nest. The male and female sit alternately; and the hatch consists of two minute white eggs, of equal thickness at both ends. When they perceive any body climbing the tree in which they nestle, they attack him in the face, attempt to strike him in the eyes, and come, go, and return, with such velocity as almost to exceed belief. Like the rest of their congeners, they are seldom caught alive. A friend of M. Dupratz having observed one of them enter into the bell of a convolvulus, and busying itself to get at the bottom, ran immediately to the spot, shut the flower, cut it from the stalk, and carried off his little captive. He could not prevail on it, however, to taste food, and it died in the course of two or three days. Charlevoix informs us, that he had one of them in his possession for twenty-four 'hours in Canada, which suffered itself to be handled, and even counterfeited death, that it might escape, but fell a real sacrifice to a slight degree of frost during the night. General Davies, by practising the following ingenious method, was somewhat more successful, for he contrived to keep some of them alive during four months. Having made an exact representation of some of the tubular flowers with paper, fastened round a tobacco pipe, and painted them of the proper colours, he ranged them in the cage in which the birds were confined, and filled the bottom of each with a mixture of brown sugar and water, as often as it was emptied. In this way he had the pleasure of seeing them perform every act, for they soon became familiar, and took their food in the same manner as when roaming at large.

Minimus. *T. minimus*, Lin. &c. *Least Humming-Bird.* Gold-green above, whitish beneath, wings and tail violet-brown. Bill of the male black; feet brown; the middle tail-feathers bluish-black, the lateral ones grey, and tipped with white. About an inch and a half in length, and weighs only twenty grains. The female is even a little smaller, and has the upper parts of the body of a green brown, with some shining reflexions on the wing-coverts, and the under parts of a dirty grey. Native of the West Indies, and Guiana. It is the most diminutive of known birds, being surpassed both in weight and dimensions by more than one species of bee. A dried specimen, mentioned by Edwards, weighed only five grains. The nest is described as rather large for the size of the bird, but this appearance is owing to its thickness. It is covered outwardly with lichens, and lined with fine cotton, or other downy substances. The eggs are not larger than coriander seeds, and of a dull white colour.

UPUPA, Lin. &c. HOOPOE.

Upupa. Bill very long, slightly arched, slender, triangular, compressed; nostrils basal, lateral, ovoid, open, and surmounted with feathers in front; a crest of a double row of long feathers, erectable at the pleasure of the bird.

Epops. *U. epops*, Lin. &c. *Common Hoopoe*, or *Hoop.* Ferruginous, wings barred with black and white; tail black, with a lunated white bar, and the crest tipt with black and white.

This beautiful bird weighs about three ounces, and measures about twelve inches in length, and nineteen in expanse of wing. It inhabits Europe, Asia, and Africa, in the last of which many of them are stationary. Some of the migrating detachments visit Britain occasionally in autumn, but they seldom breed with us. In France they arrive late in spring, and depart towards the close of summer. They are found plentifully in the deserts of Russia and Tartary, and are observed in small flocks at Gibraltar, in the month of March, on their passage northward, resting for a few hours. The female is said to have two or three broods in the year, frequently dispensing with a formal nest, and making a bed for her young by scraping together the dust in the hollow of a tree, or near the roots of trees on the ground; but she also sometimes selects the crevice of a rock, or a hole in a wall, and lines it with a few feathers or dried leaves; and, on other occasions, she seems to avail herself of the forsaken nest of some other species. The number of eggs varies from two to seven, but is generally four or five. They are somewhat oblong, bluish-white, and marked with pale-brown spots. The food of this species consists chiefly of worms, and of insects of the beetle tribe, with the refuse of which and the droppings of the young, the nest is sometimes rendered very fetid; and hence the popular but absurd notion, that the hoopoe smears its nest with dung, and even with human ordure. In some countries the species haunts meadows and moist soils in search of its food; and in Egypt, where many of them follow the course of the Nile in its retreat, they devour also frogs' spawn and young tadpoles; but in other regions they generally betray a partiality to barren and sequestered situations. The migrating individuals are particularly shy and solitary, two of them being seldom seen together, and even their migrations frequently taking place by individuals, and not by flocks. In Africa, the stationary birds associate in great numbers; and, in Egypt, they are to a certain degree domesticated; for they both build and breed on the terraces and among the houses. When they perch, it is usually at a few feet from the ground, and on a willow or osier twig, when they pronounce the syllable *poon* in a strong and deliberate tone, usually thrice in succession, turning their long bill on their breast, and erecting their head with a smart motion. Sometimes they utter a shrill and disagreeable cry; *zee, zee,* is their call of alarm; and in spring the amorous note of the male, which has been expressed by *boo, boo, boo,* is loud enough to be heard at a considerable distance. Their flight is slow and undulating, performed by jerks, and sustained by frequent percussions of the wings; and their march resembles that of our common fowl, or of the partridge. The crest usually falls behind on the neck, except when the bird is surprised or irritated, and then it stands erect; the tail, too, in that case being usually erected and spread out like a fan. Most sportsmen know that it is not so easily shot as Buffon alleges; but, if taken by surprise, when either young or mature, it is easily tamed, provided it be not kept in a cage, but allowed to roam in a house or garden, when it will also eat of many things which it would have rejected in its wild state. In captivity, however, it seldom survives the third year. The flesh of these birds has a musky flavour, which is said to repel cats; but it is in request for the table in the south of France, Italy, the Greek Islands, &c.

ORDER VII.

ALCYONIAN BIRDS.

ALCYONI-
AN BIRDS.

Bill middle sized, or long, pointed, almost quadrangular, and either slightly arched or straight; tarsus very short; three toes before, united, and one behind.

The birds belonging to this order, instituted by Temminck, like those of the next, fly with great celerity; their movements are quick and abrupt, and they neither walk nor climb. They seize their food on the wing, and often from the surface of water, and nestle in holes on the banks of rivers. They moult only once a-year; and the females and young are not very dissimilar from the males and mature birds.

MEROPS, Lin. &c. BEE-EATER.

MEROPS.

Bill of moderate size, sharp-edged, pointed, and slightly curved; legs short.

Apiaster.

M. apiaster, Lin. &c. *Common Bee-eater.* Sea green; throat yellow; back yellow-ferruginous; eye-stripe black; the two middle tail feathers elongated and acuminated. This is one of the most elegant of European birds, and, next to the roller and kingfisher, may be considered as the most brilliant in point of colour. Its size is nearly that of a thrush, being about ten inches in length, and seventeen in expanse of wing. Whether perched, or on wing, these birds utter a stridulous and somewhat disagreeable cry. They hunt for insects, especially bees, wasps, hornets, &c. among trees, flowers, and in the open air, devouring not only the hymenopterous tribes, but gnats, flies, froghoppers, &c. The situations which they select for their nests are hills of a soft soil, the sandy banks of rivers, in which, with their feet and bill, they dig holes six feet or more in depth, and in an oblique direction, with a wide entry, and round bottom. In this last the female places a nest of moss, laying from four to seven perfectly white eggs, about the size of those of the stare. In autumn, the families unite previous to migration. They inhabit the warmer parts of Europe, and many regions both of Asia and Africa; they are numerous in Southern Russia, particularly about the rivers Don and Wolga, whose banks are sometimes perforated to a great extent by their excavations. In the northern regions of Europe they are of rare occurrence. On the approach of winter, they all quit their northern tracts. At the Cape of Good Hope they are called *gnat snappers,* and direct the Hottentots to the honey which the bees store up in the clefts of the rocks.

ALCEDO, Lin. &c. KINGFISHER.

ALCEDO.

Bill long, straight, quadrangular, pointed, sharp-edged, and very rarely depressed; nostrils basal, lateral, pierced obliquely, almost wholly closed by a naked membrane; legs short, naked above the knee; tongue very short; feathers glossy.

The birds of this genus are dispersed over the whole world, although only one species is found in Europe. They are more remarkable for brilliancy of plumage than elegance of shape, their prevailing colours being blue, green, and orange; but some of the larger species are of more obscure shadings, exhibiting a mixture of brown, black, and white, variously modified. Their flight is horizontal, and, notwithstanding the shortness of their wings, remarkably strong and rapid. Most of them frequent rivers, and the vicinity of waters, and live on fish, which they catch with singular art and

dexterity, sometimes hovering over the stream, where a shoal of small fishes is seen playing near the surface, at other times waiting with attention on some low branch the approach of a single one, which may happen to move in that direction; and, in either case, dropping like a stone, or rather darting with rapidity on their prey. Having seized the latter crosswise in their bill, they retire to a resting-place to feed on it, and devour it piece-meal, bones and all, afterwards bringing up the undigested parts in pellets like other predacious birds.

A. ispida, Lin. &c. *Common* or *European Kingfisher.* Wing-coverts dark green, fulvous beneath, with the back of a brilliant blue; and the crown green, marked with transverse blue spots. The common kingfisher weighs one ounce and a quarter, and measures seven inches in length, and eleven in expanse of wing. It is diffused over the old continent, especially over the southern districts of Europe, in China, Egypt, at the Cape of Good Hope, &c. It is shy, solitary, and wary, frequenting the banks of streams and sea-shores, where it will sit for hours together on a projecting twig or a stone, now fluttering its wings, and exposing its brilliant plumage to the sun, and then hovering in the air like the kestril, watching for the moment when it may dart on its victim, which it does with almost unerring aim. Before it has gained the object of its pursuit, it will sometimes remain for several seconds under water, and then bring up the little fish, which it carries to the land, beats to death, and swallows. When sitting on the watch, the moment that it perceives the fish it will take a spring of twelve or fifteen feet upwards, and drop perpendicularly from that height. When it takes to flight, it spins its course in a direct line forwards, and with such rapidity that the motion of its wings is scarcely discernible; but it will occasionally stop short in its fleet career, at each pause remaining suspended, as it were, at the height of fifteen or twenty feet; and, when it would change its place, it descends and skims along the surface of the water, and then rises and halts again. This repeated and long-continued exercise evinces the uncommon strength of the muscles of its wings. When it falls on its victim, it utters a shrill scream, which has been expressed by the syllable *kee* frequently repeated; but, in spring, it has another song, which may be heard through the murmuring of the stream, or the dashing of the waterfall. The sexes, which keep separate, except during the breeding season, pair early in spring, when they usually take possession of a hole in the bank of a river or running stream, which had been excavated by a water rat, mole, sand martin, or land crab, and which they enlarge or contract, or otherwise accommodate to their purpose. It is formed in an ascending direction, and generally penetrates two or three feet into the bank. At the end it is scooped into a hollow, at the bottom of which there is often a quantity of small fishes' bones, nearly half an inch thick, mixed with a brown or glutinous earth, the castings of the parent birds, which repair to the spot, apparently for no other purpose than to eject this matter, and to dry it by the heat of their bodies, as they are frequently known to continue in the hole for hours together before there are any eggs. Mr. Bewick saw a specimen of a king-fisher's nest, which was entirely composed of the bones of small fishes and a brown viscid substance, and which, in the compactness of its form, resembled that of the chaffinch; but it seems to be equally well ascertained, that, on various occasions, these

Ispida.

N

birds dispense with the formality of a regular nest. The eggs, which vary in number from four to nine, are of a short oval form, and perfectly white and transparent. That the fœces of the unfledged brood, which sometimes render the nest extremely fetid, may run off, the passage is conducted in a slanting direction. As the old birds have nothing in their bills when they go in to feed the young, it is inferred that they discharge from their stomach the requisite supply. When the young are nearly full feathered, they are extremely voracious, and are often betrayed by their chirping. In our northern latitudes, the kingfishers often fall a sacrifice to intense and protracted cold ; and, in inland situations, the freezing of the rivers may prove fatal to their existence by depriving them of food. In confinement they are with difficulty kept alive, as they reject almost every thing but live fish, such as minnows, banstickles, &c. We need scarcely observe, that this species is the *halcyon* of the ancients ; that the poets placed it in a floating nest, and endowed it with power to calm the adverse winds and seas. Aristotle and Pliny gravely relate that it sat only a few days, and those in the depth of winter, and that during that period the mariner might sail in full security, whence the *halcyon days*, an expression which has descended to our own times. The flesh is strongly impregnated with a musky odour, and is not consequently relished as an article of food.

Gigantea.　*A. gigantea*, Lath. *A. fusca*, Lin. *Giant Kingfisher*, or *Great Brown Kingfisher*. Slightly crested, brown above, whitish, with black undulations beneath ; wing-coverts and rump pale sea-green, and the tail crossed by numerous black bars. This is the largest species hitherto discovered, measuring about eighteen inches from the tip of the bill to that of the tail. It is a native of New Guinea, New Holland, and several of the smaller islands of the Southern Pacific. Its singular note has been compared by the natives of New Holland to the braying of the jack-ass. The female has no crest

ORDER VIII.

CHELIDONIAN BIRDS.

Chelido-
nian
Birds.

Bill very short, much depressed, and very wide at the base ; the upper mandible curved at the point ; legs short ; three toes before, either entirely divided, or connected at the base by a short membrane, the hinder often reversible, the claws much hooked ; wings long. The flight of these birds is rapid and abrupt, their sight piercing, neck short, throat wide, bill broad, and often gaping for the reception of insects, which constitute their only food.

Hirundo, Lin. &c. Swallow.

Hirundo.

Bill short, triangular, broad at the base, depressed, cleft near to the eyes ; upper mandible slightly hooked at the tip ; nostrils basal, oblong, partly closed by a membrane, and surmounted by feathers in front ; legs short, with slender toes and claws ; wings long, the first quill the longest ; tail mostly forked.

The swallow tribes manifest a predilection to the neighbourhood of water, and those situations in which insects most abound. These last they seize with great promptitude in their long sustained and very rapid flights. They catch their food, drink, and bathe, as they glide smoothly and nimbly along the surface of the water. Their motions are easy, swift, and graceful ; and, when

not occupied with breeding or sleep, they are almost incessantly on the wing. Their nests, when dried, are hard and rough on the outside, but furnished with soft materials within. While they rid our orchards, gardens, and houses, of legions of insects, they never attack the produce of the soil. Their lively manners, twittering note, and gentle and affectionate dispositions, amply repay the shelter which our buildings afford to several of the species. Their migrations are no longer matter of doubt ; and the observations of Natterer of Vienna have established the important fact that they moult in February, which is a fresh argument against their alleged torpor in winter. All the species are more or less infested by the *Hippobosca hirundinis*, which abounds in their nests, is hatched by the warmth of the bird's own body during incubation, and crawls about under its feathers.

Rustica.　*H. rustica*, Lin. &c. *Common Chimney*, or *House Swallow*. Black-blue above, whitish beneath ; forehead and throat of a reddish aurora tint ; and all the tail feathers but the two in the middle marked with a white spot. The tail is much forked, the legs are dusky, and the lateral quill feather on each side is an inch longer than the intermediate ones : Length of the body six inches and a half, alar extent nearly one foot, and weight between five and six drachms. The colours of the male are more lively than those of the female, and the exterior feathers of his tail are somewhat longer : the colouring of the young also is much less lively than that of the adults. An entirely white variety sometimes occurs. Some have been found of a yellowish-white, with the other colours faintly impressed on some parts of the body, and others more or less speckled with white.

This well-known species occurs almost every where in the old continent. It visits us earlier in the season than any of its congeners ; usually, if the weather be mild, about the beginning of April, or a week before the house martin, and it retires about the end of September, or beginning of October. In this country it usually builds in the inside of our chimneys, at a few feet from the top ; but it will also affix its nest to the beams and rafters of out-houses ; and, in some countries, it not unfrequently constructs it against rocks, or even in trees. At Camerton Hall, near Bath, a pair built their nest on the upper part of the frame of an old picture over the mantle-piece, entering through a broken pane in the window of the room. Hither they resorted three years successively, when their access was precluded by the room being put in repair. But what is still more eccentric, a bird of the same species built its nest on the wings and body of an owl, which happened by accident to hang dead and dry from the rafter of a barn, and so loose as to be moved by every gust of wind. The carcass, with the nest on the wings, and with eggs in the nest, was brought as a curiosity to Sir Ashton Lever, who, struck with the oddity of the sight, furnished the person who brought it with a large conch-shell, desiring him to fix it just where the owl had been suspended. This was done accordingly, and the following year a pair of these birds, probably the same, built their nest in the shell, and the female laid eggs as usual. The owl, and its counterpart the shell, made a singular and grotesque appearance in the Leverian collection. Wonderful is the address which this bird exhibits in ascending and descending with security through the narrow passage of a chimney. When hovering over the mouth of the funnel, the vibration of its wings, acting on the confined air, occasions a rumbling like distant thunder. It is not improbable that the dam submits to the inconvenience of having her nest low down in the shaft, in order to secure her brood from rapacious birds, and particularly from owls, which are frequently found to fall down chimneys, probably in their attempts to get at the nestlings. The experiments of Frisch and others prove, that chimney swallows annually return to the same haunts; but they generally build a fresh nest every season; and, if circumstances permit, they fix it above that which was occupied the preceding year. Montbeillard has found them in the shaft of a chimney thus ranged in tiers, four of the same size one above another, composed of mud, mixed with straw and hair. They were of the largest size, resembling a hollow half cylinder, open above, a foot in height, and attached to the sides of the chimney, while some of smaller dimensions, and forming only the quarter of a cylinder, or even an inverted cone, were stuck in the corners. The first nest, which was the lowest, had the same texture at the bottom as at the sides; but the two upper tiers were separated from the lower by their lining only, which consisted of straw, dry herbs, and feathers. Of the small nests in the corners of the chimneys he could find only two in tiers; and he supposed that they belonged to young pairs, for they were not so well compacted as the large ones. The eggs of the first brood are four or five, white, and speckled with rusty red, and those of the second consist usually of two or three. While the female sits, the male, who sings the amorous ditty, passes the night on the brim of the nest, but sleeps little; for his twittering is heard with the earliest dawn, and he circles about almost till the close of evening. After the young are hatched, both parents perpetually carry food, and are at great pains to keep the nest clean, till the brood have learned to save them that trouble. Boerhaave relates, that a swallow returning with provisions to its nest, and finding the house on fire, rushed through the flames to feed and protect her offspring. It is pleasing to see the parents employed in teaching their family to fly, encouraging them with their voice, presenting food at a little distance, and retiring as the young ones stretch forward, pressing them gently from the nest, fluttering before them, and offering, in the most expressive tone, to receive and assist them. The young, not without difficulty, first emerge from the shaft; for a day or two they are fed on the chimney top; and they are then conducted to the dead leafless bough of some neighbouring tree, where, sitting in a row, they are attended by the parents with great assiduity. In a day or two after this they are strong enough to fly, but continue still unable to take their own food: they, therefore play about near the place where the dam is watching for flies, and when a mouthful is collected, the dam and the nestling, on a given signal, mutually advance, rising towards one another, and meeting at an angle, the young all the while uttering a short quick note of gratitude and complacency. As soon as the female has disengaged herself from the first brood, she immediately commences her preparations for a second, which is hatched about the middle or latter end of August. During every part of the summer, in short, she is a pattern of unwearied industry and affection; for, while there is a family to support, she skims along from morning to night, or exerts the most sudden turns, or quick evolutions, preferably frequenting avenues, long walks under hedges, pasture fields, and mown meadows, in which cattle graze, because in such situations

insects most abound. On downs, these birds may be seen to follow, and with great ease to fly repeatedly round a horse that is travelling at a smart trot, in order to pick up the flies roused from the turf by the motion of the animal's feet. When a fly is taken, a person may hear a snap of the bill, not unlike the noise of shutting a watch-case; but the motion of the mandibles is too quick for the eye. As the winged insects fly higher or lower, according to the greater or less degree of heat, the swallows, in pursuit of their prey, sometimes skim along the surface of the ground, and sometimes take a more elevated flight, and, when a scarcity of insects prevails, they snatch flies from spiders' webs, and even devour the spiders themselves. About the close of summer, they not unfrequently pass the night perched on alders that grow on the banks of brooks and rivers; and, at that season, numbers of them are caught in some countries for the table. They prefer the lowest branches, under the brinks, and well sheltered from the wind; and it is remarkable, that the branches on which they commonly sit during the night wither away. In our climate it sometimes happens that, after their arrival, a long tract of north-easterly wind prevails, which so benumbs the insect tribes, that thousands of swallows perish for want of food. Frisch informs us, that of all the swallows, this species has a cry most approaching to a song, though it consists only of three tones, terminated by a *finale*, which rises to a fourth, and it is little varied. Besides these inflexions of voice, however, it has its note of invitation, of pleasure, of fear, of resentment, that by which the mother warns the young of danger, &c. It rouses the house-martin, and other small birds, by announcing the approach of birds of prey; for, as soon as a hawk or owl appears, the swallow calls, with a shrill alarming voice, all his fellows and the martins about him, which pursue, in a body, and strike and buffet their adversary, until they have driven him from the place, darting down on his back, and rising in a perpendicular line in perfect security. It will also sound the alarm, and strike at cats, when they climb on the roofs of houses, or otherwise approach the nest.

Previous to their departure, the chimney swallows congregate in flocks of three or four hundred, on houses or trees, and usually steal off in the night to avoid the birds of prey, which seldom fail to harass them in their route. Mr. White relates, that as he was travelling very early on a morning of Michaelmas day, and arriving on a large heath, or common, he could discern, as a thick mist which had obscured the prospect began to break away, great numbers of swallows, clustering on the stunted shrubs and bushes, as if they had roosted there during the night. But, as soon as the air became clear and pleasant, they were all on the wing at once, and, by a placid and easy flight, proceeded on southwards in the direction of the sea; after which he could perceive no more flocks, but only occasional stragglers. About Oxford, they are usually seen later than elsewhere in England, owing, as has been supposed, to the number of massy buildings at that place, and to the many streams with which it is surrounded. Frisch more than once saw these birds take their departure in broad day, and Hebert, about the time of their retreat, observed parties of forty or fifty gliding aloft in the air, and maintaining a flight, not only much more elevated than ordinary, but also more uniform and steady. On such occasions their progress is always in a southerly direction, availing themselves, as much as possible, of favourable winds ; and, when no obstacles interfere, they usually arrive in Africa in the first week of October. If checked by a south-east wind, they halt, like the other birds of passage, on the islands that lie in their track. Adanson witnessed the arrival of parties of them, on the coast of Senegal, on the sixth of October, at half past six o'clock in the evening, and found them to be real European swallows ; and he subsequently ascertained, that they are never seen in Senegal except in autumn and winter. He adds, that they never breed there ; and Frisch accordingly remarks, that young swallows never arrive in Europe in the spring. Though generally migratory, even in Greece and Asia, some will remain during the winter, especially in the mild latitudes in which insects abound, as, for example, in the Hieres Islands, and on the coast of Genoa, where they pass the night in the open country on the orange trees.

Like the carrier pigeons, chimney swallows have been sometimes employed to convey important intelligence. For this purpose the mother is taken from her eggs, and carried to the place whence the news are to be sent ; and there a thread is tied to her feet, with the number of knots and the colour previously concerted. Immediately on being liberated, she flies back to her brood, and thus bears the tidings with incredible expedition.

Did swallows fail to make their appearance for a single summer, our houses and crops would be overrun with insects, and not merely annoyance, but famine might ensue. Hence the impolicy, as well as the cruelty, of destroying multitudes of these harmless birds, either for the table, or for improving the practical skill of the sportsman.

Urbica.

H. urbica, Lin. &c. *Martin, Common Martin, Martlet, Martinet, House Martin, Window Swallow.* Black-blue above, under parts and rump white ; tail feathers without spots. The black of the female is less decided, and the white less pure. The tail is blue-black, and forked ; the legs are covered with a white down ; and the claws are white. It is about five inches and a half in length, and rather inferior in size to the chimney swallow. It would be superfluous to describe more particularly a bird which is so familiar to our observation. The young have all the upper parts of a blackish-brown. Accidental varieties also occur ; but some writers have confounded with these different species which are natives of North America.

The martin, which seems to be intermediate between the chimney swallow and the swift, is allied to the former by its note, the familiarity of its manners, and the mode of constructing its nest, and to the latter, by the conformation of its feet, its capability of turning the hind toe forwards, for its clinging to walls, by its crawling rather than walking, and by its flying in greater flocks than usual during heavy showers of rain. Martins are more chilly than chimney swallows, courting, even in the middle of summer, the first rays of the sun, when assembled on the projections of towers or elevated houses, where they also occasionally seek for shelter in autumn : and, when cold winds or rains prevail, they press close on one another, and are sometimes so benumbed as to be caught by the hand. When molested in their asylum, however, they fly with considerable rapidity ; and although they are sensible to even slight degrees of cold, yet they survive that of frost, or, if they perish under it, it is probably from defect of food. On the occurrence of cold weather, they usually frequent the margins of pools and marshes, with

a view no doubt to catch any little prey which they can then procure, and which they would in vain search for elsewhere, and it is usually in such situations that they are found stiff or dead. Their first annual appearance in this island is about the 16th of April, and they usually sport and play about for nearly a month before they commence the important task of nidification. They delight to build their nests against the crags of precipices that overhang lakes, and seldom breed near our houses, if they can find a convenient situation elsewhere ; yet their choice often appears to be capricious, and they will sometimes begin several structures and leave them unfinished ; but when one has been completed in a sheltered situation, if not invaded or accidentally destroyed, it suffices for several seasons. As the martin often builds against a perpendicular wall, without any ledge underneath, it employs every sagacious effort to get the first foundation firmly fixed, so as to sustain the superstructure with safety. On this occasion the bird not only clings with its claws, but partly supports itself by strongly inclining its tail against the wall, and, thus fixed, it plasters the materials into the face of the brick or stone. But that this piece of workmanship may not, when soft, incline down by its own weight, the provident architect labours at it only in the morning, and thus gives it sufficient time to dry and harden. It may be seen at work before four o'clock, plastering with its bill, and moving the head with quick vibrations. About half an inch of the fabric seems to be a sufficient layer for a day, until, in the course of ten or twelve days, or if the builders are many, in half that time, a hemispherical nest is formed, with a small aperture towards the top. The shell, or crust, is a sort of rustic work, full of knobs on the outside, composed of earth or mud, picked up from the borders of stagnant waters, or the fresh morning casts of worms ; the middle is strengthened by an intermixture of chips of straw ; and the inside is rendered soft and warm by a lining of grasses and feathers, particularly those of the goose, and sometimes by a bed of moss, interwoven with wool, the whole forming a strong, compact, and comfortable abode for the parents and the young. Attentive observers have remarked that these birds carry the mortar both with their bill and their toes, but that they plaster only with the former. On some occasions, particularly when the nest has been accidentally demolished, it is reared again in a short time by the active co-operation of many individuals ; but sometimes, also, several appear to be as assiduous in pulling down as others are in rearing the fabric, a circumstance which Montbeillard insinuates may be the effect of jealousy. The common house sparrow not unfrequently seizes on the outwork of the nest, before it is completed, and adapts it to its own accommodation, after banishing the owner. But such invasions are not always submitted to without a struggle, and sometimes they are very successfully repelled. The Jesuit, Batgowiski, was an eye-witness of a sparrow thus taking possession of a martin's nest, and obstinately resisting the united efforts of a group of these birds, which the despoiled owner had summoned to her aid, when they at length immured the usurper by building up the entrance with the same mortar of which the nest was composed ; and Linné alleges that similar examples might be quoted. The young martins are sometimes hatched as early as the 15th of June. The first hatch consists of five white eggs, with a dusky ring near the large end, the second of three or four, and the third, when it takes place, of two or

Ornithology. three. During incubation, the male seldom removes from his mate, but watches for her safety and that of the young brood, impetuously darting on birds that approach too near. After the eggs are hatched, both parents fetch food to their tender offspring, and seem to treat them with the most affectionate concern. The young, on attaining their full growth, become impatient of confinement, and sit all day with their heads out at the entrance, where the dams, by clinging to the nest, supply them with food from morning to night. After this they are fed by the parents on the wing; but this feat is performed in so quick a flight, that a person must attend very exactly to the motions of the birds before he can perceive it. As soon as the young are capable of providing for themselves, the dam repairs the nest for a second family. The first flight then associate in large groups, and may be seen, on summer mornings and evenings, clustering and hovering around towers and steeples, and on the roofs of churches and houses.

These welcome and cheering visitants leave us the latest of their tribe, namely, for the most part about the beginning of October, although some have been known to remain till the 6th of November; and Col. Montagu informs us, that, in 1805, he saw them as late as the 15th of that month in the neighbourhood of Kingsbridge, in Devonshire; and Mr. White says, that he once observed in the quadrangle of Christ Church College, Oxford, a house martin flying about, and settling on the parapets, on a very warm sunny morning, which happened to be the 20th of the same month. The first broods usually begin to congregate about the first week of August; and, as the summer declines, the flocks daily increase in numbers by the accession of the second broods, till in some places, particularly among the hamlets on the Thames, they swarm in myriads, accustoming themselves to lofty flights, and apparently training for their departure. On a peculiar cry being uttered, they mount aloft and disappear. There is reason to believe that they migrate in great bodies, and too high in the air for human observation, a few unfortunate stragglers only, detained by sickness or the lateness of their birth, remaining behind. According to Mr. White, many more leave this country than retire to it in spring; but such as revisit their native seats, find their way back again to their nests, as has been ascertained, by tying coloured threads or brass wires to their legs, and setting them at liberty again. Now, by what singular faculty can a creature, apparently so helpless, direct its course, perhaps from the wilds of Africa, to the identical spot in Europe which it formerly frequented? Martins, to a certain degree, are social and familiar; and there are instances of their breeding within doors when not molested, and of their being tamed; but in this last state they are fed with difficulty, and are very apt to die. They are found throughout Europe and Asia, occurring as far north as Drontheim, in Norway, and abounding in Kamtschatka and Siberia. They arrive in Sweden about the 9th of May. In England they are more numerous than the swallows, which generally arrive in this island about ten days earlier.

Riparia. *H. riparia,* Lin. &c. *Sand Martin, Bank Martin, Sand Swallow,* or *Shore Bird.* Cinereous, or mouse-coloured above, with the throat and abdomen white; throat encircled with a mouse-coloured ring; legs black, and downy behind. Length of the body four inches nine lines, alar extent eleven inches. These are consequently the smallest of our native hirundines;

with us they are also less numerous, and more local than the other sorts. They appear about the same time as the chimney swallows, and have been sometimes observed to depart with them or the martins. They resort only to such parts as are convenient for their breeding, and hence they are chiefly seen about rivers, where they nestle in the banks, and always above the highest water-mark, occasionally in crevices of rocks, but more commonly in sand-pits, in which excavations are easily effected. These are round, horizontally serpentine, and generally two feet deep; and the nest, which is placed at the bottom, is composed of straw and dried fibres, and lined with feathers. The sand martins, however, in place of digging holes for themselves, sometimes take possession of those of the bee-eaters and king-fishers; and sometimes they build in old walls, in the cavity of a quarry, or even in the hollow of old trees. They breed once, and occasionally twice in the season, the female laying four or five pure white and very transparent eggs, which are hatched late in May. They have a low muttering voice, and in their manners considerably resemble the common martins, with which they at times associate. But they have a peculiar mode of flying or flitting about, with odd jerks and vacillations, not unlike the butterfly; and hence in Spain they are called by the peasants *mountain butterflies.* The young assume a quantity of delicate fat, which has been compared to that of the ortolan. In Malta these birds are permanent residents; and in a very warm and sheltered valley in Bugey, M. Hebert has seen them fluttering about in the winter months. Such of them as loiter too late in this country have sometimes been found stiffened with cold, and revived by the application of a gentle heat; but that they undergo any regular hybernation, appears, from the experiments of Spallanzani, to be very doubtful.

Rufa. *H. rufa,* Gmel. Lath. &c. *Barn,* or *Rufous-bellied Swallow.* Steel-blue above; forehead and throat chesnut; breast with a purple band; the tail feathers, with the exception of the two in the middle, marked with an oblong white spot. Length from the tip of the beak to that of the tail seven inches, and expanse of wing thirteen inches. This species so much resembles the common swallow, that it has often been confounded with it; but it differs in having the under parts of the body chesnut instead of white, and in building in barns, sheds, or on beams and rafters, and not in chimneys. The nest is commenced early in May, and is finished in about a week. It is in the shape of an inverted cone, with a perpendicular section cut off on that side by which it adheres to the wood. At the top there is a ridge, which seems to be intended for the old birds to perch on while tending the nestlings. The case is formed of mud mixed with fine hay, and disposed in regular layers from side to side, being about an inch in thickness; and within there is a quantity of hay profusely lined with goose's feathers. The eggs, which are usually five, are white, very transparent, and sprinkled with reddish-brown. There are generally two broods in the season, namely, the first about the middle of June, and the second about the 10th of August. These birds appear to live in great harmony; for twenty or thirty pairs often breed in the same barn; and several of their nests are within a few inches of one another, and yet no symptoms of discord are observed among them. When the young first leave the nest, they are observed to fly about within doors for some days before they venture out. On their first entrance into the open air, they are conducted by the old

Ornitho-
logy.

ones to the sides of rivers and similar places, where their food is most abundant, and there they are fed by their parents. They are easily tamed, and soon become very gentle and familiar, so that when confined in a room they quickly begin to employ themselves in catching flies, and will call out to their companions as they pass by the window. Their song is a sprightly warble, and is sometimes continued for a considerable length of time. These swallows arrive near Philadelphia the latter end of March, or the beginning of April: about the middle of August they begin to assemble and make preparations for departing, and by the middle of September there is scarcely one to be seen. They are most abundant to the east of the Alleghany mountains, and extend as far north as the river St. Lawrence. During the months of September and October they are observed in great numbers in Florida, passing southward.

Ambrosia-
ca.

H. ambrosiaca, Gmel. Lath. *Ambergrise Swallow.* Grey-brown above, paler beneath; tail much forked. It smells so strongly of ambergrise, that a single bird suffices to perfume a whole chamber: but the odour is destroyed when the skin is dried in keeping. It is a small species, and inhabits Senegal.

Pelasgia.

H. pelasgia, Lin. &c. *Aculeated Swallow*, of Pennant, Latham, and Stephens. *American Swallow* of Catesby, and *Chimney Swallow* of Wilson. Dusky above, grey-brown beneath; tail-feathers equal, their tips naked, and armed with an awl-shaped point. Total length four inches three lines. This species arrives in Pennsylvania late in April, or early in May, and builds its nest in high chimneys that are seldom used; but, in the districts inhabited by Indians, where there are no chimneys, it constructs it in hollow trees. It is in the form of the third part of a circle, and is composed of very small twigs, fastened together with a strongly adhesive gummy substance, which is said to be secreted from two glands, situated on each side of the hinder part of the head, and to be mixed with the saliva. With this substance, which Vieillot asserts proceeds from the *Liquidambar styricifolia*, Lin. and which becomes as hard as the twigs themselves, the nest, which is small and shallow, is thickly covered. It is attached by one side, or edge, to the wall, and is destitute of the soft lining with which those of the other swallows are so plentifully supplied. There are two broods in the season. The eggs are four or five, oblong, large in proportion to the bird, and spotted and striped with black and grey-brown towards the larger end, on a ground of pure white. The young are fed at intervals, even during the night. In consequence of heavy rains, it frequently happens that the nest is detached from the sides of the chimney, and precipitated to the bottom, in which case the eggs, if there are any, are destroyed; but, should there be young, they will scramble to the upper part, by clinging to the wall with their strong muscular feet, and, in this situation, continue to be fed by the old ones for a week or more. This bird is easily distinguished from the other swallows by the peculiarity of its flight, frequently shooting swiftly in various directions, without any apparent motion of its wings, and uttering the sounds *tsip, tsip, tsip, tsee, tsee,* in a hurried manner. In roosting, the thorny extremities of its tail are thrown out for its support. It never alights but in hollow trees and chimneys, and seems to be always most gay and active during wet and gloomy weather. It is also the earliest abroad in the morning, and the latest out in the evening of any of the North

American swallows. In the first or second week of September it leaves Pennsylvania for the south.

Ornitho-
logy.

H. fuciphaga, of the *Stockholm Transactions*, and of Stephens, *H. esculenta*, Lath. &c. *Esculent Swallow.* Shining dusky above, ash-coloured beneath; tail without spots. The bill is black; the wings, when closed, are an inch longer than the tail, which is slightly forked, and has all the feathers of a uniform black, and rounded at the end. The bird described under the appellation of *Esculent Swallow*, by Brisson, Linné, Buffon, &c. does not appear to be known to the naturalists of the present day, the former having taken their exemplar from a drawing by *Poivré*, who delineated many birds that were fictitious.

Fuciphaga.

The nest of this species usually weighs about half an ounce, and is in shape like a saucer, with the side which adheres to the rock flattened. The texture somewhat resembles isinglass, or fine gum dragon; and the several layers of which it is composed are very apparent, the whole being fabricated of repeated parcels of a soft slimy substance, in the same manner as the martins form theirs of mud. Authors differ as to the precise nature of the materials of which the nest is composed; but it is reckoned one of the greatest delicacies by the Chinese and other Asiatic epicures. The best sorts, which have not been occupied by a second brood, which are of a transparent white, and perfectly free from dirt, are dissolved in soup, in order to thicken it, and are said, at the same time, to impart to it an exquisite relish; or they are soaked in water to soften them, then pulled to pieces, and, after being mixed with ginseng, are put into the body of a fowl; the whole is then stewed in a pot, with a sufficient quantity of water, and left on the coals till morning, when it is ready to be eaten. These edible nests are found in vast numbers in certain caverns in Java, Sumatra, the islands of Cochin-China, &c. It has been calculated, that from Batavia alone more than twelve tons' weight of these nests are annually exported to China. A few only are brought into Europe, as curiosities and presents. The reader will find further details relative to these nests in Marsden's *Sumatra*, third edition, p. 174; and Raffles' *Java*, vol. i. pp. 51, and 205.

CYPSELUS, Illig. Tem. &c. HIRUNDO, Lin. &c. SWIFT.

Bill very short, triangular, broad at the base, inconspicuous, depressed, cleft as far as under the eyes; upper mandible hooked at the tip; nostrils cleft longitudinally at the upper part of the bill, open, and the raised margins furnished with small feathers; legs very short, with the four toes directed forwards, and quite divided, and the toes and claws short and thick; wings very long.—The birds of this genus present many analogies to those of the preceding, from which they have only recently been detached. They are still more active and unwearied in their movements.

CYPSELUS.

C. alpinus, Tem. *Hirundo Melba*, Lin. &c. *White-bellied Swift*, or *Greatest Martin.* Greyish-brown above, with the throat and abdomen white. About eight inches and a half in length. Bill black; neck with a grey-brown collar, variegated with dusky; sides dusky, variegated with white; legs flesh-coloured. In the female the collar is narrower, and the plumage less deeply shaded with dusky.

Alpinus.

This species arrives in Savoy about the beginning of April; but it flies over pools and marshes during the first fifteen days, nor visits the mountainous districts, its more permanent abode, until the end of the month.

It occurs in the mountains of Switzerland, the Tyrol, and on the shores and islands of the Mediterranean. Specimens from Africa, though differing a little in markings, appear to be only one of the varieties. Like the common swift, it flies in flocks, more or less numerous, and incessantly wheels round the precipitous rocks, which rise above the cliffs in which it nestles, uttering as it flies very loud and shrill screams. In the midst of its career it will sometimes stop and cling by its claws to the rocks, or blocks of stone, in the neighbourhood of its nest. To those which first cling to the rock others adhere, and others in succession, thus forming, for a moment, a vibrating and animated chain, when they again separate and resume their circling and clamorous flight. Among the Modenese hills, they are observed as early as the 12th of March, and soon after lay their eggs in the old nests, or prepare new ones, if the old have been destroyed. These nests are a little larger than those of the common swift, but still small for the size of the bird, lined with a light tissue of delicate feathers, under which are little bits of straw and wood, closely interlaced, in concentric circles, the interstices being filled up with the leaves of trees, and the whole varnished over with a glutinous humour, which gives it solidity and hardness. The females have two hatches, the first consisting of three or four elongated and white eggs, which are incubated in three weeks; and the young are full grown about the middle of July: and the second usually consists of only two eggs, the young proceeding from which are mature about the middle of September. They remain in the north of Italy till October. When these birds retire to rest in the night, the male and female squat down in their hole together, and in this situation will allow themselves to be touched before they fly off. They generally maintain a very elevated flight; and the period of their departure to the south is more uncertain than that of their arrival at their respective breeding stations. The young are esteemed as an article of food; but the old birds are tough and stringy.

Murarius. *C. murarius,* Tem. *Hirundo apus,* Lin. &c. *Cypselus apus,* Cuv. &c. *Micropus* and *Brachypus Murarius,* Meyer. *Swift, Screech, Screech Martin, Black Martin, Deviling,* or *Screamer.* Body black, chin white. During its residence with us, its black gloss fades to a dirty-brown. This species, which measures nearly eight inches in length, and eighteen in extent of wing, weighs only one ounce. Its folded wings project nine lines beyond the tail. Though larger than the common swallow, its bill, neck, and feet, are proportionally shorter; the head larger; the breast more ample, and the wings much longer. Owing to this conformation, it springs from the ground with difficulty, a manœuvre, however, which it has seldom occasion to practise, as it passes most of its life on the wing. Whilst it walks, or rather crawls with awkwardness, it has a strong grasp with its feet, and can readily cling to walls and other places which it frequents. From the flatness of its body, it can enter a very narrow crevice, and when it cannot pass on its belly, it will turn up edgewise to push itself through. The male is somewhat heavier than the female, and has stronger feet, with a broader patch of white on the throat; and the female is of a browner hue. We should likewise remark, that the young adult birds weigh more than the old, being much fatter, on which account they are captured for the table in Italy, and some other countries.

The swift seldom visits us before the beginning of May, nor remains later than the middle of August.

In the height of summer these very active birds are on the wing at least sixteen hours in the day, withdrawing to rest, in the longest days, about a quarter before nine o'clock in the evening, some time after all the other diurnal birds have retired. Just before they repair to their respective holes, they assemble in large groups, high in the air, screaming and shooting about with wonderful activity; but they are never so alert as in sultry lowering weather, when they manifest great alacrity. Their sight is particularly acute; and, according to the experiments of Spallanzani, they can distinctly perceive an object of five lines in diameter, at the distance of 304 feet. They generally build their nests in elevated places, such as lofty steeples and high towers, but sometimes under the eaves of roofs or the arches of bridges, and even in hollow trees, composing it of a variety of materials, as dry grass, moss, hemp, bits of cord, threads of silk or linen, small shreds of gauze or muslin, feathers, the down of poplars, and other light matters, which they frequently catch in the air, or snatch up as they skim over the surface of waters, or detach from trees, or of which they rob the sparrow and other small birds. Unless much molested, they return to the same breeding haunts, which seem to be transmitted from one generation to another. If they find their nest occupied by the sparrow, they compel the latter to resign its pretensions; nor are they in the least scrupulous of seizing on the legitimate nest of that bird, and adapting it to their purpose, lining the materials of the joint fabric with a viscid humour, which is constantly present in their throats and in their bill, and which enables them to entangle the insects which they seize. This substance, by penetrating the nest in every direction, imparts to it consistency and even elasticity. The female has only one brood in the season, and lays from two to five eggs, which are of a very lengthened and pointed form, white, larger than those of the swallow, and having a very brittle shell. The female alone performs the duty of incubation, rushing forth just before dark, to relieve her weary limbs, snatch a scanty meal for a few minutes, and then return to her charge. It should seem, however, that the male hovers about in the neighbourhood, and occasionally fetches her food, uttering his scream as he wheels about the nest. The young have a feeble cry, are fed by both parents four, five, or even six times in the course of the day; and their food, which they swallow entire, consists of insects, such as winged ants, flies, beetles, butterflies, spiders, &c. In the course of four or five weeks they quit the nest, and, contrary to the habits of some of their kindred tribe, do not return to it for a resting-place. They generally fly and feed high in the air, and range to great distances: they may sometimes, however, be observed hawking very low, and for hours together, over pools and streams, in search of phryganeæ, ephemeræ, and libellulæ, which frequent the banks and surface of waters, and which afford them a plentiful and succulent nourishment. They sometimes pursue and strike at birds of prey, but with less vehemence and fury than the swallows. Like the latter, they sip up water as they skim along its surface. During the middle of a very hot day, they are seldom seen out of their holes; but in the morning and evening they may be observed in troops, more or less numerous, sometimes describing a thousand circles in the air, sometimes defiling along a street, or wheeling round a large edifice, whilst at other times they sail along, without any perceptible motion of their wings, and then suddenly and frequently agitate them, as if impelled by some precipitate instinct. Previous to their departure, they begin to assemble early in July, when their numbers daily increase, and large bodies of them appear together. They then soar higher in the air, utter shriller cries, and fly in a peculiar style. These meetings continue till they finally disappear.

CAPRIMULGUS, Lin. &c. GOATSUCKER.

Bill slightly curved, very small, subulate, and depressed at the base; mouth extremely wide, and furnished with a glutinous humour for the retention of insects, with a series of bristles at the sides; ears very large; tongue pointed and entire; nostrils basal, wide, closed by a membrane surmounted by the front feathers; tail round or forked; legs short, the middle claw long, and serrated on the edge, but smooth in some of the foreign species. This family have their name from the ancient but erroneous notion of their sucking the teats of the she-goat. They are shy and solitary, come forth chiefly in the evening, prey on nocturnal moths and insects, and lay their eggs on the ground.

C. Europæus, Lin. &c. *European* or *Nocturnal Goatsucker,* Prov. *Night* or *Dorr Hawk, Churn Owl, Goat Owl, Fern Owl, Wheel Bird, Night Jar,* &c. The upper parts varied with black, cinereous, brown, rust-colour, and white, and the under parts reddish-white, with brown bands; the legs are short, scaly, and feathery below the knee. The male is distinguished by a large, oval, white spot, near the end of the first three quill-feathers, and another on the outer tail-feathers. Length fully ten inches; expanse of wing one foot nine inches; and weight between two and three ounces. Native of Europe, Asia, and Africa. In this island it is found, though in no great plenty, from Cornwall to the county of Ross. In the north of Europe, it has been traced as far as Sondmor; and it is common all over Siberia and Kamtschatka. With us, it is only a summer visitant, arriving about the middle of May, and departing late in August or early in September. It is no where very numerous, and never appears in flocks; even the individuals of a pair usually take their station at some little distance from each other. They perch lengthways on the branch of a tree, and not in a cross direction, like most other birds. They are partial to woods and their outskirts, but also frequent, stony, and heathy districts. Like owls, they are seldom seen in the day-time, unless disturbed, or else in dark and gloomy weather, when their eyes are not dazzled by the rays of the sun. In the dusk of the evening they prey on the larger insects, particularly on the *Scarabæus melolontha* and *solstitialis,* which emerge about that time from their earthy abode; they are also fond of the large bodied moths, and, indeed, allow few winged insects within their reach to escape from their widely distended jaws. They make no formal nest, the female depositing two or three dull white eggs, spotted with brown, in a hole on the ground, or among brakes. When perched, it usually sits on a bare branch, with its head lower than its tail, and, in this attitude, utters its jarring note. When on wing, it likewise makes a loud buzzing noise, which has been compared to that of a spinning-wheel. On some occasions, it sends forth a small plaintive note or squeak, which it repeats four or five times in succession, and which is supposed to be the call of the male. It will wheel round and round some large naked tree, with a very irregular and rapid motion, diving briskly, at intervals, as if to catch its prey, and then rising as suddenly; but it is then difficult to get within gunshot of it: for it abruptly disappears, nor can its retreat be discovered.

C. Virginianus, Gmel. &c. *Virginian Goatsucker, Mosquito Hawk,* or *Whip Poor Will.* The upper parts varied with dusky-brown, reddish, and cinereous, the under whitish, with dusky bands; throat of the male with a white crescent. Length eight or nine inches. This species arrives in Virginia about the latter end of April, and moves southward in September. The female makes no nest, but lays two greenish-brown eggs on the bare ground in May. It feeds on the larger grasshoppers, and such like insects, which it does not always catch when on the wing, but will frequently sit on a post or rail, and leap on them as they fly past. It begins its note, from which its popular name is derived, about sunset, discontinues it during the darkness, but resumes it with the first dawn, nor ceases till nearly sun-rise. Five or six may often be heard at once, to the great annoyance of the neighbourhood.

ORDER IX.

COLUMBINE BIRDS, OR PIGEONS.

Bill of moderate dimensions, compressed, base of the upper mandible covered with a soft skin, in which the nostrils are perforated, the tip more or less curved; feet, with three toes in front, quite divided, and one behind.

The Columbine family are pretty generally dispersed over the world, residing in the hottest, as well as in the more temperate climates, and even enduring the cold of Canada, Siberia, and the arctic regions. But few of the numerous species, comparatively, occur in the new continent; and warm countries, in general, seem to be most congenial with their constitution; for in them the species are both more multiplied and more varied. Although they lay only two eggs at a time, and are, besides, exposed to the depredations of beasts and birds of prey, they often pullulate in numbers, and appear in immense flocks, owing, no doubt, to the circumstance of their breeding repeatedly in the course of the year, and also to their native strength, which enables them to subsist in a wide range of soil and climate. To the vigour and warmth of their temperament, we may likewise attribute the facility with which they are transported from one place to another, and bred in latitudes remote from those whence they derived their origin. They are generally of an elegant form, of beautiful varying plumage, and of sociable, gentle, and endearing manners. In their wild condition, they are all granivorous, swallowing grains and berries entire, which are macerated and softened in the crop, before descending into the stomach. They do not digest the kernels of certain fruits, but pass them, without impairing their vegetative power, and thus prove the means of disseminating different plants. Some of the species also pick up insects. Pigeons are so strictly monogamous, that the first connection which they form is usually the only one which they contract in the course of their life, unless it is interrupted by some accident. They pair in the breeding season; and most of them unite in flocks in the latter period of that term; but each flock is composed of individuals of the same species. In their courtships the sexes coo and kiss; and they divide the task of incubation. Some nidificate in lofty trees, some in the crevices of rocks, some in copses or groves, and others in the immediate neighbourhood of human habitations. The nest is, for the most part, slightly constructed of small twigs, of a flattish form, and sufficiently broad to contain both parents, who act as nurses and guardians, feeding their tender offspring, when excluded from the shell, with aliments reduced to a sort of pap, or curd-like consistency, in their crop, afterwards providing them with grain somewhat macerated; and, lastly, with such as they swallow themselves. In order to receive their food, the young put their entire bill into that of their parent, keeping it half open, while the latter brings up and conveys into it the prepared contents of the crop, accompanying this action by a convulsive movement of the wings and body. The young pigeons are produced with a light down, and do not quit the nest till they are well fledged; and they still require the parental aid for some time after they are capable of flying. Pigeons drink much, and by a continued draught, plunging their bill into the water. They likewise devour a great quantity of food in the course of a day, and their increase is generally checked where much attention is bestowed on husbandry, on account of the waste which they occasion in fields of grain. Their voice is usually plaintive and mournful. Their instinctive partiality for carbonate of lime possibly arises from their frequent incubation, a certain quantity of calcareous matter being requisite for the formation of the shell of the egg. The natural history of the tribe has lately been admirably unfolded by M. Temminck. The subject might, indeed, furnish the materials of more than one volume; for upwards of seventy species have been recognised, and the manners of many of the European sorts have been diligently explored. In this place, however, we must restrict our notices to a few of the more remarkable exemplifications of the order.

COLUMBA, Lin. &c. PIGEON.

COLUMBA. Bill middle-sized, compressed, arched, tip-curved, base of the upper mandible covered with a soft, inflated skin; legs generally red; wings middle-sized or short.

With even tails.

Palumbus. *C. palumbus*, Lin. &c. *Ring Pigeon* or *Ring Dove*, Prov. *Queset, Cushat*, or *Wood Pigeon*. Grey, with the tips of the tail-feathers dark, the exterior margin of the primary quills whitish, and the neck white on each side; but this last mentioned character is not visible during the first year. A large species, measuring seventeen inches and a half in length, and twenty-nine inches in extent of wing, and weighing twenty ounces.

The ring dove is diffused over Europe, and though it prefers warm and temperate countries to the northern regions, it is, nevertheless, found in Sweden, Russia, and even Siberia, during the summer season. It is obviously a native of this island, in which, however, as in France, it is at least a bird of passage, shifting from the northern to the southern parts. In winter, these birds assemble in large flocks, and invariably resort to the woods, to roost in the highest trees, particularly the ash and beech. The great numbers that are seen together at this season have given rise to an opinion that many come to us from the more northern regions of the world; but if we consider how much dispersed all birds are in the period of breeding, we will be less surprised at their multitudes, when locally assembled.

In France, they are sometimes observed in winter, but much more abundantly in the fine season, generally arriving in February, and retiring in October or November. Though naturally very shy, some pairs have fixed their abode in the elevated trees of the gardens of the Thuilleries and Luxembourg, manifesting the same sense of security as domestic pigeons, and undismayed by the crowds of company; for they breed and rear their young without any symptoms of inquietude; but, when they repair to the neighbouring fields for food, they evince all the timidity of their species. They chiefly subsist on acorns, beech-mast, and various berries and grains, in default of which they will crop the tender shoots of clover, green corn, or turnips, the last of which considerably injures their flavour. They alight in numerous bands on ripe crops that have been laid by the rain; and they greedily devour the creeping roots of couch-grass, and the mountain strawberry. In several which Mr. Atkinson opened in June, the crops were full of the immature *oak-apple*, as it is called, which is the lodgement of the *Cynips quercifolia*. In England these birds most abound where the beechen woods are most extensive. When congregated in winter, they leave off cooing, but they resume it in March, when they begin to pair, at which time the male is observed to fly in a singular manner, alternately rising and falling in the air. The nest is formed of a few small sticks, so loosely put together, that the eggs may frequently be seen through them. These are two, or rarely three, white, exactly oval, and larger than those of the common pigeon. The nest, which is the joint production of the pair, is sometimes placed among brushwood, and in hedges, or large hawthorn bushes, but more frequently in the fork of a tree, or against the body of it, when encircled with ivy. The incubation lasts fourteen days, and in other fourteen the young are capable of shifting for themselves. This species breeds twice a-year. Its note is louder and more plaintive than that of the common pigeon, but uttered only in pairing time, or during fine weather. Various attempts to domesticate it, by hatching the eggs in dove houses, under the common pigeon, have proved abortive; for as soon as the young ones are able to fly, they always escaped to their proper haunts.

Arquatrix. *C. arquatrix*, Tem. *Parabolic Pigeon*. Purple-blue, breast black beneath, and varied with purple; head grey-bluish; abdomen and wings with white spots; feet feathery. Fifteen inches in length. Native of the Anteniquois forests in Africa. During the season of incubation the male and female are always found paired, but at other times they associate in flocks. They construct their nest like the stock dove, and produce ten white eggs. On commencing their flight they do not proceed in a straight line, but describe a parabola; and they continue forming a series of arcs, uttering their cry when on wing.

Œnas. *C. œnas*, Lin. &c. *Wild Pigeon, Stock Pigeon*, or *Stock Dove*. Bluish, cervix glossy green; jugulum and breast vinaceous; hinder part of the back cinerescent, with a double spot on the wings, and the tip of the tail black. Bill pale red; legs and claws black. Having been long regarded as the common source of all our domestic pigeons, this species has been very generally denominated *stock pigeon*. It appears, however, to be a distinct species, although it occasionally consorts with the common house pigeon, and may, like it, be induced to breed in dove-cots. It is about fourteen inches in length, and weighs eleven ounces. It is found more or less abundantly in Europe, Asia, and

Ornitho-
logy.

Africa. From the northern regions it migrates in great flocks on the approach of winter. Multitudes visit us in winter, and again retire in spring to their more northerly haunts; but others of them remain with us throughout the year. When beech woods occupied large tracts of ground, these birds used to frequent them in countless legions, often stretching above a mile in length, as they went forth, in a morning, to cater. In a wild state, they form their nests in the holes of rocks and old towers, or in the hollows of decayed trees, but not, as the ring-doves, on the boughs. They lay two white eggs, and breed several times in the course of the year. The male and female perform the office of incubation in turn, and feed their young by casting the contents of their crop into the mouths of the little gapers. They are partial to beech-mast, and, in default of grain or seeds, have been known to have recourse to the leaves of plants. It is, perhaps, not generally known, that they likewise feed on different sorts of snails, particularly the *Helix virgata*; for they not only regale themselves, but treat their offspring to this tender and nutritious food, the shell of which acts as a gentle stimulus to their delicate stomach, and, when ground to a powder, becomes an absorbent, and corrects the acrimonious quality of their other aliments. They may be enticed to a particular spot, by a composition of loam, old rubbish, and salt, which is termed a *salt-cat*; but as this device would decoy the pigeons of the owners of dove-cots, it is prohibited by an act of parliament.

Livia.

C. livia, Tem. *C. domestica*, Lin. &c. *C. domestica livia*, Gmel. *Domestic Pigeon*. Grey-bluish, with a double black band on the wings; the lower part of the back white; the breast pale-vinaceous, and the tip of the tail dusky. Although these characters will apply to a great many of this well-known species, it is, like most other domesticated animals, liable to an almost indefinite variety of markings. Among these, some of the most remarkable are the *White-rumped*, or *Smaller Rock Pigeon*, being of a smaller size than the more ordinary sort, and varying in its hues; the *Roman Pigeon*, of various colours, with the cere whitish; the *Rough-footed*, having hairy feathers on the feet; the *Crested*, also with hairy feathers on the feet, and a crest on the head; the *Norwegian*, with the head crested, the body snowy-white, and the feet feathered; the *Barbary*, with a naked, tuberculated space round the eyes, and a double dusky spot on the wings; the *Jacobine*, with the feathers of the occiput erected; the *Laced*, with small erected feathers, scattered over the back and wings; the *Turbit*, with the feathers on the breast recurved; the *Shaker*, with an erect open tail of many feathers; the *Tumbler*, that turns over in its flight; the *Helmet*, having the head, quills, and tail-feathers of one colour, and the body varied; the *Persian*, or *Turkish*, with a papillated red cere; the *Carrier*, or *Messenger*, with a caranculated white cere, and the palpebræ naked; the *Pouter*, with the breast inflated; the *Horseman*, with the breast inflated, and the cere caranculated; the *Smiter*, which turns over in its flight, and makes a loud noise with its wings; the *Turner*, which has the feathers in the back of the neck reversed, like a horse's mane; and the *Spot*, having the body white, and a spot on the forehead, of the same colour as the tail. These, and many other varieties, are particularly described in works which treat professedly of pigeons, as in Moore's *Columbarium*, and Temminck's natural history of the genus, in which an ample account will also be found of the management of these

birds for economical purposes. Some interesting particulars relative to the conveyance of intelligence by one of the varieties, are stated under the article CARRIER, to which we beg leave to refer.

Individuals of the present species, when unreclaimed, have two broods in the year, and lay their eggs in nests, rudely constructed in the holes of rocks, or ruined towers; but, in domestic confinement, they will breed from three to twelve times in a year, according to circumstances. They seldom lay more than two eggs at a time, one of which generally produces a male, and the other a female bird. The incubation lasts from fourteen to seventeen days. Domestic pigeons are kept in most parts of the civilized world, the young being reckoned a delicate food, while the dung serves as a good manure for certain descriptions of land, and is also used in tanning the upper leathers of shoes.

C. tympanistina, Tem. *Tambour Pigeon*. Forehead, eyebrows, and under parts of the body white; neck, back, and wings olive-brown; quills rufous, tail brown, with a black band at the tip of three of its feathers. This is an active and wild species, which inhabits Caffraria, and nestles on the summits of trees in the extensive woods of Africa. Levaillant assigned to it its specific denomination from the circumstance of its cooing resembling the sound of a tambourine at a distance.

Tympanis-
tina.

C. turtur, Lin. &c. *Common Turtle, Turtle Dove*, or *Turtle Pigeon*. Tail-feathers white at their tips, back greyish, breast vinaceous, a black spot and white stripes on the sides of the neck; abdomen white. Twelve inches long. The female is somewhat smaller, wants the white on the forehead, has the quills brownish, and the rest of the colouring less lively than in the male. Among the numerous varieties to which this species is incident, we may notice the *Portugal Dove*, which is brown, with the spot on the sides of the neck varied with black and white, the tail-feathers cinereous, and the outer ones entirely white, on the external web at the tip; and the *Luzonian Turtle*, which is greyish above, vinaceous-grey beneath, with a black spot on the neck; the feathers tipped with white, the two in the middle of the tail black, and the lateral ones white.

Turtur.

This elegant and gentle species is generally spread over the old continent, occurring in Europe, Asia, and some parts of Africa; but it migrates from the colder and more temperate latitudes on the approach of winter, quitting even Italy and Greece at that season. In this island it occurs chiefly in the south of England, arriving late in the spring, and departing about the latter end of August, frequenting the thickest and most sheltered parts of woods, and building a flat nest of sticks on the highest trees, and sometimes among brushwood. The female seldom lays more than two eggs, and in this country has only one brood in the year. During their stay of four or five months with us, they pair, build their nests, breed, and rear their young, which are strong enough to join them in their retreat. In Kent they are said to be more common than in any other county; and flocks of twenty or more will frequently injure the pea fields. In August, small groups of them are sometimes observed about Romney Marsh. They are generally very shy and retired, and yet easily tamed when captured. From their plaintive and tender note, and their winning attitudes, they have become the proverbial emblems of fond and connubial love, though it has also been alleged that they are more ardent than constant in their attachments. During

Ornitho-
logy.

Ornitho-
logy.

breeding time, both parents assist in feeding their young. For this purpose the coats of the crop put on a glandular appearance, and, for the first eight or nine days, secrete a substance much resembling the curd of milk. This is at first thrown up pure, and supplied to the young in that state; and it is afterwards mixed with the common food, in less proportions, until its secretion ceases.

With the tail wedge-shaped.

Migratoria.   *C. migratoria*, Lin. &c. *Passenger Pigeon, Migratory Pigeon*, or *Canada Turtle.* Tail cinereous, neck green-golden purple, wings with ovate spots in the middle, breast rufous, and abdomen white. Length from fourteen to fifteen inches. The female, which is scarcely so large, has the body of a grey-brown, whitish beneath, and the breast whitish-yellow.

Of all the pigeons of North America this is the most numerous, traversing, in spring and autumn, the countries which are situated between the 20th and 60th degree of north latitude. Their migratory legions will sometimes obscure the light of the sun, and cover a space of two miles in length, and a quarter of a mile in breadth. They travel in the morning and evening, and repose, about mid-day, in the forests, especially in those which abound in oaks, of the acorns of which they are very covetous. They preferably perch on dry and withered branches, and in such dense masses, that they may be shot in great numbers. Although they always shape their course in the same general direction, they seldom observe the same line of march for two seasons in succession, proceeding sometimes by the maritime, and sometimes by the more inland regions. Once in eight years they steer their way across Lake Ontario, and are so fatigued, when they alight on its shores, that hundreds of them may be knocked down with sticks. Some of their crowded squadrons are composed only of young, some only of females, and a few males; and others, again, almost entirely of the latter. Their passage, whether in spring or autumn, lasts from fifteen to twenty days, after which they are met with in the centre of the United States. When in the southern districts, they keep always in flocks, but when in the north, they pair, disperse, and nidificate in the vast forests of Nova Scotia, Canada, &c. where they commit serious havock on the newly-sown fields. When La Hontan was in Canada, they swarmed to such a degree, that the bishop, he says, had been compelled, more than once, to *exorcise* them, on account of their extensive depredations. The Indians often watch their roosting places, and, knocking them on the head in the night, bring them away by thousands. They preserve the oil, or fat, which they use instead of butter; and formerly there was scarcely a little Indian village where a hundred gallons of that commodity might not, at any time, be purchased. By the colonists these birds are generally caught in a net extended on the ground, into which they are allured by tame pigeons of their own species, blind-folded, and connected to the nets by a long string. The short flights and repeated calls of the shackled birds never fail to excite either their curiosity or their pity, and to bring them down to the spot, when they are immediately inclosed. Every farmer has a tamed pigeon at his door, to be ready against the season of flight. In Louisiana, they catch them by taking a flat vessel, and, placing some sulphur in it, set it a-light under the trees on which the birds roost, when the smoke so stupifies them that they fall down, and then the hunters pack them up in bags with as little loss of time as possible. Their flavour nearly approaches to that of the wild pigeon. Their nest consists of some sticks, arranged, apparently, without much care, on a large branch, about the middle of a lofty tree. They have two or three hatches in the season, each consisting of two white eggs, like those of the domestic pigeon. When they alight, the ground is speedily cleared of all esculent fruits, to the great injury of the hog, and other masticating animals. After having consumed every thing that has fallen on the ground, they form themselves into a great perpendicular column, and fly round the boughs of trees from top to bottom, beating down the acorns with their wings, when they again, in succession, alight on the surface, and again fall to feeding.

Ornitho-
logy.

GOURA, Steph. COLUMBA, Lin. &c. LOPHYRUS, Vieill.

GOURA.   Bill of moderate length, very slender, slightly inflated towards the tip, the upper mandible channelled on the sides, and its tip bent down; nostrils covered above with feathers, and placed in a fissure; wings short and rounded; tarsi long, and toes cleft at the base.

The species thus characterized seem to hold an intermediate station between the Columbine family and the Gallinaceous Fowls, and, in particular, to make such a near approach to some of the partridges, as to have been confounded with them. They are designated *Columbi-galline* by Levaillant, and some of the French writers. They are gregarious, and principally reside within the tropics.

Coronata.   *G. coronata*, Steph. *Columba coronata*, Gmel. &c. *Crowned Goura*, or *Great Crowned Pigeon.* Orbits black, crest erect, body bluish, shoulders ferruginous, and a white band on the wings. The head is ornamented with an erect circular crest, composed of feathers upwards of four inches and a half in length, of a loose texture, and of a fine pale-bluish ash. This species is somewhat larger than a turkey, but bills, inflates its breast, and coos like a pigeon. Its note is, however, so loud as to resemble a sort of lowing; and its mournful cries were mistaken by the crew of the Bougainville for those of savages. It inhabits the Moluccas and New Guinea, and breeds in lofty trees. Being easily tamed, it is kept as poultry in the East Indies.

Carunculata.   *G. carunculata*, Steph. *Wattled Goura.* Hoary, with the forehead and wattles on the throat red; under parts and rump white; tail brown, having the outer feathers edged with white. The female wants the naked space on the forehead, and the wattles on the throat. Length of the male ten inches, that of the female somewhat less. Native of the interior of Africa. The wattled goura makes a nest of bits of twigs and dry herbs in a hole on the ground. The female deposits from six to eight reddish-white eggs, and is assisted by the male during incubation. The young are covered with a reddish-grey down, and run as soon as they are out of the egg; but they are screened by their parents from the too ardent rays of the sun. The old birds feed them with the pupæ of ants, dead insects, and worms; but, as they acquire strength, they supply them with various sorts of grain, berries, &c. and have other habits in common with gallinaceous birds.

ORDER X.

GALLINACEOUS BIRDS.

GALLINACEOUS BIRDS.   The birds of this order have their denomination from their affinity to the domestic cock. Their anterior toes are generally united at their base by a short membrane, and denticulated along their margin, the upper mandible arched, the nostrils pierced in a broad membraneous space at the base of the bill, and invested with a cartilaginous scale. They have a heavy gait, short wings, a bony sternum, diminished by two notches, so broad and deep that they occupy almost all its sides, its ridge obliquely truncated forwards, so that the sharp point of the fork is united to it only by a ligament; circumstances which, by greatly weakening the pectoral muscles, render their flight laborious. The more ordinary number of their tail feathers is fourteen, but it varies from that to eighteen. From the simple structure of their larynx, their note is seldom agreeable. They have a very wide crop, and a very vigorous gizzard. Most of the species lay and hatch their eggs on the ground, on bits of straw, or herbage carelessly put together. Each male has usually several females, and takes no share in preparing the nest, or rearing the young, which are for the most part numerous, and capable of running as soon as they issue from the shell. The female calls them together by a particular cry, for feeding, and guides and protects them till they moult. In most species the males are furnished with spurs on their legs. Most of them walk and parade gracefully, and run nimbly, but they fly with difficulty and a whirring noise. Though they chiefly subsist on the seeds of plants, they likewise eat insects, grubs, and worms, which are macerated in their crop. It should seem that their gastric juice will not dissolve entire grains; for those of barley, for example, inclosed in tubes, or perforated spherules, are not affected by its action; but if the same grains be by any means broken, or ground, they are speedily dissolved. The food undergoes previous trituration in the gizzard, a very strong muscular viscus, whose internal coat is hard and cartilaginous. As this, however, is not the sort of animal substance suited to the reception of glands, or to secretions, the gastric juice in this family is not supplied by the stomach itself, but by the gullet, in which the feeding glands are placed, and from which it trickles down into the stomach. From this peculiarity of economy Spallanzani appears to have been struck with the resemblance between the stomachs of gallinaceous fowls and the structure of a corn mill; for while the two sides of the gizzard perform the office of the mill-stones, the crow, or crop, may be compared to the hopper. When our domestic fowls are abundantly furnished with food, they quickly fill their crop; but its contents do not immediately pass into the gizzard; and, at all times, they enter in very small quantities in proportion to the progress of trituration. Most of the species appertaining to this order are easily tamed, and are useful to mankind, on account of their flesh, their eggs, and their feathers.

Pavo, Lin. &c. Peacock.

Bill naked at the base, convex above, thickened, bent down towards the tip; nostrils open, cheeks partially denuded, feathers of the rump elongated, broad, capable of being expanded like a fan, and ocellated; tail wedge-shaped, consisting of eighteen feathers; feet furnished with four toes; the tarsi with a conical spur; the head crested.

P. cristatus, Lin. &c. *Crested*, or *Common Peacock.* Crest compressed, body of the male golden green, glossed with brassy reflexions above, the wing-coverts green-gold, with blue and brassy reflexions, the under parts of the body dusky, varied with green gold; the head with two white stripes on each side, the upper tail coverts very long, and adorned with various colourings, and auriferous eyes or arches. To recite the numerous and beautiful details of the markings of this splendid bird would require a long description, which, after all, would convey but a faint idea of the original. There are, however, we presume, few of our readers who are not sufficiently familiar with the rich and gaudy attire of the living specimen, to dispense with a minute enumeration of its dazzling and changeable hues. Like other domesticated birds, it exhibits several varieties. Thus, some have the wings transversely striated, some have the wings, cheeks, throat, upper parts of the belly, and wing-coverts, white, and others have the body entirely white, the eyes of the train being merely traceable by a different undulation of shade on the pure white of the tail. It is somewhat extraordinary, that this variety occurs in Norway unreclaimed, and migrates into Germany in winter. The ordinary length of the peacock, from the tip of the bill to that of the full-grown tail, is about four feet. The female is rather less; and her train is not only very short, but destitute of those resplendent beauties which ornament the male; her crest too is shorter, and her whole plumage partakes of a sober cinereous hue; her throat and neck are green, and the spots on the side of the head are larger than those of the male. The females of this species, however, like those of the pheasant, and of some other birds, have sometimes been known, when past breeding, to assume the male attire.

In a state of nature, the pea-hen breeds once a-year, and lays, it is alleged, from twenty-five to thirty eggs, of a whitish hue, speckled with dusky, in some secret spot, where they may be secure from the observation of the tiger and other beasts of prey, and especially from the male, which is apt to destroy them. In our climate, and when domesticated, the number of eggs seldom exceeds five or six, and the hen sits from twenty-five to thirty days, according to the temperature of the country and season. In Greece, she lays from ten to twelve eggs; and, in the absence of the male, she will also produce barren eggs, which the ancients termed *zephyrian*, as they were supposed to result from the genial stimulus of the vernal gale. When pleased or delighted, and in sight of his females, the cock erects his tail, unfolds his feathers, and frequently turns slowly round, as if to catch the sun-beams in every direction, accompanying this movement with a hollow murmuring. At other times his cry is very disagreeable, and often repeated, especially before rain. Every year he sheds his superb plumes; and then, as if conscious of his loss, he courts the most obscure retreats, till the returning spring renews his lustre. The young acquire the perfect brillancy of their plumage in their third year; but, in cold climates, they require attention in rearing, and should be fed on grass, meal, cheese, crumbs of bread, and insects, until they are six or seven months old, when they will eat wheat and various sorts of grain, like other gallinaceous birds. But the peacock is, in this respect, extremely capricious; and there is hardly any kind of food which it will not at times covet and pursue. Insects and tender plants are often eagerly sought for, at a time that it has a sufficiency of its natural food at command; and, during the indulgence of these unnatural appetites, walls cannot easily confine it; it strips the tops of houses of their tiles or thatch, lays waste the labours of the gardener, roots up his choicest seeds, and nips his favourite flowers in the bud. In India, one of its most mischievous propensities is picking at the eyes of children, which it probably takes for some glistening object of prey. According to Aristotle it lives about twenty-five years; but Willoughby and others allege that it is capable of existing for near a century. When full grown it is not readily injured by cold; and an instance is quoted of one which was found quite frozen, and had lain for some days in the snow in the courtyard of a house in Dunkirk, in 1776, and which, by the application of a gentle heat, recovered from the accident, and continued to live as if nothing particular had happened. These birds are also found to thrive in North America, notwithstanding the severity and duration of the winter season. In our cold climates, however, they seem to be incapable of very extensive flights; but they roost aloft in trees, or on the tops of houses or steeples, whence they utter their discordant scream. Though long naturalized in Europe, they are of eastern origin, occurring in the greatest profusion in the neighbourhood of the Ganges, and in the extensive plains of India, particularly in Guzerat, Cambay, the coast of Malabar, the kingdom of Siam, and the island of Java. So early as the days of Solomon, they were imported into Judea, by the fleets which that monarch equipped on the Red Sea, and which, in all probability, traded to the coast of Malabar. From India they were brought into Asia Minor, and subsequently into the Isle of Samos, where they were formerly much multiplied, and consecrated to Juno, but from which they have now wholly disappeared. In Greece they still fetched a high price in the time of Pericles. According to Ælian, thirty years after their first importation into that country, they were exhibited at Athens as a show to strangers; and he adds, that multitudes flocked to see them from Lacedemonia and Thessaly. Alexander had never seen them till he entered India, where he found them flying wild on the banks of the Hyarotis, and was so much struck with their beauty, that he decreed a severe punishment on all who should kill or molest them; but, towards the close of his reign they had so much multiplied in Greece, that Aristotle speaks of them as birds well known to his countrymen. They were introduced into Rome towards the decline of the republic; and the orator Hortensius was, according to Pliny, the first who had them presented at table, at a feast which he gave to the college of Augurs. His example was soon followed by the Roman epicures, insomuch that the price of the bird soon became exorbitant. The luxurious and effeminate emperors, refining on the extravagance of former times, took a pride in collecting large dishes of the heads or brains of peacocks, and which seem to have had nothing to recommend them but the enormous expence at which they were provided. In modern times, the young birds only are reckoned fit for the table, the flesh of the mature ones being hard and dry; but in hot countries it continues longer sweet than that of almost any other fowl. Pope Leo X. was particularly fond of white sauces, in which peacock's flesh was an ingredient. This species has now been conveyed as far north as Sweden and Norway; but there it is produced in small numbers, and not without considerable diminution of its beauty. The Europeans first fetched them to the coast of Africa, where they are now domesticated by the princes of those countries, particularly of Congo and Angola. They have been long since transported into Mexico, Peru, and the West India Islands, regions to which they could not have winged their way without the intervention of mankind.

POLYPLECTRON Tem. DIPLCETRON, Vieill. PAVO, Lin. &c.

Bill middle-sized, slender, straight, compressed; the upper mandible bent down towards the tip; nostrils lateral, in the middle of the bill, half covered by a naked membrane, but open in front; orbits and cheeks naked; legs slender, with four toes; the tarsi long, and, in the male, furnished with two or more spurs; tail broad, rounded, elongated, and composed of sixteen feathers.

P. chinquis, Tem. *Pavo bicalcaratus,* and *Pavo Thibetanus,* Lin. *Pavo Sinensis,* Brisson. *Argus polyplectron, Peacock Pheasant, Iris Peacock, Thibet Peacock,* &c. Cinereous, striated with dusky, and spotted with white above; wing-coverts sprinkled with brilliant orbicular cerulean spots, or eyes; under parts of the body grey, undulated with dusky lines; secondary quills with shining blue spots, and tail coverts with two shining green spots. From the generic and specific characters above recited, some idea may be formed of the aspect of these singular birds, which are rather larger than a pheasant, and highly elegant and beautiful. They inhabit China, and the mountains which separate Hindostan from Thibet. According to Sonnerat, they likewise occur in Malacca. The most remarkable circumstance in their natural history, is that of the tarsi being armed with several spurs, which vary in number from two to six; and frequently the same bird has a different number on each leg. Another curious fact is, that the tail is composed of two distinct ranges of long feathers, the undermost being the true tail. These feathers are capable of being erected, and displayed like a fan, when the bird is agitated, but, at other times, they remain in a horizontal position. The plumage of the female is less brilliant than that of the male, and the tail shorter. The attire of the young is of an earthy grey, with large spots, and small lines of a brown hue. After the first moult the plumage is less irregular, and the position of the spots on the wings and tail becomes visible; at the second they are more distinctly defined, and possess the fine golden-blue tint, with green reflexions; but it is not till after the third moulting, which takes place at two years of age, that all the colours are produced in perfection. In the natural state this species is not very wild, and it readily becomes accustomed to confinement, and propagates with as much facility as most of the gallinaceous fowls.

MELEAGRIS, Lin. &c. TURKEY.

Bill, short and thick; head and upper part of the neck invested with a naked, tuberculated skin; throat, with a longitudinal pendulous, and carunculated wattle; feet four-toed, tarsi of the male with an obtuse and weak spur; wings short. Only one species is known, namely,

M. gallopavo, Lin. &c. *Common Turkey.* Body, black above and beneath, and glossed with violet and gold. The female has smaller wattles, and is incapable of erecting the feathers of the tail. In its wild or original state, this bird is about three feet and a half in length, and will weigh from twenty even to sixty pounds. In consequence of domestication this species

Marginal notes: POLYPLEC-TRON. Chinquis. MELEA-GRIS. Gallopavo.

seems to degenerate, for it diminishes in size, and becomes liable to various maladies; but it also assumes a greater diversity of colouring.

Our English appellation of *Turkey* has been very improperly bestowed on the present species; but about the period when it was first introduced into the island, namely, in the reign of Henry VIII., it was customary to designate by the same name many foreign articles of luxury or rarity. We are indeed aware, that some of the elder naturalists, including Ray, and followed by the ingenious Daines Barrington, have assigned Asia and Africa as the original residence of the species, which, they allege, was known to the ancients, but they have obviously confounded it with the *Guinea Fowl*; and it is now distinctly ascertained that the bird in question is a native of North America, where it occurs from the country of the Ilinois to the Isthmus of Panama. It was formerly very common in Canada, notwithstanding the cold which prevails in that province during nine months of the year, and it abounded in the central tracts of the United States; but, with the progress of culture and population, it has gradually receded into the more remote territories.

These birds occupy the woods, in summer, in small flocks, which, when united, form bands of 100 or 200 individuals, and venture to quit their retreats, and approach near the inhabited parts of the country. They are swift runners, but fly awkwardly. About the month of March they become so fat, that they are easily run down by a man on horseback. When they are all assembled, they march in profound silence to their nocturnal haunts, and perch near one another in the large trees, manifesting a preference to branches that are withered, or stripped of their leaves. One may then approach very near to them, as they seem not to be scared either by the sight of a man, or the noise of a fowling-piece; nay, the sight of their falling and dead companions disturbs not their apparent sense of security; and the same circumstance which has been ascribed to stupidity, has been remarked of all the gallinaceous fowls of North America. During the day these birds mutually protect one another; for the first of them which perceives a bird of prey even at a distance, utters a call of alarm, and instantly all squat close down on the ground, and thus elude the sight of their adversary. About day-break they make the forests resound with their vociferous cackling, which lasts for an hour before sunrise. They then alight on the ground, and go in quest of wild berries, acorns, mast, &c. or search for insect food. The cocks among themselves are fierce and pugnacious; but, in other respects, evince little courage. As one suffices for several hens, their combats often originate in jealousy. The conqueror struts with inflated breast, expanded tail, red face, and relaxed frontal caruncle, making a singular inward noise, which seems to shake his whole frame. The disposition of the female is, in general, much more mild than that of the male, insomuch indeed that, when leading forth her young family to cater, though so large, and apparently powerful a bird, she will often afford them very little protection against any rapacious animal that may come in her way, but rather warns them to shift for themselves.

In spring the females lay their eggs, which are usually from fourteen to eighteen, and white, mixed with reddish or yellow freckles. For the purpose of incubation they select obscure and retired spots, as the male is apt to destroy them. Even the hen herself has sometimes been known to eat them; but for the most part she sits with so much perseverance, that, if fresh eggs be introduced into the nest, immediately on the young being hatched, she will continue sitting, if permitted, for two months. It should seem, however, from an anecdote related in the Memoirs of the Academy of Stockholm, that the cock turkey is not incapable of performing the duties of a nurse. M. Carlson remarks on this occasion, that the total neglect of their young, ascribed to male birds that associate with a plurality of females, is not general. Geese are of this description, and yet the gander protects the young with the greatest care. But the instance of a turkey cock sitting on eggs seems the more singular, because both in a wild and tame state the males are accustomed to destroy the nests of the females, in order that they may have them sooner free for pairing; and, for this reason, the cock is carefully separated from her while she is hatching. In some temperate and warm countries the hen also lays eggs in autumn, which are generally used in cookery, as a brood is seldom perfected from them, whereas those deposited in spring not being more numerous than the mother can hatch, are usually allowed to remain under her care. The young require to be watched with attention, as they are liable to perish from hunger or redundant moisture. In this island they are bred in great numbers, in Norfolk, and some other counties, whence they are driven to the London market in flocks of several hundreds, the attendants managing them with great facility by means of a bit of red rag tied to the end of a long stick, which, from the antipathy which they bear to that colour, effectually answers the purpose of a scourge. The quality and size of those reared in Norfolk are reckoned superior to those from any other part of the kingdom.

CRAX, Lin. &c. ALECTOR, Cuv. HOCCO.

Bill long, thick, compressed at the sides, the ridge carinated, incurved towards the tip, the base covered with a simple cere, or gibbous; nostrils lateral, placed in the cere, half covered, but open in front; top of the head ornamented with revolved feathers; feet furnished with four toes, of which the three anterior are connected by a membrane at the base; tail broad, pendant, and composed of twelve feathers.

The hoccos are peaceful, social, and familiar birds, which live in numerous troops in the vast forests of South America, and are restless and shy only in the neighbourhood of inhabited districts, where they are constantly exposed to the arms of the fowler. By some authors they have been carelessly confounded with the turkey. They generally frequent mountainous situations, but always wooded, picking from the ground the fruits on which they subsist, perching on the loftiest trees, and breeding either on the branches or the ground, forming their nest of dry twigs and stalks of herbage, lined with leaves. The number of eggs varies from two to eight. The differences which have originated in domestication, and the various provincial and local appellations, have occasioned a nominal multiplication of the species. Several of them are furnished with a singularly contorted trachea.

C. alector, Lin. &c. *Indian Cock*, or *Crested Curassow.* General colour of the body black, abdomen white, feathers on the crown curled and dark, cere yellow, temples naked, and variegated with black and yellow. Length nearly three feet. The crest, which the bird can elevate or depress at pleasure, varies in height according to age, and, in the adult, is composed of twisted black feathers. The back of the neck, breast, and tail, is enlivened with green reflexions; and the last is generally tipt with white. The intermixture of this with other congenerous species gives rise to different hybrid varieties. The crested curassows have greatly multiplied in the immense forests of Guiana; but they are also met with in Brazil, and in the other warm countries of America. Hernandez and Nieremberg have related wonderful anecdotes of their familiarity, which are not wholly without foundation; for Sonnini has seen some of the undomesticated individuals walking freely in the streets of Cayenne, without seeming to be scared by the appearance of men, and repairing to particular houses where they received food. In their native solitudes, their sense of security having been little disturbed, the traveller may easily deal destruction among their flocks, as the noise of guns does not intimidate them; but in the peopled regions of the country they are more suspicious, and have been greatly reduced in numbers. Their pace is slow and solemn, their flight heavy and noisy, and their cry hollow, as if concentrated within the body. They live on wild fruits, particularly those of *Thoa urens*, and on grain. Their eggs, which are deposited in the season of the rains, are from two to six, according to the age of the female, of a pure white, and of the size of those of the turkey. Individuals of this species are easily tamed, will readily associate with other fowls, and constitute a considerable part of the food of the planters, their flesh being white and delicate. They herd in flocks of about a dozen each, and roost on high trees during the night. They are frequently kept in our menageries; but they are unable to bear the dampness of the grass of our meadows, which renders their toes subject to rot off. Dr. Latham mentions an instance in which the whole of one foot was gone, and only part of one toe left on the other, before the bird expired.

PENELOPE, Tem. Vieill. &c. MELEAGRIS, Lin. GUAN.

Bill smooth at the base, middle-sized, broader than high, the tip compressed and arched; nostrils lateral, ovate, half-covered, but open in front; cheeks naked; the throat, with a longitudinal wattle, carunculated in the middle; feet four-toed, smooth, the tarsi reticulated; wings short.

On account of the great variations of plumage which these birds undergo at different periods, it becomes very difficult to ascertain the respective species with accuracy. Their flight is low, horizontal, and of short duration. They inhabit the most extensive and dense forests of Southern America, from Guiana to the river La Plata, perching on the inclined branches of trees, and running so quickly, by aid of their short wings, that a man cannot overtake them. They pass the day concealed in thickets; but they are astir in the morning and evening, when they resort to the outskirts of the forests, without, however, entering into the open plains, or other exposed situations. They are easily reconciled to domestication; and they subsist on grains, fruits, &c. like the other gallinaceous fowls; but, when they swallow Indian corn they seem not to digest the grains, but void them entire. They may be reared with profit in the poultry-yard, for their flesh is excellent; but they are averse to close confinement, and should be allowed to be much in the open air. They utter the sound of *pee*, in a shrill, but subdued, and nasal tone. They construct their nest of small branches, and place it in a thickly-clothed tree. The number of eggs rarely exceeds eight. In their sleeping attitude, their breast rests on their folded legs. They live in pairs, and in families, and appear to be much attached to one another, six or eight of them being often shot, in succession, on the same tree.

P. cristata, Gmel. &c. *Meleagris cristata*, Lin. Crested Guan, Guan, or Quan. Body black-green; back brown; rump and abdomen chesnut colour; neck and breast spotted with white; temples naked and violet; throat and longitudinal membrane red and hairy. About two feet seven inches in length. The feathers of the head and of the occiput are elongated into a tufted crest, capable of being erected at the will of the bird. The female differs in having a rufous reflexion on the plumage, and a shorter crest. This species frequently utters a sound, expressed by *jacco, yacoo*, or *yahoocoo*, which is feebly pronounced, and is supposed to intimate feelings of want or pain. It has likewise a still more feeble cry, which has been compared to that of the turkey. It is of very gentle dispositions, easily tamed, and, when domesticated, is apt to roost, during the night, on the tops of houses. It is in much request for the table. Its native abodes are Brazil, the forests which confine on the Bay of Campeachy, the Isthmus of Panama, Guiana, &c.

GALLUS, Ray, Brisson, Vieill. Tem. Leach, PHASIANUS, Lin. &c. COCK.

Bill somewhat thick, with the base smooth, convex above, slightly curved, and bent down at the tip; nostrils situated at the base, half covered with an arched scale, and open; ears naked; tail compressed, and composed of fourteen feathers; feet four-toed, gressorial, anterior toes connected at the base by a membrane; tarsi with a long incurved spur; wings short.

The fowls to which these characters refer, have, in conformity with the more natural arrangement of the elder ornithologists, been again detached from the genus *Phasianus*, as instituted by Linné; and our domestic cock is a pretty fair type of the manners of the race. As has happened to other animals that have undergone a long series of domestication, their varieties have been greatly multiplied, and their native abodes are not easily ascertained with precision: but they are seldom found in a wild state, except in the warmer regions of the globe, particularly in the forests of Southern Asia and America, where they subsist on worms and insects, but principally on seeds and grains, which they swallow entire. The females have many young ones at a brood, and, at the same time, take a tender charge of them, leading them abroad, sheltering them under their wings, and indicating their food. The young are, at first, invested with a thick soft down. They afford a supply of wholesome and delicate food at every table.

G. giganteus, Tem. Gigantic, Paduan, or Jago Cock. Twice as large as the common species, with red caruncles and wattles. Found wild in the forests of Sumatra, and the western parts of Java. According to Mr. Marsden, it is so much elevated on its legs, that, with its bill, it can reach to food placed on a common eating-table, and that, when fatigued, it reposes on the first articulations of the legs, and even then is higher than the common cock when standing. In a domestic state it is common in many places, particularly about Padua, in Italy; and Caux, in Normandy, where it attains to a great size, and often weighs ten pounds.

It has a very large denticulated comb, which is often double ; and the body is variegated with brilliant colouring, as in the common species. Its voice is remarkably rough and hoarse.

Sonneratii.

G. Sonneratii, Tem. *Phasianus gallus,* Gmel. *Gallus Indicus,* Leach. *Jungle Cock, Wild Cock,* or *Indian Pheasant.* Comb toothed, mouth wattled beneath, feathers of the neck elongated, spotted with white, black, and fulvous, with membranaceous tips ; throat, breast, abdomen, and back, grey, striped with white ; wing-coverts reddish-chesnut ; the tips of the feathers dilated, cartilaginous, and fulvous ; the quill and tail-feathers deep black. Female smaller, and destitute of comb and wattles ; head feathered ; body more obscure, varied with brown and red. Abounds in the large forests of India, and alleged by some, though without sufficient proof, to be the source of the domestic cock and hen.

Domesti-
cus.

G. domesticus, Steph. *Phasianus gallus,* Lin. &c. *Domestic Cock.* Comb toothed, throat wattled, feathers of the neck linear and elongated, body variegated with beautiful colours, tail compressed and ascending. Comb and wattles of the female less than those of the male. The common dung-hill cock and hen are so familiar to our daily observation, that any minute description of them would be quite superfluous, and yet inadequate to comprise the shadings and varieties ; for, with the exception of the pure white individuals, scarcely any two are perfectly alike.

The *Crested* cock has the head ornamented with a crest, in addition to the comb ; but some few are found having the latter appendage nearly obliterated, and, in place of it, a very large crest. The plumage of individuals of this variety differs as much as that of the more common sorts ; and the crest often contrasts with the rest of the feathers, some birds being white, with a black crest ; others black, with a white crest ; or the crest is black and orange, while the body is white, or varied with several colours. This breed is not uncommon in England, France, &c. In Egypt it is much in request for the delicacy of its flesh. It is said to be less prolific than some others, but to fatten more readily. The *Bantam* and *Turkish* tribes are either identical, or, at least, very nearly allied, being both of small dimensions, and attired in showy plumage ; and the legs of the bantam are sometimes so thickly feathered as to impede walking. The hen lays a great number of eggs, without sitting : and the cock is very courageous, not shrinking from measuring his strength with one of another race that is double his own size.— A *dwarf* variety, scarcely larger than the common pigeon, occurs in England, France, China, &c. and is cherished on account of the fertility of the female.— The *Dorking* cock, of Latham, and others, is of a somewhat larger size than the ordinary sort, and has *five* toes, two of which are placed behind. It is very common in England, and particularly about Dorking, in Surrey. The *Game-cock,* when in full plumage, and not mutilated for the purpose of fighting, has a fine and animated appearance. His head, which is small, is adorned with a specious red comb and wattles ; his eyes sparkle with fire ; and his whole demeanour bespeaks boldness and freedom. The feathers on his neck are long, and fall gracefully down on his body, which is thick, firm, and compact. His tail is long and arched ; his legs are robust, and armed with sharp spurs, with which he defends himself and attacks his adversary. When surrounded by his females, his whole aspect is full of animation, and he admits no competitor ; but, on the approach of a rival, rushes forward to instant combat, and either drives him from the field, or perishes in the attempt. To render his blows still more deadly, he is occasionally armed with an artificial spur, called a *gaffle.* The origin of cock-fighting is lost in the periods of remote antiquity ; yet even the polished Athenians allotted one day in the year to this barbarous sport : the Romans seem to have borrowed it from the Greeks, and the ancient Britons from the Romans. So addicted was Henry VIII. to this inhuman spectacle, that he caused a commodious house to be built for its exhibition, and which still retains the name of the *Cock-pit* ; and the practice was perversely promoted in our public schools. In China, the rage for cock-fighting is still more prevalent than in this country ; and, in Sumatra, a man will hazard not only his property, but his wife and children on a favourite bird !

Besides races, or breeds of this species, individual varieties, or anomalies, of a marked complexion, also occasionally occur, some of which may be regarded as extraordinary, or monstrous productions. " A Jew," says M. Schwartz, " exhibited for money, in 1802, at Posen, in Poland, a hen, with her face like the human, which had been hatched on a farm near Wryesnier, and which he had received in payment of a small debt." A particular account of a well authenticated case of a hen having the profile of an old woman, may be found in the eighth volume of Thomson's *Annals of Philosophy.* Various examples of defect or redundancy of organs, and of other irregularities of conformation, have been observed, especially in chickens produced by artificial hatching, but which it would be tedious to enumerate.

The cock is very attentive to his females, hardly ever losing sight of them, leading, defending, and cherishing them, collecting them together when they straggle, and eating with apparent reluctance, until he sees them feeding around him. The moment a strange cock appears within his domain, he immediately attacks him as an intruder, and, if possible, drives him away. The patience and perseverance of his mate in hatching, and her tender solicitude in protecting her young brood, are notorious and proverbial. Though by nature timid, and, on ordinary occasions disposed to fly from the meanest assailant, yet, when marching at the head of her offspring, she seems to be fearless of danger, and will dart on the face of the fiercest animal that offers to annoy her.

The domestic hen, if properly fed, and accommodated with cold water, gravel, and a warm situation, generally lays two eggs in the course of three days, and continues to do so upwards of ten months. After having laid from twenty-five to thirty, she prepares for the tedious process of incubation ; and, in about three weeks the young brood burst from their confinement. In the more northerly climates, as in Greenland and Siberia, the species does not breed.

As the chickens reared by the female bear no proportion to the number of eggs which she produces, various schemes of artificial rearing have been attempted. The Egyptian plan, which Réaumur and others were desirous of introducing into France, is principally practised in the village of Berme, and the adjacent district. The persons engaged in it spread themselves all over the country in the beginning of autumn, and each of them is ready to undertake the management of an oven. These ovens are of different dimensions ; but each is capable of containing from forty to eighty thousand eggs; and their number in different parts has been estimated at nearly four hundred. Réaumur's treatise on artificial hatching is well worthy the perusal of the curious reader; and, for the most approved modes of managing domestic poultry, we may refer to the second volume of Temminck's admirable work on the Gallinacea, and to Parmentier's excellent observations under the article *Coq*, in the *Nouveau Diction-naire d'Histoire Naturelle.*

Besides the preceding species and varieties, we might, if our limits permitted, particularize several others, as *G. crispus, Crisped,* or *Frizzled Cock,* having all the feathers curled up, and wool-like—*Morio,* or *Negro,* so denominated, from having the caruncle and wattles black—*Lanatus,* or *Silk,* with the feathers like hair, and the crest and wattles red-blue—*Ecaudatus,* or *Rumpless,* which wants the rump and tail—*Furcatus,* or *Fork-tailed,* distinguished, among other peculiarities, by a horizontal and forked tail—and *Macartnyi,* or *Macartneyan,* the *Fire-backed Pheasant* of some authors, a splendid and magnificent bird, destitute of the comb, but with a delicate tuft of feathers on the crown of the head, a native of Sumatra, very wild, and apparently incapable of domestication.

When fowls and chickens roll in the sand more than usual, and when the cock crows in the evening, or at unusual hours, we may generally infer the approach of rain.

The common poultry, which we continually employ in propagating their kind, probably soon exhaust the principles of life, and therefore, in their domestic state, are not long-lived. As it is by mere accident, however, that any of them are allowed to reach the period assigned to them by nature, we are unable to ascertain the exact term of their age. Buffon supposes that, in their domestic condition, they may live twenty years, and in their native wilds about ten more.

PHASIANUS, Tem. &c. PHEASANT.

Bill short, thickened, naked at the base, bent down towards the tip; nostrils basal and lateral; ears covered; feet four-toed and gressorial, tarsi furnished with spurs; tail elongated, cuneiform, and composed of eighteen feathers; wings short. The beautiful and elegant species comprised under this genus are all natives of Asia, frequenting woody situations, and subsisting on seeds and insects. The females produce many young at a brood, which they foster for some time, like the domestic hen. Their nests, which are rudely constructed, are formed on the ground. The young, when first hatched, are clothed with a soft down.

P. Colchicus, Lin. &c. *Common Pheasant.* The male rufous, with the head and neck blue, shining with green and gold, and variegated with black and white; tail plain and wedge-shaped. The female is smaller, and brown-grey, varied with reddish and dusky. Among the more marked varieties, we may notice the white, variegated with the colours of the preceding, and the pure white. The common cock pheasant is about three feet in length, including the tail, two feet and a half in stretch of wing, and weighs about three pounds. Hybrid individuals not unfrequently occur, the offspring of different species, or varieties of pheasants, or even from an intermixture with the common fowl, or some of the *Galli.*

The pheasant is supposed to have been originally found on the banks of the *Phasis,* in Colchis, the modern Mingrelia; but it is at present diffused over many

of the southern and temperate regions of the old continent, and has been met with even as far north as Bothnia and Siberia. We need scarcely add, that it enlivens and embellishes our parks and thickets, and furnishes our tables with a delicate article of food. Owing to the shortness of its wings, it flies heavily, and to a small distance at a time. Being naturally shy and solitary, it is tamed with difficulty, and, except in the pairing season, it seems averse to consort even with those of its own species. Yet, when these birds are in the constant habit of being attended in the coverts by a keeper, they will come to feed the moment that they hear his whistle; nay will follow him in flocks, and will scarcely allow the peas to run from his bag into the trough, before they begin to eat; and those that cannot find sufficient room at one trough, will follow him with the same familiarity to others. They are fond of corn and buck-wheat, but will often feed on the wild berries of the woods, and on acorns. The young are fed with the pupæ of ants, and with insects and worms. They are partial to the shelter of thickets and woods, in which there is long grass; but they will also often breed in clover fields. The nest, which is placed on the ground, is usually composed of a few dry vegetables, put carelessly together. The female is anxious to conceal it from the male, and lays from twelve to fifteen eggs, which are smaller than those of the common hen, and of a greenish-grey, spotted with brown. The incubation lasts twenty-three or twenty-four days; and as soon as the young break the shell, they follow the mother like chickens. If undisturbed, the parents and their brood remain for some time in the stubble and hedge-rows; but if scared or molested, they betake themselves to the woods, and come forth to feed only in the morning and evening. In confinement, the female neither lays so many eggs, nor hatches and rears her brood with so much care and vigilance, as in the fields. In a mew, she will rarely dispose her eggs in a nest, or sit on them at all; so that the domestic hen is usually entrusted with the charge of hatching and breeding the young. Even when enjoying greater freedom, the hen pheasant is less careful than the partridge to call her brood together; but she will shelter as many as seek for protection under her wings. After all, about one third of the young race never attain to full growth; for several fall a sacrifice to the first moulting, and more to a disorder called *oscitans* or *gapes,* which proceeds from the presence of a species of fasciola in the trachea. In the mowing of clover near woods frequented by pheasants, the destruction of their eggs is sometimes very considerable. As the cold weather approaches, these birds begin to fly, at sunset, to the branches of the oaks, among which they roost during the night; and this they do more frequently, as winter advances, and the trees lose their foliage. On these occasions the males make a noise called *cocketing,* which they repeat three or four times; but the hens, on flying up, utter one shrill whistle, and then are silent. Owing to their size, and their awkward and noisy flight, the sportsman reckons the pheasant a bird of easy conquest; and it is even reputed stupid, because, when roused, it will often perch on a neighbouring tree, and have its attention so rivetted on the dogs, as to suffer the sportsman to approach very near. It has been observed, however, that the old cocks have recourse to various stratagems, in thick and extensive coverts, before they are compelled to take wing; and Le Roy has remarked, that they regulate the hours of their repasts by the seasons. The crowing of the males, which begins in the first week of March, may often be heard at a considerable distance.

P. pictus, Lin. &c. *Painted* or *Golden Pheasant*. Crest yellow; feathers of the occiput brown, varied with black lines; body golden yellow above, scarlet beneath, secondary quills blue; tail cuneated. One of the most beautiful of the tribe. Total length about two feet nine inches. The female is not only smaller, and has a much shorter tail, but the whole of her plumage is less gay and splendid. The young males resemble the females, and are not invested with all the richness and brilliancy of their attire till the second moulting. The females, on the other hand, at the age of five or six years, sometimes put on the male plumage. The painted pheasants are natives of China, from which they have been introduced into the parks and aviaries of Europe. In this country they are reared with as much ease as the common species, and they seem to be more familiar in their habits. They feed on rice, hemp-seed, wheat, or barley, and they will also eat cabbages, herbs, fruits, &c.; but they are particularly fond of insects, the difficulty of procuring a sufficiency of which is supposed to be a principal cause of the many disorders to which they are liable. So early as March the female deposits her eggs, which resemble those of the Guinea Pintado, and are redder than those of the common pheasant. The flesh of the present species is reckoned superior to that of any of the others. The painted pheasant will breed with the common, but the offspring is infertile.

P. satyrus, Tem. Vieill. *Meleagris satyra*, Lin. Lath. *Penelope satyra*, Gmel. *Horned Pheasant*, or *Horned Turkey*. Red-brown, with white eyelets, ringed with black; head with a double blue horn; throat with a pendulous membrane. Of an intermediate size between a common fowl and a turkey. The most remarkable attribute of the male, is a fleshy, callous, blue substance, like a horn, which springs from behind each eye; and, on the fore part of the neck and throat, is a loose flap, of a very fine blue colour, marked with orange spots. The female wants the horns. This singular and rare species inhabits Bengal and the mountains which separate Hindostan from Thibet and Nepaul. The male possesses the faculty of dilating and lengthening the flap on the throat, so as almost to make it hang over the breast, at which time the colours are greatly heightened, appearing of a deep blue, barred across with crimson.

ARGUS, Tem. Vieill. PHASIANUS, Lin. Lath.

Bill longer than the head, compressed, straight, with the base naked, the maxilla arched, and bent down towards the tip; nostrils lateral, placed in the middle of the maxilla, and half-closed by the membrane; side of the head and the neck, featherless; feet, four-toed, slender; tarsi smooth; tail ascending, compressed, with twelve feathers, of which the two middle in the male are elongated. This genus, which has been recently detached from *Phasianus*, is, moreover, distinguished by having the secondary wing-feathers much larger than the primaries.

A. giganteus, Tem. *A. pavonius*, Vieill. *Phasianus argus*, Lin. Lath. *Gigantic Argus*, *Argus Pheasant*, *Argus*, or *Luen*. Lower parts of the neck and under parts of the body, red brown, striped with black; back and tail-coverts yellowish, and marked with rounded brown spots; secondary feathers with many eyelets, webs and quills blue, and the tail brown-black, spotted with white. The female is brown-black, spotted with

1

yellow and brown, with the webs of the quills blue-black, and the two long feathers without spots. The details of colouring in this beautiful and rare bird, though not particularly brilliant, are finely varied, and, on account of the numerous and well defined spots which they exhibit, have been compared to the eyes on the peacock's tail. The size of the body nearly corresponds with that of the turkey hen; but the total length, including that of the intermediate tail-feathers, is five feet three inches, the tail-feathers alone measuring three feet eight inches, whereas the female, though of nearly as large a body, is only twenty-six inches long, her tail being much shorter than that of the male. When the cock struts in presence of his mate, he lets down his wings nearly to the ground, and erects his tail in the form of a fan; but, when he is tranquil, the latter assumes the form of two vertical planes adjected to each other. In Sumatra, where this bird is far from uncommon, it is called *Coo-ow*, from its cry; and, in Chinese Tartary, it is named *Luen*. Its European name, *Argus*, is obviously derived from the numerous eye-like spots, scattered over its plumage, in allusion to the hundred eyes of the unfortunate guardian of Io; and, as the fable attributes this multiplicity of the organs of vision to the intervention of Juno, the Argus has likewise been called the *Junonian pheasant*. Besides the countries which we have already mentioned, it occurs in Pegu, Siam, and Malacca. In its manners it is extremely shy, being seldom captured alive, and it is so impatient of confinement, that it pines and dies in the short space of a month. Its cry is as loud as that of the peacock, and somewhat plaintive; and its flesh is as savoury as that of the common pheasant. Its eyes are dazzled by the light of day, when it appears dull and stupid; but it is very active in the dark.

NUMIDA, Tem. Lin. &c. PINTADO.

Bill thickened, arched, the base covered with a warted membrane, and a carunculated wattle hanging from the under mandible; nostrils situated in the cere, and half-covered by a cartilage; head naked, crown with a callous horn or strong crest; feet four-toed, smooth; tail short, bent down, and consisting of fourteen or sixteen feathers. The species belonging to this genus are originally natives of Africa and the neighbouring islands, have the manners of domestic poultry, except that they are less assiduous than some of the other tribes in rearing their young, and have been multiplied, for the use of the table, in various districts of Europe, Asia, and America.

N. meleagris, Lin. &c. *Guinea Pintado*, or *Guinea Fowl*. Body grey-blue, sprinkled with small white spots; head and upper part of the neck naked, a conical tubercle, with its tip reflexed on the crown, and a broad geminated membrane near the gape. The variety β of Latham and others, has the breast white, and α of Temminck, and γ of some authors, has the whole body whitish, with rounded white spots. Other varieties also occur, and a hybrid has been produced between a male pintado and a domestic hen. The young are pretty birds, somewhat resembling red partridges at an early age. The adult male is bigger than a large cock, and measures twenty-two inches in length. His loose wattle is of a bluish colour, but that of the female is red.

In a wild state, these birds associate in numerous flocks, manifesting a partiality to marshy and morassy situations, where they subsist almost wholly on insects,

RECURVIROSTRA AVOCETTA
Avocet

ORNITHOLOGY.

PLATE CCCCLV

ARGUS POLYPLECTRON
Peacock Pheasant

GALLUS SONNERATII
Jungle Cock

PHŒNICOPTERUS RUBER
Flamingo

ARGUS GIGANTEUS
Gigantic Argus

PHASIANUS SATYRUS
Horned Pheasant

ARDEA MINUTA
Little Heron

CASSUARIUS GALEATUS
Galeated Cassowary

RHEA AMERICANA
American Rhea

STRUTHIO CAMELUS
Ostrich

Engraved for the Edinburgh Encyclopædia by J. Moffat, Edin.

worms, and seeds, laying about eight eggs, but probably breeding more than once in the year. In Numidia, and many of the scorching districts of Africa, they fly in troops during the day, and perch on trees at night. According to Niebuhr, they abound in the fertile plains of Arabia, and are so numerous near Tahama, that the children knock them down with stones, and sell them in the town. Transported to America by the Genoese in 1508, they have greatly multiplied, and become so habituated to the climate, that, in the Spanish possessions, they roam at liberty in the midst of the woods and savannahs. Notwithstanding the great heat of their native country, they sustain, without injury, the cold of our northern latitudes, and might possibly be as successfully introduced into our woods and parks as the pheasant; but it is troublesome to induce them to incubate and rear their young in the poultry-yard, as they frequently desert their charge, and drop their eggs under hedges, or in other concealed places. When plentifully fed, the hen pintado will lay about a hundred eggs, if care be always taken to leave one in the nest. These eggs are smaller than those of the common fowl, of a rounder form, reddish-white, obscurely freckled with a darker colour, and are reckoned a delicate morsel. As ancient and modern epicures have vaunted the flavour of this species, it has been reared for the table in all ages, and frequently by the intervention of the common, or of the turkey hen, either of which proves a more vigilant and careful nurse than the female pintado.

TETRAO, Lin. &c. GROUS.

Bill short and thick, arched above, convex, bent down towards the tip; nostrils basal, half closed with an arched scale above, and invested with small feathers; eye-brows naked, warty, and scarlet; tarsi feathered; wings short and rounded.

An appropriate characteristic of the family is the carunculated skin over the eyes, forming a sort of eyebrow, which is more or less of a red colour. The tarsi are covered with feathers, but want spurs. Grous are polygamous, the females only taking charge of incubating and rearing the young. They make their nests on the ground, in a very artless manner, of a few small branches of pines, heath-tops, &c. They produce many eggs, usually breed only once in the year; and the young run about as soon as hatched, often with pieces of shell adhering to them. Their food consists of seeds, berries, a few insects, and the tops of heaths, and of a few evergreens. They reside in the colder and more temperate latitudes; and such of them as are found in the more southern regions, haunt the highest mountains, where, in course, the temperature is much reduced.

T. urogallus, Lin. &c. *Wood Grous, Great Grous, Cock of the Wood* or of the *Mountain, Capercailzie* or *Capercailly* of the Scots. Neck and upper parts of the body dusky, transversely waved with cinereous, dusky, varied with white spots beneath, axillæ white; breast green, glossed with brassy; tail black, and its feathers marked with two white spots towards the tip. Female transversely variegated with black and ash-colour, the throat, breast, and tail-feathers rufous, and the latter barred with black. There are several varieties, which have been briefly indicated by Nillson, in his *Ornithologia Suecica*. In size this species is little inferior to a turkey, and sometimes weighs twelve or thirteen, but, more frequently, seven or eight pounds, measuring two feet nine inches in length, and three feet in extent of wing. The female is considerably smaller, rarely measuring above twenty-six inches in length, or weighing more than four pounds. The young of both sexes, during the first year, greatly resemble the female; and the males of the second moult have the upper parts of the body greyish-black, and the green on the breast, which is afterwards so glossy, very dull.

This stately species inhabits the wooded and mountainous regions of Europe and northern Asia, occurring abundantly in the pine forests of Russia, Siberia, Norway, Sweden, &c. A smaller variety than the common sort is found in Norway and Lapland, the furthest extreme of Europe towards the Icy Sea. The wood grous is also met with in the Alps and Pyrenees, and in some of the elevated and bleak districts of France, Italy, and Greece. It was formerly not uncommon in Ireland and Scotland, but may now be said to be extirpated from both. It principally feeds on the berries of the juniper and different species of *vaccinia*, on the seeds and tops of pines, the leaves of buck-wheat, the tops of heath, &c. and on worms and insects. Like domestic poultry, these birds swallow small pebbles, and scratch the soil with their feet. In the morning and evening they resort to the copses for food, and they retire during the day into the thickest recesses of the woods. Their breeding season commences about the middle of April, when they perch with little interruption, and when the male may be seen at sunrise and in the evening, much agitated, on one of the largest branches of the pines, with his tail raised and expanded, and his wings drooping, sometimes walking backwards and forwards, with his neck stretched out, his head inflated, and his eye-brows of a deep crimson. His wooing call commences by a sort of explosion, instantly followed by a sound like the whetting of a scythe, which ceases and recommences alternately for about an hour, and is then terminated by a similar explosive noise as at the beginning. During this singular exhibition, he is apparently so deaf and insensible, that, though at other times very wild and vigilant, the sportsman may gradually approach him, and take a fatal aim. This ardour of temperament continues till June. The female deposits in an artless nest on the ground and among moss from eight to sixteen eggs, which are about the size of those of the common hen, but more obtuse at the ends, and yellowish-white, sprinkled with irregular yellow spots. When she quits them, in quest of food, she covers them over with leaves or moss. The young follow her, with great agility, immediately on their exclusion, and she leads them to procure wild berries and the pupæ of ants. The brood follow the mother for nearly two months, at the expiration of which period the young males entirely forsake her, living harmoniously together till the beginning of spring, when they separate and affect solitude, never approaching but in the spirit of hostility, every male being jealous of an intruder, and resisting him with determined obstinacy. In the provinces of Smoland and Gothland in Sweden, a hybrid but barren offspring is produced between the present species and the black grous. The flesh of the former, though very dark coloured, is much relished by epicures, when it has not contracted too much of a bitter flavour, by copiously feeding on juniper-berries; and it is often conveyed in winter, in a perfectly eatable state, from Norway to this island. The eggs, too, are much in request, and are accounted preferable to those of every other bird; but all attempts to habituate the species to confinement in a poultry yard appear to have failed.

Tetrao.

Urogallus.

T. bonasia, Lin. &c. *Hazel Grous.* Feathers on the head somewhat lengthened, a black band near the extremity of the lateral tail-feathers, under portion of the tarsus and toes naked. Accidental varieties, and the young, have given rise to the supposed species, which have been designed *Canus, Nemesianus,* and *Betulinus.* The hazel grous is between thirteen and fourteen inches in length, has about twenty-one inches of extent of wing, and flies heavily, but runs with wonderful velocity. In roosting it conceals itself among the thickest branches of pine, fir, or birch trees, and is not easily dislodged by noise. Weak, peaceful, and timid, the only two resources which, on the approach of a sportsman, or of a bird of prey, it seems to manifest, are quick running and squatting down. But it is extremely shy, and soon expires in captivity. In summer it frequents the silence and obscurity of the forest, subsisting on heath, whortle-berries, and other wild fruits, and in winter, on the catkins of the birch or hazel, the shoots of pine trees, juniper-berries, &c. These birds pair in October and November, and in spring place their nest on the ground, under the low branches of a hazel tree, or in a tuft of heath. The eggs, which vary in number, from about twelve to eighteen, are rather larger than those of a pigeon, whitish-yellow, and irregularly spotted with brown-yellow. They are incubated in three weeks, and as soon as the young are hatched they run about in all directions, and the mother rallies them around her by a low and gentle call. Though not indigenous to Great Britain, this interesting addition to the winged tenantry of our woods, might, we presume, be easily imported, for it seems to thrive in every country of the old continent that affords hills and woods, being diffused from Siberia to the extremities of Africa. The flesh, which is blackish externally, and whitish within, is highly prized by the lovers of dainty fare ; and, according to German etiquette, it is the only dish that is permitted to be served up twice in succession at the table of princes.

T. tetrix, Lin. &c. *Black Grous, Black Cock, Black Game,* Prov. *Heath Poult* or *Heath Fowl.* No long feathers under the throat, the general plumage black, with violet reflexions ; tail much forked, with the two outer feathers convoluted, and the inferior tail-coverts white. The black grous is somewhat larger than a pheasant, measuring two feet four inches from the point of the bill to the extremity of the tail, and weighing nearly four pounds ; but the female is little more than half the size. Native of the heathy, wooded, and hilly regions of Europe, especially towards the north, and remote from human culture and habitations. In this island, the progress of civilization and tillage, combined with the improved practice of shooting flying, has nearly banished this game from England, though some individuals still occur in sequestered spots, suited to their manners and dispositions, as in the New Forest, Hampshire, Dartmoor, and Sedgemoor, Devonshire, some heathy hills in Somersetshire, Staffordshire, North Wales, &c. ; but they are much more abundant in some parts of the Highlands of Scotland. They feed chiefly on the tops of fir and heath, wild berries, the grains of buck-wheat, &c. but cherries and pears are said to prove fatal to them. They perch and roost in the manner of pheasants, but never pair. In spring the males assemble at their accustomed haunts, on the top of heathy mountains, when they crow and clap their wings ; the females obey the signal, when the males become very quarrelsome, and fight like game-cocks. On these occasions, so inattentive are they to their own

safety, that two or three may often be killed at one spot, and instances have occurred of their having been knocked down with a stick. In April the female deposits from six to eight eggs, of the size of those of a pheasant, and of a dull yellowish-white colour, marked with numerous, minute, ferruginous specks, and with blotches of the same towards the smaller end. These are hatched late in the summer, and the young grow rapidly, being able in four or five weeks to perch with the mother, whom they forsake about the beginning of winter, living in small flocks till spring, when the males separate, and assume their pugnacious character. Linné has remarked, that they brave the rigour of the Swedish winter, often squatting down on a fall of snow, and remaining covered by it for fourteen days together. It is probable, however, that in this state they preserve some communication with the open air like the partridge, which, in these northern regions, will burrow with its family in the snow, but keep a passage open for egress and ingress.

T. lagopus, Lin. &c. *Lagopus mutus,* Leach, *La-* *gopus vulgaris,* Vieil. *Ptarmigan, Common Ptarmigan, White Grous, Rock Grous,* or *White Partridge.* Varied with cinereous and white ; in summer, quills white, tail-feathers black, with white tips, and the two middle ones entirely white ; a black spot between the beak and eyes of the male ; eighteen feathers in the tail ; feet covered with feathers. In winter, the body is entirely white, the change of colour in the plumage commencing, in this country, in September, and being completed in October.

Ptarmigans haunt the lofty heights of mountainous countries in Europe, Asia, and America, as the Alps and Pyrenees, the Highlands of Scotland, Siberia, Greenland, Hudson's Bay, Canada, &c. descending within the range of vegetation, to feed on the buds of trees, the young shoots of pines, and heath, mountain berries, rhododendron, insects, &c. but returning, when satiated, and even in winter, to their almost inaccessible retreats, which are generally screened alike from the sun and the wind, and are often formed of holes in the snow. During winter they live quietly, in family parties, of from six to ten individuals ; but they separate and pair in June, resorting to a lower residence on the hill, and breeding apart. Each pair scratch a circular hole, of about eight inches in diameter, at the foot of a rock or bush ; and the female, with hardly any other preparation, lays from six to twelve eggs, larger than those of the partridge, of a reddish-grey hue, and spotted with black. These are hatched in three weeks, and the young come forth, covered with down, which is brown, black, and yellowish, on the head and upper parts of the body, and of a whitish-yellow on the under. The mother defends them with great intrepidity and courage, and hesitates not to fly on those who seek to carry them off. Contrary to what has been observed of most other gallinaceous birds, the male is assiduously attentive to his mate when breeding, roaming about the nest, frequently uttering his cry, and carefully fetching her food, without, however, taking her place on the eggs. As soon as the young are produced, the parents conduct them to a more elevated station, where their growth proceeds rapidly. Many of them fall a sacrifice to eagles and hawks. At sight of these formidable invaders, the ptarmigans skulk under bushes, or projections of the rocks ; but they seem not to dread the approach of man, until they have experienced his hostile power, after which they endeavour to elude his attacks. Ac-

Ornitho-
logy.

cording to Picot La Perouse, who watched their manners in the Pyrenees, they are by no means so stupid as described by Gessner, but court independence and shun danger with the sagacity that is common to other animals. In some of our Highland districts, their gay summer attire assimilates them to their native rocks, and their winter livery to the snow by which they are surrounded, so that they are less readily discriminated by the sportsman. They fly heavily, but run swiftly. The cry of the male, which may often be heard in the night, somewhat resembles the croaking of a frog, and that of the female the call of a young fowl. In this island, they occur on the summits of the Grampian ridge, and also, though rarely, on the highest hills of Cumberland and Wales. Being naturally very shy, they are not domesticated without much trouble and difficulty; but Lord Stanley assured Colonel Montagu, that an instance of their breeding in confinement occurred in Ireland. The flavour of the young is not inferior to that of black game, and the fowler has often hunted them at the risk of his life.

Scoticus.

T. Scoticus, Lin. &c. *Lagopus Scoticus,* Leach and Vieil. *Red Grous, Red Ptarmigan, Red Game, Moorfowl, Moorcock, Gorcock,* &c. Plumage of a horse-chesnut brown hue, eyebrows toothed, and very elevated, tarsi and toes covered with grey hairs, sixteen feathers in the tail, the lateral ones blackish, and terminated with horse-chesnut brown. Caruncle on the eye-brows scarlet and lunated. The shadings of the female are less pure and deep, the brown hues being often varied with rufous, the black zig-zag lines and spots being more numerous, and the red eyebrows inconspicuous. The young are easily distinguished by their bright rufous plumage, varied with irregular blackish spots and stripes. The length of the male is about sixteen inches, its weight nineteen ounces, and that of the female fifteen ounces.

The red grous are found in extensive wastes, overspread with heaths, and not in woods, as in the mountains of Wales, in the moorlands of Yorkshire, and the north of England, but more plentifully in the Highlands of Scotland and in the waste moors of North Britain in general. They are also met with in the Hebrides, the islands of the Clyde, and in the mountains and bogs of Ireland; but those noticed by Buffon as natives of France, Spain, Italy, &c. seem either to form distinct species, or at least varieties. Linné appears to have been unacquainted with them, and Gmelin regarded them as a variety of the ptarmigan. It is not a little remarkable, that Captain Carmichael should have encountered them in the Island of Tristan da Cunha, which is situated between the Cape of Good Hope and St. Helena. In this country, they feed on the mountain and bog berries, and, in defect of these, on the tops of the heath. The female lays from eight to fourteen eggs, not unlike those of the black grous, but smaller, in a rude nest, on the ground. The young brood follow the hen till winter, when they unite in flocks, sometimes to the amount of thirty or forty, and are then very shy, and difficult to be shot. In severe winters, they sometimes descend from the hilly tracts in prodigious numbers. The shooting of them, on our Scottish moors, in autumn, is a favourite diversion of our gentry, and their flesh is esteemed a dainty, but it soon becomes tainted, especially if the birds are not drawn immediately on being killed. Several instances are recorded of their being reared in confinement.

Umbellus.

T. umbellus, Lin. &c. *Bonasa umbellus,* Steph. *Ruffed Grous, Ruffed Heathcock, Shoulder-knot Grous,*

Shoulder-knot Heathcock, or *Drumming Partridge.* Head crested, body variegated above, with fuscous, red, and black, fulvous white beneath, breast varied with brown lunules, feathers of the axillæ larger, elongated, of a deep azure; rump sprinkled with white spots, tail fasciated near the tip, a broad black band, the tip greyish-white. The tufts on each side of the neck are placed on its lower portion, near the insertion of the wings, and, when expanded, appear of a large size; they are bright black, with a fine steel gloss; and the shorter ones are slightly tipped with white or red. In the female the crest and ruff are inconspicuous.

This species is very common, not only in Canada, but in Maryland and in Pennsylvania. When the male is tranquil, he allows the crest and ruff to fall down, but, when agitated, he erects them both, especially when he expands his tail like a fan, lets down his wings to the ground, and stalks before his mate. If the latter happens to be at a distance, he recals her by a flapping of the wings, at first slow and regular, and afterwards so hurried and loud, as to have been compared to the beating of a drum, or even to distant thunder. It is in spring and autumn that he makes this thumping sound, about nine o'clock in the morning, and, again, towards four o'clock in the afternoon. The pitiless sportsman hears it at a distance, hastens to the spot, and frequently secures his prize. The female breeds twice in the year, and lays from nine to sixteen eggs, of a brownish-white, without spots, and nearly of the size of those of a young domestic fowl. Her nest is placed near the stump of a tree, among dry leaves; the incubation lasts three weeks; the young follow the mother like chickens, and the whole brood keep together till spring, feeding on all sorts of grain and fruit, and manifesting a predilection to ivy berries.

PERDIX, Lath. Cuv. Tem. &c. TETRAO, Lin. &c. PARTRIDGE.

Perdix.

Bill short, compressed, stout, base naked; upper mandible arched, convex, strongly curved towards the tip; nostrils basal, lateral, half closed by an arched and naked membrane; the three front toes united by membranes to the first articulation; tail composed of eighteen, or of fourteen feathers, short, rounded, and slanting downwards; wings short.

These birds, which are stationary in some countries, and migratory in others, are greatly multiplied in the warm and temperate regions of the globe, living in pairs, and steady in their family attachments. The greatest number reside in the fields and in open tracts of country, with the exception of some which prefer the outskirts of woods in the neighbourhood of water. They feed on grain, seeds, bulbous plants, insects, worms, &c. They run more frequently than fly, get up from the ground with an effort, and make a whirring noise when on the wing. They generally have numerous broods; and the young run about as soon as they are hatched.

Cinerea.

P. cinerea, Tem. Lath. *Tetrao perdix,* Lin. &c. *Common Partridge.* Grey, varied with red and black above, yellowish-white beneath, breast cærulescent, and varied with black lines and rufous spots; tail-feathers eighteen, the seven outer ones on each side tipped with cinereous. The ordinary length of the mature bird is about thirteen inches, its alar extent eighteen inches and a half, and its average weight fifteen ounces.

The common partridge is pretty generally spread over Europe and Asia, but most abounds in the temperate regions of these two continents. It is found, however, in high northern latitudes; and it visits Egypt and the coast of Barbary, being stationary in some countries, and migratory in others. The *P. montana*, and *P. Damascena*, Lath. are regarded by Temminck as mere varieties. According to Olina, these birds live from twelve to fifteen years. They are partial to open and ploughed fields, resorting to coppices and vineyards only when harassed by men or birds of prey; but they never penetrate into the depths of forests, neither do they readily abandon the spots which gave them birth. The extremes of heat or cold generally prove unpropitious to their increase. They are naturally sociable, always living in broods or coveys, except during pairing time; and such as have failed in maturing their hatches, again associate with the others, towards the close of summer, and continue in their company till the season of courtship returns. Should the covey happen to be dispersed, they afterwards reunite, in consequence of their well-known signal, or call, which is shrill and grating, and resembles the noise of a saw. The note of the male scarcely differs from that of the female, except that it is louder and more prolonged. On the appearance of a bird of prey, they huddle together, squat down on the ground, and continue motionless, although their enemy hovers quite near them, and tries to raise some one of them, that he may seize on it in its flight. About the middle of February the coveys separate for breeding, and the males engage in strife, the victors carrying off their respective mates, whom they afterwards sedulously attend, rising the last when flushed, whereas at other seasons they are the first to stir. About the beginning of May the female lays a considerable number of eggs, varying from eight or ten, to even so many as twenty-six, of a dull greenish-grey colour, and forbearing to incubate till they are all deposited in the nest. The latter is carelessly composed of dry leaves and grass, laid in a hole in the ground. If the nest or its contents have been destroyed, a second, but a weakly brood, is brought forth late in the season. The old birds that haunt flat grounds, select, it is alleged, a somewhat elevated spot, fenced with brushwood, to protect the nest from being flooded. During the space of twenty days, that the incubation lasts, the female undergoes a considerable moulting; for she loses all the feathers on her belly. She sits very closely and ardently on her eggs, the male attending at no great distance, and accompanying her in her hurried excursions for food. The young run about as soon as they are hatched, and the male assists in conducting them, keeping them warm, calling on them, and indicating the means of their nourishment. One of their principal regales is the larvæ of ants. At this period the sexes very reluctantly quit their range; but, when compelled to remove, it is always the male that goes off first, uttering a peculiar cry, and flying peevishly, dragging a wing, and often halting, as if lamed, with a view to deceive the intruder. The female, who starts a moment after him, removes to a much greater distance, and always in a contrary direction; but, on alighting, she returns, running along the furrows, and collecting her young, who had squatted down in different spots, and then she flies off along with them. The first food of the young family consists of small insects, the pupæ and grubs of ants, small worms, &c. nor do they subsist on grain and herbage until they are some months old. In winter, their principal resource is in the tender spikes of wheat, which they contrive to reach, even

when buried under snow. With great attention and precaution the young may be reared under the care of a common hen, and become very tame. We have only to add, that the partridge is a favourite article of game at most tables, and that many pages have been written on the details of shooting, fattening, and cooking it.

P. rubra, Tem. *P. rufa*, Lath. *Tetrao rufus*, Lin. &c. *Red*, or *Guernsey Partridge*. Grey-brown above and on the breast, rufous beneath, throat and upper part of the neck white, bounded by a black belt, spotted with white; hypochondria marked with a simple black fillet; tail-feathers sixteen, the outer ones rufous. Rather smaller than the preceding. Native of France and Italy, but not supposed to be indigenous in more northern countries, although it has been imported into England and elsewhere, and has even bred in confinement. Though termed the Guernsey partridge, it is scarcely ever found in that island; and the attempts to introduce the breed into England have uniformly failed in the course of a few years. The female lays about fifteen or eighteen yellowish eggs, spotted with red and brown. The nest is usually placed in brambles, heath, or corn; and the bird frequents the open fields, unless molested, when it takes refuge among the rocks or woods. As these partridges are addicted to a variety of food, from the particular qualities of which their flesh often receives a tincture, their flavour is sometimes reckoned highly delicate, and, at others, inferior to that of the common sort. After the breeding season they unite in large flocks; but, on the approach of winter they mingle with the first coveys. A variety entirely white, and another partially so, have been occasionally observed.

P. coturnix, Lath. *Tetrao coturnix*, Lin. &c. *Common Quail*. Body rusty grey, varied with black spots, shafts of the feathers yellowish, eye-brows and a longitudinal stripe on the crown white; throat rufous, bounded by black. Female paler, with the throat white. The young, during the first year, resemble the females, after which they vary considerably according to age. The ordinary size is seven inches and a half in length, and fourteen inches in extent of wing. Among the varieties, some are considerably larger, with more vivid colouring, and the cheeks and throat dusky brown. They also occur perfectly white, and of various intermediate shadings between pure white and the more ordinary attire. In consequence of long confinement, and of feeding on hempseed, they become of a uniform deep brown, or dusky hue.

Quails are found throughout nearly the whole of Europe, as far north as Lapland; they are likewise abundant in Asia, as far as Siberia, but not in the extreme northern parts of that vast tract of country. In China they are very common, and they are used by the inhabitants for warming their hands. They are, moreover, copiously diffused in different regions of Africa. Although more addicted to run than to fly, and although, for the most part, incapable of continuing for any length of time on the wing without experiencing lassitude and fatigue, it is nevertheless certain that they undertake pretty extensive migrations, and in immense flocks, passing from the colder to the warmer latitudes in autumn, and retracing their way in spring; and there is reason to believe that their passage, notwithstanding the opposite opinion of Col. Montagu, usually takes place in the course of the night, for they are accustomed to sleep, or at least to repose, during a considerable portion of the day, concealed in the tallest grass, when a dog may sometimes run in

Rubra.

Coturnix.

Ornitho-
logy.

upon them before they are flushed. They are met with in many parts of this island, but seldom in any considerable numbers. They leave us in August or September, are supposed to winter in Africa, and return early in spring. On their arrival at Alexandria, such multitudes of them are exposed for sale, that the crews of merchant vessels are fed on them, and complaints have been laid at the consul's office by mariners against their captains, for giving them nothing but quails to eat. With wind and weather in their favour, they have been known to perform a flight of fifty leagues, across the Black Sea, in the course of a night. On the western coast of the kingdom of Naples, in the vicinity of Nettuno, quails have sometimes appeared in such prodigious quantities, that a hundred thousand have been caught in one day, and within the limited space of three or four miles. Most of them were conveyed to Rome, where they are in great request, and fetch a high price. Clouds of them also alight, in spring, along the shores of Provence, especially on the lands belonging to the bishop of Frejus that border on the sea, where they are sometimes found so exhausted, that for a few days, at first, they may sometimes be caught with the hand. In some parts of the south of Russia, they so much abound, that at the periods of their migration they are taken by thousands, and sent in casks to Moscow and St. Petersburgh. The English import not a few from France for the table, and all of them males. The latter fight fiercely for the females, whom they abandon when incubation commences. The hen bird scrapes a hole in the ground, generally in a corn-field, and consigns to it from eight to fifteen, or even twenty eggs, of a bright green, with minute dots, or large blotches of brown or blackish. The incubation lasts about twenty-one days; and the young, which are produced covered with down, run on coming out of the shell, and are much sooner able to provide for themselves than young partridges. Drought is unfavourable to such of them as happen to be produced on a strong argillaceous soil, and in the fissures of which they are apt to get entangled, and to die in consequence. The mother continues by them till the autumnal passage, at which period solitary quails are seldom met with; but, though living in small flocks of four or five, when started, they disperse in different directions, and quickly re-assemble near the spot from which they were roused. When the young wish to flock together, they utter a feeble and plaintive cry. That of the adults is more harsh and grating, and the males are readily decoyed by the quail-pipe, with which the fowler counterfeits the call of the female. From the pugnacious dispositions of the males, they were exhibited in regular combats both by the Athenians and Romans; and the practice of quail-fighting is still cherished in China, Sumatra, and some districts of Italy. As quails are capable of receiving a considerable quantity of fat, and are reckoned delicate eating, they are killed in great numbers for the table; but they will not breed in confinement.

Excalfactoria. *P. excalfactoria*, Tem. *Tetrao Sinensis*, Gmel. *P. Sinensis*, Lath. *Chinese Quail.* Upper parts of the body brown, sprinkled with black spots and white lines, jugulum black, with a white arch, middle of the belly chesnut. An elegant little species, measuring only four inches in length. It abounds in the Manilla and Philippine Islands, and in China, where the people employ it for warming their hands, and also rear it for fighting.

TINAMUS, Lath. and Tem. TETRAO, Gmel. CRYPTURUS, Illig. CRYPTURA, Vieill.

Bill slender, straight, depressed, broader than deep, tip rounded, ridge distinct, forming a large nasal foss; nostrils lateral, pierced in the nasal foss, near the middle of the bill, ovate, expanded, and open; tarsus long, frequently with asperities behind; four short toes, the hinder one particularly so; tail wanting, or very short, and concealed by the rump feathers; wings short. This genus was instituted by Latham, who described four species; but Azara and Temminck have added eight to the list. They are all natives of South America, where they live on fruits, wild berries, and insects. They fly heavily, and run quickly, seldom perching, except to pass the night, and then only on the lowest branches of trees. They reside either in open plains, or about the outskirts of woods. Except during the pairing season, they are usually met with in small coveys. Their call, which is generally heard in the morning and evening, is a prolonged, tremulous, and plaintive whistle, which the sportsmen know how to imitate, and thus decoy them within reach of shot. They have two broods in the course of the year. They are tranquil and indolent during most of the day, and cater in the morning and evening, and frequently by moonshine. In general, they are dull, timid, and unsocial; but they have many of the habits of the other *Gallinacea.* The colonists of South America reckon them excellent eating, and carelessly denominate them *Partridges* or *Quails.*

Rufescens. *T. rufescens*, Tem. *Rufescent Tinamoo, or Guazu.* Greyish-red, transversely striped with black and white above, margin of the wings rufous red; region of the ears black, pale yellowish red, waved with brown beneath; sides and abdomen greyish. Fifteen inches and a half in length. This bird, the most beautiful of its family, is a native of Paraguay, residing among thick herbage, which it seldom quits, except on the point of being trampled on, or struck with a stone. Its cry, which is heard at a considerable distance, is a lugubrious whistle. The female conceals her nest among straw, or a tuft of grass, and lays about seven eggs of a fine violet hue, and equally thick at both ends. When alarmed, the guazu erects the feathers on the head, in the form of a crest.

Brasiliensis. *T. Brasiliensis*, Lath. Tem. *Tetrao major*, Gmel. *Cryptura magoua*, Vieill. *Brazilian or Great Tinamoo.* Olive-brown, slightly striated across, with black above, greyish-red beneath; crown rufous; the secondary quills transversely striated with rufous and black. Size of a common fowl; length eighteen inches; the body thicker and more compact than that of the pheasant. The birds of this species inhabit Brazil and French Guiana, where they roost on the low branches of trees, two or three feet from the ground. The female lays from twelve to fifteen eggs, of the size of those of a hen, and of a beautiful green colour, in a nest formed on the ground, among the thick herbage, and carelessly composed of moss and dried vegetables. The young run after the moths almost as soon as hatched, and hide themselves on the least appearance of danger. Their cry, which is a sort of dull whistle, may be heard a great way off. Many of them are shot, and many caught when roosting on the trees. The flesh and eggs are esteemed great dainties.

ORDER XI.

CURSORES, or RUNNERS.

CURSORES, or RUNNERS.
Bill middle-sized, or short; legs long, naked above the knee, and with only two or three toes directed forwards.

The birds which compose this order live always in the fields, and most frequently in desert places, remote from woods. They are polygamous, and feed on herbs, seeds, and insects. Some few of the species are incapable of flight, and others fly little, and near the ground. They run, however, with great celerity, not only when pursued, but habitually, and differ, in this respect, from the greater number of the waders, which march by measured steps. Their diet, and the nature of their residence, are also different. All of them that are capable of rising from the ground stretch their legs backwards in flight. Being very shy and cunning, their manners are not easily observed.

OTIS, Lin. &c. BUSTARD.

OTIS.
Bill straight, conical, compressed; tip of the upper mandible slightly arched; nostrils open, oval, approximated, but remote at the base; legs with three toes connected by a membrane at the base; wings of moderate dimensions.

These are heavy birds, which fly little, and are extremely shy. When fatigued in the course, or on the point of being captured, they graze along the ground with a rapid and well-sustained flight. They live in corn-fields or bushy plains, and feed on herbs, grains, seeds, and insects. One male is attended by several females, which live solitary after they are fecundated. The males of most of the species exhibit a more ornamented and varied plumage than the females; but there is reason to believe that they moult twice a-year, and that the winter attire of the sexes is nearly similar.

Tarda.
O. tarda, Lin. &c. *Great Bustard.* Waved and spotted with black, and rufous above; whitish beneath; primary quills black; under mandible with a tuft of fine elongated feathers; legs black; bill bluish. Length about four feet; extent of wing six feet eight inches; and weight from twenty to thirty pounds, being the largest of our British birds. The female is about half the size of the male, and wants the tuft or beard of slender feathers. The male is provided with a curious bag or pouch situated in the fore part of the neck, and capable of containing about two quarts of water. This singular reservoir, which seems to be unfolded only in the adult state of the bird, is probably destined for the conveyance of drink to the young, in the midst of those extensive and arid plains which the species chiefly affects. About Morocco, where it is customary to fly the hawk at the bustard, the latter has been observed to squirt the water with violence against the assailant, and thus to baffle its pursuit.

Bustards appear to be natives of the greater part of Europe, but are not of equal frequency in every district, and particularly shun well inhabited and cultivated tracts, being peculiarly shy and timid, and requiring an extensive and uninterrupted range for their erratic movements. In England, they used to be met with in flocks of fifty or more, frequenting the open country of the southern and eastern parts, from Dorsetshire as far as the Wolds of Yorkshire; but they have now become extremely scarce, even in the downs of Wiltshire, where they formerly abounded. Though not probably migratory, they occasionally shift their quarters, especially during severe winters. In Champagne and Picardy, they are observed in great numbers during spring and autumn. Their food consists of green corn, the tops of turnips, and various other vegetables, and worms; but they also eat frogs, mice, and small birds. In winter, they have been known to feed on the bark of trees, and, like the ostrich, they will swallow, indiscriminately, almost any small substance that is presented to them. In the Crimea, they are seen in large flocks, especially during winter, when the wings and crop-feathers are sometimes so encumbered with ice, that the bird is unable in the snow to take the run previously to flying, in consequence of which many are caught by the hand, or by means of dogs, and brought to market alive. The flesh, particularly of the young, when kept for a short time, is said to be excellent. Bustards pair early in spring. The female constructs no nest, but lays two eggs, as large as those of a goose, and of a pale olive-brown, marked with spots of a darker hue, in a hole formed by her feet, in a dry corn-field. The incubation lasts about a month; and the young ones follow their dam soon after they are excluded; but they are not capable of flying for some time after. They are easily tamed, and may be trained to consort with other poultry; but all attempts to rear the race in confinement have proved abortive. The quills of this species, like those of the goose, or swan, are used for writing with. The coursing of these birds with greyhounds, is said to afford excellent sport.

Tetrax.
O. tetrax, Lin. &c. *Tetrax campestris*, Leach and Steph. *Little Bustard, Field Duck,* or *Field Bustarnelle.* Variegated with black, rufous, and white; with black zig-zag markings above, white beneath; neck black, with a double white ring. Collar of the female of the same colour as the back, and the breast rufous-white, streaked with dusky. About seventeen or eighteen inches in length, and about the size of a pheasant. Native of several countries of the south of Europe, of Southern Russia, and of the deserts of Tartary; rare in the northern regions, although, according to Acerbi, it has been traced to Lapland. In this island it is extremely scarce, only a few instances of its having been shot in the south of England being on record. It manifests the shyness, and most of the other habits of the preceding. If disturbed, or alarmed, it will fly for two or three hundred paces, not far from the ground, and then run faster than a man on foot can follow. The sexes pair in May; and, about the end of June, the female lays from three to five eggs, of a beautiful glossy green. As soon as the young are hatched, the hen leads them about; and they begin to fly early in September. Before that period they squat down, on the slightest noise, and will sooner be crushed than attempt flight. The flesh of this species is dark-coloured, but much in request by the epicures.

STRUTHIO, Lin. &c. OSTRICH.

STRUTHIO.
Bill moderate, obtuse, straight, depressed at the tip, which is rounded and unguiculated; the mandibles equal and flexible; nostrils situated near the surface, and about the middle of the bill; legs very long, very robust, and muscular, with only two toes directed forwards, both of them thick and strong, but the inner much shorter than the outer, the former provided with a large and blunt claw, the latter clawless, the tibia very fleshy to the knee; wings unfit for flight, being composed of soft and flexible feathers, and armed with a

double spur. The sternum is destitute of a ridge, or keel; and the muscles of the breast are so small, as not to have power sufficient to expand the wings, so as to sustain the body of the bird in the air, whereas those of the legs and thighs are very large, and well adapted for long and powerful strides. We should add to these characters, that the birds of which they are predicated are provided with a capacious crop, a considerable ventricle between the crop and the gizzard, long blind guts, and a very ample *cloaca*, in which the urine accumulates, as in the bladder of other animals, so that they are the only birds that urinate. They swallow, almost without discrimination, any substance that is not too large to pass down the gullet, and that happens to be presented to them; but their natural food is vegetables of various sorts. They are polygamous, each male associating with three or four females, who deposit their eggs in a common receptacle, each laying about twelve or fourteen. As the genus is now constructed, only one species is known, namely,

S. camelus, Lin. &c. *Black Ostrich*, or *Ostrich*. Body black, the feathers varied with white and grey; primary quills and tail-feathers white; the female brown, or ash-grey, where the male is black. The head is small in proportion to the size of the bird, which is the largest species of the feathered tribe, weighing about eighty pounds, and often measuring upwards of eight feet in height, and as many in length, from the tip of the bill to the end of the tail; but, from the ground to the top of the back, it seldom exceeds four feet, the rest of its height being made up by its extremely long neck, the greater part of which is flesh-coloured, and sprinkled with a few hairs. The feathers on the body are lax and waving, the webs on both sides being equal, and incapable of locking into a compact whole. There are two alar spurs, namely, one on the end of the wing, and another on the spurious wing. The general aspect of the bird bears no indistinct resemblance to a quadruped, and especially to the camel, forming a sort of link in the gradation between two important classes of animals; for it is incapable of quitting the soil; the greater part of its body is covered with hair, in place of down, its upper eye-lid is moveable, and furnished with long eye-lashes, and its organs of vision are more analogous to those of man than to those of birds. The conformation of its feet corresponds, in some measure, to that of the feet of the camel; and, like that quadruped, it not only has a callosity on the breast, and another near the *os pubis*, but its back is elevated. The generative organs, too, are, in some respects, assimilated to those of mammiferous animals. The young, during the first year, are of a cinereous-grey colour, and have feathers on the head, neck, and thighs, which fall off, and are not afterwards replaced. These birds run with great rapidity, and unfold their wings in the course, less for the purpose of aiding their flight, than for the natural play of corresponding muscles, as may be proved by their raising them even when running against the wind, when, instead of accelerating, they can only contribute to retard their progress. When moving in large flocks, they have, at a distance, been mistaken for a body of cavalry.

Ostriches haunt open, sandy, and desert plains, in which they can roam at large, and which they traverse in every direction, with inconceivable speed. Thus they are found in the parched solitudes of Africa, from Egypt and Barbary to the Cape of Good Hope, and in the islands and regions of Asia which confine with those latitudes. They are less common in the neighbour-

hood of Goa than in Arabia; and they no longer appear beyond the Ganges, although, according to the ancients, they once existed there. Their natural aliment is, as we have said, entirely of a vegetable description, as grass, fruits, grain, &c. and they may frequently be seen pasturing with the zebra and quagga. Yet, so blunted is their sense of relish, so keen their voracity, and so powerful their faculty of digestion, that they will gulp down hard, and even noxious matters, as wood, plaster, glass, stones, lead, copper, &c. " I saw one at Oran," says Dr. Shaw, " that swallowed without any seeming uneasiness or inconvenience several leaden bullets, as they were thrown upon the floor, scorching hot from the mould." It is certain, however, that the idea of their digesting iron, and other metals, is quite erroneous; and we may add, that they frequently fall victims to their undistinguishing appetite, for they have been seen to die in consequence of eating quicklime, bits of copper, nails, &c. They often occasion serious injury to the farmers in the interior of Southern Africa, by coming in flocks into their fields, and so effectually destroying the ears of wheat, that, in a large tract of land, often nothing but the bare straw is left. The body of the bird is not higher than the corn, and, when it devours the ears, it bends down its long neck, so that at a little distance it cannot be seen; but, on the least noise, it rears its head, and generally contrives to escape before the farmer gets within gun-shot. According to the Arabs, the ostrich never drinks; but that which was kept in confinement at Paris drunk four pints of water a-day in summer, and six in winter. Notwithstanding their love of liberty, these birds are easily rendered tame and tractable, and become familiar with persons to whose appearance they are habituated; but they frequently attempt to push down strangers, by running furiously against them, and, when they succeed, they not only peck at their victim with their bill, but strike at him with their feet with the utmost violence. The inner claw being exceedingly strong, Dr. Shaw mentions, that he once saw an unfortunate person who had his belly entirely ripped up by one of these strokes. While thus engaged, they sometimes make a fierce hissing noise, and have their throat inflated, and their mouth gaping. At other times they utter a sort of cackling sound, like some of our poultry, especially when they have subdued or routed an adversary. During the night they often send forth a doleful cry, somewhat resembling the distant roar of a lion, or the hoarse tone of a bear, or an ox, as if they suffered great pain. The voice of the male is stronger than that of the female; and both hiss like a goose when irritated. When they run, they apparently assume a proud and haughty air; and, even when in distress, they never seem to be in a great haste, especially if the wind is in their favour, for then the swiftest horse cannot overtake them; but, if the weather is hot and calm, the difficulty of coming up with them is not so great. M. Adanson mentions two ostriches which afforded him an extraordinary sight. They were so tame, that two little negroes mounted, both together, on the back of the largest. No sooner did he feel their weight, than he began to run as fast as possible, and carried them several times round the village; nor could he be stopped otherwise than by obstructing the passage. To try their strength, he directed a full-grown negro to mount the smallest, and two others the largest: nor did this burden seem at all disproportioned to their ability. At first they went at a pretty sharp trot; but, when they became heated a little, they expanded their wings as if to fan themselves, and moved along with such fleetness that they scarcely seemed to touch the ground. The Arabs have reduced the hunting of the ostrich to a sort of science, chasing it on horseback, and beginning the pursuit with a gentle gallop; for, should they be precipitate at the outset, the matchless speed of the game would immediately carry it out of their sight, and, in a very short time, beyond their reach; but when they proceed gradually, it makes no particular effort to escape. As it does not run in a direct line, but first on one side and then on the other, its pursuers save much ground by rushing straight onwards. In eight or ten hours, or in a day or two at most, the bird's strength is exhausted, and it then either turns on the hunters, and fights with the fury of despair, or hides its head and tamely submits to its fate. The natives likewise surprise these birds by concealing themselves in ostrich skins, and thus approach them without being suspected. In Egypt, greyhounds are employed in coursing the ostrich, and running it down, while patient sportsmen lie in wait behind a bush and shoot at it as it happens to pass.

The only nest which the female makes, is a hole which she scratches in the sand, and which is studiously concealed in the most retired situation which she can find. It is about three feet in diameter; and the sand is raised to the height of a few inches, the whole being surrounded by a small furrow for the reception of the rain water. Each female usually deposits about twelve or fifteen eggs; and the incubation lasts about six weeks. It has been commonly believed that the mother, after confiding her eggs to the sand, and covering them up, leaves them to be hatched by the heat of the climate, and abandons her offspring to their own devices. Recent travellers have, however, assured us, that no bird whatever has a stronger affection for her young than the ostrich, and that none watch their eggs with greater assiduity. It happens, possibly, that in burning sands there is less necessity for the continual sitting of the female, and that she may frequently leave her eggs without any risk of their being chilled: but, though she sometimes forsakes them by day, she always carefully broods over them by night: and Kolben, who saw great numbers of this species at the Cape of Good Hope, affirms that they sit on their eggs like other birds, and that the males and females take the office by turns, as he had frequent opportunities of observing. Nor is it more consistent with fact, that they forsake the young as soon as the latter are excluded from the shell; for they are, on the contrary, very assiduous in supplying them with grass and water before they are able to walk; and they will defend them from harm even at the risk of every danger to themselves. The females, which are united to one male, deposit all their eggs in the same place, which they hatch all together, the male taking his turn of sitting on them. Unaware of this circumstance, Linné had asserted, that one female sometimes lays near fifty eggs. Levaillant informs us, that he started an ostrich from its nest, in which he found eleven eggs, quite warm, and four others at a little distance from them. Those in the nest had young in them; but his attendants eagerly caught up the detached ones, assuring him that they were perfectly good to eat, for that near the nest were always placed a certain number of eggs which the birds do not sit upon, and which are designed for the first nourishment of the future progeny. "Experience," adds this enterprizing traveller, " has convinced me of the truth of this observation; for I never afterwards

met with an ostrich's nest without finding eggs disposed in this manner at a small distance from it." Sometime after, he happened to encounter a female ostrich on a nest which contained thirty-two eggs, and twelve more were arranged at an inconsiderable interval, each in a separate cavity formed for it. He remained near the place for some time, and saw three females come and alternately seat themselves on the nest, each sitting for about a quarter of an hour, and then giving place to another, who, while waiting, sat close by the side of her whom she was to succeed. It is alleged, however, that immediately under the torrid zone little or no incubation is required; but, even in that case, the parents are the tender and faithful nurses and guardians of their young, which they watch with unceasing concern. When surprised by men, they will run a little way from the nest, describe circular movements, and expand their feathers, with a view to withdraw attention from their charge. The eggs are very large, hard, and heavy, and will sometimes weigh about three pounds each, of a dirty white, marbled with light yellow. They are reckoned a delicate article of food, and are dressed in different ways for the table. Owing to the thickness and strength of their shell, they are easily preserved for a great length of time, even at sea, and without the trouble of constantly turning them. At the Cape of Good Hope they are usually sold for about sixpence a-piece; and, from their large size, one of them will serve two or three persons at a meal. Within them are often found a number of oval-shaped pebbles, of the size of a marrow-fat pea, of a pale yellow hue, and exceedingly hard, which are frequently set, and used for buttons. Mr. Barrow says, that he saw in one egg nine, and in another twelve of these concretions. The shell is made into drinking cups, and other utensils, and is often set in silver, or gold, being very hard, and equal in appearance to the finest ivory. It is also cut into small pieces, and used for ornamental purposes. The entire shells, suspended in the domes, or arches, are among the more ordinary decorations of the mosques and of the churches of the eastern Christians; and they are used as objects of dress by the Hottentots. When the Nasamones, a people of Lybia, went to war, they had their breasts covered with ostrich hides, as some tribes of Arabs have at this day. The caravans of Nubia convey to Cairo quantities of the plucked skins of these birds, which form a very thick leather. The long white feathers of the wings and tail are in great request for parade dress, even in Europe, and form an important article of traffic at Constantinople; they are also worked into elegant fans; but it is painful to reflect that they are most valued when plucked from the live bird. The ostrich has usually a considerable layer of fat about the intestines. When the Arabs kill one, they make an opening in the throat, under which they tie a ligature, and agitate the bird with violence; they then unbind the ligature, when a large quantity of fatty, bloody, and oily matter comes out. This they use in the preparation of their dishes, and apply it in cases of rheumatism and paralysis. According to Pliny, the Romans employed it for the same purposes, and set a high value on it. In regard to the flesh of the ostrich, it is reported to be no savoury dish; but various tribes of Africans eat it without scruple; and, in ancient times, whole nations of Arabia were denominated *Struthophagi*, though now they abstain from it, Mahomet having adopted the Mosaical doctrine of its being unclean. The young are preferred to the full-grown birds; and the females to

Ornitho-
logy.

the males. The Romans introduced the ostrich at their repasts; Apicius has described the mode of dressing it; and Heliogabalus exhibited, at a single feast, the brains of six hundred of these birds!

RHEA, Lath. Vieill. Tem. STRUTHIO, Lin.

RHEA.

Bill straight, short, soft, depressed at the base, a little compressed at the tip, which is obtuse and unguiculated, lower mandible much depressed, flexible, and rounded at the tip; nostrils on the lateral surface of the bill, large, longitudinal, cleft, and open; legs long, and rather stout, with three toes before, and a callosity behind; wings short, with the phalanges furnished with feathers, more or less long, and terminating in a spur.

America-
na.

R. Americana, Lath. Tem. *American Rhea*, or *American Ostrich*. Body white, wings and back obscurely grey. Varieties entirely white, or entirely black, also occur. This is the *Nhandu* of the American Indians, but not the *Touyou*, as alleged by Buffon. It is a native of South America, in some parts of which it is very common, as in the colder mountainous regions of Peru, in the valleys of Chili, which separate the chains of the Andes, in the Magellanic territories, &c. At present, it is scarce in Paraguay, but more common in the plains of Monte Video, and in the missions and wide-spreading level tract of Buenos Ayres. It never penetrates into the woods, but ranges along the open flats. It is somewhat less than the ostrich, being about six feet in height, of which the neck is two feet eight inches. The wings stretch from tip to tip, no less than eight feet; but, on account of the webs being disunited, they are useless in flight, hanging over, and hiding the tail, which is composed of short feathers, of equal lengths. The female is a little smaller.

These birds are observed either in pairs, or in bands, which are sometimes composed of more than thirty individuals. In those parts of the country where they are not hunted, they readily approach rural habitations, and seem not to be scared by people on foot; but, where they are objects of the chase, they become very shy, and fly out of one's sight with great precipitation, so that a person requires to be well mounted in order to overtake them. When noosed, they kick with great, and even dangerous violence; and, in the midst of the chase, they sometimes wheel suddenly about, and elude their pursuer. When tranquil, their deportment is grave and majestic; for they hold their head and neck elevated, and their back in a rounded attitude. In pasturing, they lower their head and neck, and cut the grass on which they feed. They are excellent swimmers, and cross rivers and swamps with great ease. The sexes pair in July, when the males utter a sort of lowing, resembling that of the cow. The female begins to lay about the end of August, and the first young ones appear in November. The nest is a wide, but shallow hollow, scooped out on the bare ground, and without any attempt at concealment, but sometimes lined with straw. The eggs, which are equally large at both ends, and contain about two pounds of liquid each, have a very smooth white surface, mottled with yellow. They afford an excellent dish at table, and are much used in making of biscuit. The number which each female deposits is not exactly known; for, though seventy or eighty are sometimes found in one nest, these are doubtless the produce of several hens; but a single *male*, according to Azara, hatches and rears the brood, and calls them together by a hissing noise. The young which are bred in houses not only become immediately familiar, but are of such a prying disposition, that they explore every apartment, and look through the windows to observe what is passing in other houses. The flesh of the young is used at table. The domesticated individuals will eat fruits, grain, flies, or even butchers' meat; and, like the black ostrich, have been known to swallow indigestible matters that are offered to them. As they are natives of pretty cool climates, the breed might perhaps be introduced into Europe, where the eggs, flesh, and feathers, might furnish valuable articles of produce.

R. Novæ Hollandiæ, Tem. *Casuarius Novæ Hollandiæ*, Lath. *Dromaius ater*, Vieill. *New Holland Rhea, Emu, Cassowary*, or *Southern Cassowary*. Dusky, with the body hairy, crown flat, shanks serrated behind. The feathers about the head and neck are of a hairy texture, but thinly scattered on the chin and throat. When the bird is at rest, its wings, which are very short, and covered with feathers like those on the rest of the body, are scarcely discernible. About six feet high, and seven feet long. A specimen, which was dissected, had no gizzard, the liver did not exceed that of the blackbird, and yet the gall bladder was large, and distended with bile. The crop contained at least six or seven pounds of grass, flowers, and a few berries and seeds. The intestinal canal was six yards long, and the lungs were separated by a diaphragm. This singular species inhabits New Holland, where it is not uncommon, being frequently seen by the settlers, but it is exceedingly shy, and runs so swiftly, that a greyhound can scarcely overtake it. The flesh is said to taste not unlike young and tender beef.

Novæ Hollandiæ.

CASUARIUS, Lath. Vieill. Tem. STRUTHIO, Lin. &c.
CASSOWARY.

Bill straight, short, compressed, rounded towards the point; ridge keeled, and a bony rounded protuberance at the base; the inferior mandible soft, flexible, and angular near the extremity; nostrils situated in the lateral part of the point of the bill, round, and open in front; legs strong and muscular, with three toes placed forwards, the inner short, and armed with a very long and strong claw, shanks almost entirely covered with feathers; wings not adapted for flight.

CASUARIUS.

C. galeatus, Steph. *C. emeu*, Lath. *Struthio Casuarius*, Lin. &c. *Galeated Cassowary*. Black, crown galeated, body hairy, head and part of the neck naked and bluish. The helmet, or horny protuberance on the head, reaches from the base of the bill to the middle of the crown, and is three inches high, the fore part black and the hind part yellow. There are two pendent caruncles, partly red and partly blue, one on each side of the neck. On the breast is a callous bare part, on which the bird rests its body when on the ground. The rest of the body is mostly covered with brownish black, loose-webbed feathers, two of which generally arise from one shaft. On the rump, they are at least fourteen inches long, and hang down in place of a tail. The wings, if so they may be called, are not furnished with feathers, having, each only five bare shafts, that somewhat resemble the quills of a porcupine, the longest ten or twelve inches, and of a dusky hue; and at the end of the last joint, there is a sort of claw. In bulk, this bird is not inferior to the ostrich, though, from having a much shorter neck, it is not near so tall. It has short intestines like those of carnivorous animals; and there is a double cœcum, a gallbladder, &c. The eggs are narrower, and of a more elongated form than those of the ostrich, and of a green-

Galeatus.

Ornitho-
logy.

ish or greyish cast, beautifully varied with elevated grass-green spots, and marked towards their smaller extremity with white. These are deposited in the sand, and hatched by the heat of the sun and of the atmosphere, or by that of the parent, where the temperature of the climate is insufficient. The species occurs in the eastern parts of Asia, towards the south, particularly in the Molucca Islands, those of Banda, Java, Sumatra, and the adjacent countries, but seldom in plenty, nor ever, we believe, beyond the confines of the torrid zone. They are said to be most numerous in the deep forests of the island of Ceram, along the southern coast. Their food consists of vegetables; and, in confinement, they will eat bread, apples, &c. which they swallow whole, as they do almost any thing that is presented to them. They are fierce and powerful birds, defend themselves vigorously with their strong bill, and will break in pieces almost any hard substance. They will likewise strike in a very dangerous manner with their feet, at such objects as happen to offend them. They are capable of being tamed, and will even bear confinement in Europe; but they are rather objects of curiosity than of utility, their flesh being black, tough, and juiceless.

ORDER XII.

GRALLÆ, or WADERS.

GRALLÆ.   Bill of various forms, but most frequently straight, prolonged in a conical direction, and compressed, more rarely depressed, or flat; legs slender, long, more or less naked above the knee, and furnished sometimes with three, but more frequently with four toes, or at least the rudiment of a fourth.

Many of the birds included in this order are seminocturnal, stalking along the margin of the sea, lakes, or rivers, and feeding on fish, or their fry, reptiles, worms, or insects. They are furnished with long wings, suited to the extensive migrations which they undertake at stated seasons, and for which purpose they associate in numerous bands, the young and the old travelling separately. Many of them enter into the water without swimming, but they are capable of the latter, and even of diving when occasion requires.

Tridactylous, or with Three Toes.

ŒDICNEMUS, Tem. Cuv. Vieill. FEDOA, Leach, OTIS, Lath. CHARADRIUS, Lin. &c. THICK-KNEE.

ŒDICNE-
MUS.   Bill longer than the head, straight, strong, compressed at the tip, the ridge carinated, the lower mandible with the tip angular; nostrils placed in the middle of the beak, longitudinal, cleft, and open in front; legs long and slender, with three toes before, connected at the base with a membrane, which extends along the toes; tail distinctly wedge-shaped.

Crepitans.   Œ. crepitans, Tem. Œ. Europæus, Vieill. *Fedoa œdicnemus,* Leach, *Otis œdicnemus,* Lath. *Charadrius œdicnemus,* Lin. &c. *Common Thick-knee, Thick-kneed Bustard, Stone Curlew, Great,* or *Norfolk Plover.* Greybrown, with dusky longitudinal lines above, the two primary quills black and white in the middle; belly and thighs white, knees thick, as if gouty. Length eighteen inches, extent of wing twenty-six inches, and weight seventeen ounces. The young and female resemble the male, but are duller in their colouring.

These birds are found in various quarters of Europe, Asia, and Africa, frequenting open, hilly, and sandy,

or stony situations, especially heaths and large meadows, or corn fields. In France, Italy, and other southern parts of Europe, they are pretty plentifully diffused, but in Germany, Holland, and England, they are more scarce. In the last-mentioned country, they principally occur in Hampshire, Norfolk, Lincoln, and some districts of Kent. In this island, as in France, &c. they are migratory, appearing early in spring, and departing, possibly to Spain or Africa, in October or November. At the period of leaving us, which they do during the night, they congregate in troops, of three or four hundred, and seem to put themselves under the guidance of an individual, whose voice apparently regulates their movements. Being extremely shy and timid, they generally remain motionless while the sun is above the horizon, although their large eyes are not dazzled by the light, and they perfectly discern the approach of danger; but, in the evening, and during night, they fly and run about, and are excessively clamorous, resorting to the more elevated spots, or approaching houses. If roused by surprise, in the daytime, they skim over the ground with their wings, or run rapidly along the fields, and then stop short, all at once, and squat down on the ground. They feed on various insects or their larvæ, in search of some of which they turn up stones very dexterously. They likewise eat snails, the contents of land-shells, and even small lizards, toads, and snakes. In a small elliptical excavation in the sand, or among stones, the female deposits two or three eggs, of a cinereous-white, with incrusted-like spots, of dusky-olive brown, and hatches them in the space of thirty days, the male remaining by her, and assisting in rearing the young, which, though they follow their parents as soon as they are extruded from the shell, are long of acquiring the power of flight, and are, for a considerable time, covered with only a thick grey down. The hen usually conducts them to some stony field, where, owing to their resemblance, in general colour, to the stones, they are not easily discovered. In very mild winters, some have been found to remain all the year in the south of England. The grating cry of the male has been compared to the turning of a rusty handle. The young are reckoned a good game, and even the full-grown birds are deemed worthy of a place at table.

ARENARIA, Bechst. Cuv. *Calidris,* Illig. Leach, Vieill. *Tringa* and *Charadrius,* Lin. &c. SANDERLING.

Bill middle-sized, slender, straight, soft, flexible in its whole length, compressed from the base, towards the tip depressed, flatter, and obtuse; nostrils lateral, and longitudinally cleft; legs slender, with three toes before, almost entirely divided; wings middle-sized.   ARENA-
RIA.

A. variabilis, A. vulgaris, Bechst. *Calidris arenaria,* Illig. Leach. *Tringa arenaria,* Lin. &c. *Charadrius calidris,* (the young bird,) Lin. Lath. *Charadrius rubidus,* (in the summer plumage.) *Variable* or *Common Sanderling, Sanderling, Curwillet,* or *Ruddy Plover.* Bill and feet black; lores and rump greyish; body pure white beneath; shafts of the primary quills white. During the two annual moultings these birds appear in a sort of intermediate garb, so that we are not to be surprised that they should have been described as two or three distinct species, and that Temminck should have conferred on them the epithet *variable.* They are found in Europe and the north of Asia and America, frequenting the sea-shores, especially in spring and autumn, feeding on minute marine insects and worms, and supposed to breed in the arctic regions. They are not so plentiful as the purre, with which they some-   Variabilis times associate; and both are, by some, indiscriminate-ly called *ox-birds*. Col. Montagu never observed them between the months of April and July; but Mr. Boys is inclined to believe that they breed on the coast about Sandwich.

HIMANTOPUS, Meyer, Bechst. Tem. CHARADRIUS, Lin. &c.

HIMAN-
TOPUS.

Bill long, slender, cylindrical, flattened at the base, compressed at the point; mandibles laterally channelled to the half of their length; nostrils lateral, linear, long; legs very long and slender, with three toes before, of which the intermediate is united to the outer by a broad membrane, and to the inner by the rudiments of a membrane, the nails very small and flat; wings very long, the primary quills greatly exceeding the others in length.

Melanop-
terus.

H. melanopterus, Meyer, Bechst. Tem. *Charadrius himantopus*, Gmel. Lath. *Long Legged*, or *Salt Plover*, or *Long Shanks*. General plumage white; back and bill black, the latter longer than the head; legs very long.

This extraordinary species is certainly the longest legged bird in proportion of any that is known, its limbs being, in fact, thrice as long as its body, and withal, extremely slender, weak, and flexible. Though generally spread over the world, it is scarce in many countries. It is not uncommon, however, in some of the eastern regions of Europe, haunting the margins of rivers and saline lakes, migrating in flocks, and visit-ing Hungary. It is likewise common about the seas and lakes of Asia, and is a bird of passage in Germany, France, Italy, &c. Specimens fetched from Egypt, from Brazil, and from the East Indies, seem not mate-rially to differ from those of Europe. It is often met with on the shores of the Caspian Sea, by the rivers which fall into it, and in the southern deserts of Inde-pendent Tartary. In Britain it is very rare, nor have its habits been satisfactorily ascertained; but it is sup-posed to feed on the spawn of frogs, tadpoles, flies, and aquatic insects, and to breed in the extensive salt-marshes of Hungary and Russia. M. de la Motte in-formed M. Temminck, that they were known to breed, in 1818, near the town of Abbeville.

HÆMATOPUS, Lin. &c. OYSTER-CATCHER.

HÆMA-
TOPUS.

Bill long, stout, compressed, tip much compressed and cuneated; nostrils lateral, longitudinally cleft in the channel of the bill; legs strong and muscular, with three toes before, that in the middle connected with the outer as far as the articulation by a membrane, and to the inner by the slight rudiments of one; wings middle-sized, the first quill largest.

Ostralegus.

H. ostralegus, Lin. &c. *Common Oyster Catcher*, *Pied Oyster Catcher*, or *Sea Pie*. In the Hebrides, it is called *Tirma* and *Trillichan*; in Shetland, *Chalder*; and, in Orkney, *Chaldric*, *Skeldrake*, *Skelderdrake*, and *Scolder*. Upper parts of the body black, under parts, a band on the throat and wings, the rump and base of the tail, white.

This species occurs not unfrequently along the sea-coasts of Europe, on the basins of the Caspian, in some parts of North and South America, and in Senegal. In autumn they are very abundant on some parts of the coasts of Holland and Great Britain; but, in winter, they mostly retire into the interior regions of the country, or to the south. They feed on marine insects, shell-fish, and mollusca, and derive their name from insinuating their bill into the open shells of oysters, and extracting the contents. Their bill is so excellently contrived to pro-

cure their living, that, if they find a limpet but a little loosened from a rock, they bring it off in a moment; or, if the shell fish is on its guard, and more firmly fastened, they knock it off as dexterously as any fisher-man who is accustomed to use it as bait. At the recess of the tide they have been known to rip up flounders, &c. that were caught up in nets, and to pick out undi-gested shell-fish from their stomach. They are very clamorous, especially when in flocks, or when alarmed. They are capable of swimming, and will allow them-selves to be tossed on the waves, but regain the land at pleasure. The female makes no nest, but lays four eggs, of the size of those of the lapwing, of an oliva-ceous brown, blotched with black, on the bare ground, or on the grass, above high water mark, and arranged in the form of a square, with the small ends inwards, so as to give the greatest security and warmth to each. The incubation lasts twenty or twenty-one days; and the females, during the sultry time of the day, frequent-ly abandon their eggs to the heat of the sun, leaving them at nine or ten o'clock in the morning, and resum-ing their sitting at three in the afternoon, unless it should happen to rain, when they continue on them. During this season the male is very watchful, and on the least alarm utters a loud scream, and flies off, as does also the female after running to some distance. The young are at first covered with a brown-grey down, and drag their steps on the beach, but are soon enabled to run and conceal themselves among tufts of grass, &c. so as not to be easily observed. The flesh of the mature birds is somewhat black, tough, and un-savoury, but that of the young is eatable; and both it and the eggs are accounted delicious by the inhabitants of the Faroe Isles.

CHARADRIUS, Lin. &c. PLOVER.

CHARA-
DRIUS.

Bill shorter than the head, slender, straight, com-pressed, mandibles protuberant near the tip; nostrils basal and longitudinal, cleft in the middle of a large membrane, which invests the nasal foss; legs long, or moderately so, slender, with three toes before, the outer connected to the middle one by a short membrane, and the inner divided; tail slightly rounded or even; wings middle-sized and armed, either with a tubercle, which is sometimes scarcely perceptible, or with a spur.

Most plovers are partial to the muddy borders of great rivers and marshy situations, subsisting on small worms and various aquatic insects; but some of them affect dry sandy shores. They have their English ap-pellation from the French *pluvier*, deduced from the Latin *pluvialis*, because they are supposed to take plea-sure in rain, or because they arrive in France from the north during the autumnal rains. In general they live in groups, more or less numerous, and are migratory, the adults preceding the young in their periodical flights. Most of them moult twice in the course of the year, and the males and females are seldom very dissi-milar in appearance. So insensibly, too, do the species glide into one another, that their distinct extrication is attended with considerable difficulty. All nestle on the ground. They run much on the soil, pressing it with their feet, to bring out the worms and insects.

Pluvialis.

C. pluvialis, Lin. &c. *Golden*, or *Green Plover*; Prov. *Grey*, or *Whistling Plover*; and by some called *Yellow Plover*. Spotted with black and green above, whitish beneath; breast grey, with dusky spots; back and legs grey. Weight between seven and eight ounces; length ten inches and a half; and alar extent one foot and nearly seven inches. In May the female lays four eggs, of the size and shape of those of the lapwing, and of a cinereous olive colour, blotched with dusky. The young run as soon as hatched, and follow the mother to damp places in search of worms. At first they are clothed with a dusky down, and for a considerable time are incapable of flying. During the first year their upper parts are cinereous-black, with cinereous-yellow spots. In their early nonage the parents protect them with great care and courage, and will throw themselves in the way of dogs or men, and even simulate lameness, to draw off the attention of the intruder from their offspring.

The golden plover is a very common bird, being found in most parts of the known world. In this island it haunts open heathy moors and the sea-coast, in winter, repairing to the uncultivated wastes of the north for breeding. In many parts of France these birds appear in flocks in spring and autumn. As their numbers speedily reduce the living aliment on which they subsist, in a given range, they are seldom observed to remain twenty-four hours in the same spot. The first fall of snow usually induces many of them to make for a more temperate climate; and severe frost, by locking up the means of their sustenance, drives off the rest. Their manner of feeding keeps them in constant motion, while several seem to act as sentinels, and, on the approach of danger, utter a whistling scream, which is the signal of flight. In flying they follow the direction of the wind, ranged in very long and close lines, which form transverse bands in the air. The flocks disperse towards evening, and each individual rests apart during the night; but at day-break, the first that awakes sounds the call, and instantly they all re-unite. By imitating this call the bird-catchers often decoy them within gun-shot. The golden plover, when plump, is relished by some epicures; and the eggs are reckoned a delicacy.

Morinellus. *C. morinellus,* Lin. &c. including *C. Sibiricus, Tartaricus,* and *Asiaticus,* of Gmelin and Latham. *Dottrel.* Breast ferruginous, a band over the eye, and a linear one on the breast white; crown, bill, and feet, grey.

The dottrel occurs plentifully in Northern Asia, and also in various parts of Europe, frequenting the muddy borders of rivers, and breeding in the moorish and mountainous districts. It seems to make this island a resting place in its migratory flights to and from its breeding haunts, being seen on some of our heaths, downs, and moors, from April till the beginning of June, returning again in September, and halting till November. On the Wiltshire downs it resorts to the fallow ground, or to the new sown fields, for the sake of worms and beetles. They are fattest and most juicy in June, when they are most esteemed for the table. We hear of their being found in Lincolnshire, Cambridgeshire, and Derbyshire; and some of them are even said to breed in Cumberland, Westmoreland, and the Highlands of Scotland, though it is not improbable, that their alleged eggs were those of the golden plover. Their ordinary breeding stations are the north of Russia, Lapland, &c. *Morinellus,* and *Dottrel,* or *Dotterel,* are intended to denote the stupidity of the bird, which is easily enticed to the snare. The country people are said to go in quest of it in the night, with a lighted torch or candle, when it will mimic the actions of the fowler; for, when he stretches out an arm, it unfolds a wing, or, if he moves a foot, it does the same; and, meanwhile, tamely allows itself to be entangled in his net. According to Willoughby, six or seven persons used to go in company to catch dottrels, and, when they observed one,

they set their net in an advantageous position, and taking up a stone in each hand, went behind it, when, striking the stones against one another, they roused it from its sluggishness, and, by degrees, drove it into the net. But the more certain and expeditious execution of the gun has nearly suspended these devices.

C. hiaticula, Lin. &c. *C. torquatus,* Leach. *Ringed* *Plover* or *Ringed Dottrel,* Prov. *Sea Lark, Sand Lark,* or *Dulvilly.* Grey-brown above, white beneath; breast black; forehead dusky, with a white stripe; crown of the head brown; bill red, with the tip black; feet yellow. The full grown male is nearly of the size of the common lark, measuring about nine inches six lines in length, and eleven inches in alar extent, and weighing, on an average, two ounces.

Hiaticula.

The ringed plover is very generally diffused over the known world, having been observed even in New South Wales; and it enlivens the sea-shores with its hopping movements and loud twitterings, skipping nimbly along the sands, and taking short flights, and then alighting and running again; but, if disturbed, it flies quite off. That some of them may quit this country in autumn is not improbable, and has been asserted on respectable authority; but Montagu has repeatedly found some of them during our severest winters. They feed chiefly on marine insects, and worms that live in the sand; and, when a flock of them has been making a repast, the sand is perforated with numerous small holes. They pair early in May, and the female makes no regular nest, but scratches a small cavity in the sand, just above high water mark, laying from three to five, but generally four eggs, of a cinereous brown, marked all over with small black, and ash-coloured spots, and which may be overlooked by a careless observer as small pebbles. The mother is much attached to her little ones, and has recourse to various stratagems to save them from men and dogs, sometimes fluttering along the ground, as if lamed, and, if pursued, flying to a small distance, or seeming to tumble head over heels repeatedly, till it has enticed the enemy from the objects of its care, and then it flies off. In autumn these birds become gregarious, and continue to associate in small flocks all winter, mingling occasionally with purres and dunlins. According to the observations of Montagu, there are two or three varieties, or modifications, of the present species, among which he ranks *C. Alexandrinus* of Latham, and *C. Cantianus* of Lewin.

With four Toes.

VANELLUS, Tem. TRINGA, Lin. &c. SQUATAROLA, Cuv. LAPWING.

Bill short, slender, straight, compressed, tip tumid; nostrils lateral, and longitudinally cleft; legs slender, with three toes before and one behind, the middle fore one connected with the outer by a short membrane, and the hind almost obliterated, or very short, and elevated, not touching the ground; wings elongated. In some of the foreign species, the base of the wing is armed with a long and sharp spur; and a few are ornamented with wattles and a crest. The two indigenous kinds undergo a double moult, and, like other vermivorous birds in this country, are migrants. The plumage of both sexes is the same.

Vanellus.

V. cristatus, Meyer, Tem. *Tringa vanellus,* Lin. &c. *Cristatus.* *Vanellus gavia,* Leach. *Crested Lapwing, Lapwing,* or *Bastard Plover,* Prov. *Pewit,* or *Green Plover.* Greengold above, white beneath, breast black, occipital fea-

Ornitho-
logy.

thers elongated into a crest, the ten middle tail feathers, from the base to the centre, white, the outer entirely white ; feet red. A foot and a half long, two feet four inches in extent of wing, between seven and eight ounces in weight, and about the size of a pigeon. In different parts of Scotland it is called *whaap, teewhaap, teewit, peeseweep*, &c. from its querulous call ; but the male, in the breeding season, has another and a more cheerful note, which, when he feels secure, he utters with great briskness ; but, when alarmed, he pours forth the same wailing cry as the female.

The species has been traced as far north as Kamtschatka, where October is called the *month of lapwings*. Pallas met with it in a great portion of northern Asia, Sonnini in the marshes of Egypt, and other travellers in China and Persia. It is very common in Holland ; and in this country it frequents the damp shores of lakes and rivers, as also fens, moist fields, and heaths. From the extent and great muscularity of its wings, it is capable of sustaining long flights, and of moving in the air with rapidity and ease. Lapwings may sometimes be seen in flocks nearly covering low marshy grounds in quest of worms, and drawing them, with great dexterity, from their holes. When they meet with a cast, they first gently remove it from the hole, then strike the soil at the side with their feet, and steadily and attentively await the result, while the worm, roused by the shock, emerges from its retreat, and is instantly seized. In the evening they pursue a different plan ; for they then run along the grass, feeling the worms as they come forth to enjoy the coolness of the air, and thus obtaining a plentiful repast, after which they wash their bill and feet in the small pools or rivulets. " I have seen this bird approach a worm cast," says Dr. Latham, " turn it aside, and, after making two or three turns about, by way of giving motion to the ground, the worm came out, and the watchful bird, seizing hold of it, drew it forth." In France, and some other countries, the great body of lapwings is migratory ; but with us most of them seem to remain the whole year, congregating in large flocks in autumn. In spring the pairing commences, which is preceded by fierce contests among the males. On dry ground, though usually near some marsh, the female prepares a little bed of grass, on which she lays four olive-coloured eggs, spotted with black, with their narrow ends in contact, so as to occupy little room. On these she sits about twenty days ; and the young are able to run within two or three days after they are hatched, though they are incapable of flying till they are nearly full grown. The parent shows them the greatest attachment, and practises her wiles to allure boys and dogs from their retreat ; for she does not wait the arrival of intruders at the nest, but boldly sallies out to meet them. When as near them as she can venture with safety, she rises from the ground with a loud screaming voice, as if just flushed from hatching, though possibly not within a hundred yards of her nest. She now flies with great clamour and apparent anxiety, whirring and screaming round the disturbers of her peace, striking at them with her wings, and sometimes fluttering as if wounded. To complete the deception, she becomes still more clamorous as she recedes from the nest. If very near it, she appears to be altogether unconcerned ; and her cries subside in proportion as her fears increase. When approached by dogs, she flies heavily at a little distance before them, as if maimed, still bold and vociferous, but never moving towards the quarter where

her young are stationed. The dogs pursue, expecting, no doubt, every moment to lay hold of her, and thus actually lose the young ; for the cunning bird having thus drawn them off to a proper distance, exerts her powers, and leaves her astonished enemies to gaze at the rapidity of her flight. As another proof of the lapwing's sagacity, M. Gérardin mentions, that it will allow an unarmed person to approach near it, whereas it instantly flies off to a distance, if it perceives a gun in one's hand. Notwithstanding its natural shyness, it is capable of acquiring a considerable degree of familiarity in confinement ; and it is sometimes kept in gardens for the purpose of ridding them of worms, slugs, and insects. In winter, where this description of food is liable to fail, it should be fed with bread or raw minced meat. Mr. Bewick relates, that two lapwings were given to a clergyman, who put them into his garden. One soon died, but the other continued to pick up such food as the place afforded, till winter deprived it of its usual supplies. Necessity soon compelled it to draw near the house, so that it gradually became familiarized with occasional interruptions from the inmates. At length one of the maid-servants, when she had occasion to go into the back-kitchen with a light, remarked that the lapwing always uttered his cry of *peewit* to obtain admittance. He soon grew more intimate, and, as the winter advanced, he ventured so far as the kitchen, though with much caution, as that part of the house was generally occupied by a dog and a cat, whose friendship, however, he finally so entirely conciliated, that he regularly resorted to the fire-side, as soon as it grew dark, and passed the evening and all the night with his new acquaintances, sitting close by them, and partaking of the comfortable warmth. With the return of spring, however, he discontinued his visits, and betook himself entirely to the garden ; but on the approach of winter he rejoined his old associates, who gave him a most cordial reception. At last he frequently used the freedom of washing himself in the bowl which was set for the dog to drink out of, and, while thus employed, he betrayed marks of the greatest impatience if either of his companions presumed to interrupt him. He died in consequence of being choked with something which he had picked up from the floor.

As lapwings are reckoned dainty food, many of them are captured for the table ; their eggs, too, are esteemed a delicacy, and are frequently brought to the London market, where they fetch a high price.

Strepsilas, Illig. Tem. Vieill. Leach. Tringa, Lin. &c.

Bill middle-sized, hard-pointed, strong, straight, slightly bent upwards, ridge flattened, tip straight and truncated ; nostrils basal, lateral, half closed by a membrane ; legs of moderate length, a short naked space above the knee ; the three anterior toes connected at the base by a very short membrane, and the hinder articulated to the tarsus ; wings acuminated.

S. collaris, Tem. *S. interpres*, Leach, Steph. *Tringa interpres*, and *Tringa morinella*, Lin. *Turnstone, Sea Dottrel*, or *Hebridal Sandpiper*. Varied with black, white, and ferruginous above ; abdomen white ; under parts of the cheeks and neck black ; base and tip of the tail white, and the middle black. It is, however, subject to great diversity of markings about the head and neck ; but the black on the breast, and more or less round the neck, is a good distinctive character. Size of a throstle, length nine inches and a half extent of

Ornithology.

Strepsilas.

Collaris.

wing fifteen inches and a half, and the weight somewhat exceeding four ounces. The black in the female is less deep, and the other colours are paler. The young are chiefly mottled with brown and white, and have most of the feathers deeply edged with yellow.

Turnstones inhabit both the old and new continent, but are more common in the northern than in the southern regions. Though not known to breed with us, they visit some of our shores in August, and depart in spring. In the north of Scotland they are not uncommon, but much more rare in the south of England. They are usually observed in small flocks, which are supposed to constitute so many families. They make a slight nest on the dry ground, or sand, and lay four olive-coloured eggs, spotted with black. They have their vernacular name from their habit of turning up stones, to get at worms and insects; and such is the strength and vigour of their bill, that they will sometimes move a stone upwards of three pounds in weight. They are observed to occur only on sea shores.

GRUS, Tem. Vieill. Cuv. ARDEA, Lin, &c. CRANE.

Bill as long as, or longer than, the head, strong, straight, compressed, obtuse towards the tip; lateral base of the mandible deeply sulcated, ridge elevated; nostrils in the middle of the bill, and closed by a membrane behind; region of the eyes and base of the bill naked and papillated, or covered with feathers; legs long and stout, with a large naked space above the knees, the middle front toe united to the outer by the rudiments of a membrane, the inner divided, the hind toe articulated higher up the tarsus; wings of moderate dimensions.

Cranes are periodical migrants, frequenting marshy places, and rarely the sea-shore, subsisting on herbs, seeds, worms, frogs, slugs, &c. There are several species, but only one indigenous to Europe. In most the trachea of the male is of a singular construction, having several convolutions.

G. cinerea, Bechst. Tem. *Ardea Grus*, Lin. &c. *Common Crane.* Body cinereous, throat, fore-part of the neck, and occiput dusky, cap and quills black, coverts with divided webs. Size about that of the turkey, weight ten pounds, and length nearly five feet.

These birds inhabit Europe and Asia, and, in autumn regularly migrate in flocks to the southern parts of Asia and Africa. They are common in Sweden, and so numerous in Poland, that the farmers are obliged to erect huts among their fields of buck-wheat, and station people to drive them off. In the marshes of Lithuania, Podolia, and the neighbourhood of the Dnieper, they are said to remain throughout the year. They were formerly not uncommon in the fenny districts of England; but they are now hardly ever seen with us. Some years ago, during the harvest, a small flock of them appeared at Tingwall, in Shetland, and were observed to feed on the corn. In France they make their appearance from September to November, but only as passengers southward, and they return in March and April, on their way to the north, which is their breeding station. The female nestles among rushes, or alder bushes, and sometimes on the roofs of detached houses, laying two greenish ash-coloured eggs, spotted with brown. Their ordinary fare consists of slugs, frogs, worms, grain, and herbs, which grow in marshy situations, or in the fields. In winter they resort in crowds to Egypt, and the warmer parts of India. In their migratory expeditions they fly very high, and arrange themselves in a triangular form, the better to

cleave the air. When the wind freshens, and threatens to break their array, they collect their forces into a circle; and they adopt the same disposition when menaced by the eagle. They travel chiefly in the night, and betray their course by their loud screams. During their nocturnal voyages, the leader frequently calls to rally his troops, and to point out the track, and the signal is repeated by the flock, each individual answering, as if to give notice that it follows, and keeps its rank. Their cries during the day forebode rain; and their noisy tumultuous screams announce a storm. If, in a morning or evening they rise upwards, and fly peacefully in a body, we may anticipate fine weather; but if they keep low, or alight on the ground, we may apprehend a tempest. Like many other large birds, they anticipate some difficulty in commencing their flight, running a few steps, and opening their wings till they mount a little way, and then, having a clear space, they display their vigorous and rapid pinions. When assembled on the ground they are said to set guards during the night; and, in the ancient hieroglyphics, they have been consecrated as symbols of circumspection and vigilance. According to Kolben, they are often observed in large flocks, on the marshes in the vicinity of the Cape of Good Hope. He says, he never saw a flock of them on the ground, that had not some placed, apparently as sentinels, to keep a look out while the others are feeding, and to give immediate notice of the approach of danger. These sentinels stand on one leg, and at intervals stretch out their neck, as if to observe that all is safe; and, on their sounding the alarm, the whole flock are on the wing.

Although the flesh of the crane is black and tough, the Romans prized it as a delicacy; and we find it enumerated among the dishes which used to be served at the first tables in England.

G. gigantea, Tem. *Ardea gigantea*, Gmel. and Lath. *G. leucogeranus*, Pallas, *Gigantic* or *Siberian Crane.* Snowy-white, with the ten first quills black, and the bill and feet red. Stands four feet and a half high. The young of the first year are of an ochraceous hue, with the face, bill, and legs, greenish-brown; and the old have the hind part of the neck yellowish. This species occurs in the marshy plains of Siberia, near the great rivers Ischim, Irtish, and Oby, where it finds abundance of fish, lizards, frogs, &c. It is very shy and cunning, and is not easily approached, being scared at the slightest noise. During the period of incubation, however, the female assumes the most determined courage, and will fly in the face of men and dogs. She constructs her nest in the most inaccessible situations, among reeds, and lays two eggs, of the size of those of a goose, but ash-coloured, and spotted with brown. As the Siberian cranes retire southward in autumn, they are supposed to winter about the Caspian Sea.

G. virgo, Tem. *Ardea virgo*, Lin. Lath. *Anthropoides*, Vieill. *Numidian Crane*, or *Numidian Demoiselle.* Body blue-grey, the head and tip of the primary quills black; behind the eyes, on each side, a recurved, elongated, and feathery white crest. The feathers on the breast are long and depending. This is a very elegant species, nearly as large as the common crane, and measuring three feet three inches in length. It inhabits different parts of Asia and Africa, but particularly the latter, especially in the territory corresponding to ancient Numidia, in the environs of Tripoli, and on the shores of the Mediterranean. It is pretty common in Egypt during the inundation of the Nile; and, in the month of October, it appears about Constantinople. It likewise occurs on the southern shores of the Black and of the Caspian Seas, and in the neighbourhood of Lake Baikal, affecting the vicinity of rivers and marshy soils, and subsisting on small fish, reptiles, &c. In its varied movements, it seems to mimic the gestures and attitudes of mankind, whence Athenæus called it the *copyist of man*, and the ancients termed it the *player*. From the gentleness and pliancy of its manners, and the elegance of its form, it is frequently kept in menageries, and may be trained to imitate dancing, and to perform other feats for the amusement of the spectators. On such occasions it is fond of being noticed, and struts with parade, as if susceptible of vanity. It has, moreover, been known to breed in confinement, and might possibly be naturalized in the temperate quarters of Europe; for Buffon notices an instance of one which had been bred up at Versailles, from the egg, and which lived twenty-four years. In the Crimea, the female builds her nest in the open plains, and generally in the vicinity of the salt lakes. The young birds are brought to market by the Tartars, and are so susceptible of domestication, that they afterwards breed in the farm-yards.

G. pavonina, Tem. *Ardea pavonina*, Lin. &c. *Anthropoides pavonia*, Vieill. *Crowned Demoiselle, Crowned Heron, Crowned African Crane, Balearic Crane, &c.* Bluish, with the head black, hairy, adorned with a yellowish crest; wings white; tail black. This singular and beautiful species is a native of Africa, and particularly of the coast of Guinea, as far as Cape de Verd. It is of a tame and familiar disposition, easily reconciled to the society of man, and will sometimes mingle with poultry in a court-yard. Fish, worms, insects, and vegetables, are supposed to constitute its principal food. It often sleeps on one leg, runs very fast, and not only flies well, but continues on wing for a long time together. Its cry resembles that of the common crane. In confinement, it is fond of bathing in cold water, and may be fed on rice, either raw or slightly boiled; but live fish are its favourite regale. The native Africans hold it in veneration, and will allow nobody to shoot it. The flesh has the reputation of being tough.

CICONIA, Tem. Leach, &c. ARDEA, Lin. &c. STORK.

Bill long, straight, stout, even, cylindrical, in the form of a lengthened cone, acute, cutting, ridge rounded, of equal height with the head; the under mandible slightly bent up; nostrils longitudinally cleft in the horny substance, and placed in a groove; eyes surrounded with a naked space, which does not communicate with the beak; legs long, and furnished with four toes, of which the three anterior are connected at the base by a membrane, and the hind has its first joint resting on the ground; wings of moderate size.

Storks live in marshy situations, and feed principally on reptiles, frogs, and their spawn, as well as on fish, small mammiferous animals, and birds. In many countries they are a privileged race, being cherished and protected, on account of the noxious animals which they destroy. They moult in autumn, migrate in large bodies, and are easily tamed. The young of the first year do not very materially differ in appearance from the full-grown birds; but they may still be recognised, on their return in spring, by the dull black and white of their plumage. The sexes are not dissimilar in appearance. Several of the foreign species have been un-

necessarily disjoined from the present genus, and arranged under that of *Mycteria*.

C. alba, Tem. *Ardea ciconia*, Lin. &c. *Common, or White Stork.* White, with the orbits naked, and crimson; quills and upper tail-coverts dusky-green. The irides are brown; and the feathers on the breast long and pendulous. Length about three feet and a half; extent of wing upwards of six feet; size about that of a turkey. The young have the black of the wings tinged with brown, and the bill of a dusky red. A pure white variety, called *Sterchi* by the Bulgarians, occurs in the environs of Samarra.

The stork, from the familiarity of its dispositions, and its other moral habits, is one of the most popular of littoral birds, and has been generally regarded as the friend of man, attached to his dwellings, nestling on roofs and chimneys, catering on the banks of the most frequented rivers, in cultivated fields, and almost in gardens, not even shrinking from the bustle of crowded cities, taking up its abode in towers, and every where respected and welcomed. In Holland it is protected, because it checks the multiplication of reptiles in the marshes and humid flats; the Vaudois cherish and venerate it for its friendly offices; the Arabs, in like manner, treat it with the most hospitable regard; and the Turks and eastern tribes consider it as a sacred bird, which they are forbidden to kill. At Constantinople, accordingly, the storks build their nests in the streets; but, in our countries, they generally prefer a lofty situation. A mussulman cannot patiently bear to see one of them molested: and the ancient Thessalians made the killing of them a capital crime. The Moors, too, religiously abstain from offering violence to them; and hence the valley of Moukazem appears to be the resort of all the storks of Barbary, which, in this district, are more numerous than the inhabitants.

The white stork is of gentle manners, easily tamed, and manifests a sense of cleanliness, secreting its dung in some sequestered corner. Although it has a pensive and even melancholy air, it occasionally indulges in gaiety and pastime, associating even with children, and partaking of their amusements. "I saw in a garden," says Dr. Hermann, "in which the children were playing at hide-and-seek, a tame stork join the party, run its turn when touched, and distinguish the child who was to pursue the rest so well, as along with the others to be on its guard." Among the engaging attributes of these birds have been justly reckoned gratitude, conjugal fidelity, and filial and parental affection. They seem, in fact, to be very sensible of kind treatment, saluting, with a noisy flapping of their wings, the houses whose inmates had given them a friendly reception during the preceding season, and repeating the same ceremony on taking leave. With wonderful constancy, the same pair return to the same haunts, and join in mutual and fond caresses after their long voyage. The tender affection which the stork manifests towards her young, has been proverbial even from remote antiquity. She feeds them for a very considerable period, nor quits them till they are strong enough to defend themselves, and to provide for their own subsistence. When they begin to flutter about the nest, she bears them on her wings and protects them from danger; and she has been known rather to perish along with them than abandon them to their fate, an affecting instance of which was exhibited in the town of Delft, in 1636, when a fire broke out in a house that had a stork's nest on it, containing young ones that were then unable to fly. The old stork, returning with

Ornithology.

some meat for them, and seeing the danger to which they were exposed, the fire having almost reached the nest, made several attempts to save them, but finding all in vain, she at last spread her wings over them, and, in that endearing attitude, expired with them in the flames. Young storks, on the contrary, have often been observed to lavish the most affectionate and assiduous cares on their aged and infirm parents; and the ancient Greeks, observant of this striking instinct, enacted a law, to compel children to support the authors of their existence, and the guardians of their infant years.

The stork is capable of sustaining a lofty flight, and of performing long journies, even in tempestuous weather. When on wing, it pushes its head straight forward, with the feet extending backward. It returns to Alsace about the end of February, to Switzerland in the course of March, and to Germany early in May; but it rarely visits this country. If a pair, on their return, find their former nest deranged or demolished, they repair it with sticks, rushes, and other plants that grow in moist situations. It is usually placed on high roofs, the battlements of towers, and sometimes on the tops of tall trees, on the brink of streams, or on the projection of a precipitous rock. In France, it was formerly customary to lay wheels on the roofs of houses, to induce them to build on them, a practice which still subsists in some places. In Holland, boxes are placed on the roofs of houses for the same purpose. The hatch consists of two, three, or four eggs, of a yellowish sordid white, longer than those of the goose, but not so thick. The male sits on them when the female is abroad for food. The young make their appearance in the course of a month, when the parents diligently search and carry to them the requisite aliment, which they disgorge from their gullet or stomach. Both of them never leave their charge at once, but, whilst one is foraging, the other keeps watch, standing on one leg, and its eyes fixed on its offspring. The young are, at first, covered with a brown down, and drag themselves, in the nest, on their knees, their legs being too weak to support them. As their wings grow and acquire strength, the mother aids and trains them in their attempts to fly. At Bagdad, hundreds of the nests are to be seen about the houses, walls, and trees; and, among the ruins of Persepolis, every pillar has its nest. The stork rests and sleeps on one leg, with its head bent backwards on its shoulders, in which attitude it frequently fixes its eye on the reptile which it singles out for prey. Previous to migration, it makes a singular snapping noise with its bill, turning its head backwards, with the upper part of the bill placed on the rump, and the under set into the quickest motion, and made to act on the other. These birds remove southwards about the end of August; but, previously to their departure, multitudes of them assemble in the plains once a day, and make the noise with their bills which we have just described, moving and bustling among one another as if consulting on their plans. At an appointed time, and when the wind is northerly, they suddenly ascend in a body, and are quickly out of sight in the higher regions of the air. This movement is seldom remarked, because it sometimes takes place in the night-time, and always in perfect silence. Defect of food, rather than of heat, probably urges them to change their abodes; for tame individuals seem not to suffer from the severest winters. In Egypt they have a second brood; but many of them remain there throughout the year. In Japan they are likewise stationary. They proceed northward as far as Sweden,

Russia, and Siberia; and they are met with throughout Asia; but they avoid desert and parched tracts of land. Their migratory squadrons are very extensive; for Shaw, the traveller, saw three flights of them leaving Egypt, and passing over Mount Carmel, each half a mile in breadth; and he says they were three hours in passing over. We should likewise remark, that, though easily domesticated, storks never breed in confinement, and that this circumstance need the less to be regretted, since their flesh is far from savoury.

C. argala, Tem. *Ardea argala*, Lath. *Ardea dubia*, Argala. Gmel. *Gigantic Stork, Gigantic Heron, Gigantic Crane, Argil*, or *Hazeal.* Body cinereous, abdomen and shoulders white. The head and neck are naked, with the exception of a few straggling hairs, and the feathers of the breast are long and pendulous. The craw, like a pouch, hangs down on the fore part of the neck, and is thinly covered with down. This is a large species, being six or seven feet in length, five feet high, when standing erect, and measuring nearly fifteen feet from tip to tip of the extended wings. It is a native of Asia and Africa, arriving in the interior parts of Bengal before the period of the rains, and retiring as soon as the dry season commences. Though repulsive in its aspect, it is one of the most useful birds of those countries, as it reduces the number of noxious reptiles and insects. It sometimes, also, feeds on fish; and, such is its voracity, that it will eat, at a time, as much as would serve four men. On opening the body of one of them, a land tortoise and a large black cat were found entire within it, the former in the pouch, and the latter in the stomach. Being undaunted at the sight of mankind, these birds are soon rendered familiar, and, when fish or other food is thrown to them, they catch it very nimbly, and instantly gulp it down. Mr. Smeathman takes notice of a tame young one, which regularly attended the hall at dinner time, placing itself behind its master's chair, frequently before any of the guests entered. The servants were obliged to watch it carefully, and to drive it off from the dishes with sticks; yet, notwithstanding every precaution, it would often snatch off something from the table; and it one day purloined a boiled fowl, which it swallowed entire. It used to fly about, and to roost very high among the silk-cotton trees. From this station, at the distance of two or three miles, it could perceive when the dinner was carried across the court, and, darting down, would arrive early enough to enter before the dishes were all set down. When sitting, it was observed uniformly to rest itself on the whole length of the hind part of the leg. Sometimes it would stand in the room for half an hour after dinner, turning its head from side to side, as if listening to the conversation. Its courage was not equal to its voracity; for a child of eight or ten years of age was able to put it to flight, and it would not openly attack a hen with chickens. Gigantic storks are found in companies, and, when seen at a distance near the mouths of rivers, advancing towards an observer, they have been mistaken for canoes, and, when on the sand banks, for men and women picking up shell-fish on the beach. From their immense gape, they have obtained the popular name of *Large-throats;* and, from their swallowing bones, they have also been called *Bone-eaters*, or *Bone-takers.*

ARDEA, Lin. &c. but much reduced in its range.

HERON.

Bill as long as, or longer than, the head, strong, ARDEA. straight, compressed, acute, upper mandible slightly

Ornitho-logy.

sulcated, ridge rounded; nostrils lateral, placed almost at the base of the bill, longitudinally cleft in a groove, and half-closed by a membrane; orbits and lores naked; legs long and slender, with a naked space above the knee, the middle toe connected with the outer by a short membrane; wings moderate.

The birds of this family reside on the banks of lakes or rivers, or in marshy situations, subsisting on fish and their spawn, testacea, field-mice, frogs, insects, snails, worms, &c. Many of them nestle together. In flight, their neck is contracted and folded over their back, while their legs are stretched out behind. They migrate periodically in large flocks, and moult once in the year. The sexes resemble each other; but the young differ so much in appearance from the adults, that they have given rise to considerable confusion and discrepancy in the nomenclature.

Cinerea.

A. cinerea, Lin. &c. *Common Heron,* Prov. *Heron-sheugh,* or *Heronshaw,* also *Crane, Hegrie,* &c. A depending black crest on the occiput; body cinereous; lines on the neck, beneath, and pectoral bar black. Length about three feet four inches, extent of wing five feet, and average weight three pounds and a half. The young, which have been frequently mistaken for the female, are destitute of the crest and scapulary feathers, and are distinguished by appropriate markings. An accidental variety, almost entirely white, has been sometimes met with, but is reckoned very rare.

The common heron is dispersed over most of the countries of the world, having been observed in the arctic regions of Europe and America, in the East and West Indies, in Chili, on the coasts of Africa, in Egypt, Japan, Otaheite, &c. &c. In some latitudes it is migratory, and in others stationary, though it frequently changes its residence without varying the climate. It chiefly haunts tall forests, in the neighbourhood of lakes, rivers, or swamps; but it also frequently exposes itself to all the rigours of cold and tempestuous weather, when waiting for prey to come within its reach. Like savage man, and other animals which subsist by hunting and fishing, it is capable of enduring protracted abstinence, and of feeding copiously when opportunity offers. It is, moreover, gifted with powers of very rapid digestion. To the scaly tribe it is one of the most formidable of birds; for, in fresh water, there is scarcely a fish which it will not strike at and wound, though sometimes it is unable to carry it off; but the smaller fry are its staple fare. Having waded as far as it can into the water, it patiently awaits the approach of its victims, into which, when they come within contact, it darts its bill with undeviating aim. Willoughby tells us, that he saw a heron which had no fewer than seventeen carp in its belly at a time, which he would digest in six or seven hours, and then go to fish again.

Though the heron usually takes his prey by wading into the water, he frequently also catches it when on wing; but this is only in shallow waters, into which he darts with more certainty than into the deeps, instantly pinning the fish to the bottom, and thus seizing it more securely. In this manner, after having been seen with his long neck for above a minute under water, he will rise on the wing, with a trout or eel struggling in his bill, and after swallowing it entire, on the shore or in the air, will immediately return to fishing. Herons are frequently observed to feed by moonlight, when the fish come into the shoaler waters. They are, in fact, semi-nocturnal in their habits; and they prey on sea-fish as well as on those in the fresh waters. The

Ornitho-logy.

different parts of their structure are admirably adapted to their mode of life; for they have long legs for the purpose of wading, a long neck to reach their prey, and a wide gullet to swallow it. Their toes are long, and armed with long hooked talons, one of which is serrated on the edge, the better to retain the slippery spoil. The bill, too, is long and sharp, having serratures towards the point, which stand backwards, and act like the barbs of a fish-hook. Its broad and concave wings are of signal service in enabling it to convey its load of nourishment to the nest, and to transport its comparatively small and meagre body to distant regions. When to these circumstances we add the acute vision and patient vigilance of this bird, we shall see no reason for indulging in the gloomy strictures of Buffon, who would represent it as an instance of neglect and cruelty on the part of nature, as if the supremely wise and good Creator of all could ever destine animals to a life of wretchedness.

The heron has a demure and melancholy air, and is extremely shy, and impatient of confinement. The young are capable of being tamed to a certain degree; but the old ones, if captured, obstinately refuse food, and pine to death. In this state they have sometimes survived fifteen years. They fly very high in the air, especially before rain, frequently soaring beyond the reach of human vision. In the day time they are often inactive, or indulge in repose, but seldom sleep in the night, though they then perch, and are abundantly clamorous. Their cry is shrill and grating, shorter and more plaintive than that of the goose; but repeated, and prolonged into a more piercing and discordant note when the bird feels pain or uneasiness. Naturally timid and suspicious, they are often disquieted; the aspect of a man, even at a distance, greatly alarms them; and they dread the eagle and the hawk, their most determined enemies, whose attack they endeavour to elude by mounting above them in the air. As a last resource, they will, it is alleged, put their head under their wing, and, presenting their sharp-pointed bill to the invader, transfix him, as he rushes on them with all his weight and impetuosity. The bill is, in fact, a dangerous defensive weapon, to which they have recourse when their adversary least expects it; and sportsmen, accordingly, should approach them with caution when they happen to be only wounded, since, by stretching out their neck to its full length, they can strike to the distance of three feet all around. By suddenly unbending the neck from the shoulders, they dart out the bill, as with a spring, and aim at the eye of their assailant.

Although, in general, shy and solitary in their habits, herons often congregate during the breeding season; and many of them build their nests in the same place, which is called a *heronry.* Pennant mentions, that he reckoned eighty nests on one tree; and Montagu adverts to a heronry on a small island, in a lake in the north of Scotland, on which there was but a single scrubby oak, which, not being sufficient to contain all the nests, many were placed on the ground. The nest is large and flat, being composed of sticks, and lined with wool, rushes, feathers, or other soft materials. The eggs are usually four; but sometimes five or six, of the size of those of a duck, and of a greenish-blue cast. When the female incubates, the male fishes for her, and fetches a portion of his captures. Dr. Heysham has given an interesting account of a battle between a colony of herons, and a neighbouring one of rooks. The former having been deprived of their ancient premises by the removal of the trees, made an attempt to form a settlement in the rookery, which was effected after an obstinate contest, in which some on both sides lost their lives. But, after a second victory of the herons in the succeeding year, a truce was agreed on, and both societies lived in harmony together. Dr. Derham tells us, that he has seen lying scattered under the trees of a large heronry fishes several inches in length, which must have been conveyed by the birds from the distance of several miles; and the owner of this heronry saw a large eel that had been conveyed hither by one of them, notwithstanding the inconvenience which it must have experienced from the fish writhing and twisting about. Heron-hawking was formerly a favourite diversion in this kingdom; and a penalty of twenty shillings was incurred by any person convicted of taking the heron's eggs. Its flesh was also in high request, having been deemed a *royal* dish, and equal to that of the pheasant or peacock. These birds are supposed to live to a considerable age.

Purpurea. *A. purpurea*, Lin. &c. By Gmelin and Latham it has been variously designated, on account of the changes which it undergoes in its progress to maturity. Thus, it includes *A. rufa, botaurus, purpurata, Caspica,* and *variegata;* and, in English, it has been denominated the *Crested Purple Heron, Rufous Heron, Greater Bittern, Purple Heron, Variegated Heron,* and *African Heron.* Red-green above, purplish-red beneath; crown black-green; throat white; a rufous purple crest, depending from the occiput. The mature bird measures nearly three feet in length, and four feet eleven inches in extent of wing, and has the base of the neck garnished with purplish-white feathers, and the scapulars with subulated brilliant red-purple plumes. The young under three years want the crest, whose place is merely indicated by a few elegant reddish feathers. They also want the long feathers at the base of the neck and on the scapulars.

The crested purple heron, which is of singular beauty, is common in the western parts of Asia, frequenting the marshy shores of the Caspian and Black Seas, also the Lakes of Great Tartary, and the borders of the large rivers of those parts, as the Wolga and Irtisch. It likewise occurs, though sparingly, in several parts of Europe, as on the banks of the Danube, and the morasses of Holland; and a few specimens have, at different periods, been killed in England. In Africa and in Malta it is more abundant. It feeds like its congeners, and builds its nest among reeds, or underwood, but rarely in trees, and lays three greenish-cinereous eggs.

Garzetta. *A. garzetta*, Lin. &c. including the *nivea* of Gmel. and Lath. *Egret, Little Egret,* or *Snowy Heron.* Occiput crested; body entirely white; feathers of the upper part of the back elongated and silky; bill black; lores and legs greenish. A tuft of very slender and glossy feathers on the under part of the neck. Iris bright-yellow. The old, when moulting, and the young, before the third year, have no long or crest-like feathers. Length of the full-grown bird one foot, and ten or eleven inches, and weight about one pound. Not uncommon in many parts of Europe and Asia, and found also in Africa and America, about New York and Long Island, some of the West India Islands, and Cayenne. In summer, they may be traced as far north as Carolina. In Egypt, they may be seen perching, towards evening, on the trees. If we may judge from the bill of fare of the feast given by Archbishop Neville, these birds were formerly plentiful in England; for no fewer than a thousand of them are mentioned in

that list. They are now, however, if not exterminated, yet very rare in this kingdom. In their habits, they are more social than some of their congeners, and readily consort even with birds of different families, picking up their prey from the ooze of the sea-shore, &c. breeding in marshy situations, and laying four or five white eggs. They are said to be tamed without much difficulty. Their plumes, which were formerly employed to decorate the warrior's helmet, are now applied to the head-dress of ladies, and the turbans of the Turks and Persians.

A. nycticorax, Lin. &c. including, in its different *Nycticorax.* stages of growth and moulting, the *maculata, Gardeni, badia,* and *grisea,* of Gmelin. *Nycticorax Europæus,* Steph. *Night Heron, Night Raven, European Night Heron, Lesser Ash-coloured Heron,* or *Qua Bird.* The young are the *Spotted Heron, Gardenian Heron,* and *Chesnut Heron* of Latham, Pennant, &c. Crested head, occiput and back black-green, abdomen yellowish-white. Length one foot eight inches, and extent of wing three feet two inches.

This species has received its denomination from the disagreeable croaking noise, resembling the straining of a person in the act of vomiting, which it utters soon after sunset, when it comes abroad in quest of fish or insects. During the day, it keeps concealed among reeds, trees, or rocks, frequenting either sea-shores or the banks of rivers. It is met with both in the north and south of Europe, quitting our temperate climates in autumn, and returning in spring; but it is far from common in Great Britain. In America, it has been traced from Hudson's Bay to Louisiana. It likewise occurs in China, on the shores of the Caspian Sea, in Russia, particularly on the Don, and about Astrachan, in summer; but it is seldom observed in great numbers; and it is a scarce bird in the northern parts of the world. The female carelessly constructs her nest on the ground, among bushes or rushes; and, according to some authors, among rocks, or trees, and lays three or four eggs, of a dull green.

A. stellaris, Lin. &c. *Botaurus stellaris*, Steph. *Stellaris.* *Bittern,* Prov. *Bittour, Bumpy-coss, Butterbump, Bumble, Miredrum,* &c. Testaceous, with transverse spots above, paler, with oblong brown spots beneath. The full-grown male is not quite so large as the common heron, measuring two feet and four or five inches in length, and three feet ten inches in extent of wing. It inhabits Europe, Asia, and America, affecting the more temperate regions in winter, and migrating northwards in summer. Though not plentiful in England, especially since the considerable drainage which has been effected of the low swampy grounds, it is still found throughout the year; but, in winter, it leaves the more mountainous, marshy grounds, resorting to low moist situations; and, if the weather be severe, it betakes itself to the sedgy banks of rivers and streams. It is a shy and solitary bird, generally residing among the reeds and rushes of extensive marshes, continuing for whole days about the same spot, as if it sought for safety only in privacy and inaction. In the autumn, it changes its abode, always commencing its journey about sunset. During the day, it will sit among the reeds, with its head erect, by which means it sees over their tops, without being seen by the sportsman. It is with difficulty roused from its lurking-place, flies heavily, and frequently alights near the same spot. When caught, it evinces great fierceness, and strikes chiefly at the eyes of its antagonist. Though it never courts a battle, if once attacked, it defends itself with great coolness and intrepidity. When darted on by a bird of prey, it does not attempt to escape, but, with its sharp bill erected, receives the shock on the point, and thus compels its invader to retreat, sometimes with a fatal wound. Hence old buzzards never attempt to attack it; and the common falcons always endeavour to rush on it from behind, and whilst it is on the wing. When wounded by the sportsman, it often makes a determined resistance, awaiting the onset, and making such vigorous thrusts with its bill, as to wound the leg, even through the boot. Sometimes, again, especially when surprised by a dog, it turns on its back, like some of the rapacious birds, and fights with both its bill and claws. During the months of February and March, the male makes a deep booming noise, which is supposed to be his call to the females, and which is vulgarly ascribed to his putting his bill into a reed, or into the mud, and blowing through it. Both sexes assist in putting the nest together, constructing it almost entirely of dried rushes, or other herbage, placed on a stump or bush, near to the water, and yet without its reach. The female lays four or five greenish-brown eggs, and sits on them for about twenty-five days. The young, when hatched, are naked and scraggy; nor do they venture abroad till about twenty days after their extrusion, during which time the parents feed them with snails, small fishes, or frogs. In the reign of Henry VIII. the bittern was held in great esteem at the tables of the great. Its flesh, which has pretty much the flavour of hare, is far from being unpleasant; and the London poulterers still value one of these birds at half-a-guinea.

A. ralloides, Scop. Tem. Steph. including the *Comata, Squaiotta, Castanea, Marsiglii, Pumila,* and *Erythropus,* of Gmel. &c. *Squacco Heron.* Crested, with the forehead and crown yellow, marked with longitudinal black spots; upper parts of the body rufous; under parts, with the throat, rump, and tail, white.

Squacco herons abound in Asia and Africa, frequenting the bays of the Caspian Sea, and the adjacent rivers. They are also found in Poland, Russia, Turkey, the Grecian archipelago, Italy, Sardinia, and, occasionally, in Germany and Holland. An instance is said to have occurred of one having been shot in England. The female nestles among reeds, and lays from four to six greenish eggs.

A. minuta, Lin. &c. The young are the *A. Soloniensis,* and *A. Danubialis,* Gmel. *Little Heron, Little Bittern, Long-neck,* &c. The young are the *Rufous Bittern* and *Rayed Bittern* of Lath. Crown, back, quills, and tail, green black; the neck, wing-coverts, and abdomen, yellowish red. Size about that of a thrush; length thirteen inches nine lines; extent of wing one foot seven inches. Native of Europe and Asia, and has been found from Siberia to Syria and Arabia. Although not very common in France, it has been frequently observed in Lorraine and Champagne, and is by no means rare along the lakes of Switzerland. It has likewise been observed in the marshes of Holland and Germany, and, on a few occasions, in Great Britain and the Orkneys. It feeds on the fry of fish, young frogs, and their spawn, insects, and worms. During the breeding season, the male utters a cry, which resembles the distant barking of a dog. The female deposits from four to six white eggs, of the size of those of the blackbird, in a sort of nest composed of a few dried leaves and rushes, and placed among reeds.

Ralloides.

Minuta.

PHŒNICOPTERUS, Lin. &c. FLAMINGO.

Bill thick, strong, higher than broad, dentated, conical towards the point, naked at the base, upper mandible abruptly inflected, and bent down on the under at the tip; the under broader than the upper; nostrils longitudinally placed in the middle of the bill, and covered by a membrane; legs very long, with three toes before, and a very short one articulated high on the tarsus behind, the fore toes connected by a web which reaches to the claws; wings middle-sized.

P. ruber, Lin. &c. *Red Flamingo.* Quills deep black. This singular bird is scarcely so big as a goose, but has the neck and legs more disproportioned to the body than any other of the feathered race, the length from the end of the bill to that of the tail being four feet and two or three inches; but to the end of the claws six feet or upwards. The neck is slender, and of an immoderate length; the tongue, which is large and fleshy, fills the cavity of the bill, has a sharp cartilaginous tip, is furnished with twelve or more hooked papillæ on each side, which bend backwards, and it has a ball of fat at the roots, which epicures reckon a great delicacy. The bird, when in full plumage, which it does not attain till its fourth year, has the head, neck, tail and under parts of a beautiful rose-red, the wings of a vivid or scarlet red, the back and scapulars rosered, and the legs rosaceous. The young, before moulting, have their plumage cinereous, and a considerable portion of black on the secondaries of the wings and tail. At the expiration of the first year, they are of a dirty white, with the secondaries of the wings of a blackish brown, edged with white; the wing-coverts at their origin white, faintly shaded with rose-colour, but terminated with black, and the white feathers of the tail irregularly spotted with bluish-brown. At two years of age, the pink on the wings assumes more intensity.

Flamingos affect the warmer latitudes of both continents, and are not often met with higher than the 40th degree, north or south. They are common on the African coast, and the islands adjacent to the Cape of Good Hope, and sometimes on the shores of Spain, Italy, Sicily, Sardinia, and even at Marseilles, and some way up the Rhone, but rarely in the interior of the continent of Europe, and seldom on the banks of the Rhine. We trace them on the Persian side of the Caspian Sea, and thence along the western coast, as far as the Wolga. They breed abundantly in the Cape de Verd islands, particularly that of Sal, constructing on the sea-shore, but so as not to be flooded by the tide, a nest of mud, in the shape of a pyramidal hillock, with a cavity at top, in which the female generally lays two white eggs of the size of those of a goose, but more elongated. The structure is of a sufficient height to admit of the bird's sitting on it conveniently, or rather standing astride, as the legs are placed, one on each side, at full length. The female will also sometimes deposit her eggs on the low projection of a rock, if otherwise adapted to her attitude during incubation. The young are not able to fly till they are grown; but they can previously run with wonderful swiftness. In this immature state, they are sometimes caught, and easily tamed, becoming familiar in five or six days, eating from the hand, and drinking freely of sea-water. But they are reared with difficulty, being very apt to pine from want of their natural subsistence, which chiefly consists of small fishes, and their spawn, testacea, and

Ruber.

aquatic insects. These they capture by plunging the bill and part of the head into the water, and, from time to time, trampling on the bottom to disturb the mud, and raise up their prey. In feeding, they twist the neck in such a manner, that the upper part of the bill is applied to the ground. They generally shun cultivated and inhabited tracts of country, and resort to solitary shores, and salt lakes, and marshes. Except in the pairing season, they are generally met with in large flocks, and, at a distance, appear like a regiment of soldiers, being often arranged in file, or alongside of one another, on the borders of rivers. When the Europeans first visited America, they found these birds on the swampy shores quite tamed, gentle, and no ways distrustful of mankind; and we learn from Catesby, that when the fowler had killed one, the rest of the flock, instead of attempting to fly, only regarded the fall of their companion in a sort of fixed astonishment; so that the whole flock were sometimes killed in detail, without one of them attempting to make its escape. They are now, however, extremely shy, and one of them acts as a sentinel, when the rest are feeding; and the moment that it perceives the least danger, it utters a loud scream, like the sound of a trumpet, and instantly all are on the wing, and fill the air with their clamour. Flamingos, when at rest, stand on one leg, having the other drawn up to the body, and the head placed under the wing. When flying in bands, they form an angle, like geese, and in walking they often rest the flat part of the bill on the ground, as a point of support. These beautiful birds were held in high estimation by the ancient Romans, who often used them in their grand sacrifices, and sumptuous entertainments. Pliny, Martial, and other writers, celebrate the tongue as the most delicate of eatables. The flesh is not despised, even in modern times; but it is alleged by some of those who have partaken of it, that it has an oily and somewhat muddy flavour. That of the young is generally preferred to that of the adult bird.

RECURVIROSTRA, Lin. &c. AVOCET.

Bill very long, slender, feeble, depressed throughout its length, flexible, and recurved at the point, the upper mandible channelled on its surface, the under laterally; nostrils on the surface of the bill linear and long; legs long and slender, the three fore-toes united as far as the second articulation by a membrane, the hinder placed high up, and very short; wings acuminate, the first quill the longest.

R. avocetta, Lin. &c. *Scooping Avocet,* Prov. *Butterslip, Scooper, Yelper, Picarini Crooked-bill, Cobbler's-awl,* &c. Varied with white and black. It is about the size of the lapwing, but considerably taller, weighing thirteen ounces, and measuring in length from fifteen to eighteen inches. From the curvature and softness of its bill it can neither use it defensively, nor pick up with it any solid or sizeable prey. The bird is, accordingly, adapted to wading into the mud or ooze on sea-shores, or the banks of rivers, and to searching for the spawn of fish or of frogs, insects, &c. It is extremely vigilant, active, shy, and cunning, constantly on the alert, flitting about, changing its place of residence, and generally eluding the wiles of the fowler. In our continent, these birds appear to be partial to northern countries, which they quit on the approach of winter, and revisit in the spring. They are observed twice a-year in considerable numbers on the French and British coasts; and they are known to breed in the fens of Lincolnshire and Cam-

bridgeshire, and in Romney Marsh in Kent. They are far from uncommon in Zealand, Denmark, Sweden, Russia, Siberia, and in several tracts of North America, extending as far north as Nova Scotia. In a small hole surrounded with grass, or merely scooped out in the sand, the female lays two eggs about the size of those of a pigeon, and of a cinereous grey, singularly marked with deep brownish dark patches, of irregular sizes and shapes, besides some subordinate markings of a dusky hue. When frightened from her nest, she counterfeits lameness, like the plovers; and when a flock is disturbed, they fly with their necks stretched out, and their legs extended behind, over the heads of the spectators, making a shrill noise, and uttering a yelping cry of *twit, twit.* Though their feet are almost palmated, they have been seldom observed to swim.

The *R. Americana, rubricollis,* and *Orientalis,* have similar manners.

PLATALEA, Lin. &c. PLATEA, Leach. SPOONBILL.

Bill very long, much flattened, dilated towards the extremity, and rounded, like a spoon, or spatula: upper mandible channelled, and transversely sulcated at the base; nostrils approximated, oblong, open, bordered with a membrane; face and head wholly or partially naked; legs long and stout, the three anterior toes connected to the second articulation by deeply gashed membranes, the hinder one long, and bearing on the ground; wings ample.

Spoonbills live in society, subsisting on small fish and their spawn, on frogs, and other small reptiles; on fluviatile testacea, mollusca, aquatic insects, and sometimes on the grassy weeds or roots of boggy soils. According to circumstances, they place their nest on trees or bushes, or among rushes. They undergo one regular moulting in the year, and are migratory. They are but thinly dispersed over various parts of the world. Though their usual haunts are the sea-shores, or the contiguous fenny swamps, which are occasionally overflowed by the tide, or such low marshy coasts as are constantly covered with stagnant water, they are sometimes seen by the sides of lakes or rivers in the interior of a country.

P. leucorodia, Lin. &c. *Spoonbill* or *White Spoonbill.* Occiput crested, body white, throat yellow. The adult bird weighs about three pounds and a half, and measures two feet eight inches in length, and four feet four inches in extent of wing, being nearly of the size of the common heron, but with the neck and legs much shorter. One of the most striking peculiarities of these birds is the conformation of the bill, which flaps together like two pieces of leather. It is six inches and a half long, broad and thick at the base, and very flat towards the extremity, where, in shape, it is widened and rounded, like the mouth of a mustard spatula. It is rimmed on the edges with a black border, and terminated with a small point bent downwards. The colour varies in different individuals. In some, the little ridges which wave across the upper mandible are spotted, in others the insides towards the gape, and near the edges, are studded with small hard tubercles, or furrowed prominences, and are also rough, near the extremity of the bill, so as to enable the bird to retain its slippery prey. In this species, too, the trachea has a double flexure like the figure 8; but the convolutions do not cross each other at the points of contact, being united by a fine membrane.

Spoonbills are of rare occurrence in Great Britain; but they are met with more or less frequently from

Ornithology.

Lapland to the Cape of Good Hope. In Holland, they are more frequent than in most parts of Europe, especially in the marshy grounds near Leyden. Pallas observed them in Russia, on the banks of the Oka; and they are rather numerous on the Yaik, and in the country of the Calmuc Tartars. They are found also in Tartary, and in some of the maritime districts of Italy, as well as in Barbary, and on all the western coast of Africa. When agitated by fear or anger, they make a clattering noise by a quick motion of the mandibles of the bill; and, when annoyed by sportsmen, they soar aloft by an undulatory sort of flight, which is not easily disturbed. They generally feed on small fish and their spawn, frogs, insects, sedges, or other weeds that vegetate in swampy soils. They breed in trees near their ordinary haunts, making their nest of sticks, like the heron, and laying three or four white eggs spotted with reddish. According to Belon and others, they may be tamed without much difficulty. Their flesh has been compared to that of the goose.

TANTALUS, Lin. Tem. who has much circumscribed its range. *Couricaca, Ibis,* of former ornithologists.

TANTALUS.

Bill very long, straight, without a nasal foss, a little inflected at the tip, which is curved, the upper mandible arched, the base broad, sides ciliated, tip compressed and cylindrical, edges of both mandibles much inflected and sharp; face naked; nostrils basal on the surface of the bill, longitudinally cleft in the corneous substance which invests them above; legs very long; tarsus double the length of the middle toe, and the lateral toes united by a broad scalloped membrane.

Ibis.

T. ibis, Lath. &c. *Solleikel Couricaca* or *Egyptian Ibis.* Face red; bill pale yellow; quill feathers black; body reddish-white. The bill is seven inches long. This is a large bird, somewhat exceeding the stork in bulk, and measuring from thirty to forty inches in length. The fore part of the head, all around, as far as the eyes, is naked and reddish. The skin under the throat is also naked and dilatable. This species abounds in Lower Egypt, in places just freed from the inundation of the Nile, living on frogs and insects. It frequents gardens in the morning and evening, and sometimes in such flocks that whole palm trees are covered with them. It rests in an erect attitude, with its tail touching its legs, and it builds its nest in the palm trees. The Egyptians call it *Pharaoh's bird,* and Hasselquist conjectures that it is the *Ibis* of the ancients; but mummies of two other species seem to have been preserved; and it is not improbable that worship was paid to it, and to two other sorts belonging to the next genus.

IBIS, Lacépède, Illig. Tem. TANTALUS, Lin. &c.

IBIS.

Bill long, slender, arched, broad at the base, tip depressed, obtuse, and rounded, upper mandible deeply furrowed in its whole length; nostrils near the base in the upper portion of the bill, oblong, straight, and perforated in the membrane which invests the furrow; the face, and frequently a part of the head and neck, naked; legs of moderate dimensions, or slender and naked above the knee, the fore-toes united as far as the first articulation, the hind one long, and reaching the ground.

The birds of this recently instituted genus, which have been confounded with the preceding, and with the curlews, haunt the banks of rivers and lakes, where they feed on worms, insects, testacea, and often also on vegetables; but the popular reputation which they

have acquired of devouring poisonous reptiles seems to be quite unsupported by fact. They are stated migrants, and undertake long voyages.

Ornithology.

I. falcinellus, Tem. *Tantalus falcinellus,* and *T. igneus,* Gmel. &c. *Bay* and *Glossy Ibis* of Latham, *Black Ibis* of Savigny. The young correspond to *Tantalus viridis* of Gmel. and Lath. or *Green Ibis.* Head, neck, front of the body, and sides of the back, of a beautiful deep chesnut hue, the upper part of the back, wings, and tail, brassy or golden green, according to the reflexions of the light; bill greenish-black, and the tip brown; irides brown; and legs greenish-brown. Total length twenty-three inches. Before their third year the young have the feathers of the head, throat, and neck, longitudinally striped with blackish-brown, and edged with white; the under part of the neck, the breast, belly, or thighs, cinereous black; the upper part of the back and scapularies cinereous-brown, and the green reflexions on the wings and tail less lively than in the mature bird. Frequents the margins of lakes and rivers, and visits, in its passage, Poland, Hungary, Turkey, and the Archipelago. It also visits the banks of the Danube, and occasionally Italy and Switzerland, and even sometimes wanders into Holland and England. It occurs likewise in Siberia, and resorts periodically to Egypt, where it appears to have been formerly the object of divine worship.

Falcinellus.

I. religiosa, Cuv. *Tantalus Æthiopicus,* Lath. *Abou-hannes* of Bruce. *Sacred Ibis.* Part of the head and neck naked, the general plumage diversified with glossy black and white. The young differ considerably from the old birds, and have the crown of the head and the nape furnished with long pendent plumes. Common in Ethiopia and in the whole of Lower Egypt during part of the year. It sometimes lives in a solitary state, and sometimes in small bands of eight or ten. Its flight is powerful and elevated. When on wing it stretches out its neck and feet horizontally, like most of its congeners, uttering, from time to time, a very hoarse scream. Groups of them will remain close by one another, and for hours together, on ground recently abandoned by the water, incessantly busied in exploring the mud with their bill. They do not hop and run nimbly like the curlews, but walk step by step. Their breeding quarters have not been ascertained; but they arrive in Egypt when the Nile begins to swell, and diminish in number in proportion as the waters retire. For more ample particulars relative to the sacred ibis, we beg leave to refer our readers to Bruce's Travels, and to Savigny's ingenious disquisition.

Religiosa.

I. rubra, Vieill. *Tantalus ruber,* Lath. *Scarlet Ibis.* Face, bill, and legs, red; body scarlet; wings tipped with black. From twenty to twenty-four inches long. In the female the bill is yellowish-grey; a mixture of white and grey prevails in different parts of the plumage; and the tips of the two first quills are of a deep azure. The young are at first blackish, then grey, whitish just before they fly, and gradually assume their beautiful scarlet livery. These elegant birds are spread over the most of the warm countries of South America. In Brazil they are known by the name of *Guara,* and in Cayenne by that of *Flamingo.* Whether on the wing, or searching for food on low marshy shores, they are always observed in society, retiring during the heat of the day into small inlets, and courting the coolness of the shade, to which they again return at night. They begin to incubate in January, and finish in May. They lay their greenish eggs in long grass, among the brushwood, or among a parcel of sticks carelessly put toge-

Rubra.

ther. The young may be taken with the hand, are far from shy, and are readily reconciled to almost any kind of food ; but in their native state they subsist on small fish, testacea, and insects. Their flesh is reckoned worthy of a place at table. The *Tantalus fuscus* of some authors is the young of the present species.

Numenius, Lath. Cuv. Tem. Scolopax, Lin.

Bill long, slender, arched, compressed, point hard and slightly obtuse, upper mandible projecting beyond the lower, rounded at the end, and channelled through three-fourths of its length ; nostrils lateral, linear, and pierced in the chasm ; face covered with feathers ; legs slender, naked above the knee, the three fore-toes united by a membrane as far as the first articulation ; the hinder articulated to the tarsus, and touching the ground. This family of birds, which some have confounded with *Ibis*, and others with *Scolopax*, is well characterized. The individuals belonging to it frequent the neighbourhood of waters and marshes. Their food principally consists of earthworms, insects, slugs, and testacea. Their flight is lofty and well sustained. They migrate in large flocks, but live in an insulated state, during the breeding season. In general they are very shy. They moult only once a-year, and the circumstances of age and sex produce no very marked differences in their appearance. We owe principally to M. Temminck the clear extrication of this group.

N. arquata, Lath. Tem. *Scolopax arquata*, Lin. &c. *Common Curlew*, *Whaap* of the Scots, and *Stock Whaap* of the Orcadians. General plumage clear, cinereous, with brown longitudinal spots on the neck and breast ; belly white, with longitudinal spots ; feathers of the back and scapulars black in the middle and edged with rufous, and the tail whitish-cinereous, striped with transverse brown bands. The upper mandible is black-brown, and the under flesh-coloured ; the iris is brown ; and the legs are deep cinereous. The female inclines rather more to cinereous, and has the rufous tints less pure ; and the young of the first year are distinguished by the shortness and very slight curvature of the bill. This species is liable to vary considerably in size, weighing from twenty to upwards of thirty ounces, and the length of the largest reaching to twenty-five inches. The bill is generally from five to six inches long ; but Mr. Donovan alludes to an instance of one which measured ten inches, and was preserved as a curiosity. This instrument is admirably fitted for picking worms, small crabs, &c. out of the sand, and is, at the same time, successfully used as a weapon of defence against the shield-drake, and even against the common gull. The curlew occurs throughout the old continent, the specimens sent from India being perfectly similar to those of Europe ; but, in America, there is either a variety or a distinct species, which is rufous and black, and has a smaller body and longer bill.

The usual haunts of the common curlews are sea-shores and the neighbourhood of rivers and fenny grounds ; but they also visit inland heaths and moors, especially in spring, when they breed, and for which purpose they resort to the most retired situations, either on the mountains, among the heath, or in extensive and unfrequented marshes. In the north, they are found in Russia, Siberia, Kamtschatka, &c. ; and, in the south, in Italy, Greece, and Egypt. In France, they abound in the countries watered by the Loire ; and they breed on the banks of that river, or among the heaths and downs. They make no regular nest, but deposit their eggs, which are generally four, and of a pale olive,

marked with brownish spots, among the heath, rushes, or long grass. The young make use of their legs as soon as they are hatched, but cannot fly for a considerable time. In winter they congregate along our shores. They run swiftly, but seem to commence their flight with some difficulty. Though naturally very shy, they soon become docile in confinement. One that was shot in the wing was turned among aquatic birds, and was at first so extremely shy, that he was obliged to be crammed with meat for a day or two, when he began to eat worms ; but, as this was precarious fare, he was tempted to partake of bread and milk, like ruffs. To induce this substitution, worms were put into a mess of bread, mixed with milk ; and it was curious to observe how cautiously he avoided the mixture, by carrying every worm to the pond, and washing it well, previously to swallowing it. In the course of a few days this new diet did not appear unpalatable to him, and, in little more than a week, he became partial to it, and, from being exceedingly poor and emaciated, got plump, and in high health. In the course of a month or six weeks this bird became quite tame, and would follow a person across the menagerie for a bit of bread or a small fish, of which he was remarkably fond ; nor did he reject water lizards, small frogs, insects, and even barley, with the ducks. According to some, the flesh of the curlew is of a very fine flavour, whilst others talk of it in very different language ; and the fact is, that it has a delicate or a fishy flavour according as the bird feeds on inland or maritime products. The American variety, which is very common on the coasts of Labrador, is observed to fatten on the crow and whortle-berries, of which it is very fond, and which impart to it a nice flavour of game.

Tringa, Briss. Tem. Sandpiper.

Bill middle-sized or long, very slightly arched, curved, or straight at the tip, soft and flexible through its whole length, compressed at the base, depressed, dilated, and obtuse at the tip, both mandibles channelled to near their extremities ; nostrils lateral, conical, perforated in the membrane which invests the nasal sulcus in its whole length ; legs slender, naked above the knee, the three fore-toes quite divided ; but, in a few species, the middle and outer toe are connected by a membrane ; the hinder articulated to the tarsus.

We readily adopt these limitations of the genus, suggested by Temminck, who enjoyed so many excellent opportunities of studying the appearance and manners of the birds which compose it ; and we gladly also avail ourselves of his descriptive definitions of the species, both because they suffice for the purposes of discrimination, and because we cannot afford space for the enumeration of the diversities of plumage incident to most of them, from their double moulting, and different stages of growth—circumstances which have involved some of our most eminent systematical writers in a labyrinth of confusion, and given rise to a very superfluous multiplication of species. The birds in question travel in small groups, several of which unite in the breeding season, and fix on a common station. They frequent marshy soils, near rivers, lakes, and seas ; and they discuss the ooze, mud, shifting sands, or heaps of sea weed, thrown on the beach, in quest of coleopterous insects, larvæ, soft worms, mollusca, the contents of small bivalve-shells, &c. The young, before their first moulting, are very unlike their parents ; and the female is, for the most part, somewhat larger than the male.

Ornitho-
logy.

Subar-
quata.

T. subarquata, Tem. *T. cinclus*, Lin. *Scolopax Africana*, and *Scolopax subarquata*, Gmel. *Numenius subarquata*, Bech. and the young, *Numenius pygmæus* of the same author, and *Numenius Africana*, Lath. *Subarcuated Sand-piper, Red Sand-piper, Cape Curlew, Stint, Purre, Sanderling*, Prov. *Ox-Bird, Bull-eye, Ox-eye, Least Snipe, Sea Lark, Sea Wagtail*, &c. Bill arched, much longer than the head, the two middle tail-feathers longer than the lateral ones, tarsus fourteen lines long. The ordinary length of the full-grown bird is seven inches and six or eight lines. The female is rather larger than the male, and has a longer bill.

This species frequents the shores of seas and lakes, and more rarely occurs in the interior of countries. It migrates along shores and the banks of rivers in spring and autumn, and is found in the four quarters of the world, specimens brought from Senegal, the Cape of Good Hope, and America, being perfectly similar to those of Switzerland and other European countries. It feeds on insects, worms, and sea-weeds, and lays four or five yellowish eggs, spotted with brown, near the water's edge. During winter, it is found on all our coasts, appearing in vast flocks, especially affecting flat sandy shores and inlets. They leave us in April, though it is suspected that some of them remain with us all the year. These birds run nimbly near the edges of the retiring and flowing waves, and are constantly wagging their tail, while they are, at the same time, busily employed in picking up their food, which consists chiefly of small worms and insects. On taking flight, they give a kind of scream, and skim along the surface of the water with great rapidity, as well as with great regularity, not flying directly forward, but performing their evolutions in large semicircles, alternately approaching the shore and the sea in their sweep, the curvature of their course being indicated by the flocks appearing suddenly and alternately of a dark or snow-white colour, as their backs or their bellies are turned to or from the spectator.

Variabilis.

T. variabilis, Meyer, Tem. In its winter plumage, *Cinclus*, and *Cinclus minor*, of Brisson; and in its summer dress, *T. alpina*, Gmel. Lath. Wils. and *Numenius variabilis*, Bechst. At the time of its two periodical moultings, it is the *Cinclus torquatus*, and *Gallinago anglicana*, of Brisson; whilst, in some of the intermediate stages, it corresponds to *T. cinclus*, var. B. Gmel. *T. ruficollis*, and *scolopax pusilla*, of the same author. *Variable*, or *Alpine Sand-piper*, or *Dunlin*. Bill almost straight, black, slightly sloping at the tip, and a little longer than the head; the two middle tail-feathers longer than the lateral ones, and terminating in a point; length of the tarsus nearly one foot. The bird measures from seven to eight inches, and weighs from nine to eleven drachms. It occurs in Greenland, Iceland, Scandinavia, on the Siberian Alps, in Hudson's Bay, &c. Though not so plentiful as the purre, and others of its tribe, it may be seen on our shores in every month of the year, except from the latter end of June to the beginning of August, and is most frequent in the spring and autumn. The nest is composed of dried tufts of grass, or rushes, and the eggs are four, smoky-white, and irregularly marked with light and darker brown blotches, which are rather more distant and paler at the smaller end. It has been observed to breed, in company with the lapwing and ring-plover, in the islands of South Ronaldsha and Sanda, and at Loch Strathbey, near Fraserburgh, in the county of Aberdeen. "It is somewhat remarkable," observes Mr. Bewick, "that birds of different species, such as the ring-dot-

trel, sanderling, &c. which associate with the purre, dunlin, &c. should understand the signal, which, from their wheeling about altogether with such promptitude and good order, it would appear is given to the whole flock."

Ornitho-
logy.

T. cinerea, Lin. Tem. &c. including, in its different states, *T. grisea, Canutus, Islandica, nævia*, and *australis* of Gmel. *T. ferruginea*, Meyer, and *T. rufa*, Wils. *Knot*, or *Knot Sand-piper, Red, Aberdeen, Grisled Ash, Speckled*, and *Southern Sand-piper*. Bill straight, longer than the head, turgid and dilated near the tip; all the tail-feathers of equal length. Nine inches and a half long, and weight four ounces and a half. Inhabits the regions of the arctic circle in summer, living among marshes, and in spring and autumn on the sea-shores. In Holland, these birds are more numerous during their vernal than during their autumnal passage; and they are rare in Germany and France. They are gregarious, and run on the sand with great quickness. A specimen from Africa was found to correspond, in every respect, with the British. In Lincolnshire, and other fenny districts of England, they used to be caught in great numbers, in nets, into which they were decoyed by wooden representations of themselves. The season for their capture is from August to November, when the frost usually constrains them to disappear. When fattened with bread and milk, they acquire so much plumpness, that they are unable to fly, and are then reckoned a great delicacy. King Canute is said to have been particularly fond of them, and hence the trivial epithet *Canutus*, which has been corrupted into *knot*. Lewin seems to have been mistaken when he asserts that this species breeds in our island.

Cinerea.

T. pugnax, Lin. &c. The young are, *T. littorea*, Gmel. *T. Grenovicensis*, Lath. and *Totanus cinereus*, Briss.; whilst the adult females, and the young after their autumnal moult, are *T. equestris*, Lath. *Ruff*, female *Reeve*. Bill very slightly inclined, and inflated towards the tip, legs long, tail rounded, the two middle tail-feathers striped, the three lateral always of a uniform colour. The details of the markings are so variable, that two individuals are seldom found of the same pattern, and that ornithologists only begin to collect the numerous synonymes of the species. The male is distinguished by a ruff, or large tuft of feathers, which he does not acquire till the second year, and which falls off in moulting, leaving him more like his mate, till spring, when he not only resumes the ruff, but certain red tubercles on the face. Length eleven inches and from four to six lines; the female is about one-third smaller, and wants the ruff. These birds inhabit Europe and Siberia, and are particularly abundant in Holland, haunting moist and marshy meadows, and sometimes visiting the sea-shore in spring. At that season they arrive in this island; and, with a very few exceptions, which seem to be accidental, they leave it in autumn. They are even known to breed as far north as in the swamps of Lapland and Siberia.

Pugnax.

At present, the few that, comparatively speaking, visit Great Britain, confine themselves, in the breeding season, to the eastern parts, where the only extensive fens, suited to their mode of life, still exist. They were, however, in former times, not uncommon in the neighbourhood of Bridgewater, in Somersetshire, before the grounds were drained. In the county of Lincoln they have become much more scarce than usual, since large tracts of fenny soil have been drained and inclosed. Some scattered individuals still haunt the vicinity of Crowland; but the north fen, near Spalding, and the east and west fens between Boston and Spilsby, are the only spots which appear to produce them with certainty, though by no means plentifully. The trade for catching them, too, is now limited to a few individuals, who live in obscure places, on the verge of the fens, and who are little more than remunerated for their trouble, and the expence of their nets. In spring, the ruffs *hill*, as it is called, or assemble on a rising spot of ground, contiguous to the destined breeding station. There they take their stand, at a small distance from one another, and fiercely contend for the females. The fowler, from habit, discovers this resort for love and tournaments, by the birds having trodden the turf somewhat bare, though not in a circle, as usually described. Hither he repairs before day-break, spreads his net, places his decoy-birds, and stations himself at the distance of a hundred and forty yards, or more, according to the shyness of the birds. The net, which is seventeen feet in length, and six in breadth, is easily pulled over the birds within reach, and rarely fails to entangle them. As the ruffs feed chiefly by night, they repair to their frequented hill at the dawn of day, nearly all at the same time; and the fowler makes his first pull according to circumstances, takes out his birds, and prepares for the stragglers, which traverse the fens, and have no adopted hill. These are caught singly, being enticed by rudely-stuffed skins of their own species. In this country, however, the spring capture is inconsiderable; for the old birds are subject to pine, and will not readily fatten; and though they are frequently seen in the Parisian markets at that season, they are not then much prized by judges of good eating. In this island, most of them are caught in September, and particularly about Michaelmas, at which time few old males are taken, from which it has been supposed that they migrate before the females and the young. But it is more probable that such as are left after the spring fowling, like other polygamous birds, keep in parties separate from the female and her brood till the return of spring. The long feathers on the neck and sides of the head, that constitute the ruff and auricles, are of short duration, for they are scarcely completed in the month of May, and they begin to fall the latter end of June. The change of these singular parts is accompanied by a complete change of plumage; the stronger colours, such as purple, chesnut, and some others, vanish at the same time; so that, in their winter dress, they become more generally alike, from being less varied in plumage; but those that have the ruff more or less white retain that colour about the neck, after the summer or autumnal moulting is effected.

The reeves begin to lay their eggs the first or second week in May; and the young have been found hatched as early as the third of June, when the males cease to hill. The nest is usually formed on a tump, in the most swampy places, surrounded by coarse grass, of which it is also formed. The eggs are usually four, and so nearly similar in colour to those of the snipe and red-shank, both of which breed in the same wet places, and make similar nests, that some experience is required to discriminate them. They are, however, superior in size to the former, and are known from the latter by the ground being of a greenish hue instead of rufous white; but individual instances assimilate so nearly as not to be distinguished, especially as the dusky and brown spots and blotches are similar. It is a remarkable character of these birds, that they feed most greedily the moment they are taken; a basin of bread and milk, or boiled wheat, placed before them, is

instantly contended for; and so pugnacious is their disposition, that they would starve in the midst of plenty, if several dishes of food were not placed among them at a distance from one another.

Totanus, Bechst. Tem. Scolopax and Tringa, Lin. Lath. &c. Horseman.

Bill of moderate length, straight, rarely recurved, soft at the base, hard, solid, and sharp at the tip, compressed throughout its length, terminating in an acute point; both mandibles furrowed only at the base, the extremity of the upper slightly bent down on the under; nostrils lateral, linear, longitudinal, cleft in the sulcus; legs long, slender, naked above the knee, the middle toe united to the outer by a membrane, which sometimes extends to the second articulation. These birds, which travel in small troops, live indiscriminately on the banks of lakes and rivers, and in meadows adjacent to fresh-waters, and also at times frequent sea-shores, and the muddy and oozy margins of large rivers. With the hard point of their bill, they pick up worms, testaceous animals, and very rarely fish. They moult twice a-year; and the difference of their winter and summer attire often consists only in a varied distribution of spots and stripes, or in the greater or less purity of the colours.

T. calidris, Bechst. Tem. *Long-shanked Horseman.* The moulting young, assuming the winter plumage, are *Tringa striata*, Gmel. The bird, in its perfect summer garb, is *Scolopax calidris*, and *Tringa gambetta*, Gmel. *Red-shanks*, *Gambet Sand-piper*, or *Pool Snipe*. The half of both mandibles red, the rudiment of a membrane uniting the inner to the middle toe; secondary wing quills white in the half of their length. It weighs about five ounces, and is nearly eleven inches long. In spring, this species inhabits marshes and meadows, and in autumn migrates along sea-shores. It has been traced to high northern latitudes in Europe and America, is very abundant in Holland, and winters chiefly in southern countries. It is among the few species that still continue to be indigenous in the fenny districts of England, being tolerably plentiful, during the summer months, about Spalding. It makes a slight nest with coarse grass, on a tump, in the more moist or boggy parts, and begins to lay early in May. The number of eggs in each nest is invariably four, and constantly placed with their smaller ends in the centre. They are whitish, tinged with olive, and marked with irregular spots of black, chiefly on the thicker end. In Orkney, it nestles on the marshy hills, and in summer and in winter it resorts to the sea-shores, where it affects the hollows of muddy and slimy beaches, subsisting on marine vermes and insects. When disturbed, it is extremely clamorous, and flies round the intruder, uttering a shrill piping note, and rousing every bird within hearing of its screams; so that it often incurs the fowler's hate, and forfeits its life for having disappointed him of better prey. The red-shank, though similar in its habits to the ruff, will neither fatten nor live long in confinement.

T. hypoleucos, Tem. *Tringa hypoleucos*, Gmel. and Lath. *Common Horseman* or *Sand-piper*. Under parts white and spotless. Length eleven inches, and two or three lines. Inhabits Europe and North America, but is migratory, and breeds in the central parts of Europe, visiting this country in spring, and ranging as far north as Kamtschatka and Siberia. It frequents chiefly the sandy and pebbly banks of rivers, and lays, in a small cavity which it scoops out with its feet among the

Ornitho-
logy.

pebbles, four or five eggs, of a sordid white, interspersed with minute blackish spots, and so like the surrounding small stones, as often to escape observation. The young, too, though they run very nimbly, as soon as freed from the egg, squat down among the pebbles on the most trifling alarm, and are not easily distinguished. When disturbed, this bird makes a piping noise as it flies; and when running on the ground, the tail is in constant motion. In autumn it is liable to be infested with *Hippobosca hirundinis*.

LIMOSA, Briss. Tem. LIMICULA, Vieill. SCOLOPAX, Lin. OOZE-SUCKER.

LIMOSA.

Bill very long, more or less recurved, soft and flexible in its whole length, depressed, flattened towards the tip, both mandibles channelled through their length, tip flat, dilated, and obtuse; nostrils lateral, longitudinally cleft in the sulcus; legs long and slender; a large naked space above the knee; the middle toe united to the outer by a membrane, which extends to the first articulation, the hinder articulated to the tarsus.

These are tall birds, with long bills, destined to live in marshes, and on the swampy shores of rivers, their soft and flexible bill being unfit for picking food from the surface of a hard or gravelly soil, and only adapted to ransack the slime or moist sand. Hence they live in marshy meadows, and habitually resort to the mouths of rivers, where the mud is deep, and supplies them with worms, the larvæ of insects, &c. Their periods of migration coincide with those of the snipes and horsemen, with both of which they have been confounded. They moult twice a-year, and the females later than the males, which is an uncommon physiological phenomenon. The family is far from numerous, and will be sufficiently illustrated by mention of a single species.

Melanuca.

L. melanuca, Leisler, Tem. *Scolopax limosa*, Lin. *Totanus limosa*, Bechst. *Black-tailed Ooze-Sucker, Jadreka Snipe, Lesser Godwit, Common*, or *Grey Godwit*, or *Stone Plover*. Bill straight, tail black for two-thirds of its length, with the base more or less white; nail of the middle toe long, and denticulated. The young, before their first moult, correspond to the *Totanus rufus* of Bechstein; and the bird, in its complete summer attire, is *Totanus ægocephalus* of the same author, and *Scolopax ægocephala*, and *Scolopax Belgica* of Gmelin. Length of the full grown bird from fifteen to eighteen inches; extent of wing about two feet, and weight from seven to twelve ounces; for it varies much in size. Most of the individuals that are killed in spring are in the moulting state, and have a very mottled aspect. They search the mud with nice discrimination, haunting the marshy districts of Europe, Asia, and Africa, the oozy banks of ditches and pools, and, in winter, the sea-shore, on which they run with great swiftness, living chiefly on insects and their larvæ, worms, the spawn of frogs, and some aquatic and marsh plants. They usually lie concealed among the reeds or rushes during the day, being extremely shy, and venturing out at twilight, or in moonshine, flying sometimes in considerable flocks, and uttering a hoarse but feeble clamour, which Belon has compared to the stifled bleating of a goat. Their air is timid and demure, and, on the slightest alarm, they take to flight. At times, however, flocks of them will allow themselves to be shot at repeatedly without retiring to a safe distance. They breed in the tall herbage of fens and marshes, the female laying four eggs, of a deep olivaceous hue, marked with large pale brown spots. They

are much esteemed by epicures, being quite free of the rankness of some of our shore-birds, and of the fishy taste of others. They are caught in nets to which they are allured by a *stale* or stuffed bird, and in the same manner, and at the same season, as the ruffs and reeves.

SCOLOPAX, Tem. &c. RUSTICOLA, Vieill.

SCOLOPAX.

Bill long, straight, compressed, slender, soft, with the tip turgid; both mandibles channelled the half of their length, the tip of the upper projecting beyond that of the under, and the turgid portion hooked; nostrils lateral, basal, longitudinally cleft near the edges of the mandible, and covered by a membrane; legs slender, with a very small naked space above the knee; the three fore toes quite divided, or else the outer and middle rarely united. The few species which compose the reduced genus live in woods or marshes, and subsist on small slugs or worms. In some countries they are stationary, but in most migratory. They abound more in the northern than in the southern regions, and they moult twice a-year, but without inducing those remarkable changes of plumage observable in some of the preceding families.

Rusticola.

S. rusticola, Lin. &c. *Rusticola vulgaris*, Vieill. *Woodcock*. Back of the head transversely barred, lower parts barred with zig-zag lines. The ordinary length is fifteen inches, and the weight from twelve to fifteen ounces.

This well-known species inhabits the northern regions of Europe, Asia, and Africa, migrating on the approach of winter to more temperate latitudes. In this island it seldom appears in numbers till about the middle of November; but some stragglers incidentally appear as early as the latter end of September, or the beginning of October. They generally come to us with northerly or easterly winds, when their breeding stations become congealed with frost, or covered with snow; and, if intense cold suddenly overtakes them, they sometimes arrive on our coasts in large flocks, and after remaining for a day to recruit their strength, disperse over the interior of the country. Sportsmen have remarked, that there are times when these birds are so sluggish and sleepy, that, on being flushed, they will drop again, just before the dogs, or even at the muzzle of the fowling-piece that had been fired at them, owing possibly to the fatigue of a long and laborious flight across the German Ocean. In some parts of the island they are not so plentiful as formerly, when more extensive woods and marshes were spread over the soil, and the art of shooting flying was less practised. We may add, that of late years the Swedish boors bring great quantities of their eggs to the market, at Stockholm, which has had a visible effect in checking the multiplication of the species. They are, however, by no means rare in the more uncultivated parts of Cornwall, Devonshire, and Wales, and in the north of Scotland; but they are still more common in Ireland; and they seem to increase in numbers in the western parts of that island, whence it has been inferred, that the great column of woodcocks, in their passage to and from the north, fly in that latitudinal direction which is intersected by the western parts of Ireland; so that those which prosecute their route farther south, will find their resting place in Portugal. They are accordingly very plentiful in that country in November, but become scarcer as the winter advances, many of them, no doubt, moving on still in the same line to Africa. In the beginning of March, on their return northward, they are again observed in Portugal in great abundance, but disappear as the warmer season approaches. In their migrations they chiefly fly during the night, or in dark or foggy weather. They preferably betake themselves to the woods, or to places abounding in soft mould and fallen leaves, squat down in concealment during the day, and come forth in the evening and during the night to cater for worms, whose presence they seem to ascertain by the delicacy of their scent, and which they extract from the ground, or snatch from under the leaves with great accuracy and promptitude. As their eyes are constructed for seeing in the twilight, or in moonshine, they are dazzled by the glare of day. After feeding in the glades, they wash their bill in the nearest pool. Their movements are most active and lively before sunrise, and after sunset. On rising, they flap their wings, and spread out their tail. Their flight is rapid, but neither elevated nor long sustained; and they fall abruptly down, as if abandoned to their own weight. Immediately on alighting, they run nimbly to some distance, so that they are never found precisely where they fall. It has been ascertained by experiment, that they regularly return to the same winter haunts. In this country they usually pair and prepare for flight, about the middle of March, when flocks of them repair to the seacoast, and, if the wind is favourable, are soon out of sight, but, if adverse, they linger till it changes. In some countries they may be said to be stationary, only shifting from the plains to the mountains in the breeding season; and a few straggling pairs occasionally breed in our own island. The female places her nest on the ground, in solitary and hilly situations, and composes it of dry leaves and herbs, intermingled with little bits of stick, the whole put together in an artless manner, and heaped against the trunk of a tree, or under its roots; and she lays four or five oblong eggs, a little larger than those of the common pigeon, of a rufous grey, shaded with deeper and dusky undulations. She is said to be very tame during incubation; and it is mentioned, that a person who discovered a wood-cock on its nest, often stood over, and even stroked it, notwithstanding which it hatched the young, and in due time disappeared with them. When the young are hatched, they venture out of the nest, and run about, though covered only with a sort of downy hair. In cases of emergency, the parents, who never separate while the offspring requires their assistance or protection, have been seen to carry one of their young under their throat, in their feet, or on their back, to the distance of a thousand paces. During incubation, the male attends on his mate with great assiduity; and they rest, with their bills mutually leaning on each other's backs. Both male and female are mute, except in the breeding season, when their cries are variously modified, according to the emotions by which they are agitated, but their most common call resembles that of the snipe. The males are readily induced to fight from jealousy; and, when wounded, they have, it is alleged, been seen to shed tears. When the flocks are waiting for a fair wind to steer their course to the north, the sportsmen are particularly on the alert, and do great execution; but if the birds have been long detained on the dry heath, they become so lean as to be scarcely eatable. They are most plump, and in highest condition, from November to February, after which their flesh gets meagre; nor is it very tender till it has been kept for some time; and it is always served up with the trail. The inhabitants of Sweden, Norway, and some

of the northern countries, reject it from the prevalence of a foolish notion that it is unwholesome, because the birds have no crops; but they are as partial to the eggs as other epicures.

S. major, Lin. &c. *Great Snipe.* Tail composed of sixteen feathers, shaft of the first quill whitish. Bill like that of the woodcock. Weight about eight ounces. Inhabits the marshes and flooded meadows of the north, occurring in Siberia and America. In some countries it is a regular migrant, and in others a partial one. In Britain it is very rare, and in France and the south of Europe far from common. Its flight resembles more that of the woodcock than that of the snipe; and when it rises it emits a cry somewhat like that of the latter, but shorter, and of a deeper tone. It breeds among the herbs and rushes of marshes, and lays three or four eggs, of a tawny green, with large deep-brown spots.

Major.

S. gallinago, Lin. &c. *Common Snipe, Hoarse Gauk,* of the Orcadians. The tail composed of fourteen feathers, all the shafts of the quills brown. The weight of this species is about four ounces, the length nearly twelve inches, and the alar extent fifteen inches and a half. Several accidental varieties, as pure white, rufous white, and pied, have been noticed by different observers. When the head is grey, with the legs yellowish, it is *S. gallinaria* of Gmelin and Latham.

Gallinago.

The snipe is met with in marshy situations, in almost every part of the world; and it is very plentiful in our own island. In very wet seasons it resorts to the hills; but it more generally frequents the marshes of the plains, where it can penetrate the soil with its long bill in quest of worms. Some few remain with us the whole year, and breed in the extensive wet moors and mountainous bogs. The nest is made of the materials around it, as coarse grass, or heath, lined with feathers, and placed in a dry spot, contiguous to a pool, or swamp, and not unfrequently at the foot of an elm, alder, or willow, and generally inaccessible to cattle. The eggs, which are usually four or five, are whitish, spotted with cinereous and brown, and, like those of the lapwing, much pointed, and invariably ranged with their small ends inwards. The young run off soon after they are freed from the shell; but they are attended by the parent birds until their bills have acquired a sufficient firmness to enable them to provide for themselves. During the breeding season, the snipe changes its note entirely; and the male will keep on wing for an hour together, mounting like a lark, uttering a shrill piping noise, and then descending with great velocity, making a bleating sound like that of an old goat, the two notes being alternately repeated round the spot possessed by the female, especially when she is sitting on her nest. When undisturbed in its retreats, this bird walks leisurely with head erect, and moving the tail at short intervals. But it is not often observed in this state of tranquillity, being extremely watchful, and perceiving the sportsman or his dog at a great distance, and either concealing itself among the variegated withered herbage, so similar in appearance to its own plumage, that it is almost impossible to discover it, or, as happens more frequently, springing and taking flight beyond the reach of the gun. When first disturbed, and forced to rise, it utters a sort of feeble whistle, and generally flies against the wind, turning nimbly in a zig-zag direction, and sometimes soaring so high as to be lost in the clouds, when its cry is, nevertheless, occasionally audible. Though not easily shot, some sportsmen have the art of drawing it within range of their fowling-piece, by imitating its cry, whilst others are contented to catch it in the night with snares. It is much esteemed for the table, but seldom acquires its full plumpness and flavour till after the first frosts. However fat, it seldom disagrees even with weak stomachs.

Gallinula.

S. gallinula, Lin. &c. *Jack Snipe, Judcock*, or *Gid*. The tail composed of twelve feathers; a broad, longitudinal, black band, spotted with rufous, running from the front to the nape. It is less numerous than the preceding, which it resembles in aspect and manners, and with which it sometimes associates: but it is of smaller dimensions, being only eight inches and a half in length, and weighing only two ounces. It will lie among rushes, or other thick coverts, till in danger of being trampled on; and when roused seldom flies far. It comes to us later than the common snipe, and is not known to breed in this country. It is in equal request as the former for the table, and is dressed in the same manner as it and the woodcock.

RALLUS, Lin. &c. RAIL.

Rallus.

Bill longer than the head, slender, slightly arched, or straight, compressed at the base, cylindrical at the tip, upper mandible channelled; nostrils lateral, longitudinal, cleft in the furrow, half-closed by a membrane; legs long and stout, with a small naked space above the knees, the three anterior toes divided, the posterior articulated to the tarsus; wings of moderate dimensions, and rounded.

The body of these birds is compressed, and much loaded with fat: they run more than they fly; and they frequently elude their enemies by swimming over waters of inconsiderable breadth. Their chief residence is in the immediate neighbourhood of fresh waters, overgrown with herbage and shrubs; and their food principally consists of worms, insects that have no wing-cases, slugs, vegetables, and seeds. They are observed to regulate their migrations so as to avoid countries in which the soil is either bound up in frost, or parched with long and intense heat. They walk erect, run with great rapidity, conceal themselves in the herbage during the day, and come forth to feed in the morning and evening. Although habituated to the same description of soil, they do not live in flocks, but separately. They sometimes perch on the low branches of shrubs or bushes, but never on those of trees, unless pursued by some carnivorous quadruped. During flight, their legs hang down.

Aquaticus.

R. aquaticus, Lin. &c. *Water Rail, Brook Ouzel, Bill-cock, Oar-cock, Skiddy-cock, Velvet-runner*, &c. Wings grey, spotted with brown; flanks spotted with white; bill orange beneath. Length from nine to ten inches; extent of wing from fourteen to sixteen inches, and weight about four ounces. The bastard wing is armed with a spine, about an eighth of an inch in length. Inhabits watery places in Europe and Asia; and, though reputed migratory, certainly breeds with us. Perhaps it is partially migratory in most countries. The nest is made of sedges and coarse grass, among the thickest aquatic plants, or in willow beds; and, consequently, is not often found. It contains from six to ten eggs, which are either of a smooth spotless white, or yellowish and marked with brown-red spots, their colour probably varying at different stages of incubation. They are rather larger than those of a blackbird, and of a short oval form, with both ends nearly alike. By many this bird is erroneously believed to be the land rail, metamorphosed in autumn, whereas the latter leaves us at that season, and the difference of the bills

alone constitutes an essential distinction. The water rail is very shy and wily, secreting itself among the rankest grass, on the margins of pools and rivulets. It runs nimbly, and, even when pursued by dogs, seldom takes wing, until its rapid and complicated evolutions among the reeds have failed to insure its protection. It flies slowly, with its legs hanging down, and generally alights at no great distance from the spot where it first arose. When running, it flirts up its tail and exposes the white of the under tail-coverts. It wades in the water, swims, and occasionally dives, or runs along the broad leaves of the water lily. Though killed for the table in France, &c. its flesh has a muddy flavour.

GALLINULA, Lath. Tem. RALLUS, Lin. CRAKE.

Gallinula.

Bill shorter than the head, compressed, conical, deeper than broad at the base; the ridge advancing on the forehead, and, in some species, dilated into a naked plate; tips of both mandibles compressed, and of equal length, the upper slightly curved, the nasal foss very wide, the lower mandible forming an angle; nostrils lateral in the middle of the bill, longitudinally cleft, half closed by a membrane, which covers the nasal foss; legs long, naked above the knee; fore-toes long, divided, and furnished with a very narrow edging; wings of moderate dimensions.

Crex.

G. crex, Lath. *Rallus crex*, Lin. &c. *Land Rail, Corn-Crake, Crake, Crake Gallinule, Daker-Hen*, &c. Grey above, rufescent white beneath, wings reddish-rusty; bill and legs brown-ash; feathers of the body reddish-brown, the upper ones blackish in the middle; chin very pale; irides hazel. About nine inches and a half long, weight from six to eight ounces, and extent of wing sixteen inches. It inhabits the sedgy tracts of Europe and Asia. From its appearance at the same time with the quails, from its frequenting the same places, and being erroneously supposed to conduct these birds, it has sometimes been termed *King of the Quails*. Its well known cry, from which its name, in most languages, has been deduced, is first heard as soon as the grass becomes long enough to shelter it, and seldom ceases till the herbage and corn are cut down; but, as the bird skulks in the thickest cover, it is not often seen, and it runs so nimbly, winding and doubling in every direction, that it is approached with difficulty. When hard pressed by a dog, it sometimes stops short, and squats down, by which means its too eager pursuer overshoots the spot and loses the trace. The land-rail seldom springs up but when driven to extremity, and it generally flies with the legs hanging down, but never to a great distance. As soon as it alights it runs off, and before the fowler has reached the spot, it is already a considerable way from him. It will sometimes alight on a hedge, and perch, sitting motionless, until the sportsman, who fancies it to be on the ground, almost touches it. Besides corn and grass, it likewise haunts the furze or broom of commons and heaths. It is a migrative species, appearing with us about the latter end of April, and departing about the middle or close of September. In Ireland it is supposed to remain throughout the year. On its first appearance, and until the female begins to sit, the male is frequently heard to make a singular kind of noise, much resembling that of a comb when the finger is drawn along the teeth of it, and which is used as a decoy. The nest is loosely formed of moss or dry grass, generally in some hollow place among thick grass, and the female lays from seven to sixteen eggs, of a reddish-cinereous white, marked with rusty and ash-coloured spots and blotches. The young run about as soon as hatched. This species abounds in some years and is more rare in others. Besides insects, slugs, and small worms, it feeds on the seed of the furze, clover, and various plants.

Porzana.

G. porzana, Lath. &c. *Rallus porzana*, Gmel. *Spotted Gallinule* or *Spotted Water-Hen, Spotted Rail, Lesser Spotted Water-Rail*, Prov. *Skitty.* Olive-brown, variegated with spots and dashes of black and white above, ash-coloured, with white markings beneath ; bill greenish-yellow, but red at the base ; legs greenish-yellow ; iris brown. Length from seven to nine inches ; weight about four ounces and a half. This elegant species, which has many of the habits and manners of the preceding, inhabits Europe, the western parts of Siberia, and North America. It is migratory, and scarce in England, although Latham alleges that it breeds in Cumberland. We believe that it is not found farther north in Britain, but in Devonshire, Hampshire, Sussex, and Caernarvon, it has been repeatedly observed, and sometimes so early as the 14th of March and so late as the 23d of October. In this island it is seldom found far in the interior, and it chiefly resorts to the marshes and to the borders of small streams, well clothed with reeds and rushes, among which it conceals itself, so as to be with difficulty discovered. The nest is a singular construction, composed of rushes, matted together, in form of a boat, and fastened to one or more reeds, so as to float on the water and rise and fall with the stream. The eggs are from seven to twelve, and of a yellowish-red, marked with brown and cinereous spots and dottings. The young can swim and dive immediately on their exclusion from the egg, and quickly separate in different directions ; nor do the sexes associate except in pairing time. We may therefore conclude that they are of a shy and distrustful temper. Their flesh is fattest in autumn, when it is esteemed a great delicacy.

Chloropus.

G. chloropus, Lath. *Fulica chloropus*, Lin. &c. *Common Water-Hen, Moor-Hen, Marsh-Hen, Moor-Coot*, Prov. *Cuddy.* Front tawny, bracelets red, body sooty, mixed with olive above, cinereous beneath ; bill red, with a greenish tip ; irides red ; legs greenish. Weighs from fourteen to sixteen ounces ; length about fourteen inches ; extent of wing one foot seven inches ; size nearly that of a pigeon. This species inhabits various parts of Europe, America, and the West Indies, and is very commonly found on sedgy and slow rivers, streams, lakes, and ponds, but more rarely in marshes, concealing itself among weeds and rushes during the day, and swimming about in quest of small fish, insects, aquatic worms, &c. during the night. To get at seeds and other vegetable productions, it will also quit the water. On the surface, either of the water or the land, it flits rapidly on foot from one spot to another, but it flies heavily, and with its legs hanging down. In some countries it is migratory, and in others stationary, or, at least, only descends from the hilly regions to the plains in winter. The female constructs her nest with a large quantity of reeds and rushes, rudely interlaced, and carefully concealed among the aquatic herbage, but placed so near to the stream that the eggs are often swept away by the summer floods, and the young are frequently seized by predacious fishes. But there are two or three broods in the year, the first of which is always the most numerous, and consists of seven or eight eggs, whereas the others are less numerous in proportion to the lateness of their appearance. They

are of a white ground, irregularly spotted with reddish-brown. When the female quits her eggs in the evening in quest of food, she covers them carefully up with herbage, detached from the bottom of the nest, thus concealing them from sight, and keeping them warm. About the end of three weeks, the young are scarcely hatched when they swim after their mother, who teaches them to search for their food in the water, and every evening reconducts them to their floating cradle, where she affectionately places them under her until they have no longer occasion for her tender services, and have acquired strength and dexterity enough to take care of themselves. The flesh of the common gallinule is esteemed a dainty.

PARRA, Lin. &c. JACANA.

Parra.

Bill as long as the head, straight, slender, compressed, somewhat inflated towards the tip, the depressed base dilated in front into a naked plate or elevated crest ; mandibles unequal ; nostrils lateral, placed near the middle of the bill, oval, open, and pervious ; legs very long, slender ; nudity of the tibia very long ; toes likewise very long, slender, and entirely divided ; wings ample.

The birds of this family are natives of Asia, Africa, and South America. In most systems of ornithology their Brazilian name has been retained. In their natural habits and dispositions, the shortened form of their body, the figure of their bill, and the smallness of their head, they resemble the gallinules ; but they have spines or spurs on their wings, and most of them have pieces of membrane or caruncles on the forehead ; their toes are completely separated, and their nails are extremely long, straight, and slender. Owing to this configuration of the nails, and the spurs on the wings, they are called *Surgeons* in the common language of the European settlers. They are clamorous and quarrelsome ; haunt the marshes of hot countries ; walk on the broad and floating leaves of plants on the surface of the water with great nimbleness ; do not conceal themselves during the day, and fly more frequently and more vigorously than the gallinules, and in a straight and horizontal line. They are monogamous, nestle on the ground among the aquatic herbage, and lay four or five eggs. The young, as soon as hatched, follow their parents.

Chilensis.

P. Chilensis, Lath. *Chili Jacana*, or *Thegel.* Claws moderate, legs brown, hind head sub-crested. Size of a jay. Native of Chili, where it affects the plain country, feeding on insects and worms, and laying never more than four eggs, of a tawny hue, dotted with black, and a little larger than those of the partridge. The male and female are usually found together, and they fight boldly all who attack them. When they perceive a person searching for their nest, they at first conceal themselves in the grass, without manifesting the least uneasiness ; but the moment that they see him approach the spot, they dart out on him with great fierceness. They are silent during the day, and never call in the night time, unless they hear some one passing. On this account they are employed by the Araques, in war time, as sentinels, to discover during the night those who attempt to surprise them.

Jacana.

P. Jacana, Lath. *Chesnut Jacana.* Hind claws very long, legs greenish, bill of a deep yellow. The front membrane consists of three divisions, and two filaments depend from the sides. The throat, neck, and under parts are black, tinted with purple ; while the back, upper wing coverts, and scapulars, are of a rich ches-

Ornitho-logy.

nut hue. Size of the water-hen, and nearly ten inches long. It is a native of Brazil, Cayenne, and St. Domingo, and is extremely shy, frequenting swamps, marshes, and the borders of pools and rivulets, and generally appearing in pairs. Among its different cries, is that of recal, when the individuals have straggled from one another, and another when the bird is sprung, which is a shrill yelping sound, and heard at a distance.

P. chavaria, Az. *Faithful Jacana*, or *Chaza*. Toes long, legs tawny, hind head crested, bill dirty white; upper mandible like that of the dunghill cock; a red membrane on both sides of the base of the bill, extending to the temples, in the middle of which are the eyes. The irides are brown; the hind head is furnished with about twelve blackish feathers, three inches long, forming a pendent crest. The rest of the neck is covered with thick black down; the body is brown; the wings and tail are blackish; the wing spurs are two or three, and half an inch long. The belly is light black; the thighs are half bare, and the toes so long as to entangle one another in walking. About the size of a cock, and stands a foot and a half from the ground. Inhabits the rivers and inundated places near Carthagena, feeds on herbs, has a clear and loud voice, a slow gait, and easy flight. The natives keep one of these birds tame, to wander with the poultry, and defend them against birds of prey, which it does by means of its spurs. It is said never to desert the charge committed to its care, and to bring them regularly home in the evening. It will readily suffer itself to be handled by grown up persons, but not by children.

PORPHYRIO, Briss. Tem. FULICA, Lin. GALLINULA, Lath. SULTANA HEN.

Bill strong, hard, thick, conical, nearly as deep as long, and shorter than the head; the upper mandible dilated as it penetrates into the skull; nostrils lateral, pierced in the corneous mass of the bill, nearly round and pervious; legs long and stout, the toes very long in some species, the anterior quite divided, and edged with a very narrow membrane; wings of moderate dimensions.

This family of birds, like the gallinules, in which they have been often included, reside in or near fresh waters, haunt the extensive rice fields of the south, and prefer grain to aquatic herbs, their formidable bill being well adapted to remove the husks, and break the straws, while their legs, and very long retractile toes, are equally suited to lay hold of the stalks of the plant, and to carry the ears to their mouth. They walk with grace on the liquid element, and run with equal facility on the ground, or on the leaves of water plants.

P. hyacinthinus, Tem. *Gallinula porphyrio*, Lath. *Fulica porphyrio*, Lin. *Hyacinthine Sultana Hen, Purple Gallinule*, or *Purple Water Hen*. The upper mandible almost identified with the skull; the middle toe clawless, and longer than the tarsus; all the plumage blue, the frontal plate terminating behind the eyes. This definition is sufficiently characteristic of the beautiful species in question, which is about eighteen inches long, sixteen high, and which occurs on the marshy banks of rivers and lakes, and in the flooded fields of Calabria, Sicily, the Ionian Islands, Dalmatia, the southern provinces of Hungary, and, though rarely, in Sardinia. It feeds on grains, plants, and roots, and is partial to fruit and fish. The nest is placed in the thick herbage of flooded or swampy fields, and is composed of bits of sticks and fragments of plants. The female

lays three or four white, and almost red eggs. The Greeks and Romans tamed and fostered this interesting bird, introduced it into their palaces and temples, and allowed it a considerable range of flight. According to Sonnini, it abounds in Lower Egypt, appearing in the rice fields in May, and the following months, and breeding in the desert. Several other species have been enumerated, but not very accurately defined.

PSOPHIA, Lin. &c. AGAMI, or TRUMPETER.

Bill short, arched, conical, curved, much bent at the tip, the upper larger than the lower mandible; the nasal foss wide and extended; nostrils near the middle of the bill, wide, diagonal, covered in front, and closed behind by a naked membrane; legs long and slender, the middle and inner toe united, the outer separated, the hinder internally articulated, and on a level with those in front; wings short and concave; tail very short. There is only one known species.

P. crepitans, Lin. &c. *Golden-breasted Agami*, or *Trumpeter*. General plumage black, back grey, breast glossy green, orbits naked and red. The feathers of the head are downy, those of the lower part of the neck squamiform, of the shoulders ferruginous, lax, pendulous, and silky; scapulars long and hanging. Nearly twenty-two inches long, and about the size of the common domestic fowl. The young retain their down, or rather their first filamentous feathers, much longer than our chickens or young partridges; and their genuine plumage does not make its appearance until they have attained one-fourth part of their growth. Owing to the shortness of its wings and tail, the agami flies heavily; but it runs very nimbly like the partridge; and, when compelled to rise on wing, it halts every now and then on the ground, or on some branch of a tree. The female has two or three broods in the year, and lays at a time from ten even to sixteen eggs, of a light green cast, nearly spherical, and a little larger than those of the domestic hen. She places them in a hollow, which she scratches in the earth, at the foot of a tree, and without the interposition of any foreign materials. The agami will frequently stand on one leg, and it sleeps with its head drawn in between its shoulders.

These birds are spread over the warmer parts of South America, and are found, in pretty numerous troops, in Guiana. As they scarcely attempt to elude the sportsman's approach, a whole flock will sometimes fall victims to their familiar and confident disposition. But this apparent carelessness is not the effect of stupidity; for few birds are more attached to mankind, more docile in a domesticated state, more sensible to attentions, or the want of them, or more intellectual. The agami, in short, among birds, is, in some measure, the counterpart of the dog among quadrupeds. Like the latter, it is obedient to the voice of its master, follows or precedes him on a journey, quits him with regret, and hails his return with gladness. Sensible to caresses, it repays them with every expression of affection and gratitude; and, if any person approaches very closely to its master, it testifies its uneasiness and jealousy by darting on the legs of the intruder. It delights to have its head and neck scratched; and, when habituated to this indulgence, it is very importunate for its renewal. It recognises the friends of the family, and honours them with its civilities; but it harasses other people, without any apparent reason, and will even pursue them as foes. It attacks, with singular obstinacy, animals larger, and better armed than itself, and never

Ornitho-
logy.

quits them till it puts them to flight. In several districts of South America, it is entrusted with the charge of the poultry, and even of the sheep, which it conducts home every evening. Besides a shrill cry, like that of the turkey cock, it frequently utters a hollow noise, like that of a trumpet, conveyed, as if from the interior of the body, and which seems to be a signal for calling the stragglers together, for it is readily decoyed by the imitation of it. Its flesh, though dry and hard, is not unsavoury, and that of the young is still more palatable.

DICHOLOPHUS, Illig. Tem. LOPHERHYNCHUS, Vieil. PALAMEDEA, Lath. CARIAMA, or SCREAMER.

DICHOLO-
PHUS.

Bill longer than the head, strong, arched, cleft even under the eyes, depressed at the base, compressed at the tip, which is curved and a little hooked; nasal foss large; nostrils in the middle of the bill small, open in front, covered with a membrane; legs long and slender; toes very short and thick, the anterior united at the base by a membrane, the hinder articulated to the tarsus, and not touching the ground; claws short and strong; wings moderate and spineless.

Cristatus.

D. cristatus, Illig. *Lophorhynchus saurophagus*, Vieil. *Palamedea cristata*, Lath. *Crested Cariama*, or *Screamer*. Feathers of the body, and of the upper part of the head, white, those of the neck, throat, and breast, whitish-brown, long, with very feeble shafts, and lax vanes. Native of Brazil, and some other parts of South America, where it frequents the outskirts of dry and elevated forests, and particularly stony hills, feeding chiefly on terrestrial reptiles and insects. Azara seems to be convinced, that it never drinks or eats the seeds of plants. It is found either in pairs or in small flocks. It perceives a man at a great distance, and immediately takes to running swiftly; nor does it rise on wing, unless urged to extremity. Though rendered domestic it bears its head and neck erect, and assumes a haughty air, and a grave and measured step. When suspicious of danger, it explores attentively all around before it resolves either to remain or shift its station; and it never molests any other birds. Its cry is sharp, and not unlike that of a young turkey, but so loud that it is heard at the distance of a mile. On account of the delicacy of its flesh, the Spaniards rank it among pheasants.

GLAREOLA, Lath. &c. PRATINCOLE.

GLAREOLA.

Bill short, convex, compressed towards the tip; upper mandible curved from the half of its length, and notchless; nostrils basal, lateral, and obliquely cleft; legs feathered to the knee; tarsi long and slender, the middle toe united to the outer by a short membrane, and the inner separate; claws long and subulate; wings very long.

The pratincoles inhabit the warm and temperate regions of the old continent, affecting the banks of fresh and limpid waters, and very rarely appearing on the sea-shore. Their principal food is aquatic worms and very small insects. They run with great agility, and are capable of long and rapid flights. They moult twice in the year; but their winter garb is not very dissimilar from that of summer. The various species enumerated by Gmelin, Buffon, and Latham, are referable to the *torquata;* and only two others have been more recently discovered, the one in Southern Asia, and the other in Bengal.

G. torquata, Meyer, Tem. *G. Austriaca, Senegalensis*, and *nœvia*, Gmel. Lath. *Hirundo pratincola*, Lin. *Austrian Pratincole*. Grey-brown above, collar black, chin and throat white, breast and belly reddish-grey; tail much forked. Length nine inches, and from three to six lines. It is subject to considerable variety of plumage. Inhabits the banks of large rivers, inland seas, and lakes, in the provinces which confine on Asia, and in the southern countries of that vast continent; is common on the salt lakes and extensive marshes of Hungary; and is a stated or accidental passenger in some parts of Germany, France, Switzerland, and Italy, but is extremely rare in Holland and Great Britain. Mr. Bullock shot a specimen in Unst, the most northerly of the Shetland islands, and another, we believe, was shot near Liverpool. It darts, with wonderful rapidity, on flies and other insects that live among the reeds and rushes, and seizes them either as it runs or flies. It is restless and clamorous; and the female lays from three to seven eggs in the thickest and tallest tufts of herbage.

Ornitho-
logy.

Torquata

PALAMEDEA, Lath. Tem. KAMICHI.

Bill short, conico-convex, much curved at the point, compressed throughout its length; the upper mandible arched, the lower shorter, obtuse; nasal foss large; head small, covered with down, and armed with a slender and flexible horn; nostrils remote from the base of the bill, lateral, oval, open; legs short, thick, nakedness of the tibia very inconsiderable; toes very long, the lateral connected with the intermediate by a short membrane; claws moderate and pointed, that of the hinder toe long, and almost straight; wings ample, and spurs on the winglets.

PALA-
MEDEA.

P. cornuta, Lath. &c. *Horned Kamichi*, or *Horned Screamer*. Body blackish above, white beneath; under side of the wings reddish; bill and legs black; irides golden. The horn in front is three or four inches long, and two or three lines thick at the base, straight through its length, except at the tip, which bends a little forward; and its base is inclosed in a sheath, of a substance like the barrel of a quill. Independently, too, of this horn on the head, the kamichi is furnished with too strong triangular spurs on each winglet, which project when the wing is folded, and of which the upper is longer and thicker than the under, forming processes of the metacarpal bone, and having their base sheathed like that of the horn. The form of the body resembles that of the turkey; but is larger and more fleshy, the ordinary length being two feet four inches, and the expanse of wing more than five feet. This bird, though endowed with strength, and furnished with formidable offensive armour, courts solitude and repose, and seems to contend only with its own species, from jealousy in the pairing season. It resides in the half-flooded savannahs of Brazil, Guiana, and probably of other regions in South America. It rarely perches, and never enters the forest, but stalks across the plains with a sedate pace, and with the neck and head erect, occasionally uttering a very loud and horrible scream. The male and female, when paired, manifest a mutual and ardent attachment; and if one of them dies, or is taken away, the other shows every symptom of grief, and is apt to pine to death. Their nest is placed among bushes or sedges; and the female, in January or February, lays two eggs of the size of those of a goose. The kamichi pastures on grass, and eats the seeds of several sorts of plants, but never, it is alleged, live

Cornuta.

prey. The flesh of the old bird is tough and ill-tasted; but that of the young, though very dark, is frequently eaten by the natives of South America.

ORDER XIII.

PINNATIFIED, or FIN-FOOTED BIRDS.

PINNATI-FIED, or FIN-FOOT-ED BIRDS. Bill middle-sized and straight; upper mandible slightly curved at the tip; legs of moderate dimensions; tarsi slender or compressed; three toes before and one behind, rudiments of webs along the toes.

The birds included in this order are monogamous, but unite in large bands for their periodical voyages, which they perform by flight or swimming. They swim and dive with equal facility, and stretch their legs backwards in flight. In general, there is no very marked difference between the male and the female. Their food consists of insects, worms, fish, and their spawn, and occasionally of vegetables. Their body is covered with an abundant down; and their plumage is close and glossy.

FULICA, Briss. Temm. COOT.

FULICA. Bill middle-sized, strong, conical, straight, compressed, much deeper than broad at the base, the ridge projecting in front, and dilated into a naked plate; both mandibles of the same length, the upper slightly curved, and widened at the base, the lower forming an angle; nostrils lateral in the middle of the bill, longitudinally cleft, half closed by a membrane, and pervious; legs long, slender, naked above the knee, all the toes very long, connected at their base, and furnished along their sides with scalloped membranes; wings middle-sized. The coots are more decided residents in the water than even the gallinules, being rarely seen on land, living and travelling in the liquid element, and swimming and diving with equal facility. But they inhabit fresh waters, gulfs, and bays, and venture not into the deep and open seas. Although individuals of the same species vary considerably in dimensions, the sexes are scarcely distinguishable, and the young differ very little in appearance from the adults. Their food chiefly consists of insects and aquatic vegetables.

Atra. *F. atra*, Lin. &c. including the *aterrima*, Gmel. *Common, Black*, or *Bald Coot*; *Snyth* of the Orcadians. Front flesh-colour, and tinged with red in the breeding season; bracelets greenish-yellow; body blackish; outer edge of the wings white. There are, however, several varieties, which by some have been marked as distinct species. Length about eighteen inches, weight from twenty to thirty ounces; size that of the domestic fowl. Inhabits Europe, Asia, and America. In Great Britain it occurs at all seasons of the year, and is not supposed to migrate to other countries; but only changes its stations, removing from the pools, where the young have been reared, to the larger lakes, about which they flock together in winter. This species breeds early in spring, the female generally constructing her nest of a large quantity of coarse dry herbage, as flags and rushes, well matted together, and bound with softer and finer grasses, in a bush of rushes, surrounded by the water. By heaping the materials together, she raises the fabric sufficiently above the water to keep the eggs dry; but as this sort of structure frequently renders it too conspicuous to the buzzard, and other birds of prey, the old females, instructed by experience, place it on the banks of streams, and among

the tallest flags, where it is better concealed. As it is kept in a buoyant state, a sudden flood, attended by a gale of wind, has been known to drive it from its moorings, and to float it from one side of a large piece of water to the other, with the bird still sitting on it. The latter lays from twelve even to twenty eggs at a time, and commonly hatches twice in a season. The eggs are about the size of those of a pullet, and of a pale brownish-white, sprinkled with numerous dark spots, which run into blotches at the thicker end. In Holland, these eggs, before they are fecundated, are sold in the market, and fetch a considerable price. The incubation lasts twenty-two or twenty-three days. As soon as the young quit the shell, they plunge into the water, dive, and swim about with great ease; and, though they do not return to the nest, nor take shelter under their mother's wings, they still gather about her for some time, and skulk under the flags. They are at first covered with a sooty down, and are of a shapeless appearance; and before they have learned to shun their enemies, they are often sacrificed to the rapacity of the pike, the moor-buzzard, kite, &c. This species breeds abundantly in the Isle of Sheppey, where the inhabitants will not suffer their eggs to be taken, as the birds form a considerable article of food. The French eat them on meagre days; but, though skinned before dressing, they are not very palatable to every appetite. The common coot is a bad traveller, and waddles from one pool to another with a laboured, ill-balanced, and awkward gait. During the day it usually lies concealed among the water plants, rarely venturing abroad except in the dusk, or at night, in quest of herbage, seeds, insects, or fishes, the light possibly dazzling its imperfect vision. The sportsman and his dog can seldom force it from its retreat, as it will rather bury itself in the mud than spring up, or, if very closely pursued and compelled to rise, it moves with much fluttering and apparent difficulty.

PHALAROPUS, Briss. Tem. &c. PHALAROPE.

PHALARO-PUS. Bill long, slender, feeble, straight, depressed at the base, both mandibles channelled to the tip, the extremity of the upper bent down on the lower, and obtuse, point of the lower mandible subulate; nostrils basal, lateral, oval, prominent, surrounded by a membrane; legs middle-sized, slender, tarsi compressed, the anterior toes connected to the first articulation, and the rest of their length furnished with scalloped and serrated membranes; the hind toe without a membrane; wings middle-sized. The few species which strictly appertain to this genus are among the smallest of swimming birds, and flit over the waves with much grace and nimbleness, gliding, with apparently equal facility, over the smooth lake and the agitated ocean; but they seem to prefer brackish and salt water to fresh. On land they run heavily. They are often observed at a great distance from the shore; and they principally subsist on small insects and marine worms, which they pick up on the surface or margin of the waters. Like the sea-fowls, they have their body furnished with down, and their plumage thick-set and glossy.

Hyperbo-reus. *P. hyperboreus*, Lath. Tem. *P. Williamsii*, Haworth, *Tringa hyperborea*, Gmel. *Hyperborean*, or *Red Phalarope*, *Red-necked Phalarope*, or *Cock Coot-footed Tringa*. The young, before their first moult, correspond to *P. fuscus*, Lath. *Tringa fusca*, Gmel. and *Tringa lobata*, Brunn. Breast cinereous, sides of the neck ferruginous, bill black; band crossing the eyes blackish; bar on the wings white; rump with blackish

Ornitho-
logy.

band. Length six inches ten lines. Native of the arctic regions of Europe and America, and only migrating southward to shun the long freezing period of the winter months, returning in summer to breed and rear its young in Hudson's Bay, Greenland, Spitzbergen, Lapland, the shores of the Baltic, &c. Though not commonly observed in this island, it has been ascertained that it breeds in the Orkneys, the female making her nest on the dry ground, but near water, and laying four olivaceous eggs, mottled with dark spots and splashes. The male assists in the duties of incubation, and the pairs are usually found together catching insects in the water with their bill. Though they do not dive, they swim with the greatest ease, exhibiting the appearance of ducks in miniature. They are said to be easily tamed.

Platyrhyn-
chus.

P. platyrhynchus, Tem. *P. lobatus*, Lath. and, in its summer plumage, *P. rufus*, Bechst. *P. glacialis*, Lath. and *Tringa hyperborea*, and *T. glacialis*, Gmel. *Flat-billed, Lobated*, or *Grey Phalarope, Coot-footed Tringa, Scallop-toed Sandpiper*, &c. *Half-web*, of the Scots. Bill broad, depressed, flattened at the base, tail long, and much rounded. Size of the purre, weight one ounce, length between eight and nine inches. Native of the eastern portions of the north of Europe, particularly abundant on the shores of the great lakes and rivers of Siberia, migrating to the Caspian Sea. It is also said to frequent the northern regions of America, but rarely wanders to Britain or Germany, and has been found, though not often, on the Lake of Geneva. In stormy weather it appears in flocks on the surface of lakes ; but, when the atmosphere is serene, it is solitary in the fens. The details of its breeding seem to be unknown. On the 10th of June, in lat. 68° north, in the midst of icebergs, and at the distance of four miles from land, a troop of this species was observed by Captain Sabine, swimming on the sea.

PODICEPS, Lath. Tem. COLYMBUS, Gmel. GREBE.

PODICEPS.

Bill middle-sized, straight, hard, compressed in the form of an elongated and pointed cone, tip of the upper mandible slightly inclined ; nostrils lateral, concave, oblong, closed behind by a membrane, open in front, and pervious ; legs long, placed far backwards, tarsi much compressed, foretoes much depressed, connected at their base, and surrounded by a solitary scalloped membrane, hind toe compressed and scalloped, nails broad, and much depressed ; tail wanting ; wings short.

All the grebes have the under parts of their body, and especially the breast, covered with a very compact and glossy down, well fitted to resist the impressions of cold and wet, to which their residence in water, even in the most intense colds of winter, would otherwise habitually expose them. By employing their legs as oars, and their wings as fins, they swim rapidly, even under water, and pursue fish to a very considerable depth. They dive with great agility and promptitude, water, in short, being their appropriate element ; for on land their conformation obliges them to maintain an upright attitude, or to flounder about with great awkwardness. Hence, to avoid being driven on shore, they swim against the wind, and, when struggling out of the water, they may be easily caught with the hand, notwithstanding the violent strokes of their bill. They alike frequent the sea and the fresh waters ; and fishermen sometimes catch them in their nets even at the depth of twenty feet. They are usually very fat, and live on fish and their fry, wing-cased insects, small amphibious

animals, and various vegetable productions, as sea-weeds, and other aquatic plants. As pellets of feathers and other refuse have frequently been found in their stomach, it has been presumed that they disgorge these indigestible matters in the same manner as birds of prey. They moult in autumn ; but the young do not acquire their full plumage till the second or third year, a circumstance which has given rise to various nominal species, which are merely varieties induced by growth and age. The males and females seldom exhibit any very marked differences of appearance. The species which chiefly frequent the sea usually breed in the holes of rocks, whereas those which haunt pools and lakes construct their nest with interlaced reeds and rushes, and which, though half-immersed, and almost floating, cannot easily be carried off by the water.

Ornitho-
logy.

Cristatus.

P. cristatus, Lath. Tem. *Colymbus cristatus*, and *Colymbus urinator*, Gmel. *Crested, Greater Crested*, or *Tippet Grebe*. Prov. *Greater Crested Doucker, Cargoose, Greater Dabchick, Greater*, or *Ash-coloured Loon*, or *Gaunt*. Bill longer than the head, and reddish, but white at the tip ; distance from the anterior margin of the nostrils to the point of the bill, seventeen or eighteen lines. This is the largest of the grebes, weighing about two pounds and a half, and measuring about twenty-one inches in length, and thirty in expanse of wing. It occurs in almost every considerable lake of Europe, at least as far north as Iceland, and as far south as the Mediterranean ; and it is also found in various parts of Siberia and America. It breeds in some of the fens and lakes of England, particularly in the meres of Shropshire and Cheshire, and in the east fen of Lincolnshire. It is, however, rarely seen on the land ; and, though not uncommon, it is with difficulty shot, as it darts under water on the least appearance of danger, and seldom flies farther than the end of the lake it frequents. The female makes her nest of the dried fibres, stalks, and leaves of various water plants, as of the *nymphæa, potamogeton, hottonia*, and the roots of *menyanthes trifoliata*, and conceals it among the flags and reeds. The eggs are three or four, of the size of those of a pigeon, and, according to some, pure white, but, according to others, whitish-green, waved or soiled with dark-brown. The young are fed on small eels ; and the species make great havoc among the young whitings, and the fry of the sturgeon ; but they will subsist on shrimps and prawns when better fare is not within their reach. In some countries ladies' muffs, and other articles of dress, are made of the skin of the belly, which has a fine down of dazzling whiteness. It requires four skins to make a muff, which used to sell at four or five guineas. In February the skins lose their brightness, and in breeding time the breast is almost bare. The flesh of this, as of most of its congeners, though very fat, has a muddy and fishy flavour ; and specimens preserved in cabinets often retain a disagreeable musky odour for years.

Rubricol-
lis.

P. rubricollis, Lath. Tem. *Colymbus rubricollis*, and *subcristatus*, Gmel. *Colymbus parotis*, Sparrm. *Red-necked Grebe*. Bill of the length of the head, black and yellow at the base, occipital crest very short, no ruff, distance from the anterior margin of the nostrils to the point of the bill eleven lines. Chin, cheeks, and region of the ears cinereous, under part of the neck and breast rusty red, belly and secondary quill-feathers white. From fifteen to seventeen inches long, and weight about twenty-three ounces. Inhabits rivers, lakes, and sea-shores, but is most numerous in fresh waters. It is pretty common in some of the eastern districts of Eu-

1

Ornithology.

rope, and is often met with in Germany and Switzerland, but is rare in France, Holland, and Britain. The female nestles in the same manner as that of the preceding, and lays three or four whitish-green eggs, clouded with yellowish or brown. Col. Montagu, on dissecting a specimen, which was shot on the 3d of February, found its stomach distended with feathers and small seeds. " Being struck," says he, " with so singular an appearance, we carefully washed and dried the contents of the stomach, and by that means discovered that the feathers had been collected from its own body."

Cornutus.

P. cornutus, Lath. Tem. *P. obscurus*, and *Caspicus*, Lath. *Colymbus obscurus*, and *Caspicus*, Gmel. *Horned*, or *Sclavonian Grebe, Dusky Grebe, Black* and *White Dabchick*, &c. Bill strong, shorter than the head, compressed throughout its length, black, but red at the tip, iris double, distance from the anterior margin of the nostrils to the tip of the bill six or seven lines. Crown of the head, and the very broad and ample ruff, of a deep and glossy black, two large tufts of rufous feathers placed above and behind the eyes, and termed *horns*, the neck and breast of a bright shining rufous, under parts pure white, nape and upper parts blackish. Length from twelve to thirteen inches. By some of these characters this species is sufficiently distinguished from the following, with which it has been often confounded : but the young of the two species may be mistaken for one another, if attention be not paid to the circumstance of the double iris. The young of the present has also been ranked as a separate species, under the title of *obscurus*. The horned grebe is supposed to breed chiefly in the eastern and northern parts of Europe, and also in America, nestling among the reeds, and laying three or four white eggs, spotted, and soiled, as it were, with brown. M. Temminck is mistaken when he asserts, that it is pretty common in England, whereas, according to the testimony of Montagu, it is extremely rare in that country. It is found, along with some of the other species, on the Lake of Geneva.

Minor.

P. minor, Lath. Tem. *P. Hebridicus*, Lath. *Colymbus Hebridicus*, and *C. minor*, Gmel. *Hebridal, Little*, or *Black Chin Grebe, Small Dipper, Didapper*, &c. Bill very short, strong, compressed, neither crest nor ruff; distance from the anterior margin of the nostrils to the tip of the bill, five lines ; tarsi posteriorly furnished with long asperities. Length from nine to ten inches ; weight seven ounces. Rather rare in the northern regions, and preferably affects the lakes, rivers, pools, and marshes of the temperate and southern latitudes of Europe and North America, occurring also in the Philippine Isles, and the Delta of Egypt. It has been, moreover, observed in Tirey, one of the Hebrides. It seldom quits the water, and is a remarkable diver, feeding on fish, insects, and aquatic plants. With the latter it constructs a large nest, about a foot thick, in the midst of the waters that pervade it, and lays four or five eggs, of a greenish or rufous white, sullied with brown, which it covers, when it leaves the nest. A live specimen, which M. Gérardin kept in a tub of water, was content to live on the refuse of fruit, was cheerful and familiar, and amused the spectators with its diving feats, till, in an evil hour, having strayed beyond its precincts, and threatening to take an unceremonious leave, it was purposely killed, and embalmed in its master's cabinet.

ORDER XIV.

PALMIPED, or WEB-FOOTED BIRDS.

Bill of various forms ; legs short, placed more or less backwards, the anterior toes partially or wholly connected by webs, and, in some families, all the four toes united by one membrane, the hinder interiorly articulated to the tarsus, or, in some cases, wanting.

PALMIPED, or WEB-FOOTED BIRDS.

Most of the birds belonging to this numerous order dwell much in the water, and particularly in the sea. Their generally short and compressed toes easily cleave the water, and, by means of their webs, form, as it were, broad oars. Their plumage is thicker, closer, and better furnished with down, than that of other birds. In the diving species, the wings are placed forward, to increase their motion under water, by the use of four oars instead of two ; and, were the wings and feet more approximated, as in land birds, their mutual action would rather impede than assist progression. Their swimming is merely walking on the water ; for one foot succeeds the other, as on land : but, when moving under water, the impulse of the wings is combined with that of the feet, as may be seen when ducks are hunted by dogs in a clear pond. The gland at the rump, from which is expressed an oily matter for the lubrification of the feathers, is most considerable in this division of birds, and contributes to render their plumage impermeable to water. Some of this order both swim and dive, others only swim, or skim over the surface of the sea, but never plunge their heads under water, while a few are almost habitually resident in the ocean, ascending to the surface only to breathe, and repairing to the shore only to breed. They subsist on fish and their fry, testaceous animals, and marine insects ; and a few, as geese, swans, and some species of ducks, are also addicted to a vegetable diet. They breed in holes, among rocks, or sometimes on the stony beach. Most of them moult twice a-year ; and the female, in some instances, changes her feathers later than the male. The young, during the first year, and, in some cases, during several years, differ much in appearance from the full grown birds, but, with the exception of the duck and the goosander, the distinction of sex is not conspicuous. For the most part they are polygamous and prolific ; and many of them sleep in the day time, and feed at night. In many there is found an intermediate stomach ; and the anseres have a powerful gizzard. Their cry is generally harsh or mournful. The flesh of most of the species is eatable, and that of some is highly prized, while that of others savours of oil, or fish.

RHYNCHOPS, Lin. &c. SKIMMER.

Bill long, straight, flattened into a blade, truncated at the apex, upper mandible much shorter than the under ; nostrils lateral, marginal, remote from the base ; legs pretty long and slender, tarsus longer than the middle toe ; the fore toes united by a membrane ; tail forked, and shorter than the wings.

RHYNCHOPS.

R. nigra, Lin. &c. *Black Skimmer*, or *Cut-water*. Blackish above, white beneath, wings with a transverse white band, legs red. From eighteen to twenty inches long. Inhabits Asia and America, from New England to Buenos Ayres. This bird is ever on the wing, sweeping the surface of the water, and dipping in its bill, or, at least, the under mandible, to scoop out the

Nigra.

smaller fishes on which it feeds. In stormy weather it frequents the shores, and is contented with oysters, and other shell fish. It is sometimes found alone, sometimes in pairs, and sometimes in small groups. It has a disagreeable cry, which is expressed by *gaa*. There is also an African species, which is distinguished by its yellow bill.

Sterna, Lin. &c. Tern.

Bill as long as, or longer than, the head, almost straight, compressed, slender, sharp-edged, and pointed; mandibles of equal length, and the upper slightly sloping towards the tip; nostrils in the middle of the bill, longitudinally cleft, and pervious; legs small, naked above the knee, tarsus very short, the three anterior toes connected by a membrane, the hinder detached; tail more or less short; wings very long and pointed.

The terns are almost constantly on wing, seldom reposing on the land, or swimming on the water. In the course of their wheeling flights, they graze the surface of the sea, or pounce down abruptly in pursuit of small fish or insects. After the first or second month, the young do not differ from the adults. They moult twice a-year, namely, in autumn and spring; and they breed in numerous groups, so that the nests are often nearly in contact with one another. These birds, which have been not inaptly denominated *sea swallows*, seem to be seldom alarmed at the approach of man. In spring, they migrate to the sea shores and the interior of countries. Their cry is incessant, shrill, and disagreeably piercing; and they are particularly clamorous when they ascend aloft in fine weather, and during the breeding season.

S. Cantiaca, Gmel. &c. *S. Boysii*, Lath. *Sandwich Tern.* Bill long, black, yellowish at the tip, feet short and black, height of the tarsus one inch, tail long, much forked, shorter than the wings. Length from fifteen to eighteen inches. Inhabits most quarters of the world, but penetrates into inland situations more seldom than some of the other species. It breeds on the coasts of France, Holland, &c. In Kent, it appears about Sandwich and Romney Marsh, in the middle of April, and departs in September. It has also been ascertained to breed on the Fern Islands. The female lays two or three white, or whitish eggs, marked with large and small blackish spots, or marbled with brown and black, on the sand, among the pebbles on the beach, or on the bare rock.

S. Dougallii, Mont. Tem. *Macdougallian*, or *Roseate Tern.* Bill entirely black; legs orange-coloured; tarsus nine lines long, the middle toe, including the nail, shorter than the tarsus; tail much longer than the wings. The late Dr. Macdougal, of Glasgow, procured some individuals of this species, on the Cumbray Islands, in the Frith of Clyde, on the 24th of July, 1812.

M. de Lamotte, of Abbeville, has observed it associated with, and breeding along with, the *hirundo*, with which, or with the preceding, it had been carelessly confounded.

S. hirundo, Lin. &c. *Common*, or *Greater Tern*, or *Sea Swallow*. In some districts it is called the *Gull Teaser*, in New England, *Mackerel Gull*, at Hudson's Bay, *Black Head*, among the common people in Scotland, *Pictarnie, Picketarnie, Tarney, Kilmew*, &c. In Orkney it is commonly called *Rittoch* or *Rippoch*, and sometimes *Tarrick* or *Tarrack*, and in Wales, *Spurre* or *Skraye*. Bill middle-sized, red, with the tip black;

legs red; length of the tarsus ten lines; tail much forked, of the same length as the wings, or even shorter. The length of the full grown bird is from thirteen to fourteen inches; expanse of wing about two feet; and weight between four and five ounces. It has been observed in almost every corner of the world, and is very common even as far north as the coast of Greenland. In spring it arrives on our own shores, and sometimes roams a considerable way into the inland parts of the country, hovering about lakes and rivers. They are seen by mariners during the whole passage from Britain to Madeira; and immense flocks of them are said to nestle on the small islands adjacent to the Canaries. Thousands of them likewise breed in the uninhabited islets of Orkney and Shetland, and in the holmes of the lakes in high latitudes. They are common in the Isle of May, in the Frith of Forth, where, when split and broiled, they are reckoned a good relish, and their eggs, when boiled hard, and eaten cold, are deemed excellent. During the pairing season each female chooses a warm bed of sand, on which she deposits three eggs, of a size far superior to what we should expect from a bird of her dimensions. It is also deserving of remark that these eggs are of different colours, some grey, others brown, and some of a greenish hue. Nor is the manner in which they are hatched less singular; for it is, in a great measure, accomplished by the heat of the sun. If the weather be dry and warm, the female seldom sits by day, but regularly resumes her maternal functions about the time that the solar influence begins to decline. The young are not all protruded at the same time, but in the order in which the eggs were laid, and at the interval of a day between each of the three birds. If, however, during the period of laying, the weather should prove cold or rainy, the same consequence does not follow; for then the eggs that were first deposited have not been forwarded by the action of the sun-beams. The young terns are no sooner excluded from the shell than they leave the nest, and follow the parent birds, which supply them with small morsels of those fishes on which they themselves feed. As only one bird, however, appears the first day, it is led back in the evening to the nest, where the female sits to complete the hatching of the remaining two. There it shelters itself beneath her wings, and on the second evening finds a new companion. On the third the whole family is produced, and becomes, from that time, independent of further clutching; for the birds, by creeping close together, communicate a sufficient degree of heat to one another. During the whole period of incubation, the parents display great solicitude for the safety of their eggs and their young. Should a person then approach their nest, both parents tumble down from the air, and flutter about him, uttering, all the while, piercing screams, expressive of their fear, anxiety, or rage. These parental cares, however, soon cease, the young soon becoming capable of picking their food, when provided for them. For a few days at first they are fed by the mother's bill; but afterwards, what food the parents provide, they bestow without ever alighting on the ground. Fond of indulging in their airy excursions, they drop the food down on the young that are waiting below, and ready to receive it. Even then, however, the ties of parental affection are not severed, for the old birds, far above, still continue to watch over their offspring, and to warn them of the approach of danger by their cries, on hearing which, the young instantly squat down on the sand, where they continue motion-

Ornitho-
logy.

less, till, by the silence of their parents, their apprehensions are removed. Their colour so nearly resembles that of the sand that it would be difficult to find them were their pursuers not directed to the spot by those very cries by which the parents mean to protect them. The terns are provided with very large wings, from which circumstance the young are not soon able to fly, six weeks elapsing before their wings have attained sufficient length to accommodate them for flight; and during this period of nonage and incapacity, the parents continue to shower down plentiful supplies of food to their young, who already begin to fight and dispute for their prey, betraying that insatiable gluttony which characterizes their race. The mature birds are the most active fishers of all the aquatic tribes, instantaneously darting on their victim, which they descry from a great height in the air. Having dived and caught the booty, they as suddenly rise again to their former elevation. The fish is so completely digested in about an hour that the bird is ready for a fresh meal. By persecuting the smaller gulls, the terns sometimes oblige them to disgorge their food; but they, in turn, are occasionally treated in the same unceremonious manner by the arctic gull.

Arctica.

S. arctica, Tem. *Arctic Tern.* Bill slender, red, without black at the tip, length of the tarsus six lines; tail much forked, and sometimes rather exceeding the wings in length. Length of the bird about thirteen inches and a half. Was observed in great numbers within the arctic circle, particularly in Baffin's and Davis' Straits, in the course of the recent northern expeditions. Specimens killed in Scotland, and on the coasts of England, were found not to differ from those imported by Captain Sabine; but all differ from *Sterna hirundo* in the shortness of the tarsus, the limited extent of white on the abdomen, the deep cinereous of the neck, throat, and belly, the greater length of the tail, and the smaller dimensions of the bill and toes.

Anglica.

S. Anglica, Mont. Tem. *S. aranea*, Wils. *Gullhead or Marsh Tern.* Bill very short, thick, and quite black; legs long and black; length of the tarsus one inch and three or four lines; tail slightly forked; the wings extending three inches beyond its extremity; hinder toe straight. These particulars, with others which might be stated, sufficiently discriminate this from the Sandwich tern, with which it was long confounded. But the epithet *Anglica* is rather unfortunately selected; for the species is far from common in this island, whereas it abounds in Hungary, and on the confines of Turkey, and it exists both in North and South America. The Hungarians call it *hamsel.* It breeds on the borders of lakes and salt marshes, and feeds on spiders and various insects. The female lays three or four olivaceous eggs, spotted with brown, on a tuft of grass or herbage.

Nigra.

S. nigra, Lin. &c. *Black Tern*, Prov. *Stern, Car Swallow, Scare Crow, Cloven-footed Gull.* Bill black; legs purple brown; webs gashed to the half of their length; height of the tarsus seven or eight lines; tail slightly forked, and the wings extending an inch and a half beyond its extremity. The varieties which take place in consequence of nonage and double moulting have given rise to the nominal species of *S. fissipes* and *S. obscura*, Gmel. and Lath. and to *S. nævia*, Gmel. The general plumage is rather dusky than quite black. Length nine inches and three or four lines. Frequents the rivers, lakes, and marshes of the north, is numerous in Holland and Hungary, and not uncommon on the coast of Picardy, among the fens of Lin-

colnshire, &c.; but is supposed to haunt fresh water in preference to salt, and to feed principally on insects. About the middle of May the female prepares a nest of flags or broad grass, in the most marshy places, on a tuft just above the surface of the water, and lays almost invariably four eggs, weighing about three drachms each, of a clear olivaceous hue, mottled with numerous brown and black spots, which are confluent round the middle of the egg.

Minuta.

S. minuta, Lin. &c. *Minute*, or *Lesser Tern, Lesser Sea Swallow*, or *Hooded Tern.* Bill orange-coloured, but black at the tip, legs orange, length of the tarsus seven lines, tail much forked, forehead white. This is a pretty little species, resembling the common tern in miniature, but has the tail wholly white. It measures about eight inches in length, nineteen in spread of wing, and weighs little more than two ounces. Nothing can exceed the clear and glossy whiteness of the closely set feathers on the under parts of the body; but the upper plumage is of a plain sober lead grey. The young are seldom capable of flying till the first or second week in July, when their upper plumage is more or less of a pale yellow brown, intermingled with cinereous, and the tail is nearly even at the end. The minute tern chiefly haunts the sea shores, and more rarely lakes and rivers, living on marine insects, worms, the spawn and fry of fish, &c. It is gregarious in the breeding season; and the female lays two or three eggs, of a clear greenish, marked with large brown and cinereous spots, among the pebbles on the beach. It occurs in the northern latitudes of Europe, on the White and Caspian Seas, in Siberia and North America. It is rather scarce in the interior of France and Germany, but more common on the shores of Holland, France, and Britain. Though not generally so plentiful in England as the common species, it is in some districts more numerous, particularly on the coast of Lincolnshire. Belon adverts, with his accustomed simplicity of style, to its stunning clamour. In his time the fishermen used to float a cross of wood, in the middle of which was fastened a small fish, as a bait, with limed twigs, stuck to the four corners, and on which the bird darting was entangled by the wings.

Stolida.

S. stolida, Lath, &c. *Foolish Tern*, or *Noddy.* Body black, front whitish, eye-brows, bill, and legs black, hind-head cinereous. Size of the common tern, and, in conformation, approaching to the next family. It is found chiefly within the tropics, and reposes at night on the shore. At Cayenne, these birds are very numerous in the breeding season; and, if a cannon is fired, they rise from the Grand Constable's rock in such multitudes as to form a dark cloud. Nor are they less abundant about the Bahamas, Ascension, on the coasts of New Holland, New Guinea, Otaheite, &c. The females lay their eggs on the bare rocks; and, when the important duty of rearing their young is accomplished, the flocks disperse, and roam over the seas. They have their specific designation from their apparent stupidity, settling on the rigging of vessels, and allowing themselves to be caught with the hand, or knocked down with sticks.

LARUS, Lin. &c. GULL.

Larus.

Bill long, or middle-sized, strong, hard, compressed, sharp-edged, hooked towards the tip, lower mandible forming a salient angle; nostrils lateral, in the middle of the bill, longitudinally cleft, straight, and pervious; legs slender, naked above the knee, tarsus long, three fore-toes quite webbed, the hinder free, short, placed high on the tarsus; tail-feathers of equal length; wings long.

The birds of this genus are diffused over almost every maritime country; but they breed most freely, and with least disturbance, in the northern and southern extremities of the world. Flocks of them haunt the sea-shore, in pursuit of living or dead fish; and such is their voracity, that hardly any thing comes amiss to them; for they greedily feed on putrid carcasses of whales, and the refuse of the tide, and they will contend with one another for the most loathsome fare. In the eager indulgence of their ravenous propensities, they swallow the hook along with the bait, and, like other predacious birds, they throw up pellets of feathers, and other indigestible matters; nay, when harassed or alarmed, they bring up their food with great facility, and, if allowed to recover from their surprise, they will re-swallow the disgorged morsel. Martens, who had perhaps indistinctly observed some instances of such proceedings, oddly enough asserts, that, when chased, they drop their excrement, on which their persecutor seizes with avidity; and the tale has been industriously copied by various writers. Like most ravenous animals, they are also capable of enduring protracted abstinence. Among those which M. Baillon kept in confinement, some lived nine days without tasting a particle of food; and others had been gradually habituated to subsist on grain and the daily diet of the poultry. The young do not attain their full plumage till the second or third year, and before that period they generally consort with one another, apart from the full grown individuals. The latter moult twice in the year; but the females are distinguished from the males chiefly by being somewhat smaller. The summer livery is generally recognised by the absence of black spots, or bands, on the white of the tail, or on the bill. Gulls are frequently on wing, but also occasionally repose either on the surface of the water or on shore. They breed among the rocks, or downs, and some of the smaller species in meadows adjacent to the coast. When they flock in numbers to the land, and are clamorous along the coast, or, when at sea, they alight on ships, they are said to portend a storm. From the conformation of their lengthened wings, they are capable of easy, rapid, and extensive flight. The flesh of most of them is tough, fishy, and repulsive; yet many of the Greenlanders and North American Indians devour it with greediness. The use of these birds in the economy of nature is analogous to that of vultures on land; for they contribute to rid the sea and its shores of those animal remains, which, if allowed to accumulate, would multiply the foci of sickness, pestilence, and death. Notwithstanding the frequent occurrence of most of the tribe, the accurate extrication of their species is still a task of no easy performance; but, as M. Temminck has enjoyed excellent opportunities of examining many of them at leisure, and is preparing a monograph of the web-footed families, we shall here, as on various other occasions, take him for our principal guide.

Glaucus.   *L. glaucus*, Gmel. Sab. Tem. *Glaucous Gull*, and the genuine *Burgomaster* of the Dutch. Back, shoulders, and wing-coverts, bluish-cinereous; legs livid; length of the tarsus within a line or two of three inches; quill-feathers terminated by a large white space; shafts white. The bill is as long and stout as that of *L. marinus*, and of a beautiful yellow, with the angle of the lower mandible bright red. Orbits red, and the iris yellow. Length of a male specimen, described by Captain Sa-

bine, twenty-nine inches and a half, extent of wing sixty-three inches, and weight four pounds eight ounces. In immature plumage it is mottled throughout with uniform light brown and white. In winter, the mature bird has the head and neck mottled with brown, as is usual with all the white-headed gulls. This species is very common throughout Davis' and Baffin's Straits, and the north-eastern shores and gulfs, but is more rare in the temperate latitudes. In autumn the young are more frequently observed. Captain Sabine has shown that it is entitled to a place in British ornithology. The glaucous gull feeds on the carcasses and excrements of whales, young penguins, fish, &c.; and, according to voyagers, the female deposits her greenish eggs, of an oblong form, and marked with six or eight black spots, in the holes of rocks.

Marinus.   *L. marinus*, Gmel. Lath. &c. *Black Backed, Great Black and White*, or *Great Black Backed Gull*. *Swartz Back* in Orkney, and *Swabie* in Shetland. Shoulders slate-black; legs white; length of the tarsus nearly three inches, the folded wings stretching a very little beyond the tail; quill-feathers black towards the end, but tipt with white. This is the largest species of the tribe, weighing nearly five pounds, and measuring about thirty inches in length. It is spread over the seas of Europe, Africa, America, and the southern hemisphere. Though not very plentiful on our coasts, it is occasionally seen, in severe weather, in small flocks of eight or ten, and sometimes in pairs, but never associating with the other gulls. It lives chiefly on fish, but also attacks the eider-duck. As ravenous as the vulture, it greedily fastens on garbage and carrion, drives off the smaller gulls from any fishes that may happen to be thrown ashore, and seizes the whole prey to itself; but, if it miss its aim, it pounces on a piece of a dead horse or any offal that chance may bring within its reach. It has been known to tear and devour the largest fish on the hooks, when left dry by the ebbing tide. Its cry of *kak, kok, kak*, quickly repeated, is harsh and dissonant, and it utters another, both shrill and painful, when touched. Its great breeding stations are within the arctic circle, but it also propagates on Lundy Island, in the Bristol Channel, the female making her nest in the clefts of the highest rocks, and generally laying three or four olivaceous eggs, spotted with dark brown or purple, and reckoned eatable. Some of the young, when kept in confinement, have acquired a considerable degree of tameness, especially when copiously supplied with food, on which they fall with the greatest vehemence, devouring morsels little inferior to themselves in size, and retiring into a corner to digest it at leisure, when they will remain for a long time almost motionless, with their head buried in their plumage. The Esquimaux and Greenlanders not only eat the young, but make use of their fine down, and of the skins of the mature birds, in clothing.

Argenta-tus.   *L. argentatus*, Gmel. Tem. Sab. *L. glaucus*, Lin. *Silvery Gull*, or *Herring Gull* of Latham's Synopsis. Mantle bluish-cinereous; legs livid; length of the tarsus two inches and a half; wings very little exceeding the tail; quill-feathers black near the extremity, but tipt with white, and their shafts black. Its age and climate produce various changes on the plumage, and the species may very readily be confounded with the glaucous. Capt. Sabine informs us that the principal difference consists in size, the males of the present species averaging twenty-four inches in length, and from four feet five to four feet six inches in extent of wing. The female is rather less. In its mature summer plumage it was observed abundantly in Davis' and Baffin's Straits. On the shores of Holland, France, England, &c. it occurs throughout the year, although it is most numerous in the months of October, November, and December; and the young are accidental visitants of the Swiss lakes. These birds nestle in holes on the tops of downs, or on naked rocks, according to local circumstances, and are gregarious in the breeding season. The female lays two or three blunted eggs of a deep olivaceous, with some spots of black and cinereous, frequently light greenish or bluish, with brown and cinereous spots thinly scattered, and, more rarely, spotless. The live individuals in the Parisian menagerie were remarkable for their melancholy and ignoble air, the small quantity of food which they consumed, their extreme leanness, and their total silence, their habits having been entirely changed by depriving them of the use of their wings. After feeding they would remain immovable, like so many stuffed specimens. Although the flesh of this species is tough and unsavoury, it is sold in the Parisian market during Lent.

Fuscus. *L. fuscus,* Lin. &c. *Herring Gull.* Mantle slate-black, legs yellow, length of the tarsus two inches and one or two lines, the wings stretching about two inches beyond the extremity of the tail, the bill proportionally shorter and more slender than in the preceding. Weight about thirty-three ounces, length twenty-three inches. Inhabits Europe, Asia, and North America, proceeding southward in winter as far as the Black and Caspian seas, Jamaica, and the shores of South Carolina. It lives on fish, especially herrings, which it seizes with great boldness, and the shoals of which it accompanies in flocks. It is also observed to trample the soft sand, by moving its feet alternately in the same place, for the purpose of bringing up worms. It is a very common species on the British shores, makes its large nest of dry herbage on the ledges of rocks, and lays three eggs, of a dull whitish, spotted with black. On the *Black Craig,* in the Orkneys, its nests are placed as thick as they can stand on the shelves. Fishermen describe the herring gull as the bold attendant on their nets, from which they find it difficult to drive it away.

Eburneus. *L. eburneus,* Gmel. &c. *Ivory Gull.* Body quite white, legs black; a very small naked spot on the tibia; length of the tarsus one inch five lines; average length of the body twenty inches; weight twenty ounces. Inhabits the frozen seas of Greenland and Spitzbergen, and abounds in Baffin's Strait. It is likewise met with among the islands that lie between Asia and America, and on the west and east coasts of North America. Nothing can exceed the beauty of the snow-white plumage of the mature bird, which is supposed to be perfected at the end of the second year. Numbers of these birds usually associate with *Procellaria glacialis,* are attracted by whale blubber, and, being far from shy, are easily killed. According to Temminck, they accidentally roam to the coasts of Holland, and to Switzerland. The nest, rudely composed of dry grass, is generally placed on the ground, and contains four white eggs. The young are at first blackish, and afterwards spotted with that hue, chiefly on the back and wings, while the head and other parts are much mottled with brown.

Canus. *L. canus,* Lin. &c. *Common Gull.* Prov. *Sea Mall,* or *Mew.* Length of the tarsus two inches, wings reaching beyond the tail, shafts of the two outer quill-feathers black, bill comparatively small. Although this is the most common of all the British gulls, the different stages of its plumage have but lately been ascer-

tained with accuracy. Size of a pigeon, weighing about a pound, and measuring from sixteen to seventeen inches in length, and three feet five inches in expanse of wing. Inhabits Europe and America, lives on fishes, vermes, insects, and their larvæ, &c.; breeds among the rocks or stones on the sea-shore, and lays two eggs nearly the size of those of the common hen, but of an olive brown, marked with dark reddish blotches. At the mouths of large rivers, common gulls are seen in numbers picking up the animal substances which are cast on shore, or that come floating down with the ebbing tide. For this kind of food they watch with a quick eye; and such of them as are near the breakers, will mount on the surface of the water, and run splashing to the summit of a wave to catch the object of pursuit. At particular seasons they also resort to the inland parts of the country to feed on worms, &c. In winter, in particular, they are sometimes observed at a considerable distance from the shore; and in severe weather they will consort with rooks, and follow the plough for the sake of the larvæ of the chafer. When they retire from the sea, on the Norwegian coast, and take refuge behind houses, the inhabitants pretty confidently anticipate a storm. Baillon asserts, from his own observation, that they are tamed with much more difficulty than some of the other species, whereas we have been assured, on the most respectable testimony, that they are very tractable, and may be easily kept in a garden for the purpose of clearing it of snails, and almost every kind of insect, which they do very completely. Those which the gentleman to whom we allude had occasion to see thus circumstanced, paid a short visit to the sea every day, and regularly returned to their station. These apparently conflicting statements may not be irreconcilable; for, among gulls, as among other animals, individuals may manifest considerable diversity of character and dispositions, and even similar characters and dispositions may be differently influenced by different modes of treatment. Col. Montagu seems to have kept birds of this species alive without difficulty; and he observes, that, in default of fish or worms, they will, when pressed with hunger, pick up grain; but one of them will also contrive to stow within its body an eel of a foot in length. They very readily disgorge on the least alarm, and promptly re-swallow the ejected morsels when the fright is over. Some persons who live near the sea commonly eat this as they do other species of gulls, which they describe as being good for food, when they have undergone some sweetening process before cooking, such as being buried for a day in fresh mould, or washed with vinegar.

Tridactylus. *L. tridactylus,* and *L. rissa,* Gmel. &c. *Tarrock,* or *Kittiwake Gull,* Prov. *Annette,* or *Kishifaik.* Length of the tarsus one inch four lines, a clawless tubercle in place of a hind-toe. Size of a pigeon; weight fourteen ounces; length from fourteen to fifteen inches, and extent of wing from thirty-eight to forty inches. Inhabits Europe, Asia, and America, particularly the northern Atlantic, from the British Isles to the highest latitudes that have been visited. Though rare on the south coast of England, it is found on the Fern Islands, where it breeds, as also on the cliffs about Flamborough Head, the Bass, Isle of May, the rocks near Slains Castle, &c. The tarrocks leave the shores in autumn, and spread themselves over the Northern Ocean, making their chief resting places, it is alleged, on the floating islands of ice. In the spring they retire to the rocky crags. In the Faroe Isles they arrive in January, and frequent the steep cliffs, where they construct their nests of straw, sea-ware, earth, and clay, and crowd them close together. When these nests are visited by the Skua gull, the whole flock may be seen on wing, uttering loud screams, and making the air resound with their clamour. In the month of June the female lays two or three eggs, of a dingy green, or olivaceous white, marked with a great many small darker, and some less conspicuous cinereous spots. In the Orkneys they sometimes cover entire tracts of rock, so as to make them appear white at a distance. The shooting of the young, when they issue unfledged from the nest, and rest on the cliffs, is reckoned excellent sport, and the game is reputed a whet to the appetite, although an epicure, who visited the Isle of May purposely to ascertain the fact, declared, after dispatching a dozen of them, that he did not feel more disposed for dinner than usual. Even the old birds are much relished by the Greenlanders, who also make clothing of the skins. One of this species that was kept and tamed recognised its master's voice at a distance, and answered him with its hoarse piping note. It had a voracious appetite, and, though plentifully fed on bread, would rob the poultry of their share.

Sabini.

L. Sabini, Sab. *Sabinian Gull.* The thigh feathered to within three eighths of an inch of the knee; length of the tarsus one inch and a half, the hinder toe small, and placed high. Individuals were met with by Captain Sabine, and killed, on the 29th of July, 1818, on a group of three low rocky islands on the west coast of Greenland, twenty miles distant from the mainland. They were associated in considerable numbers with the common terns, the nests of both birds being intermingled. But they were not seen again during Captain Ross's voyage through Davis' and Baffin's Straits. The Esquimaux, who had accompanied the expedition as interpreter, and who possessed some knowledge of the native birds of South Greenland, had never observed them before. They flew with impetuosity towards persons approaching their nests and young; and, when one bird of a pair was killed, its mate, though frequently fired at, continued on wing close to the spot where it lay. They get their food on the sea-beach, standing near the water's edge, and picking up the marine insects that are cast on shore. This species lays two eggs on the bare ground, and hatches them the last week of July. They are an inch and a half in length, not much pointed, and of an olive cast, much blotched with brown.

Ridibun-
dus.

L. ridibundus, Gmel. Lath. who include under this designation only the bird in its summer plumage: in its winter attire, it is *L. cinerarius*, Gmel.: the young, before moulting, is the *Sterna obscura*, Lath. and after moulting, in the winter-season, *L. erythropus*, of the same author. *Laughing, Black-headed,* or *Pewit Gull.* In Shetland *Black-head,* in Orkney *Hooded Crow,* and in some other places, *Sea Crow, Mire Crow,* or *Pick Mire.* Mantle clear cinereous, a large white space on the middle of the primary quills, length of the tarsus one inch and eight or nine lines. It measures from fourteen to fifteen inches in length, and inhabits Europe, America, and the Bahama Islands, haunting the sea shore chiefly in winter, and salt lakes, rivers, and marshes, during the rest of the year. It continues to breed in the same places in Shropshire that are mentioned by Plott, and at Planisburne in Northumberland, where they are reckoned of great use in clearing the surrounding lands of noxious insects, worms, and slugs. We learn, in fact, from Gérardin, that the young may be tamed without much difficulty, and kept in a garden,

to check the multiplication of snails, &c.; and that it should be fed, during the winter months, with bread soaked in water or milk. In some of the fens of Lincolnshire they are plentiful in the breeding season, inhabiting the most swampy parts, along with snipes, red-shanks, and ruffs, whose nests are intermingled among the high tufts of bog grass. The gulls trample down the grass on the tops of the tumps, and they form a flooring for their eggs, which are usually three in number, and generally of a deep olivaceous, mottled with brown and dusky blotches; but they are liable to vary. On these the females sit insulated about a foot or more above the surface of the water or swamp. Though thus seen at a considerable distance, they can equally observe the approach of an enemy, and are not easily shot. The young, in former times, were served up at the tables of the great at their feasts of ceremony.

Capistra-
tus.

L. capistratus, Tem. *Brown Masked Gull.* A clear brown mask which terminates at the occiput; length of the tarsus one inch and a half; outer quill-feathers with white shafts. Length thirteen inches four lines. Frequents the coasts of England, Scotland, and the Orkneys, and has been traced to Davis' and Baffin's Straits. The eggs are somewhat smaller than those of the preceding, and of a greenish-cinereous colour, with darker spots.

Minutus.

L. minutus, Gmel. Lath. *Little* or *Pigmy Gull.* Length of the tarsus eleven lines; shafts of the primary quills brown; the wing-feathers tipt with pure white; the legs, when extended, reaching only to three-fourths of the length of the tail; hind toe very small, and furnished with an inconspicuous claw. Length ten inches two lines, consequently the smallest known species of the tribe, being about the size of a thrush. Haunts the rivers, lakes, and seas of the eastern districts of Europe, and also the southern parts of Siberia. It is an accidental passenger in Holland and Germany, and has rarely been observed in Switzerland. It abounds on the shores of the Caspian Sea, and is said to breed on the banks of the Wolga.

LESTRIS, Ill. Tem. STERCORARIUS, Briss. LARUS, Lin. &c. JAGER.

LESTRIS.

Bill middle-sized, hard, strong, cylindrical, sharp-edged, compressed, and hooked at the tip; upper mandible covered with a cere, the lower forming a salient angle; nostrils near the apex of the bill, diagonal, straight, closed behind; legs slender, naked above the knees; tarsi long, the three anterior toes completely webbed, the hind one nearly obliterated, and on a level with those before; claws large and much hooked; tail slightly rounded, with the two middle feathers elongated; wings of moderate size. The birds which compose this genus have been usually classed with the gulls, but they are much more bold and intrepid, persecuting the latter, and, compelling them to disgorge their food, catch it with great dexterity as it falls in the air. They likewise fasten on the carcasses of whales, which they lacerate and devour piece-meal, and have, moreover, recourse to shell-fish. Their principal abode is in the northern regions; and they may be distinguished, at a considerable distance, by their jerking and leaping mode of flight. There is no very marked or obvious distinction between the sexes, but age imprints on their plumage very different shades of colouring, of which bistre-brown and white are the prevailing. The young are very unlike the full grown individuals; but we may remark, once for all, that

Ornithology.

those of the first year may be easily discriminated by the slight elongation of the middle tail-feathers, by the rufous listing, and some irregular spots that terminate the feathers of the upper parts, and by the base of the toes and webs, which is always more or less white. In the mature state of the plumage the under parts are either totally or partially of a pure white.

Cataractes. *L. cataractes*, Tem. *Larus cataractes*, Lin. Lath. *Brown Jager, Brown*, or *Skua Gull*, or *Port Egmont Hen*, Prov. *Sea-Eagle*, or *Bonxie*. Willoughby is mistaken when he calls it the *Cornish Gannet*. Shape and dimensions of the bill similar to those of the same part in the herring gull, the projecting tail feathers broad to the end, inconspicuous asperities on the hinder part of the tarsus, which is about two inches and a half in length. Length twenty or twenty-one inches. Inhabits Europe, Asia, and America, and is met with by navigators in the high latitudes of both hemispheres, where it is much more common than in the warm and temperate parts of the globe. It occurs plentifully in Norway, Iceland, and the Faroe islands, and is met with in Shetland, but not in Orkney. When observed out at sea, it is reckoned a stupid and inactive bird, because it allows a boat to approach near it, without being apparently disturbed. When flying, the roots of the quills appear like a white spot, and the tail is spread out in the form of a fan. It is very fierce, either in pursuit of prey, or in defence of its young. A great portion of its subsistence is derived from the industry of other gulls, which it obliges to disgorge, measuring its strength with the larger sorts, and even driving away the eagle from its breeding quarters. Mr. Low and Mr. Bullock, who both, though at different periods, made an excursion to the heights of Foula in Shetland, bear ample testimony to the stout resistance which these birds make to invaders. In pouncing down on shepherds and others, who defend themselves with an iron-pointed stick, the skua gull is sometimes fatally transfixed.

Parasiticus. *L. parasiticus*, Tem. *Larus parasiticus*, Lin. &c. *Parasitical Jager, Parasitical*, or *Arctic Gull*, Prov. *Scull, Dung Bird, Boatswain, Long-tailed Labbe, Feaser, Allen, Scoutiallen, Dirten-allen, Badock, Skui, Faskidar*, &c. Bill of the shape and size of that of the *Common Gull*; the two middle tail-feathers much elongated, slender, and pointed at the extremities, a few warts on the hinder part of the tarsus, which measures one inch seven lines. Length of the mature bird from eighteen to twenty-one inches, and alar extent from forty-two to forty-three inches and a half. It inhabits Europe, Asia, and America, and has been found from the 28th degree of north latitude to the icy shores of Spitzbergen, the young sometimes accidentally roaming into Holland, Germany, France, and Switzerland. During their land excursions, these birds seem to live much on worms, insects, &c. and to be partial to the *Helix janthina*, which is said to communicate a red tinge to their dung. They are remarked for their rapacity, and they pursue the lesser gulls and the terns, not for their mutings, as has been so often asserted, but to make them disgorge what they have lately eaten, which is commonly effected by a stroke on the back. The arctic gulls are known to breed in the unfrequented heaths of the Hebrides and northern isles, constructing their nest of dried grass. The eggs are generally two, but sometimes, it is alleged, three or four, about two inches in length, much pointed, and of a dirty olive green, with irregular blotches of liver brown,

most numerous at the thick end; but, like the eggs of other water birds, they are liable to vary in colour. These gulls appear in their breeding stations about the beginning of May, and retire in the end of August, when they disperse over the ocean. In defence of their nestlings they are remarkably bold and impetuous, exhibiting movements analogous to those of the lapwing, and often feigning lameness, in order to decoy unwelcome visitors to a distance.

PROCELLARIA, Lin. &c. PETREL.

Procellaria. Bill as long as, or longer than, the head, very hard, sharp-edged, depressed, and dilated at the base, the tip compressed and gibbous; both mandibles channelled, and abruptly inflected towards the extremity; nostrils prominent at the surface of the bill, united and involved in a tube, which either forms a single opening, or exhibits two distinct openings; legs middle-sized, often long, slender, and the tarsi compressed; the three front toes entirely webbed and long, and the hinder represented by a long pointed nail; wings long.

This is a pretty numerous family, but several of the species which it includes are as yet very imperfectly known. Their habits are more or less like those of seminocturnal birds, many of them pursuing their prey during the dawn, twilight, or the luminous nights of the northern latitudes, and concealing themselves during broad day in the fissures and caverns of rocks, or the forsaken burrows of rabbits, or of other animals that live under the surface of the soil. They chiefly frequent those portions of the ocean that are the abodes of cetaceous animals, and are seldom seen along the shores, or at a distance from the sea, unless driven by violent gales from their ordinary stations. On the approach of a storm, they have often no other resource than rugged cliffs, or the yard-arms of vessels at sea; and they are often seen in the wake of a ship under sail, where they find some shelter from the wind, and are ready to surprise their prey. Although in their flight they seem to graze the billows, they are seldom observed to rest or swim on the surface of the water, and most of the species are supposed to be incapable of diving. Their English designation is derived from an allusion to *Peter* walking on the water; but, when apparently stepping on that element, their wings are fully expanded. They feed on the flesh of the morse and whales, and on such mollusca, insects, and worms, as float on the surface of the ocean. They breed in the crevices of rocky cliffs, or the deserted burrows of quadrupeds, discharging a sort of oily liquid from their nostrils on those who attack them or their young, and, by squirting it in the eyes of intruders, sometimes disconcert attempts to rob their nest. The female is rather smaller than the male, but not otherwise distinguishable; and the young are not so unlike the mature birds as in the two preceding genera.

Glacialis. *P. glacialis*, Lin. &c. *Fulmar* or *Fulmar Petrel*, Prov. *Mallmock, Mallduck*, or *John Down*. Whitish, back hoary, bill and feet yellowish; nostrils composed of two tubes, lodged in a common sheath. About the size of the common gull, and from sixteen to seventeen inches long. Inhabits both the northern and southern oceans, seldom approaching the coast except to breed, or when accidentally driven to land. While Captain Ross's ships were detained by the ice from the 24th of June to the 3d of July, in latitude 71°, fulmars were passing in a continual stream to the northward, in numbers inferior only to the flights of passenger pigeons in North America; so that multitudes of them possibly breed among the rocks and ices of the extreme north, as they are known to do in Spitzbergen, Greenland, St. Kilda, &c. They appear in the friths of Orkney, and the voes of Shetland, chiefly in the winter season. They are bold, gluttonous, very fat and fetid, subsisting on live or dead fish, or whales and carcasses, or garbage of almost any description, in quest of which they will follow ships or boats for a great way. They are often seen in the track of wounded whales, on which they pounce as often as the latter rise to breathe, and tear the blubber from their back. As soon as the *crang* is set adrift, it is covered over with these voracious birds, which then utter a loud and disagreeable noise. When the carcass is yet alongside the ship, they surround it in vast numbers, and are so eagerly intent on their prey, that they suffer themselves to be caught with the hands, and may be easily knocked down by those who are on the dead animal or in the boat. They breed in large companies among the recesses of the rocks, &c. the female depositing only one large and pure white egg. Notwithstanding their oily and rancid flavour, they are salted for food by the Greenlanders, Esquimaux, and the inhabitants of Hudson's Bay, who, with the Kurile islanders, eat them raw, dried, or boiled; and they use the expressed oil both for food and for their lamps. Even the St. Kildians partake of such loathsome fare, capturing the young about the beginning of August. The oil they value as a catholicon, and preserve it with great care. Every young bird yields about an English pint of it. Above the temperature of 52° Fahrenheit it remains very pure, but under that point it becomes turbid. The fulmar, we have to add, attends the fishing vessels on the banks of Newfoundland, and feeds on the liver and offal of the cod that are thrown overboard. It is taken by means of a hook, baited with a piece of liver, and being stretched at length on a stick, and sunk under water, it is, in a very short time, reduced to a most accurate skeleton, by the *Cancer locusta*, Lin.

P. puffinus, Lin. &c. *P. cinerea*, Gmel. Lath. *Puffin* or *Cinereous Petrel*. Bill depressed at the base, channelled above, compressed and turgid at the tip; nostrils consisting of two openings under a common sheath; bill two inches long; tarsi one inch and ten lines; tail conical. Eighteen inches long. Till lately this species had been blended with the following. It inhabits almost all seas, is not unfrequent in the Mediterranean, and is met with on the southern coast of Spain. The individuals killed in Senegal, and at the Cape of Good Hope, coincide, in all respects, with those found in Provence.

P. Anglorum, Tem. *English* or *Manks Petrel*, Prov. *Manks Puffin, Skrabe, Shear-water, Lyrie, Lyre, Lyar*, &c. Bill very slender, one inch and seven or eight lines in length; tail rounded, the wings projecting a little beyond its extremity. Length of the tarsus one inch nine lines. About the size of a pigeon, thirteen inches long, and weighing sixteen or seventeen ounces. Inhabits the southern and arctic seas, occurring plentifully in St. Kilda, the Isle of Man, the Orkneys, &c. roaming in winter along the coast of England and Ireland, but is not observed on the Baltic, and rarely on the shores of Holland or France. In the Atlantic it is every where common from the Channel to the coast of America. In its flight, it often skims along for a great length of time without any perceptible motion of its

wings. In the Orkneys its breeding haunts are said to be limited to the precipitous headlands of Hoy, and to one or two similar places in the island of Eda. The female takes possession of a rabbit's burrow or other hole, and lays one white egg, blunt at both ends, and which is hatched in August. Though the flesh is rank and fishy, it is relished by some, so that considerable quantities are killed and barrelled with salt, to be afterwards boiled and eaten with potatoes. The young are particularly fat, and in great request.

P. pelagica, Lin. &c. *Stormy Petrel, Storm Finch*, Mother *Carey's Chickens*, Prov. *Mitty, Assilag, Spency, Allamotti, Sea Swallow*, &c. Tail square, extremity of the wings a very little exceeding its tip; length of the tarsus ten lines. Head, back, wings, and tail, dull black; under parts sooty; a broad transverse and pure white band on the rump; scapulars, and secondary wing-quills, tipped with white; bill and legs black; iris brown. Length five inches and a half, about the size of a swallow, and not unlike that bird in its general appearance. The sooty hues of the young are less deep. Although more common in the American than in the European seas, this species occurs on the coast of the Faroe Isles, Shetland, Orkney, the Hebrides, and occasionally on the shores of Scotland and England, but is seldom seen on land, except in the breeding season. It is capable of flying at the rate of a mile in the minute, and is usually met with at a very considerable distance from land. Although sailors allege that its appearance portends a storm, it is no infallible indication of any change of weather; and it certainly braves the most violent tempests, skimming along the hollows of the waves, or rising on their summits. By some it is alleged to dive with great facility; but as it chiefly picks its food from the surface of the water, and is not constructed like the diving tribes, the fact seems to be at least questionable. It breeds in Shetland, St. Kilda, &c. in holes of the rocks, rabbit burrows, the deserted nests of rats, &c. and lays one purely white and nearly round egg. The species seems to be liable to some epidemical disorder in October and November, when many of them are found dead, either near to, or remote from, the shore. When one of them is caught alive, and carried home, it soon becomes so tame as to allow itself to be touched, without expressing any alarm. The flesh has a very disagreeable flavour. The Faroese draw a wick through the fat body of this bird, and use it as a candle. During the breeding season the females cater for themselves and their young in the day time, and return to their hole with a plentiful supply in the evening, when they are very clamorous, and croak like frogs. In the southern and Pacific Seas, there occurs a nearly allied species, which chiefly differs from the present in being uniformly of a somewhat larger size.

P. gigantea, Lath. &c. *Giant*, or *Osprey Petrel*, *Break-bones*. Brownish, spotted with white above, white beneath. Shoulders, wings, and tail, brown; bill and legs yellow; a naked, wrinkled, yellow membrane at the corners of the mouth. Larger than a goose; length forty inches; extent of the wings seven feet. Common in the high southern latitudes, and sometimes, though more rarely, found in the northern seas. It often sails with the wings expanded, and close to the surface of the water, yet without appearing to move them. On the beach, at Christmas Harbour, Kerguelin's Land, &c. they were so tame that they suffered themselves to be knocked on the head with a stick. Many

Ornitho-
logy.

of the sailors confound them with the albatross; but others call them *Mother Cary's Geese.* They are reckoned no unpalatable food.

DIOMEDEA, Lin. &c. ALBATROSS.

DIOME-
DEA.

Bill very long, very stout, sharp-edged, compressed, straight, suddenly curved, uppermost mandible channelled on the sides, and much hooked, the undermost smooth and truncated at the extremity; nostrils lateral, remote from the base, tubular, covered on the sides, and open in front; legs short, with only three very long toes, quite webbed; wings very long and very narrow, with the primary quills short, and the secondary longer.

Exulans.

D. exulans, Lin. &c. *Wandering Albatross,* or *Man of War Bird, Cape Sheep* of mariners. Mantle grey-brown, with black hatchings on the back and wings, and all the under parts of the body white; bill yellowish; feet reddish-brown. But the colours of the plumage are not constant. From three and a half to four feet long; extent of wing from ten to thirteen feet; size exceeding that of a swan; and weight from twelve to twenty-eight pounds. Its mode of flight is somewhat remarkable; for one cannot perceive any motion of its wings, except at the moment when it raises itself into the air, when it also frequently makes several strokes against the water with its webbed feet. This impulse being once given, it seems to have no longer occasion to flap its wings, but holds them very widely expanded whilst it glides along, balancing its body alternately from right to left, and skimming rapidly over the surface of the sea in quest of food. It is extremely voracious, preying on salmon that are found in shoals in the mouths of rivers, on the flying fish when forced out of the water by the Coryphæna, and on other fishes, which it swallows whole, and in such quantities, as to be occasionally prevented by their weight from rising. It likewise feeds on mollusca, and is itself attacked by the sea eagle, skua gull, and other birds of prey, its courage being very disproportionate to its dimensions. When encumbered with an overloaded stomach, these birds, on the approach of a boat, or other alarm, disgorge the yet undigested morsels, that they may more easily fly off. But they seldom soar aloft, except in stormy weather; and they may often be seen at a great distance from land, reposing or sleeping on the water, or alighting on the rigging of ships. Their cry has been compared to that of the pelican; and they sometimes utter a noise like the braying of an ass. Although they are met with in most seas, they chiefly occur between the tropics, at the Cape of Good Hope, and among the icy islands of the South Sea. Towards the end of June they likewise migrate in thousands to the coasts of Kamtschatka, the Sea of Ochotsk, the Kurile archipelago, and Bheering's Island, arriving in a state of extreme leanness, but soon acquiring plumpness by their abundant captures of fish at the mouths of rivers. They abandon these latitudes about the end of July or the beginning of August. On the coast of South America, they construct, in September, rude and round nests of earth or mud, on the ground, and from one to three feet high; whereas, in the Island of Tristan da Cunha, according to Captain Carmichael, they merely choose a dry spot of ground, and give it a slight concavity, to prevent the egg from rolling out of its place. The egg is white, very large, and of a peculiar shape, being very long in proportion to its diameter, and equally thick, or nearly so, at both ends. Although eatable, its white portion

is said not to coagulate by boiling. The Kamtschadales catch these birds with rude hooks, baited with fish, chiefly for the sake of the bones of the wings, which they convert to various domestic uses. In the high latitudes, mariners who have been long deprived of the comfort of fresh provisions, sometimes contrive to eat the birds themselves with relish, by previously skinning them, then steeping them for twenty-four hours in salt water, boiling them, and serving them up with some pungent sauce. A piece of sheep's skin, put on a large hook, will often suffice as a line. When taken, they toss themselves about with great violence, and endeavour to assail their captors with their bill.

D. fuliginosa, Lath. &c. *Sooty Albatross,* or *Quaker Bird.* General plumage brown; head, bill, tail, quill feathers, and claws, sooty brown; area of the eyes white. Inhabits the Southern Ocean, and chiefly within the Antarctic Circle. In November and December the sooty albatrosses are gregarious, building their nests close to one another.

Fuliginosa.

ANAS, Lin. &c.

ANAS.

Bill middle-sized, robust, straight, more or less depressed; invested with a thin skin; deeper than broad at the base, which is either furnished with a fleshy tubercle, or quite smooth, always depressed towards the tip, which is obtuse, and furnished with a nail; the edges of both mandibles divided into conical or flat lamellated teeth; nostrils almost at the surface of the bill, at some distance from the base, half closed by the flat membrane that covers the nasal foss; legs short, feathered to the knee, and placed near the abdomen; the three fore toes webbed, the hinder detached, and either destitute of a web, or having the rudiments of one; wings of moderate dimensions.

The birds which compose this numerous family are partial to an aquatic residence, swimming with ease and gracefulness, feeding on fish, testacea, insects, vegetables, and grains; some making use of their long necks to catch, with their submersed bill, the aliment most suited to their constitution, and others diving, and remaining a considerable time under water, a practice to which most of them have recourse when closely pursued. Several of the species are found on fresh, and others on salt water, or on the sea-shore. Their gait is awkward and hobbling; and some of the species drag themselves along the ground with difficulty, and seldom quit the liquid element for which they were destined. Most of them moult twice a-year, namely, in June and in November, the male only changing the colour of his plumage, assuming in June a part of that more appropriate to the female, and in November his more gay bridal attire, which he retains till hatching time. The females moult later than the males, and apparently only once a-year, while the young males, before their first moulting, greatly resemble the mature females. When journeying in Lapland, in 1732, Linné, to his utter astonishment, observed the river Calix quite covered with birds of this genus for eight days successively, migrating to the sea in pursuit of a warmer latitude. Their numbers, he tells us, exceeded those of the army of Xerxes. The larvæ of the common gnat, an insect which swarms in countless myriads in the moist and woody districts, during the short summer that is allotted to these northern regions, supply whole legions of web-footed fowls with a favourite food. Most of the tribe which we are about to illustrate, furnish wholesome and savoury aliment to mankind; and, with this view, a considerable number of the species are reduced to a state of domestication. They are conveniently distributed into *geese, swans,* and *ducks,* properly so called.

A. *Geese.*

Geese.

Bill shorter than the head, and somewhat conical; serratures of the edges conical. They reside in meadows and marshes, swim little, and never dive. They fly in wedge-shaped companies. There is no external difference between the sexes.

Hyperborea.

A. hyperborea, Gmel. &c. *Anser hyperboreus,* Pallas, Vieill. and including *A. cærulescens,* Gmel. and Lath. which is the young bird, before the fourth year; *Snow Goose, Blue-winged Goose,* Prov. *Bull-creek.* Forehead much elevated, lateral portion of the bill cut on each side by longitudinal channels and serratures. Size of the common goose, length two feet eight inches, extent of wing three feet and a half, and weight between five and six pounds. So variable are the young in their plumage, that it is difficult to meet with two that exactly coincide.

Great numbers of this species occur about Hudson's Bay, visit Severn River in May, and stay a fortnight, but go farther north to breed. They return to Severn Fort about the beginning of September, and remain till the middle of October, when they depart for the south, and are observed in immense flocks attended by their young. At this time many thousands of them are killed by the inhabitants, who pluck and eviscerate them, and put them into holes of the earth, where they are preserved quite sweet, by frost, throughout the severe season. These birds seem also to occupy the west side of America and Kamtschatka. In the summer months they are plentiful on the arctic coast of Siberia; but never migrate beyond 130° of longitude. They are supposed to pass the winter in more moderate climes, as they have been seen flying over Silesia, possibly on their passage to some other country, as it does not appear that they continue there. Those of America, in like manner, winter in Carolina. The Siberians decoy them by a person covered with a white skin, and crawling on all-fours, whom they are stupid enough, it is said, to mistake for their leader, and whom they follow, when driven by men in their rear, until he entangles them in nets, or leads them into a sort of pond prepared for the purpose.

Anser.

A. anser, Lin. &c. *Goose, Grey Lag Goose,* or *Wild Goose.* The folded wings do not reach to the extremity of the tail, and the bill is robust and thick, and of an uniform colour. Inhabits the eastern and central parts of Europe.

Flocks of this species, consisting of from fifty to a hundred individuals, are often seen flying at very great heights, and seldom resting by day; and their cry may be frequently heard when they are too elevated to be visible; but they seldom exert their voice when they alight in their journeys. On the ground they always arrange themselves in a line; and they seem to descend rather for rest than refreshment; for, after having continued in this manner for an hour or two, one of them, with a long loud note, sounds a kind of signal, to which the rest always punctually attend, and, rising in a group, they prosecute their way with alacrity. Their flight is conducted with great regularity, for they always proceed, either in a line a-breast, or in two lines, joining in an angle at the middle. In this order they generally take the lead by turns, the foremost falling back in the rear, when tired with cleaving the air, and

the next in succession occupying its place. In these lofty flights they are seldom within reach of a fowling-piece; and, even when they move in a lower track, they file so equally, that one discharge rarely kills more than a single bird. Their principal food consists of aquatic vegetables, and most sorts of grain. They breed in heaths, or in plains and marshes, as formerly in the fenny districts of England, and in various other countries, the female nestling on tufts of cut rushes, or dry herbage, and usually laying from five to eight, and very rarely so many as twelve or fourteen dirty greenish eggs, which are hatched in twenty-eight or thirty days. In some years the young ones are taken in considerable numbers, and are then very easily tamed. The old birds, however, are extremely shy, and, possessing the senses of hearing and vision in a pre-eminent degree, frequently contrive to elude the approaches of their pursuers. During the day, they often take up their abode among fields of young corn, which they seriously injure, and in the evening they resort to some lake or river, and thus escape the wily researches of the fox, which has been sometimes known to visit them in broad day. Some instances occur of tame geese uniting with bands of the wild sort, to the great disappointment of the owners. The flesh of a middle-aged wild goose, in the spring of the year, when the bird is in full feather, is very tender and finely flavoured, and differs considerably, both in taste and colour, from that of the tame variety. This species in its unconstrained state, is widely and numerously diffused over various quarters of the northern world, whence some flocks of them migrate a great way southward in winter. According to Latham, they are general inhabitants of the globe, being met with from Lapland to the Cape of Good Hope, in Arabia, Persia, China, and Japan, on the American coasts, from Hudson's Bay to South Carolina, as also in the Straits of Magellan, the Falkland Islands, Terra del Fuego, and New Holland.

The domestic breed of this species, owing to regular and copious feeding, and habits of comparative listlessness, acquire more ample dimensions and greater plumpness than those which retain their freedom and roam at large. Artificial, and often very cruel methods, are also resorted to, in order to fatten them for the table, and to enlarge their livers, so that, in the course of three weeks or a month, one of these crammed and tortured victims to sensuality, when on the point of dying of suffocation, will weigh eighteen or twenty pounds. In Upper Languedoc, there is a race of tame geese, much larger than ordinary, and characterized by a mass of fat which depends from their belly, so as almost to touch the ground when they walk. A certain family, near Highworth, in Wiltshire, were, a good many years ago, in possession of a peculiar breed of geese, which they nursed and fattened in such a manner, that they attained to a very extraordinary, and almost incredible size, insomuch that some of them would weigh from twenty even to thirty pounds. The owners could scarcely be induced, on any consideration, to part with an egg of this breed; and they sold the yearly produce of the flock to a few opulent families in the neighbourhood, at the rate of a shilling the pound. As an important department of the poultry establishment, the goose, we need hardly observe, is cultivated in almost every civilized quarter of the world, and, when under proper management, forms a profitable article of the farmer's produce, its quills, down, flesh, and even dung, being all turned to account.

3

In this island, these birds are nowhere kept in greater quantities than in the fens of Lincolnshire, several persons there having as many as a thousand breeders. They are stripped once a-year for their quills, and no fewer than five times for the feathers. The first plucking for both commences about Lady-day; and the other four are between that and Michaelmas. It is alleged that, in general, the birds do not materially suffer from these operations, except cold weather happens to set in, when numbers of them die. The old ones submit quietly to be plucked, but the young ones are very noisy and unruly. These geese breed, in general, only once a-year, but, if well kept, sometimes twice. During their sitting, each has a space allotted to it, in rows of wicker pens, placed one above another, and the *gozzard* (*gooseherd*) who drives them to water twice a-day, and brings them back to their habitations, is said to place every bird in its own nest. The numbers of geese that are driven from the distant counties to London for sale, are scarcely credible; for a single drove frequently consists of two or three thousand. In ancient times they appear to have been conducted much in the same manner from the interior of Gaul to Rome. Each driver is provided with a long stick, at one end of which a red rag is tied as a lash, and a hook is fixed at the other. With the former, of which the geese seem much afraid, they are excited forward, and with the latter, such as attempt to stray are caught by the neck, and kept in order. Such as are lame are put into an hospital cart, which usually follows each large drove. Their progress is at the rate of eight or ten miles a-day, reckoning from three in the morning till nine at night. Those which become fatigued are fed with oats, and the rest with barley.—However simple or awkward the goose may appear, it is by no means destitute of either sagacity or affection; and some singular instances are recorded of its attachment to animals of another class, and even to persons. The young, or *green geese*, as they are called, destined for the table, should be put into a place that is almost dark, and fed with ground malt, mixed with milk, when they will, very soon, and at very little expence, be fit to be killed. Should milk prove scarce, barley meal may be mixed, pretty thick, with water, which they may constantly have by them to eat as they choose, and in another part of the shed, some boiled oats and water, kept in a pan, to which they may resort when inclined to change their food. This variety is agreeable to them, and they thrive apace. With respect to *Michaelmas* or *stubble* geese, they should, immediately after harvest, be turned out on the wheat eddishes, where they pick up very fast; but, when taken up to be fattened, they should be fed with ground malt, mixed with water, or boiled barley and water; and thus treated, they grow fatter than would at first be imagined, and acquire a more delicate flavour than those in the London market. Old breeders may be plucked thrice a-year, and at an interval of seven weeks, without inconvenience; but young ones, before they are subjected to this operation, must have attained to the age of thirteen or fourteen weeks, otherwise they will pine, and lose their good qualities. It is scarcely necessary to add, that the particular nature of the food, and the care that is taken of the birds, materially contribute to the value of the feathers and the down. In the neighbourhood of plenty of water, they are not so subject as elsewhere to the annoyance of vermin; and they furnish feathers of a superior quality. In regard to down, there is a certain stage of maturity, which may

be easily discovered, as it is then readily detached, whereas, if removed too soon, it will not keep, and is liable to be attacked by insects and their larvæ. Again, the feathers ought never to be plucked long after the birds are dead, and, at the latest, before they are quite cold, else they will contract a bad smell and get matted.

Under proper management, and when unmolested by plucking, &c. the tame goose will live to a great age, even, it is alleged, to fourscore years, or, perhaps, a century. It is, however, seldom permitted to live out its natural life, being sold with the younger ones long before it approaches that period. The old ones are called *cagmags*, and are bought only by novices in market-making; for, from their toughness, they are utterly unfit for the table. The tame goose lays from seven to twelve eggs, and sometimes more, which the careful housewife divides equally among her brood geese, when they begin to sit. Those of her stock which lay a second time in the course of the summer, are seldom, if ever, permitted to have a second hatching; but the eggs are used for household purposes. In some countries the domestic geese require much less care and attendance than in this. Thus, among the villages of the Cossacks, on the Don, they leave their homes in March or April, as soon as the ice breaks up; and the pairs joining, take flight in a body to the remote northern lakes, where they breed, and constantly reside during the summer; but, on the beginning of winter, the parent birds, with their multiplied young progeny, all return and divide themselves, every flock alighting at the door of the respective place to which it belongs. The accuracy with which they thus return to their several homes, denotes more intellect than is generally ascribed to them. Another quality which they eminently possess, is vigilance; for nothing can stir in the night, but they are roused, and immediately commence cackling; and, on the nearer approach of apprehended danger, they set up their shriller and more clamorous cries. This sort of vociferous alarm saved Rome from being captured by the Gauls, and long associated feelings of respect and gratitude with the history of this watchful species.

A. segetum, Gmel. &c. *Bean Goose*, or *Small Wild Goose*. The folded wings extending beyond the extremity of the tail; bill long, depressed, and of a dusky orange hue. Length about two feet and a half, expanse of wing five feet seven inches, and weight from five to seven pounds. It has a considerable resemblance to the preceding, with which it has been often confounded, and for which it is frequently sold; but it is smaller, has the bill differently coloured, and the legs saffron. Inhabits the arctic regions, and migrates into our more temperate regions in autumn, leaving them again in May. In their passage they alight on green fields, and tear up the springing wheat. In their migrations they fly at a great height, in the same array as the wild geese, and cackling as they advance. They breed as far south as Lewis, the female laying ten or twelve white eggs, in heathy or marshy soil.

A. leucopsis, Tem. *Anser leucopsis*, Bechst. *Anas erythropus*, Lin. and Lath. *Bernacle Goose*, Prov. *Routherook, Claik, Claikis, Tree Goose,* &c. Temminck has properly cancelled the Linnéan epithet *erythropus*, because the legs are not red, but black or dusky. Cinereous, with black and white undulations above; neck black; face and belly white. Length between two and three feet. The female is rather smaller. This species is often confounded with the following; but it is somewhat larger, with more decided black in its plumage ; and it breeds only in the extreme north, visiting the more temperate latitudes in winter. When, therefore, it is said to be common on the western shores of Ireland, particularly in the Bay of Belfast, we are to understand that the *Brent*, and not the real *Bernacle* goose is meant, as was sometime ago ascertained by Sir William Elford. In the darker ages, the present species was seriously believed to be produced from the *Lepas anatifera*, or *Goose-bearing acorn-shell*. The feathery beard of the occupant of this shell passed for part of the young bird ; and as the shells were frequently found adhering to fragments of wood, they were fabled to grow on trees ; nor was it a mean mental effort to entertain doubts of this vegetable origin of the Bernacle goose. Even two centuries ago, some naturalists of name asserted that they were eye witnesses of the transformation ; and Butler, by a poetical license, transfers the fable to the gannet.

> " As bernacles turn solan geese,
> In the islands of the Orcades."

The bernacle, when taken, is very easily tamed.

A. bernicla, Lin. &c. *Brent* or *Broad Goose*, Prov. *Black Goose*, *Hora*, *Horra*, *Horrie*, *Quink*, or *Rood Goose*. Brown ; head, neck, and breast black ; collar white ; scapulars and wing-coverts ash. In the females and the younger birds, the plumage is not so distinctly marked ; and the white spots on the sides of the neck are often blended with dusky. Length from twenty-two to twenty-three inches. It is distinguished by its cry, which is a hoarse and hollow bark, frequently repeated. Inhabits the heaths and marshes of the northern regions of Europe, Asia, and America, migrating southward in winter, and sometimes frequenting our shores in great flocks. On the French coast, they are said to have been little known till 1740, when they appeared in such multitudes that they did great damage to the fields of green corn, and were knocked down with sticks and stones. A north or north-easterly wind, also, sometimes conveys them to the coasts of England, and in such dense bands that they are apt to starve for want of food. But they are more steadily plentiful in Ireland, where they are taken in nets placed across the rivers, especially in those which flow into the Irish Channel. They feed on aquatic plants and marine vermes, and are partial to *Polygonum viviparum* and *Empetrum nigrum*. They are capable of being tamed and reared in a poultry yard ; but they are extremely timid, and may be put to flight by birds much smaller than themselves. Their flesh is esteemed at table, especially in Roman Catholic countries, where it is allowed to be eaten during Lent.

B. *Swans.*

Nostrils pierced in the middle of the bill ; neck very long. Residents of the water, on which they swim with much ease and gracefulness.

A. cygnus, Lin. &c. *Wild*, *Whistling*, or *Hooping Swan*, Prov. *Hooper*, *Elk*, &c. Bill semi-cylindrical and black ; cere yellow ; body white ; head and nape very slightly tinted with yellowish ; iris brown ; legs and feet black. The female is somewhat smaller ; and the young are grey. Length of the mature male from four feet five, to four feet nine inches ; extent of wing six feet three inches ; and weight from fifteen to twenty-five pounds. The difference in respect of dimension, of the structure of the bill, of the singular flexures of the

trachea, and of the note, at once discriminate this from the next species, although Buffon and some others would represent them as identical.

The whistling swan inhabits Europe, Asia, and America, affecting chiefly the northern regions of the globe, and appearing in small flocks, of eight or ten, on the coasts of England, France, &c. in hard winters : but, on the approach of spring, they quit their southern stations, and again retire northward, to breed. A few, however, drop short, and perform that office by the way, halting in the Hebrides, the Shetland or Orkney islands, &c. In the two latter, and in the Faroe islands, large flocks of them annually arrive in October, and pass the winter about the numerous fresh water lakes. Early in spring, they take their departure for the peaceful arctic tracts, where they may incubate and rear their young without molestation. Great bodies of them occur on the large rivers and lakes, near Hudson's Bay, and those of Kamtschatka, Lapland, and Iceland. They are said to resort to the last mentioned island in flocks, of about a hundred at a time, in spring, and also to pour in on it from the north, in nearly the same manner, on their way south, toward the close of autumn, flying very high in the air, and in such compact array, that the bill of the one seems to touch the tail of the other. The young which are bred there, remain throughout the first year, and, in August, when they lose their feathers, and are incapable of efficient flight, the natives kill them with clubs, or shoot and hunt them down with dogs, on account of their flesh, which is much prized. Notwithstanding their size, these birds, when in full feather, are so extremely swift, that they are shot with great difficulty ; and it is frequently necessary to aim ten or twelve feet before the bill, when they are flying under a brisk gale, their rate of motion being then about a hundred miles an hour ; but, when they fly across the wind, or against it, their progress is inconsiderable. In their flight, they emit a note, which has been expressed by *whoogh, whoogh*, and which is very loud, hoarse, and shrill, but not disagreeable, when heard aloft in the air, and modulated by the breeze. The Icelanders oddly enough compare it to the sound of the violin ; and the ancients have unaccountably celebrated its tuneful harmony, which Lucian had the honesty to treat with his usual ridicule. The explanations which some modern authors have hazarded of the classical allusions to the musical strains of the swan, are more ingenious than satisfactory. We are equally at a loss to account for the poetical fiction which has peopled the waters of the Po and the Cayster with this family of birds. At the setting in of frosty weather, wild swans are said to congregate in great numbers, and, thus united, to make every effort to prevent the water from freezing, by constantly stirring and dashing it with their extended wings. The wild swan has been styled " the peaceful monarch of the lake," because, conscious of his superior strength, he fears no enemy, meeting even the eagle in fierce encounter, and driving off every troublesome visitor by the powerful stroke of his wing, at the same time that he preys on none of the feathered tribes. The physical force with which he deals his blows may have been exaggerated ; but a stroke of his wing has sometimes knocked a young man down. The food of this species consists of aquatic herbage, and the roots and seeds of water plants, of the myriads of insects which skim or float on the surface of the stream, and occasionally of the slimy inhabitants of its bosom. The female makes her nest of the withered leaves and stalks of reeds and rushes, and lays from four to six or seven thick-shelled ferruginous coloured eggs, with some white blotches about the middle, as if artificially stained, and which are hatched in six weeks. The flesh of the full-grown bird, though relished in some northern countries, is black, hard, and tough; but that of the young is said to be sufficiently palatable, and the eggs are reckoned a delicate article of food. The Icelanders, Kamtschadales, &c. dress the skins with the down on them, sew them together, and make them up into various sorts of garments. The American Indians have recourse to the same expedient for clothing themselves, and sometimes weave the down, as barbers do the cawls for wigs, and then manufacture it into ornamental dresses for the women of rank, while the larger feathers are formed into caps and plumes, to decorate the heads of their chieftains and warriors. They likewise gather the feathers and down in large quantities, and barter or sell them to the inhabitants of more civilized nations.

Olor.

A. olor, Lin. &c. *Tame* or *Mute Swan.* Bill red; fleshy tubercle at the base and edges of the mandibles black; the body white. Usual length of the male four feet and three or four inches, and extent of wing about seven feet three inches; weight about twenty-five pounds. The manners and habits of both species in the wild state are very similar.

The beauty, graceful motion, and majesty of the swan, when wafted along a piece of water, attract the admiration of every beholder, and have not passed unnoticed by the poets; but, out of the liquid element, the elegance of its form, and the placid dignity of its movements, entirely vanish. While the parent birds are busied with the care of the young brood, one should approach them with caution; for they will then fly on a stranger, and inflict on him repeated blows of their wings; yet they are sometimes dispatched by a slight stroke on the head. Multitudes of this species are found in Russia and Siberia, as well as farther south, in an unreclaimed state. They likewise occur, without any owner, on the Trent, on the inlet of the sea near Abbotsbury in Dorsetshire, and on some rivers and lakes in different parts of the British isles. Those on the Thames have been for ages protected as royal property; and it is still reckoned felony to steal their eggs. In former times, great numbers were reared for the table; but they are now reckoned by most a coarse sort of food. A fattened cygnet, however, is still accounted a great delicacy, and usually fetches upwards of a guinea in the poultry market. When rearing their young, or during frost, these birds should be allowed an extra quantity of food; and they will eat oats with great avidity. Twice a-year they are stripped of their down and quills, the latter of which are preferred even to those of the goose for writing. It is generally believed that the swan lives to a great age, although the term of three centuries, assigned to it by some writers, is doubtless much exaggerated. The female nestles among the rough herbage near the water's edge, lays from six to eight large white eggs, and sits upon them about six weeks. The young do not acquire their full plumage till the second year. If kept out of the water, and confined to a court-yard, they become dirty, dull, and spiritless. In their favourite element they regularly wash and clean their feathers every day, adjusting their whole plumage with their bill, and squirting water on their back and wings with the most assiduous attention.

C. *Ducks.*

Ducks.

Bill much depressed, broad towards the extremity;

the serratures long and flat; the hind toe detached and unwebbed, or with the rudiments of a free membrane. They are partial to a watery residence, and both swim and dive.

a. *With the hind toe without a membrane.*

Tadorna.

A. tadorna, Lin. &c. *Sheldrake,* or *Shieldrake.* Prov. *Burrow Duck, Skeel Goose, Sly Goose,* &c. Bill turning up at the tip; forehead compressed; head greenish black; body variegated with white. Length about twenty-two inches, extent of wing three feet and a half, and weight about two pounds and a half. The female is smaller, and less lively in her colours; and the young, previously to their first moult, differ considerably in appearance from the parent birds. The trachea of the male is furnished with a singular labyrinth, consisting of two roundish bladders, of a most delicate texture, and one of them larger than the other.

This species is dispersed, in greater or smaller numbers, over the warm as well as the cold countries, being met with as far north as Iceland in the spring, and Sweden and the Orkney islands in winter. Navigators have observed it on the coast of Van Diemen's Land, and abundantly at the Falkland Isles. In some districts of our shores it remains all the year, being partial to the margin of the sea, and breeding in rabbit burrows on the downs, and sometimes in crevices of the rocks, without making any nest. The female lays from ten to sixteen round and whitish eggs, which she covers with down from her own breast, scarcely inferior in fineness to that of the eider duck. During the incubation, which lasts thirty days, the male performs the part of a vigilant sentinel near the breeding stations, retiring only occasionally, when impelled by hunger, to procure subsistence. The female also leaves the nest on the same errand in the morning and evening, when the male takes her place. As soon as the young are hatched, or able to waddle along, they are conducted, and sometimes carried in the bill, by the parents to the sea during full tide, which shortens their journey, and are committed to the waters; nor are they afterwards seen out of flood-mark until they are able to fly, instinctively feeding on sand-hoppers, marine insects and worms, small testacea, the minute fry of fish, &c. If the family, in their march to the sea, happen to be interrupted by any person, the young ones squat down, and the parents fly off; but the mother drops down at a little distance from them, and counterfeits lameness, to divert the intruder's attention, trailing herself along the ground, and flapping with her wings. The male also has been known to have recourse to a similar stratagem. The sheldrakes are generally found only in pairs, which appear to be attached by the closest ties of affection. Although they preferably haunt the seashore, they occasionally stray to inland lakes, and, with a little care, they have been tamed, and reared in ponds; and there are instances of their breeding with the common duck. Their flesh has a rank flavour; but the eggs are in great request. When hatched under a hen the young become tame; but they seldom breed in confinement.

Boschas.

A. boschas, Lin. &c. *Wild Duck,* or *Mallard.* Cinereous; middle tail feathers of the male recurved; bill straight; collar white. Length twenty-two, or twenty-three inches, extent of wing two feet ten inches, and weight about two pounds and a half. The female is of a more sober brown hue, as are the young males before their first moult. But there are several varieties, which we cannot stop to particularize, and those produced by domestication are not readily reducible to any intelligible catalogue. Inhabits Europe, Asia, and America, frequenting the marshes and lakes of the north, &c. and migrating southward in large bodies in autumn, when they spread themselves over the lakes and humid wastes of the more temperate latitudes. Considerable squadrons of them return northward in the spring; but many straggling pairs, as well as former colonists, remain with us throughout the year, and become permanent residents in the marshy tracts of the British islands. Large flocks visit Egypt in November after the inundation of the Nile. In the opposite direction of the globe, one of their great resorts in winter is to the Loch of Stennes, and other lakes in Orkney, and, when these happen to be frozen, they betake themselves to the shores of the islands. In these districts they may be seen in great multitudes, and, on the report of a gun, they rise like clouds. They likewise abound about the subterranean lake Crickniz, in Carniola; and they are often swallowed entire by the huge pikes which frequent that singular piece of water. On the approach of a storm, they issue from the caverns of the rocks, and fly about in the country, where they soon become a prey to the peasants. Many of them are killed with clubs at the very opening of the cavities, being dazzled by the light of day. In no part of this island do they occur in greater profusion than in Lincolnshire, where prodigious numbers are annually taken in the decoys. Thus, within the compass of ten stations in the neighbourhood of Wainfleet, 31,200 have been captured in the course of a single season.

Wild ducks are naturally very shy, fly at a considerable height in the air, and in the form of inclined lines or triangles. Before alighting on any spot, they describe several turns round it, as if to reconnoitre it, descending with precaution; and, when they swim, keeping at a distance from the shore. When most of them rest, or sleep on the water, with their head concealed under one of their wings, some of the band are always awake to watch for the common safety, and to sound the alarm on the approach of danger. Hence they are with difficulty surprised, and hence the fowler who goes in pursuit of them requires to exert all his cunning, and frequently no inconsiderable degree of toil and patience. Like other swimming birds, they rise vertically from the water, and with a loud noise, while their hissing reveals their flight in the night-time, when they are more active than during the day. They generally leave their liquid residence about half an hour before sunset, and travel and feed in the dark, those which are observed in the day-time having been for the most part roused by the sportsman, or some bird of prey. During frost they repair to the outskirts of forests to pick up acorns, of which they are very fond; or else they attack the green corn. When the stagnant waters begin to be covered with ice, they shift their quarters to flowing rivers, or springs; and they seem to brave the severest cold without inconvenience, quitting our climates when the weather begins to get warm, and covering the lakes and rivers of Lapland, Siberia, Greenland, Spitzbergen, &c. They breed only once in the year, the pairing time commencing about the end of February or the beginning of March, and lasting three weeks, during which period each couple live apart, concealed among the reeds and rushes during the greater part of the day. They are ardent in their courtships, and tenderly solicitous of the comfort and protection of their offspring. The female usually selects a thick tuft of rushes, insulated in a pool, or

lake, for her breeding station, and bends, cuts, and arranges the rushes in the form of a nest, which she lines with down plucked from her own belly. On other occasions, however, she prefers heaths, at some distance from water, a rick of straw in the fields, or even the deserted nest of a magpie, or crow, on a high tree. An instance has been recorded of a female wild duck, found at Etchingham, in Sussex, sitting on nine eggs, in an oak, at twenty-five feet from the ground, the eggs being supported by some small twigs laid crossways. The eggs frequently amount to sixteen, are very obtuse and spheroidal, with a hard and whitish shell, and the yolk verging on red. The incubation lasts thirty days; and, when the female goes to feed, she covers the eggs with some of her own down. On returning, she alights at some distance from the nest, and approaches it by winding paths, which indicates her slyness and her suspicion of being discovered, but, having resumed her seat, she is not easily induced to quit it. The male all the while keeps watch near the nest, or accompanies and protects his mate in her temporary excursions for food. All the young are hatched on the same day; and, on the following, the mother issues from the nest, and calls them to the water; or, if the nest be too high, or at a distance from water, both parents convey them, one by one, in their bill; and they are no sooner consigned to the stream than they begin to feed on insects, swimming about with the greatest ease. At night the mother collects them about the rushes, and covers them with her wings. In three months they are able to fly, and, in three more, they acquire their complete growth and plumage. The moulting of the mature birds is sometimes so sudden, that they lose all the wing-feathers in the course of a single night. The males undergo this natural process after pairing, and the females after bringing their brood from the nest. Of all the properties which the ancients attributed to the wild duck, the most genuine is the superior excellence of its flesh, which is more delicate and juicy, and of a finer flavour, than that of the domestic; and the birds, in consequence, are captured by various ingenious contrivances in almost every civilized country.

The reclaimed breeds of this species assume very various markings, but the male, or *Drake*, even in confinement, retains the curling of the tail-feathers. Habits of domestication, however, have deprived the tame duck of that sprightly shape and air which distinguish the mallard. It is also deserving of remark, that ducks pair, and are monogamous in the wild state, but become polygamous when tame. The Chinese make great use of the species, but prefer the tame to the wild. We are told that most of them in that country are hatched by artificial heat. The eggs being laid in boxes containing sand, are placed on a brick hearth, to which is communicated a proper degree of heat during the time required for hatching. The ducklings are fed with cray-fish and crabs, boiled and cut small, and afterwards mixed with boiled rice; and, in about a fortnight, they are fit to provide for themselves. The proprietors then furnish them with an old *step-mother*, who leads them where they are to find provender, being first put on board a boat, which is destined for their habitation, and from which the whole flock, amounting often to three or four hundred, go out to feed, and return at command. This method is commonly practised during the nine warmest months of the year, and especially during the rice-harvest, when the masters of the duck-boats row up and down, according to the opportunity of procuring food, which is found in plenty at the tide of ebb, as the rice plantations are overflowed at high water. It is curious to observe how these birds obey their masters; for some thousands belonging to different boats, will feed at large on the same spot; and, on a given signal, will follow their leader to their respective boats, without a single stranger being found among them. No fewer than forty thousand boats of this description are supposed to ply on the Tigris.

When confined to dry situations, ducks degenerate in strength, beauty, and flavour. They feed on various animal and vegetable substances, for which they unceasingly search with their curiously constructed bills, sifting and separating every alimentary particle from the mud. They also devour worms, spawn, water-insects, and sometimes frogs and small fishes, together with various seeds of bog and water plants. They are particularly fond of *Potentilla anserina*, or silver-weed. When ducks and geese fly backwards and forwards, when they plunge frequently in the water, or begin to send forth cries, they generally intimate the approach of rain or stormy weather. The down of ducks is considerably elastic, and is used for pillows, beds, &c. being regularly sold, for these purposes, in Normandy, where large quantities of these fowls are reared. As they are excellent vermin pickers, they may be turned into the garden one or two days a-week, through the season, so as to clear away caterpillars, slugs, snails, and other insects within their reach; but, if kept longer in than two or three days at a time, they become indolent. If there is no pond or stream in the garden, they should have a little water set down to them. It will also be proper to keep them out during heavy rains, or in continued wet weather, especially if the soil be stiff; for they patter and harden the surface, to the great injury of small crops and rising seeds.

Many people in the town and neighbourhood of Aylesbury, in Buckinghamshire, derive support from their peculiar skill in breeding and rearing ducks. For the gratification of artificial wants, they reverse the order of nature, and, by a restriction of food and other means, prevent the ducks from laying till the months of October and November. Some weeks previous to the time that they wish them to lay, the ducks are fed with stimulating provisions; and, when the eggs are ready, they are put under a hen, which is frequently obliged to continue in the nest till three successive broods are hatched. By this treatment, the poor creature is generally exhausted, and dies under her compulsory duty. When the young leave the shell, they are placed near a fire, and nursed with particular care. Thus many ducklings are sent, at Christmas, to the metropolis, where they have been known to fetch from fifteen shillings to a guinea the couple.

Strepera.

A. strepera, Lin. &c. *Gadwell*, or *Grey*, Prov. *Rodge*. Head and neck marked with brown points, on a grey ground; under part of the neck, the back, and breast, with black crescents; the scapulars and flanks, with blackish and white zig-zag lines; middle wing coverts rufous-chesnut; great coverts, rump, and under tail-coverts, deep black; bill black; iris bay; tarsi and toes orange; webs blackish. Birds of this species breed in the desert marshes of the north, where they reside during the spring and summer; but, on the approach of winter, they quit the European and Siberian parts of Russia, Sweden, &c. and usually avail themselves of a strong north-easterly wind, to convey them southward, in November, when they appear on the coasts of Holland, France, &c. but they are rarely met with in this country. Over North America they are pretty gene-

rally diffused. The female nestles in moist meadows, among rushes, or in the holes of trees, and lays about eight or nine greenish cinereous eggs. These birds swim and dive with wonderful facility, seldom appearing in the day time; and they are shot with great difficulty, as they plunge down the moment that they perceive the flash of the pan. The flesh is savoury.

Acuta.

A. acuta, Lin. &c. *Pintail Duck*, Prov. *White Duck, Sea Pheasant*, or *Cracker*. Tail pointed; elongated; black beneath; a white line on each side of the occiput; the back waved with cinereous. Length of the male twenty-eight inches; weight twenty-four ounces. The female is smaller, and somewhat duller in her attire. Colonel Montagu ascertained that the males moult twice a-year, which has occasioned some discrepancy in the accounts of the colours of their plumage. Although the pintail ducks breed in the moist wastes of the north, they are very restive, sometimes wandering as far south as Italy in Europe, and Louisiana in America, while they are known to brave the severest winters of Sweden, Russia, Siberia, Canada, &c. They are seldom numerous in England; but flocks of them are frequently dispersed along the isles and shores of Scotland and Ireland; and, during hard winters, they betake themselves to the inland lakes of this and other European countries. The female lays eight or ten greenish-blue eggs. She will also breed in confinement; and Lord Stanley had a hybrid brood of the female pintail and the male wigeon. The notes of the pintail are soft and inward; the courting call is always attended with a jerk of the head, and the more ordinary one resembles that of a very young kitten. The flesh of this species is much esteemed.

Penelope.

A. Penelope, Lin. &c. *Wigeon*, Prov. *Whim, Weaver, Pandle Whew*, or *Yellow Pole*. Tail somewhat pointed; vent-feathers black; head bay; front white; back waved with cinereous. The male, like the pintail and shoveler, makes a double moult in the course of a few months. In Italy he loses the varied colours, and becomes dark ferruginous on the back, scapulars, and sides, but not so like the female as the male pintail. Wigeons inhabit the north of Europe and Asia, and migrate, in winter, as far south as Sardinia and Egypt; appearing in the latter country in November, after the inundation of the Nile. They travel and swim in bands, live on frogs, worms, small fish, insects, and water plants; and, when they fly during the night, they frequently utter a shrill piping whistle, which is a real note, proceeding from their mouth, and not, as alleged by Dampier and Salerne, produced by the flapping of their wings. They seem to be regardless of cold and stormy weather, are lively and pugnacious, and capable of being reared in confinement, when they will occasionally mingle with the pintail, and give rise to a hybrid offspring. Some of the species breed in Holland, France, &c. the female constructing a sort of floating nest among the reeds of marshes, lakes, &c. and laying from eight to ten eggs, of a dirty greenish-grey. They seem to be the most plentiful of the duck tribe that are taken in the decoys of Somerset and Devonshire. Their flesh is much esteemed; and the London markets are regularly supplied with it throughout winter, and the early part of spring.

Clypeata.

A. clypeata, Lin. &c. *Shoveler, Shoveler Duck*, or *Blue-winged Shoveler*, Prov. *Broad-bill*, or *Kerlutock*. Bill black, very broad, rounded like a spoon at the tip, with the nail hooked inwards. This species inhabits Europe, Asia, and North America, affecting lakes, marshes, and the banks of rivers. With us it is a scarce

Ornitho-
logy.

bird; and, notwithstanding the opposite assertions of some authors, it is not for certain known to breed in the island; but it is plentiful in Holland, and some parts of France, arriving in the latter country in February; and most of them seem to move farther south in March; the few which remain to breed not departing till September. The female makes her nest, lined with withered grasses, in the midst of the largest tufts of rushes, or coarse herbage, and in the least accessible parts of the slaky marsh, laying from ten to fourteen pale rusty-coloured eggs. As soon as the young are hatched, they are conducted to the water by the parent birds, who watch and guard them with the greatest care. They are at first very shapeless, the bill being then almost as broad as the body; nor does their plumage acquire its complete colouring till after the second moulting. The flesh is red, juicy, delicate, and tender; but the attempts to rear the species in the poultry-yard have hitherto failed of success. The quantities of shovelers with which the Parisian markets are supplied in the season are procured from the marshes which extend from the neighbourhood of Soissons to the sea.

Querque-
dula.

A. querquedula, Lin. &c. *Garganey*. Prov. *Cricket Teal*. A white band on the sides of the head; small wing-spot cinereous green. This species inhabits Europe and Asia, chiefly frequenting fresh waters and marshes; but it is also sometimes seen at sea, especially in stormy weather. It is of rare occurrence in England, but not uncommon in France, where it arrives early in March, and soon after pairs. The female tramples a small space of soil, about four or five inches in diameter, among tufts of rushes, and strews it with withered grasses, on which she deposits from ten to fourteen eggs, of a greenish-fawn hue. The incubation lasts about twenty-four days; and the parents conduct their young to the water almost as soon as hatched. The cry of the garganey somewhat resembles that of the land-rail. It is said to be impatient of cold. Of all sorts of grain, it prefers millet, but soaks it in water previously to swallowing it; so that it might possibly, as in ancient times, be rendered domestic without much trouble.

Crecca.

A. crecca, Lin. &c. *Teal*, or *Common Teal*. A broad glossy green band on the sides of the head; the large wing-spot half dark-green and half deep-black. Length fourteen inches and a half; stretch of wing one foot ten inches; weight about twelve ounces. Inhabits Europe, Asia, and America, and migrates from its northern stations to Britain, Holland, France, &c. Some are said to breed in the morasses in the neighbourhood of Carlisle, and in Scotland, but many more in the marshes, and on the banks of lakes, in France. Their call, which is a sort of piping or whistling note, is heard in March. In April, the female lays from seven to ten or twelve eggs, about the size of those of a pigeon, and of a dirty-white ground, marked with small hazel spots. The nest is large, and skilfully composed of soft dried grasses, lined with feathers, and concealed in a hole, among the roots of reeds and bulrushes, on the edge of the water, being so adjusted, it is alleged, as to rise or fall with the stream. The female alone incubates and rears her young, during which period the males unite, in small flocks, and do not rejoin their families till autumn. The flesh of this species was much prized by the Roman epicures, and is still in much request for the table. By putting some of the eggs under a hen, and clipping the wings of the brood, to prevent their flying off, it is presumed that they might be domesticated, as they seem to have been by the ancients.

b. Hind toe with a loose membrane.

Feed principally on the contents of bivalve shells, and on fish.

A. mollissima, Lin. &c. *Eider, Edder*, or *St. Cuthbert's Duck, Great Black and White Duck*, of Edwards. Prov. *Duntra, Duntur Goose*, or *Colk*. Base of the bill laterally prolonged into two flattened plates, bill and legs greenish-ash. Length, from twenty-two to twenty-four inches; extent of wing two feet eight inches; size about double that of the common duck, and weight six or seven pounds.

This species inhabits the high and icy latitudes of Europe, Asia, and America, and feeds chiefly on testaceous animals and fish. They are very abundant during summer, in all the islands situated in the Greenland sea, and are also met with, solitary, or in pairs, near the ice, at great distances from land. When near the coasts, they fly in large flocks, and generally arrange themselves in a regular form. Their appearance in great numbers is an indication of the proximity of land. They are capable of protracted flights in the day time, but generally return to their stations at night. They are rarely, if ever, seen in the south of England, but they breed in the north of Scotland, on Papa Westra, one of the Orkneys, on the Hebrides, the Fern Isles, on the coast of Northumberland, &c. in June and July. Two or three pair occasionally breed on Inchcolm, in the Frith of Forth; but the jackdaws frequently destroy the young. On the lonely islet of Suliskerry and its *Stack*, situated in the Atlantic Ocean, about forty miles westward from Hoyhead in the Orkneys, this species has maintained its residence at least since the days of Buchanan, who gives a lively and elegant, rather than an accurate description of its appearance and habits. The nest is made on the ground, composed of marine plants, and lined with down, of exquisite fineness, which the female plucks from her own body. The eggs are usually four, of a pale olive green, and rather larger than those of a common duck. About Iceland, the eider ducks generally build their nests on small islands not far from the shore, and sometimes even near the dwellings of the natives, who treat them with so much attention and kindness as to render them nearly tame. Two females will sometimes lay their eggs in the same nest, in which case they always agree remarkably well. As long as the female is sitting, the male continues on watch near the shore, but as soon as the young are hatched, he leaves them. The mother, however, remains with them a considerable time longer; and it is curious to observe her attention in leading them out of the nest, almost as soon as they creep from the eggs. Having conducted them to the water's edge, she takes them on her back, and swims a few yards with them, when she dives, and leaves them on the surface to take care of themselves; and they are seldom afterwards seen on land. When the natives come to the nest, they carefully remove the female, and take away the superfluous down and eggs. They then replace the mother, and she begins to lay afresh, covering the eggs with new down; and when she can afford no more, the male comes to her assistance, and covers the eggs with his down, which is white. When the young ones leave the nest, it is once more plundered. The best down and most eggs are got during the first three weeks of their laying; and it has been generally observed, that they lay the greatest number of eggs in rainy weather. One female, during the time of laying, usually yields half a pound of down, which, however, is reduced one half after it is cleaned. It is extremely soft and warm, and so light

Ornitho-
logy.

Hind toe
loosely
webbed.
Mollissima.

Ornithology.

and elastic, that two handfuls squeezed together are sufficient to fill a covering, which is used in the cold countries instead of a common quilt or blanket. According to an observation of Mr. Cartwright, these birds fly at the rate of ninety miles an hour. In spring they swim in flocks; and in a fine day it is very pleasing to see two or three dozen of them sailing by. Being very thick of feathers, they sit high on the water, which adds to the gracefulness of their appearance. Their flesh is valued as food, and their skins are made into warm and comfortable under garments.

Moschata. *A. moschata*, Lin. &c. *Muscovy, Cairo, Guinea,* or *Indian Duck,* or, more properly, *Musk Duck,* since the Latin specific appellation is significant of its musky odour, originating from the liquor secreted in the gland of the rump. Face naked, with red caruncles; the general plumage dusky brown, and glossy on the back with green; a large white spot on the wings; the bill, legs, toes, and webs red. The female is more uniformly of a dusky brown, with fewer reflexions; and she is also smaller in size. In the domesticated state, however, the varieties and shadings are indefinite. The native country of this excellent addition to our poultry-yards, is now ascertained to be South America; for Azara observes, that it is the most common species of wild duck in Paraguay and the neighbouring provinces. In these countries, the musk ducks perch on high trees, by the sides of rivers and marshes, on which they also fix their nests, breeding twice or thrice in the year, and the female laying each time from twelve to eighteen round and greenish-white eggs. The moulting commences in September, and is sometimes so suddenly completed, that the birds, rendered incapable of flight, are caught alive by the inhabitants. In general, however, they can be taken only by surprise, being as shy as our wild ducks; and yet they have readily submitted to domestication in various countries of both continents. They are larger than the common domestic species, are almost mute, easily fattened, and very fertile. The male is very ardent in courtship, and readily intermingles with the females of congenerous species, so as to occasion cross hybrid breeds. When prepared for the table, the rump and head should be removed.

Spectabilis. *A. spectabilis*, Gmel. Lath. &c. *King Duck,* or *Grey-headed Duck.* Base of the bill laterally prolonged on the forehead into two processes, which rise in the form of crests; bill and legs of a fine vermilion hue. Inhabits the extreme north, and was often observed by our navigators in the late northern expeditions, but was too shy to approach the ships. As it seldom ventures to any considerable distance southward, its history is still imperfectly known. It is a highly elegant species; and its manners are presumed to be analogous to those of the preceding; but the eggs are said to be elongated and of an olivaceous ash.

Fusca. *A. fusca*, Lin. &c. *Velvet,* or *Great Black Duck,* or *Double Scoter.* No protuberance at the base of the bill; wing-spot small and white; tarsi and toes red. Almost the whole plumage of a deep velvet black; a white crescent under the eyes, webs black. Length from twenty to twenty-one inches, and weight about three pounds two ounces. The female is rather small, and has the general plumage dusky, inclining to brown. Inhabits the arctic seas of both continents, Norway, Sweden, the Orkneys, Hebrides, &c. and retires southwards in winter to the coasts of England, Holland, France, &c. and in America, as far as New

York. They are not often found on the British shores. They consort with the *nigra;* and are sometimes taken in the fishermen's nets, but are extremely shy. They are constantly diving, chiefly in quest of shell-fish. They breed within the arctic circle, under tufts of grass or shrubs, the female laying eight or ten white eggs.

Nigra. *A. nigra*, Lin. &c. *Black Diver, Black Duck,* or *Scoter.* Wants the wing-spot; tarsi and toes brownash; a protuberance on the forehead; nail of the bill much depressed and rounded; tail very conical. Length from nineteen to twenty-two inches; extent of wing thirty-four inches, and weight about two pounds nine ounces. This species abounds in the north of Europe, Asia, and America, frequenting chiefly the sea, or its shores, and seldom flying far up into the country. It is very partial to shell-fish, for which it dives with great vigour and address. It breeds within the arctic circle, but migrates southward in autumn and winter, and is sometimes found on the coasts of Holland and France in great flocks, diving for prey. On our British shores it is either less frequent or less an object of search, its fishy flavour inducing us to reject it as a food, whilst it seems to constitute its principal merit with our continental neighbours, who are allowed to eat it during Lent. Hence numbers of them are frequently caught in nets, purposely spread for them, on the coast of Picardy, &c.

Glacialis. *A. glacialis*, Lin. &c. *Long-tailed Duck,* or *Swallow-tailed Shield-Drake.* In Shetland and Orkney, *Caloa,* or *Coal and Candle Light,* from a fancied resemblance of its long and plaintive winter-call to these words. Dr. Barry has, by mistake, applied this local appellation to *A. acuta.* Bill very short, black, with a transverse red stripe; a large patch of chesnut-brown on the sides of the neck. Length from twenty to twenty-one inches, owing to the elongation of the middle tail-feathers; but the bird is only about the size of a pigeon. Inhabits Europe, Asia, and America, frequenting both the interior lakes and the sea-shores of these quarters of the world. The birds of this species do not, like many of the other tribes, entirely quit their northern haunts in winter, but considerable numbers reside permanently in the polar regions. Numerous flocks, however, spread themselves southward in the winter, from Greenland and Hudson's Bay, as far as New York in America; and from Iceland and Spitzbergen, over Lapland, the Russian dominions, Sweden, Norway, and the northern parts of the British isles in Europe. The bands which visit the Orkneys appear in October, and continue there till April. About sunset they are seen in large companies, going to and returning from the bays, in which they frequently pass the night, making a noise, which in frosty weather may be heard at the distance of some miles. They are rather scarce in England, to which they resort only in very hard winters, and even then in small straggling parties. They fly swiftly, but seldom to a great distance, making a loud and singular cry. They are expert divers, and supposed to live chiefly on shell-fish. The female places her nest among the grass, near the water, and, like the eider duck, lines it with the fine down of her own body. According to Dr. Latham, she lays five eggs, which are of a bluish-white colour, and about the size of those of a pullet.

Marila. *A. marila*, Lin. &c. *Scaup,* or *White-faced Duck;*

Prov. *Spoon-bill Duck*. Bill broad; a small white spot on the wings. Length from seventeen to eighteen inches; extent of wing thirty-two inches; weight from a pound and a half to two pounds. The Scaup Duck breeds in the northern and cold latitudes of both continents, and migrates southwards in winter, when small flocks visit our shores; and many of them are observed on the coasts of Holland. They frequent fresh waters, and sometimes even live in subterraneous holes. The sexes keep apart from others of their congeners, make the same grunting noise, and toss their head and open their bill in a singular manner. If taken alive, put into a pond, and fed for a few days on bread soaked in water, they will afterwards eat barley freely, and become very tame. A sickly female, which was in Colonel Montagu's possession, died of an affection of the lungs. The membrane which separates these from the other viscera was much thickened, and all the internal cavity was covered with mucor, or blue mould.

Ferina. *A. ferina*, Lin. &c. *Pochard*, or *Red-headed Wigeon.* Prov. *Vare-headed Wigeon, Red-headed Poker, Blue Poker, Attile Duck, Dun-cur,* &c. Bill long; a broad, transverse, and dark-blue band on the upper mandible. Length from sixteen to seventeen inches, extent of wing two feet and a half; and weight about one pound thirteen ounces. This species leaves its native northern abodes on the approach of winter, and migrates southward as far, it is alleged, as Egypt in the old, and Carolina and Louisiana in the new continent. They arrive in the marshes of France about the end of October, and great numbers of them used to be caught in the fens of Lincolnshire during the winter season, and sold in the London markets, where they and the female wigeon are indiscriminately called *dun-birds*, and are esteemed excellent eating. The female nestles in reeds, in the northern countries, and lays as many as twelve or thirteen eggs, of a greenish-white.

Clangula. *A. clangula*, Lin. &c. *Golden Eye*, or *Golden Eye Duck*, Prov. *Pied Wigeon*. Bill very short; base broader than the tip; nostrils situated near the latter; tarsi and toes yellowish; much white on the wings. Length from eighteen to nineteen inches; extent of wing thirty-one inches; and weight from twenty-six ounces to two pounds. The golden eye is a native of the arctic regions of both continents, although some pairs have been known to breed in more temperate latitudes. In their winter migrations, they spread along our sea-coasts, and even visit inland lakes, greedily preying on testacea, small fish, and even frogs, mice, &c. They are admirable divers, and glide on the calm surface of the sea with singular gracefulness, but are proportionably awkward and embarrassed on the land. Though not clamorous in taking flight, they produce a peculiar whistling noise, by the vigorous strokes of their wings. It has been likewise remarked, that they fly low, and seldom alight on dry ground. They are far from numerous on our shores, and seldom occur in large bodies. They return northward late in the spring, and usually breed among marshy plants, but sometimes in trees. The nest consists of a heap of dried grasses, negligently enough put together, and on which the female deposits from seven to fourteen white eggs, rather smaller than those of the common hen. The incubation lasts eighteen days; and the young, immediately on escaping from the shell, accompany their mother to the water.

Histrionica. *A. histrionica*, Lin. &c. *Harlequin Duck.* Bill short, compressed; nail much hooked; nostrils closely approximated at the upper part of the base of the bill;

length seventeen inches. Inhabits the northern quarters of Europe, Asia, and America, retiring southward, or to the sea, during the intense cold of the arctic winter, but very rarely visiting this country. It breeds among bushes and herbs, near the water, and lays twelve or fourteen pure white eggs. It is esteemed more delicate game than the mallard.

MERGUS, Lin. &c.

Bill middle-sized, or long, slender, in the form of a lengthened cone, and almost cylindrical; base broad; tip and upper mandibles much hooked, and furnished with a nail; the edges of both mandibles serrated in a backward direction; nostrils lateral, about the middle of the bill, elliptical, longitudinal, and pervious; legs short, placed backwards on the abdomen, the three front toes completely webbed, the hinder detached, with the rudiments of a member; wings middle-sized. The birds of this tribe are nearly allied to the ducks, residing on the water, and usually swimming with the body submerged, the head only appearing above the surface. They dive frequently, and with great facility; while, by means of their wings, they can advance quickly under water. They are capable, too, of sustaining a protracted and rapid flight, but they walk with an embarrassed and waddling pace. They feed principally on fish and amphibious reptiles. Their appropriate and breeding stations are in the cold latitudes; and they appear in the temperate regions only in winter. The males moult in the spring; and the females and the young in autumn. All attempts to reduce them to domestication seem to have failed of success.

M. merganser, Lin. &c. *Goosander*, Prov. *Jack-saw*, or *Harl*. Wing-spot white; the mature male furnished with a short and thick tuft. Length from twenty-six to twenty-eight inches; extent of wing three feet two inches; average weight four pounds. Inhabits the north of Europe, Asia, and America; migrating, in severe winters, to more temperate climates, as the coasts of Britain, Holland, France, &c. and even penetrating to the inland lakes of Germany and Switzerland, but always returning north in spring. In quest of fish, it dives deep, and with great celerity; and it holds its slippery prey with much security by means of its serrated bill. It has been known to breed in the holes of trees, but more frequently among rocks or stones; the female laying about twelve or fourteen whitish eggs, almost equally pointed at both ends. These eggs are much relished by the Finlanders; but the flesh is rancid, and scarcely eatable. On the appearance of the young, the sexes separate; the males congregating by themselves, and the females consorting with their offspring.

M. serrator, Lin. &c. *Red-breasted Merganser, Red-breasted Goosander*, or *Lesser Toothed Diver.* Wing-spot white, crossed by two black bars in the male, and by one in the female, the mature male with a long and filamentous crest. Length twenty-one or twenty-two inches, extent of wing two feet seven inches, and weight about two pounds. This species, likewise, is a native of the northern parts of the world, where it breeds and passes the summer; but it is met with as far south as the Mediterranean, and is common about the Laguni of Venice. In Hudson's Bay, &c. it arrives early in June, when it makes its nest of withered grass, lined with the down of its own breast, on a little spot of soil that rises above the water of marshy tracts, and lays from about eight to thirteen cinereous white eggs, of the size of those of the common duck. It is said also to breed

PLATALEA LEUCORODIA
Spoonbill

ANAS SPECTABILIS
King Duck

PSOPHIA CREPITANS
Trumpeter

IBIS RELIGIOSA
Sacred Ibis

PALAMEDEA CORNUTA
Horned Screamer

LARUS MINUTUS
Pigmy Gull

FRATERCULA ARCTICA
Puffin

APTERODYTES PATACHONICA
Patagonian Penguin

DIOMEDEA EXULANS
Wandering Albatross

PELECANUS ONOCROTALUS
Common Pelican

Engraved for the Edinburgh Encyclopædia by J. Moffat Edin.

Ornitho-
logy.

bellus.

as far south as the county of Ross, in Scotland, and in Islay, one of the Hebrides.

M. albellus, Lin. &c. *Smew*, or *White Nun*. Crest pendent, occiput black, body white, back and temples black, wings variegated. Size of a wigeon, and about fifteen or sixteen inches long. Inhabits the northern tracts of both continents, and in winter advances as far south as the shores of the Mediterranean. Like its congeners, it is a frequent and excellent diver, feeds on fish, shrimps, &c. and breeds on the margins of lakes and rivers, laying from eight to twelve whitish eggs.

PELECANUS, Lin. &c PELICAN.

LE-
NUS.

Bill long, straight, broad, much depressed, upper mandibles flattened, terminated by a nail, or very strong hook, the lower formed by two bony branches, which are depressed, flexible, and united at the tip; from these branches is suspended a naked skin, in form of a pouch; face and throat naked; nostrils basal, in the form of narrow longitudinal slits; legs short and strong, all the four toes connected by a web; wings of moderate dimensions. The pelicans are large birds, which reside on rivers, lakes, or along the sea-coasts. Though excellent swimmers, they also occasionally perch on trees. They are gregarious, very fond of fish, and when harassed, or pursued, readily reject the contents of their stomach, like the gull tribe. They store up their prey in their gular pouch, from which it is gradually transferred into the œsophagus, as the process of digestion goes on. Though remarkable for their voracity, some of the species have been trained to fish for mankind. In external appearance the two sexes very nearly resemble each other.

ocro-
as

P. onocrotalus, Lin. &c. *White*, or *Common Pelican*. White, faintly tinged with flesh colour, gullet with a bright yellow pouch. The spurious wings and first quill-feathers are black. The bag at the throat is flaccid, membranous, and capable of great distension. Length between five and six feet; extent of wing eleven feet; being rather larger than the swan, though with much shorter legs. The young are distinguished by the prevalence of cinereous in their plumage, and have been erroneously designed *P. Philippensis*, and *P. Fuscus*, by Gmel. and Lath.

This bird has its specific name from its cry, which is loudest during flight, and which the ancients compared to the braying of an ass. Inhabits Asia, Africa, and South America. About the middle of September flocks of this species repair to Egypt, in regular bands, terminating in an obtuse angle. During the summer months they take up their abode on the borders of the Black Sea and the shores of Greece. They are rare in France, and unknown in Great Britain. In fishing, they do not immediately swallow their prey, but fill their bag, and return to the shore to consume at leisure the fruits of their industry. As, however, they quickly digest their food, they generally fish more than once in the course of the day, and, for the most part, in the morning and evening, when the fish are most astir. A single pelican will, at one repast, dispatch as many fish as would suffice for six men; and in confinement, it will, moreover, snap up rats and other small quadrupeds. At night, it retires a little way on the shore to rest, with its head leaning against its breast; and in this attitude it remains almost motionless, till hunger calls it to break off its repose. It then flies from its resting-place, and, raising itself thirty or forty feet above the surface of the sea, turns its head,

Ornitho-
logy.

with one eye downwards, and continues on wing till it sees a fish sufficiently near the surface, when it darts down with astonishing swiftness, seizes it with unerring certainty, and stores it up in its pouch; it then rises again and continues the same manœuvres till it has procured a competent stock. The female feeds her young with fish that have been macerated for some time in her pouch. The pelican is not only susceptible of domestication, but may even be trained to fish for its master. When a number of pelicans and corvorants get together, they are said to practise a singular method of taking fish; for they spread into a large circle, at some distance from land, the pelicans flapping on the surface of the water with their extensive wings, and the corvorants diving beneath, till the fish contained within the circle are driven before them towards the land; and, as the circle contracts by the birds drawing closer together, the fish are at length reduced within a narrow compass, when their pursuers find no difficulty in securing them. In this exercise they are often attended by various species of gulls, which participate in the spoil. The pelican generally breeds in marshy and uncultivated places, particularly about islands and lakes, making its nest, which is deep, and a foot and a half in diameter, of sedges and aquatic plants, and lining it with grass of a softer texture; but it frequently dispenses with any such formal construction. It lays two or more white eggs, of equal roundness at the two ends, and which, when persecuted, it sometimes hides in the water. When it nestles in dry and desert places, it brings water to its young in its bag, which is capable of containing nearly twenty pints of liquid; but that it feeds them with its own blood must be ranked among the fabulous assertions of antiquity. Its flesh is very generally disliked.

CARBO, Meyer, Tem. PELECANUS, Lin. &c. CORVORANT.

CARBO.

Bill middle-sized, or long, straight, compressed, upper mandible much incurved at the tip, the lower compressed, base of the bill involved in a small membrane which reaches to the throat; face and throat naked; nostrils basal, linear, and concealed; legs strong, short, situated far behind, all the toes included in a web, the middle claw serrated; wings moderate. This genus has been lately detached from *Pelecanus* and *Sula*. The birds which compose it are very expert divers, and swim with ease under water; and though far from agile or nimble on land, they walk better than the *Mergi*, yet almost in an erect attitude, and using their long and elastic tail as a point of support. They feed much on river fish, especially eels, and they are more addicted than the pelican to perch on trees. Their moulting is partially double in the course of the year.

Cormo-
ranus.

C. cormoranus, Meyer, Tem. *Pelecanus carbo*, Lin. &c. *Cormorant*, or, more correctly, *Corvorant*. Prov. *Great Black*, *Green*, or *Crested Corvorant*, *Cole Goose*, *Great Scart*, *Scarf*, *Brongie*, or *Norie*. Length of the bill two inches three lines longer than the head; the tail composed of fourteen feathers. Size of a goose, but more slender; weighs from five to seven pounds; length about thirty inches, and extent of wing from four to four and a half feet.

This species inhabits Europe, Asia, and America. It never quits the Gulf of Bothnia till that inlet is congealed, and then it may be seen on trees and houses in Sweden, resting on its passage to the ocean. On the Dutch coast, where it arrives in March, it is very nu-

1

merous; nor is it uncommon on many of our own shores, building its nest of sticks, sea-ware, and grass, on the highest parts of cliffs that impend over the sea, and laying three or more green eggs about the size of those of a goose. In the parish of North Mevan, in Shetland, are two very high inaccessible rocky pillars, on which the corvorant breeds. " What is very extraordinary," observes Mr. Laing, " the rock possessed by these birds one year is deserted the next, and returned to again after being a year unpossessed. This singular practice has been carried on during the memory of man." In winter these birds disperse along the shores, and visit the fresh waters, where they commit great depredations among the fish. They are remarkably voracious, have a very quick digestion, and, though naturally extremely shy and wary, are heavy and sluggish, and easily taken when glutted with food. The smell of the corvorant when alive is more rank and offensive than that of any other bird; and its flesh is so disgusting that even the Greenlanders will hardly taste it. In Orkney, however, the young are sometimes regarded as delicacies, especially if kept under ground for twenty-four hours, so as to make them tender, and deprive them of their fishy taste. In this state they are also said to furnish soup little inferior to that made with hare. It is not uncommon to see about a score of these birds together, on the rocks of the sea-shore, with expanded wings, drying themselves in the wind. In this attitude they sometimes remain for nearly an hour, without once closing their wings; and as soon as the latter are sufficiently dry to enable the feathers to imbibe the oil, they press that liquor from its receptacle on the rump, and dress the feathers with it, at the particular moment when it can be most advantageously spread on them. Corvorants were formerly occasionally trained in this country to catching fish for the table. For this purpose they were kept with great care in the house, and when taken out for fishing, they had a leathern thong tied round their neck, to prevent them from swallowing their prey. Whitlock tells us, that he had a cast of them, *manned* like hawks, which would come to hand. He took much pleasure in them, and relates, that the best he had was one presented to him by Mr. Wood, Master of the Corvorants to Charles I.

Colonel Montagu, in the Supplement to his *Ornithological Dictionary*, has communicated various interesting notices of a corvorant that was accidentally captured by a Newfoundland dog, and which became at once quite tame.

C. graculus, Meyer, Tem. *Pelecanus graculus*, Lin. &c. *Shag*, or *Green Corvorant*. In the north of England *Crave*, and in Orkney *Scarf*. Bill one inch and ten lines longer than the head; tail very long, graduated, conical, composed of twelve feathers. The largest of the species measures about two feet six inches in length, three feet eight inches in extent of wing, and weighs nearly four pounds. The shag is very abundant in the regions of the arctic and antarctic circles, and is a bird of passage in the eastern countries of Europe. It has much the appearance and manners of the preceding, although the two species are not observed to consort. But they are alike greedy and voracious, and after having overgorged themselves, they are often found on shore in a drowsy or stupid state; but when the torpor is over, they appear again on the water, where they are extremely alert, and not easily shot, as they dive the moment that they perceive the

flash of a gun, and take care afterwards to keep out of its reach. In swimming, they carry their head very erect, while the body seems nearly submerged. From the circumstance of their feathers being not quite impervious to water, they do not remain on that element very long at a time, but are frequently seen flying about, or sitting on the shore, flapping the moisture from their wings, or keeping them for some time expanded to dry in the sun and the wind. They nestle in the clifts of rocks, or in trees, the female laying two or three whitish eggs, much elongated, and of nearly equal dimensions at both ends. Notwithstanding the strong and offensive smell emitted by shags and corvorants, examples are not wanting of their having been eaten by people in this country; but before cooking, they should be skinned and drawn, then wrapt up in a clean cloth, and buried for some time in the earth. The crop is often infested with a species of *ascaris*.

C. Sinensis, Chinese or *Fishing Corvorant.* Tail rounded; body brown above, whitish and spotted with brown beneath; throat white, irides blue; bill yellow. This is the *Leutze* of the Chinese, who instruct it in the art of supplying its owner with fish. On a large lake, Sir George Staunton and his party saw thousands of small boats and rafts, on each of which were ten or a dozen of these birds, which, at a signal from the owner, plunged into the water, and returned with fish of a large size. They appeared to be so well trained, that it did not require either ring or cord about their throats to prevent them from swallowing any portion of their prey, except what the master was pleased to return to them for encouragement and food.

TACHYPETES, Vieil. Tem. PELECANUS, Lin. &c. FRIGATE.

Bill long, stout, sharp-edged, depressed at the base, flattened at the sides, with a suture above, the tips of both mandibles strongly curved, and the upper terminated by a very pointed hook; no nasal foss; nostrils more or less concealed, and linear; legs placed backwards, very short; tarsus shorter than the toes, and half-feathered; the three fore toes long, and half-webbed; wings very long and straight; tail much forked.

T. aquilus, Vieil. *Pelecanus aquilus*, Lath. *Frigate, Frigate Bird*, or *Frigate Pelican*. Body and orbits black; bill red; belly of the female white. The old male has a bright red fleshy membrane under the throat. Three feet long, extent of wing fourteen feet. This species has its English name from its lengthened form, rapid movement, and the spirited manner in which it attacks the birds which it compels to disgorge. In pursuit of prey, it braves the winds and tempests; but it is also capable of soaring above the region of storms; and it is often constrained to continue its flight during the night, as it can seldom repose long on the water, being unprovided with the requisite quantity of down. When intent on glutting its ravenous appetite, it is not deterred by the sight of man, and will even continue its repast when held in his hand. It preys on all manner of fish that approach the surface of the water, particularly the flying sorts, on which it darts with the greatest velocity.

As the frigate-bird rises from the ground with difficulty, it usually reposes on the point of a rock, or the top of a tree, from which it can spring at once into the air. The nest is generally placed in a tree, or the hole of a rock, at a considerable elevation, and in desert places near the sea-shore. The female lays one or two white eggs, tinged with flesh colour, and minutely dotted with crimson. The young are fed in the nest, which they do not quit till they are capable of flying. At first they are covered with a grey white down, and have the bill almost white. We know not on what authority some of the German ornithologists have ranked this species among the birds of Europe. Its ordinary residence is within the tropics.

SULA, Briss. Tem. PELECANUS, Lin. &c. MORUS, Vieil.

Bill vigorous, long, shaped like a lengthened cone, very thick at the base, compressed towards the tip, which is obliquely curved, cleft beyond the eyes, edges of both mandibles serrated; face and throat naked; nostrils basal, linear, concealed; legs short, stout, placed far behind, all the toes connected by a web, nail of the middle toe serrated; wings long; tail conical, and composed of twelve feathers.

S. alba, Meyer, Tem. *Pelecanus Bassanus*, Lin. &c. The young correspond to *Pelecanus maculatus*, Gmel. *Gannet, Solan*, or *Soland Goose*. Prov. *Gan.* Tail wedged; body white; bill, primary quill-feathers, and spurious wings, black; face blue. Length from two feet seven inches to three feet; extent of wing six feet; and weight seven pounds.

This species chiefly haunts the northern regions of the two continents. In hard winters individuals are observed on the coasts of England, Holland, France, &c. but they breed abundantly on the Bass Island, in the Frith of Edinburgh, on Ailsa, off the coast of Ayrshire, the Skellig Isles, on the coast of Kerry, in Ireland, the islands of St. Kilda, Orkney, Shetland, Faroe, &c. The rocks of St. Kilda are, in the summer season, quite covered with these and other sea-fowls, and appear at some distance like hills covered with snow. Although common in the Orcadian and Shetlandian seas, the gannets of that range chiefly breed on the stack of *Suliskerry*, which has received its name from that circumstance, *sule* being Norse for a gannet, and *skerry* meaning an insulated rock. The gannet arrives in the districts which we have just mentioned in March, and continues till September; nor is it known, in this hemisphere, to breed much farther south than the coasts of Scotland. Some few seem to stay about their breeding stations all winter; but they are supposed to be the old ones, which are unequal to the distant flight undertaken by the others. They neither arrive nor depart all at a time. A few of the forerunners are first seen about the Bass; and in some days after the main body follows, in several successive divisions. As this bird must let itself fall before it takes wing, it requires a steep and precipitous breeding place. It observes its prey from a considerable height, and darts down on it with incredible force. Its nest is a large and rude assemblage of very different materials, as it lays hold of any thing fit for the purpose, whether on the land or floating on the waters, as grass, sea-weeds, shavings of timber, shreds of cloth, and frequently articles picked up at a very great distance, or else from the nests of its neighbours. The female lays one egg, or more frequently two, which are white, of a rough surface, a long shape, and remarkably small for the size of the bird, being scarcely larger than those of a duck. The male and female incubate, and go a fishing by turns. It is currently, but erroneously reported, not only that they hatch their solitary egg by means of their foot,

but that they place it on one end, in such a manner that if a person overturn it, he cannot make it stand as before. The celebrated Dr. Harvey, who visited the Bass, and has described it in very elegant latinity, strangely enough asserts the latter circumstance. In the dilatable skin under their bill, these birds can fetch four or five herrings at a time, besides sprats, which the young extract from the mouth of the parents with their bill, as with pincers. The young begin to be taken in August, and by some are relished as an exquisite morsel; but the older ones are tough and rancid. The fowler who seizes the young, is often let down by a rope from the top of a cliff, and is sometimes stationed on the slippery projection of a rock, with a perpendicular precipice of four hundred feet or more beneath him. Gannets are said to be met with in great numbers, about New Holland and New Zealand. They also breed on the coast of Newfoundland, and migrate southward along the American shores, as far as South Carolina. When they pass from place to place, they unite in small flocks, of from five to fifteen; and, except in very fine weather, they fly low, near the shore, doubling the capes and projecting parts, and keeping nearly at an equal distance from the land. During their fishing they rise high into the air, and sail aloft over the shoals of herrings and pilchards, much in the manner of kites. When they observe the shoal crowded thick together, they close their wings to their sides, and precipitate themselves head foremost into the water, dropping almost like a stone. Their eye, in this act, is so correct, that they never fail to rise with a fish in their mouth.

S. communis, Tem. *Pelecanus sula*, Lin. *Morus sula*, Vieil. *Booby*, or *Common Booby*. Tail wedgeshaped, body whitish, primary quill-feathers tipt with blackish. The body is white beneath, and the tail brownish at the tips. But the colour is incident to considerable variety. Size between that of a duck and a goose, and length two feet five inches. This species, which has its name from its apparent stupidity, alighting sometimes when tired on one's hand, if held out to it, is often mentioned by our navigators, and is very generally spread over the sea, being found among the Faroe Isles, in North and South America, the West Indies, and New Guinea; and yet its history is very scantily unfolded. The flesh has a fishy and muddy flavour.

PLOTUS, Lin. &c. DARTER.

Bill long, perfectly straight, slender, spindle-shaped, sharp-pointed, edges of the upper mandible dilated at the base, but compressed and inflected in the other portions; both mandibles finely serrated; nostrils linear, and hid in a shallow groove; legs short, thick, and strong, tarsus much shorter than the middle and outer toe; all the toes connected by a web; wings long; tail still longer in proportion.

P. anhinga, Lin. &c. *P. leucogaster*, Vieil. *White-bellied Darter*, or *Anhinga*. Head smooth, belly white; the upper parts, abdomen, and thighs, raven black. The tail is deep black, and spotted with white. Of the size of a duck, measuring two feet ten inches in length. Inhabits the Floridas, Brazil, and other districts of South America. Subsists chiefly on fish, which it catches by darting its small head forwards; but, when at rest, it perches on a tree, with its long serpentine neck drawn in between the shoulders. It is scarcely ever seen on the ground. The anhingas associate in small parties, frequently reposing on wi-

Ornitho-
logy.

thered branches that impend over streams, expanding their wings and tail, as if for the purpose of cooling themselves, and looking at their image in the water. If approached when in this attitude they tumble down into the water, as if dead, and remain submerged for a minute or two, when, at a considerable distance, they thrust up their head and neck, the body still continuing under water. During the heat of the day, they may be seen in great numbers, high in the air, and directly above lakes or rivers. They make their nest of sticks or trees. Their skin is very thick; and their flesh, though fat, is dark-coloured, and of a disagreeable oily flavour.

PHAETON, Lin. &c. TROPIC BIRD.

PHAETON.

Bill as long as the head, thick, strong, hard, sharp-edged, much compressed, pointed, slightly sloped from the base, edges of the mandibles widened at the base, compressed and serrated in the rest of their length; nostrils basal, lateral, covered above and near the base by a naked membrane, and pervious; legs very short, placed far back, all the toes connected by a web; wings long; tail shorter, but characterised by the elongation of the two filamentous middle feathers.

Phœnicu-
rus.

P. phœnicurus, Tem. *Red-Tailed*, or *Common Tropic Bird.* Of a roseate flesh-colour; bill, and two middle tail-feathers red. Two feet ten inches long, of which the two middle tail-feathers measure one foot nine inches. The young of the first year are streaked black and white, with the under parts white; the bill black; the quill-feathers tipt with white; and those of the tail with black, constituting *P. melanorhynchos*, of some authors; but, in a more advanced state they are white, with the middle tail-feathers black at the base, corresponding to *P. œthereus*, of various ornithologists. These birds are well known to navigators, and generally announce their approach to the tropics, although they sometimes wander to the latitude of $47\frac{1}{2}°$. They are capable of supporting long flights, and of reposing on the water, feeding on the flying fish and others of the finny tribe that approach to the surface of the water. They rarely alight on the ground, and walk with awkward heaviness; but they glide through the air, or along the water, with grace and nimbleness. They breed mostly in desert or unfrequented islands, placing their nests on trees, or in holes of abrupt rocks. The female lays two yellowish white eggs, marked with rust-coloured spots. Their flesh is very indifferent food.

COLYMBUS, Tem. and including part of the Linnéan COLYMBI. DIVER.

COLYM-
BUS.

Bill of moderate dimensions, straight, very pointed, compressed; nostrils basal, lateral, concave, oblong, half closed by a membrane, and pervious; legs placed far behind, tarsi compressed, the three fore toes very long, and quite webbed, the hinder short, with the loose rudiment of a web; wings short; tail very short and rounded.

The species included under this family reside chiefly in the water, and are almost habitual divers. On the land, which they scarcely ever visit but in breeding time, they can with difficulty walk, or hold themselves in an erect position, so that they are then easily caught. They nestle on small islands or headlands, generally lay two eggs, and devour great quantities of fish and their fry, marine insects, and even vegetable productions. The sexes do not externally differ; but the markings of the young are very distinct from those of the mature birds, to which they are not assimilated till the third year. Their moulting takes place only once a-year. Their conformation, as was long since observed by Ray, is admirably fitted for making their way through the water with great expedition.

C. glacialis, Gmel. Lath. &c. *Great Northern Diver, Greatest Speckled Diver, Great Loon, Immer, Imber, Emmer, Ember Goose,* or *Great Doucker.* Upper mandible almost straight, the under bent upwards, broad in the middle, and channelled beneath; length of the bill four inches, and from one to four lines, according to the age of the individual. Length of the full-grown individual from twenty-seven to thirty inches; between four and five feet in extent of wing; and weight from fifteen to sixteen pounds, being one of the largest of the tribe. Frequents the arctic seas of both continents, and breeds among the fresh waters in Greenland, Iceland, Russia, Norway, Sweden, the Hebrides, Orkneys, &c. usually selecting the least accessible spots among the reeds and flags. The eggs resemble those of a goose, and are slightly spotted with black. The female defends her offspring with great boldness, and sometimes makes the intruder repent his rashness. The young occasionally visit the inland lakes of France, Germany, and Switzerland, but, except during severe weather, they are seldom met with in England. The northern diver is capable of sustaining a lofty flight, but resides mostly on the sea, feeding on sprats, atherines, and other small fish, or fry, on which it pounces or dives with great address and violence. Being easily scared, and instantly taking refuge under water, it is with difficulty shot; but it is sometimes accidentally caught in nets, or by hooks, at a considerable depth. Its cry is said to resemble the howling of dogs. Immediately under the skin there is a layer of fat, nearly an inch thick; but the flesh is reckoned uneatable. The skin, which is tough, and covered with soft down, is, in some of the northern countries, tanned and used as clothing.

C. septentrionalis, Lin. &c. *Red-throated Diver,* or *Loon,* Prov. *Northern Douker, Rain Goose,* or *Sprat Loon.* Bill straight, slightly curved upwards, edges of the two mandibles much bent inwards; length of the bill two inches and ten lines, or three inches. Native of the same cold latitudes as the other divers, with which, also, its habits coincide. The male and female are so constant in their attachment, that if one of them be shot, the other hovers about the spot for days together, and will sometimes venture so near the sportsman as to share the same fate. They make a howling, and sometimes a croaking noise, which the Orcadians regard as a presage of rainy or stormy weather. They are seldom seen far south, except in very severe seasons; but, in winter, they pretty regularly visit England, Holland, France, &c. In the Orkneys they statedly breed. The nest, which is placed in marshy situations, among reeds and flags, is usually composed of moss and grass, lined with down from the bird's own breast, and containing two very oblong, olivaceous-brown eggs, marked with a few dusky spots. In the harbour of Stromness, this species has been observed to make great havoc among the fry of the coal-fish.

URIA, Briss. Tem. COLYMBUS and ALCA, Lin. GUILLEMOT.

Bill middle-sized, short, stout, straight, pointed, compressed, upper mandible slightly incurved near the point; nostrils basal, lateral, concave, longitudinally cleft, half-closed by a broad membrane, covered

Ornitho-
logy.

Glacialis.

Septentrionalis.

URIA.

with feathers, and pervious; legs short, placed far behind; tarsi slender, furnished with only three toes, which are placed before and webbed; wings short. The guillemots, like the divers, are residents of the northern seas, little fitted for moving on land, and seldom venturing on shore except in breeding time, or when impelled by tempests. During the rigour of their native climates, they migrate southwards, along the coasts of some of the countries of Europe. They dive with great facility, and swim nimbly under water. They breed in company, in the holes of rocks, each female laying only one large egg. They moult twice a-year; and the complete winter plumage of the sexes is the same; nor do the young materially differ in their markings from the mature birds.

U. troile, Lath. Tem. *Colymbus troile*, and *Colymbus minor*, Gmel. *Foolish*, or *Lesser Guillemot*, Prov. *Willock, Skout, Kiddaw, Guillem, Sea-hen, Lavy, Strany, Lungy, Skuttock*, &c. Bill much compressed in its whole length, longer than the head; wings of an uniform colour, but the secondaries tipped with white; legs dusky. Length from fifteen to seventeen inches; extent of wing twenty-seven inches and a half; and weight twenty-four ounces, being a plump and heavy bird in proportion to its size. Inhabits the northern seas of Europe, Asia, and America, migrating, in large troops, in winter, to the coasts of Norway, the Baltic, Great Britain, Holland, France, &c. but more rarely wandering to the interior lakes of continents. Feeds on fish, particularly sprats, marine insects, bivalve testacea, &c. It often breeds in company with the auks, among the cliffs of the rocks, as in the Isle of Priestholm, near Anglesea, the Fern Isles, on the coast of Northumberland, and the precipitous rocks near Scarborough. In St. Kilda, it arrives about the beginning of February, and is hailed by the inhabitants as the harbinger of plenty. A rock-man of this remote island will descend in the night, by the help of a rope, to the ledge of a precipice, where he fixes himself, and tying round him a piece of white linen, awaits the approach of the bird, which, mistaking the cloth for a portion of the rock, alights on it, and is immediately dispatched. The foolish guillemot lays but one egg, which is very large, unprotected by any nest, and has such a slender hold of the rock, that, when the birds are surprised and fly off suddenly, many of the eggs tumble down into the sea. The eggs are beautifully variegated with black, white, yellow, blue, and green; and scarcely any two of them exactly resemble one another. These birds seldom quit the duty of incubation, unless disturbed, but are fed with sprats, and other small fish, by the male. In places where they are seldom molested, it is with difficulty they are put to flight; and they may sometimes be taken with the hand, whilst others flounder into the water, making, apparently, little use of their wings. In Orkney, they continue throughout the winter. They are sometimes very numerous in the Frith of Forth, where they seem to subsist chiefly on sprats.

U. grylle, Lath. &c. *Colymbus grylle*, Lin. &c. *Black*, or *Spotted Guillemot*, Prov. *Greenland Dove, Sea Turtle, Tysle*, &c. A large white patch on the middle of the wings; legs red. Black above, white beneath; and on the cheeks; iris brown. The mature male measures thirteen inches in length, twenty-two in extent of wing, and weighs about fourteen ounces. Inhabits the northern regions, and migrates in winter to more southern latitudes, but is seldom seen on shore. It is common in the Bay of Dublin, and continues throughout the

year. Mr. Henry Boys observed both the old and young birds, in the month of August, near Stonehaven, in the north of Scotland. It likewise frequents the Faroe Isles, the Bass, St. Kilda, &c. visiting them in March, making its nest far under ground, and laying one oblong egg, of a dirty white, blotched with large and small spots of black and cinereous, which are crowded near one of the ends. Except in breeding time, it keeps always at sea, lives on fish, flies low, and generally in pairs. It cannot, without considerable difficulty, rise from the ground. Its feathers are thick and close, and so damp with the quantity of oil with which the bird takes care to anoint them, as to have a very rank smell, and to be thus unfit for the purposes of bedding, for which they would otherwise be excellently suited. The Greenlanders eat its flesh, and use its skin for clothing, and its legs as bait to their fishing lines.

U. alle, Tem. *Alca alle*, Lin. &c. *U. minor*, Briss. *Mergulus alle*, Vieil. *Little Auk*, or *Small Black and White Diver*, Prov. *Little Greenland Dove, Sea Turtle, Rotche, Rodge, Ratch, Ice-bird*, &c. Bill very short, about half as long as the head, and very little arched. These birds inhabit the northern seas, at least as high as latitude 76°, where they abound among the channels between the floes of ice. During storms or intense cold, some of them are impelled into more southerly climates, but very few of them breed with us. They feed much on a small species of cancer, and breed in the holes and crevices of craggy rocks, without any formal preparation of a nest, the female laying one bluish-green egg, generally without spots, but sometimes minutely sprinkled with dusky. Captain Ross and his crew encountered myriads of these birds in the frozen seas through which they navigated. In July and August, the ship's company were daily supplied with them, and relished them as a palatable food, destitute of any fishy flavour. They were found in particular to make excellent soup, not unlike, and not at all inferior to, that made of hare. The Esquimaux make inner garments of the skins.

PHALERIS, Tem. ALCA, Lath. &c. STARIKI.

Bill shorter than the head, depressed, dilated on the sides, nearly quadrangular, notched at the tip, the lower mandible forming a salient angle; nostrils marginal, in the middle of the bill linear, half-concealed, and pervious; legs short, placed far behind, tarsus slender, with only three toes, claws much incurved, wings middle-sized.

P. cristatella, Tem. *Alca cristatella*, Lath. *Tufted Stariki*, or *Tufted Auk*. A tuft on the forehead, composed of several short feathers, from the middle of which rise six long filamentous and silky plumes, which bend forward on the bill. Scarcely larger than the missel-thrush. The young is the *Alca Pygmæa*, Lath. &c. Frequents Kamtschatka, and the islands situated between Asia and America.

FRATERCULA, Briss. Vieil. MORMON, Illig. Tem. ALCA, Lin. &c. PUFFIN.

Bill shorter than the head, deeper than long, and much compressed; both mandibles arched, transversely channelled, and notched towards the tip, the upper sharp-ridged, and elevated above the level of the skull; nostrils lateral, marginal, linear, naked, almost wholly concealed by a large naked membrane; legs short, placed far behind, furnished with only three toes, all directed forwards and webbed, claws much

Y

hooked; wings short. The birds of this family are
nearly allied to the guillemots and the penguins; with
the last of which they have been generally classed.
Though less addicted to fly than the former, they are
very seldom found on land, and they graze the surface
of the sea with considerable swiftness.

Arctica.

F. arctica, Vieil. *Mormon fratercula,* Tem. *Alca
arctica,* Lin. &c. *Puffin, Puffin Auk,* or *Labrador Auk,*
Prov. *Greenland Parrot, Tommy, Tammine, Willich,
Bass Cock, Ailsa Cock, Sea Parrot, Cockandy, Pope,
Bowger, Coulterneb,* &c. Bill compressed, two-edged,
upper mandible with three grooves, the under with
two, orbits and temples white, upper eyelid daggered,
or furnished with a pointed callus. The mature male
and female, both in their winter and summer dress,
have the crown of the head, all the upper parts, and a
broad collar, deep and glossy black, the quill-feathers
dusky brown, the breast, belly, and lower parts, pure
white. Length about twelve inches and a half, extent
of wing twenty-one inches, weight about twelve
ounces. The bill, which imparts such an appearance
of novelty to this bird, varies considerably, according
to its age; for, in the first year, it is small, weak, destitute of any furrow, and dusky; in the second year, it
is larger, stronger, of a paler colour, and discovers a
faint vestige of a furrow near the base; but in the third,
and more advanced years, it exhibits great strength
and vivid colours.

These birds inhabit, in vast flocks, the northern seas
of Europe, Asia, and America. They are very common
about the coast of Spitzbergen, but are rarely met
with at any great distance from land. In their southward progress, they have been found about Belleisle, in
the Gulf of Gascony. As they take flight with great
difficulty, they are sometimes run down by boats, or
driven ashore, when suddenly caught in a gust of
wind; but they can fly very well when once they get
wind. They appear in many parts of our rocky coasts,
about the middle of April, and commence breeding towards the middle of May. On the Dover cliffs, and
other such places, they deposit their single white egg
in the holes and crevices; but, in other situations, they
burrow, like rabbits, if the soil is light, or more frequently, take possession of a rabbit's hole, and lay
their egg some feet under ground. On St. Margaret's
Island, off St. David's, the fishermen put their hands
into the holes, and the puffins seize them so obstinately, that they allow themselves to be drawn out. The
Orcadians drag them out with a stick, to the end of
which is attached an iron hook. The flesh of the old
bird is both rank and fishy, but the young ones, which
are seized before they are quite fledged, when pickled
and preserved with spices, are much relished by some,
and are allowed to be eaten, in Roman Catholic countries, during Lent. In some places they are taken with
ferrets. The males, as well as females, perform the
office of sitting, relieving each other when they go to
feed. The young are hatched in the beginning of
July, and the re-migration of the species takes place
about the middle of August, when none remain behind, except the unfledged young of the latter hatches.
In one part of *Akaroe,* a small island off Iceland,
puffins breed in vast numbers, forming holes in the
mould, three or four feet beneath the surface. Their
principal food consists of shrimps, and a minute species
of *helix;* but they also eat small fish, and particularly
sprats. The Icelanders use their flesh for bait, and it
is alleged that the cod prefers it to any thing else.

ALCA, Lin. Tem. AUK.

Bill straight, broad, compressed, much incurved at
the tip, both mandibles half covered with feathers,
and grooved near the point, the upper hooked, the
lower forming a salient angle; nostrils lateral, marginal, linear, situated near the middle of the bill, almost entirely closed by a membrane, and covered with
feathers; legs short, placed far behind, and furnished
with three fore-toes, connected by a web; wings short.
The auks have nearly the same habits as the other marine arctic birds, seldom being seen on land, except for
the purpose of breeding, and resembling the guillemots, in particular, in their mode of life, and in laying
one large egg. M. Temminck has ascertained that
they moult twice a-year; that the sexes do not materially differ in external appearance, and that the winter
livery has been erroneously represented as the appropriate costume of the female.

Torda.

A. torda, Lin. &c. *Razor-bill* or *Razor-billed Auk.*
Prov. *Alk, Olke, Falk, Murre, Marrot, Scout, Bawkie,*
&c. Wings ending at the rump; tail lengthened, conical; size of the teal. The full grown individuals
measure about fourteen or fifteen inches in length, and
twenty-seven in extent of wing. They inhabit the
arctic seas of both continents, and migrate to the coasts
of Norway, Holland, Britain, France, &c. Not only
do they associate with guillemots, but breed in the
same places. About the beginning of May they take
possession of the highest cliffs, for the purpose of incubation, assembling on the ledges of the rocks in great
numbers, and sitting closely together, often in a series
of rows above one another. There they deposit their
single large egg on the bare rock, and, notwithstanding
the multitudes of them which are thus mixed together,
no confusion takes place; for each bird knows its own
egg, and hatches it in that situation. The sun's rays,
reflected from the bare rock, doubtless aid the heat of
incubation. But it has often excited wonder, that the
eggs are not rolled off into the sea by gales of wind, or
on being touched by the birds; and, it is alleged, that,
if they are removed by the human hand, it is impossible, or at least extremely difficult, to replace them in
their former steady situation. This is accounted for
by some ornithologists, who assert, that the egg is fixed
to the spot on which it is first laid by a glutinous substance, with which the shell is covered, and which
keeps it firmly in its place, until the young is produced.
The egg of this species is three inches long, and of a
greenish-white colour, irregularly marked with dark
spots. When eaten with salt, pepper, and vinegar, it
is reckoned palatable; but the flesh of the birds themselves is rank and fishy tasted; and yet the people in
Orkney venture over the most dreadful precipices in
quest of them.

Impennis.

A. impennis, Lin. &c. *Great Auk* or *Penguin,* Prov.
Northern Penguin or *Gair Fowl.* Wings destitute of
the feathers requisite for flight; size of a goose. The
wings are very short, not exceeding four inches and
one-fourth from the tips of the longest quill-feathers to
the first joint, and are thus useless for the purposes of
flight, but, nevertheless, very serviceable in swimming
under water. The great auks frequent the frozen seas
as far north as navigators have penetrated, seldom
straying far from land or floating ice, and yet never
quitting the water but for the purposes of breeding,
being nearly as unfit for walking as for flying, and,
when on shore, holding themselves, like the other auks

Ornitho-
logy.

and penguins, in a nearly vertical position. They visit, though in no great numbers, the Orkneys and St. Kilda, arriving about the beginning of May, and departing about the middle of June. On the ledges, or in the fissures of rocks, or in holes of its own excavation, and, frequently, close by the sea-mark, the female lays a single egg, of a very large size, being about six inches long, of a white or roan cast, marked with numerous black or purple lines and spots, which have been compared to Chinese writing.

SPHENISCUS, Briss. Tem. APTENODYTES, Lath. PEN-GUIN.

PHENIS-
CUS.

Bill shorter than the head, compressed, very thick, strong, hard, straight, hooked at the tip, obliquely grooved, edges of both mandibles bent inwards, the under covered with feathers at the base, and truncated, or obtuse at the tip; nostrils small, lateral, placed near the middle of the bill, and cleft in the furrow; legs very short, thick, placed quite behind the centre of gravity, four toes directed forwards, of which three are webbed, and the fourth is little more than a tubercle; wings incapable of being used for flight, the feathers on them being so short as to resemble scales. The birds of this genus inhabit the South Seas, from the equator to the antarctic circle, and are analogous to those of the preceding, in colour, food, and habits. They are fortified against cold by an abundance of fat; they swim very swiftly; and, on land, they cackle like geese, but in a hoarser tone.

Demersus.

S. demersus, Tem. *Aptenodytes demersa,* Lath. *Eudyptes demersa*, Vieil. *Cape Penguin.* Bill and legs black; eye-brows and pectoral band white. Black above, white beneath. Size of a small goose, and about twenty-one inches long. There are two or three varieties. Inhabits the Southern Seas, chiefly about the Cape of Good Hope. Like its congeners, it swims and dives with great expertness, but hops and flutters, in a strangely awkward manner, on land; and, if hurried, it stumbles, or makes use of its imperfect wings as legs, till it recovers its upright posture, crying, at the same time, like a goose, but with a hoarser voice. When it has scratched a hole in the sand among the bushes on the shore, it lays two white eggs, which are in request by epicures. Should a person happen to come within reach of its bill, when it is tending its eggs or young, it bites severely.

Minor.

S. minor, Tem. *Aptenodytes minor*, Lath. *Eudyptes minor*, Vieil. *Little Penguin.* Bill of the same conformation as the preceding, with the upper mandibles blackish, and the inner blue at the base. Upper plumage ash-blue, and dusky-brown at the origin of the feathers, the under parts white. Size of a teal, about fourteen inches long. Inhabits New Zealand, where it digs deep holes in the earth, in which to lay its eggs.

Chryso-
come.

S. chrysocome, Aptenodytes chrysocome, Lath. *Eudyptes chrysocome*, Vieil. *Crested Penguin.* Bill red, and three inches long; upper mandible curved at the end, the lower obtuse. These birds are inhabitants of

several of the South Sea islands. They have the names of *Hopping Penguins* and *Jumping Jacks*, from their action of leaping quite out of the water, sometimes three or four feet, on meeting with any obstacle in their course, or even without any other apparent cause than the desire of advancing by that manœuvre. This species seems to have a greater air of liveliness in its countenance than almost any of the other penguins; yet it is still a very stupid bird; and so regardless of its own safety as even to suffer any person to lay hold of it. When provoked, it erects its crest in a very beautiful manner; and we are told, that, when attacked by our voyagers, it ran at them in flocks, picked their legs, and spoiled their clothes. Their sleep is uncommonly profound, and they are very tenacious of life. They form their nests among those of the other large seafowls, making holes in the earth with their bills, and throwing back the dirt with their feet. The female generally lays only a single egg. They are often found in great numbers on the shores where they have been bred. The *cataractes*, which some authors describe as a separate species, appears to be only the young of the present.

Ornitho-
logy.

APTENODYTES, Forst. Tem.

Bill longer than the head, slender, straight, inflected at the tip, the upper mandible furrowed throughout its length, the under wider at the base, and covered with a naked and smooth skin; nostrils in the upper part of the bill, and concealed by the feathers in the front; legs very short, thick, placed far behind, four toes directed forwards, three of which are webbed, and the fourth very short; wings incompetent for flight.

APTENO-
DYTES.

A. Patachonica, Lath. &c. *Eudyptes Patachonica*, Vieil. *Patagonian Penguin.* Bill and legs black; ears with a golden spot; lower mandible tawny at the base; irides hazel; head and hind part of the neck brown; back dark-blue; breast, belly, and vent, white. Four feet three inches long; and some individuals have weighed thirty pounds. Inhabits Falkland Islands, New Guinea, and some of the islands of the South Sea. It is so stupid as to allow itself to be knocked down with sticks. M. Bougainville caught one, which soon became so tame as to follow and recognise the person who had the care of it. For some time it fed on flesh, fish, and bread, but gradually grew lean, pined, and died. This species is not only the largest, but the fattest of the genus; and its flesh, though black, is not very unpalatable.

Patacho-
nica.

M. Temminck has formed his concluding order of those birds which he terms *inert* or *sluggish*, and comprises under it the *Apteryx* of Shaw, and the *Didus* of Linné, and others; but so much obscurity still hangs on the history of these real or fictitious families, that it may be more prudent to wait for further information, than to repeat the vague and discordant statements of authors who never saw a live individual of the tribe.

Inert birds.

H. N. A.

INDEX.

ERRATA.

Page 18, col. 1, line 59, for *those* read *these*.
  32, col. 1, line 16, for *first* read *present*.
  54, col. 1, line 61, for *Rubicola* read *Rubecola*.
  66, col. 2, line 32, for *autricapillus* read *atricapillus*.
  79, col. 2, line 7, for *C.* read *F.*
  87, col. 2, line 59, for *R.* read *T.*
  88, col. 1, line 14, for *Macrorecus* read *Macrocecus*.

Page 90, col. 1, line 46, for *cossius* read *cossus*.
  94, col. 1, line 31, for *lid* read *bed*.
  105, col. 2, line 44, for *escaped* read *escape*.
  139, col. 1, line 36, for *Melanuca* read *Melanura*.
  144, col. 1, line 12, for LOPHERHYNCHUS, read LO-
PHORHYNCHUS.

OROONOKO, or ORINOCO, a celebrated river of South America, and one of the largest in the world. It is 1380 miles in length, including the windings. Its breadth, at 200 leagues from the sea, is about 2500 fathoms, and at St. Thomas, the capital of Spanish Guiana, it is 3850 fathoms. Its depth, at the same place, taken when the waters were at the lowest, was found to be 65 fathoms. The source of this river is not known with certainty, but it is supposed to be in the Ibirinoko mountains, and, according to La Cruz, it rises in the small lake of Ipava, in 55° north latitude, from whence it turns round and enters Lake Parima, to the south-east; then, taking a northerly direction, it is joined by several large rivers, from the eastern ridge of the Andes, and here forms the so long disputed junction with the great river Amazons. M. Humboldt in 1800 undertook a long and arduous journey, for the purpose of ascertaining this point, and had the satisfaction of placing it beyond a doubt. He entered the Oroonoko by the Cassiquiari, in 3° 30' north latitude, and ascended the current of the great river as far as Esmeralda, the last of the Spanish settlements in that quarter. On its southern, or left bank, it receives the rivers Maquiritari, the Cunucuma, Ventuari, Caura, Aruy, and Caroni; and, from its western bank, it acquires the still larger and more important additions of the Cassiquiari, Guariari, the Meta, and the Apure, which last is 500 miles long. The Oroonoko then turns eastward, and, dividing itself into a number of branches, discharges itself into the ocean by fifty mouths, seven of which only are navigable. The great mouth of the Oroonoko is formed by Cape Barima, to south-south-east, which is in 8° 54' north latitude, and the island of Cangrejos, lying west-north-west of the cape. They are twenty-five miles distant from each other, but the navigable part of the passage is about three.

The cataracts of the Oroonoko, at the villages Maypura and Atures, in about 6° of north latitude, are described as the most stupendous that are known. The whole scenery of the banks of this river is represented to be of the most magnificent description; vast forests are filled with aromatic trees; birds of the most beautiful plumage present themselves, and hordes of monkeys follow the steps of the traveller.

The annual inundation of the Oroonoko begins in April, and ends in August; and, in the northern part, sometimes extends twenty or thirty leagues, in a length of 200. This immense extent it retains for the whole month of September. At the distance of 1300 miles from its mouth, the rise is thirteen fathoms. The waters begin to decrease early in October, and by the end of February it is at its lowest ebb, in which state it continues till the beginning of April. The Oroonoko abounds in fish and amphibious animals of various kinds. The cayman is one of its most formidable inhabitants. Numerous Indian tribes, possessing from 500 to 2000 warriors each, inhabit the banks of this river. The Caribs boast of having 12,000 men, and the Cabarres were still more numerous. To the south of the river, the efforts of the missionaries to civilize them have been entirely fruitless. The mouth of the Oroonoko is in west longitude 59° 50', and north latitude 8° 30'. See Humboldt's *Personal Narrative*.

ORPHEUS, is the name of a real or a fabulous poet and musician of antiquity. He is said to have been an adventurer in the Argonautic expedition, and to have allured the Argonauts to row by the sound of his lyre. From a passage in Cicero, it has been inferred that Orpheus was a personage entirely allegorical,

and Dr. Cudworth has combated this opinion with much learning and ingenuity. See Cudworth's *Intellectual System*; Warburton's *Divine Legation of Moses*; Burnet's *Archæologia*; and Brucker's *History of Philosophy*.

ORRERY is the name of a piece of machinery for representing the various motions of the heavenly bodies. An account of different orreries will be found under our article PLANETARY MACHINES.

ORYCTOGNOSY. See MINERALOGY.

OSIRIS. See EGYPT, vol. VIII. p. 402, &c. &c. MYTHOLOGY, vol. XV. p. 146, &c.

OSMIUM. See CHEMISTRY, vol. vi. p. 21.

OSNABURG, or OSNABRUCK, the capital of a province of the Kingdom of Hanover, of the same name, is situated on the river Hase. It is fortified in the ancient manner, with walls and ditches, and is divided into the Old and New Towns. The houses are very low and irregularly disposed. The principal buildings are the cathedral and its relics, and the Maison de Ville, where the peace of Westphalia was concluded in 1648; four churches, two Lutheran and two Catholic; an orphan house for the Lutherans; four hospitals, a workhouse and a Catholic and Lutheran gymnasium. The Freyung is a favourite place of resort for the inhabitants, and has the advantage of an agreeable walk. There are here manufactures of coarse linen, called Osnaburgs, made in the surrounding country; of coarse woollen, leather and tobacco, besides several bleach-fields. Population, 9300. Some authors make the number of houses 1200, and the population 6000. East long. 8° 1' 11''. North lat. 52° 16' 35''. See Mangourit's *Travels in Hanover*; Catteau's *Voyage en Allemagne*, vol. i. p. 142, and the article HANOVER, vol. X. p. 633. 636.

OSSIAN[*]. The name of Ossian is now so well known, over all Europe, and, we might add, over all the world, that it might appear a defect in a work of this kind to omit noticing it. His poems, as translated by Mr. Macpherson, have acquired a celebrity of the most extraordinary kind.

We do not intend to enter largely into the controversy respecting their authenticity, which for upwards of forty years has agitated the public mind. That Ossian existed, has not been, and cannot be, called in question, while a nation exists to attest the fact. That poems ascribed to him, as well as to Oran, Ullin, Fergus, and other cotemporary bards, also existed, and have been handed down some way or other, has not, so far as we know, been disputed. On this subject positive evidence has been demanded, with a tone which indicated total ignorance of Caledonian history, or minds predisposed to resist conviction. All the evidence which the case admits, has been for years before the public; that is, the testimony of credible witnesses, and the poems themselves, in the original, as found among the papers of Mr. Macpherson.

The first thing, however, is to give a short outline of Ossian himself.

He was the oldest son of Friom, called in the poems Fingal, that is, the fair Gaul, the Fulgentius of Fordun, king of Morven, or of the west mountainous coast of Scotland, one of the best of men, one of the bravest of warriors, and the most finished character recorded in profane history. Fingal was descended of a long line of renowned ancestors. The example of some of them he quotes, as worthy of imitation by his favourite grandson Oscar. Fingal, Duan Third. Gillies, 34.

Of the extent of his dominions we have no certain, or even probable information. We doubt, whether,

---

[*] The editor has been indebted for this article to the REV. ALEXANDER IRVINE, D.D. of Little Dunkeld.

as Dr. John Smith seems to think, it comprehended almost all that territory which afterwards made up what was called the Scottish kingdom, before the Pictish kingdom was annexed to it; we however, refer to the Doctor's Seann Dana, p. 35, 36; and to Innes' Appendix to his critical Essay. From the poems of Ossian, and from tradition, we know that he was a prince of great renown.

Who Ossian's mother was, (probably Agandecca, daughter of Magnus Starno, king of Lochlin,) we are not certain, nor do we think it of any great consequence to waste time in inquiring. He was married early in life, to Everallin, daughter of Branno, king of Lego, in Ireland. She died not long after the birth of Oscar, their only son; and Ossian, who never married again, often alludes to her loss, and describes her beauty. Addressing Malvina, his daughter-in-law, in the fourth book of Fingal, he thus speaks : " Of Everallin are my thoughts, when in the light of beauty she came, her blue eyes rolling in tears." He had several brothers, whose fame he commemorates in his poems. At what period Ossian lived is disputed. If we allow Ireland the honour of giving him birth, the point is speedily settled; we have no objection, however, to give the Irish their own Ossian and their own Fingal, to command their militia and fight their battles, provided they allow us our Ossian and our Fingal, as familiar to the ear of every Highlander as Homer was to the Greeks, and Virgil or Horace to the Romans.

It seems settled among those who have investigated the subject, that he flourished towards the end of the third, or beginning of the fourth century. We refer for farther information to Mr. Macpherson's excellent dissertation on the era of Ossian, and also to that of Dr. J. Smith. Boethius, however, whose work was published in 1526, conjectures that he lived about a century later, that is, in the time of Eugenius, the son of Fergus the Second, who died in 462. On the supposition that the poems ascribed to him are really his, we are inclined to think that he lived earlier. For, in the fifth century, Christianity began to make some progress in Caledonia, to assume some settled form, and Druidism, as an established religion, was nearly overthrown. Hence, if Ossian had lived at this time, it is scarcely possible to think that he could have been unacquainted with Christianity, as his poems uniformly evince he was. The discussion he had with Patrick, a Christian missionary, one of the Culdees, still extant, and supposed to be authentic, tends to show that the Gospel was only then offering itself to the inhabitants of Caledonia. This controversy is highly amusing, and proves that Ossian had hardly any idea of a Supreme Being, at least, of one in strength and prowess superior to his father and Gaul.

His life was continually employed in wars, and to his exploits he often refers, to sooth his sorrows, when, in old age, he could no longer lift the spear. He lived to old age. He survived almost all his family and companions. Malvina alone, the daughter of Toscar, a petty prince of one of the Hebrides Isles, his son Oscar's wife, remained to attend and to comfort him, and probably survived him; to her he addressed most of his poems, or rather history. He lost his eyesight, which he feelingly laments. But, according to a poem in the possession of the writer of this article, it is said that he recovered it before he died. This may have been. The mode in which he recovered it partakes of the marvellous. We have, however, known several old men, who could see but very imperfectly for years, and yet whose sight improved some time before they died.

At what period Ossian died cannot now be exactly ascertained; as little can we ascertain with any degree of historical accuracy where he was buried. His tomb, at least a tomb called Ossian's, is believed by the natives, who cherish his memory with pious veneration, to be in Glen Almond, some miles north of Crieff, in Perthshire, next to Glenco, one of the most romantic glens in Caledonia. Considering that the scene of his warlike exploits was generally in the west and south-west of Scotland, or in Ireland, though he warred also against the king of the world, it admits of some doubt whether his body could have been deposited in the rocky and sublime valley of the river Almond.

Here it may not be improper to remark, that every tribe, at least sixteen in number, vied with one another to do honour to a prince, a poet, and a warrior, whose name to the present hour is so sacredly cherished; and to question whose poems is so keenly resented.

Many of these poems, which have made such a noise over all Europe, must have been lost. Indeed, the few that remain furnish abundant proof of the fact, that they came down to us in a mutilated state. In this state, however, we boldly venture to assert they have come down; and had it not been for the patriotic and immortal exertions of Mr. James Macpherson, to whom his countrymen, and all lovers of taste, cannot be too grateful, by this time it is probable that not a fragment of them could be found.

The authenticity of these poems has been very naturally called in question; and therefore the principal intention of this article is to place that subject in a proper point of view, premising that for our own parts it is a matter of very little consequence whether they are the poems of Ossian or of Mr. Macpherson. We must assert, however, that if Mr. Macpherson, whose abilities have not received from his adversaries their due meed of praise, could have composed such poems, so completely divested of all symptoms of imitation and modern ideas, it would be one of the greatest wonders that poetic history ever exhibited, and one of the highest attainments ever mortal bard has reached.

In stating the arguments on both sides in this controversy, and the limits of our work only permit us to state them, the situation and character of Mr. Macpherson, we should think, is the first object of consideration. That he was a man capable of writing beautiful Gaelic poems respecting the heroic age of our fathers, we do not deny; for he had a lofty genius and daring which would attempt any thing in historical literature. But knowing, as he did, the character of his countrymen, to attempt to impose upon them a spurious modern composition under the name of Ossian, would have stamped his character with a degree of audacity which must have involved him in shame and defeat. Those who knew him best, as Dr. Blair, Dr. Ferguson, Mr. Home, and Dr. Carlyle, all concur in opinion, that he was the most unfit man upon earth to attempt such a design, even if it were practicable. What has been urged against him, as unreasonable and suspicious, in not satisfying cavillers, who by the by did not understand one word of his language, is to us one of the strongest proofs of his honesty. Upon authority which cannot by any rational being be disputed, he asserted that he was merely the translator of the poems which bore the name of Ossian. He asserted that he had the originals in his possession, and invited all men to inspect them. A part of them he published. To that part no one could object, as it bore the strongest marks of ancient composition. This part, 7th book of Temora, has been examined and criticized over and over again; and by none more severely than by the author of this article, and yet every one was forced to confess, that it was a genuine composition, of an age long prior to that of Mr. Macpherson. Though it is not our purpose to draw the character of Mr. Macpherson, we must here observe, that nothing but an invincible principle of honesty could have prevented him from yielding to the opinion which attempted to make him the author of the poems which he ascribed to Ossian. Every motive urged an avowal of his poetic imposture, and we could shew that he was not insensible of the opportunity offered to him, indeed pressed upon him, to make this avowal. But though we should suppose him altogether void of honourable principle, which was far from being the case, he knew well that twenty thousand Caledonians stood arrayed against him, to oppose his claims to a sovereignty to which he had no title, but that of making it known to nations who never heard of it before.

As to his admissions that he himself was the author, because he asserted, that a translator who could not equal his original was not fit to be his translator; though we admit that this assertion should be qualified, we must at the same time admit that it is founded in reason and experience. Mr. Macpherson had the genius of Ossian. His loftiness and independence he preserved in almost every line. But we would ask the admirers of Pope's translation of Homer, if Pope could have been fit for his undertaking, if he had not had a poetic spirit; and this will apply to Madame Dacier, Cowper, Macpherson, and every one who ever tried to turn Homer to English. Nor do we suppose that Dryden, who translated Virgil, would be accused of imposture, though he should have made the same concession as Mr. Macpherson.

Had, therefore, Mr. Laing, whose historical talents rank him among the first of Scottish historians, not been blinded by prejudice, or something else, he would not, with all his forensic acumen, have construed Mr. Macpherson's consistent defence into an admission that he was the author of the poems which he ascribed to Ossian.

We regret that our limits will not allow us to enter fully into the subject. We must, therefore, now give the outline of the evidence for and against the authenticity of these celebrated poems; and this evidence we must, according to the nature of the case, divide into the external and internal. The last has never yet been properly before the public.

First, then, as to the external evidence we know nothing more complete depending on human testimony. Indeed, it is so complete to every candid person, that we feel some shame in almost reminding our readers of its nature. When we find a crowd of men, of all sentiments, and of different languages, without any visible interest but the love of truth, or any ostensible design but justice to a long unknown genius, concur in one sentiment, the opposite evidence must preponderate, indeed, before we relinquish positive facts for negative assertions.

The competency of Dr. Johnson, Laing, O'Halloran, and others, must be admitted as to the evidence of testimony. Now, a priori, we ask, is the bare unbelief of these men, and perhaps a few more, to be put in competition with the positive belief of Dr. Blair, Dr. Ferguson, Dr. Carlyle, Mr. Home, Mr. Henry Mackenzie, a most competent judge, Lord Elibank, Principal Robertson, and even Mr. Hume, who only wanted testimony, which was given, and which satisfied him? Dr. Ferguson and Mr. Mackenzie were Gaelic scholars.

But though they were, is it possible for any human being, who knew or knows sterling unimpeachable integrity, to suppose that, against honest conviction, they would attest a lie? But farther, is it possible to believe, without almost a miracle of imposture, that such bodies as the Highland Societies of London and Scotland, composed of English, Irish, Scots and Caledonians, Germans, Danes, and French, could, during a period of sixty years, have lent their aid to a daring, unprecedented adventurer, and to the present hour persist in their delusion? Is the unbelief of a few individuals of questionable motives, or no motives at all, to be weighed against such external evidence?

If these learned and honourable bodies had made no inquiry to procure satisfaction respecting the credit due to these poems, or to Mr. Macpherson, there might be some room for discussion; but whoever reads the report of the Highland Society of Scotland, and the edition of Ossian's Poems by the Highland Society of London, with the admirable dissertation by Sir John Sinclair accompanying that edition, will at once see that they were most anxious to afford all the evidence in their power, evidence which completely satisfied themselves, and ought, in reason, to satisfy others.

Here we may remark, that Cesarotti, and all other foreigners, wonder how the question, as to the authenticity of these poems, should ever have been agitated. They had no common feeling with Caledonians. They judged of the poems themselves as presented in a hurried translation. They saw every mark of antiquity and originality, such as no modern poet ever produced. Dante, Petrarch, Camoens, Voltaire, and many others, were before them, and, in comparison, fell to nothing. They saw that, without a new and unaccountable phenomenon in human nature, it was utterly impossible that Mr. Macpherson could, in so short a time, have produced poems, in all their bearings so unlike every other modern composition. See Cesarotti's *Diss. Oss.* vol. iii. See also Baron Edmund de Harold's Poems, ed. 1787, Dusseldorf.

Though we might here enlarge, our limits will not permit. We must, therefore, refer our readers to Cesarotti, and Baron de Harold, who considered the subject with all due attention and impartiality, and have decided in favour of Ossian's authenticity; and so did Mr. Hill, an Englishman, who seems to have travelled principally for the purpose of obtaining satisfaction on the subject. Both he and Cesarotti have fallen into great blunders, arising from their ignorance of the language of Caledonia. We see, then, that notwithstanding the unbelief of Dr. Johnson, who, it is admitted, was not in all respects a competent judge, as he betrays gross ignorance of the language and history of Caledonia, all foreigners, to the present hour, received the poems of Ossian as authentic compositions of the age to which they are ascribed.

We must now come to the testimony of the Caledonians themselves, who were surely the most competent judges in such a matter.

And here a few preliminary remarks appear necessary.

It is not denied that many poems, for ages under the name of Ossian and other bards, were current among the Caledonians. The Fingalian heroes were familiar to their ears from their infancy. Their bards often referred to their exploits when they wished to rouse their hearers to deeds of valour.

Now, the question is, could a whole nation, composed of men of honour and education, have been, and still be, so infatuated and so unprincipled, as gratuitously to join Mr. Macpherson in the most daring literary imposture that ever the world witnessed? On this point, Dr. Johnson's illiberal remarks deserve only reprobation; for such is the length to which he carried his partial, malignant hostility to Mr. Macpherson, and therefore to Ossian, that he broadly asserts, that, for the honour of their country, the Highlanders would sacrifice every principle of truth and probity. To believe that they would do so, requires much more faith than to believe that a bard of the third or fourth century could compose poems such as Ossian's. Here also we must remark, that they were competent judges; and that, if Mr. Macpherson, or any body else, attempted to impose upon them spurious compositions, they would be the first to detect the fallacy, and to execrate the author of it. We have been long acquainted with the irrascibility of the Highland character upon this subject. In the course of extensive inquiries to satisfy our own curiosity, or to remove what we counted reasonable scruples, we found it difficult to obtain a patient hearing, the moment we insinuated that such existed. We uniformly met the same line of conduct for which Mr. Macpherson has been so severely blamed. Said one gentleman, in answer to a question as to the authenticity of the poems translated by Mr. Macpherson, " Do you believe your own existence? We think the Highlanders insulted when such pains have been taken to convince those who will not believe the evidence of their senses." No doubt one Highlander, Mr. Shaw, a native of Arran, though once a firm believer in the authenticity of these poems, retracted his opinion, and wrote against them with a degree of violence which can scarcely be reconciled with impartiality. His unbelief seems founded upon this fact, that he could not find any, or hardly any, of the poems translated by Mr. Macpherson, any where in the Highlands or Islands of Scotland. This has puzzled more than Mr. Shaw. But we think that Mr. Clark, author of the Caledonian Bards, might have satisfied him upon this head. For further information, we refer to the notes and supplemental observations following Cesarotti's *Dissert. Ossian.* vol. iii.; and to Sir John Sinclair's Dissertation, vol. i. Mr. Shaw, however, might have found parts of the identical poems translated by Mr. Macpherson, which are referred to in the Appendix to the Highland Society's Report, and some of which have been published in 1786, by Mr. Gillies, a bookseller in Perth. We, however, here also must stop, and refer for further information to Mr. Shaw's Inquiry; his Reply to Mr. Clark; and to Clark's Defence, especially Shaw *versus* Shaw.

Before we dismiss this part of the subject, we must quote two passages from the late Dr. John Smith, minister at Campbellton, one regarding Mr. Macpherson's mode of procedure in arranging the poems, so as to form a consistent whole; another stating his own mode, from which he was led to infer that Mr. Macpherson could not have done otherwise. " With regard," says he, in one of his letters to Mr. Henry Mackenzie, published in the Appendix to the Highland Society's Report, p. 75, " to the degree of liberty used by Mr. Macpherson in his translation, it is a point on which it is difficult to decide. With better materials and superior talents, his arrangement was far beyond any thing I could pretend to. But I am convinced, from experience, that he must have followed the same process. He must have not only used a discretionary power, or critical acumen, in combining and arranging the scattered parts of poems, as was done by those who collected the books of Homer; but he must also have used his judgment in comparing one edition with another, selecting or rejecting words, lines, and stanzas, now from one, and then from another, in order to make one correct edition, from which he would make his translation. He may sometimes have added, here and there, a connecting line or sentence, or may have perhaps cast one away, without deviating, in the main, from the strict sense and sentiment of his author; but the exact degree of liberty which he took can hardly be ascertained."

In his third letter to Mr. Mackenzie, dated Campbellton, June 21, 1802, after some very pertinent observations, he writes, " that, at least, the stamina, the bones, sinews, and strength of a great part of the poems now ascribed to him (Ossian) are ancient, may, I think, be maintained on many good grounds. But that some things modern may have been superinduced, will, if not allowed, be at least believed, on grounds of much probability; and, to separate precisely the one from the other, is more than the translator himself, were he alive, could now do, if he had not begun to do so from the beginning." (P. 90.)

Dr. Smith, as we read in his addenda to his Dissertation on the authenticity of the poems which he himself had published in 1787, and a translation of which he had published some years before, candidly states the process which he himself pursued, and which every one, in similar circumstances, as we know from experience, must pursue. " After the materials were collected, the next labour was to compare the different editions; to shake off several parts that were manifestly spurious; to bring together some episodes that appeared to have relation to one another, though repeated separately, and to restore to their proper places some incidents that seemed to have run from one poem into another. I am very confident, that the poems so arranged are different from all other editions. They have taken a certain degree of regularity and of art, in comparison with the disunited and irregular manner of the original. The building is not entire, but we have still the grand ruins of it." (See Cesarotti's *Dissert. Oss.* vol. iii. and Note T.) In his preface to the Gaelic poems which were published under the patronage, and chiefly at the expence, of the Highland Society of London, in 1787, he speaks of them in the following terms: " He hopes that, with all their imperfections, these poems have still so much merit as to give the reader some idea of what they once had been; that the venerable ruins are a sufficient monument of the former grandeur of the edifice."

Considering these candid statements by so pious and so honourable a judge, how could Mr. Shaw, or any body else, find such exact poems as Mr. Macpherson or he translated and published. Mr. Macpherson, we know from a letter of his now before us, written in 1792, and from other sources to be afterwards noticed, laboured most anxiously to purify the poems which he translated from every thing modern. We are, however, far from admitting that in this he succeeded, or could have succeeded.

The other Highlander supposed or believed to have been either an unbeliever in the authenticity of Ossian's Poems, or at least sceptical about them, as translated, was Mr. Donald Macqueen, minister of Kilmuir, in Sky, a learned antiquary, and an excellent classical scholar. From his silence on a question put to him by Dr. Johnson, it has been inferred that he was not satisfied on the subject. But let us hear himself. In a letter to Dr. Blair, published in the Appendix to the Report of the Highland Society of Scotland, and dated Kilmuir, April 17, 1764, he shows the contrary. In his postscript to that letter, he adds, "I have a just esteem for the translator's genius; and, believe me, after the narrowest search I could make, that there is a foundation in the ancient songs for every part of his work; but I am apt to believe, also, that he hath tacked together into the poems, descriptions, similes, names, &c. from several detached pieces; but of this I can give no demonstration, as I met only with fragments."

From this letter, he was convinced that there was at least a foundation for the poems as translated by Mr. Macpherson. He believed that he used much freedom in the disposition of his materials. Upon this, however, he could not speak positively, as he only met fragments, that is, of the poems translated. One of them, the description of Cuchullin's chariot and horses, the most improbable of the whole collection, yet the authenticity of which is placed beyond the range of the most sceptical. Nay, we shall by and by prove, that Mr. Macpherson, so far from being the author, did not even understand it; and we question if many Gaelic scholars at this moment can.

In a letter to Captain Alexander Morrison, Mr. Macpherson's amanuensis, and an able Gaelic scholar, dated Kilmuir, August 18, 1784, and now in the possession of the writer of this article, among other matters, he says, " Though I am no correspondent of Dr. Johnson, I am made to believe that he is rather in the humour of being serviceable to ——, and Mr. James Macpherson may perhaps lend her a good word on account of old Ossian, whose character I have on my finger ends, to defend without entering into controversy, which my soul abhors." This abhorrence of controversy accounts for his silence to Dr. Johnson's question. And, perhaps, having not had time to make up his mind on a subject on which he never before thought, he suspended his judgment till such time as he could come to a rational conviction. This at least indicated, that he himself was not credulous, and had no desire to deceive. It is a proof of his integrity. And yet this is the inference which the partial and illiberal mind of Dr. Johnson, so unlike himself in all the controversy, draws, for no assignable reason, but because in the height of his glory Macpherson treated his cavils with contempt. " I asked a very learned minister in Sky, who had used all arts to make me believe the genuineness of the book, whether at last he believed it himself; but he would not answer. He wished me to be deceived, for the honour of his country, but would not directly and formally deceive me. Yet has this man's testimony been publicly produced, as of one, that held Fingal to be the work of Ossian."—*Journey*, 274, 275.

Now, we would ask any man open to conviction, whether, after all arts to make another believe the truth of a story, any answer could be given to such a question, without resenting the insult and impertinence implied in putting it? Dr. Johnson did not perceive the politeness of Mr. Macqueen, and therefore drew a conclusion which his friends and admirers should wish expunged from his works.

Now, to come to a few particulars in the chain of testimony by every individual Highlander who paid attention to the subject, we must surely reject all human testimony, if we do not admit that of witnesses sufficient to prove any other fact. Though our limits do not permit us to enter widely into the concurring evidence of so many credible witnesses, yet some parts of that evidence may be adverted to. This is the more necessary, because we are persuaded that many, if

not all of those, who affect to question the authenticity of the poems, never examined, probably never read, this evidence. If they had done so, they would find that Mr. Macpherson never could attempt to impose upon those who either saw him receive the poems, or themselves furnished them. They who were most intimately acquainted with his labours in collecting them, though distant from one another, and altogether unknown to one another, uniformly concur as to his receiving these poems through the Highlands. " It was in my house," says Mr. Donald Macleod, minister of Glenelg, in a letter to Dr. Blair, dated Glenelg, 26th March, 1764, " that Mr. Macpherson got the description of Cuchullin's horses and car in book 1st, page 11, (Fingal) from Allan Macashie, schoolmaster, and Rory Macleod, both of this Glen. He has not taken in the whole of this description, and his translation of it, (spirited and pretty as it appears, as far as it goes,) falls so far short of the original in the picture it exhibits of Cuchullin's horses and car, their harness and trappings, &c. that in none of his translations is the inequality of Mr. Macpherson's genius to that of Ossian so very conspicuous." To this description we shall again refer, in considering the internal evidence. In the mean time, suffice it to say, that Mr. Macpherson rejected what he could not understand.

Mr. Macleod, who cannot be suspected of fraud, identifies the battle of Lena, Fingal, book 2d, with those variations which tend to prove the existence of Ossian's poems, also the poem, as he calls it, in book 3d, relating Fingal's voyage to Lochlin; and the poem, book 4th, in which each of Fingal's chiefs singles out the chief among the enemy he was to fight, leaving to Fingal the honour of engaging the king of Lochlin. We refer, for the rest, to his letter appended to Report, p. 28, *et seq.* As it is impossible that we can find room for the full details of evidence contained in the Appendix to the Highland Society's Report, and in the Report itself, we must refer to it. Particularly to Mr. Gallie's letters, Mr. M'Aulay, Lieut. Dun, Mr.Mac-Nicol, Dr. John Macpherson, Mr. M'Leod of Ross in Mull, Mr. Hope minister of Rea, in Caithness, Dr. John Smith, Ewan M'Pherson's declaration, Mr. Macpherson of Strathmashie's letter, dated Strathmashie, 22d October, 1763. His letter is peculiarly important, because Mr. Macpherson himself was a superior Gaelic scholar, an excellent poet, and a most competent judge. Neither he, nor such men as Mr. M'Aulay, could be imposed upon. They knew all the process of Mr. Macpherson's labours. Though this article has extended far beyond our intentions, we must submit an extract from Strathmashie's letter to Dr. Blair. " As I hear you have made application in this country for testimonies concerning the authenticity of Ossian's poems, I make bold to send you this letter, of which you may make what use you please. In the year 1760, I had the pleasure of accompanying my friend, Mr. Macpherson, during some part of his journey, in search of the poems of Ossian, through the Highlands. I assisted him in collecting them, and took down from oral tradition, and transcribed from old manuscripts, by far the greatest part of those pieces he has published. Since the publication, I have carefully compared the translation with the copies of the originals in my hands, and find it amazingly literal, even in such a degree, as to preserve, in some measure, the cadence of the Gaelic versification. I need not aver, Sir, that these poems are taken in this country to be of the utmost antiquity."

We also refer to the letters of Sir John Macpherson,

and Sir James M'Donald, both gentlemen of rank, education, ability, and honour. The latter died several years ago in the flower of his youth, to the great regret of all men who loved genius, ability, refined taste, and moral worth; the former only two years ago, after having attained high distinction by his civil and military talents.

This part of our detail we must conclude with a single extract from Mr. Pope's letter to Mr. Alexander Nicholson, minister of Thurso, dated Rea, 15th November, 1763, Appendix, No. III. " I have perused Dr. Blair's letter to you, and would heartily wish I could be of use in that affair, in which he has taken such a concern. It was quite proper that he went to the West Highlands, as these poems have been more carefully preserved in them than with us in the North Highlands. And, from both these quarters, he can get such evidences as are sufficient to convince people of candour; so that if the literati in England will not be persuaded, they must wait till they see Ossian and his heroes in another world." We also recommend to the attention of the reader, Mr. Macpherson's letters to Mr. James M'Lagan, then minister of Amulrie, afterwards of Blair in Atholl. When the correspondence began in 1760, they had not seen one another, and consequently were attracted by similarity of pursuit. In his first letter, dated Ruthven Badenoch, 27th October, 1760, Mr. Macpherson writes: " I have met with a number of old manuscripts in my travels; the poetical part of them I have endeavoured to secure."

Captain Morrison of Greenock's testimony in favour of the honesty of his friend Mr. Macpherson is highly worthy of notice. He knew him intimately; acted as his amanuensis, and had every opportunity of detecting any fallacy, if fallacy there could be. See his answers to queries, No. XIII. Appendix to MS. Report, p. 175. 177. In addition to this answer and general observations, he wrote to the writer of this article before they were personally acquainted: " When writing Ossian's poems with James Macpherson at London, Sir James Foulis wrote me to send him the address to the Sun, which I did: And that was not the one he wanted. He wrote the poem it was in, and then I sent it to him. He knew more of the Gaelic than James Macpherson, or any man I ever saw. This you will find if you can get access to his papers."

I wrote most part of Ossian's works, with Mr. Macpherson, before I went for my family to America, in 1781." This letter is dated Greenock, 20th December, 1800.

Though we have already offered more than sufficient proof that Mr. Macpherson was nothing more than the collector and translator of only part of Ossian's poems, it would be unpardonable if we passed over in silence Sir John Sinclair's admirable dissertation upon the subject; wherein he has adduced proof conclusive enough, if no other existed; and, as we must refer to that dissertation itself, vol. i. Ossian, we shall satisfy ourselves with quoting Dr. M'Arthur's words, from his supplemental observations to his translation of Cesarotti's Dissertation on the authenticity of Ossian's Poems, published in 1807.

" The Collection of Ossian's poems, made by the Rev. Mr. Farquharson, at an early period of his life, prior to Mr. Macpherson's poetical mission to the Highlands, and the existence of the thick folio manuscript volume containing these poems, which he left at the College of Douay, at the commencement of the French revolution, has been circumstantially detailed and proved by the concurrent testimony of two bishops and three respectable clergymen now living." *Ossian*, vol. iii. p. 479.

Whoever reads Sir John Sinclair's dissertation, with the letters of these respectable clergymen, and Dr. M'Arthur's notes and supplemental observations, must be consigned to invincible unbelief, unless he believes that Mr. Macpherson was no more than the translator and editor of Ossian.

We now come to another point in the editorial evidence, which arises from Dr. John Smith's poems of Ossian, Orran and Ullin, published in 1787.

We do not think that this part of the subject has received due attention, or any weight in the controversy. He published his translation of these poems seven years before. The originals were offered to the public under every circumstance which might demonstrate their claim to belief. Dr. Smith, whom we knew well, was a man of profound piety, of singular probity, and of excellent skill in Celtic literature. Except his brother Dr. Donald, we never knew any man equal to him in that department of national literature. The authenticity of the poems edited by him was never called in question. Kennedy, who made a collection of Gaelic poems, now in the possession of the Highland Society of Scotland, claimed the merit of some of the finest passages translated by Dr. Smith, and has brought their antiquity into doubt. As we cannot enter into this strange controversy, we must refer to the Report of the Society, and to Dr. Graham of Aberfoyle's excellent essay on the authenticity of Ossian's poems, and also to Mr. Stewart's essay. If Kennedy, a poor schoolmaster, were a man of genius and talents, some attention might be due to his assertion. But Dr. Smith's opinion is so decisive against the imposture of Kennedy, that no man of common sense can, for a moment, admit it. To think that a man, who could not write three lines of any poetry, could fabricate one of the sublimest descriptions in Smith's poems, would be almost a miracle of poetic fiction. But suppose even this true, enough remains to place the poems collected and published by Dr. Smith beyond the reach of suspicion.

If they are authentic, it follows of necessity that the poems translated by Mr. Macpherson must be so too, for they bear the same character. Now, can we suppose that two men, unacquainted with one another, and quite opposite in their nature, and, I may add, in their pursuits, could nearly at the same time fabricate compositions so like one another, and ascribe them to authors perhaps of doubtful existence, while they had it in their power to take the whole merit to themselves?

We are sorry our limits do not permit us to enter largely into this part of the subject. If they did, we could show that the poems collected and edited by Dr. Smith are fully equal, and in some respects superior, to those of Macpherson. We could show, that the compositions of the different bards, though the Dr. has not attempted to class them, are easily distinguished from one another, as easily as any scholar could distinguish Ovid from Virgil, or Dante from Tasso. We refer to Dargo and Gaul, the former by Ullin, and the latter by Ossian.

Now, could any man succeed in assuming such different characters as this? If he could, it would show that Dr. Smith and Mr. Macpherson were phenomena in the literary world that never before appeared.

We find in Dr. Smith's publication some of Macpherson's poems fully identified. We also find some of those imitations called ursgeuls, or new tales, to which Macpherson likewise refers, and, to keep clear of which, he was so anxious. Now, after reading Miss Brooke's Collection, Mr. Walker's Irish Bards, and the Collections of the Highland Society of Scotland, we would ask, how could there be imitations without something to imitate? We are quite aware of an answer to this; that is, that the imitations are also fabricated. To reply to any man capable of making such an objection, would be to extinguish all reason and all virtue. They are totally different from ancient poems in style and character. A few years ago, almost every Highlander, the moment the reciter would mix any of the new tales, would exclaim, that is modern, that is not Ossian or Ullin, &c.

These imitations have continued down to our own memory. We have seen some of them of the last century, either humorous or political. We have seen others evidently intended to bring the ancient original poems to discredit, so as to destroy all the ancient associations of the people, founded on the exploits and renown of their fathers. All this arose from an idea, a very false one, that as long as these elegant compositions retained their hold of the people's mind, the gospel could have no chance of making any impression. (See Report, and Bishop Carsewell's Preface.) Before we conclude this part of the subject, it is necessary to refer to the immense collections made by the Highland Societies of London and Scotland, with a view to throw light upon the authenticity of Ossian's poems. An account of these collections will be found in the appendix to the Report of the Highland Society of Scotland, as examined by the late Dr. Donald Smith, the first Gaelic scholar of his country.

There is, however, a collection of Ossianic and other Gaelic poems, by Dr. Irvine of Little Dunkeld, a copy of which has been deposited with the Highland Society of London, and another is to be deposited with the Highland Society of Scotland, which Dr. Smith never saw, and which clearly demonstrates, as many others have affirmed, that poems ascribed to Ossian, Ullin, and others equal in merit to those collected and translated by Mr. Macpherson and Dr. Smith, existed in the Highlands. These are written just as collected during a period of nearly forty years, and any competent judge may at once see how the old and new poems were mixed together. That is, the attempt made by the successive bards to supply what was lost, or to model the story so as to please the taste of their hearers. An account of this last collection would of itself furnish an irrefragable evidence that Macpherson never could have been the author of the poems which he ascribed to Ossian.

We must now hasten to the internal evidence, which the poems of Ossian themselves, as published by the Highland Society of London, amply furnish.

Having extended our observations upon the external evidence so much beyond our intention, a few observations here must suffice.

The first is, that the originals of all the poems translated by Mr. Macpherson have not been found. Every search was made, but without success. His going to America, and his other peregrinations, may in part account for the loss of some of his collections. But we must confess, that on this head there are some difficulties which our knowledge cannot solve. They do not, however, form any argument against his honesty. The

translation, of which we have not the original, is perfectly uniform with that of which we have the original. If, therefore, we are satisfied that the one is genuine, so we must be as to the other. If Mr. Macpherson intended a forgery, he would have either left the whole entire or none at all. We know that, from the abuse he experienced from Dr. Johnson and his followers, and from other causes, he became almost indifferent about the originals, and heard the clamour of his opponents with a feeling which almost determined him to abandon a field where no further honours could be gained.

Though the originals of the whole of Ossian's works have not been found, it is but justice to say that every means have been employed by the Highland Societies of London and Scotland to discover them. Nor have we reason to doubt the integrity of Mr. Mackenzie, Mr. Macpherson's executor, in this matter. All that he got he gave to the Highland Society of London.

What became of the MSS. which certainly Mr. Macpherson had received, it is in vain now to inquire. Though we have a most sincere regard for the merits and memory of Mr. Macpherson, we must be permitted to hazard a suspicion that he himself may have destroyed them, to prevent any person from discovering or ascertaining what labour he employed in restoring their contents, to what he supposed may have been their ancient and original state. If, however, this may have been his object, it shows that he never could have been the author, and that he was a bad politician. Because we can ascertain to a demonstration how he proceeded in his labours of restoration, from fragments which still exist in their original state. Still, however, upon this part of the subject we must speak with diffidence, because we really do not know how many editions of the same poems he may have got, and because we have this moment before us editions of poems never translated, and probably never seen by him, which differ widely from one another, and yet which bear evident marks of having been originally the same. They are all ascribed to Ossian and his contemporary bards.

Most of the poems, however, we remark in the second place, we have before us, and they have been before Gaelic scholars for several years; some of them complete. Now, if they had been modern compositions, is it not strange that no one should ever have courage and probity to declare them so? We have seen them long before they were published—we examined them with a suspicious eye—we heard the opinions of many learned and competent judges upon their merit, and yet no one ever harboured a thought that they could be the composition of any modern poet.

We have the compositions of many poets for two or three hundred years back; we can easily compare these with the poems commonly called Ossian's. Yet every one of them is of a different character. There are only three, the authors of which are doubtful. The death of Fraoch, and the old Bard's Wish, and Morduth, imperfect, as published by Gillies, which bear any thing like resemblance to the composition of the ancient bards. But they also bear evident marks of their modern origin, compared with the poems translated by Dr. Smith and Mr. Macpherson.

As already mentioned, we have abundance of imitations so far down as the last century, but they are easily distinguishable from those of Ossian and others.

A third remark offers itself. If we suppose Mr. Macpherson an impostor, we must also pronounce Dr. Smith one; nay, we must go farther, we must suppose all the collectors of the poems belonging to the Ossianic æra impostors. If we do so, how can we account for the fact, that Dr. Smith and Macpherson, and all these collectors, could have written in the same style and manner, and give exactly the same characters, the same events, and the same every thing, especially as to the history and character of Fingal? So far as we know any thing of human nature and human genius, we may assert that the thing is impossible. They could not imitate Macpherson, or any body else, for Macpherson's originals, except the seventh *Book* of *Temora*, did not appear till long afterwards. These collections, which we have all examined, evidently appear to have been adulterated; they contain many modern terms which could not have been known in the fourth century. But here and there we meet passages which at once must decide, that they could not be the composition of the same authors, or belong to the same æra.

Is it likely that Macpherson could, at the time he translated or collected these poems, a young man of no experience, and no great proficient in Celtic literature, all at once form a new species of Gaelic composition, and almost a new language to himself? Could he, or almost any man, write in terms which requires much study fully to comprehend? The first Gaelic scholars, as Dr. Donald and Dr. John Smith, the two Stewarts, and several others, have pronounced these poems to be of great antiquity, not only from their style, but from the total absence of all reference or allusion to modern ideas or modern manners. Though Mr. Macpherson might succeed in one or two short poems, is it possible that he could succeed in so many poems, of such length, without being detected?

To say that he composed first in English, and then translated into Gaelic, would only subject him the more to detection—for no human being could, or can, deprive a translation of its proper characters. We have manuscripts of nearly a thousand years old. Their language, generally speaking, is the language of these poems. We have it therefore in our power to compare and determine. We have done so, and the result is favourable to Mr. Macpherson's veracity.

The poems, as published by Dr. Smith, and we may say by Sir John Sinclair, bear evident proofs of the labour taken to divest them of the spurious compositions mingled with them, so as to form a consistent whole. They clearly indicate that many pieces were tacked together, and that much had been lost. The transitions are sometimes so violent, so abrupt, so obscure, that it requires much attention to follow the speakers, or to find out who they are. Now, could all this happen if Mr. Macpherson and Dr. Smith were impostors? They had no occasion to leave the building in this unfinished state. Nay, they could not have done it.

We find also from the poems themselves that they are not all Ossian's. Dr. Smith admits this. Mr. Macpherson said nothing about it. But his collection speaks for itself. We regret that we cannot enlarge upon this important part of the subject. We therefore refer, for instance, to the very first poems in the collection of Mr. Macpherson. Cath Loda seems to be the composition of Ossian; Carrickthura, of Ullin. We could show, that throughout the whole collection, the parts of the different poets are clearly indicated by internal style and manners. Now, could Mr. Macpherson accomplish this? The attempt would be impossible—Ullin, the poet Laureate, Fergus, Carrul, Cronan, Minonn, &c. have each a peculiar characteristic style,

and all of them differ from Ossian as much as they do from one another. Ossian survived them all. There is a poem now before us, in which Patrick, the son of Alpin, is said to have come to Ossian to hear and record the history of the Fingalians. He was hospitably entertained. They had red deer venison on the table. The son of Alpin praises the size of the deer. Ossian says he saw an elk that could not be compared to it in point of bulk. This Patrick does not believe, and, in a fit of incredulity, throws all his papers into the fire. Upon this, Ossian blind breaks out into a strain of indignant lamentation at the incredulity of the son of Alpin, a Christian missionary. " Hast thou burnt every tale and poetic song? Alas! Ullin of love is no more. No more is Carrul of melodious voice. No more is Orran the strength of harmony. No more is Fergus the praise of song. No more is Annir Mor, nor Sonn." Then he breaks out into a most pathetic address to his forefathers, Cumhal, Treunmor, Luthan, and to his wife Evir.

It appears that every bard furnished his part, and recited it before the warriors when they met to hear the praises of their deeds. Now, we would ask, how could any man contrive all this, and support it throughout?

It remains now that we say a few words upon the liberty which Mr. Macpherson may have used in purifying the poems he collected. We must certainly agree with Dr. Smith, that on this subject, in the present state of our knowledge, we cannot speak with any precision. That he laboured to exclude every thing modern, as he conceived, we have his own authority already quoted. How far his judgment may on this point have been correct, this is not the place to inquire.

We may however refer to what is commonly called Malvina's Dream, as he has given it in the beginning of the poem of Croma, and as it is published in Gillies' Collection, whence we may see that his edition was not always the best. His edition is far inferior to the other, and in some instances scarcely intelligible. They differ, indeed, very materially, from which we may infer that he is not the author of the one or of the other. It is evident that his own translation was not made from the edition published. It approaches much nearer that given by Gillies, to whom it was communicated by the late Mr. Maclagan of Blair in Atholl, a first rate Gaelic scholar.

The numberless editions, however, of these poems, which have for ages circulated among the Highlanders, though generally speaking the same in substance, are so various, that it would be wrong to condemn Mr. Macpherson unless we knew exactly what edition he preferred. We could, as in the present instance, show that he did not always receive the best, and that, as in the battle of Lora, he left out, or did not possess, many terms which throw much light upon the poem. Of the chorus of the bards in Comala, beginning " Roll streamy Carun, roll in joy," we have before us a much superior edition. But it begins another poem almost altogether different from Comala, though, we think, of equal beauty. Hence we are led to believe that Mr. Macpherson selected a fragment here and there, as suited his purpose. This Dr. Smith candidly confesses he had done himself, and supposes, upon good authority, Mr. Macpherson must have done something similar. It was nothing more than restoring detached pieces to their proper places. Many pieces appear evidently to have been lost; and hence neither the skill nor genius of two such eminent men could avoid the obscurity and abruptness which mark almost the whole of their originals.

We must now hasten to a conclusion, and observe, as we have seen from the external evidence, that where Mr. Macpherson could not understand the original, he either passed over the term which he could not translate, or left it out altogether, or used some vague general terms, or circumlocution ; and we do not know how he could have done otherwise, unless he had taken more time to consult Irish dictionaries, such as Curtin's, O'Reilly's, and O'Bryan's, with which he does not seem to have been acquainted. The description of Cuchullin's chariot and horses, in the first book of Fingal, is a signal proof of his hurry, at least, if not of the little progress he made in Celtic literature, at the time he translated the Poems of Ossian. Again, however, we must say, that perhaps he translated from a different edition. But there is, in Mr. Grant of Coriemony's Thoughts on the Origin and Descent of the Gael, (p. 418) another edition of that celebrated passage, which we often heard repeated in our youth, much more full and complete, and which bears, *in gremio aut facie*, every mark of ancient composition. Some of the terms are intelligible only to Gaelic scholars of the first eminence, such as Mr. Grant. And we doubt whether many more could translate them as he has done. We would, however, point out some terms which even he had some difficulty in translating into English, and we rather think he sometimes failed. Mr. Macpherson's description is beautiful, Mr. Grant's more perfect, and we might say sublime.

It is a singular fact, that an omission occurs, and that is, the description of Cuchullin's sword, which certainly belonged to the passage, and which may be seen in Gillies's Collection, p. 211, one of the most eloquent pieces of composition in any language. But we much doubt whether any man living could do justice to it in an English translation, or whether many at this moment can fully understand it.

We think we have now established the fact, that whoever composed the poems called Ossian's, it could not be either Macpherson or Smith. We hope the Highland Societies of London and Edinburgh will soon prepare and publish their valuable collections ; and then he must be a sturdy infidel indeed who can any longer doubt the authenticity of Ossian.

Justice to injured worth and patriotic exertion demands, that we should here conclude with one single remark. That is, that the proud dignified conduct of Macpherson, resulting from conscious integrity, should, instead of forming an argument against him, for ever endear his memory to every Highlander, and raise a monument to his fame *.

OSTEND, a sea-port town in the kingdom of the Netherlands. It has four gates, and is surrounded with a great number of forts, and ten bastions, an earthen mound, and a moat. The houses, though low, are in general well built, and disposed in straight lines. The principal public building is the town-house, erected in 1711. The harbour, which is tolerably good, is formed by the tide entering the mouth of a small river, but ships of burden can only enter at high water. The town is connected by canals, with Bruges and Ghent on the

west, and with Nieuport on the east. The principal exports of this place are wheat, tallow, flax, linens, hides, and clover seed, the produce of Flanders. Its imports are, coffee, sugar, tobacco, rum, salt, British cottons, Spanish wools, French wines, dyewoods, and spices. A packet carries the mail between Dover and Ostend. The number of ships that entered the harbour in 1815 was 700, exclusive of packet boats. Population 10.800. East longitude 2° 55' 8'' ; north latitude 51° 13' 57.'.

OSTERODE, a town of Germany, in the Hartz mountains, in the kingdom of Hanover, situated on the small river Soese. It has three churches. There is here a magazine of corn, for the use of the miners, who receive it at a fixed price. The articles of manufacture are woollen goods, nails, and articles in wood. Population 4200. East longitude 10° 16' 54'' ; north latitude 51° 44' 15''.

OSWESTRY, a market town of England, in Shropshire. The town is situated on higher ground than any other in the county. The houses are chiefly built of brick, and roofed with slates. The church is spacious, with a well-proportioned tower at one end. There is also a meeting-house for the Independents, a chapel for the Baptists, and another for the Wesleyan Methodists. There is likewise an excellent free grammar school, a town hall, a prison, and a large house of industry, built at the expence of twelve neighbouring parishes. This town, which is of great antiquity, was once surrounded with strong walls, with four gates, fronting the four cardinal points. Some traces of the wall still exist. A few remains of the castle, which occupied a high artificial moat on the west side of the town, attest its former strength and importance. The town has extended on all sides considerably beyond the boundary of the wall, and continues rapidly to enlarge, particularly on the English side. Oswestry possesses a manufactory of cotton, and has a considerable trade in coarse linens, and coarse and thick woollens. Races are annually held at Cyrnybrock, in September. Population, in 1821, 844 houses ; 848 families, 719 of whom are employed in trade ; 1748 males, 2162 females, making in all 3910 inhabitants. West longitude 3° 3' ; North latitude 52° 51'. See the *Beauties of England and Wales*, vol. xiii. p. 265.

OTAHEITE, or TAITI, an island in the Pacific Ocean, lying between 17° 28', and 17° 53' South latitude, and between 149° 10', and 149° 40' West longitude from Greenwich, consists of two peninsulas, united by an isthmus about three miles in breadth. The greater of these is circular, and about twenty miles in diameter ; and the latter about sixteen miles long and twelve broad. Both are surrounded by a reef of coral rocks, and the whole island is about forty-four miles in circumference. A border of low land, seldom more than a mile in depth, encircles the island. The interior is mountainous, and rises very high in the centre, but is intersected by a number of narrow valleys, which open from the coast. Innumerable streams fall from the hills, sometimes in beautiful cascades, and supply the river which flows through the valleys. In one of the inland districts is a large lake, which the natives say cannot be sounded by any line, and which contains eels of a monstrous size. From December to March

Situation and Extent.

Appearance.

Climate.

* In confirmation of the argument urged by the author of this article, it may be proper to state, that there is not the slightest trace of evidence among the numerous letters and papers left by Mr. Macpherson, that he either composed the poems of Ossian, or wished others to believe that he did. Had he been desirous of being esteemed the author of them, he could easily have left what some would have considered as unanswerable arguments against their authenticity.—ED.

the weather is squally and rainy, with the wind frequently from the west; but during the rest of the year the wind is from the east, and the weather serene and pleasant. From March to August the thermometer was never below 65°, and seldom above 73°. The climate is peculiarly healthy and delightful.

Soil.
The soil of the low maritime land, and of the valleys, is a rich blackish mould, remarkably fertile; but, in ascending the mountains, it changes into various veins of red, white, dark, yellow, and bluish earth. The stones exhibit every where the appearance of the action of fire; and the island has evidently had a volcanic origin.

Vegetable productions.
The mountains are in most places covered to the very summits with a variety of trees, or with bamboos of great length, or with reeds and fern. In some of the higher regions is the precious sandal wood of two kinds, yellow and dark-coloured, from which the natives draw the perfume for the cocoa-nut oil, with which they anoint themselves. The more fertile spots, and even the mountainous districts, are covered with various useful vegetable productions, most of which grow spontaneously, and supply the natives with wholesome food. The most important of these are, the breadfruit tree, which seems peculiar to the Pacific Ocean, and which is found in the highest perfection at Otaheite; the cocoa-nut, which affords at once meat, drink, cloth, and oil; the plantain of various kinds; the chesnut, different in shape and size, but resembling that of Europe in taste; the *Evee*, a yellow apple, a stone-fruit, resembling a peach in flavour; yams, which grow wild in the mountains, from one to six feet in length; sweet potatoe, in great abundance, of an orange colour, resembling in taste the Jerusalem artichoke; tarro, a root from twelve to sixteen inches in length, and as much in girth, which is cultivated in wet soils, and the leaves of which are used like spinach; besides, a number of other roots and potatoes, made into pastes and puddings. The natives seldom plant the bread-fruit tree, as it springs again from the root after being cut down; but they make large plantations of cocoa-nuts and plantains. Grapes and pineapples have been introduced by European visitors; and also Indian corn, which would ripen every three months, if the natives could be brought to cultivate it. The tobacco, planted by Captain Cook, is spread over the island. There are many trees and shrubs of great beauty; and a variety of flowers, for which the natives discover a great fondness. Some of the more remarkable shrub trees are, the Chinese paper-mulberry or cloth plant, which the natives cultivate with great care, and make from the bark, when steeped, their finest white cloth; toa, a large tree of the hardest quality, of which they make their war clubs, spears, and cloth-beaters; tomanoo, a spreading tree, the wood of which resembles walnut, and of which are made, canoes, stools, pillows, pudding-dishes, and trays, all wrought out of the solid wood; hootdo, a large spreading tree, the nut of which is sometimes used for intoxicating the fish; the wild sloe-tree, the bark of which furnishes a fine grey cloth, and the branches of which hang down and take root, so as to form an enormous trunk or cluster; the silk cotton shrub, of which the natives make no use; bamboos, which grow to the height of sixty feet, and of which are made fishing rods, flutes, arrows, &c.; prickly palm, the leaves of which, six feet long, are used as thatch; the cabbage tree, of which little use is made; sugar cane, which grows spontaneously to a good size, but is not cultivated; the

yava, a shrub which has a peppery hot root, from which the only intoxicating beverage of the natives is prepared, and which is cultivated with great care; hemp, red pepper, liquorice, hops, &c.

Otaheite.

Animals.
There are multitudes of hogs which breed rapidly, and some of which are of a very large size. The dogs, also, are plentiful, and are much relished as food. Rats abound on the island, and occasion much damage. By European navigators and missionaries other animals have been introduced, namely, cows, which have run wild in the mountains, and which the natives are afraid to approach; goats, which have increased abundantly, but which, being disliked as food, and becoming destructive to the plantations, have also been driven to the mountains; sheep, which at first perished, but have been replaced with better prospect of their thriving; cats, which have multiplied, and proved useful; and rabbits, which can scarcely fail to spread.

Birds.
There are poultry in great abundance, and of the best quality; wild ducks, paroquets, doves, herons, woodpeckers, gulls, plovers, martins, sand-larks, men-of-war, tropic birds, and a multitude of others, little known to Europeans. The feathers of the tropic and men-of-war birds are held in great request as ornaments. The smaller birds of the island are caught with bird-lime made of the bread-fruit gum; and many of the natives are able to bring them down with stones thrown by the hand.

Fish.
Swarms of fish of all sorts frequent the shores of the island, and the natives are the most dexterous fishermen in the world. They have nets of all sizes, some of which are fifty fathoms long and twelve deep. They make fishing-hooks with great neatness from pearl-shells, bones, and sometimes hard wood. They use also three-pronged spears to dart at the fish which come into shallow water; and they take certain kinds, such as the hedgehog fish, which take refuge in the cavities of the coral rock, by diving, and seizing them with the hand. With their lines and hooks, they take such large fish even as the dolphin, the albicore, the skip-jack, and the shark. During the rains, they catch great quantities of small fry, at the mouth of the rivers, by large nets, or rather bags, with a wide mouth, secured by stones at the bottom. The shell fish are very abundant; oysters, crabs, cray fish, cockles of an enormous size, and many others, of peculiar beauty. There are lizards, scorpions, musketoes, butterflies, and a variety of the common insects, but none that are very troublesome or dangerous. Their houses are infested with fleas, which are the greatest pest in the island.

Govern-ment.
The government of this island is monarchical and hereditary, with this peculiarity, that the heir apparent is acknowledged as king at his birth, and the reigning sovereign thenceforth acts as regent for his son. It is the distinctive honour of the king and queen, that they are carried about on men's shoulders; and the queen alone has the farther privilege of eating the vermin, which she picks from the heads of her bearers. These sovereigns are precluded, also, from entering any house, except their own, because all the land that they touch with their feet, and every dwelling that they enter, becomes thenceforth sacred, or appropriated to their use and service for ever. It is thus only on their own lands, that they occasionally alight and walk about. The mode of saluting these royal personages, by all ranks, is to uncover the head, breast, and shoulders. Next in authority is the father of the king, or regent of the state; and, under him, are the chiefs of the different districts, who exercise a regal power in

their respective jurisdictions. The near relations, younger brothers, and chosen friends, of these chiefs, rank next to them, and are placed over portions of their territories; and, after these, come the smaller proprietors, or gentlemen. Under these are the lower class, or cottagers, who are bound to do certain services to the chiefs and gentlemen, such as building their houses, making cloth for them, and assisting in any laborious work, but who are at liberty to change their residence, and to put themselves under other chiefs. A chief is always noble, though deprived of his property, but no common man can rise higher than the rank of gentleman, or the towha of a chief. Yet the lower ranks are not in a state of slavish subjection, and are admitted to the freest intercourse with the chiefs, from whom they are scarcely to be distinguished in outward appearance. There are no records respecting property, excepting tradition and land marks; but encroachments on one another's possessions is said to be very rare, as there is nothing so much condemned among them as avariciousness and stinginess. Their litigations are often referred to any bystander, and individuals are scarcely ever known to fight in consequence of a personal quarrel. Their grounds of offence are commonly some want of customary respect; then the whole family or district take up the quarrel, and either a peace-offering is made, or a war is the consequence.

The general name for the Deity is Eatooa; and a great variety of gods are worshipped under that designation. There are three, whom they consider as supreme, but whom they think it presumptuous to address in worship, except in cases of great exigency and importance. Every island has its special divinity; and every family its guardian spirit, which was the soul of one of their deceased relatives, supposed to have been exalted to the condition of an Eatooa. They believe in the future existence of the soul, but have no idea of punishment in that state, and admit only of different degrees of felicity, according as they have pleased the Eatooa. The worship paid to the deities consists of prayers, offerings of all sorts of provisions, and sometimes of human sacrifices. At every feast, a portion is presented to the Eatooa, before any one begins to partake; and the more formal offerings are brought to the place of worship. It is on the occasion of a new king, or the commencement of a hostile expedition, or on similar public occasions, that human sacrifices are offered. The victim is said to be generally some offender deserving of death, whom the chiefs fix upon in secret council, and who is dispatched on a sudden, without being aware of his fate. On some great solemnities, every chief is required to bring a human victim, and in such cases the innocent may often suffer from their ill-will. But if any of the chiefs declare that no one deserving of death is to be found in their district, a hog may be substituted; and, on the other hand, those who may feel themselves in danger of being sacrificed on these occasions, can secure an asylum by fleeing to the places of worship. The places of worship are called ed morais; and are used also as burying places, where the dead are deposited, till the flesh fall from the bones, which are then removed, and buried. These places are approached with the greatest reverence by the natives; and some of the greater morais are used as places of meeting on solemn public occasions. There are a numerous body of priests, who, besides officiating in offering prayers at the morais, are called in on the occasion of births, deaths, festivals, sickness, and similar occurrences. They profess to know the mind of the

Eatooa, and to foretell, from various omens, the issue of any undertaking. They affect to have great power with the gods, for inflicting and removing evils. They act also as physicians, in the cure of diseases, but employ no other means of health than superstitious practices. Most of the principal chiefs act occasionally as priests, and thus hold the people in subjection by pretending to bring calamities upon them from the Eatooa. Every disease or calamity is regarded as a punishment from the gods for some offence; and they employ only prayers and other rites of worship for its removal.

The natives of Otaheite are of an olive colour, in- clining to a copper hue, but those who are most exposed to the weather are still darker; while the women, who carefully clothe themselves, and avoid the sun beams, are only a shade darker than a European brunette. The men are rather above the middle size, particularly the chiefs, who are of a larger race, and seldom under six feet in height. The women are finely formed, particularly in the limbs and arms, but have large and masculine figures. They have black, lively eyes, white and regular teeth, delicate soft skin; but, by the custom of distending the mouth, flattening the nose and forehead, and altogether widening the shape of the face, they have no pretension to beauty of feature. But the expression of their countenance is sweet and pleasing; their tempers mild and cheerful, their carriage easy and graceful; their manners affable and engaging. The dress of both sexes is nearly alike. A square piece of cloth doubled, and long enough to pass once and a half round the waist, hangs down to the knees of the men, and nearly to the ankles of the women. An oblong piece, not above a yard wide, with a hole in the middle to admit the head, hangs loosely down before and behind, as far as the knees, with the sides open, so as to leave the arms uncovered. The men also wear a narrow slip of cloth under all, which goes round the waist, and passing between the thighs, is tucked up before; while the women, again, often wear above all a square, oblong, folded piece of fine white cloth, tastily thrown round them, by way of cloak, besides a small wrapper undermost, in the place of a petticoat. The women wear also bonnets, or green shades, made in a minute, by plaiting or weaving the leaves of the cocoa-nut tree; and both sexes put on garlands of flowers and feathers. There is also a head-dress made of the hair of deceased relatives, wrapped round the head like a turban, which the women use on great solemnities. All are tatooed in various forms, and the process, which occasions great pain, usually occupies a year, at different intervals, but none are esteemed men and women till it be completed.

Their houses are commonly of an oblong form, eighteen feet along the ridge, and rounded at the ends. There are no partitions, but posts erected for hanging up the baskets, of different kinds, which contain their provisions. The furniture consists of a few wooden trays and stools, wooden pillows, a large wooden chest, matting and cloth spread on the floor as bedding. There is a separate building, where the women eat their meals, and where the servants of the family usually sleep. Part of the household frequently sleep in their canoe houses, in which they could not stand upright; and many of them, in fine weather, sleep in the open air. They do not appear to have regular hours for meals; but they usually eat as soon as they rise from bed, about day-break. They often eat voraciously, especially the chiefs, who lead a very luxurious, idle, and dissipated life, seldom failing to take a daily dose of yava. This beverage is prepared by the women, who masticate the root of the shrub of that name, and spit the juice into a bowl, mixing it with water, or cocoa nut liquor, when it quickly ferments, and is strained off for use. A gill of this liquor is sufficient to intoxicate a man ; and, while under its influence, they lie down to sleep off its effects ; the women, in the mean time, chafing their limbs with their hands. A whitish scurf covers the skin of those who are habitually addicted to the use of this liquor, which many regard as a badge of nobility, as the common people cannot procure such an indulgence. The natives in

Employ-
ments.

general, however, live without toil, and are more frequently engaged in amusement than labour. Besides the culture of the soil, which does not employ much time, their principal occupation consists in the manufacture of cloth, the making of canoes, arms, and various domestic utensils. The cloth is made from the bark of various trees, reduced to a kind of paste, by steeping it in water, and beating it out on smooth beams, with grooved beetles. This cloth they dye of various colours, and sometimes paste together pieces of different colours, in curious forms. The men provide the bark, but the women make the cloth, with the assistance of their feminine male attendants. Their canoes are of different sizes, always narrow, but frequently doubled, by lashing two of them together. The war canoes are always double, each about three feet wide, six deep, and from sixty to ninety long. These are joined together, with a space of four or six feet between them, over which a stage is erected for the warriors, with a breastwork of plank in front, about four feet high. The bows are high, and covered with carved images ; and the sterns are carried up tapering, sometimes to the height of twenty-four feet, with similar carved work on the top. Many of these are capable of carrying 300 persons ; and, besides the greatness of the work, are carved and finished in a manner that the best European workman could not exceed, with no better instruments than stone adzes and chisels, gouges and gimlets made of the arm or leg bones of a man. Their bows, arrows, and javelins, their cloth beetles, and fishing implements, their mourning dresses, war head-pieces, and breastplates, are all executed with great taste and nicety of workmanship.

Amuse-
ments.

But they have much leisure time at their disposal, and their sports are of various kinds. The people of one district contend with those of another in throwing spears, from eight to fourteen feet in length, at a mark thirty or forty yards distant ; or in shooting with bows and arrows to the greatest distance. They are dexterous wrestlers ; and challenge one another to this exercise, by striking the right hand upon the cavity in the bend of the left arm, so as to make a loud report. When the people of one district wrestle against those of another, the women commence the contest, and the men succeed. They practise from the tenderest age the exercise at quarter staff, and are very expert in defending the head and other parts of the body. They amuse themselves with the sling, and will throw a stone with such force, as to sink it in the bark of a tree at the distance of 200 yards. Their dances are various ; and are generally performed by the men and women in separate parties. They consist of slow regular movements of the hands and feet, keeping time with the music. At the conclusion of some of the public dances, the younger females exhibit various indecent gestures ; such practices are said to be unknown in private parties. After the public dances, also, there are parties of

singers, who join the music, or actors of pantomimes, in which the conduct of the chiefs is frequently satirized, and brought in some measure to the bar of public opinion. But the amusement, in which persons of all sexes, and ranks, and ages, seem to delight most, is that of swimming in the surf. They swim out beyond the place where the swell of the surf begins ; and with a small board, about two feet or more in length, to support their breast, or frequently with nothing whatever in their hands, they throw themselves on the top of the wave, and steering themseves with one leg, while the other is held up out of the water, they are carried forward with amazing velocity, till the surf is ready to break on the shore, when they wheel round with a rapid movement, and darting head foremost through the wave, rise on the outside, and swim back again to the place where the swell begins. In thus going and returning they frequently run foul of each other, and, before they can disentangle themselves, are hurled topsy-turvy on the shore, at the expence of many a bruise, but without any instance of drowning.

Customs.

There are a multitude of ceremonies and singular customs, of which the following are but a small specimen. Both sexes go naked till the age of six or seven years; and at thirteen or fourteen the operation of tattooing commences. A number of small figures and arched lines are made on the hands, feet, and hips of the females, and the men are farther tattooed on the arms, legs, and thighs : without which honourable marks, a person would be as much reproached and shunned, as if in this country he were to go about naked. About the same time, an operation, bearing some resemblance to circumcision, is performed upon the boys. After the birth of a child, both child and mother are secluded as unclean for several weeks, and various rites and offerings performed. The mother during this period is not allowed to touch provisions of any kind, but is fed by another person ; and the provisions for the use of the child must be brought into the house by a different door or opening, and carried in a distinct vessel from those of the mother. The first male child, from the moment of his birth, succeeds to all the honours of the family, and any insult offered to him is felt more deeply by the parents and relations than if offered to themselves. As the heads of the families, the children are put under no restraint, but are indulged in every thing from the day of their birth. Old age, on the contrary, is treated with the utmost disrespect, even in the persons of the chiefs ; and any thing worthless is commonly denominated " old man." The women are not allowed to eat along with the men ; and are forbidden the use of certain kinds of food. They must gather and dress their own provisions, and, were a man to touch any of them, they must be thrown away. Neither are the women permitted to enter the morais, or to touch any sacred offerings. There are a class of men called Mawhoos, of the most worthless description, who affect the dress, voice, and manners of females, who are allowed to associate with, and wait upon the women, and who are subjected to the same restrictions. The marriages are celebrated without much ceremony, but various offerings succeed it. The woman is immediately provided with an instrument, in which is fixed a shark's tooth, about a quarter of an inch of which is bare, and sharp as a lancet, with which, upon all occasions of joy or grief, even of a very trivial nature, she strikes her head till the blood flows in streams. The husband's tayo, or chosen friend, is admitted to all his privileges; but it is regarded as

Otaheite. incest in him to have intercourse with any others of the family. The higher class of females are often addicted to the most shameless and promiscuous lewdness. There is particularly an infamous society, chiefly composed of the higher ranks, called Arreoys, who live in a course of beastly concubinage, and whose female associates procure abortion when pregnant, or put to death their infants as soon as born, that they may have no interruption to their licentiousness. It is a general practice among all classes to destroy the new born children, especially the female infants, to avoid the trouble of bringing them up. The head is accounted sacred; and nothing is ever carried upon it. To lay the hand upon the head of any one is a great insult, or even to compare the size of any thing to the size of a person's head. The mode of salutation among equals is to touch noses; and before the chiefs, and sacred places, to uncover the head, breast, and shoulders. They have a great abhorrence of flies touching their food; and would throw away any provisions in which a dead fly was found. Hence they are continually provided with fly-flaps made of feathers, to keep these insects off their bodies and tables. They are remarkably attentive to personal cleanliness and neatness of appearance. They bathe three times a day in fresh water, and always wash themselves with it after coming out of the sea; nor can they be restrained from these baths even by diseases, if they are able to crawl to the water. They extract every hair from the nose, arm-pits, &c. trim their beard and hair with great attention, adjust their eye-brows and eye-lashes, and anoint themselves with fragrant oils.

Language. They are generally acquainted with the art of conversing by signs. Their voice is soft and harmonious; and their language, freed from every harsh or guttural sound, abounds in vowel combinations. They direct their voyages by the sun, moon, and stars; and have names for many of the constellations, resembling in several instances those of the Greeks.

Character. The character of the Otaheitans is a singular mixture of the savage qualities, and of certain vices and accomplishments of civilized life. They are in their general manners gentle, good-tempered, kind, hospitable, and generous to one another in a great degree. But in their wars, which frequently happen, they are ferocious and bloody, giving no quarter in battle, and putting the prisoners to a cruel death, ravaging the country of the vanquished without mercy, and killing all that come in their way, of every age and sex. They are faithless in their transactions, and strongly addicted to thieving, at least from European visitors. They have great command of their feelings, and are expert in every species of cunning. They are the most consummate flatterers in the world; and can assume such insinuating manners, and practise so many arts of endearment, as generally to accomplish their object with strangers. The population of Otaheite was estimated by Captain Cook, though probably beyond the truth, at 100,000; by the first missionaries at 15,000; and by Turnbull at 5000. This melancholy decrease of inhabitants is owing to the practice of infanticide, the frequency of their wars, the unnatural habits of the Arreoys, the custom of human sacrifices, and the prevalence of venereal distempers. But the threatened extinction of these interesting islanders, by these ruinous practices, appears now to be averted by the successful labours of the missionaries, who have at length

prevailed, by the most persevering exertions, not only in civilizing the manners of the people, but in bringing the whole community to renounce their idolatrous rites, and embrace the profession of the Christian faith. Their bloody wars, human sacrifices, murder of infants, and other unnatural practices, have ceased. Schools are every where established among them; the duties of religious worship duly observed; and the various benefits of civilization rapidly extending. The same changes have taken place in all the other Society Islands, and much of what has been said, in this account of Otaheite, must be considered as applicable to its former, not to its present state *.—See Cook's *Voyages;* Wilson's *Missionary Voyage;* and Turnbull's *Voyage round the World.*   (q)

Otchakov ‖ Ottory.

OTCHAKOV, or OCZAKOV, a town of Russia in Europe, situated on the Black Sea, at the mouth of the Dnieper, and in the government of Cherson. It is said to have been founded by a colony of Milesians, who gave it the name of Olbis. This town was once of some size, and enjoyed a considerable trade during the wars of the last century between the Russians and the Turks; to the last of whom its harbour was of great service. It has now, however, declined, since the establishment of Odessa. Its population does not now exceed 1000, and the number of ships which enter its harbour annually scarcely amounts to 100. East Long. 31° 34'. North Lat. 46° 44'.

OTLEY, a small but neat market-town of England, in the West Riding of Yorkshire. It is situated in a delightful country, on the river Wharf, over which there is a stone bridge, and is supposed to have derived its name from *Oatley,* a word signifying *oat field,* in consequence of the quantity of oats formerly cultivated in the neighbourhood. The town is built nearly in the form of a cross, consisting of four neat streets, and the houses are principally of stone, roofed with slates. The church is a spacious building, dedicated to All-Saints, and contains several ancient monuments, especially of the families of Fairfax, Fawkes, Vavasour, Palmes, and Pulleyn. It has been lately repaired, and elegantly fitted up. The principal charity is an excellent free school, which is well endowed. In the neighbourhood, at the village of Addle, the ruins of a Roman town were discovered in 1702. At the south-east extremity of Otley is the Chevin, a hill which rises high over the road to Leeds, and along with Rommald's moor, and Poolbank, form a mountainous range, extending to the river Wharf, which flows through some of the most delightful scenery in England. The population of the township is about 3065. See the *Beauties of England and Wales,* vol. xvi. p. 714.

OTTER. See MAZOLOGY. Vol. XIII. p. 418.

OTTOMAN EMPIRE. See TURKEY.

OTTORY, or OTTERY ST. MARY, a market-town of England, in the county of Devon, is agreeably situated near the bank of the river Otter. The town is large, and tolerably well built, but the streets are irregular. The church, which is very large, and of singular construction, is the principal public building. On the north and south sides there are square towers, which open into the body of the church, and form two transepts as in the cathedral of Exeter. The towers are furnished with pinnacles and open battlements, and the northern one has also a small spire. There is a richly ornamented chapel at the north-west corner, the roof of which is covered with highly wrought fan-shaped

* See the Article MISSIONS, Vol. XIV. p. 584.

tracery. The altar screen, which is of stone, is finely carved ; and most of the windows are narrow, and lancet-shaped. In Mill street, the remains of a mansion still exists, which was once inhabited by Sir Walter Raleigh ; and in one of the old collegiate houses, immediately without the church-yard, is a spacious parlour which was used by Oliver Cromwell as a convention room. Ottery possesses manufactures of flannels, serges, and other woollen goods, which were established some years ago by the exertions of Sir George Young and Sir John Dantze, Barts. Population of the parish in 1821, 3522.

OTWAY, Thomas, a celebrated tragic poet, was born at Trotton, near Midhurst, in the county of Sussex, in the year 1651. His father was rector of Woolbeding ; and, after receiving his education at Wykeham School, near Winchester, he was entered a Commoner of Christ's Church, Oxford, in 1669. Upon the death of his father, he seems to have abandoned his studies, as he left Oxford without taking his degrees, and without having formed any plans for his future life. Having repaired to London, he tried his skill as an actor, but as his talents were not fitted for this profession, he directed them, more appropriately, to the composition of tragedy. In the year 1675, he produced his first tragedy, which bore the name of " Alcibiades ;" and the same year appeared his " Don Carlos, Prince of Spain," which was highly successful, and relieved him from a state of extreme indigence into which he had fallen. The reputation which Otway had now obtained, introduced him to the acquaintance and patronage of the Earl of Plymouth, a natural son of Charles II. who procured for him the commission of cornet in a newly raised regiment. In the year 1677 he accompanied his troop to the Continent, but from his habits of dissipation, which he seems to have been unable to counteract, he soon left the regiment in a state of great poverty, and resumed his former occupation of writing for the stage. Under these circumstances, he composed the *Orphan* and *Venice Preserved*, the first of which appeared in 1680, and the other in 1682. Notwithstanding the success of these tragedies, he was again overwhelmed with poverty ; and in 1685, being compelled to avoid his creditors, he took refuge in a house in Towerhill, where he died on the 14th of April, at the early age of 34. Some of his biographers have stated, that Otway was obliged to beg a shilling from a gentleman, and that he was actually choked by devouring too eagerly the morsel of bread which it had procured him. Pope was informed that he died of a fever, brought on by the too active pursuit of a thief who had robbed one of his friends.

The merits of Otway as a tragic poet have already been estimated in our Article DRAMA, vol. viii. p. 104, 105.

OUDE, PROVINCE OF. See INDIA. Vol. XII. p. 55.58.

OUDE, or AYODHA, the former capital of the province of Oude, is situated on the south bank of the Dewah, or Goggrah river, 85 miles east of Lucknow. Abul Fazel, in 1582, describes Oude as one of the largest cities of Hindoostan ; and remarks, that it is said in ancient times to have measured 148 coss in length, and 36 in breadth. Small grains of gold, he adds, are reported to have been found, by sifting the earth round the city. In the neighbourhood of the city there are two remarkable tombs of great antiquity, which are venerated by the Mahomedans as the tombs of Seth and Job. The remains of the ancient city of Oude are adjoining to Fyzabad ; but they exhibit only a heap

of shapeless ruins. East Long. 82° 10'. North Lat. 26° 45'.

OUDENARDE, or AUDENARDE, is a small town of the Netherlands, situated on the river Scheldt, which divides it into two parts. It is situated in a valley, on the side of a mountain called Kerselaerberg, which defends the city. It contains two parish churches, five gates, and many good buildings. The inhabitants carry on some manufactures of woollen and linen goods. Population 5100.

OUNDLE, or UNDELE in Doomsday Book, is a market town of England, in Northamptonshire, situated upon a sloping ground on the River Nen, which makes a horse shoe turn almost round the town. The town, which is neat, is built nearly in the shape of the Roman letter ꓷ reversed, the body of the letter representing the principal streets. The church, which is small, but compact, consists of a nave, north and south aisles, transept, and chancel, with a square tower. The tower is 105 feet high, and the spire above it is 96 feet, making in all 201 feet. The charities consist of a free grammar school, founded by Sir William Laxton ; an alms house, and a guild or hospital. There are two bridges over the Nen, which form a communication with the roads to Thrapston and Yaxley. The last of these, viz. the North Bridge, has been generally admired, not only from its great number of arches built over the adjoining low ground, but also for an extensive causeway formed in an arcade which secures a passage by the bridge during floods. The population of the parish in 1821, was 2150.

OURFA, formerly *Edessa*, a town of Asiatic Turkey, and capital of the Pachalic of the same name, which forms a considerable part of ancient Mesopotamia. The town, which in some parts is tolerably well built, is situated partly on hills, and partly in the intermediate valley. It is about 3 miles in circumference, and is surrounded by old walls, flanked with quadrangular towers. The castle stands on the south side of the city, on the extremity of a range of hills. The ascent to it is extremely steep, and it is about one and a half miles in circumference, surrounded by a deep ditch cut in the rock, which can be filled with water. The remains of a building which the Arabs call the palace of Nimrod, stands upon the rock. It consists of two lofty and elegant Corinthian columns, and possesses some singular subterranean excavations, supposed to be of very high antiquity. A handsome Armenian Cathedral, falling to decay, and a splendid mosque, are among the other buildings of Ourfa. The caravans from Aleppo to the interior provinces of Persia, pass through this town, which thus becomes the seat of a considerable inland trade. Turkey leather is the principal manufacture of the place. The inhabitants, consisting of Turks, Armenians, Arabs, Jews, and Nestorians, have been estimated at 20,000. East Long. 38° 25'. North Lat. 36° 50'.

OUSE. See ENGLAND, Vol. VIII. p. 687, 688; and YORKSHIRE.

OUTCHANG-FOU, or VOO-TCHANG-FOO. See CHINA, Vol. VI. p. 214. Col. 1.

OUGEIN, OOJAIN, or OOJEIN, or *Ujuyini* in Sanscrit, and *Ozene* in Greek, one of the most ancient cities of Hindostan, is the capital of a district of the same name, in the province of Malwa, and is situated on the Sipperah River. The city, which is of an oblong shape, and about six miles in circuit, is surrounded by a stone wall, with round towers. Within these limits, there is some waste ground ; but the inhabited part occupies the greatest portion, and is much crowded with buildings. The houses, which are partly built of brick, and partly of wood, have a roof of lime terrace or tiles. The principal bazar is a street regular and spacious, well paved with stone, and flanked with houses two stories high. The lower story is laid out in shops, which are ascended by five or six steps from the street, and the upper stories are inhabited by the owners. The principal buildings are four mosques, erected by private individuals, and a great number of Hindoo temples. The palace of Dowlat Row Sindia, has a poor appearance, and is surrounded with other buildings. The south wall of the city, which is washed by the river Sipperah, is called Jeysingpoor, and contains an observatory, erected by Rajah Jeysingh, early in the last century.

The ancient city of Ougein, which stood a mile to the north of the present one, is said to have been overwhelmed by a convulsion of nature. Brick walls, stone pillars, and pieces of wood of great hardness, are found at the depth of 15 or 18 feet. " On digging," says the author of the article in Rees' Cyclopædia, " its walls are said to be found entire, pillars erect and unbroken, pieces of wood of extraordinary hardness, &c. The bricks thus dug up, are now applied to the purposes of building, but are much larger than any made in the present or late ages. Utensils of various kinds have been found, and ancient coins. Very little, however, has been yet done towards developing the present state of this submerged city; the interesting Herculaneum of India. Dr. Hunter noticed a large quantity of wheat that was found while he was there; it was in a charred state; a potter's kiln he also saw, filled with broken earthen vessels. Tradition imputes the destruction of the city to a shower of earth, an idea likely to have originated in superficial observation; for although Dr. Hunter observed no volcanic hills, nor scoria, in the neighbourhood, and thinks the state and position of the walls and pillars militate against the supposition of an earthquake having effected the submersion of the city, it is here difficult to impute it to any other than a volcanic cause, operating, perhaps, with less violence and convulsion than have attended similar phenomena in other countries, and combined with, or rather causing, an inundation of the river. A change in the course of the river is said to have taken place at the time, and an ancient bed is now traceable. A destructive inundation was witnessed and recorded by Dr. Hunter; and the writer of this article knows of another that occurred in a late rainy season. It would appear that the neighbourhood of Oujein is particularly subject to inundation, and when the loose friable nature of the soil is considered, it seems most reasonable to resort to an alluvial hypothesis to account for the submersion of the ancient city. But whatever may have been the real cause of the catastrophe, it cannot be supposed that the wild fancies of Hindoo historians would suffer the fact to be simply told. It must be dressed up in a mythological allegory. In fable or fact the interventions of the gods cannot be dispensed with. The following story is accordingly related.

A certain Gandharva, or celestial chorister, was condemned for an affront to the god Indra, to be born on earth in the shape of an ass; but on entreaty the sentence was mitigated, and he was allowed at night to assume the form and functions of a man. This incarnation took place at Oujein in the reign of rajah Sadasvasena, whose daughter was demanded in marriage by the ass; and his consent was obtained, on learning

the divine origin of his intended son-in-law, confirmed, as he witnessed, by certain prodigies. All day he lived in the stables like an ass; at night, secretly slipping out of his skin, and assuming the appearance of a handsome and accomplished young prince, he repaired to the palace, and enjoyed the conversation of his beauteous and happy bride.

In due time the princess became pregnant; and her chastity being suspected, she revealed to her inquisitive parents the mystery of her spouse's delectable nocturnal metamorphosis; which the rajah, (or by other accounts the mother,) being conveniently concealed, himself beheld; and unwilling that his son should return to his uncouth disguise, set fire to, and consumed, the vacant ass's skin.

Rejoiced at his release, for this event appears to have broken the spell, the incarnate Gandharva warned his beloved wife to quit the city, which he foresaw was about to be overwhelmed with a shower of earth from the resentment of Indra, thus disappointed of his vengeance in the termination of the banishment of his insolent servant. She fled, accordingly, to a village at a safe distance, and brought forth a son, named Vikramaditya; and a shower of cold earth, poured down by Indra, buried the city and its inhabitants.

It may be here noticed that this fable, wild as it is, affords still some confirmation of the supposition of an inundation during the rainy season having destroyed the city. For Indra is the god of showers, and such an event would of course be attributed to the vengeance of the Jupiter Pluvius of the Hindoo Pantheon, in the same manner as we frequently find the case in the natural phenomena mythologized in the Iliad." Adjoining the subterraneous ruins is the remarkable cave of Rajah Bhirtery. It consists of a long gallery, supported by pillars, with chambers excavated on each side, containing the figures of men carved on the walls.

Oujein imports from Surat various kinds of European and Chinese goods. Pearls and assafœtida, from Sinde, are brought here by the route of Marwar, and diamonds from Bundlecund, pass through this city to Surat. The public bazars are well supplied with grain, fruits, and vegetables. The inhabitants are chiefly Mahometans. East longitude 75° 51'; North latitude 23° 11' 13''. See Hamilton's *East India Gazetteer*, p. 625; and the *Asiatic Researches*, vol. v.

OVAL, or ELLIPSE. See CONIC SECTIONS, Vol. VII. p. 136; DRAWING INSTRUMENTS, Vol. VIII. p. 180.

OVID, PUBLIUS OVIDIUS NASO, a celebrated Roman poet, was born at Sulmo, now Abruzzo, on the 20th March, 43, before Christ. Being intended for the bar, his father sent him early to Rome, and afterwards to Athens, in the sixteenth year of his age. He made rapid progress in eloquence; but his passion for poetry interfered with those studies which his father was desirous he should pursue. Being at last prevailed upon to turn his mind to business, he pled some causes with great success, and acted as one of the triumvirs, to whom criminal jurisdiction was committed. The death of his brother seems to have freed him from the restraints of his profession, as he afterwards devoted himself entirely to gaiety and to the muses.

About the 50th year of his age, he is said to have been guilty of a shameful amour with Livia, the wife of Augustus; and in consequence of this, or some similar crime, he was banished by the emperor to Tomos, on the Euxine Sea. Here he offered the most disgusting adulation to Augustus, no doubt from the hope of

Oviedo, being recalled ; but both Augustus, and his successor
Ow. Tiberius, were deaf to all his flatteries, and resisted the
most earnest solicitations of his friends.

Ovid died at Tomos, in the 59th year of his age,
A. D. 17. His principal works are his *Metamorphoses*,
in fifteen books ; his *Fasti*, in twelve books ; his *Tris-
tia*, in five books ; his *Elegia ;* his *Heroides ;* his three
books of *Amorum ;* his three books *De Arte Amandi ;*
his book *De Remedio Amoris ;* his *Ibis ;* and the fragment of a tragedy called *Medea*.

The best editions of the works of Ovid are those of
Heinsius, Elzevir, 3 vols. 12mo. 1629 ; Burman's,
4 vols. 4to. Amst. 1727 ; that of Utrecht, 4 vols. 12mo.
1713 ; Wetstein's, 3 vols. 12mo. Amst. 1751 ; Barbou's,
3 vols. 12mo. Paris, 1762 ; and Fischer's, 4 vols. 8vo.
Lips. 1773.

OVIEDO, anciently OVIETUM, a town of Spain, and
capital of the division of the province of Asturias,
called the Asturia of Oviedo. The town is situated on
a rather elevated plain, at the confluence of the two
rivers Ovia, or Ove, and Nora, which, after their junction, fall into the Nalon. The streets are tolerably
straight, regular, and well paved, and almost all of
them open into the principal square, which is large and
handsome. The Gothic cathedral, said to have been
built in 760, is of freestone, and is very handsome.
The bones of the kings and queens were preserved in
one of the chapels. The church of San Salvador is
very beautiful. The tomb of its founder, Silo, stands
near the grand entrance. It was enriched with a great
number of relics, which are probably no longer in
existence. The university, founded in 1580, is considered one of the greatest ornaments of the town, and
contains some fine halls. The aqueduct which supplies
the town with water from the spring of Tentoria del
Boo, is of freestone, and has forty arches. There is
also here a drawing school, which is well supported.
The other public buildings are, an Episcopal palace, six convents, three colleges, and three hospitals.
The principal articles of manufacture are hides, hats,
horn combs, and bone buttons. Population about
6400. West longitude 5° 56' 22" ; and north latitude
43° 21' 55". See Laborde's *View of Spain*, vol. ii. p. 405.

OW, or Aw, Loch, a lake of Scotland, in the county
of Argyle. It is about thirty miles long, and in some
places two miles broad, though its average breadth
does not exceed one mile. The principal islands on it
are Inish-Ail, on which are the remains of a small chapel ; Inish-Eraith, the scene of one of Ossian's tales ;
Inish-Chonnell, on which are the ruins of an ancient
castle, once a seat of the Argyle family ; and Fraoch-
Elain, on which are the vestiges of another fortress,
which was granted with some adjacent lands to the
chief of the clan of M'Naughton, by king Alexander
III. on the condition of entertaining the Scottish monarch when he passed that way. On a peninsula of
Loch Ow stand the ruins of Kilchurn castle, built in
1440 by the lady of Colin Campbell, knight of Rhodes,
while her husband was fighting in the holy wars. It
afterwards was much enlarged, and became the seat of
the earls of Breadalbane ; but is now approaching gradually to ruin.

The surface of Loch Ow is 108 feet above the level
of the sea. It receives a large stream at each extremity, and discharges itself laterally by the river Awe
into Loch Etive. The lake abounds in salmon, trout,
and char. At the north-east extremity of the lake rises
the mountain of Ben-Cruachan, elevated 3390 feet above

the surface of the loch. See Pennant's *Tour in Scot-* Owhyhee.
land ; and the *Beauties of Scotland*, vol. v.

OWHYHEE, an island in the North Pacific Ocean, Situation.
the largest and most easterly of the Sandwich Islands,
a group so called by Captain Cook, by whom they were
discovered, (1778) in honour of the Earl of Sandwich,
his friend and patron. Owhyhee, which is of a triangular shape, lies in 154° 45' west longitude, and 19°
north latitude. Its greatest length, in a direction nearly north and south, is 97 miles ; its greatest breadth,
by a line drawn from east to west, is 78 miles. It is
supposed to contain 150,000 inhabitants, a number
which is daily increasing. The divisions are six, of
which Amakooa and Aheado lie on the north-west ;
Apoona and Kaoo on the south-east ; Akona and Koo-
arta on the west.

The general aspect of the island is of a mountainous General
and rugged character. The country, as it recedes from aspect.
the shore, gradually rises into heights and inequalities,
intersected by deep narrow glens, or rather chasms,
but every thing deserving the appellation of a river is
completely unknown. The two highest mountains,
Mouna Kaah and Mouna Roa, which lie on the north-
east, and the summits of which are constantly buried
in snow, must be elevated at least 16,020 feet above
the level of the sea, according to the tropical line of
snow, as determined by M. Condamine, from observations taken on the Cordilleras. The most bleak portion
of the island is the coast of Kaoo ; while the most beautiful is that of Apoona. The former, says Captain
King, " presents a prospect of the most barren and
dreary kind, the whole country appearing to have undergone a total change, from the effects of some dreadful convulsion. The ground is everywhere covered
with cinders, and intersected in many places with black
streaks, which seem to mark the course of a lava that
had flowed, not many years back, from the mountain
Roa to the shore. The southern boundary looks like
the mere dregs of a volcano. The projecting headland is composed of broken and craggy rocks, piled
irregularly on one another, and terminating in sharp
points." The coast of Apoona, on the contrary, is extremely level, and so very beautiful, that the king has
chosen it as one of his places of residence. The acclivity of the inland parts is gentle ; it is everywhere
adorned with cocoa-nut and bread-fruit trees, and exhibits the most striking appearances of cultivation and
fertility.

With the exception, indeed, of the barren, rocky, Produc-
and mountain tracts, the whole island is found to be tions.
remarkably rich ; and no spot susceptible of improvement has been left unemployed. The chief productions
are cocoa-nut and bread-fruit trees, yams, sweet potatoes, plantains, the tarrow or eddy root, and sugar
canes of an amazing luxuriance. In the manner they
manage and arrange their grounds, the natives display
considerable taste. Each class of plants is kept separate, and is either cultivated in neat rows, or formed
into groves ; while the fences, which are made of stone,
are elegantly concealed by sugar canes, thus forming
one of the most beautiful objects on which the eye can
rest. Cattle is totally unknown, so that no portion of
the soil is appropriated to pasture. No quadrupeds of Animals.
any kind, indeed, except of a very unprofitable species,
—hogs, dogs, and rats, of which the first is the most
common,—have been discovered here. The food of
the islanders consists of the vegetable productions already specified, and fish, which are very abundant in

Owhyhee.

every quarter of the coast. People of rank, however, regard the flesh of the wild boar, and of dogs, as a most delicious morsel.

Natives.

The natives of Owhyhee are of a dark complexion, but their features are pleasing. The men are above the middle size, active, and stout ; the women, some of whom are handsome, are in general, however, rather masculine, and not remarkable for delicacy, either of sentiment or demeanour. Like the other natives of Polynesia, the Owhyheans tatoo their bodies, and the females, even the tip of the tongue. Their nose is always spread at the point, owing, perhaps, to their mode of salutation, in which they press their noses together. The dress of both sexes is nearly the same,—cloth of various kinds, which the women wear loosely about them, like wrappers, while the men pass it between the legs, and fasten it to the loins. The more-dignified, both men and women, make use of a great variety of ornaments, on which, though some of them are sufficiently grotesque, they seem to set a very high value. With all their inelegancies and peculiarities, however, they are a superior race of people, devoid of the grossness and ignorance which generally characterize savage life. Captain King represents them as mild and affectionate; and it is allowed on all hands that the death of Captain Cook, of which, in the life of that celebrated person, we have already given an account, did not result from any inherent ferocity in the inhabitants, but from a sudden impulse of undeserved resentment. Their inquisitive turn of mind prompts them anxiously to acquire something new from the various vessels which visit their island. Several Europeans having settled among them, they have thus begun to exhibit some traits of civilized society ; they have made no inconsiderable progress in agriculture and manufactures ; and though they still continue to sacrifice human victims, they do not eat their flesh, like the natives of the neighbouring islands.

Religion.

But what promises most speedily and effectually to procure them the blessings of refinement and civilisation, is the introduction of the knowledge of the gospel, an object which the Missionary Society are endeavouring to carry into execution. Several of the natives have already been converted, and are now devoting their whole time to the education of their countrymen. Krimakoo, the king's prime minister, having abjured paganism, has been baptised into the Christian church ; and as the king himself, with several of his family, treat the missionaries with much kindness, and condescend to listen to their instructions, the benevolent exertions of those amiable and enterprizing men, it is hoped, will, at no distant period, be crowned with complete success.

Government.

The form of government established in Owhyhee is monarchical. There are three degrees of rank inferior to that of royalty, all of which seem to be hereditary. When Captain Cook first landed on this island, a person named Terreeoboo was king, a man advanced in years, and of mild and generous dispositions, who was soon afterwards succeeded by Maiha-Maiha, who filled the throne in 1786, when Captains Pollock and Dixon visited the island. On the death of this latter sovereign, which took place previously to 1794, Tamaahmaah was elevated to the regal dignity, whose son, the present sovereign, a person of no great promise, is denominated Tamaahmaah the Second. This island was ceded to his Britannic Majesty (1794) in the reign of Tamaahmaah the first, who, with his whole people, acknowledged themselves to be subjects of Great

Britain. This, of which the advantages are very problematical, was effected chiefly through the address and influence of Captain Vancouver, to whose Voyages we refer the reader for farther information on this subject ; and an inscription on copper, recording the circumstances relative to the cession, was deposited in a conspicuous place at the royal residence. During the stay of this celebrated navigator in the island, he caused his engineers to build a vessel of considerable size, which he called the Britannia, to be presented to his Owhyhean Majesty. The talents and ambition of the natives have already prompted them to attempt the construction of similar vessels, some of which can boast of a few light guns ; and the marine force of Tamaahmaah has now attained to such a respectable state, that he is completely master of the main in these parts. The introduction of the art of ship-building by Vancouver may, it is not improbable, form an important æra in the commercial as well as the naval history of Owhyhee. The situation of those islands, of which the one we are considering is the largest, is extremely favourable for commerce, " as all the vessels," we are told, " bound to the north-west coast on the fur trade, and also many of those bound to the coast of Asia, stop here for provisions, and to make repairs." Owhyhee, in addition to the various advantages of situation, contains also several commodious bays, of which Karakakooa, where Captain Cook landed, is the most celebrated. It is situated on the west of Akona, is several hundred fathoms in depth, and about a mile and a half in width. None of the Owhyhean towns, or rather villages, have yet been mentioned ; and it need now merely be said, that none of them are situated above four or five miles distant from the shore, and that Kirooah and Kakooa are the most considerable.

See the Voyages of Cook, La Perouse, Vancouver, &c. see also the Missionary Voyage conducted by Captain Wilson, and the *Missionary Register*. (T. M.)

Owhyhee.

Oxford.

Navy.

OXALIC ACID. See Chemistry, Vol. VI. p. 58.

OX-BILE. See Chemistry, Vol. VI. p. 145.

OXFORD, the capital of one of the midland counties of England, to which it gives its name, a city of great antiquity and some importance in British history, the see of a bishop, and more peculiarly celebrated as the seat of what may perhaps be justly considered the most splendid and extensive university in Europe. It is situated about fifty-four miles W. N. W. of London, at the conflux of two small rivers, the Isis (by far the more considerable of the two) and the Cherwell, which, by their circuitous and meandering course, almost surround the place. The city is built on a fine gravel, having as a protection on the south and west, eminences of considerable height ; to the east and north runs a low and level plain, extending through a rich and fertile country, well wooded, and on every side surrounded by the most luxuriant vegetation.

Concerning the derivation of the name of Oxford, many and varying opinions have been formed. The most common is that it was called by the Saxons Oxenford, in the same sense as the Greeks did their Bosphori, and the Germans their Ochenfort on the Oder, namely, as the *ford of oxen;* but we own, that to us no derivation appears so founded on truth and probability as the suggestion of Warton, (the historian of English poetry,) who contends, as Leland did before him, that it is a mere corruption of *Ouseneyford*, the ford at or near Ouseney, or the meadow of Ouse, *Ouse* being the general name for river or water. The city is

General description.

3

written Orsnaforda or Oksnaforda on a coin of Alfred in the Bodleian, it is Oxnaford and Oxeneford, frequently in the Saxon Chronicle, and Oxneford on pennies of the two Williams. Now Ousen, Ousn, or Osn were quickly reduced or corrupted into Orsn, Oxsn, or Okin, and the original meaning of Ouseneyford being forgot and obliterated, Oxeneford (whence Oxenford or Oxford) presented an obvious and familiar signification, which the pedantry of our ancestors Latinised into *Vadum Boum :* for, as Warton justly remarks, the great source of corruption in etymologies of names, both of places and men, consists in the natural propensity, to substitute in the place of one difficult and obscure, a more common and notorious appellation, suggested and authorized by affinity of sound *.

Antiquity.

Oxford is of very remote antiquity. There are not wanting writers who place it as early as the year of the world 2954, or 1009 years before our Saviour. These say, that it was built by Memphric, king of the Britains, and called, in honour of its founder, *Caer-Memphric,* Caer signifying, in the Celtic, a city. Others contend that it was founded by Vortigern, and called *Caer-Vortigern,* whilst a third party give it the appellation of *Bellosihem,* from its favourable situation, on a slight eminence, between two rivers, and adorned with woods. " It is indeed unknown," says Lhwyd, " what names Oxford hath borne, on account of its great antiquity." Ptolemy has been supposed to mention Oxford under the name of *Calleva,* but it may be doubted whether this was not Silchester, or Wallingford ; and it is certain that the place does not occur in the Itinerary of Antoninus, whence we may conclude that, although the Akeman Street passed in the immediate vicinity of the city, it was neither garrisoned nor inhabited by the Romans. It would be useless to dwell on the conflicting and almost fabulous reports which are met with in our early writers respecting the foundation of, and occurrences, at Oxford. Certain it is, that it was the residence of King Alfred and his three sons, Edward, Athelward, and Alfward. In 907 it was burnt by the Danes, who repeated their atrocities in 1002, 1009, 1013, and a fourth time, in 1032. The Conqueror, meeting with a refusal to his summons, stormed the city on the north side in 1067, and, taking it, bestowed his acquisitions on Robert D'Oiley. " Robertus de Olleio, that cam into England with Wylliam Conqueror, had given to hym the baronyes of Oxford and Saint Waleries. This Robert made the Castelle of Oxford, and, as I conject, other made the waulles of Oxford or repaired them. This Robert made the Chapelle of St. George in the Castelle of Oxforde, and founded a college of prebendaries there†." In the survey, commonly known as Domesday book, this Robert is rated as having within and without the walls forty-two houses inhabited, and eight lying waste ; the castle which he erected was in tolerable repair in the early part of the civil wars, but has gradually grown to decay, all now remaining being St. George's tower, of which, so much as is habitable is appropriated to the use of the county prison ; the keep, in which is a strong vaulted chamber, with a well of great depth, and a crypt, now used as a store cellar.

History.

Oxford, in the year 1139, was the place fixed on by King Stephen for the meeting of a general assembly ‡, at which a quarrel arising between the retainers of the Bishop of Salisbury, and those of Alan of Bretagne, Earl

of Richmond, one of the knights of the latter was killed, and many wounded on both sides. But the circumstance which has been more peculiarly recorded in English history as connected with Oxford, is the escape of the Empress Matilda, who, in 1142, retired to Oxford castle to await the arrival of expected succours from Normandy. Stephen, looking upon this as a favourable juncture, hastened thither in expectation of having his rival in his power, and having destroyed the greater part of the city, laid close siege to the fortress on which she relied for safety. The siege was carried on with great vigour and diligence, and the only hope of avoiding the impending disaster rested in the approach of winter, which it was thought likely would compel her adversary to retire. Stephen, however, protested, that neither the hope of advantage, nor the fear of detriment, should induce him to abandon the siege, and the garrison had already been reduced to the last extremities for want of provision, when Matilda escaped, in a manner at that time considered marvellous, and which even now we cannot contemplate without surprise and admiration. It was now Advent, the river frozen, the fields inundated, and the ice covered with snow. Taking advantage of a dark night, she ventured from her stronghold, herself clad in white linen, and attended with four knights disguised in a similar manner, she escaped through the postern gate of the castle, passed the river undiscovered, and, walking on foot to Abingdon, went from thence to Wellingford, where she was greeted with no common joy. In 1154 another great council was held at Oxford, in which all the nobility of England did homage to Henry, reserving only their fealty to Stephen for the remainder of his life. It would far exceed our limits were we to mention the several kings who have made Oxford their place of retirement at one time or at others of active political consultation, or to record the various transactions that have taken place there connected with the history of the country. The palace of Beaumont, built by Henry I., and at which Henry II. chiefly resided, is celebrated as having been the birth place of King Richard I., and the residence of succeeding princes, till Edward II. gave it to the Carmelites, who had three schools here, and a spacious church. It was situated in the north suburb of the city, and the only present remains are portions of two walls with an old door-way, and a pointed and circular window. In digging a level for a new street, from St. Giles's to Worcester College, to be named Beaumont Street, (which is the property of St. John's College,) many human bones were discovered, and some few coins, but none of a very early date.

During the civil wars, Oxford was the scene of many important transactions ; after the battle of Edge-hill, King Charles I., with his two sons, and Prince Rupert, and Prince Maurice, his nephews, came to Oxford. His Majesty, with his court and army, entered the city on the 29th of October, 1642, and he may be said to have made it his head quarters, till he delivered himself up to the Scots at Newark in 1646. The attachment of the inhabitants to the Stuart family was firm to the last. In the reigns of William and Anne, the majority was composed of sturdy Jacobites, and to this day one of the oldest and most respectable persons in the place shows, with no little pride and veneration, the arm-chair in which the pretender sat when he visited Thomas

---

* Specimen of a History of Oxfordshire. 4to. London, 1783.
‡ Will. Malmsbury, p. 182.

† Leland, *Itinerary,* vol. ii. fol. 17, in marg.

Rowney, the *honest* (as the term went) member for Oxford City.

The City of Oxford is a corporate body, consisting of a mayor, high steward, recorder, four aldermen, eight assistants, two bailiffs, two chamberlains, and twenty-four common council-men, who appoint a town-clerk and a solicitor. The mayor is chosen annually from the aldermen or assistants, and this, as well as all other offices, is filled according to the suffrages of the freemen, who amount to about 1600. The city was divided into four wards, containing thirteen parishes, viz.

St Aldate, containing at the last census, in 1821,	1871 inhabitants.
All Saints	600
St. Ebbe	1332
St. Giles	1516
Holywell	982
St. John	125
St. Mary the Virgin	383
St. Mary Magdalen	2056
St. Martin	506
St. Michael	1041
St. Peter le Bailey	1265
St. Peter in the East	1385
St. Thomas	1839

According to this, which we believe to be an accurate enumeration, Oxford contained, in 1821, 14,900 inhabitants; to these, if we add the parish of St. Clement, which is situated in the north-east suburbs, and within the jurisdiction of the university, the total population will be nearly 15,700, exclusive of the university. Each parish has its proper church, and of these the most ancient is that of St. Peter in the East, which is said to have been built by St. Grymbald in or before the year 876; and Wood, in his MS. history of the city, declares it to be " the first church built of stone that appeared in these parts." It has undergone various changes; but much of the ancient work still remains in what are called Saxon ornaments, and it has one of the finest and most perfect crypts in England. Here Grymbald intended to have been buried, but in consequence of a dispute between himself and his scholars, he removed a magnificent tomb already provided for his reception, and retired to Winchester, in which cathedral his remains were deposited. The church next in order of time is that of St. Giles, which was built in or about the twelfth century. In a vault in the north aisle lies the body of one of the university's especial benefactors, and a very singular character, Dr. Richard Rawlinson, a gentleman commoner of St. John's College, and a member of the Royal and Antiquarian Societies. He bequeathed the whole of his very valuable MSS. to the Bodleian, gave that library a large and curious collection of printed books, his coins, medals, and antiques, and founded an Anglo-Saxon professorship, leaving the residue of his property to the college in which he had received his education, and passed most of his latter years; but upon two conditions, that no Scotsman, or son of a Scotsman, no member of the Royal or Antiquarian Societies, should ever on any pretence, or by any contrivance, enjoy one farthing of his benefactions, or be eligible to his professorship. It is said that he quarrelled with the joint secretary of these societies, Mr. Gordon, who offended him in his official duties, and that gentleman being unfortunately a native of the sister kingdom, the Doctor, in a fit of ill humour has for ever excluded a whole nation from partaking of his munificence, and deprived those who enjoy his benefaction from becoming members of two societies to which he himself belonged, and was once

strongly attached. The remaining churches present little worthy of observation. St. Ebbe's and St. Martin's, (commonly called Carfax or Quatrevoix, from its standing at the division of the four ways or streets,) have been rebuilt within these few years, the latter indeed is only just completed. All Saints, which is really a very elegant and imposing building, was erected in 1708, after a design of Dean Aldrich's, in which the Corinthian order is predominant. The interior is a noble room of 72 feet by 42, and 50 feet in height, without pillars, but richly ornamented with pilasters, and the ceiling adorned with fretwork, containing the armorial ensigns of various benefactors.

It is impossible to give our readers any adequate idea of the splendour and magnificence of Oxford, considered as an object of beauty and curiosity. It must be seen to be properly appreciated. The High Street, which is undoubtedly one of the most striking and most beautiful in Europe, owes much to its peculiar formation. At about two-thirds of its entire length from west to east is a gentle curve, which occasions a variety and change of objects at every step. In this street, too, the combination of ancient and modern, the more splendid and most humble buildings, give it a character peculiar to itself, but, upon the whole, extremely grand and interesting. It is, however, much to be regretted that modern luxury and improvement are doing all in their power to lessen the general effect, by destroying a contrast so pleasing to the eye. Not twenty years ago we remember a number of low gable-ended dwellings, which, when viewed in the immediate vicinity of embattled towers, Gothic chapels, and the rich splendid edifices of the various collegiate bodies, gave the whole an irregular and picturesque character, which few other, if any, places could afford; but within the last few years many of these lowly remains of ancient Oxford have disappeared, and they are replaced with larger and more lofty buildings, which, however neat, elegant, and substantial, will not, in the opinion of the antiquary or the artist, compensate for the loss of those Elizabethan inequalities of style, with which Oxford so largely abounded. Besides the High Street, that of St. Giles's is well worthy of notice. It is irregularly built, as it consists almost exclusively of private houses, erected in proportion to the means or for the accommodation of the owners; but the street is more than 2000 feet long, and nearly 250 broad, with a row of stately elms on either side, and the view north and south bounded by the churches of St. Mary Magdalen and St. Giles, which are placed in the centre of the two extremities of the street. Nor will it, we hope and believe, be long ere another and entirely new street be added to those already possessed by the city of Oxford; for within the last few months the two colleges of St. John's and Worcester have united, to open a communication through their respective properties from St. Giles's to the front of Worcester College, the public benefit of which measure may be easily anticipated. This new street, as passing throughout the site of the old palace of Beaumont, is to be called after that name.

The UNIVERSITY of Oxford is undoubtedly of very high antiquity. It has even been contended that there were schools here in the British and Saxon times, and that king Alfred only restored these, already gone to decay in consequence of the barbarity and turbulence of these days, and causing them to be made places for public and general study, was therefore considered as the founder of the university. That king Alfred, who, we know, resided in Oxford, was a benefactor to the schools there, we can have no doubt; and indeed his own literary character, and the attentions he paid to science and learning, make it more than probable that he gave every encouragement to a place peculiarly devoted to education. "We will and command, (says he, in one of his public acts,) that all free men of our kingdom whosoever, possessing two hides of land, shall bring up their sons in learning till they be fifteen years of age at least, that so they may be trained up to know God, to be men of understanding, and to live happily; for, of a man that is born free, and yet unliterate, we repute no otherwise than of a beast or a brainless body, and a very sot." In the absence, however, of all satisfactory records, it would be useless to recapitulate the arguments for and against the antiquity and precedence of this university; suffice it to say, that it has been known and recognised as such for a long succession of ages, and governed by laws and regulations, and endowed with privileges and immunities, which were acknowledged by the sovereign and the courts of law during a period of many centuries. The statutes of the university were drawn up from time to time by the chancellor, his commissary, and the senior part of the university, and these being confirmed sometimes by papal, at others by royal authority, were entered into books appropriated to the use of the vice-chancellor and proctors, and were at all times carried to convocations, and other meetings for public business, for reference and authorities.

Statutes of the university when compiled. In process of time the code of regulations, thus formed and thus preserved, became, as may be well imagined, confused and contradictory; nor was it till the chancellorship of Archbishop Laud that a regular and well digested body of statutes was compiled. Those now in force were selected or reformed, after a careful investigation into the ancient charters and books of precedent, by a delegacy of nine doctors, and seven other the most learned and experienced members of convocation, who, after numerous meetings and much deliberation, produced the volume entitled, *Corpus Statutorum Universitatis Oxoniensis*, which was agreed to by the university at large, and finally received the royal approbation. The copy, printed upon vellum, and presented to king Charles the First, is preserved in the British Museum, and contains a Latin address in MS. to the king, by which it appears that his majesty had himself suggested the propriety of the measure, and fully approved of the mode in which it had been executed.

Officers of the university. Chancellor. The principal officer of the university is the chancellor, who, under the sovereign, possesses the supreme dignity and power. His office is to take charge of the government of the whole university, to maintain its liberties, guard over its privileges, preside in its court, and determine small matters connected with its welfare and reputation. He is elected by convocation, and the office has been held for life since the year 1484, previously to which it was an annual, or at most a biennial, election. It is unnecessary to insist upon the high consideration attached to the chancellorship of Oxford, when our readers remember that at the last vacancy, occasioned by the death of the Duke of Portland in 1809, the candidates were the Lord Chancellor of England, Lord Eldon, and Lord Grenville, the latter of whom obtained it by a majority of eleven only, although a larger number of votes polled than had ever been given on a similar occasion.

High steward. The next officer is the Lord High Steward, who is nominated by the chancellor, and recommended by his letters to the university in convocation, for their approbation. This office was instituted by a charter of Henry IV., and is also held for life. He is to assist by his advice and co-operation the chancellor, vice-chancellor, and proctors, to defend the rights and privileges of the university, and, if required by the chancellor, to hear and determine capital causes, where a scholar or privileged person is a party.

Vice-chancellor. The vice-chancellor is nominated by the chancellor from the heads of houses, subject however to the approbation of convocation. The entire business of the university is transacted by this officer, whose presence is necessary at all solemnities, and whose duty, indeed, is to represent the chancellor, and to perform, in his own person, all those acts which pertain to the regulation and due management of the body. The office is annual, but is generally held, by yearly nominations, for four years. In order to guard against any inconvenience from the indisposition or necessary departure of the vice-chancellor from the university, he appoints four pro-vice-chancellors or deputies, who are heads of houses, one of whom always presides during his absence.

Proctors. The proctors, who may be said to act as the representatives of the masters of arts, are two persons annually chosen from that body, out of the several colleges in the university. For a long succession of years, the election was made by all the masters of arts, and a northern and southern proctor were nominated, indiscriminately, from the university at large. In consequence, however, of the tumult usual on these occasions, Charles I. converted these public elections into private ones, and the proctors are now chosen out of the several colleges by turns; a cycle having been drawn up in 1629, which continues at this day, and terminates in 1835. The duty of the proctors is as general as their power is extensive. They are the preservers of the public peace, have unlimited authority over the scholars, and assist the vice-chancellor upon all occasions, their presence being absolutely necessary at all meetings, convocations, and public times. These officers also nominate four deputies or pro-proctors, who are capable of filling their posts, if themselves absent.

Orator. The *public orator*, who is the next officer in rank and antiquity, is elected by convocation, and for life. He writes all letters and addresses in the name of the university, commemorates benefactors, and presents to honorary degrees in arts. The *keeper of the archives* Keeper of archives. arranges and holds in custody all the muniments and charters, all records and registers belonging to the university. The *registrar* attends convocations and Registrar. other meetings for the purpose of recording transactions, decrees, elections, and statutes, which may take place or be enacted, and it is his duty to register them within the space of one week. The *Esquire Bedels* precede the Beadles. vice-chancellor in all solemn processions, receive the fees for the university, and execute summons and citations, call courts, and, on certain occasions, attend professors or public preachers. They have three ministri or inferior beadles, who execute the vice-chancellor's commands, warn convocations, and perform such other academical services as may seem too servile for the office of the superior bedels, who have been usually chosen from among the masters of arts.

Professors. It has been asserted, that the first public lectures in the university were founded and endowed by King Alfred, and there are not wanting some who have found professors for the various departments of learning and science in those early ages. Thus Grymbald and St.

Oxford. Neot are termed professors of theology; Asser, of grammar and rhetoric; logic, music, and arithmetic, are said to have been publicly taught by John of St. David's; and astronomy by another Johannes, a monk, and colleague of Grymbald's. The first endowed lecture on record, however, is that founded by John Duke of Bedford, in the reign of Henry VI. who gave a considerable sum of money, which, together with his books, was to be devoted to the use of a public professor, and kept in a chest, called the "chest of the seven liberal arts, and the three philosophical ones," and it was upon this donation that the university built public schools, for the better convenience of the professor and his auditors. It appears, too, from a letter of thanks written by the university to King Edward IV. that he also founded a divinity lecture, though all traces of the property, if any was ever bestowed for that purpose, have long since been extinct.

Margaret. The first professorship in point of time of foundation among those now existing, was founded by the Lady Margaret, Countess of Richmond, for a lecturer on the Holy Scriptures, to be chosen by the doctors and bachelors of divinity, and to be called by her own name. The original foundation was March 1, 1496, from which time the Lady Margaret maintained the professor, till her son, King Henry VII. in 1502, confirmed him by charter, and agreed with the abbot and convent of Westminster to pay him twenty marks annually. This payment was continued by Henry VIII. at the dissolution, and the professorship has since received the addition of a prebend in Worcester cathedral.

Regius. The regius professorships were the next as to date. They were founded by Henry VIII. who assigned to each a yearly stipend of £40, to be paid by the dean and chapter of Westminster. In order, however, to relieve themselves from so heavy a charge, they made over certain estates to the dean and chapter of Christ Church, who engaged to pay the professors of divinity, Hebrew, and Greek; those of law and physic receiving their salaries from the royal exchequer. The professorships are in the gift of the king, and have, with the exception of the Greek professor, all received augmentations of considerable value since the original foundation. Those of divinity and Hebrew have had canonries of Christ Church annexed; and the former the rich rectory of Ewelme. The professor of law is a lay prebendary of Salisbury, and the professor of physic holds the mastership of Ewelme Hospital. The regius professorship of modern history was not founded till the year 1724; that of botany in 1793.

Sedley. In 1618, Sir William Sedley gave £2000 for the purchase of land, in order to endow a professorship of Savile. natural philosophy; and, in 1619, Sir Henry Savile founded a professorship of geometry, and another in astronomy. He appointed several of the officers of state, and others holding high situations in the church and law, to be electors, and directs them to elect the ablest mathematicians, without regard to nation or university. To the honour of Oxford, it may be recorded, that her own sons have been uniformly selected, with but one exception, and this was during the civil wars, when the visitors dispossessed the actual professors, and replaced them by two mathematicians from Cambridge.

Camden. Sir William Camden, the historian and topographer, founded, in 1623, a professorship of ancient history; a chair filled successively by the present Lord Howell, and Warton, the historian of English poetry. In Music. 1627, Dr. Heather, himself a doctor of music, founded

a professorship in that science. In 1536, Archbishop Oxford. Laud gave certain lands in Berkshire for a professorship in Arabic, and, early in the last century, one exclusively appropriated to poetry was endowed by Dr. Arabic. Henry Birkhead. Dr. Rawlinson, in 1650, founded the Anglo-Saxon lecture, under certain restrictions, already noticed, as to the choice of a professor; and, in Anglo-Saxon. 1755, Mr. Viner left no less than £12,000 for a professorship, and certain scholarships in the common law. Law, &c. The clinical and Aldrichian professorships for medicine, anatomy, and chemistry, are of later date; and, within the last few years, his majesty has been pleased to lend an additional stimulus to scientific inquiry by the foundation of three readerships, one in experimental philosophy, the others in mineralogy and geology, which have already produced very beneficial effects.

Having thus briefly mentioned the public professors Course of of the university, it may not be amiss to say a few study pursued words on the general mode of education pursued in sued at Oxford, in order to attain the ultimate end, namely, Oxford. degrees in that faculty in which it is the student's intention to proceed. With respect to the studies pursued in the university, it must be observed, that the precise point at which they commence cannot be accurately defined, as much necessarily depends on the progress which a young man has made previously to his admission. With the classics most popular in public schools he has probably acquired some familiarity; he is capable of reading the less difficult tragedies of Athens, and has made acquaintance with the easier historians of Greece and Rome; the foundation of grammar has been laid, upon which a superstructure, more or less solid, has been erected, of mythology, archaiology, and ancient geography. Composition, also, to a certain extent, has been practised. In the other great branch of Oxford education, the mathematics, more, comparatively, is left untouched. With some few exceptions, the student's proficiency is confined to the elements of geometry, and the rudiments of algebra; and, owing to the exclusive study of the classics, at most of our great schools, the scholar is perhaps entirely a stranger, even to these initiatory studies. As the university grants to an undergraduate, a dispensation for residence during two terms, which are usually the two first after his matriculation, the tutor, if an opportunity occurs of ascertaining his pupil's attainments, will direct the attention of the latter to such points as he appears most deficient in, by recommending him a course of study during the half-year which generally intervenes between his matriculation and his actual residence. As soon as this commences, young men are distributed by their tutors into classes, considered suitable to their abilities, and corresponding with their proficiency. Each class attends its lecture in the tutor's apartment, at certain hours, on certain days, and each student (as called upon) has to translate the passage of a classic, or (where the class is mathematical) to solve a question, construct a problem, or demonstrate a theorem, the tutor correcting him as he proceeds, illustrating what is obscure, amplifying what is too concise, pointing out collateral objects which might have escaped the notice of a cursory or desultory reader, and proposing queries which enable him to probe the knowledge displayed, and to ascertain how far it may be merely superficial. The walks of poetry ascend, through the works of the three great tragedians, to Pindar, or to Aristophanes; after Virgil, Horace, and Terence, the student proceeds to Juvenal and Lucretius. The paths of history lead to an acquaintance with Herodotus,

Oxford.

Thucydides, Xenophon, Livy, Polybius, and Tacitus. From Cicero and Demosthenes are derived further sources of information as to the history or institutions of antiquity. As the classical pupil advances, he is initiated into the peripatetic philosophy, and reads the ethics, rhetoric, and poetics of Aristotle with the tutor, whose utmost energies are now called into exertion. The contrast between heathen morality and Christian purity, between the politics of antiquity and the constitutions of modern states, the application of those profound stores of intimate acquaintance with human nature (contained in the Treatise on Oratory,) to the confirmation of religious principles and practice, form, at the same time, the most arduous and the most fascinating department of tuition. In the mathematics, after Euclid, the pupil proceeds through plane and spherical trigonometry, and conic sections, to mechanics, care being always taken that his algebraical knowledge keeps pace with his progress. The Principia of Newton are then commenced, of which the first, second, third, and seventh sections are generally read. A treatise on optics, or astronomy, is sometimes studied by the higher classes; and as much fluxions are considered at the same time necessary as apply to those branches of science which have been attended to. Independently of instruction such as we have now detailed, as given within the several colleges, a public course of lectures is delivered annually by the university professors, on most of the above subjects, and on experimental philosophy in general. The young men are practised in writing Latin exercises of various kinds, according to their respective capacities; translations, themes, verses, or essays. Logic also must be attended to. The manual used in Oxford is so condensed, that, while it affords the greatest technical facilities to the memory of the learner, it requires much elucidation from the teacher, and can scarcely be advantageously employed except as a text-book. During the continuation of the above lectures, it is absolutely necessary for the student to follow a regular course of theological study which he pursues in private, aided by occasional lectures. The Gospels and Acts are to be read in the original with a commentary. The history, geography, and other leading features of the Old Testament are to be impressed on the memory. The various prophecies and types, with their fulfilment; the arguments for natural and revealed religion; the proofs of the Thirty-nine Articles, and explanations of the terms which occur in them; together with the doctrines contained in the Catechism and Liturgy of the established church, and the most important parts of ecclesiastical history, are to be accurately obtained and understood: to which also in some colleges is added a knowledge of the Hebrew language.

Examinations for degrees.

After a course of study such as we have now described, the academical student may be considered as a candidate for an Oxford degree, which is obtained after two public examinations. The first of these commences at one of three given periods, between the sixth and ninth term of the resident scholar, and consists of an accurate rendering of some one Greek and one Latin book at the least, together with a portion of logic or mathematics. At this trial the candidate is more especially probed as to his accurate grammatical acquaintance with the structure of the two languages; and previously to examination, every person is compelled to attend the schools during one whole day, by which means an audience is always insured. If a student fails on this occasion, it passes *sub silentio*; he

does not receive his certificate at the close of the day, and may present himself at the next *Responsions*, for so this exercise is called. The second and more formidable examinations are held twice every year, viz. in Michaelmas and Easter terms; and no one can be examined till he has commenced the fourth year from the time of his matriculation, (except the sons of peers, baronets, and knights, who are entitled to their degrees at three years' standing,) and attended the examinations himself on two distinct and entire days. At this final examination the candidate is first required to show a sufficient knowledge of the Gospels in the original Greek; he is then tried, by questions arising from the passage he has just translated, whether he has a proper view of the Christian scheme, and the outline of sacred history. He is examined as to the evidences of Christianity, in the Thirty-nine Articles, and on various other points connected with natural and revealed religion. If in this portion of his examination his answers are satisfactory, he proceeds; if not, the candidate, however great his other attainments, is precluded from his degree. The second branch, or *literæ humaniores*, requires a competent proficiency in the Greek and Latin languages, in which three authors at the least " *melioris ævi et notæ*," must be given up, although, for the attainment of honourable distinction, eight, ten, or even more, are generally offered. Rhetoric and moral philosophy, which includes the treatises of Aristotle and Quinctilian, and the philosophical works of Cicero, together with logic and Latin composition, may be said to complete this division; and the third is confined exclusively to the elements of the mathematical sciences and physics. In this latter branch candidates are examined or not at their own option, and few present themselves who do not aim at being admitted to a class. The classes are two, both in literature and science; and the second being divided into an upper and a lower, there are in fact three classes of honours in literature, and three in mathematics. The names of those who obtain either or both of these distinctions, are printed in alphabetical order, not according to merit; those who are simply adjudged worthy of their degree, receive a testimonium that they have satisfied the examiners, and, as they obtain no honour, their names are not printed, whilst, if a candidate is rejected, it passes *sub silentio*, and his certificate is not delivered to him, and he is at liberty to appear again at some future time, having again been present during two whole examinations. Such we believe to be a tolerably correct statement of the course of study and mode of examination at Oxford. For the degree of master of arts no second examination now takes place, nor is actual residence required for more than *one* term, except in those colleges, the foundation members of which are compelled to keep terms by the statutes of their founder. For superior degrees in divinity, law, and physic, certain public exercises are performed, and it is necessary that a given time, either four, five, or seven years, as the case requires, should intervene between the degree of master and bachelor, or doctor in divinity, or that of the bachelor and doctor of civil law or physic.

We shall conclude this article with a brief account of the several colleges in the university, premising that it can be little more than their names, dates of foundations, and number of fellowships and students. To begin then with *University*, which, whether founded, as has been said, by Alfred the Great, or not, was undoubtedly one of the first regular houses of education in Oxford. William of Durham, who died in 1249, left the sum of 310 marcs to purchase rents for the maintenance of a certain number of masters, who were to be natives of Durham or its vicinity; appointing the chancellor and masters of the university as overseers of his donation. For some time this money appears to have been lent out at interest, that interest being appropriated to the maintenance of the masters; but the chancellor and his colleagues willing to get rid of an office of some trouble, and which probably gave much dissatisfaction, assigned the benefaction to a certain number of masters, appointed by the regents, who purchased convenient houses, and making them fit residences for a society, did, in process of time, and by other purchases, establish themselves on the present site, calling it for a time Durham Hall, and afterwards Great University Hall; a title it retained to the reign of Queen Elizabeth. The first statutes of the society were framed in 1280; these were revived in 1292, again in 1311, and lastly in 1475. The first master, or " senior socius," as he was then called, occurs in 1219. The foundation, as now existing, is for a master, twelve fellows, (two for the county of Durham, founded by William of Durham; three for the diocese of York and Durham, by Henry IV.; three for the dioceses of Durham, Carlisle, and York, by the Earl of Northumberland; and four for any part of England, except the three dioceses just named, for Sir Simon Bennet,) and seventeen scholars and exhibitioners. In this college, the learned Sir William Jones, together with the present Lord Chancellor of England, his brother Lord Stowell, the Master of the Rolls, and Judge Richardson, received their education. The number on the books in 1822 was 188, of which 100 were members of convocation.

Baliol was founded by John Baliol, father of John Baliol, King of Scotland, and his wife, Devorguilla, about the year 1268. The old foundation, as augmented by subsequent benefactors, consisted of nine fellows and ten scholars, to which three fellowships and four scholarships were afterwards added. Two of each of these are confined to persons educated at Tiverton school in Devonshire; the remainder are not limited to any part of the kingdom. Wycliff, Archbishop Morton, and Bishop Tonstal, may be claimed as members of Baliol. Total number on the books in 1822, 183; members of convocation 66.

Merton, originally founded by Walter de Merton for twenty poor scholars, and certain chaplains at Malden in Surrey, whom he afterwards removed to Oxford, establishing his society by a charter, dated in 1264, in which he calls it *Domus Scholarium de Merton*; at the same time, he gave them statutes, which were afterwards, (in 1274,) superseded by others drawn up by the founder himself, and so judiciously, that they were recommended by the king to the Bishop of Ely, as a model for those of Peter House in Cambridge, which he was then about to erect. The foundation was afterwards increased by the addition of certain students, to be called post-masters, for whose maintenance John Willyott, chancellor of Exeter, and of the university, gave considerable estates; and their number was enlarged by a Dr. Jessop in the reign of king James I. The society now consists of a warden, twenty-four fellows, who are elected from the graduates of the whole university, fourteen post-masters, four scholars, two chaplains, and a like number of clerks. The entire number on the books is 121, of whom 59 are members of convocation. Merton College is remarkable, as containing some of the most ancient buildings in the university, a part of the warden's lodgings being consider-

ed as coeval with the foundation. The library is also a very curious specimen of the style of the fourteenth century; and the chapel, although a part only of the original design, is of the richest Gothic, although much of the fine effect of the building is lost, by its having a modern screen, wainscoat, and roof. In this spot lie the remains of Sir Thomas Bodley, the founder of the library that bears his name; and Anthony a Wood, the historian and antiquary of the university.

Exeter, founded in 1314, by Walter Stapleton, bishop of Exeter, and lord treasurer, for a rector and twelve fellows, to be chosen from the west of England. Thirteen more fellowships have been added for other counties, and one for Guernsey and Jersey, by subsequent benefactors. The numbers on the books in 1822 were 234, members of convocation 70.

Oriel, founded by Edward the Second, or rather by his almoner Adam de Brome, who having purchased lands for its erection and endowment, placed the whole into the hands of his royal master, who granted the college a new charter, and gave it additional property, and the advowson of St. Mary's church. De Brome was appointed first provost, and drew up the original statutes, which were dated in 1326. The original society consisted of a provost and ten fellows, since increased by Frank, master of the rolls, Carpenter bishop of Worcester, Smyth bishop of Lincoln, and Richard Dudley, to eighteen. This is at present one of the most flourishing colleges in the university, having 246 members, of which nearly half are young men, whose education is still proceeding: members of convocation 123.

Queen's, founded by Robert Eglesfeld, confessor to Philippa, Queen to Edward III. in 1340, for a provost and twelve fellows, who were to be natives of Cumberland and Westmoreland. The original intention of the founder, after the manner of those days, was that his society should resemble Christ and his apostles; and, in addition, he resolved to maintain seventy poor scholars, representing our Lord's disciples, who were to supply the vacancies as they might occur among the fellows, and, in the mean time, to further their education, they were directed " to be called together for their meals in the public hall, by the sound of the horn," where, kneeling on the outside of the table, they were to be examined by the fellows, sitting in purple gowns, those of the doctors being faced with black fur. The founder, however, died before he could carry the whole of his project into execution; and although the number of scholars, or poor children, never reached the founder's original intention, yet a certain number was educated, and publicly examined, even so late as the early part of the eighteenth century. The fellows were afterwards increased to sixteen, the funds admitting the expence, and this, together with two chaplains, eight taberdars, and twelve scholars, is the present number of the old foundation. In 1739 the society received a very important addition by the will of John Michel, Esq. of Richmond, who left lands and money to a very considerable amount, for eight fellows, four scholars, and four exhibitions. There are in all 264 members, 125 of whom are members of convocation. The present buildings of Queen's were begun in 1710, but not completed till 1759. They are in a style of great grandeur and magnificence: the hall and chapel form an oblong of 300 feet in length, by 220 in breadth, and, although not commonly visited by strangers, are as well worthy of admiration as any two rooms in Oxford. The proportions are admirable, and the stone roof of peculiarly good masonry. In this college, too, is one of the handsomest and most ancient pieces of plate in Oxford. It is a drinking horn, of exquisite beauty, set in silver gilt, and, according to tradition, was given to the college by Queen Philippa, as the conveyance of a valuable manor. The cover is surmounted by an eagle, of the best workmanship; and there are four circular annulets, on which is engraved the word *Wasseyl.* The extremity terminates with the head of a leopard, curved round, and the whole stands on three eagles' legs of silver. It is still used on gaudies, and contains about two quarts.

New College, in every respect one of the most magnificent foundations in Oxford, owes its existence to William of Wykeham, bishop of Winchester, and Lord Chancellor of England. He founded it in 1386, for a warden and seventy fellows, ten chaplains, an organist, three clerks, and sixteen choristers; directing that all vacancies should be filled up by persons elected from his college at Winchester, now better known as Winchester School. The numbers in 1822 were 125, of which 62 are members of convocation. To account for the disparity of this, with the numbers on the books of many smaller colleges, it must be understood that this house has not, for some years, received more than one or two independent members, (those are persons who, without any situation on the foundation of a college, resort thither merely for their education, and the sake of obtaining their degrees,) their own body requiring all the accommodations the edifice is capable of affording. The chapel of this college is even now, in spite of modern innovation, the most splendid building in the university; what it was at the period of the founder's life can only be imagined, but there is little doubt of its having been all that magnificence and liberality, piety and skill, could make it. In the earlier part of the Reformation, the images were broken and destroyed, the niches plastered up, the splendid ornaments, rich statues, and other costly decorations, removed; and even the painted windows, some of the most brilliant specimens of the Flemish school, would have shared a similar fate, had not the fellows assured King Edward's visitors that they were too poor to replace them with new and plain lattice, promising to do so whenever they should be sufficiently wealthy. In 1789, under the direction of the late Mr. Wyatt, the chapel was restored, and the old fret-work and niches at the altar imitated as nearly as possible; but the chapel still wants the original Gothic roof of open timber work, and it may be questioned whether the trifling effect produced by opening the centre of the organ, so as to make it appear a sort of frame to the painted windows in the anti-chapel, was worthy the architect or the society. Considered altogether, it must, however, be confessed, that this chapel is decidedly the most imposing of any in the university. The hall, too, is a noble room, but here again the roof is totally out of character; and the gardens are worth visiting, as they are bounded by a considerable portion of the ancient city wall, in excellent preservation, and afford a good view of the ancient edifice of St. Peter's church.

Lincoln, founded in 1427, by Richard Flemming, Bishop of Lincoln, for a rector and seven fellows, afterwards increased by Thomas Rotheram, also a bishop of Lincoln, who, whilst visiting his diocese, came to the college, where he was received by the rector and fellows, the former of whom received him with a speech, in which he complained of the want of buildings, and

of proper scholastic discipline in his society. Rotheram was pleased with the address, and promised to remedy the defects, which he did, by finishing the imperfect building, and augmenting the number of fellowships to twelve, as well as giving them a new body of statutes, dated Feb. 11, 1479; in these the fellows are limited to the dioceses of Lincoln and York, one excepted, who is to be of Wells. Members on the books 102; of convocation 45. The external appearance of this college has lately been greatly amended, by the taste and liberality of its present fellows, who, for the last few years, have devoted a considerable portion of their collegiate income to the improvement of the college. The chapel, though small, is worth inspection, as it contains some very good carving, and some of the best painted glass in Oxford.

All-Souls, situated in the High Street, near St. Mary's Church, was founded by Henry Chickley, Archbishop of Canterbury, who, in 1437, laid the foundation stone, and obtained a charter from Henry VI. in the following year, in which that king assumes the title of founder, probably at the request of Chickley, who was willing to insure his patronage. The foundation was for a warden and twenty fellows, afterwards increased to forty, and the name of the society was derived from their original occupation, which was, to pray for the good estate of Henry VI. and the archbishop, whilst living, and for their souls when dead, as well as for the souls of Henry V. the Duke of Clarence, and all subjects of England who had fallen in the war with France, together with those of all the faithful deceased. This foundation has not been increased. The number of members on the books is ninety-one, of members of convocation, sixty-six. The greater portion of the buildings of All-Souls is comparatively of modern erection; the gateways, part of the front, and of the smaller quadrangle, being all that remains of Chickley's College. The hall and chapel are indeed old, and have undergone frequent alterations, and are, notwithstanding, inferior (except in size,) to none in Oxford. No society, indeed, appears to exercise greater liberality, guided by a more correct taste, than the members of All Souls, who can boast of as handsome and convenient a hall, as splendid yet neat a chapel, as any in the University, nor can any library, (if we except the Bodleian,) at all compete with theirs, either in size and beauty, or for the excellent and well-selected collection it contains. The writer of the present article has had frequent opportunities of consulting the treasures of the Codrington library, and as frequent occasion to acknowledge the kindness with which his applications have been received, and his researches facilitated.

Magdalen, founded by William of Wainfleet, Bishop of Winchester, and Lord Chancellor of England, in 1456, consists of a president, forty fellows, thirty demies or probationers, a schoolmaster, four chaplains, an organist, eight clerks, and sixteen choristers. The fellowships are restricted to the natives of certain counties or dioceses, seven Lincolnshire, four Oxfordshire, three Berkshire, one Yorkshire, two Gloucestershire, two Warwickshire, one Bucks, one Kent, one Nottinghamshire, one Essex, one Somersetshire, one City of London, one Wiltshire, five for the diocese of Winchester, two for that of York or Durham, and two for that of Chichester. The demies, who succeed to fellowships as vacancies occur, are from any of the above counties or dioceses, with the exception of York and Durham. The founder first placed his society in the edifice till so lately used as Magdalen Hall, but, upon obtaining permission from Henry VI. to convert the ancient hospital of St. John Baptist into a college for the purposes of literature, he afterwards fitted that building for the reception of his fellows, gave them a body of statutes in 1479, and directed that it should bear the name of St. Mary Magdalene College. Two of the fellowships were founded by John Ingleden, and a third by John Foreman, but during the life, and with the permission of Wainfleet, who died in 1486. Magdalen College is situated at the last entrance to Oxford, and forms a noble object as the traveller crosses the bridge over the Cherwell. Its tower, the beauty of which cannot fail striking the eye of all who admire architectural grandeur and proportion, united with simplicity and taste, was completed in 1498, being finished in six years from the time of its commencement; and tradition relates, that Cardinal Wolsey gave the plan. It is certain that he was bursar of the college during that period; but his claim to the merit of being the architect of this noble fabric is by no means established. The cloister is coeval with the founder, as is the splendid gateway, now disused, near the president's lodgings. The hall and chapel are both of the same date, and (although subsequent alterations, and some of the decorations of the seventeenth century, might have been well omitted) contain several fine remains of the original design. The new buildings, containing three tiers of rooms for the accommodation of the members, were erected in 1733, and are 300 feet in length, the upper stories resting on an arcade. The view from these rooms is unique; one side looking towards what was the ancient building of St. John's Hospital, at this time restoring to its original appearance, and the other facing a small park filled with the finest elms, and stocked with deer. It may be added, that Addison was a fellow of this society, and a walk is still shown which tradition relates to have been his favourite retirement. The total number at Magdalen, in 1822, was 159, of which 107 were members of convocation.

Brazen Nose, founded by William Smyth, Bishop of Lincoln, and Sir Richard Sutton, Knight, in 1509, that being the year in which they commenced building their new college, although the charter bears date Jan. 15, 1511-12. It was originally for a principal and twelve fellows, natives of the old diocese of Lichfield and Coventry, with preference to natives of Lancashire and Cheshire, and particularly the parishes of Prescot and Presburg. To these eight other fellowships, and several scholarships, have been added by various benefactors. Under a late principal, Dr. Hodson, afterwards regius professor of divinity, and canon of Christ Church, this society rose from a comparatively small and inconsiderable college, to one of greater magnitude and more celebrity than any of its competitors. The numbers, in 1822, were 399 on the books, and 196 members of convocation.

. *Corpus*, founded in 1516, by Richard Fox, Bishop of Winchester, Lord Privy Seal, who gave the society a body of statutes in the following year, by which he wills that they should consist of a president, twenty fellows, twenty scholars, who should succeed to the fellowships, two chaplains, two clerks, and two choristers. Besides which, the statutes permit six independent undergraduate members, who are always " commensales superioris ordinis," *i. e.* gentlemen commoners, and there are four exhibitioners. The clerks' and choristers' places have of late years been abolished. The numbers, 109 on the books; members of convoca-

tion, 70. It may be stated, that the library of Corpus is peculiarly rich, both in printed books and MSS. and among the former are some of the finest and rarest of the early classics.

Christ Church, which is the largest and most magni-
ficent foundation in Oxford, owes its origin to Cardinal Wolsey, who, in 1524 and 1525, obtained two bulls from Pope Clement VII. empowering him to suppress twenty-two inferior priories and nunneries, and to devote their revenues to the support of his intended college. Henry VIII. concurring in these designs, gave him the priory of regular canons of St. Frideswide, and on this site he proceeded to erect *Cardinal College*, that being the original name given to the establishment. Wolsey's noble foundation was intended to consist of a dean, sub-dean, sixty canons of superior order, forty of an inferior rank, ten public lecturers, thirteen chaplains, an organist, twelve clerks, and sixteen choristers; but the Cardinal falling into disgrace, and being deprived of his power and property in 1530, the new college, (of which a dean and eighteen canons had been already appointed by the founder,) was impeded, if not dissolved, for two years. To the credit of its original author, his last and most anxious care and solicitude was for the welfare of this work, devoted to piety and learning; for, in his latest letters to Secretary Cromwell, he pleads with importunate earnestness that his majesty would be pleased to suffer his college to go on. Henry, who had seized upon the revenues, and suspended the foundation, re-established it in 1532, under the title of " King Henry the Eighth's College in Oxford," and endowed it with an annual income of £2000, for a dean and twelve canons. This was suppressed in 1545, when the charter was surrendered, and the following year the episcopal see, which, at the dissolution, had been placed in Oseney Abbey, had been removed to the new college, which was then converted into a cathedral, to be called " The cathedral church of Christ in Oxford, of King Henry Eighth's foundation," and the king consigned all the estates and property to the dean and chapter, on condition of their maintaining a dean, eight canons, eight chaplains, an organist, eight clerks, and the same number of choristers, together with sixty students, and forty grammar scholars, a schoolmaster, and usher. The forty grammar scholars were, in 1561, converted into academical students by Queen Elizabeth, who directed that they should be selected from her father's foundation at Westminster; and to this number one more student was added, by Mr. William Thurston, in 1663. The entire number at present, of dependent and independent members, is 695, of whom 345 are members of convocation. The limits of the present article will not permit us to do justice to the splendour of this college. The cathedral, which is a portion of the ancient building of St. Frideswide, has generally been referred to the time of Henry I. but it may be doubted whether many of the ornaments, the pilasters, arches, and particularly the door of entrance, as well as that to the chapter-house, are not of a much earlier date. The choir, though small, is extremely rich and beautiful, and would be still more so but for two galleries, erected for the choristers, in the vilest taste, and perfectly out of character. The kitchen, hall, and the greater part of the large quadrangle, were completed by Wolsey, and are well worthy his princely spirit. The latter is 264 feet by 261; the hall, one of the finest specimens in the kingdom, is 115 feet by 40, and 50 in height. Peck-

Oxford. water quadrangle, so called from being on the scite of an ancient hall of that name, was erected in 1705, and on the last side stands the library, a noble building, commenced in 1716, but not completed till 1761. On the basement story, besides a portion of the books, is a collection of pictures, bequeathed by General Guise; and, in the upper room, are the very valuable collections of books formed by Archbishop Wake, Lord Orrery, Bishop Fell, Dean Aldrich, and many other eminent benefactors. It would be unpardonable to conclude this brief notice without mention of the great bell, which was formerly in the high tower of Oseney Abbey, and is one of the largest in Europe, its weight being 17,000 pounds; nearly double that of the great bell of St. Paul's, London.

Trinity College. *Trinity,* founded by Sir Thomas Pope, Knight, treasurer of the court of augmentations under Henry VIII. for a president, twelve fellows and twelve scholars, to be chosen from certain parishes in which his manors and estates were situate, and in default of proper candidates from these, from any other counties in England, provided there are not more than two at the same time from any one county excepting Oxford, which may have five. There are also four exhibitions, one for a superannuated Winchester scholar. Total number of members 200, of convocation 78.

St. John's College. *St. John's,* founded by Sir Thomas White, Knight, alderman, and Lord Mayor of London, in 1557, for a president, fifty fellows, of whom twelve must take their degrees in law, and one may proceed in physic; the others are bound to enter into orders at twelve years standing, or forfeit their fellowships. Of these fellowships, six are held by kindred to the founder, thirty-seven are elected from Merchant Tailors' school, two from Coventry, two from Bristol, two from Reading, and one from Tunbridge. St. John's College owes much of its splendour and prosperity to subsequent benefactors. Archbishop Laud built the inner quadrangle, after a design of Inigo Jones, and furnished the library with some of its best books and all its manuscripts. Sir William Paddy added to the establishment an organist, five clerks, and six choristers, leaving an estate, for that and other purposes, of considerable value. Archbishop Juxon gave a sum of money amounting to seven thousand pounds, no mean contribution in those days; and Dr. Holmes, many years president of the college, left thirteen thousand, increased to fifteen by his widow. But the greatest benefactor was Dr. Richard Rawlinson, who, in addition to many kind acts performed towards the society during his life, bequeathed the whole of his property in Warwickshire and other places, to be divided amongst the fellows in shares, proportioned to their rank and degrees; besides which, he appointed the college as his residuary legatee, and gave it every fifth turn to his Anglo-Saxon professorship. His heart is preserved, according to his own directions, in a marble urn erected in the chapel; his remains, we have before said, were deposited in St. Giles's Church. The library of St. John's is one of the largest and best furnished in the university, particularly in theology, and its gardens are deservedly admired for the judicious taste by which a comparatively small spot of ground is made to confine so many beauties. This college has 204 members, 115 of whom are members of convocation.

Jesus College. *Jesus,* founded by Hugh Price, in 1571, who petitions Queen Elizabeth, that her majesty would be pleased to found a college, for the benefit and education of the natives of Wales; to which she consenting, he bestowed lands and money for that purpose, the queen giving a quantity of timber from the royal forests to Oxford. aid the building. Other benefactors have added to the original number, and the present foundation consists of a principal, nineteen fellows, and eighteen scholars, besides exhibitions. Total number of members 149, of convocation 52.

Wadham College. *Wadham,* founded in 1613, by Nicholas and Dorothy Wadham, for a warden, fifteen fellows, fifteen scholars, two chaplains, and two clerks. The scholars are to be three from Somersetshire, and three from Essex, the remainder is from any county in Great Britain, and they are to succeed to fellowships as vacancies occur. There is one peculiarity in this foundation, of which no other instance occurs in Oxford; this is, that the fellows are superannuated on the completion of eighteen years from the time of their becoming regent masters, and, if they are not fortunate enough to obtain preferment in that time, are then compelled to resign. The number on the books 161, members of convocation 48. There is a neatness, uniformity, and an air of scholastic repose, in the buildings of Wadham, not exceeded by any of the same extent and date of erection. The hall is one of the finest rooms in Oxford, and the library and chapel both do credit to the liberality of the founder. The gardens, although very confined, are tastefully laid out, and afford a very interesting view of the chapel, and northern and east sides of the fabric. By an account book preserved in the college, it appears that the whole building cost exactly £10,816. 7s. 8d., to which was added somewhat more than £500 for plate and furniture for the kitchen; the whole of which was defrayed, without any assistance, by Dorothy, who survived her husband, and devoted herself to fulfilling his benevolent intention.

Pembroke College. *Pembroke,* originally Broadgate Hall, was converted into a college in 1620, by Thomas Tesdale, Esq., and Richard Wightwick, for a master, ten fellows, and ten scholars. To these King Charles I. added a fellowship for a native of Guernsey or Jersey; Sir John Bennet two fellowships and two scholarships; and Sir John Philipps one of each, and there are certain exhibitioners added by subsequent benefactions. The fellows are either to be of the founder's kindred, or elected from Abingdon school, in Berkshire. Number on the books 137, of convocation 51.

Worcester College. *Worcester,* originally Gloucester Hall, was founded in the beginning of the last century, by Sir Thomas Cookes, Bart. for a provost, six fellows and six scholars, to be chosen from certain schools in the county of Worcester. Fifteen other fellowships, and ten scholarships have since been added by Dr. Finney, Dr. Clarke, and Mrs. Sarah Eaton. The present number of members on the books is 175, of which 83 are members of convocation.

Halls. Besides the colleges already enumerated, there are five halls, which differ from the other foundations in this particular; namely, that they are not endowed with estates, but are simply houses, under the government of a principal, for the education and residence of students; they are, however, in respect to academical privilege and discipline, on the same footing with other societies. These are,

St. Mary Hall, containing	72 members,	18 of convocation.
St. Mary Magdalen Hall,	120	27
St. Alban Hall, . . .	68	13
Edmund Hall, . . .	92	36
New Inn Hall, ...	1	1

The entire population of the university being, in 1822, 4295, of which 1956 are members of convocation, and have votes on all subjects connected with the

Oxford-
shire.

Situation
and extent.

Surface.

Rivers.

Canals.

welfare and regulation of the university. West Long. of observatory 1° 15′ 30″. North Lat. 51° 45′ 40″. See UNIVERSITY.

OXFORDSHIRE, one of the central counties of England, is bounded on the north by the counties of Warwick and Northampton; on the west, by Gloucestershire; on the south, by the rivers Isis and Thames, which divide it from Berkshire; and on the east, by Buckinghamshire. Its figure is very irregular; at Oxford, near the centre of the county, it is not more than seven miles in breadth, a little farther north it is thirty-eight, and at no part south of Oxford does it exceed twelve. Its greatest length, from north-west to south-west, is fifty miles; and its circumference, 130. The superficial extent is estimated at 742 square miles, or 474,880 acres. It is divided into fourteen hundreds, and these again into 207 parishes: it contains one city and twelve market towns; lies in the diocese of Oxford; and returns nine members to parliament.

The aspect of this county is considerably diversified. The southern district possesses much beauty and variety of scenery, being traversed by the extensive range of the Chiltern hills, which are mostly covered with thick woods of beech. The northern division is elevated and stony; the fields are inclosed with stone fences in place of hedges; and, being destitute of woods, it presents a barren and uninteresting appearance. The central division is a rich and level country, interspersed with many elegant mansions and country seats, watered by numerous streams that flow through meadows clothed in the richest verdure, and abounding in extensive forests, coppices, and plantations.

Few districts in England are better watered than Oxfordshire; some of its historians enumerate no less than seventy streams that have their course in it. The principal of these is the Isis, which rises in the north of Wiltshire, and flows in an easterly direction across the county to the town of Lechlade in Gloucestershire, where it becomes navigable, and is met by the Thames and Severn Canal; it enters Oxfordshire at Helmscot, and, proceeding in the same course between the counties of Oxford and Berks, receives the Windrush at Moorton, and the Evenlode at Ensham, after which it turns to the south-east, and is joined by the Charwell a little below Oxford; still flowing southeast it unites with the Thame near Dorchester, where they jointly obtain the name of the Thames. This river in its farther course is augmented by several streams; and, after gliding slowly through rich and beautiful scenery, leaves the county near Henley. The Thame, an inconsiderable stream, but remarkable for having been supposed to give name to the Thames, rises at Tring in Hertfordshire; and, flowing through Buckinghamshire, enters Oxfordshire near Thame, thence it flows south-west to Dorchester, where it meets the Isis. The Charwell rises on the borders of Northamptonshire, passes Bunbury, and, running south, joins the Isis at Oxford. The only other rivers of note are the Windrush, the Evenlode, the Glym, and the Ray.

The Oxford canal commences in Warwickshire, on the edge of the Coventry canal, and, after passing along the western boundary of Northamptonshire, and crossing the Grand Junction canal at Braunston, enters Oxfordshire at its northern extremity near Claydon; passing Banbury it approaches the Charwell, and proceeds at a short distance from that river to Oxford, where it joins the Isis. The advantages resulting to the county from this canal are considerable, as it opens a communication to some of the principal manufacturing counties in the kingdom; and coals, which were formerly

Oxford-
shire.

Climate.

Soil.

Minerals.

Agriculture.

brought from London at a great expence, are now procured at a moderate rate from the Wednesbury collieries.

The climate of Oxfordshire is very salubrious, but it is in general cold. The northern parts in particular, from being quite unsheltered, are chill during the greater part of the year, and disagreeably warm in summer. It is also cold on and near the Chiltern hills, and the frost is observed to take effect sooner, and continue longer on the poor white lands at their base, than on the deeper soils in the vicinity: in warm seasons the Chiltern district is usually moist with fogs.

In regard to its soil, this county has been divided by Mr. Arthur Young, in his Agricultural Survey, into four districts: the district of red land; that of stonebrash; that of the Chiltern hills; and that of miscellaneous loams. The red land, consisting of 79,635 acres, occupies the northern parts of the county. The soil is strong, deep, and friable, yet capable of tenacity; well adapted for the culture of every species of plant, and much exceeding the others in fertility. The stonebrash comprises an extent of 164,023 acres, including almost all the central division of the county, the greatest part of which is inclosed. Its general character is a surface of loose, dry, friable sand or loam, apparently formed of abraded stones, chiefly limestone; but this tract varies considerably in different parts, from a poor and light soil to one that is deep and rich. It is well fitted for turnips and wheat. The Chiltern lands contain 64,778 acres, the soil of which is chalk of almost pure calcareous earth, intermixed with a small proportion of sandy loam and clay, and abounding with flints. The district of miscellaneous loams, consisting of 166,400 acres, includes all the other varieties of soil in the county, from loose sand to heavy clay.

There are no minerals of consequence in Oxfordshire. It has been alleged, but with little foundation, that a silver mine was formerly worked in the southern part. At present no metal of any kind is found. There are, however, several freestone quarries; and limestone and slate are abundant. Excellent ochre in considerable quantities is got near Shotover; and a variety of clays in the neighbourhood of Oxford were formerly employed in pottery, but being of an inferior quality to those of Staffordshire, they are now disused. There are also several medicinal springs, chiefly chalybeate.

Oxfordshire is not remarkable for its agriculture. Of late years, however, it has made considerable improvement in this important point; the system of inclosures has been carried to a great extent, and the Norfolk husbandry seems to be well understood, and in general adopted. The annual value of a square mile is on an average £709. Landed properties are in general large; there is one estate that produces £20,000 a-year; one £12,000; one £7000; and several from 6 to £3000; but there are also many small proprietors, possessing about 4 or 500 acres, who chiefly farm their own lands. The farms vary much in extent, but they are generally smaller than in most parts of England; the rents are from £500 to £20. But what is most prejudicial to the agriculture of this county, is the shortness of the leases, few of which exceed the term of seven years; and many considerable proprietors grant no leases whatever. The rotation of crops varies in the different districts; in the red lands the customary course is one of six: 1st, turnips; 2d, barley, or spring wheat; 3d, clover; 4th, wheat; 5th, beans or peas; and 6th, oats. In the lighter lands of the stonebrash division, the general rotation is 1st, turnips; 2d, barley with clover, ryegrass, or trefoil, or mixed; 3d and 4th, clover for one or two years; 5th, wheat; 6th, oats, peas, or beans. The Chiltern district resembles the stonebrash in being well adapted for turnips, wheat, and sainfoin. Of the crops only partially cultivated are potatoes, cabbages, carrots, lentils, rape and chicory. Hemp, flax, and hops, were formerly raised in considerable quantities, but they are now almost entirely neglected. Though the rearing of corn forms the principal object of the agriculturists, grazing is by no means neglected ; and though its meadows, for which this county was formerly famed, are now greatly circumscribed, yet tracts of pasture land are found in every quarter, and particularly in the central parts in the vicinity of the Thames and the Charwell. These are chiefly appropriated to the dairy ; butter is made in considerable quantities, and some cheese of a good quality ; and a great number of calves are fattened for the London market. The long-horned breed of cattle are preferred ; and the South Down sheep are gradually taking place of the Berkshire breed.

Oxfordshire, according to Camden, was formerly famous for its extensive forests ; and even at present it is better wooded than most of the English counties. The forest of Whichwood, consisting of about 6720 acres, lies in the middle district. In this forest the oak, the ash, the beech, and elm, are intermixed, but the oak is most numerous and thriving, yet none of them will be fit for the use of the navy for a considerable time. This forest contains thirty-four coppices, averaging 100 acres, which chiefly belong to the king, and the Duke of Marlborough. The small timber of the coppices belonging to the king is usually cut at eighteen years growth, that of the duke's at twenty-one ; during the first seven of which the cattle and sheep are excluded by fences ; the deer, which are very numerous, are never excluded. The annual value of these coppices is about six shillings per acre. The beech woods of the Chiltern district are supposed to have formed a part of that extensive forest, which is described by Leland as stretching 120 miles westward from the border of Kent. They are produced almost entirely by the falling of the beech mast, very little being permitted to grow on the old stools, which are generally grubbed up. There are also numerous other tracts of woodlands and plantations in the county, particularly at Stanton, St. John, and at Blenheim, the seat of the Duke of Marlborough.

The manufactures of Oxfordshire are on a very limited scale. At Whitney the weaving of blankets is carried on to some extent ; and at Bloxham and Banbury a coarse sort of velvet is made. There are manufactures of polished steel and of gloves at Woodstock ; the latter of which affords employment to a considerable number of persons. The town of Henley sends large quantities of malt to the London market ; and, in the northern part of the county, the female poor are employed in lace-making.

Oxfordshire, together with part of Gloucestershire, was originally inhabited by the tribe called the Dobuni. When the Romans, under Aulus Plautius, invaded Britain, the Dobuni were at variance with the Cattieuchlani, a neighbouring tribe ; and, instead of joining the rest of their countrymen against the common enemy, they entreated the assistance of the Romans, and received their forces into their territory. From the inhabitants thus submitting quietly to the invaders, there are fewer traces of encampments and military stations in this county than in most other parts of England, yet there are numerous other vestiges of their establishment. Near Alchester there appears to have been a Roman station, the remains of which are of a square

form, with a ditch and mound facing the four cardinal points. Of the four great Roman roads, which stretched across the island from sea to sea, the one named the Ikeneild-street passed through the southern part of the county. It enters at the parish of Chinnor, and may be traced for several miles running in a south-westerly direction. There are also many cross roads, which passed from one colony or station to another ; the principal of these is the Akeman-street, the outline of which can be well traced. Various Roman coins and fragments of tesselated pavement have been discovered, and there are several funeral mounds which are supposed to be of Roman origin. Under the Saxon heptarchy this county formed part of the kingdom of Mercia. When Mercia was divided into five bishoprics, the name of the inhabitants was changed from Dobuni into that of Wiccii. During the Danish invasion, Oxfordshire was repeatedly ravaged ; several important battles were fought in it ; and, at the beginning of the eleventh century, it was principally inhabited by Danes. In the wars of York and Lancaster it was just once the scene of contest : an engagement having taken place between the forces of Edward the IV. and an undisciplined army, composed chiefly of the common people of Yorkshire, in which the former were defeated. In the civil wars of the seventeenth century this county did not declare for either party ; but from Oxford being chosen for the residence of the court, it unavoidably became the seat of warfare ; skirmishes took place in every quarter, and it was plundered alike whichever party was victorious : since that period nothing connected with it has occurred deserving of notice.

According to the various parliamentary returns, the population was found to be as follows : in 1801 there were 20,599 houses, and 109,620 inhabitants ; of whom 53,786 were males ; 55,834 females : 33,109 being employed in agriculture, and 16,346 in trade and manufactures. In 1811, the number of houses was estimated at 23,217, and the population at 119,191, or 160 to the square mile ; 65,555 being the amount of the agricultural population, and £40 being the average net product or rent and tithes of each family. In 1821, the number of houses was 25,594, of families 28,841, of do. employed in agriculture 15,965, of do. employed in trade and manufactures 8971 ; of males 68,817, females 68,154, and the total population 136 971.

With regard to the poor of this county, it appears from the parliamentary reports that, in 1803, the number of persons receiving parish aid was 21,525, or 20 in the 100 of the resident population ; the expense so incurred was £103,559. 10s 6d. including £2614. 19s.3¼d. expended in law suits, the removal of paupers, and charges of overseers ; and omitting a sum of about £280 spent in relieving vagrants and others not parishioners. The money raised was at the rate of 18s. 10¾d. per head on the population ; and the money expended on account of the poor averaged 16s. 8d. per head. Of the whole 21,525, there are 1131 maintained in workhouses at the expence of £12,124. 8s. 8¾d. or £10. 14s. 4d. for each person ; and 20,394 relieved out of workhouses at an expense of £91,024. 9s. 8¼d. or £4. 4s. 7d. for each person relieved. There are 69 friendly societies in this county ; the number of persons belonging to them is about 5 in the 100 of the resident population. See Young's *Agricultural Survey of Oxfordshire.*

OXIDES. See Chemistry, Vol. VI. p. 148.

OXYGEN. See Chemistry, Vol. VI. p. 9.

OYSTER FISHERY. See the Article Fisheries, Vol. IX. p. 363.

P

PADUA, a city in the north of Italy, the capital of the department of the same name, in the government of Venice. It is pleasantly situated in a fertile plain, between the Brenta and the Bacchiglione, on a small river which runs into the Brenta. It is surrounded with a mound and ditch, which are between seven and eight miles in circumference; but a great part of the inclosed space is unbuilt, and the town is very thinly inhabited, the population not exceeding 31,000. The streets are long, narrow, dirty, and ill paved; and the low porticos with which they are bordered on either side, give them a gloomy appearance. The town, however, abounds in splendid public buildings, many of them the works of the celebrated Palladio. Il Salone, or the town-house, is said to be the largest in Europe, being 312 feet long, 108 broad, and 108 high. This immense hall is ornamented with some fresco paintings, and the busts and statues of several eminent individuals. Among them there is an ancient bust and a monument in honour of Livy, who was a native of Padua. The Palazzo del Podesta, or the palace of the chief magistrate, is enriched with many valuable paintings. The Palazzo del Capitano, or commandant's palace, which formerly belonged to the Carrara family, is a fine specimen of architecture. The churches are numerous; but they are more remarkable for their interior decorations and paintings than for their architecture. The cathedral is a large heavy building, but it is reckoned one of the richest in Italy. In the sacristy there is a good collection of pictures, and among them one of Petrarch, who was a canon of this church, and who left to it a part of his library. The church of St. Justina is a fine marble edifice, designed by Palladio. It is much admired for its symmetry and proportion, and for its sculpture, paintings, and rich mosaic pavements. In front of this church is the large piazza, called Prato della Valle, which is encircled by a stream of water brought from the Brenta. The church of St. Antonio, or Il Santo, as it is more commonly termed, is a large edifice of Gothic architecture, chiefly remarkable for the tomb of St. Antony, which is adorned with fine marble and exquisite sculpture; and for its chapel, which is lined with basso relievos, representing the various miracles wrought by the saint. The university of Padua is very ancient, having been founded about the end of the eleventh century. It was at one period highly celebrated, and students flocked to it from all parts of Europe, and even from many parts of Asia: their number is said to have sometimes exceeded 18,000. Among many distinguished names that grace its annals, are those of Petrarch, Galileo, and Columbus. Its professors have always been highly eminent in science; and its establishments are on an extensive and magnificent scale. The botanical garden is rich and beautiful; the cabinet of natural history contains a curious collection of fossils; the observatory, the anatomical theatre, the hall of midwifery, and the other dependencies of the university, are well furnished and well kept up. The university consists of three faculties, viz. mathematics and philosophy, law, and medicine. The number of professors is 32; the number of students seldom exceeds 300. There is a professor of agriculture, who is allotted fifteen acres of land for the purpose of making experiments. There are also several other literary institutions, some of which were founded

so early as the beginning of the sixteenth century; the Academy of Sciences was founded in the last century by the senate of Venice. The trade of Padua is trifling. Its woollen manufactures, for which it was famous in ancient times, are now much declined, though its wool and woollen articles are still considered as the best in Italy. There are also manufactures of silk, ribbons, and leather, on a small scale.

Few of the cities of Italy have been more distinguished than Padua, and few of them can boast of such an ancient origin. If we give credit to Virgil's account, it was founded by Antenor, who, after the destruction of Troy, conducted a body of his countrymen to this part of Italy.

According to Tacitus, the Paduans were accustomed to celebrate annual games in honour of their founder. Livy (lib. x. c. 2.) alludes to a naval victory obtained by them over a Lacedemonian fleet, long before their union with the Romans. On submitting to Rome, they were treated rather as allies than as a conquered state, and were early admitted to all the privileges and honours of Roman citizens. In these times the population and resources of Padua must have been considerable; for we learn from Strabo, that it sometimes furnished 20,000 men to the Roman armies, and numbered among its citizens 500 Roman knights. On the invasion of Italy by the Goths and other barbarous nations, it shared in the common calamities, being taken and plundered first by Alaric, and then by Attila. It underwent a similar fate in the year 600 from the Lombards, and continued subject to them till the overthrow of their kingdom by Charlemagne. After having been subject to the French and Germans, it obtained its liberty, and assumed a republican form of government. In the fourteenth century it fell under the sway of the Carrara family, and in the fifteenth it was united to the Venetian territory. Besides the disasters of war, other calamities have contributed to reduce Padua. It has been several times burnt, thrice desolated by earthquakes, and once by the plague. East Long. 11° 52' 45", North Lat. 45° 24' 2".

PADUA, a province of Austrian Italy in the government of Venice, is bounded on the north by Treviso, on the west by Vicenza and Verona, on the south by Rovigo, and on the east by Venice. Its superficial extent is 860 square miles, and its population near 300,000. This territory, on account of its great fertility, and high state of cultivation, has been called the garden of Italy. It produces large quantities of corn, besides hemp, rice, wine, fruits, and silk, the last of which is a considerable article of commerce. The air is mild and salubrious, except in a few places near the salt marshes. The general appearance of the country is level, and from the fields being surrounded with rows of trees in place of hedges, it appears at a distance to be one extensive forest. The Euganean hills traverse the province, and agreeably diversify the prospect. Some of these hills, particularly Monte Rosso and Monte del Diavolo, exhibit basaltic columns, considerably resembling the Giant's Causeway, though on a much smaller scale. The farms are small, and the system of middle men universally prevails. The principal rivers are the Brenta and the Bacchiglione; the country is also intersected by several canals, which afford great facility to irrigation.

PAINTING.

The end and object of painting, viewed in its higher sphere, as a branch of the fine arts, is to convey delight by means of the power of imitation, and the pleasure we derive from the contemplation of whatever is beautiful. Not confined to the most pleasing objects in nature alone, but stretching over the wide field of imagination, it embodies whatever ideas the mind is capable of forming of beauty, in its most extended meaning—and is equally qualified to record with powerful impression the varied incidents of history, as to exhibit the workings and effects of human passion. For there are no impressions, however important or delightful, arising from the contemplation of the varied scenes of animate and inanimate nature, that cannot equally be roused by the influence of painting: thus placing in our hands a valuable and very fascinating means of instruction, and elevating the study itself far above the merit of a merely elegant and pleasing art.

It is no doubt true, that, in the fervour of their enthusiasm for a favourite study, we read in many authors of excellencies discoverable in pictures, which it is utterly beyond the power of art to produce. We are told of paintings that pourtray all the delicate blendings of mixed passion and purpose—of abstract thought and intention—the ground swell of the mental storm that is gone by, or about to arise; the distinct conveyance of which by expression, gesture, or combination, it is doubtful if the human countenance is under any circumstances capable, and which is, of course, equally little within the sphere of imitation to produce. We are, moreover, somewhat sceptical as to the extent of moral influence which pictures are said to possess, although we are far from refusing to that delightful art the power of inculcating its lessons, whether of history or morality, in the most pleasing and impressive manner; but the irresistible magic attributed to it is often overstrained.

He who explores the full range of painting, will find it sufficiently extensive to render exaggeration quite unnecessary; as, whatever becomes intelligible to the eye in nature itself, is within the scope of painting to exhibit. It may not possess the persuasive powers of eloquence or poetry, in so far as its argument is confined by time and space, and the display of simultaneous effects, within the bounds of the individual scene and instant of representation; but what it loses in the power of detail and continued history, it gains in the instantaneous and involuntary impression. Its effect is unimpaired by the fatigue of mind, and stretch of attention required to follow the descriptions of the orator or of the poet; so to retain and to arrange all the materials of poetic delineation in the mind, as to operate the desired effect.

We may describe, with all the beauty of language, or all the fascination of poetry, such incidents as act most powerfully on our feelings—the horrors arising from frantic passion—sympathy with distress and sorrow, or the delight excited by an amiable action; but how feeble is the effect likely to prove, when brought in parallel with the instantaneous impression which the actual sight and presence of the scene is capable of rousing! A person may give way to the

bitterest expressions of anger and revenge; if we only hear the words, we take time to consider of their import, and reason at our leisure on the consequences likely to ensue; but present to our view a countenance inflamed by all the vindictive workings of rage, the impression, whether of alarm or participation, becomes instantaneous—like the basilisk, it rivets our attention with an intensity beyond the power of description to excite. Accordingly, it is the great aim of the poet so to fascinate the mind's eye, as to summon it to the supposed presence of the scene he paints—to represent the incidents as in the actual course of occurrence, and his readers as actors and participators in the event. Now, this is likewise the distinctive province of the painter; for his great study is that of associating the spectator with the subject of his picture, and, by the excellence and truth of his art, so to engage attention as to excite the impressions to which the actual reality would have given birth. It is in the exercise of this higher branch of the art, which has for its object the sublime study of the moral world, that the painter takes his place beside the poet—that he renders his works not only delightful but useful, in so far as the successful effort of his genius is presented to the eye, which cannot choose but to convey a strong impression to the mind. It is exactly the same picture which the painter communicates through the eye to the mind, that the poet strives to raise in the imagination; and it cannot be denied, that the impression of ideal presence must be more favourably seconded in obtaining access through the medium of the eye than of the ear. It is a single process, and involuntary, which is not the case with the other. Painting may, in this respect, yield to theatrical representation, but to that alone.

The pleasure arising from the contemplation of a fine picture, is augmented by the very circumstance of its engaging a sense in its service which is gratified, and serves to fix the mind, that might otherwise have refused attention to any call upon its abstractive powers at that particular moment; for there is no faculty less under control than " the wayward realm of thought:" but the simple exercise of the sense of seeing is in itself a pleasing gratification, although it requires the irritation produced by any obstruction to its use, to make us sensible that we had pleasure in the exercise of it. The story told by a fine picture we read with pleasure —we enjoy the interest of the history itself—the genius of the artist—the excitement to imagination—the surprise at the happy illusion of the art—that music to the eye produced by an harmonious combination of forms and colours—the repose and concentration of the subject—the pleasure in sympathising with the feelings that animate the actors in the scene; in short, we have a feast which is exquisite, in proportion to the powers of partaking of it. We are not called upon, as in narration, to exercise fatigue of memory—the whole genius of the painter lies spread out before us—there is nothing to enfeeble the effect, as often happens in reading a poetic description, where the imagination seldom fails to outrun the words, and divine what is likely to follow. Our guess may or may not be accurate, but, in either case, the effect is injurious.

Upon this subject Lord Kames observes, that " a good historical picture makes a deeper impression than words can, though not equal to that of theatrical action. Painting seems to possess a middle place between reading and acting: in making an impression of ideal presence, it is not less superior to the former than inferior to the latter." He adds, " It must not, however, be thought, that our passions can be raised by painting to such a height as by words: A picture is confined to a single instant of time, and cannot take in a succession of incidents; its impression, indeed, is the deepest that can be made instantaneously, but seldom is a passion raised to any height in an instant, or by a single impression. Our passions, those especially of the sympathetic kind, require a succession of impressions; and, for that reason, reading and acting have greatly the advantage, by reiterating impressions without end. Upon the whole, it is by means of ideal presence that our passions are excited; and till words produce that charm, they avail nothing; even real events entitled to our belief, must be conceived present and passing in our sight before they can move us." *Elements of Criticism.*

This reiteration of impressions necessary to rouse our feelings, which Lord Kames states as the peculiar advantage denied to painting, we are not disposed to admit the deficiency of; in so far as every moment we bestow upon the contemplation of a picture, is an endless reiteration of whatever impression it is calculated to excite. Words admit of change of expression; but if a picture conveys the same sentiment with all the advantages peculiar to the art, the actual presence, as long as the mind is willing or capable of attention, is certainly equivalent in effect to any possible variety of expression. A painter, it is true, cannot state a sequence of facts or events; he cannot put his subject into different points of view; but he can select the best possible moment of action, the striking event upon which the whole tenor depends—he can call to his aid every concomitant circumstance that admits of simultaneous presence, and display them with all the attractive magic of his art—he may stamp on our minds an indelible impression of the effects resulting from human actions, either good or bad—he can show, with a truth and precision of which language is incapable, that peculiarity in our nature which commands the involuntary confession of the most secret workings of our bosom—which displays the character as a moral being, and all the changes and blendings of our passions, told with unerring accuracy by every feature of our countenance. Well may it be called the mirror of the mind, which it is the painter's peculiar province to hold up to view.

So much were the Greeks aware of the assistance to be derived from this engine, in giving a wished-for tendency to the public mind, that they made it an established principle of their policy, to encourage the exhibition of pictures in all places of public resort. They neglected no opportunity of bringing the representation of heroic actions, as well as the remarkable events of their national history, under the eyes of the people. By infusing a general taste for the fine arts among the different classes of society, they trusted to strengthen the hands of government—to sustain, in all, the sentiments of love for their native country, of admiration and pride in the glorious deeds of their ancestors, with a due veneration for their deities. And, doubtless, it would have its effect.

The Roman Catholic priesthood, at a later period, with the vigilance which characterized their proceed-

ings, did not fail to avail themselves of the influence to be derived from dexterously addressing the eyes as well as the ears of their flocks; gaining credit for the legends of departed saints, by the masterly paintings in which the stories were pourtrayed. For we willingly admit the truth of facts, the striking features of which are presented as passing before our eyes. They trusted, by this means, to maintain the sway over the public mind aimed at by themselves, who were the living aspirants to the sainthood. The devout and ignorant Catholic, kneeling down before the pictures of holy men, which invited his notice in every corner of their churches, how could he refuse belief? he lamented the sufferings of the martyr, and hoped to be admitted to a share of the reward which awaited him in another world: every altar presented to his view some memorable event in the life of our Saviour, or of the first ministers of our faith, all calculated to foster the great objects of belief. But to minister to these ends, the art of painting must be so far advanced in the road to perfection, as readily and impressively to tell its story; and by its excellence to attract admiration, engage the mind, and induce the study of the subject, so as to draw out its intended effect. In fact, it is as much to the works of the great painters, as to the eloquence of their pastors, or their acquaintance with the Bible itself, that we are to attribute the belief of Scripture history among the lower orders of the Catholic persuasion.

The essence and ground-work of poetry and painting are the same; for the painter must in mind be a poet, and join to that heavenly gift one not less rare— the gift of a painter's eye; he must have the capacity of selecting and seeing the beautiful, which is as essentially different from the mere quality of vision, as the nature of a musical ear is from the simple power of hearing sounds. It is familiar to every one that we may possess the faculty of hearing in perfection, without having any idea of that acute perception of harmony and discord, which constitutes a musical ear, or having the smallest susceptibility to the pleasure it is calculated to convey to those possessed of that talent. The distinction is not less applicable to the eye, although not so readily confessed. We laugh at the expression of extasies, if we ourselves chance not to possess internal proofs of their existence, in the consciousness of the faculty upon which the pleasure depends; yet, in the parallel case of music, we feel little reluctance to give full credit to impressions, which we either do not participate at all, or only in a very feeble degree. But when superior discernment of the beautiful is the question, the admission implies a certain obtuseness of taste, which few are willing to confess; it is not, however, the less true, and what is a singular circumstance, a deficiency in the ocular perception of the beautiful not unfrequently exists in minds possessing the highest class of poetical suceptibility. We find men of creative genius, and picturesque imaginations, utterly incapable of that delicate discrimination which is the peculiar gift of the painter's eye. Yet the object of the poet and the painter is as precisely similar as the images by which they strive to attain it. " There is necessary in both (says Mr. Barry) the same glowing enthusiastic fancy to go in search of materials, and the same cool judgment is necessary in combining them. They collect from the same objects; and the same result, an abstract picture, must be formed in the mind of each, as they are equally to be addressed to the same passions in the hearer or spectator. The scope and design of both is to raise ideas in the mind of such great virtues and great actions as are best calculated to move, to delight, and to instruct. In short, according to Simonides's excellent proverb, ' Painting is silent poetry, and poetry is a speaking picture.' These arts, or rather these branches and emanations of the same art, which is design, have, from the nature of the materials they work with, each of them its peculiar advantages and disadvantages. Nothing can give to poetry that precision of form, and that assemblage of instantaneous result, that painting has. On the other hand, poetry, if it loses by the succession of its images in one instance, it gains by it in another; and it has, besides, the power of dealing out infinite mental combinations, which no form can circumscribe." He might have added this peculiarity, that poetry speaks but one language, whereas painting addresses itself with equal success to all nations and in all languages; it requires no translators, no commentaries, no learning, to enable its meaning to be understood; it is intended for the peasant as well as the philosopher, conveying its lessons in the manner of all others the most calculated to please and to gratify.

A picture must succeed in stirring the spectator's mind to fill up and supply in the more vivid colours of imagination, what the painter has but indicated; and only indicated for that express purpose, to rouse the workings of fancy, and engage in his service their zealous co-operation to complete the impression desired. For in this no small portion of the pleasure consists that an agreeable bias is given to the exercise of imagination; by awakening such thoughts and sentiments in the spectator's breast, so suffusing his mind with the poetical inspirations of the painter, as to lead him to conceive more than the picture actually expresses. This is the true sublime of painting, as expressed by Pliny in his eulogium on the genius of Timanthes, " In unius hujus operibus intelligitur plus semper quam pingitur, et cum sit ars summa, ingenium tamen ultra artem est." It is the principle by which the merits of a clever sketch are often found superior to a more finished picture, at least to the eyes of those who are sufficiently familiar with such productions, to catch the full meaning from a hint. For the more the mind is freed from the trammels of the hand, the higher it soars. It is in fact from the drawings of the great masters that we have the best opportunity of studying their genius, as separated from dexterity in expressing it; for the drawings are the originals of which finished pictures are the copies; a circumstance in which the sister arts of poetry and painting are widely different. As the poet must finish his picture to make it intelligible, he can omit no part without prejudice to the impression aimed at; words are his only materials, and the measure must be filled up to constitute poetry: whereas the painter can, by a few lines, convey his thought in its fullest extent, with an energy, grace, and spirit, as likely to suffer by the after finishing and filling up of colour and shade, as to be improved by it. When the sketch is achieved to a painter's satisfaction, the subject in the material points of invention, design, and expression, is fully accomplished; and already in a state to transfer to the spectator's mind all the truth, sublimity, and poetic fire of the painter's fancy. Fully to enjoy and appreciate the painter's merit, the spectator must, to a certain extent, share his taste. Painting is a delightful but a difficult art, a rare gift, which cannot fail to fascinate every eye, however unlearned or unused to contemplate the works of art; but the full

measure of enjoyment to be derived from this source, is as little within the reach of all, as the capacity to produce it.

We do not mean to say that the acquirements which generate a fine taste in painting are as exclusively the gift of nature as the genius of poetry; for, though incapable of being summoned into existence at our pleasure, they are of a nature to admit of infinite improvement by study, and in all cases require its aid. But study must have the support of natural genius; it cannot work out its object alone, as in the pursuits of science; for taste is no concomitant of talent in general; they may meet, and, when they do, they result in the production of those rare and brilliant geniuses who have been the admiration of the world. But, as we have observed above, we as frequently find men of superior acquirements in every branch of science, even of acute perception in the peculiar region of the painter's genius, and producing works that abound in the most delicately and beautifully pourtrayed pictures of nature as presented to the imagination, yet singularly insensible to the beauties of painting, and utterly unable to discriminate works of merit from those that are absolutely bad. And yet what the poet thus paints to admiration cannot be intuitive; it must have resulted from a similar observation of the beauties of nature, which it is equally the province of the painter to exercise; it is difficult, therefore, to conceive why such a person should be precluded from the full enjoyment of what the successful imitation of the beauties of nature by painting is calculated to afford. He can dream the picturesque, although he is insensible to its representation.

A man of very ordinary talents may become a pleasing painter, but not only all the excellencies of the poet, as well as the painter, must be united to form the great master, but likewise that address in dexterously embodying the conceptions of his genius, which can be expected to result from assiduity alone. The hand must readily, and with truth and precision, present the images of the mind; which is an acquirement that can only be attained by painful labour. Without it, every effort of genius becomes paralyzed, and unable to quit the mind that gave it birth. The poet may start into excellence by inspiration, but the painter must toil to learn the language of his art, and to obtain the means of expressing his conceptions. Often exposed to witness the failure and disappointment of his greatest efforts,—to languish in the hopeless imprisonment with which the innumerable difficulties of the art fetter aspiring genius,—conscious how much every attempt he makes, falls short of the idea conceived; he sits down in despair to bewail the deficiency of nature, in denying the power to execute what the mind can so successfully conceive. But the accusation is misapplied; nature is not defective, but generally yields to a well-directed and persevering application, which is the price of perfection in most arts, but particularly in that of the painter; who, without dexterity of hand, labours like a person bound down by an incubus—an eagle whose wings refuse their office; or, as Dr. Franklin somewhere humorously observes, " his talent becomes as unserviceable as the odd half of a pair of scissars." In fact, a fine touch is the produce of much labour and constant practice; and, when acquired, is such that it ceases to be an effort; the hand unconsciously traces with beauty and elegance; and even in some degree it becomes itself the source of beauties, by suggesting forms and elegances in its casual exercise, which the mind did not conceive. Assiduity is therefore indispensable. " Nulla dies sine linea," is an adage well known to painters. By the same assiduity in observation, the eye will augment its powers in a surprising degree.

And as it seldom happens that the happiest work of a painter does justice to the conception of the mind, he must add an assiduous application in practice to the constant exercise of his eye upon the best models both in nature and art; and in that particular line of practice which mature deliberation shall have proved to him to be the best suited to his talents; for many a failure has resulted, after a life of great application, from having set out upon a bad or unsuitable road. Moreover, it is a journey that must be travelled in youth, when the organs are flexible, and before erroneous impressions have established their seat. The rare phenomenon of a great painter does not perhaps arise so much from nature being chary of the gift, as the necessity of so many fortunate circumstances to concur in one case, with the disposition to give them life and strength by unwearied application. In youth, our organs possess that boundless docility, so admirably ordered by nature for the wisest purposes, so that few attainments seem impossible to our early and well directed efforts. It is the particular line into which a painter is to direct his study, that constitutes the great difficulty of choice. Here is the embarrassment generally resolved by accident, and is generally proving the rock on which the promise of genius is wrecked. The germ of an historical painter is forced to grow up and bear the fruits of landscape, because, perhaps, in the outset, a landscape happened to engage his emulation; he goes on labouring in a path he was never intended to tread, and neglecting that which might have led him to eminence. It is a commendable feeling, no doubt, which excites us to strive in the highest class, whether appropriate or not; but how superior is it to reach excellence in a lower walk, than to slave on in the inferior degrees of a higher one! The misfortune is, that the failure of our misapplied efforts may easily be mistaken for those difficulties which it becomes a student's perseverance to strive, with unwearied assiduity, to overcome. He must not shrink because difficulties press on the spring of his energy; it is pressure which calls its strength into action, as success and admiration is the food provided for its reward; for a painter depends much on the encouragement arising from the taste of the times. Accordingly, in those dark ages which intervened between the decline of painting (as of every thing else) at the downfall of the Roman empire, and the subsequent revival of letters, it is impossible to suppose that nature suspended the usual supply of talent; she doubtless peopled that period with great men as profusely as any other; but the spring was withdrawn, the seed fell on a bad soil, there were none to cultivate, and as few to reward, the struggles of genius, which might as well not have existed.

We propose, in the discussion of this subject, shortly to trace the origin and ancient history of painting; an inquiry which is of considerable interest and amusement, from the degree of excellence to which, at a very early period, there is little doubt of its having attained; although the perishable nature of its evidence, joined to the remote antiquity, have left but slender traces to guide our research. We shall inquire into the state of decay, and nearly of extinction, into which painting

had fallen for so many centuries; its subsequent revival when the light of literature began again to dawn upon the long night of the dark ages; its progress in modern times, with an account of the different more celebrated schools of painting; the state of the art in the present times, with some observations on its principles, and the probable causes which influence its rise and decay. So much has been written on the biography of the celebrated painters, both ancient and modern, that we do not propose to extend our observations on that subject, farther than what the consideration of the art itself, in its different states of excellence, may render unavoidable.

As to the rise of this branch of the fine arts, we may judge, from the common propensities of our nature, that, to a certain extent, it is likely in every nation to have been nearly coeval with the origin of the nation itself. As soon as society has reached that state of leisure which results from stability of abode, and a plentiful supply of food, nature is still unsatisfied, and desires to stretch beyond its absolute wants, to seek pleasure in decorating and imitating; and human reason soon acquires a sufficient degree of development to suggest the means of gratification. For mankind is the same every where, only differing as subjected to the influence of different circumstances; in all ages, and in all parts of the world, we find the same propensities, the same objects stimulating his exertion, and giving rise to similar habits and inventions, more or less modified by casual and extraneous causes. To trace the origin of painting, therefore, is in a manner to trace the origin of nations, and to fix the period at which the faculties of observation and imitation began their exercise. It is in vain to attribute the invention of what is inherent in our nature to the ingenuity of any one people, and to point out the route by which it spread among neighbouring nations. It must no doubt have advanced by slow degrees to what we may absolutely denominate painting; but the imperceptible approaches to it are apparent in the earliest infancy of society, however rude and savage, which the course of discovery has brought to our knowledge. So as it exists in the wilds of America, at this day, or among the savage islanders of the Pacific Ocean, it doubtless existed among the infant nations of Europe when in a similar state of civilization. Savages appear particularly susceptible to the beauty of colours, with which we find them decorating their persons, their implements of war and of the chase; modelling and sculpturing the rude effigies of their superstition; bedecking themselves with the brilliant plumage of birds; and weaving the stained bark into cloth of various designs. The taste for embellishment once begun, must augment the necessary means with great rapidity; ingenuity is readily engaged in the service of its gratification, which nature seems to invite us to pursue by the beauty of all her works. It is enough to instance the brilliant colouring of flowers, which offers so palpable a hint, while the coloured juices of vegetation as readily supply the means of imitating them. The magic of light and shade, we grant, demands an accuracy of observation not to be looked for in the early stages of society; but in the process of imitation one step naturally clears the way for a progressive advance; nor can we direct our eyes to any object in nature, which does not hold out a lesson to tempt our endeavours, so that we can scarce choose but to proceed from improvement to improvement, unless opposed by extraneous events.

Whether sculpture or painting has the best claim to

precedency, appears of very little consequence to inquire; they cannot long have remained separate, and of the two, sculpture seems naturally to point itself out as the readiest means of gratifying the desire of imitation. Some rude attempts to model with clay, and to give a form to wood and stone, appear among the simplest savages; wherever superstition, under any modification, gained a footing, or wherever notions were acquired of the existence of any intelligence superior to human nature, which engaged their adoration, or excited their dread. Wherever idolatry prevailed, the art of imitation or design is implied at least; if it was not the cause, in which idolatry originated, in so far as the various attributes of the mythological personages are concerned; for as the object of fear or adoration could not be present to all its votaries, the only resource was in the representation of it, according to the capacity and inventive power of the time. These representations, however rude, would, by a natural consequence, not only soon become the direct object of worship, but in time owe the very idea of their nature and attributes to the imagination of the artist, or the extent of his power to imitate the works of his predecessors. Hence all the wild absurdities of the systems of worship recorded of ancient nations.

The Greeks strenuously assert their claim to the invention of painting, as to that of every thing else, and have forged many silly fables in support of their pretensions. However justly we may yield them full credit and admiration for the perfection to which they brought this beautiful art, (and undoubtedly in their hands it reached a degree of excellence in taste, execution, simplicity, and sublimity of conception, of which future ages can scarcely boast a parallel,) yet the exercise of the art itself was in existence long before the origin of the Greeks themselves. Imitation, indeed, is so very natural to man, that we shall find all the imitative arts to have been of very ancient invention; and of design at least, which constitutes an essential part both of painting and statuary, we have the authority of the second commandment for its pre-existence to any trace of the Greeks as a nation. When Pliny observes, that painting did not exist prior to the siege of Troy, he must have alluded to its higher sphere as a liberal art; seeing that design was in use long before. The state of the art before that period was most likely very rude, and little more than a mere imitation of established forms, which can scarcely be dignified with the appellation of liberal; but, however rude it might be, the exercise of the art undoubtedly did exist among the various nations of the East, (as a mere trade to be sure,) until transplanted into the more genial soil of Greece.

Ancient History of Painting.

Independent of the desire of imitation as tending to introduce the art of painting; its power of being rendered subservient to another equally stimulating principle in our nature, became the means of a very general extension of the practice, even in the earliest stages of society. We allude to the desire of transferring to posterity some knowledge of the transactions of our own lives, and perpetuating the memory and the deeds of our ancestors,—that mysterious principle, which leads us to solicit the feeble gratification of an ideal prolongation of our existence, by recording our deeds for the information of posterity. The most natural means that can occur to satisfy this desire, is an attempt to represent the appearance of the objects or events we strive to record by any means in our power; conscious that a few years must suffice to dissipate for ever the

fleeting substance itself, we give at least the shadow to time. Endeavours to attain this end are common to most nations in a state of infancy; and where circumstances have led to its extension or refinement, as with the Egyptians, it becomes a sort of painted language; which, in the progressive efforts to simplify, and to save time and trouble in the performance, very soon assumes the character of a symbolical representation, and ends by giving birth to writing. It depends upon circumstances, whether this event proves favourable or unfavourable to the progress of the art of painting; whether it is led to take a new flight from the useful drudgery of a record, to a more noble destination as a liberal art.

Many authors have taken the trouble to point out with precision the chronology of its progress, the exact steps by which painting advanced through every stage of discovery from the first rude essay to the highest achievements of the art. This first step they determine to have been the outline of the object to be represented, according to the mode of proceeding in the present advanced state of the art. Now, the outline is far from being the simplest process of drawing, and is the probable refinement of a much more clumsy and laborious proceeding, by an ill-defined shadow, or rude daubing of colours. But before the interchanges of commerce had begun to take place, the various facilities which the different countries had individually the means of furnishing, the nature of their climates, government, and superstitions, besides a thousand other circumstances, must in every case have contributed to render the first efforts of painting as various as they are now uncertain. In the humid and stormy climate of the north, we find the early Scandinavians transmitting the intended records of their history in the huge monumental stones, which are more a record of the imperishable nature of the substance of the monument itself, than of the motive of its erection; while the drier climates of Egypt, Hindostan, and Mexico, led their inhabitants to paint the deeds of arms, and chronicle the various revolutions of their country, in rude figures and emblems, daubed upon the sides of caverns, and the smooth surface of their rocks.

It will be sufficient for our purpose, to give a brief sketch of the earliest efforts of the art among those nations of antiquity which hold the most distinguished place in history; and in prosecuting this inquiry, we shall find that the westward march of science is not belied by the history of the fine arts. We must, therefore, turn to the east, in order to explore the source which has progressively flowed through the various regions of the civilized world, and seems still to bear on in its tendency to dawn in the west, as its light grows feebler and expires in the east. In none of the Asiatic countries, however, does painting ever seem to have attained the rank of an art; it was but a trade, and a poor trade, subservient to the more dignified calling of the potter, the weaver, or the unclean ministers to the obsequies of the dead. From generation to generation, the same grotesque figures and ornaments were painted on the potter's wares, the same imaginary flowers and whimsies, seemingly without meaning; the carpet-maker sought the brightest colours, and blended them into the form of many-headed dragons, and caricatures of natural forms, both animate and inanimate. The representation, whether good or bad, added no value to the material; the colours were there, and provided they were bright, and fancifully disposed, nothing farther was sought for. Such is the unvarying and servile adherence to ancient practice, which pervades the habits of eastern nations, and pre-

China.

cludes all chance of improvement or change, that we have little trace whereby to distinguish the history and progress of the arts they practised. We are not without specimens of great antiquity, and of very remarkable character; but the probable æra of their execution (were the discovery of any importance) remains utterly impenetrable; as no semblance of truth can be extricated from the fanciful and exaggerated chronology of these nations.

Chinese.

As to the Chinese, they seem, from time immemorial, to have possessed works abounding in singular dexterity of manipulation, without either taste or ingenuity in the design. No people ever exhibited the power of imitation in greater perfection, or showed less talent for invention or improvement of any kind. We cannot but admire the acquirements of that ancient race, whoever they were, which conferred upon the Chinese the knowledge of almost every art, which their inventive powers appear totally unequal to have discovered for themselves; but we owe them gratitude for the faithful and scrupulously accurate preservation of whatever they were taught. For it is truly surprising to observe, how absolutely strangers the Chinese seem to be to any spark of creative genius, even in its limited quality of endeavouring to improve upon any borrowed acquirement. The French, who are far from an inventive people, though surrounded by nations in whom this quality is eminently conspicuous, eagerly take up the inventions of their English or German neighbours, at the same time they strive to make some improvement upon it, or to produce some little change, enough, at least, to still the cravings of their own vanity. If they cannot so far succeed by altering the semblance as to give a colour to their claiming the merit of the invention altogether, it is satisfactory to them at least to be able to say, " Que nous y avons ajouté le sentiment ;" as happened lately when they borrowed the invention of the kaleidoscope, and added some fanciful ornaments.

With regard to the Chinese, there is no reason to suppose that the lapse of centuries, even of some thousand years, has operated the slightest difference on this most imperturbable nation. They are vain of their own imaginary importance and glory, and seem to feel an utter contempt for every thing beyond the walls of the celestial empire. The ardour of improvement can have no stimulus, where every thing, as it is, is presumed perfect; but how admirably conceived must the original principles of that government have been, which succeeded in moulding an extensive nation to such a surprising stability of purpose! Their division into casts, and the obligation imposed upon every one to follow the same trade, from father to son, through the interminable series of ages, is one great cause both of the uniformity of their workmanship in every æra, and likewise of the dexterity of execution. The familiar use of their implements of trade becomes a second nature; and that mechanical expertness implanted in childhood, grows up to perfection without the intervention of intellect, like the natural exercise of our limbs, which seems to take place quite independent of mind, and may be carried to any conceivable degree of dexterity. No vivacity of temper disturbs the patient perseverance of the Chinese : he plods on with precision, and such a perfect command of the simple implements of his work, as if they were a mere extension of the natural organs of his body; executing works which all the mechanics of Europe would be incapable of producing. Their paintings, accordingly, possess a remarkable delicacy of pencilling, with an utter ignorance of grace, composition, or perspective. The artists among them are held in no estimation, and seldom attempt any thing

beyond the regular patterns for rocks, trees, and figures. They display a most unaccountable dereliction of every thing like proportion : nature is represented in preposterous attitudes and shapes; the figures appear in whimsical masquerade, with a solemnity and gravity of deportment, even where their employment seems to indicate a playful mode, that is truly ludicrous. Chinese artists have occasionally been trained under the direction of the foreign factories of Macao, and sent to travel in China for the purpose of drawing the scenery and costume. Some of these performances which we have seen are rather of a superior cast ; but in so far as they excel their native artists, they cease to be Chinese. The same observation is applicable to those works descriptive of Chinese scenery and manners, which have been sent to Europe by the Jesuits and Missionaries. In modelling and statuary, the Chinese exhibit the same dexterity of workmanship, but their works have little merit except as specimens of the grotesque; their choice of subjects being generally either the monstrous many-armed deities of their mythology, as hideous as fancy can conceive, or the lumbering bundle of drapery under which their representations of the human figure is hid.

Persia, &c.

In so far as the human figure is concerned, the art of painting must have been much checked in Persia by the peculiar opinions which that people entertained, in common with their neighbours, the Parthians and Arabians. They considered any representation of, or even allusion to, the human figure in a state of nudity, as an abominable outrage to decency ; and so repugnant to decorum was it for man to be seen naked, that artists could have as little the means, as the inducement to study the human figure. In their statuary, the figures are almost always of men, as the representation of women seems to have been forbidden ; and these figures are, moreover, so encumbered with drapery, and with a profusion of rigid plaitings, that they present an exceedingly inelegant and clumsy semblance of man. Their religious faith was equally inimical to the arts, in discountenancing any visible representation of the Deity. It was the principle of fire which formed the chief object of their adoration, as identified with Baal or Apollo, though not in general under a visible form. This antipathy may probably account for the circumstance of their invasion and possession of Egypt having produced so little effect, in giving them any taste for the arts as practised in that country.

Persia.

Phœnicians.

We know very little of the state of art among the Phœnicians. They were a people of great enterprise both in war and trade, and so early acquainted with the use of writing as to have obtained the credit of the invention; from which it appears probable they had some notion of the arts of imitation. And as they are reported to have been a very handsome race, they are more likely to have had correct notions of beauty in their imitations of it. With them the sciences flourished, while Greece still lay buried in the shades of ignorance. Solomon, we are informed, sent for Phœnicians to build the temple of the Lord ; and even so late as the time of the Romans, the most skilful artizans were Carthaginians, a colony from Phœnicia ; for their knowledge of navigation, and the extent of the trade they carried on, even beyond the coasts of the Mediterranean, enabled their artizans to make a profitable traffic of their skill, in the various countries to which they traded. In their own country, we have the authority of sacred writ for the magnificence of the Tyrians, the splendour of their buildings, their painted chambers, and the richness of their sculptured ornaments. At this late period, however, we have absolutely nothing to guide us to any judgment of their acquirements in art, except some remaining specimens of their money; and in so far as this evidence generally records its own date, we cannot have a better; if they were more plentiful. What does exist falls very little short of the beauty and perfection of the Greek coinage; in fact, were it not for the Punic inscriptions, it would not be easy to distinguish the one from the other.

We are not to suppose from the words of the second commandment, " *Thou shalt not make to thyself any graven image,*" that the Jews were prohibited from painting or sculpture; it was the worship only which was pointed at by the sacred law: any farther extension of the prohibition would have been in the face of nature, and palpably absurd. To imitate is the common characteristic of mankind, and the means of amusement to children; so that the exercise of it is harmless. Few legislators, and certainly not an inspired one, could ever think of controlling it. We might, with equal consistency, infer, that we were condemned to regard the earth alone, like the brute creation, and never to raise our eyes to heaven, and contemplate the sun, moon, and stars; from the words that immediately follow the prohibition of images. " Thou shalt not raise thine eyes to heaven, to behold the sun, moon, and stars." But Moses himself, by God's special command, caused images to be made, and that too for the sanctuary, as we find by the following passages.

1. Two cherubims, or sphinxes, placed in the holy of holies, Exod. xxv. 18—20.

2. Ornaments in the shape of flowers on the golden lamp, Exod. xxv. 34.

3. Figures of the cherubims embroidered in the curtain of the holy of holies, Exod. xxvi. 32.

4. The same on the hangings of the sanctuary, and probably also on the other hangings which were ordered to be embroidered, Exod. xxvi. 36. and xxvii. 16.

5. To this may be added the brazen serpent. Numb. xxi. 8, 9. Ezekiel's temple, in like manner, had cherubims with the heads of men and lions. The figures of sphinxes appear on the base of the golden lamp of the second temple, which was brought to Rome by Vespasian, and a representation of which is sculptured on his triumphal arch.

But as the Jews employed Phœnician artists in all works of embellishment, it is not likely that they themselves practised the arts, if we except the manufacture of tapestry hangings; these they adorned with figure work of chimeras, arabesques, and all sorts of imaginary beings. The Greeks borrowed the taste for imaginary animals, such as griffins, centaurs, &c. from the practice of these artists. Diodorus mentions, that the bricks of which the walls of Babylon, built by Semiramis, were composed, were painted before they were burnt, so as to represent all sorts of animals. Lib. 2, chap. iv. We may infer that the more simple and easy forms of painting must have been in use before they thought of applying them by the difficult operation of fire.

The Prophet Ezekiel is desired " to take him a tile, and lay it before him, and pourtray upon it the city, even Jerusalem." Chap. iv. v. 1.—but a more remarkable passage in proof of the knowledge of painting among the Jews is that where Ananias is desired by his master, that if he could not prevail upon Jesus to accompany him, he should then bring back his picture drawn after the life. Ananias made the attempt to draw his likeness, but was prevented by a miracle from accomplishing it.

We mention the art of embroidery as demonstrating the

knowledge of the Jews in painting; for the acquaintance with that art cannot be altogether confined to the meaning modern practice gives to the word; it must admit of modification, according to the various ways by which the talent was exemplified. Painting comprehended all the modes of imitation, by means of colours and drawing, whether the matter used were paint, coloured wool, or silk, wood, or stone; we talk of a mosaic picture, and cannot deny the same appellation to embroidery. This seems, moreover, to have been an exceedingly ancient mode of painting, and certainly the first practised in Greece, as we find mention of it many ages prior to the Trojan war. The history of Philomela, although wrapt up in fable, shows the practice of tapestry pictures at a very remote period; and Homer represents Helen as embroidering the pictures of all the misfortunes and battles which her beauty had brought upon the Greeks and Trojans.

We proceed now to the Egyptians, whose practice of painting may be called the deformity of the art. It existed among them doubtless at a very remote period. There is little merit, however, to a nation, in being able to trace the antiquity of an art to a very great height, provided they cannot, at the same time, show a progressive and rapid improvement, in proportion to that advantage. The Egyptians, however, adhered with inveteracy to that peculiar characteristic of eastern nations, the strict observance of habits and acquirements, unvaried and unimproved, from generation to generation; and the aversion to change, which is so little congenial to the notions of the western world. Fashion, a word of such potency in our hemisphere, was to them unknown and unintelligible. They avoided, it is true, the frivolities of fashion, but remained, at the same time, insensible to its stimulating influence; and were content to drone through existence as their fathers had droned before them. The state of the art with them affords no indication of its age, no hint from whence to demonstrate the length of its endurance; the pictures of the earliest age and of the latest seem the works of the same artist; and a thousand years is but as a day: We must, however, allow these pictures the merit of a perfectly decided, and marked national character, immediately distinguishable from the productions of any other country, consisting of that singular rigidity of form, and absence of all grace, of which the word Egyptian is the best expletive. It is true, that the Egyptian artist had not the same advantages which nature afforded to stimulate the genius of Greece, in the beauty and elegant bodily conformation of their countrymen; for the Egyptians were an ill-favoured people, and possessed no elegance of costume to make up for the defects of nature. They were nearly of a copper colour, bandy legged, high shouldered, having the flat ungainly countenance of the Ethiopian without their freedom and flexibility of limb. The Coptish damsels were then, as they still are, far from attractive, lank, ungraceful in form, and most unbecomingly attired; however, we must allow their artists the merit of representing them with characteristic ugliness, as we may fairly infer from the very strong resemblance which the portraits on their ancient monuments bear to the present generation. They seem, however, to have been a healthy people, if we may draw that inference from a circumstance that has been remarked of all the mummies as yet opened, which is, that they exhibit a full and regular set of teeth, and in a perfectly sound and healthy state.

The monstrosity of their mythological belief, which delighted in every unnatural combination of the brute and human species, must have had a powerful influence in directing the peculiar character of the Egyptian taste in the arts; from its constituting among them, as elsewhere, the usual subject of the painter's skill. Although the difference of style between the Indian and Egyptian taste and practice in these matters is abundantly distinct, yet sufficient traces of resemblance exist to countenance the probability of their having drawn the seeds of their knowledge in the arts, as of every other acquirement, from this fountain-head of ancient science: their mutual abhorrence of change,—the establishment of hereditary and immutable casts and trades, by which every chance of advance, and every spark of genius, was so effectually neutralised,—and the same policy of excluding strangers from their country, still so pertinaciously adhered to by the Chinese,—these customs being not only common, but peculiar to both, render it probable that a close intercourse must, at an early period, have existed between the inhabitants of these distant regions.

In considering the state of painting in Egypt, it is not an easy matter to draw the line of distinction between that art and writing, as practised by them, which in its origin seems to have been more allied to the former art than to the latter; for the Egyptian letters are nothing else but disguised symbolical painting. Nor does it appear to have been so peculiarly the invention of the Egyptians as they generally get credit for. The endeavours made by any people in a low state of civilization, to embody their ideas in writing, are most likely to result in some sort of emblematical representation; accordingly this contrivance has, under certain modifications, been resorted to in the early periods of all nations, to record the simple annals of their country. There is no reason to suppose so general a coincidence to be the result of fortuitous invention, or the imitation of one people by another; it is the natural consequence of a wish to perpetuate facts, adapted to the imperfect and awkward means which most readily suggest themselves in an uninformed state of society; and we find, accordingly, the early inhabitants of all quarters of the globe attempting to communicate with posterity by means of some rude scheme of painting.

When the Spaniards landed on the coast of South America, the natives dispatched messengers to their king, Montezuma, bearing a web of cloth, upon which they had painted a representation of the extraordinary and alarming event that had taken place; as the readiest means with which their ideas furnished them to convey information of facts, the novelty of which, perhaps, incapacitated their language from transmitting verbally. It appears to have been the usual means resorted to by the Mexicans for the conveyance of information to a distance, either of time or place; as they adopted a similar style of hieroglyphics for recording their laws and history. Robertson, in his history of America, and Humboldt, in his later works, have both given curious specimens of this Mexican mode of painting. When Cortez took the temple of Mexico by assault, he found several webs of cloth, upon which all the circumstances of the assault were represented with truth; the attack of the steps, and general contest on the terrace of the temple, the subsequent defeat of the Mexicans, the conflagrations and ruin of the towers, executed with great correctness, except that the painters sought to console their countrymen by representing a number of Spaniards lying slaughtered among the ruins, which, although rather beyond the fact, was perhaps an excusable exaggeration. These

paintings, though abundantly intelligible as written descriptions, are clumsy enough in the execution; they are generally represented on wood, or as ornaments to furniture. Their mode of proceeding is to lay on, in the first place, a pretty thick coat of the colour they mean to be the ground of their work, and after being sufficiently polished, while still fresh, they trace the subject intended with a sort of etching needle, the opposite end of which is flattened like a spatula. With this instrument they proceed to scrape off the whole colour contained within the outline: on the part thus cleaned they then lay on the colours which the subject to be represented requires, not according to their proper arrangement, but successively spreading the predominating colour first over all, of which as much is then scraped off as is intended to be of a different colour; this colour is afterwards applied, and so progressively until the piece is completed. A strong varnish is then spread over the whole.

But to return to the Egyptians, to whom the history of painted writing more particularly belongs. No nation ever made so extensive a use of this medium of record: By it their laws, their mythological system, the remarkable events of their history, their private annals, and the entire scope of their knowledge in philosophy and the sciences, was conveyed; and although it has proved capable of wonderful preservation, it has shown itself greatly deficient in its chief end and object as a record to future ages, and a means of transmitting knowledge to posterity. There never was exhibited to the pride of man, a more humbling lesson of the inefficacy of his most laborious endeavours to resist the fleeting and unsubstantial nature of every thing connected with our present existence. For it was the very improvement of hieroglyphical representation which operated its defeat; the supposed perfections only served to expose the inefficacy of human foresight; so long as it retained the laborious characteristic of an absolute picture, however rude, it was still to a certain extent intelligible. But as the refinements of the art advanced, and the same object came to be received as expressive of different ideas;—as the operation in drawing was gradually simplified, to render it more easy;—and as familiarity with the style made a mere indication be at length thought sufficient, or a symbol generally received and understood at the time as the visible mark, in short, the written word for a certain meaning; it happened that, as that mark of meaning did not constitute a language, but only a conventional sign, like the gestures of a deaf and dumb person, it became for posterity an enigma, which we may guess at, but can never fully ascertain. And thus became buried in hopeless darkness the laborious chronicles of their monumental pillars, the engraved pictures which cover the bodies of some of their statues, the writings of the subterraneous vaults and galleries called Syringes; in short, all the chaos of symbolical writing preserved with so much care, and to so little purpose. There is little doubt that the system, as originally practised, was generally understood by all, and established as a matter of regular instruction to their youth; but as the extension of knowledge came to render a more correct system of writing necessary, which should admit the expression of abstract ideas, and those parts of language, as adverbs, &c. which it would be somewhat difficult to pourtray in a picture; hieroglyphics, as subservient to the more common intercourse of society, must have fallen out of use. It was, however, eagerly retained by the crafty priesthood as a means peculiarly adapted to veil the dogmas and records of their mythology in such desirable mystery, and as affording them an opportunity of rendering themselves sole possessors of all the original secrets of their faith and observances. By this means they hoped to work at pleasure on the minds of the uninitiated, and mould them to their purposes through the influence of superstitious dread, and a blind veneration for that service, which the priests were thus enabled to hide from the scrutiny of reason.

There are many who consider this circumstance as the real origin of the animal worship of the Egyptians ; as they would be naturally enough led to adore the symbolical animals thus impressed with the stamp of sacredness and of mystery, the real meaning and origin of which, their ignorance as well as superstition, forbade them to penetrate. And as the emblem of some animal generally served to designate the qualities of the ancient heroes of their race, it was of course added to the figure in various ways, as best suited the taste of the artist, but principally by substituting the head of the animal for that of the person ; thus generating the monstrous mixture of the brute and human nature, so prevalent in their mythology.

The engine with which this laborious artifice armed the priesthood, grew in strength as it became successful in excluding the people from all the treasures of knowledge, and the discoveries in natural science, of which the archives were thus placed in the hands of the priests alone. And they took especial care that the profane and uninitiated should not be instructed beyond what suited their purpose, thus occasioning the very means devised by the blindness of man for the diffusion of knowledge, to become the immediate cause of its destruction. As the second class of the Egyptian hierarchy were devoted to the duties of sacred writing, and particularly trained to the painting of hieroglyphics, they became the depositaries of the key of knowledge, and were themselves deified by the ignorant multitude, as conceiving their skill to be the result of inspiration, and their power of interpreting the divine will as implying a superior rank in the scale of beings. This serves to explain the numerous processions of figures similarly disguised with the heads of birds or beasts, that are generally represented in Egyptian pictures as attending the obsequies of the dead. Moreover, their exclusive acquaintance with natural science, and all the physical knowledge of the day, enabled them to play successfully on the credulity of the people by predictions and pretended miracles, which must have given them a very dangerous sway, and proved as detestable a consequence of this artifice, as that of depriving future generations of any benefit from the accumulated knowledge of ancient times. And yet, the ruling principle which seems to have influenced all their exertions in matters of record, appears to have been to insure perpetuity, by the singularly massive and gigantic solidity which characterizes their works in architecture and statuary. They had this object clearly in view in leaving the legs of their statues attached to each other, and the arms to the body, so as to be less exposed to accidental injury ; besides that the stone selected was the most solid and durable that could be found. Their labours are obviously for posterity, and solidity pervades every thing that remains of their works ; all sort of projections were scrupulously avoided in their statuary ; their animals are scarcely ever represented standing, but squatted solidly on their base, immoveable rocks are sculptured, and, instead of being convex, their basso-relievos are made concave.

In the durability of these, they have succeeded, but have greatly outwitted themselves with their painted records, which no doubt exist, but might as well have perished, as they only serve the tantalizing purpose of showing us that they wished to transmit information to posterity, which they conceived so important as to be engraved on the hardest stone, or painted with scrupulous exactness. But alas, not one ray appears to enable us to penetrate the utter darkness in which their ancient history is enveloped.

To perpetuate was the ruling passion of the Egyptians, and not any love of the arts, or taste for them ; so that the exercise of an elegant accomplishment did not probably form any motive in their practice of painting, as they do not appear at all to have cultivated the sister arts of music or poetry. Indeed, it is alleged by ancient authors that both music and poetry were proscribed. Strabo says that their festivals and sacrifices were performed in silence, and without the sound of instruments, as in most other countries ; but this restriction, if it ever was absolute, became probably relaxed at a later period, as in their ancient pictures we observe some representations of priests playing on musical instruments : and although the noisy pageant and hilarity of the Greek festival would have ill suited the sombre and gloomy character of Egyptian mythology, which is loaded with dark and mysterious rites ; yet their unbending adherence to ancient custom would lead us to conclude, that if at any time musical instruments appear to have been used in their service, the probability is that it was so *ab origine*.

A mere knowledge of drawing must have been exceedingly prevalent in a country where every writer was necessarily a draughtsman, but a draughtsman, in the most limited sense of the word. Forming part of the hierarchy, they were not permitted, if they had had the genius to do so, to attempt the slightest improvement or variety, or to depart in any thing from ancient practice. One generation of artists succeeded another, as wave follows wave, and might have rolled on in the same narrow tract, to the present time, had the revolutions of the world, as in China, left their progress undisturbed. Any attempt at high finishing was quite superfluous to their purpose, and also at light and shade, which would accordingly receive no attention in their performances ; nor is there any reason to suppose that they possessed the slightest idea of it. They seldom departed from the simplicity of profile, they painted the portraits of their dead upon the linen that enveloped the bodies of the mummy, and seem to have succeeded in producing a wonderful resemblance, considering the imperfection of their art, as the likeness is in general exceedingly close to the expression and countenances of their descendants of the present day. These pictures are curious, as being the most ancient specimens of portrait, and even of painting, that have reached our time ; the colouring is the part most attended to, and, considering the changeable nature of white lead, which was the pigment in use among them for the ground of their pictures, it argues an uncommon aridity of climate, to find it unaltered after so great a lapse of time. And as permanency was the great principle of their labours in the arts, this circumstance has singularly seconded their views in so perishable a means of record as painting. The esteem it was held in, was, on account of its perishable nature, quite secondary to sculpture, upon which we see that they bestowed most extraordinary labour and perseverance ; adhering, at the same time, with the most servile and scrupulous attention to the established prac-

tice, as marked by a frozen rigidity, and ponderous character, by stiffness of contour, formality of disposition,
and total want of any idea of elegance or grouping. Design, which cannot fail to accompany the practice of
statuary, naturally assumed a similar character, but
was not susceptible of that air of grandeur, which the
extraordinary bulk of their sculptured works threw
over them ; and it is a circumstance worthy of remark
in the nature of Egyptian design, that, notwithstanding
the inflexible rigidity of their figures, they seldom fail
to exhibit an uncommon accuracy of proportion, even
in subjects the most preposterous in form. We find
their gigantic monsters, and mixtures of the brute and
human creations in every possible combination, possessing, nevertheless, uncommonly accurate proportions
of limb. And this is a merit to which few nations,
either ancient or modern, can lay claim. The magnitude of their works is the only particular in which
we find the Egyptians striving to shake off the fetters of ancient practice ; but it is a clumsy attempt
to excel, when the end is not the excellence of
workmanship, but the magnitude ; it is indicative of
great poverty of invention, and a low state of the arts,
though, at the same time, it stimulated to efforts which
were productive of the most extraordinary examples of
human labour.

The skill displayed in the execution of the coins
of an ancient people, is one of the best criterions to
enable us to judge of the state of the arts among them,
in so far as they prove their own dates, at the same
time that they exhibit the existing knowledge of design. Hence we find the masterly works of the Greek
coinage bearing an exact parallel with the very great
excellence recorded of their taste and execution in
painting ; and in sculpture there is enough still extant
to speak for itself. In like manner the barbarous
coinage of other countries, as correctly quadrates with
their probable ignorance in the other branches of the
fine arts. In this particular, we have little to say in
favour of Egypt ; we shall therefore close our remarks
with some account of their mode of painting.

We should be disposed to attribute the perfect state of
preservation, in which many of the painted shrouds of
Egyptian mummies are found, retaining not only the
sharpness of outline, and minuteness of writing, but the
vivacity of colour as strong as if they had been painted
but yesterday, to the favourable circumstances under
which they have been preserved. Shut up in the
double, often treble, case of a mummy, inclosed
like fossil remains in the dry cavity of a rock, protected from the air, and external injury of every
kind, they could not fail to be preserved through
any number of ages. But when, brought to light,
exposed openly to the air, and subjected to the rough
usage of long journeys, both by sea and land, we
find them still reaching these northern climates as
fresh as ever, and continuing to withstand all the vicissitudes of our atmosphere unaltered and untarnished.
The cause commonly assigned for this uncommon degree of durability is, that the asphaltum, with which
the linen was probably impregnated, may have been
sufficiently powerful to counteract the destructive effects of time. Even the asphaltum, however, will scarcely enable us to account for the phenomenon of some
ancient painted walls to be seen at Dendera ; which, although exposed for so many ages to the open air, without any covering or protection whatever, still possess a
perfect brilliancy, and preservation of colour as vivid
as when first painted, perhaps 2000 years ago. Habituated, as we inhabitants of the moist and stormy north

are, to the keen tooth of time, in every thing that is exposed to its operation, even although sheltered under
the cover of our dwellings ; we are tempted to regard
such extraordinary preservative powers in the arid climate of Egypt as an exception to the common laws of
nature.

The Egyptians mixed their colours with some gummy substance, and applied them detached from each
other, without any blending or mixture : they appear
to have used six colours, viz. white, black, blue, red,
yellow, and green. They first covered the canvas
entirely with white, upon which they traced the design in black, leaving out the lights of the ground
colour : They used minium for red, and generally
of a dark tinge. Many of their paintings are described by travellers, who have seen them at Thebes,
and in the sepulchral grottos of Upper Egypt. Bruce
mentions his having seen some complete frescos. In
point of subject, there is, as might be expected, a very
great uniformity, and generally with reference to our
future state : they represent the body of the deceased as
swathed in linen, painted, and covered with hieroglyphical writing, laid out on the sacred boat, and preceded
by a figure of Anubis. A small winged genius seems
escaping from the body of the corpse, and a train of
figures follow, wearing the mask of the sacred bird, as
indicative, most likely, of their sacred office. It is not
easy to reconcile the anxious care with which the mummies were cased up, and secured in caverns, as if for
the purpose of being for ever hid from sight, with the
scrupulous attention and labour bestowed on the painting and decorating of the mummy itself, and the interior of the cases, which seemed intended never again to
be seen by human eye. Yet the portrait of the deceased was there, accompanied with the genealogy, and
other circumstances connected with the family, although
so industriously hid from view, that it is difficult to
conceive a motive for the seeming inconsistency. The
scrupulous care, however, attending the performance
of this religious observance, seems to indicate some
purpose connected with an idea of the future resurrec-
tion of the body ; for the furtherance of which, they
may have had the presumptive ignorance to suppose
the feeble aid of man as in some measure available. Mr.
Salt, British consul at Alexandria, had an opportunity
lately of opening one of these cases, on which the hiero-
glyphist had the discretion to be his own interpreter,
by accompanying the inscription with translations in
various languages ; as one of them happened fortunately to be in Greek, the purport admitted of being decy-
phered. It bore the name of the deceased—from
whence the body had been brought—a note of the expence attending the embalming and transport—and the
name of the person who bore the expence.

M. Denon mentions having seen some Egyptian paintings, which he describes as far from inelegant, consisting, in one apartment, of a ceiling ornamented with
figures painted of a yellow colour, on an azure ground ;
represented in different attitudes, and accompanied with
a variety of arms, musical instruments, and pieces of
furniture. In another apartment, every thing was agricultural—paintings of the plough, and various other implements of husbandry, not unlike those presently in
use—a man sowing grain on the brink of a canal—
fields of rice and harvesting scenes. Another chamber
was decorated with a person clothed in white, playing
on a harp of eleven strings—several figures were represented without heads, and one with the head cut
off, all of them Ethiopians, and painted black, while
the persons that were performing the decapitation and

held the sword, were painted red. In whatever attitude the figure is represented the heads are always in profile, and the legs in the same line, the one advanced a little before the other, and, as we have already observed, not incorrect in proportion, but without any rounding of light and shade, blending of colours, grouping, or perspective.

We shall now quit the eastern cradle of the arts, to trace their dawning in the more genial soil of Europe, where, under the fostering influence of freedom, they soon began to show the presage of their future excellence; for no fact is more surely deducible from the history of the fine arts, than their dependence on the encouragement or paralyzing power of governments. They are only found to flourish under those happy forms of rule, where neither the fetters of priestcraft, nor the weight of oppression and absolute sway, chain down the genius and energy of our nature—where merit obtains honour and reward—where the road to renown lies open to every aspirant—where wealth creates a demand for the elegancies of life, and where good taste invites the wealthy to seek the road to distinction as encouragers of talent. Such appear to have been the circumstances of the ancient state of Etruria, the most powerful and civilized of the early nations of Italy. Their dominion extended nearly over the whole range of that delightful peninsula, except some part of the northern provinces of Lombardy and Venice. They were called Terreni; and Livy, (dec. i. lib. i.) mentions their dominion, both by sea and land, to have been very extensive. We learn from Diodorus Siculus that there were many rich and powerful cities in their territories, and that for many ages their fleets ruled with uncontrolled sway over all the seas that surround Italy. They were exceedingly jealous of their liberty, the form of government being a sort of oligarchy, resembling that adopted at an after period by many of the Greek states.

Notwithstanding the rank it attained as a state among its contemporaries, there is very little known of the ancient history of Etruria—of indigenous historians not one remnant has reached our day; and the few inscriptions that remain are obscured by our ignorance of the language in which they are written. There is every probability, however, that they were not without historians of their own nation, although no notice is taken of them by the Romans, who were too intent on transmitting to posterity the record of their own triumphs only, and too anxious to veil in silence their own ignoble origin, to permit of their noticing the history of those nations whom they had supplanted in territory. We owe it most likely to the jealous policy of these invaders, that so few memorials of any kind remain of the aboriginal inhabitants of Italy. The Romans themselves had little taste for any thing but conquest, and saw clearly enough how advantageous it was to their views, to destroy whatever might tend to keep alive the national spirit of the people whom they strove to subject. They therefore industriously removed all the memorials of ancient fame, preserved by these nations, and would have blotted out their names even from the page of history, had the preservation of them not been necessary to enhance their own fame in recording the victories by which they were subjugated.

Light enough, however, remains to demonstrate the knowledge possessed by the Etrurians of the sciences, and their cultivation of the fine arts long before the Roman name existed. The peculiar practice of this ancient people in respect of the burial of their dead, had fortunately hid abundant proofs of their skill beyond the

reach of Roman jealousy; thus preserving specimens of their workmanship, and knowledge of the fine arts, both from the ravages of their conquerors, and from the later flood of barbarism that settled on this land of elegance and taste. It was reserved for modern discovery to bring to light those remarkable proofs of attainment in painting at so early a period, before it was known at all in Greece, or perhaps in any other country of Europe. Near the ancient Etruscan city of Tarquinia, ten or twelve miles from Civita Vecchia, there are a multitude of sepulchral grottos scattered about the fields to the number of some thousands, extending from Tarquinia down to the sea. Some of them are cut out of the rock, which is a tufa, and easily worked. They are of different forms—square, in the form of a cross, sometimes with three aisles like a church, and often in two stories communicating with each other. They are not deep, and generally situated under hillocks, through which a square aperture gives access to the grotto; and there is generally a communication from one to another under ground. The rock is hewn out in an architectural manner in the inside, with pilasters and cornices supporting a vaulted arch. The cornice and pilasters are covered with arabesque paintings in bad enough taste. The vault is likewise painted and divided into compartments; part of the colours remain distinct, particularly the red: the yellow is gone, but the blue and green may be distinguished. A frieze encircles the vault, which is ornamented with figures painted on it, sometimes very numerous, and painted quite in the taste of the figures upon Etruscan vases. They are generally clothed with long draperies, and have wings, bearing a spear in their hands, and in the attitude of fighting; and some of them are in cars drawn by one or two horses. There are doors represented, but no buildings, as the door seems to have served only as an indication of them, or for the symbolical mark of a house. The whole composition seems naturally enough to bear a reference to the passage of the soul into the Elysian fields. Above the frieze there are often inscribed the names of the deceased, or of the persons represented by the figures, sometimes in the Etruscan characters, and sometimes in Latin. The paintings are on the rock itself, without any preparation of plaster, so that they cannot be removed except by cutting out the piece. The peasantry, however, in search of treasure, have destroyed many of them.

The late Mr. James Byres, so generally known to all those who visited the antiquities of Rome during the latter half of the last century, has given a detailed description, accompanied with plates, of these remarkable graves. As indicative of the ideas entertained by the Etrurians on the subject of a future life, many of the friezes described are exceedingly curious. The body of the deceased is represented as laid on a chariot, drawn by two black genii, with long trailing wings; in one hand they hold a hammer, and in the other a serpent. In some of the paintings two other genii appear striking with long hammers a naked body lying on the ground, as if fallen from the chariot. What inference we are to draw from this extraordinary proceeding, it were difficult to guess: most probably some obscure notion of purification, of driving out the evil principle adherent to our corporeal existence. The means employed are no doubt far from indicative of refined ideas as to our spiritual nature; but yet it is not worse than the common belief of Mahometans, at this enlightened period of the world. With them, as soon as the body is placed in the grave, with its face to Mecca, and in a sitting posture, the Turks betake themselves to flight as speedily as possible; not to interrupt the interview which they presume to take place immediately between the corpse and two black genii, who, for that purpose, replace the soul into the body, and fix it down with an iron hook. Moukir and Nekir, the names of these visitors, forthwith proceed to interrogate the deceased as to his conduct in this world; if not satisfied with the answers, (being furnished, like the genii of the ancient Etrurians with a huge iron mallet,) they are supposed to strike the body deep into the earth; but if the interrogatories prove satisfactory to these peremptory gentlemen, they fly off, and are immediately replaced by two white genii, who remain there till the day of judgment. There are others of the ancient Etrurian pictures which pourtray combats, where the warriors are generally represented naked; and in others they consist of female dancers, which are executed with considerable grace.

The most abundant specimens of their art of design are, however, exhibited on the Etruscan pottery, which is in every body's hands; although we cannot with certainty attribute many of these vases to the ancient Etrurians, seeing so great a proportion of them are the produce of discoveries in Magna Grecia. And as both the country of Naples and the island of Sicily were colonized from Greece at a very early period, no doubt a great many of these vases are of Grecian workmanship, in imitation of the ancient Etrurian ware. But a sufficient number of examples which are not exposed to this doubt, have reached us to prove the wonderful attainments of these ancient artists in elegance of design, and dexterous management of outline. Though possessing great superiority over the Egyptian style, it is easy, in the more ancient specimens, to trace sufficient resemblance of idea and manner, to lead to the conclusion of their having acquired from that country their first rudiments of the arts. The Egyptian style, transferred to Etruria, underwent very great improvements, and latterly a total change of manner; though not to so great an extent as that to which it was subjected by the Greeks, in whose works it is not now so easy to trace the original tinge of family resemblance, though, doubtless, the debt of origin is in the one case as strong as in the other. In the preservation of their dead, there does not appear among the Etrurians any trace of the peculiar practice of the Egyptians, which leads to the inference of their having been, *ab origine*, a separate people; who had only borrowed from the Egyptians their knowledge of design, which the familiar intercourse between these two nations, by their extensive trade, would naturally lead to. But the customs of different nations, in matters regarding the interment of their dead, as they are among the earliest contracted, so they are generally the most pertinaciously observed, in the country itself, as well as among the colonists that have at any time emerged from it. People never take up the practice of foreign nations in these particulars, if they have established customs of their own, which superstition renders sacred and unassailable: It constitutes, therefore, a pretty sure guide, from which to judge of the origin of any people.

Tiraboschi, however, in his *Literatura Italiana*, supposes that the Etrurians actually did derive their origin from Egypt, and, landing in Italy, brought with them a knowledge of science and of the fine arts; but the discrepancy in their form of government, superstition, activity in trade, liberality in their intercourse with fo-

reign nations, and form of countenance as represented in their pictures, seem utterly to forbid the supposition. But whether or not their taste in the fine arts was derived from Egypt or the Phœnicians, (who generally get the credit of originating every thing about which we are left in darkness,) this at least is certain, that the ancient Etrurians were a powerful, superstitious, and luxurious people; and being for many ages in terms of friendship and commerce with both Egyptians and Phœnicians, a reciprocity of taste, and imitation of the arts as practised by each, must, to a certain extent, have been the natural consequence. Whatever the Etrurians derived from others, they must be allowed the credit of being the first nation who showed a decided and successful taste for the fine arts: the elegance displayed in the inexhaustible variety of form in the vases we have of this ancient people, evince a highly cultivated talent for design; the beauty and flowing contour of their running patterns is admirable, the tasteful placing of the handles, the playful ease and felicitous dexterity of execution; in short, every thing we have of their workmanship, has an original character of elegance, which is quite surprising for the period in which they flourished. Correct and tasteful design is one of the most difficult, as it is one of the most fascinating attributes of the art, to produce a happy effect by apparently slender means; for

" He best employs his art that best conceals."

Yet this perfection is remarkably attained in the graceful and simple lines of the Etrurian figures. Like the clever sketches of a great master, the dexterity with which the style is suited to the material used, the chaste and simple outline, heightened by a few sharp touches, and harmonized by the correspondence of two well-selected colours, could only result from a highly cultivated taste. The placing of their figures is likewise a pattern for lightness and grace. They are represented generally in motion, displaying a degree of elasticity, and successful balance in their running figures, which could not be surpassed; and they afforded to their followers the Greeks an inexhaustible fund of ideas in this field of invention, which accordingly has been copied and re-copied in every succeeding cycle of the art.

With the Etruscans themselves there seems to have been little copying, as of the very great multitude of vases that have been brought to light, there are not found any copies of the same subject; they are all originals. Although the same idea may be the subject of representation, it is always differently expressed, and with great liveliness of invention. When we consider the mechanical difficulties accompanying this mode of painting; the quickness and precision with which it must be executed, from the colours being instantly imbibed; the impossibility of retouching or altering any false line or mistake; the clean, uninterrupted, and rapid sweep of the pencil, which is the very quintessence of a draughtsman's address, and indispensable to the mode of painting in question, we cannot but admire the dexterity of these Etruscan artists. No false lines are ever detected, no interruptions, or returning upon the touch; the whole outline is dashed off with a playfulness and accuracy of pencil like the magical touch of Raphael.

They seem to have been equally attentive to secure the advantage of the finest clay, as appears by the very great tenuity and lightness of their vases. Nothing of the kind has been discovered in modern

Greece.

times of equal quality, except a vein of decomposed jasper in the neighbourhood of Montereale, in Sicily. We have had an opportunity of examining this substance on the spot, in company with the Padre Stersinger, who had been occupied for many years in the investigation of this subject. He had ascertained, that wherever the fragments of Etruscan vases so called were found in great abundance, as is often the case, and probably indicative of the former existence of a manufactory of them, he uniformly discovered veins of jasper somewhere in the neighbourhood. That of Montereale he traced down to a situation, where it was decomposed into a red earth. Of this earth he formed some vases, which we saw, fully as smooth and light as those of the ancients, which was all that depended on the earth; for in point of elegance of form, the Padre's taste and dexterity fell greatly short of his predecessors the ancient potters. Stone jasper can be pounded in the same mills as those used in our modern porcelain manufactories, and is more tenacious, smooth, and workable, than any other earth, so that we may safely infer that it really was the substance used by the ancients.

Pliny mentions some painted ceilings still existing in his day in the town of Ardea, an ancient city of Etruria, which had been executed at a date prior to the foundation of Rome. He expresses great surprise and admiration at their freshness and state of preservation after the lapse of so many centuries. At Lanuvium, another ancient city of Etruria, there was a temple decorated with pictures of Atalanta and Helen, which, although exposed to the air from the ruined state of the temple, were still in a state of great preservation in Pliny's time. They were simply painted on the wall of the building, and possessed considerable excellence of execution, according to Pliny. Caligula made an attempt to remove them, but failed from the great hardness of the plaster. At the town of Cere, another ancient Etruscan city, there were some paintings extant of a still older date.

Greece.

In the history of the various nations of the world, we find none that seems to have possessed in so eminent a degree as the Greeks, that acute susceptibility of, and taste for, the beautiful, which leads to the highest attainments in the fine arts. From the first dawning of the art among them, a correct sense of the charm of simplicity and elegance chastened the eager flights of their genius, and prevented their diverging into those extravagances into which talent is so apt to stray, so soon as it has acquired such facility in the execution of an art, as to enable it to minister readily to all the dictates of fancy. More than twenty centuries have elapsed since painting attained this state of advancement in Greece. We have accounts, not only of the painters themselves, but of their works, with detailed descriptions of their perfections, and the effects produced by them, which, unless we make very great allowance for the exaggeration naturally excited by the illusions of an art yet new, must have equalled in excellence any thing that modern genius has been able to produce. In this branch of our subject, we have not to grope in a barren wilderness, where but a few scattered and imperfect remnants of art or information is all we have to judge by; the progress of the art in Greece is no longer a mere matter of historic curiosity, but a rich mine from whence both advantage and entertainment are to be drawn. Time has no doubt enveloped much in doubt, and mowed down a great proportion of the luxuriant harvest, but valuable gleanings still remain amply to repay the consideration of the subject.

Greece.

When we advance the supposition that it was from Etruria and Egypt that Greece derived her knowledge of the arts, we do not mean to deny the probability, that some rude mode of practice common to nations in the earliest state of society, preceded in Greece the introduction of Etrurian skill, and enabled her artists speedily to improve upon their borrowed knowledge. Almost all that we know of painting at the period in question is derived from Pliny; a great deal has been written on the subject; but, with the exception of a few observations to be found in the works of Cicero and some others of the classics, Pliny is the source from which all the facts are drawn. It is easy to distinguish what he records as facts from the conjectural part of the account, such as the history of the invention of painting, where Pliny adopts the idle story of its origin from the fabulous dreams with which the vanity of the Greeks had corrupted their early history. According to them, we not only owe the discovery of this noble art to the dalliance of an amorous shepherd; but every particular step of its advance towards perfection is the distinct invention of some one of their earliest artists; and this in so very systematical a progression, that, were there no other circumstance to shake the probability of its accuracy, this consideration alone would suffice. To Cleanthes, for instance, is given the first step beyond the shepherd's shadow picture, namely, the origin of *linear* drawing, or tracing the outline; which there is little probability of ever having been the first attempt at art in any country. To this Telephanes added *hatching*, or the improvement of representing shade by crossed lines,—a merit which is likewise claimed for another artist, Ardices; but hatching is obviously a refinement of shading in its simpler form. The next step, according to the regularity of the structure, was filling up the outline, and completing the figure with one uniform colour like a shadow; to this they gave the name of *monochromatic*, and attributed its invention to Cleophanes of Corinth. The next advance was the distinction of the sexes in the representation of figures, given to Cimon of Cleona; then followed the indication of the muscles, draping, and an attempt to vary the attitude of figures, which till then had been confined to profile; and to Cimon is particularly attributed the merit of departing from the pristine stiffness, and rigid draperies, which cling to the ancient figures of Egypt, by substituting greater fulness, and a more natural disposition of folds. It must have required considerable proficiency in the art of light and shade, to give a just representation of the projections and sinuosities of the drapery.

It is of no importance to what individual the art was indebted for each step of its progress; the march of improvement advanced here, as it did elsewhere, from very rude and imperfect beginnings; and, considering the singular concurrence of advantages which Greece presented for the growth of the fine arts, it would have been surprising had they not reached great excellence. We find in Greece a number of small states occupying the finest climate of the world, full of vigour and talent, animated by the spirit of independence and emulation, striving to outstrip each other in every road to eminence, either by military glory or mental acquirements, stimulated by the fire of genius, and gifted by nature with beauty of person surpassing their contemporaries. Accordingly, in every acquirement of which human nature is susceptible, the genius of the Greeks seem to have soared above that of every other nation; whether by their valour in arms, the celebrity of their schools, their political establishments, their eloquence, poetry, statuary, and architecture. We cannot suppose, therefore, that painting should fail to join the train, although the perishable nature of its productions should deprive us of the ocular evidence of facts, which in the more permanent branches of the fine arts still remain in such profusion as to attest the masterly skill and taste of Greek artists. But there are so many essentials common to both, that the monuments of sculpture bear equal testimony in favour of the pencil; as they require the same knowledge and correctness of design, the same grace, elegance, and fire of genius. Where the one is found to flourish, we do not hesitate to admit the existence of the other. Nor have we any reason to receive with doubt the account given by Pliny, and other ancient authors, who lavish their praises on the labours of the Grecian pencil. They exalt with the same enthusiasm the excellence of their sculpture; and in this last we have abundant testimony that they do not mislead us in their judgment of them.

Yet there are many who, judging from the few imperfect specimens of painting that have reached our day, refuse to admit that the ancients really did possess any adequate knowledge of the art, compared to our ideas of the excellence attainable by it. We shall not find any difficulty, when we come in the sequel to talk of these remnants, in showing their incompetency to lead to any such conclusion. We do not deny that the praises bestowed by ancient authors on the works of art, must always be commensurate to the state of perfection it had reached at the time, and to their capacity of judging. The peasant admires the wonderful art of the sign-painter, or the wooden cuts of his collection of ballads, as great efforts of genius. Every thing is excellence that excels what we are used to, and the artist who advances a step beyond his contemporaries becomes a prodigy; but where knowledge, in all the various branches of the fine arts, has generally diffused itself over the great body of a people, as we know to have been the case among the Greeks, to a degree unequalled by any other nation, either at that time or since; we may confidently rely upon what their authors confidently assert, although the nature of the case admits of no other evidence to corroborate their opinion. When Cicero, Aristotle, Pliny, and others of the great luminaries of ancient literature, judge with precision of the beauties of writing and composition, of the excellencies of their poets and orators, we find the opinions they express on these subjects amply borne out by the testimony of their works. When, therefore, they exercise a similar discrimination of judgment as to the perfections of their painters, pointing out with all the precision and scrutiny of critics the defects of such and such individual performances; their good taste and competency to judge can be as little questionable as the fact of their having seen what they not only describe, but dwell on with the delight of amateurs. They draw with scrupulous nicety the parallel betwixt the productions of their great statuaries and painters, who are classed in an equal scale of eminence: They at the same time lament the very great decay of the art in their own day, compared to what it was some centuries before; and expose the deficiency of the Roman artists, some of whose works remain to verify the truth of their criticism.

The state of the arts in general, in the time of Homer, was probably not quite so far advanced as the enthusiasm of some of the admirers of that poet lead them to infer; but we cannot go so far as to admit, that the circumstance of his not precisely mentioning the art of painting in his poem, is sufficient to make us conclude, that painting did not exist before the period he describes; and that, in this respect, Greece, before the age of Pericles, remained in utter ignorance of the art. Much refinement in painting, or knowledge of perspective, either linear or aerial, is not to be looked for at this early age; but every authority of ancient history unites to prove, that the art was, to a certain extent, practised, and that representations in basso-relievo were much in use, which implies at least a knowledge of design.

The exquisite compositions so beautifully described by Homer, as embossed on the shields and armour of his heroes, may, in point of execution, perhaps, have been somewhat inferior to the masterly excellence of his description; but the design and composition, which is all that we argue for, is naturally implied in the circumstance of their furnishing subject for his poetic delineation. It is a subject of controversy whether these decorations were sculptured, cast, or painted; but, in so far as it proves the existence of a knowledge of design at the remotest period of Grecian history, it is immaterial for our purpose, as that was an acquirement equally requisite for them all. Neither does it avail to maintain, that painting at least was quite unsuitable to the uses to which arms and bucklers were exposed, when we recollect the early practice of dedicating votive shields as commemorative of heroic exploits, and hanging them up in the temples, where there was nothing to prevent their being of a sufficient size to admit of the representations necessary to convey the record desired. There can be no doubt of the high antiquity of this practice anterior to the age of Homer. The celebrated description which he gives of the shield of Achilles, which has called forth so much discussion, must in every view be admitted as an undeniable testimony of the usage of the age, and to the taste which existed at that epoch in matters of art, as well as one of the earliest monuments of Grecian knowledge in composition and design. As it was intended to exercise the talents of an omnipotent artist, Vulcan, whose skill might be supposed capable of giving colour as well as form to his metallic materials, we are not bound to infer, from the minute detail of colouring, that painting and not sculpture was the art contemplated by Homer. We are not even left to form a conjecture respecting the possibility of producing these metallic tints. Homer tells us that Vulcan threw brass, tin, gold, and silver into the fire, and drew from the mixture the combination of colours required, dexterously modifying them to all the delicate blendings which his subject demanded: Whatever, therefore, the execution may have been, the idea was here, and however much we may suppose it heightened by poetic hyperbole, it is impossible to read the description, without representing to our imagination a complete picture, or at least a coloured basso-relievo; for he gives no indication of a coloured sky, or of the flesh-colour required for the countenances of the figures. In fact, Homer seems willing to impress us with a notion of the omnipotent perfection of Vulcan's art, by superadding to that of the accomplished worker in metals, all the perfections and excellencies peculiar to sculpture and painting, known to, and of course practised by, that age.

This subject is treated at large in the work of L'Abbé Fraguier, and by M. Boivin, who gives a drawing of the shield, with its multifarious subjects, designed from the description. Mr. Pope likewise adds a dissertation on this subject, which he considers to have been a piece of painting; and certainly his profound knowledge of Homer ought to give great weight to his opinion. He observes, " that there is scarcely a species or branch of the art of painting which is not here to be found, whether history, battle painting, landscape, architecture, fruit, flowers, animals, &c." he adds, " I think it possible that painting was arrived to a greater degree of perfection, even at that early period, than is generally supposed by those who have written upon it. We may have a higher notion of the art from those descriptions of statues, carving, tapestries, sculptures upon armour and ornaments of all kinds, which every where occur in our author; as well as from what he says of their beauty, the relievo, and their emulation of life itself. If we consider how much it is his constant practice to confine himself to the customs of the times whereof he writ, it will be hard to doubt but that painting and sculpture must have been in great practice and repute," &c. " It is certain that Homer had, whether by learning, or by strength of genius, a full and exact idea of painting in all its parts; that is to say, in the invention, the composition, the expression," &c.

The shield was divided into twelve compartments, with a border representing the sea encircling the pictures, which were different in each compartment, meaning to represent the picture of the whole world; and so it was understood by the ancient authors, who mention it as a master-piece of picturesque sculpture or painting. The subjects were, 1. A town in peace. 2. An assembly of the people. 3. The senate. 4. A town in war. 5. An ambuscade. 6. A battle. 7. Tillage. 8. The harvest. 9. The vintage. 10. Animals. 11. Sheep. 12. The dance. Of the composition as a picture, Mr. Pope gives the following opinion: " Nothing is more wonderful than his exact observation of the contrast, not only between figure and figure, but between subject and subject. The city in peace is a contrast to the city in war; between the siege in the fourth picture, and the battle in the sixth, a piece of paysage is introduced, and rural scenes follow after. The country, too, is represented in war in the fifth, as well as in peace in the seventh, eighth, and ninth. The very animals are shewn in these two different states in the tenth and in the eleventh. Where the subjects appear the same, he contrasts them some other way. Thus the first picture of the town in peace, having a predominant air of gaiety, in the dances and pomps of the marriage; the second has a character of earnestness and solicitude, in the dispute and pleadings. In the pieces of rural life, that of ploughing is of a different character from the harvest, and that of the harvest from the vintage. In each of these, there is a contrast of the mirth and the labour of the country people. In the first, some are ploughing, others taking a cup of good liquor; in the next, we see the reapers working in one part, and the banquet prepared in another; in the last, the labour of the vineyard is relieved with music and a dance. The persons are no less varied, old and young men and women; there being women in two pictures together, namely, the eighth and ninth. It is remarkable that those in the latter are of a different character from the former; they who dress the supper being ordinary women, the others who carry baskets in the vineyards, young and beautiful virgins; and these, again, are of an inferior character to those in the twelfth piece, who are distinguished as people of condition by a more elegant dress. There are three dances in the buckler; and these, too, are varied: that at the wedding is in a circular figure; that of the vine-

yard in a row; that in the last picture a mingled one. Lastly, there is a manifest contrast in the colours; nay, even in the back grounds of the several pieces. For example, that of the ploughing is of a dark tint; that of the harvest yellow; that of the pasture green; and the rest in like manner." Virgil has given a similar testimony with Homer, to his belief of the state of the arts at the period of the Trojan war, by various picturesque descriptions in the Æneid, particularly the shield of Æneas, in imitation of that of Achilles, has all the actions of the Romans prophetically represented on it down to the age of Augustus; and he represents the whole Trojan war as painted on the walls of the temple of Juno at Carthage.

At the period of the Trojan war, and how long before we know not, embroidery, which implies a knowledge of design, was the chief employment of females of rank: it is the employment that Homer gives to Helen in the third book of the Iliad, where she is represented as exercising her talent on the extensive subject of the Trojan war. When the news of her husband's death was brought to Andromache, she is found in a small chamber embroidering coloured flowers on cloth. Now, to work flowers on canvas, the drawing must have been previously traced upon it; and if not only flowers, but the complicated subjects of history, were worked, the embroiderers must have had the model of a picture in drawing and colour to guide their work; so that tapestry, as Homer describes it to have existed, and to have been practised at that time, implies the pre-existence of painting in a considerable state of advance, and long before Pliny admits of the invention having taken place.

We have so little to guide us through the obscurity of these early times as to the real state of the arts, that inference is all we can pretend to. Many fluctuations of improvement and decay, similar to what the arts have experienced in modern times, was most probably their fate at a former era; though now we are as much in ignorance of them, as of the revolutions that may have given rise to them; but the supposition would explain the seeming inconsistency of the perfections ascribed to very ancient artists, compared with facts of a much later date leading to prove a very low state of the art. Although we are ignorant of the fact that Homer was preceded by many generations of poets of merit, who raised the art progressively; and, consistent with the usual course by which genius developes itself, to that climax of perfection which he was able to attain; there is reason to conclude that it was so, rather than to suppose the prodigy of such a luminary at once starting from the depths of ignorance. The observation applies equally to painting. We cannot suppose Homer to have anticipated by so many generations that taste for the peculiar excellencies of the fine arts.

According to Pliny, the most celebrated painters of Greece lived about seven or eight centuries before the Christian æra, when the art was in such high consideration as to constitute one of the subjects of contest at Delphos, and likewise at Corinth. In one of these, Panæus, the brother of Phidias the statuary, exhibited a painting of the battle of Marathon, in which the principal figures were as large as life, and represented portraits of the leading chiefs. This implies a pretty advanced state of the art, and likewise that portraits of these generals existed before the painting of the battle; several of them not being then in life, as the picture was painted at a period somewhat later than the æra of the battle. It is possible, however, that the painter resorted to the surer and simpler means of ascertaining the persons intended by his figures, by writing their names under each; which was not an unfrequent practice with Greek artists, and takes away not a little from the boasted merit of the resemblance. The picture was afterwards hung up for public inspection in the portico of the Pœcile at Athens. Panæus lived 448 years before the Christian era. His works were much admired in the best days of painting at Athens, yet at one of the contests for superiority in painting held at Delphos, he was vanquished by his rival Timagoras. These picturesque combats must have contributed much towards the improvement of the arts. There is a picture of a battle particularly mentioned as having been painted by Bularchus some centuries anterior to this period; the merits of which are said, though without much probability of truth, to have been such as to induce a king of Lydia to give its weight in gold for the acquisition. This story seems to have become an hereditary fable in the art, as those who have visited the cabinets of the Continent must have remarked, in most of which some legend of the kind is generally recorded.

There are many Greek artists enumerated before the age of Panæus, of whom there is little material to remark. His brother Phidias, the illustrious statuary, was likewise a painter before he devoted himself entirely to sculpture. About the same period flourished Polygnotus of Thasus, several of whose pictures were afterwards carried to Rome, and two of them are described by Pausanias, in whose time they must have been five or six hundred years old; so that their mode of painting had at least the merit of great durability. Polygnotus is much praised by Pliny for composition; and Aristotle gives him the reputation of painting the manners or character of the age with great accuracy. He worked chiefly for the decoration of the great portico begun by Panæus. His compositions were of great size; and when we find him praised for the indignant flush of modesty in the countenance of his Cassandra, it argues no mean powers of pencil. Micon, his contemporary and rival, in decorating the Pœcile, painted the battles of the Amazons, and excelled in his representation of horses, which is far from an easy part of the art. He had a rival in this particular branch, in Pauson, of whom there is an anecdote recorded by Plutarch, which, if true, says very little for the style or excellence of the painter. He had received a commission to paint the picture of a horse rolling on his back. He represented the animal, however, galloping; and when the purchaser complained that his order was not executed, Pauson desired him to turn the picture upside down, and he would find that it was so. If this was not a jest of the day upon the painter's imperfections, it seems to indicate that pictures were then painted, as we see on Etruscan vases, like basso-relievos, without either ground or sky, and quite detached, upon a dark back ground. Still the picture could have no light and shade, and must, in design, have been very imperfect, to admit of the energetic play of the muscles and limbs, in the action of galloping, having any resemblance, when reversed, to the loose motions of a horse rolling. Dionysius of Colophon, who painted in miniature, excelled in the minute accuracy of his works. Pliny enumerates various other artists who preceded the fourth century before Christ; but it was not until the ninety-fourth Olympiad, that the art reached its greatest epoch in Greece under Apollodorus and Zeuxis, at which time there shone a celebrated galaxy of competitors for the palm of painting.

Apollodorus of Athens advanced the art of painting considerably in the important matter of light and shade, by remarking that the shade always partook of the colour of the object, which he endeavoured to blend in the shading, so as merely to obscure the colour. The want of this art in his predecessors, must have occasioned great harshness in their mode of colouring; and accordingly all the ancient authors agree in giving great preference to his works, some of which were still existing in Pliny's time at Pergamo.

Zeuxis formed an epoch in the art of painting by the refinement of his composition, quitting the crowded style of the more ancient school, who sought to increase the interest of their subject, and convey its full meaning, more by accumulating figures and accessaries, than trusting to the individual perfections of their principal figures. Zeuxis studied and selected what was most beautiful in nature, which, of course, led him to the preference of the female sex. He was very proud of his famous picture of Helen, composed of the perfections of the five most beautiful girls of Crotona, who sat to the painter for that purpose. He painted Jupiter surrounded by all the deities, and the infant Hercules strangling the serpent, with his mother in alarm beside him, and Amphitrion coming to his assistance. He became so rich from the produce of his pictures, and so vain from the admiration they attracted, that at last he merely exhibited his works, alleging that they were incapable of being paid for; a resolution in which the history of the art, both in ancient and modern times, does not show that he found many imitators. The trite anecdote of the bunch of grapes which the birds came to pick, is told of Zeuxis, and argues less for his praise than is generally attributed to him from this judgment of the giddy birds, as the grapes were said to have been held up by a child, whose resemblance does not seem to have been sufficiently striking to frighten the birds away. Such attempted illusions are unworthy of the art, and have gone far to cramp the genius of some of our modern schools, which, like the older German artists, showed talent capable of accomplishing better things than to waste their ingenuity on tricks. The Italians call it *inganni*, and, among them, Bassano condescended to practise it very much. He painted a book as if laid upon one of his pictures, and met with what he conceived a glorious reward, when Annibal Caracci was deceived by it, and tried to remove the book. The painter Gennari possessed and practised this trick so successfully, as to obtain the surname of the Magician; but in fact it argues no great stretch of art to deceive animals at least, as, without demonstrating much judgment in the fine arts, dogs have often been known to recognise their master's picture, and the more readily that the portrait was that sort of daub emphatically denominated a staring likeness. Neither can we allow much discrimination, or picture knowledge, in the feathered tribe, who are so easily scared from a new sown field by the tattered effigies erected for that purpose.

To return to Zeuxis; his vanity led him upon one occasion to appear at the Olympic games in a purple robe, as indicative of his sovereignty in the arts, with his name embroidered upon it in gold letters, which obtained him the mortification of a very cold reception for the picture he exhibited. It was that of the female centaur suckling her young. The male centaur appears in the back ground, holding up a lion cub to frighten the baby centaurs. The painter had succeeded in representing a very beautiful woman in the upper part of the figure, and as beautiful a mare in the under half,

Greece.

reclining on a green field. She was represented doubly provided as a nurse, one of the little monsters being satisfied with the animal food of the quadrupeds; while the woman half caresses and nourishes the other in her bosom. Lucian, who describes this picture, of which he had seen a copy, (the original having been lost at sea when sent by Sylla to Italy,) says, that it was a masterly performance, full of a great many drolleries, very proper to the subject, and finely imagined, making the picture exceedingly gay. He particularly admires the imagination and execution of so whimsical a subject; the rough ferocity of the male, with vast shoulders entirely covered with hair, and smiling in a wild and ghastly manner at the effect of his own jest, contrasted with the exquisite beauty of the female, like a very fine woman, though ornamented with horse's ears; and so dexterously was the commixtion of natures managed, as almost to elude observation. One of the infants seems savage and fierce, while the other, with childish simplicity and alarm, stares at the lion, while it hangs on its mother's breast.

Zeuxis made use of very few colours, never exceeding four, and at times painted in the monochromatic style, with two only. His last work was that of a ridiculous old woman, as he is reported to have died of a fit of laughter at the whimsical production of his own fancy.

Parhasius.

The contemporaries of Zeuxis were Androcydes and Parhasius of Ephesus. The works of this last are much praised for expression. He painted a celebrated picture of the people of Athens, besides many others that are enumerated by Pliny. He defeated Zeuxis in a trial of skill, and seems, by all accounts, to have vied with him equally as a coxcomb in the finery of his dress, and conceit of his own talent, as he had the extravagance to paint his own portrait in the character of Mercury, alleging that he was descended of Apollo himself, and expected, accordingly, the ready adoration of his countrymen. He competed with Timanthes in painting the contest of Ajax and Ulysses for the arms of Achilles, in which he was defeated. He was, notwithstanding, a painter of great merit, as well as his adversary. Timanthes is principally known by his picture of the sacrifice of Iphigenia, so much praised on account of the judicious and beautiful idea, so often repeated since, of representing Menelaus, the unfortunate father of the victim, hiding his face in that overwhelming agony of grief, the intensity of which is thus implied as exceeding the power of art to imitate. There followed Eupompus of Sicyone, who had the merit of founding a new school, where a greater variety of colours were used than had formerly been the practice. He instructed Pamphilius of Macedonia, whose chief merit is in having been the master of Apelles, the greatest painter of antiquity.

Pamphilius.

It is a remarkable coincidence, and perhaps more than coincidence, that Pietro Perugino, who had the glory of instructing the greatest luminary of modern art, Raphael, should have resembled Pamphilius to a remarkable degree in the peculiar bent of his talent; which was that of extreme truth and accuracy, and which generated a similarly stiff, cold, and dry manner. Pliny describes him as very learned in every thing connected with his art, chiefly as relating to arithmetic and geometry, without a profound knowledge of which he maintained that a painter could not succeed. This fact is remarkable, in so far as it seems satisfactorily to refute the supposition of the Greeks being unacquainted with perspective; for in no other way can we understand the dependence of painting on geometry. About the same period, Theon of Samos gained a high re-

Theon.

putation, particularly for his picture of a youthful warrior hastening to battle. Aristides of Thebes painted the picture of a town taken by assault, and plundered; and another battle piece, for which Pliny says he received one hundred drachms for every figure in the picture: but we hasten to Apelles, the Raphael of Greece.

Greece
Aristides.

The whole of antiquity seems to unite in the praises of this great artist, and that not merely for his transcendent talents, which raised the art of painting to the acmè of perfection, which it never surpassed in the ancient world, and never equalled in modern times, until Raphael again led to that point of perfection which it seems never destined to pass;—but likewise, as was the case with Raphael, for his many amiable qualities. For Apelles, though aware of his own excellence, and sufficiently tenacious of the dignity of his art, seems to have been so without vanity or self-conceit; he was just and liberal to others, and anxious to encourage genius wherever he could discover it, without a thought of that paltry jealousy which so often tarnishes the splendour of the brightest genius. Apelles united all the great qualities of a painter, though he had the modesty to acknowledge that, in some, he was excelled by a rival; but his great excellence was the same as Raphael's, a captivating grace and simplicity, joined to a playfulness of execution, which, more than any thing, conveys the idea of a perfect master. Apelles was honoured with the friendship of Alexander the Great, as much as Titian was by that of Charles V.; although the conqueror testified his esteem for the painter in a way which might not have been so acceptable to the manners of the emperor's time, by presenting him with his beautiful concubine, Pancaste, in property; who had sat for his celebrated picture of Venus, afterwards brought to Rome. Apelles was very learned in his profession, a quality which, in Greece, was wisely esteemed essential to the successful prosecution of the art; and which was not confined to the more immediate branches of information connected with the study of painting, but embraced the general field of science. It was to this, fully as much as to their excellence as painters, that, in Greece, the professors of the liberal arts were held in such high estimation. And we shall find, when we look to the history of later times, that there were few of the great masters of the art who were not at the same time learned men. Leonardo da Vinci, in whom the art may be said to have revived, was a man of general and profound learning, as well as were most of the others whose names stand high. The diffusion of the art has now unfortunately reduced it to a state of prostitution, where a learned painter is a prodigy rarely to be found. But, learned as Apelles was, he had the modesty to court, and profit by, the criticism of the public, for which purpose he was in the practice of exposing his pictures for public inspection, close to where he prosecuted his labours, in order to have the advantage of overhearing, without being seen, any remarks that were made upon them. This practice is said to have given rise to the well known apostrophe of "Ne sutor ultra crepidam." As a shoemaker, examining one of his pictures, is said to have remarked a slight inaccuracy in the construction of the sandals worn by one of the figures in his picture, Apelles took advantage of the hint, and corrected the error. The cobler, when he saw the correction, was so elated with his own acuteness, that he bethought himself of hazarding a few criticisms on the leg, as he had succeeded so well with the foot, which drew from the judicious painter the advice that has so

Apelles.

often been used since; and it were well for the peace of society were it not so often lost sight of.

From the accounts given of the various pictures painted by Apelles, which call forth commendations in every particular quality of the art; he seems particularly to have studied the pleasing illusion of fore-shortening, which implies a degree of knowledge and address that has been often denied to the ancients. The thunderbolt held in the hand of Alexander, painted in the character of Jupiter, was said to advance beyond the picture. His celebrated allegorical picture of Calumny was likewise the subject of much praise among the ancients. The occasion of this picture was an accusation brought against Apelles, when in Egypt, by the jealousy of one of his rivals. The charge having been entertained by Ptolemy, occasioned the return of Apelles to Greece, where he took this means of vindicating his character, and teaching to the world a good moral lesson. He represents Calumny as a female of haughty mien, and magnificently attired, with a fierce and malicious expression, in one hand holding a flambeau, and with the other dragging a young man by the hair, who holds his hands up to heaven, as if declaring his innocence. Pale wasted Envy precedes, with piercing eyes, and behind is a crowd of female harpies, with artful smiles. This train approaches the judge, who readily holds out his hand to Calumny. In the back ground appears Repentance in tears, and preparing to receive Truth, who is seen coming up from a considerable distance. Much has since been borrowed from this noble composition.

Protogenes. Protogenes of Rhodes, who was the contemporary of Apelles, was a careful painter, whose merits were brought into notice through the good offices of Apelles. He is said to have finished with such laborious toil as to have been occupied seven years in the execution of one picture, which he painted several times over, in order, by giving so thick a body of colour, to secure its durability. Apelles accused him of working off the spirit of his composition by over-finishing; he was in great poverty, and painted ships to gain a livelihood. There is an anecdote mentioned of his great composure during the siege of Rhodes by Demetrius Phalereus, having been found quietly at work by the besiegers; but this story is at variance with the account of the siege given by Aulus Gellius, in the 16th Chap. 1st Book, who places the event after the death of Protogenes, and states that the possession of his famous picture of Ialysus, which the Rhodians valued as the treasure of their city, was one motive for pushing the siege with such determination. At the representation of the deputies of the town to Demetrius, that the picture would certainly be consumed if he persisted in burning the town, he is reported to have refrained from continuing the siege. If there is any truth in this story, it shows painting to have been held in a degree of estimation at that time, which surpasses any thing we know of it since. The picture represented the founder of Rhodes returning from the chase with his dog, the painter wishing to represent the foam about the dog's mouth, in which he failed of success, is said in a fit of despair to have tossed the pencil at the picture; this accidental stroke fell so fortunately on the dog's mouth, as to produce at once what he had so long laboured in vain to accomplish. Nichomacus, who succeeded Protogenes, excelled in the opposite extreme of rapidity of execution, with a light and easy pencil.

Pausias. Pausias painted ceilings and flowers, and first introduced the encaustic mode of painting; Antiphilius was

the calumniator, whose jealousy occasioned the famous picture of Calumny, by Apelles. He, as well as Pausias, painted in the taste which has been since adopted by the Dutch school. In a picture of a sacrifice painted by Pausias, he is said to have introduced a black ox, seen directly in front, but executed with such skill in perspective, as to make the whole length of the animal be distinctly perceptible, and as much so to appearance as if it had been seen sideways. The rich Lucullus gave no less a sum, according to Pliny, than two talents, about £500, for a copy of his picture of the flower girl. With Pausias originated the idea which has been so much repeated by the Dutch school, of representing the countenance of a person drinking, as seen through a glass tankard. Nothing could be more perfectly a Dutch subject than a boy blowing up a piece of charcoal with which his own countenance is brilliantly illuminated. This was the master piece of Antiphilius's performances. Euphranon painted the battle of Mantinea, so much praised by Plutarch and Pausanias, and a picture of the Argonauts, painted by Cydias, was bought by the Roman orator Hortensius for forty-four thousand sesterces.

Pliny makes no mention of Ætion, who lived Ætion. not long after Apelles. He is taken notice of by Cicero among the great painters. His principal picture, which he exhibited at the Olympic games, was the marriage of Alexander and Roxane, described at some length by Lucian, as having been remarkably happy in the allegorical employments given to a number of little Cupids. We should imagine that he was describing a composition of Albano, so close is the resemblance of style. The different pieces of the hero's armour are lying about, and occupy the attention of the little Cupids, who are seen exercising every sort of playful invention in tricking each other, and mocking the graver personages of the piece; marching about under the burden of some piece of armour, with the grotesque air of warriors, while a cunning little rogue hides himself in ambuscade within the coat of mail, impatient to play off his stratagem, and scare the warlike troop. Were we to describe the beautiful realisation of these ideas, in the loves of Cupid and Psyche, with which the divine master of modern art has decorated the Farnesiana, where colouring and the excellent disposition of light and shade seem carried to the height of perfection, it could only be in similar terms; and it is difficult to suppose any inferiority in the ancient artist with whom the conception originated.

We now draw near the close of the list of celebrated painters of Greece; for the art had already passed its meridian. It reached its greatest altitude in the age of Pericles, when Apelles flourished, and not being able to pass that point of perfection to which his powerful genius had raised it, it could not remain stationary, but, consistently with the usual tendency of human affairs, began rapidly to fall back, increasing in speed as it descended. We find the marks of languor and effeminacy where the vigour of creative genius had shone before; a degraded affectation of refinement, supplanting the noble simplicity, truth, and grace, which characterized the ascending progress of art in Greece. Having once mastered the great difficulties of an art, and possessed ourselves of the attainments in which real excellence consists, the restless principle of our nature will not suffer our remaining satisfied with the acquirement of what is possible, we strive to refine perfection, and seek for new charms to catch the eye; in search of these which assume importance as we proceed, the great principles of excellence are soon lost sight of, and we sink fast into all the trick and corruptions of a vitiated taste. Surprise, more than admiration, becomes the emotion sought to be excited; invention is occupied with mechanical facilities and puerile conceits, instead of that noble exercise of genius which gained for painting so distinguished a place among the liberal arts. Lord Kames very justly observes, that " an useful art seldom turns retrograde, because every one has an interest to preserve it in perfection. Fine arts depend on more slender principles than those of utility; and therefore the judgment formed of them is more fluctuating. The variety of form that is admitted into the fine arts by such fluctuation of judgment, excites artists to indulge their love of novelty. Restless man knows no golden mean, but will be attempting innovations without end. Such innovations do well in an art distant from perfection; for an artist, ambitious to excel, aims always to be an original, and cannot submit to be an imitator."

We may mention Nicias as having had the reputation of being a good painter; and likewise Athenion, his rival, and the philosopher Metrodorus, who attended Æmilius to Rome as tutor to his children, and had the credit of training the mind, and guiding the studies, of the great Scipio.

In Greece, the art partook more of the fixed principles of a science, than of the arbitrary exercise of an elegant accomplishment, as it has been considered in modern times; in so far as the notion of beauty assumed more of a determined quality, grounded on stated rules, and a sort of generally received standard, and not entirely left to the artist's individual feeling of taste. We know of nothing in the constitution of nature which indicates any established principles of architecture, beyond the requisite solidity and fitness for the purpose intended; and admitting of a boundless range of variety in form and proportion; yet the successive efforts of skill and genius which in Greece were for ages turned to the refinement of that art, gradually narrowed the range, until it fixed itself within the limits of certain received principles of proportion and form, which constituted the nearest approach to their ideas of perfection, and of which any infringement was universally admitted to be injurious to the object aimed at. Beyond this point, the advance of human skill seemed to be interdicted; but the aspiring genius of Greece continued, notwithstanding, to pursue the attempt with so much energy, that the apparently insignificant problem of ascertaining the exact measure best suited to the intercolumniations of the different orders of architecture, was a contest which agitated, for three hundred years, the skill of artists, and remained, notwithstanding, unsettled.

The same precision was extended to sculpture and painting, in so far as expressive of the greatest possible beauty. They classed them into the different kinds of beauty of which the human form appeared susceptible; and that they did arrive at some degree of fixed and established understanding on this seemingly undefinable subject is likely, from the perfect uniformity that is exhibited in the often repeated representations of their different deities, where they observe one fixed and uniform type of beauty, from which they seem seldom or ever to have admitted of any deviation. It was not left to the imagination of the artist to pourtray any ideal excellence of his own brain; there was an individual likeness, a combination of certain attributes, of certain perfections of form and features, which constituted the

Ideal beauty.

particular identity of beauty, of which each god or goddess was the type or enunciation. Accordingly, to those accustomed to examine the works of Grecian sculpture, there is as little difficulty in fixing upon the deity represented, as in recognizing the portrait of a well known individual: the different forms of female beauty, for instance, in the nearest approach to perfection which the purity of their taste could suggest, or the excellence of art could express, are pourtrayed in the Venus, Thetis, Juno, Pallas, and Diana, expressive of the peculiar attributes characteristic of each goddess. It required a wonderful degree of skill, and accurate observation of the effect of mind, and propensities of particular character, as enunciated by the features and form; to manage the distinct expression of them, and at the same time preserve the dignity proper to the godlike nature, requiring perfect composure and tranquillity of attitude. This search after the perfection of beauty, refined and combined from every thing that appeared the most admirable in the human form; this personification of ideal excellence, of which mankind offers but an imperfect image, became the supreme aim of every artist's genius; and has been successively taken up by the different schools of modern times, worshipped as the chief excellence by some, neglected by others, and even ridiculed as straining after a phantom.

If, with the Dutch, we consider the object and excellence of painting to consist in a close matter of fact representation of whatever in nature is presented to our view, whether elegant or homely; a painter has certainly nothing to do with this refinement of the ancients. But if painting is not rigidly confined to prose, but may have its poetry, it is then we get into the region of what the French denominate *beau ideal*, and which we find so beautifully exemplified in the exquisite remains of Grecian sculpture. It is the refinement of human nature, to the exclusion of all imperfections; impressing a sort of elevation, dignity, and intellectual grandeur, which we have delight in supposing, and would willingly believe realized. This ideal beauty, and perfect state of nature, freed from the defects and blemishes which few, if any, individual examples of beauty want, is the true basis of the great or heroic style of painting. It is the fruit of persevering study, and acute observation of nature, united with judgment to discriminate the most beautiful of every kind, and with capacity to free them from the dross of individual imperfections.

An important and difficult requisite in this art is congruity, preserving the harmony and union of the whole in all its subordinate parts. Every thing must partake of, and be consistent with, the character adopted,—a combination of excellencies not only possible but natural; for there are perfections of an incongruous nature, which, being dragged together into union, make each other ridiculous. It is a very plausible idea, but one that has given rise to more bad taste in painting than any other, that a painter who strictly follows nature must be correct; and so he will if he follows *general* nature free from individualities; but the copy of individual nature with its perfections and imperfections, such as they are, is the province of the portrait painter merely. A prejudice exists against *ideal beauty*, as if it were a desertion of reality, in order to sport in the regions of fancy and invention; but it is not so: it is simply the selection of what is beautiful in nature, to the exclusion of what is not so. It is merely choosing the most favourable point of view for our representation of nature, and clothing it in the most graceful attire. The painter tells his story like the poet, confined to accuracy and precision in substance, while the mode of expression is left to his own taste and talent for pleasing. And how much of our pleasure depends upon this is obvious to. all. The most interesting narration, anecdote, or scene, may be deprived of all its zest or merit by the mode of handling it. The painter is doubly entitled to as great latitude for the exercise of taste as the historian, and is as little bound to unadorned matter of fact, as the historian or poet to narrate in the language of mathematical demonstration.

The Greeks, with whom the best display of taste is to be sought for, adopted the practice of representing their figures either in a fanciful and more graceful attire than the usual dress of the country, or more uncovered than was at all consistent with reality. This practice furnished greater scope for the exercise of skill and genius in the delineation of the human figure, but certainly led them in time to very preposterous representations of naked philosophers, and warriors in combat, with no other covering than a ponderous helmet, a precaution which seems so needless when the rest of the body is exposed. Although the artists of Greece had the peculiar advantage of studying the human figure at their public games, and frequent practice of manly exercises, yet the usual attire of the Greeks was far from scanty, and the women particularly were very much covered, and even encumbered with drapery, as we sometimes see represented in basso-relievos.

Painting does not seem by any means to have been held in such high estimation as sculpture among the Greeks, although they were far from undervaluing either its merits or importance, as is obvious from the high honours conferred upon their eminent masters ; from the general interest taken in the competitions at the great games, where painting held a distinguished place ; and from the important influence attributed to it over the public mind, so as to occasion paintings to be considered, like the great monuments of the state, as a kind of public property. The number of painters were, however, comparatively inconsiderable to that of the statuaries, though, in proportion to the size of the state, Athens itself gave birth to more great painters than fell to the lot of many kingdoms of much greater magnitude. Pausanias enumerates one hundred and sixty-nine statuaries, and only fifteen painters, whose works he had seen and describes; but his account, though correct as an average proportion, only applies to that part of Greece through which he travelled ; for Pliny extends his enumeration to one hundred and thirty-three Greek painters, whose merits were worthy of record. The number of statues which Pausanias had occasion to examine in his journey through Greece, amounts to three thousand, which, when we consider that the Romans had already, for three hundred years, been employed in despoiling that country of its finest monuments of art, is quite surprising. He gives a particular description of many of these statues. The greater part were of marble; some of bronze ; and a few colossal ones of wood, of which the Greeks made pretty frequent use. M. de Caylus mentions having seen two statues of iron, one of them constructed of plates rivetted together with clenched nails; gold, silver, and ivory, were also used; and what of all things clearly demonstrates the energy of genius in Greece, is the circumstance that no copies appear among all the statues that have been preserved. Though frequently representing the same subject, there is no copying of one from another ; each individual statue being an original. Their portraits of private in-

dividuals were generally in sculpture, and very numerous. Accordingly, Pausanias enumerates only forty-three painted portraits, while he saw eighty-eight fresco historical pictures. Statues were not considered of such value as pictures, and sold for inferior prices ; and as some of these which have reached our day, independent of any adventitious value as objects of antiquity, are well worthy of a high price as specimens of art, we may infer what those pictures must have been which they esteemed so highly.

A Venus painted by Apelles is said to have been bought by Augustus for one hundred talents, about twenty thousand pounds Sterling. The tyrant Mnason gave about three thousand pounds for a battle piece painted by Aristides of Thebes. Nicias had the munificence to refuse sixty talents offered him by Ptolemy for his celebrated picture of the descent of Ulysses to hell, which he afterwards gratuitously presented to his native country, and was accordingly rewarded with great honours. Julius Cæsar paid eighty talents for an Ajax and Medea painted by Timomachus. The Medea was unfinished ; and as a proof that the connoisseurs of old partook of some of the absurdities of their successors in modern times, this very circumstance had the effect of greatly enhancing the value of the picture. It must no doubt be admitted, that a picture when only half-finished is sometimes in its best state, and that the finishing often proves too truly so.

Greece was for so many ages the grand and unrivalled emporium of every thing connected with taste, and the exercise of the fine arts, that it has been a matter of frequent discussion whether that excellence arose from the intrinsic genius of the people, or the accidental impetus it had so early received from the advantages of a popular government. We would say, that the history of the world has furnished no instance where so extraordinary a concurrence of every circumstance calculated to influence the development of fine taste, was realised, as in Greece. Remarkable by nature for beauty of person, the Greeks were led to appreciate its excellence, and attempt the imitation of what was constantly under their eyes. Games were established, in which the prize was given to the most perfectly beautiful ; statues were sculptured, and pictures painted of the victors, offering a subject for the exercise of genius, and a motive to stir up all the energy of emulation, as the pictures themselves became a subject for future competition. The facility of studying the human form uncovered, in their frequent games, and constant practice of the manly exercises, afforded advantages to the artists of that period, which are refused to modern nations. It roused the ambition to excel, and refined the public taste, even in that class of society to which, in our days, the very idea is a stranger; for in Greece the populace were invited, and took an animated share in the enjoyment offered to them by the exhibition of works of art. The judgment passed upon them was in a manner matter of state, and of renown to the artist whose works met with public approbation. The state and people contended with each other in honouring the successful competitor. Accordingly, the opinions of all ranks were so much consulted by artists, that they were in the practice of constantly exposing their works to public view, and attending to the observations made upon them. They had, moreover, by the means of the constant confluence of spectators assembled to see their works, an excellent opportunity of studying the manners and attitudes of the different classes, and the different effects which their pictures produced. Unless their work succeeded in

Greece. stirring the feelings of the untaught vulgar, as well as the learned, they judged that there must be a failure in some part; as there is a silent sense in every one, of the good and bad in the imitative arts, although the means of expressing it, or reasoning upon it, is only given to the learned. They thought, with Cicero, " cum ars a natura profecta sit, nisi natura moveat ac delectat, nihil sane egisse videatur."

But the extraordinary concatenation of favourable circumstances which enabled the arts in Greece to reach so high a degree of perfection, as every thing in this world has its limit, was burst asunder after the death of Alexander. Corruption fixed upon the arts, as it did on the national character and governments of that falling country. All the advantages peculiar to the nation became sterile of effect as soon as the fostering principle had withdrawn its stimulus; for it is not the possession of single qualifications, but the union of them that can rouse the vivifying spark. There are authors, who, reasoning from the principle that similar causes must always occasion similar effects, maintain, that no result so advantageous to the arts could have taken place from the prevalence of personal beauty, for instance, or from the facility afforded to artists of studying the human form at the gymnasiums, or in the constant practice of manly exercises, seeing these advantages equally exist now in Greece as in former times, without producing any such effect. But the history of the world sufficiently demonstrates how much the most distinguished qualities of our nature may lie dormant, until called into action by a favourable concurrence of circumstances. Such was the fortune that Greece experienced in the age of Pericles, when the soaring genius of the people became acted upon by every stimulus calculated to fire its ambition. Pre-eminent excellence was the result; and that not in the arts alone, but in every quality and acquirement of which human nature seems capable.

The total degradation of the arts was the work of ages. Although the spring was relaxed which had given vigour to its movements, the true principles of taste had become so firmly rooted in the Grecian character, as for a time to resist the causes that were leading to its extinction. What remained of its artists were employed not in maintaining, as their forefathers had done, the glory of their native country; but in ministering to the demands of foreign luxury. Wherever wealth, or a desire for the elegancies of life, began to create a demand for their talents, the Grecian artists eagerly sought employment; and even found the means of creating the demand where it did not before exist, by exhibiting their works, and inflaming vanity by painting the exploits of those nations whose support they solicited.

It is curious that the tide seemed at this period to set particularly towards that country whence the arts had originally emanated, as Ptolemy gave great encouragement to Greek artists; and like that unaccountable propensity of our nature, the arts seemed to have drawn towards the soil of their origin, there to expire where they first had seen the light. For in the early ages of Greece, it was from Egypt, as well as from Etruria, that the Greeks sought those acquirements which they afterwards found means to carry to such perfection. While knowledge flourished in Egypt, the Grecian youth flocked thither, as in our time, to the great seminaries of learning; but they were held in very small esteem by the Egyptian philosophers and priests, so much so as not to be judged worthy of being instructed in the sacred mysteries. The Greeks borrowed,

notwithstanding, what they could learn of these absurdities, which accounts for the very great obscurity that pervades the Greek authors as to the origin of their mythology. They seek to veil its origin, and their own ignorance of the real meaning of these legends and observances, by supplying fictions of their own, and clothing the Egyptian mysteries in fables applicable to Greece, so as to infer their origin, as founded on the heroic history of their own country; thus distorting what was already sufficiently monstrous in its Egyptian form, by adding all the absurdities of Grecian fable. While this sufficiently accounts for the preposterous nature of that mythology, it leaves us utterly unable to comprehend how a people, conscious of the delusion, and eminent for their intellectual depth and acquirements, should not only tolerate such monstrous trash, but make its observance the object of religious awe and duty,—men, who, while they sacrificed to their deities, should, at the same time, tax their artists with making them worship the pictures of their concubines. It teaches at least this lesson of humility, how very unfit a guide our reason is, when left to itself, and without the aid of revelation: for want of a better creed we are content to venerate the objects of heroic romance, the warriors and leaders of the olden time, who, seen through the veil of fable and mystery, become the usual objects of mythological worship.

Rome. We must now follow the enfeebled steps of the arts to Rome. The full tide of taste which, for so many ages, had flowed round the favoured shores of Greece, and was now fast retiring to that abyss of barbarism where, for a period equally long, it was destined to sink into utter oblivion; seemed willing, for a space, to revisit the course of its early progress. It was, however, but an emanation of the genius of Greece; for it is doubtful if the Romans can lay claim to any merit beyond that of endeavouring to copy the excellencies they had at length begun to see the value of. However much the rising power of the Roman state may have been engrossed with views of conquest solely, to the exclusion of the arts of peace, or of those acquirements cultivated by their neighbours, which were unsuitable to the austere habits of a warlike race; it is singular to find how very successfully they resisted the introduction of the ornamental arts. As no trace whatever appears for the first four centuries of their existence, of their having even given an asylum to the arts, or at all suffered the seeds of taste to be sown within their iron rule. It was not until the Romans began to despoil Greece of her treasures, and that their generals, returning to enjoy the honours of the triumph, sought to gratify their vanity by the profusion and variety of the spoils which adorned their pageant, that any specimens of the fine arts were brought to Rome; if we except the performance of Etruscan slaves, who were employed to work at the decoration of houses, even at an early period.

During the time that Rome was governed by kings, the laws of Numa were observed, which considered it as sacrilegious to have any representations of their divinities exhibited for adoration in the temples. They had some rude statues of clay, as appears by Plutarch, but merely for ornamenting their houses; and these were the workmanship of Etruscan slaves. After the arrival of the Greek artists, however, we hear no more of the Etruscans. The works of sculpture, from their more portable nature, were the first spoils of the fine arts that reached Rome, by means of every succeeding prætor or commander, as the process of subjugating Greece gradually advanced.

As the pictures were both less numerous than the works of sculpture, and as they were chiefly painted in fresco, and attached to the walls of temples and houses, the removal of them was sufficiently troublesome to defeat their purpose. The first of them found its way to Rome, from an accident, which was singularly characteristic of the very low state of knowledge of the fine arts at that time prevalent even among the higher classes of the Romans.

When the Roman general Mummius captured and sacked the city of Corinth, the works of art of every kind were scattered about as rubbish on the streets, and exposed to the licentious sport of the soldiery; the pictures they made use of as tables, which happened to bring one of them under the notice of the general; the subject was that of Bacchus, and pleased him so much, that he proposed to carry it off. As the picture was regarded as one of the public monuments, and very much valued by the Greeks, they offered a large price for its ransom, rather than be deprived of what they considered an honour to their city. The ignorant Roman, surprised at the offer of so large a sum for a mere picture, conceived, as the untaught Arabs of our day, that it must be gifted with some secret virtue; he therefore refused the price, and carried the picture to Rome, where he no doubt experienced some disappointment to find its only virtue to consist in the excellence of the artist's skill, to which his ignorance had blinded him. This accomplished Roman imposed an injunction upon the person who was charged with the transport of the picture to Rome, which might be troublesome for a carrier of our days to fulfil; namely, that if the picture was lost or injured on the way, the carrier was bound to paint one equally good.

It was about four hundred years before the Christian æra, that Greek artists began to paint in Italy. Their works were executed chiefly on plaster, the great indestructibility of which appears from what Pliny mentions of the preservation of some of them to his day.

Few works of painting are at all alluded to in the early history of Rome; and, in fact, until a love of ease and elegance had crept in, and begun to supplant the more austere habits of a nation solely bent on conquest, until the luxurious days of the emperors, decorations of any kind were considered as unbecoming of their notice. Statuary, and carvings on gems and metals, were the first species of the fine arts that obtained favour; so that the sluice once opened to admit the stream, it flowed in with constantly increasing volume. But so extraordinary was the profusion of statues in Greece, which, like a marble population, absolutely vied in number with its inhabitants, that Roman rapacity was readily supplied, without seeming to diminish, for a long time, their apparent numbers, in the great magazine of Greece.

The first native artist of Rome, whose name is recorded, was Fabius, surnamed Pictor, who lived about three hundred years before the Christian era. The account given of his performances does not say much for their excellence. Neither he nor his art were held in high estimation; for the Romans seem not only to have been quite indifferent to both, but even undervalued those persons who testified any inclination to encourage, or cultivate what appeared to them so very insignificant an acquirement. Yet their generals, on their return from conquest, found in it so ready a means of keeping their fame alive in the public mind, by exhibiting representations of their achievements; that they employ-

ed the itinerant artists of Greece to paint their battles, and hung them up in the market-places for public inspection. These were probably often indifferent enough, as it appears that the generals frequently attended in person to explain to the passengers what was meant to be represented; and to gather, themselves, whatever tribute of praise the rabble were pleased to bestow upon them. Pacuvius is mentioned as a skilful painter, whose great accomplishments, as a man of science and a poet, not only obtained esteem for himself, but went far to gain reputation for the art he practised: he is said to have contributed much towards the improvement of the Roman taste. He was followed by Turpilius, a Roman knight, and, according to Pliny's account, a good painter, remarkable for the peculiarity of painting with his left hand. Near the age of Augustus, who was the first that enriched Rome with any considerable collection of pictures, and had them publicly exhibited, there was a Roman painter of the name of Arelius, and after him Ludius, a painter of landscapes and sea-ports, who was much employed to ornament the town and country houses of the wealthy Roman citizens with trellis work. Amulus painted for Nero, who introduced all sorts of extravagances; amongst others, that Colossus of pictures, to which even the gigantic portraits of St. Christopher, which decorate the walls of German convents, must yield the palm in magnitude. It was one hundred and twenty feet high, intended as a portrait of the emperor, and painted upon cloth, from the difficulty of preparing plaster of sufficient extent of surface. This whim is supposed to have given rise to the practice of painting on canvas, which does not appear to have been in use before that period, if we except the custom of the Egyptians in painting the linen coverings of their mummies.

Historians mention Marcus Aurelius as having added to his other accomplishments that of being a good draughtsman: Labeo, the proconsul of Narbonne, was ridiculed by the Romans for condescending to seek amusement in painting. To these may be added Pinus and Priscus, which sums up the scanty catalogue of the native artists of ancient Rome.

As nearly all the works of which we have notice in history, whether in Rome or elsewhere, were the productions of Greek artists, there cannot be said to have been any Roman style of painting. Many of the performances of these itinerant artists were doubtless very indifferent, and these are what are generally attributed to the Romans; as the veneration for Grecian art occasions an unwillingness to allow that any thing inferior proceeded from their hands. Among the few pictures painted at Rome, of which the name of the artist is recorded, was the triumph of Paulus Æmilius, by Metrodorus the philosopher, whom he brought from Athens as tutor to his son Scipio. It must have been a picture of very great magnitude, if it gave a true representation of the triumph, which, for one part of the train, is said to have been attended with two hundred and fifty chariots filled with pictures and statues. This very abundant supply, which flowed from the conquest of Greece, and its colonies in Sicily, was perhaps one powerful means of paralyzing any talent for painting which might have sprung up among the Romans. So long as the demand found sufficient supply, and at the easy rate of conquest, there could be little encouragement to native artists, particularly as the Romans soon acquired skill enough to prefer the works of the ancient Greeks to any productions of their own day. The history of the arts in England and France furnish

Rome. another instance of the effect produced by a ready supply of the works of art from foreign schools.

The notion of the Greeks, as to the influence of pictures upon the public mind, was strongly taken up at Rome. Marcus Agrippa delivered an oration in favour of it, and proposed that all pictures should be considered public property, and deposited for public exhibition, so that no individual should be allowed to possess and keep a picture for private use. This policy seems to have been readily entered into, and many pictures were accordingly hung up in the market-places.

Specimens of ancient painting. As to the specimens of ancient art that have reached our day, the very small proportion is much less to be wondered at, than that any of them should have survived at all; considering how very few centuries suffice for the entire destruction of the ornamental painting of our best preserved buildings, for of that description alone are those that have been found in Italy. Of moveable pictures, such as the finer works of the Greeks are recorded to have been, no vestige has ever come to light, and probably never can. Indeed, when we consider the devastation to which Italy was exposed, and the barbarous ignorance under which that country lay for so many centuries, co-operating with the slow but sure tooth of time; it is only the singularly favourable circumstances of concealment and protection under the hermetical seal of a mass of melted rock, that could have succeeded in preserving these monuments of ancient art. But the misfortune is, that we only recover them to witness their destruction as evidence of what they were. The exposure to the air, after being buried for so many ages, soon tarnishes their colour, and destroys whatever may have existed of harmony; in fact, the very substance would have slipped from our hands, had they not been very speedily retouched, which is equally destructive of their value as evidence.

It would be a piece of injustice, in every view, to receive these specimens as testimonies of the qualities of ancient art, or a witness of the veracity of ancient authors on the subject; as they are clearly the productions of very inferior artists, (if artists they can be called,) who ornamented the walls of private houses in so inconsiderable a town as Herculaneum; and painted at Paintings at Herculaneum. a period when the art had fallen greatly from its ancient state of perfection. Yet, notwithstanding the rapid decline, and probable inferiority of the workmen, these specimens do possess traits of sufficient skill to argue strongly in favour of what the works of the more eminent artists must have been. Were we to transfer the case to our own day, and suppose the accidental discovery, at a distant period from the present time, of the very best efforts and skill of our house painters in some of the smaller provincial towns, as the only wreck of the arts left to tell the tale of our proficiency; it is to be feared, that we should scarcely come off so well as the ancients do in the comparison. We shall scarcely be able to say, as we can with truth in favour of these ancient specimens, that they are simple, correct, and in good drawing; of their merits in colouring, circumstances deny us the means to judge, as little colour could be expected to remain after being buried for nearly two thousand years under lava and volcanic ashes. They are, notwithstanding, valuable discoveries, as they have cleared up many facts connected with the manners and mode of life among the Romans. It is exceedingly probable that most, if not all, of these paintings, were merely copies by house painters of existing basso-relievos, decorating the walls of their apartments with them, exactly as we are now in the use of doing.

Those that were found in Rome were chiefly the ornamental works of baths, either in pencil or mosaic. Various collections have been published of them, and much discussion has been excited among the learned antiquaries of Italy. The piece which has principally attracted notice is called the Aldobrandine Marriage, and was found on the site of Mecenas's garden in Rome. The ancient paintings more recently discovered at Herculaneum and Portici are equally interesting. Those of Herculaneum were found painted on the walls of a temple, distributed into compartments, and representing the combats of wild beasts, real and imaginary animals, heads of Medusa, landscapes, views of houses, and architecture of various kinds; besides some historical pieces, which are the greatest curiosity of all. One represents a naked Theseus, resting on a club; he has a ring on his finger, and the *chlamys*, a sort of scarf hanging over his shoulders; between his legs lies the Minotaur, naked, whom he appears to have just killed: the body is of a human form, but the head is horned like a bull; the head is entirely seen, but the body retires in a straight line, finely foreshortened. Three little boys attend the hero, two of whom kiss his hands, and the third embraces his left arm; a virgin modestly touches the club, probably meant to represent Ariadne or Phædra, and in the air is seen another figure denoting victory. There is another picture of the birth of Telephus. A third represents Chiron, under the figure of the centaur, teaching young Achilles music. A fourth is Mercury, giving Bacchus to the nurse. The pictures found here are not all equally good: many, however, possess great merit, as to judicious composition, accurate contour, and fine colouring, which, though now much faded, was at the time of their being first brought to light as fresh as if only a few years had elapsed since they had been painted; which is perhaps to be attributed to the perfect exclusion of the air which the envelope of lava occasioned. To a certain extent, these specimens leave little doubt of the ancients having been acquainted with the leading principles of perspective and chiaro scuro, particularly if we are correct in supposing them to be copies of basso-relievos, which gave little room for a display of either.

In Stabia and Pompeia the very meanest houses seem to have been painted; and the reason why there are some paintings in the temples, theatres, and other public buildings, is, because the poverty of these bourgs, for they were not towns, did not admit of the more costly decorations of statuary and bronzes; with which it was the practice to ornament the public buildings of their towns, as well as the houses of the wealthy citizens of Rome, to the exclusion of painting on the walls, which appears only to have been resorted to when better could not be had. The very few morsels of sculpture that have been found in Stabia or Pompeii seem to prove this fact, when we find such profusion to exist among the ruins of Rome and other large cities, where, on the contrary, paintings appear to have been as rare. It seems to prove very clearly, that these paintings can have no claim to be ranked among the works of good masters, or to form any rule for judging of the state of the arts at that period; except the favourable inference to be drawn from finding such works in so insignificant a place, from which we are entitled to conclude, that those of first-rate artists must have been very superior. We find great ease and accuracy of outline, as well as much good taste in their simplicity and repose, and the display of chiaro scuro, where even the nicety of reflected lights is attended to, as is quite obvious, notwithstanding that considerable negligence is apparent in the execution : and this is a pretty conclusive fact as to their being copies. As to the colour, little can be said, nor could we have expected much from the painted walls of a village. But the mode in which Pliny discriminates the excellencies of colouring in the works of the great masters, shows that they were fully alive to all its intricacies. In discussing the merits in point of colouring of the rival pictures of Ajax, this delicate distinction is drawn by ancient critics, that the one appeared to have been fed on roses, and the other on the more substantial food of man.

As these ancient specimens were painted in fresco, it required considerable nicety to detach them uninjured from the wall ; and would have probably failed had it not been for the uncommon thickness of the plaster. The mode of proceeding was by first firmly encasing the picture in a box, before beginning to detach it ; a deep groove was then hewed out in the wall all round, so as to enable the whole mass upon which the picture was painted to be sawed off ; thin slates were then glued to the back to give it solidity. One of the pictures found at Resina is interesting, as it represents the interior of a Roman abode, with the family in various postures, and different articles of furniture in the room : we see here the style of domestic clothing in use among them, which appears exceedingly simple and loose. Another of the pictures represents a concert, which is likewise interesting and instructive. There are, besides, a great profusion of beautiful arabesques, and amusing figures in the grotesque style. Some of the manuscripts which were recovered from the lava, and are now preserved in the museum at Portici, contain a few vignettes, which are clumsy enough in point of execution, but remarkable for brilliancy of colour. There are no specimens of ancient pictures, except those preserved in this museum, upon the authenticity of which any reliance can be placed ; the avidity of gain having occasioned the fabrication of these articles of antiquarian research, to a very great extent, than which nothing can be considered as more unpardonable among the various hoaxes practised on the virtuoso. We can excuse any liberties taken with the wonted credulity of antiquaries, if it goes no farther ; but what merely tends to mislead in point of history, and for sordid motives alone, is detestable.

With the notice of these scanty remains we may close the sketch we have endeavoured to give of the ancient history of painting ; merely subjoining an enumeration of the different modes practised among the ancients, and reserving any observations on their merits, which we may have occasion to make, until we come to draw the parallel between their qualities and those of modern artists.

The more knowledge we obtain of the practice of the ancients, the more we find that there are very few things now known which they do not seem to have been equally acquainted with ; for there are wonderfully few inventions which amount to more than the revival of former discoveries. Of the various modes of painting, consisting of oil, fresco, water colours both body and transparent, mosaic, enamel, glass, porcelain, tapestry, and what the French call pastel and camayeux, there is but the first which is peculiar to modern practice ; although, even with regard to it, there is reason to suspect that the varnish used by Apelles and his successors was not very different from oil painting. If not actually in

possession, they were at least upon the very threshold, of the discovery. From the appearance of the paintings on the mummies of ancient Egypt, they must have possessed an uncommonly perfect species of oil varnish ; which completely supplied the deficiency of oil colour in their paintings. Pliny gives a description of this varnish ; but it is doubtful whether the ancients ever mixed it with the colour itself, which, strictly speaking, is what constitutes oil painting.

Until the seventh century before the Christian æra, the Greeks seem to have been confined to the simple operation of designing with only one colour, to which the colour of the ground formed a relief ; this was called by them monochromatic, and camayeux by the French, or imitation of basso-relievo in its simple shading. It is a species of painting very pleasing in its effect, if a judicious selection is made of the two colours, so as to harmonize. Some of the Egyptian hieroglyphics or picture writing is executed in this manner ; the Etruscan vases also furnish abundant examples of it, consisting of a simple coloured back ground of black or orange, upon which the figures are drawn in contrast with the ground colour. They have sometimes a little heightening of effect by sharp touches of white, a circumstance which, however, makes them cease to be monochromatic. Engraving and pencil drawing are, properly speaking, of the same species, and what the Italians call chiaro scuro drawing, as it is literally the representation of the effect of light and shade, deprived of the presence of colour. When well executed, there is a chasteness and modesty in this sort of performance which is exceedingly captivating. It was much practised by Michael Angelo, Raphael, and the great masters of those schools who did not make colouring the chief object of their pursuit. The charm of simplicity was so much increased by the use of only two colours, that when the ancients began to introduce more into their works, it was looked upon as degrading the art, and was confined at least to the use of a very few, in which case it was called polychromatic. This simplicity of colouring, which is even exhibited by the ancient specimens already alluded to, led to the idea that the ancients were not in possession of many colours. But we must not forget what the nature of these specimens are, (as probably copies of basso-relievos,) perhaps more a proof of the chasteness of their taste than of any scantiness in their knowledge of colours ; for we find both Cicero and Pliny lamenting the corruption of taste in their day, by the introduction of a gaudy mode of painting, abounding in variety of colours, more than grace and purity of taste.

In number of colours, there is probably not much difference between the ancient and modern knowledge. The ancients seem to have been possessed of some colours of which we are ignorant, while they were themselves unacquainted with some of those more recently discovered. The practice of painters upon the revival of the arts, in making a secret of their preparation of colours, has been exceedingly prejudicial to this branch of the study, as the methods of painting were then as various as the artists. The improvements in chemistry have certainly in later times enriched painters with a profusion of tints, of which, in point of brilliancy at least, no combination of the primitive colours known to the ancients could be capable. Some author, whose name we do not recollect, has taken the trouble to calculate the amount of tints which the combination of the simple colours admit of ; we should certainly have pronounced them innumerable, had he not ascertained eight hundred and nineteen to be the number of modifications. This, to a certain extent, must be fanciful, as the very nature of the thing forbids the establishing any rule of distinction, except the imperfection of the human eye, to carry the division any farther.

The colours enumerated by Pliny as in use among the ancients, amount to nine, 1st, Sinopis pontica, a sort of ochre; 2d, Parætonion, a white colour, found on the shores of Egypt; 3d, Purpurissum, a deep red; 4th, Indicus color, a fine blue; 5th, Armenium; 6th, Cinnabar; 7th, Minium; 8th, Auripigmentum, a fine green; and, 9th, Atramentum. This shows that the ancients were not ignorant of our principal colours, and might by combination have produced almost every tint. Many of their colours were so very highly priced, that it was customary for the person who commissioned the painting of a picture, to provide these particular colours, which were, 1st, Minium; and this, as appears by the paintings found in Herculaneum, they had of different degrees of intensity; 2d, Armenium; 3d, Cinnabar, of which they had two kinds, viz. the natural calx of mercury, and an artificial kind, prepared from a red species of sand found near Ephesus; 4th, Chrysocolla; 5th, Indicum; the ancients were ignorant of the origin of this pigment, being supplied with it from the east; it appears to have been indigo; and 6th, Purpurissum, a species of vermillion.

Of the encaustic mode of painting practised by the ancients, heat was the medium of application; but our information on the subject is exceedingly limited, as no specimens of that kind have reached our day, and ancient writers seem not to have bestowed such attention to the arts, as to have induced any particular examination of the practices in use regarding it. According to what Pliny says on the subject, it would appear that the colours mixed with wax were made up into crayons, and melted as used on the picture, upon which the subject was previously traced with a metal point; when the picture was finished, a waxen varnish was spread over all, in a melted state of course. By this means the colours obtained great brilliancy, and the work became protected from the injuries of the weather. After it was sufficiently dry, the surface was well polished. Various attempts have been made in modern times to revive this art, but as yet without perfect success. Indeed, the introduction of the more perfect system of oil painting, seems to supersede altogether the occasion for its re-discovery, except to gratify antiquarian curiosity. The ancients made use of encaustic painting in ornamenting their ships.

We have examples still preserved, of the ancient stucco, or fresco paintings, in the relics of Herculaneum, in which no particular is more remarkable than the very great ease of the flowing outline, which, though deeply marked, possesses all the spirit of a masterly sketch; and in fact demonstrates, not only pure taste, but an uncommon proficiency and elegance of touch. Many fine examples are preserved at Pompeii, besides what were discovered in the ancient baths of Rome; the outline, which is deeply cut, is sometimes filled up, and sometimes not. The plaster was prepared with the very greatest care, for which various articles were selected, and laid on in different coats; volcanic ashes, or terra pozzulana, was the first, and upon this a coat of calcareous matter, finely prepared, followed. Their plaster was generally allowed to dry before the paint was applied, usually consisting of black, red, or white, if brilliancy was required, to serve as a ground colour. They mixed the colours with very strong glue. The ara-

besque paintings seem to have been the favourite subject of the ancient frescos, representing capricious compositions of every variety, and generally displaying very great elegance and taste, as well as fertility of invention. They are exceedingly light and delicate; and, although painted on a plain ground, indicate, in the small details of buildings, and foreshortening of figures, no small knowledge of perspective. Raphael was much captivated by the merit of these ancient performances, and not only revived that mode of ornamental work, but made very great use of it, as his immortal works in the lodges of the Vatican testify.

For their moveable pictures, the ancients made use of wood or stone, hence the Latin term *tabula* for a picture, from whence the French derive *tableau*. They are supposed, in general, to have preferred larch-wood. They painted likewise on ivory, tracing the outline with a hot metal point. Many specimens of their paintings on glass were found at Herculaneum, and we have seen a very interesting collection lately discovered in the neighbourhood of the little town of Apt, in Provence; many specimens of which are both gilt and painted, of pure glass, and formed into globular vases of very elegant shapes. Of their painting on pottery, we have already taken notice in the mention made of the Etruscan vases.

As to the instruments of painting, they seem at first to have used the sponge, which must have been attended with many inconveniencies. It yielded to the introduction of the hair pencil, an invention so obvious, that it is not likely to have been long a desideratum in the art.

There seems no application of the art of painting in use in modern times, which was not equally practised by the ancients; even caricatures, of which several amusing specimens occur among the pictures found at Herculaneum, but frequently so gross as to forbid description. The scenic caricature, or comedy, was so powerful a political engine among the ancients, that it was quite natural for them to call in the aid of painting, for the attainment of the same object. They seem, however, to have been more abusive than witty, as we are told of a painter who, to gratify his ill humour against Stratonice, queen of Antiochus of Syria, represented her in a very indecent attitude, and exhibited the picture publicly. The queen had the good sense to despise so mean an insult. The Greeks did not even spare their gods, as Ctesilochus has represented, in one of his pictures, Jupiter dressed as a woman, and in labour of Bacchus, exhibiting ridiculous contortions, and attended by an officiating goddess. Even Apollo, the god of elegance, in another antique caricature, was represented making the most amusingly awkward endeavours to extract music from a bag-pipe, under the auspices of his instructor Pan. The merit of the performance lies in the expressions of the countenances, which are remarkably successful. The sylvan musician contemplates the efforts of his pupil with an air of mock superiority, and irritable impatience, which is most amusingly blended with the drollery of his buffoon features; while the god of harmony is obviously more sceptical as to the capacity of the instrument, than of his own musical powers.

Another species of painting, much practised by the ancients, was Mosaic, which consisted of a sort of pavement painting, with small coloured cubes of glass, marble, or wood, placed in cement. This practice, like the other branches of the fine arts, seems to have come from the East, to have been perfected in Greece, and from thence transferred to Rome. It became so prevalent in both of these latter countries, as a favourite mode of ornamenting their buildings, that remains of it are discovered wherever any vestiges of ancient towns appear. It was chiefly employed in their most indispensable luxury, the bath; and even so far was refinement carried, that moveable floors of mosaic were used by their officers in their tents when on service. Suetonius mentions, that Julius Cæsar had such pavements carried every where along with him, to exclude the damps of the northern climates which he visited. There were two kinds of mosaic, one where the morsels of marble used were pretty large, which was called *sextile*; and one where the cubes were very small, which was called *tesselated* pavement. Of this last, many magnificent specimens have been discovered in various parts of Europe, our own island not excepted. The most remarkable we have had occasion to see, is that finely restored pavement, lately discovered at Lyons. It represents a chariot and horse race, and is admirably explanatory of the practice and amusements of the Roman circus. Another valuable specimen, is the exquisite little picture of the four pigeons, at the museum of the Capitol of Rome. The pigeons are represented on the edge of a bason filled with water, out of which one of them is drinking. It is a work of singular truth and elegance, and has been frequently copied. It was found at Hadrian's villa of Tivoli, and was bought by Pope Clement XIII. for 13,000 crowns.

This species of art ran the same course of decay as the other branches; and, after its revival, was, in the seventeenth century, brought to great perfection, as exhibited in the works of St. Peter's, where the transfiguration of Raphael, and some of the finest works of the great masters, have been copied in this everlasting style. There are above ten thousand different tints made use of in mosaic work. Its greatest merit consists in the absolute indestructibility of its material, and the facility of renewing its beauty when tarnished, by polishing off and producing a fresh surface.

State of the Art during the dark Ages.

The history of the world has at all times demonstrated the intimate connection that exists between literature in general and the fine arts; in so far as regards the state of their prosperity. Dependent on the same causes, where a blight has spread over the fields of science, the fine arts are equally certain to shrink under its baleful influence. The golden ages of Athens and Rome were in this respect alike, as well as in the æras which marked the decline and downfall of their literature, in both proving equally fatal to the fine arts. It were fruitless to endeavour to assign any determined and distinct causes, as uniformly occasioning the vicissitudes observable in the state of these acquirements; as we find them flourishing and decaying under circumstances so very opposite, that what at one time seems a powerful stimulus, appears, under different circumstances, totally devoid of influence. We find, in the history of Italy, under a parallel state of affairs, the whole nation seemingly engrossed in the ardent pursuits of science and the elegant arts; while, at another time, they seem incapable of mental energy, and lie buried in ignorance and barbarism. Sometimes one species of knowledge, taste, or way of thinking, gains the ascendency; and sometimes another, without any apparent cause, either political or physical. And even when every probable cause seemed conspiring to oppress the arts, we find them flourishing; and, on the contrary, languish-

ing at another time, in spite of every endeavour to support and encourage them.

Guicciardini tells us, that, at no period since the glorious æra of Augustus, had Italy enjoyed such profound tranquillity, mildness of government, or greater promise of prosperity, than towards the year 1490. Agriculture and trade were in full activity under the encouragement of their native princes, who diffused that confidence and security, by the influence of which the genius of the country might be expected to flourish with the greatest luxuriance. The seeds may have been sown in this period of repose and prosperity, but we do not find them shooting forth with vigour, until the brilliant epoch of the next half century; when Italy was torn by intestine faction, and war raged in every corner, when the whole land had become one great field of battle, and where the powers of Europe struggled for the sceptre of the world. Neither repose nor security could be looked for, while the inhabitants were thus driven about by the vicissitudes of a doubtful war; at the mercy of that long tissue of battles, of victories, and defeats, which alternately raised and sunk the fortunes of Charles V. and Francis I. Yet this turbulent epoch was the most glorious to the fine arts. In the midst of battles, engaged even in the mortal struggle for the existence of his country, we find Michael Angelo constructing the defences of his native Florence, fighting on the ramparts, driven a fugitive from his home, and at the same time producing those marvellous specimens of art which have immortalized his name. Leonardo da Vinci, Titian, and Raphael, were the brilliant galaxy that illuminated Italy, in spite of the storm that seemed to tear it into shreds. Conjecture is here at fault; we can as little account for the phenomenon of these great masters of the art appearing, while the minds of all men were filled with conflicting passions, and tossed about by the striving powers, as that, after so long a period of barrenness, the short space of forty years should comprehend, almost exclusively, all the names that establish the glory of modern art.

It is within the course of nature that one person might have lived to see them all. Born with Titian in 1477, he might have passed his life with Leonardo da Vinci, with Michael Angelo, Raphael, Corregio, Giorgione, Tintoret, Bassano, Paul Veronese, Julio Romano, and Andrea del Sarto,—he might have outlived them all, and, even within the ordinary limits of human life, could have witnessed the close of Michael Angelo's brilliant career in the year 1563. Such was the rich harvest, which left but slender gleanings to succeeding ages. It had shot up and ripened in the midst of storms, and seemed, like the palm tree, to gather strength from the difficulties opposed to its growth, to spring into vigour in proportion to the weight employed to bear it down, " Adversus pondera resurgit." The stimulating principle which gave it life and energy to brave the adverse circumstances of the times, we can only conjecture to have been the encouragement and foresight of one enlightened family, that of the Medici.

This we may, with confidence, assert, that the encouragement of the rich and powerful is indispensable to vivify and sustain the latent sparks of genius. Adverse circumstances may, as we often see, defeat its fostering power; but, without its aid, other causes, both moral and physical, however favourable, are likely to exert their influence in vain. A taste for the fine arts is no plant of the desert, that will shoot forth unheeded, and spread its blossoms where there are none to enjoy their fragrance; nor a sturdy weed, that can struggle into vigour through rubbish and neglect: it is a plant whose seeds will remain inert until called into life by culture, and will spread into luxuriance exactly in proportion to the care taken of it. We require no other reason to account for its languor or disappearance, than the withdrawing of this culture by the cessation of encouragement. Where honour or reward fail to attend any pursuit, there will be few found to follow it.

The retrograde progress of the arts had already far advanced, notwithstanding the magnificence and splendour of the Augustan age; the dissolute and effeminate manners, joined to the degrading despotism of the successors of that emperor, helped it on in its course, when the expulsion of idolatry, which a few centuries brought about, dragged in its train those arts which had so long ministered to its support. At this crisis, moral, as well as accidental, causes seem to have combined to bear down the arts and sciences. Painting had nearly reached its lowest ebb, and was fast sinking into neglect, when, as a death-blow, the torrent of warriors issuing from the barbarous north spread devastation over the fair kingdom of Italy. They themselves, in the utter ignorance and pride of a savage state, lorded over the effeminate inhabitants of this civilized portion of Europe. Acknowledging no merit beyond the ferocity and courage of a hardy warrior, they despised the acquirements which had failed to protect the possessors from their conquering swords. It was natural to the simple manners of these bold Nordmen, to trample on and spurn that boasted superiority of knowledge, which had proved of so little avail in the hour of need. The arts and sciences were in the hands of the destroyer, and accordingly passed into oblivion along with the wrecks of the governments that had afforded them support. The Iconoclasts, moreover, instigated by mistaken notions of religion, co-operated in this blind zeal for destruction; and it is singular to reflect, that this great moral revolution, brought about by the Christian religion, which seemed to work so powerfully towards the destruction of painting, was destined, after a few centuries of darkness and neglect, to become the means of its revival.

We are not, however, to suppose, as many authors assert, that there existed a total eclipse of the liberal arts during the dark ages. Tiraboschi has collected evidence sufficient to prove, that at no period of its history was Italy totally destitute of painters, and even painters of native birth. There is every reason to suppose the curious pictures of the ancient Vatican Virgil to have been a work of the 4th century. They are executed quite in the ancient taste, are far from inelegant, and are exceedingly interesting as explanatory of ancient manners. Most of the remarkable incidents of the Æneid, Bucolics, and Georgics, are there depicted according to the existing ideas. Two ancient illuminated copies of Terence are supposed to have been executed in the time of Constantine, who, in removing the seat of empire from Rome, did more towards the destruction of the arts than any of his predecessors. He was led to this measure by the opposition of the senate and people to the reception of the Christian religion. He resolved, in revenge, to transfer the seat of government to a situation in the neighbourhood of ancient Troy, reversing the seeming course of nature, which appears to have a tendency westward in the march of dominion. In the progress of this determination, he was led, by the advantageous situation of Byzantium, to fix his empire in preference there. He proceeded forthwith to remove from Rome and Italy, not only whatever of sculpture, statuary, and painting, was valuable; but even transferred the artists to his new

4

capital, where they were to realize all the extravagant ideas he had conceived of its future grandeur. The finest buildings of Rome were pulled down, and the materials transferred to Byzantium, trusting that they would re-appear in equal splendour on their new site; but though the materials were fine, the workmen were deficient; and such was the chaos of sculptured work, that they fell into inextricable confusion, substituting the materials of one building for those of another. They tried to hide the defects by surcharging with ornament, producing a species of patchwork, of which some specimens still remain in Constantinople. St. Sophia's church was originally of this æra, though it was afterwards rebuilt by Justinian in 527. The rage for building had so seized this extravagant monarch, that he erected splendid edifices not only in Rome, Constantinople, Capua, and Naples, but likewise in the Holy Land, Egypt, and in France, as at Arles, where the remains of his palace are still visible, along with a greater number of magnificent monuments of Roman architecture than any town on this side the Alps can boast.

But however much Constantine may himself have done, the bad taste and clumsy execution introduced at this time, certainly contributed much to the subversion of the fine arts. The Goths made an attack upon Rome in the year 537, which likewise proved very disastrous to the ancient monuments. Procopius mentions, that in the assault they made upon the fortress, now called of St. Angelo, formerly the Mausoleum of Hadrian, the ample summit of which was peopled with statues of great value, the Greeks and Romans who defended the walls broke these masterly works into pieces, for the purpose of hurling them down upon the enemy. From the state in which most of the remnants of ancient art are now found, it is likely that a great proportion of these was subjected to a similar fate; more especially as the public buildings where these monuments were generally deposited, were the most of any exposed to attack, from the shelter they afforded to those who sought the protection of their strong walls.

Tiraboschi is of opinion that more destruction ensued from this cause, than from any wilfulness of the victorious Goths; as they appear to have shown considerable regard for sculpture at least, and continued to give it encouragement even after they had made themselves masters of Italy; but he doubts their having given any countenance whatever to painting, as he finds no notice taken of it. There is an enumeration given of the workmen employed in repairing and embellishing the royal palace of the Gothic monarch, in the sixth century, in which are mentioned the architects employed; the marble sculptors; founders of bronze; those who constructed the domes; workers in stucco and in mosaic: but no mention whatever is made of painters. Neither do any of the writers of the age take notice of its practice, except in the lives of the Popes, where it is recorded that some of the churches were decorated with pictures. The popes St. Sylvester and St. Leo, in the fifth century, added pictures and mosaics to the decorations of certain churches, as appears from the fresco paintings bestowed by the latter pontiff on the church of St. Paul in Rome. On the walls of the church of St. Urbain, it is still possible to distinguish traces of the frescos of the tenth century. They are now only interesting in an historical point of view, as the date 1011 appears upon them. There are some others of a similar description at Orvietto, Fiesole, and elsewhere in Italy. At Venice, for instance, the Greeks of Constantinople, in the eleventh century, ornamented that antique gem, the church of St. Mark, with the magnificent mosaics still to be seen there.

In the time of Justinian, the Bishop of Naples bestowed upon the church of St. Stephen, besides many mosaics, a particular picture of the Transfiguration, which was looked upon as marvellous. Pictures are likewise mentioned to have constituted an important article in the decoration of his own palace. So that, even at this period, it does not appear that Italy was absolutely barren of painters, however much the art may have languished.

It was not likely to have languished less under the rude government of the Lombards; but although devastation continued its course during the constant struggle which succeeded the invasion of the Goths, yet the barbarity of the Lombards proved less fatal than the rapacity of the Greeks themselves. For when the emperor Constans, in the year 663, began to follow the example of his predecessors in stripping Italy of her treasures of ancient art; he swept away every thing that he could transport to Constantinople, even the bronze covering of the roof of the Pantheon. Yet we are not without the record of pictures in the time of the Lombards; for Pope John VII. in the year 705, was employed in the decoration of some Roman churches with paintings. His example was followed by Gregory III.; besides the works in mosaic which are frequently mentioned by the writers of that period, Pope Zachary had a description of the world painted in the Lateran palace, upon a very large scale, most probably a sort of map; and the bishop of Ravenna had a series of portraits painted of himself and his predecessors in the pontificate; so that the absolute extinction of the art, at any period, seems to be a vulgar prejudice. There are many that maintain, and even some Italian authors themselves, that these examples mentioned of the practice of painting during the dark ages, were merely the remnants of some of the Greek itinerant artists who went about vending their productions. This may be the case, but there is no proof of it; and there is, moreover, decided evidence that, at that period which is generally considered as the most barbarous, painting of portraits and scriptural subjects was practised by the native Lombards themselves. Of this description is a picture in the church of St. Ambrosius, at Milan, which there is every reason to suppose a work of the seventh century. It represents the portraits of the suffragan bishops of that church.

It was towards the end of the eighth century that stained glass was introduced as an ornament to church windows. Every succeeding pope sought to surpass his predecessor in the decorations of their favourite churches, in the variety and profusion of brilliantly coloured glass, rich carved work, or fresco representations of Scripture subjects, rude enough it must be allowed, but still we owe to this fashion the preservation of the art during a period of comparative barbarism. Of the numerous list of popes who sat on the chair of St. Peter during the ninth and tenth centuries, there is not one in whose praise it is not recorded that he ornamented certain churches with mosaics and pictures. The Abbate Tiraboschi quaintly observes, that as very few of the pontiffs were themselves ornamental to the church, they never failed to endeavour to make up for the deficiency, by substituting whatever embellishment of works of art they could procure.

As to the eleventh century, we derive from the same source, (the chronicles of ancient churches,) abundant evidence of the practice of painting at least, however small was the merit of the execution; particularly in the chronicle of the celebrated convent of Monte Casino, and in the account given of the rebuilding of the Lateran palace in the twelfth century, which is particularly said to have been ornamented with pictures. The practice was not confined to Rome and its neighbourhood: for it seems to have extended to all the different parts of Italy, and even to have constituted a trade of exportation. The demand for pictures created by the newly established churches which daily arose in the different quarters of Europe, as the light of Christianity progressively diffused itself, gave full employment to the Italian and Greek artists, skilled in the hackneyed subjects of Scripture history.

The black Madonnas, and barbarous effigies of holy men, so profusely manufactured for the uses of the devout Catholics of this early period, were probably copied from the works of these Italian artists, as they seem all to have been imitated from one pattern. The incongruity of representing the Virgin as a negress, giving her three arms, and heightening the hideousness of her black countenance by a gilded back-ground, is quite overlooked in the veneration which great antiquity has acquired for these pictures. These extraordinary productions are now chiefly confined to the followers of the Greek church, and are to be found very abundantly in Russia and the Crimea, where they are held in great veneration. There are some few specimens in Italy and the bigoted quarters of Germany; but even there, they begin to change their character from the revered emblems of worship, to become simply objects of antiquarian curiosity. Dr. Clarke mentions, from some specimens he saw in the earliest churches of the Holy Land, that these were the paintings which the first Christians worshipped. As carved images were incompatible with the doctrines of the Christian faith, the first propagators of the Greek church, who came into Russia, brought with them pictures of the saints, of the Virgin, and of the Messiah, probably in the tenth century. " To protect these holy symbols of the new faith from the rude but zealous fingers and lips of its votaries, in a country where the arts of multiplying them by imitation were then unknown, (Dr. Clarke observes, that) they covered them by plates of the most precious metals, which left the features alone visible. As soon as the messengers of the Gospel died, they became themselves saints, and were worshipped by their followers. The pictures they had brought were then suspended in the churches, and regarded as the most precious relics. Many of them preserved now in Russia, are considered as having the power of working miracles. It would then necessarily follow, that, with new preachers, new pictures would be required.

The Russians, characterized at this day by a talent of imitation, though without a spark of inventive genius, follow not only the style of the original painting, but the manner of laying it on, and the materials on which it was placed. Thus we find at the end of the eighteenth century, a Russian peasant placing before his *Bogh* a picture purchased in the markets of Moscow and St. Petersburg, exactly similar to those brought from Greece during the tenth; the same stiff representation of figures which the Greeks themselves seem to have originally copied from works in mosaic; the same mode of mixing and laying on the colours on a plain gold surface; the same custom of painting upon wood; and the same expensive covering of a silver coat of mail; when, from the multitude and cheapness of such pictures, the precaution at first used to preserve them is no longer necessary."—"Many of these absurd representations are said to be the work of angels. In the Greek church, they followed the idols of Paganism, and have continued to maintain their place. They are one of the first and most curious sights which attract a traveller's notice ; for it is not only in their churches that such paintings are preserved ; every room throughout the empire has a picture of this nature, large or small, called the *Bogh*, or god, stuck up in one corner, to which every person who enters offers adoration, before any salutation is made to the master or mistress of the house." In the myriads of idol paintings dispersed throughout the empire, the subjects represented are various. Little can be said of their merit, as they are more remarkable for singularity than beauty. In the churches are seen the representations of monsters with many heads, and such a strange assemblage of imaginary beings, that they might be supposed Pagan, rather than Christian, temples. The Virgin is represented in various ways, and each have their particular votaries. There is the Virgin with the bleeding cheek, and the Virgin with three hands, both most probably originating in accident or ignorance, although the Russians themselves narrate some foolish legendary miracles on the subject.

The portrait of the Virgin which the vulgar in Italy believe, and the priests do not hesitate to assert, to be the production of St. Luke, is of the same school, or even later, if we are to judge from the mode of painting. However, as might be readily supposed, it surpasses in the power of working miracles all the multifarious editions of the Madonna. It is maintained by many authors, that this picture, attributed to the Evangelist, was the production of a Florentine painter of the name of Luke, who lived in the eleventh century, and whose works were deposited in the church of St. Maria dell' Imprimeta. Tiraboschi, however, in his *Storia della Literatura Italiana*, proves that this could not have been the case, as he finds the picture of St. Luke alluded to in authors whose works are considerably anterior to the eleventh century. This accurate historian finds that he can go no farther, and leaves the authenticity of the Evangelist's accomplishments as a painter, as open to conjecture as ever. There is less known of the private circumstances of St. Luke than of the other evangelists. St. Paul calls him, " Luke, the beloved physician ;" the scope of which appellation was probably more analogous to that of philosopher than we understand by the term physician. At all events, he appears to have been a learned man, and might have been an artist, although the picture attributed to his pencil leaves little doubt of a much more recent origin. The style of St. Luke's Gospel is considered to demonstrate greater purity and superior learning than that of the other three, which may be attributed to his longer residence in Greece, and more intimate acquaintance with the learned Gentiles. And we have already shown, that learning was considered in Greece as the indispensable qualification of an artist, so as to render them generally concomitants. The tradition of his having been a painter is of very early existence in the writings of the Fathers ; and that he had frequent opportunities of seeing and being acquainted with the blessed Virgin, the many particulars he narrates leave little reason to doubt ; which, joined to the opportunities he had of seeing works of art in Greece, removes at least any extravagance from the supposition that he might have painted a portrait of her.

After the train of evils which had for so long a period deluged Italy began to subside, when the natives of that country, worn out by oppression, felt the independence of nature stirring under the yoke, they soon discovered the possibility of shaking it off. The impulse became epidemic and simultaneous. In various quarters tyranny began to shrink into its shell, and free republican states were formed. The citizen could regard his property as his own, and exerted himself to increase it ; wealth flowed in, and brought along with it its usual concomitant, a desire for luxuries. Fortunately for the arts, munificence took the turn of embellishing the churches, as a means of extending fame, and at the same time of doing an acceptable service to the priesthood ; the priests in their turn lavished the easy requital of indulgences, and expiation of those crimes and violences which the turbulent manners of the times exposed the higher classes to fall into. This dawning of encouragement was not without its effect in preparing the way for the revival of a better taste. The emulation of the wealthy excited the invention of artists to gain favour ; and they obtained a fortunate opportunity of extending their knowledge from the increasing intercourse with foreign nations to which the crusades gave rise. They were led to borrow refinement from the elegancies and luxuries of eastern manners, to extend their observation, and gradually to improve their taste ; and, above all, they had the stimulus of an entirely new subject, to exercise their genius upon ; namely, the triumphs of Christianity. " Their religious persuasion, in favour of statues and pictures, afforded a new mine of art in the subjects of Christian story : they were desirous of ornamenting their churches with pictures and statues, upon the plan of Christianity, and there were no works of this kind in a better state in other countries than in their own. They could not now, as they had done before, in the time of the old Romans, bury and suffocate the efforts of their own people, under the more perfect arts and artists imported from Greece. The Greeks were now no better than themselves ; so that, at this time, the arts set out upon the true footing in Italy, and in all their long series of artists, from the oldest and worst to the latest and best of them, we see that every man was in his time taken for a prodigy, and his works considered as the utmost stretch of the human capacity. The artist, and the age for which he painted, were so fitted to the weakness of each other, that admiration was kept constantly alive during the whole successive progress, from barbarism to perfection. The public grew up in judgment and taste in the same progressive manner that the artist did in his practice. Another particular of the greatest consequence to them was, that there was no vicious decaying art at that time in any nation, which might be imported into Italy, to mislead and corrupt the people into the search of ornaments and fripperies, before they had regularly and solidly employed themselves upon the foundation and substance of art. This people had therefore every thing to favour them in their growth ; and they accordingly did arrive, step after step, to that degree of strength and maturity, which justly entitled them to have been the admiration of Europe." Barry's *Inquiry*.

Revival of Painting.

We have now traced the ancient history of painting from its earliest dawn, through all the migrations and vicissitudes of its progress towards perfection, and its subsequent decay. We have seen it set in the troubled ocean which overwhelmed the Roman Empire, and, after languishing in the ages of barbarism and ignorance, now again indicating the twilight of its renewed existence. An important change had taken place in the moral world, under the influence of which we are now to see the arts called into view; hitherto they had been subservient to the purposes of heathen worship, and employed, almost exclusively, in ministering to the absurdities of pagan mythology; while they rise again under the auspices of the Christian religion. Instead of imaginary deities and improbable legends, the subjects of the pencil are now to be drawn from the remarkable history of the chosen race, or the incidents of our Saviour's life, and the lives of the first ministers of our faith. The wild fables of the heathen creed did not hesitate to represent the objects of their worship, under circumstances that would have been degrading even to human nature, and giving way to sensuality and vices that would have disgraced the creatures of this inferior world; these, and the fictions of romance, were the subjects which occupied the genius of the ancient artists. But in those of Christianity, even man is always represented in an interesting situation; he is placed where the soul is raised, and moral nature subjected to trials. We see the triumphs of mind over body, and the display of that humble fortitude and resignation which it is the peculiar excellence of our blessed faith to inspire; instead of the unmeaning dreams of mythology, or the vapouring feats of romance.

It is no doubt true, that painters have nevertheless continued to be drawn to the representation of mythological subjects, and many of the finest productions of modern art are of this description. A very obvious reason can be assigned in the temptation and scope afforded to fancy, and particularly in the opportunity admitted of displaying skill in the naked and voluptuous, which does not suit the gravity of scripture history. How far these attainments are counterbalanced by the sacrifice of probability, and the interest excited by the representation of true history, may admit of doubt. An eastern tale, which we know to be the mere sport of fiction, may amuse, but it never can exercise those powers over the judgment and feelings, which the affecting incidents of reality so readily call forth. The excellence of art may fascinate the eye as much in the one case as in the other, but it must renounce all pretensions to the highest and noblest sphere of painting. Where mere fiction is the theme, it must step down from the rank of a sublime, to that of a simply pleasing art.

Dante and Boccaccio give Florence the credit of being the mother and restorer of the fine arts in Italy, but there are many other cities which do not willingly admit of this precedence. Bologna, particularly, and Siena, boast of having had painters of as great antiquity and merit as Cimabue, by whom painting was first brought into notice in Florence. Venice lays claim to the same merit, and doubtless other towns, both in Italy and beyond the Alps, have similar pretensions. As the resuscitation of learning and the liberal arts was prepared by causes of general influence, long and silently working out their effect; so was the diffusion very generally spread, and nearly simultaneous over that portion of Europe predisposed to yield to its operation. Among the older Italian writers, the question of priority in the study of the arts is a subject of bitter controversy, like the contest excited among the Grecian cities for the honour of having given birth to Homer. Champions have arisen in defence of the primacy of each of the different Italian states, who claim the honour of reviving the arts; and each, as

might be expected, boasting of having put all doubt on the subject to silence.

But as it is clear that Italy never was absolutely deprived of pictures or painters; and that, although there seems, during the whole period of the dark ages, not only to have been Greek painters practising there, but likewise native Italian artists, who competed with them for employment; we cannot correctly say that there was any distinct revival about which to contend. The art began to improve generally, and at the same time, wherever it was practised, so soon as the circumstances of the times held forth any encouragement; which, doubtless, would be more or less favourable to some states than to others. And as Florence, in particular, was happily situated in this respect, the effects naturally showed themselves more prominent. Therefore, although, perhaps, not strictly entitled to the name of Restorer of the Fine Arts, Florence decidedly took the lead in this great event.

However much the arts may have shot up in various quarters of the world, in consequence of existing circumstances propitiatory to their success, we still find that Italy is the favourite soil, where art has never failed to spring up as an indigenous plant, so soon as the obstacles to its growth are removed. Greece had its glorious age under Pericles, but the sun once set, has never risen again; while every tempest that has passed over Italy, has, like the winter storm, given place in due season to the genial influence of reviving nature. The field again began to show its verdure, and invite that cultivation which should enable it to bear fruit. With the first dawn of European history we find the Etruscans the only possessors of the fine arts. After oppression had laid waste the field, the flowers again sprung forth under Augustus. Then followed the overwhelming tide of northern barbarity. No sooner had it passed away, than the seeds which lay dormant in their native soil, sprung up afresh, and hastened to maturity, under the auspices of Leo the Tenth. The cultivation of the arts, no doubt, became general, but it was this land of genius that sent forth her artists to light up the latent sparks of taste in every quarter of Europe.

The Abbé du Bos has no difficulty in accounting for this pre-eminence of Italy, in matters of taste, from physical causes alone, and chiefly from the influence of climate. It is singular, that a notion so replete with absurdity, and which contradicts itself at every step, should have found so many followers. That climate, which is ever the same under the same latitude, should at one period be propitious, at another malign, that it should be so various in its effects upon those acting under its influence, the artists at one time rioting in all the extravagancies of fancy, at another plodding with cold and spiritless formality, and the foggy Hollander competing in excellence with the native of serene Italy, are contradictions which will not readily be admitted. But the prevalence of this opinion on the Continent is quite of a piece with the silliness of their belief as to the malign influence of the climate and coal fires of Great Britain. According to their idea, any stray spark of genius or taste that may have wandered to Britain, becomes effectually neutralized by the baneful influence of our atmosphere; our tempers are brutified, and our spirits so sunk, that in the fatal month of November, we have great difficulty in supporting the continuance of existence. It is not surprising that authors who gravely assert and reason upon such absurdities, should believe in the influence of climate, in rearing up genius as it does the native plants of the soil.

That movement of impatience so discernible in many parts of Italy towards the close of the thirteenth century, first gained vent in Tuscany, and speedily caught, like wildfire, wherever the public mind was excited by the longings for liberty and improvement. In matters of art, the productions of their own time soon fell into disrepute; they began to improve the basso-relievos destined to ornament the monuments of the wealthy. The manufacturers of Madonnas, finding the sale of their commodities flag, the old patterns despised as stale articles, saw the necessity of changing their style. Artists set about new efforts. In the mean time, the furious struggles of the Guelphs and Gibelins had thrown every thing into confusion, and so much the better, as it prepared the mass to ferment and change its nature.

We shall accompany the first steps of the revival of painting, with reference to Italy in general, as the art was considerably advanced before there was so marked a difference in the style and objects of the pursuit as to point out the distinction of individual schools. Similar features marked the early productions of Italian artists, wherever the art began to show itself; they are the works of the same class, pursuing the same route, and reaching, generally, the same state, which was far from excellent. They are all equally cold, dry, stiff, and awkward, improving as they advanced in experience, some more and some less, but still in the same predominating style of wooden rigidity. If we consider Cimabue as the father of painting in Florence, we find him anticipated by many years in Siena, and, but a few years after, Van Eyck opened a school in Flanders, and changed the whole system of painting, by the introduction of oil as the medium of applying the colours. Gio. Bellini flourished at the same period in Venice, and Andrea Mantegna in Lombardy.

There is a picture in Siena of the Virgin, bearing the date of 1221, which is nineteen years before the birth of Cimabue. It is painted by Guido of Siena. Its principal merit is the date and name, as it is the earliest instance of that practice among painters; otherwise the merit of the execution was little advanced beyond the barbarism of its predecessors. An Italian writer observes, that it was only fit to frighten children. There is another picture, attributed to the same Guido, and one at Assisa, by Giunta Pisano, dated 1236. Guido of Siena had a pupil, Ducio de Boninsegna, who excelled his master very far in the art; as he painted pictures of great size, both in fresco and mosaic, which are considered very interesting in the history of the art. The P. della Valle, in his *Lettere Sanesi* gives a detailed account of all these ancient artists of Siena.

They show pictures at Bologna of a similar antiquity, painted by natives of that town. Some of them are singular, from being painted on gilt canvas. Statues and sculpture of ancient workmanship still existed in Italy, but the artists were as yet blind to their merits. The first to burst the bonds, and grasp at something better, was Nicolas Pisano, who, in the year 1230, was attracted by the beauty of an ancient sarcophagus at Pisa, containing the body of Beatrice, mother of Countess Matilda. The subject was the story of Hypolitus, which he studied as the model by which to improve his style. The merit of the attempt began to show itself, and obtained for Nicolas extensive employment in various parts of Italy, in ornamenting with basso-relievos the monuments of the great. The admiration and celebrity of his works drew, as usual, many imitators, from a desire to share in the profits. Ancient works were sought for, and the advantage of studying them generally acknowledged. Nicolas fell far short of what he aspired to; but still, though his approach to ancient excellence was distant, he trod the same path with these great artists, and struck the first blow at the foundation of barbarism; for the reformation or advance of every art depends upon striking out some new maxim, which, adopted and worked upon by others, produces a general change of ideas, and a new theatre for the efforts of genius. This was the great merit of Nicolas, joined to the talent of being a good architect and able designer. He was followed by a few others, who made some slight progress in the art, though still adhering to a very barbarous style, as appears by the subject painted by one of them, of Christ upon the cross. He embellished his subject by representing the Virgin as placed at the extremity of one of the arms of the cross, and two other figures issuing from the other arm. There are several works of this description to be seen at Assisa, painted in fresco, of a wretched dry wooden style, but still with some attempts at expression, and a better disposition of the draperies than what was attained by their predecessors.

We have had an opportunity of seeing, in Germany, many singular specimens of such ancient monkish conceits, which were, no doubt, in these barbarous days, regarded as prodigies of ingenuity. Amongst others, there is an ancient picture of a crucifixion, where the arms of the cross terminate in a multitude of hands; on one side, tearing asunder and destroying most obscure emblems of the various sins of the human race, and on the other, assassinating death, and strangling a multitude of little objects, meant to represent the powers of darkness, though far more resembling a swarm of rats struggling in a trap. There was at Constance an ancient painting of the conception of the Virgin, a subject of all others the least adapted to the painter's art. An old man is represented seated on a cloud, from whom a beam of light issuing, penetrates a dove that flutters in mid air. At the end of the beam appears a large transparent egg, in which a fine boy, tied up in swaddling clothes, with a gold fringe of glory around his head, is seen lying. Below is the Virgin, in an arm-chair, with her mouth open, ready to swallow the egg. A sublime and dignified idea of Omnipotence! but such was the barbarous taste of the times.

As the custom gained ground of filling their churches with pictures and monuments, that class of artists who employed their talents in illuminating manuscripts began to find it more profitable to engage in works of greater size, and yielded readily to the increasing demand for frescos. Although this circumstance greatly augmented the number, it was rather detrimental to the merit and style, of the artists; as they were naturally led to transfer the pinched littleness of their former practice to the greater works on the walls of churches, so totally unfitting to the minute pencilling of the manuscript painter. There is, accordingly, little merit in any of these early productions; but we must respect their efforts, when we reflect that these primitive artists were the laborious pioneers who prepared the way for the revival of the arts in all their splendour.

It will be necessary, for the sake of perspicuity, in running over the history of modern art, to adopt the usual division of the various schools into which painting naturally divides itself, both in respect of style and locality. A school, when applied to the fine arts, means

Florentine
School.

that distinctive class of artists, who, having followed the same style of painting, partake in any respect of a common character, either as to origin, locality, particular taste, or mode of practice ; or, in a narrower point of view, who follow the mode, rules, and principles of art, introduced by a particular master. They are often distinguished by the names of the great masters in whom the style originated ; as the school of Raphael, of Michael Angelo, Titian, Rubens, or of the Carraches ; but it is more usual to take their denomination from the country where they were first established. It is equally applicable to every branch of the fine arts, as sculpture, architecture, and music. The modern schools of painting are usually distinguished into nine.   1. Florentine ; 2. Roman ; 3. Venetian ; 4. Lombard ; 5. Flemish ; 6. Dutch ; 7. German ; 8. French ; and, 9. English schools. This is no doubt somewhat an arbitrary division, and capable of modification, but we shall, for the sake of conveniency, follow it.

The Greeks adopted a similar system in distinguishing the different classes of their artists, for which, from the apparent uniformity of style, so far as our information extends, there seemed to be less occasion than when the art, upon its revival, took a new and a higher flight. There were but three schools of painting in Greece, the Athenian, Sycionian, and Asiatic ; and, although differing very slightly in style, nevertheless contending warmly for pre-eminence in reputation. In fact, this sort of *esprit de corps*, in modern times, not only kept up the distinctive character, but, by the stimulus to emulation, contributed in a remarkable degree to the general improvement of the art. There was not only an ardent competition for excellence among the individual masters, but the fame of the school to which they belonged excited feelings of rivalship, which called forth every exertion to support its reputation. There was a feeling of glory in adding to the credit and estimation of his alma mater, that made the efforts of each individual more zealous than if striving alone to rear the fabric of his own reputation. This sort of emulation among the different schools tended to counteract the mean and grovelling sentiments of personal rivalry, and to promote feelings of a more generous cast ; a desire to second the endeavours, instead of to thwart the progress, of those who laboured in the same vineyard with themselves.

Florentine School.

Florentine
School.

We have already anticipated the infant state of the arts at their revival in Florence in the course of the thirteenth century. The various branches of painting were cultivated with success, and, meeting with the judicious encouragement of some enlightened citizens, the Florentine school soon took the lead in that course in which it was destined to hold so distinguished a part. The particular character of this school, when arrived at maturity, under the genius of Michael Angelo, is accused of a certain dryness and deficiency in the richness of colouring, a want of ampleness and majesty in the draperies, and of delicacy of expression : its triumph, on the contrary, is in design, truth, historical accuracy, with grandeur and profound learning in the science of anatomy and the human figure, and skill in that difficult branch of perspective called foreshortening. The style of this school was formed under the auspices of the family of Medici, who were so instrumental in the revival and encouragement of learning as to make Florence the focus from whence the light of literature was again diffused over the world. This favoured city had to boast

at the same epoch of such geniuses as Dante, Boccaccio, Petrarch, and Machiavel ; and of artists, the not less learned Leonardo da Vinci, Michael Angelo, and Fra Bartolomeo, who lived among them, and took the impression of that great galaxy of taste and talent. The Florentine school was not satisfied with the simple copying of nature as presented to our eyes ; these learned artists sought to fix the principles upon which the effects depended, and to demonstrate the precepts to be followed, in order to produce with certainty the excellencies aimed at. We have a remarkable testimony of the laborious and profound research into the philosophy of the art, with which they accompanied their practice, in the very valuable work of Leonardo da Vinci on painting. A certain coldness and exaggerated action was the natural result of this particular bent, in so far as regarded the followers of these scientific luminaries of the Florentine school. They were considered as the sole guides worthy to be followed, from admiration of their genius, and veneration for their superior learning. But by this means, instead of becoming the allies and expounders of nature, they intervened betwixt nature and her students, and hid from their observation her more delicate beauties. Their followers applied themselves more to obtain a knowledge of their masters than to study nature, the real object of the art.

This could not fail to lead to a rapid deterioration ; accordingly, the great æra of this school lived and died in a manner with its founders, and was of very short duration.

The earliest of the Florentine masters who made the important step of shaking off the trammels of established style was Cimabue ; although, in all likelihood, instructed by that class of Greek and Italian masters whom the Senate of Florence had drawn to their city for the purpose of encouraging the arts. He had the boldness to consult nature. So much were the people astonished at the grandeur of a colossal picture which he painted of the Madonna, surrounded by angels, nothing of the kind having appeared before to equal so high a flight of genius, that they accompanied the transportation of this picture from Cimabue's house to the church with shouts and music, like a triumph. His works, although they called forth the admiration of his contemporaries, were, when compared with the subsequent attainments of the art, very rude indeed. They were stiff, dry, and monotonous, but with somewhat more of truth than his predecessors. He excelled particularly in the countenances of old men, where some expression, though of a hard severe kind, was discernible ; he had little pretension to grace or ease of any kind, and his prim starched madonnas and angels, can rarely boast of any beauty. Cimabue was notwithstanding, a man of aspiring genius, and aimed at perfections far above the grasp of his contemporaries. There are two colossal madonnas of this master at Florence, painted in a grand style ; but his talent is displayed to better purpose in his fresco paintings at the church of Assisa, which represent various subjects of sacred history. These are conceived in a bold style, and disposed with good effect ; they are likewise colossal, and possess considerable vigour of colouring. The applause which attended Cimabue's labours stirred up a desire for improvement, and was a great means of removing the languor which had so long settled on the art.

His scholar, Giotto, took a different view of the subject from the grand and severe style of his master ; preferring gracefulness and ease of outline, with a more delicate style of colouring. The sharp elongated hands and straight pointed feet, seemingly so ill adapted for

Florentine
School.

Cimabue.

Giotto.

the support of the figure; the ghastly staring eyes, which still partook of the barbarous taste, began to disappear under the pencil of Giotto. He is reported to have been a shepherd boy, and to have been discovered by Cimabue as he employed himself scratching upon a slatestone the figure of a sheep, in which he exhibited an address indicative of strong natural genius. And, much to the honour of Cimabue, whom Giotto was destined to excel, he obtained permission to take the boy under his own guidance, and trained him up in all the learning of the day. In his works, Giotto distinctly shows that he had not seen in vain the morsels of ancient sculpture preserved at Florence, and particularly in the throw of his draperies, which partake of the ancient taste. He painted at Assisa a series of pictures, descriptive of the life of St. Francis, where it is singular to observe the progressive improvement of the artist. As he advanced in his subject, we discover a more graceful composition, with increasing address in the execution; he seems to have taken courage with every additional stroke of his pencil, to aim at bolder flights and more vigorous expression, particularly in a picture, where a man, in the frenzy of thirst, throws himself upon a spring of water, which he seems that moment to have discovered.

Although Giotto's pictures still partook of the confined awkwardness of the age, and the great imperfection in the extremities of the figures, yet, as a first step towards improvement, he discovers his having been aware of the defect, as, where it is practicable, he never fails to conceal the feet and hands under the drapery of his figures. His works were in very great request in Italy, so that we find the same subject often repeated in different churches. They are easily distinguished from the dry angular performances of his predecessors, by an improved softness of colouring and outline, and by an air of graceful ease, the very reverse of which was the character of the earlier works. He was the first painter, after the revival of the art, who employed his pencil on portrait.

It was in the time of Giotto that the first discovery was made of the Etruscan vases. The superior excellence of the drawings with which many of them were ornamented seems to have excited very great astonishment, so much so, that they doubted the possibility of their being the productions of human genius. They despaired of ever being able to approach such elegance and perfection of drawing; for they do not seem for some time to have been aware in what the great merit of these performances consisted, though conscious of their superiority over what they were accustomed to see; nor how they were to set about attaining such grace and truth of design. Giotto, whose name properly was Ambro Giotto Bandone, possessed greater discernment, and seems at last to have succeeded in rousing the genius of painting from its stupor, as, towards the close of the fourteenth century, the art began to be assiduously cultivated in various cities of Italy. Though somewhat misdirected, a taste for its productions became, notwithstanding, very general, so much so, that we find it employed to every purpose of embellishment, however incongruous it might be with the real object of painting. It was liberally bestowed on the different articles of domestic furniture; beds, tables, chairs, every thing was painted, altars uniformly, and, in short, painting became a necessary appendage to works in wood.

This fashion gave rise to the barbarous mixture of sculpture and painting, which still ornament the altar-pieces of some of the more ancient churches of the Continent, by introducing painting into the minute compartments of the laborious gothic carved work which cover the interior walls. Following the same idea, where the sculptured wood was wanting, the pictures were still subdivided in an architectural manner, either by wooden pillars and pilasters, or by substituting the representation of them in painting. Many of these tall fabrics of mixed work surmounting and surrounding the altars, have a very grotesque appearance; being divided into various compartments by a confusion of arched and pillared architecture represented in perspective, with doors and windows so glaringly unsuitable to the size of the figures that represent the inmates of the building. A palace or a temple is generally the subject, and often of so exceedingly accommodating a disposition, as to display the outside as well as the inside at the same time. Friezes and pediments are represented, surmounted on the outside by statues, while the narrow compartments of the interior are crowded with groupes of cramped figures; both of so equivocal a nature, that, were it not for the unconcern of the statues above, and the exceedingly unhappy and morose countenances of the holy men painted below, who seem to fret under their constraint, it would be difficult to discover that they were meant to be of a different nature. We have, however, seen some Virgin's heads in these antique pictures, far from deficient in beauty. The gilding was as profusely bestowed on the figures as on the architecture; but the figures possessed this advantage over the architecture, that a scroll issuing from their mouths, disclosed the often very doubtful circumstances of their apparition, while the profusion of arches, pediments, and little pillars, had the exceedingly difficult task of explaining their own purpose and use. The gothic character of the letters renders the conversation of these holy men somewhat troublesome to follow, otherwise there is frequently a sort of burlesque incongruity betwixt the composure and resignation of the sentiments expressed, and the dissatisfied uncomfortable appearance of the persons themselves; accompanied with a quaintness of language that is exceedingly diverting.

By degrees the tiny columns were omitted, so as to leave the figures a little more at liberty, and what till then seemed a mere appendage of the wood work, now assumed the importance of an altar-piece. But still, so difficult is it to shake loose the trammels of custom, that, when the division of compartments was abandoned, they did not at the same time see the propriety of confining the subject to one scene. We find different scenes going on in the same picture, saints brought together who have no connection in their history, and who, moreover, perform their various parts with perfect unconcern, as if it were possible, placed as they are, not to see each other. The subject is communicated as in a law paper, item by item, with minute accuracy, but devoid of all feeling and elegance. There is no sympathy excited betwixt the spectators and the personages of the picture; even the subordinate figures themselves seem to witness with abundant composure the deeds transacting under their eyes, which in nature would call up the strongest emotions. They seem to stand as if placed there merely to fill up the pageant. Sometimes we have the preposterous idea of the same person represented as carrying on the actions of different periods of life at the same time; and sometimes the whole history of their lives is depicted, from the cradle to the grave, on the same canvas, like the shield of Achilles.

6

In fact, the painters of the fourteenth century thought that they never could load their subject too much, adding every thing which they conceived could in any way tend to the elucidation of the history represented. Deficiency in the power of painting expression was often supplied, as we have mentioned above, by the figures themselves narrating in written words what the art despaired of conveying by the pencil. Gilding was substituted for brilliancy of colour, and as a glory of light was almost always required to encircle the heads of their saints, recourse was had to burnished metal, so that the heads appear as if placed on a brazen trencher. Even the ground of the picture was often wholly gilt when great magnificence was desired ; so natural is it for ignorance to confound the rich with the beautiful, or rather to suppose that nothing can be beautiful which is not at the same time rich. Hence, the effigies of their saints all shine with gold and with fictitious jewels and baubles of every kind, which the painters of that day thought it necessary for the dignity of their art to transfer to their pictures. It is singular how reluctant the taste of that age was to abandon this false view of daubing their pictures with gilding, which necessarily destroyed any effect the colours might be able to produce. It was not entirely banished until the beginning of the sixteenth century, for we find even Raphael, in his picture of the Fornalina, did not hesitate to introduce a little gilding in her drapery.

According to Baldinucci, Giotto received very substantial encouragement from the princes of the age, with whom his talent was in great request. The Cardinal Gaetano paid to him 800 gold crowns for the picture he painted for the altar of St. Peter's ; and for his picture of St. Peter in the boat he is said to have received 2200 gold crowns. If this be accurate, it appears that both the ancient Greeks and the sub-ancient Goths, valued painting at a higher rate than it is held in our day. Giotto painted a portrait of himself by means of a mirror, which he exhibited at Florence, and likewise a picture of his friend and contemporary Dante ; for Giotto was likewise a poet and a man of learning, though originally but a shepherd boy.

Giotto had various followers, who painted much in the same manner ; and, as often happens, his very excellence was a means of retarding the progress of the art, as his successors were diffident of ever being able to do any thing better, and therefore aspired no higher than to the power of imitating his works with facility. They were numerous, and many of them possessed considerable merit ; but as our subject is the progress of the art, which remained stationary notwithstanding the efforts of these painters, it were needless to push our inquiries farther, than to mention the names of those who principally obtained a reputation as artists. Boccaccio mentions the greater part of them in the eighth day of his *Decamerone* ; and perhaps to this circumstance, fully as much as to their talent, we owe the preservation of the names of Buffalmacco, the facetious painter ; of Orcagna, and several others. Giotto's own pupils were, Stefano, who was called the ape of nature ; his son Tomasso, one of the closest imitators of Giotto, so as to obtain the surname of Giottino ; Taddeo Gaddi, of whom some pictures remain at Florence, and who excelled in colouring. There were several others, whose works still remain at Florence and Pisa, but they are only curious in an historical point of view, being all inferior in merit to their leader Giotto.

The art, indeed, which had dropped into a sort of second infancy, began to flag, and threaten a premature death, had it not been for the protection of one enlightened family, to whom it owed its preservation in the first place, and its subsequent rapid strides towards the attainment of perfection. The house of Medici had begun, from the class of merchants, to work its way, through the medium of riches, to hold an important and distinguished rank in Europe. The wisdom of this ambitious family, aspiring to the sovereignty of Florence, was in nothing more conspicuous than in their munificence and encouragement of artists ; by which, in their capacity of wealthy and enlightened citizens, they were fulfilling the duties of sovereigns. They were habituating all ranks of the people to look up to them alone for countenance and protection, and engaging that adulation in their favour which was the natural and only return that could be made by those who had benefited by their liberality. And in their turn the artists had it in their power to contribute eminently to the elevation of their patrons, by representing the different branches of the family in distinguished characters, as benefactors to their country ; placing their virtues in the best point of view. The people got accustomed to see them represented in that capacity, and were the more readily induced to assent to their assuming the reality of that of which the representation had long been so familiar to them. They experienced a feeling of pride, in perceiving that such an elevation was within the reach of one of their own class, and that they had had the discernment to bestow it so judiciously. There was nothing startling to their rights and liberties in seeing the munificent benefactor to their native country, the head of the house of Medici, occupying the reality of that station which they had been accustomed to applaud in the symbolical representations of the painters. The portraits of Cosmo de Medicis, the father of his country, are generally invested with the royal robes while he was yet a merchant citizen. Nothing could be more natural, than that he should finish the juggle by sitting down on the throne. Indeed, there are so few pictures of that period in which some one of the family is not represented in a distinguished character, as in the paintings of the adoration of the infant Jesus, where the three kings are so invariably the different members of that family, that we are led to suppose that it was one of the many political artifices by which the Medici ascended the throne.

Be that as it may, it was attended with effects highly beneficial to the arts ; and while the Medici still moved in the humble sphere of merchants, a taste for painting and sculpture became, through their means, generally diffused among the enlightened citizens of Florence. The plan was laid by Cosmo, to make Florence the great emporium of taste and literature in Europe, which was ardently pursued by his brother Lorenzo the Magnificent, and his equally distinguished grandson, Pope Leo the Tenth.

In the midst of all the turbulence of faction, all ranks of citizens seemed to unite in this great national object of embellishing Florence, and drawing to it men of eminence in every branch of literature and the liberal arts. They prosecuted the decoration of the churches with constant solicitude, and vied with each other in the elegance of their private dwellings ; creating such a demand for works of art, as became the certain presage of its future improvement.

The first important step that was gained in the improvement of the art at this period, was in the study of perspective, introduced by Brunelleschi, the architect, and taken up with ardour by Paolo Uccello. He carried his admiration of perspective to so great a pitch of enthusiasm, as to make him be considered a madman. He astonished the public, however, by the illusion of his performances, in which he succeeded in introducing within a narrow space long lines of pillars and architecture, with a truth that surprised every one. This circumstance led him particularly to the study of landscape, which had been very little practised before his time. There was another desideratum in the art as yet, chiaro scuro, the particular study of which was taken up by Massolino, which led him to soften down the dry hard style of his predecessors, and to omit the troublesome crowd of minute accompaniments with which it was usual to encumber the pictures of that period ; as attention to these was incompatible with harmony and repose in the effect of light and shade. These steps gained, prepared the way for the advance made by Maso, who, as usual with the Italians, obtained a by-name, by which he is more generally known.

Masaccio, or Masuccio, was a man of genius, and aimed at great vivacity of painting. He went to Rome to study the antique, and, by directing his pursuits in a new line, formed, in a manner, an epoch in the art. His composition and foreshortening possess great merit. His heads have grace, and he succeeded in giving the delicate tints of nature to his flesh, varying the expression of his figures, which does not seem to have been thought requisite before, at least in those which were subordinate. The legs and arms were generally the most deficient part of former pictures : Masaccio applied himself to this branch, and succeeded in placing his figures with considerable ease and truth ; and by thus boldly attacking the greatest difficulties of the art, he acquired for himself facility and address of hand. So that many authors consider that his pictures, in point of design and colouring, may stand in competition with the greater works of more modern times.

Masaccio had the talent to discern, that one of the most important objects of the art was expression, and particularly applied himself to the study of it. Without expression, a picture is but a pleasing bauble ; it may possess many qualities, but we pass them all over, to fix on that most attractive one which speaks and paints the mind. There are many subordinate requisites which a picture must possess, without which it is no picture ; but they are only the means by which to reach the great end of expression : it is that which engages every eye, the uninformed as well as the learned ; for the language of expression is universal. Those who fix on subaltern qualities, acquire a taste which is artificial : they become pedants ; and by the accident of their study being directed partially to one object, they see importance only in that particular walk they have been used to tread.

Masaccio was very harmonious in his colouring, and would probably have carried the art to considerable improvement had he not died young. He entirely changed the manner of Giotto, introducing a truth and dignity in the heads unknown to his predecessors. He varied the stiff regularity of plaits in the drapery, which formerly often resembled the regular disposition of the pipes of an organ, more than the easy flow of drapery. In fact, he renewed every thing in the art ; and although few of his works now exist, as they were painted principally in fresco, which time has effaced, yet he was very much studied by the great artists that immediately

followed him ; and was the first to introduce that modern manner, which, with the improvements of succeeding masters, has continued down to our day.

After the death of Masaccio, we find several monks occupying themselves in painting their own churches. Accustomed to the art of illuminating manuscripts, they had little difficulty to enlarge their style, so as to suit the decorations applicable to their church walls. Of these, Angelico and Gozzoli were in greatest repute, the last of whom painted in a very agreeable manner, considering the age in which he lived, except that he obscured the merit of his performance by too liberal an enrichment of gilding. The old palace of the Medici at Florence, contains a chapel painted by Gozzoli, which still remains in a state of tolerable preservation. He likewise painted at Pisa, where may be seen his picture of the drunkenness of Noah, and another of the tower of Babel. They possess considerable ease and variety in the attitudes, and are not deficient in expression. But the most remarkable of these painting monks was Fra Filippo, whose life was singularly chequered with adventures, considering the quiet and monotonous nature of his profession ; but the holy brother was at times disposed to be amorous, and fall in love with the subjects of his portraits. He had the misfortune to be taken by a Barbary corsair, in whose hands he remained for some time a slave, until he thought of making a portrait of his master, which happened to be so very resembling, that the superstitious African, for fear of the consequences, lost no time in sending so great a magician back to his own country. After many romantic adventures, Fra Filippo ended his days by poison, as might have been expected from his propensities in a jealous age, for the objects of his admiration were often of high rank, and his addresses powerfully aided by the qualifications of great personal beauty. He painted after the manner of Masaccio, with great grace and harmony of colouring.

It was about this period that an important change took place in painting, by the introduction of oil, attributed to the invention of Jean de Bruges, or Van Eyck. Before this time, painting had been confined to fresco, and the different modifications of water colours. Andre del Castagno was the first Florentine artist who began to use this mode of painting, having elicited the secret from a Venetian painter, Dominic, whom he afterwards barbarously assassinated, in order to engross the whole profit of the discovery to himself.

This invention (if so it was, for the learned are by no means at one on the subject) took place in the year 1410, as there are oil paintings of Van Eyck very near that period, in which the mellow softness peculiar to this mode of painting is not the greatest merit ; for they exhibit a wonderful truth of design, accuracy of touch, and address in the general management, with difficult and exact perspective, which would lead us to suspect that it was not in the use of oil alone that the Flemish artist had got the start of those of Italy.

In the course of the fifteenth century, that species of painting which had for its object the decoration of manuscripts, or illuminating, as it is generally termed, was carried to great perfection. It became a principal object of luxury and munificence among the princes and great men of that age, to possess splendidly illuminated copies of the books of greatest repute at the time, which, from the very great labour and expense attending these performances, could only be attained by the wealthy. The cultivation of this taste, at the particular period that it occurred, was a fortunate circumstance for the preservation of many of the literary works of the ancients, which but for the value of these embellishments, might never have reached our day. They were regarded as gems, upon which too much care could not be bestowed. The same effect would probably have followed the adoption of the splendid bindings of the present fashion. If our old charters and valuable parchments had been but handsomely illuminated, instead of being left like dirty scraps of sheep-skin, we should not have had to regret the deficiency of our ancient records. Whatever is valuable ought to have a certain degree of splendour, or fictitious merit, attached to it, to secure the regard and consideration of the ignorant.

There are many of these ancient codexes preserved in the public libraries of the Continent, which exhibit a most surprising degree of beauty and delicacy of penciling, besides much greater perfection in the other requisites of painting than consists with the generally received idea of the state of its excellence at that time. One of the most beautifully preserved of these illuminated works in the library of the King of France, is attributed to the pencil of René, the jolly old king of Provence, with every probability of authenticity; as that royal artist is recorded to have presented a beautiful manuscript of his own workmanship to one of the princesses of the house of France. There are two pictures preserved with great veneration at Aix in Provence as the reputed works of this king; there is no doubt of his having exercised the pencil, and if these pictures alluded to are of his hand, he was equal to any artist of that age; but many connoisseurs believe them to be the works of Van Eyck, who lived upon habits of intimacy with that good humoured monarch. The principal painting which is preserved in the cathedral is a good specimen of that antique style of picture called a triptick; a sort of emanation of the old architectural altar-piece, consisting of a principal picture of very tall dimensions, with two folding doors, which, when opened, extend the same subject, and, when closed for protection of the picture, represent on the back either an appropriate design, or some whimsical contrast or conceit, calculated to startle the spectator when the picture within is laid open to view. The picture in question has, on the outside, a representation of the annunciation to the shepherds, painted in camayeu; within, the centre piece represents Moses and the burning bush,—a subject which has been often tried, but seldom successfully. The prophet is here accompanied on the one side by the singularly assorted group of old René himself, Mary Magdalene, St. Antony, and St. Maurice, who gaze at the apparition of the bush; on the other side, by Joanne, René's queen, attended by St. John, St. Catherine, and St. Nicholas, who seem as much at a loss to account for what they see, as how they themselves came there.

Subjects of the same stamp are often seen in the illuminated manuscripts, which are very various in execution, some of them exhibiting not only an extraordinary degree of labour and invention, but a correctness and taste in the arabesques, which might dispute in excellence with those of Raphael. Considering the perishable nature of opaque water colours, with which these works are executed, the brilliancy and state of preservation in which they are generally found to be, is very surprising. As the subjects are often historical, and by means of the Calendar of Saints, which generally precedes the work, prove their own date by the insertion or omission of the names of certain saints, the æra of whose canonization is known; a good collection of drawings of these illumi-

nations, in chronological order, would be a valuable acquisition. There is a curious collection of them at Toulouse, by a person who makes it the sole object of his pursuit. We have seen in that collection copies of pictures not now extant, besides many indications to be gathered from them, highly interesting to the history of the art in general. We know little of the artists, as these works were generally the creation of some laborious monk, in the secrecy of his cell. Attavante of Florence is reported to have illuminated a magnificent copy of Silius Italicus, formerly belonging to a convent at Venice, besides many other works in the different public libraries of Italy. In many of these, he has painted his own name. His time was chiefly employed by the convents in embellishing the works of the Fathers.

George Merula was another celebrated illuminator, whose works possess a wonderful vivacity of colouring, graceful intricacy, and playfulness, with great truth in the figures of children, animals, flowers, festoons, and every variety of the arabesque. It was the custom for princes who aimed at literary fame, to keep some of these illuminators constantly in their service, who travelled about wherever there were valuable works to be copied, and by that means formed a collection for their employer. Some of these works are of such delicacy and richness, as to be truly magnificent, and worthy to be collected, had they no other merit than their beauty alone. But in fact the great talent in painting of that period seems to have merged in this art; it was most in request, and best paid, and would therefore naturally enough, become the pursuit of whoever felt a disposition for the cultivation of the arts.

To return to the school of Florence; Pope Sixtus IV. prepared to call forth the best talents of the age, in painting his celebrated Sextine chapel, which was begun in the year 1474. As Florence was at that time the capital of the arts, he summoned from thence the painters of the greatest reputation to undertake the work, among whom was Botticelli, Ghirlandajo, Rosselli, Lucca di Cortona, and Arezzo. This pontiff had no intelligence in the art himself, but was very desirous of the glory which it might add to his name. Of these artists, Ghirlandajo, whose real name was Dominic Corradi, obtained the greatest reputation, and was the first of the Florentines who seems to have studied aerial perspective, and by that means gave such depth to his pictures as astonished his contemporaries. It is quite surprising that this effect of aerial perspective should so long have escaped the notice of artists; so very obvious is the progressive degradation occasioned by the intervention of air, as objects are more or less removed from the eye: its effect in softening down the colour, and blending of the lights and shades, can scarce escape observation. The effect is no doubt less striking under the clear limpid atmosphere of Italy, than in a more northern climate; but still it must, in every case, be sufficiently obvious, one would think, to command attention.

It is usual to talk in raptures of the clear diaphanous atmosphere of Italy; and doubtless few can be insensible of its delicious serenity; but in a picturesque point of view, so much are we in love with the magic of aerial perspective, that we claim the preference for that climate where its effects are so much more strikingly and beautifully exemplified; where every progressive mountain reach of our own romantic valleys takes its place in the scale of distance, with a precision, and at the same time a playfulness, in the succession of vanishing tints, unknown under the clear sky of Italy. There, the visible intervention of air is so imperceptible as utterly to bewilder our northern eyes, accustomed to measure distance so accurately by that medium, and where every part of the landscape, compared to the gradations we are accustomed to, is equally bright, clear, and defined.

Ghirlandajo obtained a name for having made this discovery, the magical effect of which is denied to sculpture, and perhaps constitutes the principal advantage which painting possesses over sculpture. This power of representing distance, which is so fascinating to all, and seems so surprising to the uninformed, is seldom discoverable in any of the more ancient works. Landscape, of which it is the soul, was, however, as yet very little cultivated, and must have excited great admiration when joined to the charm of novelty. However excellent a foreground may be, of which alone an historical picture consists, it is but an approach, more or less, to truth, from its distinctness, and supposed vicinity to the eye; but when we come to look at the lovely demi-tints of the middle ground, the uncertain vanishing of the distance, it seems nature itself. It is the part of the picture where the eye reposes with perfect freedom, and the impression of which on the memory will most probably be of longest duration; it invites imagination to dwell upon the idea: whereas in the foreground there is little scope for imagination; we must take it in all the distinctness in which it is placed before us. Every one must have experienced the difficulty with which we withdraw the eye from an extensive scene in nature: there is a fascination in the progressive indistinctness of distance which rivets the mind, and transports us into a pleasing state of reverie: it is this magic which aerial perspective has the power to excite, and that in a degree scarcely inferior to nature.

There are many works of Ghirlandajo's at Florence, of which the Massacre of the Innocents, in the church of St. Maria Novella, is looked upon as one of the best. He has given in it the portraits of most of the principal citizens of Florence of his time, whether from necessity or choice is uncertain; but it must have had the effect of cramping his genius, in so far as it excluded the workings of invention. Ghirlandajo omitted much of the gilding which tarnished the works of his predecessors: he aimed at a nobler and more effectual means of producing effect and beauty. He was very partial to mosaic, and used to say that the works in perishable colours were but the drawing, whilst mosaic only constituted real painting, in so far as it was capable of eternal duration. He had a numerous school, and many pictures of the scholars now pass for those of the master. He failed, however, in that great test, the painting of hands and feet.

Such was the state of the arts at the close of the fifteenth century; in tracing it through that which followed, we shall see it arrive at the highest point of its progress, and begin again to turn towards its decay. It is lamentable to think how short-lived perfection seems to prove, or rather, to speak more correctly, our nearest approach to it. Much was still wanting in the works of Ghirlandajo and his predecessors; labour and constraint was still too obvious not to be irksome to the spectator; for to charm, a painter must seem to work with creative power, and with the ease of omnipotence. He must even sport with a degree of seeming carelessness, than which nothing is more fascinating, so that it appears the result of mere playfulness of pencil, and not of negligence. The painters of the fifteenth century were still deficient in fulness of outline, variety of composition, and harmony of colouring. They were

chained to the ground by an awkwardness in the manipulation; for a painter at once destroys the charm, if he allows in any thing the impotence of his pencil to appear. The scrupulous exactness, however, of this ancient school, was smoothing the way for the perfection about to follow; for ease is far more readily engrafted on rigid correctness, than the attainment of correctness where former practice was more loose. It is with painting as with every other art—severe precision ought to guide our first steps; the rudiments admit of no deviation from strict and measured rule. The superstructure of ease and grace becomes easily raised if the foundation be solid and good.

Had it not been from a desire not to disconnect the history of the Florentine artists, we might, with propriety, have delayed their separation from those who cultivated the arts in other quarters, as hitherto little, if any difference existed in the style generally followed. At the close of the fifteenth century, however, the diffusion of the taste for painting had reached that point which gave rise to variety of style, in proportion as the artists of different countries were led to follow the peculiar manner chalked out by their great masters, so as to become marked by features scarcely less distinctive than those of different dialects.

What we have narrated of the state of the arts since the obscurity of the dark ages had begun to pass away, falls so far short of its excellence among the Greeks, that it can scarcely be said to have yet revived. It was not till the age of Leonardo da Vinci that painting attained a degree of dignity sufficient to entitle it to be brought into comparison with the age of Pericles. Leonardo was followed by the transcendent genius of Michael Angelo, who stamped the distinctive nature of the Florentine school with the character of grandeur; profound skill in the movements and anatomy of the human body; austere solemnity somewhat at the expense of grace; and uncommon force and vigour, partaking of the supernatural, but at the same time conveying a noble and majestic conception of human nature, that excited sentiments of admiration more than of pleasure.

Leonardo da Vinci was a native of Florence, born in 1452. Tiraboschi calls him an illustrious bastard, as he happened to be the natural son of Petro, a notary at Florence. He was a man not only of superior knowledge in all the branches of the fine arts, but very learned in the sciences in general. The precocity and universality of his knowledge at a very early age was the marvel of his first instructor, Verrachio, a Florentine painter of that day. The earliest exercise of his talents was in matters of mechanism, in which he displayed a very surprising reach of inventive genius. While yet a boy, he proposed to underbuild the Church of St. John without injury to the superstructure, an architectural adventure equally new and astonishing to that age. He had the advantage to possess, in addition to all the acquirements of his genius, great beauty and elegance of person, with an amiability of disposition which made him beloved by all. He was invited to Milan by the Duke, where he charmed the court by his talents in music, which he exhibited on an instrument of his own invention; probably a sort of organ guitar, as it is described to have resembled the skull of a horse in form, and furnished with silver tubes, surpassing, in sweetness of tone, every thing known at the time. He excelled, moreover, in the quality of improvisatore.

Leonardo was particularly attached to the study of anatomy; and the fertility of his inventive genius made him impatient of the slow process of painting. He rather delighted in sketching down his fancies as they arose. There are extant some curious volumes of these jottings, filled with schemes in mechanism, observations, and drawings of every variety, particularly skirmishes of cavalry. The subjects of his pictures are generally well selected, and seemingly maturely studied.

Leonardo left at Milan many admirable specimens of his talents as an artist, which are still existing in the collections of that city; and, above all, that much celebrated and magnificent picture of the Last Supper. The subject is fortunately preserved by Morghen's inimitable engraving, as the original, the remains of which is on the wall of the refectory of the convent of Santa Maria delle Grazie, is nearly effaced by age, and deplorably injured by negligence and accident; having been exposed to the license of the soldiery while the hall was occupied as a magazine by the French troops.

There certainly could not be a more admirable subject, in every respect, for the pencil of a great master, than that important scene in the life of our Saviour, which established the mysterious rite, in the observance of which the whole world is destined one day to be united. When we reflect who the actors of this scene were, prepared by mysterious forewarnings that they had assembled for the last time; the sublime and tender sentiments which must have suffused the minds of the disciples, joined to the bewildering consciousness of inability to reconcile what they saw and heard to the usual course of reasoning, and to the melancholy forebodings of what was about to happen; the shock of so appalling a declaration of treachery in such a cause, and of such a Master, and by one of their own number,—every circumstance seemed in action to call forth the greatest vivacity and variety of expression, and all directed to one object with that intensity of attention, which the remarkable words of our Saviour must have excited. As a contrast to this ferment we have the sublime tranquillity of Jesus, the least moved of that assembly, although himself the conscious victim; contemplating with equal complacency his faithful and devoted followers, as the traitor who was destined to fulfil his dreadful doom.

Leonardo has remarkably seized that celestial purity and melancholy composure, which must have filled the soul of our Saviour when he uttered the words, "One of you shall betray me," without directing his eyes towards any one. The flush of indignation seems to mount into every countenance of his assembled followers, mixed with horror and amazement most admirably varied. The attitude of St. John, who seems greedily to listen to a hurried observation of St. Peter, from which he appears to expect some clue to the mystery, is exceedingly natural; as well as the conscious suspicion of Judas, half turning to catch by stealth what St. Peter says, expecting discovery, while the ready purpose of denial seems to settle on his expression of resolute villany. The ferment of the surrounding group, in the midst of whom the meek Jesus seems wrapt in godlike serenity, shows that the traitor is already discovered. St. James the Less seems to whisper to St. Peter, while he stretches across St. Andrew, who casts a glance of horror on the villain. St. James is in a beautiful attitude of attesting his own innocence, and love of his Master, as well as horror of what they have just heard; the same purpose is obvious in the animated movement of St. Thomas. There is an admirable mix-

ture of irresolution in many of the countenances—the natural desire to avert the horrible catastrophe announced to them—at the same time suppressed by indecision from the consciousness of their own weakness, and the power of their Master to prevent its accomplishment; the injured pride, which seems to repeat with amazement, " one of us" did he say? In the group of St. Matthew and St. Simon, they seem to refer to each other in doubt of their having accurately heard the words of our Saviour: one of them seems utterly to distrust the evidence of his senses.

Yet with all this animation of expression, it is remarkable how the genius of the painter has succeeded in making the tranquil Jesus the object upon which the eye cannot help to fix itself. The spectator's attention is drawn round the group with the same rapid anxiety of inquiry that seems to animate every countenance in the picture; but constantly returns, as by the attraction of a magnet, to the figure of our Saviour, wrapt in that composure which seems to see beyond this world, and scarcely to participate in the agitating feelings of human nature. The still serenity of evening diffuses its light with beautiful effect over these perturbed groups, in unison with the great presence of our Saviour alone, which shows the sublime conception Leonardo had of his subject. It diffuses a sort of melancholy tranquillity, like the death-bed of a saint. We seem to feel that it is the last evening of our Saviour's earthly existence; he is in mind already withdrawn from all the agitations of humanity to the serene contemplation of his higher nature.

It may with truth be pronounced a sublime composition, with all the simplicity belonging to so dignified a subject. It suited well the chaste composure of Leonardo's style. Even his formality, which in other subjects is marked as a defect, is here perfectly in character with the gravity of such an assembly. The picture now lives almost solely in Morghen's admirable engraving. We had the melancholy satisfaction very lately to see all that remains of the original, which gives but a faint shadow of its former excellence. It is thirty-two feet long by sixteen feet high in dimensions. Tradition has fixed the persons intended by each particular figure, which is probably correct, as the most remarkable of the apostles correspond perfectly with the figures allotted for them. Beginning from the left of the spectator, the figure standing is St. Bartholomew, then follows in order St. James the Less, St. Andrew, St. Peter, Judas, St. John, Jesus, St. James the Greater, St. Thomas, St. Philip, St. Matthew, St. Thadeus, and St. Simon. In one respect, no copy or engraving can approach the remarkable effect produced by the original, from the circumstance of its exactly filling up the whole space of the end wall of the apartment; and the beams and cornices represented in the picture are the exact continuation of the architecture of the hall, so as to produce the illusion of its being actually a prolongation of its length.

Leonardo appears to have proceeded with the greatest precaution in the performance of his picture. Besides painting a cartoon of the whole subject of the Last Supper, he made finished sketches of each particular figure and head, then painted pictures of each, and even went so far as to model some of them, in order to be able to study more perfectly the effect of light and shade. This was a degree of care and study that would be considered quite superfluous by our modern artists; but doubtless it was to the perseverance and care in execution, joined to profound reflection and study of the subject, that he owed that excellence which placed his work among the finest specimens of the art. We are moreover indebted to these preparatory works, which are still existing, for the perfection of the engraving, as reference was obliged to be had to them to supply the deficiency of the original. One of the reasons for its very rapid decay, was very probably the circumstance of its being painted in oil,—a mode which was then but recently invented, and perhaps imperfectly understood; as in the same apartment there are some fresco pictures of other masters, no doubt bad enough in composition, but fresh in preservation, which makes the inimitable work of Leonardo be the more regretted.

Many things seemed to conspire to bring about the rapid destruction of this picture. The plaster of the wall turned out to be defective, and began soon to scale off, leaving fearful blotches. The hall is in a low damp situation, and on the ground floor of the convent, which in rainy seasons is flooded with water, so that the brilliancy of the colours began very soon to be affected. To complete its misfortunes, the lazy monks were so regardless of their treasure, as to cut off a piece of the picture, even the legs of our Saviour's figure, for the purpose of enlarging a door-way : and sacrilegiously nailed up the imperial arms upon the face. Upon being made aware afterwards of the extent of their outrage, they endeavoured to repair the injury, by setting a dauber to work to repaint it; so that what is seen now has very little of the great Leonardo. A story is narrated in the life of this artist, but with what truth it is impossible from the present state of the picture to ascertain; that he had left the head of Jesus unfinished, from inability to conceive dignity and beauty superior to what he had given to St. James the Greater and his brother. It is abundantly obvious, that various parts have been at different times retouched. Francis I. when he made himself master of Milan, conceived the plan of carrying off the whole wall entire with its picture into France, and took measures for that purpose ; but no engineer was found bold enough to make the attempt. The simple means since adopted of securely pasting canvas over the face of a wall picture previous to detaching it, was not then thought of; which is perhaps to be regretted, as it might have proved the means of preserving this surprising work. During the French revolution the hall was converted into a stable, then a magazine, and lastly it was shut up altogether ; when the water was allowed to stagnate, and exhale putrid vapours from the floor.

Upon Leonardo's return to Florence, he found another luminary, Michael Angelo, had arisen in the same hemisphere, and moving in the same orbit, whose aspiring genius proved rather too much for him. The universality of Leonardo's talent had led him into a versatility of application, which too much attenuated the vigour of his capacity ; and prevented his coping with success against the steady tenacious purpose, and absolute fury of application, with which the uncontrollable impetuosity of Michael Angelo hurried him on to perfection. The mild and winning grace which was the merit and peculiar character of Leonardo, was overwhelmed by the force and vigour of Bonarruoti's commanding talent, steadily directed to one object. Whatever demand for grand inspiring subjects occurred, were therefore yielded up without a struggle to his powerful pencil, while Leonardo occupied himself with the gentler beauty of female portrait. Many of these still remain, the admiration of the lovers of painting. This

accomplished artist dwelt with such delight on any subject of peculiar beauty, that he is said to have employed four years on the famous portrait of Mona Lisa, the wife of Francisco di Giocondo, which Francis I. bought for 45,000 francs.

There is so much resemblance in the character, as well as occasionally in the style, of Leonardo da Vinci and Raphael, that, had the circumstances of their studies been similar, as they travelled on the same road, they would probably have reached the same point. We observe the same lovely grace and modesty, the same propriety and sedateness ; but Raphael added the magic of ease, and the elegance resulting from a more intimate study of the antique. Yet Leonardo studied with acuteness the original of the antique, nature itself ; and that with the experienced eye of an anatomist, tracing with accuracy the movements of the mind, as manifested in the body, and as indicating the rising sentiment in the delicate movement of the muscles. We never detect, in his learned works, what the more ignorant productions of modern artists so frequently display—that inexpressible something which we see to be offensive and unnatural without being able to fix on the cause ; eyes suffused with tears, where the ministering muscles remain inert ; where the painter represents a figure running without the requisite quality of making him move his limbs ; and various other incongruities, which it were needless to enumerate. Every passion and sentiment, however feeble, of which the human mind is susceptible, exercises an individual and marked influence over the whole body.—Here is the *mare magnum* of the unlearned painter, a failure in the most delicate indication of its movements, a contradiction of cause and effect, at once disenchants the scene, even to vulgar eyes. We need no *eruditos oculos* to detect any offence, however slight, against nature ; it is felt, though we may not have the power to express it. Much, indeed, is required of the painter who aspires to move our feelings.

The versatility of Leonardo's genius was his misfortune ; it interfered with his steady application to any one of the many pursuits, which, had they singly engaged the undivided capacity of his accomplished mind, he might have carried to the greatest perfection. But the consequence only a portion of his time on each, has been, that he allowed himself to be excelled in all. He is excelled by Raphael in grace, by Michael Angelo in science, and in his physical pursuits by many. But Leonardo was a distinguished benefactor to the arts, by introducing a purer style, and laying the foundation of a deeper and more accurate study of the science of painting. He was in the constant habit of committing to paper the results of daily observation and experience, on his acute, inventive, and vigorous mind, accompanied with innumerable pencil hints and studies. To this practice we owe his valuable treatise on painting ; which contains a comprehensive view of the art, accompanied with every precept, demonstration, or reasoning, suggested by the constant experience of a life passed in the active exercise of the various branches of the fine arts, as well as of the sciences.

When Leo X. obtained the pontificate, he continued his protection of Leonardo da Vinci, by inviting him to Rome, where he gave many proofs of his talent. Being brought into more immediate competition with the aspiring genius of Michael Angelo, yet a youth, and likewise at that time in the employment of the pontiff, Leonardo was induced to accept of the invitation of

Francis I. of France, in whose arms he soon afterwards expired, in the year 1518. The Ambrosian library of Milan possesses a variety of his valuable manuscripts and drawings in architecture, mechanics, and anatomy; and also of his pictures, besides notes on the various sciences, of which he was an ardent cultivator, accompanied with explanations of machines, and written in his usual manner, from right to left. Why he adopted this peculiarity is not known, but there was something original in every thing he did.

It was about the period of Leonardo's death that attention began to be drawn to the remains of ancient art, of which the ferocity of barbarian ignorance had, for the long succession of ages so ungenial to the prosecution of these pursuits, nearly extirpated all memory. The misdirected zeal of the early Christians having long continued to give vent to its fervour in the destruction of every thing connected with the worship of the Gentiles, had along with them demolished, in one undistinguishing havoc, the statues of the great men of antiquity, as well as of the gods; equally incapable, in their ignorance, of discrimination, as of forbearance. Mr. Roscoe observes that " The fury of the Iconoclasts subsided as the restoration of Paganism became no longer an object of dread; and some of the meagre and mutilated remains of ancient skill, sanctified by new appellations, derived from the objects of Christian worship, were suffered to remain, to attract the superstitious devotion rather than the enlightened admiration of the people. The remonstrances and example of Petrarca seem first to have roused the attention of the Romans to the excellence of those admirable works, by the remains of which they were still surrounded. From this period some traces appear of a rising taste for these productions, which, in the course of the succeeding century, became a passion that could only be gratified by the acquisition of them. By Lorenzo the Magnificent, this object was pursued with constant solicitude, and great success; and the collection of antiques formed by him in the gardens of St. Marco, at Florence, became the school of Michael Angelo. This relish for the remains of antiquity, whether they consisted of statues, gems, vases, or other specimens of skill, had been cultivated by Leo X. from his earliest years, under his paternal roof, where the instructions of the accomplished Politiano had enabled him to combine amusement with improvement, and to unite a correct taste with the science of an antiquarian." Although no sovereign has a more distinguished claim to the glory of encouraging the arts than Leo X. yet the constant practice of the Roman pontiffs had been to protect the arts, ever since their revival in modern times. It was a fortunate circumstance for Michael Angelo, as well as for Raphael, that the munificent and vigorous mind of Pope Julius II. took this happy turn, which so materially seconded the aspiring genius of both these great men; as some share of their excellence is perhaps due to the vast and magnificent designs of this pontiff offering so fortunate a theatre for the exercise of their talents.

Michael Angelo had worked in Bologna and Florence, principally in sculpture, where he formed his fine mind by study; but his genius was not roused to its full pitch until the return of Leonardo from Milan excited the spirit of emulation. It was this circumstance which set fire to that train of genius which was destined to illuminate Italy. The government proposed a subject for their competition in the wars that had just given to Florence the final possession of Pisa. As

such a trial was particularly calculated to exhibit the distinctive features of talent in these two great artists, thus brought into parallel with each other, we shall give the result of the competition in Mr. Roscoe's words. " The cartoons, or designs for this purpose, were immediately commenced. The preparations made by each of the artists, and the length of time employed, as well in intense meditation as in cautious execution, sufficiently demonstrated the importance which they attached to the result. From variety of talent, or by mutual agreement, they each, however, chose a different track. Leonardo undertook to represent a combat of horsemen, which he introduced as a part of the history of Nicolo Riccinino, a commander for the Duke of Milan. In this piece he concentrated all the result of his experience, and all the powers of his mind. In the varied forms and contorted attitudes of the combatants, he has displayed his thorough knowledge of the anatomy of the human body. In their features he has characterized, in the most expressive manner, the sedateness of steady courage, the vindictive malevolence of revenge, the mingled impressions of hope and of fear, the exultation of triumphant murder, and the despairing gasp of inevitable death. The horses mingle in the combat with a ferocity equal to that of their riders; and the whole was executed with such skill, that, in the essential points of conception, of composition, and of outline, this production has perhaps seldom been equalled, and certainly never excelled. Michael Angelo chose a different path. Devoted solely to the study of the human figure, he disdained to lavish any portion of his powers on the inferior representations of animal life. He therefore selected a moment, in which he supposed a body of Florentine soldiers, bathing in the Arno, to have been unexpectedly called into action by the signal of battle. To have chosen a subject more favourable to the display of his powers, consistently with the task committed to him, was perhaps impossible. The clothed, the half clothed, and the naked, are mingled in one tumultuous group. A soldier, just risen from the water, starts in alarm, and turning towards the sound of the trumpet, expresses, in his complicated action, almost every variety incident to the human frame. Another, with the most vehement impatience, forces his dripping feet through his adhesive clothing. A third calls to his companion, whose arms only are seen grappling with the rocky sides of the river, which, from this circumstance, appears to flow in front, although beyond the limits of the picture. Whilst a fourth, almost prepared for action, in buckling round him his belt, promises to stoop the next moment for his sword and shield, which lie ready at his feet. It would be as extravagant as unjust to the talents of Michael Angelo to carry our admiration of this subject so far as to suppose, with the sculptor Cellini, that he never afterwards attained to half the degree of excellence which he there displayed; but it may be asserted with confidence, that the great works which this fortunate spirit of emulation had produced, marked a new æra in the art, and that upon the study of these models almost all the great painters, who shortly afterwards conferred such honour on their country, were principally formed." Neither of these works were ever completed, and the original cartoons are not now existing. Imperfect designs and engravings of them have however been preserved. We believe there is a picture painted by Vasari from Michael Angelo's design of this subject in some one of the English collections.

After passing through this ordeal, the genius of

Michael Angelo was employed in Rome by Pope Julius II. where he found ample scope for its greatest efforts in the munificent undertakings of this pontiff. His works were held in such high estimation by Julius, that they are alleged by Vasari and others to have given rise to the idea of the great undertaking of St. Peter's Church, as a suitable place of deposit for productions of such perfection and grandeur.

Architecture and statuary were the branches of the fine arts to which Michael Angelo had chiefly bent his attention ; and it was in the exercise of these that he had hitherto raised his reputation, following design only in so far as it was connected with the main pursuit of statuary. But as Rome was now the theatre of his efforts, Raphael had by this time become his competitor in the branch of painting ; and would naturally have been called upon to undertake the completion of the paintings of the Sextine Chapel, which was at this time proposed to be accomplished. It is supposed, however, by some, that the pontiff was instigated by the friends of Raphael to impose the execution of this difficult task on Michael Angelo ; trusting that he would show his inferiority in fresco painting, in which he was unpractised, and by that means enhance the merit of his rival. It does not, however, appear that the artists themselves were actuated by any feelings of jealousy towards each other ; but, on the contrary, entertained reciprocal esteem and admiration for the private character and transcendent talents of each other. There is every reason to conclude that it was an insidious attempt of Angelo's enemies to stop him in the career of his glory as a statuary, by obliging him to paint in fresco, (of the process of which even he appears at that time to have been in ignorance) and that too a ceiling demanding a degree of skill in foreshortening and difficulty in execution, enough to overwhelm the boldest genius.

He found, however, that there was no escape from the fiat of this imperious pontiff, however reluctant he might be to undertake the task. Accordingly, he sent to Florence for the best fresco painters to assist him in the work, with whose performances he had so little reason to be satisfied, that he dismissed them in despair ; but having himself learnt the art by observing their mode of proceeding, he destroyed all that had been done, resolving to shut himself up in the chapel, and adventure boldly on the whole undertaking, unaided by any one. Preparing his colours with his own hands, he set to work, and, as might have been expected, failed frequently, but at last completed the Deluge to his own satisfaction ; but it was scarcely finished before he had the mortification to see it become mouldy and disappear, having used too much water in mixing up his colours. He was not to be daunted, however, but set to work again with that renewed determination and perseverance which is ever the presage of ultimate success. It is next to a miracle in the history of human genius, thus to stop an artist in the middle of his career, make him instantly renounce that art, the practice of which had been the employment of his whole life and mind, to tax him with the labours of a different art, to give him for his first essay, a subject the most arduous and comprehensive, in a position which united every circumstance of difficulty, in competition with the greatest master of that particular art, and yet to see him issue from such an ordeal with a success so glorious as to place him in the highest rank of artists, had he never done any thing else. This is a trait in the history of art which is, and probably ever will re-

main, unique ; the undaunted vigour of character which could contemplate such a trial, is inconceivable.

Raphael was at work at the same time on his immortal productions of the chambers of the Vatican, only a few paces distant from the Sextine Chapel. Michael Angelo completed his undertaking in twenty months, and received in payment the sum of three thousand crowns ; the subjects were very various, a detailed account of which will be found in the third discourse of the professor of painting in the Royal Academy of London, published in 1801. There is a surprising variety of form and playfulness of attitude displayed in this laborious ceiling, and of beauty in the individual compartments as soon as the eye, bewildered with their intricacy, can succeed in detaching each particular subject from the surrounding world of figures. It is, moreover, quite necessary to have previously seen a good deal before any one can derive the full enjoyment these marvellous performances of the Sextine Chapel are capable of affording. It ought to be the last to be visited of the great works in Rome, when the eye has become matured, and the mind disposed to that deliberate study which the overpowering volume of this comprehensive subject requires ; for there are here hundreds of separate subjects executed with all the learning and invention of this surprising man.

The picture of the Last Judgment, that stupendous offspring of Michael Angelo's genius, was not painted till thirty years after he had terminated the ceiling and other works of the chapel. All his paintings partake much of his early habits of the chisel ; they are bold, grand, and nervous, as different from the softer works of the Venetian school, as sculpture is from painting. The magic of light and colours has no share of Michael Angelo's creations ; he painted man and mind, disregarding every thing secondary to his ruling purpose of representing the energy of which our nature is susceptible ; and that under the most difficult attitudes and positions, giving magnitude in the smallest space, by the illusion of foreshortening, over which he possessed a miraculous power. We discover in his pictures the rare quality of interminable originality, conceptions never seen before, though often copied since.

When we look upon that colossal scene of the Last Judgment, that huge wall of fifty feet high, by forty feet wide, entirely covered with naked figures, there is something so unlike what we have ever seen before, so adventurous, that it hurries all our preconceived ideas into utter chaos ; we hesitate whether to yield to the repugnance of improbability, or to amazement at the fertility of such creative genius. Yet it is scarcely possible ever to become quite reconciled to so great profusion of nakedness, or to disembarrass our admiration from this counteracting influence ; we can submit to much nakedness in sculpture, and even scarcely experience any alloy to our admiration, from what in painting could not fail to rouse the alarm of modesty. We are disposed to wave that fastidiousness, if it is but a single naked figure ; we feel as it were alone, and unexposed to observation ; but a community of the bare must ever require long habit and familiarity to blunt the edge of the natural repugnance to immodesty. Much, however, depends on the mode of representation ; a little reflection soon satisfies the spectator, that in such a subject as the last judgment any thing else would have been quite incongruous. Yet Zucheri had the absurdity to paint a clothed judgment, and Siguorelli conceived that he had most shrewdly overcome the dilemma, by half clothing the figures in his Last Judgment. In short, it is scarcely a subject befitting the pencil; any representation, however grandiose, can but lower our idea, dark and uncertain as it must be, of that appalling event.

This picture occupied Michael Angelo eight years in painting. In it every possible difficulty of the art in design and foreshortening, seems to be exhibited, and successfully; even with a miraculous ease and playfulness of pencil, enough to spread despair among the succeeding generations of artists. There are three hundred figures, and many of them above the size of nature.

Pictures of an ordinary size, from Michael Angelo's pencil are very rare. He despised that sort of small talk, while his mind was occupied with the splendid dramas of his greater productions, and much of what passes for his, are the works of his imitators, as Daniel de Volterra, or Fra Sebastien. He made up for it, however, in the profusion of designs, which have been cherished ever since as treasures, and never fail to partake of the vigorous touch of the master. Vasari says that he never painted but one picture in oil, and resolved never to paint another after he had finished this one. The character of Michael Angelo was, grandeur of conception, profound knowledge of anatomy and foreshortening, a daring pencil, which moved on the very verge of the supernatural, marking every muscle in the extreme of action, and somewhat at the expense of that truth and delicacy with which nature indicates all the varieties of movement and expression.

He neglected, perhaps despised, the lesser elegancies and embellishments of art. One vast and lofty idea had taken complete possession of his mind, to the exclusion of every subordinate grace. Like Dante, he was an epic painter of the most masculine and daring cast.

It is surprising in how short a space from the resuscitation, the art reached that acme of perfection exhibited by the works of the great masters who were contemporaries of Michael Angelo: a point which it has never been able to surpass, if even to equal. The result of an happy combination of events may again give it a spring forward, as it is certainly not an attainment to which we can conceive final limits of perfection, beyond which human efforts must fail. It was the absence of affectation and subserviency to the fashion, tastes, and manners of the day, which enabled the earlier masters to soar so far above their successors; occupied with the study of nature in her simpler forms, and assisted by the chaste remains of Grecian taste. No sooner do painters begin to study and copy each other alone, and truckle to the taste of the times, satisfied if they succeed in pleasing the ignorant, from whose purses their labours are to be rewarded; than the art begins infallibly to retrograde, in spite of the efforts of those who may, from time to time, assume a juster view of their profession.

The reputation of the Florentine school was supported by a numerous list of artists, of whom we shall only mention a few of the most distinguished. Of the imitators of Leonardo da Vinci, Luini arrived at the closest resemblance. Although still inferior to his master, it is sometimes difficult to distinguish them. There are some fine specimens of this master at Milan, particularly one in the Ambrosian library. Pietro Perugino was an insipid painter. Fra Bartolomeo followed the manner of da Vinci and Raphael.

Andrea del Sarto excelled as a chaste and accurate painter, without much fire and genius, but always pleasing, and generally qualified with an air of melancholy. He died in the year 1530. Pontormo and Rosso were likewise followers of the style of Leonardo. Michael Angelo was imitated by Daniel de Volterra,

but in a hard and laborious manner, as it was his statues principally that were the subjects of study to most of his followers. He was followed with a degree of blind zeal that contributed very much towards the falling off of the art; as the style of Michael Angelo was of a description to be supported only by a bold, original, and powerful genius. Accordingly, in his followers, we find the turgid swollen muscles carried the length of caricature. The severity so striking in Michael Angelo's countenances, the vigour of attitude that seems to spurn the frailty of human nature, becomes, in the translations of many of his followers, a sort of prancing buffoonery, which is far from agreeable. Greatness of manner, the sublime and refined, is ever on the verge of the ridiculous, and will unavoidably fall into it, whenever it flows from any other source than that of original inspiration. It were needless to run over a number of names. It was but Michael Angelo *travestie*, varying only in proportion to the abilities of the individual artists, which continued for above one hundred years after the death of this great master. At this period, the style of painting in Florence underwent a change, and became more varied and more vigorous under the efforts of Cigoli, Allori, and Rosselli, who had extended their studies to the masters of other schools, as well as their own. They were followed by Carlo Dolce, so excellent in Madonnas and small pictures, which he finished with exquisite delicacy of pencil and feeling in the expression. Modesty and placid humility were the characters he delighted in; patient grief and resignation; penitence, or the heavenly joy that beams in the countenance of a suffering martyr. Pietro de Cortona was quite of a different taste—all fire and vivacity, with rich colouring, and clever disposition of his groups, but defective in expression. It is difficult to distinguish his pictures from those of his pupil, Ciro Ferri. For a detailed account of the Florentine painters, the work of Vasari may be consulted. He was likewise a painter, though of moderate merit.

Roman School.

In the most important and pleasing attributes of the art, in having given the first name that stands on the catalogue of its great masters, Rome may take the precedence of all other schools of painting. The stimulus of example it owes undoubtedly to Florence, and seems very early to have profited by the light that began to restore the arts to view in the thirteenth century. Specimens exist, and names are recorded, of artists, that were contemporary with Giotto, Cimabue, and the other harbingers of the Florentine school; but differing in no essential of style or merit. It is enough for the history of the art to know that they did exist. But the spring was wanting, which, under more favourable circumstances, might have enabled the early artists of Rome to contend more successfully with their Florentine neighbours, for the palm generally attributed to them, of being the first leaders of its revival. In the monuments of ancient art, with which Rome was so profusely stored, she carried in her bosom the seeds of future greatness, which, like a young shoot from an ancient stem, required only to be protected in its youth, to raise its head in the semblance of its prostrate sire; for the elements of excellence were there already, disposed to spring up into luxuriance so soon as the fostering hand of encouragement and culture should be presented. But at this period, Rome was either sunk in the mire of bigotry and mutual distrust, or abandoned altogether by her clerical masters. It was not

Roman
School.

PAINTING.

239

Roman
School.

until the re-transference of the Papal chair from Avignon to Rome, that much assistance or protection could be expected from the influence of government.

When that event did occur, it was fortunately accompanied by a reviving taste for the remnants of ancient art, of which Rome being the great storehouse, soon attracted to its school all those who felt the charms of Grecian excellence, and were prepared, by their collision, to excite that fire of emulation which soon blazed forth in splendour. It was the study of the antique which stamped the peculiar features of the Roman school. "The genius that hovers over these venerable relics, may be called the father of modern art;" and from such a source, the perfection of grace and elegance was naturally to be looked for. We may accordingly characterize the style as luxuriant, in the admirable skill, simplicity, and elegance of composition, grace and dexterity of grouping, correct design, with a noble and pathetic dignity of expression, accompanied, in the females, by the most engaging air of modesty. It wants the brilliant colouring of the Venetian or Flemish masters, but this is a defect common to all those who have made correct design the leading aim of their art. It is humiliating to the pride of human talent, to find that there is always at least some one qualifying defect to subtract from the sum of our highest attainments—that, in the exercise of an art demanding various qualities for its perfection, the limited scope of genius is, in general, so strongly impressed with the importance of one essential requisite, as to pursue the attainment of it with an ardour to the prejudice of others perhaps equally necessary—to become so dazzled as scarcely to see beyond the circle of its influence. Unqualified perfection has never yet been reached, and perhaps never will. In Michael Angelo, for instance, the greatest and most powerful genius that ever was directed to the pursuit of the fine arts, we see him entirely run away with by the strong impression he had taken of the importance of anatomy, and accordingly discover in his works that there is an *ultra* unattained, depending upon some other quality which he has overlooked.

The clerical sovereigns of Rome, reaching that eminence at a late period of life, holding it in general but for a few years of frailty, leaving no heirs to carry on their dynasty, might be presumed but little disposed towards the arts of embellishment; but the very circumstance of their leaving no family to succeed them has almost invariably excited a desire to leave some monument of taste to preserve their memory. With a few exceptions, the papal power has been the great means of furnishing subjects, and assembling competitors, for the great prizes of painting; and, while their authority was predominant in Europe, we find the brilliant æra of the arts, and Rome the theatre on which it was displayed.

Pietro Perugino. Pietro Perugino, a Florentine, and pupil of the same Veracchio who instructed Leonardo da Vinci in the mysteries of the pencil, practised his rude and dry style of painting at Rome, and derived more honour from the accident of having been Raphael's master than any merit of his own. He took a narrow contracted view of nature, pinching his figures and draperies in a manner that is far from agreeable, although his youthful and female heads often possess a degree of grace. The modest and docile disposition of Raphael led him to value the works of his master, and for some time to adhere to his style, which is even discoverable in a few of his greater works, particularly in the deep azure of

his skies, and that sort of iridescent colouring of the landscape, which gives so peculiar a tone to the simple, elegant, and graceful composure of his figures, as if it was the representation of some more ethereal nature than that of this world. Pietro had a very numerous school, in which the pupils, in their future practice, were so strictly observant of the style of their master, that collections are filled with pictures, as of Pietro Perugino, which were the performances of his scholars. Except at Perugia and Florence there are few originals of this master.

Raphael arrived at Rome about the same time with *Raphael.* Michael Angelo. He had been invited by Pope Julius II. at the recommendation of his relative, Bramanti the architect, in the year 1508, when he was still a young man. He had already gone to Florence, to study the works of Leonardo and Michael Angelo, and had at different periods of his life three distinct styles of painting; the first dry and meagre, in imitation of Pietro Perugino; the second, acquired in Florence, was characterized by grandeur; and the third, proceeding from the study of nature and the antique, formed, in his Roman manner, the nearest approach to perfection in painting which the history of the art can furnish. His first great works were in the frescos of the Vatican chambers, consisting of the comprehensive subjects of theology (erroneously called the dispute on the sacraments,) philosophy, poetry, and jurisprudence. These complex and embarrassing subjects are executed in a manner which shows a powerful stretch of mind, admirable execution, and boldness of fancy, which is quite surprising, when we consider the very arduous nature of the undertaking. In the first, we have the representation of both heaven and earth, and that on a very large scale. The Almighty, whose radiance illuminates the whole, surrounded by all the host of heaven, and supporting the earth. In a lower sphere is the Saviour, preparing to assume the fearful task of redemption, and encompassed by the righteous already in possession of heaven. Various offices of adoration employ the multitude who occupy the earth below, divided into groups, indicative of the religious ceremonies they are engaged in. This is a wonderful performance, solemn and simple, but partaking somewhat of the formality of the age in which it was painted, which, however, harmonizes not unaptly with such a subject, as in it the slightest appearance of affectation would be quite insufferable. The second subject, philosophy, is what is so well known under the name of the school of Athens. Poetry, the third subject, is of course the peopling of Mount Parnassus, where Raphael has represented himself as crowned by Virgil. Jurisprudence is depicted by a conclave of the Pope and his Cardinals, on one side of a window, and Justinian promulgating the civil law on the other, by which is meant to be represented the establishment of the civil and canon laws. The painter shows great ingenuity in the arrangement of this picture, which is so awkwardly cut through by a window, as he unites the two subjects by the figures of prudence, temperance, and fortitude, above the window, as if dispensing their influence over both, and forming the link of connection between their respective provinces. A variety of smaller emblematical subjects accompany these majestic works, which the artist intended to constitute the complete code of human science.

It is a subject much controverted by Vasari, Lanzi, and other Italian writers who treat of the fine arts, whether the merits of Raphael are entirely due to his own genius, or to his having profited by the acquirements of Michael Angelo. The progressive change and improvement of his style is a proof of his discernment and persevering study, from which it is neither to be supposed that he would omit any opportunity of advancement, or hesitate to avail himself of knowledge, by whatever means it might be acquired. Accordingly, in the peculiar modesty and candour of his disposition, he is said to have declared, that he thanked God that he had been born in the time of Michael Angelo. Mr. Roscoe says, that he did not imitate, but selected from him. " The works of Michael Angelo were to him a rich magazine; but he rejected as well as approved. The muscular forms, daring outline, and energetic attitudes of the Florentine artist, were harmonized and softened in the elegant and graceful productions of the pencil of Raphael. It is thus that Homer was imitated by Virgil; and it is thus that genius always attracts and assimilates with itself whatever is excellent either in the works of nature or the productions of art."

Raphael continued his labours in the Vatican with increasing fame after the elevation of Leo X., who was too well aware of the glory this accomplished artist was likely to shed over his pontificate, to omit the due meed of favour and munificence. He painted the expulsion of Attila from Italy, supposed to be allegorical of the overthrow of the French power in Italy by Leo X.—the liberation of St. Peter from prison—besides various other subjects in the ceilings and embellishments of these interesting apartments. Raphael was induced by a rich Roman banker, Agostino Chigi, to paint some apartments in his palace, which obtained for the admiration of future generations the lovely works of the Farnesina, descriptive of the history of Cupid and Psyche, where the painter has indulged the full luxuriance of his graceful pencil. It was during his passion for the beautiful Fornarina that he was engaged in the execution of these pictures, which would probably never have been terminated, had not the judicious banker prevailed on the young lady to attend him while at work.

He was not less distinguished for his smaller works in oil, and portraits, possessing such ineffable simplicity and grace, as to have rendered them, in general, the chief gems of every cabinet. There is a chastity of design, and unaffected purity and elegance of outline, in Raphael's works, which, joined to a modesty of colouring, and serene composure of expression, give an air of divinity to his countenances, that renders them uncommonly interesting. They are quite free of the more striking effects of boldness or brilliancy, those obtrusive excellencies that seem to challenge, at first sight, the admiration of all who look upon them. The winning graces of Raphael's more pathetic style steals upon the mind, and gains every moment we continue before them, seldom failing at last to fascinate every eye from the more commanding works of his rivals.

What is called the school of Raphael is the continuation of his pictures of the Vatican, in the execution of which he took the assistance of a number of his pupils. Of the same description is that part of the palace denominated the *Loggie*, where he has displayed that most remarkable profusion of grotesque and arabesque ornaments, whence succeeding generations have drawn the taste and the supply of all that is beautiful in that elegant and playful mode of embellishment. The idea,

as well as much of the subjects, of these arabesques are copied from the antique, which Raphael was at great pains and expence to collect from every quarter where they were to be found. Giulio Romano was principally occupied in painting the *Loggie*, and Giovanni da Udine for the stucco and grotesque works; besides several other painters who worked under the directions of Raphael. It was in this nursery of the art that Polidore de Caravaggio received the inspiration of his genius.

The cartoons, which constitute the principal treasure of Raphael's works that have reached this country, were copies for the tapestry, which, till lately, ornamented the walls of the Pope's chapel at Rome, and are said to have cost seventy thousand crowns. They were bought by king Charles the First from the Flemish workmen, in whose hands they had been left. These masterpieces of invention and genius are too well known to require any description; which, moreover, may be found at length in various works, particularly Richardson on Painting, and in No. 226. of the Spectator. His last great work was the Transfiguration, which was painted in competition with Sebastiano del Piombo, aided by Michael Angelo. This picture is understood to have been considerably damaged, when torn from its original position by the French; nor did it show so well when placed in a different light at the Louvre.

Raphael died soon after the completion of this picture, leaving his unfinished designs, of the battles of Constantine, to be completed by Giulio Romano and Francesco Penni. He had only reached the age of thirty-seven, and died in 1520, by the ignorance of a physician; thus depriving the age of its greatest lustre, and the fine arts of their most brilliant prospect.

The new style and taste introduced by Raphael, formed an epoch in the history of painting, which might have changed the whole future character of the art, had it not been for the untoward circumstances that followed his premature death. Michael Angelo, who followed a scheme of excellence in a rank so totally different, was still occupied in the ardent prosecution of his fame, accompanied by a numerous retinue of followers, who had keenly espoused his style. He survived him by many years, and succeeded in obscuring the efforts made by Raphael's school. The death of Leo, and the inattention of his successors to any thing connected with the fine arts, the devastations of the plague, and the distractions of war, finally dissolved the school of Raphael, and scattered its members to distant parts of Italy, where their works became tinged with the various tastes of other schools.

Among his more distinguished followers was Penni, called Il Fattore, who followed closely and successfully the style of his master, until he became corrupted by an overstrained taste for the colossal. But Giulio Romano was his favourite pupil, and the subsequent heir, along with Penni, of his fortune. He joined a degree of boldness and poetic fire to the milder graces of his master's style, mingling a little of Michael Angelo's vigour and daring in design, but with a harshness of light and shade, which is often at variance with the composure of his subject. He painted chiefly in fresco, of which some magnificent specimens may be seen at Mantua. Perin del Vaga was chiefly occupied with the grotesque and ornamental painting, and Polidore de Caravaggio in imitating the antique basso-relievos, which he painted in the most beautiful chiaro scuro; in this style he has

Giulio Romano.

5

Roman School.

Zuccari.

never been equalled for elegance of outline, and effect of execution. Polidore was associated in this mode of painting with Maturino.

At a later period, the Zuccari supported the reputation of the Roman school, and studied the works of Raphael; they even ventured, in some particulars, upon superior refinement, as has been observed in a picture of the annunciation by Federico. It had been remarked as a solecism, in Raphael's picture of theology, that the irradiance of the Almighty is interfered with by an extraneous light; in the picture of Zuccaro he introduces the sun in full splendour, whose beams are, notwithstanding, subordinate, and overcome by those issuing from the Deity. Baroccio was a painter of merit, and likewise Raffailin di Regio, Passignani, and Arpino, although the art had already begun to decline considerably. Arpino introduced with dexterity, great fire and bustle into his pictures, but crowded them with figures to excess. Nothing requires more judicious management than a multitude of figures assembled on one canvas, so apt are they to fatigue the eye, and distract attention, if at all offensive to the unity of action intended to be represented. The ancient artists of Greece very carefully avoided the hazard of crowding their subjects, either with many figures, or with that complication of decorations so prevalent in some of the modern works. We have several remarkable instances among our great artists, since the revival, of this difficulty being successfully overcome; where the subordinate groups, by very obviously becoming spectators themselves of the scene of action, as well as those who look at it, contribute powerfully to the interest of the subject, by their seeming sympathy with the feelings they seem to indicate.

Caravaggio.

Michael Angelo Caravaggio somewhat arrested the art in its downward progress. He aimed at great simplicity of colouring, but fell into a dark sombre manner, very fitting to the subjects he generally selected, such as nocturnal skirmishes and rencontres, treachery and murder, with strong effects of light and shade. It was not without cause that these scenes of assassination and outrage seemed to dwell upon his mind, as his life had been often exposed to hazard from the stiletto of his enemies; to escape them he fled to Naples, and thence to Malta, where he painted the picture of the decollation of St. John, which still remains in that island.

Andrea Sacchi.

The best colourist which the Roman school has to boast of after its great leader, was Andrea Sacchi. He was a learned and careful artist, painting little but well, so that his works are rare. Like Raphael, he was remarkable for graceful simplicity and correct design.

Salvator Rosa.

Salvator Rosa applied the style of Caravaggio to landscape, into which he threw a character of sombre wildness exceedingly striking, and heightened by imposing groups of figures. Sir Joshua Reynolds gives the character of Salvator's style in these words: "He gives us a peculiar cast of nature, which, though void of all grace, elegance, and simplicity, though it has nothing of that elevation and dignity which belongs to the grand style, yet has that sort of dignity which belongs to savage and uncultivated nature; but what is most to be admired in him is, the perfect correspondence which he observed between the subjects which he chose, and his manner of treating them. Every thing is of a piece; his rocks, trees, sky, even to his handling, have the same rude and wild character which animates his figures."

His talent, though generally known in landscape, was not confined to that branch; as he has left several

martyrdoms, and striking incidents of history, as the conspiracy of Catiline, &c. which are painted in a bold and vigorous style.

Venetian School.

Gaspar Poussin, although a Frenchman, may be classed in the Roman school, as it formed both the rule of his style and the constant theatre of his efforts. He painted in landscape, ornamented with figures, displaying wonderful command of every accident and appearance of nature, and suffusing a classical air over every thing he did.

Gaspar Poussin.

The Roman school had now nearly merged in the general mass into which the arts had sunk in Europe; there are but the names of Ferri, Garzi, and Carlo Maratti, as distinctive supporters of its fame. Mengs attributes this merit to the talents of Maratti alone, who was an ardent admirer and follower of Raphael; whose paintings in the Vatican and Farnesina he was employed to repair. His defect was want of vigour and originality; practising all the rules of art, he had neither manifest defects nor striking beauties.

Venetian School.

Venetian School.

The Venetian school seems to have arisen from an attentive contemplation of the effects of nature, such as they are simply presented to the eye, in all the glory of colouring—studying to seize the true tone of nature in its most beautiful moments, to catch the mellow richness and harmony of its finest tints, and to blend them together with a correct and skilful distribution of light and shade. This was the leading star of the Venetian school, by which its followers were led away from the source of ancient excellence, which had invited the Roman artists to the equally exclusive study of design, independent of the embellishment of colour. The Venetian artist sought the beauties of nature alone for his guide, and these he cultivated with surprising success. Neglectful to a certain degree of the nobler qualities of design, he was exclusively alive to the fascinating charms of harmony, as applied to his art. This he studied to excite by so skilful a disposition of colour as to show each tint to the greatest advantage, to heighten the effect by the contrast of light and shade, the magic of reflected light and reflected colour; by the judicious juxta-position of such tints as seem to bear as distinct a relation to each other as the tones of music; although we are equally at a loss, in both cases, to account for this mysterious rule of nature. They endeavoured so to dispose the subject of their picture, and to arrange the appropriate objects, as to admit naturally, and without restraint, of this melodious display of colours, (if we may so express it,) to fascinate the eye, in the same manner as the ear is fascinated by the simple effect of harmony. The powers of reflection and mind are but little appealed to by the Venetian school. Satisfied with the gratification of voluptuousness, and the passive pleasure of the eye, the spectator is seldom called upon to read and ponder such elaborate and learned works as those of the Roman and Florentine masters, or to appreciate the intrinsic merits of design and invention;—which, in fact, constitute the poetry of painting abstracted from those qualities that address the eye alone. We find the graver subjects of sacred history, the mine into which the other schools have so exclusively dug, little if at all the resort of the Venetian. Instead of the purposes of religion, to which the Italian pencil is so entirely dedicated, as to people the cabinets of Europe with saints, madonnas, and Bible subjects, from Venice we have scarcely any thing but grave senators, gorgeous feasts, and naked beauties.

Venetian
School.

Titian, Paul Veronese, Tintoretto, Giorgione, and
Bassano, were the chief ornaments of this school. Its
early progress in the arts was characterized by the same
events and circumstances, which affected the general
development of reviving taste, in those parts of Italy
which we have already considered. A marked tendency was given to the peculiar features of their style,
from two circumstances in the history of this city;
namely, the great efforts that were made at so very
early a period as the eleventh century, for the embellishment of the church of St. Mark; and the subsequent introduction of oil painting, in which Venice
took the lead of the rest of Italy. The construction
of St. Mark occasioned both Greece and Italy to be
ransacked for artists, and Constantinople for sculptured
stones, pillars, and marbles. Every splendour that the
art was then capable of, was summoned to assist the magnificence of this moresque temple; so that the rich and
gaudy ornament so profusely lavished upon this their
greatest boast, could not fail strongly to influence their
future taste in the arts in general. Accustomed to the
gay dresses and sumptuous manners of eastern nations,
with whom a long series of traffic and conquest had
brought the Venetians into contact, and confined as
they were to the narrow compass of a wretched sand
bank, hemmed in on all sides by the sea; the immense
wealth that had accumulated in the families of many
of these haughty merchant monarchs could only gain
vent in the splendour of their persons and palaces. The
fashion also of brilliant festivals and pompous processions, where it was usual to display all the gorgeous attire
of eastern princes, naturally augmented the florid tone
of their style of art.

Venice teemed with mosaics, ancient statues, and basso-relievos, besides the gaudy gilded pictures of modern
Greece, which flowed in upon them in consequence of
the capture of Constantinople, in the year 1204; but
still the moresque and florid remained the prevailing
taste. When somewhat advanced in refinement, the
discovery of Van Eyck occurred, and was communicated to the Venetian artists by Antonello de Messina,
who went to Flanders on purpose to learn the secret;
and was induced, by a salary, to make it available to
his brother artists. The advantage of oil, in facilitating
the smooth harmony and brilliancy of colouring, and the
softening and blending of tints, so much cherished by
the Venetian painters, occasioned that mode to be
greedily adopted, in preference to the severer works in
fresco.

Geo. Bellini, who had succeeded his father and brother as the leading artist of Venice towards the close
of the fifteenth century, was the first who practised
and obtained success in the new mode of oil painting.
He was not surpassed by any artist of his age in gracefulness of pencil, mellowness of colouring, or ardour
in the study of nature; but, like Pietro Perugino, his
chief glory is now considered to consist in having
guided the early studies of those destined to higher
fame than himself. He was the master of Titian,
Giorgione, and Sebastian del Piombo, in whom the
style may be said to have taken its distinctive character. But, although the seducing qualities of the brilliant and ornamental were the predominating merits
of this school, we are not therefore to suppose that they
were either ignorant of design, careless in composition,
or negligent of expression; for, as these qualities were
paramount in Rome and Florence, and at the same
time consistent with a high degree of excellence in
colour and chiaro scuro, so were these latter qualities

Antonello
de Mes-
sina.

Geo. Bel-
lini.

cultivated at Venice in preference, but not in prejudice,
of the others.

They were led from this view of the art to a more
careful and studied execution, following a different process from Raphael and others, in order to bring out
greater brilliancy of colour and softness of effect. According to Lanzi, they were in the practice of painting
on a ground purely white, which greatly aided the production of bright and transparent effect, with minuteness of detail which could be heightened to any extent.
They did not work by spreading their tints, and blending them into each other, as is usually done, but by
pointing on the colour according to the practice of miniature painters. By this means they were enabled to
go on augmenting the depth, force, and effect, without
disturbing the purity of the virgin tints, by the blendings and shadings of the usual mode. To be able to avail
themselves of the benefits which this mode of working was
calculated to convey, depending so much on confident
knowledge and correctness; not only great address of
pencil was required, but such a knowledge of the higher
qualities of the art, as design, expression, composition, &c. as can be possessed by the greatest artists only. Hence the unexpected difficulties that are experienced by those who attempt to imitate or copy the
works of the great Venetian masters, which seem to
breathe with the glowing colours of life; it arises from
the inimitable art with which their works are executed,
being so much less obvious, than when the merit consists chiefly in design and composition.

The great advantage of their mode is the avoiding of
hardness, the power of giving depth to the picture, and
heightening the illusion of a more delicate chiaro
scuro.

They did not confine their minute care to the carna-
tions alone, but extended it equally to the texture of
the draperies, to the high-wrought ornaments of their
gorgeous attire, and also to the subordinate accompaniments of the picture, with such softness, brilliancy, and
truth of representation, as to make every part of the
performance equally valuable.

The fine epoch of the Venetian school began with
Giorgione and Titian, who lived in friendship with
each other, and worked as rivals; and had not a premature death, at the age of thirty-four, arrested the
genius of Giorgione in its middle course, it is doubtful
if Titian would have carried off the palm which the
advantage of a longer life secured to him. Giorgione,
despising the minute work of his master Bellini, boldly
launched into a grand and free style of painting, strongly
marked at first, and designed for effect, but gradually refining into a masterly display of vigorous outline, with
rich and careful finishing. He painted a great deal in
fresco, which was perhaps best adapted to the boldness
of his pencil; but as these works were generally on the
outside of the walls of Venetian mansions, scarcely any
of them now remain. Many of his works in oil are still
in good preservation, painted with what artists call a
fat touch; they are principally portraits, and remarkable for strength of character and richness of attire,
glowing with life, gold, and jewellery.

Sebastian del Piombo followed the same style, and
imitated Giorgione very closely, though he fell short
of him in vigour; he likewise had most success in portraits, and particularly excelled in the admirable painting of the hands, the fine flesh tints, and, as is usual with
the Venetian masters, the lordly accompaniments that
surrounded his figures. Geo. de Udine, and Torbido,
called Il Moro, were both of Giorgione's school, as

Venetian
School.

Giorgione.

Sebastian
del Piom-
bo.

well as old Palma, and many other masters, which it were needless to enumerate here.

Titian was nothing of a poet; he was a mere painter: but as a painter of nature he had few equals in his own age or any other. In his females, it is nature in the richest bloom and full glow of beauty, and in his male figures there is a lordly dignity and splendour in which he stands unrivalled. Titian was the favourite child of nature, for he seemed to see but her beauties, and selected with admirable discrimination, both in portrait and landscape, the subjects most suitable to his pencil and particular tone of feeling. So quick and correct was his perception of the infinite modifications of light and colours, the diversities of demi-tints reflected and blended in the interminable maze of nature's colouring, as to acquire at last an exquisitely delicate and transparent mode of painting. Nothing escaped him that exists in nature, however subtle and evanescent; it is not uncommon, in his pictures, to observe the surrounding colours and objects delicately reflected by every surface capable of reflecting, even in the eyes of the figures; and at the same time that he followed nature into her most secret details, he knew how to preserve the equilibrium of colouring to a degree superior to any painter that ever existed, and which so few have been able to command. Instead of his broad shades being the dark mass generally placed for the relief of light, they are found, upon examination, to consist of that innumerable and playful shifting of shades, which is discernible in the deepest shadows of nature when minutely examined. In Titian's pictures they appear simple and easily managed, because they produce the majestic simplicity of nature; but it is a simplicity arising from infinite variety.

Shade is not the absolute absence of light, otherwise it becomes a hole in the picture; the objects under its influence must be as distinguishable in form and colour as when placed in light. In this Titian has, above all others, succeeded; so disposing them as to produce perfect repose from the judicious balancing of the picture. Shade is entirely governed by contrast and juxta-position, for what is light in one part would be shade if otherwise placed; accordingly, we find those objects opposed to a light sky acquire a degree of comparative shade, while the same tone becomes light when opposed to a darker object.

There are some brilliant pictures of Titian in the ducal palace of Venice, and in other collections of that city, where they seem so perfectly at home, in correspondence with the glowing warmth and tone of splendour that pervades the local scenery. Titian continued his labours to the venerable age of ninety-nine, and had he been spared by the plague, might have numbered a hundred years of his celebrated career, as his natural strength enabled him to wield his pencil to the last. His later works do, notwithstanding, indicate a feebler flight of genius, the failure of sight and the tremulous hand of old age. He was quite impatient of the trouble of teaching, so that he left few scholars but has always had a numerous host of imitators. He was jealous and fearful of rivals to such an extent, that he cautiously excluded Tintoretto from his study, and having discovered in his own brother remarkable capacity and predisposition for painting, he obliged him to renounce the pencil and become a merchant. Paris Bordon was among the best of his followers.

Tintoretto, though he imitated the colouring of Titian, was a painter of quite a different cast, full of fire and sprightliness. He studied the ancients, and painted with surprising expedition, and, notwithstanding in-

correctness of design, he was perhaps the first of the Venetian school. His real name was Robusti, which was not an unapt appellation for a man of his vigorous genius. Vasari stamps his taste as the excess of fantastical, which the opportunities we have had of examining his great works at Venice and elsewhere, make us disposed to controvert; bold and fanciful we admit, but we can scarcely go along with Vasari, when he asserts, " That of all the extraordinary geniuses that ever practised the art of painting, for wild, capricious, extravagant, and fantastical inventions, for furious impetuosity, and boldness in the execution of his work, there is none like Tintoretto; his strange whimsies are even beyond extravagance, and his works seem to be produced rather by chance, than in consequence of any previous design, as if he wanted to convince the world that the art was a trifle, and of the most easy attainment." There is in general an exuberance of bustle among his figures which discomposes the grouping and irritates the attention; he was neglectful of the advantage to be drawn from the introduction of groups and figures who merely look on and take no part in the action,—one of the helps so much observed by the best painters, and so useful to connect the spectator with the picture.

Schiavone and Bassano were likewise great painters of this school; the ducal palace contains some magnificent works of Bassano, particularly the humiliation of the Emperor Frederick to the Pope; he was particularly expert in his representation of animals. The tide seemed to have turned at the death of Titian, as few of the multitude of Venetian masters who laboured to maintain the fame of their school after his reign, could at all support the high rank which he had gained for it. We shall only mention Paul Veronese, who revelled in all the luxuriance of the Venetian taste for gold and glitter. His compositions are neither historically correct nor elegant in design, but possess a freshness and magnificence of colouring which is extremely attractive. Venice abounds with his works, but there are none more pleasing than his martyrdom of St. George at Verona, which was one of the spoils restored from France. He is more generally known on this side of the Alps by his picture of the feast at Cana, so placed as to be the first picture to arrest the admiring multitudes who daily visit the Louvre. Banquets are in general the best pictures of Paul Veronese, as he is not strong in expression, and the occupation of eating and drinking requires little. We may add Sebastiano Ricci, Tiepolo, and several others of a later date.

Lombard School.

In comprehending under the denomination of the Lombard school the various styles of art that have arisen under the auspices of the different great masters of the north of Italy, we are aware that they admit of little assimilation save that of locality alone. Parma, Bologna, Modena, Genoa, and other cities, obtained celebrity from the various kinds of excellence possessed by the distinguished painters who practised their art in each, and established their different schools; but the separate examination of each, where a different style gave claim to a distinctive name, would lead us far beyond the limits of the very brief sketch we propose to give of the progress of the art. Those who desire more minute detail will find elaborate and ample information in the very valuable work of the Abbate Lanzi's *Storia Pittorica dell' Italia*. The fame of these cisalpine schools arose at a much later period than those we have already considered, and, in fact, were derived from a combination of the qualities of the schools that preceded them; and, considering the acquirements of the leading masters in whom they severally originated, they might be expected to exhibit all the excellencies without any of the impurities of the sources from whence they drew. Grandeur of conception was to be sought in the bold and scientific outline of Michael Angelo; from Raphael, chaste invention, elegant composition, variety of character, sweetness and modest propriety of attire, with the exquisite diffusion of mind over every feature of his figures; and, lastly, in Titian, the magic of colouring and delightful play of light. There is but the union of these to complete the wished for perfection, of which, however, the scope of human talent is perhaps scarcely capable.

In Corregio, whose name is characteristic of the school of Parma, there is no doubt a very near approach to this ideal union of excellence. No painter ever exhibited a more graceful delicacy and lovely conception of character, a greater mellowness of colour, and that rich liquid outline, which is quite beautiful. His works were, however, somewhat defective in originality, vigour of thought, and in that air of dignity which results from a study of the antique. We shall not attempt to reduce the varied excellencies of the great painters of Lombardy to any general character, which would amount to a higher degree of perfection in a greater number of the attributes of painting than any individual school or master ever attained; a short notice of their separate attainments will sufficiently show how much the progress of the arts was indebted to their efforts.

Andrea Mantegua. Andrea Mantegua was the earliest painter of note in this quarter of the world. He was a native of Padua, and established his school at Mantua, in the end of the fifteenth century, where he has left some works of great merit, fresh and brilliant in the colours. The character given by Lanzi, of one of his pictures is, that " every head might serve as a pattern for vivacity and character, and some of them even for the imitation of antique. There is a freedom and fulness in the design, both of the naked and drapery, which contradicts the common opinion, that a dry manner, and that of Mantegua, is one and the same. The triumph of Cæsar, consisting of various pieces, was considered his principal work; these pictures are said to have found their way to England.

Corregio. Corregio, whose name was Antonio Allegri, was educated in the school of Mantegua, or rather copied his works, as Mantegua died in 1506, before he could have profited by his instruction. He had the good fortune to come into notice, at a time when it was resolved to ornament the great dome of Parma, the cupola of which he was invited to paint. To this fortunate selection the world is perhaps indebted for the great lustre that burst forth on the Lombardy republic of painting; for it has generally happened, that the great epochs in the improvement of the art, have been preceded by the opportunity of some such vast undertaking. Apelles rose under the munificence of Pericles; to the decorations of the Vatican, both Raphael and Michael Angelo owed the development of their genius, and to those of the great church of Parma we may attribute the excellence of Corregio. This great man is said to have struggled in his youth under the weight of indigence and obscurity, without the assistance of education, or an opportunity of improvement by inspecting the works of other masters, or the remains of antiquity. He worked his way into notice by the unaided ef-

forts of natural genius alone. And yet no painter that has ever appeared treads so close on the dominion of Raphael, who enjoyed all these advantages in perfection, under the protection of his powerful relative, Bramanti, and in the sunshine of royal favour. Corregio, on the contrary, is considered to have passed his short life in want and difficulties, from the burden of a large family, whom the reward of his labours scarcely sufficed to support; and to have ultimately died of chagrin at the paltry price he received for his great work at Parma.

Doubts are attached to the more early works of Corregio, arising from the circumstance of his fluctuating style before he had come to a determination of the preferable manner to be followed; he reached that perfect style so gradually, by constant advances and improvement, that it is difficult to say at what period he actually formed his manner. His great work of the cupola of the cathedral of Parma, which represents the assumption of the Virgin, was finished in the year 1530, and is painted in a manner which has commanded the unqualified admiration of future ages. It is esteemed for grandeur of design, and boldness of conception in the foreshortenings, which are very surprising, when we consider the difficulty of painting with truth and grace, what is to be looked at overhead. The immense and varied multitude of the heavenly host that surround and bear up the virgin, grouped and employed in the most skilful manner, exhibits a surprisingly happy invention. The exultation of joy and triumph seems diffused over the whole scene with that pure serenity we look for in the countenances of heavenly gladness. They seem to move in a glory of light that effectually withdraws the scene from every thing earthly. Notwithstanding the damage this magnificent picture has sustained from the effect of time, the harmony of colour and effect by which such a multitude of figures and groups are melted together into one beautiful whole is quite surprising. His picture of the Virgin and St. Jerome, likewise in Parma, is considered as one of the very finest works in Italy, and the masterpiece of Corregio, for composition and admirable sweetness of expression in the virgin. He is particularly excellent in his mode of painting children, whom he represents with such infantine simplicity and grace, and usually with such a captivating smile on their countenances, that they irresistibly draw forth expressions of endearment from all who behold them.

Corregio brought the power of foreshortening, as seen from underneath, to perfection; and exhibits a playful variety in his attitudes, that seems to tame every difficulty into perfect subjection to his pencil, and, moreover, brought out with such a luminous effect of colouring as to produce perfect illusion. His great strength was in his management of light and shade, in which he stands unequalled. There is no monotony of effect; every where is seen the shifting and play of nature itself; such depth and roundness, that we are tempted to endeavour to look behind his objects. These excellencies are conspicuous in all his performances, but particularly in that striking picture called the Night of Corregio at Dresden, representing the infant Jesus discovered by the shepherds. In this remarkable composition, the distance is discernible in the serene light of the moon, while the figures are illuminated by the miraculous effulgence of the infant God, whose body seems transparent, and shining with a mysterious sort of light that dazzles the surrounding figures, and is managed so admirably as to maintain all the dignity required by such a subject.

Since the death of this great artist his style has become the study of succeeding generations of painters, and is placed with Raphael and Michael Angelo as the summit of attainment to be aimed at. Of these followers, few have approached, and certainly none have ever equalled him. He had a son who painted, but his progress was of short duration, and his works of little note. It was the sight of Corregio's pictures that is said to have inflamed the ardour of Parmegiano, who raised himself to a very high rank as an artist; he followed the style of Corregio with devotion for some time, until having seen the works of other great masters at Rome, he formed a style for himself, in which grace and dignity were the characteristic features. His love for the graceful led him to prolong over-much the proportions of his figures; according to the opinion of many, his colouring is of a subdued and modest tone, very suitable to his graceful design; in painting children, his skill was such that his works have been often mistaken for those of Corregio.

As the diffusion of the arts had progressively spread over all the little states of Lombardy, where some leading master in each guided the taste of his townsmen, the effect became prejudicial to the general interests of painting, in so far as it became frittered into a diversity of manners, where one quality generally predominated to the prejudice of others equally essential. Many were led into false refinements from the desire of distinction, and the wish to avoid the servile imitation of any master, as almost every form of beauty in painting had been already appropriated as the peculiar study of some one of them. It became difficult to strike out any thing new, except in exaggeration of what had already been done, in caricaturing the grace and simplicity of Raphael, the anatomy of Angelo, or the foreshortening and mellow rotundity of Corregio.

The honour of correcting the prejudicial tendency of these circumstances, of arresting for a time the decay of the art, is due to that celebrated family from whom the school of Bologna derives its greatest fame. The Carracci conceived the happy design of establishing a school as a point of union, for the better study of the art, and as a check upon the extravagant taste and corruptions with which the whims of individual artists polluted its purity. The three brothers resolved to dedicate their time, fortune, and talents, to the labours of this great undertaking, and, after having travelled to every place where any thing could be learnt in the art, studied the diversified styles of all the great masters of Italy, improved their own, and stored their minds with every advantage to be derived and selected from the many sources that were scattered into waste over so wide a field, they returned to Bologna. Here they sought to concentrate all that was valuable in the practice of the arts by establishing a great school, afterwards called the Academy of the Carraccis. The undertaking was attended with the happiest effects; students flocked eagerly from all quarters; collections of pictures of good masters, and of the antique, were by degrees provided; models and anatomical preparations were furnished, with a skilful master to instruct in that science; the three brothers themselves (or rather, to speak correctly, the two brothers and their cousin Ludovico) were assiduous and eminent in the talent of teaching, so that in a very short time the eyes of the world were directed with admiration to so great a seminary of the fine arts, reared by the exertions of

private individuals alone. The great dogma of the school was the judicious union of the study of the great masters, and of the antique, with nature itself. It soon acquired so high a reputation, as to control the taste of painting in almost every quarter. It is remarkable to find at its head, a man whose early progress in the arts was so slow and unpromising, as to induce his master, Tintoretto, to recommend a change of pursuit, as his attempts in painting seemed so very hopeless of ultimate success. But Ludovico Carracci was a youth in whom solid judgment and steady purpose made up for want of promptitude in his nature. He had the sagacity early to discern in what the true merit of painting lay, and determined perseveringly to follow its pursuit, without swerving, as is usual with the generality of young artists, after its more showy and superficial parts. He pursued his studies in various parts of Italy, and returned to Bologna, where he persuaded his two cousins, Augustino and Hannibal Carracci, the sons of his uncle, who was a tailor in that city, to follow his example, and apply themselves to painting. He undertook to instruct them himself, and, upon this slender basis, was the foundation of the great school of the Carraccis laid. The school had been in activity for some time before the masters themselves had attained great celebrity as painters; and one of the advantageous effects of teaching was the very rapid improvement in the excellencies of the teachers themselves. Although their individual styles had considerable resemblance to each other, yet they were far from being alike eminent, as Hannibal excelled the other two very greatly; in style, Ludovico is said to tend towards Titian, Augustino to Tintoretto, and Hannibal to Corregio.

In all that Ludovico painted, he showed profound knowledge of the principles of his art, graceful dignified design, and chaste colouring. His cousin, Augustino, painted very little; he was a good draughtsman, and carved in metal; he showed more talent in the invention of subject than in the execution of painting.

Hannibal Carracci had acquired a beautiful style of colouring from studying the works of Titian and Corregio. He obtained from the works of Raphael knowledge of correct and graceful design, to which he added the nobleness and grandeur of Angelo. He early showed his disposition for painting, and when still a boy, accompanying his father on a journey, they had the misfortune to be robbed. Hannibal drew portraits so resembling the banditti, that they were in consequence all taken and convicted. His greatest works were the much admired paintings of the Farnese Palace at Rome, in which the grace and elegance of Raphael's style is conspicuous; in fact, they hold a rank little inferior to Raphael's finest works. The whole cieling, of above sixty feet in length of the gallery, is occupied by seven great fresco paintings of Hannibal Carracci, representing the triumph of Bacchus and Ariadne, the story of Galatea, and a variety of other subjects of mythology, equalling in the magnitude of the undertaking the great labours of Raphael in the Vatican. The subjects are varied in the most skilful manner, and accompanied with innumerable smaller works, all of which are exquisite in taste and finishing. There is a degree of gaiety and graceful splendour diffused through every part of this painted creation, that is exceedingly fascinating. So multifarious and uniformly excellent are these works, that it would seem miraculous to have been the work of one man, and of but a short period of his life; they have ever since been the

Lombard School.

chief study of succeeding artists. Hannibal Carracci was likewise exceedingly successful in the burlesque style of composition, of which there are some admirable examples in Rome. There is a picture of this description belonging to his pencil, namely, the Pan and Apollo, which we find we have by mistake placed among the works of ancient art, p. 221. To this may be added the very amusing collection of burlesques, called the " Arti di Bologna," which was the production chiefly of Hannibal Carracci.

Dominechino.

Of the many distinguished artists who issued from the celebrated school of the Carracci, Dominechino deserves particularly to be mentioned, whose name was Zampieri. He has been esteemed by many to surpass in excellence Hannibal Carracci himself, and to be second to Raphael only. This was the opinion of Poussin, who was the first to establish the superior merit of this painter, in preferring his celebrated picture in the church of St. Gregorio at Rome, where it is brought into direct competition with Guido's Martyrdom of St. Andrew, to the performance of that master. Dominechino has a bold and masterly pencil, and was in the habit of working his mind up to the feeling of the passion he meant to represent, which made him be taken for a madman, when occasionally discovered under the influence of these artificial paroxysms. The expression of violent passions was indeed his favourite study. He was engaged in painting his martyrdom of St. Andrew, and about to represent the rage of a soldier, when Hannibal Carracci came to see him, and declared that he had received more instruction from the sight of the painter himself than he had ever done from any picture. He painted generally in fresco, and somewhat in a theatrical style, from the architecture with which he was in use to accompany his subjects, and in which he excelled particularly. There is no obscurity in his subjects ; the figures speak their purpose with expression, force, and dignity ; in fact, were they gifted with speech, they would tell their story perhaps less impressively than they do in the skilful language of Dominechino's pencil.

Albani.

Albani, the great painter of nymphs and cupids, was the intimate friend and fellow labourer of Dominechino. The one engrossed the fierce and stormy passions, and the trials of fortitude which rouse the strongest energies of man ; while the other delighted in the scenes of infant sport, of gaiety, and voluptuousness. He painted the innocent and pathetic with a gay rosy tone of colour, and threw a feminine grace into his figures of Venus and the nymphs, in which he is unequalled. He was the Anacreon of painting, and seldom quitted his favourite theme, to which he had been led, not only by taste and study, but by the accident of possessing a handsome wife and twelve beautiful children, who were always at hand to sit for the subjects he delighted to paint, and to feed his appetite for the beauty of the infantine and female form. He selected the most luxuriant and beautiful scenery in nature for the subject of his pictures, which he united in the sweetest harmony with his figures. The serene repose of scenery which surrounds his sleeping Venus's, the fresh morning tints, and opening flowers, that appear around Diana and her attendants, and Galatea sporting on the placid waves, are quite charming. There is a playfulness and elegance of fancy in the employments of the little roguish cupids that people his pictures, which is exceedingly captivating

The great rival of Albani at Rome was Guido, who excited, moreover, very strongly the jealousy of the Carracci. He painted with a silvery smoothness and delicacy that gained more upon the eye than the judgment. Nothing can be lovelier or more winning than his female figures, yet when brought into parallel with the spiritual and deep feeling of Raphael and Corregio's works, they appear vapid and tame. Guido was, notwithstanding, great in his particular line, which was that of the angelic, graceful modesty, devotion, and, above all, the pathetic. The melting eyes, pious and humble resignation, of his Madonnas, is the sentiment in which he is inimitable, and which he expresses with a pearly delicacy of colouring peculiar to himself. The pictures of Guido most generally known are the Aurora in the Rospigliosi garden at Rome, and the St. Andrew already mentioned : but there are few collections without some specimen of his delicate pencil. His favourite studies were the works of Paul Veronese, Raphael, Corregio, and Parmegiano, from whom he borrowed many excellencies, and made them his own by the charm of his peculiar character. Whether he changed the attitude, the tone, or the expression, beauty attended whatever he did, and a mild grace peculiar to himself. The manner of Guido was much esteemed during his lifetime, and attracted a numerous attendance to his school, which was productive of considerable influence in softening the taste for the severer manner of his predecessors, and introducing the love for his mild and gentle beauties. But this was a taste which could not fail, in the progress of imitation, to enervate and corrupt the true principles of the art.

French School.

Guido.

Another celebrated follower of the Carraccis was Lanfranco, who attained to great excellence in design and composition, but was addicted to a very dark mode of colouring. Likewise Schidone, whose pictures are rare. Michael Angelo de Caravaggio can scarcely be called the pupil of any master, as he followed nature alone, and his own peculiar style ; his manner is black, but forcible. He was the master of Spagnoletto, who delighted in horrible subjects ; and of Gueronio, who was in every respect a pleasing artist. Castiglione, Velasques, Grimaldi, Murillos, and Luco Geordano, are likewise entitled to a place among the great masters who flourished in Lombardy, or issued from its schools.

Lanfranco.

French School.

There does not exist a greater bar to improvement or excellence in any art, than an overweaning notion of self-perfection, and an unwillingness to admit the superior acquirements of others. Many individual artists of great merit have, at different periods, existed in France ; but we fear that this masterful principle in the natural disposition of the people, will for ever exclude them from superior national eminence in any particular branch of acquirement. It is the creative fancy principally that fails in France, the powers of intuitive genius; for they have at all times exhibited an uncommon facility and adaptation of talent to the exercise of the fine arts ; a power of imitation, the ready acquirement of a skilful and dexterous execution, which might have laid the foundation of very great excellence ; but wherever any excursive effort appeared in the strength of original genius and invention, we generally find them vapouring in the unreal and vapid elegancies of sentimentality. That sort of refinement which is at war with nature, and unaffected simplicity, and is the very canker of every thing that is noble or dignified in the fine arts.

It would be difficult to assign any distinctive character to the French school of painting, where the style was liable to fluctuate from master to master, according to the person who happened to be in fashion for the

French School.

time. There were various periods of its history when the taste of France had the good fortune to be led by men of sound judgment and high acquirements in the arts, as Le Poussin and Le Sueur; and while their influence lasted, there was every appearance of the French school attaining a very respectable rank; but as stability is a rare virtue in that country, a new fashion soon drew the tide of taste into a different channel. A disposition so fluctuating is alone sufficient to counteract the best efforts of individuals; for nothing proves more prejudicial to the progress of the arts than that ephemeral tyrant fashion, whose only merit is that he did not exist a short while before, and that he shall not exist a short while hence. A painter cannot be guilty of a more foolish determination than to yield his judgment to this delusion, and join the ranks of fashion. He cannot expect otherwise than that his labours should partake of its uncertain nature, and in due time pass into the neglect, at least, if not the ridicule, which generally attends an antiquated fashion. If he expects to outlive the particular taste of the day, a painter must banish every thing from view, but those sound and fundamental principles of art that have stood the test of ages. He must generalize his subject if he expects to sympathise with the taste of other times and countries; he must separate the abstract idea of beauty from the varieties of affected and adventitious refinements with which it is at times liable to become overloaded.

The natural propensity which seems constantly urging the French taste into these forced and preposterous airs and attitudes, of which it is at the present moment more than ever a prey, seems very powerful when we consider the advantages she has had in giving birth to several artists of very superior acquirements; and latterly, the singular advantage of possessing in her own hands such an assemblage of the finest works of every age and country, as never were before collected into one place. " However the mechanic and ornamental arts may sacrifice to fashion, she must be entirely excluded from painting. The painter must never mistake this capricious changeling for the genuine offspring of nature; he must divest himself of all prejudices in favour of his age or country; he must disregard all local and temporary ornaments, and look only on those general habits that are every where and always the same. He addresses his works to the people of every country and every age; and calls upon posterity to be his spectators." " The prejudices in favour of the fashions and customs that we have been used to, and which are justly called a second nature, make it too often difficult to distinguish that which is natural from that which is the result of education; they frequently even give a predilection in favour of the artificial mode; and almost every one is apt to be guided by those local prejudices, who has not chastised his mind, and regulated the instability of his affections, by the eternal invariable idea of nature."

The earliest practice of the art that seems to have been exercised in France, was in the decoration of their church windows with portraits, armorial bearings, and subjects of sacred history, stained in brilliant colours on the glass, or enamelled on copper for the vessels of the altar. These last are much esteemed in France, as curious specimens of their ancient art, and many of them are remarkable, not only for extreme delicacy of workmanship, but as interesting compositions, descriptive of the state of art in the early ages, and of the manner and history of the times of which they are in general representations. They are of a different descrip-

tion from the enamel works of the ancients, which were either for the purpose of mosaic painting, or artificial gems. These were constructed by means of slender rods of coloured glass, applied longitudinally together, and welded into one thick rod, so disposed as to represent the device intended at each end, so that it admitted of being sliced down into as many copies of the coloured figure as was desired. The French mode was, on the contrary, actual painting, with coloured glass upon copper, which was much practised, and in great repute, in the thirteenth century, both in France and Germany. The manufactory was carried on principally at Limoge, in Guienne, where the abundance of mines of different metals, and operations of smelting, probably led to its introduction. The most ancient are done in black and white, simply representing scriptural subjects very curiously executed. The art continued to improve, and, towards the age of Francis the First, had attained great perfection, and actually possessed many of the qualities of good painting. The goldsmiths took up the idea, and, by applying it to the ornamental works on the precious metals, were the means of increasing its importance, and engaging the talents of the best artists in the prosecution of this art. It became the usual mode of portrait painting, of which there exist some exceedingly beautiful specimens, possessing the advantage of being everlasting, and little liable to accident. Having to undergo the action of fire in the process, they must either be done on metal, or some other substance that can resist its action.

The process is as follows: Having powdered a plate of metal with pounded white enamel, it is placed on the furnace until melted into a white uniform glazing; the same is then done to the other side; metallic colours are then prepared of a more fusible nature than the white enamel ground already put on; the colours are rubbed down in oil, and applied in the usual mode of painting. After this, the plate is put into the furnace, and the process of painting and melting repeated as often as is necessary, with this precaution, that some pounded transparent glass is mixed with all the colours to assist their fusion, and by increasing this fusible addition in proportion as the work is repeated: It is the last laid on colour only that melts, having been thus rendered more fusible than the one that preceded it. The greatest difficulty in this sort of painting is, like that of fresco works, many of the colours being quite different in appearance when applied, from what they become after being fused. But this is a difficulty that a little practice is able to overcome.

Francis the First was the first French monarch who seemed to consider the improvement of the arts as an acquisition desirable for the glory of his country; and accordingly, with commendable zeal, he drew to Paris all the Italian artists that his bounty could induce to settle there. Francis had the merit of carrying on a successful rivalry in this pursuit with Henry the Eighth of England, who made proposals to the same painters, but not with the same effect, as he proved unsuccessful in all his attempts. Rosso, a very excellent painter of Florence, was of this number, who passed his best days in France, decorating the palace of Fountainbleau, and painting the deeds of his patron Francis. He likewise obtained the assistance of Primaticcio, from Bologna, who was the first to introduce fresco painting into France; he likewise worked at Fountainbleau, in great rivalry with Rosso. His general knowledge in the fine arts was the means of diffusing considerable improvement into the taste of the country, by procuring for

4

the king a considerable supply of sculpture and bronzes from his native country ; thus rearing the first germ of a taste for the antique, and the style of the Roman school of painting.

The first native painter of France, whose name we find recorded, is Jean Cousin, who copied the manner of Primaticcio, and wrote on the subject of design. His pictures are not without merit in composition and expression. He painted a last judgment, of which there are engravings, and was likewise a glass-stainer and statuary.

Freminet, about the same time, imitated the manner of Michael Angelo, and Blanchard that of Titian, whose works are still to be seen pretty numerously in Paris and its neighbourhood. But the greatest painter that France ever produced, was Nicholas Poussin, although he acquired and continued to prosecute his art principally in Italy, nor did there appear any thing at all national in his manner of painting. He is, notwithstanding, called the Raphael of France. He was a correct and learned artist, and much devoted to the study of the antique, which led him to a grand simplicity of manner, though often dry and uninteresting. Mythology and ancient fable were his favourite subjects, and these his profound knowledge of every thing connected with the history and manners of the ancients enabled him to handle in a manner pure and classical, so much so, that he seemed far more at home in the society of Ovid's creation than the beings of his own age. From this circumstance, his pictures never offend by the incongruities so often exhibited in these allegorical and fabulous representations, where we find the scenes of every day life, and the familiar accompaniments of sober truth, peopled by the beings of pure fiction in all the wild transmutations of Ovid's fancy. In Poussin's pictures every thing is of a piece ; the landscape accords with its occupiers, and there is nothing to bring the mind back to reality. Poussin returned to Paris with a view to establish himself there, and would no doubt have had considerable influence in forming the taste of his countrymen ; but a disagreement with his rivals Vouet, Fouquier, and others, made him resolve to quit it again, and retire to Rome, where he continued to prosecute his art till his death in 1665.

Simon Vouet, the great persecutor and rival of Poussin, established a considerable school in France. He was a man of vigorous and active genius, painting with surprising facility and invention, but unfortunately with rather a slender foundation of knowledge or study. His ardour, however, set the energies of his pupils afloat ; and, although his manner was not much imitated, he was the means of stirring up the genius, and preparing the way for an improvement of taste among his countrymen. Like Raphael, he painted many cartoons for the tapestry works, though they do not appear to have had sufficient merit for preservation like those of the great master. Vouet would, doubtless, have become a great painter had the vivacity and promptitude of his genius allowed him to mature his talent. He was in the custom of sketching his subjects with careless rapidity, and either allowing them to be painted up by his pupils, or himself hastened through the laborious process of finishing, with the impatience of a mind that sighed for something new to exercise its fancy upon. This is a rock upon which the genius of many a promising artist has been wrecked. Run away with by the notion that the exalted merit of their art lies in the operations of invention and mental energy alone, they neglect the indispensable acquirements of practical

Nicholas Poussin.

Vouet.

knowledge and dexterity in giving that substance to their effusions which can alone render them available.

The most distinguished pupil of Vouet was Le Brun, who contributed greatly to elevate the character of the French school. He was prolific in grand subjects, nobly conceived, and executed with accuracy and skill ; the greater part of which are too intimately known to those who have enjoyed the spectacle of the Louvre to require to be mentioned. His expressions are a little theatrical and not sufficiently varied ; yet this branch was the subject of his particular study, as appears from his well known treatise on the subject ; but this very circumstance may have contributed to limit his observation on the subject, and make him the mannerist, which, in this particular, his works testify that he became. He had systematized and reduced into the narrow compass of imaginary rules, a subject which is as various as the infinitely varied modifications of passion and feelings, of which expression is indicative. The passions may admit of general classification ; but as each contains a world of indefinable diversities, it is in vain to attempt the definition of so general an idea by one specific representation. From having, however, laid down these rules, Le Brun was naturally induced to act upon them, and the consequence is a monotony of expression in which he seems even to copy himself. If Le Brun's passions were not generally announced in the representation, we might often be at a loss to give each its specific character ; in fact, instead of a representation of the human passions, we might, without much stretch of probability, write them down, The varieties of insanity pourtrayed !

The leading error in the mode of expressing character by French artists, partakes, as might be expected, a good deal of their manners in ordinary life. Instead of representing much by slight indications of expression, as is consistent with the dignified and grave demeanour of heroic character, or even of common life any where but in France, they employ violent and exaggerated expression to denote comparatively feeble movements of the mind. Like players, they overcharge the expression and attitudes, in order to make their impression discernible in the galleries, which is not only unnecessary, but destructive of effect ; as an expression which seems suppressed is of all others the most impressive, in so far as we are doubtful of its violence ; and so vigilant is the eye in reading the mind of others, that the slightest indication is as intelligible, and far more relied upon, than stronger demonstrations of feeling.

Le Brun was much attached to allegory, in which he displays great fancy ; but when mixed up in the same picture with real history and character, however dexterously managed, it cannot fail to prove revolting to that consistency and truth which is required in an art, that is the imitation of nature.

Le Sueur, who was a contemporary of Le Brun, and his rival in merit, was a far more chaste and pleasing artist, in so far as there was less affectation in his manner. He aimed at the grace and modesty of Raphael, and is entitled to rank high among his imitators for the noble and simple air of his figures, elegant flowing draperies, and correct expression of character. He despised the meretricious trickery of strong contrasts in grouping and colouring, theatrical attitudes, and overstrained expressions, with which his countrymen generally solicited admiration and astonishment. He sought to express his subject with truth, modesty, and grace, to win our admiration by concealing the art and the artist, and by that quiet harmonious repose of colour and composition, secure the undivided attention of the spectator. The greatest undertaking of Le Sueur was the event of St. Bruno's life, which he painted in twenty-two distinct pictures, for the convent of the Chartreux in Paris. They were originally painted on wood, but have been since removed to canvas, and are now exhibited at the Louvre. Although a far superior painter to Le Brun, Le Sueur was not, during his lifetime, held in such estimation in France. Le Brun was the favourite of the court; and the court of Louis the Fourteenth was omnipotent.

La Hire, Stella, and Bourdon, painted about the same period, and likewise Courtois, called Bourgignon, the prolific painter of battles and skirmishes of cavalry.

The inimitable Claud Gelee, called de Lorraine, was born in the first year of the seventeenth century, and went to Rome as a pastry cook, where, for want of employment, he entered the service of Tassi, a landscape painter, which gave the first impetus to his genius. He attained to such a degree of excellence in the particular branch of landscape painting, as to give it a more important character than it had hitherto held; the wonderful delicacy and lightness of foliage, vapoury distance, liquid transparency of sky, and motion of his light flickering clouds, was new to the art, and in felicity of execution he has never since been surpassed. The only defect of his pictures is in the figures, which are positively lumpish and bad, and not unlike the productions of his first profession. He was himself quite aware of his failure in this particular, and sometimes obtained the assistance of another hand, in general that of Lauri or J. Courtois. The subjects of his pictures are generally so extensive, varied by such an infinity of charmingly painted objects copied from nature, held in the most admirable harmony of colour and aerial perspective, that the eye never tires gazing upon them. The succession of tufty glades and extensive plains, where the distant curling smoke marks a thousand habitations, the bendings of rivers and broad bayed lakes, seems to require the length of a day's journey to reach the distant sea shore, which generally terminates his horizon, although it does not terminate the beauties of his picture; for the sky presents a scene equally varied and interesting. The learned and unlearned are alike fascinated by the pictures of Claude, for they are nature itself, decked in the most beautiful attire. There are no meaningless masses in his scenery; every tree and plant is marked by its distinctive character, and painted with accuracy and study; every beam of light, and every shadow has its cause; the period of the day and season is correctly obvious in every separate part. He is reported to have selected the beautifully extensive view from the terrace of the Villa Madama near Rome as his favourite study, and to have made it the original of his general compositions.

Mignard painted history; Parocel rencounters of cavalry; and Coypel, a family of which there were several good artists that have left works of genius, chiefly sacred subjects. To whom may be added Watteau, Le Moine, Tremoilliere, and Vernet, the painter of sea-ports.

As to the actual state of the arts in France at present, we must be allowed to withhold our assent from the feeling so generally prevalent in that country, of the superior excellence of her existing artists. We cannot do such violence to the dignity of painting, as to join in eulogising the fantastic performances of M. David, who stands at the head of the list. There is, in the

generality of his works, a sort of prancing affectation of grandeur, where, as in a phantasmagoria, the figures seem struck by enchantment into various alarming attitudes and expressions, in which nature has no share, and sympathy, of course, no place. That David copies the antique, he leaves no room to doubt; but it is, with him, the antique in masquerade, the *beau ideal* of Greece turned Frenchman—every thing is theatrical and overstrained. He generally paints in a chilly metallic sort of moon-light colouring, that gives a supernatural effect to his pictures, and distinguishes his works from the generality of his brother artists; for the Luxembourg exhibition of modern pictures of the French school is more disposed to sin in flaring brilliancy of colours. We observed lately in this collection, two pictures of portentous magnitude, that seemed particularly to attract the interest of spectators; the one representing the apparition of a single soldier of the Invincible Legion driving a host of English, Russian, and foreign warriors, in terror before him, seemingly quite unable to withstand such an alarming assailant. The other picture is the capture of a British line of battle ship by a small French corvette. It is not quite ascertained at what particular period of the late war either of these events took place. There are many of the landscape painters of France that display very considerable genius, among whom Granet may be noticed for his very successful accomplishment of striking effects of light. In the branch of history a French artist labours under very great disadvantages: He either draws his ideas from the gaudy flutter and theatrical affectation in which he has been brought up, which it would be difficult to elaborate into any thing like unsophisticated nature; or, if at all sensible of the extravagance and grimacing physiognomy of his countrymen, he must be aware how totally unfit such a caricature of nature must be as a model for painting history. He has no alternative, but either to copy the great masters of Italy, and submit to follow as a humble imitator; or try to form his taste by study of the antique. David chose the latter, but, unfortunately for his success, not so much in spirit as in fact, trimming up the ancient Greek statues, with a tame and lifeless servility, into the various personages to be represented in his subject.

German School.

There is no country in which the elements of drawing are more generally diffused among all ranks than in Germany; and none which contributes so largely to that shoal of obscure individuals who yearly pass the Alps with empty pockets, and heads filled with wild and enthusiastic bodings of future fame, in order to apply themselves to the study of the fine arts. A few years wasted in fruitless struggles with poverty and neglect, and health impaired by unwearied toil, generally serves to remove the spell; when they find the dull world insensible to their merits, and return to their native towns in order to resume the humbler trades which youthful visions of fame had induced them to abandon. The few who do chance to prove successful in this delusive game, and find their interest in prosecuting the labours of the pencil, generally connect their style more with their Italian associates, and join the prevailing manners of the day, than adopt any national character of painting; of which, in Germany, there can scarce be said, for some centuries back, to have existed any one common feature.

Consisting of so many detached and separate states, but slightly connected in manners, and not at all in government, in all of which the practice of the arts has for several ages been very generally cultivated without producing any one remarkable genius; we fear that the detailed history of its progress would be both uninteresting and diffuse. It is far otherwise at a more early age, when we find traces of a very marked character in the German taste and practice of the fine arts, and that, as far back into the obscurity of the dark ages, as we are able to trace the appearance of its revival in Italy.

In Germany, as elsewhere, the arts were first trained to the service and for the embellishments of religion; and partook of the taste of those barbarous ages we have already endeavoured to describe, in which architecture had made considerable advances, but painting so very little. We find the same gold ground in the ancient German pictures, the same constraint and defective proportions, where the figures are so awkwardly crowded on each other, and seem so unaccommodating. This continued as long as painting remained exclusively in the hands of the monks, and was never employed for any other purpose than the constant repetition of the same sacred subjects, and after the same manner of representation; but the application to profane subjects which took place in the thirteenth century, immediately effected an improvement simultaneous with what took place in Italy. The towns of Cologne and Prague seem to have produced the earliest masters whose names are known, and at the same time to have introduced a species of painting which has retained its primitive form unaltered since that time, namely, the painting of playing cards. This art, though it can pretend to very little merit in itself, was, however, a most important step in the progress of science and literature in general; in so far as it began that train of discovery, which reached by the progress of improvements through wooden stamps to wooden engraving and that on copper, to the substitution of types for stamps, to metal for wood, and ultimately to the establishment of printing itself.

The manufactory of playing cards took place in Germany about the year 1300, though the discovery is attributed to the Italians by Breitkopf in his Origin of Playing Cards. They afford a familiar specimen of the taste of that period. However barbarous the execution of these portraits, they sufficiently answered the purpose, and as effectually as if they had been more skilfully executed, so that there was no inducement to attempt any improvement in that branch; but in the other purposes to which wooden engraving was adapted, a very rapid advance took place, and that to an extent which greatly influenced the progress of the arts in Germany. Wooden cuts for various purposes, and the construction of highly ornamented letters, came to be the chief employment of artists; either in the execution of these engravings, or in preparing compositions, both historical and fanciful, for the engravers to copy. The art was carried to great perfection, and engaged the attention of the first artists of Germany, as appears from the multitude of very curious and laborious performances on wood by Albert Durer. In his hands this art seems to have reached its highest state of perfection, and to have soon afterwards yielded to the more delicate process of copper engraving for larger works; although the greater convenience, and more ample management of the wooden stamp, occasioned the employment of that mode to be long persevered in as an accompaniment to books, even after the invention of copper engraving. These early specimens of German art are

much sought after, both as interesting documents of history, and curious in respect to the composition and peculiar taste in the arts then prevalent, as they are chiefly the works of the painters themselves. For in Germany these two arts seem in their infancy to have been inseparable. Every painter exercised, at the same time, the profession of engraving; by means of which he generally extended his fame greatly more than by painting, and accordingly our acquaintance with these early artists is chiefly from their wooden cuts.

While the knowledge of art, which had so recently revived in various parts of Europe, began to advance with rapid strides towards perfection in Italy, its progress in Germany was, owing to the political circumstances of the country, and perhaps materially to the less vivacious disposition of the people themselves, comparatively slow. They continued to plod on with their laboriously minute and stiff representations of nature, without selection, grace, or elegance, but with a scrupulous adherence to truth; each hair of the beard was detailed as if seen through a magnifying medium, and yet retaining its ordinary size. Their works exhibit painful finishing, and attempts at richness of effect by the aid of gold and silver. There was no chiaro scuro, or aerial perspective at all, or breadth of light and shade; and, in short, little merit beyond a minute and servile adherence to truth. The ancient German artists sought no attainment beyond being true to nature. They had an ideal excellence in view, which was that of sincerity and innocence; so that their pictures bore a character of primitive simplicity, analogous to the moral rectitude of the people themselves. A sort of modest and bashful humility is conspicuous in their female portraits, and that of candour, upright honesty, and independence in the countenances of their men.

Almost all the more ancient specimens of painting found in Germany, are on wood, chiefly oak; they were first prepared either with a coating of white paint, or canvas glued down upon it under the white coating. The colours were mixed with the white of eggs and lime-water; but previous to being used, the subject was traced with a point on the ground, and generally gilt over these tracings, which notwithstanding remained sufficiently apparent to guide the painter. The colours were put on very thin, and with great delicacy; and they had the art to give them wonderful durability, as the freshness of the colours to this day testify. This uncommon brilliancy has often occasioned these early water-colour performances to be taken for oil paintings. It is probable that they secured every distinct coat of colour by one of transparent varnish. Of paintings on canvas alone there are no specimens beyond the period of Van Eyck, who revolutionized the whole art by his discovery of the use of oil, towards the close of the fourteenth or beginning of the fifteenth century.

The Germans did not fail to avail themselves of this discovery as well as their neighbours beyond the Alps; but, deprived of any opportunity of studying the antique, or profiting by the burst of excellence which at this juncture began to blaze forth in various quarters of Italy, they were left to improve their primitive taste in their own homely way, and to continue to follow nature as their sole instructress and guide. And this improvement consisted in refining to the full stretch that laborious minuteness and accuracy of imitation which seemed to count every hair of the beard, and express the accidental inequalities and imperfections of the skin with most odious and offensive fidelity. Of

German
School.

this class of painters was Martin Schoen, or Schoenhauer, of Colmar, called Bonmartino by Italian writers, who died in 1486, and is described by Albert Durer as the first German artist who raised for himself a lasting fame. There are some of his pictures at Munich. He was, moreover, according to the usual practice of the times, both an engraver and a goldsmith. Israel Von Mechelu was a painter of the same period and taste, some of whose pictures on a gilt ground are in the collection at Munich.

Wohlge-
muth.

The Pietro Perugino of Germany, the master of Albert Durer, who stands pre-eminent among their artists, was Michael Wohlgemuth of Nuremberg, born in 1434. Though far outshone by his pupil, Wohlgemuth was a painter of no mean merit, as his works in Nuremberg and Munich demonstrate. Lucas Kranach was one of the most celebrated of these old German masters. He was born in the year 1470. He was burgomaster of Wittemberg, and the intimate friend of Luther. Muiller was his real name, and Kranach that of the village where he was born. His works are particularly remarked for the clear and uncommon freshness of colouring, and although minute and careful to excess, are free from the littleness which might be expected to result from that mode of painting. Specimens of his laborious pencil are to be found in various parts of Germany, where they are much prized. His son, of the same name, likewise pursued the practice of painting with success, and succeeded his father in his honours of burgomaster. To these may be added the names of Burgmair of Augsburg, Gruinewald of Aschaffenburg, Manuel, who painted the first Dance of Death at Basil, and Altdorfer, all painters of the same manner.

Holbein.

Hans Holbein, whose long residence in England has brought him more into view than any other of the old German painters, was a native of Grimstadt, and practised his art in Basle. The celebrated Dance of Death in the churchyard of the Predicants of that city, is attributed to his pencil, but is doubted by some. Although a work of extraordinary fancy and merit, it is not indispensable to Holbein's credit to have painted it, as his numerous works of undoubted authenticity sufficiently support his fame. It was painted in commemoration of a destructive pestilence that raged in Basle about the middle of the fifteenth century; and was probably the work of Manuel, as mentioned above, as Holbein was not born till the end of that century. But Holbein took his hint of the drawings he executed of Death's dance from the older work, excelling it in richness of fancy, ingenuity, and that species of humour peculiar to himself. There are forty-six distinct subjects in the series, representing the various triumphs of the grim king of terrors over the human species; in which all the vicissitudes and accidents of life are pourtrayed with a degree of address and lively humour that is inimitable;—particularly in the variety of sly roguish expressions he has been able to throw into so unmanageable a subject as the bare skull of the destroyer, accompanied with the most expressive and entertaining attitudes; and contrasted with the unconscious demeanour of his victims as they busy themselves in the various transactions of life, quite unmindful of the presence of so unwelcome an intruder.

Holbein remained neglected and in poverty at Basle until noticed by the learned Erasmus, in consequence of the amusing series of caricatures he had drawn for the Moriæ Encomium, or The Praise of Folly, of which Erasmus was the author. He soon afterwards came to England, where, under the protection of Sir Thomas More, he rose to great fame as a painter in oil, as well as in distemper and water colours. He painted generally on a green ground, and sometimes on a dark blue, and has left a variety of pictures and drawings of all kinds, both in England and abroad, of which Lord Orford gives a detailed catalogue. He died of the plague in London in the year 1554.

German
School.

Albrecht
Durer.

Albrecht Durer, the Raphael of Germany, was a native of Nuremberg, and was a contemporary of Holbein. In point of genius he resembled Leonardo da Vinci more than Raphael, as he excelled in knowledge as well as in art. He published a learned work on the proportions of the human figure, accompanied with plates engraved by himself, in which the figures are more remarkable for solidity than elegance. His pictures excel in brilliancy of colour and in fecundity of composition; they are finished with all the delicacy and laborious style of his country. Durer was held in very high estimation by Raphael, and had he possessed the same advantages of studying the antique, and seeing the works of other great masters, there is little doubt that he would have approached very near to the excellence of that illustrious artist; but confined as he was to Germany, and bred up in the taste and style of his countrymen, the efforts of his unaided natural genius could do no more than reach pre-eminence in the sphere in which he was destined to move. Vasari, with all his partiality for the artists of Italy, admits that with the rare genius of Durer, had it arisen in Tuscany as it did in Germany, he would have become the first painter in Italy, as he showed himself the greatest genius of Germany. Durer's father was a goldsmith, and trained his son to the same business, which was held in great estimation at that time, as we learn from the entertaining memoirs of Cellini; and before Albert had taken to the pencil at all, his genius as a carver in silver had brought him into notice, and probably influenced his determination to the study of the fine arts. The discovery of etching on copper is attributed to Durer, by which he conferred an invaluable benefit on succeeding artists, enabling them to multiply and perpetuate their designs with as great facility as they executed the original drawing. His own works in this manner are numerous, and not less curious and valuable than his paintings.

In passing our judgment on the merits of Albert Durer, we must not lose sight of the age in which he lived, or the circumstances under which he practised. In him the art made an important step; but so wedded were the people of Germany to the stiff and primitive formality of their old gothic school, that any violent departure from its taste would have met with as little honour as support. The world is exceedingly apt to regard the successful accomplishment of difficulties as a merit, however much these difficulties may be self-created, and may arise from mistaken views of excellence; and they hold as unworthy of consideration the simple efforts of a purer taste. The old German artists, accustomed to hide the awkward and inelegant form of their figures under the refinement of minute and laborious detail, had accustomed their countrymen to consider this trickery as the chief, if not the only merit of the art; so that, had Durer done violence to their prejudices in favour of the old gothic manner, he would not probably have been so successful as he was in improving the taste of the country. The stiff formality, therefore, and overcareful pencilling of this master, is not to be laid to the charge of bad taste, so much as to judgment in uniting with his merits in colouring, and rigid fidelity to the appearance of nature, a more vigorous design, and correct composition, with an animated expression of countenance as yet unknown. His engravings are replete with fancy and deep consideration of the subject meant to be pourtrayed, and are executed with a bold and masterly touch, such as might be expected from the original works of an able master. For this art assumes a much higher character, when the painter himself possesses the power of exhibiting his compositions with all the advantages of original vigour, instead of subjecting them to be enfeebled in the translation by another hand. No artist ever possessed this advantage in greater perfection than Albert Durer; the dexterity of his touch, and the admirable execution of every part of his engravings, shows that he was equally pre-eminent over his predecessors as well as contemporaries, in this art as in painting.

The wars and persecutions of the Reformation, which at this period began to rage in many quarters of Germany, do not appear to have greatly affected the progress of art in that country. The improvements in taste introduced by Albert Durer, were carried on by his successors, among whom we may mention Schwartz, Rotenhaunmer, Elzhaimer, Bauer, Netscher, and various others. Netscher had two sons, both painters of high reputation. The productions of all three are much esteemed and sought after in Germany. But the German school loses its interest as soon as the peculiarity of its gothic character begins to become blended, and smoothed down into the purer taste which progressively diffused itself from the great focus of the fine arts in Italy. The specimens of its early manner are now collected with that veneration which attaches to objects of national antiquity, and are valued for the wonderful dexterity of microscopic neatness, more than as objects of the fine arts; yet in this view alone many of them possess a surprising degree of merit. They are principally to be seen in the collections of Vienna and Munich, and, above all, in that unique and valuable assemblage of ancient German art, belonging to M. Boiserè, at Stutgardt. A set of lithographic engravings have been lately undertaken of this valuable collection, in imitation of those recently executed of the Munich gallery, but in a much superior style of excellence. We had occasion lately to examine the first specimens of this work, which have not as yet been given to the world, and we have no hesitation in pronouncing them to be by far the finest productions that have yet issued from the Lithographic press; independent of the great curiosity to the arts, in an historical point of view, of the subjects themselves. This collection consists, exclusively of paintings, of the ancient gothic school, many of which are remarkable in various points of view; either as specimens of the different modes of practice, as demonstrative of the maners and history of the times, or of the progress of art, and many of them are valuable for their intrinsic merit as productions of art. Among these last is a remarkable head of Christ, by Heinnig; a full face in the noblest simplicity of manner, and painted with the most scrupulous delicacy and truth; in which the serene composure, and searching glance of conscious omniscience, is so irresistibly startling, that one feels overawed, and incapable of beholding it stedfastly. Of all the efforts of art, we never recollect to have experienced the force of expression so powerful and utterly discomposing, as that produced by this heavenly countenance. We seem actually in presence of the godhead, and under the influence which such an idea would excite. It is un-

usual among the innumerable pictures in which the meek Jesus is introduced, to find him otherwise represented than as the man of sorrows, and, under the influence of grief, partaking far more of his human than of his heavenly nature; but this remarkable countenance beams with an expression so remote from any mortal feeling, so unutterably divine, that it leads us unconsciously to avert the eyes from its penetrating gaze. We have seen several sculptures attributed to the ancient Gauls, representing the head of their Apollo, or god Mithros, which have a striking resemblance to the style of this head of Christ; and, in fact, have been sometimes substituted as such, and built into the walls of Christian churches, as may be seen at Geneva, Orange, and particularly at Baden; where the resemblance is so striking, that one might suppose the sculptured head the original from which the picture had been copied.

As a proof of the knowledge of chiaro scuro, possessed by the ancient German masters, there is a remarkable picture in the same collection of St. Christopher, wading in the sea with the child on his shoulder; in which the painter has ventured on the bold attempt of representing the morning sun in full splendour, and exposed to view. It is managed with such uncommon success, that the whole expanse of ocean appears in motion, with the flickering lights that dance upon the light waves, and dazzle the spectator with the horizontal beams that seem to shoot through every corner of the picture. Notwithstanding the sharp lights caught by the light airy clouds, and upon the scrupulously minute detail of plants that hang from the rocks, the harmony of the whole is admirably preserved; and with such clearness in the shadows as is seldom exhibited. Were these ancient works more known, the merits of the gothic school would doubtless become more highly prized.

Spanish School.

We are not aware that any distinctive character of painting ever existed in Spain, so as to require the classifying of its artists under the denomination of a Spanish school. Seville seems to have been the city where the arts were chiefly cultivated. The style of the Florentine school was originally followed, and subsequently that of Rubens. Like the Germans, they had not the benefit in their own country of being able to form their taste upon the models of ancient purity, and accordingly fell into a clumsy imitation of nature, and a servile habit of copying each other. Spain has, notwithstanding, produced several very excellent painters, and particularly Diego Velasquez, born at Seville in 1594, who studied in Italy, and afterwards practised with great success in Spain; he had the peculiarity of painting with brushes of five feet long, to enable him to observe the effect as he proceeded. Raphael Mengs bestows great eulogiums on the works of Velasquez, in the account he gives of the pictures contained in the Royal Palace of Madrid. Ribera, called Spagniolette, was of Spanish parentage, but, as a painter, may be considered a Neapolitan. His style is strong and vigorous, though his selection of subjects is often disgusting. Murillo, likewise of Seville, is a pleasing painter, possessing a very delicate taste in colouring with correct design, which render his works much esteemed all over Europe. He delighted in simple subjects, which he knew how to render attractive by the charms of animated expression. It is to be wished that he had selected nobler subjects than that of ragged boys, &c. which constitute the generality of his

Flemish School.

pictures. There is such a careless flow of unaffected hilarity about his beggarly urchins, and such a broad expression of natural feeling with which he animates his canvas, that Murillo may be regarded as unrivalled in representing the instinctive impulses of untutored nature.

Moralez was a painter of celebrity in Spain, and was dignified with the appellation of the Divine, as much from his merit as a painter as from the nature of the subjects he selected. He painted generally on copper, with great delicacy and taste.

Flemish School.

In Brabant, the art of painting flourished at a very early period, and moreover, to an ancient and distinguished artist of that country the world is supposed to be indebted for the discovery of oil painting. This merit is usually attributed to Jean de Bruges, or Van Eyck, towards the year 1410, although there is reason to doubt the accuracy of this point. In Germany, the contrary opinion is maintained, upon the faith of a work written by Theophilus, a monk of the eleventh century, entitled, " De omni scientiâ artis pingendi," in which he describes the use of linseed oil in painting; but his process is not correctly that of oil painting. There are some oil pictures at Vienna, by Thomas de Mutina, said to be so early as the twelfth or thirteenth century. And, in England, Lord Orford maintains the existence of oil painting nearly two centuries before the birth of Van Eyck. See a treatise on this special question, by Mr. Raspe, and a paper in the 9th vol. of the Archæologia. Lanzi investigates this subject in the first and second volume of his *Storia Pittorica d'Italia*, pages 65, and 285; and *Tiraboschi Literatura Italiana*, vol. vii. p. 407. See Williams on *Oil Painting*, and Raspe's translation of Lessings, vol. viii.

If oil painting was known in the ninth century, as is alleged, Van Eyck cannot be denied the merit at least of having brought it into successful practice, which is often far more creditable than the absolute invention; in so far as the one may be purely casual, while the other is likely to result chiefly from reflection, and well directed experiments. Oil colour was first used on wood, then on plates of copper, and finally, on canvas. It was an early practice to paint on the back of plates of glass, so that the glass should come in place of varnish for the picture, it must have been an exceedingly inconvenient mode of painting, as it became necessary to work up the whole subject at once, and without the facility of seeing properly how the process was succeeding. When the work was finished and dry, in order to give it opacity, a thick uniform coat of paint was laid over the back.

The introduction of the use of oil formed a great epoch in the history of the art, from its peculiar adaptation to the delicate blending of colours—the indestructibility of its surface when dry—the vivacity of colour, proof against the influence of the atmosphere—the facility to the artist of retouching and perfecting his work—the power of laying it aside and resuming it at pleasure—and, above all, the boldness of execution which must be inspired by the confidence of being able to rectify and change at pleasure, without being appalled by the fearful uncertainty of every bold touch destroying the work, which the painter in fresco must be exposed to. There is great advantage in the power of heightening the effect at pleasure, where the very thickness of repeated coats, by producing elevation, adds to the prominence of sharp lights; whereas in fresco, a deadening effect ensues by reason of the absorption in drying, accompanied with a change of tint.

The viscous nature of oil enables the colours to approach each other, without the uncontrollable blending of water colours, which is not in every case desirable: The artist is able, as he proceeds, to judge of the effect, the fresco painter must wait its drying; it is capable of greater transparency, and more perfect pellucidness of air and water. Oil painting does undoubtedly acquire a sombre tone in the progress of time; but in this much depends on the mode of painting, as we possess some very old works of the great masters, seemingly as fresh as the day they were painted. It is a circumstance much to be regretted, that these early painters, who, according to the mysterious habits of their day, had each some secret mode of preparing colours, or concealed process in their art, were so cautious of communicating their knowledge; that we are now entirely ignorant of what occasions the more perfect preservation of the works of some masters than of others. The preparation of the ground colour was particularly a subject of mystery, and in this there were great varieties, some using different preparations of white, others red or dark, and, in fact, every variety of colour.

But fresco painting was not without its advantages over oil; for it looks equally well in all lights: whereas the shine of oil requires a particular light, and to be seen from a particular spot. It is more durable than oil, in so far as it incorporates with the wet plaster upon which it is applied, becoming as permanent as the wall itself; for the plaster, if properly prepared, acquires the hardness of stone.

It is the most ancient mode of painting at present in use, as it was generally followed by the Greeks, and even in Egypt there are instances of it. The colours are chiefly calcined, and simply mixed with water; but it is inconvenient from the change in drying, and to a certain extent imperfect, as there are some colours which the plaster rejects. Strictly speaking, it is but the servile operation of copying, as the preparatory cartoon is in fact the painting; neither can the whole be seen at once, or the effect judged of; but each particular portion, according to the extent of day's work, must be finished up at once, and added to the preceding portion with little power of blending. The lights cannot be raised, but the shadows, when they begin to dry, may, to a certain degree, be enforced. The cartoon must be painted to the full size, through which the subject is pricked on the wall; sometimes the cartoons are fully coloured, like those of Raphael now in England, or merely traced, when they are usually accompanied by a small oil painting. Fresco loses its effect if seen very near, which is another inconvenience for the painter. It is only adapted for spacious apartments, and as an accompaniment to architecture; but it is more susceptible of general effect than any style of painting. It must be well done, and the entire effect seized in a moment; for fresco admits of no mediocrity. To succeed, a painter must be gifted with the qualities of an expert general, viz. promptitude, decision, and address in executing. The finest works of Raphael, Michael Angelo, and other great masters, are in fresco, and how brilliant is the display of generalship in some of them!

Whether it was owing to Van Eyck's introduction of the use of oil or not, the study of colouring became the principal bent of the Flemish school; and, indeed, they themselves maintain, that the Venetian school adopted the peculiarity of their taste from the Flemish artists. In consequence of Van's Eyck's having communicated his secret to Antonio de Messina, he returned to practise in Venice, where he endeavoured to conceal his art, in order to monopolize the profits and fame arising from it. It is narrated of the Venetian painter, John Bellin, that being unable to discover the cause of the uncommon brilliancy of this stranger's mode of painting, he disguised himself in the splendid attire of a Venetian nobleman, and presented himself to have his picture done: the unsuspicious painter being thus thrown off his guard, enabled Bellin, in the course of the proceeding, to discover his secret. Oil painting soon crept into general practice at Venice, and with it, according to some authors, the Flemish taste for colouring. The style, however, took a grander and more magnificent flight at Venice, while, with the exception of Rubens, the Flemish painters rather emulated the minute and close imitation of nature. Like their neighbours in Holland and Germany, it is nature, however homely, that is the ruling idea and ultimate object of their art, with very little attempt to ennoble the subject by the aid of imagination. In knowledge of colours, and extreme address in their use, in brilliancy, delicate blending, dexterity, and fineness of touch, many of the Flemish masters seem nearly to have reached the limits of perfection.

The principal works extant of Van Eyck are to be seen at Ghent, and are more remarkable for labour and care than beauty. His brother and sisters, as well as his father, were painters. Of the same class was Lucas van Leyden, whose engravings are so much sought after and so high priced, and also his friend Mabuse, who was a superior painter, and was the means of introducing a freer and better manner, though still exceedingly stiff. He was a drunken spendthrift; and, having upon one occasion pawned his coat, was obliged to appear before Charles the Fifth in a paper coat he had painted for himself, to the great entertainment of the emperor. There are several pictures of this master in England, where he resided some time. The names of the principal painters that preceded Rubens, who may be looked upon as the prince of Flemish painters, and the founder of the distinctive character of the school, were Porbus, Brill, Steenwick, Van Voss, Stradau, Spranger, Savery, Breughil, of whom there were several painters of the same name. Jean Miel, Seegers, Snyders, the painter of boar hunts, animals, and flowers; his compositions are full of skill and vigour in handling the particular subject he had selected. Crayer was a prolific painter of altar-pieces, and considered one of the best painters of the Flemish school, for chasteness of composition, and admirable blending of his colours. He died in the year 1669. His contemporary Jordaens was likewise esteemed.

Rubens, the founder of the Flemish school, was an accomplished gentleman, and son of a senator of Antwerp in the end of the sixteenth century; his works are so universally known, and his style of painting so calculated to please generally, that what we would say of him has probably been already said an hundred times. So prolific was his pencil, that his works are to be found in every quarter, and so distinguished in brilliancy and imagination, as to attract a greater share of attention than the generality of pictures that may be presented in competition with them. His subjects are familiar, and remarkably attractive by the playful and bold composition, striking effect of light and shade, luxuriance of the richest colouring, and general air of blooming profusion of every thing that is calculated to catch the eye. Rubens neither studied the antique, nor the works of the great masters of Rome and Florence, the severity of whose style was, perhaps, ill suited to the festive and splendid tone of his imagina-

tion; which was more in unison with the rich fancy of Paul Veronese, and the other masters of the Venetian school. The prevailing taste in the pictures of Rubens is so palpable and obvious as seldom to leave any doubt of their identity, and, of course, leads us to infer the charge of mannerism; but that manner is of so playful and captivating a description, as rarely to pall upon the appetite,—particularly in the rosy freshness and exuberance of health and jollity, so manifest in the flesh and countenances of his figures; which, however frequently repeated, have still the charm of novelty.

Of the learning of Michael Angelo, or the dignified grandeur of Coreggio, there is as little in the works of Rubens as of the pathetic modesty and grace of Raphael; but there is the perfection of freedom, ease, and movement, a sort of hey-day festivity, which beams in every countenance, and diffuses a charm over the whole scene. But it must be allowed, that this tone of gaiety is not unfrequently at variance with that species of decorum we require in a picture; there is often in the female figures a meretricious air, a sort of reckless defiance of modesty and feminine diffidence, that is somewhat disparaging to the purity or dignity of the female character. In his bacchanalian subjects, for instance, in his troops of nymphs, loves, and satyrs, a degree of libertinism is, perhaps, congenial enough to the scene; and flows from the pencil of Rubens with the careless and rapid facility of nature itself, as if bursting from such an overflowing source of exuberant fancy as could never fail; but still we feel disposed to yield, not without considerable reluctance, the unqualified admiration which the excellence of the execution would otherwise command. We feel conscious that the ribaldry of a drunken Silenus, accompanied by his lascivious crew of satyrs, or the meretricious excitement of a bacchanalian group, are subjects upon which we regret to see such waste of talent. The characteristics of painting ought to be truth, grace, and dignity; a certain degree of composure and gravity belongs to it, as consistent with its permanent nature; sprightliness and gaiety, however charming for a moment, fatigue by being prolonged; they become affectation, and the unskilful waste of an art directed to a nobler purpose. Painting is not adapted to the expression of sentiments that are not such as can stand the test of deliberate and continued contemplation; what pleases for a moment may soon grow contemptible if prolonged.

The knowledge of composition, and richness of fancy, pre-eminently displayed by Rubens in the fantastic variety of his allegorical groups, is another subject of admiration, the propriety of which we feel a little disposed to question. This species of composition, which is rarely if ever an elucidation of the subject, but more generally a revolting invasion of unintelligible fiction and absurdities, however skilfully executed, abounds in the works of Rubens; and particularly in that celebrated production of his pencil, meant as descriptive of the life of Mary of Medicis, in twenty-four separate pictures, now in the Louvre. As specimens of art these performances are admirable; but so utterly enigmatical and perplexing are the crowd of personified passions, qualities, sentiments, and these cross readings that bewilder the mind, that the effort required to unravel the mystery, and pick out the real from the fictitious personages, becomes exceedingly irksome. For instance, take that magnificent picture, in which we see the gorgeous assembly of the whole gods of Olympus attending the queen; Jupiter and Juno are seen harnessing some doves to a globe, and placing the reins in the hands of

Cupid, preceded by two female figures. Apollo, Minerva, Mars, and Venus, armed with their respective attributes, are employed driving away three hideous figures,—and all this, we are told, means the government of Mary of Medicis. The same subject is somewhat more intelligibly treated in another of the pictures, where the majority of her son Louis the Twelfth is indicated by the queen placing the helm of a ship into his hands; only the ship's crew are a little ambiguous, and make us alarmed for the safety of the vessel, worked by such personages as the virtues, with Good Faith, Justice, Religion, and Strength; of all the company Fame, with her speaking trumpet, is the only one that seems to know her duty.

It is always dangerous to admit of arbitrary license in allegory. It ought, if suffered at all, to be conformable to the sort of received language of symbol, with which the expression of general ideas is, by a kind of tacit consent, permitted to be conveyed, and never left to the inventions of fancy. An abstract idea is not easily expressed by any visible sign; it must be conveyed by the conventional agreement of mankind, as in words; without such agreement, no power of ingenuity could, for instance, understand the symbol of an armed woman, in the person of Minerva, to mean wisdom, or of a strapping huntress to mean chastity. There are, no doubt, some of the ancient Greek symbols that possess great elegance, and may be introduced with a very felicitous effect in pictures; conveying the idea required in a more terse and elegant manner than it is, perhaps, capable of in any other way; but it is a venture which requires very delicate handling. The Greek gems are full of those elegant allegories, and among modern painters Poussin has been the most successful in this branch of invention; of which his allegorical representation of the Nile is a happy instance, where he hides the head of his figure among the reeds, in order to indicate our ignorance of the source of that river. Another painter treats the same subject, but has the clumsy idea of setting a group of little cupids to stretch a veil over the head of the figure.

It is the unnatural mixture of truth and allegory, and the superabundance of the latter, that is so offensive in some of Rubens' pictures; but we must confess, when we see that he has the sanction of Sir Joshua Reynolds, who occasionally followed the same taste, that we speak with diffidence, although we have the authority of Lord Orford in deprecating the exuberance of allegory. He says, " I never could conceive that riddles and rebuses (and I look upon such emblems as little better) are any improvements upon history. Allegoric personages are a poor decomposition of human nature, whence a single quality is separated and erected into a kind of half deity, and then, to be rendered intelligible, is forced to have its name written by the accompaniment of symbols. You must be a natural philosopher before you can decipher the vocation of one of these simplified divinities. Their dog, or their bird, or their goat, or their implement, or the colour of their clothes, must all be expounded, before you know who the person is to whom they belong, and for what virtue the hero is to be celebrated, who has all this hieroglyphic cattle around him. How much more genius is there in expressing the passions of the soul in the lineaments of the countenance!" We know of no finer display of allegorical painting than that great work of the Caraccis, in the decoration of the Farnese palace at Rome, where the different effects of love are so beautifully and intelligibly described by a series of ancient fables. But then there is here no incongruity

by the intermixture of true history. The whole subject is the creation of fancy, in which the introduction of one real personage would be sufficient to dissolve the charm.

Rubens is perhaps as great in landscape as in any branch of the art of which he practised. There is here no alloy; every part is admirable: a sort of mixture of Salvator Rosa and Claud, uniting the vigour of wild and savage scenery with the vapoury freshness and glow of Claud de Lorraine. His general character as a painter is given by Sir Joshua Reynolds, whose opinions are always valuable and accurate. He says, that " in his composition his art is too apparent. His figures have expression, and act with energy, but without simplicity or dignity. His colouring, in which he is eminently skilled, is notwithstanding too much of what we call tinted. Throughout the whole of his works, there is a proportionable want of that nicety of distinction and elegance of mind which is required in the higher walks of painting; and to this want it may be in some degree ascribed, that those qualities which make the excellency of this subordinate style appear in him with their greatest lustre. Indeed, the facility with which he invented, the richness of his composition, the luxuriant harmony and brilliancy of his colouring, so dazzled the eye, that, whilst his works continue before us, we cannot help thinking that all his deficiencies are fully supplied."

Sir Antony Vandyke was a pupil of Rubens. His genius took the humbler path of portrait, but in that path he is unrivalled. With all the delicate precision of the Flemish school, he added the mellow tone of Titian, and a clear transparent silvery touch peculiarly his own. He is true to nature, and free from affectation of every kind. He throws into his heads an air of contemplative composure and sedateness, which adds much to their dignity, and unites all the parts with such an harmonious tone of mellow colouring, that his portraits become highly valuable as specimens of art. His subject was confined, but no painter ever possessed a more perfect command of what he undertook to represent. There is the downy softness of his flesh colours, under which we seem to see the suffusion of the circulating blood, contradistinguished from the iridescent play of colour in the satin draperies, which are quite illusory and beautiful. Vandyke seldom painted history, nor would he probably have succeeded in that class, as none of his works indicate fancy.

The father of Teniers was likewise a pupil of Rubens, and painted the familiar ale-house subjects of the Dutch school. His son, David Teniers, acquired a higher reputation in the same class, which we shall consider more at length in the sequel. He possessed a great readiness of pencil in characterizing the homely subjects of his taste. His trees are light and airy, and, in general, a character of cheerfulness is diffused over his works. The familiarity and amusement of his subjects, as well as the high merit of the execution, have made them universally prized.

There are various other painters of note belonging to the Flemish school, whose merits our limits will not admit of considering: as Schwaneveldt, so excellent in landscape; Peter Neefs, inimitable in his representations of the interior of churches; besides many others.

Dutch School.

The distinctive features of this school are abundantly different from those of Italy, arising principally from the selection of subjects in a walk of life totally different; for with regard to knowledge in the execution of their art, and dexterity in the use of their pencil and colours, the perfection attained in Holland is equal to that of any other country. The Dutch artists reject all connection with the heroic, or *beau ideal* of the Greeks and Italians; and confine their attention exclusively to a careful and almost juggling imitation of nature. Instead of selecting for the personages of their pictures those possessing beauty and elegance of person, so captivating either in nature or as represented; they seem purposely to have copied from the most homely subjects; to have preferred those figures, in which age had substituted the rugged lines of the picturesque for the beautiful of youth, or the formed grace and dignity of the meridian of life; and to people their subjects almost exclusively with the hard-weather countenances of aged fishermen and mariners, or the boisterous carousing of peasants in their cups. And even in the favourite subject of the kermis, or village festival, so often repeated by the Dutch artists, where youth, and the playful season of life, must be introduced as indispensably connected with the nature of the theme, it seems yielded to with reluctance. The personages of a younger and less sedate period of life are usually thrown into the background, to give place to a rugged group of ancient Bauers contemplating the revels in Turkish solemnity, or steeping their cares in the long tankard. We might willingly tolerate the bad taste in chusing, on account of the art displayed in executing; were it not for the edifying circumstance invariably introduced of some impure joke, in which the unceremonious proceeding of the actors is often as unceremoniously represented with the broadest vulgarity. The representation is no doubt to the life; but we shall find little in a Dutch picture to elevate our sentiments of human nature,—every thing is grovelling, debasing, and low. We cannot regard their performances without feeling that we are in bad company, and have nothing to do in such society.

It is common to cry out against the idea of not copying nature servilely, as the only legitimate end of painting; but this does not exclude the power of selecting that part, and those scenes in nature, that are most worthy of contemplation. It is the base taste of the Dutch school that makes them reject whatever is dignified in our nature, in order to offer to our admiration the lowest scenes of life. There are, no doubt, peculiarities in the manners of the Dutch, and let their artists have the full share of praise for an animated representation, whether within doors or without, of the every-day occupations and handicrafts, as well as of the holiday playing, fighting, and drinking of the common people. But we are not to suppose that we have in this a picture of society in Holland, far less a general view of human life, which ought to be the painter's theme as well as the poet's. The society of Holland is as capable to furnish subjects upon which genius might be worthily exercised, as any country of the world, were it practicable to apply the narrow principles of the taste prevalent in that country to general history, or to elevate the mean view they have taken of human character, so as to be compatible with dignity. When we hold up the mirror to nature, we must not forget that some skill is required to direct it aright; that all is not equally worthy of contemplation; and that there are many things perfectly natural which are better kept out of sight. Broad facts are often offensive. We feel disposed, when such are presented as claimants for our admiration, to visit the odium of the subject on the painter's head, who offends our eyes with the sight of them. Neither vulgar wit nor wag-

gery can ever redound to a painter's praise: they may succeed in exciting a momentary smile; but we despise the artificer of the joke who thus debases the dignity of his art.

Considered, however, merely as specimens of art, no one can deny that the Dutch paintings are in many respects admirable. So true are they to the colouring of nature, so dexterous is the manipulation, and so correct is the grouping and dispositions of light and shade, that if a true copy of nature were all that was aimed at, the Dutch school may with justice be said to have attained it in that walk of life it has chosen to select. They have the merit of perfect success in the humble style of distinction sought for, that is of precision and high finishing, and under circumstances purposely selected to display their extraordinary facility in the management of light and shade. Their candle-light scenes are very usual efforts of dexterity, in which a strong confined light shoots like a meteor through pitchy darkness with admirable truth and effect.

The objections we have ventured to make to subjects that usually meet with such unqualified admiration in this country, are not so applicable to landscape; and here we consider the Dutch artists as eminent in the skilful representation of such scenery as their country afforded. Nothing can be more delicious than the canal scenery of Vangoyen or Cuyp, the limpid crystal of the water, repeating every form and colour of the busy boating and passing sail it bears on its bosom; the old dreadnought tower, with its massive walls and weather-beaten visage projected on the light and vapoury sky, and the dexterous pencilling of the tufted bank, is making the most of the subject. But the scenery of Holland is, from its situation, devoid of dignity, variety, or any of the grand and imposing features of nature in general; and, accordingly, its painters make no attempt to convey these sentiments. We admire the vapoury atmosphere of their fenny sea-coast scenes; the dexterity and truth with which the waves, hurrying forward from their low and distant horizon, seem to swell upon the sight, and threaten to overflow the picture; and the misty forms of vessels that seem to embrace both elements, as they are borne through the scene. But still it is but one note, and however melodious, we cannot but sigh for some relief to the monotony, some of that infinite variety that supplied the glorious scenery of Claud de Lorraine, Poussin, and Titian.

It is the want of subject, however, and not of art; for such beauties as fell under the observation of the Dutch landscape painters are admirably represented. They have an air of individual locality, and topographic truth, that adds much to their value; for, like the freedom of an original, there is a charm about a real *bona fide* scene from nature, which no composition, however classical or epic, can equal. In historical painting, composition is of course inherent in the nature of the subject, and constitutes its most difficult and important requisite, as the painter has seldom if ever the means of actually seeing the subject he proposes to pourtray; but in landscape, which has for its object the scenery of nature, ever before our eyes, immeasurably varied, and so uniformly beautiful, we cannot enter into the merit of composition which we conceive must ever fall short of the reality it endeavours to imitate. The patchwork of shreds from different scenes in nature, however artificially woven into one imaginary whole, and however well executed, is but a dream, and, as such, of inferior interest to the reality. But this stamp of reality which we appreciate so highly in the painters of the Dutch school, is often degraded by the meanness of the objects upon which it is employed. When we are called upon to admire the masterly efforts of skill, by which the colours seem melted and blended together by mutual attraction, and without the intervention of human touch, we feel a sort of repugnance to observe such talent wasted on the tortuous leafing of an ignoble cabbage; the slippery slimy mass of a skate, where its hideous countenance is not omitted to be brought into distinguished observance; or on the disgusting appurtenances of a butcher's shop. Those subjects, the sight of which in reality we would incline to turn from with aversion, are surely an injudicious selection for the purpose of painting, and a degradation of the art. The talent with which they are represented renders them in fact so much the more repugnant to the feelings of the observer.

It was during the course of the fifteenth and sixteenth centuries that the most distinguished masters of this school flourished: the Hemskirks, the old and the young, both admirable in their style; and Martin Hemskirk, who followed the Italian taste, and was called Martin Tadesco; Bloemart, Both, and Metzu, the harmony of whose colouring is so much admired; Breenberg, who added the delicacy of Dutch pencilling to a more dignified description of subject, as Poelemburg did in landscape. He was often assisted by Berghem in his figures. The works of Berghem are very highly and very deservedly prized for his landscape subjects, with cattle and figures. He sometimes painted subjects of a higher class, of which there is an instance in the collection of the Collonna Palace at Rome, of an Annunciation to the Shepherds, which he treated with great skill and beauty.

Wouverman is well known for his white horses; and also Wynants, who was his instructor, as well as that of Van der Velde, who painted marine subjects to perfection. Heem painted flowers and fruit, accompanied with glasses, vases, and other similar articles, of which we see such perfect representations by many of the Dutch painters. Laar, called Bambaccio, who studied in Italy, and was the intimate friend of Poussin and Claud de Lorraine, painted huntings, robberies, and wild beasts. Gerard Douw, the most punctilious and careful of painters, Terburg and Mieris, who excelled in green grocers and kitchen subjects: His figure subjects have occasionally a dash of libertinism about them, which does not enhance their merit; but in all his works there is a degree of magical command of pencil and colour, and a closeness to nature that was never surpassed. The son of Mieris was little inferior to his father in excellence.

As to Rembrandt van Ryn, this extraordinary genius may be said to have constituted a school of his own. It was of no importance what subject, or however mean, Rembrandt selected for his pencil. He was gifted with the power of enchantment; and whatever fell within the magic circle of his genius assumed the character of his extraordinary creation. A sort of thunder and lightning conflict of light and darkness envelopes every object in maze and mystery, as if issuing from the depths of a dungeon; so that, however ignoble the subject may in reality be, under his hands it comes forth with imposing dignity, and assumes that sort of prophetic, though illusory importance, which we are apt to ascribe to the last words of any person conscious of treading on the verge of eternity. Rembrandt seemed to behold nature through the medium of a highly wrought poetic imagination, and to exhibit his visions by the sud-

den and startling light of a meteor. He had no communication with sober common-place day-light; a flaring luminary of his own creation was required to give the solemn and dazzling effect with which he delighted to make the darkness of his pictures visible. In power of execution, and dexterity in the management of his materials, this romantic painter found no curb to the exuberance of his fancy; it appears as if it had flowed from his pencil with the facility of thought. His landscapes partake of the same character, and are much and deservedly valued. What Rembrandt would have become, under the influence of different circumstances, had he been born in Rome, or even seen the works of Greece and Italy, which, to him, seem as if the beings of another world, it were hard to guess. He must have been great in whatever he attempted; and, as it is, he stands alone in the republic of painting.

But however much we may be captivated by the striking productions of Rembrandt, we must admit that his manner partakes of trick; and that at the expence of the best principles of the art, which is the truth of nature, and to the detriment of its highest object, sublimity.

We might add many names of painters of great merit, as Van der Neer, Shalker, Van der Werf, Van Huysum, and many others issuing from the prolific school of Holland, whose works are in great request.

Painting in England.

We doubt if, with propriety, we can term that a school of painting, which, though varying in some particulars of its taste and practice from those of other countries, cannot, however, be considered as having blocked out for itself any distinctive style and character, such as generally exists in the practice of the principal continental countries of Europe. The period at which the attention of the British nation was at all turned to the subject of the fine arts, was comparatively late. Like the ancient Romans, the disposition of the people seemed little calculated to relish the elegancies of life, until riches and luxury had begun to extend their influence, and soften down the austere and rugged manners of our ancestors. It happened, however, at that particular æra of our history, when the fine arts might have obtained a footing, and when they would probably have fixed those roots which were ready to shoot forth into luxuriance, that an event occurred in the political world which at once blighted its early prospects.

In the course of the foregoing sketch of the progress of the fine arts, we have seen how very dependent their prosperity seems in general to have been, on the religious institutions of the country where they were practised. Not only do there appear in the earliest times to have been the source whence they usually derived their origin, but the permanent basis of future support in all the stages of their progress. They gave dignity to the subject, which, aided by the flame of national devotion, lighted up in the minds of artists that degree of enthusiasm which was calculated to call forth the full energy of genius. But, unfortunately, the first dawnings of taste in Britain were destined to sustain the sudden deprivation of this important stimulus, at the most critical period of their existence. The Reformation, by banishing all the pageantry and show of religion, not only suspended the labours of the artists whose chief employment consisted in the decoration of churches, but rendered these harmless embellishments themselves odious in the eyes of the people. The necessity of utterly overthrowing every vestige of the ancient sin of idolatry, had rendered the first ages of Christianity fatal to the fine arts; but long before the event of the Reformation, the hostility of the Roman Catholic religion had changed into protection and favour. As Mr. Roscoe observes, she had become the foster-mother of the chisel and pencil, and supplied the noblest and most interesting subjects for the exercise of their powers. " The artist whose labours were associated with the religion of his country, enjoyed a kind of sacred character, and as his compensation was generally derived from princes and pontiffs, from munificent ecclesiastics or rich monastic institutions, the ample reward which he obtained stimulated both himself and others to farther exertions. To the complete success of the artist a favourable concurrence of extraneous circumstances is often necessary, and the mind already impressed with religious awe by the silence and solemnity of the cloister or the cathedral, dwells with additional interest on representations already in unison with its feelings, and which exemplify, in the most striking manner, the objects of its highest admiration and respect. Even the opportunity afforded the artist of a spacious repository for his productions, where they were likely to remain secure for ages, and where they might be seen with every advantage of position, were circumstances highly favourable to his success. The tendency of the Reformation was to deprive him of these benefits, to exclude his productions from the place of worship as profane or idolatrous, to compel him to seek his subjects in the colder pages of history, and his patrons among secular and less wealthy individuals."

It is much to be lamented that the spirit of fanaticism, which arose upon the introduction of the reformed religion, should, by turning its hostility so much against whatever was calculated to impress the outward senses with reverence, have proved so irreparably destructive to the fine arts. That a consequence, arising from the blind and misdirected zeal of the ignorant rabble, which never could have been the intention of the better informed and more liberal class of their instructors, should have been allowed to form itself into a dogma, and even, with many, to become a test of their faith, is quite surprising. In the circumstances of Luther's life, we find him frequently exerting his ineffectual influence to stem the torrent of destruction, which the headlong enthusiasm of his followers had misdirected from its intended course. But such is the tendency of human nature. It is often an easy matter to lay open the flood-gates of popular opinion, but a fearful uncertainty hangs over the future course of the torrent, which human power and wisdom are alike incapable to control. The Reformation exposed to the minds of the people many abuses in their faith, but the bewildered rabble sought for something more tangible than opinion to assail, and turned with fury on the harmless decorations of their former church service; although it is exceedingly doubtful if these emblems and representations of sacred story ever were considered as objects of adoration, even in the most barbarous times of the Christian æra. It is to be hoped, therefore, that, in the course of time, this prejudice against the appropriate decoration of our churches may be softened down with the decline of bigotry and the fastidious austerity of early times—that we may again see the walls of our temples ornamented with the subjects of Christian story, in the best efforts of human skill, as illustrative of the great precepts taught from the pulpit. Even in the

churches of the presbyterian worship, the bare and
homely fashion of the structure is fast giving way to a better taste; so that the time is probably not far distant, when some interior decoration may be resumed, and, perhaps, the full choired anthem once more be heard to peal within their walls.

In our estimate of the comparative progress of the arts in different countries, it is of importance, with regard to England, that we should bear in mind, that, while her efforts struggled under the blighting influence above alluded to, her neighbours enjoyed the full sunshine of public favour and ecclesiastical munificence. Foreigners very generally entertain an opinion of the inaptitude of our countrymen towards the acquisition of the arts; and we must confess, that general appearances are not much in our favour, if we judge, as they do, without regard to the very different circumstances under which a knowledge of the arts was introduced, and opportunity afforded for their cultivation. But with these important facts in view, we have no occasion to search for any cause, either in the disposition or circumstances of the British nation, adverse to as successful a prosecution of the fine arts as that of any of the continental countries of Europe. Nothing can be supposed more futile and silly than the grave and laborious reasonings of many French authors, in which they try to demonstrate the absurdities of their theory about the influence of climate in matters of genius; it is only to be equalled by the complacency with which the foreign public embrace this notion, that they are actually gifted with at least one superior quality, against the acquisition of which, by this aspiring nation, nature has interposed the insurmountable barrier of physical causes. It may be simpler, and, perhaps, is more consolatory to their authors, to say at once, that we are utterly incapable of excellence in any thing that requires taste and genius; than to investigate candidly what causes may actually have retarded the progress of the arts in Britain.

The state of the arts in Britain, at an early period, seems to have been very much the same as in the neighbouring kingdoms of the Continent, judging from the most authentic record, the coinage; as the effigies of British monarchs represented upon them are not more barbarous than those of France. Nor do the British appear to have been later in cultivating the art of stained glass, which necessarily implies the knowledge of design. That finely illuminated eastern window of York Cathedral, was the work of a native artist, John Thornton of Coventry, so early as the year 1338, according to Lord Orford, though the common account makes it sixty years later. There are various records which refer to paintings, even at an earlier date than this; and there are some historical pieces which are desired to be renewed in the reign of Henry II. It is upon the authority of some of these ancient scraps, that an argument is raised against the authenticity of Van Eyck's discovery of oil painting; as allusions are distinctly made in some of them to oil painting being practised in England so early as the reign of Edward II. in the year 1239, two hundred years before the age of Van Eyck.

The more ancient specimens of painting in England seem generally to have been heraldic, except the decorations on illuminated manuscripts, which were carried to a high degree of perfection, at as early a period as that art appears to have been practised any where else. Many of these works were rendered particularly valuable from the portraits of remarkable personages and from the historical pictures which they contain. Dallaway, in his Anecdotes, gives a detailed account of the most ancient and valuable relics of this beautiful art now existing in Britain, which are chiefly the workmanship of British artists.

There are some fresco designs of a very early date still existing in some of our more ancient churches, the workmanship of the monks themselves; but as many of these ecclesiastics were translated from foreign convents, we cannot with certainty ascribe the merit to our native artists. The specimens are no doubt rare, but when we recollect with what indiscriminating zeal the reformers obliterated every species of painting or ornament on the walls of churches, it is surprising that any were spared. The portraits that were stained on glass had a better chance of preservation, from the indestructible nature of the colour, so that even fragments retained their value; accordingly, enough of that description still remains to enable us to assert the claim of Britain to an equal share with her contemporaries, in the knowledge of art at that early period.

With the exception of these scriptural pictures on church windows, (the most remarkable of which will be found described in Dallaway's and Lord Orford's Anecdotes,) the early practice of painting in England seems to have been almost exclusively confined to portrait. These were disposed either in single heads, or family groups crowded together, and most unfancifully arranged; they were chiefly the workmanship of foreign artists, attracted to England by the prospect of gain. There appear among these, many names celebrated in the history of painting, as, Mabuse, Hans Holbein, Zucchero, Polemburg, Rubens, and Vandyk.

There was little exertion of patronage on the part of the British sovereigns, till the accession of Henry VIII. who, more from a spirit of magnificence than any knowledge or taste for the fine arts, invited various foreign artists to come to England. His pride was roused by the more successful efforts of Francis I. of France, and the Emperor Charles V. not to be behind them in encouraging the elegant and learned acquirements, as he coped with them in riches and power of arms. But Henry neither possessed sufficient skill to know how to set about the establishment of a better taste in his country, beyond the mere invitation given to celebrated artists, to settle in his dominions; nor did his proferred bounty appear to have been such as to produce the wished for effect, as neither Raphael nor Titian, who were solicited, could be induced to listen to his proposals. These great painters probably judged, that in a country where portrait painting alone had hitherto met with any encouragement, the higher branches of the art, on which they, with reason, built their fame, had little chance to be duly appreciated. However, the example of a sovereign is certain, at least, to have a powerful influence with his own court; the countenance Henry gave to the arts was the means of directing the attention of the nobility to their encouragement; and there is no reason to doubt, that, if the fostering power of the Roman Catholic religion had remained undisturbed in its protection of the arts, this country would have kept pace with its neighbours in that branch of genius, as well as in every other. But the seeds which, at the same time, began to take root both in France and England, found, in the one case, every circumstance favourable to their growth, while, in the other, they were exposed in the bud to the storm of reformation; by which, had the arts been in the very vigour of maturity, they must have been torn up and destroyed, without the necessity of any malign influence of climate, or natural disposition, to account for the effect. A tendency was given, which it requir-

ed ages, as well as the rare occurrence of powerful genius, to counteract.

The accidental taste for portrait has, unfortunately, continued to predominate in this country down to the present time, and, being so mechanical a branch of the art, in which genius has little if any scope for employment; it cannot fail materially to have depressed whatever talent for the higher branches of painting may, from time to time, have arisen in the country. When any predilection for historical painting showed itself, it was liable to wither for want of encouragement, and naturally dropped into the more lucrative course of portrait or landscape. It is in this last branch of the art that the practice of this country possesses much title to claim the distinction of a peculiar school; particularly of late years, when many artists of preeminent merit as landscape painters have appeared.

There is another style of painting, in which an English artist not only stands unrivalled, but never has, in this or in any other country, even met with a competitor. We allude to Hogarth, who struck out for himself a path entirely new and untrodden in the subject of satire; and whose genius at once raised this branch of the art to that height of perfection which has immortalised his name. Our observations on the state of British art will therefore fall to be comprised under these three heads of Satirical, Portrait, and Landscape painting.

Satirical Painting.

Hogarth is unquestionably the greatest and most original genius that England ever possessed in the sphere of painting; and in whom she can boast of a satiric artist, such as no age or country ever produced, whether he is considered as a writer of comedy or as a painter of character. His pictures are powerful satires on the morals, manners, and follies, of the age in which he lived, exposed with a degree of wit and humour, and heightened by strokes of the most comic and playful vivacity, which place his works on a par with the best comedies of Moliere. In fact, if we consider the series of pictures, in which he has represented the various acts and scenes of his subject; the manner in which the plot is carried on, and the story told, with all the eccentricities of character, and exuberance of wit in every stroke of his pencil; we must acknowledge that they are as complete comic dramas as ever were represented on the stage. Lord Orford estimates the genius of Hogarth as follows: " Moliere, inimitable as he proved, brought a rude theatre to perfection. Hogarth had no model to follow and improve upon. He created his art; and used colours instead of language. His place is between the Italians, whom we may consider as epic poets and tragedians, and the Flemish painters, who are as writers of farce, and editors of burlesque nature. Hogarth resembles Butler, but his subjects are more universal; and, amidst all his pleasantry, he observes the true end of comedy, reformation; there is always a moral to his pictures. Sometimes he rose to tragedy, not in the catastrophe of kings and heroes, but in marking how vice conducts insensibly and incidentally to misery and shame. He warns against encouraging cruelty and idleness in young minds, and discerns how the different vices of the great and the vulgar lead, by various paths, to the same unhappiness. The fine lady in ' Marriage à-la-mode,' and Tom Nero in ' The Four Stages of Cruelty,' terminate their story in blood —she occasions the murder of her husband, he assassinates his mistress. How delicate, and superior too, is his satire, where he intimates, in the college of physicians and surgeons that preside at a dissection, how the legal habitude of viewing shocking scenes hardens the human mind, and renders it unfeeling. The president maintains the dignity of insensibility over an executed corpse, and considers it but as the object of a lecture. In the print of the ' Sleeping Judges,' this habitual indifference only excites our laughter." " It is to Hogarth's honour, that, in so many scenes of satire or ridicule, it is obvious that ill-nature did not guide his pencil. His end is always reformation, and his reproofs general. He touched the folly, but spared the person. Another instance of his genius is, his not condescending to explain his moral lessons by the trite poverty of allegory ; if he had an emblematical thought, he expressed it with wit, rather than by a symbol, such as that of the harlot setting fire to the world in the ' Rake's Progress,' the spider's web extended over the poor's box in a ' Parish Church,' and a thousand in the ' Strollers Dressing in a Barn,' which, for wit and imagination, without any other end, I think the best of all his works ; as for useful and deep satire, as that on the methodists is the most sublime." We cannot, however, go along with Lord Orford in underrating the merits of Hogarth as a painter merely. The preservation of his works enables the world to judge for itself without the intervention of his lordship's meagre praise. He seems to have written the account of Hogarth contained in his "Anecdotes of Painters" with feelings scarcely worthy of an historian, by detracting from the transcendent qualities of this great man, in a few trifling particulars of character and execution, which he thought himself at liberty to question. Lord Orford, fancying himself the Mecænas of England, looked for that deference, and those assiduities, which the independence of Hogarth's disposition very probably led him to overlook. But it is always dangerous to the credit of a biographer to season the meed of praise which it was impossible to withhold, by the spicery of any little grovelling feelings of personal dislike. Lord Orford was not aware how much a greater man, in the estimation of the world, than himself, he had to deal with, so as to turn back the point of his censure more sharply on himself.

The universal and unwearied delight with which the works of Hogarth have ever been contemplated speak the most decided eulogy that could be bestowed upon them. Few painters have produced works so abundant in a rich store of intellectual food, which, like a good play, never palls upon the appetite, however frequently represented. Hogarth's merit was not confined to comedy alone, for he succeeded equally well in representing such scenes as are calculated to rouse the feelings of compassion and horror, and to act as impressive warnings of the fatal consequences arising from unbridled passions,—that species of low tragedy which, under such masterly management as that of Hogarth, strikes its warnings more surely home, than in a loftier strain, moving in a sphere with which the generality of the world experience less sympathy. Instances of such abound in his works, but we refrain from entering into any details, where the inexhaustibly varied expositions of the frailties of human nature would lead us far beyond our limits.

When we extol the works of Hogarth as original, we do not mean to overlook the inimitable production of an earlier painter : " The Dance of Death," by Hans Holbein, which presents so admirable a satire on mankind, in which the vicissitudes of human life are ingeniously and humorously pourtrayed, but in a style very different from Hogarth. That species of painting called grotesque was practised, to a certain extent, in

almost every age, both ancient and modern. Annibal Caracci left his Arti di Bologna ; even Raphael amused himself with caricature ; and the dignity of Leonardo da Vinci condescended sometimes to employ his pencil in frolic.

In the same class of composition, but more approaching to the style of caricature, are the performances of another English artist, Bunbury. Though without aspiring to the more elevated and instructive themes of Hogarth's moral pencil, Bunbury's works are replete with amusing and humorous expositions of the absurdities of character. He was followed in the same vein, and with some success, by Rowlandson.

This particular branch of art, though we have examples of its practice among the Greeks and Romans, seems, in modern Europe, to be nearly, if not altogether, peculiar to England. Private animosities, and the bickerings of party spirit, which, in the continental countries of Europe, generally armed its adversaries with the stiletto, and sought vent in assassination, appear to be quite unsuitable to the genius and tone of British feeling. No event could be supposed more calculated to call forth all the bitterness of party than the change of dynasty which took place upon the expulsion of the royal family of Stuart, and the establishment of another and a foreign family on the throne ; yet, how creditable is it to the character of the nation, to find these ranklings which, with our neighbours, would have stirred up the demon of private revenge, subsiding, as they did in this country, after the fair and open appeal to arms had settled the event. To find the hostility to the house of Hanover evaporating in political sarcasms of every kind, in which ridicule was the prevailing weapon ; a contest of wit and humour, in which the pencil was summoned to assist the pen ; for it is from this æra, chiefly, that we have to deduce the origin of caricature painting in Britain. The system has proved to be a powerful engine, either as expressive of public opinion, or as a sort of fire-ship sent forth to inflame the public mind, by exposing the conduct of the leading characters of the day, and the foibles of all ; but always attended with this good effect, that, whether it laughs at or censures, it must of necessity be in good humour, and admits of no effectual retort except by similar weapons of wit and fun. A lampoon of this kind may be ever so cutting and severe ; if it excites laughter and amusement, the sting is disarmed of its poison ; it becomes a sort of safety valve, by which the effervescence of party rancour is dissipated, and escapes as a harmless vapour. It may, at times, level the shafts of ridicule against the innocent, and even against characters deserving of the highest reverence and honour ; but while good feeling is so preeminent in the British character, such misdirected shafts will fall short of their mark. The late revered monarch of these realms was not exempt from the freedom of such licensed jokers ; but, so far from being offensive, these familiarities, in the humour of which his own good sense led him to be the first to join, only tended to endear him the more to his subjects ; who were ever as ready to join in a joke with their beloved old king, as to defend his honour at the cannon's mouth.

Strangers express much surprise at the liberties taken by caricaturists in this country, the impunity attending their attacks, and the toleration they enjoy ; but what on the Continent broods in conspiracies, party rancour, private hatred and revenge, is all above board in Britain,—and long may it be so ! Modern Rome has been much indebted to the good humoured jokes of

Pasquin and Marforio, but the window of a caricature shop answers the purpose more effectually; in so far as hilarity is more likely to be excited, and must accompany every satire, as gravity is quite incompatible with this particular mode of administering correction. It is quite surprising that a nation so remarkable for vivacity as the French, and so full of that species of wit peculiarly adapted to good humoured satire, should have utterly failed in all their attempts at the production of caricature. Nothing can be more tame and vapid than their performances of this kind. We have never seen a French caricature that was even tolerable; and so lame are their attempts at humorous drawings, that they are either burlesque extravagancies, with a total failure in seizing character, or indecent representations, without any humour to recommend them. At the same time we must allow the playful humour of an English caricature to be as little congruous with the sedate and haughty deportment of the nation, as the invincible hilarity of a Frenchman is with the clumsy failure of their pencil in the department of satirical painting.

Portrait Painting.

The great field of painting in Britain, since the time of its earliest introduction down to the present day, has been that of family memorials, confined originally to heraldic painting, but for many ages to that of portrait. Of these, ancient specimens of very great curiosity are still existing, preserved in the Royal Palaces, and more ancient baronial residences of our nobility. Accounts of them have been published in the works of various writers on the history of British painters, from whom we learn, that, among the multitude of portrait painters who filled the country with their works, there are comparatively few names of native artists. Many of these foreigners, however, became in a manner naturalized, from having passed their lives in Britain in the exercise of their art, and established their families in the country. Of that number we have to record the prince of portrait painters, Vandyck, whose works abound in Britain. Many painters of merit both preceded and followed him. So early as the reign of Queen Elizabeth, Isaac Oliver distinguished himself as a celebrated miniature painter, and his son Peter obtained a high name in the succeeding reign of James the Sixth.

Jamieson, a native of Aberdeen, studied under Rubens and Vandyck, and attained so great a degree of perfection in the art of portrait, as to be considered next to Vandyck. Were Jamieson's pictures better known, there is little doubt that he would hold a higher rank as a painter, than what is generally allowed to him. His works being chiefly confined to Scotland, and in the possession of private families in a remote part of the country, the circle of his fame has been necessarily of narrow range, though his merit is far superior to that of some English artists, whose performances circumstances have brought more into notice.

Among the classical painters of England, we have long been accustomed to consider several names of local celebrity, who are actually foreigners, though adopted by continued residence as natives, namely, Sir Peter Lely, Sir Godfrey Kneller, Sir John Medina, and others. Many of the portraits of that age were sacrificed to the absurd fashion of the times, in dress the most ungraceful as well as unnatural, that could be conceived; with full bottomed wigs, and every thing that was calculated to disfigure the human form. The tight laced gown of the ladies was equally incompati-

ble with any graceful form of drapery so desirable for a painter. They were obliged to clothe their portraits in fancy dresses, in which the taste does not always appear very judicious or appropriate. The sleepy voluptuous eye of Sir Peter Lely's ladies, with their persons but sparingly enveloped in a loose night gown, seem as if they had only that moment stepped out of bed; but leave us much at a loss to account for the garden scenery which generally surrounds them, and for which they seem so unsuitably attired. It is as injurious to the effect of a portrait to distract the attention from the countenance, by any thing very unusual in the dress, as by the introduction of obtrusive accessaries, which thrust themselves forward upon the eye.

The proper draping of a portrait is a matter of some difficulty. There are strong reasons for adopting the usual habit of the person, however inelegant; and yet, in the course of a few years, it may be the means of exciting such a degree of the ridiculous as to destroy the whole merit of the picture. At the same time, if, in our portrait, we choose to appear in masquerade, we have certainly no reason to complain of want of resemblance; for it is wonderful how small a change of dress from the ordinary habit will prove sufficient to disguise our most intimate friends; so that upon the whole the chance of appearing ridiculous in after times, is perhaps the least objection; if we are represented exactly as we appeared when living, we have little reason to complain. The more, however, the fashion of the day can be simplified, without destroying the character, the better; and yet how common it is for those who go to sit for their picture, to dress themselves up in such a manner as to aggravate the evil! It was, at one period, much the fashion to endeavour to escape this difficulty by the ingenious device of representing the person in allegorical, or even mythological characters, than which nothing could be more preposterous. Although we cannot follow the antique simplicity of the Greeks, who represented their portraits without any covering at all, yet certainly the simpler and the less ornamental the better, as the ornament forms no part of the person of whom we desire to preserve the memory.

Portrait painting has, in modern times, been suffered to lose much of its dignity, by a loose and negligent practice, with a grievous want of finishing in the accessaries and subordinate parts. There is no reason why portrait should be less carefully painted than history. In its nature it is the same, and therefore demands the same requisites; nor is perfection to be attained but by the very same qualities which constitute the perfection of an historical painter. All the difference consists in this, that the one requires the accurate study of individual character, and the other the general character of mankind, and the expression of particular sentiments and passions in individuals. It is a false view of the nature and dignity of this branch of the art, to suppose that it permits of that careless execution which constitutes the great defect of modern portrait painters, who paint for money and not for fame. Unfortunately for the credit of the art, the gain to be acquired by the most indifferent performers has occasioned the profession to swarm with the vilest daubers, who bring ridicule upon the art they are incapable of reaching. Much study and knowledge of human character are required, with correct taste, and dexterity in the practice of the art; so that the number of great portrait painters are as rare in the history of the art, as they are in the highest branch of painting.

There are peculiarities in the habits and expression of every individual, which require the nicest discernment to seize, and the greatest address to discover whether they arise from any casual motive, or are really natural and habitual to the individual. The painter must be able to draw aside the curtain of restraint, and sometimes of affectation, in which sitting for one's picture not unfrequently veils the individual. The peculiar manner of carrying the head has much influence on the resemblance. We would know our acquaintance although the countenance were hid: even the hat seems so far to partake of the influence of resemblance, as to be discernible to an acquaintance. We recognise a friend at a great distance by his mode of walking, the motion of his arms, but particularly the position of the head. All these peculiarities require the most acute observation on the part of a portrait painter, though rarely do we find their examination extended beyond the mere form of the features.

He must know, moreover, how to harmonise all those nice circumstances of character, so as not to join a haughty cast of countenance to a humble gesture, or a timid position of the head; for in nature the character is legibly diffused over every limb. Nothing is more likely to create mannerism than that usual practice of portrait painters, in subjecting their patients to the same constrained position of some elevated throne, where their natural gesture and demeanour must be kept down, where they cannot for a moment forget that they are under operation; screwed by the painter into some attitude quite at variance with their usual habits, they become strangers to themselves, and, as such, must feel and appear awkward: which the effort to retain the posture, and the whole irksomeness of the thing, cannot but tend to augment.

Besides that every individual is subjected to this particular ordeal, the light is always the same, infallibly inducing a sameness of manner; but the same light is quite unsuitable to all countenances. Some are destroyed by a strong shade, others require it; a high confined light, which is the one generally adopted, although it gives a striking contrast of light and shade, still communicates a seriousness often unsuitable to the expression. We are frequently struck with the effects of various lights upon the countenances of those persons we are in the constant habit of seeing, in changing the character, and making them unlike themselves. Great judgment is therefore necessary in choosing that light which best develops the characteristic expression.

In the generality of portraits, nothing is more discernible than that ceremonious air of constraint which we never observe in the works of Titian or Vandyck; where simple unaffected nature, the easy air and familiar gesture of the individual, shows a seeming unconsciousness of sitting to be painted.

As to effect, repose is the great object aimed at in portrait painting; therefore great caution ought to be observed in introducing any of those accidental or extraordinary effects, which tend to disturb it. Rembrandt's vivid pencil of light, shot through the dungeon darkness in which he generally places his portraits, is striking and often beautiful; but so unfrequent in nature as not to be ventured upon but with the greatest caution.

The taste of a portrait painter is in nothing more conspicuous than in the judicious selection of his point of view, so as to obtain the most favourable and characteristic aspect, which is seldom exactly the same in any two individuals. This is the legitimate mode of embellishment, which keeps faith with nature, by preserving the resemblance, and that under the most favourable circumstances.

From the time of Charles the First, portrait painting continued almost exclusively to occupy the attention of English artists, whose names or works we think it unnecessary to enumerate here, and willingly hasten to select for our theme the greatest name in the republic of British artists,—that of Reynolds, who is usually styled the founder of the English school; but the fact is, that he did not found any individual school of art; being gifted with a superior taste to what existed at that time in his own country, he had the merit of introducing more enlarged views, and a more judicious cultivation of the arts.

Few masters have been more eulogised than Sir Joshua Reynolds, and perhaps to his prejudice; as merit which is not of the most preeminent stamp is often more injured by too much being said of it than too little. The works of Sir Joshua were, like his "Discourses," in the purest unaffected taste; mild, correct, and elegant, but without those marks of transcendent genius, that irresistible vigour of talent, which shines forth in every trait of such men as Michael Angelo, Raphael, and others, whose merits we have already discussed. In Sir Joshua the fire of originality is subdued under the habitual influence of the soothing and bland temper of the man. It is, nevertheless, to his elegant mind and pure taste that the English school owes whatever is creditable in the modern practice of history and portrait painting; in so far as he was the first to extricate the art from the trammels of a dry and artificial meagreness of manner, which his predecessors sought to trick out with affectation.

The excellence of Sir Joshua was more conspicuous in portrait than in history, which is, in itself, a sufficient commentary on his genius; as implying little vigour of invention or force of drawing. His colour was soft and fleshy, but thin, without the mellow and downy roundness of Vandyck, or the Venetian painters. His attitudes have an air of posture-making, which is neither agreeable nor easy, and, of course, not graceful. This, however, is principally observable in his fancy pieces, as many of the portraits are remarkable for a happy expression of character and truth. There is a tone of accomplished manners, congenial to the elegant mind of the painter; every thing breathes the gentleman in the works of Sir Joshua. His portraits of men are superior to his women, who generally look as if acting a part, with a degree of affectation and languishing insipidity that is very far from feminine grace. His pictures of children are, in general, quite infantine and lovely; and, indeed, the undefined airy character of Sir Joshua's painting is remarkably suited to the round plump form of infancy. But still there is the same want of finishing, which is the besetting sin of the British school, and which, however excellent in other respects the portraits of Reynolds may be, would forbid their being admitted into comparison with those of Titian, or the other great masters. And still less could we adventure such a parallel in subjects of history. Whatever the reason may be we leave others to decide; but candour must admit, that, in subjects of serious history, Britain has never yet produced an artist of any general celebrity.

In the familiar subjects of domestic life there are artists of the present day who tread very close on the heels of the eminent masters of Holland, as our countryman Wilkie, and some others; but still, in the loftier walks of art, in the epic of painting, we feel that we must be silent.

Landscape Painting.

The basis on which the British school is best entitled to rest its fame, is that of Landscape, in which several of our modern artists have, of late years, attained a degree of excellence highly creditable to the country. Of these, Wilson painted in the style of Claud de Lorain with great success; the works of Smith were admired; and Gainsborough surpassed in fancy pieces of cottage scenery and rustic figures.

We might record, among the landscape painters of the present day, many names of deserved reputation, but we willingly refrain from making any comments on the works of existing artists, until the concurrence of public opinion has sufficiently confirmed their rank, and given a sanction to the estimation which each is entitled to hold. The history of the art sufficiently demonstrates the erroneous impressions that generally prevail respecting the merits of existing artists. It is not long since the insipid works of Battoni excited such admiration in Rome itself, in the very seat of taste, as to make him be esteemed a second Raphael; Mengs was extolled with equal extravagance, though they have both now found their level. Although the error has been principally in overrating, we know that many of the first geniuses lived in neglect and misery, whose names now stand high in the list of fame.

The advance lately made in the art of landscape painting, makes us augur highly of its future progress: That it should have become so decidedly the prevailing taste seems a natural consequence of the circumstances of the country, abounding in the fresh and luxuriant display of picturesque scenery. While, on the contrary, there is so little attractive to a painter's eye in the figures and dress of this country, that it is the first circumstance which strikes us with admiration, when we go to foreign countries, to observe the superior effect of colour and dress in the natives, with the splendour and frequency of their pageants and shows. The habits of the British, on the contrary, present rarely any temptation for a painter to employ his pencil on the human form. We have little taste for the stage, and no processions; the attire of our priesthood, and all our dignitaries, is simple; and the general deportment grave and sedate. There is but one opportunity in which a painter of this country can see the animal man, in the active display of his physical powers, and uncovered; but that custom is of a very questionable character. We allude to the brutal displays of pugilism, which, with all the apologies and advantages that have been pleaded in its excuse, in so far as it is a mere display of the brutal ferocity of man, undignified by mind, is a debasing spectacle; and can be acceptable alone to minds of the lowest cast. It is a mistake to suppose, that it bears any sympathy or connection with a martial spirit, or with valour. A brave soldier is a generous noble animal, as free from ferocity as from fear, capable of the highest achievements of intrepid valour, as he is incapable of the butchering ferocity of the pugilist. We doubt if such studies are ever very available to our painters, while a more inviting branch of art presents itself on every side, while nature in her most beautiful attire is spread out before them, fresh and verdant, unscorched by a vertical sun, and unscathed by the rigour of the severer north. Moreover, it is the beauty to which the rich are most alive; we are a gardening, country-loving, race. With what avidity do all ranks, from the nobleman to the mechanic, rush to the country, to plant their trees, and decorate their rural abodes! What delights in reality, must please in the imitation; and, therefore, we willingly purchase the representation of fine scenery: It is the natural food of our eye; we have comparatively little relish for the representations of allegory or ancient fable: Subjects of sacred and national history have their attractions, but they are not of long duration: while we dwell upon the fair face of nature with increasing delight.

The subjects for a landscape painter are as unlimited in extent as they are interesting from the variety of character every object is capable of assuming, whether grave or cheerful, brilliant or gloomy. We have the infinitely varied appearance of water, for instance, whether reflecting on its glassy surface all the beauties of surrounding nature, or raging and chafing against opposing rocks, whether bounding from the cliff with turmoil, or kissing in silence the flowery bank that meets its embrace. Again, we have the spreading lake, or the dark pool, and the wide expanse of ocean in all its changing forms. The nature of our scenery is uniformly soothing and beautiful, whether it be a scene of fresh smiling meadows or tufted forest; extensive plains covered with harvest, and busy trade; towns rolling their smoke, or the wild mountains of the north melting into vapour, instead of the cutting line of clear distance under an Italian sky. The ever-changing and partial lights of our varied sky, with its magnificent canopy of rolling clouds, folding into new forms of elegance as we gaze upon them, blending their rich tints in every possible gradation; from the dark thunder cloud to the gilded beams of our setting sun, offer inexhaustible food for a painter's eye. And yet, how surprising it is to observe, that, in no part of landscape painting is mannerism so prevalent as in the sky! Such is the uniformity of some painters, that they seem to have looked to heaven but once in their lives, and dress up every picture in the same artificial garb; while the inexhaustibly varied beauty of our insular sky invites their study, and offers a ready field for the exercise of taste, in form, colour, grouping, and blending of tints, in the most fascinating richness. The sky is, moreover, the key note, which ought to regulate the whole harmony of a picture, depending upon that law in nature, so difficult of imitation, and yet so obvious, of a reciprocal communication of light and colour, from every object in nature to all within the sphere of its action. Painting can but approximate to all the niceties, combinations, and intricacies, of direct and reflected light, involving the contrasted obscurities of these objects, or parts of objects, least exposed to it, and modified by the almost imperceptible gradation of intensity as it recedes from the eye. When we add to this, the infinite interchange of tints, affecting every object in nature, which may be said altogether to elude common observation, and not to be easily detected, in all their niceties, by those most familiar with the study; we shall be less disposed to underrate the merits and difficulties of landscape painting.

One of the greatest landscape painters of the present age, Mr. Turner, seems to have grappled so vigorously with this important desideratum in the art, that much may be expected from his system of study and acute observation. So far as he has gone, eminent success has attended his footsteps; and, aided by the discoveries daily making in the mysteries of light, his scrutinizing genius seems to tremble on the verge of some new discovery in colour, which may prove of the first importance to the art. His idea has been taken up by others, and the rivalry of so many men of genius is likely to work out something more definite, on the subject of light and colour, than our ideas have hitherto attained ; something to furnish a guiding clue to the infinite modifications which as yet perplex the intense observer of the effects of nature. The difficulty arises from the want of some plain guiding principle ; for in this, as in every thing else, the laws of nature are uniform and constant, were we capable of applying the rule ; but, bewildered in the immeasurable intricacies and variety, all we can at present do, is to hazard a sort of resemblance. Turner has struck out a new route, by the singular mixture of prismatic colours, with which he represents sky and water ; the idea is singularly acute and philosophical, if we consider the optical properties of the changing surface of water. So long as we are engaged with direct light, it is comparatively simple. We may interpose objects, so as dexterously to intercept the light where we wish it to fall, and thus produce an effect generally harmonious ; but exactness in the minuter parts, strictly conformable to the laws of physics, seems, as yet, beyond our reach. We can but approximate, or take advantage of a fortunate chance, as very different and unexpected results often arise from the combinations of colours, and the blending of light and shade. No one could, *a priori*, expect the neutral tint of water to result from combining the distinct and brilliant colours of the prism, upon the modifications of which, however, depend all the indescribably varied hues of that element.

The requisites of a skilful landscape are many ; and not the least indispensable, is the preservation of a due proportion betwixt the figures, trees, and various objects of which it consists ; the figures ought to have a meaning, and appear at home. Poussin excelled in this particular, by giving such interest and nobleness to his accompanying figures, that he made the landscape seem to accompany them.

Another important feature is that of the trees, in the execution of which there is much difference in the modes of different painters. Some entirely sacrifice detail to general character, while others consider distinct leafing as in all cases indispensable. If we take nature for our guide, this circumstance ought to be regulated by distance alone, and the power of vision. Trees have a general character, governed by the usual disposition of their growth, producing a certain cast of form. This, at some distance, is all by which we can judge of their kind, and the circumstance, united to the tone of colour, which ought to guide the painter. But when we approach within the sphere of distinctly seeing the foliage, it ought doubtless to be attended to, however much, in the general view of a picture, we may seem insensible to such details ; and aware of nothing beyond the general mass, until we exclusively direct our attention to that individual object. These details produce no distraction in nature, as little ought they to do so in a picture : on the contrary, when, after the first general view, we come to examine a picture more closely, the illusion becomes readily disenchanted, if we find an hazy and indefinite mass where we expected to see the animating play of foliage. Not that we would wish to find the microscopic laboriousness of some of the Dutch and German landscape painters, whose trees are painted with the most fatiguing accuracy, peopled with little birds, whose plumage is designed with the minute precision of a naturalist ; but we require the power of discerning, with the same facility we can in nature, the distinctive features of the individual tree intended.

It is not enough that we should paint the cedar of its sombre hue ; it must be unequivocally a cedar, and not a fir or holly tree ; in short, the characteristic touch of each species ought not to be less marked than its appropriate colour or mode of growth. The great difficulty in tree painting depends upon a dexterous management of these requisites, which is, unfortunately, not easily accomplished without disturbing the repose by spottiness, or tormenting the eyes by such intricacies as some of Ruysdale's and Swanevelt's otherwise beautiful forest scenery present. It is an easy matter to throw in, with grace and dexterity, the general massing and prominent characters of trees, leaving to the imagination the more difficult task of detail ; for a sketch this suits admirably, and constitutes one of its greatest charms, but it will not do for a finished picture, and destroys the merit of many of our modern productions.

The disposition of the branches, like the anatomy of the human figure, is a matter of the greatest importance, demanding much study, in so far as every species has, in this respect, a different character and conformation ; whereas the single system of human anatomy enables us to dispose all the varieties of our figures. With trees, however, each has its distinct anatomy, an accurate knowledge of which is a rare acquisition, but an important one for a landscape painter. The due balance and quantity of clothing, proportioned to the supporting arms, the disposition of all trees to supply the requisite balance, and counteract the tendency of stem; of position, of the prevailing wind, &c. require attention ; the arrangement of branches ought to be such as to show, that, if we could go round the tree, we should still find the balance preserved, some branches advance direct to the eye, and seem to overhang the frame, while others recede into the interior of the picture ; and withal a seeming chance ought to appear to rule supreme.

For a landscape painter the study of nature alone will not suffice, and that of the great masters will point out many things to which the uninstructed eye would prove a delusive guide. The illusions of vision are in every respect remarkable, and in none more than in the misconceptions of landscape. We seem to see colours, because we know them to exist. Forms are definite, and lines are straight, which the eye unconsciously sees far otherwise ; so that, when represented as such, they are unpleasing, and we know not why. Again, the degradation of distance is at constant variance with our pre-existing knowledge of the real magnitude of objects ; and it comes to be a question of some difficulty, to determine whether a painter ought to be guided by the real size and nature of objects, as geometry proves them to be, and as we see them represented by the camera lucida ; or to represent nature as we seem to see it, modified by our habits, by the influencing circumstances of light and vapour, and by all the delusions of vision.

In enumerating the requisite attainments of the landscape painter, we cannot pass over that most indispensable of all, a knowledge of perspective, although this is not the place for a minute discussion of that important subject. Its application extends to every branch of painting as well as to landscape, as there is no object in nature which presents itself to our view, not even the clouds, that is not subject to the principles of perspective, which, in so far as regards the outline, is called linear ; and, when applied to the degradation of size, colour, and distinctness of objects by distance, is called aerial. It is surprising how frequently we find artists of great merit shipwreck their fame on this rock, by neglecting the unyielding truths of perspective. A painter ought at least to be sufficiently acquainted with the rules, to be able to prove his accuracy in any doubtful point; for in general such is the truth of a well trained eye, that it instantly detects the minutest deviation from correct perspective. From the charm of perfect truth in the compositions of most of the great masters, it is easily discoverable how profoundly skilled they were in the principles of this science. And in others, on the contrary, the deficiency is quite obvious; from the negligent practice of grouping their figures at random as imagination suggested, and adjusting them as they proceeded, instead of previously establishing a distinct standard of perspective, and degradation of size, serving to regulate every object as it took its place on their canvas. Due regard must at the same time be had to the proposed position of the eye of the observer. Nothing leads more unavoidably into error, than the practice of first painting the subject, and then adding the accessaries of architecture, or whatever species of filling up the subject may require. It is a chance that they do not reciprocally destroy the merits of each other, by a disregard of some essentials in proportion and perspective. There is no surer method than to form little models of clay of the figures desired; to be placed to the height of the eye, and exactly opposite to the point of sight; removed at three times the intended breadth of the picture, where the group must be accurately drawn in the proportions which the figures respectively bear to each other. This forms a sure guide to the after painting of the picture, and to the regulation of the exact position of any large studies made for it.

The nature of aerial perspective does not admit of its being subjected to equal precision of rules, being materially governed by the actual state of the atmosphere; still an accurate observance of it is not the less indispensable. The effect of vapour produces a multitude of optical illusions, which a landscape painter must study. When augmented to the density of fog, they become exceedingly striking, and under that influence have been admirably represented by the French painter Vernet. Claude de Lorraine was likewise a great master of this art, particularly in the representation of haze as affected by the rays of the sun. Objects in a fog appear greatly larger than usual. But a more perplexing illusion takes place, from the circumstance of near objects being, by the intervention of vapour, rendered apparently at a greater distance, while at the same time they retain their magnitude. By being thus removed in appearance to a greater distance, without any alteration in the linear perspective, while the aerial is so much affected, they naturally assume the appearance of distant objects of great size.

This quality of aerial perspective is, of all the attributes of landscape, the most delightful and fascinating to a picturesque eye; and we cannot cease to wonder how its charms could possibly have escaped the notice of the Greeks. Although they had an acquaintance with linear perspective, as appears from what Euclid, Vitruvius, and other ancient authors have written, and even that most difficult part comprehending the rules of foreshortening, of their knowledge of aerial perspective there is not the slightest indication. Yet the Greeks inhabited one of the most picturesque countries of Europe, and were abundantly alive to the beauties of nature; notwithstanding which landscape never seems to have engaged their attention. But, indeed, in many things connected with the history of painting, our *a priori* conclusions are set at nought. It is not

from the uninteresting flats of Flanders, or the fenny borders of Dutch canals, that we should look for the successful cultivation of a picturesque taste; or for the countries where so many admirable landscape painters have arisen. Yet for one that has appeared in the most romantic regions of Europe, ten have risen to eminence among the sand hills and bogs of Holland. If we were to pitch upon the country in Europe where the most frippery and worst taste for landscape painting existed, we would say that it was in Switzerland, the very gem of romantic scenery.

We have now concluded what we had to say on the state of painting since its revival in the fourteenth century. We had proposed to add a short inquiry as to the comparative merits of ancient and modern art, but the subject has so imperceptibly woven itself into our account of the different modern schools, that we think it superfluous now to revert more particularly to that matter. We shall only subjoin a few observations as to the means generally esteemed most efficacious for promoting the interests of painting, although we are well aware that it is not a subject on which we have any thing very satisfactory to advance.

We may safely infer from the foregoing historical sketch, that it is little consistent with the nature of the fine arts, to remain for any length of time stationary. We have seen them invariably subjected to vicissitudes during their whole progress; nor have these vicissitudes, either of improvement or decay, followed the causes that might have been expected to induce them. On the contrary, they have only tended to prove the very fallible nature of our best exertions, and of all the expedients hitherto industriously brought into action, with a view to promote the interests of the fine arts; and that, not merely to the extent of falling short of the anticipated effects, but of producing directly the reverse of what was intended.

A great deal has been written on this subject, and many projects, both original and revived, have been keenly urged as the only infallible means of eliciting the wished for patronage. But whether that encouragement, which was to prove so efficacious, was of a public or of a private nature, there was little in experience to warrant much confidence in its effects: and accordingly the institution of academies, and other such fostering associations, has been as keenly decried by some, as being positively prejudicial. We must allow that history seems to countenance this latter opinion, when we see that wherever public institutions have been established, and exertions made for the preservation and encouragement of the arts, there they seem almost uniformly to have disappeared. At least, instead of advancing, they have generally retrograded. All the great masters of Italy had run their brilliant course before the establishment of the Della Crusca, or any other Dillettanti association; and whether it was that the busy vaunting academies which sprung up in Florence, and most of the other cities of Italy, were the mere adventitious stays of a tottering fabric; true it is, that from the period of their establishment, the art of painting sank; and has ever since remained in a state of degradation, almost contemptible. We are not aware that any improvement in the arts has resulted from the exertions of the French academy, while we must allow, that among English artists, many of the greatest names preceded the institution of our academy.

We have just witnessed the formation of a similar association for the encouragement of the fine arts in our native city. It has our sincere and ardent wishes for the successful accomplishment of its patriotic views; and we trust that, in the promotion of the arts, it may become an honourable exception to the usual fate that seems to await this system of patronage. Hitherto, whatever promise of genius or predilection for the arts, arose in this part of the island, has, for obvious reasons, generally flowed towards the southern capital, and there merged in the aggregate mass of aspirants to eminence in the British school. One advantage may therefore result from the institution alluded to, in offering some local support to native artists, who find it convenient to cultivate their profession at home, by facilitating their means of study. But let them not form unreasonable expectations, and charge, (as has often been done with acrimony,) the disappointments arising from any over-rated estimate of their own talent, upon a want of due support; where that support could neither supply defective genius, nor sustain the mistaken measure we are too apt to form of our own acquirements.

There is no country in Europe in which so much money has been lavished by private individuals on the works of art, and on artists, as in England; yet how little advantage it has operated on the improvement of the art itself is too obvious. Like bounties in general, which are often of very doubtful policy, pecuniary encouragement has, in matters of art, been found to defeat its own object, by multiplying the claimants, faster even than the means of gain are proffered; and by creating a swarm of idle competitors, whom the temptation of profit had withdrawn from more useful occupations. In fact, the multitude who now follow the profession, is one great cause of the scarcity of good artists. Every pretender who daubs the semblance of nature's image, thinks himself a painter, helps out his deficiencies with the trickeries of the trade, and conceives that he thus has mastered all the noble attainments of this delightful but difficult art. Formerly the regular apprenticeship of years of toil and study under the best masters of the day, preceded the first step to the name of painter; the variety of learning required, exhausted the scope of the then existing sciences; and a great painter was at the same time a man of great learning and general acquirements. In the present age, instead of the fertile soil of genius and learning, where alone the arts were formerly cultivated, crowds of vain and heedless pretenders, set to work with minds stuffed with dross and rubbish, out of which spring weeds profusely.

It is a dangerous thing to consider genius as omnipotent in the fine arts. Truth will divulge to every man's own mind how much we owe to the suggestions and attainments of others, however much vanity may tempt us to throw a veil over these helps; and what we consider the result of genius in the great masters, is often more the fruit of anxious labour and study, than of any intuitive quality. Those accustomed to teach in the academies of painting, have generally found that the slow and laborious student was far more likely to rise to eminence, than those who pressed forward in the confidence of genius. After every thing is acquired that experience can teach, an ample field will yet remain for the exercise of genius and invention. The scope is boundless. But the basis of painting ought to be laid on study, on an intimate knowledge of the practice and discoveries of the best masters, on acute observation of nature, and unwearied combat with the difficulties of execution. These are the substantial promoters of the art, and in so far as associations or private patronage can supply facilities of employment, and objects of emulation and of study, they have done their part.

It is not an unusual error in institutions of this de-

scription, to defeat their purpose by overshooting the mark, and endeavouring to do too much,—to present the means of encouragement uninvited, and to urge its acceptance, before the privation it is meant to supply is keenly felt, and a consciousness of its value awakened in the minds of those for whose behoof it is intended. Aids of this description must be voluntarily sought for, and earnestly wooed, before their acquisition is likely to prove effectual. There is nothing in the management of which, greater delicacy is required, than in conferring favours unasked, however much they may be needed; nor any thing more liable to rouse the jealousy of pride, (a feeling from which artists do not usually enjoy any exemption,) than those proffered kindnesses that savour of officious protection. Let the source whence it flows be ever so pure, in the eyes of those for whose benefit it is offered, it is not easily divested of a qualifying sentiment of humiliation in the acceptance, or suspicion of ostentation in the bounty, which defeats half its purpose. All that is required is not to withhold those aids and that protection which genius lays claim to as of right; and while we offer them with the hand of munificence as a tribute to the art, to preserve a due consideration for the feelings of the artist.

The objects of a painter's study are of that costly nature, that he can rarely look to any other means of acquiring them than to the public institutions of his country. And in most parts of the Continent where the fine arts have been cultivated, ample treasures have been liberally opened for the artist's use, as well as for the public gratification and general improvement of taste, which we are sorry to confess have been grievously neglected in our island. Even to this day an artist must despair of prosecuting the studies essential to his art, unless he can accommodate his means to an expensive journey and a long residence in foreign countries, where those aids are placed within his reach. Not that we are deficient in the possession of valuable specimens of ancient art; for in the numerical riches of good pictures, the sum contained in England alone, is perhaps fully greater than that possessed by any of the continental kingdoms. But to the artist as to the stranger they are alike inaccessible, except under circumstances of inconvenience and constraint, which renders the hasty contemplation of them equally fruitless of utility as of gratification; for it is only from the habitual, deliberate, and repeated study of the works of the great masters, that any benefit or improvement of taste can be expected to arise. The mere cursory transit of a gallery, however richly stored, only serves to whet the edge of our privations. We speak with reference to the arts alone, when we lament the seclusion of these great models of excellence from a more unreserved inspection; for we are well aware that it is a consequence of habits peculiar to this country, and far too valuable to its character and welfare to desire any change in that respect. While the country residences of our nobility continue to be (as we trust they ever will) their principal abode, there is little chance of seeing the valuable works of art, of which they are the chief repositories, assembled in our towns, as is generally the case abroad. But we cannot see that these valued habits are at all incompatible with such arrangements, as would occasionally enable these works to be rendered conducive to the general improvement of taste, and to the study of our artists, without either risk to the pictures or inconvenience to their possessors. A very successful experiment of this kind has already taken place in Edinburgh, and the advantages that have flowed from

PAINTING.

that effort are so conspicuous, that it cannot fail to prove highly gratifying to those who have furnished the means of its accomplishment.

We earnestly hope that the scheme may be persevered in, and meet with the essential support of those possessing pictures of acknowledged excellence. The exhibition of old pictures is the most important, but that of modern artists is not without its use; and if both exhibitions could be accomplished at the same time, we think it would be better still. We see no reason why the efforts of modern art should not be brought into fair collision with the works of admitted merit from the pencil of the first masters of antiquity; it is the only test by which modern works can find their level of merit, uninfluenced by the glare of partial estimation. The adulations or well meant commendations of friends, whose want of skill ought to disarm their praises of much weight, is notwithstanding so generally acceptable, and so much in unison with the delusions of self-conceit, as to prove highly injurious to improvement, unless effectually controlled by some surer test. In Greece the nation at large, much to the benefit of the artist, passed judgment on his works, and determined whether they were worthy to be hung up in the porticos; where, for the gratification of the people, and the emulation of rising artists, constant exhibitions of the best works took place. Even the temples of their gods were often dedicated to the same use; in which practice they were followed by the Romans at a later period. That the same usage prevailed in the Catholic world, however much it may have become the object of religious abuse, was notwithstanding of most essential service to the arts.

As yet we have access to no public collections unfettered by troublesome formalities, or more obnoxious solicitations; and of the many and valuable private collections, the habitual privacy of our domestic mode of life forbids the freedom of inspection. Whereas with our neighbours, the artist, as well as the public in general, enjoy the most unreserved and liberal access to the collections, both public and private. In the public collections, and even in some of the private ones, facilities are afforded for the copying of pictures, and the study of artists, which shows the most commendable zeal for the improvement of painting.

While we flock in thousands, and tens of thousands, to profit by the more liberal views of our neighbours in the exhibition of their picture treasures; we lavish great sums in the acquisition of similar works of art, and then send them to Britain, that they may be buried and hid from view, until they chance to stray into a sale-room, which is fortunately not an unfrequent occurrence. The hidden treasures of this description in Britain cannot but be very great; and we would venture to assert, that, were the pictures contained in the various royal residences assembled together, and arranged as a national gallery, Paris could no longer boast of her Louvre as unique in the display of the riches of art. Such a gallery, established in London, upon terms of admission and use, as liberal and judicious as that of the Louvre, would prove of incalculable benefit to the art, and worthy of the well known taste and munificence of our sovereign. The want of such an institution is a subject of reproach we have long had to submit to from our neighbours, which we would willingly have removed, seeing the means are so invitingly within our reach. We have heard a surmise, that such an idea had occurred to his majesty himself, and we look forward with hope, that it may in due time come to bear the wished-

for fruit. There are many private collections in England of great extent and value, and we have little doubt that if such a scheme as a great national gallery, founded on the riches of the royal collections, was to take effect; the liberality of the proprietors of many of the private collections would lead them to contribute to the completion of so desirable an object.

However much experience may shake our confidence in the utility of academies, and their exertions for the promotion of the arts; there can exist no doubt as to the advantages of exhibitions in general; in exalting and purifying public taste, and in affording those indispensable facilities without which the artist can never pursue his studies to advantage. They work out their object without the risk of officious protection; students are at liberty in their own way to take their use of them; and with the energy common to those engaged in the pursuits of the fine arts, there is little doubt that very effectual use will be made of such opportunities. We may with great justice attribute the backward state of the arts in this country, to the difficulty an artist has of prosecuting the study, of seeing good pictures, or of obtaining those aids and encouragements so freely proffered to the foreign artist, rather than to any want of genius or aptitude in our own countrymen. Let us then remove these depressing circumstances, and give our artists the same advantages enjoyed by their brethren in other countries, and we shall not fail to find the prevalence of a better taste, in a short time, demonstrate its efficacy.

We do not mean, however, to maintain, that exhibitions of pictures are omnipotent in the promotion of the arts, or calculated to supersede other aids; far less to assert, that wherever the facility of studying good pictures has existed, there the arts have been found to flourish. Experience has in several instances shown the contrary, and that there are other circumstances influencing the taste, energy, and progress of improvement, of sufficient force to counteract the favourable tendency of such facilities to study. But this we may with confidence maintain, that it is a means of encouragement the most safe from perversion, and the most likely to prove effectual; provided we add the indispensable stimulus to improvement and exertion, which a reasonable demand for the productions of successful industry can in no case dispense with. We are not apprehensive that the sparks of original genius will become quenched in the habits of copying, which such facilities are calculated to induce. This argument has been urged as an objection; and no doubt very conspicuous cases exist, where the profusion of first-rate works of art constantly under the eyes of the resident artists has occasioned a system of servile copying, which has superseded any efforts in original composition. But for this result there were sufficient local reasons, and where such effects take place, the original spark is probably not very vivid.

Except with a view to acquire the useful hints of experience, as to the best manner of representing particular effects and objects, a judicious student strives less to acquire the manner and mechanism of a great master, than the spirit and fire that inspired his genius. He is not, moreover, to follow with blind confidence even the greatest masters, as if perfection followed every touch, for faults are to be found in most of them; he must carefully and advisedly study their merits, nor suffer himself to be led away by any conceit of penetration. Repeated study seldom fails to point out something to which we were blind before; which ought to satisfy us of the fallacious conclusions so apt to follow that sort of first-sight acuteness which so many pretend to possess. It is accordingly not unusual to see the very worst parts of a master's works imitated, because they happened to accord with some particular view or fancy, which the copyist may have previously imbibed. It is always hazardous to imitate too closely, for what most deserves imitation in a great master, is in truth inimitable; namely, his genius and invention, his address in working, and, in short, whatever falls beyond the scope of rules to teach. It is mere buffoonery to adopt the manner of any master inconsiderately, however great his name. Profit is to be derived from great and patient study alone, from cautious decision in choosing our study, both to the master and his qualities; with acute discernment to discover the faults to be avoided. And as the great secret of art is to conceal art, we cannot expect to discover it at once, but must search out its hidden virtues.

Nothing requires the aid of a master more than to point out the proper objects for study and imitation, to direct the student to the manner of handling, instead of imitating the identical strokes of the master's pencil, which would be more the work of a forger than of an imitator. He must not attempt what is beyond his powers, which students are too apt to do; it is but a sorry employment of time to limp after any master, however perfect; and his very perfections may be so foreign to the conceptions of a student, as to render all attempts at imitation fruitless. We must previously elaborate in our own minds the ideas conceived by another, before they can be employed to purpose: we must be ourselves, for there is not one in a thousand, whose cast of genius can in all points be made to quadrate with our own. We must, therefore, be able to discriminate what is suitable from what is not, so as to profit by all we see. And, above all, we must qualify the food, by drinking at the fountain-head of nature; and, while we use the experience of others, give full sway to the bent of whatever genius we may possess. We must never lay aside our own strength to lean on the strength of others; for many are in reality capable of exertions which they never conceived to be within their reach; and he is never far distant from the mark, who resolves to strive for it. At the same time, inexperience, and the wantonness of imagination, often require a curb to temper our speed, which the careful study of the works of acknowledged excellence will furnish.

In painting, we are not to expect prodigies any more than in other arts; it must advance to perfection by progressive degrees, where every succeeding artist takes advantage of all the experience of his predecessors. And there is nothing more likely to impede its progress than that mistaken bitterness with which all imitation, even the most judicious, is inveighed against, as if the character of an artist became thereby compromised. So that excellence is attained by an artist, every means used is equally lawful and commendable, whether he draws from the pure source of genius alone, or accomplishes a judicious improvement of the experience and attainments of others. Sir Joshua Reynolds very justly observes, " that it is by being conversant with the inventions of others, that we learn to invent; as it is by reading the thoughts of others, that we learn to think." He adds, " When we have had continually before us the great works of art to impregnate our minds with kindred ideas, we are then, and not till then, fit to produce something of the same species. We behold all about us with the eyes of these penetrating observers;

and our minds, accustomed to think the thoughts of the noblest and brightest intellects, are prepared for the discovery and selection of all that is great and noble in nature. The greatest natural genius cannot subsist on its own stock. He who resolves never to ransack any mind but his own, will be soon reduced, from mere barrenness, to the poorest of all imitations; he will be obliged to imitate himself, and to repeat what he has before often repeated." An examination of the earlier works of most of the great masters will accordingly show, that they invariably worked out their excellence by industriously imitating the perfections of their predecessors, as a mine out of which they prepared to elaborate a purer metal.

We may mention, as another essential advantage of the exhibitions of good paintings, the influence it is likely to have in improving the public taste. For until a general feeling for the real excellence of art is excited, the painter's efforts will prove fruitless, as he is naturally led to work on the model of what meets with general approbation. It is only from the habitual and attentive contemplation of the works of real genius, that this purifying of public taste can take place. And however paradoxical it may appear to those whose attention has never been turned to the study of painting, it is not the less true that, although it is an art purely imitative of nature, it requires, notwithstanding, both experience and study either to understand, or correctly to appreciate its finest productions. It is no assumption of pedantry, or perversion of refinement, when we assert, that it is necessary to be familiar with the art, to derive pleasure and taste the merits of its productions. It were impossible to account for the general diffusion of taste for music and painting in Italy, not confined to the higher classes of society alone, but equally pervading those ranks which in this country never bestow a thought on such matters, but for the continued exhibitions and opportunities of freely cultivating that particular taste. Where the great bulk of society are more or less imbued with correct notions of art, there is less chance of artists stopping short in their career, as so frequently happens in this country, from overrating their own attainments. An artist who conceives he has reached an elevated point of excellence, seldom makes any farther progress, unless the persuasive voice of public opinion should dispel the delusion, and induce him to resume with modesty, but with vigour, those efforts to advance still farther, which no artist ought ever to relax. The life of a painter who aims at excellence is far from a life of repose. The moment he thinks he has done enough for fame, and may in future practise for amusement or profit, his improvement is at an end; he begins to fall off, and will inevitably settle into mannerism and insipidity.

The frequent exhibition of works of approved merit, in the excellence of which we may with safety confide, thus places a test in every one's hand, by which to try the merits of modern art. The collision may prove severe, but it is a salutary medicine, and the only one that can purify and elevate the art. In every point of view, therefore, we must commend this means of improvement, even when viewed in its narrowest sphere, as creating that taste which seeks for its gratification in purchasing the works of our modern artists, and thereby creating a powerful stimulus to emulation. In costly furniture, and in the splendid decorations of our houses, we are, perhaps, not exceeded by our continental neighbours; but with them the taste for pictures turns the chief amount of what is bestowed on embellishment towards that channel. Were the fashion of our country in this respect to take a turn, and to send some portion of that wealth towards the encouragement of art, the effect would prove of incalculable advantage : the genius, we are persuaded, exists, and wants but the impetus to rouse its energies.

There is another circumstance materially injurious in this country, to a general diffusion of taste for the fine arts, or feelings of cordial good will towards their interests, arising from the disgust occasioned by a sort of offensive pedantry, prevalent among those who have had a few opportunities of seeing good pictures. They detail their superficial dogmas and criticisms, with a degree of confidence which occasions the art itself to be undervalued ; and the acquirements contemned as frivolous and unprofitable, which tend to generate such flimsy cant. With our neighbours, where the means of information are alike familiar and open to all, the well informed classes of society are generally sufficiently conversant with the subject, to preclude the opportunity of any such vaunting pedantry. Neither are they exposed to the offensive jargon of technicalities, under which so much superficial pretension is often hid. The whole art of picture knowledge, and all the gratification to be derived to those possessing that knowledge, from the contemplation of the finest works of art, would seem, according to a very prevalent idea, to centre in the important scrutiny of fixing the originality of the work, or of degrading it to the insignificance of a copy, however masterly the performance may be. This is the experimentum crucis by which all pretensions to taste or acquaintance with the art must, in the opinion of some, stand or fall. In an historical point of view, we grant the indispensable necessity of precision in this particular, to enable us to draw a correct estimate of the progress of art under all its circumstances and vicissitudes. But as bearing upon a correct taste, and susceptibility of the pleasures to be derived from the fine arts, we consider it of the same character as that sort of black-letter pedantry which so often assumes the guise of literature.

There are several writers on the subject of painting, such as Richardson, Lanzi, Turnbull, and others, who give rules by which to distinguish original pictures from copies ; and there are no doubt a few particular indications, sufficiently known to those who have ever made pictures the subject of their attention. But, in general, there is nothing more vague and uncertain ; nor can we speak with decision as to the original character of a picture, without great practical knowledge of the art, perfect acquaintance with its history, and with the history of the artists themselves. To a person so qualified to judge, rules become quite as unnecessary as they are unavailable to a person deficient in such points of knowledge. And we generally find that the persons most capable of judging are those most cautious of pronouncing ; as experience shews that it is a matter in which we must confine our pretensions within very narrow bounds. Many instances have occurred, where the painters themselves have been deceived with regard to their own works, mistaking the copy for the original. And, in the collections of some of the first and most skilful artists, many copies have been found, of the originality of which, they had passed their lives in the fullest confidence. It is very common to despise all copies, as a sort of base coin which we view with a degree of repugnance often exceedingly misapplied ; we are perhaps at first struck with the beauties of a picture, and weigh its merits with a just appreciation ; but, rouse our suspicions of its originality, and all its beauties vanish in a moment, while innumerable faults sup-

ply their place. And, on the contrary, the picture we may have passed over as unworthy of remark, may be made to burst upon us in all its glory, by simply applying the talisman of a celebrated name.

Among the connoisseurs of Italy, there is very little of this sort of pedantry observable ; they know that there are very few collections, however choice, which do not contain copies that pass for originals, and perhaps are not of inferior merit. It often occurs, that where there are several pictures of the same subject, the question of originality has for ages remained a matter of doubt, notwithstanding the most acute scrutiny ; and the best judges in Italy do not seem to consider their knowledge as at all compromised, by expressing ignorance of the hand, while they bestow unreserved praise on the work itself. This sort of verbal criticism, (if we may apply that expression,) is in general but the subterfuge of ignorance and conceit ; it requires no talent, and rests upon the mere mechanical address which familiarity in any art supplies ; which enables the proficient to recognise the hand of the artificer, without being at all susceptible to the feelings or genius which inspired the work. We are apt to criticise and to pick out faults and imperfections in the works of art, before we have learnt to discover and judge of their beauties, which is an acquirement that ought certainly to precede the office of censuring. But these points of complaint would speedily disappear, were the means afforded of inducing a more general diffusion of taste for the fine arts, and a greater degree of attention to their advancement. Had the great works of literature and science been withheld, or of difficult acquisition, we doubt if our fame in these matters would have stood so pre-eminent as it does ; and there is every reason to suppose that equal facilities with respect to the fine arts would have been attended with similar effects. Nature may prepare the germ of genius, and must supply the necessary aptitude, but it is the facilities of study, and the stimulus to emulation, which alone can bring it to bear fruit.

We admit, with pleasure, that a very gratifying change has within these few years taken place in this country ; the public taste is rapidly improving, and we trust that the period is not far distant when the privations above alluded to may no longer be a theme of complaint to our native artists. And while we have not hesitated to remark with freedom the particulars in which we conceive our practice as yet deficient, we are far from being insensible to the great excellence of some individual artists in both quarters of the island ; and most cordially participate in the general feeling of gratification, excited by a late instance of distinguished honour conferred on our respected countryman, Sir Henry Raeburn.

There is a branch of painting upon which we have not as yet touched at all, and we fear that our limits will scarcely admit of our exceeding a very few observations ; we allude to Economical, or House Painting. Within these few years, a very remarkable improvement in this mode of embellishment has begun to appear, but a great deal still remains to be done before we can equal the proficiency of Italian artists even in this humble sphere of the art. With us, the practice is chiefly confined to that of a mere handicraft, where little refinement is sought for, beyond the simple usage of the painter's shop, the mixing up of colours, and their smooth application to the wall. Whereas, in Italy, the study and acquirements of a house painter are little inferior to what is requisite for the higher branches of

Painting in England.

the art; and, in fact, the practice of both is not unfrequently combined. They are more conversant with the science, as well as with the practice, of colouring; with the rules of harmony, and with the composition of ornamental painting in all its branches; so that their works might be transferred to canvas, and admired for their excellence. In fact, the great frescos of the first masters, which have been the admiration of ages, were but a part of the general embellishment of the churches and palaces of Italy. And the most celebrated names in the list of artists, have left memorials of their fame in the humble decorations of the arabesque, in which all the exuberance and playfulness of fancy is displayed, as well as the most enchanting harmony of brilliant colours. It is in this essential point of harmony that our practice is particularly defective; we rarely see, in the simple painting of our apartments, any combination of colours that is not in some part offensive against even the common rules of art; if there are any rules observed, save those of mere caprice or chance,—although there are certain combinations pointed out by the laws of optics, which can as little be made to harmonize as two discordant notes in music. The unpleasant effects arising from such erroneous mixtures and juxta-positions, we are often sufficiently aware of, without having the skill requisite to assign the reason, any more than the painter who chose them.

This accounts for the prevalent use of neutral colours in our ornamental painting, which is less liable to offend by whatever bright colour it may be relieved; and likewise the safer and more agreeable combination of the different shades of the same indefinite colour. But no sooner do our painters attempt any combination of decided colours, than they fail. The ornamental painting in Italy is almost entirely in decided colours, of the most brilliant hue, and yet always inexpressibly pleasing in the combinations, because the rules of harmony are known and attended to. Neither is this proficiency confined to the decorations of palaces, or the more elaborate and expensive works; we have seen in dwellings of a much humbler cast, and indeed in general practice, the most graceful designs of ornament, painted, not in the simple manner of camayeu, but displaying every possible tint of bold and vivid colouring, and melting into each other with all the skill and harmony of a piece of brilliant music.

We shall not exemplify the particular defects of harmony so conspicuous in our practice, as it would lead us into tedious details; we would only hint to our master painters, that it is a matter requiring far greater study than they seem aware of, as so few examples occur of skilful combination in their works. And as to the subject of ornamental painting, as yet we merely tread the threshold; there remains a great deal to be learnt of that pleasing art, but we fear that the means are beyond the reach of that class, from which the practitioners in the branch of house painting are usually trained. It is, notwithstanding, obvious, from the very beautiful and correct imitations of the varieties of wood, so much in use at present, that there is far from any want of capacity, were it directed to the many excellencies of which the art is susceptible. And the present seems a favourable moment, when the practice is undergoing a change, to endeavour to lead it into a still more extensive field of improvement. To

introduce somewhat of the address and elegance to which this art has been brought in Italy, in the study of their infinitely varied modes of embellishment, by combination of colours; of their superior imitations of marbles, basso relievos, and drapery, in which they display so much truth and elegance of fancy; and of their arabesques, trellis work, and the more delicate mode of entablature painting. Young men intending to prosecute this branch of art, after having acquired sufficient familiarity in the attainments of the drawing academy, would experience incalculable benefit from a few years study and practice under some of the best foreign masters. It would be the means of obtaining for the art itself a higher place in the scale than what it now holds, as a mere trade, where the skill and assiduity of a handicraftsman seems to be all that is considered necessary. With the study and acquirement of correct taste, and more extensive information, it might easily be made to resume its rank as a liberal art.

PAISLEY, a town of Scotland, in Renfrewshire, scarcely 3 miles SW. of Renfrew, about 16 SE. of Greenock, and little more than 7 of Glasgow. Paisley is, at this day, the third town of Scotland in magnitude and population. Its houses, and those of the suburbs connected with it, although arranged in comparatively few streets, are spread over a tract of ground, the length of which, from east to west, is about two miles, while its breadth, from north to south, is scarcely less than seven furlongs. The main street of the town holds a sinuous course, from east to west, receiving from the former quarter the great Glasgow road, losing itself on the latter, in the road by Beith to the north Ayrshire coast towns, and varying, as it proceeds westward, its name, from Gauze Street, successively, to Old Smith Hills, the Cross, High, Town-head, Well-meadow, New Sandholes, and Broomlands, Streets; names all borne by the principal line of street, within the limits of what may in strictness be denominated the town. Another long street line commences, also, as respects the town only, on the south; and, under the names of Causeway-side, St. Mirran's, and Moss, Streets; St. James's Place, and Love Street; crossing the other line at the quadrangular area called distinctively the Cross, merges in the road leading to Inchinnan Bridges. South of High Street, and almost parallel with it, extends, to the length of about six furlongs, a spacious, well-built, and now almost completed street, named George Street; parallel in direction with which, but yet farther south, is Canal Street, of which much remains to be built. Of the space between the main street and Canal Street, much is laid out in streets; two of which, New Street and Storey Street, are closely built and fully inhabited; while others, as Barclay Street, Barr Street, &c. are but just risen, or now rising. These all lie west of Causeway-side Street, to the east of which are also divers streets very compactly built. North of the main line again there is but little building, with the exception of a few short streets, branching from it pretty far towards the west; of the buildings upon Oak-shaw Brae, and of about a dozen regularly disposed streets and lanes, built, about forty years ago, on the lands of Snandoun, whence, as some think, a baronial title is derived to the heir-apparent of these realms. Snandoun* (vulgarly Sneddon) Street, is, with its neighbour streets and lanes, built on the margin of the river White Cart, which, entering Paisley on the south-east, makes three bold curves,

Painting in England, Paisley.

---

* The Prince of Wales is Baron of Snowdon, Snandoun, and Renfrew, as being Prince of Scotland. The titles are themselves Scottish. Now, as the Stewart family had long their chief seat in Renfrewshire, and the lands of Snandoun, near Paisley, formed, in all probability, a part of the patrimonial inheritance of that illustrious house, it does not seem at all improbable, that, as a respected friend of the writer of this article suggests, the baronial title of Snowdon actually coupled with that of Renfrew, was derived from the very lands in question.

in the general direction of north-west, and then flows northward in an almost perfectly straight line; till, on getting clear of the buildings, it begins to grow devious again. In the town, it is crossed by three stone bridges, respectively called the Old Bridge, the New Bridge, and the Abbey Bridge. On the eastern side of this stream is the New Town of Paisley, consisting, besides Gauze Street and Old Smith Hill's Street, of about fifteen others, several of them pretty long, closely built, and populous; although it is but about forty years since this important addition to Paisley was planned by James, eighth Earl of Abercorn. To this nobleman the lands which were chiefly those occupied by the gardens and out-buildings of the great monastic establishment that gave to Paisley its ancient distinction, had come, as parcel of the lordship of Paisley, acquired by his Lordship, fifteen years before, from the Earl of Dundonald, to whom the said lordship of Paisley had descended from William, first Earl of Dundonald. The term New Town is currently applied to the streets built on these lands, and that part of the town of Paisley which lies east of the river, but the other part is not so generally called the Old Town, as "The Burgh." Although not many parts of either can be said to be ill-built, yet Paisley cannot as yet cope in elegance of appearance with the other larger towns of Scotland. To this day, numerous rows and single specimens of low thatched houses, give a singular rusticity of aspect to even some of the leading streets, especially in the Burgh, out of the main street. But every year witnesses the replacing of mean by lofty and substantial tenements; in the trading streets, especially. Much of High Street, and of Moss Street, the next principal one, has been renewed in this way. It is also in contemplation to open up three new streets in the head of the town; the chief of them to run northward from the Cross, in front of the recently erected Castle. On the site of the late Town House, a very handsome pile of building, comprising shops and an inn, has been recently completed. On the northern edge of the town, a new street is in progress at this moment; and, on the eastern side, another has just been opened. *Near the former of the two, a square and several streets are laid out, and in part let on building leases.* These belong to persons whom trade has enriched; but, while Paisley was yet inconsiderable, there were in it a few mansions, the property and frequent residence of noble families. One or two of these wholly or in part remain. Than Garthland Place, at the entrance of the town from Glasgow, few more elegant rows, composed wholly of domestic edifices, could be pointed to. Gauze Street, in the New Town, is neat and spacious*. Handsome and even splendid houses are not scantily intermingled with the ordinary habitations within the Burgh, the skirts of which are graced by not a few pretty little dwellings of the villa character. The pavement is for the most part superior; but the flagged causeways are provokingly narrow, and the lighting, except in the chief streets, renders the inhabitants in general anxiously desirous that a plan for introducing gas into the town should take effect. That water for culinary purposes must be purchased from carts, which bring it from a distance, is singular in so large a town.

The public edifices of Paisley are numerous, but, with two exceptions, do not lay claim to any very particular notice, as architectural efforts. Among them are five places of worship of the establishment. The Abbey Church, a venerable remain of the olden time, demands to be first noticed. In the year 1164, according to Spotiswood, but 1160 according to Crawfurd, Walter, son of Allan, (Alan,) and Lord High Steward of Scotland, founded, on his lands of Paisley, a priory, afterwards advanced to an Abbey of Benedictines; whom, thirteen in number, he brought, along with their prior-elect, from the Cluniac Monastery of Wenlock, in the county of Salop. The founder himself liberally endowed the house, and his descendants added greatly to its possessions. Other benefactions it also, from time to time, received, so that it became one of the richest monastic foundations in Scotland. By King Robert the Third, all the abbey lands were erected into a regality, " in honorem Dei, beatæ virginis Mariæ, et beati Jacobi Apostoli, et sancti Mirini † confessoris." By King James II. this charter was confirmed. The Abbey lands were thus constituted one entire and free barony, holding "in pure and perpetual regality of the crown." In 1553, the ill-fated John Hamilton, Bishop of Dunkeld, afterwards Archbishop of St. Andrew's, resigned it, the Queen consenting, in favour of Lord Claud Hamilton, third son of James, Duke of Chatelherault. Lord Claud, generally, as Abbot Titular, styled Commendator, was at this time a mere child; but taking, when mature in years, the part of his unfortunate royal mistress, in whose cause he fought at Langside, he was attainted, and the abbey lands were held as having devolved upon the Regent Murray. By him they were bestowed on Robert, son of William, Lord Semple heritable bailie and justiciary of the regality of Paisley. To Lord Claud, they, however, soon reverted, and in his favour were, in 1587, erected into a temporal lordship. The noble proprietor was, in 1591, made a Lord of Parliament, by the title of Lord Paisley. His son, James, became first Lord Abercorn, and in the Abercorn family the lordship has since continued.

Of this great establishment few remains exist, in addition to those of the Abbey Church. Of the choir, which appears to have had no aisles, no more is left than about ten feet in height of the exterior wall. The inclosed space is, as well as a large piece of ground lying to the north of the church, used for interments. Some low trefoiled niches appear on the inner side of the southern wall of the choir, towards the east end. Of the transept, which projects northward, the walls yet stand, but are roofless and mouldering ‡. They include, nevertheless, a feature that gives to the whole fabric a peculiar grace. This is the great northern window of the church; one of noble size and excellent proportions; decorated § in character, as is indeed most of the structure; and still retaining, along with its central mullion, portions of the tracery that once adorned its head. The nave, a lofty, and, including its aisles, very spacious pile, is in pretty good repair, forming the church to a very extensive country parish, in the heart of which Paisley, with its town parishes, lies; and of which the New Town is considered a part. Four large windows to the north aisle, a porch, and a row of thickly set clerestory windows in the upper part of the building, comprise the chief exterior features of the south side of the nave. But the west end, or rather front, now laid open to Abbey Close, is an enriched

---

* The first houses were built in 1779, and in four years, the New Town contained 275 families, among whom 345 looms were kept.
† Crawfurd. Who this St. Mirin, or Mirran, was, none of our legenderian chroniclers appear to say.
‡ At the intersection of the transept with the main building, once stood a strong tower, surmounted by a lofty spire.
§ See Rickman on English Architecture.

3

and beautiful specimen of ancient ecclesiastical architecture. Its chief component parts are a door-way of early English, deeply recessed, and rich in mouldings; three large windows of decorated work, the tracery somewhat elaborate; and a couple of lancet-shaped windows. The interior of the church exhibits three tiers of arches, the lowest tier bold, pointed, and rather plain; the uppermost one pointed, narrow, and unornamented; but the middle tier at once exceedingly beautiful in effect, and, we believe, uncommon, if not peculiar, in conformation. A mean-looking window of modern insertion, at the east end of the nave, is filled with particoloured glass *. Beneath it is a large white marble monument, commemorative of the late William M'Dowall, Esq. of Garthland †. A few other monumental tablets, of recent date, appear on the walls, as do sundry rather ancient memorials of the kind, so placed with a view to their preservation. South of this part of the church is the area of the Cloisters; no part of the arcade of which, however, remains. But on the eastern side of the court is yet standing entire a building now called the Abercorn Chapel, or the Sounding Aisle. In this structure, which has a very good east window of decorated work, and the adjoining church having always been used parochially, was, we think, the private oratory of the Religious, a series of ancient mural sculptures, an elaborate altar, and tomb, the latter bearing a recumbent effigy of Marjory, daughter of Robert the Bruce, and wife of Walter the great steward of Scotland, to whom she bore King Robert the Second, merit notice. King Robert II. his first consort, Elizabeth More, and Euphane Ross, his second wife, as well as Walter, the great steward, and his lady, were among the distinguished personages interred here. The chapel is now used as a burying-place by the Abercorn family. When the abbey was in its glory, gardens and orchards lay contiguous to its multiplied edifices ‡. Around the entire precincts, which were in circuit about a mile, Abbot George Schaw, afterwards lord high treasurer of Scotland, built, in 1484, a high and strong wall, of which part remains. On this, at certain points, inscriptions were placed. One of them is yet visible, having been built into the front of a tenement constructed near Wall Neuck, a spot on which formerly stood the north-west angle of the wall. A chronicle written by the Religious of Paisley, is often mentioned in history as the Black Book of Paisley. It is thought to contain little more than a copy of Fordun.

In the town are three parishes, named from their respective churches. The High Church occupies a commanding situation towards the eastern extremity of a long terrace-shaped hill. The church, built in 1755-6, is adorned with a lofty spire. Near it is the Middle Church, built in 1781. In the lowest part of the town, towards the south, is the Low Church. This edifice was built in 1736-7. It is now occupied by a dissenting congregation; a new church, called St. George's, having been opened in 1819 for the Low Church parish. The new building is large, and has a front in a degree ornamental. The remaining place of worship of the Establishment is the Gaelic Chapel. Other places of worship are as follows: two for United Associate Dissenters; two for members of the Church of Relief; two for Baptists; and one each for Episcopalians, Roman Catholics, Original Burghers, (this is now, 1822, rising,) Congregational Independents, English Independents,

Methodists, Reformed Presbyterians, and Peculiar Independents of two distinct sorts.

Of minor sectarians, about five different bodies, generally very small, assemble for worship in rooms. In the churches, (the Gaelic one included,) about 8500 people may be accommodated with seats; in the other places of worship, of all sorts, about 12,000 §.

Of the other public buildings, the Castle, founded in 1818, and first occupied about two years ago, is at once the largest and finest. It stands on the western margin of the Cart, between the Old and Sneddon Bridges. The general form of the edifice is quadrangular; the material used in its construction excellent freestone; the style adopted in its exterior at once imposing and appropriate. It exhibits two " corps de logis," as the French style them; the western and front one comprehending a court-house, council-chambers, and a number of offices for different departments of public business. The eastern one, a prison for debtors, another for criminals, a Bridewell, and a chapel. The regulations in these prisons are at once humane and judicious. Round them is a lofty and strong quadrangular wall; armed, where necessary, with " chevaux de frise." Between the prisons and the front pile are two courts for air and exercise. The front building has a noble façade, adorned with projecting hexagonal turrets, that rise considerably above the prison roof. Over the great arched entrance, which is formed between two of these, an exterior gallery or balcony, supported on corbels, and adorned by a perforated parapet, has been constructed. The entire fabric is embattled, and the prison summits display an imitative machicolation. The building is appropriated to county, as well as burgh uses.

The steeple of the former town-house yet remains, and graces the cross. Opposite to it is a handsome structure, the upper part of which, adorned exteriorly with Ionic pilasters, includes a public coffee room, alike distinguished for size, elegance, accommodation, and comfort. On its tables, newspapers, reviews, and magazines abound. The markets, conveniently situated near the cross, are on a respectable scale. They are for butcher's meat and fish. Behind them are slaughter-houses. At Williamsburg were completed, this summer, barracks adequate to the accommodation of half a regiment of foot.

The grammar school of Paisley boasts a royal founder. From the institution charter, it appears to have been founded by King James VI. then in his eleventh year, and by him endowed with sundry former church revenues, chiefly altarages. One of the witnesses to this charter is described as his Majesty's " familiar counsellor, Mr. George Buchanane, Pensioner of Corsraguel," and " Keeper of the Privy Seal."

There are in the town four other burgh schools; five established by subscription, or by mortuaries; Hutcheson's, and seven other charitably supported ones; about forty private ones, and also about forty Sunday schools. The principal manufacture in Paisley is that of fancy muslins, which have long been unrivalled. Cotton spinning and thread-making are also carried on to a great extent. See RENFREWSHIRE, for an account of the present state of the manufactures in Paisley.

In 1821, Paisley contained 1616 houses, 5730 families; of whom 357 were employed in agriculture, and 4541 in trade and manufactures. The males were 12,133, and the females 14,295, and the total population 26,428, or 28,000, which is reckoned more accurate.

---

* Vide Rickman ut supra. † Its cost, £800, was raised by a subscription of the county gentlemen.
‡ When Crawfurd wrote his " Renfrewshire," John, Earl of Dundonald, had his principal residence at Paisley. Some remains of the apartments there yet are, adjoining to the Abbey, in the grounds of which he had a small park for deer.
§ In the Abbey parish at Johnstone, are, besides, a Chapel of Ease, and a United Secession Meeting House. These two will contain 1800 persons.

PALERMO, an ancient and beautiful city of Sicily, the capital of the island, is situated on the north-west coast, in the vale of Mazara. It stands on the western shore of a bay, near the extremity of a kind of natural amphitheatre formed by romantic rocks and mountains. Its situation is happy and picturesque in the highest degree: the sea, the hills, and lofty mountains, present on every side beautiful and striking prospects. The country between the town and the mountains is one of the most delightful spots imaginable, presenting the appearance of one extensive garden, filled with all kinds of fruit trees, and watered by numerous rivulets. Palermo is nearly of a circular form. It was formerly surrounded with a strong wall; but its fortifications are now quite neglected, except on the side towards the sea, and even on this side they are far from being strong. The interior of the town has a splendid and imposing appearance, being filled with public monuments, palaces, churches, monasteries, fountains, and statues. The principal streets are the Cassaro and Strada Nuova, which traverse the city, intersecting each other at right angles in the centre. These streets are broad and regular, consisting of lofty and uniform edifices, many of which have balconies, and fountains and statues in front. Most of the other streets are narrow, winding, and dirty, and paved only in the centre, where every one walks. The Cassaro and Strado Nuova form at their point of intersection an elegant square, called from its figure Piazza Ottangolare. Each of the sides of this space is composed of handsome buildings, and each has in front a number of statues, together with a large and elegant fountain. From this spot there is a beautiful view of these streets, and of the principal gates of the city by which they are terminated. The gates are at the distance of half a mile, the town being not more than a mile in diameter, and are fine pieces of architecture richly adorned. There are several other squares which would have a handsome appearance but for their not being paved.

Palermo is crowded with religious establishments, there being above forty monasteries, fifty convents, and an immense number of churches. The finest of these is the cathedral, or Madre Chiesa, as it is commonly termed, an old Gothic edifice erected in the twelfth century. Its exterior is magnificent and simple; the interior is supported by eighty pillars of oriental granite, and is divided into a number of chapels, some of which are very rich, particularly that of St. Rosolia, the patroness of Palermo. It contains some superb monuments of the Norman kings of the island, of the finest porphyry. The Chiesa del Palazzo is entirely encrusted over with ancient Mosaic, and the vaulted roof is all of the same. The church of St. Giuseppe is a handsome edifice, richly ornamented, and containing some beautiful columns of grey Sicilian marble, nearly sixty feet high. The palace of the viceroy is an immense mass of discordant parts, built at different periods; but the apartments are of a noble size, and richly adorned. In a square in front of the palace there is a statue of Philip IV. of Sicily, surrounded with four other statues representing the cardinal virtues, all of them of fine white marble. Many of the palaces of the nobility are much admired for their architecture; but there is commonly a great want of taste in their interior decorations. The buildings of the university are extensive, and contain an observatory, and cabinets of natural history and medals. There are professors in various branches of science, but the number of students is small. The charitable institutions of Palermo are numerous; the principal of them are the great hospital, the hospital of St. Bartholomew, and the Albergo de Poveri, or poors-house. The principal public walk is the Marina, a terrace about eighty paces in breadth, extending above a mile along the shore in front of a range of fine palaces. In the centre of this walk there is an elegant kind of temple, which in summer is used as an orchestra. Adjoining to it are the public gardens, which are tastefully arranged, and interspersed with statues and fountains. There is also a botanical garden containing a valuable collection of plants. The harbour is well fortified and capacious, being capable of containing thirty sail of the line and several hundred merchantmen. At its entrance there are a lighthouse and two citadels. It is, however, dangerously open to the swell of the sea from the north-east; and even at the anchoring place ships do not lie secure whenever a westerly wind blows. The trade of Palermo is not very extensive, consisting chiefly of silk, in which there are above 900 looms employed. The silk manufactures, and the method of rearing the worms, were introduced into the island in the 11th century by Roger, king of Sicily. Gloves and stockings, of great beauty and fineness, are manufactured of the silk thread obtained from the Pinna Marina, a species of fish which is caught on the north coast of the island. The principal articles of export are silk and satins; and the produce of the adjacent country, viz. wine, oil, and brandy, together with large quantities of fish, chiefly tunnies, the curing of which affords employment to a considerable number of persons.

The population of Palermo is estimated at 130,000; of this number the nobility, clergy, and beggars constitute a large proportion. Many of the nobility are poor, and not a few are entirely without resources to support their dignity. The streets are infested with crowds of beggars of the most wretched and disgusting description. With regard to climate, the heat in summer is very great, continuing for some months between 80° and 90° of Fahrenheit; in winter it seldom falls below 50°. During the blowing of the Sirocco, the heat is very oppressive, the thermometer being said to rise sometimes above 112°. The town has occasionally suffered severely from earthquakes.

Palermo was anciently called Panormus, a name which it derived, according to Diodorus Siculus, from the excellence of its harbour. Sicilian writers trace its origin back to a very remote period; but according to the account of Thucydides, which seems the most probable, it was originally colonized by the Phœnicians, who were induced to settle here from the convenience of the port, and the beauty of the situation. It afterwards fell into the hands of the Greeks, and then into those of the Carthaginians, who made it the capital of their possessions in the island, and a considerable place of commerce. In the first Punic war it was taken with difficulty by the Romans, who treated it as a free and allied state, and permitted it to be governed by its own laws. It always continued faithful to the Roman republic and empire, till, in 821, it fell under the power of the Saracens, who made it the metropolis of the island. In the eleventh century the Normans took it from the infidels, and made it the seat of their empire; and since that period it has been considered as the capital of the islands. It is the seat of the viceroy and the Sicilian parliament, and the residence of the principal nobility; and is the see of an archbishop, who is primate of all Sicily. The chief magistrate of Paler-

2 M

Palestine. mo is commonly a nobleman of the highest rank; his power is very extensive, inferior only to that of the viceroy. He, along with six senators, has the whole management of the civil government of the city, and is appointed yearly by the king or the viceroy. East Long. of observatory 13° 22′, 0″, North Lat. 38° 6′ 44″.

PALESTINE, formerly denoted the whole Land of Canaan, bounded on the north by Syria, on the east by Arabia Deserta, on the south by Arabia Petræa, and on the west by the Mediterranean Sea. It extended about 140 miles from north to south, between 31° 10′ and 33° 15′ of north latitude, and was of very unequal breadth. It was originally occupied by the Canaanite nations, who were conquered by the Israelites under Joshua. From this period to the Babylonish captivity it was called the Land of Israel, and the name Palestina was restricted to the maritime tract exending southward from Joppa to the frontiers of Egypt, inhabited by the Philistines, which was successively subjected to the kings of Israel, Syria, Egypt, Persia, and Macedonia. After the return of the Jews from Babylon, the whole country from Tyre to Egypt was recognised in the enumeration of the Roman provinces by the name of Palestina, consisting of four provinces, viz. Judæa, Samaria, Galilea, Peræa. In modern times, the term Palestine denotes a Turkish pachalic, which includes the territory between the pachalic of Damascus and the Mediterranean Sea; and between two lines drawn from the sea-coast, the one southward of Gaza and the other north of Joppa, so as to comprise only the country of the Philistines, together with a portion of Judæa and Samaria. But the name is generally employed to denote the whole of what is called the Holy Land, and was formerly comprehended in the Roman province of Palestina. It is generally divided into the following districts, Gaza, Hebron, Elkods or Jerusalem, Naplos or Naplousa, Harite, Jouret-Cafre-Kanna, Nazareth, Sapheth, and the country beyond Jordan.

History. After the taking and destruction of Jerusalem by Titus, A. D. 72, Judea ceased to be the residence of the Jewish people, of whom only a small remnant was left in the country. These scattered relics of the once renowned tribes of Israel having again raised the standard of rebellion against the power of Rome, the emperor Adrian completed the desolation of their capital, and built another city on its ruins, which he called Ælia Capitolina. In the reign of Dioclesian the name of Jerusalem was almost forgotten; but the scattered bands of the Jewish race were often attempting to make head against the succeeding emperors of Rome. After the unsuccessful project of Julian to reassemble the nation, and rebuild the city of Jerusalem, there is little recorded in history of their state and that of their native land till the year 501, when they openly revolted in the reign of Justinian. Jerusalem was taken by Cosroes, king of the Persians, in the year 613; but was recovered by Heraclius in 627. Nine years afterwards Palestine was subdued by the Caliph Omar, the third in succession from Mahomet; and in consequence of the contentions which arose among the rival dynasties of the Mahommedans, the country was involved in troubles and calamities for more than 200 years. In 868, Palestine was overrun by Ahmed, the sovereign of Egypt; but was again brought under the dominion of the caliphs of Bagdad about the beginning of the tenth century. Passing repeatedly through the hands of va-

rious invaders, but remaining chiefly in the possession of the caliphs of Egypt, Palestine was occupied by the Fatimites of Cyrene in the year 1078, when the Crusaders appeared on its frontiers; and Godfrey of Bouillon was elected king of its captured metropolis in 1099. Saladin, the conqueror of Asia, wrested the greater part of the Holy Land from the hands of the Christian princes in the year 1188; and the Baharite Sultans of Egypt completely expelled the remaining crusaders in 1291. In 1382, the Circassian Mamelukes, having usurped the supreme authority in Egypt, became masters of Palestine; but, in 1517, the Turks of Constantinople under Selim extended their conquests over all Syria and Egypt.

The beauty and fertility of the Holy Land, so much celebrated in ancient times both by sacred and profane writers, are scarcely discernible in its present desolate and neglected condition. The culture of its finest plains has long ceased. Its springs are buried beneath heaps of rubbish. The soil of the mountains, formerly kept up by terraces and covered with vines, is washed down into the valleys. And its eminences, once crowned with woods, have been stripped bare, and parched into barrenness. This melancholy change is not owing to any deterioration of the soil or the climate, but to the degeneracy of the inhabitants, who groan under the most intolerable oppression, and are exposed to every kind of pillage. But still there are many delightful spots to be seen, which confirm the accounts of its ancient fruitfulness, and prove its capability of being rendered a plentiful and populous country. The plain of Zabulon is every where covered with spontaneous vegetation, flourishing in the utmost luxuriance. The plain of Esdraelon is a vast meadow, covered with the richest pasture; and the country around Rama resembles a continued garden. The variety and beauty of the different kinds of *carduus*, or thistle, are sufficient indications of a fertile soil. The new globe thistle particularly (the stem and leaves of which are of a dark but vivid sky blue colour) grows to such a size in many parts of Palestine, that some of its blossoms are nearly three inches in diameter. The soil is often sandy and mixed with gravel, and, in some places, such as in the neighbourhood of Tiberias, it is black, appearing to have been formed by the decomposition of rocks, which have a volcanic aspect. The scenery is described as resembling, in many districts, the finest parts of Kent and Surrey. The crops principally cultivated are barley, wheat, doura, maize, cotton, sesamum, and linseed. The water melons of Palestine excel those of any other country in the world. " Under a wise and beneficent government," says a recent traveller *, " the produce of the Holy Land would exceed all calculation. Its perennial harvest; the salubrity of its air; its limpid springs; its rivers, lakes, and matchless plains; its hills and vales; all these, added to the serenity of its climate, prove this land to be indeed a field which ' the Lord hath blessed.' "

The country is full of wild animals. Antelopes especially are very numerous. The chamæleon, the lizard, the serpent, and all sorts of beetles, are frequently to be seen.

The inhabitants are a mixture of Christians and Mahommedans, often difficult to be distinguished from each other. The former occupy the valleys of Libanus under Maronite bishops; and the Druses, who have a religion peculiar to themselves, possess the mountains of Antilibanus. (See Druses.) The country is over-

Marginal notes, right column: Palestine. — Soil and climate. — Animals. — Inhabitants.

run in all quarters by plundering tribes of Arabs. The population is so very thin, and the aspect of the country so desolate, that a doubt has been thrown upon the accounts of its population in ancient times, which, from the statements of sacred scripture, cannot have been less than six millions. This would allow a proportion of 800 or 900 to every square league, which is thought altogether incredible. But, in the time of Vespasian, it is described by profane writers as actually containing six millions of inhabitants. The present mountainous country of the Druses is stated by Volney to contain 40,000 fighting men. The population of Barbadoes, neither the most healthy nor the most fertile part of the globe, contains at present 900 inhabitants to every square mile. The mode of living in eastern countries is favourable to the support of a numerous population on less produce than in other quarters of the world. The fertility of the country is acknowledged to be naturally very great; and the cultivation of the land is known to have been carried in former times to the utmost extent. The limestone rocks and stony valleys were covered with plantations of figs, vines, and olive trees. The hills were formed into gardens from their bases to their summits. The sides of the most barren mountains were rendered productive by being formed into terraces, whereon the soil was accumulated with astonishing labour. There are still many vestiges of this extraordinary cultivation, sufficient to prove that not a spot was neglected, and that the most unpromising situations were rendered fertile by the labours of industry. See ASPHALTITES, DRUSES, JERUSALEM, JEWS, and JUDÆA. See also Memoir by Abbé Guenée on *The Fertility of Judæa;* Clarke's *Travels,* vol. ii.; Chateaubriand's *Travels;* Buckingham's *Travels in Palestine;* Burckhardt's *Travels in Syria;* and Mr. Rae Wilson's *Travels in Palestine.* (q)

PALEY, the Rev. DR. WILLIAM, a celebrated moral, political, and theological writer, was born in Peterborough, Northamptonshire, in July, 1743. His father, then a canon-minor of that place, was afterwards elected head master of the school of Giggleswick, in Yorkshire, a situation in which he continued till his death. Previously to his leaving Peterborough, he had married Elizabeth Clapham, a lady of good family in the parish of Giggleswick, through whose friends, it is probable, he obtained this new appointment. Both parents had the happiness,—a blessing granted to few,—of seeing their son, the subject of this brief sketch, fulfil their fondest expectations, and by his elegant and ingenious writings acquire the highest reputation and honour.

Dr. Paley received his elementary instruction from his father, and he had thus combined the advantages of a public school, with the more close and vigilant discipline of private tuition. His talents were soon discovered to be of a superior order; his love of books was intense, and he early displayed that strong tendency to general and miscellaneous reading by which he was ever afterwards characterized. He entered the university of Cambridge, as a sizer of Christ's College, at the early age of sixteen. His father had even at this period been induced to cherish hopes of his future eminence. " My son," says he, " is now gone to College; he will turn out a great man, very great indeed; I am certain of it, for he has by far the *clearest* head I ever met with in my life."

Mathematical studies having long held an eminent place in the system of education pursued at Cambridge, Dr. Paley, on his return to the country,

devoted the whole summer months to the acquisition of the different branches of this science: in which he obtained so great a proficiency, that on his return to the university, Mr. Shepherd, one of his tutors, discovering that his mathematical attainments were already very considerable, excused him from attending his college lectures with the students of his own year who were not so far advanced, but occasionally proposed questions for his solution in private. With this exception, however, he attained, while at college, to no distinction in any other department of study. In theology, in ethical and metaphysical philosophy, all of which he afterwards cultivated with such happy success, he had then many superiors; classical literature he disliked and neglected both at that early period and ever afterwards; and he has been heard to say, that Virgil was the only Latin poet he could read with satisfaction. While he did not entirely neglect the several tasks prescribed him by his tutors, he was remarked chiefly for an invincible propensity for general reading, which we formerly remarked, and which may, very satisfactorily, account for the great extent and variety of his acquirements.

He was not indeed so ardent and indefatigable a student as his future celebrity may lead us to imagine. The colloquial powers for which he was distinguished, and a strong disposition he possessed for wit and sarcasm, regulated rather than subdued in after-life, caused his society to be much solicited by his fellow students, and thus interfered in no small degree with the regular distribution of his time. This mode of life is not unattended with some slight advantages; and it may have given Dr. Paley a more intimate knowledge of the human character, and have contributed, not a little, to that full development and analysis of the human heart which his writings display. Yet it is a course of life accompanied with manifold dangers, and if long persisted in, must, in all cases, undermine every hope of either moral or literary respectability. Happily for the world and for himself, the nature of the life he was leading, accidentally but powerfully submitted to his attention, was at length seen by him in its true aspect, and was the cause, when thus contemplated, of his devoting himself with renewed ardour to study, and in forming a kind of æra in his literary history. " I spent," to use his own words, " the first two years of my under-graduateship happily but unprofitably. I was constantly in society where we were not immoral, but idle, and rather expensive. At the commencement of my third year, however, after having left the usual party at rather a late hour in the evening, I was awaked at five in the morning by one of my companions, who stood at my bed-side, and said, ' Paley! I have been thinking what a —— fool you are. *I* could do nothing, probably, were I to try, and can afford the life I lead; *you* could do every thing, and cannot afford it. I have had,' continued he, ' no sleep during the whole night on account of these reflections, and am now come solemnly to inform you, that if you persist in your indolence, I must renounce your society.' I was so struck," says Dr. Paley, " with the visit and the visitor, that I lay in bed great part of the day, and formed my plan. I ordered my bed-maker to prepare my fire every evening, in order that it might be lighted by myself. I arose at five, read during the whole of the day, except such hours as chapel and hall required, allotting to each portion of time its peculiar branch of study."—And this was not a resolution formed from momentary feeling, adhered to for a few days or a few weeks, and then abandoned for ever. It was a resolution that continued to animate his future life, and was the means of elevating him to a very high degree of literary distinction. The first object of his attention were those subjects on which he was to be examined preparatory to obtaining his bachelor's degree; and so great was his success, that he was appointed senior " wrangler," and was regarded by many as superior not only to every person of his year, but even to several of his examiners.

Thus accomplished, he found it necessary to enter into active life, and to gain a livelihood by his talents and industry: The first situation he obtained, was that of second assistant in an academy at Greenwich, kept by Mr. Braken, and intended chiefly as introductory to the naval and military professions. The income, though small, which he thus acquired, was most laudably employed. While at college, he had contracted debts, which he now resolved most scrupulously to liquidate, and on this principle he restricted himself to the barest necessaries, until fully relieved from these obligations. In allusion to this circumstance, he used to remark, that " such difficulties might afford a useful lesson to a young man of good principles; and that the privations to which he then thought it his duty to submit, produced a habit of economy which had been of infinite service to him ever after." Notwithstanding his economy, however, he availed himself of every opportunity in his power to visit the metropolis, where he spent most of his time in visiting the theatres or the courts of law. In visiting the latter he was undoubtedly solicitous, at the same time, to witness the ingenuity and eloquence of the bar, and to see carried into effect those general principles of jurisprudence, with which in books he had been so long acquainted; while in the motives that prompted him to frequent the theatre, a love of amusement and dissipation of thought which he was never able fully to counteract, may have had no inconsiderable share.

Dr. Paley, in the mean time, however, was not inattentive to literary pursuits, nor unambitious of literary distinction. In 1765, he became a candidate for one of the prizes, given annually by the representatives of the university of Cambridge to senior bachelors for the two best dissertations in Latin prose. The subject proposed was a comparison between the Stoic and Epicurean systems of philosophy, with respect to the influence which they exert on the morals of their respective votaries. Paley espoused the cause of Epicurus, and defended it with so much talent, that, though with considerable hesitation, he was adjudged the first prize. This hesitation arose from a suspicion that he was not himself the author of the dissertation, or rather that the body of the essay and the notes to it were not the composition of the same person, the one being written in Latin, the other in English. There was here, we confess, much room for suspecting the candour or veracity of Paley; but the real state of the case, as himself condescended to make no communication on the subject, must now remain for ever in uncertainty.

In consequence of a misunderstanding with Mr. Braken of a pecuniary nature, he left that gentleman's service; but still continued to reside in Greenwich, as he was now employed in the capacity of tutor to a young gentleman of that place, named Ord, now Dr. Ord of Farnham, and was also, on receiving deacon's orders, engaged as assistant curate of the parish. In these situations, however, he did not long remain: in

1766, he was elected a fellow of Christ's college, (worth £100 a-year,) and the following season, having removed thither, he entered on the duties of private tuition. In 1768, he was nominated a public lecturer by Dr. Shepherd, his former tutor; and the duties of this important station he discharged with the most scrupulous fidelity and the most brilliant success. Along with Mr. John Law, his colleague, he instituted a new course of evening lectures; an innovation which at first excited considerable opposition, but which, owing to the prudence and firmness of these gentlemen, and the intrinsic merit of the plan, ultimately acquired no small degree of popularity, and added much to the reputation and importance of the college. His talents now began to be fully appreciated, and scarcely a year elapsed that did not witness him acquire some new appointment—appointments gained not by any family or political interest, but resulting entirely either from the esteem of his private friends, or from the character he had established in the world for worth and talents. In 1771, he was chosen one of the preachers in Whitehall chapel; and having, in 1775, been appointed rector of Musgrave in Westmoreland, he resigned his situation in the university, leaving behind him the character of an ingenious and useful teacher. Through Dr. Law, bishop of Carlisle, he soon afterwards obtained the archdeaconry of that place, and various other livings in the church of an inferior order: Bishop Porteus of London conferred on him the valuable prebend of St. Pancras, Cathedral of St. Paul's; and Dr. Tomline promoted him to the subdeanery of the diocese of Lincoln: But the most important preferment he obtained, was the rectory of Bishop Wearmouth, (estimated at £1200 yearly) the gift of Dr. Barrington, the present venerable bishop of Durham, and presented by him in the most flattering manner. " Be assured," says Dr. Barrington to our author, who was expressing his gratitude, " Be assured that you cannot have greater pleasure in accepting the living in question, than I have in offering it to you." He now resided, during the remainder of his days, either at Lincoln or Bishop Wearmouth.

Ere he was elevated to this last ecclesiastical dignity, he had attained to a high degree of literary celebrity by his various excellent productions. Some of his earliest compositions, which were on mathematical subjects, were printed while he was a student in the university, in the most eminent periodical productions of that time. He was the author of several pamphlets, and various occasional sermons, some of which met with a very rapid sale, and gained their author something like distinction among his brethren. But Dr. Paley was destined to produce something far greater than a short publication of transient or local interest, and, as an author, to attain to a degree of distinction to which none probably of his contemporaries in the same church can lay any claim. In 1785, appeared his " Principles of Moral and Political Science," a publication which had formed the subject of his academical lectures, and the success of which was deservedly so great, that it underwent fifteen editions in the author's life time. His next work, entitled, " Horæ Paulinæ, or the truth of the Scripture History of St. Paul, evinced by a comparison of the Epistles which bear his name with the Acts of the Apostles and with one another," was published in 1790; in 1794, his " View of the Evidences of Christianity," was given to the world: and his " Natural Theology, or Evidences of the Existence and Attributes of the Deity, collected from the appearances of Nature," appeared in 1801, at a time when the author was labouring under a disease which ultimately was the cause of his death.

His constitution, though naturally firm and athletic, had now begun to yield to the bad effects which not unfrequently result from too close an application to literary pursuits. In 1800, he had been attacked by a violent affection of the urinary system, accompanied with a species of maelena or black flux,—complaints from which, as just hinted, he never afterwards fully recovered. And though he enjoyed some short intervals free from pain, the symptoms of his disorder, at every fresh attack, became more alarming; and in May, 1805, it was evident to all that his life was in imminent danger. He was supported, in the prospect of death, by the influence of that religion which he had zealously taught and illustrated. He endeavoured to comfort his afflicted family with the hopes and promises of the gospel. His last days were spent in the exercises of devotion, and he calmly expired, on Saturday the 25th of May, in the sixty-second year of his age.

Dr. Paley had been twice married. His second wife, Miss Dobinson of Carlisle, survived him, and died so recently as March, 1819. He left behind him eight children, four daughters and four sons, of whom William the eldest, a barrister of great talents, died in 1817, at the premature age of thirty-seven.

Dr. Paley was in stature above the middle size, and, especially in his latter years, rather inclined to corpulency. The expression of his countenance was pleasing, yet there was little about it which to a stranger was very deeply calculated to shadow forth the vigour and versatility of his mind.

His moral character is entitled to praise of the highest kind. In all the private relations of life, the goodness of his heart and the undisguised simplicity of his manners were the objects of universal respect and esteem. As a minister of the gospel, also, his conduct was extremely amiable and exemplary. His devoted attachment to literary pursuits he never allowed for a moment to interfere with the conscientious discharge of his sacred duties. He was indeed a pluralist, and the benefit of his example and instructions could not be enjoyed by all with whom he was spiritually connected; but, to use his own expression, he was " a greater pluralist in children," and he uniformly took care that the clergymen placed under him were men of virtue and of faithfulness. It has been frequently insinuated that his opinions on certain articles of faith were not quite agreeable to the standards of his church. What this difference really was, it would not probably be an easy matter to determine. It is certain, indeed, that in his discourses he seldom alluded to doctrinal subjects; but a volume of his sermons, published since his death, by no means substantiate the charge of heterodoxy that has been so industriously brought against him.

To his writings the same degree of praise is due that we have paid to his moral character. " If we do not rank him," says one of his biographers, " among men of original genius, of tasteful imagination, or consummate learning, he must be allowed the first place among those *whose success has been most extensive in the moral improvement of mankind. Utility* (which in his system of ethics constitutes the essence of virtue) seems to have been his great ambition; and it is no light character of his works, that they are all eminently useful. He seems always to have clearly discerned what the age wanted. In all his works he was furnishing a desideratum; and so wisely did he calculate on the necessities of the public, that what he presented was met with the eager welcome of a seasonable supply." The distinguishing features of his works are perspicuity and simplicity,—qualities without which genius and learning are comparatively useless. He carefully avoids every thing that does not further the result he means to establish, or that may lead him into abstruse or unprofitable discussions. Readers of every class are delighted with the clearness and satisfactory nature of his reasoning; and none can rise from the perusal of his works, without feeling reverence for the character of the author, or having the better feelings of his nature improved and elevated. With regard to his ethical and political principles, there may indeed be various opinions, though Dr. Paley himself has rendered them subservient to the most amiable and salutary purposes; but of his *theological* writings there can be but one sentiment. They are alike pious, ingenious, and conclusive; the most useful certainly, on the various important subjects of which they treat; and they will ever entitle their author to a conspicuous place among the benefactors of mankind.

See *Memoirs* of Dr. Paley, by the late George Wilson Meadey, Esq. and Dr. Paley's *Works*, with his *Life* prefixed, edited by Mr. Alexander Chalmers, Lond. 1821. (T. M.)

PALIBOTHRA. See PATNA.

PALLADIUM. See CHEMISTRY, Vol. VI. p. 20. 89.

PALLAS. See ASTRONOMY, Vol. II. p. 604. 639.

PALLAS, PETER SIMON, a celebrated naturalist, was born at Berlin on the 22d September, 1741. His father was professor of surgery in the university, and young Pallas having resolved to pursue the same studies, entered upon them with zeal; and so early as 1758, in the 17th year of his age, he was able to read a course of public lectures on anatomy. Having acquired a taste for natural history from one of his preceptors, Martin Schoeling, he pursued this inviting study at the university of Halle, where he entered in 1758. In the year 1759 he went to Gottingen, where he composed an ingenious treatise, entitled *De infestis viventibus intra viventia.* He took his doctor's degree at Leyden in 1760, and he added greatly to his knowledge of natural history, by the examination of the public and private cabinets in that city.

With the view of prosecuting his medical studies, he repaired to London in 1761; but natural science engrossed all his attention, and he spent much time in examining the marine productions on the coast of Sussex. He left London in April, 1761, and when he arrived at Berlin, he began to prepare the materials for a *Fauna Insectorum Marchica.* With the permission of his father he went to reside at the Hague; and such was his scientific reputation, that he was elected a fellow of the Royal Society of London on the 7th June, 1764.

The first work which gained him distinction as a naturalist, was his *Elenchus Zoophytorum.* He afterwards published the *Miscellanea Zoologica;* and having returned to Berlin by the command of his father, and begun to publish his *Spicilegia Zoologica,* (a work which was continued in fasciculi till 1780,) he received an invitation from the Empress Catharine to become professor of natural history to the Imperial Russian Academy. Contrary to the advice of his friends, he accepted of this offer, and arrived at St. Petersburgh on the 10th of August, 1767.

No sooner had he reached that capital, than he was charged with the management of the scientific expedition to the east of the Volga, and to the remote parts of Siberia. Before his departure, however, he drew up a systematic catalogue of the zoological cabinet of the Academy; arranged the collection of Professor Breyn, recently purchased by Prince Orloff; and prepared for the press six numbers of his *Spicilegia Zoologica*.

In June, 1768, he set out on the expedition, accompanied by Messrs. Falk, Lepekin, and Guldenstaedt, and, after an absence of six years, he returned to St. Petersburgh on the 30th July, 1774, where he published, in five volumes 4to. an account of this most extensive and interesting journey.

In the year 1776, he published his collections relative to the political, physical, and civil history of the Mongol tribes. In 1777, he read at the Academy a Memoir on the formation of mountains, and on the revolutions of the globe, which was published by Mr. Tooke in his *Russia Illustrata*. In 1778, he brought out his *Novœ Species Quadrupedum e glirium ordine*. In 1781, he published his *Enumeratio Plantarum quœ in horto Procopii a Demidof Moscua vigent;* and in the same year appeared his New Northern Collections, on various subjects in geography, natural history, and agriculture; two fasciculi of his *Icones Insectarum presertim Russiœ Siberiœque peculiarium*, and the first No. of the *Flora Russica*, executed at the expence of the Empress, appeared in 1784.

Pallas was about this time appointed a member of the Board of Mines, with an additional salary of £200 per annum, and was decorated with the order of St. Vladimir. He had some time before intimated his design of disposing of his collection of natural history; and no sooner had the Empress heard of his intentions, than she informed him that she would be the purchaser, and desired him to make out the catalogue, and fix the price. He accordingly mentioned 15,000 rubles, and, when the catalogue was presented to her Majesty, she subjoined with her own hand the following paragraph:

" Mr. Pallas understands natural history much better than figures. He ought to have charged 20,000 instead of 15,000 rubles for so many valuable articles. The Empress, however, takes upon herself to correct the mistake, and hereby orders her treasurer to pay 20,000 rubles. At the same time, Mr. Pallas shall not be deprived of his collection, which shall still continue in his own possession during his life, as he so well understands how to render it most useful to mankind.'

In the year 1794, Pallas travelled to the Crimea, and after his return, he published his *Physical and Topographical Picture of Taurida*, in which he describes that interesting peninsula. His health had now begun to decline, and he felt the necessity of recovering it under a warm climate. For this purpose the Empress granted him an estate in the Crimea, and a present of 10,000 rubles to form an establishment. He accordingly removed to the Crimea, where, on his estate of Akmetchet, and in a residence more like a palace than that of a private gentleman, he spent the greatest part of his later years. Actuated by a strong desire to see his brother and his native city, he made a journey to Berlin, where he died on the 8th September, 1811, in the 71st year of his age. Besides the works which we have mentioned, Pallas communicated three papers to the Royal Society of London, which are published in the *Philosophical Transactions*, 1763, p. 62; 1766, p. 186; 1776, p. 523. He was also the author of various

Memoirs, published among those of the Imperial Russian Academy.

For farther information respecting this eminent naturalist, see Coxe's *Travels*, vol. iii. p. 203; Tooke's *View of the Russian Empire;* and Dr. Clarke's *Travels*, vol. i. p. 458, 572, 578, 579. See also our articles BOTANY, vol. IV. p. 26; ENTOMOLOGY, vol. IX. p. 65; and METEORITE, vol. XIV. p. 138.

PALMA. See CANARY ISLANDS, Vol. V. p. 356.

PALMERSTON'S ISLAND is an uninhabited island in the South Pacific Ocean, discovered by Captain Cook in 1774. It consists of eight or nine small islets, connected by a reef of coral rocks. W. Long. 163° 10', South Lat. 18° 4'.

PALMYRA, anciently one of the largest and most magnificent cities in the world, but now completely in ruins, is situated in the desert of Syria, in 34° 35' North Lat. and 38° 39' West Long. It stands 200 miles east of the Mediterranean, and 150 south-east of Aleppo, nearly on a line between that city and the Persian Gulf. Excepting on the east, where it is flanked by a ridge of mountains, it is surrounded by barren, sandy, uninhabited plains. It enjoyed the benefit of two springs, the waters of which, now nearly absorbed in the sands, are still used, though warm and sulphureous; but water seems also to have been conveyed to the city from a considerable distance, by means of a magnificent aqueduct, the ruins of which may yet be traced. *Situation.*

Of the origin of this city we can give no certain information. It is regarded by some as having risen to distinction long before the time of Solomon, who lived about a thousand years before the Christian æra; while others suppose it to have been the " Tadmor in the wilderness," built by that illustrious monarch, (1 Kings, ix. 18.—2 Chron. viii. 4.) This latter opinion is rendered not improbable, from the circumstance, that the two terms in question are synonymous. " The name of Tadmor, or Palmyra," says Gibbon, " by its signification in the Syriac as well as in the Latin language, denoted the multitude of *Palm-trees*, which afforded shade and verdure to that temperate region." A similar account is given by Josephus, no incompetent authority,—who also affords a complete refutation to the opinion, that the King of Jerusalem was too wise and prudent a prince to found a city of such extent in a distant and uninhabited corner of his dominions, when he remarks, that " the reason why Solomon built this city so remote from the parts of Syria that are inhabited, is this, that below there is no water to be had, and that it is in that place only where there are springs and pits of water," and that it was meant to form the emporium of the commerce carried on between the Persian Gulf and the mercantile cities on the banks of the Mediterranean. The pearls, cinnamon, gold, &c. mentioned in sacred history, afford ample proof that a commercial relation did subsist, from a very early period, between the places in question, because, in the countries bordering upon the Persian Gulf, could these articles alone be got; and Palmyra, situated on a straight line between the Persian Gulf and the Syrian and Phœnician cities, thus early became, it is probable, the centre of the trade of the eastern world, and attained to that degree of wealth and splendour which its ruins so powerfully indicate. It may not be improper to state, that the *original* buildings of Palmyra have been long entirely obliterated by the lapse of time; and that the edifices, the ruins of which are now so splendid, must have been erected long posterior to the time of Solomon; *Origin.*

Palmyra. because Messrs. Dawkins and Wood, to whom we owe almost all we know of this extraordinary place, discovered no inscription older than the Christian æra; and, besides, the style of architecture is all either of Greek or Roman origin.

History. But important as this city soon became, its history is almost totally unknown. This probably may be accounted for from its sequestered situation and peaceful pursuits, and the various other causes which also tended to sink in obscurity every record of the early commercial history of that interesting portion of the globe. It is transiently mentioned by an ancient historian, (John of Antioch,) that Nebuchadnezzar took possession of Tadmor ere he laid siege to Jerusalem. Pliny speaks of it as an opulent and important city—as connecting the Roman and Parthian empires by the mutual benefits of commerce, and as enjoying, from this circumstance, the privileges of a complete neutrality,—until, after the victories of Trajan, it became subject to Rome, and remained in that state for upwards of 150 years. Meagre, however, as the historical notices of Palmyra are, it can boast of one splendid æra, when, under its king, the celebrated Oudenatus, it gained various victories over the Persians, and at length stood forth as the rival of Rome herself. Oudenatus was not destined long to enjoy the honours he had won; he was, after a glorious career, murdered by a member of his own family; but on his death, Zenobia, his queen, one of the most illustrious females that Asia ever produced, assumed the government, avenged his death, and soon rendered herself formidable to all the nations within her reach. To the dominions of Oudenatus, which extended from the Euphrates to Bithynia, she added the kingdom of Egypt, derived from her ancestors. Arabia, Armenia, and Persia, solicited her alliance; the Emperor Claudius II. acknowledged her greatness, and she was universally recognized as Queen of the East. But her dignity and her power did not long continue; and Palmyra, through her, sacrificed ages of quiet and prosperity, to a moment of glory. The Emperor Aurelian, actuated by ambition, or a desire to secure the safety and tranquillity of the Roman provinces in Asia, marched a powerful army thither, attacked and defeated Zenobia, and obliged her to retire within the walls of Palmyra. The siege of this city was more tedious and more bloody than Aurelian had expected; and he thought it necessary at length to offer terms of capitulation. These terms, though favourable to the besieged, were indignantly refused. Zenobia declared that the last moment of her reign and of her life should be the same. This resolution, however, did not long continue to animate her: seeing nothing before her but defeat or death, she fled, and had got so far as the Euphrates, a distance of sixty miles, when she was overtaken and apprehended. Her courage now completely failed her, and she fixed an indelible stain on a character, otherwise glorious, by purchasing her own life at the expence of those of her subjects and her friends. Among the numbers whom, on this occasion, Aurelian devoted to death, was the celebrated Longinus, secretary to the queen, and one of the most elegant writers in the Greek language, whose works have come down to us. Palmyra was delivered over to the rapacity of the Roman soldiers; and though Valerian, with the value of the gold and jewels found in Zenobia's possession, repaired the celebrated Temple of the Sun; and though Justinian, in a subsequent age, attempted to restore it to its ancient splendour, this city gradually from this period verged in-

to decay and desolation. The Mahometans, into whose hands it afterwards fell, did nothing to save it from that ruin into which it was fast sinking; and its present mouldering remains speak to us, in the most emphatic language, of the unavoidable fate that awaits the pride of man, and the noblest monuments of human genius.

Ruins. These ruins are the most extraordinary and stupendous in the world, alike remarkable for extent and magnificence, and the romantic, wild, and desolate spot on which they are found. Architecture seems to have lavished all her ornaments, and displayed all her skill, in the construction and decoration of those splendid edifices, the very fragments of which are so massy and imposing. "We had scarcely passed," says Mr. Wood, "these venerable buildings, (the sepulchres of the ancient Palmyrenes,) when the hills opening, discovered to us, all at once, the greatest quantity of ruins we had ever seen; and behind them, towards the Euphrates, a flat waste, as far as the eye could reach, without any object which showed either life or motion. It is scarce possible to imagine any thing more striking than this view. So great a number of Corinthian pillars, with so little wall or solid building, afforded a most romantic variety of prospect." A similar account is given by Mr. Bruce, who visited these ruins before he penetrated into Abyssinia. "When we arrived at the top of the hill," says he, "there opened before us the most astonishing, stupendous sight that perhaps ever appeared to mortal eyes. The whole plain below, which was very extensive, was covered so thick with magnificent buildings, as that one seemed to touch the other, all of fine proportions, all of agreeable forms, all composed of white stone, which at that distance appeared like marble. At the end of it stood the palace of the Sun, a building worthy to close so magnificent a scene."

Of these extraordinary ruins, it is impossible, in this place, to give any thing like an adequate account. "We sometimes find a palace," says M. Volney, "of which nothing remains but the courts and walls; sometimes a temple, whose peristyle is half thrown down, and now a portico, a gallery, or triumphal arch. Here stands groups of columns, whose symmetry is destroyed by the fall of many of them; there we see them ranged in rows of such length, that, similar to rows of trees, they deceive the sight, and assume the appearance of continued walls. On which side soever we look, the earth is strewed with vast stones, half buried, with broken entablatures, damaged capitals, mutilated friezes, disfigured reliefs, effaced sculptures, violated tombs, and altars defiled by mud." These ruins, which consist chiefly of temples, palaces, and public edifices, built mostly of white marble, occupy an area of three miles in circumference; but the ancient city, the greater part of which has now disappeared, is allowed to have extended to nearly four times that space. For a farther account of this interesting place, we refer the reader to Mr. Wood's curious publication, which is accompanied with fifty plates; and to the article CIVIL ARCHITECTURE, in this work, (Vol. VI. Part II.) which contains, with other notices, a very minute account of the Temple of the Sun, the most stupendous and the most entire of these venerable remains.

Present inhabitants. The abject and sordid character of the present inhabitants of this city,—about thirty Arab families who live in huts erected in the court of the Temple of the Sun,—afford a striking and humiliating contrast to the splendid and massy ruins by which they are surrounded. These people cultivate a few olive trees, and as much corn as is necessary for their subsistence, in any vacant spot that can be found amid the dilapidations of the place; they are far removed from any inhabited district, and have no other communication with the living world, than what consists in a visit, rather of a commercial kind, paid once in two or three months, to some of the nearest villages. The caravans which travel between the Euphrates and Aleppo, keep considerably to the eastward of Palmyra—a place now so neglected, but once the very centre of the trade of the eastern world.

See Wood's *Ruins of Palmyra*, and the article CIVIL ARCHITECTURE, *ut supra*; Bruce's *Travels*, (Introduction;) Volney's *Travels*, &c.; and Swinton's *Explication of the Inscriptions at Palmyra*. Some notices may also be found in Pliny, *Hist. Nat.* lib. v.; in *Josephus*; the *Ancient Univ. Hist.*; and Gibbon's *Roman History*. (T. M.)

PALSY. See MEDICINE, Vol. XIV. p. 11.

PAMPAS. See BUENOS AYRES, Vol. V. p. 51.

PAMPELUNA, or PAMPELONA, anciently *Pampeiopolis*, a city of Spain, and the capital of Navarre, is situated in a fertile plain, on the banks of the Arga, which washes its walls. Although its fortifications are not considerable, yet it is defended by two castles, one in the town, and the other immediately without the walls. The last of these, situated upon a rock, has fine bastions, and good ditches. It has a handsome tower, several magazines, a square adorned with trees, and an armoury in the centre of the fortress.

Pampeluna contained a cathedral, three flourishing convents of monks, and two of nuns. The cathedral contains the mausoleum of Charles III. and on the side of the church is a fine cloister, of two rows of galleries, the one above the other. There is nothing remarkable in the public edifices. The city is very confused, and ill built. Two of the squares contain tolerably handsome houses, and the one used for bull-fighting is very spacious.

The commerce of the town consists only of carpets. It receives every thing from abroad, and supplies its neighbours with scarcely any thing. Parchment, leather, coarse cloth, earthen ware, and wax, are the only articles of manufacture.

Pampeluna contains 1632 houses, 2800 families, and nearly 14,000 inhabitants. West Long. 1° 41′ 15″. North Lat. 42° 59′ 57″. See Laborde's *View of Spain*, vol. ii. p. 318.

PAN, in the ancient mythology, was the son of Mercury and Penelope, and presided over those who were led by their pursuits to frequent the fields. The worship of him was particularly established in Arcadia.

PANORAMA, from παν, *every thing*, and οραω, *to see*, is the name given to pictures painted on the inside of a cylindrical surface, the eye being placed in the axis of the cylinder.

The fine panoramic paintings of Mr. Barker are well known; and we believe this eminent artist had the merit of inventing this delightful method of representing nature, and of securing, by patent, the exclusive right to the use of it.

PANTOGRAPH. See PENTAGRAPH.

PANTHEON. See CIVIL ARCHITECTURE, Vol. VI. p. 622. and Plate CLXII.

PAPA-STOUR. See SHETLAND ISLES.

History. PAPER. Before proceeding to an account of the present mode of manufacturing paper, it may be advisable to give a sketch of the history and improve-

ments of the art. Cotton paper appears to have been used in Greece about the ninth century, although no dated manuscript has been found written on this paper older than the middle of the 11th, but several of those without a date still extant appear considerably older. About the beginning of the 12th century the use of this paper was very common in Greece. It also took the place of the Egyptian Papyrus, which had been previously used in Greece. *·Paper. Cotton paper.*

Linen paper appears to have been made use of in Europe about the beginning of the 14th century. The oldest German paper-mill was established in 1390 at Nuremberg. It is uncertain if the art was invented in Germany, or imported from the east. The first paper-mill in England was established at Dartford, by a German, jeweller to Queen Elizabeth, about the year 1588. *Linen paper.*

For a long time after its establishment, the manufacture was in a very backward state in this country, so that the finer kinds used to be imported from France and Holland, till within the last fifty or sixty years. From that period, however, the manufacturers of Britain have made rapid strides, and we now find that paper of the best quality is not only made in Kent, the original seat of the manufacture, but in almost every district of the island. Till within about sixty years, paper was made by means of stampers or hammers, which still continue to be used in most of the French and Italian mills.

An account of the method then in use is not devoid of interest. In France and Holland, in the old way, the rags, after being well washed, were placed, in their damp state, in close vessels, generally tubs, and left there for about fourteen days. This caused them to become slightly putrified and destroyed, or at least injured; the fibres being then placed in large wooden mortars, they were bruised and hammered down to a fine pulp by stampers, shod with iron; two of these stampers worked in each mortar alternately; and it required about forty pair, working night and day, to prepare a hundred and twelve pounds of rags. Being reduced to pulp, or rather paste, they were made into paper by a method a good deal like that at present in use, less attention being paid to the texture and fine surface of the sheet. In England, the mode was something different. The rags being fermented nearly in the same way as in France and Holland, they were placed in a circular wooden bowl, diverging regularly towards the top; in this bowl an iron cylinder worked, the pressure on which was considerable, and acting on the side of the bowl, so that the rags were squeezed and rubbed in this way, till they obtained nearly the same degree of trituration that was given them in the French method. This is nearly the same process by which snuff is now manufactured in this country. Of these two modes, the French was the best; so that about the middle of the last century, it was commonly used in this country. *Old mode of manufacture.*

About that time, the paper engine was invented in Holland, which totally changed the mode of making paper, and paved the way for the great improvements which have since taken place in the art. *Invention of the engine.*

We now come to describe the present mode of making paper, both by the hand and by various machines. Before coming to the mill, the rags are sorted into four or five kinds, according to their fineness. This is, however, rather carelessly done. The first operation at the mill, is the cutting and re-sorting of the rags, which is generally done by women. A frame of *Present mode of manufacture.*

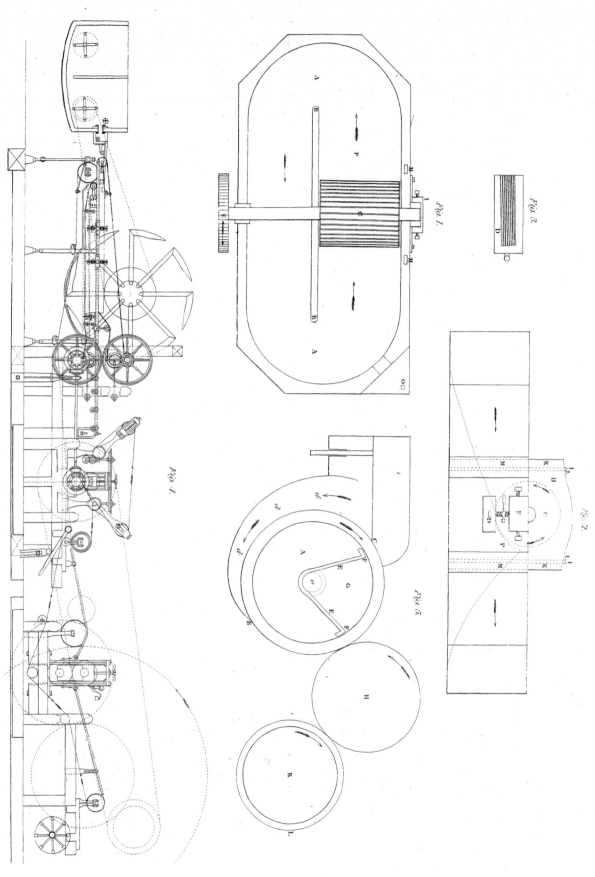

PAPER MAKING.

PLATE CCCCLVII.

Fig. 1.

Fig. 2.

Fig. 3.

Fig. 4.

Fig. 5.

Engraved for the Edinburgh Encyclopædia, for A. Moffat.

Paper.

a table is covered with wirecloth, of about three meshes to the running inch. In this frame a part of a scythe, about a foot long, is fixed, rather inclining backwards. On the left side are the uncut rags, and on the right is a box, divided into several compartments. The operator takes up a few of the rags, and shakes them on the table, so as to allow much of the dirt to pass through; she then takes up a piece and draws it along the sharp side of the scythe, so as to cut it into portions of three or four inches square, and places it in one of the compartments according to its fineness. Seven or eight sorts are in general made; the new pieces are laid aside for the purpose of making bank notes, or any paper which may require great strength. The rags are then taken to a larger table, also covered with wire-cloth, and examined by an overseer, who throws out the pieces which belong to another sort. Rags may be cut and sorted for about 1s. 4d. to 1s. 6d. per cwt. and an active woman can cut nearly that quantity in a day.

It may be well here to notice from whence the material used in this country is obtained. Next to the home collection, the supply derived from Germany, through the ports of Bremen and Hamburgh, is most considerable; and a great quantity of rags from the Mediterranean is annually imported, chiefly from Leghorn, Trieste, and Palermo. The different nature of these kinds of rags is very striking; while our home supply consists very much of cotton, and of a finer quality than the rest, that from Germany is a strong linen material, almost all unbleached, but not very fit for the paper-maker, unless bleached with the oxymuriatic acid gas, except the finer kinds, called SPFF Bremens, which are perhaps the best material for a fine writing-paper, and which brings a high price accordingly. The Tuscan rags, again, though dirty, acquire a high colour by the common way of washing, without being bleached, but are unfit for the purposes of writing-papers, from the difficulty of making them take the size. A mixture of the different kinds of rags is most esteemed by paper-makers, as it combines the good qualities of each, and as it were, neutralizes the bad effects which would result from using a particular sort unmixed.

Dusting. The next operation is the dusting of the rags. A revolving cylinder, about six feet long and four high, covered with the same kind of wire-cloth as the tables, is attached to the machinery of the mill, so that it can be set in motion with considerable velocity. In the axle of this cylinder, spokes about twenty inches long, are fixed. A part of the circumference opens, and by this door the rags are placed in the duster. The door being closed, it is set in motion. The rags are prevented from remaining in a mass by the spokes, and the dust escapes through the wire-cloth. After being driven about for half an hour or thereabouts, they are taken out to be placed in the engine, and reduced to pulp. This part of the process merits a particular description.

Engine. Plate CCCCLVII. Figs. 1, 2. The engine (see Plate CCCCLVII. Figs. 1, 2.) consists of a trough A 10 feet long, 4½ broad, and 2¼ deep, generally made of wood, but sometimes of iron. If of wood, it must be lined with lead. BB is a division in the engine, dividing it into two sides, one of 26 inches, and the other of 22 inches. CC (Figs. 1, 2.) is the roller, which is composed of wood or iron, 22 inches in diameter, and 26 inches wide. Along it, and firmly fixed in it, are bars or plates of steel 1-8th or 1-16th of an inch thick, but tapering towards the edge, and projecting

two inches beyond the wood or iron of the roller. Below the roller is the plate DD, (Figs. 2, 3.) which slides in a groove exactly under the roller, but not parallel to it. It is composed (Fig. 3.) of bars of the same kind as those of the roller, but placed close together, and 5 inches broad. The roller is supported on the box I, (Figs. 1. 2.) in which is a screw G, for the purpose of elevating or depressing it. Above the roller is a cover, which extends 6 or 8 inches on each side of it. In this cover towards the ends are two frames (Fig. 2.) I, I, covered with fine wire-cloth, and sliding in grooves in the cover, and leaving a space behind KK, communicating with the pipes M, M, (Figs. 1. 2.) Before the frames are two boards L, L, which can also be removed. We now come to describe the operation. The roller being set in motion by means of the pinion E on the same axle, with a velocity of 160 revolutions in a minute, from 112 to 130 lbs. of rags are put into the engine, with as much water as will raise the whole to within an inch or two of the brim. The roller is depressed till its bars touch those of the plate; the rags are carried through, bruised on their passage, and the greater part of them are thrown over the height P. Here they are collected and pushed round till they arrive again at the roller; are again carried through, and again carried round. This goes on continually. Meanwhile the pipe O being opened, water is allowed to run into the engine, and the boards L, L, being removed, part of the rags and water are thrown up against the frames I, I; the water passes through, and runs off by the pipes M, M. Thus the rags are bruised down and washed; **Washing.** at the same time, it is of the utmost consequence to have a regular supply of spring water. Indeed, fine papers cannot be made to advantage without this; a hogshead per minute will be an ample supply for a washing and beating engine, which will prepare about six cwt. of rags in a day, if the power of the mill is sufficient to keep them constantly at work. Both engine and roller ought to be made of elm, where iron is not used, which is better, especially for the latter, if there be power to drive them, as its weight makes it go steadier, and thus prepares a more equal stuff. The engine must be lined with lead, as the head of a nail rusting in it is sufficient to cause great numbers of those red or rusty marks often seen in paper. It is of consequence that the machinery should go equably, a heavy flywheel is hence advantageous. The power required for a 5 or 6 vat-mill is about 20 horse. The roller must make from 150 to 160 revolutions in a minute in the washing engine, and about 180 in the beating. When the rags have been about an hour in the engine they are bleached; there are two ways of bleaching used at present, one by the oxymuriatic acid gas, the other by the acid combined in the dry way with quicklime. In the first way the rags are boiled in an alkaline solution of potash and lime, for four or five hours, or if very coarse, for eight hours. The purpose of this is to destroy the coarse part of the hemp, commonly called *shon* or sheave, and which exists in a great degree in coarse linens, especially German rags. The solution is then washed out in the washing engine; the water being pressed out they are exposed to the acid, in the gaseous form, as linen is, (see BLEACHING.) The gas is then washed out as carefully as possible; this is of great importance, as if any acid remain in the rags, it causes the paper after some time to putrify and change its colour. In the other way the oxymuriate of lime is diffused in water by agitation, the insoluble matter is

Paper.

thrown out, and the liquor when clear, is diluted and put in the engine; being thoroughly mixed with the rags, it is allowed to stand for an hour or more, and the acid carefully washed out. Bleaching is not now in very common use, on account of the low price of rags. The stuff is then reduced for an hour more in the washing engine, and is then put into the beating engine. The bars of the roller in this engine are placed three together, nearly at the same distance as in the other engines. The plate has from 18 to 20 bars; it is common to make the plate of brass; then a greater number of bars, or rather grooves sawn in the brass, are necessary. The process does not go on so quickly with a plate of this sort, but the stuff prepared is clearer. The cover of this roller has only one washing frame, and even that is little used; this engine is rather smaller than the other. When the stuff has been beat, as it is called, for about three hours and a half, it is generally fine enough, and a valve placed in the bottom of the engine being opened, the stuff escapes into the chest.

We may here remark, that the greatest art in the manufacture is in the preparation of the stuff, and in adapting the state of the tackle to the material employed. The stronger the rag, the sharper must be the tackle, else the stuff would become so *wet*, that is, it would retain the water so much, that the vat-man could not, without much trouble, shake it out, and the paper would be very apt to shrink in size. This is the manner, however, to form a strong paper, and what is done in the preparing of bank-note or even cartridge stuff. The best state of the tackle consists in the bars of the roller, and those of the plate, agreeing in every respect together; those in the washing engine should be thick and blunt, where rubbing only is necessary to free the material of the dirt; and those of the beating engine are required, generally, to be sharper. But all this depends, as we have said above, on the state or quality of the material, and the thickness or thinness, &c. of the paper to be made.

Chest.

The chest is commonly a rectangular vessel, either of wood or stone; but if it is of wood, it is lined with lead. The common size may contain 300 cubic feet, or three enginefulls of stuff; but they vary very much. Round chests are, however, preferred, as they admit of agitators being placed in them, for the purpose of keeping the stuff from sinking. Agitators cannot be employed where there are angles in the chest, as the thick parts of the stuff would be driven into these angles, and rolls would be formed.

Vat.

A small quantity of the stuff is then removed to the vat, by means of a pipe, and diluted with water. The vat is a large tub, about five feet square and four deep, with sides rather inclining outwards, made either of wood or stone. On one side of this the maker stands; along the vat is laid a board, with copper ribbands fastened lengthways on it, to make the mould glide along it; this is called the bridge. To the left of the maker is a smaller board, one end of which is fastened in the bridge, the other rests on the side of the vat. In the bridge, opposite to this, is fastened a nearly upright piece of wood, called the ass. In the vat is a copper, communicating with a steam-pipe to keep it hot; there is also an agitator to keep the stuff of a uniform thickness.

Moulds.

We must now give a description of the moulds. A laid mould consists of a frame of wood neatly joined at the corners. Wooden bars run across it, about an inch and half distant from each other. Across

these, and consequently along the mould, the wires run; from 15 to twenty cover an inch. A strong raised wire is laid along each of the cross-bars, to which the other wires are fastened; this gives the laid paper its ribbed appearance.

Paper.

The water-mark is formed by sewing a raised piece of wire in the form of letters, or any device that may be wished on the wires of the mould, which makes the paper thinner in these places. The frame-work of a wove-mould is nearly the same; but instead of sewing on separate wires, the frame is covered with fine wire-cloth, of from 48 to 64 wires in an inch. On both moulds, a deckel or moveable raised edging, is used; this must fit very neatly, otherwise the edge of the paper will be rough.

Water-mark.

There are always a pair of moulds laid on the bridge, and the workman putting on the deckel, brings the mould to a vertical position, dips it about half-way up in the stuff before him, and bringing it to a horizontal position, covers the mould with the stuff, and shakes it gently. This operation is extremely difficult, for if the mould be not held perfectly level, one part of the sheet will be thicker than another. The sheet thus formed, has as yet no consistency, so that by turning the mould, and dipping the side covered with wire-cloth, in the vat, it is reduced again to pulp, if necessary; he then pushes it along the small board to the left, and takes off the deckel; here the coucher receives it, and places it resting on the ass, so as to get quit of some of the water; the vatman puts the deckel on the other mould, and makes another sheet. The coucher stands to the left side of the vat, his face towards the maker; on his right is a press in which the felts are; the felts are porous pieces of flannel; a plank three inches thick is before him on the ground; on this he lays a cushion of felts, and on this another felt; he then turns the mould and presses it on the felt, where the sheet remains, he returns the mould, and pushes it along the bridge; by this time the maker has another sheet ready, which he places on the ass, lays down another felt, and couches the sheet upon it.

Making.

Couching.

They go on in this way, felts and paper alternately, till they have a heap of six or eight quires, which is about 15 or 18 inches high. They then draw it into the press, where a pressure of from 70 to 100 tons is applied, either by a lever or machinery. When it is sufficiently pressed, they strike off the check, and, from the elasticity of the flannel, the screw flies up with great rapidity. The felts are then drawn out on the other side, where a layer stands; a board is put horizontally in the press, on which the layer places the felt; he lifts up the sheet, which has now considerable strength, and places it on another board to the other side; places on the board another felt, whence the coucher takes them, and anew puts paper on them. Two men at the vat, and a boy laying, make about six or eight reams in ten hours. In the evening, the whole is put into another press, and a moderate pressure exerted; this is to get quit of the mark of the felt and of part of the water. Next day it is all separated, which is called parting, and being again pressed, is carried into the loft. Fine papers are often twice parted and pressed, in order to give them a good surface.

Pressing.

Laying.

The next operation is the drying, which is performed in the following manner: Posts about 10 or 12 feet high, are set up at the distance of 10 feet from each other, pierced with holes at the distance of six inches one from another; two spars, with ropes stretched

Drying.

Paper.

between them, at the distance of five inches one from another, called a treble, are placed about five feet high between these posts, supported by moveable pins pushed into the holes in the posts. The workman takes up three or four sheets of paper, and puts them on a piece of wood in the form of a T, passing this T or cross between the ropes, he leaves the sheets hanging on them, and goes on till all the ropes are full; he then raises the treble, and puts another in its place, which he fills and raises in like manner. Nine or ten trebles are thus placed in every set of posts. The sides of the drying room have shutters, which can be opened at pleasure. In good weather paper is dried in a day, but in moist weather, longer time is required. For assisting in drying, steam pipes are used in some mills. When the paper is dry, it is taken down and laid neatly in heaps, to be sized. Size is made of pieces of skins cut off in tanning, or sheeps feet, or any other glutinous substance. They are boiled in a copper, to a jelly; and this jelly being strained, and set by for use, a small quantity is then dissolved, and a little alum is added. The workman then takes about four quires of paper, and spreads it out in the size, taking care to get every part of it wetted. This is rather a difficult operation. Some of the size is then pressed out, and the paper parted. Being again pressed, it is taken again to the drying room, and dried as before, care being taken not to dry it too rapidly; as in that case great part of the size would fly off in moisture. Three days are necessary for this drying. When the paper is thoroughly dry, it is carried to the finishing house, where it is again pressed pretty hard; it is then picked, which is done by women with small knives, who take out the knots, and separate the perfect from the imperfect; the paper is then again pressed, and given to the finisher, who counts it into quires and reams and folds it; it is again pressed in reams, tied up, and sent off; the whole operation takes about three weeks in general. A good finisher can count 200 reams or 96,000 sheets in a day of ten hours. It is pressed often to give it a good skin or surface, as it is called. Hot pressing is done by smoothed pasteboards, between every one of which, a sheet of paper is placed, and between every 40 or 50 pasteboards a heated plate of iron. This gives it the fine smooth surface we see in writing papers.

Fourdrinier's paper machine. PLATE CCCCLVII. Fig. 4.

We now come to give an account of the various machines invented to do away with the use of the mould. The most important of these is Fourdrinier's, Fig. 4. A is a vat in which there are two agitators, to keep the pulp suspended; from this the stuff runs by a sluice into *b*, and from that on to a web of wire-cloth *c c c c*, four feet wide, and 24 long; the two ends of which are sewed together, this wire-cloth is stretched on several rollers *k k k*; the part of it next the vat runs on a number of small level rollers, *m m* are two rollers above the wire-cloth; below these passes an endless strap *b*, which returns over the rollers above, and which forms a ledge to confine the stuff while in a fluid state. There is one of these straps at each side of the web. A rod from an eccentric wheel, shakes the part of the wire-cloth next the vat. The rollers being all set in motion, and the wire-cloth with the stuff running on it, moving on towards *d*, the rod shaking it so as to make it part with the water, forms the stuff into paper, when it arrives at the rollers *d d*, it passes between them, undergoing a slight pressure; here the paper is laid on the web of felting *e e*, the two ends of which are also sewed

together, and the web of wire-cloth returns below as is seen in the plate; the paper and felt are then hard pressed between the rollers *f f*; when the paper arrives at *g*, it is detached from the felt, and wound on the reel *h*, when this reel *h* has 16 or 18 quires on it, it is removed, and another reel *i* substituted, and the paper being cut off, the reel *h* is ready to be sent to be parted; or, if coarse paper, to the loft. The dotted line marks the passage of the paper from the vat to the reel. All this is done by machinery, which is constructed so that no part shall go too quick or too slow. There are a number of other contrivances, which our limits will not permit us to describe. For a full account of the machine, see the *Repertory of Arts*, vol. xiii. second series.

The next machine we have to give an account of, is Mr. Dickinson's.

Dickinson's paper machine. PLATE CCCCLVII. Fig. 5.

A is a hollow revolving cylinder, made of brass, and polished outside and inside. From B to C, a great number of small holes are cut in the circumference of the cylinder, and over these holes a wire-cloth is neatly sewed. The stuff or pulp fills the vessel *d*, and the water runs into the cylinder, as it revolves, and leaves a portion of pulp on the wire-cloth; the parts EE form a box in the cylinder, which does not revolve, and the edges of this box FF touches, or rubs against the interior of the cylinder, *o* is a pipe in which an air-pump works, which exhausts the box G. When the wire-cloth with the pulp on it arrives above the exhausted space G, the pressure of the atmosphere fixes the sheet on the wire-cloth, and gives it some consistency and regularity. The cylinder H, made of a hard body, covered with felt, then receives the sheet; when it reaches the point I, it adheres rather to the cylinder H than to the wire-cloth; it is then pressed between the cylinders H and K, taken off at L, and finished in the same way as paper made by the hand.

Cameron's paper machine.

Mr. Cameron's machine, near Edinburgh, is a very good one, by common moulds, fixed in a frame which has a revolving motion. The pulp runs on them as they pass by a particular place. The couching is done by the moulds as they move along, being made to turn upon their face, which comes in contact with a revolving and endless web of felting; there they receive a pressure, and, as they pass on, are again reversed to receive the stuff for another sheet.

This machine, which has been only at work for a few months, seems to have been an improvement upon that of Cobb's of London, but sufficiently improved as to entitle the present workers of it to a patent, against the opposition of Messrs. Cobb. It promises to succeed, although it cannot come into competition with that of Fourdrinier's in point of expedition or extent of work. It is better suited than the latter for a small mill, and may probably become valuable for the making of laid papers, which are necessarily at present made by hand.

There are in Great Britain about five hundred and fifty paper-mills, making paper to the amount of £2,300,000 yearly. There are about sixty of these machine mills, making about £650,000 worth of paper yearly. These last are rapidly on the increase, from the circumstance of Fourdrinier's patent having expired in August, 1822. There are three machines, and about fifty vat-mills in Scotland; and two machines in Ireland. The paper made in the United Kingdom is in general superior to what is manufactured in any other part of the world. The United States come next; then Holland.

It is curious that the manufacturers of Britain have not succeeded in making a card-paper to the satisfaction of the card-makers in England, but that that article continues to be imported from Genoa. Several imitations have been made, but not with great success, as the Genoa litteriss is still preferred by many card-makers, though at double the expence of the home-made.

In France, there are about two hundred and fifty papermills, mostly small, and about five of Fourdrinier's machines. The mill at Annonay, upon the Rhone, belonging to the brothers Montgolfier, and styled " La Papeterie Royale," is by much the most extensive, and in best order. Trade is, however, much crippled by the late restrictions on the French press. In the Austrian dominions, there are about three hundred paper-mills; in Bohemia alone one hundred and seven; and in the kingdom of Italy one hundred and five, celebrated for the manufacture of card-paper. They, and most of the foreign mills, are worked by mallets. The value of Austrian paper is about 2,000,000 florins. In the Prussian dominions there are three hundred and one paper-mills delivering about 360,000 reams annually, value £120,000 Sterling. Saxony makes 640,000 reams, but uses three times that quantity. In Hanover there are about 40 paper-mills. In Russia there are 67. In Denmark they do not make enough for the consumption. In Sweden there are about 40 paper-mills, but they also import from Holland. The duty on paper is 3d. per lb. for paper made of rags, and $1\frac{1}{2}$ for brown papers.

The manufacture of brown paper is carried on to an immense extent in Britain, not only for the usual purpose of packing paper for grocers and other tradesmen, but in a much greater degree for extensive manufacturers of linen and cotton. The consumpt in this way is prodigious in Manchester and Glasgow. In the neighbourhood of the former place, are large machine mills, constantly employed in making brown paper for these two cities. The material, old rope, costs nearly $1\frac{1}{2}$d. per lb.; the duty as much more; and the cost of manufacture not much above $\frac{1}{2}$d. per lb.

Printing papers are now most generally made by machines, and are preferred machine-made, as the thickness of a sheet is more regular, and the surface better from its passing between the smooth cylinders. One machine of the full width of 60 inches, is equal to six vats work, and consequently produces from 40 to 50 reams printing demy in 10 hours.

The cost of production of fine writing papers, exclusive of duty, is about 1s. per lb.; and that of fine printing papers about 10d. Our exports of paper are considerable, principally to the East and West Indies, Canada, and the United States of America.

PAPPUS. See Geometry, vol. X. p. 190; and the *Edinburgh Philosophical Journal,* vol. vii. p. 56. 219.

PAPUA, or *New Guinea,* is the name given to an island of great extent in Australasia, to the north of New Holland, and separated by a strait from the latter. The centre of the island is in East Long. 149⁰, and South Lat. 5°. See the article Australasia, vol. III. p. 121. 123. and 126. A very full account of the Papuans will be found in Capt. Forrest's *Voyage to New Guinea,* in 1774, 1775, and 1776. See also Pennant's *Outlines,* vol. iv. p. 20; Sonnerat's *Voyage à la Nouvelle Guinée,* vol. ii. p. 122; Fleurieu's *Découvertes*

des *Français en* 1788, 1789, *dans le S. E. Guinée,* Paris, 1790; Pinkerton's *Geography,* vol. ii. p. 631—647; and the other works quoted in the article Australasia.

PARABOLA. See Conic Sections, vol. VII. p. 154.

PARACELSUS. See Chemistry, vol. VI. p. 4; and Medicine, vol. XIII. p. 647.

PARACHUTE. See Aeronautics, vol. I. p. 169. 174.

PARAGUAY. See Buenos Ayres, vol. V. p. 51.

PARALLAX of the Fixed Stars. From the annual motion of the earth about the sun, it necessarily follows that the positions of the fixed stars differ from their positions seen from the sun; this difference of position is called the *parallax of the fixed stars.* It is evident also, that by the motion of the earth the latitudes and longitudes of the fixed stars must differ at different seasons, and also their right ascensions and declinations. But so vast are the distances of these bodies compared with the diameter of the earth's orbit, that the changes are quite insensible with inferior instruments; and it is even now a question with many, whether the instruments of astronomy have as yet arrived at such a degree of perfection, as to render the parallax of any of the fixed stars sensible.

When the Copernican system was first given to the world, the want of a sensible parallax appeared a most formidable difficulty. It necessarily followed, that if this system were true, the bounds of the universe must be extended in a manner that appeared very revolting to the notions of that age.

The discovery of a sensible parallax, therefore, was an object of great importance to the supporters of the Copernican system; and the efforts of astronomers have been unceasingly employed, either in actual attempts, or in projects of investigation. Their exertions have been productive of consequences very important to astronomy.

The above motive for the investigation of the parallax of the fixed stars, has indeed ceased since the discoveries of Sir Isaac Newton. It was no longer necessary for removing all doubts of the truth of the Copernican system; but it became an object to show by its existence the improved state of the science, and afterwards to ascertain whether it should not be adopted as one of the many corrections applied to the daily observations of the observatory.

The first attempt to examine with exactness the position of the fixed stars at different seasons of the year, appears to have been made by Tycho Brahe. He, it is well known, was quite adverse to the theory of the motion of the earth, and the result of his observations of the altitudes of the pole star seems to have confirmed him in his opinion. Kepler tells us, that the superior meridian altitude of this star always agreed to the same minute, and the same of the inferior. Kepler, however, was a strenuous advocate for the Copernican system; and remarks, as to these observations of Tycho Brahe, that neither the instruments nor observations could be exact to the fifth part of a minute.

Galileo, referring to the observations of Tycho Brahe, seems to suppose him not to have exactly understood the consequences of the earth's motion; that he imagined the constancy or change of the elevation of the *pole itself* would decide the question of the annual motion. This mistake of Tycho is not more remarkable than that of another eminent astronomer about a century afterwards.

Galileo, who, by the discovery of the telescope, was able to adduce so many powerful arguments for the truth of the Copernican system, endeavoured also to render the telescope directly subservient to proving the motion of the earth. The method he proposed he imagined would far surpass the exactness of the instruments of Tycho Brahe. He conceived he could use instruments greatly exceeding his in magnitude,—instruments, in which he tells us one degree might be of the extent of even a mile. His plan was to place on some building, on a very distant mountain, an horizontal bar, fit for just hiding or bisecting a star when viewed from a great distance through a telescope. He intended to place himself with his telescope in the meridian of this object, and at a very great distance, so that one of the stars of Ursa Major when below the pole, might be just hid or bisected by the object so placed, as to appear in the telescope like the horizontal wire in our systems of wires.

The place of the telescope was to be exactly marked, that by replacing it the observations could be repeated at the necessary times for obtaining the desired information. The deviation of the star, if any, would thus evidently be observed, and if conformable to parallax, would establish the motion of the earth.

This method is perfect in theory, but would, had it been attempted, have been found attended with great practical difficulties, and, had they been overcome, it is obvious they would have been followed by a complete disappointment as to the object intended. It is clear Galileo had no knowledge whatever of the variation of refraction, from the variable weight and temperature of the atmosphere, or of the irregularities of refraction near the horizon, both of which causes would have completely defeated his intentions. Circumstances like this are of great importance in the history of science. They afford us certain information of the true state of its advancement. The discoverer of the uses of the telescope in astronomy, besides his theoretical, must have had great practical knowledge, and yet was ignorant of what now may be observed by the most inferior instruments. The other method suggested by Galileo, of observing at different seasons the angular distance between two fixed stars very near together, is among the most promising; and it may even now be a matter of surprise that it has not hitherto succeeded. There will be an opportunity of mentioning this again.

It is well known, that the astronomers of the times that followed the revival of learning indulged themselves pretty freely in forming hypotheses. One of these, adopted by and half approved by Galileo, tended to make them less anxious to deduce by actual observation the parallax of the fixed stars; as, according to this hypothesis, it must be much less than their instruments could discern. They concluded, that as the fixed stars completed the *magnus annus* in 25,000 years, the fixed stars were necessarily 25,000 times more remote than the sun from the earth. This would have made the parallax only about eight seconds.

Here is a tolerable specimen of an hypothesis. The distances of the fixed stars have just about as much connection with the precession of the equinoxes as the motions of the planets have with the fortunes of men.

The first attempt of the discovery of the parallax of the fixed stars that seemed likely to be successful, was that of Dr. Hooke. The apparatus he constructed principally consisted of a telescope 36 feet long, which was erected at Gresham college in 1669. The result of his observations on γ Draconis, which star was within 2' of his zenith, gave him a parallax exceeding 20". The powerful instrument used by Hooke, and his known mechanical skill, seemed to have obtained for his result perfect confidence for many years. Flamstead refers to Hooke's observations for a confirmation of his own discoveries as to parallax made above twenty years after. And nearly sixty years after, the motive assigned by Bradley, for instituting those observations by which the aberration of light was discovered, were the hopes of verifying and confirming those that Hooke had communicated to the public. We now know that Dr. Hooke's observations must have been quite incorrect, as the parallax of γ Draconis certainly does not amount to half a second. His failure probably was occasioned by his telescope not having been firmly fixed; but it is inconceivable how so acute and experienced a mechanic could have been so much deceived.

Flamstead, who supposed he had ascertained the parallax of the Pole Star, by a continued series of observations made at Greenwich during seven years, also deceived himself. But his error was of a very different nature from that of Hooke. The motion that Flamstead had observed in the Pole Star, was not at all conformable to that which would have resulted from parallax. He found that the Pole Star appeared about 20" nearer to the pole in December, and about 20" farther from the pole in July, than in April and October. This it is easily understood cannot be the effect of parallax, because the effect of parallax is always towards the sun. Consequently, as the Pole Star is between the pole and sun in the beginning of April, the star must then appear most remote from the pole, and the contrary six months after. But the effects of the aberration of light afterwards discovered by Bradley, are conformable to the observations of Flamstead. Each star aberrates towards the point of the ecliptic, towards which the earth is moving; that is, towards the point 90° behind the sun.

It is remarkable, that the erroneous reasoning of Flamstead appears not to have been noticed by the mathematicians and astronomers of England. Dr. Wallis published, in the third volume of his works, the letter of Flamstead, in which a very minute account of his observations is given, without any remark as to its inconclusiveness. Even Dr. Halley appears to have acquiesced in the results, which, considering his known opposition to Flamstead, is not easily accounted for.

Roemer seems first to have pointed out the error in a letter to Flamstead himself; and afterwards James Cassini shewed at length, in the Memoirs of the French Academy, 1699, the mistake of Flamstead. Cassini himself was soon to have the inconclusiveness of his own attempts to find the parallax of Sirius shewn by Dr. Halley.

Roemer, who has so much distinguished himself by adopting and establishing the discovery of the velocity of light, after it had been abandoned by its original author, Dominic Cassini, appears to have exerted himself for many years in attempting to observe a parallax in the fixed stars. Instead of endeavouring to find the changes of declination, as Hooke and Flamstead had done, he observed the differences of right ascensions of opposite stars. He pursued this method for seventeen or eighteen years, and conceived he had found such results, as fully proved the existence of a sensible parallax in the fixed stars. He found the sum of the parallaxes of Sirius and α Lyræ, which two stars are nearly opposite in right ascension, exceeded half, but was less than three-fourths of a minute. But he died just as he was about to publish his observations and conclusions.

Horrebow, who had assisted in the observations of Roemer, published them in 1727, with the title of " Copernicus Triumphans." He himself had continued the observations, and his two sons also continued them for some years.

There can be no doubt that the discovery of Bradley put an end to these attempts in which the errors of observation, and actual changes from aberration, &c. must have been so mixed together, as to have deceived Roemer. It is otherwise difficult to account for his mistake as to the sum of the parallaxes of Sirius and Lyræ, which appears to have some reference to aberration. He had corrected the errors of Flamstead, and seems to have fallen into a similar one himself.

The two stars, Sirius and α Lyræ, from their difference of declination, were ill chosen. Even now, with the most improved transit instruments, the errors of adjustment would have too great an influence.

In 1714, James Cassini, by means of a fixed telescope, endeavoured to observe the parallax of Sirius. The futility of his attempt has been fully explained by Dr. Halley, in the *Phil. Trans.* vol. xxxi. It would not have been expected that at this period the effects of refraction were so little known, that the changes of the meridian altitude of Sirius, (the height of which at Paris is only about twenty-five degrees,) should have been attributed entirely to parallax. But the effects of refraction seem then to have been much better known by the English than by the French astronomers. Cassini concluded, from his observations, that the variation in the meridian altitude of Sirius during the whole year, was only about five or six seconds. What then can be thought of Cassini's observations, when we now know that there must, independently of the changes of refraction, have been a change of at least twenty-three seconds, the star being twenty-three seconds more southerly in the end of March than in the end of September? This objection could not have been made by Halley, as the effects of aberration were then unknown.

We now arrive at the period when the discoveries of Bradley put an end to all expectations of finding a parallax greater than a few seconds. In 1725, Mr. Samuel Molyneaux, (the son of the celebrated William Molyneaux,) and Dr. Bradley, engaged in observations on γ Draconis, with a view of verifying the observations of Hooke, in 1669, on the same star. Mr. Molyneaux adopted an instrument, (the zenith sector,) constructed nearly on the same principles as that of Dr. Hooke, but far exceeding it in exactness. This superior degree of exactness was owing to the skill of the celebrated Mr. Graham. It cannot be doubted that a vast improvement had been made in the execution of instruments since the time of Hooke.

The instrument was erected at Hesse in 1725, and was 24½ feet long. The observations having commenced in December, when the parallax was nearly greatest, no perceptible change was to be expected for some time. On the contrary, the observations having accidentally been continued, a perceptible change was soon seen, and that not according with parallax. A continuation of the aberrations for a year, exhibited a series of phenomena entirely inexplicable by any theory then known.

After the death of Mr. Molyneaux, Dr. Bradley, to pursue this inquiry with more ease and convenience to himself, erected at Wanstead an instrument 12½ feet radius by the help of the same excellent artist Graham. With this instrument he was able to extend his observations about six degrees from the zenith, whereas Mr. Molyneaux's instrument fitted up for γ Draconis, only extended a few minutes from the zenith.

About three years from the commencement of the observations with Mr. Molyneaux's instrument, Dr. Bradley completed his beautiful discovery of the aberration of light.

This discovery rendered it highly probable that the parallax of γ Draconis did not amount to a single second. All the changes of place that had been observed in γ Draconis had been exactly deduced from the theory of aberration.

Thus, as far as parallax was concerned, the observations were against its existence, as it could not be made perceptible with these most exact instruments. Dr. Bradley playfully remarks, " There appearing, therefore, after all, no sensible parallax in the fixed stars, the Anti-Copernicans have still room, on that account, to object against the motion of the earth; and they may have, if they please, a much greater objection against the hypothesis by which I have endeavoured to solve the fore-mentioned phenomena, by denying the progressive motion of light, as well as that of the earth.

" But I do not apprehend either of these postulates will be denied me by the generality of the astronomers and philosophers of the present age." (*Phil. Trans.* vol. xxxv.)

Dr. Bradley having experienced the exactness of his own observations with a telescope so much shorter than that of Hooke, expresses his surprise that Hooke, after all the care he pretends to have taken, should so egregiously have been deceived. He at the same time acknowledges the goodness of Flamstead's observations, and their accordance with the laws of aberration.

When it was found that the phenomena of the aberration had been observed so many years before by Flamstead, a claim of a prior discovery was put in for the French astronomer Picard. Indeed, it was almost impossible to suppose that observations of tolerable exactness should be made without the aberration appearing an unknown cause of irregularity. Roemer observed it; and all those who, for 50 or 60 years preceding Bradley's discovery, attempted the discovery of the parallax, must have done the same. It adds so much more to Bradley's fame, that, in so short a time, he so exactly observed the phenomena, as to enable him to discover the cause and verify the laws thereof.

Of all the stars observed by Bradley, there was only one of the first magnitude, Capella, within reach of his instrument, and the position of this star is not favourable for showing the effects of parallax in declination.

The beautiful star Sirius, has been always supposed nearer to us than any other; but the uncertain effects of refraction in this star, when observed in our northern latitudes, oppose any attempts to observe its parallax in declination. La Caille availed himself of his stay at the Cape of Good Hope, to make many observations on this star. Dr. Maskelyne, on examining these observations, found they appeared to show a parallax of several seconds. This induced Dr. Maskelyne, when at St. Helena, for the purpose of observing the transit of Venus, in 1761, to institute a series of observations on Sirius, but the result turned out quite unsatisfactory as to parallax; but here, as in almost every other attempt that had been made to discover the parallax of the fixed stars, an important advantage was gained for practical astronomy. Dr. Maskelyne discovered that the usual method of suspending the plumb-line by a loop induced very considerable errors. This was afterwards changed for the present method of making it pass over a notch.

It is to be remarked, that although by its brilliancy, even in our climate, (it must be far greater in southern latitudes,) Sirius appears to surpass all the other fixed stars; yet, from its situation, its declination is only changed by a little more than half its parallax. In this respect, then, it is not nearly so favourable for the investigation as stars of less brightness, that have considerable latitude, such as α Lyræ, γ Draconis, the stars of Ursa Major, and the Pole Star.

It is scarcely necessary to mention the speculations of Huygens, Cassini, Gregory, and Michell, respecting the distances and magnitudes of the fixed stars, as deduced from a comparison of the quantities of the light of the Sun and of the Stars. There is too much conjecture in them to obtain much confidence. All Michell's notions, however, are entitled to great respect. He computes, that were the Sun moved to such a distance that his parallax on the diameter of the Earth's orbit should be 2°, he would appear at least as bright as Saturn, which he considers to be nearly equal to that of the brightest fixed star. This conjecture turns out nearly the same as recent observations appear to point out for α Lyræ.

It may be remarked, that at this distance, the diameter of the Sun would be less than 1-100th of a second. Sir William Herschel supposes the apparent diameter of α Lyræ equal to 3-10ths of a second. These deductions, at first sight, seem opposed to each other. If we adopt the double parallax of α Lyræ to be 2″, and its apparent diameter 3-10ths of a second, its magnitude would be above three thousand times greater than that of the Sun. In this there is nothing very improbable.

Sir William Herschel himself appears to have attended a good deal to the inquiry which is the subject of this article. He resumed Galileo's method of observing the angular distance of two near fixed stars. He has explained this method at considerable length in the *Philosophical Transactions*. Sir William Herschel's discoveries as to the double stars offered great facilities of practising this method, but he does not appear to have obtained any results of importance. It is not satisfactorily explained why astronomers have not obtained more decisive information from this method. A comparison of observations, made in one part of the year after the end, and at the opposite season before the commencement, of twilight, appears to promise much. It is against all probability that two near stars of very unequal magnitudes should in general be equally distant. It may indeed happen in a few instances.

It remains now to give an account of the recent observations that have been made on the zenith distances of certain stars for examining this question.

M. Piazzi, observing at Palermo with a vertical circle, four feet in diameter, constructed by the late Mr. Ramsden, conceived he had observed a parallax in se-

veral stars. This great astronomer has given an account of his results in the 12th volume of the *Memoirs of the Italian Society*. But several circumstances tend to show that his instrument was not perfect enough for this purpose, and that the number of observations were too few for decisive results.

He makes the parallax of α Lyræ about 2″, that of α Arcturus is somewhat less. Procyon appeared by his instrument to have a parallax of 3″ in declination. This shows the unexactness of his conclusions; had Procyon a parallax of 3″ in declination, the parallax of the diameter of the earth's orbit would be 20″, a quantity that would long ago have been discovered by observations of right ascension. The application of an instrument to stars where the parallax in declination is but a small part of the whole, serves for a criterion of its exactness. If for these stars the parallax in declination appear considerable, the conclusion must be that the change of place arises not from parallax, but is an illusion either of the instrument or of the observations.

M. Piazzi, in his great catalogue of 7646 Stars, published in 1814, attributes a parallax of 1″.3 to the pole stars, from observations in right ascension. In this catalogue he attributes a parallax of 3″ only to Procyon. He could determine nothing with respect to Arcturus. The parallax of α Lyræ, he continues at 2″, and the observations that he had then made of this star appear sufficient as to number.

None of his results agree with the observations that have since been made by Dr. Brinkley at the observatory of Trinity College, Dublin. The nearest approach is that of the parallax of α Lyræ, which, according to Dr. Brinkley, is 1″.1.

The observations of Dr. Brinkley have been made with an instrument superior to those employed in the attempts of former astronomers, and have been far more numerous, so that at last we have arrived at an appearance of certainty in this interesting subject, and may conclude that all the fixed stars are not at immeasurable distances.

It is right however to state, that his results have not been confirmed by the observations at Greenwich, by the astronomer royal, Mr. Pond. On the contrary, the observations of the latter appear quite opposed to those made at Dublin.

That an opinion may be formed of the present state of this question, it appears necessary to give some account of the Dublin instrument. The account of the Greenwich mural circle, which has furnished most of the observations that are opposed to those made by Dr. Brinkley, has been given in a former volume.

The instrument at the observatory of Trinity College, Dublin, is a vertical circle, eight feet in diameter. It was planned, and partly executed, by the celebrated Mr. Ramsden, and finished by Mr. Berge. The following particulars may be sufficient to render intelligible the method of making the observations, and the degree of accuracy to be expected. (See *Transactions of the Royal Irish Academy*, vol. xii.)

The circle is supported in a frame, which frame turns on a vertical axis. The upper part of the frame is of cast iron, turns in a collar, and is connected with the lower part of the frame by four hollow brass cylindrical pillars. The lower part of the frame, which is also of cast iron, terminates in a pivot of steel, which turns in a socket of bell-metal. This socket is moveable south and north, by one screw, and east and west by another, for the purpose of adjusting the vertical axis.

The axis of the circle, a double cone four feet in length, is supported on Y's, which are themselves supported by strong bars of brass attached to the cylindrical pillars. The pressure of the weight of the circle and its axis, is relieved by an ingenious application of friction wheels and the lever. There is also an ingenious contrivance for adjusting the axis horizontal.

The limb of the circle is brass, and is divided into intervals of five minutes, which intervals are subdivided by micrometer microscopes, into seconds and parts of a second, as usual. There are three microscopes, one called the bottom microscope, opposite the lowest point of the circle; a second opposite the left extremity of the horizontal diameter, and a third opposite the right extremity of the horizontal diameter.

The frame carrying the circle turns on the vertical axis with the greatest steadiness. The circle also turns together with its horizontal axis on the Y's with equal steadiness.

The vertical axis of the instrument is adjusted by a plumb line. The plumb-line by which this adjustment is performed, is about ten feet long, and is suspended from a point about eight inches from the centre of the top of the frame, and passes over a point below eight feet from the point of suspension. By the help of this point, which is moveable by a screw, and by the moveable socket below, the axis of the instrument is made vertical. The adjustment of this axis, as to the north and south position, is, it is evident, of the most essential consequence to the exactness of the zenith distance observed. It is likewise evident, that, from the great interval between the upper and lower parts of the instrument, the relative position of the point of suspension, and of the point below, may be altered by change of temperature. To obviate this inconvenience, which would be fatal to the accuracy of the observations, the point of suspension is on a compound bar, formed of bars of brass and steel, and the point below is also placed on a similar compound bar. By this the distance of the plumb-line from the vertical axis remains always the same. This contrivance appears to answer in a very satisfactory manner.

The axis of the instrument being adjusted vertical, and the plane of the circle in the meridian, and facing the east, let b, l, and r be the zenith distances of a star, as shown by the bottom, left and right microscopes respectively. When the plane of the circle is on the meridian, and facing the west, let b', l', r' be the zenith distances of the same star as shewn by the repective microscopes. Then the true observed zenith

distance $= \frac{1}{2} \left(\frac{b+l+r}{3} + \frac{b'+l'+r'}{3}; \right)$ and the correction of the mean of the three microscopes

$= \frac{1}{2} \left(\frac{b+l+r}{3} - \frac{b'+l'+r'}{3}. \right)$

For objects above seven degrees from the zenith, the observations are frequently made both on the east and west positions of the face of the circle, at the same passage over the meridian. One observation is made just before the object comes to the meridian, and then, the circle having been reversed, the object is again observed. The observations are reduced to the meridian. This method of observing adds greatly to the exactness of the results.

By observing a star in both positions of the instrument, the zenith distance is obtained without reference to any other star. The Greenwich mural circle makes the polar distance of a star depend on the polar distance of several other stars. The polar distance of a star in the zenith, for instance, depends on the polar distances of stars many degrees from the zenith, so that, in fact, the place of a star in the zenith is affected by refraction, i. e. if we wish to compare the observed places of the star in winter and summer, we must do it by the intervention of stars affected by refraction. The stars used for comparison may not be the same stars, and then the places will be affected by the errors of the elements, such as nutation, &c. Indeed, it is quite obvious, that in this manner, it will be extremely difficult to compare with exactness the places of a star at two opposite seasons. Had Bradley used such an instrument in the observation which led him to the discovery of the aberration of light, it is highly probable he would have been unable to disentangle the complicated results met with, and so he would have missed the discovery.

These remarks appear to show, that the mural circle is an instrument by no means adapted to the discovery of minute changes in the places of the stars. The vertical circle of the Dublin observatory is free from the above objections.

Accordingly, Dr. Brinkley early applied himself to observing certain stars with a reference to parallax. An extract of a letter from him to Dr. Maskelyne, giving an account of the parallax of α Lyræ, was published in the *Philosophical Transactions* for 1810.

In March, 1815, a paper was read before the Royal Irish Academy, in which Dr. Brinkley gives a minute account of his observations relative to this subject.

The stars in which Dr. Brinkley had observed a parallax were, Arcturus, α Lyræ, α Aquilæ, and α Cygni. His observations gave no parallax for the Pole Star and γ Draconis. We must refer to the above mentioned paper and its appendix, printed in the 12th vol. of the *Transactions* of the Royal Irish Academy, for the particulars and remarks of the author on these observations.

Mr. Pond having examined his observations, made with the mural circle in 1812, 1813, and 1814, gives an account of the results in a paper printed in the *Philosophical Transactions*, for 1817. Each of the stars which Dr. Brinkley had appeared to find a sensible parallax, by Mr. Pond's observations, gave only a very small parallax, and this Mr. Pond considered to arise from some unknown cause not connected with parallax.

The unfitness, however, of the mural circle for these inquiries, appears to have induced Mr. Pond to proceed by another method. He procured two fixed telescopes to be erected at Greenwich, of considerable length. These were furnished with wire micrometers. One telescope was for observing α Cygni, and the other for α Aquilæ. For comparison with α Cygni, β Aurigæ, a star nearly opposite in right ascension, and having very nearly the same declination, was chosen. Both these stars passing through the field of view, the telescope remaining fixed, the difference of declination could be measured by the micrometer. The stars being nearly opposite in right ascension, the joint effects of parallax would be visible, or, in other words, the sum of the parallaxes would be observed instead of the difference.

Mr. Pond's observations are given in the volume of

Philosophical Transactions for 1817, and appear to prove that the parallax of α Cygni does not amount to one-tenth of a second. But, it is manifest, that as the observations of the two stars were made at intervals of 12 hours, and often at intervals of 36 and 60, &c. hours, there was a danger of the telescope, and its parts not remaining exactly fixed, and there was no means of ascertaining this. Hence there might be a constant source of error to counteract the effects of parallax. In fact, it appears, that the telescope was subject to a motion arising apparently from the change of temperature. The instrument appears to have altered its position by several seconds, between winter and summer; and if we suppose that change of temperature between day and night caused the same effect in a smaller degree, the observations would not contradict a parallax of half a second, which is the result of a numerous series of observations of this star made at Dublin.

It is a remarkable circumstance, that the change of place in the Greenwich fixed telescope, was such as might have been considered to indicate a considerable parallax in α Cygni. This is similar to what took place in Hooke's telescope; but Mr. Pond had guarded against such an error by using two stars, and so no derangement of the instrument could affect his results, excepting as far as it might take place between two succeeding observations.

In using the telescope for α Aquilæ, Mr. Pond appears not to have been able to avail himself of a star situate so as to obtain the sum of the parallaxes. The star fixed on by him 55 *l* Pegasi, (*Phil. Trans.* 1818,) although differing three hours in right ascension, is circumstanced nearly the same as to the effects of parallax in declination, as if it had only differed by a few minutes in right ascension. Consequently, in this case, no advantage was derived from using the fixed telescope.

Mr. Pond, in the same volume of the *Transactions*, has given the result of observations on the right ascension of α Aquilæ, but the objection here is, that the stars with which α Aquilæ was principally compared, were those which, according to the Dublin observations, appear to exhibit sensible parallaxes.

The most certain results, by right ascension, are to be expected, by using stars twelve hours asunder, by which the sum of the parallaxes in right ascension would be obtained, as Roemer first attempted; and, in like manner, as the sum of the parallaxes in declination are obtained by the fixed telescopes. But here we have to depend on the permanency of position of the instrument for twelve hours, which is always to be distrusted.

Dr. Brinkley, in a paper in the *Phil. Trans.* for 1818, gives some additional results, and enumerates particularly the inconveniencies and sources of inaccuracy that may take place from mural circles. In the *Phil. Trans.* for 1821, the same astronomer has given the results of numerous sets of observations made with the Dublin circle, commencing in 1818, for the purpose of examining the question in all its bearings. The number of observations amounted together to nearly 4000.

Among them are the results of observations of thirteen stars, for which both the parallax and constant of aberration are investigated.

The quantities are given in the following Table.

	No. of Observ. 1818—1821.	Constant of Aberration.	Semi-parallax, or *p*.
Polaris.	343	20″18	— 0″03
Polaris S. P.	337	20 12	+ 0 12
β Ursæ Majoris.	75	20 16	+ 0 02
γ Ursæ Majoris.	105	20 48	+ 0 39
ε — — — —	109	20 29	+ 0 33
ζ — — — —	94	20 23	+ 0 28
η Ursæ Majoris.	99	20 76	+ 0 13
Arcturus.	259	20 04	+ 0 61
β Ursæ Minoris.	131	20 49	— 0 13
α Ophiuchi.	228	20 39	+ 1 57
γ Draconis.	152	19 86	— 0 08
α Lyræ.	227	20 36	+ 1 21
α Aquilæ.	320	21 32	+ 1 57
α Cygni.	154	20 52	+ 0 33

The column containing the constants of aberration may be thought to possess considerable interest. It contains the results of probably the only direct observations that have been made to investigate the constants of aberration, since Bradley made his observations. This column, and that for the parallax, were obtained from the observations of the respective stars, by the method of making the sums of the squares of the errors a minimum.

The small negative parallaxes that appear, must be attributed to the unavoidable errors of observation. Had there appeared among these any negative parallaxes, amounting to nearly a second, it would have produced a powerful argument against a visible parallax.

Dr. Brinkley also observed several bright stars between 4 H and 10 H. AR. viz. Aldebaran, β Tauri, α Orionis, Procyon, &c. In these stars the effect of parallax in declination is only a small part of the whole. Therefore, had any of these stars shewn a considerable parallax in declination, a decisive adverse argument would have been obtained. There were nine of these stars, and in all three hundred and forty-three summer observations were compared with four hundred and fourteen made in winter. In no star was found a difference between the observations at the two seasons, greater than what might be attributed to the unavoidable errors of observation.

These stars are opposite in right ascension to those in which he had found a parallax, from which circumstance a decisive argument is deduced that the changes which appeared, and which he attributed to parallax, were not from change of figure in the instrument, or from change of temperature, because the same arches nearly were used in both sets of stars. This argument is carried somewhat farther by the observations of the pole star. By the reversing property of this instrument, the *same* arches very nearly are used for the pole star, above the pole, as for Arcturus; therefore, if the appearances of parallax in Arcturus were derived from the instrument, it must take place in the pole star observed at the same seasons, and it does not.

For some other remarks of this nature, made by Dr. Brinkley, we must refer to the paper itself.

Notwithstanding the additional evidence which Dr. Brinkley conceives he has obtained by these numerous observations, he states other conclusions obtained by him that may be thought to increase the difficulty.

Parallax.

He instituted a series of observations on stars in the same part of the heavens as those in which he had found the appearances of parallax. Of seventeen stars observed for this purpose, he only found two, γ Draconis and α Aquarii that appeared to be not affected by parallax. This circumstance will, Dr. Brinkley observes, justly, perhaps, with many, add to the difficulty of admitting his explanation. They will be unwilling to admit that many of the smaller stars are nearer to us than many of the brighter. That in a certain part of the heavens, of considerable extent, many of the stars exhibit a sensible parallax.

However, subsequent observations appear to render it probable that part of these appearances in stars of considerable zenith distance, may arise from refraction.

Dr. Brinkley also states in this paper that he considers the circumstance of the Greenwich mural circle, showing the same arch between α Lyræ and γ Draconis in summer and winter as the strongest objection that had been advanced against the results from the Dublin circle. But a recent examination having been made of the observations of the Greenwich circle, it appears that in each of the years 1812, 1813, 1814, and 1815, the arch between Polaris above the pole and Lyræ in summer being compared with the same arch in winter, there results almost exactly the same parallax for Lyræ, as has been found by Dr. Brinkley. This changes the nature of the objection. The objection, if any, against the Dublin circle, should now be that it gives no parallax for γ Draconis, whereas the Greenwich circle gives it the same as for α Lyræ.

Dr. Brinkley, anxious to obtain all possible exactness, pursued the observations, and from the great number which he had accumulated of certain stars, it occurred to him that they might be applied to finding the solar nutations, as well as the parallax and aberration. He has published a paper on this subject, in the fourteenth volume of the *Transactions* of the Royal Irish Academy.

One of the principal objections to his results, was the difficulty of ascertaining with *certainty* quantities so small. The constant of aberration had evidently been obtained by him with great exactness, but the degree of exactness was not precisely known. Now, the constant of solar nutation is known from theory with certainty to be nearly half a second, a quantity smaller than he had found for the parallax of certain stars; therefore, if the same observations should be found to give the solar nutation exact, a most satisfactory argument would be had for the exactness of the parallax.

He remarks, "The solar nutation goes through all its states twice in the course of a year; therefore, it appears impossible to suppose that if any cause should occasion the instrument to show deviations explained by parallax which did not actually exist, it should not derange the solar nutation, and cause the result of an investigation of its quantity to turn out quite erroneous.

"This method of investigation, which I have applied to several stars, has produced the most satisfactory results.

"There will not, I conceive, remain the smallest doubt with any one who examines the processes which have been used, that the observations have ascertained the quantities of parallax, with considerable exactness, of the Stars α Lyræ, α Cygni, and Arcturus, and that the parallaxes of γ Draconis and η Ursæ Majoris are extremely small. That γ Draconis is at least seven or eight times more distant than α Lyræ."

Dr. Brinkley shews that the constant of solar nuta-

tion deduced from theory does not differ one-tenth of a second from $0''51$. He shews that if the constant of lunar nutation$=9''50+y$, the constant of solar nutation$=0''506-13y$. Now y is certain to six-tenths of a second; therefore the solar nutation is certain to less than one-tenth of a second by taking it $=0''51$.

He supposes it unknown, and $= z$.
The constant of aberration $= 20''25+x$.
The constant of parallax $= p$.
The correction of the mean zenith dist. of the star known nearly, $\Big\} = e$.

From each observation he obtains an equation of the form $e+fx+gp+hz+k=0$, containing four unknown quantities, e, x, p, and z.

Thus, for α Lyræ 333 equations of this kind are obtained. These equations are reduced to 4, by the method of making the sums of the squares of the errors a minimum.

The following results are deduced:

	z	p	x
α Lyræ.	$+ 0''51$	$+ 1''14$	$+ 0''10$
γ Draconis.	$+ 0\ 42$	$+ 0\ 07$	$- 0\ 50$
η Ursæ Majoris.	$+ 0\ 58$	$+ 0\ 09$	$+ 0\ 43$
α Cygni.	$+ 0\ 56$	$+ 0\ 50$	$+ 0\ 06$
Arcturus.	$+ 0\ 44$	$+ 0\ 65$	$- 0\ 41$
α Aquilæ.	$+ 0\ 96$	$+ 1\ 73$	$+ 0\ 94$

These values of z, with the exception of that for α Aquilæ, are wonderfully near the true value. In consequence of that resulting from the observations of α Aquilæ, Dr. Brinkley leaves the former conclusions respecting this star in doubt. He considers that the irregularities of refraction have influenced the results, and assigns a reason for their having great influence on the observations of this star.

The results obtained from supposing z known, may be expected to be more accurate than those where it is taken as unknown, because then a less number of unknown quantities is deduced from the same number of observations. But it is shewn that there is no difference worth notice, particularly as to α Lyræ.

Dr. Brinkley points out, with reference to future inquiry, the difference between the constants of aberration for γ Draconis and η Ursæ Majoris.

The constant of aberration for α Lyræ, comes out $20''36$. The mean of the constants of aberration in the table of 13 stars above given, is $20''37$. Therefore those who contend, by arguments certainly of great weight, that the velocity of light of all the stars is the same, will admit that the constant of aberration has been determined with great exactness by the observations of α Lyræ.

The parallax of this star appears also established in the most conclusive manner. It is difficult to imagine a severer test for the exactness of any philosophical experiment, than that to which the observations of this star have been submitted. There are three apparent motions of this star, depending on the place of the Sun, and variously mixed together. Two of these, the aberration and solar nutation, have been separated from each other, and from the third, (the parallax,) and ascertained to the exactness probably of the 1-10th of a second. Can it be doubted that the third, the parallax appearing to amount to $1''$, 1, has also been ascertained with nearly equal exactness?

It remains to mention the method of computing the effects of the parallax of the fixed stars as to changes of declination, right ascension, &c. This may be very shortly explained. It is easily understood that by the effect of parallax, each star appears nearer the sun by

$$\text{an arch} = \frac{\text{Semi-diam. of earth's orbit.}}{\text{Star's distance.}} \times \text{sin. angular}$$

dist. of star from the sun $= p$ sin. angular dist. of star from sun.

Also, (not considering the eccentricity of the Earth's Orbit) by the effect of aberration, each star appears to approach the point of the Ecliptic 90° behind the sun

$$\text{by an arch} = \frac{\text{mean vel. of earth.}}{\text{vel. of light.}} \times \text{sin. ang. dist. of}$$

star from point of Ecliptic 90° behind the sun = 20″, 25 sin. ang. dist. of star from that point. Hence, if A represent the effect of aberration on a star when the sun's longitude is $\odot + 90°$, $\frac{p\,A}{20,\,25}$ will be the effect of parallax, when the sun's longitude is $\odot$. This is evidently true, whether the effect in declination, in right ascension, or in latitude or longitude, be required. Thus the tables of aberration are easily made to apply to finding the effects of parallax. It is only necessary to compute the aberration for (sin. longitude $+ 90°$) and the result multiplied by $\frac{p}{20,25}$ will give the effect required.

PARALLEL MOTION, or PARALLEL JOINT. See STEAM ENGINE.

PARALLEL ROADS of GLENROY. There are few of those natural appearances that attend the disposition of the earth's surface, more striking than that which is well known in this country by the name appended to the head of this article. It may at the same time be almost considered as a solitary instance; since nothing at all comparable to it has been discovered elsewhere, although slender indications of appearances arising from similar causes have been observed in a few other places. While the parallel roads, as they have long been called, are thus interesting in a physical view, and more particularly so to the cultivators of geology; they are no less striking to an ordinary spectator, or to a lover of the picturesque, from the extreme singularity of their aspect, as well as the beauty of the scenery where they lie. Though easy of access from Fort William, since the entrance of Glen Roy is scarcely more than twelve miles from that place, they are even yet but little known to the numerous travellers who visit Scotland in pursuit of the romantic and picturesque; these being contented to follow the ordinary tracks of the published tours, which are little better than copies of each other.

So little was known out of the bounds of the Highlands respecting the scenery and even the antiquities of these districts, at the time of Mr. Pennant's visit in 1772, that it is not very surprising this spot should have remained undescribed. It appears to have been even little remarked by the natives or persons in the immediate vicinity; a circumstance indeed not very extraordinary, when we consider that the taste for picturesque scenery, even among the educated, has sprung up in our own day, and that the Highlanders were as perfectly unaware of the riches of this nature in which they abound, as were the English, and even the inhabitants of the very scenes themselves, till the lakes of Cumberland and Westmoreland were first pointed out by Gray. That the parallel roads have been supposed the works of the imaginary Fingalian dynasty, is no proof of their having been observed

at any very distant period; as the personages of this ancient drama are invested with a right to all possible tombs, and hills, and caves, and streams, and mountains, throughout the whole country, even where such discoveries have almost taken place in our own days. It is a question if Staffa had ever been noticed or spoken of by a single native, when it was first pointed out to Pennant by Mr. Leach, an Irish gentleman, in 1772; yet in the course of the following year the cave acquired the name of Fingal.

Mr. Pennant himself, unfortunately did not see this remarkable spot; yet the first account of these appearances that was given to the public was in his work, in a note furnished by a minister in the neighbourhood. Still they seemed to have attracted no attention; nor was it till the publication of the statistical reports that we received any farther account of them; the report of the parish of Kilmanivaig, in which they chiefly lie, drawn up by Mr. Ross, the minister, containing the description in question. That we may give the best idea we can of the opinions then entertained respecting them, we shall quote as much of Mr. Ross's account as is necessary, and it will supersede the necessity of taking any farther notice of that handed down by Pennant.

" As there is nothing left upon record respecting the times when, the persons by whom, or the purposes for which, these roads were constructed, we can only mention the common traditions regarding them. One is, that they were made by the kings of Scotland when the royal residence was in the castle of Inverlochy, which is not above eleven miles from the nearest of them; and what gives an appearance of truth to this tradition, in the opinion of those who maintain it, is, that the construction of these roads was so vast an undertaking as could not be effected by any vassal or nobleman, however powerful. Another tradition, which is that of the natives, is, that they were made by the Fingalians, and under the name of Fingalian roads they are still known in this country. They are likewise called the Cassan, that is, the roads, by way of eminence. Of this, the natives are convinced, from this circumstance, that several of the hills have retained, from time immemorial, the names of some of the heroes of Fingal, such as the Hill of Gaul the Son of Morni, that of Diarmid, and of Fillan, and likewise of Bran, the famous dog of Fingal, &c. Now, the popular opinion cannot be considered as a direct proof of any opinion, yet we cannot help remarking that the original tradition, which in this case has always been invariable, gives a strong degree of credibility to the existence of such heroes, and renders it by no means improbable that these extraordinary roads have been the result of their labours. The purpose which they have been designed to serve, seems to have been, agreeably to the common opinion, to facilitate the exercise of hunting; for, in ancient times, and indeed till within this century, the valley was covered with wood, which made it very difficult to pursue the deer, &c. and rendered certain avenues necessary for effecting this purpose; in corroboration of which opinion, it may be observed, that on the sides of the roads, there have been found some stakes fixed in the ground, probably the remains of some of the palings or fences which in those days were made use of to confine the game till they were driven in upon a field called Dal na Sealg, or Hunting Dale, where the presumption is that they were killed." Thus far Mr. Ross.

We hear no more of them after this time, till they

were visited by Mr. Playfair, in company with Lord Webb Seymour, by Sir James Hall, and by the Earl of Selkirk, at different periods, and independently of each other. These philosophers, however, were content with giving their opinion of them in conversation, nor was any memoir published. We shall hereafter notice their different theories; and, without meaning any disrespect to names so well known, shall merely say here, that the conceptions of the whole of these observers were as superficial and indistinct, as their investigations appear to have been ill conducted; and that their several theories are quite unsatisfactory and irreconcilable to the phenomena. We need only observe, at present, as what may be considered a remarkable fact, that Mr. Playfair, long accustomed to geological investigations, and well versed in all the collateral knowledge requisite for the investigation of this subject, agreed with the Highland tradition, in so far, at least, as to consider them works of art.

The first careful examination subsequent to these was made by Dr. M'Culloch in 1814, and a paper on the subject was then drawn up, and presented to the Geological Society, but not read till 1817. In this paper, a very complete description of Glen Roy, and of all these phenomena, was given, attended with the several necessary measurements, and with views, maps, and sections for their complete illustration. A detailed view was also given of the different theories which had been proposed to explain the appearances; together with arguments drawn from them that prove these to be as unfounded as they were insufficient for the solution of the difficulties. At the same time another theory was proposed, capable of explaining all the appearances without difficulty, and supported by every one of the facts; while, by tracing the geography of the surrounding country, and comparing its present with its probable former condition, the whole subject was placed in so intelligible a point of view as to leave no difficulty to future observers.

From that paper we shall extract what is essential to our purpose, with such additions and alterations as may be necessary. A few of these are borrowed from a paper from Sir Thomas Dick Lauder, in the Transactions of the Royal Society of Edinburgh, published in 1821, from a survey made in 1817; the chief novelty of which is a prolongation of the appearances in Glen Spean into the valley that leads to Loch Treig, which had not been examined by the author above mentioned.

The lower part of Glen Roy, in particular, is exceedingly picturesque; the outlines of the hills being graceful, if not rugged, their surfaces intricate and pleasingly undulated, and occasionally sprinkled with wood, while the bottom of the valley through which the winding river runs, is scattered with clumps of wood, with cottages, and with cultivation. On the faces of these hills, in most places at least, and on the opposite sides of the valley, at heights precisely corresponding, are traced to the eye three strong lines, absolutely level, and parallel to each other and to the horizon, but at different distances from each other. So singular is the effect produced by their mathematical exactness and artificial appearance, that the spectator can scarcely conceive that they belong to the landscape; imagining them rather to be lines interposed between his eye and the hills, as in viewing an object through a telescope furnished with parallel micrometer threads. It is with some effort and study that he learns to consider them

as a part of it; and then it is that he is perhaps even more struck by their extraordinary and artificial aspect.

This seems to be a natural consequence of all those appearances in nature which most resemble works of art. It is not often that she presents us with artificial forms on a large scale; and least of all with that semblance of mathematical exactness here visible. Similar feelings are excited by the huge castellated form of the Scuir of Eyg, towering amid the clouds like a work of gigantic art, and by the columnar scenery of the Western Islands, so well known in Staffa, though displayed in far greater abundance, and on a much more various and sublime scale, in Sky, in Ailsa, and in other places. In contemplating natural objects of this character, it is with difficulty that the spectator can divest himself of the feeling that he is actually contemplating a work of art. He is constantly led to make comparisons that are ever intruding themselves on his imagination; and thus insensibly measuring the works of nature by the similar efforts of art, is struck by the magnitude of the efforts, and of the power that appears displayed, when he compares them to even the most stupendous productions of man. That this vague and unperceived metaphysical reasoning is the cause of the more powerful effect on the mind produced by them than by other species of scenery of far greater sublimity and of a much greater scale, we entertain no doubt. Where Nature can only be compared to herself, accustomed to a different scale of judgment, we pass over the sublimest scenery with comparatively little impression. There is nothing human with which we can compare the thundering cataract, the dark mountain, the beetling cliff, and the wide ocean. We measure her according to her own powers, not those of man; and our wonder is forgotten in our consciousness of her unlimited means and resources.

We must regret that we are unable to accompany the following description with such maps or plates as are almost indispensable to a due understanding of the phenomena; but as the great number of those that would be wanted renders this impossible, we must be content with referring such of our readers as may be at a loss on the subject, to the papers formerly mentioned, where all the requisite illustrations will be found. Those who are possessed of a map of Scotland, may, however, easily trace the courses and positions of the rivers and valleys which are the seats of these appearances.

All our readers know that the great glen of Scotland through which the Caledonian Canal is conducted, extends in a straight line from Fort William to Inverness, containing the connected chain of lakes, Loch Ness, Loch Oich, and Loch Lochy. The greatest height of this valley is only 94 feet above the level of the sea; and its bottom, wherever it is accessible, is alluvial, so as to have led to the not very improbable opinion that the western and northern seas once communicated through it, and that the north-western region of Scotland was a distinct island.

Between the southern extremity of Loch Lochy and Fort William, is found a wide opening, bounded on one hand by the skirts of Ben Nevis, and, on the other, by the hills near Highbridge, which separate Glen Roy from Glen Gloy. This latter glen opens into Loch Lochy at a more northern point, and extends, in a somewhat tortuous course, to the middle of Glen Roy, with which it communicates at a high level. But the wider opening forms two principal ramifications—the one into Glen Roy, and the other into Glen Spean, which, in its prolongation, is now the seat of Loch Laggan. From Glen Spean different small valleys branch off, giving access to the mountain streams that flow into the Spean. These are, however, little concerned with the phenomena in question; with the exception of that valley which leads to Loch Treig, and conducts its waters to the Spean below.

Where Glen Roy branches away from Glen Spean, it first holds a course somewhat to the northward, and then turns off to the east, where, after a course of about eleven or twelve miles, it appears to terminate. This may be called the Lower Glen; as, after suddenly rising to a higher level, it continues to hold its course eastward for about four miles, till it nearly reaches Loch Spey, on an elevation which here forms the highest water level of the country, and from which the rivers separate to the eastward and westward. We need not describe here the minor valleys that open into Glen Roy, as we could not convey a just idea of them, and as they will hereafter be noticed wherever they are required for the description of the phenomena under review.

In this whole system of associated valleys, the parallel roads, as they are called, may be traced with more or less of distinctness and continuity. But they are far more perfect and numerous in some places than in others, while in many they are altogether invisible. As they are most complete in Glen Roy, and as their effect there is far most impressive, while their origin can at the same time be more satisfactorily found, we shall commence with the description of that valley. The others will require comparatively little notice; and we shall here only premise that we have substituted the term *lines* for roads, the latter name conveying improper notions of their nature.

Commencing at the uppermost or western extremity of Glen Roy, we find a low granite hill skirting the boundary between Loch Spey, which is the source of the river Spey, and the upper valley of the glen in question. The water from the loch runs slowly eastward through a boggy plain; till, meeting with numerous other streams, it holds its way into Badenoch, and forms the noble river which finally terminates at Speymouth. The western end of this plain stretches for a few hundred yards beyond the head of Loch Spey, and then descends by a sudden step into the upper valley of Glen Roy. This valley is of an oval form, about four miles in length, as we just remarked, and one or more in breadth, being bounded on two opposite sides by high mountains. From these descend two streams, which unite about the middle of the valley to form the Roy. After this junction, the united streams flow with a moderate velocity for a space of two miles, when the glen suddenly contracts, and terminates in a rocky hill of no great elevation. The water, forcing its way for some distance through a narrow pass between approaching rocks, enters into a second glen, or into Lower Glen Roy, where the principal appearances under review are found.

But one line occurs in this upper valley, and it is most easily seen on the left bank of the stream, from the junction upwards towards the elevation that contains Loch Spey. This, when examined by the level, and duly prolonged, is found to correspond with the uppermost of the three principal lines in Lower Glen Roy, of which it is an interrupted continuation. None of the lower lines which are found in this latter glen exist in this upper division.

The flat rock just mentioned which forms the narrow entrance at the upper end of Lower Glen Roy, or which divides the upper from the lower part of the general valley, projects at right angles from the hill on the right, and then turns westward so as to form a promontory parallel to the side of the glen; thus producing a *cul de sac* on one side, and giving passage to the river on the other. This rock itself exhibits no trace of a line; but the two uppermost commence at its junction with the hill or side of the glen, whence they are seen running westward far along the faces of the mountains. The uppermost of the two, if prolonged, would just be even with the flat parts of the surface of that rock. Wherever, in a few places, it rises higher than the place where the line ought to be, it still bears no marks of it; as is an invariable rule wherever any of these lines traverse hard rocks.

It requires some previous information, or an acquaintance with these lines where they are most distinct, to discover them at first sight at the point just mentioned. They are often so faint when viewed from above, as to be scarcely distinguishable on the face of the hills. In profile they are seen somewhat more easily; but they are always distinguishable from below, or in any position in which their breadth is foreshortened to the spectator's eye, when they assume the shadowy form of strong lines. We may here remark that in this place the lines are narrower than they are in many others, and that the declination of their surfaces from the horizontal plane is very considerable. Hence it is, that, coinciding in a great measure with the declivity of the hill, they are only easily visible under the peculiar circumstances just mentioned.

This ground is rocky and irregular; the natural rock, which consists of gneiss, being visible in many places; while, in the rest of the glen, it seldom breaks through the surface; and in all such cases, wherever they occur, these lines are always least discernible; being, as in this place, less distinguished from the natural slope of the ground, and more narrow. The loose materials at this point consist of fragments that have descended from the hill, not of transported alluvia. This is rendered evident by their angular forms, and by their absolute identity with the natural fixed rock. Wherever any rock happens to interfere in the course of the lines, it interrupts them; or they are absent from that particular spot. It is evident in these cases that they have not been overwhelmed by rubbish or alluvia from the hills above, but that their absence is the result of the refractory nature of the materials in their course.

On the left side of the glen at this place, there are also seen two lines obscurely traced, but not visible on those projecting parts of the hill which are covered with alluvial matter. These correspond, both in level and relative distance, with the two on the right, as happens throughout the whole course of the valley. But besides these, some imperfect traces, or fragments of similar lines, are here seen at other levels—an appearance which is repeated also in some other places lower down.

In proceeding down the valley, we arrive at a river equal in size to the Roy, which it joins by a cascade rushing over a rocky bed. A great series of terraces here occurs, similar to those so frequent in the courses of Highland rivers, forming a large alluvium in the nature of a *terre plein* at the top of this glen. These are of different levels, and the highest of them is on a level with the third or lowest line of Glen Roy, yet undescribed. This principal one, however, declines by many successive stages of similar terraces; while

PARALLEL ROADS.

numerous smaller ones are also found descending down to the very bed of the river; skirting its banks, and accompanying its course. Here the bottom of the glen is an alluvial flat. In this place also is found one of the supernumerary lines just mentioned; appearing to be nearly intermediate between the first and second lines formerly described. These principal ones here continue their courses along the alluvial slopes of the declivities, where they also acquire their greatest breadth and distinctness.

Below this point, many great terraces become visible on the right hand; but although they do not correspond precisely in level with the third line, as that formerly described does, they do not materially differ in elevation. Many small rivers here enter laterally into the valley in several places; but it is unnecessary to mention them farther than to remark that, as in other places where no such remarkable phenomena are present, they are accompanied by their own lateral terraces. Still, as we here descend along the glen, many fragments or traces of lines are seen between the principal ones. These, however, are generally obscure, and have very short courses. In a very few places, it may also be observed, that, notwithstanding the pertinacious levels maintained by the lines, some slight errors in this respect exist. But when these are examined with care, they will be found not to affect the general question; as wherever they occur, they may be traced to the subsidence and derangement of that alluvial surface of the hill on which they were originally impressed. On the left side, about this place, one large slide may be observed which illustrates this opinion in a very distinct manner—the whole surface having descended for a space of many feet. Wherever also such appearances of a defective level occur, they will be found to arise from the laws of perspective, as they affect curved surfaces placed above or below the horizontal line.

When the faces of the hills are furrowed by descending torrents, the lines enter these cavities for a certain space; and as this rule is general, with few exceptions, it is unnecessary to mark the places where these occur. The fact, however, will hereafter be found of considerable importance in reasoning on the nature of these phenomena. They are often ploughed across and obliterated by torrents of recent origin; sometimes also they terminate abruptly in the beds of more ancient ones; but still the two upper ones may generally be very distinctly traced.

From these appearances, we can often determine the relative difference of age between the hollow or the torrent, and the line; and we may also ascertain that a part of one cavity is posterior to that mark, and another prior to it. It must also be remarked generally, that the lines are best marked on the straightest sides, or on those slopes which lie in a straight or slightly curved plane, and at somewhat high angles of acclivity; while they are most obscure where the most numerous sinuosities, torrents, irregularities, or rocky faces, occur. Among the best marked are the two upper ones on the right hand above Glen Turit, and the three above Glen Fintec on the same side.

About two miles below the head of Lower Glen Roy, a semicircular hollow opens on the right, giving rise to a considerable stream, and falling gradually into Glen Turit. The two upper lines enter a little way into the hollow, and then disappear: the third or lowest not having yet occurred. On the opposite side of this hollow, or that which adjoins Glen Turit, three lines are to be seen presenting the greatest anomaly visible

throughout their course. On a superficial view the two upper ones appear to be a continuation of those formerly mentioned; but on examining them by the spirit level, it was found that the lowest of these was continuous with the upper one of Glen Roy, and that the highest was a supernumerary one, and that it terminated abruptly at both ends, although of the same general form and appearance as the others. That one which is really continuous with the upper line of Glen Roy is prolonged into Glen Turit.

A great accumulated mass of terraces similar to those in the upper part of Glen Roy, is seen at the junction of the two streams which issue from Glen Turit, and from the unnamed hollow just described. This compound mass presents a surface of various heights; but the highest of these corresponds precisely in level with the highest terraces at the top of Glen Roy, and equally so with the lowermost line of the three for which this valley is remarkable. This line, indeed, now first comes into view distinctly; having for some time been imperfectly visible on the left side, but being here distinctly continuous on the right. The minor terraces which so frequently skirt the river are also visible here, and they accompany it for a considerable space downwards along the bottom of the glen, which still continues to present an irregular alluvial flat.

Independently of these compound and minor terraces which are accumulated below the lowest line, there are also fragments and parts of irregular terraces in various places at a level above it; besides considerable channelled alluvia, forming conoidal segments to the faces of the hills, and appearing to be the remains of more regular terraces that have been furrowed or partially destroyed by the mountain torrents.

Although the two upper lines are to be traced on the salient angle of the valley opposite to Glen Turit, they are interrupted and obscured to the very top of it. At this place, it is important to remark, the glen takes a turn so as to form a considerable angle; the opening of Glen Turit being not far from the re-entering one. At the salient angle the lowest line is first seen on the left side, as, on the right, it first occurs at the entrance of Glen Turit; into the wide opening of which it runs; together with the two upper ones, for a very short space; the whole of them speedily disappearing on this side of that glen; while, on the contrary one, the upper line runs with a well marked course till its career is interrupted by the gradual rise of the bottom of the valley.

Having at this part of Glen Roy arrived at the point where all the three lines on each side are visible, we must now remark, that there is a perfect correspondence of level between the opposite and corresponding pairs, wherever they are found. The few exceptions from anomalous or supernumerary lines were already noticed; and we may here observe that no other instances of these irregularities occur, from this point down to the termination of the valley of the Roy in that of the Spean. They are often absent altogether for a certain space, but wherever they are present they obey the general law.

The correspondence of level in question was ascertained by so many observations with the spirit level, as to leave no doubt of the truth of this fact; which is also a necessary one according to the view which we have taken of the causes of these appearances. It is by this regularity of horizontal disposition in the whole, and the continuity of the respective lines, that has produced that aspect of parallelism and regularity by which they are characterized, and to which their very peculiar effect is owing. This parallelism, it must, however, be obvious, is in the vertical plane only. On the horizontal one they cannot be parallel, because of the varying slopes of the hills or breadths of the valley, which place the corresponding ones at very different distances from each other in different places. This circumstance, it will hereafter be seen, is of importance as it regards one of the theories of their origin which has been given. It is unnecessary to give any nice account of these variations; but we may remark in a general way, that the nearest horizontal distance between the uppermost and nearest lines may be taken at 150 or 160 feet, and the greatest between the two lowermost and most distant ones at 1000; an approximation which is sufficiently accurate for any useful purpose.

Their vertical distances from each other form an important point in their history; and as they were measured by levelling, they cannot fail to be correct, as far as it is possible that they should be so, where the surfaces to be measured from are so irregular, so wide, and of a slope so much varying from the horizontal plane. The point for the level in these experiments was fixed in the middles of the lines, as a medium; and thus, omitting fractions, the distance was found to be 82 feet between the two uppermost, and that between the middle one and the lowermost, 212.

In conducting these experiments, observations were also made by the barometer, with as much care as could be bestowed on this object, for the purpose of ascertaining various other elevations connected with the due understanding of these phenomena. We need not detail the methods and precautions that were used; and as these measurements will often be referred to in the subsequent remarks on this spot, we cannot do better than give a tabular view of them in this place, as they are intimately connected with the relative vertical distances of the lines from each other. Even those which are not very immediately connected with this part of the subject, could not conveniently be omitted, as it is highly necessary towards a due appreciation of all the circumstances connected with them, to form a correct notion of the elevations of the adjoining country.

	Feet.
Upper line of Glen Roy above the western sea at Loch Eil,	1262
The same above the German Sea,	1266
The lowest line above the Western Sea,	976
The upper line above the land at Loch Oich,	1180
The lowest line above the same spot,	886
The upper line above the second of Glen Roy,	82
The second above the lowest,	212
The upper line above the junction of the Roy and the Spean,	927
The lowest line above the same place,	633
The upper line above the bottom of the glen where the Roy enters,	283
Height of the bottom of the valley at that place, above the lowest line,	11
Upper line of Glen Roy above Loch Spey,	13
The bottom of Glen Roy, at its upper end, above its bottom at the junction of the Roy and Spean; or its declivity,	644
Height from the junction of the Roy and Spean to the sea,	343
Upper line of Glen Gloy above the Western Sea,	1274
Difference of level between this line and the upper one of Glen Roy,	12
Height of Loch Spey above Garvamore,	294
Ditto above the German Sea,	1254
Height of Garvamore, or fall of the Spey, hence to the sea,	960
Depression of the eastern barrier of Loch Laggan below the upper line of Glen Roy,	304

We shall merely remark, that the only two very doubtful points in this table relate to the difference of level between the upper line of Glen Roy and Loch Spey, and the height of this last point above the German ocean. There are occasionally circumstances in the state of the weather which render it impossible to depend on barometrical measurements, when the stations of the instrument are far asunder; but whatever errors there may be here, they do not affect either the essential parts of the history of these phenomena, or the reasonings which will hereafter be deduced from them.

To return to the description of the valley. Having passed Glen Turit, the three lines now become distinct and well marked on the right side, where the hill is covered with a thick alluvium. On the opposite side, they are also distinct, although here and there slight marks of irregularity and of supernumerary lines occur. The bottom of the glen continues to exhibit an alluvial flat, for about three miles from the entrance of Glen Turit downwards; and the terraces which border the glen gradually disappear as its bottom contracts. A few interruptions occasionally occur, apparently connected with the rockiness and irregularity of the ground, and these are most remarkable on the right side; but shortly before the glen turns to the south, and till we arrive at Glen Fintec, all the three lines are strongly marked on both sides. They are particularly conspicuous on the slope of a brown hill about this place, on account of their continuity, their preservation, and the almost absolute equality of their dimensions, not only through the course of each individual line, but relatively to each other.

This circumstance also renders this part of the glen the most striking, particularly as it is seen from the south, or looking upwards; while the beauty of the picture is much enhanced by the picturesque disposition of this part of the valley. It is easy to account for this regularity, by the evenness both of the curvature and inclination of the slope of the hill on which they are marked, as well as by the form of its summit, which diverts the water courses in such a direction as to preserve this part of the hill from their action. This equality is an important feature; because it proves that the causes which produced these different lines have been similar and equal, and that the irregularities which occasionally occur are the result, not of irregularities in the action of the power by which they are produced, but of irregularities in the capacity of the ground on which that has acted.

At this place an elevated glen opens into Glen Roy on the right. No water enters from this glen, but the junction is formed by a dry plain, extending for some space, which, declining gradually in the opposite direction, carries its waters towards Glen Gloy, with which it also communicates. As the bottom of this glen is, at its entrance, at a higher level than the lowest of the lines, this latter is here interrupted; but the two upper ones enter it on each hand, and are continued for some way along its sides. It is unnecessary to pursue the course of this glen farther, as it adds no illustration to the subject; but it is proper to remark that, not only at the angles and curvatures of these lateral glens, but at the turns which the principal valley itself makes, the breadth and form of the lines is equal and similar everywhere, as well below as above the curvature.

About this place the breadth of the bottom of Glen Roy has been for some time reduced to an angle; the strath or alluvial flat, which characterized the upper part, having changed its character. The hills on the left side descend with various curvatures and irregularities, but the three lines continue well marked on them as far as Glen Glastric, on the north side of which they turn up for a short space, and then disappear. Below Glen Fintec, all the three are visible, as far as a stream which enters the Roy nearly opposite to Glen Glastric, and here the uppermost one disappears. The rapid fall of the Roy has now materially increased the vertical distance between the lowest line and the bottom of the glen. A material alteration also here takes place on the aspect of the sides of the glen, or of the including hills, and particularly on the right. A great range of deep alluvium is seen between Glen Fintec and Glen Glastric, the upper surface of which is not far beneath the lowest line, having marks of a level area continuous, but now much interrupted. This waste is owing to the action of mountain streams which have ploughed it deeply to the very river, producing a great range of semi-conoidal hillocks, similar to those mentioned as occurring in the upper part of the valley, but far more remarkable.

It is now necessary to say, that the alluvium at the top of the hill, which covers the sides of the hills, consist of sharp fragments, with a mixture of clay, precisely similar to that which occurs so generally on the declivities of mountains, and which, from the uneven nature of the fragments, and their identity with the rocks above, seems evidently to have resulted from the wearing down of the summits. But the terraces that are at the top of the glen vary in their materials; and though often composed of the same kind of sharp fragments that cover the general declivities, they also contain, as might easily be expected, various rolled and transported substances. The conoidal hillocks above-mentioned, and most of the terraces and hillocks that occupy positions much inferior to this, all along the course of the Spean, consist almost purely of transported materials. They exhibit, in their casual sections, deposits of sand, gravel, clay, and rolled stones, dispersed in a manner irregularly stratified, and inclining to the horizontal position, as is usual in similar cases elsewhere.

No traces of the lines are visible on the left hand, from Glen Glastric down the course of the valley, although no particular reasons for this deficiency can be observed, either in the form or nature of the ground; unless the gentleness of its shape may have had some share in this effect. There are no streams to which their destruction could be attributed; nor, indeed, can we properly consider the slope as the cause, as the very same lines occur again lower down, where the form and condition of the ground are exactly the same. Were it not that these lines occur at this lower point, we should, at first, be led to suppose that the action of the efficient cause had here terminated.

The upper line becomes also invisible on the right, opposite to this place, and shortly after, the whole disappear together on this side, although no material alteration takes place in the form or structure of the hills. About a mile before the junction of the Roy and Spean, the valley expands, and here the lowest line again makes its appearance, continuing its course round Meal Derig to the side of Glen Spean, where it disappears. The same line shortly after reappears on the right side, and hence it can be traced with more or less difficulty as far as Teindrish, over a various surface of very slight inclination, till it finally vanishes. At Keppoch, the Roy falls into the Spean, issuing from Loch Laggan, and here it loses its name; while the Spean holds its course westward for five or six miles till it falls into the Lochy.

4

Having thus examined the lines of Glen Roy, it is necessary to turn our attention to those found in Glen Spean.

On the left bank of this river, near the junction of the Roy, a line is visible, which was found by the spirit-level to correspond with the lowest line of Glen Roy. It runs about three or four miles down the valley, over a surface of moderate inclination, yet though the curvature and structure of the opposite hills which bound the Spean are similar, it is not always found on the other bank. It continues to hold its course westward, with more or less obscurity, from the junction of the Roy and the Spean along the declivities of the high mountains, Ben na 'Chlianach, Scuir Rinish, and Carn Derig, which bound this wide valley to the south, finally disappearing opposite to Teindrish, and nearly in the meridional direction. The valley here is of such dimensions that the opposite lines are about four miles asunder. Its bottom is extremely irregular, offering rather an accumulation of low hills than a valley properly so called. But in no place does the altitude of these low hills rise above the level of the lowest line, a fact which it will be necessary to keep in mind when we inquire into the causes which have led to the formation of these. It is also necessary to remark that through this wide and irregular space there are no streams of any note, but that the whole is drained in a manner almost imperceptible into the only river which traverses it, namely, the Spean. The opening of this valley is wider than its mean dimensions, since it gradually loses itself in the great valley of the Lochy, a part of the Caledonian Glen, which, forming a wide plain, at length terminates in the Sea, at Loch Eil.

On the north side of this part of the valley of the Spean, or on its right bank, the lowest line of Glen Roy can also be traced with more or less difficulty, round the hill of Bohuntine, which forms the angle that separates the low valleys; entering Glen Collarig, and proceeding round the base of Ben y Vaan, when it at last disappears, as nearly as possible on the same point with respect to the meridian as that on the southern side which runs along the skirts of Ben Nevis.

Near Craig Dhu, forming the angle at which Glen Roy turns round eastward into Glen Spean, the entrance of this latter valley is much contracted, and the opposite sides are steep. The hills here are not a mile asunder; but farther up they recede considerably, while their elevation also apparently diminishes. The whole length of this valley, from the point under review, to the pass of Mackull at the eastern end of Loch Laggan, is about twenty miles, including that lake, which occupies about half this space. This pass, which we formerly mentioned in the table of altitudes, forms the summit level for the waters which here flow east and west; and if our computations from the comparisons of different measurements are correct, its highest point is about ten feet above the level of the lowest line of Glen Roy, which is the one that extends up this valley. We had no opportunity of making an actual measurement of it, and have reason to think that this distance is overrated, a circumstance not to be wondered at from the circuitous mode of computation by barometers, to which we were compelled.

The mountains on the north side of Loch Laggan, are in some places of a moderate acclivity, but in a few they rise suddenly to a considerable height. Though

Description of Glen Spean.

Parallel
Roads.

not high on the south side, they are bold and rocky to the water's edge, which is indeed the general character of the sides of the lake everywhere. After the Spean issues from the lake, its course is gentle for about two miles, and through an alluvial bottom. After that it receives the water of Gulbran, and then that which runs from Loch Treig. After its union with the last, it becomes skirted with alluvial terraces, similar to those already described in Glen Roy, at various distances from its course, and in one place inclosing a considerable plain. Where this plain terminates by the approximation of these terraces below, the river enters a deep and rocky ravine; after which it again passes through another plain, similar to the former, to be again contracted lower down; and, near the mouth of this part of Glen Spean, or the upper and proper valley of that river, by another rocky interruption, through which it escapes in various falls, of which that of Munessie is the most remarkable. Shortly after this it joins the Roy, as formerly described.

Now, the lowest line of Glen Roy, which passes round Craig Dhu, runs up the valley of the Spean, but interruptedly, along its right bank, or on the north side, and so along the shores of Loch Laggan, even round its upper extremity. Near the lake it is elevated to a very small distance, not exceeding a few feet above its waters; and when it meets the alluvial terrace near the exit of the Spean, it coincides with many of them, as some of the lines of Glen Roy have been shown to do with the terraces in that valley.

From this it may be traced in a similar manner, and at the same level, along the south side or left bank of Loch Laggan and of the Spean; entering into the wide mouth of the valley that brings down the water of Gulbran for a short space, and still more perfectly and extensively into that of the Treig, which we shall presently describe. Tracing it from this place, we are conducted towards the hills formerly described under the skirts of Ben Nevis, where its existence and course have already been mentioned.

Description
of Loch
Treig.

The length of the valley of the Treig, from its exit to the lake, is about two miles, and the lake itself is supposed to be about four in length. This is a very romantic spot, and the shores are bold and rocky, and interspersed with scattered birch. The course of the water of Treig is rapid; and near its junction with the Spean, it runs through a deep ravine, forming many falls. The line which we formerly mentioned, as entering this valley, may be traced round the lake, and so down on the opposite side, till it again meets with that which properly belongs to the Spean; and throughout this course it is sufficiently well marked to permit of no doubt. In one place, a small insulated hill, called Tom na Fersit, with a double summit, near the end of the lake, rises so high as to permit the line to be marked upon it all round. In concluding this account of Loch Treig, we need only farther remark, that the line is very obscure on the eastern side, and is easiest seen on the western, and at the northern and southern extremities.

Description
of Glen
Roy.

It remains to describe Glen Roy. The general direction of this valley is about north-east, and its length is nearly eight miles. It opens into the Great Caledonian Glen, as we formerly observed, so as to pour its waters into the middle of Loch Lochy, passing by the village called Lowbridge. The hills by

Parallel
Roads.

which this valley is bounded approach so near, and the bottom of the Glen is so narrow, that in general it merely leaves room for the passage of the river. They are also very steep, particularly near Lowbridge. At about three miles upwards from its mouth, it is joined by Glen Fintec, of which the part concerned with Glen Roy was formerly described, and this little valley discharges itself into the water of Gloy. Farther above this its course is somewhat tortuous, and here it terminates after a time, by joining with Glen Turit formerly mentioned, through the intervention of which it communicates with Glen Roy.

The bottom of Glen Gloy rises rapidly to the place where it joins Glen Turit, so that it may in some measure be divided into an upper and lower valley, the upper standing at a considerably higher level than the lower. It is here that the Gloy, coming down through a deep ravine from the southern mountains, joins another in an opposite direction; their united waters forming the stream which we had traced thus far upwards from Lowbridge. But we must yet mention respecting Glen Turit, that which was deferred to this place as the account of Glen Roy. It forms a communication, as we have seen, between this valley and Glen Gloy, in such a manner that its waters are discharged on both sides. When it falls into Glen Roy it is at so high a level as to exclude the lowest of the three lines. But traces of the two upper ones enter its mouth, on the right hand side of which, (according to the course of the water) they speedily and suddenly disappear. But on the left, besides a short trace of the second, a line is to be seen, extending for the space of a mile or more, on a level with the upper one, until it is cut off by the rising of the bottom of the Glen. This line is very strongly marked; its breadth being not less than seventy feet, and its horizontal inclination being likewise very small. It is important to notice that the opposite sides of Glen Turit are very similar both in shape and composition, although so unequally marked by the lines; and it is also essential to remark, that the bottom of this glen is of solid rock, and not of alluvial formation. It will be important to remember, in the course of the following examination, that the operation of ordinary causes tends to diminish, not to augment its height.

Where this solitary line disappears in consequence of the rising of the bottom of the glen, a level space occurs without any stream; but shortly afterwards we meet with one running westward to join the Gloy, as already described. The bottom of Glen Turit may therefore be considered as a hill interrupting the communication, which might otherwise take place at an inferior level between Glen Roy and Glen Gloy. If the upper line of the former, and that of the latter were on the same level, that communication would have been formed by means of these. Respecting this we must now inquire.

On entering Glen Gloy from Lowbridge, no trace of a line can be perceived for about three miles. The marks of three then become visible in the salient angle of a green hill on the left bank of the stream, but the upper and lower soon terminate, while the middle one continues for some way up the valley. On the right side of the stream, opposite to Chew, a very strongly marked line occurs, and this may be considered as the only one which prevails in Glen Gloy, being continued with occasional obscurities and interruptions up to its extremity on both sides. Where it meets the higher part of the glen that is connected with Glen Turit, it sweeps round it, being dilated into one place into a considerable plain, analogous in its nature to the terraces occurring in other situations in the course of these lines. Between this and the lines of Glen Turit, there is a blank space of about three or four miles.

We need not trace the details of this line more nicely, as they convey no useful information. The only remaining point of importance, is, to inquire respecting the height of the line of Glen Gloy, which, on a general view, would be esteemed to correspond with the upper one in Glen Roy. From the fact that all the levels of Glen Roy, Glen Spean, Loch Treig, and the smaller communicating valleys, are continuous, it would be a natural conclusion that the same rule held good for Glen Gloy, and that all these valleys had originally formed part of one lake. This is, however, doubtful, or more. By our own barometrical measurements, it appears that the line of Glen Gloy is 12 feet higher than the uppermost of Glen Roy, and we had no opportunity of examining it by the level. Mr. Maclean's measurement, however, by the level, gave exactly the same difference; so that, however inclined to think otherwise, we are perhaps bound to believe our own observations, thus confirmed. It will hereafter be seen how much depends on their truth or falsehood.

On the na-
ture of the
parallel
roads or
lines.

We have thus described, at sufficient length, all the chief details which relate to the forms of these glens, their communications, and the disposition of the lines; but it is now necessary to give some account of their nature. This is the more requisite, as the idle question respecting their artificial origin depends very much on their form and construction.

Their extreme breadth may safely be taken at seventy feet, or a little more, and their most general one lies between that and fifty. They seldom exceed the former, or fall short of the latter dimensions. The most remarkable exceptions of this nature have been mentioned in describing the upper part of the glen; and our readers will recollect, that they were said to be always least marked on the most rocky ground. In these situations, indeed, they cannot, with the least propriety, be called roads, since they are absolutely invisible to a person standing on them.

In no case is their surface level; but it lies at various angles with the horizon, from thirty degrees and upwards, to ten or twelve. This is the reason that they are so often invisible, or difficult to see; their own inclination coinciding so nearly with that of the slopes of the hills on which they lie. Both the interior and the exterior angles are very much rounded, and the surfaces are marked by considerable inequalities, from the fall of stones, and the partial accumulation of plants and recent soil. If we were to describe their relations to the sides of the hills without the aid of figures, we would say that they resembled the sections of parallel layers applied in succession to their declivities. In only one instance we observed a slope, or superior *talus*, which was visible for about half a mile; but no marks of an inferior one were observed, as should happen if they had been roads formed by digging in the alluvial covering. As to their materials, they necessarily consist of the alluvia that happen to be present, whether these be sharp or round; and this is, therefore, a part of their history which can prove nothing respecting their causes, as some have vainly imagined, since, whether the produce of nature or art, they must have been formed out of the materials that were present.

It remains yet to say a few words respecting the communications of these glens with the surrounding country and with the sea, a subject on which we only touched at the beginning of this description. We remarked that the wide valley which forms the joint opening of the glens of the Spean and the Roy into the great Caledonian valley, was marked by an irregular bottom, interspersed with low hills, not rising to the height of the line which is continued on both sides of it. It would have been more correct to say, that there are some trifling exceptions to this rule, as we determined by levelling. The Spean falls into the Lochy through a deep ravine, well known by the wild scenery about Highbridge; but there are no other streams of any note in this tract. The opening of Glen Gloy is narrow, and its communication with the Caledonian valley is at a level somewhat higher than that of the former, as it falls into Loch Lochy.

Parallel
Roads.

On the ge-
neral com-
munication
of these
valleys
with the
sea.

The highest level of the Great Valley, already said to be 94 and 90 feet from the two seas which it joins, is at Loch Oich. This valley receives various other streams at different places; from Loch Eil, Loch Arkeig, and numerous smaller glens; while, on the northeastern declivity, it is the receptacle of the waters of Loch Garry, Glen Morison, Fyers, Glen Urquhart, and others of less note. Thus its highest level is inferior by 886 feet to the lowest line of Glen Roy and Glen Spean, and, to the uppermost, by 1180; taking the height of this above the sea at 1262 feet, as determined, for want of better means, by the barometer. The glens which communicate with this great valley are chiefly seated on the western side, and the principal ones are Glen Morison, Glen Urquhart, Glen Garry, and the valley of Loch Eil.

Though we have no means of determining this point properly, we have reason to think that the four first of these branches rise at their western ends to levels higher than those of the lines in Glen Roy. It is fortunate, however, that this point is not a material one in considering the phenomena of Glen Roy, as these would have been nearly the same, though these valleys had never existed. But the glen of Loch Eil requires some further notice, as it is probably implicated in the consequences which follow one of the theories that has been proposed for the explanation of these appearances.

The valley of the Spean, and that of the western branch of Loch Eil may be considered as opening together into the great Caledonian valley by one common wide mouth, while the southern branch of Loch Eil lies in a valley comparatively narrow, formed by the skirts of Ben Nevis on one side, and the hills of Ardgowan on the other. A valley of a dead level extends to the head of Loch Eil; and being little higher than the loch, it is of course elevated but a few feet above the sea, of which this water forms a branch. From the head of this valley a gentle rise conducts to Loch Shiel, a fresh water lake, which occupies a narrow prolonged valley that at length descends by a gentle declivity towards the sea at Loch Moidart. As the lowest of the lines of Glen Roy is 976 feet above Loch Eil, there can be no doubt that Loch Shiel is far inferior to this, though its exact height is unknown. Considering these circumstances, therefore, if, in the present state of the country, water were raised to the level of the lines of Glen Roy, it would communicate with the sea at Loch Moidart, as well as at Loch Eil and the Murray Frith.

In returning now to the head or eastern communication of Glen Roy and Glen Spean, we shall first notice the former, where we before omitted any thing essential to these general views. That line which occurs in the upper part of this glen, we consider to be the same as the uppermost in Lower Glen Roy. The author whom we formerly mentioned, Sir Thomas Dick Lauder, imagines it is the second; nor do we pretend to decide on what is, perhaps, not very material. However that be, it is some feet elevated above the source of the Spey, which, as we have seen, forms the summit level for the eastern and western waters; so that if water were now accumulated to the height of this line, it would also flow eastward, yet only to a very small depth.

The eastern outlet of Loch Laggan was already noticed. The barrier of low rocks, and a plain of nearly four miles in length, separate it here from the valley of the Spey, and this plain conducts a sluggish stream into that river at a point about ten miles from its source. The observations formerly made respecting the small differences of elevation of this barrier above the line that surrounds Loch Laggan, and which is the lowest of those in Glen Roy, show, that if water were now accumulated in Loch Laggan to a height much greater than that of the line that attends the Spean, it would tend to flow out at the eastern as well as the western extremity. If accumulated to the same height as that in which it is supposed to have stood in Glen Roy, it would have an equal tendency that way, nearly from the highest to the lowest line, or for a vertical space or depth of near 390 feet. Thus its issue in this quarter, if all these valleys once communicated, would be far more complete, supposing it had taken place at all, than by the level of the source of the Spey.

Such are the communications which these glens have with the surrounding country, and through that with the sea. They are of importance in investigating the causes of the phenomena under review; nor could the important geological consequences that may be deduced from them have been discovered or explained without considering these extended connections. We may now here terminate this minute description—a description justified as well by the singularity and extraordinary nature of the facts, as by the difficulty of apprehending all their relations and dependencies without such details. We shall, therefore, proceed to examine the several theories that have been brought forward on this subject; giving to some of them an attention which they do not merit on account of their probability or ingenuity, but which will render the general subject more intelligible, and place the geological parts of this question in a more satisfactory point of view.

Theory of
the High-
landers,
which con-
siders these
lines as ar-
tificial.

We already gave an authentic account of this theory from the best authority, that of a resident minister, Mr. Ross. The arguments used to prove either that they were made by Fingal and his followers, or by certain kings of Scotland who lived in Inverlochy Castle, are of two kinds. They are derived from supposed traditions, and also from certain physical or supposed artificial appearances, in the *Parallel Roads* themselves.

It can scarcely now be necessary to return to the much discussed question respecting the age of Fingal. But whatever opinion we entertain on this subject, we cannot see that the least stress is to be laid on those traditions which give names to the hills derived either from the great hero himself, from his friends, or from his dogs. All over the Highlands this fashion is universal, as we formerly remark-

ed. In Glenco, in Glen Lyon, in Morven, Mull, Staffa, Sky, Glen Almond, Arran, and in many other places, even as far as the Carron, we find the same names bestowed on similar objects, and the same traditions; while the very tombs of many of these warriors are pointed out in so many places that they must have possessed the property of ubiquity in death as well as in life. Such traditions know not where to stop, and can never be considered as an argument for any theory of the parallel roads.

The next class of persons to which the *Parallel Roads* are attributed, are certain kings who resided in very ancient times at Inverlochy Castle. Now, in times thus distant, it is very certain that the Highlands had no distinct kings. They were disunited from the proper and only kingdom, that of the Picts, in early times. After that they fell in equal degree under a Norwegian government; some great families or chiefs still maintaining their independence on the mainland. Next they formed various independent states, of which that of the Macdonalds was the chief; and lastly, they were multiplied or broken down into the clans who have descended almost to our own days; having been, down to a late period, almost as independent of the Scottish crown as they were of each other.

The residence of such kings at Inverlochy, is by no means established. The antiquity of this building, as we shall presently show, is not high; and the other traditions respecting it are equally absurd. It is said that it was once the seat of Bancho, the traditional head of the Stuart race, and that a league had been signed there by Charlemagne and Achaius, about the end of the eighth century. But it is well known from authentic records, that Bancho was not the head of the Stuart family. The history of the treaty between Achaius and Charlemagne has been proved to be a mere fiction. Nor was it possible that Bancho, had he existed, could have been a Thane of Lochaber. There were no Thanes in Lochaber, for the plain reason that it was not at that remote period under the dominion of the Scottish kings.

There seems little doubt that the building of Inverlochy Castle must be referred to the Cummins, who had large possessions in this country before they suffered by the parts they took in the troubles of that day. They were at the height of their power before Bruce gained the ascendancy; and every thing in the style of this castle marks the age of Edward the I. as it does that of the wealth and power of those who erected it. The western tower is still called Cummin's tower.

The castle itself is a quadrangular structure, occupying an area of about 1600 yards; and, like Harlech, and many others of the same class of buildings of Edward's time, it consists of four curtains, with flanking towers at the angles. The height of the curtain is from 25 to 30 feet, and that of the towers from 40 to 50. The scarp extends to a distance of 12 feet from the foot of the wall, and the whole is surrounded by a moat, once wet, of 40 feet in breadth. It has two principal gates, one on the land side, and another which appears to have extended to the water. There are also sally ports, and loop holes, in the towers; some of the latter being designed to cover the entrances, and others to flank the curtain. The remains of a drawbridge are also visible. It is impossible to mistake the age of a building of this kind, as the history of our military antiquities is too well known; and the circumstances which we have now described serve to show that Inverlochy Castle cannot be of a higher antiquity than that which we have assigned to it. Thus much for traditions.

With respect to the arguments from their form, materials, or appearance, we may first remark, that they are deficient in all the qualities which a road requires; neither possessing the forms nor the dimensions, nor tending to any possible point or purpose. We formerly observed, that they were broadest and most perfect where the hill was covered with loose alluvial matters; and that they could scarcely be traced where the ground is rocky. Had they ever been roads, they should have exhibited superior performance in the most durable materials. The effects of time will not explain this, since that which merely diminished the hardest should have obliterated the softest.

In other respects, they bear no resemblance to roads, nor to any work of art, as we may be satisfied by examining their profiles. There is no inferior talus, which there should have been in this case; and in only one small spot is there any trace of a superior one. No time could have destroyed these indications without obliterating the lines altogether; whereas, as we have already seen, they often preserve a breadth of 70 feet, an unusual dimension for roads. Neither, in any one instance, is the surface level, as it should have been had they been roads. The lowest inclination observed was twelve degrees; and more generally they vary from twenty to thirty; a condition of things impossible had they originally been level as any thing in the nature of a road must have been. Of the futility of attempting to ascertain their nature in this respect by examination of their materials, we have already sufficiently spoken; nor should we indeed have thought it necessary to notice it, any more than to have argued this point at so much length, had we only been to engage with the traditions and opinions of the natives. But, as this theory was adopted by Professor Playfair, and partly from this very kind of examination, it became our duty to notice these circumstances.

Their capricious arrangement, if considered as works of art, is equally an argument against the notion of their having been intended as roads. Equally impossible is it to assign any reason for their numbers, when no obvious purpose is held out, or for the various irregularities to which they are subject; or, lastly, for the extraordinary range of ground which they cover. It is almost superfluous to add to these, the uncalled for nature of an arrangement so rigidly mathematical, although it were possible to admit, which it is not, that the engineers of these days could have constructed works which, for their difficulty and expence, would alarm even those of our own times. Lastly, we may add on this head, that they are everywhere interrupted by torrents, yet are deficient in bridges, or the traces of such buildings, without which their purposes must have been entirely defeated.

As it is thus plain that they could not, at any rate, have been roads of communication, it has been said that they were constructed for the huntings of these imaginary heroes or kings. Those who have discovered this solution, seem to be less acquainted with the chace of the deer than a Highlander ought to be. They could have been of no use, either for the purpose of deer-stalking, as it is called, or for watching and shoot-

ing them in their passage. The reasons must be apparent enough to all those who either are acquainted with this variety of the chace, or will bestow a thought on the subject; nor is it worth our while to enter on them more particularly.

To get rid of this difficulty, it is said that they were used as a decoy, and that they were staked in on each side, so as to prevent the deer which had once entered from escaping. That such stakes should have been preserved for so many centuries, is not one of the least wonderful facts. This notion is, indeed, too absurd to deserve a serious examination, and seems to have been the last effort of those who were driven from all their other holds. Fortunately there are the remains of a real decoy for deer, still existing in Rum, which seems to have consisted of two stone walls, commencing in the hills, and gradually contracting till they terminated in a tall circular enclosure, in which the deer were at length confined and killed. The superfluous number of parallel roads for any purposes of this kind, as well as their mathematical arrangement, need scarcely be added to the preceding objections to a theory so very preposterous that we almost repent having bestowed so much time on its refutation.

Having thus got rid of all artificial causes, we must turn our attention to the discovery of natural ones, and these must obviously have consisted in the action of water in some manner. We think, ourselves, that the mode of action of this cause can be assigned with great certainty; although we have not succeeded in explaining all the circumstances requisite to its action, or the exact nature of the consequences which have attended it. But as other views, different from ours, have been entertained by some philosophers, and as these are attended with geological consequences of some interest, we shall give an account of these, together with the objections by which these theories are invalidated.

As Mr. Playfair considered these parallel roads to be really artificial works[*], Sir James Hall attributed them to his favourite system of debacles. Having remarked that, where a torrent hurries along mud and stones, it leaves their traces at the highest point of its past elevation, so he imagined that the lines of Glen Roy were the traces of huge deluges, or torrents on a larger scale, which at different elevations had held their courses through this and the adjoining valleys. Lord Selkirk, on the other hand, who visited them about the same time with the two last named philosophers, though he also, like Sir James Hall, considered them owing to the action of water, conceived that they had been produced by the gradual operations and descent of the rivers, which, in cutting their way downwards, and shifting their positions laterally, had left these traces. Thus he considered them as of the same nature as the terraces so generally formed on the margins of rivers; while, from the frequent coincidences of both these appearances in Glen Roy itself, he considered this opinion as fully established. In Dr. Macculloch's theory, the lines are considered to be the shores of lakes which once occupied those levels, and their present appearances are attributed to the drainage of these lakes at different intervals of time. We shall examine the arguments that relate to these different opinions.

In examining the hypothesis which attributes them to

[*] In consequence of having seen in the Vallais, near Brieg, in 1816, what he conceived to be analogous phenomena, Mr. Playfair afterwards regarded the parallel roads as aqueducts, by which the streams that descended over the face of the mountains were conveyed laterally, for the purposes of artificial irrigation. This opinion, contained in a letter to James Jardine, Esq. was read, by Mr. Playfair's desire, to the Royal Society of Edinburgh. EDITOR.

Parallel
Roads.

Examina-
tion of the
first theory
by which
these phe-
nomena
are attri-
buted to
water.

debacles or large torrents, we shall pass over any in-quiries about the general principle, and grant, what we have some doubts of, that such phenomena have been general or frequent. We must here recall the general disposition of these lines to our readers, that they may the easier understand the following arguments. They are found in Glen Roy, at its eastern extremity, com-mencing near that summit which is the common ori-gin of the Spey and the Roy, the one running east-ward and the other westward. In their progress to the west, they increase in number, and in the perfec-tion of their forms and markings, maintaining the same level throughout; while the bottom of the val-ley descends with a rapid declivity to its junction with that of the Spean. One of these lines, the low-est, ascends the valley of the Spean, surrounding Loch Laggan, and entering into Glen Turit, and fi-nally terminating in the broad common valley of the Roy and Spean, on the south side, as it does on the north also; the former being continuous with the same line on the one side of Glen Roy, and the latter being, in the same way, a prolongation of the other. The upper lines of Glen Roy enter partially into Glen Turit, as well as into other smaller ramifications of the principal valley, and one line is also found occupying a similar position in Glen Gloy.

Three distinct torrents would be required to pro-duce the three lines of Glen Roy alone, and these must be conceived as flowing from the east toward the west, as the difficulties that attend the contrary suppo-sition are even greater than those involved in this one. The causes of these debacles are conceived to arise in elevations of the land during former periods of the globe. To simplify this as much as possible, let it be supposed that there was but one line, and that in Glen Roy only. The imaginary wave, or mass of water, must therefore have flowed from the highest land, or the source of the Spey, in which case it ought to have flowed to the east as well as the west. But here there are no traces of any thing analogous to the lines in question. Nor could such a torrent have produced even the first line in Glen Roy. A mass of water re-quisite to fill the whole valley for its course of near twenty miles, must have stood at a considerable height at the summit level, and could not consequently have left its traces so very near to that as we find the pre-sent line near Loch Spey to be. The very hypothesis supposes these lines to have been formed at the mar-gin of the surface of a fluid in motion, nor could they have been produced under water.

If, under its simple form, this hypothesis is thus untenable, the difficulties are incalculably increased when it becomes necessary to adopt a series of such causes, or a succession of three similar waves at given distances of time, producing similar effects under such an inequality of circumstances. Although a more general and distant origin for the supposed diluvian wave were assumed, the same sort of difficulties occur; since the obstruction to its course, formed by the ele-vated ground of Loch Spey, would equally interfere with the wished-for effects. If the following further arguments are not absolutely necessary to the subver-sion of this ill-grounded hypothesis, they are interest-ing in a geological point of view.

As the lines, in many places, enter into the furrows which torrents have made in the hills, it is plain that many changes of the surface had been produced be-fore these singular marks were impressed on them, or the torrents at least had flowed in the same channels they do now, and that during a long lapse of time. Now, the formation of the beds of these torrents is thus shown to be prior to the lines; whereas, had these latter been caused by that general subversion of the crust of the globe to which the debacles are attributed, that could not have been the cause, nor could they have preserved their forms during disturbances of such enormous extent.

It is a supposition very improbable, that three cur-rents should have been propelled at different periods, and consisting of different masses of water, with forces so equal as they must have been to have produced effects so similar; neither does this hypothesis ac-count for the supernumerary lines, which, on such a view, could not possibly have taken place. The state of the alluvia in different places where these lines occur, offer another objection. In the upper or higher parts these are formed of the sharp untransported ma-terials of the hills, while, at lower points, they consist of rounded matters, sand, and gravel. Now, the ma-terials transported by a deluge must have been every where similar, and every where rounded alike. Nor is there any reason why such deposits should not have been formed on the rocky and hard ground as on the soft surfaces, since the inclinations of the hills are so often similar.

It is, further, a striking objection to this hypothesis, that the thickness of these lines, or alluvial deposits, are not affected by the angular turns of the valley, or its deviations from a direct line. A current thus charged with gravel and stones, flowing along a chan-nel thus bent, must necessarily have different impres-sions on the salient and re-entering angles at every flexure. The former, it is plain, must undergo the greatest change from the action of the water on the side opposed to the current, than on that which de-clines from it. The same effect will take place at the re-entering angle, but in a reverse order; and here also the deposit will be least on the side which op-poses the stream. But if the current should have con-sisted of water alone acting on an alluvium previously deposited, the effects would be contrary. The lines in this case would be most strongly traced where the ac-tion of the stream was most powerful, as in the other they would be best marked where least exposed to it. Similar effects would be found wherein the lines enter into the furrows of the hills; yet, as we have seen, no regard is paid to this in the disposition and forms of these, and that, under all these varying circumstances, their characters are consistent. The *cul de sac* former-ly mentioned at the head of lower Glen Roy, could, on this principle, have shown no traces of these lines.

The argument from the nature of Glen Fintec and Glen Turit is somewhat similar. The bottom of the former is so high as to exclude the lower line; and that of the latter, at no great distance from its junction with Glen Roy, excludes the whole three. No current could therefore have flowed through them, so as to have produced the lines now marked on their sides; and the rocky nature of the bottom of Glen Turit proves that it has not been elevated since that period by any deposits of alluvial matter; the only supposition which could be opposed to this reasoning.

A general notion of the different capacities of Glen Roy in different places has already been given; but, to simplify this argument as much as possible, we shall assume the lowest line as its groundwork. This cuts the bottom of the valley near its upper extremity, so that there is a point at which the vertical depth of the supposed current is nothing. The breadth of the valley in the same place is less than half a mile. But, at its lower end, or when it has joined the valley of the Spean, the breadth is near five miles, where the traces of this line are still visible, while its elevation above the bottom of the valley is not less than 800 feet. It must be superfluous to add to this statement, that no body of water could flow through such a valley so as to preserve a level surface, a condition requisite to the production of the line in question. We need not extend these remarks to the two upper lines, as, with some necessary modifications, they would be the same.

The case of Glen Spean presents other difficulties of its own; but we can suffer our readers to make the necessary application of the reasonings we have thus furnished. That of Glen Gloy is not less so. No current could flow from Glen Roy through it on account of the height of the bottom of Glen Turit already mentioned. None could have originated in it, nor could one have flowed from its entrance at Lowbridge towards the east, where the waters could have found no exit. We hold it quite unnecessary to pursue this unfounded hypothesis further, and shall therefore proceed to examine that proposed by Lord Selkirk.

This hypothesis presumes that the lines of Glen Roy and the neighbouring valleys are the remains of water terraces similar to those common in all alluvial straths. Such terraces are the deserted banks of the streams when they flowed at higher levels, and in different places; and their slopes and forms, resembling those of military works, are the produce of the actions of the rivers on them during their changes of place. At a distance from the sides of the hills their surfaces are flat, because they have formed part of the alluvial plain; while near these, their forms become combined with the slope of the ground.

As now the opposite lines of Glen Roy correspond at three several stages, it is plain that the action of the water to produce these effects on this system, must have consisted in cutting its way through an alluvial plain from the highest to the lowest of these stages, and so at length to the present bottom of this valley. Similar effects must have taken place in all the others that are connected with it. No set of alluvia less than this, occupying the sides of the hills on the entrances of lateral torrents, could have answered the necessary conditions; as there is no other case but that of a valley absolutely full to the highest level of any line that could have permitted the supposed river to have acted on both sides of it at such distances.

Now, if this *terre plein*, thus indispensable, be admitted, it is impossible that the lines should have acquired such an equality in breadth and appearance throughout their courses. The variety of ground which they occupy, and the unequal action which the water must have exerted on a set of terraces, the sides of which held an unequally angular direction towards its current, render such a supposition absolutely untenable. Neither could these lines have preserved this uniformity of breadth in all the sinuosities which they enter, as the very forms of these must have protected the original alluvia from the action of the river, and left, in these places, wide terraces.

The only appearance of argument on which this hypothesis rests, is the coincidence and continuity of the lowest line of Glen Roy, with the terrace at its upper end. It is not true, as has been said, that all the lines terminate alike in terraces. But the coincidence in

question proves nothing respecting the identity of the lines and the terraces; of which a very simple explanation will hereafter be given on different principles. In the mean time, we may remark, that various sets of them are seen in Glen Roy, and not those which only coincide with the lines. These are the consequences of the action of the present river, where they coincide most nearly with it; while those at higher elevations were produced by it when it held higher levels, as in all similar situations. A few are the consequences of the lateral streams flowing into the valley, and their positions are regulated by the former or present course of these.

It is admitted that the action of the present river flowing in that part of Glen Roy which has the character of a strath, does produce the abrupt forms of these terraces. But it would require circumstances utterly unintelligible, to permit a similar action, in former times, to have produced the lines, without having innumerable intermediate marks and terraces, as is the fact now wherever the river is working. As the action of water on a solid *terre plein* must have been gradual, these remains could not have been distinguished by such decided intervals. The consequences must have been the same in former times as they are at this day, which is by no means the case; nor is it difficult, on the next hypothesis, as we shall shortly see, to account for the few supernumerary and irregular marks of this nature formerly described. These, in fact, will be found chiefly in the vicinity of such torrents as have entered laterally into the valley when it was a lake. They are the remains of deltas or terraces resembling those now at the head of Glen Roy, and at the entrance of Glen Turit, which have been worn down by the action of water, and which have just the same sort of connection with the principal lines as those which now occupy the bottom of the valley. This explanation will be found to offer a solution for all the most remarkable of these cases, and very particularly for those at the entrance of Glen Turit.

It must not here be overlooked that their correspondence in altitude on the opposite side of the glen, is, on this hypothesis, perfectly unintelligible; implying a sort of regularity in the lateral wanderings of the river which is absolutely in opposition to the very essence of that action. A stream quits one side of a valley, because it finds a lower level on the other; so that opposed terraces, instead of being on the same level, are necessarily at different ones. Under this hypothesis, the lines traced round the *Cul de Sac* at the head of Glen Roy, could not have existed at all. This must have remained a solid mass of alluvia, as it is impossible that a river, under any circumstances, could have found its way into a recess of this nature. To these remarks we may add, that, in Glen Fintec, as well as in Glen Turit, there is a point of rest where no water could have flowed on any supposition, and where, nevertheless, the lines are as distinctly marked as in any part of Glen Roy, where it is supposed to have flowed freely.

The state of the surrounding country, as already described, is sufficient to prove that no river could have ever existed capable of producing the requisite changes. No river could have produced the line near Loch Spey, under any imagined former condition of the country, even had one existed; and that no river ever could have flowed in this manner, is perfectly certain, or it must have been there still. Long after this, where the Roy really begins, it is a feeble stream, utterly incapable of producing the effects in question. We think it quite unnecessary to pursue this inquiry any further. We need only add, that we have given it every possible advantage, by limiting these arguments to Glen Roy. Had we extended the same investigation to Glen Spean and Glen Gloy, it would have been only with the effect of accumulating objections of the same nature ; and, in some instances, even more insurmountable, if that be possible. We shall now, therefore, proceed to examine the hypothesis proposed by Dr. Macculloch, which attributes these lines to the drainage of ancient lakes, and which is so fully adapted to explain all the appearances, that it has set the question at rest for ever.

Examina-
tion of the
third theo-
ry, which
attributes
the parallel
roads to
water.

We admit that there are some difficulties, and of no trifling magnitude, which attend this supposition also ; but none of them are contrary, either to geological or mathematical laws, nor do they even approach to physical impossibility. Direct proof there can of course be none ; but, in cases like this, we can only reason at any time from analogies. At the same time, we may here make use of the argument by dilemma, to which we are reduced by the rejection of the former hypothesis. In reviewing the direct arguments in its favour, our readers will perceive that some of them must have been in a great manner anticipated in examining the former hypothesis, so that our details will thence admit of being somewhat the less particular.

The absolute water level which exists between the corresponding lines, whether in Glen Roy or the adjoining valleys, admits of a most ready and obvious solution, by supposing that these were once occupied by lakes, nor indeed can it be explained on any other supposition. Omitting Glen Gloy for the present, as a doubtful connection, we find that a free communication exists throughout the other valleys ; so that it is easy to imagine the water replaced in them in the same situation, at some one point, where they would form one intricate lake. The boundary of the surface of that lake would be the lowest line, which we have shewn to be the only one of which the extensive continuity can really be traced. That boundary is now, of course, deficient in this case, where the bottom of the valleys has an exit beneath that line, but this will be a subject for future consideration.

Now the lines in question must in all cases have formed the shores of this lake ; and as these are found at three distinct elevations in Glen Roy at least, it is plain that this lake existed in these different states, and that the relative depths of these three accumulations of water may be measured by the critical distances of these lines from the bottom of the valley ; allowing for such waste as the operations of the river may have produced since it was drained. The outline of this lake must, therefore, also have varied at these different elevations, as must the nature of its communication with the surrounding valleys. Without maps, we could not pretend to convey an idea of these variations and connections. From the certainty that the lake of Glen Roy thus occupied three different depths, the nature of the retaining obstacles becomes more intricate, as does that of the operations by which they must have been removed.

Now, in examining the correspondence of the phenomena in Glen Roy with the theory of a lake, it is necessary to clear away some imaginary difficulties from appearances that have originated in other causes. Those to which we here allude are the terraces. It was shown that the hills here were covered with a coat of sharp or untransported alluvium, appearing to be merely the ruins of the rocks above, and that, in other places, there was rounded alluvial matter deposited in such a manner as to indicate a transportation from places more distant. The same appearances take place in the other valleys. It was also shown that, in the lower parts of the valley, vertically considered, there were found terraces at different levels, and often with surfaces of considerable dimensions. These accompany the lateral entrances of the streams, and the principal junctions of waters ; and as they are necessarily proportioned to the magnitude and power of these, they are most considerable at the entrances of the Roy and of the waters of Glen Turit. At the upper end of the former glen, the most remarkable of these coincides with the lowest line, presenting a joint level continuously prolonged. In these places, they are still subject to the action of the river ; from which cause they gradually waste away and become diminished in their superficial dimensions. Thus also the lateral wanderings of the river multiplies their number, producing a numerous series at different levels, which accompany the course of the stream.

We may now examine how far all these appearances coincide with those which are found connected with existing lakes at the present day, and from this examination we shall see that the terraces are phenomena of an independent nature, or different from those which form the lines in question ; connected with, but not originating in, the same actions which produced these.

Where a lake is inclosed by hills of a considerable declivity, which, though formed of rock, is also covered with alluvial matters, we find it skirted by a gravelly shore, which forms an inclined plane, and constitutes a zone at the level of the water. This is of greater or less breadth, according to the declivity of the hill, the quantity of alluvial matter present, and other circumstances, by which these results are occasionally modified. When we examine such a lake by sounding, or when we enter its margin, we find that, after a short time, it deepens suddenly ; and, if the section is carefully examined by the sounding line, it will be found that the declivity from the point downwards resembles that of the hill above the water. The shallow zone is therefore a shore applied to the face of the hill, and not coinciding with its general outline.

If now rocks protrude into the water on the margin of a lake so situated, the shore in question is either imperfectly marked or altogether wanting ; these circumstances being regulated by the particular inclinations of these rocky points, and by other variations, which we need not here notice more minutely. Where the declivity is greatest, the shore is not only narrowest, but its inclination is also the greatest ; and, on the contrary, it is most level, and of the largest dimensions, where that is least. Where rivers enter the lake, there also terraces are found, which, at the water level, must necessarily coincide with the shores themselves ; and these terraces, or rather deltas, are of the greatest dimensions at the entrance of the principal stream, where, in progress of time, they even form extensive plains, so as at length to exclude the water.

Now we know not that we could have described any appearances more exactly coinciding with those of Glen Roy. If any one line and its terraces be traced, under all the modifications visible, it is in every point a perfect exemplification of this description of the shores of an existing lake. It is not, therefore, to be doubted, that, if such a lake were now to be suddenly drained, as we suppose Glen Roy to have been, it would have precisely the appearances which occur in that valley, as far, at least, as all the requisite conditions were present. The conditions which have thus led to the present state of Glen Roy, as far as regards the prolonged extent and uniform appearance of the lines, may be found in the regularity and general similarity of the forms of the including hills, in their uniform and rarely interrupted faces, and in the generally equal thickness of the alluvia by which they are covered. Whereever, indeed, these conditions are wanting, those very anomalies occur which we ought to expect on the theory thus laid down.

It is now proper to describe the manner in which the waters of a lake act in producing shores of this nature, as being the same in which the assumed waters of Glen Roy must have acted in producing its lines. This action consists, first, in the powers of the water in checking the further descent of the alluvial matters which are constantly descending from above. As these become immersed in the lake, they lose a very large portion of their weight by immersion, which, in winter, being often rendered still more buoyant from being entangled in ice, they are thrown back against the face of the hills by the incessant action of the waves. Thus they become spread along its sides, and often distributed in a very equable manner, producing an inclined shore, which is proportioned in breadth and declivity to the several circumstances already mentioned, and to the time during which this action has continued. This process may be witnessed in innumerable Highland lakes; and wherever there is a prevailing-lee shore in consequence of the course of the winds, it is rendered particularly conspicuous, from the superior action of the waves on that part. We might point out examples in so many places, that it is unnecessary to enumerate any, as they cannot be missed by those who will turn their attention to this subject. But we may here add that Loch Rannoch, which is especially exposed to westerly winds, displays an excellent example of the kind of lee shore just mentioned, at its eastern extremity.

The connection of the terraces of Glen Roy with an assumed lake, once occupying that valley, cannot now be a subject of much difficulty. The delta which we just noticed as attending the entrance of a principal stream into a lake, is produced by the same action of the waters as that which forms the shores, with the sole difference of its being exerted on a larger quantity of materials, of which also there is a perpetual supply. The joint action of the river and the waves continues to level these, until, by the growth of plants, and by detaining sand and clay in the time of inundation, they rise above the level of the water. Now, in Glen Roy, if we assume the lake to have stood at the level of the lowest line, or at its last state, it is easy to see that the present terraces at its upper extremity which coincide with that line, are the ancient deltas of the Roy, formed at the head of what may be called Loch Roy. The lateral ones, at similar elevations, are in the same manner, those which accompanied the entrance of the lateral streams into that lake.

But we must explain the cause also of their present abrupt declivities. Were a lake to be suddenly drained, its deltas would be found producing very gentle slopes, and far prolonged at their bases. But, after this operation, the river would then flow on the alluvial bottom, and would thus act on these deltas, so as to undermine and cut down their sides, just as they produce these effects on the alluvial bottoms of valleys,

where they shift their position as circumstances change. It is the present course of the Roy, in like manner, since the drainage of the lake, which has worn down the original deltas to their present forms; the various subsequent changes it has since undergone having in the same way generated the successions of smaller terraces that are found in the course of the valley. Thus have they not only acquired their present forms and dispositions, while in certain cases, where particularly exposed, they have entirely disappeared.

Thus much for the lowest state of the water in Glen Roy, as it relates to this question. Nor is it difficult to account for the absence of similar terraces at the higher levels, while the explanation itself tends to confirm the present views. The actual condition of the valley, it must be remarked, is essentially different from what it was after the two first subsidences took place which left the lines high impressed above the water. In both these cases, the bottom of the valley continued full of water, or was a lake, whereas after the last subsidence, it was entirely drained, and became dry land. It is evident that, under such circumstances, had any deltas existed at the two upper levels, they must have gradually been worn away by the action of the waters, for want of a sufficient resistance, whereas, on the final drainage of the whole, they were left in their original integrity, and exposed only to the gradual corrosive action of the river, which also by gradually lowering and changing its bed, must have shortly deserted them. Nor from the relative state of the lake, the hills, and the entering rivers, could any considerable deltas have been formed at the two upper levels. Still, though no conspicuous terraces are found at these higher levels, there are sufficient indications of them in many places; while, in all, they lie near the entrances of the torrents or rivers, so as to confirm the explanation which has here been given of their origin. By this we can also explain, as was formerly hinted, those appearances of supernumerary lines which occur in different places among the principal ones. These are the remains of such terraces, or deltas, undermined and demolished during the subsidences of the lake, from causes now sufficiently obvious.

Now, though we consider this theory as explaining not only the appearances in Glen Roy, but, with the necessary modifications, all those in the adjoining valleys, we are aware that there are some difficulties unexplained; and, as is but just, we shall here point them out. The chief of these are the deficiencies that occur in the lines in some places, when none of the more obvious causes of their absence, formerly noticed, can be traced. A few of them, indeed, as has already been shown, assist in proving the truth of this hypothesis; and it is not unlikely that, had we access to other phenomena of a similar nature, the whole of them might equally be explained. In Upper Glen Roy, as an instance of a difficulty there is only the part of one line to be seen, though there is nothing apparently in the nature or the form of the ground to prevent it from having been impressed every where. A considerable deficiency also of all the lines occurs towards the bottom of the lower valley, together with many partial ones in other places. The rocky nature of the ground, or the peculiarities of the slope, will not account for the whole of these; nor is it easy to trace marks of recent waste, by which they could have been obliterated. Similar difficulties occur in Glen Gloy and in Glen Spean. But these, however inexplicable they may yet be, are by no means sufficient to destroy, scarcely indeed to enfeeble a theory supported by so large and distinct a body of evidence; and we shall now therefore pass to another, and by far the most difficult part of this subject, to that, namely, which relates to the manner and place in which these lakes were retained during the periods at which they existed.

On the original state of Glen Roy and the adjacent valleys when occupied by water.

It has been shown, that the level of the upper line of Glen Roy is far higher than that of many of the valleys, or than much of the surrounding land which would now afford a passage to the waters of this ancient lake into the sea. No water could now therefore stand at that level, unless all these openings were obstructed, or raised to at least a higher elevation. The same holds good for the lower levels, whether in this valley or in that of the Spean. To determine the position of these barriers or obstructions is the first point necessary, and it is attended with no small difficulties; with difficulties indeed so complicated, that we cannot pretend to surmount them in our present limited state of knowledge respecting the former changes of the earth's surface. We shall first confine this inquiry to Glen Roy, as forming the principal picture. It is difficult enough here to understand the nature of this obstruction, or the former state of the ground; but that difficulty is much increased, when Glen Spean and Glen Gloy are taken into consideration.

It has been shown, that if water was accumulated as high as the uppermost line of Glen Roy, or so as to form the first Loch Roy, it would flow for a certain depth by the eastern extremity of the valley, or over Loch Spey to the eastward. There also, had it communicated at the lower extremity with Loch Laggan or Glen Spean, it might flow out at the eastern end of that lake, and that even till it had subsided to a far lower point, namely, to one not far removed above the level of the lowest line. But it would also flow, and that more completely than by the former route, into the Caledonian Glen through Glen Spean, so as to find its way into the Western Sea, either by Loch Shiel, Loch Eil, or Loch Ness, or by the whole of these openings. It is evident, therefore, that not only the condition of the present apertures of these valleys must have materially differed from the former one, but that all the adjoining country must have been different from what it is now. Every one of these apertures must at any rate have been closed by obstructions or barriers of some kind.

To attend, in the first place, to the eastern extremity; there is not much land required at Loch Spey, to elevate that point sufficiently to render it possible for water to stand at the highest level of Glen Roy, as far as this point is concerned. If there is any difficulty in accounting for the subsidence of this point, it is a mere trifle compared to the rest; nor need we dwell on it, as the loss of water by this aperture, should it have occurred, could have little effect as to the phenomena in general.

The question that relates to the eastern barrier of Glen Spean is far more difficult, if we suppose that Glen Roy and that valley formed a common lake at the highest levels. But as there are no traces of the two upper ones in this valley, there seems no necessity for adopting a supposition which only augments our difficulties. In the lowest condition of both they unquestionably formed one lake, because the lowest line is continuous through both. The two upper states of the lake may be supposed to have been confined to Glen Roy. If we were to adopt the opinion, that Glen Spean

and Glen Roy formed one common lake at the highest level, it is evident that the eastern barrier of the former, near the head of Loch Laggan, must have been much higher than it is now; namely, the difference, and somewhat more, between the highest and lowest lines, or 294 feet. Should such a supposition be adopted, it is plain that some considerable change must have taken place in the state of this barrier, and from causes which we have no means of assigning. But as the same difficulty exists in examining the western outlets, and as there is no occasion to multiply these, we think it a more safe conclusion that these formed the great exit of the confined waters, and that no very material changes have occurred either at the east end of Loch Spey or Loch Laggan.

If now we turn our attention to the western end of Glen Roy and Glen Spean, we shall find that they unite in one common valley, which communicates by a very wide opening with the great Caledonian Glen. Both Glen Roy and Glen Spean also bear the continuous marks of the lowest line, which further extends far down this common wide valley, to a point at no very great distance from where it loses itself in the great glen as it opens into Loch Eil. There has therefore been a lake at the level of the lowest line, common to Glen Roy and Glen Spean; and consequently the barrier by which it was confined, must be placed at a point at least beyond Teindrish, where this line ceases on both sides. Now, such are the nature and form of the ground, that it is impossible to imagine any such barrier placed here, without its occupying even the vale, or great flat of the Lochy. This is one of the first great difficulties that occurs in assigning the place of this obstruction, and it is possible that it ought to be removed to some point more distant. This should particularly be the case, if in Glen Gloy and Glen Roy the lines were on the same level, as these also should then have formed a common lake. But, respecting this point, it has been seen that there is yet some doubt.

Should the barrier in question have been thus distant, it must have happened that part of Glen Lochy should have been included in a common lake with Glen Roy. If also Glen Gloy is included, then that boundary must have lain to the north of the opening of this valley, and beyond the limits of Loch Lochy, which must of course have been included in this general lake. But when we attempt to determine the true point beyond Loch Lochy, we become entangled in insurmountable difficulties, nor is it possible to fix on one that will satisfy the requisite conditions.

If now we turn our attention to the southern or lower end of Loch Lochy, we find it terminating in a wide alluvial plain communicating by large openings with the sea at Fort William, and with the wide valley in which the western branch of Loch Eil lies. If it is necessary to select a place for a barrier here, and it is plain that under this view more than one is required, we should be led to chuse the narrowest part of this opening, which lies at Fort William, between the skirts of Ben Nevis and the opposite hills of Ardgowar. The aspect of the ground, the course of the waters, and the nature and disposition of the rocks, render it difficult to select any other point nearer to the opening of Glen Spean.

But as there is another free passage to the sea here through Loch Shiel and Loch Moidart, another barrier must be conceived to have existed in this place. This would imply one ancient lake, occupying Glen Roy, Glen Spean, Glen Gloy, the great Caledonian

Glen, from some unknown northern point to Fort William, Loch Arkeig, and the western part of Loch Eil, to some undefined point towards the Western Sea. This supposition rests on the probability of Glen Gloy having been included. If that is omitted, the extent of this imaginary lake becomes proportionably diminished.

One of the minor difficulties in this supposition, is the absence of water-marks or lines round those hills which include the valley of the Lochy, as these terminate even before Glen Spean joins it, and are found nowhere afterwards. That absence would not in itself, however, offer an unanswerable argument against this position of the supposed barrier; as, in so many other places, these lines are wanting where they must originally have existed. Nevertheless, those who are inclined to think otherwise, may, if they please, suppose that this barrier has existed somewhere about the place where the lines of Glen Spean now terminate. But, wherever this dam or obstruction did exist, it must, in the first instance at least, have given way suddenly, to permit the waters to quit the shore which forms the present line, however the remainder of it may have been worn away by subsequent operations. That no water remained long pent up after this first breach, is rendered probable by the absence of any lines beneath this lowest one. We must now return to Glen Roy, as far as it appears to have been independent of this larger lake occupying Glen Spean.

The complete and sudden transition from the first or uppermost to the second line of Glen Roy, and the similar transition from that to the lowest, show that Loch Roy had subsided at two different intervals, before that third and last subsidence which emptied alike the lake of Glen Spean. Now, as we already hinted, since no marks of these two upper lines are found in Glen Spean, and as it possesses no barrier to the east by which water could there have been dammed at this height, we need not suppose that it participated in this lake of Glen Roy at these two early periods. We must therefore discover a new barrier for this purpose at the west end of Glen Roy itself, on the supposition that at its two upper levels it formed a distinct lake, and that it only became united with the lake of Glen Spean at the lowest one, or after the second subsidence of its waters.

This, of course, must have existed at the very exit of Glen Roy, as the upper lines are both marked to no great distance from that point. This barrier, also, like the former, must have failed suddenly at two distinct and distant intervals. Neither could much time have intervened between these, otherwise the lines would have been less strongly marked. while intermediate ones would also have been found. We admit that by thus supposing two western barriers in different places, instead of one, the difficulties are increased; but this supposition is necessary on the foregoing view of the original state of Glen Spean.

It is proper to ask, to what causes the failure and disappearance of these barriers could have been owing; nor can we assign any, consistent with our knowledge of the actual revolutions of the earth in this place, but the corroding power of the streams issuing from these lakes; if indeed that will account for the apparent suddenness of the event, and the great decision of the intervals. Whatever causes may however have led to the first evacuations of these waters, the gradual action of the rivers on the surfaces of the ground since their drainage, is perhaps quite sufficient to account for the present appearance of the valleys

and the total disappearance of these ancient boundaries. It is possible also to conceive that these barriers might have been of such a nature as to have been suddenly broken down to the different levels by the mere weight of the water above them. Earthquakes and convulsions, as is usual on similar occasions among vulgar geologists, have also been suggested as the probable causes of these phenomena; and thus the failures of the barriers in question have been supposed to be connected with some imaginary convulsion which formed the Great Caledonian Glen. It is possible that some such event may in ancient times have separated these two parts of Scotland; but we are incompetent to reason to any purpose, where we have neither facts nor analogies to guide us. Whatever may be thought of this, it is scarcely possible that such an event should have taken place within that period, or rather those periods, which evacuated the waters of these lakes. Three such convulsions must have been produced, and these at immense intervals of time; as is indicated by the nature of the shores for each successive lake. Of such there is no probability; and most assuredly not within any period during which the present general state of the surface existed. Our present rivers, and our present alluvia, have been determined and modified to what they are now, since any great changes of this nature. Neither, if we imagine such a convulsion limited to the last failure of the barrier, could it possibly have occurred without entirely disturbing the condition of the surrounding country. More particularly, it must have disturbed the noted regularity of those appearances in Glen Roy which existed before it. This argument we think quite satisfactory against the opinion that attributes these events to earthquakes or convulsions, and therefore we shall dismiss this part of the subject.

Of Loch Treig, it is unnecessary to take any particular notice, as it is connected in the same train of reasoning as Glen Spean, of which it forms a part. But Glen Gloy still requires a few words, on the supposition that its only line is really elevated above the highest one in Glen Roy, of which we formerly expressed doubts, though shown to be so by our own observations. On this view it would require a separate barrier of its own, somewhere toward its lower extremity, as it must have formed an independent lake. One failure alone is also here requisite to answer the conditions, but we need not dwell longer on this subject. In concluding, we can only say, that though this part of the history of the ancient state of these valleys is thus beset with difficulties, we are compelled to admit the general principles, and must be for the present content to think that the foregoing views are just, however we may have yet failed in explaining all the details connected with these long past events.

Examination of the theory by which the lakes under review have been supposed to be connected with the sea.

The difficulties which we have thus stated relating to the nature of the barriers by which these lakes must have been retained, have led some persons to imagine a different mode by which the waters might have been kept at the requisite height, and by which they might afterwards have been drained. This hypothesis supposes, that the forms of the valleys have been always the same as they are at present, and that the imaginary dams or barriers were nothing else than the waters of the ocean.

If this be admitted, the lake itself must have been a portion of the sea; or Loch Roy and Loch Spean must

Parallel Roads.

have been sea lochs or friths, as well as the lake of Glen Gloy. The lines found in these valleys are therefore sea shores, or the action of the sea at different levels must have produced all the appearances which we have so minutely reviewed. It will not require much labour to examine into the truth of this opinion, as many of the arguments already used in refutation of some of the former hypotheses are equally applicable to this one.

We do not, in the first place, believe that the level of the sea has ever undergone such changes as this hypothesis would require. Even were we to admit, which we do not, that the elevation of the land above the sea has arisen from the subsidence of the latter, and not from the rising of the former, the present class of facts could not possibly be within the limits of those actions or that period of time; since they belong to that far more recent one which succeeded to these events, of whatever nature they were, and during which the present surface of the land acquired and maintained the forms it now displays. Assuredly the great revolutions that caused the present disposition of the sea and land, were long prior to the time in which Glen Roy and the neighbouring valleys acquired that permanence of form which is indicated by their phenomena of various kinds.

We as little admit that the level of the sea has undergone any appreciable changes since the time at which the present disposition of the land was determined. That the relative level of the sea and land has changed, and is occasionally changing, we do not deny. But, in many cases, as on the coasts of Italy, this has evidently arisen from the vacillations in the state of the land and its elevation, not in that of the sea. Slight changes also occur in certain seas or channels, from the gradual accumulation of materials on the bottom, but there are partial as well as trifling geologists, who, while they talk with ease about alterations of the level of the sea, as if it was the simplest of operations, forget that this cannot happen in any one place without affecting the whole ocean; and they forget also that such changes necessarily imply the destruction or generation of whole oceans, and these often within short periods of time. That the sea should, in this place, for example, have stood on a level with the upper line of Glen Roy, it is requisite that the whole ocean should also at that period have stood 1260 feet, or thereabout, higher than it does now; a state of things which must have belonged to a far different world from that which we are acquainted with.

But we know that, even in spite of such arguments as this, there are persons who still chuse to imagine such revolutions in the elevation of the sea, as will admit this cause, and inquire with what success it can be applied to the explanation of these appearances. If Glen Roy was thus open to the sea, and if its lines are to be considered as ancient sea shores, the whole ocean must have undergone three successive depressions of its level at three distant intervals; since much time is required to produce such shores as these lines must have been. At these periods also, it must have stood high in the great Caledonian Glen, as well as in a vast number of the present sea lochs and valleys of Scotland, which are exactly similar to Glen Roy in their nature. Yet, in no other place can the same kind of effects be discovered, nor any other phenomena of a similar nature which could justify such a supposition.

To these general objections we may add some of a local nature. No marine remains exist in Glen Roy, nor are there any indications of those deposits of calcareous sand or of mud, which must have existed at the

bottom of such a bay of the ocean, and in which the sea must have rested so long. Those lochs which really do belong to the sea are proved by the sounding line to contain such deposits; while, where the water has been compelled to retire in consequence of the lateral increase of the land, the alluvial lands, now laid dry, contain decided traces of their marine origin. This is remarkable in that low tract which lies between Campbeltown and Machrianish Bay, and which once rendered the Mull of Cantyre an island; and it is even more conspicuous in Isla, where a deep maritime deposit forms the neck of land which now separates Lochindaal from Loch Gruinart. If, as we formerly attempted to show, Glen Roy was once dry even before it became the receptacle of a lake, the difficulties here stated on this hypothesis become still greater. But they are already insuperable, and we shall therefore make no scruple in rejecting that which appears to us among the most gratuitous and untenable of all the theories which have been proposed on this subject. We admit that the nature of the barriers and their changes forms the most difficult part of Dr. Macculloch's Theory; but that which on this view is merely a matter of difficulty may, on the present one, be considered as fairly impossible.

If we have thus brought to a conclusion the history of the principal facts, and the reasonings which belong to this subject, there is yet ground for some useful and interesting remarks on the surrounding state of the country, as connected with these revolutions. We shall make these as brief as possible.

General remarks on the state of the country surrounding Glen Roy.

If the great Caledonian glen was once occupied by the sea, as is commonly supposed, the present land, which forms its bottom, and which is now elevated about ninety feet above the level of the water, must have been deposited by rivers, or other analogous causes, and the whole of it must be alluvial. By some partial accumulation of these, have also been formed the dams which separate the several lakes from each other and from the sea. It is plain, indeed, that these alluvia are slowly augmenting, and at some future, if far distant period, the effect will be to fill up all the lakes, and reduce the whole to a dry glen, conducting rivers to the northward and the southward. Thus, the first process here must have been that of accumulating alluvia, or raising the level of the bottom; while, at the same time, the destruction of the barriers of Loch Spean required a reverse operation. These are not, however, incompatible under conceivable circumstances, but we cannot spare any space to enter on many more of these abstruse discussions.

But there is a consequence much more puzzling than even this, to be deduced from some of the phenomena of Glen Roy, and which, being of a general nature, was reserved to this place. In many places the lines enter into the furrows on the faces of the hills for a certain space, without being prolonged all through them. It is evident from an examination of these furrows, that they have been formed by the water courses which still occupy them. But as they bear the marks of the lines through the outer, or most ancient part only, it is plain that these lines are posterior in time to that early part of the furrow, or bed of the torrent, which bears their marks, and anterior to the deeper part, where these are wanting. But if we now conceive the water of the lake to have stood at the height of the upper line, it is evident that the furrow generated by the lateral torrent could not have been formed at that level,

Parallel Roads.

and so far below it also, as is necessary to admit the depositions of these lines, or shores, on its sides; still less to have continued and repeated the same operations at the lower levels. The descent of the torrent must have ceased as soon as it met the lake, and, therefore, those parts of the furrows which are of higher or equal antiquity with this lake, as that is determined by the presence of the lines, could not have been formed by such torrents. It seems, therefore, necessary that such parts of the furrows as bear the marks of the lines, should have existed even under the waters, or before they were accumulated in the valley; while the bottoms of the same channels which now bear no marks of this nature, have been produced by the corrosive action of the same torrents since the drainage of the waters.

We are aware that this is a piece of delicate reasoning, and some of our readers may possibly think that it is over refined. But if it be just, there must have been lateral water courses in Glen Roy, flowing down the hills far towards the bottom of the present valley, and in times more ancient than the formation of the lines. They were, therefore, more ancient than the lake itself; or there was a period prior to the state of a lake, in which Glen Roy was a dry valley, or at least a lake of less depth than the most ancient one. For this end we should also require the formation of a barrier, as well as its subsequent removal; and that within a period subsequent to that at which the present distribution of hill and valley was made, and, therefore, in times comparatively modern.

Some other geological inferences of no small importance may be made from the appearances that have thus been described, and without the necessity of adverting to the precise nature of the actions which produced them, or even with the admission that any of the rejected hypotheses were the true ones.

There can be no doubt that, on any supposable case, these lines are of very high antiquity. Now, whereever they are found on similar slopes, on similar ground, or generally in the same circumstances, they present such resemblances as to entitle us to conclude, that had the ground been uniform every where, they would have been every where equal and similar. Yet, as they lie at different elevations, they are unequally subject to the action of the chief causes of waste, namely, the descent of water along the slopes of the hills, and they should, therefore, have shown distinct and different marks of waste, had these causes been of an active nature. Had such causes, indeed, been very active, they must have been obliterated, instead of having suffered, as they have done, so little injury; for, if they had suffered much, that waste, in the doctrine of chances, must have been unequal. We may, therefore, consider them as differing but little, even at this distant period, from the condition in which they were left by the subsidence of the water, or by the cessation of the generating causes. The general conclusion from this is, that the waste and descent of hills, however certain it may be, is a very tedious operation. We are here furnished with certain unknown limits, but very wide ones we are sure, within which we can estimate that little waste has been suffered by the sides or summits of the hills of Glen Roy.

Some other important facts respecting the alluvia are also deducible from these appearances. It has been remarked, that the lines are formed in two distinct sets of alluvia. The one of these occurs at the upper part of the glen, and it consists of sharp fragments that have been subjected to no distant transportation. These are the result of the tedious process of waste acting on the summits of the hills, as is proved by their identity with the natural rock, by their irregular forms, and by other circumstances. The chief of these last is the intermixture of clay with the fragments; an important character belonging peculiarly to these alluvia of descent, as they may be called. Transported alluvia, besides that their fragments are rounded and heterogeneous, alternate; the larger pieces, the gravel and the sand, forming a kind of distinct strata. If clay should happen to be present, it is disposed in a similarly separate manner, and not intermingled with the coarser materials. Now, if we consider the case of the untransported alluvia, or those which cover the faces of the hills, it is evident that a great length of time must have been required for their accumulation before the lines were formed in them. We have also seen, that, from the very little change these lines have undergone since their formation, scarcely any wearing of the hills has occurred, or any deposition of fresh alluvia of descent formed since the period at which they were traced, distant as that may be. Thus, we are necessarily carried back to a remote antiquity indeed, previous to the formation of these lines, for the deposition of the great quantity of alluvia which form such a thick covering on the hills, and which must have been produced during a very long period prior to the drainage of the lakes.

The following reasoning is no less intricate, and the consequences no less remarkable: As the alluvia of descent which form the lines in the upper part of the valley, are not much rounded, it is plain that no more violent motion than that which usually attends the margin of lakes had there existed in these waters. Neither, of course, could there be any such motion in the lower parts of the valley, since the circumstances must have been the same throughout. Yet the lines in these places are formed in a rounded and transported alluvium of pebbles, sand, and gravel. Now, we know not how such an alluvium could have been thus accumulated, except from the action of waters flowing through this valley, and this accumulation must have been formed before the presence of the lake. Thus we are carried back to a far distant time, and to a state of the valley when it contained no water, and prior even, perhaps, to the very remote time in which the alluvia of descent were deposited on the hill faces. This reasoning, it will be perceived, confirms that formerly deduced from the appearances of the furrows, however unwilling we may be to contemplate results so extraordinary and intricate.

Such are a few of the complicated conclusions which may be drawn from a proper contemplation of phenomena that must not be looked at by a careless eye, and that cannot be advantageously stated except by geologists well versed in all the complicated appearances and niceties which belong to the past and present state of the surface, and quick in seizing on the very delicate relations which belong to them. We know of no spot which requires such steadiness and minuteness of attention; and which demands so many processes of reasoning before we can derive from it all the advantages which its study is calculated to yield. We are not aware that any of the conclusions which we have here attempted to draw from them are overstrained, far less groundless. Yet, though some of them should be founded in error, there is still enough to excite our industry in the observation of similar phenomena, and in seeking for farther analogies, where to discover appearances exactly similar seems hopeless.

Of the probability of the theory here offered we need say no more; that it is simple and explanatory is certain, but that it implies some circumstances difficult to explain we have already shown. These, however, are explained by no other hypothesis; while each of those that has been proposed, and, indeed, all others of this nature that can possibly be conceived, are attended with difficulties far more complicated, and even imply impossibilities, a fault from which the theory that we have adopted is assuredly free. We have only yet to hope, that a farther acquaintance with the general changes which the surface of the earth has undergone, with the causes of them, and, perhaps, the future discovery of some analogies or resemblances to these phenomena, will ultimately remove that which yet remains difficult of explanation in the physical history of Glen Roy, and of its *Parallel Roads*.

The study to which we have alluded is difficult; it requires an eye, and a habit of reasoning, far different from those which are engaged in the comparatively trifling business of ascertaining the names and positions of rocks, and the nature of minerals. Let us hope that those who really have the requisite faculties will bestow more attention on this important and difficult branch of Geology; and that the history of the surface of the earth, and its changes, may one day be rescued from the state in which it is at present.

PARANA. See BUENOS AYRES, vol. V. p. 51.

PARASELENÆ. See HALO, vol. X. p. 614; and OPTICS, vol. XV. p. 617.

PARGA, a sea-port of Albania, is situated near the mouth of the ancient Acheron, on a rock washed by the sea, and having behind it a rugged cliff with a citadel on its summit. The town is surrounded with walls, and has a double harbour formed by a small island. " Vast screens of olive trees," says Pouqueville, " mingled with tufts of oranges grouped in the distant scene, form many points of view on which the eye rests with delight." It was given up by Ali Pacha in 1819, when most of the inhabitants, who were Albanian Greeks, removed to the Ionian Islands. Population 8000, according to Pouqueville, but only 5000 according to others. East. long. 20° 39'. North lat. 39° 22'. See Pouqueville's *Travels in the Morea*, p. 389, 395, &c.

PARHELION. See HALO, vol. X. p. 612; and OPTICS, vol. X. p. 617.

PARIAN CHRONICLE. See ARUNDELIAN MARBLES, vol. II. p. 533.

PARING AND BURNING. See AGRICULTURE, vol. I. p. 268.

PARIS, the capital of France, is built on a plain on both sides of the River Seine, which, at this place, flows in a direction nearly from east to west. Of this city, the original name, as mentioned by Cæsar, was Lutetia; a word, the etymology of which is unknown, though it is supposed by some to have been derived from a Latin term, (*lutum*, mud,) descriptive of the wet and marshy nature of the ground (*palus perpetua*, says Cæsar,) on which the town stands. Whether this opinion be fanciful or not, it would now be in vain to inquire: but of its present name, a more satisfactory account can probably be given. The Pa-

risii, who anciently inhabited that district in which Lutetia was situated, would, in process of time, naturally impart their name to the capital of the province in which they dwelt. At what time, however, this modern appellation was first applied to it, cannot be exactly determined; it could not have been earlier than towards the end of the fifth century; for Julian, who resided there for some time, speaks of it, in 458, as his *dear Lutetia* *.

Paris, built, as just mentioned, on both sides of the Seine, is situated about 260 miles south by east of London, in 48° 50' of north latitude, and 2° 20' 15" of east longitude. The country on all sides of the town is extremely level, and presents almost no diversity of physical appearance. Instead of being adorned, like the neighbourhood of other large towns, with elegant villas, gardens, and pleasure grounds, it exhibits, almost to the very gates of the city, all the features of a rural and sequestered district. Even the roads do not display any powerful symptoms that a populous city is at hand; they are enlivened, when compared with those in the vicinity of the British capital, with uncommonly few travellers; and we seem to pass at once from the silence and solitude of the country to the noise and bustle of a crowded metropolis. This peculiarity originates in the national character, in that love for social intercourse, and that aversion to quiet and retirement, for which the French, particularly the inhabitants of Paris, have always been remarkable. The approach to Paris, on one side, however, is incomparably beautiful. From the bridge of Neuilly, on the road from St. Germains, a spacious avenue of stately trees, skirted on either side by elegant houses and gardens, extend for a mile and a half in a straight line to the very gates of the city. By this entrance, some of the most splendid public edifices of the French metropolis present themselves in succession to the admiring traveller; and, in the front, the view is beautifully terminated by the yet unfinished triumphal arch, named L'Arc d'Etoile.

The air of Paris is sufficiently salubrious; the town is in general well ventilated, and is free from the humidity which its situation would lead us to expect. The winter is a little colder, though shorter, than in London; the summer is considerably milder and more genial; the weather is much less capricious; and instances of longevity are more frequent in the French than in the English metropolis. The mean temperature of Paris is 51°.08 of Fahrenheit.

The aspect of the Seine at Paris is not remarkably beautiful or interesting. It is not above half the width of the Thames at London; during the summer months its channel becomes comparatively dry, and large banks of mud are exhibited in every direction; and it is adorned by nothing that merits the denomination of shipping. Though its banks are termed quays, and though a few small boats, chiefly for the purpose of internal navigation, are frequently seen to diversify its surface, yet Havre de Grace, at the mouth of the Seine, may be regarded as the harbour of Paris, and the communication between this place and the capital takes place chiefly by land carriage, the river never being used except to transport wood, or very bulky articles. Yet the Seine is far from being deficient in beauty and ornament; its banks, or quays, which are built of stone, to the height of about 15 feet, and extend five miles along the

Side notes: Name. | Paris. | Situation. | Climate. | River, bridges,&c.

---

* The baths of Julian, the only specimen of Roman antiquity in Paris, were shown to us in 1819 by M. Chevalier. They are adjacent to the Hotel de Clugny. The part which we saw consisted of a lofty apartment sixty feet high, with huge brick arched walls. There are vaults also below, the foundations being built with small square and accurately cut stones, and the arches of brick. ED.

river on each side, form one of the most pleasant walks about Paris; they are decorated with various buildings, both public and private; and on one side, along the southern bank, there extends, for more than a mile, a row of edifices of the most elegant and massy description. Nor are its numerous and spacious bridges less deserving of notice. The Pont Neuf, the largest and the most ancient in Paris, contains twelve arches, is 1020 feet in length, and 90 in breadth. The Pont Royal, and the Pont de Louis XVI. each consisting of five arches, were built respectively by Louis XIV. and Louis XVI. In the time of Buonaparte, several bridges, of which the Pont de Jena, or des Invalides, and the Pont d'Austerlitz, are the most important, were erected, none of them deficient in elegance, and all contributing much to the convenience and comfort of the Parisians. It may not be improper to mention that the arches of the bridges are characterised by only a slight degree of elevation, as the quays or stone embankments, on which they are built, are very considerably raised above the level of the river.

Form and extent of the city.

Paris is nearly of a circular form. It stretches along the Seine about four miles and a half, and its breadth, at right angles with the river, is about four miles. It was surrounded in 1785, to prevent the illicit introduction of all exciseable articles, by a wall, seventeen miles in circumference; but as this wall incloses towards the west a considerable space of ground unoccupied with buildings, its real extent may be comprised in a circuit of not more than fourteen miles. London, with its suburbs, is extended over a much larger surface, but the French capital is more compactly built, contains much higher houses, and is more densely inhabited. The population of Paris in 1817, amounted to 715,000—about two thirds of that of the British metropolis. Paris consists of three divisions—the *cité*, which lies in the centre,—the *ville* in the north,—and the *université* in the south. The *cité*, which is built on one of the two islands, (L'Isle St. Louis and L'Isle Notre Dame) formed by the Seine, and comprises the site of the ancient Lutetia, is the original capital, and contains the greater number of important edifices. There are other subordinate divisions, designed to facilitate the administration of justice, which it is of no importance at present to specify. The Fauxbourgs of Paris, those buildings which lie between the Boulevards and the new wall, still retain their individual names; but as in every sense they form no inconsiderable part of the French capital, they are included in the foregoing description.

Streets.

The general appearance of this metropolis to a stranger is not of the most fascinating kind. With the exception, indeed, of the public edifices, which, as we shall soon see, are extremely numerous and elegant, and of the new streets, the impression which it is calculated to make is by no means favourable. The streets are crooked, narrow, particularly when contrasted with the height of the houses, ill-paved, and destitute of every accommodation for foot passengers. Every thing like regularity seems to have been studiously avoided. Paris can exhibit no long line of houses, such as you find in London, and particularly in Edinburgh, of equal dimensions, and of the same species of architecture. All the houses are indeed built of stone,—all those of an ancient date are remarkable for height, often six or seven stories, like the buildings of our Scottish metropolis,—and are inhabited by a great variety of families: but they possess no other points of similarity; and,

adjoining houses, in height, in workmanship, and in almost every other respect, often form a contrast to each other. And it not unfrequently happens, that a humble mansion, inhabited by the very meanest of the citizens, is situated beside a large edifice, the residence of some one of the most illustrious men of France. Sometimes also, a splendid gateway, which to an English traveller would suggest the idea of rank and opulence, is found to lead into a court distinguished only for filth and wretchedness. And, what a stranger regrets almost as much, some of the finest houses are completely concealed from their fronting inward, or from a high wall, erected to intercept the view from the street. In the division denominated the City, which, as formerly mentioned, was the site of ancient Lutetia, the buildings, with the exception of the public edifices, are the most inelegant, and they are found to improve gradually according to the period in which they were finished. The modern streets are, therefore, the most handsome. The Fauxbourg St. Germain, in particular, can boast of the finest streets in Paris, if not in Europe; and their beauty is much heightened by the detached villas and palaces which they contain, surrounded with gardens, in which the lilac, the laburnum, the acacia, are chiefly conspicuous. The houses, or, as they are termed, the *hotels*, of the nobility and opulent gentry, are situated either in this place or on the same side of the town, though many of the most distinguished characters still continue to reside in streets which seem exclusively devoted to the poor and the vulgar.

Boulevards.

But, to the general inelegance of the streets of Paris, there is, beside the Fauxbourg St. Germain, another remarkable exception, namely, the Boulevards, the most spacious and extensive street of the French metropolis. This street occupies the space where the ramparts of the city were placed, in an age when its circumference did not exceed seven miles. This space, unencumbered by buildings, was levelled, and converted to its present use during the reigns of Louis XIV. and his successor. The Boulevards are of a circular form, and consist of two rows of building, all of them elegant, and some of them splendid, detached palaces. The general width of the street is above 200 feet. The road in the centre is flanked by two rows of stately trees, and between each row of trees and the parallel line of buildings are elegant walks, for the accommodation of foot passengers. The effect of the Boulevards, particularly with strangers, is inexpressibly grand. The magnificence of the houses, which, from the great breadth of the street, are each seen in the most favourable aspect—the majestic trees with which the place is adorned,—the winding form of the street, which at the same time suggests the idea of its almost unbounded magnitude, and prevents the eye from being wearied with the extent of the view which it contemplates,—these, combined with the bustle and animation which on every side invite attention, form a most striking picture, and render the Boulevards of Paris one of the most interesting and splendid lines of buildings which any modern city can exhibit.

Squares.

The French capital is a good deal diversified and enlivened by the number of its squares, of which there are no less than seventy. Of these, however, none are very large or very elegant. The houses, indeed, are not unfrequently superb in point of architecture, while the area in the centre is ill-paved, and otherwise entirely neglected. This is the case in a striking manner with the Place Vendome, the largest and the finest square in Paris, which, with all the beauty of the houses, which are uniform, and decorated with Corinthian pillars, is characterized by some of the most unequivocal symptoms of vulgarity and filthiness. Of the pillar in the centre, erected by Bonaparte in honour of his successes in Germany, we shall hereafter speak. The most handsome squares, after the one already mentioned, are the Place Royale, the Place des Victoires, the Place du Carousel, the Place de Louis XV. The largest of the squares of Paris is not above 400 or 500 feet in any direction; while some places denominated squares are so exceedingly restricted as scarcely to merit that appellation.

But whatever opinion may be formed with regard to the character of the streets and squares of Paris, this capital, it is universally allowed, is superior to any other European metropolis, in the number and magnificence of its public edifices. The palace of the Thuilleries, the present royal residence, begun in the sixteenth, and completed in the following century, is a massy and venerable structure. Including the pavilion at each end, its length is upwards of 1000 feet; and though it is not probably the most chaste of Parisian buildings, though it exhibit several orders of architecture, and its height in the centre is less than at the two extremities, it has yet a very grand and imposing effect, and is worthy of the use to which it is now dedicated. The portico of the palace, and the garden connected with it, contain some admirable specimens of ancient and modern sculpture.—The palace of the Luxemberg, one of the apartments of which now forms the Chamber of Peers, is more chaste and elegant than the Thuilleries, though not so large or so striking. It is a square edifice, with an ample portico in the centre. A noble pavilion surmounts the principal building, and terminates in a dome, composed of the Doric and Ionic orders. Its interior is remarkable for a spacious staircase, adorned till lately, when they were removed to the Louvre, with the statues of some of the most illustrious generals and legislators of France.—The Palais Bourbon, where the legislative body under Bonaparte held their sittings, and where the chamber of deputies now meet, is delightfully situated on the Seine, and is characterized by some writers as the noblest building of Paris. Its front is ornamented with twelve Corinthian pillars, which support a chaste entablature, bearing, until the return of the present royal family, the inscription—*A Napoleon le Grand*, and containing a bas relief to his honour, executed in the most elegant style. In the chamber of deputies are six statues, representing Lycurgus, Solon, Demosthenes, Brutus, Cato, and Cicero; and the stair is distinguished by allegorical colossal figures, seated in calm attitudes, and exhibiting a mild, unostentatious adjustment of drapery. The Palais Royale, now more remarkable as a place of business, of amusement, and dissipation, than as the remains of a royal residence, must not be overlooked in this enumeration. It has long been vested as private property in the Orleans family; and, at the time of the revolution, it was the residence of the infamous Duke of Orleans, who, by his sensuality and depravity at least, promoted that memorable event, of which himself, ere long, was the victim. The original building is not deficient in elegance and taste; the façade, which was erected so lately as 1781, is embellished with Doric and Ionic pillars, surmounted by a finely sculptured fronton; and the whole edifice forms an oblong square, the area of which is paved and decorated with trees. The

first floor of the building is occupied chiefly with shops, small but neat, and devoted to toys, ornaments, and luxuries of every description. The second floor is inhabited by private families; it also contains coffee-rooms, reading-rooms, apartments for public exhibitions, and for the meetings of literary societies. On three sides of these buildings is a chain of arcades separated by pilasters, which form a covered walk, frequented during the day by men of business, by strangers, by the gay and the fashionable, and at night by the profligate and the sensual. There is also adjoining to the palace a garden of an oblong form, nearly 250 feet in length, with several *jets d'eau* in the centre, and terminated at either end by elegant shrubberies. The Palais Royale, with its premises, is the scene of all the dissipation and prostitution of the French metropolis; and the vices and grossness, which in other capitals are scattered over the whole town, are in Paris collected in this central spot. The Louvre, the oldest royal palace connected with Paris, is now used as a museum of painting and sculpture, and is, in every respect, a most important and interesting edifice. It is situated about a quarter of a mile to the east of the Thuilleries, to which indeed it is united by what is denominated the gallery of the Louvre. That portion of it termed the Old Louvre was erected many centuries ago; but the greater part of it, including the celebrated colonnade, was the work of the refined age of Louis XIV. It is of a quadrangular form, with an inner court of 400 feet square. Its sides present projecting building, adorned with beautiful sculptures; and altogether it forms a perfect model of architectural splendour. "It is impossible," says a sensible traveller, "for language to convey any adequate idea of the impression which this exquisite building awakens in the mind of a stranger. The beautiful proportions and fine symmetry of the great façade, give an air of simplicity to the distant view of the edifice, which is not diminished on nearer approach by the unrivalled beauty of its ornaments and detail; but when you cross the threshold of the portico, and pass under its noble archway into the inner court, all considerations are absorbed in the throb of admiration, which is excited by the sudden display of all that is lovely and harmonious in Grecian architecture." But the effect which it is calculated to produce, is much weakened by the narrowness of the open space in front, and the mean buildings with which it is so immediately associated. It is almost the only important public building in Paris that enjoys no advantages of situation. Of the use to which it is now converted, as the depôt of works of genius and art, we shall, under another head of this article, soon proceed to give an account.

Of the remaining public buildings, with the exception of the churches and hospitals, of which we mean soon to treat, the following, which we have not room to describe more minutely, are the most important. The Garde Meuble, or the depôt of the jewels and valuable furniture of the crown; the Military School; the Palace of the Legion of Honour; the Institute; the Mint, or Hôtel des Monnoies; the Royal Printing House; the Town-hall; the Hotel de Ville; the Palais de Justice, &c. The two last mentioned form an assemblage of buildings, containing the courts of justice, the public boards, and, in its lower part, the prison of the Conciergerie.

But amid all this unrivalled splendour and elegance of Paris, it is not superior to London in the size and magnificence of its churches. The two most important

Paris.

buildings of this nature which the French capital can exhibit, are those of Notre Dame and the Pantheon, neither of which is equal in grandeur or extent to St. Paul's in London. These edifices, however, are of the most massy and interesting description. Notre Dame, the metropolitan church, and the only Gothic structure of note in Paris, is situated in the city, the oldest part and centre of the capital, and rises to a stupendous height above all the buildings which surround it. It is no less than 414 feet in length; its width is 144; and it is 102 in height. Its architecture is not probably of the finest gothic; massy greatness is its distinguishing feature; and it strikes the beholder more from its immense size than from the beauty of the proportions in which it is formed. It is so old, that the date of its erection is unknown; the venerable and gloomy antiquity of its appearance affords a striking contrast to the airy brilliancy of the modern buildings with which the city is filled; its walls are crusted over with the smoke of ages; and of all the edifices in Paris, the cathedral of Notre Dame conveys to us the most lively impressions of the massiness and durability of ancient architecture. The Pantheon, or church of St. Geneviève, while it answers the purposes of a place of public worship, is used also as a place of sepulture for illustrious characters. The portal, in imitation of that of the Pantheon at Rome, consists of a superb peristyle of twenty-two Corinthian columns, each of which is five feet and a half in diameter, and fifty-eight in height. The front is adorned with elegant sculpture and colossal figures; and above the portico is the following simple inscription in reference to its being used as the burial ground of the great, *Aux grands ames, la Patrie reconnoissante*. Its situation is extremely conspicuous, being placed on an eminence; and the approach to it is by an immense flight of steps, which form the base of the building; it terminates in a dome of vast dimensions, which being the highest object in Paris, (282 feet,) is visible from any part of the city. The churches in Paris are extremely numerous, but those of St. Sulpice, St. Eustache, and St. Roche, all of which are large and elegant, are the only other ones that deserve to be particularly specified. There are four protestant places of worship in Paris, all of which were originally catholic buildings, and of which the ancient Church of the Oratory is the largest and the most splendid.

Burial grounds.

From treating of churches, the transition is natural to the consideration of cemeteries, with which till lately Paris was not very amply furnished. The Parisians were formerly accustomed to bury in the churches or in places of sepulture situated within the precincts of the city. These were so very few in number, and so limited in point of extent, that necessity at length compelled the inhabitants to adopt a mode of interment, extremely inhuman and repulsive. A deep trench was made, into which corpse after corpse was successively deposited, till the putrid heap nearly reached the level of the surface. The exhalations which these trenches emitted having become extremely disgusting and unwholesome, government at length found it necessary to interfere; the offensive practice in question was strictly prohibited; and two large burial grounds in retired situations beyond the walls have been opened, one for the southern, and the other for the northern district of Paris. In addition to these, the Catacombs, those subterraneous quarries whence the city was built, and by which a great proportion of it is undermined, have, since the latter part of the 18th century, been

Catacombs.

partially converted into a large burying repository, to which all the bones that could be collected in the ancient cemeteries within the city have been removed; and the sites of these cemeteries are now occupied as squares, or as market places. The bones, having been carefully cleaned, are regularly piled along the sides of the different passages of the Catacombs, some of which are a mile or two in length, containing the remains of several millions of human beings, and forming one of the most striking objects connected with the French metropolis.

Sepulchral monuments.

As connected with this subject, the *Musée des Monumens Français* may with propriety be mentioned. This is a collection (begun in 1790, when the property of the church was confiscated for the use of the nation) of the finest sepulchral monuments from different parts of the kingdom, particularly from the cathedral of St. Denis, in the near vicinity of Paris, which, from the earliest ages, had been the mausoleum of the French sovereigns. These monuments are arranged according to their respective dates, to illustrate the progress of the art to which they refer. The monumental relics of the most illustrious characters; of philosophers, of statesmen, and poets, are here collected under one roof, and cannot fail to excite within us the most interesting, though probably the most humiliating emotions. There is, however, we think, an evident impropriety in thus transferring those sepulchral remains from the several graves they were meant to designate and adorn. It was an act of injustice to the places which have been distinguished by the birth or the burial of eminent men; and whatever be the effect on the mind, which, in their present collected state, they produce, that individual and local interest is completely destroyed, which in their original situation they were calculated to excite and to cherish.

Hospitals.

The hospitals and charitable institutions of Paris are more numerous than in any city of the same population: the annual expence of them, which is defrayed by government, being upwards of £300,000. They have not, as in England, each its independent board of management; they are all under the control of a general board, appointed by government, and responsible to it. The situation of those established at a remote period, is found to be now nearly in the centre of the city, badly ventilated and offensive to the neighbouring inhabitants. The most celebrated of these institutions, and that on which, in time of war at least, the Parisians set the highest value, is the Hôtel des Invalides, which may be termed the Chelsea Hospital of France, instituted by Louis XIV. for the reception and maintenance of disabled and superannuated soldiers. The characteristics of this edifice are chasteness and simplicity, well suited to the objects to which it is devoted. The front is distinguished by a plain manly portico; and a dome and cupola of the finest proportions rising from its centre, form one of the most prominent objects in Paris. These buildings are very extensive; and with the adjoining grounds, which are adorned with long alleys of trees, and otherwise elegantly distributed, occupy no less a space than seventeen acres. The interior was embellished by cannon, taken at various periods by the armies of France—and innumerable standards, the trophies of many a victory, waved under its splendid dome, until 1814, when, on the approach of the allied armies, the French invalids burned and destroyed them, that they might not fall into the hands of the

Paris.

enemy. The Hôtel Dieu, or Hospice d'Humanité, which is the oldest hospital in Paris, is next to the one just described in point of importance. It is appropriated to the sick and infirm poor, of whom it contains at some periods not less than 8000. There are about twenty other institutions of this nature in Paris, accommodated to the circumstances of patients of every description, and all conducted on the most soothing and liberal principles.

Triumphal structures. Paris, amid the great variety of its institutions and public edifices, is not deficient in triumphal monuments. Of these, the column erected by Bonaparte in the centre of the Place Vendome, to commemorate his victories in Germany, deserves to be particularly mentioned. It is built in imitation of Trajan's pillar at Rome. Its diameter is 12 feet, and its height 140. But the most striking part of it, are the numerous brazen figures in bas-relief, with which it is decorated, and the materials of which were obtained by melting the cannon taken at Ulms and Austerlitz. These figures, each three feet in height, occupy the whole pillar, proceeding in a spiral direction from the base to the entablature. The name of *his majesty Napoleon* was sculptured out in a conspicuous part of the building, on the summit of which was a statue of this illustrious man grasping the imperial sceptre. But after the return of the present royal family, this inscription and effigy were destroyed, and the pillar now terminates in a gallery and dome. There is another triumphal monument, erected by Bonaparte in the Place du Carousel, originally surmounted by the figures of Venetian horses and the car of Victory; but these ornaments, and the various bas-reliefs illustrative of his victories over the Prussians, were carefully defaced or removed by the allied powers when they obtained possession of Paris. The Arc de Triomphe, begun by the same monarch, is yet unfinished. There are a few other monuments of an older date than those we have been describing. Of these, the porte or gate of St. Denis, and that of St. Martin, are the most conspicuous, and may both be regarded rather as triumphal arches than as gates of the city. The porte of St. Denis is a piece of massy architecture, seventy-two feet respectively in height and in width; and the figures in bas-relief, commemorative of the success of the armies of Louis XIV. by whom it was erected, and the various other decorations sculptured on it, add much to the beauty and majesty of its appearance.

Trade and manufactures. The country of which Paris is the capital, stands deservedly high in some departments of manufactures, such as those of wine, brandy, plate-glass, porcelain, &c.; but it is doubtful if Paris itself has attained to that degree of eminence in this respect, which its size, population, and advantages, would lead us to expect. In silks, it is greatly inferior to Lyons, and in cottons, to Rouen, and the wine made from the grapes which grow in the neighbourhood of the city is so extremely bad, that it is used only for servants: and *vin de Surenne*, so called from a village of that name, three miles from Paris, is a general expression for wine of the meanest quality. The staple manufactures of the French capital, indeed, consist chiefly of articles of taste, and all kinds of fancy works, such as jewellery of every description, watches, artificial flowers, toys, &c. But notwithstanding of this general inferiority, there are some species of manufactures in which Paris has acquired great, if not unrivalled distinction. It will at once be conjectured, that the Gobelins is here particularly alluded to,—a manufactory of the richest tapes-

try, so called from a person named Gobelin, who instituted it in the middle of the 16th century. These tapestries, the ground-work of which are webs of the finest silk or worsted, either commemorate some remarkable incident in history, or exhibit imitations of flowers or pictures, however brilliant or intricate. "The glow of colouring, fidelity of outline, and delicacy of truth," says Lady Morgan, "rival the most masterly touches of the pencil." The value of the materials of which this manufacture is made, and the tediousness of the workmanship, (not less than two years being necessary to finish a single piece,) are such, that few even of the wealthiest families can afford to purchase it. It is indeed far from being a lucrative concern, and were it not a national establishment, and conducted at the public expense, it would long ere this period have been discontinued; for the chief, if not the only consumption, consists in the government itself; the walls of the various royal palaces of France being decorated with it, and rich and numerous presents of it made to the allied sovereigns of the nation, and to foreigners of distinction. There are also manufactories of porcelain, glass, carpets, &c. conducted at the expense of government. These articles are all of the most exquisite workmanship; but so high priced, that they have never met with any thing like general sale; and, indeed, in a pecuniary point of view, are utterly unprofitable. Paris, besides, monopolizes almost the whole bookselling and printing business of France. The royal printing-office alone contains no fewer than 250 presses; and Mr. Pinkerton asserts that there are 400 respectable booksellers in the French capital, and that the total number of those who actually acquire a livelihood by this profession, though some of them in a very inferior capacity, cannot be estimated at much below 3000. The distance of Paris from the sea has always rendered it a place of no importance for foreign trade: Havre de Grace, situated above a hundred miles from it, may be regarded as its harbour; its exports consist of manufactured commodities, and its imports, neither of which is very considerable, of articles required for the consumption of the inhabitants.

Literature and literary institutions. The metropolis of France, however, distinguished as it is, is probably not more celebrated for any thing than for its literature and literary institutions. Learning and talents have uniformly, with Frenchmen of all ranks, been the objects of the greatest respect and reverence. The royal press of France, much to the honour of the government, was formerly situated in the palace of the Louvre. Printing was at a very early date introduced into Paris, and soon attained there to a degree of perfection, unrivalled at that period in any other country; one of the earliest printed books in the Greek language issued from the press of Francis Tissard; and the names of Henry, Robert, and Henry Stephens, the most accurate and learned printers of any age, are inseparably connected with the literary history of Europe. And the high character which Paris thus early obtained, it has uniformly supported; a great proportion of the scholars of France have been connected with it; and, at the present date, it stands as high in this respect as at any former period. The number of works, particularly periodical works, and some of these scientific and philosophical journals of great celebrity, is at present unusually great, and is daily increasing. And this capital, as might be expected, is extremely rich in literary institutions. The Université Royale, the oldest establishment of this kind in the kingdom, has for centuries been well known throughout Europe; and though at the Revolution it was for a time suspended, it has since been re-established on a more extensive and liberal plan. It consists of four colleges, and comprises professors in every department of science and literature. There are many similar establishments in Paris, of which the College Royale, where the admission to the lectures is gratuitous, is nearly as extensive, and is as celebrated, as the one just described. The Ecole Polytechnique, instituted principally for the education of engineers, is furnished with a large library, a drawing school, and mechanical work-shops. In the Jardin des Plantes, there are thirteen classes for botany, and the various subjects connected with natural history. There is also an academy, termed L'Ecole Royale des Beaux Arts, appropriated to the teaching of painting, sculpture, and architecture. Paris besides possesses four great public schools or Lycées, devoted to elementary instruction. There are also many private academies, and in every part of France, but particularly in Paris, several of the inferior clergy dedicate a considerable portion of their time to the instruction of youth. In addition to these, and several institutions of a similar description, the French capital is distinguished by many literary and scientific societies and associations, some of which are of great celebrity. The Institute, or Royal Society, and the Bureau des Longitudes, will, with many others, at once occur to the mind of the reader. The Institute, indeed, which was established in the reign of Louis XIV. has acquired a reputation of the most illustrious kind, and the services which it has rendered not only to French, but to European literature, are universally acknowledged. It is composed of the most eminent philosophical and literary characters in France, and maintains a correspondence with the learned of every nation. Each of the four classes, into which it is divided, has assigned it a separate department of pursuit and investigation; the first is devoted to mathematical, physical, and experimental subjects; the second to French literature and the French language—the third to universal history, and ancient literature—the fourth to the fine arts. Each of these divisions has its separate meetings; but four times a-year, the whole academy assemble, and a general report is made of the labours and progress of the institution, (see INSTITUTE, vol. xii. p. 164.) The Bureau des Longitudes, the object of which is to bring to perfection the discovery of the longitude, to make astronomical and meteorological observations, &c. can boast, in the list of its members, of some of the proudest names, and has attained to no inconsiderable degree of scientific celebrity.

The numerous and extensive libraries of Paris correspond well with the favourable description we have just given of its literature. Almost all the eminent schools and literary institutions enjoy each the advantages of a library. The royal library is the largest and most valuable in the world. It was instituted so early as the 14th century, by King John, whose collection amounted only to ten volumes; under the munificent patronage of the French monarchs, it has gradually, since that period, increased in size and importance; and it now contains no fewer than 380,000 volumes, 80,000 manuscripts, some of which are of the rarest kind, illustrative of the political and literary history of Europe; with 5000 volumes of engravings; genealogies of all the eminent French families; and a most valuable collection of medals and antiquities. Among other curious documents, it contains the original letters of Henry VIII. to Anna Boleyn, brought thither from

the Vatican. And the liberality of the principles on which it is conducted is worthy of so dignified an establishment, and highly honourable to the French character. People of every class and rank—strangers from any quarter of the globe, are allowed, without any introduction, the easiest access to it; the attendants are extremely kind and obliging; tables with every necessary accommodation are provided for the use of visitors; and the books, when required, are permitted to be taken out of the library for private perusal; a practice attended with almost no inconvenience, or risk of loss. The other libraries, which are extremely numerous, those of the Institute and the Pantheon being the largest and most important, consist either of collections in general literature, or in some particular branch of science, according to the establishment to which they severally belong. Paris besides possesses many public reading-rooms; and the number of circulating libraries, of which there was only one before the Revolution, is now much greater than in the British capital.

Nor, in speaking of the libraries of Paris, must those celebrated collections of works of art, &c. and of subjects connected with natural history, be passed over in silence. The Louvre, during the sway of Bonaparte, became possessed of every celebrated specimen of sculpture and of painting that could be procured on the continent of Europe; thither were brought all the works of genius and of art by which the various countries, over-run by his armies, were distinguished. The Louvre, however, thus enriched by conquest and by plunder, has, since the return of the Bourbon family, been stript of all the works which it had in this way amassed; and the halls of sculpture, and the gallery of paintings, now stand comparatively empty and uninteresting. A noble collection, however, still remains; and the places which this retribution left vacant, are now in a great degree occupied with paintings and statues, which either belonged to churches destroyed amid the frenzy of the revolution, or that could be procured from other collections in the various parts of the empire. The ground floor of this splendid edifice is devoted to statues, and other specimens of sculpture, ancient and modern, very limited in point of number, but judiciously arranged. From this apartment a magnificent staircase leads to the gallery of paintings, the first view of which to a stranger is unspeakably grand and imposing. It is 1400 feet in length, and notwithstanding what it has lost, it yet contains 1200 paintings, some of them the works of the most eminent masters, so arranged that there is little appearance of that vacancy and desolation, by which, from its recent fall, it must really be characterized. The specimens of the French, Italian, and Flemish schools, into which the gallery is divided, and the works of each artist, are respectively kept distinct, and thus avoid the confusion which otherwise must have taken place. The Jardin des Plantes, or royal garden, can boast of a very rich and extensive museum. Its collections of every kind are valuable and rare; in the zoological and fossil departments it is unrivalled; and it contains some curious specimens, not elsewhere to be seen, of the animal remains of the antediluvian world. The garden itself, which is of an oblong shape, and about half a mile in length, is laid out in great taste, and can exhibit groupes of plants from almost every region of the globe. The buildings belonging to it are also distinguished by a large menage, comprising animals of every climate and latitude. With the Jardin des Plantes, the names of Jussieu, Buffon, Haüy, and Cuvier, are inseparably connected. The

Pantheon contains collections in natural history, antiquities, and painting, more select than numerous. Among other curiosities, it is in possession of an original portrait of Mary Queen of Scots, in high preservation, presented by herself to the monks of St. Geneviève. There are other similar institutions in Paris, of which the Conservatoire des Arts et Métiers, a collection of the various machines invented by Frenchmen connected with the arts or with manufactures; and the Musée d'Artillerie, the repository of every warlike instrument, are the most extensive and the most celebrated.

Paris, with a small portion of the surrounding country, of a circular form, and about fifteen miles in diameter, forms what is termed the department of the Seine, and is governed by a prefect, who has under him twelve mayors, one for each division of the city, and two other substitutes, who manage the landward district. The police here is brought to a high state of perfection; the number of clerks and officers is incredibly great; and every person, whatever his character or external appearance, seems to be watched as studiously as if he were suspected of the grossest delinquencies. Paris has not inaptly been denominated the land of passports: without one, the shortest journey cannot be taken; and the circumstances of the numerous strangers, who, from all the kingdoms of Europe, visit the French capital, immediately become known, as from their passport, their name, profession, &c. are inserted in the police-books. The jurisdiction of the courts of Paris, unlike those of the English capital, extend only to the seven neighbouring departments; but, as is the case in London, it is the residence of the sovereign and royal family, it is the centre of the public business of the nation, and is the seat of the legislative assemblies.

The inhabitants of Lutetia, afterwards named Paris, as explained in a former part of this article, seem, in the time of Cæsar, to have been a resolute and bold people; for, according to that commander, they chose rather to consume their city to ashes, than allow it to fall into the hands of the enemy. Cæsar, however, finding the place advantageously situated for a military station, built a new town on the site of the old; and the Romans, from this period, retained possession of it upwards of 500 years, during which time it was visited by several of the Roman emperors, by Constantine, Constance, Julian, &c. In the year 486, it was taken by the Franks, and early in the subsequent century it was established as the capital of that people. From this period Paris, with little interruption, has increased gradually in size and in elegance. In the twelfth century, the streets were paved, and the town surrounded by a large wall. But the most memorable æra in the history of this city, is the long and glorious reign of Louis XIV. During his sway, upwards of eighty streets were opened and rebuilt; 33 elegant churches were erected; the quay was newly constructed, and four new ports were formed; the Hôtel des Invalides and the Observatory were founded; the Louvre was enlarged and repaired; the Boulevards were levelled and planted, and various other improvements were effected, which have caused the name of that illustrious monarch to be most honourably associated with the annals of the French metropolis. The same spirit continued to animate his successors, particularly Louis XVI. who not only resolved to complete the monuments and public buildings left unfinished by his predecessors, but also contemplated new improvements. These plans, however, he was not destined to carry into execution. He fell a victim to that revolution of his kingdom, which not merely subverted the ancient regime of France, but the effects

of which were felt in the most remote nations of Europe. The history of this sanguinary period may be found under the article FRANCE; and it need merely be mentioned here, that, since the revolution, the interests of Paris have not been neglected; that the ravages which were committed by the infatuated mob on some of its most splendid edifices and institutions have, as far as possible, been atoned for; and that the capital of France, during the reign of Bonaparte, made many acquisitions, both in point of external beauty and of real improvement.

See Pinkerton's *Description of Paris*, two volumes; Lady Morgan's *France*, two volumes; Millin's *Voyage en France*, five volumes; Rough's *Sketch of Modern Paris*; *Travels in France*, anonymous, Edin. 1814; *Paris*, and *Paris Revisited*, by John Scott; Mercier's *Picture of Paris*; Planta's *New Picture of Paris*. See also works on France, by Arthur Young, Birkbeck, Wraxall, &c. Of these, Pinkerton's is the most minute and authentic. (T. M.)

PARK, MUNGO, distinguished for his African travels and their unfortunate termination, was born at the farm of Fowlshiels, near Selkirk, on the 10th September, 1771. His father, a person noted for many respectable qualities, appears to have been particularly anxious to communicate the advantages of education to his family; since, though by no means in opulent circumstances, he engaged a tutor to reside with him for this special purpose. Under this domestic superintendence, Mungo (the seventh child of the family) readily acquired the first elements of learning; and was in consequence, at an early age, removed to the grammar school of Selkirk to commence his classical studies. Here, too, he showed himself equally attentive and persevering; and the same deep, calm ardour of mind, which at an after period was so conspicuously displayed, soon rendered him an object of permanent esteem to his teacher and fellow pupils.

It had been originally intended to educate Park for the church; but as he himself inclined to follow the medical profession, his friends were readily induced to comply with this desire; and at the age of fifteen, he was placed under the care of Mr. Thomas Anderson, a respectable surgeon in the town where Park was then residing. With this gentleman he continued three years, occasionally attending the grammar school to perfect his knowledge of Greek and Latin; and, in 1789, he went to the university of Edinburgh, for the purpose of completing his medical studies; where, during three successive winters, he attended the common course of lectures necessary for obtaining a surgeon's diploma. His residence in Edinburgh did not present much room for the display of superior talents; but whatever opportunities it afforded for mental cultivation were diligently employed, and Park's attainments seem to have been considerably above those usually possessed by persons in this situation. He had, in particular, addicted himself with considerable assiduity to the study of natural history. During the summer vacations, he made researches in botany among the pastoral hills of Yarrow, near which romantic stream Fowlshiels is situated; and his appetite for such inquiries was at once gratified and strengthened by a tour, which about this time he made into the Highlands, in company with his brother-in-law Mr. Dickson, whose eminence in this science had already procured him the patronage and friendship of Sir Joseph Banks.

Park had lost his father in 1790; and, so soon as his medical studies were completed, he repaired to London in quest of employment. By the brother-in-law just mentioned he was introduced to Sir Joseph Banks, who received him with the cordiality he was at all times ready to display in behalf of aspiring merit.; and, by his influence, Park was shortly afterwards appointed surgeon to the Worcester East Indiaman. He sailed for Bencoolen, in the island of Sumatra, in February, 1792; and returned next year, without any material occurrences having distinguished his voyage. It would seem, however, that his passion for natural history was still unabated, since we find in the Transactions of the Linnean Society a paper communicated by Park, and containing observations on several new species of fishes, discovered by him during his stay on the coast of Sumatra. It is dated 4th November, 1794.

Whether Park intended to prosecute the advantages held out by this new employment we are not informed; but, in a short time, objects were presented more congenial to his taste, and opening a wider scope for his ambition. Some years prior to this period, a number of individuals, with the laudable view of extending geographical knowledge, and guiding in some departments the efforts of philanthropy, had formed themselves into an Association for promoting discoveries in the interior of Africa. They had already found means to investigate the most important peculiarities in the northern part of this great continent; and had lately directed their chief attention to explore the course of the Joliba, or Niger, —a celebrated river which yet no European eye had ever seen, and concerning which the knowledge of Europeans was so vague, that different opinions existed even as to the direction of its current; some maintaining with Herodotus that it runs from east to west; others, on the contrary, from west to east. Major Houghton, whom the Association had dispatched to ascertain these points, fell in with the Moors on his journey, and came to a miserable death among them. Accounts of this occurrence had already reached England; and it was now an object to find a person properly qualified for executing the enterprize in which he had so unhappily failed. Sir Joseph Banks was an active member of the Association; and Park, who lived with him on the most friendly footing, immediately occurred to his mind, as uniting most of the requisites for such an undertaking. Park had never, indeed, particularly turned his attention to geographical inquiries; but his natural temper inclined him to long for the hazardous adventures and magnificent excitements attached to such an expedition. His constitution, naturally robust, was now, in some degree, habituated to warm climates; and the necessary previous information might be acquired without difficulty. He eagerly gave in to his patron's suggestion. Sir Joseph warmly recommended him to the Association, whose terms appeared sufficiently liberal, and, after a few additional inquiries, they willingly accepted him.

In consequence of this appointment, he left Portsmouth on the 22d May, 1795, in the Endeavour, an African trader; and arrived at Jillifree, near the mouth of the Gambia, on the 21st June. From this place he proceeded directly to Pisania, a British factory two hundred miles up the river, and was kindly received by Dr. Laidley the superintendant, in whose house he resided some months, learning Mandingo, the dialect generally spoken in those parts, and collecting information with regard to his future journey. On the 2d December, Park took leave of this last English friend, and directed his steps eastward in search of the Joliba. Soon, however, the intelligence of a war having occurred between two native chiefs, through whose territories he was to pass, induced him to bend his course to the north, into the country of the Moors. He had not proceeded far,

till a horde of that savage people surprised and took him prisoner. He was carried before Ali their leader, and treated with a degree of inhumanity, which, combined with the severe fever partly occasioned by it, would have broken any spirit less energetic than his own. He bore up, however, under the accumulated horrors of bodily exhaustion and barbarous captivity, till at length he fortunately escaped from the camp in the month of June. He reckoned his escape fortunate, though, in truth, it might seem but a change of misery. Alone in the African desert, his body worn out with sickness, and perishing for thirst, it is impossible to estimate the hardships he must have endured. Three weeks of painful wandering were at length, however, rewarded by a sight, which, in his estimation, compensated for them all. Approaching towards Sego, a considerable town on the banks of the Niger, he thus describes his feelings: " While we were riding together, and I was anxiously looking round for the river, one of the Negroes called out *Geo affilli!* (see the water!) and looking forwards, I saw with infinite pleasure the great object of my mission, the long sought for majestic Niger, glittering to the morning sun, as broad as the Thames at Westminster, and flowing slowly *to the eastward*. I hastened to the brink, and, having drank of the water, lifted up my fervent thanks in prayer to the great Ruler of all things for having thus far crowned my endeavours with success."

He had now indeed seen this mysterious stream, and ascertained the great fact of its flowing to the eastward; but more than this was beyond his power to accomplish. The presence of a white man excited jealousies among the Moorish traders of Sego: he did not find it safe to remain there, and, after proceeding onwards to Silla, where similar jealousies awaited him, a comparison of the difficulties to be surmounted, with the means he had of surmounting them, too clearly showed that he must needs return. The approach of the rainy season, whose destructive qualities he had previously experienced at Pisania, even required that he should lose no time in returning. Indeed, but for a concurrence of fortunate circumstances, he had little reason to expect to succeed in again reaching the Gambia. By the time he had arrived at Kamalia, still five hundred miles distant from the nearest British settlement, the rainy season had set in; and Park being attacked with a fever, from which he recovered slowly and imperfectly, was glad to accept the hospitality of Karfa Taura, a benevolent Negro, who proffered to entertain him in his house, till a coffle, or caravan of slaves, should set out to the European settlements. This did not occur till the latter end of April, and the journey, attended with great difficulty and distress, lasted upwards of six weeks. On the 10th June, 1797, Park once more reached Pisania. He was received by Dr. Laidley " as one risen from the dead." In a few days he went on board an American store-ship, which, after a tempestuous passage, reached the island of Antigua with great difficulty; from whence having embarked for England, he arrived at Falmouth on the 22d December, after an absence from Britain of two years and seven months. It is mentioned as a circumstance connected with his return, that having instantly hastened from Falmouth to London, for the purpose of gaining intelligence about the many friends from whom he had been so long separated, Park arrived at the metropolis before day-light, and not caring to disturb his brother-in-law Mr. Dickson's family, determined to walk about the streets till their hour of rising. Finding the door of the British Museum gardens open, he entered, and had already continued some time, when Mr. Dickson, to whose charge the gardens were committed, having gone to his post that morning sooner than usual, here found, in this strange and unexpected manner, the relative whom he had long lost and numbered with the dead.

It is easy to conceive the feeling of such a rencontre, and the joy with which the news of it were received by all immediately concerned ; but the interest excited by Park's return was not confined to his personal friends, and those who knew him individually. It was looked upon as a kind of triumph by the Association, whose hopes and projects it had in some measure fulfilled ; while the traveller's long absence, his dangerous adventures, and the extraordinary things he was said to have discovered, caused the public in general to regard him with a mingled curiosity and esteem, and to expect the appearance of his travels with no ordinary impatience. In the course of two years these anticipations were amply realised. Immediately on finishing his arrangements in London, Park returned to Fowlshiels, where, in the bosom of domestic affection, in the pastoral solitude of his native glens, he busied himself strenuously in preparing his narrative for the press. It came out in the spring of 1799. Few books of travels have acquired so speedy and extensive a reputation as this of Park's. It was sought for with an eagerness which might have done credit to a novel ; and the reader, whilst his imagination was exalted by the remoteness, the imminent perils, and strange scenes of the journey, could not help feeling something like affection for a person so kindly, so resolute, and yet so unassuming. It still continues one of the most popular works of its class ; and the qualities both of its subject and manner well deserve this pre-eminence. In perusing it, we follow the traveller with a keen anxiety ; we participate in all his toils, and dangers, and hairbreadth escapes, pourtrayed with a brief and touching simplicity, which at once awakens our sympathies by its indubitable air of truth : we are instructed and entertained by his delineation of those vast countries, and the rude tribes which people them ; we admire his modest though unshaken fortitude ; we love the honesty and benevolent candour everywhere displayed by him. Many travellers have possessed more learning, more philosophy, and greater intellectual endowments ; but none has ever known better the secret of concentrating our attention, and calling forth our esteem. It required not only extraordinary strength of mind to accomplish this undertaking ; no common powers of fancy and judgment were also requisite to describe it so agreeably *.

The profits of this publication, added to the recompense allowed him by his employers, had for the present placed Park in easy circumstances. In the autumn of this year, he married the eldest daughter of Mr. Anderson of Selkirk, his former master ; a union adding greatly to his happiness for the short period during which he enjoyed it. In the mean time, however, his way of life was undetermined, and it required some firmness to bear up under the cloud which overhung his future prospects. At one time he was applied to by government to engage in a mission which they had it in view to send out to New Holland ; at another, he was on the point of taking a farm ; and two years passed away, in the house of his mother and

brother at Fowlshiels, before he could finally determine to resume the exercise of his profession at Peebles, where a favourable opening, as he thought, occurred in 1801. The reputation attached to his name, and the amiableness of his general character, soon procured him a respectable practice. He was beloved by the poor, to whom he showed himself at all times charitable and compassionate ; and several eminent literary characters in the neighbourhood, particularly Dr. Adam Fergusson, and Mr. (now Sir Walter) Scott, were eager to number in the list of their friends a person so distinguished for his unaffected worth and great achievements. But the duties of a country surgeon, at all times laborious, and still more so in a thinly peopled district, seem never to have been much to his taste ; they were now rendered more disagreeable from the pre-existence of contrary habits, and the solicitations of those magnificent projects, which his late journey had naturally called into being. Park felt dissatisfied and impatient in the narrow circle to which he was now confined ; and while traversing the bleak moors of Tweeddale, his mind was brooding with enthusiastic hope over the image of brilliant discoveries, which he thought himself yet destined to make in the centre of Africa. He was alive indeed to all the dangers and hard vicissitudes from which he had already only escaped as if by miracle ; whilst suffering from the effects of indigestion, with which since his return he had been considerably afflicted, his disturbed slumbers used frequently to embody his pain in the shape of those miseries he had endured when in Africa ; he would dream of being in the camp of the Moors, exposed to the brutal violence of Ali, and awake in extreme agitation. But the ardent temper of his mind was not to be damped by such considerations. The evils of an African journey were distant in place, and becoming more distant in time ; whilst the disquietudes of his present situation had the painful quality of presence and reality, and he turned from them with disgust, to contemplate the more exalted prospects which imagination delighted to picture in the scene of his former adventures. Those feelings were strengthened, and in part concentrated to a definite object, by an acquaintance which about this period he formed with Mr. George Maxwell, a gentleman of that quarter, formerly an African trader, who had frequently visited the mouth of the Congo ; and from his own observations had come to the conclusion, which in time Park also adopted, that this river was nothing but a continuation of the Niger. Park longed to verify this idea, and to immortalise his name by so splendid a discovery. The obstructions under which he laboured were growing daily more irksome, when fortunately, as he judged, an opportunity occurred of putting his darling scheme into execution. In the autumn of 1803, a letter from the colonial secretary of state's office informed him that government designed to send a mission into the interior of Africa ; for the purpose of arranging which, his presence in London was required immediately.

Before finally agreeing with the terms proposed to him, on the part of government, by Lord Hobart, whom he had hastened to meet, Park requested liberty to return home and deliberate the matter with his friends. He returned accordingly, and consulted a few of them ; but his resolution was easy to anticipate.

* A question has been started, as to the share which Mr. Bryan Edwards, the historian of the West Indies, had in preparing Park's work for the public. From the evidence adduced, it does not however seem, that Mr. Edwards did more than exercise a general superintendence over the language and style, leaving the substantial merits and difficulties of the labour to Park himself.

Now at last he felt himself upon the brink of that vast enterprise on which he had longed so much to embark, and, compared with such excitements as it offered, the disquieting obstructions of his actual situation appeared insupportable. When his brother represented to him the hazard of a second African expedition, the almost certain destruction connected with it; he replied, that a few inglorious winters of country practice at Peebles would kill him as effectually as the most formidable occurrence he could meet with in the deserts of Africa.

Yet his heart was not insensible to those tender ties, which he now felt himself called upon to break asunder. He parted from his family with the most profound emotions, which he tried to enliven with the hopes of soon meeting again,—a hope, resulting more from his own vigorous determination than from any estimate of the difficulties he had to strive with. This hope was indeed fulfilled sooner than even his friends could have wished, if they looked beyond the feelings of the moment. On arriving at London, Park was appointed to sail in the month of February, 1804; but the change of ministry, already contemplated, and finally brought about by Mr. Addington's resignation, produced among its other alterations an alteration of the enterprize in question. Lord Camden, now secretary of state, gave notice that the expedition could not sail before September, if it sailed at all; and it was suggested to Park, impatient of this delay, yet obliged to acquiesce in it, that the intervening period might be profitably employed in acquiring the habit of making astronomical observations, and gaining a knowledge of the Arabic language. Accordingly, having engaged Sidi Ombac, a native of Mogadore, for the latter purpose, and taking proper instruments with him for the former, he returned to Scotland in the latter end of September. This period of leisure was employed by him in his mother's house at Fowlshiels, from which, however, he was shortly summoned; and avoiding the bitterness of a second formal separation, under pretence of a journey to Edinburgh, he quitted the paternal roof, under which so many calm and peaceful days had passed over him, and to which he was destined never more to return.

The main object proposed by Park in this second expedition, was to ascertain the course and termination of the river Niger, which, according to his own opinion, was identical with the river Congo, in the southern hemisphere. Several distinguished geographers, among others Major Rennel, had adopted the supposition that the Niger terminates in a series of lakes in the interior of the continent, and is there evaporated by the heat of the sun. The Major was so persuaded of this, and on other grounds so impressed with the forlornness and peril of the projected expedition, that when Park, before undertaking it, was directed to consult him, the Major laboured earnestly to dissuade his friend from embarking in such an enterprize. His arguments produced a transient effect; yet it was but transient; and Park, on returning to town, was still inflexibly determined to set his life on the risk of proving the Niger and Congo to be the same, or of finding means to traverse the African desert, should the Niger be discovered not to terminate at the ocean. For effecting his intentions, it was finally agreed that he should take with him forty soldiers from the garrison of Goree, having first procured fifty asses at the island of St. Jago, to transport their provisions and baggage; that in company with these men, he should penetrate as speedily as possible to Sego on the Niger; and then construct a vessel, with which it was proposed that he should proceed along the course of the river as far as it was navigable. A commission of brevet captain was bestowed on him; his brother-in-law Mr. Anderson as second in command, and his countryman Mr. Scott as draughtsman, with some carpenters and mechanics, were appointed to attend him: and he left Portsmouth in the Crescent transport, on the 30th of January, 1805.

The voyage to St. Jago, and then to Goree roads, was prosperous; and thirty-five soldiers, with a lieutenant belonging to the garrison, and Isaaco, a native priest and travelling merchant, were easily induced to accompany him. But here the prosperity of the enterprize may be said to have come to an end. The year was unluckily too far advanced for allowing them to reach the Niger before the rainy season began: but as Park preferred the alternative of setting out immediately, even with such a chance against him, to that of continuing seven months in a state of inaction, they lost no time in taking their departure. Having assembled at Kayee on the 27th April, they proceeded eastward without material difficulty to Badoo, where Park had an opportunity of writing to his friends; but long before they reached the Niger, the fatal rainy season had set in. In half an hour after its commencement, the whole troop were affected with a certain degree of sickness; and, in a few days, a horrible dysentery attacked them, and committed the most painful ravages in this little party. On arriving at Macaboo, on the banks of the Niger, no more than eleven of the forty-five Europeans who had left Goree remained alive; and before they reached Sansanding, and concluded their negociations with Mansong, the king of that country, for a free passage through his dominions, the number was reduced to Park himself, lieutenant Martyn, and three soldiers, one of them in a state of insanity. Yet even here, Park, on whom the chief toil and anxiety of a journey, obstructed by so much misfortune, had devolved, never allowed his mind for a moment to misgive him. Though finally seized with the disorder himself, he expelled it immediately by the action of powerful medicines on a vigorous constitution; and having at length adjusted the discussions with Mansong, in a manner which does equal credit to his prudence and firmness, he prepared to embark the remainder of his stores and attendants in a vessel constructed principally by the labour of his own hands, and named "his majesty's schooner Joliba," in reference to the stream which he proposed to explore by means of it. The letters which he wrote from this place to England, display well his inflexible yet modest courage, in circumstances which might have daunted the stoutest and most ardent heart. To his wife, he expressed the strong and cheerful hope of being in England next May; and to Lord Camden, with whom he had less inducement to palliate his difficulties, he thus states his determination; "My dear friend Mr. Anderson, and likewise Mr. Scott, are both dead; but though all the Europeans who are with me should die, and though I were myself half dead, I would still persevere; and, if I could not succeed in the object of my journey, I would at last die on the Niger."

This was on the 17th November, 1805. On the 19th, having first dispatched Isaaco with his letters, and a journal containing notes of the principal occurrences which had taken place, and the principal observations that had been made, during the previous journey, Park set sail ;—and here all knowledge of his history or fortune leaves us. He proceeded down the Niger, but where or how his voyage ended, is, and perhaps may long continue, a point about which conjecture is all we have to offer. It is true, some years after, when nothing was heard of Park but unfavourable though vague reports from the interior, the governor of Goree sent Isaaco, to discover, if possible, the truth or falsehood of those statements which daily reached the coast in a more decisive tone ; and Isaaco returned with a journal of his proceedings, to which was attached a narrative from the mouth of Amadoo Fatima, the guide with whom Park sailed down the river : but though this Amadoo pretended to give an account of the exact circumstances attending Park's death, his report was such as by no means to gain general credit. He stated, that after proceeding for about a month on their voyage, he himself having left Park under the guidance of another pilot, some dispute occurred with a native chief, and, in consequence, the European party were attacked at a place called Boussa, where the stream is much interrupted by rocks ; and all his attendants but one being killed, Park seized this person, and sprung with him into the river, where both quickly expired.

It is evident enough that little trust can be given to this detail. Some parts of it, indeed, particularly the theatrical circumstance of jumping into the river, are, doubtless, mere creations of Amadoo's fancy ; but the great fact, the only important one, of Park's being actually dead, cannot, for a moment, be called in question. How he died, we may perhaps never know ; all we are certain of is, that he died in the prosecution of his undertaking—most probably upon the Niger, as he had already professed to be his determination, rather than fail in the object of his mission.

The only memorial of this journey, the notes sent by Isaaco from Sansanding, together with Isaaco's own journal, were published in 1815. Being written on the spot, and under events so harassing, the information communicated by this work (never in the slightest degree intended for meeting the public) is, of course, defective and meagre. The impression produced by its simple and faithful, though hurried sketches, is perhaps unpleasant on the whole ; we are shocked with the view of such extreme wretchedness endured, with so little advantage to repay it. But the character of Park cannot fail to rise in our estimation from perusing it. The same qualities of calm intrepidity, strong resolution, and unaffected kindliness, which his former journey had brought to light, are here exhibited under circumstances of a deeper and more painful interest ; and the friends of geographical discovery, while they lament the loss of a person every way so qualified to have extended its boundaries, will be joined by the admirers of human worth, in deploring the untimely fate of a man, whose energetic yet affectionate character, did honour to the country that gave him birth.

In private life, Park was distinguished by the same mild warmth of disposition so often alluded to ; a mildness occasioned partly, perhaps, by that habit of reserve and shyness, under which the strong lineaments of his mind were usually hid. He felt little delight in general society, and the modesty of his nature was distressed whenever he became an object of particular attention. The end of all his wishes, the *beau ideal* of his thoughts, was to retire to the country, and conclude his days in the bosom of retirement and domestic affec-

tions. It may be doubted, indeed, whether the prevailing activity of his disposition would have allowed him to find much happiness in realising this *beau ideal;* but the circumstance of his having formed it, bespeaks a simplicity of taste, an honest sensibility, which it is pleasing to see united with a temper so resolute and ardent ; and Park may be pointed out as one of the most unpretending, and, at the same time, valuable specimens of humanity, that embellished the age and country in which he lived. See *Park's Travels*, first and second parts ; and *The Life*, prefixed to the latter.

PARLIAMENT. See ENGLAND, vol. ix. p. 25.

PARMA, a city in the north of Italy, capital of the dutchy of the same name, is situated in a beautiful and fertile country, on the banks of the small river Parma. This river runs through the town, dividing it into two unequal parts, which are united by bridges. It is surrounded by a ditch, and walls flanked with bastions ; and on the south side of the town is the citadel, a regular pentagon, which was formerly reckoned one of the strongest in Italy, but is now falling to decay. The streets are broad, regular, and clean, and meet in the centre, forming a handsome square, which is surrounded with arcades. The houses are of an indifferent appearance, being in general low ; many of them are painted on the outside. The public buildings are not remarkable for their architecture ; but the fine paintings with which many of them are enriched attract universal admiration. It is here, in particular, that we are to look for the masterpieces of the eminent painters, Correggio, Parmeggiano, and Lanfranco ; the two last of whom were natives of Parma.

The ducal palace is an extensive but unfinished range of buildings, without regularity and without ornament. It is occupied by several public establishments, viz. the academy of fine arts, the museum of sculpture and painting, and the public library. The library consists of 80,000 volumes, and contains many rare editions of books ; but they are mostly old. In the gallery of the academy is the celebrated fresco picture of the virgin and the child, which is accounted Correggio's masterpiece. In the same gallery there are many other fine paintings, and several ancient statues, found in the ruins of Velleia. The theatre, which also forms a part of the palace, is a building of Vignola, on the plan of the ancients, like the Olympic theatre at Vicenza. It is said to be the largest in Europe, being capable of containing 10,000 spectators : but, on account of the great expence of fitting it up, it is never used, and therefore suffered to fall to decay. There are five collegiate and thirty parish churches in Parma. The cathedral is Saxon, but lined in the inside with Roman architecture ; it is celebrated for its cupola, painted by Correggio. The Steccata, which is built in the form of a Greek cross, is the most elegant church in Parma. In the cupola of the church of St. John there is also an admirable painting in fresco by Correggio. The university was founded in 1412, by Nicolas d'Este. Its buildings, which are large and handsome, contain an anatomical theatre, an observatory, a chemical laboratory, and a museum of natural history ; there is also a botanical garden attached to it. The number of students seldom exceeds 400. The college for the sons of the nobility, founded in 1600 by Ranuccio Farneze, is fitted for the accommodation of 500 students ; but it is seldom attended by more than fifty. The royal printing press of Parma, established in 1765, has produced several elegant editions of the classics. Parma is the see of a bishop suffragan of Bologna, and the seat of the ducal administration. Its population is estimated at 28,500. Its trade consists chiefly of silk; there are also small manufactures of hats and fustian. There is an agreeable promenade on the ramparts. Near the town is the Palazzo Giardino, a ducal palace surrounded with fine gardens. This spot was, in 1734, the scene of a bloody engagement between the French and Sardinians on the one side, and the Imperialists on the other, in which the latter were defeated.

Parma was founded by the ancient Etruscans. It afterwards came into the possession of the Boii, a tribe of Celtic Gauls; and at length became a Roman colony, in the 568th year of the city. It is said to have suffered severely during the triumvirate, from the cruelties of Antony. It was several times taken and retaken by the Goths and Romans, the Lombards and Greek Exarchs. On the destruction of the kingdom of Lombardy, it was given by Charlemagne to the Holy See. It was then successively under the dominion of the house of Este, the Scaligers, Visconti, Sforzas, and the Popes: and in the sixteenth century it was given by Paul III. to his son Luigi Farnese. It remained in the Farnese family till the extinction of the male branch in the beginning of the last century, when it passed to the house of Spain, by the marriage of Elizabeth Farnese to Philip V. Their son, Don Carlos, in 1731, took possession of the dutchy; but, on his obtaining the crown of Naples, it was ceded to the Emperor. On his death, it was again claimed by Spain, and it was settled by the treaty of Aix-la-Chapelle, in 1748, that Don Philip, second son of Elizabeth Farnese and Philip V. should be put in possession of the dutchies of Parma and Placentia. In 1801, the Duke of Parma obtained the crown of Tuscany, with the title of king of Etruria; but, on his death, Parma and Placentia were occupied by the French troops, and united to France, forming the department of the Taro. On the overthrow of Bonaparte, they were given, by the treaty of Paris, in 1814, to the ex-empress Maria Louisa, reverting, on her death, to Austria and Sardinia; but, by later arrangements, it has been settled that these provinces should eventually return to Spain. West long. 10° 20'; north lat. 44° 48'.

PARMA, a dutchy in the north of Italy, bounded on the east by Modena, on the south and west by Tuscany, and on the north by the Po, which divides it from Milan. Including the districts of Placentia and Guastalla, it contains 2280 square miles. Its population, according to the census taken by order of the French government, is 377,000 or 165 to the square mile. It presents little diversity of surface, being almost an uniform plain, excepting the southern parts, which are traversed by several branches of the Appenines. The appearance of the country, however, is extremely delightful, the whole being divided into inclosures, which are surrounded with rows of mulberries, poplars, and oaks, from whose branches the vines hang in beautiful festoons. It is watered by numerous rivers, which have their source in the Appenines, and which, proceeding in a northerly direction, discharge themselves into the Po. The principal of these are the Taro, the Nuova, the Lenza, and Trebbia. The soil is a rich sandy or gravelly loam, which produces abundantly wheat, maize, vines, and olives, and likewise hemp, saffron, and all sorts of fruits. The pastures are extensive and rich, and support a great number of cattle, which are reared on account of the dairy. The Parmesan cheese has been long held in great estimation, and is exported to almost every country in Eu-

4

rope. In the southern districts, there are some mines of copper, iron, vitriol, and salt, and also some mineral springs. The trade of the dutchy is small, and consists chiefly in the exportation of the raw produce of the soil. The executive power is vested solely in the prince, whose authority is not controlled by any separate order in the state. The revenues of the dutchy amount to L.170,000. It extends from 44° 14' to 44° 59' of north latitude, and from 9° 28' to 10° 56' of east longitude.

PARMEGIANO. See PAINTING, in this volume, p. 245.

PARNELL, THOMAS, a British poet, was born at Dublin, in 1679, and educated in that capital. After taking his degree of M.A. in 1700, he was presented, in 1705, to the archdeaconry of Clogher, and about the same time he married a lady of great beauty and accomplishments. In 1712 he suffered a severe blow from the death of his wife, which is supposed to have produced those habits of intemperance which shortened his life. He died at Chester, on his way to Ireland, in July, 1717, in the 38th year of his age, and was buried in Trinity church. Some of his poetical pieces were published by Pope after his death; but though they are beautiful and pleasing, they have not placed their author in a high rank among the British poets.

PAROS, an island of European Turkey, in the Grecian Archipelago, west of Naxos, and south of Delos, situated between 36° 57', and 37° 13' of North Lat. and 25° 12' and 25° 26' of East Long. It is about forty miles in circumference; and contains a population of 2000. Its surface is hilly, but the soil is fertile, and in a higher state of cultivation than the neighbouring islands. The principal productions are wheat, barley, vines, olives, fruits and cotton. The olives are excellent, and when salted are much esteemed by the natives as an article of food. The pastures are good, and support numerous flocks of sheep. The island is surrounded with excellent natural harbours; that of Naussa, in particular, on the north-east coast, is one of the most capacious and best sheltered in Greece, being capable of containing 100 sail of the line. In the middle of the last century, it was chosen by the Russians as a naval and military station, who erected batteries to defend its entrance, and built magazines and other edifices. It is now the place of rendezvous for the Turkish galleys. Paros was formerly celebrated for its marble, which was of a dazzling whiteness, and used by the best statuaries of antiquity. The Venus de Medicis, the Belvidere Apollo, the Antinous, and many other celebrated works, are of Parian marble. There are two quarries, which are about a league to the east of Parechia, upon the summit of Mount Capresso, anciently Marpesus. These quarries were so deep, that the workmen were always obliged to employ lamps; from which circumstance, according to Pliny, the marble was called Lychnites. They have been long abandoned, and are now partly filled up with rubbish; in one of them there is an ancient bas relief engraved on the rock, representing, in three departments, a festival of Silenus. The antiquities and beautiful ruins which are every where discernible, bear testimony to the pristine opulence and splendour of Paros. The small town of Parechia, which occupies the site of the ancient Paros, and the few wretched villages scattered over the island, are all built of sculptured marble, the wrecks of former monuments and temples. The celebrated chronological tables, known by the name of the Parian or Arundelian marbles, were

Paros.

engraved in this island, and preserved in it from a very remote period. In 1627, they were purchased by the Earl of Arundel, and by him presented to the University of Oxford. The celebrated statuaries Phidias and Praxiteles, were both natives of Paros, as was also the poet Archilochus.

Paros was originally colonized by the Phœnicians, and afterwards by the Cretans. When the Persians invaded Greece, the Parians sided with them, and consequently rendered themselves obnoxious to the Athenians, who made war against them, and captured the island. In the time of Pompey, it fell under the power of the Romans, and on the partition of the empire, it was subject to the Greek emperors. In 1207, it was given to some illustrious Venetians; was afterwards taken by the Turks under Barbarossa, Captain Pacha of Soliman II.; and has languished under their sway ever since.

PARRHASIUS. See the article PAINTING, in this volume, p. 213.

PARTHIA, a country of ancient Asia, bounded on the west by Media, on the north by Hyrcania, on the south by Caramania, and on the east by Osus. According to Ptolemy, it contained twenty-five great cities, the largest of which was called Hecatompylos, from its hundred gates.

After the country had been subjugated by Alexander, and harassed by the rapacity of his successors, Arsaces, a man of obscure birth, but great military talents, headed his countrymen, and founded the Parthian empire, about 250 years before Christ. His successors in power, called Arsacidæ, extended the empire to such a degree, that it possessed eighteen kingdoms between the Caspian and Arabian seas, and was able to resist the overwhelming power of the Romans. See ARSACIDÆ, and PERSIA, in this volume, p. 391.

Parrhasius, Parthia.

PARTIAL DIFFERENCES.

Partial Differences.

1. WE have already considered, under the Article FLUXIONS, the methods of differentiating functions of two or more independent variables, and the notation which is most commonly employed to denote their differential coefficients: in considering the subject of Partial Differences somewhat more at large in this place, we shall of course take those elementary propositions for granted, merely giving such a recapitulation of them as may be necessary to give a greater degree of unity and connection to the investigations which follow.

Functions of one or more independent variables.

2. In any identical equation, where each side of the equation is identically equal to zero, or where one side of the equation contains the result of an algebraic operation, which is merely indicated in the other, being in all other respects identical in form, we may consider every symbol in the equation as equally arbitrary and independent: but if the equation is not identical, we must consider some one symbol as dependent upon all the others for its value, and as expressible in terms of them, and in the theory of equations the dependent symbol as given in terms of the others: but in the differential calculus, symbols are distinguished from each other according as they are the representatives of variable or constant quantities: thus, in the equation to the ellipse,

$$\frac{x^2}{a^2} + \frac{y^2}{b^2} = 1,$$

x and y represent the co-ordinates of the curve, which are variable between given limits, whilst a and b, the semi-axes of the ellipse, remain the same, whether known or unknown: one of them only, however, can be considered as independent, since we may express either x or y in terms of the other variable, and the constant quantities a and b. Thus,

$$y = \frac{b}{a}\sqrt{(a^2 - x^2)}, \text{ or } x = \frac{a}{b}\sqrt{(b^2 - y^2)};$$

and, in one case x, and in the other y, is the independent variable.

But if the equation should contain three variable quantities, then any one of them may be considered as expressible in terms of the other two, both of which are arbitrary and independent. Thus, in the equation,

$$\frac{x^2}{a^2} + \frac{y^2}{b^2} + \frac{z^2}{c^2} = 1,$$

which is the equation of an ellipsoid, whose semi-axes are a, b, c, we have,

$$x = a\sqrt{\left\{1 - \frac{y^2}{b^2} - \frac{z^2}{c^2}\right\}}$$

$$y = b\sqrt{\left\{1 - \frac{x^2}{a^2} - \frac{z^2}{c^2}\right\}}$$

$$z = c\sqrt{\left\{1 - \frac{x^2}{a^2} - \frac{y^2}{b^2}\right\}}$$

Partial Differences.

In this case, x, y, and z, represent the three rectangular co-ordinates of any point in the curve surface: in the first of these equations, in which we consider x as a function of z and y, the co-ordinates z and y are arbitrary and independent of each other, at least within such limits that y may not exceed b, and z may not exceed c: such limits being necessary, when the equation is considered in its geometrical representation, as belonging to a given curve surface; but if we consider it in its analytical sense only, we may give to those symbols the utmost generality of representation, of course supposing that they may become the representatives of imaginary quantities. In the same manner it may be shown, that in any equation containing n variable quantities, there are $n-1$ of them which are perfectly arbitrary and independent of each other: the consideration of such equations, however, is chiefly interesting as regards their analytical theory, for in the solution of physical or geometrical problems they are of very rare occurrence.

3. In functions of one independent variable, we have only one differential coefficient of each order to consider, the determination of which, and the consequences of such determination in the solution of geometrical and other problems, constitutes the principal part of the differential calculus: but in functions of two independent variables, we have two differential coefficients of the first order, three of the second, four of the third, and $n+1$ of the nth order: thus, if z be a function of x and y, we have

Differential coefficients of functions of two or more variables.

$$dz = \frac{dz}{dx}dx + \frac{dz}{dy}dy$$

$$d^2 z = \frac{d^2 z}{dx^2} \cdot dx^2 + \frac{d^2 z}{dx\,dy} \cdot dx\,dy + \frac{d^2 z}{dy^2} \cdot dy^2,$$

$$d^3 z = \frac{d^3 z}{dx^3} \cdot dx^3 + \frac{d^3 z}{dx^2 dy} \cdot dx^2 \, dy + \frac{d^3 z}{dx\,dy^2} \cdot dx\,dy^2 + \frac{d^3 z}{dy^3} \cdot dy^3$$

&c. &c. &c.

And, in general, in any function of m independent variables, the number of differential co-efficients of the order n is equal to

$$\frac{m \cdot (m+1) \dots (m+n-1)}{1 \cdot 2 \dots n}.$$

a conclusion which may be very easily deduced, from a consideration of the method of investigating the differential coefficients of such functions, which is given under the Article FLUXIONS in this work.

Principle
upon which
these diffe-
rential co-
efficients
are obtain-
ed.

These differential coefficients are denominated *partial* differential coefficients, being obtained by the ordinary rules of differentiation of functions of one variable, by assuming successively all but one of the independent variables, as constant quantities.

Thus, if $z = x^3 + a\,x^2 y + y^3$,

we find, $\frac{dz}{dx} = 3\,x^2 + 2\,a\,x\,y$,

considering y as a constant quantity; and, similarly,

$$\frac{dz}{dy} = ax^2 + 3y^2,$$

in this case, considering x as constant; we thus get the *total* differential, or

$$dz = \frac{dz}{dx} \cdot dx + \frac{dz}{dy} \cdot dy$$

$$= 3x^2\,dx + 2\,a\,x\,y\,dx + ax^2 dy + 3y^2 dy,$$

which is the aggregate of the two *partial* differentials of the function.

5. The preceding notation for the partial differential coefficients of z, which is the one most commonly adopted, is that of La Fontaine. Euler denoted such partial differential coefficients, by including them between brackets; thus, for $\frac{dz}{dx}$, he puts $\left(\frac{dz}{dx}\right)$, and for $\frac{dz}{dy}$, $\left(\frac{dz}{dy}\right)$, his object being to distinguish them from the ratio of the *total* differential of z to dx or dy, which is equal to

$$\frac{\frac{dz}{dx}dx + \frac{dz}{dy}dy}{dx}, \text{ or } \frac{\frac{dz}{dx}dx + \frac{dz}{dy}dy}{dy},$$

and which he represented by $\frac{dz}{dx}$ and $\frac{dz}{dy}$. It is very rarely, however, that we have occasion to consider this ratio of the total differential of z to dx or dy, which is denoted whenever it occurs, by $\frac{1}{dx} dz$, or $\frac{1}{dy} dz$. We thus appropriate the most simple notation to that quantity which is of most frequent occurrence.

Lagrange, in his *Théorie des Fonctions Analytiques*, has employed a notation for partial differential coefficients, different from those both of Euler and La Fontaine; if we suppose z a function of x and y, he expresses the coefficients,

$$\frac{dz}{dx}, \frac{dz}{dy}, \frac{d^2 z}{dx^2}, \frac{d^2 z}{dxdy}, \frac{d^2 z}{dy^2}, \&c.$$

by $f'\,(x, y), f\,(x, y), f''\,(x, y), f'\,(x, y), f\,(x, y)$. Again, if f be a function of three independent variables, x, y, and z, the differential coefficients of the first and second order of the function are denoted by

$$f'\,(x,) f'\,(y,) f'\,(z),$$

$f'\,(x,) f''\,(y,) f''\,(z,) f''\,(x, y,) f''\,(x, z,) f''\,(z, y,)$ including between the brackets, those symbols which are supposed to be variable to the differentiation or differentiations which are required to determine the coefficients.

It may be observed of this notation, that even in ordinary cases it does not speak more distinctly to the eye than the notation of La Fontaine, and becomes extremely complicated and inconvenient when the coefficients are of the third or higher orders, in consequence of the number of accents which are required: and the inconvenience is more strongly felt, when several functions are required to be considered at the same time, which can only be done, at least in conformity with this notation, by different modifications of the same letter f: it was probably for these reasons, that, in his Treatise *Sur la Résolution des Equations Numériques,* he has abandoned his former notation, and denoted the first and second differential coefficients of a function Z, of x, y, and z, by

$$\left(\frac{Z'}{x'}\right) \left(\frac{Z'}{y'}\right), \left(\frac{Z'}{z'}\right);$$

$$\left(\frac{Z''}{x'^2}\right), \left(\frac{Z''}{y'^2}\right), \left(\frac{Z''}{z'^2}\right), \left(\frac{Z''}{x'\,y'}\right), \left(\frac{Z''}{x'\,z'}\right), \left(\frac{Z''}{y'\,z'}\right),$$

a notation which seems to labour under all the inconveniences of the English notation of Fluxions, without possessing the advantage of its being part of a general system; it must be confessed, indeed, that in the choice of his notation on this as well as other occasions, particularly in the Calculus of Variations, this illustrious analyst has not shown the same profound and philosophical views of the general principles of notation which characterise his fine and original researches in almost every part of analysis.

6. The process for finding the differential coefficients of a function of two or more variables, leads to a general theorem of great importance, which is as follows: *That in deducing any partial differential coefficient of the second or higher order, where more than one symbol is considered as variable, it is indifferent in what order the operations succeed each other:* thus, in deducing the second differential coefficient of a function of x and y, by first considering x as variable, and, secondly, considering y as variable, we should arrive at the same result by first considering y as variable, and, secondly, considering x as variable: or, in other words,

$$\frac{d^2 z}{dx\,dy} = \frac{d^2 z}{dy\,dx}$$

In the same manner we should find

$$\frac{d^3 z}{dx^2\,dy} = \frac{d^3 z}{dx\,dy\,dx} = \frac{d^3 z}{dy\,dx}$$

and similarly in all other cases.

Thus, if $z = x \sin. y + y \sin. x$, we shall find

$$\frac{dz}{dx} = \sin. y + y \cos. x,$$

$$\frac{dz}{dy} = \sin. x + x \cos. y,$$

$$\frac{d^2 z}{dx\, dy} = \cos. y + \cos. x = \frac{d^2 z}{dy\, dx}.$$

Again, if

$$u = \frac{x^2 y^2}{z^2 + v^2}$$

we shall find

$$\frac{d^4 u}{dx\, dy\, dz\, dv} = \frac{32\, x y\, z v}{(z^2 + v^2)^3},$$

and the same result may be obtained by as many processes of differentiation as there are permutations of dx, dy, dz, dv, in the denominator of $d^4 u$, which are twenty-four in number.

Method of
differenti-
ating im-
plicit func-
tions of any
number of
variables.

7. If $u = 0$, be an equation containing x, y, and z, we may consider z as an implicit function of the independent variables x and y; if we suppose, therefore, y to be constant, $u = 0$, may be considered as an equation between z and x, and we shall find

$$\frac{du}{dx}\, dx + \frac{du}{dz} \cdot dz = 0,$$

or

$$\frac{du}{dx} + \frac{du}{dz} \cdot \frac{dz}{dx} = 0 ; \quad (1.)$$

from which we may determine $\dfrac{dz}{dx}$.

In a similar manner, if we consider x as constant, we shall find

$$\frac{du}{dy} + \frac{du}{dz} \cdot \frac{dz}{dy} = 0 ; \quad (2.)$$

from which we may determine $\dfrac{dz}{dy}$.

If we multiply equation (1.) by dx, and equation (2.) by dy, we shall get

$$\frac{du}{dx}\, dx + \frac{du}{dy}\, dy + \frac{du}{dz} \cdot \left(\frac{dz}{dx}\, dx + \frac{dz}{dy}\, dy\right) = 0 ;$$

which becomes, since $dz = \dfrac{dz}{dx}\, dx + \dfrac{dz}{dy}\, dy$,

$$\frac{du}{dx}\, dx + \frac{du}{dy}\, dy + \frac{du}{dz}\, dz = 0 ;$$

or, in other words, we may equate the first differential of the equation $u = 0$, taken with respect to the three variables x, y, z, to zero ; it being, of course, kept in mind, that this equation virtually includes the two equations (1.) and (2.) it being equal to their sum when respectively multiplied by dx and dy.

If it was required to investigate equations which would give *implicitly* the differential coefficients $\dfrac{d^2 z}{dx^2}$, $\dfrac{d^2 z}{dx\, dy}$, $\dfrac{d^2 z}{dy^2}$ of the second order, we should commence with differentiating the equations (1.) and (2.) with respect to x or to y ; the differential of the first with respect to x, would give us, by dividing by dx,

$$\frac{d^2 u}{dx^2} + \frac{2\, d^2 u}{dz\, dx} \cdot \frac{dz}{dx} + \frac{d^2 u}{dz^2} \cdot \frac{dz^2}{dx^2} + \frac{du}{dz}\frac{d^2 z}{dx^2} = 0. \quad (3.)$$

Again, differentiating equation (1.) with respect to y, or equation (2.) with respect to x, we should get, in both cases,

$$\frac{d^2 u}{dx\, dy} + \frac{d^2 u}{dz\, dy} \cdot \frac{dz}{dx} + \frac{d^2 u}{dz\, dx} \cdot \frac{dz}{dy} + \frac{d^2 u}{dz^2} \cdot \frac{dz}{dy} \cdot \frac{dz}{dx}$$
$$+ \frac{du}{dz} \cdot \frac{d^2 z}{dx\, dy} = 0. \quad (4.)$$

And, lastly, differentiating equation (2.) with respect to y, we should get

$$\frac{d^2 u}{dy^2} + \frac{2\, d^2 u}{dz\, dy} \cdot \frac{dz}{dy} + \frac{d^2 u}{dz^2} \cdot \frac{dz^2}{dy^2} + \frac{du}{dz} \cdot \frac{d^2 z}{dy^2} = 0. \quad (5.)$$

We have thus three equations (3,) (4,) (5,) for the respective determination of the three coefficients of z of the second order,

$$\frac{d^2 z}{dx^2}, \quad \frac{d^2 z}{dx\, dy}, \quad \frac{d^2 z}{dy^2}.$$

If we multiply the equations (3,) (4,) (5,) by dx^2, $dx\, dy$, dy^2 respectively, and replace

$$\frac{dz}{dx}\, dx + \frac{dz}{dy}\, dy \text{ by } dz, \text{ and}$$

$$\frac{d^2 z}{dx^2}\, dx^2 + \frac{2\, d^2 z}{dx\, dy}\, dx\, dy + \frac{d^2 z}{dy^2}\, dy^2 \text{ by } d^2 z,$$

we shall find, for the second total differential of the equation $u = 0$,

$$\frac{d^2 u}{dx^2}\, dx^2 + \frac{d^2 u}{dy^2}\, dy^2 + \frac{d^2 u}{dz^2}\, dz^2 + \frac{2\, d^2 u}{dx\, dy} \cdot dx\, dy$$
$$+ \frac{2\, d^2 u}{dx\, dz} \cdot dx\, dz + \frac{2\, d^2 u}{dy\, dz} \cdot dy\, dz + \frac{du}{dz} \cdot d^2 z = 0.$$

On the eli-
mination of
arbitrary
functions
from equa-
tions in-
volving
more than
two vari-
ables.

8. One of the most important analytical applications of the calculus of partial differentials, consists in the elimination of functions of variable quantities perfectly arbitrary, from equations of three or more variables in which they are involved. As the theory of the solution of partial differential equations receives a similar kind of illustration from the elimination of such arbitrary functions, that the theory of the solution of ordinary differential equations receives from the elimination of arbitrary constants from equations of two variables only, we shall proceed to explain this part of the subject by a few examples.

Let us take the equation

$$z = \varphi\, (xy),$$

where φ denotes a perfectly arbitrary function of xy. If we assume $\varphi'\, (xy)$ to denote the first differential coefficient of $\varphi\, (xy)$, considering xy as a simple independent variable u, we shall find

$$\frac{dz}{dx} = \varphi'\, (xy) \cdot y, \quad (1.)$$

$$\frac{dz}{dy} = \varphi'\, (xy) \cdot x; \quad (2.)$$

and eliminating $\varphi'\, (xy)$ from the two equations (1.) and (2.) we find

$$x\frac{dz}{dx} - y\frac{dz}{dy} = 0: \quad (3.)$$

an equation in which no arbitrary function appears. This equation (3.) is a partial differential equation of the first order, and is satisfied by making z equal to any function whatever of xy: Thus, if, for the sake of example, we make

$$z = \frac{a x y - b}{a x y + b} + \frac{c x y + d}{c x y - d},$$

we shall find

$$\frac{dz}{dx} = \frac{2\,a\,b\,y}{(a\,x\,y + b)^2} - \frac{2\,c\,d\,y}{(c\,x\,y - d)^2},$$

and

$$\frac{dz}{dy} = \frac{2\,a\,b\,x}{(a\,x\,y + b)^2} - \frac{2\,c\,d\,x}{(c\,x\,y - d)^2};$$

from which values it immediately follows, that

$$x\frac{dz}{dx} - y\frac{dz}{dy} = 0.$$

Again, take the equation

$$\frac{z-c}{y-b} = \varphi\left(\frac{z-c}{x-a}\right).$$

Differentiating, first, with respect to x, and, secondly, with respect to y, we shall find

$$\frac{\frac{dz}{dx}}{y-b} = \varphi'\left(\frac{z-c}{x-a}\right) \times \left\{\frac{(x-a)\frac{dz}{dx} - (z-c)}{(x-a)^2}\right\} \quad (1.)$$

$$\frac{(y-b)\frac{dz}{dy} - (z-c)}{y-b)^2} = \varphi'\left(\frac{z-c}{x-a}\right) \times \left\{\frac{\frac{dz}{dy}}{x-a}\right\}; \quad (2.)$$

eliminating $\varphi'\left(\frac{z-c}{x-a}\right)$ from these two equations, and reducing the result to its most simple form, we shall find

$$z - c = (x-a)\frac{dz}{dx} + (y-b)\frac{dz}{dy}. \quad (3.)$$

When more than one arbitrary function is involved in the equation, it will be necessary to proceed to differential coefficients of an order equal to the number of such functions. Thus, if it was required to eliminate the arbitrary functions from the equation

$$z = \varphi\,(y + a\,x)\,\psi\,(y - a\,x),$$

we should find, by adding together $\frac{dz}{dx}$ and $\frac{a\,dz}{dy}$, that

$$\frac{dz}{dx} + \frac{a\,dz}{dy} = 2\,a.\psi(y-ax)\varphi'(y+ax) = \frac{2\,az.\varphi'(v+ax)}{\varphi\,(y+ax)},$$

and differentiating this equation, first considering x and afterwards y as variable, we shall find

$$\frac{d^2 z}{dx^2} + \frac{a\,d^2 z}{dy\,dx} = 2\,a\frac{dz}{dx}\cdot\frac{\varphi'\,(y+ax)}{\varphi\,(y+ax)} + 2\,a^2 z\frac{\varphi''(y+ax)}{\varphi\,(y+ax)}$$
$$- \frac{2\,a^2\,z\,\varphi'^2\,(v+ax)}{\varphi^2\,(y+ax)},$$

$$\frac{d^2 z}{dx\,dy} + \frac{a\,d^2 z}{dy^2} = 2\,a\frac{dz}{dy}\cdot\frac{\varphi'\,(y+ax)}{\varphi\,(y+ax)} + \frac{2\,az.\varphi''(y+ax)}{\varphi\,(y+ax)}$$
$$- \frac{2\,a\,z\,\varphi'^2\,(y+ax)}{\varphi^2\,(y+ax)}.$$

Multiplying the last equation by a, and subtracting it from the former, we get

$$\frac{d^2 z}{dx^2} - \frac{a^2\,d^2 z}{dy^2} = 2\,a\left(\frac{dz}{dx} - \frac{a\,dz}{dy}\right)z\cdot\frac{\varphi'\,(y+ax)}{\varphi\,(y+ax)} =$$
$$\left(\frac{dz}{dx} - \frac{a\,dz}{dy}\right)\left(\frac{dz}{dx} + \frac{a\,dz}{dy}\right) = \frac{dz^2}{dx^2} - \frac{a^2\,dz^2}{dy^2};$$

a partial differential equation of the second order.

9 We shall now proceed to give Laplace's demonstration of the celebrated theorem of Lagrange, which furnishes a beautiful illustration of the application of this part of analysis.

If we suppose

$$u = \psi\,y,$$
$$\text{and } y = f(z + x\,\varphi\,y),$$

it is obvious that we may consider u as *implicitly* a function of the independent variables z and x; the object of the theorem is to express this function in an explicit form.

If we consider u as a function of x, expressible in a series proceeding according to integral powers of x, we should find by the theorem of Maclaurin or Stirling,

$$u = \underset{0}{U} + \underset{1}{U}\frac{x}{1} + \underset{2}{U}\frac{x^2}{1.2} + \underset{3}{U}\frac{x^3}{1.2.3} + \&c.$$

where $\underset{0}{U}, \underset{1}{U}, \underset{2}{U}, \underset{3}{U}$, &c. are the values of $u, \frac{du}{dx}, \frac{d^2u}{dx^2}$, &c. which arise from making $x=0$.

Since $u = \psi\,y = \psi f(z + x\,\varphi\,y) = F(z + x\,\varphi\,y)$, replacing the functional symbol ψf by F, the form of which is given, it becomes extremely difficult to ascertain the law of formation of the differential coefficients of u, after the first or second, when $x=0$, by any direct method. The following process, however, will lead to a conclusion, by which we shall be enabled to express $\frac{du}{dx}, \frac{d^2u}{dx^2}$, &c. in terms of $\frac{du}{dz}$, and given functions of y in a very simple manner.

Differentiating $y = f(z + x\,\varphi\,y)$, with respect to x and z respectively, we get

$$\frac{dy}{dx} = f'(z + x\,\varphi\,y) \times \left\{\varphi\,y + x\,\varphi'y\frac{dy}{dx}\right\}$$
$$\frac{dy}{dz} = f'(z + x\,\varphi\,y) \times \left\{1 + x\,\varphi'y\frac{dy}{dz}\right\}$$

eliminating $f'(z + x\,\varphi\,y)$, we find

$$\frac{dy}{dx} - \varphi\,y\frac{dy}{dz} = 0. \quad (\alpha.)$$

Again, since $u = \psi\,y$, we have

$$\frac{du}{dx} = \psi'\,y\frac{dy}{dx}, \text{ and } \frac{du}{dz} = \psi'\,y\frac{dy}{dz};$$

and eliminating $\psi'\,y$, we get

$$\frac{du}{dx}\cdot\frac{dy}{dz} - \frac{du}{dy}\cdot\frac{dy}{dx} = 0.$$

Or replacing $\frac{dy}{dx}$ by $\varphi\,y\cdot\frac{dy}{dz}$ its value from equation (α), we get

$$\frac{du}{dx} - \varphi\,y\cdot\frac{du}{dz} = 0 \quad (\beta.)$$

It appears, therefore, that if $y = f(z + x\,\varphi\,y,)$ and u be any function of y whatever, then

$$\frac{du}{dx} = \varphi\,y\cdot\frac{du}{dz}.$$

If, for the sake of simplicity, we put $t = \varphi\,y$, we shall have

$$\frac{du}{dx} = t\,\frac{du}{dz};$$

and therefore differentiating $\frac{du}{dx}$ with respect to x,

$$\frac{d^2u}{dx^2} = d\cdot t\frac{\frac{du}{dz}}{dx};$$

PARTIAL DIFFERENCES. 325

Partial
Differ-
ences.

Partial
Differ-
ences.

but since $t\frac{du}{dz}$ is a function of y, t being $\varphi\,y$, and $\frac{du}{dz}$ being $\psi\,y \cdot \frac{dy}{dz}$, we may consider it as the first differential coefficient $\frac{du'}{dz}$ of some function u' of y, and consequently

$$\frac{d^2 u}{dx^2}=\frac{d^2 u'}{dz\,dx};$$

or, inverting the order of differentiations,   (Art. 6.)

$$\frac{d^2 u}{dx^2}=\frac{d^2 u'}{dx\,dz}=\frac{d\cdot\frac{du'}{dx}}{dz};$$

but it appears from the result in equation (β.) that

$$\frac{du'}{dx}=t\frac{du'}{dz},$$

and therefore

$$\frac{d^2 u}{dx^2}=\frac{d\cdot t\frac{du'}{dz}}{dz}=\frac{d\cdot t\cdot t\frac{du}{dz}}{dz}=\frac{d\cdot t^2\frac{du}{dz}}{dz}.$$

In the same manner, we should find

$$u=\mathrm{F}(z)+\varphi(z)\mathrm{F}'(z)\cdot\frac{x}{1}+\frac{d\cdot\varphi(z)^2\mathrm{F}'(z)}{dz}\cdot\frac{x^2}{1.2}+\frac{d^2\cdot\varphi(z)^3\mathrm{F}'(z)}{dz^2}\cdot\frac{x^3}{1.2.3}+\&c.$$

We shall take as an example of the application of this theorem, the investigation of the series for expressing the eccentric anomaly of a planet in terms of the mean anomaly.

If u be the eccentric, and $n\,t$ the mean anomaly of a planet, and e the eccentricity of its elliptic orbit, we shall find the following equation between u, $n\,t$, and e, namely,

$$u = n\,t + e\sin.u.$$

It is required to express u in terms of $n\,t$. In this case, we have $u = y$, $z = n\,t$, $x = e$, and $\varphi\,y = \sin.u$; consequently

$$u = z + e\sin.z + \frac{e^2}{1.2}\cdot d\cdot\frac{(\sin.z)^2}{dz}+$$

$$\frac{e^3}{1.2.3}\cdot\frac{d^2\cdot(\sin.z)^3}{dz^2}+\&c.$$

Or $u = n\,t + e\sin.n\,t + \frac{e^2}{1.2.2}\cdot 2\sin.2\,n\,t+$

$$\frac{e^3}{1.2.3.2^2}(3^2\sin.3\,n\,t - 3\sin.n\,t)$$

$$+\frac{e^4}{1.2.3.4.2^3}(4^3\sin.4\,n\,t - 4.2^3.\sin.2\,n\,t)$$

$$+\&c.$$

The reader will find other examples of the uses and application of this theorem, which are both numerous and important, in Note XI. to the *Résolution des Equations Numériques* of Lagrange.

Maxima and minima of functions of two or more variables.

10. The *maxima* and *minima* of functions of two or more independent variables, are determined by making the first differential coefficients severally equal to zero, a conclusion deduced by reasoning extremely analogous to that employed in determining the *maxima* or *minima* of functions of one independent variable. We thus get as many equations as there are variable quantities, from which their values may be determined.

Thus, suppose it was required to determine the posi-

$$\frac{d^3 u}{dx^3}=\frac{d^2\cdot t^2\frac{du}{dz}}{dz\,dx};\text{ and making }t^2\frac{du}{dz}=\frac{du''}{dz},$$

we get

$$\frac{d^3 u}{dx^3}=\frac{d^5 u''}{dz^2\,dx}=\frac{d^2\frac{du''}{dx}}{dz^2};$$

and replacing $\frac{du''}{dx}$ by $t\frac{du''}{dz}$, and $\frac{du''}{dz}$ by $t^2\frac{du}{dz}$, we find

$$\frac{d^3 u}{dx^3}=\frac{d^2\cdot t^5\frac{du}{dz}}{dz^2}.$$

In the same manner, we should be enabled to replace

$$\frac{d^4 u}{dx^4},\ \frac{d^5 u}{dx^5},\cdots\frac{d^n u}{dx^n}\text{ by}$$

$$\frac{d^3\cdot t^4\frac{du}{dz}}{dz^3},\ \frac{d^4\cdot t^5\frac{du}{dz}}{dz^4},\cdots\frac{d^{n-1}t^n\frac{du}{dz}}{dz^{n-1}}.$$

Consequently, since, when $x=0$ we have $t=\varphi z$, and $\frac{du}{dz}=\mathrm{F}z'$, the series becomes

tion of a point, the sum of the squares of whose distances from four given points in space shall be the least possible. Let one of the points be the origin of the co-ordinates, and A, B, C, a, b, c, and α, β, γ, be the co-ordinates of the other three; and let x, y, z be the co-ordinates of the point whose position is to be determined. The function of x, y, z, in this case, whose *minimum* value is required, or

$$u = x^2+y^2+z^2+(\mathrm{A}-x)^2+(\mathrm{B}-y)^2+(\mathrm{C}-z)^2+(a-x)^2+(b-y)^2+(c-z)^2+(\alpha-x)^2+(\beta-y)^2+(\gamma-z)^2.$$

$$= 4(x^2+y^2+z^2)-2(\mathrm{A}+a+\alpha)x-2(\mathrm{B}+b+\beta)y-2(\mathrm{C}+c+\gamma)z+\mathrm{A}^2+a^2+\alpha^2+\mathrm{B}^2+b^2+\beta^2+\mathrm{C}^2+c^2+\gamma^2.$$

$$\therefore\ \frac{du}{dx}=8x-2(\mathrm{A}+a+\alpha)=0,$$

$$\frac{du}{dy}=8y-2(\mathrm{B}+b+\beta)=0,$$

$$\frac{du}{dz}=8z-2(\mathrm{C}+c+\gamma)=0.$$

Consequently

$$x=\frac{\mathrm{A}+a+\alpha}{4},\ y=\frac{\mathrm{B}+b+\beta}{4},\ \gamma=\frac{\mathrm{C}+c+\gamma}{4},$$

and the co-ordinates of the given point are determined.

Lagrange first pointed out completely the analytical tests, by which it may be ascertained whether a function of two independent variables, determined by this process, is a *maximum* or a *minimum*, or neither one nor the other; a question, the importance of which has been increased in consequence of its having been imperfectly solved by Euler. When more than two independent variables are involved, the application of such tests becomes extremely complicated and difficult. In geometrical questions, however, the object of the problem is generally sufficiently distinct and obvious, and leaves no doubt whatever on the mind whether the function in question is a *maximum* or *minimum*.

11. Every equation involving three variable quantities, is the equation of a curve surface, and the determination of the tangent planes, lines of greatest and least curvature, &c. of such surfaces, furnish some of the most interesting and beautiful applications of the calculus of partial differences. The limits, however, to which we are confined by the nature of this work, prevent our entering upon this subject, which would lead to details of considerable length; and we must be contented with referring our readers to the great work of Lacroix on the Differential Calculus, and the very excellent and original work of Monge, which is entitled, *Application d'Analyse à la Géometrie.*

12. We shall now proceed to the second or inverse part of our subject, the integration of partial differential equations; our notice of which must be still more brief and imperfect than that of the first.

If the equation

$$P\,dx + Q\,dy + R\,dz = 0$$

be the *total* differential of an equation $u=0$, we should have $P\,dx + Q\,dy = 0$, $P\,dx + R\,dz = 0$, $Q\,dy + R\,dz = 0$, for the differentials of $u=0$, which would arise from supposing z, y, and x, successively constant. They must, therefore, satisfy the *criteria of integrability*, (Art. 174, FLUXIONS,) that is, we must have

$$\frac{dP}{dy} = \frac{dQ}{dx}, \quad \frac{dP}{dz} = \frac{dR}{dx}, \text{ and } \frac{dQ}{dz} = \frac{dR}{dy}:$$

In this case the complete integral may always be found by the same method, as is given in the article referred to, for equations of two variables: Of this kind is the equation

$$\frac{y\,dx}{a-z} + \frac{x\,dy}{a-z} + \frac{xy\,dz}{(a-z)^2} - \frac{a\,dz}{a-z} = 0,$$

which satisfies the criteria of integrability; consequently, considering z as constant, we find

$$\int \left(\frac{y\,dx}{a-z} + \frac{x\,dy}{a-z} \right) = \frac{xy}{a-z} + f(z)$$

and $f(z) = \int \left\{ \frac{xy\,dz}{(a-z)^2} - \frac{a\,dz}{a-z} - \frac{xy\,dz}{(a-z)^2} \right\}$

$$= a \log. (a-z);$$

therefore $\dfrac{xy}{a-z} + a \log. (a-z) = $ const.

13. If the equation $P\,dx + Q\,dy + R\,dz = 0$ does not satisfy the criteria of integrability, it may, perhaps, be made to satisfy them if multiplied by some factor μ: In this case we shall find

$$\frac{d\mu P}{dy} = \frac{d\mu Q}{dx}, \quad \frac{d\mu P}{dz} = \frac{d\mu R}{dx}, \quad \frac{d\mu Q}{dz} = \frac{d\mu R}{dy};$$

which equations are equivalent to the following:

$$\mu \left(\frac{dQ}{dx} - \frac{dP}{dy} \right) + Q\frac{d\mu}{dx} - P\frac{d\mu}{dy} = 0,$$

$$\mu \left(\frac{dR}{dx} - \frac{dP}{dz} \right) + R\frac{d\mu}{dx} - P\frac{d\mu}{dz} = 0,$$

$$\mu \left(\frac{dR}{dy} - \frac{dQ}{dz} \right) + R\frac{d\mu}{dy} - Q\frac{d\mu}{dz} = 0;$$

if we multiply the first of these equations by R, the second by — Q, and the third by P, and divide the result by μ, we shall get

5

$$P\frac{dR}{dy} - P\frac{dQ}{dz} - Q\frac{dR}{dx} + Q\frac{dP}{dz} + R\frac{dQ}{dx} -$$
$$R\frac{dP}{dz} = 0, \ (\alpha);$$

an equation of condition, which, if not satisfied, shows that there is no factor μ which can make the proposed equation a complete differential; or, in other words, no one of the three variables x, y, z, can be considered as a function of the other two. Every differential equation, therefore, of three variables, does not necessarily, as in equations of two variables, admit of a multiplier by which it may be rendered a complete differential.

Equations of this kind were once considered as *absurd*, and as totally destitute of any geometrical signification. Monge, however, to whom this part of analysis is under great obligations, in the *Mémoires de l'Académie des Sciences* of Paris for 1784, first showed that such equations had a real signification, representing an infinity of curves of double curvature, possessing a common property.

The method of integrating equations of three variables, which satisfy the equation of condition (α), is to consider one of the variables as constant, and to apply the rules of integration which are given for equations of two variables. The integral which is thus found, may be completed in the same manner as for equations which are total differentials. Thus, suppose it was required to integrate the equation

$$2\,dx(y+z) + dy(x+3y+2z) + dz(x+y) = 0,$$

which satisfies the equation of condition, (α). Suppose y constant, and the equation becomes

$$2\,dx(y+z) + dz(x+y) = 0;$$

or, $\qquad \dfrac{2\,dx}{x+y} + \dfrac{dz}{y+z} = 0:$

Therefore, $2 \log. (x+y) + \log. (y+z) = \log. Y$;

or $\qquad (x+y)^2(y+z) = Y.$

In order to determine Y, we must differentiate the equation, considering x, y, and z, as variable, and we shall get

$$(x+y)\left\{ 2(y+z)(dx+dy) + (x+y)(dz+dy) \right\} = dY;$$

or, $(x+y)\left\{ 2\,dx(y+z) + dy(x+3y+2z) + dz(x+y) \right\} = 0 = dY;$

and therefore $(x+y^2)(z+y) = $ const.

is the complete integral of the equation.

In those cases in which the equation of condition (α) is not satisfied, we can no longer consider x and y as independent variables; we must assume, therefore, one of them equal to an arbitrary function of the other: It then becomes a differential equation between two variables, and may be integrated by the ordinary processes for such equations. The integral will thus be exhibited by a system of two equations, which are both of them indeterminate, as they both involve an arbitrary function. As an example, let us take the equation

$$dz^2 = a^2(dx^2 + dy^2),$$

which does not satisfy the equation of condition (α). Make x constant, which gives us $dz = a\,dy$;

and therefore $z = ay + X$, where $X = f(x)$:

Partial
Differ-
ences.

If we now suppose x variable, we find

$$dz = a\,dy + dX = a\,dy + X^1\,dx:$$

If we substitute this value of dz in the original equation, we shall find

$$2\,dy = \frac{a\,dx}{X^1} - \frac{X^1\,dx}{a},$$

and

$$2\,y = a\int\frac{dx}{X^1} - \frac{X}{a}.$$

The condition expressed by the original equation is satisfied by any curve of double curvature, whose tangents make a given angle with the plane of xy; thus the straight line determined by the system of equations

$$x = bz + c,$$

$$y = \frac{z\,\sqrt{(1 - a^2\,b^2)}}{a} + d,$$

will satisfy the equation*.

Partial differential equations involving one differential coefficient only.

14. Of partial differential equations which may be considered as arising from the elimination of arbitrary functions, the most simple are those which involve one partial differential coefficient only, with or without the variables x, y, and z; of this kind is the equation

$$\frac{dz}{dx} = \frac{xy}{x^2 + y^2},$$

whose integral is

$$z = y\log.\sqrt{x^2 + y^2} + \varphi\,y.$$

The reason of this conclusion will be obvious, when we consider that the differential coefficient $\frac{dz}{dx}$ is obtained by considering y as constant; we must suppose it constant likewise in the integration; but, in order to make the integral complete, we must add an arbitrary function of y, since such an arbitrary function would have disappeared upon differentiating the equation upon such an hypothesis.

If the equation contains z as well as x, y, and $\frac{dz}{dx}$, we must consider it as an equation between two variables z and x, and integrate it accordingly, taking care to make the integral complete by adding an arbitrary function of y; thus the equation

$$\frac{dz}{dx} = \frac{y}{x + z}, \text{ or}$$

$$dx - \frac{x\,dz}{y} = \frac{z\,dz}{y},$$

becomes a case of Bernoulli's equation, which is given under the article FLUXIONS, Art. 171; and its integral, found by that method, is

$$e^{-\frac{z}{y}}(x + y + z) = \varphi\,y,$$

replacing the constant by $\varphi\,y$.

Equations containing the two differential coefficients $\frac{dz}{dx}$ and $\frac{dz}{dy}$, with x, y, and z.

15. We shall now proceed to consider the equation $P\,p + Q\,q = R$, where $p = \frac{dz}{dx}$, $q = \frac{dz}{dy}$, and where P, Q, R, are any functions of the variables x, y, and z.

The following theorem, of which Lagrange is the author, will enable us to integrate this equation in a

great number of cases. If we integrate any two of the equations

$$\begin{array}{ll}
P\,dx - Q\,dy = 0 & (1.)\\
P\,dz - R\,dx = 0 & (2.)\\
Q\,dz - R\,dy = 0 & (3.)
\end{array}$$

and call the integral of one of them a, and of the other b; then we shall have, for the complete integral of the equation,

$$b = \varphi\,(a).$$

We shall now proceed to consider the demonstration of this important theorem: If we suppose $u = F\,(x, y, z,)$ $= 0$, to be the primitive equation of the differential equation, we shall find

$$\frac{dz}{dx} = -\frac{\dfrac{du}{dx}}{\dfrac{du}{dz}} \quad \text{and} \quad \frac{dz}{dy} = -\frac{\dfrac{du}{dy}}{\dfrac{du}{dz}}; \quad (7.)$$

by substituting these values of p and q in the equation

$$p + \frac{Q}{P}q = \frac{R}{P},$$

or $\quad p + M\,q = N,$

we get $\quad \dfrac{du}{dx} + M\dfrac{du}{dy} + N\dfrac{du}{dz} = 0. \quad (\alpha.)$

Again, since $\quad du = \dfrac{du}{dx}dx + \dfrac{du}{dy}dy + \dfrac{du}{dz}dz,$

by substituting the value of $\frac{du}{dx}$, which is given by equation (α), we find

$$du = \frac{du}{dy}(dy - M\,dx) + \frac{du}{dz}(dz - N\,dx)$$

which becomes equal to zero, as it ought to be, by supposing the equations

$$dy - M\,dx = 0$$
$$dz - N\,dx = 0$$

to obtain simultaneously.

These equations being of the first degree, their integrals, if they can be obtained, will contain two arbitrary constants, which we shall call a and b. We shall thus be enabled to express x and y, in terms of a, b, and z, which values being substituted in the primitive equation $u = 0$, will make it a function of a, b, and z; but since $du = 0$, it follows that z does not enter u. It follows, therefore, that

$$u = 0 = F\,(a, b)$$

and consequently

$$b = \varphi\,(a).$$

The success of this method will depend upon one of the equations (1,) (2,) (3,) involving two variables only. The integral of this will enable us, if necessary, to exterminate one of the three variables from one of the remaining equations, after which it may be integrated in the ordinary manner.

Let us take, as an example, the equation

$$a\,p + b\,q = 1.$$

where the coefficients of p and q are constant quantities.

---

* Monge, *Mémoires de l'Académie des Sciences*, 1784.

The equations (1.) and (2.) in this case become

$$a\,dy - b\,dx = 0 \qquad (1.)$$
$$a\,dz - d\,x = 0 \qquad (2.)$$

consequently

$$a\,y - b\,x = \alpha,$$
$$a\,z - x = \beta;$$

the integral of the equation, therefore, since $\beta = \varphi\,(\alpha)$, is

$$z = \frac{x}{a} + \varphi\,(a\,y - b\,x);$$

which is the general equation to all cylindric surfaces.

Let us take the equation

$$x^2\,p + y^2\,q = a\,x\,y.$$

In this case, the equations (1.) and (2.) become

$$x^2\,dy - y^2\,dx = 0 \qquad (1.)$$
$$x\,dz - a\,y\,dx = 0 \qquad (2.)$$

The integral of the first of these equations gives us

$$\frac{1}{y} - \frac{1}{x} = \alpha.$$

If, in the second equation, we put

$$y = \frac{x}{\alpha\,x + 1},$$

it becomes

$$dz - \frac{a \cdot dx}{\alpha\,x + 1} = 0,$$

and its integral is

$$z - \frac{a}{\alpha} \cdot . \, \log.\,(\alpha\,x + 1) = b = \varphi\,\alpha;$$

and therefore

$$z = \frac{a\,x\,y}{x - y} \cdot \log.\,\frac{x}{y} + \varphi\!\left(\frac{x - y}{x\,y}\right),$$

substituting $\dfrac{x - y}{x\,y}$ in the place of α.

Partial
differential
equations
of the first
order, but
of superior
degree.

16. Lagrange has given a general method for the solution of partial differential equations of the first order, but of superior degree, by converting them into a partial differential equation of four or more variables, which, being integrated, leads to an equation which may be treated by the preceding general process. We are compelled, from want of space, to omit all farther notice of this method, which includes nearly all the less general processes of solution of such equations, which have been invented by Euler and other analysts. We shall conclude this part of our subject by an example of such an equation, whose solution is obtained by an artifice which admits of very frequent application.

Let it be required to integrate the equation

$$\frac{d\,z}{d\,x} \cdot \frac{d\,z}{d\,y} = 1, \text{ or } p\,q = 1.$$

In this case, since

$$dz = p\,dx + q\,dy = d\,(p\,x + q\,y) - (x\,dp + y\,dq),$$

we have

$$d\,.\,(p\,x + q\,y - z) = x\,dp + y\,dq$$
$$= x\,dp - y\,\frac{dp}{p^2}$$
$$= \left(x - \frac{y}{p^2}\right) dp$$

since $q = \dfrac{1}{p}$ and $d\,y = -\dfrac{d\,p}{p^2}$.

The first member of this equation being an exact differential, the second must be so likewise; so that we must have

$$x - \frac{y}{p^2} = \varphi'\,(p) \qquad (1.)$$

and therefore

$$p\,x + q\,y - z = \varphi\,(p)$$

or

$$p\,x + \frac{y}{p} - z = \varphi\,(p) \qquad (2.)$$

by the help of equations (1.) and (2.) if we assign any form we please to φ, we may eliminate p, and thus get an equation expressing the relation between z, x, and y, which will satisfy the equation $p\,q = 1$: Thus, if

$$\varphi\,(p) = 1 + p$$

we shall find

$$2\surd(x\,y - y) = 1 + z.$$

17. In considering the theory of partial differential equations of the second order, we must keep in mind that there are three differential coefficients of the second order of a function of two variables. A partial differential equation, therefore, of this kind, of the most general form, would involve eight different quantities, the three variables, the two differential coefficients of the first order, and the three of the second. It would be almost impossible, however, to establish, *a priori*, any general rules for assisting us in the solution of equations involving so many quantities, whose relations are extremely complicated and difficult to trace. We shall confine our attention, therefore, to particular cases of the general equation.

We shall commence with equations of the form

$$\frac{d^2\,z}{d\,x\,d\,y} + \mathrm{P}\,\frac{d\,z}{d\,x} = \mathrm{Q} \qquad (\alpha.)$$

where P and Q are functions of x and y only. In this case, if we make $\dfrac{d\,z}{d\,x} = v$, we shall find

$$\frac{d^2\,z}{d\,x\,d\,y} = \frac{d\,v}{d\,y}$$

and the equation becomes

$$\frac{d\,v}{d\,y} + \mathrm{P}\,v = \mathrm{Q}$$

which may be integrated as an equation between two variables v and y, x being considered as constant in the integration, it having been considered as constant in the differentiation of v. We shall thus get

$$v = e^{-\int \mathrm{P}\,dy}\left\{\int e^{\int \mathrm{P}\,dy}\mathrm{Q}\,dy + \varphi\,(x)\right\} \; (\text{Flux. Art.171.})$$

replacing the constant by a function of x. Again, since $v = \dfrac{d\,z}{d\,x}$, we shall find

$$z = \int d\,x\, e^{-\int \mathrm{P}\,dy}\left\{\int e^{\int \mathrm{P}\,dy}\mathrm{Q}\,dy + \varphi\,x\right\} + \psi\,y$$

adding a function of y instead of a constant, since y is considered as constant in the second integration.

Thus, in the equation

$$\frac{d^2 z}{dx\,dy} = \frac{n}{y}\cdot\frac{dz}{dx} + \frac{m}{x}$$

we shall find

$$z = -\frac{m}{n-1}\, y \log. x + y^n \varphi x + \psi y.$$

There is one case of equation (α), where $P = 0$, and therefore

$$\frac{d^2 z}{dx\,dy} = Q,$$

which admits of an important application in the determination of the volumes and surfaces of solids, bounded by curve surfaces, expressed by equations between three rectangular co-ordinates z, x, and y. Before we proceed to any such application of this formula, we shall give a general explanation of the principles upon which the determination of such quantities is dependent upon the integration of an equation of this kind.

Differen-
tial expres-
sion for the
volume
and surface
of a solid
bounded by
a curve
surface.

18. Every body bounded by a curve surface may be defined by an equation between three rectangular co-ordinates, z, x, and y, two of which only can be considered as independent variables, and even their variation is confined to given limits. We may, consider, likewise, the volume and surface of this solid as functions of these same variables z, x, and y, and therefore of x and y only. The question is, to ascertain the identity of this function, or of some of its differential coefficients, with some determinate function of x and y. If we assume u to represent the function of x and y, which expresses the volume of the solid, or of a portion of it, then the increment of u corresponding to the increments h and k, of x and y, is equal to

$$\frac{du}{dx}h + \frac{du}{dy}k + \frac{d^2 u}{dx^2}\frac{p^2}{1.2} + \frac{d^2 u}{dx\,dy}hk + \frac{d^2 u}{dy^2}k^2 + \&c.$$

every term of which may be considered as representing some portion of the increments of the volume of the solid.

Now, the rectangle contained on the plane of xy by the increments h and k, of x and y, is equal to hk, and the rectangular parallelopipedon whose base is hk, and altitude z, is equal to zhk; and all the *other* portions of the entire increment of the volume of the solid are expressed by functions of x, y, h, and k, involving h and k in a different manner from z, h, k: but since the series for the increment of u must correspond to the sum of all the portions of the increment of the volume of the solid, and since the parallelopipedon zhk is the only one of those portions which involves hk alone, it follows, from a comparison of the corresponding terms of two identical series, that

$$\frac{d^2 u}{dx\,dy}hk = zhk$$

or, $\dfrac{d^2 u}{dx\,dy} = z = f(x, y)$, if

$z = f(x, y)$ be the equation of the curve surface.

Again, if we assume u to represent the function of x and y, which expresses the area of the surface of a solid, or any portion of it, the same term $\dfrac{d^2 u}{dx^2\,dy}hk$ in the series for its increment

$$\frac{du}{dx}h + \frac{du}{dy}k + \frac{d^2 u}{dx^2}\frac{h^2}{1.2} + \frac{d^2 u}{dx\,dy}hk + \frac{d^2 u}{dy^2}k +, \&c.$$

expresses an area upon a plane surface, since h and k

are lines, and $\dfrac{d^2 u}{dx\,dy}$ possesses no linear dimensions whatever.

It is obvious, that the projection of the plane surface corresponding to $\dfrac{d^2 u}{dx\,dy}hk$, is hk, for it varies directly as hk, whilst x and y remain the same: and it cannot be a portion of a plane which cuts the curve surface, for in that case the same plane would correspond to all the points in the common section of the surface and the plane, or $\dfrac{d^2 u}{dx\,dy}$, which is a function of x and y, would remain the same for the different values of x and y, corresponding to all the points of the curve of section: it follows, therefore, that it must be such a portion of the *tangent* plane of the point of the curve surface corresponding to x and y, that its projection on the plane of xy may be hk.

Now, the equation of the tangent plane is

$$z' - z = \frac{dz}{dx}(x' - x) + \frac{dz}{dy}(y' - y)$$

where z', x', y' are co-ordinates of a point in the plane. If, therefore, the projection of the portion of this plane, corresponding to $\dfrac{d^2 u}{dx\,dy}hk$ upon the plane of xy be hk, its projections on the planes of zx and zy will be $\dfrac{dz}{dx}hk$ and $\dfrac{dz}{dy}hk$ respectively.

And, therefore,

$$\frac{d^2 u}{dx\,dy}hk = \sqrt{\left\{ h^2 k^2 + \frac{dz^2}{dx^2}h^2 k^2 + \frac{dz^2}{dy^2}h^2 k^2 \right\}}$$

being equal, by a well known theorem, to the square root of the sum of the squares of its several projections: consequently,

$$\frac{d^2 u}{dx\,dy} = \sqrt{\left\{ 1 + \frac{dz^2}{dx^2} + \frac{dz^2}{dy^2} \right\}}$$

We shall now proceed to apply these expressions to two or three examples.

Problem. To find the volume of an ellipsoid, whose equation is

$$\frac{x^2}{a^2} + \frac{y^2}{b^2} + \frac{z^2}{c^2} = 1$$

$$\frac{d^2 u}{dx\,dy} = z = c\sqrt{\left\{ 1 - \frac{x^2}{a^2} - \frac{y^2}{b^2} \right\}}$$

Integrating and considering y a variable, we get

$$\frac{du}{dx} = \frac{cy}{2}\sqrt{\left(1 - \frac{x^2}{a^2} - \frac{y^2}{b^2}\right)} +$$

$$\frac{cb}{2}\left(1 - \frac{x^2}{a^2}\right) \sin.\frac{-1}{b}\frac{y}{\sqrt{1 - \frac{x^2}{a^2}}} + \varphi x;$$

but if we wish to determine the entire value of the section of the solid, which is parallel to the plane of zy at the distance x from it, we must take the integral between the extreme values of y, which are

$$+\sqrt{\left\{1 - \frac{x^2}{a^2}\right\}} \text{ and } -\sqrt{\left(1 - \frac{x^2}{a^2}\right)}$$

We shall thus find

$$\frac{d u}{d x} = \frac{\pi c b}{2}\left(1 - \frac{x^2}{a^2}\right)$$

the area of a semi-ellipse, whose semi-axes are

$$b\sqrt{1 - \frac{x^2}{a^2}} \text{ and } c\sqrt{1 - \frac{x^2}{a^2}}:$$ If we now inte-

grate with respect to x, and take the integral between the limits $x = a$ and $x = -a$, we shall find

$$u = \frac{2\pi a b c}{3}$$

and for the whole ellipsoid on both sides of the plane of $x y$, we have

$$2u = \frac{4\pi a b c}{3}.$$

Problem. To find the surface of a sphere, whose equation is

$$x^2 + y^2 + z^2 = a^2$$

$$\frac{d^2 u}{dx dy} = \sqrt{\left(1 + \frac{d z^2}{d x^2} + \frac{d z^2}{d y^2}\right)} = \frac{a}{\sqrt{(a^2 - x^2 - y^2)}}$$

$$\therefore \frac{d u}{d x} = a \sin.^{-1}\frac{y}{\sqrt{(a^2 - x^2)}} + \varphi\, x$$

$= \pi a$, between the limits of $y = \sqrt{a^2 - x^2}$ and $y = \sqrt{(a^2 - x^2)}$; $\therefore u = 2\pi a^2$ between the limits of $x = a$ and $x = -a$: and for whole sphere $2u = 4\pi a^2$.

Problem. The axis of a cylinder bisects the radius of a sphere at right angles, its radius being one half that of the sphere: to find the surface of the sphere which is cut off by the cylinder.

If $x^2 + y^2 + z^2 = a^2$ be the equation of the sphere, then $x^2 + y^2 = a x$ is the equation of the cylinder, the co-ordinates being in both cases reckoned from the centre of the sphere.

$$\therefore \frac{d^2 u}{dx dy} = \frac{a}{\sqrt{(a^2 - x^2 - y^2)}}$$

and $\frac{d u}{d x^2} = 2 a \sin.^{-1}\sqrt{\frac{x}{a + x}}$, the integral being taken

between $y = \sqrt{(a x - x^2)}$ and $y = -\sqrt{(a x - x^2)}$ the extreme values of y in the cylinder.

Again,

$$u = 2 a.\int d x \sin.^{-1}\sqrt{\frac{x}{a + x}}$$

$$= 2 a x. \sin.^{-1}\sqrt{\frac{x}{a + x}} - 2 a \sqrt{a x} + 2 a^2 \tan.^{-1}\sqrt{\frac{x}{a}}$$

$= \pi a^2 - 2 a^2$, if taken between the limits $x = 0$ and $x = a$.

It is evident, since the area of the two quadrants of the sphere which the cylinder penetrates, is one-fourth part of the surface of the sphere, and therefore $= \pi a^2$, that the remaining portion of each of these quadrants of the sphere is $= a^2$, or the square of the radius of the sphere.

It was towards the close of the 17th century, that the celebrated Viviani, one of the last of the pupils of Galileo, proposed the following problem as a challenge to the geometers of his time : " Amongst the ancient monuments of Greece, there was a temple dedicated to Geometry, whose ground-plan was circular, and which was surmounted by a hemispherical dome : this dome was pierced with four equal and similar windows, in such a manner that the remaining portion of its surface was absolutely quadrable ; it is required to determine in what manner this was done ?" It is very clear that this would be effected by piercing each of

the four quadrants of the hemisphere in the manner described in the preceding problem.

19. The equation

$$\frac{d^2 z}{d x^2} + \mathrm{P}\frac{d z}{d x} = \mathrm{Q}$$

where P and Q are functions of x, y, and z, must be treated like a differential equation of the second order between two variables z and x, the arbitrary constants being replaced by arbitrary functions of y: for y has been considered as constant in the process of deducing this equation from its primitive equation. Thus, in the equation,

$$\frac{d^2 z}{d x^2} = \frac{n}{x}\frac{d z}{d x} + \frac{a}{x y}$$

if we make $\frac{d z}{d x} = v$, and therefore $\frac{d^2 z}{d x^2} = \frac{d v}{d n}$, the equation becomes

$$\frac{d v}{d x} = \frac{n v}{x} + \frac{a}{x y},$$

and its integral

$$v = \frac{-a}{n y} + x^n \varphi\, y;$$

and therefore

$$z = \frac{-a x}{n y} + \frac{x^{n+1}}{n+1}\varphi\, y + \psi y.$$

20. We shall now proceed to the consideration of the very general equation

$$\frac{d z^2}{d x^2} + \frac{\mathrm{P}\, d z^2}{d x d y} + \frac{\mathrm{Q}\, d z^2}{d y^2} = \mathrm{R},$$

or $r + \mathrm{P}s + \mathrm{Q}\, t = \mathrm{R},$

where $r = \frac{d^2 z}{d x^2}$, $s = \frac{d^2 z}{d x d y}$, $t = \frac{d^2 z}{d y^2}$, and where P, Q, and R are functions of x, y, z, p, q.

The particular cases of this equation, which analysts have succeeded in integrating, are far from numerous, and they are nearly all of them comprehended by the following process of Monge, which is in some respects analogous to Lagrange's process for equations of the first order, which has been given above.

It may be stated as follows :—

Form the two systems of equations,

$$\left.\begin{array}{l} d y - k\, d x = 0 \\ k\, d p + \mathrm{Q}\, d q - \mathrm{R}\, k\, d x = 0 \end{array}\right\} (\alpha)$$

$$\left.\begin{array}{l} d y - k'\, d x = 0 \\ k'\, d p + \mathrm{Q}\, d q - \mathrm{R}\, k'\, d x = 0 \end{array}\right\} (\beta)$$

where k and k' are the roots of the equation

$$k^2 - \mathrm{P}k + \mathrm{Q} = 0. \qquad (\gamma)$$

If from either of the two systems of equations (α) or (β), we can deduce, either separately, or by adding any multiple of one of them to any multiple of the other, two primitive equations of the first order, such as N=a and M=b, then N=φ (M), will be the first integral of the proposed equation. We shall now proceed to the demonstration of this proposition :

Since $r\, d x = d p - s\, d y$ and $t\, d y = d q - s\, d x$, the substitution of these values in the equation

$$r\, d x\, d y + \mathrm{P}\, s\, d x\, d y + \mathrm{Q}\, t\, d x\, d y - \mathrm{R}\, d x\, d y = 0$$

gives us the equation

$$d p\, d y + \mathrm{Q}\, d q\, d x - \mathrm{R}\, d y\, d x - s(d y^2 - \mathrm{P}\, d y\, d x + \mathrm{Q}\, d x^2)$$
$$= 0 \qquad (1)$$

which is satisfied, if the equations

$$dp\,dy + Q\,dy\,dx - R\,dy\,dx = 0 \qquad (2)$$
$$dy^2 - P\,dy\,dx + Q\,dx^2 = 0 \qquad (3)$$

obtain simultaneously.

If in equation (3), we make $dy = k\,dx$, the equation becomes

$$k^2 - P\,k + Q = 0 \qquad (4)$$

which is equivalent to the two equations,

$$dy - k\,dx = 0, \qquad (5)$$
$$dy - k'd\,x = 0, \qquad (6)$$

k and k' being the roots of equation (4).

Also, if, in equation (2), we put $dy = k\,dx$, or $dy = k'dx$, the equation becomes

$$k\,dp + Q\,dq - R\,k\,dx = 0 \qquad (7)$$
or $\quad k'd\,p + Q\,dq - R\,k'\,dx = 0 \qquad (8)$

If we can find any combination whatever of equations, (6) and (7), such as the following :

$$m(k\,dp + Q\,dq - R\,k\,dx) + n(dy - k\,dx) = 0 \quad (9),$$

which is a complete differential $dM = 0$, then its integral $M = a$, will satisfy the original equation. For if we replace dp and dq in equation (9), by $r\,dx + s\,k\,dx$ and $s\,dx + t\,k\,dx$, it will become, if divided by dx,

$$m(k\,r + s\,k^2 + Q\,s + Q\,t\,k - R\,k) - n(k - k) = 0 \quad (10)$$

which is satisfied, if the equations

$$m(k\,r + Q\,s - R\,k) - n\,k = 0 \qquad (11)$$
$$m(k\,s + Q\,t) + n + 0 \qquad (12)$$

obtain simultaneously.

These equations give

$$r = \frac{n}{m} - \frac{Q\,s}{k} + R, \text{ and } t = -\frac{n}{k\,m} - \frac{k\,s}{Q},$$

which being substituted in the original equation,

$$r + P\,s + Q\,t = R,$$

reduces it to

$$s\left(P - \frac{Q}{k} - k\right) = 0,$$

or, $\quad s(k^2 - P\,k + Q) = 0,$

an identical equation, since $dy - k\,dx = 0$, or $k^2 - P\,k + Q = 0$: it follows, therefore, that $M = a$ is a particular integral of the first order of the original equation.

If we can find any *other* system of values of m and n, which would make equation (9) a complete differential, such as $dN = 0$, then it might be shown in the same manner, that $N = b$, would satisfy the original equation.

We have thus got two particular integrals of the original equation, namely, $M = a$, and $N = b$: it remains to show in what manner a general integral may be deduced from them.

If we take any constant α, the expression $dM + \alpha\,dN = 0$, is a complete differential, and its integral $M + \alpha\,N = c$, satisfies the original equation for the same reason that it was satisfied by $M = a$, and $N = b$: and the same integral would satisfy the equation even if α and c were variable, provided that $N\,d\alpha - dc = 0$, which is the only part of the differential of $M + \alpha\,N - c = 0$, which is affected by the variation of α and c: we thus get $N\,d\alpha = dc$, from whence we conclude, that N and c are functions of α, or, reciprocally, that α and c are functions of N; and $M = c - \alpha\,N$, is also a function of N, or $M = \varphi(N)$,

which is therefore a *complete* first integral of the original equation, since φ is an arbitrary function.

In many cases, we can determine the particular integrals $M = a$ and $N = b$, immediately from equations (5) and (7), without proceeding to such combinations as in equation (9). These integrals clearly satisfy the original equation, their differentials being included

in equation (9), and will therefore furnish a complete first integral of the equation.

The direct determination of the *second* complete integral from the first, frequently presents considerable difficulties, in consequence of its involving an arbitrary function of one of the particular integrals of the original equation ; it is convenient, therefore, when *possible*, to determine another first integral $M' = \varphi(N')$, from equations (6) and (8) ; we shall thus have two complete integrals of the first order of the original equation, from which we can eliminate p and q ; we thus get an equation which involves only one of the partial differential co-efficients, p and q, the integral of which is the complete primitive equation involving two arbitrary functions.

Let us take the equation

$$\frac{d^2z}{dx^2} - c^2\frac{d^2z}{dy^2} = 0,$$

or, $\quad r - c^2\,t = 0.$

The systems of equations (α) and (β), become

$$\left.\begin{array}{l} dy - c\,dx = 0 \\ dp - c\,dq = 0 \end{array}\right\} \ (\alpha)$$
$$\left.\begin{array}{l} dy + c\,dx = 0 \\ dp + c\,dq = 0 \end{array}\right\} \ (\beta)$$

From system (α), we get

$$y - c\,x = a \text{ and } p - c\,q = b.$$

Therefore,

$$p - c\,q = \varphi(y - c\,x) \qquad (1)$$

In a similar manner, from the system (β), we get

$$p + c\,q = \psi(y + c\,x), \qquad (2),$$

Eliminating q, from (1) and (2), we find

$$p = \frac{dz}{dx} = \frac{1}{2}\varphi(y - c\,x) + \frac{1}{2}\psi(y + c\,x),$$
$$z = \varphi,(y - c\,x) + \psi,(y + c\,x),$$

which is the complete integral of the equation.

It is this differential equation which occurs in the solution of some of the most difficult and important inquiries in natural philosophy, such as the vibrations of musical strings, the motion of waves, and the propagation of sound, whether in free space or in tubes, &c. The reader will have no difficulty, when he considers the extreme generality of the form of its integral, in conceiving the possibility of its comprehending the solutions of innumerable questions however apparently distinct and different in their nature.

Let us take, as another example, the equation

$$x + \frac{2y}{x}s + \frac{y^2}{x^2}t = 0.$$

In this case, k and k' are equal to each other, and the two systems, (α) and (β) are merged in one, which is

$$\left.\begin{array}{l} dy - \dfrac{y}{x}\,dx = 0 \\[2mm] dp + \dfrac{y}{x}\,dy = 0 \end{array}\right\} \ \alpha.$$

The integral of the first equation, gives us $\frac{y}{x} = a$: and if we substitute a for $\frac{y}{x}$ in the second, we find

$$dp + a\,dq = 0,$$
and $\therefore\ p + a\,q = b = \varphi(a),$

or, $v + \frac{y}{x}q = \varphi\left(\frac{y}{x}\right)$

Again, by Lagrange's process, Art. 15, we find,

$$\left.\begin{array}{l} dy - \dfrac{y}{x}\, dx = 0, \\[2mm] dz - \varphi\left(\dfrac{y}{x}\right) dx = 0. \end{array}\right\}$$

Consequently, $\dfrac{y}{x} = a$, which, substituted in the second equation, gives us

$$dz - \varphi(a)\, dx = 0,$$

and $\therefore z - \varphi(a)\, x = b = \psi\, a,$

and $z = x\, \varphi\left(\dfrac{y}{x}\right) + \psi\left(\dfrac{y}{x}\right).$

It would lead us into details much too extensive for a work of this kind, if we were to attempt to notice even the most considerable of the attempts which analysts have made to reduce other equations to integrable forms, which are either not included under the general forms already mentioned, or, if included under them, admit not of integration, by the processes which we have given; though the subject has occupied the attention of some of the most illustrious analysts of modern times—of Euler, of Lagrange, of La Place, of Monge, and of Poisson; yet, we may be said to be still in want of any luminous and connected view of the theory of such equations, and of the general principles which connect the different insulated methods, which have been adopted for their solution; the great importance however of these equations in physical inquiries, ought to present an additional stimulus for attempting to clear away the difficulties which encumber this department of analysis.   (P. P.)

PASCAL, (BLAISE) was born at Clermont, in Auvergne, on the 19th of June, 1623. Etienne Pascal, the father, was first president of the *Cour-des-aides* in Clermont, and discharged the duties of his office with a probity and discretion analogous to the calm and amiable virtues of his private character. His domestic happiness sustained a rude shock in 1626, by the death of his wife Antoinette Begon. She left him three children, one daughter elder, another younger, than the only son; and the charge of directing their education formed the chief solace, as well as the most sacred duty, of their father's subsequent life. To effect this more completely, he judged it necessary to dispose of his official situation, and remove to Paris in 1631.

Etienne Pascal was a man of intelligence and piety; the cares which he devoted to implanting the principles of both in his children's minds, were not bestowed in vain. Blaise, in particular, discovered from his earliest years a purity of disposition, and a power of understanding calculated to satisfy the fondest parent. Gifted with a retentive memory and a surprising acuteness of apprehension, he made rapid progress in every species of polite literature to which his faculties were applied. The aptitude he showed for the exact sciences was still more wonderful. The attention of thinking men was now awakened to those subjects by the discoveries of Galileo, which had already begun to operate the changes so sensibly felt before the century was

concluded. Roberval, Carcavi, with a number of other scientific men at Paris, among whom was Etienne Pascal, had formed themselves into a kind of society for discussing such matters; they met at each other's houses, subject to no law but the pleasure they felt in mutually communicating their discoveries or information; a pleasure which they continued to enjoy in this natural and simple form, till a royal charter (in 1656) converted this friendly club into the *Académie des Sciences.*

Young Pascal listened with a boundless curiosity to what passed when the meeting was held at his father's. The conversation excited all his energies towards an object fitted for his intellect, and recommended to his imagination by the esteem it gained from all whose opinion he honoured most highly. A *Treatise on Sound*, written at the age of eleven, might have gratified his father's partiality, had it not been feared that so ardent a devotion to mathematics might cut off the hope of progress in other branches of learning more suited to his age and capacity. Blaise was therefore enjoined to attend exclusively to language as a pursuit more profitable in its consequences, and better fitted for one of his years; while, in order to sweeten the disappointment, an assurance was given that if once Greek were mastered, he should be allowed immediately to begin geometry,—concerning which it was enough for him, at present, to know that its object lay in examining the properties of figures, and pointing out the various relations that subsist among their several dimensions. But the proffered hope was too distant for soothing the boy's impatience, which this vague and general description now served to direct and inflame. Blaise spent his play-hours by himself in a remote room; he traced a variety of circles, triangles and squares, on the floor, with a piece of charcoal; he arranged and combined them as fancy or judgment prompted; and, without the help of an instructor, of definitions, or even of language, he is said to have actually discovered the truth of Euclid's thirty-second proposition, that all the angles of any triangle are measured by arcs, which together amount to a semi-circumference [*]. His father detected the circumstance, and consented with tears of joy no longer to withstand the cultivation of a talent, which his son had shown so decided a disposition, and so extraordinary a power to improve. The study of mathematics, commenced under such auspices, was carried on with a corresponding success. The young man read Euclid by his own exertions without difficulty at the age of twelve; and, four years after, he composed what was then considered an admirable treatise on Conic Sections. But his efforts were soon directed to higher objects than learning, or even improving, what others had discovered. Enjoying the singular advantage of being permitted to give himself up without reserve to the prosecution of science, his ardent mind advanced with gigantic steps in this career. He profited by intercourse with the society which had originally kindled his enthusiasm, and soon repaid them by investigations of his own.

In 1641, a change in his father's circumstances caused

---

[*] Doubts have been raised as to the credibility of this fact, and contradictory doubts as to the extent of capacity displayed by it. With regard to the latter, little need be said. But, with regard to the former, in spite of M. Bossut's positiveness, it is fair to admit that such a statement is every way liable to exaggeration. We cannot imagine it to have been a continued process of reasoning that led to the result. If Pascal merely found the conclusion in a single case,—perhaps in the case of the equilateral triangle, by mechanical adaptation or otherwise, the want of *generality* would be speedily supplied; if he but suspected its *probability*, the word *certainty* was as easily pronounced, and the story was too good to be marred by such a defect. Enough remains, however, after all reasonable deductions.

young Pascal to change his residence, but not his employment. The president had first undeservedly incurred the displeasure of Richelieu, then as undeservedly acquired his favour, along with the Intendance of Rouen ; and the first year of Pascal's residence in that city was distinguished by the invention of his famous *arithmetical machine*. The present is not a fit place for describing this curious contrivance : its object was, to perform the operations of multiplying and dividing by a combination of cylinders, marked with certain columns of numbers, and turned by wheel-work. The object was gained, theoretically speaking ; but the complexity of the instrument, and the facilities attached to the use of logarithms, rendered it inapplicable to practical purposes. Like the simpler calculating machine of Leibnitz, it remains a wonderful but useless proof of its author's ingenuity.

Pascal's inventive powers were not long after exhibited in a way as striking, and far more beneficial to the cause of knowledge. We need not detail the circumstances which led Galileo to doubt the truth of Nature's abhorring a vacuum, or Torricelli to maintain that the ascent of water in the sucking pump, or of mercury in a glass tube free of air, is due to the unbalanced weight of an atmospheric column pressing on the external fluid. Torricelli died in 1646, before the truth of his conclusion could be firmly established. The experiments, but not the inference, were casually reported to Pascal, who repeated them with important variations, and asserted the same opinion in a small work published next year, under the title of *Expériences nouvelles touchant le vuide*. Yet the victory was not tamely yielded. A subtle matter, aerian spirits, every argument or hypothesis which the bad philosophy of the time could furnish, was employed to support the falling *horror of a vacuum ;* the Jesuit Noel had published his objections, when Pascal was lucky enough to devise an experiment which set the matter completely at rest. If the mercury were suspended by the weight of the superincumbent atmosphere, it was evident that the quantity suspended must diminish, as the weight, and consequently as the height of that atmosphere diminished ; hence, if Torricelli's view of the subject were correct, the fluid must sink as it approached a higher level and carried less air above it : if the mercury were not so suspended, or if the atmosphere were destitute of weight, no such effect would follow ; and at the top of the highest elevation, the fluid would rise 29 inches above its external level, exactly as it did at the bottom. Pascal fixed upon his native mountain, the Puy-de-Dôme, for exemplifying those reasonings ; and being confined by ill health, he committed the execution of the project to M. Perier, his brother-in-law. It was performed on the 19th of September, 1648 ; the mercury rose and fell as he had predicted ; the gravity of the air was proved, and Aristotle's maxim destroyed for ever.

Pascal's name is indelibly impressed on the history of the barometer ; it is also closely united with many of the most important mathematical and physical inquiries, which during the next age occupied the attention of scientific men. From considering a particular case, he was easily led to investigate the general problem relating to the equilibrium of fluids ; his principle demonstrated in two different ways, and the curious details which accompany it, were published after his death, in the *Traité sur l'equilibre des liqueurs*, and the *Traité sur la pésanteur de la masse de l'air*. The

solution of two questions proposed by an ignorant gamester, the Count de Meré, laid a foundation for the modern doctrine of probabilities : his various geometrical tracts are unfortunately lost ; but enough is known of his *Arithmetical triangle* to show, that if his pursuits had been continued, the author of so beautiful an invention might have anticipated some of the most brilliant discoveries of a subsequent age.

But the incessant application which produced results of such variety and extent, produced another consequence equally inevitable, the loss of health with all its attendant evils. From his 19th year, Pascal had laboured under the effects of excessive study ; in 1647, he was seized with a paralysis, which for three months almost entirely took away the use of his limbs. The family now returned to Paris, and forced him in some degree to relax his efforts. But his father died in 1651, his elder sister was long ago married to M. Perier, at Clermont, his younger soon after became a nun in the monastery of Port-Royal-des-champs ; and thus being left to his own guidance, he entered upon a course of labours which fast hastened the ruin of his constitution. The exhaustion of nature at length forced him absolutely to renounce every kind of mental exertion ; he had recourse to moderate exercise, he frequented society, and was beginning to receive back from it some part of the gratification which his amiable though pensive character inspired, when a fearful accident totally altered the manner of that life to which it had well nigh put a period. One day in the month of October, 1654, having gone out as usual to take the air in a carriage, he was proceeding over the Seine by the bridge of Neuilly, when the two foremost horses taking fright at a spot where the parapet was wanting, rushed furiously onward and plunged headlong into the river. Providentially their traces gave way ; the hindmost pair stood shuddering on the verge, and were led back unhurt. But the shock which such an awful occurrence must have communicated to the feeble frame of Pascal may easily be conceived. He recovered with difficulty from a long swoon ; the precipice was for weeks continually present to his imagination ; it haunted his dreams, and occasioned waking visions, one of which, in particular, made such an impression, that he wrote an account of it, and wore the paper ever after between the cloth and the lining of his coat. By degrees, however, these alarming effects subsided ; they were followed by others of a milder but more permanent nature. To the delicate, though powerful mind of Pascal, this incident appeared a direct warning from providence, a rebuke for the misuse of time, and a call to devote his talents henceforth immediately to the service of heaven. Pascal had never forgotten the precepts of religion, and his innocent unwearied life had been a constant homage to their authority ; but, in his present disposition, the arduous pursuit of knowledge, the glorious conquests achieved in that pursuit, seemed alike vain and carnal things ; they pointed but to opportunities gone by, for which a strict account must soon be given in. He determined to employ his remaining days in religious meditation. The example of his sister Jacqueline gave strength to this resolution, and perhaps invited him to Port-Royal in fulfilment of it. Here in the company of Arnaud, Saci, Nicole, and a few others of similar habits, he spent most of his time ; not indeed as a member of the establishment, but as a visitor whose stay was sometimes lengthened to many months.

In this retreat, endeared by the sanctity of its object,

and enlivened by the society of men imbued with kindred opinions, Pascal gradually recovered some tranquillity; he enjoyed intervals of comparative health, during which fresh triumphs in a new department gave farther proof of the compass and versatility of his powers. It is not our purpose to write the history of Molinism or Jansenism, or to enter on the criticism of these obscure and forgotten quarrels, which ended in the ruin of both. Pascal's work is the main plank, by means of which some memory of them still floats on the stream of time; and it is only in order rightly to understand the scope of the *Provincial Letters*, that a few words may be devoted to the controversy which gave rise to that performance. The terms Jansenism and Molinism, originated in a large unintelligible book, written by one Jansen, bishop of Ypres, in 1638, to defend St. Austin's views on necessity and free will, against the still more unintelligible book of a Spanish Jesuit Molina, regarded as a standard by the whole sect of Jesuits. The Solitaries of Port Royal were loudest in their applauses of Jansen, whose work was fast rising in public esteem, when the Jesuits, by a variety of political manœuvres, engaged Mazarin's influence, and procured from Pope Alexander VII. a bull, condemning as heretical five propositions, said to contain the abstract of Jansen's doctrine. Arnaud, the most ardent * of the Jansenists, soon published a letter denying the last assertion, and accompanied the denial with some farther expressions offensive to the Sorbonne, of which he was a member. His subsequent apology was heavy and monotonous, even by his own admission; and he gladly entrusted his cause to the abler pen of Pascal, whose first letter of Louis Montalte *to a Provincial*, appeared during the trial of Arnaud, 23d January 1657. Its effect on the public was instantaneous and powerful. Not so on the clergy, who condemned Arnaud eight days after, and expelled him from his place in the Sorbonne. But their victory was dearly paid for. A few additional observations from Montalte soon branded the whole proceeding with indelible contempt, and the Jesuits above all, whose diligence in the affair had been principally distinguished, were delivered up, without remedy, to the mockery and indignation of the world. A series of *letters* exposed their miserable shuffling casuistry, with a force of reasoning, never before or since united with an irony so playful and yet so cutting. Their replies but aggravated the evil: and though a system of intrigues at last effected the destruction of Port Royal, their quarrel with it, by calling the *Provincial Letters* into being, made straight the path which conducted themselves to an ignominious ruin.

Of a work so generally admired as the *Provincial Letters*, it is not necessary to say much. Devoted to a subject of limited and transient interest, they have had the rare fortune to outlive the question treated by them; and to unite the suffrages of men indifferent or hostile to their principles and tendency. Voltaire admits that, both in regard to fine satire and high eloquence, they stand on a level with the greatest models; and Gibbon informs us, that he repeatedly perused them, in order to acquire the power of discussing grave subjects with sprightliness, and easy though pungent reasoning. Gibbon's manner is, indeed, different from Pascal's, and their objects were still more widely different: but

the testimony is not, therefore, less decisive or sincere. Justice, however, would not be done to the talents displayed in this production, if a judgment were formed without reference to the times in which it was composed. The *Provincial Letters* were written without any model in thought or expression; and French critics still admire them as among the best specimens of composition, in a language which they contributed, more than any other work, to form and characterize.

The *Provincial Letters* were gratifying to all enemies of the Jesuits, and applauded by them. Pascal's next work promised to secure the gratitude of all Christians, by whatever name they might be called. It was his intention to examine the evidences of Christianity, on a plan which it would have required all his immense learning, and all his profound as well as comprehensive intellect, to execute rightly. He proposed to figure out a man of strong faculties, but ignorant of religious belief, as left upon the world, to choose, from the multifarious solutions of his enigmatic being, that solution which, upon the whole, was most consistent with itself and other facts. He proposed to make this unprejudiced observer acquainted with the mysteries of his own nature, to cause the successive systems of Pagan theology and philosophy to pass in review before him: and finally directing his attention towards Palestine, and the marvellous history of its people, to show the luminous distinctness which the New and Old Testament history diffuses over the secrets of our origin, our condition, and our destiny; and the strict congruity of its precepts, its representations, its promises, with the weakness and the wants of man. The idea was grand and imposing, but Pascal did not live to fill up the outline so boldly traced. A few fragments, collected into a volume, entitled *Pensées*, left behind him in the most disorderly state, are all that we possess of this mighty undertaking. The fragments appear under every disadvantage; they are often but the skeletons of future propositions, and written purely for the author's inspection: yet, judging from the noble eloquence and deep reflection which not a few of them exhibit, it seems as if nothing but a longer and more untroubled life had been wanting to enable the author to complete his design, in a manner worthy of its vast importance. Philosophy, and still more Christianity, have cause to regret that Pascal was cut off so early; and ages may elapse before another individual appears, combining such qualifications with so strong an impulse to employ them all in examining such a question.

The years which Pascal had resolved upon devoting to his favourite inquiry were soon spent, and embittered by almost incessant pain. His thoughts had long flowed exclusively in the channel of devotion, and present circumstances naturally contributed to strengthen this tendency. Yet, before his course was done, the speculations of early life resumed their sway on one occasion with a force and effect, which showed that his mathematical powers were diverted, not destroyed. It was in 1658, when an excruciating toothache had kept him long deprived of sleep, that he happened to recollect some properties formerly discovered by him respecting the cycloid; and their beauty was such, that, to procure some abstraction from his suffering, he determined to investigate their consequences. The results which he obtained, without the aid of modern

---

* The vehement stubbornness of his temper, and the zeal with which he maintained the cause, are exemplified in a well known anecdote. Nicole's milder spirit felt weary of the controversy, and he expressed a wish for rest. " *Rest!*" exclaimed Arnaud: " *Will you not have all eternity to rest in.*"

Pascal.

analysis, are still reckoned by mathematicians among the finest exhibitions of their art. Pascal was advised to publish them by way of challenge, to show that the highest attainments in a science of strict reasoning were not incompatible with the humblest belief in the principles of religion. His problems were accordingly announced under the assumed name of Amos Dettonville *; and a premium of forty pistoles was promised to whoever solved them first, of twenty to whoever solved them next. The competition, though graced by some of the first names in Europe, was not successful to any. Our countrymen Wallis and Wren were among the number; and the former having failed of success by incorrectness of execution, rather than by error of principle, accused Dettonville of injustice in not assigning him the prize. A similar complaint was made, with far less reason, and the very worst success, by the Père Lallouire, a Jesuit; and Pascal, to defend himself from such insinuations, soon published his treatise on the cycloid, containing the complete solution, which none of the claimants had succeeded in finding.

But the labours of Pascal were swiftly drawing to a close. His bodily infirmities became still more severe; and his mind was disquieted by the persecutions which his friends at Port Royal were sustaining from the Jesuits. Compulsion but made him cling with greater tenacity to the opinions he had formerly adopted in regard to the necessity of human actions. He separated from the supporters of free will even more widely than Arnaud or Nicole, whose appearance of conformity to some requisitions of the Jesuits produced a coldness in the mind of Pascal, that added to the already overwhelming chagrins of his situation. His sister Jacqueline died of grief, the *first* victim of the Port Royal controversy. When her death was made known to him, Pascal said with a deep sigh, *God give us all the grace to die like her!* His prayer with regard to himself was soon fulfilled. In the month of June, 1672, he was attacked with a sharp and almost continual cholic. It soon wore out his languid frame; and he expired on the 19th of August, tortured with pain, but full of the hopes which had long sweetened and embellished his troubled existence †.

The character of Pascal, considered as a moral or as an intellectual man, affords a bright though unequal specimen of human nature. Uniting a saint-like purity and tenderness of heart, with an understanding at once fine and capacious, his short existence was marked by the practice of benevolence and self-denial, no less than by a series of brilliant discoveries in the highest regions of philosophy. Though he lived but thirty-nine years, the longer, and what is more important, the later part of which were spent in almost continual ill health; yet such was the excellence of his powers, and such the enthusiasm which impelled them, that Pascal's name is found conspicuously engraven on all the most important scientific achievements of his time; while, in the nobler parts of literature, he occupies a rank which few of his countrymen have aimed at, and still fewer reached.

As a private man, his relations with other men were simple and restricted; but his duties, though narrowed, were not neglected. The lessons of religion which a father had impressed on his young heart, were expanded and adorned by a sublime imagination; and

Pascal
‖
Patagonia.

the precept, that matters of faith are beyond the empire of reason, sanctioned by authority so endearing, entwined itself ever more intimately with his affections, and acquired strength with his strength. It should excite not a smile but a sigh, to learn that Pascal believed in the miraculous cure of his niece by a relic at Port Royal; that he reckoned it necessary to appear cold towards his sisters, though he loved them deeply; or that in his latter years, he wore below his shirt an iron girdle studded with sharp points, which he pressed against the skin whenever any evil thought overtook him. Voltaire spoke lightly, when he advised Condorcet never to cease repeating, " that after the accident at Neuilly bridge, Pascal's head was deranged." The Provincial Letters, and the treatise on the Cycloid, written after the accident at Neuilly, might have repressed this sarcasm; and Voltaire should have remembered, that as the external colouring of our feelings depends on the associations to which we are exposed, and is changed with all their changes, so the appearance of great intellect and lofty purposes, however modified and overclouded, is always entitled to the reverence and approval of every good man.

The most valuable, indeed the only complete edition of Pascal's writings, is that of M. Bossut, Paris, 1779. A short *Life* is prefixed to it.

PASTES, Artificial. See the article Gems, vol. X. p. 128; Glass, vol. X. p. 315; and the *Edinburgh Philosophical Journal*, vol. vii. p. 370.

PATAGONIA, Land of Magellan, or Teheulia, in South America, is bounded on the north by the government of La Plata, or Buenos Ayres; on the south by the straits of Magellan; on the east by the Atlantic Ocean; and on the west by the South Pacific Ocean, extending from 64° 30′ to 74° 30′ West Longitude, and from 38° to 54° S. Lat. The boundary has been enlarged nearly 100 miles, and by extending the line to the Rio Nigro, the passes which prevent the negroes from destroying the cattle are more easily secured. The frontier includes a tract of country between Colorado and Rio Negro, which is free from the defects of the naked Pampas. *Boundary.*

Where the continent narrows, and near very high *Climate.* mountains, the country suffers from occasional snow storms: but we are not entitled to consider it so cold as Norway, since most of the inhabitants go naked. The soil is very various, for to the north of La Plata *Soil.* wood and large timber abound, while to the south scarcely a tree is seen. This part, however, has some good pastures, and numerous herds of cattle and droves of horses are to be met with. The sea-coast is a dry and sandy soil.

The inhabitants may be divided into three different *Inhabitants.* classes, and are called Cassores, Pampas, and Patagons. The first a race of common men, who live on the Terra del Fuego side, as low as opposite Cape Horn, and who were probably driven by their enemies to take shelter in this part. Of the second class, seen by Mr. Carteret, Captain Wallis, and M. Bougainville, &c. the largest measured 6 feet 7 inches; while the greatest part of the natives were only 5 feet 10 inches, or 6 feet. The third class consists of those who were seen by Commodore Byron, Mr. Falkner, &c. and whose size is said in many instances to have been from 7 feet 8 inches to 8 feet, and some say 9 or 10 feet. The com-

---

* Formed by transposing the letters of *Louis de Montalte.*

† On opening his body, the stomach and liver were found to be withered, the intestines gangrened; and it was observed with astonishment, that a large portion of the brain had become solid and very much condensed.

Patagonia. mon height was 6 feet, which was also that of the tallest women. This race was scattered from the foot of the Andes to the Atlantic Ocean, and are found as far as the Red River, at Bay Anagada, Lat. 40°; their colour is that of deep copper; their hair as harsh as hogs bristles, tied back with a cotton thread, and their hands as well as feet are small. The eye-lids of the young women are painted black. Many of the men paint their left eye with a red circle, and others their arms, and different parts of their face. They are very expert in the use of the sling, with which they entangle the legs of the ostrich and the guanaco, so that the animals are easily caught. They are of an agreeable and frequently handsome figure; and have a round flat face, very fiery eyes, with white and rather large teeth. Some of them wear long but thin whiskers. Their cloak, of guanaco's or sorillo's skins, is tied round the body with a girdle; and that part which is designed to cover the shoulders is suffered to fall back. The marrow and flesh of horses, guanacos, and vicunnas afford them their chief food; which is fastened on their horses, and sometimes eaten quite raw, but more generally roasted or boiled. They make a fermenting liquor called chucha, which causes inebriation. Their tents are covered with the hides of mares, and divided from each other by a kind of blanketing. In consequence of their frequent migrations, occasioned from want of salt, from the superstitious desire to bury their dead near the ocean, and that they may procure food by the chace, many consider them to resemble the Tartars.

Their horses are of a diminutive size, but nimble. They use bridles made of a leather thong, with a bit formed from wood, and their saddles resemble our pads. No stirrups are used, and both sexes ride in the same manner, galloping without fear over rugged roads and large loose stones.

Religion. They worship a good and a bad principle. The first is called Soucha, or chief in the land of strong drink, and by some the Lord of the dead; they consider him the creator of all things, who never afterwards troubles himself about his creatures. The evil principles are termed the wanderers without, and the dwellers in the air, who are viewed as the protectors of some and the injurers of others. The priests are regarded as mediators between the evil beings and the people who consult them about future events. Their heaven is a country where they imagine the fruits of inebriation are eternal; and they conceive their future existence will be spent in drunkenness, or in the hunting of the ostrich. After taking away or burning the flesh, &c. of the dead, a skeleton is formed of the bones, which is decked in the best robes, with various weapons, and placed sitting in a deep square pit covered with turf. A matron attends these sepulchres, keeps the skeletons clean and new clothes them every year. The priests make a libation of chucha, and drink "Long live the dead." Polygamy is permitted, and widows continue to manifest their sorrow by blackening their faces for a year after the death of their husbands. The Caziques are hereditary. They protect the property of their people, and have the power of life and death. They are obliged to pay their subjects for their services, and every Indian unprotected by them is considered an outlaw. Eloquence is in great request, and a Cazique keeps an orator if he wants this talent.

Magellan discovered this country in 1518; and during the space of 124 years, fifteen circumnavigators passed through the straits that were called after him, nine of whom bore testimony to the gigantic size of this people. From the year 1642 to the year 1766, six voyagers visited this country, and only two confirmed the account of the first discoverer. The evidence of succeeding circumnavigators has been contradictory, and our information concerning this part of America still continues to be involved in great obscurity. See Mr. Pennant's *Letter to Hon. Daines Barrington;* Magellan's *Voyage;* Hawksworth's *Voyages;* Bougainville's *Voyages.* Breckenridge's *Voyages to South America.*

PATENTS.

Patents. PATENT is the elliptical expression for *Letters patent;* the writ in the king's name and under the great seal, which secures, for a limited term, to the inventor, the exclusive right to make and sell the material product of his invention. The word *patent* has come, in common language, to signify, indifferently, the writ conveying, and the right conveyed. A patent is a monopoly, and with the exception of the copy-right of a literary publication, is the only one founded in natural right, and sanctioned by justice; all other monopolies are hostile to the principles of equality recognised in a free commonwealth, and destructive of that unrestrained competition which is essential to public prosperity. Founded on power alone, these unjust preferences have in most states, ancient and modern, occurred to despotic princes as a mode of enriching their favourites, or raising a revenue; and, although very oppressive to the rest of their subjects, they were a cheap boon from the sovereign. This blind and tyrannical policy had increased in England to such a height, during several previous reigns, to the time of Elizabeth, that it was considered by the parliament of James I. altogether incompatible with the prosperity of the country. This feeling produced the 21st of James I. c. 3, the well-known "statute of monopolies," the *nomen juris* of that most important and beneficial law. The statute suppresses monopolies, by making void the future grants of all such as do not come under the following proviso: "Provided also, and be it enacted, that any declaration before mentioned shall not extend to any letters patent and grants of privilege, for the term of fourteen years or under, hereafter to be made, of the sole working and making of any manner of new manufacture within this realm, to the true and first inventor or inventors of such manufactures, which others, at the time of making such letters patent and grants, shall not use, so as also they be not contrary to law, nor mischievous to the state, by raising the prices of commodities at home, or hurt of trade, or generally inconvenient."

The letters patent which concern printing, saltpetre, gunpowder, great ordnance, shot, and offices, are likewise saved by the same statute.

The question of literary property in printed and pub-

Patents.

Patent
right the
result of a
compromise.

Disclosure
in a specification an
essential
condition
of a patent.

Extent of
the privilege.

Objects of
patents are
new manufactures.

Not principles, processes, or
methods.

Manufactures must
be new
within this
realm.
A new invention,
what?

lished books had not then arisen. We have considered that subject under its proper head, (LITERARY PROPERTY.)

The protection conferred by a royal patent is the result of a compromise. The natural or common law right to the exclusive benefit of one's own invention, is perpetual; but it being more for the public advantage that the invention shall be thrown open, after the inventor has enjoyed the exclusive benefit for a reasonable term, he is content, in return for certain protection, to give it to the public, when that term shall have elapsed. This period, by the statute of James, which is still the law, is fourteen years. In order that, at the expiration of that period, the public may be in possession of the invention, as beneficially as it was enjoyed by the inventor, it is a condition of the patent, that the patentee shall put on public record a detailed description of the process by which the machine or substance is produced, so clear and explicit as to be intelligible to every artist conversant in practical mechanics or chemistry.

As it is important that an inventor, who is desirous of the privilege of letters patent, should know something of the law which is to regulate his right, a brief summary of the law of patents, as it now stands in England, claims the first place in the order of this article. The natural progress of meriting, soliciting, obtaining, and vindicating a patent, will keep our observations in clear arrangement, as well as within due bounds.

The statute gives the sole right of " working and making" the subject of the invention, which, by established interpretation, as expressed in all letters patent, includes vending, so as to prevent the article, when made in a foreign country, from being sold in this.

" New manufactures" are the objects of this exclusive privilege. A manufacture under the statute, is construed to mean a vendible substance, either in the form of an engine or material; the one the result of mechanical, the other, of chemical skill. Although the statute is silent on the head, the manufacture ought to be *useful;* for the inventor makes affidavit to this effect. The manufacture must farther be adequate to the professed effect, otherwise a patent for it is void. A philosophical principle, not embodied in a mechanical or chemical result, cannot be protected by patent. Neither can a mere process, or method, unless producing, as most processes and methods do, a vendible substance. It is, therefore, incorrect to give, as a title to a patent, *a method* of producing certain specified effects. Nevertheless this error is so common, that the courts of law have admitted, by indulgence, the term method to signify the thing produced by the method. Still an accurate title would avoid this style. The noblest of all mechanical inventions, the steam-engine, affords an example of the inapplicability of a patent to a mere principle. The principle discovered was the expansive force of steam; but the patent protects the *machine* called the steam-engine.

The invented manufacture must be " *new within this realm.*" This entitles to a patent right, not only the original inventor, but likewise the importer of a foreign invention. We first inquire, what is a new invention? As nobody can claim as their invention the familiar material substances—which, although many of even these, chemically speaking, are compound, we may here assume as elementary—the most original invention, either mechanical or chemical, must necessarily be a compound. The newly invented compound may be, *first,* a new arrangement of what we have called elementary substances; or, *secondly,* a new arrangement of substan-

ces already mechanically or chemically arranged; or *thirdly,* an improvement in the way of addition to a previous mechanical or chemical arrangement; or *lastly,* a new method or process of manufacturing articles already in common use, whereby they are produced in greater abundance, perfection, or cheapness. All four modes of invention may be legally protected by patent.

In the first there can be no difficulty. The original materials alluded to are free to every one. An important consideration here occurs. Many have erroneously thought, that they do not infringe a patent right, although they adopt the principle and even the arrangement, if they merely vary the material; or even if, in mechanical inventions, adopting the same materials, they vary the form of the whole, or any of the parts. If the *specified* material or form be essential to the principle, a change of either is out of the question. It is only where the material and form are not essential to the principle that such change is possible, and it is then on plain principles of justice an infringement. The patentee generally guards this point, by specifying a certain material and form, and adding, " or any others suitable."

When the invention is a new arrangement of either one or more old combinations, either with each other, or with elementary substances, if these old combinations be free, (*i. e.* not the subject of an existing patent,) the patent is good for the new arrangement, as much as if the parts had been elementary substances. If, again, one or more parts of the old combinations are the subjects of existing patents, although the patent is good for the new arrangement, the right of the previous patentee remains entire; so that the new patentee cannot practically construct or manufacture his invention, without the license of the previous patentee. If, however, the new patentee have altered the principle of any of these patent steps, he makes that step his own as a new invention.

Nearly connected with this is the *third* object of a patent, namely, an improvement on an already known engine or substance. A total variation of the principle is not an improvement, but a new invention. An improvement is built upon the previous arrangement as a basis, which is not interfered with. The patent is good for the improvement only. A patent was taken by the inventor of an improved movement in a watch, and was voided by being taken for the whole watch. It is plain, that an improvement on a *patent article,* although legally an object of a patent, is practically useless to the patentee, without the license of the previous patentee to make use of his invention as the subject improved.

A new process for refining sugar, bleaching linen, &c. (both refined sugar and bleached linen being well known,) afford examples of the fourth and last object of a patent right above mentioned.

The discovery of another use, or other uses, of a manufacture already known, is not legally the subject of a patent.

An invention, however old in a foreign country, will be secured by patent to the person who first brings it into this country. It is within the statute, in so far as it is " new *within this realm;*" and the public interest is concerned in encouraging such additions to our own manufacturing skill. But, by the present law, a revived manufacture, which, however forgotten, and therefore virtually new to the country, was in use before " within the realm," cannot obtain a patent.

Of an invention acknowledged new *quoad* the public, it is often disputed who is the first inventor. If neither claimant in a competition have published his disco-

Patents.

1. New arrangement of common materials.
Varying materials.
Varying form.

2. New arrangement of old mechanical or chemical arrangements.
When these are already patents.

3. Improvement on an old manufacture.

4. New method of making known articles.

Double use discovered, not subject of a patent.

Imported invention.

A revived invention.

First inventor, who?

Patents.

very, the priority must be determined by legal evidence. This is the case which generally occurs, when a patent is yet unobtained by either party. But an infringer of a patent, or any one having interest, may show that the thing, though likewise the invention of the patentee, was invented before. The only legal evidence of priority however is, that it was *publicly used* before. An invention kept secret, will not annul a subsequent *bona fide* invention of the same thing, as in the case of the achromatic telescope. (See 3d note on p. 179, vol. xv. article OPTICS.) Even a disclosure of the previous invention to *one* person is not sufficient; but it has been held previous publication, that it was disclosed to *two*. This point is not well settled; for it has been held that actual *public use* is necessary; and certainly when the question is, as it ought to be, who is the *beneficial* inventor, it cannot be doubted that it is the first *public* user, he always being *bona fide* inventor likewise. Sale, in the way of trade, of the patent article is undoubted public use. On the other hand, publication of the secret in any way, even accidentally or by a malicious opponent, before the patent is rendered safe *by passing the great seal*, voids the right. This is on the principle, that the disclosure, *de facto*, incapacitates the inventor from fulfilling his engagement to the public, by disclosing the invention; for no man can disclose what is already disclosed. The utmost caution is therefore necessary, in the inventor, to preserve the secret till the patent is sealed; insomuch, that the Lord Chancellor Eldon once declared from the bench, that if he were maturing an invention, and soliciting a patent, he would not entrust with the secret his own brother! We cannot help remarking, that the effect given to such disclosure, does not seem to quadrate with the principle of previous *public* use alone vacating the patent.

Public use.

Disclosure to one person.

Malicious or accidental disclosure.

Of course, the patentee must be the *sole* inventor. Even a hint from another person has been found fatal to a patent.

Patentee must be *sole* inventor.

Whenever an inventor has made up his mind to apply for a patent, he ought to lodge a *caveat*, as it is called, at the offices of the attorney and solicitor general, desiring notice of all patents applied for, for the same or the same sort of invention. This request is generally stated broadly, to be the more certain of including the particular invention. The precaution is important to an ingenious person, who is engaged in a series of difficult and expensive experiments, but who has not sufficiently matured his invention to enable him to apply for a patent. It is not less useful to the inventor, whose patent, although applied for, has not passed the great seal; and it is not unimportant to a person actually in possession of a patent, that he may oppose all subsequent applications for patents for the same invention. This is the sum of the virtue of a caveat; which has been so much mistaken as to be held to be a sort of minor patent, which, by its own operation, stays the hands of all persons engaged in similar inventions.

Caveat.

Import and effect of caveat generally mistaken.

When notice is given by the attorney or solicitor general of a rival application, the lodger of the caveat must appear personally, or by proxy, before one or both of these law officers, and lay before them his invention, with evidence, if necessary, of its date, progress, &c. The rival applicant does the same. Each case is considered separately and privately; and the law officers decide upon the question of priority, if the inventions are the same, or of difference, if different; in which last case each will be entitled to a patent. When neither point can be determined, they generally recommend a joint patent.

Discussion on caveat, in rival inventions.

Joint patent.

The inventor, even previous to his caveat, having often recourse to the aid of workmen and others, and of the capital of friends for his experiments, it is lawful to bind such persons to secrecy, under contract of paying him a sum of money for taking any undue advantage. This sum must not be called a *penalty*, but be expressly stipulated to be *liquidated damages*. So it has been decided.

Patents.

Liquidated damages for disclosure.

When the invention is completed, the inventor applies to the king by petition, accompanied by affidavit, sworn before a master in chancery, or a magistrate in the country, setting forth that he is the first and sole inventor; that the invention will be of public benefit; and that it has never been in previous use to the best of his belief. This the first document contains the title of the invention, which ought to be well considered, as it cannot afterwards be altered. The petition is referred by the king to his attorney and solicitor general. It is here that the opposition on caveat, if any, takes place, as already mentioned. If there be no opposition, or it have been met and defeated, the law officers report to the king that the invention is worthy of a patent. It is very important to observe, that this favourable report is *a matter of course* when there is no opposition; and this marked qualification is contained in the report: "*As it is entirely at the hazard of the said petitioner whether the said invention is new, or will have the desired success.*" A bill is then prepared as a warrant, and signed with the sign manual. This, after several official steps, well known in practice, and detailed in all the law books on the subject, authorizes the letters-patent to be made out at the lord chancellor's office, WHERE THE RIGHT IS SECURED, BY AFFIXING THE GREAT SEAL. It may here be observed, that the unsuccessful party, in a competition on caveat before the attorney-general, may be heard again, by the lord chancellor, on caveat lodged at the great seal, before the patent is sealed.

Petition to the king for the patent.

Here generally opposition on caveat. Attorney-general's report.

Is matter of course at hazard of grantee.

Appeal to lord chancellor.

The patentee has now to perform his part of his contract with the public, by fairly and fully disclosing his invention. This, by the present law, he must do within one, or, more generally in practice, two months after the patent is sealed, in a writing sworn to, signed, and sealed, by him, before a master in chancery, or magistrate in the country, and containing a minute description of his invention, with the relation and mode of operation of the several parts, and the union of the whole machine, so clear, that any person engaged in the same sort of manufacture, or versant in mechanics or chemistry in general, may construct or make the patent article from the description alone. Drawings or models may accompany the description, but are no legal part of it, as it must be independent of them. This description, called the *specification*, forms the last step of the proceedings, and is considered as part of the patent, being essential to ascertain and limit the patent right. It is enrolled or put on record; and any person applying is entitled, on paying the office fees, to have a copy. The reason assigned for this publicity, in so early a stage of the patent right, is, not that the public may be enabled *then* to make the article, for they cannot touch it for fourteen years, but that ingenious men may know how far they are anticipated, and may both save their labour, and avoid unintentional piracy. If the patent is of any value or public interest, its specification generally soon appears in all the scientific journals.

Duty of the patentee. Specification.

Drawings and models.

Specification open to the public.

The specification is a document of great nicety, and most of the patents, which, on judicial trial, have been lost, have been so from mistakes here. As it is the

Requires much care.

Patents.

Faults in it fatal to patents.

condition of the patent that the invention shall be fully and fairly disclosed in the specification, any part of it false, defective, or obscure, so as to mislead the public, even unintentionally, but still more designedly, any want of conformity of the description to the title of the invention, renders the patent void. Accordingly, in most prosecutions for infringement of patents, the prosecuted take their stand here; and have generally been well advised that the specification is faulty, before they venture on the infringement.

A few enumerated.

Manifold are the imperfections in specifications which are fatal to the patent right. The following are a few of them. Specifying one material and using a cheaper, not specified or included. Omitting some beneficial part of the process. Specifying something useless, superfluous, or redundant. Specifying something which will not produce the professed effect. Specifying some step that is not new, and not noting that fact, whereby the patentee is held to have assumed what he did not invent. Specifying the whole article as invented, when the patent should have been for an improvement only. Omitting to specify the old article sufficiently to identify it. Specifying articles which are meant to puzzle, and which are not essential. Specifying less extensively, not than the title of the patent, but than the mode of afterwards constructing; for example, specifying one machine, and using two. In the last case, it is plain, that the different construction or use practised by the patentee, is not protected by the patent, it is a different thing.

Common materials, utensils, &c.

Common utensils, and processes universally known, need not be described, but merely called *the common* instrument, material, utensil, or process.

The patent transferable as a vested right. Five persons.

The right once completed, by letters patent and specification, is a vested right, which descends to the patentee's heirs, and is transferable to assigns; but these must not exceed five individuals, without the sanction of an act of parliament. A patent likewise cannot be originally granted to more than five persons.

Prolongation of term.

The term of fourteen years may be prolonged, but only by special act of parliament.

Legal vindication of patent.

The vindication of the patent, or the legal remedy against infringement, comes next to be considered; and as, by the present practice, patents are granted almost, if not altogether, of course, "at the hazard" of the patentee, the legal vindication is virtually the establishment of the patent; so that it may safely be said that no patentee can feel confidence in his patent, till it is fortified by the verdict of a jury, awarding damages for infringement.

Two modes of prosecution.

There are two ways of prosecuting for infringement. 1. A bill in chancery against the infringer, to account for profits unlawfully obtained, accompanied by an application for an injunction to prevent farther piracy. The fact of infringement, however, must be sent by the court of chancery to the common law courts to be tried by a jury. 2. An action of damages at once in the common law courts, to be tried by jury,—the more common remedy.

Trial.

On the trial, the patentee must adduce evidence —slight evidence will suffice—to show the novelty and efficiency of his invention. The infringer may then show, if he can, that the patent itself is defective, in so far as it is at variance with the statute; or he may adopt the much more common course of proving a defective specification.

Repeal of patent by *scire facias*.

A patent may be repealed absolutely by a writ of *scire facias*, at any one's instance, in the king's name, with the consent of the attorney-general, on various grounds of nullity: such as, that the king was deceived by false suggestions; that the invention was not new; that letters-patent were granted to more than one person for the same invention—in which last case the first patentee may have a *scire facias* to repeal the second; or, that the king has granted the patent beyond the statute, either as to matter or duration. This writ issues from chancery, but it is sent to a court of law to be tried. The following mistakes in the grant do not vitiate the patent: 1. False recital in a thing not material, the king's intention being manifest: 2. When the mistake is the king's, and not the result of false suggestion; 3. Mistakes in law or fact not part of the consideration of the grant; 4. Grants *ex certe scientia et mero motu* of the king, which words occasion the grant to be taken in the most liberal and beneficial sense, according to the king's intention; 5. Although the recital should qualify the general words, yet, if the king's intention be clearly expressed in the body of the grant, it shall prevail.

Mistakes which do not vitiate patents.

Separate patents for the three kingdoms. Colonies.

Letters-patent must be several and distinct for England, Scotland, and Ireland, and pass under the respective great seals of these kingdoms. If wished to be extended to the colonies, a trifling additional expence is incurred. In England and Ireland the procedure in letters-patent is the same—the courts, offices, and officers, being on the same model. In Scotland, these last being different, there must be a corresponding difference in the procedure. The application is necessarily remitted to the lord-advocate, who reports upon it; the great-seal is affixed by the authority of its keeper; and the specification is enrolled in the chancery-office, the only remnant of the Scottish lord chancellor. In Scotland, we may remark, patent rights do not rest on a statutory foundation; they are only not prohibited by statute. The grievance of monopolies was felt in Scotland as well as in England; but was not done away till some time later. The statute 1641, c. 63, *discharged*, to use its expression, certain monopolies in favour of named individuals; such as monopoly of tobacco, of leather, and some others—adding, "and all other patents of *that* nature." This statute being passed during the usurpation, was, of course, included in the general act rescissory 1661, c. 15, after the restoration; but even had it not been rescinded, it is silent on patents. The English statute of James, rendered lawful in England, not only patents for new inventions, but certain other enumerated monopolies, such as printing, saltpetre, gunpowder, great ordnance, and offices. The Scots statute made no exception, and did not even reserve patents for new inventions. Patents for new inventions in Scotland are, nevertheless, acknowledged legal rights, but on no other ground than that they have, for more than 200 years, been in use to be granted by the king; and being expressly enacted in England, have evidently, by a tacit analogy, been held lawful in Scotland. Patents, therefore, rest on consuetudinary law in this northern part of the island. In the few actions on patents which have occurred in the Scots courts, the principles of English patent law have been invariably applied.

Peculiarities in Scotland.

Scots statute of monopolies.

Scots patents rest on common law.

Existing law defective.

Our readers cannot have followed us thus far, without being struck with the great imperfection of the law of patents, as it at present stands. It were well if it only baffled the patentee by utter barrenness of advantage; he is fortunate who escapes from that misfortune called a patent, short of very great loss, or absolute ruin. It is the only species of right known in law, which, seemingly created by grant and contract, is really created, not merely vindicated, by a costly law-suit, or series

Patent the only unprotected right.

of law-suits. The king grants a patent—the great seal is affixed—the grantee complies with all the conditions, and the privilege is said to be conferred. Signing, sealing, and delivering, complete any other right, but they confer not the right of patent. They amount to no more than a most unenviable privilege, or rather necessity, of being ruined in a court of law; and till the patentee comes out of court victorious,—which, from the multifarious disadvantages under which the law places him, he does once in five or six instances,—till not the king, but a jury, shall have conferred upon him a monopoly of the fruit of his ingenuity, he has no right for which any sensible person would give him a farthing! Such a privilege is a mere mockery of justice and of common sense. But this is not all: Even when a patentee has, like James Watt, expended hundreds in obtaining the seeming monopoly, and thousands in establishing, by successive law-suits, the real one—a warfare which a poor patentee could not have maintained—his specification is most unnecessarily *made public* fourteen years before it can be used by the public, and serves not only as the guide of piracy at home—so that multitudes infringe the patent who are never discovered—but is forthwith taken abroad, where, of course, the patent article is made, the foreign market shut against the real inventor, and the undue benefit given to foreigners, of the invention free, fourteen years before the patentee's countrymen can enjoy the same advantage. Those who have experience in patents, know too well the calm effrontery with which patents are pirated, if they be valuable enough, and the boldness with which the pirate laughs at the threats of an unendowed, and even of a wealthy patentee, if it chance that he has, by easy access to the specification, fixed upon one of the many trifling errors in that writing, which the present law allows to void a patent right, and by which its unfortunate holder may be baffled and ruined in a court of justice. Dishonest men in the pirating trade are well aware of the great proportion of trials which have ended against the patentee; in consequence of which piracy thrives, and prosecution is rarely attempted.

The country is itself a loser by this anomalous state of the law. Very many ingenious inventions are lost, because their owners have not courage or capital to declare the ruinous war of a patent. No person in his senses, who possesses a valuable secret, will dream of disclosing it for such a right as a patent assures to him. It is become a sort of maxim, that a secret is far more valuable than a patent. But *quoad* the public, the secret is either a perpetual monopoly to its owner and his representatives, without ever being disclosed, or it dies with him, as many valuable secrets have done, altogether. Were a patent a certain right, the monopoly of secrets might be regulated—might be limited to a patent term; but as patents are, such limitation would be the utmost injustice.

But we are not yet done with our reprobation of the present system. The courts of law themselves are most unnecessarily taxed with the labour of ascertaining the merits of mechanical and chemical inventions. This is, perhaps, the purest absurdity of all. They must have recourse to special juries, which it is very difficult to get together for such purposes; so that the jury generally comes to be composed of interested tradesmen, or ignorant persons *ex astantibus*, whom counsel, as they have often complained, cannot enlighten, and judges cannot direct—if, in all cases, these learned persons really understand the construction or composition, themselves.

The cause of these aggravated mischiefs, and the remedy, are both before our readers, when we say, 1st, That patents ought not to be granted *of course*, and " at the hazard" of the patentee that a court of law shall find *that they ought not to have been granted*, but *causa cognita*, by a sufficient and competent authority, after which they ought, like other rights, to be fixed and certain: and, 2dly, That specifications, although lodged and recorded, and that before the patent is granted—an important condition of the grant—should not be seen by the public, till they are of use to them, namely, at the end of the term of the patent.

The expression is common, that a patent may be got for any thing; but very few are found good when they come to the ordeal of a jury. Is this not saying, in so many words, that many that have, ought not to have, been granted; and that it is unworthy of this great country to pervert a valuable privilege, and confound the trash of every pretender, whose end is answered by the mere patent mark, with those inventions which illustrate the genius and exalt the character of the people?

We have not heard any objection to the first mentioned remedy, namely, that a patent shall be put on the legal footing of other rights, viz. granted for ascertained value, (in ingenuity, utility, and future conveyance to the public,) and then made absolute and secure. The reason given in the law books, for publishing the description of the invention at the beginning instead of the end of the term, is this, that the lieges shall not be led to throw away their time, talents, and labour, on the same object, or be betrayed into unintentional infringement by the concealment of the specification.

The answer to this is easy. A description, far short of a minute specification, is publication enough to inform ingenious men of the nature of inventions already protected by patents; not only in machinery, where they have the farther opportunity of comparing such description with the patent article actually in the market, but even in processes and chemical results. For this reason, the *titles* of patents should be required to be full, comprehensive, and intelligible, so as to indicate plainly what is protected, although not the mode of making the article; and a list of these titles should not only be recorded, but gazetted. With such means of information, the ingenious would have themselves to blame if they proceeded totally in the dark. In truth, *practically*, the information proposed to be offered them, would be somewhat better than any of them now take the benefit of, in all cases where the specification is not in the public journals. A list of patents, even at present, is quite warning enough; and, as a copy of a specification does cost a few pounds, no one, with the exception of the scientific journalist, thinks of having recourse to the specification record, but the deliberate, speculating, impudent pirate. But as there ought to remain, in the hands of the same competent authority which passed the specification, power to open it up privately at any time, ingenious men may have the decision of that authority, on the point whether their invention interferes with any existing patent or not.

In one trial, (*ex parte* Hoops, Vesey's Rep. vol. vi. p. 599.) the Lord Chancellor Eldon is reported to have said, that the evil of offering an undue advantage to foreigners was incurable, inasmuch as " a man has nothing more to do than to pirate your invention, in a single instance, and he will force you to bring an action, and then the specification must be produced."

Marginal notes (left column):

Patents.

A jury the virtual granters of patents.

Specification prematurely made public.

Encourages the boldest piracy.

Country suffers from present state of law.

A Secret preferable to its owner, but often lost to the public.

Courts of law perplexed with patents as now regulated.

Marginal notes (right column):

Patents.

Proposed remedy. Patents to be granted *causa cognita*.

Specifications approved of, but not published.

Patents at present too easily obtained.

No objections to patents being absolute rights. Reason given for publishing specification.

Answer.

Titles of patents should be published.

Undue advantage to foreigners not a necessary evil.

The Lord Chancellor was right as the law exists, but it is the very injustice complained of, that the specification must be produced at the command of every pirate.

We shall shortly state the modifications of the present patent law, which appear to us both just and expedient.

1. A permanent board, or judicatory of persons competent to judge of the mechanical, chemical, and legal merits of inventions, ought to be established, and be sworn to fidelity and secrecy. The members of that board should be men of eminence in practical science, assisted by persons versed in the law. Their appointment should be by no lower authority than the sovereign's.

To them alone should be committed the power of certifying new inventions to be worthy of patents; of judging of the comparative merits and priority of rival inventions; and of declaring whether or not infringement, when complained of by patentees, has been committed. From their judgment on *these* points, there ought to be no appeal either to courts of law or equity; but it ought to have the effect of a verdict, and be pleadable in all questions on patent rights in these courts.

It would necessarily come within the province of this board, to watch over and protect patent rights, from new patents for the same things; and not only to decide between the old and new applicant, but to give notice to the patentee, whenever any new application is made which is likely to interfere with his. With them, therefore, caveats ought to be lodged, and not with the law officers of the crown.

2. On the preceding supposition, a caveat could only be required to be lodged in one stage of a patentee's progress, namely, during his experiments, and downwards to the time that his patent is sealed. After that form is passed, a caveat, which at present requires annual renewal, cannot be required at all, as the patentee will be entitled, as a matter of course, to receive notice of all interfering applications. Information, or, as it is called, notice, of new applications being thus due to actual applicants for patents, and actual patentees, there will be an end of that fraudulent practice by which money is extorted from timid applicants, on pretence of withdrawing opposition, by persons who keep a number of caveats, on very general principles, on the books of the attorney-general, and threaten applicants with opposition. Certainly if obtaining money on false pretences merits the punishment of transportation, this infamous practice does so.

3. The preliminary or preparative *caveat* ought to be kept profoundly secret, while the applicant is maturing his invention. Without any assignable reason, a caveat at present is made so public, that it is scrupulously avoided by inventors, as the surest way to raise opposition, and defeat its own end.

4. The applicant having matured his invention, and prepared his specification, should submit *the whole*, at one and the same time, to the board of inspectors or commissioners. Their first duty, after examination, should be instant notice to all patentees with whom it appears to interfere. If it shall not interfere, or on trial by the board

be found to be distinct from the subject of any patent already granted, the next duty of the commissioners should be the most open publication of its title, which must be so ample and comprehensive as unequivocally to designate the invention, with an intimation to all the lieges who claim the invention, to come forward and show their grounds of preference, on or before a named day. If any competitors appear, they must prove *public* use previous to the applicant's *preparative caveat*, to which it is fair that his right shall draw back, and, because of his application for a patent, be preferable to even prior invention kept secret till brought out by the board's proclamation. Of course, prior public use, while it prevents the applicant's patent, renders the invention incapable of being the object of patent right to any one.

5. The time granted being expired, and no opposition having occurred, or having occurred and been defeated, the board should be authorized, on being farther satisfied with the specification as in all respects a full and clear disclosure, and conformable to law, to grant the applicant a certificate, which he will present with his petition to the king, upon which, if it shall please his majesty, he will warrant the passing of the patent in the usual form; the affixing the great seal being the last step, after which the patent shall be absolute, and the specification unquestionable during the whole term of the right. It follows that process of *scire facias* to set aside a patent will then no longer be competent.

6. The specification should be sealed up by the board of commissioners, as soon as approved of; and remain in their custody; with power to them, *and to them alone*, to open it up when ordered by any court of law competent to the question of infringement; or when they themselves deem a recurrence to the specification necessary. The specification thus reinspected, should be resealed, the report of the commissioners upon it having the legal force of a verdict. At the termination of the patent term, the specification should be enrolled and made open to the public.

7. In all cases of infringement, the fact should be tried by the commissioners; whose decision should be used as a verdict in actions for profits and injunction (in Scotland *interdict*) or for damages; or should operate as a verdict for the alleged infringer, the defendant, as its import may be.

The commissioners should keep an exact register of the titles of current patents, with their dates, and an explicit declaration of their objects in these titles. This should be open to public inspection for a trifling fee, and indeed ought to be regularly published in all the scientific journals *.

It may be objected that the proposed proclamation for competitors, may occasion to the applicant for a patent the loss of his labour. It is answered that, besides the great advantage he derives from his protected preparation, he is no worse than, under the present law, he remains through the whole term of his patent. And, at any rate, he ought to run the risk of anticipation to entitle him to an exclusive privilege,—for, against a patent once sealed, even previous public use ought not to be permitted to be

---

* In the above plan, we have given the substance of what appear to us the most expedient suggestions of two bills brought into parliament (by Mr. Curwen and Mr. Wrottesley) and printed in June, 1820. It seems to us that these two bills, besides both containing excellent provisions, in many particulars correct each other's defects. With much deference to their public spirited authors, we think, in what we have just stated, we have improved upon both. In what we have farther to add, our opinion will more clearly appear, that neither bill, nor both bills united, take a wide enough grasp of the important subject. We hope and trust the matter will have the early attention of the legislature.

pleaded. Again, it may be said, that too much power is proposed to be given to the commissioners. We fear, however, that this evil is essential to the due regulation of patent law, which, without such a power, must remain a sort of chartered injustice. In a country like this, however, with a free press and free discussion, there would always be sufficient check upon any thing like partiality. Such a board must, moreover, be composed of men *omni exceptione majores*, and be endowed, by regulated fees, in such a manner as to place them above all temptation to, or suspicion of, the slightest abuse of their power.

Board of commissioners should consist of three branches, one in each kingdom.

The security of the public in the fidelity, as well as in the general and local knowledge, of the commissioners, would be much increased by an arrangement well worthy of the consideration of the legislature; namely, that the court of commissioners for patents should consist of three branches, of three members each, resident in London, Edinburgh, and Dublin, respectively; that these branches should successively deliberate upon every question, both in the original granting and vindication of a patent, and a majority of two-thirds of the total individuals determine every disputed point. By an easy and expeditious mode of communication among the three branches, very little delay would be occasioned. They would obviously be a check upon each other, and their local knowledge would be of great service to the arts in all parts of the three kingdoms.

Fund for their payment.

We should propose that the three sets of commissioners should be paid by the applicants, whether these obtain certificates or not; and by the party failing in all competitions before them, or actions at law, for which their verdict is wanted. We would avoid details here, but we think the commissioners ought to be well paid, even were their fees to be over and above the present expence; as the patentee will be amply compensated by the security of his right, and the total immunity he will enjoy from vexatious piracies, and ruinous law-suits.

Reduction of office-dues.

A patent ought not to be obtained too cheaply, but it ought not to be unnecessarily enhanced by heavy sinecure dues. It is well worth the consideration of the legislature, whether or not the office-fees might not be subjected to reduction. A reduction *in London* of one-third, which is not greatly more than officers paid by government have been subjected to, would create an ample fund for the whole commissioners. But we do not think that the remuneration of the commissioners even added to the present expence, at all above the value of a patent right of the improved quality which would result from the new law.

The same sign manual to warrant the great seals of the three kingdoms.

But there is another and most desirable mode of augmenting the value and security of a patentee's right, namely, to enact that the same sign manual shall be warrant for affixing to the same patent the great seals of the three kingdoms respectively, so that for a moderate fee at the offices of the Seals of Scotland and Ireland, the right shall extend to the three kingdoms. This fee may be made much smaller than it now is in the two latter kingdoms, as the officers would be much more than compensated by *every* patent passing these seals, instead of one in five or six, the present proportion; for the increase of the market is greatly too insignificant relatively to induce patentees to extend their patents to Scotland and Ireland, at the present cost, which for each of these kingdoms is not far short of the rate already paid for England. It is more for security than profit that the

extension is at present generally applied for, to prevent the patent article from being *made* in the sister kingdoms, to be surreptitiously *sold* in England. The patent ought not to be complete till sealed in Scotland and Ireland. In this view of the expence, adding a small fee for the colonies, the patent would have the extensive range which it ought to have, and which an author's copy-right has; the commissioners, to whose establishment it owes its value, would be amply paid, as would the present officers, while the patentee would not be taxed to the amount of one half of the sum now necessary to extend his right to the three kingdoms.

Besides the changes on the law now enumerated, a few additional improvements have occurred to us. 1. The definition of previous *public* use, which, if proved, shall *prevent* a patent, ought to be explicitly laid down. This will greatly facilitate the duty of the commissioners, and afford a test of their decisions to the public, too palpable to be concealed.

Public use to be defined by law.

2. We never could reconcile to justice the principle, that *de facto* disclosure of the secret of an applicant for a patent, accidental though it be, or even by a malicious enemy, should prevent his patent. If my secret is out, I cannot, it is true, be put *in statu quo*, and must run a greater risk of infringement than if it were still in my own power. But if I am entitled to recover my property when lost, and still more when I am robbed of it, I am denied justice, if by no wrong of mine, but by accident, or by the fault or the wrong of others, I have been deprived of the property of my secret. I am nevertheless the inventor, and, as such, entitled to the statutary monopoly; and farther entitled to prosecute all who shall make such use of my secret to which they have no right, as to infringe my patent. A clause to indemnify from the effects of accidental or malicious disclosure, when established to the satisfaction of the commissioners, would be most desirable.

Accidental or malicious disclosure not to void patent.

3. When, under the new law, any person shall prefer a secret manufacture to a patent, he should be entitled to the monopoly of his secret for a certain term of years only, after which he must disclose the secret for the public benefit, and to prevent the art being lost.

Proposed limitation of secrets.

4. The commissioners may be empowered, if they see cause—but this to be entirely in their own discretion— to grant certificates for patents to those who *revive* lost or forgotten inventions of public utility, which have even been in public use in this empire, if they have long ceased and been forgotten. The public benefit which such persons confer, is certainly equal to that conferred by the importer from abroad of a useful invention.

Patents to be granted for revived inventions.

5. It is the only way of compensating to patentees, whose term is now running, the bootless expence they have incurred, and the disappointment and vexation they have endured—besides saving the credit of the great seal itself,—to make all current patents absolute and unquestionable, and subject, for the remainder of their respective terms, to the new law. The worst conceivable consequence of this measure could only be, that some very harmless monopolies, for a few years, would be given of useless articles, and some patents for useful inventions, rashly bestowed on those who did not merit them, might be confirmed; but what is this, an hundred fold repeated, to the evil that one deserving patentee should see all future inventors protected as they ought to be, while he is left to be vexed and plundered under the old *regime*. Perhaps it might be equitable to make the proposed protection to current patents, prospective with relation to infringements. Action of

Patents now current to have the benefit of the new law.

Qualification as to prosecution of past infringements.

damages or for profits should not be competent for *past* infringement, unless the action was brought before the passing of the new law; but injunction or interdict *quoad futura* should be permitted, which would stop all farther infringement, and tie up the hands of all already engaged in infringement.

The following are the advantages which will result from the proposed improvements in patent law.

1. The patentee will have an assured and marketable right in return for his labour, ingenuity, and outlay, and that over the whole empire, for an inconsiderable increase of the present expence of a patent for England alone.

2. The country will be put to no additional expence. The government will, nevertheless, have an important means of rewarding men of science. The public will be secured against the practices of dishonest patentees, who in the present blind mode of granting patents, conceal their processes, and keep back necessary parts of their inventions; and the public will be sure of reaping the full benefit at the end of fourteen years. Valuable processes in the arts, which are now used in secret and kept from the public, nay, often lost to the public, will be disclosed, as soon as security by patent can be obtained. Safety and certainty to patents will stimulate invention in this country, beyond calculation; still more increase the superiority of British over foreign manufactures, and improve the revenue by that superiority, as well as by every new article of luxury and utility brought into the market.

3. Official persons, who at present are benefited by the granting of patents, will be more benefited, even at reduced rates, by the increased number which, under a more trustworthy system, will be applied for.

See *works on Patent Law.* Hand's *Law and Practice of Patents for Invention.* Collier's *Essay on the Law of Patents, and History of Monopolies.* Davis's *Collection of cases respecting Patents of Invention, and the rights of Patentees;* and Blackstone's *Commentaries.*

PATHOLOGY. See MEDICINE, Vol. XIII. and Vol. XIV.

PATMOS, now ST. JEAN DE PATINO, is an island of the Grecian Archipelago, celebrated as the place of St. John's retirement. It is about 10 miles long, 5 broad, and 28 in circumference. Its coasts are intersected by a variety of gulfs and caves, and present many good harbours, among which that of Scola is one of the finest in the archipelago. Rabbits, pigeons, partridges, and quails, are numerous. The monastery of St. John of the apocalypse, stands on the top of a steep mountain, and is fortified by several irregular towers, which defend it, and the inhabitants who come here take refuge under it, from the depredations of the pirates. Dr. Clarke describes it as a very powerful fortress, built upon a steep rock, with several towers and lofty thick walls, which if mounted with guns, might be made impregnable. The library contains about 1000 volumes, of which about 200 were in MS. Among these Dr. Clarke discovered the Patmos Plato, and a Lexicon of St. Cyrill. He found also the curious work of Philo upon Animals, and saw an original letter from the Emperor Alexius Comnenus. Nothing can be more remarkable, says Dr. Clarke, than the situation of the town, built upon the edge of a vast crater, sloping off on either side like the roof of a tiled house. Perry has compared it to an ass's back, on the highest ridge of which stands the

monastery. The *Holy Grotto,* where the Apocalypse is said to have been written, is nothing more than a hermitage dependent on the principal monastery. The women of the island are very handsome, and keep their houses very clean. The beds, which are ten feet high, are ascended by steps. The inhabitants have twelve small vessels, with which they trade to different ports in the Euxine and the Adriatic, bringing corn for their own use. Population about 300. East Long. 26° 40'. N. Lat. 37° 30'. See Tournefort's *Voyage du Levant,* tom. ii. p. 150; Perry's *View of the Levant,* p. 483; Sonnini's *Travels in Greece,* p. 473; and Clarke's *Travels,* vol. iii. p. 348—364.

PATNA, the ancient *Palibothra,* is a city of Hindostan, and the capital of the Province of Bahar. It stands on the south bank of the Ganges, is about four miles long and one broad, and is surrounded with a brick wall, with numerous bastions. The houses are in general about one or two stories in height, and are built of wood. The principal buildings are some mosques and temples, and a small citadel, now used as a barrack and for stores. The Europeans inhabit the suburbs, called Banhypore, about a mile or two to the west of the town, where there is an immense brick granary, with a cupola roof, in the form of a bee-hive, called the *Gola,* built by Mr. Hastings, as a depôt for grain. It has two winding staircases on the outside, which have been ascended by persons on horseback. It is now used as a magazine and arsenal. The large military cantonments of Dinapore stand about 11 miles west of Patna.

Great quantities of white cotton cloths, used for chintzes and dimities, flannels and damask linens, are made in the neighbouring villages; and opium, saltpetre, sugar, and indigo, are produced in considerable quantities. Population about 150,000. East Long. 85° 15'. North Lat. 25° 37'. See Valentia's *Travels,* and Hamilton's *East Indian Gazetteer.*

PATRAS, or BALIABADRA, anciently *Aroe,* is the name of a sea-port town of Greece, situated at the mouth of the Gulf of Lepanto. It is built on the ascent of an eminence, near a bay, and contains only one good street, with a few of the houses built of brick. The principal public buildings and objects of interest, are the fort, in the form of a polygon, now falling into ruins, the synagogue, the Greek churches; part of a Doric frieze, a few small Ionic and Corinthian capitals, and a well mentioned by Pausanias as the oracular fountain of Ceres. The remains of the amphitheatre, and some antique marbles, mentioned by Shaw, have been nearly destroyed by the Turks. The part of the harbour, which is to the north of the town, is not considered safe, from its exposure to heavy seas in winter. The trade of Patras, which is considerable, consists chiefly in wine, oil, honey, currants, wax, silk, and skins. Population about 10,000. East Long. 21° 43'. North Lat. 38° 33'. See Pouqueville's *Travels in the Morea,* p. 50.

PAU, a town of France, and the capital of the department of the Lower Pyrenees, is situated on an eminence near the river, called the Gave de Pau. The town is well built. The principal public places and buildings are the square, called the Place Royale, the Promenade of the Cours Bayard, a public library, an academy of sciences, and the old castle, (now a prison and barracks) which was formerly the residence of the princes of Bearn. The principal manufactures of Pau, are linens, table-linen, and towels;

3

Pavia.

and its hams, which are celebrated, are shipped at Bayonne. Population 9000. West Long. 0° 23'. North Lat. 43° 7'.

PAVIA, a town of Austrian Italy, in the government of Milan, is situated in a delightful plain, on a navigable part of the Tesino, about four miles above the place where that river joins the Po. Its fortifications were formerly strong, but they are now neglected and falling to decay. It is nearly of a circular form, and is about a mile in diameter; the population however bears no proportion to the space which the town occupies, being estimated at not more than 25,000, in consequence of which it has a dull and deserted appearance. The streets are broad and straight, but the houses are in general low. In the centre of the town there is a large square, surrounded with arcades. There are still some remains of the numerous and lofty Gothic towers, which at a former period procured for this city the appellation of Pavia Turrita, or the city of an hundred towers. There is a beautiful marble bridge over the Tesino, which was erected in the fourteenth century. None of the public edifices is any way remarkable. The cathedral is an irregular pile of buildings, erected at different times: it contains the tomb of the celebrated Boethius, who was a native of this city, and who composed, while imprisoned here, his treatise *De Consolatione Philosophiæ*. In the immediate neighbourhood of Pavia, stands the abbey of Chiaravalle, a grand and majestic building; the architecture is Gothic and Saxon intermingled; the walls are of solid white marble, and the interior is richly ornamented. But what chiefly distinguishes Pavia is its university, which has long maintained a high reputation, and has produced many eminent individuals; among its professors it can boast the names of Spallanzani, Volta, and many others who have ranked high in the scientific world. The buildings of the university are handsome, and contain an excellent museum of natural history, an anatomical theatre, spacious lecture rooms, and a library, consisting of 70,000 volumes; there is also a botanical garden belonging to it. The number of students, however, is now much decreased.

The manufactures of Pavia are trifling, and confined chiefly to silk-weaving. Its situation on the Tesino is highly favourable for commerce; but the only articles of export are the productions of the adjacent country; wine, cheese, and rice, are sent to various parts of Italy, and an extensive trade in silk is carried on with Turin, Genoa, and Lyons. The climate is mild, but owing to the extent to which the cultivation of rice, and the system of irrigation are carried on in the neighbourhood, the air is infected with the Malaria. Pavia is the see of a bishop suffragan of Milan.

Pavia, anciently named Ticinum, from the river on which it is situated, was founded by a tribe of Cisalpine Gauls. When the Romans conquered this part of Gaul, Pavia was made a municipal town, and its inhabitants afterwards obtained the privileges of Roman citizens, and were enrolled in the tribe Papia. Hence, when the city was rebuilt in 476, after having been burnt by the Herulians, it took the name of Papia. When the Lombards became masters of this part of Italy, they made Pavia the capital of their dominions; and it continued to be the residence of their monarchs till their final overthrow in 774, by Charlemagne. From that period it was alternately subject to foreign powers and domestic tyrants, till the 12th century, when it obtained its liberty, and assumed a

republican form of government. It was distinguished at this time for the zeal with which it entered into the crusades, having supplied no less than 15,000 men to the army of Italy. In the 14th century it became subject to Galeas Visconti, duke of Milan, who, by the public edifices and charitable institutions which he founded, was one of its greatest benefactors. On the extinction of that family, their dominions became the subject of contention between the French and Imperialists; and in 1525, the decisive battle of Pavia was fought, in which the French were totally routed, and their king, Francis I. taken prisoner. In the following year, Pavia was taken and sacked by Count Lautrec, the French general. In 1706, it expelled the French garrison, and received the Austrians, who were besieging it; from that period it continued subject to Austria, till 1796, when it was taken by the French, but in 1814 it was restored to Austria. East Long. 9° 9' 48". North Lat. 45° 10' 47".

PAUL'S, St. a town of Brazil, and the capital of a district of the same name, is situated upon an eminence about fifty feet high, two miles in extent, the base of which is washed by rivulets which run into the Tieti, within a mile of the town. These rivulets are crossed with several bridges, some of stone, and some of wood. The houses, which are stuccoed of various colours, have a neat appearance, and those in the principal streets are two or three stories high. The streets are paved with an alluvial formation, containing gold, many particles of which are found in the chinks and hollows after heavy rains, when they are carefully sought after by the poor. The town contains several squares, and about 13 places of religious worship, viz. 2 convents, 3 monasteries, and 8 churches, most of which, like the houses, are built of earth. The earth is rammed into frames, which are removed. The houses are covered with gutter tiles, and the roofs project 2 or 3 feet beyond the wall.

The principal manufactures here are coarse cotton; a beautiful kind of net-work for hammocks, and lace, the making of which is the principal employment of the females. Articles of earthen ware are manufactured by the Creolian Indians in the outskirts of the town.

Population about 15,000; the clergy and religious orders amount to about 500. West Long. 46° 55'. North Lat. 23½°. See Mawe's *Travels in the interior of Brazil*, p. 65. 67. &c.

PEAS. See Horticulture, vol. XI. p. 294—296.

PEACH, Peach-Tree, and Peach-House. See Horticulture, vol. XI. p. 86, 87.

PEACH-WOOD. See Dyeing, vol. VIII. p. 229.

PEAR, and Pear Trees. See Horticulture, vol. XI. p. 111—115. 120.

PEARL-FISHERY. Pearls are hard, white, and shining bodies, usually of a roundish form, found in the body and shell of a testaceous fish, of the oyster kind. They have always been held in high estimation as ornamental gems; and the practice of fishing for them appears to have begun at a very remote period. Pliny (lib. ix. cap. 54.) enumerates a variety of places where they were obtained in his time. At present, pearls are found in different parts of Europe; in Asia, and in America. The situations in Asia, where they are got in greatest abundance, are the following: the Gulf of Manaar, the Persian Gulf, the Sooloo Archipelago; and the coast of Japan. The two first of these have been celebrated since the time of Pliny, for the number and superior quality of the pearls which they

Pearl
Fishery.

have produced. The Ceylon pearl-fishery was neglected by the Dutch from 1768, but it was resumed
in 1796 by the British, on their becoming masters of
the sea-coast. The produce has varied in different
seasons; in 1797, it yielded a revenue of £144,000;
in 1798, no less than £192,000; but in the following
year only £30,000, it having been exhausted by the
three preceding seasons. The oyster-banks extend
thirty miles from Manaar, southward of Arippo and
Condatchy, and are in general about fifteen miles from
the shore. The principal of them is opposite the bay
of Condatchy, about twenty miles from the shore, and
is ten miles in length and two in breadth. The depth
of water over the different banks varies from three to
fifteen fathoms; but the best fishing is found in from
six to eight fathoms. There are fourteen banks, of
which not more than two or three are fished in a season, in order that the oysters may attain their proper
state of maturity, which is supposed to be in seven
years. The fishing season commences about the middle of February, and continues till the end of March;
though from various interruptions there are not above
thirty days of fishing. The divers, and the boats employed in the fishing, come from Tuticorin, Karical,
Negopatam, and other parts of the Coromandel coast.
The boats rendezvous in the bay of Condatchy, where
they are numbered and contracted for; they are open
vessels, of one ton burden, about forty-five feet long,
seven or eight broad, and three deep. All the boats
regularly sail together from the bay, with the land-
breeze, at 10 o'clock, P.M.; they reach the banks at
sunrise, when the fishing is commenced; and at noon
they return with the sea-breeze. The crew of each
boat consists of ten divers, with ten manducs, or persons for hauling them up; five of the divers descend
into the sea at a time, while the other five have thus
leisure to recruit. In order to hasten their descent, a
large stone is used, with a rope attached to it, which
the diver seizes with the toes of his right foot, while
he grasps a bag of net-work with those of his left.
He then seizes another rope with his right hand, and
keeping his nostrils shut with his left, plunges into
the water, and soon reaches the bottom. Then hanging the net round his neck, he speedily collects the
oysters, and resuming his former position, he makes a
signal to those in the boat, and is immediately hauled
up, and the stone which assisted his descent is pulled
up afterwards. The time he continues under water
seldom exceeds one minute, sometimes it is one and a
half or two, and instances have been known of a diver
remaining full six minutes under water. When the
oysters are abundant, a diver often brings up 150 in
his net, but when they are thinly scattered, he will
sometimes collect not more than five; one boat has
been known to land in a day 33,000 oysters, and another only 300. The divers are all Indians, who are
accustomed to this seemingly dangerous occupation
from their infancy, and who fearlessly descend to the
greatest depths. They will frequently make from
forty to fifty plunges in a day; but the exertion is so
violent, that on coming up they discharge water, and
sometimes blood from their mouth, ears, and nostrils.
Some of them rub their bodies over with oil, and stuff
their ears, to prevent the water from entering; but
the greater part use no precautions whatever. They
take no food while in the boats, nor till they return on
shore, and have bathed themselves in fresh water.
The only danger to which they are exposed, is from
meeting, while at the bottom, with the ground-shark,
which is a common inhabitant of those seas, and of

which the divers are under dreadful apprehensions.
Some of them, indeed, are so expert as to avoid this
enemy, even when they remain under water for a
considerable time; but the uncertainty of escaping is
so great, that in order to avert the danger, they consult before they begin their priests or conjurors, in
whom they place implicit confidence. Great numbers
of this class resort to the island during the fishing
season; and two of them are employed by government, one of whom goes out in the head pilot-boat,
while the other perform certain ceremonies on shore.
After the oysters are brought on shore, they are suffered to remain together in heaps till they have passed
through a state of putrefaction, and have become dry,
when the pearl is easily extracted without being injured. Though pearls are not peculiar to one kind of
oysters, the pearl oysters of Ceylon are all of one species and one shape, being an imperfect oval, about
nine inches and a half in circumference. The body of
the oyster is white and fleshy, much fatter and more
glutinous than the common oyster, and so rank as to
be unfit for eating. The outside of the shell is smooth,
unless when covered with sea-weed; and the inside
is brighter and more beautiful than the pearl itself;
some of these animals are as red as blood, and the inside of the shell is of the same colour. The pearls are
sometimes found in the body of the oyster, but more
commonly in the shell; the round ones are always
got in the body; and many of those that are of an
irregular shape are found adhering to the inner part
of the shell, being flat on that side which is attached
to it. One can judge with some probability from the
form of the shell, whether it contains any, though the
largest shell does not always contain the greatest number, or the largest pearls; sometimes between one
and two hundred have been found in a shell, and it
frequently happens that three or four hundred shells
will be opened without a single pearl being obtained.
After being extracted, and perfectly cleaned, they are
rounded and polished with a powder made of the
pearls themselves. They are next sorted into classes,
according to their size, by being passed through brass
sieves full of holes, and are then drilled and strung.
The different classes of them are sent to different
markets; the largest meet with a ready sale in various
parts of India; those of a smaller size are best adapted
for the European market. Their colour is usually a
beautiful silvery white; but they are met with of a
variety of hues, transparent, semi-transparent, opaque,
brown, black.

The pearl-fishery at the Bahreen islands, in the Persian Gulf, is the most extensive and the most valuable
in the world. It formerly belonged exclusively to the
Persians, but a powerful tribe of Arabs have now obtained a share in it. The oyster banks extend from
25° to 26° 40' of North Lat.; they have from fifteen
to thirty feet of water over them, and some even more.
The method of fishing does not differ materially from
that practised at Ceylon: it commences in June, and
is carried on for two months; the divers employed
are Persians. The boats are all numbered; the oysters are not allowed to be opened in the boats, but are
brought ashore at a certain hour, and opened in presence of an officer. The pearls found are carried to
the collector, who receives the duty, which is one-
third, and which is daily paid in pearls or money.
The pearls of this fishery are of a golden yellow colour; and though not so much valued in Europe as
those of Ceylon, are more esteemed by the Indians, on
account of their always retaining their colour, whereas

the white ones are liable to tarnish, and soon lose their lustre. The shells are nearly of a round form, from eight to ten inches in diameter, and thick in proportion. They are the property of the divers; and are partly sent up the Red Sea, and thence to Grand Cairo and Constantinople; many of them are carried to India, and thence to China, where they are manufactured into a great variety of useful articles.

The principal situations in America, where pearls are found, are, the arm of the sea between the islands of Cubagua and Coche, and the coast of Cumana; the mouth of the Rio de la Hacha; the Gulf of Panama near the Islas de las Perlas; and the eastern coast of California. Long before the discovery of America, pearls were highly valued by the natives; and the Spaniards, on their conquest of the country, found large quantities of them in different quarters. At an early period the fisheries were very productive; in 1587, 697 lbs. of pearls were imported into Seville, among which there were some of great beauty for Philip II. The same monarch had one from the fishing of St. Marqueriti, which weighed 250 carats, and was valued at 150,000 dollars. The only places, however, where there are still fishing establishments, are the Gulfs of Panama and California; and the number of pearls which they produce is now reduced almost to nothing. The decline of these fisheries seems to be solely owing to improper management, and to the small encouragement given to the Indians and negroes, who follow the occupation of divers. The pearls of California are large and of a beautiful water, but are frequently of an irregular and disagreeable shape.

Pearls are of a calcareous nature, and consist of a number of coats or layers, regularly spread over one another like the coats of an onion. They seem to be the effects of disease, like bezoars and other stones in different animals, and are formed by an extravasation of a glutinous juice either within the body or on the surface of the animal. Such extravasations may be caused by the admission of particles of sand or other heterogeneous bodies along with the food, which the animal, in order to prevent the disagreeable effects of friction, covers with its glutinous matter; which, as it is successively secreted, forms many regular lamellæ. Accordingly, in the centre of the pearl, there is often found a small particle of sand or other extraneous matter, which may be considered as the nucleus or primary cause of its formation. When the first coat is separated, a worthless impure pearl is frequently found below, and sometimes the lamellæ are clear and impure by turns. This view of the formation of the pearl is rendered still more probable from the manner in which the Chinese are said to force the oysters to produce pearls. In the beginning of summer, when the oysters rise to the surface of the water and open their shells, five or six beads made of mother-of-pearl are strung on a thread and thrown into each of them; and at the end of the year, when the oysters are drawn up and opened, the beads are found covered with a pearly crust, so as to have a perfect resemblance to real pearls. See the article CEYLON. Percival's *Account of Ceylon; Asiatic Researches*, vol. v.; and Humboldt's *Political Essay on New Spain*, vols. ii. and iii.

PEARL, MOTHER of, Optical Properties of, and Structure. See OPTICS, vol. XV. p. 569.

PEAT. See AGRICULTURE, Vol. I. p. 229, and the *Edin. Phil. Journ.* vol. ii. p. 40, 201.

PEEBLES, a burgh town of Scotland, and county town of Peebles-shire, is agreeably situated on the north bank of the Tweed, principally on a slightly elevated ridge at the junction of Eddlestone-water with the Tweed. Peebles is a town of very considerable antiquity, and there was undoubtedly a village and a church here before the commencement of the Scoto-Saxon period. Being only twenty-one miles distance from the metropolis, Peebles was occasionally honoured by the residence of the Scottish monarchs till the death of Alexander III. It sent two representatives to the parliament which was assembled in 1357, to provide the ransom of David II. This sovereign afterwards granted the town a charter, dated September 20, 1367, in which it is styled a royal burgh; and this was subsequently confirmed by James II. and VI. with additional privileges.

The town of Peebles is divided by Eddlestone-water into two parts, called the Old and New Town. The principal street, running parallel to the Tweed, is broad and clean, and contains many excellent houses. At the west end of this street, and at the point where the Eddlestone runs into the Tweed, stands the church, which is an excellent and substantial modern structure, with a lofty spire. It occupies the site of the ancient castle. Close to it is the county jail, which is also a substantial building. There is also here a town hall; and an elegant inn, built by Tontine, which contains the assembly rooms, and other apartments where the county business is transacted.

Before the Reformation, Peebles had three churches and several chapels. The ruins of the high church, dedicated to the Virgin Mary, and erected in the 11th century, still exist in the church-yard, at the west extremity of the Old Town. When the church was destroyed at the Reformation, the Cross-church became the parochial place of worship, and continued so till 1782, when the present church was built. The remains of the cross still exist, at the east end of the Old Town. There was formerly a mint at the head of Bridge-gate, which is still known by the name of *Cunzie Nook*. The Old and New Town are connected by means of two small bridges over the Eddlestone. There is a fine old bridge of five arches over the Tweed, immediately below the confluence of the Eddlestone with the river, and which joined Peebles with a new suburb, containing many excellent houses; among which is a charity school for girls, built and supported by the liberality of Sir John Hay, Bart. Peebles possesses an excellent grammar school, which has obtained great reputation under the present master, Mr. Sloane, and is a place well fitted for the education of youth.

The principal manufactures of Peebles are those of carpets and stockings, and weaving is carried on to a considerable extent. There is an extensive brewery at Kersfield, in the neighbourhood of the town.

The town is governed by a provost, two bailies, and a council of eighteen in all; and, along with Lanark, Linlithgow, and Selkirk, it sends one member to parliament.

The principal places in the immediate neighbourhood of Peebles, are Needpath Castle, a fine old building, the property of the Earl of Wemyss and March; King's-Meadows, the residence of John Hay, Esq. Younger of Hayston; Cailzie, the residence of R. N. Campbell, Esq.; Venlaw, (where the old castle of Smithfield stood, said to have been inhabited by Darnley,) the property of J. Erskine, Esq.; Barns, the seat of James Burnet, Esq.; and Rosetta, the residence of Thomas Young, Esq. The population of the parish of Peebles in 1821, was 2701.

PEEBLES-SHIRE. This county, also known by the name of Tweeddale, is inclosed among the counties of Mid-Lothian, Selkirk, Dumfries, and Lanark; its

Peebles-shire.

greatest length from north to south being about thirty miles, and its greatest breadth, in the opposite direction, twenty-two. It is computed to contain about 184,000 Scotch acres; and the arable lands have been estimated at one-tenth of the whole. The number of parishes is sixteen.

Physical geography.

This may be considered as a purely hilly country; consisting of a group of mountains, or rather a continuous heap of mountain land, and with no other level ground than that which accompanies the courses of the rivers. Among these, notwithstanding different names, there is scarcely one mountain distinguished above its neighbours; but Broad Law, Dollar Law, and Scrape, are among the highest elevations, reaching from 1500 to nearly 2000 feet. The characters of these are every where tame and rounded, presenting no where a rugged outline, and rarely displaying naked rocks.

The principal low land is that which forms the valley of the Tweed. In this, the situation of Peebles is pleasing, but cannot be considered picturesque.

The Tweed holds its course for several miles through this county, within which it has also its origin. The spring is called Tweedswell, and is estimated at 1500 feet above the level of the sea. It first runs in a northeast direction till it receives the waters of the Lyne. It then turns east, in which course it continues till it leaves the county; entering Selkirkshire at Gatehaupburn. It nearly divides the county of Peebles into two equal parts; the length of its course in it being estimated at thirty-six miles.

Waters.

Biggar water, uniting together those of Kilbucho and Holms, rises in Lanarkshire, and is the first principal stream that joins the Tweed. After that it receives the Lyne, together with the Tarth, the water of Peebles or Eddlestone, and the Leithan, all on its left bank. On the right, it is joined by the Mannor and the Quair. The Cor, Fruid, and Tala, also join it in the higher parts of its course.

Besides these minor rivers flowing into the Tweed, some other small streams arise either in the county or in its boundaries. The Maidwan, among these, joins the Clyde. The North and the South Esks form a junction in Mid-Lothian; and passing through the picturesque scenery of Roslin, join the sea at Musselburgh. Lastly, the Megget falls into St. Mary's loch in Selkirkshire, and thus contributes to form the waters of the Yarrow.

Lakes.

There are only three small lochs in this county, although St. Mary's loch lies on its very margin. These are Gameshope loch to the south, in the parish of Tweedsmuir; Slipperfield loch in Linton parish, and Water loch in that of Eddlestone. These present no interesting features of any kind.

Soil and surface.

As the far greater part of this county lies on an argillaceous schist, properly called whinstone here, as trap is at Edinburgh, the general nature of the hill soils, at least, may be conjectured. As this schist, however, contains particles of sand and gravel in its composition, the soil is not so stiff a clay as in those districts where the finer kinds of this rock prevail. It must rather be considered as of a loamy nature, being a mixture of clay and sand, together with gravel; and, when least decomposed, containing fragments also of the hard rock of various kinds. The coarser aspect is found higher up in the hills. Farther down, as is generally the case, the decomposition of the rock is more perfect, and the consequence is a finer clayey or loamy soil. As the declivity becomes still more gentle, and as the hill faces begin to unite to the proper alluvial land below, or the haughs, the soil still improves in quality as well as in depth; but in partaking of the finer alluvial

Peebles-shire.

clay, washed along the surface by the waters, it also becomes intermixed with gravel and fragments.

The haughs or flats by the sides of the rivers present the usual character of alluvial lands in mountainous countries. In some places they are a strong clay; but more generally sandy; while in many parts a great depth of alluvial gravel is found beneath the upper soil, insuring a constant natural drainage from its absorbent nature. This is very generally the case along the broader part of the course of the Tweed.

In the northern and western parts of the county, where the coal strata are present, the subsoil displays a different character from that of the mountainous schistose tract, from the prevalence of sand; but much of the soil in these parts is also of a good quality, appearing to have arisen from the decomposition of trap rocks. There is no calcareous soil in Peebles-shire, as it scarcely contains any traces of limestone at the surface.

The old croft, or infield lands, are found about the lower declivities of the hills, and on the proper alluvial lands; above the former there is generally such outfield as is occasionally put under the plough. On the tops of some of the hills, when the decomposition of the rock is not such as to generate a true soil, or where that has been washed away, the soil is light and thin, and appears to be a mixture of moss and sand. It is so loose and light, that when dry it is blown away by the winds; and in its natural state produces heath. In some cases, as in Linton parish, where it is under tillage, and lies upon an impervious subsoil, it becomes very loose and wet in rainy seasons, so as almost to resemble mud. This soil in fact is rather peculiar to the tracts of country formerly mentioned that lie above the sandstone of the coal strata.

Peat, as might be expected, abounds in this county. It is found, as usual, in the hollows among the hills, varying from five to twenty feet in depth, forming flat bogs. Besides this, it occurs on the declivities, in the usual form of mountain peat, commonly shallow, but in some places attaining three or four feet in depth. Even this mountain peat is moist in its natural state; but after tillage and liming, it consolidates and becomes drier. When the plough can reach the subsoil in these cases, so as to turn it up, various mixtures are generated. Soils of this nature have been considerably cultivated, and have been found to yield good crops of oats, and excellent pasture for black cattle.

Agriculture and rural economy.

The chief part of Peebles-shire is divided among sixty proprietors, exclusively of some smaller ones; and the gross rent is estimated at £26,000. The valuation in the cess books is £51,927 Scotch. Some of the smaller proprietors farm their own lands, but the larger farmers are chiefly tenants. Most of the larger proprietors also farm portions of their own lands. About a fourth part is supposed to be entailed. The leases are generally for nineteen years, but longer periods are also granted. Liferents are not known.

For fine inclosed grass lands two or three guineas an acre are commonly paid. Arable farms vary from 20s. or 25s. to 50s. The number of farmers renting lands from £100 to £500 is estimated at about eighty; but there are also many smaller farms, varying from £20 to £80. The smaller sheep farms contain 600 or 700 Scotch acres; the larger range from 1000 to 4000. There are few of these sheep farms of less than £100 rent, and the highest rent paid in the county is £600. The smaller arable farms vary from 40 to 100 and 200 acres: the rents of these varying from £25 to £150.

The generality of the sheep farms have more or less arable land attached to them, but there are some of the larger where this is not the case, or where that practice is adopted on a very small scale. In these instances, the meal wanted for the support of the family is purchased, and the cows and horses in winter are kept on natural hay. The sheep, in these cases, are driven to other pastures when the snow is on the ground, or else fodder is purchased for them. In a few instances, farms are so allotted, that the sheep and the arable part are of equal importance, or the latter may even exceed the former.

In respect to the management of the sheep, Tweeddale is rather a breeding than a feeding county; but, at this time, many more are fattened for the butcher than was in use formerly. The practice with respect to selling off the stock, varies in different places. Sometimes the lambs are sold off at three or four months old. Hogs, at fifteen months, are also sold at Linton market, whence they are carried to Fife, and other places, for feeding. Some of both kinds are also sold in Roxburghshire and in England. In some of the farms they do not breed, but buy in annually lambs in June and July, which, after a twelve-month's feeding, are sold as hogs. Hogs are also bought for some high farms, and sold, after a year's feeding, as dinmonts, or else they are kept for two years and disposed of as wedders. In some, also, the greater part of the lambs are sold fat to the butchers.

Besides this, there are some fine grass farms which keep no stock in winter, buying in ewes big with lamb in March, and selling both fat to the butcher, either from the grass, or from turnip if necessary. The farms, also, which keep a stock of breeding ewes, sell off a portion of these at four, five, or six years, preserving ewe lambs to supply their places. These are commonly fattened on turnips. The number of sheep in the county is estimated at 113,000.

Most of these farms, of course, have wool to sell. Part of this goes to Stirling, some to Hawick, but the greater portion to Yorkshire, where it is used for coarse cloths, and for serges, shalloons, and carpets. Ewe-milk cheese has been, at times, made and sold on these farms, but the practice has been nearly abandoned at other times. There are a few of these farms where some black cattle and horses are reared for sale, but this practice is very limited.

The management of the arable portions attached to the sheep farms is as follows:—Where, as is commonly the case, a portion of land, from ten to thirty acres, surrounds the house, forming what is here called old croft land, the rotation is, 1. Turnips, with a portion of potatoes, and all the dung; 2. Bear, or oats, with grass seeds; 3. Hay; 4. Oats, or sometimes bear. When the land is sufficiently extensive, and of a better quality, different rotations are in use, such as, 1. Green fallow, with dung; 2. Bear, with grass seeds; 3. Hay; 4. Oats; 5. Pease, or else oats again after the pease. But, in this county, the excess of the mountain pasture over the arable land is so great, that it is not supposed that it would suffice for the winter feeding of the sheep reared, though it were all appropriated to that purpose. The outfields on the sheep farms are brought into occasional tillage, after liming, and folding the cattle and sheep on it.

Among the arable farms there are a few that are strictly so, as we already remarked, having pastures attached. Among the chief of their produce is that of the dairy. Butter is sent for the supply of Edinburgh, and hence the only cheese is from skimmed milk. The new dropped calves are also sold off, as veal is not fattened; but the old cows are sometimes sold in calf, or fattened, together with a few young cows and oxen. The farms, more especially of this kind, are those nearest to Edinburgh, as at Linton, Eddlestone, Newlands, and Peebles. This latter town also consumes a considerable part of the produce of the dairy. The milch cows are much fed in the house in summer on green clover, and in winter with turnips, as is the young stock.

Where the arable farms are all fit for the plough, and properly inclosed, they are regularly cultivated; the pasture, in this case, forming part of the rotation. Thus, if the pasture is broken up, perhaps one crop of oats and one of pease, or two of each, are taken, followed by turnip, fallow with dung, barley with grass seeds, and hay, when the land is again thrown into pasture for a longer or shorter period. Other courses are, however, used according to the particular state of the farm and the inclosures.—There are about fifty threshing mills in the county.

With respect to the nature of the crops, turnips and potatoes are chiefly used for the purpose of green fallow. Various kinds of the former are in use, and the Swedish has lately been introduced with evident advantage. The culture of both are carried on according to the most approved methods. Pease are sometimes sown upon outfields, as formerly remarked, or as part of the system of rotation upon the arable farms. They are seldom drilled. They are sown in February, March, or April, but are an uncertain crop upon the higher lands. Oats are sown in various modes of rotation, and different kinds are used on different farms. Bear is the most common variety of barley, but some two-rowed barley is also raised. Rye was once raised in small quantity, but has been abandoned. Nor is wheat much cultivated, although fine crops are produced on the farms of Sir John Hay, near Peebles. The Talavera wheat has here been successfully cultivated. Beans have been attempted, but in vain. A few tares are sown for green fodder, and cabbages sometimes come in to the fallow crop. Flax is scarcely cultivated, except on a very small scale for domestic manufactures.

There is very little natural wood in this county, nor has much been as yet planted, at least on a great scale. The chief of these plantations have been executed by Mr. Mackenzie, Sir John Hay, and Sir James Montgomery. The larch is found to thrive in the vicinity of Peebles; yet the county affords abundant shelter to trees in many places. In some, the plantations have been executed in narrow belts on the hills, as affording shelter to the sheep. This practice is of very little value, as far as relates to the growth of the wood, however adapted to these incidental purposes.

The lowest arable land on the banks of the Tweed is about 400 feet above the level of the sea, and cultivation is limited to about 500 feet above this. An average height for the pasture lands may be taken at 1200. The climate is moist, and it is also late. Sown hay is cut from the beginning to the middle of July, and that from natural grass in August. Corn harvest seldom begins till the second week in September, and it is considered early if every thing is stacked before the end of October.

In the spring months cold easterly winds frequently prevail, so that there is very little grass in May. On particular occasions, the leaves of the trees and the young shoots are destroyed by winds of this kind: an event which has also happened to the potatoe crops as late as the middle of June, and even, on one occasion, in July. The winters are severe, and hence the turnip crop is often lost, unless it is consumed before Christmas. The higher lands are also exposed to partial frosts in the end of August and beginning of September, attended with a low mist. This climate is, therefore, not favourable to fruit trees; as even the

Woods and plantations.

Climate.

hazel scarcely ripens its nut in the higher lands. The vicinity of Peebles is the most favourable in this respect, since even the bitter almond has been known to ripen there

The medium annual depth of rain appears to be about 29 inches, or less; as the registers do not seem to have been very accurately kept. The west winds exceed the east, in the proportion of four to three. The extreme vacillations of the thermometer marked, are from 81 to —14. The mean temperature of Eshiells, 500 feet above the sea, for 1821, was 45°.62; and of Tweedsmuir, about 1300 feet above the sea, 45°.13. The mean of the temperature of springs for 1821, at Tweedsmuir, as ascertained by Mr. W. Fairlie, was 45°.69; and for 1822, 45°.87.

We cannot terminate this department, without remarking, that Sir John Hay, who has bestowed much attention on experimental farming, has lately tried, on a great scale, the project recommended in a French Agricultural Report for obtaining potash from the stalks of potatoes.

The result of two trials on two separate acres was as follows:—The first acre was a rich loamy soil at King's Meadows. The potatoes were drilled, and produced a good crop. They were cut, as directed in the French communication, immediately after flowering, left ten days to dry, and then burnt in a pit. The produce was 222 lbs. of ashes; and, on lixiviation and drying, these yielded 55 lbs. of impure potash, or mixed salts.

The second acre was a clayey wet soil, with a retentive bottom; but the crop, which was also drilled, was considered moderate. These stems were treated in the same manner, but the burning was more complete, so that they contained less charcoal than the preceding. They only weighed 112 lb. and produced 28 lb. of impure potash.

Now, comparing these experiments with the French, and with some that were made in Ireland by Mr. Rice, the result is as follows:—In the French experiments the potash was said to be 2000 lb. per acre of potatoes; in that of Mr. Rice it was only 201⅓ lb. In Sir John Hay's experiments, which were conducted with every possible care, this produce was, in one instance, about the fourth, and in the other about the half, of what it was in Ireland. We must add to this, that the mixed residuum, when dry, here called impure potash, does not contain above 10 per cent. of pure alkali, the rest being muriate of potash and other ingredients.

It is impossible to reconcile these results, without considering the French trials as a mere fiction. Differences may easily be imagined that will account for the variation between the Irish and Scotch cases; and to a sufficient extent, therefore, they confirm each other, while they throw more than doubt on the French experiments. Under either of these events, it is very plain that there is no temptation to adopt this practice with a view to profit.

There is no salmon fishery in the Tweed within this county capable of paying rent, but they are caught with the rod in and out of season, in all the waters. These rivers abound also in trout, par, and eels, and the latter, in the Tweed, are esteemed of excellent quality. Perch and pike are found in the lochs already mentioned. Tweeddale does not abound in moor game; but hares and partridges are abundant in the lower lands, and pheasants have also been cultivated with success.

A woollen manufacture was established some time ago at Inverleithen, for coarse cloths. Felts for the paper mills are also manufactured on the North Esk, and a manufacture of narrow cloths was set up at Peebles. Here also there are some stocking-looms, and some hands employed in weaving linens and cottons for Glasgow and Lanark. There is no other commerce than that for agricultural produce already noticed.

By the returns in 1821, the population amounted to, males 4963, females 5061, total 10,046.

We need not describe the roads, but shall here notice the wire bridge erected by Sir John Hay, below Peebles, being the first specimen of this structure set up in Scotland. It is made on the principle first adopted, namely, that of suspending a road-way from pillars by means of wires, and which has now been abandoned in favour of the much better Catenarian principle. Where it crosses the Tweed, the breadth of the river is 110 feet. The total length of the bridge is 135, and its breadth four; the piers or columns of support rising 10 feet above the water. This bridge cost £160, and was erected by Redpath, Brown and Company, of Edinburgh*.

The far larger part of this county consists of a coarse argillaceous schist, known to mineralogists by the name of grey-wacke, and commonly called whinstone in the country. This rock, which forms the boundary of the Lammermuir hills, commences northward about Kingside, whence its boundary extends westward by Romanno and Stobo, till it passes out of the county; leaving all to the southward and eastward composed of it, or, about two-thirds of the whole.

The stratification of this rock is so irregular, that no rule can be laid down respecting it; and it even becomes difficult to distinguish its disposition in many cases. It must be considered the fundamental rock, as nothing lower in geological order is to be found. In point of quality it is exceedingly various; and, to a mineralogist, often very interesting. It differs exceedingly in aspect and general composition from the rocks of the same denomination that occur in the northern parts of Scotland, although the structure is the same.

In its simplest state it is a fine clay slate, of a dark lead blue, fissile in many cases, so as to yield roofing slate. From this it passes into a fine grey-wacke slate, in an argillaceous base containing sand and mica. In a still coarser state, it contains quartz gravel, and thus far the compounded varieties are sufficiently simple. But it is often far more compounded than this, containing fragments of former schists of the same kind, and of basalt, together with particles of limestone and other occasional substances. On the northern border it is very remarkable for containing a great variety of jasper in fragments. When these are highly coloured and intermixed with white quartz and other fragments, the conglomerates thus formed are often very beautiful, as well as of extreme hardness; being susceptible of a high polish, and forming very ornamental specimens, fit even for snuff boxes and similar trinkets.

It is quarried in many places, under the name of whinstone, for building, but is often a faulty stone for this purpose, on account of its slaty nature. In some places it is also quarried for roofing slate; and that which is wrought at Stobo is carried as far as Kelso and Edinburgh, and even into Lanarkshire.

Above this rock lies the old red sandstone, continuous with that of Dunbar; but this is traced with great difficulty in a few places on the margin of the subjacent rock. Among others it is found westward at Broomielees, where it is quarried.

This sandstone is in some places followed by that limestone which also appears near Edinburgh, and

* A full description, and a drawing of this bridge, will be found in *The Edinburgh Philosophical Journal*, vol. v. p. 241, 242.

which lies beneath the coal series; but it is not wrought any where, and has scarcely indeed been examined.

The remainder of the county, separated by the line formerly indicated, consists of sandstone, ostensibly of a whitish and yellow colour, resembling that of Edinburgh, with which it is continuous. This is, in fact, part of the coal series of that district, and it contains, besides, alternately beds of limestone and shale, as is usual elsewhere. The limestone is wrought, together with the coal, in the parishes of Linton and Newlands; but the coal workings are not carried deeper than the natural drainage will permit. The produce is consumed chiefly in the county. It is thought that this bed of coal is a continuation of that which extends on both sides of the North Esk, as far as the sea at Musselburgh. We may add to this, that ironstone occurs in this series, but not such as to pay the expence of carriage to any iron work.

Freestone quarries are wrought in this series, in the parishes of Linton and Newlands, and at Marfield on the North Esk.

Besides the limestone of this series, some slender appearances of primary limestone occur in thin beds among the grey-wacke. One of these, near Peebles, has been wrought out, and there are some also equally insignificant in two or three other places farther to the southward.

We have already mentioned ironstone. We have not found that any of the shell marl so common under peat has been discovered in the county; but some alluvial marly strata from the decomposition of calcareous rocks, are found in that part of the country where the coal series lies.

There yet remains at Linton some remains of ancient mine-workings, known by the name of the *Silver holes*. The hill itself is called Leadlaw. This silver must have been obtained from lead; and attempts were made 60 years ago to renew the mine, but without effect.

We may add, that agate pebbles, arising from the decomposition of the trap rocks of the Pentland hills, are found in this same neighbourhood.

The ancient castles of this county, of which Needpath is the most conspicuous, require no particular notice. A Roman camp remains well marked at Linton, and another at Lyre; and it is likely that this people occupied some other points in the county. In digging in the peat some years ago, there was found here, a kettle of Roman bronze, exactly resembling the iron pot common at present in our cottages, and about ten inches in height and diameter. A vessel of the same metal, resembling a coffee-pot with legs, was also dug up at Eshiells, on the estate of Sir John Hay. This specimen is eight inches high, and they are probably both Roman. Figures of them are given in the *Edin. Phil. Journal* for 1822, vol. vii. p. 55.

PEEL. See ISLE OF MAN. Vol. XIII. p. 301.

PEGU. See BIRMAN EMPIRE. Vol. III. p. 522—534.

PEKIN. See CHINA. Vol. VI. p. 206; and CIVIL ARCHITECTURE. Vol. VI. p. 588, for a very full account of this city.

PELEW, or PALOS ISLANDS, a cluster of islands in the North Pacific Ocean, lying between the Caroline and the south point of the Philippine islands, extend in the direction of S. W. to N. E. from 6° 54′, to 8° 12′ north latitude, and from 34° 5′, to 36° 40′ east longitude. The origin of the term by which these islands are denoted, has not been exactly ascertained. The most probable conjecture is, that this appellation was first applied to them by the Spaniards of the Philippine islands, (by whom, as shall soon be shown, they were first discovered,) from the tall *palm*-trees with which

they abound, and which from a distance have the appearance of masts of ships.

These islands seem not to have been known to Europeans until the beginning of last century. Some of the natives having been driven on Mindanao, and symptoms of land having been seen south-east of Samar, both belonging to the Philippine islands; the Spanish Jesuits of this place, thus instigated to explore the neighbouring seas, discovered, in November, 1710, that group of islands of which we now treat. The circumstances and character of the inhabitants, however, were comparatively unknown or misrepresented until the year 1783, when Captain Wilson of the Antelope, in the service of the East India Company, having been wrecked on the shores of one of these islands, communicated to the public, through Mr. Keate, a very excellent and minute account of the history, manners, and customs of the Pelewans. These islands have been repeatedly visited; but to Mr. Keate's valuable narrative we owe almost all the intelligence we possess respecting this interesting portion of the globe.

Of the Pelew islands, which are about eighteen in number, the most important are Babelthouap, or Panlog, Oroolong, Coorooraa, Artingall, Pelelew, Emilligne, Emungs, Pethoull, St. Andrew's. The climate is salubrious and agreeable, and the seasons are divided into the wet and dry, as in other tropical countries. None of the islands are large; they are generally long in proportion to their breadth; they are considerably high and rugged, though they are not devoid of extensive valleys, exhibiting decided marks of industry and cultivation. With few exceptions they abound in wood of various kinds, and of all degrees of height, such as the cabbage, ebony, manchineel, carambola, the palm, and the wild bread-fruit trees, plantains, bananas, bamboos, &c. Some of these trees are so large, that canoes, made of their trunks, are capable of carrying nearly thirty passengers. Of grain, the Pelewans were, when visited by Captain Wilson, entirely ignorant; their staple livelihood consisting of beetle-nuts, yams, cocoa-nuts, bread-fruit, and fish, with which the neighbouring seas are liberally stocked. Oranges, lemons, the jamboo apple, are regarded as great luxuries. The use of salt is unknown; the milk of the cocoa-nut is the usual beverage; and a species of sweet-meat is prepared from the sugar-cane, which seems to be indigenous. Every man possesses his own piece of ground, which is, in most cases, judiciously laid out, and highly cultivated, the time of the inhabitants being entirely devoted either to fishing or the cultivation of their land. But, however abundant in other articles, and though the soil, which is naturally rich, be well adapted for pasture, these islands, till lately, contained no cattle, or quadrupeds of any species, except a few grey-coloured rats, and cats of a diminutive size, neither of which it is likely are indigenous, but brought thither by some vessels that touched upon the islands. In birds of various kinds there was no deficiency; pigeons were the most numerous; and though the common cocks and hens were very plentiful, the natives never thought of using them as food till instructed by the English.

The character of the Pelewans was, as formerly hinted, entirely unknown till the publication of Mr. Keate's interesting work. The Spanish Jesuits, who first visited them, had represented them as savage cannibals, and as regarded with horror by the inhabitants of the neighbouring islands. No account can possibly be conceived more false. They are, on the contrary, characterized by mildness, politeness, and benevolence. Their humane and affectionate treatment of the English, who, in 1783, were wrecked on their coast, would have done honour to the most civilized and refined nation in the world. " They felt our people were distressed, and in consequence wished they should share whatever they had to give. It was not that worldly munificence that bestows and spreads its favours with a distant eye to retribution. It was the pure emotion of native benevolence. It was the love of man to man. It was a scene that pictures human nature in triumphant colouring ; and, whilst their liberality gratified the sense, their virtue struck the heart."

But though they are distinguished by so much genuine politeness and goodness of heart, they are nevertheless living in the simplest state of nature, ignorant of the arts and sciences, and devoid of liberal knowledge. The men go entirely naked ; the women wear two little aprons, one before and the other behind, about ten inches deep and seven wide, made of the husks of the cocoa-nut stripped into narrow slips, which they dye with different shades of yellow. They are a stout well-made people, rather above the middle size ; their complexion, though not black, is of the darkest copper colour ; their hair long and flowing, which they sometimes form into one loose curl intwined round the head, though the women often allow it to hang, in a loose dishevelled state, down the back. Both sexes are *tatooed* at a pretty early age. The men have their left ear perforated, the females both, which, according to the different ranks, are respectively decorated with beads, ear-rings of tortoise shell, or a sprig of some favourite tree. In both sexes also, the cartilage between the nostrils is bored, and is embellished with a fragrant leaf or blossom. By means of some dye, the teeth of all the children at a certain age are blacked ; but how this was effected the English could not learn, though they were told that the operation was tedious and painful. The Pelewans of all ranks, both men and women, are expert swimmers and admirable divers, and they regard bathing as a duty which every morning must be regularly performed. Their houses, situated on a pile of large stones three feet above the surface of the surrounding ground, to prevent damp, are built of wood, very closely interwoven with bamboos and palm trees. These buildings consist only of one apartment, and the fire is placed in the centre. Their bed-clothes are formed of the plantain leaf, of which also their dishes are made, though of the latter some are composed of earthen-ware, or of the shell of cocoa-nut neatly polished. Their best knives are of mother-of-pearl ; others are formed of a large muscle-shell, or split bamboo. Their warlike weapons, resembling those of the other islands of Polynesia, are the spear about twelve feet long, darts, and slings, made chiefly of bamboo. Of all kinds of fire-arms they were completely ignorant till shown by Captain Wilson. Every man has his own canoe, on which he sets a high value, and which he almost regards as sacred. They are skilful mechanics ; idleness is totally unknown ; and even the king himself, when unencumbered with affairs of state, does not hesitate to engage in mechanical operations. Any thing like religious principles seem not to be cherished among them ; but they believe that the soul survives the dissolution of the body. Polygamy is allowed ; but they are by no means distinguished for unchastity, or promiscuous sexual intercourse. Their funerals are conducted in a very solemn manner ; they have places appropriated to sepulture ; and they frequently erect unlettered monuments of stone over the spot where the body is reposited.

The form of government of the Pelew islands is monarchical ; but almost every island seems to have a distinct sovereign, whose authority is absolute. Abba Thulle, when Captain Wilson was driven on these islands, was king of Coorooraa ; a monarch of the most mild and amiable dispositions, and whose humane and hospitable behaviour to our countrymen in distress, has rendered his name dear to every Briton. His nobles were denominated *Rupacks* ; and he had instituted a singular species of knighthood, the members of which were termed knights of the bone, and were distinguished by wearing the figure of a bone on the arm. So highly did he value the superior knowledge and refinement by which he saw the English characterized, and so much confidence did he repose in Captain Wilson, that, on the departure of that commander, he permitted his son, prince Lee Boo, to accompany him. This young man was possessed of every amiable quality ; his mental endowments were rather of a superior kind ; and he exhibited an extremely ardent desire to acquire knowledge. On his arrival in England, he was put to an academy at Rotherhithe, where his talents and application, as well as the gentleness and simplicity of his manners, soon procured him the love and esteem both of his school-fellows and his teachers. His progress was extremely rapid ; and he was delighting himself with the prospect of transferring to his native islands the knowledge which he was thus acquiring. But this pleasing prospect he was doomed never to realize. In a few months after his arrival he was seized with the small-pox ; medical aid was found to be unavailing ; and on the 27th of December, 1784, this hopeful youth breathed his last in the house of Captain Wilson, in the twentieth year of his age. He was buried in Rotherhithe church-yard ; and the East India Company caused a monument, with a suitable inscription, to be erected to his memory. The East India Company, sensible what obligations they yet lay under to Abba Thulle, sent, in 1791, two vessels to the Pelew islands, under the command of Captain M'Clure, containing presents of various kinds ; cattle, goats, pigs, geese, ducks, &c. with seeds of almost every description, hardware, swords, arms, ammunition. Abba Thulle, though deeply affected at the intelligence of the premature death of his son, yet bore it with wonderful fortitude and resignation. He himself died in 1793, and was succeeded by his brother. The Pelew islands have repeatedly been visited since this period. Several Europeans now reside on them. The munificent gift of the East India Company (who have since sent presents of a similar kind) has been attended with complete success. The live stock, with the exception of the sheep, which have entirely failed, have multiplied in an incredible degree. Two crops of rice and other grain are now annually produced here ; and a small commercial connexion has been established by the English between China and the Pelew Islands.

See *Lettres Edifiantes et Curieuses*, Paris, 12mo. vols. xv. and xviii. *Histoire Général des Voyages*, vol. xv. 4to. Keate's *Account of the Pelew Islands. Narrative of the Shipwreck of Captain Wilson, &c.* one volume 12mo. (T. M.)

PELTRY. See our article CANADA, Vol. V. page 338—340, for a full account of the fur trade.

PEMBROKE, the principal town of Pembrokeshire, is delightfully situated on a navigable creek of Milford Haven, called Down Pool, over which there is an excellent bridge. It was formerly surrounded by a strong and lofty wall, which is still almost entire on the north side, where it is flanked by several bastions of considerable strength and thickness. In this wall there were three gates, on the north, east,

Pembroke. and west sides, and a postern on the south; of these
Pembroke- gates that on the north side is the only one now re-
shire. maining. The town consists chiefly of one long
street, which is wide and well built, extending from
east to west on the ridge of a hill, and terminating at
the west end in a steep precipice, on which the castle
is situated. The public buildings are a town-hall, a
free grammar-school, two churches in the town, and
one in the suburbs. The churches are of great antiquity, but they are no way remarkable for their architecture or interior decorations. The castle, though
now in a ruinous state, has an air of uncommon grandeur and magnificence. It was founded in 1092, by
Arnulph de Montgomery, son to the Earl of Shrews-
bury. In that early age it was considered as impregnable, and even so late as the 17th century, it made
a vigorous resistance to the Parliamentary forces, but
was at length taken by Cromwell. In one of its
apartments Henry VII. was born. In the rock under
the castle there is a large natural cavern, noted for its
fine echo; it is supposed to have once contained a
spring, which supplied the garrison with water, there
being a staircase from the castle communicating with
it. Pembroke is a borough town, and is governed by
a mayor, two bailiffs, and common council; and, along
with Tenby and Whiston, returns one member to Parliament, the right of election being vested in the
mayors, bailiffs, and burgesses of the three boroughs.
There are no manufactories in the town, and its trade
is trifling. The population is estimated at 2415.

PEMBROKESHIRE, a maritime county of South
Wales, is bounded on the north and west by St George's
Channel, on the south by the Bristol Channel, on the
east by Caermarthenshire, and on the north-east by
Cardiganshire. Its form is very irregular, in consequence of the numerous bays with which its coast is
indented. The greatest length from north to south
is about 30 miles; the greatest breadth 33, and the
shortest diameter 13; the circumference measures 115
miles. The superficial extent is estimated at 610
square miles, or 390,400 acres. It is divided into
seven hundreds, and these again into 145 parishes;
it contains one city, and seven market towns. It lies
in the diocese of St. David's, and sends two members
to parliament.

With regard to external aspect, this county, though
greatly diversified by an alternation of hill and dale, is
the most level part of Wales, and seems to bear a closer
resemblance to the English counties. The hills are of
moderate elevation, except in the north-east district,
where a chain of considerable height, named Percelly,
extends about 10 miles from east to west. The scenery on the banks of the Tivy, and in many places along
the coast, is beautiful and romantic; but it is in general uninteresting from the scarcity of woods and plantations, there being almost none in the county except
in some spots on the west coast.

Rivers. The rivers of Pembrokeshire are numerous; the
principal of these are the Tivy, the east Cleddau and
west Cleddau. The Tivy rises in the north-east of
Cardiganshire, and entering this county at Devy,
forms its boundary on the north-east, passes the town
of Cardigan, and falls at Kenmaes Head into the
Irish sea. The east Cleddau rises in the north of the
county, and after forming, during a part of its course,
the boundary between Pembrokeshire and Caermarthenshire, flows to the south-west and joins the west
Cleddau at Landshipping. The west Cleddau has its
source in the western district of the county, and running in an easterly direction, receives the waters of
the Hiog near Haverford west, where it becomes salt;

turning to the south-east it meets the east Cleddau at Pembroke-
Landshipping, where they united form Milford Haven; shire.
the length of which, from the junction of the two rivers
to the sea, is 16 miles, and its mean breadth one mile.

Pembrokeshire has a considerable extent of coast, Coast.
which is in general hilly, with almost perpendicular
cliffs. The natural harbours are numerous and excellent: that of Milford Haven, in particular, is reckoned the best in the kingdom; it is a deep inlet of the
sea, branching out into numerous creeks, sheltered
from all winds, and sufficiently capacious to contain
the whole of the British navy. North of Milford
Haven is St. Bride's Bay, which is also large, and
well sheltered from all winds except the west: the
other principal bays are those of Fishgard, Newport,
and Aberkikor. Near St. Bride's Bay is Ramsay Island, which is frequented by multitudes of migrating
birds, many of which are unknown in every other
part of the island; there are also some small islands
on the south-west side.

The climate is mild and salubrious, and instances Climate
of longevity are numerous and remarkable. From and soil.
being almost surrounded by the sea, this county is
more subject to rain than any other county of England, a circumstance which the great dryness of the
soil renders very beneficial. Frost seldom continues
long, and snow never lies more than a few days, except on the mountains in the north. The quality of
the soil varies considerably, but it may be divided into
four varieties; first, a strong red loam, generally from
six to fourteen inches in depth, resting on a stratum of
red argillaceous rock: secondly, a dark grey loam, from
six to twelve inches deep, on a blue and brown rock;
this earth is most abundant, the greater part of the
surface of the county being composed of it: thirdly, a
light spungy peat, usually on a clay bottom; this soil
is very unproductive, but is much improved by lime-
manure: fourthly, a rich loam of considerable depth,
on a substratum of limestone rock; this variety,
which is confined to the southern district, is well
adapted for the culture of corn.

This county is not remarkable for its mineral trea- Minerals.
sures. Several attempts have been made at different
times to procure gold and silver, but these have always proved fruitless. There are some lead mines on
the Tivy, the ore of which is said to be of a superior
quality; though formerly worked with great advantage, they are at present abandoned. Limestone and
coal are found in abundance in the southern part of
the county; the coal is by no means good, but the
limestone is of a superior quality, and equally well
adapted for manure and building. Freestone is also
plentiful, and is exported in large quantities. There are
some mineral springs, chiefly of the chalybeate kind.

With regard to agriculture, Pembrokeshire, though Agricul-
much improved of late years, is still very defective. ture.
The farms vary in extent from 50 to 500 acres; the
average size is about 200 acres. They are almost all
let from year to year, though some proprietors grant
leases usually for a term of three lives. The average
rent and tithes of a square mile amount to £284.
The farms are of a mixed description, grain being
raised on all of them, and a part of each being appropriated to the dairy and the rearing of cattle. The
system of husbandry is wretched in the extreme, it
being common to exhaust the land by four white crops
in succession, and then frequently to lay it out without any grass seeds. The grains commonly raised are
wheat, barley, and oats, and in some parts rye. Turnips and peas are cultivated on some farms, but with
no great success. The implements used in husbandry

3

Pembroke-shire. are of the most awkward and despicable description. This county produces a superior breed of jet-black cattle, with spreading horns, which are in great request in the English market, where they meet with a ready sale. Lime is extensively used for manure; and in some parts shelly sea-sand is used with advantage for barley crops. Draining has been carried to some extent, and considerable tracts of land have been reclaimed by means of it. The waste lands of the county consist of about 22,220 acres, which are chiefly used as sheep-walks.

Commerce and fisheries. This county possesses no manufactures deserving of particular notice. There were formerly some tin works on the Tivy, and a cotton-mill at Haverford-west, both of which are now discontinued. With all the advantages presented by its numerous natural harbours and great extent of coast; its commerce is very limited, being confined to a little coasting-trade, chiefly for the exportation of cheese, butter, stone, coal and culm. The fisheries are productive, but, from the want of capital, are not carried on to any extent. There are a number of fishing towns along the coast: Fishgard, in particular, is noted for its trade in herrings; the various creeks abound with oysters and other fish. There are also several salmon fisheries, the salmon being plentiful in some of the rivers; near Kilgerran on the Tivy, there is a remarkable salmon leap, where that fish is caught in great abundance.

History. Pembrokeshire anciently formed a part of the province of Dyfed, which also comprehended the counties of Caermarthen and Cardigan. Nothing of its history is known previous to the Roman invasion, and the only proofs of its being occupied by that people, are drawn from the works which they have left behind them. The great western Roman road entered the county at Llanvyrnach, and proceeded in a straight line to Menapia, at its western extremity. Another Roman road led from the great road, to the station called Ad-Vigesimum, the site of which has been lately ascertained by Mr. Fenton to be the spot called Castle Flemish. Several tumuli, the remains of a small camp and Roman bath, and other traces of their establishment, have also been discovered. After the departure of the Romans, its history is for a long period involved in obscurity. During the Danish invasions this district suffered repeatedly from their attacks. After the conquest, it was subdued by one of those military adventurers, to whom the English king William II. had given permission to hold by knights' service under himself, whatever lands they might wrest from the Welsh. In the war of the Roses, the Earl of Richmond, afterwards Henry VII. and his mother, were besieged in Pembroke castle; and in this county he landed on his enterprise against Richard III. and was immediately joined by a strong body of Welsh. In the civil wars of the 17th century, several of its castles were garrisoned for the king, and skirmishes took place in different quarters of it. From that period nothing occurred to disturb the tranquillity of the county till 1797, when considerable alarm was excited by the landing of a French force; but on the assembling of the military of the county, they capitulated on the day after their disembarkation.

Population. According to the parliamentary returns, the population of this county stood as follows: in 1801, there were 11,869 houses, and 56,280 inhabitants. In 1811, the population had risen to 60,615, or 19 to the square mile; of whom 33,338 were employed in agriculture; the average net product, or rent and tithes of a family, amounted to £24. See *The Beauties of England and Wales*, vol. xviii. p. 734, and Malkin's *Tour in South Wales*, vol. ii. p. 177.

PENDULUM.

Pendulum. PENDULUM, in mechanics, denotes a heavy body, so suspended that it may vibrate, or swing backwards and forwards about a fixed point by the action of gravity.

When a heavy body, suspended in such a manner as to be at liberty to move round a fixed axis, is drawn aside from the vertical position, and abandoned to the action of gravity, its oscillations are all sensibly equal in point of duration. It is uncertain by whom this remarkable fact was first observed; but the celebrated Galileo is universally acknowledged to have been the first who pointed out the important advantages that might be derived from it, by employing the pendulum to measure small determinate intervals of time. The general properties of the pendulum were made known by the publication of the *Systema Cosmicum*, in 1632, and more particularly by that of the *Dialogi de Motu*, in 1639, after which time the instrument began to be generally employed by astronomers; but, for want of some convenient method of counting the number of oscillations, and of supplying the loss of velocity occasioned by the resistance of the air, and the friction of the axis, no great advantage was derived from its use till these defects were obviated by Huygens. Under the article HOROLOGY, a full account has been given of the ingenious mechanical contrivance, by means of which this distinguished philosopher connected the pendulum with the wheel work of a clock; and of the methods which have since been devised to compensate the effects of a variation of temperature, on the materials of which it may be constructed, in order to render it a perfectly accurate regulator of time-pieces.

The theory of the pendulum forms a branch of mechanics, and has therefore been already considered under that article. Our principal object in the present article, is to give an account of some of the more recent and accurate experiments which have been made, with a view to determine the length of a pendulum making a certain number of oscillations in a given time,—an element of great importance in physical astronomy. But as the pendulum in such experiments is always made to oscillate in the arc of a circle, in which case the oscillations in arcs of different lengths are not exactly isochronous, it will be requisite previously to investigate the series which expresses the time of an oscillation in a circular arc of any amplitude whatever, in order to know the value of the required correction. We shall then briefly notice a few formulæ, immediately derived from the series which are required in deducing the length of the seconds pendulum, from one of which the length has been determined by experiment; referring the reader, who is desirous of information with regard to the oscillation of pendulums in cycloidal arcs, to the article on MECHANICS, already mentioned, or to the profound and elegant treatise of Huygens, entitled *Horologium Oscillatorium*.

Series for the time of oscillation in a circular arc. In order to compare with greater facility the times of the oscillations of pendulums with each other, geometricians have imagined a *simple pendulum*, composed of a heavy point of matter suspended at one extremity of a wire or thread without weight, inflexible and inextensible; the other extremity being attached to a fixed point. To determine the time of an oscillation of such a

Pendulum. pendulum in a circular arc, let BA b, Plate CCCCLVIII.
Fig. 1. be the arc in which it oscillates, C the centre of the circle, or point of suspension, CA a vertical line, and P the place of the material point in any part of the arc. Draw BD b and PE p perpendiculars to CA, and put the radius, or length of the pendulum equal l, AD$=b$, and AE$=x$. Then if t, S, and V, represent the time, space, and velocity respectively, the differential relation, according to the theory of dynamics, is $dt = \dfrac{dS}{V}$. But

PLATE
CCCCLVIII.
Fig. 1.

S$=$arc AP; therefore $dS = d$ arc $AP = \dfrac{-l\,dx}{\sqrt{2\,x - x^2}}$,

where the negative sign is taken, because the arc diminishes as t increases. Also V, or the velocity acquired by descending from B to P, is equal to that acquired by falling through DE, or equal to $\sqrt{2\,\varphi}$. DE, φ being the accelerating force of gravity. Hence, since DE $= b - x$,

$$ dt = \frac{-l\,dx}{\sqrt{(2\,x - x^2)\,.\,2\,\varphi(b - x)}}; $$

or, putting this fraction under another form,

$$ dt = -\tfrac{1}{2}\sqrt{\frac{l}{\varphi}} \cdot \frac{dx}{\sqrt{b\,x - x^2}\,\sqrt{1 - \dfrac{x}{2}}}. $$

The integral of this differential is not known under a finite form; to obtain it in a series, the factor

$$ \left(1 - \frac{x}{2}\right)^{-\frac{1}{2}} $$

must be developed according to the powers of x. The binomial theorem gives

$$ \left(1 - \frac{x}{2}\right)^{-\frac{1}{2}} = 1 + \frac{1}{2}\cdot\frac{x}{2} + \frac{1\cdot3}{2\cdot4}\cdot\frac{x^2}{4} + \frac{1\cdot3\cdot5}{2\cdot4\cdot6}\cdot\frac{x^3}{8} + $$
&c.

consequently

$$ dt = -\tfrac{1}{2}\sqrt{\frac{l}{\varphi}}\,\frac{dx}{\sqrt{b\,x - x^2}}\left\{1 + \frac{1}{2}\cdot\frac{x}{2} + \frac{1\cdot3}{2\cdot4}\cdot\frac{x}{4} + \frac{1\cdot3\cdot5}{2\cdot4\cdot6}\,\frac{x^3}{8} + \&c.\right\} $$

The integrals of the different terms of this expression are all comprehended under the general form

$$ A \cdot \int \frac{-x^n\,dx}{\sqrt{b\,x - x^2}}, $$

n being a whole positive number, or zero, and A a coefficient varying with n. To obtain the time of descent from B to A, the integrals must be taken from $x=b$ to $x=0$. Let, therefore A$_n$ be the value of the integral

$$ \int \frac{-x^n\,dx}{\sqrt{b\,x - x^2}} $$

taken between these limits, the index of A corresponding to the exponent of x, so that A$_0$, A$_1$, A$_2$, &c. may be the values of

$$ \int \frac{-dx}{\sqrt{b\,x - x^2}}, \int \frac{-x\,dx}{\sqrt{b\,x - x^2}}, \int \frac{-x^2\,dx}{\sqrt{b\,x - x^2}}, \&c. $$

taken between the same limits, and let t be the time of an entire oscillation, which is double the time of descent from B to A, we shall have

$$ t = \sqrt{\frac{l}{\varphi}}\left\{A_0 + \frac{1}{2}\cdot\tfrac{1}{2}A_1 + \frac{1\cdot3}{2\cdot4}\,\tfrac{1}{4}A_2 + \frac{1\cdot3\cdot5}{2\cdot4\cdot6}\,\tfrac{1}{8}A_3 + \&c.\right\} $$

The values of the definite integrals A$_0$, A$_1$, A$_2$, &c. Pendulum. are so related to each other, that, if one is known, the rest can easily be deduced. On diminishing the exponent of x by unity, we find

$$ \int \frac{-x^n\,dx}{\sqrt{b\,x - x^2}} = \frac{x^{n-1}\sqrt{b\,x - x^2}}{n} + \frac{b(2n-1)}{2\,n}\int \frac{-x^{n-1}\,dx}{\sqrt{b\,x - x^2}} $$

At the limits $x=b$, and $x=0$, the factor $\sqrt{b\,x - x^2}$ becomes zero; therefore, on passing to the definite integrals,

$$ A_n = \frac{b(2n-1)}{2\,n}\cdot A_{n-1}, $$

putting successively $n=1$, $n=2$, $n=3$, &c. in this equation, we obtain

$$ A_1 = \tfrac{1}{2}\,b\,A_0 $$
$$ A_2 = \tfrac{3}{4}\,b\,A_1 = \frac{1\cdot3}{2\cdot4}\,b^2\,A_0 $$
$$ A_3 = \tfrac{5}{6}\,b\,A_2 = \frac{1\cdot3\cdot5}{2\cdot4\cdot6}\,b^3\,A_0, \&c. $$

With regard to the value of A$_0$, we have

$$ \int \frac{-dx}{\sqrt{b\,x - x^2}} = \text{arc}\left\{\cos. = \frac{2\,x - b}{b}\right\} + \text{const.} $$

This integral taken between $x=0$ and $x=b$, gives A$_0 = \pi$: π representing the ratio of the circumference of a circle to its diameter. Substituting these values of A$_0$, A$_1$, A$_2$, &c. in the series, we have ultimately

$$ t = \pi\sqrt{\frac{l}{\varphi}}\left\{1 + \frac{1^2}{2^2}\cdot\frac{b}{2} + \frac{1^2\cdot3^2}{2^2\cdot4^2}\left(\frac{b}{2}\right)^2 + \frac{1^2\cdot3^2\cdot5^2}{2^2\cdot4^2\cdot6^2}\left(\frac{b}{2}\right)^3 + \right. $$
$$ \left. \&c.\right\}\ ^* $$

From this series the following formulæ are easily deduced.

1st. When the angle made by the pendulum on each side of the vertical remains constant, or when the oscillations are performed in equal arcs, the ratio $\dfrac{b}{2}$ is constant, and t varies as $\sqrt{\dfrac{l}{\varphi}}$; that is, *the time of an oscillation is directly as the square root of the length of the pendulum, and inversely as the square root of the accelerating force of gravity.*

2d. Similarly, for any other simple pendulum l', which makes one oscillation in the time t', t' will vary as $\sqrt{\dfrac{l'}{\varphi}}$, whence

$$ t : t' :: \sqrt{\frac{l}{\varphi}}\quad\sqrt{\frac{l'}{\varphi}}, \text{ or} $$
$$ l : l' :: t^2 : t'^2; $$

that is, *the lengths of two simple pendulums, oscillating in similar arcs, and incited by the same forces, are to each other as the squares of the times of their oscillations.*

3d. Let N be the number of oscillations made by a simple pendulum in the time T, we shall have $t = \dfrac{T}{N}$, the oscillations being all of equal duration; also for any other pendulum, $t' = \dfrac{T'}{N'}$. Substituting these values of t and t' in the last proportion,

$$ l : l' :: \frac{T^2}{N^2} : \frac{T'^2}{N'^2} :: T^2\,N'^2 : T'^2\,N^2; $$

* The first series for the pendulum was given by the celebrated James Gregory, the inventor of the Reflecting Telescope, in a Latin appendix to a small treatise published at Glasgow in 1672, entitled, "The Great and New Art of Weighing Vanity."

4

and supposing T and T′ to be equal,

$$l : l' :: N'^2 : N^2 ;$$

that is, *the lengths of two simple pendulums, incited by the same forces, and oscillating in similar arcs, are reciprocally proportional to the squares of the number of oscillations they make in equal times.*

The length of the seconds pendulum is obtained by the help of this proportion; for it would be impossible by any mechanical means to give such a length to a pendulum, that it would make precisely 86,400 oscillations in a day; but when l, the length of a pendulum, which makes a certain number N of oscillations in a day, is found, it is easy to deduce l', the length of the pendulum, which makes any given number N of oscillations during the same time; for $l' = l \cdot \dfrac{N^2}{N'^2}$.

4th. By the inspection of the series, it is evident that when the arc of oscillation is small, (and care is taken that this be the case in all experiments on the pendulum,) the quantity b, which expresses the versed sine of half the arc, is very small in comparison of the radius. In this case, therefore, the series will converge rapidly, so that the second, and all the higher powers of $\dfrac{b}{2}$, may be rejected without sensible error. The time of an oscillation, therefore, becomes simply $\pi \sqrt{\dfrac{l}{\varphi}} \left\{ 1 + \dfrac{b}{8} \right\}$; or, calling half the arc of oscillation A, and introducing the sine, instead of the versed sine, we obtain

$$t = \pi \sqrt{\frac{l}{\varphi}} \left\{ 1 + \frac{\sin^2 A}{16} \right\} ; \text{ for } b = \frac{\sin^2 A}{2} \text{ nearly.}$$

5th. If the arc be diminished indefinitely, the time of an oscillation becomes $\pi \sqrt{\dfrac{l}{\varphi}}$; therefore, putting $t =$ time in an arc indefinitely small, and $t' =$ time in the arc 2A, we obtain

$$t : t' :: 1 : \left\{ 1 + \frac{\sin^2 A}{16} \right\} ; \text{ whence}$$

$$t' = t \left\{ 1 + \frac{\sin^2 A}{16} \right\} ; \text{ or, substituting for}$$

t and t' their values $\dfrac{T}{N}$, $\dfrac{T'}{N'}$, as before,

$$N = N' \left\{ 1 + \frac{\sin^2 A}{16} \right\}.$$

Hence, when N′, the number of oscillations in an arc, $= 2$ A, during a given time has been observed, we obtain N, the number of oscillations which the same pendulum would have made in an arc indefinitely small during the same time.

The formula $t = \pi \sqrt{\dfrac{l}{\varphi'}}$, shows that the length of the pendulum varies as the accelerating force of gravity, when the times of oscillation continue equal. Now, it is known, that on account of the oblate spheroidal form of the earth, and its rotatory motion, this force is not a constant quantity, but increases as we advance towards the pole, both on account of the greater proximity to the centre of the mass, and the diminution of the centrifugal force. Hence, in order that a pendulum may continue to make the same number of oscillations in a given time, it must be shortened as it is carried towards the equator; and the variation of its length in different latitudes, affords an accurate measure of the force of gravity. But the force of gravity has a known relation to the figure of the earth, which, therefore, may be determined, by observing the length of the seconds pendulum at different points on its surface. In this view, the accurate determination of the length of the pendulum, is a problem not only extremely curious in itself, but highly interesting on account of its immediate connexion with one of the greatest and most important questions in the natural history of the earth. (See *Physical* ASTRONOMY, Vol. II. p. 710.)

The retardation of the seconds pendulum, on being carried towards the equator, was first observed by Richer, in the year 1672, at Cayenne, where he found it necessary to shorten the pendulum of his clock, which had been regulated at Paris, according to mean time, by a line and a quarter. This phenomenon, when announced in Europe, appeared so very extraordinary, that it did not obtain implicit credit till confirmed by the observations of Varin and Deshayes, in the islands of Goree and Cayenne, and in various places in the West Indies. It was then demonstrated, both by Huygens and Sir Isaac Newton, that the cause of the phenomenon was to be referred to the diminution of gravity occasioned by a compression of the earth at the poles; and since that time, the measurement of the pendulum has occupied much of the attention of astronomers, and formed a material part in every inquiry relative to the figure of the earth. The French academicians, Bouguer, Godin, and Condamine, when engaged in measuring the length of a meridional degree in Peru, made a great number of observations on the pendulum in places near the equator; but the results of their experiments, although they put the fact of the compression of the earth beyond all doubt, did not agree so well with each other as to give any satisfactory information with regard to its amount. Numerous experiments have since been made to determine the length of the pendulum in various parts of the world, but as the greater part of them appear to have been performed with an apparatus by no means suited to the extreme delicacy of the operation, little dependence can be placed on their results. Those of Mairan at Paris, and of our countrymen Mr. George Graham and Mr. Whitehurst, may be mentioned as being amongst the most accurate and ingenious. But the first measurement obtained by a method perfectly unexceptionable, and with the most scrupulous attention to every circumstance which could possibly influence the results, was that of Borda and Cassini, after the introduction of the " Système Métrique" in France. The immediate object which these distinguished philosophers had in view, was to determine the relation of the seconds pendulum to the metre, or ten millionth part of the quadrant of the meridian, which had been selected by the academy as the unit or basis of a consistent and philosophical system of measures.

Measurement of the Pendulum.

The apparatus which Borda employed in his experiments was constructed in the following manner. The pendulum of experiment was formed of a ball of platina, attached to a metallic wire, and suspended from the extremity of a block of stone, which rested on the top of a wall of solid masonry. It was placed at such a height, that the ball was nearly on a level with the centre of the bob of a clock pendulum placed at a little distance behind. The oscillations of the two pendulums were observed through a small telescope, placed at the distance of six feet, which, by enlarging the arc of oscillation, and augmenting the apparent velocity, enabled the observer to determine the moment of coincidence with much greater precision. In order that no disturbance might be occasioned by the influence of the external air, the whole apparatus, including the clock, was placed within a wooden case, having glass windows in front, through which the oscillations were observed. This general disposition is represented, Fig. 2.

PLATE
CCCCLVIII.
Figs. 2, 3.
The pendulum was suspended by means of a knife-edge, which oscillated on a plane of steel. AB, (Fig. 3.) represents the knife-edge, CD, an appendage to which the wire was fixed, EF a screw, furnished with a nut GH, by means of which the oscillations of the knife edge were regulated, and rendered of equal duration with those of the pendulum. When this synchronism was established, the oscillations of the pendulum could not be sensibly influenced by those of the knife-edge and its appendages, because the centre of gravity of the separate system which they formed, being extremely near the plane of suspension, an infinitely small effort was required to bring the oscillatory movement of the knife-edge into perfect accordance with that of the whole system. The plane of suspension was fixed to a plate of copper, IKL, (Fig. 4.) and attached to the block of stone, (Fig. 2.) in such a manner as to be in a position perfectly level. The knife-edge was placed over the opening ST; and when an observation was finished, it was moved aside towards S, and its place taken by a rule with which the length of the pendulum was to be compared. For suspending the ball, metallic wires were chosen, on account of their being more uniform than threads composed of vegetable substances; and the iron wire was selected as being the lightest, and presenting least surface in proportion to its strength. The ball was nearly sixteen one-sixth lines in diameter, and weighed 9911 grains—a little more than seventeen ounces.

Fig. 4.

Fig. 5.
The lower extremity of the wire was fixed by means of a pressure screw in the top of a small spherical cup of copper, Fig. 5. of the same radius as the ball; and the ball being covered with a thin layer of tallow, and then put into the cup, adhered to it in virtue of the atmospheric pressure, and the perfect contact of the surfaces. By this contrivance an opportunity was given of suspending the ball successively by opposite points of its surface, whereby any error could be corrected which might be occasioned by its unequal density or imperfect sphericity. The other end of the wire was fixed also by means of a pressure screw to the appendage CD of the knife-edge. The trial pendulum was of such a length that it made a little less than one oscillation, while the pendulum of the clock made two, so that their movements coincided only at intervals, longer in proportion as one oscillation of the trial pendulum was more nearly equal to two of the clock.

Method of
counting
the oscilla-
tions.
A small circle of black paper, crossed with two white lines, was pasted on the bob of the clock pendulum, to serve as an index; and both pendulums being at rest, the glass O was placed in the direction OPE, so that the wire of the pendulum, when seen through it, fell upon the intersection of the white lines. A dark screen was also placed at a little distance before the pendulum, the vertical edge of which concealed half the wire. This disposition being made, the clock was put in motion, and its rate having been accurately determined, the trial pendulum was also made to oscillate. Suppose, now, that at the outset the wire disappeared behind the screen before the cross; as the times of oscillation were not accurately as two to one, the interval between the disappearances would decrease, till at length both objects came to pass behind the screen at the same instant. The instant of this first coincidence was observed, the oscillations then began to disagree, afterwards to ap-

proach, till at length a second coincidence took place. In the interval between the two coincidences the clock had gained two seconds on the pendulum, so that the ratio of the times of oscillation of the two pendulums was given. The coincidences were observed till the oscillations became so small that the observations could not longer be made with sufficient accuracy. A scale was placed at a little distance behind the pendulum, graduated into minutes of a degree, to measure the amplitude.

Descrip-
tion of the
rule.

PLATE
CCCCLVIII.
Fig. 6.
The rule which was employed in the measurement was of platina, and exceeded 12 feet in length. It was covered by another rule, or sheath of copper, $11\frac{1}{2}$ feet in length, and firmly attached by means of three pressure screws to the upper extremity MN, (Fig. 6.) of the platina rule, but at liberty to slide along it at the lower. By this means, the difference of the expansion of the two rules was indicated; for their divisions being made to coincide exactly at a certain temperature, and the dilatation of copper being greater than that of platina, upon any increase or diminution of temperature the divisions would no longer coincide. The distance, therefore, between the corresponding divisions, indicated by a vernier ST fixed to the platina rule, and observed through a rectangular slit, PR, in the copper, gave the ratio of the dilatation of the two metals, whence, the dilatation of copper having been previously determined by experiment, the absolute dilatation of the platina, at any temperature, could easily be deduced. The lower extremity of the rule was armed with a graduated tongue of platina, which could be protruded by pressing on the button E. Its divisions were equal to the $\frac{1}{10000}$th of a toise, a vernier indicated the tenths, or the 1200th of a line nearly. The upper extremity of the rule was terminated by a transverse ABCD of tempered steel, by means of which it was suspended in the plane of the knife-edge, (Fig. 3.) The lower surface of this transverse had been carefully polished, and the end of the rule was brought into very close contact with it, so that, when the rule was suspended in the plane of the pendulum, its upper extremity was exactly on a level with the plane of suspension.

Fig. 3.
Fig. 2.
When a sufficient number of coincidences had been observed, and it was required to measure the length of the pendulum, the first thing necessary was to bring it to a state of perfect rest. The horizontal plane IH, (Fig. 3.) of which the support was firmly fixed to a stone projecting from the wall, (Fig. 2.) was then elevated by means of its screw, till it was brought into contact with the lowest point of the ball, and as the threads of the screw were extremely fine, the contact could be observed with the utmost precision. The knife-edge of the pendulum was then removed from the middle of the plane of suspension OP, (Fig. 4.) and the rule which had been previously suspended at QR was substituted in its place. The tongue of the rule was next protruded, till it touched the plane IH, and the contact having been carefully observed, the divisions of the vernier were read off. Accurate experiments had previously been made, to determine how much the rule was lengthened by its own weight when suspended; and the mean of these experiments gave $\frac{30}{100}$ of a division for the part of platina, and $\frac{27}{100}$ for the part of copper.

After this general exposition, an example of the method of obtaining the numerical results will serve to elucidate the whole process. In one of the observations, the interval between the first and second coincidences of the pendulums was 4394″, as indicated by the clock. The half, or $2197 - 1 = 2196$, was the number of oscillations made by the trial pendulum du-

PLATE CCCCLVIII.

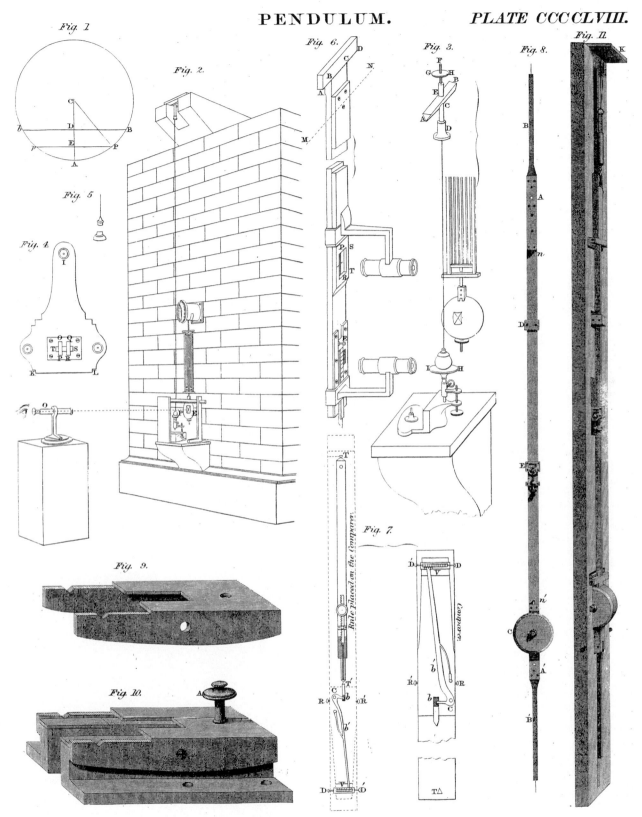

Fig. 1.

Fig. 2.

Fig. 6.

Fig. 3.

Fig. 8.

Fig. 11.

Fig. 5.

Fig. 4.

Fig. 7.

Fig. 9.

Fig. 10.

Eng.d for the Edinburgh Encyclopædia by J. Moffat Edinburgh.

Pendulum. ring the same time, for the clock gained two oscillations on the trial pendulum in the interval between the two coincidences. The clock gained 13″.4 per day on the fixed stars, and, therefore, made 86413.4 oscillations during a sidereal day, or 86650 during a mean solar day. Hence, by proportion, the number of oscillations made by the trial pendulum in a mean solar day was 43305.28. The mean of this, and of four other coincidences, was found to be 43305.30.

This was the number of oscillations in an arc of definite extent, and varying from the commencement to the end of the interval. The duration of the oscillations is, therefore, greater than it would have been had they been made in an indefinitely small arc, and must be reduced to this case, in order that the results of different experiments may be comparable with each other. If the arcs are small, and $2\,a$ be the amplitude Reduction to an indefinitely small arc. at the commencement of an interval, $2\,a'$ at the end, the mean amplitude may be considered $a + a'$, and the reduction obtained by formula 5th, which in this case

would become $N = N' \left\{ 1 + \frac{1}{16} \text{Sin.}\,^2(a+a') \right\}$. Borda, however, not satisfied with this approximation, gave a formula for the correction, which was afterwards demonstrated by Biot in the third volume of his *Astronomie Physique*, grounded on the more accurate hypothesis, that while the times increase in an arithmetical progression, the amplitudes decrease in a geometrical. Calling the required correction m, the formula is

$$m = \frac{\sin.\,(a + a')\,\sin.\,(a - a')}{32\,M\,(\log.\,\sin.\,a - \log.\,\sin.\,a')};$$

M being the modulus of the common logarithmic tables, or 2.30258509. This formula becomes the same as the former, when the arcs a and a' are so small that their first powers only need to be regarded in the development of their logarithms and sines. Borda calculated the corrections for five coincidences, and the mean obtained was 0.18. Hence the number of oscillations of the pendulum, in a mean solar day, and in an arc indefinitely small, was 43305.48.

The distance between the plane of suspension and the plane of contact, in divisions of the rule, was 203952.2, but two corrections were required; one on account of the elongation of the rule by its own weight when suspended, and the other on account of the difference of temperature during the oscillations, and at the time of measurement. We have already stated the first of these to be $\frac{3}{16}$ths of a division, which was to be added; the other was found, by experiment, to be 0.42, and required to be subtracted, the temperature being higher at the time of measurement than it had been during the oscillations. The corrected distance between the two planes was therefore 203952.08; but it remained to determine the centre of oscillation, in order to obtain the length of the isochronous simple pendulum.

For this purpose, the weight of the wire, the weight and centre of gravity of the cup, and the radius and weight of the platina ball, were all determined with the most scrupulous accuracy. From these elements, the centre of oscillation of the compound system was calculated, and found to be 51.08 divisions above the centre of the ball. The radius of the ball was 937 divisions; and the sum of these numbers being deducted from 203952.08, the distance between the plane of suspension and plane of contact, there remained 202964 for the length of the isochronous simple pendulum, in divisions of the rule. Hence, by formula third, the length of the seconds pendulum was obtained equal to 50989.55 divisions.

A correction was now necessary to reduce the length Pendulum. Correction for the buoyancy of the atmosphere. of the pendulum to that which would have been observed had the experiments been performed in vacuo. The effect of the pressure of the atmosphere upon the apparatus is to diminish the force of gravity in the ratio of the specific gravity of the pendulum to that of the air. It occasions no change in the duration of the oscillations; for if the ball is retarded while it descends from the highest to the lowest point of the arc, it is equally retarded while it ascends from the lowest to the highest; and as the effect of the retardation in the one case is to increase the time of the oscillation, and in the other to diminish it, the time of an entire oscillation is the same as if the pressure of the atmosphere were removed. Supposing the specific gravity of the pendulum to be to that of the air in the ratio of n to 1, if the square of the number of oscillations in air, during a given time, be augmented in the same ratio, the number of oscillations in vacuo, during the same time, will be obtained; and thence the addition to be made to the length of the pendulum. The specific gravity of air varies inversely as its expansion (which is about $\frac{1}{480}$ of its bulk for a degree of Fahrenheit) and directly as the height of the barometer. Borda found that when the barometer stood at 28 inches, and the centigrade thermometer at 21°, the specific gravities of the air and of the ball were as 1 to 17044, and that thus the action of gravity in vacuo, would be more powerful by the $\frac{1}{17000}$ part nearly. The addition to be made to the length of the pendulum, in consequence, was 3.02 divisions. This being corrected for the height of the barometer and thermometer at the time of observation, became 3.10, which added to 50989 55, gave 50992.65 for the length of the seconds pendulum in vacuo.

The next reduction was to obtain the length at the Correction for the temperature. fixed temperature of melting ice. At the time of measurement, the metallic thermometer stood at 181.5. The term of ice was 151, or 30.5 lower. By an increase of temperature, such as to occasion a variation of one division of the thermometer, the rule was lengthened a 216000th part; and, therefore, by the whole difference of temperature, $\frac{30.5}{216000}$, or 7.15 divisions. Consequently the length of the pendulum at the temperature of melting ice, was 50999.8 divisions of the rule. The mean of this and five other experiments, reduced in the same manner, was 50999.35. Taking afterwards the mean of two series of experiments, in which the ball had been suspended from opposite points, he found it necessary to add 0.34 on account of the inequality of the ball; and, after numerous other experiments, he finally concluded with the number 50999.6.

It has been stated that the value of a division of the rule was $\frac{1}{100.000}$ of a toise; that is $\frac{864}{100000}$ of a line.

Multiplying therefore 50999.6 by $\frac{864}{100000}$, the length of the pendulum was obtained equal to 440.63654 lines, or Reduction to English inches. in parts of the metre, $0^m.993827$. To reduce this to English inches, we take the length of the metre as assigned by Captain Kater, in the Transactions of the Royal Society for 1818, from a very exact comparison of Sir George Shuckburgh Evelyn's standard scale, with two metres of platina which had been constructed at Paris, and previously compared with the standard metre deposited in the Archives. From this comparison, it appears that the metre, taken at its normal temperature, which is that of melting ice, is equal to 39.37076 inches of Sir George Shuckburgh's standard scale, taken also at its normal temperature, or 62° of Fahrenheit. Any length l, therefore, expressed in metres, at the tempera-

5

ture of 32° of Fahrenheit, will be reduced to English inches by multiplying it by 39.37076. This multiplication being performed, we obtain 39.127724 inches.

From the experiments of Borda, therefore, it appears that the length of the seconds pendulum, at the Paris Observatory, in vacuo, and at the temperature of 62°, is 39 127724 inches of Sir George Shuckburgh's standard scale. See *Base Métrique,* vol. iii. Delambre, *Astronomie,* vol iii.

This determination of the length of the pendulum, was by far the most satisfactory that had hitherto been accomplished ; and the same method of operation was followed by Biot in his experiments to determine the intensity of gravity at several stations, both on the continent and in this country. We have already mentioned that the unit of measures adopted by the French academicians was the ten millionth part of the quadrant of the circumference of the earth. In order to determine this fundamental quantity, MM. Mechain and Delambre undertook the measurement of the whole arc, stretching between Dunkirk and Barcelona ; and, often at the peril of their lives, continued their operations during all the horrors and anarchy of the Revolution. Mechain then conceived the bold idea of extending the arc through Spain to the Balearic Isles. He himself fell a victim to his exertions in the prosecution of this splendid undertaking ; but able and not less zealous successors were found in MM. Biot and Arago, who completed it in 1807, by prolonging the measurement to Formentera, a small island about 25′ to the south of Ivica. This ample arc afforded sufficient data for determining the magnitude of the earth ; but its figure could not be inferred with equal certainty from the lengths of the consecutive degrees ; for where there is an accumulation of denser materials in the neighbourhood of any station, the plumb-line will be drawn aside from the vertical ; in other words, the direction of gravity will not tend to the centre of the earth, and thus the length of the degree will not be accurately obtained. The oscillations of the pendulum, on the other hand, are not affected by the *direction* of gravity ; they are only sensible to its *intensity.* Hence the reason for measuring a long arc, and for combining the measurement with experiments on the pendulum. A series of experiments were, therefore, undertaken by Biot to determine the length of the pendulum at the extremities, and some intermediate stations of the arc, viz. Formentera, Figeac, Bordeaux, Clermont, Paris, and Dunkirk. At Formentera he was assisted by Arago ; at the other stations by Mathieu of the Board of Longitudes.

In England an undertaking of a similar kind, but originating in other views, had been begun by General Roy, and carried on under the able direction of Colonel Mudge, till a series of triangles was extended from the south of England to the north of Scotland. On the restoration of peace, an opportunity was taken of connecting the French and English arcs, by which a meridional line has ultimately been obtained, measured with excellent instruments, from the most southerly of the Balearic to the most northerly of the Shetland Islands,—the longest that the finger of geometry has ever attempted to trace on the surface of the earth. In order to render the operations as complete as possible, the Board of Longitudes in France, were anxious that the length of the pendulum should be determined at some stations on the English arc, in the same manner as it had been done on the Continent. The governments of both countries readily acceded to this wish, and afforded every facility for carrying it into effect. Accordingly,

in the summer of 1817, Biot arrived in England, fur- nished with the same apparatus which he had employed on the Continent, and made a series of observations at Leith Fort, and at Unst, the northern extremity of the English arc.

The apparatus employed by Biot was similar to that of Borda, with some modifications, chiefly with a view to render it more portable. The length of the trial pendulum was reduced from 12 feet to less than 3, or to very nearly that of a clock making 100.000 oscillations in 24 hours ; the number of seconds into which the French academicians, in conformity with their decimal system of measures, had divided the mean solar day. The planes on which the knife-edges rested were of agate ; and the wire was of copper, in order to avoid the possibility of its being affected by terrestrial magnetism. The ball was that which had been employed by Borda. The rule was of iron, having its head of tempered steel, so that it might not be penetrated by the knife-edge, which formed the transverse, by means of which it was suspended in the place of the pendulum, and with which it was brought into very close contact. The tongue was protruded by means of a fine screw. The value of its divisions, in a function of the metre, was ascertained by a great number of experiments, both before it was carried into Spain, and during the operations at Formentera. But the principal improvement on the apparatus was the introduction of the Comparer ; an ingenious instrument invented by Fortin, a celebrated artist in Paris, for comparing lengths which differ from each other by quantities extremely small. The shortness of the pendulum rendered it desirable to ascertain the fractions of the divisions of the rule, with greater accuracy than could be done simply by means of verniers.

The Comparer is composed of a metallic rule, T R, Fig. 7. very straight, and strengthened by cross bars, to prevent it from bending. At one of its extremities is placed a heel T, with which one of the ends of the rule to be compared is brought into contact. A frame, R R′ is moveable along the rule, and can be firmly secured at any point by means of two strong screws R R′. This frame forms the essential part of the Comparer. It is furnished with a fixed pin C, which serves as an axis for the bent lever b C b'. In the instrument employed by Biot, the ratio of the arms of the lever was 1 to 10 ; hence, if the extremity of the short arm was moved forward a space $= x$, the extremity of the long arm would describe a space $= 10\,x$. A circular scale, D D′, divided into fifths of a millimetre, was fixed upon the frame, in order to measure the space passed over by the long arm ; a vernier was attached to the arm, which indicated the tenths of these divisions, or the fiftieths of a millimetre ; and the space described by the extremity V being ten times greater than that described by b, each division of the vernier indicated a variation of b equal to the 500th part of a millimetre.

From this description the use of the Comparer will be obvious. The rule and its tongue being divided equally, if, when the tongue was protruded, the divisions of the one coincided exactly with those of the other, the part protruded would be indicated precisely ; but as this coincidence of the divisions could very seldom happen, the tongue would in general be pushed out a certain number of divisions, plus a fraction, the value of which it was the object to ascertain. For this purpose, the rule was placed upon the Comparer, with its extremity resting upon the heel T. The frame was then moved till the other point T′ attached to the extremity b of the lever was brought into contact with the tongue of the rule, and V was at the middle

Pendulum. of the scale. The observer then retired till the equable temperature, which had been disturbed by his presence, was restored; after which the vernier was observed, and the tongue drawn back by means of its screw, till the divisions coincided exactly with those of the rule. The temperature having again been allowed to acquire its natural elevation, the vernier was read off; and the tenth of the space passed over by the long arm of the lever, gave the fraction whose value was required. To insure the utmost possible accuracy, the coincidences of the divisions were always observed with very powerful lenses.

Reduction to the level of the sea.

After the proper reductions had been made, and the length of the pendulum at each station deduced in the manner already described, it became necessary to make an allowance for the height of the station above the level of the sea; for since the lengths of simple synchronous pendulums are proportional to the forces by which they are incited, that is to the force of gravity, which varies with the distance from the centre of the earth, the length of the pendulum is affected by the elevation of the place at which the observation is made. Let $R =$ radius of the earth at the latitude of the station, $h =$ height of the station above the level of the sea, $l =$ observed length of the pendulum, and $l' =$ length at the level of the sea, then

$$l : l' :: R^2 : (R + h)^2, \text{ whence}$$

$$l' = l \frac{(R + h)^2}{R^2} = l \left(1 + \frac{2h}{R}\right),$$

rejecting the small fraction $\dfrac{h^2}{R^2}$. Therefore to obtain the length of the synchronous pendulum at the level of the sea, the length measured at any station must be multiplied by $1 + \dfrac{2h}{R}$.

Biot's experiments at Leith Fort.

Biot commenced his observations at Leith Fort on the 18th of June; and they were continued without interruption during fourteen days. The clock was by Breguet; the rod of its pendulum was of fir deal, and so constructed that it could be changed at pleasure from the sexagesimal to the decimal pendulum. The clock had been put in motion several days before the commencement of the experiments, and its rate carefully determined by comparison with the stars; a precaution which was taken every day during the whole time of the experiments.

At Unst.

When the experiments at Leith were finished, the whole apparatus, together with the instruments that were to be employed by Captain Colby in fixing the limit of the English arc, were embarked on board a brig of war, to be conveyed to Shetland. Biot, attended by Captain Mudge, was taken on board at Aberdeen. On their arrival in Shetland, they immediately proceeded to Lerwick, where they had originally intended to perform the experiments; but on farther consideration, they determined to proceed to the small island of Unst, on account of the advantages it offered, in being about half a degree farther to the north, and also a little to the east; and consequently nearer the meridian of Formentera. At this station, Biot conducted his experiments with greater caution, if possible, than at any of the preceding; and considering the discouraging circumstances under which he laboured, it is impossible to admire too highly his zeal and perseverance. A few days after their arrival, Captain Mudge was obliged to leave the island on account of ill health; and Biot, thus left alone, continued his observations, with unremitting ardour, for two months,

till he had accumulated no fewer than thirty-eight Pendulum. series of observations on the pendulum, each of five or six hours; fourteen hundred observations of latitude, in fifty-five series, taken both to the north and south of the zenith; and about twelve hundred observations of the absolute heights of the sun and stars, in order to regulate his clock. See *Recueil d'Observations Géodésiques,* &c. by Biot and Arago, Paris, 1821.

The results of Biot's experiments are given in parts of the metre. The reduction to English inches is made, as has already been stated, by multiplying the lengths expressed in metres by 39.37076. To obtain the length of the sexagesimal from that of the decimal pendulum, it is necessary to multiply by the ratio $\left(\dfrac{1000}{864}\right)^2$.

Results of Biot's Experiments.

Names of Places.	Latitude, North.			Length of the Decimal Pendulum at the Level of the Sea, in Millimetres.	Length of the Seconds Pendulum at the Level of the Sea, in English Inches.
Formentera	38°	39′	56″	741.25200	39.094187
Figeac	44	36	45	741.61228	39.113189
Bordeaux	44	50	26	741.60872	39.113002
Clermont	45	46	48	741.70518	39.118088
Paris	48	50	14	741 91749	39.129285
Dunkirk	51	2	10	742.07703	39.137700
Leith Fort	55	58	37	742.41343	39.155442
Unst	60	45	25	742.723136	39.171776

Captain Kater's experiments.

Sometime previous to the experiments of Biot in Scotland, a bill had been introduced into the British Parliament to establish a uniform system of weights and measures throughout the country. With a view to facilitate the attainment of this most desirable object, the attention of the scientific men, who promoted the scheme, was turned to the experiments by which the length of the pendulum could be accurately determined, as it had been proposed to assume it as the unit of linear extension; being one of the very few quantities within the reach of man, which nature preserves always of the same invariable magnitude. Among those who gave their attention to this subject, Captain Kater particularly distinguished himself by the invention of a method extremely different from that of Borda, and in some respects decidedly superior. It is scarcely to be supposed, however, that more accurate results can be obtained by any contrivance, however ingenious, than those given by Borda and Biot; but it is still extremely desirable to be in possession of different methods of determining so important an element in astronomical researches as the length of the pendulum, or the force of gravity at the surface of the earth.

In considering of the means by which the length of the pendulum could be best determined, it occurred to Captain Kater that advantage might be taken of a well known property of an oscillating body, which had been demonstrated by Huygens; namely, that the centres of suspension and of oscillation are convertible with one another; in other words, if in any pendulum the centre of oscillation be made the centre of suspension, the times of oscillation will be equal in both cases. Hence it is evident, that if the same pendulum with two points of suspension, can be brought to oscillate in the same time, the one of these points will be the centre of suspension, while the other is the centre of oscillation; and consequently their distance will be the true length of the pendulum.

On this principle Captain Kater constructed his convertible pendulum, of which a detailed account is published in the Transactions of the Royal Society of London for 1818. It was formed of a bar of plate brass, (Fig. 8.) one inch and a half wide, and one-eighth of an inch thick; which dimensions were chosen that it might be readily affected by any change of temperature. Through this bar two triangular holes were made, to admit the knife-edges, $n\,n'$, which, after a number of experiments, had been selected as the least exceptionable mode of suspension. " Four strong knees of hammered brass, A A, of the same width as the bar, six inches long, and three-fourths of an inch thick, are firmly screwed by pairs to each end of the bar, in such a manner that when the knife-edges are passed through the triangular apertures, their backs may bear steadily against the perfectly plane surfaces of the brass knees, which are formed as nearly as possible at right angles to the bar. The knife-edges had previously been tapped half way through, near the extremities, to receive two screws, which being passed through the knee pieces, drew the knife-edges into close contact with them, the surfaces of both having been previously ground together, to guard against any strain which might injure their figure. The bar is cut of such a length that its ends may be short of the extremities of the knee pieces about two inches. Two slips of deal, B B, 17 inches long, and of the same thickness as the bar, are inserted in the spaces thus left between the knee pieces, and are firmly secured there by means of pins and screws. These slips of deal are only half the width of the bar; they are stained black, and in the extremity of each a small whalebone point is inserted to indicate the extent of the arc of vibration, on a scale placed immediately behind.

" A cylindrical weight of brass, C, three inches and a half in diameter, and weighing about two pounds seven ounces, has a rectangular opening in the direction of a diameter, to admit the knee pieces of one end of the pendulum. This weight being passed on the pendulum, is so firmly screwed in its place, as to render any change of position impossible. A second weight, D, of about $7\frac{1}{2}$ ounces, is made to slide on the bar near the knife-edge at the opposite end, and this weight may be fixed at any distance on the bar, by two screws with which it is furnished. A third weight or slider, E, of only four ounces, is moveable along the bar, and is capable of nice adjustment, by means of a screw and clamp, which clamp is included in the weight. It is intended to move near the centre of the bar, through which may be seen divisions of twentieths of an inch."

By means of this moveable weight, the oscillations of the pendulum in its opposite positions were adjusted to one another, and rendered of equal duration. When this had been effected, it was secured immovably in its place.

The prisms or knife-edges, which were employed as the axes of motion, were made of the steel prepared in India, and known by the name of wootz. As the accuracy of the experiment depended materially on the uniformity and fineness of their edges, every precaution was taken to render them straight; and the hardest temper was given to the steel, to secure them as much as possible against any change during the operations. The angle of inclination of the two planes, which formed the edge of each prism, was about 120 degrees.

Plate cccclviii.
Fig. 9.

Fig. 9. represents the support of the pendulum. " It consists of a piece of bell-metal, six inches long, three inches wide, and three-eighths of an inch thick. An opening is made longitudinally through half the

length of the piece, to admit the pendulum, and the bell metal is cast with a rectangular elevation, on each side of the opening, extending through the whole length of the piece. Two plates of agate were cemented to this elevated piece, beds having been made to receive them, in order that their surfaces might be in the same plane with the bell metal. The whole was then ground perfectly flat. A frame of brass, represented Fig. 10. is attached by two opposite screws, which serve as centres to the elevated part of the support; and one end of this frame being raised or depressed by means of the screw A, the pendulum, when placed with its knife-edges resting in Ys at the other end of the frame, could be elevated entirely above the surface of the agate, or be gently lowered till the knife-edges rested wholly upon it; and thus the knife-edge was sure to bear always precisely on the same part of the agate plane, by elevating the Ys above its surface, placing the knife-edge in them, and then letting down the whole gently by means of the screw, till the Ys were completely clear of the knife-edge. The support was firmly screwed to a solid plank of mahogany."

Plate cccclviii.
Fig. 10.

With this apparatus Captain Kater commenced his experiments in the house of H. Browne, Esq. in Portland Place. The oscillations of the pendulum were compared with those of a clock of excellent construction, by Arnold, and the coincidences were observed exactly in the same manner as had been done by Borda. After the number of oscillations in a given time had been observed with sufficient care, Captain Kater proceeded to reverse his pendulum, and by means of the sliding weight E, (Fig. 8.) to bring the oscillations to an equality in the two opposite positions.

This was accomplished with such precision, that in twelve sets of experiments, each consisting of a great number of individual trials, the number of oscillations in twenty-four hours, with the one end of the pendulum uppermost, was 86058.71; and with the other end uppermost, the number in the same time was 86058.72, differing from the former only by the hundredth part of an oscillation. When this equality was obtained, the sliding weight was firmly fixed in its place; and it only remained to ascertain the distance between the knife-edges.

For this purpose the pendulum was first let in to a solid piece of mahogany, edgewise, to such a depth that the knife-edges approached to within a twentieth of an inch of the surface. This arrangement is represented Fig. 11. K is an upright piece of wood screwed to the end of the mahogany case; and to this a string is attached, passing through the ring of a common spring steel-yard, the hook of which is fixed upon the pendulum, and exerts a force rather greater than the weight of the pendulum, equal to about ten pounds. To secure the parallelism of the knife-edges, which, on account of the flexibility of the brass rod, was apt to be destroyed when the pendulum was placed in a horizontal position, two screws were passed through the mahogany case, in opposite directions, and made to act transversely on the extremity of the bar, next to the steel-yard. The microscope was then passed over the extremities of the knife-edges, and the requisite parallelism readily obtained by means of the screws. After this adjustment, four rectangular pieces of brass, each about half an inch square, were brought into contact with the knife-edges, at those points which had rested on the agate planes. On each of these pieces of brass a very fine line had been traced, the distances of which from the points in contact with the knife-edges, had previously been ascertained by means of the micrometer. The brass pieces were then fixed in their place

Pendulum. by means of springs attached to the mahogany case, and the pendulum being removed, the standard scale was placed beneath the micrometer, and the distance between the fine lines on the brass pieces was ascertained on one side of the pendulum. The scale was then transferred to the other side, and the operation repeated. The mean of the two measures will obviously correct any deviation from parallelism in the knife edges which might remain, even after the precautions already mentioned had been taken.

The expansion of the pendulum and its specific gravity were determined by accurate experiments, in order to obtain the corrections for the temperature and the buoyancy of the atmosphere. When these corrections were made, the distances between the knife-edges was found to be 39.44085 inches, and the number of oscillations in a mean solar day, was 86061.30; whence the length of the seconds pendulum, in the room in which the experiments were performed, was found by proportion equal to 39.13908 inches of Sir George Shuckburgh's standard scale, at the temperature of 62° of Fahrenheit.

Captain Kater's experiments at Unst. After this measurement had been effected, Captain Kater was requested by the Royal Society to repeat his experiments at some of the principal stations of the trigonometrical survey. Accordingly, in the month of July, 1818, he sailed for Unst, amply furnished, by the liberality of government, with every thing that could facilitate his operations. The spot he selected for the experiments, was that at which Biot had made his observations the preceding summer. To obviate the necessity of being obliged to provide a new stand for the apparatus at each station, a frame of cast iron was employed for receiving the bell metal support of the pendulum, so constructed, that it could be screwed very firmly to the wall of a building. For farther security against any lateral shake, brackets were placed below, which at the bottom spread to a distance of three feet. The clock, on the regularity of which so much depended, was by Arnold, having a gridiron pendulum for the compensation of temperature. The other stations at which experiments were made, were Portsoy, Leith Fort, Clifton, Arbury Hill, and Dunnose in the Isle of Wight.

After the explanation which has already been given of the method of making the observations, it is unnecessary to give a detailed account of his proceedings at any of the stations, as they were all exactly similar to those performed in London. The distance between the knife-edges, or the length of the pendulum, being a constant quantity, did not require to be measured at each station, as was the case in Biot's experiments; all that was necessary was to determine the number of its oscillations in 24 hours, and to observe the temperature while it was compared with the clock, in order to make a proper allowance for the dilatation. The greatest difficulty, and what required the greatest expence of time at each station, was to ascertain the rate of the clock.

Before giving the results of Captain Kater's experiments, it is proper to remark, that in allowing for the amplitude of the oscillations, he did not employ the accurate formula of Borda, considering it to be an unnecessary refinement in practice, especially as there was always an uncertainty in observing the extent of the arc, amounting to one or two hundredths of a degree. The consideration he proceeded on was this: The number of oscillations in 24 hours, in an indefinitely small arc, is known to exceed that in an arc of one degree by 1.635; and in very small arcs the times are nearly as the squares of the arcs; hence, if the mean of the arcs

observed at the commencement and end of each interval be taken, and its square multiplied by the number 1.635, the correction to be added to the observed number of oscillations will be obtained with sufficient accuracy.

The allowance which he made for the height of the station above the level of the sea, is also different from that which is obtained on the supposition that gravity diminishes simply in the inverse ratio of the square of the distance from the centre. Following out an idea suggested by Dr. Thomas Young, in a paper published in the *Philosophical Transactions* for 1819, upon the density of the earth as affecting the reduction of experiments on the length of the pendulum, he multiplies the correction obtained from the formula, by a coefficient, the value of which depends on the attraction of the matter accumulated between the general level and the place of observation. However sound this principle may be, its application by Captain Kater, who makes the value of the coefficient depend also on the geological characters of the surrounding country, is extremely arbitrary; for, unless the ratio of the density of any given mass of matter at the surface of the earth, to that of the strata below, be accurately determined, (which is perhaps impossible when the mass is extensive,) its influence cannot be assigned. The relative density of the earth at different places may be properly determined by the measurement of the pendulum; but it is unsafe to reverse the process, and assign the length of the pendulum from the assumed density of the earth.

In the following Table, therefore, which contains the results of his experiments, it is to be observed, that the correction for the height of the station above the level of the sea, is *less* than that given by the ratio of the squares of the distance from the centre of the earth.

Results of Captain Kater's Experiments.

Place of Observation.	Latitude.			Length of the Seconds Pendulum in vacuo, and at the Level of the Sea.
				Inches.
Unst	60°	45′	28″.01	39.17146
Portsoy	57	40	58 .65	39.16159
Leith Fort	55	58	40 .80	39.15554
Clifton	53	27	43 .12	39.14600
Arbury Hill	52	12	55 .32	39.14250
London	51	31	8 .40	39.13929
Dunnose	50	37	23 .94	39.13614

Comparison of the methods of Borda and Captain Kater. Captain Kater's method of determining the length of the pendulum possesses several very decided advantages over that of Borda and Cassini. Of these advantages, one arises from a very curious property of the convertible pendulum, which was not known when Captain Kater made his first experiments, but was subsequently discovered by the celebrated La Place. The property is, that if the supports of a pendulum of this kind be two cylindrical surfaces, the length of the pendulum is truly measured by the distance between those surfaces. Hence, no inaccuracy can arise from the knife-edges being blunted, for in this case they may be supposed cylinders of very great curvature, or very small diameter; and thus a circumstance which gave great alarm to Biot, becomes quite indifferent when the convertible pendulum is employed.

Another advantage attending the use of Captain Kater's pendulum, is, that it supersedes the necessity of a number of measurements and calculations, in order to determine the centre of oscillation. In Borda's pendulum, before the centre of oscillation can be found, it is not only necessary to measure the distance from the knife-edge to the plane, which is brought into contact with the ball, but also the radius of the ball, and the distance from the knife-edge to the suspension of the wire. Besides all this, the weight of the ball, of the wire, and of the cup, must be determined,—an operation scarcely less delicate than their measurement. These circumstances must render Borda's method, in ordinary hands at least, more liable to error than the other.

As experiments were made at two of the stations, viz. Leith Fort and Unst, both by Biot and Captain Kater, we possess the means of comparing their results directly with each other, independently of any hypothesis regarding the compression of the earth, or correction for the height of the station. The results given in the tables differ extremely little; but to show their agreement more perfectly, it is necessary to calculate the length of the seconds pendulum from the number of oscillations in twenty-four hours, without making any allowance for the elevation. At London, the number of the oscillations of Captain Kater's pendulum in a mean solar day, was 86061.30; at Leith Fort, 86079.22; and at Unst, 86096.84; (see Captain Kater's paper in the *Phil. Trans.* for 1819.) The length of the seconds pendulum, in the apartment at Portland Place, was 39.13908 inches; hence, from the formula $l' = \dfrac{l N^2}{N'^2}$, the length at the station of Leith Fort, at an elevation of 69 feet, is 39.15538 inches, and at Unst, at an elevation of 28 feet, 39.17141 inches. Leaving out the correction for the elevation, the lengths observed by Biot were, at Leith Fort, 39.15518 inches; and at Unst, 39.17166 inches. The differences are 0.00020 and 0.00025, and affected by contrary signs; Captain Kater's determination being in excess at Leith, and in defect at Unst. The mean difference is less than the $\frac{3}{100000}$th part of an inch, a quantity scarcely appreciable in the observations.

The first part of the *Philosophical Transactions of London* for the year 1822, contains an account of a series of experiments made at Madras in 1821, by John Goldingham, Esq. with a pendulum in every respect similar to Captain Kater's. It was constructed indeed under the immediate direction of Captain Kater himself, who also determined the number of its oscillations during a mean solar day in London, before it was sent to India, in order that they might afterwards be compared with the number at Madras. The apparatus was set up in the observatory at Madras, and the rate of the clock obtained, by comparing it with the transit clock of the observatory each day at the commencement and conclusion of the observations. The transit clock itself was regulated by transits of the sun and stars; and indeed every part of the experiments was conducted with so much accuracy, as to render the result extremely valuable.

Two series of observations were made. From the first, the mean number of oscillations in twenty-four hours, reduced to an indefinitely small arc, and to a temperature of 70° of Fahrenheit, was 86166.108; and from the second 86166.048. The height of the station above the level of the sea was twenty-seven feet; whence the correction given by the formula was 0.095; but Mr. Goldingham, after the example of Captain Kater, mul-

tiplied this number by .66, in consideration of the attraction of the interposed mass. The correction allowed was therefore 0.06, to be added to the number of oscillations in twenty-four hours. The correction for the buoyancy of the atmosphere, deduced in the manner already explained, was 6.2075 oscillations for the first series, and 6.220 for the second. These corrections being applied, the number of oscillations in a mean solar day, in vacuo, at the level of the sea, and at the temperature of 70° of Fahrenheit's scale, was obtained as follows:

By the first series of observations	86172.375
By the second	86172.328
Mean	86172.352

Before the pendulum was sent from London, Captain Kater had found, that the number of its oscillations during a mean solar day, in vacuo, at the level of the sea, and at the temperature of 70°, was 86300.226. In his own experiments, Captain Kater had found the expansion of his pendulum to be .000009959 in parts of its length, for a change of temperature indicated by a variation of one degree of the thermometer. The length of the seconds pendulum in London, at the temperature of 62°, is 39.13929 inches; at the temperature of 70°, therefore, its length is 39.142408 inches at the same rate of expansion. Hence the length of Mr. Goldingham's trial pendulum is obtained from this proportion,

$(86300.226)^2 : (86400)^2 :: 39.142408 : 39.232956.$

Another proportion gives the length of the seconds pendulum,

$(86400)^2 : (86172.352)^2 :: 39.232956 : 39.02649.$

We have been particular in stating these numbers, because the length of the seconds pendulum is stated in Mr. Goldingham's paper to be 39.026302 inches. The difference arises from his having assumed the length of the seconds pendulum in London to be 39.1386 inches when reduced to the level of the sea, as it is given in Captain Kater's first Memoir; but it was afterwards found, that a slight oversight had been committed in estimating the specific gravity, and that the true length was 39.13929 inches. On performing the whole calculation with this corrected number, the result is found to be what we have just stated.

It appears, therefore, that the length of the seconds pendulum at Madras, latitude 13° 4' 9" N. at the level of the sea, in vacuo, and temperature 70°, is 39.02649 inches. Assuming the expansion of Mr. Goldingham's pendulum to be the same with that of Captain Kater's, the length of the seconds pendulum at Madras, at the temperature of 62°, is 39.02338 inches. Captain John Warren had previously made a set of experiments, though with a very inferior apparatus, to determine the length of the seconds pendulum at the same place. His determination agrees very well with Mr. Goldingham's, being 39.026273 inches. An account of his experiments is published in the eleventh volume of the *Asiatic Researches.*

Deductions relative to the Figure of the Earth.

The experiments, of which we have now given an account, furnish some very interesting information relative to the variation of gravity, and consequently to the figure of the earth. Supposing the figure of the earth to be elliptical, it is demonstrable, from the theory of attraction, that the length of the seconds pendulum varies as the square of the sine of latitude; so

Pendulum. that, calling the latitude L, and l the length of the pendulum, the value of l will be expressed by a function of this form,

$$l = A + B \sin.^2 L;$$

A and B being two constants, of which A represents the length of the pendulum at the equator, where L is zero, and B the excess of its length at the pole. As experiments cannot be made at the pole, it is impossible to determine the value of B directly, but it may be deduced from observations made at known latitudes: thus, let l' and l'' be the observed lengths of the pendulum at two stations, L' and L'' the corresponding latitudes, we have similarly,

for the first $l' = A + B \sin.^2 L',$
and for the second $l'' = A + B \sin.^2 L'';$

whence $l'' - l' = B \left\{ \sin.^2 L'' - \sin.^2 L' \right\};$

or $B = \dfrac{l' - l'}{\sin. (L'' - L') \sin. (L'' + L')}.$

B being known, the value of A can be found from that of l' or l''.

The fraction $\dfrac{B}{A}$ expresses the diminution of gravity from the pole to the equator; and, according to Clairaut's celebrated theorem, whatever hypothesis is made respecting the variation of density in the strata of the earth, the sum of the two fractions expressing the ellipticity and diminution of gravity from the pole to the equator, is always a constant quantity, and equal to $\dfrac{5}{2}$ of the fraction expressing the ratio of the centrifugal force to that of gravity at the equator. According to the theory of dynamics, this last fraction is $\dfrac{1}{289.014}$; being multiplied by $\dfrac{5}{2}$, it becomes .00865; therefore calling ε the ellipticity, we find

$$\varepsilon = .00865 - \frac{B}{A}.$$

The hypothesis of the gravitating force increasing as the square of the sines of the latitudes, is grounded on the supposition that the spheroid is homogeneous; and if this were really the case, we should obtain the same value of $\dfrac{B}{A}$, and consequently the same compression, by substituting in the formula the lengths observed at any two latitudes whatever, abstraction being made from the errors of observation. But as we know that the strata, at least near the surface of the earth, differ very considerably in density, we may expect, *a priori*, considerable discrepancies in the results obtained, by combining the lengths observed at different stations. If we combine the lengths given by Biot at Unst and Formentera, a result may be expected very near the truth; for, on account of the distance between the two stations, the influence of any partial cause of error is greatly diminished; and as both the stations are situated on small isolated rocky islands, the difference of local density cannot be supposed great. Substituting, therefore, the observed lengths at Unst and Formentera in the above formulæ, B is found = .2091283 inches, and A = 39.012556, whence $\dfrac{B}{A} =$ .005360536, and consequently the ellipticity, or $\varepsilon =$ .003289464 = $\dfrac{1}{304}$.

Captain Kater, combining his results by two and two in the same manner, calculated the following Table:

	Diminution of Gravity from the Equator.	Compression.
Unst and Portsoy	.0053639	$\frac{1}{304\cdot 8}$
Leith Fort	.0054840	$\frac{1}{315\cdot 8}$
Clifton	.0056346	$\frac{1}{341\cdot 5}$
Arbury Hill	.0054282	$\frac{1}{310\cdot 3}$
London	.0055510	$\frac{1}{322\cdot 7}$
Dunnose	.0055262	$\frac{1}{320\cdot 1}$
Portsoy and Leith Fort	.0056920	$\frac{1}{348\cdot 0}$
Clifton	.0058194	$\frac{1}{353\cdot 2}$
Arbury Hill . . .	.0054620	$\frac{1}{313\cdot 7}$
London	.0056382	$\frac{1}{332\cdot 0}$
Dunnose	.0055920	$\frac{1}{326\cdot 9}$
Leith Fort and Clifton . . .	.0059033	$\frac{1}{364\cdot 0}$
Arbury Hill .	.0053615	$\frac{1}{304\cdot 1}$
London	.0056186	$\frac{1}{329\cdot 8}$
Dunnose . . .	.0055614	$\frac{1}{323\cdot 7}$
Clifton and Arbury Hill . . .	.0042956	$\frac{1}{229\cdot 6}$
London	.0052590	$\frac{1}{294\cdot 9}$
Dunnose	.0052616	$\frac{1}{295\cdot 1}$
Arbury Hill and London . . .	.0069767	$\frac{1}{597\cdot 5}$
Dunnose . .	.0060212	$\frac{1}{380\cdot 3}$
London and Dunnose	.0052837	$\frac{1}{297\cdot 0}$

Instead of proceeding in this manner, Biot submitted his measurements to a mode of comparison, which shows, in a very perspicuous manner, the relative intensity of gravity at the different stations. From a comparison of the terrestrial degrees, observations on the pendulum, and the values of the lunar inequalities depending on the compression of the earth, La Place found that the compression indicated by all the phenomena taken in connexion, was 00326, or $\dfrac{1}{306.75}$. Biot combining this determination of theory with the measurement at Unst, which he considered as the best of the whole, both on account of the observations having been made with all the precautions which his former experience could suggest, and on account of the great number of series from which the final result was obtained, formed a theoretic expression for the length of the pendulum, with which he compared the lengths measured at the other stations. Substituting the value of ε given by La Place in the formula $\varepsilon = 00865 - \dfrac{B}{A}$, it becomes $00865 - \dfrac{B}{A} = 00326$, whence B = A .00539.

This value of B being substituted in the general expression $l = A + B \sin.^2 L$, gives $l = A(1 + 00539 \sin.^2 L)$. But at the station of Unst, $l = 39.171776$ inches, and L = 60° 45′ 25″; therefore by substitution, the value of A will be obtained, and consequently that of B, from the ratio $\dfrac{B}{A}$. On performing the calculation, they are found as follows: A = 39.011684 inches, and B = 0.2102729 inches. Hence, for any other latitude, $l = 39.011684 + .2102729 \sin.^2 L$.

By means of this formula the following Table is constructed.

6

Names of Places.	Length of the Seconds Pendulum at the Level of the Sea.		Excess of the Calculated Length
	By Calculation.	By Measurement.	
	Inches.	Inches.	Inches.
Unst	39.171776	39 171776	0 000000
Leith Fort	39.156127	39.155442	+ 0.000685
Dunkirk	39.138809	39.137700	+ 0.001109
Paris	39.130861	39.129285	+ 0.001576
Clermont	39.119682	39.118088	+ 0.001594
Bourdeaux	39.116235	39.113002	+ 0.003233
Figeac	39.115398	39.113189	+ 0.002209
Formentera	39.093762	39 094187	—0.000425

This Table agrees with Captain Kater's, in indicating a greater diminution of gravity, on advancing towards the equator, than is given by theory; but the variation is by no means uniform. Captain Kater's Table shows it to be greater between Unst and Leith Fort than between Unst and Portsoy, greater still at Clifton, suddenly diminished at Arbury Hill, increased again at London, and diminished at Dunnose. It increases progressively through France to Bourdeaux, where its effects are most sensible; is diminished somewhat at Figeac, that station being more in the interior, and the country in which it is situated composed of denser materials. At Formentera it appears with a contrary sign, indicating a local excess in the intensity of gravity. Whether this variation from theory is uniformly in excess or defect to the south of Formentera, we want farther experiments to determine. The only experiment indeed which has been made to the south of that station which can be relied on, is that of Mr. Goldingham; for those of Bouguer, Le Gentil, and others, were not performed with an apparatus sufficiently delicate to entitle their results to be employed in deciding the question. The formula applied to the latitude of Madras, gives $l = 39.022436$ inches, and Mr. Goldingham's measurement is 39 02338 inches; so that the intensity of the gravitating force is, as at Formentera, greater that it is given by theory. On the whole, it is sufficiently obvious, that no formula can be obtained to represent, with perfect rigour, the lengths of the pendulum over the globe; and that the local variations in the density of the strata which compose the crust of the earth, prevent us from determining the true nature of the meridional curves *.

From Biot's formula we have calculated the following Table, showing the length of the pendulum at every fifth degree of latitude from the equator to the pole; and considering the data from which the numerical coefficients are obtained, we presume that it contains much nearer approximations to the absolute lengths than any that has hitherto been given.

Latitudes.	Length of the Pendulum.	Latitudes.	Length of the Pendulum.
0°	39.011684	50°	39.135344
5	39.013281	55	39.152779
10	39.018024	60	39.169388
15	39 025769	65	39.184401
20	39.036281	70	39.197359
25	39.049240	75	39.207871
30	39.064252	80	39.215616
35	39.080861	85	39.220359
40	39 098563	90	39.221956
45	39.116820		

Comparison of the Seconds Pendulum at Paris and Greenwich.

After Captain Kater had accomplished his measurement in London, the Board of Longitudes, anxious to compare the results of Borda's method with those of one so entirely different, commissioned M. Arago to make this comparison by a direct experiment. Arago was joined by the celebrated Humboldt, and the first part of their operations was, to determine the number of oscillations made during a sidereal day in the Royal Observatory at Paris, by two invariable pendulums of copper constructed by Fortin. They then proceeded to London, and being met by Biot on his return from Shetland, they made the same observations on the two pendulums at the Greenwich Observatory. After their return to Paris, MM. Arago and Humboldt determined anew the number of oscillations of their pendulums, in order to assure themselves that they had undergone no derangement by the transportation.

The mean number of oscillations made by the pendulums during a sidereal day, in an indefinitely small arc, reduced to the temperature of 10 centigrade, or 50^0 of Fahrenheit, was observed to be as follows:

First Pendulum.

At Paris	87672.33
At Greenwich	87683.87
Acceleration at Greenwich .	11.54

Second Pendulum.

At Paris	87033.37
At Greenwich	87043.36
Acceleration at Greenwich .	9.99

The acceleration of the first, reduced to seconds, and corrected for the effects of the density of the air, becomes $11''.50$; and of the second, $10''.08$: the mean of the two, therefore, or $10''.79$, will be the acceleration of a clock at Greenwich in twenty-four hours, regulated at Paris according to sidereal time. Hence it results, that the difference of length of two simple pendulums, making respectively 86,400 oscillations in a mean solar day at Paris and Greenwich, is .0098033 inches. According to Captain Kater, the length of the seconds pendulum, in the apartment at Portland Place, is 39.13908 inches. Supposing its length at Greenwich to be the same, and deducting .0098033, the length at Paris is equal to 39.12928 inches. This is precisely the length assigned in the table by Biot and Mathieu, when reduced to the level of the sea. But the allowance they made for the height of the station was .000645 inches; hence the length of the seconds pendulum, as determined by them, is less than that obtained from Captain Kater's experiments, by this quantity, or 39 128660 inches. Borda's result is less than either, being only 39.127724 inches. In the same manner, the length of the seconds pendulum at London, at a height of 83 feet above the level of the sea, is,

	Inches.
According to Captain Kater . . .	39.13908
According to Biot, Bouvard, and Mathieu	39.13844
According to Borda . . .	39.13752
Mean	39.13835

It would be extremely difficult to determine which of the three results approaches nearest to absolute accuracy. The mean, which differs from Biot's determina-

* Applying this formula to the latitude of Melville Island, 74° 47' 12".4, l is found equal to 39.20747. Captain Sabine, who accompanied Captain Parry in his memorable voyage of discovery in 1819-20, from a set of experiments made in that island, found the length of the seconds pendulum to be 39.207 inches: an agreement truly remarkable, considering the circumstances under which he operated.

tion only by the $\frac{1}{100000}$th of an inch, may perhaps be regarded as nearest the truth. It is rather a remarkable coincidence, that this mean is the precise number deduced by Mr. Watts, in a paper published in the third volume of the *Edinburgh Philosophical Journal*, from Captain Kater's measurement, by making a more correct allowance for the amplitude of the arcs.

PENNANT, THOMAS, distinguished as a tourist, and for his acquaintance with natural history and antiquities, was born at Downing, in Flintshire, in the year 1726. His school education commenced at Wrexham, and was completed at Fulham, from whence he removed to Oxford, for the purpose of studying jurisprudence, though it does not appear that he intended to pursue law as a profession. A present of Mr. Willoughby's Ornithology, when he was about the age of twelve, by John Salisbury, Esq. of Flint, the father of Mrs. Piozzi, inspired him with a taste for the study of natural history. His fondness for mineralogy commenced in the year 1746-7, in consequence of a tour through Cornwall, when he became acquainted with Dr. Borlase of Ludgvan, who communicated to him with great kindness all the stores of his own extensive knowledge in this branch of natural history. He was elected a Fellow of the Society of Antiquaries in the year 1754, when he visited the greatest part of Ireland; but the conviviality of that hospitable people prevented him from producing a journal fit to be offered to the public.

His first efforts as an author were some remarks on earthquakes, particularly one at Downing, in the year 1750, inserted in the *Philosophical Transactions*. In 1756, he wrote a paper on several coralloid bodies, collected in Coalbrook Dale, Shropshire. In 1755, he commenced a literary correspondence with Linnæus, giving an account of a recent *Concha anomia* adhering to a sea plant of the Norwegian seas, sent him by Bishop Pontoppidan. In the year 1757 he was made a member of the Royal Society of Upsal, at the recommendation of Linnæus himself.

Mr. Pennant married about this period, and passed some years in domestic retirement with a most amiable wife, his pecuniary circumstances being very limited. In 1761 he commenced his British Zoology, and dedicated its profits to the benefit of the Welsh School, Gray's Inn Lane, London. The estate of Downing, with a rich mine of lead ore, came into his possession in 1763. His domestic enjoyments were interrupted soon after by the death of his wife; and in 1765 he visited France, Switzerland, Holland, part of Germany, and formed a friendship with Buffon, Haller, the Gesners, and Gronovius. His Synopsis of Quadrupeds, a work of great value, and which was printed in 1771, was first planned at the Hague, in consequence of his interview with Professor Pallas, whose high admiration of Mr. Ray induced him to advise our author to undertake a history of quadrupeds on Ray's system improved. In 1767, he was elected a Fellow of the Royal Society, and republished next year his British Zoology, in two vols. 8vo. to which he added a third, including fishes and reptiles, in 1769.

His first acquaintance with Sir Joseph Banks commenced in 1766. He visited him at Ravesby Abbey, in Lincolnshire, and Mr. Pennant received from him many favours, and was honoured with frequent communications. Our author saw Sir Joseph on his arrival, in 1771, from his voyage with Captain Cook; and the same year had an interview with Mr. Faulkner, who had spent 38 years in Patagonia. The degree of LL. D. was also conferred on him this year by the University of Oxford. About this time he published the first volume of his tour to Scotland, which was completed, together with his

voyage to the Hebrides, in 1772. During this last tour he was presented with the freedom of the city of Edinburgh, and had great honours shown him in many of the provincial towns. A second volume of his Journey to Scotland, and his Voyage to the Hebrides, was published in 1774, which was followed by his third and last volume in 1775. A fifth edition of his Tours in Scotland was published with additions in 1790. Scotland, when he favoured the world with his tour, was very little known to our southern neighbours; since many of the preceding accounts of this part of the island were written either without candour or under the influence of strong prejudices. The great object of our tourist, on the other hand, was to conciliate the affections of the two nations, and to point out those improvements, either in the fisheries or internal commerce of Scotland, which might contribute to its benefit. Mr. Pennant has the honour, therefore, of setting an example of a faithful, accurate, and patient research into the antiquities, beauties, and resources of this part of the island, which has been so successfully followed up by Sir John Sinclair, Dr. Anderson, Sir Walter Scott, and others, who have thus immortalized themselves by perpetuating the glory of their native land.

In 1773, he published his Genera of Birds, in one volume, and made a tour on horseback, his usual mode of travelling, through the greatest part of the north of England, and kept a regular journal of the road between Downing and London. He continued his inquiries into many of the different counties in England, during 1776 and 1777. About this period he was married a second time to a very amiable consort, in consequence of which he refrained from travelling. Mr. Pennant had collected materials for a tour through Wales, by making frequent excursions with the Rev. John Lloyd, an excellent Welsh scholar, at different periods, through his native country, which he published in 1778 and 1781. He acknowledges his great obligations to his countryman for the correctness of his remarks on the language and antiquities of the Welsh counties. A great variety of very interesting anecdotes, interspersed through this Tour, afford very striking illustrations of the manners, character, and history of this part of the empire.

In his history and natural history of the turkey, published in 1781, he endeavours to prove that America alone was the place where this animal had its origin. In 1782, his "London," and "A Journey from Chester to London," were published, which contain many very instructive and amusing anecdotes. His "Arctic Zoology" was published in 1785, to which a copious introduction was added, and a survey of all the coasts of the Arctic Regions, from the Straits of Dover to the remotest north, with a variety of geographical, historical, and physical facts, that present a series of the most animated pictures. He also published about the same time a topographical account of Holywell and Downing, where he had resided more than fifty years. His "View of Hindostan," in two volumes, was the last, and one of the most original of his publications. In the year 1798 he died at Downing, in the 72d year of his age.

Mr. Pennant inherited by nature a strong and healthy constitution, which he improved by constant riding, by rising at seven during winter and summer, and refraining from supper. He was an affectionate husband and friend, an indulgent master and kind father; for he undertook one of his last tours in 1787, to the Land's End, that he might enable his son to compare the naval strength and commercial advantages of our island with those of France and Spain. He was warmly attached

Pennant, Pennsylvania.

to the political and religious liberties of his country. "Neither king nor people," he observes, "shall have the sole keeping of my political conscience. Free was I born; free have I lived; and free, I trust, will die."

His style is not very correct, but gives a lively representation of the ideas he wishes to convey. His arrangement in natural history is clear and judicious, and his descriptions luminous, concise, and energetic. The defect of his tours and travels is a want of method, which is forgotten in the midst of a great variety of amusing and interesting anecdotes, that are well calculated to enlarge the minds and improve the hearts of his readers. He blends in all his works the pleasant with the instructive, and endeavours to advance natural knowledge so as not to injure the cause of moral and religious truth. From his writings the sage may gather wisdom, and the youth instruction, without imbibing political animosity or party prejudices. He attacks the infidelity of Buffon, or the illiberality of Johnson, with the same impartiality, and always advocates the cause of religion and morality without moroseness, bigotry, or superstition. See his *Life*, written by himself.

Boundary and situation.

PENNSYLVANIA,—from *Penn*, the original proprietor, and *Sylva*, a wood,—one of the United States of North America, is situated between 39°, 42°, and 43° of north latitude, and 74° 32' and 80° 27' of west longitude from Greenwich. It is bounded on the north by New York and Lake Erie; south by Virginia, Maryland, and Delaware; east by Delaware River, New York and New Jersey; west by Virginia and Ohio; and northwest by a part of Lake Erie. The form of this state is nearly that of a parallelogram, being in length 273 miles from east to west, and in breadth 153 from north to south. The total number of acres, according to Mr. Warden is, 27,200,000, and square miles 24,500; according to Morse, 29,634,840 acres, and 46,000 square miles.

Aspect of the country.

This state is divided by the Alleghany mountains, which run from north-east to south-west, and the valleys between the different mountains are of a rich black soil. A great proportion of the state is good land, and much of it excellent.

The richest part of the state which is settled, is Lancaster, Berks, and Dauphin counties, with the Cumberland valley, from Susquehannah to Washington, resting on a bed of limestone. The finest part of the unsettled land is between Alleghany River and Lake Erie, in the north-west, and in the country on the heads of the branches of the Alleghany to the east.

Climate.

The low maritime hilly and mountainous tracts experience a great change of temperature. Winter commences from the 1st to the 15th December, and ends from the 1st to the 15th of March. The most agreeable months are April, May, the first half of June, September, and part of October. Cherries are ripe by the 25th of May, and wheat is reaped before the middle of July. The temperature of winter is severe near the sea, varying in January and February, from 14 to 28 degrees. The warm wind from the south and southeast brings on thaw, which changes immediately to frost when it alters to the north-east and north-west. The difference of temperature in summer is from twenty to thirty degrees, or even more after severe rain and thunder storms.

Principal rivers.

The principal rivers are, Delaware, on which is situated Philadelphia; Chester, West Chester; Newtown, in the county of Bucks; Easton in Northampton: it is navigable by ships of the line 20 miles; sloops of 90 tons, 35 miles; boats of 8 tons, 100 miles; and canoes 150 miles,—in all 305 miles. Susquehan-

Pennsylvania.

nah river, on which is placed Lancaster; Harrisburgh, county Dauphin; Wilksburgh, county Luzerne; York; Carlisle, Cumberland; Chamberston, county Franklin. Schuylkill, on which is situated Reading in Berks, and Norriston in Montgomery. Queensburgh, Westmoreland, and Pittsburgh, are situated on the Alleghany River. Bedford; Huntingdon; and Lewisburgh; Mufflin, are placed on the Juniata. Union Fayette is near Monongahela River, which affords a boat navigation to Morgantown, a distance of 100 miles. **Fishes.** Trouts are common in rivulets. In the eastern rivers the principal fish are roach, shad, herrings; a species of catfish abounds in the western waters, weighing from 50 to 100 lbs. as well as yellow perch and pike. Youghisgeny and Lehigh are the principal remaining rivers.

Minerals, Iron ore or iron sand is found in many of the counties. Coal on the Susquehannah near Wyoming, on Alleghany, Juniata, and Monongahela. A blind coal superior to ivory black, abounds in Luzerne. Copper, lead, black lead, flint, slate, marble, talc, are also found. **Mineral springs.** Sulphur springs are to be met with in Cumberland and York, and salt and bituminous springs near Queensburgh and in Venango county. **Forest trees.** Oak of various kinds forms the chief bulk of the woods. Chesnut, birch, sugar maple, ash, black walnut, elm, hickery, white ash, butternut, locust, and various kinds of Magnalia, abound in the western states. The greater part of the different kinds of trees, shrubs, and plants, in the United States, are to be met with in this province. **Animals.** Deer, brown bear, wolf, fox, wild cat, racoon, opossum, the grey, striped, and flying squirrel, rabbit, hare, and minx, are numerous. The musk rat is abundant, but the beaver, otter, and cougouar are nearly extinct. **Birds.** Wild turkey, ruffed grous, Pennsylvanian pheasant, Maryland partridge, wild and Carolina pigeon, and the Canvas black duck, are the most striking varieties of birds. **Insects.** Of the insects, the beetle is destructive to Indian corn. Blistering flies, grasshoppers, caterpillars, and meadow worms abound, and are pernicious both to leguminous and culmiferous crops. The Hessian fly has not been so injurious as in New England.

Population. The population of this state in 1810 amounted to 810,091, being 16 to a square mile, and has nearly doubled itself in the short space of 20 years. They are chiefly descended from German, English, Irish, Scotch, Welsh, Swedish, and a few Dutch. The Germans compose one quarter of the inhabitants, and are a very industrious, temperate, and economical people. The free blacks are 22,492, and slaves 795.

Civil division. The number of counties are 50, which contain 165 townships. **Counties and county towns.** The following are the counties and towns which we have not yet enumerated, and the names of the counties and the county towns are the same in the ten first:—Beaver, Butler, Clearfield, Erie, Green, Indiana, Mercia, Northumberland, Somerset, Warren. County Adams, town Gettysburgh; Armstrong county; Kitaning, county town; Bradford; county Cambria, Edemburgh; Centre, Bellefont; Columbia; Crawford, Meadville; Lycoming, Williamsport; Mackean, Smethport; Potter, Cowdersport; Pike, Milford; Schuylkill; Susquehannah; Tioga, Wellsborough; Venango, Franklin; Wayne, Rothany; Westmoreland, Greensburgh.

Agriculture. Agriculture has very rapidly improved during the last twenty-five years, by the use of gypsum as a manure, by the introduction of clover and of a good rotation of crops. This change has been produced by diminishing the size of the farms, and by the exertions of the members of an agricultural society. Wheat produces from 20 to 30 bushels per acre; maize and buckwheat from 25 to 40; barley and oats the same,

Pennsylvania.

Asparagus grows spontaneously in sandy soils, and the vine has been cultivated to advantage by a M. Legaux, near Philadelphia. Almost all the fruits of France are produced here. The number of horses in 1810, was 225,645, of neat cattle 612,993. Some of the farmers in the back parts have a hundred hinds, which are housed in winter. The number of sheep was 618,283. The Merino breed of sheep are succeeding very well, and yield of washed wool four pound per fleece. A farm of from 200 to 400 acres, one-third cleared, will raise a rent from 60 to 300 dollars, according to quantity, quality, and improvement; and when the rent is paid in kind, one third or one half of the crop is given by the tenant. In Centre, Bedford, and Huntingdon, many of the inhabitants live by fishing, hunting, and gathering wild honey. The price of the value of land is very various, from 120 dollars in Philadelphia County, to 5 in Beaver, Somerset, and Green. Mr. Penn's coachman, in 1681, refused a lot of land for the payment of his wages, within the present limits of Philadelphia, which was valued in less than a century at 600,000 guineas. A cart-horse brings from 85 to 180 dollars; a good cow is from 15 to 80, and a draft ox 60. In the western counties, a farm-horse brings 60 dollars.

Manufactures.

The progress of manufactures in this state have been very rapid, in consequence of the late war. The value of those of Pittsburgh in 1814, amounted to two millions of dollars, consisting of wool, cotton, iron, glass, and paper. There are six manufactories, whose machinery is driven by steam; and three companies are established for making steam-engines and steamboats. The iron founderies are very numerous and flourishing, and cotton-mills have been formed on the principle of Sir Richard Arkwright. The manufactories of silk, tobacco, snuff, maple, sugar, Glauber salts, sal ammoniac, have been successful. The whole amount of the value of manufactories in 1816, were 33,691,111 dollars. At that period there were 64 cotton manufactories, 44 blast furnaces, 78 forges, 175 nailleries, 64 paper-mills, 35 rope-walks. Nearly 200,000 hats are manufactured in this state in the space of a year.—The commerce of Pennsylvania in the

Commerce.

west is by the Ohio with the Spanish, by the lakes with the British dominions, and by both with the Indian tribes. The total value of exports from the United States, in 1801, was 93 millions of dollars, and that of Pennsylvania alone was nearly 28 millions. The tonnage of this state was almost 94,000 in 1799.

Military.

Its military strength consisted, in 1812, of 99,414, and were supported for 327,000 dollars: in 1814 they cost 470,000 dollars. The total receipts of 1813, were 492,908 dollars, and the expence 336,186 dollars, while the whole capital amounted to 6½ millions dollars.

Philanthropic societies.

This State is distinguished for a great number of humane, religious, and literary societies, which are chiefly formed in Philadelphia. They have been very active since their establishment, and productive of great advantages. The Harmonic Society, formed by George Rapp, a German emigrant, is very prosperous and distinguished for industry, cleanliness, devotion, and morality. There are four universities in this

Universities.

State. The expence of the public schools amounted to 8000 dollars in 1810, for which purpose large tracts of land have been appropriated by the legislature. There are three extensive libraries in Philadelphia, one of which contains 25,000 volumes. The same spirit of benevolence, religion, and humanity, which distinguishes London, pervades our transatlantic descendants in Philadelphia, who manifest by their conduct the love which they feel for their brethren of mankind.

The quality of the soil, the healthiness of the climate, high price of labour, and the example of industry and regularity afforded by the Society of Friends,

Manners.

have contributed to raise the moral and religious character and manners of this State. Drunkenness is much diminished. Their conduct to strangers who have not letters of introduction is reserved, but if properly introduced, their hospitality is very great. Very little preference is given to the males in the division of property. Females marry between 18 and 20, and few are unmarried at 25.

Constitution.

Few States ever enjoyed such great advantages in forming their constitution, since the act, of which the charter of Penn formed the basis, was drawn up by Sir W. Jones, one of the most distinguished scholars, lawyers, and patriots of any age, and the criminal code was modelled according to the philosophical work of Beccaria on crimes and punishments. The civil courts have adopted the greatest part of the principles of English jurisprudence; and the criminal court is the most humane in the world, endeavouring to reform malefactors by judicious treatment, rather than harden them by indiscriminately blending the veteran with the novice in crime. The prisoners also support themselves by labour, and when they leave the prison, frequently have money o receive. Great cleanliness, order, and decorum, are preserved, and corporal punishment is strictly prohibited, since the keepers are not allowed to carry even a stick. The greatest religious freedom is established; for all the thirteen denominations of Christians, all Jews, and all the believers in a God and a future state, are placed on the same footing as to offices and employments.

History.

The first settlers were Swedes and Finns, who purchased, in 1627, from the Indians, a tract of country from Cape Henlopen to the falls of the Delaware, but in consequence of want of support from Gustavus Adolphus they became subject to the Dutch until the British became its masters. In 1681, Charles II. granted all the country to William Penn, between the 40° and 43° of latitude, and extending over 5° of longitude. In consequence of the wise laws, and liberal and enlightened views, of this distinguished legislator, the colony rapidly improved, and from 1750 to 1754 not fewer than 24,000 emigrated to this State. After the defeat of General Braddock in this year, the French becoming masters of the western county, from the Ohio to the junction of the two branches of the Susquehannah river, this province suffered much from the Indians, who massacred in one night the Moravians of Guadenhutten. The village of Linisink, consisting of 43 habitations, was burnt to ashes, and seventy-one individuals perished in the flames. The militia of this State were defeated in 1777, at Germans-town, and the seat of government was removed to Washington in 1800. See Morse's *Geography;* and Warden's *United States.*

PENRITH, an ancient market-town of the county of Cumberland, England, is situated at the foot of Penrith Fell, near the river Petterel, on the north, and the confluence of the Eamont and the Lowther on the south. The houses are built of red stone, covered with blue slate; and the more modern buildings are constructed with considerable elegance. The streets are by no means regular. The town-house in the market-place is large, and the figures of bears climbing up a rugged staff reminds us of its antiquity. Wheat, barley, cattle, horses, &c. are sold in distinct parts of the town. The giant's grave in the church-yard, consists of two stone pillars 15 feet asunder, 11½ feet high, and

Pennsylvania. Penrith.

nearly 5 in circumference at the bottom, where they are morticed into round stones imbedded in the earth. The upper part is square, tapering to a point, and is ornamented with fretwork, the relievo of a cross, and the figures of some animals. These pillars are thought to have been erected in memory of Ewein Cæsarius, a gigantic warrior, and great destroyer of bears, who reigned in this country in the time of Ida, one of the Anglo-Saxon kings. The giant's thumb is a single stone not far from the pillars, 5 feet 8 inches high, and antiquarians have not agreed about its object. The church is elegant, commodious, and spacious; and its roof supported by pillars, whose shafts consist of an entire red stone, taken from a quarry in the neighbourhood. It is inclosed by a neat elliptical iron palisade about 4 feet 4 inches high. On a rising ground to the west are the ruins of a castle, which seems to have been built in an oblong shape, and fortified with a deep fosse and walled rampart. Nothing remains but the arched vaults and outside walls, the fortress having been dismantled during the civil wars. Penrith was burned by the Scotch in the 18th Ed. III. and the following year. The plague nearly depopulated it in 1597, when 2260 died in a year and a half. The Scotch Highlanders were quartered in this town for a night, without doing much injury, on their way to Preston in the rebellion of 1715; but, in 1745, they acted with the violence of enemies. The population of Penrith, according to the last census, is 5038 males, and 5896 females. The lower classes are chiefly employed in agriculture, the weaving of check, and hat-making. In 1820, the poor rates were nearly £3000; but in consequence of the appointment of a select vestry by the exertions of Mr. Shaw, churchwarden, and the adopting of great economy, they are now almost reduced to £1500. A benefit society, public library, male and female free school, national school, and other benevolent institutions, receive support and encouragement. Penrith is 18 miles south of Carlisle, and 283 north-north-west of London. West Long. 2º 45′. North Lat. 54º 40′. See Hutchinson's *History of Cumberland.*

PENSACOLA. See FLORIDA, Vol. IX. p. 377, 378.

PENTAGRAPH, PANTOGRAPH, or PANTOGRAPHER, are the names given to a very useful instrument, which seems to have been first described by Scheiner about 1631, in a tract entitled, *Pantographiæ, sive Ars nova delineandi.* A very complete description of the instrument, illustrated with figures, will be found in our article DRAWING INSTRUMENTS, Vol. VIII. p. 129.

PENZANCE, a sea port town of England, in the county of Cornwall, is agreeably situated on the north-west side of Mount's Bay. It consists principally of four streets, meeting at right angles. The streets are well paved, and contain many large and good looking houses. The church is a chapel of ease to Madron; and there are meeting-houses for Baptists, Independents, Quakers, and Methodists, and a synagogue for the Jews. There is also a grammar school and a dispensary. The Geological Society of Cornwall, and the Penrith Agricultural Society, hold their meetings here. The harbour of Penzance is fit only for receiving small vessels. The pier, which was extended in 1782 and 1813, is about 600 feet long; and a light was erected at the end of it in 1816, to show when the water was nine feet deep. From the mildness of the climate, Penzance is much frequented as a bathing-place; and hot and cold baths have been erected. The trade of the place consists chiefly in pilchards, and in shipping lead, tin, and copper of the county. The mean temperature of Penzance is 50º.05. The annual quantity of rain in 1819 and 1820 was twenty-one inches. Number of dry days on an average of thirteen years, 200.

Number of wet days 158. Number of days when snow fell 2½. Population in 1821, 5224. See the *Beauties of England and Wales,* vol. ii. p. 476; and Dr. Forbes's *Observations on the Climate of Penzance,* Penzance, 1821.

PERAMBULATOR. See ODOMETER.

PERCUSSION. See MECHANICS, Vol. XIII. p. 537. and 547.

PERFECT NUMBERS, is the name of a number such as 6, which is equal to the sum of all its divisors. See NUMBERS, Vol. XV. p. 411.

PERICLES. See ATHENS, Vol. III. p. 24.

PERIPATETICS, the name of a sect of philosophers who maintained the doctrines of Aristotle. See ARISTOTLE, Vol. II. p. 360; and METAPHYSICS, Vol. XIV. p. 83.

PERNAMBUCO, or FERNAMBUCO. See BRASIL, Vol. IV. p. 426.

PEROUSE, J. F. G. DE LA, a celebrated navigator, was born at Toulouse in 1741. He was entrusted with the command of the Boussole and the Astrolabe, that formed the expedition of discovery which was fitted out by the French government in 1785. He sailed from Brest in August, 1785, and anchored on the Brasil coast in November, after touching at Madeira and Teneriffe. Proceeding round Cape Horn, they anchored in the Bay of Conception, in 1786, reached Easter Island in April, and then proceeded to the Sandwich Islands. On the 23d June, they anchored on the American coast in latitude 58º 37′, ran down to California, crossed the Pacific, and reached Macao in January, 1787. They arrived at Manilla in February, and, passing the coasts of Corea and Japan, they touched at Chinese Tartary in latitude 42½º. They anchored in a bay in Sagalien Island, and thence proceeded up the Narrow Channel as far as 51º 29′. On their return they passed by *La Perouse*'s strait, between Sagalien and Jesso, into the Northern Pacific. On the 6th September they anchored in the harbour of St. Peter and St. Paul, in Kamtschatka, and having there refitted, they reached Navigators' Islands in December. Having gone ashore, however, to procure fresh water, M. de Langle, the second in command, and a party of sixty, were attacked by the natives, when he and eleven of his men were killed. Proceeding to New Holland, they reached Botany Bay in January, 1787; but no farther accounts have ever been received of the fate of the expedition.

The journal which La Perouse had transmitted to France, was published in 1798, in 3 vols. 4to. at the expence of the nation, and for the benefit of his widow; and it was afterwards translated into English.

PERPIGNAN, a town of France, and the capital of the department of the Eastern Pyrenees, is situated on the right bank of the river Tet. Its form is nearly circular; but is in general ill built, excepting one or two streets. The cathedral is the only public building of importance. Perpignan has extensive and good fortifications. The citadel is very strong, and stands on an eminence which commands the town. There are several fine promenades here, particularly the one on the great earthen mound, which surrounds the town. The principal manufactures of Perpignan are woollen and silk goods, soap, liqueurs, and essences. It trades principally in corn, wool, wine, and iron. Population 12,000. East Long. 2º 54′ 9″. North Lat. 42º 42′ 3″.

PERSEPOLIS, RUINS OF. See our article CIVIL ARCHITECTURE, Vol. VI. p. 528, for a full account of them; and PLATE CLIII.

PERSEES, or PARSEES. See GABRES, Vol. X. p. 65.

PERSIA.

Part I.—STATISTICS OF PERSIA.

Statistics.

Persia, an ancient and extensive empire in Asia, lies between the 26th and 40th degrees of north latitude, and the 45th and 61st degrees of east longitude.

Name.

Its name spread from one of its provinces, *Pars* or *Fars*, which at one time comprehended the dominions of the kings of Persia; but it is known to the natives and learned Mahomedans under the appellation of *Iran;* and we learn from Sir William Jones, that this term embraced within its limits the whole of Lower Asia, and thus formed one of the noblest peninsulas in the world.

Boundaries.

The modern boundaries of Persia have not been distinctly marked. In general terms, it may be said to be confined on the west by the waters of the Tigris and Euphrates; by those of the Gihon and Indus on the east; by the river Kur and the Caspian Sea on the north; and by the Persian Gulf and the Indian Ocean on the south.

General aspect.

This country is highly elevated, and has with great propriety been denominated a land of mountains. It joins the high lands of Armenia and Asia Minor on the west, and those of Central Asia on the east, having its declivities towards the Euphrates and Persian Gulf on the one side, and towards the Caspian on the other. This chain was known to the ancients under the general name of Taurus, and is interrupted by many extensive valleys and elevated plains. Extending without order in all directions, many of the mountains, after rising abruptly, gradually become flat at the summit, and present the appearance of an absolute plateau.

Division.

Persia is at present divided into two independent monarchies; Western Persia, under the dominion of the king of Persia; and Eastern Persia, or Afghanistan, ruled by the chief of the Affghan tribes. Their particular boundaries, however, are somewhat uncertain; and they differ greatly in their physical, civil, and political character. The present article will therefore be confined to an account of Western Persia.

The distinctive characters of this kingdom are its numerous mountains, and great extent of deserts, interspersed with beautiful valleys and luxuriant meadows.

Mountains. On the north are the Mount of Ararat, and a chain of very cold mountains which embrace the province of Aderbijan. From these a belt of high limestone mountains, called the Alpons, runs parallel to the southern shore of the Caspian. These are the Hyrcanian mountains of the ancients, and are described by Strabo as not only steep towards the north, but projecting " in such a manner that the rivers throw themselves into the sea, forming a liquid arch, under which men could pass on dry ground." Near the mountain of Demawend, from the top of which the eye embraces a prospect of two hundred miles, and about forty miles from the city of Teheran, is an artificial passage, called by the ancients the " Caspian Gates." It is described as a narrow road, twenty-eight Roman miles in length, and capable of admitting only a single chariot to pass. From the high black rocks on each side salt water continually trickled down; and it was rendered impassable during summer by being infested by numerous serpents. The Kurdistan range enters Persia to the south of the lake Oormia; and from thence to Ispahan

the country consists entirely of mountains. Among the most remarkable is Besittoon, celebrated for its singular sculptures, which are still in existence. The Bactyar mountains separate from the Kurdistan range, and stretch towards Shiraz. The Hetzerdera, or " thousand mountains," embrace, on the north and west, the plain, in which are situated the ruins of Persepolis and the city of Shiraz. A defile in this chain, through which Alexander the Great led his army, is called the " Persian Straits." On the south, a chain of mountains, commencing near the Persian Gulf, passes across Kerman, and, joining the range which separates Seistan from Mekran, forms, with the mountains of Sooliman and those of Wulli, a long plateau separating Persia from India. This plateau possesses great elevation even in its valleys, and joins the central plateau of Asia. The Persian mountains, when taken separately, appear of moderate height; but, from the continual snow upon their summits, they must be concluded to rest upon a very elevated base. No traveller has examined them sufficiently, so as to ascertain exactly the nature of their formation. They are supposed, however, to consist chiefly of limestone; and many of them are the most sterile and wild in the world, being merely dry rocks without wood or any herbaceous plants. Ararat and the neighbouring mountains contain a large quantity of slate; and the Alpons appear to consist of limestone, marble, and alabaster, with numerous blocks of granite. The western range is formed of sandstone, limestone, and granite, succeeding one another as in European mountains. The reefs on the coast of Mazenderan are granite.

Statistics.

Deserts.

The deserts of Persia, which are rather saline than sandy, cover nearly three-tenths of the country. The principal of these is the Great Salt Desert, lying between Khorassan and Irak Adjum, where the layer of crystallized sea-salt on the surface of the ground lies in several places an inch in thickness. It joins the Caramanian desert, which forms the northern part of Kerman; and these two stretch over an extent of nearly 140,000 square miles. The nitre and other salts with which this vast tract abounds, impregnates the neighbouring rivers and lakes. The Great Sandy Desert commences on the banks of the Heirmund, and extends to the range of mountains, which divides the province of Mekran, a distance of nearly 450 miles. Its sand is of a reddish colour, and so light that it is scarcely palpable. When raised by the wind it forms longitudinal waves, which, on the windward side present a gradual slope from the base, and on the other rise perpendicularly to the height of ten or twenty feet. Arrian tells us, that the army of Alexander, when marching through this desert, was nearly smothered in deep scorching sand. The wind, which here commonly blows from the north-west, is termed the *bade sumoom*, or pestilential wind; and during the summer months is so heated, as to destroy every thing, either animal or vegetable, with which it comes in contact. In some instances it kills instantaneously; but, in others, the wretched sufferer lingers for hours, or even days, in the most excruciating torture. The desert of *Kara-kum*, or the Black Sand, covers part of Khorassan, and forms the northern boundary of Persia towards Tartary ; and that of *Kiab* lies on the east of the Tigris, and stretches from thence to the north of Shuster.

Another striking feature in this country is its scarcity of water, which is one of the greatest obstacles to its fertility. It possesses few rivers of any importance. The Euphrates and Tigris cannot be considered as Persian ; neither can the Kur, which forms its northern boundary towards Georgia ; nor the Gihon, which divides it from Tartary. The river *Aras*, the ancient Araxes, rises in the mountains of Caucasus, and, after a long and rapid course, joins the Kur. The *Kizil-ozen* has its source in the western mountains, and, after a very winding course, reaches the Caspian. It is supposed to be the Mardus of the ancients. This river flows in a series of cataracts through picturesque ravines, and falls with such force into the sea, that its current is perceptible a considerable distance from the shore. It abounds in sturgeon, and produces numerous pike, carp, and other kinds of fish esteemed by the Persians. The *Tedzen*, the ancient Ochus, waters the province of Khorassan, and, after receiving several small streams from the mountains of Mazenderan, falls into the Caspian. The inland rivers of Persia are in general lost in the deserts. The *Zynderood* rises in the Baktyar mountains, and passing by Ispahan expends itself in the deserts of sand to the south-east. The waters of this river are at times so swollen by the melting of the snow and the rains, that they overflow their banks to a great extent.

These inundations sometimes cover several districts, and render large tracts of rich and productive land useless for the season. The injury done by one of these in 1809, was calculated to amount to three lacks of piastres. The *Bendemir* passes from north to south between Shiraz and Persepolis, and flows into the salt lake of Baktegan, which also receives another considerable stream called *Kuren*. Besides these, there are a few small streams which fall into the Persian Gulf.

The lakes of this country are very similar to those of Africa, but of greater extent. The lake *Shahee*, or

Oormia, which lies among the mountains of Aderbijan, is inclosed on the north and east by the plain of Tabreez, the salt desert, and the hills and valleys of Uzkoh ; a sublime range of snowy mountains gird it on the west ; and on the south it is terminated by the table land and extensive pastures of Maragha. It is about 280 miles in circumference, and in general very shallow, its greatest depth not being more than five or six feet, and in some places scarcely one. What is remarkable in this lake is, that it receives fourteen rivers of different sizes, without any apparent increase of its waters. Indeed, it would appear that the evaporation is greater than its supplies, as there are many visible signs of diminution. The Persian rivers, however, in general, depend much upon the mountain torrents. On the one day they are overflowing their banks, and on the other they scarcely deserve the name of rivulets ; consequently the greatest quantity of water in the lake is in the spring, when the snow melts, and the torrents flow the deepest ; and then its surface will sometimes rise about thirty feet. The waters of the Oormia seem dull, and are extremely saline, yielding, when evaporated, a bitter salt of a beautiful transparency, and one-third more in quantity than sea-water ; and are so prejudicial to fish, that when any are thrown into it by the rivers they immediately die. Lake *Erivan* lies about 100 miles to the

north. It is seventy miles in circumference, with a small island in the middle, and abounds in carp and trout.

Ten miles south-east of Shiraz is the salt lake *Baktegan*. During summer it is nearly dry, when the people who inhabit its banks collect the salt with which the bottom is encrusted, which is remarkably fine, and which is in general use throughout the province of Fars.

The climate of Persia exhibits considerable variety ; and the description given of it by the younger Cyrus to Xenophon, " My father's empire is so large, that people perish with cold at the one extremity, while they are suffocated with heat at the other," is equally applicable now as it was then. This arises, however, more from the difference of elevation and soil than from difference of latitude. There are three leading distinctions of region and climate in this country. In the *northern* pro-

vinces, on the shores of the Caspian, an excessive humidity prevails throughout the year. The inhabitants bear indelible marks of its insalubrity, having a feverish sallowness of complexion, and possessing neither strength nor spirits. Here the winter is very mild, from the temperate winds which blow from the sea ; but during summer the heats are so strong and lasting, that all who are able abandon the towns, and retire to the mountains, where they live in tents, and where the temperature is comparatively cool. Vegetation is favoured by the long lying of the snow, and a protracted spring ; and the forests are vigorous and extensive. The sides of the hills are covered with acacias, lindens, oaks, and chesnuts ; and their summits are crowned with cedars, cypresses, and pines of various descriptions. The *sumach*, so useful from its astringent virtue in the arts of dyeing and tanning, grows here in abundance ; and the flowering manna-ash is equally common. The province of Ghilan abounds in boxwood ; and the sugar cane is cultivated with some degree of success, and produces tolerable sugar. In the *central* plateau the summer is excessively hot. The

atmosphere, however, is serene, and refreshed by cool breezes during the night. A cloud is scarcely to be seen, and the light of the stars is sufficient to direct the traveller on his way. The winters are equally rigorous. Snow storms are frequent ; and instances have occurred where whole caravans have been overwhelmed by the blast. Dews are unknown in summer, and, during the rest of the year, they are of such a nature that the brightest steel, though exposed to them, would not receive the slightest rust. In spring the hails are often prejudicial to vegetation. It is then and in autumn that high winds generally prevail ; but the air is extremely dry, and thunder and lightning are rarely experienced. Among the mountains of Kurdistan and Aderbijan, however, this general character of the climate is greatly modified ; and they derive, from their great elevation and their forests, a more humid atmosphere, and more equal temperature. The province of Fars also, especially the valley of Shiraz, is exempt from excess of heat or of cold ; the thermometer in the day time seldom rising higher than 80° in summer, or sinking lower than 62° at night. In this region the elevated plains are covered with those species of plants which affect a saline soil ; but some of the open plains, which are free from sand, are covered with fertile pastures. Though the mountains of Fars are stripped of their forests, yet the beautiful walks in the valley of Shiraz are shadowed by planes, medlars, willows, and poplars, among which spring up in great beauty and luxuriance anemonies, jessamines, hypericums, tulips, and ranunculi. Descending *southward* to the shores of

the Persian Gulf, the climate undergoes a very material change. The Sumoom, though not frequent, sometimes desolates the face of nature. According to Tavernier, the people of Gombroon, when they find themselves struck by this wind, cry out, " I burn," and immediately expire. The extreme heat of the air during four months of the year is almost insupportable, and so very unhealthy, that strangers who fall sick seldom recover.

Mineralogy.

The mineralogy of this country is very unimportant, though its numerous mountains probably abound in unexplored treasures. In Aderbijan are mines of iron and copper, and also a mine of silver; but the finest silver mine is in Bokhara. These mines, however, from the want of proper artists and miners, are not wrought with much profit; and some of them have been abandoned, as the expences have been found to exceed the produce. Sulphur and nitre are found in the mountain of Demawend; and abundance of rock-salt in the province of Kerman. The only gems in Persia are the Turquoise, of which the best are obtained from a mine near Nishapore in Khorassan.

Medical springs.

Medical springs of various descriptions arise among the mountains; but they are entirely neglected by the inhabitants. Not far from Maragha, on the banks of a stream which passes near the deserted village of Chai-Bagh, are several which issue from the ground with different degrees of force. The two most remarkable are close to each other, the one cold and the other tepid. Their waters are a strong chalybeate, and of a most nauseous taste. At no great distance, another spring, of nearly the same nature, issues from the earth in bubbles, and falls into a basin of about fifteen feet in diameter. It emits a considerable volume of water; but as soon as it leaves the basin, and spreads over the ground, forming numerous ponds or plashes, it concretes and petrifies, producing that beautiful transparent

Petrifactions.

stone, commonly called *Tabreez marble*, which is so remarkable in most of the burial places of Persia, and which forms a chief ornament in all the buildings of note throughout the country

Tabreez marble.

The following account of this natural curiosity is given by Mr. Morier: " On approaching the spot, the ground has a hollow sound, with a particularly dreary and calcined appearance, and when upon it a strong mineral smell arises from the ponds. The process of petrifaction is to be traced from its first beginning to its termination. In one part, the water is clear; in a second, it appears thicker and stagnant; in a third, quite black; and in the last stage, is white like hoar frost. Indeed, a petrified pond looks like frozen water; and before the operation is quite finished, a stone slightly thrown upon it breaks the outer coating, and causes the black water underneath to exude. Where the operation is complete, a stone makes no impression, and a man may walk upon it without wetting his shoes. Whenever the petrifaction has been hewn into, the curious progress of the concretion is clearly seen, and shows itself like sheets of rough paper placed one over the other in accumulated layers. Such is the constant tendency of this water to become stone, that, where it exudes from the ground in bubbles, the petrifaction assumes a globular shape, as if the bubbles of a spring, by a stroke of magic, had been arrested in their play, and metamorphosed into marble. These stony bubbles, which form the most curious specimens of this most extraordinary quarry, frequently contain with them portions of the earth through which the water has oozed."

" The substance thus produced is brittle, transparent, and sometimes most richly streaked with green, red, and copper-coloured veins. It admits of being cut into immense slabs, and takes a good polish. So

Statistics.

much is this stone looked upon as an article of luxury, that none but the king, his sons, and persons privileged by special firman, are permitted to excavate; and such is the ascendency of pride over avarice, that the scheme of farming it to the highest bidder does not seem to have ever come within the calculations of its present possessors."

Naphtha, or rock-oil.

Another natural curiosity in this country is a mineral called *Naphtha*. Of this substance there are two kinds, the white and black. There are several fountains of the latter in Irak Arabi; but the most productive are those near Kerkook. It is procured by digging a small pit, from ten to twelve feet deep, which fills of itself, and is employed by the natives as a substitute for pitch; and is used also in lamps instead of oil. The white naphtha is supposed by some to be an entirely different substance. It is of a much thicker consistence, and greatly resembles tallow, and both affords a better light and emits a less disagreeable smell than the other. Two fountains of this kind arise near Doulakee, in the province of Fars. The oil floats like a crust on the surface of the water, and is collected by the peasantry; who daub their camels all over with it in the spring, which preserves their coats, and prevents a disease in the skin. The most remarkable, however, are those found in the neighbourhood of Baku, on the western shore of the Caspian. See BAKU.

Soil.

Persia possesses a variety of soil, from the sandy and barren tracts of the south to the rich and clayey plains on the Caspian; but scarcely a twentieth part of the land is under cultivation. In the central regions, and on the Persian Gulf, the soil is sandy or of a hard clay, which, without irrigation, is totally unproductive; yet wherever water can be obtained, the vegetation is most luxuriant. From this circumstance the industry of the farmer is chiefly directed to the watering of his land; and canals for this purpose are very common in some of the provinces. Astonishing efforts, indeed, have been made to overcome this natural defect of the country; but, in the frequent civil wars by which Persia has been torn, these canals have often been destroyed in order to cut off a supply of water from an enemy; and thus the labours of a century annihilated in a day. Indeed, the destruction of a few water-courses, made at great expense and labour, will change, in one season, a verdant valley into a barren waste.

Agriculture.

Agriculture, however, is still in its rudest state, yet abundant crops are obtained by merely sprinkling the seed upon the ground, and then scratching it with a wretched plough drawn by one ox. In the northern provinces the soil is sufficiently rich and fertile, consisting, in some places, of a fine brown mould, and cultivation is more general. Wheat is the common produce, but rice is the favourite food of the Persians; and this is cultivated with extreme care, especially in the province of Mazenderan. It is first sown like other grain, and after three months is transplanted root by root into well watered fields, which gives it that perfection which it possesses in no other part of the world. Barley and millet are also cultivated, and a few oats. A considerable bar to agriculture, however, is found in the unsettled nature of the government, which affords no protection to private property. The method also of apportioning the land tax, and the rents of the crown lands being collected according to the produce, must discourage the expenditure of capital and labour in improvements. From these causes many fertile districts are abandoned by the farmers, and consigned as pasture

Statistics.　grounds to wandering tribes, who lead their flocks over immense tracts which were once covered with grain.

Gardens.　　The gardens of Persia are both beautiful and productive. They are cultivated with great care; and few countries can surpass it in the variety and flavour Fruits.　of its fruits. Apples, pears, cherries, figs, pomegranates, almonds, peaches, apricots, walnuts, oranges, and lemons, are indigenous, and are produced in great abundance. The most succulent melons are raised in Khorassan; and are sometimes so large that two or three are a full load for a man. The quinces of Ispahan are considered the finest in the east; and the wine of Shiraz is so delicious that it is reserved for the use of the court. This country also abounds in hemp, tobacco, sesamum, rhubarb, manna, saffron, cotton, turpen-Silk worm.　tine, various gums, and gall-nuts. The silk worm is extensively cultivated, and its annual produce exceeds four millions of pounds. About a twentieth part of this quantity is used in the country, and the rest is sold in India, Turkey, and Russia.

Horses.　　The horses of Persia are of different breeds, but all of them excellent. The Arabian is still preserved pure on the shores of the Gulf; but a mixed race prevails in the interior, which, though neither so beautiful nor so fleet, are both larger and more powerful. The Persian soldier, however, prefers the Turkoman breed, which attain great size and strength. This race possesses extraordinary powers of enduring fatigue, and is capable of performing the most surprising journeys. They have been known to travel nine hundred miles in eleven successive days; and we are told, that upon one of these animals, Kurreem Khan rode three hundred Camels.　and thirty-two miles in fifty-two hours. Camels are used chiefly in those parts of the country where the soil is arid and sandy; and are preferred, as beasts of burden, to all other animals. Those in Khorassan are not inferior to the camels of Arabia. Mules, however, Mules.　are in more general use, and are next in estimation to the horse. Their breed is also an object of particular care. They are small, well proportioned, and very hardy, but require to be well fed. When we consider that there are no navigable rivers in this country, and that the roads are so bad as to prevent the use of wheeled carriages, we need not wonder at the extreme attention which is bestowed upon these animals; which are alike essential to promote the intercourse of peace, Cattle.　and give success to the operations of war. Cows and oxen are principally kept for the purposes of agriculture and the supply of the dairy. Beef is not a favour-Sheep.　ite food, and is used only by the lower classes. Numerous flocks of sheep and goats cover the plains, and constitute the wealth of the wandering tribes. The Persian sheep carries thirty pounds weight of fat upon his tail, which is flat and widest at the extremity; but no attention is paid to the improvement of the breed. Wild animals.　The more desolate parts of the country are haunted by lions, bears, tigers, wolves, hyænas, jackals, and wild boars. The antelope, the hare, the zebra, the fox, the argali, and deer of various kinds, afford ample amusement to the sportsman. The tame and wild fowl are much the same as those in Europe.

Provinces of Western Persia.　Western Persia, or the dominions of the present reigning sovereign, comprehends the provinces of Fars, Irak, part of Kurdistan, Aderbijan, Laristan, Kuzistan, Ghilan, Mazenderan, the western parts of Khorassan, comprehending the cities of Meshed, Nishapore, and Tursheez, and the western division of Kerman, including the capital of that province. As an account of some of these provinces has already appeared in this work, a reference will be suf-Statistics.　ficient; and our attention will be confined to those which have not yet been described Fars, or Far-sistan, see Vol. IX. p. 282. On the north of Fars, is Irak, which is supposed to comprehend the great-Irak.　er part of ancient Media, and occupies the central plateau of Persia. It is bounded on the east by Khorassan, and the Great Salt Desert; by Aderbijan, Ghilan, and Mazenderan, on the north; on the west by Kurdistan; and by Fars and Kuzistan on the south. This province is almost entirely covered with mountains, stretching from west to east, which are barren, and devoid of timber; and the valleys, which are of an indefinite length, and seldom exceed ten or fifteen miles in breadth, though capable of yielding abundant crops, are allowed to lie uncultivated, except in the vicinity of the towns and villages. The country around Ispahan has of late been fast advancing towards prosperity, under the management of the Ameen-a-Doulah, or second minister of the king. The small district of Linjan.　Linjan, in particular, extending about seventy miles in length, and forty in breadth, is covered with picturesque and flourishing villages, which are surrounded with gardens and pigeon-houses. It is irrigated by canals cut from the river Zynderood, and its productions are equal to those in the most fertile spots of Persia. This province contains many celebrated cities, among which are, Ispahan, Yezd, Kashan, Koom, Teheran, Casbin, Zinjan, Hamadan, Kermanshah, and Khonsar. The chief of these is Ispahan, which continued for several centuries to be the capital of the empire; but of late the royal residence has been transferred to Teheran. See Ispahan.

The city of Yezd is situated in the midst of a barren Yezd.　tract, where there is a great scarcity of wood and water; but in consequence of its being the grand mart between Hindostan, Bokhara, and Persia, it is very populous, and a place of considerable trade. It contains 20,000 houses besides those of the Guebres, or worshippers of fire, which are estimated at 4000 more, and is celebrated for its manufactures of silk stuffs, which are superior to any in Persia. Proceeding northwards about 63 miles from Ispahan, lies the beautiful valley of Natunz, about eight miles in length, and Natunz.　surrounded with rugged and lofty mountains, from which flow innumerable streams. It is famed for the salubrity of its climate, and presents to the view a continued garden of fruit trees, among which the houses of the inhabitants are interspersed and concealed. Near Kashan, the king has a beautiful hunting seat and garden at the foot of the mountains; but the road from this to Koom skirts the Great Salt Desert through a level country, depopulated by the devastations of the Turkomans.

Passing to the north-west, the district of Sava, extending nearly 80 miles, is laid out in pasture lands, and was celebrated by the ancients for an excellent breed of horses.

The route from Koom to Teheran passes over a plain, strongly impregnated with nitre and salt, and through a salt marsh, which, in some places, is above thirty-five miles in breadth, and runs from east to west about 150. On approaching the capital, however, the coun-Teheran.　try appears fertile and productive, and the surrounding scenery is particularly interesting. The lofty Demawend, with his snowy summit, overlooks it from the north; on the east it is environed by the mountains of Elburz, the traditionary abodes of demons, and on the east the extensive ruins of the once proud city of Rhé,

PERSIA. 373

the ancient Rhages, cover the plain as far as the eye can reach. Here Alexander is said to have rested five days in his pursuit after Darius. It was destroyed by the generals of Chenghiz Khan, and from its scattered population arose the city of Teheran. Teheran is between four and five miles in circumference, and, during the residence of the king, contains from 60,000 to 70,000 inhabitants; but, when the summer heats compel his majesty to remove his household, and pitch his tents on the plains of Sultanea, or Oujan, the population of the capital is reduced to little more than 10,000. This city is surrounded by a strong wall, flanked by innumerable towers, and a dry ditch with a glacis. It has few public edifices, and the only building of consequence is the citadel, which contains the palace of the sovereign and his officers. About two miles to the north-east of Teheran, is the king's pleasure house, called Tahkt-a-Cadjar. Though formed of coarse materials, and but rudely furnished, it is erected on a model admirably calculated for the heat of the summer. It is wholly built of brick, except the exterior wall, which is mud, flanked by brick turrets; and it presents a grand elevation, consisting of six successive terraces, which, at a distance, has the appearance of so many stories.

The northern frontier of Irak is formed by a lofty range of mountains, which terminates at the Caspian Strait; and an extensive valley, about twenty miles in breadth, extends as far as the city of Casbin. Here the climate is delightful, and the country is populous and well cultivated. About 70 miles to the north-west of Casbin, is Sultanea, where the king encamps during the summer months; once a splendid city, but now a heap of ruins, inhabited only by a few poor families, who live in wretched hovels, in the vicinity of the tomb of Sultan Khodahbundah, which is a large and beautiful structure, built of brick, and covered with a cupola ninety feet in height. The large and populous town of Zinjan lies about twenty miles farther to the north-west, and from thence to the river Kizil-ozen, which forms the boundary between Irak and Aderbijan, the country is very uneven and full of deep ravines. The districts between this river and the cities of Hamadan and Kermanshah, is called by oriental writers *Al Gebal*, (the mountainous.) The western part of it is almost uninhabited, though abounding in rich pastures; but the country between Sultanea and Hamadan is well cultivated, and peopled by the tribes of Giroos and Karagoozoloo; and the vicinity of the latter city for many miles is covered with productive fields and fruitful orchards, and intersected by innumerable little streams. Hamadan, the ancient Ecbatana, is situated at the foot of Mount Elwund, the Orontes of ancient geography. It has evidently been at one time an immense city, as a long succession of broken walls and sculptured fragments attest the former existence of extensive and elegant buildings. Since its capture and destruction by Tamerlane, it has been considered only as a secondary city. At present it consists of about 10,000 indifferently built houses, containing above 40,000 inhabitants; but being separated by gardens, which are watered by rivulets from the hills, it has a very agreeable appearance. Hamadan is the great mart of commerce between Ispahan and Bagdad; and numerous caravans are also constantly passing from the north to the latter city. It is consequently resorted to by merchants of various nations for the purposes of traffic. The principal manufactures of this place are a sort of felt carpet, called *nummud*, much esteemed among the Persians, and leather, in which it carries on a considerable trade. Here is the tomb of Mordecai and Esther, and also of Avicenna. Hamadan is as much celebrated for its climate as Ecbatana was in ancient times, and is said to have been the summer residence of the Persian kings from the time of Darius to that of Chenghiz Khan. A large and fruitful tract of country extends from Hamadan to Kermanshah; but the districts between Hamadan and Khonsar, a distance of 150 miles, are but indifferently cultivated. To the south-west of Khonsar, (See vol. XII. p. 449.) is the small district of Feredun, peopled entirely by Georgians and Armenians. The former, amounting nearly to one thousand families, profess the Mahomedan religion, but intermarry only among themselves.

But the richest and most fertile part of Irak is Louristan, an extensive tract of country stretching along the northern frontier of Kuzistan. It is watered by several considerable rivers, and there is scarcely a valley that is not refreshed by a number of lesser streams. It is peopled by the martial tribes of Baktyari and Fielhi, who are subject to no law but the will of their chiefs. They lead a wandering life, residing chiefly in tents, and subsisting on the produce of their flocks. Agriculture is consequently neglected, but the pasture is most luxuriant. The only town in this district is Korumabad, the ancient Corbienna, which stands at the foot of a mountain, and on the banks of a broad and rapid river, across which is thrown a bridge of twenty-eight arches. There is also a fort, built on a conical hill, in the centre of the town, sufficiently strong for its protection against the power of Persia. Between Korumabad and Hamadan lie the extensive plains of Khawa and Alister; and to the north-east are the towns of Hussar, which is large and populous, and the capital of a wealthy district; of Booroojird, a flourishing city, containing 12,000 inhabitants; and of Nahavund, celebrated for a battle which gave Persia to the Saracens.

The only part of KURDISTAN which may be said to be subject to Persia is the province of *Ardelan*. The powerful chief of this district, however, condescends to pay tribute to the Persian monarch, merely for the preservation of peace; for, in every other respect, he is completely independent. (See vol. VI. p. 512.)

ADERBIJAN, the Atropalena of the ancients, lies to the north of Irak, from which it is separated by the Kizil-ozen. It has the Caspian Sea and Ghilan on the east, Armenia and Kurdistan on the west, and the river Aras on the north. It derives its name, which signifies the " country of fire," from being the place where fire worship had its origin. This province is reckoned among the most productive in Persia, and presents a regular succession of undulating eminences, partially cultivated, and opening into plains. The villages are, for the most part, embosomed in orchards and gardens, which yield delicious fruits of every description; and no where are provisions more cheap and abundant. As the country is intersected by many small rivers, cultivation is chiefly carried on by means of irrigation, and their crops often yield from fifty to sixty fold. The climate is healthy, and the snow lies upon the mountains nine months in the year. The spring is temperate and delightful; but the hail-storms are sometimes so violent, that the cattle perish in the fields. In summer and autumn the sun has very considerable influence; but the cold of winter is severely felt from the great scarcity of fuel, for which the inhabitants have no substitute but dried cow-dung, mixed with straw. The principal towns in Aderbijan are—Tabreez, the capital, Ardebil, (Vol. II. p. 339.) Khoee, Oormia, and Mara-

Statistics.

Tabreez.

gha. Tabreez, or Taurus, is situated at the foot of a mountain in an immense plain, and on the banks of a small river, whose waters are consumed in irrigation. It was the residence of the Persian kings for several centuries; and, in distant ages, rivalled the city of Ecbatana. In the time of Chardin, it was one of the largest and most populous cities in the east, containing half a million of inhabitants. It is no more, however, the magnificent city described by that traveller. Situated near the confines of contending empires, it has been taken and sacked eight different times, and alternately in the possession of Turks, Tartars, and Persians. But its most destructive enemies were the earthquakes of 1727 and 1787, which levelled its proudest edifices with the ground, and destroyed upwards of 100,000 of its inhabitants. Out of 250 mosques, the ruins of only three can be distinguished, and nothing appears of the ancient city but an extensive and confused mass of old mud walls. Tabreez was fast declining into insignificance, when, about the year 1805, Prince Abbas Meerza, the heir-apparent of the Persian throne, having been appointed to the government of the province, made it his place of residence. He has repaired and beautified the walls, and erected a new barrack for the accommodation of his troops. The population of this city is now about 30,000. The walls are surrounded on every side with fruitful gardens, and the banks of the rivers are planted with poplars. Between Tabreez and the Kizil-ozen is a considerable territory, now uninhabited. It was formerly possessed by the tribe of Sha-Khakee, but their chief having suffered death for taking arms against his sovereign, his people were dispersed, and the majority of them retired within the frontiers of Russia. To the north of this district, is the celebrated Chowal Mogan, or plain of Mogan, where Nadir Shah assembled the nobles of Persia and received from them the crown. This plain extends from the city of Ardebil to the mouths of the river Kur; and its rich soil and luxuriant pastures have rendered it the favourite encamping ground of eastern conquerors. But the most flourishing and picturesque part of this province lies along the north and west borders of the lake Oormia. The principal cities in this district are Khoee, (see vol. XII. p. 449.) and Oormia. The former stands in a beautiful valley, about fifteen miles in length, and ten in breadth, and which, for richness, cultivation, water, and pasture, cannot well be surpassed. It is covered with fields of corn, cotton, and rice, and interspersed with well inclosed gardens. Oormia, a very ancient city, containing a population of 12,000 souls, is the Thebarma of Strabo, and supposed to be the birth-place of Zoroaster. It is situated in a noble plain, which is watered and fertilized by the river Shar, and is fortified by a strong wall and deep ditch, which can be filled with water from the river.

Chowal Mogan.

Oormia.

Maragha.

On the south-east of the lake stands the well built town of Maragha, containing 15,000 inhabitants. It lies in a low valley, at the extremity of a well-cultivated plain, and its gardens and plantations are watered by canals from a small river, which flows past the walls of the city. Many indications are visible of its having been once in a more flourishing condition; and there are several curious old tombs, in one of which are supposed to rest the remains of Hulakoo Khan. This able prince spent the last years of his life at Maragha, and erected an observatory on a hill close to the city, whose summit he levelled for the purpose. Here his favourite astronomer, Nasser-u-deen, formed those astronomical tables, so celebrated under the name of the " tables

of Eel-Khannee." The elevated tract of country stretching from the vicinity of the lake Oormia, along the course of the Kizil-ozen, towards the province of Ghilan, formed the dominions of the chief of the Hussunee, or Assassins, an abominable race, who were finally destroyed by Hulakoo.

Statistics.

LARISTAN. See Vol. XII. p. 601.
KUZISTAN. See Vol. XII. p. 489.
GHILAN. See Vol. X. p. 258.

MAZENDERAN lies between the southern shore of the Caspian Sea, and the mountains of Elburz, which separate it from the province of Irak. It has Ghilan on the west, and Khorassan on the east. This province forms part of the ancient Hyrcania, and has a great resemblance to Ghilan in its physical character, being mountainous, and intersected with swamps and forests of oaks. The valleys are abundantly fertile, and produce rice of the finest quality. Its wheat, however, is very inferior. The sugar cane is here cultivated to a considerable extent; and, what is somewhat surprising, it ripens four months earlier than in the West Indies; but there is no sugar refining manufactory in the country; and the juice of the cane is used only in the shape of a coarse syrup or thick paste. The villages are, in general, neatly built, and situated on verdant hills or in the most delightful plains, fertilized by a multitude of streams; and the natives are regarded as the most warlike of the Persians. They maintained their independence for a considerable time with much courage and ability against all the power of Tamerlane. Among the numerous useful works which Shah Abbas the Great erected, and which remain as monuments of his power, the causeway of Mazenderan is particularly worthy of notice. It extends from Kiskar several leagues beyond Asterabad, a length of about three hundred miles. The pavement is in some parts about twenty yards broad, with ditches on each side, and occasional bridges, under which the water is conveyed to the rice fields. This great work, however, is falling fast into decay. The present sovereign has been frequently petitioned to repair it, as the other roads are almost impassable in winter; but it has been the policy of the government to leave it in its present state, lest the king might be compelled in any emergency to retire there, where he could easily defend himself in the inaccessible fastnesses which the condition of the province opposes to an enemy.

Mazenderan.

Causeway.

The principal towns in Mazenderan are—Balfrosh, a meanly built town, situated in a low damp valley, and about a mile and a half in circumference. It contains 25,000 inhabitants, and enjoys a prosperous trade, particularly in silk. Sari, a small but well fortified town, surrounded by a good wall and deep ditch. It is crowded with inhabitants, among whom are many merchants, who carry on a brisk traffic with Astracan, and the interior of Persia. Amul is agreeably situated at the foot of a mountain, and on the banks of a river, over which is a handsome bridge of twelve arches. Ashraff is celebrated as the favourite residence of Shah Abbas, and enjoys the only good harbour on the southern side of the Caspian. A description of the palace is given by Hanway, but it is now in ruins. The climate of this province is rather unhealthy; and the exhalations from the fens and marshes, occasioned by the summer and autumnal heats, produce agues and dropsies, which are indicated by the sallow and bloated appearance of the inhabitants. The population is estimated at from 600,000 to 700,000. The small province of *Asterabad* is sometimes included in Mazenderan, which it resembles in climate and productions. It is

Balfrosh.

Sari.

Amul.

Ashraff.

Asterabad.

Statistics.
the paternal estate of the present king of Persia, as chief of the Kujur tribe, who have entire possession of the province. See Vol. II. p. 577.

Khorassan.
KHORASSAN. See Vol. XII. p. 448.

Meshed.
The principal cities of the Persian division of this province are Meshed, Nishapore, and Tursheez. Meshed, the capital, stands in a rich and well watered plain, and is surrounded with a strong wall. Although nearly one half of it is in ruins, it has a population of 50,000 souls. The houses are meanly built; and the palace is unworthy of the name. The bazar, which extends nearly three miles in length, is well supplied with fruits and provisions. Here is a manufactory of velvet of the finest quality; and its fur pelisses are in great estimation. This city is decorated by a very superb sepulchre, in which repose the ashes of the Imaum

Nishapore.
Reza, and the Caliph Haruun ul Reeshd. Nishapore, formerly one of the richest cities of Khorassan, is now almost in ruins, and scarcely contains 15,000 inhabitants, who occupy only a single quarter of the city. It was at one time irrigated by 12,000 aqueducts, most of which have fallen into decay, and are now destitute of water. This city was first destroyed by Alexander the Great; and after a lapse of many years was rebuilt by Sapor the First. It was taken by the Tartars in the 548th year of the Hegira, and so completely ruined that the inhabitants, on their return, could not distinguish the situation of their own houses. It, however, once more arose from its ashes, and regained its former splendour, when it was a second time pillaged by these barbarians under Chenghiz Khan, from which it has ne-

Tursheez.
ver recovered. Tursheez, with the old city of Sultanabad, to which it is united, contains about 20,000 people, who carry on a considerable trade in indigo, drugs, wool, cloth, rice, and iron.

KERMAN. See Vol. XII. p. 446.

Population.
The population of this country has been variously estimated. According to their own calculations, which are evidently much exaggerated, it is stated at upwards of 200 millions! Chardin makes it 40 millions; while Pinkerton reduces it to 10, including Affghanistan, or Eastern Persia. Malte-Brun, who professes to give a table of the different nations and tribes who inhabit this country, makes the agricultural and manufacturing class, who live in fixed dwellings, alone amount to above 10,700,000, and estimates the wandering tribes at nearly 700,000 more. This is, perhaps, as near the truth as can well be ascertained. It is supposed that the population of Persia has considerably diminished since the invasion of the Affghans. The Mahomedan portion of it, however, which comprehends nearly the whole, is greatly enlarged within the last thirty years; and when we consider the salubrity of the climate, and the cheapness of provisions, we are rather astonished at the scanty numbers of its inhabitants. There are, no doubt, many powerful checks to their increase, arising from the oppressive nature of their government, and their continual civil wars; but were these removed, the increase would be rapid and continued. The city of Ispahan has nearly doubled the number of its citizens since the commencement of the century; and this has been attributed entirely to the excellent local administration of that city. The Jews are evidently decreasing in numbers, and do not exceed twenty thousand; and the Guebres, or "worshippers of fire," may be computed at four thousand families. The Armenians, when enumerated by an order of the Bishop of Julfa, amounted to 12,383 souls.

Statistics.
General appearance.
The Persians are in general a fine race of men, as far as regards their personal appearance. The forehead high, the nose aquiline, the cheeks full, the chin large, the countenance generally oval, and the complexion varying from a dark olive to a slight tinge of yellow. They are of a middling stature, robust and active, and well adapted for military service. They shave the head, except a small tuft upon the crown, and a lock behind each ear; but the beard is sacred, and cultivated with great care. The young men long for its appearance, and grease their chins to hasten its growth; for without it they are considered incapable of enjoying any place of trust. It is almost an universal custom to dye the beard black, and also to stain with

Dress.
khenna the hands and feet. The Persian dress has very materially changed within the last century. The turban is worn only by the Arabian inhabitants, and has given place to a high black cap covered with lambs' wool, and which, till very lately, used to be encircled with a Cashmirian shawl. This, however, is now prohibited, and is allowed only as a mark of distinction, which is confined to the royal family and the principal officers of state; and this prohibition was given in order to encourage the domestic manufacture of brocade shawls. The inhabitants of the principal towns are fond of dressing richly. Their upper garments are either of chintz, silk, or cloth of a dark colour, and often trimmed with gold or silver lace; and, in winter, are lined with furs. The following account of the different parts of their dress is abridged from Morier.

1. The *zeer jumah*, a pair of very wide trowsers, either of red silk or blue cotton, and reaching below the ancle.

2. The *peera hann*, a shirt generally of silk, which, going over the trowsers, reaches a few inches below the hips, and is fastened by two buttons over the top of the right shoulder.

3. The *alcalock*, a tight vest made of chintz, and quilted with cotton, which ties at the side, and reaches as low as the thin part of the calf of the leg. It has sleeves extending to the wrist, but open from the elbow.

4. The *caba*, a long vest descending to the ancle, but fitting tight to the body as far as the hips, and buttoning at the side. The sleeves go over those of the *alcalock*, and from the elbow are closed by buttons only, that they may be opened thus far for the purpose of ablution.

5. The *shal kemer*, a bandage round the waist, which is made either of Cashmirian shawl, or of the common shawl of Kerman, or of English chintz, or of flowered muslin. It is about eight yards long, and one broad. To this is fastened a *kunjur*, or dagger, ornamented according to the wealth of the possessor, from an enamelled pummel set in precious stones, to a common handle of bone or wood.

6. The *tekmeh* and *baroonee*, outer coats made of cloth, and worn or thrown off according to the heat of the weather. The former has sleeves open from the elbow, which are generally permitted to hang behind. This coat is quite round, buttons before, and drops like a petticoat over the shawl that goes round the waist. The *baroonee* is a loose and ample robe, with proportionably ample arms, generally faced with velvet, and thrown negligently over the shoulders. Besides these, they have also coats trimmed with fur; and the warmest of their dresses is a sheep-skin with the wool inside and the leather out, of which the finest are from Bok-

hara. When they ride, they put on loose trowsers of cloth, called *shalwar*, into which they insert the skirts of the *alkalock*, as well as the silken trowsers; so that the whole looks like an inflated bladder. Their boots have high heels, are turned up at the toe, and are generally made of Russia leather."

The dress of the women is extremely simple. In summer it consists of a silk or muslin shift; a loose pair of velvet trowsers, and an alkalock or vest. In winter, a close-bodied robe, reaching to the knees, is worn over the vest. This is made of velvet or *kimcob*, is fastened in front by large gold buttons, and sometimes ornamented with jewels. The head is covered with a large black turban, over which a Cashmirian shawl is gracefully thrown to answer the purpose of a veil.

The Persians hardly wear any under linen; and, among the lower classes, the clothes they once put on are seldom taken off till worn out. Nothing could preserve the health of a people with such habits, but those ablutions which are enjoined by their religion, and the

constant use of the hot baths, which are to be found in every city, town, and village of Persia.

In describing the character and manners of the Persians, it is necessary to divide them into two classes, namely, the agricultural or manufacturing class, who reside in fixed dwellings, and the wandering tribes, who subsist by their flocks, or by fishing, and live in tents.

Among the inhabitants of the various cities and towns of Persia, there are very different shades of character, which arise from the feelings and habits which they have derived from their ancestors. The natives of Tabreez, Hamadan, Shiraz, and Yezd, who are chiefly descended from martial tribes, are famed for their courage; while those of Koom, Kashan, and Ispahan, whose forefathers have for centuries pursued civil occupations, are equally remarkable for their cowardice. As a people, however, they are, generally speaking, of a lively imagination, of quick apprehension, and of agreeable and prepossessing manners. They very much resemble the French; and an inhabitant of Shiraz, except from his dress and language, could scarcely be distinguished from a Parisian. A quick and light step, a volubility of tongue, a facility at turning a compliment, a delight in saying agreeable things about nothing, and a minute care of their clothes and manner of dressing, are common to both. The higher classes of the citizens of Persia are most carefully instructed in all that belongs to exterior manner and deportment. "Nothing," says Sir John Malcolm, "can exceed their politeness; and, in their social hours, when formality is banished, their conversation is delightful. It is enlivened by anecdotes; and their narratives and observations are improved by quotations of beautiful passages from their best poets, with whose works almost every Persian who possesses any intelligence is acquainted." They are kind and indulgent masters; and the lower ranks, as far as concerns the active performance of their duties, are the best of servants. In a state of society where there are no middle classes, and where, consequently, the actual distinction between master and servant is so great as to remove all danger of either forgetting the inequality of their condition, they often live in habits of the strictest intimacy and friendship. But the Persian character is sullied by the de-

basing vices of falsehood and duplicity; and the noble system of their ancestors, whose first care it was to teach their children to speak truth, seems to be now totally forgotten. They even attempt to defend the practice, and represent it as the natural consequence of

the state of society in which they live. The violence and oppressions of their rulers, they say, must be averted by every means in their power; and when this cannot be done by combination and strength, they can only have recourse to art and deceit. The oaths which they constantly use to attest their sincerity, are only proofs of their want of it; and it is no uncommon exclamation, when all their asseverations and oaths fail to convince a stranger of their veracity, "Believe me, for, though a Persian, I am speaking truth." Though there are many exceptions to this general description, yet their numbers are too inconsiderable to save their countrymen from this national reproach. This people are subject to extraordinary ebullitions of passion, when they conduct themselves like men altogether careless of the result; but they are of such a gay and sanguine temperament, that the most violent quarrels are often succeeded by immoderate bursts of mirth. On such

occasions a stranger is surprised at the latitude of speech which this despotic government permits in those whom it oppresses. You will hear the meanest citizen venting imprecations against his superiors, not excepting even the sacred person of the king; and this will sometimes provoke only a reproof, or a few blows. An instance of this freedom of remark is given by Sir John Malcolm, in a dialogue which passed between the governor of Ispahan, and a seller of vegetables in that city, who was remonstrating against the payment of a tax which had been imposed upon him. "You must pay it, or leave the city," said the governor. "I cannot pay it, and to what other place can I go?" "You may either proceed to Shiraz or Kashan, if you like these towns better than this." "Your brother is in power at one of these cities, and your nephew at the other: what relief can I expect in either?" "You may proceed to court, and complain to the king, if you think that I have committed injustice." "Your brother, the hajee, is prime minister." "Go to hell," exclaimed the enraged ruler, and do not trouble me any more." "The holy man, your deceased father is there," said the undaunted citizen. The crowd could not suppress their smiles at the boldness of their countryman; and the governor, who shared the general feeling, bade the complainant retire, and he would attend to his case.

The females of this class are usually placed in the situation of slaves, and possess many of those qualities which belong to that condition. Their influence in society is consequently of little importance. The lower ranks regard them in proportion as they are useful in domestic duties; while the higher ranks consider them as born for their sensual gratification. Women in this country have no assigned place in the community, but are what their husbands, or rather their lords, choose to make them. Excluded from all society except the company of their own sex, their labours and amusements are confined within the walls of the harem. There, however, their occupations are often numerous and difficult. They sew, embroider, and spin; make their own clothes, and sometimes those of their husband, and superintend all the domestic concerns of the house. As a necessary preparation for conducting their household affairs, when children they are taught at school, along with the boys, to read and write; and when too old to go unveiled, their education is finished at home by a female Moollah. Music and dancing form no part of their education. These arts are taught only to slaves, who practise them for the amusement of their owners. The Persian ladies regard the bath as the place of their greatest amusement; for there they make appointments to meet, and

Statistics. often pass seven or eight hours together in the carpeted saloon, telling stories, relating anecdotes, and eating sweetmeats. There also they employ themselves in dyeing their hair and eye-brows, and in staining their bodies with fantastic devices, such as the figures of trees, animals, sun, and planets. These artificial embellishments are spread over the breast, and exposed to view. Persian mothers are generally treated with the utmost respect and kindness by their children of both sexes during life, which often gives them an importance beyond the precincts of the haram.

Houses. The houses in this country are in general mean: the exterior being mostly built of earth or mud, one story high, with flat roofs, and no windows appearing to the view of passengers. But the form of the roofs is different in some situations. At Sultanea they are of the shape of bee-hives; and in some places in Irak those of the old buildings resemble the roofs of mosques. The generality of Persian houses consist of a large square court, lined on all sides with rooms of various dimensions and uses; and this court is laid out in walks, the sides of which are planted with flowers and refreshed by fountains. Distinct from this is a smaller court, around which are the inner apartments belonging to the females of the family; and almost every dwelling has a garden attached to it. The interior apartments of the richer classes are highly superb, yet simple in every thing that may be deno-

Furniture. minated furniture. The floor is overspread with the richest carpets; and this serves for seat, bed, table, and devotional kneeling; and the custom of kneeling on their carpets at prayers gives these articles of furniture a sacred character, which forms one reason why a native of Persia never enters a room in boots or slippers, but always leaves them at the door. " This people," says Kinnear, " never recline on cushions, in the luxurious manner of the Turks, but sit in an erect posture on a thick felt, called *nummud*. They have seldom or never fires in their apartments, even in the coldest season; and in order to be warm, fold themselves in their fur pelisse, or *baroonee*. Like other oriental nations, they rise with the sun, and having dressed and said their prayers, take a cup of coffee, or perhaps some fruit. They then enter upon the business of the day, if they have any; and if not, smoke and converse until about eleven o'clock, at which time they usually have their breakfast, and then retire into the *haram*. Here they remain until about three o'clock, when they return to the hall, see company, and finish their business; for with these people the most important affairs are discussed and transacted in public. They are passionately fond of tobacco, which they smoke almost incessantly from the moment they rise until they go to rest; it constitutes, indeed, the principal source of amusement to a man of fortune; and were it not for his *kaleoon*, or water pipe, I am at a loss to imagine how he could possibly spend his time."

The Persians are all fond of society, and, from the extraordinary cheapness of provisions of every kind, their tables are generally well furnished. Wheat is the common food of the people; but the favourite dish

Food. of the rich is pillau, or boiled rice, variously dressed; and melons, fruits, and confections, form the leading articles in their entertainments. The hog is the only animal whose flesh they are positively forbidden to eat; and wine is prohibited by their religion. The wealthier classes, however, sometimes forget the law of their prophet, and as, according to their belief, " there is equal sin in a glass as in a flagon," they

usually, when they drink, indulge to excess. Their Statistics. meals are ceremonious and silent, but short, and never exceed an hour.

We extract from Mr. Morier's work the account Entertain- of an entertainment given to Sir Harford Jones, the ments. British Envoy, by Mahomed Nebee Khan, the governor of Bushire. " In the evening we dined with Mahomed Nebee Khan. We did not go till the Khan had sent to the Envoy to say, that the entertainment was ready for his reception, a custom always observed on such occasions. When we arrived at his tent," after the usual compliments, " we sat upon the ground, where the inflexibility of our knees rendered the position more difficult than can be described. The Khan, who seemed to commiserate the tightness of our pantaloons, begged that we would extend our legs at their full length: fearing, however, to be rude, we chose to be uncomfortable, and to imitate their fashion as faithfully as possible; and really, with respect to my feelings, I thought complaisance was never carried farther."—" After having sat some time, kaleoons were brought in, then coffee, then kaleoons, then sweet coffee, (so called from being a composition of rose-water and sugar;) and then kaleoons again. All this was rapidly performed, when the Khan called for dinner. On the ground before us was spread the *sofra*, a fine chintz cloth, which perfectly entrenched our legs, and which is used so long unchanged, that the accumulated fragments of former meals collect into a musty paste, and emit no very savoury smell; but the Persians are content, for they say that changing the sofra brings ill luck. A tray was then placed before each guest; on these trays were three fine china bowls, which were filled with sherbets; two made of sweet liquors, and one of a most exquisite species of lemonade. There were, besides, fruits ready cut, plates with elegant little arrangements of sweetmeats and confectionary, and smaller cups of sweet sherbet; the whole of which were placed most symmetrically, and were quite inviting, even by their appearance. In the vases of sherbet were spoons made of the pear tree, with very deep bowls, and worked so delicately, that the long handle just slightly bent when it was carried to the mouth. The *pillaus* succeeded, three of which were placed before each two guests; one of plain rice, called the *chillo*; one made of mutton, with raisins and almonds; the other of a fowl, with rich spices and plumbs. To this were added various dishes with rich sauces, and over each a small tincture of sweet sauce. Their cooking, indeed, is mostly composed of sweets. The business of eating was a pleasure to the Persians, but it was misery to us. They comfortably advanced their chins close to the dishes, and commodiously scooped the rice or other victuals into their mouths, with three fingers and thumb of their right hand; but in vain did we attempt to approach the dish; our tight-kneed breeches, and all the ligaments and buttons of our dress, forbade us; and we were forced to manage as well as we could, fragments of meat and rice falling through our fingers all around us. When we were all satisfied, dinner was carried away with the same state in which it was brought; the servant who officiated, dropping himself gracefully on one knee as he carried away the trays, and passing them expertly over his head with both his hands, extended to the lacquey, who was ready behind to carry them off. We were treated with more kaleoons after dinner, and then departed." In an account of

Statistics. another entertainment, he says, "When the whole is cleared, and the cloths rolled up, ewers and basins are brought in, and every one washes his hand and mouth. Until the water is presented, it is ridiculous enough to see the right hand of every person (which is covered with the complicated fragments of all the dishes) placed in a certain position over his left arm: there is a fashion even in this."

Visits. In Persian visits the knowledge of etiquette is the only knowledge displayed. When visited by a superior, the Persian rises hastily, and meets his guest nearly at the door of the apartment; on the entrance of an equal, he just raises himself from his seat, and stands nearly erect; but to an inferior he makes the motion only of rising. In sitting, there is the same attention to ceremony; and he sits on his heels, or cross-legged, or in any other manner, according to the rank of the company in which he happens to be present. A common visit generally consists of three parts; first, the kaleoon and coffee; second, a kaleoon and sweet coffee; and third, a kaleoon by itself. Sweetmeats are frequently introduced at the conclusion. This practice is so uniform, and so jealous are they of their character for hospitality, that going out of a house without smoking a kaleoon, or taking any other refreshment, is deemed a high affront.

Wandering tribes. The character of the wandering tribes is very opposite to that of the other inhabitants of Persia. They are sincere, hospitable, and brave. They stand not in need of falsehood and deceit, and therefore are not in the habit of practising them; but they are rude, violent, and rapacious; and if the vices of their condition be fewer than those of the inhabitants of cities, this evidently arises from their ignorance of luxury and refinement, and the absence of temptation; for it is remarked that they never settle in towns without exceeding the inhabitants in every species of profligacy. These tribes receive the common appellation of Illiats. They constitute the military force, and their chiefs the hereditary nobility of the empire. They derive their

Their origin. origin from different nations: the Turkish from Turkistan, or Tartary; the Arabs from Arabia, and the original tribes of Persia, consisting of Kurdish, Lac, Zund, and many others. Many of them speak the language, and preserve the manners of their Scythian ancestors; and each tribe has its records, and pretends to trace its genealogy to the first generation. The Baktyari, Fielhi, and Kujurs, are the most ancient and renowned, and are probably the descendants of those ferocious bands who inhabited the country in the days of Alexander. A certain portion of land seems to have been allotted to each tribe for the pasturage of their flocks. These districts, from long and undisputed possession, are considered the property of the different chiefs; and the lines of demarcation have been strictly observed from the most remote ages. The Baktyari, who form the best infantry in the kingdom, and the Fielhi, pitch their tents in the fertile districts of Laristan; the Affshars in Aderbijan, near the lake of Oormia; the Kujurs, of whom the present king is the head, are in possession of Asterabad and Mazenderan; and the Karagoozoloo, or black-eyed tribe, who are esteemed the finest horsemen, inhabit the plains of Hamadan. It would be in vain to enumerate all the other tribes, as they are so subdivided that some of them do not exceed a thousand families. This people, for the most part, lead Manners. a pastoral life, and subsist principally on the produce of their flocks. They change their residence with

the season, pitching their dark tents during winter Statistics. in the plains, on the banks of a rivulet or a stream, and in summer on the summits and declivities of the mountains. Their tents are walled with mats, and Habitations. covered with a coarse kind of black cloth, manufactured by themselves; and the abode of the chief is only distinguished by its size from that of the lowest member of the tribe. Their encampments are generally formed in a square; the horses, mules, and sheep, are turned loose to feed; and while the women are employed in their domestic duties, or assisting the aged men and boys in tending the flocks, the young men, if not engaged in hunting, or in practising military exercises, are commonly seen sitting in circles, smoking or indulging in repose. Several of the tribes during winter settle in villages; and in Dahistan and the northern parts of Khorassan, instead of tents, they dwell in small portable wooden houses. Besides the dark coverings of their tents, they manufacture several other small articles for their own use; and the most beautiful Persian and Turkish carpets, so much admired in Europe, are the works of this wandering people. Inured from their infancy to dangers and fatigue, they are most tenacious of the honour of their tribe, and at the same time constitute the defence and glory of the empire. Each tribe is divided into branches, and each branch has a particular leader, all of whom, however, are subservient to the chief. These chiefs affect a kind of independence, and measure their deference to the authority of the monarch by their existing situation; their submission or resistance being always determined by the weakness or strength of his power. From their birth and influence they are the first men in the empire. They are mutually hostile and jealous; and the king, by fomenting their quarrels, and nicely balancing the power of the one against that of the other, insures his own safety and the peace of his dominions. During peace they usually reside with their families at court, or at the capitals of the provinces, and leave their followers, whom they occasionally visit, to the direction of the chiefs next in rank. They are thus regarded as hostages for the fidelity of their tribe; and when allowed to retire, the son is detained as security for the good conduct of the father. Being thus brought up at court, they are well educated, and polished in their manners; and, except in being more haughty, are not materially different from the other nobles and principal officers of the country. But the majority of their tribes continue in a state of the most degraded ignorance. Professing the Mahomedan religion, they circumcise their children at the proper age; and contract marriages according to the prescribed customs; but they receive no religious instruction, and are consequently ignorant and neglectful of what their law enjoins. They are all plunderers, and even glory in admitting that they are so; but they make a distinction between plundering and theft, which last they pretend to hold in abhorrence. The one, they say, is the application of force, which implies strength, and the other of fraud, which is an evidence of weakness. They are, however, remarkable for their hospitality to strangers; and their word, when once pledged, is inviolable. A hard black bread, sour milk, and Food. curds, constitute their general diet. They sometimes feast upon meat; and now and then, though not often, indulge in intoxicating liquors. They are passionately Love of romantic fond of listening to romantic tales and national songs. tales. Many an idle hour is thus spent; and the person who has cultivated this talent enjoys a great share of the

Statistics. respect of his associates. He can excite their minds to deeds of valour, by merely repeating some of the lines of Ferdosi which celebrate the renown of their ancestors; and there are instances in the history of this people, of an adventurer collecting many thousand followers, and maintaining his authority over them, by continuing to sing some favourite provincial air. The females of these wandering hordes enjoy more freedom and respect than the other women of Persia; and though they may be inferior to the natives of cities in beauty of person and softness of manners, they are superior to them in industry, in chastity, and many other virtues. They are held in more consideration, by being more useful to the community. If they are not of high rank, they perform all the domestic and menial offices; and strangers who visit their tents are certain to receive from them the kindest and most hospitable welcome. But there is nothing in their manner that can be mistaken; it is fearless but not forward; and evidently proceeds from the consciousness of security, not the absence of shame. They not only share the bed, but the fatigues and dangers, of their husbands. The masculine habits which they thus acquire do not displease, for they seem suited to their condition of life. Though, in general, their complexion is dark and sun-burnt, they have sometimes, when young, a considerable share of beauty: a sense of their free condition gives lustre to their eyes; and they often add to fine features a very graceful form. The veil is seldom used by them, but their beauty is soon destroyed by hard labour and continual exposure to the climate. Among the lower orders of these tribes, poverty and custom confine them in general to one wife. They cannot afford to support more, and unless she is old, barren, or unfit to work, they seldom marry another. The greatest respect is paid to maternal claims; and the influence of a mother over her son continues through life. It is her duty to preside over his family; and if he is rich, he usually intrusts to her not only the choice of his female partners, but their management. An anticipation of the enjoyment of this power makes the women of Persia anxiously desirous of having male children. The birth of a son is hailed with joy, while that of a daughter is always a disappointment.

Women of this class.

Arabian tribes. The Arabian tribes, who inhabit the shores of the Persian Gulf, are more assimilated in their habits to the people from which they are derived than to those among whom they dwell. They continue to use the language, and to preserve the dress and customs, of their original country. Their diet is chiefly *dates*, of which they are particularly fond. Though less rude in manners than the other tribes of Persia, they retain much of the wildness and independence of their ancestors.

Marriages. The natives of Persia are restrained by religious considerations from marrying more than four wives; but as they conceive themselves entitled to an unlimited indulgence in the pleasures of the haram, they often increase the number of females in their family to any extent that may suit their inclination or convenience; and according to law and usage this may be done either by purchase or by hire. Their marriages are conducted through the mediation of the parents; and though the female, according to the Mahomedan law, may refuse her consent when the priest comes to require it, yet this rarely happens, as the parties never see one another before they are united. The marriage ring is sent in due form; and presents are exchanged between the families. The bride is conducted to the house of her husband, attended by all her friends, and accompanied by dancers and music; and the bridegroom receives them arrayed in all the finery that his circumstances can obtain. In the marriage feast, a ruinous spirit of emulation drives many to exceed their means; and it is not unusual for a man to waste all that he has spent his life in acquiring on his wedding day. These feasts, among persons of rank, are protracted to thirty or forty days. The observance of the established forms require three at least. On the first the company are assembled: on the second the important ceremony of staining the hand with a red dye: and the third is appropriated to the nuptials. The great point in the marriage-contract is the settlement of the dower, which is made payable from the property of the husband, and is assigned over to the female or her friends before the consummation of the marriage. It becomes her entire right; and though she may exonerate her husband from any part, or even from the whole of it, yet this seldom occurs, as it constitutes the principal part of her provision in the event of her husband's death, and her sole dependence if she is divorced. Divorce, however, is of rare occurrence among this people. A Persian can institute such a proceeding at pleasure; but the expence and scandal of it renders it very unfrequent. A man of rank would consider himself disgraced by taking a step which would expose a woman who had been his wife, to be seen by others; and the difficulty of paying the dower prevents the poorer classes from having recourse to it. In the case of adultery, the woman subjects herself to capital punishment.

Statistics.

Divorce.

Among the citizens of Persia, temporary marriages are very common, in which the parties agree to live together for a fixed period, which varies from a few days to ninety-nine years. The sum agreed upon as the woman's hire, is inserted in a contract, which is legally drawn, and regularly witnessed. This contract may be dissolved by the man when he chooses, but in such a case the other party has a right to the whole amount of her hire. If the parties are willing, the deed is renewed at the period when it expires. This species of legal concubinage, however, usually takes place between persons of very unequal rank, and the woman is generally of a very inferior family. It is customary with the higher classes to purchase female slaves in considerable numbers, some of whom are appropriated to the haram, and others to the service of their wives; but, whether as servants or as sharers of their master's bed, they are alike subject to be sold again. That jealous sense of honour, however, which all Mahomedans entertain regarding females with whom they have cohabited, renders such a circumstance very uncommon.

Temporary marriages.

The funerals of the Persians are conducted with great pomp, especially among the rich. The procession is accompanied by the favourite charger of the departed warrior, carrying his arms and clothes; his boots are laid across the saddle; his cap is placed on the pique; and the *shal-kemer*, or cloth with which he girded his loins, is bound round the horse's neck. Those who desire to show their respect, send a led horse, with arms upon the saddle, to swell the mourning train of the deceased; and his memory is preserved by the erection of a splendid tomb.

Funerals.

To Persia belongs the disgrace of having introduced the use of eunuchs, and of having employed them as guardians of the purity of the haram. It is at least certain that they were as numerous and powerful at

Eunuchs.

Statistics. the ancient court of Persepolis as at the modern courts of Ispahan and Teheran. They were promoted to the first stations in the kingdom. They exercised a commanding influence in the state, and though, since the accession of the reigning family, they are very seldom employed beyond the walls of the haram, yet such as are in situations of trust are treated with uncommon attention and deference.

Amusements. Among all ranks, illuminations, fire-works, musicians, dancing-boys, wrestlers, jugglers, buffoons, and puppet-shows, are the prevailing amusements at public feasts; and riding upon horseback, walking in gardens, and sitting in groups in their houses, or under the shade of a tree, listening to a tale or a poem, are the usual occupations of their idle hours. Dancing girls were formerly introduced at every entertainment for the amusement of the guests; but at present they are not allowed at court, and are seldom seen except in the provinces at a distance from the capital.

Dexterity in riding. The higher classes in Persia never walk on foot; and as there are no wheeled carriages among them, except one or two, in the possession of the royal family, which are kept merely as specimens of European manufacture, their usual mode of travelling is upon horseback. Their women are conveyed in portable pavilions, placed on camels, or suspended between two mules. A Persian in a manner lives upon horseback, and cannot make a visit of ceremony without his charger, however inconsiderable the distance; and thus, by constant practice, he acquires a firm seat, a dexterity in the management of his horse, and a fearlessness of danger, that appears extraordinary to strangers. He rides without the least apprehension over any country, climbs the most dangerous steeps over rock and shrub, and keeps his way in defiance of every obstacle of ground. Indeed, he holds it as a fact, that a horse will find footing wherever a man can do the same. The present heir-apparent, who is governor of Aderbijan, will at full gallop shoot a deer with a single ball; or with an arrow from his bow hit a bird on the wing.

Government. The king. Perhaps no country has undergone so many revolutions as Persia, yet the nature of its government has never changed. From the most early ages, the word of the king has been deemed a law, and no monarch in the world rules with more arbitrary sway. He is absolute master of the lives and property of his subjects, and is under no restraint in the exercise of his powers, but what arises from his regard for religion, his respect for established usages, his desire of reputation, and his fear of exciting an opposition that might be dangerous to his power or his life. His family, ministers, judges, and officers of every rank, he can punish without examination, or formal procedure of any kind whatever. The general maxim is, that the king is completely exempt from responsibility; and it would be treason to affirm that he is amenable to any check but what may be imposed by his own prudence or conscience. But though the monarch may be considered as vested with authority independent of all law, yet in all capital cases among his subjects in general, where he does not personally decide, or delegate his arbitrary authority to another, the forms prescribed by law and custom are observed; and he only confirms the sentence, or pardons the criminal. The character of the Persian monarchs has often been exhibited by travellers as most tyrannical, and as reckless of the rights and lives of others. But if we consider the circumstances of their situation, and the manner in which they are educated, we should be surprised to find them possess-

ed of mercy and humanity, though these were their Statistics. natural dispositions. Ruling over reluctant tributaries, who acknowledge their authority only by compulsion, and mountain tribes who subsist chiefly by plunder; and surrounded by ambitious nobles, eager to establish their independence, their power, to be efficient, must be dreaded, and the impression of terror is necessary to secure submission. Besides, the princes of this country are accustomed, from their infancy, to the sight of human suffering. Their instructors, as if apprehensive that an indulgence in tender feelings should interfere with the performance of their future duties, carry them to witness scenes at which most men would shudder. These early lessons are uniformly successful. The habit of directing and witnessing executions must, in the course of time, harden the heart; and there is hardly one instance, in the history of this country, of a Persian king showing any uncommon degree of humanity, while there are many to prove, that by a brutal indulgence in the shedding of blood, human beings appear to lose that rank and character which belong to their species. In general they have recognised no limit to their oppressions but the apprehension of revolt; and have only measured their indulgence in pleasure by their power of enjoying it. A sovereign of Persia considers nothing as obligatory upon him but his religion; and all of them have been punctual observers of the forms of the faith which they professed. His personal His duties. duties are numerous and burdensome. He appears in public from six to seven hours every day; and is accessible to a great number of his subjects of all ranks. Early in the morning he is attended by the principal ministers and secretaries, who make reports upon what has occurred, and receive his commands. He next proceeds to his public levee, which continues about an hour and a half, and at which all affairs which are wished to be made public are transacted. When this is over, he adjourns to the council-chamber, where one or two hours are given to his personal favourites and ministers; and then retires to his inner apartments. In the evening he transacts business with his ministers and principal officers of state.

In the administration of the government, the king is His ministers. assisted by his two prime ministers, the *Vizier Azem*, or Grand Vizier, and the *Ameen a Doulah*, or Lord High Treasurer. To the former is committed the charge of every thing connected with foreign relations, and he even commands the armies in the absence of the king or prince. The latter attends principally to the internal arrangement of the empire, such as the collection of the revenues, and the cultivation of the lands. The whole Executive of the executive government is in the hands of these government. two men, and under them is a regular gradation of ment. subordinate officers, who fill situations in the household, army, and revenue departments. While they remain in power, their authority is without control; but they are dependent from hour to hour upon the favour of their master, not only for the authority which they exercise, but for the preservation of their property and their lives. Their danger increases with their charge; and their time is incessantly occupied in personal attendance upon the sovereign, in the intricacies of private intrigue, or the toils of public business. It is seldom, indeed, that they do not, sooner or later, experience a reverse of fortune. Their great object consequently is, to secure the confidence of the monarch; and their very condition often compels them to practise habits of subserviency and dissimulation. They are always men of polished manners, well-skilled in business, and of very acute observation; and are generally exalted to their high situations on account of the reputation they have attained in inferior offices. As these stations are never filled by men of high birth and rank, whose downfall might excite a spirit of discontent and turbulence among their vassals and adherents, the disgrace and execution of a minister creates no sensation among the people. From the prime minister to the lowest dependant on the government, there is a regular gradation of despotism and slavery; the inferior officers depending no less upon the favour of the prime minister than he upon the king.

Governors. The administration of the provinces is committed to officers, who receive the title of *Beglerbeg*. These situations are at present chiefly filled by the king's sons, who have their residence in the capital of the province. Under them are the *Hakim* and *Thaubet*, who severally govern a city or a town; and the *Ket-Khoda*, who is the chief of a village. Besides these is the *Kelounter*, who in every city, town, and village, superintends the collection of the tribute. This person is of considerable consequence. He is an officer of the crown, and once a-year appears in the royal presence. He is the representative of the people on all occasions. Through him their wishes and wants are made known to the king; and he brings forward the complaints of the *Rayats*, or peasants, whenever they feel oppressed. The Kelounter and Ket-Khoda must necessarily be selected from the most respectable natives of the city or village where they are to reside; and though nominated by the king, yet the wishes of the inhabitants are generally consulted upon the occasion. The character of the Beglerbegs is in general formed upon that of the reigning sovereign. The rapacity and tyranny of the one must be upheld by that of the other. However irreproachable their conduct, they know that they cannot escape the accusation of injustice and mal-administration; and unless they can satisfy the demands and avarice of the court, their punishment is certain. Aware, at the same time, that if they can only answer these demands, no inquiry will be made respecting the manner in which the money has been acquired, they have recourse to the Hakims; and they, in their turn, to the Ket-Khodas and cultivators of land. Thus a regular system of venality and extortion pervades every class, from the throne to the cottage, and the laws of order, justice, and propriety, are almost uniformly violated.

Titles. The vain love of high-sounding titles prevails in all Mahomedan governments; and, in many, this shadow of grandeur is retained after the substance has fled. One of the most common titles of the Persian monarch, and by which he is usually addressed by his subjects, is *Kebleh-Alum*. *Kebleh* is the point to which all Mahomedans turn in prayer, and *Alum* signifies the world. He is also entitled *Zil Allah*, or "Shadow of the Almighty," and *Jellal-u-Doula-ul-Deen*, "the glory of the state, and of religion;" and all his edicts are signed "by him whom the universe obeys." His arms are a lion couchant, and the sun rising at his back, which is intended to represent Sol in the constellation Leo. This device is embroidered upon all the Persian banners, and has been converted into a national order, which is conferred upon those who distinguish themselves against the enemies of their country. The common military title in Persia is *Khan*, or Lord, and civil one *Mirza*, or son of a nobleman. All chiefs of tribes are entitled to the appellation of Khan, and it is also generally bestowed upon the oldest son; but younger sons seldom receive it unless they are enrolled in the king's guards, or have performed some service. This title is creative, and is attended with few ceremonies. The king sends a *kalaat*, or dress of honour, to the person so created, and gives him a *firman*, announcing to all that the bearer is forthwith a Khan. This firman is worn three days on the top of the turban, and any person who derides this patent, or refuses to call the bearer of it by his title, is liable to the penalty of death. *Mirza* is a hereditary title, and descends to all the sons of the family without exception. It is always prefixed to the name, except in cases of the princes of the blood-royal, when it is placed after it. This appellation, however, is also conferred upon all who fill any office in the civil departments of government; and then it denotes merely a civilian, or man of business. This class are very numerous, and are usually distinguished by wearing a *kullumdan*, or small case which contains pens and ink, in their girdle.

Laws. The written law of this country, as in all states which have embraced the religion of Mahomed, is founded upon the Koran and the traditions, and is termed *Sherrah*; and in every government, strictly Mahomedan, the distribution of justice ought to be according to this law, and administered only by the priests. But the Persians, though they embraced the faith of the prophet, have retained many of the laws and usages of their forefathers, and have established another code of jurisprudence, called *Urf*, or customary law. This is administered by the secular magistrates, who decide in all cases according to precedent or custom. This law is never written, and varies in different parts of the empire, because it has reference to local as well as common usages. The prevalence of either of these codes depends entirely upon the disposition of the monarch. In the reign of Sultan Hussein, the religious zeal of the sovereign made all cases be decided according to the Sherrah; and in that of Nadir Shah the whole authority was vested in the secular magistrates. At present the decisions of ecclesiastical judges are limited to disputes about religious ceremonies, inheritance, marriage, divorce, contracts, sales, and all civil cases; while, in the Courts of Urf are instituted, all proceedings respecting murder, theft, fraud, and every crime that is capital, or that can be called a breach of the public peace.

Judges.

Court of Sherrah. The supreme judge of the Court of Sherrah is called *Scheik-ul-Islam*, or "Chief of the Faith," of which there is one in every principal city. He receives his appointment, and also a liberal salary, from the king. Under him are the *Cauzee* or judge, and the *Mufti*, whose duty it is to prepare an exposition of the case before the court, and to aid with his advice. All difficult cases, however, are submitted to the *Mooshtaheds*, an order of priests who exercise a great though undefined power over the Courts of Sherrah. These men receive no appointment, and have no specific duties to discharge; but from their superior learning, piety, and virtue, are chosen by the silent but unanimous suffrage of the inhabitants to be their guides in religion, and their protectors against the oppression of their rulers. There are seldom more than three or four priests exalted to this dignity in Persia. Their conduct is expected to be most exemplary, and their character unstained by any worldly bias. They are regarded with the greatest respect and veneration both by the king and the people; and even their habitations are deemed sanctuaries for the oppressed. The royal ear is always open to a revered Mooshtahed, when he becomes an intercessor for the

Statistics. guilty; and a city is often spared because a Mooshtahed has chosen it for his residence, and refuses to dwell in the midst of violence and injustice.

Urf, or customary law.

The Urf, or customary law, is administered by the king, his lieutenants, governors of cities, and other law magistrates. In the capital, the king himself daily sits in judgment; and he alone possesses the power of life and death. This power is never delegated to an inferior judge, unless in the time of a rebellion, or when the government is committed to one of the blood-royal. All the proceedings are conducted in open court; the decisions are summary, but not always consonant to justice; and though a suit is attended with little apparent cost, yet considerable sums are often given in bribes.

Punishments.

The punishments inflicted are most barbarous: strangling, decapitation, and stabbing, are the common modes of putting criminals to death; but in cases of enormity, when an impression of terror is to be made, or a passion of revenge to be gratified, there is no measure to their inventive cruelty. Mr. Jukes mentions the case of a slave, who, having attempted to poison the family whom he served, was sentenced to be hung by the heels in the common market-place and to be cut up in the same manner as a butcher does the carcass of a sheep; but he was denied the mercy shown to that animal, of having his throat cut before he was quartered. Rebels are burned alive, or sawed in two. Robbers are impaled, or have their limbs torn asunder by the elastic rebound of the branches of trees; and Mr. Kinnear mentions that he saw four thieves built into a wall, all but their heads, and thus left to perish. The lesser penalties are deprivation of sight, mutilation of the ears, nose, or hands, and the bastinado on the soles of the feet.

System of judicature among the wandering tribes.

Among the wandering tribes the system of judicature differs materially from that established in towns. The elders, with the Moollah, or priest of the tribe, whose duty it is to expound, when required, the holy law, form a council, where all questions of importance are fully discussed and decided by a majority of voices. In common cases, however, the chief or his deputy passes judgment in a similar manner as the lay magistrate of a city; and though they are in general careful to preserve the attachment of their followers, yet they are sometimes both cruel and oppressive. Among this class, a murderer, when the crime is proved, is given up to the heir of the deceased, who may either forgive, or take the price of blood, or put him to death. But the great object of the council is to compound for this crime, especially when the parties belong to different tribes; for if this is prevented, and the offender is screened from justice, the heirs of the deceased feel disgraced until they can obtain revenge. The most bloody feuds are often the consequence, and these are handed down from generation to generation. Should the chief of a tribe commit any open act of treason, the king, if he can seize him, deprives him of sight, or puts him to death; but, if he has merited capital punishment for any other crime, his case is referred to the Court of Sherrah, that his blood may not rest upon the monarch.

Revenue.

The revenue of Persia amounts to nearly six millions Sterling, and is derived from the following sources: the *Maleeat* or "fixed revenue," the *Sadir*, or "contribution," and the *Peish-Kesh*, or "voluntary gift."

Fixed revenue.

The Maleeat is formed chiefly from the produce of the crown and government lands, from taxes upon the Statistics. landed property of individuals, and upon every species of goods and merchandize. The government lands are generally cultivated by the peasantry of the province, and, after deducting the seed, and ten per cent. for the expences of reaping and thrashing, the remainder is equally divided between the king and the cultivator. Lands that are private property are taxed according to their situation in respect to water. When that is obtained from a flowing stream, after the above deductions, 20 per cent. is demanded; when from an aqueduct, 15 per cent.; and when from wells or reservoirs, only 5. According to the general and established rule, these duties are paid half in money and half in kind. But that depends often upon the wealth of the cultivator, as some who are poor pay the whole in kind; while others prefer making cash payments, by which they avoid the vexatious interference of the subordinate officers of the revenue. Twenty per cent. is also levied upon the sale of all vegetables, fruits, and lesser productions, besides the tax upon fruit trees and vines, which varies according to the age of the tree and the quality of the fruit. Vineyards, which have certain water, pay 6 *dinars** per vine; and those with uncertain water, five. Apple, pear, peach, &c. pay 20 dinars per tree, and walnuts 100. A considerable part of the Maleeat is derived from ground rents of houses, rents of caravansaries, baths, shops, water-mills, manufactures, and duties upon all kinds of foreign and home merchandize. Whole streets, in the principal cities, are the property of government, and are rented by its subjects. If shops, the rent is fixed in proportion to the gains of the possessor; but, if private property, the crown claims 20 per cent. upon the annual profits. To the wandering tribes arable lands are granted on very favourable terms; but they only cultivate what is necessary for their own consumption. The vast tracts of fine pasture, which they occupy, are considered as part payment of their military service; and a tax is levied upon each family according to its substance, which is collected by their chief or his deputy.

A milch cow pays annually	300 dinars.
An ass, . . .	200
A brood-mare, . .	1000
A camel, . . .	300
A sheep, . .	100

The principles upon which the Maleeat is collected are just and moderate; and the system is seldom attended either with difficulty or oppression. But this makes the inhabitants feel more keenly those irregular and oppressive exactions to which they are continually exposed.

Contributions.

The Sadir, or "contribution," is the most arbitrary and grievous. It denotes that description of taxation which is raised to provide for emergencies; and is demanded when the king desires to build a palace, or when one of the royal family is married, or when an addition is to be made to the army, or when troops are marching through the country, or on any extraordinary occasion whatever: and it is laid upon the whole kingdom, or on a particular province, according to its general or local application. The levying of this impost admits of every species of extortion. The collectors of districts are required to supply a certain sum; but the means of doing so are left to their own discretion;

* There are five hundred *dinars* in an English shilling.

Statistics.they are permitted to add on their own profit whatever they can farther exact. As these offices are bought and sold, the rate of oppression is regulated by the amount of the purchase: and every minor agent accomplishes his appointed task without any control but his own conscience.

Voluntary gifts. The Peish-Kesh, or "voluntary gift," consists of those presents which are made annually to the king by all governors, chiefs of tribes, ministers, and officers of rank, at the festival of the Nouroze, or vernal equinox. This custom has existed in Persia from the most early times. The amount is regulated by usage, and according to the wealth of the individual, and the nature of the office which he holds. Mr. Morier states, that the Peish-Kesh of the governor of Ispahan, who was also minister of Finance, amounted, in 1808, to one hundred thousand *tomauns*, which is equal to nearly three hundred and thirty thousand pounds sterling. To exceed the usual amount is increase of favour, but to fall short is loss of office. This branch of revenue is nearly equal to two-fifths of the fixed revenue of the kingdom. The receipts of the government greatly exceed the disbursements. To amass wealth has always been the policy of Asiatic despots; for where there is no public credit, a full treasury is deemed essential to the security of the state.

Army. The army of Persia comprises a considerable body of irregular horse; a numerous militia, and a corps of regular infantry and artillery, besides the king's body Cavalry. guard. The irregular cavalry are furnished by the wandering tribes, and commanded by their own chiefs. Each chief is obliged to supply a quota proportionate to the number of his tribe. Their arms consist of a scimitar, a brace of pistols, a carabine, and sometimes a lance, or a bow and arrow, all of which they alternately use at full speed, with the utmost skill and dexterity. They still preserve the mode of fighting of their forefathers; and, like their Parthian ancestors, take their aim at the enemy when apparently flying from his attack. This class of the army may amount to eighty thousand men. They perform military service in return for grants of land and liberty of pasture; and when employed, receive a small annual pay, with provisions for Militia. themselves and horses. The militia are raised and maintained by the provinces and principal cities, and is equally formed from the wandering tribes and the inhabitants of the cities and villages. They are liable to be called out on any emergency, but receive pay only when acting with the army or in distant garrisons. Their arms, which consist of a matchlock, a sabre, and a dagger; and their clothing, which is the common dress of the country, they provide at their own expence. The number of this registered militia is stated to exceed one hundred and fifty thousand men. The regular infantry and artillery amount to twenty thousand. They are disciplined after the European manner, and are clothed, armed, and paid, by government. King's body The king's body guard does not exceed three or four guard. thousand troopers, who are termed, by way of distinction, *Gholams*, or royal slaves. They are well equipped, and paid at the public expence, and are formed promiscuously from Georgian slaves, and the sons of the first nobles in Persia. They are in constant attendance on his majesty, and are more feared and respected than any other troops in his service. A few *zumbooruks*, or camel swivels, with some small fieldpieces, are their only artillery. The Persians, however, know nothing of the modern science of war, and are Statistics. entirely ignorant of fortification; and, however well adapted for predatory warfare, it can never be supposed that an army without a regular system of payment, and led by officers without experience, can ever prove formidable to their neighbours.

The Persians have few fortified towns, and though they have the complete command of an ample gulf, with the mouths of the Euphrates and Tigris, yet they do not possess one ship of war. Nadir Shah built a royal navy, and had one vessel of eighty guns, but the Persian Navy. fleet fell with the death of that usurper; and even the maritime trade of this country is now conducted by foreign vessels. The most lucrative part of this trade was Trade. formerly carried on by Ormus and Gombroon, but that is now discontinued, having been ruined by their perpetual wars. At present, however, the imports by the Persian Gulf may be estimated at the annual amount of half a million Sterling. These consist of rice, sugar, and cotton; Bengal muslins; spiceries from Ceylon and the Moluccas; white and blue coarse linen from Coromandel; cardamon, pepper, and Indian drugs; woollen cloths, cutlery, and other European goods. Two-thirds are brought by the English, and the rest by the Moors, Indians, Arabians, and Armenians. The exports to India are, tobacco, all sorts of fruits pickled and preserved, wines, distilled waters, horses, Persian feathers, and Turkey leather of all sorts and colours. To Turkey they send tobacco, galls, thread, goats hair, stuffs, mats, box-work, &c. The specie which they receive for the silks of Ghilan, and the wool of Caramania, pays for the shawls of Cashmere, and the woollens of England. From Astracan they receive cutlery, woollen cloths, watches, jewellery, and fire-arms; for which they give in return bullion, raw silk, pearls, shawls, carpets, wine, and horses. Persia, has, however, been at no time a commercial country; and the trifling trade which it now enjoys, is principally carried on by Armenians, a most industrious and respectable people, who are found in all the commercial towns in the empire, while the natives attend chiefly to their horses and the chase, neither improving their own property nor the resources of their country.

The coins current in this kingdom are mostly foreign. Money. Among these are the Turkish piastre, the ducat, and the venetian. The tomaun, which is worth nearly three pounds seven shillings Sterling, is the coin of greatest amount, except a very large piece, value one thousand tomauns, which the king has struck for the luxury and magnificence of his own treasury. The following table will show the value of the different denominations of money at present in use. It may be observed, however, that all accounts are kept in dinars and piastres, and that those in italics have only a nominal existence.

5 *Dinars*	= 1 *Ghauz.*
20 *Dinars*	= 1 Beestee.
50 *Dinars*	= 1 Shahee.*
20 Shahee	= 1 Groush = 1 Piastre.
10 Piastres	= 1 Tomaun.
2 Shahee	= 1 Mamooda.
2 Mamoodas	= 1 Abassee.
50 *Abassee*	= 1 Tomaun.
24 *Shahee*	= 1 Real or Rupee.
100,000 Rupees	= 1 Lack.

The principal Persian gold weight is the miscal, equal Weights 72 English grains; and the common commercial weight and measures. is the maund, of which there are several, viz.

---

* The present shahee is equal to three shahees of the table, and its increased value is owing to the rise of silver.

Statistics.

The Maund Tabriz   =   6⅔ lbs. avoirdupoise.
The Maund Shah   =   13½ lbs.
The Maund Corpora   =   7⅔ lbs.
The Maund of Chervy =   12.342 lbs.

The lineal measures are the large *guerze* or *arish*, equal to 38.71 English inches; and the *pic*, which is in general use, is 24.831 inches. The *parsang*, or Persian league, is equal to three English geographical miles. The *artuba*, or *ardub*, is the corn measure, which is divided into 25 *capichas*, 50 *chenicas*, or 200 *sextarios*, and is equal to 1.849 Winchester bushels; and the *legana*, or liquid measure, which contains 30 chenicas, or 120 sextarios, is equal 10⅓ English wine gallons.

Language.
Zend.

The most early dialect in Persia was the *Zend*, in which the Zenda-vesta, or sacred books of Zoroaster, were written. It has been maintained that this language was spoken in Aderbijan; but it is more probable that it never was a vulgar, but always a sacred language, like the Sanskrit. The next in antiquity is

Pehlevi.

the *Pehlevi*, or the idiom of heroes and warriors, which seems to have prevailed in Irak, and was the language of the court during the reigns of the Kaianian dynasty. Except the sacred books, (which were also translated into Pehlevi,) all works written in Persia prior to the Mahomedan conquest were in this dialect. By degrees, however, the Pehlevi was super-

Parsee.

seded by the *Parsee*, or dialect of Farsistan; and this in its turn was banished from the court by the Arabians. The Parsee was again restored by the Dilemee princes about the middle of the tenth century; and in course of time assumed its present form, which is so mixed with Pehlevi and Arabic, that it is difficult to separate the words that belong to these several languages. At the present day it is perhaps the most celebrated of all the oriental tongues for strength, variety, and harmony; but it is now giving way in the north of Persia, and even in Teheran the capital, to

Deri.

the ruder language of the Turks. The *Deri* dialect is often mentioned by Persian authors; but this term is supposed to signify only the most polished idiom of the common language of the country; and in that sense may equally apply to the Pehlevi, the Parsee, or the

Literature.

modern Persian. In general, the literature of this country approaches nearer to the European in solidity and clearness of thought and expression, than that of any other Asiatic nation. The oldest remains of Persian literature is the famous Shah Namah of Ferdosi.

Poetry.

This noble epic poem abounds with numerous passages of exquisite beauty, which would not disgrace the most eminent classic authors. Among the didactic poets, Safi ranks the highest; and Hafiz is the Anacreon of

Romances.

the east. Some of the Persian romances are exceedingly beautiful; but the greater number of their entertaining stories are known only from oral tradition. Story-telling has become an art in this country, which is attended both with profit and reputation. It, however, requires considerable talent and great study; and none can arrive at eminence in this profession, unless he possess a cultivated taste and a retentive memory. The monarch has always a story-teller in attendance, to amuse his leisure hours, to sooth his mind when disturbed with the toils of public affairs, or to beguile the fatigue of a long march; and the same tale is not allowed at any time to be repeated on pain of punishment. Poetry and romance are in fact the favourite studies among all ranks; and the finest passages of

Music and painting.

their best writers are repeated and relished by the lowest classes of the people. In music and painting, how-

ever, they have made very little progress. Their strains,

Statistics.

though often pleasing, are always monotonous, and are greatly deficient in variety of expression; and their pictures, though excelling in brilliancy of colouring, are gaudy and insipid. They are very successful in taking likenesses; but they have not the slightest idea of perspective, and very little of light and shade. Their

Histories.

historical compositions are not entitled to much consideration. They are in general written in an inflated style, and full of exaggeration and embellishment. And this character of them will not surprise us, when we are informed that a historiographer is retained by each king for the express purpose of transmitting to posterity the glory of his own exploits. The sciences are very

Sciences.

little understood in this country. They have a limited knowledge of mathematics and algebra; and they study astronomy chiefly from its connection with judicial

Astronomy.

astrology,—a science in which all ranks have the greatest faith. They are, however, totally ignorant of the Newtonian system, and follow the system of Ptolemy, both with respect to the motions of the heavenly bodies, and the shape and surface of the earth. Chemistry, in

Chemistry.

like manner, is studied only as a step to the occult science of alchemy; but the modern discoveries in that science are unknown in Persia. They are equally

Medicine.

ignorant of medicine and surgery, being totally unacquainted with anatomy and the circulation of the blood. Their physicians have a high idea of their own talents, and superstitiously adhere to their favourite theory, however opposed by the known practice of Europeans. They class all diseases and remedies under four heads, hot, cold, moist, and dry; and the great principle of their system is to apply a remedy of a quality opposite to the disease. Their skill consequently consists in ascertaining to which of the classes the disease belongs, and the remedy follows of course.

Though the sciences and learning have made but lit-

Education

tle progress, yet education is exceedingly cheap, and the knowledge of the simpler branches of learning are very generally diffused among all ranks. There are schools in every town and city of Persia, where the rudiments of the Persic and Arabic languages are taught; and the fees are sufficiently reasonable to admit the children of the poorest tradesmen. There are also *madrassas* or colleges, where are taught moral philosophy, metaphysics, and the principles of their religion. Some of these colleges are magnificent and richly endowed, and owe their origin to the piety of some of their kings or nobles, who regarded it as meritorious in the eyes of God and the prophet to employ their wealth in such charitable foundations. This facility of obtaining a certain degree of education, and the habits of indolence and indulgence which they acquire in these colleges, produce a swarm of students, who pass their useless lives in poverty and idleness. Every city

Vagrant poets.

is consequently inundated with literary mendicants and vagrant poets, who take every opportunity of dealing out their flattering verses upon all strangers, whose rank or appearance afford them the slightest prospect of a return. The art of printing is here unknown. Beautiful writing is therefore looked upon as an emi-

Penmanship.

nent accomplishment, and those who excel in it are almost classed with literary men. They are employed in copying books; and such are the acquirements of some in this art, that specimens of penmanship of a celebrated copyist have often sold for a considerable sum.

The manufactures of Persia have undergone very

Manufactures.

little variation since the days of Chardin, in the seven-

5

teenth century. Many of them are very beautiful, particularly their carpets, their gold and silver brocades, their silks, and their imitation of Cashmere shawls, which are made of the wool of Kerman. Their cottons of various kinds are inferior to those of India; and a kind of felt is their substitute for broad cloths. Manufactories of glass are established at Shiraz and Maragha, and of porcelain at Zarang; and the manufactures of leather, shagreen, and morocco, which are as old as the Parthian kings, are still in a flourishing state. Firearms are made and mounted in most of the principal towns. Excellent sabres are still manufactured at Casbin and in Khorassan, and though brittle are of an excellent temper and edge. The fine quality of the steel is known by its waving clouded streaks. They are damascened with gold; and those of Khorassan sell as high as £30 Sterling. They also enamel upon gold and silver in the most beautiful manner. Their workmanship in jewels and trinkets is admirable; and few nations surpass them in the arts of carving and gilding. Upon the whole, it cannot be said that the useful and fine arts in Persia are either in a state of deterioration or improvement. " Knowledge in this country has hitherto ebbed and flowed with the changes in the political situation of the empire, and must continue to do so, as long as its inhabitants are under the depressing influence of a despotic and unsettled government."

The national religion of Persia is Mahomedan, but in this country it has lost much of its intolerance and fanaticism. This may arise from the inhabitants professing the principles of the Sheahs, or followers of Aly, who are considered as heretics by the Turks and others of the sect of the Sonnites. Of the various

sects which have arisen among the followers of the Arabian Prophet, the most considerable is that of the *Sheahs*, who stand opposed to the *Sonnites*, or orthodox believers, and between whom there subsists an irreconcileable hostility. The principal difference between these sects arises from the Sheahs maintaining the right of Aly to have succeeded to the caliphate on the death of Mahomed, as being his first convert, his cousin and nearest male relation, and the husband of Fatima, the only offspring of the prophet. They consequently consider the three first Caliphs, Aboubeker, Omar, and Osman, as usurpers, and deny all the Sonnee traditions which rest upon their authority. The Sonnites, on the other hand, acknowledge the first caliphs as the chosen companions and legitimate successors of Mahomed, and recognise the authority of the four great Imaums or Saints, Haneefa, Malik, Shaffei, and Hanbal, who were held in reverence for their piety and learning while alive, and, since their death, have been canonized as the high priests of the established orthodox doctrine. These holy men were the founders of distinct sects, who differed considerably from each other, both in their exposition of the Koran and the traditions; but their followers, alarmed at the progress of other heresies, concurred in tolerating their respective differences, and have become consolidated into one belief. These four sects are denominated the four pillars of the Sonnee faith, and each has a separate oratory at the temple of Mecca. The Sheahs and Sonnites observe, in general, the same festivals; but the former have set aside the first ten days of the month Mohurrum to mourn over the cruel fate of the sons of Aly, and on this occasion, the lower orders particularly, pour out imprecations against the Sonnites and the usurping caliphs. There are, however, many other points of difference between these sects, both with respect to religious worship and

civil usages, which render them totally irreconcileable. Their hatred to each other is open and undisguised; and this feeling, on the part of the Sheahs, has often been of essential service to the kings of Persia, who, in all their wars with their Sonnite neighbours, have never failed to take advantage of the religious abhorrence of their countrymen, and the watch-word, that the Sheah faith was in danger, has always prevailed in rousing them to action.

The Sheah doctrines were first adopted as the established religion of the country by Ismail, the founder of the Suffavean dynasty, in 1499. Nadir Shah, when at the summit of his power, endeavoured to recall his subjects to the orthodox faith, and to abolish, by severe penalties, the Sheah worship; but his attempt failed, and the attachment of the Persians to their faith continues as decided as ever. The tenets of the contending sects differ also with respect to the priesthood. By the Sheahs, the sacred title of Imaum is bestowed only on the descendants of the prophet. The last of these, Imaum *Mehdy*, the twelfth in succession, is supposed to be concealed, but still in existence; and they conceive that the title, which belongs to him, cannot be conferred upon another. The Sonnites, however, maintain that there must always be a visible Imaum or " Father of the church," and this title is given to the four learned doctors who were the founders of their faith. It was long one of their tenets, that the Imaum must be descended from the Arabian tribe of Koreish; but the Emperors of Constantinople, who are of Tartar descent, have assumed the sacred name, and are now acknowledged the spiritual heads of all orthodox Musselmen. After the disappearance of Imaum Mehdy, his authority was exercised in Persia by the Sudder-ul-Suddoor, or chief pontiff. To this spiritual head, who resided at court,

belonged the nomination, with the approbation of the sovereign, of the principal judges of the kingdom, and the management of the immense revenues of the church. So great power vested in one individual, induced Abbas the Great to attempt the abolition of the office, and, upon the decease of the then pontiff, no successor was nominated. During the succeeding reign, however, the office was restored, but its influence was diminished by dividing its power, and two pontiffs were elected, who were distinguished by the names of the Sudder-ul-Suddoor-e-Khas, which signifies the king's chief pontiff, and the Sudder-ul-Suddoor-e-Aum, or the chief pontiff of the people. But Nadir Shah not only abolished the office altogether, but seized upon the lands that were appropriated for the support of ecclesiastical establishments, for the payment of his troops. A small pension was granted to the person then holding the situation of pontiff, which his descendants still retain, with the title of Nawab, or lieutenant of the holy Imaum. The Nawab is still treated with great respect, and receives the seat of honour from the first nobles and ministers of the empire.

The Mooshtaheds are now at the head of the hierarchy of Persia. They are holy men, raised by popular suffrage to this dignity, but this honour is seldom shared by more than three or four priests at one time, and though they receive no appointment, and have no specific duties, yet they are treated with such submission and respect by the people, that the proudest kings are led to join the popular voice, and to pretend, if they do not feel, a veneration for the man who has attained this sacred rank. It is narrated of Shah Abbas, that a person having complained to Moollah Ahmed, the Mooshtahed of Ardebil, that the king had taken his

Statistics. sister by force into the harem, received from the holy man a note to the following effect: " Brother Abbas, restore to the bearer his sister." The woman was instantly given up, and the king, showing the note to his courtiers, said aloud, " Let this be put into my shroud, for, on the day of judgment, having been called Brother by Moollah Ahmed, will avail me more than all the actions of my life." The lower orders of the Priests. priesthood, however, neither receive, nor are they entitled to much respect. They are, for the most part, remarkable for their low cunning and impudence. They beg, or rather demand alms, on the ground of their holy character, and may be said to live upon the charity of the other classes of the community, by whom they are in general feared and despised. They assume the appellation, either of *Syud,* which marks their descent from the Arabian prophet, or of *Hajee,* which denotes a pilgrim to Mecca ; or of *Moollah,* a learned man. They have great pretensions and little knowledge, and endeavour to obtain an importance with the people by a display of their bigotry and intolerance. They are often accused by their countrymen of indulging in the gratification of the worst passions of the mind ; and to say, that a man hates like a Moollah, is to assert that he cherishes towards another sentiments of the most inveterate hostility.

Sooffees. Next to the Sheahs are the Sooffees, or philosophical deists, a class of devotees, which have of late made very rapid progress in Persia. As far as regards their Mahomedan tenets, they agree with the Sheahs in upholding the rights of Aly and his family to the dignity of Imaum ; but their peculiar doctrines are involved in great mystery. They represent themselves as entirely devoted to the search of truth, and as incessantly occupied in the adoration of the Almighty—an union with whom they desire with all the ardour of divine love. But this union can be enjoyed only by those who have passed through the four stages of probation, and then " their corporeal veil will be removed, and their emancipated souls will mix again with the glorious essence from which they have been separated, but not divided." The first stage is that of *humanity,* which supposes the disciple to live in an obedience to the holy law, and an observance of all the rites, customs, and precepts of the established religion : the second is that of *power,* when he is relieved from the directions of a teacher, and from the observance of religious forms and ceremonies. He now enters the pale of Sooffeeism, exchanges practical for spiritual worship, and attains the dignity of khalifa or teacher, and a title to the sacred mantle *. The third is that of *knowledge,* when he is deemed to be inspired, and to be equal to the angels ; and the last is that which denotes his arrival at truth and complete *union* with the Deity. The Sooffees are divided into numerous sects, which it would be vain to attempt to describe ; but though differing in name, and in some minor usages, they are all agreed in the principal tenets, and particularly in those which inculcate the absolute necessity of a blind submission to inspired teachers, and the possibility, through fervent piety and enthusiastic devotion, of attaining for the soul, even when the body inhabits the earth, a state of celestial beatitude. This sect has been from the first violently opposed by the Sheahs, and have often been exposed to cruel persecution. Their num-

bers, notwithstanding, are still upon the increase, and Statistic have been calculated at between two and three hundred thousand persons.

In no part of the east are Christians better received Christian than in Persia, but their religion has, at no time, made any progress in this kingdom. There is a colony of Nestorians in the mountains of Kurdistan, who are supposed to have resided there for more than thirteen centuries. The Armenians enjoy the free exercise of their religion ; but the Jews are every where treated with contempt and scorn by the Mahomedan inhabitants. The Guebres, or " worshippers of fire," are also Guebres. treated with great rigour. They have been compelled either to emigrate or to abjure the religion of their ancestors ; and a few families in the towns of Kerman and Yezd are all that now remain of the disciples of Zoroaster.

Besides the festivals common to all Mahomedans, the Festival c Nouroze. Persians still retain the Eed-e-Nouroze, or the " feast of the vernal equinox." This festival was one of the first kept sacred by the worshippers of fire, and is to this day observed with as much joy and festivity as by the ancient Guebres. According to Richardson, the ancient Nouroze " commenced with the year in March, and lasted six days ; during which all ranks seemed to participate in the general joy. The rich sent presents to the poor ; all were dressed in their holiday clothes, and kept open house ; and religious processions, music, dancing, a species of theatrical exhibition, rustic sports, and other pastimes, presented a continued round of varied amusement. Even the dead and the ideal things were not forgotten ; rich viands being placed on the tops of houses and high towers, on the flavour of which the Peris and spirits of their departed friends and heroes were supposed to feast." This festival, however, since the rise of Mahomedanism differs from that of the Guebres, both in the diminution of its duration and in the absence of all religious observances. It commences when the sun enters Aries, and continues in general only three days. On the morning the king marches out of his capital with his ministers, nobles, and as many of his army as can be assembled. The ceremonies of the day commence with a review, and then the tribute and presents of all the rulers and governors of the different provinces are laid at the foot of the throne ; which is placed in a magnificent tent. The offerings of the principal governors are introduced to his majesty by the master of the ceremonies ; who proclaims the name and titles of the donor, and then reads a list of the articles presented. On this occasion the king sends to the chief men and officers of his court a *kalaat,* or dress of honour ; and sometimes a horse and its caparisons. The number of kalaats is reckoned at about nine hundred, and the value of each three hundred piastres. He also distributes, at his public Dewan, handfuls of money, from a vase full of gold and silver coins, to those who are lucky enough to attract his notice. The amusements, during the feast, consist of horse-racing, wrestling, rope-dancing, fire-works, and other sports. The first day, however, is considered the most important, and is observed with equal demonstrations of joy over every part of the kingdom. All ranks appear dressed in their newest apparel ; they send presents of sweetmeats to each other ; and every man embraces his friend on the auspicious morning of the Nouroze, and wishes him a happy festival.

---

* The khirka, or mantle, is a patched garment, worn by Sooffee teachers, and which is left as a legacy to their successors. Some of these mantles can be traced several centuries, their value increasing with their age, and their envied possessor has many followers who venerate the tattered garment much more than the person who wears it.

Part II.—HISTORY OF PERSIA.

History.

The early history of this country is involved in great obscurity. The only knowledge which we have of its transactions is derived chiefly from the Dabistan, or " An Account of Twelve Religions," and the celebrated poem of Ferdosi, entitled the " Shah Namah," or book of kings ; the one written by a Mahomedan traveller about a century and a half ago, and professedly compiled from the writings of the ancient Guebres, or worshippers of fire ; and the other from the remains of the Persian annals, which had been saved from the fury of their Arabian conquerors.

Persian historians entitled to little credit. Little dependence, however, can be placed on any of these histories. Truth is so mixed up with fable, that it is impossible to ascertain where the one ends and the other begins ; and the judgment of the annalist is evidently sacrificed to the imagination of the poet. Their chronology is equally extravagant, and is founded entirely on the vague tradition of the duration of each monarch's reign. To some of their princes they assign a hundred, and to others a thousand years ; but in these uncertain and remarkable periods scarcely two of their historians agree. It would be vain, therefore, to attempt any connected series of events, or offer any dates before the commencement of the Grecian histories ; and we shall merely give a short abstract of the transactions of that early period ; and for our knowledge of Persian history we are chiefly indebted to the able work of Sir John Malcolm.

Division of the ancient history of Persia, by Sir William Jones. Sir William Jones divides the ancient history of the Persians into three distinct periods : The " dark and fabulous," comprehending the ages preceding the Kaianian dynasty ; the " heroic and poetical," commencing with the Kaianian dynasty and terminating with the accession of Ardisheer Babigan ; and the " historical," which includes the reigns of the Sassanian kings.

Mahabad, the first king,

The Dabistan traces back the history of this country to antediluvian times, and Mahabad is represented as the first king and father of the present race of men. The ancient Persians alleged that it was beyond the knowledge of man to ascertain who were the first parents of the human race. They believed that time was divided into a succession of cycles or periods, to each of which was allotted its own people ; and that a male and female were left at the end of every cycle to produce the population of the succeeding one. Mahabad and his wife, therefore, were the only pair that survived the former cycle, and were blessed with a numerous offspring to people the new world. Their first habitations were caves and the clefts of the rocks. They were strangers both to social order and to the comforts and luxuries of life ; but Mahabad, aided by divine power, instructed them in many of the useful arts, and

introduces civilisation. introduced among them the blessings of civilization. He had thirteen successors who were deemed prophets, and were at once the high priests and monarchs of the country. During their reigns the world enjoyed a golden age, which, however, was disturbed by the abdication of Azer-abad, the last prince of the Mahabadian dynasty ; when his subjects, left to the free indulgence of their passions, without law or restraint, indulged in every species of excess. In the hyperbolical language of the Dabistan " the mills from which men were fed, were turned by the torrents of blood which flowed from the veins of their brethren ; the human race became as beasts of prey, and returned to their former abodes in caverns and mountains." From this state of anarchy and desolation they were delivered

by Jy-affram, who revived the neglected laws and institutions of Mahabad. He was the founder of the Jyanian dynasty, to which succeeded the dynasties of Kuleev and Yessan, which altogether comprehended a period of many thousand millions of years.

History. Jy-affram. Kuleev and Yessan.

The human race is then described as having again fallen into such excess of wickedness, that God made their mutual animosity the means of divine vengeance till they became nearly extinct ; and the few that remained had retired to the woods and rocks. While thus sunk in savage barbarity, Kaiomurs arose to reclaim and civilize them.

The world reverts to a savage state.

At this period commences the poem of Ferdosi, and indeed all the Persian histories except the Dabistan. Kaiomurs was the founder of the dynasty called Paishdadian, or " first distributors of justice ;" but his efforts in civilizing his subjects were successful at first only with his own family ; and his whole reign was spent in exertions to reclaim them from their savage habits.

Kaiomurs founds the Paishdadian dynasty.

His grandson and successor Houshung is celebrated as the inventor of many useful arts, and as being the first who introduced the worship of fire ; and Tahamurs, the son of Houshung, was engaged in constant wars against the deeves or magicians, as the enemies of this dynasty were denominated. These three princes governed Persia one hundred and ten years. Tahamurs was succeeded by his nephew Jemsheed, who is celebrated as the founder of Persepolis, which is to this day called Tukht-e-Jemsheed, or " the throne of Jemsheed." To this monarch the Persian historians attribute many important changes in the manners and usages of their countrymen. He is said to have divided his subjects into four classes or castes, and to have prohibited each class from engaging in the occupations of the other. The first were learned and pious men, devoted to the worship of God ; the military formed the second ; the third was composed of tradesmen and artizans ; and the fourth of husbandmen. He also reformed the calendar, introduced the science of astronomy, and ordered the first day of the year, when the sun enters Aries, to be celebrated by a festival, which is called Nouroze, or new year's day ; and is still the greatest festival in Persia. Many other improvements are ascribed to this prince. He constructed ships ; he invented arms ; he introduced music ; he encouraged agriculture ; and he was the first that made wine and manufactured silk. By these measures he raised his country to an unexampled state of prosperity ; but he became at last so intoxicated with power, and immersed in luxury, that, forgetting the source of all power and prosperity, he ordered statues of his person to be made, and denounced vengeance against all who did not bow down before his image and worship him as a god. This act of oppression and impiety so alienated the affections of his people, that his kingdom became an easy prey to Zohauk the Syrian, who was regarded as an instrument of divine vengeance. Jemsheed was driven from his throne ; and his wanderings and adventures as an exile have been wrought into one of the most popular romances of Persia. After many years of a wretched existence, he was at last seized by Zohauk, and cruelly put to death.

Houshung. Tahamurs. Jemsheed, divides his subjects into castes, and introduces many useful arts. He proclaims himself a god, and is deposed.

The reign of the usurper Zohauk comprehends a term of from 800 to 1000 years, and is conjectured to include that part of ancient history in which Persia is represented as subject to the Assyrians. The events of this period, as delineated by the Persian historians, are mostly

Zohauk usurps the throne ;

fabulous. All agree that Zohauk was of a most cruel and sanguinary disposition; and he is described as having upon each shoulder a voracious serpent, whose hunger could be appeased only by the brains of human beings. Two of his subjects were daily sacrificed to furnish the horrid meal, till the indignation of Kawah, a black-smith of Ispahan, whose two sons were upon the point of being put to death by the tyrant, roused his coun-trymen to resistance. Having collected a numerous army, and being joined by Feridoon, a young prince of the Paishdadian dynasty, Kawah erected his apron as a standard; and as this continually reminded them of their injuries, they fought with the greatest enthu-siasm. After several defeats, Zohauk was made prison-er, and, as some punishment for his crimes, suffered a lingering and painful death.

Feridoon was immediately raised to the throne; and the blacksmith's apron was converted into the standard of the empire, and held in great venera-tion for several centuries. The latter years of Fe-ridoon were distracted by the rebellion of his chil-dren. He had three sons, Selm, Toor, and Erij; the two former by a daughter of Zohauk, and the youngest by a princess of Persia. Desirous of repose from the cares of royalty, he had divided his extensive empire among them. To Selm, he gave the countries comprehended in modern Turkey; to Toor, Tartary and part of China; and to Erij, Persia. The older brothers, dissatisfied with what they considered an act of partiality and injustice, and enraged that the fairest portion of the empire, and the seat of royalty, should be allotted to the youngest, demanded a new division; and, to enforce compliance, they remonstrated with, and even threatened, their aged parent. Feridoon re-fused their demand, by which they were so incensed, that they soon after accomplished the death of Erij; and, adding insult to cruelty, they embalmed his head and sent it to their father. The aged monarch was seized with frantic grief at the sight of the head of his favourite son; and, uttering imprecations against his unnatural destroyers, begged of heaven that his life might be spared till a descendant of the race of Erij should arise to avenge his death. Manucheher, the son of a daughter of Erij, became the cherished hope of the aged king; and as soon as he attained to manhood, made preparations for carrying retribution upon the murderers of his grandfather. Feridoon soon had the gratification of receiving Manucheher as a conqueror, and of placing the crown upon his head; and he left this admirable lesson to his descendants: " Deem eve-ry day of your life as a leaf in your history; take care, therefore, that nothing be written in it that is not worthy of posterity."

The reign of Manucheher was long and prosperous; and, though a good and pious prince, the tranquillity of his kingdom owed its preservation chiefly to the wis-dom and courage of his prime minister Sam, the here-ditary prince of Seistan. The descendants of Sam have been much celebrated in Persian history, and his grand-son Roostum has ever been considered as the hero of the nation. The exploits of this warrior have been magnified into miracles, and his history is consequent-ly enveloped in romance; but his name is still venerat-ed and cherished by his countrymen with all the en-thusiasm of national pride. Manucheher, while on his death-bed, besought his successor Nouzer to trust to Sam and his family as the best supporters of his throne;

but that prince soon forgot his father's advice, until the rebellion of his subjects, and a threatened invasion of Afrasiab, king of Turan, or Scythia, drove him to seek that assistance of which he stood so much in need. But the death of Sam hastened the overthrow of Nou-zer; and the Scythian monarch seized the diadem of Persia, which he held for twelve years. The courage and achievements of Zal, the son of Sam, again restor-ed the fortunes of the kingdom, and placed Zoowah, a descendant of Feridoon, upon the throne. The reign of this prince was but short; and his son and successor Kershasp was soon set aside by Zal as incompetent to reign. With Kershasp ended the Paishdadian dynasty, which, according to the computation of their historians, ruled over Persia 2450 years.

In this portion of Persian history, of which the prin-cipal events are generally regarded as fabulous, there is scarcely any transaction that bears a resemblance to those of the same period as recorded by Grecian histo-rians. The usurpation of Zohauk is supposed to refer to the conquest of Persia by the Assyrians; and the duration of the Assyrian power in Persia occupies the same space of time as that assigned to the reign of Zo-hauk. Upon this supposition, Feridoon will represent the Arbaces of the Greeks, who delivered Persia from the Assyrian yoke; and there is no passage in history more fully proved by oriental writers than the revolt of Kawah, who placed Feridoon upon the throne, which event is confirmed by the undoubted fact that the im-perial standard, which fell into the hands of the Caliph Omar, consisted of a blacksmith's apron. The subse-quent events of this period may allude to the constant wars carried on against the Scythians, which led first to the usurpation of Afrasiab, and then to his expulsion from the throne of Persia; and Manucheher Nouzer, Zoowah, and Kershasp, correspond with the Mandau-ces, Sosarmus, Artia, and Arbianes of the Greeks.

We now enter upon another portion of Persian his-tory, " the heroic and poetical," where we can evi-dently discover truth to form the basis of the narrative, though often defaced and obscured by the fictions of an oriental imagination. The Persian historians make no reference to dates; so that it is only by a similarity of events that we can trace the same history as recorded by Grecian writers. After the removal of Kershasp, Zal, with the other chiefs of the empire, placed upon the throne Kai-Kobad, a lineal descendant of Manu-cheher, and the founder of the Kaianian dynasty. Dur-ing the reign of this prince, Zal held the reins of go-vernment, and his son Roostum, as yet a youth, led the armies of Persia. The Tartar Afrasiab continued to be the dreaded enemy of the empire, and seized every opportunity of disturbing its tranquillity. He had again passed the Oxus with an invading army. In the first engagement he encountered the hero Roostum, and, after a violent contest, the Tartar prince was saved only by his soldiers, with the loss of his rich crown and girdle. He immediately retreated and begged for peace.

Kai-Kobad reigned 120 years, and his son Kai-Kaoos succeeded to a powerful and prosperous sceptre. But the pride and ambition of this monarch led him into many schemes, which he wanted ability to exe-cute. In his invasion of the kingdom of Mazenderan, whose climate and fertility he had heard highly extol-led, he and his army were struck with sudden blind-ness * during a great battle, and all that were not slain were made captives. The royal prisoner was con-

* This was the eclipse foretold by Thales.

History.

fined in a strong fort, and his jailor used tauntingly to ask him what he thought of that delightful climate he was so anxious to enjoy. His captivity, however, was is liberated by Roostum. not of long continuance. Roostum, though opposed, according to Ferdosi, by all the efforts of valour and enchantment, effected his liberation, and also succeeded in adding Mazenderan to the kingdom of Persia. Kai-Kaoos again fell into the hands of his enemies. In a negociation with the king of Hamaveran to obtain his daughter Sudaba in marriage, he was invited to a feast by that monarch, and treacherously made prisoner. This event was aggravated by a new inroad of the Tartars; but Roostum once more became the deliverer of his sovereign. He led an overwhelming force against the king of Hamaveran, and his auxiliaries, the kings of Egypt and Barbary, and compelled him not only to Married Sudaba. release Kai-Kaoos, and give him the fair Sudaba in marriage, but to assist the Persians in expelling Afrasiab beyond the Oxus. A circumstance is narrated as having taken place in this reign, which greatly embittered the hostility between the Persians and Tartars, and involved them in long and bloody wars. Kai-Kaoos had married a niece of Afrasiab, who had fled into Persia, and had by her a son named Siawush, who was alike remarkable for his personal beauty and mental Intrigues of the queen; endowments. Of him the fair Sudaba, notwithstanding her marriage with his father, became deeply enamoured; and, after many vain efforts to seduce him, she endeavoured to destroy him by false accusations. Siawush, however, completely exculpated himself, it is said, by submitting to the ordeal of passing through the fire.

While these dissensions prevailed in the Persian court, Afrasiab was preparing for another invasion. But he became alarmed for his own safety by a dream which he had, and which was regarded as portentous of evil. At this time Roostum and Siawush commanded the army opposed to him, and to them he made overtures for a peace, but he was compelled to submit to hard terms, and gave 100 hostages as a pledge of his fidelity. Kai-Kaoos, who had expected nothing less than the head of his enemy, no sooner heard of the peace, than he ordered Siawush to send the hostages to court, and gave the command of the army to Toos, his son Siawush joins Afrasiab. with orders to prosecute the war. Siawush was so indignant at such a proceeding, that he joined Afrasiab with all the hostages, declaring that he would never be a party to such dishonourable conduct. In a letter to his father, however, he ascribed this step to his dread of the intrigues of Sudaba, which rendered it impossible for him to preserve his honour and his life at the court of Persia. Afrasiab, overjoyed at the accession of such an auxiliary, gave him his daughter Feringees in marriage, with Cheen and Khoten as her dowry. Siawush retired to his dominions, and diligently applied himself to the improvement of his new subjects. But his success excited only the jealousy of Gurseevas, the brother of Afrasiab, who being joined by some of the nobles of Tartary, at last accomplished his ruin. They represented to the Tartar king the impolicy and danger of allowing an enemy of their race to become acquainted with the state of his dominions, and acquire popularity among his subjects, who, as soon as he should succeed to the Persian throne, would use that knowledge and popularity to their destruction. Afrasiab long resisted their importunities, and adduced, in his behalf, his claim of hospitality and protection; Murder of Siawush. but he yielded at last, and the brave and generous Siawush was treacherously slain. The beautiful Feringees,

who was then pregnant, was also doomed to death. History. She was, however, saved by the intercession of the nobles, and her offspring ordered to be destroyed as soon as born. The execution of this order was entrusted to the vizier, Peeran-Wisa, but the heart of the minister revolted at such a deed; and when the Tartar princess was delivered of a son, he gave it the name of Kai-Khoosroo, and committed him to the care Birth of Kai-Khoosroo. of a shepherd, with secret instructions to bestow upon him an education suited to his high birth. Afrasiab was made to believe that the child had been exposed in a desert. A rumour, however, soon reached him that his grandson was alive. He immediately questioned the vizier upon the subject, who reported that the child had been found, and brought up by a shepherd, but that he had proved an idiot. The young prince was then sent for, and, being instructed beforehand by Peeran-Wisa, acted the part of a fool so well before his grandfather, that he was looked upon as perfectly harmless, and allowed to reside with his mother.

The intelligence of the murder of Siawush had no Kai-Kaoos raises an army to revenge the blood of his son. sooner reached Persia, than Kai-Kaoos assembled a large army to revenge the blood of his son. Roostum was solicited to take the command; but that chief would consent only upon the condition that Sudaba should be put to death, as it was to the wicked passions of that princess that he ascribed the exile and misfortunes of the brave Siawush. Kai-Kaoos was obliged to comply, Sudaba is put to death. and Roostum immediately took the field. After several engagements, Afrasiab was driven from his dominions, over which Roostum is said to have held sway for seven years. Every effort was now made to discover the son of Siawush, but in vain. Afrasiab, afraid of his resentment should he join the Persians, had ordered him to be conveyed beyond the sea of China. The young prince, however, was at last restored to his grandfather Kai-Kaoos, who was so overcome with joy, that he descended from his throne; and, placing Kai-Khoosroo placed upon the throne. Kai-Khoosroo upon it, ordered all present to do him homage. He was soon afterwards crowned; but, though sovereign of Persia, he paid as much attention to his grandfather as if that monarch had never resigned his power. He was a prince of the highest qualities, but his whole reign was spent in waging war against the Tartars to avenge the murder of his father Siawush. After a long and bloody struggle, with various success, it was at last accomplished by the capture and death of Afrasiab. Roostum bore a most conspi- Death of Afrasiab. cuous part in this war, and received for his services Cabul, Zabulistan, and Neemroz, as hereditary possessions.

After a prosperous reign of sixty-three years, Kai-Khoosroo resolved to devote the remainder of his days to religion. He raised to the throne Lohrasp, the son- Accession of Lohrasp; in-law of Kai-Kaoos; and, attended by some nobles, retired to a sacred spring which had been selected as the place of his repose, where, we are told, he soon after disappeared; and all those who accompanied him were, on their return, destroyed by a violent tempest. By the command of Lohrasp, an army was dispatched under Raham Gudurz, commonly entitled Bucht-ul-Nasser, the governor of Irak, to extend his dominions to the west; and, according to a Mahomedan author, extends his dominions. it was during this expedition that Jerusalem was taken and plundered, and such of its inhabitants as survived the sword carried captive into Persia. Bucht-ul-Nasser is supposed by some to be the Nebuchadnezzar of the Jewish historians; while others make the successful exploits of this army refer to the conquest of Egypt by Cambyses.

History.

Resigns his
sceptre.

Gushtasp
introduces
the worship
of fire.

Lohrasp resigned the sceptre in favour of his son Gushtasp, whose reign is celebrated chiefly for the introduction of the worship of fire by Zoroaster. This new doctrine was first taught in the province of Aderbijan, and soon spread over the whole empire. Gushtasp, who is said to have been converted by his son Isfundear, built temples of fire in every part of the kingdom, and ordered twelve thousand cow-hides to be finely tanned, that the precepts of the prophet might be written upon them. These were deposited in a vault at Persepolis, and holy men were appointed to guard them. The consequence of this change of religion was a war with Arjasp, king of Tartary, who sent a threatening message to the Persian monarch, warning him of the error into which he had fallen, and demanding that he should immediately return to the faith of his ancestors. This war was prosecuted with the exterminating fury of fanatical enthusiasm; and the devotion of Isfundear to the doctrines of Zoroaster led him to sacrifice his personal aggrandizement to the cause of his religion. The armies of Persia at first prevailed; but, in a second battle, they were completely overthrown by the Tartar king, and the daughter of Gushtasp carried into captivity. Isfundear, who had been imprisoned at the instigation of his enemies who ruled at his father's court, and who had designs against his life, was immediately released; and Gushtasp promised to resign to him his crown, should he succeed in recovering his sister. Isfundear took Roueen-deh, the capital of Tartary, by stratagem; and, having slain Arjasp, restored the princess of Persia to her father. The promise of Gushtasp, however, was not fulfilled; and the intrigues of his enemies again threw Isfundear into confinement. Upon receiving this intelligence, the Tartars again took the field, plundered Khorassan, entered Bulkh, then the capital of the empire; and, having put to the sword all the priests and followers of Zoroaster whom they found in that city, among whom was the old king Lohrasp, they carried away in triumph the apron of Kawah, the celebrated standard of Persia.

His son
Isfundear
takes the
capital of
Tartary.

Massacre
of Lohrasp
and the
priests of
Zoroaster.

Isfundear was again called from prison to lead the Persian forces; and, forgetting his own injuries, he hastened to avenge the injuries of his country. His success was complete. He took Roueen-deh, slew the Tartar king, and recovered the sacred banner. Having subdued all the foreign enemies of the empire, he now looked with confidence for his reward,—the crown of Persia. But the artful Gushtasp evaded the demand, and alleged that Roostum, who had retired to Seistan, and thrown off his allegiance, was still unsubdued. It was long before the prince could be prevailed upon to undertake this desperate enterprize, which proved fatal both to his fame and his life; and the old monarch saw too late the folly of the attempt, and long mourned his irretrievable loss.

Isfundear
slain by
Roostum.

Bahman,
the son of
Isfundear,
succeeds to
the throne;

Bahman, surnamed Ardisheer Dirazdust, the son of Isfundear, succeeded to the throne. He is celebrated for the wisdom which he displayed in the internal arrangements of his kingdom, and his minute acquaintance with the actual condition of the country. He extended his conquests to the west, deposed the son of Bucht-ul-Nasser (the Belshazzar of the Scriptures) from his government of Babylon, and appointed Koresch (Cyrus) his successor. Under Koresch the Jews were treated with great kindness, and by the express command of Bahman, whose favourite lady was of that nation. But a stain has been left upon his name and his reign by the murder of Roostum, and the invasion of Seistan. He was succeeded by his daughter Homia

Invades
Seistan,
and Roos-
tum is
slain.

who is said to have been pregnant by her own father, and who, after a reign of thirty-two years, resigned her crown to her son Darab the First. This monarch engaged in war with Philip of Macedon, and it is stated, that, though unsuccessful at first, he ultimately prevailed, and reduced Philip to such extremity that he agreed to give his daughter to Darab, and pay an annual tribute of a thousand eggs of pure gold.

History.

Homai suc-
ceeds Bah-
man, and
resigns the
crown to
Darab.

Darab the Second, from his effeminacy and his vices, fell an easy prey to the arms of Secunder Roomee, (Alexander the Great.) On his accession he sent a messenger to the Macedonian prince to demand the tribute of golden eggs; to which Secunder replied, that the bird that laid the eggs had flown to the other world. Another ambassador was immediately dispatched with the charge to deliver to Secunder a bat and ball, and a bag of very small seed, intimating by the former an amusement suited to the years of the Macedonian monarch, and by the latter the numbers of the Persian armies. Secunder took the bat in his hand, and said, " With this bat will I strike the ball of your master's dominions; and this fowl (which he had sent for, and which immediately ate up the seed) will soon show you what a morsel his numerous army will prove to mine." He then desired the messenger to tell his master what he had seen and heard, and also sent him a wild melon, as an emblem of the bitter lot which awaited him. Secunder soon after marched into Persia, and in the first great battle, Darab, according to eastern writers, lost both his crown and his life. It is said that he was slain by two of his own captains, who expected from Secunder the reward of their treason. But the soul of the conqueror was melted into tears at the sight of his fallen enemy, and kissing his cheek, assured him that he never wished to see his royal head in the dust. Darab, opening his eyes, begged of Secunder not to place a stranger on the throne of Persia, and to marry his daughter Roushunuk. The remains of the Persian king were deposited in the sepulchral vault with the most extraordinary honours; and on the same day his murderers suffered the punishment of their treachery. Secunder Roomee soon after became sole monarch of Persia, and married Roushunuk, the daughter of Darab.

Darab II.

sends a
message to
Alexander.

Invasion of
Persia, and
death of
Darab.

Secunder
becomes
monarch of
Persia.

In this short abstract of the history of the Kaianian dynasty, it is difficult to trace an exact resemblance to the history of the same period as given by the Greeks. Eastern and western writers indeed differ so materially in their narratives of the same reigns, that it is sometimes impossible to ascertain where the truth lies. In the Persian histories there is evidently much fable; but at the same time the principal historical facts are preserved. While Grecian authors, though entitled to superior credit, often throw a veil of doubt over their records by their vain exaggerations, especially in what respects the honour of their own country and achievements.

Difference
between
western and
eastern au-
thors.

The following is a table of the names of the Kaianian monarchs according to Persian and Grecian historians, from which it is evident that the Persians sometimes blend the reigns of two or more kings in one; but it may be remarked, that, though they have omitted the names of several kings, they have never interpolated one, unless Homai may be considered as such. This queen, however, may be regarded as the Parysatis of the Greeks, who was the daughter of Artaxerxes, and the wife and sister of Darius Nothus; and is represented as possessing great influence and authority in the government.

Table of
the Kaian-
ian mo-
narchs.

History.

Secunder The history of Secunder Roomee, as given by the Persians, agrees in most of the leading facts with that given of Alexander the Great by the Greeks; but upon these they have raised a superstructure of the most extravagant fable; and have filled many volumes with an account of his extraordinary adventures. But we shall give shortly what the Persians themselves consider as authentic history. Secunder, having firmly established his authority in Persia, *extends his* extended his conquests towards India. Some of its princes submitted *conquests;* without a struggle, while others were compelled by force to receive the laws of the conqueror; and even the Emperor of China offered to become his tributary. That monarch had come in disguise to the Persian camp, but being discovered, was brought before Secunder, who demanded from him the motive of such a visit. The emperor answered, that it was his desire to see the Grecian troops, and a solicitude to obtain the friendship of such a conqueror. With this answer *enters into* Secunder was so pleased, that a treaty was instantly *treaty with* concluded, by which the emperor agreed to pay an *the Em-* annual tribute. The Chinese monarch then retired to *peror of* his capital to prepare for the reception of his powerful *China.* ally. In a few days, however, he returned with an immense army, the sight of which made Secunder immediately prepare against treachery, by arraying his troops in order of battle; and when the emperor and his nobles approached, Secunder demanded why he had broken faith and collected such a force. "I wished," was the reply, "to show the numbers of my army, that you might be satisfied I made peace from other motives than an inability to make war. It was from consulting the heavenly bodies that I have been led to submit. The heavens aid you, and I war not with them." Secunder was gratified, and observed that it would ill become him to exact tribute from so great, so wise, and so pious a prince; he would therefore be satisfied with his friendship.

On the return of Secunder from his conquests in the east, he was one day seized with a bleeding at the nose, when one of his officers, unlacing his coat of mail, spread it on the ground for a seat, and held a golden shield over his head to defend him from the sun. When Secunder saw himself in this situation, he remembered the prediction of the astrologers, who foretold, that when his death approached, he should place his throne on a spot, where the ground was of iron, and the sky of gold, and exclaimed, "I no longer belong to the living! Alas! that the work of my youth should be finished; that the plant of the spring should be cut *his death.* down like the ripened tree of autumn!" He died at

the city of Zour, or, as some say, at Babylon, in the *History.* thirty-sixth year of his age.

The immediate successors of Secunder Roomee are not noticed by Persian historians. They state that, a short period before his death, he divided the provinces of Persia among the native princes whom he had deposed, to be held on tenure of a military service; each being obliged to maintain a fixed quota of soldiers. But these princes threw off their allegiance to his successors, and formed a feudal commonwealth, termed the Mulook-u-Tuaif, or "commonwealth of tribes." *The "com-* This community of small states recognised some prin- *monwealth* ciples of common policy, which led them to unite in *of tribes."* cases of common danger, and continued to exist, with various changes, for more than three centuries after the death of Secunder Roomee.

We learn, however, from the more authentic records of the Greeks, that Persia, on the death of Alexander, fell to Seleucus, who reigned also over Syria, and whose descendants kept possession of it for sixty-two years, when one of the tributary chiefs, named Arsaces, revolted, and, having slain Agathocles, the viceroy of Antiochus *The Seleu-* Theos, rescued Persia from the dominion of the Seleu- *cides expell-* cides, and established what is termed the Parthian dy- *ed by Ar-* nasty of the Arsacides. Of this dynasty there were two *saces, who* branches; the first comprehending twenty kings, who *establishes* ruled over Persia for 270 years; and the reigns of the *the Par-* eleven monarchs of the second branch included a space *thian dy-* of 221 years. This brings us down to the foundation *nasty.* of the Sassanian dynasty, at which commences "the *"Histori-* historical period;" and here we may observe, that, *cal period."* though the Persian accounts are embellished with hyperbolical descriptions, and blended with some fables, they are more correct in the general narrative than western writers, who confine their history chiefly to those transactions in which they themselves were more immediately concerned.

Arduan, the last of the Parthian monarchs, at this *About* time ruled over Persia, when Ardisheer Babigan, the *A. D. 200.* son of an inferior officer in the public service, and a *Ardisheer* descendant of Sassan, the grandson of the celebrated *Babigan* Isfundear, had so distinguished himself by his courage *founds the* and his genius, that he was appointed governor of *Sassanian* Darabjird. This rapid rise in his fortunes filled his *dynasty;* mind with more ambitious views, and soon led him to grasp at the Persian sceptre. Having represented to the Persian nobility the disgrace of submitting to a foreign yoke, and the honour and advantage to be gained by a revolution, he brought many of them over to his interest, and he and his adherents had got possession of Fars, Kerman, and Irak, before the king had taken any steps to oppose his progress. Arduan was now compelled to take the field, and, having collected a numerous army, resolved to stake his crown on a single action. The hostile armies engaged on the plain of Hoormuz, where Arduan lost both his crown and his life. This battle raised Ardisheer to the sovereignty of Persia. The other provinces soon submitted to his sway; and he assumed the proud title of Shahan Shah, or "king of kings." In extending his empire towards the west, he had to contend with the Roman armies; and though the accounts given of this war by western and eastern authors are somewhat opposite, yet, upon the whole, it would seem that the result was favourable to the Persian arms. Having established by wise *restores the* regulations the tranquillity of his dominions, he restored *religion of* to its ancient purity the religion of Zoroaster, which had *Zoroaster.* fallen into neglect and corruption during the Parthian rule. He is said to have rebuilt the city of Madain on the

History.

A. D. 240.
Resigns his
crown to
his son.
His cha-
racter.

banks of the Tigris, and made it the capital of the empire. After a most prosperous reign of fourteen years, he resigned his sceptre to his son Shahpoor.

Ardisheer is represented as a prince of extraordinary wisdom and valour. Though born in a low station, he, by his talents and intrepidity, delivered his country from thraldom, and restored the glory of the Persian name. While he was almost adored by his subjects, his friendship was courted by the greatest monarchs of the age; and his character was held up as a model to his successors.

Shahpoor.

Takes the
emperor
Valerian
prisoner.

Is defeated.

Shahpoor was a prince of considerable reputation, but is chiefly distinguished by his wars with the Romans. His first achievement was the recovery of Juzeerah, or the countries between the Tigris and the Euphrates, and the capture of the famous fort of Nisibis, which had long resisted all his efforts to subdue it. He then carried his arms into the Roman territories; he took the emperor Valerian prisoner, and compelled his captive army to receive an emperor of his own appointment. His success, however, was not of long duration. He was defeated by Odenatus, prince of Palmyrene, and driven with immense loss within his own boundaries. The latter years of the reign of this monarch were employed in decorating his dominions with many cities and public buildings. He built the city of Shuster, and erected an immense dyke, over which he brought the river Karoon, in order to supply the adjacent country with water. Nishapore in Khorassan, and Shahpoor in Fars, owe their existence to him; and the sculptured rocks, near the latter place, commemorate his capture of a Roman emperor.

Mani-
chæans.

It was during the reign of Shahpoor, that Mani, the founder of the sect of the Manichæans, first began to propagate his opinions. He attempted to reconcile the doctrines of the Metempsychosis, as taught by the Hindoos, and the two principles of good and evil of Zoroaster, with the tenets of the Christian religion; but he and almost all his disciples were afterwards put to death by order of king Baharam, and the skin of the impostor was stripped off, and hung up at the gate of the city of Shahpoor.

Hoormuz.

A remarkable circumstance is recorded of Hoormuz, the successor of Shahpoor, before he ascended the throne. He was the governor of Khorassan, and had been most successful in establishing the tranquillity of that unsettled province. But some of his enemies had excited suspicions of his fidelity in the breast of Shahpoor; of which Hoormuz was no sooner made acquainted than he made one of his hands to be cut off, and sent it to his father as a mark of his devoted allegiance. Shahpoor was so struck with horror at the deed, which his rash suspicions had caused, that he immediately sent for him to court, and treated him with the most unbounded affection and confidence. This good prince founded the city of Ram-Hoormuz, and reigned only one year.

A. D. 271.
A. D. 294.
Narsi

concludes
an igno-
minious
peace.
A. D. 310.

In the reigns of the three Baharams, nothing remarkable occurred worth noting. Their successor Narsi was a prince of a mild disposition; but he had the misfortune to engage in war with the Romans, who at that time had many great generals. His arms were at first successful. He defeated the emperor Galerius, and subdued almost all Armenia; but his subsequent discomfitures forced him to conclude an ignominious peace, by which he ceded the province of Juzeerah, and five districts east of the Tigris.

We pass over the reign of Hoormuz II. as affording no event of importance, to record the achievements of Shahpoor II. On the demise of Hoor-

muz, Persia was about to become a prey to all the troubles which accompany a disputed succession, when a lady of the harem declared that she was pregnant. The nobles of the kingdom, in order to preserve their country from the horrors of a civil war, resolved to swear allegiance to the unborn child of Hoormuz. This child proved to be a male, and the unanimous voice of the nobles bestowed upon him the name of Shahpoor. His education was conducted with the most affectionate solicitude; and every care was taken that he should imbibe those principles and views which became his high destiny. During his minority the kingdom was exposed to the insults and ravages of the neighbouring tribes, particularly the Arabs, who carried desolation into the fertile valleys of Persia. But the young monarch took signal vengeance upon these marauders; and their chastisement is perpetuated in his title of Zoolaktaf, or "Lord of the shoulders." He overran Yemen, put many of the inhabitants to the sword, and dislocated the shoulders of all his prisoners who were able to bear arms. He made no great attempt to extend his dominions on the west during the life of Constantine the Great. An improbable story is recorded of his having gone to Constantinople in the disguise of an ambassador from his own court, in order to acquire an acquaintance with the Roman empire, but being discovered he was imprisoned and treated with great indignity.

History.

Birth of
Shahpoor
II.

Chastises
the Arabs.

The disorders which followed the death of Constantine afforded Shahpoor an opportunity of recovering from the Romans those provinces which they had wrested from his grandfather. He therefore took the field; but though successful in many engagements, the fort of Nisibis defied all his efforts; and in the battle of Singara he was severely repulsed, and was forced to retire with the loss of his son. Leaving the defence of the frontiers to some of his generals, he turned his arms against the Tartar tribes, many of whom he subdued by force, while others yielded without resistance to his authority. The emperor Constans now made overtures for peace; but Shahpoor claiming Armenia and Juzeerah as belonging to the Persian empire, the treaty was broken off, and preparations made for renewing the war. Nothing decisive, however, happened during the life of Constans. But when Julian had assumed the purple, he resolved to break the Persian power so effectually, as to prevent them for ever from again disturbing the frontier provinces of the Roman empire. He therefore took the field with an immense army; but the Persian monarch, aware of his inferiority were he to risk a pitched battle, retired into the interior of his kingdom, and left his capital to be pillaged by the Romans. Julian followed, and penetrated into the heart of Persia, and, after a harassing march, and much suffering from the intense heat of the climate and the scarcity of provisions, was surprised by Shahpoor, who had collected all his forces; and in a desperate engagement which ensued, the Romans were completely routed, with the loss of their emperor, who was so badly wounded that he died the succeeding night. The consequence of this victory was, an advantageous peace, by which Persia recovered the five provinces yielded by Narsi, and the strong fort of Nisibis, which had long been the bulwark of the Roman power in the east.

Makes war
against the
Romans.

Julian in-
vades Per-
sia;

is defeated
and slain.

Shahpoor afterwards reduced Armenia into a province of the empire, and having raised his country to a state of the greatest prosperity, he died at the age of seventy-one. This prince, renowned for wisdom and valour, was alike remarkable for

Death and
character of
Shahpoor.
A.D. 381.

his knowledge of the human mind. He used to say, " that words may prove more vivifying than the showers of spring, and sharper than the sword of destruction. The point of a lance may be withdrawn from the body, but a cruel expression can never be extracted from the heart that it has once wounded."

The names of Ardisheer II. Shahpoor III. Baharam IV. and Yezdijird Ulathim, are all that is worth recording. Upon the death of Yezdijird, the succession of his son Baharam V. was opposed by the luxurious nobles at the court of Madain. This prince, while yet a child, had been entrusted by his father to the care of Noman, prince of Hirah, to be educated after the manner of the Arabs; and they could not submit to be ruled by a monarch whose habits and manners of life were so different from their own. They, therefore, raised to the throne another prince of the royal family; but Babaram, having collected an army of Arabs, obtained his right almost without a struggle. The first acts of his reign were, to reward Noman, who had educated and assisted him in regaining his crown, and to pardon those who had endeavoured to deprive him of it. These acts, and his general munificence and generosity, spread joy over Persia, and gained him the affections and esteem of his subjects. It was during his reign that musicians and minstrels were first introduced from India; and Baharam, who rejoiced in the happiness of his people, gave them such encouragement, that 12,000 were induced to settle in his dominions. This joyous disposition of the monarch impressed his neighbours with the belief that the martial spirit of the Persians had yielded to the love of merriment and ease. Acting upon this impression, the Khan of the Hiatilla, or White Huns, a tribe of Tartars who had taken possession of the country beyond the Oxus, suddenly crossed that river with a mighty army, and destruction and desolation marked his progress. Baharam saw the torrent rolling towards his capital, without possessing any means to repel it. He therefore seemed to yield to its force; and left his kingdom a prey to the conqueror. Retiring with a chosen body of Persian warriors, he passed the straits of Derbent, and, coasting the Caspian, came into Tartary. Here he refreshed his troops; and while the Tartars were feasting in supposed security, believing that he had taken refuge in the Roman empire, he silently entered Persia, surprised their camp, and, having slain their chief with his own hand, drove them with terrible slaughter across the Oxus. This victory struck awe into the Tartar tribes, and secured their forbearance during the life of the conqueror.

The Christians, who, in the former reign, had been encouraged and protected, at this time suffered much from the persecutions of the Magi. These persecutions, however, were chiefly owing to the imprudence of the Persian prelate, who in a fit of zeal burnt to the ground one of the Magian temples, which so roused the indignation of the priests, that they demolished all the Christian churches, and put the Christian bishop to death. A war with the emperor Theodosius immediately followed, which was attended with various success; but it was immortalized by the conduct of a Christian bishop, which did more to secure the goodwill of Baharam to the Christians than all the threatenings of Theodosius. In the beginning of the war, 7000 Persian prisoners, who had been brought to the city of Amida, had fallen into extreme distress. Acacius, bishop of that place, having assembled his clergy, observed that the Almighty preferred mercy to sacrifice, and proposed that the plate of their church should

be sold for the relief of these captives. The proposal was highly applauded. The Persians were liberally and affectionately treated during the war, and at last dismissed with presents to their native country.

Baharam received the surname of Gour, from his being enthusiastically devoted to the chase, particularly of the gour, or " wild ass," a diversion which he had learned among the Arabs. It was while pursuing this favourite amusement that he lost his life, by his horse coming suddenly upon a deep spring, and plunging into it with his royal master, when both disappeared. The body of the king was never found, though every search was made for it by his inconsolable mother.

Baharam Gour reigned eighteen years, and was one of the best monarchs, and most beloved by his subjects, that ever ruled in Persia. His successor Yezdijird II. was a prince of great knowledge and experience, and received the title of Sipahdost, or " the soldiers' friend," from his great attention to their wants and comforts. In the only expedition which he undertook against the emperor of Constantinople, who had refused to pay the usual tribute, he not only brought that prince to compliance, but secured the good opinion of the provinces through which he passed. He compelled his troops to pay for every thing they had, to treat the inhabitants with the greatest civility, and to conduct themselves rather like strangers who came to see the country, than like enemies disposed to destroy it.

Yezdijird, before his death, had solicited the nobles to support his favourite son Hoormuz III. on the throne, in opposition to his elder brother Firoze, who, in order to facilitate that measure, had been appointed to the command of a remote province. Firoze, as soon as he heard of the accession of his brother, took refuge with Khoosh-Nuaz, or " the bountiful monarch," one of the kings of the Hiatilla. This prince welcomed him to his court, loaded him with kindness, and supplied him with an army to recover his birthright. Hoormuz was dethroned and put to death. A seven years drought immediately followed the elevation of Firoze, which was regarded as a punishment from heaven for their crimes; but no sooner was his country relieved from this calamity, than the ungrateful prince employed all the resources of the empire to destroy the generous benefactor who had placed him on the throne. He crossed the Oxus with his troops; and Khoosh-Nuaz, unable to oppose him, retired at his approach. But the king of the Huns was saved by the patriotic devotion of one of his chief officers. This person, after communicating his plan to his sovereign, caused his body to be mangled, with the loss of some of his limbs, and to be laid on the road where the Persian army should pass. Being conveyed to Firoze, that prince demanded the cause of such cruel treatment. The artful Hun answered, that it was the tyrant Khoosh-Nuaz, who had punished him for the advice which he had given, as a faithful servant, to submit to any conditions rather than engage in war with the hero Firoze. " But I will be revenged," he added, " I will lead you by a short route, where you shall in a few days intercept the tyrant, and rid the world of a monster." The situation and words of the wounded chief established the belief of his sincerity in the mind of the Persian king; and he suffered his army to be led by the direction of the Tartar, till, thinned with hunger and fatigue, they were compelled to submit to the mercy of the enemy. The generous Khoosh-Nuaz, instead of punishing the ungrateful Firoze, offered to conduct him and the remains of his army safely back to Persia, provided he took an

Marginal notes (left column):
History.
Baharam V.
obtains the crown.
His munificence and generosity.
Invasion of the Huns;
their defeat and expulsion.
Persecution of the Christians.
Generosity of a Christian bishop.

Marginal notes (right column):
History.
Death of Baharam. A. D. 438.
Yezdijird II.
A. D. 456. Hoormuz III.
A. D. 458. is dethroned and succeeded by Firoze;
who invades Tartary.
Sufferings of the Persian army.

History.
oath that he would not again invade his dominions. With this Firoze was obliged to comply. But his soul could not brook the recollection of his degradation; and his first determination, on his return, was to wipe away his disgrace by the ruin of his benefactor. Having appointed a nobleman, named Sukhvar, regent in his absence, he, in breach of his solemn oath, and in defiance of the advice of his sagest counsellors, led his army once more against the bestower of his crown, and now the preserver of his life. On the approach of the two armies, the Tartar prince presented, on the point of his lance, the treaty to which Firoze had sworn; and besought him to desist, before he had destroyed his fame for ever. But Firoze rushed to the attack. The Huns gave way, and the Persians were received into deep pits, which had been dug for the purpose, and covered over with brushwood and earth; when the incorrigible ingratitude of the Persian monarch was punished with the loss of his army and his life.

Pallas, the son of Firoze, ascended the throne, but his reign was of short duration; and the long reign of his successor Kobad is remarkable, chiefly for the encouragement which he gave to an impostor of the name of Mazdak, who propagated the popular doctrine of a community of females and of property. The progress of this doctrine spread anarchy, rapine, and lust, throughout the kingdom. But the nobles, who cherished different sentiments from their monarch, combined for their own preservation, and having confined Kobad, they placed his brother Jamasp upon the throne. They would also have imprisoned Mazdak, but his followers were numerous, and he contrived to elude all their efforts. Kobad having escaped from prison by the dexterity and address of his sister, who, it is said, was connected with him by other ties than those of kindred, and is in fact called, by western writers, his queen, fled to the Tartar court, and by the assistance of its monarch soon regained his throne. On his return, he greatly reformed his conduct, and though still secretly inclined to the sect of Mazdak, he durst never carry his notions into practice. This prince carried on a long and successful war with the Romans; and not only extended his empire by his arms, but improved it by the encouragement which he gave to the arts, and died respected abroad and beloved at home.

By the will of Kobad, the crown was bequeathed to Chosroes, his favourite son, who was sirnamed Nousheerwan, or " The Magnanimous." This prince was distinguished by great abilities and mildness of disposition, and is considered by oriental historians as the most glorious monarch that ever ruled in Persia. His first efforts were directed to the proscription of the pestilential and abominable tenets of Mazdak, whom he ordered to be executed with many of his followers. He then set himself to reform many great abuses which had crept into the government. He fixed the revenue and taxes; and the system which was then established, continued to be followed for many centuries. For the better administration of justice, and the more easy management of public affairs, he divided the kingdom into four governments. Over each of these he appointed a governor of the blood royal, and established such regulations as seemed best adapted to prevent the abuse of power in these officers. He was indefatigable in his endeavours to promote the prosperity of his kingdom. He founded schools and colleges, and gave great encouragement to learned men of every country who resorted to his court. The famous fables of Pilpay were introduced by him

from India, and translated into Persian; and he also caused to be published a multitude of copies of a work entitled "Ardisheer's Instructions for all Degrees of Men," and obliged every family to receive one. In all these measures he was assisted by the extraordinary wisdom and virtues of his favourite vizier Abouzurg-a-Mihir, who had been raised by the discernment of his master from the lowest station to the first rank in the kingdom. Nousheerwan very early entered into a war with the Romans, during which Antioch was taken, and its inhabitants transplanted to the banks of the Tigris. We cannot enter, however, into the long wars which he waged with Justinian, and his two successors, Justin and Tiberius; but the capture of Antioch, with the reduction of Syria, the conquest of Iberia and Colchos, and his unopposed progress to the shores of the Mediterranean, testify the ability and success with which they were prosecuted. He was equally successful in other quarters. He checked the encroachments of the Huns, who had seized a large territory south of the Oxus. He drove them beyond that river, and extended his dominions as far as Ferghana. The countries to the east reaching to the Indus, some provinces of India, and the finest districts of Arabia, also acknowledged his sway.

Having settled the boundaries of his vast dominions, Nousheerwan returned to his capital, Madain, which he adorned with many beautiful buildings, among which was the palace denominated " the dome of Chosroes," which was considered one of the wonders of the East; and his court was crowded with ambassadors from the greatest potentates of the world, who came, loaded with the richest presents, to compliment him on his victories, and to court his friendship. But the prosperous reign of this monarch was clouded by the rebellion of his son Nouschizad. This prince had been educated in the Christian faith by his mother, who was a Christian captive of great beauty, and of whom the king was passionately fond, and was so impressed with the truth of its doctrines, that he could not be moved, either by the threats of the Magi or the entreaties of his father. Nousheerwan, who was a strict observer of the worship of fire, dreading the evil consequences of religious disputes among his subjects, and fearing that many might be induced to embrace the religion of the heir-apparent to the throne, placed his son in a kind of confinement. During the absence of the king in Syria, a report of his death had reached Persia, upon which Nouschizad, having effected his escape, drew together a considerable force, of which many were Christians; and continued to increase his army, even after he had been informed that his father was alive and well. As soon as Nousheerwan heard of this revolt, he dispatched one of his generals against his rebellious son; and the insurrection was quelled by the death of the prince, who fell in the first encounter.

Perhaps no monarch was ever more zealous in promoting the general happiness of his people than Nousheerwan. His impartial administration of justice, and his vigilance in detecting and punishing every act of oppression in his inferior officers, gave confidence and security to all. Many anecdotes are recorded of his strict adherence to justice, which seems to have been a principal feature in his character. He was surnamed by the Arabians Al-Malek, or, " The Just;" and Mahomed used to boast of his good fortune in being born under the reign of so just a king. A Roman ambassador, one day, admiring the noble prospect from the windows of the imperial palace, remarked an uneven piece of ground, and inquired the reason why it was not made

History.

uniform: A Persian noble replied, " It is the property of an old woman, who has objections to sell it, though often requested to do so by our king; and he is more willing to have his prospect spoiled, than to commit violence." " That irregular spot," said the Roman, " consecrated as it is by justice, appears more beautiful than all the surrounding scene." " This prince," says Khondemir, " possessed in a sovereign degree, as well the good qualities which render amiable a private man, as the exalted virtues which add lustre to a diadem." He resisted the influence of that luxury by which he was courted, neither giving himself up to indulgence, nor permitting it in others; and he remained, to the last hour of a life protracted to more than eighty years, unconquered by prosperity.

A.D. 579.

With Nousheerwan expired the glory of Persia. His son, Hoormuz III. who had been entrusted to the care of Abouzurg-a-Mihir, soon forgot the example of his father, and the instructions of his virtuous minister; and, plunging into every excess of indulgence and cruelty, rendered himself hateful to his subjects, and contemptible to his enemies. The provinces of India and Arabia, which acknowledged the power of Nousheerwan, disdained to yield obedience to his unworthy successor; and the Khan of Tartary crossed the Oxus, and demanded a free passage through Persia, under the pretence of invading the Roman empire. This chief, however, was opposed by Baharam, the Persian general, with only 12,000 chosen troops, and slain in the first engagement. In a subsequent battle, the son of the Khan was taken prisoner, and sent to Madain with 250 camels loaded with treasure. Hoormuz was at first delighted with his general's success; but a worthless favourite maliciously insinuated that Baharam had reserved the best of the spoil for his own use, or, according to the Persian expression, " he had only sent the ear of the cow." The suspicious temper of the king immediately took the alarm, and, instead of a habit of honour, the usual present of Persian kings, he sent to Baharam, as a mark of disgrace, the apparel of a woman, a distaff and a spindle. The hardy warrior, arrayed in his new apparel, presented himself to his army. " Behold," said he, " the reward of all my services." The soldiers were filled with indignation, and immediately hailed Baharam as their king. The deposition and murder of Hoormuz soon followed; and his son Khoosroo Purveez, who had collected a considerable army to support his father's throne, was completely defeated in the battle of Nahrwan, and fled for refuge to the emperor Maurice, where he met with a most hospitable and friendly reception.

Baharam assumed the reins of government; but his rule was short. Within eight months of his elevation he was defeated by Khoosroo, supported by an army of Romans, and, flying into Tartary, was welcomed and protected by a people whose armies he had often vanquished. He was soon afterwards cut off by poison, at the instance, it is alleged, of the Persian king.

Khoosroo, during the life-time of the emperor Maurice, maintained inviolable his friendship with the Romans, many of whom he treated with great favour and distinction; but upon the murder of that prince by the centurion Phocas, he dispatched an immense army into the Roman territories, under the pretence of avenging the death of his benefactor. His generals overran and pillaged Syria and Palestine; sacked the city of Jerusalem; and the true cross, attended by a crowd of captive priests and bishops, was borne in triumph to Madain. But while his arms were every where victorious, this

Hoormuz III.

His dissolute character.

The Tartars defeated by Baharam,

who is hailed king by the army.

Death of Hoormuz.

A.D. 592. Khoosroo Purveez obtains the crown.

A.D. 591.

His army successful.

monarch, who had given himself up to every species of luxury and self-indulgence, seemed to value his conquests only as they added to his pleasures. The vast territories which his generals had subdued were exhausted to add to the magnificence of his palaces, and swell the gorgeous pomp of his royal person. He built a noble palace for every season; and his principal throne, called Takh-dis, was supported by 40,000 silver columns, and in the concave over them, which was formed to represent the twelve signs of the Zodiac, and adorned with a thousand globes of gold, were seen all the planets and great constellations performing their natural revolutions. Twelve thousand females, the most beautiful in Persia, filled his haram, 6000 horses stood in the royal stables, 12,000 elephants followed his armies, and his treasures were deposited in 100 vaults. No monarch ever surpassed him in royal luxury and splendour, and for thirty years his arms were marked with complete success. His victorious troops carried the Persian banners to the frontiers of Ethiopia, and added Arabia, Egypt, and Colchos to his dominions.

But Khoosroo was aroused from his dream of happiness and of conquest by the victories of the Emperor Heraclius. This prince, who was as remarkable for his weakness and indecision in the cabinet, as for his extraordinary valour and skill in the field, had long endeavoured by negociation to avert the total overthrow of the Roman name, and had even sent deputies to express his desire to purchase peace upon any terms. He was, however, awaked from his lethargy by the insulting answer of the Persian king, " I will hearken to no terms, till your master shall renounce his crucified God, and adore the God of the Persians." Heraclius, upon this, took the field in person, and in six glorious campaigns, stript Khoosroo of all his conquests, overran the finest provinces of his empire, destroyed his magnificent palaces, plundered his hoarded treasures, and dispersed, in every direction, the countless slaves of his pleasures. The troops of Persia were overthrown in every encounter; and Khoosroo was at last deposed by his own subjects, and murdered by the command of his own son. Schiroueh enjoyed the reward of his parricide only eight months; and, during the four succeeding years, the kingdom was so distracted by intestine divisions, that seven sovereigns, two of whom were daughters of Khoosroo Purveez, were raised to the throne by the ambitious nobles, and successively murdered. Yezdijird III. the grandson of Khoosroo, was next called to wield the sceptre of Persia; and he has obtained celebrity only as being the last sovereign of the house of Sassan; and in whose reign the Arabs accomplished the subversion of the Persian empire.

The first attempt of Mahomed to extend his religion over Persia was in the reign of Khoosroo Purveez, who was so enraged at being called upon by an obscure Arabian to renounce the religion of his fathers, that he tore to pieces the letter of the prophet; and to that sacrilegious act Mahomedan historians impute all that prince's subsequent misfortunes. The next attempt was made by the Caliph Omar, who commanded a body of Arabs to pass the Euphrates. They were at first severely repulsed in several engagements; but by their valour and perseverance, they at last obtained an important victory, which laid the foundation of the Mahomedan power in that country. This action took place a few years before the accession of Yezdijird, whose first measure was to dispatch an envoy to Saad, the leader of the Arab forces. A deputation of three Arab chiefs were, in consequence, sent to Madain by order of the

History.

His luxury and magnificence.

His war with Heraclius.

Is stripped of all his conquests.

His deposition and death. A.D. 628.

Yezdijird III.

First attempt of the Arabs to extend their religion.

Obtain a victory.

History.

Holds a conference with Yezdijird.

Caliph, and after a long conference with the Persian king, one of the deputies concluded in these words, "We now solemnly desire you to receive our religion. If you consent to this, not an Arab shall enter Persia without your permission; and our leaders will only demand the established taxes, which all believers are bound to pay. If you do not accept our religion, you are required to pay the tribute fixed upon infidels; and should you reject both these propositions, you must prepare for war." Yezdijird instantly rejected these degrading conditions, and prepared for hostilities. But he was unable to uphold the declining glories of his country; and in the first general engagement, the Persian army was almost annihilated, and the famous blacksmith's apron, the royal standard of the empire, fell into the hands of the enemy. Yezdijird fled to Hulwan with all the property he could carry, and left his capital to the conqueror. The war was protracted for a few years; but the battle of Nahavund decided the fate of Persia, and Yezdijird, driven from his throne, and a fugitive in his own kingdom, dragged out a miserable existence for ten years, when he was murdered.

A.D. 641. Battle of Nahavund, and conquest of Persia. A.D. 651.

The armies of the faithful soon extended the authority of their master from the Euphrates to the Oxus, destroying with savage fury every vestige of idolatry, and the inhabitants were every where compelled to submit to the religion of the conquerors, or seek an asylum in other lands. Lieutenants were then appointed to the different districts of the country, and Persia for more than two centuries was held as a province under the Arabian Caliphs. In process of time, however, the fever of religious frenzy abated, and the power of the caliphs declined. The discontented and mutinous armies of the impotent successors of Omar and Aly were scarcely able to protect the capital, much less hold in subjection the distant provinces of the empire, whose governors exercised almost regal power, carried on war with each other, and gave no mark of allegiance to the vicegerent of the prophet, except the merely using his name in the public prayers.

Persia under the dominion of the caliphs.

A.D. 851.

While the kingdom was thus divided and distracted by the contentions of its petty rulers, the sceptre of Persia was won by the wisdom and valour of Yacoob-ben-Leis, the son of a pewterer and a robber. This daring chief was an inhabitant of Seistan, and was characterised by great simplicity of manners. He possessed the devoted attachment of his followers, and in no instance did he abuse his success by any wanton act of cruelty or oppression. Having first established his authority in his native province, he, from thence, carried his arms over the finest districts of Persia, and his ambition even led him to threaten destruction to the power and the government of the caliphs. He was, however, defeated in the vicinity of Bagdad; but, undismayed by his reverse, he recruited his army, and returned again to the attack of the capital. The caliph dreaded the result, and dispatched a messenger to the camp of Yacoob. This leader, though lying dangerously ill, having commanded that his sword, some coarse bread, and dried onions should be laid before him, desired the envoy to be introduced, "Tell your master," said he, "that, if I live, that sword shall decide betwixt us: if I conquer, I will do as I please; if he is victorious, that bread, and those onions, which thou seest, is my fare; and neither he nor fortune can triumph over a man accustomed to such diet." But the resolute chief survived only a few days, and almost the whole of Persia fell by succession to his brother Amer.

Yacoob-ben-Leis seizes the empire.

His message to the caliph.

His death.

Amer possessed few of the great qualities of his brother. While the abstemiousness of Yacoob led him to be contented with the coarsest fare, it required 300 camels to carry the kitchen furniture of Amer. He was deficient, however, neither in courage nor ambition, and he maintained with a struggle the government of Persia for more than twenty years. He was at last defeated by Ismail Samanee, a Tartar lord, who had been instigated by the caliph to invade the dominions of Amer, and carried captive to Bagdad.

History.

Amer,

defeated and taken prisoner. A.D. 902.

With Amer fell the fortunes of his family, and, for nearly a century, the houses of Samanee and Dilemee held the kingdom of Persia between them. The dominions of the former included Khorassan, Seistan, Bulkh, Samarcund, Bokharah, and Khaurizm, while those of Dilemee extended over the greatest part of Irak, Fars, Kerman, Khuzistan, and Laristan. During the period that these dynasties ruled over Persia, many chiefs maintained themselves in small principalities, which they were enabled to preserve only by balancing between these two powerful families. Among these principalities, that of Ghizni was perhaps the smallest; but from small beginnings it rose so rapidly to distinction and dominion, that its chief might be compared, in point of power, with the greatest monarch that ever wielded the sceptre of Persia. The families of Saman and Dilem were stript of their richest possessions, and Mahmood, the greatest of its princes, limited his territories by the provinces of Georgia and Bagdad, the kingdom of Bokharah and Kashgur, and Bengal and the Deccan, as far as the Indian Ocean.

Persia divided between two powerful families.

The conquests of Mahmood of Ghizni.

Mahmood was renowned, not only for his victories, but he was a munificent patron of genius; and it is to his love of literature, and the encouragement which he gave to learned men, that we owe the noble work of Ferdosi, the *Shah Namah*, or "Book of Kings," which contains almost all that remains of the ancient history of his country. A splendid reward had been promised to the poet upon the completion of his task, but Mahmood had been persuaded by envious rivals to lessen the amount. Ferdosi spurned the diminished present, and after adding to his poem a severe satire upon the king's want of generosity, left the court, and retired to his native city of Toos in Khorassan. Sometime afterwards, the monarch saw his error, but it was too late. The rich present destined for the poet entered the gates of Toos, as the body of Ferdosi was carrying to its sepulchre; and we are told that his virtuous daughter rejected the wealth which had been denied to the unrivalled merit of her father.

Encourages literature.

Ferdosi.

The conquests of Mahmood in the east were uniformly marked by religious persecution, and his bigot zeal led him not only to destroy the idols, and pillage the temples of the Hindoo idolaters, but also to cover their cities with desolation. In a popular eastern tale, the vizier of this prince is represented as pretending to be acquainted with the language of birds, and as explaining the liberality of an old owl, who, after wishing "Mahmood a long life," offered a hundred ruined villages as a dowry to her daughter. But while he was carrying the horrors of war and of persecution into every country which he visited, his own dominions enjoyed perfect tranquillity, which was greatly owing to his severe but equitable rule. The following instance of his determined justice is recorded by all his historians. "A poor man had complained that a young noble of the court came constantly to his house at night, turned him out of doors, and slept with his wife. The

Character of Mahmood.

History.

monarch bade him give notice the next time this occurred. He did as he was directed, and Mahmood went with him to his house. When he reached it, he put out a lamp that was burning, and having found the paramour, struck off his head with one blow of his scimitar. He then called for a light, and, after viewing the corpse, fell upon his knees and returned thanks to heaven, after which he bade the astonished husband bring him water, of which he drank an immoderate quantity. ' You are surprised at my actions,' said Mahmood, ' but know that since you informed me of the outrage you suffered, I have neither slept, eat, nor drank. I conceived that no person, except one of my sons, would dare openly to commit so great a crime ; resolved to do justice, I extinguished the light that my feelings as a father might not prevent me from doing my duty as a sovereign, my prayers were a thanksgiving to the Almighty, when I saw that I had not been compelled to slay one of my own offspring, and I drank, as you observed, like a man that was expiring from thirst.' "

A.D. 1028.
The family of Mahmood driven from Persia,

The successors of Mahmood were unable to maintain the glory which he had acquired, and were soon swept from the list of monarchs by the leader of a Tartar tribe, who at first had been permitted to lead their flocks over the rich pastures of Khorassan, but who soon became masters of that province, and at last drove the monarchs of Ghizni beyond the limits of Persia. The territory of this Tartar tribe of Seljookee stretched from the Oxus to the Iaxartes. But as soon as their chief, Toghrul Beg, had got possession of Khorassan, he assumed the title and state of a sovereign, and, extending his conquests to the west, overran Irak, and, by the reduction of Bagdad, became master of the person of the caliph Ul-Kaim. Having completely subdued the whole of Persia, he sought to strengthen his authority by a close alliance with the family of the successors of the prophet. Ul-Kaim had married his sister, and he himself demanded the daughter of the commander of the faithful. The dependent condition of the caliph forbade him to refuse compliance, but the aged bridegroom enjoyed his union only for a few months.

which is subdued by Toghrul Beg.

A.D. 1063.

Alp-Arselan ascends the throne.

His nephew Alp-Arselan ascended the throne, and upheld by his valour and generosity the glory of the empire which his uncle had founded. His first enterprise was directed against the tottering power of Constantinople. He invaded Georgia, and advanced into the province of Phrygia ; but he found an enemy, worthy of the name, in the Emperor Romanus. The Persian armies were forced to fall back upon their frontiers. A general engagement followed, where the troops of Romanus were at first successful ; but the treachery and cowardice of one of his principal officers, who withdrew with a large division of his forces, gave the victory to the Persians. The courage of Romanus, strengthened by despair, was unable to retrieve his fortunes ; and being at last wounded and overwhelmed by numbers, he was taken prisoner, and carried into the presence of his conqueror. " What would you have done had fortune reversed our lot ?" demanded the Persian. " I would have given you many a stripe," was the reply. Alp-Arselan smiled at his inoffensive rage ; and asked what treatment he now expected from him. " If thou art cruel," said Romanus, " put me to death. If vain-glorious, load me with chains, and drag me in triumph to thy capital. If generous, grant me my liberty." Alp-Arselan was generous. He nobly released the emperor and all his officers, and

Takes the Emperor Romanus prisoner,

and treats him with generosity.

treated them with every mark of friendship and regard.

History.

The Persian king now led his armies to the conquest of the country of his fathers. He crossed the Oxus without opposition by a bridge, which he had commanded to be thrown over that river ; but here his career of conquest was closed. The protracted resistance of a small fortress had retarded the progress of the Persian army, which so irritated the monarch, that he commanded its gallant commander into his presence; and, after loading him with reproaches, ordered him for execution. The brave soldier drew his dagger and rushed towards the sultan. The guards interposed ; but Alp-Arselan, who considered himself unequalled as an archer, seized his bow, and ordered them to stand back. He, however, missed his aim, and before he could draw another arrow, he fell under the dagger of his prisoner. Before his death, he delivered over his crown to his son Malik Shah ; and intreated him with his dying breath to entrust the management of his affairs to his celebrated minister Nizam-ul-Mulk, to whose wisdom and virtue he attributed the prosperity of his own reign.

His death.

A.D. 1072.

Malik Shah succeeds.

The accession of Malik Shah was opposed by his uncle Cawder Beg ; but that chief, having been taken prisoner, was soon after put to death ; and also by his brother Tourtousch, who, being defeated in battle, was compelled to leave the kingdom. An instance of the piety and goodness of Malik Shah on this occasion is recorded by De Guignes. In coming out of a mosque with Nizam-ul-Mulk, previous to the engagement, he demanded of his minister what had been the object of his devotions. " I have prayed," was the answer, " that the Almighty may give you a victory over your brother." " And I," said the king, " that God may take my life and crown, if my brother is more worthy than I to reign over the faithful." Having established peace at home, he directed his arms to the extension of his empire. His generals overran the whole of Syria and Egypt. Bokharah, Samarcund, Khaurizm and Kashgar were compelled to do him homage, and he prosecuted his conquests till the Mediterranean and the wall of China became the boundaries of his dominions. During his reign of twenty years the degree of prosperity which Persia enjoyed is unequalled in its history. Many colleges and mosques were built, and agriculture was promoted by the construction of canals and water-courses. The reformation of the calendar, which was entrusted to an assembly of astronomers selected from every part of his empire, and whose labours established the *Jellalean*, or glorious æra, marks the state of science at that period. The prosperity of the kingdom, however, was much owing to the excellent government of his virtuous and able minister, whose powers and attainments were entirely devoted to the glory of his prince and his country. But this devotion was at last requited with ignominy and death. Nizam-ul-Mulk had fallen under the displeasure of the principal Sultana, who feared that her plans for the aggrandizement of her infant son in opposition to the claims of his elder brother would be resisted by that faithful minister. She therefore embraced every opportunity of throwing out insinuations against him to the Sultan, who, forgetting what he owed to his exertions, was prevailed upon to demand the instant resignation of the cap and inkhorn, the insignia of his exalted station. The old man could not suppress his chagrin. " When the sea was troubled," he said, " Malik Shah honoured me with his confidence ; but all is now calm, and he listens to

An instance of his piety.

His conquests.

His prosperous reign.

His conduct to Nizam-ul-Mulk.

History.

A. D.
1092.
His death.

Sanjar
gains the
crown.

Is defeated
and taken
prisoner by
the Turko-
mans.

A. D.
1157.

His death.

Govern-
ment of the
Atta-begs.

A. D.
1221.
Chenghiz
Khan con-
quers Per-
sia.

Hulakoo
Khan,
a great pa-
tron of
science.

A. D.
1264.

His death.

my calumniators. But he will not long be ignorant that the cap and ink-horn which he has called me to resign, are connected by a divine decree with his crown and throne." Nizam-ul-Mulk was soon after-wards murdered at the instigation of his successor in office; and Malik Shah survived him but a few months. The ingratitude of the monarch has affixed a stain upon his character which all his glory will never ef-face; and the fortunes of his kingdom began to de-cline from the hour that marked the degradation of his virtuous minister.

The succession to the throne was disputed by the four sons of Malik Shah for more than thirty years, during which time they all attained power in their turns, when Sultan Sanjar became sole mo-narch of Persia. This prince is highly celebrated for humanity and valour, and is considered the best, if not the greatest, of the Seljookian kings. He recover-ed most of the territories which had been separated from Persia during the civil wars which followed the death of his father, and bestowed the kingdom of Khaurizm upon his chief cup-bearer. But the latter years of his reign were marked with the most cruel reverses. The Turkoman tribe of Ghuz had withheld their tribute of forty thousand sheep. Sanjar marched an army into their territories, but he was defeated and taken prisoner, and the barbarians overran and deso-lated the fairest portion of his kingdom. After a con-finement of four years, during which he was exposed to innumerable insults and hardship, Sanjar effected his escape from his barbarous gaolers, but was so overcome by the deplorable situation of his country, that he fell into a state of melancholy, from which he never recovered. After his death Persia continued to be the theatre of intestine wars for a period of forty years; and Toghrul the Third, the last monarch of the race of Seljook, was defeated and slain by the ruler of Khaurizm, whose descendants held the sovereignty of Persia for about thirty years.

The contests which at this time distracted the empire, raised up a number of petty princes or governors, called Atta-begs, who taking advantage of the declining for-tunes of the dynasty of Seljook, established their au-thority over some of its finest provinces, and trans-mitted them to their posterity. These chiefs enjoyed a local power, and often contended with the reigning princes, till they were all swept away by the inun-dation of the Tartars under Chenghiz Khan. This de-stroyer of the human race divided his immense con-quests among his four sons, when Persia, Khorassan, and Cabul, were assigned to Tuli Khan, who survived his father but a few years, and was succeeded by his son the celebrated Hulakoo Khan.

This monarch, having captured Bagdad, and extir-pated the race of the caliphs, fixed his residence at Maragha. In this delightful spot he spent the re-mainder of his life, enjoying the society of learned men, and promoting every work of science to the ut-most of his power. Philosophers and astronomers were assembled from every part of his dominions, who, under the direction of his favourite and learned minister Nasser-u-deen, formed these astronomical tables, known under the name of the tables of Eel-Khannee. The remains of a building situated on the summit of a low mountain near Maragha still marks the spot sacred to science, where these learned men carried on their observations. Hulakoo died before this observatory was completed, and bequeathed his sceptre to his son Abaka, a prince equally renowned for courage and wisdom, clemency and moderation.

History.

Key Kha-
tou at-
tempts to
introduce a
paper cur-
rency.

Is deposed
and slain.

A. D.
1294.

Ghazan
Khan.

His govern-
ment.

A. D.
1303.
His appear-
ance and
character.

A. D.
1316.

The reigns of this prince and of his successors, Ah-med, Arghoun, and Key Khatou, are marked by no events of importance, except the attempt of the latter to introduce a paper currency throughout his domi-nions, which however cost him both his crown and his life. This weak prince, having exhausted his trea-sury by his unexampled prodigality, listened to the schemes of one of the officers of the revenue, who pro-posed to substitute a paper exchange in lieu of specie in all commercial transactions; and by this means it was expected that all the gold and silver in the coun-try would flow into the royal coffers, and give life and vigour to the government. For this purpose banking houses were erected in every city and town in Persia, where notes of various value were regularly issued; and each note contained a positive mandate for all his majesty's subjects to receive them on pain of punish-ment. This measure, however, was so unpopular, that it lasted but a few days, when it was repealed; but it lost the monarch the confidence of all ranks; and he was soon after deposed and slain by a confede-racy of his disaffected nobles, at the head of which was Baidu Khan, the grandson of Hulakoo. Baidu, however, enjoyed the crown but a few months, when he fell by the hand of his nephew Ghazan Khan.

This prince, however, refused to ascend the throne till he was regularly elected, like his Mogul ancestors, by the assembled chiefs or ameers of the empire. He then set himself to reform the many abuses which had crept into the government during a succession of weak princes. He " not only revived and reformed the in-stitutes of Chenghiz, but framed a new and more full code of edicts; the object of which was, the reform of the administration of justice, the establishment of good regulations in the collection of the public revenue, the distribution of lands for the support of the army, the regulation of inns or caravanseries, the reform of the system of public post-houses for officers and cou-riers of government, which appear to have been es-tablished throughout the empire, the suppression of robbers, and the fixing the standard of coins, weights, and measures." These laws were founded upon principles fitted to promote the moral improve-ment of subjects, as well as the strength and safety of a government; and remain a lasting monument of the wisdom and justice of this great prince. Al-though at an early period of his reign Ghazan Khan, with a hundred thousand of his followers, had profess-ed their conversion to the tenets of Islam, yet his whole life was spent in a contest for Syria with the sultans of Egypt, the defenders of the faith which he had adopt-ed; and in friendship with Christians, whom he endea-voured to re-establish in the Holy Land. In this war he was at first successful, but latterly experienced a complete reverse, which accelerated his death, after a reign of nine years. This monarch, we are informed, was remarkable for the lowness of his stature, and the extreme ugliness of his face and person; but he pos-sessed a mind richly endowed with learning and vir-tue; and was the first of the Moghul race of kings who threw off all allegiance to the Khan of Tartary. His brother Khodah-bundah, in ascending the throne, proclaimed himself a follower of the sect of Aly, for which alone his memory is still cherished in Persia. He was succeeded by his son Abou Seyd, a youth of twelve years of age.

During the minority of Abou Seyd, the disputes among the nobles produced a general weakness and distraction, which pervaded the whole empire. Almost every province was seized by some powerful chief; and the few princes of the family of Hula-koo, who were raised to the throne after this prince, were mere pageants, whom the ameers of the court elevated or cast down as it suited the purposes of their ambition.

A kingdom thus torn by intestine divisions, could offer but a feeble resistance to the victorious Timour. This insatiable conqueror marked his progress by desolation and ruin. Many provinces were turned into deserts by the destructive ravages of his countless hordes; and even submission did not exempt their unfortunate inhabitants from pillage and massacre. Ispahan opened its gates on his approach, but a heavy contribution was levied on its citizens. An unfortunate occurrence, however, involved this city in ruin. The inhabitants were one night roused by the sound of a drum, which a young blacksmith had been beating for his amusement. They rushed together to ascertain the cause of their alarm, and, becoming irritated by the expressions of misery and distress which burst from all ranks, they vented their rage by the massacre of nearly three thousand Tartar soldiers who had been quartered in the city. On the morning the gates were shut, and the citizens called to arms; but the resistance of despair could not save them from the fury of Timour, who doomed Ispahan as an example to the other cities of the earth. He would listen to no terms. The walls were carried by storm; and, besides giving up the city to pillage, he commanded that every soldier should bring him a certain number of heads. In this horrid massacre seventy thousand heads were raised in pyramids as monuments of savage revenge.

Persia now became a province of the empire of Tartary, and continued to be ruled by the descendants of Timour, till the invasion of a tribe of Turkomans under Uzun Hussun, who became sole master of the empire in 1468. This monarch, though possessed both of valour and wisdom, is said to have owed his success over the superior forces of Persia more to his skill and activity than to his courage. He died at an advanced age, after a reign of eleven years; and the ruin of his family was accelerated by their mutual contentions for his territories, and were soon swept from the list of princes by the victories of Shah Ismail, the first of the Suffavean dynasty.

Shah Ismail was descended from a race of holy men, who were Sheahs, or adherents of the family of Aly, and who had long been settled at Ardebil, where they lived as retired devotees. Their reputed sanctity had attracted many disciples, and had acquired them the reverence and respect of the temporal rulers of their country. Among the most renowned was Sudder-u-deen, whom Timour visited in his cell, and asked what favour he could confer upon him. The pious man requested that he would release the prisoners which he had brought from Turkey. The conqueror complied; and the grateful tribes, when they had regained their liberty, declared themselves the devoted adherents of him to whom they owed it. In process of time, however, the disciples of this sect so increased in numbers, that the ruler of Aderbijan became alarmed, and banished their chief, Juneyd, the grandfather of Ismail, from Ardebil. But Juneyd found protection at Diar-bekir, where Uzun Hussun had established a powerful principality. This prince not only received him with kindness, but thinking it an honour to be connected with the holy man, gave nim his sister in marriage; and after Hussun had become sovereign of Persia he bestowed his daughter upon Hyder, the son and successor of Juneyd. Ismail was the third son of this

marriage, and was but a child when he succeeded to the mantle of his brothers; but he seems to have been more devoted to his duties, as the descendant of a race of warriors, than to those which he inherited as the representative of a family of saints. Having collected a numerous band of adherents, he marched against the ruler of Aderbijan, whom he defeated, and, having obtained possession of that province, he invaded Irak; and, after a few years, became the acknowledged sovereign of Persia. He afterwards subdued Bagdad and its surrounding territories, and drove the Usbegs from Khorassan and Bulkh. Success had hitherto attended all his movements; but he found a powerful enemy in Sultan Selim, who, advancing upon Aderbijan, completely defeated the Persian army; which reverse so affected the mind of Ismail, that, though of a cheerful disposition, he was never afterwards seen to smile. The only fruit of this victory was the plunder of the Persian camp, and the glory of defeating Ismail; for the Turkish monarch was compelled immediately to retire for want of supplies; and his death, which happened soon after, relieved Persia from a formidable foe. Ismail died at Ardebil, where he had gone on a pilgrimage to the tomb of his father, when only thirty-eight years of age.

Though Sultan Khodah-bundah, about two centuries before, had embraced the faith of the sect of Aly, yet it was to Ismail that it owed its establishment as the religion of the empire; and it was principally to the nature of its tenets that he was indebted for the rise of his fortunes. From the sanctity of his own character, and also of that of his ancestors, he was regarded by his followers as one raised up and favoured by heaven for the propagation of the new faith. They gloried in the name of Sheah, or "sectary," and vowed eternal hostility against all Sonnites. So enthusiastic were they in this feeling, that many of his soldiers disdained to wear armour when fighting under Ismail, but bared their breasts, and courted death in the midst of their enemies, exclaiming "Sheah! Sheah!" to mark the holy cause for which they fought. The memory of Ismail is still cherished with affection in Persia; and the dynasty, of which he was the founder, ruled over this country for more than two centuries.

His son Tamasp was only ten years of age when he ascended the throne. Though not distinguished by great abilities, this prince possessed a kind and generous disposition, and was not wanting either in spirit or in prudence. During a long reign of fifty-three years, which was almost periodically disturbed by the invasion of the Turks, on the one hand, and by the inroads of the Usbegs on the other, he maintained the integrity of the empire, and added Georgia to the conquests of his father. His generous reception of the emperor Hoomayoon, when driven from the throne of India, is remembered by his countrymen with national pride; and the munificent and royal hospitality which that prince experienced, and the effectual assistance which he received to replace him on his throne, called forth the praise even of distant nations. It was during the reign of this prince, that Queen Elizabeth accredited an English merchant, named Jenkinson, to visit the court of Persia, for the purpose of extending the commerce of her kingdom; but Tamasp, who was most bigoted in his religious sentiments, told him that he had no need of the aid of infidels, and bade him depart.

For nearly ten years, subsequent to the death of Shah Tamasp, the empire was torn by the contentions of his children, when his grandson Abbas was raised to the throne by the chiefs of Khorassan. The young prince was for a time held in subjection by those powerful nobles to whom he owed his elevation; and Murshud Kooli Khan, who had obtained the supremacy among them, exercised all the functions of a sovereign. But the mind of Abbas was not formed to be contented with the name of power without the reality; and the death of Murshud Kooli, which he soon after accomplished, put him in possession of an authority which he jealously retained to the end of his life. The Usbegs still continued their usual inroads into Khorassan; but Abbas in vain endeavoured to bring them to an action; for their chief object being plunder, they always retired on the approach of the Persian army. On one occasion, however, the rapidity of his movements prevented the retreat of these depredators, when a general engagement ensued, which ended in the complete overthrow of the invaders. Their prince Tulim Khan, and many of their bravest leaders, fell in this action; and the remainder saved themselves by a rapid flight across the Oxus. This victory gave a long respite to this province from such depredations; and enabled the Persian monarch to extend his territories as far as Bulkh. His generals, at the same time, had subdued the whole of the mountain province of Lar; and the islands in the Persian Gulf.

Abbas now directed his attention to the encroachments of the Turks, who not only held the fort of Nahavund in Irak, but the cities of Teflis and Tabreez, with almost the whole of Georgia and Aderbijan. His first attack was upon Nahavund, which he took and levelled its fortifications with the ground. He then marched into Aderbijan, and besought his troops to second his efforts against the enemies of their country and their faith. Tabreez and Erivan surrendered to his arms, but he was compelled to recall his general from the siege of Bagdad, by the approach of the Turkish army. The action which followed was not only glorious to the Persian arms, but the most important in its consequences which Abbas ever fought. The Turks were driven from all their possessions on the Caspian; and Aderbijan, Georgia, Kurdistan, Bagdad, Moossul, and Diarbekir, were re-annexed to the Persian empire.

This great prince had early perceived, that the internal tranquillity of the kingdom was liable to be frequently disturbed by the violent disputes of the more powerful tribes. Some of these composed the best portion of his army, particularly the Kuzel-bash tribes, whose numbers amounted to between fifty and sixty thousand horsemen. These men would only obey leaders of their own tribe; so that the king could not advance a favourite to any rank or command in his army, except he was the chief of a Kuzel-bash family. To render himself independent of these turbulent chiefs, Abbas reduced the number of their followers in his army to thirty thousand; and raised a corps of ten thousand horse and twelve thousand foot, as his body guard, who received their pay from the crown, and were commanded by officers of his own appointment. In the formation and discipline of this corps, he was greatly assisted by the counsel and exertions of two English knights of the name of Sherley, who, with twenty-six followers, had gone over to Persia as soldiers of fortune. By their instructions in the art of war, and in the use of artillery, they were enabled to cope with the janizaries of Turkey, and constituted a powerful defence to the monarch against the violence of the nobles.

Having restored tranquillity throughout the empire, Shah Abbas set himself to promote its general welfare and improvement. He fixed his residence

at Ispahan, which he made the capital of his dominions, and greatly beautified; and its population was more than doubled during his reign. "Its principal mosque; the noble palace of Chehel-Setoon; the beautiful avenues and palaces called the Char-Bagh, or "four gardens;" the principal bridge over the river Zynderood; and several of the finest palaces in the city and suburbs, were all built by this prince. He carried, at an immense expence, a causeway across the whole of Mazenderan; and rendered that difficult country passable for armies and travellers at all seasons of the year. He threw bridges over almost all the rivers of Persia; and the traveller in that country met, in every direction, the most solid and spacious caravanseries, which had been erected by the royal munificence of this monarch.

There have been few sovereigns more deserving of the title of Great than Shah Abbas, if we consider the substantial benefits which he rendered to his country. Though distinguished as a military leader, and possessed of great means, he deemed the improvement of his dominions a nobler object than the pursuit of conquest. He attended to the cultivation and commerce of Persia beyond all former monarchs, and his liberal policy attracted to his dominions Europeans from almost every country in Christendom, who enjoyed during his reign the most abundant toleration. The impression which his noble munificence in the erection of so many useful public buildings made upon the minds of his subjects, has descended to their children; and the ready answer, which is received to every inquiry respecting the founder of any ancient building in this country, is, "Shah Abbas the Great," which is given not from their knowledge of the fact, but from the habit of considering him as the author of all improvements.

During the greater part of his reign, Persia enjoyed an internal tranquillity which had been unknown for centuries; and the impartial Chardin has summed up his character in this respect in few words: "When this great prince ceased to live, Persia ceased to prosper." But notwithstanding this high eulogy, we cannot forget the many cruelties of which he was guilty, particularly towards the members of his own family, which neither the stern dictates of policy, nor the jealousy of power can ever justify. His conduct to the princes of Georgia, and the inhabitants of that province, it is impossible to palliate; and his unnatural treatment of his children, the assassination of the oldest Suffee Meerza, and the depriving the remaining two of sight, has left a stain upon his memory which his best deeds will never wash away. It is however consolatory to know, that he sincerely mourned the loss of his first-born; and that the assassin, who had at first been highly rewarded for his crime, was reserved to suffer an even more than adequate punishment. He was commanded to bring him the head of his own son. The devoted slave obeyed; and when he presented it, the tyrant demanded with a smile of bitter scorn, how he felt. "I am miserable," was the reply; "You should be happy," said Abbas, "for you are ambitious, and in your feelings you are at this moment the equal of your sovereign." This monarch died in his favourite palace of Ferrahabad, in Mazanderan, at the age of seventy, and bequeathed the sceptre of Persia to his grandson Sam Meerza, the son of Suffee Meerza.

Previous to the time of Abbas the Great, the Persian princes had been brought up as soldiers, and had often the command of armies; but the jealousy of that sovereign led him to change en-

History. tirely this system of education; and subsequent to the death of his sons, the princes of the Suffavean dynasty were from their infancy immured in the haram, and associated only with women and eunuchs. His successors consequently bore indelible marks of this pernicious system. Their characters were formed by their condition. Inexperienced and effeminate, they trusted the direction of public affairs to their ministers, and revelled in every sensual gratification. Effeminacy begat cowardice, and cowardice cruelty; and all who were at any time denounced as dangerous to their power, were immediately destroyed.

A.D. 1627. *Sam Meerza.* Sam Meerza was seventeen years of age when he was taken from the haram and set upon the throne of the Great Abbas. He was a tyrant without one redeeming quality. Every male of the blood-royal, however distantly related, and every officer of rank or reputation, were either put to death or deprived of sight; and the list of his victims was swelled by a great number of females of the highest rank, among whom were his A.D. 1641. aunt, his mother, and his queen. He died at Kashan, after a reign of fourteen years, every one of which presented the same horrid and disgusting scene of barbarous cruelty.

Abbas II. Abbas the II. was not ten years old at the death of his father, and fell of course into the hands of his ministers, who happened to be men of devout and austere habits. But the restraint in which he was kept only led him to indulge the more when he escaped from their authority: and though naturally humane and generous, yet in his drunken frolics he committed the most wanton cruelties. His excesses, however, were in a great degree confined to the circle of his court. His subjects at large knew him only as one of the most generous and just monarchs that ever ruled in Persia. During his reign the country enjoyed complete tranquillity; embassies from almost every nation in Europe, as well as from India and Tartary, visited his court, and experienced his kindness. Commerce flourished; and his hospitality and attention to strangers attracted vast numbers to his dominions. His excessive indulgence brought on an inflammation in the throat, of which he died in the A.D. 1666. thirty-fourth year of his age.

Suffee Meerza. The long reign of his son and successor, Suffee Meerza, who upon his accession assumed the name of Soliman, is not marked by any event of importance. He was characterised by the same unwarlike and dissolute habits which distinguished his father and grandfather; and his whole time was divided between the pleasures of the table and the haram. A.D. 1694. During this reign, and also the succeeding one of the *Shah Hussein.* meek but imbecile and superstitious Hussein, eunuchs were exalted to all the first offices of the state, to the disgust and resentment of the nobles of the empire. This conduct, however, provoked neither opposition nor revolt. The spirit of the nation had been gradually declining, and the peace of a century had rendered them both insensible to the approach of danger, and incapable of resistance.

The reign of Hussein is memorable chiefly for the *Affghans.* invasion and subjugation of the empire by the Affghans in 1722. This race had long inhabited the mountainous region between Persia and India. Divided into tribes, where the chief and his followers enjoyed the same savage freedom, they opposed every attempt to reduce them to one society, whose common danger and wants would have cemented their union, and rendered them formidable to their

neighbours. In consequence of this disunion, they *History.* were never able to resist any serious attack, and their country was long divided between the monarchs of Persia and India. They were, in general, however, able to maintain a considerable degree of independence by balancing between these two powerful states.

The most formidable of the Affghan tribes were those of Ghiljee and Abdallee, who had become subjects of Persia when Abbas the Great had taken possession of Candahar. The former of these tribes had their pasture lands in the vicinity of that city, and during the reigns of the successors of Abbas, had been both dangerous and turbulent subjects. They had often shown a disposition to revolt, and it was apprehended that the court of Delhi looked to the possession of Candahar through their means. In order to check this spirit of insurrection, Goorgeen Khan, the Prince of Georgia, one of the ablest and bravest officers in Persia, was appointed to the government of that province. But his *Oppressed* oppressions and injustice hastened the very catastrophe *by the Persian gover-* which he was sent to prevent. Meer Vais, an artful *nor.* and able Affghan chief, who held the high office of principal magistrate of the city of Candahar, and who had grievously suffered from the tyranny of the new governor, persuaded his countrymen to rise and revenge their wrongs. " It is better," however, said he, " to strike the lion sleeping than awake. Be secret and faithful, trust your cause to me, and be assured I will take a terrible vengeance upon our enemies." The wily Affghan so dissembled his resentment, that Goorgeen Khan accepted an invitation to a sumptuous entertainment prepared for him by Meer Vais, where he and all his attendants were murdered. The Affghans *Revolt* immediately seized the fort of Candahar, and raised the *A.D. 1709.* standard of independence. The intelligence of this insurrection came like a thunderbolt upon the effeminate court of Ispahan; but the despicable advisers of Hussein, instead of sending an army to crush the growing evil, dispatched an ambassador to persuade Meer Vais to submission. " Let thy king raise or let fall his arm as *Speech of* he pleases," said that determined chief, " if he were as *Meer Vais* formidable as thou sayest he is, it would be with deeds, *to the Per-* not empty words, he would oppose our just designs. *sian ambas-* " Our swords are now drawn, and shall never be *sador.* sheathed till your king is dethroned and your country subdued." War was now the only alternative, but the Affghans were victorious, and Meer Vais in a few years became the undisputed master of Candahar, which he constituted an independent kingdom. The death of this chief, however, delayed for a time the execution of his more ambitious plans.

His son Mahmood being only eighteen years of *A.D 1717.* age, the government devolved upon his brother Meer Abdullah. This weak and timid ruler recommended an accommodation with Persia, which excited such general discontent and indignation among the Affghan chiefs, that he was soon cut off, and Mahmood proclaimed sovereign of Candahar. This prince, who *Mahmood* was of a fierce and warlike disposition, having firm- *proclaimed* ly established his power, contemplated with high *sovereign* hopes the subjugation of Persia. This unfortunate *of Canda-* country was at this period depressed by the va- *har.* cillating measures of its pusillanimous ruler. Dangers assailed her on every side; the irruptions of the Usbegs and Abdallee Affghans into Khorassan, the ravages of the Kurds, in the western frontier, the attacks of the Arabs on the south, and the invasion of Mahmood on the west, all called for the most prompt and vigorous resistance. But the energies of the empire

History. were extinguished by effeminacy and palsied by superstition. An unusual denseness in the atmosphere, accompanied with an extraordinary redness in the appearance of the sun on the horizon, which continued for nearly two months, was converted into a symbol of divine wrath, and prince and people anticipated the destruction of the capital. Every measure which fanaticism could suggest was adopted to avert the threatenings of heaven; but their fears were confirmed by the intelligence that the army of the Affghan prince *Invades Persia.* was within a few days march of Ispahan. This army, it is said, did not exceed twenty thousand warriors, while the Persian forces within the walls of the city were more than double its numbers. But treachery and cowardice laid Persia at the feet of Mahmood, and after *A.D. 1722.* a long siege, unexampled in horrors *, Ispahan opened *Resignation* her gates, and Hussein resigned his crown to the Affghan *of Hussein.* conqueror. His son, Tamasp, who had escaped from Ispahan during the siege, and had attempted a diversion in favour of his father, but without effect, now assumed the title and state of a king; but he was unfitted to struggle with the perils of the unsettled times in which he lived, and it may be said that with Shah *His cha-* Hussein terminated the Suffavean dynasty. This weak *racter.* but virtuous prince was distinguished for great kindness of heart, and extreme gentleness of temper; but his meekness and bigotry were equally destructive to his country as the vices of his predecessors, and he had the misfortune to be surrounded by crafty and evil counsellors, some of whom sought the promotion of their own selfish views in the downfall of their country.

Mahmood The measures which Mahmood adopted at the com- *adopts mea-* mencement of his reign were such as to conciliate the *sures of* good opinion of his new subjects, and to promise pros- *concilia-* perity to Persia. His first care was to relieve the in- *tion;* habitants from famine. He received into favour all those nobles who had maintained their fidelity to Shah Hussein, while he banished or put to death those who had proved false to their duty. European factories were encouraged and confirmed in all their privileges, and Christians of all nations were allowed the public *becomes a* performance of their religious duties. But all this was *capricious* but as a gleam of sunshine before a tempest. It was *tyrant.* an effort of virtue, which his cruel and capricious nature was unable to support. He stood amidst the wreck of a mighty empire, and he became alarmed at the magnitude of the ruins with which he was surrounded. His army had been greatly reduced, and he dreaded an insurrection in the capital. In order to relieve his fears, he had recourse to measures the most cowardly and savage recorded in history. The miseries of the siege were but as a prelude to the bloody tragedy which was to follow; the different acts of which were, the murder of three hundred nobles with all their male children; the destruction of three thousand guards whom he had taken into pay; the massacre of every Persian who had ever been in the service of the former government; the plunder of European and other foreigners; and the murder of *History.* thirty-nine princes of the blood. Such horrible cruelties could only have proceeded from a mind, overwhelmed *His mas-* by the most servile fears, or under the influence of in- *sacres.* sanity; and we find that this prince soon after was seized with madness in its most dreadful form, in the paroxysms of which, according to some accounts, he not only tore off his own flesh, but ate it. He died *Dies in-* under the most excruciating tortures of mind and *sane.* body, in the prime of life, and after having sat upon the throne of Persia only three years.

Ashraff, the cousin of Mahmood, succeeded to the *Ashraff* sovereignty. He commenced his reign by cutting off *succeeds* some of the bravest leaders of his own tribe, whose am- *to the* bition he dreaded more than the resentment of the Per- *throne.* sians, and the few Persian nobles that remained at Is- *A.D. 1725.* pahan, whom he charged with being in correspondence with his enemies, shared the same fate. Having thus endeavoured to strengthen his internal government, the attention of Ashraff was called to the invasion of the Turks and Russians, who had entered into a treaty by which some of the finest provinces of Persia were to be divided between them. The issue of this war, *War with* throughout the whole of which he had displayed the *the Turks* most consummate ability, was favourable to the Aff- *and Rus-* ghans; and the title of Ashraff to the throne of Persia *sians.* was fully acknowledged. But he had now to prepare for more serious dangers.

Tamasp, whose efforts to regain the crown of his *Tamasp* father had been weak and inefficient, and chiefly con- *is joined by* fined to negociations with the Russian government, *Nadir Koo-* had fixed his small court at Ferahabad, in Mazen- *li;* deran. Many of his best friends, who had continued attached to his fortunes, had been swept away by the plague; and his hopes of success had been fast settling into despondency, when his prospects began to brighten by the accession of a powerful auxiliary in the person of Nadir Kooli. This chief was of low extraction; his sword was his only birthright, and his valorous deeds his proudest genealogy. He had commenced his career of ambition as the leader of a band of robbers. In the distracted state of his country, Nadir had risen to distinction and reputation by his valour and enterprise, and having obtained possession of the fort of Kelat, by the murder of his uncle, employed his forces against the Affghans, and recovered the important city and district of Nishapore. The tender of the services of such a chief was not to be refused in the circumstances in which Tamasp was placed; and notwithstanding the former crimes of Nadir, he was received into favour, and invested with the sole *who re-* command of the Persian army. In one season, the *ceives the* cities of Herat and Mushed were reduced, and the *command* whole of Khorassan compelled to recognise the sove- *of the* reignty of Tamasp. Ashraff, who had hitherto beheld *army,* the exertions of this prince with indifference, now perceived the coming danger, and hastened to meet it at a distance from the capital. But the genius of Nadir

---

* The dreadful extremities to which the inhabitants of Ispahan were reduced, during this siege, are described by several eye-witnesses. "The flesh of horses, camels, and mules, was so dear, that none but the king, some of the nobles, and the wealthiest citizens, could afford to purchase it. Though the Persians abhor dogs as unclean, they ate greedily of them, as well as that of other forbidden animals, as long as they were to be obtained. After these supplies were gone, they fed upon the leaves and bark of trees, and on leather, which they softened by boiling, and when this sad resource was exhausted, they began to devour human flesh. Men with their eyes sunk, their countenances livid, and their bodies feeble and emaciated with hunger, were seen in crowds endeavouring to protract a wretched existence, by cutting pieces from the bodies of those who had just expired. In many instances, the citizens slew each other, and parents murdered their children to furnish the horrid meal. Some more virtuous poisoned themselves and family, that they might escape the guilt of preserving life by such means. These evils were increased by the cruelty of the Affghans, who put to death, without distinction of age or sex, all who tried to escape from this scene of calamity."

History.
and defeats
the Aff-
ghans.

prevailed, and after two desperate engagements, one of which was fought at Damghan, in Khorassan; and the other about forty miles north of Ispahan, the Affghan power was annihilated in Persia.

Tamasp entered his capital amidst the acclamations of his people; but he is said to have burst into tears when he beheld the defaced and solitary halls of his glorious ancestors. Ashraff had led off his forces towards Shiraz, carrying with him the old men, women, and children of his tribe, upon mules and camels, and all the spoil that he could collect. Accounts, however, daily arrived of the dreadful excesses which they committed on their march, and Nadir Kooli was urged by his sovereign to pursue the fugitives. But this chief had other views than restoring a weak prince to the throne of his fathers. He saw the sceptre within his own grasp; and lost no opportunity of securing his future elevation. He therefore required the power of levying money, as essential to enable him to extirpate the Affghans. This demand opened the eyes of Tamasp to his own critical situation; but the soldiers would march under no other leader, and he was obliged to comply. Though it was the depth of winter, Nadir led his forces towards Shiraz; and in a few months Persia was relieved from her barbarous oppressors. Few of the Affghans escaped death, and hardly any returned to their native country. They either perished from want and fatigue upon the desert, or were taken and sold for slaves. Such was the termination of this extraordinary usurpation, in which a small band of foreigners, seldom exceeding thirty thousand, held in subjection the mass of a great nation; and during the seven years, in which they exercised dominion in Persia, "nearly a million of her inhabitants had perished, her finest provinces had been rendered desert, and her proudest edifices levelled with the dust"

On his return, Nadir Kooli was hailed as the deliverer of his country; and, as a reward for his great services, received the grant of Khorassan, Mazenderan, Seistan, and Kerman, with the power of exercising the privileges of an independent sovereign. The pageantry of Tamasp was now drawing to a close. Under the pretence of his having concluded an ignominious peace with the Turks, while Nadir was quelling a rebellion of the Affghans in Khorassan, he was dethroned by his victorious general, who raised the infant son of Tamasp to the throne, and accepted the office of regent of the empire. Nadir now entered into a war with the Ottoman Porte, which, after a long and doubtful struggle, terminated with the recovery of all the possessions which the Turks had seized during the Affghan invasion. The successful issue of this war stimulated the ambition of the regent; and the opportune death of the infant king presented to him a vacant throne.

On the plains of Chowal Mogan, and at the great festival of the Nouroze, Nadir had assembled the nobles and chiefs of the empire; and from them, after much affected humility, he condescended to accept the crown, upon the condition that the nation should abandon the doctrines of the Sheahs, and embrace the Sonnee faith. This desire of Nadir to change the religion of his country was evidently prompted by the hope that it would destroy that veneration and attachment which the Persians cherished for the Suffavean dynasty, by whose founder the Sheah faith was first established. The nation at large, however, continued attached to their favourite tenets, which they openly embraced at the death of Nadir Shah.

The accession of Nadir Shah was immediately followed by the reduction of the province of Candahar, which was possessed by the Affghans; and the rapid conquest of Hindostan, from whence he returned laden with the richest treasure, calculated to amount to nearly seventy millions sterling. His subjects began now to feel the benefit of their sovereign's triumphs. Taxes were remitted for three years; and Nadir was regarded as the destined restorer of Persia to its former glory. Within five years, this indefatigable conqueror had not only expelled the Affghans, but had also subdued the monarchs of Candahar, India, Bokharah, and Khaurizm, and had extended the limits of the empire to the Oxus on the north, and the Indus on the east.

Hitherto Nadir had exercised his power with comparative moderation; but a circumstance occurred at this time, which seemed to produce a dreadful change in his disposition and character. While marching through one of the forests of Daghestan, in an expedition against the Lesghees, a ball from a concealed assassin wounded him in the hand and killed his horse. His suspicions fell upon his oldest son Reza Kooli, a prince of great valour and acquirements, and who was much beloved by his countrymen; and his suspicions were so heightened by the gross misrepresentations of infamous courtiers, that in a moment of rage, he ordered the prince to be deprived of sight. "Your crimes," said Nadir, "have forced me to this dreadful measure."—"It is not my eyes you have put out," replied Reza Kooli, "but those of Persia." No sooner was the punishment inflicted than the tyrant was penetrated with remorse, and vented his fury upon all around him. Fifty noblemen, who were present, were put to death, on the pretext that they should have offered their lives to save the eyes of a prince who was the glory of their country. From this time Nadir became gloomy and irritable; and his conduct during the last five years of his life, exceeded in cruelty the deeds of the most bloody tyrants. His murders were not confined to individuals; the inhabitants of whole cities were massacred; and, according to his partial historian, "men left their abodes, and took up their habitations in caverns and deserts, in the hope of escaping his savage ferocity." The only troops that enjoyed his favour, and upon whom he placed any reliance, were the Affghans and Tartars, who were of the Sonnee persuasion; and so suspicious was he of the fidelity of his countrymen, who, in general, adhered to the Sheah tenets, that in a state of phrenzy he proposed to put to death every Persian in his army; but the bloody purpose was prevented by his death; and he was assassinated by some of his chief officers, who had been marked as his next victims.

The character of Nadir Shah may be given in few words. He worshipped at no shrine but that of ambition; and every action of his life was intended to promote or to secure his own interests. His example of usurpation had inspired every petty chief with the desire of rule; so that, at his death, Persia abounded with pretenders to regal power, and during ten years, as many sovereigns rose and fell in succession, till Kurreem Khan Zund was left without a competitor. This excellent prince was born in a low rank; but he may be numbered among the few monarchs who have risen to power without crime, and exercised it with justice

Mahomed Hussein Khan.

and moderation. His most formidable rival was Mahomed Hussein Khan, the head of the Kujurs, and grandfather of the present ruler of Persia. This chief, upon the murder of his father by Nadir Shah, had been compelled to take refuge among the Turkomans; but no sooner was he informed of the death of that monarch, than, having collected an army, he hastened to become a competitor for the empire. Kurreem Khan evacuated Ispahan on his approach, and shut himself up in Shiraz. But the troops of the Kujur chief were unprepared for the delayed hardships of a protracted siege; and daily desertions of numerous bodies of his army warned their commander of the necessity of an early retreat. Kurreem, on his return to Ispahan, was received with the most lively joy. He was the favourite competitor with the people, and possessed their sincere attachment more than any ruler that ever held the government of Persia. Hussein was soon after defeated and slain. His family fled to the country of the Turkomans, where they remained about four years, and then gave themselves up to Kurreem Khan, who treated them with great attention and kindness.

Defeat and death of Hussein.

A.D. 1762. Kurreem becomes sole ruler of Persia.

Having firmly established his authority over the whole of Persia, Kurreem Khan continued to display the same moderation in the exercise of his power, as he had shown in the attainment of it. But his government was frequently disturbed by the turbulence and ferocity of his brother Zuckee Khan, who had once openly rebelled, but had been again received into favour. This chief was employed to quell some disturbances in Damghan and Mazenderan. His track was every where marked by blood; and it was upon this occasion that his inventive barbarity made a garden of his enemies. "He directed the earth to be opened at equal distances, as if for the reception of trees, to form an avenue. Large branches were then cut, and a prisoner tied to each, with his head towards the root, which being placed where the ground was opened, the soil, as it was thrown in, produced a gradual suffocation." During the latter years of Kurreem Khan, the country enjoyed general peace and security. Under his auspices, agriculture and commerce had revived; and though unlearned himself, his court was the resort of men of liberal knowledge, whose learning he valued and encouraged. He had fixed his residence at Shiraz, which he greatly improved and ornamented with magnificent buildings and luxuriant gardens; and seemed at all times anxious to promote the happiness and prosperity of the inhabitants of that favoured city. This good prince died at an advanced age, after having ruled Persia for twenty-six years, regretted and esteemed by all his subjects.

Cruel conduct of his brother.

His government.

A.D. 1779. Character of Kurreem.

The character of Kurreem Khan has few features which naturally belong to despotism. He had never assumed the title of shah or king, contenting himself with that of vakeel or regent. He was distinguished for great lenity, and a manly simplicity of mind; and possessed that noble courage which dares to pardon. His virtues were plain and intrinsic. He was humane, pious, and just; and was enabled to carry into almost every measure of his government the best affections and feelings of human nature. His name is still venerated by the inhabitants of Persia; and they long had cause to regret his loss.

His descendants.

The descendants of Kurreem Khan forfeited by their crimes that power which he had obtained by his virtues; and were all, after twelve years of almost incessant warfare, supplanted by Aga Mahomed Khan Kujur, who

became sole ruler of Persia. The chiefs who ruled during this interval, were Zuckee Khan, the brother of Kurreem, who, to conceal his assumption of power, raised to the nominal sovereignty two sons of the late ruler; but his cruelties raised the indignation even of his own body-guard, by whom he was assassinated at Yezdikhaust. Saduck Khan, another brother, then seized the government, which he held for a short time, when he was dispossessed and put to death by Aly Moorad Khan, the nephew of Kurreem. This prince was of a firm and energetic character, and, had he lived, might have secured for a time the peace of this distracted kingdom. But being obliged, while suffering under a severe illness, to march against Jaaffer Khan, the son of Saduck, who had revolted, and was proceeding towards the capital, fatigue and anxiety hastened his death. Jaaffer Khan immediately ascended the throne, which he filled for nearly three years, when he was poisoned at the instigation of two of his nobles whom he had imprisoned. He was succeeded by his son Looft Aly Khan, whose mild and conciliatory character gave promise of better fortunes to his fallen country. Though not yet twenty years of age, his mind had been matured by continual employment during his father's reign, and he was ranked among the best and bravest soldiers of his time. But his disposition seemed to change with his exaltation; and instead of displaying those kind and prepossessing manners for which he had been formerly distinguished, he became proud, self-willed, and suspicious. He still retained, however, the heroic and enterprising qualities of a consummate soldier, and long struggled against the most fearful odds in support of his birthright. But his almost romantic exploits will find a place in the history of his more fortunate rival.

History.

Zuckee Khan.

Saduck Khan.

Aly Moorad Khan.

Jaaffer Khan.

Looft Aly Khan.

His character.

Aga Mahomed Khan was the oldest son of Mahomed Hussein Khan Kujur, and had from his infancy been inured to misfortune. When only five years of age, he was a prisoner, and was emasculated by the cruel mandate of the successor of Nadir Shah. He afterwards accompanied his father through all the vicissitudes of his fortune, and at his death fell into the power of Kurreem Khan, by whom he was treated with great favour and indulgence. During the reign of that prince, he was a prisoner at large in the city of Shiraz, with a liberal allowance to live upon, the use of the royal stud, and permission to hunt over the neighbouring country; and his extraordinary wisdom had so attracted the notice of Kurreem, that he frequently consulted him on questions of state policy. Upon the death of that ruler he fled to Mazenderan, where he had the dexterity to reconcile the jarring interests of his tribe, and to receive their support as a competitor for the crown of Persia.

Aga Mahomed Khan.

During the first years of the struggle, he employed himself in establishing his authority in his native province. But upon receiving intelligence of the death of Aly Moorad Khan, he led his followers into Irak: and before the close of Jaaffer Khan's reign, he had reduced almost the whole of that province. On the accession of Looft Aly Khan, he advanced into Fars, and having defeated that prince, laid siege to the city of Shiraz; but, after a vain attempt to make any impression upon its defences, he returned to Teheran, which he had made the capital of his kingdom. But the overbearing and suspicious temper of his rival, did more to promote his cause than his own valour, or the number of his followers.

Enters Irak.

Returns to Teheran.

Hajee Ibrahim, the prime minister, and governor

History.

of Shiraz, a nobleman of the highest talents and acquirements, and who had been the means of placing Looft Aly Khan upon the throne, had become alarmed for his own safety from the irascible disposition of his master; and, as a measure of self-preservation, seized upon Shiraz, and invited Aga Mahomed to take possession of it. A strong detachment was immediately dispatched to the support of Hajee Ibrahim, but it was attacked and defeated by the Persian prince. Another army, of superior force, and outnumbering the troops of Looft Aly more than ten to one, met with the same fate; when Aga Mahomed was under the necessity of advancing in person with an overwhelming force, which he conceived would at once terminate the war. But the brave Looft Aly was still undismayed, and, animated by the most heroic courage, he determined upon one great effort for his crown. He surprised the advanced guard of the enemy, which he defeated, and pursuing the fugitives to their camp, attacked with a band of a few hundred men an army of more than thirty thousand. Favoured by the darkness of the night, and the terror which his name inspired, he had dispersed almost the whole of the enemy, and was about to enter the tent of the Kujur chief, when he was stopped by the assurance of one of his followers, that Aga Mahomed was among the fugitives. Deceived by this report, he dispersed his troops to plunder in other directions, reserving for himself the jewels and treasures of the royal pavilion. But when the morning dawned, he was astonished to hear the public crier calling to prayers, which announced to all that Aga Mahomed Khan was still at his post. Looft Aly, awakened from his dream of victory, found himself in the midst of his enemies, and fled with precipitation, to avoid being made prisoner. Aga Mahomed marched his army to Shiraz; and from this time he may be considered the actual sovereign of Persia.

The mind of Looft Aly Khan was still unsubdued. Though struggling against the most adverse circumstances, he still cherished the hope of better fortunes. He had still a few faithful followers, who had never forsaken him; and with these this most undaunted of warriors determined again to take the field. After a variety of fortune, he took the city of Kerman by assault, and once more assumed the style of a sovereign; but this was the last of his glorious achievements. Aga Mahomed hastened with all the forces he could collect, to crush a foe who seemed to rise with renewed energy from every fall. He invested the city with an immense army; and posted a strong body of men opposite every gateway, to prevent the escape of his rival. The defence was maintained with the most heroic ardour for four months; but treachery effected what superiority of numbers could not accomplish. The citadel was given up to the Persian troops; and Looft Aly and his brave followers, after a severe contest of three hours, were overpowered by numbers, and obliged to retire. At night the young prince crossed the ditch by a bridge of planks, and, accompanied by three attendants, threw himself upon the enemy's lines with a courage strengthened by despair, and effected his escape. When Aga Mahomed found in the morning that Looft Aly was beyond his reach, he gave vent to the cruel passions of his nature, and wreaked his vengeance upon the innocent inhabitants of Kerman. All the males of mature age were commanded to be put to death, or deprived of sight; and twenty thousand women and children were granted as slaves to his soldiers.

Looft Aly Khan was soon afterwards betrayed into the hands of his merciless enemy, who, after treating him with the most brutal indignity, tore out his eyes, and sent him prisoner to Teheran. But this gallant prince, even in the wretched state to which he was reduced, was still an object of dread; and the fears of the tyrant could only be allayed by his death. Such was the fate of the last prince of the Zund dynasty, which had held the government of Persia for nearly half a century. But their implacable enemy was determined upon their extirpation; and every one, who, from his birth, could have formed the most remote pretensions to the throne, was either put to death or deprived of sight; and not only the members of this tribe, but all who had been the active supporters of the family of Kurreem Khan, were removed to the most distant quarters of the kingdom.

Aga Mahomed, having now relieved himself from all internal foes, resolved upon the conquest of Georgia. During the troubles which succeeded the death of Kurreem Khan, Heraclius, the prince of that province, had preserved it in a state of tranquillity, and had transferred his allegiance from the sovereigns of Persia to those of Russia. His motive for this measure was declared to be a desire to release his Christian subjects from the violence and oppression of Mahomedan superiors, and to place them under the protection of a great nation of their own religion. But it was not to be expected that any monarch of Persia would tamely suffer the alienation of one of the finest provinces of the empire. Aga Mahomed, therefore, was determined to insure success by the magnitude of his force. Sixty thousand men assembled at Teheran, and proceeded without resistance till within about fifteen miles of Teflis, the capital of the province, where they were met by the forces of Heraclius, amounting to one-fourth of their number. The battle which ensued was bravely contested; but the Georgians, overpowered by numbers, were compelled to fly. Teflis submitted to the conquerors, and was given up to massacre and to pillage. In describing the scene of carnage which followed, a Mahomedan historian observes, " That on this glorious occasion the valiant warriors of Persia gave to the unbelievers of Georgia a specimen of what they were to expect at the day of judgment." Youth and beauty alone were spared, and fifteen thousand of these were led into bondage.

The subjugation of Georgia was followed by that of Khorassan; and Aga Mahomed was contemplating the conquest of Bokharah, when he was recalled by the intelligence that the Russians had recovered Georgia, and were threatening Aderbijan. He hastened to Teheran; but, as the season was too far advanced to commence operations that year, he summoned the chiefs of the kingdom to meet him in the spring with all their adherents, for the purpose, as he said, " of punishing the insolent unbelievers of Europe, who had dared to invade the territories of the faithful." Persia, however, was relieved from the impending invasion by the death of the Empress Catherine, when the Russian army was recalled by her successor. But notwithstanding the retreat of the Russians, Aga Mahomed determined to overrun Georgia, and had advanced as far as Sheshah, when he was arrested by the hand of an assassin. Being one day disturbed by a dispute between two of his servants, he was so enraged at the noise which they made, that he commanded them both to be instantly put to death. Saaduck Khan Shekakee, a nobleman of high rank, having interceded for

History.

their pardon, was refused; but as it was the night of Friday, and sacred to prayer, their execution was delayed till next morning. These men knew that their sentence was irrevocable, and, as they were still permitted by their infatuated master to perform their usual avocations about his person, they, as a measure of self-preservation, took advantage of their situation, and deriving courage from despair, poniarded the monarch as

Is assassin- ated.

he lay asleep in his tent. Thus perished one of the most cruel, but at the same time one of the ablest monarchs that ever ruled in Persia.

Character of Aga Mahomed.

The character of this extraordinary man, however, must be viewed in reference to the distracted state in which he found his country, and his desire to secure its future tranquillity. The great object of his life was to acquire power, and to render it permanent in his own family; and he scrupled at no measures for the accomplishment of his purpose. In his early life he had become a profound adept in the art of dissimulation. While his success was still uncertain, he controlled every passion that could obstruct his rise; but, when the mask was no longer necessary, he gave full scope to the feelings of his savage spirit. Every chief whom he deemed in any way likely to aspire to the throne, or disturb the peace of the kingdom, was either put to death or deprived of sight; and, among his victims were two of his own brothers. To such a height did he carry his barbarous revenge, that he ordered the bones of the virtuous Kurreem Khan and of Nadir Shah to be dug up and removed to Teheran, where they were deposited at the entrance of the palace, that he might enjoy the unmanly and disgusting gratification of trampling upon the graves of two of the principal foes of his family. This monarch attempted to justify his barbarous proceedings by the plea of necessity; and, when speaking of his successor, the present king of Persia, he used often to exclaim, " I have shed all this blood, that the boy, Baba

His ava- rice.

Khan *, may reign in peace." The passion of avarice in this monarch was almost as strong as his love of power: and he had recourse to the most unjustifiable means in the gratification of it. When he wished to plunder any of his nobles, or principal officers, he was in the habit of selling them for a stipulated sum, and the purchaser, in order to enable him to raise the money, was vested with power over every thing belonging to the person bought, except his life. He is even said to have at one time combined with a religious mendicant to obtain money from his courtiers. He ordered a considerable sum to be given him in the presence of his principal officers, with the secret understanding that it was to be returned with the half of what he received from the others; but the wily beggar found means to escape with all his gains, and the courtiers inwardly rejoiced in the disappointment of their monarch's cupidity. His conduct, how-

His con- duct to Shah Rokh.

ever, to the aged Shah Rokh, the grandson of Nadir Shah, could only proceed from a heart where the love of wealth had eradicated every feeling of humanity. This weak prince was supposed to have concealed many precious stones of great value, particularly a ruby of extraordinary size and lustre, which had once decorated the crown of Aurengzebe; but as he solemnly denied the possession of them, Aga Mahomed had

recourse to torture. After a variety of pains, a circle of paste was put upon the head of his victim, and boiling lead poured into it. The ruby was discovered, which filled the tyrant with joy, but Shah Rokh survived only a few days. The person of this monarch was extremely slender, and unless upon occasions of ceremony, always dressed in the plainest manner. His beardless and shrivelled face resembled that of an aged and wrinkled woman, and the expression of his countenance, at no time pleasant, was horrible when clouded, as it very often was, with indignation. With the meanest vices, Aga Mahomed possessed the most splendid talents. During his reign, agriculture revived, and commerce flourished under his protection. He restored complete tranquillity to a distracted kingdom, and fixed his family upon a splendid throne.

History.

His ap- pearance.

Futteh Aly Shah, the nephew and appointed successor of Aga Mahomed, after a short struggle, was proclaimed king, and has hitherto been enabled to maintain the internal peace of his dominions. With respect to his frontier provinces, however, he has not been so successful. Georgia has become a province of Russia, and many of the chiefs of Khorassan yield him only a nominal obedience. Owing to the comparative mildness and justice of his rule, the inhabitants of Persia have enjoyed a state of happiness and prosperity to which they had long been strangers; and he may be regarded as holding a high rank among the sovereigns of his country. When Mr. Morier visited Persia in 1809, this prince was about forty-five years of age. " He is a man of pleasing manners, and an agreeable countenance, with an aquiline nose, large eyes, and very arched eye-brows. His face is obscured by an immense beard and mustachios, which are kept very black, and it is only when he talks and smiles that his mouth is discovered. His voice has once been fine, and is still harmonious, though now hollow, and obviously that of a man who has led a free life." He had then sixty-five sons, and it was supposed an equal number of daughters. " They are said to be affable and humane, and harmonious among themselves. Renouncing the intemperate habits of some of their predecessors, sharing in their journeys all the toils and privations of the lowest subjects with an unaffected ease, they cultivate habits which are more manly, and better adapted to persons whose duties embrace the happiness and protection of the whole society, while their taste for information is directed to all those topics which tend to the general improvement. It is possible that by their intercourse with the different polished countries of Europe, particularly through the medium of well informed men who visit them, and communicate the information and the spirit which predominate in enlightened communities, they may lay the foundation for a new æra in the national character and condition. See Malte-Brun's *Geography*, vol. ii. p. 294. Morier's *First and Second Journeys*. Sir John Malcolm's *History of Persia*. Franklin's *Observations, &c.* Sir Robert Ker Porter's *Travels in Georgia, Persia, &c.* and Kinnear's *Geographical Memoir of Persia*.

Futteh Aly Shah is proclaimed king. A.D.1796.

The cha- racter of his govern- ment.

His ap- pearance.

His fami- ly.

PERSIAN WHEELS. See HYDRODYNAMICS, Vol. XI. p. 565.

---

* Baba signifies " child," and was the name by which the present king of Persia was familiarly known till the death of his uncle. His proper name was Futteh Aly.

PERSPECTIVE.

LINEAR PERSPECTIVE is the art of delineating on a plane surface, the representation of objects, in such a manner, that to an eye properly situated, they may have, when properly coloured, the same appearance as the originals. Perspective teaches the method of tracing the outline or skeleton of a picture. The colouring and shading of it belong to the art of painting.

Perspective owes its origin to painting, and particularly to that branch of it which is employed in the decorations of the theatre. Vitruvius says, that Agatharchus of Athens was the first author who wrote upon this subject; and that afterwards its principles were more fully explained in the writings of Democritus and Anaxagoras, the disciples of Agatharchus. But none of the writings of the ancients on perspective have come down to the present time.

Bartolomeo Bramantino of Milan, and Pietro del Borgo, likewise an Italian, are the first authors who have professedly laid down rules of perspective. The latter author traced the images of the objects by supposing them placed beyond a transparent tablet; and Albert Durer constructed a machine on the principles of Borgo, by which he could trace the perspective appearances of objects.

Leon Battista Alberti, in 1540, wrote a Treatise di Pittura, in which he treats chiefly of perspective. Balthazar Peruzzi, of Siena, who died in 1536, had diligently studied the writings of Borgo: his method of perspective was published by Serlio in 1540. He is said to have been the first who discovered that the representations of lines inclined to the ground line at an angle of 45°, converge to the same point in the per-

spective plane. Such points, we may observe, are called points of distance or vanishing points, and are of great use in perspective; but not only do the representations of lines inclined to the ground line at an angle of 45° converge to a point, but the representations of all lines parallel to each other, and any how inclined, do the same. This general proposition was discovered soon after by Guido Ubaldi, another Italian, whose Treatise on Perspective was published at Pesaro in 1600. It contains the first principles of the method afterwards explained by Dr. Brook Taylor. In 1543, was published the work of Gaicomo Barozzi, commonly called Vignola, entitled, The Two Rules of Perspective, with a learned commentary, by Ignatius Danti. Maralois' Treatise on Perspective was printed at the Hague, and engraved and published by Hondius. And in 1625, Sirigatti published his Treatise on Perspective, which is little more than an abstract of Vignola's. Since that time the art of perspective has been gradually improved, but chiefly by Professor Gravesande, and Dr. Brook Taylor. In the older treatises, the rules are confined to the horizontal plane, and the constructions are exceedingly complicated; but in Dr. Taylor's treatise, and in those since published, the rules are universal, and apply equally to all planes and lines however situated, and in the constructions much fewer lines are employed. Dr. Taylor's treatise was first published in 1715, and afterwards with improvements in 1719.

The most profound and complete treatise on perspective which has yet appeared, is that of Hamilton, in two volumes folio.

THEORY OF PERSPECTIVE.

THE theory of perspective may be divided into four parts or sections. In the first section is explained the method of drawing on a plane surface the exact representation or picture of any object, the positions of the eye and the picture, and also the position and magnitude of the object being given. In the second section is explained the method of determining the original objects, the representation or pictures being given. The third section treats of the appearance of pictures when seen from a point which is not the proper point of sight. The fourth section treats of the delineation of shadows.

DEFINITIONS.

1. The plane on which the representation, projection, or picture of any object, is drawn, is called the *perspective plane*, and also the *plane of the picture*. It is supposed to be placed between the eye and the object.

2. The point of sight is that point from which the picture ought to be viewed. This point is also called the point of view.

3. If from the point of sight, a line be drawn at right angles to the picture or perspective plane, the point in which it meets that plane is called the centre of the picture; and the distance between that centre

and the point of sight, or the perpendicular above mentioned, is called the *distance of the picture*.

4. By original object, is meant the real object placed in the situation it is represented to have by the picture.

5. By original plane, is meant the plane on which any original point, line, or plane figure, is situated.

6. The point in which any original line, or any original line produced, cuts the perspective plane, is called *the intersection* of that line.

7. The line in which any *original plane* cuts the perspective plane, is called the intersection of that original plane. If the original plane be that of the horizon, its intersection with the picture, or the line above mentioned, is called the *ground line*.

8. The point in which a straight line drawn through the point of sight parallel to any original line cuts the picture, is called the vanishing point of that original line. And the distance between that point and the point of sight, is called simply the *distance* of that vanishing point.

9. The line in which a plane drawn through the point of sight parallel to any original plane cuts the perspective plane, is called the *vanishing line* of that original plane. If from the point of sight there be drawn a line cutting that vanishing line at right angles,

4

the point of intersection is called the centre of the vanishing line. And the distance between the point of sight and that point or centre is called simply the *distance* of the vanishing line.

10. If from a given point a straight line be drawn at right angles to any plane, the point of intersection is called the *seat* or orthographic projection of the given point on that plane. And if from all the points of any line or plane figure perpendiculars be drawn to any plane, the line or figure formed by their intersections with it, is called the seat or orthographic projection of the given line or figure on that plane.

PLATE
CCCCLIX.
Fig 1.

That the definitions may be fully understood, let O (Fig. 1.) represent the point of sight, ADKB the perspective plane, and AW any original plane. If from O, OC be drawn at right angles to the plane ADKB, C will be the centre of the picture, and OC will be its distance. If through O the plane QI be supposed to be drawn parallel to the original plane AW, HI, its intersection with the perspective plane will be the vanishing line of AW; and if OG be drawn at right angles to HI, G will be the centre and OG the distance of HI. If OV be supposed parallel to EF, V will be the vanishing point of EF, and OV will be its distance. AD, the line in which the plane AW intersects the perspective plane, is the *intersection* of AW.

Postulate.

In treatises of perspective it is assumed that the rays of light proceed in straight lines from the objects to the eye. This is only strictly true on the supposition that the air is of uniform density; but for the purposes of painting its truth may be safely assumed in all cases.

The reader of the following treatise is supposed to know the first six books and the 11th book of Euclid, or the article GEOMETRY in this Dictionary.

SECTION I.

On the determination of the perspective representations of given objects on a plane surface.

PROP. I. THEOR.

If straight lines be drawn from the point of sight to the several points of any object, the intersections of these with the perspective plane will mark out the perspective representation of the object.

Fig. 2.

Let O (Fig. 2.) be the point of sight, HK the perspective plane, and ABC any figure. If straight lines be drawn from O to every point of ABC, the figure *a b c*, formed by their intersection with the perspective plane HK, will be the perspective representation of ABC.

For as the rays of light proceed from the objects to the eye in straight lines, it is clear that no ray can come from the point A to an eye placed at O, except by passing through the point *a*. If, therefore, the point *a* could be coloured so as to convey to the eye at O the same impression with the point A, the absence of A would not be perceived. And as the same is true of all the other points, it is evident that the figure *abc*, when properly coloured, would have to an eye placed at O, exactly the same appearance as the original object ABC; therefore, the intersection *a b c* of straight lines, drawn from O, the point of sight, to the several parts of the original object ABC, with the perspective plane, is the perspective representation of that object.

COR. 1. If a straight line be drawn from the point of sight to any point, its intersection with the perspec-

tive plane is the perspective representation of that point.

COR. 2. The perspective representation of a straight line not passing through the point of sight is a straight line. For if straight lines be drawn from the point of sight to every point in the given straight line, they will form a *plane triangle*; whose intersection with the perspective plane is a straight line. Thus *a b* is the perspective representation of AB.

COR. 3. The perspective representation of any straight line which passes through the point of sight is a point.

COR. 4. The perspective representation of a straight line is the straight line which joins the perspective representations of its extremities.

SCHOLIUM. It follows from the above proposition, that, if the system of straight lines, or the cone of rays drawn from the point of sight to the objects be the same, their perspective representations will be the same. Hence objects of very different figure and appearance may have the same or similar perspective representations.

PROP. II. THEOR.

The straight line which joins the vanishing point with the intersection of any straight line, is the perspective representation of that line extended *ad infinitum;* and the representation of any part of that original line is some portion of the former.

Let IB, (Fig. 3) any line indefinitely extended towards B, intersect the perspective plane in I, and let V be its vanishing point; then V I is the perspective representation of the line IB, indefinitely extended towards B, and the representation of AB any portion of IB, is a portion of VI. For, let O be the point of sight, and join VO. By Def. 8. OV is parallel to IB. Therefore OV, VI, and IB, are all in one plane. Hence every straight line drawn from O to the line IB must intersect VI somewhere between V and I. If the lines be drawn from O towards the remote extremity of IB, they will intersect VI towards the point V; and though the intersections may be as near as possible to the point V, they cannot be above it, OV being parallel to IB. It is clear, then, that if straight lines be drawn from O to every point in IB indefinitely extended towards B, they will form a plane whose intersection with the perspective plane is VI; VI is therefore the perspective representation of IB indefinitely extended towards B. If straight lines be drawn from O to any two points A, B, in the line AB, they will intersect VI somewhere between V and I; and *a b*, the perspective representation of AB, is a portion of VI.

COR. 1. The perspective representations of parallel lines converge to a point in the picture. This is clear, for it has just been proved, that the perspective representation of any line passes through its vanishing point; but all parallels have the same vanishing point; their representations, therefore, pass through the same point in the picture. Thus VM, VI are the representations of the parallels IB, MN.

COR. 2. The perspective representations of all lines perpendicular to the perspective plane, pass through the centre of the picture; for the straight line drawn from the point of sight to the centre of the picture is perpendicular to the perspective plane, and is therefore parallel to the other perpendiculars. Hence the centre of the picture is the vanishing point of all the perpendiculars; but every representation passes through the vanishing point of its original line; therefore all the

Fig. 3.

PERSPECTIVE.

PLATE CCCCLIX.

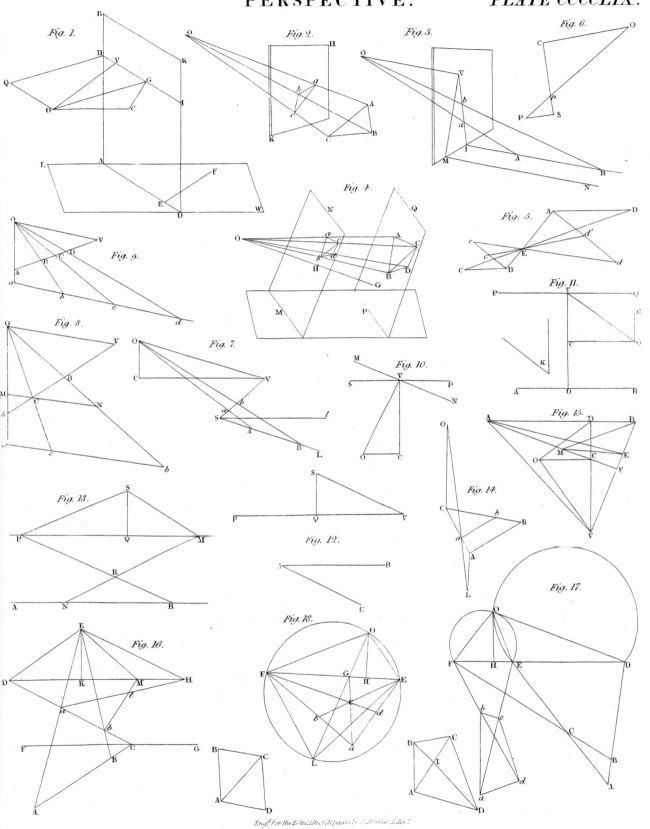

Fig. 1.
Fig. 2.
Fig. 3.
Fig. 6.
Fig. 4.
Fig. 5.
Fig. 9.
Fig. 8.
Fig. 7.
Fig. 11.
Fig. 10.
Fig. 15.
Fig. 13.
Fig. 12.
Fig. 14.
Fig. 17.
Fig. 16.
Fig. 18.

Engd. For the Edinr. Encyclopædia by J. Moffat Edinr.

representations of the perpendiculars pass through the centre of the picture.

PROP. III. THEOR.

The perspective representation of a straight line parallel to the picture, is parallel to its original; and has to it the same ratio which the distance of the point of sight from the perspective plane has to its distance from a plane drawn through the original straight line parallel to the perspective plane.

Let MN (Fig. 4) be the perspective plane, O the point of sight, and AB a straight line parallel to MN. Through AB draw the plane PQ, parallel to MN, and let OHG be drawn at right angles to the planes MN, PQ, intersecting them in the points H, G; the perspective representation of AB shall be parallel to AB, and shall have to it the same ratio which OH has to OG. For, if straight lines be drawn from O to every point in AB, they will form a plane triangle OAB, whose intersection ab with the perspective plane is (Prop. 1.) the representation of AB. But the intersections of parallel planes by a third plane are parallel (E. 12 of 11.) Therefore ab is parallel to AB. Again, by similar triangles, $ab : AB = Ob : OB$. But parallel planes cut straight lines in the same ratio (E. 11th Book). Hence $Ob : OB = OH : OC$; and $ab : AB = OH : OC$.

COR. 1. The perspective representations of all lines parallel to the perspective plane, being parallel to their originals, are parallel to each other.

COR. 2. The perspective representation of a plane figure parallel to the perspective plane, is similar to its original, and has to it the same ratio which the square of the distance of the point of sight from the perspective plane, has to the square of the distance of the same point from the plane of the original figure. Thus, $abcd$ is similar to ABCD, for the sides of the triangle acd being parallel to the sides of the triangle ACD, the triangles (E. 11th Book) are equiangular; for the same reason, the triangles abd, ABD, are equiangular. Hence the figure $abdc$ is similar to ABDC; and $abdc : ABDC = ab^2 : AB^2 = Ob^2 : OB^2 = OH^2 : OC^2$.

PROP. IV. THEOR.

The vanishing line, and the intersection or base line, of any plane, are parallel to each other.

This proposition is quite evident; for the vanishing line and base line are the intersections of parallel planes by the perspective plane. See Def. 7th and 9th.

PROP. V. THEOR.

The vanishing points of all lines situated in any orginal plane, are in the vanishing line of that plane.

For the original lines being all in one plane, their parallels drawn through the point of sight will also be in one plane; and the points in which they intersect the picture will be in the line in which that plane intersects the picture: but the points above mentioned are the vanishing points of the original lines; and the plane of the parallels being parallel to the original plane, its intersection above mentioned, with the picture, is the vanishing line of that original plane. Hence, the truth of the proposition.

COR. 1. The vanishing point of the common intersection of two original planes, is the intersection of their vanishing lines.

COR. 2. The vanishing line of a plane perpendicular to the picture passes through the centre of the picture. For the straight line drawn from the point of sight to the centre being at right angles to the picture, every

plane drawn through the point of sight at right angles to the picture must pass through that line, and consequently its intersection with the picture must pass through the centre; but the vanishing line of a plane perpendicular to the picture, is the intersection of a plane, drawn through the point of sight parallel to the original, and therefore at right angles to the picture. Hence the truth of the proposition.

PROP. VI. THEOR.

The intersections with the picture of all lines situated in any original plane, are in the intersection of that plane.

This is evident.

COR. 1. The intersection with the picture of the common intersection of two original planes, is the point in which their intersections cut each other.

COR. 2. Planes, whose common intersection is parallel to the picture, have parallel intersections, and also parallel vanishing lines. This corollary will appear evident from what follows: Suppose a straight line to be parallel to a plane. Through the straight line let any plane be drawn to intersect the given plane, and the intersection of the two planes will be parallel to the original straight line; for that intersection can never meet the given line, being in a plane parallel to it, and being also in the same plane with it, they must be parallel to each other. Hence, the intersections of the two planes, mentioned in the corollary, with the perspective plane, are each parallel to the common intersection of the two planes, and are therefore parallel to each other. The vanishing lines being parallel to parallels are also parallel to each other.

LEMMA I.

Let AB (Fig. 5.) be any straight line, and AD, BC, two straight lines drawn from its extremities parallel to each other, and let DC, the straight line which joins their extremities, intersect AB in E. Through the points A and B draw Ad, Bc, any two straight lines, also parallel to each other, and either equal to AD, BC, or having to each other the ratio of AD to BC; and either in the plane in which AD, BC, are placed, or in a different plane: then the straight line dc, or $d'c'$, will intersect AB in the same point E in which DC intersects it. For DC, dc, and $d'c'$, divide AB into parts, which have the ratio of AD to BC, of Ad to Bc, or of Ad' to Bc'; but these ratios are equal. Hence the point of intersection is the same for all.

PROP. VII. PROB.

The centre and distance of the picture being given, to find the representation of a point, whose seat on the picture, and distance from it, are given.

Let C (Fig. 6.) be the centre of the picture, and S the given seat. Join CS, and draw CO, in any direction, and equal to the distance of the picture. Through S draw SP parallel to CO; but on the opposite side of CS, and equal to the distance of the point from its seat; join OP: then p, the intersection of it with CS, is the representation required.

For the lines drawn from the point of sight to the centre of the picture, and from the proposed point to its seat, being at right angles to the picture, are parallel to each other, and in the same plane with CS; farther, they are equal to CO, SP: therefore, by Lem. 1. p is the point in which a straight line drawn from the point of sight to the point proposed cuts the picture; p is therefore the representation of the point proposed.

COR. 1. The point p may be found by means of pro-

3 F.

portional compasses, without drawing the parallels CO, SP, by dividing CS in the ratio of the distance of the picture to the distance of the point from its seat.

Cor. 2. To find the representation of a straight line by this problem, find the representation of its extremities, and the straight line joining them will be the representation required.

Prop. VIII. Prob.

The centre and distance of the picture being given ; to find the representation, vanishing point, and its distance, of a line whose seat on the picture, intersection, and the angle which it makes with its seat, are given.

Fig. 7.
Let C (Fig. 7.) be the centre of the picture, and S *l* the given seat. Make the angle LS *l* equal to that which the line proposed makes with its seat. Draw CV parallel to S *l*, and from C draw CO at right angles to it. Make CO equal to the distance of the picture, and from O draw OV parallel to SL ; join SV. V is the vanishing point, VO its distance, and VS the representation of the line proposed. For the straight lines OV and VC being parallel to SL, S *l*, the angle OVC (see Geom.) is equal to the angle L S *l*, or to the angle which the line proposed makes with its seat. But the plane passing through the straight lines drawn from the point of sight to the centre of the picture, and to the vanishing point of the proposed line, is evidently at right angles to the picture, and parallel to that plane which passes through the proposed line and its seat ; its intersection with the picture is therefore parallel to the given seat ; and the angles contained by parallel lines being equal, the angle contained by the straight line drawn from the centre to the vanishing point of the proposed line, and the straight line drawn from the point of sight to the same point, is equal to the angle which the line proposed makes with its seat, or to the angle OVC. It is therefore evident, that the triangle OVC is, in every respect, equal to that contained by the lines which join the centre of the picture, the vanishing point of the proposed line, and the point of sight ; therefore, CV is equal to the distance of the vanishing point from the centre of the picture ; and it was already proved that the straight line which joins the centre of the picture with the vanishing point of the line proposed is parallel to the seat of that line. Hence V is the vanishing point of the line proposed, OV its distance, and consequently, (Prop. II.) VS is the representation of the line extended *ad infinitum*.

Cor. 1. The same things being given, the perspective representation of any given point in the line proposed may be found. For, having made the same construction as above, make SA equal to the distance of the given point from S, the intersection of the line proposed ; join OA, meeting SV in *a* ; then *a* will be the representation required. This is evident from the Lemma,—the straight lines, drawn from the centre and the proposed point, to the points S, V, being parallel to each other, and equal to OV, SA.

Cor. 2. Hence also *a b*, the representation of AB, any portion of the proposed line, may be found.

Prop. IX. Prob.

The representation and vanishing point of any straight line being given ; to find the representation of the point which divides the original in any given ratio.

Let AB (Fig. 8.) be the given representation, and V the vanishing point. It is required to find the representation of the point which divides the original of AB in a given ratio. Draw VO anyhow through the point V, and draw *a b* parallel to, and at any distance from, VO. Take O any point in VO ; join OA, OB, and let them meet *a b* in *a, b* ; divide *a b* in *c*, so that *a c* may have to *c b* the given ratio, and join O *c*, and let it cut AB in C ; C is the representation required. For through C draw MCN, parallel to *a b*, or VO ; and by similar triangles, viz. BCN, OBV ; ACM, AVO, we shall have (E. 4. 6.) the following proportions,
$$\left\{ \begin{array}{l} CN : OV = CB : BV \\ OV : CM = AV : AC \end{array} \right\} ;$$
and hence, (by E. 22. 6,) CN : CM=CB . AV : BV.AC. But CN : CM=*c b* : *c a* ; hence *a c* : *b c* = BV × AC : BC × AV, or AC : BC = AV × *a c* : BV × *b c*. Now BV and AV are given lines, and *ac* : *bc* = the given ratio. It is evident, therefore, that the same point C will be obtained, however the lines OV, *a b*, be drawn, (provided they be parallel,) and at whatever distance from V the point O is taken. But the straight lines, drawn from the point of sight to V, and the original of AB, are parallel to each other, and in the same plane with AB ; the straight line drawn from the point of sight to the point which divides the original of AB in the given ratio, would therefore intersect the picture in the point C determined by the above construction ; C is therefore the representation of the point required.

Cor. 1. The point C may be found without the above construction, by dividing AB in C, so that CA × BV may have to BC × AV the given ratio.

Prop. X. Prob.

The representation and vanishing point of a straight line being given ; it is required to cut off, from a given point in that representation, the representation of a given portion of the original.

Fig. 9.
Let AB, (Fig. 9.) be the given representation, and V the vanishing point ; also let C be a given point in AB. It is required to cut off from AB, a portion CD, which shall be the representation of a given portion of the original of AB. Draw any line VO from V, and *a d* any other straight line parallel to it. In OV, take any point O, and join OA, OB, OC, and let them cut *a d* in the points *a, b, c* : in *a b* take *c d*, so that *a b* shall have to *c d* the same proportion which the original of AB has to the original of the portion to be cut off ; join O *d*, and let it cut AV in D ; CD will be the representation required. For it may be proved as in the last problem, that *a b* : *b c* = CV × AB : BC × AV, and   *b c* : *c d* = DV × BC : CD × BV.
Hence *a b* : *c d* = AB × CV × DV : CD × BV × AV, or DV : CD = BV × AV × *a b* : CV × DV × *c d*. But the ratio of *a b* to *c d* is given, and AB, CV, BV, AV, are also given ; hence, the ratio of DV to DC is given, the point D is therefore given. But it is evident that the point O may be supposed to coincide with the point of sight, and *a d* with the given line ; and the circumstances will not be altered. Therefore, a straight line drawn from the point of sight to the extremity of the portion of the original, whose representation is to be cut off, would pass through D : hence CD is the representation required.

Prop. XI. Theor.

A straight line, drawn from the centre of the picture, to the centre of any vanishing line, is at right angles to that vanishing line.

Fig. 10.
Let C, Fig. 10. be the centre of the picture, and V

the centre of any vanishing line SP: the straight line CV is perpendicular to the vanishing line SP. For, if not, let MN be at right angles to CV. Let O be the point of sight; and join OC, OV. Then, because OC is at right angles to the perspective plane, every plane passing throughout it, is also at right angles to that plane, (See E. 19. 11.) Therefore, the plane OCV is at right angles to the perspective plane ; but a plane is at right angles to another plane, when any straight line drawn in the one plane at right angles to their common section, is also at right angles to the other plane. Therefore MN, which is drawn in the picture at right angles to CV, is also at right angles to the plane OCV, and consequently at right angles to every line it meets in that plane; therefore MN is at right angles to OV. But the vanishing line SP is also at right angles to OV. Therefore, two straight lines, in the same plane, are both at right angles to the same line, which is impossible. Therefore, no line but SP can be drawn at right angles to CV through the point V ; SP is therefore perpendicular to CV.

Prop. XII. Prob.

The centre and distance of the perspective plane being given ; to find the vanishing line, its centre and distance, of a plane whose intersection with, and inclination to, the perspective plane, are given.

The vanishing line of any plane, being the intersection with the picture, of a plane drawn through the point of sight parallel to the original plane, must be parallel to the intersection, (See Prop. IV.) of that plane ; and the inclination to the picture of the plane drawn through the point of sight, is equal to the inclination of the original plane to the picture,—or, what is the same thing, the angle contained by the straight line drawn from the point of sight to the centre of the vanishing line, and the straight line drawn from the centre of the picture to the same point, is equal to the inclination of the original plane to the picture, and is therefore given. Hence, in the triangle formed by drawing lines from the point of sight to the centres of the picture and vanishing line, there are given all the angles and one side, viz. the distance of the picture. The triangle is therefore given, and hence the following construction of the problem.

Fig. 11.

Let AB (Fig. 11.) be the intersection of the plane proposed with the perspective plane ; C the centre of the picture ; and K the inclination of the plane proposed to the perspective plane : from C draw CD, at right angles to AB ; draw CO at right angles to CD, and make CO equal to the distance of the picture ; draw OM parallel to CD, and make the angle MOV equal to K, and let OV meet CD produced in V ; through V draw PQ, parallel to AB. PQ will be the vanishing line of the plane proposed, V its centre, and OV its distance. This is clear from what was said above ; for V is evidently the centre (Prop. XI.) of the vanishing line ; and the angle CVO being equal to VOM, is equal to K, the inclination of the plane proposed to the picture ; and OC being the distance of the picture, the triangle OCV is equal to the triangle formed by joining the point of sight and the centres of the picture and vanishing line ; and OV is equal to the distance of the centre of the vanishing line from the centre of the picture. Hence PQ is the vanishing line, V its centre, and OV its distance.

Prop. XIII. Prob.

The centre and distance of the perspective plane

being given ; to find the vanishing point of a straight line, situated in a plane, whose intersection with, and inclination to, the perspective plane are given ; the inclination of the line proposed to that intersection being also given.

Fig. 12.

Let AB (Fig. 12.) be the intersection of the plane with the perspective plane, and let BAC be the inclination of the proposed line to it; find (Prop. XII.) PV the vanishing line of the plane, and Q its centre ; and from Q draw QS at right angles to PV, and equal to the distance of the vanishing line from the point of sight ; from S draw SV, making with SQ an angle equal to the complement of BAC to a right angle, so that the angle V may be equal to BAC ; and draw it, so that the angles SVP, BAC, may look in opposite ways, then V will be the vanishing point of AC. For the vanishing point of AC is in the line PV (Prop. V.), and the triangle SQV is evidently in every respect equal to the triangle contained by the direct distance of the vanishing line, the vanishing line itself, and the line drawn from the eye parallel to the given line ; VQ is therefore equal to the distance of the vanishing point in Q, and V is the vanishing point sought.

Prop. XIV. Prob.

Having given the vanishing line of a plane, its centre, and distance, and the representation of a line in that plane, it is required to draw, through a given point in that representation, the representation of another line in that plane, which makes a given angle with the former.

Fig. 13.

Let AB (Fig. 13.) be the intersection of the plane in which the original lines lie ; PV its vanishing line, and Q the centre of that line : draw QS at right angles to PV, and equal to the distance of PV from the point of sight : also let PR be the given representation, and R the given point in it. It is required to draw through R the representation of a line, whose original makes a given angle with the original of PR. Join SP, and make the angle PSM equal to the given angle, and let SM meet PV in M ; join RM : then RM is the representation required. Since the angle formed by drawing straight lines from the point of sight parallel to the given lines, is equal to the given angle, the angle PSM is equal to the angle contained by lines drawn from the point of sight to the vanishing points of the original lines ; but P being the vanishing point of one of these lines, and QS equal to the distance of PV from the point of sight, PS must be equal to the distance of the point of sight from the vanishing point P, and the angle SPQ equal to the angle which the straight line drawn from the point of sight to P makes with the line VP. Hence the triangle SPM is equal to that formed by drawing lines from the point of sight to the vanishing points of the proposed lines ; and PM is equal to the distance of the vanishing points from each other. But the vanishing points of both lines (Prop. V.) are in the line PV : hence M is the vanishing point of the line whose representation is required. But it was proved, (Prop. II.) that the representation of any straight line passes through its vanishing point ; therefore RM is the representation required.

Cor. 1. The representation of one side of a triangle given in species, and situated in a given plane, being given, the representation of the triangle itself may be found by the above proposition.

Cor. 2. Hence also the representation of any plane figure may be found ; for every plane figure may be divided into triangles.

PROP. XV. PROB.

To find the representation of a given finite straight line parallel to the perspective plane.

Fig. 14.

Let AB (Fig. 14.) be the seat of the given parallel straight line on the picture, and C the centre of the picture; find a the representation of that extremity of the given straight line of which A is the seat, as in Prop. VII. Draw $a\,b$ parallel to AB; join C, B; and let CB cut $a\,b$ in b; $a\,b$ will be the representation required. Since the triangles BAC, $b\,a\,c$, are similar, AB : $a\,b$ = AC : a C = LO : a O = the ratio of the straight line, drawn from the point of sight to the original of a, to the straight line drawn from the same point to a. But AB is evidently equal to the line of which it is the seat, the latter being parallel to the picture; hence $a\,b$ is to the given original as the distance of a from the point of sight is to the distance of the original of a from the point of sight. Hence (Prop. III. and Cor.) $a\,b$ is equal in magnitude to the representation of the given finite straight line. But the given straight line, being parallel to the perspective plane, is parallel to its representation; now $a\,b$ is parallel to AB, and therefore to the given straight line, and passes through a, the representation of one of the extremities of the given line. Hence $a\,b$ coincides both in direction and magnitude with the perspective representation of the given finite straight line.

PROP. XVI. PROB.

The centre and distance of the picture being given, and also the vanishing line of a plane, to find the vanishing point of lines perpendicular to that plane.

Fig. 15.

Let C (Fig. 15.) be the centre, and AB the given vanishing line; from C draw CD, at right angles to AB, and from C draw CO, at right angles to CD, and make it equal to the distance of the picture; join OD, and from O draw PV at right angles to OD, and let it meet CD produced in V; then V is the point required. For if the triangle DOV be supposed to be elevated so as to stand at right angles to the plane of the picture, it is evident O will be the point of sight, and the plane AOB will be parallel to the original plane; and OV being evidently at right angles, the plane AOB will also be at right angles to the original plane, and consequently parallel to its perpendiculars; therefore V, the point in which it cuts the perspective plane, is the vanishing point of these perpendiculars. (See Def.)

COR. 1. If the points D, C, coincide, the lines OV, DV, will be parallel, and the vanishing point of the perpendiculars is infinitely distant, as it ought to be; for the vanishing line of a plane can only pass through the centre of the picture when the original plane is perpendicular to the picture, in which case its perpendiculars are parallel to the picture, and have no vanishing point.

COR. 2. If the vanishing line AB be infinitely distant, OD, DC, will be parallel, and the point V will coincide with C, the centre of the picture. This also is manifestly true; for the vanishing line of a plane is infinitely distant only when that plane is parallel to the picture, in which case the perpendiculars to it will also be at right angles to the picture, and will therefore have this vanishing point situated in its centre. (See Prop. V. Cor. 2.)

COR. 3. DC : CV = CO : CV; and CD : DO = DO : DV.

PROP. XVII. PROB.

The centre and distance of the picture being given, to find the vanishing line, its centre, and distance, of planes perpendicular to a line, whose vanishing point is given.

Fig. 15.

Let C (Fig. 15.) be the centre of the picture, and V the given vanishing point; join CV, and draw CO at right angles to it, and equal to the distance of the picture; join OV, and draw OD at right angles to OV, and let it meet CV produced in D; draw AB at right angles to DV: then AB is the vanishing line required. For let the triangle OVD be raised up so as to be at right angles to the perspective plane, and O will be the point of sight, and OV will be parallel to the given line, (See Def.) and OD being perpendicular to OV, is parallel to the proposed planes. But AB being at right angles to the plane DOV, is also parallel to the proposed planes. Therefore AOB is parallel to those planes, and AB is their vanishing line.

PROP. XVIII. PROB.

The centre and distance of the picture being given, it is required to draw through a given point, the vanishing line of a plane which is perpendicular to another plane, whose vanishing line is given; and to find the centre and distance of that vanishing line.

Find by Prop. XVI. the vanishing point of lines that are perpendicular to the plane, whose vanishing line is given. The straight line joining this point with the given point, is the vanishing line sought. For as the plane whose vanishing line is required, may be supposed to be entirely composed of perpendiculars to the plane, whose vanishing line is given, it is evident the vanishing line required must pass through the vanishing point of these perpendiculars. The straight line, which joins the given point with their vanishing point, must therefore be the vanishing line required. The vanishing line being drawn, its centre will be determined by drawing a perpendicular to it from the centre of the picture; and its distance is the hypothenuse of a right-angled triangle, of which the perpendicular from the centre is the base, the other side being the distance of the picture.

COR. 1. Let BV (Fig. 15.) be the vanishing line of Fig. 15. a plane perpendicular to the original plane, whose vanishing line is AB; draw CF at right-angles to BV, and let it meet BD produced in A: then A will be the vanishing point of lines at right-angles to the original of BV. For it is evident from Prop. XVI. that the vanishing point of lines at right-angles to the original of BV, lies in the line FC; but lines perpendicular to the original of BV, are evidently parallel to the plane, whose vanishing line is AB, and therefore have their vanishing points situated in AB. The vanishing points, therefore, of lines at right-angles to the original BV is A, the point in which FC and AV intersect each other.

COR. 2. The straight line AV is the vanishing line of a plane, which is at right-angles to the originals, whose vanishing lines are AB and BV: for the vanishing line of such a plane must pass both through A and V. Therefore AB, BV, AV, are the vanishing lines of the three planes which contain one of the angles of a cube, and A, B, V, are the vanishing points of the three lines in which these planes intersect each other.

COR. 3. If upon BV as a diameter, a semicircle be

Perspec-
tive.

described, cutting AF in M, then FM will be the direct distance of the vanishing line BV. This follows from Cor. 2. to Prop. XVI.

Prop. XIX. Prob.

Having given the centre and distance of the picture, the vanishing point of the common intersections of two planes which are inclined to each other at a given angle, and the vanishing line of one of them, to find the vanishing line of the other.

Let AB, (Fig. 15.) be the given vanishing line of one of the planes; and A the vanishing point of their intersection, which must evidently be situated in AB. Find by Prop. XVII. BV, the vanishing line of planes at right-angles to lines, of which A is the vanishing point, or, what is the same thing, of planes at right-angles to the intersection of the planes in question; find F the centre of that vanishing line, and FM its distance, (Prop. XVII.); join BM, and make the angle BME equal to the given inclination of the planes; join AE: then will be the vanishing line sought. For, if straight lines be drawn through the point of sight parallel to the intersection of the perpendicular plane with the other two planes, they will evidently contain an angle equal to the inclination of these planes, and will meet the picture in the points in which the vanishing line of the perpendicular plane intersects the vanishing lines of the other two planes. One of these lines therefore passes through B; and the angle BME having been made equal to the given angle, the other must pass through E: the vanishing line sought, therefore, passes through the point E; it must also pass through the point A, (Prop. V.) and AE is therefore the vanishing line sought.

Prop. XX. Prob.

Having given the centre and distance of the picture, also the vanishing line of one face of any given solid, and the representation of a line in that face; to find the representation of the whole solid.

The vanishing line of the face, and the representation of one of its sides being given, the entire representation of the face may be found by Prop. XIV. Cor. 2.; and the vanishing points of the sides of the face will evidently be determined by producing the corresponding sides of the representation till they intersect the given vanishing line. But the solid being given, the adjacent faces are inclined to each other at given angles. Hence the vanishing line of one face and the vanishing points of its sides or common intersections with the adjacent faces being found, the vanishing lines of the adjacent faces may be determined by the last problem; and as the representation of one side in each of these faces has been already determined, being the same with the sides of the representation already found, the entire representation of the faces may be determined by Prop. XIV. Cor. 2; and proceeding in this manner with the remaining faces, the entire representation of the solid will be determined.

SECTION II.

The perspective representations being given, to find the original figures.

Prop. I. Prob.

Having given the centre and distance of the picture, and the representation of a straight line, whose original is situated in a given plane, to determine the position and length of that original.

Perspec-
tive.

Let DH (Fig. 16.) be the vanishing line of the given plane, found as in Prop. XII.; K its centre, and KE its distance; and let *a b* be the given representation: it is required to determine the position and magnitude of the original of *a b*. Produce *a b*, and let it meet the vanishing line of the given plane in D, and the intersection FG of the given plane with the perspective plane in C; join ED. It is evident that the angle EDK is equal to the angle which the original of *a b* makes with FG; but the original of *a b* passes through the point C; therefore the original of *a b* passes through the point C, and is inclined to FG at a given angle; it is therefore given in position. Again, through C draw CA parallel to DE, and join E *a*, E *b*, and let them meet CA in A, B; then AB will be equal in magnitude to the original of *a b*. For it is evident from Lemma 1. § 1. that CA is equal to the distance of the original of *a* from C, and that CB is equal to the distance of the original of *b* from the same point C. Therefore AB is equal in magnitude to the original of *a b*.

Cor. To find the original of the point *a*, the plane in which it is situated being given, find DH the vanishing line of the given plane, K its centre, and KE its distance; and let FG be the intersection of the given plane with the perspective plane. Through *a* draw any line DC; join ED, and through C draw CA parallel to ED; join E *a*, and let it meet CA in A. The original of *a* will be placed at the distance CA from C, and in a line drawn in the given plane, and inclined to FG at an angle equal to FCA, or EDK. This is evident from Lem. 1. § 1.

Prop. II. Prob.

Having given the representation and vanishing point of a line divided; to find the ratio of the parts of the original line.

Let ACB, (Fig. 8.) be the given representation, and V the given vanishing point. It is required to find the ratio of the originals of AC, CB. Draw VO any how inclined to AB, and, parallel to it, draw any line *a b*; in VO take any point O, and join OA, OC, OB, and let them meet *a b* in the points *a, c, b*; then *a* C : *b* C is the ratio required. This is evident from Prop. IX.

Prop. III. Prob.

Having given the representation of a line, and that of a point which divides it in a given ratio; to find its vanishing point.

Let AB, (Fig. 8.) be the given representation; C that of the point which divides its original in the given ratio. Through C draw any line MCN, and make MC to CN, as the original of AC to the original of BC; join AM, NB, and let them be produced to meet in O. Through O draw OV parallel to MN, and meeting AB in V: then V is the vanishing point required.

For it may be proved, as in Prop. IX. that MC : CN = AC.BV : AV.BC. Hence V is the vanishing point required.

Prop. IV. Prob.

Having given the centre and distance of the picture, and the representation of an angle situated in a given plane; to find the original of that representation.

Let *a b l*, (Fig. 16.) be the given representation. Find (Prop. XII.) DH the vanishing line of the plane in which the original of the angle *a b l* is situated; find also K its centre, and draw KE at right-angles to DH, and equal to its distance from the point of sight. Let *a b, b l*, be produced to meet the vanishing line DH in

Fig. 15.
Fig. 16.
Fig. 8.
Fig. 8.
Fig. 16.

Perspective.

D, M; join ED, EM, and the angle DEM will be equal to the original of *a b l.*

For, (Prop. V.) D and M are the vanishing points of the originals of *a b, b l;* and the straight lines drawn from the point of sight to D, M, are parallel to the originals of *a b, b l;* and therefore, (E. 9th of 11th Book) they contain an angle equal to the original of *a b l.* But the straight lines drawn from the point of sight to D, M, are evidently equal to ED, EM, since EK is equal to the distance of the point of sight from K. Therefore the triangle DEM is every way equal to the triangle formed by drawing lines from the point of sight to the points D, M; and the angle DEM is equal to the angle contained by drawing lines from the point of sight to D and M, and is therefore also equal to the original of *a b l.*

PROP. V. PROB.

Having given the representation of a triangle, with its vanishing line, its centre, and distance ; to find the angles of the original triangle.

Let *a b l* be the given representation, DH its vanishing line, and K its centre. Produce the sides of the triangle *a b l* to meet the vanishing line in the points D, M, H ; from K (Fig. 16.) draw KE, at right angles to DM, and make it equal to the distance of DM from the point of sight ; join ED, EM, and EH: and the angles DEM, MEH, and DEH, will be equal to the originals of *a b l, a l b,* and *l a* D. This is evident from the preceding proposition. The angles of the originals of *a b l* may therefore be found as above.

Fig. 16.

PROP. VI. PROB.

Having given the representation of a triangle equiangular to a given triangle, and its vanishing line ; to find the centre and distance of that vanishing line.

Fig. 17.

Let ABC (Fig. 17.) be the given representation, and FD the vanishing line of the plane of its original ; let AB, AC, and BC, be produced to meet FD in the points D, E, F ; upon FE describe (34. 3. E.) a segment of a circle, containing an angle equal to the original of ACB ; and upon DE describe another segment of a circle containing an angle equal to the original of BAC; and let the two segments intersect each other in the point O ; draw OH at right angles to FD: then H will be the centre, and HO the distance of the vanishing line FD.

For, as circles intersect each other only in two points, there can be no point but O in the plane of the picture, and above the line FD, from which lines drawn to the points F, E, D, make with each other, angles equal to the originals of BAC, BCA ; but F, E, D, being the vanishing points of the originals of BC, AC, and AB, the straight lines drawn from the point of sight to F, E, D, being parallel to the originals of BC, AC, and AB, will contain with each other angles (Eu. 9th of 11th) equal to the originals of BCA and BAC. The lines drawn therefore from the point of sight to F, E, D, must evidently be equal to OF, OE, and OD. The segments FH, HD, are therefore equal to those which would be made by drawing a perpendicular from the point of sight to the vanishing line FD. Therefore H is the centre of the vanishing line FD, and OH is equal to its distance from the point of sight.

Cor. If BC, one of the sides of the triangle ABC, be parallel to the vanishing line FD, the construction is simpler. In that case, the point F being placed at an infinite distance, OF is parallel to DF. Consequently the angle FOE is equal to OED : but FOE is equal to the original of ACB, therefore OED is also equal to the

original of the angle ACB, and is therefore given. Hence, to find the point H, describe, as before, upon ED, the segment of a circle, containing an angle equal to the original of BAC ; and at the point E make the angle DEO equal to the original of BCA, and let EO meet the circumference of the segment in O. From O draw OH at right-angles to FD ; and H will be the centre, and OH the distance of the vanishing line DE.

Perspective.

PROP. VII. PROB.

Having given the perspective representation of a trapezium similar to a given trapezium, to find the vanishing line of its plane, and the centre and distance of that vanishing line.

Fig. 17.

Let *a b c d,* (Fig. 17.) be the given representation ; ABCD the trapezium to which its original is similar. Join AC, BD, and let them intersect each other in I. Since the original of *a b c d* is similar to the original of ABCD, the ratio of the originals of *d i, i b,* is equal to that of DI to IB, and is therefore given. Hence F, the vanishing point of *d b,* may be found by Prop. III. Sect. II. In like manner E, the vanishing point of AC, may be found ; but FE, the straight line which joins the vanishing points of *d b, a c,* is evidently the vanishing line of the plane of the original of the trapezium *a b c d,* which is therefore given. Hence, to obtain the vanishing line of the original of *a b c d,* find by Prop. III. Sect. II. the vanishing points E, F, of the originals of *a c, d b;* join EF ; and EF is the vanishing line required. Again, since the original of *b i c* is similar to the given triangle BIC, *b i c* is the representation of a triangle whose angles are given. The centre and distance of its vanishing line may therefore be found, as in Prop. VI. Sect. II.

Cor. 1. If the trapezium, whose representation is given, be a parallelogram, the problem admits of an easier construction. Let *a b c d* (Fig. 18.) be the given representation, and ABCD the parallelogram to which it is similar. Let *a b, c d,* be produced to meet in F, and *b c, a d* to meet in E. The representations of parallel lines intersect each other in the vanishing point of their originals. (See Prop. II. and Cor.) Therefore F is the vanishing point of the originals of *a b, c d;* and E is the vanishing point of the originals of *b c, c d.* But the vanishing points of lines situated in a plane, are in the vanishing line of that plane ; (see Prop. V.) therefore FC is the vanishing line of the plane of the original of *a b c d.* Again, upon FE describe a segment of a circle FOE, containing an angle equal to the original of *b a d,* or equal to BAD. Join *a c,* and let it meet FE in G ; and at the point E make the angle FEL equal to the original of *b a c,* or equal to BAC. Join LG, and let it cut the opposite circumference in O. Draw OH at right-angles to FE : then H will be the centre, and OH the distance of the vanishing line FE. For the points F, G, and E, being evidently the vanishing points of the originals of *a b, a c, a d,* if straight lines be drawn from the point of sight to the points F, G, E, (see Def. 7.) they will be parallel to the originals of *a b, a c, a d;* and will contain with each other angles equal to the originals of *b a d, b a c,* or equal to the angles FOE, FOG. But there is only *one* point in the plane of the figure, and above the line FE, to which, if straight lines be drawn from the points F, G, E, they will make the angles FOE, FOG, respectively equal to given angles BAD, BAC. It is therefore clear, that the lines OF, OG, OE, are respectively equal to the lines drawn from the point of sight to the points F, G, and E ; and consequently a perpendicular drawn from the point of

Fig. 18.

Perspective.

sight to FE will be equal to the perpendicular OH, and will intersect FE in the same point H in which OH cuts it. Therefore H is the centre of FE, and OH is equal to its distance.

Cor. 2. If two of the sides of the representation of the parallelogram be parallel to each other, they must be parallel to the vanishing line of the plane of the original parallelogram; for the representations of parallel lines can be parallel only, when the originals are parallel to the perspective plane. But, in this case, the originals being in the same plane, and being parallel to the perspective plane, are also parallel to the line in which that plane intersects the perspective plane; but the intersection and vanishing line of a plane are parallel. If, therefore, the representations of two of the sides of a parallelogram be parallel to each other, they will be parallel to the vanishing line of the plane of their originals. In this case, the centre and distance of the vanishing line may be found, as in the Cor. to Prop. VI. Sect. II.

Cor. 3. If $abcd$ the representation of a parallelogram, and H the centre, and HO the distance of the vanishing line of the plane of that parallelogram, be given; the ratio of the adjacent sides of the original parallelogram may be found as follows: Let ab, cd, and bc, ad, (Fig. 18.) when produced, meet each other in F and E; then FE will be the vanishing line of the plane of the original of $abcd$, and will therefore pass through the given point H, its centre. From H draw HO at right-angles to FE, and make it equal to the distance of FE from the point of sight; produce ac to meet FE in G; join OG, and let it mark the circumference of a circle described about the triangle FOE in L; join FL: then EF shall have to FL the same ratio which the original of ab has to the original of bc. For it is evident that the angles FOG, FOE, are equal to the angles contained by the straight lines drawn from the point of sight to the points F, G, E; but F, G, E, are the vanishing points of ab, ac, and ad. Therefore, the angles contained by lines drawn from the point of sight to F, G, E, are equal to the originals of bac, bad. Therefore, the angles FOG, FOE, are equal to the originals of bac, bad: but FOG is equal to FEL; and the angle FOE being equal to the original of bad, the supplement of FOE is equal to the supplement of the original of bad. That is, FLO is equal to the original of cba. The triangle FLE is therefore equiangular to the original of abc; and EL has to FL the same ratio which the original of ab has to the original of bc. If ab, dc, be parallel to each other, and therefore to EH, the original of abc, or adc, will be equiangular to OGE, and GE will have to EO the ratio of the original of ab to that of bc.

SCHOLIUM.

The propositions demonstrated in this section are useful in the examination of pictures. That an accurate judgment of a picture may be formed, it is necessary that the centre and distance of the picture, and the position of the vanishing line of the plane on which the original objects are situated should be known, and these may often be determined by means of the preceding propositions.

The *third* and *fourth* sections of the doctrine of perspective relate to objects of a more complex or less essential nature: into the discussion of these our limits do not permit us to enter. The reader who wishes to

investigate the subject in its widest extent, will find ample information in the following treatises, exclusive of those mentioned in p. 407.

Aleaume, *Perspective Specuiative et Pratique*, Paris, 1643. Jesuit's *Perspective*, 4to. Lond. Huret, *Optique de Portraiture*, Par. 1670. Emerson's *Cyclomathesis*, vol. vi. Molton's *Perspective*. Martin's *Graphical Perspective*, 1771. Priestley's *Perspective*, 8vo. Kirby's *Perspective*. Kirby's *Perspective of Architecture*. Clark's *Practical Perspective*. Torrelli's *Elementa Perspectivæ*, Verona, 1788. Ferguson's *Perspective*, containing plain and practical rules. Valuciennes, *Elémens de Perspective Pratique*, Par. 1777. Monge's *Géometrie Descriptive*. Edwards *on Perspective*, 4to. Lond. 1803.

PERSPECTIVE MACHINES. See Ferguson's *Perspective ;* and *Edinburgh Philosophical Journal*, vol. ii. p. 259, for an account of a very ingenious one invented by the late celebrated Mr. James Watt. See also Optics, Vol. XV. p. 655, for an account of Ramsden's Optigraph.

PERTH, the capital of Perthshire, ranks as a city; in the order of royal burghs it stands next to Edinburgh; and is, unquestionably, the finest provincial town in Scotland. Perth is a place of great antiquity, and, as such, the early periods of its history are involved in obscurity. Nothing certain is known as to the origin and etymology of the name. Lord Hailes says, with regard to it, " I have been favoured with different interpretations of the word; not knowing which to choose, I judge it best to omit them all." On the establishment of Christianity in this part of the country, a church was built in Perth, and dedicated to St. John the Baptist. From this circumstance, the town obtained, at an early period, the name of St. John's town, or St. Johnston, and by this name it is often known in history; but it is said this new name is not recognised in any ancient charters.

Tacitus, in his life of Agricola, marks the progress of that general, in his third campaign, in these words, " *vastatis usque ad Taum (æstuario nomen est) nationibus.*" And some chroniclers, anxious for the honour of Perth, have informed us, that the Roman soldiers, when they came in sight of the town, and saw the beautiful river, and the extensive plains by which the town is surrounded, exclaimed in astonishment, *ecce Tiberis ! ecce Campus Martius !* This part of its history is very apocryphal; but certainly it was paying a compliment to the Tiber, and the Campus Martius, to compare them to the Tay and the plains of Perth. Chalmers, in his Caledonia, vol. i. p. 104, has endeavoured to show that *ad Taum* cannot possibly mean *to the Tay ;* as Agricola experienced so much opposition in penetrating into Perthshire in his sixth campaign, he concludes that he could not have penetrated *ad Taum* in his third, to which the words refer. He therefore supposes that the words apply to the Solway Frith; and supports his conjecture by etymology, telling us that *tau* means any thing spread out; and was, therefore, applicable to the arm of the sea at Solway. We can only stop to say, that we do not consider his reasoning as at all satisfactory.

The first authentic information that we have respecting Perth, occurs in the reign of William, King of Scotland, who granted a charter to the town, which is still in existence. This charter was given on the 10th day of October, 1210. It is said that this king narrowly escaped being drowned in the town of Perth, by a sudden inundation of the river Tay. Hector Boece gives us a most formidable account of this inundation. He informs us that the town was entirely destroyed, and that the king's youngest son, with fourteen of his household, were swept away. He tells us, moreover, that the king built a new city about two miles farther down the river, and that this is the present city of Perth; the name of the ancient city being Bertha. Boece has been followed in this account by Camden, Buchanan, &c.; but there can be little doubt that the account is in most respects entirely fabulous. There is no reason to doubt the circumstance of the inundation; for it is particularly mentioned by Fordun, a writer of higher antiquity, and higher authority than Boece. But he says nothing of the change of the name or situation of the town; he tells us expressly that the king, with all his household, escaped, and that no lives were lost, the citizens having saved themselves either by flight, or by taking refuge in the highest parts of the houses. Still more completely to refute this story of Boece, the late Mr. Scott, an industrious antiquary, and for a long time senior minister of Perth, has shown from charters granted before and after this inundation, that the town of Perth has had the same name, and the same situation, from the earliest time that it is mentioned in history, till the present day.

Perth, from its central situation, was always considered as a military station of the first importance; as such it was strongly fortified; and has been the scene of many warlike achievements. After the unfortunate battle of Falkirk, which was lost through the jealousy which the Scottish chiefs began to entertain of Wallace, Edward I. strongly fortified Perth, which became the residence of his deputies; his son Edward resided there for some time; he was succeeded by Sir Aymer de Vallance, who gained a decisive victory over Bruce at Methven, in the neighbourhood of Perth. After the death of Bruce, Edward Baliol, by a bold enterprize, made himself master of Perth and of the kingdom of Scotland, after having fought the bloody battle of Dupplin, in the immediate neighbourhood, which was so fatal to many noble families in the country, and almost extinguished the name of Hay; the only root that was left being a child, of whom the lady of the chief was then pregnant. Perth continued to be the favourite residence of the kings of Scotland till the death of James I. who was murdered in the Blackfriars monastery; and both he and his queen were buried in the Carthusian monastery in that city.

Perth is famous for furnishing that problem in Scottish history, the *Gowrie conspiracy*. Part of the wall of Gowrie house still remains. The site of it is chiefly occupied by the county buildings and the jail. All attempts to give a satisfactory explanation of this transaction have utterly failed. The plot, if indeed a plot there was, on which side soever it originated, seems to have been most awkwardly constructed; and it is scarcely possible, on any principles of common sense, to fix a plausible imputation on either party. Public opinion has always run strong against the king; and the late Mr. Scott, in his " History of the life and death of John Earl of Gowrie," has laboured most assiduously to fix the charge of a conspiracy upon the king. His account, however, leaves an impression on the mind the very reverse of what he wished to produce; for it clearly appears that the king's attendants became anxious when he was missing; it farther appears, from the same account, that Gowrie went into his own house under the pretence of obtaining accurate information;

that he came out again and told the king's attendants, who were in the court below, *that his majesty was gone for Falkland*; and that the nobles, &c. who attended the king were calling for their horses to follow him, when he was seen struggling at a window and calling out " treason." Such are the facts stated by a zealous advocate for the innocence of Gowrie and his brother; how far they can be reconciled with such an opinion, let those who think themselves competent to the task determine.

Shortly after this transaction, James conferred several additional privileges on the town of Perth, by way of pacifying the inhabitants for the loss of Gowrie, their provost, to whom they were much attached. In April, 1601, James, by a strange anomaly in administration, was made provost of Perth. The truth of this anecdote rests on the authority of a manuscript journal, still extant, written by Dundee, a respectable citizen of Perth, who was present on the occasion. His words are, " On the XV. Apprill, in anno a thousand VI. hundred ane yeir, the kingis majestie came to Perth, and that same day he was made provost with ane great scerlane (skirling) of the courteoures, and the bankeit was meid at the crois, and the kingis majestie was set doune thereat, and six dozen glasses brokine," &c. In whatever way we are to understand this transaction, it is certain that in the Guildry Register for the year 1601, there is the following entry, *parcere subjectis et debellare superbos*; and under this motto, James R. all written in the king's own hand.

In ancient times the magistrates of Perth frequently used their power with great indiscretion. They often quarrelled with the neighbouring barons and gentry, who, in consequence, forbade their tenants and vassals to furnish provisions to the town. On such occasions, the magistrates were accustomed to sally forth with a numerous armed population at their back, to burn down the residences, and plunder the lands of the obnoxious barons. An instance of this kind occurs in the reign of James the Third, in the year 1461, of which the following record remains : " Be it kend till all men be thir present letters, we, Laurence Lord Oliphant of Aberdalgie, Knight, to have quyt, clamit, and dischargit alderman counsul and communitie of the burgh of Perth, for now and ever, of the dounecasting of the hous of Dupline, and of the spoilzeation of it and of Aberdalgie in special, and of all and sundrie actions, quarrelis and pleyis, &c. betwixt us and them, untill the day of the making of thir present writis, but reservation, fraud, or guyl." The magistrates also received a remission under the great seal, dated 5th February, 1526, for burning the house of Craigie in the neighbourhood.

Before the Reformation, Perth was a city of churches and palaces; and elegant as its present appearance is, it is nevertheless very insignificant when compared with its former splendour. The Blackfriars Monastery was a magnificent structure; it was founded by Alexander II. and served as a royal residence when the kings of Scotland were in Perth. James I. was murdered in it, as has already been stated. It stood on the grounds still called the Blackfriars, behind the present Crescent. The Carthusian Monastery, or the Charterhouse, was also a royal palace; it was the only possession which the order had in Scotland; it stood nearly on the spot where the hospital now stands, and was endowed by James I. This enlightened prince, observing the scandalous lives of the Romish clergy, invited the Carthusian Monks, one of the most rigid orders in the church of Rome, to settle in Scotland, that by their instructions and example they might rectify the abuses which had crept into the church, and especially reform the lives of the clergy. But this was an object to be accomplished by other means. The same prince also encouraged the Grey Friars, or Observantines, to settle in Perth. Their convent stood on the ground still known by the name of the Greyfriars' burying-ground. Knox tells us that the convent, when destroyed, was well provided both with comforts and luxuries; that their sheets, blankets, and table linen, were equal to those of any Earl in Scotland; and though there were only eight persons in it, there were found eight puncheons of salt beef, and wine, beer, ale, &c. in abundance. These brethren seem not to have been incommoded by their vows of poverty. The Monastery of the Carmelites, or White Friars, stood a little to the west of the town, near the place now called Dovecotland. St. Catherine's church stood on the land still called St. Catherine's; St. Paul's not far from the modern church of the same name. St. Magdalene's and St. Leonard's stood on the lands which still bear these names. There was also a chapel of Loretto, which stood on the north side of the South Street, about mid-way between the Port and Meal Vennel.

Not a vestige of any one of these buildings now remains. St. John's church is the only religious building which escaped the rage of the reformers; who began the work of destruction under the following circumstances:—The Queen Regent having heard that the reformed doctrines had been openly embraced at Perth, summoned all the Protestant preachers in the kingdom to appear at Stirling, and answer for their conduct, on the 10th day of May, 1559. The people flocked in multitudes to attend their preachers to the place of trial. The queen became alarmed; and empowered Erskine of Dun to promise to the Protestant preachers that the trial should be abandoned, provided they and their followers did not approach any nearer to Stirling. Upon the faith of this promise, they all stopped at Perth. When the 10th of May came, however, the persons who had been summoned were publicly called to appear for trial, and though they had kept away at the queen's request, they were pronounced outlaws for not appearing. Things were in this situation when Knox arrived in Perth. On the 11th of May, the day after the iniquitous proceedings at Stirling, Knox preached in St. John's church a most forcible sermon against the idolatry of the church of Rome. The most respectable part of the congregation was dispersing peaceably, when the indiscretion of a priest, who, immediately after Knox's sermon, was proceeding to decorate the altar for the purpose of celebrating mass, inflamed the mind of the multitude with ungovernable fury. They flew upon the pictures, images, and altars, and demolished them in an instant: they next proceeded to the monasteries, and in a few hours these stately buildings were nearly levelled with the ground. Such was the commencement of the demolition of the religious houses in Scotland, begun evidently without any premeditation, and condemned at first by the Protestant teachers; but continued afterwards on principle, and fortified by the maxim that, " *the best way to drive away the daws is to pull down their nests.*"

On receiving intelligence of these events, the Queen immediately marched against Perth with an army of 7000 men. So zealous, however, were the friends of the Reformation, that they instantly rallied round the Lords of the Congregation, and marched the length of Auchterarder to meet the Queen. Both parties being unwilling to risk an engagement, terms of accommodation were proposed and accepted. The substance of these terms was, that the gates of Perth should be thrown open to the Queen, that both armies should be disbanded, and that no foreign soldiers should approach within three miles of the town. The articles of agreement were instantly broken on the part of the Queen, who, on leaving Perth, introduced a garrison of 600 French troops to overawe the inhabitants. When the cause of the Reformation was every where else triumphant, Perth continued to be oppressed by this garrison. The inhabitants being no longer able to endure this injustice, rose in a body to expel the French troops by force. Lord Ruthven, and Haliburton, provost of Dundee, came to their assistance. Ruthven attacking the town on the west, and Haliburton, with the people of Dundee, attacking it with artillery from the bridge, the garrison was forced to capitulate on the 26th of June, 1559. After the loss of Perth, the Queen attempted to seize Stirling. Three hundred of the inhabitants of Perth marched to its relief, under the leaders of the congregation; and, to show their devotedness to the cause in which they were engaged, they went out of the town with ropes about their necks, solemnly denouncing, that whosoever deserted the good work should with these ropes be hanged. From this circumstance arose the proverb of *St. Johnston's Ribbands,* which, throughout Perthshire, means a halter for a malefactor.

Perth made a show of resistance against Cromwell, in favour of Charles II. It was totally unprovided with the means of defence; but, through a stratagem, it managed to conceal its weakness, and to present an appearance of determined resistance; in consequence of which it obtained honourable terms from the conqueror, who, when he knew the trick which had been practised upon him, coolly remarked that he was sorry he had not time to seize and hang the fellow who had imposed upon him. While Cromwell was at Perth, one of the inhabitants, of the name of Reid, came to him, and presented a bond granted to him by Charles II. for defraying the expence of his coronation at Scone. Reid demanded payment of the bond from Cromwell: the latter asked him whether he was not mad? and said, " I am neither Charles Stuart's heir nor executor." " Then," says Reid, in the phraseology of Scotch law, " you are a vicious intromitter." Cromwell observed to those who were with him, that it was the boldest speech that ever had been made to him. Cromwell built a strong citadel on the south side of the town. Many of the houses were demolished, to furnish materials for this work, and the inhabitants were exposed to great hardships and privations: the remains of several of the religious houses were applied to the same purpose. The citadel was surrounded by a deep ditch, which has received the rubbish of the town ever since, and is not yet completely filled up. A part of it, containing water is still to be seen in the immediate vicinity of the town.

Perth had been considered as the capital of Scotland till the reign of James III. and it was only in the year 1482 that it yielded precedence to Edinburgh. In ancient times Perth was not more distinguished as the capital of the kingdom, and as a royal residence, than as an emporium of commerce. This is evident from the following distich of Alexander Necham, an Englishman, who read lectures at Paris, in 1180, and died, Abbot of Exeter, in 1227. We quote from Camden:

" Transis, ample Tai, per rura, per oppida, per Perth;
Regnum sustentant istius urbis opes."

It is said that Perth carried on a very active and extensive commerce with the Netherlands. Of this we had an unexpected proof a few years ago. When the foundation of the Parliament House, (which stood on the north side of the High Street of Perth, in what is still called the Parliament Close,) was cleared out to make room for the present buildings, an immense number of small silver coins were dug out, in such a state of oxidation, that they adhered together in one concrete mass, and many of them crumbled to pieces on being touched : on being heated, almost to fusion, in charcoal, a great number of them were recovered, and the legend rendered quite distinct. Several of them were of Alexander of Scotland, and Edward of England ; but the great majority were Flemish, bearing the names of different Counts of Flanders ; many also had the names of Bishops, such as, *Episcopus Guido*, on the one side, and *Moneta Montes*, on the other. This circumstance, even in the absence of historical documents, would have been sufficient to prove, that a commercial intercourse had existed between Perth and the Low Countries.

Perth never having been the seat of a university, cannot be expected to be particularly distinguished as the residence of learned men. We believe, however, we may state with confidence, that Perth was the first place where Hebrew learning was taught in Scotland. It was introduced by Mr. John Row, the first Protestant minister of Perth. Row was a learned man, had been bred an advocate, and afterwards had resided long in Italy, where he was known and esteemed by several Popes and Cardinals. In 1558 he returned to Scotland, invested with the character of nuncio or legate, by Paul IV. with special instructions to oppose Knox and the other reformers. He, however, soon yielded to the force of truth, and was appointed minister of Perth. He had acquired the knowledge of the Hebrew language when abroad, and he taught it first to his own family at Perth. His children were so familiar with it, that they could read a chapter in the Hebrew Bible with as much ease as they could read English. His grandson, John Row, who was principal of King's College, Aberdeen, in the dedication of a Hebrew Grammar to the Earl of Kinnoul, says, " the Hebrew language has a claim upon me by hereditary right. It attracts me much in the same manner as my native soil, for my grandfather is reported to have been the first who introduced Hebrew learning into Scotland ; and my father, when he was a child of about four or five years of age, was taught to read the Hebrew alphabet before he knew the letters of his native tongue."

Perth seemed at one time to be in the fair way of having the honour of a university. This is a fact which seems to have escaped all our topographical writers, and we owe our knowledge of it to documents lately discovered at St. Andrew's, and now lodged with the Literary and Antiquarian Society of Perth. They relate to a negociation, which we heartily wish were resumed, of translating the University of St. Andrew's to Perth. The measure originated with the masters of the University of St. Andrew's in the year 1697, and they requested and obtained the assistance of the Earl of Tullibardine, their chancellor at that time, Principal Secretary of State for Scotland. They consulted Sir James Stewart, the Lord Advocate, and Sir Patrick Home, the Solicitor-General, as to the legality of the measure, who gave it as their opinion that there was no objection in point of law, and that it might easily be effected by a charter under the Great Seal, which

the Earl of Tullibardine pledged himself to use all his influence to obtain. But, before applying for a charter, it was judged expedient that all matters should be arranged with the town of Perth. For this purpose, the Earl of Tullibardine, and the provost of the Old College, St. Andrew's, stated to the magistrates of Perth their wishes upon the subject. The magistrates met their views with great cordiality, and made, what the Professors of St. Andrew's confessed to be a very liberal offer, for promoting so desirable an object. It is but justice to the magistrates of Perth to show the efforts which they were willing to make in order to advance the interests of literature in the town and county. By a minute of their proceedings, extracted from the records of the University of St. Andrew's, of date, April 13, 1698, the magistrates and council of Perth declare their willingness to contract with the university, to furnish them with the accommodation following, viz.

" For a divinity college, twenty convenient fashonable roumes, with kitchen, cellars, larders, brewhouse, gardens double dyked, and other apertinents necessar.

" For a philosophy college, sixtie convenient roumes for students, some whereof for noblemen's sons, some for gentlemen's sons, and the rest for men's sons of ordinary quality, with convenient schools, kitchens, cellars, larders, brew-houses, and other office-houses necessar, with ane double dyked garden, volarly, summer-house and houses of office, and ane convenient church for the whole universitie.

" And as for the other philosophy college, the magistrates and council are willing to give ane convenient spot of ground, with ane garden in such ane place of the toune as the masters of the universitie and they shall find most convenient ; and to concur with the saids masters of the universitie, to address the king, parliament and countrey, and to use all methods imaginable for procuring ane fond to build that college. For prosecuting of which design, the kindness of the nobility and gentry of Perthshire is not to be doubted."

Few towns in Britain, in the present day, would make such a stretch to obtain a university. The professors were perfectly satisfied with the terms, and appointed certain individuals of their number to meet with the magistrates of Perth, with a view to procure funds for building the third college, which was then judged necessary. But here the documents fail ; all farther traces of the transaction are lost, and no light can be cast on the subject, either from the records of the College of St. Andrew's, or of the town of Perth. Should the measure of transferring the College of St. Andrew's to any other place, ever be again seriously contemplated, Perth still possesses all the advantages which formerly recommended it, with this in addition, that the necessary buildings might be furnished with no loss to the public, and little expence to the parties concerned. The Depot, within a quarter of a mile of the town, can never again be required for the purpose for which it was built ; it is erected of the most substantial materials, and might supply ample and elegant accommodation for all the professors and students in Scotland.

Some of the reasons for transferring the college to Perth, as stated in the minutes, are curious. With regard to Perth, its central situation is obvious, and of course much insisted on ; and then its vicinity to the Highlands would, in the event of the college being placed there, afford the best means of *civilizing the*

Highland gentry. With regard to St. Andrew's, its out-of-the-way situation is equally obvious, and is urged as a prominent reason for the transfer. But we sincerely hope that some other reasons alleged for the expediency of the measure have no longer an existence. One of these is stated to be, " This place being now only a village, where most part farmers dwell, the whole streets are filled with dunghills, which are exceedingly noisome, especially when the herring guts are exposed in them, or rather in all corners of the town by themselves." Again, " It may be considered whether the dissention between the universitie and citie at present, be not a reason ; seeing it may prove impossible for us to keep gentlemen and noblemen's children from incurring great hazard, considering the dispositions of youth to be revenged, so that if the magistrates should offer to meddle, they would endeavour to tumultuate, and expose themselves to the rabble of this place, or else be in hazard of burning the toune, which this last year they had certainly done, in the case of Master Henderson, had not, by a particular providence, the design been known by one of the masters, ane hour before it was to be putt in execution." The last reason alleged against the inhabitants of St. Andrew's is, " the aversion and hatred they have to learning and learned men, (so) that since our foundation, there never was one farthing voted to the universitie by a burgess of St. Andrew's; (and) that in our knowledge there was not any capable to win his bread by learning, except our present Bibliothecar. The contrair of all these may be expected in Perth."

The situation of Perth, on the banks of the finest river in Britain, and surrounded by beautiful and picturesque scenery, is altogether delightful. From the lowness of the situation, however, it is generally supposed by strangers that it must be unhealthy. We are fully persuaded, from experience, that this is not the case, and that Perth is as healthy a residence as there is in the kingdom. The lowness of its situation, however, renders it liable to an inconvenience of a different kind, viz. to inundations of the river, which, if they have not proved fatal to the life of the inhabitants, have often filled them with no small alarm. We have already noticed the great inundation in 1210, of which Boece has evidently given an exaggerated account. One not much inferior to it occurred in the month of October 1621, by which the bridge was entirely swept away with the exception of one arch. This bridge had only been lately finished, and was built by Mylne, architect to James VI. and the ancestor of the Mylnes who have been so celebrated in the same department. An ample account of this inundation is contained in the Session Records, under the title of " A Remembrance of God's Visitation of Perth." The town was completely insulated, so that no person could either approach to it or escape from it. The inhabitants were greatly alarmed, and Mr. John Malcolm the clergyman, having called them together into the church at seven o'clock on Sunday morning, powerfully exhorted them to repent of their sins and amend their lives, as they were visited with an evident judgment on account of their iniquities. This was safe enough ground to take; but Calderwood has condescended to point out the particular sins on account of which the visitation was sent. " The people," says he, " ascribed this wreck to iniquity committed in the town, for there was held the last General Assembly; and another in 1590, when the schism in the kirk began ; and in 1606, here was held that parliament, at which the bishops were erected, and the lords

rode first in their scarlet gowns." Another formidable inundation happened in the year 1773, in consequence of the breaking up of the ice on the river after a long frost. The river was blocked up by the ice about the bridge, and the water being thrown back, soon covered the whole of the North Inch ; it then forced its way through the Blackfriars, and soon surrounded the town ; the masses of ice, which were of great size, destroyed a row of fine trees on the side of the Dunkeld road, which at that time passed through the North Inch, and great apprehensions were entertained for the bridge and the town. The water, however, subsided without doing any material damage. This may almost serve for the description of another inundation which occurred in 1814 in precisely the same circumstances. On that occasion, the broken masses of ice, which were from a foot to eighteen inches thick, were so closely jammed together below the town, that a number of horses which were on the island opposite to the quay, were led across the river, supported on the fragments of ice, as on an arch of stone. The greater part of the inhabitants of Rose Terrace were taken out of their houses in boats; but nothing worse occurred than a number of ludicrous accidents, which have been the subject of conversation ever since. Indeed we do not think that Perth has much to apprehend from inundation, beyond a little temporary inconvenience. The level of the river after it passes Perth is so little below the level of the town, that whilst this circumstance is the sole cause of inundation, it is, at the same time, a security against any dangerous current. Danger can only arise from a sudden reflux of the water in consequence of the channel being obstructed by ice; but whether this inconvenience can be remedied, is more than we are competent to determine.

The Inches of Perth, as they are called, are two beautiful fields, one on the north, the other on the south side of the town : they consist of about seventy acres each ; are adorned with fine trees, and bounded towards the east by the river. Finer walks cannot be conceived ; and they are common to the inhabitants for bleaching linen, for walking, and every species of exercise and amusement, except riding, which is strictly prohibited, except during the races, which are held on the North Inch. It is said that the two Inches were given to the town of Perth by the Mercers of Aldie, on condition of receiving a burial-place within the church, on which a wag observed that " they had made a good bargain in getting six feet for two inches."

The North Inch is celebrated for a bloody conflict, which took place in the time of Robert III. between the M'Intoshes and M'Kays. They had agreed to refer the issue to thirty combatants on each side, who were to fight it out in the presence of the king and the courtiers. When the fight was about to begin, it was discovered that the M'Intoshes wanted one of their number, who had thought proper to withdraw himself. This circumstance having created some difficulty, one Henry Wine, a saddler in Perth, came forward, and offered, for half a crown, (Buchanan says, aurei scutati Gallici dimidium) to fill the place of the deserter; his offer was accepted ; and it was agreed on all hands that the victory was decided in favour of the M'Intoshes, chiefly by his valour. This is the origin of the proverb known in Perth and elsewhere, *every man for his own hand, as Henry Wine fought.*

There are no buildings of any antiquity now remaining in Perth, except St. John's Church, which is a very ancient fabric; it now serves for three of the parish churches. Some say it was built by William the Lion; others ascribe to it a much higher antiquity, and say that it was built by the Picts, immediately on their professing Christianity. There is still extant an order from Robert the Bruce, to the abbot and monks of Scone, to allow the magistrates of Perth to dig stones out of the quarries of Kincarrachy and Balcormac, for building (it can only mean repairing) the church of Perth. It is in these words, " Robertus, Dei Gratia, Rex Scotorum, religiosis Abbati et conventui de Scona, dilectis et fidelibus suis salutem : Vos rogamus, quatenus ad instantiam nostram, concedere velitis licentiam capiendi lapicidiorum de Kynkarache et Balcormac, pro edificatione ecclesiæ de Perth, et pontium de Perth et Eryn." This order was given in 1329. Fordun tells us that Edward III. of England was standing at the altar of St. John's church, when his brother, the Duke of Cornwall, came up to him. Edward being much displeased with the accounts which he had heard of his conduct, reproved him sharply ; the duke made a haughty reply, upon which the king, in a paroxysm of passion, stabbed him on the spot. The English historians mention the Duke of Cornwall's death as having happened at Perth, but they say nothing as to the circumstances which occasioned it.

Perth formed one parish, with two ministers, and an ordained assistant, till the year 1807, when the parish was disjoined by a decreet of the Court of Teinds, and four parishes erected, with separate and independent jurisdictions ; but there is only one session (composed of the four separate sessions) for the management of the poor.

The funds for the poor are considerable. A thousand pounds a-year are raised by assessment on the town and land-ward part of the parish ; about £700 are raised by collections at the established churches ; each of the incorporated trades support their own poor, from their own funds, which are considerable. The property belonging to all the religious houses in Perth at the time of the Reformation, was consolidated by King James, and erected by charter into a new institution, designated *King James's Hospital of Perth, for poor members of Jesus Christ.* The funds of this institution are, at present, (1823) about £600 ; these funds are under the management of the ministers and elders, and arise out of the property belonging to the charterhouse, feus, ground annuals, &c. These ground annuals arise out of certain bequests to the religious houses, with which individuals burdened their property. One, for instance, left a stone of wax ; another so many pounds of wax candles, to be consumed at the altar of some favourite saint, on some particular occasion. Among other bequests to the religious houses in Perth, there is one by a proprietor in the country, of *quadraginta cartas petarum,* forty cart load of peats. All these items have been converted into money, and form part of the funds of the hospital. All the charters conveying these different articles to the religious houses are lodged in the hospital ; they were all translated or transcribed by the late Mr. Scott ; they amount to five or six huge folios, and were bought up after his death for the Advocates' Library, where they are now lodged ; they contain many curious particulars.

Besides these funds, nine-tenths of the farm of Lethendy, in the parish of Scone, were left by the proprietors to the poor of Perth ; this farm is at present let at £1100 a-year ; five-tenths of which are given to the poor, chiefly to such as have seen better days, at the rate of £30 a-year ; the magistrates and ministers

are patrons. The remainder is under particular restrictions, by the will of the bequeather.

The town is bounded on the east by the Tay, which washes the walls of some of the houses. That part of it which lies within the royalty is not of large extent, being confined between the two Inches, which are scarcely half a mile separate from each other. It consists chiefly of four parallel streets, running nearly east and west, and terminated by the river. These are Mill Street, the High Street, South Street, and Canal Street; of these, Mill Street and Canal Street are very inferior in point of appearance and importance. The South Street is the straightest and most spacious, but is greatly inferior to the High Street in the general appearance of the buildings. These four streets are intersected towards the west by Methven Street, and towards the east by George Street, St. John's Street, and Prince's Street, and partly by the Watergate, which runs parallel to St. John's Street, nearer to the river.

The principal buildings of Perth lie without the royalty or burgh. These are Athol Place, the Crescent, Rose Terrace, and Athol Street, on the north side of the town. The two first lie along the bottom, and Rose Terrace along the west side of the North Inch, and they have the advantage of a view, and of scenery, such as is not enjoyed, so far as we know, by any other town in Britain. It is matter of dispute whether they are not equalled by Marshall Place, which bounds the town on the south.

All these new streets and buildings were projected by the late Provost Marshall, whose taste and public spirit contributed most essentially to the improvement of the town and suburbs. The inhabitants were so sensible of his merits, that a subscription was entered into for the purpose of erecting a monument to his memory. It was long before the subscribers could agree upon a plan, and they found great difficulty in obtaining a proper situation. The one ultimately fixed upon is not the best that could be wished, but it is the best that could be procured. The building is now nearly finished, and promises to be an ornament to the town and a credit to the architect. The building is strictly monumental in its appearance, but the subscribers, thinking that it would be honourable to Provost Marshall's memory, to connect his name with the literary institutions of the place, have allotted an apartment in the building for a public library, and another for the Literary and Antiquarian Society of Perth. These apartments, when fitted up, will be very spacious and handsome.

The Bridgend may be considered as part of the suburbs of Perth, though it lies in the parish of Kinnoul. It is connected with Perth by means of the Bridge ; and many who carry on business in the town have houses and villas on the opposite side of the river. The face of the hill of Kinnoul, which looks down upon the town from the east, is studded with these villas, and they have the finest prospect that can be conceived. The Bridge, which connects Kinnoul with Perth, is a plain substantial structure of nine arches ; its only defect is its narrowness ; it is wide enough for carriages and loaded carts passing each other, but it admits only of a narrow footpath on one side, which, from the great intercourse which now exists between Perth and Bridgend, is often inconvenient for passengers. This is an evil which has arisen out of the increase of the population on the other side of the river, and which evidently had not been contemplated when the bridge was built. The present bridge was only finished in 1771, and the inhabitants of Perth recollect with gratitude, that the work was promoted, and completed chiefly through the active and effective influence of the Earl of Kinnoul. The former bridge, which was on a line with the present High Street, was swept away by the great inundation in 1621. It was built, as has already been noticed, by Mylne, who is called, on his monument in the church-yard of Perth, *Master Mason* to James VI. From 1621 to 1771, there was no communication between Perth and the opposite side of the river, but by a ferry; and the recollection of the inconvenience arising from this mode of transportation, makes the inhabitants of Perth set a high value on the bridge. There is a literary and antiquarian society in Perth, which was established in 1784, and numbers among its members many of the nobility and principal gentry of the county. The society has a museum and a library, and considerable additions are making to both every year. There is also a good public library, with a well-selected collection of books.

The building, containing the public schools and academy, is a very handsome structure, in which all the branches of education are ably taught.

The county buildings, containing the Justiciary Hall, Sheriff Court Room, Sheriff-Clerk's room, dancing-room, supper-room, &c. &c. &c. have lately been finished at an expense of £22,000. They are said to be an exact copy of a temple at Pæstum, in Italy.

Manufactures. The commerce and manufactures of Perth have varied so much, both in point of nature and extent, of late years, that it is not easy to give any correct general view of them. The linen trade is still a considerable branch. Ginghams for umbrellas, and linen lawns for oiling, are manufactured to a very great extent. There is also a considerable manufacture of shawls and plaids, which have already obtained a name, both for quality, cheapness, and elegance of pattern.

About thirty years ago a company was formed in Perth, for the purpose of printing cotton goods, under the firm of Young, Ross, Richardson & Co. This company has gradually extended its establishment, till it has become the most considerable in Scotland. From 500 to 1000 hands are usually employed in the work, according to circumstances; and there is a command of power, machinery, &c. which enables the Company to execute more work than any other in Scotland, when they think it advisable to extend their operations. The partners in this Company have not been more attentive to their own interest, than to the comfort and improvement of the people whom they employ. They built, by permission of the heritors, an addition to the church of Tibbermore, in which parish the work is situated, for the accommodation of their work people. They also support an excellent school, where the different branches of education are ably taught. There is another thing connected with this establishment which we cannot but greatly commend. The gentlemen who have the principal management, have made a most judicious provision for the amusement of the work people. For this purpose, they have established a band of music, composed of such of the work people as have an ear and a taste for music. They have all the instruments in use in the completest military band; and as there are the most expert artificers, in almost every department connected with the work, the greater part of the instruments are of their own making. They exercise once or twice a-week, according to circumstances; and on every festival occasion, sanctioned by the approbation of the managers, the whole population connected with the work, which

would form no inconsiderable a parish, has the amusement of music and of dancing on the green.

Trade. The foreign import trade of Perth is carried on with the following countries, viz. Russia, Prussia, Sweden, Norway, Holland, and British America. During the year 1822, there were imported from these places flax, hemp, cheese, seeds, apples, timber, deals, feathers, smalts, madders, bristles, iron, grease, Geneva, &c. &c. The duties upon which amounted to nearly £6000.

The number of vessels employed in the above trade, during 1822, was twenty; and their burthen amounted to about 3000 tons.

Perth has no direct export trade to foreign ports, but enjoys a very considerable coasting trade. During the year 1822, there were 766 vessels, measuring 35,390 tons, employed in the carrying goods coastwise from the port of Perth; and 1082 vessels, measuring 48,668 tons, in bringing goods coastwise into the port of Perth.

The principal articles sent coastwise from Perth are, grain, flour, oatmeal, potatoes, malt, paper, whisky, hardwood, printed and plain cottons, leather, yarns, wool, linseed oil, oil cake, &c. &c.

And the principal articles brought coastwise into Perth, are, coals, tea, sugars, madders, smalts, ashes, soap, candles, seeds, oils, tar, hemp, flax, bottles, glass, dyestuff, porter, ales, hardware, spirits, wines, starch, stones, slates, haberdashery, stationery, &c. &c.

Both the foreign and coasting trade of Perth are principally carried on by stranger shipping, there being very few vessels belonging to Perth. At the end of the year 1822 there were only 46 vessels, measuring 4057 tons, belonging to the port; since which time a good many have been sold to other ports and lost; and, from the present dullness of trade, there is very little chance of any increase in this department taking place soon. The foregoing statement may be taken as the average state of trade at the Port of Perth for ten years preceding 1822. West Long. 3° 25′. North Lat. 56° 23′.

The population of Perth, by the census of 1821, is 19,068, being an increase of 2120 since 1811.

PERTHSHIRE. This is the most splendid for its scenery and appearance, as it is the most extensive county in Scotland. It is of a very compact form, nearly free from angles of any note, and almost coinciding with a circle; the longest diameter, between the east and west, being about eighty miles; and the shortest, from north to south, being seventy. One detached portion alone, on the borders of the Firth of Forth, intrudes between Fife and Clackmannan. The total area is estimated at 5000 square miles.

Physical Geography.—Perthshire is, in every sense of the word, a mountainous country, although containing many considerable tracts of flat land, or of low undulating hills. It is divided between the highland and lowland districts, the latter forming about a third of the whole. The boundary between these is part of that great step which, to the southward, distinguishes the highlands from the lowlands, and is popularly known by the name of the Grampian mountains. To the south of this is a distinct ridge of hills, which, from near Stirling to near Newburgh, nearly coincides with the boundary of the county, and which, at a more northern point, is continuous with the Sidlaw ridge, leaving between it and the Tay the great and valuable alluvial flat, called the Carse of Gowrie.

The interval between the Ochil hills and the Grampians, is by far the most extensive tract of low lands in Perthshire; and being covered with agriculture, wood,

Physical geography.

and gentlemen's seats, it forms altogether the most brilliant and wealthy looking tract in Scotland. This district extends from Blairgowrie and Coupar on the east, to Comrie, Downe, and Aberfoyle, on the west; including the magnificent valley of Strathearn, with part of that of the Almond, the Tay, and the Isla. The distribution of the hills and valleys within the highland portion is very irregular, and the mountainous land bears a very large proportion to the rest. As the ridges which the hills form regulate the distribution of these valleys, the description of the one almost implies that of the other.

The principal valley is Strath Tay, commencing from the lake of that name, and attending the course of the Tay to Dunkeld, where it terminates, by the meeting of the hills, to form the pass of Birnam. This is an extremely rich and beautiful tract, while it is also of considerable dimensions. On the north it is bounded by the ridge of Ben Lawers, and on the south by an extensive group of mountains, by which it is separated from Strathearn, with the intervention, in one place, of the valley of the Braun, which also opens at Dunkeld. The latter boundary also defines its southern branch to the westward, while the eastern one is formed by another considerable mass of hill land, which separates it from Strathairdle. The dimensions of this latter valley are not considerable, and it forms a kind of notch in the line of the Grampians.

The next valley in consequence to that of the Tay is that of the Tumel, which joins at Logierait, and extends northwards to near the pass of Killicrankie. Here it terminates for a considerable space between Fascally and Loch Tumel, where the river forces its way through a very deep and narrow glen. But, at the issue of Loch Tumel, it again expands into a rich fertile woody valley, which, in its progress westward, extends to near Mount Alexander. The boundaries of this upper Glen Tumel, are, on the south, the ridge of Shehallien and Faragen, and, to the north, a group which separates it from the valley of the Garry, containing Blair in Athol, and the seat of much of the most beautiful scenery in Scotland.

Glen Lyon is the last valley of any considerable dimensions. It is bounded by the ridge of Shehallien on one side, and that of Ben Lawers on the other; losing itself gradually westward about Meggarnie, and terminating west of Fortingall; being again renewed, in some measure, as the river proceeds from this to be lost in the Tay near Dull. Many smaller glens attend the rivers and lakes in which this county abounds, but they do not require any particular description.

Among the most remarkable mountains of Perthshire is Ben Lawers; it is estimated at 4015 feet, and is indeed one of the highest mountains of Scotland. Next in elevation is Cairn Gower, part of the ridge of Ben Gloe, and it is estimated at 3700 feet or thereabouts. Ben Vualach has not been measured, but it cannot be much less, though inferior to Ben Aulder in Inverness-shire, which assists it in forming the northern extremity of Loch Ericht. Shehallien is about 3400 feet, and is conspicuous as well for its beautiful conoidal outline, as for its having been the place of Dr. Maskelyne's operations for solving the problem of the density of the earth. Ben More, a part of the southern boundary of Glen Dochart, also reaches beyond 3000 feet, as does Ben Vorlich, to the south of Loch Earn. Lastly, we may name Ben Ledi, of somewhat less elevation, and Ben Venu, which helps to constitute the exquisite scenery of Loch Cateran.

The northernmost of the Perthshire lakes is Loch Ericht, about sixteen miles in length, and scarcely any where two miles wide; but the southern half only lies in this county, the remainder belonging to Inverness. It is, in no respect, picturesque or interesting, and is situated in a country utterly wild, with scarcely a house or an arable farm near it. It has acquired, however, some historical celebrity from a cave on its margin, which formed one of the hiding places of Prince Charles after his defeat.

Loch Rannoch is upwards of ten miles long, extending from east to west, with very little variety of outline or picturesque beauty. The northern margin, in particular, is rude, and covered in many places with scattered birch of great antiquity. The southern is far more interesting, as it contains many farms, and as it is also the seat of the once extensive fir woods of Rannoch, now much reduced by cutting, but serving still to vary the scenery in such a way as to make this a very beautiful ride. There is a good wheel road all round the lake.

There are few lakes on so small a scale more beautiful than Loch Tumel. Yet as it lies in an open valley, its beauty is rather constituted by that of the surrounding magnificent scenery than by its own proper margin. The view from the high grounds at the eastern extremity is very striking, as are many of those which are obtained on all sides on descending into the valley, while the rich wooded nature of this tract confers on it a character quite distinct from that of any other Scottish lake.

The most extensive lake in this county is Loch Tay, stretching for fifteen miles, and sometimes reaching to two in breadth. Its sides are, however, straight, the northern in particular, so that it presents little of that intricacy and beauty of margin which generally constitutes the charm of lake scenery. Exceptions must be made, however, in favour of the southern shore, where an artist will discover numerous points whence exquisite pictures may be obtained. But the road on this side of the lake being abandoned, on account of the superior goodness of the other, this scenery is quite unknown. The scenery at Killin is however as picturesque as it is singular in its kind; nor is there any single spot of the same dimensions in Scotland, where an artist may equally occupy himself with scenes that seem as inexhaustible as they are unlike to every thing else. At the eastern extremity of the lake, the grounds of Taymouth are magnificent, without being picturesque; rich in wood, but disposed in an artificial English manner, ill harmonizing with the surrounding grandeur and rudeness, or with the general character of the country.

Three lakes occur in that extraordinary and desert tract, called the Moor of Rannoch, viz. Loch Dhu, Loch Baa, and Loch Lydoch; the latter being at least seven miles in length. If the most absolute solitude, and the absence of any thing like life, can give interest to a spot, these certainly possess it in a high degree. Trees might even render Loch Lydoch picturesque, since its outline is intricate and rocky, though the surrounding land is low and level; but, excepting two or three scattered firs, that have served to continue the evidence of this ancient forest, the whole is one boggy and rocky waste, without variety, extending for about twenty miles towards the entrance of Glenco.

Loch Earn, the immediate source of the Earn, is about six miles in length, and is in many places very picturesque; its margin also being in many places woody and cultivated, although but for a short space, as the hills ascend rapidly from the edge of the water. The ancient road afforded some extremely fine pictures, but these are lost on the new one, which is conducted on the north side much nearer to the margin of the lake. Loch Dochart is little worthy of notice, except for the remains of its ancient castle, situated on an island.

Loch Voil, a narrow lake about four miles long, is little known to strangers, as it does not lie in the ordinary route of tourists, but it is not deficient in picturesque beauty. Loch Lubnaig, which is also about four miles in length, is narrow, and in many places picturesque, particularly near Ardchullary, where it assumes an uncommon character from the sudden descent of the skirts of Ben Ledi by which it is bounded.

But the chief beauties of Perthshire, as far as lake scenery is concerned, is found about Loch Cateran, including in it Loch Achray, and in some measure also Loch Venachar. Loch Cateran itself is upwards of seven miles in length, Loch Achray more than one, and Loch Venachar about three, and they all communicate by means of the Teith, which forms a principal branch of the Forth. We dare not attempt to describe the beauties of this scenery, as our space would not admit of it ; but it must indeed be superfluous to describe that which is now so well known, though it is worthy of remark, that twenty-five years are scarcely passed since Loch Cateran was scarcely known even by name out of its immediate neighbourhood. Of so short a date has been the general diffusion of a taste for picturesque scenery through this country. We need only observe, that the scenery of Loch Cateran is limited to a space of little more than two miles at its eastern extremity, the remainder being tame and uninteresting.

The chain of lakes which gives rise to the Forth, including Loch Ard and Loch Chen, also presents much picturesque beauty, though little known to ordinary travellers beyond Aberfoyle. Each of these lakes is about two miles in length, and, as there is a good road even to Loch Chen, the whole is readily accessible, and well deserves to find a place in a picturesque tour. The Loch of Menteith, which is the last in this direction, is situated in a flat, and is no otherwise beautiful than from the cultivated state of the surrounding country, and the woody island bearing ancient ruins, which it contains.

On the eastern quarter of the county, there is yet a chain of lakes well deserving of notice for the beauty of the scenery. This extends from near Dunkeld towards Blair Gowrie, including the three lochs of the Lowes, Loch Clunie, and Loch Marly, an ancient house in Loch Clunie being celebrated as the birth-place of that noted quack called the Admirable Crichton. None of these exceed a mile in length, and we need take no notice of the numerous mountain lakes of small dimensions which are scattered all over this county.

Among the rivers of Perthshire, the Tay is the pride, even of Scotland. It is indeed estimated to discharge more water than any British river. Its course is, however, short, as it only acquires this name when it leaves Loch Tay ; but it is fed from more, and more discordant, sources, than any river in this country. Loch Tay itself is formed principally by the Lochy and the Dochart, which are therefore the most direct heads of this river ; but independently of these, it receives innumerable streams from the surrounding mountains. The junction of the Lyon immediately after its exit from Loch Tay, forms an addition nearly equal in dimensions, as is that branch which it receives by its junction with the Tumel. The Braun near Dunkeld, the Isla near Coupar, and the Almond near Perth, form its three last branches of any note ; as the Earn joins the firth and not the river.

Through much of its course it abounds in picturesque scenery, but that is limited to the long portion between the pass of Birnam and Loch Tay. The splendour of this noble strath is scarcely equalled by any thing in Scotland, as well for its richness in wood, houses, and cultivation, as for the grandeur and variety of its mountain boundaries. At Dunkeld the scenery assumes a new and different character, but far too well known to require any description.

Next in rank is the Earn, rising in that lake, and terminating, after a long and somewhat straight course, in the firth of Tay. This river receives no stream of any note but the Ruchil, yet is considerably augmented before its termination by numerous small streams flowing into it from the hilly land on each side. Towards its lower part, or from Crieff eastward, this valley is rather splendid and rich than picturesque, abounding in gentlemen's houses, and in many parts well wooded ; but at Crieff, and to the westward of that town, it assumes a much more wild and interesting character, yet still rich with woods and cultivation. Among the most striking parts near to Crieff are Auchtertyre and Drummond Castle, in far different styles, but highly beautiful. From Crieff westward the scenery increases in beauty ; and Menzie, near this town, but in a different valley, is also conspicuous for its beauty. The scenery at Comrie becomes of an alpine character, from the height of the hills which inclose Loch Earn. The cascades of the Lednoch are pointed out to travellers ; but by far the most brilliant part of the course of the Earn is that which reaches between Comrie and Loch Earn. St. Fillan's Hill is the principal centre of this beauty, in which Duneira also shares ; and though little known to tourists, there are few parts of Scotland more striking for singularity and magnificence of character,—a mixture of rock and wood, with high and bold mountains, traversed by an intricate and woody river, and generally of a confined nature, so as to add to the rudeness and boldness of the scene.

Tracing the Tumel from its source in Loch Rannoch, we find it receiving the Garry near Fascally, as its only principal accessory branch. If less magnificent than the Tay or the Earn, it presents a far greater variety of scenery. The first remarkable spot is at Mount Alexander, where it forces its way through a narrow rocky and wooded pass, overshadowed by the skirts of Shehallien, abounding in variety of extensive as well as close scenery, and as rich below as it is bold and rocky above. Hence it forces its way over a rocky tract, forming numerous picturesque cascades until it reaches Tumel bridge. Shortly after this it emerges into the beautifully wooded vale of Loch Tumel, joining that lake through green meadows thickly set with scattered ash trees, and bounded on each side by numerous farms that skirt the high boundaries on both hands.

On emerging from Loch Tumel it assumes a character entirely new ; being pent up for about five miles in a deep rocky and woody glen, affording no room at the bottom beyond that required for its course. Splendid as this scenery is, it is totally unknown to the public, and has indeed been visited by very few. We have no hesitation in saying, that, with the single exception of Loch Cateran, there is no spot in Scotland which contains so much grandeur, variety, and beauty, within so small a space ; nor any indeed which exceeds it in the romantic richness of its truly alpine scenes. It will well repay the labour of more days than one ; but, to see it in perfection, it must be examined on each side of the river, for which facility is afforded by good roads. Where it is about to join the Garry near Fascally, it produces the celebrated fall of the Tumel; a scene perfectly exquisite in its composition, and in the beauty of the cascade, although the height is not considerable. From this point downwards to its junction with the Tay, it passes through a narrow valley, in which the scenery about Fascally, which forms properly a part of that already described, is the most remarkable. The whole, however, is one continued series of beauties to the junction; and in diverging a little from it, we find, about the village of Moulin, views of the vale of the Tay, together with much closer mountain scenery, which ought to attract every traveller thus much out of his road.

The Garry, which at Fascally forms so large a branch of the Tumel, arises partly out of Loch Garry, near Dalnaspidel, receiving afterwards three principal branches from the Bruar, the water of Erochie, and the Tilt, besides subordinate ones. The first part of its course is through a wild uninteresting country; but above Blair it immediately assumes those beauties which are continued to its termination. Blair itself is unrivalled throughout Scotland; and scarcely any thing can exceed the beauty of the whole valley down to the pass of Killicrankie. Of the scenery of that celebrated spot it is superfluous to say any thing, except to point out to artists that it reserves the greater part of its most striking scenes for those who will pursue it with care through all its recesses. The summer's labours of the most expert artist would not exhaust half of the beauties to be found throughout this tract as far as Blair; but we have not room to describe even their places. But we must point out the grounds at Urrard, with its beautiful cascade; the views from Lude; those on the eastern side of the Garry; and those which more especially belong to Blair. Among these we must especially name Glen Tilt, affording alpine scenery of a singular character, and no less magnificent than unlike to any thing else of the kind in Scotland. When the river is about to quit the Glen, the pass which it has wrought itself through the rocks is singularly wild and romantic; and near to this place the cascades of the Fender, though in no great scale, offer specimens of this class of scenery scarcely inferior in beauty to any of the same dimensions in Scotland. The falls of the Bruar are rather rude than picturesque, but are well known, while the others are neglected.

The course of the Lyon is remarkable, from the uniformly narrow and deep valley through which it runs. Arising far west in Loch Lyon, it receives numerous mountain streams in its course to the Tay, but no river of any note. The scenery of that valley is as novel as it is beautiful; but, like many of the secluded parts of Scotland, it is alike undescribed and unknown. Where it is contracted in the narrow pass westward of Fortingall, it is particularly striking from the closeness and magnitude of the hills, and from the fine trees which cover its meandering banks. After this point it assumes a new but still beautiful character, rich in fine woods and in overhanging trees and rocks, and enclosed on each hand between high mountains.

The scenery of the Keltnie burn, which joins it near Coshiville, is exceeded by that of very few places, particularly about the ancient castle of Garth, which is placed in a most singular position at the confluence of two deep ravines. Though so accessible from Kenmore, it is quite unknown, like every thing else which has not been described in the popular tour books. Before quitting this part of the country, we must, however, mention the scenery about Moness and Aberfeldy, though that water runs into the Tay. The cascades are well known, and of these the middle one forms the most perfect scene of this nature that can be conceived, although on a very narrow scale. But the views around from the ascent to these grounds, including the noble and picturesque bridge of Tay, are equally worthy of attention.

The scenery on the Lochy and the Dochart are little remarkable except at Killin. But we must not forget to name Glen Falloch, the seat of the river of that name, which flows into the top of Loch Lomond, and which conducts us through much wild and beautiful scenery to that noted lake.

The Forth, as we have already seen, rises in the lakes of Aberfoyle, and receives no principal stream till, above Stirling, it joins the Teith flowing from Loch Cateran. After that it receives the Allan and the Devon, the most distant part of this river at least belonging to Perthshire. The most remarkable scenery of the Forth is that near Aberfoyle, already mentioned, and its course through the great plane of Stirling; where it separates these two counties, is familiar to most persons. Nor, after leaving Callander, is the scenery of the Teith particularly remarkable, except at Doune, where it is rendered highly beautiful by the majestic remains of that ancient castle, and the rich wood with which it is surrounded. But we ought not to pass over that magnificent spot, the pass of Leny, where the water of Lubnaig Loch joins it, nor that which attends the courses of some of the mountain streams in the vicinity of Callander. In this part of the Devon also which belongs to Perthshire, is situated the well known scenery of the Rumbling Bridge and of the Caldron Linn.

The courses of the Almond and the Braun present no very striking scenery amidst such a mass of beauty as we have already described; but the former contains the wild recess of Glen Almond, and in the latter also are the well known falls in the grounds of Dunkeld, and that of Rumbling Bridge on a small torrent which joins it.

The Airdle consists of two principal branches; but it is not remarkable for its scenery till it cuts through the deep ravine near Craighall, where its course is extremely romantic. The course of the Isla through Perthshire, till it joins the Tay, is however very beautiful, although in a very different style, running through a rich open woody country, backed by mountains, and bearing all the marks of wealth and high improvement.

We need describe no more of these rivers, and, as the chief beauties here, as elsewhere, attend the rivers and lakes, we shall terminate also this account of the picturesque scenery of Perthshire, of which it may be said to contain as much as nearly all the rest of Scotland, rendering it, to a stranger, by far the most interesting county of the whole. Were we to indulge further in these descriptions, we might add much more, lying apart from the lakes and rivers, but we dare not trespass further on our allotted space.

Perthshire contains every possible variety of soil, Soil and climate. nor can we pretend to enter into any very minute details on this matter, on account of the extent of the subject. The most valuable are the alluvial or carse lands, which have been deposited by the principal rivers, and sometimes in conjunction with the sea. The Carse of Gowrie is the most celebrated of them. In most places this is a rich clay of great depth, being in some interstratified with layers of peat, and also containing sand and marine deposits in its very lowest portions. Most of it is indeed alluvial; but there are some parts also of a different character, arising from the decomposition of the trap rocks, which form a dark brown soil, and others which are red and loamy, from the destruction of the sandstone which constitutes so large a part of the Sidlaw hills. The plains of the Forth, when it belongs to this county, is of the same general character, but is in many places covered with a dense coating of peat, particularly well known about Blair Drummond by the name of Moss Flanders.

Similar alluvial soils attend the course of the Earn, particularly towards the east, while higher up, the country on its margin, though still often alluvial, is more sandy and gravelly, as is the case with all the alluvia of these rivers among the mountains. The principal alluvial soils of this inferior nature was found in the upper parts of Strath Tay, Strath Tumel, and Strath Airdle, as well as on the borders of the Lyon, the Garry, and many other streams of less note. The soil around the Isla is also of this character, as is that which attends the Tay from Dunkeld to Perth, which is indeed in many places extremely bad. In others, as near Perth itself, it is very fertile.

A sandy and clayey soil, called till by agriculturists, occupies one very continuous tract from east to west, but it possesses this character most perfectly, from near Perth westward to Dunblane, originating chiefly in the destruction of the red sandstone of that district. In the higher parts it is often very barren, but many very fertile spots are found, particularly where trap rocks have existed; and in these cases the differences are very sensible.

Not to dwell on minute particulars, we shall here mention, that a tract of excellent soil, arising also from the decomposition of trap, occupies the ridge of the Ochil and Sidlaw hills; but from its elevated situation, it is only adapted to pasture, in which it is very fertile. Some soil of the same character occurs also near Dunkeld, where it is in a situation for the plough, and is marked for its fertility.

As in Scotland in general, there is very little proper calcareous soil in Perthshire. The principal tract lies in Glen Tilt and at Blair, but in such a situation as to be principally condemned to pasture, in which, however, it excels. The other tracts of this nature are too limited and scattered to deserve any notice.

The mountain soils vary exceedingly, even on those hills on which the nature of the rocks is very similar. The best of these are about Dunkeld, lying on the micaceous schist, and they seem particularly adapted to the growth of the larch and other trees. In other parts of the mountains, in various places, there are found soils of similar quality, a yellow loam, producing excellent pasture, and cultivated wherever the situation of the land and the climate permit. The worst of these mountain soils are those which lie in the quartz rock, and these are found chiefly about Ben Gloe, while much of the same character also occurs in the hill about Glen Lyon. Peat is found everywhere, and often in large tracts, but it is unnecessary to point out these places particularly. That called Moss Flanders, already mentioned, is among the largest in Britain, and has been held to contain 10,000 acres.

The climates of Perthshire are necessarily as various as its surface, and scarcely admit of any useful detail. Perth appears to be the least rainy tract, and its average water is estimated at about 23 inches annually. Seventy is among the highest summer temperatures; but a heat exceeding 65° is rare, of any continuance [*]. The tracts especially subject to rain are the several mountain glens, where the quantity is as various as it is incapable of calculation. Among these, Dunkeld, as being near the low country, is conspicuous, as is Glen Tilt in the high; but all the chief mountain tracts may be considered as in this division. In the higher valleys the summer is short, frosty nights, even at Blair, often commencing early in September. The spring is proportionally late; and these districts are, of course, much subject to snow in the winter. The higher tracts are, however, little exposed to inconvenience from the east winds, which are much mitigated or expended in its passage over them. What these districts suffer most from is a cloudy sky, to which, excluding the light of the sun, is, in a great measure, to be attributed the lateness and imperfection of their crops.

This is as various and unequal as might well be imagined in a country so extensive and various in character, inhabited in some places by opulent, enlightened, and wealthy tenants, in others by the smallest class of Highland farmers, and on the most antiquated systems. It is scarcely seventy years since the holding by runrig extended through nearly the whole county; and, under the modified form of joint farms, it is still found in many of the mountain tracts, even on the estates of the largest proprietors. Here the small farmers live, as is usual elsewhere, in their little black towns, and in a state which, except in the Highlands, would be considered one of great poverty. But improvements are daily creeping along, and chiefly from the borders of the low country; new cottages being built of stone and slate, accompanied by an increase of industry and a greater sense and desire of comfort in the people. Among these recent improvements, we wish particularly to notice the village of St. Fillan, near Loch Earn, built by Lord Gwydir on the Drummond estate, because it proves that nothing is wanting to render the cottages of Scotland as neat and clean as those of England, and the habits of the people as orderly, but a little attention and perseverance on the part of the proprietors. The rose and the honeysuckle have here taken place of the dub and the midden, and the inhabitants have learnt to think that there may be a merit and a happiness in neatness and cleanliness.

Besides these remains of the ancient system, which in many places must continue, or which can at least only be converted into small separate crofts, as in the West Highlands, there are many extensive farms in Perthshire, reaching from 30 to 500 acres and upwards. The chief of these are found in the Carse of Gowrie, in Strathearn, at its lower part, on the banks of the Isla, and on those of the Tay, chiefly between Perth and Dunkeld. The pasture farms are, of course, of much more considerable extent; and, on the borders of the hills, an arable farm generally contains a proportion of pasture.

In the agricultural system, the rotation of crops varies in different places, but the details are too minute for our limits. The chief object of cultivation is grain. Wheat is raised on most of the low alluvial lands, and in some places even on the uplands, where the soil and expence are favourable. The Carse of Gowrie, the lower part of Strathearn, and the tract near Perth, are those in which this grain is particularly cultivated. To this we must add the further parts of Stormount

Agriculture and rural economy.

---

[*] The mean temperature at Kinfauns Castle, near Perth, in Lat. 56° 24', 130 feet above the sea, for six years, was 46° 3'. The mean temperature at Kinfauns, in 1821, was 47° 3'; of Dunkeld House, 150 feet above the sea, 47° 1'; of Delvine, about 120 feet above the sea, 48° 8'. ED.

Perthshire. and Strathmore, where it lies in this county, the district of Monteith on the Forth, and some parts in the neighbourhood of Muthill, Dunblane, and the Devon, together with that portion of the county which lies detached on the Firth of Forth. It has been attempted to raise wheat, but without success, to the north of Dunkeld.

Pease and beans are not much cultivated, but some barley is grown in the better class of lands where wheat is raised. In the Highland tracts, bear is the only grain of this nature, and the practice, with respect to it, is the same as it is throughout the Highlands in general. It forms great part of the food of the common people, and much of it was also used for illicit distillation; but that practice has been lately much discountenanced by the proprietors. The cultivation of rye is so scanty as to be scarcely deserving of notice. Among oats, the most approved kinds are raised among the superior class of farmers in the best districts; but the ancient grey oat still holds its ground among some of the small Highland farms. Every thing is cut by the sickle.

The culture of flax is universal among the small farmers, and on a small scale. It is, indeed, cultivated to some extent in Stormount and Strathmore, and in some parts of Athol. This flax is manufactured in the country, partly by the common people for their own consumption, and on a small scale, and partly in Perth, Blair Gowrie, and other places, as an object of commerce. The quantity of linen stamped in 1800 was estimated at £250,000 in value, and that which was manufactured in private is supposed to have been further very considerable. Hemp is not known.

Potatoes are universal, and are yet cultivated in the Highland districts by the method of lazy-beds. The drill culture has however been introduced into these tracts; and, in the better parts of the county, the methods of cultivation are as perfect as in the most improved parts of our island. In the higher lands they are much subject to be destroyed by the early frosts before they are ripe. Potatoes, like turnips, enter into the ordinary rotation; and, in the Highlands, they are the only crop interposed with bear, oats, and flax.

Turnip cultivation, as might be expected, is widely followed in the best parts of Perthshire, and it has now also forced its way into most of the small Highland farms. Such is the advantage of the example held out by the larger and more intelligent farmers. In the west and central Highlands, where large farms are rare or unknown, it has as yet scarcely made a perceptible progress, and in many districts it is utterly unknown. Of so little use is mere precept, and so little has been the effect of premiums unassisted. Sainfoin, tares, carrots, and other rarer articles of cultivation, are nearly unknown in this county.

In the management of grass lands in this county little attention has been paid, and irrigation is nearly unknown, except on the borders of Stormount and Strathmore. In the lower lands, artificial passes are largely cultivated for hay; and the cultivation of clover, as well as that of turnips, has also reached the Highland districts. In these, however, the hay is commonly late, scanty, and ill-saved, and the greater part of it, indeed, is the produce of natural meadows and waste patches of low land.

Dairy farming does not form a conspicuous part of the rural economy of Perthshire, but the breeds of cattle are good as well as various. The pasturing of cattle in the mountain districts is practised in various places, but these tracts are principally allotted to sheep.

Nor are horses reared, excepting ponies in the Highland districts, to any extent. Some of the sheep farms are of considerable extent, and this branch is so extensive, that twenty-seven parishes are said to be almost entirely occupied by sheep. The whole number in the county has been estimated at 230,000. The blackfaced is the predominant breed, but the Cheviot and many others have been lately introduced, as have the merinos. The latter have, however, gained no footing as yet. Swine are not much cultivated, and goats have been expelled. The very fine orchards in this county require no notice; nor is the climate adapted to this purpose, except in a few very favoured spots, although the general horticulture of Perthshire is equal to that of any other part of Scotland. Neither bees nor pigeons form a specific object of rural economy in this county.

Of all the counties of Scotland, Perthshire is by far the most conspicuous for its woods. Trees of almost all kinds flourish naturally almost everywhere, since everywhere there is shelter; but, among the whole, the ash grows with the greatest vigour, and that even on very high grounds. Near Fincastle, at 1500 feet and more of elevation, there are specimens as large as in any part of Scotland. The oak and beech, however, do not grow to a large size, and the latter, in particular, is not very common. The vicinity of Duplin seems most particularly favourable to wood, producing the finest trees of all kinds anywhere to be seen in Scotland.

Most of the scattered wood of this description to which we allude, is to be found in gentlemen's parks and planted woods, in hedge rows, and about the smaller farms. But there is also much wood of this kind growing naturally about the river sides and in the Highland glens, by the margins of the lakes and streams.

Of natural wood, extensive coppices of oak occur at Dunkeld, and in various other places along the banks of the Tay and the Tumel, as well as on the skirts of different lochs throughout the county. Loch Cateran, and the other lakes in this neighbourhood, are the most remarkable in this respect. These are preserved with great care. The birch woods are fast diminishing lately, in consequence of the demand for staves for the herring fishery. That on Loch Rannoch is the most ancient, but it only contains scattered trees. On the hills that surround Loch Cateran, it abounds, and at great elevations, often, fortunately for the admirer of scenery, in places where it is inaccessible to the axe. The birch woods about Fascally were among the finest in Scotland for their extent as well as for the size of the trees, but they are fast diminishing, as are those about Blair. This is a subject of great regret as far as the beauty of the country is concerned; as, from want of inclosures, they cannot be renewed, and will not pay the expence of inclosing.

Though there is much natural fir in many parts of the county, there is only one forest. This is the great forest of Rannoch, occupying its southern margin. But it is now almost a ruin, although a century of care might easily restore it to nearly its original condition. We may point out as the most woody regions, whether from nature or art, Strath Tay, the upper and lower parts of Strath Earn, part of Strathmore, Glen Lyon, Strath Tumel, Blair, and, above all, Dunkeld; and to that chiefly is this division of Scotland indebted for its great superiority in general appearance to all the counties of Scotland.

Many extensive plantations have also been made in

Perthshire. this county. The fir woods of Meikleoure are among these, but the trees are poor, and soon cease to grow; a common defect of planted fir all through Scotland. This failure has been attributed to bad seed, to a bad variety, to bad soil, and to transplantation; to every cause, in short, but the true one. It is peculiarly the misfortune of this fir to refuse to grow in confinement, or in the dark, nor does it put forth its leaves any where except where there is free access to light. Now, it may be said of every tree, that its produce in wood, or its vigour, is exactly proportioned to the number of its leaves, which are in fact the organs by which the sap is converted into all the produce of the tree. Thus a tree stript of its leaves makes no growth; and hence the fir, in the situation to which we allude, soon ceases to thrive; since it is as effectually stript of leaves as if its branches had been trimmed off by the pruning knife. It is sufficient to examine one of these woods to be convinced of this, where firs resembling poles are seen carrying a very small bunch or head of leaves, and that wholly at the top. Such a foliage is not the hundredth part of what a tree of that height would require to insure its growth, and the consequences are too apparent.

This is the result of an improper system of planting. If at least any thing better than spars are expected, the process of nature ought to be imitated. The wild and the cultivated fir are unquestionably the same; but the former has space for all its branches, and the latter is divested of them by confinement. It is easy to trace the natural fir from youth to maturity; and in this case as in all others, the practice confirms the theory. The chief plantations of Scotch fir, besides, in this county, are those of the Duke of Athole at Dunkeld and Blair; but this tree has now been sometime abandoned in favour of the larch and spruce, which produce more than double the return in value of the timber, independently of the superiority and greater perfection of the growth and other collateral advantages.

Plantations of the Duke of Athole. The total plantations hitherto executed by his Grace, amount to 11,000 acres, of which the chief part lies in the neighbourhood of Dunkeld and on the hills. The far larger portion of this consists of larch, but within these few years much Norway spruce has also been planted. Taking the plants at 2000 per acre, this amounts to about 22,000,000 of trees; but the total number of trees planted by the Duke is about 50,000,000, as the former plantations were about from 5000 to 6000 per acre. It is found that the larch thrives in a higher region than the Scotch fir, and also grows quicker, so as far to out-top it in the same plantation. It is averse to low and wet ground, but succeeds even among the most rocky faces of the hills. The highest plantations are near Loch Ordie, at about an elevation of 1000 or 1200 feet, and at this height they promise to grow. The spruce, fortunately, shows no aversion to wetter soils, and it has the farther advantage of growing in the shade of other woods, so as to be useful in filling up their interstices. Its growth is rapid and strong; and the timber, which has been used in spars and top-masts from some of the older trees about Blair, has been found equal in quality to that imported from Norway for the same purposes.

A collateral advantage arises from the cultivation of larch, which is of no small importance in the economy of planting. Under the fir woods no grass grows. But the effect of larch is to destroy all the mountain plants, without exception, and to cover over the steepest declivities of the hills with verdure. About 20 years growth are sufficient to produce this effect; and the woods which can then no longer suffer from cattle, become pastures ten times at least more valuable than the hills were in their original state. This change alone, it is estimated, would repay the expences of the plantations. To the value of the poles and thinnings must be added that of the bark, which has been used in tanning with success, particularly when the prices of oak bark have been high. It is a further advantage in larch above Scotch fir, that it is not destroyed in winter by the weight of the snow; and that even the smaller trees below the scale required for ships, bear a better price for the ordinary purposes of common carpentry.

The first larch planted at Dunkeld were two trees, in 1738, now to be seen on the lawn. One of these measures 12 feet, and the other 11 feet in girth, at 4 feet from the ground; and they are calculated to contain 400 feet of timber. These trees were originally brought from Switzerland or the Tyrol, and being supposed delicate, were first placed in the greenhouse. The particulars of their progress are interesting.

Between 1740 and 1744, there were planted at Dunkeld nine trees, and the girths of these taken in the same manner, range from 8 feet 1 inch to 8 feet 10 inches. These trees are calculated to contain on an average, each 115 feet of timber, or the whole contain 1035 feet. During the same period, there were planted at Blair eleven trees, the girths of which, at growths from 73 to 76 years, ranged from 8 feet 2 inches to 10 feet. This lot was calculated to average 110 feet each, in the whole 1200. The total measure of this lot of 22 trees is therefore 2645 feet.

The plantation of larch between 1733 and 1759, was executed by Duke James, and amounted to 1928 trees. Of these there were cut down, between 1809 and 1816, 873 trees; 1055 being left standing in 1817, containing altogether 2883 loads, or 144,150 feet of timber.

This timber has lately been introduced into ship building, and the following are the experiments hitherto made.

The Sir Simon Taylor, a West Indiaman, was built by Sime of Leith for Mr. Sibbald, partly of the Dunkeld larch; eleven trees, measuring 1066 feet, having been cut for this purpose, with a view to ascertain the value of this timber in ship-building. Unfortunately, this vessel was taken by the Americans in her first voyage.

The Athol frigate was built at Woolwich yard, from larch grown at Dunkeld and Blair, in 1819-20, and is now at sea. The dimensions of this vessel are as follows:

	F.	I.
Length of deck,	113	8
Keel,	94	8¾
Extreme breadth,	31	6
Depth of hold,	8	6
Tonnage,	—	499¼

Since that time a brig has also been built at Perth, together with some steam-boats on the Thames.

It remains to be proved by these and other trials, what the relative value of larch is, when compared to fir and to oak for ship-building. That it is far superior to the former, is well ascertained already, but its relative value to the latter is not yet known. The price is about one half, taken as agricultural produce. It will, of course, be a question of profit or loss on the whole, when it is known what is the comparative durability of larch to oak ships. At any rate, it is desirable to command a supply of wood for this purpose,

Perthshire. free from the contingencies of foreign commerce; while, to the planter, this cannot fail to be a profitable appropriation of land, which is of very little value, even as pasture.

As the future supply of larch for building from the plantations of that wood throughout the country in general, is an interesting object of general economy, we subjoin the following tabular view, calculated from the Athole plantations alone. No estimate has yet been made for the spruce, as these plantations are but lately commenced; but there is no doubt that a considerable supply of this timber for masts, yards, and spars, may also be furnished within the course of a century.

Probable supply of Larch Wood for Ship Timber, from Athole, beginning twelve years hence from 1817.

		Load Annually.	
12 years before cutting, or in	1829	Nil.	
12 years cutting,	1841	1,250	
10	1851	8,000	Scotch Acres.
8	1859	18,000	about 2000
8	1867	30,000	
16	1883	52,000	3500
3	1886	120,000	
69 Years calculated to finish	1889	130,000	1500
3 plants marked out			
72 years		Scotch acres,	7000

N. B.—The oldest larch laid down hitherto at Woolwich yard, and several ends of which exceed 1½ load, are only 72 years of age.

Young seedlings are used in the plantations, and they are planted without pits, or by the spade dibbling. As this subject has been much studied here, it will be interesting to those engaged in similar pursuits, to see a table of six days' work, which will convey a better idea of the expedition used than any general details could do. We also subjoin a similar view of the larch cut in 1816.

1817. March and April.	Head Planter, Borrie.	Plants.	Head Planter, Browne.	Plants.
	Dowally Hill.		Dowally Hill.	
Monday, March 31.	18 men	18,000	18 men	18,000
Tuesday, April 1.	19 do.	19,000	19 do.	19,000
Wednesday, April 2.	19 do.	16,400	19 do.	16,000
Thursday, April 3.	19 do.	16,000	19 do.	16,500
Friday, April 4.	19 do.	16,000	19 do.	16,000
Saturday, April 5.	19 do.	19,000	19 do.	19,000
Total,	113 men	104,400	113 men	104,500

Total planted in six days 208,900 larch, or 34,666 daily, or rather more than 900 per man.

Upwards of 1,600,000 larch have been planted between the end of November, 1816, and 10th of April, 1817, covering at six feet apart, more than 1050 Scotch acres.

Larch cut in 1816.

Number of Trees.	Age.	Average Contents.	Charge.	
		Feet.	Load.	Feet
60	72	65	78	0
70	68	56	78	20
120	57	40	96	0
100	...	36	72	0
50	47	30	30	0
400			354	20

It is not within our power to enter on those more Perthshire. general subjects of this nature which belong to the county collectively, such as roads; objects which may be considered as belonging to the general political state of the country. Suffice it to say, that the turnpike-roads are excellent, and that the cross roads are scarcely exceeded in numbers or utility by any in Scotland. The mountain tracts are, of course, deficient, as is usual every where, but considerable improvements, even in this respect, have been lately made. The bridge at Dunkeld is a beautiful, as well as a useful piece of architecture, for which the county is mainly indebted to the spirit of the Duke of Athole. Nothing has been done towards improving the inland navigation, nor, indeed, does any thing appear practicable. The course of the Tay, from Dunkeld to Perth, is such as to render all attempts here hopeless in that most important tract. Loch Earn serves for the transport of lime from Lord Breadalbane's quarries, for the supply of Strath Earn; and the woods of Rannoch were floated down the Tumel, as was much timber from Blair. We need not describe the great operations of removing the moss of Blair-Drummond, as they are well known.

In antiquities, Perthshire does not particularly abound, Antiqui- yet it contains many interesting remains, on which, ties. however, we can touch but slightly. Many specimens of the dry stone inclosures, usually called Danish, are found about Glen Lyon, and they seem chiefly to occupy a tract of country that stretches in a line eastward to Moulin. That these were the works of the natives, rather than of their invaders, there is little doubt, as it does not appear that the Northmen ever entered this part of Scotland. Dunsinnan, the supposed castle of Macbeth, seems to have been a building of this nature, or little better; but its traces are now scarcely seen above the ground. Assuredly, what goes now by that name was not the residence of the monarch of Scotland, even in those days.

Some Druidical circles are found in different places, more or less perfect; and one of the most remarkable lies in Strath Tay. The rocking stone in Kirkmichael, attributed to the same problematical personages, is a natural phenomenon. Of antiquities later in order of time, the Roman remains are particularly worthy of notice. The principal of these is the celebrated camp or station at Ardoch, connected with which, in some measure, is that nearer to Comrie, most certainly not the scene of the celebrated battle of the Grampians, which, with far superior probability, is placed in the vicinity of Stonehaven. With these are connected the remains of a Roman road, still to be distinctly traced for many miles eastward, and in some places even used yet as a country road. The next most remarkable of these stations is at Delvin, which appears also to contain remains of a military post of a more ancient date, and by a different people. Our space will not permit us to enumerate the other places where traces of the Romans have been discovered; but on this subject we can refer to General Roy.

Considering the scarcity of ecclesiastical antiquities in Scotland, Perthshire possesses its share in the cathedrals of Dunkeld and Dumblane; both of them very perfect as ruins, though not very remarkable for the beauty or splendour of their architecture. The tower of Abernethy, similar to that of Brechin, though less lofty than those of Ireland, has long been a problem with antiquaries; nor has any rational theory of their design or object been yet advanced. This specimen, unfortunately, is hastening to ruin. Culross Abbey may be added to this list.

In Blair and Castle Huntly we have splendid specimens of the ancient castellated mansions of the country, still inhabited. The antiquity of the former is unknown, but having been built by the Cummins, it is probably not of a later date than the extinction of the power of that family, which followed the establishment of Bruce on the throne. It has been much modernized by the removal of the two upper stories ; an expedient resorted to after the affair of 1745, to prevent its re-occupation as a military post. Castle Huntly is of the date of James II. Next in magnitude and interest to these is Doune, already mentioned, which, though uninhabitable, is not irreparable, as the walls have undergone little injury. Hunting Tower, near Perth, is scarcely an object of interest. Of the smaller remains of this nature we may mention Garth, noted for the romantic beauty of its situation ; the Castle of Clunie, situated on a small island in its picturesque lake ; and the more modern Grandtully, presenting a specimen of the French or Flemish architecture, of a date and fashion corresponding to that of Glammis, but on a small scale. The baron court at Logierait, an object of some interest, has lately been nearly demolished.

The abundance of the red deer in Perthshire, now so rare almost every where else, renders this part of the natural history of Perthshire interesting. The only preserve is that of the Duke of Athole, but a few are also found in the mountains about Loch Earn. The deer forest of Athole is estimated at 80,000 acres ; but it is not absolutely a preserve, as it contains some sheep. The number of deer has generally been estimated at 6000 ; and, of these, 100 or more are killed annually—the harts in August and September, and the hinds from that time till January, when the season terminates. As Lord Fife, the Marquis of Huntly, and Mrs. Farquharson of Invercauld, are now also preserving their deer, and as all these forests join, it is supposed that their numbers are very much on the increase. The roe abounds at Dunkeld, in so much as to permit also nearly an hundred to be shot annually ; but as they are injurious to the plantations, this is done with the intent of destroying them.

Moor game abounds in this county, and no where more than in Athole, where it is unavoidably preserved together with the deer. The district round Rannoch and Loch Garry are also remarkable in this respect. Ptarmigans are also found on all the high mountains, particularly in Athole and on Benlawers ; but the black game is not abundant. Pheasants are numerous in Strathearn, and respecting other species of game it is unnecessary to say any thing.

From the multiplicity and extent of its lakes and rivers, this county also abounds in fish. The salmon fisheries of the Tay and the Earn are objects of considerable rent and commerce. The rent of the first eighteen miles of the Earn alone is £10,000 a-year, and that of the Tay is probably much more, independently of the more remote streams. When the regular fisheries cease, salmon are still taken with the rod, high up the streams of all the greater rivers, even as far as Blair. The alpine streams and narrower waters contain trout and par also, but these do not abound in the larger ones. To compensate this, however, the lakes swarm with the lake trout ; even the smallest mountain lochs being full of them. Loch Rannoch is celebrated in this respect ; and those of Loch Tumel exceed even the celebrated trout of Loch Leven in flavour. The char also is found in some of the lesser alpine lakes about Ben Gloe, small, but of a very superior quality.

Perch, pike, and eels, are also common ; the two former, in particular, in the Lochs of the Lowes, near Dunkeld. None of these are made an object of internal commerce, as they easily might be.

Of Perth we have given an account in a distinct article. The next in importance is Crieff, a neat town, with a population estimated at about 3000, and the capital of the surrounding country. Callander is perhaps the next in order, and it is also a principal point of communication with the Highlands. Doune, once the great Highland mart, and celebrated for its manufactory of pistols, has ceased to prosper. Comrie is increasing from a village to a respectable town, and is conspicuous for its neatness. Dunblane has been long at a stand, but has lately become a resort of summer visitors, on account of its mineral waters. Auchterarder presents the melancholy spectacle of an ancient inconvenient Scotch town, but is the seat of a linen and woollen manufacture. Blairgowrie has received considerable accessions within the last few years, and is a great seat of the linen manufacture. Though scattered, it bears the marks of wealth and comfort. Cupar, situated in Perth rather than in Angus, is of considerable size, yet little conspicuous for neatness. Culross might almost be enumerated under Fife, to which it approaches nearly. Dunkeld has lately undergone considerable improvements, in consequence of the building of the bridge, but is now at a stand.

Among those which are much more properly villages than towns, we may rank Alyth towards the east, and Abernethy, on the confines of Fife. Among new and old villages of no great note, we may also name Muthill, Methven, Errol, Kenmore, Killin, Moulin, Blair, and Aberfoyle, none of which require any particular remarks. Auchtergaven is a specimen of a new village built on an uniform plan, but serving little purpose but to collect in a mass those who would be much better disposed of in the surrounding country. Last of these, but chief among the villages of this class, we may name Aberfeldie, a place of some size, and a convenient centre for a fertile and populous tract that surrounds it. The numerous smaller villages require no enumeration.

Among the first articles of commerce, we may mention that in sheep and black cattle driven into the low country for sale, as well as that in wool. Grain is exported from Strathearn and Strathmore, as well as from the Carse of Gowrie, from Menteith, and from Culross. Bark is also an article of internal commerce ; at least, the produce of the numerous oak coppices in the country. To this we may add timber, chiefly fir and larch, and principally from the Duke of Athole's plantations.

Of rough produce, coals form an article of trade from Culross ; but this is rather a branch of a foreign carrying trade. Limestone is more truly an article of internal commerce, as are slate and freestone. The limeworks are, however, on a small scale, except at Clunie ; and in almost every other place the stone is purchased at the quarries, and burnt by the farmers themselves. We may include under this head the marble of Glen Tilt, used in ornamental works, but of which the sale is much limited, on account of the great expence of the land carriage. One of the chief manufactures of slate is at Dunkeld ; but much of this article is also raised near Clunie, and farther west near Comrie, Callander, and Aberfoyle. Marl, the produce of bogs that have once been lakes, may rank under the same head ; and one of the principal supplies of this article is from Auchtergaven. Sandstone for building has been little wrought, when compared with the immense tract of it, of various colours and qualities, that exists in the county.

We already took notice of the salmon fishing, and this forms a branch of internal commerce as well as of exportation. It is exported chiefly to London, both fresh and pickled. One of the principal branches of the external trade of this county is carried on at Kincardine and Culross, where seventy or eighty vessels, of small tonnage, varying from sixty to ninety tons, are employed in carrying coals to the Baltic and elsewhere, as well as to the towns on the coast of Scotland. In return, they bring back timber, corn, and other articles. Vessels are also built there. But Perth is the chief port whence are exported grain and manufactured goods, and which imports in return coal, lime, and numerous articles required for the ordinary consumption of a country. For the more particular details of this we refer to our article on that town. Some ships are also built at Perth, and chiefly from native timber.

The proper manufactures of this county are linens and cottons, of various kinds, together with shoes, of which the seat is at Perth. Linens and linen yarn are manufactured chiefly at Blairgowrie, where there are mills on a considerable scale, and at Auchterarder, Dunkeld, Crieff, and other places of less note. The cotton-spinning manufacture was established at Cromwell Park, at Deanstown, and also at Stanley, but that work has now for some time been discontinued. The cottons wove are ordinary plain and printed shawls, handkerchiefs, and muslins. The chief linens are ordinary brown, and white, and some diaper is also made. These manufactures have lately been on the decline. The printfields are at Cromwell-haugh, Hunting-tower, Stormont-field, and Tulloch; and the chief bleaching-grounds are at Luncarty, Hunting-tower, Stormont-field, Lawton, Kier, and Crieff. Besides this, sail-cloth and Osnaburghs are made at Alyth; and the latter are also manufactured in the Carse of Gowrie, together with a linen used for the linings of hats. Coarse woollens are also wove at Dunblane, as well as cottons; and there is also some cotton weaving carried on at Callander, as well as tambouring. This last branch is also established at Crieff, Culross, and Kincardine.

There are paper mills in various parts of the county, as at Crieff, Auchterarder, the Bridge of Almond, Woodend, Ruthven, and the Bridge of Allan; and oil mills have also been erected at Dunblane, Hunting-tower, Pitcairn, Auchterarder, and elsewhere. Independently of the manufacture of shoes at Perth before mentioned, much leather is dressed in the county, as at Crieff and Thornhill.

Popula-
tion, &c. The total population of the county, in 1801, was 135,093. The last returns in 1821 were

Inhabited houses,	26,718
Families,	30,970
Do. employed in agriculture,	7,779
Do. in trade and manufactures,	12,523
Males,	66,033
Females,	73,017
Total,	139,050

There are 62 parishes in the county. The freeholders are 222; and besides the county member, Perth returns one together with Forfar, Dundee, Cupar, and St. Andrew's.

Botany. Excepting in the departments of botany and mineralogy, the natural history of Perthshire offers no peculiarities that require notice, nor will much be required on the former subject. We shall only notice the rarer alpine plants.

Ben Lawers is one of the great alpine botanic gardens of Scotland, containing a greater variety of the rare plants of this division than any hill in the country. These lie chiefly on the north side of the mountain, about Loch an Nachat, but the rare Lichen croceus grows on the very summit of the mountain. To give a list of the plants of Ben Lawers, would be to enumerate two-thirds of the alpine natives of the whole country.

The Linnea borealis, yet rare in Scotland, is a native of the hill of Kinnoul. In all the lakes, even when scarcely alpine, are found Lobelia Dortmanna, and, very frequently, Isoetes lacustris, Subularia aquatica, and Scirpus lacustris. Dunkeld and its vicinity contain some of the rarer, as well as the common, orchideæ; as do Glen Tilt, and the woods in the higher part of the county. Among these we may enumerate the Orchis bifolia, mascula, morio, and conopsea, together with the Ophrys ovata, and monorchis, the Satyrium viride, and hircinum, and, more rarely, the repens, together with the Serapias latifolia.

It is rare to meet the Saxifraga oppositifolia on low grounds, but it abounds in Glen Tilt. On the surrounding hills, chiefly on the south side, the beautiful Azalea procumbens is common; and in the same neighbourhood are found the rare Cornus Suecica, Rubus alpinus, and Betula nana, together with Anthericum calyculatum. The Lichen islandicus, not very common in Scotland, abounds in the same quarter; and the nivalis, far from common any where, occurs also there, in company with all the more ordinary alpine lichens. The Rubus chamaemorus is common, as is the saxatilis. In the woods of Blair are found the Pyrola minor and rotundifolia, together with the very rare P. secunda; and the Dryas octopetala also occurs on the calcareous mountains in this neighbourhood. The Stratiotes aloides has been naturalized. One of our rarest plants, the Convallaria verticillata, is found in the Den of Rechip; and we have also discovered it near Blair, the only two places where it is yet known in this country. At Dunkeld the woods are crowded with the Saxifraga punctata; and the Trientalis Europea is there as common as daisies in an ordinary pasture. The Osmunda regalis also grows in different parts of the county; and at Birnam the Pteris crispa is found crowding the interstices of the slate rocks. Most of the rarer alpine ferns also occur on Ben Lawers, and the greater number of our agarici, together with many other fungi which we cannot here enumerate, grow about Blair, a spot particularly fertile in this tribe. But we dare not prolong this enumeration farther.

Geology and mineralogy. If the geological phenomena of Perthshire are somewhat more widely scattered, and less easy, consequently, of access than those of many other parts of Scotland, it still furnishes examples of almost all the most remarkable circumstances to be found in our part of the island. The primary rocks, however, are far predominant; and indeed were it not for the appendages which it possesses south of the Ochil hills, and on the margin of the Firth of Forth, it would be deficient in the uppermost strata. As the general geographical features have already been described in the first part of this paper, we shall proceed, without farther explanations, to examine the rocks in the order of their superposition, commencing with granite.

The first mass of granite which we shall notice in Perthshire, is limited to a small tract occurring to the north of Comrie, accompanied by a much smaller subsidiary mass to the eastward. It is grey, and of a small grain; but presents no peculiar interest, except in a few places near its junction with the neighbouring strata, where it contains imbedded fragments of gneiss, quartz rock, and micaceous schist, similar to those described by Dr. Macculloch in the *Geological Society's Transactions*, as occurring about Cruachan, Glenco, and Rannoch. Its greatest interest is derived from its having furnished materials for the obelisk erected to the memory of the late Lord Melville near Comrie. We ought, however, to add, that this rock occurs in two or three other places about Loch Tumel; but in tracts so very small, that it requires a very industrious observer to discover them. Without a map, it would be in vain to attempt to indicate their places.

The most extensive tract of this rock is that which may be considered as commencing at the western end of Loch Rannoch, whence it stretches eastward through the wild moor of Rannoch till it reaches Glenco—thus passing out of the limits of the county. From this point it also extends northerly, but in an interrupted manner, towards Loch Ericht, where it also passes out of our boundary into Inverness-shire. We have just alluded to the peculiar appearances presented by this granite, in respect to the imbedded fragments; and it displays no other phenomena admitting of detail within our narrow limits. The last granite in this county occurs on the north side of the Tilt. Near that river, it reaches from the Tarff, so as to form the northern boundary of the valley, as far down the stream as Glen Criny, where it terminates. Northward of that ridge, it is separated by a body of gneiss which occupies Benderig, and with this terminates all the granite of Perthshire.

The granite of Glen Tilt is conspicuous in many places for the great proportion of hornblende which it contains; but it presents a great variety of composition and texture. It also contains much sphene. But the most interesting phenomena belonging to it are the veins which proceed from it and penetrate the adjoining strata; appearances which excited strongly the attention of Dr. Hutton, and which are described in a minute manner by Dr. Macculloch in the *Transactions of the Geological Society*. As we cannot here enter into these in any detail, we shall only observe that the river Tilt runs, for a considerable space, precisely in the line of junction between the granite and the stratified rocks, by which means a very extensive display of the interfering veins is afforded. They are found to pass through gneiss, hornblende schist, quartz rock, and limestone; and, in all these cases, are attended by the usual well known appearances; consisting in the disturbance, fracture, and induration of the strata. The passage of granite veins through limestone had not before been observed; but we have since found similar appearances in the Shetland islands, attended with all the same phenomena of fracture and disturbance, and of the penetration of the calcareous rock by siliceous matter.

The next rock in order is gneiss, and it also occupies a very considerable tract in this county. If a line be drawn from Glen Tilt to Loch Lyon, it will, with the exception of granite, leave a body of this rock to the northward; but, without a map, we could not define it more accurately. The gneiss of Perthshire is very regularly stratified, and of a fine grain. The course of the strata is about north-east, and the dip to the southward, at angles rarely reaching to 30°: but it is always irregularly placed when it is in contact with granite. It is not unusual in various places to find it interstratified with quartz rock, micaceous schist, and hornblende schist; in portions too small and too numerous to admit of description. Otherwise it presents no very remarkable phenomena to call for a minute description; yet we ought to add, that it is sometimes found, and in considerable beds, included within the great body of micaceous schist which follows it to the southward.

Although quartz rock holds a conspicuous place among the strata of Perthshire, its extent is very inconsiderable when compared with that of the gneiss and of the micaceous schist. In a general sense, it may be considered as occupying a station intermediate between the gneiss and the micaceous schist, and it accordingly alternates in several places with both. Ben y Gloe forms one of the most conspicuous portions; and it may be traced hence with some interruption through Shehallien, and along the north side of the Lyon, till it passes out of the boundaries of the county. In Ben y Gloe it is remarkable for its variety of structure, and particularly for containing rounded pebbles and gravel, indicating its mechanical origin.

We need scarcely say, that in the remaining primary rocks, the general direction and position of the strata are the same as in the gneiss. Of these, micaceous schist is the chief, and it occupies indeed nearly all the remaining part of the primary district. As its northern boundary may be deduced from the preceding remarks, we need only add, that the southern will be found in an irregular line, drawn from a point to the north of Airly, on the eastern side of the county, to Aberfoyle at the south-western quarter. Within this space it presents many varieties, together with some of those interstratified rocks so commonly associated with it. These are, gneiss, as already remarked, with chlorite schist, and some varieties of hornblende schist. The chlorite schist is chiefly conspicuous in Ben Lawers, and in the ridge that is continuous with it; and it also appears in many other places, as in Ben y Vrackie, in Ben Ledi, and about Loch Earn and Loch Cateran. About Garth in particular, and very generally along the course of the Tay, it is conspicuous for its beauty and for the garnets which it contains. Near Dunkeld it sometimes contains tourmaline; very rarely carbonate of lime. In Glen Fernat, the garnets found in it are sometimes of an inch and more in diameter, but they are rarely of perfect forms. In some places about Blair, it is sufficiently fissile to form roofing slate well adapted to stormy situations.

Next in order to the micaceous schist follows a series of strata of a complicated nature, which, from its containing some beds of clay-slate, has been supposed to consist of that rock entirely. That however is not the fact; as this substance is only one out of many which it contains. The chief of these are coarse and fine greywacke slates, of very various aspects, with occasional portions of chlorite schist, of talcose schist, of hornblende schist, and of gneiss of different characters, which it is not here necessary to distinguish. Among these, the finer clay-slate rarely occupies above a tenth part, and very often it is altogether absent. In some places only, as we shall hereafter remark, it is quarried for use. The whole of this zone is narrow, and being the last and uppermost of the primary series, it forms the proper boundary of the mountainous district of the Highlands, or what is commonly called the Grampian ridge. The dips of the strata are somewhat uncertain; but the direction is steadily conformable to that already mentioned.

The breadth of this zone is so variable, that it is impossible to define it by a reference to any names of places alone. But a general idea of its position may be conveyed by saying, that if we begin near Airly, where the micaceous schist ceases, it may be traced hence by Cally Bridge to Dunkeld; then north of Crieff to Comrie, Callander, and Aberfoyle, where it passes out of the county. A notion of its variable breadth may be formed, by saying, that while it is three miles wide to the east of Glen Almond and to the south-west of Comrie, it is not half a mile in breadth at Monzie. Except at two or three points, where it is in contact with trap, it is immediately followed by the red sandstone series, which is the commencement of the primary strata, and which forms so extensive a district not only in this county, but in the central parts of Scotland.

Slate for roofing is quarried in many parts of this line, and may doubtless be wrought in many more, should the demand be such as to justify the opening of new quarries. One is wrought near the lochs of the Lowes, between Forneth and Dunkeld. At Dunkeld there are two, one on each side of the pass of Birnam; and, in both of these, the produce is considerable and of the best quality. Proceeding westward, it is again wrought to the south of Loch Earn, where the quarries are also very considerable. It is opened again to the east of Callander, and, lastly, between Loch Venachar and Aberfoyle, where we quit the county. We ought here to add, what should have been mentioned when speaking of the micaceous schist, that a variety of this, approaching in character both to chlorite and to talcose schist, has been wrought in the hills to the southward of Kenmore, for the purpose of building Lord Breadalbane's new house at Taymouth. It is an excellent stone for that purpose, and much resembles that of which Inverary castle is built.

We must now return to the primary limestones, which are found in so many different places, of so many different kinds, and in such small quantities where they do occur, that they could not have been conveniently treated of before. Without a map we can scarcely make our readers understand precisely where they all lie, but shall name the nearest places by which they can be marked. With respect to their position and directions, one general remark will serve for the whole. They are all thin strata, interposed among the other primary rocks, and conformable to them in direction and position. But they are often extenuated after a very short course, so as to disappear, sometimes however recurring again in the same line, so as to make us suppose that they have been continued without our perceiving it.

The most conspicuous mass in the county, as well for extent of course as for variety, is that which occurs in Glen Tilt. It forms different beds, which seem often to split, to vanish, and to meet or appear again; and in this way it can be traced to the south of Loch Tumel. The predominant colour here, as throughout the county in general, is lead-grey, but many singular varieties occur in Glen Tilt. One of these is of a pink colour, and extremely beautiful, occurring in the hills near Fealair. In Glen Tilt, near the river side, it is found of a white colour and large crystalline grain, somewhat resembling that of Paros. The white is not pure, however, or rather it is watery; nor are the beds large; but it has been quarried by the Duke of Athole. Like the Pentelic marble, it is often interstratified with mica, by which the colour is injured. This and the following were discovered by Dr. Macculloch, and the quarries were opened at his instigation and under his direction.

The next is better known, as it has been pretty largely introduced of late for ornamental work in chimney-pieces and tables. It affords blocks of any dimensions. The colours are mixtures of two or three lines of green, yellow, bright, and dark, with white, and occasionally with grey. As these colours are generally disposed in irregular alternating laminæ, a great variety of patterns arises from cutting the stone in different ways. Thus it may be striped, or mottled, or splashed with wider masses, or spotted; and it is further varied by irregular patches and veins of colour, so as to produce a great and endless diversity. The occasional presence of tremolite and of mica serves to vary it still farther. It yields in beauty to very few foreign marbles, and exceeds most of them, being at the same time of a very cheerful aspect.

Near this there also occurs a large bed, of a pure white colour and fine grain, veined and mottled with ochre-yellow. This is a tone of colour much esteemed by architects, but the quarry has not yet been opened. Other yellow marbles may be observed in various parts of the glen, but apparently in no great abundance. The green kind seems inexhaustible. On the hills to the south of the glen, at the foot of Cavin Lia, there is also a quarry of a dead white colour; and not far from that, two other portions of a grain as fine as that of Carrara; the one pink and the other ochre-coloured. These lie on the estate of Lude, but they do not promise to be worth working for ornament.

When these beds cross the Garry they become grey, and are quarried in different places for building and for agricultural purposes, as they also are on the opposite side of the water, at Shiarglas and Invervach, and farther on in the hills near Loch Vach and near Fincastle. The park of Blair stands entirely on the limestone, and hence its fertility and verdure. Not far from the house there also occurs a very beautiful variety, of a pink colour, intermixed with large spots of bright green radiating actinolite; but it is in small quantity. A variety equally singular, if not beautiful, is also found above the house under Craig Urrard. This appears to the eye to be a micaceous schist, and it splits easily into laminæ, uniformly even and flat, not above the twelfth and eighth of an inch thick. It is only on the cross fracture that the limestone is discovered; and, in this direction, it appears as if ruled with parallel lines, very much resembling music-paper. But it would be an endless task to describe all the varieties that occur in this part of the county.

To the southward of Ben y Gloe, in the hills, two or three other beds are found, which run towards the north-east, so as to appear in Glen Fernat, and on the south side of the hills of Fealair. As there is no cultivated land in this immediate neighbourhood, these are not quarried. They are of a grey colour, and, like almost all the rest, of a large crystalline grain. To the southward of this, there is still another bed, on the estate of Edradour; and it extends a good way, accompanied by other portions which we shall not detail. A probable continuation of this line is found at a considerable distance. On Edradour estate, it is wrought by Sir John Hay, and serves for the supply of the country to the southward; thus saving the carriage from Blair. There is another unnoticed bed in Strathairdle, near Kindrochet, the residence of Mr. Small Keir.

Two remarkable beds of limestone are found near the eastern extremity of Loch Rannoch. One of these crosses the water, appearing on the southern side of the Tumel at the foot of Shehallien. In many places, it is white and pink, and often of an uncommonly large crystalline grain. In others it is grey. The other bed is still more remarkable. It is also white or yellowish in many places, and of a large translucent grain. Through it are dispersed scales of a brown highly brilliant mica, and in various proportions; forming an extremely beautiful stone, and so much resembling certain kinds of gneiss as to have been mistaken for it by experienced mineralogists. For the same reason it is unknown to the country people, who fetch their lime from a considerable distance, when they have it at their doors; a circumstance by no means unusual elsewhere. The continuation of this bed, but under different features, is also found south of the Tumel, where it leaves Loch Rannoch.

Four beds of grey limestone appear between the west end of Loch Tumel and Loch Tay; and these are dispersed in various independent places. One of them is quarried for the agricultural use of a considerable tract of country in this direction. Two more are found farther south; but as the farmers go some miles to the above mentioned quarry, the existence of these is probably unknown to them. Other beds still appearing to be of the same quality, are found near Loch Tay in different places, and some are to be observed on the southern as well as on the northern side of that lake. Two more, apparently independent of all those formerly described, occur beyond the western extremity of this lake, one of them being of considerable dimensions, and the other comparatively slender. The largest is to be found to the southward; and westward of this, there is yet another, which may be traced nearly from the northern hilly range into the hills to the southward, and so on to places which it is in vain here to attempt to specify. We should have mentioned that two beds, which appear to connect these latter with those near Shehallien, occur in the western parts of the hills and valleys to the northward of Loch Tay.

The next bed that we shall notice is one that crosses Loch Earn. It is wrought largely by Lord Breadalbane, on the north side of that lake; and, by aid of the water carriage, is conveyed eastward for the supply of Strathearn. On the south side of the lake, it is found at Edinample; far beyond which we have not traced it. Lastly, primary limestone occurs in two or three places between Callander and Aberfoyle; and in others northward of this which we have no room to detail. It is probable that it also exists in other places towards the western confines of the county; but it is by no means easy to discover this rock. The space which it occupies is generally so small, that, unless every acre of land is traversed, it may easily be overlooked.

This enumeration completes the history of the primary rocks, and we shall therefore proceed to the secondary; commencing with the red sandstone.

The boundary of that deposit is, of course, the same with that of the slate series, to the northward, except where trap happens to interfere so as to render the limits obscure or doubtful. To the southward, with some exceptions, it is formed by the Firth of Tay, and by the Ochil and the Campsie hills; while to the westward and eastward, this rock passes out of the boundaries of the county. With respect to position, a reverse order, as might be expected, takes place in the dip or inclination, between this and the primary series; although this is not invariably the case. Near the primary, the angles of elevation are generally high; but at a distance, the red sandstone assumes every possible angle of inclination.

The mineral qualities of this rock vary materially in different places, as might be imagined. In the vicinity

of the primary rocks, it is generally a conglomerate, or pudding-stone, of curious aspect and composition. In other places, the beds are of fine materials; and the sandstone thence resulting presents every variety of hardness, from a tender crumbling material to one that emulates quartz rock. The colours are equally various. It is found white, passing through all shades of grey to dark lead colour, and pale red, equally passing by various hues into high red, purple, and dark brown. Not unfrequently it contains fragments of slate or shale, which often cause a deformity when it is used as a building stone. Sometimes it is so intermixed with clay as to form a highly argillaceous stone; and thus also it passes into shale, with which it is farther often interlaminated. It is largely quarried in various places for building, as near Meickleoure and Auchtergaven, and in numerous other parts of the county eastward of Perth. The celebrated quarry of Kingudie lies in the same rock. As we find it a hopeless task, without a map, to specify the other places detached from the great mass, where this rock is found, we shall here terminate this account of it.

But we must now notice a bed of limestone which occurs in this red sandstone, although of no great extent. It is of a very compact nature, sometimes white, and in many parts much mixed with the fragments of the conglomerate in which it lies. It presents some very interesting geological phenomena, which our limits do not permit us to describe, and is wrought for agricultural purposes, near to Clunie and Kincairnie.

The last of the secondary stratified rocks in Perthshire, are those which belong to the coal series. These occur to the south of the Ochil hills, as we formerly observed, and in two distinct portions; distinct, at least, in a geographical sense, as the tract round Culross is separated from the more northern one by Clackmannanshire. It is unnecessary to describe this series particularly, as it is exactly similar to that which occurs throughout Fife, as well as in many other parts of Scotland; consisting of sandstone alternating with slate and coal, and presenting also, in some places, limestone. A coal mine is wrought on the Duke of Athole's property at Blairingone; and the same place furnishes limestone, which is carried northwards into Strathallan.

We have thus disposed of all the secondary stratified rocks, in as great detail as our limits will permit, and it only remains to inquire respecting the unstratified ones. Among these, for reasons which we need not here assign, we shall include those porphyries which are probably as much primary as granite is, and which occur only among the older strata.

The best known among the ancient porphyries is that noted vein which crosses the road between Blair and Dalnacardoch, and which is remarkable, as well for its size, as for its high red colour. Many other similar ones are found to the eastward in the hills, and nearly in the same line; but whether any of these are continuous with this one, it is impossible to discover. All about Ben y Gloe, and through Glen Tilt, veins of porphyry also abound, as they do in several places in Glen Fernat. Here there is one very interesting to geologists. It crosses a bed of schist which was previously traversed by an enormous vein of quartz; and here it displays exactly the same appearances that occur in trap veins under similar circumstances; fragments of the quartz vein, of various sizes, being entangled in it, and all the junctions exhibiting the same disturbances that are so frequent at the passages of trap veins. Thus the analogy of the older and the more recent veins of this class of unstratified rocks is displayed in a very striking manner.

We cannot, however, find space to enumerate all the veins of ancient porphyry which occur to the westward and southward of these points, as we did in the case of the limestones, on account of their economical value; we shall therefore terminate this part of the subject by mentioning that an enormous vein, of a beautiful flesh-coloured compact felspar, occurs in Rannoch, which, though not porphyritic, belongs in every sense to the same family.

The trap rocks occupy a conspicuous place in Perthshire, as they form, in a great measure, the southern boundary of the county. This boundary is part of the ridge of the Ochil hills, and part of its continuation in the Campsie range. We dare not, for want of space, enter on a more minute description of the geography of this portion of that rock. Near Perth, the hill of Moncrieff forms what may be considered as a continuation of the Ochils; and, beyond it, commences the Sidlaw ridge, presenting the same rocks, but disposed in an extremely irregular and intricate manner. The great face of rock above Kinfauns is a well known and conspicuous portion of the Sidlaw trap.

The phenomena presented by these trap rocks in a hundred places, are so interesting, that they would in themselves require an essay of no small length; and in that we dare not indulge. But for some of the most remarkable of those that occur in the Hill of Kinnoul, we may refer our readers to a paper by Dr. Macculloch, in the *Transactions of the Geological Society*. For the same reason we must pass over innumerable places in this county in which trap occurs in smaller portions. There is not one of them that is not highly interesting; but even to detail the mere geography of them would occupy far more space than we can allow; much less can we enter on any description. We must, therefore, terminate this account of the trap, and, with it, of all the rocks of Perthshire, by pointing out the two extraordinary veins that occur at Drummond Castle, as in this part of Scotland they have no equals, either for their magnitude or extent.

Mines and minerals. There are no mines now wrought in Perthshire, yet there are metallic veins in different places. It is reported, in all the popular accounts and tour books, that silver, and many other metals, were once wrought in the Ochil Hills near Alva; but we have never been able to procure any definite information respecting this mine that could be relied on, neither did we succeed in finding any one who could point out the place. In Glen Lyon, there are three veins, which are known to contain copper and lead. These, together with the *snperiority* of that district, are retained by the Duke of Athole, but no attempt, even to try them, has yet been made. At Dunkeld, there is also a vein of copper; and as we tried this ourselves, we can speak of it with confidence. It lies in the micaceous schist on the southern declivity of Craig Barns, and the matrix is chiefly quartz, intermixed with clay and ochraceous iron. The total vein is about four feet wide, where it is opened on the face of the hill, but it appears to be of variable dimensions. It might be wrought with the greatest ease by a drift; and, from its place in the hill, would also admit of a lower drainage, if necessary, to a considerable depth. The surrounding rock is far from refractory. As the work was only carried on by two men, and but for one day, it is impossible to form any notion of the richness of the vein; yet it is certainly promising, since, in that short space of time, we raised

40lb. of yellow copper pyrites. The copper was found to be remarkably good, and free from arsenic.

Iron-stone, and ochre, as might be expected, occur in many places among the secondary strata, but nowhere offering any temptation to work them. As matters, also, only of interest to mineralogists, we may farther mention, that micaceous iron ore occurs in great beauty and abundance in the slate quarries of Birnam and elsewhere, and that crystallized rhomboidal specular iron is found in some of the trap veins, exactly resembling that of Vesuvius, and presenting an interesting analogy between the trap rocks and the volcanic ones, in addition to those already known.

Of other metals, thus interesting to mineralogists, we must mention, that gold occurs in the sands deposited by the Tay in many places, but in too small quantities to be sought for, except merely as an object of curiosity. The ridge of Ben Lawers is noted for the immense quantity of Rutile which it contains. This beautiful mineral is imbedded in the quartz veins of the chlorite schist chiefly, and sometimes in the schist itself; but it only occurs in the long prismatic form, although with an infinite variety of aspect. Among the specimens we have observed hollow or tubular prisms; and in some places capillary ones, not imbedded, but occupying cavities in the quartz. This mineral is often accompanied by brown spar, and the adjoining schist sometimes contains cubical crystals of pyrites of great size. We have also found Rutile in Rannoch, and in many parts of Ben y Gloe and elsewhere. Sphene also occurs in several places, as we formerly remarked, and always in the granites. The crystals are rarely large.

The list of earthy minerals occurring in Perthshire is far more extensive, and, of some of these, indeed, it produces specimens not to be found of equal splendour any where in the world. As we are indebted to Dr. Macculloch for the greater number of these, we must refer for a fuller account of them to his papers already mentioned, as we can only find room here for a very slender sketch.

In Ben y Gloe, and on its skirts, mica occurs in cavities, perfectly crystallized, both in hexagonal and rhomboidal prisms; and in this manner we believe that mineral has not yet been found elsewhere in Scotland, although not uncommon. In the same places, crystallized chlorite, resembling that of Piedmont, which accompanies the well-known garnets of that country, also occurs. The same mineral is found, less perfectly crystallized, in the slate quarries of Birnam. Talc is less common, but it occurs in one or two places in Glen Tilt, where it is also accompanied by asbestos. In the secondary limestone which accompanies the red sandstone, there is found steatite, and the same mineral also occurs in Glen Tilt, in the primary calcareous strata. In the former situation it presents great variety and beauty of colour, and often approaches in hardness to the figure-stone. It is frequently green, or yellow, or white, or orange-coloured and red; and these several tints are often mixed in the same specimen. This steatite is also accompanied by asbestos. In Glen Tilt, yellow and green noble serpentine also occur.

We already mentioned that garnet and tourmaline were found in the micaceous schists. The former is extremely abundant, and often very perfectly crystallized: the latter is not common. Pinite occurs in great abundance in the porphyry veins of Ben y Gloe. Dr. Macculloch, who first observed this mineral in

Scotland, has since informed us that it is equally common in the porphyries of Argyllshire. It is in hexagonal crystals, imbedded, and of a dark grey and brown colour. There is another analogous substance, also discovered by him, which we are inclined to consider as a new mineral; but its characters of difference are not yet satisfactorily settled.

In Glen Tilt, and on Cairn Lia, the same mineralogist has observed cyanite; and, in both these situations, it is imbedded in quartz. But the mineral for which Glen Tilt is so conspicuous, is tremolite. This occurs in the primary limestone, and with an incredible variety of character, while the magnitude and splendour of the specimens are beyond comparison superior to any to be found in the hands of dealers. Humboldt assured us that all Europe produced none at all comparable to them. We take the following varieties from Dr. Macculloch's papers above mentioned.

1. In distinct imbedded prisms, of a watery transparency, and a quarter of an inch in breadth.

2. In flat thin brilliant white prisms, radiating in large circles.

3. In accumulated small prisms radiating in circles, of which the diameter is sometimes two feet or more. The prisms are white, but translucent; and these specimens are of great brilliancy and beauty.

4. The same kind of prisms accumulated in long parallel bundles.

5. Of a silky lustre; various in fineness of texture and in brilliancy; radiated in stars of various magnitude, or in parallel forms, or curved, or variously entangled and implicated.

6. In extremely short minute prisms, forming a number of distinct concretions, which are all subsequently intermingled, so as to produce specimens of uncommon beauty.

7. Still finer and more brilliant; in strata or laminæ, which split so as to present a surface not distinguishable from white satin.

8. In radiating, sometimes almost solid globules, of the size of a musket bullet, distantly imbedded in the white marble, and of a sea green colour; highly translucent.

9. Opaque of a greenish white, radiated in globules of various sizes, and imbedded in the green marble, in which it produces some additional varieties.

10. In minute crystals, so compacted as to resemble a granular quartz, and only distinguished by its superior weight and brilliancy.

We might easily have extended this list, but the preceding include the most remarkable varieties. We must, however, add, that this mineral occurs also in the slate quarries of Birnam.

Sahlite also occurs in Glen Tilt, and in the same neighbourhood in large beds. Dr. Macculloch, to whom we are equally indebted for it, says, that it is not found crystallized. It is sometimes pure white, at others of a watery grey; and is either very distinctly foliated, or else compact. It is frequently so intermixed with minute crystals of tremolite, as to form specimens of a very puzzling nature. Crystallized sahlite, of a seagreen colour, is found in Rannoch in the primary limestone, where it is accompanied by the rutile formerly mentioned.

In Glen Tilt, in several places, actinolite abounds; of a dark or bright green colour, sometimes imbedded in gneiss; at others, in limestone. It also occurs in Ben y Vrackie and elsewhere. We have never observed that the primary limestones produce any specimens of calcareous spar; but in that which accompanies the red sandstone, it is abundant, and in very large crystals, of what is called the dog-tooth form. Quartz crystals are not uncommon about Ben y Gloe; where they are also found of considerable magnitude, though opaque. But the most beautiful specimens occur in the trap rock; and we shall now therefore proceed to consider the minerals that are nearly peculiar to that family.

The quartz of Kinnoul hill forms pendents of a stalactitical nature, sometimes having a base of chalcedony; and it also occurs in the close cavities and in the agate nodules. In the same place amethyst abounds, generally of a pale sea-green, or else white. Occasionally, very beautiful purple specimens also occur. Chalcedony is found there, as well as in many places to the westward, in numerous forms; but we will not detain our readers respecting all the varieties, called onyx, pebble, and agate, for which Kinnoul has so long been celebrated. But we must not terminate this list of the purer siliceous minerals, without mentioning, though somewhat out of place, that very beautiful specimens of red and yellow jasper are found about Alyth and Blair Gowrie, the produce of veins.

Glen Farg is the noted seat of the zeolite minerals, which were originally brought to light by the operations of making the new road. The most conspicuous of these are analcime and mesotype; and in this place they are always of a strong red, or of a flesh colour. These specimens are well known to all mineralogists, and even to the travellers who pass through this valley; and the rocks were at first productive of very fine crystals. We have rarely met with any other instances in which the analcime could be procured in insulated crystals; and they are thus found imbedded in masses of calcareous crystals, so slightly adhering, that the whole crumbles down before the fingers. We have also observed stilbite, both here and in some other places, in the trap rocks.

Prehnite, far more rare here, has been observed by Dr. Macculloch; but its occurrence is only interesting because it is accompanied by the new mineral Konilite, which he has described in his work on the Western Islands, and which, as he informs us, he has since also discovered in Sky and in the Kilpatrick hills.

These comprise the more remarkable minerals of Perthshire; and of those that occur more generally everywhere, we need take no notice. It is yet, however, important to observe, for the sake of agriculturists, that beds of marl are found in many places under the peat. A noted quarry of this nature lies at Auchtergaven. We beg to point out to those who may be interested in this subject, that such deposits exist in many other places where they are at present little suspected. These beds are always found in the seats of ancient pools and lakes, and may be sought for wherever the ground gives indications of such a former state. It is scarcely worth while to have recourse to the borer for this purpose; as the depth is seldom great, and the superincumbent matter is easily removed by the spade. It is more worthy of notice, to conchologists and mineralogists at least, that, in two or three parts of this county, marl beds occur on the surface of the ground, formed of land shells; a circumstance, we believe, that has as yet never been observed elsewhere. A particular account of the shells which produce these, and of the extent of the bed, is given in the paper on Glen Tilt already so often mentioned, and we may here add that the Duke of Athole's neighbouring tenants take it away for the purposes of manure.

Our limits warn us not to enter on the subject of the alluvia of this county; which however present a variety of interesting appearances highly worthy of the consideration of geologists. (J. M.)

PERU, a Spanish province in South America, formerly extended along the coast of the Pacific Ocean, from $1\frac{1}{2}°$ north, to 29° south latitude, being about 1900 miles in length, and 500 in its medium breadth. But in 1718 it was disjoined from Quito, and in 1778 from Potosi, and some other provinces on its southeast frontier, which were annexed to the viceroyalty of Rio Plata. Its present extent is nearly 420 geographical miles from the river Tumbez on the north, to the desert of Atacama on the south, and its medium breadth seldom more than 80 leagues. Its square contents are estimated at $33,628\frac{1}{4}$ square leagues; its population at 1,400,000. It is divided into 49 districts, and contains 1360 townships.

Peru, before its subjugation by the Spaniards, was a powerful empire, extending about 600 leagues along the coast of the Pacific Ocean. Its founder was Mango Capac, who united under his sway a number of independent tribes, whom he instructed in the useful arts of life, and placed under the regular laws of society. His successors were styled incas or lords, and were venerated by their subjects as divinities as well as obeyed as princes. In 1526, Huana Capac XII. had reduced the kingdom of Quito, and married the daughter of its vanquished sovereign. After his death, a civil war ensued between his sons Atahualpa, who reigned in Quito, and Huascaz, who succeeded to Peru; the latter of whom claimed a right to the whole of his father's dominions, on the ground of his mother having been of the royal race of Incas. Atahualpa prevailed in the field, and Huascaz, having been taken prisoner, was shut up in the tower of Cusco. At this conjuncture, A.D. 1532, the Spanish adventurer Pizarro, with his associates in arms, made their appearance in the Peruvian territories. Pizarro had discovered the coast of Peru in 1526; and having been appointed by the Spanish court governor of the whole country, which he had discovered and hoped to conquer, he set out from Panama with three small vessels and 180 soldiers, to invade the empire of Peru. Having landed at Tumbez, he proceeded to the river Puvia, where he established the first Spanish settlement on that coast, to which he gave the name of St. Michael. Without opposition he made his way into the centre of the country; and, on his reaching Caxamalia, where Atahualpa was encamped with his army, he was received in a friendly manner by that unsuspecting monarch. In the midst of a conference, the Spaniards attacked the unresisting Peruvians, and carried off the Inca as a prisoner to their camp.

After extorting immense heaps of gold as the price of the Peruvian monarch's ransom, Pizarro, by a mock trial, condemned him to the flames. One of the emperor's sons, a youth without energy or experience, having succeeded to the throne of Peru, and the governors of several provinces having assumed an independent authority, the empire was torn by intestine dissensions; and Pizarro, having received reinforcements from various quarters, made his way without difficulty to Cusco, while Benalcazar, governor of St. Michael, by a long and painful march, entered the city of Quito. New grants and fresh supplies having ar-

rived from Spain in 1534, Pizarro retired to the sea coast, where he founded the city of Lima, while his associate, Almagro, proceeded to attempt the conquest of Chili. The Peruvians, availing themselves of the security of the Spaniards, and the absence of their chiefs, attacked the garrison of Cusco, and carried on the siege during nine months with the greatest vigour; but when their efforts were on the point of succeeding, Almagro, returning from Chili, raised the siege, and made great slaughter of the Peruvian forces. Unwilling to resign the city which he had rescued, Almagro disputed the claim of Pizarro in a bloody contest on the plains of Cusco, in 1538; but his party being defeated, he himself was taken prisoner, and put to death by the conqueror. Pizarro was assaulted and murdered in his own palace at Lima, about three years afterwards, by the adherents of Almagro, who raised the son of their deceased patron to the supreme authority of Peru. But Vaca de Castro, arriving from Spain with a royal commission, appointing him governor of Peru, young Almagro was defeated and beheaded in 1542.

A short period of tranquillity was thus restored to the Peruvian provinces; but a viceroy having been sent from Spain a few years afterwards, according to a new arrangement of the Spanish settlements in America, fresh disturbances arose. Gonzalo, the brother of Pizarro, at the head of the insurgents, marched to Lima, and compelled the court of audience to nominate him governor of Peru; and the viceroy Nugnez Vela, was afterwards defeated and slain at Quito in 1546, by the daring usurper of his authority. Pedro de la Gasca was dispatched from Spain with unlimited authority to suppress these dissensions; and Gonzalo, attempting to make head against him, was deserted by his troops, and brought to capital punishment along with several of his associates. For several years the Peruvian states were distracted by the insurrections of other ambitious chiefs; but the royal authority of the Spanish monarch was at length completely established over the whole of that extensive country.

Peru is traversed by two chains of mountains from north to south, in directions nearly parallel. One is the great central chain of South America, or the Cordillera of the Andes; and the other, which is much lower, is called the Cordillera of the coast. The more inland mountains are steep and rugged, and of immense height. Their summits are perpetually covered with snow; and there are sufficient evidences of volcanoes having formerly existed in some of them. The mountains nearer the coast are partially covered with forests, and abound in mines of gold, silver, copper, tin, sulphur, &c.

The principal rivers in Peru, originating in the Andes, run eastward to the Atlantic Ocean. Those which fall into the Pacific Ocean are generally small, and some of them are dry during the half of the year. There are several extensive lakes in Peru, particularly that of Titicea, in the valley of Callao, upwards of 60 leagues in circumference.

The climate of Peru varies, of course, according both to the latitude and the elevation of its numerous districts. In the Sierra, or High Peru, between the two ranges of mountains already mentioned, the heat of summer prevails in the valleys, while the more piercing cold is felt in the mountains; but if we may judge from the longevity of the inhabitants of this district, the climate must be remarkably salubrious, the climate of Low Peru particularly. In the vicinity of Lima, the variations of temperature are very inconsiderable. The

Peru.

thermometer is never observed in winter below 60° of Fahrenheit at noon, and seldom above 85° in summer. The hottest day ever known at Lima was in February 1791, when the thermometer rose to 99°. In this district no rain falls, but the dews are heavy and regular. Hurricanes, thunder, and lightning, are little known; but earthquakes are frequent and destructive along the whole coast. The winter commences in June or July with cloudy weather; the spring opens about the end of the year; the summer is tempered by southerly winds; the autumn is short.

Soil.

Along the whole extent of coast, from Tumbez to Atacama, there occur deserts of 20, 30, or 40 leagues; and the country of Low Peru, forming an inclined plane, from 13 to 20 leagues in breadth, consists for the most part of sandy deserts, without vegetation or inhabitants, except on the banks of the rivers, and places capable of being artificially irrigated. The earthquake of 1693 was followed by such sterility in the valleys of Low Peru, that the people in many places ceased to cultivate them. The soil of the interior provinces is generally fertile; and trees of luxuriant growth are found at eight or ten leagues from the coast. As there is thus so little fertile land in Peru, it cannot become opulent by its agricultural productions. Its soil and climate are well adapted for the cultivation of sugar and cotton; but the want of roads for conveying the produce of the country to a market prevents all exertions for the improvement of agriculture. In the present state of things, one district may suffer all the extremity of want, while another is overflowing with abundance, for which no vent can be found. There are no carts or waggons for the conveyance of goods, and no other means of transporting them but on the backs of mules, which, for want of roads, are driven through the fields, over the crops and fences.

Mines.

The principal source of wealth to Peru is its mines; but these are worked by a very different class of persons from those of Mexico. In the latter country, the business of mining is carried on by persons of the greatest fortune and distinction, on a great scale; but in Peru the miner is generally an adventurous speculator, who trades with borrowed funds, and is subject to great disadvantages. The business is thus held in disrepute, as neither safe nor creditable. About the end of last century, there were wrought in Peru, four mines of quicksilver, four of copper, twelve of lead, seventy of gold, and seven hundred and eighty-four of silver. The produce of these mines, for the space of ten years, was

	Dollars.
Silver made into plate,	602,130
Silver made into ingots,	29,126,024
Gold,	4,424,035
Total produce,	34,152,189

The great mine of quicksilver at Huancavelica, which was discovered in 1566, and which has been wrought on account of the government since 1570, yielded, at an average every year, 4750 quintals of quicksilver; and has been known to produce, in two years, 17,371 quintals.

Revenue.

The revenue of Peru amounts to near five millions of dollars annually, of which 300,000 are remitted to Panama, 15,000 to the island of Chiloe, and a third sum to Valdivia. After these remittances, and after defraying the expence of the government of Peru, the clear revenue does not exceed 500,000 dollars.

Peru.

Commerce.

The commerce of Peru is divided into three branches, viz. its commerce by land with the provinces of the Rio Plata—its commerce by sea with the other colonies,—and its commerce with the mother country. To Potosi, and the other provinces of Rio Plata, its chief exports are brandy, wine, maize, sugar, pimento, indigo, and woollens. Of these, the brandy and woollens are the most important; and altogether the export trade is valued at more than two millions of dollars. From Rio Plata, it receives mules, sheep, hams, tallow, wool, cocoa-leaf, paraguay leaf, and a small quantity of tin. Of the mules, there are 20,000 annually brought from Tucuman, for the service of the mines; and the value of the whole imports is about 860,000 dollars. This traffic with the Rio Plata passes through the routes of Cusco and Arequipa. In the trade with the other colonies, forty-one vessels are employed, of which the united tonnage amounts to 351,500 quintals, and which are manned by 1460 seamen. The chief exports to Chili are European goods, sugar, coarse woollens, indigo from Guatimala, salt, cotton, pitayam. The imports are chiefly wheat, copper, negro slaves, tallow, wine, Paraguay tea, salt meat, cordage, leather, and timber from Chiloe. To Guyaquil the exports are almost entirely European goods, with a little flour, wine, brandy, and copper; and the imports are chiefly cacao and timber. The trade to Panama, which has greatly diminished since the middle of the last century, consists of an exportation of coarse woollen, sugar, flour, and brandy, and a small importation of timber, cacao, and slaves. To Guatimala are sent some woollens and wine; and indigo, with a small quantity of logwood, pitch, timber, and cacao, are brought back in return. The total value of these exports to the other colonies is 1,694,755 dollars; and of the imports 2,066,824.

The trade with Spain consists in the exportation of gold, silver, Jesuit's bark, and Vicuna wool; for which European goods are returned. The value of the annual exports is nearly six millions of dollars. This trade, which was formerly carried on by Porto Bello and Panama by the galleons, has, since the year 1748, been conveyed in register ships, by Cape Horn, which at first were insured at the exorbitant rate of twenty per cent. of their value, but now are insured for two per cent. Since 1783 this trade has been made free between certain ports in Spain, and others in the South Sea, without being subject as formerly to licenses and restrictions; a regulation which has been attended by the greatest benefits to both countries.

Natives.

The inhabitants of Peru are composed of European Spaniards, Spanish Creoles, native Indians, Mestizoes, Negroes, Mulattoes, and Samboes. The Europeans are either persons in office, in the military, civil, and ecclesiastical departments of the state, who generally return to the mother country with the fortunes which they have acquired, or mere adventurers, without credit or connexions, who have made their way to America in quest of wealth, but who often perish miserably under the effects of their poverty and vices. The Creoles have sometimes titles of nobility, and possess large estates, but are excluded from all offices of trust and honour. They are very proud of their superiority above the other castes, and fond of parade; but have naturally good talents, which qualify them for learning and science when they have the advantages of education; and they are mild, humane, and kindly in their dispositions. The Peruvian Indians, who form nearly one-half of the whole population, are, like the Creoles, remarkably long-lived, and retain their vigour to a very advanced age. In Caxamarca, a province which contains only about 70,000 inhabitants, there were found in 1792, eight persons, whose ages were 114, 117, 121, 131, 135, 141, and 147. The Mestizoes, who are the offspring of Spaniards and Indians, are next in rank to the Creoles, and next to the Indians in point of number, much attached to the former, and constantly at variance with the latter. The negro slaves in Peru are either employed in domestic service, or on the farms and sugar plantations. There are numerous free negroes, who are in general idle and disorderly. The mulattoes, whom the Spaniards call the gypsies of South America, from their resemblance in complexion and manners to the Spanish gypsies, are much employed as servants, and the women particularly as wet nurses to the children of the Creole ladies. The free mulattoes are usually tradesmen, and carry on most of the mechanical professions. The character and situation of these different castes resemble so nearly those of Mexico, that we refer to the account given of that country for fuller and more minute details. (See also LIMA.)

The progress of the late revolution in the Spanish provinces of South America, is yet too little known to admit of any correct details; but its influence may be supposed to produce many important alterations in the general state of Peru and the adjoining countries, as well as in many of the particulars which have been given in this article, as descriptive of its condition under the dominion of old Spain. (q)

PERUGIA, a city of Italy, in the states of the church. It is situated near the Tiber, on the summit of a mountain, and commands a magnificent view over a great extent of fertile country, marked by hill and dale, and enlivened by towns and villages. The town is clean and well built, though, from the number of its churches and convents, it has a general air of dullness. The cathedral is a building of indifferent architecture. The church of St. Pietro, belonging to a Benedictine abbey, is sustained by eighteen pillars of fine marble, and adorned with a splendid marble altar. The other public buildings are, the town-house, a large and handsome theatre, two public fountains, an university, and several hospitals. There are in private houses, and in some of the public buildings, several valuable paintings by Pietro Perugino and his pupil Raphael. Among the objects of antiquity here, are the gate of the Piazza Grimana, and, at the gate of St. Angelo, a Temple of Mars, adorned with pillars of eastern granite. There are here some manufactures of velvet and silk stuffs, and a considerable trade is carried on in cattle, wool, silk, corn, oil, and brandy. Population about 16,000. East Long. 12° 22′ 13″, and North Lat. 43° 6′ 46″.

PESARO, a town of Italy, in the ecclesiastical states, and department of Urbino. It is situated in a fertile country, on the river Foglia, at its influx into the Adriatic. It is surrounded with fortifications of considerable strength, and has a citadel and an excellent harbour. The town is well built, clean, and airy; the streets are regular and well paved. In the centre there is a handsome square, ornamented by a noble fountain, and formerly by a marble statue of Pope Urban VIII. which was destroyed by the French in the late war. Numerous vestiges of ancient monuments are seen in different parts of the town. Several of the churches

are remarkable for their architecture, and the many valuable paintings they contain: the principal of these are, S. Giovanni, La Misericordia, and S. Carolo. There are also some elegant palaces, containing rich collections of paintings. There is a beautiful bridge over the Foglia, of modern construction. The climate of Pesaro was formerly remarkably unhealthy, on account of some marshes in the neighbourhood; but this evil has been remedied by the marshes being drained. Pesaro has no trade or manufactures deserving of notice. It is the see of a bishop suffragan of Udino. The population is estimated at 12,000. Pesaro became a Roman colony in the consulship of Claudius Pulcher. It was destroyed by an earthquake in the reign of Augustus. It was again destroyed in the sixth century, by Totila, king of the Goths, but was soon after rebuilt by Belisarius. East Long. 12° 53′ 36″, and North Lat. 45° 51′ 1″.

PESHAWUR, a city of Afghanistan, in Cabul, and capital of a district of the same name. It is upwards of five miles in circuit, and consists of houses three stories high, built of unburnt bricks in wooden frames. The streets are paved, but are narrow, and have a kennel in the middle. There are many mosques in the town, besides a fine caravansera, and the citadel, called Bala-Hissar, which stands on a hill to the north of the town. Population about 100,000. East Long. 70° 37′, and North Lat. 33° 32′.

PEST. See BUDA, Vol. V. p. 46.

PE-TCHELEE. See CHINA, Vol. VI. p. 206.

PETERBOROUGH, a town of England, in Northamptonshire, is situated on the north bank of the river Nen, over which there is a bridge, which underwent repairs in 1790. The streets are regular. The principal one for trade is Narrow Street, which leads to the bridge. The market-place is a handsome and spacious square. The principal public buildings are the cathedral, the parish church of St. John, built in 1400, and the town-hall and market-house. The cathedral is a magnificent building, about 470 feet long. The length of the nave is 267 feet, and the transept 180. The height of the nave is 81 feet, and of the central tower 135; its whole length externally being 150 feet. The cathedral contains many old sepulchral monuments, stained glass, &c. The benevolent institutions are, a free grammar school, a charity school for twenty boys, a workhouse, a free school for sixteen boys, and Sunday schools for poor children. The stocking manufacture is the principal one in the town. Peterborough exports great quantities of millet and corn, and imports chiefly coals and groceries.

The civil government of the city is vested in seven magistrates, and in the bailiffs to the lords of the manor. The town sends two members to parliament, the number of voters being 400. The population of the town, in 1821, was 950 houses, 981 families; 306 families employed in agriculture, 665 in trade; 2108 males, 2490 females, and the number of inhabitants 4598. The population of the liberty of Peterborough, in 1821, was 8558. West Long. 0° 15′, and North Lat. 52° 35′. See the *Beauties of England and Wales,* Vol. XI. p. 228.

PETERHEAD, a sea-port town of Scotland, in Aberdeenshire, is agreeably situated on a peninsula and small island, called Keith Inch, which is the most easterly point of Scotland, being within 300 miles of the Naze of Norway. The town was originally built in the form of a cross. The principal street is an oblong and spacious square, and many of the houses are elegant, while all of them are neat and clean. The town house, built at the head of the principal street, is a spacious and handsome building, with a spire of granite 110 feet high. The established church, which is also large and commodious, has a fine granite spire, and the Episcopal chapel is a neat modern building. The Burghers, Antiburghers, and Methodists have also chapels. There is a coffee-room, and public rooms for the accommodation of those who drink the mineral waters. There are likewise friendly societies here, and a library association for purchasing books.

The mineral springs at Peterhead have long been celebrated. They contain iron, soda, muriate of lime, sulphate of zinc, sulphate of soda, and muriate of soda, and a certain quantity of fixed air.

Peterhead has two harbours, the north and the south. The south one, protected by two piers and a jetty of granite, and having an area of about five acres, has fourteen feet of water at spring tides, and could contain about 120 sail of vessels. The annual revenue is about £1425. The north harbour, with a dry dock, is now constructing with the liberal contribution of £10,000 from the Commissioners for Highland Roads and Bridges. When this is completed, ships may sail from Peterhead whatever be the direction of the wind. Peterhead has fifteen vessels employed in the Greenland fishery, amounting to about 1300 registered tons.

Peterhead was erected into a burgh of barony by George Earl Marischal in 1593. It was purchased in 1738 by the Governors of the Merchant Maidens' Hospital of Edinburgh, who, along with the council elected by the feuars, nominate the magistrates.

Peterhead had an extensive manufactory of thread, woollen, and cotton cloths, besides a salt work. See *The Beauties of Scotland*, vol. iv. and *The Edinburgh Gazetteer*, vol. v. p. 18.

PETERSBURG, St. the capital of the Russian empire, is situated at the eastern extremity of the Gulf of Finland, at the mouth of the river Neva, in 59° 56′ 23″ of north latitude, and 30° 25′ east longitude. It is built partly on islands formed by the Neva, and partly on the continent on both sides of that river ; and the ground which now constitutes the site of this large and elegant city, was formerly a vast neglected morass. The situation is so low and so level, that the town has not unfrequently been visited with considerable inundations, caused when the tides are high by a strong westerly wind blowing up the Gulf of Finland. These inundations have, at some former periods, been so formidable as to threaten the capital with complete submersion ; but of late years they have been almost totally obviated by a large wall of hewn granite with which the river has been embanked.

This capital was founded so lately as the year 1703, and derived its name from Peter the Great, to whom it owes its origin. Having wrested Ingria from the Swedes, and extended his conquests to the shores of the Baltic, this illustrious person was induced, to secure the territories he had thus acquired, to erect a fortress on an island at the mouth of the Neva. In five months, this fortress was completed, in defiance of obstacles and difficulties, which, to ordinary minds, would have appeared perfectly insurmountable. The marshy nature of the ground, the intense rigour of the climate, the almost total want of implements and materials for building, the deficiency of provisions, and the great mortality among the workmen, seem only to have rendered Peter more inflexibly fixed in prosecut-

ing his intention. The work was still carried on with unabated spirit, and most complete success. The place of those, (about 100,000,) who fell victims to the hardships just mentioned, was immediately supplied by new levies. The emperor, who now availed himself of the knowledge he had acquired in Holland, and the various countries he had visited, superintended in person, and directed every operation. By his order, morasses were drained, dykes were raised, causeways constructed, and roads, communicating with the city, were opened through forests and marshes, till that period deemed impervious. In little more than one year 30,000 houses were erected ; people of every description,—scholars, merchants, mechanics, seamen, were invited and encouraged to settle in this new metropolis ; and in eleven years from the first commencement of the work, was the seat of empire transferred thither from Moscow, the ancient Russian capital. Nor did Peter yet regard his undertaking as finished. The buildings, with few exceptions, had hitherto been formed of earth or wood ; and in 1714, he issued a mandate, declaring that every house, erected after this date, should be constructed of brick and timber ; that every large vessel navigating to the city should bring thirty stones, every small one ten, and every waggon three ; that the tops of the buildings should no longer be covered with birch-planks, and bark, so dangerous in case of fire, but with tiles, or any substance made of clay. It was also enacted, that each of the nobility and principal merchants should be obliged to have a residence in this new capital. By such means as these, the progress of the city was extremely rapid ; and its founder, before his death, which took place in 1725, had the satisfaction of seeing his favourite city flourish, and, in spite of much opposition on the part of his subjects, fully recognized as the capital of the empire. Under the patronage of the various sovereigns who have since filled the throne of Russia, it has gradually increased in size, in elegance, and wealth ; and it may now with propriety be regarded as one of the most important and interesting cities in Europe.

In giving a description of Petersburg, the Neva, on which it is built, must hold a prominent place. This river, though it runs a course of only thirty-five miles, between Lake Ladoga and the Gulf of Finland, varies in breadth from 300 to 400 yards ; the water is perfectly pure and transparent ; the current is considerably rapid ; its banks, as it passes through the city, are adorned with rows of elegant buildings ; and its surface, almost completely covered with vessels of every variety of size, presents a most busy and animated appearance. Its main stream flows in a straight line nearly through the centre of the city ; but two branches, diverging from it on the north, form the two islands on which the northern parts of the capital are built. The southern portion of the city is divided, not by the river, but by canals, (of which that named Fontanka is the finest,) which gives the Russian metropolis much the appearance of a Dutch town, particularly Amsterdam. The south bank of the Neva is embanked for three miles by a wall, parapet and pavement of hewn granite. This structure, which constitutes the Quay, is one of the most striking and stupendous works by which Petersburg is characterized. Some of the canals which pervade the city have also been embanked in a similar manner. The depth of the river, and the vast masses of ice which, in winter, are hurried down its stream, will, it is evident, never admit of a stone bridge being erected over it. About fifty years ago, however, a peasant of great mechanical genius, but of no learning, proposed a wooden bridge to be thrown over it, similar to the celebrated one over the Rhine at Shaffhausen. Of this arch, of which the artist executed a model, the length was to be 980 feet, and the height above the surface of the water 168. This extraordinary project was not reckoned altogether impracticable; it has never, however, been put in execution; nor indeed is it probable that any arch, except perhaps one of iron, will ever be stretched across the Neva. The communication between the opposite divisions of Petersburg, has hitherto been effected by pontoons or bridges of boats, which, however, in the beginning of winter, before the river is completely frozen, and in the thaw of spring, it is necessary to remove, to avoid their being destroyed by the alarming shoals of ice with which the Neva abounds. The ice in winter, which continues for five or six months successively, forms the communication between the different quarters of the city, and thus supersedes the necessity of the pontoons; and during this time the Neva affords one of the most lively and striking objects connected with the Russian capital. It is the great centre of idleness and of amusement; and the celebrated annual fair, held early in January, which continues for three days, and which is meant to supply the capital with provisions for the remaining months of winter, is held on the ice. " Many thousand raw carcasses," says Mr. Coxe, who was present at one of these fairs, " of oxen, sheep, hogs, pigs, together with geese, fowls, and every species of frozen food, were exposed to sale." No inconsiderable proportion of these provisions are brought by land-carriage from very distant quarters of the empire, even from Archangel, a place about 800 miles distant from Petersburg. Before they are fit for dressing, they must be thawed by being immersed in cold water.

The climate of Petersburg, as some of our former statements may have led the reader to believe, is extremely rigorous,—more rigorous than that of any other place of the same latitude in Europe. In winter, the cold is so intense that, unless the warmest clothing was made use of, it would be productive of the most fatal effects; coachmen indeed, and persons in a state of inactivity, have not unfrequently been known to fall victims to it. The severity of climate, however, the common people seem, in a great measure, to disregard; their dress, indeed, consists of fur or sheep-skin, but their neck and breast are almost entirely exposed; and Mr. Coxe saw some women wash in the Neva and canals, in apertures made by a hatchet in the ice, at a time when the mercury in Fahrenheit's thermometer was 60° below the freezing point. In winter, however, the intensity of the frost is all that is to be complained of; the air is extremely pure and bracing; the sky never obscured by a cloud; and the number and variety of amusements, chiefly on the ice, which distinguish that season, render it, on the whole, the most agreeable part of the year. The summer has also its charms and advantages; it is as mild and agreeable as in the south of France; and the rich and rapid vegetation for which it is so remarkable is the more delightful from the bleakness and desolation which preceded it. But this season, however pleasant, is extremely variable, abounding particularly in rain and moisture. The quantity of rain in Petersburg has been computed to be a sixth greater than in London; and of this quantity no less than three-fourths fall during the months of summer. In this capital there can scarcely be said to be either spring or autumn, at least these seasons

are unusually short; for the transition is peculiarly rapid from the rigour of winter to the mildness of summer, and the contrary. In a few days after the snow and frost begin to disappear, the fields are adorned with verdure, and the trees with foliage—a fact that is explained from the circumstance, that as the ground is covered with snow ere the frost becomes intense, vegetation is never completely checked, and thus revives instantaneously on being exposed to the genial influence of the vernal atmosphere.

Petersburg, like Paris, is nearly of a circular form; Divisions it is surrounded by a rampart of about fourteen miles of the city. in circumference. By the police ordinance of the year 1782, the capital is divided into various districts; but the original and standard divisions, which alone it is necessary to specify, are, 1. The Admiralty on the south bank of the Neva; 2. The suburbs of Moscow and Livonia, which lie between the Admiralty and the country to the south and east; 3. Petersburg; and 4. Vasili-Ostroff. The two last mentioned divisions are insulated tracts, which are situated north of the river, and constitute the site of the original buildings of the city. That part of the capital which lies south of the Neva is the largest, the most populous, and the most elegant. The insulated division named Petersburg, which comprises several smaller islands, first obtained that appellation, by which the whole city is now designated, because it contained the hut built early in 1703 for the residence of Peter; and in which he really dwelt while engaged in superintending the erection of this new capital. This hut, the oldest building in the city, which contained only three apartments, and of which the height of the roof was eight feet, is still preserved in its original state, and stands under an arched building of brick, purposely erected to save it from destruction.

The great distinguishing characteristic of Petersburg Streets. is the width and regularity of its streets, in which it is equalled by no city in Europe ancient or modern. This uniformity is discernible even in the oldest quarters of the city. From the Admiralty, which, as recently mentioned, is the most elegant and fashionable division of the town, three streets diverge in straight lines, each two miles in length. The general appearance of Petersburg is not unlike that of the New Town of Edinburgh, the streets being long and wide, and intersected at regular distances by smaller ones. In the suburbs, however, there are many blanks in the rows of building, and in the old districts of the town, particularly in the Vasili-Ostroff, wooden houses, scarcely superior to common cottages, are blended with elegant modern structures. The ancient buildings, as they gradually decay, are superseded by superb and massy edifices, that would do honour to any capital in Europe. Petersburg can boast of very few squares; with the exception, indeed, of four in the Admiralty, it contains almost nothing that deserves that appellation. The houses, originally of wood or clay, are now all of brick; there are extremely few stone edifices, though the stucco with which the buildings are ornamented, have caused some travellers to assert that they are constructed of stone. The roofs of the houses are nearly flat, and are covered with iron or copper; tiles, once commonly used for this purpose, are now only to be seen on the inferior species of buildings. The streets, which, from the low situation of the town, are, except in time of frost, wet and marshy, are for the most part paved with stone; some of them, however, are still floored with planks, with which they were all originally covered : the pavement for foot passengers is, at all seasons, considerably dry and pleasant ; but the centre of the street, set apart for carriages, is little better than a morass. In this city it is impossible to enjoy the advantages of a cellar, for in all situations water is found at the depth of several feet beneath the surface.

Public edifices.

But whatever may be the regularity and elegance of its streets, Petersburg can exhibit very few public edifices of importance : these, besides, are all *modern* buildings ; and what, indeed, a stranger regrets most in visiting the Russian capital, is the total want of *antiquity* by which it is characterized. The hut, inhabited by the emperor while the city was building, is, as recently stated, still preserved, and is an object of no mean interest. But the fortress which, ere the town was begun to be constructed, was erected in 1703, has been displaced by a more formidable and efficient citadel, which, though destitute of the important associations connected with the original structure, is yet one of the most conspicuous edifices connected with Petersburg. It is of a hexagonal form ; it occupies an island of half a mile in circumference ; its tower is 360 feet in height ; its walls of brick are faced with hewn granite, and it is defended by five strong bastions mounted with cannon. Within the walls are barracks for a small garrison ; several wards are used respectively as a common jail, and as dungeons for the confinement of state prisoners. The Imperial Palace, another public building, is deserving of notice, not so much from its architecture as from its magnitude,—being 450 feet in length, 350 in breadth, and 70 in height. Connected with this palace, by means of a covered gallery, is the Hermitage, a spacious edifice, so called from its being the scene of imperial retirement. It is constructed of brick, stuccoed white ; the apartments are large and elegant ; and it contains a valuable library, a collection of paintings, and a small museum. The Admiralty which, though distinguished by a large spire, is by no means an elegant building, comprises storehouses, and docks for the construction of ships of war. The other most important edifices are, the Marble Palace, built of marble and stone ; the Taurida, now used for barracks ; the Imperial Academy ; the Academy of the Fine Arts ; the Senate-house ; Post-office, &c.

Equestrian statue of Peter I.

As not unconnected with this subject, the celebrated equestrian statue of Peter the Great must not be passed over in silence. This monument, which is the work of Falconet, the famous French statuary, and forms one of the noblest specimens of art which the last century produced, represents that illustrious monarch on horseback, in the attitude of mounting a precipice, the summit of which he has nearly gained. " He appears," says a sensible traveller, " crowned with laurel, in a loose Asiatic veil, and sitting on a housing of bear-skin ; his right hand is stretched out as in the act of giving benediction to his subjects ; and his left holds the reins. The design is masterly, and the attitude is bold and spirited." The pedestal, a stone weighing 1500 tons—a weight not surpassed in the annals of the art to which it belongs, was brought to Petersburg from a distance of several miles. The simplicity of the inscription, (" Catherine II. to Peter I.") expressed in the Latin and Russian languages, on opposite sides of the monument, corresponds well with the stern and manly character of the extraordinary person whom it commemorates, and is infinitely more striking than a pompous detail of exalted merit.

The places for religious worship in Petersburg are considerably numerous, and comprise churches belonging to almost every denomination of Christians. The native Russians are, for the most part, of the Greek church ; though not a few of them are Roman Catholics, while some of them are Protestants ; but the vast number of foreigners, resident in this capital, account for the variety of creeds and of places of worship by which this city is distinguished. The cathedral of St. Peter and St. Paul, the metropolitan church, is a building of considerable extent and grandeur : its tower and spire, the latter of which is composed of copper, gilt with gold, are elevated to the height of 240 feet ; the interior decorations and paintings are extremely chaste and elegant ; but, with all its beauty, this edifice is chiefly remarkable from its containing the bones of Peter the Great, by whom it was founded,—of Catherine, his wife and successor, and of several others of the imperial family. The tombs are of marble, and are decorated with inscriptions, which, with one exception, are all written in the Russian language. The church of St. Alexander Newski, connected with the monastery of the same name, is also distinguished as a royal cemetery, Catherine II. having formed a vault underneath it to contain her own ashes and those of her imperial successors. The church, dedicated to St. Isaac, which is built of marble, jasper, and porphyry, on a basement of granite, would probably have been regarded as the most costly and superb sacred edifice belonging to this capital, had not the late emperor, in utter contempt of taste and propriety, caused the dome, which was not completed till his time, to be constructed of brick. The Lutheran churches of St. Anne and St. Catherine are conspicuous, merely for the neatness and simplicity of their architecture.

Manufactures.

In the department of manufactures, Petersburg, though it has attained to eminence in various other respects, is a city of very inferior importance. The inhabitants, though not devoid of enterprise, have not hitherto enjoyed the advantages of capital. The Russian nobility are abundantly opulent ; but the great body of the citizens are, to a degree unknown in other towns of the same extent, remarkable for poverty and indigence. Hence the government has found it necessary to step forward to afford an example ; and thus the chief manufactories of this city are national establishments. Of these, the most important are, a celebrated tapestry work, a bronze work, foundries of metal and of cannon, powder-mills, &c. Notwithstanding this general poverty of the inhabitants, however, there are not wanting manufacturing establishments the property of private individuals,—of whom no small proportion, it must not be denied, consist of enterprising foreigners, attracted by the many facilities and advantages of the Russian metropolis. These establishments, some of which are of great extent, and the number of which is rapidly increasing, are of various kinds, such as manufactures of silk, cotton, woollen, paper and cards, wax-cloth, snuff, tobacco, leather, watches, mathematical and musical instruments, and soap. Notwithstanding this enumeration, however, there is no species of manufactures in which Petersburg *excels ;* so much, indeed, is the contrary the truth, that many of the simplest articles of manufacture, such as cottons, hardware, and pottery, are annually imported.

Commerce.

But, in compensation for this inferiority in manufactures, this capital is, in a commercial point of view, one of the most important cities of Europe. Its eminence

Petersburg. in this respect is owing chiefly to its being the only great maritime outlet in the Gulf of Finland, and to an extensive and almost unrivalled communication with the interior of the empire. From 1000 to 1700 ships annually enter the Neva; and a canal having been constructed between this river and the Wolga, a communication is thus opened between the Russian capital and the Caspian Sea, a distance of no less than 1400 miles. The foreign trade of Petersburg is, it must not be concealed, almost entirely in the hands of foreigners, (of whom nearly one-half are British,) as the poverty of the Russians have, in a great degree, incapacitated them hitherto from engaging in any extensive speculation. The trade of the interior, however, is by law secured to the natives, who, from want of money, can with difficulty avail themselves of this privilege, as, on the delivery of goods, they require part at least, if not all, of the price to be paid, while yet they expect very long credit from those from whom they purchase. But this disability is now beginning to be removed; and the Russians will, it is hoped, ere long be in a condition to profit by the commercial advantages by which their country is distinguished. The exports of Petersburg consist chiefly of the simplest produce of the soil, such as hemp, flax, leather, tallow, bees-wax, iron, the skins of hares and foxes, &c. To these, however, may be added canvas, and all kinds of coarse linen—articles easily manufactured, and in which, from the cheapness of the raw material, the Russians can afford to undersel most other nations. The imports, on the contrary, consist of every species of colonial produce, of all the luxuries, and not a few of the necessaries and comforts of life. The total amount of the annual imports is about six millions—nearly a third more than that of the exports; and the foreign trade of Petersburg is equal to one-half of that of all the other ports of the Russian empire.

Literature. This capital, however, with all its importance, has as yet attained to no literary distinction. Its celebrated founder, indeed, invited men of genius and talents to it from every quarter, and was a devoted admirer and patron of learning; but none of his successors have shown themselves possessed, in any degree, of similar dispositions; and the cause of literature, if it has not languished, has certainly not flourished since the death of that wonderful man. Petersburg, however, can boast of several libraries, and not a few societies and establishments of a literary description, such as the Academy of Sciences, the Academy of the Fine Arts, the Academy for promoting a Knowledge of the Russian History and Language. But the libraries, the best of which are very imperfect, were not open to the public till 1812; and the literary societies, though the names of some of them are extensively known, are little better than nominal, as most of the members that compose them are foreigners. The native and resident scholars are, in general, so ignorant or so careless, that some of these most important institutions are shamefully neglected. The observatory, for instance, is often in so damp and ruinous a state, that observations cannot, without great difficulty, be made in it, particularly during the winter season. Though this capital was not, till 1819, distinguished by a university, it yet contained a considerable number of inferior seminaries, some of them of no mean importance, such as military schools, schools for medicine, navigation, mining, &c. But, notwithstanding of the number of these institutions, the department of medicine is almost the only one in which the Russians have attained to any thing like eminence;

and this result has been owing, in no mean degree, to Dr. Petersburg. Erskine, a Scotch physician, who settled in Petersburg under the patronage of Peter the Great, and to various other medical gentlemen of this country, who, since that period, have held the dignified office of physician at the Russian court. This capital contains also a botanical garden, and several scientific collections, of which the most valuable are those belonging to the Academy of Sciences, the Mining Schools, and the Medical Society. The inhabitants of Petersburg, though they have not yet acquired any very high literary reputation, will, it is hoped, soon be roused to avail themselves of the advantages which, from the above enumeration, it is evident they enjoy. Government besides, has, much to its honour, lately stepped forward to encourage learning: A university, as just mentioned, was established in 1819; and above thirty charity schools are supported at the public expence, in which not fewer, it has been computed, than 7000 children are educated: a fact which, in a few years, cannot fail to have a most beneficial effect on the intellectual and literary character of this celebrated city.

By a survey made in 1817, the population of Petersburg was found to amount to 285,000; of whom, it ants. was stated, 55,000 were connected with the land and sea service, and 25,000 were foreigners. Of the character of the people hospitality is a prominent feature. A mania for gaming pervades all ranks. The lower orders are addicted to the intemperate use of spiritous liquors: and they are not very remarkable for honesty. The female character is much more respectable here than in most cities of the same size, particularly in Paris; unmarried ladies seldom go into mixed companies, and the married pride themselves chiefly in the neatness and economy of their domestic establishments. In Petersburg there are three theatres, a German, a French, and a Russian. The actors are paid by government, and do not depend, in any degree, on their audience; but none are permitted to attend without having obtained a ticket of admission. In winter, the ice on the Neva is the great centre of pleasure and relaxation. Skating, sledge-racing, sliding down artificial elevations, form the daily and favourite amusements of the citizens. These elevations, generally about thirty feet in height, are composed of snow, and are encrusted with ice; and down the declivity thus formed, the Russians descend on a sledge with such velocity, that they are often driven on the surface of the ice to a distance of 300 or 400 feet.

After having gradually undergone various improve- Police. ments and modifications, the police of Petersburg was finally organized in 1782; the system then established has been uniformly adhered to since that period; and there are indeed few cities of equal extent where the peace and property of the inhabitants are so completely guarded and secured. The officers are, a grand-master, two inspectors, eleven presidents of quarters, with various other dignitaries of an inferior description. Sentinels being stationed in the streets at the distance of 150 yards from each other, the least disturbance is thus easily prevented; and few, while the town is so guarded, have the hardihood to attempt a breach of the peace. Russia, like France, is quite a land of passports; and a stranger, to save much disagreeable trouble, must, immediately on his arrival in Petersburg, deliver his passport at the principal police-office, and must, besides, publish his arrival three different times in the public papers: And a similar process must be submitted to on his departure from the capital. The officers of po-

Peters-
burg.
Petrarch.

lice here, as in most other cities, are invested with various judicial functions of a subordinate nature, such as deciding differences between master and servant; and in spring they are deputed to superintend the breaking up of the ice on the Neva, a work of no small difficulty and danger. The police have also the superintendence of the various hospitals of the city—of which there are a considerable number, and which are all liberally endowed.

The neighbourhood of Petersburg, though it is distinguished by several imperial palaces, is devoid of every thing like natural beauties; on the contrary, it presents to the view a dead uncultivated flat, diversified only by forests and marshes of the most hopeless and gloomy description. These marshes, however, government is at present endeavouring to drain; and other improvements will undoubtedly be attempted; but the rigour of the climate, and the level and barren nature of this district of the Russian empire, will for ever, it is feared, render it totally unproductive and unprofitable. Cronstadt, though situated on an island, in the Gulf of Finland, twenty-two miles distant from Petersburg, may be looked upon, from its commanding the entrance to the Neva, as the fortress of the city; it is, besides, the principal naval station of the Russian fleet, and contains great magazines of naval stores, and extensive docks and yards for ship-building.

See the various *Lives of Peter the Great;* particularly those by Voltaire and Gordon; *State of the Russian Empire,* by Perry, who was contemporary with Peter the Great; Tooke's *View of the Russian Empire,* 3 vols.; Wraxall's *Tour,* &c. *Travels in Russia,* &c. by Dr. John Cook, M.D. 2 vols. Edin. 1773; Coxe's *Travels in Poland, Russia,* &c. 5 vols. see vol. 2d. (T. M.)

PETRARCO, or PETRARCH, FRANCIS, a celebrated Italian poet, was descended of an ancient and respectable family of Florence, but was born (1304) at Arezzo in Tuscany, whither his parents had fled for refuge in consequence of some internal commotions to which that republic was then subjected. His father and grandfather, who followed the profession of the law, were equally esteemed for the probity of their character, and the eminence of their talents *. The mother of Petrarch, about seven months after his birth, ventured to return with the child to Ancise, a villa belonging to her husband in the vale of Arno, fourteen miles from Florence. The family of Petrarch afterwards settled at Carpentras, in the vicinity of Avignon, then the residence of the Pope, where the subject of this sketch received his scholastic education. Displaying at an early age great talents and a decided taste for literature, he made much greater proficiency in his studies than any of his contemporaries; he made himself acquainted when at school with books known to few at his age; and among other works which caught his youthful admiration, Cicero was his greatest favourite, and continued to be so at every future stage of his life. His father, who intended him for the law, sent him at the age of fourteen to the University of Montpelier; whence he afterwards removed him to Bologna; at both which places, instead of applying himself to the study of law, he devoted his time to the cultivation of poetry and elegant literature. In vain was parental authority interposed. Petrarch, though distinguished for filial affection, found the natural tendency of his

mind altogether irresistible; and had his father lived, his good principles would undoubtedly have induced him to sacrifice his own views and wishes to those of so affectionate and promising a son.

But Petrarch was not destined long to enjoy the advantages of parental tenderness and wisdom. His mother died in 1324; and his father, overwhelmed with grief at the sense of his loss, survived her only a short time, and left two sons, who had scarcely reached the age of manhood, without friends and almost without fortune.

In such circumstances, Petrarch left Bologna, and settled at Avignon, a place distinguished at that time for luxury and licentiousness, where he soon became remarkable, as much for the magnificence of his dress and the gaiety of his life, as for the brilliancy of his talents, and the intensity of his application. But though a votary of fashion, he was never insensible to the charms of literature. Every leisure hour he could command, he devoted to the study of ancient learning and of poetry, and shewed at that time a trait of character by which he was ever afterwards distinguished; namely, that of collecting manuscripts of classical authors, and of taking new copies of them, many of which he transcribed with his own hand.

And this devotedness to literature was cherished and confirmed by the character of some of those eminent personages whose friendship he at this time acquired. The individual, whose salutary advice and warm encouragement first gave him confidence in his own genius and talents, was the venerable Canon of Pisa, a person eminent alike for an intimate acquaintance with ancient literature, and for purity of character. But the most important incident in the life of Petrarch at this time was, his introduction into the illustrious family of Colonna, to whose kind and patronising attention he owed some of the happiest moments of his existence, and most of the preferments and honours to which he was afterwards raised. After having spent a summer with James Colonna, bishop of Lombes, in the bishoprick near the foot of the Pyrennees—a place, and the delights it afforded him he never ceased to remember,—he was kindly solicited to reside with that prelate in the house of his brother, Cardinal Colonna, then at Avignon. This invitation he did not hesitate to accept; and he thus found an agreeable home, where he enjoyed every opportunity for the indulgence of his favourite studies, and where he became known to the most distinguished persons of that period; and the friendship of all to whom he was introduced, his amiable manners and exquisite genius never failed to secure.

But an event about this time took place, certainly the most important in the life of Petrarch, and which had a powerful effect on his future history. On the morning of April the 6th, 1327, he saw, for the first time, the beautiful *Laura,*—a name immortalized in his verses, and which, in the mind of every reader, is connected with the most interesting and romantic ideas. Various have been the conjectures concerning the identity of this celebrated lady, and in what circumstances she was placed, when Petrarch became her admirer. Referring the reader to the works mentioned at the end of this article, we shall here only state, that she seems to us to have been born of an honourable family

Petrarch.

---

* Garzo, the grandfather of Petrarch, it may not be uninteresting to state, " after having passed one hundred and four years in innocence and good works, died like Plato on the day of his birth, and in the same bed in which he was born."—*Dobson's Life of Petrarch,* p. 1.

in the neighbourhood of Avignon, in the parish in which Vaucluse is situated, and that, when Petrarch first beheld her, she was not only not married, but was only in her thirteenth year.

Whatever conflicting conjectures, however, have been made relative to the identity of Laura, all writers concur in representing her as distinguished by all that is beautiful and elegant in the female form. " Her face, her air, her gait, were something more than mortal."—" The expression of her whole figure is that of a very young girl, of amiable ingenuity of countenance, much sweetness of disposition, and extreme bashfulness."—" Nature formed you," says the poet himself, " the most striking model of her own power : when I first beheld you, what emotions! nothing can efface the impression you then made."

But the love of Petrarch, though of the most pure and ardent kind, did not experience a suitable return. Unmoved by the most devoted affection, or by the unrivalled beauty of those verses which it breathed, Laura treated him with unkindness or neglect. Some expressions of regard, indeed,—something like return of affection, she seems, in a favoured hour, to have condescended to bestow—which he felt deeply, and on which he expatiated with rapture—but her general demeanour was marked by coyness and indifference ; and it is one of the most remarkable facts in the history of the tender passion, that a female, young and unengaged, should thus remain uninfluenced by the affection and admiration of a lover, distinguished, as Petrarch was, by every grace of external form, by every accomplishment which can constitute a gentleman, and by the most brilliant genius. Yet, extraordinary as it is, and painful as it may have been to Petrarch, posterity, we think, has no great reason to regret it. For, to this indifference, the world is indebted for those elegant verses which have shed a lustre over the names of Petrarch and Laura, and which, for exquisite and romantic tenderness, stand unrivalled.

Petrarch, though, as is evident from his letters and works, he enjoyed positive pleasure in the indulgence of a tender melancholy, and though he experienced so much kindness as to induce him to cherish the hope of one day possessing his beloved Laura, yet felt that his days, capable of more noble undertakings, were ingloriously consuming in painful anxiety, and had the courage to make a vigorous effort to break the fetters by which he was enchained. He abandoned Avignon, and undertook a tour through France, Germany, and Flanders, partly from a wish to gratify natural curiosity, and partly from the hope, by removing from the object of his adoration, to abate the ardour of his passion, and to restore the peace of his mind. The attempt, however, was unavailing. " Laura," he confesses, " appeared in every object, and was heard in every breeze ;" and, after an absence of several months, he returned more enamoured, if possible, of Laura than before.

Another attempt, however, he yet resolved to make. Aware that the best years of his life were passing away unimproved, and remembering the delights he had once enjoyed in literary seclusion, in the remote bishopric of Lombes, he retired, at the age of thirty-four, to the solitude of Vaucluse, a place fifteen miles from Avignon—beautiful as the vale of Tempe—surrounded by rocks of prodigious elevation, and intersected by a stream, the banks of which formed beautiful meadows

and pastures of perpetual verdure *. Here, in a small house, the humble dwelling of a shepherd, did Petrarch remain for many years ; and, following the natural tendency of his genius, devote his mind with the closest application to the pursuits of literature. He extended his acquaintance with ancient writings ; collected rare and valuable manuscripts, many of which would undoubtedly have been lost had it not been for his care in preserving them,—and composed the most celebrated of his works, both in prose and verse. Of this latter kind, the epic poem of *Africa*, in honour of the great Scipio, gained him, though printing was then unknown, the reputation of being the greatest poet of his time. And it may be mentioned, as a singular proof of his celebrity, that, on the same day, in his remote hermitage at Vaucluse, he received an invitation from the senate of Rome, and the University of Paris, soliciting him to accept of the laureate's crown. A feeling of patriotism, seconded by the advice of Cardinal Colonna, induced him to accept this honour from Rome ; " and thus," says an elegant writer, " the dignity of poet laureate, which, from the scanty appearance of genius in these dark ages, had not been conferred for some centuries, was now revived in honour of Petrarch."

Notwithstanding, however, the ardour with which he prosecuted his studies, and the seclusion to which he had retired, the image of Laura was ever present to his thought, and his love for her seemed but to be strengthened by time. It has indeed been conjectured that he had withdrawn to Vaucluse for the express purpose of seeing her often, as Cabrieres, her father's country seat, was in the neighbourhood. If this opinion be correct, Vaucluse was calculated rather to increase than to remove the ardour of his love. " Here," says he, " the fire which consumed me having its free course, the valleys, and even the air itself, resounded with my complaints."

But the time had now arrived when all hopes of becoming possessed of his adored Laura were at an end. This lovely lady died on the 6th April, 1348, the same day, the same hour when, twenty-one years ago, he first saw her and became her admirer. Petrarch was, as may easily be supposed, inconsolable at this event ; and he spent several days without food, giving way to the bitterest sorrow. " I dare not think of my condition," says he, " much less can I speak of it.' " Since the strongest cord of my life is broken, with the grace of God I shall easily renounce a world where my cares have been deceitful, and my hopes vain and perishing." In this state of anguish he complains that the source of his genius was now dried up for ever; and yet the sonnets and *Canzoni*, written after this event, are, if possible, the most elegant of his effusions, and " are so beautifully varied, so tender, and so affecting, that he seems to have exhausted the whole powers of pathetic composition."

Nor was this the only cause of his grief; for while his tears were flowing for the loss of Laura, he was deprived by death of Cardinal Colonna, the man who had been his warmest friend and benefactor. The Bishop of Lombes had died a short time before, and ere long he saw the last of this illustrious family drop into the grave, their name extinguished, and their wealth pass into the hands of strangers. Thus disengaged from the world, he saw it was necessary for him either to enter into the active business of life, to

---

* This celebrated valley derives its name from the character of its situation,—*vallis clausa*, Vaucluse.

Petrarch. dissipate the gloom by which he was overwhelmed, or return into retirement, to undermine by grief the sinews of his existence, and to be laid in an untimely tomb. He chose the former; and, removing to Milan, he entered the service of the powerful family of the Visconti, the sovereigns of that place, by whom he was greatly honoured, and frequently employed in state negociations. He took a warm interest in the extraordinary and unsuccessful attempt of Nicola Rienzi, who, on the wild pretence of restoring the ancient liberties of his country, usurped the government of Rome under the title of tribune. Petrarch had before this time obtained some ecclesiastical preferments: he was canon of Lombes, archdeacon of Parma, and canon of the Cathedral of Padua. He also held the office of domestic chaplain to Robert, King of Naples, and to his grand-daughter, Queen Joanna. But he was not ambitious of holding distinguished situations. He refused the offer of secretary to the Pope, and subsequently another eminent establishment in the court of his Holiness; and he declined accepting a bishoprick, which was more than once offered by the Popes, his contemporaries. He was indeed never higher in the church than a secular clergyman; he never entered into the order of priesthood, from a desire to preserve his freedom, and follow unrestrained that course of life most congenial to his taste. It is not improbable, indeed, that his views with regard to his beloved Laura may have had some influence on this determination; since, by not entering the priesthood, he was at liberty, merely by resigning, as has often been done, the ecclesiastical situations he held, to accept of her hand at any time she might think proper to offer it.

The high estimation in which he was held, and the flattering proofs of friendship he obtained from the most illustrious men of his time, must have formed to him a source of the most rational delight. But no incident of his life afforded him such deep satisfaction as the honour paid him by the citizens of Florence, to which, as formerly mentioned, his family originally belonged. They sent an embassy, at the head of which was the great Boccaccio, intimating to him the restitution of his paternal estate, forfeited by the political offence of his father, and requesting him to honour them by spending the remainder of his brilliant career at Florence, as the president of their newly instituted university. This flattering invitation, which he felt most deeply, he thought it proper to decline. He knew he was fast approaching the end of life, and his love of studious retirement was superior to every other consideration.

Petrarch had, in the meantime, resided in various places, Naples, Milan, Venice, &c. He had also paid several visits to his favourite Vaucluse; and now, when old and infirm, he built a neat villa at Arqua, three miles from Padua, where he was destined to spend the evening of his days. His constitution, from his nervous sensibility, from incessant study, and from age, had now begun to exhibit symptoms of decay; his friends were afraid that his death could not be far distant; and he himself looked forward to that event with a degree of resignation and hope, illustrative of the innocence and piety of his life. He delighted in his studies even at the moment of his greatest debility, and he was found dead in his library, sitting upright, with one arm leaning on a book. His death, which was witnessed by none, took place on the 18th of July, 1374, in the 70th year of his age; and he was buried in the parish-church of Arqua, where a monument was erected to his memory.

The character of Petrarch is every thing that is amiable and interesting. Every action of his life, and every sentence of his composition, bespeak the man of virtue, of benevolence, and of piety. His feelings were almost of too delicate a contexture, his sensibility too nice and acute, his heart too warm and unsuspecting, for encountering without uneasiness, the selfishness and the apathy by which our nature is generally characterized. His love of Laura is something more than human; it seems to have become more ardent in proportion as the hope of its being successful diminished; and in purity, intensity, and duration, is without a parallel in the records of the passion to which he was devoted.

As a man of genius, Petrarch is entitled to the veneration of all succeeding generations. The exquisite beauty and tenderness of his sonnets and *Canzoni*, by which he is best known to us, have never been surpassed; and his other works, though now comparatively little read, do honour to the age in which he lived. But, valuable as his writings are, he is probably entitled to commemoration, chiefly as a promoter of learning, and as inspiring a taste for literature. To him we owe the preservation of some MSS. which might otherwise have been lost; the multiplying of copies, which he often did with his own hand; and the proof which, in his own person, he afforded his contemporaries and the succeeding ages, of the high advantages to be derived from the study of the classical authors of Greece and Rome.

His works are extremely numerous. His *Sonnets*, having been translated into our language by Lord Morley, Mrs. Anna Hume, and others, are well known to the English reader. His other productions, which we cannot at present characterize more minutely, are, *De Remediis utriusque fortunae; De Vera Sapientia; De Vita Solitaria; Secretum, seu de Contemptu Mundi; Epistolae Familiares; Africa; De sui ipsius et Multorum Ignorantia*, &c. &c. These works have been published in every variety of form. His *Latin* works were first printed at Basil, in one vol. folio in 1496. His *Italian*, at Milan, in one vol. folio, in 1512; and both these, in a collected form, at Basil, in two vols. folio, in 1581.

Accounts of the life of Petrarch have been published in every possible shape. The best continental publications on this subject are, *Memoirs of Petrarch*, written by M. de la Bastie, and inserted in the *Memoires de l'Academie des Inscriptions et Belles Lettres*, vols. xv. and xvii.; and *Memoires pour la Vie de Petrarche*, by the Abbé de Sade. In English, the best are Mrs. Dobson's *Life of Petrarch*, 2 vols. 1807, which is professedly an epitome of de Sade; and an *Essay on the Life and Character of Petrarch*, one vol. Edin. 1810, supposed to be written by the late Lord Woodhouselee. See also Watt's *Bibliotheca Britannica*, article PETRARCH. (&)

PETRIFACTIONS. See ORGANIC REMAINS, in Vol. XV. p. 681.

PETWORTH, a town of England, in Sussex, is agreeably situated on the river Rother and the Arundel canal. The houses, which are tolerably built, are disposed in a long street, and in a smaller one setting off nearly at right angles from it. The church has a square tower, and contains the tombs of many of the Earls of Northumberland. The market-house, in the centre of the town, is a handsome building. The bridewell is a high edifice, on Howard's plan. Petworth-house, the splendid seat of the Earl of Egremont, is close to the town, having an extensive park, about 12 miles in circuit. Population of the parish in 1821, 2781. See the *Beauties of England and Wales*, vol. xiv. p. 24.

PHANTASMAGORIA. See OPTICS, Vol. XV. p. 630.

PHARMACY. See MATERIA MEDICA, Vol. XIII. p. 355.

PHIDIAS. See SCULPTURE.

Situation.

PHILADELPHIA, the capital of Pennsylvania, in the United States of America, is situated on the western bank of the Delaware, or rather on a narrow isthmus formed by the Delaware and the Schuylkill, about six miles above their confluence. It lies in 39° 57' North Lat. and 75° 10' West Long. about 120 miles from the Atlantic, by the course of the river, but in a straight line not above half that distance. The ground on which it stands, extending between the two rivers, which are a mile distant from each other, is elevated, where highest, but a little above the level of the water, and is extremely uniform: the country in the neighbourhood is fertile, and highly cultivated, and the numerous roads which communicate with the city are of the best and most approved construction. The appearance of Philadelphia, in any direction you approach it, is favourable, except in that of the Delaware, whence nothing is seen but a confused heap of wooden storehouses, built on platforms of artificial ground, and wharfs which project a considerable way into the river.

Origin.

This city owes its origin to William Penn, the illustrious founder and proprietor of the province of which it is the capital, and was begun to be built in 1682. In the course of a few years it became an extensive and populous place; and though it was originally meant to consist of an oblong or parallelogram, of two miles by one, it soon exceeded these dimensions, and was regarded as the most important city on the continent of North America. In 1701, Penn granted a charter to the inhabitants, conferring on them the privilege of electing a mayor, recorder, eight aldermen, twelve common-councilmen, a sheriff, and a clerk. This charter, however, was superseded at the revolution, and a new one granted in 1789; and Philadelphia is now governed by a mayor, a recorder, fifty aldermen, and thirty common-councilmen. The mayor is elected annually by the aldermen out of their own body; the recorder every seven years by the mayor and aldermen; the aldermen and common-council-men are chosen by the citizens—the former every seventh year, the latter every third. These magistrates enjoy various judicial functions, and take cognizance of cases of misdemeanour and small felonies; and under them the police of the city has attained to a very high degree of perfection. Philadelphia was considered the capital of the United States till the year 1800, when the seat of government was transferred to Washington. The bank of the States is still in this city, and the mint, in which the national money is coined.

Streets.

The original parts of Philadelphia, built according to the plan of Mr. Penn, consist of long, wide, and regular streets, intersecting each other at right angles. Nine streets, according to this plan, extend between the two rivers, and are crossed by twenty-three, which run in the contrary direction. The city is now much larger than was originally intended, and the new streets are as regular, and certainly more elegant, than the old. This place is not more distinguished for the length and uniformity, than for the width of its streets: Broad Street is 113 feet wide; High Street,

100; Mulberry Street, 60; while almost none are less than 50, and the greater number much more. The town is well lighted, and for the most part well paved, with a foot-path on each side of the street, composed of brick, elevated about eight or ten feet, and defended on the outside by a range of hewn stones. The number of squares, according to Penn, was 184; but that number has been increased to about 300. The houses are, in general, three stories high, are constructed of brick, and though devoid of ornament, have the appearance of neatness, cleanliness, and comfort, if not of opulence.

Public edifices.

The appearance of Philadelphia is highly improved by the number and simple elegance of its public edifices—in which it is equalled by no other city in the United States. The State House, used as a museum since the seat of government was transferred to Washington, is a large and superb building: adjoining to it is an elegant square, used as a public walk, decorated with trees, shrubs, &c. and enclosed on three sides by a high wall, the building itself occupying the other side. There are here no fewer than sixty places of public worship, belonging to an uncommon variety of religious denominations, some of which edifices are massy and spacious. The churches belonging to the Episcopalians, to the German Lutherans, and to the Roman Catholics, are severally furnished with an organ, and one of the Episcopal churches can boast of a high steeple. The other public buildings, of which we have not room for a more full enumeration, are the two city court-houses, a county-house, a state-penitentiary, a bridewell or jail, an hospital, two alms-houses, one of them belonging to the Friends or Quakers, three dispensaries, a medical theatre, a university, the hall belonging to the Academy of Natural Sciences, the hall belonging to the Philosophical Society, a public library, the Washington hall, two theatres, a masonic hall, ten incorporated banks. Of these edifices the most important are the national bank, built of marble; the masonic hall, of gothic architecture, ornamented with a handsome steeple; the Washington hall, 73 feet in front, and 138 feet deep, with a saloon capable of containing 4000 persons, and a dining room 117 by 30; the hospital, an extensive structure, nearly 300 feet in length, and remarkable for the excellence of its internal accommodation; connected with it is another building of three stories, calculated to contain 40 or 50 patients, the whole number of patients being usually between two and three hundred.

Benevolent institutions.

Nor is this the only hospital of which Philadelphia can boast; for its institutions of this and of a similar kind are extremely numerous, and are conducted on the most liberal and philanthropic principles; a circumstance which results in no mean degree from the worth and active benevolence of the society of Quakers, who form about a fourth part of the whole population. "In the city of Philadelphia," says Mr. Warden, "there are eight public charitable institutions and two private; three female societies for general charity; eight free schools; fifteen mutual benefit societies; associations for the relief of foreigners; and eleven mutual benefit societies for foreigners and their descendants.—St. Andrew's Society, German incorporated Society, St. George's Society, Hibernian Society, French Benevolent Society, the Cincinnati Society, composed of officers of the army of the revolution, for granting relief to the distressed members, their widows and orphans. The mutual benefit societies are: the Ship-master's Society, the Franklin Society, the Caledonian Society, the Union Society, the Friendly Society, the Provident Society, and some others." (Warden's *Account of the United States*, vol. II. p. 88.) Several of these institutions are large and extensive. In the Alms-house and house of employment, included in the above enumeration, there were in 1810, 735 patients, and it is not likely that, since that period, the number has diminished. It may not be uninteresting to mention, that the Abolition Society, also comprehended in the foregoing list, and which has for its object the abolition of slavery, and the relief and education of negroes, was instituted so early as 1774, a period when the important object it has in view had scarcely begun to be contemplated in any other portion of the globe. Of this Society, Dr. Benjamin Franklin, who had deeply at heart the cause it was meant to promote, was long president.

But Philadelphia, remarkable as it is for its charitable and benevolent associations, is still more remarkable for its literature and literary institutions. In this respect indeed, it is incomparably superior to any other city in the western hemisphere. Not only can it boast of Dr. Franklin, and many others, whose names would do honour to the most celebrated nations of Europe; but, what is probably of as much, or of more importance, liberal knowledge has long been diffused throughout the whole community, and forms the distinguishing characteristic of the citizens. In addition to the public chartered seminaries of learning, (of which we shall soon speak,) and various others of a private description, Philadelphia possesses the advantages of eight charity schools; so that education is put within the reach of the meanest and most destitute; and it is thus a thing of extremely rare occurrence to meet with a single individual, a native of the city, who is not a proficient in the ordinary branches of learning,—reading, writing, and accounts. The number of printing houses, of booksellers' shops, and of newspapers published daily, weekly, &c. is uncommonly great: even so early as the year 1795, this city was distinguished by no fewer than thirty-one printing houses, and produced four daily newspapers; facts which, more than any other thing, give us a correct view of the intelligence and reading habits of a people. Philadelphia, indeed, may justly be denominated the emporium of the literature of America.

And the number and variety of its literary, philosophical, and scientific institutions, correspond well with the account which we have just given. The benevolent founder of the city did not neglect the real interests of the inhabitants: he established seminaries of education for their benefit; and the Friends' Public Schools, incorporated by him, and which have uniformly been in a flourishing state, enjoy considerable funds, and support a great many inferior seminaries. This institution possesses an observatory, and extensive philosophical apparatus; and under its direction are taught, besides the more common branches of education, the Latin and Greek languages, mathematics, and natural and experimental philosophy. The college of Pennsylvania was instituted in 1735, by some of the most public-spirited citizens of Philadelphia, among whom was Dr. Franklin, who drew up the original plan and proposals for carrying it into effect. In 1769, this institution was erected into a university, denominated "the University of the State of Pennsylvania." By an act of the legislature in 1791, it was considerably new-modelled and liberally endowed; and it has now for a long period held an eminent rank among similar institu-

tions. The number of professors are seventeen; the course commences in October, and terminates about the beginning of April; the amount of students it is not easy to ascertain, but we may form a pretty correct conjecture, since we are informed that the number of medical students is no less than 500: and the institution embraces every department of literature and science, except divinity. Its medical school, which commenced in 1764, is the most extensive and celebrated in America. Connected with the university are the academy, in which youth are instructed in the learned languages preparatory to college, and a charity school for the education of poor children. The American Philosophical Society was formed in 1769, by the union of two former societies, and was incorporated by a charter in 1780. It has produced several valuable volumes of Transactions, and in the list of its members are enrolled the names not only of the most eminent Americans, but those also of the most distinguished foreigners. The other most useful literary institutions, which we cannot at present specify more minutely, are the Medical Society, established in 1790; the College of Physicians, formed in 1787; the Medical Lyceum, instituted in 1804; the Academy of the Fine Arts, in 1805; the Linnean Society, in 1806; and the Academy of Natural Science, founded in 1812, and incorporated in 1817. It possesses a library of above 2000 volumes, and valuable collections in natural history, and publishes from time to time a Journal, the first number of which appeared in May 1817. There is also a society for promoting agriculture, formed so early as 1784, which, incorporated in 1809, still continues to flourish, and which has given the world three excellent volumes of memoirs. Philadelphia is also distinguished by various libraries, some of which are of considerable value and extent. The Philadelphia library originated with Dr. Franklin, and was incorporated in 1742. It contains about 25,000 volumes, and is rich in rare editions of the classics. It is open for the use of the public, and the character of its management is the most liberal and accommodating. In the front of the building in which it is contained, is a statue of the illustrious Franklin, to whom the city owes the most invaluable obligations. The other large libraries are the Friends' and the Loganian, so called from a Mr. Logan who bequeathed his library to it. In addition to these, the university, and almost all the literary institutions of the city are possessed of libraries, consisting of books illustrative of the particular departments of science or literature connected with the establishments to which they severally belong.

The Delaware, which is a mile broad at Philadelphia, is navigable to the city for ships of 1200 tons, and small vessels can ascend almost 150 miles nearer its origin. The port of Philadelphia, though 120 miles from the sea, and though inaccessible on account of ice for several weeks in winter, is yet, being large and commodious, well adapted for the purposes of commerce. The river contains 16 public landings, about 500 feet from each other, and private wharfs sufficient for 200 vessels at a time, and room for ship-building to almost any extent. The Schuylkill too, which is not entirely devoid of similar advantages, has ten public landings. Philadelphia may, in some respects, be regarded as the centre of the trade of several of the neighbouring states; for by means of canals and excellent turnpike roads, a connexion is opened with the most distant parts of the interior; a canal is now constructing between the Swetara branch of the Sus-

Philadel-
phia.

quehannah, which is to communicate with the Schuyl-kill and the Delaware; and a communication was at one time contemplated, and may yet be carried into effect, between this latter river and Lake Erie, a distance of 560 miles. In 1816, the shipping belonging to this port amounted to no less than 101,830 tons. The principal exports are iron, brass, copper, iron utensils of every description, candles, paper, ropes, with the productions of the soil, such as wheat and flour, beef, pork, wool, leather, furs, hemp. The imports, on the other hand, consist of all kinds of British manufactures: wine, gin, glass from France and Holland; rum and sugar from the West Indies; teas, nankeens, silks from China and the East Indies. With all the other states Philadelphia holds a regular interchange of productions and manufactures.

Manufactures.

Philadelphia, thus eminent in a commercial capacity, is yet probably more distinguished for the extent, variety, and excellence of its manufactures. The steam-engine was early introduced into this town, and is now invariably used in all large manufacturing establishments. Steam-engines and steam-boats are indeed more common, if possible, in every district of the United States than in Great Britain. In Philadelphia are several iron and brass founderies; manufactories of steam-engines, of lead, copper, &c. to a great amount, also of glass, leather, ropes, earthen-ware, &c. The number of paper-mills in the city and neighbourhood is very great; and printing is carried on to a higher extent here than in any other town of the United States. Philadelphia is also celebrated for its distilleries and breweries, particularly for an excellent porter brewery. Many vessels, some of considerable size, are built of pine at this port.

Climate.

Philadelphia, though it lies in the same latitude as Naples, partakes nothing of a similar climate, except probably for a month or two in the middle of summer. It has indeed been not very inaccurately characterized as a compound of all climates, varying at the different seasons of the year, from the severity of Norway to the heat of the torrid regions. The warmth of the summer at Philadelphia is unknown in the correspondent latitudes of Europe and Asia; while the intense cold of winter can hardly be conceived by the inhabitants of Scotland, though this country is situated above 16 degrees farther north than the city which we are considering. The most agreeable months are April and May,—September, October, November.

Salubrity.

Philadelphia, as may be supposed from the variable nature of the climate, is not very remarkable for salubrity. There are indeed not wanting instances of persons who attain to extreme old age, who even have outlived a century; and the members of the Society of Friends, a class of men distinguished everywhere for regularity and temperance, are in general healthy, and see more than the average terms of years. But, with these exceptions, the climate of this city is not favourable to health and longevity. Dr. Morse mentions,

what is unknown in the country parts of Pennsylvania, that nearly one-half of the children born in Philadelphia die under two years of age, chiefly from a disease in the stomach and bowels. In the autumns of 1793 and 1797, the city was visited by yellow fever; at the former period 4000, and at the latter 1200 persons fell victims to its ravages. In July and August, the warmest months in the year, the greatest number of deaths take place.

Inhabitants.

The inhabitants of Philadelphia consist of people from almost every quarter of the world, though those of English, Irish, and German extraction predominate. They all retain an unshaken attachment to the respective countries from which they emigrated, as the enumeration of their benovolent institutions, given in a former part of this article, decidedly shows; and it may yet be several ages ere this spirit be entirely removed. The citizens, whatever be their country or their origin, are all characterized by industry, correct conduct, and a deep respect for religion. Every thing like abject poverty is unknown; and the richer classes, in the article of dress and the luxuries of the table, rival the inhabitants of the great towns of Europe. The variety of religious denominations is extremely great; Presbyterianism is the most common. This city has long been the chief residence of the Friends or Quakers; their number, however, is rather diminished; but they are distinguished by the same pure and virtuous conduct which, whatever opinions we may form of their theological principles, has long gained them the respect of all nations. The population of Philadelphia in 1790 was 43,525.; in 1802, 62,000; and in 1810, the date of the last census, 92,247; this number is now, it is thought, much augmented.

See Morse's *American Geography*; Mease's *Picture of Philadelphia*; Clarkson's *Life of Penn*; and Warden's *Account of the United States*. (T. M.)

Philadelphia, Philippine Isles.

PHILIPPINE ISLANDS, or MANILLAS, a large group of islands, lying south-east from China, and north of what has been termed the Eastern Archipelago, are situated between 5° and 20° north latitude, and 114° and 126° east longitude. They are extremely numerous, amounting to about twelve hundred, of which four hundred are of considerable extent and importance. They were first discovered by Magellan *, who took possession of them in the name of the King of Spain, and, as he landed on them on the anniversary of St. Lazarus, denominated them the Islands of St. Lazarus, in honour of that Saint. This appellation they retained for little more than half a century, as in 1564, in the reign of Philip II. a Spanish fleet having been sent out to make a conquest of them, they were named the Philippine Islands, after that monarch. The Manillas is a term which has also been long applied to them, and which Pinkerton regards as the most popular and correct. They have also been denominated the Bisayas or Islas de Pintados or Painted Islands, the inhabitants having been accustomed to paint their bo-

Situation and names.

* The island first visited by Magellan was Zebu, in which he was received with great kindness, and the king of which, with his principal nobility, he persuaded to embrace the Christian religion. He afterwards sailed to the small island Mactan, east of Zebu. This island was governed by two kings, one of whom having refused to pay tribute to the king of Spain, Magellan had recourse to arms, and in an engagement which in consequence took place, this celebrated navigator lost his life, ere he had accomplished, what he uniformly had regarded as practicable, the circumnavigation of the globe. He was succeeded in the command by Sebastian, a person who proved himself worthy of the appointment; and under his direction, the ship Vittoria, the only one remaining of five, of which the squadron at first consisted, arrived at Seville on the 7th September, 1522, after an absence of within fourteen days of three years, being the first ship that circumnavigated the globe. Before their arrival, the crew were reduced to eighteen out of two hundred and thirty-seven, the number to which the expedition originally amounted. The Vittoria is calculated to have sailed 14,000 leagues, and to have crossed the equator no less than six times.

dies before the arrival of the Spaniards. The name, in honour of Philip, however, is that by which they are now generally designated.

Of these islands the largest is Manilla, or Luzon, being about 500 British miles in length, by a medium breadth of 100. A chain of mountains extends towards the east, the whole length of the island; it is traversed by many beautiful rivers, and is distinguished by a vast number of lakes, some of them large, particularly that from which the river Manilla takes its rise. The physical appearance is thus considerably diversified, and it is characterized by the most luxuriant fertility, and with due cultivation might soon become one of the most valuable islands connected with this part of the world.—" Manilla, the capital of this island, as well as of all the Spanish settlements in the Philippines, is," to use the words of an acute writer, " a tolerably large city. It is well built, the houses are handsome, and there are magnificent churches. It is a fortified city, situated in a most advantageous position, on the banks of a considerable river, which washes its walls, and whose divided branches completely traverse the island of Luzon. The entrance of the river is shut by a bar, which becomes dangerous when the sea is rough. There was a plan of no great labour to have, instead of the bar, a commodious bason, which would have been perfectly calm and safe. They began it, but, soon fatigued, they abandoned the design!" Small vessels only can come up to the town; and Cavite, nine miles distant, at the mouth of the river, is regarded as the port of of Manilla. The town has frequently been visited by earthquakes, which have proved very destructive. The number of inhabitants is above 30,000. The other chief towns of this island are, Caceres, New Segovia, Bondo, Passacao.—Of Magindanao, or Mindanao, which is next to Manilla in size and importance, an account has already been given, (Vide MAGINDANAO, Vol. XIII. p. 243.) and it need here merely be mentioned, that the capital, which is of the same name as the island, and is neither large nor celebrated, is situated on the eastern coast,—and that the Spaniards, though masters of but a small portion of it, have succeeded in planting several colonies on it, the chief of which is Sambuang on the south-east.—Palawan, 180 miles in length by about 30 in breadth, is the most westerly of the Philippine islands, and the largest of the group termed Calamianes. The Spaniards, though they have made several attempts, have not yet been able to make a conquest of this island. They have, however, succeeded in establishing a garrison on the north-east end of it, at a place called Tatay. The king of Borneo possesses very extensive settlements on it, while the natives, now comparatively few in number, can hardly be said to enjoy any fixed abode, their situation being determined by the movements and operations of their invaders.—Sooloo, which lies nearly in a straight line between Mindanao and Borneo, is about thirty-six miles long and twelve broad. It is chiefly remarkable for its populousness, containing about 60,000 souls,—a number accounted for, from the advantageous situation of the island, which renders it, in some respects, the emporium of the commerce of the adjacent islands. The inhabitants are Mahometans, and are distinguished, as shall afterwards be shown, by the piratical life which they have for centuries led; the island is governed by a Sultan, whose territories include a variety of small islands in the neighbourhood.—Of the other islands, which we have not time to specify more minutely, the

most important are, Mindoro, Pani, Buglas, Zebu, Leyte, Samar, Mactan. They are all characterized by the same features as those already described, beauty, fertility, diversity of physical appearance, resulting from the variation of mountains, rivers, lakes, valleys, with which they are embellished. They all also present volcanic appearances, and most of the islands abound with lava and volcanic glass, sulphur, and hot springs; though these appearances are so trifling and minute, as not materially to diminish the beauty of the physical scenery which these islands every where present.

These islands, with all their fertility and natural capabilities, remain still in a comparatively desolate state. The natives are indolent and inactive, and prefer living on the simplest and coarsest productions, rather than submit to exertion to improve their condition, or enlarge their comforts; and the Chinese, who were remarkable for industry, they always regarded with jealousy, and at length expelled. The insecurity of property, and the hurricanes with which the islands are so often visited, may also, in some measure, be regarded as the cause of this indolence and want of enterprize.

These islands, as already mentioned, were discovered by Magellan, and were afterwards made a conquest of by a Spanish fleet sent thither from Mexico. The islands are so numerous and so extensive, that in one expedition, or even in one age, it would not be possible to conquer them; and accordingly the Spaniards became possessed of them slowly, island by island; nor are they yet masters of the whole group. Zebu was the first which they attacked and subdued; and a few years afterwards they effected a settlement at the mouth of the Manilla river, and constituted the town of Manilla, (the metropolis of the island of the same name,) the capital of the Spanish possessions in the Philippines. The Spaniards, in the mean time, continued to extend their conquest in this immense group; but they did not on every attempt experience success. The island of Gooloo, for example, repulsed the assailants with great slaughter; and the inhabitants of this island, in defiance of every attempt to crush them, have for nearly three centuries been the piratical scourges of that quarter of the world, and have proved most destructive to its commercial and social interests. Nor have the Spaniards merely been unsuccessful in their endeavours to obtain possession of all these islands. The possession even of those they have conquered they have not been allowed to enjoy in tranquillity or in safety. The colony of Manilla was attacked by Chinese pirates in 1574, who were indeed repulsed, but not without the loss of much blood on both sides. When the Dutch established themselves in India, a war commenced between them and the Spaniards, which was not terminated for nearly half a century. Natives of China had, in the meantime, emigrated thither to such an extent, that in 1639 their number amounted to 30,000, most of whom had settled in Calamba and Binan. Though these emigrants were remarkable for industry and inoffensiveness, the Spaniards had long entertained a deep-rooted dislike to them; and, at the period last mentioned, made an attack upon them, and effected so dreadful a havock of them, that in a short time they were reduced to 7000, who surrendered at discretion. This dislike, however, still continued; and in 1757, the Viceroy of the Philippine Islands dispatched all the Chinese to their own country; and, in order to prevent their return, he appropriated a certain place for the reception of such Chinese as should come in a commercial capacity; and no natives of China have since been permitted to establish themselves in these islands, except such as were converted to the Christian religion.

A war having in 1761 broken out between this country and Spain, forces were sent the following year from the East Indies, under the command of General Draper and Admiral Cornish, to attack the Spanish settlements on the Philippine Islands. They arrived in the bay of Manilla, where, their visit being unexpected, the Spaniards were unprepared, and, after a siege of twelve days, the city surrendered at discretion. The inhabitants were admitted as prisoners of war upon their parole of honour; but all the native Indians, to conciliate their affections, were dismissed in safety. Manilla, with the port of Cavite, remained in the hand of the English till 1764, when, peace having been concluded between the two nations, these conquests were restored to the Spanish. Since this period, these colonies have not been disturbed by any European enemies, though they have been much infested by the piratical forces of those islands not subject to the Spanish government, Sooloo, Mindanao, &c.; and such is the illiberal policy of the government, that, though from these cruizers extensive damage is sustained, their ships captured, their coast plundered, their people massacred or carried into slavery, they will not allow the native Indians to carry arms. The Spaniards are not at present, nor ever have been, possessed of one-half of these islands. Those of them that remain unconquered have each its own sovereign and its own laws; but the aboriginal inhabitants of the whole are of the same race, and are still distinguished by similar manners, customs, and institutions.

Climate.

These islands, though they lie within the tropics, are not distinguished by that intense heat which is generally found in places of the same parallel of latitude. This has been accounted for from the vast number of extensive lakes, and consequent moisture with which they abound. They possess, however, all the other peculiarities of a tropical climate. The rains begin in May, and continue till September, or even longer, and are succeeded by a general and uninterrupted spring, which prevails till the ensuing May. Vegetation of every description is peculiarly luxuriant, insomuch that it is a work of almost insuperable difficulty to keep the cultivated lands free from weeds and insects, the latter of which are a source of great annoyance, if not of danger, to the inhabitants. The winds are periodical; and violent storms and hurricanes are very frequent, and are productive of great devastation. These islands are also, as stated above, subject to earthquakes. By an earthquake (1645) a third of the town of Manilla was destroyed, and 3000 of the inhabitants perished.

Productions.

Of these islands, the productions are not essentially different from those of the other Asiatic islands of the same latitude; rice, different kinds of pulse, as mongos, patani, kidney-beans, and millet; the palm tree, the sugar-cane, the bread-fruit tree, the plantain, the orange, and mango trees, the areca or betel nut, and various others, common to a tropical climate. The tobacco of these islands was long reckoned the best in Asia, and was exported in great quantities. The mountains afford excellent timber, both for ship and house-building; and the bamboos, of which the houses of the natives are constructed, attain here to an unusual size. Pigs, fowls, ducks, goats, and buffaloes are reared under the same roof as the inhabitants. The mountains abound with deer; the woods and fields with quails, pigeons, partridges, &c. and the sea is stocked with an almost endless variety of fish, of which the islanders do

not fail to avail themselves. To these indigenous productions, the Spaniards have added horses, horned cattle, which have multiplied to such an extent that they now run wild in the mountains: sheep, geese, grapes, figs, wheat, &c. The islands have never been infested with tigers, or any strong carnivorous animals. Mines of gold and iron are very common, and gold is likewise found by washing the sand on the mountain streams; advantages of which the natives are too indolent to avail themselves.

Commerce.

In a commercial capacity these islands have not as yet attained to much eminence. They form, however, in a considerable degree, the centre of intercourse between China, Japan, and the Spice Islands, and they connect the Asiatic and American commerce. They are thus destined, at no very distant period, to form the great emporium of trade between these two continents, and the islands in the Pacific and South Seas; but at present their importance is limited chiefly to two or three ships which pass annually between them and Acapulco, on the western coast of Spanish America. They also carry on a small trade with the Chinese, with the Malays of Borneo, and the British in our settlements in India. The extent of their connexion with the latter, (for with regard to the rest we have no information,) may be known from the following statement. From 1802 to 1806 inclusive, there was imported into Manilla from British India, goods and treasure to the amount of only £286,000; while the exports, during the same period, amounted to about double that sum, or to £516,356. The native Indians, besides, carry on among themselves, in the different islands, a barter for their respective productions. Gold is the representation of value and medium of exchange. Their imports consist of India piece goods, particularly cloths, handkerchiefs, chintz; also European cutlery and iron of all descriptions. From the Chinese they obtain silk goods, lackered ware, teas, China ware,—most of which they again export by the ships for Acapulco. Their exports, which have not been so extensive as they must soon become, are casia, gold-dust, pepper, tortoise-shell, wax, wild honey, amber, marble, tar, cochineal.

Character of the inhabitants.

The character and condition of the inhabitants may be inferred from what has been already advanced. Their houses are formed of bamboos, covered with palm leaves, and raised on pillars to the height of eight or ten feet. Their chief food is rice. They have laws, and punish crimes, of which adultery is reckoned the chief. They have ever been distinguished by indolence and want of enterprize; but though living in a state of barbarism, they afford interesting examples of mildness and benevolence. Very few of them have been converted to Christianity; and the illiberal treatment they have uniformly experienced from the Spaniards, have inspired them with no ambition to acquire the spirit and manners of a refined people. But the great characteristic of these people is a universal tendency to piracy,—which no exertions, not even the authority of their chiefs, have yet been able to counteract, and in which they exhibit the greatest enterprize and dexterity. Vessels of a peculiar shape and size they make for the express purpose of piratical expeditions. However little they may disregard the property of others, they have laws and regulations by which they are themselves connected together, and which it is reckoned dishonourable to violate. These islanders are generally tall and handsome; in some places they go naked; in others they wear a kind of loose shirt with loose drawers; and in other respects they exhibit slight variations of character, as may indeed be expected from a people, (though of the same origin,) so little connected, and scattered over so great a number of islands.

See *Voyages* of Magellan, Dampier, De Pagés, La Pérouse. See Forest's *Voyage to Papua*; Sonnerat's *Voy-*

age de la Nouvelle Guinée; and the article MAGINDANAO, *ut supra.* (&)

PHILOSOPHY. See MORAL PHILOSOPHY, Vol. XIV. p. 673, and NATURAL PHILOSOPHY, vol. XV. p. 159.

PHOSPHORESCENCE.

THIS is a name that has been applied to a property which many substances possess of emitting light under certain circumstances. Though the term would lead us to imagine that it depended on the presence, or rather on the slow combustion of phosphorus, it has no connection with that, in any of the instances where it occurs, as far at least as chemical examinations have yet proceeded. Indeed, in every case, the whole of these processes are so mysterious, that we cannot pretend to throw any light on their real nature, and must, therefore, content ourselves with treating of phosphorescence merely as a fact; as a branch of natural history, noting those circumstances with regard to it that are the most interesting.

We must, however, caution our readers against imagining that the various phosphorences which we shall describe arise from a common cause, or have any connection; or that we have here placed them together from conceiving that they were all parts of one subject. On the contrary, it is most evident that the phosphorescence of minerals must depend on circumstances utterly different from those which cause vegetable matters and animals to yield light. In these two departments also there appears no analogy in the source of the luminous appearance; nor are we even sure that among the animal creation possessed of this remarkable property, we have any reason to refer the light to a common cause. In truth, all these phenomena seem to be united by little more than a common term; and, therefore, following the general usage, we shall proceed to treat of them in one article.

But if we cannot distinguish the causes of this appearance, we can at any rate distinguish those by which it is excited, or the circumstances under which it appears. These seem to be five. Some substances emit light when their temperatures are raised; and this is more particularly the case with mineral substances; whether these are natural compounds, or minerals, properly so called, or chemical ones, such as the earthy metallic and alkaline salts, or the metallic oxides; or, lastly, the simple earths. Others emit light after having been previously exposed to its action without any elevation of temperature; a phenomena which is also confined to the same classes of substances. Electricity excites it also in certain cases; but the action of this cause is comparatively rare. As it is excited, in the fourth place, by friction, pressure, or percussion, it is far better known, not only in many minerals, but, familiarly, in the case of sugar; and, finally, it appears to occur spontaneously, or, at least, without any exciting cause which can be ascertained; as is the case for the most part in animal and in vegetable substances.

In making these experiments by means of heat, it is generally sufficient to place the substance to be tried on an heated body of iron or baked clay. The exceptions we shall note in their proper places hereafter. The heat must not be red, lest that light should interfere with the phosphorescence, and the substances must be examined in a dark room. When bodies are to be

examined for their powers of absorbing light, it is sufficient to expose them to the direct rays of the sun for a few minutes, or even seconds. The mode of producing the results by electricity or friction, require no notice, except that the force or quantity of the latter that is required in different cases is very various.

Phosphorescence of Insects.

In the animal creation, the property of emiting light is confined to the insect tribe and to fishes; appearing to be very limited in the former, but, as we hope to show hereafter, universal in the latter. We shall first describe the insects which possess this quality, premising at the same time that we do not imagine all the luminous species to be yet known.

This property has been observed in the genera Elater, Lampyris, Fulgora, Scolopendra, Pausus, Limulus, Galathia, and Lynceus; but the observations of naturalists on most of these have been slight. We may notice the most remarkable. The Lampyris noctiluca is our common glow-worm, being an insect tolerably well known to most persons. In this animal the light proceeds from a pale spot on the under side of the abdomen towards the tail. Though without wings, it is the female of a winged beetle so unlike, that the two would never be imagined to belong to one species. But the male also gives light, as has lately been ascertained; yet not nearly so brilliant as that of the female. It is produced from four small points on each of the two last segments of the abdomen. Both the male and female have the power of extinguishing the light at pleasure; and they can also render it for a short time more brilliant than common. The Lampyris splendidula and hemiptera are also luminous; and, in the former, the light is visible when the insect is on the wing.

To these observations, long since made, we must add a few very recent ones from Monsieur Macaire, whose experiments agree in some points with those of former observers, and differ in others. These observations were made on the Lampyris noctiluca, and we prefer recording them in as brief a manner as we can, to any attempt to reconcile them with former ones; as we know not to whom, among all the naturalists who have investigated this subject, credit is most due.

The abdomen in this insect consists of ten segments, the three last of which are of a yellowish colour beneath, the last of all being of the same colour above, while all the rest of the body is brown. On the back there is a remarkable ridge, running from the thorax to the end of the tail. The most brilliant light is emitted from the middle of the two antipenultimate segments, and from the sides of the last. The light exhibited by the other parts of the abdomen is feeble, and as if it was obscured by some covering, except that there is a single luminous point on the fourth segment. A faint light is also displayed by the hinder end of the dorsal line. When the animal is at liberty, the light is consequently downward, but it turns the tail up and agi-

tates, apparently for the purpose of display. At sunrise, the light disappears, with the exception of the
two bright points of the last segments; and it begins
first to be visible at seven or eight o'clock in the evening. M. Macaire is further of opinion, that the luminous points of the last segments are far less under the
will of the animal than the other portions.

He objects to the opinion that the light of the glow-
worm is intended as an attraction to the male, not
only because the male is itself luminous, but because
this property continues throughout the season when
there is no intercourse of this nature. Even at the
very moment that the insect quits the egg, when it is
a little greenish worm, not more than the twelfth of
an inch long, it displays the two luminous points at
the end of the tail. As it grows, the body becomes
black, though no change of shape takes place, and the
light continues to increase during the whole of this
process.

Our author's remarks on the powers of the animal's
will over the light, appear much more particular and
accurate than those of his predecessors. Sometimes
noise or agitation cause it to extinguish the light, yet
this does not always happen. A sudden blow generally
has that effect, but if the insect is, on the contrary, much
teased, the light is augmented instead of being diminished. The light of candles or lamps has no effect
on it, but that of the sun seems in some way accessory,
if not necessary, to the luminous effect, as in the cases
of the minerals which phosphoresce from exposure to
it. When the insects were inclosed in a box, they seldom showed their light when this was opened at night,
particularly on the first day. But by covering one
side of it with a glass, and treating them in the same
manner, they always yielded a brilliant light at night.
When the light is about to be extinguished voluntarily,
it first disappears from the foremost segments and proceeds backwards; though the two luminous points on
the last often continue to shine after the rest has ceased.
M. Macaire attempted in vain to discover by what
means this observation was produced. He is confident
that no membrane is drawn over it; but having traced
some flesh-coloured filaments into the luminous organ,
he considers that the cause consists in some species of
nervous action. No effect on the strength of the light
was produced, as far as his observations went, by deprivation of food, or by thundery or stormy weather.

The Lampyris Italica is far more brilliant than these,
and is the common fire-fly of Italy. The ladies in that
country, according to Sir James Smith, stick these insects into their hair at night as ornaments; and a similar practice with regard to some other luminous insects, is followed by females in India. It is probable
that all the species of this genus have the same property, but it has not been absolutely ascertained.

Elater.

In the genus Elater, the Noctilucus is the common
fire-fly of the West Indies. This insect is about an
inch long, and one-third of an inch broad, and it gives
out its principal light from two transparent tubercles
on the thorax; there are also two luminous patches
under the elytra, which are not visible except when
the insect is flying, when it appears adorned with four
brilliant gems of a most resplendent colour, besides
which the whole body is so luminous that the light
shines out between the abdominal segments when they
are separated by stretching the body. The light is so
considerable that the smallest print may be read by it;
and it is said that in former times the inhabitants of
St. Domingo not only used them as lights for domestic
purposes, but used to tie them on their persons in tra-

velling, in hunting, and in fishing. They are also
used as decorations on holidays; the young men fas-
tening them to their persons and horses, and thus galloping about the streets so as to present a moving blaze
of light. The ladies are also adorned with them as
gems. In the same genus the ignitus, and many
others, are known to be luminous; but it is not certain
if all the species, which amount to twelve, have this
property.

Phosphor-
escence.

Among the Hemipterous insects, the Fulgora is next
conspicuous for its light. It is not known how many
of the species possess that quality, but it has been observed in the Lanternaria, the Candelaria, and the Pyr-
rarinchus. The first, or the lantern-fly, is a native of
South America. In this tribe the luminous matter is
contained in a transparent snout, or projection of the
head, which is differently shaped in the different species. The lantern-fly is two or three inches in length,
and the luminous organ is so large, that the light which
it produces is very considerable; quite sufficient for
reading the smallest print. In the Scolopendra, the
Electrica and Phosphorea are both luminous, and the
former is a common insect in our gardens. It is suspected that other species in this genus have also the
same property. In the genus Pausus, which we mentioned, the Sphærocerus is known to be luminous, and
the light, which is feeble, proceeds from the antennæ.
Other genera, besides those which we first mentioned,
also exhibit these faint partial lights; as the Noctua
psi, the Bombyx cossus, and some other moths, and in
these it is produced in or about the eye. It is also
suspected by Lamarck, that the Chiroscelis bifenestrata
has a luminous organ; and it has further been observed, that the Ocelli, in the Elytra of Buprestis ocellatæ,
are luminous. The same is suspected to be the case in
the Gryllotalpa vulgaris; and we have little doubt
that it will be found in many others where it has not
yet been observed.

Fulgora.

Pausus

The observations on the nature of the luminous matter are very scanty, and we are indebted for some of
the principal ones to Mr. Macartney. That it is in
some cases a permanent substance, independent of the
will of the insect, is ascertained by the fact, that the
boys in the West Indies rub their faces with the dead
body of a fire fly to make them shine in the dark. In
both the glow-worms, the Elater noctilucus and the ignitus, Mr. Macartney found that the light proceeded
from a substance resembling the common fat, or interstitial matter of insects, but of a yellower colour. Besides this, he found under the last abdominal segment
two minute oval sacs, formed of an elastic spiral fibre
similar to that of the tracheæ, containing a soft yellow
substance, of a closer texture, like that which lines the
adjoining region, and affording a more permanent and
brilliant light. This light is less under the control of
the insect than that from the adjoining luminous substance, which it has the power of voluntarily extinguishing, not by retracting it under a membrane, as
Carradori supposed, but in some other manner which
could not be ascertained. It is further suspected that,
in this animal, the whole interstitial matter is luminous; and De Geer observed, that there are two luminous patches under the elytra, and that the intervals between the abdominal segments gave light when the
animal was stretched.

On the na-
ture of the
luminous
matter.

M. Macaire's observations on the luminous organ do
not differ very materially from those of Mr. Macartney,
but are more minute, and apparently more accurate.
The inner surface of the three last abdominal segments
is covered with a pale yellowish substance, which ap-

pears semi-transparent. But the microscope discovers it to be formed of numerous minute fibres, ramifying in a complicated manner, and phosphorescent. When this substance has been removed, the luminous appearance of the tail ceases; and it is owing to the transparency of the segments under which it lies that the light is at all visible. In the two posterior luminous points the same fibrous substance is found, but of a more compact texture.

The immediate cause of the light has not been ascertained in the Fulgoras, nor in the Pausus. But in the Scolopendra electrica there is a luminous matter secreted over the surface, which may be taken off on the hand, where it continues to shine for a few seconds. The chemical cause has rather been guessed at than ascertained. It is known that phosphoric acid is an ingredient in animal substances, and therefore it has been supposed that this luminous matter was phosphorus. This is doubtful.

It is a secreted substance, in the first place, because when extracted from the receptacles, it was restored in two days. Being dried, it becomes glossy like gum, and loses its luminous property, but recovers it again on being moistened. When kept moist after extraction, it continues luminous for some time. By some naturalists it is said to have its brilliancy increased by heat, and by being placed in oxygen gas, and to be extinguished by cold, and by hydrogen and carbonic acid gases. Hence Spallanzani, and others following him, concluded that the phenomenon arose from the slow combustion of phosphorus. But Carradori, on the contrary, observed that the luminous matter of the Lampyris Italica shone alike in vacuo, in oil, and in water; a fact which is sufficient to set aside this hypothesis. Mr. Macartney's experiments coincide with Carradori's, and as he further found that the luminous substance was not susceptible of inflammation by applying flame, or a hot iron to it, and that it had no effect on the thermometer, it is very certain that it is not phosphorus, and that the light is not produced by any combustion.

Thus far former observers; but we must now notice the most recent observations made by M. Macaire. On immersing a glow-worm alive into warm water, of the temperature of 11° Reaumur, it became restless; and when the heat was raised to 22° it began to give out light. At 33° it became still brighter, but shortly after this the animal died; yet the light was not extinguished. But at 46° it ceased altogether. The same experiment, frequently repeated, gave mean results, from which it was deduced that the light appeared at a heat varying from 20° to 25°, and ceased at one varying from 47° to 50°. When the heat of the water was maintained at 28°, the phosphorescence continued, although the animal was dead: and when it was suffered to subside below 20°, the light went out. When the insect was thrown into water heated to 35°, or 40°, it died instantly, but shone very bright: but, on raising the heat ten degrees, the light was extinguished, and nothing could revive it again.

Corresponding appearances took place when the animal was heated to similar temperatures in sand, or whenever moisture was not present; except that in these cases the phosphorescence ceased at lower temperatures, as invariably happens whenever the luminous matter becomes dry. The same results were obtained from dead glow-worms, provided they had neither been dried up nor exposed to a greater heat than 45° or 50°. The rays of the sun, concentrated by a lens, produce the same effect as heat, and excite the phosphorescence

immediately. If, on the other hand, a glow-worm is exposed to cold when in a luminous state, the light diminishes, and is extinguished as soon as the temperature has fallen below 10°. At 0° the insect dies; but even then a heat of 25° will make the light re-appear. If it is killed by cutting off the head, or if the luminous part is cut off, the light ceases in about five minutes; but after a short time it begins again to recover, and the light may then be maintained or re-produced for two or three days by the application of heat. The insect that dies a natural death preserves, in the same manner, a feeble phosphorescence for two or three days.

It had been remarked by former observers, that when a glow-worm, in the act of shining, was plunged into water, the phosphorescence ceased in a few minutes if it was alive, and in an hour or two if dead. M. Macaire considers this to be a mere case of temperature, similar to these above mentioned. But if it is placed in alcohol, it is extinguished in two minutes, and the light cannot again be restored by heat. In the same way it is extinguished by the mineral acids, and that in proportion to their strength.

When this insect was placed in a receiver, and the air exhausted, it died, and of course swelled, so as sometimes to burst. No light could then be excited by the application of heat, but, on letting in air, it immediately appeared; while these results were invariable in a great number of experiments. If the insect was introduced while in a luminous state, and the air exhausted gradually, the light was diminished in proportion, until it was totally extinguished. On letting the air again in it is restored; and this experiment may be repeated with the same results many times in succession on the same insect.

Both in oxygen and in azote the light appeared to be increased; but the insect seemed to suffer inconvenience, and it was soon extinguished. In chlorine it died immediately, with the loss of its light; but on applying heat the light re-appeared, not however as before, but of a red colour, which also soon ceases. Hydrogen, carbonic acid, nitrous gas, with carburetted and sulphuretted hydrogen, extinguish the light quickly, and it is not in any of these cases restored by heat. It will be seen how these experiments stand when compared with those of former observers; and, as far as we can judge, from the manner in which this communication is drawn up, we should feel no hesitation in giving superior credence on all disputed points to M. Macaire's experiments.

No effects were produced by electricity, in whatever mode it was applied. But the effect of galvanism was to excite the luminous action in the living animal, while it also ceased when the circuit was interrupted. The same effects were produced on the dead insect, and even on the luminous part of the body when separated; and that happened even where no effect was produced by ordinary electricity. But in the vacuum, galvanism was ineffectual, and the light could not be renewed by it.

M. Macaire found that the luminous matter itself, when separated, was translucent and yellowish, that it became dark on drying, and appeared to consist of grains having an organic structure. Its specific gravity was somewhat greater than that of water. Exposed to the effects of dryness and moisture, it gave the same results as in former experiments, and was also excited by heating as far as 42° of Reaumur, when it was extinguished. It also ceases to shine in vacuo,

4

and is re-excited by the admission of air; in other respects being affected by the different gases as it is when in the animal. When heated before the fire it ceases to shine, and when it is burnt, gives the smell of burnt horn, with a slight trace of ammonia. The mineral acids dissolve it when warm, and it communicates a bluish-green colour to the sulphuric; but on saturating the acid with an alkali, no light is re-produced. It is not soluble in oils, either hot or cold; but ceases to shine, and, as is supposed, from the exclusion of air. Ether and alcohol render it white and opake, and destroy the phosphorescence. Pure potash dissolves it, and acquires a light orange colour; and saturation with an acid does not restore it. It is also destroyed by corrosive sublimate, and other metallic salts. So far from being soluble in boiling water, it appears to acquire from it a greater degree of consistence.

M. Macaire concludes, strangely enough, as it appears to us, by determining that this luminous matter is chiefly composed of albumen.

With respect to the use or design of this provision, it seems fully as obscure as the cause. It has been supposed, indeed, (and the poets have made use of the thought,) that the female glow-worm made the signal to the other sex. But the male is also provided with it, and in the other luminous flies both sexes have the property alike. It has been thought a mode of defence; but surely it is much more likely to be the reverse. So at least thought the author of the well known fable of the nightingale and the glow-worm. That it should assist the animal in pursuing its prey, or in avoiding injuries, is very possible; but we fear that we must still confess our ignorance of the real designs of this, as well as of the ten thousand varieties in the forms and properties of the animal creation, which almost seem to us as if they were meant to show the exhaustless resources of nature, the wantonness, we might almost say, which she displays in the means of procuring happiness to myriads of different animals, when, for aught we can conjecture to the contrary, a very few would have served the same purposes.

On Luminous Marine Animals.

There are few phenomena in nature much more striking than the luminous appearance exhibited by the water of the ocean, particularly in tempestuous weather; terrific, in particular, to landsmen in these cases, as it is splendent and beautiful in the calms of summer. It has accordingly not only been an object of much remark among common observers, but has excited the attention of naturalists at all times, so as to have led to much discussion. From the time of Pliny downwards, frequent inquiries have been made respecting the cause, and accordingly many different theories have been proffered. Some of these, as usual, have been pure hypotheses, even in modern times, where experiment was easy, and its necessity in all such cases acknowledged. Were this not a frequent resource of philosophers in many other departments of natural science, we might be surprised that such explanations should have been offered even within a few years, and in a case in which investigation was so easy.

With these persons, as with naturalists in general, it was long taken for granted, as it is even yet by some, that this property belonged to the water itself, not to any bodies contained in it. Hence, instead of examining into its real seat, they were induced to speculate on its cause. A few of these theories deserve

notice, because we are fully sensible that they have not yet been quite abandoned, in spite of the evidence respecting the real cause which has been produced, and which ought to satisfy the most speculative or incredulous.

Mayer, and others who followed him, considered that this phenomenon depended on the same cause as the light emitted by the diamond and other substances after exposure to the sun's rays. He supposed that the sea-water absorbed light which it afterwards gave out. Others were content with calling the light phosphoric, and with supposing that sea-water was endowed with the property of phosphorescence; a solution just as satisfactory as all those in which words are substituted for meaning, or in which one term is changed for another. As if these hypotheses were not unintelligible enough, this phenomenon was also attributed to electricity, although the slightest attention to the nature of this power might have shown that, under no circumstances, could the electric action be excited within a body of water, and by the mutual collision of its own parts. Another party attributed the light to the putrefaction of sea-water, although it was not explained what the connection was between putrefaction and phosphorescence. But the least knowledge of sea-water might have shown, that except in some few rare cases, such as in calms in the tropical latitudes, where many animals are present, the waters of the sea are not subject to this change. On the contrary, and for reasons as obvious as on the land, nature has made ample provision in the sea as she has done in the atmosphere, for the speedy decomposition and dissipation of all such dead animal matter as might render that element noxious to its inhabitants. The waves, the tides, the currents, and probably other causes, effect in the ocean what storms do in the air, a renewal of a perpetual state of purity. The experiments of Dr. Hulme made a nearer approximation to the true cause, by showing that the luminous secretion or matter attached to the mucus of certain fishes, was diffusible in water. But that even this is not the true one, we shall shortly show.

The luminous appearance of the sea has, by mariners and fishermen, as by philosophers, been attributed to some inherent property in the water itself, and, like all splendid and striking phenomena has been supposed to arise from mysterious and recondite quality which it was fruitless to inquire further about. Hence they have neglected investigations more within their reach than in that of philosophers, or they might long since have not only shown what the real seat and origin of this appearance was, but have assisted us at this moment in the enumeration we shall attempt to make of those bodies in which the property really does reside. To mariners, professionally and hereditarily superstitious, the light elicited by water has been a fruitful source of prognostics, as all meteoric phenomena are respecting changes in the weather. That a high degree of phosphorescence in the sea is the forerunner of a storm, is a creed as firmly fixed among them as it is, that changes in the weather are governed by periods in lunation, are directed by the moon, although every day's experience contradicts them—not less in the one case than in the other. That it may be fortuitously connected with peculiar states of the atmosphere we do not however deny; and thus therefore it may really sometimes forerun changes of weather sufficiently, when added to the prevailing prejudices, to perpetuate this common error.

Later, or more accurate naturalists and seamen also, have, however, observed that some marine worms and insects were luminous; and thus it was admitted that some at least of the luminous appearances of the sea might be produced by these. Still this was held to be independent of the general luminous property so widely extended through the ocean; while many naturalists, who had ascertained the phosphorescent power of some species of marine animals, denied it to all the rest, and persisted in affirming that this quality depended on something inherent in the ocean itself. At one time, and that not very long ago, the Nereis noctiluca was supposed to be the only luminous creature in the sea, and thus it was thought that wherever the light depended on an animal, it was produced by this worm. By degrees, however, others were added to the list by voyagers and naturalists; yet even when it had been considerably increased, the popular belief was not shaken. Such a persistence in wilful error might have excited surprise, had it not also happened, that not only was the general subject overlooked, but that even the very existence of the myriads of minute animals that crowd the waters of the ocean to a degree that appears almost miraculous was unsuspected. We shall immediately show, not only that there are many luminous animals in the sea that were not suspected to possess this property, but that probably it belongs to every marine animal living as well as dead, and that uncounted and uncountable myriads of minute creatures reside in the ocean, which, with scarcely any exceptions, have been overlooked by all naturalists.

We are indebted to Dr. Macculloch for having first brought the whole of this question into one clear point of view, in his work on the Western Islands of Scotland, and for so great an extension of the luminous property to the marine species, as to have erected this into a general law; and we shall therefore borrow from his writings, the following facts relating to this curious subject, as well as the conclusions which he has drawn from them.

It must, in the first place, be remarked respecting sea-water, that it is far less frequently pure than is imagined. Within the vicinity of land it is so very rarely in that state, that it will not often fall to the lot of an observer to find it so, although this is generally believed to be the case, and that it appears sufficiently bright and clear on a superficial view, not only to a common observer, but even to one long practised in optical researches, and alive to minute distinctions of this nature. We have observed on several occasions, that not only it may contain animal matter in a state of solution without any sensible diminution of its transparency, but that it may abound with animalculae without showing, from this cause, the slightest degree of turbidness or opacity, and consequently without exciting the smallest suspicion respecting its purity. It is probable, however, from our own observations, as well as from those of Mr. Scoresby, that there is an optical effect produced by the presence of animalculæ, which has hitherto been a source of difficulty to philosophers. It is known that the colour of sea-water varies absolutely, and independently of any effects arising from the state of the atmosphere. On our own coasts, and generally in the vicinity of land, it is green, supposing that it is clear or transparent, and free from mud or any visible matter mechanically suspended in it. To judge of that colour truly, we must however view it in a bottom of white sand, or receive white light through it; and no where is it seen so bright as in the breaking of a wave in the sunshine, when the white foam is intermixed with the thin edge of the surf. Now in the ocean, on the contrary, or far from land, the green colour disappears, and it becomes blue; and that also independent of colour derived from the sky. This distinction appears to depend on the presence or absence of minute animals, which are to be found in the green water, but are wanting in the blue.

When the water is green, however, it is also not uncommon to find that it has undergone a loss of transparency. Sometimes this is so slight that it cannot be discovered without care; at others it is very sensible, and the effect resembles that which would follow from introducing into it a small quantity of milk. Now, if we attend to these appearances, when examining the luminous property of the sea, we shall find that it always yields most light in proportion as its transparency is least perfect; and we shall also discover in such cases that it contains the greatest number of animals. Further, when the opacity or milkiness is considerable, the microscope detects, besides living animals, a quantity of delicate fibrous matter diffused through it. In a few instances, this is so abundant as to be rendered highly sensible by re-agents, and to be even discovered by evaporation, and heating the residuum to burning. In making these experiments on sea-shores, we must however be careful not to confound with this kind of opaque matter, the fine mud which is brought down from the land by rivers, or forced up from the bottom of shallow seas by gales of wind.

When the sea-water is, on the contrary, blue instead of green, it is neither opaque, nor does it contain animals. In the same cases it gives out no light; but as errors may arise in the examination of this property, we must here make some distinctions. When we say that it gives out no light, we only mean that this is the case as long as it contains no visible animals. It does not present that diffused and faint phosphorescence so general in green water; but the presence or passage through it of any marine animal may still be attended by luminous appearances. It also happens that even in the wide ocean, and in the midst of a blue sea, tracts of light will occur at night when all the surrounding water is dark; but, in such instances, it will always be found that in these places the sea is discoloured or turbid, and the microscope will then also show us that it abounds both in living animals and in diffused animal matter.

If we have thus succeeded in establishing these propositions, the water of the sea, when in a state of purity, yields no light, supposing also that it contains no visible animals. In proportion as it becomes green, which seems to be the result of some admixture of foreign matters, living or dead, or both, its tendency to show light increases, and is greatest when it is milky, at which time it is easy to discover that it contains dead and living matters, both invisible to the naked eye. Hence it is a legitimate conclusion, that the phosphorescence of sea-water is a property, not belonging to itself, but to substances accidentally contained in it.

That we may attempt to ascertain what those substances are, we may first remark, that at a certain period after the death of fishes, they become luminous, even before putrefaction. In fact this property disappears before the proper putrefaction process has commenced. It is at the same time more remarkable in some fish than in others, although it occurs in the whole as far as our observations go. It is popularly remarked to be especially prevalent in the whiting; but we think that the reason of this is not only very intelligible, but that in assigning it we shall also explain why it has been overlooked in the other fishes in which it occurs. Among fishes, the whiting is one of those which goes quickest into the putrefactive state, while in others that process is far more tedious; in some indeed that is so much the case, that they may even be dried without experiencing it at all. This, in particular, is true of the salmon, the skate, and some others, while the turbot, the sole, the dory, and many more, can be preserved for days without undergoing any change. Now, as we have shown that the luminous process occurs in a stage intermediate between the death of the animal and the first occurrence of the putrefaction process, it is not difficult to see how that has been overlooked in those fish which take it in slowly. In fact, these fishes are eaten long before it has commenced; and as it is, when intended for this purpose, that observers are chiefly familiar with them, it is not surprising if this phenomena has been so often overlooked. It is only necessary to keep the whole of them a sufficient length of time, to find that they will all become phosphorescent.

Now it happens, that during this luminous stage, as well as after it, there is a solution of some of the solid matter of the fish going on; or, if not an actual solution, a disintegration of the cellular or muscular fibre. This is diffusible through the water, and may easily be examined by the microscope; at times indeed by the naked eye. For a short time after it has been thus separated, it retains the luminous property, provided it was in a phosphorescent state before; and it is in this way that a portion of water may be rendered luminous for a short time merely by agitating a luminous fish in it. This is the explanation of the experiments of Dr. Hulme, which led many persons to imagine that the luminous appearance of sea-water was derived from putrescent animal matter. But, in the first place, there is no putrescence in this case, as that term is generally understood; besides which the light is very transitory. It is a mistake, moreover, to suppose that the light resided in the mucus of the skin, and that in agitating the fish in water this was the substance that carried the light with it. In succession, all the muscular and cellular matter of the animal becomes luminous, though the surface alone may appear so at first, because there the first change occurs. It is easy to see this by watching the progress in any fish, and it will be found that, at one period, the whole animal is luminous throughout, and as if transparent.

It is now plain, that if all the fibrous matter thus separated from fish at a certain stage after death, were permanently luminous, we might thus account for the phosphorescence of turbid water, or of that in which the milkiness above-mentioned is discernible. But that is not the case; since, as we just remarked, the luminous property of this matter speedily disappears. We have also often succeeded in procuring water thus turbid and abounding in fibrous matter, which was utterly dark or incapable of phosphorescence: and in these instances, as in others, we have also ascertained, as we shall hereafter fully show, that no phosphorescence was present unless the water contained living animals, and that in this case it was invariably luminous.

We observed above, that it was supposed by some,

that the luminous matter resided in the mucous secretions of the skin, and that thus being diffused through the water, even from the living animals, it was the cause of the luminous property of the sea. We were at one time inclined to adopt this opinion ourselves, not indeed with regard to all the light which the sea exhibits, but to a particular feeble diffused phosphorescence which we shall presently describe. But we have since found reasons for withdrawing this opinion, at least in a great measure, and for recurring to a different cause, even for this kind of light, which is intermixed with those more brilliant sparklings that the ocean exhibits. We do not profess indeed to be quite satisfied respecting the extent, either in the durability or the intensity of the light which does reside in the surface of fishes, nor of the degree to which it is diffusible when removed from the animal. We have, however, ascertained that the whole surface of a living fish does become luminous, if not always or permanently so, as in some cases it appears to be; and we therefore think it possible, that if the luminous matter is a secretion, it may be washed off together with the mucus, so as to be diffusible through the water, as it is in the case of the dead animal. Even in this case, however, we should no more expect to find it permanent or durable, than when separated from a dead fish; and we must add, that we even doubt whether such an event ever happens, as we have never succeeded in rendering water diffusely luminous by means of a living fish, unless when we could ascertain that animals of a minute kind were also present.

Now, the conclusions that we would derive from these statements are the following: We think there is no reason to doubt, that, in certain situations, and under certain circumstances, the water of the sea may be phosphorescent, in consequence of dead phosphorescent animal matter diffused through it, though we will not here pretend to determine whether that is to proceed solely from dead fishes, or occasionally also from living ones. But as we have shown that the property is very transitory in matter so detached, as the animal matter, from its mere deficiency in quantity, cannot be diffused very far from its source, and as the sea cannot be supposed so to abound in dead fishes, or even in living ones, as to be rendered extensively luminous from this cause, we think that very little need be allowed to it in inquiring respecting the origin of the phosphorescence of sea water.

We must here also distinguish, what we shall have occasion to do more fully immediately, between the several kinds of light which the sea affords. Sometimes it seems generally luminous, shining with a very pale and feeble whitish light; at others it exhibits wide flashes, like a particular sort of lightning; and at others again it is filled with brilliant sparks of different sizes and colours. Now it is only the first of these, or the faint diffused light, which is caused by diffused dead matter, so that we have still the other two sorts left unaccounted for and to be referred to other causes. But here also we do not admit that all the faint diffused lights are produced by dead animal matter. On the contrary, we have ascertained by numerous observations, that this kind of light is produced by living animals though of a very minute size; by animalculæ, in short, to use the common term, or microscopic creatures; and in this we are supported by the remarks of many voyagers who have described the sea as appearing at night to be like a sea of milk, or a plain of snow, while these phenomena have at

the same time been discovered to be produced by minute animals. In the green water also, when no turbidness at all could be discovered, we have often found
the diffused luminous appearance, and have in these
cases ascertained that animalculæ were present, but
either too minute or too transparent in themselves to
affect the clearness of the water. Hence our final conclusion is, that though sea-water may at times be rendered phosphorescent by detached and dead animal
matter, that circumstance is so rare that it need scarcely enter into our calculations respecting the causes of
the luminous appearance. With this slight exception,
therefore, we shall now proceed to inquire into the
causes which are most efficient and common, and describe the several appearances that occur, adding a description or enumeration of the animals, as far as we
have yet ascertained those by which it is produced.

It has been so positively asserted by so many observers, that they had seen, not only the general diffused light, but the sparkling appearance in sea-water
when no animals were present, that we must first show
that this assertion is founded in erroneous observation.
We say, on the contrary, and without hesitation, that
this never happens, and that the mistake has arisen
from negligence or ignorance of the subject where observations have been made, and from preconceived
opinions where they have not. The sources of error
require to be pointed out, as well as the method, not
only of ascertaining the fact generally, but the very
animals in which the luminous property resides in
these more obscure cases.

In the first place, a very few bright lights dispersed
through the sea are sufficient to produce a very brilliant effect, and to make observers imagine that the
water is universally luminous. The phenomenon is in
itself dazzling, particularly in a dark night; and the
general impression is also not a little augmented by a
slight feeling towards the marvellous, so apt to exag-
gerate every thing that is new or uncommon. Now, it
is quite easy to take up from such a sea, and that repeatedly, as we have often experienced, a bucket full of
water without a single animal in it, while at another
time two or three of the very medusæ, or other creatures yielding the light, are obtained. There is another
reason why they so often escape, and that is, their slippery nature; so that, floating on the surface, as they
generally do, they are washed out by the wave that
takes place on hoisting the bucket on board. Hence
one great source of the errors of careless observers
with respect to the presence of these animals, and the
consequent cause of the sparkling appearance of the
sea.

In the next place, a great many animals that yield a
very bright light, even in the form of distinct and
brilliant sparks, are so transparent, although of visible
dimensions, that it is quite impossible to see them,
either in a ship's bucket, particularly at night, or in a
vessel of earthen ware. Nay more, there are many,
even among the medusæ, reaching to the tenth or
eighth of an inch in diameter, that cannot easily be
seen, although in a glass, and by candle light. If there
is even half an inch of water between them and the
eye, or sometimes less, they are quite invisible, because
their refractive density is exactly equal to that of the
water. We have often been employed for half an hour
or more in searching for such an animal in a common
tumbler, where we had previously ascertained its presence, and it had merely escaped from the reach of the
eye. Hence it is not surprising if an impatient ob-

server determines that nothing is present, merely because it is not visible at the very moment he expects.
Had the nature of these animals been better understood, such errors could never have taken place. In
all investigations, of whatever nature, it is useful to
recollect that we cannot always succeed unless we are
provided with more than one kind of information.

Further, a great many of the animals that yield distinct and bright sparks, are either of microscopic dimensions, so as to be utterly invisible to the naked
eye, or if not so very minute, are rendered thus invisible by the combination of their transparency with their
very limited dimensions. Those which produce a
general diffused light, are, in particular, thus microscopic, while they are also abundant, so as to crowd the
water like the common infusoria. Among those which
we have examined, there are innumerable animals, and
of many species, that do not reach to the hundredth of
an inch in dimensions; there are even many not larger
than the two hundredth of that measure, and perhaps
many more that we have never discovered, still smaller.
The transparency and low refractive density of these,
contribute, no less than their minuteness, to render
them difficult to discover, while there are difficulties
in managing the lenses, the light, and the objects
themselves, which throw no small additional impediments in the way of the investigation.

It is not possible, in the first place, to conduct these
inquiries by means of the compound microscope in the
usual manner, and in a single drop of water; because,
although such animals may abound in the sea, it is
perfectly easy to take out many successive drops
without entrapping one. Moreover such a drop dries
quickly under the lens, even while the lights and foci
are arranging; and whenever that happens, all the
animals which it may include disappear for ever, so
small is the quantity of solid matter which they contain. They must therefore be sought for in a large
glass, where they may swim at liberty by the aid of a
simple lens. Even here it is difficult to find them,
though we should have previously ascertained that they
were present, and that for many reasons. The water,
in the first place, is commonly turbid where they
abound, or even where they exist. Those also alone
come into view which approach so near to the fore
part of the glass as materially to diminish the column
of water between them and the eye; and thus also
they often escape observation, while the spectator is
surprised to find that he can discover nothing in the
light, when, in the dark, the water has abounded in
luminous sparks. When a lens is used, it is also only
in the observer's power to gain a sight of those which
pass immediately through its focal point; so that, in
this case also, he is apt to underrate their numbers, or,
if rare, to doubt their existence altogether. By the
mere light of day it is scarcely possible to discover
them at all, and that of the sun is too bright for the
eye to bear. It is not then very surprising if, under
these difficulties, incautious, or hasty or inexpert observers, should fail to discover them even where they
most abound.

Another cause yet has tended to deceive naturalists
respecting the presence of minute animals in sea-
water, and that is their speedy solution or disintegration after death. That many of them consume much
oxygen, and that all consume some, is from analogy
probable. Hence it is, probably, that they shortly die
when confined to a limited quantity of water. This is
very remarkable in the case of the medusæ; and thus

if, where smaller animals are present, the water is laid by till the morning for examination, nothing will be found but milky fibres floating about in it.

To these various and neglected sources of error, we must yet add two more, by which the luminous animals themselves contrive to deceive the observer. There is no doubt that the light is under the command of the animals, and that from this, perhaps from other causes also, it is subject to intermissions. Thus, whether from caprice, or fatigue, or a voluntary effort, or some other causes yet unknown, they often refuse to show their light even when violently agitated or injured; if we are right respecting the final causes of this property, which we shall hereafter suggest, any injury is precisely what would tend to make them extinguish it, for the purpose of escaping from the pursuit of their enemies. Hence, although they have been luminous when in the sea, or have even shown their lights after being taken, they afterwards refuse to shine again in spite of all our attempts. Thus a naturalist, finding that his prize abounds with animals, and that he cannot nevertheless procure any light from them, is apt, perhaps naturally enough, to imagine that the cause of the phosphorescence lies elsewhere, not in the animals, but in the sea-water itself.

The last of these sources of deception which we shall here point out, arises from the nature and magnitude of the light compared to that of the animal; and this operates in two ways. A naturalist who happens to know that a dead medusa, lying on the beach, is luminous all over, expects to find the same animal displaying the same light when alive. Yet the two cases are perfectly distinct; and this is an important fact to notice, as it relates to the light itself, independently of the object now under consideration. The luminous part of even a large medusa, or other animal, is sometimes extremely small; a single bright spot, perhaps not equal to an hundredth part of its dimensions. Hence the observer who has seen in the water a bright spot, not larger than a pin's head, and has taken a medusa of three or four inches in diameter, cannot imagine that it proceeds from such an animal, particularly when he cannot induce it to make a display again; and thus he returns to his favourite hypothesis of luminous water. He is equally subject to be deceived by a circumstance precisely the reverse of this. In many of the very minute animals, from its brilliancy and power of radiation, as happens in a star, the spot of light appears so large as far to exceed the animal in dimensions. It is by no means uncommon, thus, in some of the luminous species, to find that a light, which seems in the sea as large as a pea, is caused by a creature not the twentieth of an inch in diameter. In this way an observer brings on board a bucket of water, which he sees, when over the ship's side, to be full of such large lights, and examining it afterwards by candle-light, finds nothing but a crowd of transparent creatures nearly microscopic, and of course, under these circumstances, unwilling to shine, or exhibiting no light. Thus he falsely concludes that the animals which he is inspecting are not the cause of these lights, and once more returns to his favourite mysterious property of sea-water.

These, then, are the principal circumstances with regard to the animals themselves, which the naturalist should have in view in his attempts to investigate the water of the sea for the purpose of discovering the luminous animals which it may contain, and for satisfy-

ing himself that our statements are correct. In this way, also, he will succeed, and in this only, in discovering the mere existence and nature of these animals, as well as in ascertaining the fact of their luminous nature. The more particular directions respecting individuals we shall give immediately. Besides these deductions, however, the foregoing facts will serve to add something to our knowledge respecting the natural history of these much neglected animals generally; for that they have been much neglected we hope shortly to prove. But should these remarks serve no other purpose, they will serve to assist others, as they did ourselves, in these examinations. They are deductions made from our own repeated experience, and they will probably serve to prove most fully to others, what we ourselves think completely ascertained, namely, that luminous animals abound in the waters of the ocean, even when, from their minuteness, from their not actually emitting light, or from other causes, they are least suspected; and that the property of phosphorescence is granted to every one of these neglected inhabitants of the deep.

It is now necessary to point out somewhat more particularly the method used in examining these animals, so as to enable us to decide on the luminous property of any species.

With respect to the larger kinds, there is seldom any difficulty. With sufficient care, a large medusa, a beroe, a nereis, or any of the distinctly visible animals, may be secured in the very act of emitting light, and then examined at leisure. Should not an animal, as is usual, extinguish its light as soon as it is taken, it is only necessary to place it in a sufficiently large receptacle of water, and to leave it for some hours at peace. On then agitating the water, or irritating it slightly, it will immediately show its light, so as fully to remove all doubt from the observer's mind. If more than one species of these should occur together, they are easily separated, and afterwards examined. When the species are smaller, and more numerous, and where many kinds occur together, it becomes a much more difficult task to satisfy ourselves that all the individuals are luminous. Yet, even in this case, by sufficiently multiplying the examinations, we may approximate at least to something like accuracy; while, where a property like this is observed in so many instances to exist, and where it has probably been conferred for certain universal purposes, which we shall hereafter point out, it is not a rash conclusion to infer that no species is exempt from the general law, or deprived of this power; since, in all essential circumstances, the habits and pursuits of these marine animals are the same.

In making these observations, at least in a small vessel, it is requisite that the water should be calm; as any agitation of the ship renders the investigation impossible, from the motion of the observer's person, as well as that of the water under examination. It is difficult enough, under the most favourable circumstances, to catch and retain the smaller species within the focus of the lens. They are themselves no less rapid and restless in their movements than they are minute; so that he who is determined to investigate them must not only be freed from all unnecessary inconveniences, but be armed with no small share of patience. When such examinations can be made on shore, it is most convenient; but in this way we are very much limited as to the number of species, as many of them are only found at considerable distances from the land. In the deep harbours and sea-lochs of our own country, we can generally both examine them easily, on account of the smoothness of the water when at anchor; besides which it will be found that their situations present a very great variety.

There is something in their localities, which, though not ascertained fully, appears constant at least within certain limits, independently of mere climate. As to this latter circumstance, we have reason to believe, from the observations of the very few navigators who have attended to this subject, that many species exist in the ocean, in the polar, the temperate, and the tropical seas, which are confined to those particular tracts, as are the larger fishes of the same regions. Yet this subject has met with so little attention, that we can scarcely give the description or name of any one species of the minuter kind. That our readers may be enabled to judge of this neglect, we need only say, that in the space of six summer weeks on our own coasts, we have examined upwards of 200 different animals, and that of these not less than two-thirds were undescribed species.

We have no doubt that we could have tripled our own list in one season, had this formed a principal pursuit, instead of being, as it was, only an incidental amusement for idle hours; and have every reason to suppose that we should even then have been very far short of knowing those which belong to our seas. Our readers who reflect on the infinite variety of larger marine animals which have been discovered in various parts of the world, may well conceive the numbers of these also that would have been ascertained, had naturalists, favoured with such opportunities for observation, paid greater attention to a subject which they seem to have almost universally agreed in neglecting. Excepting the labours of Muller, there is not much that is worthy of notice in the writings of naturalists on this subject; and even he appears to have been far from suspecting the existence of numerous species that must have passed through his hands. Of animals purely microscopic, we scarcely find ten that have been described by all naturalists united; and, in a single bay of the Highlands, we have found twice as many in one evening. We mention these circumstances, not to boast of our discoveries, since we scarcely consider ourselves as deserving to be ranked among this class of naturalists; but with the hope of stimulating the curiosity and activity of those who have the means of consistently pursuing a train of investigation, which, to us, was purely accidental.

Now, excepting some particular cases, such as those described by Mr. Scoresby, and by Cook, Horsburgh, Perouse, and other voyagers, where such minute animals were found in immense colonies in the wide ocean, we have reason to think that they are far more numerous near land than in the open sea. In our own observations on the coasts of Scotland, this was invariably the case. Within eight or ten miles of land, they always appeared to become most numerous, and in harbours they were still more abundant. With few exceptions also we found them in the greatest quantity and variety in narrow creeks, among rocks, or under high cliffs, where the water was sheltered from the sea and wind, and when, at the same time, it was least disturbed. A large proportion of them seemed indeed to be exclusively limited to situations of this nature, as we never observed them at all in the open sea, or at any considerable distances from the shore. Many of them also seemed peculiarly to affect those shallow and

rocky places where sea-weeds abound. It was only at the end of the season in which our principal observations were made, that we happened to be thus situated; and we discovered thus, in one day, as many species as we had found before in the course of a whole fortnight. Not to specify more minutely the places where these observations were made, we shall only say that they were confined to a few of the lochs on the west coast of Scotland, to one or two places on the coast, north of Inverness, and to some of the bays of Orkney and Shetland. These are the situations, then, and that chiefly in summer weather, and in calm seas, where the naturalist who may undertake this pursuit is most likely to meet with success.

Some of these species, however, seem utterly to disregard boisterous weather; while there were many, on the contrary, that almost invariably disappeared on the coming on of a fresh gale, and were only found again when the weather moderated. In the same manner, other changes of wind or weather, even when there was not a strong breeze, or perhaps no wind at all, caused them to disappear entirely in the course of a few hours. It is probable that these animals, like the leech and many others, are highly sensible to atmospheric changes, and that they retire to the deeper water from some warning which they have of that which might be injurious to them; probably to avoid that agitation which, to many of the larger kinds, would be fatal from their tenderness and bulk. We have no doubt that many of them are destroyed, in bad weather, by the agitation of the sea at the surface. These hints, like the others, will be useful to the naturalist in his labours.

But, besides this, these remarks will serve to throw light on that part of the subject which relates to the uncertainty and the apparently capricious occurrence of the phosphorescence of the ocean. That this is very variable, is well known, even from day to day, or indeed from hour to hour; when we are sure that the animals cannot have had time to remove to any distance, and when we know that they were abundant but a short time before. Thus when the sea has been quite dark, or sparingly luminous, or exhibiting only a few sparks, it will on a sudden become bright and crowded with lights; and, in a contrary manner, a bright sea will become dark, even though no change from calm to storm, or the reverse, should happen. This, among others formerly enumerated, has been one of the causes which has served to mislead observers; and which has induced them to imagine that the phosphorescent property belonged to the water, and that it was under the influence of the atmosphere. It has equally given rise to many of the prognostics relating to the weather; which, whether they are just or not, are the prophecies of living animals, and neither those of the water nor the air.

We already noticed that seamen were accustomed to draw their own prognostics from these appearances, and we then professed to disregard them as founded in erroneous views of the phosphorescence of sea water. We have not, however, the least doubt that some true prognostics might actually be drawn from such phenomena, provided all the collateral causes were duly considered, as may be done by studying the motions of leeches. But we are quite sure that the popular ones are unfounded; while it is equally plain that many things must be considered before we could hope to arrive at true conclusions on this subject. Thus the mere abundance of these animals at one time, and their absence at another, would, to an incautious observer, seem to foretel the same changes as those which are indicated by their appearance at the surface, or by their retiring, or else by their showing or obscuring their light in consequence of other causes. It is from this last circumstance that is derived the erroneous opinion, that a very luminous state of the sea is the forerunner of bad weather. This, however, is a consequence of the mere agitation of the water, which always excites the luminous action of these animals; so that a luminous sea is the concomitant, and not the forerunner of an agitated one. So far indeed is the prognostic from being true, that it is by no means uncommon for the sea to be extremely brilliant in a calm, and to become dark at the approach of a gale of wind; the animals retiring to the deeps for the reasons stated above. But even in calm weather, and when we can ascertain that these animals are actually present, and that also in abundance, there is often no light to be seen; another circumstance which has equally led to fallacious prognostics, as well as to unfounded opinions respecting the seat of the light. Very often we have found the water crowded, even with the large medusæ, yet scarcely betraying themselves by an occasional twinkle, when the dash of an oar, or any accidental agitation, was sufficient to involve the whole water in a blaze of light. Many other circumstances already mentioned, as well as this, prove that the light is under the guidance of the animal's will; and all our observations concur in confirming this opinion. We have often observed the usual locomotions performed by millions of these animals, of all kinds, for a whole night, without the slightest indication of their presence; or perhaps some one individual might emit an occasional spark, when the least alarm excited, even by mere noise in some cases, was sufficient to render the whole luminous.

The incredulity of naturalists on this subject, or their unwillingness to believe that the light was produced by animals, has been confirmed by two other circumstances. For this reason it is necessary to take notice of these; besides which, they form an important part of the history of the phosphorescence of the sea. These things are, the apparently perfect diffusion or the abundance of the light, in some cases, through every part of the water, both in sparks and otherwise, and the distinction between the sparkling lights, which are commonly very bright, and the more faint light which seems inherent, and, as it were, incorporated with the whole fluid. We hope to show that, for the most part at least, these different appearances are owing to the same class of causes—to the phosphorescent powers of animals.

If naturalists had been aware how numerous or abundant these creatures were, it would never have appeared extraordinary to them that the water should be so generally or extensively luminous; no more than that, when their minuteness is considered, they should have escaped ordinary observation. When even only one species is present, the numbers are sometimes such as even to confound the imagination; when there are many, it has sometimes appeared as if there was as much space occupied by the animals as by the water. On one occasion a single species was observed extending all the way from the Mull of Cantyre to Shetland, and occupying the breadth of sea which our vessel was obliged to traverse in beating against the wind; a space probably of four or five miles broad. How much wider than that it might have been we had no means of knowing, but it is probable that this animal was far from being limited to that narrow space. To what-

ever depth the eye or the ship's bucket could reach the water appeared equally crowded with this animal; which was an unknown species of what Muller has thought proper to include under the genus Vibrio. In the sunshine the water appeared almost opake, and as if filled with minute scales of mica; and, at night, there was no difficulty in ascertaining that this creature was the cause of the general luminous appearance. It would be a very moderate computation indeed, to say, that an hundred of these were contained in every cubic inch of water; were we to say a thousand we should probably be nearer to the truth. To attempt to form a conception of their numbers, only for the space of a few yards, would be fruitless; and the endless myriads of them existing throughout the extent of sea thus navigated baffles all the powers of imagination.

In the same seas, and nearly at all times, the water was found crowded with many different species of other genera; many of them not visible without the lens, or truly microscopic. This very transparency of the sea was affected by these, so numerous were they; besides which, ten or twenty animals of various kinds, visible to the eye, were found in the same water, and in the space of a common drinking glass. Such facts as these, which are, as far as our experience goes, of common occurrence, are sufficient to account for all the light of the sea without the necessity of seeking for any other causes.

In all these cases, where the animals were very minute, or microscopic, the sea was universally and diffusedly luminous; and when they were more visible, it abounded in bright sparks. That the sparks were produced by these latter, admitted of no doubt, because they could be taken out of the water by means of a feather, in the very act of shining, and transferred to other water for examination. At the same time, the general luminous appearance was destroyed when the animals died, either from keeping the water too long, or by warming it, or by the addition of spirits. The facility, indeed, by which the phosphorescence of water is extinguished by all those means which kill its inhabitants, is in itself a sufficient proof that this property resides in these.

With some attention, it is even easy, to a certain extent, to distinguish the different sparks of light yielded by different animals; as far, at least, as they differ in dimensions. In the larger kinds, the bright spot is quite distinct, and very often varies in colour, being white, or yellowish, or bluish, or reddish. In the smallest, agitation produces a general luminous appearance; the light of each separate individual being so small, or so faint, as not to be separately distinguishable. Thus, wherever sparks are observed, we may expect to discover visible animals. These sparks are frequent in the vicinity of sea-weed. They are also found adhering to these plants, as well as to oysters and crabs, and to the larger fishes; and by examining these by a lens, the animal itself is easily discovered. Small monoculi, poduræ, cyclopes, nereides, scolopendra, squillæ, and other animals of considerable dimensions, will thus be frequently detected, as well as minute hydræ, and other creatures which it is unnecessary to enumerate; as, in fact, we have never observed one that was not phosphorescent.

Now it also appears to us, that, in those cases where the dash of an oar produces a flash of pale light, without distinct sparks, or where the well-known stream of light accompanies the descent of a fishing line, these effects arise from the microscopic animals already described, and neither from any imaginary detached secretions of fishes, nor from decomposing animal matter; because, in all such cases, the water abounds with those minuter creatures. Though we cannot add many testimonies in support of our own on this subject, we shall quote the very few that have occurred to us in the course of our reading, as bearing on this part of the question. In the late voyage of Captain Tuckey, in the narratives of Riville, Newland, and Langstaff, as well as in those of Cook, La Perouse, and Horsburgh, formerly noticed, it was remarked that great tracts of sea were sometimes found diffusedly luminous, shining without sparks, and with a faint general light. Some of these observers compare the effect to that which might be produced by a plain of snow; others have thought that the sea resembled milk. By some of these persons, it has further been observed, that this appearance was produced by myriads of minute animals. Their characters, however, have seldom been described; and it is more than probable that many different kinds have been found, though no attention was exerted in discriminating them. Professor Smith appears to have fallen into an error, in considering this luminous diffused matter as dead, or a detached substance, consisting of solid spherical particles. Such particles are indeed common; but, instead of being dead matter, they are living animals; belonging, as it appeared to us, sometimes to the genera Vorticella and Volvox, and at others to genera not yet named; to new and neglected animals, in short. It is easy to account for this error from the use of the compound microscope, and from operating on a single drop of water; as, by this, their motions become checked, so that they may easily be mistaken for dead inorganic particles.

On this account, to warn future observers against similar errors, and to enable others to save themselves trouble by profiting from our experience, we will not terminate this part of our subject without describing particularly the mode we followed in our attempts to draw these animals, and to discover their forms and distinctions.

They are very commonly found in milky or turbid water, where they are abundant; and on examining such water, it is found filled with floating fibres, that appear to have been produced by their own destruction after death. In the Vibrios, among which, taking this ill-contrived genus as it now stands, we have discovered about fifteen new species, it is easy to witness the death of the animal, and its gradual dissolution; since that takes place in the course of a few minutes, or in the larger in a quarter of an hour. That opacity sometimes interferes a good deal with these observations, and is therefore better avoided, if possible. In the same way, they are more difficult to examine when numerous, as they disturb each other by their rapid movements, and prevent the observer from keeping any of them within the focus of the lens. Some species of a genus which has yet received no name, are so extremely troublesome in this respect, from the rapidity of their motions, that if they happen to be present, it is almost hopeless to attempt to make any accurate observations.

It is preferable to examine all these animals by candle light, as ordinary day light is not sufficient for the purpose; nor can the light of the sun be managed in such a manner, as, at the same time, to be endured by the eye, and to serve the purpose of illuminating the objects. It is desirable to use more than one candle, as it is convenient to have more than one luminous spot

under command; the rapid motions of these animals carrying them so quickly out of the limits of one spot as to cause considerable trouble to the observer, who has many things to distract his attention at the same time. Some of them are best examined in the brightest light; others at its borders; and very often it is necessary to examine the same object in different lights before a just idea of its form can be obtained. A separate light is also required to illuminate the paper on which the drawings are to be made; the eye being so far paralyzed by the excess of light required to view them, as not to be able to see, in a moderate degree of illumination; and it being absolutely necessary to draw them without losing the least practicable interval of time after viewing them through the lens. A few seconds are sufficient to cause the observer to forget the exact figure of the parts which he is to delineate.

The most convenient receptacle in which they can be placed for examination is a rummer, or conoidal glass, of such dimensions as to contain about half a pint. It is, in the first place, quite necessary that they should be at liberty; as it is only when in motion that many of them can at all be discovered; and as the peculiar nature of their motions, which, in all, are very different, and highly characteristic, is of great use in discriminating individuals otherwise much resembling each other. It is true, that this is productive of great inconvenience, from their passing so quickly out of the field of view; and thus it often requires a long time, and examinations patiently repeated, to ascertain the exact figure of one individual.

It is impossible to confine them in a single drop of water in the usual manner, unless absolutely microscopic, and as small as the Infusoria, without losing sight of their forms. In this way they come to a state of rest, and their fins, legs, antennæ, and other fine parts, become invisible, generally collapsing close to the body. Moreover, the affection of light produced by the contact of the animal with the surface or edge of the drop, or of that of the drop with the glass on which it stands, totally destroys distinct vision, and renders their forms quite unintelligible. A glass of less dimensions than that above-mentioned, or a wine glass, is also far less convenient than a rummer; as the smallness of the circle, or nature of the convexity, produces a far less useful spot of light.

In many cases, where, from their excessive activity, it is difficult to catch these objects for a sufficient length of time in the field of view, to study their parts, we have found it useful to diminish their powers of motion. This may be done by slightly warming the water, by suffering it to stand for a few hours in the glass, or by the addition of a small quantity of spirits, and probably of other substances. But slight injuries are sufficient to kill them; and, as they then become invisible, the observer must be on his guard not to exceed in the application of these means.

From the necessity of thus using a large glass to contain them, and from the freedom of motion thence allowed, it is evident that a high magnifying power cannot be applied. It is scarcely possible, indeed, to make effective use of one greater than that produced by a simple lens of half an inch focal distance; and as, with this power, the field of view is very contracted, it is often convenient to have two other lenses at hand, of one inch and of two inches in focal distance. The very minute ones may, indeed, occasionally be secured under a compound microscope, in a single drop of water; but the observer will be disappointed much oftener than he will succeed, in his attempts to examine them in this way; partly from the chance of his failing to find any in many successive portions of water thus separated, and partly for the reasons that have just been stated.

Having thus far proved, as we imagine, that both the general luminous appearance and the bright scintillations emitted by the waters of the sea, are produced by the smaller or more imperfect and obscure marine animals; and having described all the general circumstances relating to them which are most important, we shall, as far as lies in our power, give a list of those that have been ascertained to be luminous, reserving the consideration of the fishes to a future part of this essay. That this list is not larger, must be attributed to the inattention and prejudices of the observers, which we have already noticed; and that it is longer in number than in names, arises from the discovery of many new animals by Dr. Macculloch, which he has not yet arranged or described, or rather has not published. That this list will ultimately be extended to perhaps every inhabitant of the ocean, we entertain no doubt; but while opinions are yet unsettled on this subject, we think it best to limit ourselves to such particulars as have really been ascertained. We shall place these animals without any order; as there is not a sufficient number of them to render an arrangement of any use, and as we have rather chosen to name them according to the authorities by which their luminous properties have been ascertained. Having very little confidence in the principles of arrangement by which many of the new genera have been formed, and considering that the whole subject requires a thorough revisal and reform, we shall use indiscriminately the ancient and the new names, just as they happen to occur. Naturalists will easily know the animals that are meant, under any nomenclature.

Among the crustaceous animals, several species have been found luminous by different observers, such as the Galathea amplectens of Fabricius, by Sir Joseph Banks, and the Astacus fulgens of the same author. Several luminous species have also been found in the divisions of Gammarideæ. The Beroe fulgens, of a genus now most improperly united to the Medusæ, derives its name from its luminous property; and Sir C. Giesecké informs us, that he has found, in Greenland, many undescribed species of the same genus, which are also luminous. To these Dr. Macculloch has added eight new species, all equally possessed of this property. Some Beroes were also found to be luminous in Captain Tuckey's voyage. Sir C. Giesecké also mentions a Cyclops, which he calls brevicornis, possessed of the powers of phosphorescence. That is a genus, however, respecting which naturalists are not agreed; as, indeed, they seem little satisfied, in general, with each other's arrangements respecting these animals. But, in the mean time, and for want of a better place, Dr. Macculloch has added to Sir C. Giesecké's animals thirty-three new species, and all of them highly luminous. The Monoculus lynceus is also said, by the same naturalist, to be luminous; and, in that genus, Dr. Macculloch has introduced five new species, all luminous. The Nereis noctiluca has been often described as luminous; appearing, indeed, as we formerly remarked, to have been the animal in which this property was first very generally noticed; and, into that genus also, the last named observer has introduced three or four new and luminous species. The Limulus noctilucus is described as a phosphorescent animal in Captain Horsburgh's voyage.

Monsieur Peron has described, in very splendid colouring, a newly discovered luminous animal, which he calls Pyrosoma Atlanticum; and more recently it has been ascertained that the whole of that newly separated genus emits light. By Spallanzani we are informed that four of the genus Pinnatula are phosphorescent; namely, the Grisea, Argentea, Phosphorea, and Grandis; and it has since been remarked, that the whole of this family are endowed with the same property. He also mentions five other luminous marine worms, of which he had not ascertained the genera; while, among those that inhabit shells, the Pholades have been observed to exhibit light. In Captain Tuckey's voyage, we are informed that some species of Holothuria, and one of the genus Scyllarus, was found to be luminous, as was a species of Sulpa. In the latter genus, Dr. Macculloch has discovered a new species on the west coast of the Highlands, which he calls Moniliformis, and which is also luminous.

From Captain Tuckey's narrative we also learn, that twelve crabs were found to be possessed of this property; but neither the species are described, nor the particular divisions in the new arrangement to which they belong. Probably Professor Smith had as little made up his mind on that subject as Dr. Macculloch, who has ascertained nine new and luminous animals of this wide genus on the coasts of Shetland and Orkney.

In the genus Medusa there appear to have been more luminous species described than in any other. It would have shortened the matter to have said, what we believe to be the fact, that every one of them is so; we, at least, have never seen a species that was not. Mr. Macartney, who has betowed some trouble on this subject, has pointed out the Hemispherica and Scintillans as possessed of this property, but has, we know not why, supposed it to be limited. The Medusa pellescens has been described as luminous by Sir Joseph Banks, the Noctiluca and Dorsa by Forskahl; and two others, one in the Mediterranean, and the other at the Cape of Good Hope, of which no specific characters are given, are mentioned by Spallanzani and Forster. We are surprized that these observers should have limited themselves to so scanty an enumeration, as they could neither have failed to see many more species, nor, if they had inquired, to have found them all luminous. In the same manner have almost all our recent voyagers neglected this subject. Not one luminous Medusa or other animal is mentioned in any of the Polar expeditions, nor in Kotzebue's long expedition, although provided with two naturalists. On our own shores many species are found, and the whole are invariably phosphorescent; the most abundant, in point of numbers, among these, being the Aurita and the Cruciata. Very recently Dr. Macculloch has added twenty-one new species to this genus, and has also ascertained that the whole of them were luminous.

We shall terminate this miscellaneous list, by mentioning some other animals ascertained by the observer last mentioned, to be equally phosphorescent, all of them being found on the northern coast of Scotland and the islands. As many of these are new species, and some of them new genera, to which he has not yet given names, we can only make this enumeration in a general manner.

Besides the species of the genus Nereis above mentioned, he found some Scolopendrae which appear to be non-descript kinds. In the genus Phalangium there was one, together with some in the genera of Oniscus and Iulus. Of the animals of the genus Vibrio, formerly mentioned, taking that genus as it is now constituted, there were nineteen species, of which seventeen appeared to be new. Sixteen of those belonged to that department of luminous animals which do not emit sparks, but produce a pale and diffused light. But he considers the whole as properly divisible into four genera, to one of which he also proposed to add three or four more non-descript animals, similar in their leading characters to some which Müller has disposed of without any regard to their essential distinctions.

In the genus Vorticella six or eight new species were found; and these also were ascertained to be among the animals which cause the general diffused light formerly described. A similar number was found in the genus Volvox, and equally unknown; microscopic, like the former, and in the same manner assisting in producing that kind of general phosphorescence. Two or three new species were also observed in the genus Cercaria. Others, equally minute, might be referred, as Müller has done with some corresponding animals, to other genera in the division of Infusoria; but being dissatisfied with the construction of these genera, Dr. Macculloch declines to arrange them in that manner. We can only therefore add, in terminating this list, that in this very short course of observations, amounting only to six weeks, 190 luminous species were ascertained; none of them having been observed to be luminous before, and a great number of them being undescribed animals. Those wanting to complete that number, in addition to what has already been enumerated, must be thrown into new genera: and among them is included one fish, which in itself must form a new genus.

Having thus disposed of all the invertebrate animals, of whatever nature, which have been proved to be luminous, we must inquire how far that property belongs to the fishes properly so called. In this our information is still more deficient, yet we doubt not to render it probable that it is possessed by the whole tribe. We have ourselves observed it in the conger, the gilthead, the bream, the pollack, the pilchard, the sardine, the herring, the coal-fish, the whiting, the mackerel, and the gar; a list which is only scanty, we believe, because of our want of more opportunities for observation. Many of the genus Squalus have been observed to shine at night; and the flying fish emits a pale light resembling that of the moon. The same has been observed by many persons respecting different fishes at St. Helena, but we have not been able to procure their names. In *Anburey's Travels* it is mentioned that the porpoise is luminous in the river St. Lawrence.

This is a scanty list we must admit, but it is not difficult to assign other reasons besides our own inexperience, and the neglect of those who have had better opportunities than ourselves. There is no great chance of discovering it except in those fish that are taken by the hook at night, which form but a limited number. We cannot take in the day, so as to keep and examine them as we do the marine worms, those which are only caught at that time; so that we have not much hope of discovering whether the day fish are luminous or not. But it is extremely common at night to see great flashes of light deep in the water, and these have been observed by many people. Pere Bourzes speaks of luminous vortices, as he calls them; a phenomenon which we have no doubt are like the flashes of light produced by the motion of large fish. That this is really the fact in the pilchard, the herring, and the coal-fish, we have ascertained; but it is very seldom possible to conjecture what fish are swimming alongside at night, and equally difficult to take them.

Thus far, however, the fact is ascertained of a sufficient number, to render it probable that it exists in all; particularly when the purposes for which it seems to have been intended are recollected. On that we shall offer a few remarks immediately. A question may indeed arise here, which we cannot easily solve, except on the same grounds of utility; of a purpose to be served by the phosphorescent powers of fishes. As we have already shown that the general luminous effect produced by the microscopic marine animals was excited by agitation, it might be conceived that when a large fish seems to emit light, that may exist in the water around it, and not in the animal, and that it is only caused to appear in consequence of his motion. We can only answer this doubt by saying, that the fact might be ascertained without risk of error, if fishes were thus found luminous when no such animals were present; and it is to be hoped that future naturalists, paying hereafter more attention to this subject than they have hitherto done, may so ascertain it. In the mean time, if it is really a useful, and even a necessary, property to all marine animals, as we hope immediately to show, we may be very well assured that nature would not have trusted it to chance in this manner. We shall also presently show that it proceeds from a voluntary act on the part of the fish, and with an obvious design; a further metaphysical argument, in defect of better physical ones, to prove that it is a property of the animal, because that act indicates consciousness.

But as on this part of the subject we can now proceed no further for want of more facts, we shall terminate it by remarking, that the property of emitting light, so far from being inherent in the water of the sea, belongs to its inhabitants; and that so far also from being limited to a few species of marine worms or insects, it is in all probability extended to every inhabitant of the ocean.

We have already shown that, in the invertebrate animals, this property seems to be under the guidance of the will, even more than it is in the glow-worm. None of them are perpetually luminous,—all of them are occasionally, and, as it appears to us, capriciously so; irritation or alarm excites it in all at first; yet when that is repeated they extinguish themselves, and nothing can excite them again to display their light until they chuse to do it. Such an alarm, in fact, both causes them to show their light and to withhold it; and that unquestionably from certain designs or reasonings, or instincts, on the part of the animal, the purposes of which do not seem difficult to comprehend. In the larger fishes, the same effort of will produces similar effects. If fish are swimming alongside, it will be perceived that they sometimes show light, and at others not. If an alarm be excited, it is immediately displayed, although but for a moment. But the most remarkable effect of this kind may be witnessed by striking on the bottom or gunwale of a boat when among a shoal of herrings or pilchards, probably of all other fish. In an instant the whole sea exhibits one broad flash of bright light, producing a most splendid appearance. This is again in a moment extinguished, but is renewed on repeating the same alarming sound. We noticed this circumstance slightly before, in inquiring about the seat of the light in this case, and may now add, that as we have seen this effect produced when we could not excite it ourselves in the same manner by the oars, we think there is no reason to doubt that it is the property of the fish itself, and not of the surrounding water.

If now, as we have thus attempted to prove, no marine animal, be its species or nature what it may, has yet been fairly examined for this purpose without being found possessed of phosphorescence; and if, as is probable. it is therefore extended to the whole of these uncountable races of beings, while it is also under the control of their wills, it is worth our while to inquire what purpose is served by this very singular provision, or what, in ancient phraseology, is the final cause of this arrangement. That it is destined for wise ends, we have no reason to doubt; nor do we think it difficult to show what these are. If we have taken a correct view of them, we cannot sufficiently admire the resources of nature, who, in depriving so large a portion of her dependent creatures of the light of the sun, has compensated for that loss by a power derived from their own internal resources.

While the property of emitting light is, among the land animals, confined to a very few insects; in the ocean, it is not only extended to very many, probably to every individual that exists, but in the latter, the superiority in numbers of the different races is such that while, in a few climates, the twinkle of an insect is occasionally seen, the nocturnal darkness of the immense ocean is illuminated by its inhabitants. Though, among the former, we have not yet succeeded in discovering the uses of this provision, we may be sure that they are very partial; while in the latter they must be such as are alike interesting to the whole; and without which the business of life could not be carried on. These ends are mutual communication: as far as the wants of these animals are concerned; this light is a substitute for that of the sun; and as their great and hourly wants are mutual self-preservation, or, alternately, prey and defence, so by these lights they are guided to each other for attack; while, by their power of obscuring them, they are also furnished with the means of resisting it. Betraying their existence by their light, they become the object of pursuit to their enemies; while nature, providing them at the same time with the means of quenching it, has given to them those compensating powers which, in the article of defences, she has in some manner or other bestowed on all her creation.

The great business of fishes, as it has sometimes jestingly been said, is to eat each other, and a great part of it must be carried on in the dark, or, at least, without the light of the sun. From the experiments of Monsieur Bouguer, it has been deduced that the transmission of light through sea-water is diminished in a ratio so rapid, that at the depth of 723 feet it ceases to be transmitted any longer. Now, we do not think that the method adopted by this philosopher was a correct one, or capable of determining this question. But as the general principle is unquestionable, we are willing to allow 1000 feet instead of 723; and it will immediately be seen that the main purpose of our argument will not be affected though we should adopt a still higher limit. At some depths, therefore, and that probably not very great, there is absolute and perpetual darkness. But fishes are not thus limited to the surface or near it, or even to depths of a thousand fathoms, much less to one of as many feet. There does not indeed seem to be any limit of depth for the habitable ocean. Innumerable fishes are known to reside, to

breed, and to prey, in regions to which light can never penetrate. This is the case in particular with the pelagie fish, which form in themselves numerous tribes. It would indeed be a strange supposition were we to imagine that the dark regions of the sea were uninhabited. In Captain Ross's voyage, shrimps were brought up by the sounding line from depths of 1300 feet; and other animals of various kinds were found in the same manner at 6000. It is difficult to prove this fact in many particular instances, because soundings seldom extend very deep, nor do fishermen fish at great depths. The greater number of our own seas are shallow; and it is the character of some of our principal fish to frequent the banks, or shoaler parts, where woods grow, and where they probably find their prey. Besides this, it is tedious and expensive to fish in deep water. But we can quote one positive fact to this purpose. It is the habit of the ling to frequent the deep valleys of the sea, while the cod, like many others, resides on the hills, or banks, as they are commonly called. In the Shetland seas, one of the most productive spots for this fish, is a valley about 1200 feet deep, bounded on each side by hills that must be nearly precipitous; since, in sounding, the water suddenly deepens from 20 and 30 to 200 fathoms. In this place, as well as in others, where this kind of fishery is carried on, it is found that the best fishing exists at the greatest depths; nor is it unusual to sink the long lines in water of 250 fathoms deep. But the time required for setting and drawing up from this depth, the enormous length of line that is used, is so great as to prevent the fishermen from making any attempts in deeper water; but they are all of opinion that this fish abounds most in the deepest places, and might advantageously be fished for at much greater depths. Thus the ling, for one, is proved to reside in places which must be perpetually dark, although we were to double M. Bouguer's estimate of the point of non-transmission.

But so far we have only examined the one-half of this question. It is perfectly known to fishermen that many species, which, in summer, frequent the shallow seas, apparently for the purpose of spawning chiefly, retire to the great depths in winter; and, as these persons suppose, to avoid the cold. The regions of darkness seem to be their proper residence; while, like the salmon and other migratory fishes, they are merely visitors in those of light. But, besides this, a very large proportion of all the fishes of the sea only preys by night, while there are some that do so by day, and others are ready for their food at all times. In the polar regions, and in the depths of winter, there can for a long period be no light in the sea, whatever faint glimmering the atmosphere, the planets, or the aurora, may yield for the inhabitants of the land. Yet here many fishes, and most conspicuously, some of the whales and the sword-fish, have their perpetual residence. These animals can have no light for a long time, particularly in their deep waters, unless they find it in their own bodies or in that of their prey. The food of the great whale, consisting of various insects and worms, very commonly shrimps, such as the Cancer oculatus, resides at the bottom as well as on the top of the sea; and there cannot, therefore, be any doubt that, even in summer, but most assuredly in winter, it feeds in regions that are inaccessible to light.

Our readers may now see the conclusions, which we are inclined to draw respecting the final cause or purpose of this property of phosphorescence in fishes. It is necessary to their general intercourse, and indispensibly so in those particular cases just mentioned. Without it, in the deeper seas they would be unable to discover their prey at any time ; nor, in our shallower ones, could they do so at night. Whatever diminution of light is felt by us during that period, must, in a far greater degree, be experienced in the sea, even at small depths. Without such a provision, all intercourse between fishes must cease in the night ; whereas we know that it is then often most active. We do not, however, mean to say, that the light of fishes supplies the place of the sun, or that it is intended to produce a general illumination of these obscure regions. The main purpose of it seems to be, to indicate the presence of the object which forms the prey, to point out where the pursuit is to be directed. For that reason it seems to be particularly brilliant and decided in those inferior animals which, from their astonishing powers of reproduction, and from a state of feeling apparently little superior to that of vegetables, appear to have been in a great measure created for the supply and food of the more perfect kinds. Thus also it is diffused through every, even the minutest animalcula, as all these seem in their turns to be destined to the same end, among others ; mutual enjoyment and mutual destruction.

It is also not improbable that the light which fishes possess enables them to discover their own food, or to guide themselves, as well as to betray themselves to their enemies. We might conclude this from the effect which any alarm produces in causing them to display their powers, as if it was for the purpose of discovering danger. This may be observed even in the most minute ; but it is extremely remarkable in the larger fishes, as we formerly noticed respecting the pilchard and the herring. Unfortunately we can never become very intimately acquainted with this department of creation ; and must, therefore, be content to draw our conclusions in the best manner that we can.

We must now recal to our readers' minds the remarks which we made at the beginning of this subject respecting the phosphorescence of dead fishes. We have no doubt that the object of it is the same ; namely, to point these out as a prey to others. By this means they are not only removed, so as to prevent the inconveniences which would arise from their putrefaction, as terrestrial animals are by birds and beasts of prey, but they serve the purpose of food to numbers. It is worthy of notice, too, that this phosphorescence immediately succeeds death, while it precedes putrefaction ; so that the dead animal becomes of as much use as the living one would have been. Surely such a provision is not casual ; and most probably its objects are those which we have here stated. It is in the same way also that we must probably explain the desire which fishes show to follow light at night ; a feeling which is turned to account by fishermen in many well known instances, and which might probably be used still more extensively with advantage. That they are then in pursuit of an imaginary prey, can admit of little doubt.

Such, then, are our opinions respecting the uses of the phosphorescent property in fishes. We had imagined them new and peculiar to ourselves for some time, till we found a passage, not, however, in the writings of a naturalist, which seems to prove that he at least, if not others in his day, had entertained something like the same notions on this subject. In his well known collection of Poesies, called the Mistress, Cowley compares his fair one when bathing to a luminous fish, and insinuates at the same time the purpose for which these lights are hung out. The simile

is among the most outrageous ; but it will not much alarm those who are accustomed to the writings of the metaphysical poets.

> " The fish around her crowded, as they do
>   To the false light which treacherous fishes show."

As there can be no doubt, from the various preceding remarks, that the light of all these animals is under the control of the will, it is a proper object of inquiry how this matter is managed. Here, however, we are fully as much at a loss as in the case of the luminous terrestrial insects. The whole question of its cause, its seat, and its chemical nature, is equally obscure ; and till these are explained, it is almost useless to think of the manner in which it is either exerted or controlled.

Professor Smith, in Captain Tuckey's voyage, thinks he ascertained that, in a certain crab which he examined, the seat of the light was in the brain. That is possible ; but we are much more inclined to imagine that there is a special organ provided for this purpose, wherever it is confined to a limited space ; as it is in many of the worms, and among others in the Medusæ and the Beroes, as well as in the shrimps and other insects. We have always observed that in these it occupies a single spot, often very small in proportion to the size of the animal, but we have in vain endeavoured to discover what that was. In some of the larger Beroes and Medusæ, we could distinctly ascertain at night, by the feel, that the luminous point was at the anterior or rounded end. Yet, on examining the same place by the light, we could discover no peculiar organization where it could have resided, as the whole substance was alike transparent. Yet we still think, from some observations, that it resides in the stomach or intestine ; an opinion farther confirmed by observing that in the shrimps also it lies within the thorax, and probably equally in that organ. We are persuaded that Professor Smith mistook this for the brain. But we must leave this point for future investigations. In the larger fishes, however, it occupies the whole surface of the skin ; and hence it is that they show a general diffused and faintish light, while the various invertebrate animals exhibit distinct and defined sparks.

This much respecting the seat of the light, which, however, gives us no assistance towards explaining how it is controlled by the will. But we must, for the present, be content with our ignorance ; nor have we any great reason to be surprised at it, if all the naturalists that have laboured this subject, with an abundance of specimens, and the most ample means of investigation, arising from the vitality of the animal, and the facility with which it can be preserved and examined alive in any manner, have as yet been unable to determine this point for the glow-worm.

We have last to inquire, respecting the phosphorescent substance itself, if substance it be, and its chemical nature. Here it appears to us that we are in a state of absolute ignorance ; no less so than in the phosphorescent terrestrial insects. Those who have published their experiments on this subject, have, in the first place, assumed that the phosphorescent matter of the dead animal was the only thing to be examined ; a conclusion which we think by no means warranted. It may possibly be so, but that is not necessary. As far as our own trials go, we have been able as yet to devise no method of getting at the phosphorescent matter in the living animal. The experiments of Dr. Hulme on the luminous substance of the dead fishes are worthless, and lead to no information. Those of M. Dessaignes have an air of more accurate research, and there is in them a principle of proceeding. We shall barely record them, without pretending to decide on their accuracy ; because, even if they are correct, we consider that we are as far as ever from the cause of phosphorescence in living fishes.

A piece of phosphorescent fish was put into a saline solution favourable to the production or maintenance of this property, but which had previously been deprived of its air by ebullition. After two hours the substance became dull, or lost its light. But on introducing a bubble of air, the phosphorescence was restored in a few minutes, and this effect was continued as long as fresh bubbles were introduced, and till the water was perfectly saturated with air, when it remained permanently bright. He considers it, therefore, as a true combustion ; and, as in the phosphorescence of rotten wood, he thought that carbonic acid was produced, so phosphoric acid must have been the result in this case.

We shall conclude this part of our subject with one remark, not less important as a question in natural history and in animal physiology generally, than it is on the subject of the final cause of the phosphorescence of marine animals as we have already stated it. Like all that has preceded, we are indebted for it to Dr. Macculloch.

It might be objected to this view of the final causes, that, although the larger or true fishes, and the insects of the sea, are provided with organs of vision, a very large part of the maritime creation has none, and could not therefore profit by the light. Assuredly there is no appearance of eyes, nor indeed of organs of any sense at all, in numerous genera ; and, in particular, of those commonly called worms or vermes, whether these are naked or the inhabitants of shells. Nor have we any doubt that there are many animals in the sea which have no use for light nor any concern with it. Yet, that some of these imperfect animals have the means of seeing or feeling light, if we may chose to term it so, without appearing to be furnished with any special provision for that purpose, seems fully proved by the experiments of the observer above mentioned. He convinced himself by many trials, that some of the Beroes and the Medusæ, when confined in a glass at night, were attracted by the light of a candle. In one large Beroe this was so remarkable, that the animal could be conducted by the light in a circular direction round the glass for any length of time, while its motions could be reversed by changing that of the candle. In this case it always presented the anterior extremity, yet there is no organ of any kind situated there, any more than in the Medusæ. In fact, this genus, like the Medusæ, seems to possess no organs of any kind but the stomach and the swimming machinery. It was impossible to try this experiment on the smaller tribes with any chance of success, so that these trials were necessarily limited to a few species. Yet it is highly probable that a similar sense is widely diffused among the analogous animals, since all have the same habits and wants, and that they all affect the light of day, is most evident from their invariably swimming near the surface, except when atmospheric changes drive them below. In a physiological view, we need have no objections to the existence of this power. The eye is an optical machine, intended to produce an image ; but light alone may be perceived by an arrangement of nerves, similar to that of the retina, so

that the perception of light, which is all that is here contended for, may as well belong to the Medusæ and Beroes as to any other animals provided with a nervous system.

Phosphorescence of Vegetables.

We know not of any authentic instance of a luminous appearance arising from living vegetables which can be referred to phosphorescence. It is true that some authors have seen, or imagined, that the tuberose, and one or two other flowers, give out a light, under peculiar circumstances, at the moment of their expansion, which some have referred to this cause, and which others have attributed to electricity. But the instances of this occurrence are as yet so rare, that although we have no reason to distrust the accuracy of the reporters, we are in no condition to reason on this phenomenon ; if, indeed, it belongs to the division of luminous appearances under review.

In wood, under certain states of decay, however, this phenomenon is known to every school-boy. Yet neither the peculiar circumstances requisite for its production, nor the cause of the light, have been satisfactorily ascertained. Neither is it well known to how many kinds of wood it is limited, or whether, if the same kind of decay can be produced, it may not occur in all. In the soft woods, such as willow, hazel, and birch, it appears, at any rate, to be most frequent. It has also been observed in the sugar-cane. When wood is thus luminous on decay, it is spongy and somewhat moist, being also very tender, of a white colour, and often stained with green and blue tints, that seem to be the result of some process of fermentation similar to that which, in so many vegetables, produces indigo. This effect is, however, transitory, and it appears to be limited to some very particular stage of the progress of decay, as it seldom lasts above two or three days. M. Dessaignes considers that humidity and the contact of air are both necessary, and that the effect does not take place unless the temperature is 8° or 10° of the centigrade thermometer. The light is extremely pale and gentle, with a slight bluish tinge, and is not very unlike to that which is given out by dead fish in their luminous stage. It is accompanied by no smell, or any heat, and the cause has as yet eluded the investigations of chemists. Yet the same author thinks that a chemical combination is going on, analogous to that by which lime unites to water, in which light is, in the same manner, generated.

As analogous to this, we must consider the light that is sometimes yielded by peat, which we have observed in the Highlands of Scotland, but which has not been noticed by authors, except by Dr. Macculloch in his Account of the Western Islands. This also appears to be a transitory light ; and, from that cause, as well as from its minuteness in size, and its feebleness, it may easily escape observation. We have only found it in that kind of fine and smooth naked peat so common in wet mountains, which occupies these deep channels and cuts, well known to sportsmen as well as mountaineers, for the impediments they produce in wandering over such regions. It is not even visible at the ordinary distance of the eye from the ground, but may be seen by close inspection. We have never found it otherwise than in small spots, not exceeding the head of a pin in size, and of a dark blue colour, resembling that of burning sulphur. At first we had imagined these lights were produced by some minute luminous animal, and were only convinced of our error by a careful microscopic examination. Respecting the cause we have no conjectures to offer.

These cases, according to M. Dessaignes' theory, must both equally proceed from a species of combustion in which water and carbonic acid are formed. Wood loses half its weight during the process; and, according to him, though not at first extinguished in airs that contain no oxygen, it at length ceases. It is also destroyed by boiling water, and ceases at the freezing temperature.

Miscellaneous Sources of Phosphorescence.

We have been obliged to adopt this division for the purpose of including some luminous appearances that do not well fall under any of the other heads, but which, for want of more knowledge, have been classed under this sweeping term. In all, the causes are as obscure as in any of the instances already pointed out, and more inexplicable they need not be.

The case of white sugar is universally known, and its phosphorescence is extremely brilliant, while it is excited by a very moderate friction. In the breaking of the lumps by the common nippers, it is extremely familiar, and it is also readily excited by rubbing two lumps together. No smell is yielded, nor does any circumstance occur by which we can be led to conjecture the cause or real nature of the light.

In one instance, not long since, a light analogous to phosphorescence was observed to be produced by ice. This happened in Switzerland, when the Glacier of the Weisshorn fell. As it struck on the valley below, a bright light was given out, respecting which there could be no mistake, as it was witnessed by many persons. It was suggested that this might be either electrical or phosphoric, but we are rather inclined to rank it under the latter head. More facts of the same nature are however required, since this is, as yet, as far as we know, a solitary case.

It is well known that the skunk, (*Viverra putatoria*,) the zorrillo of the Spaniards, which inhabits South America, has the power of discharging, to a distance of six feet or more, its urine, as a means of defence against its pursuers. This liquid is so peculiarly offensive as to exceed in that respect all things that can possibly be imagined. It is at the same time so acrid as to inflame the skin, and produce a sensation of burning, which lasts for many hours. Azara, who improperly calls this animal Yagouaré, since Jaquar is the American leopard, says, that when this secretion is discharged in the dark, it is phosphorescent. Whatever the cause may be in this case, it is not likely that it will soon be investigated more narrowly.

According to M. Dessaignes, whose experiments on this subject are very numerous, it was found that glass and porcelain shone when heated to a temperature of 325° of the centigrade thermometer, as we also notice under the head of mineral phosphorescence. The same happens with respect to many of the alkaline or earthy salts, but at different degrees of temperature. In some of the metallic oxides, provided they be in a vitrified state, and also in some of the metallic salts, it equally occurs. Among these we may enumerate the sulphate and muriate of soda and of potash, the metallic phosphates, nitrate of lime, and sulphurate of lime, the last familiarly known as the phosphorescent substance of Canton's phosphorus.

The phenomena presented by this latter substance are somewhat remarkable, and require a little additional notice. It shines equally whether it has been exposed to the light of the sun, or to any of the coloured rays of the prism, or to the light of the moon, or that of a lamp. Most other substances which shine by absorbing light require that of the sun.

The property of phosphorescing by the application of heat, has also been observed in some vegetable and animal substances; and we have thought fit to separate these cases from the former, as appearing to be of a different nature, and to proceed from a different cause.

If linseed oil be heated to 125° of the centigrade thermometer, although that should be in a vacuum or under water, it becomes luminous; but when the light ceases, it does not recover again in the same circumstances. If it be heated in the open air to the boiling point, or near it, a very bright light is produced. This, however, appears to be of a different nature, since it is extinguished by carbonic acid and restored by the access of atmospheric air. The first appears to be a simple phosphorescence, similar to that of mineral substances; whereas the latter is probably a species of combustion, analogous to the slow burning of phosphorus.

Mr. Heinrich, one of the latest writers on this subject, has remarked, that many other vegetable substances became phosphorescent by exposure to light. His method was, to remain himself in a perfectly dark room for half an hour or more, and to expose the substances under experiment to the light of the day for about ten seconds, taking care not to expose them to the rays of the sun, in order to prevent them from being heated. They were then observed in the dark chamber, where his eyes had become sensible to the least quantity of light. With respect to woods, he found those of hot climates more luminous than those of our own. The wood of the hazel was amongst those which displayed the most of this property. Cotton was very feebly phosphorescent, as were most dried plants; and he found that paper and linen, or other bleached vegetable matters, were more luminous than the same substances in a natural state.

With respect to animal matter, he found many to be phosphorescent in which this property had not before been suspected. Such of the harder substances of this nature as contained carbonate of lime, were observed to possess this quality in a higher degree than those which contained the phosphate. Thus, egg shells, corals, and the shells of fish, gave a more striking light than bones. Other vegetable and animal substances, which did not phosphoresce in exposure to light, acquired that property by being cooled or heated. Thus, flesh, tendons, bones, and the yolks of eggs, became luminous after drying or burning; and the same was observed with regard to toasted cheese. Among vegetable matters, coffee, pease, chesnuts, and other substances, became also phosphorescent after roasting.

We remarked above, that a light had been observed on the falling of a glacier, and that it was questioned whether it was of an electrical nature, or to be referred to this class of phenomena. As Mr. Heinrich has remarked that ice phosphoresces on exposure to light, it is probable that these appearances are both of the same nature. He remarked also in this case, that heat augmented the intensity and diminished the duration of the light, and that cold had a contrary effect. In no case did he succeed in causing transparent fluids to shine.

In Dessaignes' experiments we find no fluid recorded as phosphorescent but linseed oil; and, in Mr. Heinrich's, this branch of the subject has also, as we have this moment seen, been passed by. Here Dr. Brewster assists us with a catalogue by which we may enlarge this enumeration of the miscellaneous phosphorescences, for the present; as we are unable to do much towards generalizing or arranging them, for want of a sufficient number of substances, exhibiting this property, to admit of an useful classification. His experiments were performed by heating the different fluids on a hot iron, in the manner practised with the minerals that were thus treated.

Saliva, the white of egg diluted in water, and the solution of isinglass, were thus found to be phosphorescent. So was a solution of soap, and also one of rhubarb; there appearing to be little analogy between any of these except the saliva and the solution of albumen. Oil of olives, like the linseed oil in M. Dessaignes' trials, was found to be possessed of the same property, as was the essential oil of Dill. The phosphorescence of tallow was so obvious as to be visible in extinguishing a candle. Of saline solutions he found those of common salt, nitre, and alum, to be luminous; and it is probable that this catalogue might be considerably extended. Lastly, alcohol exhibited a beautiful light on the heated iron, on which *it never inflames*, but it is probable that this is an instance of slow combustion, analogous to that of phosphorus, and resembling the second kind of light, which is shown by linseed oil, when it is heated up to near the boiling point.

But we must terminate this part of our subject, on which much information is still wanted, and proceed to consider the phosphorescence of mineral substances.

Phosphorescence of Minerals.

That phosphorescence was a property belonging to various minerals, had long been known; but it was not till the experiments of Dessaignes in France, and those of Dr. Brewster in our own country, that we were acquainted either with the numerous circumstances by which it is excited or modified, or with the minerals in which it exists. But as those of the former philosopher apply chiefly to general principles, affecting not only minerals but many other substances, we shall reserve an account of them for the end of this article, except where they may particularly apply to any of the cases now to be mentioned.

Dr. Brewster thinks that the phosphorescent property of minerals was first remarked by the noted Benvenuto Cellini. In his essays on *Orificeria*, he says, that he had seen a carbuncle (garnet) shine in the dark, and that one of these stones had been found near Rome by means of the light which it emitted in the night. Mr. Boyle, some time after this, observed that a diamond emitted a light in the dark, equal to that of a glow-worm, either when heated or rubbed, or sometimes when simply pressed. Other authors have remarked, that a diamond acquired this property only in consequence of a previous exposure to the sun's rays; while many persons have repeated the same experiment without success. In our own trials, we have been uniformly unsuccessful; and it has now indeed been observed, that a very few diamonds only are possessed of this property; although, by what particular circumstances in the crystallization or aspect of the stone it is indicated, is not yet known. But this is equally true of many other minerals; since, among the tremolites, for example, where the eye can trace no reason for the difference, some are found to phosphoresce and others not. In consulting the subjoined list, therefore, which we have borrowed from

Dr. Brewster, (*Edin. Phil. Journal*, vol. i. p. 383.) it is necessary to remember this circumstance; lest an inaccuracy should be suspected in the reporter. With regard to this very mineral, tremolite, nothing can be more notorious, or generally believed, than that it phosphoresces by friction; yet among the numerous specimens we have examined from Glen Tilt, we have never yet in one instance observed it.

That the diamond and garnet have been long observed to possess this property, is probable from the occasional mention of them that is made in the Oriental tales. The dark subterranean caverns of the genii and enchanters, are often lighted by carbuncles; and the diamond which Saad took out of the fish that he had caught, serves his household for a lamp. So general a belief must have had a foundation; and, indeed, if we examine all the phenomena described in these tales, which are not absolutely extramundane and supernatural, we shall find them all founded on facts, exaggerated and inverted.

The minerals which phosphoresce on friction are far less numerous than those which exhibit the same property when heated. We have already mentioned the diamond and the garnet, although we have ourselves succeeded with neither. But the phosphorescence of quartz on friction or collision, is very remarkable and lively; while it is also attended with a peculiar smell, as if some combustion took place. It was once imagined that it produced black globules on being thus treated; but that ultimately proved to be a fallacy. We already mentioned the occasional phosphorescence of tremolite, and in some cases, it is such as to be excited even by a feather; while, in many more, it cannot be produced at all. In the harder crystalline minerals, the friction or the abrasion produced by a file, is necessary to excite the light; while, in some, it is only discovered by pounding them in a mortar. We have observed it to take place in the carbonate of lime, provided the surfaces are rough, and the force considerable; but, in making experiments with rocks, it is necessary to take care that we are not misled by the presence of particles of quartz.

The phosphorescence of minerals by heat is well known, with regard to fluor spar at least, as it is the substance commonly exhibited for this purpose at popular lectures. Mr. Wedgewood was among the first to enlarge the list of minerals in which it existed. His experiments were performed by reducing the substance under trial to powder, and strewing it on a plate of iron heated just below the visible redness, and removed into a dark place. In this way he found that this property was possessed by the following substances, namely:—

Fluor spar	Marbles
Red felspar	Diamond
Ruby	Calcareous (Iceland) spar
Steatite	Flint (black)
Rock crystal	Asbestos
Red ferruginous mica	Alabaster.

To which list Haüy afterwards added;

Arragonite	Apatite
Tremolite	Carbonate of barytes
Carbonate of strontian	Harmotome
Dipyre	Wernerite.

But Dr. Brewster's experiments have materially enlarged this list; so that the property of phosphorescence, used by Haüy as one of the distinguishing characters for minerals, has almost ceased to be of any use in this respect. If Dr. Brewster has thus deprived mineralogists of one of their convenient empirical marks, he has conferred a greater benefit on them by preventing them from deceiving themselves by trusting to it. In some of these experiments, he followed nearly the same plan, namely, that of placing a fragment of the mineral in question on a hot iron, and then carrying it into a dark room. When the light was not perceptible in this manner, the fragment was placed in a pistol-barrel, which was then heated to a point short of redness, and the phosphorescence observed by looking down the bore. On other occasions, the barrel was first heated, and when the red heat was gone, the mineral was introduced into it, and examined in the same manner.

We extract from his communications on this subject, the following table, where the results are exhibited in a condensed form.

Minerals.	Colour of Minerals.	Colour of the Light.
Fluor Spar, . .	Pink.	Green.
Do. Do. . .	Purple.	Bluish.
Do. Do. . .	Bluish White.	Blue.
Compact, do. .	Yellowish.	Fine Green.
Sandy, do. . .	White.	White sparks.
Calcareous Spar, .	Yellow.	Yellow.
Do. Do. .	Transparent.	Yellowish.
Limestone, Irish, secondary,	White.	Yellowish Red.
Apatite, . . .	Pink.	
Arragonite, . .	Dirty White.	Reddish Yellow.
Carbonate of Barytes,	Whitish.	Pale White.
Harmotome, . .	Colourless.	Reddish Yellow.
Dipyre, . . .	White.	Specks of Light.
Tremolite—Glen Tilt,	Do.	Yellow.
Do. Cornwall,	Do.	Bluish.
Topaz—Aberdeenshire,	Blue.	Do.
Do. Brazil, .	Yellow.	Faint Yellowish.
Do. New Holland,	White.	Bluish.
Rubellite, . .	Reddish.	Scarlet.
Sulphate of Lime, .	Yellowish.	Faint Light.
Do. of Barytes, .	Yellow.	Pale.
Do. Do. .	Slate colour.	Do.
Sulphate of Strontian,	Bluish.	Bright.
Do. of Lead, .	Transparent.	Faint by fits.
Anhydrite, . .	Reddish.	Faint.
Sodalite, . .	Dark Green.	Brightish.
Bitter Spar, .	Yellowish.	Faint White.
Red Silver Ore, .	Red.	Bright, flitting.
Bary Strontianite, .	White.	Faint.
Arseniate of Lead, .	Yellowish.	Bright White.
Sphene, . .	Yellow.	Do.
Mica, . . .	Greenish.	Whitish.
Do. Waygatz Strait,	Black.	White specks.
Do. Do.	Brown.	Pretty bright.
Titanium—Menachanite,	Black.	Feeble specks.
Hornstone, . .	Grey.	Yellowish.
Tafelspath, . .	Whitish.	Do.
Lazuli, . .	Blue.	Faint.
Spodumene, . .	Greenish.	Do.
Titanite—Rutile, .	Reddish.	Very Faint.
Cyanite, . .	Yellowish White.	Bluish.
Calamine, . .	Brown.	Faint.
Augite, . .	Green.	Pretty bright.
Petalite, . .	Reddish.	Bright and Blue.
Asbestos-rigid, .	Do.	Pretty bright.
Datholite, . .	Transparent.	Bright.
Corundum, . .	Brown.	Do.
Anatase, . .	Dark.	Reddish Yell. flame.
Tungsten, . .	Yellowish white.	Brilliant, like a coal.
Quartz, . .	. . .	Very faint.
Amethyst, . .	. . .	Faint.
Obsidian, . .	. . .	Dull Blue, brightish.
Mesotype. Auvergne,	. . .	Very faint.
Actinolite, . .	Observed in the pistol barrel.	Small specks.
Muriate of silver, .		Rather bright.
Red, ruby do. .		Blue.
Carbonate of copper,	. . .	Very faint.
Green telesie, .	. . .	Pale Blue, pretty br.

It was asserted by Mr. Wedgewood, that minerals could not be deprived of this property by many heatings, nor by any degree of heat. Dr. Brewster found, on the contrary, that a specimen of green fluor, which was highly phosphorescent, having been wrapped in a leaf of platina, and exposed for an hour to the heat of a common fire, lost not only its green colour, but its power of phosphorescence, although it had not flown to pieces, as it usually does on the iron plate. Neither the ordinary rays of the sun, applied for several days, nor even the focus of a burning-glass, restored this property; and it is farther worthy of remark, that when placed on the hot iron, it no longer flew in pieces, as it always does while it possesses the phosphorescent property. We have tried the same experiment with other varieties of fluor, and with corresponding results.

We may now add to these experiments of Dr. Brewster, that we have farther observed that the phosphorescence was, in some minerals, excited by a high degree of heat when inferior ones produced no such effects. Not having had this object in view in these researches, we neglected to record the substances, having been at that time pursuing a different train of investigations. We also noticed that the phosphorescence, in some minerals, was excited with peculiar facility in melted nitre, or upon its surface when far short of a red heat. Among others, which, for the same reason, have escaped our memory, we noticed some specimens of crystalline primary limestone, of tremolite, of chlorite, and of chalcedony. In some of these cases the light was as bright as the sun, and seemed to pervade the whole of very large fragments.

M. Dessaignes has also remarked, that many minerals which shine at 200°, (centigrade,) refuse to give light when heated to a higher point; and, of course, he concludes that it is not the consequence of incandescence, as we had done from our own trials with melted nitre. He has also observed, like ourselves, that different substances require different temperatures to enable them to give out light. Thus, fluor-spar, apatite, and adularia, shine at 100° or 112°, (centigrade,) while quartz and many of the harder crystalline minerals, as well as glass and porcelain, do not give out light till they are raised to 375°. He also asserts, that, at a mean heat, or about 256°, a point easily marked by the melting of bismuth, all these phosphorescent substances become luminous.

Farther, it is remarked by the same observer, that the light yielded is in a direct ratio to the degree of temperature, but that its duration is in an inverse one. Farther, if any mineral, such as fluate of lime, which shines at a low temperature, is exposed to a higher heat, it will no longer emit light at a lower one, but will do so at a temperature still higher than the first. Dr. Brewster's experiment agrees with the first of these, and does not contradict the second. The same substance, also, being subjected several times in succession to a temperature of 300°, gave a bright light, which, at the first trial, lasted 30 seconds, at the second 15, and at the third 10. Thus the power of giving light seemed for a time gradually to diminish; but still it was not destroyed, as in fifteen more successive trials it continued of the same strength.

Farther, " vitreous bodies," including certain of the crystalline minerals, lose their phosphorescent properties with great difficulty, and not without heating them strongly for half an hour, or an hour; while the metallic substances and their salts, together with their phosphorescent oxides, lose their luminous quality immediately after they are strongly heated. Lime, barytes, strontian, alumine, magnesia, and silex, cannot be deprived of it at all. Also, if these are first heated to 100^0 or 125^0, they do not emit any light if they are afterwards placed on a hot body heated to 250°; whereas, if thrown on it cold, they shine without difficulty. The carbonates of lime, barytes, and strontian, lose their power of phosphorescing when moderately calcined; but if after that they are heated to whiteness for half an hour, they resume this property; apparently in consequence of the loss of their carbonic acid.

The power of absorbing light is not a property of all the minerals which give it out on heating. Yet it belongs to some of them. We have already observed, that it belongs to some diamonds and some garnets. It has also been observed in blende, in the cat's-eye, in apatite, in hyaline quartz, in some emeralds, in lapis lazuli, according to Brugnatelli, and, according to Beccaria, in almost all substances. The power of phosphorescing on heating appears to be most common in the imperfectly transparent minerals, and in the coloured ones; but the colour of the light has no relation to that of the mineral. It is not necessarily connected with the power of giving light by friction; and substances which have been deprived of the property of phosphorescing by heat will still yield it by attrition.

But some farther remarks on the phosphorescence produced in minerals by exposure to light are requisite, and we shall quote those of Mr. Heinrich made in the manner already mentioned.

He observed, as others had done before him, that some diamonds were phosphorescent after exposure to light, and others not; although there was nothing in their external appearance to indicate, *a priori*, what effects were to be expected. In some of these also, it was found that the light continued for a short time, while in others it was very durable. These differences were so great, as to vary from five seconds to an hour. On exposing farther the phosphorescent diamonds to the red rays of the prism, it was found that they acquired no luminous power at all; while, when exposed to the blue, a durable phosphorescence was induced.

After remarking generally, that the fluates and carbonates of lime became phosphorescent in this manner, it was observed that the luminous appearances, in all the saline combinations of lime, varied with the acid in the salt. The fluates were the most phosphorescent, and their light continued for an hour on some occasions. The carbonates were the next in point of luminous power, in intensity at least, if not in duration. The light which these emitted, was, in some instances, so clear and white, that it was possible to read by it; but it did not last more than from thirty to forty-five seconds. The sulphates were found to shine but for a short time, and very faintly, while the phosphates proved to be the most feeble of the whole. The siliceous, argillaceous, and magnesian earths were not found to phosphoresce under these circumstances; but some of their natural combinations were observed to possess this property in a very slight degree.

Dr. Brewster remarks, that the light of these phosphorescent bodies is similar to that of the sun, or any other luminous body. In the blue fluor spar, he also remarked, that the phosphorescent part of the mineral was arranged in strata or veins, parallel to certain veins diverging from a central line, by which the structure of this mineral is determined. Each of these strata emitted a distinct light, as well in colour as in intensity. Some were purple, others yellowish-green, and others, again, white; while some of them displayed no light whatever. It was also remarkable that these different strata of light were beautifully defined, and far more numerous and minute than the strata of the mineral itself seemed to be when subjected to a microscopic examination. Thus the phosphorescence of fluor detects a structure which could not be discovered in any other manner.

The same philosopher discovered, that in the Brazilian topaz, the colour was often of a fine orange, and that, in many cases, the external parts were phosphorescent, while the nucleus, or internal ones, displayed no light whatever. In general, it was also most brilliant in the outer laminæ; but, in other instances, again, the light was brightest in the laminæ between the nucleus and the outer parts of the crystal. In one specimen, a faint phosphorescence appeared and vanished at intervals in the nucleus, while the outer parts shone with a bright and steady lustre [*]. The singularity of all these facts serves to teach us that we have yet much to learn on this subject, and to point it out as one that requires to be thoroughly examined, in the hopes that some more general laws may be established, such as to lead to a more satisfactory knowledge of its nature than we yet possess.

M. Dessaignes has also remarked, that the light of phosphorescent bodies is decomposed by the prism like ordinary light. He thinks that it is of a blue colour in all the phosphorescent bodies which do not contain metallic oxides, and that it may be rendered so when bodies which yield light of other colours are forced from them. Thus, if phosphate of lime from bones, which has a yellow light, the Spanish apatite, which shows a green one, and the green fluor, the light of which is also green, be freed from their iron by means of muriatic acid, they all yield blue lights.

The phosphorescence of minerals is proved to be independent of combustion, because it is not affected by immersing them in various gases. Lime, farther, is very luminous in dry, and very dull in damp weather; and, in general, the substances which attract moisture strongly, do not shine except when they are united to a quantity of water less than that which would saturate them; but it is not necessary that they should be totally deprived of it. If lime, strontian, and barytes, are thrown on sulphuric acid in a dry state, they do not phosphoresce, nor are they immediately dissolved. But if the breath, or a moist vapour, be applied, they immediately phosphoresce, and are, at the same time, dissolved. But we dare not pursue this curious subject farther without the hazard of far transgressing our limits.

General Observations on Phosphorescence.

We must now take notice of some particulars belonging to this class of phenomena which could not

---

[*] Dr. Brewster has remarked, that none of the Mesotypes or Needlestones, including *Natrolite* and *Thomsonite*, are phosphorescent by heat, excepting the Auvergne mesotype.

well have been included under any of the preceding heads.

M. Dessaignes, after saying, what we willingly admit, that the phosphorescence of mineral substances is not affected by the nature of the gases in which they are placed, goes on to remark, that the light emitted by vegetable and animal bodies is increased in oxygen, and disappears in hydrogen, azote, and carbonic acid. With respect to the insects, we have already said, that the contrary has appeared the case to many accurate chemists, and the same is the fact respecting the marine luminous animals. It is easy to commit errors in this case by adopting an hypothesis, because these luminous bodies lose their light after a short time, in whatever air they are confined.

M. Dessaignes conceives that he has established a certain relation between electricity and phosphorescence; and we shall here select a few of his most remarkable facts. Some of them, however, do not appear to us to bear much on the subject of this connection or analogy, or by whatever name it is to be called. Among the " metallic powders," those of zinc and antimony are the most phosphorescent, and those of gold and silver are least so. In a damp state of the atmosphere, all these, as well as the metallic oxides, lose their luminous qualities. Even in dry weather, antimony loses its power of phosphorescing, if it be rubbed in a metallic mortar; whereas, in an insulated vessel, the light is very much increased. If glass be pounded in dry weather, it is far more luminous than when this is done in a damp state of the air. In wet linen, it loses that property entirely; but it is not deprived of it, like antimony, by being bruised in a metallic mortar; because it is, in a certain sense, self-insulated. Adularia, that it may phosphoresce briskly, must be pounded in an insulated or insulating mortar; and, in all these cases, the handle of the pestle should also be an insulating substance. If, farther, glass be " calcined" till its phosphorescence is diminished, it resumes that property by being exposed on an insulated support, and subjected to a few electrical discharges, or to a current of electrical matter. The same method succeeds with any other substances that have lost their luminous property by similar treatment. It is also remarked, that electricity does not succeed in restoring the phosphorescence of those substances that have been deprived of it by the light of the sun.

From numerous experiments made on phosphorescent substances exposed to that light, this philosopher is of opinion that those which are imperfect conductors of electricity are all susceptible of the luminous property, from the action of the solar rays; that non-conductors shine imperfectly, or not at all; and that most conductors give no light whatever. Orpiment, and some of the oxides of arsenic, tin, zinc, and lead, are, however, exceptions to this rule; as are the muriate of tin, and the sulphate and phosphate of lead. It appears, in addition to all this, which we confess we can reduce to nothing like an agreement with any electrical hypothesis, that there are effects of this nature even more anomalous and unintelligible. Thus the non-conductors, and the conductors which refuse to phosphoresce by feeble electrical discharges, become luminous after strong ones; while the imperfect conductors, that phosphoresce by means of weak discharges, give no light whatever if the strength of the explosions is increased. We forbear to quote any more of these experiments, partly because we can discover no conclusions to be drawn from them, and partly because we think that they require to be repeated and generalized in some other hands.

But, in support of this analogy between phosphorescence and electricity, M. Dessaignes farther observes, that the former property is affected by the presence of points. If fluor spar has the asperities that are produced by fracture, it phosphoresces with great ease, whereas the entire and smooth crystal remains dark. The same happens to carbonate of lime, adularia, apatite, emerald, and common salt.

Similar results were obtained from rough and from smooth glass. But there is another remarkable circumstance in this case, namely, that if both sides of the plate of glass thus used be rough, it becomes phosphorescent throughout; whereas, if one side be rough, and the other polished, it only shines when the former surface is in contact with the heated support.

It is still more remarkable, that the hexagonal lime spar, terminated by three faces, in which the laminæ of the primitive rhomb are placed at 45° to the axis of the prism, shines throughout its whole substance, when one of these faces is in contact with the heated body; but if the crystal be split, so that the face of the lamina be applied in the same manner, it emits no light. In a similar manner, arragonite phosphoresces when the side of the prism is laid on the heated plate, but refuses to do so if the base be placed on it. Diamonds, in the same manner, did not show any light when the sides of the primitive octohedron touched the plate, but phosphoresced in any other position.

These phenomena are assuredly interesting in a great degree; and they are, at the same time, more intelligible than the preceding. They are also confirmed by other experiments, in the phosphorescences that are excited by exposure to light, and not to heat; which seem similarly connected in some manner with the electrical susceptibilities of the same bodies.

If transparent Iceland crystal be exposed to light, it acquires very little phosphorescence, while its faces are polished; but if one of these be rendered rough, and then presented to the rays of the sun, it readily becomes luminous. In a similar manner, prismatic arragonite acquires very little light when the smooth natural crystal is exposed; but if it be broken, it easily becomes luminous, in whatever manner the fracture may have been made. Phenomena of the same kind, but less strongly marked, are observed when apatite and chrysolite are treated in a similar way. These, and similar experiments, were multiplied and repeated with diamonds, and other minerals; and the relations between the phenomena of electricity and of phosphorescence were thus rendered more evident. All the faces parallel to the primitive form were most easily and strongly electrified, but produced least phosphorescence when exposed to the rays of the sun; while the other faces, whether these were natural or artificial, formed on the edges of the lamina, were feebly electrified by friction, and soon lost their electricity; but were, on the other hand, highly phosphorescent. These results are singular and interesting; and they tend to prove what we suggested at the beginning of this article, that the term phosphorescence was a word of very vague signification, applied to phenomena distinct in their natures as in their causes, and connected by no other bond than the common property of giving light under peculiar modes of treatment.

All the bodies, nearly, that are suceptible of phosphorescence by friction, become luminous by heating, by electrization, and by exposure to light. This property is generally diminished by overheating, as is the ordinary phosphorescence of the same bodies which is excited by more moderate degrees of heat ; yet glass thus treated still emits light when rubbed by a file. The phosphorescence on friction takes place alike in all the gases, and in vacuo. Our author has an hypothesis on this subject which we do not well understand, and of which we do not see the necessity. He supposes that the phosphorescence is produced by a particular fluid, which is set in motion by light, by heat, by electricity, and by friction ; and that the process of overheating, or of long exposure to light, causes it to be dissipated. But this hypothesis will not explain how electricity restores this fluid when once lost ; nor indeed is it in any way tenable. We can only conclude, that whatever connection between the power of phosphorescence and electrization may exist, we are yet incapable of understanding its true nature ; and that it is necessary to accumulate many more facts before we can arrive at any rational determination respecting any part of this very curious subject.

Some general remarks of Mr. Heinrich, on the phosphorescence excited by exposure to light, belong also to this division of our article ; and they serve to explain a point of the subject which Dessaignes and others have left somewhat imperfect. The first relates to the duration of the light, which varies exceedingly in the different substances susceptible of this property, to whatever class of bodies they may belong. Thus, for example, while the diamond and fluor spar will continue to display their light for an hour, there is scarcely another mineral in which it lasts for a minute. No relation has been observed between the brightness and the duration of the light.

In all cases, except that of the diamond, where light is emitted by minerals, it is white ; and this result is not altered, whether they are caused to shine in consequence of the white light of the sun or the day, or by exposure to the coloured rays of the prism. Although the direct rays of the sun have greater power in exciting the luminous action, than the light of day only, long exposure to these is injurious, as, by exciting heat in the substance, it diminishes the phosphorescent power. The white substances are more active in their powers of yielding light than the coloured ones, and this property also diminishes as we approach nearer to the darkest or black substances. Immersion in water does not extinguish the light of bodies that are in the act of emitting it ; nor is any very sensible difference produced by change of temperature.

In cases of exposure to heat, we formerly remarked, that the whole substance throughout was luminous ; and the same was observed in those experiments where the phosphorescence was excited by light. Grooves being cut deeply into the substances when in a luminous state, it was observed to be emitted by the deepest of these as strongly as by the surface. Mr. Heinrich has also remarked, in confirmation of Dessaignes's observations, that, in some cases, polishing destroyed the phosphorescent quality in those substances which were luminous when rough, while in others the light was only diminished.

On the subject of the phosphorescence of fluor spar from exposure to light, it has been observed by this philosopher, that, after it has ceased to be luminous, the property may be re-excited by warming it slightly,

either by the breath or by the hand. This effect may also be renewed several times after one exposure, particularly if, at each time, the temperature be slightly increased. This, however, at length ceases to act ; but the mineral then recovers its property by a fresh exposure to the light, or to the sun's rays.

It was long ago observed by Beccaria and Kircher, that if the diamond which became luminous after exposure to light was fully excited, and then covered with a coating of black wax, or any other substance capable of excluding light, it did not lose this power, but retained it for several days ; displaying its phosphorescence as soon as the coating was removed. The same happens with fluor-spar ; as well with the ordinary kinds, as with the chlorophane, the light of which is of so brilliant a green.

From all these experiments, it might be concluded, as Mr. Heinrich has done, and as many others have done before him, that the light emitted by bodies which phosphoresce from this cause, is that which they have previously absorbed. It is impossible to reconcile some of them to the electrical hypothesis of M. Dessaignes Nor is it very easy to see how this species of phosphorescence is connected with that which is excited merely by heating, and where no light is present ; although, with respect to some of the substances, the power of phosphorescing from each of these causes very nearly corresponds in energy. But, in truth, the whole subject is full of obscurity ; and, if the experiments and observations which we have thus collected and recorded from various sources, are as yet insufficient to enable us to form a theory on the subject of phosphorescence, they are, in themselves, highly interesting, as adding to our knowledge of the history of many departments of nature. By multiplying and varying such observations, and by the addition of new experiments, which it would not be difficult to suggest, we shall probably one day arrive at a method of reconciling and explaining all these phenomena, and of classing, under their proper heads, all the discordant subjects which, from mere necessity, are now included under one wide term. For farther information on this subject see—

Benvenuto Cellini, *Due Trattati dell Orificeria.*

Baldwin, *Phil. Trans.* 1676, vol. xi. p 788.

Beccaria, *De Phosphoris,* 4to. Bologna, 1744 ; see also *Phil. Trans.* 1746, p. 81.

Hulme, *Phil. Trans.* 1801.

Wedgewood, *Phil. Trans.* 1792, vol. lxxxii. p. 28, 270.

Haüy *Traité de Mineralogie,* tom. i. p. 235, 273.

Dessaignes, *Bulletin de la Soc. Philomathique,* and *Phil. Magazine.*

Dr. Macculloch, *Account of the Western Islands;* and *Quarterly Journal,* vol. xi. p. 248.

Dr. Brewster, *Edinburgh Phil. Journal,* vol. i. p. 383.; vol. ii. p. 171. ; vol. iv. p. 180.; *Transactions of Cambridge Philosophical Society,* vol. ii. ; and unpublished MSS.

Riville, *Mémoires des Sçavans Etrangers,* tom. iii. p. 267.

Heinrich, *Bibliotheque Universelle,* vol. xv. p. 247.

Maçaire, *Bibl. Universelle,* 1821.

Scoresby, *Account of the Arctic Regions,* and *Journal of a Voyage to Greenland in* 1822.

PHOSPHORUS. See CHEMISTRY, Vol. VI. p. 12.

PHOTOMETRY. See OPTICS, Vol. XV. p. 623.

PHYSICAL GEOGRAPHY.

Physical Geography.
To describe the general appearances of the earth; to trace the connexions and mutual relations of the diversified objects of which it consists; and to explain the causes, whether of a chemical or mechanical nature, which regulate the changes of form and condition they incessantly undergo, is the province of PHYSICAL GEOGRAPHY.

Outline of the subject.
In the view which we propose to give of this important branch of geography, we shall proceed, after laying before the reader a general sketch of the external appearance of the earth; to consider, 1st, Its figure, density, composition, and structure. 2dly, We shall examine the nature of the atmosphere, including under this head a summary account of the various effects, which are connected with the pressure, elasticity, and chemical agency of that great aerial fluid. 3dly, We shall describe the aqueous portion of the globe, comprehending under this department of the subject, a description of the ocean, its depth, currents, saltness in different latitudes, &c. together with an explanation of the origin and progress of springs and rivers. 4thly, We shall investigate the various physical causes which affect the climates of the different regions of the earth, so far as it depends upon temperature, humidity, or circumstances of a local nature. 5thly, We shall take a general survey of the products of vegetation, in so far as these are connected with geographical position. 6thly, We shall take a similar view of animal beings. 7thly, We shall conclude with some general observations on the changes which the earth has undergone by physical convulsions, or the gradual operation of human industry.

General view of the earth.
The beauty and magnificence of nature cease to be viewed with the interest they are fitted to excite, in the same proportion that we become familiarly acquainted with the appearances and mutual relations of her works. This indifference is not to be ascribed to any defect in the constitution of external things, but to that process of the human mind, which gradually sinks into commonness, whatever is the object of its frequent contemplation. The objects around us, infinitely diversified as they are, have been too frequently observed, and are too well known to call forth, for the most part, any other emotion than a mere perception of their existence. The slow and gradual manner in which we acquire a knowledge of the properties and habitudes of bodies, seldom exposes us to astonishment, or any of those sudden emotions which rouse the curiosity, and command the attention. Hence the extreme apathy with which we generally view the beautiful and harmonious system of things around us.

Let us only, however, conceive for a moment the surprise and delight which an intelligent being would experience, who from a distant region of the universe, should be suddenly transported to our earth, and gradually made acquainted with the endless variety of objects, which on every hand would solicit his attention. Suppose such a being, after contemplating the magnificent appearance of the starry vault, over which so many shining bodies are scattered with boundless profusion, should have his curiosity withdrawn from the heavens to the earth by the opening dawn, and the grateful approach of day. What a multitude of forms, living as well as inanimate, would on every side excite his wonder and rouse his anxious inquiry, when the sun, emerged in all his grandeur from the far-spreading ocean, and diffused over the face of things his exhaustless stream of light. The most obvious beauty that would every where strike the eye of an observer, in these circumstances, would be the verdant covering of the earth, and the ever-varying appearance of its surface, stretching on the one hand, as far as the eye can reach, into extensive and fertile plains, and bounded on the other by lofty and swelling ridges, whose inaccessible summits are covered with perpetual snow. The inequalities of the surface he would perceive to be so diversified, that seldom would he find two landscapes offering a similarity of outline. Every change of place would produce a change of prospect, and present new objects to delight and refresh the imagination.

To add to the beauty of nature, and facilitate the intercourse of social life, lakes and rivers are interspersed over the varied scene; the former collecting, and the latter carrying off the superfluous moisture of the land to the great reservoir of the ocean. In that vast collection of water, too, how much is there to fix the attention, and stimulate the inquiries of a rational being! The daily flux and reflux of its tides, its mighty currents, and unfathomable depths, at once excite our astonishment, and furnish ample materials for exercising the speculative principles of our nature. Even the air by which we are surrounded, though its particles, on account of their extreme subtilty, escape the cognizance of several of the senses, exhibits, in different conditions of its existence, qualities of so opposite a kind, that they can scarcely be conceived to belong to the same substance. In a state of cloudless serenity, for example, when it transmits unimpaired the pure light of heaven, how different is it in aspect from that gross and impenetrable haze which sometimes shrouds the face of day, and wraps in gloomy obscurity every object around us. How different, too, in a state of repose, when it moves not the bending stalk of the most delicate plant, from that powerful agent which lashes into fury the foaming billows of the deep; lays prostrate the mighty oak of the forest, and everywhere marks its destructive course with havoc and desolation.

Should our observer enter upon a more minute examination of the various objects by which he was surrounded, his curiosity would find, on every hand, abundant materials for its exercise. What a boundless field would the mineral kingdom present for examination, not only in regard to the external characters and chemical constitution of particular fossils, gems, and metals, but also in respect of their geognostic arrangement and distribution! The vegetable world furnishes a still more extensive and interesting subject for contemplation and inquiry, whether we consider the unlimited variety of external forms which it exhibits, or the wise and beautiful contrivances by which the various functions of plants are rendered conducive to their nourishment and vigour. Should we ascend a step higher in the scale of organization, and direct our researches to the living beings, which, under every conceivable form, people the earth, and the waters, and the air, what a multitude of creatures do we discover. How diversified in structure, as well as in magnitude! How different in habits and disposition! And yet how admirably are all of them suited to states of existence the most dissimilar!

Proceeding in this manner, not one part of the terraqueous fabric alone, but every production of nature, becomes the object of rational speculation. The most familiar appearances are divested of that aspect of commonness, which renders us indifferent even to things of the utmost importance, and acquire in our estimation an interest which they never before possessed. We begin to inquire in what manner, and for what purposes, the surface of the earth has come to have those elevations and depressions by which it is every where marked; to demand the origin of springs and rivers; to examine the cause of that alternate rising and falling of the waters of the ocean, denominated the tides; and to investigate the nature of the extensive changes in the atmosphere, upon which so much of our comfort depends. Nor are our inquiries confined entirely to the surface. The internal structure of the earth, as well as the depths of the ocean, must be explored; and though conjecture here must often supply the place of facts, we must be satisfied with the deductions of well-grounded analogies, when we can no longer be guided by the light of experience.

Sect. I.—*Of the Figure, Density, Composition, and Structure of the Earth.*

Difficulty of determining the true figure of the earth.

The determination of the true figure of the earth, is one of those physical problems, which, involving little difficulty when general results are sought after, require the finest resources of analysis, and the utmost nicety of observation, when they are attempted to be solved with rigid precision. Hence, though it has been known from the remotest times that the earth possessed a spherical form, it can scarce be affirmed that the efforts of the ablest mathematicians of Europe, aided by the most delicate astronomical instruments, have hitherto succeeded in ascertaining, beyond all controversy, its actual curvature.

First idea of the roundness of the earth, how suggested.

The first idea of the roundness of the earth seems to have been suggested by the varying appearances which the heavens exhibit to a spectator, at different points on its surface. It must have been perceived, at a very early period, that on advancing in the direction of the meridian, either toward the north or the south, many stars came within the field of observation, which before were unseen; while others, which at the former position obtained a considerable altitude in the heavens, ceased entirely to be visible by the change of situation. From these appearances, which were every where observed, it was easy to infer that the surface of the earth was convex. This conclusion, which was gradually strengthened by other considerations, is now so completely established by a variety of concurring phenomena, as well as by the deductions of physical science, that it no longer admits of the slightest degree of doubt.

Proofs of its globular form.

One of the most decisive proofs of this globular figure is, that the earth has been actually circumnavigated by different individuals. This enterprize, which,

in the early history of maritime discovery, was accounted extremely arduous, was first attempted about the beginning of the sixteenth century, by Ferdinand Magellan, a native of Portugal, who, though he did not live to accomplish it, at least prosecuted the undertaking to a sufficient extent to demonstrate its practicability. Since that period, the earth has been successfully sailed round, in various directions, by many distinguished navigators.

To the irresistible argument for the roundness of the earth, may be added others of a more familiar, but not less convincing kind. As ships recede gradually from the coast, for example, it is observed that the hull and lower parts of the rigging disappear first from the view, while the contrary takes place as they approach it; and that this is not owing to any indistinctness of vision, on account of the vapours which may be supposed to hang over the surface of the ocean, is demonstrated by the fact, that when the sight is aided by the telescope, we only perceive more distinctly the parts which we formerly saw without its assistance, while those which were invisible remain equally concealed from our view. Nor is a great extent of water necessary for exhibiting this convexity of its surface; since we can easily satisfy ourselves of its actual existence, by raising the head at different elevations above the surface of a smooth lake or river. It is on account of the roundness of the earth, too, that when water is to be conducted from one place to another by means of pipes, or canals, it will not flow in the direction of the apparent level, at either extremity; but a suitable allowance must, in all cases, be made for the deflection of the earth's surface, before the actual level can be obtained.

The spherical form of the earth is confirmed by other proofs of a more refined, but equally satisfactory nature. Among these we may notice the appearance of the moon, during a lunar eclipse; and the excess of the three angles of a spherical triangle, measured on the surface of the earth, above the angles of a plane triangle. The moon, which, as her monthly phases demonstrate, derives her light entirely from the sun, exhibits from time to time a partial or total obscuration of her disc, which is denominated an eclipse. This phenomenon, which only happens when her orb is fully enlightened, and when, with respect to the earth, the sun is in a quarter of the heavens diametrically opposite, is produced by the projection of the earth's shadow on the lunar disc. Now the boundary of this shadow being at no time a straight line, but always a curve, proves that the body which occasions it must possess a globular form. The other proof alluded to, drawn from the *spherical excess* of terrestrial triangles, (See Spherical Trigonometry,) could only be obtained from very extensive geodesic measurements, and only from these, too, when they were conducted by means of instruments of the most accurate and delicate graduation. Had any portion of the earth's surface been a perfect plane, nothing is more certain than that the three angles of a triangle described upon it, would have amounted exactly to two right angles; whereas, if it be spherical, it is no less demonstrable that the amount of these angles must always exceed two right angles, by an assignable quantity, or at least by a quantity which implies a certain relation between the whole surface of the sphere, and that of the triangle which is applied to it. The difference, which is entitled the spherical excess, may, in the case of small triangles, be too minute to be detected by our best instruments; but no extensive geographical survey can be carried on,

Physical
Geography.

with any degree of accuracy, without affording the most convincing proofs of its reality.

Considering all these facts and appearances, we are warranted to infer, from actual observation, that the earth is a detached body, floating in free space, and possessing a figure which approaches to that of a sphere. The true form and magnitude of this stupendous mass can only be ascertained by the deductions of geometry, from the measurement of lines traced on its surface, or the investigation of such physical phenomena as may bear upon this interesting but difficult problem.

The general figure of the earth slightly affected by the irregularities of its surface.

When our observation is confined to a small portion of the earth's surface, the irregularities which every where prevail might seem to render it impossible to detect, amidst such a multitude of hills and valleys, its real curvature; but a more enlarged view of the matter soon convinces us that these irregularities, great as they appear to be, are very insignificant in comparison of the magnitude of the globe, and affect but slightly its predominating aspect. In fact, the figure of the earth differs but little from the general form it would possess, if its solid parts were entirely covered with the waters of the ocean. Most of the large continents are intersected by inland seas, which penetrate many hundred miles into the interior of these extensive tracts of land, and approach so nearly their most elevated regions, that none of them can be said to be far removed from the borders of the ocean. The moderate velocity with which rivers descend from these lofty eminences is sufficient to prove that the inclination of their beds is inconsiderable, and that in no instance, perhaps, do they flow from a height of five, or at most six miles, above the level of the sea. Hence the surface of the ocean may be regarded as indicating the general figure of the earth.

The curvature of the earth, how determined at a particular point.

The nature of this figure, or at least its curvature at any particular point, may be determined from the relative position of lines cutting its tangential direction at right angles. For since the waters of the ocean, when they are in a state of repose, assume, by the influence of gravity, (see HYDRODYNAMICS, p. 427.) such a form, that a tangent at any point of their surface is always at right angles to the direction of a plummet-line, it is evident that a comparison of the relative inclination of the vertical lines, at different places on the earth's surface, must serve to point out the curvilineal direction at these places.

assume on the same meridian a number of points at measured intervals, and thus determine the angles which the several vertical lines form with each other at these points.

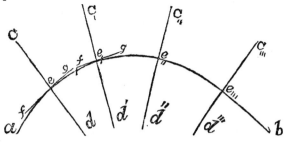

By following out this method with all the accuracy which the nature of the problem requires, the true figure of the earth will be ascertained with considerable precision. If at equal distances on the surface of the earth the vertical lines were always found to make equal angles with each other, this would imply that the earth was an exact sphere; but, on the other hand, if any deviation from that equality should be observed at different points, it would show that the curvature belonged to some other solid, the convexity being always greatest when the convergency of the vertical lines was so. The determination of the figure of the earth by the method we have briefly sketched, depends upon the measurement of two quantities; 1st, The inclination of the vertical lines at two different points on the earth's surface; and 2d, The length of the intercepted arch, in reference to the curvature which the ocean would possess if it flowed freely between the two stations. The difference of latitude between two places, or the difference of their zenith distances from the elevated pole, affording an easy method of ascertaining the inclination of two vertical lines at these places, it is usual to select two stations lying under the same meridian, and then to determine the distance between them, either by actual measurement, or by means of a series of triangles connected with some accurately measured base line.

We shall first shew that the inclination of the vertical lines at the two stations, is equal to the difference of latitude, or, what is the same thing, the difference of elevation of the nearest celestial pole, as observed at the two stations; and then describe the method of computing the intermediate distance by triangular measurements.

Thus if the lines CD, C' D' &c. were firmly attached to the flexible line AB, so as always to retain a direction at right angles to the tangents $fg, f'g'$ &c. when the line AB was bent in the form ab, the various inclinations of the lines $cd, c'd'$ &c. would serve to indicate the degree of curvature possessed by the intermediate portion of the curve. To apply this view of the matter to the earth, it will only be necessary to

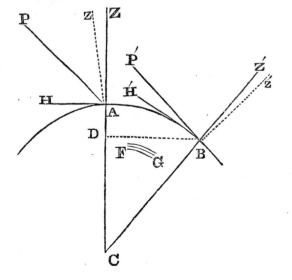

Let A and B denote the two stations, the arch AB being the intercepted portion of the terrestrial meridian; let CZ and CZ′ represent vertical lines at each of the stations respectively; then HA and HB′ being drawn at right angles to HZ and CZ′, will be horizontal lines at A and B. Now if BD be drawn parallel to HA, and AB and BP′ represent the direction of the elevated pole, the angle HAP will be equal to the latitude of A, while the angle H′BP′ will be equal to that of B. But the angle DPB′ being equal to the angle HAP, and the angle H′BD being equal to the difference of the angles DBP′, and H′BP, it is evident that the angle H′BD is equal to the difference of latitude of A and B. Again, since the angle H′BC is a right angle, and the angles DBC and BCD are together equal to a right angle, it follows that the angle ACB is equal to the angle H′BD. *Hence the inclination of the vertical lines, at the two stations, is equal to the difference of latitude of the stations.*

Influence
of local at-
tractions.

The only circumstance that can affect the accuracy of the result, in its application to determine the figure of the earth, from the inclination of the vertical lines, is the influence of local attractions, exerted either at the surface of the earth, or below its external crust. Thus, if an accumulation of very dense materials, as FG, should exist under the surface, and between the two stations, the direction of the vertical line ZA might be changed to zA, while that of Z′B might, in like manner, be changed to z′B. A double effect would thus be produced on the inclination of the vertical lines, by an invisible and unknown agent, the operation of which could only be detected by a careful examination of the angles formed by other vertical lines, in situations not greatly remote from each other, or at different points in the same meridional line. In the great trigonometrical surveys, for determining the figure of the earth, which have lately been prosecuted with the utmost accuracy, in various parts of the world, anomalies of the kind we have alluded to have frequently occurred.

Having proved that the inclination of two vertical lines, at different points on the same meridian, is equal to their difference of latitude, or what is the same thing, the difference of the zenith distance of the same stars at the two stations, it now remains to describe the method of measuring the intercepted terrestrial arch, or the lineal distance between the stations. The first thing to be determined for this purpose, is the exact direction of the meridian. This is obtained by means of a transit instrument, which, after being duly adjusted to the plane of the meridian by observations of circumpolar stars, is brought to a horizontal position, and directed to a distant terrestrial object, such as an upright post erected on purpose, and placed as far off as it can be distinctly discerned in coincidence with the vertical wire of the instrument. Another post being substituted for the instrument, the latter is removed from its first position, and a line is then continued in the direction of the two posts, as far as the measurement is to be extended. In some cases, however, it will become necessary to verify the meridional direction by observations with the transit instrument.

Base line,
how to be
chosen.

When the nature of the ground permits, the stations should be chosen, so that as great a portion as possible of the intermediate line may be measured, without the aid of trigonometry; and a vast deal of labour will be saved, both in direct measurement and future calculation, if the surface should be horizontal, or have nearly the convexity of the ocean. It was nearly in such circumstances as these that the direction of a meridian line was traced in Pennsylvania by Messrs. Mason and Dixon, for an extent of 538077.94 English feet. The latitude of the most southerly point of the terrestrial arch thus measured, was found to be 38° 27′ 34″, and that of the most northerly point 39° 56′ 19″, so that the portion of the meridian, intercepted between the two stations, was 1° 28′ 45″. The proportional length of a degree, by this measurement, turned out 363771 English feet; and if the earth were an exact sphere, its circumference would accordingly be about 24,802 miles, a result which, though it cannot be regarded as perfectly correct, may yet serve as a useful approximation in subsequent measurements, particularly when allowances are to be made on the lines actually measured, on account of the curvature of the terrestrial spheroid.

Physical
Geography.

When a large arch, however, is to be traced, the above method could not be resorted to. All that can be done in this case, is to fix upon the two extreme stations, as nearly as possible under the same meridian, and afterwards to ascertain the distance between them by commencing with a good base line, measured with great care, in a favourable situation, and then connect it with the most remote points of the survey by means of a series of triangles, in which it would only be necessary to measure the angles, and the bearing of their sides with the meridian.

Corrections
to be at-
tended to,
when a
large arch
is measur-
ed.

In carrying into effect the various operations which the measurement requires, and reducing the sides of the resulting triangles, certain corrections must be applied, which are founded on the supposition of the globular figure of the earth. The corrections deduced from the suppositions, (even though the true figure and magnitude of the earth were imperfectly known,) are indeed of such a nature that a considerable error respecting its form and dimensions, can seldom lead to any great inaccuracy in the ultimate result; but, at the same time, they are too important to be altogether overlooked, without affecting very materially the correctness of the measurements. Thus, the base line itself, from the manner in which it is determined, is neither a straight line nor a continuous curve; but is made up, in the most favourable circumstances in which it can be measured, of the sides of a polygon inscribed on a circle, the radius of which is the radius of curvature of the terrestrial arch. Hence the line to be determined, namely, the distance between the two extremities of the base line, must be somewhat longer than the length of the measured base, which is obtained either by means of inflexible rods, or uniformly distended chains, placed consecutively at the extremities of each other, and whose real length can only be accurately found by converting the polygonal into a curvilineal base, having the same convexity as the earth.

For the
base line.

The magnitudes of the angles of the connecting triangles are equally affected by the rotundity of the earth, and must undergo a corresponding correction to prepare them for the calculation of the unknown sides. For since the triangles on the surface of the earth can, from what has been stated, no longer be regarded as plane triangles, neither can the horizontal angles at one station be considered as in the same plane with the horizontal angles at another. Thus, let AB be the original base line, the point A being one extremity of the meridian line AM; and let the point C be supposed on the same level with A and B, after the suitable allowances are made for the earth's sphericity. In the

For the
angles.

triangle ABC, besides the base line AB, the angles at A and B must be measured, and even the third angle at C, as a means of verifying the other two. But these angles being the angles formed by tangents to the earth's surface, at the points A, B, and C, must, from the convexity of that surface, exceed two right angles, by a quantity which, on the supposition that the earth is an exact sphere, can always be accurately assigned; and though a slight deviation from this excess in the amount of the angles obtained by actual measurement, does not absolutely prove that these angles have been inaccurately determined, either on account of imperfections in the instrument, or carelessness on the part of the observer, it forms a check on their magnitude, which, in the case of great anomalies, ought never to be entirely disregarded. In computing the length of the two sides, AC and BC, by means of the side AB, and the two angles at A and B, we should evidently come nearer the truth, by treating ABC as a spherical triangle, rather than a plane one.

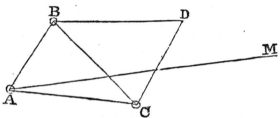

Theorem of Legendre for simplifying the calculation.

The labour of the calculation would, no doubt, be thus increased, but the greater accuracy to which it would lead, would more than compensate for the additional trouble it would occasion. But even in this case the labour of the calculation is greatly abridged by means of a beautiful approximating theorem of Legendre, who first demonstrated that if each of the angles of a small spherical triangle, such as those usually employed in geodesic operations, be diminished by a third part of the spherical excess, their sines become proportional to the opposite sides of the triangle, considered as spherical. This conclusion, though it is one which might have been inferred by a rude examination of the analogy which subsists between spherical and plane triangles, was deduced from the most refined geometrical considerations, and is of the utmost value in extensive trigonometrical surveys. In fact, the computation of the sides AC and BC is rendered by this theorem nearly as easy as if they had been the sides of a plane triangle. Another method of calculation has been proposed, which, though less direct, is preferred by several geometers; it consists in reducing the angles, obtained by actual measurement, to the angles formed by the chords of the arches which constitute the sides of the triangles, that is, to the angles of a plane triangle, whose angular points coincide with those of the spherical triangle. The sides of this triangle being computed by the rules of plane trigonometry, the arches of which they are the chords are afterwards deduced from them, by the usual methods of determining an arch from its chord. This method, which is not without its advantages, is recommended by Delambre, and has been generally adopted in the surveys conducted by British mathematicians, both in this country and Hindostan.

Whichever of these methods is employed for finding the length of the arch BC, this line becomes, in its turn, the base of the triangle BCD, so that with the angles CBD and BCD the lengths of the arches BD and CD

are obtained by calculation. It often happens, however, that the three angular points of the triangle are not in the same horizontal plane, and hence it becomes necessary to reduce the angles actually observed to the magnitude which would have belonged to them if this had been the case. Let B and C, for example, be in different horizontal planes from D, the angle BDC is reduced to a horizontal plane B'DC', passing through D, by measuring the angles of elevation of the points B and C, viz. angle BDB' and angle CDC' and then forming a spherical triangle BZC with their complements BZ and CZ, and BC the measure of the observed angle BDC. The angle BZC, computed from these data, being the same as the angle B'DC', gives the magnitude of the angle BDC, reduced to a horizontal plane passing through D.

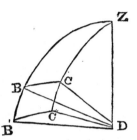

If the angles at each station are reduced in this manner to the horizon, the several stations of the survey may be considered as projected on the surface of the terrestrial sphere, and thus constituting a series of spherical triangles, in which all the angles are known. By means of these data, and the original base-line, it will be easy to compute all the other sides, and to deduce at last the length of the meridional arch between the two extreme stations. The necessary calculations may be greatly simplified, in particular cases, by modifications of the general formula; but we cannot enter upon details, and must refer for a full view of the subject, in all its bearings, to the *Base du Système Métrique Decimal*, published by Mechain and Delambre, in their account of the measurement of the great arch between Formentera and Dunkirk. See also Colonel Mudge's *Account of the Trigonometrical Survey of England and Wales*; *Astronomie par Delambre*, chap. xxxv. *Phil. Trans.* vol. lxxv. lxxxv. and xc.

First measurement of a portion of the terrestrial meridian by Eratosthenes.

The measurement of the length of a portion of the meridian, together with the corresponding celestial arch, for the purpose of determining the magnitude of the earth, seems to have been first made by Eratosthenes. This distinguished astronomer, by comparing the difference of latitude between Alexandria and Syene, with the distance of these two places, concluded, as we are informed by Cleomedes, that the circumference of the earth was 250,000, or according to the account of Pliny, 252,000 stadia. Now the stadium being stated by the latter writer to be 125 Roman paces, or 625 Roman feet, if we estimate the Roman foot, with Sir George Shuckburgh, at 11,6074 English inches, the circumference of the globe, by the measurement of Eratosthenes, should be, according to Pliny's statement, 30,467 English miles, or about one-sixth part of the whole in excess. Freret indeed is inclined to believe, that the stadium used by Eratosthenes was the Olympic stadium, a conjecture the more probable, as the result, by adopting it, would coincide very nearly with the measurements of modern times.

Measurement of Picard.

The first measurement of a degree of the meridian, of a recent date, that has any claim to precision, is that of Picard. This measurement, which embraced a line stretching between the parallels of Malvoisine and Amiens, was executed in 1670, and prepared the way for the more accurate trigonometrical surveys which have since been made in various parts of Europe. The most extensive, and perhaps the best executed of these surveys, is one which was carried on during the late revolution in France, by Mechain and Delambre. The terrestrial arch which it embraced, extended nearly over 10 degrees; and what was of some importance, it was almost exactly bisected in the parallel of 45°. Next in importance to it, in point of extent, and not inferior to it in point of accuracy, we may reckon the trigonometrical survey of Great Britain, begun by General Roy, and afterwards prosecuted by Colonel Mudge and Major Colby.

Length of a degree of the meridian, in different latitudes.

The length of a degree of the meridian, in different latitudes, as deduced from the most accurate measurements, is thus stated by Biot.

Place of Observation.	Mean Latitude of the Arch.	Length of a Degree in Toises.	Names of the Observers.
Peru, . .	Equator.	56753	Bouguer.
Pennsylvania,	39° 11′ 57″	56888	Mason and Dixon.
Italy, . .	42° 9′ 58″	56979	Boscovich and Lemaire.
France, .	46° 11′ 58″	57018	Delambre and Mechain.
Sweden, .	66° 20′ 10″	57192	Melanderhielm.

These results obviously indicate an increase in the length of a degree of the terrestrial meridian from the equator to the pole, and consequently a smaller degree of convexity at the latter than the former. By a comparison of the different measurements, it appears that the increase in the length of a degree is nearly proportional to the square of the sine of the latitude, from which it has been inferred that the earth is not an exact sphere, but an ellipsoid, having the shorter axis for the axis of revolution. At the same time the eccentrity of the generating ellipse appears to be so small, that in most of the corrections which it is necessary to employ, in deducing from observation the real figure of the earth, it is sufficient to consider its form as that of a perfect sphere; though it ought not to be concealed, that even the ellipsoidal figure is incompatible with the results of some of the most accurate measurements which have been made, both in the northern and southern hemisphere. The ellipse, however, being the curve next in simplicity to the circle, which possesses the conditions that accord best on the whole with the form of the meridian, it has been selected by geometers with the view of comparing its curvature with that of the terrestrial arches, as inferred from actual measurement in various latitudes. The comparison is made by means of a well-known geometrical relation, viz. that at every point of a curve, whatever be the nature of its curvature, a circle may be found which approaches nearer to that curvature than any other circle. This arch, which blends itself with the curve, to a small extent on either side of the point of tangency, is called the osculatory, or equi-curve circle; and so intimately does it coalesce with the curve to which it is applied, that for a limited portion of the arch, they may be regarded as coincident. In the ellipse the radius of the equicurve circle varies with the curvature at different points, but its magnitude may be determined for each latitude, in terms of the two axes; and if it be multiplied by 2×3.1415926, &c. and the product afterwards divided by 360°, the result will be the length of a degree of the meridian in that latitude. Hence if two equations be formed, expressing in terms of the two axes, the length of a degree measured in two different lati-

tudes, it will be easy to determine by elimination the length of each axis. By employing this method, it has been ascertained that the hypothesis of the elliptical form of the meridian is, to a certain extent, reconcileable with observation, and, with the exception of those cases in which the result is evidently affected by local peculiarities, may be regarded as exhibiting the true figure of the earth. From a comparison of the measurements of a degree of the meridian, on which the greatest reliance can be placed, Delambre has deduced the following results.

	Toises.
Half the greater axis or radius of the equator =	3271864
Half the shorter axis or radius of the pole =	3261265
Difference . . . . =	10599

This difference, divided by half the longer axis, considered as unity, is called the *compression*, and amounts, according to that celebrated astronomer, to $\dfrac{1}{308.65}$

A comparison of a degree of the meridian, in any two latitudes, ought to lead to the same relation between the axis, provided the measurements from which it is deduced can be relied upon for their accuracy; but a careful examination of the different surveys, best entitled to confidence on account of the precision with which they have been executed, by no means confirms this conclusion. Thus, La Place assigns for the compression $\dfrac{1}{322}$; M. Sejour from $\dfrac{1}{307}$ to $\dfrac{1}{320}$; M. Carouge and La Lande $\dfrac{1}{300}$; and, lastly, Mr. Playfair $\dfrac{1}{312.5}$. The circumference of the elliptical meridian is, according to the result deduced by Mr. Playfair, 24855.84 English miles, and that of the equator 24896.16 miles, so that a geographical mile, of which there are 60 in the mean degree, should be 6075.6 English feet.

Notwithstanding the seeming coincidence of the above results, all of which were deduced on the supposition that the terrestrial meridian is of an elliptical form, it is certain that the trigonometrical operations for the measurement of a large portion of the meridian in France and England, with respect to the accuracy of which it is impossible to entertain the slightest doubt, give, by a rigid comparison of the length of a degree on different parts of the arch, a compression of $\dfrac{1}{150.6}$. From this result, which was deduced by La Place, it has been inferred by that distinguished analyst, that the earth cannot be considered an exact ellipsoid of revolution; but that irregularities exist in its internal structure which sensibly affect its form, and cause the meridians to deviate from continuous ellipses. He is disposed to think that the great compression, inferred from the osculatory ellipse in France, is not to be ascribed to the attraction of the Pyrenees, and the mountains to the south of France, but to the operation of causes of a more extensive influence, the effects of which are felt in the north of France, as well as in England, Austria, and Italy. " The azimuthal observations," says he, " which have already been made, do not accord with each other; and if the degree measured at the Cape of Good Hope be compared with the degrees measured in the northern hemisphere, there will be grounds for believing that the northern

Physical
Geography.

Method of
determin-‑
ing the
figure of
the earth
by the
length of
the pendu-
lum.

and southern hemispheres differ in form from each other." *Mech. Cel.* II. 144.

The variation of gravity at the surface of the earth affords another method of determining its actual figure. This subtile and pervading power, which acts upon all matter with a force directly as the mass, and inversely as the square of the distance, tends to communicate to bodies exposed to its influence equal velocities in equal times. One of the modifications of this action is the oscillation of the pendulum, which is of longer or shorter duration, according to the energy of the attractive force, and the square root of the length of the pendulum. If the earth were an exact sphere, destitute of the motion of rotation, and possessing the same density throughout its whole mass, the force of gravity, by which bodies at its surface are drawn towards the centre, would be uniform, and invariable in every latitude. But the elliptical form of the earth destroys this uniformity, and causes the attractive force at the poles to preponderate over that at the equator. This inequality in the force, by which bodies at the surface of the earth retain their positions, is augmented by the diurnal rotation, which, by its centrifugal tendency, impresses a greater disposition on bodies to recede from the centre of the earth at the equator than at the poles, where its effects cease to be felt. By the joint operation of these two causes, one of which acts with a force proportional to the square of the sine of the latitude, a sensible difference ought to be observed in the velocity acquired by heavy bodies, in falling through the same space, as we advance from the equator to the poles. An important relation between the time of the vibration of a pendulum, and that of the descent of a heavy body, according to which the lengths of pendulums, vibrating sychronously, are directly as the force of gravity, enables us to submit this conclusion to the test of experiment. Newton long ago demonstrated, that if the earth were perfectly homogeneous, the same fraction, viz. $\frac{1}{230}$, would express both the compression of the terrestrial ellipsoid, and the increase of gravity from the equator to the poles. This conclusion, which was deduced from the supposition of an uniform density, was afterwards modified, with singular address, by Clairaut, who showed that the two fractions expressing the compression, and the increase of gravity, though not exactly equal, must always together amount to $\frac{2}{230}$. Assuming the compression, therefore, to be equal to $\frac{1}{312}$, the increase of gravity from the equator to the poles, or the indication of that increase, as given by the length of the pendulum, should be $\frac{2}{230} - \frac{1}{312}$, or $\frac{1}{182}$ nearly. The correctness of this conclusion, if not completely established, is, at least, to a certain extent, confirmed, by the experiments which have been made with the pendulum in different latitudes. La Place having selected fifteen of the best of these observations, and applied to them the necessary corrections, on account of the resistance of the air, difference of temperature, and elevation above the level of the sea, deduced the following results, in which the length of the pendulum at Paris is considered to be unity:

Latitudes.			Length of the Seconds Pendulum.	Names of the Observers.	Places of Observation.
Equator			.99669	Bouguer	Peru
9°	32′	56″	.99689	Do.	Portobello
11	55	30	.99710	Gentil	Pondicherry
18	0	0	.99745	Campbell	Jamaica
18	27	0	.99728	Bouguer	Petit Grave
34	7	15	.99877	La Caille	Cape of Good Hope
43	35	45	.99950	Darquier	Toulouse
48	12	48	.99077	Liesganig	Vienna
48	50	0	1.00000	Bouguer	Paris
50	58	0	1.00006	Zach	Gotha
51	30	0	1.00018	. .	London
58	14	53	1.00074	Mallet	Petersburgh
59	56	24	1.00101	Do.	Ponoi
66	48	0	1.00137	Grischow	Arensberg.
67	5	0	1.00148	Mapertuis	Fornea

The above results indicate obviously an increase of the force of gravity from the equator towards the poles. La Place has shown that, in whatever way they are combined, it is impossible to avoid an error of less than .00018, on the hypothesis of the variation of gravity at the surface of the earth increasing as the squares of the sines of the latitude from the equator to the poles. The expression for the ellipticity, which connects best the different equations of condition, is $\frac{1}{335.78}$, a result which accords in a very remarkable manner with the compression deduced from the measures of the French mathematicians in France, and at the equator.

It may be inferred from these experiments with the pendulum, that the compression of the earth is greater than is compatible with the supposition of an uniform density. The same anomalies, too, which are discernible in the measurement of a degree of the meridian, and which are undoubtedly owing to the dissimilar structure of the globe, may be traced in the results of these experiments. The beautiful property of the pendulum, first discovered by Huygens, that the centre of oscillation and the point of suspension are interchangeable with each other, and which has been so happily applied by Captain Kater to determine the length of the second's pendulum, renders this mechanical contrivance infinitely better fitted to ascertain the true figure of the earth, than the complicated methods which were formerly employed for the same purpose. The facility with which the observations may be made, and the certainty of the results with which they are attended, may be expected to furnish much interesting information, not only with respect to the general form of the globe, but also with respect to its structure and composition in particular situations. See *Phil. Trans.* for 1819, p. 420.

Captain Kater has already applied his method of determining the length of the pendulum at several of the most important stations of the British Survey, and deduced from his observations among others the following results:

Physical
Geography.

Names of the Stations.	Diminution of Gravity from the Pole to the Equator.	Compression.
Unst and Leith Fort . .	.0053840	$\frac{1}{315.8}$
Clifton . .	.0056340	$\frac{1}{331.5}$
Arbury Hill . .	.0054282	$\frac{1}{310.3}$
London . .	.0055510	$\frac{1}{322.7}$
Leith Fort and Clifton . .	.0059033	$\frac{1}{364}$
Arbury Hill .	.0053615	$\frac{1}{304.1}$
London .	.00561816	$\frac{1}{329.8}$
Clifton and Arbury Hill . .	.0042956	$\frac{1}{229.6}$
London . .	.0052590	$\frac{1}{294.9}$
Arbury Hill and London .	.0069767	$\frac{1}{597.5}$
Dunnose .	.0060212	$\frac{1}{380.3}$
London and Dunnose . .	.0052837	$\frac{1}{297}$

It appears by these results that the compression deduced from each pair of observations approaches nearer to the mean results obtained by the measurement of the meridian, the more remote the two stations are from each other. This was to be expected, and must be ascribed to the operation of local causes, which are more liable to affect observations made at two places at no great distance from each other, than when they are separated by a more extensive interval. Thus it may be seen in the preceding table, that the number expressing the diminution of gravity from the observations at Unst and Leith Fort, is less than that deduced from the arch between Unst and Clifton, and that this number afterwards decreases at Arbury Hill, and again increases at London. It may also be inferred in general from these observations, that, in advancing from the north of Great Britain to the south, gravity decreases in a more rapid ratio than is assigned by theory,—a circumstance which is perhaps best explained by the supposition that there exists a mass of materials of greater density than common near the northern extremity of the island, while the contrary is the case in the vicinity of Clifton. The sudden increase of gravity at Arbury Hill is worthy of notice, both on account of its intensity, and the limited space to which it extends; for while the arch between Arbury Hill and London gives ·0069767 for the diminution of this force, from the pole to the equator, that between London and Dunnose gives only ·0052837. It has thence been conjectured that the strata in the neighbourhood of Arbury Hill consist of materials of extraordinary density.

M. Biot, by a comparison of his experiments at Unst, with those made at Formentera and Dunkirk, has deduced $\frac{1}{310}$ for the resulting compression. This agrees in a remarkable manner with the fractional expression for the ellipticity of the terrestrial spheroid, derived by La Place, from data of a very different kind. That profound geometer has shown, in his theory of the moon, that one of the inequalities of the lunar motions, which depends on the longitude of the moon's node, amounting to 20″·987, as

deduced by Burg, from a vast number of observations of Maskelyne, gives a compression of $\frac{1}{305.05}$; while another, depending on the sine of the moon's true longitude, and indicated by an inequality of the lunar motion in latitude, gives $\frac{1}{304.6}$. These inequalities, as La Place remarks, are deserving of the attention of observers, inasmuch as they possess the advantage over geodesic measurements of affording the means of deducing the compression of the earth in a way less apt to be affected by any irregularities of its density or contour in particular situations. *Mech. Cel.* III. p. 173. See the article PENDULUM in this volume.

Having thus described the various methods which have been employed to determine the figure of the earth, we shall now give a brief outline of the attempts which have been made to ascertain its mean density. The limited knowledge we possess of the internal structure of the globe, and the small depths to which human industry has penetrated below the surface, might seem to render any inquiry into this subject altogether hypothetical. The operations of mining have scarce, in any instance, been carried half a mile perpendicularly into the solid crust of the globe, and even though they had been prosecuted to a much greater depth, the information they would have furnished of the subterraneous regions would have been too partial to permit us to draw any general conclusion respecting the nature of the unexplored parts of this dark and unknown mass. But the problem, though attended with much difficulty, admits of an approximated solution, derived from the principles of universal gravitation. From the observations of Dr. Maskelyne on the attraction of the mountain Schehalien, it was found that the zenith distances of stars observed on opposite sides of that mountain, gave a difference of latitude between the two stations, which exceeded that deduced from the actual distance of the latter, by a quantity amounting to 11.6 seconds. The deflection of the plummet line on each side amounted, therefore, to about 5″.8, from which it was easy to conclude that the force exerted by the mountain was to that exerted by the whole earth as 1 to 35608 nearly. From the data thus furnished by astronomical observation, Dr. Hutton deduced, by a series of nice and laborious calculations, which are very fully described in the *Philosophical Transactions* for 1778, that the mean density of the earth was to that of the mountain as 9 to 5. To reduce this result to the common unit of density, that of water, it was assumed that the mean specific gravity of the rocks which compose Schehalien is $2\frac{1}{2}$, which gave the mean density of the earth to that of water, as $4\frac{1}{2}$ to 1. In this estimate, however, as has been justly observed by Mr. Playfair, the specific gravity of the mountain was reckoned too low, Schehalien belonging to the class of primitive rocks, and possessing a specific gravity considerably above 2.5. From an actual survey of the mountain, of which an account is given in the *Phil. Trans.* for 1811, it is inferred by that distinguished philosopher, that the mean density of the earth probably lies between 4·558 and 4·867, the mean of which is 4·713.

Mr. Cavendish has inferred, from the effects of attraction on small masses of matter, that the mean density of the globe is $5\frac{1}{2}$ times that of water. The experiments from which he drew this conclusion, though of a very delicate nature, were performed with all the

Mean density of the earth.

Physical Geography.

attention to extreme accuracy, which distinguished the physical researches of that illustrious philosopher. The limits of this article will not allow us to describe the very ingenious contrivances to which he had recourse in prosecuting this interesting subject, but a minute account of them will be found in the *Phil. Trans.* for the year 1798. It is worthy of remark, however, that Newton, with that intuitive sagacity which characterized all his conjectures, thought it probable, that the mean density of the earth might be five or six times as great as water. See ATTRACTION, p. 80.

Probable condition of the internal mass of the globe.

Since the mean specific gravity of the earth is, according to these experiments, about double the average density of the substances which compose the external crust, or at least of that portion of it which is within the reach of our examination, we are forced to conclude, that the central parts must abound with metallic substances, or some other species of heavy matter, to counterbalance the lighter bodies at the surface, and produce so great a mean density as that which actually exists. Assuming the mean specific gravity of the metallic bodies to be 10, it would require, according to Dr. Hutton's computation, 16 parts out of 27, or somewhat more than one half of the matter in the whole earth to consist of substances of that relative weight, in order that they might constitute a mass of the mean density, which, according to the experiments of Dr. Maskelyne, the earth seems to possess. Hence we may conclude, that unless the central parts of the earth be composed of substances, differing greatly in density from those found at the surface, no considerable portion of them can either be hollow, or occupied by water. If, indeed, we admit the compressibility of that fluid, and take for granted that it obeys the same laws of compression with elastic fluids, its density might be several thousand times greater at the centre than at the surface; for, as Dr. Young remarks, even steel in that situation would be compressed into one-fourth of its bulk, and stone into one-eighth, if it were subjected to the weight of the whole superincumbent mass. The cohesion of the solid parts, however, must, in a great measure, render each of the concentric shells, of which we may conceive the globe to consist, independent of the rest, and thus secure them from the effects of the enormous compression which would otherwise, at great depths, result from the statical pressure of a fluid mass.

General view of the two great continents.

Our knowledge of the internal constitution of the earth being almost entirely conjectural, we must confine the observations we have to offer respecting the materials of which it is composed, to the external crust. The surface of the earth exhibits an irregular distribution of land and water, the latter predominating over the former in the proportion of about three to one. The solid parts which rise above the ocean form two extensive tracts of land, to which geographers have given the name of *Continents;* one of them being sometimes termed, for the sake of distinction, the *Old,* and the other, the *New World.* These continents, though of different aspects, have yet certain features in common which give to their general outline a considerable degree of similarity. Both of them stretch from the same parallel of latitude in the north, to nearly the same parallel in the south; and both are contracted towards the middle into narrow isthmuses or necks of land. Each of them is studded along the eastern boundary by numerous detached portions of land of moderate extent, called *Islands,* while both of them are alike desti-

tute of these insular appendages on their western skirts. Even the extremities of these great divisions of the globe have no small resemblance to each other; the boundaries on the north, running in both nearly along the same parallel of latitude, and terminating on the south in pointed promontories or capes. The geographical position of both tracts is remarkable, for, whereas they extend in the northern hemisphere nearly to the pole itself, neither of them reaches in the southern hemisphere beyond the 50th degree of latitude.

Physical Geography.

The coasts or outline of the land present sometimes an abrupt and sudden termination, skirting, like a mighty wall, the solid parts of the globe; but more frequently they shelve down to the level of the ocean, from the encroachments of which they are only defended by a slight difference of elevation. From the coasts the land rises, by a succession of steps, into lofty eminences, to which we give the name of *hills* or *mountains,* according to the degree of their elevation above the level of the sea, or that of the plains, on which their bases repose. The ascent of the land from the ocean, to the highest ridges which crown the interior of continents, is sometimes very gradual, as in the case of the interminable Savannahs of North America, and the steppes, or central plains of Asia; while at other times it is exceedingly abrupt, as in the Cordilleras of South America, and suddenly carries the traveller to the loftiest pinnacles of the globe. It even frequently happens that the inclination is very different on opposite sides of the same mountain; thus the summits of the Andes, which, on the western side, are only about 100 miles from the borders of the Pacific, are, in some cases, upwards of 2000 miles from the shores, which are washed, on the eastern side, by the waves of the Atlantic.

Outline of the coast, and general aspect of the surface of the land.

The usual method of exhibiting the features of a country, by maps or horizontal projections, is but ill calculated to convey a representation of the inequalities of its surface. This can only be successfully accomplished by means of vertical sections, in which the form of the mountains, their relative heights, and varying declivities, are accurately outlined. These sections, in the case of a particular portion of the earth's surface, may either consist of several planes differing in direction, according to the importance of the positions to be included in the profile, or of a single plane, on which each plane is laid down by orthographic projection. In the latter case, the distances on the physical or sectional map will often differ considerably from the absolute distances, particularly when the mean direction of the points whose height and position have been determined, deviates greatly from the direction of the plane of projection. In all cases, the scale of distance must necessarily differ from the scale of elevation. Were we to make these scales of the same magnitude, we should be compelled, either to give to the profile an inconvenient length, or to assume a scale of elevation so small, that the most remarkable inequalities of the surface would be insensible.

Method of exhibiting an outline of the surface.

Sectional maps.

Physical maps of this description demand for their construction, not only the latitudes and longitudes of places, but their elevation above the level of the ocean; so that it is only by uniting barometrical measurements with astronomical observations, that the true physiognomy of a country can be exhibited. This kind of projection may be expected to become more frequent in proportion as travellers devote their attention to barometrical observations. At present, as Humboldt

Necessary elements for their construction.

Physical Geography. justly remarks, few provinces of Europe offer the necessary materials for constructing profiles analogous to those which he has published of equinoxial America.

Having made these preliminary remarks on the surface of the globe in general, and the method of representing in profile the irregularities of its outline, we shall proceed to consider a little more in detail the physical character of the mountains, valleys, and plains, of which it consists.

Mountains. Mountains are, properly speaking, masses of considerable elevation, and which have, at the same time, a pretty rapid ascent. They must not be confounded with those more extensive portions of the earth's surface, which constitute large tabular masses, and are Table land. usually denominated *table land*. A portion of the surface of the earth to which this term is applied, may sometimes rise very abruptly from the ocean, by which it is either wholly or partially bounded, but the small difference of elevation which it afterwards exhibits for a great extent, distinguishes it essentially from the more limited masses to which we give the epithet of mountains. The most extensive tracts of table land are to be found in the inland parts of continents, such as Tartary, Persia, Thibet, and the central regions of Africa. These portions of the globe have their general level more elevated than the rest of the continent of which they form a part, and are accordingly regarded by some geologists as of more ancient formation.

Designations of mountains. Though mountains resemble one another in regard to their general aspect, their individual forms are considerably diversified. Some of them have accordingly received the name of *peaks*, while others, whose summits are still more angular, have been denominated *needles*. One mountain, from the flatness of its top, is compared to a *table*, and another, from its serrated outline being conceived to resemble a *saw*, is thence called a *sierra*. These geological appellations are less numerous in our language, than in the languages of the continent, where the face of nature presents a greater variety of contours for discrimination. The external appearance of a mountain is often determined by its internal structure and composition. Thus the mountains denominated primitive, in which granite, gneiss, and mica slate predominate, commonly exhibit a bold denticulated outline, exposing their naked tops to the heavens, while those of the secondary formation are not only less elevated, but of a more gentle acclivity, and clothed with vegetation to their summits. See MINERALOGY, p. 394. 405.

Mountain chains. Mountains seldom exist in insulated or detached masses, but are usually found in continuous groupes, or connected chains, traversing the surface of the earth to a great extent. Thus the enormous chain, composed of the Stoney Mountains and the Andes, run from one extremity of America to the other ; and, in like manner, another chain, of still greater extent, is pretended to be traced on the eastern skirts of Asia and part of Africa, from Bherings Straits to the Cape Their great extent. of Good Hope. These two vast chains having been at one period united together at the north and the south, are represented to have constituted the sides of an immense basin, which inclosed in its capacious bosom nearly the whole of the habitable part of the globe. In this supposition, however, there is more of splendid hypothesis than sound philosophy. The continuity of this imaginary circular wall is, in many places, very indistinctly traced, and between Cape Horn and the Cape of Good Hope every vestige of it disappears. At Physical Geography. the same time, it must be admitted, that when our attention is confined to a more limited portion of the earth's surface, mountain groupes frequently exhibit the appearance of a circular arrangement. In such cases, a similarity of structure and composition may be traced, not only in the internal nucleus of the group, but also in the order and distribution of the rocks which cover it, sufficiently great at least to to render it extremely probable, that the whole range has had a common origin. See MINERALOGY.

Direction of mountains. From this view of the distribution of mountain groupes, we may expect to find them traversing the surface of the globe in all directions. Thus, the Andes run, for many hundred miles, nearly in the direction of the meridian, while the central chain of Africa, commonly denominated the Mountains of the Moon, is represented to proceed at right angles to that line. On the other hand, the Himalayah range, the loftiest in Asia, runs from north-west to south-east, while the Alps, the highest mountains in Europe, cannot be said to affect, for a great extent, any well-defined direction whatever. See ALPS, ANDES, &c.

Elevation of mountains. The general direction of the principal mountain chains is better known than their elevation, at particular points, above the level of the ocean. Nor need we wonder at this circumstance, when we consider how much labour and time are necessary to determine the difference of level between two places, at no great distance from each other, and how much the difficulties of doing this are increased, when extensive tracts of irregular ground intervene. The ordinary mode of levelling is, in such cases, altogether incapable ; and, even if the method by the barometer should be employed, though admirably adapted to the purpose, it yet requires either contemporaneous observations at other places whose height has been previously ascertained, or a series of observations for a longer period than is usually convenient for travellers, at the place whose height is to be found. The barometrical method of determining Best determined by the barometer. difference of elevation is nevertheless of the greatest value in obtaining the necessary data for the construction of physical maps, and should never be neglected in extensive surveys. The barometer, in a portable form, is so easily conveyed from one station to another ; the requisite observations with it are made with so much facility ; and the computations for deducing the difference of altitude between the places of observation are so short and simple, that every person who visits unknown regions, or even places whose heights are inaccurately ascertained, should be supplied with at least one of these valuable instruments. If we except the thermometer, there is no philosophical contrivance, of equal simplicity in point of construction, which is fitted to furnish so much useful and valuable information, respecting the general physiognomy of the globe. For the method of measuring heights by the barometer, see PNEUMATICS.

Situation of the loftiest mountains. The loftiest mountains are to be found within the Torrid Zone, or at no great distance from that artificial belt of the earth's surface. To account for this remarkable state of things, it has been conjectured by La Place, in defiance of all sober induction, that our globe was, at one period, surrounded, like the planet Saturn, by a ring, which encircled it nearly in the plane of the equator ; but that this ring having, by some accident, lost its equilibrium, and being unable to retain any longer its annular form, fell in detached masses to the

Physical
Geography.

Attempt
to explain
the reason
why the
loftiest
mountains
are to be
found in
the tropi-
al regions.

earth. The ruins of the ring thus scattered over the tropical regions gave rise, according to this visionary hypothesis, to the elevated land which exists in that portion of the globe. The following considerations will afford, we conceive, a more rational explanation of the fact. In the equatoreal regions the loftiest mountains are covered, to the height of 15,000 feet, with a mantle of vegetation which protects the subjacent soil, and the rocks over which it is spread, from that incessant waste and removal to which they must otherwise have been exposed ; whereas, in the temperate zones, where the point of perpetual congelation is much less elevated, the line which separates the habitats of vegetables from the regions of absolute sterility and nakedness, being only 6000 or 8000 feet above the level of the ocean, the summits of the lofty mountains in these zones are continually suffering a species of disintegration and decay, which, however slow in its progress, must, in the lapse of ages, produce the most extensive effects. If we assume, therefore, that the mountains had, at any one period, nearly the same elevation, over the surface of the globe, (a supposition which may be admitted by the advocates for the most opposite geological opinions,) the reason we have assigned would be sufficient to account for the diversity of altitudes which they now exhibit, without having recourse to the operation of any other cause. In many instances, indeed, even within the temperate zones, the flanks of the highest mountains are covered with a thick coating of ice, which is no less fitted to defend them from the violence of the destructive agents by which they are assailed, than the more genial covering which preserves the tropical mountains from demolition ; but this covering seems to be confined within a certain range of elevation, and while it stretches, with its lower skirts, a little below the line of perpetual frost, its highest limits seldom extend many hundred feet above it. Besides, the fluctuations to which these icy coverings are liable, are often attended with consequences which powerfully contribute to the disintegration of the mountains on which they rest, as they frequently carry along with them, when detached from the integrant masses of which they constitute a part, immense blocks of the rocks to which they adhered, and hurry them to the plains below. The cause we have briefly alluded to may be expected to operate with the greatest effect, in situations where the fluctuations of temperature are at once frequent and extensive ; and, particularly, where the maximum temperature of the day rising above the point of congelation, the minimum temperature of the night sinks considerably below it. In these circumstances, the water existing alternately in the liquid and the solid state, is first insinuated between the fissures of the rocks, and being afterwards converted into ice, produces, by its expansion, a gradual enlargement of the crevices in which it is lodged, till the external masses against which it exerts its disruptive force, having lost their equilibrium, tumble from their bases, and descend, by their own gravity, to a lower situation. This process being frequently repeated, occasions a progressive degradation of the summits of mountains, the extent of which is, perhaps, best indi-

cated by the massy fragments, as well as the comminuted materials, which are scattered around their bases.

Having offered these general observations on the causes which contribute to the disintegration of mountains in different climates, we shall now exhibit a tabular view of the heights, above the level of the sea, of the most remarkable points on the surface of the globe. Various modes of arrangement might have been adopted. We have distributed them, merely in reference to their altitudes, on both sides of the Atlantic.

Physical
Geography.

Heights of the most remarkable points in both continents.

OLD WORLD. Names.	Altitude in Feet above the level of the Sea.	NEW WORLD. Names.	Altitude in Feet above the level of the Sea.
Dhawala-giri ⎫ Himalay-	26,862	Chimborazo . . .	21,458
Jamautri ⎭ ah range	25,500	Cajambe	19,360
Mon Blanc (Alps) .	15,662	Antisana . . . ;	19,290
Karbec (Caucasus) .	15,346	Catopaxi . . .	18,862
Monte Rosa (Alps) .	15,084	Popocatepetl . . .	17,903
Aiguille d'Argentiere		Mount St. Elie . .	17,883
(Alps)	13,402	Orizaba	17,390
Pic of Teneriff . .	12,175	Mowna Roa, in Owhyhee	16,416
Gros Klockner (Tyrol)	12,796	Pichincha	15,670
Pic d'Ossana (Pyrenees)	11,700	Silver Mine of Chata,	
Mount Etna . . .	10,954	Peru	11,830
Glacier de Buet (Alps)	10,124	Mean height of Andes	
Pic du Midi (Pyrenees)	9,300	according to Humboldt	11,820
Canigou (do.) .	9,247		
Mount Cenis (Alps) .	9,212	Quito, City of . . .	9,515
Gondar (City of) . .	8,440	El Pinal, do. . .	8,362
Monte Velino (Appen.)	8,297	Las Vigias, do. . .	7,820
Mount Cenis, Pass of	6,776	Perote, do. . . .	7,723
Simplon, (do.) .	6,562	St. Marten . . .	7,711
The Dole (Mount Jura)	5,523	Mine of Valenciana .	7,582
Puy de Dome . . .	4,920	Mexico, City of . .	7,468
Mount Hecla . . .	4,887	Acaxete, do. . .	7,275
Pauda (Uralian chain)	4,512	La Puebla, do. . .	7,200
Benmacdouie, (highest in		St. Antonio, do. . .	7,192
Britain)	4,390	Tula, do. . .	6,733
Ben Nevis ⎫ Inverness-	4,370	St. Juan del Rio, do.	6,484
Brae Riach ⎭ shire.	4,304	Queretano, do. . .	6,362
Whern-side . . .	4,050	St. Miguel el Saldado	5,761
Ingleborough . . .	3,987	Xalapa	4,335
Vesuvius	3,875	Masatlan	4,168
Ben Lawers . .	3,858	Caraccas	2,558
Ben More	3,723	Mescala	1,694
Ben Gloe*	3,690		
Snowdon	3,555		
Shehallien	3,461		
Table Mount . . .	3,454		
Helvellyn	3,324		
Skiddaw	3,270		
Soracte	2,271		
Madrid, Plains of . .	1,920		
Geneva	1,278		
Arthur Seat . . .	803		

The Himalayah range.

The principal chain or system of mountains in the Old Continent, both in regard to elevation and extent, is undoubtedly that which, in modern times, has received the name of the Himalayah Range, supposed to be the Imaus of ancient geographers. This vast stony ridge, which separates Hindostan from Thibet, has not yet been completely explored, but the numerous large

* Determined by the writer of this article, in reference to a mean of 10 barometrical observations, taken near the base of the mountain ; the contemporaneous observations having been made at Kinfauns Manse by the Rev. Mr. Gordon. The height of Kinfauns Manse above the mean level of the German Ocean, was ascertained by levelling, and connected with a level line, extended by Mr. Jardine, from the mouth of the Tay to the town of Perth. The measurement of General Roy, which assigns for the height of Ben-gloe 3472 feet, is certainly 200 feet below the truth.

rivers which have been ascertained to flow from it, in all directions, demonstrate its great elevation, and leave no doubt that it must be regarded as the loftiest mountain chain on the face of the globe. It occupies, with its various ramifications, a vast space in the central part of Asia, between Persia, India, China, and Tartary, stretching, with little interruption, for upwards of 1500 miles from south-east to north-west, and sending off several lateral branches from the main chain, of considerable extent. From the flanks of this immense upland tract, proceed the rivers Oxus and Iaxartes on the west, the Amur on the east, the Indus, the Ganges, and Burrhampooter, on the south, and the Obi and Jennisay on the north, insomuch, that the countries through which these mighty rivers wind their way, may be said to hang on the skirts of this mass of elevated land. Some geographers attempt to trace this chain along the south-east of the Caspian, and pretend to discover it, after several interruptions, in the Alps and the Pyrenees. It is certain, however, that it sends out a mountainous ridge towards the south-east, which separates India from China, causing the principal streams of the latter to descend eastward, while it compels those of the former to run towards the south. The northern flank must have a gradual slope towards the Arctic Ocean, as the whole system of rivers on that side pursue the same general course, and discharge themselves into the Frozen Sea. *Hamilton's Account of Nepaul*, p. 87. *Rennel's Herodotus. Elphinstone's Account of Caubul*, p. 636.

The Uralian chain. The Uralian Chain, though of moderate height, may be deemed, on account of its great extent, the next, in point of importance, to the Himalayah Range, on the Old Continent. Extending nearly 1000 miles, in the direction of the meridian, it forms a barrier between Europe and Asia, the more remarkable, on this account, that the rivers on each side of it, though running parallel to each other, flow in opposite directions. To account for this singular disposition of the basins of these rivers, it is affirmed that the Siberian waters not only rise from a more elevated level than those of Russia, on the western side of the Uralian Mountains, but continue their courses along a descent, which is every where higher, until they approach the Frozen Ocean. (See *Rennel's Geog. of Herodotus*, p. 182.) The Uralian Mountains have been stiled by the Russians the girdle of the world, an appellation to which they are but little entitled for their height, which rarely exceeds 4000 feet. The highest ridges are described to be of the primitive formation, and consist of granite, gneiss, and micaceous schistus.

The Altaian chain. The Altaian Chain, the most distinguished in Siberia, crosses, according to Pallas, the head of the Irtus, and running between that river and the sources of the Obi, it afterwards pursues a winding direction among the springs of the Jennisay. Passing to the southward of the sea of Baikal, where it is termed the Mountains of Sayansk, it bends in a more northerly direction towards Ochotsk, and terminates in the Daourian Mountains. From this quarter a low ridge proceeds nearly due south towards China. The Altaian chain is stated to extend for 5000 miles, though this is extremely doubtful. It is described to be chiefly of primitive formation, but few of its loftiest summits attain the height of 6000 feet.

Chain of Caucasus. The Chain of Caucasus extends between the Euxine and the Caspian Seas, and overlooks, on the north, the Deserts of Astrachan and the country of the Don Cossacks, while, on the south, it constitutes a side of the vast basin in which are contained the countries of Syria, Mesopotamia, and the Arabian Desert. The Mountains of Caucasus form properly two chains, which run nearly parallel to each other. The highest ridge, which is covered with perpetual snow, rises, in some places, to the height of 15,000 or 16,000 feet. The summits of these lofty peaks, like the most elevated points of the Andes, are represented to consist of porphyry. The Mountains of Caucasus constitute a branch of the stupendous rocky chain, known to the ancients under the name of *Saurus, Emodus,* &c. which, originating in the south-western extremity of Asia Minor, and passing near the skirts of the Levant, separated in its course eastward, Armenia from Mesopotamia; the Greater Media, from the narrow tract along the south border of the Caspian Sea; and, finally, India from Scythia. From the body of Taurus, according to Rennel, near the place where the Euphrates effects a passage through it, a lateral chain stretches to the south, with a slight inclination to the west, and first falling in with the Mediterranean at the Gulf of Issus, it afterwards runs along the shores of that sea, like a mighty wall, under the names of Lebanon, Amanus, &c., till it reaches the southern borders of Palestine. Quitting the Mediterranean, it proceeds towards the eastern coast of the Red Sea, and finally terminates in Arabia Felix. From another part of Taurus proceeds, according to the same distinguished geographer, separate ridges on the north-east quarter of Assyria, forming the eastern side of an immense basin, of which Amanus and Lebanon constitute the western, and Taurus itself the northern side. At the eastern border of Susiana it approaches the Persian Gulf, which it shuts up on the side towards Persia, and at length terminates at the neck or entrance of that inland sea. (*Rennel's Geog. of Herodotus*, p. 180.)

The Ghauts. The Ghauts form a mountainous ridge, which runs along the western coast of the Deccan, though the same appellation is occasionally applied to the elevated land, which skirts the eastern shores of that vast promontory. This rocky chain extends, with little interruption, from the Gulf of Cambay to Cape Comorin, seldom retiring more than sixty miles from the coast, and forming an abrupt termination on the west, of an extensive tract of table land, which gradually declines eastward to the Coromandel shore, and gives a corresponding direction to the waters of that part of Hindostan. The Ghauts are of moderate elevation, seldom extending 5000 feet in height, but the influence they exert on the climate of the southern provinces of India, gives them an importance in physical geography, which they would not otherwise have possessed.

The Alps The Alps, the most remarkable mountainous ridge in Europe, extends for upwards of 500 miles, in the form of a crescent, commencing at the Gulf of Genoa, and stretching through Switzerland to the eastern shores of the Adriatic. This chain, which, in different places receives distinctive appellations, may be regarded as forming two separate ridges, which, to a certain extent, run nearly parallel to each other, from south-west to north-east. The most northern ridge, denominated the Helvetian Alps, presents several peaks of great elevation, some of which rise to the height of more than 10,000 feet, and are covered with perpetual snow. The southern ridge extends from Mont Blanc, the pinnacle of Europe, to the Tyrolese territory, where it terminates in the Rhaetian Alps, on the south of the river Inn. The Alps are more distinguished by their elevation than their extent. As the Himalayah Range gives rise to the principal rivers on the eastern part of the Old Continent, the Alps contain the sources of the largest streams which take their rise on the western side. Thus, the Rhine, the Rhone, the Danube, and the Po, which flow in very different directions, all descend from this lofty mass, and return to the ocean by channels, whose mouths are separated many hundreds of miles from each other. See ALPS.

The Pyrenees. The Pyrenees, which separate France from Spain, run for about 200 miles in a north-west and south-east direction. This ridge has many elevated peaks, some of which, though they attain the height of 11,000 feet, abound, on the very summit, with many marine productions. The calcareous rocks of Mont Perdu, one of the highest of the range, present, in some places, a perpendicular front of 600 feet, and appear to be inaccessible on every side. La Perouse, who examined the Pyrenees with much attention, states, that this lofty range of mountains contains beds of granite, porphyry, trap, horn-blende, and petro-silex, alternating with primitive limestone, and surmounted by calcareous rocks of secondary formation, in which abundant traces are discovered of shells and other marine exuviæ.

Carpathian mountains. The Carpathian Mountains bound Hungary on the north and the east, and extend, in a winding direction, from the sources of the Oder on the west, towards the confines of Buckovina, on the south-east, where they divide into two branches, one of which shoots out to the east, the other to the west of Transylvania. The whole extent of this mountainous range is estimated at 500 miles. The summit of the Lomnitz, one of the loftiest of its peaks, is stated by Dr. Townson to be 8640 feet above the level of the sea.

The Appennines. The Appennines form a continuation of the Alps, though they are greatly inferior to the latter in point of elevation. This secondary chain stretches, with little interruption, along both sides of the Gulf of Genoa, and running afterwards in a south-east direction, terminates in the southern extremity of Italy. The most elevated points of the Appennines rarely reach the height of 8000 feet above the level of the sea, and are found to consist, for the most part, of a grey compact limestone, having a stratified structure. Il Velina and Il Gran Sassa, the most considerable mountains of the chain, have been ascertained to be, the former 7872, and the latter 9577 Paris feet, above the level of the sea. The country on the two sides of the Appennines presents a good deal of difference in geological structure; that next the Adriatic, consisting almost entirely of secondary rocks, while, on the side of the Mediterranean, an extensive tract stretches along the coast, consisting of primary and transition rocks, with occasional portions of secondary strata. Between the loftiest mountains and the sea, a succession of hills intervenes, which seem to be of more recent formation than the main ridge. These hills are composed of marl, with a covering of sand and gravel, and are found to contain the trunks of trees, nearly in their natural state, with leaves of vegetables and skeletons of fishes, on many of which the dried flesh is still to be seen. See *Brocchi's Geology of the Appennines.*

Norwegian mountains. The Norwegian chain of mountains, which separates Norway from Sweden, receives various names in its progress, and is scarcely known to geographers by any distinctive appellation. Commencing with the mountains of Joglefield on the south, it runs in a north-east direction towards the North Cape, seldom bending far from the ocean, and often projecting into it

with bold promontories. Pennant asserts, on apparently good authority, that its highest points are 7000 or 8000 feet above the level of the sea. Snähäda, the centre of the great chain, was ascended in 1800 by Esmark, and ascertained to be 8120 feet above the level of the sea; and Sulitelma, the highest of all the mountains of Lapland, was measured by Dr. Wahlenberg about the same period, and found to be nearly 6000 feet above the same point. The Norwegian mountains repose on gneiss, which, according to Von Buch, is the prevailing fundamental rock in the north of Europe. See *Von Buch's Travels in Norway and Lapland.*

Mountains of Africa. The African mountains have been so imperfectly examined, that we can scarcely venture to give even an outline of their distribution. Geographers, in general, agree in representing a great central chain, as extending from the mountains of Kong, on the west, to those of Donga, on the east. The sources of the Niger, the Senegal, and the Gambia, are contained in the mountains of Kong. This chain of mountains, the existence of which is established on very slender authority, is affirmed to send off a lateral branch to the south, but nothing is known with certainty respecting its exact position or extent. It seems to be better ascertained, that a lofty ridge proceeds from the southern promontory of the African Continent to Cape Gardafui, at the entrance of the Arabian Gulf; though, even of this chain, little is known excepting the name. The Portuguese, the only Europeans who have visited these mountains, have denominated them the Mountains of Lupata, but they have furnished no information respecting their position, their altitude, or their structure.

The mountains which skirt the western side of Southern Africa have been described by Barrow and Lichtenstein, but with little geological precision. The sandstone rocks, which prevail a considerable way to the northward of the Cape of Good Hope, along the western coast, are stated to present the most fantastic shapes, frequently towering one above another, till they seem to touch the sky. From the decay of this stone arises the vast accumulation of sand, spread over the low lands, which form the Karroos or barren plains, that stretch for an unknown extent towards the north. The Nardow Mountains, which were crossed by Lichtenstein, are represented to exhibit a slaty structure, and to contain, in some places, the impressions of marine animals, but it is not mentioned whether they consist of argillaceous or calcareous schistus. *Lichtenstein's Travels in Southern Africa; Barrow's Travels in Southern Africa.* The geognostic relations of the mountains in the immediate vicinity of the Cape have been described, with much accuracy, by Professor Jameson. *Edin. Phil. Journal,* vol. i. p. 283.

Mountains of Atlas. The Mountains of Atlas, so celebrated in ancient classical story, constitute a ridge, which, according to the best authorities, extends from Cape Geer, in a north-east direction, separating the Kingdom of Algiers from Zeb and Bilidulgerid, and terminating near Tunis. The most elevated peak of this chain is behind the City of Morocco, and is estimated, from the height of the line of perpetual congelation in that latitude, to be 12,000 feet above the level of the sea.

Mountains of Abyssinia. The Mountains of Abyssinia have been more minutely explored than those of any other portion of Africa. They seem to be connected with the great chain, which, traversing the central regions of this extensive continent, gives birth, at its two extremities, to the most remarkable elevated masses, consisting of various ranges of mountains, the highest of which are towards the centre. The loftiest points are stated by Tellez to be those of Amhara and Samena, from which streams descend in all directions. Gojam, in which Bruce placed the source of the Nile, was computed by that enterprizing traveller to be upwards of 10,000 feet above the level of the sea. In Upper Egypt, the mountains which run along the shores of the Red Sea, are of primitive formation, and consist chiefly of granite and porphyry. They appear to constitute one of the sides of that extensive basin which contains the desert and low lying lands of Arabia.

Having given a general sketch of the principal mountain ridges in the Old World, we shall next endeavour to exhibit a similar view of those which exist in the American Continent. Of these, the most important, by far, is the stupendous chain, termed the Andes, this range being not only the most elevated and extensive, but abounding with volcanic peaks of a more towering magnitude, than any to be found elsewhere on the face of the globe. This lofty chain, which may be said to commence in the kingdom of New Mexico, and terminate in the southern extremity of South America, possesses an extent of nearly 5000 miles. The Andes stretch, on the whole, from north to south, though in some places they deviate considerably from the meridional direction ; and their general construction is somewhat different on the two sides of the equator, which crosses some of the loftiest summits of the chain. In the southern hemisphere, the Cordilleras, (for such is the term usually applied to this lofty range,) are frequently interrupted by deep chasms or transverse valleys, whereas, on the north, the ridge of the mountain may be said to constitute an expanded plain, of great elevation, which stretches for an extent of 1500 miles, with a declivity so gentle that the surface never descends lower than 5000 feet above the level of the sea, and rarely rises 9000 feet above it. From this elevated table land, several volcanic peaks raise their frowning summits above the clouds, but they are inferior in height to some mountains of a similar description, on the south side of the equator. The most gigantic of those stupendous masses are those which rise out of two parallel ridges, into which the chain is divided by an extensive longitudinal valley, which begins at the equator, and continues to the south of Quito, where the two ridges are again united. The western chain contains Chimborazo, the loftiest mountain in the New World, Pichincha, Illinissa, and Corazon, the least elevated of which is upwards of 15,000 feet above the level of the sea, while the western contains Cayambe, only inferior in height to Chimborazo, Cotapaxi, and Tungurahua. Capac-Urca, a volcanic mountain, the summit of which has sunk into the crater, is affirmed to have been, at one period, higher than Chimborazo ; and the appearance of Illinissa, which is that of a double pyramid, renders it probable that its height, which is still 17,000 feet above the level of the sea, had also been considerably greater than it is at present. Many of these stupendous mountains exhibit the singular contrast of throwing out eruptions of fire and smoke, from under a covering of perpetual snow.

The composition of the rocks which constitute the Cordilleras of the Andes, is similar to that of other extensive mountainous chains. Granite seems to be the great basis on which the other formations repose. Over this rock lies gneiss, which is succeeded by the different formations of primitive schistus. The sum-

mits of the Andes are everywhere covered with porphyry, basalt, greenstone, and other kindred rocks. At their bases are observed two different kinds of limestone ; the one with a siliceous base, inclosing primitive masses, and occasionally cinnabar and coal ; the other with a calcareous base, uniting the secondary rocks. Upland plains, of a vast extent, are covered with an ancient deposit of limestone, over which rests the Alpine limestone, abounding with marine petrifactions at a great elevation. Next appears a lamellar gypsum, impregnated with sulphur and salt ; above this another calcareous formation, whitish and homogeneous, but sometimes cavernous. Then calcareous sandstone, and lamellar gypsum mixed with clay ; and, lastly, calcareous masses, involving flints and hornstone, with which the series terminates.

One of the most remarkable facts connected with the structure of these elevated masses is, that the secondary formations are not only of an enormous thickness, but frequently at an immense height above the level of the sea. Beds of coal are observed in the neighbourhood of Santa Fé at the height of nearly 9000 feet, and even at Huanaco in Peru, which is about 6000 feet higher. Fossil shells, which in the Old World have not been discovered at a greater elevation than the summit of the Pyrennees, have been traced on the Andes, to the height of 14,000 feet. In like manner, the basalt of Pichincha, possesses an elevation of 15,000 feet, while the greatest height, in Europe, where that species of rock has been observed, is little more than 4000 feet above the level of the sea. Again, granite, which generally crowns the loftiest summits of mountain peaks, in the old world, does not occur on the Andes above the height of 11,500 feet ; the highest points of the chain consisting chiefly of porphyry, sometimes 10,000 or 12,000 feet in thickness. *Tab. Physique des Regions Equatoriales.* Par Humboldt. *Edin. Review*, No. XXXI.

Towards the north of Mexico the Andes gradually decline in height, and on Chili, their elevation, according to Ulloa, is not more than a seventh part of the height of the Cordilleras of Peru. From the great chain already described, it appears by the statements of Humboldt, that there are three remarkable lateral chains, which run nearly east and west, or at right angles to the principal ridge ; 1st, That of the north coast, between the latitude of 9 and 10 north ; 2d, That of Parime, or of the great cataracts of the Orinoco ; and, 3d, That of Tiquitos, which separates the branches of the Amazons from those of la Plata.

The littoral chain, or Cordillera of the Coast, stretches, in the 10th degree of north latitude, from Quibor and Barquesimato, as far as the point of Paria, and is linked by the Paramo de las Rosas to the Nevado de Merida, and the Andes of New Grenada. The mountains of Parime, a less elevated but more extensive group than that of the Coast, may be traced over a space of more than 700 miles in length ; but it is rather a succession of granitic mountains, separated from one another by small plains, than a continuous chain, pursuing, without interruption, the same general direction. This chain is not connected with the Andes of New Grenada, but is detached from the main ridge, by an interval of 80 leagues. The last of these chains, the Cordillera of Tiquitos, unites, in the parallel of 16° and 18° of south latitude, the Andes of Peru to the mountains of Brazil, and forms a barrier between the systems of tributary streams which supply, on opposite sides of it, the waters of the Amazon and La

Side notes: The Andes. / Their structure and composition. / Immense height at which the rocks of secondary formation occur in the Andes / Physical Geography.

Plata. These three transverse chains are entirely destitute of active volcanoes. None of their summits ascends above the limit of perpetual frost ; and the mean height of the two northernmost ridges does not reach 4000 feet, though some of their summits rise upwards of 8000 feet above the level of the sea. *Humboldt's Pers. Nar.* IV. 203. See also ANDES.

The Stony mountains. The mountainous chain, in the American continent, next in importance to the Andes, is perhaps the extensive ridge, denominated by the inappropriate designation of the Stony Mountains. Of this lengthened range, which some geographers regard as a prolongation of the Andes, little is known, excepting that it commences in the northern parts of New Mexico, and terminates near the Arctic ocean. This chain was crossed in 1804 by an expedition sent out by the United States to explore the Missouri and the Columbia, but the party having no barometer, and being scantily provided with philosophical instruments of every description, the information they brought back of the regions they visited was of no great value to physical geography. From other authorities, on which little more reliance can be placed, we learn that the Stony Mountains are in general about 3500 feet above their base, which is supposed to be nearly as much above the level of the ocean. *Pinkerton's Geog.* Vol. II. 531. Humboldt conjectures that their absolute height may be reckoned 6000 or 7000 feet. *Humboldt's New Spain,* Vol. I. 19. *Mackenzie's Travels,* Vol. III. 331.

The Apalachian chain. The Apalachian chain, another important range of mountains in North America, commences in Georgia, and running in a north-east direction, terminates near the banks of the river St. Lawrence, in New Brunswick. The extent of the range may be estimated at nearly 1000 miles. The most elevated points are towards the northern extremity, where some of the loftiest peaks attain the height of more than 6000 feet above the level of the sea. The principal part of the range consists of primitive rocks, particularly that portion of it which passes through Virginia, North Carolina, and Georgia. In Pennsylvania and Maryland the primitive rocks are less abundant, the most elevated parts of the chain being composed of transition rocks, with some intervening patches of secondary formation. Besides the principal range, there is, according to Mr. Maclure, an extensive district, occupied by primitive rocks, on the west of Lake Champlain, joining the primitive rocks in Canada to the north and north-west, and following a line from the Thousand islands in St. Lawrence, which runs nearly parallel to the Mohawk river, till it meets Lake George on the southwest. It appears, by the same authority, that from near Kingston on Lake Ontario, to some distance below Quebec, the whole tract is nearly primitive ; and that the great mass of continent lying to the north of the 46th degree of latitude, for a considerable distance to the west, consists of the same formation. *Maclure's Geology of the United States.*

Arctic mountains. Of the Arctic mountains little is known. Their structure on the sea coast, according to Parry, is that of a horizontal stratification, presenting a number of regular projecting masses, broad at the bottom, and tapering towards the top, having a resemblance to so many buttresses raised by art at equal intervals. This remarkable structure, we are informed by this enterprizing navigator, continues with little variation, along the whole northern shore which he explored. It is not easy to determine the composition of these mountains, from this very vague description of their appearance, but they are probably basaltic, and of volcanic origin. The Byam Martin mountains are of considerable height. One of them was measured trigonometrically by Captain Parry, and found to be 3382 feet above the level of the sea. *Parry's Voyage for the Discovery of a North West Passage.*

Volcanic mountains. We shall conclude our account of these stony ridges which traverse the surface of the earth, with a brief description of the principal volcanic mountains. It is difficult to trace, in the geographical distribution of these mountains, any thing of a precise nature. They are found in both hemispheres ; in all latitudes ; and in the old as well as the new world. They seem in general, however, to be situated near the sea coast, and rarely or never in the interior of large continents. Cotopaxi, in South America, is perhaps, of all volcanic mountains, the most distant from the ocean, and yet it is only 140 miles from the shores of the Pacific.

Form of volcanic mountains. Volcanoes are generally of a conical or pyramidal shape, and possess a considerable regularity of form. Their summits always terminate in a large concavity, called the *crater,* sloping down to a contracted aperture, from which melted matter is ejected, when the central fire is in a state of activity. The size of the crater does not depend, as we might at first suppose, on the magnitude of the volcanic mountain, of which it is the vent. The diameter of the crater of Vesuvius is five times that of the Peak of Teneriffe, though the height of the latter is four times the height of the former. Nor will this appear surprising, if we reflect that the loftiest volcanoes frequently throw out less matter from their summits than from the lateral openings by which they are pierced ; and indeed it might be laid down as a very general fact in geology, that the most elevated volcanic mountains have the smallest craters at their summits, had it not been ascertained by Humboldt, that the craters of the colossal volcanoes of Cotopaxi and Ruenpechincha are nearly a mile in diameter. *Humb. Pers. Nar.* I. 172.

Volcanoes in the old world. In the old continent, the most remarkable volcanoes are those of Ætna, Vesuvius, and Hecla, all of which are in the immediate vicinity of the sea. The eastern coast of the Asiatic division of the globe abounds with volcanoes, many of which, in the peninsula of Kamschatka, are in a state of activity. *Cook's Voyages.* The Indian Seas also contain a great number of islands, which are the seats of these magazines of destructive matter, particularly Japan, the Manillas, Borneo, Mindanao, Sumatra, Ternat, Celebes, Java, Bourbon, Amsterdam, &c. The western coast of Africa presents no remarkable volcano, unless we include under this extensive range the Canary isles and the Azores.

Volcanoes in the new world. In the American continent, volcanoes are not only more numerous, but of a more stupendous magnitude than in the old world. Several of the volcanic mountains in this quarter of the globe, ascend, even within the tropical regions, far above the limits of perpetual snow. In 1802, the cone of Cotopaxi was heated to such a degree, that almost in one night it lost the enormous mass of snow by which it had long been covered. *Humb. New Spain,* ii. 113. Popocatepetl, the loftiest volcano of New Spain, is, with the exception of the Himalayah range, 2000 feet higher than the most elevated summit in the old world, and yet it is more than 1000 feet lower than Cotopaxi. Humboldt seems to consider the different volcanic mountains in South America, more especially on the south side of the isthmus, to be so intimately connected, as to constitute rather a single swollen mass, than groups of distinct volcanoes. *Pers. Nar.* iv. p. 29. Volcanic mountains occur both in the northern and southern extremity of America, as well as in the equatorial regions ; but never, as we already remarked, at a distance from the sea. Of these, we may mention Mount St. Elie, which rises nearly to the height of 18,000 feet, and the volcanic peaks of Terra del Fuego.

The slope or inclination of mountain ridges, is generally different on opposite sides of the chain, being usually bold or precipitous on one side, and gentle on the other. Thus the Himalayah mountains, the loftiest in the world, are extremely precipitous on the side of Hindostan, while they decline with a very gradual descent toward the elevated plains of Thibet. In like manner, the Alps, which rise abruptly on the side next Italy, present a more easy ascent on the side of Switzerland. A similar remark is applicable to the Andes, which, though extremely steep on their western flanks, gradually sink away, on the eastern sides, into the immense basins of the Amazon and Oroonoko.

One of the most precipitous mountains which has been accurately measured, is perhaps the Silla of Caraccas. Though not exactly perpendicular, the slope of it, which is about 60°, is sufficiently great to give the side of the mountain next the sea the appearance of an inaccessible rock, rising to the enormous height of 7000 feet. The mean slope of the Peak of Teneriffe, notwithstanding its extreme steepness, is only 12° or 13°, and that of Mont Blanc toward the Allée Blanche, does not exceed 45°, though in the greater number of geological works, that stupendous mountain is described as presenting a perpendicular front on the south side. No rock in Europe has been discovered which rises perpendicularly to the height of 1500 feet. The Pyrenees, though abounding with calcareous cliffs, exhibits no precipice of more than 600 feet in height. *Humboldt's Pers. Nar.* III. 508. A slope of 5° is a marked inclination, and if it amount to 15°, becomes too great for carriages. When it reaches 37°, it is inaccessible on foot, if the bottom be a naked rock, or a turf too thick to form steps ; and a declivity of 42° can only be climbed when it is covered with firm sand, or volcanic ashes. An inclination of 44° or 45° cannot be scaled, even though the ground should admit of thrusting the foot into it for the purpose of forming steps. The cones of volcanoes have an average slope from 33° to 40° ; and the steepest parts of them are from 40° to 42°. A slope of 55° is quite inaccessible, and if viewed from above, would be estimated at 75°. These remarks on mountain slopes, which we have given on the authority of Humboldt, seem to be agreeable to experience. *Humboldt's Pers. Nar.* I. 204.

The quarter of the
heavens
faced by
the precipitous sides
of mountains.

As mountain chains have no determinate direction, neither do their most precipitous flanks always look toward any particular quarter of the heavens. The most abrupt sides, however, of the principal mountains seem to face the south and the west, though occasionally they look to the opposite points of the horizon. They may be expected, indeed, to front the quarter from which the most copious rains, and the most violent storms of wind proceed in the particular regions in which they are situated ; but the dip of the stratification seems also to have a powerful influence on the form of the outline, as mountains frequently decline gently towards the side where the bed dips from the horizon, and exhibit a precipitous aspect on the opposite side where the edge of the stratum breaks out to the day.

The most elevated mountains, and those which present the greatest continuity of extent, consist, as we have seen, almost entirely of granite, in which no vestige can be traced of the remains of organic beings. The flanks of these lofty masses are usually covered with a succession of rocks, which, though differing in particular cases as to the order of arrangement, are sufficiently definite in character to entitle them to be classed by the general denomination of *Primitive Rocks.* Granite never being found resting on any other species of rock, is considered by geologists, as constituting the shell, if not the internal nucleus of the globe, on which the other fossil bodies repose. It is occasionally observed, in detached masses, at a great distance from granite mountains, a fact which we shall endeavour to explain in a subsequent part of this article ; but for the most part, it exists in extensive masses of vast continuity and unknown depth. At the bottom of the primitive mountains, though sometimes at a considerable elevation on their sides, a species of rock, denominated calcareous rocks of *transition*, occurs to a great extent. These rocks consist of pure calcareous earth in a crystallized state, with the remains of living beings of the lowest order, in point of organic structure ; and form an intermediate link between the primitive rocks, which rarely exhibit a stratified appearance, and those in which that structure is clearly discernible. The transition rocks include a considerable variety of earthy substances ; but they are generally composed of the primitive rocks, reduced to a state of disintegration, apparently by a mechanical cause, and afterwards reunited into conglomerate masses by some kind of cement, of an argillaceous or calcareous nature.

The *secondary rocks* are generally distributed into regular layers or beds termed strata, inclined at small angles to the horizon, and composed chiefly of calcareous and argillaceous earths, intermixed occasionally with the wrecks of animal and vegetable products,— the types of which, in many instances, are no longer to be recognized among the living beings which now exist at the surface. The argillaceous schistus, in particular, frequently contains impressions of vegetables, which must have existed previous to their consolidation. In like manner, while the strata of bituminous marl contain numerous specimens of petrified fishes, and other marine productions ; the calcareous rocks abound no less with the remains of terrestrial animals. These rocks, and others of a similar structure and composition, usually succeed each other in such a manner, that the impressions of vegetables are lowest in the arrangement, and those of animals nearest the surface.

To these rocks, possessing a generic character, are to be added a variety of others, which seem to have no fixed order of arrangement, or distribution, but graduate, at one time, into rocks of the primordial class ; and at another, are found associated with rocks of the most recent formation. Of these may be mentioned gypsum or sulphate of lime, which, though found most frequently in connexion with the secondary, occurs, under a slight modification of condition, among the primitive as well as the transition rocks. In like manner, the different kinds of sandstone, which mineralogists have divided into various orders, is seen alternating with gypsum, limestone, trap, marl, and clay.

Under the article MINERALOGY we have described the various kinds of alluvial works, including under

Physical
Geography.

Primitive
mountains.

Rocks of
transition.

Secondary
rocks.

Remains
of organized beings
in rocks.

Physical Geography.

Plains, Steppes, Llanos, &c.

this head the alluvial formations of the low or flat lands, such as clay, sand, &c. and given, at the same time, a general view of the extensive tracts of the earth's surface, which have been denominated, *Plains, Steppes, Llanos, Savannahs*, &c; we shall, therefore, confine the few additional observations we have to offer on the subject, to those relations which are more immediately connected with physical geography. The alluvial deposits, composing the low-lands or plains which extend from the bottoms of mountains, are generally found to be derived from the debris of these elevated masses, and to possess a depth proportionate to the mouldering nature of the adjacent rocks. In some cases the soil, thus formed, consists of successive layers of alluvial earth several hundred feet in thickness, while in others, it is so thinly spread over the subjacent rocky basis, that it affords with difficulty a covering to the roots of a few hardy plants, which are capable of vegetating in circumstances so unfavourable. Lewis and Clarke observed, in the vast solitudes of Louisiana, a hill of clay of a quadrangular form, the sides of which were a mile in extent, and whose height rose 100 feet above the surrounding savannahs; and Humboldt noticed similar beds of clay in New Spain. On the other hand,

Karroos.

the soil of the Karroos of Southern Africa, and many of the Llanos of America, is so exceedingly shallow, that scarcely have the plants which it nourishes exhibited the appearance of vegetation when they begin to languish and decay; insomuch that, in these barren regions, a few days after a rich verdure had adorned the plains, a brown-red dust, formed of the leaves and stalks of the dried and withered plants, covers the desert, cracked, as it then becomes, in every direction by the heat. *Lichtenstein's* Travels in S. Africa. *Humboldt's* Pers. Nar. IV. 336.

Soil of valleys.

The soil of extensive valleys is generally of considerable depth, and affords strong grounds for believing, that, at one period, it had been covered by the waters of a lake. It usually consists of an intermixture of the argillaceous and calcareous earth, with carbonaceous matters; though occasionally the siliceous earth, in the state of sand, constitutes one of the principal ingredients, and greatly diminishes its fertility.

Steppes.

The most extensive plains in the old continent, termed steppes, occur in central Asia and European Russia. These tracts of level land sometimes stretch, with little interruption, over a vast extent of territory, and are characterized, not more by the unvarying monotony of their surface than their extreme sterility. In some instances they are intersected by sluggish rivers that discharge themselves into inland seas of salt water, which, though unconnected with the ocean, are supposed, not without reason, to have a lower level than the mass of its waters.

Slight elevation of the Russian steppes.

On the left bank of the Volga commences one of the most extensive of these level plains, which stretches towards the south as far as the Caspian sea and Lake Aral, and toward the north and east, till it reaches the confines of the Steppe of Issim and the river Sarasou. This vast plain, which is almost destitute of vegetation, is about 700 miles from east to west, and nearly of the same dimensions from north to south. From the Uralian chain to the Caspian a ridge of low sandy hills runs across this desert, which, in many places, abounds with sea-shells and salt pools. Its slight elevation above the level of the sea, together with the numerous marine productions which are scattered over it, seem to countenance the idea that it had been covered at no very remote period by the ocean. A rise in the waters of

the Mediterranean, to the extent of 200 or 300 feet above its present level, would probably connect that sea with the Baltic, and inundate the whole of this barren tract as well as many of the finest provinces of Russia. *Humboldt's* Pers. Nar. I. 22.

Physical Geography.

The north-eastern part of this steppe, which is called the steppe of the Kalmucks, from the wandering tribes of that name who roam over it, is connected with the steppe of the Irtish, and is even regarded, by some geographers, as extending to the Ob, where it receives the name of the steppe of Barabbin. The latter, viewed as a distinct plain, is about 400 miles in length, and 300 in breadth. It contains a few salt lakes, but the quality of its soil is greatly superior to that of the steppe of the Kalmucks. Between the parallel of 56° N. and the Arctic sea we find another of these dreary plains, bounded on the west by the Ob, and on the east by the Lena. This extensive tract, which, though exceeding in surface the whole of Europe, contains only three or four millions of inhabitants, is denominated the desert of Siberia—an appellation which has long been associated with desolation, cruelty, and oppression.

Central land of Asia.

Between the Altaian chain and the lofty range of the Himalayah mountains, there exists a great extent of high table land, which contains several sandy deserts of considerable magnitude that have hitherto been little explored. Some parts of this elevated region are said to abound, even in the latitude of 27°, with large frozen lakes; and the soil, in general, is as barren as the climate is chill and inhospitable. A portion of this tract, lying between the Himalayah mountains and the parallel ridge of Caillus, which separates them from Thibet, has been partially examined by British travellers from Hindostan. It is described to decline gradually from each chain towards the middle, in a rugged and broken surface, sometimes presenting deep ravines of considerable breadth, remarkable for nothing but their sterility, and the entire absence of all vegetable productions. In these elevated regions hot springs are not uncommon; but no trace is observed of any volcanic action. *Quart. Rev.* XVI. 416.

Plains of China and Hindostan.

The plains into which this upland tract graduates, towards the north-east, the east, and the south, are not inferior in extent to the vast steppes of Siberia, into which it declines towards the north, while they constitute, in point of fertility, the richest portion of the habitable globe. China, a part of this alluvial formation, is esteemed by its inhabitants, with better reason than can be given for any of the pretensions set up by that vain and ignorant people, to be the most distinguished region of the earth; and, indeed, it must be admitted that the mighty streams which wind in every direction through its fertile plains, the richness of its soil, and the general salubrity of its climate, all contribute to justify that opinion. Every vegetable production which can be rendered subservient to the use or the luxury of man, may probably be cultivated in some quarter or other of this extensive country. Hindostan, which stretches from the bottom of the Himalayah mountains, on the south, to the Indian Ocean, is no less celebrated for the extent and fertility of its plains, and the numerous majestic rivers by which it is watered. This vast tract contains, within a range of 500,000 square miles, few hills which rise to the height of 3000 feet; and, in many places, the plains consist of a black vegetable mould, which is not less than six feet in depth. A soil so excellent is fitted, in such a climate as India possesses, to rear, in the utmost luxuriance, every product of the vegetable kingdom. In some parts of Hin-

Physical
Geography.

dostan, indeed, along the banks of the Indus, tracts of considerable extent are to be found in which scarce a trace of vegetation can be observed, and where the only diversity of scene arises from the different elevations of the hillocks of sand, which shift their position, and alter their shapes, according as they are affected by the whirlwinds of the desert. In the midst of these arid regions it is singular to observe, that the water melon, the most juicy of fruits, is the only vegetable product to be found. One of these deserts, in the Caubul territory, about 400 miles in length, is composed of sand hills, or still more barren plains of indurated clay. *Elphinstone's* Account of Caubul, p. 5.

Quitting the Plains of Hindostan, and advancing westward along the shores of the Persian Gulf, we find, between the Indus and the Euphrates, a wide region which consists of an alternate succession of elevated ridges and extensive flat deserts; the latter consisting, either of arid sands, or of a hard sterile clay, which is equally unproductive. One of these deserts, the great Salt Desert of Persia, stretches away into the interior towards the Caspian Sea, over an extent of about 500 miles. The sand of this desolate region is, according to Pottinger, of a reddish colour, and so exceedingly fine, that, even when closely examined, the particles of it are barely descernible on account of their minuteness. It is raised by the wind in the form of longitudinal waves, presenting, on the windward side, a gradual rise from the bottom to the top, but on the other, an abrupt slope of ten or twenty feet in height. This dreary waste produces nothing but a few saline and succulent plants. The wind which traverses it usually blows from the N. W. and, during the hot summer months, the temperature of the air is so elevated as to destroy any thing, either animal or vegetable, with which it comes in contact. *Kinneir's* Journey through Persia, &c. p. 223.

After doubling the head of the Persian Gulf, we descend into the Plains of Arabia; the greater part of which may be described to be an immense desert of barren sand impregnated with sea-salt, nearly destitute of rivers, and containing, only here and there, a scanty spring of brackish water. The Arabian Desert bears every mark of having been recently a part of the bed of the ocean; and its little elevation above the level of the sea would require but a small rise of its waters to restore this desolate tract to its former condition. Its subsoil, like that of the other deserts, is a greyish clay, with a large proportion of sand, intermixed with marine exuviæ, extending to a great distance from the sea. It contains large strata of salt, (the muriate of soda,) which, in some places, rise up into hills of considerable elevation. Its gentle and uniform slope towards the sea seems to indicate, that it has gradually emerged from the ocean; which is still receding from it. The retreat of the watery element, however, promises to be attended with little advantage to man, as the newly formed lands are not more productive than the desolate tract whose bounds they are slowly enlarging.—*Niebuhr's* Travels. Sect. xxix. chap. 2.

Having taken a general view of the plains which surround the Himalayah mountains, and the other lofty ridges connected with that mass of elevated land, we shall proceed to give a similar sketch of the flat lands, or alluvial formations, which lie around the principal ranges of mountains, on the northern and western side of the old continent.

The most extensive plains in Europe are to be found in Hungary, between the Danube and the Theiss. This vast tract of level land, which is elevated only 200 feet above the ocean, is more than 240 miles distant from the nearest sea. The line of division, constituting the ridge between the two rivers, was ascertained by an accurate survey, taken with the view of connecting their waters, to be only thirteen toises above the height of the Danube. The area of these plains is, according to the computation of Humboldt, about 3000 square leagues. Between Czegled, Snolnok, and Katsemel, this plain may be compared to a sea of sand. *Humboldt's* Pers. Nar. IV. 294.

In Russia, between the Borysthenes, the Don, and the Volga, plains of a vast extent are to be found, which rival in magnitude the Asiatic steppes. Some of these plains possess a considerable degree of fertility, and abound, not only with rich pasturages, but yield abundant crops of every species of grain. Others are of a more barren character, and are only covered, here and there, with a few detached saline plants. The small elevation of some of these plains above the level of the ocean, and the probability of their having, at no very remote period, been covered with the sea, have already been noticed.

The most elevated plains in Europe occur in Spain. The interior of that country constitutes an extensive tract of elevated land, which is about 2000 feet above the level of the ocean. The plains of La Mancha, if placed between the sources of the Niemen and the Borysthenes, would form, even in that inland situation, a group of mountains of considerable elevation.

An extensive plain, of moderate height, embracing the most fertile provinces of Europe, and intersected by the largest rivers which drain that quarter of the globe, stretches, with little interruption, from the banks of the Rhine to the source of the Volga. This wide-spreading plain possesses a great diversity of soil; exhibiting, in some places, particularly in Holland, the appearance of a flat marsh which has lately been rescued from the ocean, and in others, as in Prussia, that of sandy deserts of considerable extent, in which few traces of vegetation are to be observed. Large tracts of this low-lying land, however, consist of a rich and fertile clay, from which the most abundant crops are raised.

Of the interior of Africa too little is yet known to enable us to describe any thing beyond its most general features. A large portion of this division of the earth seems to consist of barren sandy plains; which are, probably, increasing in extent, and contracting within still narrower limits the few scanty tracts which have hitherto been subjected to human industry.

Of these sandy regions the most distinguished is that known by the appellation of *Sahara* or the *Desert*. This immense barren tract stretches, nearly with the same monotonous aspect, from the shores of the Atlantic to the confines of Egypt, and includes a space of about 2500 miles in length, and 700 in breadth; the whole of which, excepting a few insulated spots of comparative fertility, occurring here and there in the midst of this ocean of sand, appears to be condemned to the most hopeless sterility. These detached spots, which are called *Oases*, generally abound with springs, to which they owe much of that luxuriant verdure which causes them to form so very striking a contrast with the barren wastes around them. Major Rennel seems disposed to ascribe the existence of an oasis entirely to the gradual accumulation of vegetable mould, derived from the decay of the numerous plants which are nourished by an abundant supply of waters, in regions where the climate is extremely favourable to vegetation. Whatever there may be in this opinion, there can be little doubt that the springs, by which they are so plentifully watered, have their origin in the elevated land which surrounds them on every side; while it is no less probable, that the barrenness of the Great Desert is to be ascribed, in no small degree, to the total want of mountains in that part of Africa. These elevated masses not only afford, by their disintegration, a suitable soil for the nourishment of plants, but, by intermixing the aerial currents, produce those occasional depositions of moisture from the atmosphere, without which the richest soil would be altogether unfit for vegetation. *Rennel's Geog. of Herodotus*, p. 545.

The gradual encroachment of these sandy tracts on the habitable portions of the African continent, furnishes matter of interesting speculation to the geologist. By comparing the accounts we have, in modern times, of Tripoli, Tunis, and Algiers, with what appears to have been the state of the Carthaginian empire, before it had sunk under the power of Rome, we must admit that great physical changes have taken place in these countries, within the last twenty centuries. These changes are chiefly to be ascribed to the slow advance of the sands towards the shores of the Mediterranean. The vast Desert of Sahara is doubtless the source of those desolating clouds of siliceous particles which, borne along by the whirlwind of the wildnerness, must continue to enlarge the bounds of a region of sterility already too extensive to be limited by the utmost efforts of man. From the same cause, it is no less certain, that the bounds of vegetation have been greatly contracted in Nubia, and the confines of lower Egypt.

With respect to the origin of the Great Desert itself, it is difficult to form even a plausible theory. Some have conjectured that the ocean at one time covered this sandy tract, and gradually retired, leaving the surface to be dried and pulverized by the tropical winds to which it has been exposed for ages. This opinion would receive some confirmation, were it ascertained, as we are strongly inclined to believe, in this case, that the average level of the desert is below that of the ocean. Others are disposed to think, that it is the debris of an extensive range of sandstone rocks, which, at one period, overspread the African continent, and have been gradually crumbled down by the action of the weather. This hypothesis derives no small support from the accounts we have received of Southern Africa, where the formation of sandy tracts of great extent, from the demolition and decay of rocks of sandstone, has been described as still going on, by Barrow and Lichtenstein.

The physical geography of America is, owing to the indefatigable exertions of Humboldt, perhaps better known than that of Europe. This celebrated naturalist has delineated, in his various works, a comprehensive sketch of the most interesting portion of the New world, of which we shall endeavour to give a general outline. The two basins, placed at the extremities of South America, are described by Humboldt to be savannahs, or steppes, pasturages without trees; while the intermediate basin, which receives the collected waters of the Amazon, and its tributary streams, is represented to be almost one vast forest, through which there is no other route for the traveller but that of the rivers. These three capacious basins are characterized, in the language of the colonists, by terms which are sufficiently distinctive of their prominent features.

Thus we have the *Llanos* of Varinas, and of Caraccas; the *Bosques* or forests of the Amazon, and the *Pampas* of Buenos Ayres.
When we consider the slight elevation of these extensive valleys above the surface of the ocean,
they may be regarded as immense gulfs in the dry land, stretching across the American continent, and possessing a level so little raised above the waters of the Atlantic, that a tide of 500 or 600 feet at the mouth of the Amazon, would reach the base of the Andes, and cover more than the half of South America. Several appearances seem to indicate that the great plains of the Lower Oroonoko, the Amazon, and the Rio de la Plata, were, at one period, the basins of ancient lakes. The plains of the Rio Vichada and the Meta appear to have been the channel through which the waters of the most elevated of these lakes, those of the Amazon, found their way toward the inferior basin, the Llanos of Caraccas separating the Cordilleras of Parima from that of the Andes. The ground, which is perfectly level, between the Guaviare, the Meta, and the Apure, exhibits no trace of a violent eruption of the waters; but, on the borders of the Cordilleras of Parima, between the latitude of 4° and 7°, the Oroonoko, which flows in a western direction from its source to the mouth of the Guaviare, has forced a passage through the rocks, directing its course from south to north. When it has reached the north of the Apure, in that very low ground where the inclination towards the north is intersected by a counterslope towards the south-east, the Oroonoko receives a new direction, and flows towards the east. The circuitous route of this river illustrates some important facts connected with the inclination of the different regions through which it flows.

One of the most distinguishing peculiarities of the Great elevation of
the table
land of
South
America. new continent is the great elevation of some of its plains. While few level countries in Europe, of any considerable extent, rise to the height of 1800 feet, several of the plains in South America stretch for many hundred miles, at the immense elevation of 10,000 feet above the level of the ocean. The Cordilleras of the Andes exhibit, at the height of more than 8000 feet, the extraordinary sight of well-cultivated plains, adorned with populous cities, and yielding abundant crops of wheat. The great plains of Antisana approach in height to Mont Blanc, the loftiest mountain in Europe, and yet they are so level that the inhabitants of those elevated regions seem not to be aware of the remarkable situation in which nature has placed them. Many of these lofty plains crown the very summits of the mountains; and in some instances are separated from each other by transversal valleys, whose perpendicular depth is nearly a mile, and which constitute an aerial barrier between them, nearly as impassable as an arm of the sea. Others are so little disjoined by inequalities in the surface, that they form but a single plain on the lengthened ridges of the Cordillera. Thus the plains of Mexico stretch, with little interruption, from the 18th to the 40th degree of latitude, with a gentle slope, which declines towards the north, and graduates into the plains of Louisiana.

The plains of Louisiana, like the vast basins of the
Amazon, the Oroonoko, and the Rio de la Plata, have a gradual inclination towards the east. These extensive plains, which in some places do not exhibit the smallest discernible rising over a range of 800 miles, are almost entirely destitute of trees; but they are everywhere covered with a rank coarse grass. The soil is of various descriptions; and though, in general,

Physical
Geography.
it is a rich brown loamy earth, it occasionally degenerates into a yellowish clay, which is more or less intermixed with sand. Over these vast regions, the dominion of man is in a great measure unknown; and
countless flocks of buffaloes roam undisturbed. Clarke
and Lewis mention that, on one occasion, they descried,
from a small eminence on the banks of the Missouri, a
herd of about 20,000 of these wild cattle.

Plains of
North
America.
The alluvial country to the eastward of the Alleghany mountains consists of beds of sand, gravel, and
clay, which vary with the nature of the adjacent rocks,
from the disintegration of which they have originated.
In many instances, they contain animal and vegetable
remains, which are found at the depth of nearly 100
feet below the surface.

The northern parts of America, beyond the 50th
degree of latitude, may be described, in general terms,
as an extensive tract of marshy land, abounding with
lakes and small rivers. Its elevation above the level
of the ocean is inconsiderable, except towards the
western shores of the continent, where the primitive
mountains are observed, in some cases, to rise abruptly
from the water's edge, and to attain a stupendous
height.

Character-
istic fea-
tures of
Austra-
lasia.
The great division of the globe to which modern
geographers have given the name of Australasia, is
characterized by certain geognostic peculiarities, the
nature of which we cannot altogether pass over, in a
general survey of the earth's surface. In New Holland, for example, the elevated land which, in other
parts of the world, is generally found in inland situations, forms here a sort of rampart, which surrounds
the whole of this insular continent, at a small distance
from the coast. The rivers, too, instead of flowing
into the sea, direct their course towards the interior,
where they are lost in lakes, or large marshy plains,
overspread with reeds, and other aquatic plants. The
soil of these inland tracts is described to be, in some
places, a red tenacious clay, and in others, a dark hazel-
coloured loam, so rotten and full of holes, that it is almost impassable. It remains to be determined whether the lakes into which the principal rivers of New
Holland discharge themselves have any communication with the ocean, or whether the waters they receive from the surrounding mountains are again dissipated by evaporation. Many ages must elapse, in
the ordinary state of things, before the alluvial matters
conveyed into these muddy magazines can produce
any sensible change in their elevation; but a sudden
convulsion, by raising the interior a few hundred feet
above its present level, might instantly convert them
into rich and fertile plains.

Fissures,
veins, and
caverns.
As we have already described, under MINERALOGY,
the nature of the materials which compose the solid
crust of the globe, we must refer to that article for a
detailed account of every thing connected with the
composition, and geognostic situation, of mineral substances, and confine our attention, at present, to a few
of the more remarkable appearances which fall to be
mentioned under Physical Geography. The immense
fissures or crevices which, in many places, traverse the
solid strata to an unknown extent, claim our first consideration. These rents, which, on a small scale, are
denominated veins, receive the name of caverns, or
grottoes, when they exceed certain dimensions.

In general, the rocks of primitive formation exhibit
few caverns of any great magnitude. The largest cavities observed in the oldest granite, called *Ovens* in
Switzerland, are occasioned, for the most part, by the

union of several contemporaneous veins of quartz, of
feldspar, or of fine-grained granite, and rarely exceed
four or five feet in diameter. They are to be regarded
rather as partial and accidental phenomena, than as
general appearances belonging to an extensive formation.

In what
species of
rocks most
frequent.
In the calcareous rocks of the secondary order,
grottoes occur of the largest size, and in greatest abundance; but they are also frequent in primitive as well
as transition limestone. The species of limestone to
which mineralogists have applied the appellation of
Jura limestone, so abounds with caverns, in both continents, that several followers of Werner have given it
the name of cavern-limestone. (HŒHLENKALKSTEIN.)
In this rock are to be found the grottoes of Boudry, of
Matiers-Travers, and of Valarbe, in the Jura; the
grotto of Baume, near Geneva; the caverns between
Muggendorf and Gailenreuth, in Franconia; of Sowia
Jama, Ogrodzimiec, and Wolodowica, in Poland; and
the Cueva del Guacharo, and the other grottoes of the
valley of Caripe, in South America. It is this rock, too,
which, by its cavernous nature, frequently interrupts
the course of small rivers, by engulfing them in the capacious recesses with which it abounds.

The muriatiferous gypsum presents, also, on account
of its great solubility, enormous cavities, which sometimes communicate with each other, over an extent of
several leagues. Among the secondary rocks, besides
the limestone and gypseous formation, we may notice
a third formation, that of the argillaceous sandstone,
as occasionally containing caverns; these, however,
are limited in extent, and progressively contract toward their extremities.

Form of
caverns.
The form of grottoes, though affected chiefly by the
nature of the rocks in which they occur, is frequently
modified, in no small degree, by accidental causes.
Humboldt has, in reference to their most general appearance, divided them into three classes. Some have
the form of large clefts, or crevices, like veins not filled
with ore, such as the cavern of Rosenmuller, in Franconia; Eldenhole, in the Peak of Derbyshire, and the
Sumideroes of Chamacasapa, in Mexico. The depths
of some of these clefts is enormous: that of Eldenhole is unknown, it having been sounded by a line of
1600 fathoms, without reaching the bottom; and the
depth of a similar abyss, near Frederickshall, in Norway, is so great, that a stone requires two minutes to
descend through it, which would make its depth, if the
stone received no interruption in its fall, upwards of
20,000 feet.

Fissures or
clefts.

Perfora-
tions,
through
mountains.
The second class of caverns, according to Humboldt's
arrangement, are open to the light at both extremities,
and may be said to be natural galleries, through the
mountains in which they occur. Of this description
of caverns are the Pierre-Pertuise, in Jura; the Pausi-
lippo, near Naples; the Holeberg of Muggendorf;
and the celebrated cavern called Dantœ, by the Otto-
mite Indians, and the Bridge of the Mother of God, by
the Mexican Spaniards. The Torgnat in Norway,
another of these stupendous perforations, has an extent
of nearly a mile, and presents an opening of about 150
feet in height, through which the sun may be seen at
certain seasons of the year.

Caves, or
grottoes.
The third form of caverns, being the one of most
frequent occurrence, exhibits a succession of cavities of
various extent, running nearly in the same direction,
and communicating with each other by passages of
greater or less breadth. It often happens with grottoes
of this description, that the entrances are extremely

disproportionate to the magnitude of the internal cavities to which they afford access, it being frequently necessary to creep under very low vaults to reach the deepest, and most spacious, of these subterraneous works of nature. One of the most extensive caverns, or rather series of caverns, of the class we are now considering, which has yet been discovered, is the Mammoth Cave, in Kentucky, for a particular description of which, see KENTUCKY, p. 441. This wonderful assemblage of caverns, which, with its various ramifications, has an extent of more than ten miles, occurs in the limestone formation. The cavern of Guacharo, another of the same description, of which an accurate account was first given by Humboldt, is so well described by that accomplished traveller, that we shall offer no apology for giving the following extracts from his interesting sketch of it: " What gives most celebrity," says Humboldt, " to the valley of Caripe, beside the extraordinary coolness of the climate, is the great *Cueva*, or cavern of the *Guacharo*. In a country where the people love what is marvellous, a cavern that gives birth to a river, and is inhabited by thousands of nocturnal birds, the fat of which is employed in the missions to dress food, is an everlasting object of conversation and discussion. Scarcely has a stranger arrived at Cumana, when he is told of the stone of Araya for the eyes ; of the labourer of Arenas, who suckled his child ; and of the cavern of Guacharo, which is said to be several leagues in length ; till he is tired of hearing of them. A lively interest in the phenomena of nature is preserved wherever society may be said to be without life ; where in dull monotony it presents only simple relations, little fitted to excite the ardour of curiosity.

" The cavern, which the natives call a *mine of fat*, is not in the valley of Caripe itself, but at three short leagues distance from the convent, towards the west-south-west. It opens into a lateral valley, which terminates at the *Sierra del Guacharo*. We set out toward the Sierra on the 18th of September, accompanied by the Alcaids, or Indian magistrates, and the greater part of the monks of the convent. A narrow path led us at first, during an hour and a half, toward the south, across a fine plain, covered with a beautiful turf. We then turned toward the west, along a small river, which issues from the mouth of the cavern. We ascended during three quarters of an hour, walking sometimes in the water, which was shallow, sometimes between the torrent and a wall of rocks, on a soil extremely slippery and miry. The falling down of the earth, the scattered trunks of trees, over which the mules could scarcely pass, the creeping plants that covered the ground, rendered this part of the road fatiguing.

At the foot of the lofty mountain of Guacharo, we were only 400 steps from the cavern, without yet perceiving the entrance. The torrent runs in a crevice, which has been hollowed out by the waters ; and we went on, under a cornice, the projection of which prevented us from seeing the sky. The path winds like the river ; at the last turning, we came suddenly before the immense opening of the grotto. The aspect of this spot is majestic, even to the eye of a traveller accustomed to the picturesque scenes of the Upper Alps. I had before this seen the caverns of the Peak of Derbyshire, where, extended in a boat, we traversed a subterraneous river, under a vault of two feet high. I had visited the beautiful grotto of Tresemienhiz, in the Carpathian mountains ; the caverns of

the Hartz, and those of Franconia, which are vast cemeteries of bones of tigers, hyenas, and bears, as large as our horses. Nature, in every zone, follows immutable laws in the distribution of rocks, in the exterior form of mountains, and even in those tumultuous changes which the external crust of our globe has undergone. So great an uniformity led me to believe, that the aspect of the cavern of Caripe would differ little from what I had observed in my former travels. The reality far exceeded my expectations. If the configuration of grottoes, the splendour of the stalactites, and all the phenomena of inorganic nature, present striking analogies, the majesty of equinoxial vegetation gives, at the same time, an individual character to the aperture of the cavern.

The Cueva del Guacharo is pierced in the vertical profile of a rock. The entrance is toward the south, and forms a vault eighty feet broad, and seventy-two feet high. The elevation is but a fifth less than that of the colonnade of the Louvre. The rock that surmounts the grotto is covered with trees of gigantic height. The mammee tree, and the genipa, with large and shining leaves, raise their branches vertically toward the sky, while those of the courbaril, and the erythrina, form, as they extend themselves, a thick vault of verdure. Plants of the family of pathos, with succulent stems, oxalises, and orchideæ, of a singular structure, rise in the driest clefts of the rocks ; while creeping plants, waving in the winds, are interwoven in festoons, before the opening of the cavern. The entrance of grottoes, like the view of cascades, derive their principal charm from the situation, more or less majestic, in which they are placed ; and which, in some sort, determines the character of the landscape. What a contrast between the Cueva of Caripe, and those caverns of the north crowned with oaks and gloomy pines !

" But this luxury of vegetation embellishes not only the outside of the vault ; it appears even in the vestibule of the grotto. We saw with astonishment plantain-leaved Heliconias eighteen feet high ; the praga, palm-tree, and arborescent Arums, follow the banks of the river, even to those subterranean places. The vegetation continues in the Cave of Caripe, as in those deep crevices of the Andes, half-excluded from the light of day, and does not disappear till, advancing in the interior, we reach thirty or forty paces from the entrance. We measured the way by means of a cord ; and we went on about 430 feet, without being obliged to light our torches. Day light penetrates even into this region, because the grotto forms but one single channel, which keeps the same direction, from southeast to north-west. Where the light begins to fail, we heard from afar the hoarse sounds of the nocturnal birds ; sounds which the natives think belong exclusively to these subterraneous places.

" It is difficult to form an idea of the horrible noise occasioned by thousands of these birds (the Guacharo) in the dark part of the cavern, and which can only be compared to the croaking of our crows ; which, in the pine forests of the north, live in society, and construct their nests upon trees, the tops of which touch each other. The shrill and piercing cries of the Guacharoes strike upon the vaults of the rocks, and are repeated by the echo in the depth of the cavern. The Indians showed the nests of these birds by fixing torches to the end of a long pole. These nests were fifty or sixty feet high above our heads, in holes in the shape of funnels ; with which the roof of the grotto is pierced like a sieve. The noise increased as we advanced: and the birds were affrighted by the light of the torches of copal. When this noise ceased a few minutes around us, we heard at a distance the plaintive cries of the birds roosting in other ramifications of the cavern. It seemed as if these bands answered each other alternately."

" The Indians enter into the Cueva del Guacharo once a-year, near midsummer, armed with poles, by means of which they destroy the greater part of the nests. At this season several thousands of birds are killed; and the old ones, as if to defend their brood, hover over the heads of the Indians uttering terrible cries. The young, which fall to the ground, are opened on the spot. Their peritoneum is extremely loaded with fat; and a layer of fat reaches from the abdomen to the anus, forming a kind of cushion between the legs of the bird. This quantity of fat in frugivorous animals, not exposed to the light, and exerting very little muscular motion, reminds us of what has been long ago observed in the fattening of geese and oxen. The Guacharo quits the cavern at night-fall, especially when the moon shines. It is almost the only nocturnal frugivorous bird that is yet known. The conformation of its feet sufficiently shows that it does not hunt like our owls. It feeds on very hard fruits—as the Nut-cracker and the Pyrrhocorax."

" We followed, as we continued our progress through the cavern, the banks of the small river which issued from it, and is from twenty-eight to thirty feet wide. We walked on the banks as far as the hills formed of calcareous incrustations permitted us. Where the torrent winds among very high masses of stalactites, we were often obliged to descend into its bed, which is only two feet in depth. We learnt with surprize, that this subterraneous rivulet is the origin of the river Caripe, which, at a few leagues distance, after having joined the small river of Santa Maria, is navigable for canoes. It enters into the river Areo under the name of *Canno de Terezen*."

" The grotto of Caripe preserves the same direction, the same breadth, and its primitive height of sixty or seventy feet, to the distance of 472 metres, or 1458 feet, accurately measured. I have never seen a cavern, in either continent, of so uniform and regular a construction. We had great difficulty in persuading the Indians to pass beyond the outer part of the grotto; the only part which they annually visit to collect the fat. The whole authority of *Los Padres* was necessary to induce them to advance as far as the spot, where the soil rises abruptly at an inclination of 60°, and where the torrent forms a small subterraneous cascade. The natives connect mystic ideas with this cave, inhabited by nocturnal birds; they believe that the souls of their ancestors sojourn in the deep recesses of the cavern."

" At the point where the river forms the subterraneous cascade, a hill covered with vegetation, which is opposite the opening of the grotto, presents itself in a very picturesque manner. It appears at the extremity of a straight passage 240 toises in length. The stalactites, which descend from the vault, and which resemble columns suspended in the air, display themselves on a back ground of verdure. The opening of the cavern appeared singularly contracted when we saw it about the middle of the day, illumed by the vivid light reflected at once from the sky, the plants, and the rocks. The distant light of day formed somewhat of magical contrast with the darkness that surrounded us in those dark caverns."

" We climbed, not without some difficulty, the small hill whence the subterraneous rivulet descends. We saw that the grotto was perceptibly contracted, retaining only forty feet in height; and that it continued stretching to the north-east without deviating from its primitive direction; which is parallel to that of the great valley of Caripe. In this part of the cavern the rivulet deposes a blackish mould, very like the matter which, in the grotto of Muggendorf, in Franconia, is called the *earth of sacrifice*. We could not discover whether this fine and spongy mould falls through the cracks which communicate with the surface of the ground above, or be washed down by the rain-water that penetrates into the cavern. It was a mixture of silex, alumine, and vegetable *detritus*. We walked in thick mud to a spot where we beheld, with astonishment, the progress of subterraneous vegetation. The seeds which the birds carry into the grotto, to feed their young, spring up wherever they can fix in the mould that covers the calcareous incrustations. Blanched stalks, with some half-formed leaves, had risen to the height of two feet. It was impossible to ascertain the species of plants, the form, colour, and aspect of which had been changed by the absence of the light."

" The Missionaries, with all their authority, could not prevail on the Indians to penetrate farther into the cavern. As the vault grew lower, the cries of the guacharo became more shrill. We were obliged to yield to the pusillanimity of our guides, and trace back our steps. The appearance of the cavern was indeed very uniform. We find that a bishop of St. Thomas, of Guiana, had gone farther than ourselves. He had measured nearly 2500 feet from the mouth to the spot where he stopped, though the cavern reached farther. The bishop had provided himself with great torches of white wax of Castile. We had torches composed only of the bark of trees, and native resin. The thick smoke which issued from these torches, in a narrow subterranean passage, hurts the eyes, and obstructs perspiration."

" We followed the course of the river to go out of the cavern. Having at length reached the entrance, and seated ourselves on the banks of the rivulet, we rested after our fatigues. We were glad to be beyond the hoarse cries of the birds, and leave a place where darkness does not offer even the charm of silence and tranquillity. We could scarcely persuade ourselves that the name of the grotto of Caripe had hitherto remained unknown in Europe. The guacharoes alone would have been sufficient to render it celebrated. These noctural birds have been nowhere yet discovered, except in the mountains of Caripe and Cumanacoa."

Such is the account of this remarkable grotto given by Humboldt. It would be inconsistent with the nature of our work to dwell longer on the descriptive part of these subterraneous recesses; and we shall, accordingly, now proceed to offer a few remarks on the origin of caverns.

While, on the one hand, the frequency of the occurrence of caverns in calcareous rocks indicates a similarity of origin, the variety of form and structure which they exhibit, in both hemispheres, would seem to imply, that different causes have contributed to their formation. Two leading opinions are held by physiologists on the subject: one ascribing the production of caverns to violent and instantaneous convulsions—such as might arise from the elastic force of vapours, or the commotions of volcanic action; and the other, to the slow but uninterrupted operation of less powerful causes —as the gradual erosion of water, or the solution and

Physical Geography. abstraction of enormous masses of muriate of soda. The horizontality in the direction of the larger caverns is considered, by Humboldt, to be favourable to the hypothesis of their having been excavated by water. The effects produced by this agent would be alike applicable to account for the origin of caverns which form an uninterrupted range, or several ranges lying one over another, as happens almost exclusively in gypseous mountains. The extrication of carbonic acid, by the agency of the mineral acids on carbonate of lime in a semi-fluid state, might also have contributed to the formation of cavities in limestone rocks. Captain Flinders ascribes the production of a cavern, in the Isle of France, to a mass of glance iron having been melted and carried away by a volcanic eruption.

General appearance of the interior of caverns. The caverns observed in the gypseous rocks are generally extremely beautiful, on account of the varied and brilliant tints which are reflected, on every side, from the innumerable facets of crystallized selenite with which they abound. Vitreous crystalline plates of brown and yellow display themselves on a ground of alabaster; and are viewed with the more amazement, as, notwithstanding their picturesque and diversified forms, they are known to be the mere productions of nature, displaying, in these dark and solitary abodes, the most splendid and magnificent of her works.

The calcareous grottoes are more uniform in their aspect; but they, too, are frequently adorned with stalactitical concretions, whose imitative forms equally excite the curiosity of the naturalist, and of the less attentive observer of external objects. The most remarkable stalactites occur in caverns of small dimensions, where the circulation of air is considerably obstructed by the narrowness of the galleries through which they communicate with one another. The calcareous matter, which is held in solution by water impregnated with carbonic acid, is thus allowed to crystallize in a more regular manner, and to assume, during its solidification, a greater variety of grotesque and fanciful forms.

Temperature of caverns. There is no circumstance connected with caverns more difficult to explain, than the depressed temperature of the air which prevails within some of them at all seasons of the year. In the chain of Jura two caverns have been long known, the mean temperature of which is so low, that abundance of ice is to be found in Ice caverns. them even during the summer months. Caverns which contain ice throughout the whole year, also occur in the mountains of Faucigny, at an elevation far below the line of perpetual congelation, and at Fondeurle, in the great calcareous sub-Alpine range in the south-east of France. The cavern of La Baume, one of those alluded to as existing in the chain of Jura, was examined with much care in 1743, by M. de Cossigny, and afterwards with equal attention by M. Prevost, in 1789. According to the account of Cossigny, this cave is sixty-four toises in length, and twenty-two in breadth at the widest part. It declines considerably from the entrance to the farthest extremity, the slope forming an angle of 30° with the horizon. The height varies from ten to fifteen toises.

Ice cavern of Baume. When M. Cossigny first examined this cave, in August, 1743, he observed that the thermometer stood a degree of Fahrenheit above the freezing point in the interior, whilst at the entrance it was at 77°. At the time of his second visit to it, in October 1745, the thermometer was at 32° in the inside, and at 50° at the outside of the cave. On both occasions he remarked, that the bottom of the cavern was incrusted with ice, containing here and there a shallow pool of water; and Physical that icy stalactites were in the act of forming at the Geography. farthest extremity by the congelation of the water which dropped from the roof. Similar appearances were noticed in this cave in 1711, by M. Billerez, of Bezançon, who visited it in the month of September; so that the existence of the ice cannot be ascribed to the operation of an accidental cause acting with more than ordinary vigour during a particular season. It appears, indeed, from an account of this cave, drawn up by Professor Pictet of Geneva, and published in the *Edin. Phil. Journal*, (Vol. VIII. p. 2.) that not only is the ice renewed after removal, but that it is more copiously produced in summer, when the weather is warm, than in winter, when the temperature of the external air is less elevated. The icy incrustation at the bottom of the cave is formed, however, in the opinion of M. Prevost, not by direct congelation, but by the fall of the icicles generated at the roof, which drop, from time to time, by their own weight.

Ice cavern of St. George. The other ice cavern of the Jura, that of St. George, is situated in a wood of thinly scattered pines, about 430 toises above the lake of Geneva. This cavern was lately visited by Professor Pictet, from whose description of it we have been enabled to draw up the following account of its most remarkable features. The entrance to the cave is by two natural pits of about twelve feet in diameter; which it is necessary to descend by ladders, one of these being greatly inclined, and the other almost vertical. After a descent of forty-six steps, a short inclined plane conducts to the grotto; the floor of which is covered with a mass of ice, lying nearly in a horizontal position. The length of the icy surface is about seventy-five feet, and extends over the whole cavern; the mean width is forty, and the height of the most elevated part twenty-seven feet. At the utmost extremity of the cavern numerous concretions are observed, which, at first sight, might be taken for stalactites of the carbonate of lime, but which prove, on examination, to be icicles of an opaque white. A thermometer which, suspended in the shade, stood on the outside at 63° Fahrenheit, being placed in the middle of the grotto, two feet above the floor, marked the temperature of that situation $34\frac{1}{2}°$. The work-people employed in breaking up the ice, for the purpose of having it conveyed to Geneva, assured Professor Pictet, that, if they left two blocks of it in contact near the bottom of the cave, they found them frozen together next day—a sufficient proof that the process of congelation went on without intermission, even during the hot season. The temperature of a spring, which issued from an enormous mass of rock, about a gun-shot from the grotto, was observed to be 51°; a fact which, as Professor Pictet remarks, renders the cold which pervades the cavern only the more remarkable. It is evident, indeed, that the low temperature which prevails in the grotto must be owing to some cause of partial operation, as a large cave in the immediate vicinity is, at all times, totally destitute of ice.

Explanation of the low temperature of particular caverns. In endeavouring, therefore, to account for the great cold which has been observed in particular caverns, an explanation of this singular fact must be sought for rather in local peculiarities than in relations of a more general nature. A phenomenon noticed by Professor Pictet, in the neighbourhood of one of those caves, is calculated to throw some light on the subject, though we are by no means disposed to admit that the conclusion he has drawn from it is altogether free from objection. At the ice cave of Brezon, in the Alps, a current of cold air was observed to issue, with considerable force, from several crevices near the cavern, which depressed a thermometer exposed to its influence from 51° to 38¾°. In applying this fact to the solution of the cause of the phenomenon in question, M. Pictet cites the observations of Saussure on the air rushing from the cavities of Monte Testaceo, near Rome; where a little hill, composed of the fragments of urns, and other vases of earthen ware, produces an effect similar to that of the calcareous sides of these icy caverns. Round the base of this artificial mound several caves have been dug, in the back walls of which a number of perforations have been formed, running upwards like chimneys, and through which a current of cold air constantly descends in summer. On the 1st of July, 1773, the external air being at 78.1 Fahrenheit, the thermometer stood at 44¾° in one of the caverns, and at 44° in another. " It is certainly a very singular phenomenon," says Saussure, " that in the middle of the Campagna of Rome, where the air is always burning hot and suffocating, there should be found a little insulated hill, from the base of which should issue, on all sides, currents of air of an extreme coolness." Saussure mentions several other places where he observed, that a current of air rushing from crevices in the rocks, which formed the sides of caves, was accompanied with a great degree of cold. The caverns in which the cold was the most remarkable, were generally situated in calcareous rocks, at the foot of a mountain. In short, these grottoes appear, in many instances, to be the mouths of natural galleries, communicating with upright shafts, through which a stream of air flows downward, when the temperature of the external air exceeds that of the cavern. The current of air thus determined, must acquire, during its descent, the temperature of the vertical portion of the crevices through which it passes; and that temperature must in general be, at least, as low as the mean temperature of the place. Professor Pictet supposes that the air descending through these fissures in the strata must be still farther cooled by the refrigerating effect of evaporation, from the moistened materials which it encounters in its progress; but that process, though capable of producing, in certain circumstances, a great diminution of temperature, can contribute, in our opinion, very little to the effect under consideration. Air completely charged with humidity, at the temperature of 44° for example, the temperature of one of the caves of Monte Testaceo, must have possessed an extraordinary degree of dryness at the temperature of 78°, before it entered the vertical perforations which conducted it to the caves, to allow it to be cooled at all by evaporation; and if we assume, that when it reached the cave, it had not been brought to a state of perfect dampness, this supposition would involve us in greater difficulties, as it would imply that the external air was in a state of dryness, which can rarely occur at Rome. At the temperature of 44°, a cubic inch of air is capable of holding in the vaporous condition .002032 grains of water, and at the temperature of 78°, no less than .005878 grains; so that air, at the temperature of 78°, charged with the quantity of water it could hold in solution at 48°, would possess a relative humidity, represented by $\frac{2032}{5878}$, or 346, which would correspond to 23° of De Luc's hy-

grometer; a degree of dryness which is seldom observed, except in high latitudes. It would seem, therefore, that, to whatever cause the low temperature is owing, which prevails in the caves of Monte Testaceo, and the icy caverns formerly described, no part of the effect can be ascribed to evaporation. On the contrary, we have not the smallest doubt it will be found, by a more particular examination of the state of these caves, that a deposition of moisture takes place from the external air before it reaches the cavern. At the same time, it is difficult to conceive in what other way the air could be reduced to a temperature so low as 44°, in the latitude of Rome, at a place so slightly elevated above the level of the sea, merely by passing through a quantity of loose materials, whose mean temperature cannot be less than * 46°.

In the case of the icy caverns, however, there is room for a wider range of conjecture. Among the various opinions which might be advanced to explain the cause of their depressed temperature, it would imply no extravagance of supposition to take it for granted that these subterraneous recesses are connected by means of horizontal crevices, running inwards to a great extent, with vertical fissures ascending in some adjacent mountain, to a height above the line of perpetual congelation. The great distance under ground to which several of the caverns in calcareous rocks have been traced, permits us to indulge the conjecture that in many instances they may proceed far beyond the limits to which they have actually been explored; and as we are certain that, in some cases, they penetrate several miles through the solid strata, it is easy to imagine that rents proceeding from them may branch off, in a vertical direction, to the very summit of the mountain in which they occur, or at least to a height beyond the regions of perpetual congelation. This state of things would be quite consistent with the fact, affirmed to be observed in all the icy caverns, that more ice is formed in them during summer than in winter; as the current of air flowing downward ought to be most powerful, and consequently the cold induced greatest, when the difference between the temperature of the atmosphere at the mouth of the cave, and at the opening of the vertical crevices, where the air is supposed to enter, is greatest. Nor does this hypothesis exclude the influence of evaporation in contributing to the effect; on the contrary, it admits its operation in the only circumstances in which it could possibly act, namely, when the humidity of the air, before it entered the crevices which conduct it to the cavern, is less than what it possesses at the freezing point. In no other case could evaporation reduce the temperature of a moistened surface to that point.—See *Edin. Phil. Journ.* vol. viii. p. 1.

In some caverns, organic remains occur in great abundance; while, in others, not a trace of them is observed. It is a curious fact, that though many of the caves in the old world are absolutely filled with these wrecks of living beings, only a single instance has yet presented itself of the skeleton of an animal being buried in a cavern of America. This solitary example of a phenomenon by no means of rare occurrence in Europe, is described by Mr. Jefferson as having been observed in the caverns of Green Briar, in Virginia, in the case of the bones of the Megalonyx, a kind of sloth, of the size of the rhinoceros. The fossil bones of the Megatherium, the Mastodontes, and other large animals which

---

The mean temperature of Rome is, according to Humboldt, 45.9 in the three winter months; and 75.2 in the three summer months.

Physical Geography. have been brought from South America, were all found imbedded in alluvial soil. See ORGANIC REMAINS.

Much important information respecting the materials and constitution of the solid crust of the globe, will be found under the articles CHEMISTRY, MINE, MINERALOGY, ORGANIC REMAINS, THEORY OF THE EARTH, and the various geographical articles contained in this work.

Of the Atmosphere.

General view of the atmosphere. The earth is every where surrounded, to an unknown height, by a thin, invisible, elastic fluid, consisting of a mixture of oxygen and nitrogen gases, in the proportion of about one part of the former to four of the latter. This aërial shell, which envelopes the globe, is denominated the atmosphere. In this vast magazine of attenuated matter, both animals and vegetables perform the various functions of life. Deprived of the due portion of it, they soon languish and die; nor can they long enjoy health and vigour, when its purity, or even its mechanical condition, undergoes a material change.

Ends which it serves in the great processes of nature. The great processes in nature which give rise to the formation of rain, hail, and snow, are conducted entirely through the medium of this fluid, which, while it conveys to the vegetable tribes a proper supply of moisture, is, at the same time, the vehicle by which the noxious exhalations arising from combustion, and the decomposition of organized beings, are gradually carried off, and prepared for new forms of existence.

Its uses as a moving power. In a state of active motion, it constitutes *wind*; and if, in this condition, it sometimes occasions the most extensive and deplorable calamities, it enables us, under a milder form, to waft, with safety and expedition, the productions of one hemisphere to another, where nature may, in some respects, have been less profuse in her bounty. As a moving body, too, it is the great agent by which the Author of nature has established nearly an equal allotment of temperature over the various climes of the globe, and rendered almost every portion of it a suitable abode for the living beings which are dispersed over its surface.

Essentially necessary for the propagation of sound. Moreover, without air, sound could have no existence; so that, to the intervention of this subtile and attenuated fluid, we owe all the advantage and delight which we derive from the easy interchange of thought by means of articulate language; as well as all the pleasure which we receive from the exquisite combinations of musical harmony. Even the operations of vision, the most excursive and unfettered of all the senses, would be greatly limited, were they not assisted by the aërial particles which compose the atmosphere; for, though these particles have no inherent light in themselves, they possess the power of reflecting and dispersing, in every direction, the light of shining bodies, by which we are enabled, not only to perceive objects which are exposed to the direct rays cast upon them by a luminous body, but also such as are in the shade, and receive their illumination from the soft and mellow light, reflected upon them by the air.

And to the process of combustion. Lastly, the process of combustion, which is so intimately connected with most of the arts of life, depends essentially on the union of the oxygenous principle of the atmosphere with the basis of combustible matter; so that, had the air either been entirely wanting, or differently constituted, such an arrangement must have had a powerful influence on the physical, as well as the moral condition of our species.

Physical Geography. Pressure of the atmosphere, though continually varying, is nearly the same over all the globe. The pressure of the atmosphere, though incessantly varying, is nearly the same in its mean state, over the whole globe; and is found, when the observation is made on the sea coast, to correspond very nearly to 30 inches of mercury. This fact has been verified by numberless observations made with the barometer in both hemispheres, from the equatorial to the Polar regions; and, in illustration of it, it will be sufficient to cite a few of the best observations which have been made in different latitudes. We shall, accordingly give the result of observations with the barometer in the northern hemisphere, at Calcutta, London, Edinburgh, and Melville Island, corrected for temperature, elevation above the level of the sea, and the influence of the earth's rotation on its axis.

	Lat.	Bar. Pressure.
Calcutta,	22° 35′	29.776
London,	51° 31′	29.827
Edinburgh,	55° 56′	29.835
Melville Island,	74° 30′	29.884

The observations at Calcutta were made in the years 1784 and 1785, by Mr. Trail, and are given in the second volume of the *Asiatic Researches*. They have been reduced to the freezing point, by making a suitable allowance for the expansion of mercury, and also to the level of the sea by the formula, log. $b =$ log. $b' + \dfrac{h}{10,000}$, in which b is the altitude of the barometer at the level of the sea, b' its mean altitude, obtained by observation, and h the height of the plane above the level of the sea, in fathoms. The mean height of the barometer at the level of the sea, thus deduced, was afterwards corrected for the latitude of the place of observation, by means of the coefficient of La Place. $(1 + .00284 \cos. 2 \psi) b$, in which ψ denotes the latitude.

The observations at London are derived from the meteorological tables of the Royal Society of London, for a period of nine years; those at Edinburgh, from the meteorological tables of the Royal Society of Edinburgh, for a period of three years; and those at Melville Island, from the register kept by Captain Parry, during his residence in the Arctic regions, from the beginning of Sept. 1819 to the end of August the ensuing year.

Mean height of the barometer declines from the equator to the poles. The mean of the whole would give for the medium pressure of the atmosphere 29.83; but it deserves to be noticed, that, in these observations, which have been reduced to the same condition, for the purpose of an accurate comparison, a gradual increase of the atmospheric pressure may be traced from the equator toward the pole. This must be owing, either to the correction of La Place for the latitude being too small; or, perhaps with more probability, to the influence of humidity, which gradually diminishes from the equatorial to the polar regions. It may be partly ascribed, also, to a greater quantity of the carburetted hydrogen which ascends into the upper regions of the air being destroyed by the operation of electricity, over the warmer than over the colder zones of the earth.

The variations of the barometer in different places. But, though the mean pressure of the atmosphere is nearly the same, at the level of the sea, over the whole globe, the extent of the variations to which it is liable is exceedingly different, in different parallels of latitude. At the equatorial regions, the range of the barometer is much more limited than within the polar circles; and, in the polar zones, it seems to be still more confined than in those usually denominated temperate. Within the tropics, the interval between the greatest and least altitude of the barometer seldom exceeds half an inch. Thus, at Quito, the range is about 1 line; at Peru, it amounts to a third of an inch; and, at Calcutta, it extends to half an inch. As we advance beyond the tropical regions, the oscillations become more variable, as well as more extensive. At Kathmandu, the capital of Nepaul, in latitude 27° 30′, the difference between the greatest and least altitude of the barometer, for a year, appears, by the observations of Mr. Hamilton, to be .85 of an inch. It ought to be remarked, however, that, on account of the elevated situation of Nepaul, the variations of the barometer there must be more extensive than under the same parallel, near the level of the ocean. By a register of the state of the weather, from October to April inclusive, which was kept by Krusentern, at Nangasaky, the capital of Japan, in latitude 32° 43′, we learn that, during that time, the highest state of the barometer was 30.25, and the lowest 29.4 inches; so that the range was .85 of an inch. The extreme range at Paris, as deduced by Rohault, from observations during a period of 15 consecutive years, was .04737 metre, at the temperature of 12° centigrade, being 1.86 inch English; but the mean annual range is only about $1\frac{1}{4}$ inch. The mean annual range over the whole of Great Britain, may be stated at 2 inches. At Petersburgh, it exceeds that quantity, amounting to about $2\frac{1}{4}$ inches; but the oscillations of the barometer seem to become more limited in the higher parallels of latitude, if we may judge from the observations of Captain Parry, which give the annual range at Melville Island 1.86 inch. The most extensive variations seem to take place between the parallels of 30° and 60′, being the zone within which the annual changes of temperature and humidity possess the widest range,—the two circumstances which chiefly affect the atmospheric pressure.

In the northern hemisphere, the greatest fluctuations of the barometer are observed to take place in December and January; and, in the opposite hemisphere, it may be inferred that a condition of the atmosphere attended with similar results, occurs in June and July. In this country, the barometer has been observed to stand as low as $27\frac{1}{2}$ inches, and as high as 31 inches. Mr. Townly of Lancaster observed it on the 4th of February 1703, to descend so low as 27.39 in. (*Phil. Trans.* Motte's Abridg. II. 52), and the writer of the present article observed it at Perth, on the 9th of January 1820, to stand at the unusual height of 31.074. Even within the tropics, the barometer has occasionally been observed, in the Indian seas, below 27 inches; and the Abbé Rochon affirms, that during a hurricane in the Isle of France in 1771, the mercury sunk to 25 inches French (26.643 in. English). On account of a species of reaction in the atmospherical columns, it not unfrequently happens that the greatest depression of the barometer succeeds to an extraordinary rise of it; and *vice versa.* Thus, in the course of ten days after the barometer had reached the remarkable height it attained at Perth, mentioned above, it sunk to 28.830, being a diminution of nearly $2\frac{1}{4}$ inches of pressure within that short period.

Besides the more extensive oscillations to which the barometer is liable, during considerable intervals of time, it appears to be subject to a diurnal variation, which undergoes some alternations in the period of twenty-four hours. These daily changes in the atmospherical pressure are most readily detected within the tropical regions, where, on account of the slight variations of the barometer, they are less apt to be confounded with the other vicissitudes in the flux and reflux of the atmosphere. They seem to have been first noticed by Mr. Trail, at Calcutta, who remarked, in the course of his meteorological observations, that the mercury rose every night till about eleven o'clock, when it became stationary. The fact was subsequently confirmed by the observations of Mr. Farquhar, who also ascertained, that from six in the morning till about seven or eight it remains stationary; that it then rises till nine or ten, after which it continues stationary till noon. From noon it begins to descend, and attains a minimum state at three; from three till eight it remains stationary, when it begins to rise, and continues to do so till eleven, being at that hour at the same height as in the morning. To these periods of rising and falling in the twenty-four hours, a fourth was added by Dr. Balfour, who observed that a minimum state of the barometer occurred between ten o'clock at night and six in the morning, analogous to that which Mr. Farquhar had observed between eleven in the forenoon, and six in the evening. In order to determine, with some precision, the progress of these four states of maxima and minima, by actual observation, Dr. Balfour submitted to the task of observing and recording the changes of the barometer, as far as he was able, every half hour, day and night, during the interval of a complete lunation, from an opinion that the cause of these periodical changes was, in some way, connected with the position of the moon. The result of his observations was,

1*st,* That in the interval between ten at night and six in the morning, there existed a prevailing tendency in the mercury to *fall.*

2*d,* That in the interval between six and ten in the morning, there existed a prevailing tendency in the mercury to *rise.*

3*d,* That in the interval between ten in the morning, and six in the evening, there existed a prevailing tendency to *fall.*

4*th,* That in the interval between six and ten in the evening, there existed a prevailing tendency in the mercury to *rise.*

These different prevailing tendencies to rise and fall periodically, at certain times of the day and night, necessarily imply, as Dr. Balfour remarks, a proportional corresponding cause; but the only conclusion he has drawn on the subject is, that they seem to be connected with the diurnal revolution of the earth. (*Asiat. Res.* vol. iv. p. 201.)

But whatever may be the cause of these remarkable anomalies, their existence has been too well established to admit of being called in question. M. Lamanon, an ingenious naturalist, who accompanied the unfortunate Peyrouse, has furnished a few observations, which lead to the same general results as those obtained by Dr. Balfour. In compliance with the instructions of the Academy of Sciences, M. Lamanon kept an exact account of the state of the barometer, near the equator, at different hours of the day, with the view of determining the extent of the diurnal variation of the atmospheric pressure due to the action of the sun and moon, that quantity being there probably at its maximum, while the aberrations arising from other causes are at their minimum. About the 11th degree of north latitude he began to perceive a certain regular motion of the mercury, by which it stood higher about two hours before mid-day; descended till about four in the afternoon; rose again till about ten o'clock in the evening; and afterwards declined till about four in the morning. As they approached the equator, these alternations were more distinctly observed; and on the 28th of September, the ship being then in latitude 1° 17' north, a succession of observations was begun, and continued for every hour till the 1st of October, at 6 A. M. The following abstract shows the result of the observations on the 28th and 29th of September.

		line.
September 28.		
From 4 to 10 A. M. Barometer rose	.	1.9
10 A. M. to 4 P. M. . fell	.	1.2
4 to 10 P. M. . rose	.	0.9
10 to 4 A. M. (29th) fell	.	1.3
September 29.		
From 10 to 4 A. M. Barometer fell	.	1.3
4 to 10 . . rose	.	1.5
10 to 4 P. M. . fell	.	1.3
4 to 10 P. M. . rose	.	1.0

Hence it is concluded that, at the equator, the diurnal flux and reflux of the atmosphere causes in the barometer a variation of about 1.2 line, corresponding, as M. Lamanon remarks, to a difference of elevation of nearly 100 feet. These reciprocations cannot be ascribed to the action of the sun and moon, whose joint influence, according to Bernouilli, could produce an atmospheric tide of only seven feet; and, according to La Place, a tide not nearly so great. With still less probability can they be regarded as the effect of the land and sea breezes, in the tropical climates,—another cause to which they have been ascribed; as the observations of the French navigators were made too far from the coast to be affected by any cause of that nature. We find, moreover, that the observations of Dr. Francis Hamilton, made in the Nepaul territory, at the distance of about 1000 miles from the ocean, though they were not intended to verify the diurnal reciprocations which take place in the atmospherical pressure near the equator, show that corresponding changes in the height of the mercurial column occur in inland situations, even beyond the tropics. Dr. Hamilton's observations were made at Kathmandu in lat. 27° 30' N. at the dawn of day, noon, 3 P. M. and 9 P. M. The mean results for a year are the following:

Dawn.	Noon.	3 P. M.	9 P. M.
25.229	25.227	25.178	25.219

These results so far coincide with those deduced from the observations already noticed, in indicating that a minimum state of pressure occurs at three or four hours past noon. The observations at the dawn, at noon, and at 9 P. M. differ but little from each other, the times when they were made being nearly at equal distances from the periods when the maximum state is found to take place. (Hamilton's *Account of Nepaul.*) Similar fluctuations on the state of the barometer, within the period of twenty-four hours, have been noticed by M. Chanvallon, in Martinique; and by Mr. Horsburgh in the Indian seas. The latter, however, remarks, that the diurnal changes were performed with more regularity at sea than on land; and indeed he mentions several instances in which the periodical ascent and descent of the mercury ceased entirely on approaching the coast. During a voyage from Canton to Prince of Wales Island, Mr. Horsburgh observed the

diurnal oscillations of the barometer with the utmost care, and he states, among other instances which he gives of the influence of the vicinity of land, that on entering the strait of Sincapore, which is about 3½ leagues wide, the mercury in the barometers became a little obstructed, and did not perform the equatropical motions, in the same quantity of rise and fall, as in the China Sea. But on the following day, he adds, after passing the narrow part of the strait, the mercury resumed the daily fluctuations, and continued to exhibit them regularly, until the ship arrived in the harbour of Prince of Wales Island. The whole time the ship remained at that place, the diurnal variations of the mercury were very slight, being in general not more than half the quantity that is observed in the open sea, or at a considerable distance from land. On leaving the harbour of Prince of Wales Island, the daily motions of the mercury were again observed, in the usual quantity experienced at sea, and no interruption of them occurred till the ship reached Diamond Harbour, when the mercury inclined to be nearly stationary during the twenty-four hours, as was observed to happen, on former occasions, at Canton, Bombay Harbour, &c. *Phil. Trans.* 1805.

It may be inferred from these observations of Mr. Horsburgh, that the diurnal variations of the atmospherical pressure, to whatever cause they are owing, are more distinctly perceived at sea than on land, but this may be explained, without having recourse to any peculiar influence of the ocean, by the obvious fact, that at sea the cause of the phenomena in question must operate in a more undisguised manner than on land, where its effects are more closely interwoven with the results produced by local and adventitious causes.

One of the most interesting facts which has been ascertained by comparing the observations made with the barometer at places considerably remote from each other, is the corresponding state of the atmospherical pressure, at the same instant of time, in regard to the variations to which it is liable. This coincidence of the elevations and depressions of the mercurial column, at different places, is best perceived by the happy contrivance, introduced more than a century ago by Dr. Lister, according to which a graphical declination of the pressure is exhibited, by the intersection of two ordinates, one of which represents the day of the month, and the other the altitude of the mercury in the barometer. By examining the state of the barometer at different places in Great Britain, it appears, that though the barometer is not always affected exactly in the same manner, on the same day, a greater similarity exists between the varying conditions of the pressure than might be expected to prevail over so wide a portion of the atmosphere. Observations are yet wanting to determine the extent to which this sameness of affection may be traced; but on making a comparison between the state of the barometer at London and Kathmandu for the same year, no indication of a similarity in the undulations of the barometrical curve can be perceived. A like comparison of the observations of Captain Parry at Melville Island, with those made in this country for the years 1819—20, proves that though a remarkable state of the atmospherical pressure occurs nearly at the same time, both in the Arctic regions and the north of Britain, the slighter changes are by no means coincident, either in regard to time or degree. Thus the great elevation of

Observations of Dr. Hamilton in Nepaul.

Difference between the diurnal variations at sea, and on land.

Simultaneous state of the barometer, at different places considerably distant from one another.

Extent to which the same elevations and depressions may be traced.

the barometer, which was observed in this country on the 9th of January, 1820, occurred ten days earlier at Melville Island, viz. on the 30th of December, 1819; and an elevation, nearly as great, which took place here on the 24th of the ensuing April, was followed by a corresponding state of the barometer, at Melville Island, on the 27th of the same month. For the most part, however, the undulations of the barometer, at stations so very remote from each other, have little similarity of outline; and, indeed, if any general inference can be drawn from a comparative view of the atmospherical pressure over Britain and the Arctic regions, we should be disposed to conclude that a depressed state of the barometer, at the latter, is accompanied with an elevated state at the former, and contrariwise. A careful comparison of the meteorological tables, kept in this country and the north of India, seems also to justify the conclusion, that a high state of the barometer near the tropics is produced by the removal of a portion of the atmosphere from the northern parts of the temperate zone in our hemisphere.

Whether
the atmos-
pheric pres-
sure has
undergone
any change
since ob-
servations
were first
made with
the baro-
meter.
The mean pressure of the atmosphere seems to be the same now that it was when observations were first made with the barometer. Thus we learn from a meteorological journal kept by the celebrated Mr. Locke, at Oates in Essex, that the mean annual pressure for the year 1692 was 29.58, which, making allowance for the altitude of the place of observation above the level of the sea, would be nearly the same as the mean height observed at present. The extreme range, too, appears to have remained unaltered; and the greatest and least altitudes occurred, as is still generally observed, in the month of December. Hence we may conclude, that notwithstanding the extensive and important changes which have taken place in the physical condition of the globe, and the alternate absorption and evolution of the constituent elements of the atmosphere by the growth and decay of vegetable productions, the great mass of that fluid has undergone no perceptible change in point of quantity. The atmospheric pressure, therefore, though perhaps of too variable a nature to be adopted as a standard of measure, seems to be one of those physical quantities which are continually oscillating on either side of a mean state, that may be regarded as permanent.

Causes of
the changes
which take
place in the
atmosphe-
ric pres-
sure.
Having considered the variations which take place in the atmospheric pressure over the different zones of the earth, we shall now endeavour to trace the principal causes by which these variations are produced. The first, and perhaps the most general cause to which they can be ascribed, is change of temperature in the inferior strata of the atmosphere, which, by increasing or diminishing the elasticity of that portion of the aërial columns to which its influence extends, must necessarily affect in a corresponding degree its pressure on the barometer. The effect of humidity, though subordinate to that of temperature, must also be assigned as one of the most powerful means by which variations in the atmospheric pressure are produced. In the next place, the influence of electricity, whether that subtile principle exerts its agency in a chemical or a mechanical manner, must be regarded as giving rise to important changes in the atmosphere, more especially when the effects are sudden, and limited in extent. Lastly, winds blowing in a particular direction, though originating themselves from one or other of the three preceding causes, or all of them combined,

must also be assigned as one of the most frequent causes which occasion these changes.

The temperature of the atmosphere, as well as that which prevails at the earth's surface, being derived chiefly from the sun, must evidently vary with the latitude and the season of the year. Within the tropics, the sun's rays impinge at noon, during the whole year, nearly at the same angle, and produce their greatest effect in communicating heat. The atmosphere, therefore, is more expanded over the torrid zone, than over the less genial regions of the earth; and the dilatation thus produced is still farther augmented by the diurnal rotation, which, being most rapid at the equator, cannot fail to give a greater centrifugal tendency to the aërial particles which float above it, than it communicates to those which press on the temperate and the polar zones. Hence within the tropics the height of the atmosphere must be considerably greater than over the temperate zones; while over the latter, it must, in like manner, be greater than beyond the polar circles. On this account it is inferred that the upper surface of the atmosphere possesses a greater degree of curvature at the equator than at the poles, and that it consequently declines from the former towards the latter, but in a manner which varies with the sun's declination. The uniformity of temperature which prevails within the tropics, joined to the great height of the atmosphere in that quarter, seems to be the cause why the oscillations of the barometer are so limited within a certain range of the equator, just as a stone which is sufficient to agitate violently a small pool, would produce little commotion if dropped into a larger mass of water. Beyond the tropics the alternations of temperature, by the vicissitudes of the seasons, begin to be felt, and to occasion considerable differences in the density of the air, both by their own immediate operation, and the indirect influence they exert over the exhaled vapour which exists in the atmosphere. The range of the barometer is accordingly extended, and the effect is increased till we reach the 55th degree of latitude, where it seems to attain its maximum state. This appears to be the reason why the variations of the barometer are greatest in the zone intervening between the space where the temperature is nearly uniform throughout the whole year, and where it is so powerfully affected by the alternations of summer and winter.

Why the
oscillations
of the ba-
rometer are
so limited
near the
equator.

The influence which the moisture existing in the air, in the state of vapour, exerts over the atmospheric pressure, is distinctly indicated by the fall of the barometer, which almost always precedes rain. The quantity of moisture maintained in the vaporous form varies with the temperature; and we have shown, under the article HYGROMETRY, p. 575, that the elasticity which it acquires is liable to change from the same cause. The weight of a certain volume of vapour, however, being less than that of an equal bulk of air, in similar circumstances with respect to temperature and pressure, in the ratio of 5 to 8, it follows that an increase of the humidity of the atmosphere must tend to diminish the height of the barometer, by displacing the air above it, and substituting a lighter for a more dense fluid. Hence the prevalence of a south wind is accompanied with a low state of the barometer in the northern hemisphere; a current of air from that quarter being always warmer and more rarefied, and consequently bringing along with it a greater quantity of moisture, while a north and a north-east wind produce, from an opposite cause, a contrary effect. It may easily be conceived, indeed, that on certain occasions, the vapour which mingles itself with the atmosphere may, before an equilibrium is established between the aërial columns, raise the barometer by the increased elasticity which it is capable of communicating to dry air; and, in like manner, that when a large portion of it is suddenly reduced to the liquid state, by the intermixture of strata having different temperatures, the change of condition which it suffers depriving it of its elasticity, and causing it, at the same time, to descend to the earth, must produce a corresponding effect, and depress the barometer. In the latter case, the place of the precipitated moisture being quickly supplied by the influx of air from the surrounding portion of the atmosphere, the equilibrium is soon restored, and the barometer begins to rise. This seems to be the reason why that instrument frequently indicates an increase of the atmospheric pressure immediately after the commencement of rain, and occasionally a short time before its fall.

But though it cannot be doubted that the varying humidity of the atmosphere contributes in a considerable degree to produce the changes which are observed in its pressure, it has probably much less influence than some of the other causes to which we alluded. To be convinced of this, we need only recollect that the changes in the atmospheric pressure are most limited in those zones where the elasticity of vapour is greatest; and that in this country a difference of pressure, to the extent of two inches in the height of the barometer, is not unfrequently observed in the interval of a few days, at a season of the year when the precipitation of the whole of the moisture contained in the atmosphere could not produce a change of more than a quarter of an inch in the length of the mercurial column. It seems probable, therefore, that in every case where the change of pressure amounts, in the temperate zones, to that of an inch of mercury, the effect must be ascribed either to electricity, or the translation of the atmospherical columns from one place to another, by the action of winds. In whatever way the atmosphere is affected by the electric fluid,—whether by the immediate operation of that subtile agent, or through the chemical effects which it is capable of producing, (such as the union of large portions of the gases of which the air is composed) the remarkable variations in the barometrical pressure which accompany the more vivid appearances of the aurora borealis, render it extremely probable that an intimate connexion subsists between them. It is difficult, indeed, to account on any other principle for the separation of carburetted hydrogen from the atmosphere. Without some agent like electricity to produce explosions of that gaseous body when it reaches to a height above the surface of the earth, where it settles by its specific gravity, there would be apparently no provision in nature to prevent its indefinite accumulation in the upper regions of the atmosphere, and no arrangement to restore the elementary substances of which it is composed, for the purpose of again renewing the vegetable products, from whose decomposition it is incessantly derived. The changes which the atmosphere undergoes in the general economy of nature are thus counteracted, and the permanency of its constitution secured, amidst the diversified processes which are daily going on in that vast magazine of aërial matter.

But the principal cause of the fluctuations which occur in the pressure of the atmosphere, is the removal

Probable influence of electricity.

Influence of winds.

of the air itself from one portion of the earth's surface to another. From the remarks which have already been made respecting the influence of temperature and humidity in causing variations in the length of the mercurial column, the effect of winds, in producing similar changes, will be readily admitted. Thus a south wind in the northern hemisphere, and a north wind in the southern hemisphere, usually occasion a sinking of the barometer, because they come from a warmer region, and convey a greater quantity of vapour in admixture with the air which they waft along, than the portion of the atmosphere in the latitudes to which they extend. On the contrary, the north and north-east winds produce an elevated state of the barometer, because they proceed from regions where, on account of the reduced temperature, the air which they transport is both drier and more dense. This air being exposed to an increase of temperature, its elasticity is also increased, which must continue to affect the barometer, until an equilibrium is again established between the action and re-action of the pressure exerted by the columns of the atmosphere. Winds which blow for a season in a direction contrary to that of the prevailing atmospherical current in any particular zone, occasion an accumulation of air which produces an elevated state of the barometer; but the effect is greatest at first, and gradually diminishes in degree the longer the anomalous wind continues, till at length it is scarcely perceptible. Thus, the prevailing wind in the temperate zones being from the west, an east wind, when it first begins to blow, seldom fails to be accompanied with a rise of the barometer.

The extensive depressions which take place in the barometer before violent storms of wind, and during their continuance, seem to proceed from great rarefactions of the air, occasioned, in all probability, by the destruction of large portions of it in the higher regions of the atmosphere. The great extent over which those depressions prevail on the same day, and often apparently at the same instant of time, evidently implies the operation of some powerful cause; and no physical agent with which we are acquainted seems more adequate to the effect than electricity, acting upon the combustible gases which ascend from the earth to the upper regions of the atmosphere.

Sudden depressions of the barometer probably occasioned by the destruction of a portion of the air.

From the observations we have already made on the atmospherical pressure, it would seem that the columns of air over the various regions of the globe are seldom in a state of equilibrium. This want of stability in the different parts of an elastic fluid, capable of being set in motion by the slightest impulse, is the great cause of the currents of air from one point to another, which we denominate *winds*. Change of temperature, the introduction of moisture in the vaporous state, and its extrication in the form of water, or any of the other conditions in which it is separated from the surrounding air; the condensation of extensive portions of the atmosphere by chemical union; and probably other circumstances still unknown to us, all conspire to disturb the equilibrium of statical pressure among the particles which compose that vast fluid, and give rise to a great diversity of aërial currents, which are still farther modified by the varying surface of the earth, over which they flow.

Winds produced by a want of equilibrium among the atmospheric columns.

Winds have been classed, in regard to their duration, under the heads of *Constant* and *Variable*; and under those of *General* and *Local*, in respect of their extent.

A wind which may be denominated constant and general prevails within the tropical regions, moving

Classification of winds.

round the globe from east to west, with scarcely any interruption. This wind is generally called the *Trade wind*, and is styled by some writers "*the wind of the rotation of the earth.*" Under the article NAVIGATION, p. 196, we have given an explanation of the causes of this wind, together with a description of the local circumstances by which its general direction is influenced in particular cases; and at present, therefore, it is only necessary to give an account of certain species of winds which are more immediately connected with geographical situation.

Beyond the tropics, the prevailing wind on either side of the equator blows from the west. A current of air, having that direction, seems to be necessary to restore the equilibrium of the atmosphere, which is so incessantly disturbed by the action of the trade winds. This wind, which prevails along the western shores of Europe, is somewhat modified by the irregularities of the surface as it passes over that continent to the eastern coasts of Asia. Thus, while it predominates on the western coasts of Portugal, France, and the Netherlands, it appears to be considerably affected by the two great inland seas, the Mediterranean and the Baltic, each of which gives birth to particular systems of winds. The winds are extremely variable in the different cantons of Switzerland, on account of their Alpine situation; but though they blow on both sides of the meridian, their general direction is towards the east. At Rome, and along the shores of the Mediterranean, a northerly wind is frequently experienced; and the same wind prevails over Egypt during the greatest part of the year. In Syria the winds are extremely irregular, owing, it is supposed, to its extensive sea coast and high mountains in the interior. In the north of India the western winds are most frequent, and their influence extends to the Asiatic coast.

In the northern hemisphere of the New World, a westerly wind blows the greater part of the year in the country about Hudson's bay; and the same wind is most prevalent in Nova Scotia. A wind from the west and the north generally prevails in the United States. In the higher latitudes of the southern hemisphere, winds from the north-west and south-west prevail in the Pacific Ocean, as well as generally in all seas beyond the natural limits of the trade winds, to the south of the parallel of 28° and 30°. "By means of the south-west winds," says Humboldt, "during my stay in Peru, English vessels came from the Cape of Good Hope to Val Paraiso in Chili, in ninety days, although they had to run from west to east nearly two-thirds of the circumference of the globe. In the northern hemisphere," he adds, " the north-west facilitates the passage from the coast of Canada to Europe, as well as that from the east of Asia to the western coast of America." (Humb. *New Spain*, iv. 71.) The westerly winds blow almost without intermission on the coast of Magellan's land; and hence the difficulty which mariners have always experienced in their attempts to double Cape Horn. It would appear by these statements, that the most prevalent winds in the temperate zones blow from west to east,—a fact to which we shall afterwards advert, in endeavouring to explain the remarkable difference of temperature which is observed on the west and the east sides of continents and extensive islands.

In a general view of the currents of the atmosphere, it may be proper to notice briefly a kind of periodical winds, observed in some parts of Europe. The winds to which we allude resemble the monsoons which take place within the tropics, and blow from opposite points at different seasons of the year. They are styled *Etesian* and *Ornithian* winds, it being observed that birds of passage take advantage of the periods at which they begin to blow, to assist their flight from one clime to another. The former of these winds commences about the middle of July, and continues to blow for a period of six weeks, their direction being from north to south. The tract over which they spread comprehends the countries which skirt the northern shores of the Mediterranean, and even the opposite coasts of Africa. These winds seem to be occasioned by the same causes that determine the current of air which flows from the poles to the equator. At the season of the year, when the Etesian wind begins to blow with steadiness, the northern parts of the torrid zones have acquired their maximum of temperature, which being considerably greater than that of the zones, having a higher latitude, a current is thus established from the places where the superincumbent atmosphere is more dense towards those where it is more rare.

The Ornithian winds commence about the beginning of March, and continue to blow, with occasional interruptions, for a period of five or six weeks. These winds blow from the south-west, crossing the Mediterranean, and sweeping over Greece and Macedonia. They are supposed to be owing to the melting of the snow on the mountains of Syria, and the northern parts of Africa.

A wind blowing alternately from the land and the sea, is observed to prevail in most places which have a maritime or insular situation. This wind, which is most distinctly felt within the tropics, changes its direction with great regularity every twenty-four hours, flowing from the sea to the land during the day, and from the land to the sea during the night. Hence it has been denominated the *sea and the land breeze*. This breeze blows with considerable violence on mountainous coasts, insomuch that during the time it proceeds from the land there is no access to shipping, which are therefore detained by it till the return of the sea breezes. These breezes are evidently owing to the unequal effect of sun upon the atmosphere over the land and the ocean. The air over the land being much warmer during the day than that which is over the ocean, the denser air over the latter overcomes, by its greater statical pressure, the resistance of the air over the former, and thus occasions a flux of the atmosphere from the sea towards the land. During the night the state of things is reversed, and a current of air is determined by the denser air rushing from the land towards the sea. This explanation is finely illustrated by the phenomena of these winds on several of the South Sea islands, particularly in such of them as contain elevated peaks. Notwithstanding the smallness of extent of these insulated portions of land, they attract so strongly towards them from all sides the surrounding air, that the general current of the trade wind is counteracted by their influence, and a brisk breeze continues to blow during the day from the sea to the central and elevated parts of the islands. During the night the air flows from the interior, as from a centre, dispersing itself in all directions, and thus producing a diverging land breeze from every part of the coast.

Having thus described the more common phenomena of winds, we shall briefly consider the character of the atmospherical currents, which are either of a local nature, or of less frequent occurrence. In every country there are winds which may be said to be peculiar to it, and hence may be called *local winds*. Thus in the spring season, the dense atmosphere from the summit of the

Alps generally pours down on every side from these towering masses, and spreads itself in all directions over the plains below, sometimes with so much violence as to stretch across the Mediterranean. Chains of lofty mountains, by opposing the current of air which prevails where they are situated, frequently contribute to increase the strength of the winds in particular places. It is to this cause we are to ascribe the stormy state of the sky so generally observed at the extremities of the continents and large islands, such as Cape Horn, the Cape of Good Hope, and other remarkable promontories. There are winds of a still more topical description, the cause of which can only be ascertained by a reference to local circumstances, which the limits of this article do not permit us to enter upon. In the province of Dauphiné, for example, we are informed by the Abbé Richard that a tract exists, where local winds are so prevalent that it may be styled the cavern of Æolus. One of these partial currents takes its rise in the woods in the vicinity of Noyons, and spreads over the adjacent country to the extent of four leagues in length, and a league in breadth. It is represented to be intensely cold; but it is of short duration, and takes place at no regular period.

Among the remarkable winds which occur occasionally, we may include the hurricane or typhon, the whirlwind, the sirocco, the harmattan, and the simoom. The hurricane is most commonly experienced in the West Indies, on the western coast of Africa, and in the Indian Ocean; but though it happens more frequently within the tropics, there is perhaps no region of the earth where its effects are altogether unknown. The hurricane generally lasts only a few hours; but the devastation and ruin which it occasions in so short a period almost exceeds belief. The most substantial buildings are unable to withstand its fury; the largest trees are torn up by the roots; and every where the signs of desolation and distress mark its destructive course. The thunder rolls without intermission; the rain descends in torrents; and the ocean, agitated to its lowest depths, and forced far above its natural bounds, seems to conspire with the heavens for the destruction of nature. Hurricanes are always preceded, and accompanied by a very low state of the barometer; and the blast is not unfrequently directed from every quarter towards the point where the atmospherical pressure is least. They commonly advance to windward; that is, their influence is first felt at the place towards which the current flows, and is gradually extended in an opposite direction until the influx of air restores an equilibrium of pressure.

In illustration of this important fact, Dr. Franklin has given us an account of a violent storm from the north-east, which he observed at Philadelphia in the year 1740. At that place it began to be felt about seven o'clock in the evening; but by examining its progress, he ascertained that it did not come on at Boston till about eleven o'clock, and by comparing the various accounts which he received from the different places over which it passed, he found that its effects were felt an hour later for every 100 miles towards the north-east. To account for this, he gives the following familiar illustration: " I suppose a long canal of water," says he, " stopped at the end by a gate. The water is at rest till the gate is opened; then it begins to move out through the gate, and the water next the gate is first in motion, and moves on towards the gate; and so on successively till the water at the head of the canal is in motion, which it is last of all. In this case all the water moves indeed towards the gate; but the successive times of beginning the motion are in the contrary way, viz. from the gate back to the head of the canal. Thus to produce a north-east storm," he adds, " I suppose some great rarefaction of the air in or near the Gulf of Mexico; the air rising thence has its place supplied by the next more northern, cooler, and therefore denser and heavier air; a successive current is formed, to which our coast and inland mountains gave a north-east direction." Franklin's *Phil. Letters*, p. 389. This explanation of the reason why hurricanes are first felt to leeward appears to be highly satisfactory; but it may be questioned how far mere rarefaction, produced by the processes to which it is commonly ascribed, is sufficient to account for the tremendous violence with which these winds sweep over the surface of the earth. It seems probable, as we hinted in another part of this article, that hurricanes are principally owing to the sudden destruction of large portions of the atmosphere by electricity, and the subsequent rushing of the surrounding air into the partial void, which is thus found. This hypothesis would also serve to account for the sudden calm which often occurs during the interval of a hurricane changing its direction; for it is often observed that violent gales, after blowing with great fury from a particular quarter, cease for a short time, and then blow with equal impetuosity in an opposite direction. The first direction might be regarded as the effect of the expansion of the detonated air; the temporary calm would be accounted for, by supposing that it took place at the time when the elastic force of the expanded air was balanced by the resistance of the surrounding atmosphere; and the subsequent change of direction would be explained, by ascribing it to the collapsing of the air after detonation by the electric fluid.

The whirlwind, though more limited in point of extent than the hurricane, often exhibits effects no less terrific and appalling. It is generally preceded by an uncommon stillness of the atmosphere, and a sultry heat. In an instant the deceitful calm gives place to a whirling motion of the air, which appears to be produced by a sudden impulse that causes it to flow from all directions towards the circumference of a cylindrical column of the atmosphere over a particular spot. A rotatory motion is thus communicated, which gradually increases in rapidity, till the revolving column is able to raise in its vortex bodies of considerable weight from the ground, and transport them along with it to a great distance. The diameter of the column varies from a few feet to several hundred yards, but the whirling motion seems to be greatest at the circumference. The following account of a whirlwind, which occurred in Burgundy in the year 1755, is given by Abbé Richard, and will convey some notion of the nature of this violent meteor. " An extremely dark cloud, hanging low in the atmosphere, and driven forward by a north wind, was observed to cover the surface of the territory in which the small town of Mirabeau is situated: it occasioned very singular appearances for about a league in length, and the half of that space in breadth. Different whirlings appeared at once in this dark mass of condensed vapours; some hail fell, and thunder was heard; the quickset hedge rows, and most of the trees in the vineyards, were rooted up; the little river of Mirabeau was carried more than sixty paces from its bed, which remained dry; two men were enveloped in the whirlwind, and carried to a distance without experiencing any injury; a young shepherd was lifted high in the air, and thrown upon the banks of the river, yet his fall was not violent, the whirlwind having placed him on the verge where it ceased to act. In the woods within its circle its effects were traced, by finding the trees either twisted or torn up by the roots. Some sheep that were in the fields were enveloped and carried to a distance; several of them were killed. It unroofed the farm-houses; and, after raging in this manner for half an hour, the wind shifted to the south, when the tempest immediately ceased."

Water-
spouts.

When whirlwinds take place over the sea, they are commonly attended by waterspouts, which are still regarded as among the most remarkable and perplexing phenomena in meteorology. The appearances of a waterspout are the following: At its first formation it appears in the shape of a dark cone, protruded downwards from a black cloud, from which it seems to be suspended; as the cone extends itself towards the sea, the water begins to be violently agitated immediately below it, boiling and smoking like a furnace. At length the conical cloud having nearly reached the surface of the sea, the smoke-like appearance rises higher and higher till it reaches the cloud with which the spout is connected. The waterspout now assumes its most dreadful appearance, striking with amazement and terror those who, for the first time, have witnessed its awful and magnificent effects. Towards the end, it begins to appear like an immense tube, black at the borders and white in the middle, discharging a vast quantity of water, with a rushing noise, into the dark overhanging clouds; turning with a rapid spiral motion, and occasionally bending its huge trunk, as it is variously affected by the winds which now blow from every quarter of the heavens. When the spout begins to disperse, the black cloud generally draws itself up in a ragged form, leaving, however, a thin transparent tube, which reaches to the water where this smoky appearance still continues. If it should happen to burst in the middle, which not unfrequently is the case, it gives way with a rushing noise, like that of a cascade descending into a deep valley, and in a short time the whole is dissipated in the clouds, or precipitated in heavy rain, which, on being examined, is found to be perfectly fresh. The length of the spout is sometimes nearly half a mile, so that the water, which is raised by it, must be carried up by some powerful mechanical impulse, totally different from any thing that could be produced by atmospherical pressure. The existence of a vacuum, therefore, in the inside of the column, is quite inadequate to account for the ascent of the water to the great height which it seems to reach; and in the present state of our knowledge with regard to this curious phenomena, we can only ascribe its origin vaguely to the influence of electricity, or the mechanical action of a whirlwind. Some persons, indeed, who have observed the appearances of waterspouts with attention, maintain that the column does not consist of a continuous stream of water, but merely of dense vapour. This opinion, if well founded, would greatly diminish the difficulty of explaining their formation. See *Phil. Trans.* 1695, xix. 28.; *Ib.* 1701, xxii. 805.; *Ib.* 1702, xxiii. 281.; *Ib.* 1733, xxxviii. 75.; *Ib.* 1751, 477.; Cavallo's *Nat. Phil.* ii. 305.; Young's *Lect.* ii. 488.; *Edin. Phil. Journ.* vol. v. 39, 275.; vol. vi. 95.; and the article WATERSPOUT.

Pillars of
sand raised
by whirl-
winds.

Another variety of the whirlwind is exhibited in the vast pillars of sand which are frequently observed in the deserts of Africa. Bruce describes an appearance of this kind which he witnessed in his journey to Abyssinia, in the following terms: "At one o'clock we

alighted among some acacia trees at Waadi el Halboub, having gone twenty-one miles. We were here at once surprised and terrified, by a sight surely one of the most magnificent in the world. In that vast expanse of desert from west to north-west of us, we saw a number of prodigious pillars of sand, at different distances, at times moving with great velocity, at others stalking on with majestic slowness. At intervals we thought they were coming in a very few minutes to overwhelm us, and small quantities of sand did actually more than once reach us; again they would retreat, so as to be almost out of sight, their tops reaching to the very clouds; then the tops often separated from the bodies, and these once disjoined, dispersed in air, and did not appear more; sometimes they were broken in the middle, as if they were struck with large cannon-shot. At noon they began to advance with considerable swiftness upon us, the wind being very strong at north. Eleven ranged along the side of us, about the distance of three miles: the greatest diameter of the largest appeared to me at that distance as if it would measure ten feet. They retired from us with a wind at southeast, leaving an impression upon my mind to which I can give no name, though surely one ingredient in it was fear, with a considerable deal of wonder and astonishment. It was in vain to think of flying; the swiftest horse, or fleetest sailing ship, could be of no use to carry us out of this danger; and the full conviction of this rivetted me to the spot." A similar account of these moving pillars of sand is given by M. Adanson, who had an opportunity of observing one of them in crossing the river Gambia. It passed within eighteen or twenty toises of the stern of the vessel, and seemed to measure ten or twelve feet in circumference, and about 250 feet in height. Its heat was sensibly felt at the distance of 100 feet; and it left a strong smell, more like that given out by saltpetre than sulphur, and which remained a long time.

The sirocco.

The sirocco, the harmattan, and the kamsen, or simoom, seem to be modifications of the same species of wind, all of them being accompanied by a dry and sultry state of the atmosphere. The fatal effects of these winds, when inhaled incautiously, particularly those of the simoom, have been greatly exaggerated by some travellers, though it cannot be doubted that all of them possess noxious qualities. The wind

Places
where the
sirocco is
felt.

termed the sirocco seems to take its rise from the deserts to the south-west of Egypt, where it commonly makes its appearance a few days before the swelling of the Nile. It is attended with a suffocating heat, and a hazy obscureness of the air, which causes the sun to appear of a blood-red colour. From Egypt it spreads over all the Mediterranean, and even penetrates into Arabia, Persia, and some parts of Hindostan. It is also experienced in Italy and Spain; but, in these countries, its effects are less deleterious than in Egypt and the places adjacent, where it is sometimes charged with such quantities of sand, that it darkens the air as with a thick cloud. Brydone supposes that the sirocco has its origin from the highly rarefied air over the burning sands of Africa, a conjecture which seems to be confirmed by the observations of Volney, as well as by the fact that this wind, wherever it makes its appearance, always deposites an impalpable powder on the leaves of trees, and other substances exposed to its influence. During the continuance of this wind, respiration is attended with difficulty, and a certain degree of pain, which occasions languor and depression of spirits. The best remedy against its pernicious effects is found

Its effects.

from admitting the sea breeze, or inspiring the vapour of water sprinkled copiously over the floors of the apartments into which it penetrates, a proof that its unwholesome qualities are chiefly owing to its extreme dryness. The harmattan, which is experienced on the coast of Guinea, seems to differ little from the sirocco, and probably has its origin from the same cause. The simoom is represented to be extremely dangerous and sudden in its operation, but its malignity, as we already hinted, has been greatly exaggerated and heightened by all the frightful images that could impress the imagination. Thus, we are gravely informed by Goldsmith, that this terrible blast instantly kills all those that it involves in its passage; that it frequently assumes a visible form, and darts in a kind of bluish vapour, along the surface of the ground; but that none can tell in what its malignity consists, as none have survived its effects, to give information. (Goldsmith's *An. Nat.* I. 286.) The best authenticated accounts of this wind are to be found in the writings of Bruce and Burckhardt, who both witnessed its effects. The account of Bruce partakes of the usual love of the marvellous, so often to be traced in his descriptions of uncommon occurrences and rare phenomena. We shall give it in his own words: " At eleven o'clock, while we were contemplating the rugged tops of Chigre, where we expected to solace ourselves with plenty of good water, Idris called out, with a loud voice, ' Fall upon your faces, for here is the simoom.' I saw from the southeast a haze come, in the colour like the purple part of the rainbow, but not so compressed or thick. It did not occupy twenty yards in breadth, and was about twelve feet high from the ground. It was a kind of blush upon the air, and it moved very rapidly; for I scarce could turn to fall upon the ground, with my head to the northward, when I felt the heat of its current plainly upon my face. We all lay flat upon the ground till Idris told it was blown over. The meteor or purple haze which I saw was indeed passed; but a light air which still blew was of heat sufficient to threaten suffocation For my part," he adds, "I found distinctly on my breast, that I had imbibed a part of it, nor was I free of an asthmatic sensation till I had been some months in Italy."

Such is the description which Bruce gives of the simoom. The account of Burckhardt is more minute; and as it differs, on some points, from that of Bruce, we consider it proper to subjoin it in his own words: " I again inquired, as I had often done before, whether my companions had often experienced the simoom, (which we translate by the poisonous blast of the desert, but which is nothing more than a violent southeast wind). They answered in the affirmative; but none had ever known an instance of its having proved fatal. Its worst effect is, that it dries up the water in the skins, and so far it endangers the traveller's safety. I have repeatedly been exposed to the hot wind in the Syrian and Arabian deserts, in Upper Egypt and Nubia. The hottest and most violent was at Suakin, yet even there I felt no particular inconvenience from it, although exposed to all its fury in an open plain. For my own part, I am perfectly convinced that all the stories which travellers, or the inhabitants of the towns of Egypt and Syria relate of the simoom of the desert, are greatly exaggerated; and I never could hear of a single well-authenticated instance of its having proved mortal, either to man or beast. The fact is, that the Bedouins, when questioned on the subject, often frighten the town's people with tales of men, and even of whole caravans, having perished by the effects of the wind, when, upon closer inquiry, made by some per-

son, whom they found not ignorant of the desert, they will state the plain truth. I never observed that the simoom blows close to the ground, as commonly supposed, but always observed the whole atmosphere appear as if in a state of combustion. The dust and sand are carried high into the air, which assumes a reddish, or bluish, or yellowish tint, according to the nature and colour of the ground from which the dust arises. The yellow, however, always more or less predominates. In looking through a glass, of a light yellow colour, one may form a pretty correct idea of the appearance of the air, as I observed it during a stormy simoom at Esne, in Upper Egypt, in May 1813. The simoom is not always accompanied by whirlwinds; in its less violent degree, it will blow for hours with little force, although with oppressive heat. When the whirlwind raises the dust, it then increases several degrees in heat. In the simoom at Esne, the thermometer mounted to 121° in the shade; but the air seldom remains longer than a quarter of an hour in that state, or longer than the whirlwind lasts. The most disagreeable effect of the simoom on man is, that it stops perspiration, dries up the palate, and produces great restlessness. I never saw any person lie down on his face to escape its pernicious blast, as Bruce describes himself to have done, in crossing the desert; but, during the whirlwinds, the Arabs often hide their faces with their cloaks, and kneel down near their camels, to prevent the dust from hurting their eyes. Camels are always much distressed, not by the heat, but by the sand blowing into their large prominent eyes. They turn round to endeavour to screen themselves by holding down their heads: but this I never saw them do, except in case of a whirlwind, however intense the heat of the atmosphere might be. In June 1813, going from Esne to Siout, a violent simoom overtook me upon the plain between Farshiout and Berdys. I was quite alone, mounted upon a light-footed hedjin. When the whirlwind arose, neither house nor tree was in sight; and while I was endeavouring to cover my face with my handkerchief, the beast was made unruly by the quantity of dust blown into its eyes, and the terrible noise of the wind, and set off at a furious gallop. I lost the reins, and received a heavy fall; and not being able to see ten yards before me, I remained wrapt up in my cloak on the spot where I fell, until the wind abated, when, pursuing my dromedary, I found it at a great distance, quietly standing near a low shrub, the branches of which afforded some shelter to its eyes.

Bruce has mentioned the moving pillars of sand in the desert; but although none such occurred during my passage, I do not presume to question his veracity on this head. The Arabs told me, that there are often whirlwinds of sand; and I have repeatedly passed through districts of moving sands, which the slightest winds can raise. I remember to have seen columns of sands moving about like water-spouts, in the desert,—the banks of the Euphrates,—and have seen at Jaka terrible effects from a sudden wind. I therefore very easily credit their occasional appearance in the Nubian desert, although I doubt of their endangering the safety of travellers."—Burckhardt's *Travels*, p. 204.

It is by no means easy to assign a distinct cause for the origin of these winds; but, as we already remarked, their extreme dryness evidently indicates that they take their rise in regions where the air cannot be supplied with the quantity of moisture which, in ordinary cases, it holds in the vaporous state. The simoom has been referred to volcanic action, it being general-

Marginal notes:
The harmattan.
The simoom.
Bruce's account of it.
Burckhardt's account.
Physical Geography.
Difficulty of explaining the cause of these winds.

ly observed, that an offensive suffocating air accompanies severe earthquakes and volcanic eruptions; but if we can trust to the account of it given by Burckhardt, there is no reason for having recourse to any explanation of its origin, different from that to which we usually ascribe the cause of winds in general.

In giving a view of the winds which prevail in particular regions, it may not be improper to notice briefly the tracts in which long-continued *calms* prevail. The portion of the Atlantic Ocean denominated the *Rains* has been long known to navigators as being remarkable in this respect. This tract, which forms a zone of about 350 miles in breadth, is comprised between the meridians of Cape Verde and the eastermost islands of the groupe which bear that name. It is affirmed to be condemned to perpetual calms, attended occasionally by the most dreadful storms of thunder and lightning, and such copious rains, as to be considered a sufficiently distinctive appellation for it. The feeble winds, which are sometimes felt in this region of calms, are only sudden and uncertain puffs, of very little continuance, and less extent, insomuch that the wind blows from every quarter in the course of an hour, each breeze dying away into a calm before another succeeds; and instances are not wanting of ships being detained whole months in it, for want of wind. Similar calms prevail under the equator, in the western hemisphere, between Cape St. Francis and the Galapagos Islands; and Humboldt informs us, that the same sluggish state of the atmosphere is experienced on the western shores of America, between 13° 30', and 15° of north latitude, and 103° and 106° of west longitude, during the months of February and March. In the year which preceded that in which he visited those seas, a dead calm of 28 days, with a want of water in consequence of it, forced the crew of a ship newly built at Guayaquil, to abandon a rich cargo of cocoa, and save themselves in their boat, by making for the land, eighty leagues distant. Humb. *New Spain*, iv. 66. These calms seem to be owing to a suspension of the great equatorial current of the atmosphere, occasioned by the superior temperature of continents over that of the contiguous ocean.

Manner in
which heat
is trans-
mitted
through
the atmo-
sphere.

Having thus considered, at some length, the nature of the currents of the atmosphere, we shall now proceed to examine the manner in which heat is distributed through the mass of that fluid. When the sun's rays pass through a diaphanous medium, it is well known that they are not found to impart to it the slightest elevation of temperature; and hence a fluid like our atmosphere, if it were endowed with perfect transparency, could receive no heat from the sun by direct radiation. It is only where the solar rays encounter, in their progress, dark and opaque substances that the heat they are capable of communicating is disengaged from them, in a way fitted to affect terrestrial matter. The surface of the earth being thus warmed by the immediate influence of the sun's rays, the temperature which it acquires is slowly imparted to the superincumbent air, which, being rarefied, ascends upwards, gradually giving off its heat during its ascent, till it reaches a situation where its specific gravity becoming equal to that of the surrounding mass of air, its tendency to ascend ceases, and, for a moment, it remains stationary. The place which it originally occupied being supplied by a fresh stratum of air, the same process is repeated, and incessantly renewed with portions of air. But the ascending air, as it mounts aloft in the atmosphere, having its volume enlarged, in consequence of the pressure to which it is now exposed being diminished, acquires, in its new situation, an in-

creased capacity for heat, by which its sensible temperature is, in a like degree, reduced. The descending portions of air are affected in a way the reverse of this; giving out a portion of their latent heat as they sink lower and lower, till they arrive at the surface, where, being heated by coming in contact with the ground, they re-ascend, to begin anew the same round of changes in their thermal condition. It appears by this explanation that the sun warms the atmosphere by first heating the surface of the earth, from which the heat is gradually communicated to the air immediately over it, and afterwards to the more elevated parts of the atmosphere, by means of the alternate ascent and descent of the air, and the different capacity of that fluid for caloric in various states of density. The heat at the surface gives birth to a succession of ascending and descending currents; but these currents being once established, the principal cause of the inequality of temperature at the top and bottom of a column of the atmosphere seems to be, the evolution and absorption of heat by the alternate condensation and rarefaction of the air. The imperfect manner in which heat is conducted through fluids, agreeably to the fine discoveries of Count Rumford, effectually secures the lower strata of the atmosphere from any loss of heat by transmission; and hence a diminution of temperature is observed as we ascend above the surface of the earth.

The law which regulates the distribution of heat as we ascend in the atmosphere, appears to be different at different distances from the equator, as well as at different seasons of the year. Saussure observed, that by ascending from Geneva to Chamouni, a height of 347 toises, Reaumur's thermometer fell 4°.2, being 1° of Fahrenheit for 236 English feet. On another occasion, the same accurate observer found, that on ascending from the same place to the summit of Mont Blanc, an elevation of 1941 toises, Reaumur's thermometer sunk 20°.7, being at the rate of 1° Fahrenheit for 266 feet. From these observations, and others of the same kind, Saussure has assigned, as a mean result, 1° Fahrenheit for 292 feet in summer, and 1° on the same scale for 419 feet in winter. M. Ramond has given 299 feet, and M. d'Aubuisson 315 feet, for 1° Fahrenheit. These results do not differ greatly from those obtained by Gay Lussac during his aeronautic ascent. This intrepid naturalist found, that, for an elevation of 22,960 English feet, the mean decrease of temperature corresponded to 1° Fahrenheit for 341 feet, at a time when the heat in the vicinity of Paris was nearly equal to that of the equatorial regions.

Decrement
of heat dif-
ferent in
different
seasons,
and in dif-
ferent lati-
tudes.

But it is to Humboldt we are indebted for the most precise, as well as the most extensive observations connected with the diminution of heat in the atmosphere. From the results which he has stated in his dissertation on the distribution of heat over the globe, we learn not only that the heat does not decrease uniformly, but that the rate of its diminution must be greatly modified by local circumstances. Thus, in the Cordilleras, he observed that the decrease became slower between 1000 and 3000 metres of ascent, particularly between 1000 and 2500; and that it afterwards increased between 3000 and 4000 metres. This will be perceived by the following Table, which exhibits the partial results of his observations at the back of the Andes.

Height in Metres.		Fahr.	Eng. Feet.
From 0 to 1000	.	1°	309
1000 2000	.	1	536
2000 3000	.	1	423
3000 4000	.	1	239
4000 5000	.	1	328

The mean result, in reference to the entire length of

Physical Geography.

the column, is one degree of Fahrenheit for 346 feet; which differs only 5 feet from the mean result deduced from the observations of Gay Lussac. The slowness with which the heat decreased in the stratum of air between 1000 and 3000 metres of elevation, Humboldt ascribes to the joint effect of the extinction of light, or the absorption of the solar rays by the clouds, which are chiefly formed in that region; to the production of rain; and to the obstruction which the clouds present to the dispersion of heat from the inferior strata by radiation. *Edin. Phil. Journ.* vol. iv. p. 278.

From the above observations it may be inferred, that the diminution of heat in the atmosphere, for the greatest heights we can reach, is nearly uniform; but that the rate over any particular place may be so affected by the circumstances of its situation, as to give rise to considerable deviations from an uniform decrease by

Various hypotheses respecting the diminution of heat in the atmosphere.

arithmetical progression. La Grange is inclined to adopt this hypothesis, not only on account of its simplicity, but as most conformable, on the whole, to actual observation. *Berlin Memoirs* for 1772. On the other hand, Euler considers a harmonic progression as most reconcileable with appearances; and Mr. Leslie has given a formula, deduced from experiments on the capacity of air for heat, under various degress of density, which differs from both the preceding[*]. According to this formula, if b denote the pressure of the barometer, at the lower station, and β that at the higher, the difference of temperature, expressed in centesimal degrees, will be $25\left(\dfrac{b}{\beta} - \dfrac{\beta}{b}\right)$.

To apply this expression Mr. Leslie assumes, that the heat in every part of a vertical column is the same; and that the decrease of heat is entirely produced by a diminution of the density of the air at different elevations. He admits that the constant coefficient may require alteration; and that in many places it may be better to assume 30 for the multiplier in the summer months, and 20 in the months of winter.

In consequence of the diminution of temperature, which is experienced as we ascend in the atmosphere, it is evident that in every climate a point of elevation may be reached where it will be continually freezing. The altitude of the point above the surface of the earth will depend partly on the temperature of the lower regions of the atmosphere, and partly on the decrement of heat belonging to the column at the period of observation. Thus, near the equator, it was observed by

Line of perpetual congelation.

Bouguer, that it began to freeze on the sides of the lofty mountain Pinchincha, at the height of 15,577 feet above the level of the sea, whereas congelation was found by Saussure to take place on the Alps, at the height of 13,428 feet. By tracing a line, on the plane of the meridian, through the points at which it constantly freezes, a curve is obtained which has been denominated the line of *Perpetual Congelation.* The height at which this curve intersects a vertical line, in the various latitudes, has been computed by Kirwan, partly from observation, and partly from the mean temperature of the parallel, and the decrement of heat, as we ascend in the atmosphere. The following table exhibits the result of his calculation; and though it is constructed on the erroneous supposition that the mean annual temperature of the pole is 31°, which, according to the observations of Captain Scoresby and Captain Parry, must be far beyond the truth [†], it is tolerably accurate for the more accessible regions of the globe.

Lat.	Mean height of Term of Congelation.	Lat.	Mean height of Term of Congelation.
0	15,577	45	7,658
5	15,457	50	6,260
10	15,067	55	4,912
15	14,498	60	3,684
20	13,719	65	2,516
25	13,030	70	1,557
30	11,592	75	748
35	10,664	80	120
40	9,016		

Physical Geography.

These numerical relations are best perceived at a glance by means of a diagram. Let AB therefore represent the rectified meridian, from the equator to the pole, divided into intervals of 10°; and from each of the

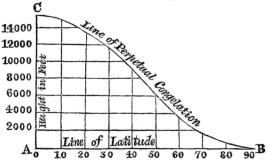

points, 0, 10, 20, &c. let perpendiculars, or ordinates be drawn to represent the height of the freezing point at the equator, and at 10°, 20°, &c. of latitude, the curve BC, which has a contrary flexure about 60°, will exhibit the general form of the line of perpetual congelation, from the equator to the pole.

The following formulæ have been given by Dr. Brewster, upon the supposition established by Humboldt, that the line of 32° is different from that of perpetual snow. Calling T the mean temperature, in degrees of Fahrenheit, and L the latitude in degrees, then 310 (T — 32°) = height of line of 32° in English feet, and 310 (T — 32°) + 48 L = height of the line of perpetual snow. For the meridian of the west of Europe, or for the Alps, the formulæ in terms of the latitude only will be 310 (81½° cos. L — 32) = height of line of 32°, and 310 (81⅕° cos. L — 32) + 48 L = height of line of perpetual snow.

Changes in the line of perpetual congelation.

The line of perpetual congelation must obviously assume a change of curvature at different seasons of the year, rising higher in summer, and descending lower in winter. The limits appear to be separated by a small interval, within the tropical regions; but in the higher latitudes, where the annual range of temperature is more considerable, they are disjoined by a wider range,

Circumstances which affect the quantity of moisture in the air.

—a circumstance which affects, in no small degree, the appearance of the heavens in the temperate, as well as the polar zones, during the different seasons of the year. Hence within the tropics, the clouds when they appear, are generally seen at an immense height in the atmosphere; whereas in the more fluctuating climates of the temperate zone, they often descend to the earth, and conceal for days the azure vault of the sky.

Under the article HYGROMETRY, § 92, we established a fact, which had frequently been called in question, that the moisture existing in the atmosphere in the state of vapour, is maintained in that condition by the influence of heat alone, and quite independently of any kind of chemical solution by the aerial medium in which it floats. This being the case, it is evident that the quantity of moisture which is thus mechanically

---

[*] In a masterly paper, on the *Astronomical Refractions*, just published, by Mr. Ivory, in the *Phil. Trans.* for 1823, he maintains, that "there is no ground in experience for attributing to the gradation of heat in the atmosphere, any other law than that of an equable decrease as the altitude increases," p. 436. The extreme accuracy with which his formula, founded on this supposition, represents the results of astronomical observations, may be considered as a strong proof of its correctness.—ED.

[†] See the *Edinburgh Transactions*, vol. ix p. 212, &c. and the article POLAR REGIONS in this work, Vol. XVII. Sect. *Climate.*

combined with the air over different regions, must depend, in the first place, on the mean temperature; and, secondly, on the presence of a sufficient quantity of water, at the surface of the earth, to afford an adequate supply of moisture to the atmosphere by evaporation. The latter condition may be said to determine the degree of dryness of the air; the former sets bounds to its absolute humidity, and prevents the indefinite accumulation of water in that aerial fluid. In all places, therefore, it will be found, that the absolute quantity of moisture held in the state of vapour by the atmosphere, ranges between the maximum quantity of it which is due to the greatest and least annual temperature of the situation. HYGROMETRY, § 52.

Mean humidity of the air over the ocean.

The humidity of the air over the ocean, and places having an insular situation, is nearly as great as the mean temperature is capable of maintaining in the condition of vapour, though for reasons we have stated in the article HYGROMETRY, it generally corresponds to a point from 6° to 10° lower. The following Table, drawn up from observations made at the request of the writer of this article, at noon, in various parts of the Atlantic, exhibits the gradual increase of humidity from the parallel of 50° to 23°. The fifth column contains the absolute quantity of moisture in 100 cubic inches of air, deduced from the formula laid down in § 63 of HYGROMETRY, which we have since verified by numberless observations; the sixth the point of deposition, or the temperature below which the moisture of the air would begin to return to the state of water; and the seventh the relative humidity of the air, complete dampness being denoted by 100, and perfect dryness by 0*. See METEOROLOGY, p. 168.

Hygrometrical observations on the Atlantic ocean.

Lat.	Long.	Temperature of the Air.	Temperature of the Atlantic.	Grains of Moisture in 100 Cubic Inches.	Point of Deposition.	Relative Humidity. Perfect dampness 100.
50°.22′	9°.32′ W.	50	57½	.1893	42°	60°
50 9	10 29	62	59	.2513	50½	70
48 57	10 58	64	60	.3116	57¼	74
46 37	12 51	61	60½	.2400	49	68½
44 23	15 38	60½	62	.2346	48½	68
42 23	17 20	63	64	.2997	56	81
39 49	18 41	64	65	.2933	55⅓	76½
36 40	19 42	65	68	.3056	56¾	77
34 6	21 47	65	68	.3145	57¼	79½
31 51	23 51	68	70½	.3262	58½	75
30 12	25 45	70½	72	.3338	60	71
29 8	26 19	70	72½	.3540	61	79¾
27 49	26 46	72	74	.3834	64	78
26 3	26 46	72	74½	.3834	64	78
24 12	27 47	75½	75	.3956	65	74
23 6	29 9	76	75¼	.4325	67¾	78
22 40	31 22	75	76	.4125	66	76¾

The observations from which the above table was constructed were made from the middle to the end of October 1819. It appears by the results which it contains, that the quantity of moisture, held in admixture with the air, is regulated in the different zones solely by temperature; but it deserves remark, that though the absolute quantity of moisture is nearly double, in the parallel of 23°, of that in the parallel of 50°, the relative humidity upon which the health and vigour of living beings chiefly depend, is nearly the same in every latitude; increasing, however, in a slight degree towards the equator.

The relative humidity of the air nearly the same in every zone.

Great dryness of the air in elevated regions.

On elevated table lands the dryness of the air is generally excessive. Thus, at the back of the Cordilleras of Mexico, on the banks of the Lake Tezcuco, Humboldt observed the hygrometer of De Luc to stand so low as 15°, when the temperature of the air was 23°.4 centigrade, or 74° of Fahrenheit. This very depressed state of the instrument would, by sect. 88. HYGROMETRY, correspond to .123 of vaporous tensions; which, by the table in sect. 39 of the same article, indicates .1673 grains of moisture in 100 cubic inches of air, and gives the point of deposition so low as 27°. On the other hand, extensive plains, abounding with trees, are usually characterized by a humid and foggy atmosphere. This is the case particularly with Brazil, Guiana, and the great central basin of South America, which receives the waters of the Amazon. In the middle of a continent overspread with forests, and watered by the equatorial rains, the humidity is nearly the same as on the ocean.

The humidity of the air, in every place, affected by the winds.

The humidity of the air, in every place, is greatly affected by the quarter from which the wind blows. Within the tropics, it is observed that the driest tracts are situated to the westward of elevated lands; whereas within the temperate zones, an opposite state of things is found to exist. In illustration of this remark, it may be mentioned that the confined regions on the west of the Andes are dry; while the wide countries on the east side of that chain are exposed to a damp atmosphere, from the trade winds blowing over the Atlantic. On the contrary, we find that in the northern temperate zone, the country to the westward of the Stoney mountains is remarkable for the dampness of its climate, while Louisiana, and the northern parts of America lying to the eastward of the same elevated ridge, possess an atmosphere comparatively dry. In like manner, the western shores of Europe are more humid than the eastern coasts of Asia We shall afterwards advert to this important fact in explaining the great inequality of temperature which is observed on the east and west sides of continents.

The temperature of the atmosphere diminishing at an average about 1° for every 300 feet of ascent, it follows that the absolute humidity of the air must decrease rapidly as we mount into the higher regions of

* The following results are extracted from a Table which Humboldt has given in his *Personal Narrative*. The weight of the moisture which is expressed in the original Table, in the number of grammes contained in a metre cube, has been reduced to English grains in 100 cubic inches. The observations were made in June and July 1799. The results are stated to have been deduced by D'Aubuisson by an intricate formula of La Place. Their agreement with the corresponding quantities which are contained in the Table given in the text is the more satisfactory, as they have been derived by methods totally different.

Periods of Observation.	Latitude of the Place in the open Sea.	Temperature of Air by Fahrenheit's Therm.	Grains of Moisture in 100 Cubic Inches.	Relative Humidity.
9th June 1799	39° 10′	58	.2902	65
15	30 36	68	.3413	71
16	29 18	68	.3309	68
30	18 53	70	.3371	63
4th July	16 19	72½	.4087	75
10	12 34	75	.5469	77
12	10 46	77¾	.5982	79
14	11 1	77	.6058	83

the air. In the article HYGROMETRY, § 97, we have given a table, calculated from theoretical principles, in which the weight of the moisture in a cubic inch of air is exhibited for various elevations above the surface of the earth, adapted to the mean temperature of the parallel of 45°. From numerous observations we have made since that table was computed, we are satisfied that it expresses with great accuracy the mean hygrometric state of the air at different heights; and that it may be applied to the calculation of the moisture contained in a column of air for any other latitude, by simply multiplying the absolute quantity of moisture existing in a given volume of air at the surface, by the successive multipliers in the column of "relative tension of the vapour."

Formation of clouds. On account of the decreasing progression of humidity as we ascend in the atmosphere, it must be obvious that a certain volume of air at the surface, so charged with watery vapour that the point of deposition is only a few degrees below its own temperature at the time, must, on being raised to a moderate height, arrive at a situation where it will be reduced to absolute dampness; and that on being elevated a little higher, a portion of the moisture which it holds in the state of vapour must be converted into water, and assume a visible form, more or less opaque, according to the extent of the diminution of temperature to which it is exposed, below the point of deposition.

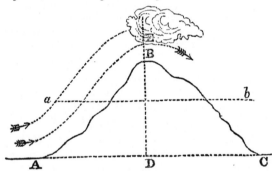

Thus let ABC represent the contour of the section of a mountain, and let BD, its altitude above its base, be 2000 feet; then if the air at the bottom of the mountain be supposed to be charged with humidity, so that the point of deposition is only 5° below its temperature at the time, on being raised to the height of 5 × 300 or 1500 feet, the moisture it contains will begin to appear in a visible form, and to envelop the summit of the mountain with a fog, the bottom of which will not descend below the line *a b*, supposed to be 1500 feet above AC. If the air is more partially charged with moisture, so that the point of deposition is, we shall say, 12° below the temperature at the bottom of the mountain, then 12 × 300 being 3600, the fog or cloud occasioned by the condensed vapour will be formed above the mountain, as at the point E; and it will be perceived by those who examine the phenomenon with attention, that however violently the wind may sweep over the summit B, the cloud or condensed vapour always remains stationary over the mountain, new portions being added to it, on the windward side, as the parts driven to leeward are dissolved, in consequence of descending to a lower region in the atmosphere, where the temperature is higher *. Hence the origin of the vulgar prejudice, that mountains attract the clouds; and hence too it may be inferred, that when the sides and tops of these elevated masses are free from fogs and clouds, the air must possess great dryness, especially if it be in motion at the time. The influence of mountains, indeed, in producing rain, has been universally remarked. Barrow informs us, that he was prevented from ascending the Pic of Teneriffe, by a storm of wind and rain, while not a drop had fallen in the lower part of the island.—Barrow's *Voyage*, p. 44.

Causes which regulate the formation of clouds. The formation of clouds, viewing the subject in its most general aspect, must depend essentially on the causes which produce a transition of the atmospheric moisture from the vaporous to the liquid state. Various circumstances may contribute indirectly to this effect; but the immediate cause, by whatever means it is induced, is change of temperature. Now, all the

---

* As the account of the formation of clouds has been stated hypothetically in the text, it may not be improper to give the following illustration of the subject from actual experiment and observation. On the 17th of August 1818, the writer of this article ascertained, by a set of observations made with great care, that, at a point near the base of Bengloe, elevated 502 feet above the level of the sea, the temperature of the air was 62¼°; the quantity of moisture in 100 cubic inches of air, .2479 grains; the point of deposition being 50°, and the relative humidity 68°. The air was cloudy, but tranquil, and rather dry. After ascending to the height of 2374 feet above the sea, as ascertained by an excellent barometer of Adie's construction, and graduated to the $\frac{1}{1000}$th part of an inch, the state of the air was again examined, when the temperature was found to be 51¼°; the quantity of moisture in 100 cubic inches of air .1989 grains; the point of deposition 43½°, and the relative humidity 77°. Lastly, on reaching the summit of the mountain, which is elevated 3690 feet above the level of the sea, the thermometer sunk to 45°, while the quantity of moisture in 100 cubic inches was determined to be .1819, the point of deposition 41°, and the relative humidity 87°. Though contrary to what is usually observed, the relative humidity had risen from the bottom to the top of the mountain, progressively from 68° to 87°, the air retained for some time the most perfect transparency, and afforded a fine opportunity of viewing the surrounding mountain groups. In about half an hour, during the course of which a set of observations were made with Wollaston's apparatus for determining the boiling point, a gentle breeze sprung up from the south, and wafted the air from the base to the summit of the mountain, where it soon gave rise to a dense fog, or cloud, so very close that objects could barely be discerned through it at the distance of five or six yards. By attending to the hygrometric state of the air along the slope of the mountain, we shall be able to point out, in the most distinct manner, the various circumstances connected with the transition of the vapour to the liquid, or vesicular state. At the bottom, as already stated, 100 cubic inches of air were found to contain .2479 grains of moisture; and the same volume of air, near the middle of the ascent, where the first traces of the fog appeared, .1989 grains.

Hence 100 cubic inches of mixed air must have held in solution, $\dfrac{.2479+.1989}{2}$ or .2234 grains, which by the Table in § 39. HYGROMETRY, gives 47°, as the point of deposition. But the temperature of the air at the top of the hill was 45°, so that the difference between the quantity of moisture capable of being held in the vaporous state at 47° and 45°, which by the Table referred to is .01398 grains in 100 cubic inches, was detached from the air to constitute the fog or cloud.

As the vapour passed to the visible state, it was observed that it frequently sent out *cirri*, or ramifications in a horizontal direction, in the very face of the winds with a velocity which, when first observed, excited much surprise. This was found to proceed from the strata of the vaporized air reaching successively, during their ascent, their respective points of deposition, and thus producing the appearance of motion in the mass of vapour previously condensed. In fact, had the inferior strata of air, as they ascended, reached the point of deposition at the same instant, the condensation would have taken place at once over the whole of their extent; but the different portions of it holding more or less moisture in solution, had also different points of deposition, and as they reached the height where the temperature corresponded to these, a succession of precipitations took place, which if they happened to be nearly in the same plane, exhibited the appearance of an actual motion of the fog against the direction of the wind.

Physical Geography.

more important changes of temperature, which occur in the atmosphere, may be classed under the following heads: 1st, The diurnal change, produced by the rotation of the earth; 2dly, the annual change, produced by the varying declination of the sun; 3dly, the change of temperature occasioned by winds, or the translation of the aerial columns from one parallel of latitude to another; and, 4thly, the change of temperature produced by the elevation or depression of the atmospherical strata.

The formation of clouds, how far affected by the diurnal changes of temperature.

The first of these causes of change of temperature exhibits its effects on the clouds and vapours, which sometimes form, near the surface of the earth, in the evening, and again disappear the following morning as the heat of the day advances. It is true, indeed, that at certain seasons of the year, the reverse of this is observed to take place with clouds of moderate elevation, a cloudy day being sometimes followed by a clear starry night; but this result, the explanation of which has been in no small degree perplexing to meteorologists, seems to be connected with a very unusual dryness, in the upper regions of the atmosphere, and a partial subsiding of the strata of air in which the clouds exist, during the night, in consequence of which they are brought nearer the surface of the earth, and exposed to a temperature sufficient to dissolve the visible vapour of which they are composed.—De Luc, *Idées sur la Meteorologie*, vol. ii. pp. 16, and 97.

By the annual changes of temperature.

The annual change of temperature produces effects upon the transparency of the atmosphere, which give a peculiar character to the aspect of the sky at certain seasons of the year. The period of the seasons when the air is driest and least charged with humidity, either in a visible or imperceptible state, is the spring; while on the other hand, the dampest and most cloudy weather occurs at the close of autumn. During the former of these seasons, the temperature of the air being on the increase, its capacity for moisture seems to augment in a faster ratio than the additions which are made to its humidity, by evaporation; whereas, during the latter, the temperature undergoing a very rapid decline, the relative humidity is maintained at all times, nearly in a maximum state. Hence the origin of the dense fogs which in autumn overspread the north of Europe.

By the change of temperature occasioned by winds.

The change of temperature occasioned by winds, and the translation of large portions of the atmosphere from one parallel to another, must be regarded as one of the most powerful causes by which the transparency of the air is affected. In both hemispheres, a wind blowing from the nearest pole, brings with it air charged with a smaller quantity of moisture than belongs, in its mean hygrometric state, to the air of the region to which it is conveyed; and hence the north-east winds, which generally prevail in this country during the months of April, are attended with great dryness and a cloudless atmosphere. The reverse happens in the case of a current of air blowing from the equator, the dampest weather to which we are exposed being uniformly produced by south, south-west, and south-east winds. The hygrometric effects of particular winds are greatly modified, however, by local circumstances. Thus the sky of Xalapa, in New Spain, which is beautiful and serene in summer, assumes a gloomy appearance from the month of December to the month of February. Whenever the north wind blows at Vera Cruz, the inhabitants of Xalapa are enveloped in a dense fog. The thermometer then descends to 55° or 60° of Fahrenheit, and during this period the stars are often invisible for two or three weeks together. Humboldt's *New Spain*, vol. ii. p. 268. At Lima the

cloudy state of the atmosphere commences about the beginning of July, and continues till the end of November, the wind then blowing chiefly from the south and south-south-east.—*Ulloa*, vol. ii. p. 64.

Physical Geography.

By the change of temperature produced by the elevation and depression of the atmospherical strata.

The last cause to which we adverted, as influencing the formation of clouds, is the elevation and depression of the atmospherical strata. One of the principal means by which these alternations of altitude are produced, in particular portions of the air, is mountain ridges, and elevated table-land. We have already illustrated, by statements of a precise nature, the effect which lofty mountains have on the formation of clouds; and on this head, it is quite unnecessary to add any arguments, of a general description, in support of the conclusions to which we were led by the facts we adduced. It may be sufficient to affirm, that in conformity with these conclusions, the windward sides of extensive tracts of land have always a more cloudy atmosphere than their leeward sides; and that countries having a diversified and rugged surface, uniformly possess a dark lowering state of the heavens, while the extensive level plains, denominated steppes and llanos, are no less distinguished by a clear and parched sky. The aerial currents, when they arrive from the ocean, being nearly at the maximum state of humidity, are compelled, as they advance into the interior, to ascend higher and higher by the slope of the land; in consequence of which their temperature is diminished; the vapour is condensed; fogs and clouds are formed; and the absolute quantity of moisture contained in the air becomes less and less. After being wafted over a succession of high table lands and elevated summits, rising gradually above one another, the air is deprived of a large portion of its humidity, and it descends on the opposite side, with an increasing capacity for moisture. It therefore becomes relatively drier in its progress, till at length the point of deposition is so far depressed below the actual temperature as nearly to preclude the possibility of clouds being formed, unless in very particular cases. Within the tropics, for example, from the eastern shores of America to the ridge of the Andes, the sky is almost always cloudy, and an opportunity is seldom afforded, except on the llanos, of observing the heavenly bodies. " From the 30th of April, to the 11th of May," says Humboldt, " I had not been able to see any star on the meridian, to determine the latitude of places. I watched whole nights in order to make use of the method of double altitudes, but all my efforts were useless." " The fogs of the north of Europe," he adds, " are not more constant than those of the equatorial regions of Guiana." *Pers. Nar.* v. 253. Yet the same air, which exists in so humid a state in the great basins of the Oroonoko and the Amazon, is so much deprived of moisture after it passes over the summits of the Cordilleras, that, when it reaches Lima, it is no longer in a condition to produce rain. *Ulloa*, ii. 64. The Ghauts, in the Peninsula of India, afford a still better example of the effects produced by mountain chains on the hygrometric state of the air over the plains which stretch below at their bases. On the one side of that chain is Malabar, on the other Coromandel. On the Malabar side, between that ridge of mountains and the sea, it is summer, as it is called, from September till April; during which time there is always a clear sky, and very rarely any rain; while, on the other side of the hills, on the Coromandel coast, the same period of the year is termed winter; and there, at that time, it rains almost incessantly. From the month of April to the month of September, the state of things is reversed, it being clear and dry weather on the Coro-

Changes in the humidity of the air by passing over elevated land.

Cause of rains on the Malabar and Coromandel coasts.

mandel side, and cloudy and rainy along the coast of Malabar.

Now, if the direction of the monsoons be kept in view at the time these opposite effects are produced, it will be found that the results are just what should be expected, in conformity with the fact we have endeavoured to establish, viz. that the windward sides of extensive portions of the earth's surface possess a more humid atmosphere than the leeward sides, the air being deprived of its moisture by passing over elevated land.

But though the origin of clouds, so far as it is connected with the elevation and depression of the atmospherical strata, must be ascribed chiefly to the inequalities of the earth's surface; it cannot be doubted that electricity exerts, on many occasions, an important influence in their formation, by producing similar effects. This subtile fluid has been found to be, at all times, more abundant in the elevated parts of the atmosphere than near the surface of the earth; where it is known to be developed by a variety of processes. It has been proved by Mr. Canton that dry air, when heated, becomes negatively electrified, but that it assumes the positive state when cooled. He has also shown that it undergoes changes in its electrical condition, as it is exposed to various degrees of pressure; and Beccaria, Cavallo, Achard, and other experimental inquirers, have ascertained that these changes are connected with other meteorological phenomena. On this subject we quote the following observations from Humboldt, which that illustrious traveller made in the valleys of Aragua: " Being sufficiently habituated to the climate," says he, " not to fear the effects of tropical rains, we remained on the shore to observe the electrometer. I held it more than twenty minutes in my hand, six feet above the ground, and observed that, in general, the pith balls separated only a few seconds before the lightning was seen. The separation was four lines. The electric discharge remained the same during several minutes; and having time to determine the nature of the electricity, by approaching a stick of sealing wax, I saw here on the plain what I have often observed on the back of the Andes during a storm, that the electricity of the atmosphere was first positive, then null, and then negative. These oscillations from the positive to the negative state were often repeated. We had already observed," he adds, " in the valleys of Aragua, from the 18th and 19th of February, clouds forming at the commencement of the night. In the beginning of the month of March the accumulation of the vesicular vapours became visible to the eye, and with them signs of atmospheric electricity, augmented daily. We saw flashes of lightning to the south, and the electrometer of Volta displayed constantly at sunset positive electricity. The separation of the little pith balls, null during the rest of the day, was from three to four lines at the commencement of the night; which is triple what I generally observed in Europe * with the same instrument in calm weather." Again he remarks, " about the end of February and the beginning of March, the blue of the sky is less intense, the hygrometer indicates by degrees greater humidity, the stars are sometimes veiled by a thin stratum of vapours, and their light is no longer steady and planetary; they are seen twinkling from time to time at 20° above the horizon. The breeze, at this period, becomes less strong, less regular, and is often interrupted by dead calms. The clouds accumulate toward the S. S. E. They appear like distant mountains, with outlines strongly marked. From

time to time they detach themselves from the horizon and traverse the vault of the sky with a rapidity which little corresponds with the feeble wind that reigns in the inferior strata of the air. At the end of March the southern region of the atmosphere is illumined by small electric explosions. They are like phosphorescent gleams circumscribed by one group of vapours. The breeze then passes, from time to time, and for several hours together, to the west and south-west. This is a certain sign of the approach of the rainy season; which begins at the Oroonoko about the end of April. The sky begins to be obscured, the azure disappears, and a grey tint is spread uniformly over it. At the same time, the heat of the atmosphere progressively increases; and soon they are no longer clouds, but condensed vapours, that cover the whole vault of the sky." *Personal Narrative*, iv. 400. It would appear, however, from some queries which Humboldt afterwards proposes, that he is disposed to doubt that electricity has any influence in the formation of vesicular vapours; or rather, that he is inclined to embrace the opinion, that it is the formation of these vapours which augments and modifies the electrical tension. But, though this may be true to a certain extent, it cannot be denied that the partial and unequal distribution of electricity, throughout the different strata of the atmosphere, must produce attractions between them, and give rise to changes in their altitude, which must often be attended with the formation of vesicular vapour.

The form and density of clouds vary exceedingly with the extent as well as the degree of condensation of the vapour which accompanies their formation; and so diversified are the appearances they assume, that a distinct classification of them might well seem impossible. Of late, however, attempts have been made to reduce them under specific forms; and, though a certain degree of vagueness is inseparable from the subject, a more systematic distribution of them has been obtained than appeared to be possible with objects that seemed so little susceptible of precise and accurate description.

Clouds have been divided by Mr. Howard into seven kinds, which are considered sufficiently different from one another in appearance to constitute distinct species, and yet so generic in character as to include, under their combined forms, all the varieties of condensed vapour to which the term cloud is applied. The nomenclature, though not remarkable for elegance, is not altogether destitute of precision. It includes, 1st, The Stratus, or Fall-cloud; 2d, The Cumulus, or Stacken-cloud; 3d, The Cirrus, or Curl-cloud; 4th, The Nimbus, or Rain-cloud; 5th, The Cumulo-stratus, or Twain-cloud; 6th, The Cirro-stratus, or Wane-cloud; and, 7th, The Cirro-cumulus, or Sonder-cloud.

The stratus, or fall-cloud, includes fogs, mists, and extensive sheets of vapour, in contact with the surface of the earth. This cloud is commonly formed by the condensation of vapour, at the close of the day, in consequence of the diminution of the daily temperature. It reaches its greatest density a little before sun-rise, and generally disappears as the temperature of the day advances. In some instances, however, it assumes a more permanent character, and spreads over a great extent of country, for several days together. A particular modification of these clouds hovered over the greater part of Europe during a considerable portion of the year 1783.

The cumulus, or stacken-cloud, is distinguished by its flattened base and towering structure; and is com-

Margin notes:

Influence of electricity on the formation of clouds.

Classification of clouds.

Howard's distribution of clouds.

The stratus, or fall-cloud.

The cumulus, or stacken-cloud.

---

* At Salzbourg, at Bareith, and at Jena, in Germany; in the plain of St. Denis, near Paris; and on the table land in Castille.

posed of detached clouds collected together into an accumulated mass. Its formation generally commences a little after sunrise; and it disappears towards the evening, when it is resolved into the stratus, or fall-cloud. The cumulus seems to owe its formation chiefly to electricity.

The cirrus or curl-cloud, so denominated from its resemblance to a distended lock of hair, is distinguished from other clouds by its thin fleecy appearance, and the continual changes of form to which it is liable during its existence. The cirrus-clouds are generally at a very great height in the atmosphere, their elevation being seldom less than four or five miles above the surface of the earth. The *Comoid* cirrus, which, among the vulgar, has received the name of the *grey mare's tail*, affords a good example of this species of cloud; and when it retains its general form for a considerable length of time, is regarded as a prognostic of a gale of wind from the quarter to which the cloud is directed.

The nimbus, or rain-cloud, is affirmed to be a uniform precursor of rain. Any of the three clouds already described, as well as the combinations of those termed cumulo-stratus, cirro-stratus, and cirro-cumulus, may exist in the atmosphere without being accompanied by rain; but this can never happen, we are told, with the nimbus, the formation of which always produces that phenomenon. The appearance of the nimbus is described with little precision by the author of the new nomenclature of clouds; and indeed it seems to be rather a modified state of the other forms, than a distinct species. To assert, therefore, that rain never falls unless this cloud be previously formed, is little better than to maintain, that whatever be the aspect of the sky, it never rains while it is fair weather.

The cumulo-stratus, or twain-cloud, differs from simple cumulus by a greater degree of density, and by consisting of several congregated masses of clouds, piled one above another. The lower part of this cloud is generally horizontal, while the upper part is composed of large swelling protuberances, which sometimes tower, in the most gigantic manner, to a great height. The twain-cloud is frequently resolved into the nimbus, already described, and descends in rain.

The cirro-stratus, or wane-cloud, is commonly of an elongated form, possessing a great horizontal extent in proportion to its thickness or depth. Like the cirrus it is continually changing its appearance, and seems to derive its origin from that cloud as it subsides into the lower regions of the atmosphere. From its changeable nature it has been called the wane-cloud. The cirro-stratus assumes a considerable variety of aspects. At one time, it seems to consist of a number of undulated bars in close connexion,—a form which graduates into what is termed the mackerel-back sky; at another, it puts on the appearance of a sword-fish, and hovers over the summits of the cumulo-stratus, with which it seems at last to coalesce. The *cymoid* cirro-stratus, which consists of small rows of little detached clouds, waved in a funicular-like manner, is considered a certain precursor of stormy weather.

The cirro-cumulus, or sonder-cloud, is composed of a great number of distinct clouds of moderate size, having a roundish form. It is distinguished from the cirro-stratus, which in some respects it resembles, by the greater density and compactness of the orbicular masses of which it consists.

These distinctions of clouds, it is to be suspected, have more of the semblance than the reality of scientific arrangement; and, therefore, without dwelling longer on a branch of meteorology, which is scarcely recommended to our attention by the precision of its nomenclature, we shall proceed to examine the more important phenomena which are connected with the formation of rain. The circumstances upon which that formation depends have already been so fully explained under the articles HYGROMETRY, vol. XI. p. 597, METEOROLOGY, vol. XIV. p. 164, and PNEUMATICS, in this volume, p. 701, that it is altogether unnecessary to give any additional illustration of the theoretical principle laid down in these articles, farther than to remark, that the four causes of change of temperature in the atmospheric strata, to which we have ascribed the origin of clouds, may also be extended, to explain the cause of rain in every case of its occurrence.

The rainy season takes place within the tropical regions, when the causes which concur to produce an intermixture of the atmospherical strata operate with the fullest effect. In some tracts, indeed, within the tropics, it rains almost incessantly the whole year. Thus, in the immense forest of Guiana, the sun and the stars are seldom visible, and it often rains five or six months without the smallest interruption. Humboldt measured the rain which fell on the 1st of May in that humid region, and found that during the space of five hours it amounted to 21 lines in depth. The 3d of the same month he even collected 14 lines in three hours; and he assures us, that the observations were made not during a shower, but in an ordinary rain. *Pers. Nar.* v. 248.

Phenome-
na by which
it is pre-
ceded.
In general, however, the season of rains and storms within the tropics coincides with the period when the sun passes through the zenith of the place. At the time, on the north side of the equator, the regular north-east winds cease; dead calms succeed; and these are afterwards followed by strong gales from the south-east and south-west, accompanied by a cloudy atmosphere. During the continuance of the north-east winds in that hemisphere, the aerial currents are continually bringing vast masses of relatively dry air towards the tropics; the atmosphere over the equinoxial regions is thus kept in a state of humidity, such that the point of deposition is considerably below the mean temperature of the season; and the hot air of the torrid zone thus partially charged with moisture mounts aloft, and flows in opposite directions towards the two poles. While this state of things continues, the moisture, instead of being accumulated over the zones where it is evaporated, seems to be wafted towards the temperate regions of the earth, where the quantity of water that descends in the form of rain, probably exceeds that which is raised by evaporation. On the other hand, as the sun approaches the zenith of any particular parallel, the trade winds become less regular; the temperature increases; and all the causes which contribute to the humidity of the atmosphere act with the fullest vigour. The superincumbent columns of air are soon saturated with vapours, the production of which is accompanied with a great accumulation of electricity in the higher regions of the atmosphere. At length an intermixture of the strata begins to take place, produced chiefly, it would appear, by the electrical explosions; the precipitation of the condensed vapour commences, and proceeds, especially during the day, with scarcely any interruption. The rain now descends in vast sheets of water,—the rivers, raised above their ordinary level, can no longer be confined within their banks, and the supply they receive from the clouds exceeding the discharge by their channels, they spread far and wide over the adjacent fields, and exhibit, on every hand, a dreary expanse of muddy and discoloured waters. This state of things undergoes little alteration, until the sun returns to the signs of the other he-

misphere. At that period the aerial currents from the *homonymous* pole are renewed; and the air which flows from it, being very far from the point of saturation, the rains cease, and the sky resumes its former clearness and serenity. Humboldt's *Pers. Nar.* iv. 404. In India the most remarkable rainy season occurs at the time of the south-west monsoon. It extends from Africa to the Malay peninsula, and deluges all the intermediate countries, within certain lines of latitude, for four months in the year. "In the South of India," we are informed by Mr. Elphinstone, "the monsoon commences about the beginning of June, but it gets later as we advance towards the north. Its approach is announced by vast masses of clouds that rise from the Indian ocean, and advance towards the north-east, gathering and thickening as they approach the land. After some threatening days, the sky assumes a troubled appearance in the evening, and the monsoon, in general, sets in during the night. It is attended with such a thunderstorm as can scarcely be imagined by those who have only seen that phenomenon in a temperate climate. It generally begins with violent blasts of wind, which are succeeded by floods of rain. For some hours lightning is seen almost without intermission; sometimes it only illuminates the sky, and shows the clouds near this horizon; at others, it discovers the distant hills, and again leaves all in darkness, when, in an instant, it appears in vivid and successive flashes, and exhibits the nearest objects in all the brightness of day. During all this time the distant thunder never ceases to roll, and is only silenced by some nearer peal, which bursts upon the ear with such a sudden and tremendous crash as can scarcely fail to strike the most insensible heart with awe. At length the thunder ceases, and nothing is heard but the continued pouring of the rain, and the rushing of the rising streams. The next day presents a gloomy spectacle; the rain still descending in torrents, scarcely allows a view of the blackened fields; the rivers are swollen and discoloured, and sweep along with them the hedges, the huts, and the remains of the cultivation which was carried on during the dry season, in their beds.

"This lasts for some days, after which the sky clears, and discovers the face of nature changed as by enchantment. Before the storm the fields were parched up, and except in the beds of the rivers, scarce a blade of vegetation was to be seen; the clearness of the sky was not interrupted by a single cloud, but the atmosphere was loaded with dust, which was sufficient to render distant objects dim, as in a mist, and to make the sun appear dull and discoloured, till he attained a considerable elevation; a parching wind blew like a blast from a furnace, and heated wood, iron, and every other solid material, even in the shade; and immediately before the monsoon this wind had been succeeded by still more sultry calms. But when the first violence of the storm is over, the whole earth is covered with a sudden but luxuriant verdure; the rivers are full and tranquil; the air is pure and delicious; and the sky is varied and embellished with clouds. From this time the rain falls at intervals for about a month, when it comes on again with great violence, and in July the rains are at their height; during the third month they rather diminish, but are still heavy; and, in September, they gradually abate, and are often suspended till near the end of the month, when they depart amidst thunders and tempests as they come.

Diversities
in the state
of the pe-
riodical
rains in
India.

"Such," continues Mr. Elphinstone, "is the monsoon in the greater part of India. It is not, however, without some diversity, the principal feature of which is the delay in its commencement, and the diminution of

the quantity of rains as it recedes from the sea. In the countries which are the subject of the present inquiry, (Caubul,) the monsoon is felt with much less violence than in India, and is exhausted at no great distance from the sea, so that no trace of it can be perceived at Candahar. A remarkable exception, however, to the rule is to be observed on the north-east of Afghaunistan, which, although much farther from the sea than Candahar, is subject to the monsoon, and what is equally extraordinary, receives it from the east." To account for this anomaly, Mr. Elphinstone suggests the following considerations, which seem to afford a good explanation of it: "Most part of the tract in which the kingdom of Caubul lies, is to leeward of Africa and Arabia, and receives only the vapours of the narrow sea between its southern shores and the latter country, which are but of small extent, and are exhausted in the immediate neighbourhood of the coast. India, lying farther east, and beyond the shelter of Africa, the monsoon spreads over it without obstruction. It is naturally most severe near the sea, from which it draws its supplies, and is exhausted after it has passed over a great extent of land. For this reason the rains are more or less plentiful in each country, according to its distance from the sea, except in those near high mountains, which arrest the clouds, and procure a larger supply of rain for the neighbouring tracts, than would have fallen to their share, if the passage of the clouds had been unobstructed.

"The obstacle presented to the winds and clouds by the mountains has another effect of no small importance. The south-west monsoon blows over the ocean in its natural direction; and though it may experience some diversities after it reaches the land, its general course over India may still be said to be towards the north-east, till it is exhausted by the western and central parts of the peninsula. The provinces in the north-east receive the monsoon in a different manner: the wind which brings the rains to that part of the continent originally blows from the south-west over the bay of Bengal, till the mountains of Hemalleh, (Himalayah,) and those which join them from the south, stop its progress, and compel it to follow their course towards the north-west. The prevailing wind, therefore, in the region south-west of Hemalleh, is from the south-west, and it is from that quarter that our provinces in Bengal receive their rains. But when the wind has reached so far to the north-west as to meet with Hindoo Coosh, it is again opposed by that mountain, and turned off along its face towards the west, till it meets the projection of Hindoo Coosh and the range of Solimaum, which prevent its farther progress in that direction, or at least compel it to part with the clouds with which it was loaded. The effect of the mountains, in stopping the clouds borne by this wind, is different in different places. Near the sea, where the clouds are still in a deep mass, part is discharged on the hills and the country beneath them, and part passes up to the N.W.; but part makes its way over the first hills, and produces the rains in Thibet." Elphinstone's *Account of Caubul*, p.126.

Extent of
the effects
of the
monsoon,
in regard
to the pe-
riodical
rains.

The effects of the south-west monsoon, which begins to be perceived on the Malabar coast in May, are felt later in the Mysore territory. At Delhi, the rains make their appearance about the end of June, and the fall of water is considerably less than at Calcutta or Bombay. Their influence extends even to Nepaul; but in that country, though showers are experienced in May and June, the periodical rains are chiefly felt in July and August. In the north of the Punjaub, near the hills, more rain falls than at Delhi; but in the southward of that district, where a greater uniformity of surface prevails, the rains are more scanty. The regular monsoon, however, seems to extend itself as far west as the utmost boundary of the Mekraun; and though the rains by which it is generally accompanied in its progress are little felt over Lower Sinde, they are more plentiful in Upper Sinde and Domaun, where they are the principal rains of the year. Beyond a line drawn through the northern part of the table land of Kelaut, and the northern boundaries of Shoraubuk, of Pisheen, and of Zhobe, to the source of the Koorum, the effects of the monsoon have scarcely been traced; but on the eastern coast of Asia, it determines the rainy season as far to the northward as the Japan islands.

Winter rains in India.

In the northern parts of India, a second rain is experienced about the time of the winter solstice, which assumes the form of rain or snow according to the temperature of the place. This rain, which is partially felt in the low country, extends over all the countries west of the Indies as far as the Hellespont. A spring rain is also experienced over the same tract, during a period which extends in some places to a fortnight, and in others to a month. Both this and the winter rain are said to come from the west.

Rainy season within the temperate zones.

In the two temperate zones, the causes which give birth to the precipitation of moisture from the atmosphere are more influenced by local circumstances than within the tropical regions; but, in each of these artificial divisions of the globe, the principal rains occur nearly at the same time with the periodical rains in their respective hemispheres. The most copious rains in Europe, for example, take place in June, July, and August, and are uniformly heaviest in the vicinity of mountains. As the rains in equatorial America (where the general direction of the trade wind is not disturbed as in India by monsoons,) are first experienced on the eastern shores of the continent, and gradually extended to the table land of the interior, so in the temperate zones, where the prevailing current is westerly, the rains begin to windward, being first felt on the coasts of Portugal, France, and the British isles, and afterwards more sparingly in the countries to the eastward. The same remark may be applied to that part of the transatlantic continent which lies between the tropic of Cancer and the arctic circle. The Altaian chain in Europe, and the Rocky Mountains in America, both following nearly the direction of the meridian, seem to produce similar effects upon the hygrometric state of the atmosphere to the eastward of them; and after the views which we have already given of the manner in which moisture is separated from the air, as it is transported over elevated land, it will be easy to perceive the reason of its great dryness in both cases.

Quantity of rains in different parallels.

In the article HYGROMETRY, vol. IX. p. 597, we have given a table of the quantity of rain, which, agreeably to the theoretical principles there laid down, ought to fall in the different parallels of latitude. On account of the powerful effect of mountains in producing that intermixture of the atmospheric strata by which rain is chiefly occasioned, it cannot be supposed that the table alluded to is strictly applicable in all cases *. It will be found, however, to exhibit, with considerable accuracy, the mean results, when these are not affected by local and adventitious circumstances. Thus at Vera

Cruz, in latitude 19° 12′, the quantity of rain by theory should, according to the table, be 63.5 inches; now it appears by the accurate observations of M. de Costanzo, (Humboldt's *Pers. Nar.* v. 347.) that the actual quantity was 62⅕ inches. Again, at Charleston, in South Carolina, in latitude 32° 40′, the quantity of rain is, by a mean of fifteen years † 48 inches, (*Phil. Trans.* vol. xlviii.) and by the table 43¼. The quantity of rain observed to fall in Madeira, which lies under the same parallel, varied, by the observations of Dr. Heberden, from 22 to 49 inches. Lastly, to take an example in the higher latitudes of the temperate zones, the quantity of rain observed to fall at Perth, in lat. 56° 23′, was, by an average of six years, 21.5 inches, and, by the table referred to, it ought to be 21 inches. These coincidences are sufficiently exact to show, that the table indicates, with considerable accuracy, the mean quantity of rain corresponding to the different parallels of latitude; but the correctness of the principles from which it is deduced will be still better perceived, by comparing the mean quantity of rain which it gives for the whole globe with the mean quantity as determined by actual observation. Now, if the sum of the quantities in the table be divided by the number of parallels to which they refer, the mean result will be found 36.17 inches, which, according to the table, should be the mean annual quantity of rain for the globe. But the same quantity deduced by Cotte, as the mean of the observations for 147 places, is 34.7 inches; which differs from the above result only about 1-30th part of the whole quantity.

Mean quantity of rain over the globe in general.

It ought to be mentioned, however, that the quantity of rain which has been observed to fall in some particular places greatly exceeds the quantity given by the table as due to the latitude; thus, 105 inches of rain have been observed to fall during a year in the island of Grenada, and even 150 inches at Leogane, in the island of St. Domingo. (Malte-Brun, *Geog.* vol. i. p. 368.) At Bombay 110 inches were observed in the year 1790 to fall between the 15th of May and the 18th of October. But these results are uncommon, and must be ascribed either to peculiarity of situation or the concurrence of very remarkable circumstances.

Extraordinary quantity of rain at some places.

In some instances a very great quantity of rain has been observed to fall, during a short time, even at places where the annual quantity is inconsiderable. Thus 13 inches 2 lines have been observed to fall at Viviers in the space of eighteen hours—a quantity which exceeds in degree the tropical rains on the banks of the Oroonoko, where, Humboldt informs us, he observed 18 lines in three hours, and 48.2 lines in nine hours. (*Pers. Nar.* v. 347.) But even this quantity, great as it is, is surpassed by a rain at Montpellier, which produced an inch of water in an hour ‡. (*Journ. de Phys.* viii. 437. *Ibid.* ix. 391.) In India, the quantity of rain which descends in a short time perhaps exceeds any thing that we have stated; but as it has seldom been measured by a rain-gage, it can only be conjectured to be very great from the instantaneous effects which it produces upon small streams and rivulets. Mr. Elphinstone, in his account of the mission to Caubul, mentions a remarkable instance of the sudden swelling of a brook which is well calculated to illus-

Remarkable falls of rain within a limited time.

---

* How very much the quantity of rain, which falls at a place, may be modified by local circumstances, we learn by a striking fact mentioned by Humboldt. "The port of Cumana is only seven nautical leagues from Cumanacoa. It scarcely ever rains at the first of these places, while in the second there are seven months of wintry (rainy) weather." *Pers. Nar.* iii. p. 54.

† By taking a mean of the rainiest year, in which the quantity of rain was 65.962 inches, and of the driest, in which it was only 36.006 inches, Dr. Young (*Nat. Phil.* ii. 477.) has stated the annual quantity of rain at Charleston to be 50.9 inches.

‡ On the 7th of October, 1823, a rain, which continued at Perth for fifteen hours, yielded 2.1 inches, which, though greatly less than the quantity mentioned in the text, has seldom been surpassed in this country, at that season of the year. In Silliman's *Journal*, vol. iv. p. 375, it is affirmed that twelve feet seven inches of water fell at the Isle of Cayenne, from the 1st to the 24th of Feb.

Physical Geography.

trate this. It occurred in his journey between the Indus and Hydaspes, and is described in the following terms: " On one occasion, the rear guard, with some gentlemen of the mission, were cut off from the rest by the swelling of a brook, which had been a foot deep when they began to cross. It came down with surprising violence, carrying away some loaded camels that were crossing at the time, and rising about ten feet within a minute. Such was its force, that it ran in waves like the sea, and rose against the bank in a ridge like the surf on the coast of Coromandel."—Elphinstone's *Caubul*, p. 78.

The annual quantity of rain varies in different seasons.

The annual quantity of rain which falls at the same place, in different seasons, is subject to some irregula-

Lunar periods of nineteen years.

rity. Toaldo, indeed, has endeavoured to show, from a great number of observations, that the very rainy seasons return after an interval of nineteen years, according to the terms of the cycle of Saros; but this opinion, though countenanced by some striking resemblances between the seasons quoted in support of it, is far from being established by a sufficiently extensive induction of facts, to render it more than a plausible hypothesis. At the same time, as the subject is not destitute of interest, and merits the attention of other observers, we shall subjoin a table from the meteorological works of Cotte, in which the characteristic seasons are distributed, according to the cycles referred to, in periods of nineteen years.

Physical Geography.

First Period.	Second Period.	Third Period.	Fourth Period.	Fifth Period.	Sixth Period.	Seventh Period.	Eighth Period.	Ninth Period.	Tenth Period.	Eleventh Period.	Twefth Period.	Character of the Seasons.
1681	1700	1719	1738	1757	1776	1795	1814	1833	1852	1871	1890	Warm and dry.
1682	1701	1720	1739	1758	1777	1796	1815	1834	1853	1872	1891	Variable, moist.
1683	1702	1721	1740	1759	1778	1797	1816	1835	1854	1873	1092	Variable.
1684	1703	1722	1741	1760	1779	1798	1817	1836	1855	1874	1893	Warm and dry.
1685	1704	1723	1742	1761	1780	1799	1818	1837	1856	1875	1894	Do.
1686	1705	1724	1743	1762	1781	1800	1819	1838	1857	1876	1895	Do.
1687	1706	1725	1744	1763	1782	1801	1820	1839	1858	1877	1896	Cold and moist.
1688	1707	1726	1745	1764	1783	1802	1821	1840	1859	1878	1897	Mild and dry.
1689	1708	1727	1746	1765	1784	1803	1822	1841	1860	1879	1898	Ordinary.
1690	1709	1728	1747	1766	1785	1804	1823	1842	1861	1880	1899	Cold and moist.
1691	1710	1729	1748	1767	1786	1805	1824	1843	1862	1881	1900	Cold, tolerably dry.
1692	1711	1730	1749	1768	1787	1806	1825	1844	1863	1882	1901	Ordinary cold and moist.
1693	1712	1731	1750	1769	1788	1807	1826	1845	1864	1883	1902	Cold and moist.
1694	1713	1732	1751	1770	1789	1808	1827	1846	1865	1884	1903	Rather cold and moist.
1695	1714	1733	1752	1771	1790	1809	1828	1847	1866	1885	1904	Ordinary.
1696	1715	1734	1753	1772	1791	1810	1829	1848	1867	1886	1905	Do.
1697	1716	1735	1754	1773	1792	1811	1830	1749	1868	1887	1906	Cold and dry.
1698	1717	1736	1755	1774	1793	1812	1831	1850	1869	1888	1907	Variable, moist.
1699	1718	1737	1756	1775	1794	1813	1832	1851	1870	1889	1908	Warm and dry.

How far the recurrence of certain rainy years is determined by the influence of the moon.

The similarity which is supposed to exist between the seasons, of years returning after an interval of nineteen years, is principally ascribed to the influence which the moon exerts upon the atmosphere of the earth, it being well known to astronomers that the moon's nodes make almost exactly nineteen complete revolutions in 223 lunations; so that, after a lapse of a little more than eighteen years, the sun, the moon, and the node are again nearly in the same position. To this period Toaldo has added another, depending upon the angular position of the axis of the lunar orbit. This line has a progressive motion, like that of the earth's orbit, and makes an entire revolution, relatively to the fixed stars, in a little more than nine years. Toaldo was led to infer some connexion between this period, and the recurrence of similar seasons, by finding from observations, during a considerable length of time, that the amounts of the quantities of rain for nine successive years were always equal, or nearly so, both at Padua and Paris. It remains, however, to be determined, to what extent these conclusions, admitting them to be well founded with regard to these places, can be applied to other parts of the globe whose geographical situation is different. If we compare the years in which, according to Humboldt, the greatest quantity of rain fell at Mexico, viz. the years 1553, 1580, 1604, 1607, 1629, 1648, 1675, 1707, 1732, 1748, 1772, and 1795, we neither discover a coincidence of seasons between these years and the corresponding years of the cycle, nor, unless in one instance, any thing like an approach to a period, either of nine or nineteen years. For an excellent dissertation on the influence of the moon upon the weather, see a paper of Dr. Horsley, in the 65th volume of the *Phil. Trans.*

But whatever foundation there may be for the opinion,

of rainy seasons occurring at regular periods, it is certain, that the quantity of water which descends from the sky varies greatly in different seasons at the same place. Thus, the quantity of rain observed at Lyndon, in Rutlandshire, for 1740, 1741, 1742, and 1743, was 66.361 inches, whereas, that observed at the same place in 1772, 1773, 1774, and 1775, was nearly double, being 124.957 inches. (*Phil. Trans.* for these years.) The quantity of rain which is experienced in the Karroo, or Caffrarian desert, is affirmed to be much less now than in former years; and a change of the same kind is affirmed to have taken place in the Steppes of central Asia, and even in the humid regions of Guiana. In the arid plains of the great desert of Africa these vicissitudes are unknown, because, in that barren waste, it is rare that rain ever falls at all. " When I was at Tozer," says Dr. Shaw, " we had a small drizzling shower that continued for the space of two hours; and so little provision was made against accidents of the kind, that several of the houses (built only with palm branches and tiles baked in the sun) fell down by imbibing the moisture." *Shaw's Travels*, p. 219. The desert of Muerto in New Spain, a plain 30 leagues in extent, appears to be nearly as destitute of water as the Sahara of Africa. The whole of this country, is, in general, in a frightful state of aridity; for the mountains de Los Marsos, situate to the east of the road from Durango to Santa Fé, do not give rise to a single brook. Humb. *New Spain*, ii. 310. Along the coast of Peru rain is so rare a phenomenon, that its appearance in any particular season is noticed as a remarkable event; but an ample supply of moisture is afforded by the *garuas*, or dense fogs, which prevail during the greater part of the year in that extraordinary region. Ulloa has attempted to explain the reason of this singular state of the atmosphere over that

Remarkable changes in the humidity of particular places.

Regions of great dryness.

Reason why it does not rain at Peru.

Physical
Geography.

part of Peru, by assuming, that at a certain height above the surface of the earth, the winds blow with more violence than either above or below it; that rain is formed a little above the lower limits of this ventose region; but that the vesicular vapour which either remains below, or mounts above it, cannot be reduced to a state to produce rain. By a gratuitous accommodation of facts to this hypothesis, he afterwards endeavours to explain why the vapour is kept at one season of the year below the region where rain is formed; and why at another it is wafted above it, without being in either case followed by that copious precipitation of condensed vapour which constitutes rain. (*Ulloa,* ii. 67.) The true cause, however, of the want of rain in this part of Peru, is to be sought for in the general fact, which we have already stated and illustrated; namely, that the leeward sides of extensive tracts of land, must always be less subject to rain than the parts to windward. The coast of Peru receives the air which has been transported by the trade winds over the summits of the Andes, and consequently after it has been deprived of almost the whole of its moisture. Hence though the absolute quantity of vapour, which the air holds in admixture with it, is by this means greatly diminished, the relative humidity must be maintained all the time that the air is ascending the Cordilleras in a maximum state; so that the air, when it reaches the tops of these mountains, though it may no longer contain a sufficient quantity of moisture to produce rain, is still sufficiently humid to occasion perpetual fogs and mists, at the reduced temperature to which it is brought in those elevated regions.

Hail and snow.

Having described, under METEOROLOGY, vol. XIV. p. 167, the manner in which hail and snow are supposed to be formed, it is only necessary at present to advert briefly to some circumstances connected with these modes of the condensation of atmospheric vapour in different zones. In the case of hail there are some difficulties to be solved, to which an explanation of the origin of snow does not seem to be liable. If the air contain the requisite quantity of humidity, snow is generally observed to fall when the mean temperature of the place descends below the freezing point; whereas hail is most frequently experienced at seasons, when the temperature of the lower regions of the air is farthest removed from that point. Nor is this the only difficulty connected with the history of hail: it is a well-established fact, that hail seldom or never falls within the tropical regions or plains, whose height above the level of the sea is less than 1500 or 2000 feet. The only supposition we can make to reconcile this fact with our knowledge of the constitution of the atmosphere is, that the hail, after being formed at the same height above plains and elevated table lands, is again melted in passing through the lower strata of the air, the mean temperature of which in these regions is from 75° to 80°. This explanation, however, is far from being completely satisfactory. In many parts of the temperate zone, the heat of the plains is little inferior to that which is experienced within the tropics; and during the heat of summer, the decrement of heat follows, in both cases, nearly the same law. If then the absence of hail within the torrid zone, at the level of the sea, be produced by the melting of the hailstones in crossing the lower strata of the air, we must assume with Humboldt (*Pers. Nar.* iv. 537.) that these hailstones, at the moment of their formation, are larger in the temperate than the torrid zone. How far we are entitled to assume this supposition, must be determined by future observation. It is certain, that in some cases at least the magnitude of the hailstones, which have been seen

Hail never observed to fall on the equatorial plains, near the level of the sea.

to fall in various parts of Europe, has been such, as to render it impossible for complete liquefaction to take place during their fall through 2000 feet, even though the temperature of the lower strata of the atmosphere at the time had greatly exceeded that of the tropical regions. In the Transactions of the Royal Society of Edinburgh, we find an interesting account, by Mr. Neill, of a hail shower which fell in Orkney, on the 24th of June, 1818, from which we learn, that some of the masses of ice were nearly half a pound in weight, and that though the weather was warm, many of these remained undissolved on the ground for more than an hour. (*Trans. Roy. Soc. Edin.* ix. 187.) Dr. Halley gives a description of a similar storm which took place in Wales, on the 29th of April, 1697, in which he states that some of the hail stones weighed five ounces, and produced much damage over a tract of country nearly sixty miles in extent. (*Phil. Trans.* Lowthorpe's *Abridg.* ii. 145.

Physical Geography.

But if we are unable to give a satisfactory account of the formation of hail, it is no less difficult to explain the origin of showers of various kinds of organized matter, which have been affirmed to descend from the upper regions of the atmosphere. The only plausible hypothesis that can be offered to account for phenomena so extraordinary, as showers of vegetable productions, reptiles, fishes, &c. (*Phil. Trans.* No. 21, p. 377. No. 188, p. 281. No. 243, p. 289. Sigaud Lafond, *Dict. de Merv. de la Nature*, iii. p. 196.) is, that the substances observed to fall had been previously caught by a whirlwind, and borne aloft in the air, from which they had afterwards descended in the form of showers.

Showers of organized matter.

We shall conclude the account of the atmosphere with a few observations upon its relations to light. In every region of the earth, the face of the sky presents an aspect which is in some measure peculiar to its geographical situation. The imaginary vault to whose concave surface we refer the position of the heavenly bodies, seems to be most elevated in the equatorial regions, and diminishes in apparent altitude as we advance towards the poles. This is evidently owing to the decrement of heat in the atmospheric columns being more rapid as we recede from the equator, and the vapour they contain being less perfectly dissolved. The region of clouds becomes depressed in a corresponding degree, especially in situations where the inequalities of the earth's surface contribute to intermix the different strata of the air. Travellers who have visited the various regions of the globe, agree in representing the sky which prevails over the scattered isles of the Pacific ocean, as possessing a serenity and a purity which is altogether unknown in less genial climes. This remarkable purity of the atmosphere is even to be found, in particular situations, at a considerable distance from the equator. Thus the sky of California, where the soil is, in the highest degree, sandy and arid, is constantly serene, and of a deep blue; and should any clouds appear for a moment, at the setting of the sun they display the most beautiful shades of violet, purple, and green. "All who have been in this country," says Humboldt, "preserve the recollection of the extraordinary beauty of this phenomenon, which depends on a particular state of the vesicular vapour, and the purity of the air in these climates." (*New Spain,* ii. 326.) In like manner, the dryness of the columns of air, which incessantly rise over the great desert of Africa, and which are wafted by the east wind across the Atlantic ocean, gives to the atmosphere of the Canary islands a transparency which surpasses that of the boasted sky of Italy and Naples, and even rivals in beauty the serene and cloudless air which is experienced in most of the Pacific isles. It is this

Appearance of the sky in different regions of the earth.

Remarkable purity of the atmosphere within the tropics, over the Pacific Ocean.

Over the Canary islands.

1

Physical Geography. purity of the atmosphere which heightens the brightness of the vegetable colouring within the tropical zones, and imparts to the face of nature that indescribable softness of outline, that richness of hues, and that harmonious contrast of light and shade, which so rarely charm the eye of the painter in our variable climate. Its influence over the moral qualities of our species, though greatly over-rated by some writers of reputation, is far from being inconsiderable; for it cannot be denied, that a serenity of the sky is calculated to inspire a corresponding frame of mind, while a dark and lowering atmosphere is no less fitted to fill the soul with gloomy and melancholy ideas.

The greatest transparency of the sky not observed at the tops of mountains. The greatest transparency of the sky is not to be found, even within the tropics, at the summit of mountains. With the exception of a few barren plains in Mexico and Peru, the very elevated table lands which crown the tops of the Cordilleras, possess a cloudy and variable climate. An extreme purity of the atmosphere, such as prevails in the low regions during the dry season, compensates for the greater tenuity of the air, produced by elevation, while the higher strata of the atmosphere, when they envelop the summit of lofty mountains, are always liable to suffer sudden changes in their transparency, which more than counteract the advantages derived from the more partial extinction of light.

Over the ocean the sky exhibits a paler blue than over the land. When, from the summit of the Andes, the eye is directed toward the Great South Sea, a haziness, uniformly spread to about 10,000 feet in height, is observed to cover, as with a thin veil, the surface of the ocean. This appearance takes place in a season when the atmosphere, viewed from the coast or at sea, appears pure and transparent, and the existence of the opaque vapour is announced to navigators only by the little intensity of the azure colour of the sky. (Humboldt's *Pers. Nar.* ii. 99.) For the cause of the blue colour of the sky we refer to CYANOMETER; and for other optical appearances exhibited by the atmosphere to FATA MORGANA, and MIRAGE, under the article OPTICS, Vol. XV. p. 617. See also ATMOSPHERE, HALO, &c.

For the mechanical properties of the atmosphere we refer to PNEUMATICS; and for its chemical constitution, to CHEMISTRY.

SECT. III.—*Of the Aqueous Parts of the Globe.*

Ocean. The great reservoir of water from which that fluid is distributed over the surface of the globe, under the form of atmospheric vapour, and through all the modifications of its existence, till it is again reduced to the liquid state, and rolled back in rivers to its original source, is the ocean. As almost all rivers discharge themselves into the sea, so it is chiefly from that immense volume of water that they incessantly receive their supplies. The vapour, which is slowly but continually raised by evaporation from the surface of the ocean, is afterwards wafted by the aerial currents we have already described, and diffused over the face of the land. The change of temperature to which it is thus exposed, during its progress from the warmer to the colder regions, partly by the current of air, which always flows in the higher regions of the atmosphere from the equator towards each pole, and partly by the variable winds which transport it over mountainous tracts of the earth's surface, causes a portion of the vapour to return to the liquid condition, and resume the form of water. The precipitated vapour, in whatever state it descends, is gradually united after it reaches the ground into numberless rills, which, by their junction, give birth to rivulets, and these, in their turn, to larger collections of water. In this manner rivers

Rivers, how connected with the ocean.

are formed, some of which, after receiving from a great extent of country an innumerable multitude of tributary streams, roll on towards the ocean with a volume of water that excites the utmost astonishment when we contrast it with the little murmuring streamlets from which it is derived.

Extent of the ocean. The ocean occupies by far the most considerable portion of the surface of the globe. This immense collection of fluid matter seems entirely to surround the solid parts of the earth, encircling the eastern and the western continents, and reducing them to the condition of two extensive islands. But though it forms only one united body of water, and stretches from pole to pole, it has been divided by geographers into a certain number of subordinate oceans, which are conceived to be separated from one another, rather by artificial lines than by natural boundaries. The most extensive of these is the Great South Sea or Pacific Ocean, which comprizes more than a hemisphere of water, and is subdivided into, 1. The Southern Pacific Ocean; 2. The Northern Pacific Ocean; and, 3. The Equatorial Pacific Ocean, to which the designation of Pacific Ocean should perhaps be exclusively applied. The other principal division of water constitutes the Atlantic Ocean, which is subdivided into the Northern and Southern Atlantic. To these we may add the Indian Ocean, regarded by some geographers as a portion of the Pacific, and the Arctic and Antarctic Oceans, the former of which is sometimes denominated the Northern Polar Basin.

Pacific Ocean. Of the extent of the Pacific Ocean we may form some idea from the fact, that if we fix upon the Society Islands, as a central point in this vast collection of water, there is scarcely any direction in which a ship might not sail five or six thousand miles, without experiencing any interruption of her course by opposing barriers of land. This great expanse of water, however, merits the epithet of Pacific only between the parallels of 30° south and 10° north. Within the zone, bounded by these parallels, an undisturbed serenity prevails. Gentle winds, generally from the south-west, blow in this peaceful tract during the whole year, and such is their regularity that they are scarcely ever affected by the change of the seasons. The Atlantic Ocean has a more definite outline than the Pacific; and it is also more limited in its extent. Separating the two great continents, which compose nearly the whole of the solid parts of the globe, it forms a vast basin between them, towards which they both seem to decline; the one towards the west, and the other towards the east. The Pacific and Atlantic Oceans are disjoined by a narrow isthmus in equatorial America, the breadth of which is so inconsiderable that the proposal of establishing an artificial communication between the two seas is by no means a visionary project. The accomplishment of an object, so interesting to the civilized world, will, it may be hoped, speedily engage the attention of the American republics, which have lately secured their independence. For a view of the various lines of communication, we refer to Humboldt's *Account of New Spain,* i. 16.

Atlantic Ocean.

Relative quantity of water in the two hemispheres. The quantity of water in the northern and southern hemispheres is exceedingly different, and gives to each of these portions of the globe a peculiarity of physical character. In the former, the proportion of land and water is nearly as 72 to 100; whereas, in the latter, it is only as fifteen to the same number. This unequal distribution of land and water, in the two hemispheres, led the geographers and naturalists of the last century to conclude, that a great continent existed near the south pole, to counterbalance the mass of land in the

Physical
Geography.

opposite regions of the globe. By the voyages of Cook and other navigators, these conjectures have been proved to be unfounded; and, indeed, according to the more rational view which is now taken of the subject, the general equilibrium of the globe can be but little affected by the slight inequalities which are observed at its surface. The ocean may be less deep in the southern than in the northern hemisphere, while the solid strata upon which it reposes may possess an unusual degree of density sufficient to compensate for any defect in their quantity. This hypothesis is strengthened by the result of the measurements of La Caille, near the Cape of Good Hope, which assign a different convexity to the meridians in the southern, from that obtained for the northern hemisphere. *Geographie Phys. par* Malte-Brun, i. 167.

Connexion between the form of the coast and the bottom of the ocean.

In a preceding part of this article we gave a general description of the boundary which separates the land from the water, denominated the *coast*. This common limit varies greatly in appearance, being at one place low and shelving; and, at another, bold and precipitous. For the most part, when the coast is abrupt, the bottom of the ocean possesses a similar character; and, on the other hand, a flat shore is generally regarded by navigators as an indication of a shallow and dangerous sea. Thus, the German Ocean, opposite to the low lying shores of Holland, has rarely a greater depth than twenty fathoms; whereas, on the broken and abrupt coast of Norway, the depth is increased to 140 fathoms. *Edin. Phil. Journ.* vol. iii. 42.

Depth of the ocean.

The knowledge we have obtained respecting the depth of the ocean in various places, though sufficient for the purposes of navigation, is too limited to satisfy the inquiries of the physiologist. The greatest depth that has been reached by actual sounding has seldom exceeded a mile; an immense depth, indeed, when we consider the means that must be employed for the purpose, but greatly inferior to the heights above the level of the ocean, which have been attained by ascending with the balloon, in a fluid more inaccessible to man. In latitude 57° 4′ north, longitude 24° 34′ west, about 100 leagues from the nearest land, Captain Parry found no bottom with the deep sea clamms, and a line of 1020 fathoms*, being the greatest depth of soundings ever attempted, and more than a quarter of a mile deeper than was reached by Lord Mulgrave. On another occasion, the same intrepid navigator, found no soundings with a line of 890 fathoms, at a place in Davis' Straits, in lat. 68° 24′ north, longitude 63° 8′ west. Along the eastern coast of America, the average depth of the ocean, at the distance of 100 leagues from the land, appears to be about 50 or 60 fathoms; but the theory of the tides seems to require that the mean depth of the Atlantic should be about 3 miles. In no instance have we reason to conclude that the greatest depth of the ocean exceeds 4 miles. Young's *Nat. Phil.* i. 581.

Nature of the bed of the ocean.

Of the nature of the bed of the ocean we know still less than of its depth below the surface. Like the dry land, it appears to present the utmost variety of outline, sometimes stretching for a great extent, nearly parallel to the surface of the ocean, and at other times rising suddenly into perpendicular rocks. The portions of it which have been explored by sounding, are found, in one place, to contain immense collections of the wrecks of testaceous animals intermixed with sand and gravel, and in another to consist of soft alluvial mud, several feet in depth. Donati found the bottom

Physical Geography.

of the Adriatic to be composed of a compact bed of shells, not less than a hundred feet in thickness; and it is well known, that a great part of the bottom of the South Sea is covered with coral rocks, which, though the production of small insects, frequently rise like stupendous walls to the surface, and constitute extensive islands. The eastern coast of New Holland is almost wholly girt with reefs and islands of coral rock, rising in some instances a thousand feet perpendicularly from the bottom of the abyss. Barrow's *Voyage*, p. 165.; Flinders' *Voyage to Terra Australis*, vol. ii. pp. 88—115. Nicholson's *Jour.* vol. xxxiii. p. 136.

Coral rocks.

In Cook's *Voyage to the Pacific*, we find the following interesting account of the appearance of one of these submarine formations: "At one part of the reef, which bounds the lake within, almost even with the surface, there was a large bed of coral, which afforded a most enchanting prospect. Its base, which was fixed to the shore, extended so far that it could not be seen, so that it appeared to be suspended on the water. The sea was then unruffled, and the refulgence of the sun exposed the various sorts of coral, in the most beautiful order; some parts luxuriantly branching into the water; others appearing in vast variety of figures; and the whole greatly heightened by spangles of the richest colours, glowing from a number of large clams, interspersed in every part. Even this delightful scene was greatly improved by the multitude of fishes, that gently glided along, seemingly with the most perfect security. Their colours were the most beautiful that can be imagined; blue, yellow, black, red, &c. far excelling any thing that can be produced by art. The richness of this submarine grotto was greatly increased by their various forms; and the whole could not possibly be surveyed without a pleasing transport, accompanied, at the same time, with regret, that a work so astonishingly elegant should be concealed in a place so little explored by the human eye." Cook's *Voyages*, vol. i. book ii.

Coral rocks not found in the Caribbean Sea.

It is sufficiently remarkable, as Barrow observes, that although different kinds of what are called corals, or corallines, are found on the shores of the West India Islands, no extensive masses of rock, nor reefs, nor islands wholly composed of this material, have been discovered. We might suppose that an undisturbed tranquillity, like that which prevails in the part of the Pacific Ocean where these formations are most numerous, was necessary for the unremitting operations of the minute insects, by which large and continuous masses of coral rocks are brought into existence, did we not know that creations of the same kind occur in the Chinese Seas, a portion of the ocean which is no less exposed to storms and tempests than the Caribbean Sea. From their situation with respect to each other, their union in particular places in large groups, and their total absence in other parts of the same seas, Dr.

General level of the ocean.

Chamisso is disposed to think, that the corals have founded their buildings on shoals of the sea; or, to speak more correctly, on the tops of mountains lying under water. *Edin. Phil. Journ.* vol. iv. 38.

The level of the ocean, from its constant agitation, can seldom be exactly the same, even at places not very distant. In gulfs and inland seas especially, where the deviation from the state that ought to result from the equilibrium of pressure is increased by local peculiarities, differences of level may be supposed to exist to a very sensible extent. Accordingly it is affirmed, that the Gulf of the Zuyderzee is considerably more elevated

---

* In latitude 74° 30′ north, and longitude 78° 1′ west, Captain Parry sounded with the deep-sea clamms, and found 1050 fathoms by the line, on a bottom of mud and small stones, but the ship's drift at the time being considerable, the real depth was not supposed to exceed 800 or 900 fathoms. Parry's *Voyages*, p. 30.

Physical Geography.

than the waters of the German Ocean, (Malte-Brun, *Geog.* i. 526.) and that the Red Sea, in like manner, has a higher level than the Mediterranean. (Rennel, *Geog. of Herodotus,* p. 476.) The barometrical observations of Humboldt, at the mouth of the *Rio Sinu,* on the Atlantic, and on the coast of the South Sea, in Peru, prove, that the difference of level between the two seas, cannot exceed 40 feet.— *New Spain,* i. 32.

Specific gravity of the waters of the ocean.

The specific gravity of the waters of the ocean, when examined at a sufficient distance from the coast, appears to be nearly the same in every latitude. The best observations, however, seem to give an increase of density from the polar seas to the equator, though the discrepancies are, in some cases, greater than can be ascribed to inaccuracies in the mode of experimenting. Dr. Marcet, has given the following results of his examination of seventy different kinds of sea water.

Conclusions drawn by Dr. Marcet.

1. That the Southern ocean contains more salt than the Northern, in the ratio of 1.02919 to 1.02757.

2. That the mean specific gravity of the waters of the equatorial zone is intermediate between that of the northern and southern hemispheres.

3. That there is no notable difference of sea water under different meridians.

4. That there is no satisfactory evidence that the sea at great depths contains more salt than at the surface.

5. That the sea, in general, contains more salt where it is deepest, and most remote from land ; and that its saltness is always diminished in the vicinity of large masses of ice.

6. That small inland seas, though communicating with the ocean, are much less salt than the open sea.

7. That the Mediterranean contains rather larger proportions of salt than the ocean. (*Phil. Trans.* 1807, ii. 296, and 1819, ii. 161.)

Not confirmed by other observers.

The first of these conclusions is directly at variance with the experiments of Dr. Davy, (*Phil. Trans.* 1817, ii. 275.) who has given the result of an almost daily examination of the waters of the ocean, during a voyage from England to Ceylon. From 49° of N. lat. to 40° W. the specific gravity increased from 1.0251 to 1.0277 ; and from 35° of E. lat. to the equator, it increased from 1.0253 to 1.0264.

Humboldt concludes, from a few accurate observations on the waters of the Atlantic, that their specific gravity augments regularly from the coast of Portugal to Teneriffe, that is, from the parallel of 43° to that of 28° ; but that it diminishes again from 22° 52', to 18° 45'. " It seemed to me," he remarks, " that in the part of the Atlantic, comprised between the coast of Portugal and Cumana, the water is a little salter * to the south of the tropic of Cancer, than under the temperate zone ; and I should be induced to generalize the fact, he adds, if the experiments made during Cook's last voyage, did not peremptorily prove that this difference does not exist in every meridian." *Pers. Narr.* vol. ii. p. 130.

The density of the water of the ocean less near the equator than near the tropics.

All the observations we have quoted, give a slight increase † of density from the Arctic regions to the tropic of Cancer ; but it is a singular enough circumstance, that the specific gravity of the ocean, in the vicinity of the equator, seems to be less, by the experiments of Marcet and Davy, than near the tropics. The former of these results may easily be explained, by ascribing it to the greater evaporation which takes

place from the surface of the ocean, in the warmer zones, in consequence of which the remaining portion of the water is increased in density ; but it is not so easy to perceive why the same cause should not operate with still greater efficacy, in situations where the temperature may be presumed to be higher, and thus render the specific gravity of the equatorial waters the greatest of all. Perhaps this anomaly, however, may be, in some measure, accounted for, by referring it, partly to the immense quantity of water which is discharged into the Atlantic, by the Congo, and the other rivers of Africa, within the tropics, and, partly, to the more copious rains, which fall near the equator. " Once," says Dr. Davy, " the specific gravity of the water seemed diminished by a heavy fall of rain, viz. in lat. 4° N. and in long. 18° 13' W. where we experienced a quick succession of tropical squalls."—*Phil. Trans.* 1817, Part ii. p. 280.

The specific gravity of the water of the ocean at different depths.

The specific gravity of the water of the ocean, when brought up from various depths, appears, by the experiments of Dr. Marcet, to be nearly the same as at the surface. This conclusion was also deduced by Captain Scoresby, from his examination of the waters of the Arctic seas, brought up from different depths, as far as 660 feet below the surface. The contrary, however, is affirmed by Dr. Traill (*Edin. Phil. Journ.* vol. iv. p. 186.) who maintains, as the result of his experiments, that the specific gravity of sea-water increases with the depth from which it is drawn.

The same opinion is given by Bergman, who states in support of it, that the water of the Euxine contains less salt at the surface than at the bottom, in the ratio of 72 to 62 ; and that the water of the Mediterranean, examined in similar circumstances, affords saline matter, in the proportion of 32 to 29. (*Geog. Phys.* I. p. 431.) Watson's *Chem. Essays,* vol. ii. essay ii.

Salts held in solution by the water of the ocean.

The quantity of foreign ingredients contained in the water of the ocean varies with its specific gravity. The substance which it holds in solution in greatest abundance is the muriate of soda. Besides this salt, chemists have detected in it the sulphates of lime and magnesia ; and lately Dr. Wollaston has discovered in it a small portion of potash, existing, as he supposes, also in the state of a sulphate. It appears by the researches of Dr. Marcet, that sea-water contains the same ingredients over all the world, and that the saline matters which it holds in solution, differ more in quantity than in the relative proportion which they bear to one another. The following results exhibit the quantity of saline matter which he obtained by evaporation, from the waters of different seas, the quantity operated upon being, in each case, 500 grains.

Places from which the Water was procured.	Residuum after Evaporation.	Relative Situation.
Arctic Sea .	14.15 Grains.	From surface.
	19.3	From a depth.
	1.75	Sea-ice water.
North Atlantic .	21.3	
Equator .	19.6	
South Atlantic .	20.6	
Mediterranean .	19.7	
Sea of Marmora .	14.11	From surface.
Do. . .	21.	From bottom.
Black Sea .	10.8	
Baltic . .	3 3	
‡ Dead Sea .	192.5	

* This opinion is far from being countenanced by facts quoted by Humboldt himself. See *Pers. Narr.* vol. i. p. 65.

† This fact is still further corroborated by the late experiments of Dr. Traill.—*Edin. Phil. Journ.* vol. iv. p. 187.

‡ By the analysis of Gay Lussac, (*Edin. Phil. Journ.* vol. i. p. 417.) the waters of the Dead Sea hold in solution the following salts: Muriate of soda 6.95, Muriate of lime 3.98, Muriate of magnesia 15.31, Total 26.24.

Cause of
the salt-
ness of the
water of
the ocean.

There is perhaps no subject connected with the physiology of the globe, that has excited more attention
than the origin of the saltness of the ocean. But though
in every age it has engaged the speculative inquiries
of learned men, the opinions entertained concerning it
are still as unsatisfactory as when the question was first
agitated. We are even ignorant whether the saline
substances, which the waters of the ocean hold in solution, exist in it now in the same proportion as formerly,
or in greater or less abundance.

Halley's
hypothesis.

Dr. Halley having observed that river water, in its
greatest purity, is always impregnated with a minute
portion of saline matter, has endeavoured to account
for the saltness of the ocean, by ascribing it entirely to
the soluble substances which are incessantly washed
into it by the rivers. The water, after reaching the
ocean with a certain quantity of salt, is again evaporated, and being dispersed over the atmosphere by
aerial currents, it afterwards descends in rain or vapour upon the surface of the earth, from whence it
hastens to pour into the bosom of the ocean the fresh
tribute of salt which it has collected in the course of its
progress through the soil. Thus, according to the opinion of Dr. Halley, the salt conveyed into the sea, not
being a volatile substance like the fluid by which it is
dissolved, must perpetually increase in the great storehouse of waters, and render the ocean more and more
salt. That eminent mathematician, with little of the
caution of genuine philosophy, has even carried his speculations so far on this subject, as to pretend that the
rate of increase of the saltness of the ocean afforded
sufficient data for determining the age of the world.
Phil. Trans. No. 344, p. 296. The absurdity of this
opinion has been well exposed by Dr. Watson, *Chemical
Essays*, vol. ii. essay iv.

Other opi-
nions re-
specting
the saltness
of the
ocean.

Other naturalists (Boyle, vol. iii. p. 221.) observing
that extensive beds of sea-salt occur in almost every
quarter of the globe, and concluding from analogy that
the bottom of the ocean must be similar in its formation to the surface of the land, have concluded that the
saltness of the sea is derived from the continual solution of beds of the muriate of soda,—a hypothesis
which, like that of Dr. Halley, necessarily implies a
progressive saltness of the ocean. On the other hand,
many modern geologists consider the waters of the sea,
in their present state, as the remains of a primitive cha-
otic fluid, which at one period held in solution the various materials of which the globe is composed; and
that this fluid having deposited all the earthy and metallic substances with which it was originally charged,
now retains in a state no longer susceptible of crystallization, the few saline ingredients which are found to
exist in combination with it, constituting the ocean,
such as we find it, under every clime.

Several branches, or portions of the great ocean, denominated seas, have been distinguished from each
other by epithets which have a reference to the peculiar
colour they commonly possess; such as the Red Sea,
the Yellow Sea, the White Sea, the Black Sea, &c.
The differences of colour of the waters of these seas, are
owing, it is believed, to accidental circumstances; as the
nature of the bottom, the earthy substances they hold
in solution, &c. In some instances the colour is permanent, and must therefore depend upon causes of a similar description; while in others it is superficial and
transitory, and is derived from the reflection of the fugitive tints of the sky.

Colour of
the waters
of the
ocean.

It is affirmed, that the upper part of the Mediterranean sometimes assumes a purple tinge; and the vermillion sea near California, has received its name from
the beautiful red colour which it occasionally exhibits.

In the Gulf of Guinea the Atlantic is of a whitish appearance; and in the Indian Ocean, around the Mal-
dives, the sea is black. The prevailing colour of the
ocean, however, is a deep green, inclining to blue.
Humboldt attempted to apply the cyanometer to measure the colour of the sea. In fine calm weather, he
found the tint to correspond to the thirty-third, the
thirty-eighth, and even the forty-fourth degree of that
instrument, at a time when the vault of the sky was
pale, and reached only the fourteenth or fifteenth degree. When, instead of directing the cyanometer to a
great extent of open sea, the eye is fixed on a small
part of its surface by means of a tube, the water exhibits a beautiful ultramarine colour. Towards evening,
on the contrary, when the edges of the waves illumined
by the sun are of an emerald green, their surface on the
shady side has a purple reflection. *Pers. Nar.* ii. 108.

Independ-
ent of the
colour of
the sky.

The colour of the ocean seems to be independent of
the reflection of the sky, though doubtless it proceeds
from the same causes which impart a blue colour to the
distant mountains, and spread an azure tint over the
face of the heavens. Humboldt informs us, that he
frequently observed the waters of the Atlantic, when
no change could be perceived in the appearance of the
atmosphere, to pass suddenly from an indigo blue to
the deepest green, and from the latter to a grey state;
and Captain Scoresby remarks, that the colour of the
Greenland seas varies from ultramarine blue to olive
green, and sometimes from the purest transparency to
great opacity. These appearances, we are farther told,
are not transitory, but permanent; not depending on
the state of the weather, but on the quality of the water

Colour of
the ocean
within the
tropics.

In general, the tropical seas possess a more intense
and a purer azure colour than the ocean in high latitudes; and so marked is the difference, that the waters
of the Gulf Stream can be readily distinguished by colour from those of the ocean, through which they flow
like a vast sea-river.

In the
Arctic
seas.

Between the parallels of 74° and 80°, the colour of
the Arctic Sea is chiefly green. Captain Scoresby, to
whom we are indebted for most of the observations
that have been made in the colour of that part of the
ocean, informs us, that the green waters often constitute long bands or streams, lying north and south, or
north-west and south-west. The dimensions of these
bands are extremely variable. In the year 1817, he
informs us the sea was observed to be of a blue colour,
and transparent, the whole way from 12° east, in the
parallel of 74° or 75°, to the longitude of 0° 12' east,
in the same latitude, where it became green, and less
transparent. Sometimes, he adds, the transition from
the green to the blue water is progressive, passing
through the intermediate shades in the space of three
or four leagues; at others it is so abrupt, that the line
of separation is perceived like the rippling of a current.

The food
of the
whale oc-
curs most
abundantly
in green
coloured
waters.

The food of the whale occurs in greatest plenty in
the green-coloured waters, and is therefore the general
resort of these huge animals. On submitting a portion
of these waters to examination, Mr. Scoresby found
that it contained a great number of semi-transparent
globular substances, which appeared to belong to a species of Medusa. He discovered the same animalculæ in
great abundance in the waters of an olive-green colour;
but more sparingly in those of a bluish-green tint.
He is disposed to ascribe the opacity of the green water to the presence of these insects; as in the blue
water, where few of them are to be found, the sea is
so transparent, that the bottom may sometimes be distinctly discerned at the depth of 80 fathoms. (*Edin.
Phil. Journ.* vol. ii. p. 14.) Captain Parry is inclined to
think, that the brownish tinge, sometimes remarked

Physical Geography.

Temperature of the ocean.

Temperature of the ocean within the tropics.

in the waters of the Arctic seas, is owing to the admixture of large portions of fresh water, supplied by the melting of the snow and ice. (Parry's *Voyage*, p. 6.)

The temperature of the ocean in different parallels of latitude, and at various depths below the surface, forms a subject of inquiry still more interesting than that of its colour; and happily it is a subject, respecting which the voyages of discovery that have been undertaken, in modern times, by almost every maritime state in Europe, have furnished much important information. The temperature of the ocean, like that of the air, varies with the latitude and the season of the year; but its range is far more limited in point of extent, and less liable to daily vicissitude. We have given, under NAVIGATION, p. 198, an extensive table of the temperature of the ocean, in different parallels of both hemispheres, and pointed out some important applications of it, for the determination of a ship's place by means of the thermometer. In the present article, we have also given a table, one column of which exhibits the temperature of the waters of the Atlantic, for a considerable number of positions, between the parallels of 20° and 50°, to which we must refer for the farther elucidation of the subject.

Near the equator, the maximum heat of the equator varies but little in different seasons. M. Churruca found it in 1788, in the Atlantic Ocean, 81.7 Fahr.; M. Perrins, in 1804, at 80.75; M. Quevedo, in 1803, at 81.5; M. Humboldt, in the South Sea, at 82.75; Dr. Davy, in 1816, at 80.5; and Dr. Horner, in 1817, at 80.8. The difference between these results is remarkably small, when we consider that they were obtained, not only in different years, but at different seasons of the year. It may be presumed, indeed, that if the equinoctial ocean had no communication with the seas of the temperate zones, its temperature would undergo scarcely any sensible variation by the change of the seasons. Within the tropics, the temperature of the ocean is generally higher than that of the air in contact with it; a fact which is easily explained, partly by the great mobility of the atmosphere, and partly by the great quantity of heat abstracted from the air, to carry on the process of evaporation at the surface of the ocean.

In the temperate zones, the temperature of the ocean is lower in summer, and higher in winter, than the diurnal temperature of the air in the same parallel. The range of temperature is accordingly very limited, and oscillates but a few degrees on either side of the annual mean, as will be best perceived from a synoptic view of the thermal state of the ocean in different months.

Physical Geography.

Temperature of the ocean within the temperate zones.

North Latitude.	Fahrenheit's Thermometer and West Longitude.						
	Jan. & Feb.	March.	April & May.	June & July.	October.	October & Novemb.	Annual Variation.
18°		† 72.9 Long. 28° 32'	‡ 73.7 Long. 41° 17'	§ 72.3 Long. 32° 10'	‖ 79.5 Long. 22° 10'	¶ 79 Long. 29° 50'	7°.2
26°		† 69.3 Long. 26° 20'	‡ 68.2 Long. 39° 54'	§ 68.4 Long. 19° 45'	‖ 74.5 Long. 26° 46'	¶ 77 Long. 35° 20'	8°.6
30°	* 69.3 Long. 9° 30'	† 66.7 Long. 23° 15'	‡ 69.3 Long. 38° 40'	§ 65 Long. 16° 50'	‖ 72.8 Long. 16° 4'	¶ 72 Long. 25° 45'	7°.8
34½	* 64 Long. 66° 10'		‡ 65.8 Long. 41° 11'	§ 63.3 Long. 16° 55'	‖ 72 Long. 10° 37'	¶ 75.75 Long. 52° 40'	11°.75
45°	* 61 Long. 14° 14'	** 52 Long. 14° 10'			* 61 Long. 16° 10'		9°.
50°	* 48.5 Long. 18° 35'				* 59 Long. 10° 29'		
55°				‡‡ 44.25 Long. 35° 56'			
59°				‡‡ 38.5 Long. 48° 12'			
68½°				‡‡ 30 Long. 62° 0'	31° Long. 63° 33'		
73°				‡‡ 34 Long. 58° 42'			

General inferences.

It appears by the above Table, that the mean annual variation of the temperature of the Atlantic for the temperate zone, is about 9°. The mean difference of temperature under different meridians, from the parallel of 18° to that of 45°, may be taken at 12°, being a mean decrement of nearly half a degree of Fahrenheit's thermometer for each degree of difference of latitude. From the parallel of 45° to that of 73°, which embraces about an equal range of the meridian, the mean decrease of heat appears to be about 30°, being more than one degree of Fahrenheit for each degree of difference of latitude. The most rapid diminution of temperature occurs between the parallels of 45° and 55°, where the decrement of temperature is nearly two degrees of Fahrenheit for each degree of difference of latitude. In these respects, the temperature of the ocean seems to obey the same laws as that of the atmosphere.

The decrement of temperature, however, seems to be somewhat different in the two hemispheres. From the equator to the parallel of 25°, the decrease of heat is slower in the southern than in the northern hemisphere; but from that parallel to the limits of the polar zones, the temperature declines more rapidly in the former than in the latter. Humboldt's *Pers. Nar.* ii. 79. *Trans. Irish Academy*, viii. 422. *Phil. Trans.* 1817, part ii. p. 277. The parallel of 25° in the southern

Decrement of temperature varies in the two hemispheres.

* Captain Anderson. † Perrins. ‡ Quevedo. § Humboldt. ‖ Churruca. ¶ Rodman. ** Dr. Davy. ‡‡ Parry.

Physical Geography. hemisphere appears to possess a mean temperature which is nearly equal to that of the equator ; but from that parallel to the parallel of 35°, the decrease is about 18°, being nearly two degrees of Fahrenheit for each degree of difference of latitude, and indicating a diminution of temperature more than twice as great as that which is observed for the same zone in the northern hemisphere. From 35° to 40°, the rate of decrease is still greater, insomuch that, while the southern parts of New Holland are exposed to sultry winds, Van Dieman's Land, which is separated from it by a narrow strait, has its mountains covered with perpetual snows. Cook's *Voyages.* Peron, *Voyage aux Ferr. Aust.* Labillardiere, *Voyage a la recherche de La Peyrouse.*

Cause of the difference of the temperature of the ocean on the two hemispheres. The remarkable difference between the temperature of the ocean in the higher latitudes of the two hemispheres has been ascribed, 1st, To the shorter continuance of the sun in the southern than in the northern hemisphere ; 2d, To the greater radiation of heat ; 3dly, To the vast extent of the Antarctic ocean, and the particular form of the land, which, in both continents, terminates towards the south in pointed headlands. It is not easy to perceive, however, why the effects of the first of these causes should only begin to be felt beyond the tropic of Capricorn ; nor does it appear to be at all conformable to observation, that the radiation from the surface of water is greater than that from land in similar circumstances. In the third reason which has been assigned, we have, it is said, a state of things by which a free outlet is opened up to the polar currents of the ocean, and through which they are permitted to push, in all directions, numerous ice-bergs from the pole towards the limits of the southern tropical zone. These floating masses of ice, fraught as they are with cold, having reached the parallel of 40°, are prevented from advancing farther northward, partly by the action of the great equatorial current, and partly by the variable winds to which they are exposed in that parallel. They therefore undergo a rapid dissolution ; but the quantity of sensible heat which passes into the latent state during their liquefaction, cannot fail to reduce, in a very great degree, the temperature of the zone, where the change takes place. It is extremely probable, too, that the elevated mountains of the newly-discovered southern continent may contribute very essentially to affect the temperature of the adjacent seas.

Temperature of the ocean at various depths. When the temperature of the ocean is examined at various depths, by means of a self-registering thermometer, it is found, in most cases, to differ considerably from the temperature at the surface. In general, the cold increases with the depth, but in the higher latitudes, the reverse of this is often observed to hold. The most extensive observations on the difference of temperature, in these circumstances, have been given by Dr. Horner and Captain Parry*. From their results it may be inferred.

General conclusions. 1st, That in the tropical seas, as well as in the temperate zones, the temperature of the waters of the ocean diminishes as the depth increases. The decrement of temperature is subject to some anomalies in different parallels but the law which connects the greater number of Dr. Horner's observations is, that if the depth be in arithmetical progression, the temperature diminishes nearly in geometrical progression.

2dly, That in the Arctic Seas, the decrease of temperature is extremely small ; or rather that in most cases, the temperature, at great depths, exceeds the temperature at the surface in these seas. Physical Geography.

3dly, That from the equator to the parallel of 75°, we have no reason to infer from actual observation, that the temperature of the ocean, at great depths, descends below 30° of Fahrenheit's scale*.

For an account of the currents of the ocean, we refer to the article NAVIGATION, Vol. XV. p. 194 ; and for a minute description of icebergs, to the article ICE, Vol. X. p. 636.

Origin of springs and rivers. Besides the water of the ocean, the aqueous portion of the globe consists partly of collections of the same fluid, more or less pure, as it exists in rivers and lakes. Rivers, we have already stated, are the natural canals by which the superfluous water evaporated from the surface of the ocean, is conveyed back to the place of its origin, to renew without interruption the beneficent round of operations, which the Author of nature has assigned to it in the economy of vegetation. The beginnings, or the sources of almost all rivers, may be traced to springs of water which gush out from the sides or bottoms of mountains. The origin again of these feeders of rivers, is doubtless to be ascribed to the slow but ceaseless filtration of water through the fissures and crevices of rocks, especially of such as possess a schistose or lamellated structure, and a porous texture. When these fissures commence near the summits of lofty mountains, and traverse their whole mass from top to bottom, the quantity of water which they discharge is very considerable. In such cases, the percolating moisture, augmented as it descends by the supplies which it derives from an innumerable multitude of invisible veins, at length emerges from its confinement, and issues in a powerful stream. Lewis describes a Remarkable springs. spring of water he observed on the banks of the Missouri, near the Great Falls, which afforded so abundant a discharge, that its beautiful transparent stream was discernible for half a mile down the river, in spite of the rapidity of its course at the point of junction. In like manner, we are informed by Barrow, that the spring from which the river Kourmanna, in Southern Africa, takes its rise, forms, at not more than a hundred paces from its source, a stream of water at least thirty feet wide and two feet deep †.

Various opinions respecting the origin of springs. Some springs seem, by the uniform regularity of their discharge, to draw their supplies either from natural reservoirs in the hearts of rocks, where the water is collected in large abundance, or the infiltration of the waters of the ocean through unknown tubes or crevices in the earth. Springs of fresh water in the sea. The springs of fresh water in the island of Bermudas rise and sink with the flux and reflux of the sea, as well as those which are impregnated with salt, and on that account more obviously connected with the ocean ; and instances are not wanting, of copious streams of fresh water spouting out from the very bed of the sea. Humboldt informs us, that in the northern coast of Yucatan, at the mouth of the Rio Logartos, many powerful springs of fresh water occur at the distance of 400 metres from the shore. The same phenomenon is observed in the bay of Xagua, in the island of Cuba. A remarkable spring of a similar description occurs in the harbour of Bridlington, the

---

* On November 13, 1822, in 83½° W. long. and 20½° N. lat. Captain Sabine found that at a depth of 6000 feet the temperature was 45°.5, that of the surface being 83°, the difference amounting to 37½°. M. Perron had formerly found this difference to be 38° in 5° of N. lat. at a depth of 1200, and 42° in 4° N. lat. at a depth of 2144 feet. See *Phil. Trans.* 1823. p. 208. ED.

† The hot springs of La Trinchera, which have a temperature of 198½, form a rivulet which, in the time of the greatest drought, is two feet deep and eighteen feet wide. Humboldt's *Pers. Narr.* iv. 194. The celebrated fountain of Vaucluse is too well known to require description.

discharge of which is evidently affected by the hydrostatic pressure of the sea as the tides rise and fall. (*Phil. Trans.*) The bay of Naples, and the Gulf of Carraco, also afford examples of submarine hot springs. (Humb. *Nar.* iii. 200, and *New Spain*, iii. 246.)

Circumstances unfavourable to the formation of springs.

When the hydrostatic pressure is too feeble to force a vein of water to discharge itself at the surface, or when the strata are too compact to permit its egress from the bowels of the earth, the stream must advance towards the ocean, or towards the bed of the nearest river, in subterraneous channels. Even an open sandy soil seems unfavourable to the existence of springs, on account of its bibulous nature. The water in such situations, instead of being discharged by a single orifice, oozes through the bed of loose gravel, and thus spreads itself slowly below the surface. On the other hand, when a subterraneous vein of water runs under an argillaceous bed, the water is still more effectually prevented from reaching the surface; but the moment the clay is pierced, the confined liquid bursts forth in a powerful and continued stream. It is probably on account of the substratum of clay which lies at a small depth below the savannahs of Louisiana, that so few springs are to be found in these extensive plains. Lewis states, that he only observed two springs along the banks of the Missouri, from its junction of the Mississippi to the Stony Mountains, an extent of more than 1500 miles.

The sources of springs not far below the surface.

It does not appear that springs have their sources at any considerable depth below the surface of the earth, whether their discharge is occasioned by the pressure of a more elevated column of water, or the action of elastic fluids. When mines are sunk to a certain depth, it frequently happens that all traces of water disappear; insomuch that one of the principal inconveniences which is felt in deep mines, is the parching dust which pervades the different galleries that traverse these subterraneous excavations.

Reciprocating fountains.

The discharge of certain springs varies at different times within short intervals, and hence they are called *Intermitting or Reciprocating Fountains.* The periods at which they intermit are sometimes pretty uniform, but more frequently they appear to be influenced by no constant law. One of the most remarkable of these fountains is the Geyser in Iceland. See ICELAND, Vol. XI. p. 653. and HYDRODYNAMICS, vol. XI. p. 486.

Formation of rivulets and large rivers.

The water of springs has no sooner emerged from the earth than it hastens to return to the ocean. By the action of gravity it runs to the lowest situation; and if it finds not a channel already prepared for its conveyance, it soon produces, by its restless activity, one fitted for the purpose. It thus proceeds towards the ocean by a path more or less direct; but seldom does it advance far on its journey before it is joined by other collections of water, having the same destination with itself. The united streams, gathering strength in their progress, move onward with a force which gradually becomes less subject to control, as it seems more able to overcome the obstacles it encounters. Yet it has not altogether lost that infantine gentleness which characterizes the efforts of a new-born stream. It still winds with placid murmurs through its native vale; or, obedient to the despotic authority of man, it refuses not to enter the artificial channels which he prepares for its reception, and to perform, under his guidance, a thousand nameless offices which administer to the necessities of his nature. As it advances onward, however, and receives new accessions to its magnitude, it begins to set the control of man at defiance, and disdains to be confined within the limits which he has assigned to it. Rising at times

above its ordinary level, it throws down the barriers which human power has erected against its encroachments; rushes with impetuous violence over the cultivated plains, and spreads ruin and desolation on every side. Happily this is not its usual state; for, though occasionally it is the minister of evil, it in general retains much of its original gentleness, and continues to render the most essential services to man. At length, after wandering over a large extent of the earth's surface, and receiving on every hand numberless auxiliary streams, it rolls onward, in majestic grandeur, to the ocean, and finally pours into that vast reservoir its widely-collected tribute of water.

Basin of a river.

The principal stream of a river, as well as its tributary branches, necessarily flows from a higher to a lower level. The general receptacle of the whole is denominated the *basin*. The basins of different rivers being separated from one another by mountains, the sloping sides of which determine the direction of the streams by which they are fed, it is easy to conceive that they must frequently approach one another. Thus, the upper parts of the basins of the Rhine, the Rhone, and the Danube, are disjoined by the Alps, while the lower parts of those of the Volga and the Don, and of the Ganges and the Burrampooter, are separated near the embouchures of these rivers by ridges of elevated land. In certain cases, the basins of rivers have a sort of communication with each other, which produces a singular distribution of their waters.

Bifurcations of rivers.

A remarkable example of this kind to which we allude is to be found in the case of the Amazons and the Oroonoko, a branch of the one inosculating with a branch of the other, and affording a free communication between these majestic rivers. This celebrated bifurcation, with others no less remarkable, is minutely described by Humboldt, *Pers. Narr.* v. pp. 376, 449. Something similar to it may be observed in North America, where geographers have represented an imaginary chain of mountains between the great lakes of Canada and the country of the Miamis. At the seasons of inundations, the waters flowing into the lakes communicate with those which run into the Mississipi; so that it is possible to proceed by boats from the sources of the river St. Mary to the Wabash, as well as from the Chacago to the Illinois. Humboldt's *Pers. Narr.* iv. 159. Drake's *Cincinnati*, p. 222.

The bed of a river.

The lowest part of the basin of a river, or the channel through which it flows, is called its *bed*. In some instances the beds of rivers are immense chasms, or transverse ravines, cutting the longitudinal direction of the mountains through which they pass, at right angles. Thus, the bed of the Missouri, where it makes its exit from the Stony Mountains, is represented to be a vast sluice, the sides of which rise perpendicularly, according to the report of Lewis and Clarke, to the enormous height of 1200 feet from the surface of the water. This remarkable defile is stated by the same travellers to be six miles in length, and so narrow that it barely contains the river, and seldom affords a spot where a man could stand between the water and the tremendous cliffs. Most of the great rivers quit the mountains in which their sources are situated by similar transverse openings through the solid strata. Thus, the Sutledge, the Ganges, and the Burrampooter, pierce the chain of the Himalayah, in the same manner as the Amazon, the Paute, and the Pastaza, break the Cordillera of the Andes. It is impossible to determine whether these deep chasms have been formed, after a long lapse of time, by the rivers to which they afford a passage, or have been suddenly produced by some great convulsion of nature. Perhaps it would be nearest the truth to

Physical Geography.

suppose that both causes have contributed to their formation, some convulsive operation having first given birth to an extensive fissure, and the ceaseless action of the stream having afterwards reduced it to its present condition.

Elevation of the beds of rivers by alluvial deposites.

In Alpine countries the lower part of the beds of rivers generally consists either of hard rocks, or of gravel derived from their decomposition. The more soluble parts of the rocks, which suffer disintegration by the action of the stream, are gradually conveyed toward the sea, and, during their progress downwards, give rise to various alluvial formations, which not only affect the banks by which the waters are confined, but frequently modify both the velocity and general direction of the stream. The quantity of loose materials carried down by rivers is probably much greater than is generally imagined. The disintegration which they are able to accomplish, though gradual, and almost imperceptible in its progress, continues to advance without intermission, and is forcibly indicated by the vast accumulation of sand and mud which is to be found at the mouths of all great rivers. It is to the operation of this slow but uninterrupted process, that we ascribe the gradual elevation of the beds of rivers, near their embouchures, as well as the formation of deltas and islands.

Dangerous consequences resulting from it.

The retardation in the velocity of rivers, as they approach the sea, arising partly from the diminished inclination of their beds, and partly from the frequent deflections of their courses through the soft alluvions which they have deposited, is extremely favourable to the subsidence of the earthy particles they carry along with them. Their beds are thus slowly raised, and require a corresponding elevation of their banks, to confine them within their former limits. In illustration of this fact, it may be stated that the Rhine, the Rhone, the Po, and even the Mississippi, now flow on beds greatly elevated above their ancient level; insomuch that artificial embankments of great extent are necessary to prevent these rivers from passing beyond their ordinary channels, and inundating the adjacent countries. These embankments, however, afford only a temporary and insecure defence against the evils they are intended to obviate; and already, in many instances, have been the means of producing the most extensive and deplorable calamities. By raising a river above its natural bed, and thus preventing the adjoining plains from sharing in the gradual elevation, which is produced by alluvial depositions, a state of things is established that is pregnant with much danger, and may be followed by the most fatal consequences. The devastations occasioned by the overflowings of the Rhine and other rivers, which have been raised by *dikes* above their original level, are too frequent not to be generally known*. From Bologna towards Ravenna, on the east, and Ferrara on the west, a great extent of rich territory, amounting to 26 square leagues, is now entirely desolated by the Po, in consequence of the great elevation to which the bed of that river has been raised by its own alluvial depositions, and the constant oozing of its waters through its banks. The only effectual remedy that can be adopted against the increase of these evils, is either to deepen the beds of rivers, or to strengthen and elevate their embankments.

Physical Geography.

Origin of deltas.

The formation of deltas, by the accumulation of alluvial matter at the mouths of rivers, is one of the most interesting phenomena which hydrography offers to the consideration of the naturalist. Rivers which, in a flooded state, are much discoloured by the earthy matters they carry along with them, frequently enter the sea by two or more mouths, and thus form, at their embouchures, considerable spaces of land, which have received the appellation of deltas, from their resemblance to the Greek letter of that name. As these triangular islands consist entirely of sand and other alluvial matter deposited by rivers, it is scarcely possible to entertain the smallest doubt with respect to their origin. The formation of deltas, however, is by no means universal; for though most of the great rivers of the Ancient continent are furnished with them, it is not a little remarkable that they are rarely to be found at the mouths of the American rivers. This difference appears to be owing, as Major Rennel has remarked, to the original conformation of the adjacent coast, and to the depth of the sea beyond it. If the estuary of a river, and the part of the ocean into which it flows, are extremely deep, the alluvial matter is lost in the abyss; whilst in a shallower sea, it not only fills up the bed of the inlet itself, but affords sufficient materials to form a projecting tongue of land, which gradually advances outward, and lays the foundation of future islands.

Deltas of the Nile.

The Nile, the Ganges, the Danube, and the Volga, are the most remarkable among the class of rivers which exhibit the formation of deltas on the largest scale. The delta of the Nile, in particular, on account of the information we possess of its condition from a very remote period, is extremely interesting, and its history is well calculated to illustrate the nature of these curious formations. When we examine the extreme flatness of this delta, the peculiar quality of its soil, so different from that of the adjacent country; the promontory of low land which it forms, projecting beyond the general contour of the coast; and with all this, keep in view the probability from appearances, that it now fills up a great inlet or gulf of the sea, which, in ancient times, washed the base of the rock on which the pyramids of Memphis are erected, we are amazed at the vast results capable of being produced by a process apparently so tedious as that by which deltas are formed. Rennel's *Herodotus,* p. 482.

Different kinds of deltas.

Humboldt notices three kinds of deltas; 1. *Oceanic deltas* at the mouths of great rivers where they enter the ocean. 2. *Deltas* on the shores of *inland seas,* like those of the Volga, the Oxus, and the Sihon. 3. *Deltas of tributary streams,* like those at the mouth of the Apure, the Arauca, and the Branco; but these distinctions relate rather to a slight difference of the circumstances in which the formation of a delta takes place, than to any essential difference in the general process itself. *Pers. Narr.* v. p. 466.

Rivers which have a moderate length of course, and

---

* The effects of the inundations of the Mississippi are not less formidable, when that river bursts its embankments, and overflows the adjacent grounds. The following account of that occurrence is given by Mr. Brackenridge in his work on Louisiana: " The waters rush from the river with indescribable impetuosity, like the noise of a roaring cataract, boiling and foaming, and tearing every thing before them. To one who has not seen this country, it is almost impossible to convey any idea of the terrors excited by a *crevasse,* or breaking of the levée. Like the breaking out of fire in a town, where no one knows when his dwelling may be assailed, it excites universal consternation; every employment is abandoned, for miles above and below; and all hasten to the spot, where every exertion is made, night and day, to stop the breach, which is sometimes successful, but more frequently the hostile element is suffered to take its course. The consequences are, the destruction of the crop, the buildings, and sometimes the land itself is much injured, which the current has washed over, carrying away the soil, or leaving numerous logs or trees drawn into the vortex as they are floated down the river; these must be destroyed before the land can be again cultivated. The effects of a breach in the levée, he adds, are even more desolating than those of fire."

The bar of a river. carry along with them an inconsiderable quantity of alluvial matter to the sea, deposite at their mouths only as much mud and sand as is sufficient to form a bank or shoal. This bank varies in extent with the form of the coast; but the additions made to its breadth being always towards the sea, the increase of its magnitude in that direction is only checked by powerful currents in the sea itself. When the accumulation of alluvial matter raises the bank nearly to a level with the surface of the water, the river, finding its discharge impeded, is compelled to form a passage through this obstacle of its own creation, and produces what is technically termed a *bar*. The position of the bar of a river may, in general, be determined, from a simple inspection of the state of the shores at the embouchure. The shore on which the deposition of the principal portion of alluvial matter is taking place, will be found to be flat, whilst the opposite one is steep. It is along the side of the latter that the deepest channel of the river lies; and in the line of this channel, but beyond the parts that form the mouth of the river, will be the bar. (Rennel's *Herodotus*, p. 490.)

In some cases, the alluvial matter is not allowed to settle at the embouchures of the rivers, by which it is discharged into the sea, but it is transported by currents of the ocean, and spread along the coast, so as to give birth to a connected chain of shoals, which in process of time become islands of an elongated form. Thus the alluvions conveyed by the rivers, which fall into the Gulf of Mexico, being extended along the shore by the action of the gulf stream, have produced the long stripes of insular land which run parallel with the coast from the latitude of 22° to 29° north.

The length of the courses of rivers. The length of the courses of rivers, as well as the magnitude of their streams, is immediately connected with the form and extent of their basins, not less than with the height of the mountain ridges by which their direction is determined. Rivers which traverse flat countries, necessarily receive few tributary streams in their progress; and hence though they may flow over a great extent of surface, the quantity of water which they discharge is extremely small in comparison of the length of their courses. Thus the Missouri, while it continues to flow through the extensive savannahs of Louisiana, a tract of more than 1600 miles in extent, is all along nearly of the same breadth, and but little different in depth; and, like many of its tributary branches, it would probably disappear entirely by evaporation long before it joined the Mississippi, were it not for the occasional supplies which it receives during its progress from a few of its more permanent auxiliary streams. On the other hand, the Amazon, which flows through a basin of vast extent, and derives its supplies from rivers which have their sources in the most elevated regions of the earth, advances onward with increasing grandeur, and at last pours into the ocean the collected streams of more than a tenth part of the habitable surface of the globe. The lengths of the most distinguished rivers in the world, taking the length of the Thames as unity, are stated by Major Rennel to be in the following order: The river Amazon $15\frac{3}{4}$; the river Kian Ku in China $15\frac{1}{2}$; the Hoango $13\frac{1}{2}$; the Nile $12\frac{1}{2}$; the Lena $11\frac{1}{2}$; the Amur 11; the Obi $10\frac{1}{2}$; the Jenissey 10; the Ganges, the Burrampooter, the Ava, and the Volga, each $9\frac{1}{2}$; the Euphrates $8\frac{1}{2}$; the Mississippi 8; the Danube 7; the Indus $5\frac{1}{2}$; and the Rhone $5\frac{1}{4}$. If the relative importance of rivers be estimated by the quantity of water they discharge, a different arrangement must be adopted, and they will stand in the following order: The Amazon, the Nile, the Senegal, the St. Lawrence, the Hoango, the La Plata, the Jenissey, the Mississippi, the Volga, the Obi, the Amur, the Oroonoko, the Ganges, the Euphrates, the Danube, the Don, the Indus, the Dneiper, the Dwina, &c. Some idea will be formed regarding the absolute lengths of these rivers, by recollecting that the Amazon, the largest in every respect that is known, has a course of nearly 4000 miles. This mighty stream, whose length is nearly equal to a sixth part of the circumference of the globe, enters the ocean with a channel which is 150 miles in breadth, while its depth in some places is represented to exceed 100 fathoms.

Periodical floods of rivers. Almost all rivers are subject to occasional changes in the magnitudes of their streams; but it is chiefly within the tropical regions that the most remarkable overflowings and contractions of their waters are exhibited in a regular and periodical manner. The Nile, so long celebrated for its annual inundations, was at one time supposed to be the only river which was subject to periodical floods; but since the torrid zone has been more fully explored, it has been ascertained that various other rivers are liable to the same alternate rising and falling of their streams. This phenomenon is influenced in some degree in the rivers where it occurs by circumstances of a local nature; but it is chiefly to be ascribed to the periodical rains which take place, at certain seasons of the year, in all the mountainous countries within the tropics. Malte-Brun has made a distinction between rivers which run parallel to the equator, and those which flow in the direction of the meridian; and hinted that the former must be less liable to inundations than the latter, particularly when the course of their streams stretches through extensive plains. In support of this opinion, he cites the Oroonoko, the Senegal, and the Niger, the last of which he takes for granted has a course lying nearly east and west. The first of these rivers, however, affords any thing but a confirmation of the opinion in question; as its course, so far from being parallel to the equator, is remarkable for its spiral form. The Senegal, which has something of a similar form, is not a river of sufficient magnitude to afford a proper example of great inundations; and we know too little of the actual course of the Niger, to pronounce any thing with certainty respecting its overflowings. Besides, it is well known that the Oroonoko is as subject to periodical floods as any other of the tropical rivers. M. de Pons fixes the rising of this river at 13 fathoms, and Humboldt states that foreign pilots reckon it even 90 feet in the lower Oroonoko. (*Pers. Nar.* v. p. 750.) The periodical inundations of large rivers, therefore, though they may be affected, in certain cases, by the directions in which they flow, must be explained by referring them to causes more immediately connected with the origin and formation of rivers themselves. All great rivers must take their rise in mountainous countries, which are most favourable, at all seasons of the year, for bringing about that intermixture of the atmospherical strata by which rain is produced; and hence if the feeders of the tributary streams, which unite in the formation of a large river, are situated in a latitude which does not exceed 30 or 35 degrees, the limit of the great periodical rains, the main stream, in whatever direction it flows, must be subject to annual overflowings.

Rivers in which inundations usually occur.

Periods of the inundations. The inundations of the rivers in the same hemisphere occur nearly at the same season of the year; but the period of the greatest height of the waters in particular situations, is considerably modified by their distance from the mountains, where the rains which produce the floods take place. Thus the inundations of the Ganges and the Nile in the old world, and of the Oroonoko and the Mississippi in the new, happen when the sun has

PHYSICAL GEOGRAPHY.

*518

Physical
Geography.

north declination; while those of the Amazon, the Rio
Plata, and the larger rivers of New Holland, occur
when the sun has south declination. The annual inundations of the Ganges, it need scarcely be remarked,
are produced by the great rains which deluge the whole
of India during the south-west monsoon, and those of
the Nile by the rains which fall at the same time in
Abyssinia and the neighbouring countries.

In general, it is some time before the effects of the
rains which fall near the source of a river are felt near
its mouth: the rising of the Nile, for example, is observed to commence at Cairo, about ten or twelve days after the rains have begun to fall in Abyssinia; and, in
like manner, the inundation does not attain its maximum state at the former place, till the middle of September, when the rains have considerably abated along
the whole course of the river.

Malte-Brun affirms, that no rivers in the temperate
zones are subject to periodical overflowings. This assertion is far from being correct, as the inundations of
the Mississippi are greater than those of the Nile, which
are only 35 feet at Cairo, whereas the rising of the Mississippi is 55 feet at Natchez. Humboldt's *Nar.* v. 750.

The period when the inundations of a great river
take place, affords the means of forming a conjecture,
when direct information is wanting, with respect to
the position of the sources of the principal streams by
which its waters are supplied. In illustration of this
remark, it may be stated that the mouth of the Congo
being situated in the southern hemisphere, while the
overflowings of that river occur at a season when the
rains happen in the northern hemisphere, it may be
inferred, with much probability, that most of the tributary streams of the Congo flow from the northern
side of the equator. *Edin. Phil. Journ.* iii. 105. *Quart.
Review*, vol. xviii. 348.

Important purposes served by mountains in causing inundations.
From the influence of mountains in separating aqueous vapour from the atmosphere, it must be evident
that these stupendous masses, though themselves consigned to perpetual cold and sterility, are the immediate causes of the inundations which impart fertility to
the plains; and that without them, the surface of the
earth could not have enjoyed that grateful supply of
moisture which is necessary for the support of the various orders of organized beings with which it is every
where so abundantly stored. Mountains are not to be
regarded, therefore, as useless excrescences upon the
surface of the globe, encroaching upon the abodes of
animated beings, and limiting the range of happiness
and enjoyment; but as essential parts of a harmonious
whole, every element of which contributes its share to
produce the wisest and most beneficent purposes.

Velocity of rivers.
The velocity of rivers is affected by so many circumstances, that without having recourse to actual
experiment, it is nearly impossible to determine, with
much precision, what it may be in any particular
stream. So uniform, however, is the relation between
the length of the bed of a river, and the altitude of
the most elevated point of it above the level of the sea,
that less difference of velocity is observed in the streams
of various rivers, than might be anticipated. Few rivers flow, for any length of course, with a velocity
which exceeds five or six miles an hour, and the most
sluggish streams seldom or never at less than half that
rate. The velocity at any particular point must evidently vary with the inclination of the bed, and the
hydraulic mean depth; though it would seem that the
rapidity of currents frequently depends nearly as much
upon the impulse which they receive from the waters
by which they are pressed, as even upon these primary
conditions. Thus the Ganges, which according to

Major Rennel has scarcely any apparent declivity in
its bed from Hardwar to the sea, a distance of 1350
miles, yet moves, in that part of its course, with a
velocity of three miles in the dry, and five or six miles
per hour in the wet season. The Amazon, too, the
declivity of whose bed for 200 leagues does not exceed,
according to Condamine's estimate, ten or 11 feet, has
also a very considerable velocity.

We have already stated, that the mean velocity of
rivers varies from three to six miles per hour. In particular cases, however, when the bed has a considerable inclination, the motion of currents is proportionally increased, and amounts to eight miles per hour.
According to Clarke and Lewis, the velocity of the
Missouri, a little above the point where its waters
mingle with those of the Mississipi, is seven feet, and
in some places even twelve feet, per second, exceeding
that of the Cassiquiare, which Humboldt determined
to be in some places, which he navigated, eleven feet
eight inches per second. At the famous Pongo de Man-
zeriche, where the Amazon forces its way through the
rocky barriers of the Andes, the velocity of that majestic river is about eight or nine miles per hour. It
has been affirmed that no boat could ascend a stream,
the velocity of which exceeds three feet per second,
(*Encyc. Brit.* art. RIVER,) but it has been abundantly
proved by the ascent of the Cassiquiare and Missouri,
the velocity of whose streams exceeds, in many places,
three times the supposed limit.

Inclination of the beds of rivers.
The inclination of the beds of rivers, when they
flow through extensive plains, is, in general, very
small; that of the Amazon has been estimated for the
last 600 miles of its course, at one-fifth of an inch per
mile; and that of the Nile, from Cairo to Rosetta, at
1⅓ inch per mile. The descent of the Seine, between
Valin and Serres, is reckoned about ten inches per
mile; and that of the Loire, between Pouilly and Briare,
at 4½ feet per mile, but between Briare and Orleans,
it diminishes about 2⅔ feet for the same distance. When
the inclination of the bed of a river becomes eight or
ten feet per mile, the velocity of the stream which flows
over it is greatly augmented, and the waters, instead
of gliding silently along, rush forward with tumultuous
impetuosity, and are converted into foaming torrents
by the obstacles they encounter.

Cataracts or falls of rivers.
But rivers do not always descend from one elevation
of table-land to another by inclined beds. They occasionally precipitate themselves over abrupt declivities
of great height, and pass suddenly from one inclined
plane to another. These descents generally occur in
situations where nature exhibits scenes of the utmost
sublimity and grandeur; and hence *cataracts* have always been reckoned among the most interesting objects of a landscape. The number of cataracts belonging to different rivers generally varies with the lengths
of their streams, and the elevations of their sources
above the level of the sea; but few rivers of any magnitude are altogether destitute of these abrupt changes
in the position of their beds. The most stupendous
falls are to be found in secondary countries, where rivers, having acquired a considerable size, rush with irresistible fury over perpendicular walls of calcareous rocks.

Their situation of great importance.
The situation of the falls of rivers is of the utmost
importance to their successful navigation. In the case
of the Amazon, for example, the cataracts are not more
than five or six hundred miles from its source, so that
five-sixths of the course of that stupendous river are
perfectly navigable. The falls of the Missouri are still
more advantageously situated in that respect, being
only about 250 miles from its source in the Stony
Mountains; whereas the great falls of the Oroonoko

form, on the contrary, a barrier to the navigation of that river, which is placed nearly at equal distances from its extremities.

The heights of cataracts have generally been much exaggerated, probably more from the astonishment produced upon the minds of the persons by whom they have been described, than from any wish to deceive, on the part of those who have witnessed for the first time those scenes of appalling grandeur. In alpine regions they are loftiest, and most abrupt; in countries of secondary formation they are less elevated, and generally of the description of falls termed rapids. The falls of Tequendama, formed by the river De Bagota, in South America, which was estimated by Bouguer to be of the enormous height of 1500 feet, has been reduced by Humboldt to little more than a third part of that height. A little way above this extraordinary fall, the stream is about 150 feet in breadth, but immediately before its descent it is suddenly contracted to forty, when it passes, at a double bound, to the depth of 574 feet. Humboldt's *Researches*, vol. i. 76. This fall was, at one time, esteemed the loftiest in the world; but it is greatly inferior in height to the cascade of the Ache, which rises in the cavern of the glacier of mount Tauren, runs through the valley of Achentall, and after reaching the Gulf of Tauren, throws itself over an elevation of 2000 feet. There are five great falls, the last of which forms a most magnificent arch of water, and is resolved into spray before it reaches the ground. The noise of the rushing water is so loud, that it is heard at the distance of more than a league, and the current of air which it sets in motion is so violent, that it forcibly drives back those who attempt to advance towards the top of the gulf. *Edin. Phil. Journ.* vol. iii. 203. The greatest fall in Europe, and perhaps in the world, if both the height and the mass of water be considered, is that of the river Lulea, in Sweden, which is one-eighth of a mile broad, and 400 feet high. *Edin. Phil. Journ.* vol. ii. 199. The great fall of Niagara, the noise of which is heard at the distance of thirteen miles, is 400 yards across, immediately before the descent, and its height is 150 feet.

The excavations which are formed by large rivers when they precipitate themselves over high rocks, are often of an immense depth. The abyss into which the river of Gottenburgh rushes from a high precipice is so enormously deep, that large pines floating down the stream are often dashed in pieces when they are projected over the cataract; and such of them as descend vertically, penetrate to so great a depth, that they sometimes disappear for upwards of a quarter of an hour before they return to the surface.

The chasms through which rivers occasionally flow in alpine countries, seem to have been formed, at least in part, by the unceasing action of torrents gradually eroding the solid rocks over which they are projected. The falls of Niagara are, by this wasting process, advancing slowly up the stream, and, if sufficient time be allowed for the action of the waters, the period must arrive when the entire demolition of the rocky barrier which lies between the fall and Lake Erie, will drain off the waters from that extensive basin, and convert the alluvions, which they now overspread, into a rich and fertile plain. In support of this assertion, it may be stated, that the falls of the Nile at Syene do not at all correspond now with the description which the ancients have left us of the stupendous cataracts, represented to have existed there in former times.

Instances are not wanting of some large rivers disappearing partially, and others entirely, in their course. The waters of the Oroonoko are almost lost at the

Randal de Cariven, beneath the immense blocks of granite which rise here and there in the bed of the river, and leaning against one another, form so many huge and shapeless arches, under which innumerable tumultuous torrents rush with the most horrible noise. In like manner, at the Rapids of *Atures*, the same river is every where deeply engulfed in caverns, in one of which Humboldt assures us he heard the waters rolling at once over his head and beneath his feet. But the total disappearance of a river, though an occurrence more fitted to excite astonishment, is also occasionally observed. As examples of this, we may mention the sudden disappearance of the Rhone between Seyssel and Ecluse; of the Cedar-creek in Virginia, &c. This subterraneous descent of rivers is ascribed to their encountering in their progress a bar of rocks, which, obstructing their waters, compels them either to flow over them, and form cascades, or find a passage below, where the materials may be softer, and afterwards work their way, for a longer or a shorter space, under ground. In the year 1752, the entire bed of the Rio del Norte, a considerable river in New Mexico, became suddenly dry for an extent of sixty leagues. The water of the river had precipitated itself into a newly-formed chasm, and disappeared for a considerable time, leaving the fine plains on its former banks entirely destitute of water. At length, after a lapse of several weeks, the water returned to its former channel, probably because the chasm, and the subterraneous conductors connected with it, had been filled up. A similar phenomenon is said to have occurred in the river Amazon, about the beginning of the eighteenth century. At the village of Puyaya the inhabitants saw, with terror and surprise, the bed of that vast river completely dried up for several hours, in consequence of a part of the rocks near the cataract of Rentena having been thrown down by an earthquake. Humboldt's *New Spain*, ii. 312. The Guadiana in Spain, and many of the tributary branches of the Missouri, lose themselves, after a long drought, amidst the bibulous sands over which they flow. All the great rivers of New Holland seem to direct their courses towards the interior, where they disappear in an extensive inland marsh.

Rivers are often distinguishable by the peculiar colour of their streams. The Danube retains a yellow colour the whole year round; and the waters of the Traun and the Ens, which hold in suspension a great deal of schistose and calcareous sand, possess a beautiful green colour. Other rivers, as the Rhone, near Geneva, have a colour which is decidedly blue. We learn from some of the ancient writers on geography, that the Greeks were struck with astonishment when they beheld the blue waters of Thermopylæ, the red waters of Joppa, and the dark-coloured waters of the baths of Astyra, opposite to Lesbos. Some naturalists, who have examined the purest waters of the Glaciers, and the rivers which flow from mountains covered with perpetual snows, where the earth is destitute of the relics of vegetation, seem disposed to adopt the opinion, that the proper colour of water is a bluish-green. Humboldt, who appears to have examined with much attention the colour of the waters of the tropical rivers, distinguishes them only by the epithets of *white* and *black*. The black waters, he informs us, are the purest and most limpid, such being their transparency, that the smallest fish are visible in them to the depth of twenty or thirty feet. The colouring principle of these waters seems to be too sparing in quantity to be detected by analysis; but is conjectured to be an extractive vegetable matter. It is not a little remarkable, that both the crocodiles and moschettoes, the greatest pests of equatorial America, carefully avoid the black waters. When the smallest breeze plays upon the surface of these dark-coloured rivers, they appear of a fine grass green, like the lakes of Switzerland. Humboldt's *Pers. Narr.* v. 91, 185, 419.

Quantity of waters discharged by rivers.
The quantity of water discharged by rivers into the sea has been imperfectly examined. From facts, which we have already stated, the mean annual quantity of rain over the globe may be estimated about three feet; which would give no less than 16,000,000,000,000,000 cubic feet for the quantity of rain over the whole surface. If we suppose that a third part of this falls upon the land, we should have upwards of 5,000,000,000,000,000 cubic feet for the supply of rivers, and the economy of vegetation. Now, to compare this with the quantity of water discharged by all the known rivers of the world, we shall take, with Buffon, the example of the Po. This river, according to Riccioli, before it divides into branches, has a mean breadth of 1000 feet, and a depth of ten feet, with a velocity of four miles per hour. Consequently, it conveys into the sea about 5,000,000,000 cubic feet per day, or nearly 2,000,000,000,000 cubic feet annually; so that if we suppose a fifth part of the water which descends in rain upon the land, to be dissipated again by evaporation, and another fifth to be decomposed by the processes of vegetation, we should still have remaining as much water as would supply 1500 rivers equal in size to the Po. Or if we take this view of the subject: the Po appears to traverse a country about 380 miles in length, and the rivers which flow into it on each side arise from sources which are about sixty miles distant from the main stream. Thus the Po, and the rivers which it receives, water a country of about 45,600 square miles. But the surface of the dry land being, according to Buffon's estimate, 63,728,938 square miles, (Buffon's *Nat. Hist.* i. 136;) if we suppose that each portion of the earth's surface, equal in extent to the basin of the Po, is furnished with a river of the same magnitude, we should have by this computation about 1400 rivers of the same size with the Po to drain the surface of the globe.

It appears by some late experiments of M. Escher, that the annual discharge of the Rhine at Basle is 1,046,763,676,000 cubic feet; that of the Tay appears from observations made at Perth, by the writer of this article, to be about 100,000,000,000 cubic feet, being only about a tenth part of the quantity of water conveyed by the Rhine. The basin of the Tay is 2315 square miles, and the annual supply of rain which it receives about 130,000,000,000 cubic feet; so that, for that extent, about 30,000,000,000 cubic feet of water return to the atmosphere by evaporation or decomposition. In July 1819, after a long drought, the discharge of the Tay was found to be reduced to 457 cubic feet per second, being only about a-tenth part of the average quantity which it conveys to the sea.

Number of rivers of considerable size.
In the old continent, there are, according to Buffon, about 430 rivers which fall either into the ocean or into the Mediteranean and Black Seas; and in the new continent, about a third of that number. In this estimate, which assigns 565 rivers, for the whole number of rivers of both continents, none are reckoned which are not as large as the Somme in Picardy.

Phenomena of river tides.
The limits of this article allow us to describe very briefly some of the phenomena of river tides. The flux and reflux of water which occur periodically in the ocean, twice a-day, are felt in some rivers at a very great distance from their mouths. Condamine observed a regular rise and fall of the waters of the Amazon at the distance of 600 miles from the mouth of that river; and, by noticing the time of high water as he descended towards the sea, he found that there were several simultaneous points of high water, with corresponding points of low water intervening, between Para and the confluence of the Madera. This connected series of tides, which Condamine erroneously ascribed to the immediate action of the sun and moon, was merely the successive undulations produced by the tides of the ocean at the mouth of the river, and propagated up the stream in the form of immense waves, whose curvature was imperceptible for an inconsiderable extent. This phenomenon is observed in all rivers flowing through extensive plains. It was long ago pointed out by Newton, that the high water of the Thames, at London Bridge, takes place when it is low water at the mouth of the river, the surface of the water being then at London actually forty feet above its level in the German ocean; and, indeed, all large rivers, in which tides are observed, never exhibit a regular descent of surface towards the sea, but a waving outline in continual motion from their mouths to the farthest limit of the river tide. When a river is suddenly enlarged or contracted in breadth, these inundations in its waters are attended with remarkable appearances. Below Dundee, the breadth of the Tay, where it joins the inlet of the German Ocean, is about a mile; but, above that town, its bed enlarges very considerably and forms a capacious frith, which may be considered as the bed of a lake, whose waters are alternately withdrawn and restored by the sea. The tides from the German Ocean, which enter the river through the narrow channel at its mouth, not finding sufficient vent for themselves at time of flood, the level of the water in the frith never attains the same level as at the mouth of the river by fifteen inches, it being high water at the latter before this can be effected. In its progress up the river, however, the tide wave suffers a considerable contraction of its breadth by the narrowing of the river at Newburgh, and is again elevated about a foot above its level, near the middle of the frith, opposite to Mylnefield. When it reaches Perth, where the river is still more contracted by its banks, the water rises to the same level as at the mouth of the river *. Similar effects have been observed in other rivers. At La Reole, for example, it has been ascertained by M. Bremontier, that in the bed of the Garonne, the oscillations of the tides ascend an inclined plane, far above the level of the waters of the Atlantic, at the mouth of the river. At La Reole the tides appear to flow ten toises, at Bourdeaux five toises, above the low water mark, near Royan; and yet the tides rise to the same apparent height at Royan and Bourdeaux. Humboldt's *Pers. Narr.* v. 737.

Successive tides in large rivers.

Elevation of the tide-wave above the level of the water at the mouth of a river.

Several rivers present, near their junction with the ocean, a peculiar phenomenon, depending upon the flux and reflux of the tides, which is attended with much danger. The phenomenon to which we allude is termed the *bore* of a river, and is found to exist chiefly in large rivers, which have a wide outlet, and in which the greatest tides occur. In rivers of this description, the accumulated water of the gulf or outlet not being entirely discharged before the return of the ensuing tide, it encounters the rising waters of the ocean flowing in an opposite direction, and produces, by the mutual reaction of the conflicting surges, an elevation of

Bore, or accumulation of water at the time of flood.

---

* For these interesting facts we are indebted to James Jardine, Esq. civil-engineer, who verified them by a series of very accurate levellings, and well-conducted observations.

Physical Geography.

the water far above its natural level. The wave formed in this manner rolls up the channel of the river with an irresistible force, overwhelming in its progress every thing which it encounters, till exhausted by its own exertions, it dies away into a feeble undulation. In some rivers the *bore* rushes along with a head of water which appears almost incredible. In the Severn it even swells to the height of ten feet; but in the great rivers of America, particularly the Amazon, where it receives from the Indians the name of the *Pororaca*, it becomes a rolling mountain of water, which is stated to attain the height of 180 feet. Malte-Brun, *Geog.* i. 306. About the time of the fall and change of the moon, when the tides are at the highest, the bore assumes its most formidable appearance; and if we can rely upon the descriptions which are given of it, must be truly terrific.

Its great height in some rivers.

Having thus taken a general view of the origin of rivers, and of the features which they exhibit during their progress to the ocean; we shall conclude our account of these natural canals, by a brief sketch of their distinctive characters, in the great divisions of the globe.

Rivers in the different quarters of the globe.

The largest rivers in the world are undoubtedly to be found in America. The highest land in this quarter of the globe, running along the western shores of the continent, an uninterrupted descent is formed by a succession of declining basins from west to east, which is extremely favourable to the existence of large rivers. The Amazon, which is not only the noblest of the American rivers, but the largest in the world, takes its rise in the eastern cordillera of the Andes, and has a course which extends almost from the shores of the Pacific to those of the Atlantic. All the rivers which run eastward from the Andes, between the equator and 15° or 16° of south latitude, pour themselves into this mighty stream; and many which flow in the direction of the meridian are connected with it by lateral valleys, which communicate on either side with its capacious basin. Several of its tributary streams vie in magnitude with the largest rivers in the old world, and are yet so inconsiderable in comparison with it, that they are scarcely known to geographers by a uniformity of name. Amidst the multitude of small rivers which flow into the Amazon, the main trunk is with difficulty recognized. The most received opinion is that which places its remotest source in the jurisdiction of Tarma, and represents it as issuing from the lake of Lauricocha in 11° of south latitude. From this elevated point it proceeds southward almost to 12°, where it takes a gradual circuit till it assumes an easterly course, and flows in that direction through the country of Juaxa. After quitting the cordillera of the Andes it flows northward, and pursues the same course to the city of Jaen. Here, by a second flexure, it turns towards the east, and continues to flow with little change in its direction till it reaches the Atlantic Ocean, where its channel is 150 miles in breadth, and its depth of corresponding dimension. The whole course of this immense river, including all its windings, cannot be reckoned less than 3600 miles. See the art. AMAZONS, Vol. I. p. 596.

American rivers.

The Amazon.

Another American river, almost rivalling the Amazon, is the St. Lawrence in Canada. One of the most remarkable features of this stream is its uniform breadth and depth. Below the great falls, at the base of the rocky mountains, its breadth was found to be 800 yards, and its depth, in most places, ten feet; while nearly 1000 miles farther down, after it had received the waters of

St. Lawrence.

a number of considerable rivers, it was only 500 yards wide, without any increase of depth. The small change in the dimensions of this river, from its source in the Stony Mountains to its junction with the main stream, must be ascribed to the excessive dryness of the Savannahs through which it flows, and to powerful evaporation *. See CANADA, Vol. V. pp. 328, 329, &c.

Physical Geography.

The next of the American rivers in point of magnitude is the Oroonoko, already described in Vol. XVI. p. 176. The course of this river is rather peculiar. The bifurcations and intertwinings of the tributary streams of the Oroonoko are perhaps more numerous and varied than those of any other system of rivers in the world,—a circumstance which is evidently owing to the small undulations of the extensive plains on its left bank. Humboldt remarks, that the course of this river displays three peculiarities: 1. The constancy with which it remains near the group of mountains round which it turns, at the south, the west, and the north. 2. The situation of its sources on ground which would seem to belong to the basins of the Rio Negro and the Amazon. 3. Its bifurcations, sending a branch to another system of rivers. The whole length of the Oroonoko may be estimated at 2000 miles; but on account of its spiral form, after it has flowed 1350 miles, it has scarce receded the third part of that distance from its source. Humboldt's *Pers. Narr.* v. 451.

Oroonoko.

All the great rivers of America are characterized by an extreme degree of muddiness. The waters of the Oroonoko, according to Don Ulloa, communicate a muddy tinge to the ocean, which is perceived at the distance of 60 or 70 leagues from its mouth. Humboldt's *New Spain*, ii. 312.

Muddiness of American rivers

The Rio de la Plata, the last of the American rivers we shall notice, though one of the largest streams in the world, is not known by that name many miles above its junction with the ocean. It is composed of the united streams of the Paraguay, the Panana, the Pilcomayo, and the Uruguay; the first of which may be regarded as the main trunk. The Paraguay takes its rise in the transverse range of mountains which separate the basin of the Amazon from that of the La Plata. Its course, which is nearly from north to south, is about 1600 miles in length. The Panana, which is esteemed by some geographers the principal stream, rises in the mountains of Brazil, at a small distance from the shores of the Atlantic, from which it proceeds in a south-west direction, till, after a course of 1200 miles, it joins the Paraguay, in lat. 27° 20' south, long. 58° west. The grand cataract of Panana is situated in lat. 24° south, near the city of Cuayna. It is described to be rather a succession of rapids than a single fall of the river, and extends over a space of twelve leagues amidst rocks of the most terrific grandeur. The Panana is navigable to the town of Assumption, being about 1000 miles from the sea. The estuary of this noble river, where it bears the name of La Plata, is so spacious, that its banks cannot be descried on either side from the middle of the stream.

Rio de la Plata.

The principal rivers of the Asiatic division of the globe are, the Kian Ku, the Hoango, the Lena, the Amur, the Obi, the Jennisey, the Ganges, the Burrampooter, the Euphrates, and the Indus. The two first, the Kian Ku and the Hoango, have their origin towards the eastern extremity of the lofty ridge of mountains which bounds the north of Hindostan, in a district of Tartary called Kokondar, from two lakes about 200 miles asunder; and, after embracing, in

Asiatic rivers.

Kian Ku and Hoango.

---

* The American travellers, Clarke and Lewis, though unprovided with a hygrometer, state some facts which leave no doubt respecting the extreme dryness which prevails in the Steppes of Louisiana. They inform us that their sextants warped and shrunk in the joints; and that a table spoonful of water was dissipated in a few hours by evaporation. Clarke's *Voyage up the Missouri*, i. 300, 302, 322.

their course, a large portion of the most fertile provinces of China, fall into the Yellow sea at a distance from each other, nearly equal to that which separates their sources. The lengths of these majestic streams differ but little from each other, and are only exceeded by those of the Amazon and Mississippi; the course of the Kian Ku being reckoned 2150 miles, and that of the Hoango 2200. At the points where they are most widely disjoined they are upwards of 1000 miles distant from each other. These rivers are more remarkable for their velocity, which, in some places, approaches to eight miles an hour, than for the body of water which they discharge. The Kian Ku, at the distance of seventy miles from the sea, is about a mile in breadth, with a depth of nine or ten feet. Staunton's *Embassy to China*, iii. 234.

The Lena, Obi, and Jennisey.   The Lena, the Obi, and the Jennisey, have their sources at no great distance from one another, in the elevated chain of mountains which bound the Chinese empire on the north; and all of them, pursuing a northerly course, discharge their waters into the Atlantic ocean, by mouths separated widely from one another; the estuary of the Lena being nearly 2000 miles from that of the Obi. The course of the Lena is reckoned 1600 miles, that of the Obi, 1900, and that of the Jennisey, 1800. The Amur, a kindred river, rises near the Yabloni mountains, and, having collected, in its widely-expanded basin, the greater part of the waters of eastern Asia, falls into the sea of Ochotsk, after a course of about 1850 miles.

Ganges.   The Ganges, though inferior to several of the Asiatic rivers in point of magnitude, is, in many respects, the most interesting of them all. See the article GANGES, where it is fully described. The Indus and Burrampooter have also been described in our article INDIA, Vol. XII. p. 61, 62. See also Elphinstone's *Caubul*, iii. 652; and *Edin. Phil. Journ.* vol. iii. p. 37.

The Euphrates, the principal river of Asiatic Turkey, rises in the mountains of Armenia, a few miles from Erzeroon. Its course is at first towards the south-west, as if it were to proceed to the Mediterranean; but, after running in that direction for about 350 miles, it is diverted from it by a range of mountains which force it towards the south. On reaching the borders of the Syrian desert, it assumes a more easterly line, and at last enters the Persian Gulf, after a course of about 1400 miles. The Tigris, its largest tributary branch, joins it about 100 miles above its principal outlet. In the days of Herodotus, both these rivers seem to have discharged themselves by separate courses into the Red Sea.—Herodotus, *Clio*, 180, 189.

African rivers. Niger.   The African rivers are very imperfectly known to geographers. The Niger, about which so many disputes have arisen, is conjectured by some to be the western branch of the Nile; while, by others, it is supposed, with more appearance of probability, to be the main stream of the Congo, or Zaira. A third hypothesis, not less plausible than either of the two preceding, is, that this mysterious river either falls into a great inland lake, or loses itself amidst the bibulous sands of the African deserts. The small elevation of its source renders it extremely improbable that its course is very extensive; and seems to preclude the possibility of its joining either the Nile or the Congo. Of the latter river, any information we possess is so very scanty, that we can scarcely form a rational conjecture respecting the place of its origin, farther, than that its periodical floods seem to imply, that it takes its rise on the north side of the equator. All that we know with certainty concerning it is, that it is an immense river which discharges itself into the Atlantic

Congo.

ocean, in the lat. of 6° 10′ south, with a stream so powerful, that it may sometimes be traced to the distance of 200 miles from the shore. According to the account of Mr. Maxwell, this river, 150 miles from its mouth, is a mile and a half wide, having from thirty feet deep of water, from the very edge, to 300 feet about the middle of the stream; where its velocity is five or six miles per hour. The Senegal, according to Park, rises in the mountains of Jallonkadoo, in lat. 11° 10′ north, long. 7° 34′ west, at a very small distance from the source of the Niger, where it bears the name of Kokoro. Its course at first is towards the north-west; in this direction it proceeds till it reaches the lat. of 16° north, and the long. of 12° east, after which it bends more towards the west; and, having been joined in its progress by a few inconsiderable streams it empties itself into the Atlantic at the isle of St. Louis.

Senegal.

The Nile has been fully described in our articles ABYSSINIA, Vol. I. p. 40, and EGYPT, Vol. VIII. p. 393.

Nile.

The European rivers are greatly inferior in magnitude to the rivers which drain the other great divisions of the globe; but, winding through the regions where the effects of human industry and civilization have, in all ages, been conspicuously developed, their importance is not to be estimated entirely by the length of their courses, or the abundance of their waters. The principal rivers of Europe are, the Volga, the Danube, the Dneiper, and the Don, on the east; the Rhone, and the Ebro, on the south; the Vistula, the Oder, the Elbe, the Rhine, the Loire, the Tagus, and the Douro, on the west; and the Dvina and Pachora on the north. We shall notice, in this general sketch, only the most remarkable of these rivers.

European rivers.

The Volga, by far the most majestic of European streams, is distinguished from all the great rivers of both continents, by discharging itself, not into the ocean, but into an extensive inland sea. The river takes its rise from several lakes in the mountains of Valday, between the ancient and the modern capitals of the Russian empire. From these lakes it proceeds in an easterly direction, inclining a little southward till it reaches the Kama, a large tributary stream proceeding from the Uralian mountains, when it advances more towards the south, and, after a winding course of about 1700 miles, falls into the Caspian Sea, at Astracan. The fall of the Volga from Ostachkow to Astracan, has been recently determined by Dr. Pansner, to be 957.97 French feet. *Edin. Phil. Journ.* vol. iii. 408. This extensive stream, running through a flat alluvial country, which in some places has undoubtedly a lower level than the surface of the ocean, has no cataracts, and so few shoals, that it is navigable as far as Twer, being about 1000 miles from its mouth. It is affirmed, though we know not upon what authority, that the waters of the Volga have been sensibly diminished since the commencement of the eighteenth century. Pinkerton's *Geog.* i. 321. The Don, and Dneiper, kindred rivers to the Volga, receive the waters of the various streams which flow from the fertile and extensive plains lying to the north of the Black Sea. The former has a course of 800 miles, the latter of about 1000 miles.

Volga.

Don. Dneiper.

The Alps, the highest land on the western side of the old continent, give birth to three of the most distinguished rivers in Europe, the Danube, the Rhine, and the Rhone. The first of these rivers flows towards the east, collecting in its progress the various streams which descend from the Carpathian ridge, on the one hand, and the mountains of Illyria and Rumelia, on the other. After watering Suabia, Bavaria, Austria Proper, Hungary, and part of Turkey, it enters the

Danube.

Physical
Geography.

Black Sea, by several mouths. Its course is computed to be about 1300 miles. The Rhine proceeds in an opposite direction, and after flowing through some of the most fertile provinces of Europe, discharges itself by several channels into the German Sea. Its course is only about 600 miles. The Loire, the Tagus, and the Douro, drain the western parts of Europe ; as the Dvina and Pechora carry off its waters in the north.

Lakes.

We shall conclude the history of the aqueous parts of the globe with a brief description of lakes. These collections of water may be classed under two general heads : according as they are connected with, or entirely disjoined from, the ocean. Lakes of the former kind may be regarded as the expansions of rivers, in situations where their beds originally possessed a great depth ; and those of the latter kind, as small inland seas cut off from all communication with the ocean, on account of their want of water to flow over the elevated land by which they are surrounded.

Lakes through which rivers flow.

Lakes of the first kind are of very common occurrence, and indeed few rivers are without them. The rivers of North America, however, furnish the most remarkable examples of these enlargements of their beds, many of them flowing through lakes which, in magnitude, resemble seas, and yet retain all the purity and freshness of mountain streams. Lake Superior, the largest collection of fresh water in the world, is about 125 leagues long, and 50 broad, with a depth in many places of 300 fathoms ; and Lake Huron, which is connected with it, is nearly of equal dimensions. Besides these collections of fresh water, North America contains several other lakes of the same kind, which, though of inferior magnitude, are yet of great extent. Among these we may mention Lake Michigan, Lake Erie, Lake Ontario, Lake Champlain, the lake of Assiniboils, the Slave Lake, &c. In the old continent, lakes of fresh water are less numerous than in America ; but not a few are to be found of considerable extent. Among the most remarkable of these we may notice Lake Ladoga, and Lake Onega, in Russia, and the lakes of Geneva and Constance in Switzerland. Several extensive fresh water lakes are also found in China, and various parts of the north of Asia.

Lake Superior the largest fresh water lake in the world.

Lakes which have no communication with the ocean.

Lakes which have no communication with the ocean are less numerous than fresh water lakes, but generally exceed the latter in point of extent. The largest lake in the world, of this description, is the Caspian sea ; which extends from south to north about 300 leagues, with a mean breadth of fifty leagues. This lake receives, as we already noticed, the Volga, besides several other rivers of considerable extent. It is no longer a matter of doubt that the surface of this inland sea is nearly 200 feet below the medium level of the ocean.— *Edin. Phil. Jour.* vol. iii. p. 409. Hence the waters carried into the Caspian must disappear by evaporation. Lake Aral, which is situated in the same sandy region with the Caspian Sea, possesses a similar character, receiving the Gihon, and some other rivers of inferior note, without having any apparent communication with the ocean. The geological constitution of the soil seems to indicate, that, notwithstanding the difference of level in these waters, the Euxine Sea, the Caspian, and Lake Aral, communicated with each other, at a period beyond the times of authentic history. See the article BLACK SEA, Vol. III. p. 553.

Caspian Sea.

Lowness of its level.

Probable communication of the Caspian Sea and Lake Aral with the Euxine.

America contains a few lakes of a similar character, but situated on a higher level. The lakes of Mexico, and of the valley of Aragua, are supplied by various streams, without having any outlet to the ocean.

Lakes having no communication with the sea.

Lakes which have no communication with the sea, are uniformly impregnated with some kind of saline mat-

ter. The lakes of Mexico are found to hold in solution the muriates and carbonates of soda. The same salts exist in the waters of the Caspian Sea and Lake Aral, as well as in the Natron lakes of Hungary.—Humboldt's *New Spain,* ii. 36. *Edin. Phil. Jour.* vol. vi. p. 260.

Physical Geography.

Lakes, in general, but especially such as have no outlet for the waters which flow into them, must gradually become less deep, by the alluvions they receive. The process may be slow, but it is never retrograde. Besides the instance of the Palus Mareotis, record furnishes several examples of the filling up of lakes by depositions. The Tigris and Euphrates, in the time of Nearchus, formed an extensive lake near the sea. That lake is no longer to be found. The upper part of the *Paludis,* into which the Pallacopa led, below Babylon, now forms a plain, although it retains its former name of *Bahr Nedjuff ;* that is, the sea or lake of Nedjuff. It has also been remarked, that the site of the Lake Mareotis still bears the name of Baheira, or the Lake.—Rennell's *Herodotus,* pp. 69. 542. Humboldt's *New Spain,* ii. 115.

Disappearance of lakes by the filling up of their beds.

The level of the waters of lakes is considerably affected by winds, as well as by fluctuations in their supplies. When the east wind blows with any violence, the water of the Lake Tezcuco, on which the city of Mexico stands, withdraws towards the western bank of the lake, and leaves an extent of more than 600 metres (1968 feet) dry. (Humboldt's *New Spain,* vol. ii. p. 35.) The Lake of Geneva is affected in a similar manner. The waters of lake Ontario are subject to periodical elevations, to the extent of seven or eight feet perpendicular, which are, perhaps, partly owing to the same cause. (Howison's *Upper Canada,* p. 50.) Mr. Dalton informs us, that the surface of Derwent Lake is sometimes agitated, when no wind can be perceived, in so violently a manner that it exhibits large waves with white breakers. The phenomenon is denominated a bottom wind, but the cause of it is utterly unknown. (Dalton's *Meteor. Essays,* p. 52.) Lake Wetter, in Sweden, is occasionally affected in a similar manner. (Malte-Brun, *Geog.* i. 311. *Phil. Trans.* No. 298, p. 1938.)

Changes in the level of the waters of lakes.

Some lakes are subject to periodical changes in their condition, which seem to imply the existence of vast subterraneous excavations below their beds, which act upon their waters in the manner of reciprocating fountains, swallowing them up at one time, and forcibly rejecting them at another. One of the most remarkable lakes of this description is the lake of Circhnitz, in Carniola, already described under that article, Vol. VI. p. 519. We know not how far the explanation given in that article is satisfactory ; but the existence of the subterraneous cavity, into which the waters retire, seems to be proved by the fact, that fishes and aquatic birds, which descend with the water, are afterwards ejected alive. Some of the ducks, thus cast out with the water, are supposed by Dr. Brown to be hatched under the mountain Javornick, as, when they make their appearance, though they can swim well, they are quite blind, and without feathers. *Phil. Trans.* No. 53, p. 1083.

Disappearance and reappearance of lakes.

We cannot dismiss the subject of lakes, without taking notice of the floating islands which, in some cases, are to be found on their surface. In the Mexican lakes these singular islands are called *Chinampos,* and are of an artificial nature. " The ingenious invention of chinampos," says Humboldt, " appears to go back to the end of the 14th century. It had its origin in the extraordinary situation of a people surrounded with enemies, and compelled to live in the midst of a lake little abounding with fish, who were forced to fall upon every means of procuring subsistence. It is even probable, that nature itself suggested to the Aztecs the first idea of floating gardens. On the

Floating islands in lakes.

Physical Geography. marshy banks of the lakes of Xochimilco and Chalco, the agitated water in the time of the great rises carries away pieces of earth covered with herbs, and bound together by roots. These, floating about a long time as they are driven by the wind, sometimes unite into small islands. A tribe of men, too weak to defend themselves on the continent, would take advantage of those portions of ground which accident put within their reach, and of which no enemy disputed the property. The oldest chinampos were merely bits of ground joined together artificially, and dug and sown upon by the Aztecs. These floating islands are to be met with in all the zones. I have seen them in the kingdom of Quito, on the river Guayaquil, of 8 or 9 metres (26 or 29 feet) in length, floating in the midst of the current, and bearing young shoots of bambusa, Pistia stratiotes, pontederia, and a number of other vegetables, of which the roots are easily interlaced. I have found also in Italy, in the small *lago de aqua solfo,* of Tivoli, near the hot baths of Agrippa, small islands formed of sulphur, carbonate of lime, and the leaves of the *ulva thermalis,* which change their place with the smallest breath of wind." *New Spain,* ii. 97.

Some floating islands appear and disappear periodically. The Lake of Ralang, in Smaland, a province of Sweden, contains a floating island, which, from the year 1696 to 1766, appeared ten times, commonly in the autumn. A similar floating island is said to exist in Ostrogothland. Malte-Brun, *Geog.* p. 311.

One important purpose which is served by lakes, is to equalize the distribution of the waters which are conveyed by rivers, and to counteract the destructive consequences of their inundations. Thus, the Rhine falls into the Bodensea, the Rhone into the Lake of Geneva, the Reus into the Lake of Lucerne, the Adda and Macra into the Lake of Como, the Lent into the Lake of Zurich, the Aar into the Lakes of Brientz and Thun: And, in general, it will be found, that the more considerable the rivers are, and the more impetuous their streams, so much the larger are these receptacles of water in which they are to lose their force and rapidity. For an account of the Lake Iberi, formed by infiltration, see BUENOS AYRES, Vol. V. p. 49.

PHY

Physiognomy.

Definition.

PHYSIOGNOMY, derived from φυσις, nature, and γινωσκω, to know, is that science which teaches to judge of the temper, dispositions, habits, and intellectual endowments, by the conformation of the body, but particularly by the lineaments and expressions of the countenance. This is the precise sense in which the term was originally used, and is now understood; but, for some time in the middle ages, it was applied in a more extensive signification, and denoted that knowledge of the internal properties of *any* material substance, which could be obtained from the external appearances which they severally exhibited.

History.

This science, whether we regard the principles on which it is founded as fanciful or otherwise, has, we must allow, occupied, from a very early period, the attention of the learned, and has formed the subject of many an elaborate production. Its warmest supporters assert that it was cultivated in Egypt and India; that a knowledge of it was introduced into Greece by Pythagoras; and that, in the time of Socrates, it had been elevated to the dignity of a distinct *profession.* These opinions are not unsupported by evidence; but it is certain, at least, that physiognomy engaged much of the attention of Aristotle, who lived scarcely a century posterior to Socrates, and whose ingenious theory on this subject is known to all scholars; and that, after his time, it was zealously studied by Theophrastus, Polemon, and other Greek philosophers. Physiognomy was also regarded as an important branch of erudition by the Romans, but it shared the fate of other sciences on the overthrow of that ingenious people, and continued neglected or unknown till the revival of learning in the beginning of the sixteenth century. From this period it has, on the continent in particular, been most assiduously cultivated, though it was considered very much in conjunction with the *occult* sciences; and it can exhibit in the list of its supporters many illustrious names, such as Baptista Porta, Cardan, Spontanus, &c. Nor was it entirely overlooked in this country; for Dr. Guyther, Dr. Parsons, and others, have given it the sanction of their authority, and have promoted it by their learning. But whatever degree of importance had been previously attached to this science, and how numerous and ingenious soever its advocates had been, it may yet be regarded as in its infancy, till the appearance, in 1775, of the celebrat-

PHY

Physiognomy.

Lavater.

ed publication of M. Lavater of Zurich—a work which forms an era in the history of physiognomical science. Lavater had, from his earliest years, been in the habit, not only of observing with extreme attention the endless variety and expression of the human countenance, but of taking drawings of such as appeared peculiar and striking. He at length discovered, or thought he discovered, a correspondent relation between the form and lineaments of the body, particularly of the face, or rather of the nose and forehead, and the qualities of the mind; and that, not only the transient passions, but the permanent principles of action might, in this way, be clearly ascertained. He thus became a firm believer in physiognomy, and felt convinced that the data on which it was founded were so invariable and demonstrable, that it was fully entitled to be considered as a *science.* His work, written under this impression, was read with uncommon avidity. It is, indeed, more fanciful and lively than solid and scientific; yet, it displays so intimate a knowledge of the human heart, so much discrimination, so much delicate feeling, and its illustrations are so happy and so striking, that it gained proselytes wherever it was read, and physiognomy soon formed the fashionable study of Europe. This effect, however, was far from being permanent; and Lavater had the mortification, before his death in 1801, of seeing his favourite opinions, and the work in which they were so beautifully illustrated, notwithstanding the labours of Hunter, Holcroft, and others, fast verging into neglect or forgetfulness.

That the system, however, which this celebrated writer endeavoured to establish, is totally fanciful or absurd, no man will venture to declare. On the contrary, there is none who, in his intercourse with the world, does not *practise* it in a greater or less degree. But our estimate of the character of a stranger, from his physiognomical indications, we often find to be the very reverse of the truth.

Lavater's first publication on the subject of physiognomy was a small pamphlet in 1772. The first volume of his great work appeared three years afterwards, under the name of Fragments, and was soon followed by three other volumes, which completed the work. To this celebrated publication the reader is referred, and to the Article LAVATER in this work. (&)

PHYSIOLOGY.

CHAPTER I.

INTRODUCTORY OBSERVATIONS.

Physiology. Definition. PHYSIOLOGY, according to the modern use of the term, may be defined, the science which treats of the functions of the living animal body, and of the powers upon which these functions depend.

Remarks on the history. Although it is impossible to enter into any speculations, either medical or pathological, without pre-supposing a certain acquaintance with the operations of the body in its healthy and natural state, yet the contrary plan has been pursued in the medical sciences. Until about the middle of the last century, we had no writers who made physiology an exclusive, or even a direct object of their attention; so that we are to collect our information, respecting the hypotheses or opinions that were entertained before that time, from the incidental notices or observations that occur in works written professedly either on pathology or on the practice of medicine. As we have given a sketch of the authors of this description in the history of MEDICINE, we shall refer to this article for an account of the physiological opinions and hypotheses of the earlier writers; and shall, in this place, only offer a few remarks upon the progress of the science from the period when it was brought before our notice, as a distinct department of natural philosophy, by Haller.

Haller. This celebrated individual is, in every point of view, entitled to be considered as the father of modern physiology, whether we regard the unremitting assiduity with which he cultivated the science, or the actual advancement which he effected. Every circumstance, both of talent, character, and situation, conspired to promote his great object; in learning, in industry, in discrimination, and in candour, he has seldom been excelled; he devoted a large portion of his life to the cultivation of physiology, while his rank and fortune gave every facility to his exertions. What, however, more especially entitles him to the highest commendation, is the method which he introduced and established, of investigating the phenomena of the living body solely by observation and experiment, and keeping hypothesis entirely in subjection to these two leading principles. So powerful an effect have his influence and example produced, that, since his time, the science has assumed altogether a different aspect; and, from the publication of his " Elements," we may date the commencement of a new era in physiology.

Cullen. This great monument of learning and industry was still in progress, when Cullen entered upon his career; a man of a very different, and, in some respects, of an almost opposite turn of mind, yet one who was eminently useful in this department of knowledge. He excelled in general views rather than in minute researches; and, without adding many new facts to our previous stock of information, he arranged, into a very beautiful and interesting system, those of which we were already in possession. Few persons have contributed more than Cullen to sweep away the useless rubbish of antiquity; and there is a spirit of philosophical scepticism that pervades his writings, which, very for-

tunately, coincided with the inquiring genius of the Physiology. age in which he lived.

Hunter. Among the authors who have been most successful in the cultivation of this branch of science, we are necessarily led to class John Hunter. He possessed a remarkable share of boldness and originality of conception; and, in addition to these qualities, he manifested the most patient industry in the examination of nature under all her forms, and under every aspect in which she presents herself to our notice. He professed to proceed entirely upon the result of experiment and observation; but, in this respect, he exhibited an example of self-deception which is by no means rare, for his writings are, in fact, full of hypothesis, and abound with theories expressed or implied. He has unhappily introduced into physiology a kind of metaphysical language, which has certainly tended to impede the progress of science, by substituting new expressions for new ideas, thus leading us to suppose that we had made an addition to our knowledge, when, in fact, we were merely employing new forms of speech. Upon the whole, however, since the time of Haller, there is, perhaps, no one to whom the science is more indebted than to Hunter for important facts; and upon these his fame will be amply supported when his speculations are forgotten. In all his physiological hypotheses, Hunter makes perpetual reference to the existence and energy of what he calls the vital principle. It is not easy, on many occasions, to determine how far his expressions are to be received in a literal, or how far in a metaphorical sense, but many of them strongly resemble the Stahlian doctrine, of an intelligent principle, connected with the body, directing its motions, and preserving it from injury or destruction. In his explanation of the functions and operations of the living animal, he not unfrequently confounds physical with final causes, and attributes to the specific effects of life, actions that ought to be referred to the powers belonging to inanimate matter.

Bichat. Among the modern physiologists there is no one who has more just claim to our attention than Bichat, whether we regard him as an observer of facts or as an improver of theory. In the course of a short life he acquired a very accurate and extensive knowledge of anatomy, and made many discoveries in this department of science, which seemed to have been so entirely pre-occupied by his predecessors. In his views of the animal economy he proceeded upon the principles of correct philosophy; he regarded the vital functions as of a description essentially different from any other natural phenomena, and diligently applied himself to obtain an accurate knowledge of them, to observe their relation to each other, and to arrange them accordingly. His classification will, probably, in many of its parts, appear too refined, and his speculations to savour too much of metaphysical subtilty, but we must still consider him as possessing an unusual share of genius and acuteness, and as, perhaps, having added more to the actual stock of physiological knowledge than any of his contemporaries.

Appropriate powers of the living body. In order to obtain an insight into the true principles of physiology, we must begin by inquiring, what are the appropriate and specific powers which distinguish the living animal from all other beings; these we shall find to be two—spontaneous motion and sensation. Wherever spontaneous motion and sensation are found, we do not hesitate to regard them as connected with the living body; and we can have no idea of animal existence which does not possess one or other of these powers. These two specific properties of animal life are conceived to depend upon two principles inherent in the body, contractility, or the power of muscular contraction, and sensibility, or the power of nervous sensation; the former, the origin of motion, the latter of feeling. Haller had the merit of clearly ascertaining the nature of these two powers, and of pointing out their differences; and to him we are indebted for the development of the important fact, that they are distinguished as well by their seat as by their mode of action; contractility being exclusively confined to the muscular fibre, and sensibility residing only in the nervous matter. To the action of the one or other of these principles every change that is effected in the animal system must be referred, and it is through their immediate operation that all the functions are performed. Although, perhaps, in every case they both conduce to this end, yet, as we generally perceive one to be more essential than the other, the subjects of physiology may be divided into two classes, according as they primarily depend upon the contractility of the muscular fibre, or the sensibility of the nervous matter. To this division we propose to adhere in the following article; and we shall begin with those functions which are more immediately dependent upon contractility. The functions which fall under this description are, the circulation of the blood, respiration, animal temperature, secretion, digestion, absorption, and generation.

Plan of the article.

Contractile functions.

But before we enter upon a description of the individual functions, it will be proper to give a more particular account of the nature of contractility and sensibility, and of their appropriate organs—the muscles and the nerves. For the full understanding of the subject it will be necessary to begin by a description of membrane and bone, because these substances are essential ingredients of the basis of the body, and serve, as it were, for the ground-work of every other part. With respect to contractility in particular, they are so connected with the muscular fibre, and contribute so directly to muscular action, that, without being previously acquainted with them, it would be impossible to comprehend the functions of the muscles, or the effect of their contractions.

Sensitive functions.

After going, in succession, through the different contractile functions, we shall proceed to the other great division of the science—the functions which are more immediately connected with the nervous power. The connexion between the mental and corporeal parts of our frame is so intimate, that it will be impossible to acquire a complete knowledge of the one without paying some attention to the other; and, therefore, although we shall be anxious to encroach, as little as possible, upon the province of the metaphysician, we shall feel it necessary to take a brief view of some of the intellectual operations, as well as of those that depend upon different modifications of the power of sensation. We shall conclude by some observations upon the natural progress which the living system manifests to a state of dissolution, by which its component parts necessarily fall into decay, and its functions become impaired and finally destroyed.

CHAPTER II.

Of Membrane.

Organization defined.

BEFORE we proceed to give an account of any of the individual parts of the body, it will be proper to explain the term organization, as it is of frequent occurrence in physiology, and one, with the import of which, it is proper for us to be acquainted. In its most extensive acceptation, it may be regarded as nearly synonimous with the word arrangement, signifying that the parts of the organized body are placed according to some specific structure which is visible to the eye. Thus the serum of the blood, when coagulated and dried, in its chemical and mechanical properties almost entirely agrees with membranous matter, yet its texture is obviously different. The serum is not organized; it has a perfectly homogeneous fabric, is cut or broken with equal facility in every direction, whereas, in a tendon which is organized, there is a regular distribution of the particles in a specific form, and according to a determinate arrangement.

The word organization is used by physiologists in a more restricted, but, at the same time, in a more correct sense, when it is applied to a system composed of a number of individual parts, possessing each of them appropriate powers and functions, but all conducive to the existence and preservation of the whole. An animal body is thus said to be organized, or to consist of a number of organs or instruments. A vegetable, in like manner, is an organized being, composed of separate parts, as the root, the sap vessels, and the leaves; each of them constituting a separate organ or instrument for performing some appropriate action, yet all composing one connected system. It is this species of organization which properly distinguishes living from dead matter; and, where we are able to ascertain its existence, it may be regarded as a sufficient characteristic of the presence of life.

Membrane defined.

Under the term membrane, we propose to include, not merely those parts to which this name has been usually applied, but all those substances, whatever be their form, which possess a similar mechanical structure, and the same chemical properties. They nearly coincide with the *white parts* of the older anatomists, and with the cellular texture of Haller; but the former of these terms is obviously too vague, and we conceive the latter to be objectionable, as implicating a theoretical opinion respecting their nature, which is at least doubtful, if not incorrect.

Its extent.

According to this method of employing the term, we shall find the membranous matter to be the most simple in its properties, of any of the organized parts of the body, while, at the same time, it is the most extensively diffused, and exists in the greatest proportion. The coverings, not only of the whole body at large, but of each of its individual parts, both internal and external, are principally composed of membrane, and it lines all the cavities in which the different organs are situated. It constitutes the main bulk of the bones, and determines their figure, the earthy matter upon which their strength and hardness depend, being deposited in a tissue of membranous cells. Membrane also enters into the structure of the muscles, not only affording them an external sheath, in which they are each of them enclosed, but the same matter is also interspersed between their fibres, separating them into bundles, to which it, in like manner, affords a distinct covering, and these into still smaller bundles, until it appears at length to envelop each individual fibre. The membranous matter composes very nearly the whole substance of the tendons, by which the muscles are attached to the bones; the ligaments, by which the bones and solid parts are connected to each other, and the cartilages, which form the basis of many parts of the body, and supply the place of bone, and which also cover the ends of the bones, and assist in the formation of the joints. It enters very largely into the composition of horns, hair, feathers, nails, and other similar substances. It likewise composes what is called the cellular texture, a series of cells or interstices, which have been compared to those of a sponge, which extends over a great part of the body, fills up its intervals, and serves to unite the different parts to each other. The membranous matter chiefly forms the glands, and the viscera of all kinds; the brain is also enveloped in a covering of membrane, and it is probable that the matter of which the nerves are composed is deposited in a series of membranous cells. The pouches or bags, which are found in different parts of the body, such as the stomach and the bladder, are almost entirely composed of membrane; and what perhaps must be regarded as the most important of all the purposes which it serves, membrane composes the principal part of the tubes or vessels of various kinds, with which the animal body is so plentifully furnished.

From this account of the extent and distribution of membrane, it will be found that it exceeds in quantity all the other solids of the body taken together, and enters as a principal ingredient into almost every portion of the animal frame. It serves indeed as a connecting medium between all the different organs by which they are held together, the basis to which they are all attached, and the mould into which the particles of the other kinds of matter are deposited.

Structure of membrane. The mechanical structure of membrane is a subject which has exercised the ingenuity of many of the modern anatomists, and has also formed a conspicuous feature in some of the most celebrated pathological hypotheses. In tracing the history of opinions, it will be necessary to take some notice of the theory that was

Boerhaave's account. formed on this subject by Boerhaave; which, although in itself highly improbable, and scarcely supported by a single fact, or by any fair analogy, was at one period very generally embraced, and was even adopted as the basis of much pathological and physiological reasoning. He conceived that there was a kind of hypothetical fibre, almost infinitely minute, and that by the union of these fibres, a membrane is composed of the first order; and that this, when coiled up, forms a vessel of the first order. These vessels, by being placed in contact, form a membrane of the second order, and these again are coiled up into a vessel of the second order; and, by a repetition of this process, we obtain vessels and membranes of any assignable magnitude. It follows, as the direct consequence of this hypothesis, that, except the earth of the bones, no part of the body is properly solid, besides the coats of the vessels, and that all the parts which appear to be solid, are in fact nothing more than a congeries of vessels, arranged in these regularly ascending series. Although this doctrine was directly in contradiction, both to the results of anatomical injections, and of observations made by the microscope, and, in fact, may be considered as resting solely upon the credit of its inventor, yet so powerful was the authority of Boerhaave, in every point con-

nected with medical science, that it required all the Physiology. force of Haller's reasoning, as well as that of his most acute contemporaries, to controvert the doctrine.

The opinion which Haller endeavoured to substitute Haller's. for that of Boerhaave was, that the membranous matter is composed of a vast assemblage of infinitely minute lines or fibres, connected together by either lines or plates, according to the structure of the parts to which they belong. He was at much pains to exhibit this fibrous structure in all parts of the body, and to trace their connexion with each other, by means of what he calls the cellular web, which he conceived to form the mechanical basis that unites all the various parts into one whole.

This doctrine of Haller is no doubt much more correct than that of his preceptor, but still it must be regarded as, in some measure, hypothetical, and as partaking of that metaphysical spirit, which is not yet entirely banished from our physiological reasoning. He speaks of the original or fundamental fibre as being inorganic, and seems to consider it necessary that we should possess a certain number of these inorganic fibres, before we arrive at one which is entitled to be considered as properly organized matter. He also supposed that, in the formation of the larger parts from these ultimate fibres, there are intervening spaces, which are filled up with an inorganic concretion, a doctrine which we apprehend to be quite inconsistent with any correct conception of the nature of the living body. The fibre itself may be conceived not to be vascular, but still we must suppose that there is no part which is not within the action of some of the vital organs, and is not therefore properly alive; although with respect to the degree, and even the nature of their vitality, the different parts may be essentially different.

With respect to the actual appearance which the Fontana's. membranous matter presents to the eye, when assisted by the microscope, we learn from the observations of Fontana, that it consists of a number of flattened plates, which he calls primitive fasciæ, and which are connected together by a cellular web of a more lax texture. These fasciæ, when macerated, or divided as much as possible by mechanical means, are found to be made up of cylinders in the form of solid threads, of a spiral or waved form, which are neither hollow nor vascular, and which appear to be of the same kind in all parts of the body. These tendinous threads are said to be about the 13,000th of an inch in diameter. Ample experience has proved, that all microscopical observations are to be received with great caution; but the account of Fontana is given with so much candour, and appears in itself so reasonable, that we are disposed to place some confidence in it.

The physical properties which more especially belong Physical properties of membrane. to membrane, are, cohesion, flexibility, extensibility, and elasticity. By its strong cohesive power, it is well Cohesion. fitted to strengthen and support the different organs of the body, and to render their union firm and durable, to serve as a complete covering for them; and, in short, to perform all those offices where much strength is requisite. Its flexible nature peculiarly adapts it for Flexibility. the structure of those parts where much motion is exercised, as about the joints and muscles, in the large blood vessels, and in the cellular substance. Besides affording a capacity for motion in general, the flexibility of the membranous matter enables the different parts to yield to external violence, and thus to sustain much less injury than if they had possessed a more rigid texture. The advantages which we derive from

Extensi-
bility.

the flexible nature of membrane; are intimately connected with its extensibility. This property is essential to the structure of a system, which is principally composed of soft parts, perpetually in motion, and constantly altering their form and bulk, where some are contracted, while others are necessarily stretched beyond their ordinary size, and which are all surrounded and held together by membranes. This quality is peculiarly important in the different organs which are destined for the reception of fluids, whether in the form of pouches or of tubes; the quantity of fluid which they contain is perpetually varying; and, according to their present constitution, the size of the recipient is always exactly fitted to the bulk of the contents. No

Elasticity.

less important to the animal system is the elasticity of the membranous matter. As we advance in our knowledge of the subject, we shall be better able to estimate the importance of this property; at present it will be sufficient to remark, that it serves an important purpose in the action of the organs of circulation and of respiration, that it frequently co-operates with the muscles in the motions of the joints, and that it is employed to restore the situation of parts which had been previously removed by muscular contraction from their natural position.

Vital properties of membrane.

Besides the above properties which membrane possesses in common with various kinds of matter, it has been thought by some physiologists, especially those of the French school, to exhibit qualities which are more properly of a vital nature, or such as belong only to bodies that form part of the living animal system. Bichat conceives that membrane is contractile, and adduces some facts in support of his opinion *; but, we

Membranes not contractile.

apprehend, that when they are duly considered, they will be found to be all referable to elasticity. Blumenbach, to whom the science of physiology is so much indebted, also ascribes to membrane a specific power, which he terms the vis cellulosa, which consists in the reaction of a membrane that has been distended, when the stretching force is withdrawn †; but all cases of this kind, when carefully examined, may, we conceive, be referred, like those adduced by Bichat, to the effect of elasticity.

Not sensible.

The sensibility of membrane is a point respecting which very various opinions have been entertained by physiologists, and especially by those of the last century, when it became the subject of a warm controversy between Haller and his pupils on one hand, and Whytt, in conjunction with his countrymen, on the other. Haller instituted a variety of experiments on living animals, from which he deduced the conclusion, that mere membrane is altogether without sensation, as he was unable to excite any appearance of it, by applying the most powerful stimuli, either chemical or mechanical. Whytt, in opposition to the experiments of Haller, brought forward a number of well known facts, connected with the diseased condition of these parts, where, by being inflamed, they produce the most acute pain. Upon the whole, the opinion of Haller is to be regarded as the one that is literally correct, because it is generally admitted that sensation is confined to the nervous matter; and it is known that membrane is very sparingly furnished with nerves, and must therefore have a corresponding degree of insensibility. To what cause we are to ascribe the extreme pain which attends certain morbid conditions of tendons and other similar

structures, is a question to which, at present, we are, perhaps, not able to give a satisfactory answer.

Errors of the ancients.

It is probable that the erroneous opinions of the modern anatomists, at least of those who lived shortly after the revival of letters, were, in a considerable degree, produced by the mistaken notions of the ancients respecting the nature of membranes, and the relation of this substance to the nerves. They had generally but a very imperfect acquaintance with the nervous system, and were in the habit of confounding tendons with nerves; and hence it was laid down as a principle, that the tendons are among the most sensible organs of the body. Long after the distinction between these parts was clearly ascertained, the influence of the old doctrine was felt, not only in our physiological speculations, but even in the details of surgical practice, and gave rise to operations which were extremely painful and dangerous, and which were employed for the purpose of avoiding the problematical evil of dividing a membrane.

Chemical composition of membrane.

So very imperfect was the knowledge of animal chemistry, even as late as the time of Haller and Cullen, that they supposed all the soft parts to consist of the same chemical substance, differing only in its mechanical arrangement.

Opinion of Haller.

Haller had an opinion, that membrane, being the least complicated part of the body, consisted principally of simple fibres, which served as a kind of basis to the whole system, and that the fibre itself was composed of earthy particles, cemented by gluten. The discoveries of the pneumatic chemists, and especially of the French, who have assiduously cultivated this branch of the science, proved that Haller's opinion is totally fallacious, and that earth is not an essential constituent of membrane. The hypothesis of the connecting gluten is equally gratuitous, and quite contrary to the more correct notions of modern chemistry. The particles of membrane, as well as those which compose any other solid, are held together by their affinity for each other, not by any connecting medium. Membrane, indeed, acts mechanically in uniting the different parts of the body to each other, and in maintaining the proper form of the substances, which are of so delicate a consistence as not to afford a sufficient degree of adhesion between their particles to keep them in a compact state. The soft pulp of the nerves, for example, and the adipose matter seem to be retained in their present form, merely by the membrane in which they are imbedded; but this is altogether independent of the consistence of the membrane itself.

Of Fourcroy.

The ideas of the French chemists, and more particularly of Fourcroy, although much more accurate than those of Haller and his contemporaries, do not, however, appear to be perfectly correct. Finding that a large quantity of jelly could be extracted by boiling from many membranous bodies, he was disposed to regard membrane as essentially composed of jelly, or at least as differing from it rather in its physical than its chemical properties.

Of Hatchett.

We are indebted to Mr. Hatchett for much valuable information on this subject; from his experiments we learn, that what may be regarded as the basis of membranous matter, is a substance which, in its chemical properties, resembles coagulated

Consists of albumen.

albumen, and which seems to differ from the pure albumen of the blood, or the white of an egg, solely in its mechanical structure. Albumen appears, therefore, to be the proper basis of membranous matter, that

* Traité des Membranes, p. 54; Anatomie, Gen. t. i. p. 80.   † Inst. Physiol. sect. 40, 59.

which gives it its general form, and determines its peculiar texture, yet it probably always contains a portion of jelly, and, in many cases, even in greater proportion than the albumen itself.

Jelly is very soluble in water, especially when heated; it is thus separated from the albumen, and by the evaporation of the water, may be obtained in a state of purity. The most characteristic property is that which has obtained the specific name of gelatinization, or jellying, where a solution of the substance in hot water concretes as it cools, and is again dissolved by increasing the temperature, without undergoing any farther change. Another peculiarity of jelly is the change which it experiences by putrefaction; instead of acquiring the highly fœtid odour of most animal substances, and generating ammonia, it becomes acid. The nature of the acid thus produced has not been accurately ascertained, but it is supposed to be the acetic.

Mucus, or mucilage, appears likewise to enter into the composition of membranes, or at least to be always attached to it. This substance, like jelly, is soluble in water; yet it does not possess the property of gelatinizing, and differs from jelly in many of its chemical relations. It is, however, a substance of rather an indefinite nature, at least the term mucus has been hitherto applied in an indefinite manner, and has been used rather as a popular than as a scientific, or a technical appellation.

A considerable proportion of membrane, as well as of all the other soft parts, consists of water, and it has been supposed by many eminent physiologists, that upon the relative quantity of the water and the solid matter depend many of the morbid changes of the body, as well as the varieties of the constitution and temperament of different individuals. These speculations formed a prominent part of the theories of Boerhaave, and his successor Gaubius; and, to a certain extent, were adopted by Cullen. It is obvious, that when membranous matter no longer forms a part of the living body, its properties are much affected by the quantity of water with which it is combined; and it is probable that this may be the case during life, with some of the external parts, and those that enjoy only a small portion of vitality, but it is very doubtful how far these principles will apply to the great bulk of the animal body, and affect its powers and functions, as it was conceived to do by the Boerhaavians.

With respect to the ultimate elements of membrane, we know indeed that it consists of carbon, hydrogen, oxygen, and azote, but we are not accurately acquainted with the mode of their combination, or with the proportion in which they exist. From its being less disposed to undergo the putrefactive fermentation than most of the other soft parts of the body, it has been supposed by the French chemists to contain less azote, but this opinion seems to be founded rather upon hypothesis, than deduced from any exact facts, and is not supported by the recent experiments of Berzelius, (*Med. Chir. Trans.* vol. i.) who was unable to detect any material difference between the chemical constitution of fibrin and albumen.

The greater fixedness of membrane must be immediately attributed to a stronger attraction between its particles, and this probably, in some measure, arises from its being more free from the admixture of heterogenous bodies, especially from its containing but a small proportion of either blood or fat, substances which seem always to have a strong tendency to decomposition. The circumstance of membranous matter generally containing less water than most of the solids of the body, may also be one cause why it is less disposed to become putrid. There are, indeed, some reasons for supposing that jelly contains less azote than other animal compounds; and, so far as jelly forms a constituent of membranous matter, the same remarks will apply to this substance. It is from this supposed constitution of jelly, that it is frequently said to be less completely animalized than most other of the constituents of the body, as the chemical composition of animal matter differs from that of vegetables principally in the latter containing little or no azote. In connexion with this substance, it is deserving of our attention, that if we examine the corresponding organs of animals of different ages, those of the young animals will be found to contain a greater proportion of jelly, and those of the older of albumen. It is on this account that the parts of young animals, such as the feet of the calf, are principally employed in the preparation of jelly as an article of food; and upon the same principle it is that soups prepared from veal differ so much from soups prepared from beef, in the great quantity of jelly contained in the former. We perceive, therefore, that the young animal, not only in its physical and mental powers, but even in its chemical constitution, is less completely possessed of its specific characteristics than when it has arrived at a more mature age, an observation which we shall find to be supported by many other facts, besides the one which has been stated above, respecting the membranous matter.

After this account of the properties of membranous matter in general, we shall proceed to make some observations upon the different species of it, reserving, however, for their appropriate places, descriptions of those parts that derive their distinguishing character from some other substance superadded to the membrane, such as muscle and bone, or those that, in consequence of their peculiar organization, serve for the performance of some specific function, as the blood vessels and glands.

All animals, except those of the simplest structure, possess an outward covering, which connects their parts together, protects them from injury, and prevents the too powerful impression of the various external agents to which the body is exposed. In the human species, and those of the most perfect organization, it is called the cutis, or skin. It has been divided by anatomists into three layers, or rather into three distinct organs, which possess peculiar and distinct functions. These are, the epidermis, the rete mucosum, and the cutis. The epidermis, or cuticle, is the external part; it is thin, and semi-transparent; it seems to possess no sensation, and is not furnished with blood vessels that are visible to the eye. It is frequently destroyed, and is easily re-produced, without causing any material derangement in the functions of the subjacent parts.

As the cutaneous perspiration is supposed to issue from the whole of the surface of the body, it has been inferred that the cuticle must be furnished with pores for its transmission, yet we have no satisfactory evidence of these pores having been ever actually detected. We have indeed little knowledge respecting the minute structure of the epidermis; and it would appear, from the best observations which we possess, that it consists merely in a thin expansion, in which no specific texture can be perceived. Most of the older anatomists, and even Haller and Bichat among the moderns, were induced to regard it simply as a crust or film, spread over the

Marginal notes:
Physiology.
jelly,
and mucus.
Membrane contains water.
Ultimate elements.
Physiology.
Various species of membrane.
Skin;
epidermis,
Cutaneous perspiration.
Texture of the epidermis.

Physiology. surface, and supposed it to be formed by an exudation from the cutaneous vessels, merely hardened by exposure to the air. But such an opinion seems scarcely compatible with our ideas respecting the nature of any organ which forms a part of the animal body, and appears inconsistent with that extreme minuteness with which the cuticle is spread over the whole surface, and applied with perfect accuracy to all its inequalities. In some of its morbid states the cuticle is obviously connected with the vascular parts of the system; and the analogy of the inferior animals would lead us to the same conclusion; for the scales of fish, the thick folds with which the elephant is covered, and other similar substances, are properly productions of the cuticle.

Thickened by pressure. There is a remarkable fact respecting the epidermis, that, independent of any morbid state, it becomes increased in bulk under certain circumstances. It is always found to be naturally thicker in some parts than in others, as, for example, in the soles of the feet; and we likewise find that it may be still farther thickened or increased by pressure. This affords one instance among many others, of that admirable adaptation of the organs to their appropriate uses, by which they are not only fitted for performing certain actions. but possess the property of accommodating themselves to incidental circumstances. The physical cause by which this change is effected, may perhaps be referred to the increased action of the cutis, which we may conceive is excited in these cases, but it must be confessed that this explanation is, in some measure, conjectural, and at best is only supported by a loose analogy.

Rete mucosum. There has been much controversy respecting the next layer of the skin, the rete or corpus mucosum. Its existence was first announced by Malpighi; he described it as a layer of soft matter, disposed in the form of fibres, crossing each other in various directions. Some of the later anatomists have conceived it to be merely a thin stratum of pulpy matter, without any distinct reticulated structure, while Bichat seems altogether to doubt its existence, as a proper layer or membrane, and supposes that the net-work which Malpighi described, is merely an extremely delicate congeries of vessels, which, after having passed through the cutis, ramify on its surface in all directions, and produce the appearance of a number of reticulated fibres.

Gives the skin its colour. A circumstance which renders the rete mucosum an object of considerable interest, is, that the peculiar complexion of different individuals is conceived to depend upon the colour of this part; and this would appear to be the case, whether it be actually a proper membrane, as Malpighi supposed, or simply an assemblage of vessels, according to the doctrine of Bichat. It seems as a matter of fact, that in the Negro it is black, in the Asiatic yellow or tawny, in the native American reddish brown or copper-coloured, and in the European of different shades of olive. The primary cause of this difference of colour in the rete mucosum has been popularly ascribed to the operation of the sun's rays, as referable to the same action by which the skin is browned in consequence of exposure to a bright light. But this tanning of the skin has no connexion with the permanent colour of the negro, and probably exists in a different organ. The blackest complexions are not found in the hottest regions; and there are considerable tribes, nearly under the equator, whose skin is whiter than many Europeans. Besides

the brownness of the skin, which is produced by the Physiology. sun, is not transmitted from parents to their offspring, whereas the children of negroes are equally black in whatever climate they are born, and their complexion is not altered by a change of climate during any number of successive generations. It has not been precisely ascertained upon what part of the skin the sun acts, but it is probably upon the epidermis, because there are certain applications, as blisters and various mild corrosives, which are stated to have the effect of removing tan, and which, it may be inferred, act principally upon the external surface.

In connexion with the colour of the skin, we may **Albinos.** advert to a singular variety of the human species, which is also found among other classes of animals, where the skin is entirely without colour, producing a perfect opaque whiteness. Of this peculiarity, which is supposed to depend upon the absence of the rete mucosum, we have already given an account under the article ALBINO, in an early part of this work; we shall at present only remark concerning it, that this condition of the skin appears both to confirm the existence of a proper substance upon which the colour of the complexion depends, and likewise tends to prove that the shade of the complexion is independent of the immediate operation of the sun's rays.

Under the rete mucosum, lies the true skin, the **Cutis.** cutis or corion, a body of considerable thickness, tough, flexible, of a dense texture, composed of a number of small fibres or plates, closely interwoven together. Its external surface is nearly smooth, while internally it is more loose or irregular, as it is connected with the parts below it by the cellular texture, into which substance it passes by almost insensible degrees. Besides the proper membranous basis of the skin, there is an extensive surface of nerves and blood-vessels, which are connected with it, and which are spread over every part of it with so much minuteness, that it is impossible to insert into it even the smallest point of a needle, without both exciting a sensation and producing a discharge of blood. With the exception of some of the organs of sense, it perhaps possesses more feeling than any other part of the body, and it is accordingly observed in surgical operations, that the most severe pain is experienced during the division of the skin.

The surface of the skin, when minutely examined, **Papillæ.** is found to be rendered unequal by a number of little eminences or projections, which have obtained the name of papillæ. They are said to contain each of them a small branch of an artery and a nerve, of which they constitute the ultimate ramifications, and are supposed to be the immediate seat of the organ of touch, and of the other sensations which reside in the surface of any part of the body. They are observed to be the most numerous, and to be of the largest size, in those parts of the body where the touch is the most delicate, as in the points of the fingers, or in the organs which exercise any peculiar function, as the tip of the tongue.

The minute structure of the skin is described by **Structure** Haller as consisting of threads or plates, which are **of the skin.** short, intricate, and closely interwoven together, the external parts being more dense, and the internal more spongy. This texture may be easily detected by maceration in water, when a tissue of fibres will be obtained, which are intimately connected together with a number of areolæ between them, through which the nerves and vessels pass that ramify on the external surface. Except in this state of partial decomposition it is very difficult, if not impossible, to exhibit these pores to the eye, yet there can be no reasonable doubt of their existence. The difficulty with which they are rendered visible, probably depends upon their not piercing the cutis in a straight direction, but following a winding course, and passing between the folds or plaits, of which the skin is composed.

Properties of the skin. The properties of the skin may be considered under two points of view, either as depending upon its physical structure, or upon its action as a part of the living body, plentifully furnished with blood-vessels, and nerves. The properties of its membranous basis are the same with those of other membranes, and are entirely mechanical, while its blood-vessels and nerves render it subject to many of those changes and actions which are possessed by the parts of the body which have the greatest share of vitality.

Chemical composition. Although the chemical composition of the skin has been much attended to by the moderns, our knowledge respecting it is still imperfect. It is generally described as consisting of a solid jelly, differing from jelly as procured from other substances, solely in being more dense and less soluble in water. M. Seguin, who has particularly attended to the nature of the skin, in connection with the process of tanning, describes it as consisting of two distinct structures; one which forms its basis, composed of a number of minute interlacing fibres, nearly similar to the muscular fibres, and the other a semi-fluid mucus, or gelatinous matter, mechanically interspersed through these fibres. Considered generally, the idea of Seguin appears to be supported by observation, although it must be admitted that it is somewhat hypothetical.

Art of tanning. The valuable art of making leather depends upon the property which the solid texture of the skin possesses of uniting with the tan, and forming a new chemical compound, without having its mechanical texture destroyed, so that while it retains its original form, its nature is so far changed as to be no longer soluble in water, and but little susceptible of the action of moisture. The art of forming leather from skins, is one of very ancient date, and there are few nations which do not possess some kind of process of this description; but it was not until of late years that the theory of tanning was understood, and for this knowledge we are much indebted to the French chemists, and especially to M. Seguin. Considerable light has also been thrown upon the subject by Mr. Hatchett, and some improvements have consequently taken place in our manufacture of leather; but it is, we believe, generally admitted, that by expediting the operation, as was proposed by Seguin, we materially injure the nature of the article that is produced.

Proper membranes. Nearly allied to the external skin, both in their texture and their uses, are the membraneous coats or tunics, which line the internal parts of the body, and cover the different viscera. In consequence of their being less exposed to injury, and of the necessity of a greater delicacy of structure, the proper membranes are much thinner than the skin of the external surface; they are also, for the most part, homogeneous in their texture, and are not divisible into different layers. They are generally thin, transparent, and of considerable tenacity; they possess but little sensibility, and are scantily supplied with blood-vessels. It was to these bodies that the name of membrane was originally applied, from which it has been extended to the whole class of substances that exhibit a general similarity in properties and composition.

The proper membranes have been made the subject of a very elaborate treatise by Bichat, in which he has arranged them into different classes, has minutely examined the structure and functions of each, and pointed out their relation to the other parts of the system. The three principal divisions which he lays down are the mucous, serous, and fibrous; of each of these we shall give a short description. The mucous membranes are characterized by the peculiar semifluid substance with which their surface is covered; they are always found lining those cavities that are disposed in the form of irregular passages or canals, that open externally, and are connected at their termination with the cutis. Of these the principal are the mouth, the nostrils, the œsophagus, the urinary passages, and the whole of the digestive organs. Their external surface is soft and pulpy, and is diversified by various projections, which serve different purposes, according to the functions of the part where they are found. The mucous membranes are the immediate seat of some very important operations in the animal economy; they constitute the organs of taste and smell, of digestion, of assimilation, and of various secretions. On this account they differ from most membranous bodies in being plentifully supplied with blood-vessels and nerves, as well as in possessing an extensive apparatus of glands and absorbents.

The serous membranes differ materially, in almost all respects, from the mucous. They are always found in close cavities that do not communicate with the atmosphere, as, for example, in the thorax and abdomen, and they form coats for many of the most important organs, as the heart, the lungs, and the abdominal viscera. In their texture the serous membranes are smooth, compact, and thin, but of considerable strength in proportion to their bulk; they have their surface always moistened by a fluid which exhales from them, but as no glands have been detected, and as it differs very little in its chemical nature from the serum of the blood, it is supposed to be produced rather by a kind of infiltration through very minute pores, than by what can properly be regarded as secretion. The fluid that is thus produced is always in health absorbed as speedily as it is formed, but in certain states of disease it is liable to accumulate, when it gives rise to the different species of dropsy. The serous membranes have scarcely any vessels of sufficient size to convey red blood, and have very few, if any, nerves; they are therefore without sensibility, and possess only in a small degree the general powers of vitality. They have a considerable share of elasticity, and are capable of great extension, but they are not properly contractile, nor do they possess any powers except those that are common to many other parts of the body.

The fibrous membranes are named from their obvious texture, as consisting of a visible assemblage of fibres, united into a continuous extended surface. They differ from the mucous and serous in not being moistened by any fluid, but they bear a considerable resemblance to the latter in their general aspect, being dense, thin, and smooth, although, according to their situation, and the uses which they serve, they are more varied in their form and consistence. Among the most important of the fibrous membranes are the periosteum, the dura mater, the aponeuroses, which are found in different parts of the body, the capsules of the joints, and the sheaths of the tendons. The texture of these membranes is obviously fibrous, without blood-vessels, nerves, glands, or any specific apparatus. Their use in the animal economy is purely mechanical; to enclose the soft parts and preserve them in their proper form, to separate them from each other, and to keep them in their relative position. The chemical composition of membrane appears to differ in the different species; but they all of them consist of a basis of albumen, united to certain proportions of jelly and mucus.

Cellular texture.

Immediately below the skin, and connected with the subjacent parts, is a series of membranous cells, which have been called the cellular texture, and which is extended through nearly every part of the body. It not only unites the cutis with the muscles over which it is extended, but it fills up the interstices between the muscles, and occupies all the spaces that intervene between the different viscera. The cells of which this texture is composed appear to be of all shapes and sizes, adapted to the peculiar parts in which they are situated. They have a communication with each other, so that air introduced into them, either intentionally or accidentally, is soon diffused over every part of the body. This occurrence sometimes takes place in wounds of the chest, where a puncture having been made in the lungs, and a communication formed with the neighbouring cells, the air received in respiration is admitted into the membraneous texture, and becomes diffused through the whole body, puffing it up in an extraordinary degree. These cells are destined for the reception of a serous fluid, which, in the healthy state, exists in small quantity only, but in dropsical affections is much increased, so that the body sometimes becomes distended to a great size.

Adipose membrane.

It is in this system of cells that the fat is deposited; but it appears that the fat and the serous fluid are not actually in contact, in consequence of each globule of fat being provided with a distinct vesicle in which it is contained. On this account fat cannot pass from one part to another, as we observe to be the case with the water of dropsy, or with air introduced into the cellular texture, but the same particles of fat always remain stationary in the same cells.

Tendons, ligaments, &c.

The tendons and ligaments bear a close relation to the fibrous membranes, and indeed are conceived to differ from them solely in their external form, for, like them, they consist entirely of strong fibres, closely united together, without nerves, and possessing very few blood vessels. Cartilages are of a more uniform texture than tendons and ligaments, so that no fibres can be perceived in them. They consist principally of albumen, with only a small proportion of jelly or mucus, and at the same time a small quantity of the earth of bones enters into their composition. They are harder than tendons, but generally more elastic. Their principal use is to supply the place of bones where strength and elasticicity are both necessary, particularly in the chest, the wind-pipe, the gullet, and about the joints. They may be regarded as forming a kind of intermediate link between membrane and bone, and accordingly it is found, that many parts of the body which are cartilaginous in the young animal, become converted into perfect bone as it advances to maturity.

How connected with the other parts.

As the fibrous membranes, the tendons, ligaments, and cartilages, are without nerves, are very scantily supplied with vessels of all kinds, and possess neither contractility nor sensibility, it may be asked, How are they connected with the vital system, or in what sense are we to regard them as possessing life? The question is one which it is not very easy to answer, and which, perhaps, must depend more upon the definitions which we give to certain words and expressions, than upon any facts which we have it in our power to advance. Some eminent physiologists conceive life to be always connected with vascularity and sensibility, and, in conformity with their views, they do not hesitate to style the dense membranous matter dead or inanimate, seeming to regard it as only mechanically attached to the more vital parts. But to this it may be objected, that there is no portion of the animal body which has not a regularly organized structure, and that this can only be produced by some vascular action, analogous to secretion, by which the matter that composes them may be deposited in its proper position. There are many facts, which would seem to prove, that all these parts are under the influence of the absorbents, by which their substance is gradually removed, particle by particle, in the same gradual manner in which it was deposited, and there are likewise other facts which show that these extravascular parts are subject to various diseased actions, which prove their connexion with, and dependence upon, the arterial system. We may therefore conclude from analogy, that all these structures are, in some manner, under the influence of the secretory and absorbent vessels, or of vessels which possess similar powers, although it is admitted that we cannot demonstrate their existence, or bring forward any arguments in favour of it, except the effects which are produced.

Nails, &c.

There is a class of bodies, connected with the external surface of all animals, which, although very different in their shape and appearance, are analogous to each other in their origin and uses. They may be divided into two varieties, the first consisting of nails, claws, hoofs, scales, &c., the second consisting of hair, bristles, wool, quills, and feathers. The first variety may be considered as weapons of defence or protection, they are either productions of the skin, or at least are so intimately united to it, that it is often difficult to trace the exact line of demarcation between them. We may generally perceive in them a kind of fibrous or laminated texture, although this cannot be detected in those that are the most dense, which are nearly homogeneous. They are composed of coagulated albumen, united to different proportions of jelly and mucus.

Hair, &c.

Hair and feathers differ materially from the bodies just described, both in their origin and in their organization; they proceed from a kind of root or bulb, that is situated below the skin, and they pass out through its pores. They consist essentially of an external tube and an internal pulp; in hair the tube is very delicate, and is entirely filled with the pulp; in the quill the tube is denser, and the internal pulp is much smaller in quantity. Although hair is so smooth to the touch, it is stated to possess an imbricated or bristled texture, the processes all pointing in one direction, from the root to the point, analogous to the feather part of the quill. It is upon this texture that the operation of felting has been supposed to depend, in which the hairs are entangled together, and are retained in this state by the inequalities on their surface. The basis of all these bodies is coagulated albumen, generally mixed with small quantities of jelly and mucus. The pulpy part of hair contains an oily substance, which produces its peculiar colour, and generally corresponds to the shade of the complexion, as

Physiology. depending upon the rete mucosum of the skin. In their natural state all these bodies are without sensation, and possess no visible blood-vessels, but, under certain circumstances, many of them are subject to a species of inflammation, when vessels may be detected in them, and they become acutely painful.

CHAP. III.

OF BONE.

General description.

BONE, in its ordinary state, is a hard inflexible body, in the human species of a whitish colour, without sensibility or contractility, and very little subject to decay. It serves as a defence and a support to the soft parts of the body, either affording them a solid case, in which they are lodged and protected from injury, as takes place with respect to the brain and lungs, or as a basis to which the different parts may be attached, as is the case with the muscles. The bones are also fixed points, against which the muscles react when they commence their contractions; they form a system of levers, by which the movements of the body are effected, and they very essentially contribute to the function of locomotion, by the share which they have in the formation of the joints. The total number of bones is about 260, exhibiting every variety of figure and size, according to the structure and uses of the parts in which they are found. They may, however, be arranged under two great divisions, the broad and flat, and the long and round bones; to the first class belong the bones of the skull, and to the second those of the arms and legs.

Two kinds of bones.

These two kinds of bones differ not merely in their external shape, which may be conceived to be an incidental circumstance, and one of little importance, but likewise in the more essential points of the mode of their growth and their mechanical structure. They also serve very different uses in the animal economy; the long bones are adapted for the purposes of motion, either enabling us to shift our position from place to place, or to act upon other bodies that are contiguous to us, while the object of the flat bones is simply to protect the parts which they inclose.

Particular examples.

It would be carrying us far beyond the proper subject of this article to enter into any minute description of the individual bones, but it may be proper to make a few general observations upon this part of the animal fabric, and especially to show how admirably each of its individual parts is adapted to its particular uses. For this purpose we cannot take a better example than that of the upper and lower extremities. In the human subject, the arms are obviously intended, not for support but for prehension. They are therefore attached to the trunk in such a manner as to be easily applied to contiguous bodies in all directions, the upper part admitting of free motion, but at the same time possessing considerable strength, while the extremity is formed of an assemblage of small bones, that are so connected together as to form an apparatus by which we can execute all the necessary offices of life with a degree of quickness and accuracy, which would be almost inconceivable, were we not so familiar with it.

The lower extremities are equally fitted for their specific object, the support of the body and its progressive motions. They are so situated as to bear the weight of the body in the most advantageous manner, the feet afford a firm basis to the pillars which are placed upon them, while its smaller parts possess that Physiology. degree of motion upon each other, which is the best calculated for promoting this end, without exhibiting that variety of minute actions, which are necessary for the hand and fingers, but which would have been inconsistent with the greater firmness that is requisite in the parts destined to support the whole body.

Joints.

The form and structure of the joints are among the most interesting parts of the animal economy. Technically speaking, every part is styled an articulation where two bones unite together, but at present we shall only notice those which are moveable, where the bones are united by ligaments, or other membranous bodies of a flexible nature, so as to be capable of changing their relative position. They present a great variety of forms, but they may be all reduced to two divisions, the ball and socket, and the hinge. In the first of two kinds. kind of joint the moveable bone is furnished with a round end, which plays in a corresponding hollow in the fixed bone, while in the hinge, both the bones are furnished with processes and depressions, which are mutually adapted to each other; the hip and shoulder are examples of the first, the knee and elbow of the second kind of articulation. It is obvious that the ball and socket admits of motion on every side, while the hinge is moveable in one direction only.

Mechanism of the joints.

Although the general form and outline of the joints is observable in the solid body of the bones, yet, as we have already stated, the cartilages contribute materially to the accurate completion of the parts, and the whole extent of articulating surface is covered with this body. Thus, a greater degree of motion is admitted than could have taken place if the joints had been entirely composed of a hard substance, and the bad effects of concussion are, in a considerable degree, prevented. Still farther to facilitate motion by preventing friction, the joints are all inclosed in a kind of bag, which is filled with a dense fluid, called synovia. To complete the mechanism of the joints, they are provided with a number of ligaments, which serve to keep the bones in their relative places, and to regulate their motions, so as to prevent their displacement, except under circumstances of extraordinary violence. The bones of the ball and socket joint are united together by a ligament which passes through their centres, while in the hinge joint the ligaments are placed at the sides of the bones; but it would be encroaching on the province of the anatomist to enter upon a minute description of these parts. We shall only farther observe, that in none of the organs of the body is the adaptation of means to ends more remarkable than in the construction of the joints and the apparatus connected with them.

Physical properties of bone.

In its physical properties, bone is the most simple of any of the components of the body. Membrane, as we already remarked, is not possessed of any properties that are peculiar to the living system, and which do not belong to many other substances, but bone is neither flexible nor extensible, and, except elasticity, has scarcely any physical properties which are not common to every kind of solid matter.

Structure of bone.

The mechanical structure of bone formed a part of the interesting investigations of Malpighi; and it was discovered by him that the basis consists of animal matter, arranged in the form of cells. Duhamel still farther advanced our knowledge on this subject; but it appears to have been Herissant who first announced, that bone contains earthy matter, and that upon this ingredient depend its hardness, and most of its peculiar properties. By means of diluted muriatic acid, we can dissolve the earth of the bones without acting upon the membranous cells ; if a bone, therefore, be immersed in this fluid, we shall deprive it, in a great measure, of its earthy matter, and reduce it to a soft, flexible, and elastic substance, retaining its former shape and bulk, but having exchanged the properties of bone for those of membrane. In this process, we have removed the earth and left the membrane ; but, to make the experiment complete, we must reverse the operation, and remove the membrane. This we accomplish by burning the bone, for in this operation it is the membrane alone which is consumed, the earthy matter being left untouched ; and if sufficient caution be used, it may be preserved without having its texture materially injured.

Of the membranous part.
The membranous part of bone appears to be, like the other soft solids, essentially composed of fibres ; these, by their union, form horizontal plates, lying parallel to each other, and united together by smaller plates, crossing the others at different angles, forming, by their intersection, the cells into which the earth is deposited. Some writers have described the plates as held together by small processes, like nails ; but this seems to be a fanciful conjecture, and is not supported by correct observation. Even the laminated structure of bone has been denied by Bichat, who has endeavoured to prove that the facts which have been adduced in favour of its existence are all of them fallacious. To a certain extent, the observations and reasonings of Bichat appear to be correct ; and we think that there has been much fanciful conjecture exercised upon the subject, which probably had its origin from Duhamel, who thought that the substance of bone was composed of a succession of concentric layers, arranged like those which form the trunk of a tree. But, on the other hand, there appear to be many reasons for supposing that bones possess a proper plated texture ; of this, however, we shall have occasion to treat more fully hereafter.

Almost all bones, whatever be their shape, are the hardest on the external surface, and become less and less dense in their internal portion, until we arrive at a perfect cavity, or at least, at a part where there are only a few plates, crossing in different directions, and leaving cells that are proportionally large. These have obtained the denomination of cancelli, or lattice-work. In the flat bones, both the external surfaces are hard, and the internal lattice-work is extended between the plates, presenting, in some measure, the same form with the bone itself. In the round bones, there is, of course, only one external surface, which is hard, like that of the flat bones, and a cellular cavity is left, which is more or less occupied by the cancelli, besides which there is also another network of membrane, which does not contain earthy matter. It is on this membrane that the marrow is lodged ; like the fat of the cellular texture, it is contained in distinct cavities, which have no communication with each other.

Use of the cavities.
One use of the internal cavities of bones is, by increasing their external surface, to afford a greater space for the insertion of muscles and ligaments, and we accordingly find, that the ends of bones, to which the tendons are principally fixed, possess most extent of surface. But this structure likewise serves the still more important purpose of increasing the mechanical strength of the bone, without adding to its weight. The absolute strength of a bone may indeed be considered as depending upon the quantity of solid fibres which it contains ; but its power of resistance may be mathematically demonstrated to be augmented in proportion to its diameter, so that the same number of fibres placed, as it were, in the circumference of a circle, produces a bone more capable of resisting external violence, than if they had been united in the centre, and the diameter of the bone had been proportionally diminished. Conformably to this principle, we find that the cylindrical bones, which possess the largest cavities, are in the extremities of the body, where, from their position, they are the most exposed to violence.

Vessels and nerves of bones.
The bone is everywhere surrounded by a proper membrane, which is supplied with blood-vessels ; the membranous part of the bone itself seems also to possess a set of vessels for its support, and the bones are pierced with numerous holes, through which arteries enter to nourish the internal membrane, and probably to secrete the marrow. Few nerves have been traced into the bones, and, in their natural state, they are without sensation, yet like other parts, into the composition of which dense membrane enters, they become extremely painful in certain states of disease.

Ossification.
The process by which bone is formed, called ossification, is one of the most curious that occurs in the animal economy, and respecting which there has been an abundance of speculations and hypotheses. In the fœtal state, the body is without any proper bones, those parts which afterwards acquire the osseous texture, possessing the general figure of the future bones, but being composed merely of soft membranes. These membranes seem to become gradually more and more dense, until at length they acquire the nature of cartilage ; then small points of bone appear on their surface ; from these, as from centres, bony fibres radiate in all directions, and these ossified spots gradually enlarge, until at length they unite, and the whole becomes a solid body. These facts were ascertained by Haller, who minutely examined the gradual evolution of the chick in ovo, during the different stages of its incubation, and it appears that the same changes occur in the embryo of viviparous animals.

Duhamel's hypothesis.
Before the nature of bone was thoroughly understood, it was conceived that the membrane became converted into bone by some mechanical means, as by the compression of the contiguous muscles, by the evaporation of its watery parts, or the condensation of the membrane by the heat of the body. Duhamel formed an hypothesis, which professed to be founded upon experiment, and was, for a long time, very generally received. He supposed that there was an analogy between the bones of animals and the stems of trees, and imagined that bone was generated by the condensation of successive layers of the investing membrane, in the same manner as the annual rings of wood, in the trunk of a tree, are formed from the bark of the preceding season. He founded his experiments upon the fact which had been discovered, that if the root of madder was mixed with the food of animals, it communicated a red tinge to their bones ; and he affirms that, by feeding animals for a certain period with madder, and then omitting it for some time, again resuming its use, and again discontinuing it, the bones of animals that had been thus treated were composed of successive rings of red and white matter. Mr. John Bell shrewdly remarks, that when speculators perform experiments, they generally find exactly what they desire to find, and so it seems to have been with Duhamel. We are now assured that the membrane surrounding the bone is of a totally different nature from the osseous part of the bone, and could never be formed from it, without

found to be erroneous.

an entire change of its nature; that the different parts of the bone are tinged with the madder, in proportion to the quantity of earthy matter which they contain; and that the membrane which surrounds the bone is not itself affected by it. Dr. Rutherford discovered that this curious effect of madder depends upon the attraction between this body and the earth of bone, by which they unite and form a compound of a reddish purple colour. When the particles of madder are received into the stomach, like many other extraneous substances, they are absorbed and carried into the blood; and when, in the course of the circulation, they arrive at the bones, they are separated by their affinity for the earthy matter. As the external layers of the bone contain the most earth, they will soonest acquire the red colour, will exhibit the deepest shade, and retain it longer than the other parts.

Deposition of the earthy matter. With respect to the manner in which the earth is carried into the cartilage, so as to convert it into bone, it seems to be a case of secretion analogous to many other operations in the body, where the arteries possess the power of either separating particles already existing in the blood, and appropriating them to some specific purpose, or forming new combinations, which may be afterwards detached from the mass, and employed in different ways.

As to the cause which determines this effect to be produced at particular periods of our existence, we can say little more than that we find it to be a matter of fact. It is a part of the general constitution of the animal system, that at regular times, certain changes should take place, without our being able to assign any physical cause for them. The final cause of the present order of things is sufficiently obvious, and we cannot conceive of an arrangement better adapted to the situation of the animal at the commencement of its existence, or to the alteration which it afterwards experiences. In the first instance, softness and flexibility are absolutely requisite, and hardness would be injurious; while, as the necessity for resisting external violence gradually arises, the capacity for resistance is proportionably produced.

Alteration in the membrane. But, independent of the deposition of earthy matter in the bone, the membranous part itself undergoes a complete change in its structure. The original cartilage is of a uniform consistence in all its parts, whereas, in the fully formed bone, the centre is nearly hollow, and the more solid parts which surround it have their density much increased as they approach to the surface, while the whole is composed of plates disposed in a specific manner, with numerous cavities or interstices between them. How then, it may be asked, is the cartilage converted into the membranous matter which enters into the composition of bone? The only way in which we can well suppose this change to be effected, is by the gradual absorption of the cartilage, and the deposition of other particles of animal matter, which may constitute the future bone; but upon this supposition we are at a loss to explain by what means the vessels have their actions or powers so directed, that the mechanical structure of the part should be so much altered, or that the position of the new particles should be so different from that of the former matter.

Reparation of bone. The manner in which bones are repaired, when they have suffered from external violence, is as remarkable as that by which they are originally formed; and this process has, in like manner, given rise to much speculation and controversy. The common opinion among the older writers was, that a soft mucus or jelly is, in the first instance, deposited between the ends of a broken bone, that it is condensed by heat or pressure into a hard gluten, which they called callus, and they conceived that it always retained its membranous state, and was never converted into proper osseous matter. Some physiologists supposed that this callus was produced from effused and coagulated blood, and others that it was derived from the membrane inclosing the old bone. It is now, however, generally understood that the reparation of bone is effected by a process very similar to that by which it was originally produced. The arteries of the divided bone throw out a soft matter, of a mucous or gelatinous nature, which gradually hardens into a cartilaginous substance, or is replaced by it; in this the earthy matter is deposited, and the whole is new-moulded, in the manner which has been described above. What is the immediate cause by which this process is effected, why the arteries throw out this substance, how it is moulded into the proper form, whence the supply of earth is derived, just at the exact period when it is required by the wants of the system, are questions that have not yet been satisfactorily answered. The hypotheses that have been formed upon the subject have been, in some cases; the mere expression of the fact in different words; in others, the substitution of the final for the efficient cause, or they have proceeded upon the assumption of some imaginary agent, created by the fancy of the writer, to meet the present emergency. We cannot doubt that there is a proper efficient cause for this, as well as for every other change which occurs in the system; and that, were our knowledge of the animal economy complete, we should be able to refer it to the general laws by which the body is directed. At present, however, our acquaintance with many of the minute operations of nature is extremely limited, and we are only retarding the advancement of knowledge by premature attempts at explaining them.

Chemical nature of bone; phosphate of lime. The chemical nature of bone was very imperfectly understood until about forty years ago, when Gahn discovered that it contains an earthy salt, composed of phosphoric acid and lime. Later and more accurate researches, especially those of Berzelius, have shown that the salt is in the state of a sub-phosphate, and that it is mixed with a small quantity of phosphate of magnesia, and fluate of lime. The earth of bones is insoluble in water, bears a high temperature without being decomposed, and is, in all respects, of a very imperishable nature. We accordingly find, that the compact bones of animals are frequently met with in a tolerably perfect state, after the lapse even of many centuries, and after having been exposed to all the revolutions to which the surface of the earth has been subjected. Indeed, from some of the discoveries that have been lately made by Cuvier and other modern naturalists, we are induced to believe that bones still remain belonging to animals that must have existed before any traditional or historical records of which we are in possession, and when the earth was peopled by animals of a different kind from any of its present inhabitants.

Albumen, We are indebted to Mr. Hatchett for the discovery of the nature of the membranous part of bone, which he found to possess all the characters of coagulated albumen; the substance which has been already stated to be the basis of membranous matter of all descriptions. **and jelly.** We find, also, that bones contain a quantity of jelly,

3

Physiology. which can be extracted by boiling; and that this jelly is much more abundant in the bones of young than of old animals.

Oil in bones. Besides the marrow, which is contained in the cavities of the round bones, there is a quantity of oil in the solid part of the bone. The use of this oil, as well as of the marrow, does not appear to be well understood. The idea that the oil of bones serves to render them less brittle, and more flexible, appears to be too mechanical, and does not accord with the nature of the body in question; for it is probable, that the oil is not diffused through the general body or substance of the bone, but is lodged in small cells like the marrow and the fat. Upon the whole, this is a point respecting which we are not able to give any very satisfactory opinion.

Deposition of the earth. In considering the composition of the bones, an interesting question presents itself respecting the origin of the phosphate of lime: Is it received into the system along with the food, or have the organs of assimilation and secretion the power of generating this salt? Then, if we suppose this point to be satisfactorily explained, we have still to inquire respecting the mode in which the earth is deposited in the bones. If we conceive it to be present in the blood, we have still to learn what causes it to pass into those particular vessels that go to the bones; and how is it disposed of at those times when it is not required for the growth or the reparation of these parts? There is also very considerable difficulty in conceiving of the manner in which the earth quits the vessels and is deposited in the membrane. We may suppose it to be poured out from the extremities of the vessels, or that it might be extravasated from their sides, or we may suppose it possible that it may remain lodged in them, so as, in fact, to convert the arteries themselves into the osseous fibres. Perhaps, of these operations, the first is the most probable, and the one most analogous to the other operations of the animal economy; yet this affords no explanation of the fibrous form which the bony matter is disposed to assume; nor is it easy, upon any supposition, to reconcile this mechanical disposition of the bones with any mode in which we can conceive their formation to be effected.

How connected with the membrane? Another subject of inquiry is concerning the manner in which the earthy matter is attached to the membranous part of the bone. It has been supposed by some physiologists, and it appears to have been the prevailing opinion among the older writers, that the particles of earth existed in the blood, and that, being poured out from the secreting arteries, they were deposited between the interstices of the membranous matter, and lodged there almost after the manner of extraneous bodies. Yet this has been thought by other writers to afford too mechanical a view of the subject, and not to accord with the ideas of vitality which must belong to every part of an organized body.

Vital properties of bone. With respect to the vital properties of bone, it appears that they exist only in a very imperfect degree. Bones are scantily supplied with blood-vessels, few if any nerves are distributed to them, and we judge of the presence of absorbents rather from observing effects, which cannot be ascribed to any other cause, than from being able actually to demonstrate their existence. Bone is, therefore, necessarily devoid of sensibility, and is without contractility; it partakes, in a small degree only, of the actions of the system; its changes of all kinds are effected slowly, and often in an imperceptible manner. There are, however, many circumstances which prove to us, that bones are under the influence of the arterial and absorbent systems; for there are Physiology. many facts which render it highly probable, that the earth of bones undergoes a gradual change, so that all the particles which enter into its composition at one period, are, after some time, replaced by others. The diseases to which bones are subject also show that they are under vascular influence, and are connected with the vital actions of the system. They have affections which are analogous to the inflammation, swelling, and suppuration of the soft parts, although considerably modified by their situation and structure. Under these circumstances, also, bones are not unfrequently found to possess very great sensibility to pain; and they exhibit, in an obvious manner, the power of separating the living from the dead parts, and of repairing those portions which have been separated or destroyed.

CHAPTER IV.

OF MUSCLE.

Arrangement. In treating on the subject of the muscles, we shall arrange our remarks under four heads: we shall, first, describe the structure and composition of muscles; secondly, their properties and uses; thirdly, their mechanism; and, lastly, we shall make some remarks upon the hypotheses that have been formed to explain their action.

Sect. I. *Structure and Composition of Muscles.*

Description of muscles. Muscles constitute what is usually termed the flesh of animals, and, in their most usual form, they are composed of masses of fibres, lying parallel to each other, intermixed with a quantity of membranous matter. We may obtain an accurate idea of the structure of a muscle by cutting it transversely, and boiling it for some time. We shall, in this way, perceive, that the whole muscle is inclosed in a sheath of membrane, which covers it in every part, except where its ends are attached to the base. The fibres, we shall find, are disposed into small bundles, each of which is enclosed in a sheath of membrane, while these bundles are divisible into still smaller bundles, apparently without any limit except the imperfection of our instruments.

Minute structure. By the aid of microscopes, the ultimate fibre, as it is called, or that which is no longer capable of farther subdivision, has been observed and described; but as is too often the case in microscopical observations, the Microscopical observations by Leeuwenhoek. account of the different observers differ, both with respect to its size and its structure. Leeuwenhoek, who is so celebrated for the use which he made of the microscope in anatomical researches, describes the ultimate filaments as almost inconceivably minute, some thousands of them uniting to form one visible fibre. We learn from him, that the ultimate fibres are serpentine and cylindrical bodies, lying parallel to each other, that they are of the same figure in all animals, but differ considerably in their size; and he says that their size bears no relation to that of the animal to which they belong. In some instances, we are informed, that the smallest animals have the largest fibres, that of the frog, for example, being larger than that of the ox.

Muys. Muys paid particular attention to the minute structure of muscles, and his descriptions, in many respects, agree with those of Leeuwenhoek, except that he re-

Physiology. gards the ultimate filament as being always of the same size. He supposes that the fibres are divided into regular gradations or series; and estimates that the smallest fibrils of which the last series is composed, are some hundred times less than the finest hair, a proportion larger indeed than that assigned by Leeuwenhoek, yet still too minute to enable us to form any distinct conception of it.

Prochaska. Among the more modern anatomists, the labours of Prochaska seem to be entitled to our particular notice, as there is every reason to suppose that he examined the subject with great care, and has given us an accurate detail of what he observed. To the smallest division of the muscle, which can be separated by mechanical means, he gives the specific name of fibre, while the still more minute divisions, which are only to be detected by the use of glasses, he styles threads or filaments. He informs us, that each of the fibres, as well as the larger portions of the muscles, or lacerti, is furnished with a distinct membranous sheath, but it does not appear that this is the case with the filaments. The fibre, when carefully separated from all extraneous matter, he conceives to be of a uniform thickness, through its whole extent, and continuous from one end to the other. He differs from Leeuwenhoek, Muys, and other preceding anatomists, respecting the form of the fibre, which they have described as being cylindrical, whereas Prochaska says that it is obviously of a polyhedral form, and is generally flattened, or thicker in one direction than the other. He farther observes, that they are not always of the same diameter, being thicker in some parts than others; also, that they are smaller in young subjects, and increase in size as the body increases in bulk generally. With respect to the filaments, their shape and extent are said to be similar to the larger fibres, being flattened polyhedrons, but they differ from the proper fibre in being always of the same magnitude; and this he conceives to be about 1-50th part the size of the red globules of the blood. The filaments are solid and homogeneous; when prepared for examination, a number of depressions or wrinkles are observable on their surface, which give them a waved appearance; and, when viewed in certain directions, cause them to assume a serpentine or zig-zag form; these he conceives to be produced by the blood-vessels, nerves, and membranous bands which cross them.

Fontana. Fontana's account of his observations on the ultimate fibre, is not very different from that of Prochaska. The smallest filaments into which he could divide the muscular fibre by means of a needle, he considers to be the primitive fibres, and a great number of these collected together, he conceives to form the primitive fasciculus; but it seems somewhat doubtful whether by this he means the same division which Prochaska names a fibre. Fontana describes his primitive filament as a solid cylinder, marked externally with transverse lines or bands. The filaments lie parallel to each other, and are not twisted together, as he says is always the case with membrane, and therefore affords a means of easily distinguishing between them. The smallest vessel capable of containing red blood, is about three times larger than the muscular filament, and the smallest nerve about four times larger than the smallest blood-vessel.

Carlisle. The observations of Sir A. Carlisle differ, in many respects, from those of preceding writers, especially of Prochaska and Fontana. He describes the ultimate fibre as a solid cylinder, the covering of which is a re-

ticular membrane, and the contained part a pulpy substance irregularly granulated; and, when dead, of little cohesive power. He does not specify its exact size, but speaks of it as not being so inconceivably minute as has been hitherto supposed. The extreme branches of the blood-vessels and nerves may be seen ramifying on its surface, but they do not appear to enter into its substance. Upon the whole, we feel disposed to place confidence in the statements of Sir A. Carlisle; but it is desirable that the observations should be repeated, as they differ so materially from those of former anatomists, whose authority is too respectable to be hastily abandoned.

Besides the descriptions of the muscular fibre, which profess to be the result of actual observation, many accounts have been published of their nature and structure, derived from mere speculative opinions. Some writers have spoken of them as being hollow tubes, some as being jointed, and others as composed of a number of parts connected together like a string of beads. Borelli announced that the muscular fibre consists of a series of hollow vesicles, and deduced from this structure a theory of muscular contraction, which he supported by a long train of mathematical problems; and, while mathematical reasoning was admitted into physiology, his demonstrations were conceived to be incontrovertible.

Another opinion entertained respecting the nature of the muscular fibre was, that it is entirely composed of vessels, either possessing some peculiar structure, or consisting of the small branches of arteries. This hypothesis, which appears to have been first broached by Hooke, was afterwards adopted by many learned physiologists, especially those of the mathematical sect, and was made the foundation of some of their speculations concerning muscular contraction. The celebrated names of Willis and Baglivi are attached to an erroneous opinion, that besides the longitudinal fibres, muscles possess transverse fibres, crossing the others at right angles, and that these are important agents in muscular action. The sagacity of Haller perceived the futility of these fanciful opinions, and his authority greatly contributed to effect their downfall.

Among the more noted hypotheses that have been formed respecting the nature of muscles, independent of their visible appearance, we must not omit to mention one which prevailed very generally about fifty years ago, and was supported by Cullen, that muscles are, to use his own expression, the moving extremities of nerves. The nerves are supposed to be continuous with the fibres of the muscles, and to be absolutely the same substance, but that they experience a change in their structure, so that, when the nerve is converted into muscle, it loses the power of communicating feeling, and acquires that of producing motion. In answer to this hypothesis, it may be sufficient to observe, that substances which differ in their appearance and structure, as well as in their physical and chemical properties, can have no claim to be regarded as identical. The same remark will apply to a similar kind of hypothesis, that muscles and tendons are the same substance, differing only in the more condensed state of the latter; an opinion which was transmitted from the ancients, embraced by Boerhaave and his disciples, and was so generally adopted, even in the last century, that Haller scarcely ventures to give a decided opposition to it.

The figure of muscles is infinitely varied according to their situation and uses, but they may be described

Margin notes: Physiology. Hypothetical remarks. Borelli's. Hooke's. Cullen's. Figure of muscles.

Physiology. as approaching to an oval form, swelling out in the centre, and tapering towards the extremities, and commonly having a tendon attached to one at least of their ends. There are considerable spaces between many of the muscles, which are occupied either by fat or membrane; and a safe lodgment is afforded in these intervals for the trunks of blood-vessels and nerves. Most of the larger muscles are situated near the surface, covering the bones, and filling up the interstices between them, so as to produce the general form or outline of the body.

Muscular coats.

Besides these, which are more properly styled muscles; muscular fibres are found under a different and less obvious form, but are not less important in the animal economy. Many of the minute, although most important operations of the body, are performed by muscular fibres, not collected together into bundles or masses, but placed in a less regular and connected manner on the surface of membranes. This arrangement is generally found in the tubes and pouches with which the body is furnished, and it is by this structure that these organs are enabled to propel and discharge their contents; these are called muscular coats, and will be described more minutely when we treat of the different organs, of which they compose an important part.

Uses of them.

The uses of these two classes of bodies are as different as their structure, and bear an obvious relation to it. The proper muscles are always intended for the motion of some part, by altering its relative position with respect to some other part, while the motions that are caused by the fibres of the muscular coats are destined to operate solely upon the contents of the organs to which they belong, and consist in a number of small contractions, in each of which a few fibres only act at the same time. These two kinds of organs differ in the relation which they bear to the other parts of the system, and particularly to the nerves; for while the nerves of the proper muscles are derived either from the brain itself, or from the spine, which may be considered as an immediate appendage of the brain, and are, for the most part, more or less dependent upon the will, the muscular coats are generally supplied from the ganglia, and their action is altogether involuntary.

Preparation of pure muscle.

In man, and the more perfect animals, muscles generally possess a red colour, but this seems not to be essential to them, as by maceration in water and alcohol, this colour may be removed. By this means a quantity of albumen and jelly is carried off, as well as some saline bodies, which are always present in the animal fluids; and if the fibre be then cleared as much as possible from the membrane and fat, it may be considered as brought to a state of purity. In consequence of the abstraction of these heterogeneous substances, the fibre is rendered much less susceptible of putrefaction, and if it be secured from moisture, it may be preserved for a long time without any sensible alteration.

Colour of muscles.

It has been doubted whether the peculiar colour of muscles depends upon something which is attached to the fibre itself, or whether it merely arises from the blood, which is so plentifully sent to them. Bichat labours to prove that it is not owing to the blood, but to some proper colouring matter, independent of any fluid that is contained in the vessels; and, upon the whole, there seems reason to acquiesce in his opinion. It may be observed that the voluntary muscles are, for the most part, those that possess the deepest shade of

colour, and that the colour is frequently found to be Physiology. increased the more the muscles are exercised.

Cellular substance.

Besides the membranous matter which encloses the whole muscle, and forms the coverings or sheaths of its individual parts, there is in the interstices of the lacerti, a portion of the same kind of cellular texture, which is dispersed through the body generally, and which here, as in other parts, serves the purpose of containing the oily and adipose secretions. Some writers have contended that, besides this kind of fatty deposit, muscles are furnished with a quantity of oil, which is diffused through their substance, and tends to render their motions more easy; but this we apprehend to be an idea unsupported by any well authenticated facts or analogies.

Albumen, jelly, and salts in muscles.

By digesting muscles in water, a quantity of albumen, jelly, and saline matter, may be extracted from them; but it does not appear whether these substances actually entered into the composition of the fibre itself. It is probable that the saline matter is rather contained in the fluids which circulate through the vessels, than the proper fibres; and, as far as it has been examined, it appears to be the same with the saline matter in the blood. It is principally composed of the phosphates of soda, ammonia, and lime, the carbonate of lime, and the muriate and lactate of soda. If the water in Extract. which muscles has been macerated be evaporated, and afterwards digested in alcohol, the extract alone is dissolved, and by removing the alcohol, may be procured in a separate state. This substance was first obtained by Thouvenel. It has a brown colour, an acrid taste, an aromatic odour, is soluble both in water and in alcohol, and is thought to be the ingredient which gives its specific flavour to the flesh of different animals.

Effect of nitric acid.

The strong mineral acids, and the caustic alkalies, readily dissolve the muscular fibre; but the only circumstances that are deserving of any particular attention, are the effects of the nitric acid. The same gases are extricated during the solution, as from many other animal substances, but with this difference, that the muscular fibre yields a larger proportion of azote. As this is the element which predominates in animal substances, and which particularly distinguishes them from vegetables, muscles are said to be the most completely animalized part of the system, thus affording an example of what has been already alluded to, that the chemical composition of the body bears a certain relation to its specific powers. Diluted nitric acid has the power of producing a very peculiar change in the muscular fibre, which is also capable of being brought about by other means. When it is digested either in an acid of this description, or is kept for a length of time at a certain temperature, instead of undergoing the usual process of putrefaction, it nearly preserves its original form, but loses its colour and consistence, and is converted into a substance very similar to spermaceti.

Formation of adipocire.

A well known and very remarkable example of this kind of change occurred between thirty and forty years ago in Paris, where, in consequence of an order from the police, it was determined to remove the contents of an immense burial ground, when, to the surprise of those engaged in the undertaking, the bodies were found to be, for the most part, converted into this peculiar substance. Fourcroy examined it with much minuteness, and from its appearing to possess properties intermediate between those of fat and wax, named it adipocire. This substance is very similar in its properties to spermaceti, differing from it princi-

PHYSIOLOGY. 535

Physiology. pally in melting at rather a lower temperature, and not exhibiting any degree of the crystalline or laminated texture. By observing what takes place when we employ nitric acid in the formation of adipocire, it would seem that the change consists in the abstraction of part of the azote, and the addition of a quantity of oxygen. When the acid is employed in a concentrated state, and its action is promoted by heat, the muscle is dissolved and decomposed; carbonic acid, nitrous, and azotic gases, are disengaged, and several new compounds are produced.

Sect. II. *Properties and Uses of Muscles.*

Properties and uses of muscles. We must now proceed to give an account of the properties and uses of muscles. As a large quantity of membrane always enters into their composition, we find that they partake of the qualities of this substance, as well as of those which belong more exclusively to the proper muscular fibre. Accordingly, muscles are always, in some degree, elastic; but it is impossible to ascertain whether this elasticity belongs to the fibre itself, because the fibre cannot be detached from the membrane which encloses it, without having its structure much injured; but, from its consistence and texture, as described by Sir A. Carlisle, we may conjecture that it is not so. The properties, however, which the muscular fibre may have in common with membrane, or with any other form of matter, are little worthy of our attention, compared with that power which it exclusively possesses, and from which all its actions are immediately derived, what has been designated under *Contracti-* the name of contractility. Contractility may be defin-*lity.* ed, the power which the fibre possesses of shortening *Stimuli.* itself upon the application of a stimulus. Under the appellation of stimulus are included a variety of things, which seem to have scarcely any common property, except that of acting upon the muscular fibre. It has been asserted, and is indeed literally true, that every body in nature is a stimulus to the muscular fibre, because, independently of any other quality, the mere contact of a material substance produces this effect. Stimuli have been arranged in various ways; but perhaps the most convenient and comprehensive is into the three classes, of mechanical, chemical, and what may be termed, physiological. Mechanical impulse of all kinds, beginning with the slightest touch that is capable of being perceived, and proceeding to any force short of what absolutely destroy the texture of the part, are of the first class; a great variety of chemical substances, alcohol, acids, alkalies, metallic salts, and many vegetable acids, that have few properties in common, are of the second class, while, in the third class, we may place those agents that seem to operate through the intervention of the nervous system, as the electric fluid, and particularly that modification of it which is styled galvanism. Independent of any external agents, the muscles are thrown into the strongest contractions by a variety of affections, which arise from internal causes, and, above all, from the act of volition. By a process which has hitherto proved inexplicable, we no sooner will the motion of any muscle, than the desired effect is immediately produced.

Effect of stimuli. When, by means of any of these stimulating powers, a muscle is thrown into action, the middle or belly swells out and becomes hardened, the ends are brought nearer together, and the surface, which was before smooth and shining, now becomes furrowed and wrinkled. In consequence of this swelling out of the middle and approximation of the extremities, the more moveable of the two ends is drawn towards that

which is the most fixed, and the bones or other parts *Physiology.* which are attached to it, are moved in the same direction. It has been a question, whether the contraction of a muscle increases its specific gravity, or whether they do not exactly gain in thickness what they lose in length. On this point Sir G. Blane made the fol-*Blane's* lowing experiment: he enclosed a living eel in a *experi-* glass vessel, filled with water, the neck of which was *ments.* drawn out into a tube; then by a wire introduced into the vessel, he irritated the animal, so as to produce strong contraction, but he found that the water in the tube remained stationary during the operation. An experiment of a similar kind was performed by *Carlisle's.* Sir A. Carlisle on a man's arm, but with a different result, for here the volume of the muscle appeared to be increased by the contraction, indicating a consequent diminution of specific gravity. But such experiments probably do not admit of a very decisive result, for it may be supposed, that while one muscle, or set of muscles, is contracting, the effect may be counterbalanced by the relaxation of a corresponding muscle or set of muscles.

When the stimulus ceases to act upon the muscle, or *Relaxation.* when the muscle ceases to obey the action of the stimulus, contraction likewise ceases and relaxation ensues; the fibres no longer exercise their power of shortening themselves, and the muscle is reduced to its former state. The replacement of the parts is brought about in various ways; sometimes by the elasticity of the membranes contained in, or immediately connected with, the muscle, by that of the ligaments and cartilages attached to it, by the action of antagonist muscles, or by the weight or reaction of the parts that were moved, being now left at liberty to exercise their powers. We are therefore to consider relaxation as altogether a passive effect, or a negative quality, merely consisting in the absence of contraction.

There is a circumstance respecting muscular con-*Exhaus-* traction, which it is important to notice, that the power *tion.* of contraction is limited in its duration. When a stimulus is applied to a muscle, although the application be continued as at first, or even increased, after a certain time it ceases to act, and relaxation necessarily follows; the muscle is then said to be exhausted, and it requires some time to intervene before the part is recruited, or can so far regain its power as to be again capable of obeying the action of stimuli. In general, the degree of exhaustion corresponds with the previous degree of stimulation, but they are very far from being in an exact ratio to each other. It is not perhaps very easy to ascertain the exact amount of contraction of which muscles are capable; in ordinary cases, we should consider it a powerful exertion which could reduce a muscle to two-thirds of its natural length, but there are instances where it would seem to go far beyond this limit.

Now that we are become familiar with the concep-*Contracti-* tion of contractility, as a distinct property inherent in *lity distinct* muscle, and peculiar to it, we can scarcely imagine any *from elas-* physical quality which is of a more specific character, *ticity.* yet it was only of late years that its nature was properly understood; for although Baglivi, Glisson, and others, entertained some correct notions upon the subject, Haller was the first who clearly pointed it out as a distinct quality, and announced it as the exclusive property of the muscular fibre. Before his time contractility had been more or less confounded with elasticity, yet the difference between them is sufficiently obvious. Elasticity is the mere effect of re-action; it is never the origin or source of power, but only restores,

Physiology. in a contrary direction, the force which had been previously impressed. Even when acting to the greatest advantage, it cannot afford any real increase of power, nor can it produce an effect, in the smallest degree greater than the cause; nor can reaction take place as long as the force continues to be applied. But the contrary to all this occurs with respect to muscular contractility. The mechanical effect bears no proportion to the cause producing it, and at the very time that the cause is still acting, the effect takes place, and infinitely surpasses the force of the agent. Although no facts occur more frequently to our observation than those here alluded to, yet so difficult is it to detach the mind from a wrong direction into which it may have once swerved, that, until the last century, all the attempts to account for muscular contraction were derived from the laws of mechanical impulse. The most learned men of the age, profound mathematicians, and acute reasoners, invented various hypotheses of this description, which were brought forward with all the parade of geometrical demonstration, and supported by a series of problems, theorems, corollaries, and lemmas. To all such misapplied learning it is sufficient to reply, that a mechanical force of an indefinite extent is frequently produced without the intervention of any mechanical cause whatever, and must therefore be referred to a power of a totally different nature.

Connexion between contractility and volition. We have mentioned above, that one of the most frequent causes of muscular contraction is the exercise of volition; but it is observed that different muscles bear a different relation to this faculty. Some muscles are almost entirely under the power of the will, while there are others over which the will has no control. Hence arises a division of muscles into voluntary and involuntary, the first including the muscles of locomotion, and those immediately concerned in the action of the external senses; the second including the muscles employed in the internal functions, such as the heart, the parts about the lungs, and the stomach. The law of contractility, by which relaxation always succeeds to contraction, is the most observable in those muscles that are affected by the stimulants that act independently of the will; when the stimulating power is applied to them in a regular and uniform manner, the alternations of contraction and relaxation proceed with perfect regularity, and give rise to some of the most important operations of the animal economy.

Habit influences muscular motion. There is no part of our frame over which habit has more influence than the muscles, and especially those which are directed by the will. All those actions by which we maintain a voluntary intercourse with our fellow-creatures, and with the external world, are effected by complicated trains of muscular contractions, which are originally acquired by long practice, and after many unsuccessful attempts, but which by degrees become so familiar, through the operation of custom, that they are at length performed without one being conscious of them. The same remark applies to our associated muscular motions, which may be traced up to the effect of habit, connecting different actions, which, in the first instance, seem to have no necessary dependence upon each other.

Use of muscles. It is not necessary to make many observations upon the use of the muscles, as this is sufficiently obvious from the consideration of their characteristic properties. They are the organs of motion, both of that kind of motion by which the body is moved from place to place, constituting locomotion, that by which each of its separate parts is moved when we act upon contiguous bodies, and that by which many of the minute actions of the animal are performed, which are essential to the exercise of the vital functions. All those effects are brought about by the simple act of contraction, or the shortening of the fibres, by which the ends are approximated, and the parts moved to which they are attached. The action of the muscular coats is no less efficient than that of the muscles, although it is less obvious to the eye. The fibres in this case not being collected in large masses that act simultaneously, the effect of their contraction is not the motion of any large organ, but as the different fibres appear to act more independently of each other, they produce in the organ to which they belong a peculiar kind of undulatory, or, as it is termed, vermicular motion, which serves to keep their surface in a state of continued agitation, and to communicate it to their contents.

Are all spontaneous motions contractile? There is one question connected with this part of the subject, which has often been discussed, whether all the spontaneous motions that occur in the body are to be referred to contractility, or whether every motion which cannot be accounted for by the laws of elasticity or of gravity, or any of the general physical powers of matter, may be explained upon the principles of muscular contraction. A difficulty has arisen in certain cases, because we observe very obvious motions to take place in some organs, and yet we are not able to detect any muscular fibres in them. One of the most remarkable cases of this description, which has been appealed to as sufficient to decide the controversy, is the motion of the iris. In this organ, which is so large as to be quite open to our inspection, and in which the motions are considerably extensive, no muscular fibres have yet been satisfactorily demonstrated, nor, if they were so, is it very clear in what way they could be disposed, so as to produce the desired effect. To account, therefore, for the motion of the iris, it has been thought necessary to have recourse to some other principle *.

Blumenbach's hypothesis. Blumenbach has attempted to solve this problem, by ascribing to this and some other parts, in which a similar kind of anomaly exists, a peculiar property or power, which he terms vita propria, and supposing that this vita propria causes the contractions of these organs. But this hypothesis of Blumenbach cannot be regarded in any other point of view than as a mere form of speech, which throws no light upon either the phenomenon itself or its causes, and which neither tends to generalize analogous facts, nor to show how they bear upon each other. Nothing, however, can be more injurious to the progress of knowledge than to form hypotheses which are merely verbal, and which really give us no insight into the nature of the subject. Every one must be conscious that there are many parts of physiology which are yet unexplained, and we conceive the motion of the iris to be one of these, nor are we to regard it as in any respect humiliating, that, on so abstruse a subject, we are frequently under the necessity of confessing the insufficiency of the present state of our knowledge.

Sect. III. *Mechanism of Muscles.*

Muscular motion depends upon contraction. In considering the mechanism of muscles, we must refer to the description which was given of these organs, as consisting of bundles of fibres lying parallel to each other, which possess the power of shortening

* The microscopical observations of Mr. Bauer have decided the controversy respecting the iris, by clearly detecting its muscular structure. See *Phil. Trans.* 1822.

Physiology. themselves, and, in this way, bring their extremities nearer together. The ultimate object of this shortening of the fibres is, to move the ends of the bones to which the fibres are attached; but, in order to promote the symmetry of the form, or to facilitate motion, it frequently happens that the flesh of the muscle itself is not inserted into the part which is to be moved, but that a membranous body intervenes, which, according to its situation, or the use of the organ, is either condensed into a strong cord, constituting a tendon, or is spread out into a membranous expansion. The motions of the bones, depending upon the shortening of the muscular fibres, are generally performed by means of joints; and it will be found that the bones are acted upon by the muscles in the manner of levers; the part where the muscle or tendon is inserted into the bone representing the power, the joint the fulcrum, and the part that is moved constituting the weight. With a few exceptions only, the bones form levers of that description which are styled by mechanicians of the third kind; in which the power is placed between the fulcrum and the weight. The motion of the fore-arm may be taken as an example of the effect of muscular contraction, and the manner in which it is produced. When we wish to raise a weight by bending the elbow joint, it is effected by muscles situated below the shoulder, which have tendons inserted into the top of the bone of the fore-arm near the elbow.

Bones constitute levers.

Example of the arm.

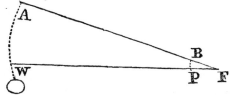

Let AB represent the fore-arm, BD the shoulder bone, C the muscle, E the tendon, F the insertion of the tendon into the fore-arm, and B the elbow joint. The contraction of the muscle tends to bring F to D, and, as D is a fixed point, this is effected by bending the joint B, raising up the point F, and, consequently, the weight A. By considering the manner in which the muscle acts in this case, and referring the action to the mechanical principles of the lever, we find that the mechanism of the animal body is calculated to produce a great loss of power. This depends upon the principle in mechanics, that in the action of levers, the power is to the weight as the distance between the weight and the fulcrum is to the distance between the power and the fulcrum. In the present case, the power of the muscle will be to the effect produced by it as AB is to FB; and, supposing FB to be $\frac{1}{10}$ of the length of AB, $\frac{1}{10}$ only of the power of the muscle is exerted in raising the weight, the rest is expended in acting against the disadvantage of the position. We shall find it to be a law of the animal economy, with respect to the action of muscles, that power is always sacrificed to convenience. Had the object been to raise the weight in the hand with the least possible power, the muscles would have been placed near the wrist, and the tendon inserted into the lower part of the shoulder bone; but, in this case, the awkwardness of the limb would have much more than counteracted the supposed advantage of a saving of muscular power. The remark applies with still greater force to the fingers; they are moved by the contraction of muscles placed on the fore-arm, and connected to them by long and delicate tendons, which pass over the wrist and the hand. But if this order had been inverted, and the flesh of the muscles had been placed on the fingers, the hand would have been almost useless from its clumsy form.

Loss of power in muscular action.

Power sacrificed to convenience.

Velocity gained.

There is, moreover, a decided advantage in the present arrangement, that, although we lose power we acquire velocity, and this in the same proportion.

Physiology.

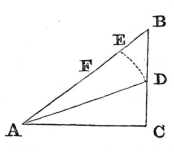

Let WPF represent the bone of the fore-arm, in which W is the weight, P the power, and F the fulcrum. Now, let us suppose that the elbow-joint is moved, so as to bring the arm into the position ABF; from the centre F draw the arcs AW and BP, and it will appear, that, while the power is passing through the small arc PB, the weight is describing the large arc AW. Now the arcs are to each other, as the lines WF and PF, and the arcs are passed over in the same time, the velocity will therefore be as the lines WF and PF, or, in this case, as ten to one.

There is another circumstance in the mechanical structure of the muscles which causes a large expenditure of power, but which is compensated by the advantage of its saving the quantity of contraction, or in enabling a muscle to perform more by the same degree of contraction than could otherwise have been done. We refer to the oblique position of the muscular fibres.

Oblique insertion of the muscles saves contraction.

Let A and C be two fixed points in a bone, and let B be a moveable point, which is to be brought down to D. If this were done by a straight fibre, passing in a perpendicular direction, BC, it would be necessary that the fibre should contract equal to half its whole length, supposing BD equal to DC; but if we employ the oblique fibre AB, the effect is produced by its contracting through the space EB only, which is less than half its length by EF. AB being bisected in F. It is evident that the smaller is the degree of the contraction of the fibre, and the less alteration the muscle consequently experiences in its general form, the more conveniently will the action be performed. There will be less displacement of parts, less pressure upon the vessels and nerves, the antagonist muscles will be less stretched, and, in short, there will be less change in the relative position of the organs, or of the different parts of the same organ.

A third source of loss of power depends upon the circumstance of two or more muscles concurring in the same object, and, therefore, having a certain degree of obliquity to each other, and, in so far as this is the case, acting as antagonists. When two oblique muscles act upon the same point, the effect will be to draw it down through the diagonal; we, therefore, have it in our power to alter the direction of the motion with great facility, by throwing a little more or less energy into one or other of the muscles, and thus moving the body into any of the intermediate positions, so that a number of motions may be performed by two muscles only.

Co-operation of muscles.

Physiology.
Oblique insertion of the tendons.

A great loss of power, likewise, arises from the tendons being generally inserted into the bone at a very acute angle, whereas, in order that the power might have been exerted to the most advantage, the muscles ought to have acted upon the lever in a perpendicular direction; and, upon the same principle, power is lost by having the muscular fibres inserted obliquely into the tendons. But, in these cases, it is obvious, that the present arrangement is much more convenient, and conducive to the symmetry and beauty of the form. It is generally stated by writers on the mechanism of muscular motion, that half the power of the muscles is lost in consequence of the two ends pulling against each other. Where one end of a muscle is attached to a fixed point, as much power is expended on this as on the moveable extremity; and, before the latter can produce any effect, it must counteract and overcome the resistance offered by the former.

Other causes of loss of power.

There are probably other causes, besides those which have been mentioned above, by which there is a loss of power in the contraction of the muscles; but, in all cases, this loss of power will be found to be compensated by some corresponding advantage. It may be conjectured, that, in proportion as the contraction of the fibre advances, a great force becomes necessary to produce each successive degree of contraction, and the more the fibre is shortened the more painful the exertion becomes, and the more fatigue is induced by its continuance. Hence we may perceive why power is always sacrificed for the purpose of diminishing the quantity of contraction necessary for effecting a certain change of position, as well as for increasing the velocity of the motion, or promoting the symmetry of the form.

Borelli's estimate.

Borelli, who explained the mechanical action of muscles with so much ingenuity, and had the merit of first placing the subject in a correct point of view, has made many elaborate calculations to estimate the quantity of power which is lost by the different circumstances that have been pointed out, and some others which he mentions in addition to them. He concludes that, in many cases, not more than $\frac{1}{60}$ part of the power exerted is actually employed in performing the effect required; and, although we may doubt whether all his calculations be equally well-founded, yet, perhaps, upon the whole, the estimate is not exaggerated.

Saving of power.

After pointing out so many circumstances in the animal mechanism, which contribute to the expenditure of muscular power, we must not omit to notice, that there are a few instances of a contrary kind, where the structure of the parts tends to assist the muscles, and produces a saving of power. The heads of the bones into which the tendons are inserted frequently swell out so as to form a considerable projection, by which means the muscles act upon the bones at a less oblique angle; and we observe this structure to exist more remarkably in those cases where the greatest exertion of muscular power is required, as about the trunk and the lower extremities. For the same purpose some bones have processes of considerable length, which appear to be intended solely for the insertion of muscles; and the same would seem to be the use of the small detached bones which are occasionally found about the joints, such as the patella of the knee.

SECT. IV. *Hypotheses of Muscular Contraction.*

Cause of contractility.

The cause of contractility, or the relation which it bears to the other powers or properties of matter, has given rise to many hypotheses and conjectures, some of which it will be proper for us to consider. The subject must be regarded in two points of view: we may first inquire, what is the physical cause of the contraction of the fibre? and, second, what is the cause or nature of that property of the fibre which enables it to contract? Both these questions are obscure and of very difficult solution; and we shall find, that, notwithstanding all the attempts that have been made to solve them, very little light has been thrown upon the subject. With respect to the efficient cause of muscular contraction, every explanation which depends upon mere mechanical principles must be necessarily abortive, nor shall we be more disposed to place confidence in the opinions of those who refer it to some chemical operation, as fermentation, or effervescence, excited by the mixture of an acid and an alkali; or some occult or mysterious operation of the animal spirits distending the fibres; or to any electrical or galvanic arrangement which causes muscular contraction by its explosion. It may not, however, be uninteresting to give a short account of one theory, not so much from any merit which it possesses, as from its being a specimen of the manner in which the most learned men of the seventeenth century misapplied their learning, by permitting themselves to confound a train of reasoning with a deduction of facts. The theory to which I refer is that of Keill, a man of considerable ingenuity; and who was well versed in the mathematical sciences, which were then deemed the basis of all physical knowledge.

Keill's hypothesis

Keill began by adopting the notion of Borelli, that the muscular fibre consists of a series of rhomboidal vesicles which communicate with each other. He observes, that if these vesicles be distended, the length of the fibre must be diminished, and the muscle consequently shortened. The blood and the animal spirits were made the agents for effecting this distention, which it was supposed was done by the fluids contained in the muscle being rarefied. To produce this rarefaction the author has recourse to the supposition, that a quantity of condensed air is attached to the fluid particles of the blood, which is retained in its present state by the pressure of the vesicle exactly balancing the distending force of the air; but when a quantity of the animal spirits are brought into contact with the blood containing the condensed air, the two fluids unite together, and a sudden rarefaction or increase of elasticity is the consequence, which distends the vesicle and produces contraction. Having thus explained the nature of the effect that is produced, the author enters upon a long and abstruse train of mathematical reasoning, to show how the degree of effect may be indefinitely increased, without increasing the quantity of the elastic fluid which is set at liberty. He observes, that by diminishing the size of each vesicle, and proportionally increasing their number, the same shortening of the fibre will be produced at the same time that the capacity of the vesicles taken together will be diminished in proportion as their number is increased, and as there is no limit to this operation, it follows that any bulk of gas may produce any quantity of contraction, in the ratio of one to several millions. It is scarcely necessary to remark, that the whole of this hypothesis is built upon suppositions which are entirely gratuitous, and that the whole is consequently without the slightest foundation.

General remarks.

Although we should not be tempted to examine any more of the hypotheses which have been formed on this subject, it may be proper to consider in what de-

Physiology. gree the cause of muscular contraction is a legitimate object of inquiry, and towards what points we ought particularly to direct our attention. The simple act of contraction must consist in the diminution of the length of the fibres, of which the muscle is composed; but we have no proof, either from the evidence of our senses, or from any correct deduction of reasoning, of any specific structure or composition of the fibre, which can, in any degree, explain the manner in which this diminution is effected. It is not likely that any farther discoveries can be made on this subject, by the aid of microscopes, for it appears that there is a limit to the employment of high magnifiers, beyond which the liability to ocular deception is so great, as to counteract any supposed advantage of the increased size of the object. If we are unable to account for the shortening of the fibres, still less are we able to explain why the various things which we call stimuli, so extremely heterogeneous in their nature, and which have no common property, should coincide in this single point of acting in the same manner upon the fibre. This is so unlike the operation of any other physical cause with which we are acquainted, that we must, at least for the present, consider it as an ultimate fact, one of those mysteries in nature, which daily present themselves to our observation, but which elude all our attempts to refer to any more general principle.

Cause of contractility. The attempts that have been made to explain the cause of contractility are no less numerous than those respecting the mode in which the contraction is effected, but they have hitherto been equally unfounded; nor indeed do we possess the least insight into this part of the subject. Because it was observed that there is an intimate connexion between the temperature of an animal and the degree of its contractility, some physiologists have conceived that contractility depends immediately upon caloric interposed between the fibres. Others, perceiving how remarkably the muscles are affected by the electric fluid, supposed that this was the immediate source of muscular contractility, while other writers have contented themselves with saying, that contractility depends upon structure. The fibre, they say, does not differ in its general properties from many other forms of matter, but it possesses a peculiar structure, this must therefore be the immediate cause of its contractile power.

Referred to chemical composition. An hypothesis respecting contractility, which at one time excited considerable attention, was, that this property depends upon the chemical composition of the fibre; whenever the different elements are combined in such proportion as to form the fibre, contractility is one of the properties which necessarily results from the combination. Humboldt published a train of experiments, which were directed to this point, and which, if correct, would seem to prove, that apparently slight changes in the chemical composition of the muscle entirely destroy its contractility, and that by restoring the original composition of the muscle, the contractility is also restored.

To oxygen. A modification, or peculiar form of the chemical hypothesis, was brought forward a few years ago, according to which oxygen was regarded as the principle of contractility, or was that substance which, by being imparted to the system, or removed from it, gave the muscles their contractile power. The source of the oxygen thus obtained was conceived to be the air inspired by the lungs, which was united with the arterial blood, and in this way Physiology. carried to the muscles. For some time this opinion acquired a considerable degree of popularity, and it appeared to be supported by many pathological facts, but we apprehend that it is now generally admitted to be entirely without foundation. Nor indeed can any of the above mentioned speculations afford us a satisfactory reply to the proposed question. They teach us that contractility can only exist under a certain range of temperature, and as attached to a certain mechanical structure and chemical composition, and they likewise prove that the electric fluid is one of the most active and powerful stimulants, but they do not establish that kind of connexion between the supposed cause and its effect, which can induce us to regard them as bearing this kind of relation to each other. Indeed there are many well known facts, which seem to lead to an opposite conclusion. Many circumstances affect the contractility of a muscle, which cannot be supposed to alter either its chemical or its mechanical properties. A muscle, immediately after death, as far as we can judge, is similar in its structure and composition to a living muscle, yet, upon the application of stimulants, we find it to be no longer contractile. If it be argued that the chemical or mechanical composition are different, but that the difference is too minute to be detected, we should reply, that where the difference is too minute to be observed, we can have no proof of its existence.

Other hypotheses. In tracing the history of opinions, we must not overlook a doctrine which has been sanctioned by some distinguished physiologists, especially by Haller and Cullen, that contractility is nothing more than a peculiar mode of attraction which subsists between all kind of matter; nor that of Fordyce and Hunter, who ascribe it to what they term the attraction of life. But these, when stripped of the peculiar language in which they are conveyed, amount to nothing more than the expression of the fact in new terms, for still the fundamental difficulty remains, what is it that determines the attraction between the particles of matter to exert their force in this peculiar manner, and under these peculiar circumstances.

Conclusion. We have therefore no hesitation in concluding, that, in the present state of our knowledge, contractility ought to be regarded as the unknown cause of known effects, a quality attached to certain forms of matter, possessed of specific properties, which we cannot refer to any more general principle.

CHAP. V.

OF THE NERVOUS SYSTEM.

Nervous system. AFTER having described in the last chapter one of the appropriate powers of the animal system, contractility, and the organ by which it is exercised, we must proceed to the other exclusive property of animal life, sensibility. We shall arrange our remarks on this Arrangement. subject into three sections; in the first, we shall offer a brief description of the organ of sensibility, the nervous system, of its anatomical structure, and of its physical and chemical properties; secondly, we shall inquire into its vital properties, and, particularly, we shall examine the nature of sensibility; in the third place, we shall treat of the use of the nervous system.

SECT. I. *Description of the Nervous System.*

Description of the brain.

The nervous system consists of four principal parts, the brain, the spinal cord, the nerves, and the ganglia. The brain is an organ of a pulpy consistence, resembling a soft coagulum, lodged in and filling the hollow bone called the skull, which forms the main bulk of the head. It is of an extremely irregular figure, having a great number of projections and depressions, corresponding partly to the irregularities of the skull, and partly formed by convolutions and cavities in the brain itself. There are also some considerable cavities in the interior of the brain, which are called ventricles; they are lined with a serous membrane, secreting an albuminous fluid, which is generally absorbed as rapidly as it is produced, but in certain morbid states is accumulated in the part, and gives rise to the formidable disease of hydrocephalus. With respect to the use of the different projections and depressions of the brain, nothing certain is known; but there are two points connected with its form, which it is important to attend to, as they appear to throw some light upon the physiology of the organ; first, the division of the encephalon, or cerebral mass into the brain, properly so called, or cerebrum, and into the lesser brain or cerebellum; and, second, its division into the two hemispheres. By much the greatest part of the nervous matter within the skull composes the proper brain or cerebrum: it occupies the whole of the upper part of the head, and is separated from the cerebellum by a dense membrane, called the tentorium, except at the common basis of both, where they are united. There is also a dense membrane projecting downwards to a considerable depth from the upper part of the skull, called the falx, which stretches from the fore to the back part of the head, and divides the brain into its two hemispheres; there is also the same kind of division in the cerebellum.

Cortical and medullary matter.

When we cut into the brain we find it to be composed of two substances, that differ in their colour and consistence; the one external, called the cortical or cineritious matter, the other occupying the central part, named the proper medullary matter. The cortical is of a brownish colour, and contains a great number of blood-vessels that are visible to the eye, while many more are brought into view by means of the microscope. Ruysch went so far as to conceive that it is entirely composed of vessels, together with the connecting membrane, an opinion which is obviously incorrect. Malpighi, probably influenced rather by his hypothesis than by actual observation, announced the existence of a glandular structure in this part of the brain. The medullary matter is less vascular than the cortical part, and may be regarded as consisting of the nervous matter in a purer or more perfect state.

Fibrous structure.

When we minutely examine the medullary part of the brain, it will be found to exhibit a fibrous texture, or to be composed of a number of longitudinal striæ, and these striæ are disposed in such a manner as that they meet in the centre of the brain, and form what are styled the commissures. It has been supposed that they proceed still farther in the same direction, actually decussating or crossing each other, and a variety of pathological facts are adduced, which seem to favour this opinion; as where an injury or disease exists on one side of the brain and manifests its effects on the opposite side of the body. With respect to the fact itself of the decussation of these fibres, it may be doubted how far it is established by dissection, but

undoubtedly the morbid phenomena are satisfactorily explained by this supposition.

Membranes.

The brain is covered with two principal membranes, an external one, thick and dense, which lines the skull, and the other thin and delicate, which is more immediately attached to the brain itself, and follows it through all its convolutions; these membranes are called respectively the dura and pia mater, from a whimsical notion of the older anatomists, that they were the origin of all the membranes of the body. Between these two membranes lies the third, of a texture still more delicate than the pia mater, which, from its fineness, is termed the arachnoid membrane.

Spinal cord.

From the lower part of the brain, and connected with it by the intervention of a medullary mass, called the medulla oblongata, proceeds the spinal cord, or, as it has been improperly termed, the spinal marrow; this is a quantity of nervous matter, filling up the hollow which is continued through the centre of the chain of bones composing the spine. Like the brain, it is inclosed in membranes, and possesses both cortical and cineritious matter, but the relative situation of the two is reversed. It has a depression on its back part, analagous to the division of the brain into the two hemispheres, but the effect of injuries of the spinal cord is different from those of the brain, in as much as the loss of power is on the same side of the body.

Nerves.

From the base of the brain, or the parts immediately connected with it, proceed a number of white cords, called nerves, composed of medullary matter, contained in membranous sheaths, and apparently possessing a fibrous structure, which are sent to the different organs of sense. The same kind of bodies pass from the spinal cord to all the muscles, and to the different viscera of the thorax and abdomen; both the cerebral and the spinal nerves are disposed in pairs, and proceed in corresponding directions to the opposite sides of the body. There are originally nine pair of cerebral, and thirty of spinal nerves, but soon after their commencement they branch out in various directions, and form numerous anastomoses; these are in some cases so complicated, as to compose a complete network, to which the name of plexus has been applied. From these plexuses new nerves arise, which often seem to be quite independent of those which produced them, and are some of them evidently formed by the union of the two nerves, which probably originated from a different quarter. When the nerves arrive at their ultimate destination, they ramify into small branches, which become more and more minute, until at length they are no longer visible to the eye.

Plexuses.

Ganglia.

The ganglia are small masses of nervous matter, situated along the course of the larger nerves, frequently where two or three of them form an angle, and especially in the different parts of the thorax and abdomen. They consist of a mixture of both cortical and cineritious matter, and are generally more plentifully supplied with blood-vessels than the nerves. With respect to their texture, we are informed that the filaments of the different nerves which compose the ganglia proceed without interruption, but that they are all twisted together into an irregular bundle, and that filaments of different nerves are united together so as to compose one nerve as it proceeds from these parts; the viscera of the thorax and the abdomen are principally supplied with nerves from the ganglia.

Distribution of the nerves.

The organs of sense and the muscles of voluntary motion receive the greatest proportion of nervous matter, the viscera are supplied more sparingly, the glands

Physiology. still more so, while the membranous parts are nearly without nerves. For the most part, the organs of sense receive their nerves from the brain, and the muscles from the spinal marrow, while the viscera generally are supplied with nerves from the ganglia or the plexuses. These latter are connected with each other, and with the other parts of the body in a variety of ways, as if for the purpose of insuring a communication between all the different parts. If we conceive of the body as divided by a plane passing perpendicularly through its centre, the nerves of the two halves will be found almost exactly similar to each other.

Blood sent to the brain. Anatomists have remarked upon the great quantity of blood that is sent to the brain; although this organ is only about one-fortieth part of the weight of the whole body, yet it is estimated, that at least one-tenth of all the blood is immediately sent to it from the heart, and there are many curious contrivances in the structure of the brain, by which the force of the blood is diminished, or at least so modified as to prevent the danger of its pressing with too much violence upon any part of this organ, and thus injuring its texture.

Minute structure. The minute structure of the brain and nerves has been examined and described by different anatomists, but it must be confessed that considerable difficulty still attaches to the subject. When we inspect the brain shortly after death, we can readily distinguish in its medullary part a number of furrows with ridges between them, which run parallel to each other, and the same kind of fibrous or striated texture may be perceived in the nerves. It seems, however, that we are capable of detecting much more minute divisions in the nerves than in any part of the brain, those of the former, according to the microscopical observations of Fontana and Reil, being far too minute to be visible to the naked eye, whereas, it does not appear that we are able, by the aid of glasses, to separate the visible fibres of the brain into any smaller fibres.

Chemical properties of brain. For our knowledge of the chemical properties of medullary matter, we are principally indebted to Fourcroy and Vauquelin. We learn from the experiments of the latter, that brain consists of a proper adipose substance, the peculiar animal principle called osmazome, a quantity of albumen, a minute portion of phosphorus, and some salts. The adipose matter is so connected or combined with the albumen, as to form a kind of saponaceous substance, so that when brain is agitated with water it forms an emulsion, which continues for a long time without being decomposed. The albumen is capable of undergoing an imperfect coagulation by heat, or by the addition of various re-agents, but it seems, independently of the presence of the other ingredients, to differ somewhat from the albumen of the blood. Brain contains about three-fourths of its weight of water, and when this is removed by a careful evaporation, the residuum is converted into a half solid friable mass. The salts that are found in brain are chiefly the phosphates of lime, soda, and ammonia; the muriates, which are in such large quantity in the blood and many other animal fluids, appear not to be present in the brain, or at least to exist in much smaller quantity.

Sect. 2. *Vital Properties of the Nervous System,— Sensibility.*

Sensibility. We proceed, in the second place, to consider the properties of the nervous system, and the connexion which it has with the other parts of the body. It is obvious that the office of the nervous system is to produce sensation; but it is extremely difficult to comprehend the **Physiology.** manner in which this is accomplished, and it is equally difficult to ascertain the relation which the different parts of the nervous system bear to each other. The general doctrine on the subject is, that the brain is the centre of the system, the part to which all the rest are subservient; that the spinal cord is merely a prolongation or continuation of the brain; that the nerves receive impressions from external objects, and transmit these impressions to the brain, where they become sensible to the mind, and the intellectual faculties. This view of the subject is probably in the main correct, although the experiments and discoveries of the modern anatomists have led to some modifications which deserve to be noticed.

Nervous action obscure. All questions respecting the action of the nervous system are involved in much obscurity, which appears, in some measure, necessarily attached to the nature of the subject. Although there are many difficulties connected with the operations of the muscular system, yet we can form a plausible conjecture respecting the mode in which it acts, and we can distinctly trace it from its commencement in the fibre to the part that is moved; so that we are able to see the connexion between the shortening of the fibre and the ultimate effects, although we cannot assign any reason why the application of stimulants should produce this immediate effect upon the fibre. But we have no analogy of this kind to guide us in explaining the phenomena of the nervous system; so that, although we have sufficient evidence that the nerves are the media by which external impressions are conveyed to the brain, we are unable to account for the mode of the conveyance.

Sensibility defined. Sensibility, the term which is generally employed by physiologists to express the power which the nervous system possesses of producing sensation, is here used in a metaphorical sense, its original import implying a certain state of the mind or character, and having no express relation to the physical state of the nerves. When, however, we adopt it as a physiological term, we restrict its operations to the nervous system, and define it to be, the power which this system possesses of receiving and transmitting impressions. The affection of the nerves appears, in some cases, to be confined to themselves, and at other times to be transmitted to the mind, when it constitutes a perception; but this is **Perception.** not a necessary consequence, as there are many instances in which the nerves transmit impressions to distant parts, of which our feelings give us no indication. Hence we perceive the distinction between a simple sensation and a perception, a distinction which nearly coincides with Bichat's division of sensibility **Bichat's organic and animal sensibility.** into organic and animal; for this division would appear to have a real foundation in nature, although we may conceive that he is not always correct in the classification of the different cases which he notices.

Haller and Whytt's controversy. In relation to this subject, we may notice the learned and animated discussion that was carried on about sixty years ago, between Haller and Whytt, respecting the mode in which the muscular and nervous systems are connected with each other. The question at issue was, whether the nerves are necessarily concerned in muscular contraction; whether, when a stimulant acts upon a muscle so as to produce contraction, it acts directly upon the fibre, or always produces its effect through the intervention of the nerve. Before the time of Haller, no clear conception had been formed of the living body, as endowed with distinct faculties or powers, but as simply possessing life. He very accu-

Physiology.

Haller's hypothesis.

rately examined the nature of the vital power, and showed that it may be referred to the two heads of contractility and sensibility, which are exercised by two sets of organs. And he did not rest here, but he endeavoured to show, that these functions not only differ in their nature, but that they are independent of each other in their operation: and he concluded that the muscular fibre, without the co-operation of the nerve, possesses the power of being directly acted upon by stimulants; to this power he gave the name of irritability.

Whytt's.

Whytt, on the contrary, denies the existence of this innate irritability, but supposes, that in all cases, stimulants act primarily upon the nerves connected with the muscle, and that the impression is conveyed from the nerve to the muscular fibre.

Arguments of Haller.

The great argument of Haller was an appeal to the anatomical structure of the body. He pointed out many parts that are extremely contractile, but which are possessed of very little sensibility; and he endeavoured to show generally, that these two properties bear no relation to each other, which they should do were they necessarily connected together.

Condition of the heart;

The heart was particularly referred to by Haller in this controversy, as being a muscular organ in perpetual motion, and capable of strong contraction, yet scantily furnished with nerves, and almost destitute of feeling.

separated parts remain contractile.

It was also advanced, as a strong proof of this doctrine, that muscular parts remain contractile for a considerable time after they are removed from the body; and, of course, when their communication with the brain is destroyed; and this is particularly the case with the heart itself; which, in many of the amphibia and cold-blooded animals, remains susceptible of the impression of stimulants for some hours after its separation from the body; yet now, it was asked, can the nervous system be affected since the seat of sensation is removed?

Acephalous fœtuses;

Upon the same principle, and in furtherance of the same train of reasoning, cases were adduced of acephalous fœtuses, which had yet grown to their full size, and seemed to possess the various vital functions in a perfect state, so that they must have enjoyed muscular contractility, although totally destitute of a brain.

animals without nerves;

It was also urged, that, among the lower classes of animals, there are many that are entirely without a nervous system; yet where the muscles are easily excited by stimulants, and capable of very powerful contractions. It was also remarked, that, in the more perfect animals, if we watch the progress in which the different parts are formed, and of course the order in which the different functions are developed, we shall find that the heart exists before the brain; and, of course, that there must be contractility without sensibility.

heart formed before the brain.

And this circumstance accords with our ordinary opinion upon the subject; for we can easily conceive the possibility of mere life being continued without sensation, while we could not imagine any species of existence to which some kind of internal motion was not essential.

Arguments of Whytt; general diffusion of nerves;

The reasoning that was employed by the neurologists was, in like manner, founded upon the structure of the animal body. They asserted that nerves are dispersed through every portion of the muscular system; and that, although some parts are more plentifully supplied than others, yet that the quantity of nerve in each case is in proportion to the wants of the part, and are adequate to produce all the contractions of which it is capable. With respect to the particular case of the heart, it was asserted that it possesses nerves, although perhaps less than some other muscles, and that the use of these nerves is to receive the first impression of the stimulants, which ultimately cause its contraction.

Physiology.

and of feeling;

As a proof of the general diffusion of nerves, it is affirmed, that there is no part of the body in which we can produce a contraction, where we cannot, at the same time, excite a sensation, for that it is impossible to insert the finest point of a needle, where we shall not as easily feel pain or produce motion. Whytt seems to have had some difficulty in accounting for the contraction of a muscular part after its removal from the body, and its separation from the nervous centre, and he found no better method of explaining this circumstance than by supposing that the sentient principle is divisible, which in fact amounts to the position that different parts of the body can individually feel the impressions that are made upon them. It must, however, be admitted, that this consequence does not necessarily attach to the hypothesis of the neurologists, for we allow that nerves may be affected, and may transmit the impression to the muscular fibre, without producing a perception.

Muscles acted on through the nerves.

Many facts of perpetual occurrence were adduced, where muscular contractions were excited by causes which could only operate through the nerves, such as passions of the mind, and more especially the act of volition, which is the immediate cause of so large a proportion of our motions. Numerous experiments were also adduced to prove that physical agents, both stimulants and sedatives, operate through the medium of the nerves. If the nerve which communicates with a muscle be immersed in a solution of laurel water, or, on the other hand, be submitted to the galvanic influence, the muscle is as much, or more affected, than if these agents were applied to the fibres themselves. There are, likewise, a variety of morbid phenomena which favour the opinion that the nerves are immediately concerned in muscular action, both those circumstances which immediately affect the brain, or any part of the nervous system, and still more those which only operate through the intervention of the intellectual functions.

Experiments of Le Gallois,

And besides the numerous considerations which were adduced by Whytt and his contemporaries in favour of the nervous hypothesis, some elaborate experiments, which were lately performed by Le Gallois, have been supposed to afford a still more direct proof of this doctrine. His object was to ascertain what are the respective effects of the different parts of the nervous system upon the powers of life; and, in the course of this inquiry, he conceived that he had demonstrated, that every muscular part is under the influence either of the brain or spinal cord, both of these parts being centres of nervous sensibility. One powerful objection to the hypothesis of Whytt is therefore removed, that the heart is capable of contraction after its separation from the brain; for, according to Le Gallois, the spinal cord is the part from which the heart derives its energy. He also endeavoured to show, by direct experiments, that when both the brain and spinal cord are removed or destroyed, all muscular contraction ceases; and he hence concludes, in opposition to the doctrine of Haller, that the nervous system is necessarily concerned in all cases of muscular contraction.

controverted by Philip.

But notwithstanding the elaborate and varied nature of Le Gallois's experiments, many of his deductions have been called in question by Dr. W. Philip, who, from experiments no less elaborate, has attempted to show that muscular parts, and in particular the heart, can continue to contract for an indefinite period after the complete destruction of both the brain and spinal cord, so as entirely to destroy the force of Le Gallois's reasoning, and to go far towards establishing Haller's hypothesis.

We may therefore conclude, that, notwithstanding the weight of argument in favour of the opinion of the neurologists, which has, at least of late years, given it a preponderance in the public estimation, they have not proved the point under discussion ; and that, although we admit the facts which they adduce, we may still doubt whether the nervous influence be a necessary step in the production of muscular contraction. In order to establish this point, we must not only show that the nerves may be concerned in the operation, but that their action is essential to the process. It is admitted that the nerve is frequently a necessary intermedium between the application of the stimulant and the contraction of the fibre, but is this always the case ? To this question we are disposed to reply in the negative ; and we conceive it to be clearly proved by Dr. Philip, that there are a large class of muscular parts which have but little connexion with the nervous system, or are only occasionally subject to its influence. This is the case with the parts which are not under the control of the will, and especially with the organs which are concerned in those functions, which, in their ordinary and healthy action, do not produce perception.

This very circumstance affords some presumption in favour of this opinion, as well as their being little affected by those causes which act so powerfully upon the voluntary muscles, and still more from the anatomical facts which were adduced by Haller, as well as those more recently brought forwards by Dr. Philip, many of which, we presume, it would be difficult to reconcile with the hypothesis of their antagonists. The result of the Galvanic experiments, which have been much insisted upon, when duly considered, must be regarded as less favourable to the nervous theory than has been supposed by its advocates. It is indeed true, that, in the contraction of the voluntary muscles, the influence may be applied through the medium of the nerves, but the case is different with those parts that are not under the control of the will ; for we find that we can produce no effect upon these muscles by transmitting the Galvanic influence to them through their nerves, or at least no effect at all proportional to the contractility of the parts. The fair inference from these experiments therefore is, that Galvanism is one of those stimulants that act principally through the medium of the nerves, while they throw no light upon the nature of the connexion between the muscular and the nervous systems. We may farther remark concerning this controversy, that no facts or experiments are strictly applicable to it, except those which refer to the involuntary muscles ; and that it is not enough to prove that, in certain cases, the stimulant acts primarily upon the nerve, but to show that it does so in every instance.

Sect. III. Uses of the Nervous System.

The uses of the nervous system are two—to maintain a connexion with the external world, and to unite the different parts of the body into one whole. No point in physiology is better established, than that the nerves are the media by which the external impressions are conveyed to the brain. The eye, for example, is an optical instrument adapted for receiving the rays of light and bringing them to a focus, so as to form an image of the object on an expansion of nervous matter, which communicates by the optic nerve with the under part of the brain. Now it is found to be as necessary for vision that the nerve should be in a perfect state as

that the eye itself should be sound ; and blindness is as certainly produced by a defect in the one part as in the other. With respect to the muscles of voluntary motion, if the nerve which passes to them from the brain be divided in its course, or even if it be pressed upon, or have its action in any way impaired, motion is as certainly destroyed as if the muscle itself were injured. As we always find that the effect of a stimulant upon a muscle is completely obstructed by the division of the nerve, although the muscle itself be in a perfect state, it follows, that the action of the nerve, whatever it may be, is something propagated successively from the extremities to the centre of the system. It is by a reference to this principle that we account for the different paralytic affections in which a part of the body, without any apparent injury, loses its power of motion. In some cases the disease occupies exactly one half of the body, when it is found that one of the hemispheres of the brain is injured, and that all the parts connected with it have their functions impaired ; often it is only a single limb, or even a single muscle, that loses its power of motion, and here we are generally able to detect some morbid cause situated between the brain and the injured part.

The second use of the nervous system which we pointed out is, to connect the different parts of the animal together, and to compose one whole out of its various powers and faculties. The functions, which more immediately originate in contractility, are all necessarily dependent upon each other ; but still it is a kind of mechanical dependence, where we may conceive the effect to be produced by the mere operation of the laws of impulse and chemical affinity, and yet where the animal may have no consciousness of identity, and where there may be no connexion between the various operation except what arises from the ordinary properties of matter. This is, probably, very much the case with vegetables, which possess some functions that appear to be analogous to those of animals, but where we have no evidence of a nervous system. In animals, on the contrary, the brain and nerves produce a connexion of a different nature, where the effect is transmitted from one part to another without any change being produced which can be referred to mere physical agency, and which is of that kind usually denominated sympathetic. The analogy of the inferior animals leads us to the same conclusion respecting this use of the nervous system ; we find, in general, that they possess many of the individual functions in great perfection, but they have not that intimate connexion with each other, so that their separate parts are more tenacious of life ; they can sometimes even be completely re-produced when they have been destroyed by external violence ; and, in some cases, the whole animal may be multiplied by being cut into a number of parts, in the manner of a vegetable. In these cases, we always find that the nervous system is either altogether wanting, or that it is defective, consisting of a number of nervous cords, without any centre in which they unite ; or, if there be a brain, it is small in proportion to the nerves that proceed from it.

This view of the use and operation of the nervous system may throw some light upon a question which has been frequently agitated, whether there be a sensorium commune, a part of the nervous system to which all impressions are referred before they excite perceptions ? Another question has been stated, which is very nearly of the same import, whether, when an impression be made upon an organ of sense, as, for example,

Physiology. upon the eye, the perception exists in the eye or in the brain? The general result of our experience leads us to believe, that there is a common centre of sensation; and that, in the human subject, it exists in the brain. We have no consciousness of any impressions made upon the organs of sense when their nervous communication with the brain is destroyed; and, farther, it has been found, that, when a change has been produced upon the brain, similar to an impression that had been previously transmitted to it from an organ of sense, it has been mistaken for a recent impression; this is a well-known occurrence in dreams, and in various morbid states of the brain, where we frequently mistake ideas for perceptions. We likewise find that persons who have had the eyes entirely destroyed after they have arrived at years of maturity, can form as perfect conceptions of visible objects as those whose eyes are in a sound state, when any associations tend to recal such perceptions to the mind, making due allowance for the length of time that may have elapsed since the impressions were originally received.

Where situated. Many of the facts which were mentioned above, when we were considering the nature of the connexion between the muscular and the nervous systems, lead us to the conclusion, that there is a sensorium commune, and that this has its seat in the brain. Physiologists have not, however, been satisfied with assigning the brain in general as the common centre of sensation; but they have endeavoured to find out some particular part of it, which may be regarded as the essential organ to which all the rest are subservient. The investigation is certainly a curious one; and, although it may have been rendered ridiculous by the whimsical opinions to which it has given rise, it is in itself a legitimate object of inquiry.

Effect of injuries of the brain. Two plans have been adopted to ascertain the seat of this supposed centre of our sensations; the first has consisted in examining the brain after its different parts have been injured by accident or disease, and noticing what effects were produced on the faculties; the other proceeded upon the principle of actually tracing up the nerves to some one spot within the cranium, where, it was supposed, their actions might terminate. With respect to the first of these methods, the correspondence between the injury of the brain and the loss of any particular faculties, we have not yet been able to obtain any very decisive results. It seems, indeed, to be established, that the external cineritious part of the brain is less sensible than the medullary part; and we have many examples, in which large portions of the former have been removed or destroyed without any material injury to the powers or functions either of the body or the mind. There are also many curious and well-authenticated cases on record, where different parts of the medulla of the brain have been destroyed; and even such as, from their form and texture, or from their situation with respect to the organs of sense, might have been supposed the most essential, and yet the faculties have remained. It occasionally happens that water collects in the ventricles at the base of the brain, and, if the effusion be not too rapid, or if the skull yields to the distending force, so that the pressure be not too suddenly applied, life may be preserved for a long time. When such cases are examined after death, the form and texture of the brain is found to be completely altered; and it has been even supposed, that a considerable portion of the cerebral matter has been removed by the action of the absorbents. An alteration of this kind must be extremely slow, so that we may ven-

Hydroce- phalus.

ture to assert, that, for some time before death, the head must have been nearly in the same state as it is found upon dissection, yet the faculties, both physical and intellectual, have remained in tolerable perfection, and the patient has suffered rather from general indisposition, and from the inconvenience of an unwieldy head, disproportioned to the rest of the body, than from any direct injury or diminution of the nervous powers.

Nor has any great degree of success attended the attempts which have been made to discover the sensorium commune, by tracing the nerves of the different organs of sense up to one spot within the brain, although this has been attempted by some very learned and skilful anatomists. Indeed the general result of our inquiry respecting the sensorium commune is, that it is rather the brain in its whole extent which is to be regarded as the common centre of sensation, than any particular part of it; on the contrary, it is probable that different portions of the brain have different functions, or are more immediately subservient to different faculties, and therefore that the integrity of the whole is, at least to a certain extent, necessary for the due performance of the nervous functions.

Attempts to trace the nerves to one point.

This doctrine, of the different parts of the brain exercising different functions, was first explicitly advanced by Willis, who thought that he had proved this to be the case with respect to the cerebrum and the cerebellum, the one belonging more immediately to the organs of sense and the mental faculties, the other to the muscles. Willis's particular hypothesis is not now conceived to be correct, but the principle upon which it was founded is generally admitted, that the cerebrum and cerebellum serve different purposes in the animal economy, although it may not be in our power to assign the nature and extent of their respective powers. It is well known that this idea has of late been carried to a much greater length than it was by Willis, even so far as to assign separate organs, not only for the powers which are more particularly dependent upon sensation and motion, but even for all the different mental faculties; this subject, however, will be more fully considered in a subsequent part of the article.

Various functions of the brain.

The metaphysicians of the seventeenth and eighteenth centuries were very anxious to discover the seat of the soul, an inquiry which every one is now well aware must be entirely fruitless. It would be an absolute waste of time to relate all the different discussions that took place on this subject, or to attempt to rescue them from the merited oblivion into which they have fallen; but, as a matter of literary history, it may not be improper to allude to an opinion which was maintained by Descartes, and which, from the celebrity attached to his name, was for some time favourably received, viz. that the seat of the soul is in the pineal gland. The situation of this gland, and the manner in which it is protected from external injury, appeared to point it out as serving some useful purpose; and upon examining the brain of certain idiots, it was discovered in these cases to contain a quantity of silex. This earthy matter was conceived to be a morbid deposition, and it was hastily concluded that it must have the effect of interrupting the functions of the part, and that the idiotism of the subjects in question depended upon this cause, hence affording us a proof of its being the proper seat of the intellect. We have, however, learned since the time of Descartes, that earthy matter is always found in the gland, so that the hypothesis of

Seat of the soul.

Physiology.

6

Physiology. this philosopher is entirely without foundation. But although it may appear that we are not able to point out any one part of the cerebral mass, as the more immediate centre of sensation, there are certain points connected with this subject which it is important to attend to.

Opinions of Dr. Philip. Dr. Philip, whose researches on the nervous system are peculiarly valuable, has shown that the action of the nerves is different from, and independent of that of the brain; and he designates them respectively by the names of the nervous and the sensorial power. It would appear that the former of these consists simply in the transmission of certain effects from one part of the system to another, which takes place without the intervention of the brain, while the latter consists in the functions of perception and volition, in which the nerves and the brain are both concerned. It is obviously to the latter of these powers alone that the inquiry respecting the common centre of sensation can refer; and there are certain circumstances which seem to render it probable that different parts of the encephalon are respectively concerned in the functions of perception and volition.

Experiments of Mr. C. Bell. An analogical argument in favour of this opinion may be derived from a very curious observation which has been lately made by Mr. C. Bell, on the spinal nerves. These nerves have a double origin; one set of their filaments proceeding from the anterior, and the other from the posterior part of the spinal column; and it has been discovered by this eminent anatomist, that if the anterior filaments are divided, the part to which the nerve is sent is deprived of voluntary motion, while the division of the posterior filaments destroys its sensation. Now there appears some ground for supposing that the anterior part of the column is more directly connected with the cerebrum, and the posterior with the cerebellum; and hence we may conjecture, that these two parts are respectively the more immediate seats of the two faculties.

His classification of the nerves. Mr. Bell has also brought to light another very interesting circumstance in the anatomy of the nerves, which throws considerable light upon their operations and upon their connexion with the other parts of the animal economy. He arranges all the nerves into two classes; to the first of these he gives the title of symmetrical or original, and to the second of irregular or superadded. The first set consists of the fifth pair of the cranial and of all the spinal nerves: they resemble each other in the mode of their origin, and in the circumstance of their passing laterally to the two halves of the body, the two sides having no connexion with each other, and are distributed to all the voluntary muscles. The second set, which arise principally from the medulla oblongata, or the parts contiguous to it, proceed, in a very irregular manner, to all the organs which are concerned, either directly or indirectly, in the function of respiration; hence they may be called the respiratory nerves. They pass from one organ to another in the most irregular manner, connecting them together, crossing the symmetrical nerves, and uniting the two halves of the body. The parts to which they are distributed, are not under the control of the will, and they appear to be principally concerned in what, according to Dr. Philip, may be styled simple nervous action, i. e. in transmitting the nervous influence from one part to another without exciting perceptions.

General conclusions. The conclusion then that we form respecting the nervous system, and its functions, are, that it has two distinct powers, that of transmitting impressions, which

is exercised by the nerves and spinal cord, and that of perception and volition, more immediately depending upon the brain, or upon the brain in conjunction with the nerves. To these two powers or classes of functions, we must add a third class of intellectual; but the nature of these, as well as the connexion which they have with the physical part of our frame, is generally regarded as being essentially different from the two former classes. With respect to these two classes, the mere nervous and the sensorial functions, as contrasted with the intellectual, we observe that they exist in very different degrees in different classes of animals; and it has been a subject of investigation by anatomists, whether we can trace any correspondence between the respective states of these functions and the different parts of the nervous system. Many of the inferior animals possess the nervous and sensorial functions in a more acute state than man, but man decidedly excels them all in his intellectual powers.

Great size of the human brain. The great size of the human brain, compared to that of other animals, was observed by Aristotle; and he laid it down as a general principle, that the faculties of the brain are in proportion to its size, when considered in relation to that of the whole body. But although this rule appears to hold good with respect to many of the animals which fall under our daily observation, there are several important exceptions. The moderns have discovered that in some of the mammalia, the proportion of the size of the brain to the body is equal to that of the human subject, and that there are certain species of birds, in which the proportionate size is even greater. In man, the average ratio of the weight of the brain to that of the whole body, is about 1-28th; in the dog, about 1-160th; in the horse about 1-400th; in the elephant about 1-500th, while in the Canary bird it is 1-14th; but these numbers evidently bear no ratio to the faculties of the respective animals.

Proportion of the brain to the nerves. An observation has been made by Sœmmerring, which appears to be much more correct, and to which we have hitherto met with no exceptions, that the functions do not correspond to the size of the brain compared with that of the body, but to the size of the brain compared to the aggregate bulk of the nerves that proceed from it. In those cases where the size of the brain is as great or even greater than that of man, comparing it with the bulk of the whole body, we shall find it to be very small when compared with the size of the nerves that proceed from it, thus seeming to prove that acuteness of the organs of sense, or of the sensorial functions, is more particularly connected with the nerves, and that the intellectual powers have their seat in the brain, or that these are the organs to which the respective nervous operations are more especially attached. It may, however, be supposed, that the size of the nervous system is a less important circumstance than the perfection of its organization; but this is a subject which is entirely involved in obscurity, for although considerable pains have been taken to develop the minute texture of the brain, so far as we are aware, no attempts have been made to establish any comparative observations on this point.

Use of the ganglia. The use of the ganglia is a question which has given rise to much discussion, but which still remains undecided. From their situation, and the manner in which they are composed, it has been thought that they serve to produce a more perfect connexion or sympathy between the different parts of the body; but this, so far

Physiology. as we are able to judge, might have been accomplished by the mere union of the nerves, as in the plexuses, without the additional apparatus which is found in the ganglia. Many writers of considerable authority have supposed that these organs are to be regarded as small subsidiary brains, affording independent sources of nervous power, and constituting a number of minor seats of sensation; but we have no sufficient evidence of this being the case; and, upon the whole, it appears the most prudent to confess our ignorance of the subject.

CHAP. VI.

OF THE CIRCULATION OF THE BLOOD.

Circulation of the blood.

AFTER these remarks upon the nature of contractility and sensibility, we must proceed to the consideration of the different functions which depend upon the action of these powers; and, according to the plan which has been laid down, we shall begin with those operations which are more particularly referable to the contraction of the muscular fibre. Of these, the circulation of the blood, on every account, holds the first rank.

Its import-ance.

Although the animal functions act as it were in a circle, and are so intimately connected together, that the intermission of any one of them is followed by some disturbance of the system, yet the circulation of the blood seems to be that from which all the rest derive their origin, and which is the most essential to the well-being of the whole.

Compared with respi-ration.

In the more perfect animals, respiration is indeed as necessary for existence as the circulation; but if we may be allowed the expression, it is, as it were, only incidentally so, because by respiration we induce that state of the blood which imparts to the muscles, and to the ventricles of the heart among the rest, their power of contraction. In many of the inferior animals this change in the blood is brought about by a different kind of apparatus, so that the function of respiration is altogether superseded; but there is no animal, in which we have distinct organs and a vascular system, where the fluid is not carried about by something equivalent to the circulation.

Early for-mation of the heart.

We have already remarked that the circulation is, in respect of time, the first function which we are capable of observing in the young animal during its fœtal existence. Haller informs us that he was distinctly able to trace the rudiments of the future heart in the chicken during incubation, for some time before he could clearly observe either the brain or the lungs.

Relative importance of the heart and the brain.

With respect to the relative importance of the heart and the brain, it may be remarked, that although both of them are equally necessary for the functions of the most perfect animals, yet we can easily conceive that simple existence may, for some time, be sustained without the intervention of any of the faculties which originate from the nervous system, but that the nervous system cannot act for the shortest interval without a due supply of blood from the heart, or some analogous organ. Upon the whole, therefore, we are to regard the heart as the centre of the animal frame, which serves to unite the various functions, however different in their nature and operations, into one connected vital system.

Description of the heart.

The organs of circulation may be divided into three parts, the heart, the arteries, and the veins. The heart is a hollow muscle, composed of masses of strong longitudinal fibres, forming an irregular cone, and leaving an internal cavity. The outside of the heart is covered with a strong membrane, and the internal cavity is also lined with the same substance; the muscular part is copiously supplied with blood-vessels, but it is generally described as possessing few nerves in proportion to its bulk. It is suspended from its base by the great blood-vessels, which form the trunks of the sanguiferous system, and it is enclosed in a membranous purse, called the pericardium. The interior of the heart is divided into two distinct cavities, named ventricles; and there are two membranous bags at the base of the heart, called auricles, forming in all four separate cells, each of the auricles communicating with its corresponding ventricle, while neither the auricles nor the ventricles have any direct communication with each other. Although the auricles may be denominated membranous bodies, when compared with the ventricles, yet they are plentifully furnished with muscular fibres, and possess the power of contraction.

Use of the heart.

The use of the heart is to receive the blood that is brought to it from the veins, and to propel it along the arteries, and this it accomplishes by the contraction of its fibres, in consequence of which its cavities are diminished in size. But the simple diminution of the cavities, and the pressing out of the blood, would not be sufficient for the purpose of the circulation; for it is not only necessary that the blood be moved, but that it be moved in the proper direction. For this purpose the heart is furnished with a curious mechanism of valves, which are attached to the orifices of the ventricles and the arteries, and which are so arranged, that when the heart contracts, and the blood is forced out, the current is necessarily directed in the proper course.

Arteries.

When the blood leaves the heart, it is sent with considerable force into the large trunks of the arteries; these vessels soon begin to ramify in various directions to all parts of the body, until at length they are reduced to vessels too small to be traced by the eye, or even by the microscope. There are in the body two distinct sets of arteries, which are distributed to different organs, and serve very different purposes in the animal economy; one of these is sent to the lungs, the other to all the remaining parts of the body; the former constitutes the pulmonic, the latter the systemic circulation. On this subject we shall at present only observe, that before the blood can be employed in the various functions of the body, it is necessary for it to undergo a certain change, which is effected in the lungs. After it has undergone this change, it is brought back to the heart, and is again propelled from this organ, along the arteries of the systemic circulation, to all parts of the body. The arteries which perform this office of conveying the blood from the heart, are flexible elastic tubes, principally composed of membrane, but, as is generally supposed, containing also a quantity of muscular fibres, which give them, to a certain extent, the power of contracting, and consequently of propelling their contents.

Veins.

When the blood has been transmitted by the arteries towards the extremities, it is returned to the heart by the veins, being first received into their minute extremities, and carried from larger to smaller branches, contrary to what takes place in the arteries, until at length it arrives at the large trunks, and is poured from them into the heart. The veins resemble the

Physiology.

arteries in being membranous tubes, but they differ from them in possessing a less firm texture, in being without muscular fibres, and in having a number of valves in different parts of their course, whereas the arteries have no valves, except at their commencement.

Course of the blood.

We shall now trace the progress of the blood through the heart and along the vessels ; and it will be perceived, that every portion of it makes two complete circuits, before it arrives again at the same point in the circulation. We may conveniently begin with that part where the blood enters the heart, when it leaves the systemic veins, or those which belong to the greater circulation. It is received into the right auricle, and is poured from this into the right ventricle ; when the ventricle becomes distended, it contracts, and the valves which are at its mouth, closing up the passage into the auricle, it is necessarily forced into the pulmonary artery. The pulmonary artery carries the blood through the lungs, along what is called the lesser or pulmonic circulation, where it undergoes that peculiar change which fits it for the support of life ; it is brought back in this altered state to the left auricle, and from this into the left ventricle. The left ventricle, when filled with blood, contracts ; and the valves, preventing the fluid from returning into the auricle, it is sent into the aorta, or the grand trunk of the systemic arteries. It is transmitted by this through the minute arterial branches, to all parts of the body ; from these it is received by the extremities of the veins, passes from them into the large veins, and so to the vena cava, the main trunk of the systemic veins, whence it is finally delivered into the right auricle of the heart.

Discovery of the circulation of the blood.

A very casual observation of the phenomena of the living body was sufficient to prove that the blood is perpetually in motion ; but the nature of this motion, or the course which it pursues, was unknown to the ancients. They had many unfounded speculations upon the subject, which it is not necessary to relate, although they are sanctioned by very high authority. Some approaches to the true theory of the circulation were made by Cesalpini, who flourished in the sixteenth century ; but the honour of this great discovery, which is generally regarded as the greatest that ever was made in anatomy or physiology, is due to our illustrious countryman Harvey. He completed the discovery about the year 1620, but, with a rare degree of philosophical forbearance, he spent eight years in digesting and maturing his ideas, when they were at length given to the world, in a short tract, written with remarkable clearness and perspicuity, which has been justly characterized " as one of the most admirable examples of a series of arguments deduced from observation and experiment, that ever appeared on any subject." The manner in which this discovery was received by the public forms a curious and instructive occurrence in the history of philosophy. Harvey, for some time, scarcely obtained a single convert, and he was assailed by a violent clamour for having ventured to call in question the authority of Aristotle and Galen. After some time, however, it was found that the doctrine was true, and his opponents were then driven to a new species of attack ; they asserted that what had been brought forward as a new discovery was in fact only borrowed from the writings of the ancients ; and passages were produced, although warped and strained in a thousand ways, to meet this allegation. It is even said that Harvey suffered in his medical practice, in consequence of the prejudice that was excited against him ; but he lived long enough to witness the triumph of truth over the cavils of his enemies, and finally saw his doctrine almost universally adopted.

Physiology.

Proofs adduced by Harvey.

Although it might seem unnecessary to adduce a formal train of arguments in support of a theory which is no longer opposed, yet it may be useful to review the nature of the proofs which were brought forward by Harvey, as they constitute a series of important facts, which throw considerable light upon the structure and properties of the sanguiferous system. The proof that the circulation proceeds in the course which has been described above, is derived partly from observations and experiments made on living animals, and partly from the anatomical structure of the organs concerned.

Inspection of the living heart.

If we open the chest of a cold-blooded animal during life, and bring the heart into view, we may observe its alternate contraction and dilatation proceeding with considerable regularity. For a short space of time, the heart lies at rest, and suffers itself to be distended with blood ; then it is suddenly seen to rise up on its basis, to shorten its fibres, and to expel its contents. During this period it strikes the ribs, and produces what is called the beating of the heart.

Action of the valves.

From an inspection of the mechanism of the valves, we perceive that it is impossible for the blood to return into the auricles, but that there will be no obstacle to its entrance into the arteries ; they therefore become distended with blood. The valves, which are at the commencement of the arteries, will prevent any blood which has once entered them from returning to the heart ; it must consequently be carried forwards into the minute extremities of the arteries, and from these it must pass into the veins, proceeding from the smaller to the larger vessels, until it arrives at the vena cava, whence it is delivered into the right side of the heart. As there is no direct communication between the two auricles and the two ventricles, it cannot pass from the right to the left cavities without traversing the pulmonic circulation, which may be regarded as a smaller circle, interposed, as it were, between the right ventricle and the right auricle. The valves of these parts point out the current to be, as we have described it in the systemic circulation, from the ventricle, first along the artery, and afterwards through the veins.

Effect of ligatures and wounds.

That the passage of the blood along the arteries is from the heart towards the extremities, is well illustrated by the effect of ligatures placed upon them ; for in this case we find that the part of the artery between the ligature and the heart is distended, while the more remote part becomes partially emptied of blood. The same circumstance is exemplified in wounds of the arteries, where the upper part of the vessel is seen to send out jets of blood, corresponding with the action of the heart, while only a slight discharge issues from the lower part of the divided vessel. The reverse of all this happens from ligatures, or wounds of the veins : here the distention, or the stream of blood, occurs in the part of the vein more remote from the heart, while the part contiguous to the heart becomes relaxed and emptied.

Operation of transfusion.

The curious operation called transfusion, proves the course of the blood to be, as we have described it, from the arteries into the veins. In this process, which seems to have been first practised by Lower, the artery of one animal is connected by a tube with the vein of another, when we find that the first animal is emptied of blood, while the second becomes preternaturally distended with it. By permitting the blood of the

Physiology. second animal to escape through an opening from its veins, the greatest part of the blood in the body may, in this way, be changed, and at a time when diseases were thought to depend upon some morbid qualities residing in the fluids, the operation of transfusion was held up as a most important method of restoring the health ; and, repugnant as it now appears to our feelings, the blood of lambs or calves was actually transmitted into the vessels of persons labouring under different diseases, or debilitated by old age.

Microscopical observations.
Besides these proofs of the direction of the blood through the sanguiferous system, the observations that were made by the microscope may be mentioned among the points that were insisted upon by Harvey and his contemporaries. Malpighi taught us the method of rendering the circulation visible to the eye, by applying this instrument to the web of a frog's foot, or other transparent membrane in the cold-blooded animals, when we have the interesting appearance presented to us, of the arteries projecting the blood in successive waves, which is returned in a uniform stream by the veins. But although the two kinds of vessels may be distinctly perceived, as well as the difference in the motion of their contents, we are not able to trace their connexion with each other, nor the relation which they bear to the other parts of the sanguiferous system.

Regular motion of the heart.
The regularity with which these actions succeed each other was a circumstance that excited great surprise among the earlier physiologists, and gave rise to many speculations. Bellini, who was a strenuous advocate for the mathematical doctrines, conceived that the auricles and ventricles were antagonists to each other. Baglivi, a very ingenious physiologist, whose premature death was a real loss to science, accounted for the regularity of the action by an alternation of pressure on the brain and nerves, in consequence of the alternate distention and relaxation of the ventricles, and an opinion something similar to this was maintained by Boerhaave. But these, and many other refined theories, were all discarded by Haller, who reduced the action of the heart to the simple effect of a stimulus, acting at successive intervals, on a contractile organ, the mechanism of which is so adjusted that each part, when relaxed, receives the stimulating power from the neighbouring part.

Period of a circulation.
A calculation has been made by Blumenbach of the length of the time which the whole mass of blood requires to pass through the entire circulation, a point which admits of being reduced to numbers with tolerable accuracy. Supposing the whole mass of blood to be thirty-three lbs. that the heart contracts seventy-five times in a minute, and expels two ounces at each contraction, the blood will complete the circuit in two minutes and thirty-six seconds, and will be carried through the vessels nearly twenty-three times in an hour.

Controversy between Vesalius and Dubois.
To describe the minute anatomy of the heart and blood vessels would be foreign to the object of this article ; but there is one fact, which we may notice as a remarkable, although not an unexampled instance, of the bigotted attachment of many of the moderns to Galen. Vesalius, the great restorer of anatomy, perceived that the description of the vessels connected with the heart, which was left by Galen, did not quite correspond with what he found in the human subject, while it exactly resembled the structure of this part in apes and monkeys ; hence he naturally concluded that Galen had employed these animals in his dissections. A learned French anatomist, Du Bois, a warm advocate for the ancients, and a violent antagonist of Vesalius, in his zeal to support the honour of his master, seriously maintained that the human form had undergone a change in its structure since the age of Galen, and that formerly the vessels were distributed as he described them.

Use of the circulation.
With respect to the use of the circulation, it is sufficient for the present to say, that it is necessary for all parts of the body to be provided with a regular supply of arterial blood, as it is termed, or blood that has undergone its appropriate change in its passage through the lungs. The object of the lesser, or the pulmonic circulation, is to effect this change ; and the object of the larger, or the systemic circulation, is to convey the blood, when changed, to all parts of the body.

Cause of the heart's contraction.
Many causes have been assigned to account for the power by which this great machine is primarily moved. Some of the ancients conceived that there was an innate fire in the heart which produced its motion : Sylvius, who is celebrated as being the founder of a noted chemical sect in medicine, attributed it to the effervescence excited by the mixture of the different kinds of blood, and many other equally absurd ideas prevailed, until the publication of Senac's treatise on the heart. He correctly ascribed the power by which the circulation is carried on to muscular contractility, principally residing in the heart ; and he showed that, by the blood being poured into its cavities, and causing a certain degree of distention of its fibres, the heart is stimulated to contraction, and by this act expels its contents. The stimulating cause being thus removed, the heart relaxes ; but, in the mean time, the blood having traversed the vessels, is poured into the auricles, and from them into the ventricles, which being again distended, are again made to contract and expel their contents into the artery. We frequently observe, that even in human contrivances, the most important effects are produced by the most simple means, and the same remark will apply to the mechanism of the heart.

Senac's opinion.

Cause of the regularity of the heart's action.
An important point connected with the motion of the blood, and one which has given rise to much controversy, is the inquiry into the cause of its regularity and constancy. How, it has been asked, can the heart proceed for years together, pulsating at equal intervals, and propelling the same quantity of blood? Willis, who was one of the first physiologists that was fully sensible of the importance of the nervous system in the animal economy, advanced the opinion to which we have already alluded, that the nerves of the heart, as well as of all the muscles which are in constant motion, are derived from a different part of the brain from the nerves of those parts which are called into occasional action only, and which are under the control of the will. There are no doubt some facts which countenance the opinion, that the nerves which supply the voluntary and the involuntary muscles, are derived from different sources, but there is some doubt how far these facts will apply to the heart, and even were they admitted, they would scarcely solve the difficulty. Other hypotheses have been proposed, to which it will not be necessary for us to advert ; but we must not pass by without noticing the remarkable doctrine which was maintained on this subject by Stahl. He ascribed the regularity of the heart's motion to the agency of the *anima*, or principle of intelligence which resides in man, and superintends all his functions, though without exciting any sensation, or producing any consciousness of its existence. This principle,

Hypothesis of Willis;

of Stahl.

Physiology.

Remarks upon it.

aware of the fatal consequences that would ensue from the intermission of so important an operation as the circulation of the blood, is careful always to preserve it in due action, and at all times to regulate its operations according to the demands of the system.

The doctrine of a superintending intelligent principle residing in the body, and directing its operations, seems to have originated with Vanhelmont, who gave it the name of *archeus;* Stahl refined upon Vanhelmont's notion, and applied it to many parts of the animal economy under the title of *anima,* and it has borne a distinguished share in the hypotheses of many learned physiologists down to the present day. An agent of this kind, although not so distinctly brought into view as by Stahl and some of his immediate followers, forms a leading feature in the writings of John Hunter; and many of Darwin's speculations, when divested of their poetical garb, must be referred to the same principle. Yet nothing surely can be more contrary to the spirit of true philosophy, than to assume the existence of an intelligent agent in the body, of which we are entirely unconscious, or to adduce as the cause of certain effects, a power of which we have no knowledge or intimation, and which is only had recourse to as a commodious method of removing the present difficulty. The Stahlian doctrine in all its ramifications, and under every form in which it has been exhibited, seems to have originated, partly from the want of an accurate discrimination between the physical and the final causes of the operations of the body, and partly from an indistinct conception of the difference between the agency of the first great cause of all things, and the secondary or physical cause, into which alone it is the province of natural philosophy to inquire. It affords no explanation of the physical cause, or the nature of any phenomenon, to say, that the Supreme Being has thought fit to order it so; the object of our researches is to examine to which of the general laws that he has impressed upon matter the action in question is to be referred.

Conclusion.

In the present instance, as far as respects the heart, the only answer that can be given to the proposed question, is one that is itself, in some measure, an acknowledgment of our ignorance. We know that distention excites a muscle to contract, and that when a muscle has contracted, relaxation ensues. We must conclude then, that in the original formation of the body, the degree of contractility bestowed upon the heart, the quantity of distention which it receives from the blood, the size and strength of the arteries which are to transmit the blood, and the quantity of resistance which it has to overcome, are so nicely balanced, that each individual action is kept in due subjection to the rest, and contributes to the perfect performance of the function.

Contractility of the arteries.

I have already stated that the heart is the great source of motion to the circulating system, and the main cause of the transmission of the blood to all parts of the body, but other powers have been pointed out which are conceived to assist in the operation, some of which at least have probably a real efficacy. The principal of these is the contractility of the arteries, a point which, although it has been much controverted, and has even been denied by some very eminent physiologists, is now generally admitted to exist. Between the coats of membranous matter which compose the principal substance of the arteries, there is a layer of transverse fibres, which bear a considerable resemblance to the fibres of muscles, and have been generally conceived to possess a contractile power. The action of these fibres, if muscular, must be to diminish the cavity of the vessels, and, by the alternation of contraction and dilatation, to propel their contents.

Experiments on the muscularity of the arteries.

Haller performed many experiments on the muscularity of the arteries, which consisted in applying to them the stimulants that produce the contraction of the proper muscular fibres; but his results were, for the most part, unsuccessful. Other experimentalists, however, since his time, have been more fortunate; in the first instance, Verschuir, and more lately Drs. Philip, J. Thomson, and Hastings, have in the most unequivocal manner, proved that the arteries possess a power, in all respects, analogous to that of muscular contraction; and it may be fairly presumed that the transverse fibres, or as they have been usually termed, the muscular coat, is the seat of this power. Probably one cause of Haller's failure was, that he performed his experiments principally upon the larger vessels, which appear to possess this property in a small degree only, while it is the minute capillary extremities of the arterial system that are the most contractile, and where the operations are principally carried on that depend upon this power.

Cullen's hypothesis.

Before the contractility of the arteries had been proved by direct experiment, or rather, while experiments seemed adverse to the doctrine, a very ingenious physiological argument in support of it was advanced by Cullen. This acute physiologist remarks, that if the motion of the blood depended entirely upon the impetus impressed on it by the heart, its force and velocity, in the different parts of the body, must, at all times, bear the same ratio to each other. If the quantity and velocity of the blood in any two parts, as for example in the two arms, be the same, provided the arteries were membranous tubes, the momentum of the blood in the arms must always be precisely similar, and this will continue to be the case, whatever be the strength or velocity of the heart's motion, and however these may vary at different times.

Observations on the action of the capillaries.

But we do not observe this constant ratio to exist; on the contrary, the relative momentum of the blood in the different parts of the body is always varying, so that the quantity of blood and the velocity with which it moves, are perpetually altered, both from the effect of external stimuli, and from a number of internal causes. The variable state of the contraction of the capillary branches of the arteries, constitutes what is termed the action of the vessels, a circumstance which forms a very prominent feature in the modern doctrines of medicine, and for which we are chiefly indebted to Cullen, who substituted this action in place of the humoral or mechanical pathology of his predecessors. It is to an altered state of the capillaries that we refer many of the phenomena of fever and local inflammation, the morbid changes in the secretions, and the derangement of most of the functions which serve for the growth and nutrition of the body.

Hunter's experiments.

Hunter performed an elaborate set of experiments upon the vessels, by which he endeavoured to discriminate between their elastic and their muscular power. They consisted in examining portions of the artery of an animal that had been bled to death, by which it was supposed that the vessels would be reduced to a state of extreme contraction, for the purpose of ascertaining how far they were able to recover themselves from a certain state of distention. Dead membranous matter retains the whole of its elasticity, and after being stretched, will restore itself to its

Physiology. former size, but the contractile power of muscles ceases with life; and therefore when a muscular fibre is stretched, it remains permanently distended. The results of Hunter's experiments sanctioned Cullen's hypothesis, that the elasticity of the arteries diminished, and their elasticity increases, as we recede from the heart.

Elasticity not the source of power.

Besides the muscularity of the small branches of the arteries, many of the old writers conceived that the elasticity of the vessels contributed to the motion of the blood; but this idea depended upon an erroneous conception of the nature of elasticity, which can never actually generate power, but only restore what has been impressed upon the blood in a contrary direction. Even if the arteries were perfectly elastic, they could only re-act upon the blood with exactly the same degree of force which the heart had expended in their dilatation; and so far as the mere motion of the blood is concerned, it would have been more promoted if the arteries had possessed a rigid texture similar to that of metallic tubes. But the loss of power which is occasioned by the flexible and imperfectly elastic nature of the arteries is no doubt amply compensated by other advantages.

Effect of contraction of the muscles.

The passage of the blood along the veins is accelerated by the contraction of the muscles. The veins, as has been remarked above, are furnished with numerous valves in different parts of their course, which are so constructed that they permit the blood to pass in one direction only towards the heart; and as many of the large veins are so situated that when the muscles contract they are pressed upon, and their contents partially expelled, we perceive how the circulation of the blood is actually promoted by the contraction of the muscles. The contraction of the heart, that of the capillaries of the arteries, and the pressure of the muscles upon the veins, are all of them causes obviously contributing to the motion of the blood; but it may be questioned whether there are any other circumstances which are to be considered as real sources of power to the circulation, for although the elasticity of the parts concerned in this function may tend to distribute the force in a more commodious manner, yet it cannot actually generate power.

Retarding causes.

The causes which retard the blood's motion along the vessels are numerous, and some of them very efficient, so that the force employed very greatly exceeds the effect produced. The following may be considered as some of the most important of the retarding causes: the resistance which the quantity of blood previously in the vessels opposes to the entrance of a fresh quantity, the imperfect elasticity of the vessels, their flexibility, their winding course, the adhesive nature of the blood, the friction which it must occasion in passing along the vessels, the ramification of the arteries into smaller branches which go off at considerable angles from the trunk, the union of two streams of blood at a large angle with each other, and the increased diameter of all the branches compared to that of the trunk. We know from the laws of hydraulics that these are real causes of retardation, which must act powerfully on the motion of the blood; but they are all independent of the vital actions of the organs, and apply to them as they would do to a system of tubes, possessed of the same physical properties, but without any of those powers which are peculiar to the living animal.

Application of mathematics to physiology.

The degree in which the sanguiferous system is subjected to the physical laws of matter, induced the mathematical physiologists to bestow an unusual share of attention upon every circumstance connected with the action of the heart and the motion of the blood. There is little doubt that, by the cautious application of mathematical reasoning, we have arrived at some physiological truths which we could not have attained by other means, and which are beyond the reach of actual observation. But when we call in the aid of mathematics to assist us in our researches, it is essential to our success that the data which we employ be well-founded, and that we are not misled by false analogies, or by the misapplication of principles which may be in themselves correct. Unfortunately, however, the mechanical physiologists fell into all these errors; and the consequence was, that, compared to the labour employed, the advantage resulting from it was very inconsiderable; while the mistakes which they committed, and the erroneous statements which they advanced, which were for a long time received with little hesitation, were both very important and very numerous.

Estimates of the force of the heart.

A point which was very minutely attended to by the mathematicians, was the estimate of the force of the heart, or the power which it exerts upon the propulsion of the blood along the great arteries which immediately communicate with the ventricles. Some of the most learned men of the seventeenth and eighteenth centuries engaged in this investigation, and employed upon it all the force of their genius; yet it may be confidently asserted that they entirely failed in their object, and have, in fact, given us little or no information upon the point in question.

Borelli's.

But, although the attempts that were made to solve this problem were in themselves of little value, some of them may be considered as deserving of our attention, both in consequence of the celebrity which they at one time acquired, and, also, because they afford us a good specimen of the nature of the reasoning which was employed by the most eminent physiologists of the age. Borelli, proceeding upon the gratuitous hypothesis which he had formed, that the power of the muscles is in proportion to their weight, estimated that the force of the heart was equal to the enormous sum of 180,000lbs.

Keill's.

Keill perceived the extravagance of Borelli's estimate, and attempted to arrive at the truth by a more complicated process. He stated, that the force of the heart produces two effects; it propels a quantity of blood from its cavities, and communicates motion to the contents of the arteries. He first endeavoured to estimate the quantity of blood thrown out of the heart at each of its contractions; and, by taking the diameter of the aorta, he could then calculate the velocity with which it passes along this vessel. He found the quantity of blood to be about two ounces, the area of the great vessel to be about three-quarters of a square inch, while the actual contraction of the ventricle was conceived to occupy the 200th part of a minute. Hence it follows, that the blood sent into the aorta would compose a cylinder of eight inches in length, and be driven along with a velocity of 156 feet in a minute. But, in producing this velocity, the heart has to overcome all the resistances which the blood meets with in its passage along the vessels; and the next step was to determine their amount. For this purpose he opened a living animal, and laid bare the iliac artery, together with the corresponding vein. He laid down the position, that all the blood which is transmitted by the artery must return by the vein in the same time, but with a diminished force; the arterial blood having the force which

Physiology. is necessary to overcome all the resistances, and the venous blood having only that degree of force left which remains after all the resistances have been overcome. He then opened the artery, and received all the blood which passed through it in a given time; and he next received the blood which flowed through the vein during the same time, when he found that these quantities were to each other in the proportion of $7\frac{1}{2}$ to 3. From this he drew the conclusion, that the actual force of the heart is to the force given to the blood in the artery as $7\frac{1}{2}$ to 3, and, consequently, that the real quantity of force exercised upon the blood would be sufficient to propel it 390 feet in a minute had it no obstacle to overcome. From this datum he estimates the force necessary to move a given column of blood with a known velocity in a given time; and this he determines to be in man $5\frac{1}{2}$ ounces—a quantity about half a million of times less than the calculation of Borelli.

Remarks upon it.   We may admit a certain share of ingenuity in the experiment and reasoning of Keill; but they are obviously incorrect in many particulars. In the first place, there is a great resistance offered to the blood at its first entrance into the aorta, which must have been overcome before it arrives at the artery on which he made his experiment. In the second place, the quantity of blood which flows from a divided vessel is no measure of what passes through it at other times, because blood will be sent from all the neighbouring parts to a point where the resistance is diminished. In the third place, it is by no means correct to suppose, that, exactly what passes along an artery is returned by what we call the corresponding vein; besides that, in Keill's experiment, a greater quantity than ordinary would pass off by the vein from the anastomoses which the veins have with each other. However, it is unnecessary to dwell longer upon this experiment, as the remarks which we have made are sufficient to show that it does not afford even an approximation to the truth.

Hales's experiments.   The only other calculation of this kind which we shall notice is that of Hales. He attempted to estimate the relative force of the arteries and veins, by inserting tubes into the great vessels near the heart, and observing the comparative height to which the blood was impelled into them. Although he found it to vary in different experiments, yet it was always greater in the arteries than in the veins, upon the average as about 10 to 1. In order to obtain the absolute force of the heart, Hales inserted tubes into the aorta, soon after it leaves the left ventricle; and he found the column of blood projected into the tube to be of such a height, that, by comparing it with the cavity from which it proceeded, and by taking into account the time and the area of the vessel, the force of the heart would be about 50lbs.

Remarks.   We may conceive that the estimate of Hales is nearer the truth than that of any of his predecessors; but still there are many points in which it is defective, even regarding the heart merely as a hydraulic machine; and when we consider contractility as a variable power, depending upon a number of causes connected with life, which it is impossible to appreciate, we shall be convinced of the futility of all such calculations. Hales, however, was a man of a truly philosophical cast of mind, who was far from being blindly devoted to any set of opinions; and whose experiments, considering the period in which he lived, exhibit a powerful understanding. But the genius of the age was so decidedly turned to the employment of mathematical reasoning in every department of philosophy, that he was led to

apply it to many parts, both of the animal and vegetable economy, which depend altogether upon different principles. Physiology

CHAPTER VII.

OF THE BLOOD.

Having described the course which the blood pursues along the different parts of the sanguiferous system, we must now proceed to consider the nature of this fluid. Blood may be regarded both in a chemical and a physiological point of view; either as it is a substance possessed of certain chemical properties, or as an agent which materially influences the vital powers of the system, and is intimately connected with the performance of its most important functions. The first of these subjects we shall pass over in a very cursory manner, as it has already been treated of under the article CHEMISTRY; while we shall consider more in detail those properties of the blood which are especially connected with it as forming a constituent of the living animal body. Introductory remarks.

Blood, when first drawn from the vessels, is a tenacious fluid of a thick consistence; in man, and the more perfect animals, of a red colour, of a homogeneous consistence, of a specific gravity greater than water, and of the temperature of the animal from which it is taken; this, in the human species, is about 98°. Very soon after it leaves the vessels, it separates into two distinct parts; a solid mass is formed of a red colour, called the clot or crassamentum, which floats in a yellowish fluid, named the serum; each of these bodies, however, are composed of various other substances: these we shall describe in succession. The crassamentum generally appears under the form of a soft solid, of such a consistence as to bear cutting with a knife. When formed under particular circumstances, especially if it be gently agitated during the time of its coagulation, it exhibits a fibrous appearance, and, by proper management, nearly the whole of it may be converted into an irregular net-work of a dense fibrous substance; in this case it is generally deprived of its red colour. The red colour may also be removed from it by long-continued washing; and, in this case, the same fibrous texture is also developed. The substance thus obtained, consisting of the coagulum deprived of its red colour, was formerly called coagulable lymph or gluten; but lately it has obtained the more appropriate name of fibrin. The washing removes from the coagulum a quantity of serum which was entangled, as it were, between its fibres, and also the substance to which it owes its red colour; the fibrin is then left nearly white, of a firm consistence, and possessed of a certain degree of toughness and elasticity. It is upon this part that the separation of the clot depends; a process which has been termed the spontaneous coagulation of the blood. Spontaneous coagulation. Crassamentum. Fibrin.

So singular a change could not but excite great attention among physiologists; and very numerous experiments have been made, both to explain its occurrence, and to observe what causes tended to promote or to retard it. Two of the most remarkable circumstances which might be supposed to operate as constituting the chief difference between the blood while in the vessels, and after it is discharged from them, are rest and exposure to air. If blood, when newly drawn from the vessels, be briskly agitated, the process of coagula- Cause of coagulation. Effect of rest and air.

Physiology. tion is entirely prevented from taking place; either in consequence of a more complete union of its constituents, which prevents their subsequent separation, or from the fibrin losing the property by which its parts are attracted to each other. Hewson performed a number of experiments on the effect of air upon the spontaneous coagulation of the blood; and, although they are, perhaps, not very decisive, nor always uniform, yet the general conclusion is, that the contact of air promotes coagulation. Hunter opposed the opinion of Hewson; but his facts go no farther than to show, that air is not essential to the process. This point is indeed proved by the consideration, that the blood occasionally coagulates within the vessels, where it must be completely excluded from the air; and, indeed, this change has been found to exist, to a certain degree, during life, as seems to be the case in aneurisms, where a part of the blood is removed from the direct impulse of the heart's action. Many wonderful stories that are on record, of worms being found in the heart, the brain, or other internal organs, are to be explained upon the idea, that the spectators were imposed upon by portions of coagulated fibrin, which had assumed the form of long strings.

Hewson's and Hunter's experiments.

The air of the atmosphere being a compound body, it was natural to examine the effects of its constituents separately upon the blood, as well as of the other factitious gases. A number of experiments have accordingly been performed on this subject, but, perhaps, without any very decided result. In experiments of this kind much manual dexterity is required; and there are many circumstances connected with the state of the animal itself—the manner in which the blood flows from the vein, the kind of vessel in which it is received, the temperature and other conditions of the atmosphere, and the manner of applying the gases—which may all produce a notable variation in the effects. Upon the whole, the most respectable authorities would lead us to conclude, that oxygen retards the process of coagulation, but that it is promoted by carbonic acid, and by some other of the unrespirable gases. The coagulation of the blood is much retarded, or entirely prevented, by the addition of certain salts; and if blood be diluted with twelve times its bulk of water, the clot no longer separates. The process of coagulation takes place more slowly in venous than in arterial blood; but it is asserted that the coagulation of venous blood is more complete, and the clot firmer.

Effect of different gases.

The cause of the coagulation of the fibrin has never been satisfactorily explained. It is a phenomenon which does not exactly resemble any other with which we are acquainted, and the effect of external agents is not so well marked as to enable us to refer it to any general operation of the physical properties of bodies. What renders the subject peculiarly difficult is, that there are some circumstances which affect the process, and which operate in a way that we are quite unable to explain. Many causes of sudden death prevent the usual coagulation of the blood from taking place; yet, except in this one particular, they do not appear to have the least resemblance to each other. Among others we may enumerate lightning and electricity, a blow upon the stomach, an injury of the brain, the bites of venomous animals, some acrid vegetable poisons, excessive exercise, and even violent mental emotions. In all these cases there has been found to be a remarkable coincidence between the want of coagu-

Cause of the coagulation of fibrin.

lability in the fibrin, and the loss of contractility of Physiology. the muscles immediately after death. The muscles are found to be relaxed, and are incapable of being excited by the ordinary stimulants, while, at the same time, the body has been found much disposed to run into the state of putrefaction. These facts have been supposed to identify, to a certain degree, the operation of muscular contraction with the coagulation of the blood; and this idea has been farther urged, from the consideration, that the chemical composition of fibrin is exactly similar to that of the muscular fibre.

It was probably from facts of this kind that Hunter Life of the was led to form his celebrated hypothesis of the life of blood. the blood. He supposed that the blood was not merely the substance which gives life to the animal, by carrying to all parts what is necessary for their support and preservation, but that it is itself a living organized body, and even the peculiar seat in which the vitality of the whole system resides. The question concerning the life of the blood cannot be fully examined until we are farther advanced in our view of the animal economy, and especially until we have endeavoured to give a correct definition of the manner in which the term life ought to be employed. But we may remark, that even were the Hunterian doctrine of the life of the blood to be fully established, it would not afford any real explanation of the cause of its coagulation, for the same difficulty still remains, in what manner the presence of life operates, so as to produce either the coagulation of the blood, or the contraction of the muscles. Perhaps the most consistent view of the subject is, that the fibrin has a natural disposition to assume the solid form, but that as it is added to the blood, particle by particle, while this fluid is rapidly circulating through the vessels, it has no opportunity of concreting; but it exerts its tendency to assume the solid form, as soon as it is at rest, either within or without the vessels.

There is a subject connected with the coagulation of Buffy coat. the blood, which is of great importance in the practice of medicine, that the nature and appearance of the coagulum varies very much according to the state of the body at the time when the blood is drawn. The most important of these varieties is the formation of what is called the buffy coat, a term which is used to express that state of the coagulum, when the upper part of it contains no red particles, but exhibits a layer of a buff-coloured substance, lying upon the top of the red clot. This buffy coat is generally formed when the system is labouring under inflammatory fever, and when, according to the modern doctrines of pathology, there is an increased action of the capillary vessels. The immediate cause of this appearance is obvious; the red particles which give the crassamentum its red colour, begin to subside before the coagulation is completed, so that the upper part of the clot is left without them. The remote cause of the buffy coat is still undecided, although many experiments have been made to discover it, especially by Hewson, Hunter, and Hey.

Hewson thought that the fibrin became specifically Experi- lighter, and the red particles, of course, comparatively ments of heavier, whence they were disposed to fall to the bot- Hewson, tom of the clot. Hunter seemed disposed to account &c. for the appearance from the firmer coagulation of the fibrin, as it were, squeezing out the red particles; but this would not explain why the upper part of the clot

Physiology.

alone is left without them. Hey's opinion seems to be better founded; that by the increased action of the vessels, the different constituents are more intimately united together, the fibrin therefore requires a longer space of time for its coagulation, and thus the red particles have an opportunity of partially subsiding. It is, however, not improbable that Hunter's opinion is also in part correct; for we find that the clot of inflamed blood obviously possesses a firmer texture than it exhibits in its ordinary state, thus affording an additional analogy between the coagulation of the blood and the contractility of the muscles; for it appears that in this state of fever, the force of muscular contraction in the organs of the circulation is augmented in the same proportion with the coagulating powers of the fibrin.

Red particles. The red particles, which together with the fibrin compose the crassamentum, from the peculiarity of their appearance and organization, have been the subject of almost innumerable observations and experiments. Soon after the introduction of the microscope into physiological researches, these substances were minutely examined by Malpighi, and afterwards by the indefatigable Leeuwenhoek. They were at first described simply as spherical bodies, floating in the serum, and giving the blood its red colour; but as observations were multiplied, errors and absurdities were advanced in almost an equal proportion. Leeuwenhoek himself invented a fanciful hypothesis, which had a long and powerful influence over the most enlightened physiologists, that the red particles of the blood were composed of a series of bodies descending in regular gradations; each particle was supposed to be made up of six particles of serum, a particle of serum of six particles of lymph, &c. This hypothesis, for which there does not appear to be the slightest foundation, was so suited to the mechanical genius of the age, that it was generally adopted, and even formed a leading feature in all the doctrines of Boerhaave. Its futility was exposed, in the first instance, by Lancisi and Senac, but it still maintained its ground until the time of Haller.

Observations of Hewson, &c. When objects can only be detected by lenses of highly magnifying powers, it is so extremely difficult to avoid being misled by ocular deceptions, that all descriptions of this kind are to be received with the greatest caution. The necessity for this caution is sufficiently proved by the discordant accounts of the red particles that have been given by the different observers, who, as far as we can judge, could have no motive for intentionally imposing upon their readers. Hewson published a very elaborate description of these bodies, professing to be the result of accurate observation; he informs us that they consist of a hollow vesicle, containing a solid body in its centre. The Abbe Torré described the red particles as being in the form of rings, while Monro thought that they were flattened bodies, in the shape of coins, with a dark spot in the centre. Cavallo, after reviewing the opinions of those who had preceded him, concluded that they were all deceptions, owing to the peculiar modification of the rays of light, and imagines that the real figure of the particles is a sphere, while Dr. Young, from the result of his observations, has been induced to adopt an opinion nearly similar to that of Hewson. The particles of the blood of the skate, from their size and distinctness, are the most proper for observations of this kind; and he announces them as being composed of an external envelope, containing a central nu-

cleus, the two bodies having but little adherence to each other, and seeming to be of a very different nature and consistence. Dr. Young has also observed in the globules of the human blood an appearance which partly coincides with that stated by Monro, as they are said to be flattened and to have a depression in the centre.

Size. Very various statements have been made respecting the size of the red particles; Leeuwenhoek says it differs much in different animals; but later writers have thought that they are more nearly of the same size. Haller estimated them at about the five-hundredth of an inch in diameter, and this estimate is sanctioned by the observations that have been more recently made by Dr. Young and Captain Kater; while, on the contrary, the still later researches of Mr. Bauer make them considerably larger, as much as the two-hundredth of an inch in diameter.

Composition. The nature and composition of the particles have been the subject of nearly as much controversy as their figure. The older writers supposed them to be of an oleaginous nature, but this idea is incompatible with the more correct observations that have been since made upon them, according to which they bear no resemblance to an oily body, either in their physical or their chemical properties. A part at least of the uncertainty which attaches to their nature depends upon the difficulty which there is in procuring these bodies in a separate state, detached from the other constituents of the blood; this objection applies to the analysis of Berzelius, although it is probably the most correct that we possess. The result of his experiments is, that the red globules do not materially differ from the other parts of the blood, except in their colour, and in the circumstance of a minute quantity of oxide of iron being found among their ashes after combustion.

Iron in the blood. The discovery of iron in the blood is generally attributed to Menghini; the fact has been very fully confirmed by later observers, although they have differed very much as to the amount of the quantity of the iron. Menghini, and most of the earlier writers, appear to have very much over-rated the quantity. Berzelius informs us that the colouring matter of the blood, separated from the other parts, leaves about 1-80th of incombustible matter, of which rather more than one half is the oxide of iron. We are still quite uncertain in what state the oxide of iron exists in the blood: Fourcroy brought forward an opinion, professing to be the result of experiment, that the iron was in combination with phosphoric acid, but some late experiments, especially those of Mr. Brande, show that this opinion is untenable. Various saline bodies, when added to the blood, produce considerable effects upon the red particles, some dissolving them, others causing them to shrink up into a small bulk, some brightening their colour, and others rendering it deeper. Many experiments of this kind were performed by Hewson, and it is probable that he has accurately detailed the results; but as they lead to no important conclusion, we shall not enter into any detail of them.

Action of the air. Perhaps the most interesting fact with which we are acquainted respecting these particles, is the change which is produced in their colour by the contact of the atmosphere. It had been long observed that the upper part of the clot was of a bright scarlet colour, while the lower part was of a purplish red, but no one seems to have been aware of the true cause of this ap-

PHYSIOLOGY.

Physiology. pearance, until Cigna of Turin announced it as depending upon the action of the air. The idea was immediately embraced by Priestley, who, after verifying the statement of Cigna, discovered that the action of the air depended solely on its oxygenous portion, while the azote, as well as the unrespirable gases generally, had no effect of this kind upon the colour of the blood, but even, on the contrary, tended to deepen the colour of scarlet blood. Upon examining the air which had been employed in these experiments, he found that it had lost a part of its oxygen, and was no longer capable of supporting life, the same change having been induced upon it as upon air that had passed through the lungs in the natural process of respiration. It was generally concluded, although perhaps without any very sufficient evidence, that the action of the air in these cases was upon the iron in the blood; there are, indeed, many reasons for supposing that the red globules are the part of the clot upon which the air more particularly acts; but how this action is effected, whether the iron has any share in it, or what change it undergoes, are questions that at present we are unable to answer.

Serum. The liquid which separates from the clot, when the spontaneous coagulation of the blood takes place, is called the serum. It is a viscid fluid, of a dull straw colour, of considerable specific gravity, a saltish taste, and when warm of an odour resembling milk. It consists of water, holding in solution different animal and saline substances, the principal of which is albumen, a body which possesses the singular property of becoming solid at a temperature of about 160 degrees. This process, like the concretion of the fibrin, has obtained the name of coagulation, yet it is in fact a very different kind of operation, not indeed exactly similar to any other with which we are acquainted. If the serum, after being coagulated, be cut into small pieces, a quantity of a brownish fluid gradually drains from it, which has been named the serosity; this consists of water, holding in solution an animal substance, different from albumen, together with a quantity of saline matter. The albumen after coagulation being no longer soluble in water, by sufficient ablution the other constituents of the serum may be removed from it. In this state, however, a large quantity of water still remains attached to it; and if this be slowly evaporated, the albumen is converted into a hard, semi-transparent, brittle substance, which resembles membrane in all its physical and chemical properties, except that it is destitute of any appearance of organization.

Cause of coagulation. Albumen is coagulated by various chemical re-agents as well as by the application of heat, particularly by the mineral acids, by alcohol, by various metallic salts, and, according to the curious discovery of Mr. Brande, by the action of the galvanic pile. It is probable, however, that, in these different cases, neither the substances procured are similar, nor is the operation the same by which they are produced. Many conjectures have been formed to account for the action of heat in coagulating albumen, but, as we think, without affording any just explanation of it; and, upon the whole, we are disposed to attribute it to a specific action, which is not referable to any general principle.

Composition of serosity; The substance which drains from the albumen after it has been coagulated, called the serosity, exists in small quantity only in comparison with the other ingredients of the blood, and there has been much controversy respecting the nature of the animal matter

contained in it. Cullen, who was one of the first chemists that paid much attention to it, speaks of the serosity as a solution of fibrin in water; and Hewson conceived it to be similar to the mucus of the lungs. Parmentier and Deyeux, in the year 1790, published an elaborate set of experiments upon the subject, from which they concluded that the animal matter in serosity is jelly. Their account of it had so much the appearance of correctness, that their opinion was generally adopted, until, in 1805, Dr. Bostock found that it was without foundation, and that the blood contains no jelly, a discovery which has been since confirmed by Professor Berzelius, Dr. Marcet, and Mr. Brande. Dr. Bostock named this substance the uncoagulable matter of the blood; while Dr. Marcet, from a reference to its chemical properties, calls it muco-extractive matter.

All the fluids of the animal body are furnished with a quantity of salts; and, as they are soluble in water, they remain, at least for the most part, in the serosity. Guglielmini appears to have been one of the first who distinctly announced the presence of salts in the blood; they have been since examined by different chemists, but by none with so much accuracy as by Berzelius and Marcet. From their experiments we learn, that they consist principally of soda, muriate of soda, and some of the phosphates. Since we find that a certain quantity of saline matter is always present in the animal fluids, it is natural to conclude that they perform some important office in the animal economy; it has been supposed that they may stimulate the muscular fibres to contraction, that they may contribute to the operation of the secreting organs, or that they may aid in the process of digestion; but all these are mere conjectures, for which we have no certain foundation.

We have now described the blood, as it exists in its ordinary state, without regarding the changes which it occasionally experiences from the operation of peculiar circumstances. Of these the most important is the difference between the venous and the arterial blood. The most obvious difference is the colour, which, in the larger trunks of the systemic arteries, is a bright scarlet; and, in the systemic veins, of a purplish red. We have very different statements of the comparative temperature of the two kinds of blood; for, simple as the experiment may appear, writers of equal authority give us very opposite statements. But the most important circumstance in which the arterial and the venous blood have been supposed to differ from each other, is the one which was announced by Crawford, that arterial has a greater capacity for heat than venous blood: but this point will be considered more fully in the next chapter, on respiration and animal temperature.

CHAPTER VIII.

OF RESPIRATION.

In the more perfect animals, or those which are furnished with the greatest number of distinct organs, respiration is almost as essential to their existence as the circulation of the blood. This function consists in the alternate reception and emission of air into and out of the lungs; while, at the same time, the blood is transmitted through a set of vessels so formed as to enable the air to act upon it, and to produce that change in its nature and properties which fits it for the support of life. We shall arrange our remarks upon this subject into three heads: 1st, The mechanism of respiration;

Physiology.

diaphragm.

2d, Its direct effects; and 3d, The remote effects of respiration upon the living system.

Sect. 1.—*Mechanism of Respiration.*

Organs of respiration; trachea,

The organs of respiration are the trachea, with its ramifications, the lungs, and the diaphragm. The trachea, or wind-pipe, is a long tube, composed of cartilaginous rings, and furnished with muscular fibres, which extends from the mouth into the chest. It there divides into two branches, called bronchia, which pass respectively into the two lungs; here they subdivide into smaller branches, and these again into branches still smaller, until at length they terminate in minute cavities, which are called the air vesicles. These vesicles, which are destined for the ultimate reception of the air that is taken in by the trachea, are composed of a delicate membranous substance, and lined with a fine mucous membrane, on which the pulmonary arteries ramify that proceed from the right side of the heart; those which compose the pulmonic circulation. This distribution of the blood was first minutely described by Malpighi, and has been generally received as correct, although there has been considerable difference of opinion respecting the form of the vesicles, and their connexion with the branches of the trachea. Some anatomists, as Willis, conceived that each air-tube terminated in a separate rounded cell, which had no connexion with any other cavity, whereas others supposed that the lungs consist of an irregular tissue of membranous matter, the different parts of which, like those of the common cellular texture, have a communication with each other.

Air vesicles.

Lungs.

The lungs are two spongy bodies, each of them of an irregular oval form, united at their upper part by the trunks of the bronchia: they are kept distinct from each other by the mediastinum, a membranous body, which divides the thorax into two cavities, that do not communicate with each other. Each lung is divided into three principal parts, called lobes, and these into a number of smaller parts, or lobules, each lobule consisting of a branch of the air-tubes, with the accompanying blood vessels, and the connecting cellular substance. The lungs entirely fill up the two cavities of the chest, so as to leave no vacant space between the pleuræ, or the membrane which encloses the lungs and that which lines the thorax, although, in the healthy state of the chest, these membranes have no connexion, except at their origin, and admit of free motion upon each other.

Thorax.

The thorax itself is composed partly of bone, and partly of cartilage; its sides are formed by the series of arched bones called the ribs; the spaces between which are filled up by the intercostal muscles. The lower part of the chest, which is contiguous to the abdomen, consists of the diaphragm, an expanded membrane, furnished with muscles, which give it the power of contraction, and constitute it the principal organ in the mechanism of respiration.

Act of respiration; contraction of the diaphragm.

The mechanical act of respiration consists essentially in increasing the cavity of the chest. The diaphragm, in its natural state, forms an arch, which is convex towards its upper surface, so that when its muscles contract it becomes flattened, and in this way increases the capacity of the thorax. The thorax is likewise increased in size by the contraction of the intercostals, although in a much less degree than by the flattening of the diaphragm; and indeed it is generally conceived that the principal use of these muscles is to fix the ribs, and prevent them from being drawn down by the con-

traction of the diaphragm, and thus counteracting the effect which is produced by its action.

Physiology.

Capacity of the thorax increased.

As the lungs are every where in contact with the cavity containing them, they are necessarily expanded in an equal degree with the thorax. In consequence of this expansion, their capacity is increased, and as there is a free communication with the atmosphere by means of the trachea, a portion of air enters them equal to their increased capacity. After some time the muscles of the diaphragm and the intercostals relax, and the elasticity of the cartilages of the thorax brings back the parts to their former bulk, and the capacity of the lungs being thus diminished, the additional portion of air which they had received is expelled. In a short time, however, the muscular contraction is renewed, and is again succeeded by relaxation; and this alternation, which continues to the end of life, constitutes the mechanical process of respiration. Hence it appears that the state of expiration is what may be termed the natural condition of the respiratory organs, or that in which they are found when the position of the parts is not affected by muscular contraction. We also perceive, that the air enters the lungs solely in consequence of the increase of the capacity of the thorax, which is affected by muscular contraction; that this is the only step in the process which can properly be regarded as a vital action; and that the rest of the mechanism of respiration depends upon the elasticity, or other physical properties of the parts concerned.

History of opinions.

The above account of the mechanism of respiration is the one generally adopted by the modern physiologists, and appears to explain all the phenomena, without having recourse to any occult agents or gratuitous suppositions. It was not, however, until after many premature attempts, and without numerous and even violent controversies, that the correct theory was established; for while the physical properties of air were not understood, it is not surprising that errors should prevail respecting the action of the atmosphere on the human body. Boyle, who was so successful in his investigations on the subject of pneumatics, first explained upon correct principles why the air enters the lungs; but his simple doctrine was not suited to that age, where refined hypotheses were so much in vogue, and where every thing was to be explained by some abstruse mathematical problem. We find, therefore, that for a century or more after he wrote, a variety of learned speculations continued to prevail upon the subject, which were derived either from false principles of philosophy, or from incorrect opinions respecting the anatomy of the organs. Some of these notions were even attempted to be proved by experiment; such, for example, as that a quantity of air is contained in the cavity of the chest, between the pleuræ, which by its spring compresses the lungs, and produces expiration; or that the lungs themselves are furnished with pores, through which the air is alternately discharged and reabsorbed in the different states of respiration. Most of the older anatomists supposed, that the lungs possess an innate power of motion, by which they draw in and expel the air; but all these opinions are now entirely discarded.

Action of the intercostals.

Few points in anatomy have been the subject of more warm and protracted discussion than the action of the intercostals. Between each of the ribs are two sets of muscular fibres, one external and the other internal; both of which are situated obliquely, but in opposite directions. The older anatomists conceived, that the contraction of the external layer would tend to raise the ribs, and thus, by increasing the angle which they form with the spine, enlarge the capacity of the thorax, while the internal layer had the contrary effect of depressing the ribs, and consequently diminishing the chest. Mayow appears to have been the first who decidedly adopted the opinion, that the contraction of both the external and the internal intercostals raises the ribs,—the opinion which is now generally embraced; but the contrary idea continued to prevail until the middle of the last century, when it was successfully refuted by Haller, and has not been since revived.

The nature of the diaphragm, its muscular action, and its importance in the mechanism of respiration, were very imperfectly understood by the ancients, and even by the earlier modern anatomists. By some, it was supposed to be the immediate seat of the soul; by others it was thought to have a kind of independent life; and it was generally regarded as being possessed of some mysterious power, until Fabricius explained its operation upon rational principles, referring it solely to the combined action of muscular contractility and the elasticity of membrane,—the first producing a change in its form, and the latter bringing it back to its original position after the contraction had ceased. It is now universally regarded as the great agent by which the size of the cavity of the thorax is regulated. In its natural or relaxed state it is arched upwards, so as to protrude into the chest and diminish its size; and when, by the contraction of its muscles, it is flattened, the capacity of the thorax is proportionably increased.

Many attempts have been made by physiologists to ascertain the quantity of air that is taken into the lungs at one time, or the bulk of a single inspiration. Respiration is, however, so much under the control of the will, that all we can obtain by our experiments is the average quantity; for, although we cannot suspend the action of the lungs for more than a very limited period, we can at pleasure receive into them a greater or less quantity of air. There is also a considerable difference in the form of different individuals with respect to the size of the chest; and it is probable that peculiar states of the constitution, and perhaps of the air itself, may affect the quantity received into the lungs. And besides the question respecting the bulk of a single inspiration, there are others which deserve our attention. We may inquire, not only what is the average bulk of an ordinary inspiration, but what is the amount of the greatest quantity of air that we are able to take into the lungs by the most powerful voluntary effort, what is the quantity of air left in the lungs after an ordinary expiration, what farther quantity we are able to expel by the most powerful effort, and what quantity still remains in the lungs.

With respect to the bulk of an ordinary inspiration, the first writer who gives us any very accurate information is Jurin. By breathing into a bladder, and making the necessary allowance for temperature and pressure, he estimated the quantity at forty cubic inches. Goodwyn employed a peculiar apparatus, in which he measured the bulk of an inspiration by the quantity of water raised up from one vessel to another. Sir H. Davy endeavoured to find the quantity, by examining the chemical changes which a certain portion of air had experienced by passing through the lungs; and other methods have been employed, which gave results that varied from a few inches to above fifty. But of all the experiments of this kind that have been performed, those of Menzies seem to be entitled to the

greatest confidence, both from the nature of the apparatus, and from the general uniformity of the results. He performed two sets of experiments. In the first, he employed a membranous bag, of such a size as to enable him to take the average of a number of inspirations, and so fitted with valves as to keep the inspired and expired air distinct from each other. In the second set of experiments, a man was immersed up to the chin in a vessel of water, which was closed at the top, and furnished with a projecting tube, in which any alteration in the level of the water might be readily perceived, and thus the corresponding changes in the bulk of the body be accurately estimated. By employing every necessary precaution, he found the result of both sets of experiments to be nearly similar, and also to correspond with the simple process of Jurin, indicating the average bulk of a single inspiration to be forty cubic inches.

The quantity of air that can still be expelled from the lungs after an ordinary expiration, depends upon the size of the individual, and the peculiar formation of the chest. It appears, however, that a middle-sized man can expel between 150 and 200 cubic inches by a powerful voluntary effort. But it is obvious, from the formation of the lungs and chest, that no voluntary effort can expel all the air from them; and here again, as on all the other points, the opinions of anatomists and physiologists have been very various. Perhaps the experiments of Goodwyn are the most to be relied on, which make this quantity somewhat more than 100 cubic inches. From these data, which, although confessedly imperfect, seem to be the best which we possess, it may be estimated, that, by each ordinary expiration, between one-sixth and one-seventh of the whole contents of the lungs is discharged; and that, by the most violent effort of expiration, two-thirds, or even a greater proportion of the air, is evacuated. Supposing that each act of respiration occupies about three seconds, a bulk of air, nearly equal to three times the contents of the lungs, will be expelled in a minute, or about 4000 times their bulk in 24 hours. This quantity will amount to between 600 and 700 cubic feet.

There are two curious subjects of inquiry connected with the function of respiration, which have abundantly exercised the genius of physiologists—what is the cause of the first inspiration in the newly born infant? and what is the cause of the regular successions of inspiration and expiration during the remainder of life? With respect to the first of these points, Harvey asks the following question, Why is the animal, when it has once breathed, under the necessity of continuing to respire without intermission, when, if the air had never been received into the lungs, the same animal might have remained some time without exercising this function? Whytt gave an answer to this question, which at the time was very generally acquiesced in. He supposes that, immediately after birth, an uneasy sensation is experienced in the chest from the want of air, which may be regarded as the appetite for breathing. To supply this appetite, the intelligent principle with which the body is endowed, produces the expansion of the chest, being aware of the fatal consequences that would result from the exclusion of fresh air. It is sufficient to remark concerning this hypothesis, that it labours under the defect of all the speculations of the metaphysical physiologists, that it confounds the final with the efficient cause, and supposes the agency of a principle, the existence of which is itself a point which requires to be proved.

Perhaps it would be difficult to give any answer to

Harvey's query, which should be altogether satisfactory; but there is one point which may tend to throw some light upon this obscure subject. We refer to the mechanical change which the chest experiences when the young animal leaves the uterus. Before this time, in consequence of the position of the fœtus, the lungs are squeezed up into as small a space as possible, and are nearly impervious to the blood; but when the trunk is extended, and the parts are allowed to exercise their natural elasticity, the ribs rise up, and the diaphragm descends, so that the dimensions of the chest are extended in both directions. The thorax being thus brought into its state of average distention, and there being a free passage through the mouth, the air necessarily rushes in to supply the vacancy thus produced.

Cause of the alternation.

The second subject of inquiry that was pointed out, regards the regular alternation of inspiration and expiration. The attempts that have been made to solve this problem are very numerous; but we are disposed to regard them all as inadequate to the end in view; nor are we able to afford any explanation which is entirely satisfactory. We are indeed disposed to consider this action as depending upon different principles, according to the manner in which it is carried on, whether in the ordinary process of respiration, or when the lungs, from any cause, are excited to an extraordinary effort. In the first case, it would appear that when the blood has passed through the systemic circulation, it undergoes a change which renders it no longer fit for performing the functions necessary for the continuance of life. In some way or other, which we shall not now attempt to explain, when the blood comes into this state, an uneasy sensation is experienced about the heart, which sensation is removed by taking a portion of fresh air into the lungs. Whether the sensation itself serves as a stimulus to the muscles, or to the nerves connected with the organs of respiration; or whether the blood produces some more complicated train of changes, which eventually ends in the contraction of the diaphragm, is a point which we are unable to determine; but the result is, that a necessary connexion is established between these actions, in consequence of which the diaphragm contracts, wherever the blood is returned to the heart in the venalized state.

Remarks.

On certain occasions, however, there is a necessity for an extraordinary quantity of air to be received into the lungs, either for the performance of some mechanical operation, or to produce a greater degree of effect than ordinary upon the blood. In these cases, it would seem that the organs of respiration are influenced either by an instinctive feeling or by the direct efforts of volition. The act of sneezing commences by a powerful inspiration, for the accomplishment of which all the muscles of the thorax and diaphragm are brought into a state of strong contraction, and this is done in the most complete manner by the newly born infant, who must necessarily be quite unconscious of the end in view, and ignorant of the means by which it is brought about. There are, on the contrary, many actions of the respiratory organs that are completely voluntary, such as sighing, straining, &c. in which different muscles are called into action to produce a specific effect, in consequence of previous experience, in the same manner with the motions of the arms and legs. According, therefore, to the degree in which the lungs are called into action, the muscles connected with the thorax appear to be influenced by different powers; in ordinary cases by some impression upon them, depending on the state of the air and the blood; while in extraordinary inspirations, the principles of instinct and of volition, as in other parts of the body, produce muscular contractions, which tend directly to produce some useful purpose in the animal economy.

Effect of respiration upon the heart.

Most of the older physiologists, and even several of the moderns, have supposed that the varying bulk of the chest, in the different states of expiration and inspiration, must have a considerable effect upon the circulation. This opinion was maintained by Hales and Haller, and many experiments were adduced by which it appeared to be countenanced. But it is probable that in these cases the effects of ordinary and of extraordinary respiration have been confounded together. When experiments are made on living animals, we may presume that the respiration must be rendered laborious, that the air will be taken in at longer intervals, and consequently in a larger bulk at once, at the same time that the circulation being in a languid state, is more liable to be affected by slight causes acting upon it. That the circulation is not affected by the state of the lungs in ordinary cases may be inferred from the fact, that although the heart contracts four or five times as frequently as the diaphragm, and that consequently the blood must pass through the lungs in all their different states of distention, yet the pulse remains the same, without any alteration corresponding to the changes in the lungs. Upon the whole, therefore, we may conclude, that when the organs are in their natural condition, the different states of the lungs do not materially affect the circulation of the blood.

Sect. II.—*The direct Effects of Respiration.*

Effects of respiration.

We now proceed to the second division of our subject, the direct effects of respiration. These are to be considered in two points of view; 1st, The effects upon the air; and, 2d, Those upon the blood.

Upon the air.

From the inspection of the anatomy of the pulmonary organs, and particularly of the complicated apparatus by which the air and the blood are brought within the sphere of their mutual action, it was natural to conclude that the use of the lungs is to effect a change in the blood through the operation of the air. The ancients had some rude conception of the existence of this action, although their idea of its nature was very imperfect. Perhaps the most generally received opinion among the earlier physiologists was, that the immediate effect of respiration is to remove from the blood a quantity of heat and water, for it was a fact too obvious to be overlooked, even by the most superficial observers, that air which is expired from the lungs, differs from that which is taken into them, by the addition of warmth and moisture. During the prevalence of the mathematical sect, there was a great controversy respecting the question, whether respiration has the effect of rarefying or of condensing the blood. One party conceived that the blood must necessarily be condensed, because a quantity of water is evaporated from it, while their opponents, who supposed that a portion of air is absorbed by the blood in passing through the lungs, were equally strenuous in maintaining that it must be rarefied.

Boyle's observations.

Although nothing could be more obvious than the necessity of the uninterrupted continuance of respiration, yet this was attributed more to some mechanical effect which it produced upon the motion of the blood, than to any change in its qualities, and it was not until the time of Boyle that we became fully sensible of the fact, that a constant supply of successive portions of

Physiology. fresh unrespired air is essential to life; a fact which he discovered in the course of his experiments upon the air pump. His investigations, however, were principally directed to the knowledge of the mechanical properties of the air; and it was in this point of view that he almost exclusively regarded its action upon the lungs. Yet he did not entirely overlook the other physical changes which it experiences; he noticed the moisture which is exhaled along with it, and farther observed, that it carries off, what he calls recrementitious steams; but he does not enter into any explanation of their nature. He also observed, that, under certain circumstances, the air in which an animal has been confined is diminished in bulk; and this he accounts for by saying that it has lost its spring.

Mayow's. Mayow made an important addition to Boyle's hypothesis, by supposing that the air, besides carrying off these vapours, imparts something to the blood; and he even attempted to explain the nature of this substance which is abstracted from the atmosphere. By performing comparative experiments on portions of air before and after it had been respired, he concluded that, during its passage through the lungs, it imparts to the blood a certain volatile matter, which he calls nitro-aerial spirit, and which was also concerned in combustion, as well as in many other chemical operations. Most of the contemporaries of Mayow, as Borelli, Lower, and Willis, adopted opinions that were not very dissimilar with respect to the part which the air acts in the process of respiration, some of them imagining that a portion of the whole mass of air, and others that some particular part of it, entered the blood. This hypothesis was, however, after some time, gradually abandoned, and what may appear more remarkable, the discoveries and experiments of Mayow, which were extremely curious, and calculated to throw great light upon natural philosophy, were entirely forgotten.

Hales's. Our knowledge respecting the change which air undergoes by respiration, remained without any addition, or rather may be considered as retrograde for some years, when the inquiry was again resumed by Hales. He instituted a number of experiments upon this point, and was led to form a conclusion nearly similar to that of Boyle, that the change consists in the air acquiring a noxious vapour, and losing part of its elasticity; the same doctrine was also maintained by Haller. It was

Black's. shortly after this period that Black commenced his investigations on the chemical nature of air; and after discovering the existence of carbonic acid, as a gaseous substance, possessed of distinct and specific properties, he found that a quantity of it was generated in the lungs by respiration. The labours of Black in this department of science were zealously seconded by Cavendish, Scheele, and Priestley, whose successive discoveries led to the knowledge of the chemical composition of the atmosphere, as consisting principally of the two aeriform substances to which the names of

Priestley's. oxygen and azote have been since applied. Among the great variety of subjects to which the last of these philosophers directed his attention, he carefully examined the nature of the effect produced upon the air by respiration, when he found that it had lost a part of its oxygen, or had experienced nearly the same kind of change as by combustion, fermentation, and other analogous operations, which, in conformity to the hypothesis then prevalent, he styled phlogistic processes; he therefore concluded that the air, in passing through the lungs, loses oxygen and acquires phlogiston and aqueous vapour.

Not long after the publication of Priestley's experiments, the subject of respiration was taken up by Lavoisier. He examined the opinions of his predecessors with his accustomed address; he agrees with Priestley in the essential circumstance of the diminution of the oxygen in air that has been respired; but he points out an important distinction between the different phlogistic processes that had been hitherto confounded together; and with respect to the effect of respiration, he concludes that the air loses part of its oxygen and receives an addition of carbonic acid. The opinion of Lavoisier has been generally assented to by succeeding physiologists, and the object of the experiments which have been lately made, has been either to ascertain the amount of these several changes, or to account for the operation of the lungs in effecting them. Physiology Lavoisier's

With respect to the first of these changes, the consumption of oxygen, there are two points to be ascertained. 1st, What proportion of it in air that is respired is necessary for the support of life? and, in the 2d place, what is the actual quantity that is consumed under ordinary circumstances? Although our experiments have enabled us to acquire much information on these subjects, yet considerable difficulty attends all our investigations, and we are obliged, in most cases, to make allowance for various intervening circumstances, before we can apply our results to the solution of the question under discussion. We find that different classes of animals affect the air in very different degrees, and that this is likewise the case with different individuals of the same class, or even with the same individual under different circumstances. We find that the degree of purity in the atmosphere necessary for the continuance of life, depends very much upon the constitution of the animal as to its ordinary temperature, and the structure of its organs of respiration. Birds would appear to require the greatest proportion of oxygen, and to be incapable of subsisting when more than two-thirds of the usual proportion is removed. A mouse can live until nearly three-fourths is consumed; frogs, and the cold-blooded quadrupeds will exist in an atmosphere that contains considerably less oxygen, while worms and snails are not destroyed until very nearly the whole is abstracted. It is, however, necessary to bear in mind, that the death of the warm-blooded animals, in these cases, depends not so much upon the deficiency of oxygen, as upon the presence of carbonic acid; and, accordingly, it is found, that when the experiments are so conducted, that the acid is absorbed as fast as it is produced, a mouse can live, without apparent uneasiness, when no more than one-fifteenth of the original proportion of oxygen is left in the air. The temperature of the human subject, and the general structure of his organs of respiration and circulation, are similar to those of the mouse, so that it is probable a man might exist in air of this standard; but it would only serve for his support while in a state of perfect rest, and without the unnecessary action of any of the functions, for, as we shall afterwards find, the consumption of oxygen is materially augmented by these circumstances. Quantity of oxygen consumed.

The first attempts to estimate the absolute quantity of oxygen consumed, were those of Menzies. He found that one-twentieth part of air that has once passed through the lungs is removed, and this he supposed to be oxygen; hence he concludes that 52,000 cubic inches, or between 17,000 and 18,000 grains, are consumed in 24 hours. This calculation, however, being derived from insufficient data, can only be regarded as Experiments of Menzies.

an approximation to the truth; and the results of some experiments which were performed by Lavoisier, in conjunction with Seguin, seem to be much more entitled to our confidence. They were conducted upon a large scale, with an apparatus more complete than had hitherto been employed in physiological researches, and every circumstance seems to have been attended to which could ensure their accuracy. We learn from them, that a man, under ordinary circumstances, consumes in 24 hours about 46,000 cubic inches, or 15,500 grains. Since the death of this philosopher, who, as is well known, was sacrificed to the barbarous fury of Robespierre, some experiments on the same subject have been performed by Sir H. Davy; and although he made use of a very different kind of process, his results nearly coincide with those of Lavoisier. We may, therefore, conclude, with considerable confidence, the quantity to be between 45,000 and 46,000 cubic inches, or about 2lb. 8 oz. Troy.

The next point to be ascertained with respect to the chemical change produced in the air by respiration, is the quantity of carbonic acid that is produced. We have already stated, that the general fact of its existence in air that is emitted from the lungs is due to Black; but he does not appear to have made any attempt to estimate its quantity. Menzies calculated that nearly 4lbs. of carbonic acid are produced by a man under ordinary circumstances in twenty-four hours; whereas Lavoisier and Seguin, in the experiments referred to above, reduce the quantity to rather more than 3lbs.; and in their later experiments, which, it it may be presumed, were performed with greater accuracy, the carbonic acid was still farther diminished to only half that quantity. The estimate of Sir H. Davy, on the contrary, nearly agrees with the first of Lavoisier's.

In these experiments, as well as in all the others that were performed until lately, the oxygen consumed always appeared to be greater than the carbonic acid that was generated; and although the difference between these amounts varied considerably in different experiments, yet the difference was found to exist in all those upon which the greatest confidence was to be placed. We have, however, a series performed by Messrs. Allen and Pepys, which were conducted, as it would appear, with the most scrupulous attention to accuracy, where the amount of oxygen consumed exactly coincided with the carbonic acid produced; and, in consequence of these experiments, the opinion has been pretty generally adopted that these quantities always coincide. It is, indeed, difficult to conceive how experimentalists of acknowledged address and dexterity, such as Lavoisier and Davy, could have fallen into so considerable a mistake, yet is is, perhaps, still more so, to detect any probable source of error in the operations of Allen and Pepys.

Besides the general causes of uncertainty that must attach to all experiments performed upon the living body, there is a specific difficulty in ascertaining the amount of the chemical changes produced upon the air by respiration depending upon the circumstance, that different states of the functions cause the changes to be produced in different degrees. This fact was first noticed by Priestley and Crawford, with respect to the operation of external temperature: they observed that an animal consumed less oxygen, and produced less carbonic acid, when exposed to a warm medium, than the same animal when placed in a lower temperature. Subsequent experiments have confirmed this discovery, and Jurine

of Geneva extended the observations to other circumstances besides temperature. He found that the production of carbonic acid was increased by the process of digestion, by violent exercise, and by the state of fever; and Lavoisier met with the same results in his elaborate researches. The experiments in this case were performed upon the person of Seguin; and, so far as the proportionate quantities are concerned, they appear to deserve great confidence. When the stomach was empty, the body at rest, and the temperature considerably elevated, it was found that 1210 cubic inches of oxygen gas were consumed in an hour; whereas, when the temperature was reduced to 25° of Fahr., the other circumstances remaining the same, the amount of oxygen was increased to 1344 cubic inches. During digestion the oxygen was found to be between 1800 and 1900 inches; and, if violent exercise had been used when digestion was going forwards, the quantity was increased to 4600 cubic inches in an hour. It is to be observed, that, in all these different cases, the temperature is not affected, but that the circulation and respiration are much accelerated.

We meet with the same kind of discordance of opinion respecting another change which the air has been supposed to experience by its passage through the lungs, viz. the diminution of bulk. The earlier physiologists very much over-rated this diminution in bulk, in consequence of obvious sources of inaccuracy in the mode of conducting their experiments: but the same change, although in a less degree, has been admitted to take place by Goodwyn, Lavoisier, and Davy. Lavoisier, in the first of his memoirs, stated it at 1-60th, and Davy found it to vary from 1-70th to 1-100th. But, powerful and direct as this evidence must appear in favour of the fact, a contrary result was obtained by Messrs. Allen and Pepys; who, in all cases, found the bulk of the air to be the same before and after the experiment. The difference of opinion that exists respecting this matter of fact is the more important, as it very materially affects our hypothesis of the nature of the action of the lungs. When oxygen is converted into carbonic acid by the addition of carbon, it experiences no change of volume; therefore we are led to conclude, that, if the bulk of the air remain unaltered after passing through the lungs, the only effect of respiration will be, to remove a portion of carbon from the blood; whereas, if the quantity of oxygen which disappears be greater than what is necessary for the formation of the carbonic acid, a portion of it must be employed for some other purpose in the animal economy.

Some chemists, and even Sir H. Davy himself, have supposed, that a quantity of azote is absorbed in the lungs, but the general result of the experiments are against this supposition; and it is now almost universally admitted, that this gas, which composes so large a proportion of the air, is not affected by respiration, although the contrary supposition would be a very convenient addition to our hypothesis, by furnishing us with an obvious source of azote for those animals who do not receive it through the medium of the stomach.

The exhalation of a quantity of aqueous vapour from the lungs, mixed with the expired air, was too obvious a phenomenon to be overlooked, even by the earliest physiologists; but, except the general fact, little certainty has been obtained respecting it. Hales attempted to ascertain the quantity of this vapour, by breathing through wood ashes, and finding how much they had increased in weight. His experiments led him to

---

Marginal notes (left column):

Physiology.

Lavoisier.

Carbonic acid produced.

Is there an excess of oxygen?

Experiments of Allen and Pepys.

Effect of temperature, &c.

Marginal notes (right column):

Physiology.

Diminution of bulk in the air.

Absorption of azote.

Exhalation of water.

Experiments of Hales;

Physiology.
conclude, that the water exhaled in twenty-four hours would amount to about 20 oz.; while Menzies, who attempted actually to collect the water, reduced it to 6 oz. Lavoisier endeavoured to solve the problem less directly, by instituting a calculation founded upon the composition of water, compared with that of the other substances which are received into, and discharged from, the lungs. We have already stated, that he supposed there was an over-proportion of oxygen after the formation of the carbonic acid; and this oxygen, he imagined, was united to a quantity of hydrogen in the lungs, and thus formed water, the amount of which might be known from that of the oxygen employed. Ingenious, however, as this method of Lavoisier's may appear, there are some obvious considerations which will prevent us from placing any confidence in it. Indeed, the foundation of all the reasoning, the disproportion between the oxygen and the carbonic acid, is itself a very doubtful point. Besides, the exhalation of hydrogen from the lungs, and its union with oxygen, under these circumstances, is not analogous to any other operation in the animal economy; while, at the same time, there is a much more obvious source for the water in the fluid which is secreted by the mucous membrane which lines the respiratory organs.

Recapitulation. After having thus examined in succession all the different changes which are supposed to be produced in the air by respiration, it may be desirable briefly to recapitulate the result of our inquiries. 1. Air that has been respired loses a portion of its oxygen; the quantity varies according to circumstances; but it may be estimated, upon the average, that a man consumes between 45,000 and 46,000 cubic inches, or about 15,500 grains, in twenty-four hours. 2. A quantity of carbonic acid is generated, the amount of which also varies according to circumstances, probably in proportion to the consumption of the oxygen; but there is a considerable difference of opinion respecting the relation which these quantities bear to each other, whether the quantity of oxygen that disappears be precisely equal to that of the carbonic acid which is generated. If we admit that all the oxygen is employed in the production of carbonic acid, the quantity will be as before, between 45,000 and 46,000 cubic inches, or above 21,000 grains. 3. A quantity of water is emitted from the lungs, mixed with, or diffused through, the air of expiration; but the amount of the water is still undetermined. The two next supposed changes, the diminution in the bulk of the air, and the abstraction of a portion of azote from it, are points concerning which there has been a considerable diversity of opinion; but, upon the whole, it appears that they are not supported by sufficient evidence. Hence we may conclude, that the only changes which are certainly known, as being produced upon the air by respiration, are the removal of a portion of its oxygen, and the addition of carbon and water.

Changes in the blood. We now proceed to consider the change which is effected in the blood by respiration, an inquiry attended with much more difficulty than that respecting the air, in proportion to the greater difficulty there is in ascertaining the exact chemical composition of the blood. The large quantity of blood which the lungs always contain, induced even the earliest physiologists to suppose that some important effect was produced upon it by this organ; and the conjecture was strongly confirmed by the discovery of Harvey, that every part of the blood passes through the lungs in each circulation. The opinions that were entertained respecting the nature of the change were extremely various, but they may be all reduced to three heads. It was supposed by some, that the change was merely mechanical; that it consisted in mixing the different parts of the blood intimately together; that it was condensed by pressure, or rarefied by the addition of a portion of air. A second set of physiologists, among whom we find Lower, Hooke, Mayow, and many of the Italians, conceived that the air imparts something to the venous blood, by which it is converted into the arterial state; while a third class, in which are included Harvey, Boyle, Hales, and Haller, supposed that the blood discharges some noxious matter, which is carried off by the air. Considered in its general outline, we shall probably find the third of these opinions to be the most correct; but they were all of them advanced rather as hypotheses than as deductions from facts; and when their respective advocates attempted to go into any minute detail, they soon degenerated into false, or even absurd speculations.

Lower endeavoured to prove by experiment, independent of any theory, that the scarlet colour which the blood acquires in the lungs is due to the action of the air. By opening the thorax of a living animal, he discovered the precise point in the course of the circulation where the change of colour takes place, and proved that it was not effected in the heart, as had been previously supposed, but when the blood passes along the capillaries of the lesser circulation. He kept the lungs distended, but without renewing the air, and he observed that the blood in this case returned to the heart without any change of colour; but when there was a continued supply of fresh air introduced into the lungs, the purple was converted into scarlet blood, exactly as in natural respiration. Lower enforced his opinion respecting the action of the air upon the blood by observing the change which it produces in the crassamentum out of the body; and he proved that the redness of the upper part of the clot is owing to its being exposed to the atmosphere, not, as was imagined, to the red particles subsiding to the bottom. Notwithstanding the direct nature of Lower's experiments, they made but little impression upon the minds of his contemporaries; the mathematicians thought that the change of colour might be referred with more plausibility, to some mechanical operation; and even Haller decidedly opposed the doctrine of Lower.

After a long interval, Lower's opinion was revived by Cigna, and supported by a train of experiments which may be regarded sufficient to establish the point; but they seem to have produced little conviction, until Priestley took up the subject, confirmed Cigna's experiments, added many of his own, and finally disclosed a series of facts which has served as a basis for all that has since been discovered upon the subject. After having unequivocally proved the action of the air in converting purple into scarlet blood, as in natural respiration, he proceeded to examine the effects of the constituents of the atmosphere, taken separately, and also of the other gases which had been lately discovered. He found that purple coagulum was reddened more rapidly by oxygen than by the air of the atmosphere, while azote, hydrogen, and carbonic acid, gave to scarlet crassamentum the purple colour of venous blood. The conclusions from these experiments were direct and highly important; they showed that the alteration of colour which the blood experiences in the lungs depends upon the oxygen in the atmosphere, and conversely, that the change

Physiology. which the air undergoes in the lungs depends upon the action of the blood in the pulmonary vessels. As we have stated above, Priestley conceived that change to consist in the addition of what he termed phlogiston to the air, and the consequent abstraction of this substance from the blood.

Lavoisier's. We have already given an account of the modifications which Lavoisier introduced into the doctrine of Priestley, partly in consequence of his more correct views of the nature of what had been styled phlogistic processes, and partly from the theory he adopted of the formation of the water which is exhaled from the lungs. His idea was, that the air, in passing through the pulmonary vessels, acquires carbon and hydrogen; and consequently he concluded, that these elements were given out by the blood, and constituted the difference between the arterial and the venous state of this fluid, thus converting the phlogiston of Priestley into hydro-carbon. So great was the authority of Lavoisier, that his opinion was almost universally received by his contemporaries; although, as we have seen above, the proof of the discharge of hydrogen was quite defective, and the opinion is now generally abandoned. We are therefore reduced to the conclusion, that the venous blood, in passing through the lungs, loses a portion of its carbon, which is carried off by the air, in the form of carbonic acid.

Union of oxygen and carbon. We may therefore consider the fact, that the venous blood loses carbon in passing through the lungs, as fully established, but there is some difficulty in explaining the manner in which this change is effected. On this subject two hypotheses have been proposed, each of which has been supported by the authority of great names, and by a variety of ingenious and plausible arguments. According to the original idea of Black, which was the one adopted by Priestley, Lavoisier, and Crawford, the oxygen simply attracts carbon from the blood, as it passes through the lungs: while, according to the hypothesis of Lagrange, which was adopted by many physiologists both in this country and in France, the operation is more complicated. Here it is supposed that the oxygen is absorbed by the blood, is mixed with it, and gradually unites with a portion of the carbon. When, in the course of the circulation, the compound of oxygen and carbon is again brought to the lungs, it is discharged in the form of carbonic acid, while at the same time a fresh portion of oxygen is absorbed. The essential difference between the two hypotheses is, that, according to the first, the change induced by respiration is entirely completed in the lungs, while in the other the change is effected in the body at large, the lungs serving merely as the organ where the ingredients are absorbed or discharged. Our judgment respecting them must be decided partly from investigating the source of the carbon that is emitted from the lungs, and partly from considering the effects which must be produced by the union of the oxygen and carbon.

Crawford's hypothesis. Crawford was the first who proposed any consistent explanation of the method in which the blood is supplied with the carbon which is discharged from the lungs. He observed that the matter of which the body is composed has a constant tendency to change: after some time, it appears to become incapable of serving for the purposes of the animal economy, and is therefore removed, while at the same time fresh matter is deposited in its room. The arteries are supposed to be the instruments by which this interchange is effected.

They convey the nutritious matter to all parts of the Physiology. body, so as to repair the necessary waste; while, at the same time that the blood loses its nutritive particles, it receives the effete matter, which is now become useless to the system, is conveyed to the lungs by the veins, and is there discharged. It is to this change of matter, which is supposed to be carried on in the capillaries of the systemic circulation, that the blood is converted from the venous to the arterial state, while the opposite change, from venous to arterial blood, is produced in the capillaries of the lungs. Hence it follows, upon this hypothesis, that the matter which is received by the systemic veins, contains a greater proportion of carbon than that which is employed in the growth and nutrition of the body.

Crawford's hypothesis accords with many well known Remarks facts, and seems to afford a simple and natural explana- upon it. tion of them; yet there are several parts of it that are decidedly objectionable. We have no evidence of any set of vessels, by which carbon can enter the veins at their extremities, while, on the other hand, there is an obvious source, from which this matter is conveyed into the blood in a different part of the circulation. We have every reason to suppose, that the only supply which the blood receives is by the thoracic duct, which pours its contents into the systemic veins, just before they arrive at their termination in the right auricle, previous to the transmission of the blood through the lungs. Hence, as it appears, we are necessarily reduced to the conclusion, that arterial blood becomes venalized, merely in consequence of the loss of what is removed from it by the capillary arteries for the purpose of nutrition and secretion, and not from any additional matter that it receives when it undergoes the change.

Some observations have been made upon this change, Hypothe-which must materially influence our hypothesis re- sis of La-specting the mode in which it is effected. It has been grange. found, that, in certain cases, the blood has been converted from the scarlet to the purple colour, while it has remained in the same system of vessels; thus seeming to prove, that the alteration depends, not upon any thing which it receives or discharges, but upon some change which is effected by the action of its constituent parts upon each other. It has been remarked in surgical operations, that after the blood has been confined by the tourniquet in a large arterial trunk, when the instrument is first removed, the fluid has acquired the venous appearance; and Hunter found, that the same change was effected when a portion of an artery was inclosed between two ligatures. It was also found, that arterial blood, when extravasated into the cavities of the cellular substance, gradually acquired the venous character, and that the same change took place when a portion of scarlet blood was confined out of the body in glass tubes. From these facts, together with the supposed disproportion between the oxygen absorbed and the carbonic acid produced, as well as from certain considerations to be hereafter mentioned, respecting the equable diffusion of animal heat, the second hypothesis of respiration was proposed by M. Lagrange, and illustrated by the experiments of M. Hassenfratz, in which the oxygen is supposed to be absorbed in the lungs, to be gradually united with the carbon in the course of the circulation, and to be afterwards expired in the form of carbonic acid. In some respects, this hypothesis affords an easy explanation of the leading phenomena; but as it rests upon facts which are of an

4 B

Physiology.

Observations on the absorption of oxygen.

equivocal nature, and is much less simple than the old theory, it has not been generally received.

To those who are acquainted with the doctrines of the modern physiologists, it will be obvious that many of their favourite speculations must fall to the ground, if we reject the absorption of oxygen by the lungs. The very extensive influence which this element has been found to possess over the operations of chemistry, and more particularly the part which it seems to act in the function of respiration, induced many persons to conceive, that its agency must extend to every part of the animal economy. Thus oxygen has been thought by one, to be the immediate cause of contractility; by another, of sensibility; by some, it has been assumed as the chief agent in digestion and secretion; and it has even been identified with the vital principle itself. In pathology it has acted a no less conspicuous part. Some diseases have been attributed to its excess, others to its deficiency; some medicines have been supposed to operate, by imparting this element to the body; others by abstracting it: so that we find the terms oxygenation and deoxygenation of the system familiarly employed, as operations which were quite within our power to accomplish. But we think it may be safely asserted, that all these speculations are completely without foundation; the arguments alleged in their favour are derived from loose analogies, the experiments inapplicable, and the facts of questionable authority.

Proportion of carbon in venous and arterial blood.

As venous seems to be converted into arterial blood by the discharge of carbon, we are naturally led to conjecture that the opposite change, from arterial to venous, must be produced by a reverse operation. Yet as no addition of carbon can be obtained from the blood in this part of the circulation, we are reduced to the necessity of supposing, that the nutritive and secretory matter, which is separated by the capillary arteries, contains a smaller proportion of carbon than the general mass of blood, and consequently increases the proportion of carbon in what is left. We have indeed no positive evidence that this is the case, nor perhaps will it be ever possible to prove it by any direct experiments; but the conclusion appears, notwithstanding, to be sufficiently warranted, that there must be some outlet from the sanguiferous system to balance that of the lungs; and we know of none except the secretory and nutritive arteries. Upon the whole, then, we may venture to draw the probable conclusion, that venous differs from arterial blood in containing a larger quantity of carbon.

On what part does the air act?

An interesting question occurs to us in this part of our investigation,—upon what part of the blood is it that the air more immediately acts? According to one hypothesis, the immediate subject of inquiry will be, from what part does the oxygen abstract the carbon? and, according to the other, by what part is the oxygen attracted? Although we are obliged to form our conclusions rather from conjecture than from any direct facts, yet it appears natural to suppose, that the red particles are the immediate agents in this operation. These globules are the only constituents of the blood which possess any specific characters, and which can therefore impart any specific properties to it, while, at the same time, they are known to be easily decomposed, and to be more readily affected by various chemical re-agents than either the serum or the fibrin. The nature of the action is indeed obscure; for there does not appear to be any foundation for the idea that prevailed at one time, that these red particles attract the

Physiology.

oxygen in consequence of the iron which they contain. All the most recent experiments tend to discountenance this idea, which is farther objectionable, as involving the doubtful hypothesis of the absorption of oxygen by the blood.

More crassamentum in arterial blood.

One circumstance still remains to be noticed, in which arterial has been supposed to differ from venous blood, that the former contains a larger proportion of crassamentum. Although we have perhaps no very decisive evidence of the fact, yet it is not in itself improbable; for when the arterial blood is sent into the minute arteries of the muscles, we imagine that one operation which it performs is to afford a supply of fresh fibrin, to repair the waste which is continually going on in all these organs. It may indeed be said, that the membranous parts will require the same supply of matter from the serum; but there are reasons for supposing that membrane is a substance of a more fixed nature than fibrin, and that there is a less frequent change of its constituent particles.

Recapitulation.

We have now reviewed in succession the various changes which are supposed to be produced in the blood by respiration, and it will be perceived, that notwithstanding the discovery of many important facts, the subject still remains involved in much obscurity. This depends, in a great measure, upon the difficulty of performing experiments on a substance like the blood, composed of a number of ingredients, connected together by a complicated system of affinities, which is liable to be disturbed by the operation of almost every external body. The difference between arterial and venous blood is therefore rather inferred from the comparison of a number of observations that have been made upon it in different states of the body, or from its operation on substances that are subjected to its action, than from the direct result of experiment. The present state of knowledge may, we think, be comprised in the following propositions: 1. The blood, when it leaves the right side of the heart, is of a purple colour; during its passage through the lungs it is converted to a bright scarlet, and it again acquires the purple hue when it enters the capillaries of the veins. The change from purple to scarlet would appear to be effected by the oxygenous part of the atmosphere, which is received into the vesicles of the lungs. 2. The blood, in passing through the lungs, emits a quantity of carbon, which is expired in combination with oxygen, under the form of carbonic acid gas. 3. The change of colour from purple to scarlet may be produced in the crassamentum of venous blood out of the body by exposure to atmospheric air, or still more to oxygen, while scarlet blood is rendered purple by exposure to azote, hydrogen, or carbonic acid. 4. A quantity of aqueous vapour is expired from the lungs; but there is no proof that it is formed there by the union of its component parts. On the contrary, it is more probable that it proceeds from the evaporation either of a portion of the water that is united with the blood, or with some of the mucous secretions with which the pulmonary organs are furnished. 5. There is no direct proof of the absorption of either oxygen or azote by the lungs, nor is it probable that hydrogen is discharged from them, although experiments have been adduced in favour of each of these points.

SECT. III. *The Effects of Respiration upon the Living System.*

We now proceed to the third division of the subject, the effects of respiration upon the living system. As

Physiology. the generation of animal heat has been supposed to be one of the most important of these, we shall inquire into the nature of this function.

Animal heat.

One of the most obvious circumstances in which different classes of animals differ from each other, is their temperature. All those which possess the greatest variety of organized parts, and whose functions are the most perfect, possess the power of maintaining their temperature at a uniform standard, and one considerably above that of the atmosphere. The temperature of birds is the highest, that of man and the mammalia is about 98°, and these experience little alteration, except near the surface, while fish and reptiles possess what is called cold blood, being of a variable temperature, only a degree or two above that of the media in which they are immersed. The subjects of inquiry respecting animal heat, are 1. What is the cause or source of it? 2. By what means is its uniformity preserved? To which we may add in the 3d place, How is the body cooled, when placed in a temperature higher than that which is natural to it?

General observations.

Of all the functions of the living body, none is perhaps more calculated to excite our admiration than its power of producing heat. The body is surrounded by an atmosphere generally 40 or 50 degrees colder than itself, and heat must necessarily at all times be rapidly abstracted from it; yet a supply is found sufficient to repair the loss. This appeared to the ancients so much beyond the reach of all physical action, that they attributed animal heat to the direct agency of omnipotence itself; or it was spoken of as something mysterious or inexplicable, beyond the reach of human intellect to explain or comprehend. It remained for the present age to attempt the solution of this curious problem.

Account of opinions.

With respect to the cause of animal heat, the ancients were so far from adopting any rational views respecting it, that, as we have just remarked, they seem to have regarded it as scarcely forming a legitimate subject for physiological research. Galen says that it is a primary innate quality of the body, contemporary with life, and that it has its origin in the heart; indeed, so far was he from conceiving that it originated in the lungs, that he considered the cooling of the blood to be the principal use of the function of respiration. After the revival of letters, when physiologists were divided between the chemical and the mechanical sects, the doctrine of animal heat was viewed in various lights, according to the theory of the writer. By some it was supposed to depend upon the fermentation of the blood; while others imagined that it was produced by the friction of its particles as they passed through the minute vessels; and the effect of respiration, in both cases, was not to impart heat but to remove it from the system.

Black's hypothesis.

Although particular expressions may be occasionally met with which hint at a more correct opinion, the first real information that we obtain upon this subject, is derived from the researches of Black on latent heat. After having shown that bodies indicating the same temperature to the thermometer, actually contain different quantities of caloric, he proceeded to apply this principle to explain the phenomena of combustion, and other chemical processes, in which heat is extricated. In the burning of charcoal, this substance is united to oxygen, and forms carbonic acid; while, at the same time, heat is generated. Here we conclude, that the oxygen and carbon, in their separate state, have a greater capacity for heat, than the same bodies when united in the form of carbonic acid; so that a part of their capacity is destroyed upon their union. After he

had found that the same kind of chemical change is produced by respiration as by combustion, and that heat is also generated, he concluded that it was due to the same cause, to the formation of carbonic acid; and hence, that respiration was the cause or source of animal heat, being literally a species of combustion.

Physiology.

Objections.

Black's conclusion was received as the fair deduction from the facts, and was regarded as at least a considerable approximation to the true nature of the hitherto inexplicable function; yet it was found that there were still formidable difficulties to be removed, before it could be adopted as a correct theory. It was objected, and apparently with justice, that if the union of the carbon and oxygen took place in the lungs, their temperature ought to be much greater than that of any part of the body, whereas all the internal organs were supposed to be nearly at the same temperature; and this objection appeared so forcible, as almost to induce Black himself to relinquish the theory, when the investigation was taken up by Crawford. The result was, the formation of an hypothesis, professing to be the direct result of experiment, which seemed to remove the difficulties that had occurred to Black, and afforded one of the most beautiful speculations which had hitherto been presented to the world on any subject connected with the animal economy.

Crawford's theory.

Crawford, taking Black's doctrine of latent heat as the basis of his inquiries, proceeded to examine the relative capacities for heat of all the substances concerned in the process of respiration. He found that the capacity of the air, before it had been received into the lungs, was greater than after it had been expired, in this way explaining the liberation of heat under these circumstances. In the next place, he examined the respective capacities of arterial and venous blood, and, after a long and careful investigation of this point, he announced that the specific heat of arterial was greater than that of venous blood, in the proportion of about 11 to 10. The conclusion appeared obvious and important, that when the blood is converted from the venous to the arterial state, it absorbs and renders latent a part of the heat which would otherwise have been extricated by the union of the oxygen and carbon, and these operations would appear to be so nicely adjusted to each other, that the actual temperature of the blood, as it passes through the lungs, is not elevated; a part of the heat produced by the formation of the carbonic acid being required for warming the inspired air, and for evaporating the aqueous vapour, which is mixed with the expired air, while the remainder is employed in supplying the arterial blood with a sufficient quantity of heat to compensate for its increased capacity. In conformity with that nice adjustment of the different operations to each other, which forms so remarkable a feature in the animal economy, it will follow that the more carbon is consumed, and the more heat consequently extricated, the more perfectly is the blood arterialized, the more is its capacity necessarily increased, and the greater proportion of caloric will it require to maintain its temperature. According to Crawford's hypothesis, the blood is not warmed in passing through the lungs, but during the course of the circulation, when it is converted into the venous state. In proportion as this effect is brought about, the blood loses its increased capacity; its heat, which was before latent, then becomes sensible, and is thus diffused over the body, preserving every part at its proper temperature.

Remarks upon it.

This theory has the merit of being consistent in all its

parts, and of easily explaining the phenomena; and it was announced as being supported in every part by direct experiments. It rests principally upon the three following data: that the temperature of the blood is nearly uniform in all parts of the body; that the capacity for heat is greater in the arterial than in venous blood; and that the capacity of oxygen is greater than carbonic acid. Every one of these points has, however, been called in question; and some of them are contradicted by experiments, the results of which are precisely the reverse of Crawford's. Thus we are informed by writers of respectability, that the arterial blood is always about one or two degrees warmer than the venous blood. With respect to their relative capacities, the experiments of Dr. John Davy do not indicate that difference which was announced by Crawford; while, in the third place, we learn from M. M. De la Roche and Berard, that the capacities of oxygen and carbonic acid are at least much less different than they had been previously supposed to be. It is not easy to decide upon points where opposite facts are brought forward by individuals, whose authority is so respectable as that of Crawford and his opponents. In the present state of the question, we conceive it the most prudent plan to suspend our judgment until the experiments have been repeated, or some new ones adduced which may be more unexceptionable.

Brodie's experiments. We must not, however, pass by without noticing a train of experiments which have been performed by Mr. Brodie; the results of which have been supposed to be directly opposed to the chemical doctrine of animal heat in all its parts. He opened the chest of an animal soon after death, and kept the lungs inflated with atmospheric air, when he observed that the blood underwent the usual change from purple to scarlet, and that carbonic acid was produced in the same manner as during life; yet, notwithstanding these changes, the heat of the body diminished as rapidly as if it had been left at rest. The experiments appear to have been performed with considerable address, and are certainly entitled to much attention; but there is one important circumstance which seems to have been overlooked, that no more air should be admitted into the lungs than they have the power of acting upon, otherwise the directly cooling effect of the air will more than counteract the operation of any chemical change which it may experience. Dr. Philip accordingly found, that, Philip's experiments. when the air was admitted into the lungs, in very small quantities only, the cooling of the body after death was sensibly retarded. And although, in Mr. Brodie's experiments, the blood experienced the same change of colour as in the act of respiration, and carbonic acid was produced, still many circumstances were wanting to render the state of the animal exactly similar to what it is during life, particularly with respect to the manner in which the blood is afterwards disposed of through the body, and the re-conversion of it from the arterial to the venous state.

General observations. Independent of direct experiment, there are many circumstances connected with animal temperature which would lead us to conclude, that it is intimately connected with the function of respiration. In the first place, all animals that have a temperature much superior to that in which they are immersed have their lungs constructed in the most perfect manner, and possessing the most elaborate organization; while there is an obvious relation between the quantity of oxygen which they consume and the heat which they evolve. Thus, what are styled the warm-blooded animals, have lungs of a large size, and so formed as to permit the blood and the air to exercise the most extensive influence over each other. In amphibia, the pulmonary vessels of the lungs are much more scanty; while the circulation is so arranged, that only a part of the blood passes through them during each circulation. The temperature of these animals is proportionally low; and in fish, where there is only a small quantity of blood to receive the action of the air, and that in a less direct manner, the temperature is only a degree or two above that of the medium in which they live. In the second place, it is observed, that, in the same species of animals, or even in the same individual under different circumstances, whatever quickens the circulation raises the temperature; and that, when the respiration is impeded, either from disease or from an original mal-conformation of the organs, the temperature is proportionally lowered. Lastly, it may be urged in favour of the chemical theory of animal heat, that oxygen is actually united to carbon; and that, according to the ordinary effect of this union, caloric must be liberated, so that it would be difficult to explain how it is disposed of, if it be not employed in raising the temperature of the body. There is also a farther circumstance to be held in view, that, if we reject the hypothesis of the lungs being the source of animal heat, we have no other adequate cause for its production; for, although some writers have supposed that the stomach, and others that the nervous system is concerned in this function, yet these have been thrown out as mere conjectures, without being digested into any regular system, so as to point out, in either case, in what manner the effect follows the supposed cause. Upon the whole, therefore, we think ourselves warranted in concluding, in the present state of our knowledge upon the subject, that animal heat is derived, in the first instance, from the union of oxygen and carbon, which takes place in the lungs during the process of respiration.

Uniformity of the animal temperature. If we have found it difficult to arrive at any certain conclusion on the first point that we proposed to discuss, we shall probably find it still more so with respect to the second—By what means is the uniformity of the animal temperature preserved? because any speculation which we may form upon this subject must, in a great measure, depend upon our ideas of the means by which animal heat is produced. With the general fact we are well acquainted, that, in warm-blooded animals, each species has a temperature that is natural to itself, from which it deviates very little while in its healthy state. The temperature of the internal parts of the human body is between 98° and 99°; and this temperature is preserved with as much regularity by the Greenlander as by the African. There are, no doubt, many circumstances in their modes of life by which the inhabitants of these different regions endeavour to counteract the extremes of heat and cold to which they are exposed; but after making allowance for all these circumstances, some system of adjustment of the functions will be necessary in order to preserve that uniformity of temperature which is so essential to life.

Different quantities of oxygen consumed We have already referred to the experiments of Priestley and Crawford, which first threw some light upon this intricate subject, and which were repeated and considerably extended by Lavoisier. They led to the same conclusion, that the union of oxygen and carbon in the lungs is influenced by the temperature of the inspired air; the lower the temperature the more tendency there is to their union, there is a greater consumption of oxygen, and a more rapid generation of carbonic acid. Hence, according to our usual notions upon this subject, there must be a greater evolution of animal heat; and this will naturally have the effect of counteracting the lower temperature in which the body, in this case, is conceived to be immersed. According to Crawford's theory, the greater quantity of carbon is removed from the blood, the more perfectly is it converted from the venous to the arterial state, the more is its capacity for heat increased, and the more will it require to supply this increased capacity, which will be afterwards liberated during the course of the circulation to maintain the due temperature of the body. Although this explanation proceeds in part upon the principles of Crawford's theory, and may be so far considered as of doubtful authority, it depends, to a certain extent, upon the direct results of experiments that were performed without any view to this hypothesis, and which appear to be entitled to our confidence; while, it must be admitted, that the admirable manner in which they explain the phenomena, affords at least some presumption of their truth. But although the experiments that have been performed are favourable to the hypothesis—that the formation of carbonic acid in the lungs is so regulated by the temperature of the air as to produce heat according to the demand for it in the system—still they are not sufficiently numerous or decisive to amount to a demonstration of its truth. Should it be confirmed by subsequent facts and experiments, it must be admitted to be one of the most beautiful examples of the adaptation of means to ends that is to be met with in any part of the animal economy.

Effect of
high tem-
peratures. It was an opinion generally received among the older writers, and it was maintained even by Boerhaave, that life cannot exist in a temperature higher than that which is natural to the body: but many facts have been lately brought to light which completely disprove this position. The first of them, which rested upon good authority, was communicated by Tillet and Duhamel. They gave an account of some young women, in the service of a baker, in one of the provincial towns in France, who were accustomed to enter the hot ovens for the purpose of turning the loaves; and this, it was said, was done without any apparent inconvenience, provided they were careful not to touch the heated surface. The narrative was scarcely credited at the time, but subsequent facts have fully established its credibility. A set of experiments were performed in London, by Blagden and Fordyce, in which a chamber was heated to a temperature higher than that of boiling water, and these gentlemen found that they could easily remain in it for an indefinite length of time. It is, however, to be regretted, that they almost exclusively directed their attention to the effects of the heated air upon the various substances in the room, and unfortunately neglected to observe its action upon the living body itself. We are, indeed, informed that they perspired very copiously, but we have no information respecting the most important point, whether their temperature was actually raised; or, at least, what we are told on this subject is too vague to allow us to place much confidence in the statement. Some experiments have been lately performed by M. De la Roche which give us some insight into this intricate subject. He found that the body was capable of remaining in a temperature considerably higher than that which is natural to it, as long as there was a free access to the surrounding air; but that, when the animal was con-

fined in a small space, an uneasy sensation was produc- Physiology. ed, and the temperature was elevated. Hence it may be conjectured, that the evaporation of aqueous vapour from the lungs, and perhaps also from the surface of the body, is the means by which the superabundant heat is carried off in these cases, so as to form a kind of balance to that operation, whatever it be, by which heat is generated under ordinary circumstances.

There is, however, much left for us to inquire into Remarks. in this process. In the first place, we have to ascertain, to what degree a mass of matter, of the same capacity with the body, and of equal bulk, would have been heated at the same temperature with that to which the individuals were exposed in the above experiments. We know, that when air is much heated, it is proportionably rarefied; fewer particles of it, therefore, come into contact with the cold body, and hence the communication of heat will be much slower. Then, with respect to the animal functions taken in connexion with each other, we should examine what effect the respiration has, in these cases, upon the air taken into the lungs; is there any carbonic acid formed? and, if there be, what quantity is generated? We should be led by analogy to suppose, that the amount of oxygen consumed must be very small, so that the usual supply of heat would be cut off. Our next object should be, to discover whether the quantity of aqueous vapour discharged from the lungs would be sufficient to counteract the operation of all the sources, either internal or external, by which the body acquires heat, and we should then be able to decide upon a point which has been much agitated, whether there be any specific function for the purpose of cooling the body, or rather, whether the evaporation of the cutaneous and pulmonary vapour be alone sufficient for that purpose. There has been much vague speculation employed by physiologists, on the power of the body in generating cold. No part of the animal economy has been treated of in a more mysterious manner, and different metaphysical notions have been formed to account for an operation, the existence of which has not yet been satisfactorily proved. What, however, we do know upon the subject, seems to warrant us in pointing out this part of the animal system, as an additional example of that beautiful adjustment of the functions to each other upon which we have already taken occasion to remark; for it appears, that not only have the lungs the power of evolving heat in greater or less quantity, in proportion to the demands of the system, but that the same organ, when necessary, can even produce the contrary effect, and generate cold.

It will be evident, that this account of animal tem- Animal
heat an ef-
fect of re-
spiration. perature is a necessary step in our examination of the effects of respiration upon the living system; for, if it should appear that the modern doctrines on this subject are in any degree well-founded, we must conclude that the evolution of heat is one of the most important of the indirect effects which are brought about by the action of the lungs. The direct effects, as we have already seen, are the discharge of carbon and water, and these are the only changes of which we can be said to have any immediate evidence, either from experiment or observation; and it will now appear, that, among the secondary, or indirect effects, are the evolution of heat, by means of the discharge of carbon, and the regulation of the heat thus generated by the evaporation of water. But it is impossible to observe these operations without contemplating the farther effects which they may produce on the living system, more especi-

ally as, in the case of the discharge of carbon, it does not appear very obvious why it is so essential to life, or why so extensive and complicated an apparatus should be provided, for what we might be tempted to regard as a comparatively unimportant object. That there is some farther purpose to be served than the mere discharge of carbon, for the purpose of producing animal heat, is evident from the consideration, that if an animal be plunged in warm water, so as to have its temperature kept at the natural standard, there is the same necessity for the regular supply of oxygen to carry off the carbon, as under ordinary circumstances. The sense of suffocation which takes place, when the supply of fresh air is not regularly preserved, seems to depend upon the stagnation of the blood in the ventricles of the heart, and this stagnation is owing to the muscles of the heart having lost their power of contraction, in consequence of their not receiving the due supply of arterial blood. The same loss of contractility occurs in other parts of the body under the same circumstances; and hence we draw the inference, that one important indirect effect is to support the contractility of the muscles.

Respiration prevents the body from decomposition.

Having now proceeded so far as to conclude, that one indirect use of respiration is to produce that change in the blood which enables it to preserve the muscles in a contractile state, and that this object is attained by transmitting to them a quantity of arterial blood, which is returned from them in the venous state, we are led to inquire what is the nature of the operation that is here carried on, or in what way are the muscles rendered contractile by the abstraction of a portion of their carbon? On this subject we can be guided only by analogy, and that of a vague and uncertain nature; but, proceeding upon such grounds as we possess, there would appear to be some connexion between the effects of respiration, and those changes by which animal matter is preserved from spontaneous decomposition. Now, the first step in the process of decomposition would appear to be, the discharge of a portion of carbon, which combines with the oxygen of the atmosphere, and forms carbonic acid; and it may be inferred, that if the superabundant portion of carbon be continually removed from a body which has a tendency to putrefaction, its decomposition may be obviated. We have already had occasion to make the remark, and farther proofs of it will occur in the course of our investigations, that all the matter of which the body is composed, after it has performed its appropriate functions, seems to experience some change, which renders it no longer suitable for the purpose; that it is carried off, and its place supplied by fresh matter. It is this interchange of particles which preserves the living body in its healthy state; and when it is suspended by death, so that the effete matter is no longer duly removed, complete decomposition ensues. The blood appears to be the medium by which this change is immediately effected, the veins are the channels by which the matter is carried from the mass of fluids, and the lungs the outlet by which it is finally discharged. The chemical effect of respiration is therefore similar to the first step in the process of the putrefactive decomposition; hence it appears that an important indirect effect of respiration is to carry off from the body the particles of matter which would produce a putrescent tendency in the blood, were they not removed from it as rapidly as they are deposited.

Comparison of ancient and modern opinions.

From what has been said above respecting the history of opinions on the subject of respiration, it will appear that this doctrine amounts very nearly to the hypothesis of Priestley, that the use of respiration is to carry off phlogiston from the blood. To the same principle, although still more indefinitely expressed, we might refer the *recrementitious steams* of Boyle, and even the *fuliginous excrement* of Galen, and indeed he goes so far as to speak of respiration as a species of combustion, and describes the lungs as a kind of vent or chimney for the emission of vapour. He farther attributes the dark colour of venous blood to the mixture of a black or sooty matter with it, and the change to scarlet to the discharge of this matter, so that certain individuals who have been disposed to exalt the knowledge of the ancients, have not hesitated to ascribe to Galen a very correct acquaintance with the modern doctrines of respiration. But, unfortunately for the argument, Galen supposed this combustion to occur, not in the lungs, but in the heart, and conceived that a main object of respiration was to cool the blood, or, as he expresses it, to quench the fire of the heart.

Conversion of chyle into fibrin.

There is still another indirect effect of respiration to be mentioned, the conversion of chyle into fibrin. It may be presumed that as this change consists in taking from the blood a substance which has an undue proportion of carbon, a superabundance of this element will be left in the blood from which the fibrin has been secreted, and this blood will be carried to the lungs, where it will part with its excess of carbon. And here we are presented with another instance of the reciprocal action of the different functions upon each other. Arterial blood contains the elements of the muscular fibre; when the blood has parted with its fibrin, it becomes venalized, and now contains the matter which, by uniting with oxygen in the lungs, evolves caloric; this gives energy to the muscles and nerves, and imparts to the whole machine its capability for action.

Mechanical effects of respiration.

We have hitherto said little respecting the mechanical effects of respiration, although, until lately, these were what entirely engrossed the attention of physiologists. Boyle dwelt much upon the power of the lungs in destroying the spring of the air, and the same effect was insisted upon by Mayow and his contemporaries. But since we are become better acquainted with the nature of the atmosphere, we know that a great part of what was formerly attributed to mechanical, really depends upon chemical causes, and that, when they supposed that the air lost its spring, and was, in this manner, rendered unfit for respiration and combustion, it was owing to the conversion of part of its oxygen into carbonic acid, and frequently to the absorption of the acid thus formed. As they were ignorant of the chemical properties of the air, and of the changes which it experiences in passing through the lungs, they imputed all the effects of respiration to the changes of bulk in the thorax; and from observing that, when respiration ceased, the motion of the heart was also suspended, they concluded that one principal object of respiration was to expand the lungs, so as to permit the blood to arrive at the left side of the heart. Numerous experiments were instituted to establish this position, and so little were physiologists in the habit of making experiments, or of drawing correct deductions from them, that this opinion was adopted even by Hales and Haller. It had indeed been observed by Boyle, a century before, that the expansion of the lungs was of no avail unless the air was perpetually changed; but ingenious conjectures were always at hand to disguise the truth, and for a long time these prevailed over what we should now consider the obvious inference from the facts

CHAPTER IX.

OF SECRETION.

Definition.

THE literal meaning of the word secretion, is separation; and it was used nearly in this sense by the older physiologists, who considered this function to consist merely in the separation from the blood of certain substances that were previously contained in it. By the moderns the term is employed in a more technical manner, to designate the faculty by which certain organs produce from the blood substances different from the blood itself, or from any of its constituents. In the following chapter we shall first give an account of the organs of secretion; in the second place, we shall describe some of the more important of the secreted substances; and, lastly, we shall offer some remarks upon the hypotheses that have been proposed to explain the nature of the operation.

Description of the organs of secretion.

The organs of secretion are so infinitely varied in their form and structure, that it is impossible to give any description of them which shall not be subject to numerous exceptions; but, taking them in their most perfect, and, at the same time, in their most general form, they consist of a rounded body, which, from its shape, has obtained the name of gland. A gland may be said to consist essentially of a number of arteries, which ramify in various directions through a mass of cellular texture; from these proceeds another set of vessels, which contain the secreted substance; and these vessels commonly unite in one or more trunks, which are named excretory ducts. The gland usually consists of distinct masses or lobes, which may be successively divided into smaller and smaller lobes, until we arrive at what have been termed the acini, the smallest portions into which a gland can be mechanically separated. The glands, in common with other parts of the body, have veins, nerves, and absorbents, but these do not appear to be immediately concerned in their appropriate functions.

Intimate structure of glands.

There is still much obscurity concerning the intimate structure of glands, especially respecting the question, whether there be any intermediate part between the secreting artery and the excretory duct. Malpighi supposed that the secreting artery terminated in a small cavity or follicle, which was the immediate organ of secretion. Ruysch, in prosecuting his delicate injections, supposed that he had disproved the doctrine of Malpighi, and that he had established the point, that there is no intervening follicle between the artery and the duct; and as he professed to derive his opinion from the simple exposition of facts, without any view to theory, his account has been in general preferred to that of Malpighi. Upon the whole, however, it may be questioned, whether in this, as in so many other controverted questions, either party be absolutely correct.

The structure which we have now been describing, belongs to the more perfect of the glands; but the complete apparatus is comparatively seldom met with, even in those instances where what appears the most elaborate operations are performed. In some cases we can detect nothing more than a vessel leading to a pouch, in which the secretion is lodged, and which is sometimes provided with an excretory duct, and is sometimes without one. Many secretions are poured out on the surface of membranes, where no specific structure can be detected, except a small vessel which

terminates externally; and there are a number of cases, in which a substance is produced and separated from the blood, where we are not able to discover any appropriate apparatus for the purpose. We may observe that the nature of the substance produced, so far as respects its resemblance to any of the constituents of the blood, bears no relation to the simplicity of the apparatus by which it is formed. The saliva, for example, is secreted by a large gland, while no organ has been detected for the secretion of the adipose matter, yet the latter is much more unlike any part of the blood than the former.

Classification of the glands.

Glands have been arranged by anatomists in different ways, sometimes according to their structure, and at other times according to the nature of the substance which they produce; but no arrangement has yet been formed to which there are not many objections. The older writers divided them into conglobate and conglomerate; the first consisting, as they supposed, of one lobe only, the others of a number of lobes connected by cellular texture. It is not, however, always easy to draw the line of distinction between the two kinds; and it is obvious that many of the most important secretions are produced by organs to which neither of these terms will apply. But we shall be better able to understand the structure of the glands when we have reviewed the various substances that are secreted by them, which was the second point that we proposed to consider.

Account of the secretions. Arrangement.

Before we attempt to give an account of so numerous a class of bodies as the secretions, it will be necessary to adopt some kind of classification of them. The earlier anatomists divided them into recrementitious and excrementitious; the first comprehending those substances, which, after they are formed, serve some useful purpose in the system; the second, such bodies as are secreted for the purpose of being rejected, as either useless or noxious. There is a foundation for this division, but it is neither sufficiently comprehensive nor minute to be of much advantage in our investigations respecting the nature of the substances. As the knowledge of physiology advanced, more scientific arrangements were constructed, founded upon the chemical or physical properties of the substances, but still they were all incorrect or defective. Haller classed the secretions under four heads; the aqueous, the mucous, the gelatinous, and the oily. Fourcroy, in conformity with the improved state of chemistry when he wrote, formed them into eight divisions, the hydrogenated, the oxygenated, the carbonated, the azotated, the acid, the saline, the phosphated, and the mixed. This arrangement, although it may be considered as more scientific than any which had preceded it, and in some measure corresponds with the improvements of modern chemistry, is yet, upon the whole, rather founded upon theory, than upon the actual nature of the substances concerned.

Of Haller.

Substances separated from the blood.

There is one question, which it will be necessary to inquire into in this place, whether there may be not certain bodies to which the term of secretions literally applies, according to its original acceptation, viz. substances which exist ready formed in the blood, and which are merely separated from it, without undergoing any change in their chemical composition. This we may conceive to be the case with the muscular fibre, for it would appear that it resembles the fibrin of the blood in every respect, except its mechanical structure, the muscle having its particles regularly arranged and organized, whereas the fibrin is dissolved or suspended in the blood, without any regular organization, a circumstance which necessarily results from the latter being in a fluid state. The same remark applies to the earthy salts which compose the bones, for it may be conceived to be more probable that these are merely separated from the blood, than that they undergo any chemical change through the action of the vessels by which they are deposited.

Transudations.

There are likewise a number of fluids, respecting which it may be doubted, whether they are properly entitled to be considered as secretions, or whether they are only separated from the blood by a kind of transudation. Of this kind is the fluid in the pericardium, and the different species of dropsical effusions, which would appear to contain the same ingredients with the serum of the blood, except that they are diluted with a greater quantity of water.

Preliminary remarks.

Had we a perfect knowledge of the nature and composition of all the secretions, the most correct method of arranging them would be, according to their chemical composition or their chemical relation to the blood; and although at present any attempt of this kind must be necessarily imperfect, yet, as this is the case with every other arrangement that has been proposed, we think it proper to employ it as the least exceptionable. On the subject of arrangement there are a few preliminary remarks which we must attend to. We may observe that most of the secretions consist of more than one ingredient, and that the properties of the compound occasionally depend so much upon both the substances that enter into their composition, that it is difficult to determine which is to have the preference. We may remark, in the second place, that the same gland often furnishes a substance of very different properties in different states in the system, and this without the occurrence of what can be strictly termed disease. Then it is obvious that the nature of the secretion is materially affected by disease, and from this cause new substances are occasionally formed that did not previously exist. In order to take a perfect view of the subject, we should mark the gradations from the healthy to the morbid condition, and observe all the intermediate states which the secretions assume; this, however, would require a more advanced state of the science than we at present possess.

Arrangement.

Making a due allowance for all these circumstances, and excluding those substances which appear to be merely separated from the blood, without undergoing any change, we may arrange the secretions into seven classes; the aqueous, the albuminous, the mucous, the gelatinous, the oleaginous, the resinous, and the saline.

Aqueous secretions.

The aqueous secretions are those that consist almost entirely of water, or of which the water composes so large a proportion as to give them their specific characters. The most important of these is the matter of perspiration which is thrown off from the surface of the body. Attempts have been made to collect the cutaneous perspiration, in order to examine its properties; and from these it would appear to consist of water, containing animal and saline matter, the quantity of which is so small as to render it very difficult to ascertain their nature. Probably no other substance strictly belongs to the class of the aqueous secretions; for the exhalation from the lungs is to be regarded as nothing more than water evaporated from the mucus which lines the pulmonary vesicles. We are entirely ignorant of the nature of the apparatus by which the cutaneous perspiration is produced; and indeed there is some reason to doubt whether it is not to be regarded rather as the effect of transudation than of secretion.

Physiology.

Albuminous secretions.

The second class of secretions, the albuminous, are more numerous and better defined than the aqueous. All the cavities of the body, which have no natural communication with the atmosphere, as those of the thorax and abdomen, the ventricles of the brain, the pericardium, and all the parts of the cellular texture, are lined with what is denominated a serous membrane, which secretes a fluid that, except in the proportion of its ingredients, seems to be exactly similar to the serum of the blood. These constitute the albuminous secretions, and, like serum, possess the characteristic property of being coagulated by heat and various chemical re-agents. In diseased states of the serous membranes, these fluids are often disposed to accumulate in their respective cavities, and sometimes their quality as well as their quantity is changed. In some of these secretions, as in that which is found in the cavities of the brain, the quantity of albumen is so small, that we are scarcely able to detect it; the liquor pericardii contains more animal matter, while the dropsical effusions that are poured into the cavity of the abdomen, differ but little from the serum of the blood. The most minute anatomical investigation has not been able to detect any appropriate organ for the production of this class of fluids; and, in consideration of their nature, it may be doubted whether these, as well as the aqueous secretions, are not more properly to be regarded as transudations.

Mucous secretions.

The third class of substances, the mucous, are more strictly entitled to the appellation of secretions, than either the aqueous or the albuminous, as they derive their most characteristic physical and chemical properties from an ingredient which does exist in the blood. They are distinguished by their viscidity, or the capability of being drawn out into threads, and by being with difficulty dissolved in water, although they are always combined with a large quantity of it. In some respects they are decidedly different from the serum of the blood, and the immediate cause of this difference would appear to be, that they contain a substance which resembles albumen in the coagulated state. The mucous secretions differ from the albuminous in their seat, as well as in their properties; for while the latter are found on the surface of the membranes which line the close cavities of the body, the mucous are poured out over the surfaces which communicate with the atmosphere, as those of the mouth, the nose, the œsophagus, the stomach, and the whole course of the alimentary canal, the trachea, and its ramifications through the interior of the lungs. A glandular apparatus may be generally detected in these parts, although we know little of its minute structure. In some cases, as in that of the saliva, the gland that secretes the mucus is unusually large, and possessed of all the parts which enter into the composition of the most perfect glands. The bladder and the urinary passages are lined with membranes which secrete a mucous fluid; and it is probable that the tears and the synovia also belong to this class of substances.

Gelatinous secretions.

The fourth class of secretions which we enumerated are the gelatinous. We have had occasion to give an account of the properties of jelly, the most characteristic of which is its solution by heat, and concretion by cold, producing the phenomena to which the term gelatinization has been appropriated. Jelly was formerly supposed to be one of the ingredients in the blood;

but this we now know is not the case. There are some circumstances which would lead us to suspect that albumen is converted into jelly by the addition of oxygen; and we may conceive that some interchange of the elements of the blood may take place, so as to produce this conversion. No apparatus has been detected by which jelly is produced; and it may, upon the whole, appear more probable, that it is actually formed in the parts where it is deposited, than that it is separated by the medium of a gland. On this point, however, we have scarcely any thing to guide our opinion, either of fact or of analogy. Jelly does not appear to form a component part of any of the animal fluids, but it enters largely into the composition of many of the solids, especially of the parts of young animals.

Oily secretions. The fifth class of secreted substances, the oleaginous, are removed still farther from the natural state of any of the constituents of the blood. All animals that possess a temperature much superior to that of the atmosphere are furnished with a quantity of oily matter, which varies in its consistence from the fluid state, as it exists in the whale, to that of a soft solid, as in suet and tallow, while it agrees in its other chemical and physical characters. Oil differs from blood in containing no azote, and a larger proportion of hydrogen; so that the secretion of oil must consist in separating from the mass a substance which has a basis of carbon, with an excess of hydrogen, and a small quantity of oxygen. We are entirely ignorant of the apparatus by which these secretions are produced, but they appear to be formed with great facility, because there is no animal substance which is so rapidly generated as fat; and we not only find that fat is very readily deposited, but that it is more quickly removed than any other of the components of the body. Whenever the absorbents act more powerfully than natural, or rather, where their action is not counterbalanced by that of the nutritive arteries, the fat first disappears, and this is equally the case whether it be the effect of disease or of old age.

Use of the fat. There is considerable obscurity respecting the use of the adipose matter. Probably, in the first instance, the secretion of fat is an operation of that kind which has been denominated excrementitious, where a substance is separated from the blood because it is superfluous, or useless; for it would appear that this fluid contains a less proportion of carbon and hydrogen than chyle. But, although the primary object of this secretion may be to separate from the blood its excess of carbon and hydrogen, it is analogous to the other operations of the animal economy to suppose that fat, when once formed, may perform some important secondary purpose. Now it has been stated above, that the inflammable matter which is consumed in the process of respiration is derived from the chyle, and it may be presumed, that, in ordinary cases, the demand and the supply are in due proportion to each other. If, from any cause, the supply be too considerable, we may conjecture that it contributes to the formation of the adipose matter, which then accumulates in the system; but if, on the contrary, the demand is increased, and the stomach does not furnish it in adequate quantity, by the usual process of digestion, the fat which had been deposited in its appropriate cells is then taken up by the absorbents, is returned into the blood, and being carried to the lungs, is there employed in the evolution of animal heat.

Milk. Besides the oil or fat, in its more simple form, there are some other secretions of a more compound nature, but which may be referred to this class, as they derive

their most characteristic properties from their oily part. Physiology. Among these we may place milk, a fluid which is secreted by the female after parturition, and which is destined for the first nourishment of the offspring. Although the milk differs considerably in the different classes of animals, yet its principal constituents are always the same, and it is found to consist essentially of albumen, oil, and a peculiar saccharine matter, the albumen and the oil being united in the form of an emulsion, and the whole dissolved in water. We may suppose that the albumen is immediately derived from the serum of the blood; but neither the oil nor the sugar previously existed there. The glandular apparatus by which it is produced is large and well-defined in all its parts, but we are ignorant of the nature of the minute operations which are carried on in it, or what relation its different parts bear to the different constituents of the fluid.

Another substance, still more important to animal Brain. existence than milk, which may be classed among the oleaginous secretions, is the matter which composes the brain and nerves. It appears to be formed of a combination of albumen and oil, the albumen being in a state of imperfect coagulation, and the oil approaching to the nature of adipocire. Except in the absence of saccharine matter, brain may therefore be regarded as bearing a near resemblance to milk; yet there appears to be no glandular structure appropriated for its formation, nor can we form any conception of the mode in which it is produced.

As we proceed with our examination of the secretions, Resinous we come to those which are more remote from any of secretions. the constituents of the blood, and which, while they are the most complicated in their nature, derive their characteristic properties from the greatest number of ingredients. This remark applies to the sixth class, the resinous substances, of which the principal is the bile. Bile is the product of the liver, a very large gland, and Bile. one possessing the most elaborate structure of any of the organs destined for secretion. This fluid has been very frequently made the subject of chemical analysis, and is found to be composed of a great number of substances; but it would appear that its specific properties depend upon a peculiar resin which it contains. To this resin the colour, taste, and odour of bile are probably owing, as well as its action upon the stomach and bowels. There are certain facts, and some analogies, which would lead us to conjecture that the resin of the bile is immediately derived from the red particles of the blood; and we are farther led to conceive that this conversion is effected by the addition of oxygen to these particles.

Much has been written upon the use of the bile, or Use of rather upon the relative action which the liver possesses the liver. in the system at large. Many of the speculations that have been formed on this subject have been obviously derived from incorrect principles, and we are still unable to advance any thing that may not be liable to objections; but there are many facts in medicine and pathology which lead to the following conclusion. When venous blood becomes loaded with inflammable matter, which the lungs cannot discharge, and when circumstances are not favourable to the deposition of fat, the liver is the organ by which this matter, after it has undergone certain changes, is removed from the system. Hence we are to regard bile, like fat, as, in the first instance, an excrementitious substance, although, in conformity with the usual arrangements of the animal economy, the different organs and functions

Physiology. are so admirably adapted to each other, that a variety of important objects are accomplished by the same operation. Although, therefore, the primary purpose of the liver be to remove the excess of hydrogen and carbon from the blood, yet the bile appears to exercise a salutary action upon the digestive organs, and perhaps also upon some other parts of the system. Hence we may explain the frequency of bilious disorders in warm climates, where the body, being continually immersed in a high temperature, a sufficient quantity of carbon cannot be discharged from the lungs, and where, from certain causes, there is no tendency to the formation of adipose matter.

Saline se- The seventh and last class of secretions are the sacretions. line. The most important of these is phosphoric acid, which, when united with lime, forms the earth of bones; the same acid also forms a considerable proportion of the salts of the urine. A curious question, and one that is of difficult solution, here presents itself; whether the saline substances that exist in different parts of the body are formed there, or whether they are not received into the stomach, and carried by the absorbents into the blood. This investigation is intimately connected with many important points in the physiology of some of the inferior animals. A large part of the whole substance of several of the mollusca and the crustacea consists of calcareous matter; and it appears that many of the large masses of limestone which occur in different parts of the world, have originated from the decomposition of immense numbers of these animals. What is the origin of this lime? Did it exist previous to the formation of these animals, and did they receive it into their system, and organize its particles, so as to form their shells and crusts, and afterwards, by their destruction, compose the masses in which it is now found? or have their digestive and secreting organs the power of actually generating lime? Each of these opinions has had its advocates, and experiments have been advanced on both sides; but we conceive they have not been of that unequivocal nature as to warrant our drawing any decisive conclusion from them. Upon the whole, however, the result of the experiments that would seem the least exceptionable are in favour of the generation of lime by the powers of the living body; but it must be acknowledged that this is a conclusion which would involve many suppositions that are at variance with our ordinary ideas respecting the economy of nature.

Theory of After this attempt to form a classification of the sesecretion. cretions, we must proceed to consider the nature of the operation by which they are produced. The opinions that have been entertained on this subject are very numerous; but they may be reduced to five distinct hypotheses; that of the older chemists, who ascribed secretion to fermentation; that of the mechanicians, according to whom the substances are separated from the blood by filtration; the doctrine of the Animists, who conceive it to be a sufficient explanation to ascribe it to the immediate operation of the vital principle; that of the modern chemists, who suppose that the elements of the secretions exist in the blood, and that, in the passage of this fluid, or some of its component parts, through the glands, new affinities are called into action, which produce new combinations; and lastly, the hypothesis which attributes secretion to the influence of the nerves.

Hypothesis The doctrine of ferments, as the cause of secretion, of fermen- was advanced by Van Helmont; it was farther matured tation; by Sylvius, and received various modifications from

Willis, and other eminent physiologists of that period. Physiology. Each gland was supposed to possess a peculiar species of fermentation, which assimilated to its own nature the blood that passed through it, as is the case in the formation of vinegar. Respecting this hypothesis it will be sufficient to remark, that the resemblance between secretion and fermentation is rather apparent than real; and that, since we are become better acquainted with the circumstances that are necessary for the production of this latter process, and with the substances that are generated by it, we find the phenomena of the two operations to be very different from each other.

When the chemical physiology began to be exploded, of filtra-and mechanical doctrines were had recourse to, the tion; hypothesis of filtration was adopted. It was supposed that the secretions were all ready formed in the blood, and that, when portions of this fluid were carried to the different glands, the respective secretions were separated from it as through sieves or filtres. In order to explain how so many different substances could be separated from the same fluid merely by filtration, two conjectures were formed by the earlier physiologists. The first to which we refer is that of Descartes, who supposed that the particles of the secreted fluid were of a particular shape, for example, circular, triangular, four-sided, &c. and that the gland which separated them had pores of a similar form. Every one in the present day must regard this opinion as completely whimsical, and as altogether without any support of facts; it is obviously less philosophical than the hypothesis which was opposed to it, and which appears to have originated with Leibnitz. He compared the action of the gland to that of a filtre which had its pores saturated with a particular fluid, so as not to permit any other to pass through them, in the same manner as paper moistened with water will not permit oil to pass, and vice versa. But this explanation, although ingenious, appears to be purely hypothetical; and it proceeds upon the supposition that the secretions exist ready formed in the blood, of which we have no evidence, or rather a strong presumption that it is not the case.

The doctrine of Haller on the subject of secretion is Haller's fundamentally that of filtration, although much modi- hypothesis. fied, and considerably more consonant to our modern notions than that either of Descartes or Leibnitz. As it is merely mechanical, it cannot be admitted; but, we must acknowledge, that it displays his usual caution in drawing conclusions where the premises are of doubtful authority. He proceeds upon the supposition that the secretions are all ready formed in the blood, and he then inquires what are the circumstances that are likely to effect their separation from it? He points out seven. 1. A difference in the nature of the blood itself; 2. Its velocity as affected by the size of the vessel; 3. The transmission of the fluid from one vessel to another of a different size; 4. The angle at which the secreting vessel passes off from the artery; 5. The winding course of the vessel; 6. Its density; and, lastly, the structure of the excretory duct. Haller himself principally insists upon the different sizes of the vessels, and the different velocities of the fluids; and conceives that, in proportion to the existence of these causes, the four classes of secretions which he points out will be produced; and we may go so far as to allow, that these, as well as the other mechanical causes enumerated above, may considerably influence the action of the glands, but we are of opinion that they are alone quite inadequate to their production.

The hypothesis of the Animists, of which Stahl was the great defender in the seventeenth century, and which has been received, with some modifications, by Hunter, Blumenbach, Darwin, and others in our own times, will not require any long discussion, because the remarks that have been offered on the other parts of this doctrine will equally apply to the subject of secretion. Even supposing the existence of the intelligent or vital principle, as assumed by these physiologists, we have no account given us of the mode of its operation, nor are we informed whether it acts upon chemical or mechanical principles.

The fourth hypothesis, that of chemical affinity, seems to have been suggested by Keill, but it has received its principal support from the numerous discoveries that have been made of late years in the science of chemistry, and especially from our knowledge of the great variety of changes which a compound body may undergo, by having its components combined in different proportions, or exposed to the action of various external agents. Thus oxygen and azote, when united in one proportion, form atmospheric air, in other proportions, nitrous and nitric oxide, and in others, nitrous and nitric acid, substances which differ from each other most materially in both their physical and chemical properties. Now the blood is composed of several ingredients, which are held together by a weak affinity, and are very liable to be disunited by slight causes. There is reason to suppose that its constitution varies in the course of the circulation, partly from the action of its components upon each other, and partly from the addition and subtraction of various substances. If, to these circumstances, we add the mechanical actions indicated by Haller, and, perhaps, some additional ones of a similar kind, which may affect the passage of the fluids through the vessels, and the degree of their action upon them, we may conceive of as great a variety of products as there are secretions, and differing as much from each other. How far any considerations of this kind may be thought capable of affording a satisfactory solution of the difficulty that attends this question, we are not disposed to decide; but, upon the whole, we consider this hypothesis as more tenable than the mechanical doctrine, and we conceive that the objections which have been raised against it arise rather from our ignorance than from its own insufficiency.

The last hypothesis of secretion, is that which attempts to account for it by the action of the nerves. It may be regarded in two points of view: 1st, As professing to explain the nature of the function generally; and, 2dly, As showing how particular glands prepare their specific fluids from the blood. There are many facts which show that there is an intimate connexion between the influence of the nerves and the action of the glands. Certain secretions are increased in quantity, and have their quality affected by the various agents, both mental and corporeal, which operate through the medium of the nerves. This is so well known with respect to different articles of diet and medicine as to require no illustration, and the power of the mental affections is, likewise sufficiently obvious; for example, every one knows that the flow of the saliva is increased by the sight of food, a fact which may be observed in the lower animals as well as in man. It is therefore to be regarded as a well established point, that nervous excitement promotes secretion; but although this may prove the connexion which subsists between the muscular and the nervous systems, it does not throw any light upon the nature of secretion. An increase of ner-

vous energy produces an increased contractility of all the muscles, and, among the rest, of those which are immediately concerned in the circulation; hence the blood is propelled more freely to all parts of the body, and the glands being more plentifully supplied with it, are more disposed to produce their appropriate secretions.

The hypothesis which refers secretion to the action of the nerves, has been lately made the subject of an elaborate and very ingenious set of experiments by Dr. Philip; and from their results it is fully established, that, by dividing the par vagum in such a manner as to prevent the transmission of the nervous influence, the digestive power of the stomach is almost entirely destroyed. The conclusion deduced from the experiment by Dr. Philip is, that secretion is a nervous function, or one, in the due performance of which the nervous influence is the prime and essential agent. But although this might, at first view, appear the natural and necessary inference from the facts, it has been remarked by Dr. Alison and others, that it does not necessarily follow from them. They prove, indeed, that the nerves which go to the stomach have the power of affecting the secretion of the gastric juices, but they do not prove that they are essential to the formation of this fluid, much less to the function of secretion generally. There are, indeed, certain facts which would seem to demonstrate that secretion is, under ordinary circumstances, altogether independent of the nervous system, especially those to which we have already referred, where foetuses have been born in a state approaching to maturity, in which the brain and spinal marrow were entirely wanting.

Some of the modern physiologists have not been satisfied with the general reference of secretion to the power of the nerves, but have endeavoured to shew how particular glands produce particular secretions, by imparting to the different organs what they term specific sensibilities, so as to enable them to select from the blood these elements which may produce the different secreted substances. This we regard as one of those refined speculations which it is not easy to put to the test of experiment, and which must rest upon analogy and its intrinsic plausibility; upon the whole, however, it appears to us to be too vague and indefinite to require any more minute examination.

With respect to the nature of secretion, it appears to us that there are two leading points to be ascertained before we can arrive at any perfect theory upon the subject. We must learn, in the first place, how the elements of the blood can be so changed as to produce the secretion; and, in the second place, how the substance, when formed, can be separated from the blood. Although, in the present state of our knowledge, we are not able to give a decisive answer to either of these questions, yet we may, perhaps, go so far as to conjecture, that the first of these effects depends more upon chemical, and the second upon mechanical causes. We cannot form any conception of a mere mechanical action producing a new chemical affinity, although it may favour the union of elements which had a previous affinity for each other. But, when the compound is once formed, we may conceive how the size or shape of the vessels, or the velocity with which the fluid passes through them, may tend to favour its separation from the blood. With respect to any share which the action of the nerves may have in secretion, we consider it as depending altogether upon their influence on the living system generally, and not upon any specific operation on the glands.

CHAP. X.

OF DIGESTION.

Definition and division of the subject.

THE two last functions which have been described, those of respiration and secretion, consist essentially in the separation of certain substances from the blood; we are now to give an account of the means by which the waste thus occasioned is repaired. This is effected by the function of digestion, a process by which the food that is taken into the stomach is made to undergo certain changes, which adapt it for the purposes of nutrition. After the process of mastication, the aliment is reduced by the action of the stomach into a kind of pulpy mass called chyme, and afterwards it experiences a still farther change into a substance resembling cream in its appearance, which is called chyle. This is the ultimate product of the proper digestive organs; it is then fitted for its reception into the thoracic duct, and is poured into the trunk of the subclavian vein, where it is mixed with the blood, and becomes assimilated to this fluid in all its properties. In treating on the subject of digestion, we shall arrange our remarks under four heads: In the first place, We shall describe the organs of digestion; in the second place, We shall make some observations on the different substances employed as food; 3dly, We shall detail the successive changes which the food experiences, from the time it is taken into the mouth until it becomes converted into chyle; and, lastly, we shall give some account of the different hypotheses of digestion.

Organs of digestion;

The organs subservient to digestion may be arranged in three divissions: Those by which the food is mechanically divided into small parts; those in which the different substances lose their specific properties, and are reduced to a pultaceous mass, called chyme; and those

in man.

in which chyme is converted into chyle. In man, these three parts are the teeth, the stomach, and the duodenum. Of the teeth it is unnecessary to give any description in this place. The stomach is an irregular oval bag, which lies across the upper part of the abdomen; although principally composed of membranous matter, yet it is furnished with numerous muscular fibres, which give it a great degree of contractile power, and it is lined with a mucous membrane, thickly studded with glands. It is plentifully furnished with blood-vessels, and has so many nerves distributed to it as to render it one of the most acutely sensible parts of the body. The orifice by which the food is discharged from the stomach, the pylorus, communicates with the duodenum, the first part of the long winding tube which forms the intestinal canal. The intestines, like the stomach, consist of three principal parts, or coats—the membranous, the muscular, and the mucous; the first giving them their general form, the second their contractile power, and the third affording their secretions.

We have hitherto confined ourselves almost exclusively to the various organs and functions as they exist in the human subject. In the present instance, however, we shall digress so far as to make some remarks upon the digestive apparatus of some other species of animals, that differ essentially from man, because, by observing the peculiarities of their structure, we obtain a good illustration of the uses of the corresponding parts, and of their relation to each other. Birds are

in birds,

without teeth, or any part in the mouth by which the food can be comminuted, yet many of them feed upon hard vegetable substances, which cannot be digested in their entire state. The want of teeth in these animals is supplied by the crop and the gizzard. The crop is the receptacle for the grains when they are first swallowed, and where they remain for some time for the purpose of being macerated, so as to prepare them for the action of the gizzard. The gizzard is a cavity of a flattened form, the sides of which are composed of strong muscles, so connected together by ligaments, that, when they contract, whatever is placed between them is strongly pressed upon and triturated with considerable force. This force is, indeed, almost inconceivably great, and, at the same time, the muscles are lined with a firm cartilage, so as to be able not only to reduce the hardest grains to a perfect pulp, but even to grind to powder pieces of glass, and to blunt the edges of lancets, that had been introduced for the purpose of experiment, without the organ itself receiving any injury. The action of the crop and the gizzard are altogether mechanical, and is equivalent to the effect of mastication in animals that are provided with teeth.

in ruminating animals.

There is another class of animals, which includes some of the largest quadrupeds, who are furnished with teeth; but as they live upon vegetables, which require much mastication, while, at the same time, their bulk, and the nature of the food, renders it necessary for them to take in large quantities of it, the economy of their organs is so arranged, that the food, in the first instance, is swallowed nearly as it is taken into the mouth. It passes immediately into a large reservoir, called the paunch, or the first stomach, and, after going through a second stomach, it rises up into the mouth, in the form of a rounded ball, and is then masticated by the animal at its leisure for a length of time, constituting what is called chewing the cud, or rumination. When the food is sufficiently masticated it is again swallowed; but it is now carried directly to the third, and afterwards to the fourth, or proper digestive stomach, where the process is completed in the usual manner. When ruminant quadrupeds take in fluids, these pass immediately into the third and fourth stomachs, without entering the first and second; and the milk, which nourishes the young animals, goes in the same course, obviously because, in these cases, mastication is not necessary. There are many other varieties in the digestive organs of other classes of animals, and we observe, in all cases, that the parts are most admirably adapted to the wants and condition of the individual.

Elements of substances used in diet.

The articles of diet may be arranged under the two great divisions of animal and vegetable substances, both as it appears competent to the support of life, although the different kinds of animals possess organs that are more peculiarly adapted to one or the other of them; while, in man, the most perfect nutrition is produced by a certain combination of both animal and vegetable diet. The ultimate chemical elements to which animal substances may be reduced, differ considerably from the elements of vegetables; the first are reducible into oxygen, hydrogen, carbon, and azote; the latter contain oxygen, hydrogen, and carbon, but the proportion of carbon is greater and of hydrogen less, while they either contain no azote, or only a small quantity of it.

Diet of different countries.

The inhabitants of the northern countries live almost entirely upon animal diet; those of the torrid zone, on the contrary, chiefly employ vegetables; while, in the temperate climates, the food is composed of a mixture

Physiology.

Sugar.

Primary
animal
compounds.

vegetable.

Gluten.

Farina.

Mucilage.

Nutritive
and digest-
ible sub-
stances.

of the two. This arrangement, which is, in a great degree, the result of necessity, appears likewise to be the most favourable to the health of the respective individuals. An animal diet probably affords a species of nourishment which gives the body more vigour, and enables it to evolve a greater proportion of caloric, while a vegetable diet seems equally appropriate to the warm climates, which abound in fruits and esculent plants.

The primary animal compounds that are used in diet are fibrin, albumen, jelly, and fat, and they are generally taken combined together in different proportions. The flesh of quadrupeds and birds consists chiefly of fibrin and albumen; that of fish, and of young animals of all descriptions, contains more jelly; while every one of them contains more or less of oil or of fat. The primary vegetable compounds are farina, gluten, mucilage, oil, and sugar. The vegetable products that compose any considerable share of our diet, are seeds, roots, fruits, and the stalks and leaves of plants. In Europe, and in the most civilized parts of the world, the main bulk of vegetable food consists of seeds, and especially of the different cerealea. Among these, wheat has always been considered the most important; and this is not to be attributed merely to its being the most palatable, but also to its being the most nutritive; and this depends principally upon the great quantity of gluten which it contains.

Gluten has been termed the most animalized of any vegetable product, as it consists of the same chemical elements with animal matter, and nearly in the same proportion; when it is duly mixed with other vegetable matter, and especially after it has undergone the process of fermentation, as is the case in wheaten bread, it affords an article of food perhaps more universally nutritious to the various classes of animals, than any with which we are acquainted. Gluten is also found in some other seeds besides wheat, and likewise in some roots; but these owe their nutritive quality chiefly to their farina. Farina, or starch, is the next most nutritious of the primary vegetable compounds, and constitutes the most important part of those seeds that do not contain gluten, and also of many of the roots, or tubers, that are employed as food, especially of the potato. A considerable proportion of the bulk of these substances consists of mucilage, which likewise affords nutrition, although still less than farina. Farina and mucilage are the principal components of fruits: in the chesnut, farina is the main ingredient; in the pulpy and acid fruits mucilage predominates; in the oleaginous fruits the oil is sometimes mixed with mucilage, as in the olive, while in the various species of nuts it is united to albumen. Mucilage also enters largely into the composition of stalks and leaves, although combined with other principles, which give them their specific flavour, and contribute to their nutritive qualities. Sugar and oil are primary vegetable compounds, which are found in different parts of many plants, and, although generally regarded rather as condiments than as articles of diet, yet they are commonly supposed to be highly nutritious substances. Nearly all the sugar and oil that are employed in this country in a separate state, are procured from the sugar cane and the olive respectively; but there is a considerable quantity of both these substances in many of the vegetable products that are in common use.

In considering the effect of different articles of food upon the stomach, it is necessary to remark, that there is a great and a very essential difference between what is the most nutritive and what is the most digestible. It indeed not unfrequently happens, that those bodies which, bulk for bulk, are capable of furnishing the greatest quantity of chyle, are not very easily acted upon by the stomach. It would appear also that a certain quantity of what may be considered as diluting matter contributes to digestion, or enables the stomach to extract and prepare the chyle with greater facility, and that in this way, what would afford little or no nourishment when taken alone, becomes useful when properly mixed with other substances. We also find, at least in the human subject, that a mixture of several substances is more salutary than any single article, although it may unite in the highest degree the two properties of nutrition and digestibility. In some elaborate experiments, which were performed by Stark upon his own person, he found that one of the most nutritious substances was a compound of suet and wheaten flour; but when he attempted to live upon this alone, the stomach soon became deranged. We may farther remark, that there are very great differences in the digestive powers of different individuals, and although these differences are often so singular as to appear more like the effect of caprice, or of some accidental association, than any original peculiarity in the condition of the digestive organs, yet there can be little doubt, that besides the effects which can be traced to these causes, there actually exists an original difference in the digestive powers of different individuals, in the same way as there is between different classes of animals. The difference that exists between different kinds of animals in this respect is sufficiently well known; besides the two great divisions, of carnivorous and graminivorous, we find in the carnivorous animals some feeding entirely upon the flesh of quadrupeds, others upon fish, and others upon insects. Among the graminivorous, we have some feeding entirely upon seeds, others upon fruits, and others upon the leaves of plants. In these cases we may always perceive something in the structure of the animal which determines or indicates the nature of its food; the peculiar form of the teeth, some adapted for biting or tearing, others for mastication or for rumination; the beaks of birds are some of them pointed, others flattened; the structure of the stomach, sometimes formed for trituration, sometimes for solution, and a variety of other circumstances may be observed, all suited to the mode of life and general habits of the species.

The liquids of various kinds constitute an important part of diet. These may be considered either as consisting of water, holding in solution or suspension substances of a nutritive nature, forming soups and gruels, or, as what may be more strictly speaking, called drinks; fluids which are employed, not for the purpose of nutrition, but to quench the thirst, or to promote the digestion of the solids. Of these the most important is water, which is indeed the basis of all the rest. They may be divided into the two classes of vegetable infusions and fermented liquors. Of the former of these tea and coffee are in the most general use in this country, and, to most individuals, form a refreshing and salutary beverage. The same epithet may be applied to the weaker fermented liquors, if taken in proper quantity, and with due regard to the state of the stomach and the nature of the constitution; but it is probable that distilled spirits, although very valuable as medical agents, must be always more or less pernicious when employed habitually in diet.

A third class of substances remains to be noticed,

Physiology.

Drinks.

Stark's experiments.

Graminivorous and carnivorous animals.

Liquids.

Condiments.

Physiology. which are very extensively used in diet, the articles that are not in themselves nutritive, but which are employed for the purpose of giving flavour to our food, styled condiments. These are very numerous and of very various descriptions, but they may all be reduced to the two classes of salts and spices. Their selection seems, in many cases, to depend upon very singular habits and caprices, so that we find those substances which are the most grateful to certain individuals and classes of people, the most disagreeable or even nauseous to others. There is such a very general relish for sapid food that we are induced to suppose some useful purpose must be answered by it, more than the mere gratification of the palate. It is to be observed that this kind of taste does not seem to exist among the inferior animals, as, for the most part, they all prefer that kind of food which is best adapted to their organs in a simple state. Man, however, differs from other animals in the capacity of subsisting in all climates and situations, a circumstance which renders it necessary for him to be omnivorous, able to subsist upon any substance which contains the elements of chyle. Now, as it seems essential, that whatever is taken into the stomach must undergo the same kind of change previous to digestion, it is reasonable to suppose that some assisting or correcting substances may be required to aid the action of the stomach, in reducing the various species of aliment to one uniform standard. Hence vegetable food, for example, may require the addition of warm aromatics to prevent it from running into the acid state, while animal food may have its putrefactive tendency corrected by acids and salts. It would appear, as a general rule, that the corrections are found in those situations where they are the most wanted; and we generally find that they are naturally agreeable to the palate. Brute animals, being only found in those climates or countries where there is a supply of the food which is most suitable for them, and being likewise guided in their choice of the articles of diet by instinct, do not require these correctives to adapt their food to the digestive process.

Medicaments. There is a very important class of substances which are analogous to the condiments in their relation to aliment, although very different in their effects upon the palate, the various species of medicaments. These are not themselves properly nutritive, as they do not contain the elements of chyle, but they produce changes on the stomach, which enable the system to regain its state of health, when any of the functions have been deranged. The knowledge of these substances, and of their action upon the body, constitutes the science of medicine, which has already been treated of under the appropriate articles. (See Materia Medica and Medicine.)

From the review that we have taken of the various kinds of food, it will appear that they embrace the whole range of organized substances, taken from both the animal and vegetable kingdoms, and that they scarcely agree in any property, except in their being easily decomposible, and being resolved into the same ultimate elements.

3. Changes which the food undergoes; We must now proceed, in the *third* place, to describe the successive changes which the food undergoes, from the time it is received into the mouth, until it is converted into perfect chyle. The first step which is necessary for this purpose is a due degree of mechanical division, in order to prepare the aliment for the action of the proper digestive stomach; and, according to the structure of the animal, this is accomplished,

either by mastication, trituration, or maceration, or by a combination of these processes. After the requisite mechanical change, the food is received into what has been called the proper digestive stomach, and is there reduced to the state of a soft pultaceous mass, which has obtained the name of chyme. It has been asserted, that the specific odour and other sensible properties of the alimentary matter no longer exist in chyme, but that, whatever kind of food be employed, the resulting mass is always the same. As far as respects the same class of animals, where the nature of the food is not very dissimilar, and where all the functions are in a natural state, the position is, generally speaking, correct; but we learn from experiment, that the chyme from vegetables differs from that of animal origin, and it is likewise probable, that in different states of the stomach of the same individual, and where the same kind of the aliment has been used, the chyme does not always possess precisely the same qualities.

Physiology.

formation of chyme.

Although the nature of chyme has been examined with considerable accuracy, we are not able to explain very satisfactorily the mode by which it is produced. It is, in some respects, similar to chemical solution, in which a body is not only divided into its most minute parts, and has its aggregation completely destroyed, but also acquires new chemical properties. This solution is proved by numerous experiments, and especially by those of Spallanzani, in which different kinds of food were included in metallic tubes perforated with holes. These were introduced into the stomach, and were suffered to remain there for a certain length of time, when it was found that the inclosed substances were more or less dissolved, without the tubes being acted upon.

Spallanzani's experiments.

The common opinion with respect to the production of chyme, and the one which appears to be sanctioned by facts, is, that the glands of the stomach secrete a peculiar kind of fluid, named the gastric juice, which is the proper solvent of the food. This may be considered as having been proved by direct experiment. The gastric juice has been obtained from the stomachs of animals in various ways, sometimes by introducing sponges, which were afterwards withdrawn, and the fluid pressed from them, at other times by causing the animals to vomit after fasting. Alimentary matters were then subjected to the liquid thus procured, and kept at the temperature of the human body, the result of which was, that a kind of imperfect digestion took place, perhaps as nearly resembling the natural process as could be expected from the manner in which the experiment was conducted. Yet it is not a little remarkable, that when the gastric juice has been examined, no properties have been detected in it, which would seem adequate to produce the effects which we observe. It seems indeed to differ very little from saliva, which we are disposed to regard as a substance very inert in its chemical relations. Yet many circumstances tend to show that the stomach has the power of secreting a substance, which possesses an operation similar to chemical affinity, because its action on bodies bears no proportion to their mechanical texture or other physical properties. Thus not only can the fluids of the stomach act upon dense membranes and bones, but have even been found capable of dissolving iron; yet, at the same time, many bodies of comparatively delicate texture, as the skins of fruits, and the finest fibres of cotton and flax, are not attacked by the gastric juice.

Gastric juice.

There are two properties of the gastric juice, which

Coagulating power.

Physiology. indicate still more decisively its chemical action, the power of coagulating albumen, and of resisting putrefaction, although it may be difficult to explain how these properties can be attached to such a substance as analysis indicates it to be. It is upon the coagulating power of the gastric juice, as residing on the surface of the stomach, that the method of making cheese depends. What is called *rennet* consists of an infusion of the digestive stomach of the calf, and by adding this to milk, we reduce the albuminous part to the state of curd, from which the cheese is prepared. It is admitted that we are unable to explain the mode of its action in this case; but the process of coagulation is itself one of the most mysterious operations in chemistry, and one which we find to be produced by a variety of agents that have little analogy with each other, and probably do not operate upon the same principle.

Antiseptic power. The antiseptic power of the gastric juice is no less difficult to explain than its coagulating quality; but there is no doubt of its existence, as it has been ascertained, that in carnivorous animals, who frequently take their food in a putrid state, the first operation of the stomach is to remove the fœtor from the substances received into it. Experiments made upon the gastric juice out of the body, likewise demonstrates its power of resisting putrefaction, or of stopping the process when it has commenced.

Chyme, how produced. It appears then that we are warranted in concluding, that when the food has undergone a sufficient degree of mechanical division, it is acted upon by the stomach, or rather by the fluids secreted from its surface, so as to experience a complete change in its properties. This change is so far analogous to a chemical process, as that the chemical nature of the substance is affected by it, yet we are but imperfectly acquainted with the agent which produces these changes, or with the successive steps by which they are effected. A degree of heat appears to be extricated during the formation of chyme, gas is frequently discharged, and there is sometimes an acid produced, but these effects, the two latter of them at least, would seem rather to be deviations from the natural operation, than an essential part of it.

Vermicular action. In some cases, either from accident, or for the purpose of experiment, the stomach has been exposed to view during the process of digestion, and it has been observed to be in constant motion, the different portions of it alternately relaxing and contracting, in a way which has been termed vermicular, from its supposed resemblance to the crawling of worms. This motion is evidently intended to mix all parts of the mass intimately together, and to apply each of them, in succession, to the surface of the stomach, so as to bring it in contact with the gastric juice. The mass is, at the same time, gradually pushed on towards the pylorus, and is finally propelled into the duodenum, where it is to receive a further alteration of its properties.

Chyle. The alteration referred to, is the conversion of chyme into chyle. The nature and properties of chyle have been examined with considerable minuteness. It is opaque and white, resembling cream in its consistence when first discharged from the vessels; by degrees it concretes, and after some time separates into a dense coagulum, which is surrounded by a colourless fluid, an operation which appears to be analogous to the spontaneous separation of the blood into crassamentum and serum. The chemical properties of the two constituents of the chyle are, in many respects, similar to the corresponding parts of the blood; and the chyle has been likewise found to have the same kinds of salts in it, but it differs from the blood, in containing a quantity of sugar and of oily matter. Upon the whole, we may conclude, that both the physical and chemical properties of chyle, indicate it as a substance intermediate between chyme and blood.

Process of chylification. The mode in which chylification is effected, is altogether very obscure; we know little more than the general fact, that the contents of the duodenum, soon after they leave the pylorus, begin to separate into two parts; the white substance, constituting the chyle, and the refuse matter, which is afterwards rejected from the system in the form of fæces. The chyle is gradually taken up by a set of small vessels, called from the appearance of their contents, the lacteals, by which it is transmitted to the blood. We find upon examination, that there is no proper chyle formed in any part of the stomach; that it first makes its appearance soon after the alimentary mass passes out of this organ, that the greatest quantity of chyle exists at a short distance from the pylorus, and that it gradually disappears as we advance along the small intestines.

Difficult to explain. The bile is poured into the duodenum from its appropriate duct about the part where the chyle is found in the greatest quantity and the most perfect state; and the fluid from the pancreas enters the intestinal canal about the same place. It has been supposed, therefore, that the bile and the pancreatic juice are concerned in the process of chylification; but except this coincidence, there is no proof of this action, nor can we give any account of the way in which it is effected. All that we can say upon the subject is, that the conversion of chyme into chyle must be brought about either by the reaction of the component parts upon each other, by the operation of the bile and the pancreatic juice, or of some secretions from the duodenum itself; but we are unable to say which of these causes is concerned in the operation, which is the most efficient, or whether others may not co-operate with them, or be even more powerful.

Is alimentary matter rendered soluble? It has been a question, whether by this conversion, first into chyme and afterwards into chyle, the alimentary matter is rendered soluble in water. It is perhaps not easy to decide upon this question, but we are disposed to answer it in the negative, although it is essential that it be reduced to a state of minute division, to enable it to enter the mouths of the absorbents. It has been farther questioned, whether any part of the food passes into the system unchanged, without being decomposed and entering into new combinations. To this also we should reply in the negative: that it must be the case with vegetable aliment of every kind is sufficiently obvious; and even the animal substances employed in diet, seem to have all their properties entirely altered, so that none of them can be exempt from the operation of the gastric juice. And were this not the case, the power which the absorbents possess, of separating the matter which is adapted to them from the whole mass that is in contact with their extremities, renders it very probable that if any substance had escaped decomposition in the stomach, it would not be received by the lacteals.

Is the whole decomposed? But although it appears that no part of the proper alimentary matter passes into the blood unchanged,

Use of salt in diet.

yet there are some substances which are taken into the stomach, and mixed with our food, that are carried into the circulation without being decomposed. This is probably the case with some of the salts, that are either intentionally or incidentally mixed with the food, and also with some of those bodies which give the specific flavour to both animal and vegetable substances. Common salt is one of the constant constituents of the blood, and exists there always in the same quantity, so that we are led to conclude it must serve some useful purpose in the animal economy. The necessity for a due proportion of salt in the system is well illustrated by the extraordinary efforts which certain classes of animals make to obtain it, when it is not easily procured. We are informed, that in the interior of the vast continents of Africa and America, beasts of prey will traverse immense distances to get at the brine springs which are occasionally found there. We have under our eyes daily examples of the salutary operation of salt, as entering into the diet of animals, when they are suffered to feed on salt marshes, or still more directly, by mixing salt with their provisions. At the same time that we observe animals to be led by instinct to the use of salt, so the human species are induced to employ it from its grateful effect upon the palate; for it may be remarked, that there is no description of people, the most barbarous or the most refined, who do not relish a certain proportion of salt along with their food.

Lime in the body, whence derived?

With respect to common salt, therefore, we have no difficulty in accounting for its introduction into the body, but the case is different with some of the other components of the body, and particularly with the calcareous earth. The salts of lime form so large a proportion of the solids, and are so essential to their existence, that the inquiry becomes a very interesting one, whence this earth is originally derived. As lime exists in various articles, both animal and vegetable, which are employed in diet, it has been supposed, that the whole of what is received into the stomach may be retained, and that in the course of time, a sufficient quantity may be accumulated to answer all the necessary demands of the system. But the difficulty increases as we proceed in the investigation, for when we examine the great masses of limestone which are found among the upper strata of the earth, whence the calcareous matter might be supposed to be derived, which enters into the composition of animals, these masses afford strong indications of having been themselves the remains of former organized bodies.

Experiments.

In order to solve the problem, recourse has been had to experiment. Animals have been confined, and the composition of their food carefully ascertained, and the amount of lime which they could obtain from this source was compared with that existing in their bones. The same kind of difficulty occurs with respect to plants; and as it is much easier to subject them to trials of this kind, analogous experiments have been performed with them; and it appears that, in both cases, making due allowance for unavoidable sources of inaccuracy, the earthy matter found in them is more than could be derived from the water with which they are supported. But it must be allowed, on the other hand, that experiments of this kind are very liable to error, from the length of time and unremitted attention which they require, so that we ought to pause before we venture to draw a conclusion so much at variance, not merely with the ordinary operations of chemical affinity, but with our conceptions of the general powers of nature, as they are observed to operate under other circumstances.

The theory of digestion has afforded a very fruitful subject of speculation, no less than seven hypotheses having been formed to account for the operation; for in this, as in many other parts of physiology, it may be observed, that the more obscure is the subject, the greater is the number of explanations of it that have been proposed.

Theory of digestion.

Hippocrates ascribes digestion to what he calls concoction; a term which was employed to designate the operation by which substances undergo a degree of solution and a change in their properties, when they are confined in close vessels, and subjected to a certain degree of temperature; but this obviously affords no explanation of the nature of the operation.

Concoction.

The next hypothesis was that of putrefaction. The food, after being received into the stomach, was observed to have its texture broken down, and to acquire an unpleasant odour; and this was, without hesitation, considered by the older physiologists as a species of putrefaction, in conformity with the loose method of reasoning which they were in the habit of employing. It is not necessary to enter into a refutation of this opinion, because it is now well known that putrefaction and digestion are operations totally different from each other.

Putrefaction.

The mechanical physiologists endeavoured to account for all the phenomena of digestion by trituration; and they advanced many curious facts in support of their doctrine, derived from those animals who possess what are called muscular stomachs. But, in the view which they took of the facts that fell under their notice, they committed two great errors: first, in extending to all classes of animals an action which belongs only to certain classes, and second, in regarding the mechanical operation of grinding down the food, which is performed by the gizzard of birds, and is merely the first step of the operation, to supply the place of teeth, as constituting the proper act of digestion. The experiments of Spallanzani and others have satisfactorily shown, that the appropriate change which the food undergoes in the stomach is altogether independent of trituration; while we learn, at the same time, that, in those animals whose digestive organs are provided with muscular appendages, the process of chylification is carried on in a different part of the apparatus, and after the usual manner, by the operation of the gastric juice.

Trituration.

The experiments that we have alluded to above, which proved the fallacy of the doctrine of trituration, were supposed to establish the chemical hypothesis, according to which digestion is merely a case of chemical solution. The stomach, it is supposed, secretes a fluid, which is the proper solvent of the substances introduced into it, and that nothing farther is necessary to complete the process than to bring the aliment and gastric juice into contact, so as to enable them to act upon each other. The experiments that were brought forwards by Spallanzani, where he imitated digestion out of the body, were conceived to be decisive in favour of this hypothesis, and no doubt, to a certain extent, warranted the conclusion that was deduced from them. But we do not consider them as competent to explain the whole of the operation. Even were we to suppose that the gastric juice possesses properties which enable it to dissolve all the variety of substances which are taken into the stomach, we can scarcely conceive how it

Chemical solution.

3

could reduce every thing to the same consistence, and form the same, or very nearly the same, species of chyme from bodies that differ so much in their chemical constitution.

In consequence of these objections, and of the difficulty which there is in accounting for digestion either upon mechanical or upon chemical principles, most of the modern physiologists have attributed digestion to the direct agency of the vital principle. The interior surface of the stomach is said to be endowed with a specific property, unlike any other that exists in nature, which belongs to it solely as a living substance, and which enables it to digest food. We have had frequent occasion to advert to the doctrines of the Animists in different parts of this article; and the same kind of remarks which we have already employed may be used in this place. The foundation of their doctrine is the impossibility of accounting for the facts upon any other principle. They assume it as proved, that no modification of the powers of chemistry or mechanics can explain the effect in question; and they, in consequence, assume the existence of a new power to meet the difficulty. But this proceeds upon the supposition, that our knowledge of the nature of digestion is much more complete than we are disposed to allow it to be. We have only an imperfect acquaintance with the successive steps of the operation of the stomach, and scarcely a sufficient knowledge of the compounds that result from them; and it is essentially necessary to inform ourselves upon these points before we proceed to introduce new powers or principles to explain these difficulties. This method of prematurely generalizing facts is always injurious to the progress of science, as it tends to conceal our ignorance by leading us to substitute new words for new ideas.

An hypothesis of digestion which has been recently brought forwards, and supported by direct experiment, is, that this function depends immediately upon the action of the nervous system. The experiments are those of Dr. Philip, of which we have already given some account, where it was found that digestion was suspended by dividing the nerves that go to the stomach. The effect of this operation is the stoppage of the secretion of the gastric juice; the nervous influence is, therefore, no farther essential to digestion than as it is supposed to furnish the agent by which the food is converted into chyme. It is, in fact, therefore, rather an hypothesis of secretion than of digestion, and the remarks upon it, when considered in that point of view, will consequently apply to this subject.

The last hypothesis of digestion which remains to be considered is that of fermentation. It appears to have been invented by Van Helmont; and when expressed in modern language, and divested of all the unessential parts, is supported by strong analogies, and is, we conceive, the most consonant to established facts. Fermentation consists in a change which the elements of a body experience by their action upon each other, or by the addition of a small quantity of some foreign ingredient, by which the nature of the compound is materially altered, and all its component parts assimilated into a homogeneous mass. Different kinds of fermentations are enumerated by chemists, of which the principal are the vinous and the acetous; these differ from each other in the materials that are the most favourable for their production, the nature of the operation itself, and the properties of the product. To an analogous operation we are disposed to attribute the conversion of alimentary matter into chyme, the gastric juice acting the part of the ferment.

The objection that has been urged against the hypothesis of fermentation is, that the products of digestion are not similar to those of the other fermentations, neither alcohol nor acetous acid being formed by the stomach. But this objection proceeds upon the principle, that fermentation is confined to those operations, where either alcohol or acetous acid is produced. Yet this is not the case. For example, a mixture of flour and water, by the addition of yeast, undergoes a change which is properly entitled to the appellation of fermentation, although differing specifically from either the vinous or acetous. The principal circumstances in which digestion and fermentation resemble each other are the following: 1. Substances possessed of various properties are all reduced to one homogeneous state, by the addition of a minute quantity of an extraneous body. 2. The quantity of the fermentative substance, which is the immediate agent in this process, is often extremely minute in proportion to the effect which it produces. 3. The subjects of the operation are organized bodies alone, and those consisting of the elements united in very various proportions. 4. The process may be suspended, or entirely destroyed, by very minute circumstances, which would previously have appeared inadequate to the effect. 5. When the ultimate change is effected, and the new substance has acquired its specific properties, if it be kept under the same circumstances as at first, a new operation commences, by which it becomes disposed to undergo a second change, and to form a new substance, also possessed of peculiar and specific properties. The analogy might be extended; but we conceive that enough has been pointed out to show the essential resemblance between the two operations of fermentation and digestion.

There is indeed one difficulty which attaches to this view of the subject, although not more to this than to the other theories of digestion, that the action of the stomach in the formation of chyme is only the first step in the process, and that there still remains to be accounted for the farther change of chyme into chyle. But, respecting this point, we are left so very much in the dark, that it appears almost undesirable to attempt any explanation, until we have made ourselves better acquainted with the facts. We may, however, remark, that there is one point which ought to be ascertained, before we enter into any speculations upon the subject, whether the chyle exists in chyme, and is afterwards merely separated from it, or whether the chyle be actually produced in the duodenum. If we find that chyle does not exist in chyme, the next point will be to ascertain, whether the continuation of the same fermentative process, by which aliment is converted into chyme, will not convert chyme into chyle, in the same way as in the fermentation of sugar and mucilage, we first procure alcohol, and, by continuing the operation, convert the vinous fluid into acetous acid. In the next place, if we find that chyle does not bear this kind of relation to chyme, we must inquire whether the bile and the pancreatic juice can act, either separately or conjointly, as a ferment to convert chyme into chyle, or whether any other addition is made to them, or any change in their situation or circumstances, which can account for this change. Until these inquiries have been made, we have no right to complain of the intricacy of the subject, or to speak of the process of chylification as of something mysterious, and which cannot be effected without ascribing to matter new laws, which are supposed to direct its operations.

CHAP. XI.

OF ABSORPTION.

Absorption.

After having given an account of the means by which fresh matter is provided, to repair the waste that is continually going forward in the system, it remains for us to consider the function by which the particles that are intended for the future supply of the body are conveyed into the blood, while, at the same time, those that have performed their appropriate offices, and are therefore become useless or noxious, are removed from the body : this constitutes the process of absorption. We shall first describe the apparatus by which this function is carried on; 2. The use of the absorbent system ; and, in the 3d place, we shall offer some remarks upon the mode in which the absorbents are supposed to act.

Arrangement.

Description of the absorbent system.

The absorbsent system consists of four parts ; the lacteals, the lymphatics, the conglobate glands, and the thoracic duct. The lacteals are a system of vessels, the object of which is to take up the chyle from the intestines, and convey it into the circulation. They seem to have been imperfectly known to Galen, although he was mistaken as to their destination, which he supposed to be the liver. For some centuries they were entirely forgotten or disregarded, until they were again discovered, in the beginning of the seventeenth century, by Asselli. They obtained the name of lacteals, in consequence of their contents having the consistence and appearance of cream. The lacteals are described as opening into the intestine by a number of small capillary tubes, termed villi, which radiate, as it were, from a centre, several of them uniting to form one vessel ; but there is still some uncertainty respecting the nature of these villi, and their connexion with the proper lacteals. The lacteals themselves are then carried along the mesentery. During their passage the small branches run together, and form larger and larger vessels, until at length they are all reduced to a few principal trunks, which terminate in the thoracic duct. The lacteals are characterized by the thinness and transparency of their coats, and by the circumstance of their being furnished with numerous valves. From this structure, it follows that when they are distended either by chyle or by injections, they assume a jointed appearance, something like a string of beads. During their course they frequently inosculate, and the inosculations are sometimes so numerous and intricate as to form a complete plexus. They are supposed to possess a considerable degree of contractility, although, from their transparency and delicacy of texture, it is impossible to demonstrate their fibres.

Lacteals.

Lymphatics.

The lymphatics, both in their functions and their destination, are analogous to the lacteals, except that whereas the latter are confined to the intestines, the former are dispersed over all parts of the body. They originate from every surface, external and internal, communicate with every organ, and at length terminate in the thoracic duct. In their structure they much resemble the lacteals, being, like them, possessed of muscular contractility, and provided with numerous valves ; but the fluid which they contain being, like themselves, nearly without colour, they are not easily detected ; and they were accordingly not discovered until some time after the lacteals. There has been a good deal of controversy respecting their discovery ;

but it is now generally agreed that the merit belongs jointly to Rudbeck and Bartholine, who, each of them, published their observations about the middle of the seventeenth century, and seem to have pursued their investigations without any concert or communication. This department of anatomy has of late years been assiduously cultivated in this country, particularly by Hunter and Monro, from whose observations we learn that the lymphatic system is distributed to every part of the body.

Both the lacteals and the lymphatics, in their course to the thoracic duct, meet with a number of glands, which have been termed, from their supposed structure, conglobate ; but the relation which they bear to the vessels themselves is obscure ; nor indeed is their structure thoroughly understood, for it has been a much agitated question, whether they contain proper cavities, or consist altogether of a net-work of vessels. Upon the whole, the evidence appears to be in favour of the opinion, that the glands are entirely vascular, except the cellular substance necessary for connecting the vessels together. The glands are much more numerous in some parts of the body than in others ; but it is admitted as a general fact, that no lacteal or lymphatic arrives at the thoracic duct without passing through one or more glands in its course. This remark, however, is only true so far as respects the human species, and those animals who possess a structure and organization the most nearly resembling him ; for these glands are said to be rare in birds, and in fish to be altogether wanting.

Conglobate glands.

The lacteals and lymphatics all terminate in the thoracic duct,—a vessel of considerable size, that is situated along the back part of the thorax. It receives at its lower end the contents of all the absorbents, and pours them into the left subclavian, not far from the termination of the venous system in the right auricle of the heart. The thoracic duct, in its structure and functions, agrees generally with the other absorbent vessels ; like them it is thin, elastic, and contractile, and possesses numerous valves.

Thoracic duct.

With respect to the use of the absorbent system, their office is literally expressed by their name ; it consists in taking up certain substances, which they transport from one part of the body to another. The action of the lacteals is confined to the chyle, while the lymphatics receive a variety of substances that are presented to them. The thoracic duct is to be regarded merely as a receptacle, where the contents of the smaller vessels are lodged until the veins are able to receive them. So far we appear to proceed upon certain grounds ; but the office of the glands, which form so important a part of the absorbent system, is not so obvious : nor indeed can it be expected that we should understand this point, while we are still unacquainted with their structure. It is yet undecided whether the gland is merely a convolution of the absorbent vessel itself, or whether it consists of other vessels derived from the artery, and only communicating with the absorbents. Upon the whole, the results of the most minute investigations seem to favour the opinion, that the gland is formed by a convolution of the absorbent system itself, and the office of these organs is rather to effect some change in the chyle or lymph, by the action of its components upon each other, than to add to them any extraneous substance.

2. Use of the absorbents.

But although it is admitted as a general fact, that absorption is carried on by the lacteals and lymphatics, it has been a very warmly controverted point, whether

Do the veins absorb?

this operation be exclusively performed by these vessels? It was supposed, that the veins likewise possessed the power of absorption ; and, in some parts of the body, and in some animals, they were conceived to be the principal, or even the sole agents in this process. This was the common opinion until the middle of the last century, and is the doctrine that was maintained both by Boerhaave and by Haller. Since that time, however, the lymphatics have been discovered in many organs where they were not then known to exist, and, in consequence, partly of the universal distribution of these vessels, and partly of direct experiments that were performed by Hunter, Monro, and others, the doctrine of venous absorption was almost universally abandoned, and there were few facts in physiology which seemed to be more completely established, than the exclusive absorbing power of the lacteals and lymphatics. The old opinion, however, has been of late brought forward by M. Magendie, and supported by arguments and experiments which, it must be allowed, will render it necessary for us to pause, and carefully review our former conclusions.

But whatever we may think upon this point, we know that the use of the lacteals and lymphatics is to absorb; and we are now to inquire, what is the respective office of each, or what kind of substances are they each of them destined to convey? That of the lacteals is obviously confined to the absorption of chyle ; and as this is the direct source whence the blood receives its supply, we are to regard these vessels as the immediate organs of nutrition. The lymphatics may likewise occasionally contribute to the same end, but the nutrition of the body would not appear to be their ultimate object, because the substances which are taken up by them have been, for the most part, previously organized, and have already entered into the composition of the body, so that it would reduce their action to a mere alternation of the processes of decomposition and reproduction. We must, therefore, look for some other and more remote object in the lymphatics than the supply of nutrition ; and we are led to suppose that their principal use is that of moulding and fashioning the body, and enabling it to acquire an increase of size without deranging its form. When we reflect upon the manner in which the body grows, we must be aware that it cannot be either by the distention of the parts already formed, or from the mere accretion of new particles to their surfaces, by an operation similar to crystallization ; for neither of these processes are applicable to organized bodies, where the change consists not in an increase of bulk only, but in a change of the whole internal structure, and a corresponding change in the external form.

If we take the case of a muscle, one end of which terminates in a tendon, while the other is immediately attached to a bone, this, in the infant, is of a certain length, and afterwards attains to two or three times its former size, while its general form and the relation of its different parts remain the same. Now it is obvious that this increase of bulk is not produced by the distention of its parts, because the muscle, when at its full size, exhibits no appearance of this kind. Nor can the growth be effected by accretion, because the situation of the different parts with respect to each other is obviously inconsistent with this supposition. We must, therefore, conclude, that the growth of the muscle and tendon can be accomplished in one way only—the gradual removal of all the particles of which they originally consisted by the lymphatics, and the deposition of new particles by the secreting arteries. The new matter which is deposited does not occupy precisely the same place with the former, but its situation is adapted to that of the neighbouring parts. The fibres of the muscle, and the cells and plates of the membrane, are thus continually growing more numerous, and, perhaps, each of them likewise becoming larger, while, at the same time, all the surrounding parts change their position, so that the new matter is exactly adapted to the place which it is intended to occupy.

We shall be still more convinced of the correctness of this mode of viewing the subject, when we apply it to the growth of the hard parts. The bone of a young animal has a certain figure, is furnished with a certain number of eminences and depressions, projecting spines and cavities, and, as a general rule, the shape of the bone in the adult is the same with that of the infant, but it is much larger. Now, it is obvious that bone is incapable of distention, and that, by the mere addition of more matter to the original bone, we should have a body of a totally different form. Nothing, in fact, can produce the effect in question except the process we have described above—the removal of the old bone, particle by particle, and the substitution of new particles in a situation different from the former. This reciprocal change appears to be connected with a principle in the animal economy to which we have already alluded, that the matter of which the body is composed gradually undergoes some alteration, by which it becomes unfit for the performance of its proper functions, and requires, from time to time, to be replaced by fresh matter. We are ignorant in what this change consists, and what are the ultimate purposes which it serves, but it seems to be intimately connected with the process by which the body is moulded into its proper form. The conclusion to which we arrive is, that both the lacteals and the lymphatics are employed in the formation of the body, but that they contribute to this end in different ways ; the lacteals convey the nutritive matter to the blood, while the principal office of the lymphatics is to dispose of this matter, so as to give the body its proper form, and enable each individual part to increase in size without affecting the relation which they bear to each other.

We are now to inquire, in the third place, into the mode in which the absorbents act ; and here several interesting questions present themselves to us. We must endeavour to ascertain, first, how the substances enter the mouths of the vessels ; and second, how they are carried along them. We should examine into the nature of the substances that are adapted for the action of the absorbents, and into the changes which they undergo before they are in a state proper for absorption. We have already spoken of the minute vessels termed villi, which are described as constituting the mouth of the lacteals ; a structure which would seem to favour the opinion, that the operation is merely that of capillary attraction, were it not that the thinness and flexibility of the vessels appear inconsistent with this effect, so as to lead to the idea that the vessels must be endued with some specific power, different from that of mere inorganic tubes. But before we can decide upon this point, it is necessary to determine the exact sense in which we employ the term capillary attraction. If we regard it as not a mere mechanical action between the tube and the contained fluid, but as farther partaking of an elective attraction, which varies according to the nature of the tube and the fluid, we may perhaps be able to explain the effect which is produced by the absorbents upon the matter that is presented to their orifices. And there are, indeed, several circumstances which seem to render it probable that this kind of selection actually takes place, and that the absorbents receive certain particles and reject others, not from any relation to their physical properties, but from something specific in their chemical nature. But it would still appear, that the mouths of the absorbents could not permit the particles to enter without exercising some kind of vital action, by which they may be alternately contracted and relaxed, such as we have reason to believe the vessels themselves possess, and which it is therefore natural to attribute to their extremities.

General conclusion. The conclusion, therefore, to which we are brought is, that the mouths of the absorbents possess contractility, and likewise a power something analogous to elective attraction, by the continued operation of which the appropriate particles are enabled to enter the vessels. When they have once entered, the vessels carry them forwards by their contractile force, assisted by external pressure, and by the valves with which they are furnished; the contractility and external pressure forcing the matter from one part of the vessel to another, and the valves determining this motion to be always in one direction.

Absorption of solids. Our remarks have hitherto referred principally to the lacteals, as concerned in the absorption of the chyle, but a more difficult point still remains to be considered, how the absorption of the solids is effected. We have every reason to suppose that this absorption actually takes place, so that there is not a single particle of the hardest bone, which is not, in due course of time, taken up by the lymphatics, and, in short, that after a certain period, not a single atom remains of the former individual. Yet this effect is brought about so slowly, and the particles are removed in so imperceptible a manner, that the identity is not destroyed, and it even requires a considerable degree of accurate observation to become sensible of the effect. Many particular cases of the absorption of solids daily present themselves to our observation; constant pressure upon a part causes it to waste away, even although the part pressed upon be harder than the part producing the pressure. The pulsation of an artery will even cause the removal of bone, and by the gradual operation of certain medical agents, large solid tumours are occasionally dispersed. In all these cases the lymphatics are the immediate agents; and it is a curious speculation to inquire in what manner these vessels act, how the texture of the part is broken down, and reduced to a state proper for absorption. Most writers, when treating upon this subject, have employed language which can only be regarded as metaphorical, although they have not expressly stated this to be the case, as where they speak of the lymphatics eating away or corroding the hard body. When we come to consider the nature of the operation, it must, we conceive, be admitted as a necessary step in the process, that the solid, before it can enter the vessel, must either be reduced to a soluble state, or to a state of very minute comminution. We are indeed ignorant how this is brought about, whether by the intervention of any solvent, or in short, by what other means, yet it seems scarcely possible to dispense with this operation.

Absorption of dead matter. There is one fact that has been ascertained on this subject, that dead matter is absorbed more readily than the same matter while it is possessed of life, although agreeing with it in every other property, and indeed a moment's reflection must convince us that no part can be absorbed until it is first deprived of life. Physiology. This has been spoken of as depending upon some mysterious power of the vital principle, by which it enables a part to resist the action of the absorbents, but perhaps a little reflection may enable us to view this subject in a more comprehensible manner. It is obvious, that while a solid retains its state of aggregation it cannot enter the absorbents, and therefore, whatever process adapts it for entering these vessels must previously decompose it. If we suppose a part to be simply deprived of life, and, at the same time, to retain its physical structure and chemical properties unaltered, the absorbents could have no effect upon it. It would therefore appear that the death of the part, although the first step in the process, is not properly the effect of the absorbents, and that they cannot act until the decomposition has commenced. How far we are able to trace a connexion between these two effects remains to be considered; in the case of absorption, as resulting from external pressure, we probably have it in our power to do so. We may conjecture, that in consequence of this pressure the secreting arteries are prevented from performing their functions, while the same action may not affect, or may even promote, that of the absorbents; the consequence will be, that the old particles of the solid are removed more rapidly than ordinary, while no fresh ones are provided to supply the deficiency. The balance is therefore destroyed between the powers of accumulation and of expenditure, and when the latter prevail, the necessary consequence must be absorption. The difficulty which attends the investigation is to explain the manner in which the old materials are reduced to a state proper for absorption, what share the absorbents have in this part of the process, or rather, what are the powers by which it is effected.

There is one part of the subject of absorption which Cutaneous remains to be considered, the power which the external surface of the body possesses of taking up extraneous substances that are presented to it. We learn from the researches of the anatomists, that lymphatics are very copiously distributed to all parts of the skin, and that they appear to terminate under the cuticle; we likewise know that various medical substances applied to the skin, particularly if we use the aid of friction, will enter the circulation, exhibiting the same action upon the system, as if they had been received into the stomach. In these cases there is sufficient proof of the existence of cutaneous absorption, but it is a question that has given rise to much controversy, whether, when water is applied to the surface, as in the warm bath, or the aqueous vapour which exists in the atmosphere, it can be absorbed by the skin, simply in consequence of the body being immersed in it. A number of circumstances led us to believe in the reality of this absorption, particularly those that were brought forwards by Sanctorius, who was conceived to have proved, in the most decisive manner, that, under certain circumstances, the weight of the body is sensibly augmented by the water which it imbibes by the skin. Until very lately, the doctrine of cutaneous absorption was universally assented to, and many important pathological speculations were founded upon it, but the progress of modern discovery has thrown a doubt upon our former conclusions; and the opinion, perhaps at present the most generally adopted is, that when the surface of the body is in its sound state, and where no external force is employed, the skin is impervious to moisture, but that various substances may be

3

forced into it by friction, and even by long immersion in warm water, by which the epidermis becomes softened and perhaps partially destroyed, at the same time that the mouths of the lymphatics are relaxed and rendered more disposed to receive what is presented to them.

CHAP. XII.

OF GENERATION.

Of genera-
tion. IF we have found it difficult to account for the series of actions which constitute the functions that have lately passed under our review, still more so shall we find it to explain the mysterious operation by which a succession of individuals is produced for the continuance of the species. It will not be necessary for us to give any description of the appropriate organs, nor of the process by which it is accomplished; we shall confine ourselves to a detail of some of the more important changes which take place in the production of the fœtus, to which we shall add a few remarks upon the theories that have been proposed to explain these changes.

Functions
of the two
sexes. In all those animals, whose structure and functions bear a general resemblance to the human, generation is performed by the concourse of the two sexes, the office of the male being to introduce a portion of the fluid which is secreted by the testes, into a part of the body of the female, appropriated for its reception. It is probable that the emission of the semen from the male may be referred to the same kind of action by which secreted fluids are ordinarily discharged, the excitement of the termination of the excretory duct. But the series of actions which take place in the female are much more complicated, and are involved in much more obscurity. She has not only to contribute her share of the matter which may serve for the formation of the embryo, but she has likewise to protect and nourish it during the fœtal state, until its own organs have acquired sufficient maturity to support its independent existence. This appears to be the result, in part, of a certain operation which is performed by the vascular system of the mother, and in part by the production of certain membranes which essentially belong to the fœtus, and are attached to the parent during a limited period only, for the purpose of keeping up the communication between them. In order to furnish the rudiments of this temporary apparatus, the
Ovarium. female is provided with an organ called ovarium, from the analogy of the oviparous animals, and by a complicated and hitherto inexplicable connexion between this part and the entrance of the seminal fluid into the uterine system, the first change which occurs in the female is the production of a small glandular body in the ovary, which, after a certain interval, is discharged from its nidus, and is transmitted along the Fallopian tube into the cavity of the uterus. At this period the quantity of blood sent to the uterus is augmented, so that both the embryo and the uterus itself gradually increase in bulk until their final separation takes place. But although we may conceive, that what has now been stated constitutes the essential part of the process, there are many points respecting it which are very obscure. In the first place, it may be assumed, as a necessary part of the operation, that the female must contribute, along with the male, to the ma-

terials of the fœtus, yet we have no knowledge of any secretion which can serve for this purpose, or of any organ by which it is furnished, unless we suppose it to compose a part of the vesicle which produces the connecting membranes. Another question which has been much agitated respects the mode in which the male secretion acts upon the female ovary; is it brought into actual contact with the part, or does it produce some change in the uterus, which is propagated to its appendages, and operates upon them? Many observations, as well as direct experiments, have been performed for the purpose of ascertaining this point; the result of which renders it probable, that the formation of the vesicle does not require the immediate application of the semen. It appears, on the contrary, that the evolution of the vesicle and its transmission into the uterus depend upon a remote action, propagated to the part, which causes the succession of changes to take place in their due order.

There is likewise another important question, re- Descent of specting the formation and subsequent detachment of the vesi-
the vesicle, whether this process, although we may cle.
conceive that it usually depends upon the concourse of the sexes, is essentially connected with it, or whether it may not occasionally take place from other causes. Upon the whole, it appears probable that this is the case, and that, at least, under peculiar circumstances, the vesicle is detached from the ovary without the co-operation of the male, and deposited in the uterus, where it remains, for some time, ready to be impregnated with the seminal secretion. Some physiologists have of late gone so far as to maintain that this is always the case; that the evolution of the vesicle is due to the powers of the female alone; and that the sole effect of the male is to impregnate the ovum already lodged in the uterus. This, it must be acknowledged, presents a much more simple view of the operation; but we conceive that the observations and experiments adduced in its favour scarcely warrant its adoption.

When the vesicle has received its impregnation from Evolution the male, the next operation is to attach itself to the of the fœ-
internal surface of the uterus, by means of vessels pro- tus.
duced for this purpose, which are afterwards prolonged into the umbilical cord, and consist of an arterial and a venous part, connected with the circulating system of the fœtus. To the uterine termination of the cord is attached the placenta, a mass of loose cellular substance, containing a considerable quantity of blood, part of which appears to be more immediately connected with the mother, and part with the fœtus; the object of this structure is to produce the same change in the blood of the fœtus, which, after birth, is effected by the lungs. There is, however, some doubt respecting the mode in which this is accomplished; anatomists have not been able to detect any communication between the maternal and fœtal vessels in the way of direct anastomosis, and it has therefore been conjectured, either that the blood is conveyed from one set of vessels to the other by a system of minute absorbents, or that, without any actual transmission of the fluid, the blood-vessels attached to the mother are brought into contact with those of the fœtus, so that their contents, being separated merely by thin membranes, are enabled to act upon each other, in the same way that the blood in the lungs is affected by the air that is received into the pulmonary vesicles.

It remains that we say a few words respecting the

Physiology.

Hypothesis of seminal animalcules;

degree in which the two sexes contribute to the production of the fœtus. And on this point two very celebrated hypotheses, for a long time, divided the opinions of physiologists, one ascribing the essential part to the male, the other, on the contrary, supposing the greater share to belong the female. The first of these opinions originated with the microscopical discoveries of Leeuwenhoek and his friends, who found the male secretion to contain a number of animalcules; these they conceived to be the rudiments of the fœtus, and that the only office of the female is to afford them a suitable situation, where they might be deposited and brought to maturity. The existence of these animalcules is generally admitted, although many of the accounts that have been published concerning them must be received with some caution, and it is extremely doubtful what connexion they have with the continuance of the species. It has been stated, that similar kinds of bodies may be found in various other fluids; even though it may be admitted that the substance in question is more disposed than many others to give rise to them.

of pre-existing germs;

The second hypothesis to which we have alluded, that of pre-existing germs, was the one that was adopted by Haller and many of his friends, and was at one time very generally embraced. It supposed that the ovary contains, ready formed, the rudiments of the fœtus, and that the only office of the male is to impart life to it, not by the addition of any new matter, but merely by operating as a stimulus, and exciting into action its dormant faculties. It follows, as a necessary consequence from this doctrine, that the original female of every species contained in her ovaries the germs of every one of her descendants, enveloped in each other, by a species of *emboîtement*, as it has been termed! The arguments in favour of this doctrine were derived from experiments, which proved the extreme minuteness of the quantity of male fluid which was sufficient to impregnate the female, and also from some anatomical considerations in regard to the manner in which the fœtus of oviparous animals is attached to the parts composing the contents of the egg. The main bulk of the egg is evidently the produce of the female, and as some of these parts seem to be continuous to the chick, this, it is argued, must likewise be derived from the same source. But, in answer to these arguments, we may reply, that the first is simply a consideration of quantity; that we have no means of ascertaining *a priori*, how much matter is necessary to compose the first rudiments of the fœtus; and that, for any thing we know to the contrary, the smallest particle may be amply sufficient for this purpose. And, with respect to the anatomical argument, we may observe that the parts in question, although they appear continuous, may not have been originally so, but that they are united by close apposition, so as to form one continuous body, as soon as they become visible to the eye, although, in the first instance, they were derived from different sources. We are then reduced to the most obvious and natural hypothesis, that which

of Epigenesis.

was defended by Harvey under the title of Epigenesis, which supposes that the fœtus is produced by the union of a certain quantity of matter derived from both parents. In this way alone can we conceive why the offspring should be equally disposed to partake of the properties of both parents,—a fact established by daily observation, and which it appears impossible to reconcile with the hypothesis of animalcules, or of pre-existing germs.

CHAP. XIII.

OF VISION.

Sensitive functions.

AFTER having considered, in detail, the various functions which depend upon the contractility of the muscular fibre, we must now proceed to those which originate in the sensibility of the nervous system. These may be divided into the two classes of physical and intellectual: The first comprehending those which immediately originate in the operation of some external or physical agent; the second, in the powers of the nervous system re-acting upon each other.

External senses.

The physical functions of the nervous system are what we usually denominate the external senses, which are generally, although not very correctly, classed under five heads. They are distinguished from all other faculties, both by the causes which produce them, and the instruments by which the causes operate; both the cause and the instrument being, in each case, appropriate, and not applicable to any other function. No organ, except the eye, can give us any conception of light, nor except the ear, of sound; the first is produced by an agent of a subtile nature, that acts exclusively on the eye; the second by undulations in the air, the operation of which is equally restricted to the ear. The primary effects which are produced upon these organs have received different names, but, perhaps, the most correct and comprehensive term is perception of impressions, implying both an effect produced by an external agent, and the transmission of the effect to the sensorium. We shall begin by considering the sense of vision, as it constitutes the most numerous and important class of the perceptions of impressions; we are also the best acquainted with the action of the exciting cause, and of the mechanism of the instrument by which it operates.

Vision.

In giving an account of vision, it will not be necessary for us to consider the nature and properties of light, as this subject is amply treated of in other articles. We shall, therefore, begin by describing the structure of the eye, the uses of its different parts, and the manner in which light acts upon it, so as to produce vision; and we shall afterwards enter upon the consideration of what have been termed the acquired perceptions of sight, and the associations which are formed between the sight and the other classes of physical sensations. The eye is an optical instrument,

Description of the eye.

consisting of three orders of parts. The most important is a transparent sphere, or lens, through which the rays of light pass, and are conveyed to a focus, producing an image of the object, similar to that in the camera obscura. The next point is to transmit the impression to the sensorium; for this purpose it falls upon a nervous expansion, termed the retina, which is connected with the optic nerve, and this with the brain. In the third place, there are many auxiliary parts, by which the eye is protected from injury,—is preserved in its proper form,—is furnished with the necessary secretions, and enabled to perform all its various motions.

Humours.

The ball, or globe of the eye, consists of what have been termed the three humours; these are, the crystalline, the aqueous, and the vitreous. The crystalline is a firm, transparent body, having the shape of a double convex lens, which is placed perpendicularly in the eye, behind the pupil. Its average density has been found to be intermediate between that of glass and of

Physiology. water. It appears to be composed principally of albumen; it is softened by maceration in water, and is then divisible into a number of layers. Between the crystalline and the cornea, which constitutes the fore part of the eye, there is a small space which is filled with the aqueous humour, a substance composed almost entirely of water, holding in solution a small quantity of albumen and some salts: this alone, of the different parts of the eye, is properly entitled to the appellation of humour. Behind the crystalline, and occupying the greatest part of the ball or globe, is the vitreous humour,—a transparent substance, nearly of the consistence of the white of the egg, and composed of nearly the same materials.

Formation of the image on the retina. The humours are inclosed in dense membranes, which preserve the eye in a spherical form, the convexity of the fore part of which is such, that parallel rays of light entering it are refracted to a focus exactly at the back part. Kepler demonstrated this to be the case, by removing a portion of the membrane from the back part of the eye, and covering it with oiled silk; we then perceive a small inverted picture of the object towards which the eye is directed. The principal refraction takes place when the rays first enter the cornea; it increases until they arrive at the centre of the crystalline, and afterwards is diminished a little when they pass into the vitreous humour, in proportion to the respective densities of these bodies.

Use of the crystalline. When we consider the situation, the structure, and the appendages of the crystalline, we find that it is the most elaborate part of the eye, and that to which the others seem to be subservient. It was, on this account, supposed by the earlier anatomists to be the immediate seat of vision, until Kepler discovered its refractive power, and showed that it possessed all the physical properties of a lens of the same form and density. Yet we conceive that its use, as forming a part of the eye, is still somewhat obscure. After the lens has been removed, in consequence of disease, if there be no displacement of the other parts, and no circumstance occurs to prevent the healing process, the eye retains the faculty of vision, almost as perfectly as before the loss of the part. Yet it would be quite inconsistent with our notions of the animal economy, to suppose that there should not be some specific use for an organ that holds so conspicuous a situation; and, accordingly, three different purposes have been assigned to it, although, perhaps, rather upon theoretical grounds, than as the result of observation or experiment.

To correct aberration. The first of these uses that has been proposed for the crystalline, is to correct the spherical aberration of the eye. When rays of light pass through a sphere, and form a focus behind it, provided the sphere be of uniform density in all its parts, the focus will be imperfect; but if we suppose the sphere to consist of concentric layers, which gradually increase in density as we approach the centre, this imperfection or aberration in the focus will be corrected, and this structure has been supposed to exist in the crystalline. The same structure has been applied to correct what has been termed the Newtonian aberration, the defect which would ensue from rays passing through a sphere, in consequence of the different refrangibility of the component parts of the entire ray. The different refractive powers of the different layers of the crystalline, it is said, will render the eye an achromatic instrument, and thus prevent the mixture and confusion of colours which would take place without this contrivance. These remarks are founded upon correct mathematical princi-

ples, yet it has been questioned, both on theoretical and on practical grounds, how far they apply to the actual condition of the eye. It has been calculated, that no perceptible degree of aberration could take place in an instrument similar to the eye; and in those persons who have had the crystalline removed, it is stated that the defects from the two kinds of aberration have not been observed.

To adjust the eye to different distances. The third use that has been assigned to the crystalline, is the adaptation of the eye to distinct vision at different distances. In the natural state of the organ, and when its structure is perfect, we know that those rays alone can form an accurate image which enter the cornea in nearly a parallel direction, yet we have the power of seeing objects distinctly which are so near to us, that the rays proceeding from them must enter the eye in a diverging state. If we attend accurately to our sensations when we view near objects, we shall perceive that we exercise a voluntary power, by which the conformation or shape of the eye is altered, and we shall find that a specific effort is necessary for the purpose, and that a certain length of time must elapse before the effect is produced.

Remarks on the adjustment of the eye. The nature of this power, or the means by which the adjustment of the eye is effected, has been a very fertile field for controversy, and is a point which we can scarcely consider as even yet quite decided. Since the time of Porterfield, who made many experiments upon this subject, it is generally agreed that it must depend either upon a change in the general form of the eye, or in the relative position of its parts; and the structure and situation of the crystalline immediately pointed it out as the probable agent by which the effect was produced. Leeuwenhoek, by employing his microscope, thought that he had discovered muscular fibres in the lens, which, by their contraction, would render it more or less convex, and thus contribute to form an accurate image on the retina, whether the rays entered the cornea in a parallel or a divergent direction. Descartes adopted this opinion, and it has been more lately supported by Dr. Young. Porterfield thought there was a muscular ligament attached to the crystalline, which had the power of bringing it forwards, and thus increasing its distance from the retina, when the ray enters the cornea from a very near object; but Haller controverts Porterfield's doctrine, upon the principle that the ligament in question is not muscular, and that its action, if it were so, from the general structure of the eye, would not permit this change in the disposition of the parts to take place. But to all these hypotheses an objection of very great weight has been started, that those persons who have lost the crystalline, still retain the power of altering the focal distance of the eye, an objection which, if it could be maintained, would evidently be decisive against them.

Eye from which the crystalline is removed. In order to ascertain this point, upon which the whole controversy may be said to turn, several experiments were performed with great care upon an individual who had lost the crystalline, in order to ascertain how far he retained the power of adjustment; but easy as it might appear to come to a conclusion on this subject, great difficulties occurred, and nothing decisive was accomplished, Dr. Young conceiving that the trials which were made confirmed his view of the subject; while Sir E. Home adopted a contrary opinion, and supposed that the adjustment was effected by the external muscles of the eye pressing upon the sides of the ball, and thus increasing the distance from the cornea to the retina. But this hypothesis would seem to

Physiology.

Young's experiments.

be disproved by a subsequent experiment of Dr. Young's, in which the eye was immersed in water, through which the sight was directed, when it did not appear that the power of adjustment was, in any degree, impaired by this means ; yet here it is obvious, that no change in the external figure of the cornea could produce any effect, but that the change must consist in an alteration of the relative position of the internal parts of the eye. Upon the whole, therefore, we consider the opinion of Dr. Young as the most probable ; but we do not think that the muscularity of the crystalline has been sufficiently established.

Nerves of the eye.

The next order of parts in the eye are those composed of nervous matter, by which a sensation of the image is produced, is transmitted to the brain, and constitutes a perception. This is accomplished by means of the retina and the optic nerve. The retina is an expansion of nervous matter, which lines the posterior part of the membranes enclosing the humours, and which receives the image formed by the rays that enter the cornea. From the analogy of the nervous system generally, and from the connexion of this part with the optic nerve, it has generally been considered

Seat of vision.

as the immediate seat of vision. This opinion was, however, controverted about a century ago by many physiologists, in consequence of the discovery of Marriotte, that the part of the retina, which lies over the commencement of the optic nerve, is not sensible to light. It was argued, that because in this part, which is insensible, the retina is present, while the choroid is not so, the choroid and not the retina must be the seat of vision ; and, as the sensibility of membrane was a favourite doctrine of the Stahlians, the hypothesis of Mariotte gained many followers. The fact indeed, as discovered by him, is generally admitted ; but the conclusion is so repugnant to the other analogies of the animal economy as to be now universally discarded. The inference which we should draw from it is, that there is a difference in the functions of nervous matter, according as it is in the form of a thin expansion, or a dense cord, the first being adapted for receiving impressions, the latter for transmitting them to the brain.

Iris.

The third order of parts in the eye is very numerous, and contains many curious and elaborate structures. One of the most important of these is the iris, the coloured ring which surrounds the pupil, or aperture through which the rays are admitted into the interior of the eye. The use of the iris is to regulate the quantity of light which enters the pupil. For this purpose it has the power of contracting in a bright light, and thus excluding part of the rays which would otherwise enter the eye ; while, on the contrary, in a feeble light, it expands so as to admit a greater number of rays. Physiologists were, for a long time, unable to decide upon the nature of the mechanism by which this effect is brought about ; but it is now proved that the iris is a muscular part, and that its fibres contract

when they are exposed to the stimulus of light ; this opinion is supported by the fact, that certain individuals have a voluntary power over this organ. Fontana has made an important observation concerning it, that the light does not act directly upon the iris, but upon the retina ; for he found, that when a small beam was made to fall upon a part of the iris, no contraction ensued, but that the effect was produced when it was directed through the pupil, so as to fall upon the retina.

Physiology.

Cause of vision.

After this account of the form and structure of the eye, and the uses of its principal parts, we must inquire into the manner by which the sensation of sight is produced. The image of the object being formed upon the retina, a conception of it is transmitted to the brain, and the object of our investigation will be to ascertain in what manner this is effected, or more generally what change takes place in the nerve and the brain, which immediately precedes mental impressions. Two hypotheses have been advanced on this subject : the first, and the one most generally known, is that of animal spirits ; the other that of vibrations. According to the first, it was supposed that the brain is a species of gland, which secretes a subtile fluid, termed the animal spirits. The nerves were conceived to be tubes, which convey these spirits to all parts of the body, and when an impression is made upon the extremity of a nerve, the animal spirits are so affected as to transmit the impression to the brain. The ancients had an opinion somewhat resembling this. It was very generally adopted at the revival of letters, and still maintains its ground ; yet it appears to be entirely destitute of direct evidence ; it is difficult to form any distinct conception of it, and it does not correspond with the structure of the part concerned, or with the usual analogies of the animal economy.

Animal spirits.

The hypothesis of vibrations, which was much extended and illustrated by Hartley, supposes that when an impression is made upon the extremity of a nerve, a peculiar kind of vibration is excited among the particles of the nervous matter ; this is transmitted to the brain, and these produces a corresponding vibration, which is the immediate cause of perception. This hypothesis is more easy to comprehend than that of the animal spirits, and, in some respects, accords better with the nature of the action that is excited ; but it is, like the other, wholly devoid of direct evidence, and appears inappropriate to the nature of the organ. It accordingly met with but few advocates when it was first proposed, and is now almost totally neglected, so that we are reduced to the necessity of confessing our ignorance of the mode in which sensations are conveyed to the brain, and are there rendered perceptible to the mind *. With respect to the eye in particular, although we are well acquainted with the physical properties of light, and with the manner in which the rays enter the eye, and form a focus upon the retina, yet

Vibrations.

Conclusion.

* There is a recent speculation on the subject of the nerves, to which we think it necessary to advert, both in consequence of the interesting discussion to which it has lately given rise, and also from the curious experiments which have been performed in support of it. We have already given an account of the experiments of Dr. Philip, in which it appeared, that by dividing the nerves which go to the stomach, the secretion of the gastric juice was suspended, consequently the food was prevented from undergoing its proper change. He found, however, that the digestion was restored, by interposing the galvanic apparatus between the stomach and the divided end of the nerve ; and hence he concluded, that galvanism and the nervous influence are identical. Experiments were indeed performed by Mr. Brodie, Mr. Broughton, and others, which were thought to disprove the correctness of Dr. Philip's ; but by repeating the experiments with the proper precautions, it appears that his original statement of the facts is correct. We conceive, however, that there are many points to be settled, and a variety of considerations to be taken into account, before we come to the conclusion, that the nervous power is identical with galvanism. The experiments show, that, in this instance, the electric fluid has the power of acting upon the secretions of the stomach, so that, under certain circumstances, it can produce upon them an effect similar to what, at other times, is brought about by the operation of the nerves. There are likewise a number of examples, which demonstrate that the electric fluid is a very powerful and subtile agent in exciting the action of the nerves ; but we do not think that the facts warrant us in carrying our conclusions beyond this point.

we are quite unable to explain how this picture operates in producing vision, how it acts upon the retina, how the retina communicates with the nerve, and how this affects the brain.

Permanency of the impression. But although we are ignorant of the nature of the process by which sensation is produced, there are some points respecting it which require to be noticed, and which particularly apply to the sense of sight, as we have the specific cause of this sense entirely under our command, and can accurately observe the direct effects produced by it. When an impression has been made upon the extremity of a nerve, the sensation remains for some time after the cause is removed, as is often observed with respect to the eye, where, after the application of a bright light, the impression continues for some time after the light is removed. If a burning body be rapidly whirled round, it will produce the appearance of a complete circle of fire; or if the seven prismatic colours be painted upon a card, and the card be made to spin upon its centre, no individual colour will be seen, but the eye will merely receive the impression of whiteness, arising from the combined impression of the whole. These effects depend upon the principle, that the eye retains the impression of the object, in each particular part of the circle, until it arrives again at the same part, and the different impressions are thus all confounded together.

Ocular spectra. Analogous to these phenomena, although acting in a somewhat different way, are those which have been termed ocular spectra. These appearances were noticed by Buffon, who styled them accidental colours, and they have been since more minutely described by Darwin. If the eye be steadily directed to a bright spot on a dark ground, and then turned aside, an image of the spot will be perceived; but the spot will now appear dark and the ground white, and the reverse will take place if we view a dark spot on a bright ground. This alternation takes place likewise between different colours, as well as between different degrees of light. If we look at a blue object, the eye acquires a yellow spectrum, if at a yellow object, a blue spectrum; green produces a red, and red a green spectrum; in short, every colour has its appropriate spectral colour, which is inseparably connected with it, and is produced, with more or less intensity, according to the brilliancy of the object and the peculiar condition of the vision. It is probable that the harmony of colouring, as it exists in paintings and in the arrangement of furniture and drapery, depends very much upon this affection of the eye, although we are guided in these cases by experience, without any conception of the principle on which it rests. See ACCIDENTAL COLOURS, Vol. I.

Supernatural appearances. There is reason to believe, that the formation of these spectra, aided by mental impressions of various kinds, have frequently given rise to the belief of supernatural appearances. There are certain diseased states of the system generally, and of the nerves in particular, when the retina is peculiarly disposed to retain these images, so that even after the object has been removed for some time, if the light be withdrawn, the spectrum will still be visible. The surprise which such appearances must occasion to those totally ignorant of their nature, the terror which is often associated with darkness, and other concurrent causes, may be conceived to operate powerfully upon weak minds, perhaps farther debilitated by fatigue or disease.

Exhaustion. The cause of this peculiar state of vision is obscure. It has been referred to a property of the nervous system, by which a part is unable to persevere in the same kind of action beyond a limited period, producing, what has been styled, exhaustion. The term exhaustion must be regarded as metaphorical; it was derived from the hypothesis of animal spirits, upon the principle that there is a limited supply of these spirits in the nerve, which, by a too long continuance of the action, becomes expended, and that it is necessary for some time to elapse before the nerve can again acquire the due quantity of this agent to renew its functions. But it is scarcely necessary to observe, that this reasoning presupposes the existence of the animal spirits, an hypothesis, which is itself without foundation.

Pressure on a nerve. If a nerve be confined by a ligature or firmly pressed upon, it loses the power of transmitting impressions, but regains it on removing the pressure, provided the structure of the part be not injured. Now we have no proof of the existence of any substance attached to the nerve, or proceeding from it, which is concerned in the production of sensation, so that we are led to conjecture that some kind of change must take place in the relation of the parts of the nerve to each other; and as it appears to be propagated successively along the nerve, we may farther conjecture, that this change consists in the motion of its particles. So far we may coincide with Hartley, that there is a certain degree of plausibility in the general doctrine of the propagation of impressions by motion, but when he attempts to describe the kind of motion, and to explain how it operates, he goes farther than either the evidence of facts or sound reasoning will authorize.

Sensations of sight from galvanism, &c. We have hitherto spoken of the sensation of sight as produced solely by light falling upon the eye; but although this is the appropriate cause, it appears that the sensation may be occasioned by other causes, as by galvanism and by external pressure. When a weak galvanic discharge is passed through the eye, a flash of light is perceived, and the same effect is produced by a smart blow or by friction. The sensation of light is also excited if the ball of the eye be firmly pressed upon, and it is observed, that the apparent situation of the light is on the side of the eye exactly opposite to that part upon which the pressure is made. It is difficult to conceive how a ray of light, the galvanic influence, and external pressure, can all produce the same effect, but it may be thought to indicate that they all operate by exciting some kind of motion in the nervous matter, although they afford us no indication of its nature.

Insensibility to colour. There is a singular state of vision, in which the eye possesses a perfect sight, so far as respects the form and position of objects, but it has only an imperfect conception of colour. The defect exists in different degrees; but in most cases of this description, the individual can perceive certain colours, but is entirely insensible to others. We have a minute account of this affection given us by Mr. Dalton, as existing in his own person; he informs us, that when he looks at the prismatic spectrum, he can distinguish only three colours, which would seem to be blue, yellow, and purple, while he is incapable of seeing either the green or the red rays. The cause of this defect is not well explained; we are not acquainted with any physical state of the eye which should have this effect upon the rays of light, nor have we any analogies to guide us derived from the other senses.

Short-sightedness. A very common defect of the eye, and one which is easily explained upon optical principles, is the state that is named short-sightedness. Here the refractive power of the eye is greater than ordinary, so that when parallel rays enter the cornea, they converge to a focus

Physiology. before they arrive at the retina. It depends upon the form of the eye being too convex, and is accordingly remedied by the use of a concave lens. We notice this state of the eye principally because it has been thought to throw some light upon the power which this organ possesses of accommodating itself to distinct vision at different distances. Numerous observations prove to us that short-sightedness is more frequently met with among persons of studious habits, or who are accustomed to examine minute objects. Young children appear to be seldom short-sighted, while the defect commences about the period when they first begin to apply themselves to books. It prevails much more among the higher classes, which probably depends in part upon the frequent use of glasses, by which any tendency that the eye might have to assume this form is confirmed, the efforts being thus prevented, which would be otherwise necessary to produce distinct vision. Now it has been supposed that the state of the eye, in these cases, is similar to that which it acquires when we adapt it to near objects, and as in those who are short-sighted, there is an obvious degree of increased convexity in the cornea, it has been concluded that there must be the same convexity in the natural adjustment of the eye. There is some foundation for this reasoning, but it must be remarked, that the experiments of Dr. Young, to which we referred above, are in opposition to this conclusion, and seem to prove that the eye is accommodated to near objects by some change which does not affect its external figure.

Acquired perceptions of sight. We now proceed, in the second place, to consider the acquired perceptions of sight, and the associations which are formed between this sense and the other classes of the perceptions of impressions. One of the first inquiries that presents itself on this subject is the mode by which our visible ideas of distance, magnitude, and position, are obtained. It was formerly supposed that the eye judged of distances by an original law of the constitution, until this opinion was controverted by Berkeley, who demonstrated that our knowledge in this respect is derived solely from experience. This conclusion is sanctioned by many circumstances of daily occurrence, where we fall into the greatest errors, in attempting to form our judgment of distance by the mere action of the eye. Berkeley's doctrine was also remarkably confirmed by the well-known case of Cheselden, where a young man that was born blind, was restored to sight by a surgical operation, when he was of an age to give an account of the impressions made upon him, after he had acquired the new sense. It appears that at first he had no ideas of distance, but that he was obliged to correct the mistakes of his sight by the touch, until he gradually gained more correct notions.

Means by which we judge of distances, Proceeding, therefore, upon the principle, that our perceptions of visible distances are all acquired, we find that there are a number of circumstances, which assist us in forming our judgments, some of them depending upon peculiar sensations in the eye itself, and others upon the appearance of the object. With respect to the peculiar sensation excited in the eye, we have already offered some remarks upon the mode in which the organ accommodates itself to distinct vision at short distances, and in these cases we learn to associate certain distances with the feelings that are excited in the eye by the voluntary efforts that we use for this purpose. When an object is viewed at a moderate distance, but not such as to render it necessary to alter the figure of the lens, the eyes are directed straight forwards, but are turned inwards, so that the centre of each eye, on the optic axis, may point exactly to the object; in this case also a peculiar sensation is excited, connected with the relative direction of the optic axes, which by habit we learn to associate with certain distances. This appears to be the mode which we the most frequently employ in judging of the distances of objects that are within our reach, and, as a proof of this, we find that those individuals who are deprived of the sight of one eye possess this power of judging of distances in an imperfect degree only. The circumstances in the objects themselves, which enable us to judge of their distances, are the apparent size of the object compared with what we know of its real size, the clearness with which it is seen, the vividness of its colour, and the number of objects interposed between it and the eye.

of magnitude, It is generally admitted, that we judge of the magnitude of objects entirely from experience. We learn, from the principles of optics, that the farther an object is removed from the eye, the smaller is the image which it forms upon the retina, and it appears that our judgment is derived entirely from our supposed knowledge of the real size obtained by other means, and not from the size of the image. We are perpetually liable to fall into the greatest errors about the actual magnitude of objects, when we are unacquainted with their distance, so that we are aware that we can only judge of objects that are beyond our reach by experience and association. The art of landscape and architectural painting, and the science of perspective, depend upon this principle, and we immediately refer every object to the size which it is intended to represent, without any regard to the space which it occupies upon the canvas.

of position. The third point which we proposed to investigate is not so easily resolved,—the mode in which we acquire our ideas of the visible position of bodies. When the rays of light form the picture upon the retina, we know, from the laws of optics, that the image must be reversed, and it has been asked, why does the object, which is reversed upon the retina, appear to us in its natural position? If a man were born blind, and were suddenly restored to sight, would he conceive of objects as being inverted or erect? When we speak of two points, as being one above the other, do we employ these terms in consequence of some innate principle, or of something in the structure of the eye, which directly leads us to form the conclusion, or does it depend upon knowledge which is gradually acquired by experience and association? Berkeley supposes that our ideas of visible position, like those of visible distance and magnitude, are acquired perceptions, and that the blind man, referred to above, would have no conception of the relative situation of the two points, until he had learned by means of the touch, or of information derived from other sources, that one of them was more distant than the other from the surface of the earth, and had thus learned to associate visible with tangible position. Porterfield and Reid, on the other hand, maintain that we possess ideas of visible position, independent of experience or of association with the touch, and they lay down certain general principles, which they consider to be laws of the animal economy, or original principles of our nature, by which objects are necessarily seen in certain situations with respect to each other.

Remarks. We are disposed to think that no arguments have

been yet brought forward in this controversy, which are decisive in favour of either opinion. Berkeley's doctrine would appear to be more in conformity with the general principles of vision, but there are certain facts which seem rather incompatible with it. In those persons who have been born blind, and have acquired their sight at a mature age, we have not perceived those erroneous conceptions respecting the position of objects, which might have been expected upon this view of the subject; while the effects of pressure upon the ball of the eyes favour the opinion that there is some natural connexion between the position of objects, and the part of the ball on which the impression is made. We conceive, however, that the greatest part of the difficulty has arisen from some inaccuracy in our mode of considering the subject, in consequence of our not discriminating between the impression made upon the retina and the idea conveyed to the mind. It is true that the image is inverted, but we do not see the image, and we can perceive no reason why the inversion of the picture should convey to the brain the impression of an inverted rather than of an erect object. We apprehend, therefore, that the question which has been so often asked, why do not objects appear to us inverted, might be answered by asking in return, why should we expect this to be the case? The more general question, how do we acquire our ideas of the relative position of objects, as proposed by Berkeley, is of a different aspect, and highly deserving of attention, but we are disposed to regard it as one to which we are at present unable to return a satisfactory answer.

Single vision with two eyes.

A more difficult problem remains to be considered, and one which has long exercised the ingenuity of the metaphysical physiologists, the cause of single vision with two eyes. When we look at an object we direct both the eyes to it, and of course have an image formed on both the retinæ, yet the mind receives only one perception. The question is, whether this depends upon any thing in the organization of the eye, or whether it is merely the result of experience and association? An opinion has indeed been maintained, and not without a degree of plausibility, that although both the eyes are turned to an object, we in fact only employ one of them at once, the attention being directed to each of them alternately. But against this opinion there is an experiment of Jurin, who found, that when the eyes are both directed to the same object, it is seen with considerably more vividness than when viewed with only one eye.

Opinions of Porterfield and Reid.

Porterfield proceeds upon his general principle, that every object is necessarily seen in the place where it actually exists, and as both the eyes see the object in its real place, only one object can be perceived. Reid lays it down as a principle of vision, that where the objects fall on what he terms corresponding points of the retinæ, the eyes can perceive only one object, while Smith, on the contrary, argues that the eyes, each of them receive a distinct impression, capable of exciting a distinct idea, but that by habit, and by comparing visible with tangible sensation, we correct the errors of the sight, and finally learn to associate the double impression with a single object.

Remarks on Porterfield.

Wells's observations on Reid.

The opinion of Porterfield we regard as clearly disproved by the frequent mistakes into which we fall with respect to the position of objects, thus showing that there is not that necessary connexion between their real and their apparent situation which the hypothesis would require. Against Reid's doctrine of corresponding points some direct experiments have been brought

forward by Dr. Wells, which seem to prove its fallacy; and the same ingenious physiologist likewise objects to it, that it is contrary to the analogy of the anatomical structure of the body, that these corresponding points should be both on the right or both on the left side of the retina, because the parts which might be supposed to correspond would be either both without or both within the centres of the eye; and there is an experiment, originally performed by Du Tours, which has been conceived to be decisive against Reid's doctrine. If we look through a tube, at the other end of which are placed two glasses lying over each other, one blue and the other yellow, we perceive a green colour. Now it is argued, that if we apply a tube to each eye, and at the end of one have a blue, and at the end of the other a yellow glass, we ought, as in the other case, to perceive a green colour, as the images are here conceived to fall upon corresponding points of the retinæ, where the sensations will unite as if they had both fallen upon one eye. But we do not find this union to take place; we, in fact, see one colour at once, first the blue, and then the yellow, or *vice versa*; or they sometimes seem to lie one over the other, but they never amalgamate so as to produce the idea of green.

Remarks on Smith.

The objections to Smith's doctrine are perhaps still more decisive. There is said to be no instance on record where a person ever had the power of single vision with two eyes, when the eyes were not similarly directed to the object, so that the images might fall upon points similarly situated with respect to the centres of the retinæ. It is farther stated, that, in Cheselden's case, the patient did not see objects double when he first received his sight; and we generally observe that infants and blind persons move the eyes together, as if from some sympathy or natural connexion between them. The effects of intoxication have been referred to as favouring Smith's opinion, for here the vision frequently becomes double, depending, as it has been supposed, upon the temporary loss of the power of association. But the double vision of intoxication has been accounted for in a different way, not upon the disturbance of the usual train of associations, but upon the eyes not moving parellel to each other, so that the images fall upon points of the retinæ which do not correspond. The same effect is always produced when the eyes are affected by accident or disease, so that they do not move together; whereas, in insanity, where all the ordinary trains of our ideas are destroyed, provided the eyes be not especially affected, we do not find that double vision exists.

General conclusion.

Upon the whole, therefore, we must conclude that the present state of our knowledge does not enable us really to come to any conclusion on this point; there are some circumstances which lead to the opinion, that the eyes do not actually convey two perceptions at the same time, but that they are always in a state of rapid alternation, an opinion to which Haller inclines, yet this hypothesis is not without its difficulties; but there are greater objections against the hypothesis of corresponding points as advanced by Reid, and perhaps still greater against the doctrine of Smith.

CHAP. XIV.

OF HEARING.

Hearing.

THE sense of hearing comes next to that of sight, both as to its real importance, and the elaborate structure of its appropriate organ. We have also a tolerably

Physiology. accurate knowledge of the nature of sound, and of the process by which the ear receives the impression, although less so than we possess concerning the eye, and the action of light upon it ; we have likewise less correct ideas of the acquired perceptions of hearing.

Ear described.
The essential parts of the ear are, a cavity in the temporal bone, the membrana tympani stretched across this cavity, by which it is divided into two parts, called, respectively, the meatus auditorius and the tympanum, a number of small bones or ossicles connected with the tympanum, the auditory nerve, and the Eustachian tube passing from the tympanum to the fauces. On the internal surface of the tympanum, or drum as it is popularly styled, the termination of the nerve is spread out in a manner analogous to the expansion of the optic nerve at the back of the eye ; and this, like the retina, is supposed to constitute the imme-

Nature of sound.
diate seat of the impression. Sound is excited by the vibration or oscillation of the particles of certain bodies, named, from this circumstance, sonorous, and is capable of being transmitted from one body to another until it arrives at the tympanum, and strikes upon the nerve. Sonorous bodies are of various kinds, but the medium by which sound is usually conveyed to the ear is the atmosphere ; liquids and solids are, however, better conductors than the air, both with respect to the strength of the vibration and the velocity with which it is conveyed. When a gun is fired at sea, if we apply the ear to the surface of the water, we receive two successive impressions of sound, the first the one that is carried by the water, the other through the air. The same thing occurs if a sound be produced in the immediate vicinity of long metallic rods or tubes, the sound being conveyed by these bodies more quickly, and with greater intensity, than by the air which is contiguous to them. The different states of the atmosphere affect its power of transmitting sounds ; but we find that all sounds, whether loud or weak, are conveyed by the same medium with the same velocity. The vibration of the air which constitutes sound, travels at the rate of about thirteen miles in a minute, very nearly a mile in five seconds.

Reflection of sound.
.Sound is capable of being reflected from the surface of bodies at a determinate angle, so as to be concentrated into a focus, although in a less precise manner than the rays of light. Upon this principle echoes depend ; and, as modified by the form of the surface, the increase of sound is produced in speaking and hearing trumpets, domes, whispering galleries, &c. The external parts of the ear probably act in the same way by affording an elastic surface on which the undulations of the air impinge, and which, after a number of successive reflections, are collected in the tympanum. We have continual opportunities of observing the use of the external ear among the inferior animals, where this part is large and is furnished with muscles, which give it the power of being readily turned to the sounding body, and thus conveying the impression with more force to the seat of sensation.

Membrana tympani.
The membrana tympani, from its size and position, would appear to be a part of considerable importance in the economy of the ear, yet it must be acknowledged that its use is but very imperfectly known. Boerhaave conceived that we possess the power of contracting and relaxing this part, by means of the ossicles attached to it, according as we are more or less attentive to sounds. This conjecture may be considered as, in some measure, verified by the observations of Sir E.

Home upon the ear of the elephant, where, in conse- Physiology. quence of the size of the parts, he was able to detect a muscular structure so connected with the membrana tympani, that, by the action of the muscle, the membrane would be contracted or relaxed. In consequence of the delicacy of the mechanism, he was led to suppose that this is the part of the organ which is adapted to receive the impression of musical sounds ; but the hypothesis was overthrown by a case which occurred to Sir A. Cooper, in which the membrane of one ear was entirely destroyed and that of the other nearly so, and yet the person retained the complete power of perceiving musical sounds. It may appear not a little remarkable, that we should be ignorant of the uses of that part, both of the eye and the ear, which, from their structure and situation, might be supposed to be among the most important to the respective organs.

Acquired perceptions.
The acquired perceptions of hearing are less numerous than those of sight, and are principally useful as enabling us to supply the deficiencies of the latter. That this is the case will be obvious when we observe what takes place with respect to the blind, who learn to substitute audible for visible impressions in a variety of instances where it would previously have been conceived to be impossible. In this way they not only acquire correct ideas of the position of the bodies which immediately surround them, but they judge of distances which are far beyond their reach, as of the size of rooms and buildings, the vicinity and approach of bodies, and of other circumstances for which we exclusively employ the sight. This they accomplish by the associations which they form with certain undulations of the air that strike upon the nerves of the ear, and their attention being exclusively directed to these impressions, they learn to distinguish them with much more accuracy than the generality of mankind. But we must be aware that a great part of the knowledge which the blind thus acquire depends upon their intercourse with those who can see, as without this they would not be able to form those associations between audible and tangible impressions upon which their knowledge depends.

Position of sounding bodies.
Among the acquired perceptions of hearing, some of the most useful are those by which we judge of the position of sounding bodies—a subject which appears to have been but little attended to until it was examined by Mr. Gough. He observes, that it cannot depend upon the mode in which the vibrations strike the auditory nerve, because, before they reach the internal cavity of the ear, they must have been reflected out of their original direction. He conceives that the bones of the skull, in the neighbourhood of the ear, are capable of receiving the vibrations of sound, and that we judge from the part of the head which is thus affected, and especially upon the comparative effect produced upon the two sides of the head. It is on this account that persons who have lost the use of one ear are less able to judge accurately of the position of sounding bodies ; presenting a kind of analogy to the defect which is produced by the loss of one eye.

Musical tones.
There are two kinds of sounds, those that merely produce a perception of sound generally, and those that produce what are termed musical tones. The difference between simple sounds and musical tones is supposed to depend upon the regularity of the vibrations of the sounding body. When the body is irregular in its texture or its figure, so that its vibrations or oscillations are not isochronous in all its parts, the effect is

Physiology. simply a noise; when, on the contrary, the vibrations all coincide, we have a musical tone. Musical tones are generated by metallic wires, rods, or plates, by membranous cords or expansions, and by air, when confined in tubes—the two former constituting stringed, the latter wind instruments. Sounds of all kinds differ from each other according as they are strong or weak, a difference which probably depends upon the force of the vibrations; but musical sounds have a specific difference, independent of strength, by which they are denominated high or low, acute or grave—a property which is supposed to depend upon the rapidity of the vibrations of the minute particles of the body, those which are the most rapid constituting the high or acute sounds.

Harmony.
The mental feelings that are associated with certain sounds are very powerful, and often appear to depend entirely upon accidental circumstances; but we learn from experience, that there are certain combinations of sounds which are naturally agreeable to the ear, and others, on the contrary, that are naturally harsh and unpleasant. The effect of musical sounds of the same description appears to depend principally upon the number of vibrations which occur in a given time, and the proportion which the vibrations of the different tones bear to each other. The proper combination of these tones constitutes the science of harmony, one of the most curious branches of mechanical philosophy, and which, when united with the different kinds of tones, and their adjustment to each other, combined with certain mental impressions, gives rise to one of the

Musical ear.
most refined and elegant of the polite arts. The power of distinguishing musical tones is a distinct faculty from that by which sound in general is perceived; we frequently observe deaf persons who possess an accurate knowledge of music, and, on the contrary, we find other persons who have a quick perception of sound, but who are entirely destitute of a musical ear. On what this difference depends, or by what part of the ear this faculty is exercised, is a matter of mere conjecture.

CHAPTER XV.

OF TOUCH, TASTE, AND SMELL.

Touch.
THE sense of touch is the most important after those of sight and hearing. The term has been frequently applied indefinitely, to express every sensation of impression which could not be referred either to sight, hearing, smell, or taste. The sensations of touch are, however, strictly speaking, merely those of resistance, excited by a body pressing upon certain portions of the skin. Although every part of the surface seems to possess some degree of touch, yet there are specific organs by which it is exercised with peculiar acuteness and delicacy—such are the points of the fingers in the human subject, and in many animals, the lips and the tip of the tongue. The greater sensibility of the fingers is probably owing principally to the finer texture of the skin, and to the greater quantity of nervous matter distributed to the part; but it must be partly ascribed to our dexterity in recognizing the sensations impressed upon it, which we acquire by habit: for there are examples of individuals born without hands, who acquire a delicacy of feeling in the toes not very much inferior to that of the fingers.

Relations of touch.
Some eminent metaphysicians have advanced the opinion, that the touch is the most certain of all the

Physiology. senses, and that it is essentially useful in correcting the errors of the sight and hearing. This remark is, to a certain extent, true, for the organ of touch is necessarily brought into contact with the body upon which it acts, whereas, in the action of the eye and the ear, the impression is conveyed by a peculiar medium, which may, and frequently does, affect the nature of the original impression. But, although we may allow that the perceptions derived from the touch are more correct, we must admit that they are very limited, and that our knowledge would be confined within a very narrow range were we to acquire no ideas through any other medium.

Case of Mitchell.
An interesting detail has been lately published, of a young man in this country, who appears to have possessed a competent share of intellect, but was born both blind and deaf, the principal part of whose knowledge of the external world has therefore been derived from the sense of touch. It is curious to observe with what patience and perseverance he has laboured to obtain a certain degree of knowledge of the external world, cut off, as he necessarily is, from almost all intercourse with his fellow-creatures; while, at the same time, we must be strongly impressed with the very limited information which, with all his exertions, he has been enabled to acquire.

Acquired perceptions.
We so seldom employ the touch without likewise making use of some of the other senses, that it is difficult to determine what ideas we originally derive from it, and what are its acquired perceptions. Locke appears to be successful in showing that the conception of solidity is altogether gained by the touch, but we think that the ideas of motion and figure originate at least as much from visible as from tangible impressions. The touch has been generally supposed to afford us the ideas of distance and extension; but with respect to these we are much aided by the sight, and also by the peculiar sensations that originate in the motion of the joints—sensations that are essentially different from those that depend upon resistance.

Taste and smell.
The senses of taste and smell are much less important to our existence, and to our intercourse with the external world, than those of sight, hearing, and touch. In the human species they are to be regarded as rather conducive to our gratification than to our utility; but in the lower animals they are of more importance, as being connected with some of the instincts which are directly essential to the existence of the individual, and to the continuance of the species. They are deserving of notice as affording some remarkable instances of the power of association, partly as derived from very early impressions, and partly as acquired by subsequent habits. It appears indeed probable that certain flavours and odours are naturally agreeable to us, but, at the same time, our daily experience proves, that our tastes in this respect are principally acquired.

There are many sensations of impressions, besides those derived from the five senses, which have been either incorrectly arranged with those of touch, or have been altogether overlooked. Of these we may point out three; the sensations which attend the motion of the joints, the sensations of heat and cold, and that of hunger. The least reflection upon our own feelings will convince us, that these are quite different from the impressions of resistance produced upon the ends of the fingers by a hard body. Some metaphysical writers have supposed, that we derive our idea of what is termed the third dimension of bodies, not so much by the

Idea of third dimension.
touch, as from the sensations which we experience by opening the joints of the hand, and that from the same

Physiology. kind of sensations in the joints of the extremities we derive our ideas of distance and extension. We are probably much assisted by the sight on these occasions; but with respect to the blind, there is every reason to suppose that their ideas of tangible distance are principally derived from the associations which they form with particular motions of the joints.

Sensations of heat and cold. The sensations of heat and cold are essentially different from those of touch, as well as from every other class of impressions. It is remarked by Darwin, that the sensations of touch, and those of heat and cold, are possessed in different degrees of acuteness by the same part of the body, and that the parts which are the most sensible to each class of sensations are different. He also relates a case, and other cases of a similar nature are upon record, where the body became insensible to mechanical impulse, but retained its full sensibility to heat and cold.

Their cause. The sensations of heat and cold are caused, ultimately, by the passage of caloric into or out of the body; but the degree of effect does not depend upon the absolute quantity of it, but upon the quantity gained or lost, compared to the previous temperature of the body. The general fact seems to be, that we feel the sensation of heat, when the body is receiving caloric, more rapidly than it did the moment before; and the sensation of cold, on the contrary, when it is losing its heat more rapidly; and that these sensations may take place, even although the body may be, in both instances, absolutely gaining or losing caloric. There are, however, many individual cases in which this rule does not apply, where sensations of heat and cold are quite independent of the actual temperature of surrounding bodies, but depend upon particular conditions of the sanguiferous and nervous systems. Some of these, where they are connected with morbid states of the body, are among the most curious and inexplicable parts of pathology.

Sensation of hunger. The peculiar sensations connected with the stomach, especially that of hunger, is essentially different from that of touch, although frequently confounded with it. Yet every one who reflects upon his own feelings, must be conscious that hunger no more resembles the resistance of a hard body pressing upon the skin, than sight resembles pressure upon the eye-ball. The immediate cause of the sensation of hunger has been much discussed, and there are two opinions that have been very prevalent, one among the mechanical, the other among the chemical pathologists. The former of these sects ascribed it to the friction of the sides of the stomach against each other, an opinion which is disproved by the slightest acquaintance with the anatomy of the organ. The chemical sect accounted for the sensation of hunger to the action of the gastric juice, as they conceived tending to corrode the part by its powerful action upon organized matter. But upon this hypothesis we may observe, that we have no reason to suppose that the erosion of acrid chemical agents is at all similar to that of the gastric juice, or that any degree of actual erosion takes place upon the stomach during the life of this part. Upon the whole, we are to regard the sensation of hunger as a specific effect produced upon the nerves connected with the stomach, the final cause of which is sufficiently obvious, but with the efficient cause of which we are totally unacquainted. We may remark with respect to the stomach, that there is no organ possessed of specific sensations, the feelings of which are more under the influence of habit. This is apparent, both with respect to the time of taking food, and the quantity of it which is required to satisfy the calls of hunger. The accidental associations of the stomach are no less remarkable than those of the palate, so that we often experience the sensation of nausea, where there is nothing in the body in question to produce vomiting, except its possessing a taste or odour, or some other external quality, which resembles a substance that has a directly emetic effect.

Physiology.

CHAP. XVI.

OF ASSOCIATION, HABIT, IMITATION, &c.

Association defined. WE have frequently had occasion to refer to the effects of association, and it will therefore be proper to give some account of its origin and mode of operation. When two impressions of any kind have been made upon the nervous system, and repeated together for a sufficient number of times, if one of them be afterwards excited, the idea of the other necessarily succeeds. Although this principle was not overlooked by the ancients, Locke appears to have been the first who clearly saw the full extent of its operations, and arranged them in a systematic form. A still more minute attention was afterwards paid to it by Hartley, who made it the basis of his system, and extended it to all parts of the animal economy, both physical and intellectual. It is, indeed, generally admitted that he carried his favourite doctrine to an unreasonable length; yet we are disposed to admit that its influence is very extensive, and of almost constant occurrence. Our object, in this place, is to consider association so far only as it relates to physiology; and, proceeding upon this ground, we may point out the following varieties, or modes, in which this principle operates. Perceptions may be associated with other perceptions; they may also be associated with ideas, and ideas may be associated with each other. Perceptions may likewise be associated with mechanical actions, mechanical actions with ideas, and with other mechanical actions; the combination which is the most connected with our subject, is the association of muscular motions, either with each other, or with some affection of the nerves.

Associated muscular motions. With respect to the associated muscular motions, it has been laid down as a general rule by Darwin, " that all animal motions which have occurred at the same time, or in immediate succession, become so connected, that when one is reproduced, the other has a tendency to accompany or succeed it." Many of the ordinary actions of life are composed of a number of individual operations, which, in the first instance, had no necessary connexion with each other; but yet, if the conjunction be sufficiently repeated, an indissoluble association is produced. On this account it becomes extremely difficult to determine, in many cases, whether any particular train of actions is connected together by association, or by some natural law of the constitution. This difficulty may sometimes be removed by ascertaining how these complex actions are acquired. In the case of progressive motion, as in walking, we employ a number of muscles in different parts of the body, which individually serve very different purposes; we alternately contract the muscles of the lower extremities; by an effort of the loins we throw the weight of the body, first to one side, and then to the other, while we move the upper extremities in order to assist in preserving the body in a perpendicular position. The act of walking, which consists of this complicated train of

Act of walking.

actions, we know can only be acquired by long practice; and we may affirm, that a person born without legs, who should afterwards be furnished with them, would be no more able to walk without instruction, than to play upon a musical instrument. Yet these motions become so firmly associated together, that it requires a powerful effort of the will to perform them in a different order; and they proceed with almost as much regularity as the motion of the heart, or any other function over which the will has no control.

Act of swallowing.

There are, on the contrary, some actions strictly voluntary, and which also require the co-operation of many muscles, but which seem to have a necessary connexion with each other. In the act of swallowing, the muscles of the mouth, lips, cheeks, tongue, neck, and gullet, are all concerned, and they act in such a manner, and in such an order with respect to each other, as all to contribute to produce the desired effect in the most appropriate manner. Yet we find that the newly-born infant, immediately after birth, swallows the mother's milk as readily as at any subsequent period: this cannot, therefore, be the effect of association.

Habit.

Another principle of the animal economy, which is nearly allied to association, is habit, which consists in a peculiar state of the system, induced by the frequent repetition of the same act. The force of habit is too well known to be insisted upon, and we have perpetual illustration of the truth of the remark, that habit is a second nature; for there is scarcely any impression, however disagreeable, to which we do not become reconciled by habit. The effects of habit are the most observable in those operations which recur only after certain intervals, such as taking food and going to rest.

Periodical actions.

When the usual period arrives, we experience the accustomed sensations; but, if we powerfully resist the calls of hunger, or the inclination for sleep, the hunger or drowsiness cease, and some time elapses before they are again experienced, thus showing that they do not altogether depend upon the state of the stomach, or the exhaustion of the nervous system. It is difficult to assign a cause for these periodical accessions of habitual feelings, and more especially, why they should observe the diurnal period of twenty-four hours. It would be curious to inquire, whether, by any voluntary effort, we could so far change our modes of life, as to go through the ordinary routine of the diurnal actions in a longer or shorter space of time, for example, in thirty, or eighteen hours. A remarkable effect of habit upon the corporeal organs is to blunt or diminish impressions of all kinds, so that not only do we acquire, in a great measure, an indifference to those that were originally agreeable; but we even become, within certain limits, insensible to pain. There are, on the contrary, trains of actions which were originally almost indifferent, that, by habit, become essential to our enjoyment, and sometimes almost so to the continuance of life.

Imitation.

Another very important principle in the animal economy is the tendency which we have to imitation. Strictly speaking, imitation is rather a complicated series of actions than a principle or faculty, yet it seems to depend upon a peculiar condition of the system, or some of its organs, which is not easily to be referred to any more general principle. The tendency to imitation appears to be natural to the constitution; for, we observe, in children, that one of the first symptoms of intellect which they display, is to imitate the actions of those about them. This has generally been regarded as an ultimate fact, a circumstance which we are unable to explain, although we cannot doubt of its existence. We may go so far in our attempts at accounting for this series of facts as to assume, that when an action has been once performed, the repetition of it becomes more easy, and farther, that it is more easy to imitate an action that passes under our observation than to invent a new one. But although the physical cause of imitation be obscure, the final cause is obvious; it is in this way that we acquire the first rudiments of our knowledge, and profit by the information of those who have preceded us. In this way it is that we learn to form the articulate sounds which constitute speech, which is the basis of all education.

Speech.

Speech is altogether a voluntary act, and affords an example of a process composed of a train of actions, the connexion between which is obscure, although the different steps of the operation are easily explained. The mechanism of speech has been accurately examined and satisfactorily explained by the writers on anatomy; it is sufficient for our purpose to remark, that it depends upon a number of complicated motions of various muscles belonging to the tongue and lips, while the inflections of the voice are produced by another set of muscles connected with the upper part of the larynx.

Imitation of articulate sounds.

The power which we possess of imitating articulate sounds and the inflections of the voice, is so far different from the ordinary kinds of imitation, as the parts concerned are concealed from the eye, so as to render it very difficult for us to conceive how we acquire a knowledge of the muscles necessary to perform the proper actions. We can only judge of them through the medium of the ear, and without knowing in what the actual change consists, yet by an act of volition we produce a certain state of the muscles of the part, which enables us to form the same tone or articulation. It has been conjectured that, by repeated trials, we discover what sensations in the tongue or larynx are accompanied by particular sounds, and whenever we wish to produce these sounds, we excite the same sensations. But even admitting the truth of this hypothesis, it scarcely explains the difficulty.

Sympathy.

Some of the most remarkable actions of the animal body are those which we refer to the effect of sympathy. There is scarcely a motion or affection that takes place in any part which does not give rise to a motion or affection of some other part, in some cases depending, as it appears, upon mere contiguity, at other times being conveyed through the medium of the nerves, and frequently, as far as we can judge, connected merely by association. But there are also cases in which none of these causes can be supposed to operate; where no association can be traced, and where there is nothing in the physical structure of the body which can account for the effect. We may instance as an example the act of sneezing. Here, in order to remove an irritation from the nose, we force a current of air through the nostrils, which is accomplished by the involuntary contraction of the diaphragm. As this act takes place in the newly born child, and is independent of the will, it cannot be referred to association, and we are not acquainted with any circumstance in the structure of the nervous system which can account for this connexion *.

* Considerable light has been thrown upon this and other similar operations by the interesting discoveries of Mr. Charles Bell on the Nervous System. In this particular case the effect may probably be explained by nervous connexion.

But we not only observe the effects of sympathy as operating between different parts of the same individual, but also as affecting different individuals. And this not merely in the intellectual operations, but in the physical actions of the system, for it is well known, that by witnessing pain or suffering in another, the body sometimes actually becomes affected in a similar manner. The tendency to fainting, which is experienced by the sight of blood, or by being present at surgical operations, and still more, those cases in which convulsions are excited by the sight of an individual labouring under such diseases, are to be regarded as examples of this kind of transferred sympathy. To this head likewise must be referred many of the examples of enthusiasm and fanaticism, where violent gestures are propagated through large assemblies of people, in such a manner as to prove that they are, at least in a certain degree, beyond the control of the will.

There is another class of actions, which are of a peculiar nature, and are generally classed together as depending upon the same principle, which are styled instinctive. Instinct may be defined a capacity for performing actions which are voluntary, and immediately conduce to some useful purpose, but which are not acquired by experience, and of the object of which the animal is entirely ignorant. The case of the bird building its nest has been frequently referred to as an example of an instinctive action. The animal, although it may have been taken from its mother immediately after it left the shell, and been since kept confined in a cage, previously to laying its eggs, will prepare its nest with as much skill as if it had lived among other birds, and built a nest for a number of successive seasons ; yet it cannot be directed either by imitation or by reason, nor can we suppose that there is any direct impression made upon any part of the body which can bring about the effect. It would seem that in this case a particular state of the brain exists, which leads to a certain action, similar to what in other cases is induced by imitation, association, or by reason. There are other kinds of instinct, where we can trace the effect produced to a direct impression upon a nerve or organ of sense, such as where the smell prevents an animal from eating food which is not adapted to the state of its digestive organs. Here the impression upon the olfactory nerve is alone sufficient to produce an effect, which in the human species is derived from a more complicated feeling, partly from instruction, partly from association, and in part from reason, combined probably, in some degree, with an immediate effect upon the organs of sense.

The phenomena of instinct appear to be so clearly marked among the inferior animals, that its existence, as applicable to them, has been seldom doubted, and except Darwin, there is perhaps no writer who has attempted to argue directly against it. He proceeds upon the principle, that as instinct is a kind of blind impulse, directly the reverse of reason, it should always proceed in the same uniform track, and he endeavours to show that in those actions, which are generally regarded as instinctive, such as the building of nests, we discover some symptoms of reason, in the adaptation of means to peculiar and extraordinary circumstances. But to this argument it may be replied, that in contending for the operation of instinct we do not propose entirely to exclude that of reason, on the contrary, it is more probable that they both co-operate to the same

end, the one supplying the deficiencies of the other. But there is no ground for concluding that instinct consists in this blind direction to certain objects, it seems rather to prompt the animal to perform the action in the manner the best adapted for the object in view, so far resembling the effect of reason, but differing from reason in the mode in which the impression is received into the mind.

It has been a subject of discussion among metaphysicians, whether man possesses the faculty of instinct, or whether the actions, which at first view resemble instinct, may not with more propriety be referred to other principles. The disciples of Locke are, for the most part, disposed to deny the existence of instinctive actions, and refer to association, habit, sympathy, or to some other principle, the effects which other writers have referred to instinct. Reid, on the contrary, and his followers, suppose that many of our operations are innate or instinctive, depending upon the nature or original laws of our constitution, independent of any circumstances either internal or external. That the latter class of philosophers have unnecessarily multiplied these innate actions, and even, on some occasions, carried them to a ridiculous excess, is generally admitted, but, on the other hand, we conceive that their antagonists have not unfrequently failed in their attempts to explain various operations of the animal economy by their favourite doctrine of association. We are disposed to conclude, with respect to this point, that while brutes are guided principally by instinct, combined with some portion of reason, man, although possessed of an infinitely higher degree of reason, is not without some share of instinct.

Although the imagination is a faculty of a purely intellectual nature, yet its action upon the body and its functions is so remarkable, as to render it necessary for us to notice it in this place. It acts not only upon the nervous system, which might be supposed more adapted for its operations, but likewise upon the circulation, the respiration, and the digestion; in short, it is one of the most powerful agents over the animal economy. The history of medicine abounds with examples of the effect of the imagination, so that it frequently requires the greatest sagacity in the practitioner to distinguish between the physical effects of remedies and their effect upon the imagination. Some of the most remarkable illustrations of the power of the imagination were afforded by the operations of animal magnetism, and more lately by those of the metallic tractors. Indeed, so powerful was the influence of the tractors over the body, and so much beyond any thing that could have been anticipated, that it was a long time before the imposition was detected, not indeed until it had been proved that, by proper management, similar effects might be produced without the aid of these supposed agents. In this point of view, the experiments of Dr. Haygarth are of great value, where he imitated the operation of the tractors, in the removal of severe and obstinate diseases, by applying bits of wood to the patients, while their minds were impressed with the belief that they were to receive some mysterious influence from the application. He found, that in this way obstinate pains of the limbs, that had long resisted all remedies, were suddenly removed, joints that were immoveable were restored to motion, and, in short, it became difficult to say how far its operations might not extend. We can have no doubt, that in this way we are to account for some of the pretended miracles of the ignorant and dark ages; many of the wonderful tales that are on record are actually true, but the inference that was drawn from them is false, and we must ascribe to the imagination of the patients themselves, the effects which they attributed to supernatural agency.

CHAP. XVII.

OF VOLITION, AND THE PASSIONS.

Of volition. WE have frequently had occasion to refer to the operations of the will, and to the connexion which it has with the action of the muscles, upon which is founded the division of muscular motions into the two classes of voluntary and involuntary. It will be necessary for us to make a few observations upon both these points; first upon the mode in which volition produces its effects upon the muscles, and, in the second place, upon the cause of the difference between the voluntary and the involuntary muscles.

Voluntary motion. The act of volition is connected with the brain, while the exercise of it depends upon the co-operation of the nerves and muscles, and no volition can become effective, unless the brain, the nerve, and the muscle, be each of them in a sound state. The nature of the connexion between them is very much concealed from our view, but we know that when the mind forms a volition, we acquire a feeling of power, and that the effect instantly follows without our being at all acquainted with the nature of the process, or with the mode in which the different parts of the operation are connected together. We have sufficient proof that the nerve is the medium through which the impression is transmitted from the brain to the muscle, and indeed we have every reason to suppose, that the great use of the nerves that are sent to the voluntary muscles is to place them under the control of the will. It follows that some change must be induced upon each of these three parts, and that in regular succession; first upon the brain, then upon the nerve, and, lastly, upon the muscle; but we are totally ignorant of the nature of the change that takes place in the two first, as well as of the mode in which they are connected together. *Hartley's hypothesis.* Hartley has indeed attempted to explain this point, by referring the actions of the nervous system to vibrations, but we conceive that his system is without proof, and, even if it were adopted, would throw little light upon the subject. In order that the hypothesis of Hartley be established, it would be necessary to show, that the changes of the nervous system consist in a vibratory motion among its particles. Now we apprehend that no proof of this kind has ever been adduced. We conceive that they do not exhibit any characteristic of this kind of motion, and that there is not a single circumstance which affords any direct evidence of its existence. Nor do we think that any light would be thrown upon the subject by admitting the existence of this motion among the particles of the nervous matter, or that we can have any clear conception of the manner in which this vibratory motion could produce those effects which originate in the action of the brain and nerves, or that it tends to explain the connexion between the material and the intellectual parts of our frame.

Objects of volition. It appears then, that although we are so well acquainted with the phenomena of voluntary motion, we are ignorant of the series of changes by which it is effected. The ultimate objects of voluntary motion are

certain actions of the organs of speech and of the muscles connected with the joints; and we may class them under two divisions, or consider them as existing in two states, which may be termed direct and remote; the first comprising those cases where the will is immediately directed to the contraction of the muscle; the second, where we overlook the action of the muscle, and only regard the effect that is to be produced by it. These two varieties are well illustrated in the learning of any mechanical art; here, in the first instance, we only think of the particular motion of the hands or fingers, whereas afterwards, as these become familiar to us, our attention is directed solely to the effect that is produced by them.

It has been remarked that the idea or consciousness *Power, in* of power always enters into our volitions; and it may *what it* be proper to inquire in what this consists, or how it is *consists.* exercised. The effect to be produced is the contraction of certain muscles, but these are not the objects of the will, because, in most cases, we are entirely unconscious or ignorant of their existence. We know, by previous experience, that certain feelings are associated with certain motions, and we seem to have the capacity of reproducing these feelings at pleasure, so that the idea which we have of power would appear to consist in the recollection of these feelings; beyond this we have no knowledge of the nature of the operation.

The second class of muscular motions are the involuntary, or those which originate in something *Involuntary motions.* which acts upon the muscle independently of the will; to this class belong the contraction of the heart and of the diaphragm, and generally of those muscles which are subservient to the vital functions. The contractions of the muscular expansions are involuntary, as well as of the muscular fibres that are attached to vessels of all descriptions. Although there are some muscular organs that partake of both these kinds of motions, yet, for the most part, each one has its appropriate action, either voluntary or involuntary. It *Difference* hence becomes a question on what this difference de- *between* pends; whether there be any thing in the structure of *voluntary* the muscle itself, or in its connexion with any other *and involuntary* part, which can account for this difference of action. *motion.* Although there is a considerable difficulty in determining this point, as indeed is the case with every thing that respects this department of physiology, it appears probable that the difference depends, in part at least, upon the kind of nerves that are sent to the muscular fibres, and especially, whether the nerves proceed immediately from the brain and spinal marrow, or from some of the ganglia. As a general fact, it may be stated, that the nerves which place a muscle under the control of the will, proceed from the former source, while the mere sensibility of a part is produced by its nervous connexion with the ganglia. The muscles of speech and of locomotion, in a sound state of the body, are completely voluntary; those that belong to the vital functions are involuntary, while the organic functions are immediate between the two in this respect; and it will be found that the origin of their nerves corresponds generally to their degree of voluntary power.

Among the parts of the animal economy which *The passions.* serve as a connecting link between the physical and intellectual functions, we may place the passions. Although, in the first instance, they belong exclusively to the intellectual functions, yet they depend so much upon our corporeal organization, and have so powerful

Physiology. an influence over it, that they become an interesting object of attention to the physiologist. The passions depend for their existence upon the combined operation of impressions made upon the external senses, and the previous state of the nervous system, either as derived from original organization, or from the effect of previous impressions. But in whatever way the passions be themselves excited, it appears to be on the organic functions that they exert their influence. An impression made upon the eye, combined with some previous idea of pain or danger, produces the passion of fear, and the effects of fear manifest themselves upon the action of the heart, causing it to throb violently, or almost to suspend its motion, according to the constitution of the individual, and the degree of effect produced. Nor is it upon the circulation alone that the influence of the passions is experienced; the respiration is no less under their influence, and is affected in an equally evident manner by surprise, while there are other emotions which produce their appropriate operation upon the digestive or secretory organs. It follows, from these considerations, that the passions are, in a great measure, innate, or that different individuals, although placed in the same circumstances, will have different passions excited, or, at least, different degrees of the same passion. But it is not only the organization which influences the passions, the reverse of this operation takes place; the passions have the power of affecting the organization, and, of course, the functions depending upon it. If a violent emotion of any kind produces a temporary derangement of the stomach, it is easy to suppose that a continued action, or frequent recurrence of these feelings, may permanently affect it, producing, in the first instance, a functional, and at length a structural disease of the organ.

Craniology and Cranioscopy. The remarks which have been made above, respecting the connexion between the physical structure and the intellectual functions, lead us to the subjects of craniology and cranioscopy—topics which have of late exercised so much of the ingenuity both of the anatomists and the physiologists. These sciences are founded upon the position, that the character of the individual depends upon the structure of the brain; that this affects its external form; and that this form, and consequently the character, may be detected by an examination of the skull. Many insulated facts had been observed which appeared to countenance this doctrine, but it was not until the publication of Dr. Gall that these speculations assumed a regular form, and were entitled to the rank of a scientific hypothesis. This writer, in conjunction with Dr. Spurzheim, endeavours to prove, that particular faculties of the mind have their seat in particular parts of the brain, and that the individual will be distinguished for certain faculties, according to the proportional size of the appropriate cerebral organ. It is farther maintained, that these organs are seated in the convolutions of the cerebrum; that they impress their form and size on the skull; and may be perceived by an external examination of the head.

Remarks. This subject involves several topics of inquiry, which are, to a certain extent, independent of each other. We must first inquire, whether there actually be this division of the brain into distinct parts, each serving as the seat of an intellectual function; in the second place, whether these organs be situated in the external part of the cerebral mass; and, thirdly, whether they can impress their form upon the skull, so as to admit of being detected by an examination with the hand. The controversy which has been excited on this subject can only be determined by the careful examination of facts, Physiology. and the proper deductions from them. We should observe the effects of partial diseases or injuries of the brain, noticing their connexion or correspondence with the different faculties; and conversely, in those cases where individuals have exhibited very strongly marked characters, either from the undue manifestation of certain faculties, or from their absence, we must endeavour to learn how far the brain and the skull have possessed a figure which would have enabled us to detect them. To a certain extent this has been attempted by Drs. Gall and Spurzheim, and is professedly the basis on which they have built their hypothesis; but we conceive that they have been two little careful in the selection of facts, and too hasty in their generalization of them. At present, therefore, we shall not venture to decide upon the truth of the doctrine, and shall only remark concerning it, that we think there are some strong facts which tend to the conclusion, that the functions of the brain are rather attached to the whole, as one organ, than to each of its individual parts; that it is antecedently more probable that the internal parts of the brain should be the seat of its different functions, provided this division of functions actually exists; and farther, we are disposed to regard the classification and arrangement of faculties, which have been proposed by the advocates of the doctrine, as not those which would follow from a correct knowledge of the human understanding. It will be obvious that some of these objections apply to the doctrine itself, while others are rather to be considered as belonging to the method in which it has been developed by Dr. Gall and his disciples.

The science of physiognomy is nearly allied to that Physiognomy. of cranioscopy, so far as it professes to judge of the internal faculties by external characters; but it employs a different set of parts for this purpose, viz. the form and expression of the face. It must be admitted as a matter of fact, that all persons of any degree of reflection are physiognomists; that they form an opinion of the character of individuals from the inspection of their countenance; and that they do this, as it were, involuntarily, by having acquired an experimental conviction of the truth of their observations. And it is not difficult to account for this correspondence between the character and the expression of the countenance. The muscles of the face are the great instruments for expressing the passions; and when any passion is strongly excited, and frequently repeated, the soft parts acquire a tendency to certain positions, even when the corresponding emotion no longer exists. Nor is it going beyond the limits of probability to assume, that the tendons, and even the hard parts, may have their form permanently altered by the action of the muscles, so as not merely to produce a permanent change in the expression of the features, but even, in some measure, to alter the shape of the face.

CHAP. XVIII.

OF TEMPERAMENTS AND VARIETIES.

BESIDES these differences in the form and structure Temperaments. of the brain and the contiguous parts, there are other original differences, of a more decided and less equivocal nature, in the general organization of the body. When these belong to a certain number of individuals only, they are styled temperaments; but when they ex-

Physiology. ist in large communities, and appear to be attached to peculiar countries or climates, they are termed varieties. The ancients were very attentive to the discrimination of temperaments, and traced out their distinguishing features with considerable acuteness. A large part of the pathology of Hippocrates and of Galen is founded upon the supposed knowledge of temperaments, and of the influence of external agents upon them. As is usually the case on these subjects, we find, in the writings of these authors, a mixture of correct observation with false hypothesis. The four temperaments were formed upon the principle of their being a disproportion between the four constituents of the blood, and they were accordingly named, sanguine, choleric, phlegmatic, and melancholic—names which are still retained, although the hypothesis whence they were derived has been long discarded.

Account of. Various writers among the moderns have formed classifications of temperaments, some professing to proceed entirely upon new observations, while others have taken Hippocrates's arrangement for their basis, only attempting to adapt it to the modern improvements in science. We conceive that there is a real foundation for all the temperaments of Hippocrates, although, as they depend upon such very erroneous opinions, it may appear absurd to retain the old appellations. We should be disposed to substitute for them the following, vascular, tonic, atonic or relaxed, and muscular, corresponding to those above mentioned, and, if we add to these the nervous, after the example of Dr. Gregory, we conceive that we shall possess a classification, in which we may arrange all those individuals who possess any peculiarities that are sufficiently well marked, and are, at the same time, common to any number of individuals. The cause of the different temperaments may be attributed partly to an original difference in the physical structure of the body, and partly to a difference in the powers of contractility and sensibility. Without going into minute detail, we may conceive of the vascular temperament as depending upon the fluids existing in too large a proportion to the solids, while, at the same time, the system possesses a considerable share of both contractility and sensibility. The tonic temperament appears to be the one in which the structure of the body, as well as its appropriate powers, are the most correctly balanced, while in the relaxed or atonic, we have the excess of fluids, as is the case in the vascular, but along with this, a deficiency of both contractility and sensibility. The muscular and the nervous temperaments derive their respective characters from the disproportion between these two powers, the first having an excess of contractility, and the second of sensibility. Few individuals possess these characters in the extreme degree, and in those cases where they have been the most strongly marked by nature, education, peculiar modes of life, and various other causes, have so far modified or counteracted them, as materially to diminish their effect, but still there appear sufficient ground to admit of their existence, as entering into the original elements of our constitution.

Varieties. The classification of mankind into the different varieties, and the description of the circumstances in which they differ from each other, belong rather to the province of natural history or anatomy than to that of physiology; but there are some points connected with the subject which will properly fall under our notice.

And the first, as well as the most interesting inquiry Physiology. which presents itself, respects the common origin of the different varieties; whether, for example, the European and the African proceed from one common stock, or whether they are derived from different parents, each of whom were possessed of the characters of their respective descendants?

The above question is one of very difficult solution, Remarks in which we have little to guide us except doubtful on the ori- analogies, and considerations which apply only in an gin of the indirect way to the subject under consideration. In different varieties. the first place, it may be remarked, that we are not acquainted with any natural causes now in operation, which would appear adequate to effect the change in question. It is also asserted, that from the earliest records of history, the same varieties existed among the individuals of the human species as at the present day *. Nor do we see those gradations which might have been expected to take place, were the varieties the mere result of external causes, which may be supposed to operate upon the human body in all different degrees. There are likewise instances of tribes belonging to different varieties, living in the same country, and even pursuing the same habits and modes of life, yet where they each of them retain their peculiar character, without any approach to the production of an intermediate species.

But although these considerations may weigh in fa- Probably vour of the hypothesis which supposes the human race from one to have proceeded from more than one origin, there are pair. some powerful arguments which induce us to conclude that they are all the descendants of one pair. These arguments principally consist in analogies taken from the inferior animals, where we observe varieties produced, more considerable than those among the human race, yet all derived from a common stock. The different kinds of dogs, which are so familiar to us, differ more from each other than the European does from the African, and they seem equally disposed to be permanent, and to be unaffected by external circumstances, yet naturalists are generally agreed in referring them all to one origin. And although we are disposed, when speaking of the general fact, to remark upon the permanency of the varieties of the human race, and upon the little effect which external circumstances produce upon them, yet this is not absolutely the case. There are some instances, where the changes produced by civilization upon man, are almost as obvious as those of domestication upon brutes, and although it would be very difficult to conceive of the metamorphosis, as occurring in the course of only two or three successive stages, it may be conceived to take place through a sufficient number of gradations.

If we are then to admit of the possibility of this How pro- change, our next inquiry will be into the means by duced? which it is accomplished; and there appear to be two methods in which we may conceive of this effect, although we may doubt whether they be altogether adequate to the object, and whether there may not be some farther principle in operation which is still unknown to us. The two circumstances to which we refer are the effects of what is called domestication, and the tendency which there seems to be to the perpetuating any accidental variety which may occur in the form or organization of the body. It will be unnecessary for us to make any remarks upon the change which is produced by domestication, its power in al-

---

* This fact has been remarkably confirmed by the paintings in the Egyptian tomb, discovered by Belzoni.

Physiology. tering both the form of the body, as well as its functions, being too well known to require illustration. Our object at present will be, to inquire whether we are warranted in extending the analogy to the human species. It is admitted, that we are not able to adduce any facts of so direct and striking a nature, as applicable to man, but still we conceive that here the operation of refinement and a high state of civilization is sufficiently apparent. In those countries where the difference of habits between the higher and lower classes exists in the greatest degree, and where, from moral and political causes, the classes are kept the most distinct, an obvious difference may be observed in the form and organization, although the whole community may have originally belonged to the same variety.

With respect to the other principle to which we referred, there are some individual facts that bear very strongly upon the question, although it perhaps may be doubted whether it be of general operation. The art, which has been carried to so great an extent in this country, of improving the breed of cattle, depends upon the power which we possess of perpetuating in the offspring any peculiarity in the parent. But the most curious facts are those in which a deviation from the ordinary form or organization of an animal, which might appear purely casual, has a tendency to become hereditary. Two series of phenomena of this description have been lately brought under our notice, which may serve to illustrate the point in question; the American family, of which an account has been written by Sir A. Carlisle, several members of which have a supernumerary thumb and toe on each extremity, and the individual who lately exhibited himself in London under the appellation of the Porcupine Man, in consequence of his skin being covered with hard processes, several of whose relations were possessed of this peculiarity.

Which is the original variety?
A curious question will here present itself for our consideration, whether any of the varieties of the human race, as they now exist, is to be regarded as the parent stock whence all the rest are derived, and if so, to which of them we are to give this pre-eminence? In this inquiry there are scarcely any documents derived from history; and any conclusions that we may form from physiological considerations, must be almost entirely conjectural. Upon the whole, it would appear more probable, that the changes induced upon mankind have been in consequence of a progress from a state of barbarism to a state of refinement than the reverse; and here we are led to suppose that variety to be the primary one, which, through all the vicissitudes of human affairs, has remained in the most degraded state, and which, in its structure and functions, differs the most from that variety which has uniformly enjoyed the greatest degree of civilization. Upon this principle, we must regard the African as the type of the original pair, from which have sprung the Malay, the Tartar, the aboriginal American, and lastly, the variety which at present occupies the greatest part of Europe and the western parts of Asia, and which we are entitled to regard as the most perfect form of the human race.

Gradation of animals.
It has been a favourite object with many naturalists, to establish a regular gradation among the different classes of animals, so as to form the whole into one chain, the successive links of which closely resemble each other, and carry us on from the least perfectly organized, to that which is the most so, by almost insensible degrees. By this kind of gradation it has been attempted to connect the human race with some of the simiæ, and so far as the shape of the skull is concerned, we find, that if we place at one end of the series a very perfect European skull, and proceed through the other varieties to the African, and so on to the ourang-outang, there is actually a degree of resemblance between the two latter, with respect to some of the most remarkable features in the form of the bones. Nor is this difference altogether confined to the shape of the skull, although it is the most obviously marked in this part; so that, upon the whole, we may be justified in the assertion, that the African constitutes a less perfect specimen of the human form than the European. How far this inferiority of form may be extended to the intellectual faculties it does not belong to our subject to investigate.

CHAP. XIX.

OF SLEEP, AND DREAMING.

WE have now been considering the functions and powers of the living body as acting according to certain general laws, and proceeding in a regular course without interruption or deviation. But this, we are aware, is by no means the case; we are not only subject to a variety of accidental injuries, constituting disease, but the very nature of the body itself is such as to lead us, by an inevitable progress, through the successive stages of growth, maturity, decline, and decay. But before we enter upon this subject, there is a peculiar kind of interruption to the actions of the system, which we must attend to,—that which constitutes sleep.

In considering the phenomena of sleep, two topics especially present themselves for our consideration; 1st, In what does sleep essentially consist? and, 2d, What physical change takes place in any part of the muscular or nervous system, which ought to be regarded as the efficient cause of sleep? With respect to the first query, if we watch the approach of sleep, and compare this with the state after it is fully formed, we shall find that its most obvious characteristics are the loss or diminution of the power of the will, and the incapacity of receiving impressions from external objects. The functions that serve for the support of life, both physical and intellectual, are many of them continued with full activity; the circulation, the respiration, and the digestion, proceed nearly in their ordinary manner, and our ideas often flow with great rapidity, and are perhaps even more vivid than in our waking hours. But during this time we are insensible to the impression of external objects; and the power of volition is altogether suspended. It is upon the loss of power over the voluntary muscles that the complete relaxation of all the parts of the body depends which occurs in sleep, for every position which we assume during our waking hours, although from habit we are unconscious of it, requires the constant exercise of the will. It is, however, to be remarked, that although we are so nearly insensible to all external impressions in sleep, we retain our sensibility to internal stimuli, as appears both by the continued action of many of our functions, and by the various feelings of pain and uneasiness to which we are subject at this time.

It is upon this combination of circumstances that the curious phenomena of dreaming seem to depend; we are insensible to external objects, while the nervous system retains a considerable degree of activity, and is

Of sleep, and dreaming.

Sleep.

Dreaming

5

Physiology. liable to be affected by various internal feelings. Dreams consist of a succession of ideas, that pass rapidly through the mind, and frequently excite very vivid emotions, but which differs from our train of waking thoughts in being independent of external objects, and, as it appears, not under the control of the will. Hence, in dreams, we have no conception of time and place, we confound past and present events, annihilate distances, and fall into all kinds of inconsistencies and incongruities. In dreams our ideas would appear to follow each other principally in consequence of association, whereas, while we are awake, although our thoughts are much influenced by association, still they are perpetually diverted into new channels by the intervention of external impressions, or by our voluntary control over them. Dreams are, in many cases, influenced by those circumstances which have produced the strongest impression upon us during our waking hours, but we do not find this to be invariably the case ; and it is frequently no easy matter to explain how the first link in the chain of associated ideas has been excited. It probably depends upon some accidental impression made upon the nervous system, at the moment of dropping asleep, by which the previous series of ideas being once broken, the new train acquires complete possession of the mind, to the entire exclusion of the former. It must, however, be remarked, that we are not altogether insensible to external impressions during sleep, and that, on some occasions, our dreams are evidently derived from some sources of this kind.

Nightmare. There is a peculiar form of sleep that is styled incubus or nightmare, where a great degree of pain and uneasiness exists, but where sleep still continues, and this in opposition to our efforts to dispel it. We appear to have a kind of imperfect consciousness of our state, and to be aware that, if we could execute our volition we should remove the uneasiness, yet this we are unable, for some time, to accomplish. The accession of incubus is supposed to be generally attended with some local pain or uneasiness, frequently arising from an affection of the stomach or the organs of respiration ; not unfrequently it is to be regarded as a morbid affection, or at least as a symptom of disease in some of the organic functions.

Sleep-walking. There is another kind of dreaming, which is still more peculiar, where the sleep, so far as respects the effect of external impressions, is unusually profound, but where the voluntary power over the muscles is only partially suspended ; it is styled somnambulism or sleep-walking. Although it requires a great degree of external violence to rouse the individual from sleep, yet he is able to perform many of his ordinary occupations ; he can move about the house, utter sentences, and can even write or play upon an instrument of music. To perform these actions, it is necessary that the organs of sense should be in exercise ; yet it appears that they are almost, if not altogether, insensible to other impressions. Where, for example, a person in this state is engaged in writing, the sight must be directed to the paper and to the writing implements, yet the eye has been found to be insensible to all other surrounding objects. In one respect somnambulism essentially differs from common dreaming, that whereas, in this latter state, the ideas appear to pass from one circumstance to another, in the most unconnected manner ; in the former, they are firmly directed to one object. Although somnambulism, when it exists in a slight degree, seems often to arise from some casual or incidental circumstances, yet, when more confirmed, it

has appeared to originate in, or to be connected with, *Physiology.* a morbid condition of the nervous system, and even to terminate in derangement of the mental faculties.

The second subject which we proposed for inquiry, *Cause of* the efficient cause of sleep, is one which is involved in *sleep.* much obscurity. There are many circumstances which lead us to conclude that sleep is an affection of the nervous system, and that the state of muscular action is only so far affected by sleep, as that we lose our voluntary power over the muscles. A favourite hypothesis with the earlier physiologists was, that sleep depends upon an exhaustion, as it was termed, of the nervous power ; that this power, existing in a limited quantity only, and being expended by the ordinary occupations of life, a certain period of time is required for it to accumulate, in order that it may perform its appropriate functions. There is no doubt a portion of truth in this hypothesis ; but it must be acknowledged, that it is rather a simple expression of a general fact than an explanation of it. It gives us no light respecting the nervous power, or the mode of its production ; it does not inform us whether the state of sleep, in any way, favours this production, or whether it merely prevents its expenditure. Some of the most eminent modern physiologists, as Haller and Hartley, conceive, that the physical cause of sleep consists in an accumulation of blood in the vessels of the brain, thus pressing upon the organ and impeding its functions, an hypothesis which was supposed to be proved by the effect of morbid collections of fluid within the skull in producing a state of lethargy or coma. But, upon this opinion, we may remark, that the state produced by pressure upon the brain, only resembles sleep in the circumstance of the partial or total abolition of the nervous faculties, while it differs from it essentially in many of its other phenomena ; at the same time that it is highly improbable that a daily occurrence, and one of the most salutary operation, should be identical with a morbid affection of a very dangerous nature, and which is generally followed by an irreparable injury to the functions of the part. We may, upon the whole, conclude, that we have no certain knowledge respecting the efficient cause of sleep, and that we are not acquainted with the physical change that takes place in the nervous system.

In a medical and pathological point of view, it often *Sleep, how* becomes a matter of great importance to ascertain *promoted.* what are the circumstances which tend to promote sleep ; and, according to the view of the subject which has been taken above, we may arrange them under two heads ; 1*st,* Those which consist in removing every circumstance which may excite the nervous system into action ; and, 2*d,* Those which render it less sensible to the impression of ordinary stimuli. With respect to the first head, we may remark, that every function requires a certain portion of stimulating power in order to produce its action ; for, without this stimulus, neither sensation nor motion would take place. If we, therefore, carefully abstract all external impressions, and as much as possible prevent the mind from dwelling on its own ideas, sleep generally ensues, unless it be counteracted by some morbid cause. Among the other causes of sleep, those which act by diminishing the sensibility of the nervous system, we may place as the most effectual a moderate degree of fatigue, both mental and corporeal, by which the nervous power is expended, and thus less easily excited. Various narcotic drugs appear to have the power of directly acting

Physiology. upon the nervous system, and diminishing its sensibility; and if it be not carried to too great an extent, the same effect appears to ensue by preventing the blood from experiencing its due change during its passage through the lungs. Hence we may conclude that the most favourable combination of circumstances for the promotion of sleep, are moderate fatigue, absence of pain, light, noise, and other circumstances calculated to produce a strong impression upon the nerves or organs of sense, and, above all, a tranquil state of mind. This last is indeed probably the most important of all the circumstances that have been enumerated, for we find that persons in a rude state of society, and young children, immediately fall asleep when the body is at rest; but that, on the contrary, while the mind continues in agitation, no attention to external circumstances will induce sleep.

CHAP. XX.

OF THE DECAY OF THE SYSTEM.

Decline of the system. ALTHOUGH we have found it difficult to ascertain the efficient cause of sleep, its final cause is obviously to afford rest to the nervous system, by which it may repair the waste that necessarily occurs during our waking hours. This reparation, in the first instance, is applicable to the nervous system only; but it is also experienced in the organic functions, although in a less direct manner. Still, however, under the most favourable circumstances, the process of expenditure is more rapid than that of reparation; and both the structure of the body and its functions begin to exhibit symptoms of that tendency to decay, which forms a necessary part of our constitution. We shall offer a few remarks upon the progress by which the body, after having arrived at its state of maturity, passes through the different stages of decline, until its powers become finally extinguished.

Progress to old age. The progression from youth to maturity, and from maturity to decay, is visible in all the solid parts—as the membranous matter, the bones, and the muscles. In infancy, membrane contains a large proportion of jelly and water, whereas, as age advances, these constituents are much diminished in quantity, so that at length it consists almost entirely of albumen; to which, in some parts, is added a portion of earthy matter. The mechanical properties of membrane experience a corresponding change; at first it is soft and relaxed, it gradually becomes firmer and more elastic, until at length it is so rigid and inflexible as to be no longer adapted for its appropriate functions. From the important part which membrane acts both in the circulation and in locomotion, we may easily conceive how much they must be impaired by any cause which materially changes its structure and composition; and, with respect to the former of these, we may conceive how it must affect every part of the system, by altering the distribution of the blood, or the quantity which is sent to the different parts of the body. An important alteration is likewise induced upon the bones; they contain a larger proportion of the phosphate of lime, by which they appear to be rendered harder and more brittle; but, what is more important with respect to the animal economy in general, some parts which are tendinous or cartilaginous in infancy become osseous as age advances; and, in this way, many of our motions become less free, and some parts connected with the

vital functions, as the valves of the heart, and even the Physiology. arteries themselves, acquire a texture which renders them no longer adapted for the purposes of the circulation. Nor is the mechanical structure of the brain and nerves exempt from its appropriate changes. Their substance becomes firmer, it contains a less proportion of fluid, and has less blood sent to it. And we observe that a corresponding change takes place in the functions of the nervous system. In infancy it appears merely adapted to receive external impressions, conveyed to it either from the organs of sense or from the action of some of the organic functions; and some time elapses before the intellectual powers are able to unfold themselves. In youth they acquire the state of greatest activity, while, as age advances, although the understanding is improved by the knowlege which it has been gradually acquiring through life, still the functions of the brain and nerves are exercised with more difficulty, and at length become entirely dormant.

Progress to decay. Every one must be aware that the successive stages of growth, maturity, and decline, are necessarily connected with our constitution; and it would appear that the most active agent in bringing about the successive steps of this process is the circulation. Some ingenious speculations on this subject were formed by Cullen; he supposes that in youth the arteries are in a state of plethora, and are endued with a capacity for powerful action. Hence the growth of the body is rapid, the secretory vessels furnishing a copious supply of materials; this enables the digestive agents to elaborate a large quantity of blood, which, being sent to the muscles and nerves, enables them to exert their powers with unusual energy. But after some time this operation tends to counteract itself; the vessels become extended to the utmost limit which they are able to sustain, while the quantity of matter added to them renders them less moveable, and, consequently, less capable of propelling their contents. In the most perfect state of the human body, when it has completed its growth, and when all its functions are in their most vigorous state, the force of the arteries may be conceived to be precisely balanced by the resistance which the vessels oppose to it; but this balance is soon destroyed by the increasing strength of the arteries, so that the plethoric state which they formerly experienced becomes transferred to the veins, in consequence of their being more distensible than the arteries, and being less liable to have their texture affected, as less under the immediate influence of the active operations of the system. This state of venous plethora seems to be proved by many observations that have been made on the state of the body in old age, and explains very satisfactorily many facts in pathology. The consequences that must ensue from this diminished activity of the arterial system are apparent in every part of the system. When the blood is sent with less force and in less quantity to any part, the deficiency is first experienced in the capillaries; and, as these are the most active organs of the circulation, a diminution of their number, or in their capacity, must directly impair the functions of every part of the system, and induce a state of diminished activity of both the corporeal and mental powers.

Conclusion. There is another circumstance which indirectly tends to hasten the decay of the system, the want of a due correspondence between the different functions, and especially between those of assimilation and absorption. In the perfect state of the system, these functions always maintain their due relation to each other, and,

Physiology. while the absorbents are employed in removing the old materials, the secreting arteries furnish a due supply of fresh matter. But as life advances, this balance of action is destroyed, and, although the more usual effect is a deficient action of the secretory vessels, yet, either irregularity disturbs the general order of the functions and accelerates the progress towards decline, or even induces premature dissolution. Thus, even under the most favourable circumstances, and where every cause of injury is the most carefully excluded, the animal body is, after a certain period, doomed to destruction; its powers cease to act; its fabric is destroyed, and the matter of which it is composed enters into new combinations.

INDEX.

PIANO-FORTE.

601

Piano-Forte.

PIANO-FORTE, a musical instrument of the keyed kind. The name is composed of two Italian words, signifying *soft*, and *strong* or *loud*, intimating its distinguishing property from the harpsichord and spinet, which from this superiority it has now entirely superseded. It is an instrument strung with wires, which are struck with hammers through the medium of finger-keys.

History.

Stringed instruments, played with finger-keys, were invented, it would seem, for the purpose of adapting to the harp or cymbal the key-board of the organ.

Virginal.

One of the earliest of these inventions was the *Virginal*. In this the strings were struck with hammers, which were simply a piece of strong wire, with a leather head screwed into the farther end of the finger-key. But as this simple hammer, even with the most dextrous and staccata touch, did not instantly quit the string, it had the effect of deadening, in a great measure, the tone of the instrument. On that invention

Harpsichord.

the *harpsichord* was an improvement, the strings being struck by a quill fixed on a jack, which rested on the farther end of the finger-key. The quill by the stroke was forced past the string, its own elasticity giving way, and remained above it so long as the finger was pressed on the key, giving the string liberty to sound. In returning, by a very ingenious but simple piece of mechanism, the quill opposed extremely little resistance; and a little bit of cloth fixed on the top of the jack, rested on the string, and served as a damper. Still it was impossible to get quit entirely of a scratching noise, occasioned by the quill passing the string in returning, which was a material defect in the quality of the instrument.

Piano-forte invented by Schroëter.

The piano-forte, in which the strings are struck by hammers, of such a construction as to produce a quality of tone superior to that of the harpsichord, and instantly to quit the string entirely, leaving it free to vibrate, was the invention of Christopher Gottlieb Schroëter, a native of Hohenstein, on the frontiers of Bohemia. This ingenious man was born in 1699, and having received a good musical education under Schmitt, chapel-master at Dresden, obtained without solicitation the place of organist in the principal church of Minden in 1726, and of Nordhausen in 1732, where he remained till his death in 1782. So early as 1717, he had made a model of his invention, which he exhibited at court in 1721. He published a detailed description of his new invented instrument, " on which the performer may play *piano*, or *forte*, at pleasure," with plates, in 1763.

The merit of this instrument was not immediately acknowledged, at least by the musical public in general. The ingenious inventor reaped no personal advantage from it, nor was it in his own country that it first came into vogue. The elder Broadwood, at that time a manufacturer of harpsichords in London, by executing the mechanism in a superior style, and by producing instruments of a better tone than had formerly been made, first put the superiority of the piano-forte over the harpsichord beyond question; and though some maintained the orthodoxy of the latter, the innovation gradually forced its way in this country, and it had in a great measure taken possession of the public taste here, while the generality of musicians on the Continent still clung to the harpsichord. In the course of years, however, the piano-forte made its way every where, and is now universally established.

Great improvements.

Ever since the piano-forte came into general use, the ingenuity of rival makers has been exerted to improve the instrument in power and quality of tone, and in the delicacy and effectiveness of the touch. New inventions are bringing forward up to the present hour, insomuch that when one compares what was reckoned a capital instrument a dozen or twenty years ago, with one of the same class now-a-days, the difference is very striking, after making every allowance for the wearing out of the instrument. These improvements have been effected chiefly by enlarging the instrument in general, by extending the scale, and increasing the weight of the strings, by correspondently strengthening the frame-work, and by improving the mechanism of the *movement*.

Three kinds of piano-fortes made at present.

Piano-fortes are at present of three kinds, 1st, small or square; 2d, grand; these two may be conceived as representing the spinet and harpsichord of former times; and, 3d, the cabinet piano-forte, a medium between the two first. The square and cabinet piano-fortes have two strings in unison, and the grand piano-forte has three unisons to each finger-key. One end of the string is hung on a fixt pin, and the other is wound round a tuning pin, which turns in a wooden block. The length of the sounding part of the string is determined by two bridges, over which it passes, one on the block in which the tuning pins are inserted, and the other is placed on the *sound-board*. This last bridge is now divided into two, one for the steel-strings, that is, from the top of the scale down to A on the first space of the bass, and the other for the brass strings. The reason of this division is, that the steel strings require a greater degree of tension than the brass, and the division of the bridge favours both the tone and the keeping in tune.

Extent of the scale.

The original scale of the piano-forte was from FF (octave below that immediately under the staff of the bass) up to f in *alt.* comprising five octaves; and this has been gradually extended. The first addition was of half an octave upwards to c in altissimo. Then the scale was carried down to CCC; that is, half an octave lower than FF. And latterly, extra additional keys in the treble have carried it up to f in altissimo, comprehending six octaves and a half. These gradual extensions have improved the tone of the instrument both in quantity and quality, though the extra notes below are generally in themselves so indistinct, as to deserve the name of noise rather than that of musical notes.

Sizes of wire employed.

While these extensions of the scale have been taking place, the weight of the strings has been continually increasing. The sizes at present made are as follows: From pitch C to the top, steel wire No. 10; from pitch C to middle C (the octave below) No. 11; and from middle C down to D 3d line of the bass No. 12. and thence to A♯ No. 13. A is a brass string, No. 12.; and the sizes increase very fast in going downwards. The largest size in the grand piano-forte is No. 17. Formerly the smallest steel strings were small No. 9. and the largest No. 11.; the largest brass was No. 14. about half the present sizes. In the square and cabinet piano-fortes a sufficient length of string cannot be obtained. Strings *covered* with small brass or copper wire are used, in order to obtain the depth of tone from about half an octave above FF down to the bottom of the scale; and, in the grand piano-forte, from FF downward. The quality of these covered strings has been greatly improved by making the covering wire smaller, but laid close together like that of the bass string of the violin.

Great strain on the instrument.

Few people are aware of the immense strain which the framing of the piano-forte has to sustain. In

VOL. XVI. PART II.

4 Q

Piano-forte.

order to be able to speak with some precision on this subject, the writer of this article made, or rather witnessed, the following experiment: A wire of the size of that used for pitch C, was hung at one end on a pin fixed in a board, and laid over two moveable bridges, which were placed so as to make the sounding part of the string the same length with that in the instrument. Weights were then appended, till the string became unison with the tuning fork: the weight required was found to be 50lb. The same experiment being made with middle C, the weight was found to be 57lb. and with A♯ the weight was 81lb. The brass strings were found to require a weight of 40lb. Now, taking the average of these four 57, as the average of the whole, which cannot be very wide of the truth, the strain on a grand piano-forte with 3 unisons and 78 finger-keys, is 13,338 lb. that is, nearly six tons.

Framing.

To sustain so great a strain, the small piano-forte is built of a strong square frame, with a very thick bottom upwards of three inches of white Swedish pine. The grand and cabinet piano-fortes, instead of a solid bottom, are built with a frame-work of strong beams, four inches in depth by two in breadth, running the length way of the instrument, and tied with cross beams at several distances in the length to prevent them bending. This framing lies immediately below the sound-board.

Mr. Stodart's metal tubes to resist the strain.

Notwithstanding every precaution, so great is the strain, and so much are the wood framing and strings affected by the changes of the weather in opposite directions, that the grand piano-forte especially stands very ill in tune. In order to remedy this defect, chiefly in instruments sent abroad, Mr. Stodart, of London, conceived the idea of substituting metal tubes instead of the wood framing, which, he imagined, being similarly affected by changes of temperature with the strings, would tend to keep the instrument better in time; and he found that he had not only obtained his end, but a very great unlooked for improvement in the power and quality of the instrument. In order to adapt his tubes more nicely to the end, he makes them of iron over the steel strings, and of brass over the brass strings. They are placed over the strings instead of below the sound-board, in order to allow the vibrations of the latter to act on a greater body of air below it. But in whatever way the effect is produced, it is unquestionable that he has obtained a very superior tone, both in point of quality and quantity. The lowest notes in the extra finger-keys below, instead of a chaos of sound, are as clear and distinct as any part of the scale; and in a concert room, the instrument *tells* in a style to which the piano-forte formerly had no pretensions. At the same time the advantage in point of keeping in tune is very remarkable.

Sound-board.

The sound-board is a part of the instrument on which the quality of tone in a great degree depends. It is generally made of Swiss fir, which at one time was believed to be the only wood fit for the purpose. While the British ports were shut, however, during the revolutionary war, necessity obliged the makers to try the substitution of other kinds, and the American white pine was found frequently to give as good a tone. The sound-board is about one-fifth of an inch in thickness, and in the square piano-forte occupies about two-fifths of the length of the instrument. In the grand and cabinet net it occupies the whole area; but part of it is deafened by bars of wood glued on the underside.

Movement of the hammers.

The quality of tone depends also on the rapidity

with which the hammer strikes the string. The mechanism of Schroëter's hammers was simple. The hammer consisted of a lever, of about 3½ inches in length, moving on a pivot with a leather head. The lever rested near the pivot, on a pin with a leather head screwed into the farther end of the finger key; and the pin was of such a length, that, when the key was slowly pressed down, the face of the hammer came within about a quarter of an inch of the string; but when the key was struck smartly, the hammer, by the rapid motion communicated, was thrown up to give the string a blow, and, instantly recoiling, fell on the leather head of the pin, and left the string free to vibrate. And this form of the mechanism continued for a long while after the piano-forte was in general use. It has subsequently become more complex, for the purpose of attaining more rapidity and smartness in the blow; and this for the sake of enabling the performer to produce greater contrast of loudness and softness, and greater delicacy in the shades, on which the expression of the instrument chiefly depends. The mechanism consists of an additional lever, placed under that of the proper hammer; the object of which is to apply the moving power as near as possible to the pivot of the hammer, which, it is evident, increases the rapidity of the blow. The end of the under lever rests on a little piece of mechanism, fixed in the finger-key, called a *grasshopper,* not unlike, in its object and contrivance, to that of the jack of the harpsichord. When the key is struck, the upper end of the grasshopper, which is about ⅛th of an inch in thickness only, is carried past the end of the under lever, which rested on it, but communicates its impulse in passing, and receives the end of the lever on a little block of wood, glued on about a quarter of an inch below. In returning, the grasshopper, which is kept in its upright position by a slight spring of brass wire, yields, and passes the end of the lever again to its original position.

There is a nicety in the structure of the head of the hammer of great importance to the quality of the tone; and many experiments have been made, and are, we believe, daily making, to attain improvement. The head is made of many folds of leather glued over each other. The best outside cover is found to be doe-skin; and there is even a nicety in the degree with which this is stretched.

In the grand piano-forte the whole key-board is moveable towards the left hand; and, by means of a pedal, the performer has it in his power to make the hammer, which, without the use of the pedal, strikes all the three unisons, at pleasure strike two or only one of them. The cabinet piano-forte has a similar pedal, affecting its two unisons. This is an additional source of variety and expression.

To each string there is a *damper,* which is a bit of cloth glued on a little block of wood, and rests on the unisons; a bit of wire attached to the block passes down, and nearly touches the farther end of the finger-key. When the key is pressed, it raises the damper, and so long as the key is held down, the string has freedom to speak; when the finger is released, the damper falls down and silences the string. A pedal raises all the dampers at once, and allows, at the performer's pleasure, the sound of the strings to continue after the fingers are removed.

Among the many improvements offered to the public, Clementi and Co. have lately brought forward one which they call the harmonic swell, and which promises to furnish still additional variety of effect and expres-

Piano-forte.

Original movement.

Grasshopper movement.

Hammers.

Pedal.

Dampers.

Pedal to raise the dampers.

Clementi's harmonic swell.

sion. In the usual construction of the instrument there is between the bridges on the sound board, and the pins on which the strings are hung, a considerable space; and it is usual to pass a narrow piece of cloth alternately over and under this portion of the strings, behind the bridges, to prevent any sound being propagated among them. Clementi and Co. have placed an additional bridge on the sound-board between the others and the pins on which the strings are hung, which they call the bridge of reverberation. A general damper lies on all these back strings, which, at the pleasure of the performer, is raised by means of an additional pedal. This new bridge is in a curve somewhat similar to that of the proper bridge; but there does not seem to be any principle observed in proportioning the new reverberating string to the length of the proper string to which it belongs.

Mott's sostenente.

Messrs. Mott of Pall-Mall have added to the grand piano-forte what they call a *sostenente*, which holds the note while the finger is kept on the key. It resembles the celestina stop long ago applied to the harpsichord; but the effect is produced, not by drawing a skein of silk over the strings, as in that invention, but on a different and very curious principle. A strong silk thread is stretched across the strings of the grand piano-forte, and to each finger-key there is a strong silk thread, to which is attached a skein of silk; which skein passes over a cylinder of about two inches diameter, and is ultimately attached by three threads to the cross thread above mentioned. When the finger-key is pressed, it stretches the skein over the cylinder, and brings the cross thread to press on the string. At the same time the cylinder is turning on its axis, and being touched with the dust of fiddle rosin, communicates vibration to the string. The patentees say that the sostenente requires no separate tuning. But when the piano-forte is tuned to twelve equal semi-tones, the thirds are so harsh that they would find it a real improvement to tune the instrument more on the organ principle, that is, to flatten the fifths so as to make the thirds better.

Tuning.

For the temperament or tuning of the piano-forte, see Music, Art. 267.

PICTS. See Britain.

PIEDMONT. See Italy, Vol. XII. p. 361.

PIETRA MALA, a small town of Tuscany, twenty-four miles north by west of Florence, remarkable for having a mountain in its neighbourhood which discharges streams of bright flame, which rise to the height of several feet. The cause of the flame is hydrogen gas in a state of combustion.

PILE Engine. See Mechanics, Vol. XIII. p. 615, 616.

PILLAU, a small sea-port town of eastern Prussia, situated on a tongue of land which projects into the Baltic at the entrance of the Frische Haff. The streets are broad and straight, and the houses are in the Dutch style. It is defended by a regular pentagonal fortress with bastions. The harbour, which is the port of Olburg and Konigsburg, from which it is thirty miles distant, has only thirteen feet of water, but several hundred vessels arrive annually. In 1817, 1096 vessels sailed from the port, of which 309 were Prussian, 269 Flemish, 444 English, and 101 Swedish. There is a good sturgeon fishery here. Population of the town about 3000.

PINDAR, one of the most celebrated lyric poets of ancient Greece, was born at Cynoscephalæ near Thebes, and flourished about the year 480 before Christ, and is said to have died in the public theatre at the advanced age of eighty-six, in the year 535. In the early part of his life he was instructed in the kindred studies of music and poetry, and was taught the composition of verses by Myrtis and Corinna. He was afterwards patronized by Theron of Agrigentum and Hiero of Syracuse, and had every sort of honour paid to his talents, both during his life and after his death. Few of his works have escaped the ravages of time. His book of odes in praise of the victories at the Olympic, Pythean, Nemean, and Isthmian games is alone extant; and these are distinguished by boldness and force, and by a great wildness and irregularity of character, so as to characterize a particular species of poetry known by the name of Pindaric.

The best editions of Pindar are those of Heyne, 4to. printed at Gottingen in 1773; of Glasgow, 12mo. 1774; and of Schmidius, 4to. Wittsberg, 1616.

PIN Manufacture. The manufacture of pins has been long carried on with great success in England, and so great is the consumption of this small article, that several tons of pins are made annually by some of the principal manufactures.

The brass wire of which pins are made, is first drawn to the proper thickness, and after being straightened it is cut into different lengths, each of which is sufficient for making several pins. The ends of these lengths are then well pointed on small grinding-stones, and the length of a pin is cut off from each end, and the process repeated till the length of wire is exhausted. In order to make the head, a piece of metallic wire is spun on another, so as to form a hollow spiral when taken off. This spiral wire is then cut by shears into smaller parts of two coils each, which is sufficient for making the head. In putting on the head, the workman thrusts the blunt end of the pin among the heads, and then immediately placing it under a heavy weight or pressure, the head is made secure by a blow, and the pin completed in its form. It is then whitened, by putting it in a copper colouring tin and the lees of wine. Twenty workmen are said to be employed on each pin, from the drawing of the wire to the arrangement of the pins on the paper.

Great improvements have recently been made in heading pins, as the excellency of the article depends chiefly upon the nicety with which this is effected. The old method has received great improvements; but these, we have no doubt, will be superseded by the machine lately invented by Mr. Church, for raising a head upon the wire itself, so that the whole pin consists of one piece of brass. The pins made in the usual manner are put into a sort of hopper, which permits only one to escape at a time. The pin is seized as it escapes, and has a head raised upon it by the machine, and this head is perfected by another operation.

We have now before us some of the pins manufactured by Mr. Church's machine, which are remarkably beautiful, and must give great satisfaction to those who use them. We expect to be able to give a drawing and description of Mr. Church's machine in the Supplement to this work.

PINE Apple and Pinery. See Horticulture, Vol. XI. p. 234.

PIPES, on the motion of water in. See Hydrodynamics, Vol. XI. p. 509.

PISA, a city of Italy, in the grand dutchy of Tuscany, is situated in a fertile plain, on the river Arno, about five miles from the sea. This river flows through the town, dividing it into two nearly equal parts that are connected by three bridges, one of which is of white marble. The town is between six and seven miles in circumference, and is surrounded with a wall and ditch, and fortified with a castle and modern citadel. But, like many of the cities of Italy, the population bears no proportion to the space within the walls, so that it has a solitary and deserted appearance. The number of inhabitants, which, at one period, amounted to 140,000, does not now exceed 17,000. The streets are broad and well paved; the houses are in general lofty, and, though they are chiefly ancient, appear remarkably fair and new. The principal street is the Lungarns, which extends along both sides of the Arno from one extremity of the town to the other, and is composed of elegant houses and several noble palaces; some of which were built by Michael Angelo. The public buildings are on a magnificent scale, and many of them built entirely of marble. The ducal palace and the exchange are both splendid edifices: several of the churches are elegant and enriched with fine paintings. But the great boast of Pisa is the cathedral, with its baptistery, belfry, and campo santo, forming, perhaps, the finest group of buildings to be found in Italy. These edifices are all detached, and occupy a considerable space; they are all of the same era, viz. the 12th century; all built of the same marble; and varieties of the same architecture, being that called, by the Italians, Gotico Moresco. The plan and elevation of the cathedral are basilical; the roof is supported by noble pillars of oriental granite. The interior is adorned with statues and fine paintings; and the doors, which are of bronze, are much admired for their rich sculpture. The baptistery is a large rotunda, finely carved, and embellished with columns and arcades. The campo santo, or burial ground, is an oblong enclosure, surrounded with corridors filled with various Grecian and Roman sarcophagi, basso relievos, busts, &c. many of which are of great beauty. The belfry, or celebrated leaning tower of Pisa, is of a cylindrical form, and consists of eight circles of columns, all supporting arches, which are smaller and more numerous as you ascend. It is about 180 feet in height, and is extremely graceful in its proportions; but it is chiefly remarkable for an inclination of more than fourteen feet from the perpendicular. It has occasioned much discussion whether this striking phenomenon has been owing to accident or design. The most probable account seems to be, that the foundation ground gave way before the edifice was finished, and that the architect completed his work in the direction thus accidentally given to it. The university of Pisa was one of the first established in Italy, and long maintained a high reputation; but after the subjugation of Pisa to Florence it gradually declined, and, though partially restored by Lorenzo de Medici, it has never recovered its former fame. It consists of three colleges, and possesses an extensive library, a botanical garden, a cabinet of natural history, and an observatory. It is resorted to by the greatest part of the Tuscan youth. There is also a public hospital, which is calculated for the reception of 300 patients. The trade of Pisa is very limited, and there are but few manufactures. The climate is extremely mild and bland, and attracts great numbers of invalids; winter is the finest season, and is fully as mild as spring. The town is supplied with water by a long aqueduct, which is carried as far as Leghorn, and consists of 1,000 arches. The hot baths of Pisa were formerly more frequented than at present: they are about four miles from the city, and occupy 100 houses, situated at the foot of a calcareous mountain.

Pisa, according to Strabo, was founded by a colony of Arcadians from the Grecian town of that name in the Peloponnesus, and Virgil assigns to it the same origin,

> " Alpheæ ab origine Pisæ,
> Urbs Etrusca solo."

In the year of Rome 572 it was colonized by the Romans, and at a later period it became a municipal town. On the decline of the Roman empire Pisa shared in the common sufferings; after being long subject to foreign or domestic tyrants, it, in the 10th century, asserted its liberty and assumed a republican form of government. During the following century it attained the highest pitch of power and opulence, and even rivalled Venice and Genoa in commercial greatness. Together with these states it furnished transports to the armies of the crusaders, and contracted with them for military stores and provisions, by which means it acquired immense sums; while, at the same time, it obtained a large share of the commerce which had been engrossed by Constantinople and the other ports in the east of the Mediterranean. About this period Pisa subdued Carthage and took the king prisoner, Corsica and Sardinia were subject to it, and its fleets rode triumphant on the Mediterranean. This state of prosperity continued till the end of the 13th century, when it received a fatal blow from the victories of the Genoese. The usurpations of domestic tyrants next broke the spirit of its citizens, and paved the way for its subjugation to Florence; which took place in 1406; and since that time it has been gradually on the decline. Pisa is the see of an archbishop. North lat. 43° 43' 11"; east long. 10° 24'.

PISE', the name of a method of building used in some parts of France, with stiff, earthy materials of a loamy quality.

PITCAIRN ISLAND is the name of an island in the South Pacific Ocean without a river or harbour. It was discovered in 1808 by an American vessel which touched at it, and has recently become very interesting as the site of a colony founded by the mutineers of the Bounty. The history of the mutiny, and of Admiral Bligh's second expedition, communicated to us by Admiral Bligh himself, has already been given in our article BREAD-FRUIT TREE, Vol. IV. p. 445. A very curious account of the colony will be found in the *Quarterly Review*, vol. xiii. The island was visited in 1819 by Captain Henry King of the Elizabeth, who has given a very interesting account of it in the *Edin. Phil. Jour.* vol. iii. p. 380. West long. 133° 20' 45" and South lat. 25° 22'.

PITT, WILLIAM, Earl of Chatham, the second son of Robert Pitt, Esq. of Boconnock, in the county of Cornwall, was born on the 15th of November, 1708. The family was originally of Blandford in Dorsetshire; Christopher Pitt, the translator of Vida and Virgil, and Thomas Pitt, governor of Madras in the reign of Queen Anne, were both of this place. The latter was Chatham's grandfather; and likewise remarkable as having purchased, during his residence in the east, the jewel known by the name of the *Pitt diamond*, which weighed 127 carats, and was afterwards sold by him to the King of France for £135,000, having originally cost £20,400. It may also be worthy of mention, that, by the wife of this gentleman, Chatham was descended from the Regent Murray, natural son of James V. of Scotland.

Of Chatham's youth and early habits little is recorded, except that he studied at Eton as a foundation-scholar, was removed to Trinity College, Oxford, in 1726, and left the University without taking any degree. His proficiency in the attainments usually acquired there may, however, be inferred from the circumstance, that some Latin verses of his were judged fit to appear in the collection printed by that learned body on the death of George I.; and still more, certainly, from the predilection for classical pursuits which he displayed in after life, and the decidedly classical tincture which pervades all his compositions. Demosthenes is said to have been so great a favourite with him, that he repeatedly translated certain of his orations into English.

The immediate cause of his removal from Oxford was a hereditary gout, which had already attacked him at Eton in his sixteenth year. He sought to expel the disorder by travelling; he made the tour of France, and visited Italy, but without realizing his purpose; his gout still adhered to him, it preyed upon his constitution throughout life, and never left him till it gained the mastery. To an ordinary mind this malady would have proved a severe misfortune: Pitt found means to convert it into almost an advantage. Excluded by it from the gaieties and dissipations of common life, he applied himself the more earnestly to the acquisition of knowledge; he read, and wrote, and studied, endeavouring by every method in his power to cultivate those faculties, which were one day to become the ornament of his age and nation.

In the mean time, however, his immediate prospects were by no means magnificent. He had lost his father in 1727; a scanty fortune and a sickly frame made him anxious for some fixed appointment, and he was glad to accept a commission of cornet in the Blues, which some of his friends had interest enough to procure for him. But his inclinations pointed to a different scene. The leisure which his duties left him was still sedulously consecrated to the improvement of his mind; and he longed to employ in public life those talents he had been so careful to perfect. In 1735, this opportunity was granted him; he was that year returned member for Old Sarum, to serve in the ninth parliament of Great Britain. The appearance he made there was such as to justify all his hopes, and to awaken hopes still more glorious. His eloquence soon became the pride of his friends and the terror of all that opposed him. A fine voice and figure prepossessed the hearers in his favour; and the sentiments and opinions which he uttered bespoke a great and noble mind. There was in him a stern inexpiable contempt for meanness in whatever shape; a fervid enthusiasm for the cause of freedom, for the honour of his country, for all good and worthy things; the whole tempered and matured by a strong commanding intellect, the force and justness of which might have seemed scarcely compatible with so much youthful ardour. His acquired advantages gave full scope to those gifts of nature. The style he employed was chaste, regular, and argumentative, yet both splendid and impassioned; and the energetic graces of his delivery gave new power to what he spoke. When warmed with his subject, when pouring forth his own glowing feelings and emphatic convictions, in language as glowing and emphatic, the attitude of conscious strength which he assumed, his lofty looks, his indignant glance, would dismay the stoutest and most subtle of his opponents; and the veterans of parliament have stood abashed in the presence of a youth. Sir Robert Wal-

pole, in his pride of place, with all the dexterity of ministerial management which a life had been spent in acquiring, was awed before this champion of simple virtue. Detected in his sophistries, stigmatized for his corruptions, baffled in his attempts at retaliation or defence, this intriguing statesman came at length to dread, as the signal of defeat, the very sound of his adversary's voice. "Let us before all things," said he, "try to muzzle this terrible cornet of horse."

But the enterprize was ineffectual, the cornet was not to be "muzzled;" and if Sir Robert still believed in his favourite maxim, *that every man has his price*, it must have mortified him to discover that the price of Pitt was not within the compass of his gift. Unable to gain over, he took the imperfect satisfaction of alienating still farther. Pitt was deprived of his commission in the army; and this stroke of official severity, while it confirmed him in his opposition, rendered him still dearer to the public, whose rights he was asserting. It strengthened him also in the favour of Frederick Prince of Wales, the centre at that period of all who aimed at a change of men and measures. Pitt was appointed groom of the bed-chamber to the prince, in the year 1737. He continued in the successive sessions of parliament, to support the same liberal principles which he had at first adopted; the increase of years increasing his experience in the principles of policy and government, without seeming to abate the ardour of his zeal. He distinguished himself by his animated hostility to the *Spanish convention*, in 1738 *; and generally by his aversion to every measure that appeared likely to injure the rights of the subject, or the lasting interests of the country. His speeches contributed not a little to the downfall of Sir Robert Walpole. One of his most brilliant displays is preserved in the reported debate on a motion for an inquiry into the last ten years of that statesman's administration. The motion, though carried in the House of Commons, was defeated of its object by a ministerial manœuvre; but it sealed the ruin of the Walpole party, and yet affords a striking indication of the powers of this young, and ardent, and enlightened politician.

The Pelhams, who succeeded Walpole, wishing to secure the co-operation of Pitt, attempted to get him brought into office; but a formidable obstacle stood in the way. The king was offended at Pitt for joining with the heir apparent to oppose the favourite minister and his Hanoverian politics; he refused to consent to his admission. The Pelhams resigned in consequence; but were shortly after reinstated, and brought Pitt along with them, as vice-treasurer of Ireland, in 1746. This post was soon converted into that of treasurer, and then exchanged for the place of privy counsellor, and paymaster-general of the forces. His conduct in this latter situation served to display the disinterested integrity of his nature; he disdained to retain any portion of the public money in his hands to profit by its interest, or by speculating with it in the funds, though his predecessors had acted thus without scruple; he even refused the usual perquisites of his office, when they seemed unmerited by the duties of it. Such a manner of proceeding seemed to exemplify in practice the high principles which he had professed as an orator; it sanctioned and augmented the favour, in which he had long stood over all the empire. With the king it was less successful: George II. still viewed Pitt with a jealous eye, and Pitt was still inflexible in maintaining

---

* It was in the course of this debate that he pronounced his spirited reply to Horatio Walpole's sneers against his youth and declamatory manner. Translated into the language of Dr. Johnson, this piece is familiar to every reader.

what he thought the true advantage of Britain, against all the frowns of royalty and the intrigues of court. In the beginning of the seven years war, when his majesty returned from the Continent, and presented the subsidiary treaties he had made with Hesse Cassel and Prussia, for the defence of his beloved Hanover, Pitt did not hesitate to speak in parliament against their ratification. He was, in consequence, dismissed from office; and Mr. Legge, who had partaken in his fault, partook also in his punishment. This was in 1755.

Pitt was now again a private man, but surrounded with a blaze of reputation, which few ministers would not have envied. The long and brave struggle he had made in defence of their privileges endeared him to the people; his virtue, proved alike in place and out of it, gave a new and more steady lustre to the splendour which his high talents shed around him. In 1744, the Dutchess of Marlborough had left him a legacy of £10,000, "upon account," as her testament expressed it, "of his merit in the noble defence he has made for the support of the laws of England, and to prevent the ruin of his country." Eleven years had now elapsed since the date of this splendid testimonial; nine of which had been spent in office, amid temptations such as have ruined the fame of many a patriot, yet still his popularity had continued to augment; and his late disfavour at court, by investing him with something of the grace of a martyr, had raised it to a higher pitch than ever. Men called him the *Great Commoner*: he was listened to by the nation as its guardian and father.

Happy in these circumstances of his public situation, Pitt was also happy in his domestic circle. In 1754 he had married Hester, only daughter of Richard Grenville, Esq. and of the Countess of Temple—a lady whose accomplishments, and graces, and affection, formed a permanent solace to him throughout the remainder of his life. In a short time, also, he had reason to applaud the wisdom of his own anticipations, and to pity the incapacity of the actual ministers. He spoke loudly against the policy of sending English money to defend Hanover by subsidies; he reprobated the idea of introducing Hanoverian soldiers to defend England. The course of events strongly seconded his reasoning: the beginning of the seven years war was marked to Britain by nothing but disasters; the nation murmured, addresses and petitions called vehemently for a change, and the universal voice named Pitt as the man. His majesty was again obliged to treat with this discarded servant: a new ministry was formed in 1756, in which Pitt took the post of secretary of state, his friend Mr. Legge being chancellor of the exchequer. His majesty's repugnance and difficulties are strongly marked by the fact, that having a second time dismissed Pitt, for his inflexible opposition to the Duke of Cumberland as general of the German war, he was again forced by the public opinion to recall him, with the most ample concessions. Pitt resumed his place of secretary on the 29th of June, 1757, and formed a cabinet according to his own choice. His personal influence, of course, was the predominating; he was unfettered by conflicting colleagues; even the king's prepossessions began to abate. Pitt, in their preliminary interview, had said to him, "Sire, give me your confidence, and I will deserve it." His majesty had answered, "Deserve it, and you shall have it;" there was at least, henceforth, no visible discordance between them.

It was now that the genius of Pitt shone forth with unclouded splendour in the eyes of all Europe. Unconstrained in his movements, the vigour of his own mind seemed to pervade every department of the public service; its influence was soon felt in the remotest corners of the globe. He found the nation depressed and degraded; in three years, he raised it to a height of greatness which it had never before attained. Devoting himself wholly to the duties of his office, entirely avoiding the pageantry of levees and public exhibitions, he bent himself with all his might to mature the plans he had formed for the national advantage, and to discover fit instruments for realizing them. The extent of his information, the quickness of his understanding, enabled him at once to discover where the enemy was most assailable; his projects, magnificent as the mind that conceived them, were examined and provided for with the most scrupulous accuracy, and put in execution with an energy that insured success. The people were averse to any interference in the continental war: Pitt objected less to the fact of interference, than to the actual manner of it. Dismissing the Duke of Cumberland from the command of the army, to which the convention at Kloster-sieben had shown too well that he was unequal, he assisted Frederick of Prussia by subsidies, and gave the English troops to be led by Ferdinand of Brunswick. Some outcry was raised against him at first; it was thought he should have shaken off the interest of Hanover entirely; but he underwent these censures, persevered in his measures, and "conquered America in Germany," as he predicted. The French being occupied in these continental expeditions, and Frederick assisted by British gold to make head against them, their colonies and distant possessions were left ill guarded, and fell an easy prey to the vigorous attacks of the English. Before 1760 they had lost nearly all their foreign settlements; they were banished from Africa and Asia, and the Canadas had yielded to the heroism of Wolfe: the navy of France had scarcely an existence; her own coasts were continually insulted, and her people kept in constant terror of invasion. The talents and diligence of Pitt, the skill with which he administered the resources of Britain had raised her to be the arbitress of Europe.

But all his triumphs abroad were insufficient to secure him against the vicissitudes of faction at home. In 1760 the king died, and the dependents of his successor George III. began to look with eagerness for a change. It is hinted also, that Pitt was not too agreeable to some of his colleagues. The great and uniform success of all his enterprises had exalted his reputation to a height, which it was painful for a competitor to contemplate; and his habit of seeing every obstacle give way to the commanding effort of his will, had strengthened in him that rigidness of manner, that imposing inflexibility of purpose, which his friends might dignify as the natural expression of a lofty and self-dependent mind, but which his enemies did not fail to brand with the name of arrogance, or domineering ambition. The court sought a cause of quarrel with him; and one was not long in occurring. By the accuracy of his intelligence, he had discovered the existence of that *family-compact* between the French and Spanish branches of the house of Bourbon, the secret influence of which had rendered abortive some recent attempts at making peace. With his characteristic decision, Pitt immediately moved for a declaration of war against Spain, and a vigorous attack on her foreign possessions: he judged it better to surprize the enemy than be surprized by him; and the treachery of Spain seemed to authorize the omission of preliminary complaints and negociations. The rest of the cabinet thought otherwise; the question was debated keenly, Pitt's opinion was overruled, and hints were given that his concurrence was no longer indispensable. The popularity of a young king, and the national desire for peace, warranted them in such proceedings ; but it was against the minister's principle to incur responsibility where he had not the management : he resigned his office in October, 1761. The applauses of all good men accompanied him in his retreat ; he had the character of the most able and virtuous of statesmen. His private fortune was likewise increased by an annuity of £3000, conferred on him at his resignation, to last during his life, and that of his lady. The total inattention he had always manifested to his individual interests, while managing the concerns of the public, rendered this annuity a necessary gift. His lady was farther honoured with the rank of the peerage, conferred on her by the title of Baroness of Chatham.

Again reduced to a private station, Pitt attended chiefly to his duties in parliament ; and, without uniting himself to any party in the state, he kept a watchful eye over the public conduct of ministers, delivering his sentiments in the same fearless spirit, which had hitherto distinguished all his public exhibitions. When the peace of Paris, which his own exertions had done so much to bring about, was to be concluded in 1762, he expressed himself warmly against the terms of it,—against the smallness of the benefit likely to result to England from the commanding attitude she had maintained throughout the latter years of the war. On the question of *General Warrants*, arising from the case of Wilkes, in 1764, he delivered an animated speech against the legality of such exertions of official prerogative,—reminding his hearers " that an Englishman's house was his castle, defended not indeed by battlements and bulwarks, but by the impassable though unseen barrier of law : it might be a straw-built shed, into which every wind of heaven might enter ; but the king could not, the king dared not." That his popularity remained undiminished was evinced by a fact striking enough in itself, and more so as it regarded him. Sir William Pynsent of Burton-Pynsent, in the county of Somerset, passed over his own family, in order to bequeath an estate of £3000 a-year to this distinguished patriot. Already had the commencement of his political life been dignified by a similar tribute of approbation : it must have been doubly gratifying to find the same testimony still more unequivocally renewed, when the busiest and most dangerous part of it was past.

Pitt was again to be a minister, but never so happy a one as he had been already. In 1766, the necessities of the government once more called him to a share in it ; the formation of a new cabinet was entrusted to him, but the undertaking did not prosper in his hands. His brother-in-law and old associate Lord Temple, his friend the Marquis of Rockingham, could not enter into his views, or act along with him ; and the *Great Commoner* had offended many of his favourers by accepting of a peerage. He was made Earl of Chatham, and Baron of Burton-Pynsent, prior to his entrance upon office. Of his ministry Mr. Burke has left us a curious and often-quoted description. The members of it were the most heterogeneous and discordant ; the results they produced betrayed the feebleness of their union. Chatham resigned in two years,—disgusted with the untowardness of his coadjutors, and tired of useless exertions to bend their clashing principles to a conformity with his own.

This was the last time he appeared in office : his strength and health were exhausted ; years and exces-

sive labour had increased the violence of his constitutional disorder ; he wanted retirement and repose. His peerage had shut against him the habitual scene of his parliamentary exertions ; he was not a constant attendant in the house of Lords : but when some great question called him forth from his retreat, the fire of his genius still shone with unabated brilliancy. The chief theme of his oratory, from this period, was the quarrel with the American colonies, the interests and claims of which now began to occupy the principal share of the public attention. Chatham resisted the imposition of taxes on them ; he warmly seconded the repeal of the *stamp act.* But when war had been undertaken, above all when France had taken part in it, he was resolute for continuing in arms at whatever risk. The memorable scene in which he displayed his anxiety on this head is well known. On the 7th of April, 1778, the Duke of Richmond having moved an address to the king, in which the necessity of admitting the indedendence of America was broadly insinuated, Chatham deprecated such a consummation in the strongest terms. " I rejoice," said he, " that the grave has not closed upon me, that I am still alive to lift up my voice against the dismemberment of this ancient and noble monarchy. Pressed down as I am by the load of infirmity, I am little able to assist my country in this most perilous conjuncture ; but, my lords, while I have sense and memory, I never will consent to tarnish the lustre of this nation by an ignominious surrender of its rights and fairest possessions. Shall a people, so lately the terror of the world, now fall prostrate before the house of Bourbon ? It is impossible ! In God's name, if it is absolutely necessary to declare either for peace or war, and if peace cannot be preserved with honour, why is not war commenced without hesitation ? I am not, I confess, well informed of the resources of this kingdom, but I trust it has still sufficient to maintain its just rights, though I know them not. Any state, my lords, is better than despair. Let us at least make one effort ; and if we must fall, let us fall like men." The duke replied, and Chatham made an eager effort to rise that he might speak farther—but in vain—his voice was never more to be heard in that senate which it had so often dignified and delighted ; he staggered, laid his hand upon his bosom, fainted, and was caught in the arms of the lords who sat near him and sprang to his assistance. They carried him into an adjoining room, and the house immediately adjourned. Medical assistance being procured, he was conveyed to his villa at Hayes, in Kent ; where he lingered only till the following 11th of May, and then died, in the seventieth year of his age.

The circumstances of his death combined with the general character of his life to render that event peculiarly impressive. News of it being conveyed to London by express, Colonel Barré reported the intelligence to parliament, where it suspended all other business. The sense which the public entertained of their loss was manifested by the honours done to his memory. Party differences seemed to be forgot ; all joined in voting that his debts should be paid by the nation, and that a yearly sum of £4000 should be permanently added from the civil list to the title he had borne. He was buried in Westminster Abbey with all the pomp of a public funeral ; and a piece of sculpture was afterwards erected by way of monument, representing the last scene of his parliamentary life, and inscribed as the tribute of the King and Parliament to the Earl of Chatham.

The chief lineaments of Chatham's character may be

gathered from the most meagre chronicle of his actions. That he was a man of a splendid and impetuous genius —adapted for the duties of an orator by the vehemence of his feelings, and the rich gifts of his intellect; for the duties of a statesman, by his vastness of conception, his unwearied assiduity in ordering, his inflexible energy in execution—the highest and the humblest qualities that should combine to form a public man— may be learned from contemplating any portion of his public life. A survey of the whole will better show in how extraordinary a degree he possessed these requisites, and how richly he adorned them all by a truly noble style of sentiment, a rigid adherence to the great principles of honour and generosity, and every manly virtue. And as his mind was singularly elevated, so has his fortune been singularly good. Few men that have acted so conspicuous a part, have united so great a plurality of suffrages in their favour. The reason is, that he founded no sect, was the father of no party, but of the party that love their country and labour for it; and having thus been a genuine *catholic* in politics, his merits are admitted by all. Accordingly, the clamours that assailed him in life, the voice of obloquy and opposition, the memory of his failings have long since died quite away; and Chatham is one, in praise of whom the bitterest of partymen forget their bitterness. He stands in the annals of Europe, " an illustrious and venerable name," admired by countrymen and strangers, by all to whom loftiness of moral principle and greatness of talent are objects of regard.

" His private life," says Lord Chesterfield, " was stained by no vice, nor sullied by any meanness. All his sentiments were liberal and elevated. His ruling passion was an unbounded ambition, which, when supported by great abilities, and crowned by great success, makes what the world calls a great man. He was haughty, imperious, impatient of contradiction, and overbearing; qualities which too often accompany, but always clog, great ones. He had manners and address; but one might discover through them too great a consciousness of his own superior talents. He was a most agreeable and lively companion in social life, and had such a versatility of wit, that he could adapt it to all sorts of conversation. He had a most happy turn to poetry, but seldom indulged, and seldom avowed it. His eloquence was of every kind, and he excelled in the argumentative as well as the declamatory way. But his invectives were terrible, and uttered with such energy of diction, and such dignity of action and countenance, that he intimidated those who were most willing and best able to encounter him. Their arms fell out of their hands, and they struck under the ascendant which his genius gained over theirs."

If Chatham's faculties had not been more worthily employed, we might have regretted that he left so few memorials of them in a literary shape. Many of his speeches, under all the deformities of incorrect reporting, are full of beauty; and a volume of " Letters" to his nephew, published some years ago, may be read with a pleasure independent of their author. See *Life of Chatham*, in 3 vols. and the public histories of the time.

PITT, WILLIAM, second son of the last mentioned Earl of Chatham, was born on the 28th of May, 1759. The early promise of his childhood was not unmarked by his father, and no means were left unemployed to realize it. Influenced partly by the delicate health of the boy, and still more by his own sense of a parent's

duty, Lord Chatham had his son educated at home under his own immediate inspection. A tutor was engaged to instruct him in the elements of school learning; and the great statesman himself devoted a portion of his leisure to form the principles and direct the understanding of his child. His manner of conducting this employment was suitable to the feeling which had prompted him to undertake it. He studied to sink the character of father in that of friend: he encouraged William and his other children to converse with him freely upon every topic; each day he made a point of delivering to them some instruction or advice; and every evening he closed this paternal exercise by reading, in their presence, a chapter of the Bible. It is also mentioned, that William being intended for a public speaker, one of his customary tasks was to declaim on some given topic in the presence of his father; a practice to which he doubtless in some degree owed the remarkable fluency and correctness of diction, which afterwards characterized his speeches in parliament.

Under such tuition, the young man made a rapid proficiency: at the early age of fourteen, he was found advanced enough for attending the university, and was entered accordingly at Pembroke-hall college, Cambridge, in 1773. His progress here was equally rapid; he enjoyed some peculiar advantages, and profited well by them. To the valuable gifts of nature, a quick apprehension and a retentive memory, he added the no less valuable habit of steadfast and zealous application; and, by his father's request, each of the two college tutors devoted an hour every day to his improvement. One of these tutors was Dr. Prettyman, now Dr. Tomline, bishop of Winchester. His connexion with Mr. Pitt began here; it gradually ripened into a closer attachment, and continued unbroken till death divided it. This circumstance speaks favourably for the feelings of Mr. Pitt; except in acts of mutual kindness, there could be little sympathy between them. The learned prelate is now writing a life of his illustrious pupil, three volumes of which have already been published.

Mr. Pitt was too young to acquire much distinction by his academical exercises, among competitors grown up to manhood. But his residence at Cambridge was marked by qualities much more valuable than such distinctions imply. His diligence and regularity continued unabated; he was gradually enriching his mind with the treasures of learning, and forming his conduct on the principles of virtue and sobriety. Indulging in few relaxations, and no excess, he pursued his studies with such intensity, that his naturally feeble health was frequently in danger; and the chief care of his affectionate parent was not to excite his ardour, but to restrain it. " All you want at present," he writes to him on one occasion, " is quiet; with this, if your ardour αριστευειν can be kept in till you are stronger, you will make noise enough. How happy the task, my noble amiable boy, to caution you *only against pursuing too much* all those liberal and praiseworthy things, to which less happy natures are to be perpetually spurred and driven! I will not teaze you with too long a letter in favour of *inaction* and a competent *stupidity*, your best tutors and companions at present. You have time to spare; consider there is but the Encyclopædia, and when you have mastered all that, what will remain? You will want, like Alexander, another world to conquer."

This excellent father he lost in 1778; a circumstance which, to a less sound and steady mind, might have

3

proved of fatal consequence. But Mr. Pitt, in his nineteenth year, was equal to the guidance of himself; his plan of life had already been chalked out for him; and he possessed the qualifications necessary for pursuing it with success. Intended for the bar and the senate, he busied himself unweariedly in preparing for the duties of both. After quitting the university, and spending a winter at Rheims in France, having completed his terms at Lincoln's Inn, he was made a counsellor in 1780, whenever he became of age. In the ensuing western circuit, he followed the court, and appeared in several minor causes with great approbation. But brighter prospects opened to him elsewhere; he never made another journey of this kind. The parliament being dissolved in the autumn of the same year, he started as a candidate for the university of Cambridge. Here, indeed, he was unsuccessful; the interest of his competitors appeared so decidedly superior, that he withdrew without coming to a poll; but a few months afterwards, the interest of Sir James Lowther procured him a seat for the borough of Appleby, and he took his place accordingly, in January, 1781.

In this scene of his father's early triumphs, Mr. Pitt was destined to secure as brilliant triumphs at an age still earlier. He had not yet completed his twenty-second year; and, in a few weeks, his talents had forced their way into notice, in spite of all the claims of the many distinguished orators who at that time swayed the House of Commons. His first speech was during the debate on Mr. Burke's bill for an economical reform in the civil list. He is said to have been in some degree surprized into speaking; but the appearance he made indicated no such want of preparation. Mr. Byng, the member for Middlesex, knowing the sentiments of Mr. Pitt to be decidedly in favour of the bill, had requested him to reply to Lord Nugent, at that moment addressing the House in its favour. Mr. Pitt gave his friend a dubious answer, which was construed into an assent, and the notice of it was circulated round in whispers. In the interim, however, he had come to the resolution *not* to rise; and it would have agitated a man of less self-possession to notice, that when Lord Nugent sat down, a universal pause ensued, and then a loud call from various quarters of the House for "Mr. Pitt." He stood up in consequence: his last biographer thus describes what followed, " Though really not intending to speak, he was from the beginning collected and unembarrassed; he argued strongly in favour of the bill, and noticed all the objections which had been urged by the Noble Lord who immediately preceded him in the debate, in a manner which greatly astonished all who heard him. Never were higher expectations formed of any person upon his first coming into Parliament, and never were expectations more completely answered. They were indeed much more than answered: such were the fluency and accuracy of language, such the perspicuity of arrangement, and such the closeness of reasoning, and manly and dignified elocution—generally, even in a much less degree, the fruits of long habit and experience—that it could scarcely be believed to be the first speech of a young man not yet two-and-twenty." Mr. Pitt spoke only thrice during this session; but he acquitted himself so well, as, before the end of it, to secure the reputation of a most able orator, from the best judges of his time. One of Mr. Fox's friends, about this period, observed to him, that Mr. Pitt promised to be one of the first speakers ever heard in the House

of Commons; to which Mr. Fox instantly replied, " He is so already." A still warmer tribute of applause was paid him not long after, by Mr. Dunning: " Almost all the sentiments," he said, " which he had collected in his own mind on the subject, (the misconduct of our naval affairs,) had vanished away like a dream, on the bursting forth of a torrent of eloquence, from the greatest prodigy that ever was seen in this, or perhaps in any other country—an honourable gentleman possessing the full vigour of youth, united with the experience and wisdom of the maturest age."

The removal of Lord North and his adherents might have opened the way for Mr. Pitt's admission into office. The Rockingham party, anxious to appropriate the benefits of his eloquence, had even offered him the vice-treasurership of Ireland, a place of some consequence formerly held by his father. But Mr. Pitt, with a consciousness of great abilities, which succeeding events amply justified, had made up his mind from the first to accept of no situation which did not give him a place in the cabinet. He therefore refused this offer, though he continued to support the measures of the ministry, whose liberal system of government was naturally accordant with the principles of a son and pupil of the great Chatham. About this time, also, he brought forward the famous question of *Parliamentary Reform*. It appears that about that period he had felt a considerable interest in this important subject; he had encouraged the combinations formed in various parts of the kingdom in favour of it, and had himself sat as a delegate at a meeting convened in Westminster for this express purpose. He supported the same cause with great eloquence in his place in parliament. His motion (May, 1782) " for a committee to inquire into the state of the representation in parliament, and to report to the House their observations thereon," was lost by a majority of twenty; he again spoke earnestly in favour of reform in 1783; and, lastly, while a minister, in 1785, he presented a specific plan for effecting this object, which also was rejected. These proceedings were long afterwards contrasted with his subsequent proceedings in the same matter, and much loud accusation was drawn from the comparison.

By the Marquis of Rockingham's death, Lord Shelburne became prime minister; and Mr. Pitt was associated with him as chancellor of the exchequer, in June, 1782. The task which devolved on him was one of great difficulty. Lord Shelburne's elevation had converted several of his friends into bitter enemies: his peace with America and France was at best but a humiliating affair; and the whole charge of managing the House of Commons was entrusted to Mr. Pitt. Scarcely arrived at the age of twenty-three, he had thus to make head against the most formidable opposition. Lord North was still in his place, with ability or extent of connection undiminished; and the hostility of Mr. Fox, who had left the ministry at Rockingham's death, was at once strong and implacable. The quarrel of Lord Shelburne and Mr. Fox is a well-known event; the mode in which the latter sought for justice or revenge, is also well known, and very diversely judged of. We need only at present remark, that the combination of Lord North and Mr. Fox overpowered the new and unstable minister: he was compelled to resign, and Mr. Pitt went out with him, in the beginning of 1783. Prior to this event, we are told, a reconciliation had been attempted. " Neither Mr. Pitt nor Lord Shelburne," says the Bishop of

Winchester, "saw any reason why they should not act with Mr. Fox. It was therefore agreed that an offer should be made to him to return to office, for which purpose Mr. Pitt waited upon him by appointment. As soon as Mr. Fox heard the object of Mr. Pitt's visit, he asked whether it was intended that Lord Shelburne should remain first lord of the treasury; to which Mr. Pitt answered in the affirmative. Mr. Fox immediately replied, that it was impossible for him to belong to any administration of which Lord Shelburne was the head. Mr. Pitt observed, that if such was his determination, it would be useless for him to enter into any farther discussion, "as he did not come to betray Lord Shelburne;" and he took his leave. This was, I believe, the last time Mr. Pitt was in a private room with Mr. Fox; and, from this period, may be dated that political hostility which continued through the remainder of their lives." The same feeling of integrity towards his colleague, induced Mr. Pitt respectfully to decline the offer of succeeding him, which the king condescended to make him in person. He again would not "betray Lord Shelburne;" and, under the Duke of Portland, the united party of Lord North and Mr. Fox came into office in their stead.

This famous coalition ministry was offensive at once to the king and to a great portion of the country. Mr. Fox's share in it was entirely approved of by none but his very warmest partisans. Mr. Pitt, though he was of those who thought it "monstrous, in the ardent defender of the people's rights, to unite with the lofty assertor of the prerogative," yet pledged himself not systematically to oppose their measures. They had his support on more than one occasion; but, on the first motion of Mr. Fox's celebrated India bill, he expressed his unqualified dissent from it, and resisted it in all its stages. We need hardly mention the fate of this bill; it was pushed through the House of Commons by overpowering majorities; but the king took the alarm at the great and permanent accession of influence which it seemed to confer on the ministers; Lord Temple made known his Majesty's feelings, and the bill was thrown out in the House of Lords. Mr. Fox and his colleagues were, in consequence, displaced.

The prospects of a prime minister at this juncture, were far from inviting: the highest talents in the country, supported by the most powerful parliamentary interest, and embittered by defeat, were like to be arrayed against him; he could have nothing to rely on but the king's favour and his own abilities. Mr. Pitt, however, did not hesitate to accept this office; he was appointed first lord of the treasury, and chancellor of the exchequer, in December, 1783. The appalling state of matters soon became apparent. The new minister's India bill was rejected by a majority of 222 to 214; and a similar fate attended all the subsequent motions on which he divided the house. Nevertheless, Mr. Pitt stood his ground. Strong in the favour of the king, in the consciousness of his own abilities, and firmly believing in the goodness of his cause, he exerted himself with the most extraordinary diligence to vanquish the opposition made to him, and fix himself securely in the confidence of the nation at large. In this contest, the versatility of his talents, the dexterity of his argumentation, the sharpness of his sarcasm, the ingenuity of all his measures, were not less wonderful than the firmness of mind, which prompted him at an age so early, to encounter, single-handed, some of the most formidable obstacles that ever minister had to strive with. By dint of unwearied exertions, he at

length succeeded in reducing the majority which supported his opponents, to a single voice; and, finally, in drawing over that voice also to his own side. Having prospered so far, and what was more important, having now, as he thought, convinced the public of the rectitude of his measures, he determined to appeal more immediately to the general sense of the nation, and the parliament was dissolved in March, 1784. The new election justified his hopes; there was now a decided majority in his favour; his India bill passed, and he became prime minister in substance as well as form. He had earned his power with difficulty, and he kept it steadfastly. For the next seventeen years he was constantly in office.

His conduct during this long administration was marked by great caution and skill; and, for a considerable period, by the almost universal approbation of the country. The few faults found with it indicated how completely he had mastered the failings most likely to beset him. It was not the ardour of youth, its passion for dazzling schemes, or the indiscriminate zeal for splendid improvements, natural to one who had already declared himself so warmly in their favour, that were blamed; it was rather a circumspectness, bordering on jealousy, a reverence for existing institutions, a coldness or hostility to innovation, which looked like political apostacy in the once powerful advocate for reform; the errors, in short, of an old and narrow-minded statesman, not of a young and highly-gifted one. If these features of his public character gave little testimony as to the extent of his enthusiasm, or the warmth of his feelings, they indicated favourably respecting his prudence and the clearness of his judgment. Mr. Pitt had still a strong, though no longer a triumphant opposition to encounter in parliament; the public confidence was yet but partially merited; and it seemed good policy to avoid all extraordinary movements which might expose him to misrepresentations, or put his still wavering stability in danger. Accordingly, though continuing to patronise the principles of freedom and liberality, which he had at first announced, he abstained from making any of them what are called cabinet questions; he spoke and voted in their favour, but did little more. He no longer took a lead among their abettors; some of them he came at last resolutely to oppose. The friends of parliamentary reform expected, that now, when the power was in his hands, the schemes he had twice proposed were at length to be realized; but his motion for this purpose, in 1785, having, as we mentioned already, been rejected in the House of Commons, he never more recurred to the subject, except as a decided opponent of those who pushed it forward. His conduct underwent censures on this head; they were augmented by his opposition to the repeal of the test act—a piece of management which many stigmatized as a homage done to bigotry and popular prejudice, unworthy of the son of Chatham. The same party who blamed him for his indifference to the cause of improvement at home, also blamed him for the minute jealousy of his conduct with foreign powers. His disputes with Catharine of Russia about the fortress of Orchakow, and with Spain about the fur-trade of Nootka Sound, were exclaimed against as trifles which he was magnifying into causes of war. With the great body of the nation, however, he was still a decided favourite; they forgot these alleged blemishes in his character, or reckoned them as beauties, while they felt the substantial good he was affecting in many departments of domestic policy, and participated in the steady prosperity which the country enjoyed under his administration. The improvements he had made in collecting the revenue, his plans for preventing contraband trade, his general skill as a financier, were universally applauded. The probity and zeal with which he served the public had gradually secured him its confidence; and his admirable talents for debate, the unrivalled clearness of his expositions, the sagacity of his management, enabled him to influence, in the requisite degree, the deliberations of parliament, and verified, in the common opinion, the high expectations at first entertained of him. His ministry, if not brilliant, had hitherto been fortunate; a few disappointed reformers might murmur, but the voice of the country was yet with him.

The king also had long cordially approved of his measures; and the conduct of Mr. Pitt, during the famous regency question, is said greatly to have strengthened this sentiment. In 1788, his majesty was seized with the first attack of that awful malady, under which his days were destined to close; the head of the government was declared to be incapable of discharging his functions; and the mode of supplying his place became an object of keen discussion, involving some of the most dubious principles of the constitution, and quickened by hopes and fears which had no reference to the general question. As the Prince of Wales then favoured the Whig party, it was their interest to have him appointed regent with as few limitations as possible; Mr. Pitt's, on the contrary, with as many. The prevailing opinion appeared to sanction the views of the latter. Mr. Fox, in maintaining that the unrestricted regency should devolve on the heir apparent independently of the two Houses of Parliament, was accused of forsaking those maxims of popular right which it had been the great object of his public life to support. During the discussion Mr. Pitt was countenanced by numerous addresses from various parts of the kingdom, and at length succeeded in passing a bill of such a kind as he desired. His Majesty's recovery happily rendered this superfluous; but the minister's prudence and firmness were rewarded by an increase of confidence from his former adherents, and particularly from the master whose interests he watched over with such care.

Hitherto Mr. Pitt had proceeded without violent opposition, so as to gain the toleration of all ranks, and the warm applauses of many. But the next great event in which he took a share, while it united him more closely to his own party, made an irreparable breach between him and those who adopted the contrary side. In 1789 the French revolution broke out, convulsing all Europe by its explosion; and it became a momentous question to determine what measures England should follow in a crisis so terrible. For the arbitrary monarchs of the Continent, it was natural to view with horror and aversion this formidable display of democratic principles: Was Great Britain to join in their league against the dishonoured cause of freedom, to check the disseminators of such doctrines by coercion and punishment at home and abroad; or, standing aloof from the contest, to guard her own internal quiet, and study to promote her own interest, by the favourable conjunctures of a struggle, which she might contemplate without mixing in it? The latter was in part the opinion of one class, at the head of which was Mr. Fox; the former was the plan adopted by Mr. Pitt. He embarked with great zeal in the continental war of 1792; and Britain became involved

in that quarrel, the disasters of which overspread Europe with misery for five-and-twenty years. The commencement was eminently unsuccessful; the allied armies were defeated in every direction; the voice of discontent grew clamorous at home; commercial distress pressed heavy on the country; reformers came forward with wild and dangerous schemes, which the government met by treatment of unexampled severity. The *habeas corpus* act was suspended, and political prosecutions multiplied without end. The events of the war continued to be unfortunate abroad; and at length a bloody rebellion broke out at home. Mr. Pitt's conduct in this universal commotion deserved the praise of steadfastness at least; he persevered in his resolution amid every difficulty; he strained every nerve to strike an effective blow at France; he met the danger of national bankruptcy by the suspension of cash payments; he prosecuted reformers; he quelled the rebellion in Ireland, and united that kingdom to our own. For these exertions he was by many venerated as the saviour of the British constitution; by a few he was almost execrated as its destroyer. One party fondly named him "the pilot that weathered the storm;" another reckoned that the "storm" was yet far from being "weathered." Agitated and tired by these incessant conflicts, he must have viewed as a kind of relief his retirement from office, which took place in 1801. Various reasons have been assigned for this step: some say it was by reason of differences with the king in regard to the proper mode of treating the Irish Catholics; others assert that, being hopeless of making any peace with France, at all suitable to the high tone with which he had begun the war, he was willing to leave to others the ungracious task of completing this unprosperous enterprise. He was succeeded by Mr. Addington, now Lord Sidmouth.

That both causes had some influence in his resignation was rendered probable by the line of conduct which Mr. Pitt pursued when out of office. He justified the peace of Amiens in his place in Parliament; but, in various important points, he voted with the opposition. This peace was of short duration; a new war was declared, and the existing ministry being found inadequate for the support of it, Mr. Pitt was again called to the supreme charge in 1804. He formed a cabinet by introducing several of his own friends, and retaining many of those already in place. His own station, as formerly, was that of first lord of the treasury.

Mr. Pitt was now to become a war minister in earnest; he prepared himself for the most vigorous efforts to acquire the same reputation in this new department of public service, as he had before acquired in that of finance. By his exertions, Russia and Austria entered into a new confederacy against France,—which, it was at last hoped, these two formidable powers would succeed in reducing to subjection. The battle of Austerlitz put an end to such expectations. Mr. Pitt's plans again became abortive; he was again beset with difficulties; and the state of his health rendered this stroke of misfortune peculiarly severe. The news of the French victory found him at Bath, to which he had been forced to retire in the end of 1805. His disorder originated in a tendency to gout, which he inherited from his father, and which his own anxious and overlaboured life, as well as his somewhat exuberant convivial habits, had of course strengthened rather than abated. The Bath waters gave him no permanent relief; and in the beginning of January he returned to his villa at Putney, in a very weak state. Still his physicians saw no cause for immediate alarm; but, before the twentieth of the month, various apprehensions were entertained for him, and a few hours of that day converted these apprehensions into mournful certainty. A short while previous to his decease, Dr. Tomline, then bishop of Lincoln, who watched affectionately over his illness, communicated to him the unfavourable opinion of Sir Walter Farquhar, his medical attendant. Mr. Pitt inquired of Sir Walter, who then stood beside his bed, "How long do you think I have to live?" The physician expressed a faint hope that he would recover; a languid smile on the patient's countenance showed that he understood the reply. When the bishop requested leave to pray with him, he answered, "I fear I have, like too many other men, neglected prayer too much to have any hope that it can be efficacious on a deathbed; but," added he, making an effort to rise as he spoke, "I throw myself entirely on the mercy of God." He then joined in the exercises of devotion with much apparent meekness and humility. Of his death he spoke with calmness; arranged the settlement of his private concerns, and recommended his nieces to the gratitude of the nation; "I could wish," he said, "a thousand or fifteen hundred a-year to be given them, if the public should think my long services deserving of it." He died about four o'clock on the morning of the 23d of January, 1806, in the 47th year of his age. The parliament decreed him the honours of a public funeral, and granted the sum of £40,000 to discharge his debts. A monument was afterwards erected to his memory in Westminster Abbey; and similar testimonies of the public feeling are to be met with in various quarters of the kingdom. His death, so unexpected, and at so gloomy a period, was deeply regretted at home, and created a strong sensation over all Europe.

Of his character it is difficult to speak so as to escape contradiction; he passed his life in contests, and their influence extends beyond his grave. In his private relations it is universally admitted, that, under a cold and rather haughty exterior, he bore a mind of great amiableness and sterling worth. The enthusiasm with which his intimate friends regarded him gives proof of this. "With a manner somewhat reserved and distant," says Mr. Rose, "in what might be termed his public deportment, no man was ever better qualified to gain, or more successful in fixing, the attachment of his friends than Mr. Pitt. They saw all the powerful energies of his character softened into the most perfect complacency and sweetness of disposition, in the circles of private life; the pleasures of which no one more cheerfully enjoyed, or more agreeably promoted, when the paramount duties he conceived himself to owe to the public admitted of his mixing in them. That indignant severity with which he met and subdued what he considered unfounded opposition; that keenness of sarcasm with which he expelled and withered, as it might be said, the powers of most of his assailants in debate, were exchanged, in the society of his intimate friends, for a kindness of heart, a gentleness of demeanour, and a playfulness of good humour, which no one ever witnessed without interest, or participated without delight."

His merits as a public man are yet a matter of vehement discussion, and bid fair long to continue so. That he was a powerful speaker—unrivalled for the choice of

his words, the lucid arrangement of his statements, the address and ingenuity of his arguments—appears to be universally granted. That he was a skilful financier—distinguished for the sagacity of his plans and the diligence with which he reduced them to practice—appears also to be granted, though less universally. But with regard to the wisdom of his foreign and domestic policy, there is no unanimity of opinion even among those best qualified to judge him. His friends have exalted his merits to the highest pitch of human excellence; his enemies have represented him as destitute of great ideas, a narrow seeker of temporary expedients, who sacrificed the cause of freedom to a love of place and kingly favour. No doubt there is much exaggeration in this. The change of his political sentiments after his accession to authority is certainly a circumstance unfavourable to his general reputation; but the impartial observer will hesitate before adopting so mournful a solution of it. In this world of vicissitudes, it is not necessarily owing to unsoundness of moral principle that the opinions of our first age cease to be those of our last. Mr. Pitt, in his twenty-fourth year, arrived at the highest station which a subject can hope for, without any violation of sincerity; it was natural that he should look on the business of reform with very different eyes when he viewed it as a minister and as a popular orator—on the side of its benefits and on the side of its inconveniences; that, as he gradually accustomed himself to the exercise of power, and grew in years, and influence, and strength of habits, the ardent innovator should pass by degrees into the wary minister, for whom the machine of government was less a thing to beautify and improve than to keep moving with steadiness and quiet. There seems no need for more sinister imputations in all this; and Mr. Pitt's general conduct proved too well the independence of his mind to admit of such being formed. His treatment of Lord Shelburne, the total inattention he uniformly showed to personal profit or aggrandizement, should acquit him of such charges. When the jarrings of Whig and Tory have given place to other causes of discord, as they succeeded others, a distant posterity will join the names of Pitt, and his rival Fox, to the names of the Chathams, the Oxenstierns, the Colberts, and other great statesmen of Europe; it will be for the same posterity to decide what rank they shall occupy in that august series—to trace with clearness the influence due to their actions, and assign to each the proper share of gratitude or blame.—See *Gifford's Life of Pitt, Tomline's Life,* &c. &c. &c.

PITCAITHLEY, a village in the parish of Dumbarney, and county of Perth, celebrated for its mineral springs. The principal ingredients in the water are, muriate of lime, and muriate of soda, with sulphate of lime, and carbonate of lime. They have been found very serviceable in dyspepsia and other complaints. As the country is beautiful, and the accommodation for visitors, both at Pitcaithley and at the Bridge of Earn, very excellent, the place is much frequented.

PITTSBURG, a town of North America, and the capital of Alleghany County, Pennsylvania. It is situated on a broad point of land, at the confluence of the rivers Alleghany and Monongahela, whose united streams form the Ohio. It stands on a triangular piece of ground, which is now nearly filled with houses. Its public buildings are a court-house, a jail, an academy, a library of about 2000 volumes; a national armoury, five banks, and eight places of worship. Three newspapers are published here. In 1816, the number of houses was 960, besides 300 in the suburbs and adjacent villages, making a total population of 12,000. The country around is one great bed of fossil coal; and iron ore and various minerals are found in abundance. Hence various manufactures have been established, among which are those of steam-engines; five green and white glass-houses; four air furnaces; three breweries; 67 flour-mills, &c. In 1814, the manufactures of Pittsburg amounted to 2,000,000 dollars; consisting of wool, and cotton, iron, glass, and paper. At some seasons, vessels of 200 or 300 tons descend the Ohio from Pittsburg. From New Orleans, a distance of 2000 miles, a steam-boat proceeds up the Ohio at the rate of 60 miles a-day; and will therefore reach Pittsburg in 60 days. See Warden's *Account of the United States,* vol. ii. West Long. 80° 81', and North Lat. 40°. 32'.

PIVOTS. On the form of. See MECHANICS, Vol. XIII. p. 600.

PLACENTIA, a city of the north of Italy, in the goverment of Parma, and capital of the former dutchy of Placentia. It is situated in a rich and extensive plain, at the confluence of the Po and Trebia. It is a large and handsome town, surrounded with fortifications; the streets are, in general, broad and regular; the houses and public buildings are mostly constructed of brick; and many of the ornaments are of the same materials, and have a good effect. Few of the public buildings are remarkable. In the great square is the townhouse, a large building in the Gothic style, with Saxon arches and reticulated brick-work. In the same square there are two bronze equestrian statues, which are much admired for their attitude, animation, and drapery. The best of them represents the celebrated Alexander Farnese, who commanded the Spanish army in the wars of the League. The cathedral is an ugly Gothic building, but enriched with many paintings of great celebrity; and the dome, painted by Guercino, is admired for the richness of its colouring. Several of the churches are of fine Roman architecture, and adorned with numerous paintings; that of St. Augustine is remarkable for the beautiful proportions of its façade. The religious establishments were formerly very numerous, but many of them have been suppressed; the clergy, however, still form a tenth part of the population. The university of Placentia is of no great celebrity. The theatre, though small, is a handsome and commodious edifice. Placentia is not a trading town; the few manufactures carried on consist chiefly of silk stuffs, woollen, fustian, stockings, and hats. It has given birth to Pope Gregory X. Cardinal Alberoni, the celebrated prime minister of Spain, and several other eminent persons. The population is estimated at 15,000. Placentia derives its name, according to Pliny, from the beauty of its situation. It was founded by a Roman colony 219 years before Christ, being the first town that the Romans built in Cisalpine Gaul. Shortly after its foundation Placentia sheltered the remains of the Roman army after the disastrous battle of Trebia, and was afterwards besieged by Hannibal, but without effect. In the war between Otho and Vitellius its spacious and magnificent amphitheatre, which stood without the walls, was destroyed by fire. It was taken in the sixth century by Totila after an obstinate siege. On the overthrow of the kingdom of Lombardy, Placentia obtained its liberty, which it enjoyed for a very short period; after having frequently changed masters it was annexed to Parma. In 1799 a bloody

engagement was fought in its neighbourhood between the French and the Russians, under Marshal Suwarrow; in which the former were defeated. North lat. 45° 2' 44''. east long. 9° 42' 32''.

PLAGUE. This formidable disease, though always originating in countries far remote from us, is brought so much within our reach, by our extended commercial intercourse, as to be an object of interest, even to ourselves, if less so than to the Christian nations of the Mediterranean. There are few of these indeed that have not at some period suffered from it; and assuredly there are no diseases, the characters of which are more formidable, as well for the extent and rapidity of its progress, as for its incurable nature.

We must, however, thank our own care and prudence that we are still enabled to keep it at a distance; and it is right at the same time to remember, that it is only by such exertions that we can insure ourselves from it at any time. That it can spread widely, even where it does not originate, sad experience has shown; and that it is constantly tending to do so even now, there are recent proofs. In 1818, it had penetrated from the Adriatic even into the Lazaretto of Venice, and into Naples. The Illyric coast is, indeed, in constant danger of it, from the commerce carried on in Albania by the Dalmatians, and more especially by the inhabitants of the Bocca di Cattaro. We are also held in continual fear of it, by its permanent residence on the Barbary coast, and by the constant system of piracy carried on by these nations in the Mediterranean, and on the coasts of Spain and Italy. Hence it has appeared not very long ago at Malta, as it has in Greece, and even in Gibraltar; in former times, as we shall presently see, its ravages in these quarters were much more frequent and decisive. That its communication is not now limited, even to those maritime countries, is further but too certain; since in 1819, it appeared at Nuremberg, having been imported in some bales of cotton from Smyrna; many persons having died of it notwithstanding the most rigid precautions taken by the Austrian and Prussian governments.

Introduction of the Plague into Christian Europe.

The seat of the plague has been almost uniformly referred to Egypt. The great plague of Athens is considered by Thucydides, as having been imported from the borders of that country by a circuitous course through Libya. It appeared first in many of the Greek islands, particularly at Lemnos, and first shewed itself, at Athens, in the Piræus. This, the first instance on record of its appearance in Europe, took place in the year 430, A. C. Procopius also traces a plague, which spread over an enormous extent of country for fifty-two years, from Pelusium, the modern Damietta, and thence in succession to Alexandria, Palestine, and Constantinople, whence it was lastly propagated to almost all known Europe.

Its first introduction into modern Europe was by means of the Crusades, and there is here no difficulty in tracing it to the same sources. Since that, it has appeared in various places, and by many different routes; yet always imported from some part or other of the Turkish empire, where it is effectually preserved by the necessarian creed of Mohammedanism. Among these examples, we may name its introduction into Marseilles in 1720, where, in the short space of seven months, 60,000 people fell victims to it; and that into Messina, where, in three months, 43,000 people perished.

It is more interesting to ourselves to recal to mind its appearance in our own country, which has also suffered most severely from it at different times. It appeared in London in 1593, and at that period it destroyed 11,503 persons. In this case, it was proved that it had been imported from Alkmaar. Again, in 1603, 36,269 people fell victims to the plague; and, in this case, the contagion was introduced from Ostend. Six years after this it appeared again at Alkmaar, as well as in Denmark; but in consequence of the communication between these countries and England having been suspended, Great Britain escaped at this time. But in 1625 it broke out again in London, at which time it was traced to Denmark. On this occasion its ravages extended to about 35,500 people. In 1636, it again destroyed 13,480 persons in London, when its origin was traced to Leyden. In 1665, its severity was still greater; as, on the smallest calculation, 68,600 inhabitants died of it. Here, however, our own experience of it terminates; as quarantine laws, added to a variety of improvements in the state of society, have, since that, protected us from these calamitous visitations. On its appearances at Petersburg and elsewhere, in modern times, we cannot here pretend to enter.

Origin of the Contagion of the Plague.

That this disease is of Egyptian origin, seems universally admitted, though we may not be able to define exactly the circumstances by which it is generated. From the nature of the Egyptian territory, the low and maritime parts of that country have been a perpetual source of pestilential miasmata, even in the best times of that extraordinary nation. In more recent ones, the disturbed state of things, bad government, perpetual wars, and all their ruinous consequences, have led to the neglect of those canals, embankments, and other works, which confined and regulated the course of the Nile, and which also assisted in regulating the contests of the sea and land at the mouth of that river, not less injurious in their ultimate effects. Hence have originated marshes, stagnant waters, and wet lands, that were formerly unknown. But, even in far distant times, Herodotus speaks of the diseases consequent on these and similar causes; accusing the priests of neglecting the state of their lands between the plain and the sea, while they were employed in studying the heavens. He then also tells us, that, at the time of his visit, Egypt had just terminated a ruinous war, in consequence of which the country was infested by robbers and ravaged by diseases. That the sacred writers, who so often denounced threatenings to Egypt, alluded to this disease, is more than probable. It would seem as if Isaiah had even known the country from personal experience.

There are authors nevertheless, and among others Monsieur Olivier not long ago, who have asserted that the plague does not originate in this country, but that it is annually imported from Constantinople through Alexandria. That such an event as this may have actually happened, is not improbable; but Olivier's opinion is little worthy of attention; from his incapacity of judging on this subject, as well as from our knowledge, that it was part of his business, employed as he was by the French government, to do away all the fears likely to interfere with the expe-

dition to that country. It is not only on this occasion that even the name of the disease has been suppressed, from interested views of a similar nature, and that its contagious property has been denied. It is not longer ago than 1818, that a physician was bastinadoed at Tunis for having declared a disease to be the plague; and with such ruinous consequences as may easily be apprehended.

If the French had thus made up their minds to be at ease on this head, they were not long in being compelled to form a different opinion. When their army disembarked at Alexandria, in 1796, the first symptoms broke out in the naval hospital there, from which it was communicated to two others in the same city, and at length to Damietta, Rosetta, and the surrounding country. At that time it is very certain that no vessel arrived at Alexandria. But it is indeed the universal belief of the inhabitants of this city, whether Copts or Mussulmen, that the plague originates in Alexandria every year, and that it lasts from autumn till the next summer heats, extending its ravages along the whole of the sea coast.

But in fact the same opinion is universal, not only throughout Lower but in Upper Egypt; and in the latter division it is believed, uniformly, to spread from the low country. It has been particularly remarked, that the disease had not appeared at Gaza for forty years; and that, when it did appear, about the period above mentioned, it was brought by some Mamelukes who had fled from the French armies. Degenettes, whose personal experience renders him a good authority in this case, is decidedly of opinion that the plague is endemic in Lower Egypt, and along the coasts of Syria, and that for these two centuries past it has been observed to spring up in many places in this tract, where there was no external communication of any kind.

According to Mr. Larrey, chief surgeon to the French army in Egypt, that part of the year which lies between the vernal equinox and the beginning of June, is extremely pernicious to the inhabitants, and still more so to strangers. At this period, for about two months, the south winds are very violent and hot, blowing for three or four hours at a time from the immense sandy deserts. These winds are also charged with miasmata from the pools and marshes of the Nile. In June the north winds commence, and produce that state of the air in which Egypt is entirely free from diseases. Not to dwell longer on this, the conclusion is, that the plague is both endemic and contagious in Lower Egypt, but that it is merely contagious in Upper Egypt, as well as in Syria and all the more distant countries, to which it is carried by personal communication or inanimate substances. That it should not always be easy to trace its immediate origin to the district in question, is no cause for surprise, when we recollect that for so many ages it has continued to prevail, and that its contagion is probably permanent, however temporarily inactive in countries deriding all precautions, and impressed with the fatal doctrines of fatality.

It has been asked, and naturally, why the same disorder does not originate in other countries, in the same or similar regions that appear to be in the same circumstances. It was not found any where else endemic, by Bruce, Lord Valentia, or Salt, where it might have been expected, nor by any other oriental traveller. It is equally unknown in southern and middle Africa, where the situation appears favourable to it; although these regions are subject to the most destructive of the fevers produced by marsh miasmata, and arising from lands of the same character. Thus also India produces its jungle fevers, and the West India islands their yellow fever; while the same classes of disease, but no plague, are equally abundant in all the hot marshy districts of the American continent.

Answers have been attempted to this question, yet with little success. It is said that the course of the Nile is peculiar, and that it traverses fifty or sixty lakes and marshes in Abyssinia and Sennaar; that it thus flows through Upper Egypt, charged with putrescent matters, and that when it arrives at the lower country it begins to deposit these. Here it is also said that the river is much checked at its junction with the sea; thus generating new marshes, which, partly fresh and partly salt, are exposed to the action of a burning sun.

But the reply to all this is easy. The history of the Nile, as far as this point is concerned, is that of an hundred rivers. The mouth of the Ganges is no better, nor is that of the Oroonoko, or the Amazon, or the Yellow river, nay, we may add, of the Rhine. But in a thousand situations, where no rivers of such magnitude are concerned, the circumstances are precisely the same. Yet these produce fevers enough; never the plague. The characters of these diseases, severe as they are, are utterly distinct from those of that formidable disease. But the most fatal objection to this view of the causes of the plague is, that these fevers are not contagious. They are simply epidemic, and can neither be communicated from one person to another, nor can their poison be preserved in inanimate substances. Thus the poison of the plague is analogous to that of typhus fever, which is generated by animal bodies, by human subjects, and which is quite independent of marsh miasma. It is still a contagion *sui generis*; but if it is generated merely by land under the peculiar circumstances stated, it is as solitary an instance as it is an inexplicable one, of a miasma which is also a contagion. A confession of ignorance as to its real causes, is at present our safest conduct.

Contagious Nature of the Plague.

This is a question which has often been agitated, and its decision is obviously an object of the greatest importance. It is far from a new subject; although some persons, actuated apparently more by the love of notoriety than of truth, have recently brought it under the review of the British Parliament. If they were not very well occupied in this inquiry, the result has, we trust, been to set it at rest again, at least till some new lover of paradox arises.

In the sixteenth century, it was proved by Massaria, that the plague was not only different from common pestilential fevers, but that it was communicated both by the contact of persons and things. After that, Gerstmann, a physician of Cremona, maintained that it was produced by fear; and, during the plague of Marseilles in 1725, it was also determined by Messrs. Vernier and Chicoyneau, commissioners appointed for this purpose by the government, that it was not contagious. These persons were answered by Deider, who found clearly that it could not arise from mere epidemy, or from poisonous matters diffused through the atmosphere; because all those persons who were shut up in the Abbey of St. Victor and in the convents, remained exempt

from it. But even this plain demonstration, together with the advantages that arose from separating persons, and the dreadful consequences that followed that neglect, did not prevent the same heresies from being repeated by numerous persons, and even by the French Encyclopædists. This is such an important question that we shall give a sketch of the evidence respecting it.

It is of little consequence for the present purpose, whether it is originally generated from marsh effluvia or not, as we have here to inquire respecting its propagation. However endemic it may be in Egypt, it is assuredly not so either in Turkey or in Christian Europe. Contagious fevers, in these countries, have also been produced at various times, and in extreme degrees of virulence; particularly in a state of war, in sieges, after general actions, in winter quarters, and after famines. Yet in no one instance has the plague been produced in this manner in these places, any more than it is at Walcheren, or in Italy, or the West Indies, by miasmata. In every case where it has appeared, it has been an imported disease; however much its progress after importation may have been favoured by a peculiar state of the season or of the atmosphere, by negligence, poverty, want of cleanliness, alarm, or bad food.

There is not an instance on record, and we have formerly named a few, where it could not be traced to the communications between the Christian Europeans and the Saracens, Arabs, Turks, or Moors. It is perpetually imported now from Egypt and the Levant, as it has been, quite recently, into Malta and Corfu; and it is preserved by the fatalism of these nations, in their clothes, their furniture, and their houses, whence it is transmitted in a thousand ways whenever the season and circumstances are favourable to its propagation. Thus it travels, from port to port, checked only by the severe laws that all sensible people have established for this purpose. That these remedies are effectual when they are carefully attended to, and that the neglect of them has always been followed by its introduction, should be proof enough of its contagious nature.

Where and however the original poison is produced, that substance gives rise to a disease by which it is multiplied and propagated; so that, from generation to generation, new cases are produced precisely similar to the former, and always reproducing the same disorder with the same symptoms; a character peculiar to all contagious diseases. To such a progress as this, no less in ordinary contagious fevers than in the plague, there could be no end but the destruction of the human race; were it not that the very seats and foci of these diseases are destroyed from time to time, and were it not that they exhaust themselves in some manner unknown to us, consisting probably in conditions of the atmosphere, respecting which we cannot form the slightest conception.

To those names which we formerly mentioned, we may add, Dr. Skoll of Vienna, who wrote against the contagion of the plague. Howard, the great philanthropist, has ably controverted his opinion, and has adduced the most unquestionable proofs of its contagious nature, from living sources of great experience, who all coincide in representing it as communicated both by the contact of persons and things. Among these authorities we may quote Fra Luigi di Pavia, of Smyrna, an observer of eighteen years' practice at that perpetual seat of the disorder. Drs. Raymond and Demollins, of Marseilles, were of the same opinion; both observing that it proceeds only from contact, and has always been imported. Such also was the opinion of Giovanelli of Leghorn, and of many others.

In Malta the plague has always been considered as contagious. From the sixteenth century to its visit in 1813, the same system of precaution and interdiction has been used to check its progress; and whenever this plan has been fairly acted on, it has always been successful. Ciantaro, in his description of Malta, gives a distinct account of the introduction of this disorder at four different periods. The first was in 1592, by means of four gallies belonging to the Grand Duke of Tuscany, who had procured pilots in this island. They had taken two ships from Alexandria, laden with rice and flax for Constantinople, and containing 150 Turks. Hearing of the plague at Alexandria, they brought their prizes into Malta, introducing the disease along with them, followed by a great mortality.

The second event of this nature occurred in 1623, and it originated, as far as could be traced, in the house of the harbour-master. But almost as soon as it was discovered, precautions were taken, and the diseased were sent to Lazarettos, so that it made no progress. The third broke out, in the same manner, in 1633, in a house near the Porta Maggiore, where the ships from the Levant usually anchored. This was traced to the ships themselves. The whole family was soon infected, but, by transferring them immediately to a lazaretto, the disorder was immediately extinguished.

The fourth attack, about the latter end of 1675, was far more destructive, lasting seven months. It was traced to the house of a shopkeeper; but, having been at first unsuspected, many families became infected. The usual precautions were adopted, but with less success than on former occasions. A census of the people was taken; and the town was divided into twenty-four districts, each placed under the superintendence of a nobleman, with an adjunct from the inferior citizens, and a secretary. These commissions visited their allotted houses daily, and had also charge of the arrangements of the Lazarettos. But from some differences of opinion, sufficient precautions were not taken to separate the infected and the suspected persons, and hence the disease continued to spread. In the Lazarettos, also, and floating hospitals, great neglect took place. In the town, the people broke out of their bounds, disseminating the evil which they finally could not escape; so that all the efforts of the government proved ineffectual. It was found then necessary to send for physicians from France. In consequence of their regulations, all the people were confined rigidly to their houses, with the exception of the infected and suspected, who were sent to the Lazarettos. From this moment the disease diminished, and within three months entirely disappeared, after destroying about 10,000, or a sixth of the whole population. No stronger evidence than this of its contagious nature could well be imagined.

The history of the last visitations of this nature here, is not less interesting and satisfactory. At this period the population of Malta was greater than at any former time in its history, being then the great emporium of commerce in the Mediterranean. One of the great branches of that trade was with the Levant, and the usual long established precautions against the disease were adopted, except that the situation for performing quarantine was a thoroughfare for boats, so that it was not very difficult to evade the regulations. In March, 1813, the

brig St. Nicholas arrived from Alexandria; and, from the evidence of the captain, it appeared that two of his crew had died from some pestilential disease, while the plague was known to be in existence at the port whence she had sailed. Two more ships arrived at the same time from the same place, one with two sick and suspected persons, and the other having lost one man by the plague. As the cargo of the St. Nicholas also consisted of flax, considerable alarm was excited by the continuance of these vessels in the harbour.

In consequence of this the crew was transferred to the Lazaretto on the next day, and the ship placed in charge of the proper officers. In the mean time the captain and one of the crew died, and no doubt remained of the nature of the disorder. The ship was therefore sent back to Alexandria, but in vain. By this time the contagion had found its way into the town, destroying some persons; and on the 3d of May it was declared to be in great danger, by a report of the Committee of Health. The alarm immediately caused the people to leave their houses, and many embarked; but, on the following day, strict regulations were put in force. Notwithstanding these it continued spreading slowly till the 19th, and after that much more rapidly; not having been finally extirpated till the 7th of January in the capital, and remaining till March in the village of Curmi. It was also communicated to Gozza.

During the whole progress of this attack the contagious nature of the disorder was manifested by every circumstance which occurred, with regard either to its spreading, or its diminution and final extinction. It did not spread from one house to its neighbour, merely from vicinity, but was traced to distant houses through relations and friends. All the early cases were, therefore, dispersed through various parts of the town, and its progress was irregular and straggling. In the country it was the same; and, in almost every instance, the cases could be traced to communication with the capital. It was much hastened and aggravated by a false confidence in the people, that it must subside as the summer advanced. Its eradication was equally the consequence of the adoption of more vigorous measures, viz. proper classification and absolute separation of the healthy, the sick, and the suspected. It was owing to the opposition which many of the inhabitants had shown to these measures that its progress was so destructive; and this was particularly proved by its protracted residence in the village of Curmi. When once it had become confined within walls, all farther danger ceased. It was farther one of the leading causes of the great progress of this attack, that the people could not for a long time be induced to believe in its nature, while their incredulity was supported by the dissemination of documents in support of that opinion.

It is remarkable also, in this case, that, though Gozza, owing to the strictness of its regulations, was free from the plague during its progress in Malta, it appeared there after it had been overcome in the latter island. Its introduction was clearly traced to a box of clothes brought from Malta after the restrictions had ceased. The disease, in this case, was speedily arrested by the rigid enforcement of precautionary measures, only ninety-six altogether having died of it. This history of success offers a strong evidence in favour of the contagious nature of the plague, as does the former, where the precautions were for so long a time ineffectual.

In Albania, in the same year, the same results took place. The introduction was traced to an inhabitant who brought it frum Romelia; and the progress was similar, as were the effects of the cautions adopted.

Now it is very important to remark, in this instance, that the Mahometans themselves became sensible of the value of these precautions, and profited by them. These principles are indeed speedily gaining ground in many other parts of the Turkish empire, and more particularly in those which are less connected with Constantinople, and which have the most direct commercial intercourse with the Christian nations. Tripoli has been long secured from the disease by the exertions of the present Pacha, assisted by medical persons from Europe. It is not many years since it appeared in the arsenal of that city, but was stopped by the exertions of an English physician. That these more enlightened views of the subject are still spreading, is as probable as it is desirable.

We may add to these instances its recent appearance at Corfu and Cephalonia. It appeared first at Marathia, in the former island, in December, 1815; and was traced to the introduction of some infected goods from Albania. This attack was quelled with some difficulty by the active interference of the British government, and in the usual manner. In Cephalonia it was also introduced from Albania in some clothes taken from two Turks who had died of the disease.

It is a strong confirmation of the contagion of the plague, that the troops employed on all those occasions as guards continued healthy. Had it been an epidemic merely, that could not have been the case, as they were in the very focus of the disorder. In such cases as the epidemic remittent, new comers suffer, while the natives comparatively escape; the very reverse of which was the case here. This happened remarkably enough at Argostoli; that fever breaking out about the same time as the plague, and destroying many soldiers while the inhabitants escaped.

If any thing could be supposed established by evidence, it is the contagious nature of the plague. It has been traced to the contact of infected persons, and to infected goods; it is propagated from hand to hand, and preserved dormant in proper substances for an indefinite length of time; while it is completely prevented by any precautions that are effectual enough to prevent this kind of communication. By shutting themselves up in their houses, the European consuls and merchants escape it annually in Smyrna, Tripoli, Algiers, and elsewhere; while the inhabitants, who neglect these precautions, are dying all around them. It has also been propagated by inoculation, as in the case of Dr. White.

It has been argued, on the other hand, against the contagious nature of the plague, that, if this were the case, its ravages should never cease in those countries like Turkey, where no measures of precaution are taken against it. But this argument applies alike to all contagious diseases, which exhaust themselves, and are again renewed on favourable occasions, owing to circumstances which we have never yet ascertained. But in truth it never entirely ceases in Turkey; it slumbers but to break out again, and under favourable circumstances is re-excited, as other contagions are, without fresh importation from what we have considered its native seat. Were it not that the measures resorted to in Christian countries exterminate it, the case would be the same in these; and that it admits of being so exterminated is proof enough of its contagious nature.

The efficacy of the quarantine laws is an argument of the same kind, since these have always been found effectual in preventing the importation, except when accidentally infringed; and there can be no doubt that all these means, duly enforced, would produce the same effects in all the Turkish states as they have been known to do in Tripoli. Occasional exemptions from the plague form no arguments against its contagious nature, because this happens equally in every disease of that kind.

It is next important to remark, that, although the disorder is thus contagious by communication, it is not propagated generally through the atmosphere. Were this the case, all the usual precautions would be useless, nor could they have the effects which has been shown to follow them. Thousands of persons in Turkey, daily, and in those cases where it has been imported into Christian countries, have breathed the atmosphere of an infected city, or even of an infected house, without injury. It is a serious mistake to suppose that a single person, or even many infected persons, can contaminate the air of a city.

It is farther an important mistake to imagine, that the propagation of the plague depends entirely on the season, whatever may be the fact respecting Egypt as we formerly stated it. It is proved by much and sad experience, that neither extremes of heat nor cold have succeeded in checking its progress in the countries into which it has been imported, whether in Europe, or Africa, or Asia. The mortality from this disease has been experienced in every season of the year. In Malta and the Ionian islands this was sufficiently remarkable, as it has been in other cases of European importation. In Egypt and Turkey it has, for these last twenty years at least, been found throughout the year at many periods; and it is not very long since the mortality in Constantinople amounted to 2000 daily when the streets were covered with snow.

Nevertheless, instances do occur which justify this opinion to a certain extent. We have already seen what happens in Egypt on the occurrence of the north winds in summer. It is also remarkable, that, although a great commerce by caravans is carried on between Palestine, Syria, Arabia, and the East Indies, from infected places, and that the crews of ships navigating the Persian Gulf have been known to die of the disease, the plague has very rarely been received at Guzzerat, Surat, or Bombay.

The establishment of these opinions is a matter of the highest importance. It is always when the plague has been mistaken for other diseases, or when its first steps have been overlooked, that its progress has been most secure, and, ultimately, most fatal. These errors have been frequent and destructive. It is when the disease has manifested itself in an unquestionable manner, so as to excite a salutary terror and a conviction of its contagious nature, that it has been counteracted and checked. The great mortality at Marseilles arose from the obstinate disbelief in its contagious nature; those in London from its having crept in unperceived till it had spread itself over the whole town, and from the consequent difficulty of adopting the necessary regulations. In both, it was at length checked, though late, by the same means as those which we have already described. In these cases it was sufficiently proved that the air was not infected; since, in the former city, the Monastery of the Visitation, which was situated between the Plague Hospital and the burying ground, escaped, as did another convent, which lay in the way of that hospital, and past which the sick and suspected were carried every day. In Cambridge, the colleges remained uninfected by keeping apart from the town's people, and, in a plague at Rome in 1656, the monasteries were similarly exempt.

The substances capable of transmitting the contagion of the plague are various. The most efficacious in this respect, and therefore the most dangerous, are soft porous bodies, and, first among these, animal substances, such as wool, feathers, furs, hair, and silk. After these follow cotton, flax, hemp, paper, and all manufactures into which these materials enter. It has been said that metal and wood do not convey it; but it is suspected that foul and rusty metals, such as money, can transmit it, and that wood, unless varnished, is doubtful or suspicious. It is thought in the Levant that it is not conveyed in bread, but at Marseilles the physicians are of a different opinion. It is said that it cannot be attached to plants, but that it does attach itself to odoriferous flowers, and that it is conveyed in this way. Dogs, cats, rats, and other domestic animals, form other modes of communication, and are therefore destroyed wherever proper precautions are adopted.

All these substances are no less dangerous for the facility with which they part with the contagion to the human species, than for the pertinacity with which they retain it, and that for a great length of time. It has been found more than once, that ropes, bed-clothes, and other similar articles, which had been used about patients, infected with the plague, have communicated the disorder even many years after they had been laid by and forgotten. It is sufficient merely to touch such an object to become infected, and in fact they are even more dangerous than the bodies of persons labouring under the disease. In this way an individual may carry the contagion in his clothes without being himself infected; and some remarkable instances have occurred, where a person has carried infected clothes about him for a considerable time without suffering, when the casual contact of them, after being taken off, had excited the disease in another person.

It is an important question to ask, whether the contagion of the plague can be communicated through the air alone. This is the question between infection and contagion, which has been the subject of so much controversy. The most prevailing opinion, however, is, that the disease is exclusively contagious, and not infectious, or that it can only be communicated by contact. Whatever the truth may be in this case, the doctrine may become inconvenient and dangerous. There is no doubt that, if there is a free circulation of good air, a sound person does not receive the infection from a diseased one, provided that he keeps at a small distance. This is experienced every day in the plague countries.

But this is not the case when the air is stagnant or foul, charged with various exhalations, or with miasmata and other seeds of disease. Such air, it is undoubted, acts the part of a conductor to the poison, and produces the same effects as immediate contact would do. Thus in the case of common typhus, the air of an ill-ventilated hospital will transmit or produce the fever, even at great distances from the bodies of the patients. In a similar manner it has been found that the same contagion, as well as that of the plague, has been propagated rapidly, and with the most pernicious effects, in low grounds, then subject to marsh miasmata, when the same people in more elevated and in more ventilated situations, escaped.

These remarks apply to the plague considered inde-

pendently. That disorder has its three periods of rise, of severity, and of decline. At the two extremes, nothing of this kind can take place. But when the disease is at its height, and the infected numerous, and when some neglect and disorder are the necessary consequence, it is more than likely that some accumulation of pestilential matter, to a dangerous degree, may take place in an air which, at all times, in narrow streets and similar situations, must be considered a favourable conductor, from the quantity of various impurities which it contains. In these cases ventilation is not easy, as every day's experience proves, from the smells thus accumulated in the narrow streets and close parts of all great towns in particular. This was fully proved in Vienna, when, about the height of the plague in that city, the air was so contaminated, that the disease was taken by merely passing through the streets. That it has been communicated a thousand times by the breath of a patient, there is no doubt; and thus physicians and nurses have fallen victims to the disease in hospitals, even when the greatest precautions against contact were used.

To this foul state and consequent conducting power of the atmosphere, we must attribute the bad effects that have been experienced from burning various matters in apartments, and lighting fires in the streets; a practice as old as the time of Hippocrates. This practice was tried at Toulon, so that the air was thick with smoke, and the consequence of it was materially to increase the rapidity of the progress of the disease. In houses, the same consequences have been produced by the use of perfumes and fumigations, a fashion so common in all diseases; but the utility of a pure air produced by a free ventilation is now well understood.

It is a question how far a person who has received the contagion, but in whom the disease has made no progress, can communicate it. Notwithstanding some ancient opinions that have prevailed on this subject, it does not appear that the body alone can communicate it, at least if washed and shaved. It appears rather that the contagion is retained in their hair and clothes, as *fomites*, and that in this way the poison is communicated to others, long before the infected person suffers from it, or even when he escapes its action altogether. An exception, however, seems required respecting the body when suffering from the disease, or when in a febrile state, or in a heated or perspiring one; in which cases there seems no doubt that the contact of the naked skin will communicate the disease. All the excretions of the body, as well as the perspiration and the breath, seem to be impregnated with the poisons at the same time, and to communicate it readily. That some persons have thought otherwise, will scarcely be considered an argument against this doctrine, when we know that this is the case with all other contagions, and when the fact is itself supported by the experience of innumerable persons, physicians, and others. Were it even otherwise, it would be a safe error to adopt this belief and to act on it; nor is it easy to see what advantages those persons have proposed to themselves or the community by circulating doctrines that can only tend to danger; actuated apparently by vanity, or by the love of singularity, or opposition.

It has also been a question whether this contagion can be communicated by the dead body. Mons. Desgenettes thinks that it cannot; but this is also a dangerous doctrine. This may be true enough in particular cases ; but in a disease subject to so many varieties, and often so anomalous, it is better to regulate ourselves on a far wider experience. Whatever might have happened in the French Egyptian army, this opinion is contradicted by all the experience of Marseilles, and indeed by the examples in general that have occurred in Christian Europe. In these cases, it has always been found very difficult to get persons to bury the dead ; and the persons so employed always died speedily afterwards. At Marseilles, in consequence of this, the galley slaves were employed in this service, and they also died. The particular instances of this nature were numerous ; and that the general principle is true of other contagions, is proved by the same having occurred in cases of typhus and of small-pox. These facts seem to prove two things, namely, that the poison is communicated from dead bodies, and that it is transmitted by the air.

It is unnecessary to inquire by which of these methods the poison is rendered most active in exciting the disease, and by what road it is conveyed into the system. It is supposed that all contagion is introduced through the lungs or the skin, or both, and that it cannot enter by the stomach, as it is destroyed by the digestive powers. The same has been judged true of the plague, because dogs have swallowed the poison in this way without injury, when they received the disease by means of inoculation.

Substances and means of destroying the contagion have been anxiously sought after in all times ; and innumerable substances have been proposed and used. Fumigations and perfumes of all kinds have had their several reputations, as in other contagious diseases. These are inefficacious, to say the least ; and we have already shown, that, in some cases, they may be injurious. But we have no manner of doubt that this contagion, like all others, is destroyed by the vapours of the mineral acids, the nitrous, muriatic, and sulphureous, and by oxymuriatic gas. The sulphureous acid, however, is not applicable to living bodies, on account of its destructive properties to life ; but the nitrous and oxymuriatic have been found both effectual and admissible in all contagious fevers, and would doubtless be equally so in the plague.

These methods are, however, so little known as yet, even to physicians, except in a few places, and so much neglected by ordinary practitioners, even at home, that it is no cause for surprise that they have never been introduced into the plague countries, as they unquestionably might, with advantage. In the Levant, exposure to a free air is the great expedient, both for things and persons. Water is also found efficacious ; but this cannot be used except for particular sorts of goods and objects. For these, it is usual in all houses that are insulated in an infected place, to be provided with a vessel of water, or vinegar and water, through which every thing that comes into the house is passed. It is quite agreed, however, that water is as efficacious as vinegar.

This fact proves, that the matter of this contagion is dissolved or decomposed by water. So valuable is this practice, that it is proper to keep, in all wards and infected houses, buckets of water ; often changing them for fresh ones, and passing through them every object which has communicated with a patient, and which may be capable of conveying the infection.

It is probable also, since so many persons who are exposed to the plague escape it, that there are constitu-

tions and particular states of the system unsusceptible of the poison. This condition is the reverse of that which forms the predisposition to disease, in this case, as in all others of contagious disorders. To investigate what these conditions are, is a matter of great importance, as giving confidence in the midst of danger, and as rendering us capable of availing ourselves of the services of such persons, always wanted in conducting the treatment and prevention of the plague. A few instances of this indisposition to the disease will not be misplaced.

In the plague of Vicenza, in a poor family of six persons, two only took the disease, although the whole lived in constant and free communication. A similar case occurred to Massaria, in his own house. In Marseilles, the two commissioners who were incredulous respecting the contagion, and Deidier, who believed in it, communicated freely with the patients, as in ordinary diseases, even to the opening of the bodies after death, and without injury ; this being one of the circumstances which confirmed the belief of many respecting the non-contagious nature of the plague. The same happened to the curate, the surgeon, and the notary, in one of the villages ; even though the latter had lost two sons by the disease, whom he was obliged to carry to the grave on his back. A more remarkable instance was that of a child, which was placed in the coffin with its dead mother, with the expectation that it must die at any rate ; yet being afterwards removed, it did not take the disease, and lived. Many instances of the same kind occurred in the French Egyptian army, even among husbands, wives, and children, but we need not detail more of them.

No reasonable conjectures have been offered respecting these predisposing or indisposing causes : but the facts themselves serve to confirm our doubts of the efficacy of all the pretended preventatives for this disorder. It will be proper, however, to inquire into some of the collateral circumstances which attend the propagative inactivity of the disease, and the reverse.

It was already seen, that, in Egypt, the disease suddenly ceased when the hot south winds ceased, and the north winds began to blow. It is also remarkable in this country, that the inhabitants of Matwrieh, situated on the margin of water, are nearly exempt from the plague ; a fact, however, which applies to the endemic rather than to the communicated disorder. As to this latter, daily experience seems to prove, that the state and temperature of the air have no effect on it, or at least very little. To the instance of Constantinople, we may add, that it raged in Russia during the most severe cold ; nor, in Marseilles, did it cease, as was expected, during the heats of summer. It is thus an important point to make the distinction in this case between the endemic and the communicated disease.

It is generally thought that fear assists in the propagation of the plague, as in that of all contagious diseases. It may certainly, in timid persons, render a slight attack fatal ; it may even facilitate the reception of the contagion. But it is a great and fatal mistake, on the other hand, to imagine that it may be braved with impunity, or that fear is necessary to its propagation, as the reverse of this is experienced every day.

It is also thought that old persons, from the dryness of their skins, are less susceptible of the plague, and that its reception is facilitated by the use of the warm bath. Water carriers, or persons much exposed to cold, have been said to be comparatively free from it ; and it is also thought that, among the working classes, it attacks most readily bakers, cooks, smiths, and others, subject to violent heat and changes of temperature.

It has been supposed that the free use of wine was a preventative. This notion is as old as the plague of Athens, yet it has been decidedly opposed by Desgenettes, and others, who farther say, that drunkards are particularly susceptible of it, and that with them it is always fatal. Certain chronic diseases, issues, the lues venerea, and the itch, have also been thought to ward off this poison; but that these, on the contrary, facilitate its ravages, is decidedly asserted by the French physicians employed in Egypt. Respecting the power of the small-pox in this respect, there is some doubt; as strong instances in its favour are given; but we have great hesitation in believing that the vaccine infection, as has been asserted, is a preservative against the plague.

On the Practical Prevention of the Plague.

Of preventative medicinal practices, it has already been seen that we entertain strong doubts. Bleeding has been supposed a means of prevention, as has the exhibition of various medicines that must be considered trifling, or absolutely inert. The most effectual precaution is flight, or seclusion; and, after that, the cautiously avoiding contact with infected persons, or infected objects, or with any thing which is even suspected. The use of water we already noticed. For those who are employed about the sick, it is recommended to keep a fearless mind, fully occupied in the business; to touch no body, even in the streets; never to sit down in a house; not to stay a moment longer near the sick than is necessary; to avoid their breath, and to dip the fingers in water after feeling the pulses, to change the clothes outside the house in returning, and to cause them to be washed or ventilated; to wash all the body at the same time: and lastly, to avoid all intemperance, fatigue, or other debilitating causes, and to live well.

Much has been said of frictions with oil, or of the external use of this substance, as a preservation against the plague. It is said that those who are employed as carriers of oil in Alexandria and Tunis, always escape. They are so convinced of its efficacy, that they will not lay aside their oily clothes during the continuance of the pestilence, and when this has happened, or that they have cleaned themselves in the warm bath, they have taken the infection like others. It was also remarked in Marseilles, that tanners, curriers, soap makers, and others accustomed to handle oily substances, were least infected with the disease. In opposition to this, it must be stated, that, in the plague of Malta, in 1812, this practice was tried without success; and that, were the remedy as efficacious as has been said, the Armenians, Jews, Greeks, and others, who, in the plague countries, do not believe in predestination, would undoubtedly have recourse to it. We must think that this is a very doubtful preservative indeed.

On Public Methods of Prevention.

We have no reason to doubt that, as long as the wise laws which Christian Europe has established to prevent the introduction and spreading of the plague, are rigidly obeyed, they will continue to be as efficacious as they have hitherto been in this respect. The many plagues, however, which have appeared among these nations, and, among others, one that was introduced into Gressenber in Siberia, as lately as 1820, prove that neglect of these regulations is at any time sufficient to permit this formidable poison to establish itself among us. In these cases, the original evil arises in the ports where cotton and other goods are shipped; and it appears too, that the precautions always resorted to in case of sea-carriage, are very much neglected when these articles are conveyed overland.

The most pernicious neglect of this nature is that which takes place among the ports of the Turkish empire itself, though it appears that they are at length becoming sensible of the value of preventative means, and that such, more or less perfect, have already been adopted in many of the towns of the Levant. This has been the case particularly at Salonica and Cyprus: and in Egypt, the new Pacha has built a lazaretto at Alexandria, among many other improvements in the general condition of that country. If Egypt, however, continues, as it always has been, the original nursery of the disease, these precautions can at least never exterminate it; and, under the Turkish government, it is scarcely to be expected that measures of prevention will ever be generally adopted. It is our duty, therefore, never to relax, since our safety must depend on ourselves.

As the plague has lately been raging all round the Mahometan shores of the Mediterranean, the strictest regulations have been enforced, particularly on the coasts of France and Spain. Troops are established along the shore at various places, and guard boats are employed in keeping off every vessel that might approach the land. It is a capital crime for any one to enter, or to introduce merchandize privately. Nor is any vessel arriving from Barbary, Egypt, or Turkey, allowed to enter a port, except under the regulations of the quarantine, or any vessel which has, at sea, communicated with others from these ports. At Marseilles, the same strict regulations are extended to fishing boats that are suspected to have dealings with vessels at sea. These, and other regulations, have always been found effectual wherever the plague has been raging violently; and wherever that disease has been introduced, it has been when its existence was not suspected in the Mahometan states; a proof that the misfortune has arisen from relaxing or neglecting the regulations. This shows the necessity of strictness; particularly as these nations always conceal the existence of the disease among them as long as they can.

Whatever details be adopted in these regulations, their object is to prevent communication between all persons or things in a state of suspicion, and those who are in health; the same general principles being applicable as in all cases of specific contagion in other diseases. The efficacy of all the regulations which commonly go by the name of quarantine, was fully established in the French army in Egypt as long as they could be adhered to; and the reverse took place as soon as the disturbances arising from the state of war prevented them from being duly enforced.

One of the most difficult parts of the quarantine regulations consists in the treatment of infected goods. These are received in lazarettos, and subjected to purification by water, and by exposure to the sun and air, or to artificial heat. When this is effectually done, the time required for this purification need not exceed a few days, though fear and prejudice have not generally concurred in this belief. The tents employed for the plague patients lately in Cephalonia, were returned into the stores safely, after being merely washed four or five times successively in sea water and dried in the sun. We may therefore conclude, that all bale goods received into lazarettos might equally be purified in a few days, and that fourteen, with proper care, are fully as much as can ever be required. Making allowance for some neglect on the part of the officers employed, twenty ought to be sufficient for all purposes; as, far within this time, should the disease be present, it must be communicated, since it cannot lie dormant in the human body.

The present period of quarantine for goods is therefore far too long; and as it lays heavy restraints on commerce, the laws are the more apt to be infringed. Thus their very severity defeats their object, by encouraging smuggling and all other methods of evasion. The rigidity of these regulations seems far more censurable, when extended, as is done, to vessels in ballast and ships of war. It is an evil effect, also, of the severity of these laws, that no provision is left for the exercise of the judgment in particular cases. As long, however, as the general practice continues thus strict, and the period of quarantine thus long, no state dares to differ from it. In such a case, particular restrictions would be placed on its foreign commerce; and its vessels, instead of a modified quarantine, would be subjected to the same treatment as that used towards ships arriving from ports in a state of disease. Thus, if any modifications are attempted, as has often been suggested, they could only result from some general concurrence of all the governments concerned. Such a modification as would remove all temptations to evasion, would probably add to our security instead of diminishing it, which it would also be of material benefit to commerce. As to the quarantine of persons, it is very plainly far too long; and thus also evils arise from the great temptation to infringe the regulations. It is quite certain that the disease cannot lie dormant in the constitution. If the clothes of the individuals are subjected to the proper treatment in the lazarettos, the person himself, after proper washing, may be considered safe from the power of the disease, and of course incapable of communicating infection, after a very few days.

Description of the Plague.

The definition of this disease is, that it is a contagious fever, very severe, generally, and rapid in its progress, accompanied by buboes, carbuncles, and petechiæ. It spreads rapidly by contact, and is generally fatal to about two-thirds of those attacked by it. The attack is very commonly sudden, and begins with headach in the forehead and occiput. There is either no shivering, or there are violent and short tremors, alternating with heats. If the patient feels a burning heat within, that is not perceived at the surface, and very often that heat is succeeded by great cold. The physiognomy becomes immediately affected; the eyes become red, and acquire a ferocious aspect. The headach then increases, and is sometimes very severe, though more generally dull and heavy, with a sensation of numbness. The pain also extends along the spine, to the joints and to the limbs. These symptoms are followed by vertigo, with threatening of syncope, and afterwards delirium, which is at first mild but afterwards becomes fierce. The tongue is dry and yellowish, but without thirst; there is nausea, with ineffectual efforts to vomit, or, if any thing is brought up, it is green bile. The respiration is laborious, with general uneasiness. During this time flying pains are felt among the muscles and glands, and buboes appear in the groins, the arm-pits, or the parotids, together with carbuncles. Petechiæ also occur, generally numerous and of large size, sometimes with vibices, which more frequently, however, come out immediately after death. There is nothing particular in the alvine excretions, though they are sometimes liquid. The urine is often turbid, with an oily aspect. The smell of the patient is occasionally nauseous, but if the disease has lasted a few days, the perspiration has often a sweetish disagreeable smell, which attaches itself to the surrounding objects, and can only be got rid of by washing or ventilation. The disease varies in duration from three to seven days, although the patients sometimes die within a few hours of the attack. If it passes the eighth day there are hopes of recovery. The pulse varies extremely, being sometimes frequent and hard, sometimes feeble and irregular, and, in some cases, it is found to vary little from the healthy state.

In these cases the disease is sometimes not easily discovered. The patient appears labouring under debility, becomes melancholy, morose, or anxious, with unpleasant sensations about the heart, and pains in the loins, and acquires the peculiar physiognomy which attends this disease. In other cases of this nature, the patient dies suddenly at the first attack, as if by apoplexy; a fact which has been known to occur among the persons employed in opening infected bales. Some also die at periods from one to three or four days, without any affection of the pulse, and without buboes or eruptions, complaining of nothing but faintness and weakness, but still with the peculiar physiognomy by which this disorder is recognised even at a distance, sparkling eyes, and an expression of countenance resembling that of persons under the hydrophobia.

Though the prostration of strength is a very common symptom, it is by no means universal, as many persons have been known to walk within a few hours of their death; and even the soldiers in the French army in Egypt often marched for many hours after they were attacked. The same indeed happens in severe remittent fevers. In a few instances in the plague, even the intellect has been preserved till near the time of death.

The appearance of buboes and carbuncles decides the nature of the disease wherever there may be any doubt. The bubo is an inflammation of the glands, already mentioned, which it attacks, sudden and painful. It terminates by resolution, suppuration, or gangrene, the latter being always fatal. There are often as many as four buboes, sometimes many more, and perhaps as many carbuncles; and nothing but great inattention can confound these with the same affections proceeding from other causes, though, in some cases, on their first appearance, they have been mistaken for venereal affections. The appearance of the carbuncle is also sudden, but it sometimes vanishes and returns again. When it breaks, it is by many points discharging a yellow or black fluid, which destroys the neighbouring skin and even the muscles. Sometimes the carbuncle is single, at others it consists of many pustules, which at length join, and form a large ulcer.

Putrefaction occurs speedily after death; the limbs remain flexible, hæmorrhages take place, and petechiæ or vibices appear. On dissection, the gall-bladder has been found distended with greenish-black bile, the inside of the intestines and stomach have been covered with a yellow mucus, and the conglobate glands indurated. But dissections, for obvious reasons, have not been numerous.

It has been asked, whether the buboes and other eruptions are a favourable effort of nature; and, of course, what their treatment ought to be. It is commonly thought that their disappearance is a bad sign; yet there are many instances of recovery under these circumstances. The plague has sometimes a crisis at three, five, or seven days, marked by the urine and perspiration; but it does not appear that the eruptions are ever critical. Nothing is known of the proximate cause of this disease, more than that of fever, and we will not waste upon this subject what, after all, are nothing but words.

It is very important to be able to distinguish this disease with certainty, even in the slightest cases, and on the first attack; as it is in these that its progress is most dangerous. Unfortunately the first symptoms are often very equivocal; but, in the Levant, where physicians are always on the watch for it, the slightest marks of debility, sickness, or pain of the head, are carefully watched. In our own country, these would naturally pass for common fever, should the presence of the plague not be suspected. Many imaginary signs, peculiar to this disease, are talked of in the Levant, particularly among the Turks; but European physicians consider them as unmeaning. The presence of buboes, or petechiæ and carbuncles, leave no doubt: but in all cases the physician must be guided by many circumstances united, and by such collateral considerations as may be derived from the presence or probability of this contagion.

Prognosis in the Plague.

The disease may be divided into three periods, its rise, vigour, and declension. It is in the first stage that cures are chiefly effected, and often, it is likely, by the hand of nature, even when medicines have gained the credit. All general attacks of the disease are most fatal to people during the times when there are most sick. During its decline at Marseilles, about one-half recovered, but during its more general prevalence not more than one-third were saved. It does not prevent the occurrence of the usual remittents and other diseases of a country, and, by careless persons, these have sometimes been confounded with it.

In individual cases, the prognostic depends on the violence of the symptoms. At Marseilles, the favourable cases were attended only with slight shivering at the time of the attack, pain in the epigastrium, nausea, vomiting, headach, and vertigo, with a moderate fever that terminated in five or six days, by sweat or alvine dejections, but without buboes or eruptions. But even in some of these, there were buboes that suppurated quickly, or of which the suppuration was protracted without inconvenience for twenty or thirty days, or which were resolved and disappeared.

In the next class, besides the symptoms above enumerated, there were pains about the region of the heart, great prostration of strength, fainting, oppression, coma, delirium, phrenzy, hæmorrhages, and diarrhea, with buboes that suppurated with difficulty, carbuncles, pustules and petechiæ. But even in these cases, if the patients survived four days, about one quarter of them recovered. In the last and most severe cases, the patients were suddenly attacked with violence, as already remarked, and generally died in a few hours, from one even to twenty-four, although the pulse was but slightly or not at all affected. These patients complained of little but debility, but were always known by their peculiar physiognomy already described.

In Egypt, in the French army, those who had a slight fever, with delirium and buboes, almost always recovered; the delirium abating on the fifth day, and the fever disappearing on the seventh, was attended with a considerable proportion of recoveries. In the more severe cases, where there was much delirium and fever, with carbuncles, buboes, and petechiæ, very few recovered, and death took place between the third and fifth days. In the Levant, it is esteemed a good sign if there are many buboes; and even thirteen have been known: but when there are buboes and carbuncles together, the cases are esteemed nearly hopeless. A firm hard bubo is esteemed favourable; a flaccid or soft one the contrary; particularly if it is attended with convulsions, hiccup, cardialgia, diarrhœa, or sweatings. It is farther said that a bright red inflammation in all these tumours is a fatal sign, and that a violet colour is favourable.

Strong robust persons die in a greater proportion than the feeble, the women, and the children: menstruation in women is also said to terminate the plague favourably. In the celebrated plague of Morocco in 1808, the young, strong and healthy, were first attacked; then women and children, and lastly valetudinarians and aged persons. This is similar to what happens in ordinary contagious fevers.

It has been a frequent, and is an important question, whether the same individual is subject to the plague more than once.

The opinions differ, unfortunately, on this subject. In Marseilles, it is said that the convalescents, who, with this expectation, were employed to attend the sick, all relapsed and died. The same happened in the French army in Egypt, according to the reports of their physicians. On this view, inoculation, which has been proposed as a means of diminishing the violence of the disease, must be useless.

But Mr. Tully, our latest writer on this subject, who was employed with the British army in Malta, and in the Ionian islands, in this department, maintains an opinion directly the reverse, as far as his own experience is concerned. At Corfu, twelve persons who had had the disease at different periods, were employed by him in the hospitals and lazarettos, and they all escaped; as did four soldiers who were employed as orderlies in the same situations. Among the expurgators in the lazarettoes, there were also many persons who had had the plague many years before, in Smyrna and at other places. These all escaped infection; and indeed such was their own confidence in their immunity, that they made use of no precaution. Mr. Tully concludes by remarking, that he never witnessed a single relapse, nor any instance where a person took the plague a second time. Some irregular febrile symptoms were indeed observed during the period of convalescence, but in no case was it any thing like a relapse.

It is admitted that, in any febrile attack, ancient pestilential buboes have become painful and inflamed. These affections seem often to have been mistaken for attacks of the plague, and have probably given rise to the opinion of its return when it has not been present. In this state at present remain the notions of physicians on this part of the subject.

Treatment of the Plague.

That this disease does sometimes terminate by the assistance of nature alone, gives ground to hope that medical treatment may really be of use. The two chief errors hitherto seem to have been, that a specific

Plague.

against the plague might be found, and that, being a highly putrescent disorder, it was to be treated by cordials and stimulants. Others, again, finding the symptoms variable, have been content to attack these as they arose, without adopting any fixed principles of cure. The treatment, in short, has been chiefly of an empirical nature.

In the plague which appeared in the French army at Jaffa, bark, tamarinds, coffee, and camphor in large doses, were among the remedies employed, but without success, as were sudorifics, emetics, and blisters. Bleeding was thought to be of advantage when the season was coldest. At Damietta, the same means were all resorted to with as little success, though it was thought that blisters were useful. From these reports, bleeding and blisters appear to be the only remedies that have been attended with any advantage.

In the plague of Vicenza, in 1576, Massaria found that bleeding was of great use, and that purgatives were injurious. Laxatives alone were admissible. In a subsequent plague in Italy, in the following autumn, advantages were also derived from bleeding by Septal, a Milanese physician. Yet this practice had not the same success at Rome at the same time; and Fallopius relates, that out of a thousand persons bled by one physician, only two were saved. The same uncertainty has appeared in the current practice of the Levant; the Greek physicians having sometimes found bleeding advantageous, and, in other cases, quite ineffectual.

Whether these differences are to be attributed to the climate or the season, is uncertain; but it is probable that, from some cause or other, the condition of the disease varied on those different occasions. Clear indications for this practice seem to lie in the circumstances of a youthful and plethoric habit, a strong pulse, violent headach, and oppressed respiration. This practice is also indicated if there have been previously suppressed hæmorrhages or other evacuations, and if the season is cold, as in winter and spring. But without the presence of these symptoms, it is probably an inefficacious or dangerous remedy.

When the stomach or intestines are loaded, emetics or laxatives seem to be indicated, according to the circumstances. In small-pox and in fevers, this practice is alike useful; but unless these symptoms were present, it does not seem safe to adopt it in the plague. That the stomach is not necessarily affected in this disease, is certain; since, even when buboes are present, the patients have been sometimes known to preserve their appetite. As diarrhœa is a dangerous symptom, it seems judicious to avoid any thing which may bring it on.

The slighter cases seem best abandoned to nature; supplying the patient only with light aliment and the ordinary drinks in fevers. When the nervous system seems much affected, or the vital forces are much depressed, with faintings, violent delirium, or convulsions, and when the eruptions do not appear, or there are only petechiæ, it becomes a question, whether the common cordials and alexipharmaes are really advantageous or not. It seems safest at present to regulate our practice on these occasions by that usual in the typhus.

Sweating has been recommended, but apparently on theoretical grounds, and the practice has not been attended with any success. Neither has the use of cold water, which some have recommended as a specific in this disease. The use of oil has also been much celebrated. At Tangier it is said to have been very successful, used as a friction, lately in 1819. This practice was recommended by our Consul Mr. Baldwin, and by Father Louis of Pavia, whom we formerly mentioned as for so many years resident at Smyrna. This application excites sweating. The method is to apply the oil by means of a sponge, and in such a manner as to cause the skin to absorb a pound of oil, as it is said, in about three minutes. This practice is resorted to on the first day, and continued daily till there is a favourable change. It has also been used at Smyrna, and, as it is said, with great success. Vegetable diet alone is used.

Even on this subject, however, testimonies differ. Dr. Frank thought it successful in Egypt. Messieurs Renati and Rozel did not find that effect from it which they expected from Baldwin's account, but they thought that it was sometimes attended with advantage. In Malta lately, the oil frictions were thought of use in the first and last states of the disease, but were of no advantage when it was at its height. This perhaps will explain the secret of this boasted remedy, which appears efficacious only when the disorder would retire without aid.

It is generally recommended to open the buboes, and to treat them and the carbuncles in the simplest possible manner by emollient applications. No advantage was ever derived from more violent practice, or from remedies founded on the notion that these were of a critical nature.

The list of authors on the plague amounts to two hundred and forty. We cannot enumerate what would occupy one of our pages, and shall content ourselves with referring to Russel's Treatise as among the most complete.

PLANETS. See ASTRONOMY, Vol. II. p. 607—649.

PLANETARY MACHINES.

Planetary Machines.

History.

THE machines contrived for exhibiting the motions of the planetary bodies, in different ages of the world, have been mechanical representations of the particular systems that prevailed at the respective times of their construction, and the names given to them seem to have been dictated by circumstances of an arbitrary nature. The appearance of certain *wandering* bodies traversing the regions of space, by motions sometimes direct and sometimes retrograde, in very early ages attracted the notice equally of shepherds and philoso-

Planetary Machines.

History.

phers; and for centuries before telescopes were invented, continued series of observations on the comparative changes of place had determined the various periods of seven primary bodies, with a degree of accuracy that has excited the admiration of succeeding generations. The different suppositions on which the phenomena arising out of these varying motions were attempted to be accounted for, gave rise to different planetary systems: and the principal difficulty to be solved was, whether the sun or the earth was to be considered as the planet next to Mars ; or, in other words, whether the duration of the *year* depended on the revolution of the sun round the earth, or of the earth round the sun. And also, whether the moon, and two inferior planets, revolved round the body that produced the change of seasons, or round the centre of the system. But whatever opinion predominated in any age, it is pretty certain that the mechanism contrived to illustrate that opinion produced corresponding motions. History informs us that astronomy was cultivated by the Chinese, Brahmins, Chaldeans, and Egyptians, many centuries before the Christian era ; and there can be no doubt but that celestial mechanism, of one construction or another, formed one of the many images which superstition, if not philosophy, pointed out as a proper representative of celestial objects.

The three spheres, made more than 2000 years before our Saviour by the Chinese sages Yu-chi, Xuni, and Chun, appear to have contained each seven planets, viz. the Moon, Mercury, Venus, Sun, Mars, Jupiter, and Saturn, with the earth in the centre, round which they probably revolved in different periods of time by some species of mechanism not sufficiently described. The idea that the sun was the fourth planet continued a part of the Ptolemaic system, and the astronomers of the present day, though greatly enlightened, and advocating a system that accounts for all the various changes among the celestial phenomena, yet retain a variety of terms that are calculated to confuse rather than rectify the natural notions of man in his attainment of correct information on the subject of planetary motions, while they continue to bear testimony to the former existence of a system which is now exploded. We still speak of the *sun's* longitude, latitude, right ascension, declination, motion in the ecliptic, &c. as if we still believed him to be actually a planet, and the earth at rest ; and these expressions having become familiar, will probably be transmitted to future generations as appropriate terms in the science of astronomy.

The veneration in which works of genius have been held in all ages has been marked in no instance more clearly than in cases where the celestial sphere has been imitated by human ingenuity. The sphere of Archimedes formed a subject for the Roman poet Claudian, about two hundred years before the Christian epoch ; and Cicero made the invention of Possidonius' sphere the theme of his admiration in his second book " *De Naturá Deorum,*" in which he entertains no doubt but that the *barbarous* Scythian or *Britain* would acknowledge its workmanship to be a proof of the perfection of reason.

We do not find that Ptolemy, who, in the second century, rejected the Egyptian system that gave rise to the Latin names of our week, and who substituted his system of cycles and epicycles, ever attempted the mechanical construction of a machine that should represent these motions, though, in his Almagest, he has given an account of a sphere on which he depicted the constellations, and to which he could refer the apparent paths of the planetary bodies, as Eudoxus had done nearly 500 years before him.

Chromatius, however, the governor of Rome, constructed a machine in the third century, which, probably, was intended to represent the Ptolemaic system ; it is recorded, both by St. Sebastian and St. Polycarp, as being a chamber composed of glass, (*cubiculum holovitreum,*) on which was explained the knowledge of the heavenly bodies, and in the construction of which two hundred pounds weight of gold was employed ; it

is said to have had an ecliptic circle divided into twelve signs, and that the different phases of the moon were shown by mechanism ; but how far this could be considered as a planetary machine does not appear. It has been affirmed, that the saints of that day, either from a supposed *impiety* attaching to this representation of the heavens, or from the known value of the materials of which it was composed, took the liberty of converting the erection into some purpose more agreeable to their own wishes. Their veneration for the heavenly science yielded, probably, to their more powerful attachment to the building made with hands.

The celebrated Chinese astronomer Y-tang had a machine constructed about the year 721, which, according to Father Gaubil, contained many wheels, put into motion by water, that gave motion to the sun, moon, and five planets, and indicated the *ke* or hundredth part of the Chinese day by pointers, one for the day, and the other for the night ; this contrivance also gave notice of the arrival of the *ke*, by making a little image step forwards, and give an audible stroke on the face of a wooden board ; which mechanism must have been anterior to the invention of clocks, except the clepsydræ, or water-clocks, of which this may have been a specimen ; for we find, down to the present day, an evident disposition, in the more scientific mechanics, to apply the maintaining and regulating powers of a clock to produce the recurrence of the day of the month, of the moon's age and phases, and, occasionally, the motions of the planets or satellites, in addition to the indication of the current time.

Of a similar nature must have been the contrivance of William, the abbot of Hirsham, who, in the eleventh century, is said " to have invented a natural horologe in imitation of the celestial hemisphere," (*naturale horologium ad exemplum cœlestis hæmispherii excogitâsse.*) Besides these, we read of various other horologes in the thirteenth, fourteenth, and fifteenth centuries, which have partaken of the joint construction of clocks and planetary machines ; one of which was given by one of the Sultans of Egypt to the Emperor Frederic II. of Germany, in the year 1232. Another was made by the learned Abbot of St. Albans, Richard of Wallingford, which, Leland says, exceeded, in ingenious contrivances and expensive workmanship, every other machine in Europe. And a third was constructed by John Dondi, afterwards styled *Horologius*, from his great skill in horological mechanism. But the first, perhaps the only machine that exhibited the Ptolemaic system, was made by Heirlin, under the direction of the ingenious Werner of Nuremberg, about the year 1500. We are not, however, aware, that any particular description of this piece of mechanism has been recorded, so that we may gain access thereto.

Having arrived at the time when Copernicus, in opposition to all the prejudices of a long established opinion respecting the motion of the sun, made the earth a planet, and fixed the sun in her place, at the centre of what is now called the solar system, we might naturally have expected to meet with some variation in the structure of its mechanical representation ; particularly as clockwork had begun to be cultivated at that time ; but we find that new systems, however plausible, when proposed by humble individuals, are not suddenly adopted by prejudiced minds. The well known clock of Oronce Fineé, in the library of the Pantheon at Paris, was constructed in 1553—1560, several years after the demise of Copernicus, and yet shows the planetary periods on a supposition that the

Planetary
Machines.

History.

Rheita's
planeta-
rium.
A.D. 1650.

Huygens'
automaton.
A.D. 1665.

earth is placed in the centre, with the sun revolving between her and Mars, and carrying his secondaries, Mercury and Venus, along with him. The periods are produced by wheelwork, with a degree of accuracy that does credit to the inventor; and for the first time we find the period of the retrogression of the moon's node included. In a printed *Recueil*, No. $\frac{V}{68}$, in the library already mentioned, it is stated, that the increase and decrease of the planetary velocities are alternately produced by the mechanism, as well as the eccentricities, motions of the nodes and apogees, and deviations from the ecliptic; all which are indicated on the different faces or dials of the machine.

Even so lately as in the year 1650, we are told by Schott, in his "*Technica Curiosa*," that P. Schirleus de Rheita, constructed a planetarium, that represented all the true and mean motions of the planets then known, with their stations, retrogradations, &c. by means of wheelwork actuated by a water wheel, on a supposition that the sun is a planet, accompanied by Mercury and Venus as his satellites. Hence it is evident, that the true solar, or Copernican system of the world, was not generally received at the middle even of the seventeenth century.

The *Automaton* of Christian Huygens was, in all probability, the first planetary machine that represents the motions of the heavenly bodies agreeably to the true system. It is supposed to have been contrived and constructed during the ingenious mechanist's residence at Paris, between the years 1665 and 1681, though its description was not published till the year 1703. The world is indebted to this author for his beautiful method of determining such trains of wheelwork, as shall produce the planetary periods with great precision; which method will be explained presently: but some doubt may be entertained whether he made the best use of his knowledge in the construction of his own mechanism. After he had computed numbers for the teeth of his wheels and pinions for an exact *solar year*, he adopted a train that gave motion to his annual arbor, or prime mover, in 365 days, instead of 365.242, &c. thereby vitiating all his original computations; and Benjamin Martin informs us, that this machine was the *original* from which the orreries of his time derived their chief constituent parts. Many of the larger wheels of the automaton were composed of rings placed a little eccentrically, and kept in their places by rollers, so that an alternate increase and decrease of velocity was effected by a variation in the lengths of the radii, by means of long pinions lying across the contrate edges of the indented rings; while some of the last wheels of certain trains had their teeth cut into unequal sizes, so as to produce the same effect by that inequality. In this machine, all the trains were kept in constant natural motion, by a clock regulated by a balance and balance spring, before the pendulum had yet been applied as the regulating agent. The places of the aphelia and ascending nodes of the planets, as given by Huygens, were taken from the tables of Ricciolus, for the 1st Jan. 1682, which, therefore, was probably the time when the machine was finished, and ready for rectification.

Roemer was mathematician to the French King, (Louis XIV.) at the time when Huygens resided at Paris, and probably caught from him a fondness for astronomical mechanism; for we find him presenting

Planetary
Machines.

History.

Roemer's
satellite
instru-
ment.
A.D. 1679.

Flamsteed with a satellite instrument of his contrivance in the year 1679. It is not improbable but that Huygens may have been consulted by Roemer on the eligibility of his plan, which, being calculated to produce the motions of Jupiter's satellites only, was sooner made, and did not interfere with Huygens' calculations. The construction, too, was different; for Roemer introduced a set of concentric tubes, revolving within one another, which received on their lower extremities, each the second wheel of as many pairs, while the first wheel of each pair was made fast to one common arbor, from which the motion commenced, on a supposition that its revolution was performed in an exact week: hence the periods of the four satellites were produced by four pairs of wheels in as many corresponding revolutions of the arms carrying the satellites round their primary, when attached by friction to the upper ends of their respective tubes. The method of determining the values of these periods will be explained hereafter. As Huygens' automaton was the prototype of the orreries that followed it, so Roemer's satellite instrument dictated the construction, subsequently adopted, for the common Planetarium, where a system of revolving concentric tubes constitutes the basis.

Roemer's
planeta-
rium.
A.D.1735.

In 1735, Roemer published his "*Basis Astronomiæ*," in which he gives a description of a planetarium constructed under his direction, which was finished in 1697, and which appears to have been the very model from which the ordinary planetarium has had not only its form of construction, but its numbers copied. Like the satellite instrument, it has the system of concentric tubes, carrying each a single wheel below, and an arm or radius vector above, in periods produced by as many pairs of wheels, that constitute so many fractions of a year, which is the period fixed on for the revolution of the common arbor, that has all the first moving wheels affixed to it. This is certainly a much more simple construction than that of the automaton, but then it admits of no other than mean, or equable motions, and constant distances.

Martinot's
armillary
sphere.
A.D. 1701.

About the beginning of the eighteenth century, spheres began to be constructed in France, containing planetary motions, and put in motion by clockwork. Martinot's armillary sphere was made, with the sun in the earth's place, in the year 1701; while Pigeon's sphere had the sun in the centre, which is said to have been constructed about the same time; hence, it should seem, the struggle between the two systems of Ptolemy and Copernicus had not been finally relinquished at the commencement of the eighteenth century. In Martinot's sphere the computations made the year only 365 days, but in Pigeon's the year consisted of $365^d.$ $5^h.$ 49^m; so that the latter must have been preferable in more respects than one.

Pigeon's
sphere.

Orrery of
Rowley.
A.D. 1715.

About the year 1715, when Rowley and Graham distinguished themselves in London, by their mechanical skill, the former was applied to by the Earl of Orrery to make a grand machine for representing the motions of the planets in their true periods and orbits, as nearly as could be effected by mechanical means; and when the complex machinery was finished, with some deviations from the construction of the automaton of Huygens, the maker called it, in honour of his noble employer, an ORRERY, which appellation has continued to designate those more complex machines, in which both the revolutions round the sun, and also some of the rotations round the axes, have been mechanically effected at the same time; whereas those which exhibit only the periodic revolutions, or motions in circular concentric orbits, have been called Planetaria, according to the name originally selected by Roemer. By the accounts that have been transmitted to us, some of the contrivances in Rowley's grand orrery, of which there is a specimen preserved at the Royal Observatory at Kew Gardens, were introduced by Graham; but the weight of metal and complexity of the parts, chiefly concealed from the sight, will probably prevent so expensive a machine from being constructed in future; and particularly as five additional planets have been discovered since its formation; and as the general principles of calculation and construction of planetary mechanism are better understood in the nineteenth, than they were in the eighteenth century. Some of the orreries that have been recently made, are calculated not to astonish, but to instruct the student in astronomical science. And, for this reason, we propose not to waste our pages in the minute description of inventions that no longer interest the reader, but to describe those machines only, which, from their improved constructions, are best calculated to convey, at the same time, both amusement and instruction.

Our countryman Ferguson, and his cotemporary genius, Ben. Martin, ought not to be passed over in silence, as they both contributed largely to explain the construction of the different orreries and planetaria, which they themselves improved from time to time, but which remain as specimens only of their ingenuity, since the modern discoveries of five additional primary planets has rendered their best labours defective. The improvement of instruments is a natural consequence of discoveries in any art or science; and it is the fate of those that have long been in use, and much esteemed, to sink in estimation in proportion as more appropriate substitutes are brought forward to supplant them. While a celebrated mechanist in Paris, Antide Janvier, was employed, in Bonaparte's reign, to construct a planetary machine for the instruction of his son, an instructor of British youth directed his attention to the construction of more simple, but equally accurate machines for explaining the phenomena of the solar system, as it includes all the planets hitherto discovered. The instructor we allude to is the Rev. W. Pearson, LL.D. and F.R.S. at present the treasurer of the Astronomical Society of London, which is greatly indebted to his co-operation for its existence as an useful society. As we have been favoured by this gentleman's permission to describe some of the planetary machines constructed under his superintendence, by the late artist Fidler, we presume we shall render a more acceptable service to the public, than if we attached greater importance to more expensive, but less instructive pieces of mechanism, that have survived the estimation in which they were originally held. Of course we do not wish to bring into disrepute those scenic representations of the heavenly bodies, which are produced by moving transparencies, of any description, for the amusement rather than the instruction of a wondering audience; but our aim is to present to our readers, whom we must consider as composing the scientific class of British inhabitants, an account of machinery equally calculated to amuse the learned, and to instruct the learner.

Examination of Planetary Wheelwork.

Every person who purchases a planetary machine,

of any description, ought to make himself acquainted with the powers and properties of that machine; but few persons would be able to do this without some previous general instruction how to proceed. When the mechanism consists of as many single pairs of wheels as there are heavenly bodies to be actuated, which is the case with Roemer's satellite instrument and planetarium, the first thing to be done is to ascertain in what assumed period the driving, or first moving wheel, is intended by the maker to revolve; which generally may be done by noticing the index and dial, if any, that are connected with the arbor that carries the said first wheel; but if there be no such index, then the handle itself may be considered as the index, and its connexion with the first wheel will show, after a few turns, whether an increase or decrease of velocity is produced in the arm or lever that carries the body, which is usually the last mover. In this way, it will be readily discovered whether the handle turns in a day, a week, or a year. Let us take Roemer's satellite instrument for examination, as one of the simple cases: here it is immediately perceived that the first and second satellites move with a velocity exceeding that of the handle; that the third satellite has apparently the same velocity, or nearly so; and that the velocity of the fourth is slower than the motion of the handle: hence it may be concluded, that as the third satellite revolves in nearly a week, seven days may be taken as the period of the handle's revolution, from which the periods of the satellites are to be derived by the wheelwork. Indeed this would appear at first sight, if a dial, indicating the seven days of the week, were observed in connexion with the arbor of the handle. In the next place, the teeth of each wheel must be counted carefully, and the wheels must be put down in pairs, as they are observed to act together, in the form of as many fractions, with the driven wheels as the numerators, and the driving wheels as the denominators: then in each pair the numerator will be in the same proportion to the denominator, as seven days (the period assumed for the common arbor of all the first moving wheels,) are to the respective periods of the revolving planetary arms. Hence if the assumed period be multiplied by the numerators of each fraction, and divided by the denominators respectively, the resulting numbers carried into days, hours, minutes, and seconds, in the usual way, will be the times of the periodic revolutions produced by the wheels in question; and the times deduced may then be compared with the true periods, as in the subjoined small table.

Roemer's Satellite Machine.

Satellites.	Wheels.	Periods by the Wheels.				True Synodic Periods.				Errors in a Period.	
		d.	h.	m.	s.	d.	h.	m.	s.	m.	s.
1	$\frac{22}{87}$ of 7 days.	1	18	28	57.93	1	18	28	35.95	+ 0	21.98
2	$\frac{32}{63}$ of do.	3	13	20	0	3	13	17	53.75	+ 2	6.25
3	$\frac{43}{42}$ of do.	7	4	0	0	7	3	59	35.87	+ 0	24.13
4	$\frac{67}{28}$ of do.	16	18	0	0	16	18	5	7.09	— 5	7.09

In this examination it might appear, at first sight, that the error in the synodic period of the fourth satellite is the greatest; but when it is considered, that the motion of that body is much slower than that of any of the rest, it will be found that $+2'\ 6''.25$ in the period of the second satellite, is a greater error than $-5'\ 7''.09$ in that of the fourth; and accordingly we find among Ferguson's improvements* the substitution of $\frac{33}{65}$ for $\frac{32}{63}$, thereby producing a period in $3^{d.}\ 13^{h.}\ 17'\ 32''.3$, in which the error was reduced to $-0'\ 21''.45$. In this machine the wheel-work was contained in a long box, carrying a dial on the cover divided into the seven days of the week, to which a hand, fixed on the common arbor of the four driving wheels, constantly pointed, to indicate the day as the handle revolved; but we do not learn that there was any hour-circle, to shew the position of the satellites at any given hour of the day.

About the termination of the last century, the Rev. Dr. Pearson contrived a simple machine to answer the same purpose as Roemer's, but without knowing that Roemer had ever made one; and as the assumed period was a solar day, it will afford a second example for our method of determining the periods produced by the wheel-work.

Dr. W. Pearson's first Satellite Machine.

Satellites.	Wheels.	Periods by Wheels.				True Synodic Periods.				Errors in a Period.	
		d.	h.	m.	s.	d.	h.	m.	s.	m.	s.
1	$\frac{39}{69}$ of 24 h.	1	18	27	41	1	18	28	35.95	— 0	54.95
2	$\frac{27}{69}$ of do.	3	13	20	0	3	13	17	53.75	+ 2	6.25
3	$\frac{18}{129}$ of do.	7	4	0	0	7	3	59	35.87	+ 0	24.13
4	$\frac{8}{134}$ of do.	16	18	0	0	16	18	5	7.09	— 5	7.09

It is somewhat remarkable, that the errors in this construction are, in three out of the four periods, the same as in Roemer's; but this machine had the advantage of a dial of 24 hours, as well as a spiral face to indicate each day of the year, by the simple addition of one wheel of 73 teeth, and an endless single screw. We shall have occasion to show hereafter, that a more correct satellite machine was afterwards made by the same contriver.

As a third example, we will examine the periods produced by the wheel-work of Roemer's Planetarium, in which a pair of wheels for each planet at that time known, may be taken as the fraction of a solar year. The numbers of the wheels employed, and the revolutions produced thereby, when the denominators are fixed on one common arbor, and the numerators attached to each a separate concentric tube, will appear from the following arrangement.

Roemer's Planetarium.

Planets.	Wheels.	Periods by Wheels.				True Tropical Periods.				Errors.			
		d.	h.	m.	s.	d.	h.	m.	s.		h.	m.	s.
Mercury	$\frac{13}{54}$ of 365.2422	88	2	44	30	87	23	14	35.2		+3	29	51.8
	$\frac{33}{137}$ of do.	87	23	28	19	.	.	.	.		+0	13	33.8
Venus . .	$\frac{24}{39}$ of do.	224	18	20	48	224	16	41	30		+1	39	18
Earth . . .	$\frac{36}{36}$ of do.	365	5	48	48	365	5	48	48				
Mars . .	$\frac{47}{25}$ of do.	686	15	44	20.6	686	12	18	37		+3	25	43.6
	$\frac{42}{79}$ of do.	687	0	4	38.3	.	.	.	.		+11	46	1.3
Jupiter . .	$\frac{83}{7}$ of do.	4330	17	30	3	4330	14	40	30		+2	49	33
Saturn . .	$\frac{147}{5}$ of do.	10738	2	54	43	10746	19	20	0	d. —8	16	25	17
	$\frac{206}{7}$ of do.	10748	13	21	49.6	.	.	.	.		+1 18	1	49.6

The true tropical periods, which are contained in the fourth column, are derived from the tables of La Lande; and if we were to compare the numbers that compose the wheels of the common planetarium, exhibited for sale by the different mathematical instrument makers, we should find the greatest part of them bearing testimony to the computations of the original contriver. In the instances of Mercury, Mars, and Saturn, the instrument maker is at liberty to choose either of the two pairs offered him, according to the size of the wheels he means to employ. It is hardly necessary to remark, that the diameters of the two wheels that act together, must be to each other in the same proportion that their respective numbers of teeth are to each other, *exclusively* of the *acting portion* of the teeth, which will be more or less according to the fineness of the teeth employed; and also that the teeth and spaces should fit each other well, that no loss of time may be occasioned by improper shake; but it may be proper to observe, that the sum of the acting radii of all the pairs thus employed, should be separately the same constant quantity; hence the sum of the teeth in each pair should not differ considerably from the sum of the numbers of the mean pair taken for the assumed motion of the earth; which requisite Roemer has not sufficiently attended to, though he might have increased or diminished any of his numerators, provided that its own denominators were also increased or diminished in the same proportion. It is only necessary that the value of the fraction should be retained.

When the revolution of a planet is occasioned by a train consisting of several wheels and pinions, which is usually the case in orreries, where the rotations are effected as well as the revolutions of certain planets, the periods may be ascertained without difficulty, by considering the whole train as a compound fraction of the assumed period of the first mover, and by reducing it

* See Ferguson's *Tables and Tracts*, or the edition of his *Works*, newly published, by Dr. Brewster, vol. v. p. 260.

into a simple fraction in the following manner: Select all the *driving* wheels and pinions, which generally are found in the alternate places, viz. in the first, third, fifth, &c. each actuating its fellow, and having counted the teeth of each in succession, multiply them into each other, and let the product be taken as the denominator of a large reduced fraction; then do the same with the *driven* wheels and pinions, which will be found to occupy the second, fourth, sixth, &c. places, and make their product the numerator of the same large fraction; and the reduced fraction thus obtained, must be considered as a pair of large wheels, the period produced by which may be determined in the same manner as the periods of Roemer's satellite instrument and planetarium have been ascertained. For instance, in the automaton of Huygens, a clock movement with a balance impels all the planets, by first giving motion to a common annual arbor, from which all the planets derive their periods

thus: A pinion of four leaves, revolving in as many days by means of the clock-work, drives a wheel of 45 teeth, on the arbor of which another pinion of 9 teeth is made fast, which drives another wheel of 73 teeth round in $\frac{45}{4}$ of $\frac{73}{9} = \frac{3285}{36}$ of 4 days, $=365$. Here the two pinions are the drivers, and the two wheels are driven, which consequently are made the numerators in the compound fraction, and the velocity is thereby diminished; but if it had been required to increase the velocity in the same ratio, the wheels must have been the drivers or denominators of the fraction. Again, the annual arbor, which carries all the driving wheels of the planetary pairs, and of the trains for Mercury and the Moon in this machine, must be considered as the first mover, from which the periods of all the last wheels are derived by their respective fractions of 365 days, according to the subjoined explanation.

Automaton of Christian Huygens.

			d. h. m. s.
Mercury's movement $\frac{12}{121}$ of $\frac{17}{7} = \frac{204}{847}$ of 365 days	=	87 21 50 47.4
Venus' do. . . . . $\frac{32}{52}$ of do. . . .	=	224 14 46 9.2
Earth's do. . . . . $\frac{60}{60}$ of do. . . .	=	365 0 0 0
Mars' do. . . . . $\frac{158}{84}$ of do. . . .	=	686 13 8 34.2
Jupiter's do. . . . . $\frac{166}{14}$ of do. . . .	=	4327 20 34 17.1
Saturn's do. . . . . $\frac{206}{7}$ of do. . . .	=	10755 17 8 34.2
Moon's lunation $\frac{12}{137}$ of $\frac{12}{13} = \frac{144}{1781}$ of do. . . .	=	29 12 16 34.49

In this machine the annual arbor does not revolve in an assumed solar year, but in 365 days only, as limited by the train of connexion.

Whenever a screw is met with, which will be frequently the case when a very slow motion is wanted, it will always be found to be a *driver*, and must be made a denominator of 1 or 2 to its wheel, according as it is a single or a double screw; and in some cases, a single wheel will be introduced merely for the purpose of changing the *direction* of motion, from direct to retrograde, or the reverse. In such case, the number of this wheel, which may be considered both as a driver and driven wheel, may stand both as numerator and denominator of a component part of a compound fraction, to shew that such wheel is employed; but in computing the value of the period produced by such train, the wheel may be omitted, as increasing the products, without altering the value of the fraction.

In machines where the rotation of any planetary body is introduced, some additional wheelwork will be found placed on the revolving bar or arm, that carries the said body round in its periodic time according to its appropriate train. When such additional mechanism is used, the motion of the rotation is usually produced by a central *fixed* wheel, round which its fellow wheel or pinion is carried in the course of the revolution of the revolving arm. In this case, the period of the rotation will depend on the two wheels, or train of wheels, considered as the fraction of the time of revolution of the bar. If the numerator and denominator, *i. e.* in this case, the moveable and fixed wheels, have

their teeth equally numerous, the period of rotation will be the same as the period of the revolution; but if the fixed wheel, which may be considered always as the driver, is larger than the driven one, or carried round it, while their teeth are in connexion, then the period of revolution, multiplied by the driven wheel, and divided by the driver, will give the period of the rotation. But sometimes it will happen that the central wheel, round which the revolving bar is carried by its appropriate train, is itself one of the rotation train, and is consequently always in motion. When this happens, the period of the rotation is affected thereby, and either an addition or subtraction may take place, according as the wheel carried round the central one has its motion, derived from the train, direct or retrograde, as compared with the additional motion it receives by virtue of its connexion with the central wheel. An example will render this observation more intelligible, and at the same time shew the necessity of a rigid notice with respect to this particular.

If we suppose a wheel A of 50 teeth, placed on one of the central revolving tubes of any machine, to have 80 revolutions given it in a solar year, in a direction from west to east; and another smaller wheel B of 25 teeth, placed on a moving bar, and carried round it once in the same period in a contrary direction, or from east to west, while their teeth are in connexion. The consequence would be, that the motion given to B would be derived from two sources; for first, this small wheel would have $\frac{50}{25}$ of $80=160$ rotations, communicated in the ordinary way, supposing the bar on which it is placed stationary; and, secondly, it will rotate twice more by virtue of the motion of the bar that carries it in a contrary direction while their teeth are connected, and the whole number of rotations will be $160 + 2 = 162$. On the contrary, if the motion of the larger wheel A be from east to west, with the arm carrying B moving once in the same direction as before, the wheel B will receive 160 rotations in a direction contrary to that of wheel A, and two in the same direction, by virtue of its journey round the central wheel A, and the whole number of its turns will be $160 - 2 = 158$ only.

The Tellurian of Benjamin Martin, which is seen in the different shops of mathematical instrument makers in London, has an error, arising from a want of attention to this source, in the rotations of the earth round its axis. The train which turns the year into days in this machine, is $\frac{59}{365} \times \frac{10}{20} \times \frac{8}{40} \times \frac{10}{59} = 365^{d.} \ 0^{h.} \ 0^{m.}$ only; according to which computation one day will be deficient in every four years; but this is not the only source of error. The first wheel 365, though fixed in the form of an indented plate, gives motion to the rest of the train, that is carried round it in a year by the annual bar, and the last pinion 10, which was intended to rotate in a solar day, may be called the diurnal pinion. One condition with respect to this pinion is, that it shall turn from west to east, in order that the earth may rotate in the proper direction. An additional arbor is introduced therefore, and the numbers $\frac{10}{20}$, which might have been omitted if $\frac{8}{40}$ had been made $\frac{8}{80}$, may be considered as answering no other purpose than changing the direction of motion of the diurnal pinion; or the two wheels of 59 teeth each might have been omitted, so far as the computation of the train is concerned, one being a multiplier and the other a divisor, if the direction of motion had not been a condition. But while the earth rotates on its axis, during its progress in its annual orbit, another condition is, that its inclined axis should be kept parallel to its original situation during the whole year, which is done by giving one retrograde motion in a year to the small bar that supports the earth, which bar is called the bar of *parallelism*. On this bar of parallelism are placed two additional pinions, every way similar to the diurnal pinion of 10 teeth, to afford the means of giving inclination to the earth's axis, and of transmitting the motion of the diurnal pinion to the said axis *unaltered*; but unfortunately the annual retrograde motion of the bar of parallelism round the diurnal pinion, produces a *deduction* of one revolution of the two additional pinions, and consequently diminishes the number of the earth's rotations by one in each year; so that instead of $365\frac{1}{4}$ days there are only 364 in each year produced by the train of wheelwork, and therefore an index to point out the hour, will always be at variance with the position of the earth in such a construction. But there is yet another cause of error in this machine, independently of what is produced by the operation of the two additional pinions of the train. The same contrivance which preserves the parallelism of the earth's axis, makes her turn round from east to west in each year, while the train makes her turn, as we have explained, 364 times only from west to east, so that in fact another day is deducted in each year; and an inhabitant of any given spot on the earth will transit the sun,

or the sun will appear to transit him, only 363 times in the year. In the more perfect machines these sources of error have been guarded against, as will be seen hereafter.

Another case, in which a planet's motion in its orbit is not altogether produced by its own train, is, when it has a part of its train in common with another planet, and the remainder carried by that other planet's revolving arm; which is generally the case when the *synodic* revolution is represented by the mechanism. We have an instance of this sort in Ferguson's orrery, where the motions of Venus and Mercury are so connected, that the latter derives its motion from the former in a two-fold manner. The train that actuates Venus is $\frac{25}{8} \times \frac{69}{7} \times \frac{73}{10} = 224^{d.} \ 20^{h.} \ 47^{m.} \ 1^{s.}$, and Mercury's revolution is occasioned by only two additional wheels in $\frac{18}{28}$ of Venus' period. Hence the revolutions of Mercury would be to those of Venus as $1 : 1.555$, if the wheels were all placed on a bar at rest; but the $\frac{18}{28}$ of Mercury are fixed on the moving arm of Venus, which carries Mercury round once, without reference to the operation of the train, in every revolution of Venus. Hence the period of Mercury's revolution round the sun is $\frac{244.86606^{d.}}{1 + 1.55555}$, or $\frac{244.86606^{d.}}{2.55555} = 87^{d.}$ $23^{h.} \ 47^{m.} \ 24^{s.}$; but as it regards Venus, the synodic revolution will be $\frac{244.86606^{d.}}{1.55555} = 157.414$ days. Hence it is of the utmost importance in the examination of a planetary machine, not only to count the teeth of the wheels and pinions with care, but to notice particularly whether the whole train be so situated as to position, that the intended effect is correctly produced. The small orrery of Ferguson is more correct than any of its predecessors; we shall therefore subjoin a table of its trains, and of their corresponding values in time, as an example that includes almost all the different modes of computation that are likely to occur in any one machine.

The Trains of Ferguson's Orrery.

Motions.	Wheelwork.	Periods.
		d. h. m. s.
Earth's diurnal motion,	$\frac{25}{8} \times \frac{69}{7} \times \frac{83}{7}$	365 5 48 58.78
A Lunation, . . .	$\frac{30}{64} \times \frac{63}{1}$	29 12 45 0
Solar Rotation, . .	$\frac{25}{8} \times \frac{69}{7} \times \frac{64}{78}$	25 6 35 36
Revolution of Venus,	$\frac{25}{8} \times \frac{69}{7} \times \frac{73}{10}$	224 10 47 8
Revolution of Mercury,	$\frac{18}{28}$ of Venus + 1	87 23 47 24
Rotation of Venus, .	$\frac{8}{7\frac{1}{4}}$ of its revolution.	24 22 31 8
Moon's node, . . .	$\frac{56}{59 - 56}$	$18\frac{2}{3}$ years.
Earth's parallelism, .	$\frac{40}{40} \times \frac{40}{40}$ of a year.	1 revolution.

Planetary Machines.

It may be proper to notice here, that when a retrograde motion, as compared with another motion, like that of the moon's node, is produced by mechanism, the effect is estimated by dividing the number of teeth in the driver by the *difference* of the two wheels, or products, if there be a train; but if the motion is progressive, like that of the moon's apogee, then the difference of the two wheels, or products, contained in the teeth of the *driven* wheel, or wheels, will be the value, and in the same denomination of time as to years, months, or weeks, &c. as the period is, in which the first wheel or driver revolves. In the table before us, $\frac{56}{3}$ years is the period of the node's motion; and in another of Ferguson's machines the wheels for the apogee are $\frac{55}{62}$, and the progressive period $\frac{62}{7} = 8\frac{6}{7}$ years.

In examining whether the earth's axis has its parallelism preserved during the whole year, it is only necessary to notice whether the wheels employed, if only two, (with an intermediate one to change the direction of motion,) have the same number of teeth each; or, if a train be used, whether the products of the numerators and of the denominators are alike. In Martin's tellurian, the train for this purpose is

$$\frac{59}{365} \times \frac{62}{10} = \frac{3658}{3650} = 1.002192,$$

which is therefore erroneous. In Ferguson's orrery, which we have examined, the portion $\frac{25}{8} \times \frac{69}{7}$ of the train which converts the year into a day, is common to the trains of the sun's rotation, and of Venus' revolution, which circumstance diminishes the number of wheels and pinions required by the computations.

Computation of Planetary Wheelwork.

Computation of planetary wheelwork.

Having explained how the value in time may be ascertained for any given pair of wheels, or train of wheelwork, acting under different circumstances, we shall next proceed to show, how wheelwork may be computed to produce revolutions or rotations in any given time. The operations required for this purpose are just the reverse of those that have been explained for determining the time, when the wheels and pinions are examined, as to their number of teeth and position. But before any computation can be effectually entered upon, the plan of the intended machine, and disposition of all the parts employed to produce the respective motions, must be clearly comprehended and determined upon, otherwise the mechanism may not effect the calculated periods. Of this there is a remarkable instance in the small common orrery to be met with in the shops, said to have been contrived by one **Errors of Ryley's orrery.** Ryley, who computed his wheelwork for the periodic revolutions of Mercury, Venus, and the Earth, as they regard the Sun, but placed them on planetary arms in such a way, that they actually produce *synodic* times instead of *periodic*, i. e. they overtake one another in their orbits, in the same time that they ought to have employed in going round the Sun; for instance Mercury overtakes Venus in $86\frac{1}{3}$, instead of 115.877 days, and Venus overtakes the Earth in $219\frac{1}{2}$, instead of

585.923 days. In the latter case the velocity of the planet is more than double what it was computed to be, and would have been, if the wheels had been placed in a stationary position; hence the machine becomes nothing more than an expensive toy, calculated to mislead rather than to instruct the juvenile student in astronomy. It is a disgrace to the venders of such an imperfect piece of mechanism, that they have never examined and detected the errors arising out of its construction. For the sake of method, we will follow the same order in our computations, that we observed in our preceding examination of the different motions effected by wheelwork. The first and simplest case is that where a wheel and pinion, or two wheels only are required to act together for the productions of a motion to be effected in a given period, say in seven days; here, if the driver, or first mover be assumed to have a revolution in one day, and to have 15 teeth, or any convenient number, the wheel to be driven by it, must evidently have $15 \times 7 = 105$ teeth, in order to revolve in $\frac{105}{15}$ days. An instance of this sort may happen where a weekly index is introduced in conjunction with a daily hand, to indicate the 24 hours of each of the seven successive days as they recur. But it will hardly ever happen, that any planetary motion can be correctly produced by a computation so simple. The periodic or synodic times of any two planets to be compared together, must first be reduced into the lowest denomination; and if the large simple fraction, composed of such high numbers, could be brought, by continual division, into terms low enough to constitute the numbers of two wheels, without a remainder, the value would thus be retained, and the reduced fraction would at once give the respective numbers for the teeth of the required wheels, or wheel and pinion. But two periods taken in this way will very rarely be found exactly *commensurate*, and therefore some method of approximating to the truth must be adopted in the practical computation of such planetary numbers as shall in all respects answer the best purpose.

The most direct mechanical method of determining a series of approximate fractions, is by means of two logarithmic lines of a long sliding rule, if one of the high numbers taken on the slider (A) be placed in coincidence with the other, taken on the stock (B), then every pair of coincident strokes, read along the rule, will be so many fractions of nearly the same value with each other, and with the high numbers from which they are derived; and if they are written down in succession as they occur, their comparative values may be ascertained by considering them as so many fractions of the assumed period of the first mover, and by examining such fractional parts of the said period in succession. Thus let the tropical revolution of Mercury be given, as compared with the revolution of the earth, viz. 525948.8 : 126674.585 minutes, then their velocities will be to each other as 1 : 4.151967, or as 1 : 4.152 very nearly; if therefore 1 on A be put into coincidence with 4.152 on B, as before directed, the pairs of coincident numbers, read on the rule in succession, will be $\frac{6}{25}$, $\frac{7}{29}$, $\frac{13}{54}$, $\frac{33}{137}$, and $\frac{46}{191}$, with several others nearly coincident. The values of these fractions may be determined and arranged thus;

	d.	d.	h.	m.	s.
$\frac{6}{25}$ of 365.24222 =		87	15	47	42
$\frac{7}{29}$ of do. =		88	3	52	17
$\frac{13}{54}$ of do. =		88	2	44	10
$\frac{33}{137}$ of do. =		87	23	28	19
$\frac{46}{191}$ of do. =		87	23	8	10
True tropical period =		87	23	14	35.2

Hence it appears that the numbers $\frac{46}{191}$ would produce a tropical revolution of mercury within 6' 25″ of the truth itself, and that the errors of the other numbers increase as the numbers themselves diminish. If the driving wheel of 191 teeth were placed on an annual arbor, and 46 on Mercury's tube, in a planetarium, the planetary arm carried thereby would perform a revolution in the period above specified. If, however, the numbers in any of the pairs are too small, they may both be increased in the same proportion, so as to give wheels of a proper diameter for construction; for instance $\frac{13}{54}$ may have its numbers doubled, and $\frac{26}{108}$ will make a pair of wheels of convenient practical dimensions; but in the last pair, 191 being a *prime* number, cannot be diminished; and the computation that is best in theory, is frequently inconvenient to be introduced in practice, as the constituent portion of a simple machine, where the common distance between the arbors is limited. If we were to compare the tropical period of Venus, in like manner, with a solar year, the only small fraction procured by the sliding rule would be $\frac{8}{13}$, which may be made $\frac{16}{26}$, $\frac{24}{39}$, $\frac{32}{52}$, $\frac{40}{65}$, or $\frac{48}{78}$, accordingly as the numbers are both multiplied by 2, 3, 4, 5, or 6, till the wheels become of a suitable diameter to answer their proposed purpose. The value of $\frac{8}{13}$ of a solar year, is 224$^{d.}$ 18$^{h.}$ 20$^{m.}$ 10$^{s.}$ and the true tropical period of Venus 224$^{d.}$ 16$^{h.}$ 41$^{m.}$ 30$^{s.}$, so that the error in each period would be + 0$^{d.}$ 1$^{h.}$ 38$^{m.}$ 40$^{s.}$ In a similar manner, the approximate fractions of a year may be obtained for all the other planets with very little trouble; and the wheels derived from them, when duly proportioned, and cut with suitable cutters for equalizing the tooth and space, will constitute a planetarium of Roemer's construction.

When, however, the periods are intended to be exhibited with great accuracy, a train must necessarily be substituted for a single pair of wheels. In this case, when the high fraction, consisting of the periods of the two planets to be compared together, is reduced to a common denomination, and diminished into its lowest terms, each part of such fraction must be considered as a *product*, arising out of two, three, or more *factors*, according to the number of wheels intended to be employed in such train; and if each part of the fraction, reduced into its lowest terms, is found to be divisible into factors, having numbers suitable for constituting wheels, then such factors, put into the form of a com-

pound fraction, in which the numerators and denominators must keep their respective places, will be the train required. But as it will very seldom be found, that a large portion is *commensurable*, when days, hours, minutes, and seconds, are all taken into both parts of the portion; and as the occurrence of a large *prime* number, as a factor, renders the train *impracticable*, the direct method of approximation devised, as is generally understood by COTES, must be substituted for the two logarithmic lines, for determining a series of approximate fractions, out of which to choose a practicable pair of numbers for the composition of a train. The method of procuring a continuous series of fractions, or ratios, by common arithmetic, may be easily practised by attending to the following rules:

1. Reduce the periods of the two heavenly bodies, to be connected by a train into one common denomination, either in seconds, or in decimal parts of their comparative periods, where unity will represent the shorter period.

2. Divide the greater number by the smaller, and reserve the quotient; then make the division a new dividend, and the remainder a new division, to procure a second reserved quotient; and continue the same process until seven, eight, or more quotients are obtained, according to the usual mode of obtaining a common measure in vulgar fractions.

3. Put $\frac{0}{1}$ for the first ratio, or fraction, and $\frac{1}{0}$ for the second, and then the succeeding fractions may be obtained from the reserved quotients, taken successively in the order of their occurrence: thus, multiply the numerator of the last fraction by the first quotient, and add to the product the numerator of the next preceding fraction, and the number so obtained will be the numerator of the next following new fraction; treat the denominators in the same way, that is, multiply the last denominator by the same quotient, and add thereto the denominator of the next preceding denominator, and the amount will constitute the denominator of the said new succeeding fraction. Let this process be continued till all the quotients are involved in so many successive fractions, which will approach gradually to the true fraction wanted; and if the division is continued till there happens to be no remainder, the last quotient will produce a fraction representing the truth itself; namely, the two numbers constituting such fraction, will be to each other in precisely the same ratio as the two periods themselves, from which the succession of quotients was derived by the continual division.

As an exemplification of this method of determining a series of planetary numbers, for the wheelwork of a planetarium, or orrery, either for single pairs, or for trains, we shall take the periods of Mercury and the Earth, as before proposed for the sliding rule, and from the accordance of the two methods, as to the results, it will appear that the arithmetical process has so far the advantage over the mechanical operation, that the fractions can be carried into terms of a higher denomination than can be read on a sliding rule, however large its logarithmic scale; and, consequently, the arithmetical series is preferable, as it affords a greater variety for the choice of practical trains, which must be derived from some single fraction composed of high numbers.

Computation of Mercury's Train of Wheelwork.

Divisors.	Dividends.	Quotients.	Formulæ.	Fractions.
				$\frac{0}{1}$
				$\frac{1}{0}$
1.000000	4.151967 / 4000000	4	$\frac{4\times1+0}{4\times0+1}$	$\frac{4}{1}$
151967	1000000 / 911802	6	$\frac{6\times4+1}{6\times1+0}$	$\frac{25}{6}$
88198	151967 / 88198	1	$\frac{1\times25+4}{1\times6+1}$	$\frac{29}{7}$
63769	88198 / 63769	1	$\frac{1\times29+25}{1\times7+6}$	$\frac{54}{13}$
24429	63769 / 48858	2	$\frac{2\times54+29}{2\times13+7}$	$\frac{137}{33}$
14911	24429 / 14911	1	$\frac{1\times137+54}{1\times33+13}$	$\frac{191}{46}$
9518	14911 / 9518	1	$\frac{1\times191+137}{1\times46+33}$	$\frac{328}{79}$
5393	9518 / 5393	1	$\frac{1\times328+191}{1\times79+46}$	$\frac{519}{125}$
4125	5393 / 4125	1	$\frac{1\times519+328}{1\times125+79}$	$\frac{847}{204}$
1268	4125	3	$\frac{3\times847+519}{3\times204\times125}$	$\frac{3060}{737}$

The same quotients would have been obtained, and consequently the same series of fractions, if the two periods reduced into seconds had been used as the first divisor and dividend, viz. $\frac{525948.800}{126674.580}$. In the last column the same small fractions succeed one another, as are given by the logarithmic lines, as far as to $\frac{191}{46}$, but

beyond this fraction the numbers become too high. It is fortunate that the last fraction $\frac{3060}{737}$, which is the most correct, is divisible into the factors $\frac{90\times34}{11\times67}$, which will constitute a train, of which the value differs almost imperceptibly from the truth; for $\frac{11\times67}{90\times34}=\frac{737}{3060}$ of 365.24222 days, gives 87^d. 23^h. 14^m. 35.726^s for Mercury's tropical period; in which train the error is only 0.526^s in the whole period.

If the last fraction is found to contain a prime or incomposite number, too large to constitute a wheel, one of the preceding, but less accurate fractions, must be taken in stead; or another quotient may be substituted for the last quotient in the formula, provided that it be nearly of the same value. In this case, the quotient 2 or 4 might have been put for 3, and then $\frac{2\times847+519}{2\times204+125}$ $=\frac{2213}{533}$, and $\frac{4\times847+519}{4\times204+125}=\frac{3907}{941}$ would have been the resulting numbers, of nearly equal value with $\frac{3060}{737}$; but, on consulting a table of prime numbers, it will be seen, that 2213 is not divisible into any two factors, and that both the numbers in the latter fraction are incomposite; on which account, they must have been rejected as impracticable, and another quotient, 1 or 5, must have been substituted for the 3, in case practical numbers had not been otherwise obtained from one of the direct fractions of the series.

In like manner, a series of continuous fractions of a solar year may be obtained for all the planetary system; and the trains, arising out of the last fractions of each series, or out of fractions of nearly the same value, (to be substituted by means of a change in the last quotient,) may be procured for the construction of a very perfect machine, so far as the mean motions are concerned. It may not be unacceptable to some of our readers to have a list of continuous fractions, which we have taken the trouble to compute, according to the mode which we have just laid down and exemplified; and we, therefore, subjoin the results in the form of a table.

A List of Planetary Continuous Fractions of a Solar Year.

Planets.	Tropical Periods.	Continuous Fractions.
	d. h. m. s.	
Mercury	87 23 14 35.2	$\frac{1}{4}$, $\frac{6}{25}$, $\frac{7}{29}$, $\frac{13}{54}$, $\frac{33}{137}$, $\frac{46}{191}$, $\frac{79}{328}$, $\frac{125}{519}$, $\frac{204}{847}$, $\frac{737}{3060}$.
Venus	224 16 41 30	$\frac{1}{1}$, $\frac{1}{2}$, $\frac{2}{3}$, $\frac{3}{5}$, $\frac{8}{13}$, $\frac{243}{395}$, $\frac{251}{408}$, $\frac{5514}{8963}$, $\frac{5765}{9371}$.
Earth's Rotation	365 5 48 48	$\frac{1}{365}$, $\frac{4}{1461}$, $\frac{29}{10592}$, $\frac{33}{12053}$, $\frac{128}{46751}$, $\frac{161}{58804}$, $\frac{450}{164359}$.
Mars	686 22 18 37	$\frac{1}{1}$, $\frac{2}{1}$, $\frac{15}{8}$, $\frac{32}{17}$, $\frac{47}{25}$, $\frac{79}{42}$, $\frac{205}{109}$, $\frac{899}{478}$, $\frac{1104}{587}$.
Vesta	1335 0 23 0	$\frac{3}{1}$, $\frac{4}{1}$, $\frac{7}{2}$, $\frac{11}{3}$, $\frac{95}{26}$, $\frac{106}{29}$, $\frac{5395}{1476}$.

Table—continued.

Planets.	Tropical Periods.				Continuous Fractions.							
	d.	h.	m.	s.								
Juno	1590	17	35	0	$\frac{4}{1}$,	$\frac{9}{2}$,	$\frac{13}{3}$,	$\frac{61}{14}$,	$\frac{135}{31}$,	$\frac{196}{45}$,	$\frac{331}{76}$,	$\frac{3175}{729}$.
Ceres	1681	6	15	0	$\frac{4}{1}$,	$\frac{5}{1}$,	$\frac{9}{2}$,	$\frac{14}{3}$,	$\frac{23}{5}$,	$\frac{267}{58}$,	$\frac{1892}{643}$.	
Pallas	1681	10	26	0	May be taken the same as for Ceres.							
Jupiter	4330	14	40	30	$\frac{11}{1}$,	$\frac{12}{1}$,	$\frac{71}{6}$,	$\frac{83}{7}$,	$\frac{5217}{440}$,	$\frac{10517}{887}$,	$\frac{10734}{1327}$.	
Saturn	10746	19	20	0	$\frac{29}{1}$,	$\frac{59}{2}$,	$\frac{147}{5}$,	$\frac{206}{7}$,	$\frac{765}{26}$,	$\frac{971}{33}$,	$\frac{1736}{59}$,	$\frac{11387}{387}$.
Herschel	30589	8	27	0	$\frac{83}{1}$,	$\frac{84}{1}$,	$\frac{335}{4}$,	$\frac{23869}{285}$,	$\frac{24204}{289}$.			
Moon's Lunation	29	12	44	3	$\frac{1}{12}$,	$\frac{2}{25}$,	$\frac{3}{37}$,	$\frac{8}{99}$,	$\frac{11}{136}$,	$\frac{19}{235}$,	$\frac{334}{4131}$,	$\frac{353}{14366}$.
Sun's Rotation	25	8	20	0	$\frac{1}{14}$,	$\frac{2}{29}$,	$\frac{3}{43}$,	$\frac{8}{115}$,	$\frac{19}{273}$,	$\frac{27}{388}$,	$\frac{181}{2601}$,	$\frac{208}{2989}$.

In this table, if the numerators of the different fractions be taken as so many solar years, the respective denominators will express the number of tropical revolutions made by the corresponding planets in those years nearly ; and if the last fractions be taken in each line, the coincidence of the two periods will be very exact. In the instance of the earth, the numerators are years, and the denominators days, and, what is extraordinary, the seventh quotient leaves no remainder in the continual division ; consequently, the value of $\frac{164359}{450}$, is $365^{d.}\ 5^{h.}\ 48^{m.}\ 48^{s.}$ and is reducible into the compound fraction, or train, $\frac{269}{10} \times \frac{47}{9} \times \frac{13}{5}$, or into either of the following equivalents, $\frac{269}{10} \times \frac{47}{9} \times \frac{39}{15}$, or $\frac{269}{10} \times \frac{10}{26}$ $\times \frac{18}{94}$, the last of which Dr. W. Pearson has availed himself of in one of his new machines, hereafter described. From this remarkable coincidence between 164359 days and 450 solar years, we arrive at a perfect correction of the Calendar, or can reconcile the solar with the civil years, by simply omitting seven and retaining two centenary leap-years in every 900 years; instead of omitting 9, as the practice is now established : for $365 \times 450 + 109 = 164359$; hence in every 450 solar years there should be 109 intercalary days, or 118 in 900 such years ; but if we count 24 leap years only in each of nine successive centuries, there will be only 116 intercalary days, instead of 118, and therefore every fourth (or fifth) and ninth century should alternately retain the 29th day of February, in order to make the solar years and civil days accord at the termination of every nine centuries.

Should any, or all of the *synodic* revolutions be fixed

upon for the wheelwork of an orrery, for the sake of connecting the revolving arms without the assistance of tubes, as Dr. W. Pearson has done in his large orrery with equated motions, the fractions and trains for such periods may be computed by means of the converging series, as well as any other train. With the inferior planets the numerators will be found the same for both periods, but the denominators of the synodic revolutions will be equal to the denominators of the periodic revolutions, after their numerators are subtracted therefrom, provided that the earth be one of the two planets from which the synodic period is computed. In this case, a part of the synodic train must be placed on the earth's bar, or arm, which, by its annual motion, while the train is in action, will convert the synodic into a periodic revolution. This effect we have already noticed in the instance of Venus in Ferguson's orrery. If we take $\frac{8}{13}$, which is one of her fractions, for producing a periodic revolution, when placed in a stationary position, her corresponding fraction for a synodic revolution will be $\frac{8}{13-8} = \frac{8}{5}$, provided the 5 revolve in a year, and be placed on the earth's revolving arm in connexion with the 8, which 8 being central, will, under these circumstances, carry Venus in her periodic time as she has reference to the sun, but in her synodic period as she regards the earth ; hence a periodic becomes a synodic train when *unity is ejected.* In the computations for the inferior planets, the solar year was the dividend, but in those for the superior planets, it was the divisor ; hence the synodic train of Mars, or other superior planet, is derived from its periodic train by considering the denominator as unchangeable, and taking the *difference* for the numerator.

The following TABLE *contains the Mean Synodic Periods of all the Primary Planets as they have reference to each other, expressed in Days and Decimal Parts.*

Planets.	Herschel.	Saturn.	Jupiter.	Ceres and Pallas.	Juno.	Vesta.	Mars.	Earth.	Venus.
Mercury .	88.290	88.694	89.792	92.825	93.118	94.174	100.888	115.877	144.566
Venus .	226.358	229.493	236.993	259.355	261.654	270.169	333.917	583.923	
Earth .	370.713	378.091	398.892	466.606	474.101	502.813	779.938		
Mars . .	702.713	733.836	816.434	1161.394	1208.955	1415.002			
Vesta . .	1395.950	1524.347	1930.007	6480.000	8302.370				
Juno . .	1678.104	1867.166	2514.552	2952.164					
Ceres and Pallas	1779.242	1993.233	2748.674						
Jupiter .	5044.960	7253.595							
Saturn .	16568.625								

When the synodic period, from conjunction to conjunction, of any two planets is required, look for one planet at the top, and the other at the side of the table, and the square which is common to both will contain the period sought for. For instance, the time which Mars will require in passing from his conjunction with Jupiter to the same relative situation again, will be 816.434 days in mean motion, but this period will be lengthened or shortened according to the sum or difference of the equations of the two planets at the termination of the mean period. In all cases where synodic revolutions form the data for the computation of wheelwork, the resulting trains must connect the two arms of the planets in question, and then the slower moving arm will *push* the quicker round *once* in the time of its own periodic revolution, without reference to the direct effect produced by the computed train.

In like manner, the synodic revolution naturally arises out of the periodic revolutions of two planetary arms, by reason of the difference of their velocities; and though such synodic period is not contemplated in computing the periodic revolutions, it is a natural consequence of the relative velocities, provided the trains are in a permanent situation that produce the respective motions.

When a graduated dial and its index are both revolving in the same direction, but with different velocities, so that either a direct or retrograde quantity is indicated by the difference, in given periods; as is the case in some orreries, where the moon's apogee and node have their motions pointed out; the period must be first reduced to its lowest terms, in the form of an improper fraction, and then the numerator will be the driven wheel, and the denominator must be subtracted from, or added to the numerator, to constitute the *driver*, according as the motion is comparatively progressive or retrograde: for instance, if the moon's progressive motion of the apogee be taken at $8\frac{6}{7}$ years, the improper fraction, reduced in the usual way, will be $\frac{62}{7}$ and $\frac{62}{62-7} = \frac{62}{55}$ will be the required wheels; and when the fraction is in high numbers, for the sake of accuracy in the period, the difference may be applied

in a similar manner, and the high fraction thus obtained may afterwards be broken into factors for a train, as has been already explained. As another instance, let us take the moon's node, the period of which is nearly $18\frac{2}{3}$ years, or $\frac{56}{3}$ when reduced; hence $\frac{56}{56 \times 3} = \frac{56}{59}$ will be the proper wheels; and if 56 revolve in a year, 59 immediately connected with it will revolve in $\frac{56}{3}$, or $18\frac{2}{3}$ years. In this case, also, if higher numbers were taken as the improper fraction, for the sake of greater precision in the period, after the difference has been applied, the high numbers may be broken into factors for a train retaining the same value as the high simple fraction. Examples where trains have been used, for both the motions of the moon's apogee and node, will occur hereafter, when we come to describe Dr. W. Pearson's Tellurian and Lunarian united in one perfect machine. With respect to the computation of numbers for preserving the parallelism of the earth's axis, any numbers will do for the wheels, provided that the products of the numerators and of the denominators are the same, and provided that the earth is made to rotate *backwards* once in each year, or in the period during which the annual bar carries it *forwards* round the sun.

The Description of a Complete Planetarium for Mean Motions.

The common planetarium is not only imperfect with respect to the numbers that constitute the wheelwork, but defective as it regards five out of the eleven primary planets; so that we should not perform our duty to the public, if we did not lay before them the model of a machine that will represent the various motions in their periodic times, and in a much more perfect manner. The model that we have to offer was recently contrived by a mechanist, who has been much accustomed to exercise his talents both in the computation and construction of planetary machines, and we anticipate, that the boon we here offer to the instrument-makers will be gratefully received. The greatest

The description of a complete planetarium for mean motions.

Planetary
Machines.

Complete
planeta-
rium for
mean mo-
tions.

portion of the planetary numbers are derived from the fractions of a solar year, which we have already presented to our readers ; and the diameters of the respective pairs of wheels employed for giving the periods of the different planets, are put into proper proportions, as well as practicable sizes ; so that any mechanic, who has access to a good cutting-engine, will have no difficulty in preparing the mechanism. The construction also is so simple, that any workman, who has seen a common planetarium, may put all the parts together. Each planet has only one pair of wheels, forming the fraction of a solar year, except Herschel, which, from its slow motion, is incapable of being actuated by the same means, and therefore its revolution is derived from Saturn's, but in a way that is very simple, and will be easily understood and practised. In order to render the tropical mean periods as correct as can be done by simple fractions of a moderate denomination, the sum of the teeth of each pair of wheels has been assumed on an average at about 170, so that the common distance from their respective centres may be 2.7 inches, and the number of teeth in an inch about 10, which are sufficiently strong, and not liable to unnecessary shake, when the teeth and spaces are made equal, and laid at a proper depth for action. We have compressed all the necessary information, for the use of the maker, into the form of a table, which affords him, at the same time, the means of ascertaining the order in which the different pairs of wheels follow one another in their respective positions, as well as the requisite dimensions to be attended to for each separate wheel, and also the cutters that will be proper to be used when the engine is employed. When we speak of the diameter of any wheel, it must be understood to mean the geometrical diameter, or diameter measured from what is practically called the *pitch-line*, exclusive of the ends of the teeth, that take hold of one another ; allowance must therefore be made for the additional acting parts of the teeth in each wheel, which will be more or less according to the coarseness or fineness of the teeth, as every workman accustomed to manufacture and put together wheelwork cannot but comprehend.

The mechanism of this planetarium is contained in an oblong frame of brass, having the upper plate connected with the lower one by four pillars at the respective corners, which are made fast with screws in the usual way ; each of the plates of this frame is eight inches long, and four wide ; and the length of the pillars may be from three to four inches, according to the thickness of the wheels and the distances between them. The long annual arbor carries round with it nine fixed wheels, or pinions, for ten of the planets ; Ceres and Pallas having both the same wheel in common, and Herschel's not being included ; this arbor is pivoted into the two plates of the frame, and its upper pivot is prolonged, so as to receive the annual index above the circular, or rather cylindrical box, in which the frame is included when fixed on a tripod of brass. A long stem of tempered steel, turned on a lathe perfectly cylindrical, is fixed to the lower plate in a vertical position, round which the system of concentric brass tubes revolve within one another, so nicely fitted, that while there is but little friction there is as little play as possible. These tubes are of different lengths, varying about a quarter of an inch from each other, the innermost being the longest, and the outermost the shortest ; but all

Planetary
Machines.

Complete
planeta-
rium for
mean mo-
tions.

of them long enough to ascend through the cover of the cylindrical box, in which the frame is screwed fast, that each tube at its superior end may receive its respective planetary arm, or radius vector. As the wheels and pinions fixed fast to the annual arbor are the *drivers* in each pair, the *driven* wheels corresponding thereto have each its separate tube, which therefore revolves in its proper period, and carries along with it its planetary arm exactly as in the orrery hereafter described. The tube which carries Herschel's arm, as we have before said, derives its motion from Saturn's, and is thus effected : A wheel of 61 teeth is screwed fast to the under face of Saturn's large wheel of 206, and thus moves in Saturn's period ; then two wheels, of 112 and 60 teeth, are fixed on a short piece of small tube, and placed on the annual arbor loosely as on a stud, and while the 112 is connected with the 61, and is made to revolve thereby, the 60, moving along with the 112, drives the large planetary wheel 93 of Herschel, which therefore is made fast to the lower end of his tube, and revolves

in $\frac{61}{112} \times \frac{60}{93}$ of 10748.566 days, (Saturn's period by

the wheelwork) ; and the period thus effected is very near the truth, viz. 30589.333 days ; the revolution also is performed in the proper direction from west to east like all the other revolutions. There is moreover a bridge of brass, with a tube fixed at right angles on its centre, which surrounds the two tubes of Venus and Mercury, so as not to impede their motion, and which forms a fixed stud, round which the earth's tube and all the other surrounding tubes revolve. The use of this *fixed* tube is twofold : first, it separates the two innermost tubes, which are slender, from the more weighty tubes without, which it supports, while it lessens the friction ; and secondly, it supplies the means of giving motion to the moon, and of holding a graduated dial for the indication of the sun's place, while the annual bar carries the index at its remote end to point to it ; the dial itself being indented into 235 teeth, and driving a pinion of 19 on the annual bar round the earth's stem in a lunation. The moon's stem, fixed to the small revolving tube connected with the pinion of 19, becomes moreover the index to a small plate of $29\frac{1}{2}$ divisions, carried by the earth's stem, and points out, in a distinct manner, the day of the moon's age, while the annual hand points out as clearly the day of the month engraven on a circle on the cover of the machine. Indeed, if a quadruple spiral were drawn instead of a circle, the leap year would also be indicated, as the annual train gives a period not varying more than a single second, if so much, from the true solar year.

Lastly, an arbor for the handle, to give motion to the different pairs of wheels at the same time, has a double screw cut upon it, so as to act with Venus's wheel of 104 teeth, not much rounded ; and as this wheel revolves in a year, it will require 52 turns of the handle to produce an entire revolution of it, and consequently of the annual arbor to which it is made fast ; hence a turn of the handle will give very nearly seven days motion to the whole planetary system ; and all the eleven primary planets and the moon will preserve their respective velocities with considerable precision from year to year, with as many pairs of wheels only as there are planetary bodies.

Synopsis of the Wheelwork employed in the New Planetarium.

Planets.	Fractions.	Periods by the Wheels.	Wheels.	Diameters in Inches.	Teeth in the Inch.
	d.	*d.*			
Mercury .	$\frac{33}{137}$ of 365.24222	87.978	33	1.05	10.0
			137	4.35	10.0
Venus .	$\frac{64}{104}$ of do.	224.764	64	2.05	9.9
			104	.35	9.9
Earth .	$\frac{75}{75}$ of do.	365.242	75	2.70	8.8
			75	2.70	8.8
Mars .	$\frac{79}{42}$ of do.	687.003	79	3.52	7.1
			42	1.88	7.1
Vesta .	$\frac{106}{29}$ of do.	1335.023	106	4.24	8.0
			29	1.16	8.0
Juno .	$\frac{135}{31}$ of do.	1590.571	135	4.39	9.8
			31	1.01	9.8
Ceres and Pallas	$\frac{138}{30}$ of do.	1680.114	138	4.43	9.9
			30	0.97	9.9
Jupiter .	$\frac{166}{14}$ of do.	4330.729	166	4.98	10.6
			14	0.42	10.6
Saturn .	$\frac{206}{7}$ of do.	10748.556	206	5.20	12.5
			7	0.20	12.5
Herschel .	$\frac{61}{112} \times \frac{60}{93}$ of 10748.556	30589.333	61	1.90	10.1
			112	3.50	10.1
Moon .	$\frac{19}{235}$ of 365.242	29.5302	60	2.12	9.9
			93	3.28	9.9
			19	0.45	13.5
			235	5.55	13.5

According to this table of dimensions, the earth's stem must stand at three inches exactly from the sun, or central fixed stem which supports the sun; and the dial with 235 teeth will be 5.55 inches in diameter, and will admit of an ecliptic circle to be divided into twelve signs, and each sign into 30°. The arms of Mercury, Venus, and Mars, may be in their due proportions; but the other superior planets must have their arms in fractional parts of their due distances. In the second column, the numerators of the fractions are those which are attached to the revolving tubes, and the denominators are those made fast on the annual arbor, which communicate the motion to their numerators respectively, with the exception of Herschel's. The usual apparatus for showing the direct and retrograde comparative motions, and stationary places, when viewed from any one planet, as it regards any other, may be applied to this machine with great advantage, as its structure is firm, and its parts all sufficiently compact. The mechanism and external appearance of this new machine resembles the planetarian portion of the orrery, which we have yet to describe, so much so that the drawings of the one which we have to give will suffice to explain the construction of the other, when the parts not belonging to the planetarium are omitted, and when the numbers designating the teeth are taken, as we have here given them, in their most simple form.

A short Account of Planetaria with equated Motions.

To give a minute detail of all the constituent parts of the various planetary machines that have been invented, and to illustrate the principles of their construction by reference to engravings, would occupy a large volume: we have consequently been obliged to abridge our article into such compass, as will render it admissible into a work that embraces all the various departments of science. We were unwilling to pass over in silence the more complex machinery that has been contrived to represent the *equations* of the mean planetary motions; but we have to regret, that our plan will not allow us to extend our plates and descriptions beyond what our readers *in general* may be disposed to approve.

Soon after the Royal Institution of London was founded, the managers had occasion to procure a planetarium among other apparatus for the lectures, when Dr. Garnett ceased to be the lecturer; and a plan was suggested about the year 1801, by one of its original proprietors, (to whom we are indebted for this short account,) for exhibiting the *equated* motions of all the planets at that time discovered. This suggestion, being soon after the two planets Ceres and Pallas had been discovered, was adopted; and Kenneth M'Culloch, an aged workman brought up under James Ferguson, was employed in the construction of the machine in the workshops of the institution. The inventor was aware, that, if a small arm carrying a planet was by any means made to revolve backwards at the remote end of a radius vector, while the radius vector itself revolved forwards in the same period, the planet would have an

A short account of planetaria with equated motions.

Planetary Machines. eccentric orbit, in which the variable distances would be preserved, and also one-half of the grand equation would be produced, provided that the small arm bore the same proportion to the radius vector that the planet's eccentricity does to its mean distance from the sun. The plane of the planetary orbits was therefore made vertical in this machine, in order that small weights, suspended on the small revolving arms, under certain limitations, should keep them always parallel; that is, always pointing in one direction, by the simple effect of gravity. In this way, the variations of distance, and one-half of the alternate increase and decrease of velocity were occasioned, and the remainder of the equation depended on the eccentric cutting of the planetary wheels into teeth of unequal sizes. A train of four wheels, or wheels and pinions, was employed for each planet except for Ceres and Pallas, whose periods are very nearly the same, and therefore required only one train. The annual arbor, which we will call A, without reference to any figure, had all the first driving wheels made fast on it; and the second and

third wheels, pinned together, revolved in as many pairs on a fixed stem B; while the fourth or planetary wheels, revolving with unequal teeth in the proper periods of the different planets, were fixed on the lower extremities of as many concentric tubes, revolving round C, the sun's stem, and carrying as many radii vectores attached to their superior or projecting ends. In this construction, the common plane of the orbits was presented to the audience in the lecture-room, and the person who turned the handle stood behind a vertical wooden frame, which supported the small brass frame of the wheelwork. But though the natural position of the machine was vertical, whenever the small arms representing the eccentricity were removed, the radii vectores might be put into the usual horizontal position by simply discharging a bolt, and fixing it again in the horizontal position. The mechanist, who may wish for information respecting the farther particulars of the construction, will obtain it from the contents of the subjoined Table.

Planetarium at the Royal Institution of London.

	Trains, or Fractions of a Year.	Periods produced.				Wheels on Arbor A.	Wheels on Stem B.	Wheels with Tubes.
		d.	h.	m.	s.			
Mercury .	$\frac{22}{90} \times \frac{67}{68}$	87	13	14	35.8	90	$\left.\begin{array}{l}22\\68\end{array}\right\}$	67
Venus .	$\frac{32}{113} \times \frac{63}{29}$	224	16	42	1	113	$\left.\begin{array}{l}32\\29\end{array}\right\}$	63
Earth . .	$\frac{60}{60} \times \frac{60}{60}$	365	5	48	48	60	$\left.\begin{array}{l}60\\60\end{array}\right\}$	60
Mars . .	$\frac{56}{53} \times \frac{89}{50}$	686	22	20	41.2	53	$\left.\begin{array}{l}56\\50\end{array}\right\}$	89
Ceres . ⎱ Pallas . ⎰	$\frac{121}{21} \times \frac{48}{60}$	1683	14	14	26.6	21	$\left.\begin{array}{l}121\\60\end{array}\right\}$	48
Jupiter .	$\frac{111}{22} \times \frac{94}{40}$	4330	14	39	17.6	22	$\left.\begin{array}{l}111\\40\end{array}\right\}$	94
Saturn .	$\frac{124}{7} \times \frac{98}{59}$	10746	18	54	20	7	$\left.\begin{array}{l}124\\59\end{array}\right\}$	98
Herschel .	$\frac{105}{7} \times \frac{67}{12}$	30589	0	52	0	7	$\left.\begin{array}{l}105\\12\end{array}\right\}$	67
Sun . .	$\frac{19}{137} \times \frac{25}{62}$ of Mercury's Revol.	25	10	0	0.2			

In adjusting this machine, the lecturer must attend particularly to the manner in which the trains are put together, viz. that the smaller teeth of each tubed wheel may be in action, when its planetary arm is pointing to the aphelion point of its orbit, and the larger teeth when the motion produced is for the perihelion portion. If this rectification is not attended to, the equations will be improperly represented; and if the contrary positions are given, the wheels will counteract the effect of the backward revolutions of the small arms, and the motions will become equable; and if this should happen to be the case with some of the planets, and not with the others, the want of due adjustment of the position of the trains will occasion a confusion of anomalous motions.

The inventor of the preceding planetarium has noticed with regret, that the astronomical lecturers who have had occasion to use it, have not made themselves acquainted with the mixed principles on which its construction is founded, and therefore have never attended to its requisite adjustments, so that its value has never yet been duly appreciated, nor its best properties been properly displayed. In this machine, as in chronometers, regulators, musical instruments, &c. the superiority can only be known when the nicer adjustments are attended to, or the instruments properly tuned.

To avoid the necessity of particular attention being required to the putting together of the wheelwork with unequal teeth, which must always be for a *given time*, a dial was added to the back part of the machine, to show at all times the particular year for which the rectification is proper, at any subsequent period, when once it has been duly adjusted; and if this dial is consulted, there is no necessity for a new adjustment, provided that the index, and all the planetary arms, are allowed to keep their proper places given them by the machinery; but in a public institution, while all the members have access to the apparatus, such precaution can never be insured, and therefore the machine, as might be expected, is never in proper order.

Another planetarium for exhibiting the *equated* motions, was afterwards made under the direction of the same gentleman, by the late Fidler, which the inventor has yet in his own possession, and which is free from the objection above stated, arising out of the inequality of the teeth of certain planetary wheels. It may be acceptable to several of our readers, to have a succinct account of this machine, without engravings, as may enable them to comprehend its peculiar properties. The computations of this second planetarium are founded on the synodic periods, and the system of tubes, introduced into all former planetaria, is entirely left out of the construction. The wheelwork is consequently all in sight, interposed between the different long arms, or radii vectores, of the respective planets; and one portion of each train is carried round the sun by one or other of the two contiguous arms, from which the synodic period is derived, while one of the wheels belonging to each train is made fast to a strong stem of steel, that supports the sun in the centre; and in this way each planet, including two of the recently discovered ones, has its appropriate train partly fixed and partly circulating; but all the wheels in the machine are so connected together, that no one wheel can perform its office, without at the same time compelling all the rest to perform also their respective offices; and whenever the handle is turned, the planetary arms commence their several mean motions round the sun, and perform their tropical periods in their exact relative times. The nice fitting of the teeth of the several trains, where they are all in due proportion, prevents the play, which otherwise would have rendered the commencement of all the motions successive, instead of contemporaneous. The table, or stand of this planetarium, is the same as that on which the tellurian and lunarium united is mounted, and also the satellite instrument; and the large ecliptic circle is equally subservient to all the different machines, when the superstructures are properly placed. This machine however has its central stem perforated by a round hole, through which an arbor ascends, connected with the handle at the table up to the sun's train, which is the uppermost, and which communicates all the motions

downwards through the conical stock of wheels that constitute the various trains. If the stems that support the planetary balls were inserted into the remote ends of the radii vectores, when put into mean motion in the manner that has been described, this would be a complete planetarium for mean motions, and indeed might be made such at pleasure; but the inventor's object was to represent the *equated* motions without the unequal teeth of planetary wheels; and this required some appendages, which we shall now endeavour to render intelligible. A grooved circle of brass, or pulley, is fixed on the sun's stem by friction, between each pair of the radii vectores; and a similar pulley at the extreme end of each radius vector, admits an endless silk cord to embrace both the pulleys in such way, that the motion of the radius vector forwards turns the pulley carried by the radius vector backwards once in every revolution of the planet; and a short arm representing double the eccentricity, and connected with the revolving pulley, carries the planet's stem in an eccentric orbit, with an equated velocity that always keeps the planet in its true heliocentric plane, as referred to the large ecliptic circle. According to this construction, the motions of all the planets are represented agreeably to their alternate and gradual increase and decrease of velocity from the aphelion to the perihelion, and back again in each revolution; but the change of distance is not so correctly effected, nor is it of importance, as the mean distances themselves cannot be duly preserved in any machine whatever. The revolving pulley of each radius vector is made adjustible by a screw and sliding piece, for the purpose of tightening the silk cord, and, when sufficiently tight, the cord acts as a brace to each of the radii, and prevents their tendency to bend. The longest radius, which carries Herschel, has a small roller resting on that edge of the table which bears its weight, and allows the scale of lengths to be greater than they would otherwise admit. The proper variation of distance might also be represented in each orbit, if a second short arm, one-half of the length of the first, were made to revolve twice in each period by another pair of pulleys, which the inventor effected; but this addition renders the adjustments troublesome, and increases the complexity of the mechanism. The equation of the centre would however still be exhibited, as well as the variation of distance, by this last addition. We shall not attempt to detail all the particulars in the construction of this machine, which would require an entire plate to explain it minutely; but will give such a table of its trains, and of their values, as may suffice and gratify the curiosity of our astronomical readers.

A Table of Synodic Trains, with their Tropical Periods.

		d.	h.	m.	s.
The Revolution of the Handle is performed in		7	0	0	0
Sun's Axis . $\frac{61}{18} \times \frac{30}{28}$ of seven days, ...	.	25	10	0	0
Mercury's Revolution $\frac{61}{18} \times \frac{35}{53} \times \frac{73}{13}$ of do.	.	87	23	14	36
Venus's do. . $\frac{30}{76} \times \frac{63}{16} = \frac{945+608}{608} = \frac{1553}{608}$ of Mercury's period, .	.	224	16	41	56
Earth's do. . $\frac{26}{126} \times \frac{97}{32} = \frac{1261+2016}{2016} = \frac{3277}{2016}$ of Venus's do. .	.	365	5	48	39

A Table of Synodic Trains, with their Tropical Periods—continued.

						d.	*h.*	*m.*	*s.*
Mars's Revolution.	$\dfrac{28}{142}$	$\times \dfrac{134}{30}$	$= \dfrac{938+1065}{1065}$	$= \dfrac{2003}{1065}$	of the Earth's period,	686	22	17	11
Pallas's and Ceres's do.	$\dfrac{53}{166}$	$\times \dfrac{154}{34}$	$= \dfrac{4081+2822}{2822}$	$= \dfrac{6903}{2822}$	of Mars's do. .	1680	7	43	23
Jupiter's do. .	$\dfrac{40}{182}$	$\times \dfrac{122}{17}$	$= \dfrac{2440+1547}{1547}$	$= \dfrac{3987}{1547}$	of Pallas's do.	4330	14	28	28
Saturn's do. .	$\dfrac{43}{126}$	$\times \dfrac{178}{41}$	$= \dfrac{3827+2583}{2583}$	$= \dfrac{6410}{2583}$	of Jupiter's do.	10746	20	52	36
Herschel's do. .	$\dfrac{39}{129}$	$\times \dfrac{171}{28}$	$= \dfrac{2223+1204}{1204}$	$= \dfrac{3427}{1204}$	of Saturn's do.	30589	7	18	58
Moon's do. .	$\dfrac{62}{107}$	$\times \dfrac{12}{86}$	of 365.242 &c. days,		. . . .	29	12	44	0

In this construction, the wheels fixed on the sun's stem are 171, 178, 122, 154, 134, 97, and 63; the wheels attached to the under faces of the radii vectores are 129, 126, 182, 166, 142, 126, and 76; and the small wheels in each train are made fast together in pairs, that revolve round as many studs on the upper faces of the respective radii vectores, and form the connexion between each adjoining train. In order that each pair of small wheels may have their direction of motion right, a small wheel is interposed in each train that does not enter into the computation. The arbor of the handle lies under, and parallel to the face of the table, and has a pinion 18, which turns a contrate wheel 61, on the arbor that ascends through the sun's stem, and forms part of his train; and the days of the week are indicated by a hand placed on the arbor of the handle at the front edge of the table. The heliocentric place of each planet is seen at any time on the large ecliptic circle surrounding the table, by holding a plumb-line so that the eye, the planet, and the sun, are in the same straight line, when the plumb-line is suspended above, and close to the edge of the table. The remote ends of the radii vectores are graduated, to show the mean anomaly, the equations of the centre, and heliocentric latitudes of the corresponding planets, by the aid of hands fixed on the revolving pulleys respectively; and, by these contrivances, the mean and equated anomalies are both rendered conspicuous, and illustrate even the formation of the planetary tables themselves; for the small arm at all times subtends the angle at the sun, which constitutes the grand equation belonging to the planet's angular distance from the perihelion position of the small arm, which distance is now called the mean anomaly.

Tellurian and Lunarium united.

Tellurian and Lunarium united.

A machine to explain the phenomena arising out of the joint motions of the earth and moon, had long been a desideratum, when, in the year 1805, the author of the present article computed all the requisite trains, and devised a plan for uniting them, on a scale of magnitude, and with a degree of correctness, that leaves nothing more to be wished for. Formerly the changes of day and night, and the vicissitudes of the seasons, were explained separately on a tellurian that had not the means of correctly indicating the time from day to day as the year advanced, in consequence of the earth's rotations not being true solar days; and the lunarium, when separately applied to the stand of the tellurian, exhibited indeed the phases, conjunctions, oppositions, longitudes, and latitudes of the moon in a general way, but without reference to either time or place, so that it did not appear *when* or *where* the lunar phenomena would be *visible*, nor yet were the motions so correctly represented by the wheelwork as the numbers more recently computed will give them. In fact, all the most interesting problems arising out of the various eccentric relative situations of the sun, earth, and moon, were thus incapable of being solved in any thing like a satisfactory manner. The occurrence of a solar or a lunar eclipse, for instance, might be pointed out as a phenomenon likely to take place in a given lunation; but the relative positions of the earth, sun, and moon, at the moment of such occurrence, and its visibility or invisibility to an inhabitant of a given country, were left entirely to conjecture; the machine, however well computed and constructed in separate portions, that required to be united, was quite incompetent to exhibit effects depending on a union of three different motions—on the earth's annual and diurnal motions, and on the moon's motion in its orbit; which body is constantly varying both in velocity and the direction of its path. The machine, however, which we now proceed to describe, comprehends all the essential parts for showing the various phenomena resulting from a combination of these different motions, and, at the same time, points out the times and places of their occurrence in the most natural manner. We shall first give a synopsis of the wheelwork employed in this curious machine, as we did of the planetarium, and afterwards point out how these wheels are disposed of, to perform their different offices in the most convenient and correct manner.

Revolutions produced by the Wheelwork.

	Trains of Wheels.	Periods corresponding.
		d. h. m. s.
Earth . . .	$\dfrac{269}{10} \times \dfrac{26}{10} \times \dfrac{94}{18} = \dfrac{657436}{1800}.$	365 5 48 48
Moon's Lunation, or Moon's Nodes .	$\dfrac{10}{269} \times \dfrac{43}{13} \times \dfrac{48}{73}$ of a solar year.	29 12 44 3.28765
	$\dfrac{94}{18} \times \dfrac{26}{10} \times \dfrac{43}{13} \times \dfrac{48}{73}$ of a day.	29 12 44 3.28765
	$\dfrac{16}{74} \times \dfrac{179}{42}$ of a lunation.	27 5 5 36.9
Moon's Apogee .	$\dfrac{67}{64} \times \dfrac{41}{46}$ of a lunation.	27 13 18 32
Handle . . .	$\dfrac{10}{269} \times \dfrac{10}{26} \times \dfrac{94}{18}$ of a solar year.	1 0 0 0
Weekly hand . .	$\dfrac{18}{18} \times \dfrac{56}{8}$ of a day.	7 0 0 0

Table of Dimensions.

Motions.	Wheels.	Diameters.	Teeth per Inch.
Earth and Handle.	269	12.0 In.	7.1
	10	0.45	7.1
	26	1.20	8.0
	18	0.385	8.0
	94	3.70	8.0
	18	0.71	8.0
Lunation.	13	0.60	7.0
	43	1.96	7.0
	73	3.33	7.0
	48	2.18	7.0
Nodes.	74	2.05	11.5
	16	0.44	11.5
	42	0.67	20.0
	179	2.86	20.0
Apogee.	64	2.05	10.0
	67	2.14	10.0
	46	1.46	10.0
	41	1.30	10.0 .
Hand for a Week.	18	0.71	8.0
	18	0.71	8.0
	8	0.2	15.0
	56	1.22	15.0

	Ft. In.
Diameter of the Circular Stand	2 6
Distance from the Earth to the Sun	1 8
Distance of the Moon from the Earth . . .	0 8
Diameter of the Globe	0 9
The distance of its Centre from the Table . .	1 0
Small Ecliptic Plate	0 9
Fixed Plate for the Moon's Age	0 10¼

ters of reference; and the parts that support them will be seen from the situations in which they are placed, without a minute and tedious detail of particulars that will be obvious from an inspection of the figure.

Upon the plane of the circular table is screwed fast a broad rim of silvered brass, to receive the graduations that will be explained presently. A long bar of brass, braced by edge-bars, extends entirely across the table, and revolves round a solid stem of steel, made fast into the large wheel 269, under this bar, which may be called the *annual* bar, as it carries all the mechanism placed on it once round the said wheel and rim in each solar year, by means to be hereafter described. The steel stem passes through the centre of the table, and is kept close down by a tapped nut and collar under the table, so that the large wheel may be fixed in any position, as it regards the graduations on the circumscribed rim. On the upper end of the steel stem, above the annual bar, a contrate wheel, 62, is made fast, by a side screw passing through its piece of tube into the solid part of the steel, so that it may give motion to the small pinion 8, in contact with it, while the annual bar carries this pinion round it. The sun's stem is also carried round the central stem, by being erected a little out of the centre, behind the central wheel 62, and a crank-piece is attached near the sun's stem, to the remote end of the annual bar, which, therefore, partakes of its motion, and a silken thread stretched across the open part of the crank-piece, forms an index to all the divided circles and quadruple spiral on the face of the large brass rim attached to the table. Upon the nearer, or projecting end of the annual bar, are made fast several bridges and cocks, to support the remainder of the wheelwork, and to keep each wheel in its proper place of action; which we shall describe in separate trains, and in the order of their transmission of motion. The handle is seen withdrawn from its squared arbor to the left of the annual bar; the horizontal arbor to which it belongs is concealed, and carries a vertical wheel, 18, which drives the wheel 94 under the first large bridge, by acting with its contrate teeth; then the arbor of 94, being pivoted into the said bridge above, descends through a hole cut in the annual bar,

Description of the tellurian and lunarium united.
PLATE
CCCCLX.

A perspective view of the principal parts of the tellurian and lunarium united in one machine, is given in Plate CCCCLX; where some of the wheels that would otherwise be concealed by the surrounding plates, bars, or bridges, are dotted, or withdrawn from their true positions, so as to be exposed to view. We propose to describe the various wheels by the numerals that belong to their teeth, instead of letters of reference; and the parts that support them will

PLATE
CCCCLX.

4

Planetary
Machines.

Description
tion of the
Tellurian
and Luna-
rium
united.
PLATE
CCCCLX.

and rests on a small cock under the said bar ; a pinion, 10, fixed on this vertical arbor, drives the contrate wheel 26, the long arbor of which lies parallel to and under the annual bar, till it reaches the teeth of the large wheel 269, with which it is connected. That portion of the long arbor just mentioned, which projects beyond the edge of the table, is displaced in the figure, together with the pinion 10, and small cock over it, which otherwise could not have been seen, nor easily comprehended ; but the remainder of this arbor is concealed by the annual bar, as well as its pinion 10 that acts with the large wheel. This long arbor is carried by two cocks, one seen, out of its place, at the extreme end of the annual bar, and the other not seen, but fixed under the said bar, above the large wheel, in such a way that a screw with a milled head, seen within the cranked part of a small bridge carrying a long vertical stem, will draw up or let down the pinion borne by it, so as to put it into or out of action with the large wheel at option. Now, when the handle is inserted on its arbor of pinion 18, (concealed,) and turned round, the wheels 94 and 26 both commence moving by means of their impelling pinions ; but the last pinion 10, meeting with a large wheel made fast to the table, cannot turn it round, but, as sufficient force is applied to the handle, the annual bar itself is obliged to move forward instead of the large wheel, and its revolution round the central stem is effected by the train in an exact solar year. Thus, in $365^{d} \cdot 5^{h} \cdot 48^{m} \cdot 48^{s}$ the cranked index, attached to the annual bar, travels gradually over the graduations of the rim, as the handle gives the corresponding motion through the train ; and, what is an important consideration, no time is lost during this transmission of motion—the handle and the index have their motions contemporaneous. When our readers have seen how the annual bar is put into a steady regulated motion, they will easily conceive that the other wheels carried by it must also be put into their respective motions. We shall next explain how the motion of the handle is transmitted to the earth's axis.

The earth is placed over a long steel rod screwed fast into the annual bar, which, in being turned in the lathe, is left a small trifle thicker at the two ends, in order that a long tube revolving round it may have its friction reduced to the ends only. This tube, which is nearly six inches long, carries at its lower end a pinion, 18, acting with the edge of wheel 94, which is cut into teeth that are so rounded as to act both on the points and edges ; and its motion, therefore, is precisely the same as that of the handle : it carries, moreover, at the upper end, a small wheel, 40, which drives another 40, attached to the earth's axis by the intervention of another similar or third wheel 40, that only changes the direction of the motion. These three similar wheels are all bevelled a little, for the purpose of allowing the earth's axis to have its proper inclination ; and, so far as their connexion with the handle is concerned, it is obvious that the earth's axis must have a revolution every time that the handle is turned round, provided that no cause interfere to alter this effect : but, as the earth's inclined axis must necessarily continue to point, as in nature, to the north pole of the heavens, in order to produce the requisite change in the seasons, while the rotations effect the succession of day and night, a contrivance becomes indispensable for preserving the parallelism of that axis on every part of the earth's course round the sun. For this purpose the contrate wheel 62 is fixed at the centre of the table with its teeth pointing downwards, to catch the pinion

Planetary
Machines.

Description
tion of the
Tellurian
and Luna-
rium
united.
PLATE
CCCCLX.

8, which has a long arbor passing under a bridge, and extending above and parallel to the annual bar, till its similar pinion 8 takes hold of another contrate wheel, 62, with its teeth pointing upwards, in order that its motion may be in a retrograde direction just once in every year. As it is of no importance what the number of teeth of these two wheels and of these two pinions may be, provided that they be respectively alike, we have left them out of the table of trains, and consider them only as an appendage, that do not affect the trains otherwise than by giving the earth an additional rotation, as we shall now explain. The long bridge standing lengthwise over the pinion 18, of which two or three teeth only can be seen, has a tube fixed in it, which ascends towards the earth ; and the tube of the latter 62 moves round it, and, at its upper end, supports the small ecliptic ring, to which the bar is screwed fast that carries the three similar wheels of 40 teeth each above described ; this bar, therefore, in common with the small ecliptic ring, has a retrograde motion, which amounts to a revolution in each year, by virtue of its connexion with the revolving tube of wheel 62 ; but the first small wheel 40 is fast to the diurnal tube, round which the second and third similar wheels are carried backwards once every year ; the second wheel, therefore, receives a revolution in consequence of its circuit round the first, and, in the same direction as its revolutions from the train are performed, and the joint effect of these two causes of motion is the performance of 366.24222 turns, in 365.24222 revolutions of the handle, consequently, the third wheel, immediately impelled by the second, gives the earth 366.24222 rotations in a solar year ; which, with respect to a star, or other fixed point in the heavens, is exactly according to nature. But, though the absolute rotations of the earth are 366.24222, the relative rotations, as they regard the sun, are only 365.24222 in so many solar days, for the apparatus that preserves the parallelism, by giving one retrograde revolution to the bar that supports the earth, deducts one rotation in each year, by turning the earth backwards as it proceeds in its annual course, thereby affecting the difference between solar and sidereal time ; and when a dial of 24 hours is borne by the upper end of the diurnal tube, an index, made fast to the fixed rod of steel, shows solar time, while another index, placed on the retrograde bar, shows sidereal time on the same graduated circle ; and, on any day, the difference between the two times, thus indicated, is equal to the sun's mean right ascension, provided that the two hands are adjusted to indicate the *same time* at the moment of the vernal equinox. This combination of the mechanism produces, in a beautiful manner, and with perfect accuracy, all the changes of summer and winter, day and night, both as to solar and sidereal time.

The lunation, or synodic period of the moon, as she has reference to the earth, comes next to be considered. The value of the lunar train may be ascertained by taking it as the compound fraction of either a day or a year, accordingly as we reckon from the handle or from the great wheel. For the sake of diminishing the number of wheels, and of rendering all the motions dependent, as much as possible, on the same wheels, a part of the diurnal and annual train is made common to the moon's wheelwork. If we count from the great wheel, $\frac{10}{269}$ is the common part, but if from the handle, $\frac{94}{18} \times \frac{26}{10}$ is the common portion ; in either case

Planetary
Machines.

Description of the
Tellurian
and Luna-
rium
united.
PLATE
CCCCLX.

$\dfrac{43}{13} \times \dfrac{48}{73}$ are all the additional wheels and pinions required for completing the lunar train for its lunations. When motion has been communicated from the handle, so as to cause the long concealed arbor to revolve with the contrate wheel 26, a pinion, 13, fixed on the same arbor, revolves in the same time, and compels a contrate wheel, 43, and also the wheel 73, fixed on its vertical arbor, to turn together; while the latter drives the last wheel of the lunar train, 48, round in a month, this last wheel, 48, rests on a cross bridge, having a tube fixed to it that ascends above the monthly bar, and a tube fixed to the wheel 48 revolves round the said fixed tube, and carries the monthly bar round in each lunation. If the moon's stem had been screwed into the remote end of the monthly bar, as is usual in common machines, there would have been no variation of either latitude, velocity, or distance, from the earth in her motion; and, to effect these purposes, two additional trains are introduced, which respectively derive their motions from the lunation. The train for exhibiting the moon's variable velocity and distance has reference to the period of the progressive motion of the moon's apogee, and is thus arranged. The wheel 64 is made fast on the upper end of the cross bridge's tube, round which the monthly bar revolves, while the wheel 67 is connected with it; the latter, therefore,

being carried by the monthly bar, revolves in $\dfrac{64}{67}$ of

a lunation. On the arbor of 67 is made fast a smaller wheel, 46, which ought to reach the 41, so as to impel it; but, in that case, either the wheels must have been inconveniently large and heavy, or the distance of the moon would not have allowed a nine inch globe to represent the earth; the motion is, therefore, conveyed from 46 to 41, by two similar pinions on the same horizontal arbor, which take the motion from 46, and give it unaltered to 41, the last wheel of the apogeal train. Above the last wheel, which has, as its arbor, a piece of brass tube, squared within, is a light dial, borne by the small cock of wheel 41; and a hand inserted on the revolving tube, or short arbor, indicates thereon the moon's equation of the centre, and the place of the apogee and perigee, in each month. The stem of the moon is squared, so as to fit nicely into the squared bore of the short tube, forming the arbor of wheel 41, and the moon's weight makes the squared stem descend till it rests on a small edge bar of steel, connected with the train of the moon's nodes, to be noticed again presently. The crank-piece, which bears the upper part of the moon's stem, fits the lower squared part, and performs a revolution every time that the wheel 41 turns round; that is, once during the period of an anomalistic revolution. The length of the horizontal part of the crank-piece of the moon's stem is equal to twice the eccentricity of her orbit, to radius eight inches, the length of the monthly arm from the earth; and the motion thereof being retrograde, as it regards the direct motion of the moon round the earth, is continually increasing or diminishing the mean motion of the moon, by carrying her alternately forward or back, round the squared portion of the stem. The equation thus arising will keep the moon continually retarding or accelerating her velocity in her orbit, as the greatest equation is subtended by a line equal to twice her eccentricity. The distance also is as constantly varying, and would vary very nearly in conformity to her true orbit, if the upper part of the

stem were screwed into a small hole, made at the distance of once the eccentricity, denoted by the head of a pin; but as the true distances and sizes of the heavenly bodies cannot be represented mechanically in due proportion, this part of the stem may keep its situation for giving the equation of the centre without detriment to the distance; a change in which will thus be rendered still more perceptible to the eye.

With respect to the train for giving the proper retrograde motion to the moon's nodes, and for showing her latitude at all times, this is also derived from the lunation in the following manner: The wheel 74 is made fast, under wheel 64, on the same fixed arbor of the cross bridge, and a concealed pinion 16 revolving in

$\dfrac{74}{16}$ of a lunation; this pinion has a short vertical arbor

descending through a hole perforated in the monthly bar, and the small wheel 42, fast to the same, acts with the large contrate wheel 179, which has a horizontal arbor, pivoted into the end of a screw, at the lower end of a small cock fixed to the under face of the monthly bar. This part of the train is visible in the drawing, though the first portion is not. On the back face of the wheel 179, which revolves in the period of the moon's return to the node, is soldered an epicycloidal rim of brass as an edge-bar, in an eccentrical position as it regards the wheel's arbor; and a forked piece of steel, on which the lower end of the moon's squared portion of the stem rests, catches the epicycloidal edge-bar, which, during the wheel's motion, makes the remote end rise and fall alternately a proper quantity for giving the moon her due latitude, north or south of the ecliptic, in every position of the earth: the centre of motion of the forked bar being a pin in the small cock into which the wheel's arbor is pivoted. According to these arrangements, the three motions of the moon are so united, as to produce the lunation, and the requisite variations of latitude, velocity, and distance at the same time; a union which has probably never before been so completely effected by such simple means. The broad edge of the wheel 179 has the graduations for the latitude, which are indicated by the edge of the monthly bar. Above the trains on the monthly bar a large dial is fixed, along with the wheels 64 and 74 on the top of the cross bridge's tube; and a cranked index, similar to the annual index, has a thread stretched over its open part to mark the day of the moon's age, and other graduations relating to the tides, which may be inserted or omitted according to the wish of the maker or purchaser. This large dial has been considered as transparent in the drawing, in order to show the situation of the dotted ovals, representing the concealed wheels and portions, which could not otherwise have been intelligibly described. The graduations on the table are such as have reference to the sun, namely, a divided ecliptic, and corresponding circle of the sun's declination; with the day spaces laid down in due proportion and position, so that there are nearly eight days more in the summer than in the winter half-year; and yet all the circular motions and periods, connected with the indication by unequal divisions, are free from errors, notwithstanding the earth's motion in its circuit round the sun has its actual velocity constantly varying. This apparent paradox may be thus easily solved: the large wheel 269 has the size of its teeth varying from the aphelion to the perihelion points of the ecliptic, each way round, by this simple contrivance in the

Planetary
Machines.

Description
tion of the
Tellurian
and Luna-
rium
united.
PLATE
CCCCLX.

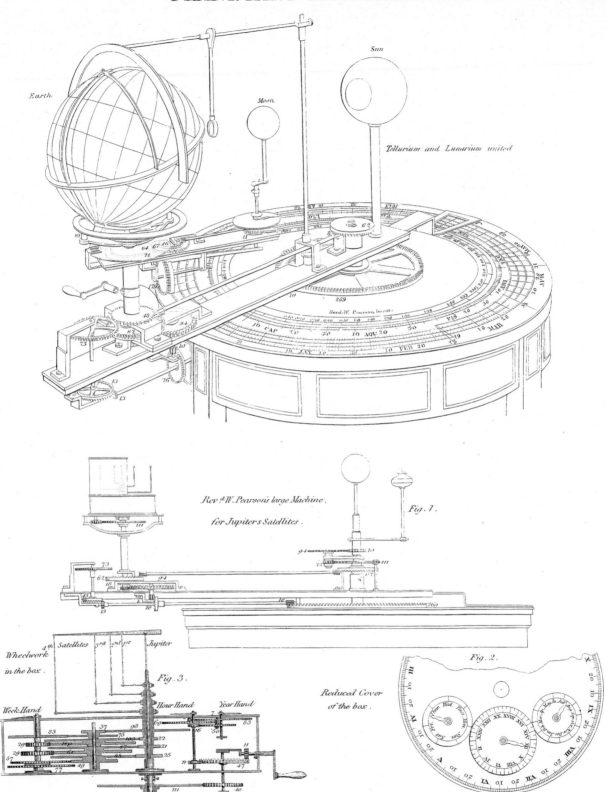

Earth

Moon

Sun

Tellurium and Lunarium united

Revd. W. Pearson Invent.

Revd. W. Pearson's large Machine.

for Jupiter's Satellites.

Fig. 1.

Fig. 2.

Wheelwork
in the box.

4th Satellites 3rd 2nd 1st Jupiter

Fig. 3.

Reduced Cover
of the box.

Week Hand

Hour Hand

Year Hand

Engraved for the Edinburgh Encyclopædia by J. Moffat Edin.

Planetary
Machines.

Description of the
Tellurian and Luna-
rium
united.
PLATE
CCCCLX.

cutting and dividing of the teeth : a point was determined out of the centre of the wheel, which bore the same proportion to its radius that the earth's mean radius does to its eccentricity, which we believe in this wheel was two tenths of an inch, and in this point a hole was drilled and broached, just large enough to admit the arbor of the cutting engine, and then the blank wheel placed upon this hole, as a centre, had its contrate teeth cut by the engine in the usual way, and the regular increase and decrease of the size of the teeth, throughout each respective semicircle, was thus mechanically insured, without any skill on the part of the operator, or powers of the engine, beyond what the *prime* number of teeth required to be done during the common operation of cutting. This work, we understand, can be easily performed by Fayrer of Pentonville, near London, whose apparatus will enable him to cut a wheel into any number of teeth, prime as well as composite, and to round the teeth, without a file, at the same operation.

A globular lamp, of Argand's construction, is made the representative of the sun, and the rays of light are rendered parallel, or nearly so, by a couple of lenses, one of which is adjustable, as in a magic lantern ; and by these means one half of the globe nearly is illuminated, while the other is in the shade, behind the semicircular terminator, and a lens, of small diameter and form, is interposed between the sun and earth, which, being properly adjusted, condenses the light it receives to a focus on the surface of the globe, the luminous point being just one half of a degree in diameter. This luminous index shows at all times the place where the sun is vertical ; and the addition of adjustable meridian and horizon circles, properly graduated, afford the means of working various problems connected with the sun's place, such as the time of his rising, setting, and culminating, his declination, the length of the day, and end of twilight, &c. ; besides which, a small graduated quadrant applied at the zenith, and passing through the luminous point, which always represents the sun's place at any moment, (as seen from the centre of the earth,) will indicate his altitude, and show his azimuth on the horizon circle, at any hour of any day in the year, so that the approximate solution of many interesting spherical triangles may be performed in the most natural way, from hour to hour, as the earth proceeds in her annual course, and at the same time turns round her inclined axis, which is always kept parallel to itself.

There is also a small lamp carried occasionally by the moon's stem, with a corresponding lens to give another luminous point for describing the moon's path on the face of the earth ; which lens is kept in its parallel situation in every part of the month, and rises and falls together with its lamp, so as to show the variation of both latitude and longitude of the luminous point thus occasioned. If a celestial globe were substituted for the terrestrial, the moon's appulse to and passage over the zodiacal stars might thus be pleasingly represented, while both the solar and sidereal times would be pointed out, and nothing but the proper parallax of the moon would be wanting to produce the times (nearly) of the occultations.

There is, lastly, a contrivance, by means of a circular plate of brass, for projecting the moon's shadow upon the surface of the earth, to show on what part of the terrestrial globe an eclipse of the sun may be expected to be visible ; and a velocity is communicated to this plate by a lever, sufficient to make the shadow pass

over the globe, large as it is, in the requisite time, or nearly so. In fact, the various problems usually worked on the terrestrial globe, will be solved during the progress of the year, by the mere turning of the handle, when the meridian and horizon circles are properly placed for the given longitude and latitude. The train at the handle, that gives motion to the weekly hand, resembles the dial-work of a common clock or watch ; the pinion 18 on the daily arbor drives another 18, together with a smaller pinion of 8 leaves fast to it, and this latter again drives the wheel 56 fixed on a tube, that revolves in 7 days round the arbor of the handle, and its tube carries the weekly hand over the same dial that the hour hand points to, near the handle. When the annual index is required to be carried to a given day on the large graduated rim, the pinion on the long arbor is detached from the large wheel by its lifting screw, and the mechanism for preserving the parallelism is then all that remains in a state of action, in which situation the annual bar may be pushed round without using the handle, and the change of seasons may thus be explained separately from the other phenomena. If the luminous point is properly adjusted, and placed over the first degree of Aries on the globe, while the annual index points to the same, it will travel along and cover the ecliptic circle all round, as the annual bar is pushed round the table, and will thus show that the ecliptic circle itself is formed by uniting all the points where the sun is seen at noon of each successive day, into one continued circular line, which intersects the equator at an angle equal to the inclination of the earth's axis. At the same time, it will appear, that the two poles of the earth are each presented to the sun's rays by turns, till the circle of illumination gradually extends to $23\frac{1}{2}$ degrees beyond the polar point, and then as gradually recedes, till the same appearance begins to take place at the opposite pole. Thus it may be explained, by means the most simple, viz. by a union of the *parallelism* with the *inclination* of the earth's axis, how all the beautiful variety in the face of nature, and the regular succession of bountiful supplies for the use of man and beast, are wonderfully produced by the power and wisdom of the omnipotent Creator and Preserver of the universe.

Satellite Machine.

Planetary
Machines.

Description
tion of the
Tellurian
and Luna-
rium
united.
PLATE
CCCCLX.

We have already given an account of the wheelwork of some of the machines that exhibit the revolutions of Jupiter's satellites by single pairs of wheels, and that produce the proper periods *nearly ;* but we have reserved to this place an account of a machine, into which a train of wheels is introduced for each separate satellite, and which produces all the requisite motions for not only explaining, but even computing the occurrence of the various Jovian phenomena, with a degree of exactness that is truly surprising. The machine in question was contrived and constructed in the year 1805, by the Rev. Dr. W. Pearson, and may either be used as a portable machine, without reference to the motion of Jupiter and the earth, or may be applied to the stand of the Tellurian and Lunarium united, when some of its parts are dismounted, and other appendages substituted. We propose to describe this machine first in its detached state, mounted on a small tripod, without the motions of Jupiter and the earth ; and also as forming a more extended piece of mechanism acting in conjunction with the trains that give motion to the two primaries, Jupiter and the Earth. Fig. 1. of Plate CCCCLXI. is a section of a cylindrical brass box, con-

Description
tion of Dr.
Pearson's
satellite
machine.

PLATE
CCCCLXI.
Fig. 1.

Planetary
Machines.

Description
tion of Dr.
Pearson's
Satellite
Machine.
PLATE
CCCCLXI.
Fig. 2.

Fig. 3.

taining the wheelwork that constitutes the trains for producing the respective revolutions of the four satellites,
as they regard Jupiter seen from the earth. The different arbors are placed in a straight line, that none
of the wheels or pinions may be concealed behind one
another; but Fig. 2, which represents a portion
of the circular cover, and explains the calliper, will
convey a clear idea how the wheels are placed in
the interior of the box, so as that each pair shall be situate properly for due action. If we begin with the
handle, we shall be able to trace the transmission of
motion through the separate trains to each satellite;
and, as in our preceding descriptions, if we use the
numerals belonging to the respective wheels, instead
of letters of reference, the drawing will be less encumbered. The first pinion 11, Fig. 3. is fixed on the horizontal arbor of the handle, and the time of its turning
round is assumed to be a solar day; this impels another similar pinion 11 on a vertical axis, through the
medium of a wheel 47, of which we shall take no farther notice at present, than that its teeth are formed to
act with both pinions, by being rounded on the edge,
and also on the face of the wheel; the latter pinion,
therefore, revolves also in a solar day, and carries the
hour-hand on its upper pivot, pointing to the hour-
circle on the cover: this second pinion 11 appears in
the figure removed almost the whole length of the
section of the box from the weekly arbor, though in
the box it reaches wheel 77, when brought round into
its place depending on the calliper, and drives it round,

together with its arbor, in $\frac{77}{11}$, or 7 days. This week-

ly arbor, the upper pivot of which carries a hand to
point out the seven days of the week, is common to
four other driving wheels, ranged one above another,
namely, 57, 29, 29, and 83, all which are fast to the
said weekly arbor: between this arbor and the centre
of the box, but drawn a little to one side, is made fast
a steel cylindrical stem, rising perpendicularly from
the bottom of the box, round which stem four pairs of
wheels separately revolve with appropriate velocities,
being respectively impelled by the four wheels on the
weekly arbor already specified: the lower wheel in each
pair is driven, and the upper one is a driver, giving
motion to a fourth wheel, attached to a revolving tube

in the centre. Hence it is not difficult to perceive,
that the four concentric tubes, that carry the bent arms
of the satellites, have each the fourth or last wheel of
its own train attached to its lower extremity; and that
all the periods are separately produced by as many
trains of four wheels each, acting on a uniform system; the second and third wheels in every train being
pinned together, and at liberty to revolve together
round the common fixed stem. The little ball, which
represents Jupiter, is small enough to be taken as unity
in the scale of distances given to the arms; but a conical piece of brass wire may be inserted on the bearing stem, instead of Jupiter's ball, with notches made
at the under side for the small satellites to pass through,
at the times of their falling into Jupiter's shadow, while
a paper screen attached to the box receives the shadows of the moving small bodies, and exhibits the various appearances occasioned thereby, while a steady
lamp, of Argand's construction, properly adjusted,
is made a substitute for the sun. The train which
gives motion to the annual hand, that indicates the
months, remains yet to be described; and as its only
use is to regulate this hand, wheels of moderate dimensions, such as Ferguson employed, are chosen for
effecting this purpose, without regard being had to extreme accuracy. On the diurnal vertical arbor is fixed
the pinion 16, that drives the contiguous wheel 50
round a small stud descending from the cover; then
the pinion 7, made fast to the wheel 50, and revolving
with it, impels the wheel 69 round a similar small stud
under the cover with its attached pinion 7; and, lastly, this latter 7 turns the last wheel 83 and its arbor
along with it, that bears the annual hand, in the requisite period, namely, in a solar year. Thus each turn
of the handle gives the proportionate quantum of motion to each of the four satellites and three indexes, and
these motions are all performed with such precision,
that when the machine is once adjusted for the respective places of the arms and indexes, no new rectification will be necessary for several centuries back, or to
come. The subjoined table contains all the particulars
necessary for affording full information as to the dimensions and value of the trains contained in the box,
which are all that are required when the box is mounted on a small tripod, as a portable machine.

Planetary
Machines.

Description
tion of Dr.
Pearson's
Satellite
Machine.
PLATE
CCCCLXI.

Satellites.	Trains.	Periods from the Trains.				Wheels.	Diameters.	Teeth per Inch.	Wheels.	Diameters.	Teeth per Inch.
		d.	*h.*	*m.*	*s.*						
1	$\frac{49}{57} \times \frac{25}{85}$ of 7 days.	1	18	28	36.41	57	1.68	11.2	29	0.59	18.3
						49	1.46	11.2	139	2.49	18.3
2	$\frac{61}{29} \times \frac{21}{87}$ of do.	3	13	17	54.44	85	2.38	11.6	103	2.53	14.2
						25	0.74	11.6	22	0.57	14.2
3	$\frac{139}{29} \times \frac{22}{103}$ of do.	7	3	59	35.89	29	1.05	9.5	83	1.63	16.8
						61	2.11	9.5	75	1.46	16.8
4	$\frac{75}{83} \times \frac{98}{37}$ of do.	16	18	5	2	87	2.48	11.4	37	0.87	14.3
						21	0.65	11.4	98	2.23	14.3

When this machine is placed on its small tripod, and
fixed by means of a slit tube and clamping piece, made
fast to the under face of the box, the lamp, which represents the sun, must stand at the same height on a
table that the satellites and screen are, and must occasionally be moved to the right or left; so that the geocentric place, or shadow of Jupiter's body, may fall to
the right or left of a small circle described on the cen-

tre of the screen, as the heliocentric place, accordingly
as the Nautical Almanack gives immersions or emersions
at the time for which the machine is rectified.

When the box is dismounted from its small tripod,
and made an appendage to the table of $2\frac{1}{2}$ feet diameter, which carries the united mechanism of the tellurian
and lunarium, the motions of Jupiter and the earth
are then superadded to the trains of the satellites,

Planetary
Machines.

Description of Dr.
Pearson's
Satellite
Machine.
PLATE
CCCCLXI.

which we have described above; and a small lamp, carried round the sun by the earth's revolving arm, while Jupiter himself has also his proper motion, throws the shadow of Jupiter at all times on its proper geocentric place on the screen, for exhibiting transits and occultations as they occur naturally in the heavens, and thus supersedes the necessity of manual rectification of the lamp. We shall now proceed to explain what additional wheelwork is required to give the machine the advantage we have here stated, together with other advantages, which will presently be manifest. The velocity of Jupiter in his orbit is to that of the earth as $440 : 5217$, as may be seen in our " list of planetary continuous fractions," and the fraction $\frac{5217}{440}$ is reducible into the train $\frac{47}{11} \times \frac{111}{40}$; if therefore the velocity of the annual index, or earth's bar, in the tellurian and lunarium be diminished in this ratio, it will become the radius vector of Jupiter, and the ecliptic circle will serve to point out Jupiter's heliocentric place instead of the earth's ; but the spiral and circle of the sun's declination will become useless. The train for 365.24222 days, which was explained in its place, will become a part of the train of Jupiter, if we add thereto the other portion $\frac{47}{11} \times \frac{111}{40}$, to diminish its velocity in the due proportion. Thus the two trains taken as one, will be

$$\frac{47}{11} \times \frac{111}{40} \times \frac{94}{18} \times \frac{26}{10} \times \frac{269}{10} = \frac{3429843612}{792000}.$$

$4330^{d} \cdot 14^{h} \cdot 39^{m} \cdot 17.6^{s}$. In this case, the handle which revolved in a solar day, when inserted on the arbor of 18, the first pinion of the earth's train, will still revolve in the same time as it regards Jupiter's period, when immediately connected with the arbor of 11, Jupiter's first pinion. Accordingly, when the handle is applied to the side of the small box, containing the trains of Jupiter's satellites, the arbor which it turns has a pinion of 11 teeth driving the contrate wheel 47, which we before passed over in silence ; and the driving wheel 40, fixed to its vertical arbor, drives another wheel 111, which completes the additional portion of Jupiter's long train. The wheels 40 and 111 are

Figs. 1.
and 3.

seen under the box in both the Figures 1 and 3. The connexion with the earth's, or now the second portion of Jupiter's train, is thus effected: The wheel 111 is clamped fast to the upper end of the tellurian's diurnal tube, that has the pinion 18 at its lower end, driving the wheel 94 ; and while its pinion 10 actuates the contrate wheel 26, the second pinion 10, as was before explained, takes hold of the large wheel 269, which by its resistance occasions the annual bar, now the radius vector of Jupiter, to revolve with its due velocity in the period above specified. In the mean time, the trains, which carry Jupiter's satellites in their proper synodic periods, continue in action, and thus all the motions commence with the first turn of the handle, and all the revolutions are performed with reference to the diurnal handle in their exact relative times, and without any perceptible error in the indication arising from the length of the trains, and the play that is necessary to prevent friction. In Fig. 3. the lunar wheels connected with the earth's train are not dismounted, viz. wheels 13, 43, and 73, because they do not interfere with the new arrangement ; but the other parts of the lunar apparatus, (which are fixed only by clamping

pieces of slit tube with screws,) are necessarily removed, and leave the tube of parallelism and its little ecliptic circle in their places, together with the two contrate wheels 62 and 62, and their respective pinions before described. As this small ecliptic circle is always kept parallel to the first position given it, namely in such a way that its divisions continually accord with the same divisions on the large fixed ecliptic, it becomes very useful in showing the geocentric place of Jupiter at any time by the help of a silk thread stretched from the earth's stem to the stem of Jupiter, standing over the centre of the box, while the heliocentric place of the planet is pointed out on the large ecliptic by the cranked index. Also the angular distance of each satellite from Jupiter may be seen, by referring its arm to the circle surrounding the box beneath it.

We have seen, that when the annual bar of the tellurian and lunarium united is converted into Jupiter's radius vector, the diminution of velocity is effected by means of the pinions 11 and 40 driving their wheels 47 and 111 ; therefore the same train, if the wheels be made to drive the pinions, will increase the velocity of the earth's arm, that carries the lamp, in the same proportion ; or will convert the period of Jupiter back again to the period of the earth without any further computation ; which we find to be the case in the machine we are now describing. Three small columns ascend from Jupiter's radius vector, at equal distances from the circumference of a circle described round the central contrate wheel 62 under the sun, and form the fixed supports of the wheel 111, which wheel therefore turns round the sun once in Jupiter's period ; then a horizontal arm is clamped to the sun's stem, and bears at its extreme end a pinion 22 under it, in connexion with the wheel 111 ; and the wheel 94, attached to pinion 22 by a short piece of revolving arbor without pivots, drives the tubed pinion 40, and with it the earth's (or lamp's) arm in a solar year. Thus a lamp, carried by the small annual bar round the sun, projects the shadows of Jupiter and of his four satellites on the paper skreen, attached to the opposite side of the box ; and when the geocentric places of the satellites are viewed by day-light without the lamp, the eye viewing them must be situate in the place of the lamp. The distances of the satellites from the body of Jupiter are given in diameters of Jupiter's little ball, so as to correspond with the configurations given in the Nautical Almanack ; but as the distance of the earth from Jupiter cannot be made in a machine in the same proportion, a small hole is drilled and tapped in the earth's arm at a short distance from the sun, into which the lamp's stem is made to screw, and from which the projections on the skreen will fall more correctly, for exhibiting the places where the immersions and emersions take place to the right and left of Jupiter's body, or small circle on the screen, agreeably to his relative position with respect to the time of his opposition. The synodic period of Jupiter will, however, be affected very sensibly by the grand equation of the centre, and may accelerate or retard the day of opposition by several weeks ; on which account, the inventor of this machine applied a new wheel of 269, adapted for the eccentricity of Jupiter's orbit, instead of the one adapted for the earth's eccentricity. The teeth of this fixed wheel for Jupiter are so distributed, by the eccentric cutting in the engine, that 143 are contained in one semicircle, and only 126 in the other ; so that the radius vector has what is called the *equated* motion of Jupiter thus me-

Planetary
Machines.

Description of Dr.
Pearson's
Satellite
Machine.
PLATE
CCCCLXI.

chanically produced, without affecting the motions and periods of the satellites. The earth's arm, however, which is destined to carry the lamp, derives its motion from Jupiter's radius vector, and would also be an *equated* motion, constantly varying its velocity, if no provision were made to prevent such improper effect ; but the wheel 111 is also cut into teeth, gradually varying in size throughout each of its two semicircles, from an eccentric point duly proportioned to counteract the inequality of motion given to Jupiter's radius vector. The motion of the earth's arm is rendered equable, by reversing the position of the two wheels 269 and 111, so that the smallest teeth of wheel 111 shall be acting with the pinion 22, when the largest teeth of wheel 269 are in action with its pinion 10, and *vice versa*. The pinions are so proportioned, as to work well enough with both the largest and smallest teeth, which individually differ almost insensibly from each other ; but contiguous teeth, taken by a number together, occupy larger and smaller arcs in the circumference of the respective wheels, and produce the desired effect in the motions. The small bearing piece over wheel 111, which carries the pinion 22, may be clamped to the sun's stem in any position, to bring the said pinion into action with the large or small teeth of 111 as the adjustment may require.

In adjusting the positions of the four satellites, the mean places may be computed from the Tables, and the arms placed accordingly ; or the monthly, weekly, and hourly hands being adjusted for the immersion or emersion of the first satellite, its shadow may be moved to the proper edge of Jupiter's shadow by a manual adjustment of the arm, according to the time given in the Nautical Almanack ; and then as many turns and parts of the handle, as will bring the other satellites in succession to their respective times of immersion or emersion, must be successively made before the other arms are in like manner adjusted to the proper edge of Jupiter's shadow ; and when all the adjustments are finished, any number of turns given to the handle will cause the corresponding motions of Jupiter and of his satellites, as well as of the earth, from whence they are viewed ; and all the variety of the Jovian phenomena will be represented in the most natural and pleasing manner, as well as with the utmost precision as to time, for ages past and to come.

The Orrery.

The difference between a PLANETARIUM and an ORRERY is now understood to consist in this, that a planetarium exhibits by wheelwork the periodic or tropical revolutions of the primary planets round the sun, without any reference to their rotations, whereas the orrery gives, besides the revolutions of the primary planets, the revolutions of some or all of the secondaries, and the rotation of the earth, together with the moon's anomalistic revolution, and her revolution with respect to the period of the retrograde motion of the nodes. Hence the orrery, when constructed on its

comprehensive plan, may be said to comprise within itself the planetarium, the tellurian, the lunarium, and the machine for Jupiter's satellites. As we have given descriptions of these different machines in their detached states, we shall now be able, we trust, to render intelligible our account of a machine, that unites in itself the properties of all the others, and that is adapted for explaining the various phenomena of the solar system, as far as can be done by mechanical representation.

The orrery which we propose to describe, is at the same time the most comprehensive, the most correct, and yet the most simple, considering the numerous motions produced, of any that has yet been contrived. It was constructed in the year 1813, by the same artist, and under the same superintendent, as the machines that immediately precede it, and includes the proper motions of the two small planets last discovered, Juno and Vesta. In this machine, for the sake of simplicity, all the motions are equable, except those of the moon and Mercury, the latter of which was at first carried round by an equable motion in the plane of the ecliptic, but was afterwards made to move in an eccentric orbit, and in its own plane, as a specimen of planetary motion, by means of which equal areas are passed over in equal times. We shall first give a synoptic table of the wheelwork contained in this machine, with the periods produced by them, and their errors, and then proceed to explain, by reference to engravings, the positions of the different pairs and trains of wheels that are employed in the different parts of the machine. The construction is founded on the principle of concentric tubes carrying the respective planetary arms, or radii vectores, and in this respect resembles the planetarium for equable motions ; but the planets that move much faster and much slower than the earth, have trains, while those between the earth and Jupiter inclusive have only pairs of wheels, instead of trains, in consequence of their velocity admitting of simple fractions of a year. Some of these pairs of wheels are the same which we have recommended to be adopted in the planetarium, and the mode of applying them is also the same ; so that the description of certain parts of the present machine will illustrate the construction of the planetarium also, which is our reason for not having given an engraved drawing of the planetarium in a separate plate. Indeed, the present orrery is so contrived, that its planetarium portion may be used either with or without the tellurian, lunarium, and Jovian portions, by a temporary disengagement of their respective trains, without dismounting them ; and on many occasions it may be desirable to confine the attention of an audience to certain parts of the system, in succession, before a display of all the motions is made at once ; which otherwise would be liable to confound the mind, not yet prepared to comprehend the separate effects produced by the distinct parts of the machine. The first orrery of this construction was made in the short space of two months ; and the price put upon it by the maker, without profit for the sale, was eighty-five guineas.

Synoptic Table of the Wheelwork of Dr. Pearson's Orrery.

	Trains or Pairs of Wheels.	Periods produced.				Errors in each Period.					
						In Time.			In Space.		
		d.	h.	m.	s.	h.	m.	s.	′	″	‴
Solar year . . .	$\frac{120}{15} \times \frac{61}{23} \times \frac{241}{14}$ of 24^h.	365	5	48	49	+0	0	1	0	0	2.5
Mercury	$\frac{97}{78} \times \frac{34}{108}$ of Venus's period.	87	23	14	37	+0	0	1.8	0	0	18
Venus . . , .	$\frac{63}{113} \times \frac{64}{58}$ of a solar year.	224	16	41	53	+0	0	23	0	1	32
Earth	$\frac{85}{85}$ of a solar year.	365	5	48	49	+0	0	1	0	0	2.5
Mars	$\frac{79}{42}$ of do.	687	0	4	38	+1	46	1	2	19	0
Vesta	$\frac{106}{29}$ of do.	1335	0	23	32						
Juno	$\frac{135}{31}$ of do.	1590	13	37	32	Not perfectly ascertained.					
Ceres . . . . . Pallas	$\frac{138}{30}$ of do.	1680	2	44	27						
Jupiter	$\frac{166}{14}$ of do.	4330	17	30	1	+2	51	31	0	35	36
Saturn	$\frac{50}{53} \times \frac{121}{46}$ of Saturn's period.	10746	21	18	25	+1	28	25	0	10	0
Herschel.	$\frac{46}{86} \times \frac{149}{28}$ of Saturn's period.	30589	8	32	25	+0	5	26	0	0	6
Lunation	$\frac{12}{107} \times \frac{62}{86}$ of a solar year.	29	12	44	1.2	−0	0	1.6	0	0	52
Moon's Node . .	$\frac{24}{62} \times \frac{76}{31}$ of do.	*y.* 18	23	14	29	0 −4	52	24	0	39	0
Moon's Anom. Revol.	$\frac{67}{64} \times \frac{46}{41}$ of do.	27	13	18	32	−0	0	1.9	0	1	2
Saturn's Satellites, 1.	$\frac{29}{90}$ of 5.493014 days.	1	18	28	45.49	+0	0	9.49	1	24	25
2.	$\frac{33}{51}$ of do.	3	13	18	11.78	+0	0	17.78	1	15	4
3.	$\frac{60}{46}$ of do.	7	3	57	18.8	−0	2	17.2	4	45	51
4.	$\frac{61}{20}$ of do.	16	18	5	19.5	+0	0	12.05	0	10	5.0
A Week	$\frac{120}{15} \times \frac{70}{80}$ of 24 hours.	7	0	0	0	.	.		.	.	
5½ days . . .	$\frac{55}{70}$ of 7 days.	5	12	0	0	.	.		.	.	

Planetary
Machines.
Dr. Pear-
son's Or-
rery.

PLATE
CCCCLXII.
Fig. 5.

Plate CCCCLXII. Fig. 1. exhibits the wheelwork contained in the preceding Table, given in section, on longitudinally, and that one half of each is removed, to show the sun's stem in the centre. In our description of this comprehensive machine, we propose to direct the attention of our readers to each separate portion in succession, and to begin with that which would constitute a *Planetarium*, if the other portions were not included. AABB is a cylindrical brass box, twelve inches diameter and three deep, supported by a tripod or claw-pillar of brass, as represented in Plate CCCCLXII. Fig. 5. within which the wheelwork, supported on a strong brass plate CC, is made fast by four small pillars, of which one is dotted, another made black, and the two others concealed from view. The handle that is assumed to revolve in a solar day, enters the side of the box, and taking hold of a horizontal arbor H, gives motion to the diurnal arbor F, by means of two small bevel wheels of 24 teeth each. At the lower end of this diurnal arbor (which rests on a small cork below, and carries the daily index on its superior pivot) a pinion 15 is fast, which is the first of the annual train for producing a revolution of the arbor E in a solar year. This train lies below the strong plate CC, the wheel 120 and pinion 23 being fast together, and revolving on an arbor descending from the under face of the said plate, and wheel 61 revolving together with pinion 14 on a stud under cock L, (seen in Fig. 3. more clearly,) while the annual wheel 241 is made fast to the annual arbor E. Thus the communication of motion from the diurnal handle to the annual arbor does not interfere with the planetary wheels, which are placed above the plate CC. When the wheel 241 is put in motion, it carries round with it the annual arbor, and all the wheels and pinions attached to it, as being the denominators of all the simple fractions from the earth to Jupiter, both inclusive, viz. 85, 42, 29, 31, 30, and 14. These eight denominators, revolving in a solar year, drive each its numerator in the corresponding planetary periods; and as the driven, or planetary wheels, have each a tube at their superior ends, they also carry their respective planetary arms in their true periods. In the planetarium above recommended, Venus, Mercury, and Saturn, have each a pair of similar wheels acting in the same manner, so that this part of our description will equally apply to that more simple machine. The first driver, or denominator of Venus's train, 113, is attached to the tubed wheel 85 of the earth, instead of the annual arbor, and drives wheel 63, and under it 58, made fast together round the annual arbor used as a stud, and the 58 in its turn impels the tubed wheel 64 in the period of Venus; and, in like manner, 78, the first driver of Mercury's train, is made fast to the 64 of Venus, and drives 97 and 108 fast to it, round the annual arbor, as round a stud, loosely, while the 108 is connected with the small wheel 34. This last wheel, therefore, being fast to the innermost tube, revolves in the period of Mercury, and carries his arm next to the sun. This innermost tube is the longest, and each succeeding tube decreases in length at both ends, for the purpose of making room for the arms above, and wheels below, successively. The motion of Saturn is derived from Jupiter's last wheel thus: The first driver 53 is attached to Jupiter's 166, and, revolving in Jupiter's period, drives 50 and 46 over it together round the annual arbor, while 46 drives the tubed wheel 121 round in Saturn's period; and, lastly, Herschel's wheel 86 is fast to Saturn's 121, and

drives 46, together with 28, round the annual arbor; and the latter, being connected with 149, carries it round, together with its tube, in Herschel's period. Thus all the primary planets perform their respective revolutions, while the annual index, placed on the upper pivot of the revolving annual arbor, indicates the sun's declination and reduction of the ecliptic to the equator; the day of the month in a quadruple spiral, and the sun's (or earth's) equation of the centre, being shown on a circular plate, seen under the sun, in Figure 5. not yet described.

Planetary
Machines.
Dr. Pear-
son's Or-
rery.
PLATE
CCCCLXII.

Hitherto we have considered the revolutions of the planets as derived from the diurnal handle, which is the case only when all the different portions of the orrery are in motion together; when the planetarium part alone is used, the diurnal handle is disengaged, and a weekly handle is substituted, which actuates those wheels only that are not connected with the diurnal motion of the earth, nor with Jupiter's moons. This handle is more convenient than the diurnal handle when the revolutions alone are exhibited, on account of the increased velocity thus given to the moving bodies. We shall now explain how this change of motion is effected; which will require some consideration to understand, as some of the parts are not visible in the principal figure. The annual train, under the plate CC, is represented as having the calliper, or pivot, in a straight line, that the wheels essential to be shown might all be in view; but in reality these pivots, or studs, round which the wheels revolve, are situate round the central stem D, which is a piece of strong steel wire nine inches long. The wheel 120, and the pinion 23 fast to it, revolve in $\frac{120}{15} = 8$ days, and the common arbor on which they are fixed carries, above the plate CC, another wheel, 80, not seen in the principal figure, but exhibited in a detailed state in Fig. 2. without the dotted cock M, which is partly seen in Fig 1.; then this wheel 80 impels a weekly wheel 70, on a separate arbor, which is also seen in Fig. 2, and the weekly hand V, placed on its upper pivot, is seen on the lid of the box in Fig. 5. which will explain the relative position of this arbor. The pinion 23, which we have said revolves in 8 days, impels another similar pinion, 23, on a stud, seen only in Fig. 3, and that impels a third similar one on a vertical arbor passing through a brass bar LL, the cranked part of which bar is seen obliquely in Fig. 1.; this vertical arbor, therefore, turns in eight days also, and a bevel wheel of 32 teeth, fixed on its superior end, drives another bevel wheel of 28 teeth round in seven days, $\left(\frac{28}{32} \text{ of } 8\right)$ together with its horizontal arbor, which extends nearly to the edge of the box; and when the handle is inserted on this last arbor, it consequently gives seven days' motion to each of the planets in each turn. The wheel 61, which has been shown to be one of the annual train, being supported by a stud on the lower face of bar LL, is capable of being brought into action with the pinion 23 on the arbor of wheel 120, as in Fig. 1. or of being disengaged from it, while, in both cases, it remains in action with the second pinion 23, carried by the stud under the bar LL; for this bar has a limited motion round a stud, near the annual arbor, which takes the wheel 61, carried by this bar, out of the teeth of pinion 23, attached to 120, but suffers the connexion to remain with pinion 23, carried also by the said bar; hence this wheel 61 can be made to de-

PERSPECTIVE VIEW OF THE IMPROVED ORRERY FOR MEAN MOTIONS

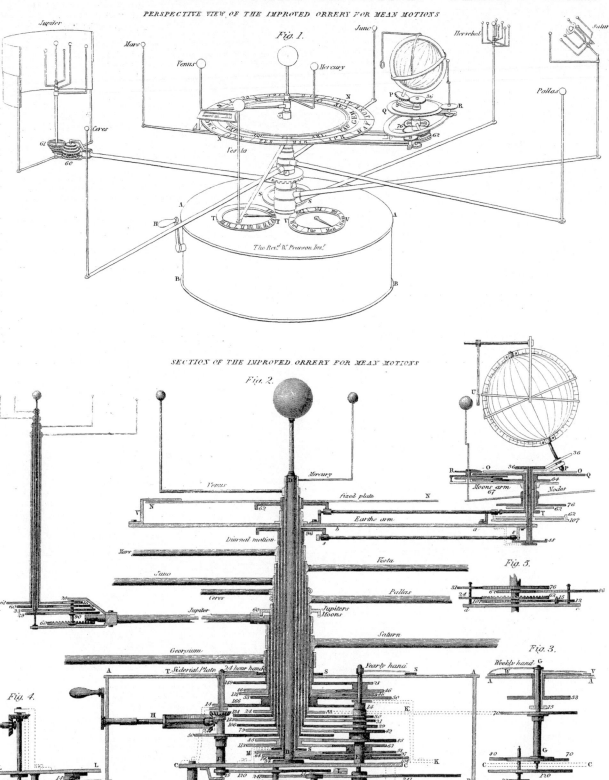

Fig. 1.

Tho. Rev.ᵈ W. Pearson, Inv.ᵗ

SECTION OF THE IMPROVED ORRERY FOR MEAN MOTIONS

Fig. 2.

Fig. 5.

Fig. 3.

Fig. 4.

Eng.ᵈ by J. Moffat Edin.ʳ

Planetary
Machines.

Dr. Pear-
son's Or-
rery.
PLATE
CCCCLXII.

rive its motion from either the diurnal or weekly handle as may be required, by the mere partial displacement of the bar LL, the exterior end of which is fixed to either of its two positions by a pressing screw under the box ; and in either situation the handle will only take that arbor which corresponds to the given position of the bar. It might be expected that the pinion 14, made fast to wheel 61, would also be disengaged from the large wheel 241 with which it acts, but this effect is not produced by the motion of the bar that bears it; and that is occasionally displaced, because the centre of the bar's motion is close to the centre of the large wheel, and the pinion 14, instead of being disengaged, only rolls round the circumference of the large wheel, while their teeth continue engaged ; and thus it is always in a state to perform its office, whichever of the two handles may be used.

The next portion of the orrery is the *tellurian*, on which the changes of day and night, and vicissitudes of the seasons depend, as well as various other geocentric phenomena. Near the middle of the vertical diurnal arbor F, is a wheel, 50, which we have not before noticed, and which drives another of 100 teeth, having a long tube attached to it; this latter wheel stands next above the annual wheel 85, and its tube surrounds that of 85, but its motion is much quicker ; its revolution being performed in two solar days. Immediately under the wheels 85 and 113, which revolve together in a solar year, a cock M, seen dotted in Fig. 1. carries another tube, which has no motion, but which ascends above the annual tube, and holds a circular plate, NN, for containing the days of the month, the ecliptic circle, and the sun's equation, corresponding to his mean anomaly ; the earth's motion being equable in this machine. The earth's arm is clamped fast to the annual tube of wheel 35, and a contrate wheel, 96, is made fast by friction on the tube of wheel 100, revolving in two days ; then two equal pinions, of eight leaves each, at the opposite ends of a horizontal arbor, lying under and parallel to the earth's arm, take the motion from wheel 96, and give it to another contrate wheel 48 under the earth ; this smaller wheel, therefore, would revolve in an exact solar day if the earth's arm had no motion round the sun, and the bevel wheel 36, at the upper end of its vertical arbor, would give the same motion unaltered to a similar bevel wheel 36, attached to the earth's inclined axis ; and thus, a turn of the diurnal handle would produce a rotation of the earth. But the earth's arm makes a revolution in the period of the annual wheel 85, or in 365.2423 days, while the pinion 8 is connected with the contrate wheel 96 ; this

pinion consequently revolves $\frac{96}{8} = 12$ times in a year,

by virtue of its circuit round the sun, and these twelve revolutions are given to the wheel 48, by the similar pinion of the opposite end of the long horizontal arbor ;

hence the wheel 48 receives in each year $\frac{12 \times 8}{48} = 2$

revolutions, in addition to the 365.2423 derived from the diurnal handle; and therefore makes 367.2423 turns, which it communicates to the earth's axis in the manner above stated ; and the earth would thus make 367.2423 rotations in a year if there existed no other modification than what has hitherto appeared. But we shall see presently, that one rotation in a year is lost by a cause very similar to that which adds two annually. A contrate wheel, 62, is screwed to the fixed plate NN, and the annual arbor carries another long

horizontal arbor above it, with a couple of similar pinions at the opposite ends, one of which is made to revolve by means of its connexion with the fixed wheel 62, and the other pinion gives the same motion to a second contrate wheel 62, on a tube that surrounds the arbor of the 48 above described ; and as the teeth of the second 62 stand in an opposite direction to those of the fixed 62, it revolves once in a year in a direction suitable for preserving the parallelism of the earth's axis, which, therefore, is retrograde ; and as the piece P, which supports the earth's axis, is carried backwards once in a year by the second wheel 62, on the tube of which it is fixed, the wheel 36 on the axis is carried round the revolving wheel 36 that is placed on the arbor of 48, and thus receives one backward revolution in a year, and deducts a single rotation from the 367.2423 rotations above explained, and, in this way, the resulting number of the earth's actual rotations is 366.2423, viz, a rotation in each sidereal day as in nature.

Planetary
Machines.

Dr. Pear-
son's Or-
rery.
PLATE
CCCCLXII.

The sidereal rotation of the earth is converted into a solar day, without any regard to the wheelwork, in this way : the retrograde contrate wheel 62 carries a small ecliptic circle OO, to which the bearing piece P already referred to is fixed, and the earth, carried backwards by this small ecliptic while its parallelism is preserved, exposes every meridian line on it in succession to the sun, as it proceeds in its annual orbit, while a vertical solar ray travels once round the globe in the course of the year ; and if the earth had no rotation on its axis, the effect of the parallelism of the earth's axis, as it regards a star, or other fixed point in the heavens, would be an *annual solar day* given to the inhabitants of the earth, but in such a way, that the sun would appear to rise in the west, and to set in the east six months afterwards. This effect takes place gradually ; and if we conceive it to exist, while the earth is making her regular rotations in a contrary direction,

we shall perceive that $\dfrac{1}{366.2423}$ the part of a day, or

$3^m. 56.5^s$ will be deducted from the time of each rotation ; hence the earth makes 366.2423 rotations in 365.2423 solar days, the sidereal day being an absolute, and the solar day a synodic or relative period. This mode of producing the proper number of sidereal rotations of the earth in a solar year, renders the machine perfect, so far as the earth's position at any given time has reference to the lunar and planetary phenomena to be viewed from her surface. The solar time at which any of the phenomena will occur is indicated by a hand on the pivot of the diurnal arbor, pointing to a fixed rim, or dial on the lid of the box ; and sidereal time is pointed out by the same hand on a dial, consisting of a small circular plate that revolves backwards once in a year, and meets the hand sooner every day by a space equal to $4^m. 56.5^s$. This annual retrograde motion of the sidereal dial is produced by a very simple contrivance, thus : the revolution of Jupiter is

produced by the wheel and pinion $\dfrac{166}{14}$, as we have

already seen ; hence, reversing the position thus, $\dfrac{14}{166}$,

and making 166 the driver, in Jupiter's period, will give just a year's motion to the pinion 14 ; therefore Jupiter's wheel 166 has a pinion 14 acting with it, when fixed to a tube that revolves round the diurnal arbor as a stud, and the upper end of this annual tube

4 N

Planetary
Machines.

Dr. Pear-
son's Or-
rery.
PLATE
CCCCLXII.
Fig. 4.

carries the sidereal dial in its proper direction and due period, without farther contrivance, and in the most correct manner.

We come next to describe the *Lunarium* portion of the Orrery. The moon's lunation is derived from the revolving wheel of parallelism 62, which, we have said, moves once backwards in a year. This part of the mechanism will best be explained by reference to Fig. 4, which gives the trains for the lunation, and the period of the nodes, in a detached state, so that all the wheels may be seen. Wheel 107 revolves in a year, by being fast to the retrograde wheel of parallelism 62, and drives the pinion 12, through the medium of a pinion 15, to change the direction of motion; and the tubed arbor of pinion 12 takes wheel 86 at its upper end, which wheel drives the lunar wheel 62 round in the lunation, and together with it the moon's arm fixed on the upper end of its tubed arbor. In like manner, the period of the moon's node is derived from the annual wheel of parallelism 62; thus, the contrate wheel 62 has its teeth rounded also on the edge, and carries the small wheel 24, together with 31, on the same revolving arbor, which 31 impels the last wheel of the train 76 in the period of the nodes. The wheel 76 is made fast to a short tube, which revolves round the lunation tube, and which supports the node's plate, that has the moon's latitude engraved on it, and is inclined in an angle equal to the angle that the lunar orbit makes, on an average, with the ecliptic; then the cranked stem of the moon being squared, descends through the moon's arm, and rests on the inclined plane, so as to be at liberty to rise or fall as the moon is carried forwards, accordingly as the inclined plate directs. The anomalistic revolution of the moon, on which the change of distance and velocity depends, is effected by the train carried by the moon's arm; the wheel 64 is attached to a fixed plate Q, on which the moon's age is indicated, which plate is borne by a long tube ascending from a cock under the moon's arm, a part of which is seen dotted; then as wheel 67 is carried round the 64, thus fixed, in every lunation, the 41 pinned to it drives the 46, in the period of an anomalistic revolution. The revolving arbor of the last wheel 46 is perforated with a square hole, so as just to admit the moon's squared stem to pass without friction; and from this combination the moon performs her lunation in the proper period, but undergoes all her variations of latitude in the period of the nodes, and her variations of velocity and distance, as occasioned by the revolving crank of the stem, in the proper anomalistic period. Above the small cock at the remote end of the moon's arm, which supports the upper pivot of the perforated arbor of wheel 46, is a small circular dial R fixed, to which an index borne by the said arbor points, to show the apogeal and perigeal points of the moon's orbit, and also her grand equation at any specified time of her lunation.

Fig. 2.

We proceed, lastly, to describe the *Jovian* portion of the machine now under consideration. Fig. 2. exhibits the weekly arbor GG, which we have before had occasion to mention, as an arbor revolving in seven days. On the middle of this arbor a wheel 70 is seen, which drives another wheel 55, having a tube revolving next to and within Jupiter's tube, in $5\frac{1}{2}$ days, or $\frac{55}{70}$ of a week: to the upper end of this tube a contrate wheel 60 is clamped fast, with its teeth pointing downwards, to take the pinion 8 on a long arbor that lies within

Planetary
Machines.

Dr. Pear-
son's Or-
rery.
PLATE
CCCCLXII.

the horizontal tube, which constitutes Jupiter's radius vector, and another similar pinion 8 at the remote end of the concealed arbor drives another contrate wheel 60, with its teeth pointing upwards, in order to have the proper direction when moving; a piece is cut away at each end of the tube, or radius vector, to allow the pinions to be engaged. Now, as the first contrate wheel of 60 teeth revolves in $5\frac{1}{2}$ days, the second wheel having 60 teeth and a similar pinion would also revolve in the same period, if Jupiter's radius vector had no motion; but as Jupiter makes a revolution in his proper period, the first pinion 8 makes $\frac{60}{8}=7\frac{1}{2}$ revolutions during this time by means of its circuit round the central wheel 60 while their teeth are engaged, and these $7\frac{1}{2}$ revolutions are given by the remote similar pinion 8 to the wheel 60 at the remote end of the radius vector, which therefore has its motion accelerated so as to gain an additional revolution in Jupiter's period, or in 4330.72916 days, which is the period produced by $\frac{166}{14}$ of a solar year. The true time employed by each turn of the latter wheel 60 may therefore be thus ascertained;

$$\text{as } 4330.72916 : 4325.22916 :: 5\frac{1}{2} : 5.493014.$$

Hence 5.493014 must be taken instead of $5\frac{1}{2}$ days, as the period in which the four contemporary wheels revolve, which are made fast to the common arbor of the wheel 60, just mentioned; and if the acceleration or difference .006986 be multiplied by the days and parts of Jupiter's period above stated, the product will be $5\frac{1}{2}$ days, the whole amount of the acceleration. The four wheels 90, 51, 46, and 20, or the common arbor of wheel 60, drive their corresponding wheels 29, 33, 60, and 61, fixed to as many separate tubes, in the respective periods of the four satellites, and the arms carried by those tubes perform their revolutions round Jupiter whenever the weekly arbor is made to revolve. The distances of the satellites from Jupiter are taken from a scale of which his diameter is the unit, and a small lamp, substituted for the earth, will project their shadows on a paper screen made fast to a slender bar that is adjustable on the lower end of Jupiter's stem. The time of Jupiter's meridian passage is moreover shown on an horary dial surrounding the weekly arbor, by means both simple and accurate: a pinion 14 driven by Jupiter's wheel 166, in a solar year, like the one we before described as carrying the sidereal plate, has a tube revolving round the weekly arbor G, which carries an annual index V round the horary dial W, which dial is made to revolve within the weekly rim in Jupiter's period, by means of a second wheel 53, which by its connexion with Jupiter's 53, turns in Jupiter's period; the annual hand, therefore, passes over Jupiter's dial in his synodic period; and when the hand is put to XXIV at the time of Jupiter's conjunction, the distance in time of the planet from the sun, or the time of his southing, on any subsequent day will be pointed out on this dial, while the day of the week is indicated on the divided rim surrounding it.

It would enlarge our article far beyond our prescribed bounds, if we were to enter into a detail of all the variety of phenomena that may be illustrated, and problems that may be worked by this comprehensive machine, when in a proper state of rectification, with a three inch terrestrial globe and its appendages, which were described in our preceding account of the "Tellurian and Lunarium united." This machine is properly, what Benjamin Martin denominated one of his less accurate and less comprehensive machines, "a Microcosm," or world in miniature. We shall conclude our description by giving such a Table of Dimensions of this machine, as will enable any clock-maker to undertake and accomplish its construction.

Table of Dimensions.

	Radius Vector in Inches.	Wheels.	Diameters in Inches.	Teeth per Inch.		Wheels.	Diameters.	Teeth per Inch.
Mercury ..	2.89	78	2.00	12	Sun's parallelism	62	2.16	9.16
		97	2.50	12		62	2.16	9.16
		108	3.42	10	Diurnal motion	50	1.50	9.4
		34	1.08	10		100	3.00	9.4
Venus ...	5.45	113	2.00	12	Do. on annual bar.	90	3.00	9.5
		63	2.50	12		45	1.50	9.5
		58	3.42	10	Weekly motion	80	2.17	11.7
		64	1.08	10		70	1.90	11.7
Earth ...	7.5	85	2.35	12	To Saturn's moons	70	2.51	8.75
		85	2.25	12		55	1.99	8.75
Mars ...	11.45	42	1.56	8.5	Lunation ...	107	2.25	15
		79	2.94	8.5		15	0 31	15
Vesta ...	$\frac{5}{8}$ of 15.3	29	0.97	9.5		12	0.25	15
		106	3.53	9.5		86	1.81	15
Juno ...	$\frac{4}{5}$ of 19.9	31	0.84	11.8		62	1.31	15
		135	3.66	11.8	Nodes	62	2.16	9.1
Ceres .. } Pallas .. }	$\frac{4}{5}$ of 20.7 }	30	0.80	11.8		24	0.84	9.1
		138	3.70	11.8		31	0.87	11.3
Jupiter ..	$\frac{1}{2}$ of 39.2	14	0.35	12.6		76	2.13	11.3
		166	4.15	12.6	Anom. Revolution	64	1.14	17.8
Saturn ...	$\frac{3}{10}$ of 73	53	2.32	7.25		67	1.20	17.8
		50	2.18	7.25		41	0.74	17.8
		46	1.24	11.8		46	0.82	17.8
		121	3.26	11.8	Saturn's Arm .	60	optional	
Herschel ..	$\frac{1}{6}$ of 144	86	2.93	9.3		60	do.	
		46	1.57	9.3	1 Satellite ..	90	1.77	16
		28	0.71	12.5		29	0.58	16
		149	3.79	12.5	2 do. ...	51	1.43	11.4
Annual Train		15	0.41	12		33	0.92	11.4
		120	3.29	12	3 do. ...	46	1.02	14.3
		23	0.63	12		60	1.33	14.3
		61	1.65	12	4 do. ...	20	0.58	11
		14	0.385	12		61	1.77	11
		241	6.60	12				

P L A

PLANING MACHINE, as the term implies, is an engine for effecting by machinery the operation of planing timbers, boards, &c. Of all the manual performances of a carpenter or joiner, there is perhaps no one that is more laborious, that employs more time, or requires less skill, than that of planing; and consequently no one, in which a machine may be more advantageously employed to perform the functions of the artist. It is, however, only within a few years that any attempt has been made to produce an engine capable of this kind of operation; the planing machine of General Bentham, for which he took out a patent in 1791, having been, we believe, the very first essay that was ever made; and this was not attended with all the advantage the ingenious projector had anticipated. The principal object in this patent was to exonerate the joiner from the charge he had of his tool in the operation of planing, by so adjusting the cutting-iron, that it could not but perform the operation intended without requiring any of the skill of the workman, and thereby rendering a common labourer equally as serviceable as the best joiner for this purpose. With this view, the plane is made the full width of the boards,

P L A

and on each side of it are fixed fillets or cheeks, which project below the face of the plane just as much as it is intended to reduce the board in thickness, serving thereby to guide the plane sideways, and to gage its thickness; because, when the boards are reduced to this amount, the fillets then rest on the bench on which the boards are placed, and will no longer apply its edge to the plank. The plane is kept down by its own or by additional weights when necessary, which latter are so contrived as to be capable of having their position shifted during the time the plane is making the stroke, the pressure at first acting forwards, and lastly on the hinder part, to prevent the fore-end dipping down the instant it leaves the board. By another contrivance, the plane is lifted up on its return, so as to clear the cutting edge from the wood; this is effected by a piece of wood which acts as a handle to the plane, and to which the power is applied; it is placed by this upon an axis extending across the width of the plane, and carrying on each side a short lever, provided with rollers at their extremities; the handle projects upwards from the plane, which, being forced forward by it, assumes an inclined position, as do also the short levers, and their rollers then rise above the cheeks of the plane; but when the plane is drawn back into an erect position, and the levers moving with it, their rollers project beneath the cheeks of the plane, and raise it off the bench, the plane being on its return borne by them.

The bench for supporting the board during the operation, has also some peculiarity in its construction, which it may be proper to describe. In cases where the boards to be planed are winding and irregular on the lower side, so that they will not lie flat upon the bench, it is provided with two sides that may be brought close upon the edges of the board, and hold it steady between them, being furnished with two or more rows of flat teeth to penetrate the wood and retain it; these sides being so contrived as to rise and fall with the bench to accommodate the whole to different thicknesses of board. When a very thin board is to be planed, it would be liable to spring up to the iron, so as to be reduced even after the plane came to rest with its cheeks upon the bench; to avoid which, the edges of the board are to be held by the sides of the bench above mentioned; but as it would still be liable to spring up in its middle part, heavy rollers, or rollers loaded with weights, are fitted in apertures made in the plane, as near as possible to the cutting edge, which answer the intended purpose of keeping the board down close to the bench. For planing pieces of greater thickness at one end than at the other, the cheeks of the plane are borne upon rulers of wood, laid on the bench on each side, the wood being as much thicker at one end as the board is to be at the other; therefore, when the plane has reduced the wood, the cheeks come to their bearing on these rollers, and cause it to move, not parallel to the bench, but inclined, according as they are thicker at one end than at the other. In like manner, by using them of different thicknesses at the different sides, the boards may be made what the workmen call featheredged.

This planing machine may be put in motion by means of a crank turned by a mill to give it a reciprocating motion; or, on a smaller scale, it may be worked by hand in the usual manner, but as all the adjustments are made by the machinery, none of the skill of the joiner is requisite in the process.

Planing Machine in the Royal Arsenal, Woolwich.—Notwithstanding the machine above described possessed several advantages in comparison with the manual operation of planing, yet it was far from being so perfect, or so powerful an engine, as seemed requisite where large and heavy works were going forward. Accordingly, in the year 1802, the late ingenious Mr. Bramah invented a planing engine upon a principle altogether different from the former, and in which the operation was performed by the rotation of a vertical spindle, and a horizontal wheel furnished with cutters and planes. The first machine of this kind was erected on Mr. Bramah's own premises at Pimlico, where it is still in action; and a second, which differs in many important points from the former, was set up in the Royal Arsenal, Woolwich, and which has been since considerably improved by various ingenious additions and alterations by General Millar, the superintendant of the carriage department in that establishment. Our drawing of it

Plate
cccclxiii.
Figs. 1. and
2.

exhibits the machine in its present improved form, Fig. 1. and Fig. 2. Plate CCCCLXIII. showing the elevation and plan; and the rest of the figures, sec-

tions, and delineations of such parts as require particular illustration.

In Fig. 1. *aa*, is a solid bed of brick and stone work, intended to form a foundation for the machine, and rising one foot above the ground-floor; *bb* are iron slides fixed firmly to the foundation stones, as shown in Fig. 2. and inclining half an inch from the horizontal line in the whole length (forty feet) towards B; *cc*, *dd*, are the moveable carriages, on which the wood *ee*, intended to be planed, is supported; *ff* is the cylinder of an hydraulic press, having two entrance pipes, *g* and *h*, one at each extremity. The piston rod of this press is furnished with a rack *ii*, which works a pinion *j*, under and attached to the wheel *w*. Round this wheel and the three smaller wheels, W, W, W; passes an endless chain, which may be stretched at pleasure, so as to keep it to its work by means of a screw attached to the moveable slider carrying the centre wheel. The cylinder containing the condensed or compressed water is in an adjacent room, and therefore not shown in the drawing; the water is, however, conveyed by pipes to the cocks at *k*, which are so contrived as to admit of the compressed fluid being directed through the pipes *g* or *h*, and such that, when the pipe *g*, for example, is opened to the compression, the pipe *h* is made to communicate with the waste; hence, when the water enters at *g*, the piston is urged forwards, and the rack, working on the pinion, under the wheel *w*, gives motion to the chain and to the carriages attached to it, by a contrivance which will be explained below. This motion serves to bring the carriage *cc*, from the extremity A towards B; and, at the same time, the carriage *dd* towards A; at least when this latter is also attached to the chain, but generally only one carriage is attached at a time; the contrivance for attaching and detaching the chain and carriages will be explained in a subsequent paragraph. The carriage *cc* having been advanced as far as requisite towards B, the cock at *k* is turned, the pipe *g* is opened to the waste water, and the pipe *h* to the compression; the carriage then returns towards A, the pipe *h* is then opened to the waste, and the pipe *g* to compression, when the carriage again returns.

Having thus explained, in general terms, the means employed to give motion to the carriages, it remains, in like manner, to illustrate the operation of the planing wheel. In the elevation, Fig. 1. CC is a strong vertical iron spindle, carrying the horizontal iron wheel HH, which in its circumference, or rim, is pierced with thirty holes, furnished with twenty-eight gouges, or cutters, and two planes. This wheel, which is preserved horizontally by twelve braces, *m l*, *m l*, is made to revolve by means of the wheel-work shown in the figure, at the rate of about ninety revolutions per minute, FF being the principal shaft, or axle, connected with a steam-engine in an adjacent apartment. DD, Fig. 1. are the sections of two principal beams across the workshop; EE, EE, two uprights, or pillars, which with the wood-work shown above in the figure, and two other pillars shown in the transverse section, Fig. 6. serve to give stability to the machine, and to support the stout wire guard *n n n n*, intended to protect bystanders from accident, to which they might be otherwise exposed.

The operation of the machine is now, in its general character, pretty obvious; while the carriages are passing from one end of the slider to the other, by the action of the hydraulic press above explained, the wheel

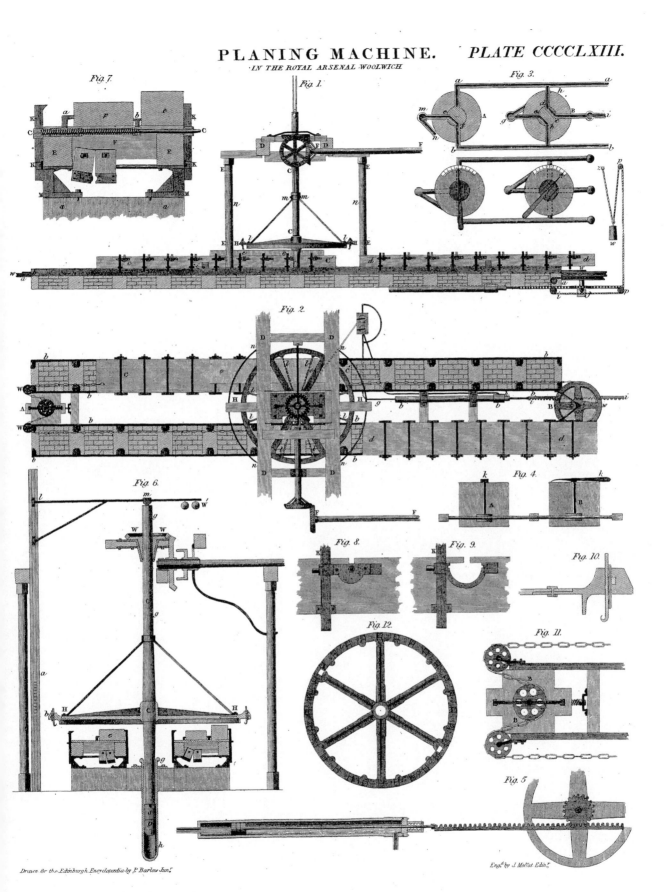

Fig. 7.

Fig. 1.

Fig. 3.

Fig. 2.

Fig. 6.

Fig. 4.

Fig. 8.

Fig. 9.

Fig. 10.

Fig. 12.

Fig. 11.

Fig. 5.

Drawn for the Edinburgh Encyclopædia by P. Barlow Jun.

Engd. by J. Moffat Edin.

is put in rapid rotation, and so adjusted by means of another hydraulic press, shown in the transverse section in Fig. 6. that the gougers and planers attached to the horizontal wheel HH just catches the surface of the piece of wood e e, in its passage under it. The gouges being arranged in its rim, at different distances from the centre, and these being followed by the two planing irons in the rotation, render the surface thus exposed to the operation beautifully plane and smooth.

Operation of the Cocks.—We have stated generally, that, by exposing the front, or back of the piston, in the hydraulic cylinder *ff*, Fig. 1, 2. to the action of the compressed air and water in the condensing vessel, the piston, with its rod and rack, are driven either way at pleasure; let us now endeavour to explain the very ingenious contrivance adopted for the purpose of producing this change of action.

The cocks *k*, seen in Plate CCCCLXIII. Fig. 2. are shown enlarged in Figs. 3. and 4. the former being a plan, and the latter an elevation of the same. Referring to Fig. 3, *a a* represents a pipe called the *entrance pipe*, which is open to the condensing cylinder in another apartment, and in which the water is constantly kept under a pressure of about 1400 lb. per square inch. The other pipe *b b* is called the *waste*, and is connected with a vessel open to the atmosphere, and exposed only to its pressure. The smaller circle in the cocks A and B is a sort of brass plug, having, the former one and the latter two, curving holes *e f, a b*, and *c d*. This plug (confining our remarks at present to the cock B) may be turned by means of the handle shown in Fig. 4. the other end of the same serving as an index to the workman, the upper plate having engraved upon it, *open, shut, backwards, forwards*, to indicate the position of the handle in these cases. In Fig. 3. the pipe *g h* leads to the back of the cylinder towards *h*, (Fig. 2. Plate CCCCLXIII.) and the pipe *c i* to the front of the cylinder towards *g*. In the position, therefore, in which the handle is supposed to be placed in the figure, the plug, or cock, is so situated, that there is an open communication between the entrance pipe *a a*, and *c i*, leading to the front of the cylinder *g*, while the pipe *g h* is open to the waste *b b*. In this case, therefore, the motion of the piston in the hydraulic cylinder is from *g* towards *h*; the water which had previously been forced in between the piston and the end *h* being now returned to the waste. The piston having arrived at *h*, the handle *k* (Fig. 4. Plate CCCCLXIII.) is turned, and with it the brass plug *c d a b*, in such a way that *c* takes the place of *d*, *d* the place of *a*, and, of course, *a* the place of *b*, and *b* that of *c*. In this new position, therefore, the pipe *g h* will be open to the entrance pipe *a a*, and *c i* to the waste *b b*; the water, therefore, which in the former position was under compression in the hydraulic cylinder *ff*, between *g* and the piston, is now relieved of that pressure, and is open to the waste; and the compressed water, now entering at *h*, will return the piston, with its rod and rack, back again towards *g*; when the cock is again turned back, and the former motion repeated. To effect this, the handle moves through a quadrant, as is obvious; and if it be made to move through only half a quadrant, then it is evident that the bores in the centre plug being excluded from any communication with either pipes, the machine will be at rest. The hydraulic cylinder, rack, pinion, and wheel enlarged, are shown in Fig. 5.

Of the Method of Raising and Lowering the Principal Cutting Wheel and Spindle.—This is effected by means of the cock A, Figs. 3. and 4. which acts on precisely the same principle as that last described, except that the centre plug has but one passage through it. Here the pipe *m n* is that which passes to the bottom of the hydraulic cylinder *g h*, (seen in the enlarged transverse section) Fig. 6. under the piston *h*, and which may be opened to the waste, or entrance pipes, at pleasure, by means of the handle *k*, Fig. 4. as explained in the last case. In the position shown in the figure, the pipe *m n* is open to the waste; and, consequently, the piston *p*, the spindle C, and wheel HH, are down, and the cutters, when the wheel is in motion, will act upon the wood *e*. When it is necessary to raise the wheel, in order to pass the carriages and wood under it, or for any other purpose, the handle *k* is turned so that the hole or passage which now connects *m n* with the waste pipe *b b*, may then connect it with the entrance pipe *a a;* in this latter case the pressure passing under the piston at *h*, raises the former, and with it the steel socket *s*, in which a pin projecting from the end of the spindle turns, whereby the latter and the attached wheel are also elevated at pleasure. So again, when it is required to lower the wheel to any proposed quantity, according to the thickness of the wood to be planed, the passage in the cock must be again opened to the waste, till the wheel sinks to its proper place, and then the cock being shut, by turning the handle a semi-quadrant, it will be retained at that height till some new arrangement is called for. To assist the workmen in this determination, the long ruler *b l m*, Fig. 6. rests on the upper point of the spindle, and rises and falls with it; and at *a b*, is a scale of inches and parts, by which he regulates the elevation and depression of the wheel. In order that this motion may take place without throwing the wheel WW out of geer, a contrivance is had recourse to, which it may not be improper to explain.

Referring to the enlarged section, Fig. 6. there will be seen under the wheel WW, two conic frustums, the inside one of which is fixed to, and forms one piece with, the wheel, and the exterior one is attached to the timber frame above, and serves as a socket for the inside cone to turn in, and which thereby preserves the spindle steady as it revolves. The interior of the interior cone, has on one side what the workmen call a feather, and which slides freely in a groove in the spindle, so that the former cannot revolve without carrying the latter with it; at the same time the cone and spindle being free in their motion up and down, the latter may be raised while the machine is in motion, without lifting the wheel, and consequently without throwing the work out of geer. The groove in the spindle is shown at *g g*, the sections being made to pass through it.

The other part of the wheel-work, and the method of throwing the wheel out and into geer, differs in no respect from common mill-work, and therefore requires no particular description.

Method of attaching the Timber to the Carriage, and the Carriage to the endless Chain.—In Fig. 7. is shown a section of the carriage enlarged, passing through one of the transverse screws, of which there are seven seen in each carriage of the plan, Fig. 2. In this figure *a a* is the masonry, to which is fixed by screw-bolts and nuts, the sliders MM. EE are the sides of the carriage, which are strengthened at intervals by cross pieces; one of which, F, is seen in the figure; KK are pieces of iron, shown also in Figs. 8. and 9. fixed to the timber of the carriage, and serving to guide it along on the sliders, and to prevent it from coming off. The upper part K is furnished with a row of flat teeth; and pieces of iron of a similar make are seen at *a* and *b*. The piece *a* has an interior screw, in which works the exterior screw C *c*, running in a collar at C, so that by turning this screw by a wrench for the purpose, the piece *a* is drawn up towards C, and presses the timber, when this is of sufficient breadth, against the flat teeth in K, and thereby holds it fast. But when the breadth is not equal to this, then an intermediate piece of timber *p* is introduced, and the flat-toothed piece *b* is screwed into a slider, and the whole brought up together by the screw C, as before.

To attach or detach the carriage to or from the endless chain, a *clip* Q L is fixed to the cross-piece F; Q being wholly a fixture, but the other piece L capable of motion; into this passes the screw, whose end is seen at K, and by means of which the jaws LM may be opened or shut at pleasure: when open, the chain passes between them, and the carriage remains at rest; but when they are shut close, they catch the chain, and the carriage then partakes of its motion. Fig. 10. shows the method of fixing the gouges to the rim of the wheel; and Fig. 12. is the wheel itself to the same scale as the transverse section; Fig. 6. and Fig. 11. shows the system of wheels at the end A of the plan, Fig. 2. also on an enlarged scale. The line and weight *p p z*, and W are attached to a plane wheel, under the large wheel *w*, its purpose is to regulate the motion of the carriages; for when their motion coincides with that of the revolving cutters, the action of the latter has a tendency to urge the carriage along too quick, and when it returns the motion is too slow; the line therefore which is attached to the circumference, serves by its weight to retard the motion of the carriage in the former case, and to accelerate it in the latter. During the late war, when there was great demand for gun-carriages, this fine machine was kept in constant employment, and both carriages were in perpetual action; it is now but seldom in operation, and never with more than one carriage going at a time.

PLANTS. See BOTANY, FILICES, FUNGI, MUSCI, HORTICULTURE, and *Vegetable* PHYSIOLOGY.

PLASTIC, from πλάσσω, *to form*, is a name applied to nature, as supposed to have the faculty of forming a mass of matter after the shape of a living body.

PLATA, LA. See BUENOS AYRES, Vol. V. p. 48.

PLATINUM. See CHEMISTRY, Vol. VI. p. 17; METALLURGY, Vol. XIV. p. 68; and the *Edin. Phil. Journal*, vol. x. for an account of Dobereiner's recent discoveries respecting this metal.

PLATO, a celebrated Athenian philosopher, was the son of Aristo, an Athenian, and Parectonia. He was born in the island of Ægina, about 428 or 430 before Christ. His original name was Aristocles; but, on account of the breadth of his shoulders, he received the name of Plato, (from the Greek word πλατυς, *broad*.) Related on his father's side to Cadmus, and on his mother's to Solon, his education was conducted with great care. His body was strengthened with athletic exercises, and the study of painting, poetry, and geometry, formed the occupation of his youthful mind. The poems and tragedies which he composed at this time were on the eve of being laid before the public, when his acquaintance with Socrates banished all his hopes of acquiring fame from his poetry, and induced him to commit his productions to the flames, and to devote himself entirely to the study of philosophy. During the period of eight years he received

instructions from this great master, and after his death he retired from Athens, with the view of improving his mind by travelling. He visited Megara, Thebes, and Elis. He went to Magna Græcia, to visit Philolaus, Archytas, and Eurytas, the supporters of the Pythagorean school, and he afterwards passed on to Sicily, to examine the volcanic phenomena of Mount Etna. From that island he went to Egypt to see the mathematician Theodorus of Cyrene; and, in the disguise of a merchant, he travelled through the whole kingdom of Artaxerxes Memnon, and made himself acquainted with the astronomical observations and computations of the Egyptian priests.

Having thus enlarged his mind by travelling, Plato returned to the groves of Academus, in the vicinity of Athens, where he established that celebrated school, over which he presided for forty years. He lived to the advanced age of eighty-one, and he is said to have expired while he was writing, on his birth-day, about 348 years before Christ.

The works of Plato, which are numerous, are all written in the form of a dialogue, excepting twelve letters. The best editions of them are those of Francof. folio, 1602; and of Bipont. 12 vols. 8vo. 1788.

For farther information respecting Plato and his philosophy, see Brucker's *History of Philosophy*, by Enfield, vol. i. and ii.; the Article ACADEMICS, Vol. I. p. 71; and ASTRONOMY, Vol. II. p. 588.

PLAUTUS, M. ACCIUS, a celebrated Latin comic poet, was born at Sarsina in Umbria. Having gone to Rome, he obtained both fame and emolument from his dramatic compositions; but engaging in unsuccessful commercial concerns, he was reduced to the greatest poverty, and was obliged to enter into the service of a baker, who employed him in grinding his corn. He wrote twenty-five comedies, of which twenty are extant, though some are in a state of considerable mutilation. He died in the year 184 before Christ.

His comedies were composed in pure and energetic language. His wit, though sometimes coarse and indelicate, was considered by Cicero as elegant, refined, ingenious, and facetious; and during five hundred years his plays commanded and received the highest applause.

The best editions of his works are those of Gronovius, 8vo. Lugd. Bat. 1664; of Barbou, 12mo. 3 vols. Paris, 1759; Ernesti, 2 vols. 8vo. Leips. 1760; and that of Glasgow, 3 vols. 12mo. 1763.

PLAYFAIR, JOHN, a celebrated Scotch mathematician and natural philosopher, was the eldest son of the Rev. James Playfair, minister of the united parishes of Liff and Benvie, in the county of Forfar. He was born at Benvie, on the 10th of March, 1748; and after receiving a classical education under the roof of his father, he entered the university of St. Andrews at the age of fourteen. At this ancient seat of learning Mr. Playfair soon distinguished himself by the excellence of his conduct, as well as the ardour of his application; and so great was his progress in natural philosophy, that Professor Wilkie, (the author of the *Epigoniad*) who taught that branch of knowledge in the university, selected him to teach his class during his indisposition.

In the year 1766, upon the death of Mr. Stewart, Professor of Mathematics in Marischal College, Aberdeen, seven candidates appeared for the vacant chair. Among these were the Rev. Dr. Trail, Dr. Hamilton, and Mr. Playfair. The professorship was a private foundation, by a Dr. Liddel, and a clause in the deed of foundation was considered as a direction to fill up the vacancy by a disputation or comparative trial. Dr. Reid of Glasgow, Mr. Vilant of St. Andrews, Dr. Skene of Marischal College, and Professor Gordon of King's College, accepted the office of judges on this occasion; and after a severe examination, which lasted for a fortnight, Dr. Trail was appointed to the chair. Mr. Playfair was excelled only by two out of six candidates, viz. Dr. Trail and Dr. Hamilton, who now fills the same chair; but when it is considered, that Mr. Playfair was two years younger than Dr. Trail, the result of the election must have been greatly affected by that circumstance alone; and Dr. Trail himself has modestly remarked, in a letter to the writer of this article, that he has always attributed his own success to this disparity of years.

In the year 1772, when the chair of natural philosophy became vacant by the death of Dr. Wilkie, Mr. Playfair again cherished the hopes of a permanent appointment; but his expectations were a second time frustrated; a disappointment which was the more severe, as the death of his father in the same year had devolved upon him the charge of his mother and her family. This circumstance appears to have determined Mr. Playfair to follow the profession of his father, to which he had been educated, but which his ardent attachment to mathematical pursuits had induced him to think of abandoning. Having been presented by Lord Gray to his father's living of Liff and Benvie, of which, however, he did not obtain possession till August, 1773, in consequence of a dispute respecting the right of patronage, Mr. Playfair devoted his time to the duties of his sacred office, to the education of his younger brothers, and to the occasional prosecution of his own favourite studies. In 1774 he went to Schehallien, where Dr. Maskelyne was carrying on his interesting experiments on the attraction of the mountains; and while he was enjoying the acquaintance of that eminent astronomer, he was little aware that he should himself contribute, at some distant period, to the perfection of the result which it was the object of this experiment to obtain.

In the year 1777, Mr. Playfair communicated to the Royal Society of London an essay *On the Arithmetic of Impossible Quantities*, which appeared in the Transactions for that year, and which was the first display of his mathematical acquirements. In this ingenious paper, which is strongly marked with the peculiar talent of its author, Mr. Playfair has pointed out the insufficiency of the explanation of the doctrine of negative quantities given by John Bernouilli and Maclaurin, viz. that the imaginary characters which are involved in the expression compensate or destroy each other; and he has endeavoured to show that the arithmetic of impossible quantities is nothing more than a particular method of tracing the affinity of the measures of ratios and of angles, and that they can never be of any use as an instrument of discovery, unless when the subject of investigation is a property common to the measures both of ratios and of angles.

The late Mr. Ferguson of Raith having held out to Mr. Playfair a very advantageous offer to superintend the education of his two eldest sons, the present Robert Ferguson, Esq. of Raith, and Sir Ronald Ferguson, he was induced, in 1782, to resign his living for this purpose, and we believe he never afterwards exercised any of the duties of the clerical office.

In the year 1785, when Dr. Adam Ferguson exchanged the chair of Moral Philosophy for that of Mathematics, which was then filled by Mr. Dugald Stewart, Mr. Playfair was appointed Joint Professor of Mathematics, a situation which had been the highest object of his ambition, and which he was in a peculiar manner qualified to fill.

As Mr. Playfair was a member of the Philosophical Society of Edinburgh, he became one of the original fellows of the Royal Society at its institution by royal charter in 1783, and by his services as an office-bearer, as well as by his communications as a member, he contributed most essentially to promote the interests, and to add to the renown, of this distinguished body. His memoir *On the Causes which affect the accuracy of Barometrical Measurements* [*] was read on the 1st March, 1784, and on the 10th January, 1785. The mensuration of heights by the barometer was involved in many errors. M. De Luc had applied the important correction, depending on the temperature of the atmospherical column; but when the height was great, and the difference of temperature at the two extremities of the column considerable, his method of estimating the temperature was liable to considerable error. Mr. Playfair was therefore led to give an accurate formula for this purpose, and to investigate new ones, in order to express those other circumstances by which the density of the atmosphere is affected. The manner in which he has executed this task deserves high praise, and though the memoir is written with much perspicuity, and contains many original and sagacious views, it has not been referred to, as it ought, by those who have followed him in the same field of inquiry.

On the 3d of April, 1786, Mr. Playfair read to the Royal Society a *Biographical Account of the Rev. Dr. Matthew Stewart*, in which he has displayed those talents for elegant composition for which he was afterwards so highly distinguished.

In the year 1789, Mr. Playfair succeeded Dr. Gregory as Secretary to the Physical Class of the Royal Society; and as Dr. Robison, who then filled the office of General Secretary, was unable, from indisposition, to attend to its peculiar duties, the management of the society, and the arrangement of its memoirs for publication, devolved principally upon him.

The appearance, in 1787, of the *Traité de l'Astronomie Indienne et Orientale*, written by M. Bailly, the eloquent historian of astronomy, attracted the particular notice of Mr. Playfair, who became a complete convert to the fascinating views which it contains respecting the antiquity of the Indian astronomy. He was therefore desirous of presenting to his countrymen that particular view of the argument which had appeared to himself the most striking, and hence he was led to compose his *Remarks on the Astronomy of the Brahmins* [†], which was read to the Royal Society on the 2d of March, 1789. The views which this paper contains have given rise to considerable controversy; and (though we have maintained the opposite side of the question in our article ASTRONOMY) we believe it is now universally admitted by the most acute, as well as by the most learned astronomers, that the Brahmins had skilfully adapted their tables to the fictitious epoch of the Calyoughan.

Mr. Playfair's next communication to the Royal Society was his paper *On the Origin and Investigation of Porisms* [‡], which was read on the 2d April, 1792. The account which he has here given of this class of geome-

---

trical propositions is in every respect philosophical, and removes all the difficulties which had been so long attached to them. This paper, however, contains only their geometrical analysis; and though the algebraical investigation was promised as a second part, there is no reason to suppose that he ever prosecuted the subject any farther. This loss, however, is the less to be regretted, as, in the article PORISMS, which Mr. Babbage has written for this work, (Vol. XVII.) this distinguished mathematician has endeavoured to supply those observations on the algebraical part of the subject which might have been expected in the continuation of Mr. Playfair's paper.

In the year 1795, Mr. Playfair published his *Elements of Geometry*, which consisted of the first six books of Euclid, with three additional ones containing the rectification and quadrature of the circle, the intersection of planes, and the geometry of solids, with plane and spherical trigonometry, and the arithmetic of sines. The notes to this work possess a peculiar value; and hence the work itself has been held in high estimation for the purposes of elementary instruction.

During the same year, Mr. Playfair communicated to the Royal Society his *Observations on the Trigonometrical Tables of the Brahmins* * ; and some time afterwards, on the 5th February, 1798, he read to the same body his *Investigation of certain Theorems relative to the Figure of the Earth* +, one of the principal objects of which, was to consider the advantages of comparing a degree of the meridian with a degree of the circle perpendicular to it, and also with a degree of the parallel of latitude by which it is crossed.

The death of Dr. James Hutton in the winter of 1797, gave a new direction to Mr. Playfair's studies; and, with some exceptions, rendered necessary by his professional occupations, the rest of his life was devoted to geological investigations, or to those kindred pursuits from which this fascinating study derives either support or illustration. Attached by long acquaintance and similarity of opinion to the celebrated author of the Huttonian theory, Mr. Playfair was led by inclination, as well as by duty, to compose a biographical memoir of his departed friend. Having been in the daily habit of discussing with Dr. Hutton the difficult questions which this theory involved, Mr. Playfair had acquired a more correct knowledge of its principles than could have been derived from the writings of its author; and he was therefore peculiarly qualified to appear as its illustrator and defender.

After five years' labour, Mr. Playfair produced, in 1802, his *Illustrations of the Huttonian Theory*, in one volume 8vo.; and on the 10th January, 1803, he read to the Royal Society of Edinburgh his *Biographical Account of the late Dr. James Hutton*. These two works added greatly to the fame of their author; and whether we consider them as models of composition or of argument, we cannot but regard them as the productions by which the name of Mr. Playfair must be handed down to posterity. All his other writings, beautiful and profound as they are, can be considered in no other light than as able and perspicuous expositions, which illuminate the obscurities of science without extending her domains. But his illustrations of the Huttonian theory are marked with a higher character. Though brought out under the modest appellation of a

commentary, it is unquestionably entitled to be regarded as an original work; and though the theory which it expounds must always retain the name of the philosopher who first suggested it, yet Mr. Playfair has in a great measure made it his own, by the philosophical generalisations which he has thrown around it; by the numerous phenomena which he has enabled it to embrace; by the able defences with which its weakest parts have been sustained; and by the relation which he has shown it to bear to some of the best established doctrines, both in chemistry and astronomy. In the execution of this great work, and in the subsequent improvements which it had undergone during the last seventeen years of the life of its author, he received great assistance from Sir James Hall, Lord Webb Seymour, Dr. Hope, Sir George Mackenzie, Mr. Allan, and Mr. Jardine; and many of the happiest of his days were spent in the society of these eminent individuals, who either accompanied or aided him in all his geological journies and investigations. The deep interest which these gentlemen, in common with all Mr. Playfair's scientific friends, took in the appearance of the second edition of the *Illustrations*, may therefore be readily conceived; and it is not easy to express the regret which they feel, that literary labours of a more fleeting kind should have interfered with the completion of a work, which would have shed a new lustre over his already honoured name.

Upon the death of Dr. Robison, in 1805, Mr. Playfair was elected General Secretary to the Royal Society, and he was also appointed his successor in the chair of natural philosophy,—a situation which his mathematical acquirements, and his powers of perspicuous illustration, rendered him peculiarly qualified to fill. This event, however, though in every respect advantageous to himself, interrupted in no slight degree the progress of his general studies. The preparation of a course of lectures on subjects which he had only indirectly pursued, and the composition of his Outlines of Natural Philosophy, which he considered necessary for the use of his students ‡, occupied much of that valuable time on which the higher interests of science possessed so many claims. Notwithstanding these avocations, however, he read to the Royal Society, in January, 1807, his paper *On the Solids of greatest Attraction*, ||—a subject to which his attention had been necessarily directed during his lithological survey of Schehallien, which he made in conjunction with Lord Webb Seymour, and of which he has given an account in the *Philosophical Transactions* for 1811 §. The object of this survey was to obtain an estimate of the specific gravity of the mountain, in order to correct the deductions of Dr. Maskelyne respecting the mean density of the earth; and the conclusions which this survey authorized, were deduced by means of the formulæ investigated in the memoir already alluded to on the solids of greatest attraction. The leading problem in this paper had been previously treated by Boscovich, and also by M. Sylvabelle; but Mr. Playfair had never seen the labours of either of these mathematicians.

On the 6th of March, 1809, Mr. Playfair submitted to the Royal Society an ingenious paper *On the Progress of Heat, when communicated to Spherical Bodies from their Centres* ¶. This paper originated from an argument urged by the late Dr. Murray against the fun-

---

Edinburgh Transactions, vol. iv. p. 83—106.   † *Ibid*. vol. v. p. 3—30.
‡ Two volumes of this truly valuable work appeared in 1814; the third was left unfinished, to the great regret of all his scientific friends.
|| *Edinburgh Transactions*, vol. vi. p. 187—243.   § Page 347—377.   ¶ *Ibid*. vol. vi. p. 353—370.

Playfair,
John.

damental principle of the Huttonian theory. Although Mr. Playfair's defence was unanswerable, Dr. Murray, who could not be supposed to appreciate the mathematical argument, replied to it at considerable length. A second and more popular paper was again read by Mr. Playfair; but he did not think it necessary to strengthen his original defence by any additional illustration.

In the year 1805, Mr. Playfair laid before the Royal Society a *Biographical Account of the late John Robison, LL. D.* * and he left behind him an unfinished memoir of the late John Clerk of Eldin, the inventor of the naval tactics, which has been published in the 9th volume of the *Edinburgh Transactions*.

In addition to the works which bear Mr. Playfair's name, he wrote various articles in the *Edinburgh Review*, which he never hesitated to acknowledge, and some of which have been reprinted among his works. Of these reviews, *three* are particularly memorable, as indicating the peculiar character of Mr. Playfair's talents, as well as the great versatility of his powers. His analysis of the *Mécanique Céleste* of Laplace, while it evinces the highest powers of composition, is at the same time one of the choicest specimens of perspicuous illustration. His review of *Leslie's Geometry* (the ablest, perhaps, that he ever wrote) is distinguished by a masterly argument in one of the most difficult topics of abstract mathematics, and has been no less celebrated for the force and the dignity of its satire †. The review of Madame de Stael's *Corinne* in the same work affords the clearest evidence that its author was equally fitted to shine in the field of elegant literature and in the walks of abstract science. Several other reviews from Mr. Playfair's pen would have been entitled to notice in a more extended memoir of his life, but those already mentioned have been selected as particularly characteristic of his powers as a natural philosopher, a profound mathematician, and a cultivator of the lighter branches of literature.

At the restoration of peace in 1815, Mr. Playfair undertook a journey to the Continent, for the purpose of examining the stupendous phenomena presented in the geology of the Alps,—of studying the recent effects of volcanic eruptions in Italy, and of developing those of more ancient convulsions among the extinct volcanoes of Auvergne. Excepting the phenomena exhibited in our own island, which he had personally examined, Mr. Playfair had acquired his geological knowledge principally from books; and it was therefore desirable, before the republication of his favourite work, that his views should receive those modifications which the study of nature in her grandest forms could not fail to suggest. With this view he spent about seventeen months in France, Switzerland, and Italy, busily engaged in geological observations; and he returned to Edinburgh in the end of 1816, eager to embellish and

complete the great fabric which it had been the business of his life to rear.

Unfortunately, however, for the Huttonian School, Mr. Playfair had been urged to draw up a dissertation on the progress of mathematics and physics for the Supplement to the Encyclopædia Britannica; and the composition of this paper, as his nephew informs us, interrupted the execution of the second edition of his Illustrations ‡. This dissertation, the first part of which Mr. Playfair did not live to finish, is marked with the able but now faultering hand of its distinguished author. In the 70th year of his age, and haunted with the image of his unfinished work, the drudgery of compilation must have been irksome to a mind less anxious than his, and conscious that it was exhausting its powers on an arena where no laurels could be gained. The history of the mathematical and physical sciences had been already exhausted by the voluminous and profound labours of Montucla. The Abbé Bossut had gleaned its choicest flowers, and prepared them in nervous and simple rhetoric for the taste of less laborious students;—and that branch of the history of physics, for which Mr. Playfair's talents were peculiarly adapted, namely, the history of astronomical discovery, had been illustrated by the brief yet powerful narrative of Laplace, by the rich and discursive eloquence of Bailly, and by the varied and searching erudition of Delambre. A field thus pre-occupied, and on which learning and genius had cast their richest offerings, was not likely to be chosen by Mr. Playfair for the display of his own powers. He undertook the task to which he had been urged; and that part of it which Providence allowed him to execute, he executed with his usual judgment and discrimination.

Some time after his return from the Continent, Mr. Playfair read to the Royal Society a paper *On Volcanoes*, which excited great interest, but which is neither mentioned in his life, nor printed along with the rest of his works. On the 3d December, 1818, he likewise communicated to the same body his *Description of the Slide of Alpnach*, which has been published as an appendix to his life. These two communications were an earnest of the stores of valuable information which he had accumulated during his travels, and which he meant to give to the world in a series of detached papers. His health, however, had been for some time on the decline; and in the winter of 1818—1819 his labours were often interrupted by a severe attack of a disease in the bladder, which, at his advanced period of life, it was not easy to subdue. An interval of health soothed for a while the anxieties of his friends; but it was only a deceitful precursor of the fatal attack which carried him off, on the 19th July, 1819, in the 72d year of his age. The various public bodies with which he was connected followed his re-

* *Edinburgh Transactions*, vol. viii. p. 495—539.

† M. Legendre, one of the first of modern geometers, has, both privately and publicly, expressed his particular admiration of this criticism. See his *Elements of Geometry*, English edit. p. 237.

‡ " The other, which was the first conceived, but interrupted in the execution by the dissertation, was a second edition of the Illustrations of the Huttonian Theory of the Earth. This edition, of much greater magnitude than the former, was likewise completely different in the arrangement of its contents. It was intended to commence with a description of all the well-authenticated facts in geology, collected during his extensive reading and personal observation, without any mixture of hypothesis whatever. To this followed the general inferences which may be deduced from the facts, an examination of the various geological systems hitherto offered to the world, and the exclusion of those which involved any contradiction of the principles previously ascertained; while the conclusion would have presented the development of the system adopted by the author, and the application of it to explain the phenomena of geology. It must be viewed by every one as a great loss to science that this design was never completed; for such an analysis of voyages and travels, such a description of geological phenomena, such a system of physical geography, as would have been contained in the first division of this work we can scarcely hope to see; and where is to be found the geologist, who will bring to the execution of the theoretical part the candour in the search of truth, the habits of accurate reasoning, and the power of employing the mathematical sciences as a test of the soundness of his conclusions, all possessed in so high a degree by Mr. Playfair." *Biographical Account, &c. prefixed to the Works of the Author*, p. xxiv.

mains to the grave, and testified the respect which they cherished for that rare union of worth and talents which marked the character of this much esteemed and deeply lamented philosopher.

For a fuller account of the life, writings, and character of Mr. Playfair, the reader is referred to an edition of his works published by his nephew Dr. Playfair, in 3 vols. 8vo. and to a biographical memoir which will probably appear in the tenth volume of the *Transactions of the Royal Society of Edinburgh.*

PLEIADES. See Astronomy, vol. ii. p. 759.

PLEURISY. See Medicine, vol. xiii. p. 753.

PLICA Polonica, or *Trichoma*, is the name of a disease of the hair endemic in Poland, and some of the neighbouring countries, in which, from the deposition of morbid matter, it becomes matted together, so as to form masses which cannot be unravelled. The most palpable signs of the commencement of this disease, are clammy sweets and a sensation of lightness about the head. A greasiness collects on the hairs, and their smell becomes disagreeable. A morbid matter is deposited upon them, and sometimes in such a quantity that they burst; but it is not true that blood either flows out of them, or that they bleed when cut. The hair on the other parts of the body is sometimes affected. This very remarkable disease prevails at present in Tartary, White and Red Russia, Lithuania, and in the country from the source of the Vistula to the Carpathian mountains. See Colebert's *Précis Théorique et Pratique sur les Maladies de la Peau*, p. 92, and the *Manchester Memoirs*, vol. iv. part ii.

PLINY the Elder, Caius Plinius Secundus, a celebrated Roman author, was born at Verona in the reign of Tiberius, in A. D. 23. Pliny distinguished himself early in the field, and after having been made one of the augurs of Rome, he was appointed governor of Spain. Though he was not inattentive to his public duties, yet every leisure moment that he could command was devoted to literature and science. His habits of industry were so great, that he availed himself of every portion of his time. At his meals, and while he was dressing, one of his servants read to him: He constantly inserted in a memorandum book notices of all the information which he thus acquired, and he went from place to place in a sedan, that he might read on the road.

When he commanded the fleet at Misenum in the month of August, A. D. 79, he was startled at the sudden appearance of a cloud of dust and ashes, and being ignorant of its cause, his curiosity was so great that he instantly set sail in a small vessel towards Mount Vesuvius, which he observed in a state of violent eruption. Although the inhabitants were flying from the coast to avoid the danger, yet he ordered his pilot to steer directly across to Stabiæ, where his friend Pomponius had a villa, and having landed, he passed the night at his house. Fresh showers of ashes, however, had nearly blocked up his apartments, and the walls of the house were shaken with earthquakes, so that he was compelled to quit it early in the morning. A contrary wind preventing him from returning to Misenum, and the violence of the eruption having increased, the fire at last approached the place where he had taken shelter to make his observations. He now endeavoured to escape; but though supported by two of his servants, he at last fell down, and was suffocated by the sulphureous flames by which he was enveloped. Three days after, his body was found, and decently interred by his nephew, who happened to be

then at Misenum with the fleet. The death of Pliny took place in the 56th year of his age. His works are as follows: 1. On the Use of the Javelin on Horseback. 2. On the Life of Pomponius Secundus. 3. Of the Wars in Germany, 28 books. 4. On Oratory, 3 books. 5. On Grammar, 8 books. 6. On the History of his own Times, 31 books. 7. On Natural History, 37 books. The only one of these works which is extant is his *Natural History*, which is regarded as one of the most valuable remains of antiquity. Pliny is said to have written 160 volumes of annotations on the different authors which he read; and one Lartius Lutinus is said to have offered a sum equal to £3242 Sterling for these notes.

The best editions of Pliny are that of Hardonius, 3 vols. fol. Paris, 1723; that of Frantzius, 10 vols. 8vo. Lips. 1778; of Brotier, 6 vols. 12mo. Paris, 1779; and the Variorum edition, 8vo. in 8 vols. Lips. 1778—1789.

PLINY the Younger, Caius Plinius Cæcilius Secundus, was the son of L. Cæcilius, by a sister of the elder Pliny, and was born at Como, in the reign of Nero, A. D. 62. Having been adopted by his uncle, he inherited his estates and his MSS. He was educated under Quintilian, and at the age of nineteen he went to the bar, where he distinguished himself to such a degree, that he and Tacitus were reckoned the greatest orators of the age. In the reign of Domitian he filled the offices of questor, tribune of the people, and prætor. Nerva made him president of the Saturnian treasury; and in the third consulate of the emperor Trajan, he was named one of the honorary consuls. He was next appointed to the care of the channel and the banks of the Tiber, and afterwards he obtained the augurate, and then the proconsulate in Bithynia, in which last situation he wrote his famous letter to Trajan, respecting the primitive Christians. The history of Pliny, after his return from Bithynia, is not known; but it is supposed that he died about the year A. D. 113, in the 53d year of his age.

The works of Pliny consist of his Epistles in ten books, and his Panegyric on Trajan, which was pronounced at his appointment to the honorary consulship. The best editions of his works are that of Gesner, 8vo. Lips. 1770, and of Lallemand, 12mo. Paris. The Variorum edition of the Epistles, by Veenhusius, Lugd. Bat. 1667, is excellent, and also Schwartz's separate edition of the Panegyric, in 1746, in 4to. The Epistles of Pliny have been translated into English by Lord Orrery and Mr. Melmoth. The translation of the latter has been much admired.

PLOTTING. See Surveying.

PLOUGH. See Agriculture, Vol. I. p. 249.

PLUM-TREE. See Horticulture, Vol. XI. p. 206.

PLUMBAGO, or Graphite. See Chemistry, Vol. VI. p. 11. and Mineralogy, Vol. XIV. p. 517. An account of the black lead mines of England and Scotland, by Professor Jameson, will be found in the *Edinburgh Philosophical Journal*, vol. i. p. 130; and an account of the fusion of plumbago, by Professor Silliman, will be found in the same Journal, vol. ix. p. 179.

PLUTARCH, an eminent Greek author, was born at Cheronea, in Bœotia, about the beginning of the reign of Nero. He is supposed to have first visited Rome, and other parts of Italy, in a public capacity; but he afterwards re-visited that capital, and established a school, which was well frequented. The Em-

3

PLYMOUTH.

Plymouth. peror Trajan raised him to the office of consul, and appointed him governor of Illyricum. Upon the death of his benefactor, he returned to his native village, where he lived respected by all around him, and composed in peaceful retirement his moral pieces, and the celebrated Lives which have immortalized his name. He died at an advanced age, in the year A. D. 140. The best editions of his works are those of Frankfort, 2 vols. fol. 1599; and of Stephens, 6 vols. 8vo. 1572. The Lives were edited separately by Reiske, in 12 vols. 8vo. Lips. 1775.

PLUVIMETER. See METEOROLOGY, vol. xiv. p. 152.

PLYMOUTH, a large and populous sea-port borough and market town, in the hundred of Roborough, and deanery of Plympton, is situated at the extreme south-west corner of the county of Devon, between the estuaries of the rivers Tamar and Plym, and from the latter of which it takes its name. Its mean latitude is 50° 22′ 14″ north, and mean longitude 4° 7′ 31″ west; it is 214 miles from London, and 43 from Exeter, the county town.

Its ancient name was Sutton, (i. e. Southtown); but as early as 1383, it appears to have been occasionally called Plymouth. According to Leland, the town in the reign of Henry II. was "a mene thing as an inhabitant for fischars." In 1253, a market was established; and in 1377, 1388, 1400, and 1403, it was attacked by the French, and at the latter period 600 houses were said to have been destroyed In 1588, the celebrated Spanish armada appeared off the port; and the spot is still shown, where the great Sir Francis Drake first received intelligence of it, being engaged in playing at bowls. So confident was the Spanish admiral of victory, that there is a tradition of his having selected the beautiful seat of Mount Edgecumbe for his future residence.

During the whole of the civil war, Plymouth was in the hands of the Parliament, and even at a time when all the west was in the possession of the royal forces.

Plymouth, under the name of Suteton, sent members to parliament in the reign of Edward I. but there was an intermission from the reign of Edward II. to that of Henry VI. The elective franchise is at present vested by decisions of the House of Commons in the body of freemen only, though it is well known to have been enjoyed by the freeholders of the town, as well as the freemen, prior to the year 1739.

Plymouth having gradually risen from a humble fishing town to a place of considerable magnitude and importance, the buildings have been erected as circumstances required, and hence little regularity will be found in the streets. The modern improvements of the town present a striking contrast to the central and more ancient districts.

To the illustrious navigator before mentioned, the inhabitants are indebted for an ample supply of fresh water, brought from the borders of Dartmoor, through a circuitous and winding channel of twenty-four miles.

The mayor is chief magistrate of the borough, and is assisted in his public duties by other officers of the corporation.

The town is divided into the parishes of St. Andrew and Charles. Prior to the reign of Charles the First, that of St. Andrew embraced the whole borough; but in the reign of that monarch, the present division was made, and a new church built, dedicated to him. The old church is a venerable structure, and is known to have existed as early as 1291, having been included in the survey of the western churches of the kingdom, made by order of Pope Nicholas. The tower was erected in 1440, by a generous merchant of the town. At the present moment a beautiful chapel of ease is erecting, to accommodate the increasing population of the parish. Charles Church, before the recent alterations, was an interesting structure. Its steeple, of Dartmoor granite, is particularly light and elegant. There are also several excellent chapels for the different denominations of dissenters. These are, the Presbyterian Chapel; the New Tabernacle Independent Calvinist Chapel; the Ebenezer Methodist Chapel; the Unitarian Chapel; the Baptist Chapel; the Old Tabernacle; the Quakers' Meeting; the General Baptist Chapel; and the Jews' Synagogue. The churches and chapels are in general exceedingly well filled; and a spirit of piety appears to prevail in the majority of the people.

The workhouse is an excellent establishment to relieve the wants of the aged and the poor. It is particularly distinguished for order and cleanliness; and while a proper attention is paid to the claims of humanity, a rigid economy is at the same time maintained. An annual election of fifty-two guardians takes place from among the inhabitants of the borough, and out of this number a governor and other subordinate officers are elected.

Plymouth is particularly distinguished for the number of its charitable institutions. Among these may be mentioned, the General Dispensary, the Eye Infirmary, Kelway's Trust for educating boys at the Grammar School and at Oxford; Hele and Lanyon's Charity, and orphan's aid for educating and clothing poor boys; alms houses for the reception of infirm and aged women. The Grey School for the education of children of both sexes; Lady Rogers' School for the education of girls in household arts; the School of Industry; the Household of Faith; the public subscription schools, and many Sunday schools; the Lying in Charity; the Female Benevolent Society; the Merchants' Hospital; the Female Penitentiary; the Misericordia; the Corpus Christi Society; the Provident Society; the Auxiliary Bible Society; the Society for Promoting Christianity among the Jews; the Religious Tract Society; the Peace Society; Society for Promoting Christian Knowledge, and several auxiliary missionary societies. To the credit of the town it may be stated, that, in general, these societies are actively supported. In few places are the wants of the poor better attended to, or the sufferings of humanity more effectually allevi. ted. Benevolence is the general characteristic of the inhabitants, and the exercise of Christian philanthropy no inconsiderable object of their lives.

Within the last twelve years, Plymouth has been much improved. A taste for architecture has contributed to the external appearance of the town; and several splendid buildings evince the public spirit of the inhabitants. Of these, the Royal Hotel and Theatre may be mentioned first, on account of their magnitude and beauty. The northern front of this noble building extends 275 feet; and in the centre is a magnificent portico of eight Ionic columns. At the eastern end is another portico of smaller dimensions, but of the same beautiful proportions. A superb ball-room is adorned with columns of the Corinthian order; and the classical observer will perceive, that the taste of the architect has directed him to the chorasic monument of Lysicrates, at Athens, for the model of the capital and entablature. The cieling is enriched by the pencil of Ball, a native artist of considerable talent. The theatre occupies the western division of the building, and for beauty is rivalled by none out of the metropolis. The scenic decorations are of the most excellent kind. To guard against the effects of fire, the roof is entirely constructed of wrought iron; and the frame-work of the interior, together with the pillars supporting the tiers, are of cast iron.

The public library is also another elegant and spacious building. It is of the Doric order, and contains a valuable collection of books. A news-room is also connected with the institution; and the stranger finds ready and immediate access to it. The inhabitants are indebted to the active exertions of Mr. Eastlake, for this useful establishment. This gentleman was the friend of genius in its most enlarged and liberal sense.

The Athenæum is a chaste and beautiful building, dedicated entirely to the purposes of literature and science. It is of the Doric order, the portico being formed on the model of the temple of Theseus at Athens. The interior is adorned with splendid casts from the Elgin collection, presented by the king. Casts also from the Apollo Belvidere, the Medicean Venus, and the young Antinous, add to the beauty of the building. A society, consisting of 40 ordinary, and 150 extraordinary members, meet weekly, from October to March, when lectures are delivered on subjects of a literary and scientific nature. The lectures are always discussed, and generally with liberality and candour. The essays delivered are mostly of a literary nature; but occasionally papers of considerable scientific merit are read. At some future period, the society, from its possessing several members of known talent and ability, may look forward to the publication of a volume of Transactions, and which, from the number of local objects meriting a particular examination, could not fail to be acceptable to the public. The formation of this society has had a sensible influence on the habits and pursuits of the inhabitants; and the same may be perceptibly traced even in the surrounding villages. The love of literature has increased, and a taste for the sciences been displayed, which, before this useful institution was formed, had scarcely an existence. The investigations of Newton and Laplace become more extensively diffused by the creation of societies of this kind; and the splendid discoveries of the nineteenth century are melted down in their ingenious and instructive discourses into the simplest and most elementary forms, ultimately becoming blended with the ordinary realities of life.

In the month of August, an exhibition of paintings is opened in the hall of the Athenæum, consisting of the works of artists and amateurs of the town and neighbourhood, and pictures of the Italian, Flemish, Dutch, and British schools, furnished from the collections of the neighbouring nobility and gentry. This also has had a powerful influence on public taste, and contributed essentially to the improvement of the town.

Some attempts have also been made to establish an observatory; and although it has not hitherto been successful, the same energy and zeal that has created so many useful institutions within a few years, may raise an edifice consecrated to the stars, and by its means perhaps add a fragment to the lofty pyramid of astronomical science. In a great naval establishment, indeed, the practical utility of such a structure would be of im-

mense importance. At the present moment, ships take their chronometers to sea without knowing the exact longitude of the place for which their time is determined.

The custom-house is another modern structure. The front is of granite, and the colonnade of five arches is supported by rusticated piers. The building is well adapted to the purposes of business, and presents a substantial and handsome appearance.

The exchange is conveniently situated near the custom-house, the quays, and the principal warehouses. From an open area, surrounded by a spacious piazza, proceeds a massive staircase of granite, leading to the Sales Room, Chamber of Commerce, Marine Insurance Society, and other apartments connected with the establishment.

The market covers a surface of three acres; and the convenience of the public has been consulted, by the erection of numerous colonnades for the butchery, and markets for fish, butter, vegetables, and corn. The abundant supplies from the surrounding country render provisions exceedingly cheap. Excellent fish is at all times to be had; and large quantities are sent off by the coaches at proper seasons for Bath and the metropolis. Above fifty large fishing vessels, called trawlers, sail almost daily, and return with immense supplies.

Below the eastern rampart of the citadel is a public establishment named the victualling office, for the purpose of supplying the royal navy with provisions. It contains immense granaries for corn, and storehouses equally commodious for beef, pork, butter, and cheese; and extensive lofts for biscuit, and capacious cellars for wine and spirits. Eight large ovens for baking biscuit were in continual activity during the war. At the present moment, it is in contemplation to unite the victualling office, brewery, cooperage, and slaughter house, at present detached from each other, into one great establishment at Stonehouse,—a situation better adapted for the purpose, and from which the ships of war can draw their supplies with more ease and expedition.

The commerce of Plymouth is chiefly confined to an extensive coasting trade, and with but a small intercourse with foreign nations. The chamber of commerce has in some degree quickened the spirit of commercial speculation; and some ships have in consequence been fitted out for the South Sea whale fishery. The principal imports are timber, iron, tar, coals, culm, corn, Irish provisions, wines, spirits, and fruit; and the exports are granite, marble, slate, copper, tin and lead ores, antimony, manganese, fish, soap, sail-cloth, and earthenware.

Sutton Pool is an excellent harbour for the smaller sort of merchantmen, and is nearly surrounded with quays. In Catwater, mooring chains are laid for 1000 sail of a larger class. During the war, the latter harbour was so filled with vessels captured from the enemy, as to have the appearance of a forest of masts.

The Hoe is a favourite promenade of the inhabitants to the south of the town, above which it rises by a gentle ascent. From its level summit, the most charming variety of marine and land scenery is presented to the eye. The beautiful groves of Mount Edgecumbe are on one side, and on the other the rugged and barren heights of Staddon. Midway the dark line of the Breakwater stretches across the Sound; and in the distant horizon may be clearly seen the Eddystone, the noblest of the works of Smeaton. At the eastern extremity is the citadel, which,

Plymouth. from its commanding situation, is well calculated to protect the town and harbour. It was built after the restoration, by king Charles. The western extremity of the Hoe commands a fine view of the towns of Stonehouse and Dock, the barracks for the marines, the extensive buildings employed for prisoners during the war, the naval and military hospitals, Hamoaze the harbour for the men of war, and the scattered villas and ornamental cottages with which the neighbourhood is adorned.

Of the literary and scientific characters produced by Plymouth, may be mentioned Huxham, Bidlake, and the family of the Mudges. Mr. Thomas Mudge contributed, in no inconsiderable degree, to the early improvement of time-keepers, and for which Parliament voted him a handsome reward. Many beautiful specimens of his mechanical skill are still in the possession of Mr. Rosdew, a descendant of the family. Dr. Huxham was celebrated for his skill as a physician, and for several valuable papers published in the *Philosophical Transactions.* Dr. Bidlake was the author of many interesting poems, and distinguished for his friendly attachment to indigent merit; and of which the town is at the present moment proud to boast of more than one example. Mr. Haydon, the historical painter, and who has obtained so high a celebrity by several grand compositions, is a native of the same place; and so also is the venerable Northcote, whose long life, consecrated to the highest and noblest walks of the art, has shed a high lustre on his native town.

Plymouth is much subject to southerly winds, in consequence of its being exposed in that quarter, but is sheltered on other sides by the surrounding land. The vapours of the Atlantic having an uninterrupted passage over the town, and becoming condensed by the cold and bleak hills of Dartmoor, occasion a considerable precipitation of moisture. The average quantity of rain for thirteen years amounts to $32\frac{1}{3}$ inches; a quantity much less than is afforded by many other towns in England. Nevertheless, a considerable humidity exists at all times in the air; and which is the frequent cause of dense mists, and also of considerable depositions of dew. The quantity of rain which falls at any one time is in general not considerable; it chiefly descending in gentle showers. For many days the hygrometer exhibits almost absolute humidity, without any fall of rain; and, at other times, there is scarcely a day without a shower, for some weeks together. According to Captain Rotheram's accurate register, the number of days in which rain fell was, in 1820, one hundred and fifty-two; in 1821, one hundred and eighty-four; and in 1822, one hundred and forty-one.

The mean temperature, deduced from the average of six years' observations, is 51°.31 of Fahrenheit; and, according to Dr. Brewster's formula, given in his paper on the Mean Temperature of the earth in the 9th volume of the *Transactions of the Royal Society of Edinburgh,* it amounts to 51°.99, agreeing within half a degree of that deduced from observation.

The town enjoys on the whole a considerable share health; and its mortality has decreased, in common with the whole country. In 1800 the mortality was one in twenty-seven, and in 1810 one in twenty-eight; but the mean of the last five years only afforded one in forty-five.

The following is an abstract of the population returns for 1821:

Inhabited houses	.	.	.	2384
Families occupying them		.	.	5150
Houses building	.		.	29
Houses uninhabited		.	.	233
Families employed in agriculture		.	176
Families employed in trade and manufactures		2976
Other families	.	.	.	1998
Males	.	.	.	.	9269
Females	.		.	.	12322
Total population		.	.	21591

There are several extensive and important improvements in a rapid state of advancement in the town and neighbourhood. The most extensive of these is a magnificent rail-road, proceeding from Sutton Pool to Dartmoor; a space of from twenty-five to thirty miles. The country through which it passes is, perhaps, one of the most difficult for an undertaking of the kind, in consequence of the innumerable inequalities of its surface. A ride over it presents some of the most striking and picturesque scenes, and from which the lover of the bold and irregular aspect of nature may draw the most exquisite enjoyment. The object of its formation is to afford a facility of transport for the fine granite with which the Tors of Dartmoor abound, and to convey into the interior, manure, coals, &c. for the line of country through which it passes.

Two suspension bridges are also in contemplation; one across the estuary of the Plym, to open a new line of communication with the more southern parts of the county; and the other across the Tamar, at Saltash, to afford a readier communication between Cornwall and Devon. The latter will be of magnificent dimensions; the distance between the points of suspension of the chains exceeding 800 feet.

From the diversified country and soil around Plymouth, the botanist can enrich his herbarium with species of almost every genus in the British flora. The woods of Manadon, Tamerton, and Warleigh; the heaths of Buckland, the rocky district of Shaugh, together with the rich vale of Bickleigh, the banks of the Tamar and Plym, and an extensive range of sea-coast, present full scope for the exertions of the naturalist, and are such as will amply reward him for his research.

Of phenogamous plants, upwards of one thousand species have been discovered by Mr. Banks of this place, (author of an introduction to the study of English Botany; and in whose intended *Flora Plymouthiensis* it will be seen that the greater part of English Cryptogamia abounds in this neighbourhood.

At this place the account of Plymouth might with propriety have ended; but as no account has appeared in the Encyclopædia, of the large and flourishing town of Plymouth Dock, in which the great naval arsenal is situated, and as it has been usual to include it under the general denomination of Plymouth, it may be proper to furnish a brief description.

Plymouth Dock is situated at a short distance to the west of Plymouth, its mean latitude being 50° 22' 19" north, and mean longitude 4° 9' 58" west. It owes its origin to the advantages possessed by the noble estuary of the Tamar, called Hamoaze, for a safe and commodious harbour for ships of the largest class. Its length is four miles, and its depth, at low water, fifteen fathoms, and contains moorings for ninety-two ships of the line. The town rises from the eastern shore of the harbour, by a gentle and uniform ascent, and its higher parts commanding the most varied and extensive prospects. Its form is that of an oblong, the longest side of which measures three thousand feet, and the breadth fourteen hundred, and is surrounded by fortifications. A considerable degree of regularity has been observed in the construction of the houses, and in the formation of the streets; most of which intersect each other at right angles. Their general width is from thirty to fifty feet.

The principal public building unconnected with the government establishments, is the town hall, which has been very recently erected. It is a fine specimen of the Doric order, and does great credit to the judgment and taste of the architect. The parish church is situated at Stoke, at an inconvenient distance from the town. Within the walls are St. Aubyn's and St. John's chapels, for the members of the church of England, and several places of worship for the dissenters. Of these may be named three Independent Calvinistic chapels, two Baptists, two Methodist chapels, and one for the Moravians.

Of the charitable institutions may be mentioned, with particular approbation, the Public Dispensary, the public schools for poor boys and girls; several Sunday schools among the dissenters, who display a laudable activity in training the lower orders to habits of virtue and industry. The members of the Lying-in Society, the Female Benevolent Society, the Dorcas Society, the Association for the Indigent and Distressed, and the Religious Tract Society, are particularly active in alleviating the miseries of humanity, and in attending personally to the many wants of the poor. A savings bank, on a very extensive scale, is also established.

The military establishments at this place are very considerable. A cordon of barracks is continued in an almost uninterrupted series, from the northern side of the town to the southern, sufficient to contain 3000 men. The government house on Mount Wise, is a considerable edifice, and is the usual residence of the lieutenant-governor, who is at the same time commander-in-chief of the western-district. The whole is defended by extensive fortifications.

The principal object of interest in the town is the dock-yard. This extensive and important establishment commenced in the reign of William III., and from that period to the present has been in a progressive state of improvement. It lies on the eastern border of Hamoaze, and is bounded by it on the western and southern sides. On the north and east it is separated from the town by a lofty wall. Its area amounts to more than seventy acres.

The immense docks are the first objects that attract the attention of the visitor. The new north dock is the only one at present without a roof. Its length is 240 feet, its breadth 85, and depth 29 feet. It remains uncovered, in consequence of its being necessary, occasionally, to take ships into it with their masts standing. This dock is the largest in the kingdom. The double dock is also an object of interest, and is so called from the two docks being constructed, one within the other, in a straight line. The inner dock is provided with gates, and is so entirely unconnected with the outer, that ships may be taken in or out of the latter without interrupting the operations in the former. Four docks are covered with immense roofs, having numerous windows in them.

The jettées also are well worthy of attention. They are immense platforms projecting from the harbour

wall, supported upon piles driven deep into the mud. By these expedients, the largest ships are brought within floating distance of the yard, and enabled to receive or discharge their stores and ballast without the interposition of boats.

The building ground is a particularly interesting part of the yard. It is divided into three slips, covered with immense roofs. They are constructed on what is called the balanced system in carpentry, and exhibit some of the finest examples of construction in that useful art, perhaps in the world. They were first recommended by Mr. Pering, the inventor of the excellent patent anchor, now generally adopted in the navy. These immense structures not only afford shelter and protection to the workmen from the inclemency of the weather, but contribute also to the preservation of the ships. At the present moment, the London, a ship of an immense size, has all her frame together; and when her interior is viewed from one of the extremes, the great assemblage of timbers presents an imposing spectacle. Such an example will not be lost on the cultivator of perspective. The Lancaster, a sixty gun frigate, embracing the latest improvements of Sir Robert Seppings, is on another slip. This ship has a round stern, and now joins beauty of external form to the essential attributes of strength. Near these slips are various workshops, plank houses, store cabins, boiling kilns, and a long line of saw-pits, to afford a convenient and ready supply of all the materials for building.

The various ranges of workshops for the different classes of artificers, the rigging house, sail loft, the immense ranges of storehouses, attract also the attention and curiosity of the stranger. One of the latter is constructed entirely of stone and iron. The floors are of Yorkshire slate, and the beams and supports of cast iron. The attention also that has been displayed in obtaining a maximum of strength, with a minimum of materials, is most perfectly exemplified in the iron employed in this building. The two rope houses are also constructed with the same attention to security. They are each 1200 feet in length. Cables are formed here for ships of 120 guns, of 100 fathoms in length, and 125 inches in circumference. The mast houses are a range of buildings of considerable extent; and there are, at all times, a number of masts in a state of readiness for any emergency. Near these buildings are immense ponds for the reception of timber, communicating with the sea by convenient gates.

The blacksmith's shop is a spacious rectangular structure, 160 feet by 140. The operations performed in it are at once astonishing and terrific. Forty-eight forges throw forth at once deep and powerful volumes of fire and smoke. Immense masses of glowing iron shower myriads of sparks, as the dark and brawny workmen wield their ponderous sledges. The roaring of the bellows, and the incessant clanking of chains, always produce a powerful impression on a visitor. Masses of iron are sometimes required, which defy the unaided power of man, and a mass of metal, called a Hercules, of nearly 8 cwt., suspended over a pulley, descends in a perpendicular direction on the glowing mass, to shape it to the desired form.

The commissioner, and principal officers of the yard, reside in a handsome row of buildings, adorned with naval trophies. The number of artificers amounts to about 3000.

Near the dock yard is the gun wharf. It stands on

Plymouth Dock.

a surface of nearly five acres. The armoury is a large building, filled with the various implements of war. The intervening spaces between the different edifices are occupied by large piles of ordnance belonging to the ships in the harbour, and immense pyramidal heaps of cannon shot.

A well-supplied market occupies a convenient and central situation in the town, and is plentifully supplied with the different necessaries of life. Fish is very abundant.

Many vessels are employed in the coasting and coal trades, and other ships trade with the Mediterranean, North America, &c.

Excellent hot and cold baths are situated on a pleasant beach, below Richmond Walk, immediately opposite to Mount Edgecumbe.

A few years since, a respectable literary and philosophical institution existed in the town; but it has latterly gone to decay. From the unquestionable utility of such institutions, and the influence they exercise on society, it is hoped that it will again revive, with increased usefulness.

Plymouth Dock, as has been already remarked, is bounded on one side by the sea, and on the other by an extensive line of fortifications. This has given birth to the adjacent village of Stoke Dameral, now containing a very considerable population.

A little to the south is the military hospital, a spacious and extensive structure, consisting of four distinct buildings of marble, with a noble piazza of forty-one arches, supporting a terrace, and on which convalescents enjoy the beneficial effects of gentle exercise in the open air, without the fatigue of descending and ascending numerous stairs.

Another village, which has grown out of the overflowing population of Plymouth Dock, called Morice Town, is situated to the north of the gun wharf. The great London road, which terminates at this place, recommences at the opposite shore of Tor Point.

Two dissenting chapels have been lately built; but there is no place of worship belonging to the establishment nearer than the parish church of Stoke Damarell.

At a short distance from Morice Town is the powder magazine, for the supply of the government establishments at this port. It is completely insulated from all other buildings, and protected by numerous conductors from the effects of lightning.

Between the towns of Plymouth and Plymouth Dock is the pleasant little town of Stonehouse. Its streets are straight and commodious, and the buildings neat and handsome. There is one chapel devoted to the established religion, one Independent Calvinist, one Methodist, and one Baptist meeting. There is also a Roman Catholic chapel, which is the only place dedicated to the Catholic worship in the neighbourhood.

In this little town there are several charitable institutions, which do much credit to the inhabitants. Of these may be mentioned the public school for poor boys and girls, the Lancasterian schools, a Sunday school open to children of all denominations, the adult school, and the Benevolent Society, for the sick and infirm poor.

The principal public establishments at this place, are the Royal Naval Hospital, and the Royal Marine Barracks. The former of these stands on a pleasant ascent, and contains an area of about twenty-four acres, thirteen of which are occupied by a beautiful lawn, forming a delightful place of exercise for convalescents. The hospital consists of ten buildings, surrounding an

extensive quadrangle, and is capable of accommodating twelve hundred sick. Every branch of the establishment is conducted in the most perfect way; and, when visited by the immortal Howard, called forth his warm admiration. From January, 1800, to the same month in 1815, no less than 48,452 seamen and marines were admitted into the hospital; by far the majority of whom returned to the king's service as effective men.

The Royal Marine Barracks are regularly and handsomely built, and contain accommodations for nearly a thousand men. Near these are the Long Room Barracks, capable of holding nine hundred men.

Stonehouse will most probably increase in a rapid manner, if the intended removal of the victualling office from Plymouth should take place.

The following is an abstract of the population returns of Stoke Dameral and Stonehouse for 1821.

Inhabited houses	3864
Families occupying them	9315
Houses building	31
Houses uninhabited	210
Families employed in agriculture	142
Families employed in trade and manufactures	3834
Other families	5339
Males	17,188
Females	22,433
Total population	39,621

PLYMOUTH BREAKWATER. Plymouth Sound is very much exposed, and the heavy swell that is almost constantly rolling in, is much increased when the wind blows fresh from any point between south-east and south-west. In consequence, therefore, of the danger arising from the anchoring of large ships of war in a situation so entirely unprotected, it was necessary, during the latter part of the last war, for the fleet destined to watch the movements of the enemy at Brest, to seek for shelter in Torbay, when the tempestuous state of the weather would no longer permit them to hover round that port. This circumstance led to an idea of improving the anchorage of Torbay, by affording it the protection of a breakwater; and a proposal was accordingly submitted to Lord Spencer, then at the head of the Admiralty, in the year 1799, by Mr. Whidbey. This proposal, although approved of by the noble Earl, was nevertheless lost sight of until the year 1806, when the idea of improving Plymouth Sound, by the erection of a proper breakwater, was suggested to Earl Grey, then first Lord of the Admiralty, by the late Earl of St. Vincent; and in the same year Messrs. Rennie and Whidbey were directed to survey the Sound, and to report on the possibility of affording a safe anchorage to ships of the line by the erection of such a structure.

This report, drawn up by two persons so eminently qualified, from their practical knowledge and experience, to investigate a subject of so difficult and complicated a nature, decidedly proved the possibility of protecting the Sound, and of making it a good harbour for at least fifty sail of the line. Unfortunately, however, from various changes in the ministry, those able reports and plans were neglected until 1811, when Mr. Yorke, then presiding at the Admiralty, resolved to carry the important work into immediate execution; and thus to secure to our fleets that security, and those advantages of position, which the glory and the safety of the British navy so essentially demanded.

The choice and situation of materials for the construction of the work was the next object of consideration. It was recommended as the most practicable and best mode of forming it, to sink very large blocks of stone in the line of the intended breakwater, allowing them to find their own base, and assume those positions which gravity would permit them ; and that irregular masses of stone, from one and a half to two tons in weight, would be sufficiently heavy to resist the action of a stormy sea. The immense beds of limestone on the eastern shore of Catwater *, were found capable of producing blocks even much greater than the weight here alluded to, and this, together with the convenience of the shores for the loading of vessels, and the sheltered situation of the harbour, immediately pointed it out as the most eligible for the purpose.

On the 7th of August, 1812, the quarries were opened, Mr. Whidbey having been appointed to superintend the works in October of the preceding year. Five days after the opening of the quarries, the first stone was deposited in the Sound, amidst the acclamations of hundreds ; and on the 31st of March, 1813, the Breakwater was first seen above the face of the sea, at low water of the spring tide. From that time the work has progressively advanced, and with so little ostentation and display, that the stranger wonders when he arrives in Plymouth, to find that a work, which ranks among the proudest of our national monuments, should be carried on with so much quietness and ease. At the present time, (July, 1823,) there have been one million eight hundred thousand tons of stone deposited.

The Breakwater consists of a central part of one thousand yards in length, and two wings, each of three hundred and fifty yards, forming, with the middle portion, angles of 158°, the angular points being turned towards the ocean. At the distance of sixty fathoms from the eastern extremity of the central part, are the St. Carlos Rocks ; and these, together with the Shovel Rocks, extend to 640 fathoms, so that considerably more than half the central part of the Breakwater rests on masses of rock, which at all times impeded the navigation of the Sound. The transverse section is of the form of a trapezoid, whose base, on an average, extends to about 290 feet, its breadth at the top 48 feet, and its average depth about 56 feet. The sloping sides of this trapezoid have different inclinations ; that towards the harbour forming with the horizon an angle of 33°, and that towards the sea one of 22°, the stability of the structure being much increased by diminishing the inclination on the latter side. On the top it is proposed to build a pier, with breast-walls, and a light-house, at each extremity. The place of the latter is at present supplied by a light placed in a vessel, which is kept constantly moored at the western end of the works.

The average depth of water in the immediate vicinity of the Breakwater is 36 feet at low water spring tides ; and it is carried in height above that to 20 feet, which is somewhat more than the general rise of spring tides in the port. On the central part of the top, the huge blocks are so arranged as to form a convenient path from one end to the other ; and to which hundreds resort during the summer to enjoy the surrounding scene : the water covered with numerous boats presenting a changing picture of perpetual interest ; and the land, rising into lovely hills, bounded on one side by the lofty summits of Dartmoor, and on the other slowly melting into the distant tors of Cornwall.

The quantity of limestone required for its construction, as originally estimated by Messrs. Rennie and Whidbey, amounted to 2,000,000 tons ; and the probable expence to £1,171,100.

The blocks of stone are transported to the Breakwater in vessels of a strong and peculiar construction. They weigh, on an average, from three to five tons, and are placed on trucks at the quarries, and run down from thence, on iron railways, to the sterns of the vessels, which are turned towards the quays to receive them. Iron railways are also fixed on the deck, and in the hold, for the purpose of receiving the trucks. A cargo sometimes consists of 80 tons, though frequently, on account of the weather, it varies to 60, and even 40 tons. Instances have been known, however, of cargoes of 80 tons being discharged in 40 or 50 minutes. By means of very powerful cranes, the stones, notwithstanding their great diversity of form, are so singularly accommodated to each other, as to call forth the admiration of the beholder.

The experience of eleven years has fulfilled the expectations of the warmest advocates of the Breakwater. The second year after its erection, its good effects were plainly perceptible ; and every winter has increased the testimonies in its favour. In the early part of 1817, a decided proof was afforded of its benefit, by its sheltering the Sound and Catwater from the fury of one of the most tremendous hurricanes remembered by the oldest inhabitant. The water rose six feet above the usual height of the spring tides, and the most desolating effects must have ensued, if the raging of the ocean had not been checked by this noble structure. A fine though melancholy contrast was exhibited in the fates of the Jasper and Telegraph, which were anchored in a part without shelter from the Breakwater, and a deeply laden collier lying under its protection. The former, though possessing every advantage that the cables and anchors of the king's service could afford, were totally wrecked ; whereas the latter, with but feeble means, rode out the fury of the storm, and presented to the few, who might before that time have doubted of the efficacy of the Breakwater, a most convincing and undeniable proof of its advantages.

Another great work, connected with the Breakwater, is the noble reservoir at Bovisand, for the purpose of supplying the navy with water. It contains 12,000 tuns, and the water is conveyed in iron pipes to Staddon point, a distance of 1200 yards, a great portion of which is a tunnel, cut through the high surrounding land.

PLYMOUTH, a sea-port town, and the capital of Plymouth county, Massachusetts. The town, which is the oldest in New England, is chiefly built of wood, and has five churches, a court-house, a bank, and a jail. There are in the town considerable manufactures of cotton, woollen, and iron, the machinery of which is driven by a small rivulet which passes through the town. The town is defended by a fort, and there is a lighthouse nine miles east by north of it. In 1816, there was shipping belonging to the port amounting to 18,875 tons, which was principally employed in the fisheries, and in the West India and European trade. Population 4228. Distance from Boston 36 miles south-south-east. West Long. 70° 30′, and North Lat. 41° 58′.

---

* It is in these quarries that the caverns have been discovered containing the bones of the Rhinoceros, the Hyæna, and other animals, which have so much interested the geological world. The bones and caves are described in the *Philosophical Transactions*, and in Professor Buckland's interesting work, entitled, *Reliquiæ Diluvianæ.* See also the *Edin. Phil. Journal*, vol. ix. p. 225, 226.

PNEUMATICS.

Pneuma-
tics.

THIS word is derived from the Greek term πνευμα, *spiritus*, and is the name given to that science which treats of the mechanical properties of compressible fluids.

Origin of the science.
The circumstance which successfully directed the attention of philosophers to this subject, was a failure on the part of some mechanics who had been employed to erect a pump upwards of thirty feet long. This incident perplexed them so much that they had recourse to Galileo, the most ingenious philosopher of his time, for an explanation. The bold and original genius of Galileo, though it had enriched science with many new discoveries, was unable to divest itself at once of prejudices which had acquired strength from their antiquity. Instead of totally relinquishing the Aristotelian aphorism that " nature abhors a vacuum," and inquiring, upon mechanical principles, into the cause of this anomaly, he contented himself with adjusting his prepossessions to experience, and concluded that the *fuga vacui* obtained only within 32 feet of the earth.

This accommodation of the hypothesis to fact did not long continue. It appears to have proved unsatisfactory to Galileo himself; for while it shook the ancient philosophy to its basis, in as far as the truth of the physical axiom was concerned, it assigned no general principle by which the phenomenon might be explained. The adherents of the old philosophy were displeased to see their doctrines compromised; whilst the ardent followers of the new philosophy were dissatisfied with an explanation so fanciful and incomplete.

Torricelli's explanation.
Torricelli, a disciple of Galileo, has the honour of having exploded the maxim of the schoolmen, and of substituting, in its place, a natural explanation. It occurred to him that the fluid was maintained in the barrel of the pump by the pressure of the external atmosphere. To verify this conjecture, he perceived that it would be necessary to employ a fluid of a density different from that of water, and observe to what height it could be supported; for he was aware that the elevations at which two fluids of different densities can be maintained by the same pressure are inversely proportional to their densities. For this purpose he made use of mercury, a fluid whose specific gravity is to that of water as $13\frac{1}{2}$ to 1. Having filled a tube which was hermetically sealed at one end, and open at the other, with this fluid he immersed the open end in a cistern containing the same, and found that it did not occupy the whole tube, but descended until it reached a height of about 30 inches. This experiment completely overturned the opinion of Galileo, and confirmed his own conjecture. For,

$13\frac{1}{2}$: 1 : 33 feet : 30 inches : the exact height at which, according to hydrostatical principles, the fluid ought to stand when maintained by a pressure capable of supporting a column of water 33 feet long.

This experiment was not only important in affording an accession to human knowledge, but also in dispelling the plausible, though crude opinions, which had been previously entertained concerning the nature of the atmosphere. The tenuity of air distinguishes it so much from every other modification of matter, that the ancients appear to have considered it as a distinct principle.

" Ignea convexi vis, et sine pondere, cœli
Emicuit, summaque locum sibi leget in arce.
Proximus est aer illi levitate, locoque;
Densior his tellus.
OVID, *Metamorph.*

The facility with which the feathered tribes appeared to glide through it, and the ease with which the other animals transferred themselves from one place to another, led to the conclusion that it opposed no resistance, but yielded to the slightest impulse. It was also supposed to have been endowed with an inherent levity, because it occasioned no sensible incumbrance to those who lived beneath it. To consider, therefore, this substance as a fluid, at a time when its very names were appropriated to express ideas the most refined and remote from human apprehension, was truly philosophical, and to attribute to its agency the support of a considerable weight of dense and ponderous matter, betokened an originality of mind and boldness of conception, which, perhaps, in the present advanced state of knowledge, we cannot justly appreciate.

This striking discovery of Torricelli was communicated by him to his friend Viviani, who performed the experiment successfully in 1643.

He again repeated it himself, and varied it in such a manner as to bring into operation the several causes which contribute to the result.

Having taken a glass tube, of moderate width, and about four feet long, after sealing it at one end, he filled it with mercury, and inserted it in a cistern containing mercury, covered with a portion of water. Whilst the lower end was immersed among the mercury in the cistern, the column was maintained as usual at the height of about 30 inches. On raising the tube, however, from among the mercury, as soon as it reached the water, the mercury flowed out of it, and its place was supplied by a column of water which occupied the whole length of the tube. Experiments of this kind not only demonstrated that the atmosphere exerted a pressure, but, by being frequently repeated, they soon pointed out to Torricelli that this pressure was subject to variations. The result of the whole of his inquiries was published in 1645, but he did not live to enjoy the renown of his great discovery, having been cut off by a fever in the midst of his philosophical pursuits, and in the flower of his age.

Pascal's discovery.
The next individual who devoted himself to this science was the celebrated Pascal, who, from his earliest years, had displayed a strong predilection for physical studies, in which he was encouraged by his father, who was himself distinguished for his learning. While residing at Rouen, he obtained, through means of father Mersenne, a learned mathematician, who maintained an extensive correspondence over Europe, an acquaintance with the famous Italian discovery. Pascal immediately undertook to repeat it upon a larger scale, but appears to have been ignorant of the explanation which had been given of it by Torricelli. With this view he provided a glass tube about fifty feet long, sealed at one end, and having first filled it with water tinged red, he inverted the open end into a basin containing the same fluid; immediately the inclosed fluid subsided, leaving a vacant space of about fifteen feet. He next took a syphon or bent tube, which he filled

with mercury, and having immersed its extremities in two basins containing the same fluid, it subsided in both branches, and stood at a level of about thirty inches above its surface in each of the cisterns. On placing the instrument in such a position that the elevation of the highest point was less than thirty inches above the extremity of the shorter branch, he perceived the fluid to rush out in a continued stream through the longer branch. In a disputation upon this subject he decidedly maintained the existence of a vacuum, a doctrine which provoked the opposition of the schoolmen, particularly of father Noel, rector of the Jesuits' College at Paris. During the polemical discussions in which he was thus involved, he became acquainted with the cause which had been assigned by Torricelli for the phenomenon. The method which he proposed to render manifest its influence, was in itself most ingenious, and led to one of the most beautiful applications of the science of pneumatics.

It occurred to him, as the column of mercury was supported in the tube by the atmospherical pressure, that whatever cause might affect the latter, would also induce a change upon the former. The means of removing the atmospherical pressure directly had not yet been discovered, so that he was obliged to have recourse to an indirect manner of accomplishing this. By ascending into the higher regions of the atmosphere, the superincumbent mass would obviously be lessened, and of consequence its pressure ; and accordingly he was led to expect that, in this manner, the column of mercury, which forms a counterpoise to it, might be made to diminish. From the rarity of air, however, he seems to have anticipated that it would require no ordinary elevation to cause a diminution of the mercurial column in any degree perceptible ; for, instead of making the experiment himself, he committed the accomplishment of his views to his brother-in-law, Perier, who usually resided at Clermont in Auvergne. This place was particularly favourable for the purpose, as there stands in its neighbourhood the Puy de Dome, a lofty mountain, at the bottom and summit of which Pascal requested that the height of the mercurial column might be observed. This request was made in November, 1647 ; but Perier, by absence from home, and other impediments, was prevented from attending to it until the 19th September in the following year.

Early in the morning of that day, he invited a few curious friends to meet him in the garden of a monastery, situated in the lowest part of Clermont, where he brought a quantity of quicksilver, and two tubes hermetically sealed at the top. These he filled, and inverted as usual, and found the mercury to stand in both at the same height of about 28 English inches. Having left one of the tubes in this situation, he proceeded with the other towards the mountain, on the summit of which he repeated the experiment ; when his party was equally astonished and delighted to find that the mercury stood only at about 24.7 inches. In his descent he found the mercury gradually to rise, so that, on reaching the monastery, it was observed to stand at the same height with the barometer which he had left behind. This was a most decisive proof to Pascal of the truth of the explanation given by Torricelli. He received intelligence of the result when residing at Paris, and finding, contrary to his conjectures, that the depression was so considerable for an ascent of 500 toises, or about 3000 English feet, he resolved to see the effect that would be produced by raising the instrument to some of the most considerable eminences about

that city. For this purpose he selected a high house, on the top of which he remarked that the mercurial column was much shorter than in lower stations. It immediately occurred to him to apply this principle to determine the difference of level between places situated at any distance from each other.

This ingenious idea was not overlooked by philosophers. The nature and constitution of the atmosphere now became an object, not merely of curious but useful speculation. The discoveries which had already been made on this impalpable substance roused the attention of mankind, and although many who had imbibed the Aristotelian philosophy did not acquiesce in the explanations which were given, the facts were undeniable, and excited speculation amongst all.

In this manner a spirit of inquiry burst forth, which was eminently rewarded by several beautiful discoveries and inventions.

When the air came to be considered as a substance possessing weight and fluidity, and capable of being excluded from a well compacted vessel, as was learned from the vacuum produced by Torricelli, the ingenious soon employed themselves in devising a contrivance by which it might be exhausted mechanically. The first who succeeded in this attempt was Guerické, a burgo-master of Magdeburgh, who devoted much of his leisure to philosophical pursuits. He first endeavoured to produce a vacuum in a cask filled with water, which he employed the common sucking-pump to empty. This was a work of considerable labour, and proved unsuccessful, for, after a considerable portion of the water had been extracted, a hissing sound was heard, produced by the air insinuating itself through the interstices of the vessel. He then substituted for the cask a copper ball, to the lower part of which he attached a syringe ; and, after securing its joints by water, he at length succeeded in emptying the vessel. It was in this manner that he performed the famous Magdeburgh experiment, which was not below the attention of the deputies and ambassadors who were assembled at the diet of Ratisbon, and to whom it was first exhibited in 1654.

Having taken two hemispheres which exactly fitted each other, by employing the syringe he exhausted them so completely, that they were retained together by the pressure of the external air with such a force, that it required the energy of twelve horses pulling in opposite directions to sever them from each other.

This method of producing a vacuum was extremely rude, as it required the unremitting labour of two strong men for several hours together ; and, besides, the vessel to be exhausted was composed of one entire globe, with a narrow neck, so that it became a matter of difficulty to introduce into it the substances upon which experiments were to be made. To remedy these inconveniencies, the celebrated Boyle, aided by the ingenuity of Dr. Hooke, whom he employed as an assistant in his philosophical researches, invented an instrument, of which Plate CCCCLXIV. Fig. 1. is a representation.

PLATE
CCCCLXIV.
Fig. 1.

The principal parts of it are the glass-vessel A, which is usually called the receiver, and the pump SVG. It differed chiefly from the instrument which had been invented by Guerické, in the construction of the receiver. That employed by Boyle is stated as having been capable of holding about thirty wine quarts. At the top of it is a round hole EC, whose diameter is four inches, and which is encircled by a lip of glass about one inch in breadth. Upon this was closely cemented a brass ring, the interior of which was of a conical form, that it might receive a brass

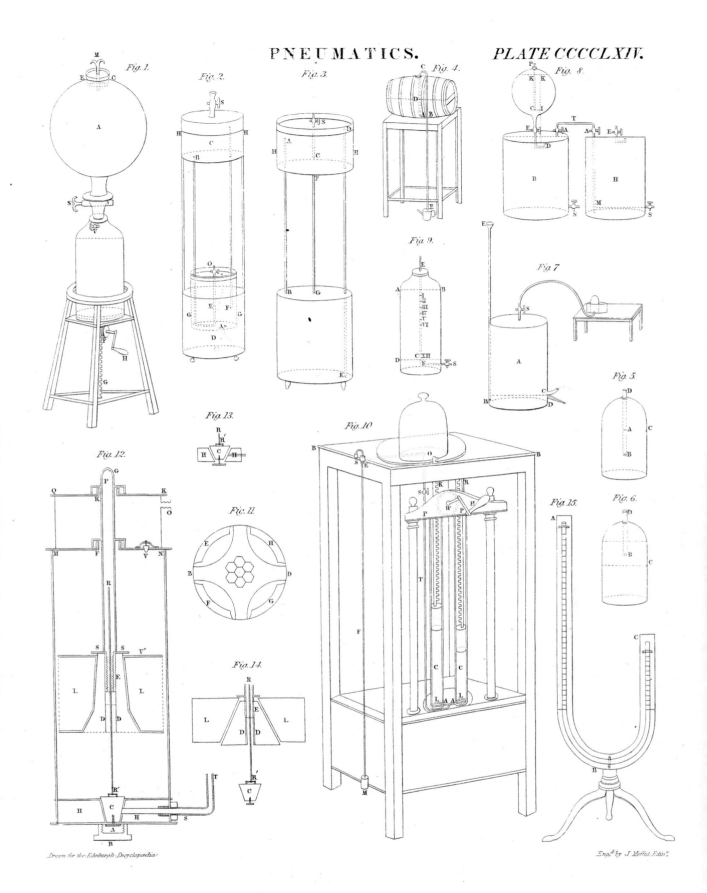

Drawn for the Edinburgh Encyclopædia. Engd by J. Moffat, Edinr.

stopple. These were so accurately fitted to each other, that though the stopple might be made to revolve within the ring, no air could enter between them. In the middle of the stopple was a small orifice, to which the stop-cock M was carefully adapted. These were also rendered tight by means of oil. The receiver was cemented upon a tin plate, which was soldered to the stop-cock S. This stop-cock was connected with the cylindrical vessel VG, within which a piston was made to move by means of the rack-work FGH. In the upper part of the vessel was the valve V.

The method of exhausting by means of this machine was extremely laborious and irksome. The stop-cock S is supposed to be shut, and when the piston is made to ascend, the valve V is opened in order to allow a passage for the air which the piston drives before it. When the piston has reached the top of the vessel, the stop-cock S is opened and the valve shut. On withdrawing the piston, the air included in the receiver falls down, and occupies the whole interior of the apparatus. The stop-cock S is again shut, and the same process is resumed until the vessel is exhausted to the degree required.

This instrument appears rude and obvious in the present improved state of science; but it must be recollected, that its inventors knew almost nothing of the fluid upon which they were to operate, except its existence. The ingenious mechanical improvements which have since been made upon the air-pump, depend upon principles which were first unfolded by the simple contrivance of Boyle. He was the first who seems to have been acquainted with the elastic force of air.

This idea was suggested to him by the manner in which the air issues from the valve V. We shall express his observations on the subject in his own language:—" Upon drawing down the sucker, the valve being shut, the cylindrical space deserted by the sucker is left devoid of air; and, therefore, upon the turning of the stop-cock, the air contained in the receiver rusheth into the empty cylinder, till the air in both the vessels be brought to about an equal measure of dilatation. And, therefore, upon shutting the receiver by turning the key, if you open the valve and force the sucker again, it will be found that, after this first exsuction, almost a whole cylinder full of air will be driven out; but, at the following exsuctions, you will draw less and less out of the receiver into the cylinder, because there will remain less and less in the receiver itself, and, consequently, the particles of the remaining air, having more room to extend themselves in, will less press out one another. On the receiver being almost emptied, if at such a time, the valve being shut, you let go the handle of the pump, you will find the sucker forcibly carried up to the top of the cylinder by the protrusion of the external air, which being much less rarefied than that within the cylinder, must have a more forcible pressure upon the sucker than that contained in the receiver. For the more easy understanding the experiments made by our engine, I thought it not superfluous, in the recital of this first of them, to insinuate the notion by which it seems likely the most, if not all of them, may be explained."

You will easily suppose, that the notion I speak of is, that there is a spring, or ελατηρ, in the air which we live in, by which I mean, that our air consists of parts of such a nature, that in case they be bent, or compressed, by the weight of the incumbent part of the atmosphere, or by any other body, they do endeavour, as much as in them lieth, to free themselves from that pressure, by bearing against the contiguous bodies that keep them bent."

With this instrument Boyle was enabled to make several very interesting experiments, and, among others, to obtain a direct evidence that the pressure of the air supported the mercury in the barometrical tube. This was done by filling a tube after the manner of the Torricellian experiment, which he placed within the receiver. The stopple was then let down into its place, by causing the part of the tube which projected from the receiver to pass through its orifice. A luting was then applied round the orifice to render it air-tight. On exhausting the receiver, the mercury was found to descend, until it came nearly upon a level with that contained in the cistern; and on allowing the air to reenter, it was found to ascend to nearly its former height. He next employed water instead of mercury, and, after working the pump for some time, it was also found to subside. Upon this occasion he observed small bubbles ascending from the water, and which, like air, he found to be possessed of elasticity. We need not observe that this was merely air, which had been mechanically united with the water, but which made its escape upon the pressure at the surface having been removed.

The elasticity of air, which Boyle had thus the merit of discovering, serves to explain several useful and curious inventions.

I. JETS OF WATER.

Plate CCCCLXIV. Fig. 2. represents what has been called the Fountain of Command. It consists of three cylindrical vessels, D, E, and C. The upper vessel is filled with water to a certain height, and then the stop-cock S is shut to prevent the access of air. The water begins to flow through the tube BGO, and rises from the orifice O with the velocity due to the height HO. As the water subsiding descends in the vessel C, it ascends in E, and though a portion of it escapes at the orifice O, it gradually accumulates here until it covers the lower extremity of the tube F. No air is now admitted into the vessel C, and as the level line HH descends, the air which is contained above it becomes attenuated, and loses its elasticity. The column of fluid HO, and the diminished pressure of the confined air is no longer equivalent to the elasticity of the external air, which stops the jet at O. The water in the vessel E receiving no addition, continues to flow through A into the lower vessel, until it sinks below F. The air then gains admission through the tube CF into the upper vessel, and the jet is recontinued. Thus the fountain alternately plays and stops; and as a person, by observing when the lower level reaches F, can know when it is to flow, it has received the name of the Fountain of Command.

PLATE CCCCLXIV. Fig. 2.

Plate CCCCLXIV. Fig. 3. represents Hiero's fountain. AC and BE are cylindrical vessels, connected together by the tubes AB, DE, and the support EG. The vessel AC is surmounted by a rim, made to contain the water which falls from the jet. This water is received into the orifice D, and transmitted through the tube DE into the lower vessel. As the water ascends in this vessel it condenses the included air, and thus augments its elasticity until it become equivalent to the atmospheric pressure, together with the weight of the column of water DE. As the tube AB allows the air in the lower vessel to pass up into the higher, the elasticity of both is the same. The water, consequently, contained in the latter is pressed by the superincumbent air with a force equivalent to the weight of the atmo-

Fig. 3.

sphere, together with that of the column DE. It is
thus forced up into the tube CS, and, on turning the
cock at S, it ascends with the same velocity as if it
were issuing from an orifice in the bottom of a vessel
filled with water to a height equal to DE.

The way to prepare this fountain for playing, is to
pour water into the lower vessel through the tube DE,
then to invert it that the water may flow through AB
into the upper cistern, until it be filled. On setting
the fountain again upright, water is poured into the
tube DE, until it can receive no more, when, upon turning the cock S, the jet commences.

II. Syphon.

Plate
cccclxiv.
Fig. 4.
The syphon is a bent tube, represented as in Fig. 4.
Plate CCCCLXIV. which is employed in conveying a
fluid from one vessel or place to another. By immersing one extremity of the tube in the fluid to be transferred, and extracting the air from it by means of a
pump, the pressure of the atmosphere acting upon the
surface of the fluid causes it to ascend into the tube;
and if the issuing leg CE be longer than the driving
leg CA, the fluid will continue to flow through the
tube. The reason of this is, that the force employed
in raising the fluid is the atmospheric pressure, diminished by the weight of a column of fluid having for its
height CD; whereas the pressure which is exerted
against the fluid when issuing from E, is the atmospheric pressure diminished by the weight of a column of
fluid, having for its altitude CE. From this it is obvious that the fluid will flow at E with the velocity
due to the difference of level DE.

As the atmospherical pressure is the cause why the
water ascends in the syphon tube, it is apparent that
the point C ought never to exceed 32 feet in height
above the surface of the fluid at B in the case of water,
or 30 inches for mercury. In conducting water from
one place to another, by means of this instrument, a
forcing pump is usually connected with the end of the
issuing leg, in order to fill the syphon; when the place
has been drained, a stop cock is turned in order to prevent the water from issuing, until there be again occasion for the syphon. It is obvious, that if the issuing
and driving leg be of the same length, the fluid will
cease to flow, and not only so, but the air will gradually ascend into the tube, and occupying the highest
parts of the bend, will detach the two columns of fluid
and cause them to fall through their respective orifices.

Every thing, consequently, which has a tendency to
this effect in the construction of syphons ought to be
avoided. The driving leg ought always to be as nearly vertical as possible, in order to furnish a plentiful
supply of water: and the issuing leg ought always to
have a gentle inclination throughout.

A syphon having the issuing leg to pass in a concealed manner through the bottom or handle of a cup, as
represented in Hydrodynamics, Figs. 13, 14, 15. of
Plate CCCXVII. has received the name of Tantalus'
cup. For an account of various syphons, see the article
Hydrodynamics, Vol. XI. p. 485.

III. Gasometer.

The pressure of air, like that of all other fluids, is
exerted in every direction. Hence it happens, that
every part of the surface of a body which is inclosed
in air, is subject to a weight equivalent to that of a
column of water 32 feet long. Calculating upon this
principle, the pressure upon every square inch is $14\frac{1}{2}$
lbs. If the surface of the human body be supposed to
be 11 square feet, the pressure exerted upon it will be

25056 lbs. or upwards of 11 tons; and the pressure
upon the surface of the whole, earth, which in round
numbers, is 5,575,680,000,000,000 square feet, is equal
to about 1,164,201,840,000,000,000 pounds. These results may perhaps appear incredible, and it may be
conceived that such an immense pressure would completely destroy all motion. In science, however, it is
proper to reason before coming to a decision; nor ought
a result to be rejected merely because it is astonishing.
The following fact, though more obvious, is still more
wonderful. Fishes are sometimes caught at a depth of
2560 feet; and are consequently compressed with a
force equivalent to about 80 atmospheres; yet they are
not burst by this immense weight, nor impeded in their
movements. The reason of this is, that the fishes are
filled with fluids, which from their impenetrability oppose a sufficient resistance to the immense pressure
from without, 'and preserve the slightest membranes
from being broken. With regard to their facility of
motion, as the pressure which they support acts in
every direction, it neutralises itself, by promoting as
much as it impedes their endeavour to move themselves.
The reason why man and the other animals suffer no
inconveniencies from the atmospheric pressure is precisely the same. The vessels of the body, together with
the bones, are filled with fluids capable of supporting
any degree of weight, or with air, whose elasticity
being equal to that without, proves an exact counterbalance to it. Most of the fishes who live in the depths
of the sea, are provided with a vesicle filled with a particular kind of air or gas, produced and secreted by the
economy of their nature. The elasticity of this is so
great as to resist the pressure of several atmospheres;
on drawing up the animal therefore to the surface, the
diminished pressure which it now sustains is no longer
a counterpoise to the gas inclosed in the vesicle, which
consequently dilates and bursts it. In like manner, to
remove the atmospheric pressure from off the human
frame would destroy life instantaneously. That the
air presses equally in all directions is proved by
the following ingenious experiment devised by Mariotte. DB (Fig. 5.) is a tube introduced into the
neck of the glass bottle AB, and fitted to it so as to
be air-tight, the bottle having previously been filled Fig. 5.
with water. If a small orifice be opened in the side of
the vessel as at C, about 1-10th of an inch in diameter,
the water will immediately subside in the tube to the
level A, and a portion of it will flow from the orifice equal to that which has been displaced from the
tube. Should the lower extremity of the tube be above
the orifice in the side of the vessel, as in Fig. 6. the air Fig. 6.
will ascend through it to the top of the bottle, and cause
the water to flow until its surface descend upon a level
with the orifice.

The reason why the water ceases to flow in the
first case is, that the lateral pressure of the air on
the orifice is an equivalent to its vertical pressure in
the tube at A. This principle is employed in the construction of a vessel for the purpose of receiving
gases, (Fig. 7.) EB is a tube, with a conical piece Fig. 7.
soldered at the top that water may be the more easily filled into it. This tube descends to within a very
small distance from the bottom of the vessel A. This
vessel has, at the top, a tube fitted with a stop-
cock, and at C another tube inclined upwards, with a
spout below to carry off the water which may be made
to issue at D. By shutting the tube at D, and opening
the stop-cock at S, the vessel A may be filled by pouring water in at E. By shutting the cock at S, and
opening that at D, after the vessel has been filled, only

as much water will flow off as is contained in the tube above the level of the orifice C. In order to admit gas into the gasometer it is only necessary to introduce the tube of a retort, or whatever vessel the gas is formed in, into the orifice at C; from which it will ascend by its levity to the surface of the water which is let off at C. The gas is drawn from the gasometer by means of a tube connected with the orifice at S, and received beneath the pneumatic trough.

This principle, for which we are indebted to Mariotte, has been ingeniously applied by Dr. Wollaston in the construction of an apparatus by which an uniform current of air is made to pass from one vessel into another.

PLATE
CCCCLXIV.
Fig. 8. Let B and H (Fig. 8. Plate CCCCLXIV.) be two vessels having each a stop-cock and spout at S, and a stop-cock at E, and let them be connected by a tube T, proceeding from the vessel B, containing the gas to within a small space of the bottom of the vessel C, into which the gas is to be transferred. To the stop-cock E of the vessel containing the gas is screwed the vessel KC holding water. The water is represented as standing at the level KH; and the stopple P, being placed in its proper cavity, the pressure of the external air is removed from its surface. The tube KC, open at both ends, descends into the water. The vessel C is also filled with water. The stop-cocks E, A, A, S, are now opened. The water descends into the vessel B with the velocity due to the height ID, which consequently is constant. The air contained in the receiver B is, therefore, compressed with the atmospheric pressure, together with the weight of the column of water ID, and is thus made to pass through the tube T. It presses at M with its whole elastic force, and is opposed by the atmospheric pressure, so that it overcomes this resistance by a pressure equivalent to the weight of the column of water ID. If, therefore, the vessel KC contains a supply of water sufficient to fill B, the air will be expelled from this vessel into C with a constant force. The air may be again replaced after the same manner in B, by screwing the vessel KC to the tube E', shutting the stop-cock S, filling the vessel B with water, and opening the cock S.

A clepsydra, or water clock, might be fitted up on this principle, where the hour might be marked by equal divisions on the tube CE, (Fig. 9.). For, until the water reaches the level line DC, it obviously issues uniformly at the cock S with the velocity due to the difference of level CF.

Fig. 9.

IV. AIR PUMP.

The elasticity of air having been ascertained by the experiments of Boyle, the ingenious soon availed themselves of it in the construction of air-pumps. The principal objections to that which Boyle employed were, the inconvenience of alternately shutting and opening the stop-cock and valve, and the great difficulty of making the piston descend when the internal air is considerably rarefied. The first of these was surmounted by employing the air itself as a mechanical agent; and the second by employing two pistons connected in such a manner that the one was depressed when the other was elevated, by which means the pressure of the external air which opposed the descent of the one favoured the ascent of the other. An improved machine of this nature is represented in (Fig 10.) which receives the name of Hawksbee's pump, from the individual who contrived it. KR are the two piston rods which move by the revolution of the wheel W in their respective cylinders CC. PL PL are two pistons

Fig. 10.

which are fixed perpendicularly to the frame work of the instrument; over these is placed the transverse bar of wood PP, into which the upper extremity of the cylinders are fixed, and to which the wheel W is attached, which is turned by the handle H. Their lower ends rest upon two circular pieces of brass, which contain each a valve covering the extremities of the horizontal tube AA. The valves were formed by covering two very small holes pierced through the brass by a slip of limber bladder which was fastened by a silken thread wound around the circumference, and embracing its extremities.

These valves are so constructed as to be distended upwards by the elasticity of the internal air, and resemble in every particular the two valves which are at the end of the piston rods. The tube AA is connected with the pipe T, which passes up through a hole in the board BB, over which the receiver is placed. This tube is usually fitted with a stop-cock, which is shut after a vacuum has been made, in order to prevent any air which may enter at AA, or any other part of the pump, from getting access to the receiver. The manner in which the air is exhausted, is obvious from the construction of the machine; when the handle is turned, one of the pistons is raised and the other depressed. The air contained in the cylinder of the ascending piston is dilated, for no external air can enter, as its pressure shuts the valve of the piston rod by compressing the bladder upon the puncture; hence its elasticity becomes less than that of the air contained within the receiver and tube AA, which, of consequence, opens the lower valve and expands itself into the cylinder until the density of both become equal. On turning the handle in a contrary direction, the elevated piston is made to descend, and by compressing the air beneath it, which cannot force itself back into the receiver owing to its increased elasticity, it at length exceeds in density the external air, and, opening the piston valve, makes its escape. The same process is repeated until any required degree of exhaustion is obtained.

From the manner in which the air is exhausted a formula may be given, by which the degree of exhaustion produced after a given number of strokes may be found. For let V be the capacity of the receiver, v that of the barrel, and δ the density of the air. Then, as on raising the piston for the first time, the volume v is exhausted, V is the portion of air which remains, and as this expands and fills the space $V+v$,

$$\frac{\delta V}{V+v} \text{ is its density.}$$

By raising the piston a second time, the volume v of the density $\dfrac{\delta V}{V+v}$ is exhausted, so that there will remain as before the volume V; and, as this air is dilated so as to fill $V+v$, its density becomes $\dfrac{\delta V^2}{(V+v)^2}$.

Hence the density of the air which remains after the nth stroke is $\dfrac{\delta V^n}{(V+v)^n}$.

And $\delta \div \dfrac{\delta V^n}{(V+v)^n} = \left(\dfrac{V+v}{V}\right)^n$ is an expression for the degree of rarefaction produced.

Such was the state of the air-pump when it engaged the attention of Mr. Smeaton. The imperfections of Mr. Hawkbee's pump, which he endeavoured to remedy, arose from the difficulty in opening the valves at the bottom of the barrels, and from the pistons not fit-

Pneuma-
tics.

Mr. Smea-
ton's im-
provement.

ting exactly when put close down to the bottom, which left a lodgement of air which could not be got out of the barrel. The first of these defects was owing to the small orifice through which the air passed in raising the slip of bladder, and which opposed a considerable resistance, from the circumstance of its having been necessary to keep it moist with oil or water. The diameter of the hole was about 1-10th of an inch. Now, suppose the air to have been rarefied 140 times, which was nearly the maximum effect of the machine, and $\frac{30}{140}$ inches of mercury will represent its elasticity; or, in other words, a column of mercury of this height would have prevented the air from expanding. But, as the specific gravity of mercury is about $13\frac{1}{2}$, and the weight of the cubic inch of water is 252 grains,

$$\frac{3}{14} \times \frac{1}{10^2} \times 13\frac{1}{2} \times 252 \times \cdot7854 = 5.\ 5\ \text{grains nearly,}$$ is

the pressure which the air could exert in this attenuated state. This force was incapable of overcoming the cohesion of the bladder to the plate, by which means the process of exhaustion was discontinued. To obviate this, Mr. Smeaton resolved to expose a greater surface to the action of the air; with this view, instead of one hole, he "made use of seven, all of equal size and shape, one being in the centre, and the other six round it, so that the valve was supported at proper distances by a kind of grating made by the solid parts between these holes." To expose a sufficiently great surface the holes were made hexagonal as represented (Fig. 11. Plate CCCCLXIV.) and the partitions filed almost to an edge. The letters E, F, G, H, show where the metal was a little protuberant, to hinder the piston from striking against the bladder. To prevent any lodgement of air in the lower part of the barrel, he removed the external pressure from the piston valve, by making the piston move through a collar of leather, and forced the air out by a valve applied to the plate at the top of the barrel which opened outwards.

PLATE
CCCCLXIV.
Fig. 11.

Cuthbert-
son's air-
pump.

The latest improvement which has been made on this machine is due to Cuthbertson, a philosophical instrument maker of Amsterdam, who has ingeniously contrived to allow the air to escape, by opening a passage to it mechanically without the assistance of its elastic force. We shall give a description of a machine of this contrivance as constructed by Miller and Adie, instrument makers, Edinburgh. GB (Fig. 12.) is a section of the barrel of the pump, where T represents a tube connected with an orifice in the plate of the pump, and screwed to the barrel at S. C represents a frustum of a cone which is made to fit exactly an excavation in the piece HH. At R' this conical valve is connected to a solid rod R'R, having a loop at its lower extremity, which is made to embrace a horizontal bar in such a manner as to allow it a little play. When the cone is placed in its receptacle, a screw A is driven home from below, whose head is large enough to prevent the cone from being drawn out by pressing against the plate HH. By drawing the rod the cone can be raised a certain degree out of its cavity, as represented in (Fig. 13.) by which means a communication is opened between the interior of the receiver and the barrel. On pressing down the rod, on the other hand, the cone is restored to its place, and, being ground quite tight, it completely shuts up all communication. DD represents another cone, with an aperture about half an inch in diameter, in order to receive collars of leather which are represented in Figs. 12 and 14, as shaded. These collars occupy about two-thirds of

Fig. 12.

Fig. 13.

the channel, and are pierced through so as to embrace very lightly the rod R'R, on purpose to raise the cone C. This cone is received inverted into the piston LL, which is hollowed out into a conical form so as to fit it exactly. When so placed the rod PSE, which is hollow in order to contain R, is screwed into the cone at E. The rod PSE is provided with the flanch SS, to prevent the cone, when pressed down, from being driven from its cavity altogether. By depressing the rod the cone DD is at first lowered so as to open a communication between the part of the barrel which is above and that which is below the piston; and then the flanch SS, acting upon the piston LL, forces it down also. F and K are collars of leather contained in nuts which are screwed upon the plates MN, QK, V is a conical valve ground into an aperture in the plate MN; it is raised up by the pressure of the part V' of the piston, and is prevented from escaping by means of the contrivance represented in Fig. 12, which Mr. Adie has the merit of inventing. O is an aperture in the side of the barrel, fitted with an exterior screw, to which a tube may be attached for the purpose of condensing air. Having thus explained the parts of the pump, let us now attend to the manner in which it operates. On raising the rod G (which is done precisely in the same manner as in Hawksbee's pump,) the collars of leather DD, which closely embrace the rod RR', raise it, and consequently lift the cone C from its cavity, so as to allow the air confined in the tube T and the receiver to expand itself into the lower part of the barrel. The cone D is also raised to fill its cavity and shut up all communication between the upper and lower part of the barrel. In this manner the air contained in the part of the barrel above the piston is condensed, and is driven through the valve V, which is acted upon by the elasticity of the air, and completely raised by the action of V' against it. On depressing the piston rod, the valve V' falls back into its former place, and prevents the air from re-entering into the barrel: by continuing the descent of the rod, the cone C is also replaced in its socket, and thus prevents the air contained in the lower part of the barrel from rushing back into the receiver; the cone D is now displaced, however, and opens a passage by which this air can ascend so as to occupy the upper part of the barrel. On raising the piston a second time, the same movements take place, by which means another portion of air is expelled through the passage V. It is obvious that this machine may also serve for condensing air into a vessel connected by a tube to the orifice O, by allowing the orifice S to communicate with the atmosphere, or the gas which it may be required to condense.

Pneuma-
tics.

Fig. 12.

The experiments of Boyle not only prepared the way for these improvements, but also suggested a method by which the operator might always judge of the degree of exhaustion which he had obtained. We have already seen how, by introducing a common barometer beneath the receiver, he was enabled to verify the theory of Torricelli; it only remained, therefore, that the law which connected the density of the air inclosed in the receiver, and the altitude of the barometer, should be discovered in order to render the indications of the one a criterion of the other. Mr. Boyle, whose genius was more successful in detecting the chemical than the mechanical properties of air, appears to have overlooked this subject; at least from his writings there is no evidence that he ever attempted it.

The honour of this discovery has been usually given

Method of
estimating,
by the ba-
rometrical
gage, the
degree of
exhaustion
produced.

to Mariotte, whose method of inquiry was as follows :—
Having taken a bent tube, (Fig. 15, Plate CCCCLXIV.)
hermetically sealed at the extremity of the shorter branch,
but open at the extremity of the longer, which was
about six feet in length, he attached to it a wooden
frame and support ABC. The frame was formed into
a scale of inches, which, as the bore of the cylinder
was of uniform diameter, indicated equal volumes.

Having poured mercury into the longer branch, it
rose to a certain height in the other, which was observed. The air contained in the shorter branch was
now compressed by the weight of the external air, as
shown by the barometer at the time, and also by the
excess of the mercury in the longer branch above that
in the shorter. Let V be the column which the air occupied, h being the height of the barometer in inches,
and δ the difference of level at which the mercury stood
in the two branches also in inches; then is $h+\delta$ the
force by which the air was compressed. After these
observations were made, an additional portion of mercury was introduced; and the volume occupied by the
air was again observed, as also the difference of level at
which the mercury stood. Suppose the former were
V′, and the latter δ', then the law which Mariotte found
to obtain was that $h + \delta' : V :: h + \delta : V'$, or that the
compressive force varied inversely as the spaces which
the included air occupied. But as the space occupied
by the air also varies inversely as its density, the compressing force is always proportional to the density of
the air which it compresses.

From the manner in which the experiment was made,
it will be seen hereafter, that although the observations might favour this general law, they could not exactly confirm it, at least beyond a certain range; for
the elasticity of air has been found to be greatly affected by the presence of vapour, a circumstance which
was then unknown, and consequently not guarded
against. The law of Mariotte was employed to determine the degree of rarefaction which was produced in
the air-pump, by connecting with the orifice O a tube
OE, communicating with the vessel S, which was cemented to a cylindrical tube F, made of glass. (See
Hawksbee's pump.) The lower extremity of this tube
was immersed in the vessel M containing mercury. Before the pump is worked, as the density of the air
contained in the tube F is the same as that of the external air, the mercury remains at the same level within
and without the tube. On placing the receiver over
the orifice, and exhausting a portion of the included
air, its density and its elasticity become less: accordingly, the pressure of the external air causes a portion
of the mercury to ascend into the tube. Suppose that,
after the pump has been worked for a short time, the
mercury stands at a height of p inches above its level
in the cistern; then, if the barometer stands at the
height of h inches, the included air is compressed by a
force of $h - p$ inches.

And, if unity be assumed to express the density of
the external air, as

$$h : h - p :: 1 : \frac{h - p}{p},$$

$\frac{h - p}{p}$ will express the degree of rarefaction which
has been obtained.

This discovery of Mariotte was extended by the learned Cotes, who proved, in his *Harmon. Mens.* that the
density of the atmosphere, at uniform distances from

Pneuma-
tics.

PLATE
CCCCLXV.
Fig. 1.

Cotes's dis-
covery.

the earth's surface, diminishes in geometrical progression.

Let LAB, (Plate CCCCLXV. Fig. 1,) represent a
column of air whose base, AB, rests upon the earth's
surface, and let it be divided into strata of uniform
thickness, by the lines CD, EF, GH, which are to be
taken so that the density of the air in each stratum
may be equable. Let the densities of the several strata
be represented by δ, δ', δ'', &c. &c. and the weight of
the air by which they are pressed by W, W′, W″.

Then, from the experiment of Mariotte, it is known
that

$$W : W' : \delta , \delta'$$
$$\text{and } W' : W'' : \delta' : \delta, \&c.$$

But the weights of equal columns of matter are in
proportion to their densities.

Hence δ, δ' : weight of stratum CB : weight of stratum FD.

$$\text{or, } \delta : \delta' :: W - W' : W' - W'',$$
$$\text{wherefore } W : W' : W - W' : W' - W'',$$
$$\text{and } W' : W'' :: W' - W'' : W'' - W'''.$$

By alternation and composition,

$$W : W' : W' :: W'' : W'' : W''', \&c.$$

Now, $W : W' :: \delta : \delta$, and $W' : W'' :: \delta' : \delta''$

Hence $\delta : \delta' :: \delta'' : \delta'''$, &c. Q. E. D.

Now it has been ascertained, by the experiments of
Perier upon the Puy de Dome, that, by ascending
about 3000 feet, the barometer fell from 28 to 24.7
inches. The density, consequently, at the earth's surface, is to the density at this height in the ratio of 28 to
24.7. By taking 12 terms, in a decreasing geometrical
progression with 28 and 24.7, the least will be the height
at which the barometer should stand at an elevation
of 36,000, or nearly seven miles. To find this, we know,
from the principles of geometrical progression, that

the least term, or $a = \dfrac{l}{r(n-1)} = \left(\dfrac{28}{\frac{28}{24.7}}\right) 11 = 3.972$,

or 4 inches. At this height, therefore, the density is
only $\frac{1}{4}$ of what it is at the earth. From this fact the
following table of the atmospheric density at different
elevations is easily found.

Altitude in miles.	Corresponding density.
0	1
7	$\frac{1}{4}$
14	$\frac{1}{16}$
21	$\frac{1}{64}$
28	$\frac{1}{256}$
25	$\frac{1}{1024}$
42	$\frac{1}{4096}$
49	$\frac{1}{16384}$
56	$\frac{1}{65536}$

From this it would appear, that even at an infinite
height, the density of the atmosphere, though small,
does not become nothing. This curious circumstance
was first remarked by Dr. Brook Taylor, who thought
it so improbable, that he was inclined to believe, that
when the air became highly rarefied, its density decreased in a much higher proportion than the compressive force; which would have the effect of circumscrib-

Pneumatics.

On the density of the atmosphere.

ing the whole within narrower limits. Were the density of the air to be concluded from the principles laid down by Cotes, so great as sensibly to disturb the motion of the planets, it would be necessary to have recourse to such an hypothesis.

This, however, is by no means the case. The following remarks have been made on this subject by an ingenious philosopher : " I know not for what reason mathematicians have been afraid to admit the infinitude of the atmosphere of the earth, whether they thought it would bear hard upon the Newtonian doctrine of a void, or impede the planetary motions. But neither the one nor the other of these consequences is to be apprehended ; for neither the phenomena of nature, nor the principles of the Newtonian philosophy, require that there should be any where a chasm in the universe, or that the whole material world should be actually circumscribed within any finite space. A large proportion of interspersed vacuity is sufficient for all purposes." The air, even at a comparatively small elevation, becomes exceedingly rare, and could not produce a sensible resistance upon the motions of a planet after very many ages. The table annexed, and which was calculated by Bishop Horsley, who made the observations quoted above, will show this distinctly.

Height in Miles.	Volume.	Height in Semi-diameters.	Volume.
0.0.0	1	1	3069^{50}
40	3069	1.5	3069^{60}
80.8	3069^2	$2.\frac{1}{3}$	3069^{70}
122.6	3069^3	4	3069^{80}
165.0	3069^4	9	3069^{90}
208.5	3069^5	49	3069^{95}
252.1	3069^6	62	$3069^{98.36}$
298.2	3069^7	&c.	&c.
344.5	3069^8		
391.9	3069^9		
440.3	3069^{10}		
489.7	3069^{11}		
540.6	3069^{12}		
990.6	3069^{13}		
1698.1	3069^{14}		
2641.7	3069^{15}		

PLATE CCCCLXV. Fig. 2.

In order to illustrate the manner in which the density of the atmosphere diminishes, as we recede from the earth's surface, let CD, Fig. 2. Plate CCCCLXV. be a curve so connected with the abscissa AB, that the ordinates CA, FE, which are removed from each other by any common distance AE, are in geometrical progression.

Then if CA be taken to represent the density of the surface of the earth, and one-fourth CA the density at L, distant seven miles from A, the ordinate at any other point whatever will represent the density at that point. This curve has received from mathematicians the name of the Logarithmic Curve, because the abscissæ are the logarithms of the ordinates ; and it will be necessary to investigate a few of its properties in order to understand the application which has been made of Cotes' discovery to the measurement of heights by the barometer.

Proposition I. If any three ordinates be drawn to the curve which are equidistant, the intercepted areas are to each other in the same ratio as the middle ordinate is to either of the extreme ordinates. Let DF, FE, Plate CCCCLXV. Fig. 3. be each divided into any number of small portions, each equal to D*m* or F*n*.

Fig. 3.

Then if A, B, C, D, be the ordinates drawn from those points which are situated between D, F, and A', B', C', be the ordinates drawn from the corresponding points between FE: it follows that the space HDKF = (A + B + C + D + &c.) D*m*.
And the space KFEL=A'+B'+C'+B'+, &c.) FN.

But from the nature of the curve
DH : KF : A : A'': B : B'', &c.
And by Euclid 12th Prop. Book V.
DH:KF : A + B + C +, &c. : A' + B' + C' +, &c.
that is, in the same ratio as the space HDFK to the space KFLE.

Cor. HD : KF : : space HDC : space KFC. For KF : LE : : space KE : space LB. Therefore by equidistant ordinates, the area is divided into spaces in geometrical proportion.
Hence HF : KE or HD : KF : space HDC : space KFC.

Proposition 2. Let the tangent BC, Fig. 4. Plate CCCCLXV. be drawn to any point of the log. curve B, then is the area of the whole curve = BA . AC.

PLATE CCCCLXV. Fig. 4.

For let the abscissa be divided into very small equal parts, from which ordinates are drawn to the curve. Let AE be one of these. Then calling the ordinates A, B, C, D, and the area will be (A+B+C+D+, &c.) AE.

But $A+B+C+D+, \&c. = \dfrac{A}{1-B} = \dfrac{A^2}{A-B} = \dfrac{AB^2}{Bo}$,

from the principles of geometrical progression.

Hence the area is $\dfrac{AB^2.AE}{BO}$. But AE : BO : AC :

AB. Wherefore $\dfrac{AB^2 . AC}{BA} = AB . AC$.

Cor. 1. The subtangent AC is a constant quantity. For, by the proposition, the area FG *nm* = FG . GH. But B *nm* A : F *nm* G : BA : FG. Hence BA × AC : FG × GH : BA : FG, or AC=GH.

Cor. 2. The area, intercepted between any two ordinates, is equal to the rectangle contained by their difference and the subtangent.

PROP. III. The distances between two equal ordinates in two or more logarithmic curves are in the same ratio as the subtangents of these curves.

Because the ordinates AB, ED (Fig. 5. Plate CCCCLXV.) are equal to A'B', E'D' respectively, it follows that the area ABED is to the area A' B' E' D', in the ratio of CB to C'B'. Let B'D' be supposed to be divided into any number of parts, all equal to B' *m'*, and let BD be divided into the same number of equal parts, whereof B *m* is one. Then, because the same number of means is inscribed between the equal extremes AB, ED : A'B', E'D', in both cases, it follows that the means are themselves equal. Now, as *m'* B' is very small, the area A' *m'* = *m'* B' . B'A' ; for the same reason, *m* A = *m* B . BA, but as AB=A'B', A *m* : A' *m'* : : B *m* : B' *m'*. In like manner, the corresponding portion of the two areas can be proved to be to each other as their bases, that is, as *m* D : *m'*D'.

Fig. 5.

Wherefore, the area AD : area A'D' :: BD : B'D', And, consequently, BD : B'D' :: CD : C'B'.

Cor. 1. BD=Log. $\dfrac{AB}{DE}$, in that system whose subtangent is CB ; and B'D'=Log. $\dfrac{A'B'}{D'E'}$, in the system whose

4

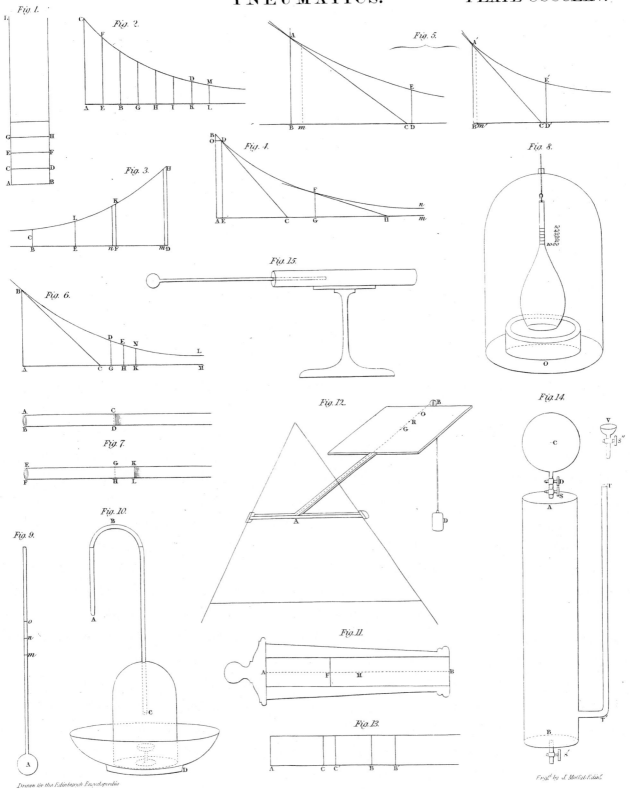

Pneuma-
tics.

Halley's
formula.
PLATE
CCCCLXV.
Fig. 6.

subtangent is C'B'. But as $\frac{AB}{DE} = \frac{B'A'}{D'E'}$, it follows that the logarithms of the same number for different systems of logarithms, are in the same ratio as the subtangents of their respective systems. The two most remarkable logarithmic systems are the Naperian and Briggian. In the former the subtangent is unity, and in the latter it is 0.43429448.

Let BL (Fig. 6. Plate CCCCLXV.) be the curve whose ordinates represent the atmospheric densities at the several distances from the earth's surface A, and which is, therefore, called the atmospheric logarithmic. Then let equal spaces GH, HK, be taken, within which the density is equable. It follows, since DG is the density, and GH the measure of the volume, that

DG . GH=weight of air contained in the space GH.

In like manner, EH . HK=weight of air contained in the space HK.

Hence the area of the curve BLMA represents the weight of the whole column ; but as BA . AC is equal to the area, it also is a measure of the weight of the atmospheric column. If, therefore, the atmosphere were of a uniform density throughout, its height must be equal to the subtangent AC, that its pressure may be the same with that which it possesses as at present constituted. Now, as from hydrostatical principles it is known that the lengths of two columns of fluids, whose densities are uniform, and which maintain each other in equilibrio, must be inversely proportional to their densities ; we can ascertain by the altitude of the barometrical column, and the specific gravities of mercury and air, the length of the atmospherical subtangent. For if 30 inches be assumed as the mean height of the mercurial column, which can be maintained by the atmospherical pressure, it has been found, by a method to be pointed out hereafter, that .001306 is the specific gravity of air, that of mercury being 13.6 ; and the length of the subtangent will be found thus,

.001306 : 13.6 :: 30 : 312692.1 inches = 4342.945 fathoms, or 5 miles — 342.325 feet.

The length of the subtangent having been thus determined, Halley, from the properties which are demonstrated in the preceding paragraphs, deduced a formula for finding the difference of level between two stations, by observing the height of the barometer at each of them. For if BDL be the atmospherical logarithmic, and BA . DG be in the same ratio as the altitude of the barometers at the two stations, AG will be the height which it is required to determine. But AG = Log. $\frac{DG}{BA}$, in a system whose subtangent has been found to be 4342.945 fathoms. Now, Log. $\frac{DG}{BA}$ in Briggs' system, is to this logarithm as .43429348 : 4342.945, or as

1 : 10000.

Hence the height required is to the common logarithm of $\frac{DG}{BA}$: 10000 : 1, and is therefore found by the formula H = 10.000 (Log. DG — Log. B'A) ; which was first employed by Halley in determining the height of Snowdon ; but, upon comparing the results obtained by means of it with those which were derived by trigonometrical measurement, it was found to be imperfect.

Pneuma-
tics.
De Luc's
formula.

The next individual who successfully directed his attention to this subject was De Luc, whose discovery we shall proceed to unfold. Previous to his inquiries, measurements by means of the barometer were made, by the formula delivered in the last paragraph, without taking into consideration the temperature of the atmosphere. Reflecting, however, that the temperature affects the density, and of consequence the elasticity of air, he was induced to attend to it while making his observations. The results were found to depend so much upon this cause, whose agency had not hitherto been appreciated, that he found himself under the necessity of introducing a correction depending upon it into the formula. He found, that when the temperature of the heights to which he ascended among the mountains in the neighbourhood of Geneva was uniform, his thermometer standing at $16\frac{3}{4}°$ of Reaumur, the difference between the tabular logarithms of the barometrical altitudes at the two stations, when multiplied by 10.000, gave him the elevation in Paris toises. But when the temperatures at the two stations differed from each other, he found that, by taking a mean between them, and calling its difference from $16\frac{3}{4}°$ n, the height would be given also in Paris toises by the formula

$$10.000 \left(L \pm \frac{n}{215} L\right).$$

When L marks the difference between the logarithms of the barometrical altitudes at the two stations, the upper sign being employed when the mean is greater than $16\frac{3}{4}°$, and the lower when it is less. That we may possess a clearer idea of these results, we shall reduce them to English measures. The temperature at which water boils is variable, and depends upon the intensity of the atmospherical pressure to which it is submitted. When it is heated to such a degree that the elastic power of vapour is equal to the superincumbent pressure, it boils. Let the temperature of water, when it boils under a pressure of 30 inches of mercury, be 180° above that of freezing, which is the notation of Fahrenheit's scale as used in this country, then, from the experiments of Dalton, we learn that

Log. F_t = 1.477123 — 0.0153741955 t — 0.000067427352 t^2 + 0.0000000033 t^3.

On the boiling point under different pressures.

Where F expresses the elasticity of vapour at t degrees below 212°. This formula enables us to find the temperature, according to Fahrenheit's scale, at which water will boil under any given pressure. For as F is the elasticity of vapour at the temperature 212° — t°.

Conversely, 212° — t° is the boiling point when the superincumbent pressure is F.

It is obvious from the nature of the formula, that as F diminishes t increases. Hence, in high stations and elevated countries, the temperature at which water boils is less than in valleys and low situations. Accordingly we find, that the boiling point was fixed upon the thermometers employed by De Luc when the atmospheric pressure was 27 French inches, or 28.7739 English inches. By substituting this quantity for F_t in the formula given above, and deducing from it t, we can obtain the temperature on Fahrenheit's scale, which corresponds to the boiling point in De Luc's

4 P

Pneumatics.

thermometer. For this purpose, let the formula referred to be put under the form

$$\text{Log } F_t = 1.477123 + a\,t + b\,t^2 + c\,t^3,$$

or making Log. $F_t - 1.477123 \quad \delta$,

$$\delta = a\,t + b\,t^2 + c\,t^3.$$

Then, as an approximation of t, we have $t = \dfrac{\delta}{a}$, and substituting this in the equation, omitting the last term

$$\delta = \left(a + \frac{\delta\,b}{a}\right) . t \text{ and } t = \frac{\delta}{a + \dfrac{\delta\,b}{a}}.$$

Substituting again this expression, we find

$$\delta = \frac{\delta}{1 + \dfrac{\delta\,b}{a^2}} + \left(b + \frac{c\,\delta}{a}\right) t^2,$$

and

$$t = \delta \sqrt{\frac{b}{(a^2 + b\,\delta)\left(b + \dfrac{c}{a}\,\delta\right)}}.$$

From this equation t is found $= 1.178064$; and the boiling point on De Luc's scale corresponds to 210.822 on Fahrenheit's.

De Luc's formula reduced to English measure.

The graduation of De Luc's thermometer was according to the method of Reaumur. Hence, 178.822 of Fahrenheit's $= 80^0$ of De Luc's, and $16\frac{3}{4}°$ of the latter $= 69°.41$ of the former; at this temperature, therefore, our author found the subtangent of the atmospheric logarithm equal to the subtangent of Briggs' logarithm in Paris toises.

The formula $10.000 \left(L \pm \dfrac{n\,L}{215}\right)$ becomes, then, according to Fahrenheit's scale, $10.000 \left(L \pm \dfrac{n \cdot 80 \cdot L}{215 \times 178.822}\right)$ The subtangent, consequently, for any other temperature,

$$\text{is} = B \pm \frac{n\,B}{480.6}.$$

when B is the subtangent of Briggs' system, and n the number of degrees which the mean temperature of the atmospheric column is above or below 69°.41.

The French toise bears to the English fathom the ratio of 1.0657 : 1. The subtangent therefore expressed in English fathoms $= B \left(1 \pm \dfrac{n}{480\cdot6}\right) \times 1\cdot0657$.

From this expression, let us now find at what temperature the atmospherical subtangent will be equal to the subtangent of Briggs' system, considered as English fathoms. For this purpose, we have to find n B $\left(1 \pm \dfrac{n}{480\cdot6}\right) \times 1\cdot0657 = B$. Hence $n = -29°.64$. and $69.41 - 29.64 = 39°.77$.

At the temperature of $39°\ 77'$ Fahrenheit; the difference between the tabular logarithms of the barometrical altitudes at the two stations, will, when multiplied by 10.000, be equal to their difference of level.

Let $B \left(1 \pm \dfrac{n}{480.6}\right) \times 1\cdot0657 = B \left(1 \pm \dfrac{n'}{480.6}\right)$.

Then $.0657 = \dfrac{n'-n}{480.6}$ or $n'-n = 29.64$. and $n' = 29°\ 64 + n$.

Hence $B \left(1 \pm \dfrac{n'}{480.6}\right)$ is the expression for the subtangent of the atmospherical logarithm, in English

fath. when n' is the difference between the mean temperature and 39.77, and De Luc's formula for finding the height of the barometer is $10.000 \left(z \pm \dfrac{n'\,L}{480.6}\right)$.

Pneumatics.

Sir George Shuckburgh's observations.

The work in which this correction was given to the world attracted general admiration, and induced Sir George Shuckburgh, an English gentleman, when setting out for his travels upon the Continent, to provide himself with proper apparatus, that he might verify the discoveries of De Luc in the very place where they were made. An account of his proceedings is given by himself in vol. lxvii. of the *Philosophical Transactions*. To ascertain the heights trigonometrically, he carried along with him an equatorial instrument, the circles of which were about seven inches diameter, made by Ramsden, a fifty feet steel chain, and three three-feet rods, two of deal, and one of brass, in order to examine and correct the chain; these last made by Boradelli at Paris. The barometers he employed were also made by Ramsden, the specific gravity of the mercury at the temperature of 68°, being 13.61, the diameter of the base of the tube being 0.20 inches, and that of the reservoir 1.5 inches. In taking the temperatures of the thermometers, he availed himself of a little bell-tent. De Luc, on the other hand, in his experiments, placed his thermometers directly in the sun's rays, conceiving that, as only one half of the instrument was in this case exposed to the solar heat, while it shaded the other, the mercury would indicate the mean temperature. After a comparison of the two methods, Sir George found that they gave nearly the same results.

The first object of his inquiry was to determine the height of Mont Saleve, one of the Alps, situated about two leagues south of Geneva. He found it by a very accurate trigonometrical measurement 2833.41 English feet. Having ascertained this, he next proceeded to take the barometrical altitude at the top and bottom. This was taken by two observers at intervals of three quarters of an hour, that the instruments might acquire the true temperature of the air.

The following is a specimen of his method of calculation.

Observations at the Summit of the Mountain.

	Barometer 25.7120 inch.	Ther. Attached.	Ther. Detached.
Correct for } Ex. of ☿ }	162	78.°0	65°.0
Barom. at top 25.6958	Log. 4098621		
Below . 28.3911	Log. 4532434		

          433.813 Height in Fathoms.

Correct for 29.°7 of excess above 39.7=28.728

          462.541
          6

Height in feet = 2775.246

Observations Below.

	Barometer 28.3990 inch.	Th. Attached.	Th. Detached.
Correct for Exp. } of ☿ }	39	72°.1	73°.9
	28.3951		65°

          69 4 mean.
          39.7
          + 29.7

The corrections for the expansion of the mercury, and the excess of the mean temperature above 39.7 were taken from tables calculated by Dr. Horsley in the *Philosophical Transactions*.

Pneuma-
tics.

Compari-
son be-
tween the
trigono-
metrical and
barometri-
cal results.

The following Table presents a comparative view of the accuracy of the barometrical and trigonometrical methods of measurement; and if the results obtained by the latter be considered as exact, it points out to us the imperfections of De Luc's theory.

Place of Observation.	HEIGHT.		Error as a Fraction of the whole.
	True Height.	Barometrical Height.	
Mont Saleve	2831.3	2775.2	.0198
		2763.2	.0240
		2759.4	.0254
The Mole	4211.3	4132.7	.0187
		4140.1	.0169
		4115.1	.0228
		4111.9	.0235
		4113.7	.0231
		4104.9	.0252
Mont Saleve	2828.9	2755.6	.0259
		2754.9	.0262
		2748.9	.0282
		2752.8	.0269

The data from which these heights were calculated, are as follows.

Place of Observation.	Barometer.		Ther. Attached.		Ther. Detached.	
	Above.	Below.	Above.	Below.	Above.	Below.
Mont Saleve	25 7120	28.3990	78°.	72°.1	65°.	73°.9
	25.7025	28.3940	73.4	71.6	64.	73.
	25.6900	28.3935	69.7	71.1	62.	72.5
Mole.	24.1437	28.1295	57	60.4	54.8	61.9
	24.1420	28.1300	56.9	60.4	56.	61.8
	24.1676	28.1320	56.	60.9	56.	63.
	24.1780	28.1360	57.2	61.8	56.	63.9
	24.1840	28.1350	59.6	62.4	57.	64.
	24.1900	28.1310	61.	62.6	57.	63.6
Mont Saleve	25 6533	28 4040	58.	58 1	56.2	58.8
	25.6550	28.4040	56.2	58.5	57.	60.8
	25.6620	28.4040	56.2	59.3	57.2	62.
	25.6600	28.4040	56.4	59.3	57.4	62.2

Sir G. Shuck-
burgh's
improve-
ment of De
Luc's for-
formula.

To remedy this defect in the formula of De Luc was the next object to which Sir George directed his attention. For this purpose he instituted a series of manometrical experiments. The manometer, an instrument for determining the expansibility of air by heat, consists of a straight tube, whose bore is from $\frac{1}{15}$th to $\frac{2}{15}$th of an inch, and whose length varies from four to eight feet. One end of it is left open, and upon the other is blown a bulb. The tube must be graduated, so that the cylindric space between any two of the divisions may be a certain aliquot part of the capacity of the bulb. This is done by weighing the instrument when empty, and again weighing it after the bulb has been filled with a fluid whose specific gravity is known. The difference of weight shows the weight of the fluid which has been introduced, and consequently the space occupied by it, or the capacity of the bulb. By inserting a small additional portion of fluid so as to fill the tube to a certain height, and weighing the instrument in this state, the weight of the fluid which has been added is ascertained, and consequently the volume which it occupies. If the tube be truly cylindrical, by dividing the distance between the surface of the fluid and the bulb into equal parts

it will be graduated into parts of equal capacity, whose relation to the capacity of the manometer is known.

Pneuma-
tics.

The instrument is now emptied of the fluid, whose place is occupied by the air which is to be submitted to experiment. By applying heat to the bulb, the internal air may be rarefied to any degree required. Having reduced the density of the air as much as may be deemed necessary, let the open end of the tube be immersed in a basin of mercury, and as the bulb cools, a portion of the mercury will be forced up into the tube. Let the instrument now be held in a vertical position, having the bulb undermost, then p being the height of the barometer at the time, and h the length of the small column of mercury contained in the tube, $p+h$ will be the pressure upon the air inclosed in the manometer. Let the volume into which it is compressed by this force, when at a certain temperature be marked, then by applying different degrees of heat, the law, according to which the air expands, may be learned.

By an instrument of this kind, Sir George derived the following results. The pressure was $30\frac{1}{2}$ inches, and the volume of the inclosed air at the temperature of freezing was 1000.

No. of degrees the air was heated.	Expansion for 1 degree.	No. of degrees the air was heated.	Expansion for 1 degree.
22°	2.38	14°.6	2.30
28	2.50	32.2	2.43
21.5	2.34	49.7	2.48
30.1	2.44	51.1	2.51
22.6	2.44	32.2	2.43
Mean Expan.	2.42	Mean Expan.	2.44

From this table it appears that the air, at least between the temperatures of 32° and 83°, expands uniformly. The experiments were repeated with air subjected to various pressures from $23\frac{3}{4}$ to 40 inches, and the same remark was applicable, for whatever variations were observable, Sir George was inclined to impute rather to incorrectness in the observation than to a change in the expansibility.

It remains now to point out the manner in which this experimental inquiry can be employed in improving the formula.

Suppose AD, EL, Plate CCCCLXV. Fig. 7. to PLATE CCCCLXV. Fig. 7. be sections of two tubes in every respect alike, and containing equal quantities of atmospheric air, separated from the external air by two thin films of mercury CD, GH. It is obvious, that while under the same pressure and of the same temperature, the included air will in both tubes be of the same density, and will occupy equal spaces, AD, EH. Assume this pressure to be equivalent to that of 30 inches of mercury, and let it be represented by p; also let the common temperature be 32°. Now suppose one of the tubes, EH for instance, to be removed to a higher station where the atmospheric pressure is p' and the temperature $t°$. The density of the air contained in EL is affected by two causes, viz. a change of pressure and of temperature. Let v represent the original volume which it occupied, and then, agreeably to the expansive power of air, the volume which it is made to occupy by the increased heat, the pressure remaining the same, will be

$$v\,(1 + \overline{t-32}\,.\,m),$$

where m is .00243.

But when air of the same temperature is exposed to different pressures, the densities are proportional to the pressures.

Hence $p:p'=v(1+\overline{t-32}.m):v'$,

and the volume which the air occupies under the pressure p', and at the temperature t' or $v'=\dfrac{p'}{p}v$ $(1+\overline{t-32}.m)$.

From this equation, there results, $p'=\dfrac{p\,v'}{v(1+\overline{t-32}.m)}$.

Now as v is the volume which the air occupied when at the lower station, and v' is the volume which it now occupies under the pressure p', and when of the temperature $t°$,

$\dfrac{v'}{v}$ will be the density under these circumstances. Let this be denoted by y, the height to which the tube has been raised being x, then the atmospheric pressure at any height x will be $p'=\dfrac{p\,y}{1+\overline{t-32}.m}$. (A.)

It is obvious that p' will also be expressed by $p-y\,dx$, provided the gravitation of all the strata of the aerial column be considered as equal, which is the case in moderate heights. From this we derive the equation,

$$p-\int y\,dx=\frac{p.y}{1+(t-32)m},$$

and, taking the fluxions $-y\,dx=\dfrac{p.dy}{1+(t-32)m}$.

Hence $-\dfrac{dy}{y}=\dfrac{dx}{p(1+\overline{t-32}m)}$, and taking the fluents

$$-{}^{*}\log.y=\frac{dx}{p(1+(t-32)m)}+c.$$

When x is nothing, let y become $y'=$ the density at the lower station; then Log. $y'=c$.

Hence $\log.y'-\log.y=\log.\dfrac{y'}{y}=\dfrac{x}{p(1+\overline{t-32}.m)}$

But, according to equation (A), as t is supposed to be constant, being the mean temperature within the range of observation, $y\doteq p'$, that is, the atmospheric pressure as measured by the barometrical altitude. Let then the corrected height of the barometer, at the lower and upper stations be expressed by b and β, then

$\log.b-\log.\beta=\dfrac{x}{p(1+\overline{t-32}.m}$, and assuming L to

denote $\log.b-\log.\beta$,

$x=p(\mathrm{L}+\overline{t-32}.m\mathrm{L})$. Now, according to De Luc's formula,

$x=10{,}000\left(\dfrac{\mathrm{L}+t-\overline{39.77}.\mathrm{L}}{480.6}\right)$: at 32° the value of the subtangent, consequently, according to De Luc, is

$10{,}000.\mathrm{B}\left(\dfrac{1-7.77}{480.6}\right)$, which is $=p$; B being the subtangent of Briggs' system of logarithms. Or, if L be employed to denote Log. $b-$ Log. β, being the logarithms of b and β according to Briggs' system.

$10{,}000\left(\dfrac{1-7.77}{480.6}\right)=p$; and hence we derive

$10{,}000\left(\mathrm{L}+\dfrac{t-\overline{39\ 77}.\mathrm{L}}{480.6}\right)=10000\,(\mathrm{L}+\overline{t-32}.m\,\mathrm{L})$ $\left(\dfrac{1-7.77}{480.6}\right)$.

From this equation the value of m may be found for De Luc's formula. For

$1+\dfrac{t°-39°.77}{480.6}=(1+\overline{t-32}\,m)\left(\dfrac{1-7.77}{480.6}\right)$, or

$1+\dfrac{t-32\,m}{480.6}-\dfrac{7.77}{480.6}=1+\overline{t-32}.m-\dfrac{7.77}{480.6}-\dfrac{t-32\,m}{480.6}\times 7.77.$

Hence $\dfrac{1}{480.6}=m\left(\dfrac{1-7.77}{480.6}\right)$, and

$m=\dfrac{1}{480.6-7.77}=\dfrac{1}{472.83}=.00212.$

We are now able to perceive the defect in De Luc's formula, and to apply a proper correction for it. The expansion of air for 1° of Fahrenheit has been found to be .00243 of its bulk at freezing, instead of .00212, an approximation, however, which reflects the highest credit upon the ingenuity and exactness with which De Luc had conducted his experiments. The formula then will assume the form $x=p(\mathrm{L}+\overline{t-32}\times .00243\,\mathrm{L})$, where p (or the value of the quantity which, multiplied into the subtangent of Briggs' system ought to produce the atmospherical subtangent in English fathoms) is indeterminate, and must be fixed by observation. For this purpose Sir George Shuckburgh employed his trigonometrical measurements.

From those which he made upon Mont Saleve, he obtained the following equations, where p is expressed in feet.

1. $2831.3=p\,($Log. $28.399\ -$Log. $\overline{25.712}\ (1-.00102\times 6)\ (1+37.4\times .00243)$
2. $2831.3=p\,($Log. $28.3940-$Log. $\overline{25.7025}\,(1-.00102\times 1.8)\,(1+36.1\times .00243)$
3. $2831.3=p\,($Log. $28.3935-$Log. $\overline{25.69002}\,(1-.00102\times 1.4)\,(1+39.9\times .00243)$

Here we have applied the correction for the expansion of the quicksilver in the barometers only to one of them, for, as it is the ratio of their heights which enters into the equations, it is apparent that to reduce the height of one of them to what it would be, were it of the same temperature with the other, is all that is necessary.

According to the observations made upon the Mole,

1. $4211.3=p\,($Log. $28.1295-$Log. $\overline{24.1437}\,(1+.00102\times 3.4)\,(1+26.3\times .00243)$
2. $4211.3=p\,($Log. $28.1300-$Log. $\overline{24.1420}\,(1+.00102\times 3.5)\,(1+26.9\times .00243)$
3. $4211.3=p\,($Log. $28.1320-$Log. $\overline{24.1670}\,(1+.00102\times 4\ 9)\,(1+27.5\times .00243)$
4. $4211.3=p\,($Log. $28.1360-$Log. $\overline{24.1780}\,(1+.00102\times 4.6)\,(1+28.\ \times .00243)$
5. $4211.3=p\,($Log. $28.1350-$Log. $\overline{24.1840}\,(1+.00102\times 2\ 8)\,(1+28.5\times .00243)$

* Note, by log. is meant the Naperian Logarithm, and by Log. the Briggian or common Logarithm.

By reducing these equations, they become,

$$2831.3 = p \times .04999937$$
$$2831.3 = p \times .06113086$$
$$2831.3 = p \times .04698980$$
$$4211.3 = p \times .06907461$$
$$4211.3 = p \times .06917736$$
$$4211.3 = p \times .06807858$$
$$4211.3 = p \times .06687522$$
$$4211.3 = p \times .06044915$$

$$\overline{29550.4 = 8\,p \times .49177495}$$

Hence $p = 60092.9$ feet $= 10015.5$ fathoms; and the formula as corrected by Shuckburgh is

$$x = 10015.5\ \mathrm{L}\ (1 + \overline{t - 32} \times .00243)$$

After correcting the formula in this manner, Sir George concludes his inquiry by finding at what temperature the logarithms of the barometrical altitudes at the upper and lower station would, when multiplied by 10,000 give the height in English fathoms. This is easily done; for, according to the corrected formula,

$$H = 10015.5\ (\mathrm{Log.}\ b - \mathrm{Log.}\ \beta)(1 + \overline{t-32} \times .00243).$$

which is by supposition equal to

$$10,000\ (\mathrm{Log.}\ b - \mathrm{Log.}\ \beta).$$

Hence $10015.5\,(1 + \overline{t - 32} \times .00243) = 10,000$ and

$$t - 32 = -\frac{155}{243} = -.63 .\ \text{and}\ t = 32 - .63 = 31° 27'.$$

The coincidence between this and the freezing point is so remarkable, that from the corrected formula Shuckburgh concludes, that at 32° the difference of the barometrical altitudes at the stations being multiplied by 10,000, will give the height in Eng. fathoms.

We have given in detail the improvements which had been made upon the method of taking altitudes by means of the barometer, before the science of hygrometry had made any progress. The effects produced by moisture upon the elasticity of air had not attracted the attention of philosophers until Mr. Nairne pointed it out in a paper communicated by him to the Royal Society. The pear-gauge of Smeaton was the instrument by which the elastic force of vapour was detected. The following is a description of this instrument, as given by the inventor.

"It consists of a bulb of glass, (Fig. 8. Plate CCCCLXV.) something in the shape of a pear, and sufficient to hold about half a pound of quicksilver. It is open at the one end, and at the other is a tube hermetically sealed. By the help of a nice pair of scales may be found what proportion of weight a column of quicksilver of a certain length, contained in the tube, bears to that which fills the whole instrument. By this means I was enabled to mark divisions upon the tube answering to $\frac{1}{1000}$th part of the whole capacity; which being about $\frac{1}{20}$th part of an inch, each may, by estimation, easily be subdivided into smaller parts. This gage, during the exhausting of the receiver, is suspended therein by a slip-wire. When the pump is worked, as much as shall be thought necessary, the gauge is pushed down till the open end is immerged in a cistern of quicksilver placed underneath; the air being thus let in, the quicksilver will be driven into the gauge till the air remaining in it becomes of the same density with the external, and as the air always takes the highest place, the tube being uppermost, the expansion will be determined by the number of divisions occupied by the air at the top."

Whilst comparing the indications of this instrument with those of the barometrical gauge, Mr. Nairne was

astonished to find by how much they differed from each other. The pump with which he operated was not capable, according to the barometrical gauge, of exhausting above 1000 times, and yet, according to the pear-gauge, the exhaustion must have been at least four times greater. To obviate this disparity, he resolved to see whether the fault might not be in the gauges, and for this purpose he provided himself with recently made glass tubes, which he filled with the greatest care. The anomaly being altogether inexplicable by him, he showed the experiment to the Hon. Henry Cavendish, Mr. Smeaton, and other Members of the Royal Society, at a time when the pear-gauge indicated an exhaustion some thousand times more complete than the barometrical gauge. On this occasion Mr. Cavendish pointed out to him the true cause of the phenomenon, by attributing it to the influence of vapour. His father, Lord Charles Cavendish, he stated, had found by some experiments, that water, whenever the pressure of the atmosphere upon it is diminished to a certain degree, is converted into vapour, and is as immediately converted into water on restoring the pressure. The degree of pressure varies according to the temperature of the water; when the temperature is 72° the water is converted into vapour under a pressure of $\frac{3}{4}$ inches of quicksilver, but when the temperature is only 41°, the pressure must be reduced to $\frac{1}{4}$th of an inch before the water passes off into vapour. Hence, at the temperature of 72°, when the pressure or elasticity of the air inclosed in the receiver is reduced below $\frac{3}{4}$ths of an inch of quicksilver, the moisture adhering to the different parts of the machine will be converted into vapour, and the united pressure of the vapour so formed, and of the air contained in the receiver, will affect the barometrical gauge. On re-admitting the air into the receiver, the mixture of air and aqueous vapour which filled the pear-gauge will be reduced in volume, but as the vapour of the supposed temperature cannot exist under the incased pressure, it will be converted into a film of water, so that the pear-gauge will only indicate the pressure of the atmospheric air which the receiver contained.

This explanation appeared satisfactory to Mr. Nairne, who, having taken precautions that as little moisture as possible might adhere to the machine, found that the indications of the two gauges were more alike. By introducing, on the other hand, moist substances into the receiver, the difference between them was found to be increased. This happened particularly in the case of moist leather, when the pear-gauge indicated 100,000. Having inclosed a quantity of sulphuric acid beneath the receiver, the barometrical gauge was found to indicate a rarefaction of 340, whereas the pear-gauge indicated only 240. This was a decisive proof that the elastic force of vapour occasioned the difference between the two gauges; for, owing to the strong affinity which this acid has for moisture, we may suppose that it almost completely dried the included air. When the air contained in the receiver was compressed into the pear-gauge, as the portion of moisture it contained was exceedingly small in comparison of the whole, it would still retain the gaseous form, and have its elastic force increased by the compression; so that, in this case, the pear-gauge would indicate a less degree of exhaustion than the barometer gauge, as was observed.

General Roy was about this time eagerly engaged in pneumatical researches. The two principal objects which he had in view were to ascertain the laws according to which air and mercury expanded. By several experiments, he found the former to be .00245 of its bulk, at 32°, and under a pressure of 30 inches of mercury. This result is only a mean of those which he obtained, and which were so irregular as scarcely to be comprehended under a general law. A tabular view of them was given by him in Vol. XLVII. of the *Philosophical Transactions*, and has been transferred by Cavallo into his *Elements of Natural Philosophy*, Vol. I. The following conclusions may be deduced from these manometrical experiments.

I. " 1000 equal parts of common air, loaded with two atmospheres and a half, being affected with a heat of 212°, expand 434 of those parts.

II. " 1000 equal parts of air pressed only with ⅖ths of an atmosphere, and suffering 212° of heat, expands nearly 484 of those parts. Also common air pressed with a single atmosphere has the same expansion with air of only ⅚ths of that density.

III. " The maximum expansion corresponds to that section of the scale between 52° and 72°."

IV. When the compressing force is small, as for instance, one-fifth of an atmospheric, the expansibility of air by heat is much diminished.

The unit of measure which he adopted was the volume at the temperature of zero on the scale of Fahrenheit. Consequently, if we suppose that the expansion is uniform, the mean expansion for a degree, taking the temperature at the volume of freezing as the standard of measure, is .00190 when the pressure is two and a half atmospheres. As under this great pressure the elasticity of vapour would have but little influence upon the experiment, we may conclude, that .00190 is the value of the expansion of dry air for 1° of Fahrenheit, as found by Roy. By reducing the number given for the expansion in the second conclusion after the same manner, the mean rate for each degree is .00228. Upon the third conclusion Gen. Roy makes the following observation, " whether this maximum of expansion of air compared with that of quicksilver, be owing to moisture or any thing else which is mixed with the former, which is brought into its greatest degree of action about the temperature of 57° of Fahrenheit must be left to the investigation of future experimenters. From the first and last conclusions he was led to infer, that the expansibility of air was a maximum under the pressure of thirty inches of mercury.

Inconsist-
ent with
Mariotte's
law.
PLATE
CCCCLXV.
Fig. 9.

This last deduction was completely at variance with the law which had been established by Mariotte. For let (Plate CCCCLXV. Fig. 9.) A be the manometer, and A n the volume of air which it contains at 32°, under a pressure P ; also let A o be the expanded volume which it occupies when the temperature is raised to (32 + t°.) Now, let us suppose that an additional pressure p is imposed upon the expanded air so as to reduce its volume to A n, the temperature being still (32 + t°.)

Then, according to Mariotte,

$$P + p : P = A o : A n.$$

Let it now be supposed, that the temperature descends from (32 + t°) to 32°, and that the volume being compressed by P + p is reduced to A m, then, by the same law, we have

$$P + p : P = n A : m A,$$

Wherefore A $o : n$ A = n A : m A, and by division,

O $n : n$ A = $n m : m$ A, that is the expansion of a portion of air under any pressure for any increase of temperature is always a proportional part of its volume at the temperature of 32°.

This proposition, which was in opposition to the experiments of Roy, has been completely confirmed by the observations of Mr. Dalton, who took precautions that the object of his inquiries should be air thoroughly dry. This was effected in the following manner : He took the bent tube ABC, (Plate CCCCLXV. Fig. 10.) with which the experiment was to be performed, and having first wiped it, and exposed it to a considerable heat, in order to free it from moisture, he placed the open end beneath the receiver C, which was inverted into a cistern of dry mercury over a portion of muriate of lime. After remaining in this position for a few days the desiccative was withdrawn, and the tube having been depressed among the mercury, a piece of finely polished glass was introduced among the mercury beneath its open extremity. On inverting the apparatus, the mercury inclosed in the tube fell to the lower part B, and prevented all communication between the dry inclosed air and the external. The receiver was then removed.

Mariotte's
law estab-
lished by
Dalton.
PLATE
CCCCLXV.
Fig. 10.

In his experiments upon air thus prepared, he found, that if V represented the volume under the pressure p, and V' the volume under the pressure $p + a$, that the equation

$$\frac{V}{V'} = \frac{p + a}{p} \text{ held universally.}$$

Still, however, it might be doubted whether the same law obtained with regard to air, the pressure upon which is considerably smaller than the atmospheric pressure, or whether the deviations from it observed by Roy might not exist. To decide this, Dalton employed the following process. Having taken a common barometrical tube of an uniform bore, which was graduated into equal parts, he filled it to a certain height with mercury, which he then boiled in order completely to exclude the air and moisture. The upper part of the tube was occupied by air which was rendered dry by means of muriate of lime. Having observed the number of divisions which the air possessed whilst it existed in its common state under the atmospheric pressure, as indicated by the barometer at the time, the open end of the tube was covered by a well polished plate of glass, and inverted into a cistern containing mercury. The air now ascended, and after several oscillations occupied the highest part of the tube.

Now, agreeably to the law of Mariotte, an expression can easily be found for the number of divisions which the air ought to occupy. For let h be the height of the barometer as observed, h' the height of the tube above the level of the mercury contained in the cistern, V, the volume occupied by the air when compressed by the atmosphere, and x the volume or number of divisions which it now occupies. Then the remainder of the tube, or $h' - x$, is filled with mercury, which serves in part as a counterpoise to the atmospheric pressure. The elasticity of the included air is the other part; but as this, by supposition, is inversely proportional to the space in which the air is contained, we have, in order to find it, the analogy,

$$x : V = h : \frac{h V}{x}.$$

Hence $h' - x + \frac{h V}{x} = h$ and by resolving the equation $x = \frac{h' - h \pm \sqrt{(h' - h)^2 + 4 h V}}{2}$.

The root with the upper sign is that which answers the conditions of the problem, as it is always positive ; for, as the lower sign gives the value of x negative, it would serve to indicate, that the air, instead of depressing, attracts the mercury above the height of the barometer at the time.

Now it was found that the air, in this attenuated state, while under the pressure, $h - h' + x$ gave always such a value of x as confirmed the truth of the principle upon which the construction of the equation rests. The results obtained by General Roy, therefore, which would appear to overturn it, must be accounted for by the influence of vapour, whose elasticity follows, within certain limits, a different law from that of pure air. For, by an accession of heat, so long as a portion of moisture remains, it is converted into vapour, whose tension appears to increase rapidly but irregularly; nor does it follow the law according to which air expands, until the whole has been evaporated.

Mr. Dalton also availed himself of the following method of verifying his results. Having provided a tube, sealed at one end, and whose bore was about one-twentieth of an inch in diameter, he divided it into parts of equal capacity, and introduced into it a small column of mercury, which inclosed a portion of air. The tube, although inverted on account of the smallness of its bore, does not allow the mercurial column to break so as to permit the air to get entrance. While in this state, accordingly, as the mercurial column is suspended, it descends until its weight, together with the diminished elasticity of the inclosed air, becomes equivalent to the upward pressure of the atmosphere. On reversing the tube, the mercurial column, together with the weight of the external air, both press upon the portion which is inclosed in the tube. Let a denote the number of inches contained in the length of the mercurial column, p the height of the barometer at the time, V the volume which is filled by the included air when the instrument is erect, and V' that which it occupies when dilated, the instrument having been reversed; then the equation, which he always found to obtain, is

$$\frac{V}{V'} = \frac{p-a}{p+a} \qquad (A)$$

This experiment may be somewhat modified by placing the tube in a horizontal position, and observing the number of divisions which are occupied by the air, which we may call v. When the instrument is in this position, it is obvious that, as the mercury exerts no pressure either way, the confined air will be of the same density as the common atmospheric air at the time; p, denoting the force, therefore, by which it is compressed, it will be found that

$$\frac{V}{v} = \frac{p}{p+a} \text{ and } \frac{V'}{v} = \frac{p}{p-a}.$$

An instrument of this kind may obviously be employed as a barometer. For, from the equations delivered in the last paragraph, we can easily deduce the following analogy:

$$V : V' = p - a : p + a,$$

By conversion $V' - V : V = 2a : p - a$, and
By composition $V' + V : V = 2p : p - a$. Wherefore
Ex æquali $V' - V : V' + V = a : p$.

Hence p, or the height of the barometer $= \dfrac{V' + V}{V' - V} \cdot a$.

where all the quantities are known.

The next subject in which Mr. Dalton occupied himself, after having fully confirmed the law of Mariotte, was an inquiry into the elasticity or tension of vapour, both while it existed by itself and in union with atmospheric air. Before, however, giving a view of his discoveries, connected with vapour, it may be necessary

Pneuma-
tics.

On the
elastic
force of
gunpowder
gas.

to advert to the nature of a compressible fluid, whose great elasticity, together with its application, forms as interesting an object of study almost as steam, and its subserviency to mechanics. It was known so early as the days of Roger Bacon that a mixture of five parts of powdered nitre, one of sulphur, and one of charcoal, composed a substance which yielded, on being heated, a very powerful gas. Its energy was so great, that it was soon applied to the purposes of war, and from this received the name of gunpowder. The first who appears to have attempted to measure the tension of this air was the ingenious and celebrated Benjamin Robins, engineer to the East India Company. In order to this, he inclosed a red hot iron within a receiver, placed upon the air-pump, and having exhausted it, a quantity of powder was allowed to fall upon the iron; after the explosion the mercurial gauge suddenly descended, and after a few oscillations it remained stationary below its former height. He was enabled to prove, in this manner, that the elasticity of the fluid was always in proportion to its density. Having taken a receiver containing about 520 cubic inches, and let fall upon the red-hot iron one-sixteenth of an ounce avoirdupois, the powder having been all fired, the mercury in the gauge subsided two inches exactly. He then heated the iron a second time, and having exhausted the receiver as before, two drams were let down at once, which caused the mercury to sink $3\frac{3}{4}$ inches. In this experiment a part of the powder, sufficient to have caused the mercury to subside one-fourth of an inch more, had fallen beside the iron without exploding.

He next determined the relation between the weight of the fluid and that of the powder which yields it. From the experiment which has been related, it appeared that $\frac{1}{16}$th of an oz. avoirdupois, or about 27 troy grains of powder, sunk the mercury in the gauge two inches, from this it follows that $\frac{15}{16}$th of an oz. or 410 troy grains, would have filled the receiver with air whose elasticity would have been equivalent to 30 inches of mercury. And as the receiver contained 520 cubic inches, it appears that 410 troy grains are capable of yielding this volume of gas under a pressure of 30 inches. He was of opinion, however, that the elasticity of the gas was increased about one-fifth by the excess of temperature in the receiver, and that the volume, consequently, which it would occupy at an ordinary temperature, would be 416 cubic inches. From this he inferred, that an ounce avoirdupois of powder yielded $443\frac{1}{11}$ cubic inches, and assuming its specific gravity to be the same as that of atmospheric air, the weight of this volume was found 135 grains, while it appeared that the weight of this fluid was $\frac{3}{10}$ths nearly of the quantity of powder. Since 17 drams avoirdupois of powder filled two cubic inches, he inferred that the ratio of the volume of powder to that of the gas produced from it was 1 to 244; and that, as condensed in the powder, its elastic force is 244 times that of common air.

To find the elasticity of this gas at the temperature of 212°, he employed a piece of a musket barrel, about six inches long, closed at one end, and having the other end drawn out conically, and terminated in an aperture about one-eighth of an inch in diameter. The cavity of the barrel contained 796 grains of water. The tube was heated to the extremity of red-heat, and immersed in a bucket of water, where it was kept until it had cooled. He found that the water which it took in at three different trials was 610, 595, and 600 grains; whence it appeared that the whole capacity of the tube was to the respective spaces occupied by the cool air as 796 to $194\frac{1}{3}$, taking a mean of the results. As atmospheric air and this fluid appear to be affected after the same manner by a change of temperature, the same increase of heat which raises the elasticity of the former from $194\frac{1}{3}$ to 796, will raise the latter in the same proportion; and as

On the ve-
locity with
which a
ball is pro-
pelled from
a piece of
artillery.

$194\frac{1}{3} : 796 = 244 : 999\frac{1}{3}$, this, or in round numbers, 1000, is the number of times that the air evolved from fired gunpowder exceeds the elasticity of common air.

These results he employed to investigate a rule, by which *a priori* the dimensions of any piece of artillery, the density of the ball, and the quantity of charge being given, the velocity of the ball might be known. In the solution of this problem he assumed the following principles: 1st, That the action of the powder upon the ball ceases as soon as it has got out of the piece; and 2d, That all the powder of the charge is fired, and converted into an elastic fluid before the bullet is sensibly moved from its place. Let the whole length of the piece, Plate CCCCLXV. Fig. 11. $AB = a$, the length of the space in which the charge is contained $AF = b$, the diameter of the ball c, and its specific gravity $= n$; also let the distance of any point in FB from F be called x. When the ball has advanced to M, the space which the elastic fluid occupies is $b + x$, and its elasticity is $\dfrac{b}{b+x}$, that which it possessed on being fired being represented by unity; or is $\dfrac{1000\, b}{b+x}$ if the elasticity of common air be that referred to. But the elasticity of air is equivalent to the weight of a column of water 33 feet high. Hence $\dfrac{33 \times 1000\, b}{b+x}$ is proportional to the moving force by which the ball is impelled at any point M.

PLATE
CCCCXLV.
Fig. 11.

But the weight of the spherical ball is proportional to $\frac{2}{3}\, nc$; wherefore the accelerative force is $= \dfrac{33 + 1000\, b}{b + x} \div \frac{2}{3}\, nc$. Now, from the principles of dynamics, it is known that if v be the velocity, f the accelerative force, and x the space

$$v \cdot dv = f \cdot dx.$$

Hence, in the present case, $v\, dv = \dfrac{33 \times 1000\, b}{\frac{2}{3} \cdot nc} \cdot \dfrac{dx}{x+b}$,

and $\dfrac{v^2}{2} = \dfrac{33 \times 1000\, b}{\frac{2}{3} \cdot nc} \cdot \displaystyle\int \dfrac{dx}{x+b}$. But $\displaystyle\int \dfrac{dx}{x+b}$ is an expression for the hyperbolic logarithm of $\dfrac{x+b}{b}$, as shall be proved geometrically hereafter; hence

$$\dfrac{V^2}{2} = \dfrac{33 \times 1000\, b}{\frac{2}{3} \cdot nc} \times \text{hyp. Log.}\ \overline{\dfrac{x+b}{b}}.\ \text{or,}$$

$$V = \sqrt{\dfrac{33 \times 1000\, b \times 64.23 \times \text{Tab. Log.}\ \overline{\dfrac{x+b}{b}}}{\frac{2}{3} \cdot \times .43429448 \cdot n \cdot c}}.$$

Now, when $x = FB$, $x + b = a$. and the velocity with which the ball leaves the piece is

$$\sqrt{\dfrac{33 \times 1000\, b \times 64.23}{\frac{2}{3} \times .43429448 \times n\, c.}\ \text{Log.}\ \dfrac{a}{\cdots b}}$$

To illustrate this formula, let us take the following example from our author. The length of the piece was 45 inches $= a$, the space occupied by the charge $2\frac{5}{8}$ inches $= b$, the diameter of the ball $\frac{3}{4}$ of an inch $= c$, and its specific gravity being lead $11.345 = n$.

$$\text{Log.}\ \dfrac{a}{b} = 1.234084.\ \text{Log.} = 0.0913447$$

$$\text{Log.}\ \dfrac{33 \times 1000}{\frac{2}{3} \times .43429448} = 11397.8.\ \text{Log.} = 5.056821$$

$$\text{Log.}\ \dfrac{b}{n \cdot c} = \dfrac{2.625}{8.508} = .3085 \quad \text{Log.} = 1.489255$$

$$\begin{array}{r} 2 \times 32\tfrac{1}{6}\ \text{Log.} = 1.808436 \\ \hline 2\,)\,6.445856 \\ \hline 1670.85\ \text{feet}\quad 3.222928 \end{array}$$

Mr. Robins illustrated this theory by musket balls only; but it afterwards engaged the attention of Dr. Hutton, who has, from a series of experiments made with cannon balls, been able to deduce the following facts.

I. That gunpowder fires almost instantaneously.

II. That the velocities communicated to shot of the same weight, with different charges of powder, are nearly as the square roots of those charges.

III. That when shot of different weights are fired with the same charge of powder, the velocities communicated to them are nearly in the inverse ratio of the square roots of their weights.

IV. That it would be a great improvement in artillery, occasionally to make use of shot of a long shape, or of heavier matter, as lead; for thus the momentum of a shot, when discharged with the same charge of powder, would be increased in the ratio of the square root of the weight of the shot; which would both augment proportionally the force of the blow with which it would strike, and the extent of the range to which it would go.

V. That it would also be an improvement to diminish the windage; since by this means, one-third or more of the quantity of powder might be saved.

The second and third of these remarks are easily deducible from the formula given above for the velocity. For as Log. $\dfrac{x+b}{b}$ is always a small factor, and not susceptible of great changes, V is proportional to $\sqrt{b}$, that is, to the bulk, and consequently to the weight of the charge, when $n \cdot c$ is a constant quantity. On the other hand, when b remains constant, it is equally obvious from the formula, that V varies inversely, as $\sqrt{\dfrac{2\, n\, c}{3}}$, that is, as the square root of the weight of the ball.

The rule which Mr. Robins thus deduced *a priori*, he ingeniously contrived to verify by experiment. He proposed to discover the momentum of the ball at any period of its flight, by opposing to it a large block of wood, suspended in the manner of a pendulum, to which he gave the name of the Ballistic Pendulum. To the lower part of the block was attached a chord, which passed through a slit in the frame work of the instrument. When the pendulum was repelled by the action of the ball, it carried along with it the chord; and as it was divided into inches, it shewed the length of the chord of the arc through which the pendulum moved.

Before employing this instrument in determining the velocities of projectiles, it is requisite to find first the centre of gravity of the block. This may be done in the following manner:—Knowing the weight of the pendulum, which may be represented by W, and the weight D, which is capable of retaining it in a horizontal position, we have to find AG, Fig. 12, Plate CCCCLXV. the distance of the centre of gravity from the centre of suspension, the analogy

PLATE
CCCCLXV.
Fig. 12.

Pneuma-
tics.

On deter-
mining the
centres of
gravity and
oscillation
in the bal-
listic pen-
dulum.

$$W : D = AB : AG = \frac{D \cdot AB}{W}.$$

The second thing to be determined is the centre of oscillation of the pendulum, or that point which moves with the same velocity, as though the whole matter contained in the block were collected into it, and formed what is called a simple pendulum. For the method of finding this theoretically, we refer to the article MECHANICS; the following practical method has been employed: The pendulum, after having been suspended, is put in motion, and the number of vibrations which it performs in a given time are observed. Let the duration of the observation be t seconds, and the number of vibrations n, then the time of one vibration will be $\frac{t''}{n}$. But the time of a vibration, if o be considered as the centre of oscillation, is also $=$ $\pi \sqrt{\frac{SO}{2\,l}}$, when l is the length of the second pendulum, or 193 inches. Hence

$$\frac{t}{n} = \pi \sqrt{\frac{SO}{2\,l}}, \text{ and}$$

$$SO = \frac{2\,t^2\,l}{n^2 \cdot \pi^2}.$$

By making $SR = \sqrt{SG \cdot SO}$, we determine a point R, which has this remarkable property, that if the system, when in equilibrio, be put in motion by any external force, the momentum acquired by it will be the same as though the whole matter were collected in the point R. Now, it is known from the principles of rotatory motion, that two masses which can be moved with the same velocity by a given force are inversely proportional to the squares of their distances from the centre of suspension. The resistance, therefore, opposed by the block to an impulse directed against the point D, is precisely the same as the resistance which would be opposed by the mass $\frac{W \cdot SR^2}{SD^2}$ placed in this point.

Having ascertained these three points, viz. the centres of gravity, oscillation, and gyration or percussion, let us suppose that the pendulum is struck by a bullet, and that its extremity describes an arch whose chord is measured according to the method alluded to. After the impulse of this force has been expended, the pendulum falls through the same arch through which it rose, under the influence of gravity, and acquires at the lowest point of its descent, the velocity which it possessed the moment in which it was struck by the ball. Let $A°$ be the angle through which the pendulum has moved, let $SO = s$, and $SD = d$; then the velocity acquired by the centre of oscillation, in describing from rest any arch, being the same as that acquired by a body descending freely through a space, equal to the versed sine of that arch, if b be assumed as the versed sine of the angle $A°$ for the radius 1, $b\,s$ will be the versed sine of the arch described by the centre of oscillation, and $\sqrt{2\,g\,b\,s}$ will be the velocity which this point acquires by falling through the angle $A°$, and, consequently, the velocity with which it commenced its motion. As the velocity communicated to every point of the pendulum is proportional to its distance from the centre, that communicated to D will be expressed by

$$\sqrt{2\,g\,b\,s} \times \frac{d}{s} = \sqrt{\frac{2\,g\,b\,s \cdot d^2}{s}}.$$

Let this be called V. Then, since action and reaction are equal and opposite, if W′ be taken to denote the weight of the ball, and x its velocity, we have

$$W' \times x' = \left(\frac{W \cdot SR^2}{SD^2} + W'\right) V,$$

$$\text{and } x = \frac{W \cdot SR^2 + W' \cdot SD^2}{W' \cdot SD^2} \cdot V.$$

Pneuma-
tics.

On finding
the velocity
of projec-
tiles by it.

To illustrate these formulæ. The pendulum employed by Mr. Robins weighed 56 lb. 3 oz. or 675 oz. The distance of the point of impact from the centre of suspension was 66 inches $= 8$ D, SO $= 62.66$, SG $= 52$. The chord of the angle through which the pendulum was impelled by the stroke, was found to be 17.25 inches to a radius of 71.125 inches, and the weight of the ball employed was 1 oz.

From these data we find $A° = 13° 55' 48''$,
$$b = .02941057.$$

Whence $V = \sqrt{\dfrac{2\,g\,b\,d^2}{S}}$, or the velocity of D $=$ 39.729 inches.

$$\text{and } x = \frac{W.SR^2 + W'.SD^2}{W' \cdot SD^2}.V = \frac{675 \times 52 \times 62.66 + 1 \times 66^2}{66^2}$$
$$\times 39.729 = 505.9 \times 39.729 = 20100 \text{ inch.} = 1675 \text{ feet.}$$

The result obtained by Mr. Robins from these data is 1645 feet. This difference was occasioned by an assumption which the ingenious author had too precipitately made, viz. that the velocity which every point of a pendulum acquires by falling through any angle into a vertical position, is the same as that which would be acquired by a heavy body falling freely through a space equal to the versed sine of the arch described by that point. This error was pointed out by Euler in his judicious commentary. This profound mathematician has also estimated corrections which it might be necessary to make on the velocities, which are derived by means of this formula, on account of the resistance of the air upon the pendulum. After an elaborate investigation, he finds, however, that it only amounts to $\frac{1}{440}$th of the whole. By taking this into consideration, the velocity of the ball, in the example which we have given, becomes 1679 feet.

Having in this manner confirmed the truth of his theory by experiment, Mr. Robins next proceeded to investigate the velocity with which the elastic air of gunpowder would expand itself, supposing it to be fired in a given piece of artillery, without either a bullet or any other body before it. This problem has been solved by Euler in his ingenious commentary, by assuming as an axiom, that the elasticity of the air is uniform throughout during the whole of its motion. Let AB Fig. 13. represent the space occupied by the air, immediately upon being fired, and AB′ the space which it occupies at a given time after. Then, as the elasticity remains uniform throughout during the whole of the motion, while B expands to B′, the middle lamina C expands to C′, the middle point between A and B′. Hence the velocities of the several laminæ are proportional to their distances from A. If, therefore, S be the height due to the velocity of B, the velocity itself will be represented by

PLATE
CCCCLXV.
Fig. 13.

$$\sqrt{2\,g\,S}.$$

Calling the distance AB′, x, and the distance of any other lamina from A, z, its velocity consequently will be expressed by

$$\frac{z\sqrt{2g\,S}}{x}$$

and the square of the velocity by

$$\frac{2\,z^2 . g\,S}{x^2}.$$

The increment of the square of the velocity is

$$\frac{2\,z^2 g . d\,S}{x^2}, \text{ and } v . d\,v = \frac{z^2 . g . d\,S}{x^2}.$$

In like manner, if $d\,x$ represent the space passed over by B' in any increment of time, $\frac{z . d\,x}{x}$ will be the increment of space passed over by the lamina, while the increment of velocity $\frac{z\sqrt{2g} . d\,S}{2\,x . S}$ is acquired. Now, from the principles of dynamics, it is known that the increment of half the square of the velocity is equal to the accelerative force into the increment of the space. Representing, then, the accelerative force by f, there results

$$\frac{z^2 . g . d\,S}{x^2} = \frac{f . z . d\,x}{x}.$$

Let the air, immediately after the gunpowder has been fired, be supposed to have been of the density m, then its density in its present expanded form, calling AB b, will be expressed by $\frac{m\,b}{x}$.

If G be the specific gravity of common atmospheric air, the weight of the lamina will be

$$\frac{m\,b\,G . d\,z}{x}.$$

Let the moving force upon the lamina be called $d\,y$, then as the moving force, divided by the quantity of matter moved, is equal to the accelerative force, we have

$$f = \frac{x\,d\,y}{m . b . G . d\,z}.$$

The equation delivered above, becomes then, by substituting for f, this value,

$$\frac{z . g . d\,S}{x} = \frac{x . d\,x . d\,y}{m . b . G . d\,z}.$$

Hence $d\,y = \frac{m . b . G . g . d\,S . z . d\,z}{x^2 . d\,x},$

and taking the fluent

$$y = \frac{m . b . G . g . d\,S . z^2}{2 . x^2 . d\,x}, \text{ (when } z = x.) = \frac{m . b . G . g . d\,S}{2\,d\,x},$$

an expression for the moving force of the included air when it expands to B'. Now, as g H is the moving force, which is equivalent to the momentum of air of the common density, when H is the height of the homogeneous atmosphere, $\frac{m' G . H . b}{x}$ will be another expression for the moving force of the included air when it has expanded to B', if its elasticity be denoted by $\frac{m' b}{x}$. Here m' is different from m, as the latter expresses only the density of the air immediately on being fired, or 244, as it was found; whereas the former is employed to express the elasticity as affected by temperature as well as density, or 1000.

Stating these two expressions for the moving force as equal, we have

$$\frac{m' H}{x} = \frac{m . d\,S}{2 . d\,x}, \text{ and}$$

$$\frac{d\,S}{2} = \frac{m' . H}{m} . \frac{d\,x}{x}. \text{ Hence S} = \frac{2\,m' H}{m} . \log. x.$$

But as when $x = b$, the velocity of B, and consequently $S = 0$, the equation when corrected becomes

$$S = \frac{2\,m' H}{m} (\log. x - \log. b) = \frac{2\,m' H}{m} \log. \frac{x}{b}.$$

And when $x = a$, the length of the bore,

$$S = \frac{2\,m'}{m} H . \log. \frac{a}{b}.$$

Now, the velocity is $= \sqrt{2g\,S}$, wherefore the velocity is

$$= \sqrt{\frac{4\,g . m' . H}{m}} . \log. \frac{a}{b}.$$

If, instead of the Naperian logarithms, Briggs' be taken, the expression becomes

$$\sqrt{\frac{4\,g . m' H}{m \times .4342998}} \log. \frac{a}{b}.$$

But as H in fathoms was found to be nearly 4342.945, the velocity is

$$\sqrt{\frac{24 \times 10000\,g . m'}{m}} \log. \frac{a}{b} = . \sqrt{1000000\,g} . \log. \frac{a}{b}.$$

Let us illustrate this formula by an example. The length of the bore a was $= 45$ inches. The length of the charge b was $= 2\frac{5}{8}$ inches.

Log. $\frac{a}{b} = 1.23408$. log. $= 0.091343$

Log. $g = $ log. 32.166 $= 1.507316$
Log. 1000000 $= 6.000000$
2|7.598659

Velocity $= 6300$ feet, log. $= 3.799329$

In this investigation no account has been taken of the resistance of the air. Were it, however, taken into the calculation, the result would scarcely differ from 6000 feet. Euler, who has given the same calculation, gives the result 3215; but he has omitted the consideration of temperature; and of course m and m' being equal, gives a velocity less than the actual velocity in the ratio of

$$\sqrt{1000} \text{ to } \sqrt{244}.$$

The velocity which Mr. Robins found by experiment was about 7000 feet. The subject does not seem to admit of greater accuracy; so that instead of following Euler through his very elaborate commentary, we shall content ourselves with extracting from the experimental inquiry of Dr. Hutton a few of his results, to show the velocities with which balls issue from pieces of different lengths with the same charge, and also the charges that gave the maximum velocity for the same piece.

The lengths of the bore were for No. 1. 28.5 inches, No. 2. 38.4 inches, No. 3. 57.7 inches, No. 4. 80.2 inches, the calibre of each being $2\frac{3}{5}$ inches, and the medium weight of the ball 16 oz. 13 drams.

Table of Initial Velocities.

Powder.	The Guns.			
Oz.	No. 1.	No. 2.	No. 3.	No. 4.
2	780	835	920	976
4	1100	1180	1300	1370
6	1340	1445	1590	1680
8	1430	1580	1790	1940
12	1436	1640	- -	- -
14	- -	1660	- -	- -
16	- -	- -	2000	- -
18	- -	- -	- -	2200

By increasing the quantity of the charges continually for each gun, it was found that the velocities continued to increase till they arrived at a certain degree, different in each gun, as shown by the following Table:

Gun. No.	Length of the Bore.	The Charge.		
		Weight of Powder. Oz.	Length	
			Inches.	Part of Whole.
1	28.5	12	8.2	$\frac{3}{10}$
2	38.4	14	8.5	$\frac{3}{13}$
3	57.7	16	10.7	$\frac{3}{16}$
4	80.2	18	12.1	$\frac{3}{20}$

Having made these few observations on the elastic force of gunpowder, a subject which is more fully treated of in the article GUNNERY, we now proceed with our account of Mr. Dalton's discoveries.

The elastic force of a mixture of air and aqueous vapour.

The next subject with which he occupied himself, after having fully confirmed the law of Mariotte, was an inquiry into the tension of vapour, both when it exists by itself, and in union with atmospheric air. The tension of unmixed vapour at different temperatures as obtained by him are to be found in the article HYGROMETRY, and which, together with the equation derived by Biot, it is unnecessary here to deliver.

The most striking fact which his experiments have unfolded, regards the tension of air and aqueous vapour when in a state of combination. This he has found to be equal to the tensions which they exert, when they exist separately, the temperature being the same in both cases. To illustrate his researches upon this point, we shall describe the contrivance employed by Gay-Lussac in repeating his discoveries. AB (Plate CCCCLXV. Fig. 14.) is a cylindrical tube, divided into parts of equal volume, and shut at the two extremities by the stop-cocks SS′ A little above the lower stop-cock the tube TT is connected with the tube AB, so as to be air-tight. After having dried and heated the apparatus well, the stop-cock S is opened, and the tube AB is completely filled with dry mercury. The mercury will ascend in the small tube TT until it has reached the same level in both. The spherical ball C, which contains the dry air, is then screwed to the plate S, and the stop-cock D is turned, which opens a communication between them. If the air contained in the ball be of the same density with the external air, the mercury will still remain in equilibrio. On opening, however, the lower stop-cock S′, it flows off and leaves room for the air to expand itself. After a sufficient quantity of air is in this manner introduced, the two stop-cocks SS′ are shut, but as the air inclosed is of less density now than the external air, it is obvious that the

Plate CCCCLXV. Fig. 14.

mercury will stand higher in AB than in the tube TT. In order to bring it to a level in both, or reduce, in other words, the internal air to the same density with the external, a small quantity of mercury is poured into the tube TT. The spherical ball C is now removed, and its place is supplied by the small stop-cock S″, surmounted with the vessel V, made to contain the water which is to be evaporated. The cock S″ is not bored completely through, but has only a small niche, in order to receive a drop of the fluid, which, on being turned round, falls among the dry included air. By this means as many drops of water may be introduced into the tube as may be deemed necessary. These, in a very short time, are converted into vapour, which begins to manifest itself by depressing the mercury in the tube AB. This is promoted for a while by the addition of fluid, but after a certain number of drops have been added, the effect ceases. When in this state, the air is said to be saturated. The mixture of air and aqueous vapour, from its increased elasticity, depresses the mercury. Let a portion of the mercury now escape, by the aperture below, so that the mixture may expand until its elasticity become equal to that of the external air; and let the number of divisions which it occupies be N′, that which the dry air occupied itself, when of the same density with the external air being N. Then h being the height of the barometer at the time of the experiment,

$$\frac{N \cdot h}{N'}$$

is the elasticity of the air which composes the mixture. But this, together with the tension of the vapour combined with the air is equal to h; hence the tension of the vapour is expressed in inches of mercury by $h - \dfrac{N \cdot h}{N'}$; a quantity which is invariably found equal to the tension of vapour when it exists by itself at the temperature at which the experiment may happen to be made.

To illustrate this, let us conceive the length of the tube AB to be divided into 100 equal parts, which also mark equal volumes, as the diameter is uniform throughout. After the dry air has been introduced, and condensed until it has become of the same density with the atmosphere at the time, let us suppose that it occupies 8 divisions, then N = 8. Let the barometer, during the experiment, stand at the height of 29.5 inches, and the thermometer at 77°; also let the number of divisions which the composition of air and aqueous vapour occupies, when reduced to the same density with the external air be N′; then, according to Dalton's theory, as the tension of vapour or f at 77° = .910 inches of mercury, we have the equation

$$h - \frac{N}{N'}, h = .910 \text{ and } N' = \frac{hN}{h-f} = 8.2544;$$

a value of N′ which was verified by experiment.

Such was the result which he obtained from his experiments upon air completely saturated with moisture. When, however, the mixture was expanded by heat, and allowed to occupy a larger space, he found that its elasticity varied inversely as its volume, provided there was no accession of vapour. This fact may easily be established by means of the instrument which has been described. For let a portion of the mercury flow off by the lower stop-cock, then the moistened air will expand, and occupy an enlarged volume. Its elasticity

3

Pneumatics.

by this means is diminished, and consequently the mercury stands higher in the tube AB than in TT. Let the difference of level be observed in inches, and called d; then is $h - d$ the pressure to which the inclosed air is subjected, and consequently the measure of its elastic force. If N'' denote the volume which the composition now possesses, the equation

$$\frac{N''}{N'} = \frac{h}{h-d}$$ will be found to obtain always.

To discover from this the change which the tension of the vapour has undergone by being dilated, let it be called f', then we have $h - d - f'$ as the measure of the elasticity due to the portion of air with which it is united. But $h - f$ was the elasticity of this portion of air when it occupied the space N'; hence, according to the law of Mariotte, its elasticity, when it occupies the space N'' is $(h-f) \cdot \frac{N'}{N''}$. By stating these two values for the elasticity of air as equal, we obtain the equation

$$(h-f)\frac{N'}{N''} = h - d - f',$$

Now it is ascertained by experiment, that

$$h - d = \frac{N'}{N''} h,$$

hence $f' = f \frac{N'}{N''}$, that is

$f' : f :: N' : N'''$, or the elasticity of vapour varies inversely as the space which it occupies.

The expansion of moisture, or of a mixture of dry air and moisture, having thus been discovered by Dalton to follow a very different law from that of pure dry air, it became necessary to determine the law according to which it expanded; for, as no endeavour had been made to separate these two substances in the experiments which were formerly made on this subject, they could no longer be relied upon. The following Table shows the results obtained by Mr. Dalton:

Law according to which dry air expands.

Fahren.			Fahren.			Fahren.		
32	.	1000	59	.	1064	86	.	1123
33	.	1002	60	.	1066	87	.	1125
34	.	1004	61	.	1069	88	.	1128
35	.	1007	62	.	1071	89	.	1130
36	.	1009	63	.	1073	90	.	1132
37	.	1012	64	.	1075	91	.	1134
38	.	1015	65	.	1077	92	.	1136
39	.	1018	66	.	1080	93	.	1138
40	.	1021	67	.	1082	94	.	1140
41	.	1023	68	.	1084	95	.	1142
42	.	1025	69	.	1087	96	.	1144
43	.	1027	70	.	1089	97	.	1146
44	.	1030	71	.	1091	98	.	1148
45	.	1032	72	.	1093	99	.	1150
46	.	1034	73	.	1095	100	.	1152
47	.	1036	74	.	1097	110	.	1173
48	.	1038	75	.	1099	120	.	1194
49	.	1040	76	.	1101	130	.	1215
50	.	1043	77	.	1104	140	.	1235
51	.	1045	78	.	1106	150	.	1255
52	.	1047	79	.	1108	160	.	1275
53	.	1050	80	.	1110	170	.	1295
54	.	1052	81	.	1112	180	.	1315
55	.	1055	82	.	1114	190	.	1334
56	.	1057	83	.	1116	200	.	1354
57	.	1059	84	.	1118	210	.	1372
58	.	1062	85	.	1121	212	.	1376

Experiments on the expansion of dry air were also made by M. Gay Lussac with the greatest accuracy.

Pneumatics.

In order to obtain the air dry, he filled a manometer with mercury, and then made it to boil, as is done in constructing thermometers. The manometer was then connected with a tube of considerable diameter, as represented in Fig. 15. Plate CCCCLXV. which was supported in a horizontal direction. This tube was filled with muriate of lime, or some other desiccative, which completely absorbed the aqueous vapour contained in the air. After this was done, M. Gay Lussac employed a very slender iron rod, by means of which, on inclining the apparatus, he was enabled to cause a portion of the mercury to flow from the tube. Its place was immediately supplied by the dry air. In this manner the whole mercury was allowed to escape, except a thin film, which served as a barrier against the admission of moist air.

Plate CCCCLXV. Fig. 15.

The tube having been thus filled, it only remained to expose its contents to different temperatures, and observe the results. For this purpose a metallic vessel was employed, filled with water, of the form of a parallelopipedon, which rested upon a furnace. From the circumstance that the different horizontal strata of a fluid which is exposed in a vessel to the action of fire, partake of different degrees of heat, it was found necessary to introduce the tube into the vessel by an aperture in its side, so that every part of the air might have the same temperature at the same time. The temperature was indicated by a thermometer similarly situated with the tube, at the opposite side of the vessel. By drawing out the thermometer after a certain time, until the mercury appeared, the temperature was known, and in the same manner were the number of divisions observed, which the air occupied in the manometer at that temperature.

In deducing the actual from the apparent expansion of the air, at different temperatures, there are two circumstances to be attended to.

Corrections to be made for finding the true from the apparent expansion.

1. The changes that take place in the atmospheric pressure. 2. The dilatation of the glass which composes the manometer.

As to the first of these, it has been found by the experiments of Lavoisier and La Place, that the lineal dilatation of glass tubes from the freezing to the boiling point is ·00087572, the volume at freezing being represented by unity, and also that the expansion is uniform. Now let c be the capacity of a glass vessel at the temperature of 32°, and c' its capacity at a temperature of t^0 above 32°. It is obvious, that as all the dimensions expand uniformly, the volumes are in both cases similar. Let the number ·000004865, or the lineal expansion for 1°, be denoted by k, and let l be one of the lineal dimensions of the vessel at 32°; then at t^0 above 32°, l becomes $l + k t l$. And since similar figures are as the cubes of their homologous sides,

$$c : c' :: l^3 : l^3 (1 + k t)^3.$$ Hence

$$\frac{c'-c}{c}$$ or the expansion of volume $= (1 + kt)^3 - 1 =.$

By expanding $(1+kt)^3$, it becomes $1 + 3kt + 3k^2t^2 + k^3t^3$;

Wherefore $\frac{c'-c}{c} = 3kt$, as the higher powers of k may be rejected without incurring any sensible error;

and $c' = (1 + 3kt) c$.

Let us now suppose that V is the number of divisions of the manometer occupied by air, at 32°, and that V' is the number of divisions, when the temperature is raised $t°$ above 32°. If δ be assumed to represent the expansion of air, conceiving the volume at 32° to be the unit, then

$V(1+\delta)$ will be the space occupied by the dilated air. But the space as observed is V', which being corrected for the dilatation of the glass, becomes

$$V'(1+3kt).$$

Wherefore $V(1+\delta)=V'(1+3kt)$ and

$$\delta=\frac{V'-V}{V}+3kt\cdot\frac{V'}{V}.$$ where the first part of the

expression is the dilatation, were there no change produced upon the glass by heat; and the second part is the correction to be made when this circumstance is to be taken into account.

The second thing to be attended to in finding the absolute expansion of air, is the force by which it is compressed at the time of observation. Let us suppose this to be p when the observation is made at 32°, and p' when at the temperature of $32°+t°$. It will be necessary in the formula given above for δ, when the pressure varies in this manner, to substitute for V, V', the values which these quantities would have, were the air compressed by the same force in both cases. Now, if 30 inches of mercury be the pressure which is to be regarded as the standard,

V will become $\dfrac{Vp}{30}$,

and V' . . . $\dfrac{V'.p'}{30}$.

Hence $\delta=\dfrac{V'p'-Vp}{Vp}+3kt\cdot\dfrac{V'p'}{Vp}$. is the general formula by which the expansion of the unit of volume for $t°$ above 32° is calculated when the observed volumes are V, V', and the observed pressure p, p'.

The coincidence between the experimental inquiries of Dalton and Gay Lussac on this subject is remarkably striking. The expansion obtained by the former by heating air from 32° to 212° was .376, of the volume at 32°, and that obtained by the latter is .375. Biot relates in his *Traité de Physique Experimentale et Mathematique*, that Tobias Mayer, the celebrated astronomer, had arrived also at the same result. From this well ascertained fact, therefore, it is concluded that the expansion of air for 1° of Fahrenheit, is .00208 of the volume at 32°.

To ascertain with precision the specific gravity of air is an important object, from its use in many of the applications of pneumatical science. For the best conducted experiments on this subject, we are indebted to the accurate researches of MM. Biot and Arago, which are delivered in detail by the former in his *Traité de Physique*.

Specific
gravity of
air.

By the specific gravity of a body is meant the relation which the weight of a given volume of it bears to the weight of the same volume of water, at a certain temperature. In the case of air and the other gases, there are three causes which affect the density, and of consequence the weight of a given volume, viz. pressure, temperature, and moisture. In order, therefore, to find the specific gravity of these substances, the circumstances which tend to modify the result must be observed, and enter into a formula, which evolves the specific gravity, when the air is under a certain pressure, at a given temperature, and in a given hygrometrical state. The general principle upon which experiments relative to this subject have been conducted, is, that the weight of a hollow exhausted sphere *in vacuo*,

being subtracted from the weight of the same when filled with any gas, also weighed *in vacuo*, will give the weight of the gas which has been included; and, as this must always be small in comparison with that of water, it has been proposed to determine the specific gravity of the various gases, that of dry air having been ascertained, by referring to it as a standard, when under a pressure of 30 inches, and at the temperature of freezing.

Let V be the capacity of the hollow sphere at the temperature of 32°, p the height of the barometer, and t the temperature above 32°, when weighed empty. It is obvious that if V be a volume of air at 32°, $V(1+.00208t)$ is the volume occupied by the same portion, when of the temperature $(32°+t)°$; also $\dfrac{V(1+.00208t)}{p}$ 30, is the volume where the pressure is p. Were this volume of air to be inclosed in the sphere at 32°, as it can undergo no dilatation from the increase of temperature or change of pressure which the atmosphere has suffered, its weight will be the same as that of the volume $\dfrac{V(1+.00208t)}{p}$ 30, of external air, in the circumstances specified. Let the weight of this portion of air be called X, then the weight of the unit of volume is,

$$\frac{pX}{V(1+.00208t)30}$$

On account of the expansion of glass by heat, V becomes

$$V+3ktV;$$

hence the weight of air which can occupy this enlarged volume at the temperature $(32+t)°$, under the pressure of p inches is

$$\frac{pX(1+3kt)}{(1+.00208t)30}.$$

If, therefore, the hollow sphere, when completely exhausted, be weighed, and its weight be found to be W; then its absolute weight, or weight in vacuo, will be,

$$(1.)\quad (W)=W+\frac{pX(1+3kt)}{(1+.00208t)30}+e;$$

For a body, weighed in a fluid, loses as much weight as the portion of fluid weighs which it displaces. In this equation e denotes the weight of the thin spherical shell of air which is displaced by the matter of which the vessel is composed, and which must necessarily be very small.

Let us now suppose that the exhausted sphere is connected by means of a screw with the vessel V, which contains the gas, or dry air, whose specific gravity is required, and that the stop-cocks S, S, are turned, so as to open a communication between them. The air or gas will now ascend and occupy both, and by lowering the vessel V in the pneumatic trough, until the surface of the fluid which it holds be on a level both around and within V, the gas will be of the same density as the atmosphere at the time, and the pressure will be p'. Suppose the temperature at the time this takes place to be t', and Y to be the weight of the gas or air, the capacity of the sphere V can hold at 32°, then $\dfrac{p'.Y(1+3kt')}{(1+.00208t')30}$ is the actual weight which it contains.

After the vessel has been filled in this manner, let it be weighed a second time, when the atmospheric pressure is p'', and the temperature t''. Then, if W'' be the weight,

$$(W) = W'' + \frac{p''\,(1 + 3\,k\,t'')\,X}{(1 + .00208\,t'')\,30} + e'' - \frac{p'\,Y\,(1 + 3\,k\,t')}{(1 + .00208\,t')30}.$$

By stating the value of (W) thus obtained as equal to that found in equation (1), there results

$$W + \frac{p\,X\,(1 + 3\,k\,t)}{(1 + .00208\,t)\,30} + e = W'' + \frac{p''\,X\,(1 + 3\,k\,t)}{(1 + .00208\,t'')\,30} + e'' - \frac{p'\,Y\,(1 + 3\,k\,t')}{(1 + .00208\,t')30}$$

But as e is very small, and $e - e''$ totally inappreciable in any case,

$$0 = W'' - W + \frac{p''\,X\,(1 + 3\,k\,t)}{(1 + .00208\,t'')\,30} - \frac{p\,X\,(1 + 3\,k\,t)}{(1 + .00208\,t'')30} - \frac{p'\,Y\,(1 + 3\,k\,t')}{(1 + .00208\,t')30}$$

And when dry air is employed as $Y = X$, there is obtained,

$$X = \frac{(W'' - W)\,30}{\dfrac{(1 + 3\,k\,t)\,p}{(1 + .00208\,t)} - \dfrac{(1 + 3\,k\,t')\,p'}{(1 + .00208\,t')} - \dfrac{(1 + 3\,k\,t'')\,p''}{(1 + .00208\,t'')}}.$$

Since all the quantities in the second term of the equation are known, X, or the weight of the volume V of dry atmospheric air at the temperature of 32°, and under the pressure of 30 inches of mercury, is also known ; it only remains, therefore, that V, the capacity of the vessel, be known, in order to deduce the specific gravity. Biot and Arago found $X = 7.25323$ grammes, and $V = 5.581375$ Litres. Hence the weight of the litre is,

$$\frac{7.25323}{5.581375} = 1.299541 \text{ grammes.}$$

Now the weight of a litre of water, at the maximum of condensation, is 100 grammes. Wherefore, the specific gravity of air is .001299541. Now, the weight of the cubic inch of water is 253.175 Troy grains ; hence the weight of 100 cubic inches of atmospheric air, at the temperature of 32, is 32.901 grains. According to the experiments of Mr. Kirwan, it was found to be 32.6996, and of Sir Humphry Davy 32.5878 grains.

From the discoveries of Dalton, Gay-Lussac, and the experiments of Biot, it may be proper to investigate analytically the formula for measuring heights by the barometer.

Let a column of air be conceived to be divided into an infinite number of small strata, having $d\,x$ for their thickness. Let y represent the actual density of each of these strata, their distances from the earth's surface being x. Since the accelerative force of gravity diminishes as we recede from the earth's surface, if r be the earth's radius, the pressure on each strata will be

$$c - \int \frac{r^2\,y\,dx}{(r + x)^2}, \text{ or } - \int \frac{r^2\,y\,dx}{(r + x)^2}$$

If this column possessed uniformly throughout the temperature of 32°, and were composed solely of atmospheric air; then, according to the law of Mariotte, the densities would be in proportion to the compressing forces ; but when the volumes are equal, the densities are directly as the weights, and inversely as the accelerative forces ; wherefore the pressures are also as the weights directly, and inversely as the accelerative forces. Now, let p be that compressive force under

which, at the temperature of 32°, one of these strata is reduced to the standard density of 1, the accelerative force being also 1, and let its weight be W' ; that of any of the other strata being W, then

$$(A) \ldots \ldots p : - \int \frac{r^2 y\, d x}{(r + x)^2} : : \frac{W' \cdot r^2}{(r + x)^2} : W \times 1 : :$$

$$W' : W \frac{(r + x)^2}{r^2}.$$

According to what has been already shown, air expands for 1° of Fahrenheit, .00208 of its bulk, when at the temperature of 32° ; if, therefore, the temperature be raised throughout the column $t°$, the weight of each of the strata will no longer be W, but

$$W\,(1 - .00208\,t)$$

Now, let us suppose that this column is not composed of pure air, but that it contains a portion of aqueous vapour. The vapour is diffused irregularly, abounding most in the lower strata, while the upper strata are less humid. Its tension, or elastic force, varies too in the different strata, depending upon their temperature and upon the quantity in which it exists. As, however, in regard to temperature, so also in respect of humidity, it will be found to hold that the average tension is nearly a mean between those of the extreme strata of the column. Let this mean tension be named F. Then as Investigation of the
formula for
finding
heights by
the baro-
meter, from
the data
furnished
by Dalton,
&c.

$$- \int \frac{r^2 y\, d x}{(r + x)^2} \text{ is the compressing force on each of the}$$

strata, the elastic force of the portions of air of which they are severally composed will be expressed by

$$- \int \frac{r^2 y \cdot d x}{(r + x)^2} - F.$$

As for the same volume, the weights are proportional to the densities, and the densities to the compressing forces, since $W\,(1 - .00208\,t)$ is the weight of air in each stratum, when the compressing force is

$$- \int \frac{r^2 y\, d x}{(r + x)^2},$$

it follows that

$$(B) \ldots \ldots - \int \frac{r^2 y \cdot d x}{(r + x)^2} : W(1 - .00208\,t) : : - \int \frac{r^2 y \cdot d x}{(r + x)^2} - F : W(1 - .00208\,t)\left(- \int \frac{r^2 y\, d x}{(r + x)^2} - F \div \int \frac{r^2 y\, d x}{(r + x)^2} \right) = $$

the weight of air actually contained in each.

Again, if F were the compressing force on each of the strata, the weight they would contain would be

$$\frac{W(1 - .00208\,t)\,F}{- \int \frac{r^2 y\, d x}{(r + x)^2}},$$

consequently the weight of vapour contained in each

of the strata (see HYGROMETRY, Art. 34.) is expressed by

$$\frac{W(1 - .00208\,t)\,F}{- \int \frac{r^2 y\, d x}{(r + x)^2}}$$

Adding together this quantity, and the expression for

the weight of the air contained in each stratum, we
have

$$\frac{W(1 - .00208\,t)\left(-\int\frac{r^2\,y\,d\,x}{(r+x)^2} - \frac{3F}{8}\right)}{-\int\frac{r^2\,y\,d\,x}{(r+x)^2}},$$

for the actual weight of each stratum.

If this weight were estimated when the accelerating
force is 1, it would be

$$\frac{\left(\frac{r+x}{r}\right)^2 W(1 - .00208\,t)\left(-\int\frac{r^2\,y\,d\,x}{(r+a)^2} - \frac{3F}{8}\right)}{-\int\frac{r^2\,y\,d\,x}{(r+x)^2}}.$$

But the weight of the same volume under the same accelerative force is W', regarding the density as 1,
hence

$$(C)\dots\frac{\left(\frac{r+x}{r}\right)^2 W(1 - .00208\,t)\left(-\int\frac{r^2\,y\,d\,x}{(r+x)^2} - \frac{3F}{8}\right)}{W'\times -\int\frac{r^2\,y\,d\,x}{(r+x)^2}}$$

is the expression for the density of each stratum, and
is therefore equal to y.

Recurring to equation (A),

$$W' : p :: W\left(\frac{r+x}{r}\right)^2 : -\int\frac{r^2\,y\,d\,x}{(r+x)^2}, \text{ or}$$

$$1 : p : \frac{W}{W'}\left(\frac{r+x}{r}\right)^2 : -\int\frac{r^2\,y\,d\,x}{(r+x)^2}, \text{ wherefore}$$

$$\frac{1}{p} = \frac{W}{W'}\left(\frac{r+x}{r}\right)^2 \div -\int\frac{r^2 y\,d\,x}{(r+x)^2}.$$

Substituting this value of $\frac{1}{p}$ in the equation (c),
there results

$$(D)\dots y = \frac{1 - .00208\,t)}{p}\cdot\left(-\int\frac{r^2\,y\,d\,x}{(r+x)^2} - \frac{3F}{8}\right).$$

Let $\dfrac{1 - .00208\,t}{p}$ be represented by A, then, by taking the differential, we have

$$dy = A\times d\left(-\int\frac{r^2\,y\,d\,x}{(r+x)^2}\right)$$

and $\dfrac{dy}{y} = -\dfrac{A\,r^2\,d\,x}{(r+x)^2}.$

Hence (F) $\dots$ log. $y = \dfrac{A\,r^2}{(r+x)}.$

Making $x=0$; let us suppose y in this case, which is
the density in the lower station, to be expressed by y',
and we have

$$\text{log. } y' = A\,r.$$

Subtracting E q . (F) from this equation, we obtain

$$\text{log. } y' - \text{log. } y = A\,r - \frac{A\,r^2}{(r+x)}$$

or log. $\dfrac{y'}{y} = \dfrac{A\,r\,x}{r+x}$

Hence $x = \dfrac{1}{A}\left(\text{log. } \dfrac{y'}{y}\cdot\overline{1 + \dfrac{x}{r}}\right)$ (G).

In this equation, as r is the radius of the earth, y' is

obviously the density of atmospheric air at the level of
the sea. Let us now assume another height above the
level of the sea, and represent it by n, where the density of the air is y_i, then, by the formula, we have

$$x_i = \frac{1}{A}\left(\text{log. } \frac{y'}{y_i}\right)\left(1 + \frac{x_i}{r}\right);$$

and by subtracting E q . (G) from this, there results

$$x_i - x = \frac{1}{A}\left(\text{log. } \frac{y'}{y_i}\overline{1 + \frac{x_i}{r}} - \text{log. } \frac{y'}{y}\overline{1 + \frac{x}{r}}\cdot\right)$$

Let $x_i - x = \delta$, then this expression becomes

$$\frac{1}{A}\left(\text{log. } \frac{y'}{y_i}\overline{1 + \frac{x'}{r}} + \text{log. } \frac{y}{y'}\overline{1 + \frac{x_i}{r}} + \text{log. } \frac{y'}{y}\cdot\frac{\delta}{r}\right)$$

As the height of the lower station above the level of
the sea is in general very small, y' may be considered
as equal to y, and

$$\text{Log. } \frac{y}{y'} = \text{log. } \frac{y'}{y} = 0.$$

Hence $\delta = \dfrac{1}{A}\left(\text{log. } \dfrac{y}{y'}\cdot\overline{1 + \dfrac{x+\delta}{r}}\right).$

By means of this formula, the difference of level between two stations in the atmosphere may be known,
by finding the values of y_i and y_i at those stations.

We assumed $\dfrac{1}{A} = \dfrac{p}{1 - .00208\,t}$, where p is the

height of an aerial column of uniform density, whose
temperature is $32°$, and by whose pressure a volume of
air at the earth's surface may be reduced to the standard density. To determine this quantity, as t, the excess
of mean temperature of the column above $32°$ is not very
great, we may bring $1 - .00208\,t$ from the denominator to the numerator, and, by rejecting $(.00208\,t)^2$
and the higher powers, it becomes $1 + .00208\,t$,

so that $\dfrac{1}{A} = p(1 + .00208\,t).$

According to the experiments of Biot and Arago,
which we have described above, the specific gravity of
dry atmospheric air, under a pressure of .76 metres,
and at the temperature of freezing in the latitude of
$45°$, is .001299075, considering the specific gravity of
water in the same circumstances as the standard. Its
density consequently for the latitude of any place, and
under the pressure of .76199 metres, or 30 inches, will
be

$$\frac{.001299075(1 - 0 . 002837 . \cos. 2\,l)\times .76199}{.76},$$

when l is the latitude. By assuming this as $56° = $ latitude of Edinburgh, the value of the density then becomes

$$\frac{.001299075(1 + 0.002837 \times .37461) \times .76199}{.76}$$

$$= .00130386.$$

Now, according to the same authority, the specific
gravity of mercury is 13.597190; the column of atmospheric air, therefore, which is a counterpoise for 30
inches of mercury, of this specific gravity, must be in

length $= \dfrac{13.597190\times 30}{.00130386} = 312852.37$ inches.

Hence $\delta = 312852.37(1 + .00208\,t)\left(\text{log. } \dfrac{y}{y_i}\overline{1 + \dfrac{x_i}{r}}\right).$

In the logarithmic curve, if t denote the sub-tangent, y the ordinate, and x the abscissa, the differential equation is

$$t = y \frac{dx}{dy}.$$

Hence $dx = dy \cdot \frac{t}{y}$, and by taking the fluents $x = $ log. $y \times t$; wherefore $\frac{x}{t} = $ Naperian logarithm y; that is, the logarithm of any system divided by its sub-tangent, is equal to the corresponding logarithm of Na-pier's system. Instead, therefore, of the hyperbolic logarithms log. $\frac{y}{y}$, log. $\left(1 + \frac{x_i}{r}\right)$, let us take the corresponding logarithms in Briggs' system, divided by the subtangent T, and

$$\delta = \frac{312852.37}{T}(1 + .00208\, t)\left(\text{Log.}\frac{y}{y_i} + \left(1 + \frac{x_i}{r}\right)\right).$$

Now $\frac{1}{T}$ is the modulus, or 2.302585; wherefore

$$\delta = 10005.127(1 + .00208\, t)\left(\text{log.}\frac{y}{y_i} + \right)\left(1 + \frac{x_i}{r}\right) \text{ in English fathoms.}$$

It appears that the value of δ, the quantity sought, is itself involved in this equation. We can easily disengage it, however, by the following process:

The product $\left(1 + \frac{x_i}{r}\right)$ may be resolved into two factors $\left(1 + \frac{\delta}{r}\right)$, $\left(1 + \frac{x}{r}\right)$; for that part which is multiplied into $\frac{1}{r^2}$, may be regarded as inconsiderable.

Now, according to a supposition by Biot, x may be assumed as $= 1200$ metres, being the mean height at which observers may have occasion to take their lower station.

This number is obviously too great, and has been adopted for the purpose of making the constant multiplier correspond with that derived by M. Ramond from observation. We may assume the mean height of the lower station as 300 feet, or 50 fathoms; from which we obtain $\left(1 + \frac{x}{r}\right) = 1.0000142$, and the constant multiplier becomes 10005.269.

Let us now represent $10005.269(1 + .00208\, t)$ by N, and we have

$$\delta = N\left(\text{Log.}\frac{y}{y_i} + \cdot \overline{1 + \frac{\delta}{r}}\right).$$

$$\text{or } \delta = \frac{N \cdot \text{Log.}\frac{y}{y_i}}{1 - \frac{N}{r}\left(\text{Log.}\frac{y}{y_i}\right)}.$$

The latter term in the denominator is of very small value, for $\frac{N}{r}$ amounts only to $.002866$. The log. $\frac{y}{y_i}$ when y is 30, and y 24, which corresponds to an altitude of nearly 6000 feet, is only $.09691$. According to these assumptions, therefore,

$$\frac{N}{r}.\text{Log.}\frac{y}{y_i} = .00027716.$$

The constant multiplier is therefore found to be 10008.0402, and

$$\delta = 10008.0402 \times \text{Log.}\frac{y}{y_i}(1 + .00208\, t).$$

By recurring to E q (C), we have

$$y = \frac{\left(\frac{r+x}{r}\right)^2 W(1 - .00208\, t) \times \left(-\int \frac{r^2 y \cdot dx}{(r+x)^2} - \frac{3F}{8}\right)}{W' \times -\int \frac{r^2 y\, dx}{(r+x)^2}}.$$

In like manner for $y\, y_i$, we have, by changing x into x_i and W into w_i,

$$y_i = \left(\frac{r + x_i}{r}\right)^2 \cdot w \cdot (1 - .00208\, t) \times \left(-\int \frac{r^2 y_i\, dx}{(r+x)^2} - \frac{3F}{8}\right) \div W' + -\int \frac{r^2 y_i\, dx}{(r + x_i)^2}$$

$$\text{Hence } \frac{y}{y_i} = \frac{\left(\frac{r+x}{r}\right)^2 W \times \left(\int -\frac{r^2 y \cdot dx}{(r+x)^2} - \frac{3F}{8}\right) \cdot - \frac{r^2 y_i\, dx}{(r+x_i)^2}}{\left(\frac{r+x_i}{r}\right)^2 w \times \left(\int -\frac{r^2 y_i\, dx_i}{(r+x_i)^2} - \frac{3F}{8}\right) \cdot - \frac{r^2 y\, dx}{(r+x)^2}}$$

$$\text{But } \left(\frac{r+x}{r}\right)^2 W : \left(\frac{r+x_i}{r}\right)^2 w = -\int \frac{r^2 y\, dx}{(r+x)^2} : -\int \frac{r^2 y_i\, dx}{(r+x')^2}.$$

$$\text{Wherefore } \frac{y}{y_i} = \frac{-\int \frac{r^2 y \cdot dx}{(r+x)^2} - \frac{3F}{8}}{-\int \frac{r^2 y_i\, dx}{(r+x_i)^2} - \frac{3F}{8}}.$$

Now $-\int \frac{r^2 y\, dx}{(r+x)^2}$ and $-\int \frac{r^2 y_i\, dx}{(r+x)^2}$ are respectively the values of the superincumbent pressures upon the lowest and upmost stratum. These pressures are proportional to their effects. It is well known, that the support of the column of mercury in the barometer tube is caused by the compression of the atmosphere. The variations in the altitude of this column indicate, therefore, the changes incident to the cause, and consequently are the measures of them.

Let b and β be the observed barometrical altitudes at the lower and upper station, then

$$-\int \frac{r^2 y\, dx}{(r+x)^2} \text{ and } -\int \frac{r^2 y\, dx_i}{(r+x_i)^2}$$

are expressed by b and β. In order to this it is necessary, however, that the mercury in both barometers have the same density and the same gravitation. The former of these is affected by a difference of temperature at the two stations, and the latter by the difference of elevation.

It has been already remarked, that for every degree

PLATE CCCCLXVI.

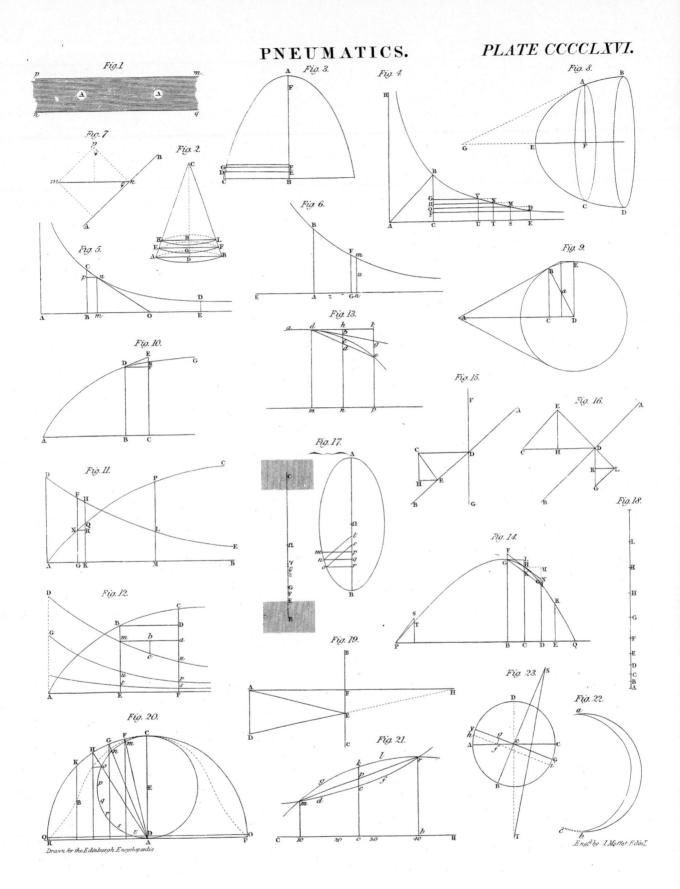

Fig. 1.
Fig. 3.
Fig. 4.
Fig. 8.
Fig. 7.
Fig. 2.
Fig. 6.
Fig. 5.
Fig. 9.
Fig. 10.
Fig. 13.
Fig. 15.
Fig. 16.
Fig. 11.
Fig. 17.
Fig. 14.
Fig. 18.
Fig. 12.
Fig. 19.
Fig. 23.
Fig. 22.
Fig. 20.
Fig. 21.

Drawn for the Edinburgh Encyclopædia

Eng.d by J. Moffat Edin.t

of increase of temperature, mercury expands the $\frac{1}{9733}$ part of its length. It will be necessary, therefore, by means of thermometers attached to the barometers, to ascertain their temperature at the two stations, and reduce their columns to what they would be were the temperature the same. This may be done, by increasing β, the length at the upper and colder station, to

$\beta + \beta \cdot \dfrac{t'}{9733}$, t' denoting the difference of temperature indicated by the two attached thermometers. Instead of log. β, we shall then have, in the formula,

$$\text{Log.}\left(\beta + \frac{\beta t'}{9733}\right) = \log.\ \beta\ (1 + .0001027\ t').$$

By receding from the earth's surface, the force of gravity diminishes, and consequently the same height of fluid does not indicate an equal pressure at a high and low station. In moderate heights it would be affectation to introduce any correction on the barometrical columns for this cause. In great heights it may be necessary to attend to it. By the formula,

$$\partial = 10008.\ \text{Log.}\ \frac{\left(b - \frac{3}{8}\ \text{F}\right) \times (1 + .00208)}{\text{Log.}\left(\beta\ \overline{1 + .0001027\ t'} - \frac{3}{8}\ \text{F}\right)},$$

we can obtain an approximate value for the height which we may call h; then, by applying the formula,

$$\partial = 10008.\ \text{Log.}\ \frac{\left(\frac{r^2}{(r+h)^2}\ b - \frac{3}{8}\ \text{F}\right) \times 1 + .00208\ t}{\text{Log.}\left(\beta\overline{1 + .0001027\ t'} - \frac{3}{8}\ \text{F}\right)},$$

we obtain the true value.

In order to compare this formula with that derived from observation, it will be necessary to recollect that Shuckburgh and General Roy measured the expansion of air without adopting any precautions for having it dry. As their experiments were made at different times, and a mean of them was taken for the true expansion, we may conceive that the air employed was of the mean state of humidity.

F or the tension of vapour for 77° = .910 inches.
and . . . . 32° = .200 .

Now within this range we may regard the increase of tension as uniform, and as being for $t°$ above 32° equal to $.200 + .0158\ t$.

Considering the air as containing a mean quantity of moisture, F will become equal to $.100 + .0079\ t$, and

$$\frac{3}{8}\ \text{F} = .0375 - .002962\ t.$$

Hence the formula for taking heights by the barometer, derived from the experiments made upon dry air, is

$$\partial = 10,008.\ \frac{\text{Log.}(b - .0375 - .002962t) \times (1 + .00208\ t)}{\text{Log.}\ \beta\ (1 + .0001027\ t') - .0375 - .002962\ t)}.$$

On the resistance of air. For a table of some of the most remarkable heights which have been found by the barometer, we refer to the article PHYSICAL GEOGRAPHY.

The resistance of fluids from the time of Des Cartes has been an important subject of consideration to phi-

losophers. According to his theory of the planetary motions, the heavenly bodies were wheeled round in the vortices of a thin aërial fluid. To overturn this opinion, it became necessary for Newton to inquire into the mechanical laws according to which fluids act. The subject is now interesting to us, however, not as a refutation of an exploded theory, but as it explains to us the movements of bodies propelled through the air.

The term "resistance," in regard to retarded motions, is of similar import with the expression "moving force," as applied to accelerated motions. The moving force is estimated by the product of the "tendency" of each particle in a mass into the number of particles which it may contain, and is synonymous with the word *weight* in common language. Resistance to a body is measured by its loss of momentum, or is equal to the product of the retardation of each particle into the number of particles. Thus, to a body descending *in vacuo*, its *weight* is the *moving force;* but to an ascending body its weight is the resistance.

In this motion the moving force or resistance is constant, when the space passed through is small ; the case is different, however, when the moveable has to ascend or descend through a fluid. According to the third law of motion delivered by Newton, the loss of momentum in one body is equal to that acquired by another to which it is opposed. Let us now suppose the body A Fig. 1. to be projected with any velocity through the fluid $p\ m\ n\ q$; and let us suppose that its velocity at A is the double of that which it possesses when it reaches A'. Then it is obvious that it displaces each of the particles which oppose it at A, with double the velocity which it imparts to those at A'. From this consideration, therefore, the resistance at A must be the double of what it is at A'. But the term "momentum" expresses the quantity of motion lost in a given time. Now it appears that at A the body will displace twice as many particles in the same time as at A'. The resistance, on this account, will also be in the former case double of what it is in the latter. Hence the actual resistance at A is quadruple of what it is at A'; and, in general, we conclude, that the resistance to a body moving through a fluid is proportional to the square of its velocity.

Having ascertained this law, we shall now proceed to deduce from it certain dynamical conclusions ; and for this purpose we shall throw out of view at present the quantity of matter resisted.

PLATE CCCCLXVI. Fig. 1.

PROBLEM I.

What is the relation betwixt the space, time, and velocity of a body propelled through a fluid, and subject to no force except its resistance?

To solve this problem, we shall premise the following lemmata :—

LEMMA I.

Let a, b, c, d, &c. be a succession of quantities constituting a decreasing series in geometrical progression, then

$$a^m (a - b) + b^m (b - c) + c^m (c - d) + \&c. = \frac{a^{m+1}}{m+1},$$

when a exceeds b by an infinitely small quantity *.

Because $a : b : c : d : e : f : g : h$, &c.,

it follows by dividing,

that $a : a — b : b : b — c : c : c — d : d : d — e$, &c.

and (by Prop. IV. Book V. Euc.) that

$a^{m+1} : a^m . \overline{a—b} : b^{m+1} : b^m . \overline{b—c} : c^{m+1} : c^m . \overline{c—d}$. &c.

and by Prop. XII. that

$a^{m+1} : a^m . \overline{a—b} :: a^{m+1} + b^{m+1} + c^{m+1} +$ &c.

$: a^m . \overline{a—b} + b^m . \overline{b—c} + c^m . \overline{c—d}$, &c.

But as a, b, c, d, e, &c. are in geometrical progression, $a^{m+1}, b^{m+1}, c^{m+1}, d^{m+1}$, must also be in geometrical progression, and

$$a^{m+1} + b^{m+1} + c^{m+1} + \&c. = \frac{a^{m+1}}{1 - \dfrac{b^{m+1}}{a^{m+1}}} =$$

$$\frac{a^{2m+2}}{a^{m+1} - b^{m+1}}.$$

Hence $a^m . \overline{a—b} + b^m . \overline{b—c} + c^m . \overline{c—d} + \&c. =$

$$\frac{a^{2m+1} . \overline{a—b}}{a^{m+1} - b^{m+1}}.$$

But $\dfrac{a^{m+1} - b^{m+1}}{a—b} = a^m + a^{m-1} b + a^{m-2} b^2$

$+ \quad \cdots \quad . \quad a^{m-m} b^m.$

Wherefore $a^m . \overline{a—b} + b^m . \overline{b—c} + c^m . \overline{c—d} =$

$$\frac{a^{2m+1}}{a^m + a^{m-1} b + a^{m-2} b + \&c.} =$$

(when $b = a$) $\dfrac{a^{2m+1}}{m+1 . a^m} = \dfrac{a^{m+1}}{m+1}$.   Q. E. D.

LEMMA II.

Let BDG be the equilateral hyperbola, having for its plate assymptotes AE, AH ; or, in other words, let it be a ccclxvi. Fig. 4.

Plate
CCCCLXVI.
Fig. 2, 3.

* This lemma we conceive to be a strictly geometrical as well as synthetic demonstration of the principles of the integral calculus. For let the quantities a^m, b^m, &c. be represented by the general symbol x^m, and $a—b$, $b—c$, $c—d$, &c. by dx, then the lemma contains a demonstration of the algebraical proposition that the fluent of $x^m dx = \dfrac{x^{m+1}}{m+1}$. It appears to us, that in teaching the elements of mathematical science, this demonstration, which is entirely elementary, as it involves no previous proposition which is not either contained in the Fifth Book of Euclid's Elements, or may be easily deduced from it, might be successfully extended, so as to put the student in possession of a great number of important truths, the evidence for which appears far-fetched and inconclusive, when founded, as it frequently is, upon the arithmetic of infinites, or the abstract though ingenious speculations on velocity, constituting the science of fluxions.

1. Thus, to find the solidity of a cone, we have only to conceive the altitude of the solid to be divided into the parts CG, CH, &c. in geometrical progression ; and representing these by a, b, c, d, &c. ; the expression for the areas AB, EF, &c. will be $m \pi a^2$, $m \pi b^2$, $m \pi c^2$. if AD be assumed $= m a$. Hence the sum of the cylinders having these areas for their bases, and $a—b$, $b—c$, &c. for their altitudes, will be

$$m \pi (a^2 \overline{a—b} + b^2 . \overline{b—c} + c^2 . \overline{c—d} + \&c.) = \frac{m \pi . a^3}{3} \text{ by the lemma.}$$

Here it is evident that as GD is infinitely less than CD, the excess of AD above EG is also infinitely less than AD, and consequently the excess of the cylinder constituted upon AB exceeds by an infinitely small quantity the solid EFBA. Hence $\dfrac{\pi a^3}{3}$ is also an expression for the solidity of the cone.

2. To find the surface of a parabola.

Let the abscissa AB be divided into the parts AB, AE, AF, &c. in geometrical progression, then from the nature of the curve $CB = p \sqrt{a}$, $DE = p \sqrt{b}$, $GF = p \sqrt{c}$, where p denotes the parameter. Hence the sum of the rectangles having CB, DE, GF, &c. for their base, and $\overline{a—b}$, $\overline{b—c}$ for their altitudes, is expressed by

$$p (\sqrt{a} . \overline{a—b} + \sqrt{b} . \overline{b—c} + \sqrt{c} . \overline{c—d} + \&c.)$$

Now, since $a : a—b : b : b—c : c : c—d : d : d—c$, &c. it follows by (Prop. IV. Book V. Euc.) that $a \sqrt{a} : \sqrt{a} \ \overline{a—b} : b \sqrt{b} : \sqrt{b}$. $\overline{b—c} : c \sqrt{c} : \sqrt{c} : \overline{c—d}$, &c. ; and (by Prop. XII. Book V. Euc.) that $a \sqrt{a} : \sqrt{a} : \overline{a—b} : a^{\frac{3}{2}} + b^{\frac{3}{2}} + c^{\frac{3}{2}} + \&c. : \sqrt{a} . \overline{a—b} + \sqrt{b} . \overline{b—c} + \&c.$

$$\text{Now } a^{\frac{3}{2}} + b^{\frac{3}{2}} + c^{\frac{3}{2}} + \&c. = \frac{a^{\frac{3}{2}}}{1 - \dfrac{b^{\frac{3}{2}}}{a^{\frac{3}{2}}}} = \frac{a^3}{a^{\frac{3}{2}} - b^{\frac{3}{2}}}.$$

Hence $\sqrt{a} . \overline{a—b} + \sqrt{b} . \overline{b—c} + \&c. = \dfrac{a^2 . \overline{a—b}}{a^{\frac{3}{2}} - b^{\frac{3}{2}}} = \dfrac{a^2 (a^{\frac{3}{2}} + b^{\frac{3}{2}}) . (a—b)}{a^3 - b^3} = \dfrac{a^2 (a^{\frac{3}{2}} + b^{\frac{3}{2}})}{a^2 + a b + b^2} = $ (when b is assumed $= a$) $= 2 a^{\frac{3}{2}}$.

But when b differs by an infinitely small quantity from a, DE differs also by an infinitely small quantity from CB, that is, the rectangles differ from the corresponding parabolic spaces by an infinitely small quantity. Wherefore the area of the parabola is

$$\tfrac{2}{3} p \sqrt{a} . a.$$

We might proceed to show how this strictly geometrical process might apply in a great number of cases ; as, for instance, to find the solidity of the sphere of the parabolic conoid, &c. The example in the text shows with what neatness and brevity it leads to the important formula for the hyperbolic logarithm of any quantity. With the demonstration of Taylor's theorem, to be given hereafter, this lemma affords a *new* and *simple* exposition of the principles of fluxions.

curve line, so related to AE, that $BC = \frac{1}{AC}$, then is the

area $BCDE = CE - \frac{CE^2}{2} + \frac{CE^3}{3} - \&c.$

Let $CE = a$, $CS = b$, $BC = CA = 1$.

Make $CE : CS : CS : CT$, and $CS : CT :: CT : CU$, or

$$a : b : b : c ; \quad b : c : d, \&c.$$

Then, $DE = \frac{1}{1+a} = 1 - a + a^2 - a^3 + a^4 - a^5 + \&c.$

and $BF = 1 - DE = a - a^2 + a^3 - a^4 + a^5 - \&c.$
Hence it may be shown, in like manner, that

$$BQ = 1 - MS = b - b^2 + b^3 - b^4 + b^5 - \&c.$$
$$BR = 1 - NT = c - c^2 + c^3 - c^4 + c^5 - \&c.$$

By taking the differences between BF, BQ, BR, &c.
we have

$$FQ = \overline{a-b} - \overline{a^2 - b^2} + \overline{a^3 - b^3} - \overline{a^4 - b^4} + \&c.$$

$$QR = \overline{b-c} - \overline{b^2 - c^2} + \overline{b^3 - c^3} - \overline{b^4 - c^4} + \&c.$$

Wherefore, the rectangles

$$QD = a . \overline{a - b} - a . \overline{a^2 - b^2} + a . \overline{a^3 - b^3} - \&c.$$

$$MR = b . \overline{b - c} - b . \overline{b^2 - c^2} + b . \overline{b^3 - c^3} - \&c.$$
$$\&c. \qquad \&c. \qquad \&c. \qquad \&c.$$

Now $a . \overline{a - b} + b . \overline{b - c} + c . \overline{c - d} + \&c. =$

ultimately to $\frac{a^2}{2}$.

$$a . \overline{a^2 - b^2} + b . \overline{b^2 - c^2} + c . \overline{c^2 - d^2} =$$

$$2 a^2 . \overline{a - b} + 2 b^2 . \overline{b - c} + \&c. = \frac{2 a^3}{3}.$$

$$a . \overline{a^3 - b^3} + b . \overline{b^3 - c^3} + c . \overline{c^3 - d^3} =$$

$$3 a^3 . \overline{a - b} + 3 b^3 . \overline{b - c} + \&c. = \frac{3 a^4}{4}.$$

But the sum of the rectilineal areas QD, MR, &c. $=$
curvilineal area BFD. Hence

$$BFD = \frac{a^2}{2} - \frac{2 a^3}{3} + \frac{3 a^4}{4} - \frac{4 a^5}{5} + \&c.$$

Now area $EF = a - a^2 + a^3 - a^4 + \&c.$ Hence
the hyperbolic area,

$$BDEC = a - \frac{a^2}{2} + \frac{a^3}{3} - \frac{a^4}{4} + \frac{a^5}{5} - \&c. \text{ Q. E. D.}$$

This is a general expression for the hyperbolic logarithm of the quantity $\overline{1 + a}$.

Cor. Let us assume, as a general symbol, for a, b, c,
&c. x, and for $\overline{a - b}$, $\overline{c - d}$, in the ultimate state dx,
then we have

$$d x - x d x + x^2 d x + \&c. = \int \frac{d x}{1+x} = \text{Log.} \overline{1+x}.$$

Having premised these lemmata, we now proceed to
solve the problem in reference to which they were introduced.

It is a general proposition in Dynamics, that if f denote the accelerative or retarding force, and s the space
described, v being the velocity acquired after passing
over s, that

$$f . d s = v . d v.$$

But, in the case of a body passing through a fluid,
we know that

$f \doteq v^2$, hence $v^2 . d s \doteq - v . d v$, or $d s = - \frac{d v}{v}$.

From this relation among $d s$, $d v$, and v, we conclude that s is the abscissa of the logarithmic curve, v
being the ordinate, or that

$$s = - \text{log.} \, v + c.$$

Let s be conceived as equal to o, and let the initial
velocity be represented by V, then $o = - \text{log.} \, V + c$,
and $c = \text{log.} \, V$.

Hence $s = \text{log.} \, V - \text{log.} \, v = \text{log.} \, \frac{V}{v}$. Q. E. F.

Relation
among the
space,
time, and
velocity,
when a
body is
projected
horizontal-
ly in a re-
sisting me-
dium.

Cor. 1. Let CD be a hyperbola, of which AE is an

assymptote, and let $\frac{1}{AE}$ or DE be assumed as the mea-

sure of v, and $\frac{1}{AB}$ or CB as the measure of V, then

$\text{log.} \, \frac{V}{v} = \text{log.} \, AE - \text{log.} \, AB = $ space CBED.

Cor. 2. It is also a proposition in Dynamics, that if
t be taken to represent the time of a body's motion,

$$v . d t = d s.$$

Wherefore, in the present case, $v . d t = - \frac{d v}{v}$, and

$$d t = - \frac{d v}{v^2}.$$

Taking the fluents $t = \frac{1}{v}$.

Now v, or the velocity, is measured by the ordinates
CB, DE, &c. ; wherefore t, or the times of describing
the spaces CBED, CFEG, will be measured by the abscissæ AE, AG, &c. reckoned from the centre of the
hyperbola.

Cor. 3. The space which can be passed over, whilst
the velocity at any point is destroyed, by the retardation at that point being continued constant, is a constant quantity.

For, let CB be any ordinate, and let the corresponding abscissa be called x, then $CB = \frac{1}{x}$. Let $n m$ be
another ordinate taken so near to the former, that $d x$
may be the portion of the abscissa between them, then

$m n = \frac{1}{x + d x}$ and $CB - n m$ or $C p = \frac{d x}{x^2 + x . d x} =$

ultimately to $\frac{d x}{x^2}$.

Wherefore $\frac{C p}{p n} = \frac{1}{x^2}$. But $\frac{C p}{p n} = \frac{1}{\text{tang.} \angle BCO}$
Hence tang. $\angle BCO = x^2$ (the radius being unity) and
$BO = \frac{1}{x} \times x^2 = x$.

But the area CBO will express the space passed over,
while the velocity CB is destroyed by the retardation
at B being continued constant ; and it is equal to

$\frac{CB . BO}{2} = \frac{1 \times x}{2 x} = \frac{1}{2}$ a constant quantity.

Fig. 5.

Fig. 5.

We have remarked that the resistance is equal to the mass into the velocity. This expression may be rendered more useful by the following modifications. During a body's progress, however great the initial velocity be, it is obvious, from the nature of the hyperbolic curve, that it will gradually diminish in a continued manner, until it differs insensibly from nothing. The retardation, from being proportional to the square of the velocity, must also decrease. To a body ascending or descending perpendicularly through the air, there is consequently a degree of velocity, such that the retardation consequent upon it is equal to the accelerative force of gravity. It is obvious that when a descending body has once acquired this velocity, it can acquire no increase of velocity in its future descent, as the retardation and acceleration are equal; hence it has been called the terminal velocity.

Let the terminal velocity be represented by U, and the accelerative force of gravity by g; also let any other velocity which the moveable may possess during its motion be represented by V, and the corresponding retardation by f. Then from the relation which has been shown to subsist between the velocity and retardation, we have

$$g : U^2 :: f : V^2.$$

Hence the retardation, when the moveable possesses the velocity $V = g \cdot \dfrac{V^2}{U^2}$.

And the resistance (denoting by W the weight of the body) $= g \dfrac{V^2}{U^2} \cdot W.$

The most general differential equation by which the relation between the space, and velocity of a body moving through a fluid can be expressed, is

$$g \frac{V^2}{U^2} \cdot ds = V \cdot dV.$$

We shall now proceed to consider in what manner the retardation of the air affects the perpendicular ascents and descents of bodies.

Problem II.

What is the relation between the space and velocity, when a body is projected perpendicularly upwards through the air?

Employing the symbols introduced still in the same sense; the retardation to an ascending body will be expressed by $g + g \dfrac{V^2}{U^2}$, where the first term is the retardation caused by the weight of the body, and the second that arising from the resistance of the air. Substituting this value in the dynamical equation $f ds = v \, dv$, and there results

$$\frac{g}{U^2}(U^2 + V^2) \cdot ds = -V \cdot dV, \text{ and}$$

$$ds = \frac{-V \cdot dV}{U^2 + V^2} \times \frac{U^2}{g}.$$

Now by division $\dfrac{1}{U^2 + V^2} = \dfrac{1}{U^2} - \dfrac{V^2}{U^4} + \dfrac{V^4}{U^6} - \dfrac{V^6}{U^8}$ &c.

hence $\displaystyle\int \frac{-V \cdot dV}{U^2 + V^2} = \frac{-V^2}{2U^2} + \frac{V^4}{4U^4} - \frac{V^6}{6U^6} + \frac{V^8}{8U^8} -$

&c. $= -\frac{1}{2}\left(\dfrac{V^2}{U^2} - \dfrac{V^4}{2U^4} + \dfrac{V^6}{3U^6} - \dfrac{V^8}{4U^8} + \&c.\right) =$

$$-\frac{1}{2} \cdot \log. \left(1 + \frac{V^2}{U^2}\right).$$

Wherefore $s = -\dfrac{U^2}{2g} \cdot \log. \left(1 + \dfrac{V^2}{U^2}\right) + c.$

If V' be the initial velocity, then the equation becomes

$$o = -\frac{U^2}{2g} \cdot \log. \left(1 + \frac{V'^2}{U^2}\right) + c, \text{ and } c =$$

$$\frac{U^2}{2g} \cdot \log. \left(1 + \frac{V'^2}{U^2}\right).$$

Wherefore $S = \dfrac{U^2}{2g}\left(\overline{\log. 1 + \dfrac{V'^2}{V^2}} - \overline{\log. 1 + \dfrac{V^2}{V^2}}\right) =$

$$\frac{U^2}{2g} \log. \frac{U^2 + V'^2}{U^2 + V^2}.$$

If S be the maximum height to which the body can ascend with the initial velocity V', then $V = o$ and

$$S = \frac{U^2}{2g} \cdot \log. \frac{U'^2 + V'^2}{U^2} = \frac{U^2}{2g} \cdot \log. \overline{1 + \frac{V'^2}{U^2}}.$$

Problem III.

What is the relation between the velocity and the time in which it is acquired by a body ascending perpendicularly?

Substituting in the dynamical formula $V \cdot dt = ds$, the expression for ds, given in the preceding problem,

We have $V \cdot dt = \dfrac{U^2}{g} \times \dfrac{-V \, dV}{U^2 + V^2}$, and $dt =$

$$\frac{U^2}{g} \cdot \frac{-dV}{U^2 + V^2}.$$

But $\displaystyle\int \frac{-dV}{U^2 + V^2} = -\frac{V}{U^2} + \frac{V^3}{3U^4} - \frac{V^5}{5U^6} + \frac{V^7}{7U^8} =$

$$-\frac{1}{U}\left(\frac{V}{U} - \frac{V^3}{3U^3} + \frac{V^5}{5U^5} - \&c.\right).$$

Now $\dfrac{V}{U} - \dfrac{V^3}{3U^3} + \dfrac{V^5}{5U^5} -$ &c. is the value of the arch whose tangent is $\dfrac{V}{U}$;

Wherefore $t = -\dfrac{U}{g} \times$ arch whose tangent is $\dfrac{V}{U} + c.$

Let $t = o$, then V becomes the initial velocity or V', and

$$o = -\frac{U}{g} \times \text{arch whose tangent is } \frac{V'}{U} + c \text{ or}$$

$c = \dfrac{U}{g} \times$ arch whose tangent is $\dfrac{V'}{U}$. Hence $t = \dfrac{U}{g}$

$(A' - A)$; when A is the arch whose tangent is $\dfrac{V}{U}$, and

A' that whose tangent is $\dfrac{V'}{U}$. The time, therefore, in which a body projected upwards with the initial velocity V' will reach its maximum height, is

$$t = \frac{U}{g} A' \text{ as V is } = o.$$

Problem IV.

What is the relation between the space described, and the velocity acquired by a body in falling perpendicularly through the air?

For descending bodies the acceleration will be expressed by $g - g\dfrac{V^2}{U^2}$, where g is the accelerative force of gravity, and $-g\frac{V^2}{U^2}$, the retardation caused by the resistance of the air. Substituting this expression for f in the formula,

$$f \cdot ds = V \cdot dV, \text{ and it becomes } g\left(\frac{U^2 - V^2}{U^2}\right) \cdot ds = V \cdot dV.$$

Hence $ds = \dfrac{U^2}{g} \times \dfrac{V \cdot dV}{U^2 - V^2}$. But $\dfrac{1}{U^2 - V^2} =$

$$\frac{1}{U^2} + \frac{V^2}{U^4} + \frac{V^4}{U^6} + \frac{V^6}{U^8} + \&c.$$

Wherefore $\displaystyle\int\frac{V \cdot dV}{U^2 - V^2} = \frac{V^2}{2\,U^2} + \frac{V^4}{4\,U^4} + \frac{V^6}{6\,U^6} + \&c.$

Now $\log. \left(1 + \dfrac{V}{U}\right) = \dfrac{V}{U} - \dfrac{V^2}{2\,U^2} + \dfrac{V^3}{3\,U^3} - \dfrac{V^4}{4\,U^4} + \&c.$

And $\log. \left(1 - \dfrac{V}{U}\right) = -\dfrac{V}{U} - \dfrac{V^2}{2\,U^2} - \dfrac{V^3}{3\,U^3} - \&c.$

Hence by addition $-\frac{1}{2}\log. \left(1 - \dfrac{V^2}{U^2}\right) =$

$$\frac{V^2}{2\,U^2} + \frac{V^4}{4\,U^4} + \frac{V^6}{6\,U^6} + \&c.$$

And $s = \dfrac{-U^2}{2\,g} \cdot \log. \overline{1 - \dfrac{V^2}{U^2}} + c.$ When $V = o$, $s = o$, hence $c = o$; and the general equation is $s = -\dfrac{U^2}{2\,g}\log. \dfrac{U^2 - V^2}{U^2} = \dfrac{U^2}{2\,g} \cdot \log. \dfrac{U^2}{U^2 - V^2}.$

PROBLEM V.

What is the relation between the time and the velocity, when a body descends perpendicularly in a resisting medium?

Substituting in the equation $V \cdot dt = ds$, the value assigned to ds in the preceding problem, there results

$$dt = \frac{u^2}{g} \cdot \frac{dV}{U^2 - V^2} = \frac{U^2}{g}\left(\frac{dV}{U^2} + \frac{V^2 \cdot dV}{U^4} + \frac{V^4 \cdot dV}{U^6} + \&c.\right)$$

Hence $t = \dfrac{UV}{g} + \dfrac{V^3}{3\,U^4} + \dfrac{V^5}{5\,U^6} \cdot + \&c.$

$$= \frac{U}{g}\left(\frac{V}{U} + \frac{V^3}{3\,U^3} + \frac{V^5}{5\,U^5} + \&c.\right)$$

But $\log. \left(1 + \dfrac{V}{U}\right) = \dfrac{V}{U} - \dfrac{V^2}{2\,U^2} + \dfrac{V^3}{3\,U^3} - \dfrac{V^4}{4\,U^4} + \&c.$

And $\log. \left(1 - \dfrac{V}{U}\right) = \dfrac{V}{U} - \dfrac{V^2}{2\,U^2} - \dfrac{V^3}{3\,U^3} - \dfrac{V^4}{4\,U^4} - \&c.,$

by taking the difference,

$$\log. \frac{U + V}{U - V} = 2\left(\frac{V}{U} + \frac{V^3}{3\,U^3} + \frac{V^5}{5\,U^5} + \&c.\right)$$

Wherefore $t = \dfrac{U}{2\,g} \cdot \log. \left(\dfrac{U + V}{U - V}\right).$

Cor. Let us suppose $V = U$ in this equation, then $\dfrac{U + V}{U - V}$ is infinite, and consequently t is infinite. From this it appears, that a body cannot, by descending for

any finite time, acquire the terminal velocity V, although it constantly approaches to it as a limit.

The conclusions at which we have arrived on this subject cannot be employed to any practical purpose, until the resistance of the air, or the terminal velocity which depends upon it, be first determined. Resistance, as has been stated, is correlative to the term moving force. The latter is always estimated by weight. To ascertain the former, therefore, is to discover what weight is an equivalent to the pressure exerted by the air against a body moving through it with a given velocity. This subject has called forth the ingenuity of almost every philosopher of eminence since the days of Newton; nor does it yet appear to be settled with a precision suited to its importance. In treating of it, we shall first deliver the theoretical, and then the practical results which have been obtained.

PROP. VI. THEOREM.

If a body move through a fluid, exposing a plane surface to its action, the resistance will be equivalent to the weight of a column of the fluid having the plane for its base, and for its altitude twice the height which must be fallen through by the body in vacuo, under the influence of gravity, in order to acquire the velocity with which it moves. *On the measure of resistance to a body moving in a fluid.*

It has been already shown, that if a body moves through a fluid, the velocities at the different points of its path will be represented by the hyperbolic ordinates, and the spaces by the included areas. Let us assume c^2 as the area exposed to the fluid, p the length of the parallelopiped, and m its specific gravity; then its weight is $m\,p \cdot c^2$, that of the same volume of water being unity. Also let $\sqrt{2\,g\,h} =$ velocity of the moveable at $A = BA$, and $n =$ the specific gravity of the fluid. *PLATE CCCCLXVI. Fig. 6.*

The analytical equation for the curve BC is $y = \dfrac{1}{x}$; let the physical equation be $y = \dfrac{r}{x}$; then $AE = \dfrac{r}{\sqrt{2\,g\,h}}$, which, for the sake of brevity, may be represented by a.

Let the equation be taken from A, as the centre of the perpendicular co-ordinates, then expressing the ordinates by u, and the abscissæ by z, we have

$$m\,n = u = \frac{r}{a + z}.$$

Let us suppose that, for the small space $F\,n$, the particles are displaced with the same velocity, then their number being $n \cdot c^2 \cdot dz$, and the velocity of impulse being u, the momentum communicated to them will be

$$n \cdot c^2 \cdot dz \cdot u^2 = \frac{n \cdot c^2 \cdot dz \cdot r^2}{(a + z)^2} =$$

$$n \cdot c^2 \cdot r^2\left(\frac{dz}{a^2} - \frac{2\,z \cdot dz}{a^3} + \frac{3\,z^2\,dz}{a^4} - \&c.\right)$$

Wherefore, by taking the fluent, the sum of the momenta communicated to the fluid in the time z, is

$$r^2\,n \cdot c^2\left(\frac{z}{a^2} - \frac{z^2}{a^3} + \frac{z^3}{a^4} - \frac{z^4}{a^5} + \&c.\right) =$$

$$\frac{r^2 \cdot n \cdot c^2}{a} - \frac{r^2 \cdot n \cdot c^2}{a}\left(1 - \frac{z}{a} + \frac{z^2}{a^2} - \frac{z^3}{a^3} + \&c.\right)$$

But as action and reaction are equal and opposite, this must be equal to the momentum lost by the solid. Representing, therefore, the velocity lost by $\sqrt{2\,g\,h'}$, we have

$$\frac{r^2 \cdot n \cdot c^2}{a} - \frac{r^2 \cdot n \cdot c^2}{a}\left(1 - \frac{z}{a} + \frac{z}{a} + \frac{z^3}{a^3} + \&c.\right)$$
$$= m\,p \cdot c^2 \sqrt{2\,g\,h'}.$$

Since $1 - \dfrac{z}{a} + \dfrac{z^2}{a^2} - \dfrac{z^3}{a^3} + \&c. = \dfrac{1}{1+\dfrac{z}{a}}$, the equation becomes

$$\frac{r^2 \cdot n \cdot c^2}{a} - \frac{r^2 \cdot n \cdot c^2}{a} \cdot \frac{1}{1+\dfrac{z}{a}} = m\,p \cdot c^2 \sqrt{2\,g\,h'}.$$

Let us now suppose that z, or the time, becomes infinite, then $\dfrac{1}{1+\dfrac{z}{a}} = 0$, and as the whole velocity is lost, h' becomes

$= h$; hence $\dfrac{r^2 \cdot n \cdot c^2}{a} = m \cdot p \cdot c^2 \sqrt{2\,g\,h}$. But $a = \dfrac{r}{\sqrt{2\,g\,h}}$, wherefore $r \cdot n \cdot c^2 = m\,p \cdot c^2$. and $r = \dfrac{m\,p \cdot c^2}{n \cdot c^2_i}$.

From this we infer, that $y = \dfrac{m\,p \cdot c^2}{n \cdot c^2 \cdot x}$ is the physical equation for the curve.

According to the principles of dynamics,
$$g \cdot f \cdot d\,t = d\,v;$$
and, from the principles of fluxions, $-\dfrac{n \cdot c^2 y^2 \cdot d\,x}{m \cdot p \cdot c^2} = d\,y$. Now since y represents the velocity, and x the time, $d\,y = d\,v$, and $d\,x = d\,t$. Hence, by comparing together these two equations, we have

$$g\,f = \frac{-n \cdot c^2 \cdot y^2}{m \cdot p \cdot c^2} \text{ and } f = \frac{-n \cdot c^2\,y^2}{g \cdot m\,p \cdot c^2}.$$

But the retardation f is equal to the resistance divided by the quantity of matter resisted; and as $m\,p \cdot c^2$ is the quantity of matter resisted, it follows that $\dfrac{n \cdot c^2 \cdot y^2}{g}$ expresses the resistance, and $\dfrac{y^2}{g}$ the retardation. From the principles of uniformly accelerated motions, the square of the velocity, divided by twice the accelerative force, is equal to the height fallen from, wherefore $\dfrac{y^2}{g}$ is double the height from which a body must fall so as to acquire the velocity y. Q. E. D.

COR. It is obvious that the resistance will depend upon the surface which is exposed to the action of the fluid. Let us investigate what must be the resistance when the surface is a plane inclined at any angle φ to the direction of its motion.

PLATE
CCCCLXVI.
Fig. 7.

Let $AB^2 = c^2$ be the surface, also let $m\,n$ represent the direction and intensity of the pressure of the fluid. When the surface is perpendicular to the direction of its motion, the resistance is according to the proposition $= 2\,n \cdot c^2 \cdot h$. But when the surface is inclined, the quantity of fluid which it intercepts is diminished in the ratio of

$$\text{Rad} : \text{Sin}. \varphi.$$

Also the force with which each particle acts against the surface is diminished in the ratio of Rad. : Sin. φ. Hence the action of the fluid, when estimated perpendicularly against the surface, is diminished in the ratio of Rad.² : Sin.² φ.

Now the part of this force, which is efficient in retarding the surface, will be found, by reducing $p\,n$ to the direction $m\,n$ in which the body moves; so that the pressure against a surface perpendicular to the direction of its motion, is to the pressure against the same surface when inclined to it at any angle φ, in the ratio of Rad.³ : Sin.³ φ.

PROP. VII. PROB.

What is the expression for the resistance of a fluid against any surface of revolution?

Let BED be any surface of revolution, and let it be required to find an equation for the resistance opposed to it. Assume $EF = x$, and $AF = y$, then the surface of any small ring will be equal to

$$2\,\pi\,y\sqrt{(d\,x)^2 + (d\,y)^2}.$$

Were the surface perpendicular to the direction of its motion, the resistance to it would be

$$4\,\pi\,y\sqrt{(d\,x)^2 + (d\,y^2)} \cdot n\,h.$$

Being, however, inclined to it at the angle AGF, the resistance will be diminished in the ratio of Fig. 8.

$$\overline{(d\,x)^2 + (d\,y)^2}\Big|^{\frac{3}{2}} : (d\,y)^3;$$

and is therefore expressed by

$$\frac{4\,\pi\,y \cdot d\,y}{\left(\dfrac{d\,x}{d\,y}\right)^2 + 1} \times n\,h.$$

Wherefore the resistance to any surface of revolution is equal to $4\,\pi \cdot n \cdot h \cdot \displaystyle\int \dfrac{y\,d\,y}{\left(\dfrac{d\,x}{d\,y}\right)^2 + 1}$

COR. For the sphere; the equation between x and y is,

$$y = (2\,a\,x - x^2)^{\frac{1}{2}}.$$

Taking the fluxion of this equation,

$$d\,y = \frac{\overline{a - x} \cdot d\,x}{\sqrt{2\,ax - x^2}}, \text{ hence } \left(\frac{d\,x}{d\,y}\right)^2 = \frac{2\,a\,x - x^2}{(a - x)^2}.$$

The resistance, consequently, $= 4\,\pi \cdot n \cdot h$

$$\int \frac{\overline{a - x^3}}{a^2} \cdot d\,x = \frac{4\,\pi \cdot n\,h}{a^2}\left(a^3\,x - \frac{3\,a^2\,x^2}{2} + a\,x^3 - \frac{x^4}{4}\right).$$

Which, when $x = a$, becomes $\pi \cdot n\,h\,a^2$. Hence the resistance to a sphere is $\frac{1}{2}$ of the resistance to a cylinder having the same diameter.

Newton's
experi-
ments on
the resist-
ance of the
air.

It has been ascertained by experiment, that the resistance to a sphere is only $\frac{1}{2}$ of the quantity which has been here assigned to it. This is distinctly shown by experiments made at the request of Newton, and detailed in the Principia. This circumstance however admits of a satisfactory explanation. In our reasoning, it was assumed, that the particles of the fluid were completely at rest, until they came into immediate contact with the moving body, and that they were then displaced with a velocity equal to that which it possessed. The most casual observation however shows, that a solid does not move in this manner through a fluid; or, in other words, that a fluid does not thus act upon a solid. Whilst the particles of a fluid approach to any obstacle, they begin to take a direction sideways, and glide past it, communicating their impulse not to the solid, but to a portion of the fluid which remains stagnant about it. In esti-

Pneumatics.

mating the resistance, therefore, regard must be had not to the actual surface of the solid, but to the surface upon which the impulse of the fluid is directed. Knowing, therefore, the resistance to a sphere, let us inquire in what manner the fluid impinges upon it. Let it be assumed that the motion of the particles after impulse is along the line AB, whose equation is $y = m x$, reckoning A the origin of the co-ordinates, then $d y = m \cdot d x$; and the general formula for the resistance delivered in Proposition VII. becomes, in this case,

PLATE
CCCCLXVI.
Fig. 9.

$$4 \pi n \cdot h \int \frac{m^4 \cdot x \cdot d x}{1 + m^2} = \frac{\pi \cdot n \cdot a^2 h}{2} \text{ by supposition.}$$

Hence $2 \cdot \dfrac{m^4 \cdot x^2}{1 + m^2} = \dfrac{a^2}{2}$ and $\dfrac{m^2 \cdot x^2}{1 + m^2} = \dfrac{a^2}{4}$.

But $x = \dfrac{y}{m}$ and $x^2 = \dfrac{y^2}{m^2}$, consequently $\dfrac{m_2 \cdot y^2}{1 + m^2} = \dfrac{a^2}{4}$;

and supposing $y = a$, $\dfrac{m^2}{1 - m^2} = \dfrac{1}{4}$, hence $3 m^2 = 1$ and

$m = \sqrt{\dfrac{1}{3}}.$

The equation, therefore, of the line AB must be $y = \dfrac{x}{\sqrt{3}}$. Now $y = x \times$ cotang. $\angle ABC$, wherefore,

cot. $\angle ABC = \dfrac{1}{\sqrt{3}}$, and $\angle ABC$ or $BDA = 60^0$.

The fluid, therefore, when resisted by a sphere, will begin to diverge in the direction AB, the point A being at a distance from the sphere equal to its radius.

The experiments alluded to were performed by Dr. Desaguliers, by dropping from the summit of St. Paul's Cathedral, a height of 272 feet, spheres composed of such light substances as would render the resistance of the air appreciable. The method employed for finding the times of descent, was to station observers with seconds' pendulums both above and below. Those above dropped, at the same time, a leaden ball, and a dry spherical bladder, and observed the time of the descent of the ball; whilst those below observed the difference of time between the descent of the ball and that of the bladder. The following table shows the result of these observations.

Weight of Spheres.	Diam. of Spheres.	Times of Descent.
128 Gr.	5.28 Inches.	19″
156	5.19	17″
$137\frac{1}{3}$	5.30	$18\frac{1}{2}$″
$97\frac{1}{2}$	5.26	22″
$99\frac{1}{2}$	5.—	$21\frac{1}{2}$″

In order to illustrate the problems given above, we shall introduce here the calculations for the spaces which the several spheres ought to have described, as found from theory. The experiments having been made in the month of July, we may assume the temperature at 60°, and the weight of 100 cubic inches of air at 30.78 grains.

I. The capacity of a sphere whose diameter is 5.28 inches = 77.07 inches.

The weight of air contained by a sphere of this capacity = 23.722 grains.

Hence the ratio of $n : m = 23.722 : 128$.

Pneumatics.

The resistance of the air, agreeably to Newton's theory, a being the radius of the sphere expressed in feet, is $= \dfrac{\pi \cdot a^2 \cdot h \cdot n}{2}$. And the quantity of matter moved is $\dfrac{8 \pi \cdot a^3 \cdot m}{6}$, wherefore the retarding force, or

$$f = \frac{3 \pi \cdot a^2 h n}{8 \pi \cdot a^3 m} = \frac{3 h n}{8 a m} = \left(\text{since } h = \frac{v^2}{2 g} \right) \frac{3 v^2 n}{16 a m g}.$$

Now, since the retardations are proportional to the squares of the velocities, we have to find the terminal velocity.

$$1 : f : U^2 : v^2, \text{ or } 1 : \frac{3 U^2 n}{16 a m g} :: U^2 : v^2.$$

Hence $U^2 = \dfrac{16 a m g}{3 n}$. and $U = \sqrt{\dfrac{16 a m g}{3 n}} . = 4 \sqrt{\dfrac{a m g}{3 n}}.$

Substituting in this expression for a, m, g, n, their respective values,

$$U = 4 \sqrt{\frac{32\frac{1}{6} \times 128 \times 5.28}{3 \times 23.722 \times 24}} = 14.268 \text{ feet.}$$

Now, by Problem V, $t = \dfrac{U}{2 g} \log. \dfrac{U + V}{U - V}$, or

$19 \times 4.509 = \log. \dfrac{U + V}{U - V}$

From this we infer, that V differs from U by an infinitely small quantity, and may consequently be regarded as equal to it.

The equation $t = \dfrac{U}{2 g} \log. \dfrac{U + V}{U - V}$, may be put under the form $U \cdot t = \dfrac{U^2}{2 g} \log. \dfrac{(U + V)^2}{U^2 - V^2}$. But by Problem IV. $S = \dfrac{U^2}{2 g} \log. \dfrac{U^2}{U^2 - V^2}$. Hence $S - U t = \dfrac{U^2}{2 g} \log. \dfrac{U^2}{(U + V)^2} = \dfrac{U^2}{2 g} \log. \dfrac{U^2}{U^2 + 2 U V + V^2} = \dfrac{U^2}{2 g} \log. \dfrac{1}{4}.$

and $S = U t + \dfrac{U^2}{2 g} \log. \dfrac{1}{4} = 19 \times 14.268 - 3.165 \times 2.302585 \times .60205 = 266.706 \text{ feet.}$

Newton's conclusion from this experiment is, that the height fallen through, according to theory, should be 271 feet 11 inches. In this computation, the density of the air is assumed much smaller than it has been found by the accurate experiments of later philosophers. He considered it as $\dfrac{1}{860}$, that of water being unity, whereas Sir Humphry Davy has found it to be $\dfrac{1}{819.3}$, at the temperature of 60°, the barometer standing at 30 inches.

II. We shall calculate the space, by the second experiment, from the data assumed by Newton.

The capacity of the sphere whose diameter is 5.19 inches = 73.198 inches.

The weight of air contained by a sphere of this capacity = 21.477 grains.

$$U = 4 \sqrt{\frac{a \cdot m \cdot g}{3 n}} = 4 \sqrt{\frac{32\frac{1}{6} \times 156 \times 5.19}{3 \times 21.477 \times 24}} = 16.412.$$

$$S = U t + \frac{U^2}{2 g} \cdot \log \cdot \frac{1}{4} = 16.412 \times 17 - 4.187 \times$$
$$2.302585 \times .6020 \times 273.285 \text{ feet.}$$

The resist-
ance of air
moderates
the veloci-
ty of rain.

The resistance of the air, like every other arrangement of nature, points out to us the beneficent character, and unerring wisdom of its Creator. He has formed it of such a density as is the best possible for supporting animal existence, and at the same time for supplying a due quantity of moisture to the vegetable
creation. Had the air been much less dense than it is,
the drops of rain would descend with such a velocity
as would completely destroy that delicate organization
which they are designed to refresh. The earth would
no longer grow green under the influence of the summer showers, but would be converted into a barren
waste, where the most hardy plants could not flourish. As at present constituted, even the heaviest drops
of rain are so much retarded in their descent that they
do not injure the tenderest shoot.

According to the principles which have been laid
down, U, or the terminal velocity $= 4 \sqrt{\dfrac{a \cdot m \cdot g}{3 \, n}}$

Let us suppose that a drop of rain has its diameter
$\frac{1}{10}$th of an inch, which appears to be the usual magnitude, and inquire what is the greatest velocity which
it can attain. The ratio of $m : n$ in this case is that of
the density of water to air, and is equal to the ratio of
$1 : .00130386$ as found by Biot.

Hence $U = 4 \sqrt{\dfrac{32\frac{1}{6}}{3 \times .00130386 \times 120}} = 4 \sqrt{6.877} = 10.48$
feet.

Now, were there no atmosphere, and this particle to
drop from the same height as at present, its momentum
would be incomparably greater, and could be sustained
by no object without the greatest injury.

We now proceed to investigate the nature of the
curve described by a moveable projected at a given
angle of elevation, and with a given impetus through a
resisting medium. Before entering upon this subject,
it may be proper to demonstrate, in the form of lemmata, a few truths, which, although elegantly treated
of by the Continental writers, according to the analytic
method, have never been presented in so simple and
obvious a point of view as their importance requires.
For the assumptions which are made in this kind of
reasoning, however allowable, are with difficulty con-
ceded unless by those who have become expert analysts. The third lemma to be delivered has received
the name of Taylor's theorem, from the profound and
original mathematician who first demonstrated it in his
Methodus Incrementorum. It was originally discovered,
however, and first applied by Newton, and is perhaps
the most general as well as useful proposition in the
higher geometry.

PLATE
CCCCLXVI.
Fig. 10.

Definition. By the angle of curvature is meant the
angle which a tangent to a curve makes with the abscissa. Thus, the angle EDF, Plate CCCCLXVI.
Fig. 10. is the angle of curvature at D. The tangent of
this angle (the radius being unity) we call the tangent
of curvature for the sake of brevity.

LEMMA I.

A curve whose equation is $y = p \, x_m$, has for the tangent of curvature the general expression $m \, p \, x^{m-1}$.

According to Lemma I. Prop. I. $a^m = m \, a^{m-1}(a - b)$
$$+ m \, b^{m-1}(b - c) + \&c.$$
and $b^m = \qquad + m \, b^{m-1}(b - c) + \&c.$

Hence $a^m - b^m = m \, a^{m-1}(a - b)$ and $\dfrac{a^m - b^m}{a - b} = m \, a^{m-1}.$

Let ADG be the curve, and let the abscissæ AC, AB, be represented by a, b; then from the equation we obtain,
Fig. 10.

$$HC - DB = p(a^m - b^m), \text{ and } \frac{HF}{DF} = p \cdot \frac{(a^m - b^m)}{a - b}.$$

But $p \dfrac{(a^m - b^m)}{a - b} = p \, m \cdot a^{m-1}$, when b becomes equal
to a; and as, in this case, $HF = FE$, it follows that
$\dfrac{FE}{DF} = m \, p \, a^{m-1}.$

COR. 1. The area of this curve is obviously represented by

$$p \cdot a^m (a - b) + p \, b^m (b - c) + \&c. = \frac{p \, a^{m-1}}{m+1}.$$

COR. 2. In general, if $y = p \, x^m + q \, x^m + \&c.$ be the
equation of a curve, the expression for its tangent of
curvature will be

$$m \, p \, x^{m-1} + n \, q \, x^{m-1} + \&c.$$

and the expression for its area will be

$$\int p \, x^m \, d \, x + \int q \, x^n \, d \, x + \&c.$$

where x is a general symbol for the terms of the geometrical series a, b, c, &c. into which the abscissa is
supposed to be divided, and $d \, x$ for their differences
$a - b$, $b - c$, &c. Wherefore, by the lemma quoted
above, the area will be expressed by

$$\frac{p \, x^{+1}}{m+1} + \frac{q \, x^{n+1}}{n+1} + \&c.$$

LEMMA II.

Let DE, AC, (Fig. 11. Plate CCCCLXVI.), be two
curves so connected that the areas DAGF, DALM, of
the one, are expressed by the ordinates GN, PM, of the
other, then will the ordinates FG, LM, of the former
be the tangents of curvature of the latter.
Fig. 11.

According to supposition DAGF = ordinate NG,
            and   DAKH = ... KQ *.

Hence, by taking the differences, FGHQ = QR.
But FGHQ is ultimately equal to FG . GK; wherefore FG . GK = QR, and FG = $\dfrac{QR}{GK}$ = tangent of
curvature at N.

In like manner, it might be shown that LM is the
tangent of curvature at P, and so on of the other ordinates to the curve DE.

LEMMA III.

Let the tangents of curvature to the curve Ac (Fig.
12. Plate CCCCLXVI.), be expressed by the ordinates to the curve $m n$; and let the tangents of curvature to the curve $m n$ be expressed by the ordinates to
the curve $u p$, and so on; then will the difference
between any two ordinates to the first curve as
Fig. 12.

---

* Both quantities are conceived to be expressed by the same abstract number. It is on this principle that, in dynamics, we imagine
the space described by a body to be represented by an area.

Pneuma-
tics.

PNEUMATICS.

689

Pneuma-
tics.

$$CD = m\,E\,.\,EF + u\,E\,.\,\frac{EF^2}{1\,.\,2} + t\,E\,.\,\frac{EF^3}{1\,.\,2\,.\,3} + \&c.$$

Or let the tangent of curvature at the point B be represented by $\frac{dy}{dx}$, at the point m by $\frac{d^2\,y}{dx^2}$, at the point u by $\frac{d^3\,y}{dx^3}$, &c. also let EF be represented by h; then

$$CD = \frac{dy}{dx}h + \frac{d^2\,y}{dx^2}\frac{h^2}{1\,.\,2} + \frac{d^3\,y}{dx^3}\frac{h^3}{1\,.\,2\,.\,3} + \&c.$$

According to Lemma II. the curvilineal space $EFmn$ $=CD$. But $EFmn = EE\,.\,Em$ — area man. Hence $CD = \frac{dy}{dx}h$ — area man. In order to find the area man, let us suppose the abscissæ to be reckoned from m, and called z, and the ordinates bc, an, to be called v, and the equation of the curve to be

$$v = A\,z^m + B\,z^n + C\,z^p + \&c.$$

Then the expression for the tangent of curvature to this curve becomes $m\,A\,z^{m-1} + n\,B\,z^{n-1} + \&c.$ which, when $z=0$, should be equal to $u\,E$. Hence $m-1=0$, $m=1$, and

$$A = u\,E = \frac{d^2\,y}{dx^2}.$$

The expression for the tangent of curvature is therefore

$$u\,E + n\,B\,z^{n-1} + p\,c\,z^{p-1} + \&c.$$

which consequently is also an expression for the ordinates to the curve up, which are situate between $u'E$ and pF.

Again, the expression for the tangent of curvature to this arch becomes

$$n\,.\,\overline{n-1}\,B\,z^{n-2} + p\,.\,\overline{p-1}\,.\,c\,.\,z^{p-2} + \&c.$$

$$v = \frac{d^2\,y}{dx^2}\frac{h}{1.} + \frac{d^3\,y}{dx^3}\,.\,\frac{h^2}{1\,.\,2.} + \cdots \cdots \frac{d^m\,y}{dx^m}\frac{h^{m-1}}{1\,.\,2\,.\,3\,..\,(m-1)} + P\,h^{m+\frac{1}{n}}$$

Hence $$CD = \frac{d^2\,y}{dx}h + \frac{d^2\,y}{dx^2}\,.\,\frac{h^2}{1\,.\,2} + \cdots \cdots \frac{n\,.\,P\,h^{\frac{nm+m+1}{n}}}{nm+m+1}.$$

This theorem gives the value of CD, developed in terms of the powers of h in every case in which it is possible, and in every case shows what terms it is possible to develope in this manner.

PLATE
CCCCLXVI.
Fig. 13. LEMMA IV. Let ae (Plate CCCCLXVI. Fig. 13.) be any arch of a curve, and $mn = np$, also let ab be a tangent to the point a; when mn is infinitely small, the ratio of $bc : cd$ is that of equality.

Produce ab to meet pe produced in g, and draw ak parallel to mp. If mn be called h,

$$hd = \frac{dy}{dx}h + \frac{d^2\,y}{dx^2}\frac{h^2}{1\,.\,2} + \&c.$$

But $hb = \frac{dy}{dx}h$,

hence $$bc = \frac{d^2\,y}{dx^2}\frac{h^2}{1\,.\,2} + \frac{d^3\,y}{dx^3}\frac{h^3}{1\,.\,2\,.\,3} + \&c.$$

Again, since $mp = 2h$, we have in like manner

$$ge = 4\,.\,\frac{d^2\,y}{dx^2}\frac{h^2}{1\,.\,2} + 8\,\frac{d^3\,y}{dx^3}\,.\,\frac{h^3}{1\,.\,2\,.\,3} + \&c.$$

But $ge = 2bd$, hence

$$bd = 2\,.\,\frac{d^2\,y}{dx^2}\,.\,\frac{h_2}{1\,.\,2} + 4\,\frac{d^3\,y}{dx^3}\,.\,\frac{h^3}{1\,.\,2\,.\,3} + \&c.$$

Taking $z=0$, this expression should become equal to $t\,E$. Hence $n-2=0$, $n=2$. and

$$2\,B = t\,E,\; B = \frac{t\,E}{2} = \frac{d^3\,y}{dx^3} \times \frac{1}{1\,.\,2}.$$

In this manner, we may proceed to determine the co-efficients C, D, &c. so long as there is a tangent of curvature, as $t\,E$. When it becomes $=0$, the remaining terms of the equation

$$v = A\,z^m + B\,z^n + C\,z^p + \&c.$$

become $=0$.

This equation may therefore be expressed generally thus,

$$v = \frac{d^2\,y}{dx^2}\,.\,z + \frac{d^3\,y}{dx^3}\,.\,\frac{z^2}{1\,.\,2} + \frac{d^4\,y}{dx^4}\,.\,\frac{z^3}{1\,.\,2\,.\,3} + \&c.$$

and the area $man =$

$$\frac{d^2\,y}{dx^2}\,.\,\frac{z^2}{1\,.\,2} + \frac{d^3\,y}{dx^3}\,.\,\frac{z^3}{1\,.\,2\,.\,3} + \frac{d^4\,y}{dx^4}\,.\,\frac{24}{1\,.\,2\,.\,3\,.\,4} \&c.$$

which, when h is taken instead of z, becomes

$$\frac{d^2\,y}{dx^2}\,.\,\frac{h^2}{1\,.\,2} + \frac{d^3\,y}{dx^3}\,.\,\frac{h^3}{1\,.\,2\,.\,3} + \&c.$$

Hence

$$CD = \frac{dy}{dx}h + \frac{d^2\,y}{dx^2}\frac{h^2}{1\,.\,2} + \frac{d^3\,y}{dx^3}\frac{h^3}{1\,.\,2\,.\,3} + \&c.\;Q.E.D.$$

We have here connected the quantities by the sign $+$, for in every particular case the proper sign will always be ascertained by finding the tangents of curvature, or, in other words, by taking the differentials of the equation of the curve. Should the tangent of the angle of curvature become infinite in any case, then z must occur in the denominator; or, in other words, one of the indices m, n, p, must be a mixed number, and

and $$cd = bd - bc = \frac{d^2\,y}{dx^2}\frac{h^2}{1\,.\,2} + \frac{3d^3y}{dx^3}\,.\,\frac{h^3}{1\,.\,2\,.\,3}$$

Wherefore $bc : cd =$

$$\frac{d^2\,y}{dx^2}\frac{h^2}{1\,.\,2} + \frac{d^3\,y}{dx^3}\frac{h^3}{1\,.\,2\,.\,3} : \frac{d^2\,y}{dx^2}\frac{h^2}{1\,.\,2} + \frac{3\,.\,d^3y}{dx^3}\frac{h^3}{1\,.\,2\,.\,3}$$

Now when h is infinitely small, the two last terms are obviously in the ratio of equality; hence

$$bc = cd.$$

We shall now proceed to apply these results to the determination of the path of a projectile propelled through the air with any velocity, and at any angle to the horizon, under the influence of the force of gravity.

Let PGQ (Plate CCCCLXVI. Fig. 14.) be the curve PLATE
CCCCLXVI.
Fig. 14. in which the projectile moves. Let GB, HC, ID, KE, be four ordinates at equal distances from each other; also let GL, HN, be tangents to the curve at the points G, H, and HM a line parallel to PQ. From N draw N o perpendicular to HI. If t, t', be assumed to express the times in which the projectile moves over GH, HI, the velocities with which it describes these small arches will be expressed by

4 s

$$\frac{GH}{t} \text{ and } \frac{HI}{t'}.$$

The velocity of the moveable has been increased, while passing over HI, by the force of gravity; and as it has been carried over the space NI by this force in the time t', the velocity which has been thus communicated is expressed by $\frac{2\,NI}{t'}$. Reducing this velocity into the direction HI, it becomes $\frac{2\,OI}{t'}$, which is the increase of velocity acquired by the projectile from the force of gravity in passing over HI. Since the triangles ONI, HMI, are similar, $OI = \frac{MI \cdot NI}{HI}$; and consequently the velocity with which the projectile would move in the direction HN, were it not deflected by the force of gravity, is

$$\frac{HI}{t'} - \frac{2\,MI \cdot NI}{HI \cdot t'}.$$

Hence the velocity lost by the resistance of the medium through which the projectile moves, is expressed by

$$\frac{GH}{t} - \frac{HI}{t'} + \frac{2\,MI \cdot NI}{HI \cdot t'}.$$

Now since the velocity which a body, by falling under the influence of the force of gravity, would acquire in the time this retardation takes place, is expressed by $\frac{2\,NI}{t'}$, it follows that the retardation of the medium is to the accelerative force of gravity in the ratio of

$$\frac{GH}{t} - \frac{HI}{t'} + \frac{2\,MI \cdot NI}{HI \cdot t'} : \frac{2\,NI}{t'}; \text{ that is}$$

$$\text{of } \frac{t'\,GH}{t} - HI + \frac{2\,MI \cdot NI}{HI} : 2\,NI.$$

Let CD be represented by h, CE by $2\,h$, and CB by $-h$; then, according to Lemma III. MI may be expressed by the series $A\,h + B\,h^2 + C\,h^3 +$ &c. and NI by the series $B\,h^2 + C\,h^3 +$ &c. Also, if CH$=$P, the ordinates DI, EH, and BG, will be severally expressed by

$$P - A\,h - B\,h^2 - C\,h^3 - \&c.$$
$$P - 2\,A\,h - 4\,B\,h^2 - 8\,C\,h^3 - \&c.$$
$$P + A\,h - B\,h^2 + C\,h^3 - \&c.$$

To the difference of the squares of BG, CH, let us add the square of BC or h^2, and there results,
$$GH^2 = h^2 + A^2\,h^2 - 2\,AB\,h^3 + \&c.$$
In like manner,
$$HI^2 = h^2 + A^2\,h^2 + 2\,AB\,h^3 + \&c.$$
By taking the square roots of these series, neglecting the terms where h occurs in a higher power than the square, we have

$$GH = h - \frac{AB\,h^2}{1 + A^2} \text{ and } HI = h + \frac{AB\,h^2}{1 + A^2}.$$

Again, if an arithmetical mean be taken between the ordinates GB, ID, the difference between it and HC will give $HR = B\,h^2 + \&c.$

In like manner, the sagitta to the arch HK will be found equal to $B\,h^2 + 3\,C\,h^3$.

According to the fourth lemma, $B\,h^2$ and $B\,h^2 + 3\,C\,h^3$ have to each other the same ratio as LH and NI. But as the spaces described under the influence of a constant force are proportional to the squares of the times, it follows that

$$\frac{t^2}{t'^2} = \frac{B\,h^2}{B\,h^2 + 3\,C\,h^3} \text{ and } \frac{t'}{t} = 1 + \frac{3\,C\,h}{2\,B}.$$

By substituting for GH, HI, MI, NI, $\frac{t'}{t}$ their values, in the expression given above for the accelerative force, and omitting those terms which contain powers of h higher than the square, there results

$$\frac{t'}{t}\,GH - HI + \frac{2\,MI \cdot NI}{HI} = \frac{3\,C\,h^2}{2\,B}\sqrt{1 + A^2}.$$

Since $2\,NI = 2\,B\,h^2$, by dividing $\frac{3\,C\,h^2}{2\,B}\sqrt{1 + A^2}$ by this quantity, we obtain $\frac{3\,C}{4\,B^2}\sqrt{1 + A^2}$ as an expression for the retardation of the medium through which the projectile moves, considering the accelerative force of gravity as the unit.

Again, the small part of the curve HI may be considered as a parabola; now, from the parabolic theory, (see Art. GUNNERY,) the velocity, in any part of the curve, is the same as would be acquired by a heavy body in falling through one fourth of the parameter at that point. The parameter at the point H is $\frac{HN^2}{NI} = \frac{HI^2}{NI} = \frac{h^2 + A^2\,h^2}{B\,h^2} = \frac{1 + A^2}{B}$; consequently the velocity acquired by falling through one fourth of this space is $\sqrt{\dfrac{1 + A^2}{2\,B}}$

It has already been shown that the retardations are proportional to the squares of the velocities; suppose, then, that a is the height due to the terminal velocity, and we obtain

$$1 : a :: \frac{3\,C}{4\,B^2}\sqrt{1 + A^2} : \frac{1 + A^2}{4\,B}. \text{ Hence } a = \frac{B\sqrt{1 + A^2}}{3\,C}.$$

From Lemma III. we know that A is equal to $\frac{dy}{dx}$, B, $\frac{d^2y}{dx^2} \times \frac{1}{1 \cdot 2}$ and C, $\frac{d^3y}{dx^3}$,

hence $a = \dfrac{\dfrac{d^2y}{dx^2}\sqrt{1 + \left(\dfrac{dy}{dx}\right)^2}}{2 \cdot 3 \cdot \dfrac{d^3y}{dx^3} \times \dfrac{1}{1 \cdot 2 \cdot 3}} = \dfrac{\dfrac{d^2y}{dx^2}\sqrt{1 + \left(\dfrac{dy}{dx}\right)^2}}{\dfrac{d^3y}{dx^3}}.$

We shall now proceed to deduce from this fluxional property an equation for the curve. For this purpose, let us suppose P to be the centre of the perpendicular co-ordinates, or the point from which the values of y and x are calculated, also let $\angle$ SPQ $=$ angle of elevation be represented by θ. Then will $\frac{dy}{dx}$, when $x = 0$, become equal to tang. θ. Let U be taken to represent the initial velocity, then, according to the parabolic theory,

$$U = \frac{PS}{\sqrt{2\,ST}} \text{ and } \sqrt{2 \cdot ST} = \frac{PS}{U}.$$

But ST is equal to NI, or $-\frac{d^2y}{dx^2} \times \frac{h^2}{1 \cdot 2}$ when x becomes equal to 0 ; hence, on this supposition,

$$\frac{d^2 y}{d x^2} \cdot \frac{h^2}{} = \frac{PS^2}{U^2} = \frac{-\text{Sec.}^2 \theta \cdot h^2}{U^2} = \frac{-h^2}{U^2 \cdot \cos.^2 \theta}$$

and $\dfrac{d^2 y}{d x^2} = \dfrac{-1}{U^2 \cdot \cos.^2}$.

If b be the height due to the velocity U, then

$$\frac{d^2 y}{d x^2} = \frac{-1}{2 b \cdot \cos.^2 \theta}$$

Recurring to the equation, $a = \dfrac{\dfrac{d^2 y}{d x^2} \sqrt{1 + \left(\dfrac{d y}{d x}\right)^2}}{\dfrac{d^3 y}{d x^3}}$, let

$\dfrac{d y}{d x} = p$, then we have $\dfrac{d^2 y}{d x} = d p$, and $\dfrac{d^3 y}{d x} = d^2 p$, and

$a = \dfrac{\sqrt{1 + p^2} \cdot d p \cdot d x}{d^2 p}$; consequently, $d^2 p =$

$$\sqrt{1 + p^2} \cdot d p \cdot \frac{d x}{a}.$$

Representing $\dfrac{d x}{a}$ by c, this equation takes the form

$$\frac{d^2 p}{d p} = c \sqrt{1 + p^2}$$

Taking the fluxion of this expression, we have

$$\frac{d^2 p \cdot d p - (d^2 p)^2}{(d p)^2} = \frac{c \cdot p \cdot d p}{\sqrt{1 + p^2}} \text{ and}$$

$$d^3 p = \frac{c \cdot p(d p)^2}{\sqrt{1 + p^2}} + \frac{(d^2 p)^2}{d p}.$$

Again, taking the fluxion of this equation, we derive

$$d^4 p = c \left(\frac{((d p)^3 + 2 p \cdot d p \cdot d^2 p)(1 + p^2)) - c p^2 (d p)^3}{(1 + p^2)^{\frac{3}{2}}} \right.$$

$$+ \frac{2 \cdot d p \cdot d^2 p \cdot d^3 p - (d^2 p)^3}{(d p)^2}.$$

By taking the fluxion of this equation, we find the value of $d^5 p$, and so on.

By substituting for c, $d p$, $d^2 p$, $d^3 p$, their values, when $x = 0$, we find,

1. $\dfrac{d^2 p}{d p} \cdot \dfrac{d^2 y}{d x^2} = \dfrac{d^3 y}{d x^2} = \dfrac{d x}{a} \sqrt{1 + \text{tang.}^2 \theta} \cdot \dfrac{d^2 y}{d x^2}$

$\dfrac{d^3 y}{d x^3} = \dfrac{1}{a} \sqrt{1 + \text{tang.}^2 \theta} \cdot \dfrac{d^2 y}{d x^2} = \dfrac{-1}{2 a \cdot b \cdot \cos.^3 \theta}$.

2. $\dfrac{d^3 p}{d x^3} = \dfrac{d^4 y}{d x^4} = \dfrac{\sin. \theta}{4 a b^2 \cdot \cos.^4 \theta} - \dfrac{1}{2 a^2 b \cdot \cos.^4 \theta}$.

3. $\dfrac{d^4 p}{d x^4} = \dfrac{d^5 y}{d x^5} = \dfrac{4 \cdot \sin. \theta}{4 a^2 b^2 \cdot \cos.^5 \theta} - \dfrac{1}{8 a b^3 \cdot \cos.^5 \theta}$

$$- \frac{1}{2 a^3 b \cdot \cos.^5 \theta}.$$

&c.   &c.   &c.

As a, b, the heights due to the terminal and initial velocities, are very great, and as they occur in the denominators, they will render each successive term of less value than that preceding it; hence as a very exact approximation, we have

$$y = \text{tang.} \theta \cdot x - \frac{1}{2 \cdot p \cdot b \cdot \cos.^2 \theta} \cdot \frac{x^2}{1 \cdot 2} - \frac{1}{2 a \cdot b \cdot}$$

$$\cos.^3 \theta \cdot \frac{x^3}{1 \cdot 2 \cdot 3} - \frac{1}{2 a^2 b \cdot \cos.^4 \theta} \cdot \frac{x^4}{1 \cdot 2 \cdot 3 \cdot 4}, \text{ &c.}$$

By adding to and subtracting from this series the quantity $\dfrac{a}{2 b \cdot \cos. \theta} \cdot \dfrac{x}{1 \cdot 1}$, we obtain

$$y = \text{tang.} \theta \cdot x + \frac{a}{2 b \cdot \cos. \theta} \cdot \frac{x}{1 \cdot 1} - \frac{a}{2 b \cdot \cos. \theta} \cdot \frac{x}{1 \cdot 1} -$$

$$\frac{1}{2 b \cdot \cos.^2 \theta} \cdot \frac{x^2}{1 \cdot 2} -, \text{ &c.}$$

$$= \left(\text{tang.} \theta + \frac{a}{2 b \cdot \cos. \theta} \right) x - \frac{a^2}{2 b} \times$$

$$\left(\frac{1}{a \cos. \theta} \cdot \frac{x}{1 \cdot 1} + \frac{x^2}{a^2 \cdot \cos.^2 \theta \cdot 1 \cdot 2} + \frac{x^3}{a^3 \cdot \cos.^3 \theta \cdot 1 \cdot 2 \cdot 3} + \text{&c.} \right).$$

Let the series $\dfrac{x}{a \cdot \cos. \theta} + \dfrac{x^2}{1 \cdot 2 \cdot a^2 \cdot \cos.^2 \theta} + $ &c. be expressed by P, then it is known by means of recurring series *, that

$\dfrac{x \cdot \cos. \theta}{a} = \log. (1 + P).$ Now if $e = 2.718281$, or

that number whose hyperbolic logarithm is 1, then

$$\log. e^{\frac{x \cdot \cos. \theta}{a}} = \frac{x \cdot \cos. \theta}{a} = \log. (1 + P).$$

Wherefore $y = \left(\text{tang.} \theta + \dfrac{a}{2 b \cdot \cos. \theta} \right) x - \dfrac{a^2}{2 b} \times$

$\left(e^{\frac{x \cdot \cos. \theta}{a}} - 1 \right)$ is the equation for the curve.

OF AIR IN MOTION.
I. THE WIND.

The impulsive force of air is subject to the same law with that of the incompressible fluids. Its tendency to produce motion upon the sails of a windmill was found by M. Parent to be 54° 44'. This is the complement of the angle of weather, as it is called, or of the angle which the plane of the sail makes with the direction of its motion. The demonstration of this truth is very simple. Let CD (Fig. 15. Plate CCCCLXVI.) represent the velocity and impulsive force of the wind against a plane whose section is AB. By reducing this force into the direction CE, we obtain the efficient force with which the fluid strikes against the plane ; and by reducing this again into the direction CH, we obtain that force which imparts a rotatory motion to the sail.

If CD be called a, and $\angle$ CDE, x, then CE $= a$. sin. x, and CH $= a$. sin. x . cos. x . But as the number of particles which strike against the plane is also diminished on account of its inclination in the ratio of rad. : sin. x, it follows that the action of the fluid against the plane is expressed by a . sin.$^2 x$. cos. x .

To find when this is a maximum, we have by taking the fluxions

$2 a$. sin. x . cos.$^2 x$. $d x - a$. sin.$^3 x$. $d x = 0$

or 2 . cos.$^2 x - $ sin.$^2 x = 0$; hence sin. $x = \sqrt{2}$. cos. x

and tang. x (radius being unity) $= \sqrt{2}$.

Wherefore $x = 54° 44'$.

It is obvious that this determination proceeds upon the supposition that the plane is at rest. We shall now

The action of wind upon a sail at rest.

PLATE CCCCLXVI. Fig. 15.

* See La Grange's " Théorié des Fonctions," chap. iii.

5

Action of
wind upon
a sail in
motion.
PLATE
CCCCLXVI.
Fig. 16.

proceed to inquire at what angle the impulsive force produces the greatest effect when the plane has acquired a determinate velocity.

Let CD (Fig. 16. Plate CCCCLXVI.) as before, represent the direction and impulsive force of the wind, DG the direction and velocity of the sail's motion. By reducing the velocity of the wind and sail into the direction AB perpendicular to the plane, the relative velocity of the wind, or that with which it strikes the plane, is ED — DL. Hence the effect of the wind in producing a rotatory motion will be expressed by EH — DK.

Let CD, as formerly, be represented by a, and DG by c, then $EH = a . \sin. x . \cos. x$, and $DK = c . \cos.^2 x$ obviously. Hence the impulsive force is expressed by $a . \sin. x . \cos. x — c . \cos.^2 x$. But, as before, the number of particles of fluid which strikes against the plane is diminished in the ratio of rad. : sin. x, wherefore the whole momentum against the sail is expressed by $(a . \sin. x . \cos. x — c . \cos.^2 x) \sin. x$.

Let $\sin x = y$, then $\cos. x = \sqrt{1 — y^2}$, and
$$(a . \sin. x . \cos. x — c . \cos.^2 x) \sin. x =$$
$$(a y \sqrt{1 — y^2} — c . \overline{1 — y^2}) y.$$ By taking the fluxion of this quantity we obtain

$$\left(a . \sqrt{1 — y^2} . dy — \frac{a . y^2 . dy}{\sqrt{1 — y^2}} + 2 c y . dy \right) y +$$
$$(a y \sqrt{1 — y^2} — c — \overline{1 — y^2}) \, d y = o;$$

and dividing by $d y$,

$$2 a y \sqrt{1 — y^2} — \frac{a y^2}{\sqrt{1 — y^2}} + 3 c y^2 — c = o,$$ or

$$2 — \frac{y^2}{1 — y^2} + \frac{c}{a} . \frac{3 y^2 — 1}{y \sqrt{1 — y^2}} = o .$$

But $\frac{y^2}{1 — y^2} = \text{tang.}^2 a,$

wherefore $2 — \text{tang.}^2 x + \left(3 — \frac{1}{\sin.^2 x} \right) \frac{c}{a} . \text{tang.} x = o;$ and by reducing this quadratic equation

$$\text{tang.} x = \sqrt{ 2 + \frac{3 — \frac{1}{\sin.^2 x}}{2} \times \frac{c^2}{a^2} + \frac{3 — \frac{1}{\sin.^2 x}}{2} \times \frac{c}{a} }.$$

On the supposition that $c = a$, or, in other words, that the velocity of the sail is equal to that of the wind, we have

$$\text{tang.} x = \sqrt{ 2 + \frac{3 — \frac{1}{\sin.^2 x}}{2} + \frac{3 — \frac{1}{\sin.^2 x}}{2} }.$$

Assuming as an approximation, in order to find x from this equation, that its value is 54° 44′, we find as a nearer approximation $x = 65°$ 24′. Taking the sine of this angle, and substituting it as an approximation in the second number of the equation, we find, as a still more correct approximation, $x = 68°$ 54′. Substituting this again for x, we find, as a fourth approximation, $x = 69°$ 4′, which we consider as the correct value.

Let us again suppose that $c = 2 a$, or that the velocity of the sail is double the velocity of the wind, then the formula becomes

$$\text{tang.} x = \sqrt{ 2 + \left(3 — \frac{1}{\sin.^2 x} \right)^2 + 3 — \frac{1}{\sin.^2 x} }.$$

Substituting 75° as the value of x, we obtain as a first approximation $x = 77°$ 3′. Substituting again this value, we deduce as a second approximation $x = 77°$ 7′,

which may be considered as the true value of x in this case.

Those who desire a theoretical acquaintance with the principles of machinery impelled by wind, we would refer to Euler's work upon this subject. All his conclusions, together with many other useful observations, are contained in Dr. Brewster's edition of Ferguson's *Lectures on Select Subjects;* and also in the article MECHANICS, vol. xiii. p. 566—570.

The theory of winds has not arrived at that degree of perfection which renders science subservient to the purposes of life. We can as yet only attribute them in a vague manner to the operation of a few general causes. From what we have seen of the expansibility of air by heat, one may easily conceive how the atmosphere must always be in a state of commotion, some parts of it being exposed to an intense temperature, while others are comparatively cold. That portion which encircles the torrid zone, by receiving the rays of a vertical sun, is much rarer than that which surrounds the higher latitudes. Hence, in order to maintain a due equilibrium, the aerial column at the equator must be higher than it is in colder climates. This was found to be the case by Mr. Casson, who observed that, for the same elevation, the barometer falls only about half as much in the torrid as it does in the temperate zones.

The air being thus expanded by means of heat, it is displaced by means of the denser air which rushes in from higher latitudes. The winds which are occasioned in this manner are called the trade-winds, and are so uniform in their action, that they render the greatest service to those who navigate the tropical seas. From October to May, the north-east trade-wind continues to blow, and from April to October the south-west.

M. De Luc has advanced a very ingenious explanation of the oblique direction in which these winds approach the equator. This he has attributed to the rotation of the earth. The air at any place when apparently calm, or in a state of rest, possesses obviously the same velocity of rotation, with which that place revolves. Now the rotatory velocity of any point on the earth's surface is proportional to the parallel of latitude which passes through it; that is, to the cosine of the latitude, as may be easily shown; hence, were the whole atmosphere in a tranquil state, the actual velocity of every section of it would be proportional to the cosine of its angular distance from the equator. Let us now suppose, that from the influence of heat, the condensed air of the north begins to move towards the south. Its rotatory motion, being the same with that of the region which it has left, is less than that of the place into which it has come. Hence, as the direction of the earth's motion is from west to east, it will appear to blow from east to west with a relative velocity equal to the difference between the velocities of the parallel left and that come to. The same explanation obviously applies to the westerly direction of the wind which rushes towards the equator from the south. In confirmation of this theory, it may be observed, upon the authority of Mr. Dalton, that in sailing northwards, the trade-winds veer more and more from the east towards the north, so that about their limit they become nearly N. E.; and *vice versa*, in sailing southwards, they become at least almost S. W. These winds are seldom perceptible in a higher latitude than 30°. Their place of concourse appears to be a little to the north of the equator, from the circumstance that the sun, the source of heat, is longer in the northern than in the

Theory of
winds.
Trade
wind.

De Luc's
explana-
tion of
their
oblique di-
rection.

Pneuma-
tics.

southern hemisphere. About the equator, they blow about 4° from the east or west points.

This influx of air towards the equator appears to be counterbalanced by a current in the higher regions of the atmosphere towards the poles. The heated air at the equator continues to ascend until it reaches an altitude where its elasticity exceeds that of the air which surrounds it. It then begins to diffuse itself towards the poles, maintaining an equilibrium in the atmosphere, and moderating the intense cold of the climates towards which it is wafted. "Such would be perhaps the only fluctuations in the atmosphere, were the whole globe covered with water, or the variations of the earth's surface in heat regular and constant, so as to be the same every where over the same parallel of latitude. As it is, however, we find the irregularities of heat, arising from the interspersion of sea and land, are such, that though all the parts of the atmosphere in some sort conspire to produce regular winds round the torrid zone, yet the effect of land is such, that striking inequalities are produced; witness the monsoons, the sea and land breezes, &c. which can be accounted for upon no other principle than that of rarefaction, because the rotatory velocity of different parallels in the torrid zone is nearly alike *."

Anemome-
ter.

We shall conclude these observations by referring to the article ANEMOMETER, vol. ii. p. 69—77, for the description of instruments for measuring the velocity of winds, referring for a more particular account of their origin to the article PHYSICAL GEOGRAPHY.

The consideration of the law which connects the difference of elevation at which the fluid stands in the tubes of Dr. Lind's anemometer, and the velocity of the wind by which it is occasioned, leads us to the second branch of our inquiry into the properties of air in motion.

II. ON THE VELOCITY OF AIR RUSHING FROM A DENSER INTO A RARER MEDIUM.

On the velocity of air rushing from a denser into a rarer medium.

It may be demonstrated of air as of water, that it rushes into a vacuum with the velocity which would be acquired by a heavy body in falling through a height equal to the head of pressure. Now, it has been shown of air, that if its density were equable throughout, its elevation, in order that its density might be the same at the earth's surface as at present, would be 312852.37 inches, or 26071.03 feet. But if $32\frac{1}{6}$ feet be represented by g, the velocity acquired by falling through any space S, is represented by $V = \sqrt{2gs}$; by substituting for S in this expression, the number 26071.03, V, or the velocity with which common atmospheric air rushes into a vacuum, will be found equal to 1295 feet per second.

This principle serves also to determine the velocity with which air will rush from a denser into a rarer medium. The height of a homogeneous atmosphere is always proportional to its density; hence we may consider the denser air as a fluid rushing into a vacuum with the velocity due to the atmospherical subtangent reduced in the ratio of the density of the heavier air to the relative density.

Let Δ be the density of the heavier air, H the atmospherical subtangent corresponding to it; also let δ be the density of the rarer air. The air having for its density Δ will obviously, when mixing with the air whose density is δ, have the same velocity as though it were rushing into a vacuum with the density $\Delta - \delta$.

Now the atmospherical subtangent corresponding to this density is found by the analogy

$$\Delta : \Delta - \delta :: H : H\left(\frac{\Delta - \delta}{\Delta}\right).$$

From the dynamical relation $V = \sqrt{2gs}$, it appears that the velocities acquired by falling from different heights are proportional to their square roots. If, therefore, V′ be taken to represent the velocity of common air rushing into a vacuum, or the number 1295 feet, and H′ the common atmospherical subtangent, or 26071.03 feet, we have

$$H' : H\left(\frac{\Delta - \delta}{\Delta}\right) :: V'^2 : V'^2 = V'^2 \cdot \frac{H}{H'}\left(\frac{\Delta - \delta}{\Delta}\right).$$

$$\text{and } V = V'\sqrt{\frac{H}{H'}\left(\frac{\Delta - \delta}{\Delta}\right)}.$$

If Δ' be assumed to express the density of common air; since $\Delta' : \Delta :: H' : H$, we have $\frac{H}{H'} = \frac{\Delta}{\Delta'}$, and $V = V'\sqrt{\frac{\Delta - \delta}{\Delta'}}$, when Δ is the density of the denser medium, δ of the rarer, and Δ' of the atmosphere.

It is by means of this formula that we are enabled to obtain a knowledge of the velocity of wind by the anemometer. For since the air in the horizontal tube is maintained in its state of superior density by the velocity of the wind, it is obvious that if the wind were to abate instantaneously, the air contained in the tube would rush out of it with the same velocity as the wind possessed. But by means of the difference of level at which the fluid is held, we can ascertain the density of the air contained in the horizontal tube, and consequently can calculate, by means of the formula, the velocity possessed by the wind. Thus, suppose that the difference of level were observed to be $\frac{9}{10}$ths of an inch; then the density of the air in the horizontal tube will be expressed by 33 feet $+ \frac{9}{10}$ths of an inch, that of common air being expressed by 33 feet. Hence in the formula we have $\Delta = 33\frac{9}{120}$, $\Delta' = 33$, and in the present case $\Delta' = \delta$, wherefore

$$V = V'\sqrt{\frac{9}{120 \times 33}} = 1295\sqrt{\frac{1}{440}} = \frac{1295}{2.1} = 61 \text{ feet.}$$

Of air rushing into a vessel.

The expression given for the velocity with which air rushes from a denser into a rarer medium, may be employed to determine the time in which common air will fill a vacuum of any dimensions. Let Δ' be the density of the atmosphere, δ the density of the air in the vessel after any time t, and C the capacity of the vessel in cubic feet, O being the area of the orifice in square feet. The accession of air during the time dt, may obviously be expressed by $C \cdot d\delta$. But the influx of air is also measured by the velocity, multiplied into the product of the time by the area of the orifice, that is, by

$$O \cdot \Delta' \cdot V'\sqrt{\frac{\Delta' - \delta}{\Delta'}} \cdot dt. \text{ Hence we derive the equa-}$$

tion $O \cdot \Delta' \cdot V'\sqrt{\frac{\Delta' - \delta}{\Delta'}} = C \cdot d\delta$, and

$$dt = \frac{C \cdot d\delta}{O \cdot \Delta' \cdot V'\sqrt{\frac{\Delta' - \delta}{\Delta'}}}. \text{ By taking the fluents,}$$

there results $t = \frac{2C}{O.V'}\int \frac{d\delta}{2\sqrt{\frac{\Delta' - \delta}{\Delta'}}}.$ But $\int \frac{d\delta}{2\sqrt{\frac{\Delta' - \delta}{\Delta'}}}$

---

* Dalton's Meteorological Observations and Essays.

$= \sqrt{\dfrac{\Delta' - \delta}{\Delta'}}$. Hence $t = \dfrac{2\,C}{O.V'}\sqrt{\dfrac{\Delta' - \delta}{\Delta'}} + A$ When

$\delta = O$, $t = O$ also; wherefore $A = \dfrac{-2\,C}{O.V'}\sqrt{\dfrac{\Delta'}{\Delta}}$, and

$t = \dfrac{2\,C}{OV'\sqrt{\Delta'}}\left(\sqrt{\Delta'} - \sqrt{\Delta' - \delta}\right)$.

To illustrate this by an example. In what time will a cube of 27 feet be filled with air of half the common density by an aperture whose area is a square inch?

$t = \dfrac{2\,C}{OV'\sqrt{2}}\left(\sqrt{2} - \sqrt{1}\right) = \dfrac{2 \times 27 \times 144}{1295}\left(1 - \dfrac{1}{\sqrt{2}}\right)$

$= \dfrac{7776 \times .7071}{1295} = 4.2426''$.

When the vessel is to be filled with air of the common density as $\delta = \Delta'$ the formula becomes $t = \dfrac{2\,C}{OV'}$.

It is obvious that $\dfrac{C}{O.V'}$ is the time in which the quantity C of air would be expelled through the orifice O into a vacuum. Hence to expel this quantity into a vessel requires double the time of expelling it into a vacuum.

These propositions are true only when the moving force is constant. When this varies, the air makes its escape according to a different law. Suppose a vessel were to contain air of the common density, and that by means of an aperture the air were allowed to rush into a void. It is obvious that the velocity with which the first particles would make their escape, would be the same as that acquired by a heavy body falling through a homogeneous atmosphere. The density, however, and of consequence the elasticity of the remaining air is diminished. Hence the moving force is diminished in the ratio of the original density to the present density. But the quantity of matter expelled through the orifice is also diminished in the same ratio, wherefore the accelerative force is a constant quantity; that is, the particles escape with a uniform velocity, until the vessel is emptied.

Of air rushing from a vessel into a vacuum.

Let us now investigate an expression for the quantity of air ejected in a given time. Suppose the density of the air contained in the vessel to be represented by Δ, and that C is its capacity; then the quantity of air which it contains will be expressed by $C\Delta$. Also let δ be the density after the time t, and O the area of the orifice. Since the velocity of efflux is constant, and is equal to V', we have as an expression for the quantity of air which escapes in the increment of time dt,

$$O.V'.\delta.dt.$$

The same quantity is also expressed obviously by $-C.d\delta$; hence we derive the equation

$$O.V'.dt.\delta = -C.d\delta \text{ and } dt = \dfrac{-C.d\delta}{O.V'.\delta}.$$

By taking the fluents, we have $t = \dfrac{-C}{O.V'}.\log.\delta + A$.

When $t = O$, $\delta = \Delta$, consequently $A = \dfrac{C}{O.V'}.\log.\Delta$,

and $t = \dfrac{C}{O.V'}.\log.\dfrac{\Delta}{\delta}.$ and $\log.\dfrac{\Delta}{\delta} = \dfrac{O.V'.t}{C}.$

It is obvious from the investigation, that the time in which the vessel will be emptied is infinite. For as δ must, in this case, be $= O$, $\dfrac{\Delta}{\delta}$ will be infinite, and so also will its logarithm. Hence t is infinite.

It is by a train of reasoning precisely similar, that we ascertain the quantity of condensed air which will make its escape from a vessel into the atmosphere in a given time. Let Δ represent the density of the condensed air, and Δ' the density of the atmosphere, then the velocity at the commencement of the motion is expressed by

$$V'\sqrt{\dfrac{\Delta - \Delta'}{\Delta'}},$$

Of condensed air rushing from a vessel into the atmosphere.

as we found when treating of air rushing from a denser into a rarer medium. Let Δ'' be the density of the condensed air after the time t, C the capacity of the vessel, O the orifice; then $O.V'.\Delta''\sqrt{\dfrac{\Delta'' - \Delta'}{\Delta'}}.dt$ is an expression for the quantity which escapes when of the density Δ''. This is also expressed by $-C.d\Delta''$. Hence

$$O.V'.\Delta''\sqrt{\dfrac{\Delta'' - \Delta'}{\Delta'}}.dt = -C.d\Delta'', \text{ and}$$

$$dt = \dfrac{-C.d\Delta''}{O.V'\sqrt{\dfrac{\Delta'' - \Delta'}{\Delta'}}\Delta''} = \dfrac{-C\sqrt{\Delta'}}{O.V'}.\dfrac{d\Delta''}{\sqrt{\Delta'' - \Delta'}.\Delta''}$$

Let $\sqrt{\Delta'' - \Delta'} = x$, then $\Delta'' - \Delta' = x^2$ and $\Delta'' = x^2 + \Delta'$ and $d\Delta'' = 2x.dx$. Hence

$$\dfrac{d\Delta''}{\sqrt{\Delta'' - \Delta'}.\Delta''} = \dfrac{2x.dx}{x(x^2 + \Delta')} = \dfrac{2dx}{x^2 + \sqrt{\Delta'}^2}.$$

Now $\int\dfrac{dx}{x^2 + \sqrt{\Delta'}^2} = \dfrac{1}{\sqrt{\Delta'}} \times$ arch, whose tang. is $\dfrac{x}{\sqrt{\Delta'}}$ (rad. being 1); wherefore $t = \dfrac{-2\,C\sqrt{\Delta'}}{O.V'} \times \dfrac{1}{\sqrt{\Delta'}} \times$ arch, whose tang. is $\dfrac{\sqrt{\Delta'' - \Delta'}}{\sqrt{\Delta'}} + A$. When $t = O$, then $\Delta'' = \Delta$, and

$$A = \dfrac{2\,C}{O.V'} \times \text{arch, whose tang. is } \sqrt{\dfrac{\Delta - \Delta'}{\Delta'}}.$$

Let the former arch be represented by a, and the latter by A, then

$$t = \dfrac{2.C}{O.V'}\,(A - a).$$

When the time is required, in which the density of the air contained in the vessel shall be reduced to that of the external atmosphere, as $\Delta'' = \Delta'$, it follows that $a = O$, and

$$t = \dfrac{2.C.A}{O.V'}.$$

To illustrate this by an example. In what time will air of double the atmospheric density confined in a vessel, whose capacity is 12 feet, expand into the atmosphere through a circular aperture one tenth of an inch in diameter, so as to be reduced to the common density?

$$t = \dfrac{2 \times 12^3 \times 100}{.7854 \times 1295} \times \text{arch, whose tang. is } 1, =$$

$$\dfrac{2 \times 12^3 \times 100}{1295} = \dfrac{345600}{1295} = 268'' = 4'\,28''.$$

Even although the density of the confined air were infinitely greater than that of the atmosphere, the time in which it would be reduced would be a finite quantity. For Δ being infinitely greater than Δ', the tang. $\sqrt{\dfrac{\Delta - \Delta'}{\Delta'}}$ is also infinite, and corresponds to the arch of 90°. Hence in this case

$$t = \frac{2 \cdot C}{O \cdot V'} \times 2 \times .7854.$$

If the capacity of the vessel, and the area of the aperture, be the same as in the example, the time in which this infinitely condensed air would be attenuated, so as to be of the same density with the atmosphere, is

$$8' \cdot 56''.$$

III. ON SOUND.

On sound.

One of the most remarkable properties of air in motion is its capacity for transmitting sound. The variety and delicacy of the sensations which are acquired through this medium, are no less admirable than the wise and beautiful arrangement by which they are communicated. The first who appears to have considered this subject in a philosophical point of view was the illustrious Newton, who explained with very great precision the nature of the phenomenon. The continental writers, though they admit his conclusions, have called in question the accuracy of his demonstrations. Euler, La Grange, and several others, have engaged in the subject, but have added nothing new to our information; for they have been under the necessity of restricting themselves to the cases which Newton has supposed. The labours of La Grange have claimed the highest praise. Without, however, pretending to disparage his efforts, it may be proper to obviate the allegations which have been brought against the validity of Newton's reasoning, by presenting it in a more detailed manner than that in which it is delivered in the *Principia*. Sound is produced by a sudden condensation of air, which gradually extends itself in the form of a pulse, or spherical shell, having its density greater than that of the surrounding medium. The first proposition delivered by Newton concerning these pulses is, that the particles of which they are composed advance from and recede to their state of quiescence, under the influence of a force which varies as their distance from the point of greatest condensation. He assumes, however, in his reasoning, that the greatest condensation differs only by a very small quantity from the condensation of common air; an assumption which will be found agreeable to fact, except perhaps in the case of violent explosions, where the condensation of the adjacent particles will be considerably greater.

PLATE
CCCCLXVI.
Fig. 17.

Let E, F, G, Plate CCCCLXVI. Fig. 17. be three particles of air in a state of quiescence, which are immediately to be put in motion by a pulse, whose centre, place of greatest density, is at C. Also let ε, φ, γ, be the position of the particles after a certain interval of time. It is apparent, that as the particles are acted upon precisely in the same manner, the same curve will express the relation between the spaces which they describe and the times in which the spaces are described. Let the curve A m B be one such, that when the abscissæ B, p, &c. represent the spaces, the corresponding arches B, m, represent the times. Then, since the interval of time between the commencement of the motions of E and F must be equal to the interval between the commencement of the motions of F and G, if this be represented by mn or no, and if B p be equal to E ε, B q will be equal to F φ, and B r to G γ. Hence

$$B p - B q = p q = E \varepsilon - F \varphi = EF - \varepsilon \varphi,$$

and in like manner

$$B q - B r = q r = F \varphi - G \gamma = FG - \varphi \gamma.$$

Wherefore $\varepsilon \varphi = EF - p q$, and $\varphi \gamma = EF - q r$; for EF and FG are equal.

Now the force which accelerates the particle φ is obviously the excess of the elasticity of the particles behind it above those which precede it. Let the elasticity of two particles of air at the distance 1 be represented by unity, then will the elasticity of air of the common density be expressed by $\frac{1}{EF}$, since the elasticity is inversely proportional to the distance between the particles. In like manner, the force by which φ is propelled is expressed by $\frac{1}{\varepsilon \varphi}$, and the force by which it is retarded is expressed by $\frac{1}{\varphi \gamma}$; wherefore the excess of the former above the latter, or $\frac{1}{\varepsilon \varphi} - \frac{1}{\gamma \varphi}$, expresses the accelerative force which impels the particle φ. From the values given above for $\varepsilon \varphi$ and $\varphi \gamma$, we find

$$\frac{1}{\varepsilon \varphi} - \frac{1}{\varphi \gamma} = \frac{1}{EF - p q} - \frac{1}{EF - q r} = \frac{q r - p q}{EF^2 - EF (p q + q r) + p q \cdot q r}.$$

But, according to the assumption of Newton, the greatest condensation differs only by an infinitely small quantity from the condensation of common air; that is,

$$EF - \varepsilon \varphi, \quad FG - \varphi \gamma$$

differ by an infinitely small quantity from EF. Wherefore the accelerative force of φ is expressed by $\frac{q r - p q}{EF^2}$ the elasticity of common air being denoted by $\frac{1}{EF}$. If, however, the latter be expressed by unity, the former will be expressed by $\frac{q r - p q}{EF}$.

Let the normals os, nt, be drawn from the points o, n, to meet the line of the abscissæ AB, then from the property of similar triangles, we have

$$q r : o n :: o r : o s \text{ and } q r = \frac{o n \cdot o r}{o s},$$

$$q p : m n :: n q : n t \text{ and } p q = \frac{m n \cdot n q}{n t},$$

hence $\frac{q r - p q}{EF} = \frac{o n (o r - n q)}{EF \cdot n t}$, for $m n = n o$, and as the points m, n, o, are infinitely near to each other, $o s$ is ultimately equal to $n t$. Again, let Ωr be represented by x, the ordinate at this point by y, and the normal of the curve by F (x) a function of the abscissa Ωr; then if f be taken to express the accelerative force which acts upon φ, we have $f = \frac{o n \cdot d y}{EF \cdot F(x)}$, considering $d t = o n$ as a constant quantity. From the principles of dynamics, it is known that $d s = v \cdot d t$ and $f \cdot d s = v \cdot d v$. By applying the first of these propositions, we have $v = \frac{d s}{d t} = $ (from similar triangles) $= \frac{y}{F(x)}$; and by applying the second

$$\frac{o n \cdot d y \cdot d x}{EF \cdot F(x)} = \frac{y}{F(x)} \cdot d \frac{y}{F(x)}$$

But $d x : d t :: y : F(x)$, wherefore $d x = \frac{d t \cdot y}{F(x)}$ and $\frac{a \cdot y \cdot d y}{F(x)^2} = \frac{y}{F(x)} \cdot d \frac{y}{F(x)}$, where a represents the constant multiplier $\frac{o n \cdot d t}{EF}$. Dividing both sides of the equation by $\frac{y}{F(x)}$, it becomes $\frac{a \cdot d y}{F(x)} = d \frac{y}{F(x)}$

and consequently $\frac{dy}{F(x)} = d\frac{y}{F(x)}$ and F (x) is a constant quantity. If the last inference be not admitted, then $\frac{a.dy}{F(x)} = \frac{dy}{F(x)} - y.\frac{dF(x)}{F(x)^2}$ and $(1-a)$ F $(x) = d$ F (x), which is absurd.

From this, it appears that the curve B m A is a circle, since the normal is a constant quantity; also that the accelerative force by which φ is impelled, is proportional to dy. But as dy, when dt is a constant quantity, is proportional to x, it follows that the particle is impelled by a force which varies as its distance from Ω, the point of greatest condensation. Upon reasoning of this kind, Newton advanced the 47th Prop. of the 2d Book of the Principia, which he thus enunciates: "Pulsibus per fluidum propagatis, singulæ fluidi particulæ, motu reciproco brevissimo euntes et redeuntes, accelerantur semper et retardantur pro lege oscillantis penduli."

The expression for the accelerative force f was found to be

$$\frac{on.dy}{EF.F(x)}.$$

At the commencement of the motion, as on and dy approach to a ratio of equality, this expression becomes $\frac{on^2}{EF.F(x)}$ or $\frac{on^2}{EF.\Omega B}$, since F (x) has been shown to be equal to the radius. The elasticity of common air is regarded as the unit to which this measure of the accelerative force refers. In order to reduce it therefore, to the accelerative force of gravity as a standard, let this quantity be represented by $g = 32\frac{1}{6}$ feet, also let the elasticity of two particles of air at the distance 1 be called m.

PLATE
CCCCLXVI.
FIG. 18.

Conceive A, B, C, &c. Plate CCCCLXVI. Fig. 18. to form a column of particles of atmospheric air extending to the height of the atmosphere from the earth's surface. Then the elasticity of the particle A$= \frac{m.A}{AB}$; which is obviously equal to the pressure sustained by B, since action and re-action are equal and opposite. Now, if the particles B, C, D, be supposed to have the same gravitation, their united pressure will be expressed by g (B+C+D+), &c.

Hence $\frac{m A}{AB} = g$ (B+C+D+), &c.

As B, C, D, &c. are all equal to one another and to A, let their number be expressed by n, and $\frac{m}{AB} = g.n$. Wherefore $m = g.n.AB$. But $n.AB$ is obviously the height of the homogeneous atmosphere, which we may denote by H'; hence, the elasticity of common air, when referred to g as a standard, is $\frac{g.H'}{AB}$, or in reference to the preceding figure $\frac{g.H'}{EF}$. The expression $\frac{on^2}{EF.\Omega B}$, consequently, when referred to the same standard, becomes $\frac{g.on^2.H'}{EF^2.\Omega B}$.

Let V be assumed as the radius of a circle whose circumference is EC'(see the preceding fig.) or the space passed over by the pulse during the vibration of the particle E. As the aerial particles are perfectly elastic,

the motion of the pulse will be uniform. Wherefore the time of describing EF is to the whole time in which the pulse moves to C' as EF to EC'. But the time in which EF is described by the particle E is expressed by on, and the time in which the pulse passes to C' is expressed by the circumference of the circle AB. Hence $on : \pi.AB :: EF : EC'$; or $on^2 : EF^2 :: \Omega B^2 : V^2$, and consequently the accelerative force by which φ is impelled at the commencement of its motion, is $\frac{g.H'.\Omega B}{V^2}$.

In order to obtain a formula for the velocity with which sound is conveyed, it will be necessary to find an expression for the time in which the particle E performs its vibration. For this purpose let us assume γ as the accelerative force at the unit of distance from the centre of motion, and x as the distance of the particle from this point at any time t; then the accelerative force at this distance is $\gamma.x$. By employing the general dynamical formula $f.ds = v.dv$, we obtain,

$$-\gamma x.dx = v.dv,$$

and by taking the fluents

$$-\gamma x^2 = v^2 + A.$$

But when $x = r = \Omega B$, $v = o$. Hence $-\gamma r^2 = A$, and the complete fluent becomes $\gamma (r^2 - x^2) = v^2$, so that $v = \sqrt{\gamma.(r^2 - x^2)}$. Again, by employing the dynamical formula $v.dt = ds$, we obtain

$$\sqrt{\gamma (r^2 - x^2)}.dt = dx, \text{ and}$$

$$dt = \frac{dx}{\sqrt{\gamma (r^2 - x^2)}} = \frac{r.dx}{r\sqrt{\gamma (r^2 - x^2)}}. \text{ Taking the}$$

fluents, we have $t = \frac{1}{r\sqrt{\gamma}} \times$ arch, whose cosine is x, from which we conclude, that the time in which E performs a complete vibration is $\frac{2\pi\Omega B}{\Omega B\sqrt{\gamma}}$. As the accelerative force at the commencement of the motion, or at the distance BΩ, is $\frac{g.H'.\Omega B}{V^2}$, the accelerative force at the distance 1, or $\gamma = \frac{g.H'}{V^2}$. Wherefore the time of a vibration is $\frac{2\pi V}{\sqrt{g.H'}}$. Hence also the time in which the pulse, with a uniform motion, describes the space EC', or $2\pi V$ is $\frac{2\pi V}{\sqrt{g H'}}$; and consequently the velocity is equal to $\sqrt{g H'}$.

This is the result which Newton obtains in the 49th Prop. of the second Book, when he proposes the problem, "Datis medii densitate et vi elasticâ, invenire velocitatem pulsuum."

The conclusion which has thus been deduced from a theoretical view of the subject, differs from the results obtained by experiment. For the atmospherical subtangent, according to Biot, is 26071.03 $(1 + .00208\,t)$ in English feet, wherefore the velocity of sound, according to theory, is $\sqrt{g \times 26071.03\,(1 + .00208\,t)} = 944$ feet per second, when t is taken $= 28°$, the temperature of the atmosphere being 60°. Newton, who assumed the ratio of the density of mercury to air, greater than it has been found by later experiments, determined the velocity of sound to be about 979 feet,

Pneuma-
tics.

Velocity of
sound, as
determined
by experi-
ment.

which, although greater than that obtained by the formula given above, falls considerably short of the true result.

Before giving a view of the methods which have been adopted for reconciling the theory with experiment, it will be proper to collect together the results which experimental philosophers have arrived at. They have all adopted the same principle in conducting their observations, viz. that the motion of light from one place to another upon the earth's surface is performed instantaneously. By employing fire-arms, they were enabled to perceive exactly from the flash, the time when the report was given, whereupon, at the place of observation, a second's pendulum was put in motion. By reckoning the number of vibrations which was performed before the report was heard, the time in which the sound passed over the intermediate space was ascertained, and by measuring this space, the velocity with which it moved was discovered. The following list is extracted from a paper by Mr. Derham, given in the *Phil. Trans.* and shows the results which were in this manner obtained by several distinguished individuals.

Authors.	Vel. in feet.
Roberts	1300
Boyle	1200
Mersenne	1474
Flamsteed and Halley	1142
Florentine Academy	1148
French Academy	1172

Upon the first three observations, great reliance cannot be placed, both on account of the imperfection of the instruments which were used, and of the small distance at which the observations were made, which scarcely exceeded 700 feet. In the last three observations, a greater coincidence appears, which undoubtedly arose from the improved instruments which were employed. The pendulum was connected with clockwork, so that the ear alone could judge of the vibrations, whilst the eye was intent upon the flash of the gun. The interval was also very considerable. Halley and Flamsteed's observations were made at the distance of about three miles from the Royal Observatory, and the sound was transmitted in $13\frac{1}{2}$ seconds. The Florentine academicians made their observations at nearly the same distance, whereas the French academicians had an interval of about $1\frac{1}{3}$ mile only. According to the Florentine academicians, the wind was found to have no effect in accelerating or retarding the velocity of sound, a conclusion which Dr. Derham discovered to be erroneous, by a series of experiments made upon a very extensive scale. By a great number of observations made at the distance of about 25 miles N.E. from Blackheath, where cannons were fired from time to time, he found that when the wind was from the N.E. the report reached him in 120 seconds, whereas, when it blew from the S.W. the time which elapsed was only about 13 seconds, and was found to depend very much upon the force of the wind.

The result which appears to be the most correct is that which Flamsteed and Halley have obtained. It was found by Dr. Derham to hold most exactly. Having measured a very extensive line along the shore upon the coast of Essex, he found that sound travelled with a uniform velocity, passing over a mile in $9\frac{1}{4}$ semi-seconds, two miles in $18\frac{1}{2}$ semi-seconds, and three miles in $27\frac{3}{4}$ semi-seconds, being at the rate of 1141.6 feet per second. This conclusion exceeds, by a very small quantity, that obtained by M. Biot. In prosecuting his researches upon this subject, he availed himself of an opportunity afforded him for measuring the velocity of sound, by transmitting it along cast-iron tubes, which were formed into a pipe for conducting water into Paris. The number of tubes was 376, the mean length of each being 2.515 metres. After having been connected, they formed a pipe $951\frac{1}{4}$ metres in length. At one extremity of the pipe there was fixed, within the tube, an iron ring, of the same diameter with it, supporting at its centre a bell and a hammer, which one could allow to fall at pleasure. The hammer, in striking against the bell, struck also the tube through the medium of the circular ring of iron ; so that a person situated at the other extremity of the pipe might have heard two sounds, the one transmitted through the air within the pipe, and the other more rapidly through the metal of which it was composed.

Pneuma-
tics.

The result
obtained by
the experi-
ments of
M. Biot.

Having made this arrangement, the interval of time between the transmission of the two sounds was first carefully observed. This, after no less than two hundred observations, was found to be 2.5 seconds. His next object was to find the time in which the sound was transmitted along the tube. For this purpose, two observers, provided with watches, which preserved the same rate of going, were stationed, one at each end, to strike the tube, and observe in what time the sound was communicated. It was of no consequence whether the watches showed exactly the same time. For, suppose that one of the observers, whose watch is before that of the other r'', strikes the tube when he observes it upon his own watch to be $30''$. At that instant, the watch of the other observer indicates $(30 - r)''$. Let p'' be the number of seconds in which the sound is transmitted, then $(30 + p - r)''$ is the time at which he hears the first sound. Again, let us suppose that the second observer strikes in his turn when his watch is at $40''$; then the watch of the first observer is at $(40 + r)''$, and the time when he hears the sound is $(40 + p + r'')$. Having, by means of these two observations, found the values of $p - r$, and $p + r$ by taking an arithmetical mean between them, we find p''. In this manner, by a great number of observations, M. Biot found the mean value of p to be $0.26''$. Adding this to the interval of time which elapsed between the transmission of the sound through the air, and along the metal, he found $2''.76$ to be the time in which the former took place. From this, it appears that the velocity of sound, when conducted through the air, is, according to the determination of this author, 1131 feet per second, which differs from Dr. Halley's result by 11 feet, an error which corresponds with an error in time of the $\frac{1}{104}$th part of a second.

Methods
adopted for
reconciling
theory with
experi-
ment.

Having thus pointed out, very briefly, the conclusions which have been deduced from theory and experiment, we now proceed to consider the various hypotheses by which it has been attempted to reconcile them. The formula for the velocity of sound derived from theory is $V = \sqrt{g H'}$, H' being the height of the atmospherical subtangent. As this, however, is a variable quantity, depending, as we have seen, upon the height of the barometer, and the temperature of the air, it will be necessary to substitute instead of it the expression $\frac{\Delta h}{\delta} (1 + .00208 \, t)$, where Δ is the density of mercury, δ of dry air, and h the height of the barometer. The formula then becomes $V = \sqrt{\frac{g \cdot \Delta h}{\delta} (1 + .00208 \, t)}$, where it is obvious that the only variable part of the expression which cannot be

Difference
not atti-
butable to
moisture.

directly observed is ∂. The causes which may affect this quantity are two, viz. the moisture contained in the atmosphere, and a change of temperature.

It may be easily seen that the disagreement does not depend upon the former. When investigating a formula for measuring heights by the barometer, founded upon the data furnished by Mr. Dalton, it was shewn, that if F expressed the mean tension of the vapour contained in the atmosphere, the density of the vapourized air would be $= \int \frac{r^2\,y\,.\,d\,x}{(r+x)^2} - \frac{3\,\mathrm{F}}{8}$; or $= h - \frac{3\,\mathrm{F}}{8}$; if $.\,h$ be the height of the barometer, and 30 inches be assumed to express the density of dry air at the earth's surface. Since the latter, however, is expressed by .00130386, it follows that the former, or

$$\partial = \left(h - \frac{3\,\mathrm{F}}{8} \right) \times .00130386.$$
$$\overline{30}$$

By substituting this value of ∂ in the formula for the velocity, it becomes

$$\mathrm{V} = \sqrt{26071.03 \,.\, g \,.\, \frac{h}{h - \frac{3\,\mathrm{F}}{8}}}.$$

The mean value of $\frac{3\,\mathrm{F}}{8}$ was found to be $.0375 + .00296\,t$, wherefore the additional velocity communicated to sound by the union of vapour with air is expressed by $\sqrt{\dfrac{h}{h - .0375 - .0029\,t}}$. Let h be taken $= 30$ inches, and $t = 28°$, then this quantity is found to be

$$\sqrt{\frac{30}{29.8785}} = 1 + \frac{1}{497}.$$

From this we conclude, that the presence of vapour in the air accelerates the velocity of sound $\frac{1}{497}$th part, or about 2 feet only.

Nor to the
develop-
ment of
heat by
means of
the con-
densation
of the
pulses.

The next cause which may affect ∂, is the temperature of the aerial pulses by which sound is produced. To it M. La Place has attributed the difference between the results derived from theory and experiment. It is well known, that by compressing air, it is made to give out heat; and that, on the contrary, by dilating it, it absorbs heat. This may be seen by suspending a thermometer within a receiver, and then exhausting it rapidly. The rarefied air absorbs caloric from the adjacent bodies, and among the rest from the bulb of the thermometer. Hence it follows that the mercury falls sometimes a degree or more. This experiment merely illustrates the fact which we have stated, but cannot be considered as an evidence of the quantity of heat disengaged or absorbed. For the surrounding bodies absorb almost instantaneously the heat which is given out on condensing air, and supply the heat which is absorbed by rarefied air. During this rapid operation the mercury in the thermometer has not time to indicate the full extent of the change of temperature, for in order to obtain true results by means of this instrument, it is necessary that it be immersed in a medium for a considerable time in order to indicate its proper temperature. That, however, the heat disengaged by condensing air to a great extent is considerable, may be learned from the circumstance, that combustibles, as phosphorus, &c. may be inflamed in this manner. Also, in filling a glass ball with condensed air by means of a syringe, flashes of light are frequently perceived, and a temperature is excited capable of kindling a piece of match.

From these well established facts, it must be admitted, that the very rapid compression of the surrounding particles of air, produced by the vibrations of sonorous bodies, disengages caloric, which, from the rapidity with which they succeed each other, is prevented from dissipating; yet it will be found that this cause is inadequate to produce the effect attributed to it. In estimating the velocity of the pulses of air, when we attend to the temperature thus excited, we cannot suppose, as heretofore, that the elasticity is in proportion to the density, for the disengaged caloric increases the elasticity, although the density remains constant. To introduce, therefore, into the formula, a correction depending upon this cause, let us assume ∂ as the initial density of a spherical shell of air, and that while forming a part of a pulse, its density becomes $\partial(1+\omega)$, ω being a small quantity, which expresses the increase of density. If this change of density took place, without the extrication of heat, then the elasticity would be expressed by $g \triangle h (1+\omega)$; and the density by $\partial (1+\omega)$. Let us suppose, moreover, that by means of the heat which is evolved, the elasticity is increased by the quantity $g \triangle h \,.\, \mathrm{K}\,\omega$, K being a constant quantity to be determined, then the whole elasticity is

$$g \triangle h \,(1 + \omega + \mathrm{K}\,\omega).$$

Introducing this quantity, together with the expression for the increased density $\partial\,(1+\omega)$ into the formula for the velocity, and we have $\mathrm{V} = \sqrt{\dfrac{g\,.\,\triangle\,.\,\partial\,.\,h\,(1+\omega+\mathrm{K}\,\omega)}{\partial\,(1+\omega)}}$. By dividing both numerator and denominator by $1 + \omega$, and neglecting the higher powers of ω on account of their smallness, we obtain the velocity equal to $\sqrt{\dfrac{g\,.\,\triangle\,.\,h\,(1+\mathrm{K}\,\omega)}{\partial}}$. But $\sqrt{\dfrac{\triangle h}{\partial}} = \sqrt{26071\,.\,03}$, hence the velocity $= \sqrt{26071.03 \,.\, g\,(1+\mathrm{K}\,\omega)} = 1142$ by experiment. By deducing from this the value of K$\,\omega$, we find it equal to $.555$. Again, the formula for the velocity, when t is assumed as the excess of the temperature of the medium above 32° is

$$\sqrt{26071.03\,g\,(1 + .00208\,t)}.$$

Wherefore, by comparing together the two formulæ, we obtain

$$.00208\,t = .555 \text{ and } t = \frac{.555}{.00208} = 267°.$$

Such is the very great degree of heat which would require to be developed by the condensation of air, in order to account for the disagreement between the theory and experiment. If we were to give the result to which M. Biot's investigation leads, it would be 217°. By an oversight which he has committed in rejecting the quantity $1 + \omega$ from the numerator and denominator of the expression $\sqrt{\dfrac{g \triangle h(1+\omega+\mathrm{K}\,\omega)}{\partial\,(1+\omega)}}$, he has rendered it $\sqrt{\dfrac{g \triangle h\,(1+\mathrm{K})}{\partial}}$. He then states this quantity as equal to 337.18 metres, which is the velocity of sound as determined by the members of the Academy of Sciences in 1738; and deduces K instead of K$\,\omega$ equal to $.4254$. In continuing his investigation, he proceeds to inquire what additional temperature is requisite to increase the elasticity of the pulses of air to the degree required. With this view, he assumes a thin shell of air, whose temperature is t and density ∂, and conceives it to be condensed until its density be-

Pneuma-
tics.

comes $\delta\,(1+\omega)$. Its elasticity, when of the density δ, being $g\,\Delta h$, its present elasticity will consequently be $g\,\Delta h\,(1+\omega)$, as it is supposed to retain still the same temperature t. He again conceives that being still kept of the same density, its temperature is increased t' degrees; and then remarks that its elasticity will become $1+(t+t')\,.00375$, the elasticity of air, at the temperature of zero, being regarded as the unit: or

$$\frac{1+(t+t')\,.00375}{1+t\,.00375}$$

if the elasticity of air at the temperature t be referred to as a standard. From this, he concludes that the elasticity of the air, when its density is $\delta\,(1+\omega)$, and its temperature $(t+t')$ will be expressed by

$$g\,\Delta h\,(1+\omega)\left(\frac{1+(t+t')\,.00375}{1+t\,.00375}\right).$$

In the formation of sound, as the increase of temperature t' is necessarily very small, he remarks that it may be considered as proportional to the change of density ω; and may, therefore, be assumed as equal to $a.\,\omega$, a being a constant quantity. By substituting this value of t' in the formula for the elasticity, it becomes

$$g\,\Delta h\,(1+\omega)\left(1+\frac{.00375\,.\,a\,\omega}{1+t\,.00375}\right).$$

In comparing this formula with that formerly given for the elasticity, viz. $g\,\Delta h\,(1+\omega+\mathrm{K}\omega)$, he concludes that

$$\mathrm{K}\,\omega=\frac{.00375\,.\,a\,\omega}{1+t\,.00375}.$$

In this equation he substitutes .4254 as the value of K, whereas it is properly the value of K ω, and finds $a\,\omega$ instead of a equal to $115°.\,99'$ on the centigrade scale. Hence, he concludes, $t'=115°.\,99'\,\omega$, whereas t' itself is equal to this quantity.—(Biot's *Traité de Physique*, vol. ii. p. 20.)

Corrections
introduced
by Newton.

Having thus shewn that the imperfection of the theory of sound cannot be attributed either to the existence of moisture in the air, or to latent caloric, which is evolved by the condensation of the pulses, we shall now advert to the explanation given by Newton. He takes into consideration the space occupied by the particles of air, through which he supposes that sound passes instantaneously. This supposition is perfectly consistent with facts; for, according to M. Biot's experiments, it passed along a metallic tube 951.25 metres long in .26″, or about 10,000 feet per second; and its velocity, when transmitted along liquids, is unquestionably as great. He next supposes, that a particle of air has the same weight with a particle of water, and that the specific gravity of air is less than that of water, on account of the distance among its particles. If this supposition be admitted, it follows that the diameter of an aërial particle is to the distance between two adjacent particles in the ratio of $1^{\frac{1}{3}}:727^{\frac{1}{3}}-1$, or of $1:8$. To the space through which sound is transmitted in a second, according to the theory, an eighth part must be added through which it passes instantaneously, as a correction for the density of the particles of which the atmosphere is composed. He farther supposes, that the vapour which exists in union with the air is one-tenth of its bulk, by which the velocity of sound will be increased in the sub-duplicate ratio of 11 to 10, or in the direct ratio of 21 to 20. By means of these two corrections, he increases the velocity from 979 feet to 1142 feet, so as to agree with the experimental result obtained by Dr. Halley. It may be remarked concerning these suppositions, that the second is entirely gratui-

tous; for the weight of a particle of air might be supposed to be equal to that of a particle of mercury, or any other fluid as well as of water: and that the third is too great; for the elasticity of vapour cannot be $\frac{1}{20}$th part of the elasticity of air, unless when the atmosphere is saturated with moisture, and of the temperature of 95° Fahrenheit.

Pneuma-
tics.

The intensity of
sound.

From inspecting the formula which gives the velocity of sound, it appears that it is transmitted with the same celerity in all directions, when the temperature is the same throughout its range; for, in that case, the only variable quantities are h and δ, which preserve always the same ratio, since the density of air is proportional to the pressure which it sustains. The intensity of sound follows a different law; for it is less, *cæteris paribus* in lofty regions than in those which are low; and diminishes as we recede from the point where the sound originates. The intensity is proportional to the velocity into the number of particles which strike against the ear, and is therefore expressed by the formula

$$\sqrt{g\,.\,\Delta\,.\,h\,.\,\delta(1+.00208t)}.$$

Since $\sqrt{h}$ is proportional to $\sqrt{\delta}$, the intensity of sound is proportional to the density of the medium through which it is conveyed. This explains to us a fact stated by Saussure, that on the summit of the Alps the report of a pistol is no louder than the sound of a cracker at the earth's surface. The connection between the intensity of sound and the density of the medium in which it is excited, may be easily illustrated by means of the air-pump. Take a receiver, and suspend within it a bell, then place it upon the plate of the air-pump. In order to render the experiment the more striking, it may be proper to cover the plate with a piece of moist leather, which will have the effect of intercepting any vibrations which might be conveyed through it. On exhausting the receiver to a certain degree, it will be found that when the clapper is made to strike the bell, the intensity of the sound will be considerably diminished. When the receiver is exhausted as much as possible, the sound of the bell will with difficulty be heard at all.

Reflection
of sound.

Since the particles of air are perfectly elastic, when they strike against an opposing surface, they are reflected after the manner of light, and other elastic bodies. The angle of incidence is equal to the angle of reflection. In a room of a spheroidal form, therefore, if a person situated at one of the foci articulate sounds, they will be heard with the same distinctness with which they are uttered by a person situated at the other focus, however great their distance from each other may be. When sound is reflected in this manner, it occasions the phenomenon called an echo. To illustrate the manner in which it is produced, let A be the centre from which the sound is propagated, and BC any obstacle against which it strikes. Draw AF perpendicular to BC, and produce it to H, so that AF=FH; then the reflected sound will be perceived as coming from H. For let AE be an incident ray, impinging against the obstacle at E; join HE, and produce it towards D. It is obvious, from the principles of geometry, that the angles AEB, DEC, are equal, consequently DE is the direction in which the ray AE is reflected. The same sound is thus heard twice by an auditor at D, first by the direct ray AD, and secondly by the reflex ray DE, provided the difference between AD and AED be sufficiently great; for if the reflex sound arrives at the ear before the impression of the direct sound ceases, the sound will not be double, but

To PLATE
CCCCLXVI.
Fig. 19.

Pneuma-
tics.

only more intense. It is known by experience, that if more than eight or nine syllables be pronounced in a second, the sounds will not be distinct and articulate; therefore, that the reflex sound may not be confounded with the direct sound, there ought to be at the least the eighth part of a second between them. As sound travels at the rate of 1142 feet per second, the space passed over by the reflex sound should be 160 feet, and the distance of the obstacle which occasions the echo should be 80 or 85 feet. That a reflecting surface may produce a dysyllabic echo, it should be at twice this distance, or 170 feet, and so on.

By means of an echo, a general idea may be sometimes obtained of the distance of an inaccessible object, the width of a large river, &c. Thus Dr. Derham, standing upon the bank of the Thames opposite to Woolwich, observed that an echo of a single sound was reflected back from the houses in three seconds. Consequently $1142 \times 3 = 3426$ feet, the half of which, viz. 1713 feet, is the breadth of the river there, being somewhat more than a quarter of a mile. After the same manner, we can find the depth of a well, by dropping into it a stone, and observing the time in which we hear it striking the bottom. For this purpose, let the depth of the well be x, the time in which the body descends t; then we have

$$16\tfrac{1}{12} : x :: 1^{12} : t^2 = \frac{x}{16\tfrac{1}{12}}.$$

Again, let the time in which the sound ascends be t', then

$$1142 : x :: 1 : t' = \frac{x}{1142}.$$

If the time which elapses between dropping the stone and hearing the sound be c, we have

$$c = \sqrt{\frac{x}{16\tfrac{1}{12}}} + \frac{x}{1142};$$

and by solving the equation $x = \dfrac{s - b^2}{4\,a}$, where $a = 16\tfrac{1}{12}$, $b = 1142$, $s = \overline{b^2 + 4\,a\,b\,c}^{\frac{1}{2}}$, we find x. Suppose the time in which the sound is heard to be $10''$, then $c = 10''$; also we have $4\,a\,b\,c = 736460$, and $b^2 + 4\,a\,b\,c = s^2 = 2040624$. Whence $s = 1428.5$, and $s - b = 286.5$; consequently

$$x = \frac{286.5^2}{64.488} = 1273 \text{ feet.}$$

The speaking trumpet is an instrument employed for transmitting sound in a particular direction, with more energy than when it is allowed to diffuse itself around on all sides. The best contrivance for effecting this, has been found to be a hollow cone, with a mouthpiece at the narrow end to receive the lips, and confine the voice of the speaker. The beat of a watch may be heard to twice the distance through a speaking trumpet as without one. For an account of this instrument we refer to the article Acoustics.

Air con-
sidered as
the medi-
um of heat
and mois-
ture.

Having given a brief view of the most important statical and dynamical properties of air, we now proceed to consider it as the medium through which heat and moisture are conveyed to us. Owing to the rarity of air, the solar rays in their direct transmission impart to it little or no portion of their heat. The temperature of the atmosphere depends chiefly upon the heat radiated from the earth's surface. From this it arises, that the temperature of the lower strata of air exceeds that

of the higher. It was found by Dr. Hutton of Edinburgh, that a thermometer kept on the top of Arthur's Seat, a height of about 800 feet, indicated a temperature 3° lower than one placed at the bottom of the hill. Bouguer also, when making his barometrical measurements on some of the lofty mountains in South America, observed that a thermometer raised 15,564 feet above the level of the sea, fell about 54°. From these facts, it appears that the temperature of the atmosphere decreases as we ascend, and that the thermometer falls 1° for an elevation of 270 feet, or about 3°.7 for 1000 feet. The experiments of De Luc with the barometer show that the diminution of temperature follows an arithmetical progression. In fact, if the mean temperature of each stratum throughout the year be considered as a constant quantity, which it is, we can easily prove, upon abstract principles, that this law ought to obtain. For let h, h', h'', be the heats of three adjacent strata of air, and Δ, Δ', Δ'', their densities respectively. Then since the quantity of heat communicated by a warmer to a colder body in a given time is in proportion to their densities,

$$\Delta : \Delta' :: h - h' : (h - h')\frac{\Delta'}{\Delta} =$$

the heat communicated in an instant from the first stratum to the second. In like manner we find

$$(h' - h'')\frac{\Delta''}{\Delta'}$$

to be the degree of heat communicated by the second to the third. But as the temperature of the middle stratum is, by supposition, constant,

$$(h - h')\frac{\Delta'}{\Delta} = (h' - h'')\frac{\Delta''}{\Delta'}.$$

As the strata may be conceived to be indefinitely thin, Δ, Δ', Δ'' may be regarded as equal. Consequently h, h', h'' form a decreasing arithmetical progression.

The mean temperature of the atmosphere, at the equator has been found by observation to be 85°, and at the pole it is computed to be 31°. The mean temperature for any latitude L is given by the formula $t = 68 + 27 \cdot \cos 2\,\mathrm{L}$, from which we conclude, that in this latitude it is about 48°. By combining this formula with the rate according to which the temperature diminishes as we ascend above the earth's surface, we obtain a formula for the mean temperature at any latitude and at any elevation. Let the height be expressed by H, then

$$t = 58 - \frac{\mathrm{H}}{270} + 27 \cdot \cos 2\,\mathrm{L}.$$

By assuming $t = 32°$, we deduce from this formula the height of that particular point in every latitude where the temperature throughout the year is at freezing.

$$\mathrm{H} = 270\,(58 - 32 + 27 \cdot \cos 2\,\mathrm{L}), \text{ or}$$
$$= 270 \times 27 + (27 \cdot \cos 2\,\mathrm{L}) - 270.$$

The locus of the point H, or the curve in which it is always found, has received the name of the line of perpetual congelation. It may be easily represented by the following construction. Take CA, and upon it describe a circle; from A, with the distance AC, describe a semicircle. Divide the semicircle CA into nine equal parts in the points m, n, o, &c. From the point A, draw through these points lines meeting the quadrant CR in the points F, G, H, &c. From these points let fall perpendiculars upon AR; through the points m, n, o, &c. draw lines parallel to AR to meet

Pneuma-
tics.

PLATE
CCCCLXVI.
Fig. 20.

the perpendiculars; their intersections will constitute so many points in the line of perpetual congelation.

Make AD = $\frac{1}{27}$th of AE, and through D draw DQ parallel to AR; then the ordinate drawn through any point B in the curve of perpetual congelation to the line DQ, will show the height of that curve above the earth's surface at the latitude represented by the arch CK. The reason of the construction is obvious from the nature of the formula.

Causes
which af-
fect the
mean tem-
perature.

The mean temperature at the earth's surface is best found by taking the temperature of springs, which are not found to vary in summer or winter. It may also be found by taking the temperature of the ocean, which preserves at all seasons nearly the same temperature, on account of its fluidity. In this latitude, the temperature about the latter end of April is considered to be the mean temperature of the year. The maximum cold takes place about the 21st of January, and the maximum heat about the 21st of July. The mean temperature of a place is found to be affected by several other circumstances besides latitude. Thus small seas, in cold climates, are warmer in summer and colder in winter, than the standard ocean, being influenced by the temperature of the adjacent land. The Gulf of Bothnia is an instance of this, being frequently frozen in winter, whereas in summer its temperature is sometimes as high as 70^0. The German Sea, likewise, is found to be 3° colder in winter, and in summer 5° warmer than the Atlantic Ocean. The Mediterranean Sea has always its temperature lower than the Atlantic; a circumstance which produces a current from the latter into the former.

The mean temperature of a place is also affected very considerably by the state of the soil. The cultivation which modern Europe has received appears to have rendered the climate much milder than it was in former times. To this cause is to be attributed in some degree the severity of the climate in North America. The surface of the earth is covered there with immense forests, or consists of swamps and morasses, which imbibe the solar heat, and promote evaporation, which is always attended with cold. Places situated to the windward of lofty mountains are always found to be much warmer than those to the leeward, which may be thus accounted for. As evaporation produces cold, so, on the contrary, the condensation of vapour is attended with heat. We have already remarked, that the quantity of vapour which can be held in solution by the air at a given temperature, and under a given pressure, is a constant quantity. When a wind, therefore, loaded with vapour, has to pass over a lofty ridge of mountains, it is blended with the colder air at the summit, by which means its temperature is reduced. The vapour which it carries along with it can no longer exist at the reduced temperature, and is deposited in the shape of rain. The extrication of heat which is thus produced, contributes to increase the temperature of the windward side of the mountain. After this process has taken place, the air which composes the current of wind is carried along in a dry state, and imbibes in its passage over the country to the leeward as much moisture as it can retain; by which means the temperature is there diminished.

Dr. Hut-
ton's theo-
ry.

These remarks lead us to the consideration of air as the medium of humidity. A striking, though common, appearance connected with this subject excited the attention of Dr. Hutton, who, by endeavouring to explain it, was led to the formation of his theory of rain.

It is the breath of animals becoming visible, in being expired into an atmosphere which is cold or moist, and the transformation of steam into the state of mist, when mixed with air, which is of a colder temperature. He considers the air inspired by an animal as a menstruum dissolving water upon the warm and humid surface of the lungs, until it has become saturated. When this solution is expired, it may be cooled down so, that, according to the known laws of condensation, water may be separated from the menstruum, and become visible by reflecting light. In like manner, water may be rendered an invisible elastic fluid by means of heat alone. But, he observes, when breath or steam become visible in mixing with the atmosphere, this effect is not produced in consequence of the general principles of heat and cold, but requires, for its explanation, the knowledge of a particular law, viz. that the capacity of air for moisture does not increase at the same rate with its temperature.

To verify this law, it may be proper to attend to the several suppositions of which the case can admit, and these are,

I. That the capacity of air for moisture increases at the same rate with its temperature; or, that equal increments of heat may be accompanied with equal increments of dissolved vapour.

II. That the capacity of air for moisture varies at a less rate than its temperature; so that when the temperature increases by equal differences, the quantity of vapour which can be absorbed increases by differences continually diminishing.

III. That the capacity of air for moisture increases at a greater rate than its temperature, or that equal increments of heat may be accompanied with increasing increments of moisture.

These three suppositions may be represented geometrically in the following manner. Draw the straight line CH to represent the thermometrical scale, and let the ordinates to it represent the quantities of moisture which the air may imbibe at the corresponding temperatures, agreeably to the three hypotheses. The ordinates to the straight line $m\,r$ correspond to the first supposition which has been made, for their increments are in a constant ratio to the increments of temperature; those belonging to the curve $m\,g\,k\,l\,r$, which is concave towards CH, correspond to the second supposition, for their increments are in a less ratio than the increments of temperature; and those belonging to the convex curve $m\,d\,e\,f\,r$, relate to the third supposition, for their increments increase in a greater ratio than the increments of temperature. Let us now consider these three rates of aqueous solution, with a view to know the effects of mixing together saturated portions of the atmosphere of different temperatures. For this purpose, it may be observed that the ordinates of the straight line $m\,r$ will always represent the quantity of vapour which belongs to a unit of the mixture, whether it can be held in solution by it or not.

On the first supposition, let a portion of saturated air, at the temperature of 40°, be mixed with an equal portion of saturated air of the temperature of 10°. The moisture contained in the former is expressed by $r\,b$, and that contained in the latter by $m\,a$. The temperature of the compound is obviously 25°; and the quantity of vapour which air of this temperature can hold in solution is expressed by $p\,o$. But $p\,o$ is precisely the quantity of vapour which belongs to a unit of the mixture; hence the mixture remains still saturated, but deposites none of its moisture. In like manner, two

PLATE
CCCCLXVI.
Fig. 21.

parts of the temperature of 10°, combined with one of 40°, will produce a compound of the temperature of 30°, still saturated without any excess of vapour. Every mixture, therefore, according to this law, will be found equally saturated as are its constituents, and will have neither excess nor deficiency of the dissolved substance.

On the second supposition, let, as before, a saturated portion of air, of the temperature 40°, be combined with another saturated portion of the temperature 10°. The temperature of the mixture is obviously 25°; and the quantity of moisture which air of this temperature can hold in solution is expressed by $k\,o$. But the quantity of moisture belonging to a unit of the mixture, is expressed by $p\,o$; hence the mixture will be capable of absorbing an additional portion, which is represented by $k\,p$. In like manner, we will find that, according to this law, upon mixing together any quantities of saturated air, the compound will always have a capacity for more moisture.

Capacity of
air for
moisture
greater
than its ca-
pacity for
heat.

On the third supposition, let a saturated portion of air, of the temperature 40°, be united with another saturated portion of the temperature 10°. The temperature of the mixture is obviously 25°; and the quantity of moisture which air of this temperature can hold in solution is expressed by $e\,o$. But the quantity of moisture belonging to a unit of the mixture is expressed by $p\,o$; hence a portion of it, expressed by $p\,e$, must be deposited in the form of dew or water. In like manner, we shall find that, upon mixing together any quantities whatever of saturated air, provided they are of different temperatures, a deposition will always be found to take place.

From these considerations, it appears that the third hypothesis is the only one which serves to explain the phenomena of breath and steam becoming visible on being mixed with air which is colder than themselves. It also explains the various appearances which may occur in mixing together several portions of air more or less saturated with moisture. For, however cold the component parts of the mixture may be, they do not necessarily form a visible condensation on being combined. To produce this effect, it is necessary that they hold in the aggregate as much vapour in solution as will saturate the unit of mixture at the temperature to which they are reduced. On this account it is, that during summer, although the air contains generally much more moisture than it does in winter, the breath of animals is not perceptible. For then the air is of a higher temperature, and its capacity for moisture is consequently greater than during the winter season, so that it is able to retain in solution the vaporous particles which are exhaled.

Having, upon these general principles, selected that law which alone can explain the atmospherical phenomenon of visible mist, Dr. Hutton then proceeds to employ it as the foundation of his theory of rain. He remarks, that the most convincing experiment in favour of the theory would be to have rain or snow produced by a mixture of portions of the atmosphere, properly conditioned for the condensation of the contained vapour. An instance of this is adduced by him from M. de Maupertuis, who observes, that at Tornea, upon the opening of a door, the external air immediately converts the warm vapour of the chamber into snow, which appears in what he calls " de gros tourbillons blancs." A similar appearance has been observed by Dr. Robison to take place at Petersburgh. In a crowd-

ed assembly, when the company was suffering from the closeness of the room, a gentleman broke a window for relief, whereupon the cold air rushing in formed a visible circumgyration of a white snowy substance.

To these facts we may add another proof in confirmation of this law, and the theory which it supports, from the recent discoveries which have been made in HYGROMETRY. By referring to that article, Vol. XI. p. 577, § 39, we there find the maximum quantity of vapour which can be held in solution by a cubic inch of air, at all the intermediate temperatures between 1° and 100° Fahrenheit. It may be observed, that the temperatures increase by equal differences, whereas the quantities of moisture increase by differences continually augmenting, agreeably to the law which has been adopted. The application of the law to the theory may also be illustrated by the table which is there given. Let us suppose that saturated air, of the temperature of 60°, is combined with an equal portion of saturated air of the temperature of 80°. The weight of vapour which a cubic inch of the former contains is .00338832 grains, and the weight which a cubic inch of the latter contains is .00623919 grains. By taking an arithmetical mean of these two quantities we have .00481375 grains, the weight of vapour which belongs to a cubic inch of the mixture. But at the mean temperature 70°, which is that of the mixture, the weight of vapour which can be held in solution is only .00461639. Hence it appears that from every cubic inch of the compound there must be precipitated, in the form of water, a portion of vapour whose weight is .00019736 grains.

Had the capacity of air for moisture increased in the same ratio with its increase of temperature, no deposition could have taken place, unless by a diminution of heat after the whole atmosphere had become saturated. The summer's heat would have only caused the atmosphere to imbibe moisture, but would never have been attended with rain. Stores of humidity would thus have been accumulating during the time when they could have been most beneficially expended, and would have been reserved until the winter, when the rigour of the season would have produced deluges of rain. According to the present constitution of things, however, heat, which renders the air a better recipient for moisture, also creates currents in it of different temperatures, so that we have refreshing rains even when the atmosphere has its greatest capacity for humidity.

This theory also points out to us another beautiful arrangement in the constitution of the earth. Every thing which has a tendency to promote the mixing together of currents whose temperatures are different is favourable to the production of rain. Thus mountains the most barren have an influence upon the fertility of the surrounding plains; for, by opposing the course of a moist current of wind, they cause it to ascend to a colder region, where it produces clouds or rain. That the clouds which surround mountains are chiefly formed in this manner may be learned from the circumstance, that the most experienced seamen always consider the appearance of a cloud at a distance as an indication of an island or lofty land. Previous to Dr. Hutton's theory, the explanation given of this fact was, that the clouds were attracted towards the mountains by electricity; an opinion which is altogether fanciful.

According to Dr. Hutton's theory, the clouds produced in this manner should be formed at a less or greater elevation, depending upon the humidity of the wind. Thus, should air of the temperature of 60° form a cloud at the height of 1500 feet, we may infer that its temperature requires to be reduced $\frac{1500}{270}$ or 6° before the moisture which it contains be sufficient to saturate it. But by inspecting the table given in § 39. Hygrometry, we find that the weight of vapour contained in a cubic inch of saturated air at the temperature of 54° is .002280358 grains. Hence the altitude of clouds, together with the temperature of the air from which they are formed, may be considered as data sufficient for determining the quantity of vapour which winds contain. When the wind is moist, the clouds which it occasions are always low; when, on the other hand, it is comparatively dry, the clouds are proportionably high.

Clouds are composed of small spherules of water, whose diameters are so small that they are prevented from falling through the air on account of its resistance. To find what their diameters must be, in order that they may remain sensibly suspended in the air, we have only to take the expression for the terminal velocity

$$v = 4 \sqrt{\frac{g \cdot m \cdot a}{3 n}}$$ by means of which we can find the radius of a sphere corresponding to any terminal velocity. If we apply it to the small globules composing mist or clouds, we shall find that their diameter must be about .00004 of an inch in order to fall one foot in twenty-four hours. Thus a denser fluid, by being divided into exceedingly small portions, is made to float in a much rarer fluid, and, by the agitations of the latter, is wafted from one place to another, in order to produce the most beneficial effects. When clouds subside in an atmosphere saturated with moisture, the particles of vapour conglomerate, and thus acquire a greater terminal velocity. It is in this manner that drops of rain are formed; when, on the other hand, they subside into a warmer stratum of the air, the vapour is re-dissolved, and the clouds disappear. When this operation takes place near to the earth's surface, the particles, on account of the small space through which they fall, descend in a very minute shape, and form dew. The condensation is in this case produced by cold alone. During the day a quantity of moisture is absorbed by the heated atmosphere, which cannot be retained by it at the temperature to which it is reduced during the night. It is a curious fact, that the greatest cold which can happen upon any night may be predicted with very considerable precision during the preceding day. For this purpose we have only to observe, by a hygrometer, the quantity of moisture which the atmosphere contains, and calculate the temperature at which it will deposit it; this will be found upon trial to be the minimum temperature of the night. The heat given out by the condensation of the vapours existing in the atmosphere appears to set a limit to the reduction of temperature. When the air, accordingly, is in a comparatively dry state, it may be expected that this counteracting cause will be less powerful, and that the cold will be severe; whereas, on the contrary, when the air is moist, it may be presumed that the nocturnal temperature will be high. In this manner, the same process which moderates the temperature of the day tends to increase that of the night, and preserve a uniformity which is necessary for maturing the fruits of the earth. The same causes also moderate the change from the intense heat of summer to the severe cold of winter. During summer the absolute quantity of moisture contained in the atmosphere is much greater than during winter. At the latter end of harvest, when the temperature decreases, it is condensed, which is the reason that, at this period of the year, the air generally appears to be saturated with moisture. The vapours which are reduced to the form of water give out heat, and tend to equalize the temperature. On the other hand, during winter the absolute quantity of moisture contained in the air is small. At the commencement of spring, therefore, when the heat of the sun begins to be felt, the atmosphere has its capacity for moisture increased. This occasions a tract of dry weather which is best suited for the labours of the husbandman, and promotes evaporation, which renders the passage from winter to summer gradual.

This important fluid, which forms the medium of heat and moisture, is not peculiar to the globe which we inhabit. We have already seen how, from its elasticity, it must extend to an infinite distance from the earth's surface. It will be interesting, however, to attend more particularly to the manner in which it exists in the remote regions of space. It is obvious that the atmosphere partakes of the diurnal revolution of the earth, and that the portion of it which is in contact with the earth's surface accompanies it with the same velocity. As we ascend into the atmosphere the strata move with an increased velocity, proportional to their distance from the earth's centre, whilst, at the same time, their gravitation becomes less. From this it appears that there must be a certain point in the aërial fluid where the centrifugal force will be equal to the centripetal force, so that the particles will have no weight whatever. Beyond this point the aërial particles, if they have a rotatory motion at all, will always recede in a curve of the spiral form from the earth's centre. Their places will be occupied by other particles, which will distend themselves, from their elastic nature, into the vacant space. These, in their turn, will begin to withdraw themselves from the earth's centre, and thus, in the progress of time, the atmosphere which surrounds our globe will float away into the empty regions of space.

To avoid this conclusion, which is contrary to fact, although logically deduced from the principles of mechanics, it will be necessary to retract the supposition which has been made, of the aërial particles having a rotatory motion beyond that point where their gravitation is just sufficient to preserve them in a circular orbit around the earth's centre. Beyond this point, we must conceive that the whole extent of space is occupied by an elastic fluid at rest, which is capable of repressing the expansive force of the particles which compose the terrestrial atmosphere. To render admissible the existence of such a fluid, however, it must be shown that its elasticity is not required to be so great as to retard or derange the motions of the celestial planets. For although barometrical observations point out to us that the density of the atmosphere remains unaltered, and direct us to some cause by which it is prevented from dissipating by means of its elasticity and rotatory motion, yet at the same time the celestial motions require that this cause should not be such as to interfere with their regularity. If the cause by which the atmosphere be restrained, be, as is conceived, an attenuated fluid, which occupies the whole extent of space, its elasticity and density must be the same as the elasticity and density of our air at the point where its gravity is in equilibrium with its centrifugal force. In order to determine this point, let its distance above the earth's surface be x, and the radius of the earth be r, then the space described by the centripetal force in 1″ at the height x, will be $\left(\dfrac{r}{r+x}\right)^2 \times 16\frac{1}{12}$ feet. But the arch described by the rotatory motion of the aërial particles at the height x in 1″, is

$$\frac{2\,\pi\,r\,(r+x)\times 5280}{r\times 86400}\ \text{feet.}$$

When a body revolves in a circle, the diameter multiplied into the space described by the influence of the centripetal force in a second, is equal to the square of the arch described by the moveable in a second, or

$$\frac{2\,r^2\times 5280\times 16\frac{1}{12}}{(r+x)} = \left(\frac{2\,\pi\,.\,\overline{r+x}\,.\,5280}{86400}\right)^2$$

hence $r+x=26600$, and $x=22610=$ about 6 radii of the earth.

We may conclude, that at this great height the density of the air can oppose no resistance to the planetary motions, for even at the comparatively small height of 500 miles, its rarity is so great, that a sphere, having its diameter equal to that of Saturn's orbit, could contain as much of it as would occupy only a cubic inch, were it reduced to be of the same density with the air at the earth's surface. The density at the height of 22,610 miles is inconceivably less, and cannot sensibly affect the planetary motions after the lapse of millions of years.

Dr. Wollaston's arguments against the indefinite extent of the atmosphere.

This attenuated fluid which compresses our atmosphere, will occasion atmospheres around all the other planets. For, if its existence be admitted, we know from the law of gravitation that it must be collected and condensed by the attractive force of these bodies. Accordingly, astronomers have observed appearances in almost every planet of our system, which can only be explained by the existence of an atmosphere around them. Before proceeding to state them, however, it may be necessary to attend to an argument advanced by Dr. Wollaston, against the existence of atmospheres about the sun and Jupiter. "Assuming the sun's mass as 330,000 times that of the earth, and his radius 111.5 times that of the earth, he finds that the distance from the sun's centre, at which his atmosphere will have a density fully equal to our own, and therefore capable of refracting a ray of light more than a degree, is $= \sqrt{330,000} = 575$ times the earth's radius; that is, a point whose angular distance from the sun's centre is $15'\ 19'' \times 5.15 = 1°\ 21'\ 19''$."—*Edinburgh Philosophical Journal*, No. XIII. p. 159. But, according to several observations made by himself and other astronomers, the heavenly bodies have not been found to be refracted when much nearer than this to the sun's centre. It may be objected to this argument, that the temperature at the sun, and at the earth's surface, is supposed to be the same. If it be reasonable, however, to assume that the temperature of the sun is much greater than that of the earth, it must be admitted that the sun's atmosphere is not so dense as has been here concluded. For if we suppose the temperature of the sun to be only eight times the mean temperature of the equator, its atmosphere will have only half the density which is ascribed to it. But, as the solar temperature must be much higher than this, it may be presumed that the solar atmosphere will be so much rarefied by means of it, that any refraction which it may occasion will not be perceptible unless when a body approaches much nearer to the disc than has been hitherto observed.

His argument drawn from the eclipses of Jupiter's satellites is not open to the same objection; we shall therefore state it along with the conclusion which he deduces from it. "These bodies advance regularly, and without any retardation, from refraction to the very disc of the planet; so that Jupiter cannot possess that extent of atmosphere which he is capable of attracting to himself from an infinitely divisible medium filling space. For, taking Jupiter's mass at 309 times that of the earth, and his diameter at 11 times that of the earth, then $\sqrt{309}=17.6$ times the earth's radius $= \dfrac{17.6}{11} = 1.6$ times his own radius, which will be the distance from his centre at which an atmosphere equal to our own should produce a refraction of 1°. To the fourth satellite, this distance would subtend an angle of about 3° 37′; so that an increase of density to 3.5 times our common atmosphere would be more than sufficient to render the fourth satellite visible to us when behind the centre of the planet, and consequently to appear on both or all sides at the same time." Hence Dr. Wollaston concludes, that the earth's atmosphere is of finite extent, limited by the weight of ultimate atoms of definite magnitude, no longer divisible by repulsion of their parts.

Mr. Schroëter's observations.

Allowing this fact to have its full weight, for the subject can only admit of probable reasoning, as we cannot assign the temperature at the surface of Jupiter, we now proceed to state some phenomena which can only be accounted for by conceiving the planets to be surrounded by atmospheres. In the *Philosophical Transactions*, vol. lxxxii. Mr. Schroëter details the observations which he made respecting Venus and the Moon, from which he infers the existence of an atmosphere. We shall give a brief outline of his observations, reasonings, and conclusions.

His observations on Venus for this purpose, commenced on the 9th of March, 1790, when the planet was very near to her inferior conjunction. The appearance which it presented to him is sketched in Plate CCCCLXVI. Fig. 22. The southern cusp did not appear precisely of its usual circular form, but, as represented at a, inflected in the shape of a hook, beyond the luminous semicircle into the dark hemisphere of the planet. The northern cusp was terminated at b, in the same tapering manner as the southern, but did not extend in its bright luminous state into the southern hemisphere. From its point, however, the light of which, though gradually fading, was yet of sufficient brightness, a streak of glimmering light proceeded into the dark hemisphere from b to c, which, though intermittent as to intensity, was of permanent duration, and, although very faint, could be seen by a telescope magnifying 74.95 times. This light seemed to twinkle in various detached portions, and appeared throughout not only very faint, when compared with the light at the point of the cusp, but also of a very peculiar kind of faintness, verging towards a pale greyish hue. Its appearance, in short, was as faint as the dark limb of the moon three days after and before the new moon, when it is illuminated by rays reflected from the earth. The apparent diameter of the planet was, by means of the projecting table and the mean of several observations, all of which agreed to within 1″, found to measure 59″; but the greatest breadth of the illuminated part did not exceed 2.6″.

On the following evening he repeated his observations, when he perceived that the southern cusp had still its luminous prolongation, though not quite so dis-

PLATE CCCCLXVI. Fig. 22.

tinct as on the preceding night. He also perceived, that both cusps, but chiefly the northern one, had now most evidently a faint tapering prolongation of a bluish-grey cast, which, gradually fading, extended along the dark hemisphere, so that the luminous part of the limb was considerably more than a semicircle. On the evening of the 11th of March, the same appearance was again presented to his notice. He repeated his observations on the subsequent evening, and ascertained the following facts:

I. That the faint streak at the northern cusp, as represented by $b c$ in the figure, extended at least 8″ of a degree along the limb of the dark hemisphere.

II. That the prolongation of the southern cusp measured likewise full 8″, its inflected hooked form appearing now very distinctly; and,

III. That the apparent diameter of Venus subtended an angle of between 59 and 60″ *.

The planet, after these measurements were taken, was approaching too near its conjunction to admit of farther observations. This phenomenon occurred on the 18th day, at 4 P. M. On the 23d day, at 5 hours 10′ in the morning, M. Schroëter resumed his observations, when the same emanation of light was again perceived; it continued visible to him until the 30th, when all traces of it disappeared.

Upon these observations he institutes the following reasoning. As Venus, like the Moon, cannot be said to receive some light on its dark side from the earth, or any other heavenly body, it follows that these streaks of light must either proceed immediately from the sun, being occasioned by the illumination of the tops of a ridge of lofty mountains, or else result from an atmosphere in Venus, which refracts the rays proceeding from the sun, so as to fall upon the dark hemisphere of the planet, and produce an effect analogous to our twilight.

To overturn the first hypothesis, he remarks,

I. That this light does not appear, as on the mountains Leibnitz and Doerfel, in the moon, in single detached and distant points, but as a continued streak of light proceeding from the extremities of the cusps, and continuing along the limb of the dark hemisphere to a distance of about 8″, or in proportion to the apparent diameter of the planet 15° 19′ of its circumference.

II. That were this the light of the illuminated summits of a chain of mountains, it would not appear so even, regularly connected, and spherical as we behold it.

III. That this light is extremely faint, and forms as great a contrast with the whitish and more vivid light of the cusps, as the ash-coloured light, reflected from our earth on the dark limb of the moon, does with the solar light on its phase. Had this faint streak, like the more livid light, been an immediate emanation from the sun, the light in the dark part immediately contiguous to the points of the cusps, must have been nearly of the same degree of brightness as the points themselves, which is not the case.

After having concluded that this phenomenon is nothing less than a twilight, which Venus possesses similar to our own, he explains the reason of the hooked appearance of the southern cusp, on the evening in which he commenced his observations, by attributing it to the solar light illuminating a high ridge of mountains, which was situated in that region. The ash-coloured streak was not visible on that occasion, because the twilight which must have existed at this part would be eclipsed by the much greater brightness of the light immediately derived from the sun, in the same manner as in our earth, mountains that face the rising or setting sun are known to darken the twilight that ought to illuminate the regions situated behind them.

From the length of the streak of light which proceeded from the two cusps, he deduces certain inferences concerning the constitution of the atmosphere of Venus. The length of the streak was found to be 8′, of such parts as the apparent diameter contained 60°. The arch consequently corresponding to this chord, is 15° 19′. This, however, must not be understood, as the extent of the twilight at the surface of Venus. For let s (Fig. 23. Plate CCCCLXVI.) be the sun's place, T that of the earth, and c the centre of Venus. Join these three points. In the plane of the triangle thus formed, describe a circle FABGCD to represent a projection of Venus; and draw the diameters FG, AC, perpendicular to the lines S c, T c respectively. It is obvious that FDG is a projection of the illuminated half of Venus, and that C c G is a projection of that part of her disc which is visible to an observer at the earth. Let us suppose that the twilight extends beyond FG to hi, then it will appear to extend from the cusps to the diameter $f c =$ 15° 19′. To deduce from this quantity the true breadth of the twilight, or the arch whose projection is $f g$, we must know in the right-angled triangle $f c g$ two of the parts.

By means of the heliocentric longitude of Venus and of the earth, we can find their difference. With this datum, and the heliocentric latitude of Venus, we can determine the angle c ST. In the triangle c ST, we have the radii vectores of Venus and the earth, viz. S c, ST, as also the included angle c S T, from which we can determine the angle S c T. The supplement of this angle is the angle B c T $= g c f$. Mr. Schroëter finds this quantity to be 17° 49′ 45″. In the right angled spherical triangle $f c g$, he then has $f c$ and angle $f c g$ given, to find $f g$, which he calculates to be 4° 38′ 30″, the breadth of the twilight. This computation leads us to remark, that the breadth of the twilight cannot be observed at any other point of the terminating border, except the cusps, because it only amounts to 2.45 seconds, and is eclipsed by the superior brightness of the adjacent luminous hemisphere. Even at the extremity of the cusps, it cannot be seen, unless for a few days before and after the inferior conjunction. For in proportion as the angle $f c g$ increases, since $f g$ is a constant quantity, $f c$ will diminish. During the time of the inferior conjunction, therefore, $f c$ is a maximum.

From the success which attended his observations upon the atmosphere of Venus, Mr. Schroëter was led to make similar observations upon that of the moon. From what has been already stated, it appears that the best time for conducting this inquiry is about the time of new moon. Accordingly, on the 24th of February, 1791, two days and twelve hours after the conjunction, he observed, at the extremities of the lunar cusps, emanations of light, having a faint ash-coloured appearance, precisely similar to those which he perceived in Venus. The same figure, therefore, which was employed by us to illustrate his former discovery, will

PLATE CCCCLXVI. Fig. 23.

---

* Though Dr. Herschel, in the 83d vol. of the *Transactions*, criticises some of Schroëter's assertions, he does not deny the accuracy of these observations.

also serve to explain that which he now made. The length of the emanation from both cusps was found to be the same, and amounted to 1′ 20″. The apparent diameter of the moon was also measured, and found to be 31′ 18″. From this it appears that $f c$ is the projection of an arch of 4° 53′ 13″. Farther, he was also able to measure the apparent breadth of the twilight, or the arch whose projection is $c k$; this he found to be about 2″. By calculating the value of this arch, in the same manner as he did the corresponding one upon the disc of Venus, he obtained the same result, viz. 2″. The true breadth of the twilight of the moon is therefore 2° 34′ 35″.

From these observations, the reason appears why this twilight cannot be perceived at the terminating border of the falcated phase, and why, on the succeeding evening, it disappeared even at the cusps. From a long series of observations, M. Schroëter has been led to the conclusion, that the lunar atmosphere is much rarer than that of Venus.

Although phenomena similar to these cannot be observed in the superior planets, yet their appearance is such as can leave no doubt that an atmosphere exists around them. The variations which take place in the aspect of Jupiter and Mars can only be accounted for by the existence of clouds hovering around these bodies. The former appears to be encircled with belts, or zones, parallel to its equator, of various degrees of brightness, which are probably owing to differences in its climate. These zones are not of a uniform brightness, but are interspersed with spots, which plainly move from east to west. Such, perhaps, would be the appearance which our earth would exhibit to a spectator stationed in another planet. Mars possesses an interesting resemblance to the earth, having an atmosphere which appears to carry clouds and deposit snow. Around his poles there is a white appearance, which begins to fade away when they are for some time directed towards the sun. These analogies lead us to believe that all the planets of our system may be the residences of living beings, who, like ourselves, have their summer and winter season, their day and night; and whose existence may be supported by breathing the same air.

PŒSTUM. See CIVIL ARCHITECTURE, Vol. VI. p. 601, 602. and Plate CLXXXVI.

POETRY.

POETRY, POESY, is a term derived from the Greek ποιητρία, ποιησις of ποιεω, *I make*, intimating, that the art which it denotes was regarded of unrivalled eminence, or of peculiarly difficult execution. In nothing have critics differed and disputed so much as about the definition of this divine art, each succeeding writer rejecting altogether, or essentially qualifying, the definition given by his predecessors. The father of criticism has denominated it " a mimetic or imitative art." Others have characterized it as " the art of expressing our thoughts by fictions," a definition supported by the authority of Aristotle and Plato. Neither of these definitions is correct. The former is defective, inasmuch as it does not discriminate poetry from other arts which depend equally on imitation; for, not to mention sculpture and painting, " an imitation of human manners and characters," says an excellent critic, " may be carried on in the humblest prose, no less than in the more lofty poetic strain." The latter is equally defective, and for similar reasons, because, though fiction be one of the characteristics of poetry, yet many of the happiest poetical effusions may be literally descriptive of real life, and of things which actually exist; while fiction forms also one of the great lineaments and features of prose as well as of poetical composition. There have been numberless other definitions more or less objectionable; but that given by our countryman Dr. Blair may probably be regarded as the most just and comprehensive that has yet been submitted to the public, " that it is the language of passion, or of enlivened imagination, formed most commonly into regular numbers." " The historian, the orator, the philosopher," says the same author, " address themselves for the most part primarily to the understanding; their direct aim is to inform, to persuade, or to instruct. But the primary aim of a poet is to please and to move; and therefore it is to the imagination and the passions that he speaks. He may, and he ought, to have it in his view, to instruct and to reform; but it is indirectly, and by pleasing and moving, that he accomplishes this end. His mind is supposed to be animated by some interesting object which fires his imagination, or engages his passions; and which, of course, communicates to his style a peculiar elevation suited to his ideas, very different from that mode of expression which is natural to the mind in its calm ordinary state." This definition, so clearly expressed, and so admirably illustrated, may probably be made yet more simple and accurate by being rendered more minute. And poetry may therefore be defined, as the language of passion, or of enlivened imagination, expressed in the most elegant and rich terms, whether in regular numbers or otherwise, ornamented with similies, metaphors, tropes, figures, episodes, allegories, and hyperboles; in which fiction and imagination may, with propriety, be indulged beyond the strict limits of truth and reality. This definition, we presume, is free from the defects by which those quoted above are characterized, and yet, at the same time, combines their truth and excellencies.

Verse or regular numbers, it is evident, are not essential to the existence of poetry. Verse is, we grant, the common external distinction of poetry, and probably may be regarded as contributing much to its beauty and fascination; yet poetry consists not in the form or dress in which it is presented to the eye; it consists in the soul and spirit by which this form is animated, and which imparts to it all its native fire. There is, besides, a species of verse scarcely distinguishable from prose, as that of the comedies of Terence; and there are various productions, apparently written in prose, of so elevated and impassioned a character, as virtually and undeniably to belong to the highest and purest kind of poetical composition. The Telemachus of Fenelon, and the English translation of Ossian, will at once occur to every reader. Hence it is, since verse and prose are not inherently and radically distinct, but like light and shade run on some occasion into each other, that the exact limit between poetry and eloquence (the art most closely connected with poetry) cannot with precision be determined. They both depend essentially, though probably in somewhat different degrees, on the same principles, on deep susceptibility of feeling, on boldness

Poetry.

and originality of invention, on animated and figurative language. The exact boundaries of the two arts, therefore, it would be difficult, and at present we have not time, to ascertain; and it need merely be mentioned, as one of the greatest distinctions between them, that study and discipline are more necessary in the one than in the other; or, in other words, that to an orator, whatever be his natural genius, study, education, and rigid discipline, are indispensably necessary; while a poet may attain to the very perfection of his art without education, without the benefit of human learning, merely by the innate force of genius alone. An orator must necessarily be a student and a scholar, ere he can gain distinction; a poet, though learning and reading may be useful, may reach to eminence without the assistance of either. Homer is known to us as the greatest of all poets in consequence of natural endowments alone: Demosthenes enjoyed the same distinction in eloquence as the result of human learning and the most inflexible study, united with genius,—a result which genius of itself would have been insufficient to accomplish.

Music and poetry coeval.

But, though verse be not essential to poetry, a certain melody or modulation of voice, analogous probably to verse, seems to have been the dress in which poetical composition first appeared. So correct is this opinion that poetry and music are allowed by all to have had the same origin. " The first poets sung their own verses; and hence the beginning of what we call versification, or words arranged in a more artful order than prose, so as to be suited to some tune or melody. The liberty of transposition or inversion, which the poetic style would naturally assume, made it easier to form the words into some sort of numbers that fell in with the music of the song. Very harsh and uncouth, we may easily believe, these numbers would be at first. But the pleasure was felt; it was studied; and versification by degrees passed into an art." (*Blair's Lectures*, ii. 223.) Music and poetry, being thus coeval, continued intimately connected till music began to be studied as a separate art, divested of the poet's song, and formed into the artificial and intricate combinations of harmony, thus losing all its ancient power of inflaming the heart with strong emotions, and becoming an art of mere amusement among polished and luxurious nations.

Origin of poetry.

The origin of the art which we have thus endeavoured to define and characterize, must be referred to the remotest antiquity. The Greeks, indeed, have given a mythological account of its origin, and have ascribed the honour of it to their ancient deities, or to their first distinguished bards, to Apollo and the muses, to Orpheus, Linus, Musæus. But this opinion is evidently fabulous. To explore the rise of poetry, we need not have recourse to refined and accomplished nations. Poetry has its origin in the nature of man, and belongs to every age and to every country. It belongs in particular to the simplest and most unsophisticated manners. It first appeared in the deserts and the wilds, among hunters and shepherds, in the first generations of the world, or in the rudest state of society, before refinement had polished or learning had illumined mankind. And, consistently with this opinion, we find poetry, not only more common, but more pure and impassioned, in those nations, the inhabitants of which are the farthest removed from the luxury, learning, and refinement of civilized life. Poetry, indeed, seems to lose its original character of boldness, originality, and enthusiasm, and to become timid, unnatural, and artificial, in proportion as the people by whom it is culti-

vated are removed from the state of rude and savage existence. Hence it is that we find the wild Indians of America employ in their treaties and public transactions, bolder metaphors, more splendid gorgeousness of style, than the civilized nations of Europe in their most elevated poetical productions. Having concluded a treaty of peace with the British, the Five Nations of Canada expressed themselves by their chiefs in the following language. " We are happy in having buried under ground the red axe, that has often been dyed with the blood of our brethren. Now, in this sort, we enter the axe and plant the tree of peace. We plant a tree whose top will reach the sun, and its branches spread abroad, so that it shall be seen afar off. May its growth never be stifled and choked; but may it shade both your country and ours with its leaves! Let us make fast its roots, and extend them to the utmost bounds of your colonies. If the French should come to shake the tree, we should know it by the motion of its roots reaching into our country. May the Great Spirit allow us to rest in tranquillity upon our mats, and never dig up the axe to cut down the tree of peace! Let the earth be trod hard over it where it lies buried. Let a strong stream run under the pit to wash the evil away out of our sight and remembrance. The fire that had long burned in Albany is extinguished. The bloody bed is washed clean, and the tears are wiped from our eyes. We now renew the covenant chain of friendship. Let it be kept bright and clear as silver, and not suffered to contract any rust. Let not any one pull away his arm from it." (Cadwallader Colden's *History of the Five Indian Nations.*)

Nor is this a solitary and unsupported instance. Of the principle we are labouring to establish, the poems of Ossian afford a striking illustration: and innumerable other references might be made, (see particularly an Essay on Sclavonic poetry, published in *Letters on Poland,* 1823, and Von Troil's *Letters on Iceland,*) as a proof how inseparably, in rude periods of society, poetry is connected with the feelings and principles of every class and condition of men, particularly on moving and interesting occasions. Among all savage tribes indeed with whom we have yet had any intercourse, poetical effusions, rude probably, but true to nature, obtain in an extraordinary degree. This fact has been established by the minute and concurring accounts of travellers. Their religious rites are celebrated in song. By songs they lament their public and private calamities, the death of friends, or the loss of warriors. By these they express their joy on their victories, record and embalm the bravery of their heroes, excite each other to perform feats of valour, and to encounter death or torments with inflexible firmness. Agreeably to this opinion, Moses and Miriam, the first authors known to us, offered upon the banks of the Red Sea a song of praise to the Almighty, for the deliverance which, through his miraculous assistance, they had experienced from Egyptian bondage. This song has been transmitted to us, and forms not only the most ancient monument, but an unrivalled specimen, of poetical composition. * * * " Thy right hand, O Lord, is become glorious in power: thy right hand, O Lord, hath dashed in pieces the enemy. And in the greatness of thine excellence thou hast overthrown them that rose up against thee: thou sendest forth thy wrath which consumed them as stubble. And with the blast of thy nostrils the waters were gathered together; the floods stood upright as an heap, and the depths were congealed in the heart of the sea. The enemy said, I will pursue, I will overtake, I will divide the spoil: my lust shall be satisfied

Poetry.

Poetry.

upon them: I will draw my sword, my hand shall destroy them. Thou didst blow with thy wind, the sea covered them: they sank as lead in the mighty waters. Who is like unto thee, O Lord, among the gods? Who is like unto thee, glorious in holiness, fearful in praises, doing wonders?" * * *

Poetry of greater antiquity than prose.

From these varied examples, it is evident that poetry, except in common conversation, or in reference to every-day occurrences, is of greater antiquity than prose. History, law, theology, were all embodied and transmitted from age to age in poetic numbers. The prophets of the Hebrews "prophesied," we are told, "with the psaltery, tabret, and harp before them." With the Arabians and Persians, poetry was the earliest form and medium of all their learning and instruction: their proverbs and moral maxims were moulded into verse like the writings of Solomon or the book of Job. Minos and Thales sung to the lyre the laws which they composed and disseminated. Tacitus mentions the hymns of the Germans, at a time when that rude people lived in the woods in circumstances of savage existence; and the Runic songs of all the Gothic tribes formed the source whence the more early writers of their history drew their most important information. Among the Celtic nations poetry was, if possible, more assiduously cultivated and more deeply venerated: their bards were held in such high estimation, that even their persons were regarded as sacred. So much, in ancient times, was poetry the vehicle in which national, local, and individual history was embodied, that even in periods comparatively recent, historians, imbibing the ancient spirit, have clothed their compositions in a similar dress,—a fact of which our countrymen Lermont, Barbour, Winton, form conspicuous instances. In short, history, eloquence, poetry, were coeval, and synonimous or at least analogous terms. Whoever, in these rude ages, wished to move or to persuade, to instruct or to interest his friends or his countrymen, whatever was the subject on which he descanted, had recourse to the harmony of numbers and the melody of song.

Progress of poetry.

Poetry thus having its foundation in the nature of man, may be expected to exhibit similar features during the primitive ages of every country. The circumstances which caused it to be cultivated and cherished were every where nearly the same. The praises of gods and men, individual or national glory or calamity, joy or lamentation, which constituted the early subjects of poetry, are topics common to every tribe and nation. But though, in the first stages of society, mankind in every country resemble each other, they gradually vary: climate and modes of living form and develop principles and habits among one people which are unknown or despised by another. Thus, though in every nation, the source of poetry and its great general lineaments, were at first similar, it by degrees, among different tribes, exhibited distinct and peculiar characteristics; and was mild or impetuous, martial or tender, unpolished or refined, according to the circumstances and institutions of the different nations of the world. Hence the great national division of poetry, the Hebrew, Chinese, Arabian, Gothic, Celtic, Grecian, each kind being powerfully descriptive of the circumstances of the people, and the natural scenery of the country, where it obtained. Nor was this general division the only change that poetry underwent. Poetical composition at first embraced the whole impulses of which the human soul is susceptible, the unrestrained range of the human imagination; and every species of the art lay confused in the same mass, according as circumstances or enthusiasm directed the poet's strain. But now, in ad-

Different kinds of.

dition to the national division just spoken of, the different kinds of poetry were severally discriminated, each being assigned its separate character and importance, and subjected to rules and restrictions unknown in the earlier stages of the art. History, eloquence, and poetry, long so closely connected, were now disjoined, and each regarded as distinct from the others, and independent of them. The historian now laid aside the garb and brilliancy of poetry; he wrote in sober, elaborate prose, and was ambitious of no praise but that of candour and authenticity. The orator, though he did not altogether relinquish the splendid and flowing ornaments by which he was formerly characterized, laboured to gain his point, as much by ingenuity, and arguments addressed to the understanding, as by his warm and impassioned appeals to the feelings and the heart. "Poetry," says an elegant critic, "became now a separate art, calculated chiefly to please, and confined generally to such subjects as related to the imagination and the passions. Even its earliest companion, music, was in a great measure divided from it." It now indeed assumed a comparatively tame and uninteresting aspect. The bard, instead of pouring forth his song as the native and irresistible effusions of an ardent and inspired heart, had recourse to study and to rules, affected to be actuated by what he did not feel, and supplied the want of native emotions by pompous and artificial ornaments, chosen to dazzle and to deceive.

Divisions of.

The divine art, therefore, of which we are treating, has, in the more civilized countries, been divided into different departments or professions, a thing unknown in the poetic compositions of a rude state of society. It must not be denied, however, that, even at the earliest periods of the art, we may trace symptoms and indications of that division which we are now contemplating. Thus, what we now denominate the Ode or Lyric Poetry, may, with propriety, be reckoned the first species of composition. As the word Ode denotes, it was a species of poetry intended to be sung or accompanied with music; a distinction, however, at first peculiar, as formerly shown, to no one mode of poetical writing. But of that which we now call the Ode, the earliest productions, such as the Song of Moses and Miriam, the Psalms of David, &c., are correct and regular specimens. The Elegy would at a remote period be introduced, lamenting the death of friends, of chiefs, and of warriors. Nor would Epic Poetry be long uncultivated. To celebrate the exploits of heroes is a task which the bard would early be excited to perform; and his effusions on such an occasion would literally give birth to the epic or heroic species of poetic composition. And if, while reciting a production of this nature at any of the public meetings of the tribe, the different bards should endeavour to personate the different heroes and personages, and should feel, and speak, and act, agreeably to the several characters they had assumed, this representation would necessarily be the origin and the first outlines of dramatic composition. Thus early, therefore, may we trace the undefined, original appearances of the different kinds of poetry, of which the most ancient tribes (though this division was not nominally known to them, and though poetry of every description was then indiscriminately blended together) afford some striking indications; but it was left to more civilized nations to effect, by study, by rigid definition, and by criticism, what the early bards did not fully understand or wilfully neglected, preferring, as they did, to give utterance to the strong movements and sympathies of their souls in such wild and impetuous language as nature spontaneously dictated, rather than do violence to

Poetry.

the noble warmth of their feelings by study or by artificial arrangements. The remainder of this article shall be employed in giving an analysis of the different kinds of poetic writings, and in enumerating some of the more eminent authors, in the several departments of the art.

Poetry of the Hebrews.

But before entering on this portion of our subject, we shall treat of the poetry of the Hebrews, not because it is the medium of divine revelation,—we shall not at present consider its awful dignity and importance in this respect,—but because it is the most ancient, as well as the most curious and perfect specimen of poetical writing handed down to us. Though the books of the Old Testament, being the production of various individuals and different ages, are characterized by great diversity of style, it is not difficult to ascertain which of them belong to the department of poetry. Of this class, undoubtedly, are the Book of Job, the Psalms of David, the Song of Solomon, the Lamentations of Jeremiah, a great proportion of the prophetical books, with innumerable detached passages in the historical writings. Whether these compositions were originally written in verse has long been a subject of dispute with biblical critics, and is yet undetermined. Our knowledge of the correct pronunciation of the language in which they are written is so imperfect, that the dispute can never be expected to be settled. Many learned writers, however, such as Dr. Lowth and Dr. Blayney, are decidedly of opinion, that in the poetical-books the arrangements of the words and the cadences of the sentences are so essentially different from those in the historical, as to warrant the inference that they were originally composed in regular numbers. Music and poetry, among the Hebrews, as well as among all other people, seem to have been inseparably connected. In the earlier notices on this subject in the Old Testament, it is mentioned that praises were offered up to the Lord in songs accompanied with various instruments of music. We are told by Samuel of the prophets " prophesying with the psaltery and harp before them." " Sing unto the Lord a new song," is an expression every where to be found, and is evidently conclusive with respect to the intimate connexion formerly stated as existing between poetry and music. But whatever opinions may be entertained on other points, Hebrew poetry, it is allowed by all, is of a peculiar description, unlike that of any other nation with which we are acquainted. And this peculiarity consists in no mean degree in its artificial external structure, in its repetitions, amplifications, alternation and correspondence of parts. Every period is divided into two members, either tautological, or forming a contrast to each other, and always the same in point of sound and measure. Our English version, though in prose, being literally word for word after the original, retains all the characteristic marks of metrical and poetical composition, and may with propriety be quoted for the benefit of those unacquainted with the Hebrew language. Thus, in the twentieth chapter of Job :

" The triumphing of the wicked is short,—and the joy of the hypocrite but for a moment.
Though his excellency mount up to the heavens,—and his head unto the clouds ;
Yet he shall perish for ever like his own dung :—they which have seen him shall say, where is he ?
He shall fly away as a dream and shall not be found,—yea, he shall be chased away as a vision of the night.
The eye also which saw him, shall see him no more ;—neither shall his place any more behold him."

This method of composition, which forms the peculiar and distinguishing feature of Hebrew poetry, became at length so familiar, and so much the character of the language, that it prevailed more or less in every other species of composition. In the prophetical writings this idiom is conspicuously remarkable. In Isaiah, chapter fifty-fifth, the reader will find striking specimens of this, as well as in innumerable other places.

The origin of this idiom in the Hebrew tongue may probably be traced to the nature of their music. Their hymns or odes, like those of other nations, were uniformly sung ; but with them this was accomplished in a way somewhat peculiar. Their singers and musicians did not all perform together, but each individual, or the different divisions of the band, had their respective parts to accomplish, so as to obtain a varied but uninterrupted melody. Thus, for example, one band sung, " The Lord reigneth, let the earth rejoice;" the chorus or semi-chorus immediately succeeded, " let the multitude of the isles be glad thereof." " Clouds and darkness are around him," was sung by one, while the other replied, " judgment and righteousness are the habitation of his throne." Of this peculiarity, the 24th psalm may be adduced as, probably, the most striking and satisfactory instance. It is supposed to have been composed on the important and solemn occasion of the ark of the covenant being brought back to Mount Sinai. " Who shall ascend unto the hill of the Lord, and who shall stand in his holy place ?" is sung by a semi-chorus, and the response is made by a full chorus, " He that hath clean hands and a pure heart, who hath not lifted up his soul to vanity, nor sworn deceitfully." As the procession approached the door of the tabernacle, the full chorus is supposed again to join in the exclamation, " Lift up your heads ye gates, and be ye lifted up, ye everlasting doors, and the king of glory shall enter in." " Who is the king of glory ?" is a question by the semi-chorus, and the answer is returned by the whole chorus, as the ark is introduced into the tabernacle, " The Lord, strong and mighty, the Lord, mighty in battle." These examples, while they illustrate the nature of Hebrew poetry, show, at the same time, how much of the beauty and magnificence of this portion of the sacred volume is lost to those who understand not the genius of the original tongue, or who know not the different circumstances for which these compositions were severally written.

It may be here remarked, that this practice of the Hebrew poets, of always amplifying the same thought by repetition or contrast, does not in the least degree tend to enfeeble their style—a result which, at first sight, we would suppose unavoidable. In managing this extremely difficult point consist their merit and their eminence. The same thought is never dwelt upon long ; their sentences are short ; and, except with regard to the peculiarity which we have just contemplated, they use no superfluous words, no artificial embellishments. There is nothing else very peculiar or idiomatical in the mode of construction of Hebrew poetry. It is certainly characterized by beauties of every description to a degree altogether unrivalled. Simplicity, strength, boldness, magnificence, sublimity, pathos, are its distinguishing features. With the Hebrew poets there are no far-fetched allusions and illustrations, no false feeling, or studied and artificial magnificence. The pastoral life, and the parched ground of Judea, the palm-trees and the cedars of Lebanon, are almost the only sources from which they draw their figures and their associations.

Having thus treated of the poetry of the Hebrews, we proceed to give such an account of the different species of poetic composition as our limits will admit.

Lyric poetry, or the Ode.

Lyric Poetry, or *the Ode*, is probably the first that will suggest itself to the mind of every reader. As its name imports, it is intended to be sung or accompanied with music—a distinction, as formerly shown, not originally confined to any one kind of poetic writing, as music and poetry were coeval, but which the ode was allowed to retain when these two arts were separated. The ode, therefore, may justly be regarded as the form of the earliest poetical effusions; and, consistently with this opinion, it is required to be more fervid, more impassioned, more directly the offspring of natural feeling, than any other department of the art. Following the dictates of natural emotion, it may be abrupt in its transitions, it may make bold digressions, and give way to enthusiastic and energetic flights, incompatible with every other species of composition, and which, at least, can never be justified in verses written for simple recitation. The subjects, too, on which it may descant, are more akin to those which originally formed the song of the poet.

> " Musa dedit *fidibus* divos, puerosque deorum,
>   Et pugilem victorem, et equum certamine primum,
>   Et juvenum curas, et libera vina referre."—*Ars Poetica.*

The ode, therefore, is necessarily a composition in which dignity, energy, and passion, are conspicuous; it is usually meant to be a warm transcript of the poet's heart—a character which it still, in a great measure, retains, though, in modern times, it has been divided into four denominations, each more or less distinct and different from the others. These are sacred odes; heroic odes; moral and philosophical odes; festive and amatory odes. The two first possess the distinction by which the ode was originally marked, elevation and pathos; while the two last are of a more subdued and tame description, in general elegant and nervous, though sometimes gay and sportive. To the festive and amatory ode belong songs of every character, and of every degree of merit. The most celebrated writers of odes of antiquity are Pindar, Anacreon, Horace. In England, the names of Cowley, Dryden, Collins, Gray, Smollett, will at once occur to every poetic reader. " Dryden's Ode to St. Cecilia," " The Tears of Scotland," by Smollett, and " Collins's Ode to the Passions," may be mentioned as, probably, the finest specimens of lyric composition which the country has yet produced.

As not unconnected with the ode, or rather as a species of it, *the Elegy* may be mentioned. " It is," says Johnson, ": the effusion of a contemplative mind, sometimes plaintive, always serious, and, therefore, superior to the glitter of artificial ornaments." It was originally appropriated to mourn the death of a friend, a benefactor, or a distinguished character; but it was afterwards used in a wider sense, and came to express the grief of lovers, and every species of distress and disappointment. Poets of almost every age and nation have cultivated, with various success, elegiac composition; but " The Country Church-yard" of Gray probably stands unrivalled in ancient or modern times. " It abounds," says the author just quoted, " with images which find a mirror in every breast, and with sentiments to which every bosom returns an echo."

But though lyric poetry be regarded as the first species in use among savage tribes, yet *the Epic* has a claim to nearly as remote an origin, and certainly at least it retains its original characteristics as unpolluted as any other division of the art. The recital of the achievements of heroes and of ancestors, of warriors who had fallen, or who had conquered in battle—and

this recital would literally constitute epic poetry,— would naturally be a subject which, in the earliest periods of society, would call forth the poet's powers, and which he would wish to embalm and perpetuate in song. And this mode of poetic writing, besides being old, is allowed to be the most dignified, elevated, and majestic, fitted only for the cultivation of men of the finest and most diversified genius. A story, or the achievements of a single hero, are regarded as indispensable requisites in an epic poem, both to excite the interest and admiration of the reader, and to connect the subsidiary narratives and episodes of the work. It has been compared to tragedy, and indeed the only essential difference between the two is, that the epic employs narrative, and in some respects partakes rather of the character of historical composition; while tragedy represents incidents as appearing before our eyes, and her heroes and actors speaking their own sentiments, and engaged in all the bustle and fervour of active existence. Tragedy, therefore, displays characters chiefly by means of sentiments and passions which seem to pass under our review; epic poetry chiefly by actions. Epic poetry, besides, is a less animated and impassioned composition, and deals more in narrative and description than tragedy. It requires indeed occasional bursts of energetic and overpowering emotions, but these are not its leading characteristics. The emotions, however, which it does excite, if not so frequent or so violent as those of dramatic composition, are more prolonged and more developed by actual occurrences; for it embraces a wider compass of time and action than the kind of writing with which we are contrasting it. The action of the Odyssey, for example, extends to eight years and a half; that of the Æneid about six years. The epic poet is not obliged to confine himself to historical truth; fiction, invention, imagination, may be admitted almost to any extent, at the expence of scrupulous accuracy, provided always the poet sin not against the *unities*, or that his work, according to the language of critics, embrace an *entire action*, or have a beginning, a middle, and an end. This is the distinguishing quality of the great epic poems. The object, for example, of the Odyssey, is the return and establishment of Ulysses in his own country; and amid all the ramifications of the poem, every portion of it has its proper and suitable dimensions; the great object is steadily kept in view, and every sentence and every apparent departure from the subject, is made powerfully and directly conducive to the interest and progress of it. In this department of writing, in addition to the work just mentioned, the most distinguished are Virgil's Æneid, Tasso's Jerusalem, Lucan's Pharsalia, Statius's Thebaid, Camoens' Lusiad, Voltaire's Henriade, Cambray's Telemachus, Ossian's Fingal and Temora, Milton's Paradise Lost, Glover's Leonidas, Wilkie's Epigoniad.

Pastoral poetry, the species which we next proceed to consider, is not of so ancient an origin as those we have already contemplated. Figures and descriptions of a pastoral kind indeed occur in the earliest poems that have been handed down to us; but these descriptions are incidental only; and it is now allowed by all critics that pastoral poetry was not cultivated as a separate and distinct branch of the art till towns and cities had been built and inhabited, till gradation of rank had been established, and men had become comparatively luxurious and refined. Rural peace and tranquillity were not known or not appreciated till they could be contrasted with the bustle and anxiety of courts and large cities. "Men, then," to use the words of an elegant writer, "began to look back on the more simple and innocent life which their forefathers led, or which they supposed them to have led; they looked back upon it with pleasure; and in those rural scenes and pastoral occupations imagining a degree of felicity to take place superior to what they now enjoyed, conceived the idea of celebrating it in poetry. It was in the court of King Ptolemy that Theocritus wrote the first pastorals with which we are acquainted; and in the court of Augustus he was imitated by Virgil." But to whatever date we may assign the origin of pastoral poetry, it is agreed on all hands that no species of the poetic art is more fascinating, sweet, and natural. It brings before our minds the most ancient, the most innocent, the most happy, and the simplest form of existence. It recals to the imagination of most of us the place of our birth, and the haunts of our childhood, " the green pastures and the still waters," hallowed and endeared to us by many a tender association, and on which at every period of our life memory lingers with peculiar fondness. Flocks, trees, flowers, streams, rural love and rural peace, carry charms to every bosom.

In writing pastoral poetry, however, rural life must be painted, not literally as we find it in the present age, but in reference to those innocent and simple times described so exquisitely by the earlier pastoral poets. It is this pleasing illusion, probably more than any thing else, which has shed such inexpressible beauty and sweetness over this species of poetry.—Of pastoral compositions, the language, it is evident, must be humble, devoid of floridness and pomp; the figures simple, concise, and taken from rural scenery and rural occupations; the sentiments, the result of natural and unsophisticated emotions. Apostrophes to inanimate objects, if not turgidly executed, may be frequent; digressions may be allowed, if short and directly connected with the circumstances in which the parties are supposed to be placed.

There is a form of pastoral poetry that has been introduced in recent times, and which it would be improper to overlook, namely, that in which it assumes the character of the regular drama, founded on the sympathy and innocence of rural manners. Of this kind the Pastor Fido of Guarini, and Tasso's Aminta, are well known. But our own country has produced a pastoral drama which will bear a comparison with any composition of the kind. We allude to the "Gentle Shepherd" of Ramsay, which abounds with beauties of the highest and most varied order. It is completely free from offensive rusticity or coarseness; it uniformly sustains the genuine character of rural simplicity; while, at the same time, the affecting incidents, tender sentiments, and natural description, by which it is characterized, would do honour to any poet.—Among the ancients, the most celebrated writers of pastorals are Theocritus and Virgil. Various authors of our own country have applied their genius to pastoral composition,—but with no eminent success; and, with the exception of Ramsay, Britain can boast of no great poet in this department of writing but Shenstone, whose "Pastoral Ballad" has challenged the praise and admiration of every critic. Of all the moderns, however, Gesner, a native of Switzerland, has cultivated pastoral composition with the most brilliant success. He excels chiefly in the description of domestic sympathy and felicity, the mutual affection of husbands and wives, of parents and children, of brothers and sisters,

and of lovers. There is throughout his Idyls such sweet and tender sentiments, such genuine touches of nature, as must make a deep impression on every heart susceptible of pure and simple, yet elevated emotions.

The object of *Didactic Poetry*, which is the next species that claims attention, is to convey knowledge and instruction. It has been employed chiefly on moral, philosophical, and critical subjects. In works of this nature, method and arrangement are indispensably necessary, so as to give a connected strain of instruction; and yet in no department of writing are such privileges allowed. Digressions and episodes of all kinds, historical or fabulous, every embellishment and illustration may with propriety be introduced, provided they originate naturally in the subject, and tend to elucidate or enforce it. The great art of a didactic poet, indeed, is to relieve the reader by digressions and collateral discussions; and to make, as it were, the ostensible object of his composition subservient to illustrations and episodes which are susceptible of higher poetry and deeper interest than can be communicated to a continued series of grave instructions. It is this in which the chief interest of Virgil's Georgics consists, and the genius of the author is most eminently displayed. This celebrated production, with all the merit which in other respects it possesses, and all the valuable information it conveys, would be comparatively uninteresting and prosaic, were it not for the beautiful and highly poetical digressions by which it is characterized; such as the praises of Italy, the felicity of rural life, the fable of Aristaeus, the story of Orpheus and Eurydice. Nor is the talents of Virgil less remarkable in connecting his episodes happily with his subject: they are all made directly subservient to the great purpose of his treatise, and they are introduced and terminated so happily, that we believe the two to be perfectly inseparable,—and a didactic poem is entitled to praise, not for any one quality more than for its resembling, in the points just specified, the Georgics of Virgil. This kind of poetry, it may be remarked, is one of the highest species of the art. It does not merely require elevation of sentiment, and richness and dignity of language, but it embraces almost every other mode of poetical writing, the descriptive, the pathetic, the tender, and the sublime; and is therefore to be cultivated only by poets of the highest and most varied endowments. Didactic poetry has been cultivated both in ancient and modern times, by Lucretius, Virgil, Horace, Vida, Boileau, Pope, Akenside, Young, Rogers, Campbell.

Descriptive Poetry. though we have so long delayed treating of it, is probably as difficult of execution, and requires as high powers of genius as any of the kinds we have yet analyzed. Descriptive poetry, however, does not mean exclusively any one particular form of composition. There are few poems purely descriptive; and still fewer in which description does not form a large and prominent part. Shakespeare, for example, though his excellence lies in manners and characters, may justly be denominated a descriptive poet, as in his works are instances of scenery painted with exquisite taste and beauty. But there are poems, such as Thomson's Seasons, or Milton's Allegro, more professedly descriptive than others, as description is their predominating and distinguishing characteristic. A writer of ordinary talents is evidently unfit to attain even respectability in this species of poetry. To him nature, which is the great field for the display of the descriptive powers, has nothing striking or interesting, or she seems exhausted by those who have preceded

Poetry.

him; and his language, being copied from others, instead of being the result of his own lively impressions, is vague, general, and languid; and though his descriptions may be decked with the drapery of poetry, we find, after perusing them, that nothing has been felt, and nothing has been accomplished. A true poet, on the contrary, sets the object painted distinctly and visibly before us. He makes a proper selection of circumstances; all the interesting tints, and beauties, and associations, make a deep impression on his own breast, and he transmits a warm impress to the breasts of others. We see before us scenery, and life, and reality, something in short from which a painter might copy. This praise is peculiarly the praise of Thomson. Thomson had a warm imagination, and a feeling heart; was deeply enamoured of the beauties of nature, and was possessed of genius to catch what was attractive and pleasing, and to reject what was superfluous or uninteresting; and he was thus enabled to produce the noblest poem of the kind we are considering, of which any language can boast. It need merely be mentioned farther, that in portraying inanimate natural objects, the description should be enlivened by the introduction of living beings to excite our interest and sympathy. It is this which gives description its highest charms, and brings the subjects of it home to the business and the bosom of every class of readers. The force of this opinion will be fully seen from the following quotation from Ossian: " I have seen the walls of Balclutha, but they were desolate. The fire had resounded within the halls; and the *voice of the people is now heard no more.* The stream of Clutha was removed from its place by the fall of the walls; the thistle shook there its lonely head; the moss whistled to the wind. The fox looked out at the window; the rank grass waves round her head. *Desolate is the dwelling of Moina: Silence is in the house of her fathers.*" Nothing can be conceived more exquisitely touching than the thought conveyed in the sentence with which this description terminates. It finds a way direct to every bosom.—Description, as already mentioned, prevails more or less in every poetical production, ancient and modern. The British poets who stand highest in this department, are Ossian, Milton, (particularly in his Allegro and Pensoroso,) Blair, (the author of the Grave) Denham, Falconer, Thomson, Grahame, Scott,—of whom Milton and Thomson are unrivalled.

Allegory.

A poetical composition, in which *allegory* is the prevailing feature, can scarcely be regarded as forming a distinct and separate division of the art, as allegory is nothing but a continued metaphor, and, therefore, does not change the inherent nature of the work in which it is used. An amatory, or a pastoral poem, for example, may be allegorical, and its character as a pastoral or amatory production remains unchanged. Allegory has a reference only to the machinery employed, and its effect, therefore, is confined to the drapery in which poetry is veiled, not to the spirit by which it is animated. It is merely external, and is more remarkable than any other figure, merely because it is not so common, and because, when once introduced, it can be terminated only with the subject which it is employed to embellish or illustrate. Allegory, however, whatever be its influence on the nature of poetical writing, is recommended to us, as it forms the medium through which some of the most important truths in holy writ are conveyed to us. A very fine example of it may be found in the eightieth psalm, in which the Israelites are represented under the image of a vine.

Poetry.

The parables in the prophetical writings, and in the New Testament, are all allegorical, and are supported and managed with incomparable felicity. Allegory seems to be of oriental origin, where it still prevails. It was early introduced into Europe. It was the great charcteristic of the Provençal poets. Nor is it unknown in British literature. In the fourteenth and fifteenth centuries indeed, it was the prevailing taste, as the work of Chaucer, Gower, Lydgate, James I. of Scotland, and various others, amply testify. Thomson's Castle of Indolence, various prose essays in the Spectator, Rambler, and Adventurer, partake of the same character; but the progress of learning and refinement has banished this false taste; and no poet is now so blind to his reputation or success, as to attempt to revive and perpetuate it.

In the foregoing enumeration we have not introduced *Dramatic Poetry,* referring for a full discussion of that subject to our article DRAMA.

Living English poets.

We have hitherto also said nothing of the nature and progress of poetry in Britain; nor have we scarcely alluded to any of the great poets of the present day. The former topic is far too extensive for our present purpose, and besides (in addition to its being familiar to every reader from the writings of Warton, Johnson, Ellis, Campbell, and others), it will be found collaterally discussed in this work, in the lives of the various poets that this country has produced. The latter subject is of a nature too delicate and difficult for present consideration. Of living merit, indeed, it is peculiarly hazardous to speak, lest partial feelings should lead us to undue panegyric, or to unwarranted disapproval. With regard, therefore, to both these subjects, (though extremely important and interesting) we shall in this place merely mention that England is inferior to no country in the number and excellence of her poetical productions; that in every age, from the days of Chaucer and Gower, she has in this art produced writers of the highest endowments; that, though after the death of Goldsmith an interval elapsed more barren than any previous era in the history of English poetry, yet the subsequent age has been, if possible, more eminent than any former period for the variety and superior character of its poetical compositions. The present, indeed, has been denominated one of the most flourishing epochs of English poetry; an opinion of which no person can fail to be convinced if he reflect for a moment on the illustrious names by which it is adorned. We have, indeed, lost Cowper, Grahame, Leyden, Keats, Bloomfield; but we can still boast of Scott, Byron, Campbell, Southey, Rogers, Moore, Crabbe, Wordsworth, Coleridge, Montgomery, and a multitude of others—each distinguished by his own peculiar genius and characteristics—all of them possessed of the highest and richest endowments, and not a few of them unrivalled in the departments of poetry which they have severally chosen to cultivate and adorn.

Venimus ad summum fortunæ * * *
Psallimus * * Achivis doctius unctis.

The reader, besides the works already mentioned, may consult Beattie's *Essay on Poetry and Music;* Boileau, *Art Poetique;* Lowth, *De Sacra Poësi Hebraeorum;* Blair's *Lectures,* and his *Essay on the Authenticity of Ossian; Letters on Iceland,* by Dr. Von Troil, § xvii. on Icelandic Poetry; *An Essay on Sclavonic Poetry,* in a work entitled, *Letters, Literary and Political, on Poland.* 1823. (&)

POGGY ISLANDS. See SUMATRA.

POISONS.

THIS is a most important subject, in many points of view. The history of poisons, like that of all the other properties of natural bodies, forms an important and interesting subdivision in their natural history, independently of the uses or abuses that may be made of these substances. Their action on the animal economy, whether considered as poisons or remedies, is also an important branch of medicine and physiology. In a legal point of view, as far as criminal jurisprudence is concerned, the knowledge of these substances is indispensable, as is that of the effects by which they may be detected after death; and in this manner the history of poisons is an essential branch of medical jurisprudence. Lastly, it is not only of great consequence that all the poisonous substances should be well known to men of science, but that this knowledge should be as widely diffused as possible; since much more extensive mischief proceeds from the ignorance of the public respecting them, than from any abuse which is made of those that are known. The antidotes to poisons, or the medical treatment of sufferers under them, ought also to form a branch of this subject.

The poisonous substances may be divided between the mineral, vegetable, and animal kingdoms as usual; but it appears also necessary to notice those, the true nature of which is nearly unknown, which are diffused through the atmosphere, producing diseases and death. If to these we add the chemical gases possessed of this property, we shall have a fourth division, or one of atmospheric poisons; and under these four divisions the whole of them may be comprised.

Every thing is considered as a poison which, in small doses, injures the health, or destroys life. This is a vague definition; but it cannot well be otherwise, since the limits of doses are indefinable, and since that which is injurious in one dose, is innocent or salutary in another. It is, therefore, difficult to know where to stop in such an enumeration; and, with all our care, it must be taken subject to the provision thus named. To study the nature of poisons thoroughly, requires an attention to their several relations as connected with natural history, chemistry, pathology, and physiology, whether living or anatomical. Such a view as this holds out, implies a far more extensive treatment than we can bestow on this subject. We can only pretend to give a very condensed view; and for the mineral department shall be partly indebted to Monsr. Orfila's work. The completion of this treatise as to the other departments, is very much desired. But instead of following his method of division, which appears to us not very good, we shall adopt that which alone belongs to the most obvious part of their natural history, as before laid down.

MINERAL POISONS.

These are generally considered as corrosive poisons, as they inflame and destroy the parts to which they are applied. Their power varies much, according to the dose,—to their solid or liquid state,—or to their internal or external application. They are amongst the most active and dangerous.

In a physiological view, their effects on the system vary exceedingly. Sometimes they act as stimulants to the brain and nervous system, and at others their efforts appear to be of a sedative nature. In some cases they augment the natural secretions, in others they interrupt them. Hence it is that, in safe hands, they become medicines of great efficacy. When in very strong doses, they produce speedy death, the immediate cause of which is not always the same. Sometimes the poison is absorbed, and acts on the brain, the heart, and other organs. Sometimes the primary action on the stomach is communicated by sympathy to these, without any apparent absorption; and, in other cases, death seems to be the consequence of their immediate operation on the stomach.

Symptoms produced by these Poisons.—The common ones are burning heat in the mouth, œsophagus, stomach, and intestines, with thirst; pains through the whole alimentary canal, and chiefly in the stomach and œsophagus; hiccup, nausea, painful and obstinate vomitings, sometimes bloody, with tenesmus and bloody excretions; the pulse small, frequent, and often imperceptible; coldness sometimes, at others violent heat; dysuria, strangury, and cold sweats. Sometimes petechiæ, and at others miliary eruptions, break out. Delirium, blindness, convulsions, or loss of the intellectual faculties, complete the horrible catalogue.

Anatomical effects. Inflammation of the alimentary canal, strictures, gangrene or sphacelus, and corrosions, are the most obvious appearances on dissection. Sometimes the skin is affected with gangrenous spots; or the white skin for a large space has been found black. The lungs have also been found in a state of gangrene from arsenic. In some cases, however, death occurs, and yet no obvious injuries can be discovered.

Medical treatment. In some cases, antidotes may be administered on just chemical principles, as we shall mention in treating of the different substances. Of ancient, and often inefficacious or imaginary antidotes, the catalogue is immense; as few objects have engaged the attention of physicians more, in the dark ages of medicine. Evacuants, and the antiphlogistic systems, are employed in our own days on more rational principles. These are subject to no errors in the hands of ignorance, as antidotes often are; since the proposed decomposition may be impossible, or the treatment as injurious as the poison.

For the chemical history of the following substances we must refer to our article CHEMISTRY.

CORROSIVE SUBLIMATE. This substance, given in a dose of the eighth part of a grain, acts as a general stimulus on the alimentary canal and the secretions. Sometimes there is a sense of heat and pain in the stomach. If the dose is larger, or long continued, it produces colics and vomitings, with salivation and ulcerations of the mouth and tongue. This is followed by loss of the teeth and affections of the bones in these parts; and, besides these effects, there occur cardialgia, dyspepsia, dysentery, dyspnœa, hæmoptysis, and violent pains in the bones and muscles, or in the joints, with trembling, palsy, tetanus, mania, and death. The quicksilver, in these cases, is sometimes deposited in a metallic form in many cavities. If given in an extreme dose, it produces death quickly; and, in this case, physicians are not agreed respecting the mode in which it

Poisons. operates on the functions. We need not recite their various opinions.

This substance has been known to produce death also on several occasions when used externally, as an ointment to the entire skin, or as a plaster, or as a dressing for ulcers. The symptoms are nearly the same; salivation sometimes, or, without that, the usual affections of the stomach, and convulsions.

To discover if a patient has taken this poison, as it is always necessary, if possible, to ascertain the cause of the injury first, either the remains of the substance taken, or the matter vomited, if these cannot be procured, must be examined by the usual chemical tests. After death, the same investigation required for judicial purposes must be made of the contents of the stomach. For the detail of these, and all others of the same nature hereafter mentioned, we must refer to the history of the several substances under the title CHEMISTRY.

Treatment of the patient. The remarks to be made here on chemical antidotes to this poison, are of general application to all the mineral poisons. A substance, to be an antidote, should possess the following properties:

It ought to admit of being taken in large doses without danger.

It ought to act on the poison at the animal temperature, or at one inferior to that.

Its action ought to be speedy.

It should be capable of combining with, or decomposing the poison, in spite of the mucus or other secretions in which it may be entangled.

Lastly, it ought to deprive the poisonous substance of all its deleterious qualities.

Experiments made on animals have proved that the alkalies, the sulphuretted alkalies, and sulphuretted hydrogen, did not prevent the poisonous effects of this substance. Sugar, bark, and metallic mercury, have been recommended, but they produce no effect. Albumen decomposes corrosive sublimate, so as to produce an innoxious compound, and, when given in sufficient quantity, has succeeded as an antidote.

The practice therefore recommended is, to give large quantities of the white of egg mixed with water, as it may be given to any extent. If this cannot be obtained, linseed tea, rice water, sugar and water, broth, or even plain water, may be given. This practice also encourages vomiting, and must be continued till the symptoms abate. In case that vomiting cannot be excited, it is recommended to empty the stomach by means of an elastic bottle and tube passed into it. The more fluid of any kind that can be given, the better; and, in many cases, this has proved sufficient for the cure. They should be forced down, therefore, whether the patient is willing to drink or not.

Oily substances, often had recourse to, are useless, and may be injurious, by impeding the action of other substances. The remainder of the treatment must resemble that adopted in gastritis, or enteritis; local bleeding, fomentation, emollient injections, general blood-letting, the warm bath, and in general, the antiphlogistic system.

RED PRECIPITATE OF MERCURY. This, whether procured by heat or nitric acid, is a violent poison, and produces nearly the same symptoms.

TURBITH MINERAL. In practice, is scarcely known as a poison, but it is such. All the other active salts of mercury may be considered in the same light, and require no particular detail.

QUICKSILVER. Mercury in the state of vapour is poisonous, and is well known as such, in gilding and some other arts, where the workmen are exposed to it. Tremour of the limbs leading to palsy are the most common effects. The more violent are, salivation with ulceration, colics, asphyxia, hæmoptysis, asthma, atrophy, apoplexy, and death. On some occasions, quicksilver taken internally has proved a poison. On others it has proved innocent, and these differences of result seem to depend on the state of the intestinal fluids, and the length of time it remains in the body.

ARSENIC. Some of the salts of this metal form the most violent poisons with which we are acquainted. It is the poison also whose effects are best known, as it is the most frequently resorted to for purposes of murder or suicide; being often also swallowed by mistake. The poisonous preparations from it are, the white oxide, or arsenious acid, the arsenical acid, the arsenites, and the arseniates, the red and the yellow sulphurets, the black oxide, and the vapour. Of these the white oxide, commonly called arsenic, or the arsenious acid, is the most common.

ARSENIOUS ACID. This acts both externally and internally, and produces death in a very short time. The exact mode in which it operates on life is not well agreed on, but the general symptoms produced are the following: An austere taste, with spitting, constriction of the throat, grinding of the teeth, hiccup, nausea, and vomiting, the matters being brown or bloody. Then anxiety, fainting, burning heat in the stomach, with inflammation of the mouth and throat, great irritability of the stomach, and black evacuations. The pulse is small, frequent, irregular, sometimes slow and intermittent, with a burning heat over the body, and an inward sense of the same; yet occasionally there is a feeling of icy cold. Palpitations, thirst, fainting, difficulty of respiration, cold sweats, dysuria, or bloody urine, may be added to these. The physiognomy is affected, presenting a lucid circle round the eyes; the body swells, and is covered with a red eruption, sometimes with petechiæ; and, to complete this frightful list, we may add prostration of strength, delirium, convulsions, priapism, loss of the hair and epidermis, and finally death. It is rare, however, that many of these effects are present in one patient; and sometimes death has been produced without any other symptom than previous faintings.

The visible effects of arsenic on the body after death resemble those of corrosive sublimate. Erosion, or inflammation of the stomach, is not necessary for the production of death. Such symptoms must not therefore be depended on in cases of judicial examination.

The poison which has been used must be procured in the way recommended for corrosive sublimate, and examined by the now well-known tests to be found in the chemical history of this substance.

Treatment of the patient. No chemical substance yet tried is an antidote to arsenic in its solid state. All solutions are rendered inert by the hydrosulphurets; but the poison is so rarely given in this form, that these are of no practical use.

The first part of the treatment is to expel the poison by vomiting, and by the same substances recommended in the case of corrosive sublimate; to which may be added tickling the throat by means of a feather. This alone has sometimes proved successful. In all cases, the fuller the stomach is of any fluid, the less violent are the effects of this poison. The metallic emetics only add to the mischief. Oils and fat substances are injurious, as has been fully proved by experiments on animals. In the liquid state of the poison, lime water may be useful, but not in the solid. Theriaca, and the numerous vegetable antidotes recommended, are useless, except for the quantity of fluid in which they may be given. The medical treatment, as in the case of mercury, is formed on the antiphlogistic plan.

The arsenical acid, and the arsenites and arseniates, are all attended by similar symptoms, but they require no farther remarks.

SULPHURETS OF ARSENIC. Yellow artificial orpiment is poisonous in the quantity of even three or four grains. The native has been given in considerably larger doses with little injury. The native red sulphuret is also comparatively inert, while the artificial one is poisonous. These effects imply chemical differences not yet examined.

BLACK OXIDE OF ARSENIC. This has been found to poison dogs in doses of five or six grains. Taken by accident, it has had the same effects on the human species.

ARSENICAL VAPOURS. The breathing of these produces effects very similar to those caused by mercury, excepting the salivation. When very slowly taken, as in certain arts, tremors, with shrinking of the muscles of the arms and hands, are the common effects. It appears that the arsenite of potash can be taken in smaller doses medicinally for a great length of time without producing injurious consequences. Red eruptions of the skin are the most common consequences of an overdose.

ANTIMONY. This is a poisonous metal, and its chief preparations are the following: Tartar emetic, oxide of antimony, sulphuretted oxide, and muriate, to which we may add antimonial vapours.

Tartar emetic is proved to be a poison, because, when dogs that had taken it were prevented from vomiting, they always died. Thus also it has happened in the human species, when considerable doses of this substance were given, and little or no vomiting followed. When evacuated, no inconvenience has followed it. In cases of death, the intestinal canal is affected with inflammation throughout, as well as the lungs. It is remarkable also, that whether this substance is injected into the veins or taken into the stomach, the same affections take place; a fact which occurs alike when arsenic is injected in the same manner. The symptoms are vomiting, heat, and pains in the stomach and bowels; diarrhœa, cramp, and pains of the muscles, and lastly death; effects similar to, though less violent than those produced by the poisons above mentioned.

Treatment of the Patient. If there is much vomiting, little more is requisite than to encourage it by large quantities of warm water. No additional advantage is derived from the vegetable substances often added to these. If there is no vomiting, that should be excited by tickling the throat with a feather, and by warm water at the same time. If oil excites vomiting it will be useful. If, with all these attempts, vomiting is not produced, large quantities of the decoction of bark should be given; which has the property of decomposing this salt, and may be taken in any dose. It is also to be observed that the yellow bark is a better precipitant for this salt than the red. Tea, galls, and other astringent vegetables, may be substituted, if this is not at hand. The alkaline substances and the hydrosulphurets are injurious. When the vomiting is

very violent, opium is useful; and if there is much constriction about the throat and pains of the stomach, or symptoms of any inflammation, the antiphlogistic treatment must be resorted to.

The symptoms produced by the other antimonial preparations are similar, but vary in violence according to their nature. The muriate is the most violent, and the treatment is the same for all. The vapours of antimony, under any form, have been found to produce cough, oppressed respiration, hæmoptysis, and colics: there can be no doubt that if long continued they would be a cause of death.

COPPER. All the preparations of copper are poisonous. The most common are the acetate, the sulphate, the nitrate, the muriate, the ammoniuret, as chemical poisons. In domestic use, those of ordinary occurrence are solutions of the metal in wine or vinegar, and its combinations with oily matters.

In many countries, and particularly in France, where copper vessels are much used in cooking, this poison is very frequently called into action, and it is therefore important that it should be well known. These poisons, however, are always taken inadvertently, never given with design to kill. There is no doubt that milk also acts in copper vessels in particular cases, and produces poisonous effects. A case is related by Dr. Darwin, where the mistress of a dairy farm suffered, merely from a custom of frequently tasting the cream at the edges of the milk pans. Verdigris is one of the most active of these poisonous preparations.

The ordinary symptoms are an acrid metallic taste, with dryness of the mouth and tongue and constriction of the throat. Spitting, nausea, with vomiting, or vain efforts to vomit, follow. There are pains in the stomach and bowels, alvine dejections, sometimes black or bloody, with tenesmus, and the abdomen is inflated. The pulse is small and irregular, and generally hard and frequent; with debility, burning thirst, difficulty of breathing, cold sweats, dysuria, headach, vertigo, cramps, convulsions, and death. These do not, however, often occur in the same person; and the most common ones are vomiting with colic pains. Gangrene sometimes takes place, and is easily known by its common symptoms.

The appearances, after death, are an inflamed or gangrenous state of the alimentary canal, and sometimes they are corroded into holes, as happens with arsenic.

Treatment of the Patient. The alkalies and alkaline sulphurets are not antidotes to copper, because, though they decompose the salts, they leave the oxides, which are equally destructive. Nor has the infusion of galls been of any use. Sugar has very unexpectedly been found an antidote, as it renders the soluble acetates insoluble, and comparatively innocent.

The best practice, therefore, if sugar can be procured, is to give it in large quantities dissolved in water, by which means vomiting is at the same time encouraged. If that is not at hand, warm water, or broth, or any vegetable drink, must be given, and that in large quantities. It is unsafe to use emetics, and they should only be adopted in case it is impossible to excite vomiting in any other way. If, however, the poison has been so long taken that vomiting has ceased, and there are pains in the abdomen from its having passed into the intestines, vomiting must be avoided, and we must have recourse to emollient injections, and to the usual antiphlogistic remedies. When spasms and convulsions are present, anodynes and antispasmodics are proper.

This treatment applies alike to all the other preparations of copper.

TIN. Although this metal, under any form, is never given as a poison designedly, yet, being used in medicine and in many manufactures, it is necessary to be aware of its effects. The muriates and the oxides are the only preparations likely to become poisons in these ways. The former are by far the most active.

The symptoms do not differ much from those produced by the other metallic poisons; being namely, a metallic taste, constrictions and thirst, vomiting, pains, diarrhœa, an oppressed pulse, convulsions, and palsy. After death, the same effects have been observed in the alimentary canal as are produced by mercury.

Treatment of the patient. Milk has been found useful in diminishing the effects of this poison, and should therefore be given in large quantities; and, in defect of it, warm water and mucilaginous decoctions. The poison will thus be diluted and discharged, and the remainder of the practice resembles that described before.

The action of the oxide resembles that of the muriate, but it requires considerable doses.

ZINC. The sulphate and the oxide are the most common forms of this metal likely to operate as poisons; and as it is much employed in medicine and in the arts, it is proper to be aware of its properties.

The sulphate of zinc is the least dangerous of all the active metallic salts, as it is generally immediately expelled by vomiting. When this does not happen, or when, in experiments on animals, it is prevented, death follows quickly. Injected into the veins, the same consequences are produced.

The usual symptoms produced by the sulphate when given in an over dose, are a metallic taste, with constriction of the throat, vomiting, purging, pains in the epigastrium and abdomen, difficulty of respiration, an accelerated pulse, paleness, and coldness of the extremities. After death, the mucous membrane of the stomach and intestines has been found inflamed.

Treatment of the patient. To favour the rejection of the poisons by large quantities of warm water, is the first object, or, what is better, by means of milk. Chalk and the alkalies decompose this salt in the stomach, but are in danger of adding to the irritation. The antiphlogistic and antispasmodic treatment must lastly be adopted wherever the symptoms may require it.

Though the oxide of zinc is poisonous, it is never given in doses sufficiently large to produce death.

SILVER. The only preparation of this metal likely to act as a poison, is the nitrate, which has been used in medicine; particularly of late in epilepsy.

When injected into the veins, it produces death speedily, and without our being able to ascertain the cause. But we shall notice these effects no more; as there is scarcely any substance, apparently the most simple, which does not in the same way produce death, and with the same trains of symptoms. The action on the animal economy, in these cases, is not understood; but, in a practical view, it is of no moment, as death does not occur, either accidentally or designedly, in this way, unless in the case of experiments on animals.

The symptoms which nitrate of silver produces when taken into the stomach in a large dose, are exactly the same as those caused by the other metallic poisons. Blueness of the lips, from the change induced on this salt from exposure to light, is an additional symptom,

which, when it is present, serves to indicate the nature of the poison. The appearances after death differ in nothing from those caused by the other metallic poisons.

When nitrate of silver has been given medicinally in small doses for any length of time, it is deposited between the skin and epidermis, producing a livid stain which can never be discharged, and which causes a great deformity through life. This has frequently happened in the hands of ignorant practitioners, but it begins to be more generally known. This consequence is so disagreeable, that the medicine ought to be rejected in medical practice, as it possesses no advantage over the other metallic tonics to compensate for this inconvenience.

Treatment of the patient. The muriate of soda, or common salt, decomposes this substance, and destroys its deleterious qualities.

Salt should therefore be given immediately, diluted in much warm water. Mucilaginous drinks may then be given to diminish irritation, followed by the antiphlogistic practice where necessary.

GOLD. The muriate has lately been used in French practice, and, even in small quantities, has been found poisonous. Given in the dose of a tenth part of a grain daily, it excites fever, without producing any other bad effects; but if that be increased, general erethismus, with local organic inflammations, is apt to follow. It does not, however, appear to be so active as corrosive sublimate. As there is no instance on record, however, of any person having been killed by this salt, its further effects are not known. Fulminating gold has been said, in doses of three or four grains, to produce all the usual symptoms of the metallic poisons, attended by salivation, and death.

The medical treatment should resemble the general practice formerly described.

BISMUTH. This, in the state of the nitrate, or of the subnitrate, (white oxide) has been used in medicine as a tonic and antispasmodic, and the latter is used as a paint for the skin. There is no doubt respecting its poisonous properties, as it has been found to produce diarrhœa, constipation, vomiting, heat, tremblings, coma, and vertigo. On animals it has also been found poisonous. Both the nitrate and the white oxide produce inflammations and corrosions of the stomach and bowels, attended with the usual symptoms, which we need not repeat.

The treatment in such cases of poisoning, should they occur, consists in large draughts of milk, or mucilaginous drinks, together with fomentations and the general antiphlogistic practice.

IRON. We have known the muriate of iron to produce the usual symptoms of poison, and it was treated successfully by alkalies and hot water.

LEAD. This is one of the most fearful poisons in the catalogue, on account of the numerous accidental ways in which it is introduced into the body, whether in the way of food or medicine, or in the various arts in which, in some form or other, it is used. Even where it does not produce death, its consequences are most pernicious.

The most common forms in which this substance is apt to be swallowed are the following: the acetate, litharge, ceruse, and the red oxide; as also in water, wine, cider, vinegar, pickles, &c. and in the form of vapour. Thus it finds its way into our food every where. In the arts, those who suffer chiefly from it are painters, lapidaries, glass-grinders, workers in smelting houses, and in ceruse works and paint mills, makers of shot, and so forth. It is this which renders it so important an object of investigation to medical men.

It is well known that wine was formerly much treated with lead in France to correct undue acidity; but it is said that the practice has long been abandoned. Still, there is no doubt that, from design or inadvertence, it often finds its way into wine. When used in the metallic state in wines abounding in tartar, it forms an insoluble tartrite, which is precipitated; so that if the wine is fined, little inconvenience follows. When the acetite is used, or the wine is acescent from acetous fermentation, the danger is considerable.

It is known to have been frequently found in cider, from the use of lead in the presses, but that practice has been rectified. In all cases it may be introduced into wine or cider from shot remaining in the bottles after cleaning.

Some waters, kept in leaden cisterns, have been known to corrode them so as to become poisonous. This is particularly the case on long standing, or when vegetable matters are present at the same time.

The usual manner in which lead is introduced into cookery, is by means of vessels glazed with the glass of lead. Pickles preserved in this kind of earthen ware are frequently highly poisonous. Thus also fish, potted in vinegar, and many other articles in common use, become poisons. It is said that, in France, syrups and sweet cordials are clarified by means of acetate of lead. Children have died from eating red wafers, which are coloured by means of the red oxide.

The methods by which it gets access to many of the artists employed on lead, are sometimes very obscure. In many cases it seems to produce its effect by acting on the skin. Thus lapidaries and glass-grinders become paralytic in the hands and arms, from the putty used in polishing, which is a mixed oxide of tin and lead. Many artizans probably suffer from mere exposure to vapours or dust of lead in some form or other. The medical application of lead externally has produced the same effects, and must be considered a very unsafe practice.

The poisonous effects of lead sometimes come on quickly, if the substance has been taken in quantity; but more generally the attacks are insidious and slow; and very often, when the quantity is very small, the effects are so gradual, that the cause is not suspected.

The most ordinary symptoms are vomiting, chiefly at the beginning of the attack, pains in the abdomen rising to violent colic, and accompanied by retraction of the external muscles which is relieved by strong pressure, and constipation. There is no fever nor inflammatory action, but the attack of colic is generally followed by paralytic affections, and, commonly, of the arms. These are sometimes the only symptoms, but they affect other parts also, while there are tremors and shrinking of the muscles. These symptoms are commonly incurable, and they occur most frequently among artizans of various kinds, when the action of the metal in small quantities has been long continued.

The symptoms, on dissection, show that there is inflammation of the mucous membrane, with occasional slight extravasations of blood, but only when a large quantity of the poison has been taken at once. In other cases, nothing has been found but contractions of the colon.

Treatment of the patient. If the poison has been just swallowed, the first thing to be done is to give sulphate of soda, or magnesia, with much water. The sulphate of lead thus produced does not appear noxious.

Otherwise, the practice is to give purgatives of senna, or salts, or both, or of other medicines, according to the state of the bowels. Opium is also found necessary to relieve the spasms and constrictions of the intestines. But for the more minute details of this practice we must refer to our article MEDICINE.

The paralytic affections generally defy all attempts at a cure.

SULPHURIC ACID. This is unfortunately too common a poison, being often swallowed from design, or taken inadvertently. From being so much used in many manufactures and arts, it is always within reach of the people. It is by no means an uncommon expedient among suicides, extraordinary as it may appear; and it has also frequently been taken accidentally by children and others.

The symptoms which it produces are, an austere styptic taste, with a burning heat through the œsophagus and stomach, pain in the throat, an insufferable smell, with insupportably fetid breath, black vomitings, constipation, or bloody diarrhœa, colic pains, and tenderness of the abdomen, dyspnœa, anxiety, a small hurried pulse, with a sense of coldness in the skin, restlessness, oppressed respiration, spasms, and sometimes a pustular eruption all over the body. The mouth and throat are always inflamed, and generally ulcerated.

Inflammations and gangrene of the throat and alimentary canal in general, are the common appearances after death.

Treatment of the patient. Pure magnesia proves the best counterpoison in this case; but unless it is administered very early it is inefficacious, as it cannot counteract that inflammation and destruction of parts which has already been determined. It should be given as soon as possible, diluted in abundance of water. Should it not be at hand, alkalies, or even soap and water, may be given. Every thing here depends on promptitude and activity, as there is no time to lose. Supposing the poison to be thus neutralized, the local injuries must be treated in the same way as if they had arisen from any other causes, by proper surgical and medical remedies and applications.

We must remark here, in closing this account of the sulphuric acid, that its external application has been known to produce death.

NITRIC ACID. This is even more frequently used by suicides than the sulphuric, and has also been often taken accidentally so as to produce death. From its large use in many arts, it is often at hand, and too easily obtained for either of these purposes.

Its effects on the animal economy are extremely violent. The symptoms are burning heat in the throat and stomach, with violent eructations, nausea, and hiccup, pains in the throat and epigastrium, vomiting, diarrhœa, tension and pain of the abdomen, and most other of those symptoms which attend the metallic poisons. The mouth and tongue are of a pale white or yellowish colour, and sloughs come away from them. It appears that the pains are most severe when the dose has been least; when very large, immediate destruction of all the sensible parts is the consequence. The vomiting is most violent when the pains are greatest.

When death is not immediate, it sometimes occurs at many days' or weeks' interval; and the parts then slough away before the patient dies. Sometimes the patients continue to live, but in extreme ill health, and subject to pains and burning heats.

The appearances after death are the yellow colour of the parts affected, the teeth loosened, with inflammation, sloughing or gangrene, and perforations of the alimentary canal.

Treatment of the patient. Pure magnesia, diffused in water, ought to be administered immediately in considerable doses, and the vomiting is to be encouraged by mucilaginous drinks. If magnesia is not at hand, soap dissolved in water may be used. Oil has also been found useful, if given in large quantities. If the poison has been taken in small quantities, or has had time to act on the parts, the emollient method is alone of use ; and the antiphlogistic practice is to be adopted wherever the symptoms require it.

MURIATIC ACID. This is a poison, under the same circumstances as the former. The effects and the symptoms are very similar, and need not be repeated. The treatment is also the same as in cases of poisoning from nitric acid.

PHOSPHORIC ACID. This also admits of no other remarks. Its poisonous quality has only been experienced on animals.

FLUORIC ACID. This appears to be a most powerful poison. Externally applied, it is one of the most corrosive substances known, acting on the animal fibre with great violence. No sooner does it touch the skin than it excites violent pain, and the parts become white and ulcerated. Even the smallest quantities produce these effects, although they take a longer time to appear. It has not been, and need not be tried internally.

FLUO-BORACIC ACID. The action of this appears even more violent than that of the former, the ulceration and affection of the skin being also of a very singular character. Applied even externally, it produces death. No opportunity has offered as yet respecting the treatment of these cases, and we must have recourse to general principles.

OXALIC ACID. The poisonous effects of this substance have been frequently experienced of late in this country, from its use for domestic purposes, and from its being sold or mistaken for Glauber's salts. The doses that have been taken with these consequences, have, however, been large, amounting commonly to an ounce. The symptoms and effects are the same as those produced by the other mineral acids. Magnesia treated in the way formerly mentioned, seems to be the most convenient remedy, accompanied by plentiful dilution.

TARTAROUS AND ACETIC ACIDS. It is probable that these are equally poisonous; but we have no practical experience respecting them.

POTASH. The poisonous nature of pure potash must be sufficiently evident, from the extreme energy of its action on animal substances. But the subcarbonate, or common salt of tartar, has been also found to produce the same effects when taken by mistake in doses of an ounce. The symptoms are scarcely different from those produced by all the other mineral poisons, and need not be detailed. These substances produce perforations of the stomach and intestines, even more readily than any of those formerly mentioned.

Vinegar, with abundance of water and other diluents, is the most efficacious antidote in those cases.

SODA. The effects and the treatment are the same; but we have seen a considerable dose of the subcarbonate given by mistake without injury.

AMMONIA. Pure water of ammonia, or ammonia mixed with oil in the form of the volatile liniment, is not unfrequently taken by mistake. It has been known to produce death in the short space of a few minutes. It destroys the mouth, œsophagus, and stomach, and its action is accompanied by hæmorrhages from the nose and intestines, and by fever. Besides that, there are the other symptoms so often enumerated. When the dose has been small, the inflammation of the mouth and throat are the chief effects, and they often prove fatal.

There is little to be done in these cases if it is not done quickly ; and the same practice, by means of vinegar, is the best that can be adopted.

BARYTES. This is a most active poison, and apparently in all its states; whether in that of the pure earth, the carbonate, or the neutral salts. The muriate has been employed in medicine, in scrofulous and glandular affections. It is very commonly used for poisoning rats in the countries where it is found.

Its action on the stomach does not seem to account for the sudden and violent death which follows its use ; and it is supposed that it is absorbed so as to act on the nervous system. No particular details of the symptoms have been given, except violent pains and convulsions observed in animals.

In treating a case of this nature, the best practice seems to be to give either the sulphate of soda or magnesia in large doses, with plenty of water, and to induce vomiting by the most gentle means.

LIME. Though this is an active poison, we are not aware that its effects have been observed, except on animals made the subjects of experiment. The symptoms both before and after death resemble those produced by the caustic alkalies. Should such a case happen in the human subject, the same treatment by means of vinegar would be the most appropriate.

NITRE. This is a dangerous poison, although only acting in large doses, because it is often sold instead of Glauber's salts by careless apothecaries. We have seen it taken to the extent of half an ounce without any obvious consequences. In doses of an ounce, it generally produces death, accompanied by the usual symptoms of poison. In some cases where the patients have recovered, there have remained cramps and pains of the limbs, particularly of the legs, with shrinking of the muscles, and tremors. We doubt if any chemical antidote is applicable, and can only recommend vomiting and dilution, together with the antiphlogistic practice.

OXYMURIATE OF POTASH. This is sometimes used in medicine, and there can be no doubt that it is an active poison. In doses of twenty or thirty grains it produces fever, with a white tongue, and inflammatory action. In somewhat larger quantities, it produces pains in the stomach, and would probably cause death if much increased. We can only recommend the same treatment in this case as in the former.

We are not aware, that poisonous effects have been experienced from any other of the alkaline neutral salts.

MURIATE OF LIME. This is also an active poison in small doses, and it has been used, like the muriate of barytes, in glandular affections. In cases of poison from it, we should be tempted to use carbonate of soda with dilution.

We do not know that any trials have been made with any other of the earthy neutrals.

PHOSPHORUS. This substance has been introduced

into medical practice in France, in chronic diseases of various kinds, and in particular in palsy and epilepsy. Its effects in this way are very doubtful, and it is a very active poison. In experiments on animals it has been used dissolved in oil, and is equally deadly in this manner. When injected into the veins, phosphoric acid in vapour is speedily disengaged through the lungs. In the stomach, it produces inflammation and corrosion; and these injuries are attributed to the production of phosphoric acid.

If it be taken in a solid state, the symptoms are not produced for some time. If in solution in oil, or in ether, they appear quickly, and are chiefly vomiting, violent pains, and nervous affections.

In case of poisoning by phosphorus, emetics are first necessary. If taken in a dissolved state, magnesia must also be given to neutralize the acid which is produced. Plentiful dilution, and the antiphlogistic practice, must be superadded.

GLASS. Pounded glass is vulgarly reckoned a poison; but it only acts mechanically, and is therefore not entitled to a place among these substances. That many solid matters, much more likely to be offensive, are often swallowed with impunity, is most particularly proved by the well-known case of the sailor admitted into St. Thomas's hospital, who had been in the habit for many years of swallowing pocket knives. The remains of many were found on dissection; and he admitted the having thus disposed of ten or twelve. (See *Edin. Phil. Journ.* vol. vii. p. 204.)

CHLORINE. This gas dissolved in water has been given in venereal cases, with the effect of curing the disease. Its action resembles that of the oxymuriate of potash; and it is unquestionably highly deleterious, although no instances of death from it have occurred. We should be inclined to treat such a case with chalk and water, besides the more ordinary means.

PRUSSIC ACID. This has lately been introduced into medicine, and it is among the most active poisons known. It seems to differ in its action from all the other mineral poisons, its effects being sudden, and in the highest degree sedative. In under doses it produces syncope, or temporary apoplexy, with vertigo, nausea, and other symptoms. It is equally dangerous when respired. Ammonia has been found to counteract its effects; but this can be of little use, from the suddenness with which it acts in producing death. Its destructive effects, when introduced by punctures or injection, are particularly sudden.

IODINE. This has lately been introduced into medicine, chiefly in the form of the hydroiodate of potash. In all its forms it is an active poison. In small doses, given in glandular affections, and particularly in the enlargement of the thyroid gland, it excites fever, which, if pushed to excess, becomes fatal. On animals, in larger doses, it produces death, with inflammation and ulceration of the intestinal canal. We are not aware of any proper counterpoison for it.

Although it is highly probable that there are yet many other poisons in the mineral kingdom, there is no experience respecting them. We are willing to believe, that all the metallic substances are so, in a greater or less degree. This is a long catalogue, and will probably yet lead to many experiments on animals among those who have cultivated this branch of pathology and chemistry. It is a safe rule in the mean time, to avoid the whole tribe under whatever form. But as we have no positive facts to bring forward, we shall proceed to the animal poisons.

OF THE ANIMAL POISONS.

We may consider those first, which commonly operate by being taken into the stomach; and then those which must be admitted into the circulation by puncture or otherwise to produce their effects.

CANTHARIDES. The *Lytta vesicatoria* is the most noted of the animal poisons, and is much used in medicine as a local or general stimulant. It is commonly given in the form of tincture.

It even produces death on animals when injected into their veins, with the usual symptoms of convulsions, oppressed respiration, &c. It has also produced grievous symptoms and death, merely when applied in the form of blisters.

The ordinary symptoms in poisoning from cantharides, are a nauseous smell and taste, nausea, vomiting, bloody evacuations, with violent pains, strangury, bloody urine, and priapism, with heat and thirst, a hard and frequent pulse, sometimes hydrophobia, convulsions, tetanus, and delirium.

The internal appearances resemble those produced by other poisons, adding to them inflammatory affections of the urinary organs.

We have no means of treating this poison by chemical antidotes as yet, as the true nature of all the animal compounds is still little known. Gentle emetics with oil are recommended, so as to evacuate the substance if possible; and for the rest we must trust to the ordinary medical means applicable to the symptoms that arise.

Poisonous substances resembling that of cantharides are so common among the insect tribe, that there are doubtless many more of this nature; but we are not likely to become acquainted with them.

FISH. There are many fishes poisonous, particularly in the tropical climates; but we are very ill informed respecting their names. It appears also, that many are poisonous at one season and not at another; and that in some cases the liver alone is the noxious part. It has also been remarked in the West Indies, that the same species are poisonous in one place and not in another, and that there is even a particular tract of sea throughout which this quality prevails.

The yellow-billed sprat of Barbadoes is the most notedly poisonous fish that has been ascertained; and it is said to have even produced death, even when it had been spit out after being taken into the mouth. It is supposed to communicate the same properties to the fish that feed on it.

In our own country, muscles are sometimes poisonous, at least to particular individuals; but this property varies also according to seasons or other circumstances not yet ascertained. It is a popular opinion that the beard, as it is called, or the gills, are the poisonous part; but there seems to be no ground for this notion.

The symptoms vary in violence, even to death. The usual ones are swelling of the surface with exanthemata, and with nausea, pains of the abdomen, purging, vomiting, and torpor. The exanthemata generally relieve the affection of the stomach.

Evacuants, as they may be required, seem to be the most efficacious remedies; but brandy, opium, and similar stimulants, have been found useful.

PUTRID MEAT. This operates as a poison in many cases, and particularly if long continued, or taken in considerable quantity. Its immediate effects are nausea and diarrhœa, with fever, sometimes followed by death.

Poisons. If used more gradually, it produces carbuncles, petechiæ, and appearances of scurvy, sometimes attended
by typhus and death. Evacuations, in the first instance, and the ordinary treatment of the symptoms
afterwards, are the only remedies to which we can have
recourse. Among savage nations, habit seems to render
such a diet innoxious; as putrid fish are eaten from
choice in many of the South Sea islands.

PUTRID EGG. This seems to be the most active and
noxious of all the putrid substances. Taken to the
amount of even two or three grains, it sometimes brings
on dysenteric affections very difficult of cure. We
know of no remedies but such as will occur on reflection to every one.

We might have added to this list, many substances
of an animal nature which are poisonous, although in a
slight degree, to particular persons. But as they are not
uniformly so, these cases must be ranked among the
idiosyncracies. Medical men ought to be aware of
them, lest they mistake one thing for another. The
effects produced by salmon on many individuals are
well known. Fattened poultry, a very common article of diet, often produces considerable derangement in
many persons, even when taken in the smallest quantities. But on these we need not dwell. It is sufficient
if patients and practitioners are aware of them.

The list of animal poisons which act through the
circulation by puncture is very considerable; but we
shall only name the best known.

SERPENTS. The list of poisonous serpents is not
very considerable when compared with their total numbers; but we need not give it. It is sufficient to name
the most remarkable, as the effects produced by the
whole are similar, varying only in intensity and rapidity.

The best known poisonous species are the rattle-snake,
the Cobra di Capello, the whip snake, the Egyptian
snake, and the common viper. All the poisonous snakes
have a particular apparatus for that purpose, consisting
of a poison bag attached to two tubular and jointed
fangs, through which it is infused into the punctures
which these form. It appears that these poisons will
preserve their virulence even when dry, and for a great
length of time.

The symptoms in all cases are the same, if there is
time for them to appear; and they are chiefly, pain in
the bitten part, affections of the stomach, convulsions,
vertigo or coma, and death. In some violent cases,
death is produced in less than a minute.

It has been attempted to check the progress of the
poison, where a limb has been bitten, by a ligature;
or to destroy it by caustic substances, or by excision.
Oil externally applied, has also been considered a remedy, as has ammonia. This last substance is also given
internally, and, as it is said, with good effects. Savage
nations possess many other antidotes, real or imaginary;
but we have no very solid information respecting any
of these remedies.

SCORPION. All the species are poisonous, but in different degrees, by means of a sting in their tail emitting
poison. The effects resemble those produced by the
bites of serpents. One or two kinds are said to be very
deadly. The injury produced by others is not greater
than that from the sting of a bee. Oil is here also held
out as a remedy; and what is less probable, the body
of the animal bruised, and applied to the part.

CENTIPEDE. Some of the American kinds are very
deadly. Most of them appear to be poisonous in different degrees, and with the same effects as the serpent
tribe.

SPIDERS. It is believed that some of the larger kinds   Poisons.
found in hot climates are poisonous. The effects respecting the tarantula are now admitted to be fabulous.

BEES, WASPS, HORNETS. These are all poisonous
by means of a peculiar sting, and stand in order of violence as we have here placed them. The hornet has
been known to produce death.

ANTS. In hot climates, many of this family seem
to be very poisonous, though we have no instances of
death from them. The bite of our own red ant is painful, and the poison here seems to be nothing but acetic
acid.

EARWIGS. The forfex at the tail of this insect is
slightly poisonous; but it is only capable of penetrating very soft parts of the skin.

We need not notice particularly our domestic torments, such as bugs, &c. nor the numerous flies, tabani,
conopes, culices, &c. with which all countries swarm.
If these are not more injurious, it is probably rather
from the very small quantity of the poison admitted,
than from any want of virulence in it.

FURIA INFERNALIS. We have thought fit to mention this extraordinary worm, on account of the violent
effects which Linnæus attributes to it; but we consider
the whole history as fabulous, notwithstanding that authority. We believe that he suffered his credulity to
deceive him, as he has not described it from his own
experience.

MAD DOG. If not the most rapid, this is, to us, among
the most terrific of the animal poisons. The nature of
the disease which enables the dog to secrete this poison is
unknown. It cannot well be called a fever, as sometimes neither the appetite nor any other functions are
impeded, even to the moment of death. The obvious
symptoms, however, at the beginning, imply some sort
of febrile state with great irritability. Towards the
end there are convulsions, vertigo, and tetanus. Hydrophobia is not a symptom in the dog itself. This
erroneous opinion has often led to fatal consequences.
All the animals which most resemble the dog are supposed capable of generating this disease. In the wolf
at least, it appears to have been well ascertained.

The poison is communicated by the saliva. The
time which it takes to operate in exciting the disease
in the human subject, varies from a few days to three
months, or even more. Six weeks appear to be a
common period. When once it has appeared, its operation is rapid, generally killing in three days. The
dread of water, and the impossibility of swallowing
fluids, are the most obvious symptoms, but they are not
indispensably present. Anxiety, delirium, convulsions,
and tetanus, precede death.

Excision and caustics to the parts should be resorted
to in the first instance. Every remedy which physic
possesses has been tried in vain when once the disease
has commenced; and there are nostrums beyond all
number. One or two cases have recovered; but it was
impossible to attribute the cure to the medicines used.
We must refer to medical works, and to our own article
MEDICINE, for further particulars. The appearances
on dissection are next to nothing.

VEGETABLE POISONS.

This is a very numerous class, but is as yet imper-   Vegetable
fectly known, as there are numerous plants of whose   poisons.
properties we are still ignorant. We shall here enumerate the most important, and the best ascertained.

Poisons.

Their actions are so little understood, that we do not think it worth while to attempt a classification of them. Of the medical treatment, little is known beyond evacuating the poisonous matter. The symptoms are also but little varied, and the appearances after death are generally very trifling. On these subjects we can afford to be brief.

CORN. Damaged corn has been known, on various occasions, to prove the cause of disease; and the ordinary symptoms have been gangrenes of the extremities. The immediate cause is unknown, as is the exact nature of the change in the grain which is thus injurious.

RYE. In this, as well as in some other grains, a vegetable disease, without damage, has been known to produce similar effects. An obscure disease of that grain in particular, known by the name of *Ergot* in France, has been found to produce destructive effects in that country.

LOLIUM TEMULENTUM. DARNEL. This grass has a narcotic seed, and it is said to have produced poisonous effects when ground inadvertently among corn. This also has been chiefly remarked in France, where this plant is known by the name of *Ivraie*.

No remedies have been proposed for these diseases, beyond the common treatment, and change of food.

IATROPHA MANIOC. The cassada root. The juice of this is extremely acrid and poisonous; but it is decomposed below the boiling heat, and the root is then made into coarse bread.

ARUM. The whole genus, it is believed, is poisonous; but these are also destroyed and rendered innocent at the same temperature. Some of them are used after this process as aliment; among the rest our own *Arum maculatum.*

THE YEW TREE. TAXUS BACCATA. It is not known by experience that this is a poison to the human subject; but horses, asses, and cows, die in a few hours from eating the leaves, which they nevertheless like.

TOBACCO. One of the most virulent of the vegetable poisons, though, like other narcotics, the body becomes habituated to large doses without apparent injury. The symptoms are coma, convulsions, vertigo, nausea, vomiting, and sometimes purging. There is no remedy in the nature of an antidote known. Both the species of the *Nicotiana*, the *tabacum*, and the *glutinosa*, have the same properties.

TEA. Green tea is a deadly poison to small animals. Unquestionably, in a sufficient dose, it would prove the same to the human species, as its effects are decidedly noxious. It seems to operate quickly as a sedative.

SCAMMONY. An acrid poison, as well as a purgative, although safely used in medicine.

GAMBOGE. Still more active, exciting vomiting as well as purging, with burning heat in the throat. Convulsions and death follow extreme doses of these substances, attended by cold sweats. There are no remedies known but evacuation and antispasmodics.

RICINUS PALMA CHRISTI. The seeds are a purgative, and they poison in doses of from ten or twenty to forty grains. Another Ricinus from India is still more virulent, though its oil is now used as a purgative, in doses of a single drop.

MOMORDICA ELATERIUM. The most active of the poisonous purgatives, and operating in extremely small doses. It is used in medicine with caution.

CUCUMIS COLOCYNTHIS. Stands in the same class, but its action is less violent. Its extract is a common medicine.

VERATRUM ALBUM and NIGRUM. The roots of both

these rank among the acrid poisons. They are now little used in medicine.

STAPHISAGRIA. This is believed to be poisonous, but does not appear very active.

RHODODENDRON CHRYSANTHUM. The whole plant is poisonous.

ARNICA MONTANA. This ranks in the same class, and has been sometimes used in medicine.

CHELIDONIUM MAJUS. This is an active acrid poison, though it has not been named as such by botanists. It is frequently given by the common people for jaundice, on account of the yellow colour of its juice,—a relic of the Rosicrucian doctrine of signatures. We have seen speedy death produced by it.

COLCHICUM AUTUMNALE. An extremely virulent poison; the root is the active part. It has lately been introduced as a remedy for the gout. It appears that the peculiarly poisonous part is first dissolved in wine, and after some time precipitated, whence we learn to diminish or avoid its injurious effects.

SCILLA MARITIMA. THE SQUILL. The effects are apparently very similar; but in moderate doses it is successfully used in medicine.

ABRUS PRECATORIUS. The scarlet seeds of this tree are well known in necklaces. It is not however generally known, as it ought to be, that they are a violent poison. A single one swallowed by a child has been known to produce death.

CONVOLVULUS ARVENSIS. The root is poisonous, as appears to be the case with the whole genus. It is acrid and purgative.

ASCLEPIAS. More than one of this genus are poisonous, and among the rest the *vincetoxicum.*

APOCYNUM. Some in this genus are known to be poisonous.

DAPHNE MEZEREON. Is unquestionably poisonous, though used in medicine. Its acrimony affects the throat with constriction.

DAPHNE LAUREOLA. Similar in its poisonous effects.

ŒNANTHE FISTULOSA and CROCATA. These are virulent poisons, but their effects are rather narcotic than stimulant. The roots are the most active, and the *crocata* is sometimes mistaken for parsley.

CLEMATIS. The *erecta, flammula,* and others are acrid poisons.

ANEMONE. The *pulsatilla, nemorosa,* and others of the genus may be added to this list.

ACONITUM NAPELLUS and LYCOCTONUM. The former has been used in medicine, and it appears, in small doses, to act on the skin, or organs of perspiration.

RHUS TOXICODENDRON and others in this genus. The very exhalations from the living plant are said to be poisonous.

EUPHORBIA. Every species in this genus. Their juices are also active vesicatories, or caustics.

RANUNCULUS. Many of this genus are very acrid, producing ulcerations of the stomach and intestines. They are also escharotics externally, causing obstinate ulcers, and therefore used by beggars for extorting charity. Of our own species, the *sceleratus, bulbosus,* and *arvensis,* appear the most active.

PHYSALIS ALKEKENGI. The roots are poisonous.

SOLANUM. A good many species in this genus appear to be poisonous in some part or other of the plant. It is doubtful if the berries of the *dulcamara* are so, as commonly thought. Those of the *nigrum* are, as are sometimes the *melongena* and the *lycopersicum.* These, like the *Physalis,* are narcotic poisons.

ATROPA BELLADONNA. The berries of this plant

Poisons.

possess no sensible properties, yet are highly poisonous. From their beauty and taste, they have frequently been eaten by children. They are very narcotic.

ATROPA MANDRAGORA. Less known, but the roots and leaves are poisonous.

DATURA STRAMONIUM. Every part of the plant is a narcotic poison, but the seeds and seed vessel appear the most active. The smoke of the seeds is a remedy for toothach. That of the leaves inhaled has been found useful in some dyspnœas, commonly called asthma. The delirium produced by this poison is of a very singular character. Some peculiar effects of this plant, whether real or imaginary, are noticed in Hudibras. Such, at least, was the popular belief—

—————— " with Dewtry
Commit fantastical advowtry."

LACTUCA VIROSA. A powerful narcotic. The *sativa* is also a narcotic, but of a mild character, and is used in medicine instead of opium.

PARIS QUADRIFOLIA. The berries and the plant are narcotic.

MERCURIALIS PERENNIS. The plant is narcotic.

CICUTA VIROSA. One of the most virulent of the narcotic poisons. The whole plant is poisonous. It is remarkable that all the narcotic plants are eaten by goats with avidity and impunity. No quantity, even of tobacco, appears to injure them. Deer and sheep also eat tobacco wherever they can get it, without any bad effects.

CONIUM MACULATUM. Much used in medicine as a sedative, and is a strong narcotic poison. Giddiness is one of the first symptoms it produces. Many of these plants produce blindness, vertigo, delirium, and convulsions. Such symptoms are indeed the only very remarkable ones; and, in great excess, are the forerunners of death.

HYOSCIAMUS NIGER. Has the reputation of being very poisonous: but its extract, used in medicine, may be taken to the amount of ten grains with little sensible effect.

APIUM GRAVIOLENS. Celery in its wild unblanched state is a pretty active narcotic. Parsley is a mild one.

LATHYRUS CICERA. The seeds are narcotic. We may remark here, that many of the seeds of the papilionaceous plants, that are little suspected to be so, are more or less poisonous. Even those of the common furze are a powerful emetic. So are some in the genera Ervum, Vicia, Spartium, and many others chiefly foreign, which have hitherto been but little noticed. The leguminous plants must therefore be suspected whenever they are unknown.

CALTHA PALUSTRIS. This is an acrid poison.

ANAGALLIS ARVENSIS. This is supposed a poison to sheep and cattle, and the Hydrocotyle vulgaris is also supposed a poison to sheep. We are inclined to doubt of both.

ÆTHUSA CYNAPIUM. A narcotic poison, common in gardens, and sometimes mistaken for parsley.

There are other narcotic poisons among the umbelliferous plants, which are as yet little known. The whole race is suspicious.

BRYONIA ALBA. The roots are narcotic.

MANCHINEEL. A well-known poisonous tree of tropical climates.

TICUNAS. A celebrated poison.

There are many other poisonous plants in hot climates
4

with which we are little acquainted, and of some of which even the botanical names are unknown. We should swell this list unnecessarily by adding them, as it is chiefly important to be aware of those which are most likely to come in our way.

DIGITALIS PURPUREA. One of the most singular of our native poisons, though much used in medicine. Its action seems peculiar to itself. The effects are to reduce, and ultimately to stop the action of the heart, without producing the ordinary effects of the sedative poisons on the sensorium. Its action is so capricious and uncertain, that it is a very dangerous medicine.

The bitter plants, of whatever natural orders, seem all to be narcotic poisons in different degrees. The poisonous genera are of course numerous, but we shall limit our list to a few of the most remarkable.

PRUNUS LAUROCERASUS. This is amongst the most active of the whole. The effects of laurel water have long been familiar to the public. It is not known that it produces any great effects when taken in an under dose, but when the quantity is sufficient, it causes almost instantaneous death. Its action resembles exactly that of the Prussic acid, and as it contains that singular substance in large proportions, it is not improbable that this is the active ingredient.

The distilled oil is the most active poison known; as it kills animals even when applied to the tongue, or introduced by a slight puncture, like the poison of snakes.

PRUNUS OCCIDENTALIS. Is probably not less active. It is the ingredient used for flavouring noyau, which, in large quantities, would probably prove a poison.

Others of this genus possess the same poison, particularly in the young leaves.

AMYGDALUS COMMUNIS. The bitter almond is poisonous, and gives, on distillation, the same poisonous oil as the laurel. The young leaves are also possessed of the same property, as are those of the Amygdalus persica, or peach tree.

STRYCHNOS NUX VOMICA. One of the most potent of the bitter poisons. To this we may add the Faba Sancti Ignatii. In tropical climates, there are many others of this class yet little known.

PAPAVER ORIENTALE. Apparently, all this genus is narcotic. Opium is the best known, but its effects, both as a medicine and a poison, are so familiar, that we need not dwell on them. Death, in these cases, is produced by the usual effects, marked by nausea, vomiting, vertigo, coma, convulsions, and delirium.

If taken in the tincture, as laudanum, it is frequently its own antidote by exciting vomiting, particularly if the dose is large. To evacuate, is the chief remedy. Acetic acid is supposed to be a perfect antidote. Even the weaker acids, such as lemon juice, have been found useful.

It is not our intention here to notice the peculiar essential salts which recent chemistry has extracted from this and many other of the poisons; as they are not yet well known, and are not likely to fall in our way in ordinary life.

CANNABIS SATIVA. Our own hemp, and the oriental, called bang, are highly narcotic. The smoke, frequently used in Egypt and the east, is said to be more powerful than tobacco. It appears that the ancients had a practice of intoxicating themselves with some such plants, by sitting round smoking fires made of them.

Many of the Fungi are known to be poisonous, but the species are not at all determined. Their actions also differ; some being narcotic, and others acrid. They are all held in great fear in this country; but many species are eaten in France and Italy that are rejected by us. The only ones in use with us are the *Agaricus campestris*, and *oreades*, the *deliciosus*, more rarely, and the truffle and morel. The Russians eat the whole race, using the poisonous ones as means of intoxication. It appears, however, that these are used after a species of fermentation, so that their noxious effects are probably diminished.

The *Agaricus piperatus* and *muscarius* are the two which seem most acrid among our species. The narcotic ones have not been ascertained; though, as death from their use is not an uncommon occurrence, it is probable that many different species possess this property.

We shall here conclude this list of the vegetable poisons. But we have yet to remark on these and the animal ones, that they appear to be all destructive when brought into the circulation even by punctures. Hence the practice of poisoning arrows. Savage nations are each attached to particular substances for this purpose, but their numbers are probably far greater than is suspected. The Euphorbias are amongst those used. We believe that all the active, acrid, and narcotic plants are equally poisonous in this way. As to animal poisons, the deadly effects of putrid animal matter introduced, even slightly, during dissections, are but too well known. These remain active even when dry, and may be effectually used for poisoning arrows.

ATMOSPHERIC AND GASEOUS POISONS.

These may be divided into the animal, vegetable, and chemical, if it is thought necessary; but we shall describe them all as briefly as possible, without any further subdivisions.

PUTRID ANIMAL EXHALATIONS. There are various situations in which these occur, such as in church-yards, or after general actions in war. It is thought by some that they generate contagious fevers, while, by others, this has been denied. It seems, however, undeniable, that epidemic and contagious diseases do occur very often in conjunction with these circumstances, and it is more than probable that these effluvia are in some manner, direct or indirect, the cause.

When more concentrated, it is certain that they produce nausea, often with vomiting, diarrhœa, or dysentery, vertigo, and fainting. In an extreme degree of concentration, they are often the cause of instantaneous death. It is possible that the gaseous matter in these cases may be of a different nature, as chemistry neither has analyzed, nor probably ever will analyze these invisible and extraordinary compounds. Such accidents occur in London sometimes, and probably elsewhere, to sextons; and a grave of this nature is there technically called a green grave. They also happen to nightmen occasionally; and that trade is unquestionably pernicious at all times, as may be seen in the sallow countenances of the people employed in it.

The acid gases decompose and destroy this poisonous matter. The sufferers can only be treated medically on general principles.

PLAGUE. This volatile poison is unquestionably the produce of animal bodies labouring under the disease, whenever it is propagated in those countries where it is not endemic. Its original production in Egypt is still, however, a matter of great obscurity. It is very fully treated of in our article on the PLAGUE, so that we need not dwell further on it in this place.

CONTAGIOUS FEVER. This is still more certainly a produce of animals in a state of disease, and, properly, of man alone, whatever analogies to it the epidemics of some animals may have. But it appears also to be generated, without previous fever, merely by the close confinement of many healthy persons in one place, or by the long accumulation of human effluvia from want of care and cleanliness. There are not wanting analogies in the animal creation; since, if healthy sheep are crowded together for a considerable time, they generate a contagious and deadly fever.

Like the poison of the plague, that of fever, and indeed of all the contagious diseases, admits of being permanently attached to many substances, and more particularly to wool, so as even to gain virulence, and to excite the specific disease at great distances of time. It may be remarked here, that ordinary putrid effluvia admit of the same attachment, whence our clothes retain the smell of such matters for a long time. Whatever be the nature of these compounds, they are destroyed by heat, by ventilation, by water, and by exposure to the mineral acid vapours.

It is important to note this as a means of preventing the propagation of diseases so fatal. To destroy all matters of contagion in houses, ships, or generally in inanimate substances, the most efficacious and cheap substance is the sulphurous acid. This is readily produced by burning a mixture of two parts of sulphur in powder with one of nitre, which burns out without the necessity of admitting air. It should be placed in iron pots, in such places, that every part of the house, or ship, should be filled with it, taking care to stop all orifices or crevices by which it might escape. Furniture and clothes should be opened in such a manner as to give it free access to every thing; and the same should be done with all recesses where the contagion might be suspected to remain. As the materials are cheap, it is better to err by excess than defect of quantity; and with respect to that we can only give general rules. From four to six pounds of the mixture may serve for a room of ordinary size, so that what is required for a house may be computed accordingly. The rooms should be kept hermetically closed for twelve hours. For a ship of 200 or 300 tons, from forty to fifty pounds may suffice. In ships, in particular, this practice is attended with many other advantages; as it kills equally all rats and insects, such as cockroaches, bugs, &c. We may add that, after we had introduced this practice into the transport service during the late war, not a single instance occurred of a fever breaking out in the ships, though, before that, such accidents had been frequent and fatal.

This acid cannot be used for fumigations when human beings are present, on account of its poisonous effects; but in these cases we can safely have recourse to the nitric and oxymuriatic acid vapours. The muriatic is not more efficacious, and is much more intolerable to the lungs. The vapours of the nitric acid are easily produced by sulphuric acid and powdered nitre, and those of the oxymuriatic by the same substance, with a mixture of two parts of common salt and one of manganese. The latter seems to be the most efficacious, and is the most convenient, as it requires no heat. As fumigations for inanimate objects alone, these are as efficacious as the sulphurous acid, but they are more expensive. We cannot recommend this practice too strongly; as, since we have used it, we have never yet seen one instance where any contagious disease has been propagated, even in schools and hospitals.

As we need not enter into those minute details on this subject which rather belong to treatises on medicine, we shall content ourselves with barely naming the diseases which owe their propagation to similar substances. The same general rules, whether as to their propagation or their antidotes, apply alike to all; and that their chemical natures must all differ, can admit of no doubt, however impossible, and, we may add, however hopeless, it may be to discover in what they really consist.

The specific contagions best acknowledged, therefore, are those which produce smallpox, measles, scarlatina, and hooping cough. Dysentery belongs to fevers, and of others we need take no particular notice.

It is however interesting here to remark, that besides these specific poisons which act on the human body, there seems to be others peculiar to many classes of animals. But as in these cases it is not easy to distinguish between epidemic and contagious diseases, it may be most safe to refer these poisons to the next species, or the vegetable atmospheric poisons.

MIASMA. This is an atmospheric diffusible poison, exciting diseases, but not capable of being reproduced or communicated by the diseased individual, or of being preserved in inanimate substances. It is supposed to be of a vegetable nature, or, more properly, of a vegetable origin, because it is produced from vegetating surfaces under peculiar circumstances.

The most obvious of its sources are marshes, whence it is also known by the name of marsh miasma. It is most frequent and virulent in hot climates, and in warm weather; whence the diseases arising from it are, in such countries, marked by uncommon severity. The exact conditions of the ground required to generate it, are not well understood, but we may mention them briefly.

All swamps and marshy grounds, whether fresh or salt, together with low meadows, ponds, ditches, and the æstuaries of flat rivers generally, are among the most pestilential, particularly in hot climates. So are close and damp woods. Hence the jungle fevers of the mouths of the Ganges. Hence also those of lower Egypt, of the African coast, of the West India islands, of the Mississippi, the Demerara, and other American rivers, and of the woods and swamps of the interior of America. In Europe, the fevers of Greece and the much-talked of Malaria of Italy, depend on similar causes, as do those of Holland, among which Walcheren stands a memorable example. In our own island, agues are the produce of the same poison.

It is here important to observe, that, in all these cases, stagnant water intermixed with vegetable matters are the obvious circumstances present. Yet the same poison is in some places generated in dry soils, as in the Maremma of Tuscany. It is also produced from lakes and ponds, where no apparent vegetable decomposition is going on; and it is very essential to remark, that the smallest quantity, or space, favourable to its production, is sufficient to produce it, so as to cause these diseases. Hence many places are subject to the disorders which it produces, when the cause remains unsuspected.

This poison is capable of being transported by the winds, and more particularly by the east wind, to great distances, and hence very often arise many obscure ailments produced by that pernicious wind. In other respects its power and mode of spreading appear very capricious. In some cases it is limited to very short distances from the generating source, and it is even known to be entangled among the plants of a soil. Hence inhabitants of the upper stories of a house escape, while those below are affected. Yet on other occasions it ascends, while the lower tracts are exempt. Towns generally interrupt its career, or destroy it, yet at this moment Rome is suffering from it through more than half its extent, while it is rapidly increasing its ravages: so uncertain are all these general rules.

The diseases produced by miasma are all connected and convertible into each other, and are therefore probably distinct cases rather than distinct diseases. They are, the remittent or yellow fever of the West Indies and elsewhere, the jungle fevers of India, the common remittents of Europe, with the whole tribe of intermittents, the disease known by the name of Neuralgia, dysentery, and cholera, and obstructions and inflammations of the liver and spleen. The treatment and symptoms of these belong to medicine.

There appears to be no antidote against this poison but that of avoiding it and its causes. Many chemical attempts have been made to procure and analyze it, but hitherto without the least success. It has been supposed to be hydro-carbonate, because the same grounds generate that gas; but this substance produced by chemistry has no such effects. It is probable that we shall never discover its nature. It has been lately said, that the simple wearing of a gauze veil will prevent it from affecting the individual, even in the most dangerous situations; but the experiments in favour of this opinion have not as yet been sufficiently numerous to admit of this conclusion.

The next division of aerial poisons are the gases produced by chemistry.

AMMONIA. This substance breathed in quantity, or not too much diluted, produces sudden death. In a minor degree, it merely produces strictures of the bronchiæ and catarrhs. To inhale the vapour of vinegar and of warm water is useful; and in all cases of much spasm in the lungs from this or other pernicious gases, the vapour of ether may also be breathed with advantage.

OXYMURIATIC GAS. This also is deadly in large quantities, and pernicious even in the smallest ones. The minor symptoms are catarrh, with stricture of the bronchiæ, which sometimes terminate in incurable dyspnœa. Diluted vapour of ammonia and of water are useful in diminishing and removing these effects. Bloodletting and opium may also be necessary.

SULPHUROUS ACID. The effects, and the remedies for this, are exactly the same.

MURIATIC ACID. We may make the same remarks on this acid.

NITRIC ACID. The vapours of this are little injurious in small quantities, though deadly in a large dose. The fluoric and phosphoric are little known as gaseous poisons; but there is no reason to doubt of their possessing the same properties.

NITRIC OXIDE. There can be no question of the poisonous nature of this gas, though when breathed in small quantities it only produces a temporary delirium resembling a pleasing intoxication. It seems then to leave no bad effects behind.

HYDROGEN. Appears to act as a direct poison on the system in large quantities, while it seems innocent in small. If azote acts as a poison, it seems to be rather in a negative manner. Pure oxygen appears injurious, exciting inflammations of the lungs.

HYDROCARBONATE. All the gases of this nature are

Poisons. direct and active poisons when in large doses, and the olefiant gas appears the most active of the whole. We also suspect that the gradual use of this gas in a very diluted state is destructive to the health. To this we would attribute what is technically called the grinder's rot, a disease common to all those who grind iron even under water. It has been supposed to rise from dust entering the lungs. But this cannot happen in wet grinding, while it is certain that hydrocarbonate is here generated in consequence of the oxidation of the steel, which is the proper object of most of this kind of grinding. Those who flatten saws are especially subject to it; and so dangerous indeed is this branch, that the workmen can earn a guinea in the day by it.

ARSENIATED HYDROGEN. This is only produced occasionally in the laboratory, and, as might be expected, it is peculiarly destructive, deranging the constitution very much, even when it does not produce death.

GAS FROM BURNING ANIMAL SUBSTANCES. We can give this no chemical name, because its true composition is unknown. It is generated in many of the large chemical manufactories on a great scale, as in that of Prussian blue for example. It excites nausea, headach, and vertigo, so that there can be no doubt respecting its poisonous nature; but we cannot produce any instance of death from it. It is extremely offensive.

CARBONIC ACID. This is a direct and active poison in large, though innocent in small quantities. Its effects are death, with the symptoms of apoplexy. It is a very frequent cause of accidents in breweries and wine cellars, in places where charcoal is burned in close rooms, and in wells or other places that have been long shut up. In small doses it excites headach and vertigo. The remedies are the same as in the case of drowning, or other kinds of suffocation.

POITIERS, a town of France, and the capital of the department of Vienne, occupies a large space within its walls, on a rising ground near the river Clair; but much of this space is occupied with gardens. The streets are commonly steep, crooked, and ill paved; and the houses have a mean and antiquated appearance. The *Place Royale*, the finest of the squares, stands in the centre of the town, and contains some good buildings. The churches are here the only public buildings of note. The principal ones are the Gothic cathedral and St. Hilair's. Among the Roman antiquities are some arches of an aqueduct, the ruins of an amphitheatre, and portions of a triumphal arch. Its literary institutions are a sort of university, a royal college, a provincial school, an atheneum, a public library, and a botanic garden. The principal manufactures of the place are those of woollen caps, stockings, leather, and gloves. Population about 21,000. East Long. 0° 20′ 43″, North Lat. 46° 35′.

POLA. A full account of this town is given under ISTRIA, Vol. XII. p. 331, 332.

POLAND.

Poland.

Name. POLAND, formerly a large country of continental Europe, derived its name (*Pohlen*, a plain,) from the general aspect of its surface, which, with the exception of a few diminutive eminences, is so extremely level, that, after a rainy season, the waters of different rivers, inundating large portions of the country, flow into each other. The vast tract of land which this name originally designated, exists no longer as an independent country. A small part of it, in the centre, has lately been erected into a kingdom tributary to Russia; but by far the greater proportion, by rapacity and conquest, has become subject to the sovereigns of Russia, Prussia, and Austria respectively. In the present article, we shall first communicate every information respecting ancient Poland which cannot with propriety be given in the description of the countries to which it now belongs, and then conclude with an account of *the kingdom of Poland* as constituted by the Congress of Vienna.

Situation and extent. Poland was bounded on the west by Germany and Silesia; on the south by Hungary and Turkey; by Russia on the east; and on the north by Prussia and the Baltic. Situated between 48° 30′ north latitude; and between 16° and 32° 10′ east longitude, its greatest length, from Domes Ness on the north-west, to the extreme south-east point, was 660 miles; and its greatest breadth, from east to west, was 620,—its superficial extent being estimated at 284,000 square miles; and as the population amounted to 15,000,000, averaging about 53 to the square mile.

Ancient constitution. The crown of Poland, with the exception of five centuries previous to the year 1370, was purely elective. Its sovereigns, whose authority before the era just mentioned was unlimited and absolute, were originally termed *duces*, dukes, or generals, in reference to the almost invariable practice of their conducting the armies of the state to the field in person. In the 14th century, the nobles availed themselves of the weakness of a female reign to diminish the power of their sovereign, and to extend that of their own order. They enacted that no taxes should be levied, that no new laws should be passed,—in short, that no measure of any importance should, as formerly, be effected by the king, but by representatives chosen from among themselves. Hence the origin of the Diets of Poland, of which there were two kinds, Ordinary and Extraordinary, the former statedly assembled once in two years, while the latter was summoned by the king only on great emergencies. The Diets consisted of the king, the senators, and deputies from provinces and towns, amounting altogether to about four hundred members. These assemblies could sit only for a limited time, and any individual, however humble, had the power of calling for a division of the meeting on any question, and one dissentient voice had the effect of rendering the whole deliberations ineffectual. This latter right, which was termed *liberum veto*, and which was repeatedly exercised, was the cause of the greatest calamities, and often of much bloodshed. Without the unanimous consent of the Diet, the king could determine no question of importance, could not declare war, make peace, raise levies, employ auxiliaries, or admit foreign troops into his dominions, with other restrictions, which almost extinguished the regal authority. Nor did the nobility stop here. Having thus undermined the power of the king, there was but one step more to gain to themselves the uncontrolled government of the nation, namely, to render the throne elective. This was accordingly accomplished; and the king of Poland enjoyed now the title, but little of the power or dignity of a free sovereign. Liberty, so much boasted of by the Poles, seems from this period to have been confined to the nobles

Poitiers, Pola.

Poland.

Poland.

alone. They arrogated an unlimited sway over their respective territories; some of them were hereditary sovereigns of cities and villages, with which the king had no concern; they exercised a power of life and death over their tenants and vassals; they were exempted from taxes; and could not be arrested and imprisoned but for a few crimes of the basest kind. But the most dangerous of all their rights, and one which made their situation analogous to that of the German princes, was the power of constructing fortresses for their private defence, and of maintaining a military force, which, in imitation of regal dignity, they caused to keep guard round their palaces. The election of the king was vested in them alone; and none but they, and the citizens of a few particular towns, possessed the privilege of purchasing or inheriting property in land. The nobility, amounting to about 500,000 individuals, Malte-Brun emphatically terms the *sovereign body* of Poland.

The senate, however, which owed its origin (in the eleventh century) to Boleslaus I. formed an intermediate authority between the king and the nobles. This body, composed of the ministers of state, of the representatives of the clergy, of palatines and castellans, consisted of 149 members, until 1767, when four new members were added to the number, as representatives of the province of Lithuania. The senators, except the representatives of the clergy, were nominated by the king, but continued in office for life, and after their appointment were totally independent of royal authority, to which indeed they were regarded as a valuable counterpoise. The duty of the senate was to preside over the laws, to be the guardians of liberty, and the protectors of justice and equity, and, conjunctly with the king, to ratify laws made by the nobility. A Diet could not, as previously hinted, be constituted, without the junction of the senate to the national representatives: a portion of the senators, indeed, acted as a committee for facilitating and conducting the public business of that assembly. The president of the senate was the archbishop of Gnesna, who, during an inter-regnum, discharged the functions of king, and enjoyed all the royal prerogatives but that of dispensing justice. His duty also was to summon the extraordinary diet when the throne became vacant, and to preside at that assembly.

The diet which thus assembled on the death of a king of Poland to elect a sovereign to occupy the vacant throne, was not unfrequently characterized by the most sanguinary proceedings. This assembly, which consisted of the senate, of the representatives of districts, of the clergy and the nobles,—the latter, a most numerous body,—met on horseback in a plain adjoining the village of Wohla in the neighbourhood of Warsaw. Though the electors were prohibited from appearing at the meeting attended by any body guard, they yet uniformly came armed with pistols and sabres, prepared to perpetrate the greatest excesses. Every member of the diet, as previously mentioned, was entitled to call for a division of the assembly on any question, or to put an end to the deliberations, or even the existence of the assembly, merely by protesting against its proceedings. This singular and absurd privilege, which was frequently exercised in those meetings of unenlightened and violent men, was productive of the most fatal consequences. It often led the stronger party to attack, on the spot, their antagonists, sword in hand; and it not unfrequently formed the origin of civil wars, by which the resources and the stability of the nation were undermined, patriotism extinguished, and the progress of

liberal knowledge retarded. Before the successful candidate was proclaimed king, he had to sign the *pacta conventa*, or the conditions on which he obtained the crown, which, on his knees, he had to swear never to violate.

Such was the ancient constitution of Poland,—monarchy blended with aristocracy, in which, for several centuries previously to its dissolution, the latter prevailed. The Poles, indeed, denominated their government a *republic*, because the king, so extremely limited in his prerogative, resembled more the chief of a commonwealth than the sovereign of a monarchy. But it wanted one of the necessary characteristics of a republic: The people were kept in a state of slavery and vassalage, and enjoyed not even the semblance of any civil privilege: the whole power was engrossed by the nobles; and thus the Polish constitution possessed not that community of interests, that general diffusion of political privileges which are the very life and stamina of a republic, as well as of a mixed monarchy, and with which, in spite of much internal misrule, and of the aggressions of foreign enemies, Poland might have flourished till this day.

The administration of justice, and the execution of the law in Poland, was characterized by the grossest abuses. The judges, nominated by the king, were chosen without the most remote regard to their talents or integrity; the decision of the courts of law were openly and unblushingly sold to the highest bidder; and no cause, whatever its merits, could be successful, unless supported by the all-prevailing power of money. Nor was this corruption, for which no redress could be obtained, confined to cases in which the litigants were wealthy, or in which, as resulting from some base and unprincipled transaction, the most ample and liberal payment ought to have been demanded. Actions for which a man deserved the thanks of the state, were, when brought before a legal tribunal, the source of much unjust expence to the person performing them. "If a man apprehended a murderer," says a writer quoted by Malte-Brun, "and brought him before the proper officer, he was charged ten ducats for his trouble; which, if he were unable or unwilling to pay, the murderer was immediately set at liberty." Had he submitted to this payment, the sums that would, on some pretence or other, have been exacted of him, ere the offender was brought to justice, no man unacquainted with the history of Poland could conjecture. "It has cost," says the same writer, "a merchant of Warsaw 14,000 ducats for apprehending two thieves." Nor was the expence of a plea more to be execrated than the duration of it. No litigation, even the simplest,—one, for example, between a debtor and creditor,—could be brought to a termination in less than four years. In so short a time, however, was almost no case decided. Vautrin mentions that he knew cases which had been pending for sixty years, and which, so far as he could foresee, might continue undetermined "till the last generation." The nobles, disgusted with this fatiguing tediousness, not unfrequently withdrew their pleas from the decision of the courts of law, and settled them by force of arms,—of which some instances occurred even so recently as the middle of last century.

The Polish nobles, as recently stated, paid no taxes; and the national revenue, which never exceeded £1,000,000 of our currency, was drawn from the most sterile sources: from the royal domains, which were always held as fiefs by noblemen, at an extremely low rate; from taxes extorted from the miserable peasantry; from the capitation impost on the Jews; from the cus-

Poland.

Administration of justice.

Revenue.

toms, excise, and stamps of a country without commerce; and from other departments of industry equally unproductive. The revenue, thus small in its amount, and the collection of which was distinguished by the grossest injustice and cruelty, exhibited the striking features of an unprosperous country. In 1767, it did not cover the expenditure by £250,000; in nine years afterwards, the annual deficiency was double that sum; and though at various periods new taxes were imposed, the revenue, at its most flourishing state, (only £936,000) did not come within £130,000 of the expenditure.

Military force.

It is impossible that, in such circumstances, the military state of the nation could be adequately supported. This evil, which was felt in every age of the republic, proved peculiarly disastrous towards the end of last century, as the neighbouring powers then possessed a regular standing army, before which the rude, undisciplined troops of Poland, with all their bravery, were obliged to give way. In 1788, when it was determined to raise the army to 100,000 men, the measure was found totally impracticable, on account of the niggardly scantiness of the revenue. And called upon, as the Poles then were, by every inducement calculated to alarm and arouse a brave and suffering people; when not merely the glory of their nation, but its very existence, was at stake, all the troops they could muster, after three years' exertion, never exceeded 60,000, of whom, it is thought not more than 40,000 actually appeared in the field.

Pospolite.

But the true constitutional force of Poland was the *Pospolite*, that is, the union of the whole inhabitants capable of bearing arms, under the banners of their several palatinates. This force, when it could be called into action at the very moment it was required, was found to be irresistible. The privilege of summoning the pospolite belonged originally to the sovereign; but when the nobles, in the frenzy of their zeal to add to their own power at the expence of that of their king, deprived him of this privilege, they rendered the assembling of this force a process so tedious and complicated, that the danger which they were intended to avert had often taken place ere they could be brought into action. The pospolite, besides, probably from the same circumstances, lost at length that high character for courage and patriotism given them so liberally by ancient historians. Their celebrated defeat, under the Duke D'Ostrog, palatine of Sandomir, in 1647, and their conduct under King Casimir, in 1651, have rendered them almost ridiculous even in the eyes of the Poles themselves. They were assembled, for the last time, about twenty years after the period last mentioned, to the number of 100,000, but they no sooner beheld the enemy advancing, than they fled tumultuously before them, though they had their king at their head, and though the illustrious Sobieski, with 35,000 regular troops, was with them to support and encourage them.

The Poles, it may be stated, had anciently no military force except the pospolite. The first *standing* army, called *Kwarciane*, was organized in 1562, and paid out of the fourth part of the revenues of the crown lands. The Cossacks, in the reign of Stephen Batthori, performed a regular service in guarding the frontiers of the Ukraine and Podolia from the inroads of the Turks and Tartars; and, finally, the royal guards, with their military attendants and the staff of nobility, formed a considerable regular force ready for the field on the shortest notice. These bodies, however, the Poles never regarded as of great or permanent importance;

and the pospolite formed the protection of the kingdom till, as just mentioned, they forfeited all confidence by their ignorance and pusillanimity.

Poland formed a district of ancient Sarmatia; and was successively ravaged by those various hordes of barbarians who plundered the south of Europe, and overturned the Roman empire. Its early history, like that of most other nations, is involved in obscurity and fable. That it originally consisted of several independent principalities is sufficiently evident; but the period when it became incorporated under one sovereign is not clearly ascertained. It was, for many ages, according to the opinion of the best writers, governed by an elective chief, bearing the title of *duke*, or general; but no regular dynasty was established until the accession of Piaste in 840. Of this election, which however did not take place till the state was on the very verge of ruin, in consequence of the hostility and obstinacy of two rival factions, the Polish nation had much reason to be proud. The wise administration of this prince restored peace and tranquillity among all orders of the state; and, after a reign of twenty years, spent in advancing the true interests of his subjects, he died in 860, at a very venerable old age. So dear was his memory to the Poles, that, until last century, they gave his name to his successors in the throne (Piastes) who were natives of the kingdom.

The family of Piaste filled the throne of Poland for upwards of five hundred years. The most illustrious princes of this house were Miécislaus, who, towards the end of the 10th century, introduced Christianity into his dominions,—Boleslaus, his son, a warlike and intrepid prince, who was the first that obtained the title of *king*, an honour conferred on him by the Pope,—Casimir I. a virtuous and pacific sovereign, who was called to the throne after he had assumed the monastic habit in the abbey of Cluny,—Casimir II. surnamed the Great, who was a liberal patron of letters, and founded the academy at Cracow,—who encouraged industry, commerce, and the arts, and furnished the nation with a code of written laws. He died in 1370, and was doomed to be the last of his illustrious family.

He was succeeded by his nephew Louis, king of Hungary, at whose death the Poles elected his youngest daughter, Hedwigua, in his room. To obtain the hand of this princess, Jagellon, grand duke of Lithuania, embraced the Christian faith, and was baptized by the name of Uladislaus. With Jagellon commenced a new line of princes, who swayed the sceptre of Poland for two hundred years. He united his hereditary dominions to those of Poland, conquered Samogitia, and defeated the knights of the Teutonic Order in the great battle of Tannenberg, in 1410. Casimir took Western Prussia under his protection, and forced the Teutonic knights to pay him homage for the remainder. Under Sigismond I. Prussia was changed into a secular dukedom. Sigismond Augustus effected the same thing in regard to Courland: the empire of the Teutonic order was at the same time placed under the government of a duke, and made entirely dependent on the crown of Poland. In the reign of this monarch, Poland had reached its highest pitch of dominion and glory. He saw Lithuania, Livonia, Volhynia, Podolia, and Kiow submit to his sovereignty. But with him terminated, in 1572, the male line of the house of Jagellon,—" a family," says a learned writer, " as wise and virtuous as celebrated and brave,—a family under whom Poland saw herself enjoy internal tranquillity and the respect of neighbouring nations—under whom she was ruled by wise, established laws, and was rendered eminent by the multitude of her scholars in every department of human knowledge." (*Tableau de la Pologne*, par Malte-Brun, p. 448. Paris, 1807.)

Henry de Valois.

After an inter-regnum of about a year, two powerful candidates appeared for the throne, Henry de Valois, brother to Charles IX. king of France, and Maximilian of Austria, of whom the former being elected, he soon, by his youth and accomplishments, gained the affections of his people. But he had not enjoyed the sceptre of the Jagellons above four months, till he inherited, in consequence of the death of his brother, that of Valois; and he abandoned the cheering hopes which the esteem and confidence of his adopted subjects held out to him, for the troubles with which his natural subjects were convulsed, and of which he soon became the victim.

Batthori.

On the abdication of Henry, the contentions of rival factions again revived; and it was not without considerable difficulty that Stephen Batthori, prince of Transylvania, was elected his successor; an honour which he gained not more on account of his own many qualifications, than of his having married Anne, daughter of king Sigismond Augustus. Batthori, a prince equally eminent for bravery and virtue, restored peace to Dantzick, the inhabitants of which had rebelled against him; retook Livonia; chastised the Czar of Russia for having invaded his dominions, carrying cruelty and devastation along with him; and raised a new militia, composed of Cossacks, a tribe brave and barbarous, whom he united to his kingdom by granting them a territory on the Dnieper, and by conferring on them several important privileges; favours which they abundantly repaid by defending Poland from the incursions of the Tartars, and by making the Turks and Russians respect her. He died in 1586, leaving behind him a character for wisdom, intrepidity, and patriotism, which few Polish sovereigns have been enabled to outshine.

Sigismond III.

The death of Batthori was a signal for the renewal of civil commotions. Four candidates appeared for the crown*, each supported by a separate party, brave and resolute; and much blood was spilt ere the successful candidate, Sigismond of Sweden, nephew to the widow of Batthori, could be put in possession of the throne. Having soon afterwards obtained the crown of his native dominions, Sigismond neglected not to avail himself of the assistance of Poland against the Swedes, with whom he was extremely unpopular, and who were endeavouring to throw off his yoke. But the Poles, jealous of their liberty, were not much devoted to the cause, and felt no great disappointment in their king's being deprived of his hereditary states. This loss, however, which the subsequent monarchs of Poland wished to repair, gave birth to almost continual wars with Sweden, equally fatal to both nations; for though, on the one hand, they brought Poland to the very verge of submission to the Swedish yoke, they conducted, on the other, the Swedes to Pultowa, that tomb of their glory and their power.

Sigismond, having lost the throne of Sweden, aspired to that of Russia, but without success. But he was more unfortunate still in a war in which he was engaged with the great Gustavus Adolphus, king of Sweden; for he was compelled to forfeit to that monarch Livonia, and the towns of Elbing, Memel, Braunberg, and Pillau. He died in 1629, worn down with cares and misfortunes, and was succeeded by his son Uladislaus, who established public tranquillity, and reigned not without glory; but the inter-regnum that followed his death was characterized by a disastrous and bloody war with the Cossacks, occasioned by several perfidious attempts on the part of the Polish nobles to make encroachments on their privileges and independence. That barbarous people, who felt that their very existence as a separate tribe was endangered, becoming desperate, vanquished their enemies in two great battles; and John Casimir, successor of Uladislaus, was obliged to conclude with them a dishonourable peace. Poland was again ravaged by the Swedish army, and Charles Gustavus would undoubtedly have made the conquest of it, had not the bad policy of Denmark drawn into that country, almost to the total ruin of it, the whole military force of the common enemy. Nor did this circumstance, favourable as it unquestionably was, prove the entire safety of Poland. By the treaty of Oliva, (1660,) Casimir was forced to cede Livonia to Sweden, Smolensko and Kiow to Russia, and to Brandenburgh the sovereignty of Prussia. With this diminution of her territory, Poland experienced a diminution also of her power; and from this period she ceased to be regarded as one of the first nations of Europe. Casimir indeed gained several decisive victories in a war with the Russians; but these came too late, either to gratify the king, or to prove advantageous to his people. He had already verged into a state of melancholy and despair, and Poland was delivered over to all the horrors of a civil war.

In such circumstances, Casimir, who, at every period of life, had shown a deep-rooted attachment to the exercises of devotion, and the pursuits of literature, resolved to renounce his crown, and to spend the remainder of his days in solitude and peace. Though undaunted in opposing the public enemies of his country, he shuddered to encounter the agitations and enormities of internal rebellion. His abdication took place in 1668, and the Diet absolved him from all the engagements he had made to his people, and particularly from the oath of the *pacta conventa*; obligations entered into by every sovereign at his election. Casimir survived this event four years, when he died in the abbey of St. Germains in France, whence his body was removed to be interred at Cracow.

Wisniowiecki.

After an inter-regnum of a year, Casimir was succeeded by Michel Coributh, duke of Wisniowiecki. Though the reign of this prince was short, he alienated the minds of the nation and the army on account of his lethargy in defending the republic against the invasion of the Turks, and of the shameful treaties which he ratified with them. The glory of the Polish arms, however, was well maintained by John Sobieski, a warrior of extraordinary merit, and than whose there occurs not a more illustrious name in the annals of his country.

Sobieski.

Sobieski, raised to the sovereign authority on the death of Wisniowiecki, did not long want an opportu-

John Casimir.

---

* It may not be uninteresting to mention that, on the death of Batthori, Sir Philip Sydney, "the jewel of Queen Elizabeth's court," was put in nomination as his successor. His supporters, however, were not very numerous, and, besides, Elizabeth, from envy, or from a wish to retain so accomplished a person in her own service, opposed his advancement. Sydney's days were doomed to be few; for he was cut off (17th October, 1586,) in the battle of Zutphen at the early age of 32, a few months after the death of Batthori. "As Providence seems to have sent Sir Philip Sydney into the world to give the present age a specimen of the ancients, so did it, on a sudden, recall him, and snatch him from us, as more worthy of heaven than of earth." (*Biographia Brittanica*, article *Sydney*.)

nity of increasing his own glory, as well as that of his nation. The Turks had, at this time, carried their conquering arms into Austria, and were laying siege to Vienna. The fate of Christendom was thought to be involved in that of the Austrian capital; and had not the exorbitant power of that empire been a source of uneasiness and fear to the neighbouring states, almost all the nations of Europe would have been in arms to chastise these infidels. Sobieski, however, either did not experience these feelings, or was enabled to overcome them. He levied 40,000 men for the assistance of the emperor; put himself at their head; and his valour and genius decided the terrible battle (1683,) which forced Soliman to raise the siege of Vienna, and eventually, with the loss of almost his whole army, to withdraw into his own territories.

The inhabitants of Vienna received their deliverer with the most lively demonstrations of gratitude; and exclamations of joy accompanied him to the very threshold of the chapel, whither he went to return thanks to the God of battles for the success of his arms. When *Te Deum* was chaunted, he himself joined very cordially in the service. A sermon was delivered on the occasion from a text, which the clergyman, in extremely bad taste, seems to have selected as peculiarly appropriate: "*There was a man sent from God, whose name was* JOHN."

But the joy which Sobieski must have felt in having performed so important a service to the Austrians, and in receiving their congratulations, was moderated by his unpopularity with his own subjects. In this foreign expedition the Poles found that their treasury had been drained, and that many of their countrymen had perished; while, as a compensation for these evils, no substantial advantage to the republic had resulted, or could be expected to result from it. His wish to make the crown hereditary in his own family exasperated and disaffected the nobles; and the consequence was, that, after his death, which took place in 1696, after a reign of twenty-three years, his children were ungratefully excluded from the throne*. Another great cause of his unpopularity was the cession of certain lands to Russia; for which, however, in return, he was promised assistance in the meditated conquest of Moldavia and Wallachia,—schemes which a new aspect of affairs made it not necessary to prosecute.

Whatever suspicions, however, the Poles may have attached to his memory, Sobieski was undoubtedly a great man. Endowed with strength of body, and vigour of mind,—skilled in the laws, the constitution, and political relations of his country,—as eloquent and wise in council, as enterprising and enthusiastic in the field, he possessed all the virtues and qualities necessary for a great warrior or an accomplished monarch. The nobleness and elevation of his mind were clearly shadowed forth in the lineaments of his countenance, and the dignity of his personal appearance. He possessed a peculiar art of profiting by the least advantage, and was characterized by a sure and quick sagacity of foreseeing and preventing danger. Reading and study formed the amusements of his private hours: he was master of several languages, and he delighted in conversing with men of letters. His court was brilliant, and filled with strangers of rank and distinction. All

the powers of Europe sent ambassadors to him; he received an ambassador even from the king of Persia to congratulate him on his victories, and to ask his friendship and alliance.

Enthusiasm, which was a predominant feature in his character, imparted an oracular tone of authority and majesty to all his words and expressions, which, on this account, are still commemorated and applauded. When taking his departure from Warsaw in his campaign against the Turks, he said emphatically to the ambassadors at his court, "Tell your master that you have seen me mount my horse, and that Vienna is safe!" In this expedition, though the greater part of his army were well mounted, one battalion was so extremely ill clothed, that prince Lumboriski advised him, for the honour of Poland, not to exhibit it before the allies. Disregarding this suggestion, he exclaimed, when the battalion was passing before the allied troops, "Examine these men attentively: they are invincible; and have sworn, that in time of war they will wear no other dress but that of the enemy: in the last war they were clothed after the Turkish fashion." After the defeat at Vienna, a gilt stirrup which had belonged to Mustapha having been found, "Take that stirrup to the queen," cried he, "and tell her, that he, to whom it belonged, is conquered." And at the same time he wrote to the queen, "that the grand vizir had made him his heir, and that he had found in his tent the value of several millions of ducats. So," added he, "say not of us what the Tartar women say when they see their husbands return empty-handed, *You are not men, since you come home without booty!*"

Such was John Sobieski, the last illustrious monarch that filled the throne of Poland. His character, with all its defects, we delight to contemplate, as it affords us a bright spot on which to pause amid the general gloom. "The spirit of discord and anarchy," says Mr. Coxe, "was laid for a time by his transcendent genius. Under his auspices Poland seemed to revive from the calamities which had long oppressed her, and again to recover her ancient splendour: such is the powerful ascendancy of a great and superior mind." The contentions and commotions which followed his death we have no time at present to describe. It may be sufficient to remark that, though the prince of Conti had been elected by a majority of votes, Augustus, elector of Saxony, backed by a powerful army, was ultimately declared successor to Sobieski. Augustus began his reign auspiciously by concluding a peace with the Turks, by which Kaminieck and Podolia were added to his dominions. But this was the only favourable transaction in which, during a long reign, he was engaged. Charles XII. the celebrated king of Sweden, having invaded his territories, compelled him to surrender the crown to Stanislaus Leczinski, a Pole of noble rank, whose elevation, however, was but of short continuance. The battle of Pultowa dissipated the Swedish power, and Augustus was restored through the friendship of Russia, though not without making the most inglorious concessions to that nation. Surrounded by Russian and Saxon troops, bound to obey every order he received from the court of Petersburg, his reign was without authority and without honour. He was succeeded, at his death, in 1733, by his son of

* This result, however, was owing not less to the unnatural conduct of the queen, who disliked her eldest son, and endeavoured too successfully to prevent his accession, than to the ingratitude of the Poles. The name of Sobieski is now extinct; but by the female line his family is still represented by the houses of Lorraine and Saxony. It may not be improper to state that Clementina Mary, daughter to James his eldest son, was married (1719) to James Edward Stuart, the Pretender, and was mother of Charles, celebrated for an unfortunate attempt to obtain the throne of his ancestors,—and of Henry, Cardinal of York, who both died without issue.

Poland.

the same name, though not without the most formidable opposition on the part of the French king, who espoused the cause of Stanislaus, whose daughter he had married. Augustus II. had even less merit than his father. His reign was an unvaried scene of anarchy and rebellion. So extremely unpopular was he, and so completely divested of any thing like power, that,.when driven from Saxony, his patrimonial dominions, the Poles would scarcely afford him an asylum among them. And after an inefficient and unhappy reign, he died at Dresden in 1764, and was, not unfortunately, doomed to be the last of his family who attempted to wield the sceptre of Poland. This ill-fated country had been for some time regarded by Russia, and not without reason, as a tributary province; and accordingly Catherine II. when the throne became vacant, compelled the diet to elect for king Stanislaus Poniatowski, under the name of Stanislaus Augustus,—

Stanislaus Augustus.

a Pole of noble rank, who, having resided in Petersburg, had by his address and abilities rendered himself agreeable to the empress. He was an amiable and patriotic, though not a very energetic character. Whatever had been his talents, however, Poland before his time was rapidly hastening to decay; and during his reign he saw it completely erased from the chart of the world.

Dissidents.

The causes which led to this catastrophe, though known to every reader, it may not be improper shortly to investigate. The reformed religion, though early introduced into Poland, was not for two centuries very generally adopted. The Protestants, called *Dissidents*, (a term which also comprised those of the Greek church,) were tolerated, though they were obliged to labour under many civil disabilities. During the inter-regnum that preceded the election of Poniatowsky, a decree had been made by the diet, by which the dissidents were, in a great measure, forbidden the free exercise of their worship, and totally excluded from all civil and political privileges. The history of almost every nation in Europe has established the impropriety and danger of such a step. As liberty of conscience, and the undisturbed freedom of worshiping God publicly according to its dictates, are privileges the most dear, and of which no earthly power has a right to deprive us, a decree, like that in question, is calculated to divide the interests of the community, to unsheath the sword of civil war, and thus to render the nation an easy prey to the ambition of a foreign foe. This was precisely the result in the present instance. The dissidents could not submit without a struggle to the deprivation of their most invaluable privileges. They combined unanimously to endeavour to accomplish the repeal of this decree, and, for this purpose, applied for advice and assistance to some of the most eminent powers of Europe. And accordingly Russia, Prussia, Great Britain, and Denmark, made remonstrances to the government of Poland on this subject. These remonstrances, however, were without effect; for the decree was confirmed by the coronation diet held after the king's election. The dissidents in the meantime presented to the government petitions and memorials; and the decision of the question was at last referred by the diet to the bishops and senators. And upon a report from them, the diet made some concessions, which, however, were far from satisfying the dissidents, who thought it absurd that the redress of their grievances should be entrusted to those very persons who were the *authors* of them. The dissidents, whose cause was now openly espoused by Russia, Prussia, and Austria, were not to be flattered by the

concessions of these persecutors, nor overawed by their power. They formed confederacies for their defence in every province, and were determined to resist unto blood in support of their rights and privileges. Nor were the Popish clergy and their adherents slow in making preparations. *The Confederation of the Barr,* the hope and bulwark of their party, took up arms. The cries of liberty and religion became every where the signal of a war, the true object of which with the Catholics, was, not only to disperse or destroy their opponents, but to dethrone Stanislaus, whom they regarded as friendly to the dissidents, and to rescue Poland from the influence of Russia. The *confederates,* as the Catholics were now termed, feebly supported by Saxony and France, were vanquished in almost every battle; and the dissidents would have been secured in the open and unshackled profession of their faith, had the sovereigns to whom, in no mean degree, they owed their success, been actuated by any regard to their cause, or had not trampled under foot every principle, which the law of nations,—which the law of nature should have taught them to cherish and reverence.

These sovereigns, however, instead of being animated in the cause of civil and religious liberty, were, under the falsest pretences, labouring solely to extend the boundaries of their respective dominions, and to promote the aggrandizement of their power. Nothing less than the dismemberment of Poland, and the partition of it among themselves, was their object in the assistance they afforded the dissidents,—an object which could only be attained, or at least more easily attained, by fomenting internal divisions, and thus undermining the resources and unanimity of the kingdom. This plan, it is thought, was first contemplated by Prussia; but Russia and Austria readily enough embraced it, though all these kingdoms at different periods owed much of their glory, and even their very existence, to the country which they thus resolved to destroy. A great proportion of Poland was thus seized upon by these kingdoms, and a treaty to this effect was signed by their plenipotentiaries at Petersburg in Feb. 1772. The partitioning powers having forced the Poles to call a meeting of the diet, threatened, if the treaty of dismemberment was not unanimously sanctioned, that the whole kingdom should immediately be laid under military execution, and be treated as a conquered state. The glory of Poland was past; and though some of the nobles, rather than be the instruments of bringing their country to ruin, chose to spend their days in exile and poverty, the measure was at length agreed to; and Stanislaus himself, threatened with deposition and imprisonment, was prevailed upon to sanction it. Europe, though astonished at what was taking place in Poland, remained inactive. The courts of London, Paris, Stockholm, and Copenhagen, indeed, sent remonstrances against this usurpation; but remonstrances without a military force, will, as in the case before us, be always unavailing.

Partition of Poland.

" Oh bloodiest picture in the book of time,
Sarmatia fell, unwept, without a crime !"

A large portion of the eastern provinces were seized by Russia; Austria appropriated a fertile tract on the south-west; while Prussia acquired a commercial district in the north-west, including the lower part of the Vistula. Poland was thus robbed of 70,000 square miles, or about a fourth of her whole territory.

Stanislaus, thus deprived of a great part of his dominions, did not, however, give way to unavailing sorrow and despondency: he exerted himself strenuously to promote the happiness and prosperity of that por-

Internal improvements.

tion which was left him. He made various improvements in the internal economy of the state; he introduced and cherished a taste for agricultural pursuits; the peasantry, so long neglected or enslaved, were the objects of his most anxious solicitude, and now began to assume that rank and importance in the state to which their usefulness entitled them; and a national system of education was established on the most advantageous principles. That Stanislaus effected such great improvements is much to be wondered at; for, with all his merit, he could never acquire the esteem of his subjects, and his power was extremely circumscribed. Availing herself of the hatred which the grandees of Poland felt towards their sovereign, Russia introduced into the constitution an executive power, thus rendering him little less than a simple president. This power was confided to a permanent council, composed of eighteen senators and an equal number of the equestrian order, over the election of whom Stanislaus had little or no influence. The command of his own body guard was wrested from him; and other innovations were introduced, which deprived him of almost all dignity and authority.

New constitution.

But the great body of the nation were by no means satisfied with the nature of their constitution, and with the spirit of rivalry and opposition which universally prevailed. The present state of things they regarded as incompatible with their prosperity and security, either as individuals or as a nation. For three years previously to 1791, various attempts had accordingly been made to establish a new constitution upon more liberal and more unexceptionable principles. *This* the diet effected at the period last mentioned, to the great satisfaction of the king, and of almost the whole of his subjects. This new constitution was so admirably constructed, that Mr. Burke remarked of it, that the condition of all was made better, and the rights of none were infringed; and Kant, the celebrated German philosopher, emphatically observed, *nisi scirem opus humanum esse, divinam crediderim.* The king now enjoyed the executive power in all its plenitude; he nominated all the great officers of state, even the senators; a council was allowed him, composed of the archbishop of Gnesna, five ministers, and two secretaries; the senate, and the *national representation,* consisting of the provincial deputies and the representatives of towns, formed the two legislative chambers; the *liberum veto* was abolished; a general toleration proclaimed; the civil liberty of the peasantry, now no longer *adstricti glebæ,* was guaranteed by law; freedom was extended to every man the moment he entered the Polish territory; and the privilege of purchasing the lands of the nobility, when exposed to sale, granted to burgesses. The greatest defect of their former constitution, elective monarchy, was also removed; and the throne declared hereditary in the house of Saxony.

Invasion by Russia.

The hopes of happiness and independence, however, which this new order of things was so well calculated to afford, was but of very short continuance. Poland had been too long the scene of anarchy and opposition, to be so easily reconciled to obedience and tranquillity. A few of the nobles, irritated at the sacrifice of some of their privileges, repaired to the court of Petersburg; and their representations corresponding with the ambitious views of the empress, she immediately dispatched an army into Poland, under the pretext of guaranteeing the constitution as established in 1772. The Poles were not backward in making preparations to oppose her. All animosities were forgotten in the desperate struggle; the nobles hesitated not to surren-

der their plate and valuable jewels to enrich the treasury; every rank and class of men in the state were resolved to conquer or die in the defence of their liberties and independence. In vain, however, prince Poniatowsky, general of the army, (nephew of the king,) supported by the intrepid Kosciusko, performed prodigies of valour. Catherine was almost every where triumphant. And a letter, written by her to Stanislaus, threatening to double or triple her forces unless he yielded, induced that benignant monarch, in order to prevent the farther effusion of human blood, to surrender at discretion. He was removed to Grodno, to await the determination of the empress. Nor did she allow her intention to remain long concealed. In the beginning of 1793, a manifesto was published by the courts of Russia and Prussia, declaring that, to remove from their respective frontiers the dangerous influence of the anarchical principles recently proclaimed in Poland, they had resolved to unite to their dominions several of the provinces of that kingdom.

Second partition.

This resolution, than which nothing can be conceived more arbitrary and base, was communicated to a diet, summoned by the Russian ambassador for the express purpose. The members, disgusted with the cruel and insulting proposition made to them, refused to sanction it with an obstinacy as honourable as it was unavailing. The question was soon decided; for an *ultimatum* terminating in these words was submitted to the diet by the Russian ambassador: " The undersigned must moreover inform the states of the republic assembled in general diet, that he has thought it absolutely necessary, in order to prevent every kind of *disorder,* to cause two battalions of grenadiers with four pieces of cannon to surround the castle, *to secure the tranquillity of their deliberations.* The undersigned expects, that the sitting will not terminate until the demanded signature of the treaty is decided." And these threats were immediately put into execution. The castle was surrounded by the Russian soldiers. Some of the officers even entered the assembly, under the false and absurd pretence of guarding the person of the king against conspirators. In such circumstances the Poles had no alternative but submission, though the treaty was not agreed to till three o'clock in the following morning, and not till after much discussion, and many successive divisions. They appealed, however, to the right of nations, and to every power of Europe, and declared, that, deprived of their liberty, and surrounded by a foreign army, they were compelled, contrary to their feelings and their principles, to sign this treaty of dismemberment. It was towards Prussia that the Poles felt the strongest aversion. Prussia had guaranteed the independence of Poland so recently as 1790, and had, at the same time, entered into a treaty, by which she bound herself to furnish her new ally with 36,000 auxiliary troops. These conditions, however, were not only not adhered to, but Prussia had used them in subservience to her ambitious designs. Russia, to which in some degree the Poles had for a considerable time been reckoned tributary, was regarded as less deserving of their hatred; but the result showed that the views of both these powers were the same, though the latter adopted more honourable and ingenious means in the prosecution of them.

Nor were the views of either any longer concealed. The constitution of 1791 was ordered to be annulled, and every paper relative to it to be delivered up. These orders the council hesitated to obey; and Iglestrom, the Russian ambassador, to deprive them of all power of resistance, immediately issued a mandate to reduce

Poland. their military force to 16,000 men. The army was as inflexible and patriotic as the council; the gallant Madalinsky put himself at the head of the troops, who refused to lay down their arms. The spirit of resistance was inveterate, and was widely diffused; and the Russians, to see their orders put into execution, marched into Poland with a numerous army. The ruthless conduct of these invaders drove the Poles to desperation: the peasantry were compelled to lodge, to feed, to transport their enemies from place to place without remuneration. Such degradation roused the spirit of the **Kosciusko.** nation; and the brave Kosciusko, whose name will ever adorn the history of his unfortunate country, suddenly appeared, (1794,) surrounded by a very considerable number of the armed peasantry, and by his skill and intrepidity supported for a while the falling honour of his country. This great man having driven the Russians out of Cracow, this city became the centre of the patriotic army; and having issued a proclamation, expressed in the most energetic terms, calling on every rank and class of men to shake off their disgraceful fetters, and to conquer or perish in defence of their country, the appeal was not made in vain: he was immediately elected generalissimo of the national troops, and received the support of the nobility, who, having proclaimed the constitution of 1791, departed for their respective estates to arm and assemble their vassals. And the success of Kosciusko corresponded for a while with the justness of his cause, and the bravery with which he supported it. A body of troops amounting to 6000 men, having marched towards Cracow to give him battle, was completely defeated; they lost 1000 men, with eleven cannon, and their general Wononzow was taken prisoner. This was the signal for general hostility. The Russians, who had seized upon Warsaw, and were attempting to become masters of the arsenal, were resolutely attacked by the inhabitants, and, after three days of the most bloody engagements, were driven from the city. Similar achievements were performed in other towns. Poland was all in arms; and her troops amounted to 60,000 men, exclusive of the peasantry, who were armed with pikes. Russia and Prussia in the mean time marched 110,000 troops against Poland; and Kosciusko made a skilful retreat upon Warsaw, which he defended for ten weeks against the Prussians, who, after losing 20,000 men in an inglorious and unavailing siege, found it prudent to withdraw into their own territories.

Kosciusko, thus freed of the Prussians, marched to oppose the new Russian troops, who, during the siege of Warsaw, had conquered Lithuania and Volhynia. The eyes of all Europe were placed upon him; but fortune had declared against him; and though he and his brave companions in arms performed feats of valour, the Russians (19th October) gained a signal victory,

Kosciusko himself being dreadfully wounded, and taken prisoner[*]. The fate of Poland was now irrevocably **Poland.** sealed, the whole kingdom being in the power of the Russians, with the single exception of Warsaw, whither they immediately marched their victorious army. The Polish troops in that city, " few but undismayed," resolved to make a desperate resistance; but how could 10,000 men withstand the impetuosity of five times that number? The suburb Praga was taken by assault, and, after eight hours of the most obstinate defence, Warsaw was obliged to surrender at discretion. But the implacable Russians, commanded by the infamous Suwarrow, were not yet satisfied. About ten hours after the battle was finished, they set fire to the city, and plundered and massacred the inhabitants in the most brutal manner; no age or sex escaped their violence; they perpetrated deeds at the bare idea of which humanity shudders, and of which even the history of Poland affords few examples.

Poland being thus overthrown, the two usurping **Dismem-** powers were about to form a partition of it betwixt **berment.** them, when Austria unexpectedly stept forward, and declared that she could not permit the entire destruction of Poland, unless she were allowed to share in the division. The consequences of a refusal they were not willing to encounter; and Austria had thus her ambitious views realized, without having incurred the smallest danger or expence. Stanislaus, who had all this while remained in his capital, was at length removed to Grodno a second time, where he was compelled to resign his crown, and was thence carried to Petersburg, where he resided as a state prisoner in solitude and exile till his death, which took place in February, 1798.

The result of this partition was as follows:

			Square Miles.	Population.
To Austria	.	.	64,000	4,800,000
To Prussia	.	.	52,000	3,500,000
To Russia	:	.	168,000	6,700,000
			284,000	15,000,000

Of this territory, the partitioning powers appropriated to themselves those districts that lay most convenient to their respective dominions, the acquisitions of Russia being larger than those of the other two taken collectively.

Such was the fate of Poland; and the arrangements made by the partitioning powers have remained more stationary than their unjust nature, or the convulsed state of Europe, could have led any one to suspect. The first alteration which they sustained was made by Bonaparte, who, having carried his conquering arms into Poland, (1807,) stripped Prussia of a part of her Polish dominions. Of these he assigned a small portion to Russia, who had already obtained so much; and he erected the remainder into a new state, denominated **Duchy of** *the Grand Duchy of Warsaw,* which he bestowed on the **Warsaw.**

---

[*] The subsequent fate of this brave man it may not be improper to state. Having recovered a little from his wound, he was advancing forward a few steps, when a Cossack aimed at him a dreadful blow, which would inevitably have proved mortal, had not a Russian general (to whose wife Kosciusko, when she was his prisoner, had shown the most disinterested generosity) stopped his arm; and when the officer was requested, (if he really wished to render him a service,) to allow the soldier to put an end to his existence, he spared his life, but made him a prisoner. Kosciusko having been removed to Petersburgh, was confined in the fortress there, till, on the accession of Paul the late emperor, (1796,) who showed great liberality to the persecuted Poles, he was set at liberty, and permitted to remain either in the Russian dominions, or to emigrate to America. He preferred the latter. He afterwards returned to France. When the allies entered Paris in 1815, he was then residing in that capital; and some Polish soldiers having recognised him, could not sufficiently express their gratitude and veneration for a man, who, then weighed down with years and misfortunes, had done and suffered so much to redeem the fading glory of their country. He died in France; but through the intervention of the emperor Alexander, (king of Poland,) his remains were restored from a foreign grave, and reposited at Cracow in a vault, which formed the cemetery of the kings of Poland, and which contains the ashes of the illustrious Sobieski. On the summit of Mount St. Bronislawa, near Cracow, a tumulus of the Carpathian marble has lately been raised to the memory of Kosciusko. The emperor Alexander, who seems to wish to make amends to Poland for the barbarous rapacity of his predecessors, has also removed to the same cemetery the dust of Stanislaus Poniatowsky.

king of Saxony. Having forced Austria, in 1809, to relinquish Gallicia, he conferred part of that province on Russia, while the rest was added to his new duchy. But the fate of this extraordinary person, as finally decided in the great battle of Waterloo, affected in no inconsiderable degree the history of Poland, and settled it in those circumstances in which we at present behold it. The congress of Vienna (1815) restored to Austria and Prussia part of what they had lately ceded, in obedience to the order of Bonaparte, and while they confirmed to Russia all her former acquisitions, conferred upon her in addition the sovereignty of the central provinces, under the name of *the kingdom of Poland*, of which we now proceed shortly to give an account.

Kingdom of Poland.

Extent.

The kingdom of Poland thus recently erected, and the only portion of the country just described, that officially retains the ancient name, comprises the greater part of that district which formed the duchy of Warsaw. It consists of the central provinces, comprehending the palatinates of Cracow, Sandomir, Kalisch, Lublin, Plock, Masovia, Podlachia, and Augustow, and is bounded by the respective acquisitions of Russia, Austria, and Prussia. And with the exception of a detached tract extending in a north-east direction towards Lithuania, it resembles a square of 200 miles, of which Warsaw, the capital, stands nearly in the centre, and it contains about 2,800,000 inhabitants.

Climate.

The climate of Poland is by no means so mild and salubrious as the geographical situation of the country would lead us to expect. Vegetation is considerably later than in the parallel latitudes of Germany and France; and the winter in Poland is frequently as rigorous as in Sweden, though the latter country is situated nine degrees north of the former. The air is always strongly impregnated with moisture, originating in the vast extent of marshy ground hitherto uncultivated; but the deleterious effects which this moisture has a tendency to produce, are, to the natives at least, in a great degree counteracted by the high winds for which Poland is so remarkable. Comparatively ungenial, however, as the climate of Poland is, it is remarkable also for another quality, equally unfavourable to health and vegetation,—it is extremely changeable and capricious. The crops in the neighbourhood of the Carpathian mountains have frequently been destroyed in the middle of summer by snow-showers, which are very common in all seasons of the year on these heights. The rivers have sometimes continued frozen from the beginning of October till the vernal equinox; while, on the contrary, the months of winter have not unfrequently exhibited the phenomenon of a second vegetation, which, however, a single night's frost has been known to blast and destroy. The climate of this country, however, like that of every other place in a state of nature, is susceptible of great improvement; and this change might be effected by cutting down the forests, so abundant in Poland, by draining the marshy lands, by constructing canals, and by the general introduction of agricultural pursuits. By these means the climate of Poland, it is supposed, might be rendered as genial and mild as that of any of the corresponding latitudes of Europe.

Physical appearance and soil.

Poland is an extremely level country, diversified by few or no eminences, except a ridge of hills branching off from the Carpathian mountains, which anciently formed the southern boundary of the country. The rivers are unadorned with banks, and flow lazily in a flat monotonous course, insomuch that when, as previ-

ously stated, heavy falls of rain take place, the country for many miles is completely inundated. The number and extent of marshes and forests, neither of which the Poles have hitherto seemed very anxious to remove, uniformly strike strangers as one of the great characteristics of Poland. The soil, which is chiefly either of a clayey or marshy description, is, in many places, so extremely fertile, that, with the least cultivation, it is calculated to produce the most luxurious crops of corn; and it is distinguished for the richest pastures in Europe. Agriculture with the Poles, however, is completely in its infancy. For many ages they neglected this useful art, as they neglected every art of peace and domestic comfort; they were a warlike people; and, besides, the produce of the fields was not the property of the peasants, but their *masters*, and they were themselves doomed, without hope of advancement, to continue in the same rank of life, whatever had been their industry or their skill. But, though these disabilities have now been greatly removed, though the Poles are rapidly emerging from that state of laziness and inactivity in which they remained so long sunk, yet, in the department in question, they have nearly every thing to learn. Of the use of manure they are almost entirely ignorant; their common practice is to crop a field till it be exhausted, and then for a few years to abandon it. Their ploughs are scarcely sufficient to penetrate the *surface* of the ground; and their fields, when reaped, exhibit from this circumstance as rich a verdure as if they had remained for years unbroken. This ignorance, however, is diminishing every day. Some portions of Poland have been denominated the garden of Europe; and a period may not be far distant, when the term may, with much propriety, be applied to the whole territory. Societies for the encouragement of agriculture have been established in Poland; and the vast tracts of forests and marshes with which it abounds certainly open up an extensive field for the display of skill and enterprise.

Trade and manufactures.

The same causes which influenced the Poles to neglect agriculture, operated as forcibly in counteracting the interests of commerce. A Polish nobleman could not engage in traffic, even on the most liberal and extensive principle, without immediately forfeiting his rank and dignity; and the wealth of burghers was either so limited, or so much at the mercy of the nobles and of the government, that they had no encouragement for entering on speculations which, with all their enterprise or success, might not to them be productive of any emolument. The natural facilities and resources of a country, great as these may be, will never succeed in obviating and surmounting disadvantages such as these; and, by consequence, the spirit of commerce in Poland has yet hardly displayed itself. What has been effected in this department has been accomplished chiefly by the Jews, a race of people of whom we shall soon speak, and who, in every country, are remarkable for the same characteristic features,—love of money, industry, and wealth. The number of manufactories in Poland are, as may be expected, extremely few, and these few are by no means on an extensive scale, or brought to any thing approaching to perfection. Towards the end of last century, the Poles made attempts to manufacture silks, fine woollen cloths, &c. but these succeeded only so far as Stanislaus protected them, and were in a great measure relinquished when he was forced to resign his throne. In Warsaw, a considerable eminence has been attained in Polish productions.

Several manufactories in linen and woollen cloth, black soap, carpets, stockings, and hats, have been established there. The great manufactory of what has been denominated *Turkey* carpets, situated about half a league from the city, is still in a very flourishing condition. But the only articles they make well in Warsaw are all kinds of carriages and harness work. In this capital there are indeed no fewer than fifty coach-making establishments, of no inconsiderable extent. There are several branches of industry to which the soil, the climate, the natural productions of the country, are favourable, and which they are now beginning to cultivate, namely, glass, leather, linen and coarse cloths, distillation, &c. With the exception of coaches, however, their exports in the mean time consist almost entirely of raw produce, corn to a great amount, about 4,000,000 of English quarters annually, hemp, flax, cattle, timber, honey. An account of the trade of Dantzick, Elbing, and Thorn, may be found under the article PRUSSIA.

Among the many natural facilities with which ancient Poland abounded, and which might have raised her high in the commercial world, her rivers may well be mentioned. This advantage, however, the present Poland does not possess in any very eminent degree. The only great river now belonging to her is the Vistula, which cannot, indeed, be permanently counted upon for any other purposes but those of internal navigation, as, before it reaches the sea, it passes for 200 miles through the Prussian dominions. It rises in the circle of Teschen, on the north of the Carpathian mountains, becomes navigable at Cracow, and after passing Warsaw, Plock, &c. it falls into the Baltic at Dantzick. In its course, it receives the waters of several tributary streams, of which the Pilica, the Narew, and the Bug, are the most considerable. Poland can yet boast of no canals; a mode of conveyance to be found only in rich, civilized, and commercial countries. It may be mentioned here, that conveyance by land is cheap and expeditious; the roads are good, and posting has been brought to considerable perfection; but (what may be expected in a country where there are few travellers) the inns are wretched, insomuch that travellers are obliged to carry with them their bed and provisions.

The towns of Poland are not of a very elegant or interesting description. Warsaw, the capital, affords a sickening contrast of magnificence and meanness, the public buildings, the churches and palaces, being large and beautiful, while the houses of the ordinary citizens are small, mean, ill-constructed hovels. It consists of a long street, strait and dirty, intersected at right angles by cross ones, all ill paved, and otherwise entirely neglected. The houses originally were formed of wood, but these are gradually disappearing, being supplanted by new and splendid edifices of stone covered with tiles; and it is no longer lawful to erect buildings of wood. The castle, situated on an imposing eminence, commands the Vistula, and its opposite banks. It contains many superb and interesting apartments, adorned with pictures, marbles, and bronzes. Many of the streets, squares, and *places*, are spacious and beautiful; some of them ornamented with statues and pillars. A statue of the illustrious Copernicus, who was a native of Poland, is about to be erected; and Thorwaldson is employed on a bronze equestrian statue in memory of Prince Joseph Poniatowski, to be placed in one of the principal squares. The usual public promenades in Warsaw are the gardens of Saxe and Krasinski, both occupying a considerable space within the city. The

avenue of trees, conducting to Uiazdow, may rival in effect those of the Prater near Vienna; and, on Sundays and festival-days, is crowded with citizens, who resort thither for recreation. At Uiazdow is a well-provided botanic garden. Twice a year there is a fair at Warsaw, when the city is filled with merchants from the remotest corners of the kingdom, and from foreign countries. Its manufactories, of which we have formerly spoken, have not of late increased in number or in value, except, probably, in the department of coach-making. The fine collection of pictures which the late king commenced and patronised, have been removed to Russia. His library, which contained 45,000 volumes, and the library established by two brothers (Bishops,) of the family of Zaluski, comprising 200,000 volumes, in which were many rare books and MSS. relative to Polish history, have experienced the same fate. This capital, however, still possesses many distinguished advantages. It can still boast of a university, founded in 1766, by Stanislaus Augustus, in which are taught the Polish, the French, the German, and Latin languages, mathematics, fortification, drawing, military tactics, history, &c. It was meant at first to receive only the sons of the nobility. Nor do we know that the original intention was ever departed from, though for the sake of literature, and of the social intercourse of the nation, such a plan is extremely impolitic and destructive. This university seems to have been abolished, or to have been re-modelled, and, as it were, re-instituted, in 1816, by the present sovereign, the Emperor Alexander. Few universities in Europe are more flourishing than that of Warsaw. It is composed of five faculties, Divinity, Law and Administration, Medicine, Mathematics and Physical Science, and Literature and the Fine Arts. There are no fewer than forty-two professors in it, many of them writers of considerable learning and celebrity; though we are led to believe that the number of students have not yet corresponded with the advantages and endowments by which the seminary is characterized. Warsaw is yet possessed of other literary recommendations. It is distinguished by fifteen printing presses, with a suitable number of book-shops, two lithographic establishments, several schools for the instruction of engravers, academies for designing after nature, an annual exhibition of paintings, an academy for the deaf and dumb, and schools on the Lancastrian mode. It has, besides, several benevolent and charitable institutions, conducted on sufficiently liberal principles. Warsaw also produces various newspapers and literary magazines, written with no mean ability, and circulating through the different districts of the kingdom. This capital, which is an open town, having neither walls nor gates, is situated partly on a plain, and partly on a gently rising ground on the western banks of the Vistula, which flows from south to north, and is hardly so deep or so broad as the Thames at London. The river separates it from Praga, reckoned its suburb, but which may be regarded as a considerably large town of itself. In 1782, it contained 7000 inhabitants; but, in consequence of the barbarous visit of Suwarrow, that number was reduced fully one-half. The united population of the two places amounts to nearly 100,000 souls, independent of the garrison, which contains about 20,000. In addition to Praga, there are other three conterminous towns, regarded as suburbs to Warsaw. Their names are Leszno, Szolec, and Grybow. They have each their exclusive privileges, and their respective town-houses.

Villanow, a palace in the Italian style, remarkable as having been built by the illustrious Sobieski, and as having formed his favourite residence, stands within a league from Warsaw. To it he retired while not engaged in the active services of war, and in it he closed a life uniformly devoted to the honour of his country. Having been sold at his death, it went into the noble family of Zartoriski, who granted it to Augustus II. a monarch who considerably enlarged it, and ornamented it with various bass-reliefs, illustrative of the principal victories of Sobieski. It is now the property of Count Potocki. In the extensive park by which it is surrounded, there still exist various poplars, planted by the hand of its distinguished founder. There is also another remarkable palace in the neighbourhood of Warsaw, namely, Lazienki, the country seat of the last king, Stanislaus, which is adorned with numerous paintings of the first masters, and with marble busts of all the Polish kings.

Lublin, a town of eminence, is the capital of the palatinate of that name, is the see of a bishop, and can boast of a citadel. It is, however, particularly remarkable for three great annual fairs, each lasting a month, which are frequented by merchants from all the neighbouring nations.—Sandomir, on the Vistula, between Cracow and Warsaw, is delightfully situated on a hill, was once the residence of the Polish kings, and contains several colleges. But the most agreeable and lively town of Poland is Plock, surrounded with orchards, and washed by the Vistula, which is here animated with crowds of fishermen, and with boats which convey into Dantzick the exports of Poland *.

Poland, though a level country, is not deficient in mineral productions. Almost all the morasses and meadows, according to Malte-Brun, abound in iron. Podolia produces various species of marble. That large district lying between the Vistula and its tributary stream Pilica, famous for its mines, contains lead, iron, copper, calamine, marble, and slate. In various provinces is found a kind of clay, peculiarly well adapted for earthen-ware. Poland, though not remarkably abundant in stone, produces granite, and several other kinds well fitted for building; yet the houses are for the most part constructed of wood, an article neither so durable nor so comfortable, but which the ignorance and laziness of the Poles cause them to prefer.

There is nothing, however, very important or peculiar in the mineral kingdom of Poland, excepting the salt mines of Wielitska, near Cracow, the most productive and the most celebrated in Europe. According to some historians, these mines were known so early as the thirteenth century. It is ascertained, however, that they have been wrought since the fifth, since which period they have formed one of the richest sources of revenue which Poland ever enjoyed. The entrances to the pits are a few miles from Cracow, but the city is completely undermined, and is suspended, as it were, on pillars of salt. The vaults are uncommonly large and spacious; some of them contain chapels, of

which that of St. Anthony is 30 feet high, and contains images of saints cut out of the solid rock; some of them are used as magazines for depositing the salt when put in barrels, &c. while others are set apart respectively for stables, and for keeping hay for the horses, of which a great number are in daily use. " Many of the excavations, or chambers from whence the salt has been dug," says Mr. Coxe, " are of an immense size; some are supported with timber, others by vast pillars of salt, which are left standing for that purpose. Several of vast dimensions are without any support in the middle. I remarked one of this latter sort in particular, which was certainly 80 feet in height, and so extremely long and broad as almost to appear, amid the subterraneous gloom, without limits. The roofs of these vaults are not arched, but flat." " We found these mines as dry as a room, without the least damp or moisture; observing only, in our whole progress, one small spring of water, which is impregnated with salt, as it runs through the mine." (Vol. I. p. 246.) The air is bracing and salubrious; and the miners, of whom there are regularly about 700 employed, and who work, as in most other mining countries, about six or eight hours at a time, enjoy good health, and attain to the ordinary length of human life.

The salt, at the various stages of its depth, presents different appearances. At its highest elevation, it is found in large irregular rocks, from which are frequently cut masses of the size of 400 or 500 cubic feet. Here, also, it exhibits the greatest impurity, being intermingled with various kinds of stone: and it assumes a grey, dark, or green colour, according to the nature of the marl in which it may be imbedded. At this stage, also, is found the crystal salt, which is generally dug up in the shape of a cube or rectangular prism. The purest and most close is at the bottom of the pit, and is sparry; and the quality of all is found to improve in the direction of the Carpathian ridge, which, it is not improbable, lies on beds of salt; a fact the more likely, as the salt mines on the opposite side of these mountains are of a similar kind, and exhibit similar appearances.

" Such an enormous mass of salt," says the accurate traveller just quoted, " exhibits a wonderful phenomenon in the natural history of this globe. Monsieur Guetard, who examined these mines with great attention, and who has published a treatise upon the subject, informs us, that the uppermost bed of earth, at the surface immediately over the mines, is sand; the second clay, occasionally mixed with sand and gravel, and containing petrifactions of marine bodies; the third calcareous stone. From all these circumstances, he conjectures that this spot was formerly covered by the sea, and that the salt is a gradual deposit formed by the evaporation of its waters." Vol. I. p. 246.

The Poles, as has been incidentally mentioned before, continue still to be divided into four classes: those of nobles or gentlemen, of clergy, of citizens or burghers, and peasants. The Poles set no value on

---

* The town of Cracow, with a small adjacent territory, is not included in the present Polish dominions. By the Congress of Vienna, it was declared a free and neutral city, under the denomination of *The Bishoprick of Cracow*. Russia, Prussia, and Austria, have engaged to respect its neutrality, and to cause it to be respected by others; and no armed force, on any pretext, is allowed to enter its territory. Cracow is situated on the Vistula, was formerly the capital of the palatinate of the same name, and at a very remote period the capital of Poland. It enjoys the advantages of an ancient and celebrated University, which contains eleven colleges, and which has the superintendance of fourteen schools, situated within the city. It is a Bishop's see, as its name denotes; it formerly was the burial-place of the Polish kings; and the ancient royal palace is still pointed out on a rock on the banks of the river. The kings of Poland were formerly crowned at Cracow, but the last monarch was crowned at Wilna. It is a town of great antiquity; but it now bears all the marks of neglect and decay; and though at one time its population amounted to 70,000, it was in 1810 only 25,736. (See the article CRACOW, in this work.)

736

POLAND.

Poland.

titles of honour: all who possess a freehold estate, or can trace their descent from ancestors formerly possessing a freehold estate, and who have engaged in no trade or commerce, are, whatever be their titles, equal in point of rank; they are termed brothers, and the appellation of *a gentleman of Poland* is regarded as the highest name by which they can be distinguished. The clergy are possessed of as great civil as well as professional influence, as at any former period, and enjoy various immunities and privileges. The privileges of the citizens were formerly few, and these few, in many instances, were undermined and wrested from them: while the peasants, born slaves, attached to the soil, were doomed to unavailing toil and misery, and treated by their cruel masters as belonging to an inferior species of beings. The condition of the peasantry and citizens, however, are now highly meliorated; and are, as rapidly as their late bondage and exclusion will allow, advancing to that state of freedom and refinement which the same classes enjoy under the most enlightened governments of Europe. Every disability has now been removed from them.—The richer inhabitants of the cities, as well as the nobles, have all their chateaus or country houses, with parks and gardens, which rival in beauty and in the works of art which adorn them, those of France and Germany. The peasantry in particular, so long sunk in a state of iron depression, but declared free by the constitutions of 1791, 1807, and 1815, though not far advanced in civilization, abound in good qualities, and are daily rising in importance and respectability. "Every peasant," we are told on the authority of a Polish writer, "may quit his landlord if injured or dissatisfied. In some districts the peasants rise to be farmers, both hereditary and for terms of years." "The houses of the better order of peasants," says the same author, "contain spacious and commodious apartments. Of late years houses of stone are often met with."

Jews.

In giving an account of the different classes of society among the Poles, however, the *Jews*, a peculiar race of men, and in this country extremely numerous, must not be overlooked. In Poland, indeed, the Jews are supposed to be more numerous than in Palestine, and amount to about a seventh part of the whole population. They were introduced into this country in the time of Casimir the Great, whose favourite mistress was a Jewess, and who was thus induced to confer upon them privileges, many of which they still enjoy. The nobility, too, encouraged their settlement in their respective dominions, because it was soon discovered that, through their instrumentality alone, they could obtain the comforts, the luxuries, and even some of the necessaries of life. They hence soon became people of importance; and while, with great reluctance, the Poles allowed the rank of nobility to the most distinguished strangers, a converted Jew was regarded by them as virtually a gentleman; and if he possessed wealth enough to purchase property in land, he was capable of being elevated to the highest situation in the republic. Such an event has sometimes taken place, though, in spite of this inducement, few Jews have been found inclined to abandon the religious principles of their forefathers. In Poland, they were for ages the only persons who engaged in any thing like commerce, or who seemed to appreciate the value of money or of property. Almost all the current coin of the realm was in their hands; the nobility have often been known to mortgage to them a great proportion of their lands: they have sometimes taken a lease of

Christian baptisms, and have had in their possession the baptismal fonts, for the use of which they took care that they were liberally remunerated. But with all their enterprise, they were fradulent, avaricious, and immoral. The great object of their existence was to acquire wealth, but whether honestly or otherwise they seemed not to care. Seldom has a law-suit occurred in Poland in which a Jew was not a party, or a theft in which a Jew was not more or less directly concerned. Such indeed is their love of money, and such the baseness of their principles, that, for a pecuniary compensation, they have been known to submit their wives and their daughters to the embrace of strangers.

Dress, and mode of salutation.

With the character of the Poles the reader must already be well acquainted; the following account of their mode of salutation and of their dress, related on the authority of a late accurate traveller, will not prove uninteresting. "The Poles seem a lively people, and use much action in their ordinary conversation. Their common mode of saluting is to incline their heads, and to strike their breast with one of their hands, while they stretch the other towards the ground; but when a common person meets a superior, he bows his head almost to the earth, waving at the same time his hand, with which he touches the bottom of the leg near the heel of the person to whom he pays his obeisance. The men of all ranks generally wear whiskers, and shave their heads, leaving only a circle of hair upon the crown. The summer dress of the peasants consists of nothing but a shirt and drawers of coarse linen, without shoes or stockings, with round caps or hats. The women of the lower class wear upon their heads a wrapper of white linen, under which their hair is braided, and hangs down in two plaits. I observed several of them with a long piece of white linen, hanging round the side of their faces, and covering their bodies below their knees; this singular kind of veil makes them look as if they were doing penance. The dress of the higher order, both men and women is uncommonly elegant. That of the gentlemen is a waistcoat with sleeves, over which they wear an upper robe of a different colour, which reaches down below the knee, and is fastened round the waist with a sash or girdle; the sleeves of this upper garment are in warm weather tied behind the shoulders; a sabre is a necessary part of their dress as a mark of nobility. In summer, the robe, &c. is of silk; in winter, of cloth, velvet, or stuff edged with fur. They wear fur caps or bonnets, and buskins of yellow leather, the heels of which are plated with iron or steel. The dress of the ladies is a simple polonaise or long robe, edged with fur." This account, though written forty years ago, is almost in its most literal acceptation applicable to the Poles of the present day, and will, it is likely, be applicable in a greater or less degree for ages to come. The natural and unavoidable consequences of a revolution; their subjection to a foreign power; their freedom from a state of oppression and slavery; and their intermixture with strangers, all tend to render the Poles of the present day more refined and civilized than at any former period, and to approach more nearly to the manners and habits of the various nations with which they have continual intercourse. But their national character is still sedulously cherished, and will not soon cease to predominate. A people, situate like the Poles, maintain with unshaken tenacity the customs, even the prejudices, of their ancestors, as affording them no inconsiderable consolation for the ruin and desolation in which their country has been involv-

Poland. ed. It need now merely be added, in reference to the foregoing subject, that the personal appearance of the Poles is dignified and prepossessing, that their complexion is fair, and their figure well proportioned. They are lively, hospitable, honest, brave, patriotic. The women are beautiful, modest, chaste, and dutiful to their husbands.

Literature. From the circumstances already narrated, it may with propriety be inferred, that Poland cannot have attained any great eminence in science and literature. Such an opinion is literally correct, as far at least as regards the great body of the people. She possessed indeed no regular seminaries for the education of the lower classes, till the reign of Stanislaus Poniatowski; and while schools in the country are still few and inefficient, those in the villages and towns can hardly be regarded as more useful and respectable. The truth indeed need not be concealed. The Poles in the lower ranks are either totally ignorant, or their acquaintance with books is uncommonly limited and superficial. In short, there is no current and common literature among the great body of the nation; and though the cause of education is not neglected by the present government, ages must elapse ere the Poles attain to that degree of intelligence and taste for reading, by which the common people in the more civilized nations of the Continent are characterized. Notwithstanding this, however, Poland has produced many celebrated scholars and writers, whose names would shed a lustre over any nation. Mathematical and physical science in particular was cultivated at an earlier period, and with happier success in Poland than in any other country in Europe. Vitellio, a Pole, who lived in the thirteenth century, has been regarded as the first in Europe who investigated the Theory of Light and understood its principles. (See the article OPTICS, Vol. XV. p. 464.) The illustrious artronomer Copernicus, of whom any nation might boast, was a native of Poland, being born at Thorn, which, though now in Russia, was situated for time immemorial in a Polish province. The names of Brudzewski, Martin of Olkusz, Grzebski, Broscius, are intimately connected with the literary history of Europe. Nor was Poland deficient in writers in other departments of literature. Her theologians, poets, historians, particularly the two last, are extremely numerous, many of them of superior learning and endowments, but whose works, with few exceptions, are not extensively known beyond the boundaries of the kingdom. Her poets indeed are so numerous, that in a " Dictionary of the Polish Poets," published in 1820 by Juszynski, the lives of upwards of fourteen hundred are described, including of course versifiers of every degree of merit. And this dictionary is not completed; for it comprises only the poets anterior to the reign of Stanislaus Poniatowski. Nor have the fine arts been neglected in Poland. The government encourages them equally with science and literature; and there is in the university of Warsaw a professorship for instruction in this department, besides academies and inferior seminaries. There is also in this capital an annual exhibition of paintings and engravings, and the government awards prizes. In addition to many of a subordinate rank, Poland has produced two first-rate painters, Czechowicz and Smuglewicz, both educated in Italy, the fountain of the fine arts. " The paintings of the latter," says Mr. Szyrma, " adorn the cathedral of Wilna; several of them are to be found in the churches at Warsaw, also in St. Petersburg, whither he had been invited by the emperor Paul. He excelled in strong original conceptions. His sub-

jects are for the most part religious, taken from the Poland. Bible, like those of the English West. Some few of them are historical. The assassination of St. Stanislaus, the tutelary saint of Poland, by king Boleslaus the Bold, and his Cain and Abel, are master-pieces of art, and much admired by connoisseurs."—Music, both profane and sacred, is much cultivated; and the national airs and dances have long been regarded as elegant, dignified, and striking.—The theatre is also under the patronage of the government. There is a dramatic school in Warsaw for educating aspirants for the stage. The dramatic writings of Poland have not hitherto attained to any great height of perfection; but Boguslawski, who has long been regarded as the Kemble of Poland, is devoting his retirement and old age to the publication of his dramatic writings, which are to extend to twelve volumes, and will undoubtedly be gratifying to his countrymen, as they have for a long time afforded them delight on the stage. Of the Polish language, a dialect of the Sclavonic, and which the works it has produced will not allow to perish, a copious grammar has been compiled by Kopezynski, and a dictionary in six quarto volumes by Linde, an author who has not inaptly been compared to Adelung, the famous German philologist. The literary institutions of this country, though yet not very numerous or very efficient, may be expected rapidly to improve and increase, as they are liberally patronized both by the nobility and the government. Her national libraries have been transferred to Petersburg, and though there are several extensive private collections, the only public library is that belonging to the Society of Friends of Science at Warsaw. With the exception of the University of Warsaw, this Society is the most learned and celebrated institution in Poland. Its origin is interesting. Stanislaus Poniatowski, we are told by Mr. Szyrma, soothed the misfortunes of his life with the healing balm of literary pastime, destining every Thursday evening to social conversation with men of learning. After the partition of Poland, when the name of that country was to be for ever obliterated, the same *literati* who were thus accustomed to hold these literary meetings with the king, actuated by patriotic feelings, united themselves into a society for the object of rescuing from oblivion whatever related to the history and literature of their unfortunate country. The members have since exerted their powers in different departments of learning, and have originated many literary productions that have excited a deep and general interest over the nation. The transactions of this society are published under the title of Annals, and are now grown voluminous. No institution promises to do more for the interests of science and literature in Poland than that which Mr. Szyrma has thus described.

Poland, as already known, exists no longer as an in- Constitution. dependent kingdom, but maintains its existence in an unequal conjunction with a mighty empire. The Emperor Alexander, however, has done all in his power to prevent the Poles from regarding their dependence on Russia as a burden, or as a dereliction of their national independence. In a letter addressed to the president of the Polish senate immediately after the Congress of Vienna, he says, " The kingdom will be united to Russia by the bond of *its own constitution*. If the great interest of general tranquillity has not permitted the union of all the Poles under the same sceptre, I have at least endeavoured to alleviate as much as possible the pain of the separation, and to obtain for them every where the peaceful enjoyment of the nationality. Conformably to this promise, he granted them in 1815, a constitutional charter, embracing as nearly as possible the admirable principles of the constitution of 1791, with as much of the ancient spirit and ancient forms of their old dynasty as were consistent with the safety of the nation and the improvements made in legislation. There are now as formerly, a king, a senate, and a diet. The czar is represented by a viceroy, in whom, and in a cabinet of ministers, the executive government resides. The chief ministerial departments are those of war, finance, police, law, and national education; and the ministers, as in Britain, are responsible to the senate. The senate consists of thirty members, namely, ten bishops, ten palatines, and ten castellans named by the king for life. The Chamber of Representatives contains seventy deputies from the provincial nobility and gentry, and of the members of the cabinet, who have seats in it in virtue of their office. The diet, analogous to the ancient ordinary Polish diet, consists of the senate and House of Representatives. Its sittings cannot extend beyond a fortnight; the king is not obliged to convoke it oftener than once in two years, its sanction being necessary only for certain measures, for the imposition of taxes, for the passing of new laws, or the abrogation or alteration of old ones. There are numerous provincial courts both civil and criminal, in which the laws are wisely and impartially administered; and there are besides two courts of appeal, with one supreme court, whose decisions are final. The established church is the Roman Catholic, which is the religion of the majority; but Protestants of every denomination are extremely numerous; a considerable number belong to the Greek church; and the Jews, as formerly mentioned, amount to a seventh part of the population. The most unshackled toleration is established, embracing not merely every denomination of Christians, but Jews and Pagans. It need only farther be mentioned, that the revenue of Poland amounts to £900,000 sterling; that of this sum £180,000 goes to the civil list; and that the military force is considerable, especially in cavalry.

See *Tableau de la Pologne*, par Malte-Brun, Paris, 1807, 8vo.; Reichard's *Guide des Voyageurs; Guide du Voyageur en Pologne et dans la République de Cracovie;* Reinhard's *Guide des Voyageurs dans le Nord ;* Coxe's *Travels in Poland*, &c.; Dr. Connor's *History of Poland ;* Palmer's *Authentic Memoirs of the Life of John Sobieski ;* Rulhiere's *Hist. de la Pologne ; Letters Literary and Political on Poland*, Edin. 1823, 8vo. published anonymously, but known to be written by Mr. Szyrma, a Polish gentleman at present residing in Edinburgh: it is an interesting production, deserving the attention of every reader.   (T.M)

GENERAL EXPLANATION

OF THE

PLATES BELONGING TO VOLUME SIXTEENTH

OF THE

EDINBURGH ENCYCLOPÆDIA.

PLATE CCCCLIII.

Illustrative of ORNITHOLOGY, contains Figures of
Vultur Gryphus, Condor.
Falco Imperialis, Imperial Eagle.
Serpentarius Africanus, Snake Eater.
Strix Passerina, Little Owl.
Buceros Rhinoceros, Rhinoceros Hornbill.
Glaucopis Cinerea, Cinereous Wattlebird.
Paradisea Major, Great Bird of Paradise.
Menura Superba, Superb Menura.
Pipra Carunculata, Carunculated Chatterer.

PLATE CCCCLIV.

Illustrative of ORNITHOLOGY, contains Figures of
Sylvia Regulus, Golden Crested Wren.
Parus Pendulinus, Penduline Titmouse.
Loxia Curvirostra, Crossbill.
Fringilla Paradisea, Whidaw Bunting.

Ramphastos Viridis, Green Toucan.
Psittacus Cristatus, Broad Crested Cockatoo.
Psittacus Alexandri, Alexandrine Parakeet.
Trochilus Minimus, Least Humming Bird.
Upupa Epops, Hoopoe.
Alcedo Gigantea, Giant King Fisher.
Hirundo Fuciphaga, Esculent Swallow.
Oriolus Galbula, Golden Oriole.
Oriolus Baltimore, Baltimore Oriole.

PLATE CCCCLV.

Illustrative of ORNITHOLOGY, contains Figures of
Argus Polyplectron, Peacock Pheasant.
Phasianus Satyrus, Horned Pheasant.
Argus Giganteus, Gigantic Argus.
Struthio Camelus, Ostrich.
Rhea Americana, American Rhea.
Casuarius Galeatus, Galeated Cassowary.
Ardea Minuta, Little Heron.

Phœnicopterus Ruber, Flamingo.
Recurvirostra Avocetta, Avocet.
Gallus Sonneratii, Jungle Cock.

PLATE CCCCLVI.

Illustrative of ORNITHOLOGY, contains Figures of
    Platalea Leucorodia, Spoonbill.
    Ibis Religiosa, Sacred Ibis.
    Psophea Crepitans, Trumpeter.
    Palamedia Cornuta, Horned Screamer.
    Larus Minutus, Pigmy Gull.
    Diomedea Exulans, Wandering Albatross.
    Anas Spectabilis, King Duck.
    Pelecanus Onocrotalus, Common Pelican.
    Fratercula Arctica, Puffin.
    Aptenodytes Patachonica, Patagonian Penguin.

PLATE CCCCLVII.

Figs. 1, 2, 3. Represent the Common Paper Engine.
Fig. 4. Represents Fourdrinier's Paper Machine.
Fig. 5. Represents Dickinson's Paper Machine.

PLATE CCCCLVIII.

Fig. 1. Diagram for finding the time of the Oscillation of a Pendulum in a Circular Arc.
Figs. 2—5. Represent the Apparatus of Borda for measuring the Length of the Pendulum.
Fig. 6. Represents the Rules for measuring the Length of the Pendulum.
Fig. 7. Represents the Comparer, an Instrument invented by M. Fortin.
Figs. 8—10. Represent the new Pendulum invented by Captain Kater.
Fig. 11. Shows the method of measuring the length of the Pendulum.

PLATE CCCCLIX.

Contains various diagrams illustrative of the Article PERSPECTIVE.

PLATE CCCCLX.

Is a Perspective View of the principal parts of the Tellurian and Lunarium, united in one Machine.

PLATE CCCCLXI.

Figs. 1—3. Exhibit the construction of the Satellite

Machine invented by the Rev. W. Pearson, LL. D.

PLATE CCCCLXII.

Fig. 1. Is a Perspective View of the Orrery invented by the Rev. W. Pearson, LL.D.
Figs. 2—5. Contain a Section of the Machine and of its different Parts.

PLATE CCCCLXIII.

Figs. 1—12. Represent the Planing Machine in the Royal Arsenal of Woolwich, as constructed by the late Mr. Bramah.

PLATE CCCCLXIV.

Fig. 1. Represents Boyle's Machine for extracting air.
Fig. 2. Represents the Fountain at command.
Fig. 3. Represents Hiero's Fountain.
Fig. 4. Shows the Syphon for conveying a fluid from one place to another.
Figs. 5—7. Show Mariotte's Experiment for proving that air presses equally in all directions.
Fig. 8. Represents Dr. Wollaston's Apparatus for making uniform currents of air pass from one vessel into another.
Fig. 9. Shows a Clepsydra, or Water Clock.
Fig. 10. Is a representation of Hawksbee's Air Pump.
Fig. 11. Shows Mr. Smeaton's Improvement on the Air Pump.
Figs. 12—14. Represent an Air Pump of the best construction, as made by Messrs. Miller and Adie, Edinburgh, on the principle of Mr. Cuthbertson.
Fig. 15. Represents the Barometrical Gage for estimating the degree of exhaustion, as first practised by M. Mariotte.

PLATE CCCCLXV.

Figs. 1—7. Are diagrams for illustrating the principles of PNEUMATICS.
Fig. 8. Represents the Pear Gauge for detecting the elasticity of vapour.
Figs. 9, 10. Are diagrams illustrative of Mariotte's Law.
Fig. 11. Is a diagram for illustrating the elastic action of gunpowder.
Fig. 12. Shows the Principle of the Ballistic Pendulum.
Fig. 13. Is a diagram for illustrating the Expansive Force of Gunpowder.
Fig. 14. Shows Gay Lussac's Contrivance for Repeating Dalton's Experiments on the tension of a Combination of Air and Aqueous Vapour.

2

Fig. 15. Shows Gay Lussac's method of determining the Expansion of Dry Air.

PLATE CCCCLXVI.

Figs. 1—14. Are diagrams illustrative of the Velocity and Resistance of Fluids.

Fig. 15. Is a diagram for illustrating the action of Wind upon a Sail at Rest.

Fig. 16. Is a diagram for illustrating the Motion of Wind upon a Sail in Motion.

Figs. 17, 18. Are diagrams for illustrating the Theory of Sound.

Fig. 19. Is a diagram for illustrating the Reflexion of Sound.

Fig. 20. Shows a Construction for representing the Mean Temperature at different Altitudes.

Fig. 21. Is a diagram for illustrating the Capacity of Air from Moisture.

Fig. 22. Shows the Appearance of Venus as observed by Schroëter.

Fig. 23. Is a diagram illustrative of Schroëter's inferences respecting the Atmosphere of Venus.

END OF VOLUME SIXTEENTH.

Printed by A. Balfour & Co.
Edinburgh, 1823.